CATALOGUE

OF THE

LIBRARY

OF THE

BOSTON ATHENÆUM.

1807–1871.

PART V.

BOSTON.

1882.

Note. The recent publication of Vol. 1 of Halkett and Laing's "Dictionary of anonymous and pseudonymous literature of Gr. Britain" has enabled me to give in the following list the previously unknown names of the authors of a considerable number of works.

2 **Abbey** of Kilkhampton, *etc., is by* [H. Croft].
Abbeys. *See also.* Add **Dryburgh**; — **St. Savin.**
5 **Abnaki Indians.** VETROMILE, E. Sande. *After* 1867 insert *n.p.*, [1866]. Broadside.
7 **Academician.** *After* Picket *insert* Vol. 1. 1818-20.
8 **Accompt** of all, *etc., is by* [R. Baxter].
13 **Adams, J.,** *Pres.* Works. *Contents.* Vol. 3. Instructions of the town of Boston. *For* representatives *read* representative.
— Correspondence. *Same.* *Omit the entry.*
— Essay, *etc.*, is *also in* True sentiments of America. 1768. (B 462)
15 **Adams, J. Q.** Speech on his. *For* June *read* Jan.
18 **Address** to Prot. diss. 1774 *is by* [J. Priestley].
Address to the bishops *is by* [J. Disney].
Address to the Cocoa-tree *is by* [J. Butler].
Address to the dissidents *is by* [J. Aikin].
20 **Adorno.** *For* **Cattarina** *read* **Caterina Fieschi.**
Advice and reproof, *etc., is by* [T. Smollett].
Advice to a painter *is by* [A. Marvell].
Advocate of revealed. *For* July *read* Jan.; *omit* Vol. 2; *after* 1804 *insert* 2 v.
21 **Æginetan marbles.** *For* Bayern *read* Baiern.
22 **Æschylus.** BINAULT, L. *For* v. 4, 1853 *read* déc. 1843.
Æsopus, *Chinese.* Sloth *is pseud. for* R. Thom.
26 **Africa.** *Nat. hist.* BURMAN. *For* 1788 *read* 1738-39. 2 v.
27 **African** repository. *For* 1824 *read* 1826.
Afternoon of, *etc., is by Mrs.* [S. J. Penny].
Agassiz, L. Various articles. *For* v. 1, 2, 4, 6 *read* v. 1-6.
28 **Agate, J.** The plain truth. *For* 1808 *read* 1708.
— WITHERS, J. Truth. *For* 1708 *read* 1709.
Age of frivolity *is by* [T. Beck].
Agreement between, *etc., is by* [J. Gother].
38 **Albumazar** *is by* [D. Garrick].
39 **Alciati, A.** De magistratibus. *For* Galenio *read* Gelenio.
40 **Alcott, W. A.** The young wife. *Before* Boston *insert* 8th ed.; *for* 1837 *read* 1839.
43 **Alexandria.** BARTHÉLEMY ST. HILAIRE. *For* B. *read* J.
46 **Algeria.** TEMPLE. *For* 1853 *read* 1835.
48 **All** for greed *is by* M. P. Rose, Baroness Blaze de Bury.
49 **Allen, E.** SPARKS, J. *Same.* *For* Chipman, N. *read* Chipman, D.
50 **Allen, J.,** *alias* **Walton, G.** Add *Another copy, bound in Allen's skin.*
55 **Almeida Pimenta** *should come after* **Almeida, M.** de.
Almeyda, T. de. *After* t. 2 insert 3 *and after* 85 insert 3 v.
Alofsen. *For* S. *read* Salomon.
58 **Amari, M.** *For* Frammenti *read* FRAMMENTI; *before* Dei recenti *insert* VANNUCCI, A.
77 **American** journal of education. *After* Hartford *for* 1855 *read* 1856.
78 **American** med. intelligencer. *For* 1837-40 *read* 1838-41.
American mineralogical journal. *After* Vol. 1 *insert* [1810].
American monthly magazine. New series. *For* 1836-37 read 1836-38.
79 **Amer. Orient. Soc.** Journ. *Contents.* Vol. 3. *For* **Vassullo** *read* **Vassallo.**
84 **American** review. *Note.* *For* v. 2 *read* v. 11.
85 **American** state papers. *Contents.* Class 1. *For* 35th *read* 20th.
86 **American** system, *etc., is by* [N. Hale].
American Temperance Soc. *After* Temperance manual *insert* [with 6th-8th report].
91 **Anadol** *is by* [J. H. Skene].
Analecta Scotica *was edited by* [J. Maidment].
Anam. *Lang.* TABERD, J. L. *After* 1838 *insert* 2 v.
99 **Andree, K. T.** *Omit the note.*
101 **Andromeda,** L'. *For* 1639 *read* 1638.
Andros, *Sir* E. JAMES II. *For* 1836 *read* 1846; — MATHER, I. Revolution. *For* 1836 *read* 1846.
Andry, —. *For* Vallisneri *read* Vallisnieri.
102 **Aneurisms.** VOSE, J. *For* 1819 *read* 1809.
103 **Anghiera, P. M. d'.** Sommario. *For* 1574 *read* 1565.
Angler, *etc., is by* [— Belton].
107 **Anne Gray** *is by* [T. H. Lister].
110 **Answer** to a disc. *is by* [G. Tully].
Answer to a late, *etc., is by* [J. Williams].
Answer to a pamphlet *is by* [T. Randolph].
Answer to a paper printed *is by* [G. Burnet].
111 **Answer** to one, *etc., is by* [N. Amhurst].
Answer to some, *etc., is by* [J. S. Barrington].
Answer to the anon., *etc., is by* [J. Peirce].
Answer to the Bp. *is by* [W. Lloyd].
Answer to the late, *etc., is by* [J. Welwood].
112 **Antidote** against, *etc., is by* [E. Bagshaw].
113 **Antiquities.** ROCHETTTE, D. R. *For* 1864 *read* 1846.
116 **Apologie** for the, *etc., is by* [E. Bohun].
117 **Apology** for the liturgy, *etc., is by* [S. Horsley].
Apostate, The. *For* Shiel *read* Sheil.
118 **Appeal** on, *etc., is by* [M. Davidoff].
Appeal to the people of Eng. *is by* [C. Fleming].
Appeal to the unprejudiced *is by* [T. Gordon].
Appellate jurisdiction *is by* [G. Moir].
121 **Arabia.** *Hist. and Antiq.* *See also.* *Add* **Zin-ud-Din.**
124 **Arborea.** *For* VESME *read* BAUDI DI VESME.
Arcana Gallica *is by* [J. Oldmixon].
132 **Argumentum** *is by* [E. Cooke].
136 **Aristoteles.** RAUMER, F. L. G. von. *For* 1827 *read* 1828.
138 **Arithmetic.** WALGRAVE, W. *For* 17— *read* 167-.
142 **Arnott, J.** *Same.* *For* hand *read* fluid.
146 **Artists.** VASARI, G. *Eng.* *For* 1851. 2 v. *read* 1850-52. 5 v.
149 **Arts, Useful.** URE, A. Dictionary. *For* 1839 *read* 1839-44.
— *Same.* *Before* Boston *insert* 4th ed.
152 **Asher.** *For* G. M. *read* Georg M.
156 **Assolant, J. B. F.** Un Quaker. *For* 1867 *read* 1866.
157 **Astronomical** journal. *For* 1829 *read* 1849; *for* 1849 *read* 1851.
161 **At home,** *etc.*; by B. Taylor. *For* 1862 *read* 1860-62.
167 **Atterbury, F.** Letters. *After* 1869 *insert* v. 8. 1806.
168 **Aubert, J.** DUCHESNE, J. *is author of* AD ejus, *etc.*
Audubon, J. J. Birds. *For* 1827-38 *read* 1828-39.
174 **Austria.** VIENNA. AK. D. WISS. Monumenta. *For* 1853 *read* 1854.
175 **Authentic** narrative, 1810 *is by* [G. Veeson].
Authority, The, *etc., is by* [E. Synge].
Autobiography. *For* N. G. Chamberlain, *read* N. H. Chamberlain.
176 *For* **Avezac-Macaya** *read* **Avezac de Castera Macaya.**
180 **Babylon's** fall. *For* 1565 *read* 1655.
Bacchanalia *is by* [C. Darby].
182 **Bacon, F.** Works. *Same.* Ed. by J. Spedding. *For* 1857-56 *read* 1857-59.
183 **Bacon, L.** *For* Answer *read* Reply.
194 **Ballou, H.** WHITTEMORE, T. *For* 1854 *read* 1854-55.
203 **Banford, Joseph.** B.'s lib. ser. *For* 6 v. *read* 8 v.
206 **Baratariana** *was ed. by* [Rev. — Simpson].
210 **Barfoot, P.** *After* directory *insert* (Vol. 1, 3, 3d ed.); *for* 1790 *read* 1790 [—97].
212 **Barnard, J.** *For* Letter *read* LETTER.
216 **Barrell,** *Miss.* *For* 1806 *read* 1800.
Barrell, Joseph. *Before* Statement of facts *insert* BARRELL, C., *and others.*
Before True statement *insert* JOY, B.
Barrier treaty *is by* [F. Hare].
219 **Barthélemy, J. J.** Voyage. *After* Paris *read* an VII [1798].
Barthold, F. W. *For* Mullenweder *read* Wullenweber.
222 **Barton,** *Brig. Gen.* Wm. On the device. *For* 1869 *read* 1866.
Baruffaldi, G. De poetis. *For* 1699 *read* 1723.
224 **Bastile.** RAVAISSON, F. *For* 1866 *read* 1866-79. 10 v.
228 **Baviera, M. A. W.** *Omit the entry.*
230 **Bayonet.** *Omit the entry* MCCLELLAN, G. B., *etc.*
235 **Beauties** of Fox, *etc., is by* [G. Chalmers].
239 **Beechdale.** *For* 1867 *read* 1868.
241 **'Beggynhof'** (*sic*) *is by* [Mrs. W. P. Byrne].
242 **Belgium.** *Descr.* NARRATIVE, *etc., is by* EATON, C. A.
— - TROLLOPE, F. *For* 1835 *read* 1834.
243 — *Hist.* RELIGION *is by* DESROCHES, J.
Belgrand. *For* E. *read* Marie François **Eugène** *and for* **Paris** *read* **Seine, Préfecture de la.**
247 **Belles-lettres** rep. and mag. *For* 1819-20 *read* 1820.
249 **Beneden, P. J. van.** *For* v. 1 *read* v. 2.
254 **Bentham, J.** HAZLITT, W. *For* v. 5. 1859 *read* 1825. *After* Bentley, R. *insert d.* 1742.
— Designs *is by* **Bentley, R.,** *Jr., d.* 1782.
255 **Benton, T. H.** *For* 1789-1856 *read* 1789-1836.
262 **Berridge, J.** *After* *Same* *insert* New ed.; *for* Cheerful *read* added, Chearful.
265 **Bethell, S.** *For* N., W. *read* W., W.
266 **Beust, F. F.** The Austro-Hungarian Empire *is by* DE WORMS, H.
Beverley, R. Hist. of Va. *French.* *For* Paris *read* Orléans.
268 **Biarmland.** *Omit the entry.*
274 **Bible.** DWIGHT, T. *Same.* *For* **Melmoth,** C. *read* **Pratt, S. J.**

 CORRECTIONS

284 **Bible.** *N. T. Criticism.* WETSTEIN, J. J. *For* 1746 *read* 1764.
295 **Bibliomania,** 1867, *is by* [J. T. Brown].
Bibliotheca Amer., 1789, *is by* [A. Homer].
299 **Bigamy.** *For* Fielding *read* Feilding.
302 *For* **Bingham,** *Capt.* read **Bingham,** *Hon. Capt.* D. A.
303 **Biography.** *Biographies.* BOYHOOD *is by* EDGAR, J. G.
304 — *Dictionaries.* THOMAS, J. *After* 1870 *insert* 2 v.
307 **Bishop of Oxford** *is by* C. E. K.
308 Bit o'writin *is by* [J.(?) Banim].
311 **Blackstone,** *Sir* W. BIOG. hist. *is by* [D. Douglas].
314 *For* **Blakeley,** *Rev.* A. *read* **Blakely,** *Rev.* A.
317 Blome. *For* Robert *read* Richard.
318 **Blood-letting.** TURNER, W. *For n.p.*, 1851 *read n.t.p.* [N. Y., 1851.]
324 **Bohemia.** TRAVELS. *After* 1857 *insert* 2 v.
328 **Bollman,** Erick *and* **Bollman,** Justus Erick *are the same man.*
Bologna. *For* ZECCHI, J. *read* ZECCHI, G.
329 *After* **Bonaparte,** C. L. J. L. omit *Prince of Canino.* Charlemagne, *etc.*, *and* Memoirs *are by* Bonaparte, Lucien, *Prince of Canino.*
330 **Bondone,** G. di. *For* Canzone, *etc.*, *read See* **Giotto.**
331 **Bonifacius** *or* **Winfred.** Opera. *For* 1845 *read* 1844.
332 **Book** about, *etc.* *For* **Hope,** A. R. *read* **Moncrieff,** R. H.
Book, The. *After* N. L. R. *insert* [Mrs. Ellen Ranyard].
352 **Boston** republican. *Before* republican *insert* daily; add *Note.* Continued as Congregational review.
Boston weekly messenger. *For* 26–27, 29 *read* 26–29.
Boswell, H. For *n.d. read* [1785].
Botany. PULTENEY, R. Hist. of botany. *Omit the entry.*
355 — *For* WILLDENOW, D. C. *read* WILLDENOW, K. L.
369 **Bradshaw,** A. *For* v. 4 *read* v. 15.
375 **Brazil.** *Descr.* YVES. For *d'Evreaux* read *d'Evreux.*
377 **Bremen** lectures. *Contents.* *For* **Zockler,** O. *read* **Zoeckler,** O.
Brentano, L. *For* **Smith,** T. *read* **Smith,** J. T.
379 **Brewer,** J. S., *and* **Bullen,** W. *For* 3 v. *read* 5 v.
For Brewer, John *read* Brewer, John M.
381 **Brief** exam. into, *etc.*, *is perhaps by* [G. Rose].
386 **British** and f. med. rev. by J. Forbes. *For* 1836 *read* 1836–47.
396 **Brown,** A. G. Sketches, *etc.* *Omit the entry.*
398 **Brown,** J., *d.* 1787. An exposition. *For* 1827 *read* 1824.
403 **Brucker,** J. J. Notitia. *For* 1627, 1628, 1629, 1630 *read* 1727, *etc.*
404 **Brunnich,** M. T. *For* Morton *read* Martinus.
405 **Brunswick,** [Theatre], The *is by* [C. Thomson].
Brutus, *pseud.* WEAKNESS *is by* WEBSTER, P.; *add Same.* (*In his* Polit. essays. 1791.)
406 **Bryant,** J. C. *For* 1849 *read* 1847.
411 **Budget,** The, *is by* [Col. R. Torrens].
422 **Burke,** E. Beauties *is* [by G. Chalmers].
429 **Burr,** *Col.* A. WOOD, J. *Before* N. Y. *insert* 2d ed. corr. with notes.
Burrill, J. LETTER *is by* B—t, F—l.
430 **Burrows,** *Sir* J. *Omit the entry.*
432 **Bush** wanderings *is by* [H. W. Wheelwright].
439 **Cabinet,** The. *For n.d. read* [1811].
442 **Cæsar,** C. J. Quæ extant. *Eng.* Tr., [with] disc. *For* 1774 *read* 1755.
443 **Cairn,** The, *was ed. by* [Lady N. H. Nicholas].
Calabria. CALABRIA *is by* TAVEL, D. de.
447 **Caledonian** comet *is by* [J. Taylor].
451 **Calumet Co.** Omit *Cal.*
452 **Calvin,** J. *For* TOMLIN, G. read TOMLINE, G.; *before* London *insert* 6th ed.
Calvinus, A. Add *See also* **Servetus,** M.
458 **Campagne** du roy. *Omit* P. V.
464 **Canada.** *Hist.* Smyth, *Sir* J. C. *For* 1775 *read* 1755.
466 **Canale,** M. G. *For* Michel *read* Michele; *for* 1856 *read* 1857.
467 **Candid** investigation *is by* [G. Rous].
Candid retrospect. *For* 1830 *read* 1780.
473 **Capital punishment.** *For* PHILANTHROPOS *pseud. read* LADD, W.
— SIMON, J. *For* 1867 *read* 1869.
476 **Carey,** H. C. Principles of social sci. *For* 1853 *read* 1858.
477 **Carey,** M. The crisis. For *Same* read The crisis; an appeal to the good sense of the nation; *and after* No. 1, 2 *add.* 3d ed. Phila., 1832. 8°.
— Protecting system. *For* Phila., 1829 *read* [Phila., 1829.]
484 **Carson,** A. Answer. *For* 1807 *read* 1809.
488 **Case** of allegiance *is by* [S. Marsters]; *for* 1789 *read* 1689.
Case of an, *etc.*, *is by* [G. Legh].
489 **Casey,** S. *For* 1862 *read* 1863, 62.
Cashmere. IRELAND. *For* W. H. *read* J. B.
490 **Casserius,** J. *After* Linder *insert* v. 1.

491 **Castel,** W. Petition. *For* 1636 *read* 1836; *for* 1836 *read* 1844.
492 **Castle** builders. *For* 1844 *read* 1864.
Castil Blaze, B. *Omit the entry.*
496 **Cathedrals.** WINKLES, B. *Before* London *insert* (Vol. 3 new ed.); *for n.d. read* [1835-] 1851.
497 **Catholic Church.** *Prayer books.* GARDEN of the soul, *etc.*, *is by* CHALLONER, R.
498 — *Doctr., etc.* WILMOT, *Judge.* Transfer the entry to *Doctr., etc. Protestant authors.*
— AGREEMENT *is by* GOTHER, J.
— - ANSWER *is by* J. WILLIAMS.
499 — - DEFENCE *is by* MATHER, S.
501 — *Periodicals.* U. S. Cath. mag. *For* C. L. White *read* C. I. White.
Cath. Ch. in Gr. Brit. ADDRESS *is perhaps by* C. P. Cooper.
503 **Catholic** emancipation, 1805, *is by* [— Corneille].
505 **Cause,** *etc.*, *is by* [J. Allen].
506 **Cavalier,** The. *is ascribed by Halkett and Laing to* T. Roscoe, Jr.
507 **Caveat** against the, *etc.*, *is ascribed by Halkett and Laing to* J. Peirce.
508 **Cayet,** P. V. P. **Michaud.** *Dele* v. 13.
509 **Cecil** Dreeme. *For* S. *read* T.
511 **Censura** temp. *Before* London *insert* [by S. Parker]; Oct. 1708, July 1709; *for* 1708 *read* 1708–09. 2 nos.
512 **Certain** cases, *etc.*, *is by* [J. Scott].
515 **Chalcocondyles,** L. *Same.* *For* v. 42 *read* v. 45.
520 **Chandler,** T. B. What think ye. *For* S. Galloway *read* J. Galloway.
522 **Channing,** W. E. REVIEW of [his] disc. *For* 1826 *read* 1825.
525 **Character** of a trimmer. *For* 1687 *read* 1688.
Character of an honest, *etc.*, *is by* [R. Peers].
Character of an independent, *etc.*, *is by* [T. Gordon].
Characteristics of men, *etc.*, *is by* [A. A. Cooper]; *dele* the.
526 **Charles I.** WAGSTAFFE, T. *For* Βασιλική *read* Εασιλική [*sic*].
— WORDSWORTH, C. King Charles I. *For* Ikon *read* Icon.
531 **Charleston** mercury. *After* 61 *add* 63.
536 **Chatsworth** *is by* [P. G. Patmore].
539 **Cheetham,** J. WOOD, J. *Omit* 2d ed. N. Y. *and insert after* 1802 (*In his* Correct statement.)
547 **Chevalier** de St. G. *For* no. 67 *read* no. 68.
549 **Child,** F. J. Obs., *etc.* Gower's Confessio. *Note. Omit* 1864.
555 **China.** *Descr.* WRIGHT, G. N. *For n.d. read* [1843].
557 **China.** *Literature.* ÆSOPUS. After Sloth *add* [R. Thom].
564 **Christianissimus,** *etc.*, *is by* [M. Nedham].
568 **Christianity.** *Evid.* POWELL, B. *For* 1738 *read* 1838.
— TINDALL, M. Address. *Same.* *For* 1830 *read* 1730.
572 **Chrysal.** *For* C. Johnstone *read* C. Johnston.
574 **Church,** The, in perils *is by* [S. Wright].
575 **Church of Eng.** *Liturgies.* ACCOMPT *is by* BAXTER, R.
— - APOLOGY *is by* HORSLEY, S.
— - DEFENCE is *by* FOWLER, E.
— - DIALOGUE *is by* TOWERS, J.
576 — *Bibl.* *After* FRÈRE, E. *insert* B.
577 — *Convocation.* DISCOURSE *is by* TENISON, T.
578 — *Establishment.* BRIEF *is by* COLLIER, J.
— *Doctrine.* AGREEMENT *is by* GOTHER, J.
581 **Church** review. *For* Vol. 1 *read* Vol. 1–20; *for* 1848, *read* 1848–69. 20 v.; *add Note.* From Vol. 11 called American quarterly church review.
582 **Churchill,** C. *Before* London *insert* 3d ed; *for* 1744 *read* 1744–46.
Churchman, J., *of Nottingham* is author of ACCOUNT, *etc.*
Churchman, The. *Before* Mar. *insert* Vol. 5–28.
596 **Clark,** C. On the edge. *Omit the entry.*
599 **Classical** antiq. *For* VOIGHT, G. read VOIGT, G.
Classical philology. VONCK, C. V. *For* 1844 *read* 1744.
602 **Clayton,** J., *d.* 1773. *For* v. 17, 1673 *read* v. 17, 18, 1694–95.
605 **Clergy** (Ch. of Eng., *etc.*). APPEAL *is by* FLEMING, C.
— CLERGY-MAN'S advocate *is by* LEWIS, T.
606 **Cleveland,** a tale *is by* [Mrs. M. Gartshore].
610 **Clyffards,** *etc.*, *is by* [J. Payn].
613 **Cobbett,** W. *For* ROGERS, J. E. K. *read* ROGERS, J. E. T.
— WATSON, J. S. *For* Wilks *read* Wilkes.
621 **Col.** of scarce tracts. *Contents.* *For* **Whateley,** T. *read* **Whately,** T.
625 **Collier,** J. P. Shakespeare's lib. *Contents.* v. 2. *For* Story *read* Tale; *for* of *read* in.
627 **Colloquies.** M. A. Manning. *The initial M. is doubtful.*
630 **Colombia.** COLOMBIA *is by* WALKER, —.

631 **Colomer**, V. M. *For* 2 de Junio *read* 28 de Junio.
Colonies. *After* SAINTE-CROIX *for* C. E. J., *etc.*, *read* G. E. J., *etc.*
633 **Columbiad**, The, a poem, *etc.*, *is by* R. Snowden.
634 **Combe**, G. Constitution. *For* 1829 *read* 1838.
Comedian *is by* [T. Cooke].
Comedias. *Contents.* *For* Oliveriza *read* Olivenza; *for* dotor *read* doctor.
635 **Coming** rest *is by* [D. Pae].
Coming struggle *is by* [D. Pae].
636 **Commerce.** Considerations *is by* RAIKES, J.
637 **Commerce.** *General works.* *For* USTERIZ *read* USTARIZ.
642 **Conchology.** *Dictionary.* TURTON, W. *For* 1831 *read* 1819.
649 **Confederate.** *Periodicals.* MISCEL. newspapers. *Namely.* *For* Aug. 7 *read* June 11; *for* Oct. 10 *read* Oct. 11.
652 **Congregational** review. *Omit the Note.*
657 **Conscience**, H. Les heures. *For* 1864 *read* 1867.
Conscience. *Cases, etc.* CASE *is by* LEGH, G.
658 **Considerations** on the late, disturbances, *is by* [T. L. O'Beirne].
Considerations on the pract., *etc.*, *is by* [J. Shore].
Considerations on the pres. Germ. war *is by* [I. Mauduit].
Considerations on the propr., 1774 *is by* [E. Law].
Considerations upon the American, *etc.*, *is ascribed by Halkett and Laing to* J. Galloway.
660 **Constipation.** Obstinate constip. *is by* WARTON,—.
665 **Cook**, *Rev.* F. C. *For* **Thomson, T.** *read* **Thomson, W.**
672 **Copenhagen.** **K.** Comm. *Contents*, v. 3. **Repholtz**, M. G. P. *For* Barontie *read* Baroniet.
694 **Crack** upon crack *is by* [R. L'Estrange].
697 **Crasso**, N., *the younger.* *For* pt. 1 *read* pt. 4.
Craven. DIALECT *is by* CARR, *Rev.* W.
698 **Crayon**, The. *For* 1861 *in both cases read* 1860.
700 **Crèvecœur**, J. *After French* read *with add.*; *for* 2 v. *read* 3 v.
703 **Crisis** of the, *etc.*, *is by* [J. Stephen].
Critical obs. on books *is by* [T. Howes].
713 **Cultivator.** *For* 1834–53 *read* 1834–54.
Culloden papers *was ed. by* [— Duff].
717 *Before* **Cup** of tea, *etc.*, *insert* **Cuoq**, *Rev.* **A.** Etudes philologiques sur quelques langues sauvages de l'Amérique; par N. O. Montreal, 1866. 8°.
718 **Cursory** animad. *is by* [A. Moseley].
Cursory obs. *is by* [W. Stevens].
724 **Cyrus**, *the younger.* *Same.* Mit Anmerk. *For* 1851 *read* 1854.
728 **Dalton**, J. *Prof.* WILKINSON, T. T. *For* v. 17 *read* v. 12.
732 **Danegeld.** SHORT account *is by* WEBB, P. C.
Dangerous guest, *etc.*, *is by* [H. Jackson].
735 **Danubian** principalities. DANUBIAN, *etc.*, *is by* SKENE, J. H.
736 **Dapper.** *For* Olfert *read* Olif.
737 *For* **Barracott**, R. *read* **Darracott**, R.
Dartmouth, The. *Before* Vol. 5 *insert* **1843–44.**
738 **Darwin**, C. R. Zoology. *For* the Beagle *read* H. M. S. Beagle; *for* 1838–43 *read* 1838–42.
739 **Dati**, C. R. Prose. *Contents*, v. 5. **Varchi**, B. *For* 23, 24, 25 *read* 33, 34, 35.
741 **Davenport**, R. A. Narratives, v. 1. *For* Vertibi *read* Viterbi.
Davers, M. M. Inquiry *is by* B., J.
743 **Davies**, S. Sermons. 6th ed. *For* 1777 *read* 1767.
754 **Defence** of Dr. Clarke's 'Demonstration,' *etc.*, *is by* [J. Clarke].
767 **Derby** ministry. M. Rochester *is pseud. for* W. C. M. Kent.
770 **Desor**, Edouard. Esquisse. *For* 1847 *read* 1861.
Destiny. *For* Mary *read* Susan Edmonstone.
776 **Dialogue** between a clergyman, *etc.*, *is by* [J. Disney].
Dialogue between two gentlemen, *etc.*, *is by* [J. Towers].
781 **Didron.** Annales. *For* 1854 *read* 1844.
787 **Directions**, *etc.*, *is by* [J. Wesley].
Discourse of the, *etc.*, *is by* [E. Robinson].
789 **Dissenters.** ADDRESS *is by* AIKIN, J.
791 **Dissertation** on Jacob's, *etc.*, *is by* [J. Skinner].
Dissertation on the ancient *is by* [J. Towne].
793 **Dobson.** *For* Wm. *read* Thomas.
798 **Domestic economy.** *After* WARREN *read* Mrs. E.
806 **Dragoon.** *For* MONDSIÉR *read* MONDÉSIR.
816 **Du Couret**, L. L'Arabie. *Eng.* *Before* N. Y. *insert* [by A. Dumas, pseud.].
822 **Dumas**, A. D. *For* Aveuglement *read* Avengement.
824 **Dumas**, A. D. Une vie. *Before* Paris *insert* Nouv. éd.
834 **Duty** of praying, *etc.*, *is by* [W. Romaine].
835 **Dwight**, T. Theology. *For* 1828 *read* 1827.
836 **Dyspepsia.** *For See* **Indigestion** *read See* **Digestion.**
838 **Early English Text Soc.** *Namely.* v. 10. *For* **La Courdrette** *read* **La Coudrette**; v. 23. Dan Michel's *is by* **Lorens**, *Frère.*
— *After* **Earnshaw**, T. *insert and* **Arnold**, J.; *for* E. *read* them.
840 **East** and West India sugar *is by* [Z. Macaulay].
842 **Eastern Empire.** *For* WILKEN, — *read* WILKEN, F.
848 **Ecclesiastical** polity. AUTHORITY, *etc.*, *is by* SYNGE, E.
849 — ESSAY, *etc.*, *is by* ALEXANDER, J.
850 — WALCH, C. G. F. *For* G. *read* W.
851 **Eclectic** journal of med. *After* Nov. *insert* Dec.
855 **Edmonds**, C. R. *For* 1835 *read* 1835–36. 2 v.
859 **Education.** Amer. educ. year-book. *For* Boon *read* Boston.
864 **Egypt.** *Antiq. and Arts.* ANTIQUITIES *is by* OSBURN, W.
— WILKINSON, *Sir* J. G. Manners, *etc.* *Before* London *insert* Vol. 1, 2d ed.; *for* 1837 *read* 1842, 37.
870 **Elgin marbles.** *For* HEYDEN, B. R. *read* HAYDON, B. R.
874 **Ellicott**, C. J. Scripture. *For* **Thomson, T.** *read* **Thomson, W.**
876 **Ellis**, G. E. Life. *For* v. 12. 1846 *read* v. 22. 1847.
881 **Emerson**, *Mrs.* E. *For* 1808 *read* 1809.
Emerson, G. B. Remarks. *For* 1831 *read* 1839.
884 **Emery**, W. H. Report. *For* 1848 *read* 1857–59. 2 v.
889 **England.** *Antiq.* BOSWELL, H. *For n.d. read* [1785].
896 **England** and France *is by* [B. Disraeli].
England's conversion *is by* [R. Manning].
898 **English ballads**, *etc.* *Polit. songs.* WRIGHT, T. Polit. poems. *For* 1859 *read* 1859–61.
902 **English** humor. *For* p. 912 *read* p. 914.
905 **Eng. lang.** *Gram.* WELLS, W. H. *For* Andover, 1846 *read* Boston, 1854.
910 — - WORCESTER, S. *After t.p.w. insert* [1834.)
911 **Eng. period. lit.** Collegian. *Omit the entry.*
915 **Englishwoman** in America, The, *is by* [Miss I. Bird].
916 **Enquiry** into the conduct of a, *etc.*, *is by* [H. Cotes].
Enquiry into the conduct of our, *etc.*, *is by* [W. Pulteney].
Enquiry into the present state of affairs, *is by* [G. Burnet].
Enquiry into the reasons, *etc.*, *is by* [B. Hoadly].
920 **Episc.** ordination. EPISCOPAL, *etc.*, *is by* HAMILTON, W.
Epistle to Curio *is by* [M. Akenside].
926 **Essay** in, *etc.*, *is by* [A. Lee]; *for* 1765 *read* 1764.
Essay on church government, *etc.*, *is by* [J. Alexander].
Essay on ways, *etc.*, *is by* [F. Fauquier].
Essay towards preventing, *etc.*, *is by* [S. Berkeley].
Essay towards vindicating, *etc.* *For See* **Sykes, A. A.** *read* [by T. Church]. London, 1737. 8°.
927 **Essays** on public, *etc.*, *is by* [D. Williams].
Essential principles, *etc.*, *is by* [J. Gray].
928 **Essex Inst.** Hist. col. *Contents*, v. 2, 7, 9. *For* W., E. S. *read* **Waters**, E. S.; — v. 2. Materials for a hist. of the Ropes family *is by* **Waters**, E. S.; — Notices of S. Ingersol *is by* **Bentley**, W.
943 **Europe, North of.** *Descr.* *For* STEWART, C. W. V. *read* VANE, C. W. S.
947 **Everett**, E. Address, Dec. 19. *After* **Winthrop**, T. *add* L.
— Speech on the proposed, *etc.* *For* 1854 *read* 1832.
948 **Every** Saturday. *After* 1866–69 *add* 72, 73.
950 **Excellent** woman *is by* [T. Dorrington]; *for* 1692 *read* 1692–95. 2 v.
951 **Experienced** angler *is by* [R. Venables].
Eyck, J. and L. van. *For* Lambert *read* Hubert.
Eye, A. v. Das bürgerliche. *For* 1866 *read* 1868.
Eye. ART, *etc.*, *is by* BEER, G. H.
952 **Eyre**, Jane. *Omit the entry.*
963 *For* **Farmer**, A., *etc.*, *read* **Farmer**, A. W. *See* W., A.; *and omit the next entry.*
For **Farmer's** monthly journal *read* **Farmer's** library and monthly journal; *for* Vol. 1–3, *etc.*, *read See* **Monthly** journal of agriculture.
966 **Fathers** and sons. *For* I. *read* J.
971 **Female education.** WILLARD, E. Address to the public. *For* 1809 *read* 1819.
976 **Ferreira**, A. Poemas. *After* 1771 *insert* 2 v.
Ferri, A. De sclopetorum, *etc.* *For* 1590 *read* 1610.
983 **Fielding**, H. Works. *For* 1813 *read* 1816.
989 **Fishbough**, W. *After* Pt. 1 *for* Microcosm *read* Macrocosm.
992 **Fitchburg.** FACTS. *Omit the entry.*
993 **Flaccus**, V. *The 2d entry belongs under* **Flachat**, E.
996 **Fletcher**, A. Lectures. *For* Vol. 3 *read* Vol. 2, 3 *and for* 1830 *read* 1829, 30.
997 **Fletcher**, Phineas. *For* Grossart *read* Grosart.
1002 **Florian**, J. P. C. de. Claudine. *For* Sinclair *read* Sainclair.
1003 **Florida.** *Hist.* The impartial inquirer *is not by* MADISON, J., *but anonymous.*

For GARCILASO DE LA VEGA *read* VEGA, G. de la.
1006 **Folard**, J. C. de. For *See, etc., read* (*In* **Traverse**, J. V., *baron* de. Etude militaire, v. 2. 1758.)
Folra, J. J. *Omit the entry.*
1010 **Force**, P. Col. of tracts. *For* 1836 *read* 1836-46.
1018 **Foster**, *Sir* M. ANDREWS. *After Dr. insert* J.
Foster, T. Obs. *For* **Foster** *read* **Forster**.
1024 **Fraehn**, C. M. *For* v. 1. 1836 *read* v. 3. 1836.
1026 **France**. *Codes.* MAURICE, —. *For* 1840 *read* 1841.
1043 — *History.* VOLTAIRE, F. M. A. de. *Eng. For* 1780 *read* 1779–81.
1044 — - NÉGOCIATIONS: *Omit the entry.*
— - RIVAROL, A. *After* national *insert* [1789].
1048 — - VAULABELLE, A. de. *This entry should be under the heading Restoration, etc.*
1049 — - STERN, D. *Omit the entry.*
1057 — *Period.* Indépendance. *For* P. *read* B.
— - Nord. *For* P. *read* B.
1059 — *Philosophy. Note. For* **Deslisle** *read* **Delisle de Sales**, J. B. C. I.
1063 — *Statistics.* SCHNITZLER. *For* P. *read* H.
1065 **Francis**, P. *For* SCOTT, J. *read* WARING, J. S.
1068 **Franklin Co.**, *Mass.* WILLIAMS, S. W. *For* v. 1. 1808 *read* v. 7. 1848.
1073 **Free trade.** AMERICAN system *is by* HALE. N.
1073 — *After* WALTER, E. *insert pseud. for* DELMAR, A.
1074 **Freeman**, J. Descr. of Truro. *For* v. 5 *read* v. 3.
1079 **Freund**, W. *For* 1855 *read* 1855–56.
1093 **G.**, J. Journey, *etc.*, *is by* **Green**, J.
G., R. Instructor, *etc.*, *is by* **Gardiner**, R.
G., R. Virginia's cure. *For* 1836 *read* **1844.**
1095 **Galaxy.** *For* 1866 *and* 1868 *read* 1867; *before* N. Y. *insert* Vol. 3-18.
1098 **Galland**, A. Bibliothèque, *etc. Omit the entry.*
1105 **Garnet**, H. *For* 1678 *read* 1679.
1110 **Gaul.** THIERRY, A. S. D. Histoire. Nouv. éd. *Omit the entry.*
— VERDY DU VERNOIS, A. M. F. de. *For* 1812 *read* 1802.
— **Gay**, C. *Contents.* Documentos. *For* 1844–54 *read* 1844–52.
1136 **Germany.** *Hist. Corr. After* SODEN, C. T. von read *and* TOBIESEN, H. A.
1137 — *Dict. Lat.* SCHELLER, I. J. G. *After* 1805 *insert* 5 pts.
1149 **Gibson**, E. ADDRESS *and* SECOND address *are by* TINDAL, M.
1156 **Girard**, S. For *Same* read OUTLINE of the case and heads of argument by counsel of appellants].
1163 **Gloucestershire.** *For* WASHBURN *read* WASHBOURN.
1164 **God.** ARGUMENT *is by* LOWMAN, M.
1169 **Goethe.** *Biog.* VIEHOFF, H. *After* Leben *insert* 3e Aufl.; *and for* 1828 *read* 1858.
1170 **Golden** legacy. *For* H. F. Moore *read* H. J. Moore.
1176 **Gordon**, *Ld.* G. *For* VINCENT, W. *read* HOLCROFT, T.
1178 **Gorton**, S. *Same. For* 1836 *read* 1846.
1180 **Gothic architecture.** YOUNG, M. *For* v. 15. 1828 *read* v. 3. 1789.
1181 **Gould**, H. F. *For* 1841. 2 v. *read* 1839–41. 3 v.
Gouldbourn, E. M. *Omit the entry.*
1184 **Grace.** *After* WHITEFIELD, G. *insert* Letter to Wesley. Boston, 1740. 8°.; — *For* Free grace, *etc.*, *read* FREE grace, *etc.*
1206 **Gr. Brit.** *Court of Exchequer.* MODERN practice *is by* Y., B.; *for* in *read* of.
1218 — *Parl. Accounts, etc.* East India. *For* Sir T. *read* Sir C.
1220 — - *Acts, etc.* Chronolog. table. *For* Shute *read* Chute.
1227 — *Biog. See also. For* p. 590 *read* p. 960.
1234 — *Financial disc.* CAUSE, [1660–1846] *is by* ALLEN, J.
1238 — *Hist.* WRIGHT, T. *For* the reign of Henry VIII. *read* that of Richard III.
1239 — ROGERUS *de Hoveden.* Chronica. *For* 1861 *read* 1868–71. 4 v.
1240 — - VERGILLIO, P. *For* 1864 *read* 1844–46.
1250 **Gr. Brit.** *Politics.* DUTCH. 1713 *is by* WITHERS, J.
— - ESSAY, 1721 *is by* BERKELEY, G.
— - ENQUIRY, 1727 *is by* HOADLY, B.
— - DEFENCE, 1729 *is by* HOADLY, B.
— - CONDUCT, 1734 *is by* HERVEY, J.
— - ENQUIRY, 1734 *is by* PULTENEY, W.
— - APPEAL, 1739 *is by* GORDON, T.
— - CONSIDERATIONS, 1739 *is by* LYTTELTON, G.
1251 — - CHARACTERISTICS, 1758 *is by* WALLACE, R.
— - CONSIDERATIONS, 1763 *is by* RUFFHEAD, G.
— - ENQUIRY, 1766 *is by* COTES, H.
— - EXAMINATION, 1766 *is by* LLOYD, C.
— - CONSTITUTIONAL, 1766 *is by* JONES, W.
1252 — - TICKELL, R. 1778. *For* M----ty's *read* M----y's; *after* P--l-----t omit 1778.
— - TICKELL, R. 1779. *For* M----- *read* M----y's; *for* P--l---- *read* P--l----t.
— - CANDID, 1784 *is by* ROUS, G.
1253 — - YORKE, H., 1793. *For* to *read* that.
1255 — *Politics.* COMPRESSED. 1814 *is by* ATCHESON, N.
— - COUNTRY, 1830 *is by* BROUGHAM, H.
1256 — - ENGLAND, 1832 *is by* DISRAELI, B.
1257 — *Registers.* BARFOOT, P. *After* Vol. 1, *insert* 3; *for* [1791, 90] *read* [1790–97].
1268 **Greece.** *Philosophy.* ZELLER, E. *After* 59 *insert* 62, *and for* 4 v. *read* 3 v. in 4 pts.
1269 — *Religion.* SMITH, W. For *See Biography* (p. 1260) read *See* **Classical biography** (p. 599).
1270 — *Education. For* WILLIARD, E. *read* WILLARD, E.
1272 **Greeley**, H. The Amer. conflict. *For* 1861–64 *read* 1860–65; *and for* Hartf., 1864 *read* Hartford, 1864–66. 2 v.
1293 *For* **Guarda**, J. M. *read* **Guardia**; *for* 1869 *read* 1867.
1310 **Hagenbach**, K. R. Compendium. *For* 1858 *read* 1858–59.
1325 **Hamilton**, J., *b.* 1814. Life in earnest. For *n. d.* read [1845].
1327 **Hamor**, R. *After* 1614 *read* London, 1615, [*reprinted* Albany, 1860].
1328 **Hampshire Co.**, *Mass. For* BLISS, C. *read* BLISS, G.
1329 **Handbook** for Switzerland, *etc. After* Piedmont *insert* [by W. Brockedon].
1332 **Hanway**, —. Advice *is by* **Hanway**, Jonas, *the next author.*
1344 **Harris**, J. Navigantium bibl. *Contents*, v. 2, b. 1. *After* **Willoughby** *read* F. *for* T., *and* through *for* thro'.
1345 **Harris**, J., *d.* 1719. *For* 1708 *read* 1708–10.
1355 **Harv. Coll.** *President.* Addresses, 1869. *For* J. S. Wright *read* J. S. White.
1364 **Hawkins**, *Sir* J. Last voyage. *For* 1562 *read* 1595.
1378 **Heeren**, A. H. L., *and* **Ukert**, F. A. *Contents. For* **Lappenberg**, F. M. *read* **Lappenberg**, J. M.
1385 **Henrietta Maria**, *Q. of Eng.* LA FAYETTE, M. M. P. Histoire, *etc.*, *is about* **Henrietta Anne**, *of Eng.*, *Duchesse d'Orléans.*
1390 **Heraldry.** *Before* BOUTELL, *etc.*, *insert* — BOKE of St. Albans. *See* **Heraldic** miscellanies (p. 1389).
1396 **Hernia.** WARREN, J. *For* Cure *read* Case.
1401 **Heuschling.** *For* Theodore *read* Theodose.
1403 *For* **Heyward**, J. H. *read* **Heywood**, J. H.
Hialmar. *Omit the entry.*
1405 **Hieronymus Sophronius**, E. *For* BOECKLER, O. *read* ZOECKLER, O.
Hierophant. *Before* N. Y. *insert* 1842–43.
1410 **Hill**, H. A. Decision. *For* senate *read* state.
1413 **Hilton**, Wm. *For* 1836 *read* 1846.
1425 **Hobson**, Wm. *For* JOHNSTON *read* JOHNSON.
1426 **Hodges**, R. M., *M.D.* Modern surgery. *For* Med. comm., v. 2, 1810 *read* Pub., v. 2. 1867.
1433 **Holland.** *Politics.* DUTCH, *etc.*, *is by* WITHERS, J.
1440 **Homerus.** WELCKER, F. G. *For* 1835–45 *read* 1835–49.
1450 **Horncastle.** *For* lake *read* soke.
1454 **Hosmer**, J. K. *For* 1861 *read* 1864.
1456 **Hour**, The, *etc. For* 1856 *read* 1860.
1459 **Howe**, R. To their excell. *For* 1796 *read* 1776.
Howe, *Sir* W. REPLY, *etc.*, *is by* GALLOWAY, J.
1475 **Hunt**, J. W. *For* 1856 *read* [1855].
1484 **Hydraulic engineering.** LEUPOLD, J. *After* 1774 *insert* 2 v.
1486 **Hydropathy.** WATER cure. *For* Augusta, [1798] *read* N. Y., London, 1848.
1493 **Ichthyology.** *For* BUSHMAN *read* BUSHNAN.
1499 **Independent.** *For* 1871 *read* 1875.
1504 **India.** *Hist.* REVIEW. *For* **1807** *read* **1806.**
1505 — *Missions.* BUCHANAN, C. Observations *is by* WARING, J. S.; *for* [1806] *read* [1807].
— - WARING, J. S. *After* strictures *insert* on the preface to Observations.
1507 — *Religion.* RAMMOHUN ROY. 2d defence. *Add Same.* Calcutta, 1844. 12°. **(E 133)**
— - SELLON. *For* v. 3. 1870 *read* v. 2. 1866.
1508 **Indian Ocean.** VINCENT, W. *After* 1807 *insert* 2 v.
1512 **Indians.** *Language. Gen. and miscel. After* O., N. insert *pseud. for* A. Cuoq.
— *Legends.* SCHOOLCRAFT, H. R. *After* 1839 *insert* 2 v.
1513 — *Origin. For* WORSLEY, J., *read* WORSLEY, I.
1514 **Inductive sciences.** WHEWELL, W. Philosophy. *After* sci. *read* New ed., with corr., add., and app. London, 1847. 2 v. 8°; *and add the new title* Novum organon renovatum; 2d pt. of Philos. of inductive sci. 3d ed., with add. London, 1858. 16°.
1517 **Ingleby.** *For* C. *read* Clement.
Ingomar *is by* E. F. J. von Muench-Bellinghausen.
Inman. *Before* London *insert* 2d ed.
1527 **Iona.** *Before* London *insert* (Vol. 1. 2d ed.).
1532 **Ireland.** *History.* SMITH. *Before* Oxford *insert* 2d ed.
— *Language.* SCURRY, J. *For* v. 16. 1830 *read* v. 15. 1828.

1534 — *Politics.* BARATARIANA. *After* [1767–62] *insert* [ed. by Rev. — Simpson].

For WELLESLEY, W. R. A. *read* WELLESLEY, W. P. T. L.

1539 **Istorie.** *For* 1723 *read* 1733.

1541 **Italy.** *Biography. See also. For* **Renata** *read* **Renée.**

1552 **Jackson,** James, *M.D.* Observations. *For* v. 7. 1848 *read* v. 6. 1841.

1554 **Jacobites.** *For* BEAUMONT, W. *read* BEAMONT, W.

1557 **Jamaica.** *Descr.* WILLIAMS, C. R. *For* in *read* through; *before* London *insert* 2d ed.

1558 **James,** E. P. Account. *For* 2 v. *read* 3 v.

1559 **James,** G. P. R. The stepmother. *After* 1845 *insert* 2 v.

1560 **Jameson,** *Mrs.* A. *Before* London *insert* 3d ed.

1562 **Janson,** O. Terror. *For* Voightland, *read* Voigtland.

1568 **Jefferson,** T. *For* LYNN, P. *read* LINN, W.

1570 **Jenkins,** J. S. Lives. *Contents. For* Gates, J. C. *read* Yates, J. C.

1571 **Jennie** Juneiana. *Omit the entry.*

1573 **Jesse,** Edward. Scenes. *After* hist. *insert* New. ed.

1575 **Jesuits.** (*Against the Jesuits.*) *See also. Add* **Campion,** E.

1577 **Jesus.** *Against the Deity.* ACCURATE *is by* NYE, S.

1579 — *Second Advent.* For *See* **Second Advent** read *See* **Millennium.**

1581 **Jews.** *Conversion.* CASE *is by* LESLIE, C.; *so also under Judaism and Christianity* (p. 1582).

1588 **Johnson.** *After* Lorenzo *add* D.

1590 *For* **Johnson,** G. *read* **Johnston,** G.

1594 **Jones,** J. H. *For* The knowledge *read* The kingdom.

1597 **Joseph** and his friends. *For* 1871 *read* 1870.

1601 **Journal** officiel. *Before* jan. *insert* juil. - déc. 1870.

— *Same. After* 1869 *insert* jan. - sept. 1870.

1606 **Jury.** Add *See also* **Trials.**

1608 **Juvarra,** F. Modello *is by* TAVIGLIANO, G. P. B., *conte* di.

1614 **Kazan.** *For* TERNEVELLI *read* TURNERELLI.

Keach, B. *Before* London *insert* 5th ed., corr. with add.

Keating, W. H. Narrative. *For* of the *read* of an.

1615 **Keenan,** S. *For* Montpelier *read* Montpellier.

1619 **Kennedy,** Q. *For Crosraguell* read *Crossraguell.*

Kennett. Antiquities. *Before* 1731 *insert* 9th ed.

1623 **Kertbeny,** K. M. *For* Karl *read* Károly.

1626 **King,** C. W. Natural history. *After* metals *insert* [2d ed.].

1638 **Knox,** J. Works, v. 3. *For* exhortation *read* exposition.

1639 **Koehler.** *For* K. F. *read* Karl Franz.

For **Koeklenyesdi** *read* **Koekenyesdi.**

1641 **Korff.** *For* M. *read* Modeste Andréevitch de.

1644 **Kutuzof,** M. L. G. SCHNITZLER, J. H. *For* 1865 *read* 1863.

Kyd, T. **Spanish.** Before *in* **Dodsley,** R. *insert in* Scott, *Sir* W. Anc. Brit. dr., v. 1. 1810.

1647 **Labor.** SIMON. *Before* Paris *insert* 3d ed.

1651 **La Cruz,** J. de. *Omit the entry and insert See* **Cruz Cano y Olmedilla,** J. de la.

Ladd, Wm. *After* Poems *add Note.* For five pamphlets *see* **Philanthropos.** *pseud.*

1658 **Lamb,** —. Stop. *Before* London *insert* 2d ed.

1660 **La Mennais.** Défense. *For* 1828 *read* 1321.

Lami, H. *For* Mirpickel *read* Mixpickel.

1663 **Land tenure.** *See also. For* **Inclosure** *read* **Enclosures.**

1664 **Land's End.** WHITE, W. *Before* London *insert* 2d ed.

Landscape painters. *For* HAMMERTON *read* HAMERTON.

1666 **Langsdorff.** Voyages. *For* 1813 *read* 1813–14. 2 v.

1667 **Language.** *Compar. Philol.* VEMBERGUE. *For* v. 12 *read* n. s., v. 7.

1669 **Lankester,** E. Vegetables. *Omit the entry.*

1670 **Lapham,** I. A. After *Same insert* entitled Wisconsin, its geography and topography.

1674 **Lascelles,** P. For *See* **Proceedings,** *etc.*, read *See* Cope, *Sir* J.

1676 **Lathrop,** Joseph. Stedfastness. *For* 1706 *read* [1806].

1678 **Latin language.** *Dict.* YOUNG, W. *The title should read* Lat.-Eng. and Eng.-Lat. dict. 9th ed. Dublin.

— *Dict. with def. in lang. other than Eng.* SCHELLER. *Before* Leipzig *insert* 3e Aufl.

1681 — *Synonyms.* RUTLAND. *For* 1613 *read* 1646.

1683 **Latrobe,** C. J. *For* Rambles in N. A. *read* Rambler in N. A.; *and before* London *insert* 2d ed.

1684 **Latter** day luminary. *For* Boston *read* Phila.

1685 *After* **Laurent** *insert* Pierre Louis.

1688 **Law.** *History.* PASTORET. *For* 1817–34 *read* 1817–37.

1690 **Law of nature.** ZACHARIAE, T. M. *Before* Breslau *insert* 2e Aufl.

1696 **Lechford,** T. Plain dealing. *The* Introd. and notes *are in the ed.* of 1867.

1697 **LeClerc,** N. G. C. 2d entry. *For* 35 *read* [94].

1700 **Lee,** T. J. For *See, etc.*, read 2d ed. Wash.,1853. 8°.

1704 **Leidy,** J. Descr. *For* 1853 *read* 1852.

1705 **Leighton,** R. Whole works. *For* 1823 *read* 1828.

1709 **Lennep,** J. D. von. *Same. For* 1808 *read* 1805.

Lenni Lenape Indians. *Language.* ZEISBERGER, D. *For* 1825 *read* 1830.

1712 **Leroux,** L. C. P. *Before* Dijon *insert* 2d ed.

1715 **Leslie,** *Sir* J. Omit *See also, etc.*

1716 **Lestrange,** B. de. *For* London *read* Londres.

1717 **Leti,** Gregorio. *Before* 12°. *insert* 2 v.

1721 *After* **Letters** addressed to C. Strong, *add* — *Same.* 2d ed. Phila., 1817. 8°.

1722 **Lettsom,** J. C. Apology. *Omit* 2d ed; *For* 1804 *read* 1803; *add* — *Same.* 2d ed. London, 1804. 8°. (B 821)

1725 **Lever,** C. J. Life. *For* 1855–57 *read* 1852–54.

1726 **Levy,** A. *For* v. 12 *read* v. 1, 2.

1729 **Liberator.** *For* 15 v. *read* 32 v.

1730 **Liberty.** REMARKS *is by* FERGUSON, A.

1731 **Liberty of conscience.** CHRISTIAN, **1664** *is by* FARNSWORTH, R.

— DIALOGUE, 1792 *is by* DISNEY, J.

1732 **Liberty of the press.** ESSAY, **1755** *is perhaps by* HAYTER, T.

— *For* SETIER, **181-** *and* **1815** *read* SÉTIER.

1733 **Libraries.** *Misc.* CASE *is by* COCHRANE J.

1757 **Literary** journal. *For* nos. 4, 11 *read* nos. 4, 6, 11.

Literary mag. and Amer. register. *For* 1807 *read* 1808.

1760 **Liver.** WEBER, J. E. *For* Hyatids *read* Hydatids.

1761 **Livermore,** E. St. L. *For* NEW HAMPSHIRE *read* UNITED STATES.

1766 **Locke,** D. S. *For* Swinging *read* Swingin; *for* circle *read* cirkle; *for* 1866 *read* 1867.

1768 **Locomotive engines.** SEWELL, J. *After* 1852–53 *insert* 2 v.

1769 **Loebell,** J. W. Ueber die Epochen. *For* 1831 *read* 1841.

— *For* **Locher,** F. von *read* **Loeher,** F. von.

1770 **Logeais.** — *Before* Tours *insert* 7e éd.

1774 **London.** *Bridges.* THOMSON, R. *For* 1837. 8°. *read* 1839. 16°. (Fam. lib., v. 66.)

1778 — ECCLES, *etc.* ROBERT *de W. For* 1722 *read* 1222.

1779 — INTERNAT. EXHIB. 1851. WYATT, M. D. *For* 1852 *read* 1851.

London and Edin. journ. of med. sci. *For* 1843–44 *read* 1843.

1780 **London** med. gaz. *For* 1827–51 *read* 1828–51.

London spy. *For* **Word,** E. *read* **Ward,** E.

1781 **Long Island.** THOMPSON, B. F. *Before* N. Y. *insert* 2d ed.

1782 **Longacre,** J. B. *For* 1835–39 *read* 1837–39.

1783 **Longobardi.** TROYA, C. *For* 1845 *read* 1844.

1784 **Lord,** B. *For* 1844 *read* 1744.

1791 **Louis** XIV., *of France.* VOLTAIRE, F. M. A. de. *Eng. For* 1779–80 *read* 1779–81.

1792 **Louis** XV. VOLTAIRE, F. M. A. de. *For* 1780 *read* 1779–81.

1793 **Louis** XVI. VALORI. *For* H. *read* F. F.

1805 **Lundy,** Benj. *Before Phila. insert* 2d ed. enl.

Lungo, I. del. *For* v. 11, p. 2 *read* v. 11, p. 1.

1818 **MacCarthy,** J. *For* 1821 *read* 1821–22.

1819 **McClellan,** G. B. Manual. *Omit the entry.*

M'Clure, D. Settlement. *For* 1798 *read* 1816.

1820 **McCulloch,** J. *After* 1813 *insert* 4th ed.

1825 **Mackenzie,** A. S. Life of O. H. Perry. *Before* 18°. *insert* 2 v.

1828 **M'Leod,** A., *d.* 1833. *After* WARE, H. *insert Jr.*

1829 **Macmillan's** mag. *For* Vol. 1, Nov. 1860 *read* Vol. 1–36, Nov. 1860 - Oct. 1877; *for* 3 v. *read* 36 v.

1832 **Madeira.** *Descr. Before* ed. *insert* [**1851**]; 2d.

Mlle. Mori *is by* [Miss Roberts].

1834 **Maffei,** G. P. Opera. *For* Bergo *read* Bergomi.

— Historiarum. *For* Cadoni *read* Cadomi.

1852 **Manchester,** *Eng.* WHITAKER, J. *Before* London *insert* 2d ed; *for* 1783 *read* 1773.

1855 **Mann,** Horace. MANN, M. *Before* Boston *insert* 2d ed.

Mann, *Mrs.* M. Life. *After* Mann *insert* 2d ed.

1857 **Mantell,** G. A. Geological. *Before* London *insert* 3d ed.

1858 **Manufactures.** URE, A. Dict. *Same. Before* Boston *insert* 4th ed.

1863 **Marcus,** *pseud.* WOODS, L. *For* 1800 *read* 1806.

1866 **Marion;** by Manhattan. *Before* London *insert* 2d ed.

1870 **Marquette,** J. Unfinished. *For* Dublin *read* C. Dablon.

Marquis de P. *For* Pasaval *read* Pazaval.

1871 **Marriage.** *For* M. Ferrier *read* S. E. Ferrier.

1873 **Marsh.** *For* O. C. *read* Othniel Charles.

1874 **Marshall,** John. Life. *For* 1804 *read* 1804–07.

1878 **Martin de Moussy.** *Before* V. *insert* J. A.

1879 **Martini,** G. H. *Contents. For* ἀνεδότῳ *read* ἀνεκδότῳ.

1882 **Maryland.** *Hist.* WHITE, A. *For* 1836 *read* 1846.

1903 **Mass. Hist. Soc.** Col., v. 1. *For* **Bangs**, E. *read* **Paine**, T., *and others.*

1907 — Proc., **1858–60. Interpretation** of the title, *etc., is by* **Winthrop**, R. C.

1912 **Mass. Med. Soc.** Med. comm. *Contents.* **v. 7. Mackie**, A. *For* Reed *read* Read.

1913 **Mass.** quarterly review. *For* **1846** *read* **1848.**

Mass. teacher. *Add* 1859, 69; *for* 1848–68. 8 v. *read* 1848–69. 10 v.

1917 **Matériaux.** *For* Carolilhac *read* Cartailhac.

1925 **Maunior.** *After* Charles *add* Jean.

1926 **Maurice**, —. *For* Vort *read* Voet.

1927 **Maurice** and Berghetta *is by* [Wm. Parnell].

1928 **Maximillian**, *Prinz.* For *Wied-Nieuwied* read *Wied-Neuwied.*

1930 **May**, S. J. Rights. *For* sermon, *etc., read* [sermon, Syracuse], Nov. 8. Syracuse, [1846], *etc.*

1933 **Mead**, M. The almost Christian. *Before* Boston *insert* 16th ed.

1938 **Medical jurisprudence.** Taylor, A. S. On poisons. *Before* Lond. *insert* 2d ed.

1941 **Medicine.** *History.* SCHWARZ. *For* des *read* der.

— - SPRENGEL. *Before* Halle *insert* 3e Aufl.

1943 **Medicine.** *Periodicals.* ECLECTIC. *After* Nov. *add* Dec.

1944 **Meditations** on life. *For* H. *read* J. H. D.

1047 **Mejov.** *For* V. I. *read* Vladimir Ismaïlovitch.

1948 **Mélingue**, E. M. *Before* Paris *insert* Nouv. éd.

Melish, J. Geog. descr. *For* 1814 *read* 1822.

Mellon, M. TRIAL *is by* MORTIMER, I. (*In his* Report of trials. 1830.)

1949 **Melville**, H. Omoo. *After* Sea *insert* 5th ed.

1951 **Mémorial** topog. *Omit the entry.*

1956 **Meredith**, G. Vittoria. *For* 1866–67 *read* 1866.

1965 **Meusel**, J. G. Litteratur. *Before* Lpz. *insert* 2e Ausg.

1966 **Mexico.** *Boundary.* EMORY, W. H. *For* **1848** *read* 1857–59. 2 v.

1968 — *War with the U. S.* REPUBLIC, *etc., is by* RANTOUL, R.

— *Language.* PIMENTEL, F. *For* 1863 *read* 1862–65.

1971 **Michelet**, J. La sorcière. *For* Paris *read* Brux., Leipzig.

1972 **Michigan.** *History.* LANMAN, J. H. The red book *is by* LANMAN, C.

1975 **Middleborough.** WALLING, H. F. *For* 1853 *read* 1855.

Middlesex Co. *Eng.* GENERAL view *is by* BAIRD, T.

1980 **Military art and sci.** *Gen. and miscel. works. After* SANTA CRUZ *insert* DE MARZENADO, A. de N. O.

1987 **Millennium.** COMING, **1583** *is by* PAE, D.

1994 **Mineralogy.** PHILLIPS. **1823.** *After Same* insert 3d ed. enl.

1995 **Mines.** *For* VALIÈRE *read* VALLIÈRE.

2005 **Mitchell**, D. G. Wet days. *Note. For* **v. 12** *read* v. 11.

2009 *For* **Mofras**, — *read* **Mofras**, Eugène Duflot de.

2017 **Money.** CURRENCY, **1858** *is by* SAMPSON, M. B.

2026 **Montolieu.** Le Robinson suisse. *For* **Wiss**, P. *read* **Wyss**, J. D.

2029 **Moore**, T. Rebellion record. *For* 1861 *read* 1861–68.

Moore, J. B. Memoirs. *Contents. For* J. Winslow *read* J. Winthrop.

2035 **Morales**, G. de. *For* prosiedades *read* propiedades.

2036 **Morcelli**, S. A. *Before* De Napoleone *insert, and* Schiassi, F.

2038 **Moreau**, P. *For* Notre *read* Notré.

2040 **Morgante.** *Before* 12°. *insert* 3 v.

2047 **Morton**, M. REPLY *is another copy of the preceding.*

2048 **Moseley**, B. Comment. *Before* London *insert* 2d ed.

— Treatise. *Before* London *insert* 2d ed.

2050 **Moulton**, J. W. *For* **Gates**, J. V. W. *read* **Yates**, J. V. N.

2052 **Mozart.** *For* Chrystomus *read* Chrysostomus.

Mrs. Jerningham's journal *is by* [Mrs. Hart].

2053 **Mudge**, Wm., *and others. For* 1784–1800 *read* 1784–96.

Muegge, T. Der Voigt. *For* Sett *read* Silt.

2054 **Mueller**, F. M. *See also. For* **Rig-Veda-Sanhita** *read* **Veda-Sanhita.**

2056 **Mueller**, W. *Contents. For* R. Weckherlin *read* G. R. Weckherlin.

2058 **Munich. K. B. Ak. der Wiss.** Chroniken. *Contents.* v. 2. *For* **Tucker**, E. *read* **Tucher**, E.

2064 **Murphy**, H. C. *For* C. *read* Crisse.

2066 **Muscat.** MUSCAT. *For* **Notes** *read* **Osgood**, J. B. F. Notes.

2070 **Musset**, L. C. A. de. Selections. *After* M. *insert* tr. by S. B. Wistar.

2074 **Nani**, G. B. F. G. *Eng. For* H. Honywood *read* R. Honywood.

Nanni, G. *The title should read* Berosi antiquitatum libri quinque; cum com. J. Annii.

2078 **Napoleon.** *Biography. For* WHATELY, H. R. *read* WHATELY, R.; *for* Eng. ed. *read* Amer. ed.

2080 **Napoleon** I. *Miscel works.* MORCELLI, S. A. *For* Schiassi, R. *read* SCHIASSI, F.

2083 **National** mag. *After* Vol. 1–3 *insert* 1845–46.

National preacher. *For* 1826–53 *read* 1826–54; *after* 28 v. *insert* (Vol. 12–14, 17–21, 23–26 w.); — *Note. For* Vol. 3–22 *read* Vol. 3–28.

2084 **Natural hist.** *General and miscel. works. For* VALISNERI *read* VALLISNIERI.

2088 **Naturalization.** UNITED STATES. *For* 1818 *read* 1816.

2096 **Nepos**, C. *For* RINCK, G. F. *read* RINCK, W. F.

2097 **Nervous system.** *Anat., etc.* PROCHASKA, G. *For* London, **1851.** 8°. *read* (*In* **Unzer**, J. A. Principles of physiology. **1851.**)

2098 **Netherlands.** *Art.* TAINE. *For* Duran *read* Durand.

2099 **Netherlands.** *Hist. and Pol.* WITT, J. de. *For* 5 v. *read* 4 v.

2104 **New England.** *Maps.* ALEXANDER, W. *For* 1530 *read* 1630.

2105 — *Hist. and Pol.* WINTHROP, J. *Same. For* **1630–44** *read* **1630–49.**

— GORTON, S. *For* 1836 *read* 1846.

2106 **New Eng.** Bapt. register. *For* Jan. 5, Dec. 26 *read* Jan. 5 - Dec. 28.

2113 **N. J. Hist. Soc.** Proc., v. 4. List of judges, *etc., is by* **Johnson**, R. G.

New Jerusalem, Church of the. *For* WELMER, J. *read* WILMER, J.

2114 **New Mexico.** *Politics. For* WRIGHTMAN, R. H. *read* WEIGHTMAN, R. H.

2115 **New Plymouth Colony.** *Hist.* BAYLIES, F. *For* 1830 *read* 1866.

2116 **New York** (*City*). *City Inspector.* Annual report of deaths. *For* 1824 *read* 1825.

2017 **Money.** WHATELY. **1853.** *Before* London *insert* 13th ed.

2123 **New York** (*State*). *History. Colony.* **1492–1732.** *For* SMITH, H. *read* SMITH, W.

— - SMITH, W. History. *Omit this entry.*

2126 **N. Y. Hist. Soc.** Col., 2d ser., v. 1. VRIES, D. P. de. *For* Twost *read* Troost.

2129 **Newfoundland.** *Descr. For* WHITBOURN, R. *read* WHITBOURNE, R.

2130 *For* **Newman**, *Sir* J. *read* **Newnan**, *Sir* J.

2133 **Nicaragua.** *Desc. For* PIM, B. *read* PIM, B. C. T.

2134 **Nicholas**, G. *Before* Lexington *insert Printed* Phila., *reprinted.*

2141 *For* **Nismes** *read* **Nimes** *and tr. to p.* 2140.

2142 **Noble.** *After* Birdsey *insert* G.

2145 *For* **Nordenskiold**, A. E. de *read* **Nordenskiold, Nils** Adolfe Erik de.

2150 **North Amer.** archives. *For* 1835–36 *read* 1835.

2154 **Northampton County**, *Eng.* SIMPSON, J. *For* Boston *read* Stamford.

— - *Same. Omit this entry.*

2155 **Northwest.** *For* **Kinsie** *read* **Kinzie.**

Norton, C. B. *For* B. *read* Benjamin.

2157 **Norwood**, *Col. For* 1836 *read* 1844.

2160 **Nova Britannia.** *For* 1806 *read* 1836.

2161 **Nova Scotia.** *History and Politics.* FRANCE [*and* GR. BRIT. Mém. des commissaires. *For* 3 v. *read* 2 v. in 3 pts.

2162 **Now** and then. *For* Warner *read* Warren.

2166 **Nyerup**, R., *and* **Kraft**, J. E. *For* Almingeligt *read* Almindeligt.

2167 **O.**, N. is *pseud.* for A. Cuoq.

2169 **O'Callaghan**, Edmund Burke. *For* Burke *read* Bailey.

2173 *For* **Ogden**, — *read* **Ogden**, *Rev.* John C.

2174 **Ohio.** *Descr.* EXPLANATION *is by* CUTLER, M.

2180 **Olivier**, G. A. *Before* London *insert* 2d ed.

2182 **Ontwa** *is by* [H. Whiting].

2183 **Ophthalmia.** WARE, J. *Before* London *insert* 5th ed.

2185 **Oration** on the beauties, *etc. Insert Note.* Attributed to Isaac Skillman.

2187 **Ordnance.** SHORT account *is by* TREADWELL, D.

2190 **Oriental** philanthropist. *For* Boston *read* Portsmouth.

Oriental Trans. Fund. Misc. *Contents. For* **Sakad** *read* **Sakaa.**

2193 **Oronoko.** *For* 1792 *read* 1799.

2196 *For* O'Shea H. A. *read* **O'Shea, Henry.**

Ossawattomie. *For* J. Swaayze *read* Mrs. J. C. Swayze.

Ossoli, S. M. F. Woman. *Before* Boston *insert* 3d thous.

2199 **Ovaries.** WELLS, T. S. *Before* London *insert* Vol. 1.

2203 **Oxford Univ.** *Biog.* WOOD, A. *Same. After* Oxon *insert* New.

2209 **Paine**, Thomas, *b.* 1737. *After* Letter to Abbé Raynal *add* — *Same.* Boston, 1782. 4°. (B 321)

2210 **Painters.** RUSKIN. *Before* London *insert* (vol. 1. 3d ed.); *for* 6 v. *read* 5 v.

Painting. *Gen. and miscel. works. For* HAMMERTON *read* HAMERTON.

2211 — *Theory and practice.* *Before* London *insert* New ed.
2214 **Palestine.** *Descr.* *For* VAN DER VELDE, C. W. M. *read* VELDE, C. W. M. van der.
2217 Palloni, G. S. *For* La *read* Se la; *for* Licorno *read* Livorno.
2219 **Pamphleteer.** *Contents.* v. 8. *For* **Onslow,** S. *read* **Onslow,** A.
2222 — - v. 23, *For* **Gr. Brit.** *Parl., etc., read* **Gr. Brit. Artisans.** Summary of report of committee, *etc.*; — v. 29. *For* **Westerna** *read* **Westenra.**
2224 **Panoplist** and Missionary mag. *After* Vol. 1 *insert* no. 9.
Panoplist, The; or, The Christian's armory *should be Same* under Panoplist, 1806–20.
2232 **Paris.** *Hist.* BINGHAM. *After Capt. insert* D. A.
2244 **Paris Soc. Central de Vaccine.** Disc. *For* W. Husson *read* [H. M.] Husson.
2250 **Parker,** A. A. *Before* Concord *insert* 2d ed.
2254 **Parkman,** S. Relations. *After* 1852 *insert* Phila., 1852. 8°.
2256 *For* **Parish,** *read* **Parrish.**
2257 **Parsons,** *Rev.* Jonathan, *Funeral sermon on. For* 1785 *read* 1776.
2258 **Partisan** leader. *After* 1861 *insert* 2 v.
2260 **Passages** from the history *is by* J. R. Dix.
2266 **Patmore,** P. G. *Before the entry* My friends, *etc., insert* Chatsworth; or, The Romance of a week. N. Y., 1844. 8°.
2268 **Paul,** *St.* WHATELY, R. *For* Essay [2d ser.] *read* Essays 2d ser.; *for* St. *read* the apostle; *before* London *insert* 6th ed.
2279 **Pelagianism.** WIGGERS, G. F. *After* 1833 *insert* 2 v.
2282 **Peninsular War.** *For* STEWART, C. W. Vane *read* VANE, C. W. S.
2283 **Penn,** Wm. *is pseud. for* J. Evarts.
2290 **Percy** anecdotes. *For* **Robinson,** J. C., *and* **Byerley,** T. *read* **Byerly,** T., *and* **Robertson,** J. C.
2291 **Pereia.** For *Father* read Thomas.
2293 **Perkins,** Wm. *Before* Camb. *insert* Workes.
2293 **Perkins,** W. *Insert* Workes; *for* 1608–31 *read* 1608–13.
Perkins Inst. *Note.* *For* **Massachusetts** *read* **New England.**
2298 **Persia.** *History. See also.* *Omit* **Persepolis.**
2303 **Peru.** *Hist.* VEGA. Hist. *Same.* *Before* Madrid, 1722 *insert* 2a imp.
— *Same.* *For* Madrid, 1800–03 *read* Nueva ed. Madrid, 1800–01.
2304 **Perugia.** *Bibliog.* Principe. *Before* Perugia *insert* 2a ed.
2305 **Petau,** P. Veterum. For numorum *read* nummorum; *for* Parisiis *read* Parisius.
Peters *or* **Peter,** H. HISTORICAL *is by* **HARRIS,** W.
2312 **Pharmacopœias.** WOOD, G. B. *Before* Phila. *insert* 10th ed.
2313 **Phemie.** *For* Kellar *read* Keller.
2316 **Phila. Soc. for Prom. Agriculture.** Memoirs, v. 3. Bakewell, W. *For* French ploughing *read* Trench ploughing.
2317 **Philanthropic** results *is by* BROCKETT, L. P.
2320 **Phillips,** C. A. B. *For* Camb. *read* Brighton.
2320 **Phillips,** S., *d.* 1771. PARK, E. A. *For* 894 *read* 891; *for* Taylor's Mem. Boston *read* Bibliotheca Sacra, Oct.
2324 **Philopolites.** *For* provinces *read* provinc.
Philopolities is *pseud.* for **B. Prescott.**
2326 **Philosophy.** *Hist., Anc.* VOSSIUS, G. J. *For* 1657 *read* 1658.
2329 — *Periodicals.* Journal. *For* 1867–76. 10 v. *read* 1867–79. 13 v.
2329 — *See also. Study.* Omit **Empiricism.**
2332 **Phrenology.** SPURZHEIM. **1833.** *Before* Boston *insert* 2d Amer. ed.
2338 **Physiology.** *Gen. works.* *After* 2 v. *read* (v. 1. w.). 12°.
2343 **Piedmont.** *Descr.* HANDBOOK for P., *etc., and* HANDBOOK for Switzerland, *etc., are by* **BROCKEDON,** W.
2353 **Pitt,** Wm., *Earl of C.* FREE. *For* 1776 *read* 1766.
2356 **Planters'** plea. *Same.* *After* v. 2 *insert* 1838.
2363 **Plymouth County.** THOMAS, J. *For* 1817 *read* 1811.
2363 **Plymouth,** *Mass.* (*Town.*) Russell. *Before* Boston *insert* 2d ed.
2367 **Poetry.** *Dict.* VANIÈRE, J. *Before* Lugd. *insert* 2a ed.
2370 **Poland.** *Hist.* WYDZIAŁ. *For* Paryżu *read* Paryż.
2372 **Political** ballads. *For* p. 989 *read* p. 897.
Pol. econ. *Gen. and miscel.* SMITH, A. *Same.* 9th ed. *Omit the entry.*
— ESSENTIAL, **1797** *is by* GRAY, J.
2373 **Political economy.** *Gen. and miscel. works.* SCROPE, G. P. **1833.** *For* Boston *read* London.
2373 — - SAY, J. B. **[1828–30.]** *For* 5e éd. *read* 3e ed.
2375 — *See also.* Omit **Protective system.**
Political gazette. *For* Oct. 15 – Sept. 24, 1795 *read* Sept. 10, 1795 – Aug. 4, 1796; *for* 1795 *read* 1795–96.
2376 **Polit. sci.** *Gen. and miscel.* THOMAS. *For* J. *read* T.
2377 — - WILLIAMS, D. *For* politics *read* politeness [*sic*].
2382 **Pompeii.** ZAHN. *For* Herculaneum and Stabia *read* Herkulanum und Stabiæ.
2387 **Pope,** A. WARTON, J. *Before* London *insert* 5th ed.
2388 **Popes.** VOIGT, J. *For* 5n *read* 15n.
2389 **Popish** plot. ADVICE *is by* **MARVELL,** T.
2391 **Port Royal Abbey.** SAINTE-BEUVE. *Before* Paris *insert* 10e éd.
2393 **Porter** *alias* **May,** J. TRIAL *is by* **MORTIMER,** J. (*In his* Reports of trials. 1830.)
2394 **Portrait** monthly. *After* no. 4 *add* 7; *before* Apr. *insert* Jan.
2397 **Portugal.** *Dict.* *After* VIEYA *insert* TRANSTAGANO; *before* London *insert* New ed.
2402 **Potts,** T. *For* Lancashire *read* Lancaster; Manchester *should be in brackets.*
2406 **Prayer.** CERTAIN, **1683** *is by* **SCOTT,** J.
— WARDLAW, G. **1880.** *The title should read* The obligations and efficacy of prayer; three discourses. 2d Amer. ed., *etc.*
— DUTY, **1757** *is by* **ROMAINE,** W.
2411 **Prescott,** B. *See the correction on p.* 2324, **Philopolities.**
2417 **Priestley,** J. Institutes. *Omit* Vol. 2; *after* 1794 *insert* 2 v.
2431 **Proudfit,** A. M. *For* 1815. 4 v. *read* 1806.
2434 **Prussia.** *Educ.* WYSE, T. Present state, *etc., is* (*In* v. 3, 1859.)
2435 — *Hist.* VARNHAGEN VON ENSE. *For* 1868 *read* 1868–69. 5 v.
2442 **Punch.** Shilling's worth. *Before* London *insert* 6th ed.
2442 **Pulse.** *For* Valleix, — *read* Valleix, F. L. I.
2445 **Purves,** J. *Before* Edin. *insert* 2d ed.
2455 **Quint,** A. H. Record of the 2d Mass. *For* [1661–65] *read* 1861–65.
2457 *Before the entry,* **R., M.,** *etc., insert* **R., L. N.** *See* Ranyard, *Mrs.* Ellen.
2460 **Raffles,** *Rev.* Thomas. Memoirs. *Before* Boston *insert* 3d Amer. ed.
2464 **Rammohun Roy.** 2d defence. *For* Valdas *read* Veds.
2469 *Before the entry* **Raoul,** *Duke of N. insert* **Ranyard,** *Mrs.* Ellen. The book and its story; by N. E. R. Phila., 1855. 12°.
2472 **Ravenstein,** E. G. *For* E. *read* Ernst.
Rawlet, J. *Before* London *insert* 20th ed.
Ray, F. *After* stamp-duty *insert* by W. Bollan.
Rawlinson, G. Genuineness. *For* T. *read* W.
2478 **Redemption.** WATSON, T. *The title should read* Redemption through the blood of Jesus.
2481 **Reformation.** *Biography.* TULLOCH, J. *Before* London *insert* 2d ed. Edin.
2482 — *Gen. and miscel.* ZOLLIKOFER, G. J. *For* Camb. *read* Boston.
2483 **Refuge.** *Before* Phila. *insert* 1st Amer. ed.
2492 **Remarks** on a pamphlet by Dr. Price. *After* Parliament *insert* [by A. Ferguson].
2497 **Republic** of the U. S. *Add Note.* Probably by J. F. Cooper.
2498 **Republican Party.** *Note.* *After* of *insert* 1831 *see* **Baltimore** (p. 195).
2502 **Revolutions.** VOLNEY, C. F. *Before* Paris *insert* 5e éd.
2503 **Revue** moderne. *For* 45, 55 *read* 45–55.
2503 **Reybaud,** M. R. L. Etudes. *Before* Paris *insert* 5e éd.
2508 **Rhode Island.** *History and politics.* STONE, E. W. *Before* Prov. *insert* 2d ed.
2509 **Rhymes.** *Dict.* WALKER, J. *Same.* *For* 1857 *read* 1851.
2514 **Richelieu,** A. J. du P. VAZQUEZ DE ACUÑA. *For* H. *read* A.
2517 **Rigby,** E., *of N.* On, *etc.* *Before* London *insert* 5th ed.
2519 **Riol,** S. A. Informe. *For* v. 3 *read* v. 6.
2532 **Rodriguez,** A. J. *Omit the entry.*
2533 **Roger,** F. *For* saisée-arrêt *read* saisie-arrêt.
2534 **Rogers,** R. STARK, C. *For* 1810 *read* 1861.
2538 **Roman** nights. *For* 1835 *read* 1825.
2540 **Rome.** *Antiquities.* WILCOCKS, J. *Before* London *insert* 2d ed.
2548 — *Descr.* VENUTI, R. *After* [1763] *insert* ed. 3a.
2557 **Rotation of Crops.** SKETCHES *is by* B., J. B.
2574 **Rubruquis.** *For* Willehm'von *read* Willem van.
2578 **Rush,** Benj. Effects. *Same.* *Before* Phila. *insert* 4th ed.
2582 **Russia.** *Descr.* HAMEL, J. *For* 1774 *read* 1835.
2583 — - CLARKE, E. D. *For* 1811 *read* 1816.
2594 **St. Albans, Abbey of.** SOME *is by* **NICHOLSON,** H. I. B.; *the title should read* The Abbey of St. Alban; extracts, *etc.*

2598 **Saint Martin.** *Before* Vivien *insert* Louis.
2599 **Saint Petersburg.** *For* RAIKES, S. *read* RAIKES, T.
2635 **Sanscrit literature.** *Coll.* WILSON, H. H. Hindoo theatre. *Omit the entry*; for *Same* read WILSON, H. H. Select specimens of the theatre of the Hindus.
2639 **Sargent, E.** Mod. stand. drama, v. 14, *etc.* *For* **Fitzball, E.** *and* **Fitzbald, E.** *read* **Ball, E.**
2641 **Sarracoll, J.** *For* Withington *read* Withrington.
2646 **Savonarola.** VILLARI, P. *Eng.* *For* G. Homer *read* L. Horner.
Savorgnano, G. *For* Friula *read* Friuli.
Savoy. *Descr.* Handbook. **1843, 1863** *is by* BROCKEDON, W.
Sawkins, James G. *For* G. *read* Gay.
2650 **Scandinavia.** *Mythology.* THORPE, B. *For* 1851 *read* 1851–52.
2656 **Schiller.** Works, v. 4. *For* Fresco *read* Fiesco.
2657 **Schlagintweit-Sakülünski.** *For* Hermann Adolph Robert *read* Hermann, Adolph, *and* Robert.
2663 **Schroeder-Devrient, W.** Ein Beitrag *is by* WOLZOGEN, A. F. de.
2671 **Scotland.** *Hist.* TYTLER, P. F. *For* 10 v. *read* 9 v.
2674 **Scott, John,** *b.* 1638 *After* life *insert* 6th ed. corr.; *for* 2 v. *read* 3 pts. in 4 v.
— - *Same Before* London *insert* Vol. 1, 2, 12th ed.; 3, 4, 6th ed.; 5, 8th ed.
2678 **Scribe, A. E.** *Before* Zoé insert *and* **Duveyrier, A. H. J.**; — For *and* **Duveyrier, A. H. J.** read *Polish.*
2680 **Scrope, G. P.** The geology. *Before* London *insert* 2d ed. enl.; *for* Volcanoes, *etc.*, *read* Considerations on volcanoes, the causes of their phenomena, *etc.*; After *Same insert* Volcanoes *and bring here* with descr. cat., *etc.*, *from previous entry*; *for* forms *read* form.
2683 **Sebellian language.** *Omit the entry.*
2684 **Second** letter to a friend. *For* Chauncey *read* Chauncy.
2684 **Secrets** du diable. *For* 1857 *read* 1858.
2686 **Sedgwick, J.** *After* preaching *insert* Pt. 2.
2694 *For* **Seraglia** *read* **Seraglio.**
2696 **Serious** address to the inhabitants of the colony. *For* 1784 *read* 1774.
2699 **Servants.** *For* HANWAY, — *read* HANWAY, J.
2702 **Sewall, D.** *For* 1784 *read* 1810.
2705 *For* **Shahcoolin** *read* **Shahcoolen.**
2715 **Shedd, J. H.** *For* 1866 *read* 1865.
2719 **Sheridan, R. B. B.** School. For *Spanish* read *Portuguese.*
2725 **Shrewsbury,** *Mass.* WARD, A. H. *For* 1717–29 *read* 1717–1829.
Shrine, The. *For* Vol. 2 *read* Vol. 1, 2.
2729 **Sydney, A.** WINTHROP, R. C. *For* 1853 *read* 1854.
2739 **Sin.** TAYLOR, J. **1741.** *Before* London *insert* 2d ed.
2741 **Siljeström, P. A.** Educational, *etc.*, *is the English translation of* Resa, *etc.*
2741 **Singing.** *For* JEBB *read* WEBB.
2744 **Skilton.** *For* **Skillman,** *see the correction given in the* 1st *column*, *for* p. 2185, **Oration** on the beauties.
2746 **Slater, S.** WHITE, G. S. *Before* Phila. *insert* 2d ed.
2748 **Slavery.** *Gen. and Miscel.* ESSAY, 1764 *is by* LEE, A.
2749 — - ESSAYS. **1825.** *For* Virginius *read* Vigornius.
2750 — - GR. BRITAIN. **1831–32.** For *Ho. of Com.* read *Ho. of Lords.*
2753 — - WRIGHT, H. C. **1846.** *Before* Rochdale *insert* 3d thous.
2755 — - **1860.** SOUTH, The, *etc.*, *is by* TOWNSEND, J.
2756 — - *See also.* Hildreth, R. *For* 1852 *read* 1812.
2759 **Smedley, E.,** *and others.* Encycl., v. 7. *After* **Edwards, T.,** *add and* **Don G.**
2761 **Smith, Adam.** *Same.* 9th ed. *Omit the entry.*
2768 **Smith, T. A.** *For* EARDLEY-WILMOT, *Sir* J. E. *read* WILMOT, *Sir* J. E. E.
2778 **Sniadecki, J.** Trigonometrya. *Before* Wilnie *insert* Wydanie 2e.
2804 **Somersetshire.** *For* BUTTON, J. *read* BRITTON, J.
2808 **Soul.** DESCARTES, R. *For* (*In his* Pensés. **1811.**) *read* [1641.] (*In his* Pensées, 1811.)
2809 **South, J. F.** *For* Clarke, *read* Clark.
2812 **South Carolina.** *Descr.* PURRY, P. *For* v. 1. *read* v. 2.
— *Hist.* YONGE, F. Force, P. *For* 1836 *read* 1838.
2818 **Spain.** *Descr.* WILLOUGHBY. **1664.** *For* T. *read* F.; *for* thro' *read* through.
— TOWNSEND, J. 1787. *Before* London *insert* 2d ed.
2820 **Spain.** *Hist.* **711.** ZURITA, G. *For* 1604, 10, 68–70 *read* 1669, 10, 69, 68, 70, 04.
2836 **Spirit** of the pilgrims. *For* 1838 *in both places read* 1833.
2837 **Spiritual** mirror. *Omit the entry.*
Spoerer, *For* J. *read* Julius.
2839 **Spotted fever.** *For* WILSON, J. C. *read* WILSON, J.; *for* London, **1817** *read* Boston, **1815.**
2843 **Staelin, C. F.** *For* 1800 *read* 1808.
2844 **Stamp Act.** CONDUCT *is by* LLOYD, C.
2857 **Sterling** and Penruddock. *For* 3 v. *read* 2 v.
2867 **Stone, W. L.** Life. *For* Brunt *read* Brant.
2871 **Strachey, W.** For the colony. *For* 1836 *read* 1844.
2872 **Street, G. E.** Architecture. *For* 1866 *read* 1866, 67.
2875 **Strother, D. H.** *For* v. 38-41. 1868–70 *read* v. 33–35. 1866–67.
2877 **Stuart, M.** WHITMAN, B. *Same.* *Before* Boston *insert* 2d ed.
2879 **Subscription,** *etc.* DIALOGUE, **1772** *is by* TOWERS, J.
— CURSORY *is by* STEVENS, W.; *for* 1772 *read* 1773.
— CONSIDERATIONS, **1773** *is by* MANNING, O.
2880 — ARCANA, **1774** *is by* ROBINSON, R.
— CONSIDERATIONS, **1774** *is by* LAW, E.
— DEFENCE, **1774** *is by* PALEY, W.
2886 **Sumpter,** *steamer.* *For* **Sumpter** *read* **Sumter.**
2887 **Sunday.** WHATELY, R. **1854.** *Before* London *insert* 4th ed.
2891 **Surgery.** WARREN, J. M. **1866.** This entry should be *Same* to the 4th entry above.
2893 **Surveying.** WILSON, H. *For* Geodæsia *read* Geodœsia; *before* London *insert* 4th ed.
2898 **Swedenborg.** Economy. *For* 1860 *read* 1868.
2902 **Switzerland.** *Descr.* WILLIAMS, H. M. **1798.** *For* by *read* par.
— HANDBOOK, **1843, 46, 63, 67** *is by* Brockedon, W.
2903 — *Hist.* VERDEIL, A. **1475.** *For* Bourgoyne *read* Bourgogne.
2908 **Syria.** *Hist.* YANOSKY, J. Add *and* DAVID, J. A.
Szymanowski, J. Pisma. *For* v. 4 *read* v. 26.
2915 **Tangletown.** *Omit the entry.*
Tanguy de la B. *Eng.* *For* 1796 *read* 1797.
2916 **Tappan, L.** *Same.* *For* 1832 *read* 1828.
— WARE, H., *Jr.* *Same.* *After* 2d ed. *insert* Bost., 1828. 12°.
2927 **Teatro** nuevo. *Contents.* v. 3. *For* **Harleville, C.** de *read* **Colin d'Harleville, J. F.**
2934 **Temple** family. *For* 1855 *read* 1856.
2939 **Test laws.** ANSWER, **1688** *is by* LLOYD, W.
— ANSWER to some queries, **1732** *is by* BARRINGTON, J. S.
— ANIMADVERSIONS on a paper, **1733** *is by* SLADEN, J.
— CHURCH, **1733** *is by* WRIGHT, S.
2940 — ADDRESS, **1790** *is by* DISNEY, J.
2942 **Texas.** PHILLIPS. *Hist.* *For* [1845–46] *read* [1861].
2955 **Theology.** WILLARD. *Systematic works.* *For* **1607** *read* **1707.**
2975 **Thornton, R. J.** Pastorals. *Before* London *insert* 3d ed.
2989 **Toledo,** *Ohio.* *For* 1864–66. 2 v. *read* 1863–65. 3 v.
3005 **Tredgold, T.** Principles. *Before* London *insert* 2d ed.
3012 **Trinity.** ANSWER, **1721** *is by* PEIRCE, J.
3021 **Tryal,** *etc.* *For* twenty-one *read* twenty-nine.
3023 **Tuckey, J. K.** *For* Kingston *read* Hingston.
3038 **Turkey.** *Politics.* APPEAL, **1854** *is by* DAVIDOFF, M.
3048 **Ulster** county gazette. *For* Jan. 14 *read* Jan. 4.
3051 **Unitarians.** *Gen. and Misc.* DIALOGUE, **1792** *is by* DISNEY, J.
3058 **U. S.** *Army.* HARDIN, B. **1836.** *The entries from* HARDIN, B. *to* WISE, H. A. *should be transferred to* U. S. *Fortification* (p. 3121).
3071 — 6*th Cong.* For *March* read *May.*
2972 **Thompson, Z.** *Before* Burlington *insert* 3 pts.
3075 — 8th *Cong.* For *Nov.* 8, 1804 – *March* 1 read *Nov.* 5, 1804 — *March* 3.
3095 **United States.** *President.* *G. Washington.* Coll. *For* 1776 *read* 1796.
3110 — *Female biog.* ELLET, E. F. *Before* N. Y., *insert* 2d ed.
3121 — *Finance.* **1843.** *After* ought *insert not.*
3124 — *Hist.* WASHINGTON, G. 1774. *Omit the* 2d *Same.*
3139 — *Periodicals.* **Volunteer.** *For* 1832–23 *read* 1832–33.
3143 — *Politics.* ESSAY, **1764** *is by* LEE, A.
— - DEFENCE, **1765** *is by* HOWARD, M.
3144 — - CASE, **1769** *is by* BUSHE, G. P.
— - APPEAL, **1774** *is by* LEE, A.
3146 — - ANSWER, **1776** *is by* LIND, —.
3152 — - COMPRESSED, **1814** *is by* ATCHESON, N.
3155 — - WILSON, H. **1856.** *For* 1856 *read* 1857.
— - WORCESTER. **1857.** *For* CONVENTION *read* CONVENTIONS.
3162 — *Tariff.* WINTHROP, R. C. **1842.** *Omit the entry.*
3183 **Varnhagen, F. A. de.** *Add vicomte de Protoseguro.*
3235 **Wahn, Der.** *For* **Ueller** *read* **Mueller.**
3251 **Ward, R. P.** Chatsworth. *Omit the entry.*
3294 **West Indies.** *Politics.* CRISIS *is by* STEPHEN, J.
3303 **Whipple, E. P.** Essays, *etc.* *For* 1848 *read* 1848–49.
3324 **William IV.** The reform. *After* 1867 *insert* 2 v.
3352 **Woman.** *Character, etc.* 1692. EXCELLENT *is by* DORRINGTON, T.
3354 — *Misc.* AFTERNOON *is by* PENNY, *Mrs.* S. J.
3365 **Worship.** ESSAYS, **1773** *is by* WILLIAMS, D.

CHRONOLOGICAL LIST

OF THE

PROPRIETORS OF THE BOSTON ATHENÆUM,

FROM

ITS FOUNDATION TO JANUARY 31, 1882,

ACCORDING TO THE CERTIFICATE BOOK.

Note. When several names are attached to the number of a share, the *last* is that of the present holder. The certificates of the shares taken by the original subscribers in 1807 were not issued till 1815.

No.	Name	Year
1	Harrison Gray Otis	1815
	Charles Thacher	1849
	Mary Elizabeth Holmes	1869
	Fan'il Hall Nat. B'k, Bost.	1878
	Mary Elizabeth Holmes	1878
2	John Lowell	1815
	Rebecca Amory Lowell	1842
	Anna Cabot Lowell	1874
3	John Lowell	1815
	John Amory Lowell	1817
	Anna Cabot Lowell	1852
4	Josiah Quincy	1815
	Joseph Brown Tilton	1876
5	Josiah Quincy	1815
	Josiah Quincy, Jr.	1823
	Lemuel Edward Pope	1853
	Stephen H. Williams	1860
	Charles Vose Bemis	1864
	Thomas Lang	1878
	George Cabot Lee	1879
6	Josiah Quincy	1815
	George Burroughs	1815
	Henry Burroughs	1852
7	Samuel Eliot	1815
	William Havard Eliot	1821
	Nathaniel Greene	1832
	Nathaniel Curtis, Jr.	1841
	Francis Alger	1842
	Frank Wrisley	1866
	Helen Williams Wrisley	1876
8	James Perkins	1815
	Samuel Cabot	1831
	Francis Skinner	1839
9	John C. Brown	1815
	John Coffin Jones	1820
	Anna P. Jones	1839
	Oliver H. Perry, Guardian	1864
	George W. Pettes	1868
	Frances Ann Moseley	1874
10	Thomas Perkins	1815
	William Powell Perkins	1829
11	Daniel Sargent	1815
	John H. Cabot	1820
	Amos Binney	1833
	Samuel Woodbury Swett	1840
	Russell Sturgis	1846
12	Joseph Head	1815
	Moody Kent	1837
	New Hampshire Asylum for the Insane	1867
	Arthur Earl Jones	1869
13	Thomas Handasyd Perkins	1815
	Stephen Cabot	1852
	Eben Dyer Jordan	1866
14	William Pickman	1815
	William M. Vaughan	1857
	Sidney Brooks	1864
	Susan Warner Hardy	1879
15	Uriah Cotting	1815
	Ebenezer Francis	1815
	Elizabeth Frances Fay	1859
16	Benjamin Bussey	1815
	George Livermore	1843
17	Thomas Coffin Amory	1815
	Thomas Coffin Amory	1818
	Thomas Amory Dexter	1820
	Jeffrey Richardson	1822
	Wm. Lambert Richardson	1879
18	Thomas W. Storrow	1815
	Jacob Tidd	1817
	George Minot Dexter	1828
	Samuel G. Williams	1830
	Enoch Martin	1837
	Arthur Scholfield	1841
	Otis Drury	1854
19	Peter Oxenbridge Thacher	1815
	Charles Pelham Curtis	1828
	Margarett Stevenson Curtis	1864
20	Samuel Torrey	1815
	Daniel Pinckney Parker	1821
	Edwin Percy Whipple	1855
21	Samuel Dexter	1815
22	Charles Lowell	1815
	Charles Russell Lowell	1859
	Anna Cabot Jackson Lowell	1871
	Edward Jackson	1874
23	John Hancock	1815
	John Hancock Moriarty	1862
	Clara Erskine Clement	1874
24	Cornelius Coolidge	1815
	Samuel G. Williams	1821
	James Allen	1822
	Joseph M. Marsh	1824
	James Allen, Jr.	1826
	Eben Billings	1828
	Robert B. Allen	1830
	Charles Allen	1834
	Geo. Washington Warren	1836
	Edward Sprague Rand	1839
	Edward Sprague Rand, Jr.	1864
	William Frederick Duff	1876
25	Francis Johonnot Oliver	1815
26	Oliver Putnam	1815
	Daniel Parkman	1827
	Samuel A. Bemis	1827
	Amos Adams Lawrence	1842
27	Nathan Appleton	1815
	Franklin H. Story and others, Trustees	1862
	Thomas Gold Appleton	1864
28	Stephen Higginson, Jr.	1815
	Francis John Higginson	1828
	Howard Sargent	1831
	Mrs. C. K. Sargent	1834
	Nath'l Ingersoll Bowditch	1834
	Elizabeth Brown Bowditch	1862
29	Stephen Higginson, Jr.	1815
	George Sullivan	1816
	Henry Lee	1817
	Francis Lee	1821
	Henry Lee	1830
	Samuel Torrey Morse	1867
30	John Richards	1815
	Francis Richards	1826
	George Henry Richards	1868
31	Stephen Codman	1815
	Henry Codman	1818
	Charles Henry Isburgh	1866
32	Samuel May	1815
	Samuel May	1871
33	James Lloyd	1815
	John Borland	1832
	Alida Livingston Borland	1876
34	John Gore	1815
	Thomas Perkins, Guard.	1819
	John C. Gore	1827
	Arthur Goar	1861
	John C. Gore	1861
	Edwin Faxon	1869
35	Allan Melville	1815
	Charles Russell Codman	1820
	Wm. Gardiner Prescott	1863
	Francis Augustus Osborn	1866
36	Joseph Coolidge, Jr.	1815
	Tasker H. Swett	1841
	Elizabeth B. Swett	1842
	William B. Swett	1860
37	Eben Preble	1815
	Ralph Randolph Wormeley	1826
	James Blake	1828
	John Harrison Blake	1849
38	John Prince, Jr.	1815
	Wm. Howard Gardiner	1831
39	Samuel Parkman	1815
	Thomas Davis	1832
	William Davis Bliss	1850
40	Kirk Boott	1815
	John Wright Boott	1817
	William Boott	1831
	John Wright Boott	1834
	Kirk Boott	1850
	Alfred Hemenway	1879
41	Edward Tuckerman, Jr.	1815
	Edward Tuckerman, Jr.	1839
42	Thomas Lindall Winthrop	1815
	George Stillman Hillard	1843
	M. Fayette Dickinson, Jr.	1881
43	Timothy Williams	1815
	Joshua Huntington Wolcott	1842
44	William Smith Shaw	1815
	Joseph Barlow Felt	1826
	John S. Barstow	1864
	William Spooner Smith	1878
45	William Sawyer	1815
	Hannah F. Lee	1859
	Mary Gorham Palfrey	1871
46	Judah Hays	1815
	Boston Athenæum	1822
	Thomas Beale Wales	1823
	Arthur Welland Blake	1868
47	John Parker	1815
	John Parker, Jr.	1825
	Charles Beck	1845

Anna L. Möring 1878
48 Samuel D. Harris 1815
Samuel Salisbury 1826
Alexander Parris 1826
Stephen Codman 1847
Wm. Sohier Dexter 1862
49 Gardiner Greene 1815
John Singleton Copley Greene 1835
Samuel Austin 1840
Ezra Wilkinson 1856
50 Edward Blake, Jr. 1815
Samuel Parkman Blake 1851
William Sanford Rogers 1861
John E. Allston 1873
Charles William Baker 1878
Edward Russell 1880
51 Nathaniel Goddard 1815
Martin Gay 1843
Eleanor A. Gay 1853
Richard Hildreth 1854
George D. Oxnard 1856
Gordon Bartlet 1862
Frank Parker Appleton 1868
52 Samuel Salisbury 1815
Josiah Salisbury 1819
Edw'd Elbridge Salisbury 1833
Thomas Minns 1859
53 Joseph Tilden 1815
George W. Tilden 1856
John Revere 1869
54 Peter Chardon Brooks 1815
Peter Chardon Brooks 1849
Susan O. Brooks and others, Executors 1881
55 Thomas K. Jones 1815
Samuel James Bridge 1832
Bradford Lincoln, Jr. 1833
Robert Treat Paine 1837
56 Nathaniel R. Sturgis 1815
Russell Sturgis 1818
Samuel Henshaw 1845
James M. Murdock 1861
Lyman Mason 1863
57 William Ingalls 1815
Caleb Stimson 1824
Caleb Morton Stimson 1841
Chas. Frederick Crehore 1868
58 Israel Munson 1815
Le Baron Russell 1844
59 William Rufus Gray 1815
William Gray 1831
James Freeman 1833
Charles Torrey 1836
James H. Hicks 1838
Josiah Parsons Cooke 1842
Mary P. C. Nash 1881
60 Ebenezer T. Andrews 1815
William Turell Andrews 1830
Robert Codman 1881
61 Thomas Cushing 1815
Benj. Marston Watson 1818
John P. Rice 1824
Benj. Wm. Crowninshield 1832
George Caspar Crowninshield 1853
Harriet Sears Crowninshield 1859
Fanny Crowninshield Adams 1873
62 Isaiah Thomas 1815
Frederic Tudor 1831
William Tudor 1870
William Storer Eaton 1877
63 Theodore Lyman 1815
Theodore Lyman 1820
64 Caleb Loring 1815
Charles Greely Loring 1836
Charles Greely Loring 1872
65 John Pickens 1815
Henry Lienow 1826
Hartley Hezekiah Wright 1838
Charlotte Wright 1852
Richard Black Sewall 1875
66 Benjamin Pickman, Jr. 1815
Clarke Gayton Pickman 1821
Peter P. F. Degrand 1839
Charles Torrey 1844
Ebenezer Rockwood Hoar 1850
67 Francis Cabot Lowell 1815
John Lowell, Jr. 1821
Jacob Abbott 1838
Francis Brown Hayes 1844
Lemuel Stanwood 1846

Otis Clapp 1863
68 Nathaniel Amory 1815
Joseph Linzee Cunningham 1822
Henry Bromfield Rogers 1822
69 Benjamin Weld 1815
Charles Barnard 1823
James Munson Barnard 1854
70 John Warren 1815
Edward Warren 1833
Charlotte Louisa and Annie Storrow Ware 1879
71 Joshua Davis 1815
Robert Farley 1843
Stephen Henry Phillips 1847
John Avery 1858
William Sewell Gardner 1873
72 Benjamin Rich 1815
John Bellows 1822
Benjamin Rich, Jr. 1824
Samuel H. Rich 1827
Francis Brown Hayes 1846
73 Micajah Sawyer 1815
Thomas Sawyer 1824
Henry Fowle Durant 1865
74 Joseph Hall 1815
Charles Cunningham 1848
William and Francis E. Parker, Trustees 1872
Frederic Cunningham 1874
75 Seth Knowles 1815
William Taylor 1831
Thos. Buckminster Curtis 1837
John Albree 1850
William Parsons 1850
76 William Prescott 1815
William Hickling Prescott 1827
Wm. Gardiner Prescott 1869
77 Thomas Hill, Jr. 1815
Francis Boott 1817
Mark Healey 1848
78 George Gardner Lee 1815
David Sears 1816
David Sears 1871
Leverett Saltonstall 1873
79 Jonathan Davis 1815
Edward Gardiner Davis 1829
Pickering Dodge 1835
Jona. Ingersoll Bowditch 1836
80 John Heard, Jr. 1815
Benjamin K. Hough 1864
Elizabeth Hough 1880
James Adams 1881
Arthur Rotch 1881
81 Samuel Salisbury, Jr. 1815
Nancy Salisbury 1850
82 Stephen Higginson 1815
Henry Higginson 1834
Thomas Butler Pope 1839
John Stevens 1840
William Joseph Hubbard 1852
83 Samuel G. Perkins 1815
Thomas Handasyd Perkins 1833
Stephen Higginson Perkins 1833
Elizabeth W. Perkins 1878
84 John T. Apthorp 1815
George Bruce Upton 1849
85 Timothy Bigelow 1815
John Prescott Bigelow 1817
86 Adam Babcock 1815
William Edward Payne 1831
Edward W. Payne 1831
Edward Greely Loring 1832
Richard C. Cabot 1835
Francis Davis 1845
J. Amory Davis 1857
Ann Wainwright Davis 1865
87 Andrew Craigie 1815
Daniel Hastings 1816
John D. Winslow 1820
Daniel Hastings 1824
Charles Pelham 1839
M. B. Hamilton 1868
Abraham Firth 1869
88 Charles Davis 1815
Josiah Marshall 1823
Thomas Motley 1831
Edward Motley 1865
89 Richard C. Derby 1815
Charles Lyman 1855
90 Isaac P. Davis 1815
William S. Tuckerman 1847

John Brooks Parker 1869
91 Benjamin Joy 1815
Daniel Austin 1855
Andrew Preston Peabody 1866
92 Jonathan Mason 1815
Robert Bennett Forbes 1832
George Bancroft 1838
Nathaniel H. Emmons 1850
Arthur Brewster Emmons 1878
93 Joseph W. Revere 1815
94 Abraham Touro 1815
Charles Taylor 1823
95 Russell Sturgis 1815
Mass. General Hospital 1817
John Belknap 1822
Edward Belknap, Trustee 1856
Henry Belknap 1881
Ellen Neville Wheelwright 1882
96 Robert Hallowell Gardiner 1815
Rob't Hallowell Gardiner 1875
97 Thomas Bartlett 1815
Thomas Bartlett Hall 1855
98 Jonathan Phillips 1815
Silas Atkins Bancroft 1862
99 Stephen Jones, Jr. 1815
John Richards, Jr. 1834
Francis Richards 1850
Francis Gardiner Richards 1852
100 Samuel Welles 1815
Peter Parker 1816
James Walker Austin 1873
101 James Lamb 1815
Thomas Lamb 1822
102 Isaac Parker 1815
Daniel Parkman 1828
Cyrus Alger 1828
John Prince Bayley 1856
103 William Smith Shaw 1815
George Searle 1826
Benj. Marston Watson 1829
Samuel Jackson Gardner 1833
Jesse P. Richardson 1834
Isaac Parker 1836
Richard C. Cabot 1849
Mary G. Loring 1868
104 Henry Gardner Rice 1815
Caleb Adams 1819
Benjamin Adams 1829
James Bowen 1859
105 Ralph I. Reed 1815
Jacob Gates 1816
Boston Athenæum 1821
Henry Alexander Scammell Dearborn 1822
George Leonard Chandler, Jr. 1832
Giles Henry Lodge 1835
106 Joseph Hurd, Jr. 1815
William Hurd 1842
Francis Wm. and Joseph Hurd 1862
Francis William Hurd 1868
107 William Vincent Hutchings 1815
James Trecothick Austin 1820
Ivers James Austin 1871
Charles Levi Woodbury 1882
108 Nehemiah Parsons 1815
Thomas Wigglesworth 1818
Thomas Wigglesworth 1855
109 Nathaniel G. Snelling 1815
George Cheyne Shattuck 1815
George Cheyne Shattuck Morison 1854
110 James Bowdoin 1815
James Bowdoin 1832
William C. Tyler 1835
Edward Blake 1835
111 George Higginson 1815
James P. Higginson 1819
H. Frederick Higginson 1878
112 Henry Andrews 1815
Thomas G. Chase 1819
Henry Gardner Rice 1820
Samuel Buckminster Rice 1826
Henry Gardner Rice 1827
Geo. Middleton Barnard 1853
113 William Whitwell 1815
John Bumstead 1817
Lloyd W. Wales, Exec. 1867
William Story Bullard 1868
114 John Clarke Howard 1815
John Clarke Howard 1841
115 Eben Larkin 1815

Henry Rice 1819
Whitwell, Bond, & Co. 1829
Henry Rice 1835
John McLean Bethune 1841
George Amory Bethune 1873
116 William Oliver 1815
Boston Athenæum 1821
Rezin D. Shepherd 1822
Gorham Brooks 1844
Shepherd Brooks 1858
117 Benjamin Whitwell 1815
Henry Cabot 1818
George Bond 1820
Benjamin F. White 1837
Samuel Whitwell 1845
118 Samuel G. Williams 1815
Charles Pelham Curtis 1819
Nathaniel Bowditch 1824
Henry Ingersoll Bowditch 1839
119 Richard Sullivan 1815
Richard Sullivan 1879
120 Francis Johonnot Oliver 1815
John S. Capt 1817
121 John Codman 1815
William Appleton 1820
Edwin Forbes Waters 1862
122 Thomas Williams 1815
Francis Henry Williams 1834
Frederick Howes 1837
Susan Burley 1841
Joseph Sebastian Cabot 1863
Susan Burley Cabot 1880
123 Samuel J. Prescott 1815
John Brown 1818
Boston Athenæum 1821
Joseph Coolidge 1822
Joseph Coolidge, Jr. 1826
Elijah Lowell 1834
Abby M. Loring 1861
Peter Benton, Guardian 1864
John Lowell, Guardian 1865
Abby R. Loring 1877
124 William Phillips 1815
Gustavus Tuckerman 1827
Henry H. Tuckerman 1837
Henry Gardner 1837
Benjamin Worcester 1870
125 William Phillips 1815
Samuel Hurd Walley 1822
John Welles 1827
Arnold Welles 1835
Robert Charles Winthrop 1852
George Derby Welles 1865
Edward Daniel Hayden 1870
126 William Phillips 1815
Edward Phillips 1822
William Phillips 1853
Arnold W. Conant 1863
Eben Denton 1867
Charles Storrow 1875
127 John Thornton Kirkland 8118
James Freeman, Jr. 1828
Henry H. Tuckerman 1831
John Homans 1844
Charles Dudley Homans and others, Trustees 1870
128 William Cochran 1820
Caleb Andrews 1822
Charles L. Andrews 1854
John Jeffreys, Jr. 1858
129 Samuel Appleton 1822
Franklin Darracott 1854
Francis S. Carruth 1863
Henry Martyn Saville 1864
130 George Searle 1822
Washington P. Gragg 1825
Martin Brimmer 1830
Martin Brimmer 1849
131 Lewis Tappan 1822
Charles Bowen 1827
John Hancock, Jr. 1827
George Hancock 1870
132 Joseph P. Bradlee 1822
Franklin Haven 1843
Edward Belknap Haven 1875
133 Thomas Wigglesworth 1822
Edward Wigglesworth 1822
George Wigglesworth 1877
134 Josiah Bradlee 1822
Fred. Wainwright Bradlee 1849
William Hilton 1865
135 Daniel Hammond 1822
George Hammond 1873
Ellen Hammond 1876
136 Asa Whitney 1822
Benjamin Duick Whitney 1831
Cornelius Conway Felton 1838
Benjamin D. Whitney 1848
James H. Foster 1851
Caroline M. Barnard 1876
137 Pliny Cutler 1822
Charles Brown 1841
Joseph W. Homer 1841
Sydney Homer 1852
Thomas J. Homer and others, Trustees 1878
138 John Hooper 1822
Samuel Hooper 1824
Alice Sturgis Hooper 1878
139 Richard D. Tucker 1822
William Story Bullard 1840
Franklin Howard Story, Jr. 1847
140 Francis Lee 1822
Rufus Wyman 1826
Jeffries Wyman 1843
Susan Wyman 1876
141 Thomas Lee 1822
142 George Ticknor 1822
William Foster Otis 1854
George William Bond 1859
143 John Hubbard 1822
Caleb Reed 1845
William Prescott Hunt 1855
Margaret S. Eveleth 1858
Uriah Atherton Boyden 1860
144 John S. Ellery 1822
Samuel W. Waldron 1836
Lemuel Shattuck 1836
Sarah Baxter 1838
Lemuel Shattuck 1845
Clarissa B. Shattuck 1860
145 Jonathan Amory 1822
Jonathan Amory, Jr. 1830
Henry Grew 1831
Zelotes Hosmer 1836
Henry Roby 1837
James Frothingham Hunnewell 1851
146 Jesse Putnam 1822
Benjamin W. Putnam 1862
Dupee, Beck, & Sales 1869
Elbridge Gerry Cutler 1870
147 Charles Jackson 1822
Samuel George Snelling 1864
148 Samuel Pickering Gardner 1822
Peter Thacher Homer 1844
149 Patrick Tracy Jackson 1822
Lydia Jackson, Trustee 1860
Elizabeth H. Webster 1865
Arthur Reed 1876
150 Charles Bradbury 1822
Charles Browne 1855
Edward Ingersoll Browne 1879
151 Horace Gray 1822
William Story Bullard 1849
152 Francis Calley Gray 1822
William Gray 1858
William Gray, Jr. 1858
Chester Guild, Jr. 1860
Francis Batcheller 1877
153 John Chipman Gray 1822
James Beck 1864
Edith Doane Beck 1875
Charles Edward Wilson 1876
154 Thomas Wren Ward 1822
Charles L. Field 1858
John S. Davenport 1867
Augusta Kimball Horton 1876
155 William Sturgis 1822
William Hurd 1866
Alex. Strong Wheeler 1866
156 John Bryant 1822
Waldo Higginson 1868
157 Henderson Inches 1822
Henderson Inches 1858
158 Isaac Winslow 1822
Benj. Pollard Winslow 1862
159 Gorham Brooks 1822
Peter Chardon Brooks 1858
Ellen Brooks 1865
160 George Hallet 1822
Caleb Cushing 1828
161 Charles Thorndike 1822
Charles Greeley Loring, Adm'r. 1846
Ezra A. Bourne 1851
162 Augustus Thorndike 1822
Wm. Cranch Bond Fifield 1860
163 Benjamin Guild 1822
Eliza Guild 1861
Edward Chipman Guild 1861
164 Edward Brooks 1822
Francis Brooks 1878
165 Alden Bradford Weston 1832
Peters & Parkinson 1878
Francis Manning Stanwood 1879
166 Ebenezer Rollins 1822
167 Abbott Lawrence 1822
William Nye Davis 1857
Annah Delano 1863
James D. Thomson 1866
Robert Hooper 1866
Joseph Hurd 1867
168 Marshall Binney Spring 1822
169 Amos Lawrence 1822
William Richards Lawrence 1836
170 Israel Thorndike 1822
Edward Greely Loring 1844
Geo. Washington Warren 1844
171 William Pratt 1822
William P. Winchester 1845
Eliza G. Winchester and others, Trustees 1851
172 James Hall 1822
James Trecothick Austin 1841
Susanna Williams 1847
Edward A. Williams 1860
Sarah A. E. Williams 1872
Thomas W. Williams 1875
Charles Merrick Gay 1879
173 John Tappan 1822
John Gallison Tappan 1872
174 David W. Child 1822
Artemas Ward 1835
Henry Artemas Ward 1848
Edward Alexander Strong 1866
175 Robert Gould Shaw 1822
John Haven Cheever 1855
David Williams Cheever 1869
176 Thomas Cordis 1822
Thomas Aspinwall 1856
Francis Henshaw & Co. 1880
Charles Smith Bradley 1880
177 John Bellows 1822
George Alexander Otis 1826
John Brazer Davis 1827
James M. Robbins 1835
178 Abijah Fisk 1822
Hercules M. Hayes 1824
John Williams 1829
Hercules M. Hayes 1830
Simon Eliot Greene 1830
Samuel G. Goodrich 1831
John Henry Jenks 1832
Samuel G. Goodrich 1833
John Mackay 1840
William Davies Sohier 1845
William Sohier 1872
179 Samuel Dorr 1822
Charles Hazen Dorr 1845
180 Samuel Whitwell 1822
Benjamin F. White 1837
Charles R. Bond 1839
Thomas Wm. Parsons, Jr. 1840
181 Frederic William Paine 1822
Gardiner L. Chandler 1835
David B. Tower 1837
Rufus Choate 1839
Mary Ann Palfrey Russell 1865
182 Francis Stanton 1822
Joshua Blake 1840
Charlotte Caldwell Hubbard 1867
183 Jonathan Chapman 1822
George Chapman 1831
Jonathan Chapman 1834
Ozias Goodwin, Trustee 1849
184 Lot Wheelwright 1822
Wm. Wilson Wheelwright 1827
Chas. Henry Wheelwright 1835
Edward Blanchard, Jr. 1838
Elizabeth L. Nichols 1878
185 John Davis Williams 1822
George Foster Williams 1849
Ellen V. Sears 1873
186 Charles Torrey 1822
Frederick Augustus Cobb 1829
Amos Adams Lawrence 1838
Francis Boott 1841

No.	Name	Year
	Benjamin Robbins Curtis	1843
	Francis Bowen	1852
187	Samuel Torrey	1822
188	John Odin	1822
	Reuben Richards, Jr.	1833
	George E. Richards	1856
	Anna Mitchell Richards	1876
189	David Ellis	1822
	Samuel B. Barrell	1839
	Alvan Lamson	1843
	Artemas Ward Lamson	1865
190	Samuel Calley Gray	1822
	Freeman Allen	1852
	Henry Freeman Allen	1862
191	Gorham Parsons	1822
	Theophilus Parsons	1822
	George W. Swett	1858
	Samuel Woodbury Swett	1870
192	James Jackson	1822
	James Jackson Storrow, Trustee	1868
193	Edward Cruft	1822
	Annah Pickman Cruft	1866
194	Peter Roe Dalton	1822
	Samuel T. Armstrong	1826
	Abigail Armstrong	1879
195	Edward Everett	1822
	Helen C. Everett	1865
	Edward Everett	1881
196	William Lawrence	1822
	Josiah Dwight Whitney	1850
	David W. Holmes	1855
	Stephen Higginson	1866
	Agnes G. Higginson	1871
197	Elbridge Gerry	1822
	Daniel Parkman	1828
	John Parkman	1828
	Samuel Gridley Howe	1835
	Lee, Higginson, & Co.	1880
	Robert Hale Bancroft	1880
198	Benjamin Wiggin	1822
	Moses Whitney	1827
	Warren Jacob Whitney	1836
	Samuel Downer	1841
199	Samuel Atkins Eliot	1822
	Charles W. Cunningham	1858
	Lynde C. Ferris	1858
	Hawes & Henshaw	1880
	Thomas Buckminster Curtis	1880
	William Burdick Stevens	1882
200	David Henshaw	1822
	George Winslow	1853
	Erving Winslow	1865
201	Samuel Swett	1822
	George H. B. Hill	1867
	Josiah Dwight Whitney	1868
202	John Dorr	1822
	Theodore Haskell Dorr	1856
	George Snell	1870
203	Benjamin Russell	1822
204	Daniel Webster	1822
	Moses Kimball	1864
205	Seth Bass	1822
	George N. Faxon	1849
	Mary Josephine Faxon (Mrs. Forbush)	1855
	Samuel Baker Rindge	1881
206	Jacob Bigelow	1826
207	William Ingalls	1826
	Henry Clark, Admr.	1853
	Junius S. Morgan	1853
	Charles Torrey	1855
	Samuel Edmund Sewall	1856
208	Samuel Atwood Shurtleff	1826
	Augustine Shurtleff	1861
209	John Ware	1826
	Grenville Temple Winthrop Braman	1865
	George Henry Torr	1877
210	Zabdiel Boylston Adams	1826
	James Thomas Fields	1866
211	Enoch Hale, Jr.	1826
	Geo. Washington Wales	1852
212	Edward Reynolds, Jr.	1826
	Thomas William Parsons	1836
	Alfred Greenough	1838
	Samuel Dunn Parker	1858
	Alfred Greenough	1863
213	Woodbridge Strong	1826
	Henry H. Iles	1874
	Sarah L. Adams	1876
214	Josiah Foster Flagg	1826
	Rufus Wyman	1854
	Elizabeth Wyman	1875
	Margaret C. Wyman	1881
215	Joshua Henshaw Hayward	1826
	Thomas Graves Cary	1832
	Mary Perkins Cary	1866
	Elizabeth Cary Agassiz	1880
216	John Gorham Coffin	1826
	Ambrose S. Courtis	1829
	Thomas Courtis	1844
	James Diman Green	1844
	James Chandler Braman	1856
217	George Parkman	1826
218	George Hayward	1826
	Mary Ann Hayward	1872
	Nathaniel Dana Carlile Hodges	1881
219	Walter Channing, Jr.	1826
220	John Gorham	1826
	Samuel Kettell	1839
	Wm. Howard Hinckley	1856
	Katharine G. Hoffendahl	1868
221	Horace Bean	1826
	Richard Fletcher	1827
	Eben Farrington	1870
	Charles Frederick Farrington	1872
	Charles Chauncy Burr	1874
222	John Dixwell	1826
	Epes Sargent Dixwell	1864
223	Geo. Washington Otis, Jr.	1826
	Grenville Temple Winthrop Braman	1881
224	George Bates	1826
	Hermann Jackson Warner	1852
225	David Osgood	1826
	George Stillman Hillard	1863
	Henry Dwight Hyde	1870
226	Anson Hooker, Jr.	1826
	Thomas J. Whittemore	1830
	Thomas Sherwin	1834
	Thos. Coffin Amory, Jr.	1846
227	Chandler Robbins, Jr.	1826
	Samuel R. Putnam	1835
	Mary Lowell Putnam	1875
228	Thomas Foster	1826
	John Foster	1831
	James Hayward	1841
	Edmund S. Clark	1866
	Richard Manning Hodges	1868
229	Charles Wild	1826
	Mary C. Atkinson	1867
	Edward Atkinson	1880
230	Amos Farnsworth	1826
	Charles Knapp Dillaway	1835
	Robert Henry Eddy	1836
231	John Collins Warren	1826
	James H. Beal	1858
232	William Johnson Walker	1826
	John P. Rice	1835
	Samuel Lawrence	1835
	Uriah Atherton Boyden	1841
233	Asa Bullard	1826
	Simon Eliot Greene	1827
	Ammi B. Young	1840
	James Francis Thomas	1880
234	Solomon Davis Townsend	1826
	Solomon Lincoln, Jr.	1862
	Robert Shaw Perkins	1864
	William Edward Perkins	1878
	John Codman Ropes, Admr.	1880
	James Edward Radford Hill	1880
235	John Randall	1826
	Elizabeth Randall	1846
	John Witt Randall	1868
236	John Clark	1826
	Richard Cobb	1829
	Matthias Plant Sawyer	1836
	Charles Inches	1860
	Thomas Joseph Lee	1863
	Albert Gallatin Browne, Jr.	1866
	Richard Leeds	1870
237	Benjamin Ropes Nichols	1826
	John Eugene Tyler	1859
	Charles Amos Cummings	1869
238	Samuel Hubbard	1826
	Jas. Mascarene Hubbard	1870
239	William Ellery Channing	1826
	William F. Channing	1849
	Charlotte L. Inches	1858
	Martin B. Inches and Edward Dexter Sohier, Trustees	1873
	Richard and Alfred Ela	1875
	Francis Snow Hesseltine	1881
240	William Parsons	1826
	William Parsons	1838
	Theophilus Parsons	1863
	William Parsons	1865
241	William Sullivan	1826
	Francis Bassett	1839
242	Benjamin Willis	1826
	Benjamin Willis	1854
	Hamilton Willis	1872
	Samuel Baker Rindge	1879
	Henry Woods	1880
243	Henry Sigourney	1826
	Henry Sigourney	1854
244	Alexander Bliss	1826
	William Grigg	1828
	Nathaniel Faxon	1836
	Horace Hopkins Coolidge	1861
245	William Ropes	1826
	George Williams Lyman	1830
	Samuel Leonard Crocker, Jr.	1860
	James D. Thompson	1867
	Charles H. Bennett	1872
	Henry Taylor	1874
	Samuel Guild Child	1875
246	Jonathan Porter	1826
247	Abiel Chandler	1826
	George Minot Dexter	1833
	William Gibbs	1834
	William Richardson	1847
	Horace Richardson	1857
248	Edmund Dwight	1826
249	Robert Waterston	1826
	Helen Ruthven	1829
	Robert Waterston	1830
	George Clement Lord	1872
250	Charles J. Cazenove	1826
	John Eliot Thayer	1834
	Oliver White Peabody	1858
251	John Davis	1826
	Andrew Alexander	1848
252	Josiah Loring	1826
	Henry Russell Cleveland	1842
	Sarah Perkins Cleveland	1844
253	Benjamin Loring	1827
	George Brooks Young	1861
	John Collamore	1865
254	John Randall	1827
	James Andrews	1827
	Charles Henry Ferdinand Moring	1851
	John Goodnow	1858
	John Rogers	1862
255	John Quincy Adams	1829
	Charles Francis Adams	1829
256	Thomas H. Cabot	1830
	Samuel Cabot, Jr.	1836
257	John Guardenier	1831
	George Howe	1839
	Charles Mixter	1843
	Catharine H. Pierce	1869
258	Israel Thorndike	1831
	William Joseph Loring	1831
	John Ellerton Lodge	1841
	Nathaniel Amory	1864
259	George Minot Dexter	1842
260	John Guardenier	1842
	Joseph Bell	1843
	Jabez Baxter Upham	1853
261	Luther Stearns Cushing	1842
262	Oliver Wendell Holmes	1843
263	John Guardenier	1845
	John Redman	1845
	John Bromfield	1846
	Henry Bromfield Pearson	1852
	James Schouler	1864
264	Josiah Bradlee, Jr.	1844
265	Thomas Beale Wales	1844
	Henry George Spaulding	1868
266	Robert Hooper	1844
267	John Parker	1844
	Robert William Hooper	1845
268	William Edward Coale	1844
269	George Cheyne Shattuck, Jr.	1844
270	Thomas Wren Ward	1844
	John Gallison Ward	1844
	Thomas Wren Ward	1859
271	Thomas Wren Ward	1844
	George Cabot Ward	1844
	Philippe Wolff	1878
272	Samuel Fales	1844

Charles Henry Parker 1850
273 James Sullivan Amory 1844
274 Charles Barnard 1844
John Parker Tarbell 1854
John F. Tarbell 1859
John Parker Tarbell 1863
275 John Borland 1844
James Lloyd 1844
John Nelson Borland 1849
276 Edward Blanchard 1844
Andrew Cunningham Wheelwright 1853
277 George Theodore Lyman 1844
James Diman Green 1859
Addison Child 1865
Charles Edward Sampson 1881
278 William Amory 1844
279 Francis Cabot Lowell 1844
Chas. Cotesworth Beaman 1875
280 George Gardner Lowell 1844
281 George Baty Blake 1844
282 John Wiley Edmands 1844
Alvah Augustus Burrage 1877
283 Phineas Upham 1844
Benjamin Leeds 1861
Benjamin Leeds, Jr. 1866
Frank Shaw 1866
284 Sidney Bartlett 1844
Francis Bartlett 1866
285 Samuel Leonard Abbot 1844
286 Joseph Balch 1844
Anna Loring Balch 1850
Francis Vergnies Balch 1882
287 John Chipman Gray 1844
Horace Gray, Jr. 1848
288 John Chipman Gray 1844
Francis Augustus Brooks 1849
George Higginson 1852
289 John Chipman Gray 1844
Nathaniel Hooper 1849
Charles Henry Hamm 1865
290 Abbott Lawrence 1844
James Lawrence 1846
James Lawrence 1875
291 Abbott Lawrence 1844
Timothy Bigelow Lawrence 1846
Abbott Lawrence and others, Trustees 1869
292 Abbott Lawrence 1844
Abbott Lawrence, Jr. 1846
293 Amos Lawrence 1844
William Richards Lawrence 1853
Frederick West Holland 1854
294 Amos Lawrence 1844
Jerome Van Crowninshield Smith 1849
295 Joshua Huntington Wolcott 1844
Charles Sumner 1845
Charles Follen Atkinson 1875
296 Charles Hamilton Parker 1844
Chas. Phelps Huntington 1857
297 Ozias Goodwin 1844
298 Benjamin Ropes Nichols and others, Executors 1844
Sarah P. Pratt 1845
Mary and Sarah P. Pratt 1855
Henry Wilder Foote 1862
299 Benjamin Adams 1850
Sam'l Hammond Russell 1852
Seth E. Brown 1860
Lincoln Flagg Brigham 1861
Frederic Beck 1866
Lucy Doane Beck 1873
300 John Bryant, Jr. 1844
301 Jacob Sleeper 1844
302 Daniel Pinckney Parker 1844
Henry Tuke Parker 1845
Charles Devens 1855
Arthur Lithgow Devens 1878
303 Henry Baldwin Stone 1844
Isaac Orr Barnes 1850
Gustavus Vasa Fox 1868
James W. King 1879
Mary Sarah Thomas 1882
304 George Washington Coffin 1844
William Spooner Coffin 1881
305 Caleb Curtis 1844
Henry Clay Weston 1865
306 Henry Sidney Waldo 1844
Theodore Parker Adams 1880
307 Thomas P. Cushing 1844
Howard Payson Arnold 1865

Agnes Gordon Balch 1870
308 Samuel R. Putnam 1844
Robert B. Storer 1850
Charlotte Avery Kennard 1871
309 Charles Amory 1844
Edward Linzee Amory 1864
310 William Lawrence 1844
James Bicheno Francis 1856
311 William Lawrence 1844
Benjamin Daniel Greene 1850
312 William W. Stone 1844
Charles Torrey 1851
Daniel D. Brodhead 1853
Edward Sprague Rand 1854
313 Thomas Wetmore 1844
William J. Reynolds 1862
Charles W. Cunningham 1865
Charles Deane 1865
314 Gardner Colby 1844
315 Jonathan French 1844
316 James Ingersoll 1844
Alexander Thomas 1852
Rufus Ellis 1874
317 Robert Chamblet Hooper 1844
Adeline Denny Hooper and others, Trustees 1881
318 John W. Trull 1844
John Hunt Welch 1849
John Trull Heard 1853
John Theodore Heard 1881
319 John Davis Williams 1844
John D. W. Williams 1849
Henry Bigelow Williams 1874
320 John Davis Williams 1844
David W. Williams 1849
Arthur Lincoln 1876
321 John Davis Williams 1844
David W. Williams 1849
Edwin Lamson 1850
Benjamin Smith Rotch 1868
322 Stephen Ball, Jr. 1844
Francis McLennan 1876
Charles Lowell Thayer 1879
323 John P. Thorndike 1844
George Quincy Thorndike 1850
324 Benjamin W. Crowninshield 1844
Edward Augustus Crowninshield 1849
Caroline Maria Crowninshield (Mrs. Arnold) 1860
325 Daniel Sargent Curtis 1844
326 Addison Gilmore 1844
Geo. Baty Blake, Guard'n 1852
George Morey 1859
Elisha W. Willard 1869
327 Francis Henry Appleton 1844
Francis Henry Appleton 1871
328 Samuel Cabot 1844
James Elliot Cabot 1855
329 Charles F. Hovey 1844
Richard Cranch Greenleaf 1859
330 Samuel Batchelder 1844
John M. Batchelder 1881
331 William Rollins 1844
John Steele Tyler 1856
Robert Amory 1868
Copley Amory 1870
Charles Fletcher Dole 1876
332 Charles B. Shaw 1844
Ellen Twiselton Parkman 1880
333 William Blake 1844
Joshua Richardson Bigelow 1867
334 John James Dixwell 1844
Elizabeth Boardman Ingersoll Bowditch Dixwell 1877
335 George Basil Dixwell 1844
336 Joshua Sears 1844
Susan Warner Hardy 1859
Sarah C. Sears 1879
337 Joseph Whitney 1844
Joseph Cutler Whitney 1871
Nat. Bell Telephone Co. 1879
Amer. Bell Telephone Co. 1880
338 Samuel Frothingham 1844
Samuel Frothingham 1863
Augustus Howe Buck 1873
339 David Stoddard Greenough 1844
Isaac P. Rand 1852
John Lowell Gardner, Jr. 1866
340 Aaron Hobart 1844
William Story Bullard 1847
Charles Eliot Norton 1849

341 George Robert Russell 1844
Sarah Shaw Russell 1876
342 George Callender 1844
Henry Stone Hovey 1863
343 William F. Whitney 1844
Dio Lewis 1868
344 Henry Hall 1844
Matilda Stewart Buck 1875
345 William Perkins 1844
346 Willard Sayles 1844
Maria F. Sayles 1848
Henry Sayles 1858
347 Isaac Livermore 1844
Franklin Hall 1858
348 John Adams Blanchard 1844
Sarah Harding Blanchard 1873
349 Francis Fisher 1844
Benj. Franklin Stevens 1874
350 Charles Storer Storrow 1844
351 Hugh R. Kendall 1844
William H. Shailer 1853
Kate Frazer 1865
Waldo Maynard 1871
Sarah S. Fay 1874
352 James Parker 1844
Charles Sprague 1878
353 Sumner Hudson 1844
Lyman Perry 1848
James Tuttle 1850
Maria Louise Brackett 1882
354 John S. Wright 1844
Willard C. Van Derlip 1875
James Wheeler Edgerly 1879
355 George Gardner 1844
356 Charles E. Miller 1844
George Tyler Bigelow 1874
Lewis Stackpole Dabney 1879
357 Gardner Brewer 1844
Caroline A. Brewer 1875
358 Benj. G. Wainwright 1844
Farnham Plummer 1849
Eliz'th Chandler Fletcher 1880
359 Charles Francis Adams 1844
John Quincy Adams 1854
360 John Murray Forbes 1844
Robert Forbes Perkins 1873
361 George Francis Parkman 1844
362 Timothy C. Leeds 1844
Charles William Moseley 1875
363 Sampson Reed 1844
James Reed and others, Trustees 1880
James Reed 1881
364 Andrew Eliot Belknap 1844
James H. Weeks 1859
Joseph N. Sturtevant 1869
Thomas Leggett and Edward Lewis Sturtevant 1881
365 John Lowell Gardner 1844
Joseph Peabody Gardner 1856
366 John Lowell Gardner 1844
Geo. Augustus Gardner 1856
367 John Lowell Gardner 1844
Thomas Groom 1845
368 George Horatio Kuhn 1844
369 James Bowdoin Bradlee 1844
370 William Gray 1844
Jonathan French 1859
371 Caleb Eddy 1844
Samuel Barrett 1847
Willard Phillips 1848
Alexander Young 1866
Samuel Swan Arnold 1871
Francis Lee Higginson 1878
372 Francis Low 1844
Daniel Swan Gilchrist 1848
Nathaniel Greene 1849
Daniel Kimball 1851
Sereno Dwight Nickerson 1856
373 William Whiting 1844
Wm. Goodwin Russell and Abraham Firth, Trustees 1878
374 Benjamin Seaver 1844
Charles M. Seaver 1858
375 Henry Augustus Page 1845
376 Theodore Metcalf 1844
377 Lucius Manlius Sargent 1844
Susan M. Lawrence 1880
378 Nathan Carruth 1844
Simon Greenleaf 1846
James Greenleaf 1857
Mary L. Greenleaf 1866
379 Jabez C. Howe 1844

John Green Cary 1870
380 Joseph N. Howe, Jr. 1844
Charles James Morrill 1870
381 George Alfred Whitney 1844
George Alfred Whitney 1868
James Phineas Whitney 1871
Charles Franklin Dunbar 1871
382 Jeffrey Richardson 1844
Charles Tallman White 1879
383 John Douglas Bates 1844
384 Francis S. Carruth 1844
Charles Homer 1845
Charles Alfred Welch, Trustee 1881
385 Edward Hutchinson Robbins 1844
William Henry Swift 1856
William Tennant Hart 1862
386 Abel Kendall, Jr. 1844
Ann M. Kendall 1870
Henry Warren Torrey 1871
387 Charles Sprague 1845
Ezra Lincoln 1851
Charles Uriah Cotting 1881
388 William Minot 1845
Francis Minot 1868
389 George Barrell Emerson 1845
Lincoln F. Emerson 1854
390 John D. Gardner 1845
Jonathan Peele Dabney 1852
Thomas Morong 1868
George Young 1871
391 William Thomas 1845
Mary T. Guild 1873
392 John Templeman Coolidge 1845
393 John Lamson 1845
Daniel S. Lamson 1859
Boston College 1865
394 Erastus Brigham Bigelow 1845
Harvey Drury Parker 1880
395 Andrew Townshend Hall 1845
Charles H. Mills 1869
396 Charles Lyman 1845
Peter P. F. Degrand 1845
Samuel R. Spinney 1857
Joshua Clapp Stone 1860
Edmund T. Hastings 1861
John Joseph May 1862
397 Francis Caleb Loring 1845
Samuel W. Rodman 1859
Frederick W. Tracy 1860
Caroline T. Hubbard 1880
398 Marshall Spring Perry 1845
399 Nathan Cooley Keep 1845
400 Francis Boardman Crowninshield 1845
Georgiana Phipps Munroe 1878
Otis Munroe 1882
401 Robert Caldwel Mackay 1845
402 Josiah Quincy, Jr. 1845
Southworth Shaw 1852
Henry S. Shaw 1875
Alfred Hubbard Batcheller 1877
403 James Johnson 1845
Josiah H. Cobb 1860
Gardner S. Langton 1860
Elizabeth Eaton 1862
404 Ebenezer Chadwick 1845
Elizabeth Chadwick 1854
Sewall Tappan 1856
Robert Oliver Fuller 1879
405 William Cushing Aylwin 1845
Charles F. Aylwin 1852
George O. Hovey 1857
John Torrey Morse, Jr. 1879
406 Jeremiah Mason 1845
Charles Mason 1849
Mary Hemenway 1863
407 James Paul 1845
Otis Daniell 1847
Jas. C. Fisk, Sarah F. Daniell, Emily Longfellow 1873
408 Benjamin Bangs 1845
Samuel Bradstreet 1859
John Kimball Rogers 1865
409 Thomas Greenleaf, Trustee 1845
Wm. Greenleaf Appleton, Trustee 1856
Thomas Pember 1857
Samuel D. Talbot, Jr. 1858
John Dean 1861
410 Thomas Greenleaf, Trustee 1845
Wm. Greenleaf Appleton, Trustee 1856
Eliza Appleton 1871
411 Thomas Greenleaf, Trustee 1845
Ezekiel Price Greenleaf 1856
412 Thomas Greenleaf 1845
Ebenezer Woodward, Trustee 1856
Alanson Tucker 1870
413 Francis Calley Gray 1845
William Gray 1858
George B. Jones 1859
Joseph Rowe Webster 1859
Mary Phillips Webster 1880
414 Nathan Appleton 1845
Franklin H. Story and others, Trustees 1862
Thomas Gold Appleton 1864
415 Nathan Appleton 1845
Franklin H. Story and others, Trustees 1862
Mary Mackintosh 1864
James L. Goodridge 1864
Dupee, Beck, & Sayles 1869
Edward Holzapfel 1869
Sarah Henshaw Hunt 1872
416 Nathan Appleton 1845
Thomas Gold Appleton 1847
417 Edward Austin 1845
William Austin 1854
Francis Aldworth Hooper 1867
George Edward Brown 1877
Morrill Wyman, Jr. 1878
418 Theodore Chase 1845
George Bigelow Chase 1865
419 Martin Brimmer 1845
Nathaniel Whiting 1849
420 John Stearns 1845
John Stearns 1865
421 Oliver Eldridge 1845
Edward H. Eldredge 1863
Amariah A. Taft 1879
Peters & Parkinson 1879
John Larkin Thorndike 1879
422 Charles Fred. Adams 1845
Emily M. Adams 1862
Emily Matilda Curtis 1878
423 Samuel Appleton 1845
Noble Maxwell 1854
Sidney Brooks 1864
John Goddard Stearns, Jr. 1879
424 Robert Gould Shaw 1845
Francis George Shaw 1849
425 Peter Chardon Brooks 1845
Abigail B. Adams 1849
Brooks Adams 1870
426 Peter Chardon Brooks, Jr. 1845
Susan O. Brooks and others, Executors 1881
427 Daniel C. Bacon 1845
Daniel G. Bacon 1857
Florence Maria Cushing 1877
428 Charles C. Little and James Brown 1845
429 Peter Chardon Brooks 1845
Gorham Brooks 1849
Peter Chardon Brooks, Jr. 1852
George Abbott Osborne 1881
Joseph Bangs Warner 1881
430 Amos Binney 1845
Henry P. Binney 1863
Eliza Cabot 1864
431 Caleb Chace 1845
Edward Gilchrist 1865
Wm. Frederic Matchett 1870
432 Jonathan Chapman 1845
Francis Bacon 1849
Elizabeth J. Tuck 1876
433 Jonas Chickering 1845
Daniel Denny 1854
Henry Gardner Denny 1860
434 Edward Codman 1845
Horatio Chickering 1862
Lucy Lee Chickering 1876
435 Samuel F. Coolidge and Elisha Haskell 1845
Jonathan Brown 1849
436 Charles Pelham Curtis, Jr. 1845
437 Thomas Dixon 1845
B. Homer Dixon 1850
George P. Kettell 1858
Andrew Nickerson 1865
George Abbott James 1872
438 John Guardenier 1846
Benjamin Tyler Reed 1850
John Hooper Reed 1874
Lucy Ann Woodbridge 1879
439 James Davis, Jr. 1845
Henry Winsor, Jr. 1881
440 Samuel Atkins Eliot 1845
Enoch Redington Mudge 1858
William Burdick Stevens 1881
Marie Louise Joy 1882
441 Edwards & Stoddard 1845
Charles Stoddard and J. S. Lovering 1847
Joseph Swain Lovering 1854
442 John Earle, Jr., & Co. 1845
William Pearce Parrott 1849
Collateral Loan Co., Bost. 1875
Mrs. Wm. Pearce Parrott 1876
443 Stephen Fairbanks 1845
William O. Moseley 1867
444 Samuel Atkins Eliot 1845
Francis E. Faxon 1858
Joshua Cleaves Dodge 1867
Henry Augustus Gowing 1879
445 Richard Sullivan Fay 1845
William D. Pickman and others, Adm'rs. (of R. S. Fay) 1867
446 John Gardner 1845
447 Horace Gray 1845
Tristram B. Mackay 1849
Henry B. Goodwin, Trus. 1873
Tristram Barnard Mackay 1875
448 Prince Hawes 1845
Benjamin Lincoln 1849
449 George Hallet 1845
Benjamin Franklin Wing 1845
450 James H. Hicks 1845
Charles Eliot Ware 1849
451 Robert Gould Shaw 1845
Robert Gould Shaw, Jr. 1849
George W. T. Riley 1874
John Wesley Lindsay 1878
452 Patrick Tracy Jackson 1845
Lydia Jackson, Trustee 1848
John H. Foster 1869
Samuel Savage Shaw 1870
453 Eliphalet Kimball, J. H. Jewett, & Co. 1845
Eliphalet Kimball 1849
Augustine Heard 1849
George W. Heard 1852
Albert Farley Heard 1868
George James Harris 1875
454 Henry Lee, Jr. 1845
455 Arnold Welles 1845
Charles Davenport 1852
Daniel A. Patch 1868
Charles Lothrop Smith 1877
456 James L. Little, Paul Alden, & Co. 1845
James Lowell Little 1852
457 John Amory Lowell 1845
Elizabeth Rebecca Lowell 1852
Elisha Pomeroy Cutler 1874
458 Robert Means Mason 1845
Ida Means Mason 1879
459 James K. Mills 1845
Susan Bulfinch Lyman 1858
460 Charles Callahan Perkins 1845
William Nichols 1873
461 Edward Newton Perkins 1845
John Weiss 1859
Charles Henry Newhall 1880
462 John Amory Lowell 1845
John Lowell 1852
Andrew Robeson 1868
Mary Arnold Robeson 1882
463 Samuel Phipps 1845
Charles Russell Lowell 1860
Anna Cabot Jackson Lowell 1871
Edward Henry Whorf 1873
Arthur F. Estabrook 1875
Edward Henry Whorf 1875
Frank Wm. Hunt 1875
Samuel Bradley Noyes 1876
Charles P. Coffin 1880
Henry Francis Greenleaf 1880
464 George Pratt 1845
465 William C. Eayrs and Josiah L. Fairbanks 1845
Francis Cogswell 1861
Alfred Ely 1874
466 Thos. Handasyd Perkins 1845
Thomas Handasyd Per-

kins, Jr. 1849
Holmes Ammidown 1856
William Frederic Match-
ett 1863
Robert I. Lee 1866
Cyrus Sargeant 1866
467 George R. Sampson 1845
Langdon Williams 1865
John S. Crisp 1867
John Spencer Clark 1868
Luther Clark 1870
468 Robert Gould Shaw 1845
Gardner Howland Shaw 1849
Charles Heath 1855
469 Francis Skinner & Co. 1845
Henry Kenney Horton 1847
Eleanor Goddard May 1872
470 Josiah Stickney 1845
Sidney Brooks 1864
Emily Sever 1879
471 Philo S. Shelton 1845
Harvey Jewell 1856
472 Ignatius Sargent 1845
473 James W. Smith 1845
George O. Carpenter 1881
Grant Walker 1881
474 Matthias Plant Sawyer 1845
George Means Mason 1854
Edward Wyman 1866
William P. Lawrence 1874
Augustus Lord Soule 1880
475 John L. Tucker 1845
Samuel K. Williams 1848
Samuel Johnson and Geo.
H. Peters, Trustees 1875
Elizabeth S. N. Goodall 1876
476 Adam Wallace Thaxter 1845
Francis Jewett Parker 1863
477 John Eliot Thayer 1845
Nathaniel Thayer 1858
Christopher Toppan
Thayer 1858
478 Henry Timmins 1845
George Henry Timmins
and others, Executors 1864
Cyrus Moors Warren 1865
479 John Collins Warren 1845
Jonathan Mason Warren 1858
Edward Page 1874
480 John Welles 1845
Jane Welles 1856
Isabella P. Shaw 1881
481 John Welles 1845
Horatio Hollis Hunnewell 1847
482 Moses B. Williams 1845
Silas Emlyn Stone 1868
483 J. Simmons & Son 1845
George Abbott Osborne 1873
John Murray Forbes 1874
484 Lewis William Tappan 1845
Amos L. Frothingham 1863
485 Michael Hodge Simpson 1845
486 James Savage 1845
487 John Amory Lowell 1845
Augustus Lowell 1852
Allen Melanchthon Sum-
ner 1874
488 Charles Francis Adams 1850
Chas. Francis Adams, Jr. 1856
489 Lemuel Shaw 1845
Lemuel Shaw 1862
490 H. M. Holbrook, J. B. Carter,
& Co. 1845
William Endicott, Jr. 1868
491 Samuel Appleton 1845
Mary Appleton 1853
Frances Elmira Bangs 1868
492 Samuel Appleton 1845
Edward Bangs 1853
493 David Sears 1845
Emily E. Sears 1874
David Sears 1874
494 Peter Chardon Brooks 1845
Francis Boott Brooks 1849
Richard Chamberlain
Nichols 1863
495 Frederic Richard Sears 1845
496 Mercantile Library Assoc. 1845
497 Knyvett Winthrop Sears 1845
498 Thomas Handasyd Perkins 1845
Charles Perkins Gardiner 1851
499 Thomas Handasyd Perkins 1845
Augustus Thorndike Per-
kins 1851
500 Thomas Handasyd Perkins 1845
Richard Cary 1851
501 Charles Amory 1850
John Louis Clarke 1850
Charles Amory 1855
Copley Amory 1867
Henry Pickering Walcott 1870
502 Charles Amory 1850
503 William Amory, Jr. 1850
504 Nathan Appleton 1850
Franklin H. Story and
others, Trustees 1862
Mary Mackintosh 1864
Henry Allen Rice 1864
Delano Alexander God-
dard. 1869
L. B. Stone 1870
Elijah B. Phillips 1880
505 Robert Appleton 1850
Nathan Matthews 1852
Charles Mayo Ellis 1855
Helen T. Ellis 1878
Arthur Dixwell 1879
506 Samuel Appleton 1850
Thomas Tracy Bouvé 1854
Charles H. Wheelwright 1860
Susan Candler 1867
William Latham Candler 1880
507 Samuel Appleton 1850
Nathaniel Curtis, Jr. 1854
Madeleine Curtis Mixter 1875
508 Samuel Appleton 1850
Caleb Gould Loring 1854
Joseph Willard 1856
509 Samuel Appleton Appleton 1850
Nathan Matthews 1855
510 William Appleton, Jr. 1850
511 Abigail Armstrong 1850
Barney Cory 1872
512 Samuel Austin 1850
William A. Rea 1851
Henry Rice 1861
Dexter T. Mills 1868
Nathaniel A. Shute 1868
Mary E. Holbrook 1871
Helen W. Shute 1873
513 George Williams Lyman 1854
Philip Howes Sears 1858
514 Ebenezer Bacon 1850
515 James F. Baldwin 1850
George R. Baldwin 1871
516 George Pemberton Bangs 1850
Jerome George Kidder 1855
517 James Bayley 1850
Harriet K. and Caroline
L. Bayley 1852
518 Charles Beck 1850
John H. Comer 1867
Isaac S. Cruft 1868
519 Joseph Bell 1850
Joseph Mills Bell 1853
520 John Adams Blanchard 1850
George Henry Blanchard 1854
Laura Smith Blanchard 1873
521 John W. Blodget 1850
Caleb William Loring 1856
522 Jonathan Ingersoll Bow-
ditch 1850
Chas. Pickering Bowditch 1876
523 Dwight Boyden 1850
Charles Alfred Welch 1855
524 Josiah Bradlee 1850
George B. Cary 1850
Oliver Ames 1881
525 Josiah Bradlee 1850
James Bowdoin Bradlee,
Jr. 1851
Mary M. Bradlee 1860
526 Josiah Bradlee 1850
Frederick Hall Bradlee 1851
527 Elijah Dana Brigham 1850
Mary Wheeler Bowles 1869
528 Francis Augustus Brooks 1850
529 Peter Chardon Brooks 1850
Sarah Anne Cheever 1865
James Freeman Clarke 1870
530 Henry Bryant 1850
Edward Dexter Sohier and
William Minot, Trustees 1870
531 William Story Bullard 1850
Stephen Hopkins Bullard 1852
Elizabeth Lyman Bullard 1873
532 Benjamin Burgess 1850
Charles F. Sawyer 1865
Estes Howe 1866
William Taggard Piper 1878
533 Fred. Howes, Exec. 1850
William Burley Howes 1850
Elizabeth Howes 1880
534 Joseph Burnett 1850
John Adams Bates Cutter 1853
Joseph Burnett 1854
James Madison Beebe 1856
Esther Elizabeth Beebe 1876
535 T. O. H. Perry Burnham 1850
536 Theophilus Burr 1850
Theophilus Burr 1864
Chas. Townsend Hubbard 1865
537 Thomas Graves Cary 1850
Robert Howard Cary 1859
Gamaliel Bradford 1868
538 Ebenezer Chadwick 1850
Elizabeth Chadwick 1854
John W. James 1856
Julia Bradford Hunting-
ton James 1863
539 Walter Channing 1850
Nathaniel Francis 1852
Anson Joseph Stone 1867
540 Rufus Choate 1850
Dwight Foster 1865
541 Benjamin Cutler Clark 1850
Robert Farley Clark 1867
B. P. Chamberlain 1868
John A. Alley 1870
Augustine Jones 1875
542 Charles Russell Codman 1850
Samuel W. Rodman 1863
Charles Merriam 1866
Robert Gould Shaw 1871
Hannah B. Shaw 1875
543 Edward Codman 1850
Edward Wainwright Cod-
man 1859
544 George Washington Coffin 1850
James Chrystie Rogers 1851
Benj. Franklin Burgess 1857
545 William E. Coffin 1850
Charles S. Lynch 1856
John Calvin Dodge 1875
546 Joseph H. Cotton 1850
Arria Cotton 1873
547 John A. Cunningham 1850
C. Loring Cunningham 1850
Edward Cunningham 1858
548 Benjamin Robbins Curtis 1850
Edward Jackson 1854
549 Wm. Whitwell Greenough 1850
550 Thomas Buckminster Curtis 1850
Caroline Wells Healy
Dall 1872
Abraham Firth 1878
551 Thomas P. Cushing 1850
Edmund Munroe 1853
Dupee, Beck, and Sayles 1869
John W. Draper 1869
552 Samuel Turner Dana 1850
Mary Elizabeth Dana 1878
553 Edmund W. and Stephen
W. Dana 1850
Richard Frothingham, Jr. 1854
Thomas G. Frothingham,
Admr. 1881
Benj. Loring Young 1881
554 George Darracott 1850
John Turner Welles Sar-
gent 1853
George Edward Brown 1878
Helen Augusta Dodge 1879
James Gilchrist 1881
555 Frederick W. Davis 1850
Samuel Thomas Snow 1863
556 Otis Turner 1850
Peter P. F. Degrand 1855
Francis H. Peabody 1857
Charles Lowell Andrews 1862
Wallis S. Chase, Guard. 1878
557 William Dehon 1850
Joshua William Davis 1866
558 Franklin Dexter 1850
559 John R. Dow 1850
John D. Gardner & Co. 1851
Thomas Tolman 1852
Mary Lowell Stone 1876
560 Levi A. Dowley 1850
Clarence W. Jones 1858
Francis Parkman Hurd 1859
561 Daniel Draper 1850

Ada A. Draper 1867
562 William C. Eayrs and Josiah L. Fairbanks 1850
William Mountford 1861
Frederick Alex. Lovering 1877
563 Edward Everett 1850
William Everett 1865
564 George N. Faxon 1850
Henry M. Leeds 1867
565 Harrison Fay 1850
James Harrison Fay 1858
Arabella Rice 1864
Alice W. Parker 1873
566 William C. Fay 1850
Jacob Albert Dresser 1862
567 Fay & Farwells 1850
Thomas F. Curtis 1867
Wm. Bordman Richards 1870
568 Albert Fearing 1850
Francis Vose Parker 1871
Caroline W. Tebbetts 1871
William Carr Tebbetts 1877
569 Charles B. Fessenden 1850
Edward Belknap Haven 1857
Thomas Dwight 1865
George Golding Kennedy 1866
570 Richard Fletcher 1850
Joel Prentiss Bishop 1870
571 William B. Fosdick 1850
572 Jonathan French 1850
573 Nathaniel Langdon Frothingham 1850
Thomas B. Frothingham 1863
Edmund Dwight 1880
Arnold A. Rand 1880
Jennie Lathrop Rand 1880
574 Addison Gage 1850
575 William Howard Gardiner 1850
576 Henry Joseph Gardner 1850
577 John Lowell Gardner 1850
Henry Barney Smith 1851
Edmund Burke Otis 1861
Sarah S. Dunn 1875
James Anson Lawrence Whittier 1878
578 Ozias Goodwin 1850
Rich'd Chapman Goodwin 1854
579 Moses Grant 1850
Moses Pierce Grant 1856
J. Y. McClintock 1876
James M. Codman 1881
580 John Chipman Gray 1850
Wm. Channing Appleton 1863
581 Thomas Gray 1850
Cassius Darling 1854
Enoch S. Johnson 1864
Benjamin Faxon Field 1878
582 Andrew Townshend Hall 1850
Lydia Y. Hall 1877
Hales Wallace Suter 1881
583 Henry Hall 1850
Quincy Tufts 1852
William Tufts Brigham 1874
584 Henry S. Hallet 1850
Harrison Otis Briggs 1869
William Rudolph Griffiths 1882
585 Peter Harvey 1850
John Cauldwell Sharp 1863
586 Franklin Haven 1850
Franklin Haven, Jr. 1853
587 William Hayden 1850
John Hartshorn 1852
Charles Bunker 1854
John Alden Loring 1854
588 William A. Hayden 1850
David Hyslop Hayden 1876
589 George Hayward 1850
George Hayward, Jr. 1853
Uriel Crocker 1858
590 Augustine Heard 1850
Edward Olcott Shepard 1869
Frances Lewis Wilson 1874
591 Peter Thacher Homer 1850
Gerard Curtis Tobey 1880
592 George Howe 1870
George Dudley Howe 1873
593 Samuel Johnson 1850
Charlotte Abagail Johnson 1869
594 Horatio Hollis Hunnewell 1850
Jane W. Sargent 1881
595 James Ingersoll 1850
George Morgan Browne 1851
596 Charles Jackson 1850
Charles Cushing Paine 1854
Helen, Mari Anne, and Sarah C. Paine 1874
597 Charles Jackson, Jr. 1850
Susan Cabot Jackson 1871
598 Anna P. Jones 1850
John Coffin Jones 1851
Anna P. Jones, Guardian 1863
James Jackson Storrow 1865
Joseph Cutler Jones 1870
Wm. Frederic Freeman 1870
599 George B. Jones 1850
George William Gordon 1851
600 George Horatio Kuhn 1850
Francis Henry Brown 1865
601 Abbott Lawrence 1850
William A. Hovey 1857
William H. Thompson 1874
Ida Agassiz Higginson 1882
602 Abbott Lawrence 1850
Charles Torrey 1857
Daniel H. Treadwell 1859
603 Abbott Lawrence 1850
Thomas Gaffield 1857
604 Samuel Kirkland Lothrop 1850
605 Samuel Lawrence 1850
William B. Spooner 1860
William Mixter 1865
606 Amos Lawrence 1850
Amos Adams Lawrence 1853
Hetty Sullivan Lawrence (Mrs. Cunningham) 1877
607 James Lawrence 1850
William T. Eustis 1851
George Smith Burton 1874
Daniel Low Winchester 1877
608 Samuel Lawrence 1850
George Lawrence 1854
Frederick Almy 1872
William Theodore Wardwell 1872
609 William Richards Lawrence 1850
Joseph Scholfield 1851
610 James Lee, Jr. 1850
John Dandridge Henley Luce 1878
611 Thomas Lee 1850
William W. Baker 1868
George Dennie 1869
Edmund Sanford Clark 1872
612 Sargent S. Littlehale 1850
Ednah Dow Littlehale Cheney 1876
613 Giles Henry Lodge 1850
Walter Baker 1851
Eleanor J. W. Baker 1854
614 Henry Cabot 1850
Anna Cabot Lodge 1870
Henry Cabot Lodge 1879
615 Ammi Cutter Lombard 1850
Joseph Beale Glover 1852
William Wilder Wheildon 1863
616 Israel Lombard 1850
617 Elisha T. Loring 1850
Ellen H. Childe, Guardian 1870
John Healey Childe 1879
618 Francis Caleb Loring 1850
Pelham W. Hayward 1851
George P. Hayward 1863
James Elliot Cabot 1864
Thomas Crane Wales 1870
619 Francis Cabot Lowell 1850
Ellen Frothingham 1875
620 Francis Cabot Lowell 1850
Willliam Henry Swift 1875
621 Francis Cabot Lowell 1850
Henry Frederick Teschemacher 1876
622 John Amory Lowell 1850
Francis Tucker Washburn 1872
Samuel Jennison 1873
623 John Amory Lowell 1850
Arthur Theodore Lyman 1859
Effie Wood Palmer 1873
624 John Amory Lowell 1850
Sarah Putnam Lowell 1859
Andrew Gerrish Webster 1874
James Henry Whitman 1882
625 John Amory Lowell 1850
Susan Cabot Sohier 1852
Sophie W. Dana 1873
Albert Fleetford Sise 1876
626 George Theodore Lyman 1850
James Cutler Dunn 1859
Harriet Stillman Hayward (Mrs. Winslow) 1862
627 George Williams Lyman 1850
Arthur Theodore Lyman 1851
628 Thacher Magoun and Thacher Magoun, Jr. 1850
Charles Parker Lombard 1865
Jos. Randolph Coolidge 1867
629 William Powell Mason 1850
George Dexter 1865
630 John M. Mayo 1850
Abby W. Pulsifer 1856
Mrs. Gridley James Fox Bryant (Louisa Bryant Bryant) 1858
631 Charles Merriam 1850
Charles Merriam and others, Executors 1866
632 Charles H. Mills 1850
Hales Wallace Suter 1851
John Wallace Suter 1876
633 Charles H. Mills 1850
Henry William Domett 1851
Charles Henry Minot 1851
634 Charles H. Mills 1850
John Q. A. Williams 1858
Charles Henry Dalton 1863
635 George Williams Lyman 1854
Charles William Eliot 1858
636 James K. Mills 1850
Samuel Baker Walcott 1851
Martha P. Walcott 1856
Charles Folsom Walcott 1880
637 Lawrence Nichols 1850
George Foxcroft Haskins 1863
638 Nathaniel H. Osgood 1850
Mary Channing Eustis 1852
639 James W. Paige 1850
Abbott Lawrence, Jr. 1869
640 Daniel Pinckney Parker 1850
Henry Tuke Parker 1852
William Nye Davis 1852
Samuel Bass King 1853
Samuel Crocker Cobb 1854
641 John Brooks Parker 1850
Annie B. Parker 1870
Charles A. Parker 1878
William Tennant Hart 1880
642 William F. Parrott 1850
Augustus E. Bachelder 1869
643 Arthur L. Payson 1850
James Diman Green 1857
Thomas Cushing 1858
Sarah Mason 1868
Hasket Derby 1880
644 George Peabody 1850
645 John H. Pearson 1850
David Miller Balfour 1852
646 Charles Callahan Perkins 1850
647 Edward Newton Perkins 1850
Benjamin F. Nourse 1859
Edmund F. Bradlee 1863
Josiah Putnam Bradlee 1875
648 Thomas Handasyd Perkins 1850
Rob't Bennett Forbes, Jr. 1851
Pliny Merrick 1858
Daniel Waldo Lincoln 1868
Benjamin W. Whitney 1874
Walter Hastings 1875
649 Thomas Handasyd Perkins 1850
George Cabot Perkins 1851
George N. Dana 1869
650 Thomas Handasyd Perkins 1850
Louis Cabot 1851
Edward Clarke Cabot 1857
Louis Cabot 1866
651 Lyman Perry 1850
Isaac Warren Danforth 1854
652 Edward D. Peters 1850
James H. Barnes 1858
Alfred Ellingwood Giles 1867
653 William Dudley Pickman 1850
654 Samuel S. Pierce 1850
Clement Hugh Hill 1881
655 William Hickling Prescott 1850
Peleg Whitman Chandler 1851
656 Josiah Phillips Quincy 1850
657 James Read and Christopher C. Chadwick 1850
James Read Chadwick and James Read 1868
James Read Chadwick 1871
658 Lewis Rice 1850
659 Henry Bromfield Rogers 1850
Daniel Dennison Slade 1853

660 William Ropes 1850
John Codman Ropes 1869
661 George R. Sampson 1850
Catherine Stevens 1863
662 William Sawyer 1850
Hannah F. Lee 1859
Julia Bryant 1864
663 David Sears 1850
William C. Rives, Jr. 1852
664 William Washburn 1850
665 Timothy Farrar 1850
Anna B. Crane 1875
666 Horatio Bigelow 1850
667 Nathaniel J. Bradlee 1850
Peters & Parkinson 1876
Seth James Thomas 1876
668 Gardiner Howland Shaw 1850
Charles Russell Codman 1863
Gardiner Howland Shaw 1864
Cora Lyman Shaw 1867
669 Robert Gould Shaw 1850
John Ham Williams Page 1858
Francis Minot Weld 1860
670 Robert Gould Shaw 1850
William B. Greene 1852
671 Quincy Adams Shaw 1850
Francis Parkman 1853
Francis Parkman 1880
672 Robert Gould Shaw, Jr. 1850
Charlotte Bartlett and Emily Hallowell 1874
673 Michael Hodge Simpson 1850
674 Francis Skinner 1850
William S. Lincoln 1851
William Leavitt Lincoln 1863
Arnold W. Conant 1867
George Browning Wilbur 1869
675 Jarvis Slade 1850
Charles Folsom Coffin 1860
676 Richard Soule 1850
Edwin Augustus Warren Harlow 1876
677 Paran Stevens 1850
Frederick H. Stimpson 1853
Susan Storer Stimpson 1876
678 Joshua Thomas Stevenson 1850
Jennie Porter Mills 1878
679 Henry Parkman Sturgis 1850
Elizabeth Orne Paine Sturgis 1871
680 Henry Jacob Bigelow 1850
681 Lewis William Tappan 1850
Silas Peirce 1866
Edward Clarke Cabot 1867
682 Enoch Train 1850
Frederic Walker Lincoln 1857
683 Nathaniel Thayer 1850
Sarah Harris Mills 1865
684 William Thomas 1850
Peter Butler, Jr. 1852
685 Charles Torrey 1850
John Colby Abbott 1851
Frederick W. Thayer 1854
Maria Wilder Thayer 1870
686 Frederic Tudor 1850
Henry James Tudor 1854
Fanny H. Tudor 1865
687 William Underwood 1850
Sara Hale Siedhof 1879
688 Thomas Beale Wales 1850
Frederick Lothrop Ames 1869
689 Samuel Gray Ward 1850
Charles H. Bennett 1878
690 Thomas Wren Ward 1850
Catherine Scollay 1858
Sullivan Whitney 1863
691 George Washington Warren 1850
Harriett Atwood Warren 1873
692 Aaron Davis Weld 1850
693 William F. Weld 1850
Caroline Langdon Weld (Mrs. Wm. G. Weld) 1880
694 John Welles 1850
Susan Jones Welles 1856
Jane Welles 1871
Jane P. Hunnewell 1881
695 Alden Bradford Weston 1850
Ezra Weston 1850
Henry Grew 1854
696 Charles Octavius Whitmore 1850
697 David Rice Whitney 1850
698 Edward Wigglesworth 1850
Edward Wigglesworth 1874
699 James Christie Wild 1850

700 Solomon Wildes 1850
Josiah Quincy, Jr. 1853
701 Charles Wilkins 1850
Samuel Hurd Walley 1858
James Ellison 1864
Ellen M. Shumway 1880
702 John Hubbard Wilkins 1850
George Hughes 1864
Harriet M. Harding 1881
703 David W. Williams 1850
William Harrington Mann 1856
704 George Foster Williams 1850
Ezra Farnsworth 1870
705 John E. Williams 1850
James Tucker Fisher 1851
Thomas Joseph Lee 1856
Samuel Devens 1858
Charles Torrey 1860
John Bronson Meer 1874
706 Hamilton Willis and Lucian Skinner 1850
Abel Goodrich Farwell 1852
Hamilton Willis 1853
Henry Willis 1856
Samuel Dennis Warren 1874
707 William Sohier, Trustee 1850
708 Joshua Huntington Wolcott 1850
Henry Allen Rice 1850
Richard Baker, Jr. 1852
709 Selectmen of Templeton, Ms. 1854
710 " " " 1854
711 " " " 1854
712 " " " 1854
713 " " " 1854
714 Selectmen of Littleton, Mass. 1854
715 " " " 1854
716 " " " 1854
717 " " " 1854
718 " " " 1854
719 Mary Ellen Russell 1854
720 Samuel Bass King 1854
Edwin Leonard 1860
721 Charles Barnard 1854
George Middleton Barnard and James Barnard, Trust. 1870
George Middleton Barnard and Samuel Barnard, Trust. 1872
722 Exec. of Samuel Appleton 1854
Zelotes Hosmer 1854
John J. Clarke 1862
Joseph Story Fay 1863
723 Exec. of Samuel Appleton 1854
George Bemis 1854
Frederick G. Bemis 1879
724 Exec. of Samuel Appleton 1854
Simon Willard 1854
725 Exec. of Samuel Appleton 1854
William Brigham 1854
John Pickering Lyman 1879
726 Exec. of Samuel Appleton 1854
Henry Grafton Clark 1854
James Jackson Storrow 1874
727 Exec. of Samuel Appleton 1854
William Courtis 1854
Henry Dawes 1862
Benjamin Cushing 1863
728 Exec. of Samuel Appleton 1854
John Bumstead Fessenden 1854
George Frederick Wilde 1871
729 Exec. of Samuel Appleton 1854
John H. Eastburn 1854
Caroline Hubbard Blatchford 1875
730 Exec. of Samuel Appleton 1854
William Jenkins Niles 1854
731 Exec. of Samuel Appleton 1854
Ephr'm Whitman Gurney 1854
732 Henry Ware Wales 1854
733 John Amory Lowell 1854
John Lowell 1867
734 John Amory Lowell 1854
Eliot Channing Clarke 1881
735 John Amory Lowell 1854
Augustus Lowell 1882
736 John Amory Lowell 1854
Katharine Bigelow Lowell 1882
737 John Amory Lowell 1854
Elizabeth Putnam Sohier 1882
738 John Amory Lowell 1854
Susan Cabot Sohier 1867
739 John Amory Lowell 1854
Arthur Theodore Lyman 1867
740 John Amory Lowell 1854
Augustus Lowell 1867
Percival Lowell 1882
741 John Amory Lowell 1854
Elizabeth Rebecca Lowell 1867
742 John Amory Lowell 1854
Sarah Putnam Lowell 1867
743 George O. Hovey 1854
Jacob Wendell, Jr. 1856
744 Charles Beck 1854
James Clarke Davis 1878
Jona. Ingersoll Bowditch 1878
745 Thomas Wren Ward 1854
William Downs Austin 1858
Catherine D. Austin 1861
Elven Dean Hall 1865
746 Samuel Gray Ward 1855
Jonas Harrod French 1878
747 John Borland 1854
Melancthon Woolsey Borland 1854
748 Henry Wainwright 1854
James Henry Davenport 1868
749 William Powell Mason 1854
Jeannie Ursula Dupee 1873
John Lawrence 1874
750 William Richards Lawrence 1854
Peter P. F. Degrand 1845
Henry Purkitt Kidder 1857
751 Francis K. Fisher 1854
Walter Howard Sweet 1874
752 Eliza Brimmer 1854
Martin Brimmer Inches 1860
753 Charles Stoddard 1854
754 Adeline Davis 1854
755 Moses L. Hale 1854
George Punchard 1862
Moses L. Hale 1865
Cyrus King Hale 1868
Josiah Little Hale 1874
756 Samuel Russell Payson 1854
Mrs. Samuel Russell Payson (Hannah Gilbert Payson) 1854
757 Paschal Paoli Pope 1854
Isa'c Danforth Farnsworth 1868
758 Rebecca W. Dearborn 1854
Samuel Worcester Bates 1868
Chauncey Smith 1870
759 Paschal Paoli Pope 1854
William H. Boardman 1868
Peters & Parkinson 1877
Mary L. Cochrane 1879
760 William Picard 1854
Samuel Eliot 1859
761 Benjamin Apthorp Gould 1854
Lucretia D. Gould 1864
762 Nathan Appleton 1854
Wm. Sumner Appleton 1864
763 Nathan Appleton 1854
Wm. Sumner Appleton 1864
764 Wm. Sumner Appleton 1854
765 Nathan Appleton 1854
Nathan Appleton 1864
Eliza Ingersoll Bowditch 1877
766 Nathan Appleton 1854
Nathan Appleton, Jr. 1857
Alfred Bowditch 1877
767 Nathan Appleton 1854
Nathan Appleton 1864
Henry Dorr Sullivan 1865
768 Nathan Appleton 1854
Henry Wadsworth Longfellow, Guardian 1864
Charles Appleton Longfellow 1865
769 Nathan Appleton 1854
Franklin H. Story and others, Trustees 1862
Henry Wadsworth Longfellow, Guardian 1864
Ernest Wadsworth Longfellow 1866
770 Nathan Appleton 1854
Franklin H. Story and others, Trustees 1864
H. H. Stevens 1865
Eben S. Stevens 1868
George H. Appleton 1871
Robert Sedgwick Watson 1876
771 Nathan Appleton 1854
Franklin H. Story and others, Trustees 1864

John Chandler Bancroft 1865
772 David Sears, Jr. 1854
Emily E. Sears 1874
Henry Francis Sears 1874
773 George Callender 1854
Timothy Bigelow 1862
Amelia S. Bigelow 1874
Edward Farmer 1876
George Lothrop Bradley 1882
774 George Francis Parkman 1854
775 William Warren Tucker 1854
776 Edmund L. S. Benzon 1854
George Parsons King 1869
777 Edward Cruft 1854
Samuel Breck Cruft 1854
778 Eben C. Stanwood 1854
Samuel Hall, Jr. 1868
Mary E. Hall 1873
779 James Davis, Jr. 1854
Louise Brooks 1881
780 Joshua Henshaw Hayward 1854
John Henry Jenks 1858
781 Albert Fearing 1854
John Morehead Clark 1871
782 Thomas Wigglesworth 1854
Ann Wigglesworth 1855
783 Thomas Wigglesworth 1854
Thomas Wigglesworth, Trustees, 1855
Mary Wigglesworth 1861
784 Thomas Wigglesworth 1854
Jane Grew 1855
Thomas Wigglesworth 1869
785 Samuel Appleton Appleton 1854
Amos William Stetson 1862
786 William Amory 1854
Charles Walter Amory 1866
787 Jonathan Ellis 1854
James Clarke White 1868
788 George Richards Minot 1854
789 Jacob Bigelow 1854
Herman Brimmer Inches 1854
790 Rufus Ellis 1854
791 Edward Reynolds Hall 1854
792 Elizabeth Gair Bradlee 1854
Elizabeth Gair Abbott 1856
793 Lucy Hall Bradlee 1854
794 Josiah Bradlee 1854
Frederic Stone 1854
Mary I. Hooper 1872
Eunice Hooper 1874
795 Josiah Bradlee 1854
Randolph Marshall Clark 1855
Henry Willard Williams 1874
Charles Herbert Williams 1879
796 Josiah Bradlee 1854
John De Wolfe Smith 1854
John Gray Rogers 1860
John Rogers 1879
Andrew Sigourney Bird 1879
797 Josiah Bradlee 1854
Charles Torrey 1854
Lydia E. E. Greene 1854
Benj. Greenleaf Boardman 1859
798 Josiah Bradlee 1854
Edward Wheelwright 1854
799 Josiah Bradlee 1854
Henry Van Brunt 1855
Annie W. Whitney 1859
Mary Whitney 1871
800 Jared Sparks 1854
801 Mrs. William Pratt 1854
Mary Pratt, Jr., and Sarah P. Pratt 1855
Mary Pratt 1865
802 Mrs. William Pratt 1854
Mary Pratt, Jr., and Sarah P. Pratt 1855
Sarah P. Pratt 1865
Mary Pratt 1867
803 Mrs. William Pratt 1854
Mary Pratt, Jr., and Sarah P. Pratt 1855
Robert M. Pratt 1865
Charles Henry Miller, Jr. 1878
804 George Washington Wales 1854
Gardner Paine Gates 1854
805 Thomas Beale Wales 1854
Charles Theodore Carruth 1871
806 John Wiley Edmands 1854
Benjamin G. Gay 1877
Jona. Ingersoll Bowditch 1881
807 Thomas Jefferson Coolidge 1854
808 Charles Hook Appleton 1854
John Appleton Burnham and Franklin Gordon Dexter, Trustees 1879
809 Franklin Gordon Dexter 1854
810 Charles Amory 1854
John Singleton Copley Greene 1854
Mary A. Greene 1873
Charles Albert Whittier 1873
J. H. Chadwick 1874
Joseph Veazie 1877
811 Mary Anne Wales 1854
812 Elizabeth W. Emmons 1854
George Foster 1871
Augustus Floyd Webster 1874
Edward Henry Whorf 1876
Augustus Floyd Webster 1878
813 Joseph Iasigi 1854
Eulalie Iasigi 1878
814 James Leeds 1854
John Chipman Gray, Jr. 1875
815 Edward Montagu Cary 1854
816 Thomas A. Goddard 1854
John Adams Bates Cutter 1869
Wm. Henshaw Horton, Jr. 1875
John Templeton Bowen, 1880
Robert Ralston Newell, Trustee 1881
817 Thomas Goddard 1854
818 Daniel F. Child 1854
Henry Walker Frost 1860
819 Hugh R. Kendall 1854
Benjamin F. Kendall 1856
Moses Bradstreet Wildes 1868
820 Exec. of Robt. G. Shaw, Sr. 1854
Benjamin Franklin Atkins 1854
821 Exec. of Robt. G. Shaw, Sr. 1854
James McGregor 1855
Robert Roberts Bishop 1876
H. C. Wainwright & Co. 1881
Charles Smith Bradley 1881
822 Exec. of Robt. G. Shaw, Sr. 1854
George W. Crockett 1855
William Albert Crockett 1860
823 Exec. of Robt. G. Shaw, Sr. 1854
Alexander Wadsworth 1855
824 Exec. of Robt. G. Shaw, Sr. 1854
Supply C. Thwing 1855
Edw. Britton Townsend 1879
825 Exec. of Robt. G. Shaw, Sr. 1854
John Colby Abbott 1855
826 Exec. of Robt. G. Shaw, Sr. 1854
Gardiner Howland Shaw 1855
Cora Lyman Shaw 1867
827 Exec. of Robt. G. Shaw, Sr. 1854
Arthur Webster Tufts 1855
828 Exec. of Robt. G. Shaw, Sr. 1854
Jonathan Brown Bright 1855
829 Exec. of Robt. G. Shaw, Sr. 1854
Charles B. Dana 1854
John N. Turner 1863
Nathaniel Dana Turner 1868
830 George Williams Lyman 1854
Julia Lyman 1880
831 George Williams Lyman 1854
Arthur Lyman 1880
832 George Williams Lyman 1854
Herbert Lyman 1880
833 George Williams Lyman 1854
Sarah Pratt Sears 1880
834 George Williams Lyman 1854
Sarah Pratt Sears 1880
835 George Williams Lyman 1854
Annie Lyman Sears 1880
836 George Williams Lyman 1854
Lydia Williams Paine 1880
837 George Williams Lyman 1854
Lydia Williams Paine 1880
838 George Williams Lyman 1854
Edith Paine 1880
839 George Williams Lyman 1854
Robert Treat Paine, Jr. 1864
840 Sidney Bartlett 1858
841 George Horatio Kuhn 1854
William Putnam Kuhn 1870
842 Thomas C. Smith 1854
Frances B. Smith 1881
843 Charles W. Cartwright 1854
James H. T. Adams 1873
Mary Anne Catharine Livermore 1873
844 Ebenezer Dale 1854
Ebenezer Dale 1872
Lucy Kimball 1876
L. Cushing Kimball 1878
David Pulsifer Kimball 1879
845 Theron J. Dale 1854
Edward A. W. Hammatt 1874
Grace Meserve Coolidge 1878
846 Henry Upham 1854
John Appleton Burnham and Geo. P. Upham, Trustees 1876
Henry Upham 1881
847 Gardner Brewer 1854
Thomes Mayo Brewer 1855
Sally Rice Brewer 1881
848 George L. Pratt 1854
Henry D. Austin 1868
William Eben Stone 1880
849 James Hayward 1854
Tilly B. Hayward 1866
George Frederick Farley 1881
850 Seth W. Fowle 1854
Robert Ingalls Burbank 1860
William L. Beal 1861
George Stark 1872
Daniel Augustus Patch 1880
851 Francis Skinner & Co. 1854
Thornton Kirkland Lothrop 1874
852 Charles Uriah Cotting 1854
Daniel Davies 1857
Charles Albert Whittier 1877
853 Alexander Hamilton Vinton 1854
Alexander Hamilton Vinton 1856
John C. Potter 1859
James E. Root 1865
Susan Tillinghast Kimball 1878
854 William H. Milton 1854
Richard S. Milton 1880
855 James Lodge 1854
Mary G. Lodge, Executrix 1870
Beck Brothers 1870
Cyrus Woodman 1870
856 Isaac Thacher 1854
857 William Ropes 1854
Joseph Samuel Ropes 1869
858 James Sturgis 1854
Dexter David Bowman 1878
859 Adam Wallace Thaxter 1854
William Cowper Peters 1862
860 Blake, Howe, & Co. 1854
Blake Brothers & Co. 1859
861 Glidden & Williams 1854
John Murray Glidden 1872
862 Abner Kingman 1854
Greely Stevenson Curtis 1881
863 Henry Lawrence 1854
Frederick Almy 1872
Charles A. Phelps 1872
864 Joseph Whitney 1854
Ellerton Pratt Whitney 1871
865 William Benjamin Bacon 1854
866 Levi B. Meriam 1854
Charles Greenleaf Wood 1869
867 Elijah Dana Brigham 1854
Daniel L. Furber 1869
868 Richard Baker, Jr. 1854
869 Francis Boardman Crowninshield 1854
Benj. Wm. Crowninshield 1857
870 William F. Parrott 1854
Andrew Bigelow 1869
Edwin Wright, Trustee 1878
871 George Bruce Upton 1854
George Bruce Upton 1865
872 William Shimmin 1854
Chas. Franklin Shimmin 1857
873 William Goodwin Russell 1854
874 Isaac Livermore 1854
Silas A. Quincy 1861
875 Cyrus Alger 1854
Charles Hickling 1856
Edward Hickling Bradford 1878
876 Francis Alger 1854
Cyrus Augustus Bartol 1859
877 Edward C. Bates 1854
Josiah H. Cobb 1867
Catharine Lawrence Appleton 1868
Anne Parker Appleton 1878
878 Charles C. Little 1854
John D. Parker 1870

No.	Name	Year
	Joseph Stone	1870
	Oliver Ditson	1881
879	George Henry Timmins	1854
	Benj. Barnard Appleton	1875
	Jane W. Appleton	1881
880	George Barrell Emerson	1854
881	Charles Linzee Tilden	1854
882	John G. Torrey	1854
	John Revere	1869
883	Nathaniel Goddard	1854
	Peters & Parkinson	1875
	Joseph Cook	1878
884	George Walker Weld	1854
885	Richard T. Sprague	1854
	George Darius Sargent	1881
886	John Lowell Gardner	1854
887	George Ticknor	1854
	John Wells	1873
888	Robert Charles Winthrop	1854
	Robert Charles Winthrop, Jr.	1878
889	Augustus Flagg	1854
	Charles Jackson Paine	1868
890	John L. Payson	1854
891	Octavius Brooks Frothingham	1854
892	Moses Field Fowler	1854
	Hattie L. Stevens	1869
893	Augustine Heard	1854
	George Otis Shattuck	1872
894	Andrew Townshend Hall	1854
	Lydia Y. Hall	1877
	Joshua Montgomery Sears	1881
895	Joseph Coolidge	1854
	Charles John Whitmore	1880
896	Joseph W. Revere	1854
897	John Welles	1854
	Hollis Hunnewell	1872
898	John Welles	1854
	Jane Hubbard Hunnewell	1881
899	John Welles	1854
	Henry Sargent Hunnewell	1881
900	Adolphus Davis	1854
	James W. Davis	1862
	Joseph Beale Glover	1863
901	Calvin W. Clark	1854
902	Junius S. Morgan	1854
	J. Pierpont Morgan	1854
	George Bartlett	1855
	Henry Bromfield Pearson	1865
	W. B. Townsend	1865
	Catherine M. Bissell	1866
	BenjaminFranklin Nourse	1868
	Alice Helen Buck	1875
903	Benjamin Welles	1854
	Benjamin S. Welles	1860
	Henry W. Wellington	1865
	Charles Fairchild	1871
904	Benjamin Welles	1854
	Russell Sturgis, Jr., Guardian	1871
905	Benjamin Welles	1854
	John Osborne Sargent	1870
906	Powell Mason Parkman	1854
	David W. Cunningham	1860
	Oscar Gassett	1861
	George William Baldwin	1864
907	John Phelps Putnam	1854
	Frederick Dexter	1869
908	David Sears	1854
	Frederick Sears Grand d'Hauteville	1871
909	David Sears	1854
	Harriet Sears Crowninshield	1871
	Caspar Crowninshield	1873
910	David Sears	1854
	Harriet Sears Crowninshield	1871
	Cora Crowninshield	1873
911	David Sears	1854
	Frederick Richard Sears	1871
912	David Sears	1854
	Frederick Richard Sears	1871
913	David Sears	1854
	Grace W. Rives	1871
914	David Sears	1854
	Knyvett Winthrop Sears	1871
915	David Sears	1854
	Grace W. Rives	1871
916	David Sears	1854
	Anna S. Amory	1871
	Ellis Loring Motte	1880
917	David Sears	1854
	Anna S. Amory	1871
	John Lewis Bremer	1880
918	Thomas P. Cushing	1854
	Ebenezer Francis Parker	1865
919	James Savage	1855
920	Octavius Pickering	1855
	Henry Pickering	1864
921	Justin Winsor	1855
922	William Rounseville Alger	1854
923	Samuel Miller Quincy	1854
924	Edmund Quincy, Jr.	1854
925	Henry Parker Quincy	1854
926	Amos Adams Lawrence	1854
	Howard Stockton	1879
927	Amos Adams Lawrence	1854
	Amory Appleton Lawrence	1869
928	Amos Adams Lawrence	1854
	Charles Folsom	1856
	Amos Adams Lawrence	1873
	William Lawrence	1873
929	William Lincoln	1854
	Benjamin Robbins Curtis	1858
	Walter Curtis	1876
	Benjamin Robbins Curtis	1877
	Seth C. Chandler, Jr.	1879
930	Martin Brimmer	1855
931	" "	1855
932	" "	1855
933	" "	1855
934	" "	1855
935	" "	1855
	Andrew B. Almon	1864
936	Martin Brimmer	1855
	Franklin W. Pitcher	1864
	Quincy Adams Shaw	1873
937	Martin Brimmer	1855
	William Gray Brooks	1858
	Otis Everett Weld	1875
938	Martin Brimmer	1855
	Elias Hasket Derby	1858
939	Martin Brimmer	1855
	Edward Dexter Sohier	1857
940	Francis Bassett	1855
	Elisha Bassett	1856
	Francis Josiah Humphrey	1876
941	John Reed Brewer	1855
942	Henry Weld Fuller	1855
	Edmund Farwell Slafter	1857
943	Charles Gordon	1855
	Frank William Hunt	1874
	Charles Greenough Chase	1874
944	David Stoddard Greenough	1855
	Edmund Sanford Clark	1869
	Francis Augustus Brooks	1872
	Francis Vose Parker	1875
945	Isaiah B. Libbey	1855
946	Robert Means Mason	1855
	Ellen Francis Mason	1879
947	Benjamin White Nichols	1855
948	Lyman Nichols	1855
	Lyman Nichols	1879
949	Robert Williams	1855
	Arthur Williams	1865
	Antoinette O. Williams	1877
	Horace H. Stevens	1877
	John Charles Phillips	1878
950	John Chipman Gray	1855
	Jacob Willard Pierce	1856
951	Giles Henry Lodge	1855
	Isaac Osgood	1857
	Edward John Biddle	1866
	Josiah H. Cobb	1869
	John Barber Winslow	1870
952	William P. Pierce	1855
	Samuel Hatch	1870
	Samuel Baker Rindge	1875
953	Alexander Hamilton Rice	1855
954	Isaac Rich	1855
955	William D. Swan	1855
	John Dickinson	1861
	James H. T. Adams	1873
	Robert Williamson Lovett	1876
956	S. Benton Thompson	1855
	John Heath Whitney	1867
957	Edmund P. Tileston	1855
	Abel Camp Martin	1866
958	Edmund P. Tileston	1855
	Charles Stratton Dana	1873
959	Edmund P. Tileston	1855
	Eustace Carey Fitz	1873
960	George Washington Warren	1855
	George Willis Warren	1860
961	George A. Whitney	1855
	James P. Whitney	1868
	Francis Amory	1871
962	David Whiton	1855
	Hugh Montgomery	1858
963	John Hubbard Wilkins	1855
	William Rogers	1864
	Anna Lothrop Rodman	1870
964	John Eliot Thayer	1855
	Ephraim Peabody	1855
965	John Eliot Thayer	1855
	George Putnam	1855
	George Putnam, Jr.	1858
966	John Eliot Thayer	1855
	Ebenezer Francis Thayer	1855
	James Henry Blake	1865
967	John Eliot Thayer	1855
	Nathaniel Thayer	1858
968	John Eliot Thayer	1855
	Nathaniel Thayer	1858
969	John Eliot Thayer	1855
	Nathaniel Thayer	1858
970	John Eliot Thayer	1855
	Nathaniel Thayer	1858
971	John Eliot Thayer	1855
	Nathaniel Thayer	1858
972	John Eliot Thayer	1855
	Nathaniel Thayer	1858
973	John Eliot Thayer	1855
	Nathaniel Thayer	1858
974	John Chipmam Gray	1855
	William Rotch Robeson	1856
975	John Chipman Gray	1855
	Levi Bartlett	1856
	Henry C. Angell	1865
976	John Chipman Gray	1855
	Edward H. Green	1856
	Nathan Matthews, Jr.	1872
977	John Chipman Gray	1855
	George S. Winslow	1856
	John Andrew Henshaw	1856
978	Edward William Hooper	1855
979	William Sturgis	1855
	Samuel E. Sawyer	1859
	Thomas E. Dorr	1862
	Mrs. Richard Price Hallowell	1865
980	William Sturgis	1855
	John Benjamin Hench	1864
981	William Sturgis	1855
	W. A. Kimball	1864
	Henry Saltonstall	1866
	William Sheafe	1869
	William Sheafe, Jr.	1880
982	William Sturgis	1855
	Joseph Cotton Hovey	1864
	Ellen R. Motley	1875
983	William Sturgis	1855
	James O. Murray	1864
	James Haughton	1871
	Austin Daniel Kilham	1876
984	William Sturgis	1855
	Georgiana E. Cooley	1859
	William Henry Hill	1863
985	William Sturgis	1855
	Andrew Bigelow	1859
	Edwin Wright, Trustee	1878
	John Tucker Prince	1878
986	William Sturgis	1855
	Nathan A. Tufts	1859
	Samuel Hastings	1874
987	William Sturgis	1855
	William Sturgis Hooper	1856
988	Executors of Thomas Handasyd Perkins	1855
	William Ferdinand Cary	1855
	Nancy Perkins Cary	1880
989	Executors of Thomas Handasyd Perkins	1855
	William Ferdinand Cary	1855
	Nancy Perkins Cary	1880
990	Executors of Thomas Handasyd Perkins	1855
	Thomas Graves Cary	1855
	Mary Perkins Cary	1866
	Thomas Graves Cary	1880
991	Executors of Thomas Handasayd Perkins	1855
	William Howard Gardiner	1855
992	Executors of Thomas Handasyd Perkins	1855
	Israel Whitney	1856
993	Executors of Thomas Handayd Perkins	1855
	Thos. Handasyd Perkins	1855

994	Executors of Thomas Handasyd Perkins	1855
	Thomas Graves Cary	1855
	Mary Perkins Cary	1866
	Sarah Gray Cary	1880
995	Executors of Thomas Handasyd Perkins	1855
	William Howard Gardiner	1855
	Samuel Lothrop Thorndike	1876
996	Executors of Thomas Handasyd Perkins	1855
	Samuel Cabot	1855
	Walter Channing Cabot	1857
997	Executors of Thomas Handasyd Perkins	1855
	Charles Follen	1855
	John Higginson Cabot	1873
998	Henry Melville Parker	1855
	Francis L. Lee	1857
	Harriet W. Phillips	1868
999	Frederic Tudor	1855
1000	Frank William Andrews	1856
1001	John Barnard Swett Jackson	1856
1002	John Chipman Gray	1856
	Russell Gray	1881
1003	John Chipman Gray	1856
	George Shattuck Cushing	1865
1004	John Chipman Gray	1856
	John Appleton Burnham	1857
1005	John Chipman Gray	1856
	George Brooks Bigelow	1857
	Samuel Bigelow	1879
	Wm. Richardson Dupee	1879
1006	John Chipman Gray	1856
	Perkins Institution for the Blind	1864
1007	Joseph Hobson Phipps	1856
	Edward Sawyer	1867
1008	Algernon Coolidge	1856
1009	Edward Jackson Lowell	1856
1010	George Winslow	1856
	William Henry Winslow	1859
	Joseph B. Morss	1863
1011	Georgiana Lowell	1856
1012	Executors of James Brown	1856
	James Alexander Dupee	1857
	John Bacon	1860
1013	Executors of James Brown	1856
	Edward Austin	1857
1014	Executors of James Brown	1856
	Samuel Langley, Jr.	1857
1015	James Perry Brown	1856
	Adams Sherman Hill	1870
1016	Francis Edward Parker	1856
1017	Master of the Latin School	1856
1018	Master of English High School	1856
1019	Samuel Austin	1856
	Edward Austin	1860
	Henry Austin	1881
	Henry W. Cunningham	1881
1020	Chandler Robbins	1856
	Hamlin Rand Harding	1866
1021	William Turell Andrews	1856
	John Taylor Clark	1856
	Daniel Collamore Heath	1882
1022	William Turell Andrews	1856
	Edward Reynolds Andrews	1856
	William Scollay Whitwell	1880
1023	Charles Eliot Norton	1856
	Arthur George Sedgwick	1868
	Eliot Norton	1880
	Thomas Emerson Proctor	1881
1024	Charles Callahan Perkins	1857
1025	Edward Newton Perkins	1857
1026	Josiah Quincy	1857
	Robert Cassie Waterston	1859
1027	Josiah Quincy	1857
	Eliza Susan Quincy	1861
1028	Josiah Quincy	1857
	Helen Frances Quincy	1861
	Lewis Wm. Tappan, Jr.	1876
1029	Josiah Quincy	1857
	Abby Phillips Quincy	1864
1030	Josiah Quincy	1857
	Mary Sophia Quincy	1864
1031	Edmund Quincy	1857
	Sarah Rhea Bowditch	1878
1032	Edward Blake	1857
	William Payne Blake	1867
1033	Thomas Motley, Jr.	1857
	William Henry Greeley	1877
1034	William Hickling Prescott	1857
	William Henry Greeley	1862
	Francis Vergnies Balch	1874
	Levi Lincoln Thaxter	1878
1035	William Hickling Prescott	1857
	Jonathan Preston	1862
	Emily West Preston	1876
1036	Clarke Gayton Pickman	1857
	George Walker	1860
	Charles A. Stevens	1867
	George Ropes	1876
1037	John Pickering Putnam	1857
	Charles Ammi Cutter	1879
	Anna W. Huntington	1880
1038	William Dwight	1857
	Geo. Washington Morse	1879
1039	Francis Caleb Loring	1857
	Otis Norcross	1872
1040	William Gray, Executor	1857
	William Gray	1858
	Nathaniel Ingersoll Bowditch	1859
	Elizabeth Brown Bowditch	1881
1041	William Gray, Executor	1857
	William Gray	1858
	Leverett Saltonstall	1859
	William Minot	1860
1042	William Gray, Executor	1857
	William Gray	1858
	Francis Henry Gray	1859
	Hedwiga R. Gray	1880
1043	William Gray, Executor	1857
	William Gray	1858
1044	William Gray, Executor	1857
	William Gray	1858
	Jonathan French	1859
1045	Andrew Eliot Belknap	1857
	Robert Trueman	1859
	Theodore William Snow	1859
	Charles M. Delano	1860
	William B. Stearns	1861
	James Alexander Dupee	1862
1046	Charles H. Mills	1857
	Arthur Lithgow Devens	1859
	James Clarke Davis	1873
1047	Joseph Swett Coolidge	1857
1048	Joseph Swett Coolidge	1857
1049	Charles William Storey	1858
	Elizabeth B. Inches	1858
	William Barry Wood	1875

ALPHABETICAL LIST

OF THE

PROPRIETORS OF THE BOSTON ATHENÆUM,

FROM

ITS FOUNDATION TO JANUARY 31, 1882,

ACCORDING TO THE CERTIFICATE BOOK.

Note. The numbers *within parentheses* denote shares *formerly* held by the persons to whose names they are annexed.

A

Abbot, Elizabeth Gair 792
Abbot, Samuel Leonard 285
Abbott, Jacob (67)
Abbott, John Colby (685), 825
Adams, Abigail B. (425)
Adams, Benjamin (104, 299)
Adams, Brooks 425
Adams, Caleb (104)
Adams, Charles Francis (359, 488), 255
Adams, Charles Francis, Jr. 488
Adams, Charles Fred. (422)
Adams, Emily M. (422)
Adams, Fanny Crowninshield 61
Adams, James (80)
Adams, James H. T. (843, 955)
Adams, John Quincy (255), 359
Adams, Sarah L. 213
Adams, Theodore Parker 306
Adams, Zabdiel Boylston (210)
Agassiz, Elizabeth Cary 215
Albree, John (75)
Alexander, Andrew 251
Alger, Cyrus (102, 875)
Alger, Francis (7, 876)
Alger, William Rounseville 922
Allen, Charles (24)
Allen, Freeman (190)
Allen, Henry Freeman 190
Allen, James (24)
Allen, James, Jr. (24)
Allen, Robert B. (24)
Alley, John A. (541)
Allston, John E. (50)
Almon, Andrew B. 935
Almy, Frederick (608, 863)
American Bell Telephone Co. 337
Ames, Frederick Lothrop 688
Ames, Oliver 524
Ammidown, Holmes (466)
Amory, Anna S. (916, 917)
Amory, Charles (309, 501, 810), 502
Amory, Charles Walter 786
Amory, Copley (331, 501)
Amory, Edward Linzee 309
Amory, Francis 961
Amory, James Sullivan 273
Amory, Jonathan (145)
Amory, Jonathan, Jr. (145)
Amory, Nathaniel (68)
Amory, Nathaniel 258
Amory, Robert (331)
Amory, Thomas Coffin (17)
Amory, Thomas Coffin (17)
Amory, Thomas Coffin, Jr. (226)
Amory, William (786), 278
Amory, William, Jr. 503
Andrews, Caleb (128)
Andrews, Charles Lowell (128, 556)
Andrews, Edward Reynolds (1022)
Andrews, Ebenezer T. (60)
Andrews, Frank William 1000
Andrews, Henry (112)
Andrews, James (254)
Andrews, William Turell (60, 1021, 1022)
Angell, Henry C. 975
Appleton, Anne Parker 877
Appleton, Benjamin Barnard (879)
Appleton, Catharine Lawrence (877)
Appleton, Charles Hook (808)
Appleton, Eliza 410
Appleton, Francis Henry (327)
Appleton, Francis Henry 327
Appleton, Frank Parker 51
Appleton, George H. (770)
Appleton, Jane W. 879
Appleton, Mary (491)
Appleton, Nathan (27, 414, 415, 416, 504, 762, 763, 765, 766, 767, 768, 769, 770, 771)
Appleton, Nathan (765, 766, 767)
Appleton, Robert (505)
Appleton, Samuel (129, 423, 491, 492, 506, 507, 508)
Appleton, Samuel, Executors of (722, 723, 724, 725, 726, 727, 728, 729, 730, 731)
Appleton, Samuel Appleton (509, 785)
Appleton, Thomas Gold 27, 414, 416
Appleton, William (121)
Appleton, William, Jr. 510
Appleton, William Channing 580
Appleton, William Greenleaf, Trustee (409, 410)
Appleton, William Sumner 762, 763, 764
Apthorp, John T. (84)
Armstrong, Abigail (511), 194
Armstrong, Samuel T. (194)
Arnold, Mrs. *See* Crowninshield, C. M.
Arnold, Howard Payson (307)
Arnold, Samuel S. (371)
Aspinwall, Thomas (176)
Atkins, Benjamin Franklin 820
Atkinson, Charles Follen 295
Atkinson, Edward 229
Atkinson, Mary C. (229)
Austin, Catherine D. (745)
Austin, Daniel (91)
Austin, Edward (417, 1019), 1013
Austin, Henry (1019)
Austin, Henry D. (848)
Austin, James Trecothick (107, 172)
Austin, James Walker 100
Austin, Ivers James (107)
Austin, Samuel (49, 512, 1019)
Austin, William (417)
Austin, William Downes (745)
Avery, John (71)
Aylwin, Charles F. (405)
Aylwin, William Cushing (405)

B

Babcock, Adam (86)
Bachelder, Augustus E. 642
Bacon, Daniel C. (427)
Bacon, Daniel G. (427)
Bacon, Ebenezer 514
Bacon, Francis (432)
Bacon, John 1012
Bacon, William Benjamin 865
Baker, Charles Wm. (50)
Baker, Eleanor J. W. 613
Baker, Richard, Jr. 708, 868
Baker, Walter (613)
Baker, William W. (611)
Balch, Agnes Gordon 307
Balch, Anna Loring (286)
Balch, Francis Vergnies (1034), 286
Balch, Joseph (286)
Baldwin, George R. 515
Baldwin, George Wm. 906
Baldwin, James F. (515)
Balfour, David Miller 645
Ball, Stephen, Jr. (322)
Bancroft, George (92)
Bancroft, John Chandler 771
Bancroft, Robert Hale 197
Bancroft, Silas Atkins 98
Bangs, Benjamin (408)
Bangs, Edward 492
Bangs, Frances Elmira 491
Bangs, George Pemberton (516)
Barnard, Caroline M. 136
Barnard, Charles (69, 274, 721)
Barnard, George Middleton 112
Barnard, George Middleton and James, Trustees (721)
Barnard, George Middleton and Samuel, Trustees 721
Barnard, James Munson 69
Barnes, Isaac Orr (303)
Barnes, James H. (652)
Barrell, Samuel B. (189)
Barrett, Samuel (371)
Barstow, John S. (44)
Bartlet, Gordon (51)
Bartlett, Francis 284
Bartlett, George (902)
Bartlett, Levi (975)
Bartlett, Sidney (284), 840
Bartlett, Thomas (97)
Bartol, Cyrus Augustus 876
Bass, Seth (205)
Bassett, Elisha (940)
Bassett, Francis (940), 241
Batchelder, John M. 330
Batchelder, Samuel (330)
Batcheller, Alfred Hubbard 402
Batcheller, Francis 152
Bates, Edward C. (877)
Bates, George (224)
Bates, John Douglas 383

C

I

J

K

LIST OF LIFE SUBSCRIBERS.

N. B. This list embraces the names (in Italics) of all the members of the Anthology Club except *Arthur Maynard Walter*, who died before the incorporation of the Athenæum. They became entitled to life-shares by a vote of the Proprietors, passed in 1807.

Alden, Timothy
Bigelow, Jacob
Boott, Kirk
Brimmer, George Watson
Buckminster, Joseph Stevens
Burroughs, Charles
Cabot, Frederick
Clap, Elisha
Codman, John
Colman, Henry
Dana, Edmund Trowbridge
Dana, Samuel Luther
Danforth, Blowers
Eaton, Asa
Emerson, Ralph Waldo
Emerson, William
Everett, Alexander Hill
Field, Robert
Freeman, James
Frothingham, Nathaniel Langdon
Foster, Leonard
Gardiner, John Sylvester John
Gardiner, Robert Hallowell
Gore, Christopher
Gorham, John
Gray, Thomas
Greene, Benjamin Daniel
Greenwood, Francis William Pitt
Harris, Thaddeus Mason
Head, Joseph, Jr.
Holmes, Abiel
Jackson, Charles
Jackson, James
Kirkland, John Thornton
Lowell, Edward Jackson
Lowell, Francis Cabot
Lyman, William
McKean, Joseph
McKean, Joseph William
Mansfield, Isaac
Minister of King's Chapel
Moody, David
Moody, David J.
Moody, Paul
Norton, Andrews
Parkman, Francis
Payne, William Edward
Pickering, Octavius
Pierce, John
Porter, Eliphalet
Ritchie, Andrew
Sales, Francis
Sargent, Winthrop
Savage, James
Shaw, William Smith
Smith, Isaac
Stickney, John
Stuart, Gilbert
Tappan, Charles
Thacher, Peter Oxenbridge
Thacher, Samuel Cooper
Thorndike, Israel
Ticknor, George
Tuckerman, Joseph
Tudor, William, Jr.
Warren, John Collins
Welles, Benjamin
Wells, William
Willard, Sidney
Willard, Solomon

LIST OF OFFICERS.

PRESIDENTS.

Theophilus Parsons	1807–13
John Davis	1814–15
John Lowell	1816–19
Josiah Quincy	1820–29
Thomas Handasyd Perkins	1830–32
Francis Calley Gray	1833–36
George Hayward	1837–45
Thomas Graves Cary	1846–59
John Amory Lowell	1860–76
Charles Francis Adams	1877–79
Samuel Eliot	1880–

VICE-PRESIDENTS.

John Davis	1807–13
John Lowell	1814–15
Josiah Quincy	1816–19
James Perkins	1820
John Richards	1821–22
Peter Oxenbridge Thacher	1823–25
Francis Calley Gray	1826–32
George Ticknor	1833
George Hayward	1834–36
Thomas Graves Cary	1837–45
John Amory Lowell	1846–59
George Livermore	1860–65
Andrew Townshend Hall	1866–75
Charles Francis Adams	1876
Charles Deane	1877–

TREASURERS.

John Lowell	1807–10
Joseph Tilden	1811–15
Nathan Appleton	1816–27
Thomas Wren Ward	1828–36
Josiah Quincy, Jr.	1837–51
Samuel Hooper	1852–53
Henry Bromfield Rogers	1854–67
Arthur Theodore Lyman	1868
Henry Bromfield Rogers	1869–76
Charles Pickering Bowditch	1877–

SECRETARIES.

William Smith Shaw	1807–23
Henry Codman	1824–27
Josiah Quincy, Jr.	1828–30
William Turell Andrews	1831–45
Henry Tuke Parker	1846–50
Charles Pelham Curtis, Jr.	1851–52
William Sohier Dexter	1853–54
Henry Melville Parker	1855
William Appleton, Jr.	1856
Lemuel Shaw, Jr.	1857–61
Arthur Theodore Lyman	1862–67
Charles Francis Adams, Jr.	1868–72
Brooks Adams	1873–79
Charles Herbert Williams	1880–

DIRECTORS, 1807.

William Emerson,
John Thornton Kirkland,
Peter Oxenbridge Thacher,
Robert Hallowell Gardiner,
Joseph Stevens Buckminster.

Note. At the meeting of the Corporation of the Boston Athenæum, April 7, 1807, it was voted that the officers of the Corporation should consist of a President, Vice-President, Treasurer, Secretary, and five Directors, and at a meeting held July 17, 1807, the Board of five Directors was changed to a Board of six Trustees. At a meeting of the Proprietors held February 4, 1822, the number of Trustees was raised to nine, and at a meeting held January 5, 1852, it was increased to fifteen.

TRUSTEES.

William Emerson	1807–10
John Thornton Kirkland	1807–10
Peter Oxenbridge Thacher	1807–22
Robert Hallowell Gardiner	1807–15
Joseph Stevens Buckminster	1807–12
Harrison Gray Otis	1807–21
James Perkins	1807–19
Samuel Eliot	1807–10
Samuel Dexter	1811–15
Richard Sullivan	1811–21
John Lowell	1811–21
Josiah Quincy	1813–15
John Richards	1814–20
John Davis	1816–21
Joseph Tilden	1816–22
David Sears	1819–22
Theodore Lyman, Jr.	1821–26
Edward Everett	1822–23
Francis Calley Gray	1822–25
Amos Lawrence	1822–25
Charles Jackson	1822
Henry Codman	1823–27
Samuel Swett	1823–27
William Sturgis	1823–25
Thomas Wigglesworth	1823–28
George Ticknor	1823–32
Nathaniel Bowditch	1826–33
Samuel Dorr	1826–27
Edward Brooks	1826–29
George Hayward	1827–33

Israel Thorndike	1828
Henderson Inches	1828–31
Joseph Coolidge, Jr.	1828–29
Franklin Dexter	1828–35
Charles Pelham Curtis	1829–34
John Lowell, Jr.	1829
Isaac P. Davis	1830–44
Edward Wigglesworth	1830–50
Samuel Atkins Eliot	1831
William Hickling Prescott	1832–47
William Joseph Loring	1832–35
William Turell Andrews	1833–54
Thomas Graves Cary	1834–36
Nathaniel Ingersoll Bowditch	1834–44
Samuel May	1835–44
John Amory Lowell	1836–45
Samuel Lawrence	1836–38
Thomas Buckminster Curtis	1837–45
Enoch Hale	1839–48
Martin Brimmer	1845
Samuel Austin, Jr.	1845–51
George Stillman Hillard	1845–52
Amos Binney	1846–47
Oliver Wendell Holmes	1846–53
Charles Amory	1846–50
John Lowell Gardner	1848
Henry Bromfield Rogers	1848–51
George Theodore Lyman	1849
William Richards Lawrence	1849
William Phillips	1850
George Livermore	1851–59
Samuel Hooper	1851
Edward Newton Perkins	1851–52
J. Ingersoll Bowditch	1852–54
Andrew Townshend Hall	1852–65
William Thomas	1852–63
Albert Fearing	1852–59
Adam Wallace Thaxter, Jr.	1852–55
Amos Adams Lawrence	1852–53
Edward Augustus Crowninshield	1852–59
Gardiner Howland Shaw	1852–57
Erastus Brigham Bigelow	1852–57
Charles Eliot Norton	1852–64
James Brown	1853–55
Samuel Gray Ward	1853–55
Martin Brimmer	1854–61
Henry Tuke Parker	1854
Charles Eliot Ware	1855–79
Robert William Hooper	1855–
Uriah Atherton Boyden	1855–56
Edward Newton Perkins	1856–
Francis Edward Parker	1856–76
William Appleton, Jr.	1856
Edward Clark Cabot	1857–75
James Elliot Cabot	1857–
Francis Parkman	1858–
Charles Russell Codman	1858–63
Gardiner Howland Shaw	1860–67
Francis Boardman Crowninshield	1860–75
George Washington Wales	1860–
Lemuel Shaw	1862–
Alexander Hamilton Rice	1864–
Charles Storer Storrow	1864–78
Christopher Toppan Thayer	1865–80
Charles Deane	1866–76
Samuel Eliot	1866–79
Benjamin Smith Rotch	1868–
Arthur Theodore Lyman	1876–
Ephraim Whitman Gurney	1877–
John Chipman Gray, Jr.	1877–
Henry Cabot Lodge	1879–
Howard Stockton	1880–
Thomas Buckminster Curtis	1880–81
Clement Hugh Hill	1881–

LIBRARIANS.

William Smith Shaw	1813–22
Seth Bass	1825–46
Charles Folsom	1847–56
William Frederick Poole	1856–68
Charles Ammi Cutter	1869–

ASSISTANT LIBRARIANS.

Micah W. Hill	1820–21
Joseph Backus	1822–25
Seth Bass	1846–47
Charles B. Fairbanks	1847–53
William Frederick Poole	1851
Ezra Abbot	1854–56
Manton Malone Marble	1856
William J. Adams	1856–66

T., A. Letter from a blacksmith to the ministers and elders of the Ch. of Scotland, 1758. 4th ed. London, *printed*, Phila., *reprinted* 1765. 8°. (C 43)

— *Same.* 7th ed. London, *printed*, Newburyport, *repr.*, [17—]. 8°. (B 157)

— *Same.* 3d ster. ed. Boston, [1828]. 16°.

— MODES of the Presbyterian church worship vindicated, in a letter to the Blacksmith; by a Presbyter of Ireland. Dublin, 1761. 8°.

— *Same.* 4th ed. London, *printed* Newburyport, *reprinted* 1789. 8°. (B 157)

T., D. Account of what was trans. in the Commons when Dr. Jenkins and F. Butler were voted guilty of high treason. (*In* **Somers**, J. Col. of tracts, v. 5. 1811.)

T., F. Letter to a Bishop. 1768. *See* **Francklin**, T.

T., F. Poésies gasconnes recueillies. Nouv. éd. 17e siècle, J. G. d'Astros. Vol. 1. Paris, 1867. 8°.

T., S. Letter to Dr. Snape. *See* **Fleetwood**, W.

T., W. Memorial of W. Darlington. West Chester, 1863. 8°.

Ta'abbata Sarran, Tâbit Ben Gâbir von Fahm, *called.* BAUR, G. Der arabische Held und Dichter Ta' abbata Sarran, nach seinem Leben und seinen Gedichten. (*In* **Zeitschr.** d. D. morg. Ges., v. 10. 1856.)

Ta hio, ou La grande science. (*In* **Mémoires** conc. l'hist., *etc.*, des Chinois, v. 1. 1797.)

Tabari, Abu Ja'far Muhammad ibn Jarir. Chronique; tr. sur la version persane d'Abou-Ali Mohammed Belami, par L. Dubeux. Vol. 1. Paris, *Orient. Trans. Fund*, 1836. 4°.

— Conquest of Persia by the Arabs; tr. from the Turkish by J. P. Brown. (*In* **Amer. Orient Soc.** Journ., v. 1, 2. 1849-51.)

— ROSEN, G. Ueber die in Constantinopel gedrückte türkische Uebersetzung von Taberi's Geschichtswerke. — Nachrichten über Taberistan aus dem Geschichtswerke Taberi's. (*In* **Zeitschr.** d. D. morg. Ges., v. 2. 1848.)

Tabarrani, Pietro. FABRONI, A. (*In his* Vitæ Ital., v. 19. 1804.)

Tabarrini, Marco. Di alcune tavolette scritte in cera retrovate in una antica torre di Porta Rossa di Firenze. (*In* **Archivio** stor. ital., app., v. 3. 1846.)— Necrologia di E. Repetti. (*In* v. 8.) — Degli studi stor. in Ital. e del più fruttuoso loro indirizzo. (*In* n.s., v. 4, pt. 2.) — Della Chronica di Fra Salimbene. (*In* v. 16, pt. 1.) — Relazioni dello stato di Milano fatta dal cav. B. Guarini. (*In* ser. 3, v. 5, pt. 2. 1867.) — Lettere di J. da Volterra a papa Innocenzo VIII, 1467. (*In* v. 7, pt. 2. 1868.) — Necrologie di G. Canestrini e A. Sagredo. (*In* v. 13, pt. 3.) — Necrologia di L. Cibrario. (*In* v. 14. 1871.)

— *and* **Milanesi**, C. Necrologia di G. P. Vieusseux. (*In* **Archivio** stor. ital., n.s., v. 17. 1863.) — Necrologia di G. La Farina. (*In* v. 18. 1863.)

Taber, Azor, *and others.* Address. (*In* **Albany. Young Men's Temperance Soc.** Proc., 1836. B 1718)

Taberd, J. L. Dictionarium Anamitico Latinum primitus incep. ab J. Pigneaux. Serampore, 1838. 4°.

— Dictionarium Latino-Anamiticum. Serampore, 1838. 4°.

Note. An Anamese-Latin grammar is prefixed.

Tabernæmontanus, Jacob Theodorus. *See* **Theodorus**, J.

Tabes dorsalis. *See* **Consumption.**

Table-book. *See* **Hone**, W.

Table moving. *See* **Spiritualism.**

Table talk. LUTHER, M. Tischreden von Gottes Wort. [1652.] (Vol. 57-62 *of his* Sämmtliche Werke. 1854.)

— - *Eng.* Table talk; tr. by W. Hazlitt. New ed. London, *Bohn*, 1857. 8°.

— SELDEN, J. Table talk. [1689.] London, 1868. 16°. (Arber's Eng. reprints, v. 2.)

— - *Same.* Edin., 1819. 12°.

— - *Same.* With an acc. of the life of S. (*In* **Young**, A. Lib. of Eng. prose writers, v. 2. 1831.)

— COWPER, W. [1782.] (*In his* Works, v. 8. 1836.)

— HAZLITT, W. Table talk; or, Essays on men and manners. [1821.] Lond., 1824. 2 v. 8°.

— - *Same.* (*In his* Miscel. works, v. 1, 2. 1859.)

— - *Same.* Pts. 1, 2. N. Y., 1845. 12°.

— TABLE-TALK; or, Selections from the ana. Edin., 1827. 18°. (Constable's miscel., v. 10.)

— BOOK of table talk; illust. with wood cuts. Vol. 1. London, 1836. 16°.

— ROGERS, S. Recollections of the table-talk of R. N. Y., 1856. 12°.

Table traits with something on them. *See* **Doran**, J.

Tableau de la campagne de 1813, en Allemagne; par [— de Boutourlin]. Paris, 1817. 8°.

Tableau de la vie. *See* **Rétif de la Bretonne**, N. E.

Tableau de l'Europe en nov. 1795; [par C. A. de Calonne]. Londres, [179-]. 8°. (B 1848)

Tableau de Paris; [par L. S. Mercier]. Amst., 1782-88. 12 v. 8°.

Tableau du mariage, Le; en un acte; par **A. R. Le Sage.** (*In his* Œuvres, v. 13. 1823.)

Tableau historique et pittoresque de Paris; par [J. M. B. B. de Saint Victor]. Paris, 1808-11. 3 v. 4°.

Tableau historique et pol. des rév. de Genève, 18e siécle; par [F. de Ivernois]. Genève, 1782. 8°.

Tableaux historiques de la Révolution Française. Paris, 1804. 3 v. f°.

Tableaux hist. des campagnes d'Italie; suivis du précis des opérations de l'armée d'Orient, *etc.*, jusqu'à la paix de Presbourg; d'après les dessins de C. Vernet. Paris, 1806. 8°.

Tables. MILLERS', merchants', and farmers' ready reckoner. London, *Weale*, 1861. 12°.

See also **Annuities**; — **Barometer**; — **Commerce**; — **Decimal system**; — **Ecclesiastical chronology**; — **Engineering, Civil**; — **Exchange**; — **Insurance**; — **Logarithms**; — **Longitude**; — **Mathematics**; — **Mortality**; — **Navigation**; — **Weights and measures.**

Tables and calculations resp. the plan of finance proposed to Parl. in 1807. *n.t.p.* [18—.] 4°. (A 21)

Tablet, The; devoted to the belles lettres. Vol. 1, no. 1-11, May 19-June 28, 1795. Boston, [17—]. 4°. (A 18)

Tablet, The; weekly newspaper. N.s., v. 3-24 (o.s., v. 35-56). London, 1870-80. 22 v. f°.

Note. Also 3 nos. of 1869 cont. 'The Vatican, a weekly record of the Council'.

Tablet of memory, showing every event in history to 1807. 11th ed. London, 1807. 12°.

— *Same.* 13th ed., to 1817. London, 1818. 12°.

Tablets. *See* **Alcott**, A. B.

Tablettes de Themis. 3e partie. Paris, 1755. 32°.

Taboada, Melchior Emmanuel Nunez de. *See* **Nunez de Taboada**, M. E.

Tabor, *Miss.* Early piety; recollections of H. B—; by one who knew and loved her well. 2d ed. Boston, *A.U.A.*, 1857. 18°.

Tabor, *Miss* Eliza. Nine years old. London, N. Y., 1872 [1871]. 16°.

— When I was a little girl; illust. by L. Frölich. London, 1871. 16°.

Tabouet, Julien. NICERON, J. P. (*In his* Mém., v. 38. 1737.)

Tabourot, Etienne. Poésie. (*In* **Auguis**, P. R. Poètes français, v. 5. 1824.)

— Poésie. (*In* **Annales** poétiques, v. 11. 1779.)

Tabulæ curiales. *See* **Foss**, E.

Tachard, Gui. Reise nach Siam, [und] Ostindien. (*In* **Allgemeine** Hist., v. 10. 1752.)

Taché, Jean Charles. The seigniorial tenure in Canada and plan of commutation. Quebec, 1854. 8°. (E 149)

Tachygraphy. LINDSLEY, D. P. Elements of tachygraphy. 2d ed. Boston, 1871. 8°.

Tacitus, Caius Cornelius. Opera Latina cum versione Germanica J. *Micylli.* Francof., 1612. 8°.

— C. C. Tacitus et in eum M. Z. *Boxhornii* et H. *Grotii* observationes. Venetiis, 1676. 12°.

— Opera. Edin., 1792. 2 v. 12°.

Contents. Vol. 1. De vita et scriptis Taciti e pref. G. Brotier. — Annalium lib. I-VI, XI-XV. 2. Lib. XVI. — Historiæ. — De moribus Germanorum. — De vita Agricolæ.

— Opera. Vol. 1: Annales instr. a G. A. *Ruperti.* Gottingæ, 1804. 8°.

— Opera; ex recens. I. A. *Ernesti*, cur. J. J. *Oberlinus*; cum notis selectis. Bostoniæ, 1817. 3 v. 12°.
Contents. Vol. 1. Vita, per J. Lipsium. — Annalium lib. I-VI, XI-XII. 2. XIV-XVI. — Historiæ. 3. Germania. — Agricola. — De oratoribus. — Stemma Cæsarum. — Index.

— C. C. Tacitus qualem pub. J. J. *Oberlin* cui annot. et add. subj. J. *Naudet*. Parisiis, 1819-20. 5 v. 8°. (Lemaire. Bibl. class. Lat.)
Contents. Vol. 1. Vita, per Justum Lipsium conscripta. — Veterum scriptorum de Tacito testimonia. — Annalium lib. I-VI. 2. XI-XVI. 3. Historiarum libri quinque superstites. 4. De moribus et populis Germaniæ. — Julii Agricolæ vita. — De oratoribus.— Excursus variorum. 5. Excursus variorum. — Stemma Cæsarum. — Anecdota de imperatoribus. — Præfatio G. Broterii. — Exempla imitationis e tragœdiis variorum poetarum Gallicorum collecta. — Editions et traductions de Tacite, par Bardier.

— Opera; ed. F. *Haase*. Ed. ster. Lips., *Tauchnitz*, 1855. 2 v. 8°.
Contents. Vol. 1. F. Haasii de vita, *etc.* — Annalium lib. I-VI, XI-XVI. 2. Historiarum lib. I-IV. — Germania. — Agricola. — De oratoribus.

— Libri que supersunt; rec. C. *Halm*. Lips., *typis Teubneri*, 1858-59. 2 v. 16°.
Contents. Vol. 1. Annales. 2. Historiæ. — Germania. — Agricola. — De oratoribus. — Index.

— *Eng.* Works; with notes, *etc.*, by A. *Murphy*. New ed. London, 1807, 05-07. 8 v. 8°.
Contents. Vol. 1. Essay on the life, *etc.*, by A. Murphy. — Annals, I-II. 2. III-VI. 3. XI-XIV. 4. XV-XVI. — Chronological table. 5. History, I-II. 6. III-V. 7. Germany. — Agricola. 8. Dialogue conc. oratory. — Geographical table.

— - *Same.* With essay, notes, *etc.*, by A. *Murphy*. Phila., 1836. 8°.

— - Works; pref. political disc. upon that author, [by T. *Gordon*]. 2d ed. London, 1837. 4 v. 8°.
Contents. Vol. 1. Discourses. — Annals, I-III. 2. IV-VI, XI-XVI. 3. History, I-II. 4. III-V. — Germany. — Agricola. — Index.
Note. Vols. 1-3 have continuous paging.

— - *Same.* Oxford tr. rev. London, *Bohn*, 1854. 2 v. 8°.
Contents. Vol. 1. Annals. 2. History. — Germany. — Agricola. — Dialogue on orators.

— *French.* Tacite; nouvelle traduction, par *Dureau de Lamalle*. Paris, 1790. 3 v. 8°.
Contents. Vol. 1. Disc. prélim. — Annales, liv. I-VI, XI-XII. 2. XIII-XVI. — Histoire, lib. I-II. 3. Histoire III-V. — Vie d'Agricola. — Mœurs des Germains. — Dialogue sur les orateurs.

— *Germ.* *See, above,* Opera. 1612.

— *Ital.* Tacito volgarizzato da *Davanzati*; riv. da G. *Biagioli*. Parigi, 1804. 3 v. 12°.
Contents. Vol. 1. Annali lib. I-V. 2. VI, XI-XVI. 3. Storie. — Germania. — Agricola.

— - *Same.* Annali. (*In* **Davanzati**, B. Opere, v. 1. 1853.) — Storie. — La Germania. — Agricola. — Della perduta eloquenzia. (*In* v. 2.)

— C. C. Tacite, historien du roi, de Buonaparte, *etc.*; avec une version française. Paris, 1815. 8°. (B 801)

— Julii Agricolæ vita. *n.t.p.* [Colophon:] Venetijs, 1497. f°.

— *Eng.* Life of Agricola; with interlinear trans. 2d ed. London, 1832. 12°.

— *French.* Vie de A.; tr. de P. *Boullon de Martel*. (*In* **Abbéville. Soc. Imp. d'Emulation.** Mém., 1861-66.)

— Annales.] C. Tacitus; erklært von K. *Nipperdey*. 2. verb. Aufl. Berl., 1855-57. 2 v. 8°.
Contents. Vol. 1. Lib. I-VI. 2. XI-XVI.

— *Eng.* Annales; description of Germanie; [tr. by R. *Grenewer*. London,] 1604. f°.

— *French.* Tacite; avec des notes politiques et historiques par A. de la *Houssaye*. Paris, 1724. 4 v. 12°.
Contents. Vol. 1. Discours critique. — Annales, liv. I-II. 2. III-VI. 3. XI-XII. 4. XIII.

— Germania; Agricola et De oratoribus; ex editione Oberliniana; acc. notæ Anglicæ; cura C. K. *Dillaway*. Bostoniæ, 1840. 18°.

— *Eng.* Germania; with ethnological dissertations and notes by R. G. *Latham*. London, 1851. 8°.

— Colophon] Historię Augustę; nec nõ de situ, moribus, et populis germanie libellus, ac de oratoribus dialogus. *t.p.w.* Venetijs, 1497. f°.

— Histoire de Tacite en latin et en français avec notes par J. H. Dotteville. Paris, 1772. 2 v. 12°.
Contents. Vol. 1. Introd. — Histoire, liv. I, II. 2. III-V. — Suite du ve livre.

— Historiarum libri V; acc. De moribus Germanorum, Agricolæ vita, De oratoribus; cum var. not.; [ed. J. L. Kingsley]. Novi-Portus, 1832. 12°.

— *Eng.* The end of Nero and beginning of Galba; Foure bookes of the Histories; Life of Agricola; [tr. by H. Savile]. 3d ed. [London,] 1604. f°.

— - Five books of the history; Manners of the Germans and Life of Agricola; with English notes by E. B. Williston. Hartford, 1826. 12°.

— *French.* Traduction du 1er liv. de l'hist. de Tacite. (*In* **Rousseau, J. J.** Œuvres, v. 14. 1782.)
See also, above, 'Histoire'.

— Selection. Morceaux de Tacite; en *lat.* et en *français*. (*In* **Alembert, J. le R. d'.** Œuvres, v. 12, 13. 1805.)

— Orationes ex T. collectæ. (*In* **Conciones** ex historicis Latinis excerptæ. 1805.)

— Burnet, J. The style of T. (*In his* Origin and prog. of lang., v. 3. 1786.)

— Dirksen, H. E. Die römisch-rechtlichen Mittheilungen in des Tacitus Geschichtbüchern. (*In* **Berlin. Ak. d. Wiss.** Abh., 1860.)

— Hill, J. Principles of historical composition, with an application of those principles to the writings of Tacitus. (*In* **Roy. Soc. of Edin.** Trans., v. 1. 1788.)

— Lerminier, E. (*In* **Revue** d. Mondes, jan. 1834.) — Nisard, D. Les historiens romains: Tacite. (*In* jan. 1847.)

— Niceron, J. P. (*In his* Mém., v. 6. 1728; *and, Germ.*, v. 7. 1753.)

— Ponce de Leon, P. Censura sobre los Anales é Historias. (*In* **Valladares**, A. Seman., v. 13. 1788.)

— Ruperti, G. A. Commentarius in Taciti annales. Londini, 1825. 8°.

— Weguelin, J. Sur la psychologie de Tacite. (*In* **Berlin. Ak. d. Wiss.** Abh., 1779.) — Sur l'art caractéristique, moral, et politique de Tacite. (*In* 1780.) — Suevern, J. W. Ueber den Kunstcharacter des Tacitus. (*In* 1822-23.)

Tacitus, *pseud.* *See* **Evans, T.**

Tactics. Ælianus *tacticus*, *fl. circ.* 100. Tactics; tr. with a prel. discourse by Visc. Dillon. London, 1814. 4°.

— Hanson, T. Manual exercise. (*In his* Prussian evolutions. 17—.)

— Le Blond, G. Elémens de tactique. Paris, 1758. 4°.

— Guibert, J. A. H., *comte* de. Essai général de tactique; préc. d'un discours sur l'état actuel de la politique; et de la science militaire en Europe. Londres, 1772. 2 v. 8°.

— - *Same.* (*In his* Œuvres mil., v. 1, 2. 1803.)

— - *Eng.* General essay on tactics. Lond., 1781. 2 v. 8°.

— New system of military discipline, founded upon principle. London, 1773. 4°.

— Silva, M. de. Remarques sur l'Essai général de tactique [de J. A. H. Guibert]. Turin, 1773. 8°.

— Mesnil-Durand, F. J. G. d'O., *baron* de. Fragmens de tactique. Paris, 1774. 4°.

— GRIMOARD, P. H., *comte* de. Essai théorique et pratique sur les batailles. Paris, 1775. 4°.
— ELÉMENS de tactique démontrés géometriquement; ouvrage allemand, tr. par de Holtzendoff. Paris, 1777. 2 v. 8°.
— NAPOLEON I. Maxims of war. [179-.] Richmond, 1862. 8°.
— SIMONS, J. A new principle of tactics practiced by armies of France; illustrated and recommended to be practiced by armies of the U. S. Charleston, 1797. 8°. (B 420, W 57, 64)
— MILITIA soldier's pocket companion; extract from Steuben's regulations. Worcester, 1807. 12°. (D 11)
— MEUNIER, H. A. J., *baron*. Evolutions par brigades. Paris, 1814. 8°.
— OKUNEF, A. Mém. sur les principes de la stratégie. [182-.] (*In his* Considérations, *etc.* 1841.)
— TERNAY, C. G. d'A., *marq*. de. Traité de tactique; rev., corr., aug. par F. Koch. Nouv. éd. Brux., 1840. 8°.
— DUFOUR, *Gen*. G. H. Strategy and tactics; tr. by W. P. Craighill. [1842.] N. Y., 1864. 12°.
— WILLIAM I., *Emp. of Prussia*. Regulations for the great manœuvres of the Prussian army, 1861; tr. from the German by C. Staveley. London, 1870. 18°.
— COPPÉE, H. Field manual of evolutions of the line. Phila., 1862. 32°.
— STEFFEN, W. Digest of U. S. tactics. Boston, 1862. 16°.
See also **Artillery**; — **Cavalry**; — **Infantry**; — **Military art and science**; — **Naval tactics**; — **Rifle**; — **United States**.
Taddei, Rosa. Alla contessa Farini, dolente per la morte del padre. — A novello parocco. (*In* **Poeti** ital. contemp. 1843.)
Tadeuskund, the last king of the Lenape; hist. tale, by N. M. Hentz. Boston, 1825. 12°.
Tadman, Lana, *pseud*. To the editor of the Brit. review, in answer to his remarks on the pamphlet of W. Edmeades, resp. commuting the tithes. (*In* **Pamphleteer**, 1818; v. 12 of **B 838**)
Taeping rebellion. *See* **China**. *History* (p. 555, 556).
Tafel, Gottlieb Lukas Friedrich. Dilucidationum Pindaricarum volumina duo. Berol., 1824–27. 2 pts. 8°.
Contents. Pt. 1. Olympia. 2. Pythia.
— *and* **Thomas**, G. M. Urkunden zur älteren Handels- und Staatsgeschichte der Republik Venedig, mit besonderer Beziehung auf Byzanz und die Levante. Wien, 1856–57. 8°. (Fontes rerum Austr., 2. Abth., 12–14. Bd.)
Tafel, Johann Friedrich Immanuel. Documents conc. the life of Swedenborg; tr. by I. H. Smithson. New ed., with add. by G. Bush. N. Y., 1847. 8°.
— Life of Jesus from the gospel record, vindicated and defended against the attacks of Dr. Strauss; from the German [by R. L. Tafel]. Chicago, 1868. 12°.
— Verzeichniss deutscher Werke von und nach Swedenborg, nebst Vorwort über die theologischen Werke desselben. Neu hrsg. Basel, 1869. 18°.
Tafel, Rudolph Leonhard. Emanuel Swedenborg as a philosopher and man of science. Chicago, 1867. 12°.
Taffin (*Lat.* **Taffinus**), Pierre. De veterum Romanorum anno seculari. (*In* **Grævius**, J. G. Thes. antiq. Rom., v. 8. 1698.)
Tafiletta. SHORT and strange rel. of part of the life of Tafiletta the conqueror and Emperor of Barbary. London, 1669. 4°.
Taft, Alphonso. Oration; life and public services of D. Webster, Dec. 18, 1852. Cincin., 1853. 8°. (**B 1727**)
Tafuri, Giovani Bernardino. Censura sopra i Giornali di M. Spinelli. (*In* **Gravier**, G. Rac. di scr. di Napoli, v. 16. 1770.)
Tafuro, Angelo. Descriptio belli a Venetis 1484 inlati Provinciæ Hydruntinæ. (*In* **Muratori**, L. A. Rer. Ital. scr., v. 24. 1738.)
Tagart, *Rev*. Edward. Memoir of Capt. P. Heywood; with extracts from his diaries and correspondence. London, 1832. 8°.
— Sermon, May 26. London, 1833. 8°. (**B 1346**)
— Sermon, the parables. (*In* **Beard**, J. R. Sermons. 1832.)
— Two sermons, Jan. 22. London, 1832. 8°. (**B 1346**)
Tagault, Jean. Institutiones chirurgicæ. (*In* **Uffenbach**, P. Thes. chirurg. 1610.)
Tagebuch eines armen Fräulein; von M. Nathusius. Boston, [18—]. 8°.
Taggart, *Rev*. Samuel. Address on impressments. *n.t.p.* [1813.] 8°. (**B 453, 2530**)
— Address to electors of Hampshire north district. Greenfield, 1811. 8°. (**B 440**)
— Discourse, Colrain, Feb. 22, [on] Washington. Greenfield, 1800. 8°. (**E 48, W 50**)
— God's visitation of sinful nations; two sermons, Colrain, fast day July 23, and in Shelburne, Aug. 20. Greenfield, 1812. 8°. (**B 1259**)
— Oration, Colrain, July 4th. Greenfield, 1803. 8°. (**B 342**)
— Oration. Conway, July 4. Northampton, 1804. 8°. (**B 342**)
Tagliacarne (*Lat.* **Theocrenus**), Benedetto. NICERON, J. P. (*In his* Mém., v. 33. 1736.)
Tagliazucchi, Girolamo. Discurso. (*In* **Raccolta** di prose ital., v. 1. 1808.)
Taglioni, Paolo. Electra; a ballet. Lond., 1849. 12°. (**E 5**)
Tagus and the Tiber. *See* **Baxter**, W. E.
Tâhir Muhammad, *Mir* Tâhir Muhammad Nasyâní bin Saiyid Hasan. Táríkh-i Táhirí. (*In* **Elliot**, H. M. History of India, v. 1. 1867.)
Tahiti *formerly* **Otaheite**. GARNIER, J. Excursion autour de l'île de Tahiti. (*In* **Paris. Soc. de Géog.** Bul., 5e sér., v. 16. 1868.)
— NEUESTE Nachrichten aus Otaheite. (*In* **Sprengel**, M. C., *and* **Forster**, G. Neue Beiträge, v. 3. 1790.)
Tahureau, Jacques. NICERON, J. P. (*In his* Mém., v. 34. 1736.)
Tahzib ul mantik; extracts from a Persian translation of the T. (*In* **Asiatic** researches, v. 8. 1808.)
Tailer, *Col*. Wm., *Funeral sermon on*. 1731. *See* **Cooper**, W. (**B 85, 216**)
Tailer. *See also* **Tailor**; — **Tayler**; — **Tayleur**; — **Taylor**; **Taylour**.
Tailfer, Patrick, *and others*. True and hist. narrative of the colony of Georgia. Charles-Town, 1741. 8°.
— *Same*. (*In* **Force**, P. Col. of tracts, v. 1. 1836; — *and in* **Georgia Hist. Soc.** Col., v. 2. 1842.)
Taillandier, Alphonse Honoré. Introduction. — Loi de la procédure du Canton de Genève. (*In* **Foucher**, V. A. Col. des lois, v. 5. 1837.)
— Nouvelles recherches hist. sur la vie et les ouvrages du chancelier [Michel] de L'Hospital. Paris, 1861. 8°.
Taillandier, Gaspard Ernest Saint René. *See* **Saint René Taillandier**, G. E.
Taillasson, Jean Joseph. Observations sur quelques grands peintres. Paris, 1807. 8°.
Tailor. *See also* **Tailer**; — **Tayler**; — **Tayleur**; — **Taylor**; — **Taylour**.
Tailor, Robert. The hog hath lost his pearl. (*In* **Dodsley**, R. Col. of plays, v. 6. 1825; — *in* **Scott**, *Sir* W. Anc. Brit. dr., v. 3. 1810; — *and in* **Lamb**, C. Spec. of dram. poets. 1854.)
Tailor, Thomas. *See* **Taylor**, T.
Tailors. DORAN, J. (*In his* Habits and men. 1855.)
Tailors, The; or, a tragedy for warm weather. (*In* **London** stage, v. 4. 182-.)
Taine, Hippolyte Adolphe. L'art en France. (*In* **Paris** guide, v. 1. 1867.)
— Essai sur Tite Live. Paris, 1856. 12°.
— Essais de critique et d'histoire. Paris, 1858. 12°.
Contents. Pref. — Macaulay. — Fléchier. — Dickens. — Guizot. — Thackeray. — Les jeunes gens de Platon. — Saint-Simon. — Mme. de La Fayette. — Michelet. — M. Troplong et M. de Montalembert.
— Histoire de la littérature anglaise. Paris, 1863–64. 4 v. 8°.
Contents. Vol. 1. Introd. — Les Saxons. — Les Normands. — La nouvelle langue. — La renaissance païenne. — Le théâtre. 2. Ben Jonson. — Shakspeare. — La renaissance chrétienne. — Milton. — La restaura-

tion. — Dryden. 3. La révolution. — Addison. — Swift. — Les romanciers. — Les poëtes. — Les idées et les œuvres. — Lord Byron. — Le passé et le présent. 4. Le roman: Dickens. — Thackeray. — La critique et l'histoire: Macaulay. — La philosophie et l'histoire: Carlyle. — La philosophie: Stuart Mill. — La poésie: Tennyson.

— *Same*. Tome 5: Les contemporains. 2e éd. Paris, 1869. 16°.

— *Eng*. History of English literature; tr. by H. van Laun. Edin., 1871. 2 v. 8°.

Contents. Vol. 1. Introd. — The Saxons. — The Normans. — The new tongue. — The pagan renaissance. — The theatre. — Ben Jonson. — Shakspeare. — The Christian renaissance. — Milton. — The restoration. 2. Dryden. — The revolution. — Addison. — Swift. — The novelists. — The poets. — Ideas and productions. — Ld. Byron. — The past and the present. — The novel: Dickens. — Thackeray. — Criticism and history: Macaulay. — Philosophy and history; Carlyle. — Philosophy: Stuart Mill. — Poetry: Tennyson.

— *Same*. With a [new] preface. N. Y., 1871. 2 v. 8°.

— De l'idéal dans l'art. Paris, 1867. 18°.

— *Eng*. The ideal in art; tr. by J. Durand. N. Y., 1869 [1868]. 12°.

— L'idéalisme anglais; étude sur Carlyle. Paris, 1864. 16°.

— De l'intelligence. 2e éd. Paris, 1870. 2 v. 8°.

— Italy: Florence and Venice. *See, below*, 'Voyage'.

— Italy: Naples and Rome. *See, below*, 'Voyage'.

— Notes sur Paris; vie et opinions de F. T. Graindorge. 2e éd. Paris, 1867. 8°.

— Nouveaux essais de critique et d'histoire. Paris, 1865. 12°.

Contents. Philosophie religieuse [par] J. Reynauld. — La Bruyère. — Balzac. — Jefferson. — Renaud de Montauban. — Racine. — Les Mormons. — Marc-Aurèle. — Le Bouddhisme. — F. Wœpke.

— Philosophes français du 19e siècle. Paris, 1857. 12°.

Contents. Laromiguière. — Royer-Collard. — Maine de Biran. — Cousin, écrivain. — Cousin historien et biographe. — Cousin philosophe. — Théorie de la raison par Cousin. — Cousin érudit et philologue. — Jouffroy, psychologue. — Jouffroy, moraliste. — Pourquoi l'éclectisme a-t-il réussi? — De la méthode.

— Philosophie de l'art. Paris, 1865. 18°.

— Philosophy of art: art in Greece; tr. by J. Durand. N. Y., 1871. 12°.

— Philosophie de l'art en Italie. Paris, 1866. 12°.

— Philosophy of art in the Netherlands; tr. by J. Durand. N. Y., 1871. 16°.

— Le positivisme anglais; étude sur Stuart Mill. Paris, 1864. 16°.

— Voyage aux Pyrénées. 5e éd. Paris, 1867. 12°.

— Voyage en Italie. Paris, 1866. 2 v. 8°.

Contents. 1. Naples et Rome. 2. Florence et Venise.

— *Eng. of v.* 1. Italy, Naples, and Rome. London, 1867. 12°.

— *Eng. of v.* 2. Italy, Florence, and Venice; [tr.] by J. Durand. N. Y., 1869. 8°.

— Several articles.] (*In* **Revue d. D. Mondes**, août 1855–mai 1866.)

— JANET, P. La philosophie de Taine. (*In his* La crise philos. 1865.)

— MAZADE, C. de. Du realisme dans la critique. (*In* **Revue** d. D. Mondes, juil. 1867.) — PLANCHE, G. Le panthéisme et l'histoire, à propos des Essais de critique de T. (*In* avr. 1857.)

— VANNUCCI, A. Tito Livio e la critica storia e la scienza moderna a proposito del Saggio di T. (*In* **Archivio** stor. ital., n.s., v. 5, pt. 1. 1857.)

Tainsh, Edward Campbell. One maiden only. London, 1870. 3 v. 16°.

— Study of the works of Tennyson. London, 1868. 16°.

Tainter, Dean Willis. History and geneal. of the descendants of J. Taynter who settled in Watertown, 1638. Boston, 1859. 8°.

Taintor, Charles Micaiell, *transcriber*. Extracts from the records. *See* **Colchester**, *Conn*.

Taisnier, Joannes. NICERON, J. P. (*In his* Mém., v. 39. 1738.)

Tait. *See also* **Tate**.

Tait, Peter Guthrie. Treatise on natural philosophy. *See* **Thomson**, *Sir* W.

Tait, Wm. Magdalenism; an inquiry into prostitution in Edinburgh. Edin., 1840. 8°.

Tait, *Rev.* Wm. Meditationes Hebraicæ; exposition of the epistle to the Hebrews. New ed. London, 1855. 2 v. 8°.

Taitt, Alexander. Roman account of Britain and Ireland. (*In* **Tracts** illustrative of antiq. of Scotland. 1836.)

Tâittiriya-Prâticakhya, The; with its commentary, the Tribhashyaratna; text, trans., and notes. (*In* **Amer. Orient. Soc.** Journ., v. 9. 1871.)

Tajo *or* **Tajus** *Cæsaraugustanus*, Samuel. Epistola. — Sententiarum libri v. (*In* **Florez**, H. España sagrada, v. 31. 1776.)

Talabot, Edmond. MORT de T. *n.t.p.* [1832.] 8°. (**B1660**)

Talæus, Audomarus (*French* Omer **Talon**). Rhetorica e P. Rami prælectionibus observcita. Amst., 1666. 12°.

Talaing. MASON, F. The Talaing language. (*In* **Amer. Orient. Soc.** Journ., v. 4. 1854.)

Talanta, La; commedia, da P. Aretino. (*In* **Teatro** ital. ant., v. 8. 1811.)

Talavera. HERMOSILLA Y SANDOVAL, I. de. Noticia de las ruinas de Talavera la vieja; [con] contin., por J. Cornide. (*In* **Madrid. Ac. d. l'Hist.**, v. 1. 1796.)

Talba, The; by A. E. Bray. (*In her* Novels, v. 6. 1845.)

Talbot, *Miss* Catharine. Works. 8th ed., first published by E. Carter, republished with add. papers by M. Pennington. Lond., 1812. 8°.

Contents. Acc. of the life of C. T. — Reflections on the days of the week. — Essays. — Letters. — Dialogues. — Prose pastorals. — Imitations of Ossian. — Allegories. — Poetry.

— Reflections on the seven days of the week; [with her] life. Boston, 1813. 12°. (**C 118**)

— Series of letters between E. Carter and C. Talbot, 1740–70; pub. by M. Pennington. London, 1808. 2 v. 4°.

Talbot, Charles John, *Viscount Ingestre*. Meliora; or, Better times to come. 1st, 3d ser. London, 1852–53. 2 v. 16°.

Contents. Ser. 1. **Osborne**, S. G. Beer-shop evil. — **Girdlestone**, C. Rich and poor. — **Hook**, —. Institutions for adult education. — **Nicolay**, C. G. On dwellings of working classes in British North America. — **Gore**, M. Sailor's homes. — **Goderich**, *Visc.* Adulteration of food and its remedies. — **Guy**, *Dr.* Policy of prevention. — **Beames**, T. Plea for education of the million. — **Baker**, R. Words for the working classes. — **Owen**, J. B. Popular investments. — **Fulford**, —. On prison discipline. — **Talbot**, C. J., *Visc. Ingestre*. Letter to a friend. — **Denison**, W. B. Model lodging-houses. — **Nutt**, J. Model *vs.* common lodging-houses. — **Byng**, F. On improving the dwellings of the poor. — Gaol revelations. — **Leaves** from the lives and opinions of working men; by themselves. — **Mayhew**, H. Home is home, be it never so homely. — **Truths** from a pawnbroker. — **Tupper**, M. F. Homes of the poor. — **Howard**, G. W. F., *5th Earl of Carlisle*. Address, at meeting in aid of evening classes for young men in London and its suburbs. — **Osborne**, S. G. Immortal sewerage. — **Thomson**, A. Our treatment of the lower and lowest classes of society. — **Mackenzie**, H. Ideas of the parish. — **Shore**, C. J., *Ld. Teignmouth*. Ragged and indust. schools. — **Bell**, G. Few observations on principles of social reform. — **Beames**, T. Education as it is, and as it ought to be. — **Leigh**, J. Juvenile offenders and destitute pauper children. — **Talbot**, C. J., *Visc. Ingestre*. Social evils; their causes and their cure. — **Leaves** from the lives and opinions of working men. 2d series. — **Thomson**, A. Prevention is better than cure. — **Field**, J. Hints on imprisonment and penal labour. — **Stooks**, T. F. Sunday in London. — **Model** lodging-houses and the working classes. — **Gore**, M. Notes of a residence in Paris in the spring of 1853. — **Parker**, J. Literature of the working classes. — **Legge**, W. W., *Visc. Lewisham*. Thoughts upon town and country. — **Proposal** for establishment of a company for affording loans to distressed poor. — **Beggs**, T. Maine law; with suggestions for its application to Gr. Britain. — **Guy**, *Dr.* Rescued from the beggars; or, How to support our hospitals. — **Truth** from a top room.

Talbot, Edward Allen. Five years' residence in the Canadas; incl. a tour through part of the U. S. London, 1824. 2 v. 8°.

Talbot, Elizabeth, *Countess of Shrewsbury*. BACON, *Sir* F. Charge against the Countess of Shrewsbury. (*In his* Letters and life, v. 4. 1869.)

Talbot, Eugène. Introduction et notes. (*In* **Xenophon.** Œuvres complètes. 1859.)

Talbot, Frederic. Causes of the defective condition of national education. (*In* **Nat. Assoc. Prom. Soc. Sci.** Trans., 1857.)

Talbot, Gerald F. Analysis of the organization of the Prussian army. London, 1871. 8°.

Talbot, Guillaume H. French translation self-taught. Boston, 1855. 12°.

— Philosophy of French pronunciation. N. Y, 1854. 12°.

Talbot, Israel Tisdale. Annual address, 1861, 'The common sense of homœopathy'. (*In* **Mass. Homœop. Med. Soc.** Pub., 1861.) — Tracheotomy in croup. (*In* 1862.)

Talbot, John, *Earl of Shrewsbury*. Letter to A. L. Philips, descriptive of the estatica of Caldaro and the addolorata of Capriana. 2d ed.; add., Three visits to the estatica of Monte Sansavino. London, 1842. 8°.

Talbot, *Sir* Robert, *pseud*. *See* **Maubert de Gouvest, J. H.**

Talbot, *Com.* Silas. TUCKERMAN, H. T. Life of T. N. Y., 1850. 18°.

Talbot, Thomas H. Constitutional provision resp. fugitives from service; and the act of Congress, Sept. 18, 1850. Boston, 1852. 8°.

Talbot, Wm. Sermon before the Queen, at St. Paul's, May 1; thanksgiving for the union of the kingdoms of Eng. and Scotland. London, 1707. 4°. (B 98)

— Sermon, coronation of George I., Oct. 20. Dublin, 1714. 8°. (C 79)

— Sermon in the parish-church of St. Sepulchre, June 13, anniv. meeting of the Charity Schools. London, 1717. 4°. (B 97)

— Speech, impeachment of H. Sacheverell. (*In* **Fisher,** J. Speeches. 1710.)

Talbot, Family of. SANFORD, J. L., *and* TOWNSEND, M. (*In their* Great govern. fam., v. 1. 1865.)

Talbot de Malahide, James, *Lord*. On public health. (*In* **Nat. Assoc. Prom. Soc. Sci.** Trans., 1861.)

Talboys, D. A. Bibliotheca theologica; catalogue of theological books. Oxford, 1835. 12°.

Talcott, *Rev.* Daniel Smith. Jesus Christ himself the all-sufficient evidence of Christianity. (*In* **Boston** lectures, 1871.)

Talcott, John. Letter to Sir E. Andros, 1687. (*In* **Mass. Hist. Soc.** Col., v. 23. 1833.)

Talcott, Joseph, *Gov. of Connecticut*. Address of condolence to him; with his answer. (*In* **Mass. Hist. Soc.** Col., v. 21. 1825.)

Tale of a box, The. Boston, 1820. 12°. (C 119)

Tale of a tub; a comedy, by B. **Jonson.** (*In his* Workes, v. 2. 1640; v. 5. 1756; v. 6. 1816.)

Tale of a tub; [by J. Swift]. 3d ed. corr. London, 1704. 8°.

Tale of adventure, A; the Siberian sable hunter; by [S. G. Goodrich]. N. Y., 1843. 18°.

— *Same.* (*In his* Works, v. 3. 1812; v. 10. 1824.)

Tale of eternity. *See* **Massey, G.**

Tale of the Tyne; by H. Martineau. London, 1833. 18°.

Tale of two cities, A; by C. Dickens. Lpz., *Tauchnitz*, 1859. 2 v. 16°.

Note. From All the year round, v. 1-2. 1859.

Talea, Ermelinda, *pseud*. *See* **Maria Antonie Walpurgis,** *Electress of Saxony*.

Talebearing. BENTOM, C. Talebearing a great sin; sermon, Feb. 22. Quebec, 1801. 8°. (B 213)

Talentoni, Giovanni. Lezione. (*In* **Dati**, C. R. Prose flor., pt. 2, v. 4. 1751.)

Tales, Livonian. *See* **Livonian** tales. 1846.

Tales and sketches; by [C. M. Sedgwick]. 2d ser. N. Y., 1844. 12°.

Tales and sketches; by the Ettrick Shepherd [J. Hogg]; illust. by D. O. Hill. Edin., [1836]. 6 v. 12°.

Tales and sketches of Christian life; by [Mrs. E. R. Charles]. N. Y., 1865. 12°.

Tales and stories from history; by A. Strickland; with illust. Phila., 1848. 16°.

Tales and traditions of Hungary; by F. and T. Pulszky. London, 1851. 3 v. 8°.

Tales by the O'Hara family; [by J. Banim]. Phila., 1827. 2 v. 12°.

Tales, essays, and sketches; by R. Macnish; with life by D. M. Moir. 2d ed. London, 1844. 2 v. 8°.

Tales for mothers; tr. from the French of J. N. Bouilly. N. Y., 1824. 12°.

Tales for the times; a selection of stories, by [S. G. Goodrich]. N. Y., [1840]. 16°.

Tales from Bentley. London, 1865. 6 v. 16°.

Tales from history; by A. Strickland. Phila., 1748. 16°.

Tales from Shakspere for the use of young persons; by C. and M. Lamb. Lpz., 1846. 16°.

— *Same.* N. Y., 1869. 12°.

Tales from the Eastern land. *See* **Grimm, A. L.**

Tales from the German; [by K. F. van der Velde]; tr. by N. Greene. Boston, 1837. 2 v. 12°.

Tales from the parsonage; by A. Stevens. Boston, 1845. 12°.

Tales of a barrister; by F. Liardet. 2d ed. London, 1847. 3 v. 12°.

Tales of a grandfather; by Sir W. Scott. 1st ser. Phila., 1828. 2 v. 18°.

— *Same.* 3d ser. Phila., 1830. 2 v. 18°.

— *Same.* (Vol. 22-28 *of his* Prose works. 1836.)

Tales of a traveller; by W. Irving. Phila., 1824. 2 v. 8°.

— *Same.* (Vol. 7 *of his* Works. 1860.)

Tales of a voyage to the Arctic Ocean. London, 1826. 3 v. 12°.

Tales of a wayside inn. *See* **Longfellow, H. W.**

Tales of all countries; by A. Trollope. London, 1864. 12°.

Tales of fashionable life; by M. Edgeworth. (Vol. 7-10 *of her* Tales and miscel. 1825; 5, 6 *of her* Tales and novels. 1848.)

Tales of my landlord; by Cleishbotham [Sir W. Scott]. 4th ser. Phila., 1833. 3 v. 12°.

Tales of old time, Five. *See* **Five** tales. 1844.

Tales of old travel re-narrated. *See* **Kingsley, H.**

Tales of Peter Parley about America; [by S. G. Goodrich]. Boston, 1832. 24°.

— *French.* Les contes sur l'Amérique. Boston, 1832. 24°.

Tales of real life; by A. Opie. *n.t.p.* [Boston, 1827.] 12°.

Tales of the Crusaders; by Sir W. Scott. Phila., 1825. 4 v. 12°.

Tales of the good woman; by a doubtful gentleman, otherwise J. K. Paulding; ed. by W. I. Paulding. N. Y., 1867. 8°.

Tales of the Great St. Bernard; by G. Croly. N. Y., 1829. 2 v. 12°.

Tales of the grotesque and arabesque; by E. A. Poe. Phila., 1840. 2 v. 12°.

Tales of the manor; by B. Hofland. N. Y., 1822. 2 v. 12°.

Tales of the mountains. London, 1851. 2 v. 12°.

Tales of the Northwest; [by W. J. Snelling]. Boston, 1830. 18°.

Tales of the passions; by G. P. R. James. Phila., 1839. 12°.

Tales of the priory; by B. Hofland. N. Y., 1820. 2 v. 12°.

Tales, romances, and extravaganzas; by T. Hood. N. Y., 1866. 8°.

Talfourd, Francis. The household fairy; a domestic sketch. (No. 64 *of* DeWitt's acting plays.)

Talfourd, *Sir* Thomas Noon. Attempt to estimate the poetical talent of the present age; incl. a sketch of the hist. of poetry. (*In* **Pamphleteer**, 1815; v. 5 of **B 838**)

— The Castilian; a tragedy. London, 1853. 16°.

— Critical and miscellaneous writings. [Repr. from periodicals.] 3d Amer. ed. Boston, 1856. 8°. (Mod. Brit. essayists, v. 6.)

Contents. British novels and romances. — Mackenzie. — The author of Waverley. — Godwin. — Maturin. — Rymer on tragedy. — Colley Cibber's Apology for his life. — J. Dennis's Works. — Modern periodical literature. — Genius and writings of Wordsworth. — North's Life of Ld. Guilford. — Hazlitt's Lectures on the drama. — Wallace's Prospects of mankind, nature, and providence. — Pulpit oratory. — Recollections of Lisbon. — Lloyd's poems. — Oldaker on modern improvements. — A chapter on 'Time'. — On the profession of the bar. — The wine cellar. — Destruction of the Brunswick theatre by fire. — First appearance of Fanny Kemble. — The melo-dramas against gambling. — Intellectual character of W. Hazlitt. — The late dowager Lady Holland. — Addr. at the anniv. of the Manchester Athenæum. — Ld. Eldon and Ld. Stowell. — Speech for the defendant in the prosecution of the Queen *vs.* Moxon, for the publication of Shelley's works, (Court of Queen's Bench, 1814). — Speeches on copyright, (Ho. of Commons, 1837, 38, 39). — The Westminster play, 1845.

— Dramatic works. 11th ed. London, 1852. 16°.

Contents. Ion; a tragedy. — The Athenian captive; a tragedy. — Glencoe; a tragedy. — Minor poems. — Sonnets. — Alum Bay. — Verses.

— Ion, a tragedy. N. Y., 1837. 12°.

— *Same.* (*In* **Sargent**, E. Mod. standard dr., v. 1.)

— Speech for the defendant in the prosecution of the Queen *vs.* [E.] Moxon for the publication of Shelley's works, London, 1841. 8°.

— Thoughts on the late W. Hazlitt. (*In* **Hazlitt**, W. Lit. remains, v. 1. 1836.)

— Vacation rambles and thoughts. London, 1845. 2 v. 12°.

See also **Lamb**, Charles. Literary sketches and letters, 1848; — Works. 1838.

— Blanchard, L. (*In his* Saunders' portraits, v. 1. 1838.)

— Horne, R. H. (*In his* A new Spirit of the age, v. 1. 1844.)

— Redding, C. (*In his* Personal reminiscences, v. 2. 1867.)

— Tuckerman, H. T. The dramatist. (*In his* Characteristics of lit., 2d ser. 1851.)

— Whipple, E. P. (*In his* Essays, v. 1. 1848.)

Taliaferro, John. Extract from a poem entitled 'Old Virginia Georgics'. Wash., 1840. 8°. (D 20)

Taliessin. The book of T.; in Welsh; [with tr. by R. F. Williams]. (*In* **Skene**, W. F. Four ancient books of Wales. 1868.)

— Turner, S. (*In his* Vindication of the genuineness of the anc. Brit. poems. 1803.)

Tallack, Wm. Friendly sketches in America. London, 1861. 8°.

— George Fox, the Friends, and the early Baptists. London, 1868. 16°.

— Ought the principles of the reformatory system, including voluntary management, to be extended to adults? (*In* **Nat. Assoc. Prom. Soc. Sci.** Trans., 1868.)

— Thomas Shillitoe, the Quaker missionary. London, 1867. 8°.

— Several articles.] (*In* **Nat. Assoc. Prom. Soc. Sci.** Trans., 1865-67.)

Tallard, Camille d'Hostun, *comte* de. Campagne en Allemagne, 1704. Amst., 1763. 2 v. (v. 2 w.). 12°.

Tallemant, Paul. Niceron, J. P. (*In his* Mém., v. 22. 1733; *and, Germ.*, v. 16. 1758.)

Tallemant des Réaux, Gédéon. Historiettes; mémoires pour servir à l'hist. du 17e siècle. 2e éd., augm. [avec] des notes par Monmerqué. Paris, 1840. 10 v. 8°.

— Monmerqué, L. J. N. (*In* **Revue** d. D. Mondes, juil. 1835.)

Talleyrand Périgord, Charles Maurice de, *prince de Bénévent.* Eloge hist. de le comte Reinhard. (*In* **Paris. Inst.** *Ac. d. Sci. Mor.* Mém., v. 2. 1839.)

— Mémoires sur les relations commerciales des Etats-Unis avec l'Angleterre. — Essai sur les avantages à retirer de colonies nouv. dans les circonstances présentes. (*In* **Bulwer, H. L.,** *Ld.* Hist. char., v. 1. 1868.)

— *Eng.* Memoir conc. the commercial rel. of the U. S. with Eng.; [with] an essay upon the advantages to be derived from new colonies, *etc.* London, 1806. 8°. (**B 680**)

— *Same.* Boston, 1809. 8°. (**B 411, 536, 2521**)

— *Same.* (*In* **Pamphleteer, 1814**; v. 4 of **B 838**)

— Rapport sur l'instruction publique. Paris, 1791. 4°. (**A 10**)

— Brougham, H., *Ld.* (*In his* Statesmen in the time of George III., v. 2. 1839.)

— Bulwer, *Sir* H. L. (*In his* Historical characters, v. 1. 1868.)

— Capefigue, J. B. H. R. (*In his* Diplomatists of Europe. 1845.)

— Catalogue of a splendid library [Talleyrand's] sold 1816. London, [1816]. 8°.

— Loménie, L. L. de. (*In his* Gallerie des contem. illust., v. 1. 1840.)

— Mignet, F. A. A. (*In his* Notices et portraits hist. et lit. 1854; — *and in* **Revue** d. D. Mondes, mai 1839.)

— Pichot, A. Souvenirs intimes sur M. de T. Paris, 1870. 18°.

— Sainte Beuve, C. A. Essai sur T., par H. L. Bulwer. (*In his* Nouveaux lundis, v. 12. 1871.)

— Sallé, A. Vie politique de T. Paris, 1834. 8°.

— Villemarest, C. M. de. Life of T. London, 1834-36. 4 v. 8°.

Tallien, *Mme.* Thérèse Cabarrus. *See* **Chimay**, T. C., *princesse* de.

Tallmadge, *Gen.* Benjamin. Speech, Jan. 27, providing an additional military force. *n.p.*, [1809]. 8°. (**B 410, 553**)

— Speech, on removing the seat of government to Phila. (*In* **Gardenier**, B. Speeches. 1808. **B 398**)

— Sketch.] (*In* **Longacre**, J. B., *and* **Herring**, J. Nat. portr. gal., v. 3. 1836.)

Tallmadge, Frederick Augustus. Speech at the Litchfield County centennial celebration. (*In* **Litchfield Co.**, *Conn.* Centen. celebration. 1851.)

Tallmadge, *Gen.* James. Address before the Amer. Inst., at the 14th, 16th, 18th, 23d fair. (14th, 16th, 2d ed.) N. Y., 1841-50. 4 pam. 8°. (**B 1586**)

— Speech on giving the choice of presidential electors to the people, Aug. 5. Albany, 1824. 8°. (**B 1805**)

— Speech on slavery. N. Y., 1819. 8°. (**B 448**)

— West, The, vindicated; review of [his] address before the Amer. Inst., Oct. 25, 1841. Buffalo, 1842. 8°. (**B 1586**)

Tallmadge, Nathaniel P. Appendix. (*In* **Edmonds**, J. W., *and* **Dexter**, G. T. Spiritualism. 1853.)

— Introduction and appendix. (*In* **Linton**, C. The healing of the nations. 1855.)

Tallmadge Colonization Soc. Whittlesey, E. Addresses before the Soc., July 4, 1833. Ravenna, 1833. 8°. (**B 1483**)

Talloires. Vernazza di Freney, G. Considerazioni sopra la salvaguardia di Talloires. (*In* **Turin. Ac. d. Sci.** Mem., v. 34. 1830.)

Talmud. Kohut, A. Was hat die talmudische Eschatologie aus dem Parsismus aufgenommen? (*In* **Zeitschr.** d. D. morg. Ges., v. 21. 1867.)

— Lightfoot, J. Horæ Hebraicæ, or Hebrew and Talmudical exercitations upon [the Gospels], Acts, Romans, [and] I. Corinthians. (*In his* Works, v. 2. 1684.)

— Neubauer, A. La géographie du Talmud. Paris, 1868. 8°.

— Schindler, V. Lexicon pentaglotton, Hebraicum, Chaldaicum, Syriacum, Talmudico-Rabbinicum, *etc.* Hanov., 1612. f°.

Talon, Omer, *b. about* 1510, *d.* 1562. *See* **Talæus**, A.

Talon, Omer, *b.* 1595, *d.* 1652. Mémoires de Omer Talon, continués par D. Talon. (*In* **Michaud.** Col. des mém., v. 30. 1854; — *and in* **Petitot.** Col., 2e sér., v. 60-63. 1827-28.)

Talon, Jean, *successively baron D'Orsainville, des Islets, and d'Ormale.* Mémoire sur l'état présent du Canada. (*In* **Lit. and Hist. Soc.** of **Quebec.** Col. 1840.)

Talvi, *pseud.* *See* **Robinson**. T. A. L. von J.

Tam O'Shanter. *See* **Burns**, R.

Tamaris; par G. Sand [Mme. Dudevant]. Paris, 1862. 12°.

Tamaulipas. Colonization law of T. (*In* **Texas.** Laws and decrees of Coahuila and Texas. 1839.)

Tambien hay duelo en las damas. *See* **Calderon de la Barca.**

Tambien la afrenta es veneno; comedia. *See* **Guevara, L. V. de.**

Tambour nocturne, Le; comédie. *See* **Destouches, P. N.**

Tamburlaine. 1850. *See* **Marlowe, C.**

Tamerlane. *See* **Timur.**

Tamerlane; a tragedy, by N. **Rowe.** (*In his* Works, v. 1. 1756.)

Tamil language. HOISINGTON, H. R. Brief notes on the lang. (*In* **Amer. Orient. Soc.** Journ., v. 3. 1858.)

— *Conversation.* PHRASE book to assist the Tamil youth in the study of the Eng. language. 2d ed. Jaffua, 1841. 16°.

— *Dictionary.* WINSLOW, M. Tamil and English dictionary. Madras, 1862. 4°.

— *Grammar.* RHENIUS, C. T. E. Grammar of the Tamil lang. 3d ed. Madras, 1853. 8°.

See also **Bible** (p. 270).

Taming a tiger; a farce, adapted from the French. (No. 31 *of* **DeWitt's** acting plays.)

Taming of a shrew, The old, upon which Shakespeare founded his comedy; ed. by T. Amyot. London, 1844. 8°. (Shakespeare Soc.)

Taming of the shrew. *See* **Shakespeare, W.**

Tamizey de Larroque, Philippe. Preuves que Thomas à Kempis n'a pas composé 'l'Imitation de Jésus-Christ'. Paris, 1862. 8°.

Tammany, *Indian chief.* MITCHILL, S. L. Life, exploits, and precepts of T. N. Y., 1795. 8°. (**B 744**)

Tammany Soc. Account of the interment of the remains of 11,500 American seamen, soldiers, and citizens, who fell during the revolution; and an oration at the tomb of the patriots, by B. DeWitt. N. Y., 1808. 8°. (**B 407**)

— Address of the Soc. to its absent members, and members of its several branches throughout the U. S. N. Y., 1819. 8°. (**B 568**)

Tanaro. DURANDI, J. Delle antiche contese de pastori di Val di Tanaro, e de' politici accidenti sopravvenute. (*In* **Turin. Ac. d. Sci.** Mem., v. 19. 1811.)

Tancred. RAOUL *de Caen.* Gesta Tancredi principis in expeditione Hierosolymitana cum obs. E. Martene et U. Durand. (*In* **Muratori, L. A.** Rer. Ital. scr., v. 5. 1724.) — Histoire de T. (*In* **Guizot, F. P. G.** Col. des mém., v. 23. 1825.)

Tancred; ein Trauerspiel nach Voltaire. (*In* **Goethe, J. W. von.** Werke, v. 5. 1816.)

Tancred and Gismunda. *See* **Wilmot, R.**

Tancred and Sigismunda; a tragedy. *See* **Thomson, J.**

Tancrède; tragédie. *See* **Voltaire, F. M. A. de.**

Taney, Roger Brooke. Decision in the Merryman case. Phila., 1862. 8°. (**B 1724**)

— MAURY, S. M. (*In her* Statesmen of America. 1847.)

— U. S. *Circuit Court.* Notice of his death. Boston, 1864. 8°. (**B 1540**)

— VAN SANTVOORD, G. (*In his* Lives of the Chief-Justices of the U. S. 1854.)

Tanfani, Leopoldo. Due carte inedite in lingua sarda dei secoli 11, 13. (*In* **Archivio** stor. ital., ser. 3, v. 13, pt. 3. 1871.)

Tanganyika Lake. BURTON, R. F. Tanganyika, Ptolemy's western lake reservoir. (*In his* Nile basin. 1864.)

— SPEKE, J. H. Journal of a cruise on the Tanganyika Lake. (*In his* Discovery of the Nile. 1864.)

Tangents. APOLLONIUS *Pergæus.* Two books concerning tangencies, as restored by Vieta and Ghetaldus, with supplement by J. Lawson. Camb., 1764. 4°. (**A 33**)

Tangiers. DUMAS, A. Impressions de voyage: Le véloce, ou Tanger, *etc.* Paris, 1855. 2 v. 18°.

Tangletown letters. Buffalo, 1856. 12°.

Tanglewood tales for boys and girls; by N. Hawthorne. Boston, 1868. 18°.

Tanguy de la Boissière, C. C. Observations sur la dépêche écrite le 16 jan. Phila., 1797. 8°. (**B 634**)

— *Eng.* Observations on the dispatch by Mr. Pickering, Jan. 16; tr. by S. Chandler. Phila., 1796. 8°. (**B 423, 1699**)

Tanis et Zélide; tragédie-opéra. *See* **Voltaire, F. M. A. de.**

Tankerville, *Earl of.* *See* **Bennet, C.**

Tannahill, Robert. Poems and songs. Revised ed.; with a life of the author and of R. A. Smith, by P. A. Ramsay. Glasgow, 1838. 12°.

Tanner, Henry S. Map of Connecticut. [Phila.,] 1845. 8°.

— New picture of Philadelphia. 4th ed. N. Y., [184–]. 18°.

— New universal atlas. Phila., 1844. 4°.

— Pocket map of Connecticut. N. Y., [184–]. 12°.

Tanner, John. Narrative of the captivity and adventures of T. among the Indians. N. Y., 1830. 8°.

Tanner, Thomas Hawkes. Signs and diseases of pregnancy. London, 1860. 8°.

Tannhaeuser; a poem. *See* **Fane, J. C. H.,** *and* **Lytton, E. R. B.**

Tannhaeuser. GRAESSE, J. G. T. Der Tannhaeuser und Ewige Jude; zwei deutsche Sagen mythologisch und bibliographisch verfolgt und erklärt. 2e Aufl. Dresden, 1861. 8°.

Tanning. RUBIGNY DE BERTEVAL, —. Extrait du mém. sur l'abus de la marque des cuirs, *etc.* [Colophon:] Brux., 1788. 4°. (**A 74**)

— – Mémoire pour les tanneurs de France sur l'abus du droit et de la marque des cuirs. Brux., 1788.] 4°. (**A 74**)

— COPPINGER, J. The American practical brewer and tanner. N. Y., 1815. 8°.

— ANGUS, T. C. Tanning trade. [1862.] (*In* **Armstrong,** *Sir* W. G., *and others.* Industrial res., *etc.* 1864.)

— PERRAULT, A. Matériel et outillage mécanique de la tannerie et de la mégisserie. (*In* **France.** *Com. Imp. de l' Expos. de* 1867. Rapports, v. 8.)

Tanquerel des Planches, L. Lead diseases; tr. with notes and add. by S. L. Dana. Boston, 1850. 8°.

Tansillo, Luigi. Egloghe. (*In* **Ferrario,** G. Poesie pastorali. 1808.)

— The nurse; tr. from the Italian by W. Roscoe; [with Ital. text]. 3d ed. Dublin, 1800. 8°.

— *Same.* [English only.] N. Y., 1800. 18°.

— Poesie. Londra, 1782. 12°.

— Sonetti. — Canzone. (*In* **Gironi,** R. Rac. di lir. ital. 1808.)

— NICERON, J. P. (*In his* Mém., v. 18. 1732; *and, Germ,* v. 14. 1756.)

Tans'ur, Wm. Elements of musick. London, 1772. 8°.

Tantara-rara, rogues all; by J. **O'Keeffe.** (*In his* Dram. works, v. 3. 1798.)

Tante Eloi; par le comte de Montferrier. Paris, 1869. 18°.

Tap, John. Arte of navigation; first written in Spanish by M. Curtis and tr. by R. Eden; corr. and augm. by T. [London, 1596.] 4°.

Taparelli, Massimo, *marchese d'Azeglio.* *See* **Azeglio.**

Tapestry. BARBIER DE MONTAULT, X. Rome chrétienne, tapisseries. (*In* **Annales** archéol., v. 15. 1855.)

— BASCHET, A. Négociation d'œuvres de tapisseries de Flandre et de France. [1610–21.] (*In* **Gazette** des beaux-arts, v. 11, 12. 1861–62.)

— DEVALS, J. U. La tapisserie de Montpezat. (*In* **Annales** archéol., v. 3. **1845.**)

— BADIN, —. Tapis et tapisseries. (*In* **France.** *Comm. Imp. de l'Exposition de* **1867.** Rapports, v. 3.)

See also **Bayeux** tapestry; — **Gobelin** tapestry.

Tapeworms. *See* **Cestoids.**

Tapia, Andrés de. Relacion sobre la conquista de México. (*In* **Icazbalceta,** J. G. Col. de doc., v. 2. 1866.)

Tapia, Gomez de. Egloga. (*In* **Sedano, J. J. L.** de. Parnaso esp., v. 3. 1782.)

Taplin, Wm. Gentleman's stable directory. 10th ed. enl. [London, 179–.] 8°.

— *Same.* Modern farriery. 12th ed. Phila., 1794. 8°.

— Sporting dictionary and rural repository. London, 1803. 2 v. 8°.

Tappan, Arthur, *and others.* To the people of the U. S., or, to such as value their rights, and dare to maintain them. (*In* **Collection** of documents. 1836. **B 1718**)

— Tappan, L. The life of A. Tappan. N. Y., 1870. 8°.

Tappan, Benjamin, *Funeral sermon on.* 1790. *See* **Forbes,** E. (**B 314**)

Tappan, Benjamin, *of Ohio, b.* 1773, *d.* 1857. Speech, permanent prospective pre-emption law. Wash., 1841. 8°. (**B 1663**)

— Speech, resolution to limit the term of office of the judges of the supreme and inferior courts, Jan. 16. Steubenville, 1843. 8°. (**B 1499**)

— Speech, U. S. fiscal bank bill, July 14. Wash., 1841. 8°. (**B 1664**)

Tappan, *Rev.* Benjamin, *d.* 1863. Address, Kennebec, March 2. Hallowell, 1815. 8°. (**B 1168**)

— Sermon, interment of J. Appleton. Hallowell, 1819. 8°. (**B 283**)

— Abert, J. J., *and* Markoe, F. Reply to Tappan. Wash., 1843. 8°. (**B 1449**)

Tappan, *Rev.* Benjamin. Discourse commem. of E. P. Mackintire, Feb. 14. Boston, 1864. 8°. (**B 1540**)

Tappan, Christopher, *Jr.* Sketches of the weather and progress of vegetation in Ulster Co. (*In* **Soc. Prom. Useful Arts in N. Y.** Trans., v. 4, pt. 2. 1819.)

Tappan, *Mrs.* Cora L. V. Address. (*In* **Free Religious Association.** 2d an. meeting. 1869.)

— Discourse on faith, hope, and love. N. Y., 1858. 8°. (**B 1200**)

— Discourse on the immutable decrees of God and the free agency of man. N. Y., 1858. 8°. (**B 1200**)

Tappan, David, *D.D.* Beauty and benefits of the Chr. Ch.; two sermons, Plymouth, Jan. 5, [after] ordination of Mr. Kendall. Boston, 1800. 8°. (**B 166, 232, E 212**)

— Character and death of the servant of God; sermon, Byfield, Jan. 18, [on] the decease of M. Parsons. Newburyport, 1784. 8°. (**B 232**)

— Character of unregenerate sinners; discourse. Newburyport, 1782. 8°. (**B 150**)

— Christian thankfulness, *etc.*; sermon, Charlestown, Feb. 19, thanksgiving. Boston, 1795. 8°. (**B 232, 855, 856, 1833, W 38**)

— Connexion between faith in God and a suitable regard to Christ; disc., Portsmouth, before the Assoc. of Cong. Ministers. Portsmouth, 1792. 8°. (**E 212**)

— Discourse, Boston and Charlestown, Apr. 5, fast [day]. Boston, 1798. 8°. (**B 232, 2508, E 212**)

— *Same.* 2d ed. Boston, 1798. 8°. (**B 170**)

— Discourse, funeral of S. Phillips, Feb. 15. Boston, 1802. 8°. (**B 174, 232, E 212**)

— Discourse, Harvard Coll., June 17. Boston, 1794. 8°. (**B 232, H 2**)

— Discourse, Harvard Coll., June 19. Boston, 1798. 8°. (**B 197, E 212**)

— Discourse, Harvard Coll., Sept. 16. Boston, 1794. 8°. (**B 171, 232, 1833**)

— Discourse, Harvard Coll., Sept. 6. Boston, 1796. 8°. (**B 333, E 212**)

— Discourse, Newbury, May 1, ratification of a treaty of peace between Gr. Britain and the U. S. Salem, 1783. 8°. (**B 232**)

— *Same.* London, 1783. 8°. (**B 333**)

— Disconrse, Nov. 17, death of J. Russell. Boston, 1795. 8°. (**B 913, E 212**)

— Discourse [on] Washington, Feb. 21, 1800. (*In* **Willard, J.** Address in Latin. 1800.)

— Funeral discourse, Providence, on the Lord's day after the interment of E. Hitchcock, who died Feb. 27. Camb., 1803. 8°. (**B 174, 913, E 212**)

— Lectures on Jewish antiquities, Harvard Univ., 1802–03. Boston, 1807. 8°.

— A minister's solemn farewell to his people; disc., Newbury, on his removal to the Univ. at Cambridge. Portsmouth, 1793. 8°. (**B 913, E 212**)

— The question answered 'Watchman, what of the night'; discourse, May 15, fast. Salem, 1783. 8°. (**B 232, E 212**)

— Sermon before the Convention of Cong. Ministers, June 1. Boston, 1797. 8°. (**B 167, 232, E 212**)

— Sermon, Cambridge and Charlestown, Apr. 11 [fast]. Boston, 1793. 8°. (**B 151, 232, 855, 1833, E 212**)

— Sermon, general election. Boston, 1792. 8°. (**B 176, 179, 182, 187, 855, E 212**)

— Sermon, Kennebunk, Sept. 3, ordination of N. H. Fletcher. Camb., 1800. 8°. (**B 124, 166, 1313, E 212**)

— Sermon, ordination of J. T. Kirkland, Feb. 5. Boston, 1794. 8°. (**B 164, 168, 232, 2508, E 212**)

— Sermon, ordination of T. Dickinson, Holliston, Feb. 18. Boston, 1789. 8°. (**B 169, 1312**)

— Sermon, third parish in Newbury, July 24, on the sudden death of eight persons of the Soc. Newburyport, 1794. 8°. (**B 913**)

— Sermon, Wiscasset, Sept. 8, installation of H. Packard. Camb., 1802. 8°. (**B 333, 913, E 212**)

— Sermons; [with] a biog. sketch of the author, and a sermon preached at his funeral, by A. Holmes. Boston, 1807. 8°.

— Two friendly letters to S. Spring, on his 'Nature of duty'. Newburyport, 1785. 8°. (**B 150**)

— Bradford, E. Answer to Tappan's remarks on his thanksgiving sermon, Feb. 19, 1795. (*In his* Nature of humiliation. 1795. **B 873**)

— Spring, S. A friendly dialogue, between Philalethes and Toletus, upon the nature of duty. Newburyport, 1784. 12°.

— *Funeral sermon on.* 1803. *See* **Kendall, J.** (**B 203, 282**)

Tappan, Henry Philip. Mutual responsibilities of physicians and the community; an address. Detroit, 1856. 8°. (**B 1563**)

Tappan, Lewis. The fugitive slave bill, its hist. and unconstitutionality, with account of the enslavement of J. Hamlet. N. Y., 1850. 12°. (**C 259**)

— Letter from a gentleman in Boston to a Unitarian clergyman [H. Ware, Jr.]. 2d ed. Boston, 1828. 8°. (**C 184, D 63**)

— *Same.* 3d ed. Boston, 1882. 8°. (**C 226**)

— *Same.* 4th ed. Boston, 1828. 12°. (**D 61**)

— Life of A. Tappan. N. Y., 1870. 12°.

— Remarks on prisons and prison discipline. Vol. 3, no. 3. Boston, 1826. 8°. (**B 928, 1794**)

— Reply to charges brought against the American and Foreign Anti-Slavery Society; introd. by J. Scoble. London, 1852. 8°. (**C 257**)

— Dunbar, E. E. Statement of the controversy between Tappan and Dunbar. N. Y., 1846. 8°. (**B 1449**)

— Quincy, E. Examination of the charges of J. Scoble and L. Tappan against the American Anti-Slavery Soc. Dublin, 1852. 8°. (**B 1479**)

— Remarks on the 'Letter from a gentleman in Boston', *etc.* Boston, 1828. 12°. (**C 242**)

— Review of 'Letter from a gentleman in Boston', *etc.* 2d ed. Boston, 1828. 12°. (**C 184, 242**)

— *Same.* 3d ed. Boston, 1828. 8°. (**C 226**)

— Ware, H., *Jr.* Reply of a Unitarian clergyman to the 'Letter of a gentleman in Boston'. Boston, 1828. 12°. (**C 226, D 63**)

— — *Same.* 2d ed. (**C 242, D 61**)

— Webb, R. D. The national anti-slavery societies in England and the U. S.; strictures on a 'Reply to charges against the American and Foreign Anti-Slavery Society', *etc.* Dublin, 1852. 8°. (**B 1479**)

Tappan, Lewis W. Communication. *See* **Sampson & Tappan.**

Tappan, *Rev.* Wm. Bingham. Poems and lyricks. Boston, 1842. 12°.

— To my mother in New England. (*In* **Boston** book, 3d col. 1841.)

Tappy's chicks. *See* **Cupples,** *Mrs.* G. *Note.*

Tar. Prince, T. Observations of the several sorts of tar used in Boston. (*In* **Prior,** T. Authentic narr. of tar water. 1749. **B 655**)

— Account of tar and directions for using the different kinds of coal tar and varnish. N. Y., 1788. 8°. (**B 747**)

— Crichton, A. Account of some experiments made with the vapor of boiling tar, in the cure of pulmonary consumption. Edin., 1817. 8°. (**B 831**)

Tar water. Berkeley, G. Siris; or, virtues of tar water. 2d ed. impr. Dublin *pr.*, London *repr.*, 1744. 8°.

— — *Same.* (*In his* Works, v. 2. 1871.)

— — Farther thoughts on tar water. [Dublin,] 1752. 8°.

— — *Same.* (*In his* Miscellany. 1752; — *and in his* Works, v. 3. 1871.)

— Prior, T. Success of tar-water in curing distempers. London, 1746. 8°.

— — *Same, abridged.* London, *printed* 1746, Boston, *reprinted* 1749. 8°. (**B 655**)

Tara Hill. Petrie, G. Hist. and antiquities of Tara Hill. (*In* **Roy. Irish Acad.** Trans., v. 18, pt. 2. 1839.)

Tarakanof, Elizabeth, *Princess.* Challemel Lacour, P. Hist. d'une aventurière russe au 18e siècle. (*In* **Revue** d. D. Mondes, mai 1870.)

Taranto, *Italy.* Giovane, G. De antiquitate et varia fortuna Tarentinorum. (*In* **Grævius.** Thes. antiq. Ital., v. 9, pt. 5. 1723.)

— ROCHETTE, D. R. La numismatique tarentine. (*In* Paris. Inst. *Ac. d. Inscr.* Mém., v. 14, 2e pte. 1840.)

Tarantula. BAGLIVI, G. De anatome, morsu, et effectibus tarantulæ. (*In his* Opera. 1714.)

— – *Ital., abridged.* Historia de la T. *n.p.*, [17—]. 4°. (B 1896)

Tarare; opéra, par P. A. C. de Beaumarchais. (*In his* Œuvres, v. 2. 1826.)

Tarascon, Junr., James Berthoud, & Co. Address to the citizens of Phila. on the trade of the western country. Phila., 1806. 8°. (B 422)

Tarasia, *St.* MACEDO, F. de S. A. (*In* **Acta sanct.**, v. 24. 1867.)

Tarassenko-Otreshkof, Narcès. De l'or et de l'argent. Vol. 1. Paris, 1856. 8°.

Tarazona, *Spain.* FUENTE, V. de la. La iglesia de Tarazona. (*In* **Florez, H.** España sagrada, v. 49, 50. 1865-66.)

Tarchun. GRAY, *Mrs.* E. C. Tarchun and his times. (*In her* History of Etruria, v. 1. 1843.)

Tardes americanas; gobierno gentil y catolico; noticia de toda la hist. indiana; trabajadas por un Indio y un Español; sacalas a luz J. J. Granados y Galvez. Mexico, 1778. 4°.

Tardieu, —. Choix d'édifices publics, *etc.* 1828. *See* **Gourlier, P. C.**

Tardieu, Auguste Ambroise. Treatise on epidemic cholera; tr. by S. L. Bigelow; with app. by [W. W. Morland]. Boston, 1849. 12°.

— La morgue, les morts violentes, crimes, et suicides. (*In* **Paris** guide, v. 2. 1867.)

Tardieu, Eugène Amédée. Sénégambie et Guinée. Paris, 1847. 8°. (Univers.)

Tardieu, Jules Romain. Pour une épingle; legende, par J. T. de Saint Germain [pseud.]. Paris, [1863]. 8°.

Tardieu, P. A. F. Carte des routes de postes de l'Empire Franç., du Royaume d'Italie, et de la Conféd. du Rhin. Paris, 1814.

Tardieu, Pierre Alexandre. GALICHON, E. (*In* **Gazette** des beaux-arts, v. 14. 1863.)

Tardif, Jules. Monuments historiques. *See* **France.** *Archives* (p. 1026).

— Sur les notes tironiennes. (*In* **Paris. Inst.** *Ac. d. Inscr.* Div. sav., 2e sér., v. 3. 1854.)

Tarduzzi *or* **Tarduccius,** Achille. Turca vincibilis in Ungaria. (*In* **Conring, H.** De bello contra Turcas. 1664.)

Tarella, Pietro. AMATO, G. d'. (*In his* Panteon, v. 2. 1851.)

Tarentum. *See* **Taranto.**

Targioni Tozzetti, Giovanni. Relazioni d'alcuni viaggi in diverse parti della Toscana. Firenze, 1768-79. 12 v. 8°.

— *French.* Voyage minéralogique, philos., *etc.*, en Toscane, [1742]. Paris, 1792. 2 v. 8°.

— VICQ D'AZYR, F. Eloge de T. (*In his* Œuvres, v. 3. 1805.)

Tarif général, ou Comptes faits pour faire et recevoir des paiemens en monnaies des Pays Bas, de France, d'Allemagne, et d'Angleterre. 4e éd. augm. Brux., [1825?]. 12°.

Tariff. DESROCHES, M. Tarifs des douanes de l'Europe, 1 jan. Paris, 1860. 8°.

See also names of countries as **Great Britain**; — **France**; — **Mexico**; — **United States**; — *also* **Sound tariff**; — *also* **East and West India sugar**; — **Sugar**; — **Taxes**; — **Free trade.**

Tarin, Vincenzo. Description d'un ancien ouvrage en mosaïque, suivie des remarques sur ce genre de peinture. — Discours sur l'utilité des grandes collections de médailles antiques et specialement par rapport aux beaux arts. (*In* **Turin. Ac. d. Sci.** Mem., v. 13. 1803.) — Discours sur l'utilité des sciences, littérature, et beaux-arts. — Explication d'un bas-relief antique. (*In* v. 15. 1804.)

Tarleton, Banastre, *Lieut. Col.* A history of the campaigns of 1780-81 in the southern provinces of N. America. London, 1787. 4°.

— *Same.* Dublin, 1787. 8°.

— Reply to Col. de Charmilly. Lond., 1810. 8°. (B 1420)

— MACKENZIE, R. Strictures on T.'s 'History of the campaigns'; *etc.*, added, The siege of '96, and re-capture of the island of New-Providence. London, 1787. 8°.

— VENAULT DE CHARMILLY, *Col.* Letter to T. London, 1810. 8°. (B 1420)

Tarlton, Richard. Tarleton's jests and News out of purgatory, with some account of his life by J. O. Halliwell. London, 1844. 8°. (Shakspeare Soc.)

— Tarleton's jests. (*In* **Hazlitt, W. C.** Shakespeare jest books, v. 2. 1864.)

Tarnowski (*Lat.* **Tarnovius**), Jan, *count.* De bello cum Turcis gerendo. (*In* **Conring, H.** De bello contra Turcas. 1664.)

Tarquinius Superbus, Lucius. MALVEZZI, V. Tarquinio Superbo. (*In his* Romulo. 1634.)

— ROWE, T. (*In* **Plutarchus.** Vies, v. 11. 1778.)

Tarr family. VINTON, J. A. (*In his* Giles memorial. 1864.)

Tarraga, Francesco de. La enemiga favorable. (*In* **Ochoa, E. de.** Tesoro del teatro español, v. 1. 1838.)

Tarragona, *Spain.* FLOREZ, H. Las memorias eclesiasticas de Tarragona. (*In his* España sagrada, v. 24, 25. 1769-70.)

Tárrega, Francisco. El prado de Valencia. — La sangre leal de los montañeses de Navarra. — La duquesa constante. — La enemiga favorable. (*In* **Mesonero Romanos,** R. de. Dramaticos contemporaneos a Lope de Vega, v. 1. 1857; v. 43 of Aribau. Bibl.)

Tarsia, Paolo Antonio di. Historiæ Cupersanensium. (*In* **Grævius.** Thes. antiq. Ital., v. 9, pt. 5. 1723.)

Tartagni, Alessandro. PAPOTTI. T. Elogio di T. (*In his* Elogi d' illust. Imolesi. 1841.)

Tartar emetic. LEPELLETIER, A. R. J. Le l'emploi du tartre stibié dans le traitement des maladies en général, *etc.* Paris, 1835. 8°.

Tartarotti, Girolamo. De auctoribus ab A. Dandulo laudatis in Chronico Veneto. (*In* **Muratori, L. A.** Rer. Ital. scr., v. 25. 1751.)

Tartary. *Agriculture.*

— PALLAS, P. S. Account of sheep in [Russia and Tartary]. Edin., 1794. 8°.

Description.

— DESCRIPTION of Korea, Eastern Tartary, *etc.*, [1202-1720]. — TRAVELS through Tartary, [1246-1698]. (*In* **Green, J.** Col. of voy., v. 4. 1747; — *and, Germ., in* **Allgemeine Hist.**, v. 6, 7. 1750.)

— VOY. of an Englishman into Tartaria, *etc.*, **1243.** (*In* **Hakluyt, R.** Col. of voy., v. 1. 1809; — *and in* **Kerr, R.** Col. of voy., v. 1. 1824.)

— CARPINI, J. de P. Long and wonderfull voy. into Northeastern [Tartary], **1246.** (*In* **Hakluyt, R.** Col. of voy., v. 1. 1809; — *and in* **Kerr, R.** Col. of voy., v. 1. 1824.)

— DUE viaggi in Tartaria per alcuni frati, **1247.** (*In* **Ramusio, G. B.** Raccolta, v. 2. 1573.)

— RUBRUQUIS, W. von. Remarkable travels into the East, partic. Tartary, **1253.** (*In* **Harris, J.** Col. of voy., v. 1. 1705; — **Green, J.** Col., v. 4. 1747; — **Hakluyt, R.** Col. v. 1. 1809; — **Pinkerton, J.** Col., v. 7. 1811; — **Kerr, R.** Col., v. 1. 1824; — *French, in* **Montémont, A.** Biblioth. univ., v. 31. 1836; — *and, Germ., in* **Allgemeine Hist.**, v. 7. 1750.)

— POLO, M. [1272.] (*In his* Le livre. 1865.)

— SCHILDTBERGER, J. Travels into Tartary, **1394.** (*In* **Kerr, R.** Col. of voy., v. 1. 1824.)

— VEER, G. de. Schipvaerde der Hollandsche ende Zeeusche schepen by noorden Noorwegen, Moscovien, ende Tartarien, **[1594].** (*In* **Commelin, I.** Begin, v. 1. 1646.)

— – *Eng.* Three voyages by the north-east towards Cathay and China by the Dutch [under W. Barentsz], **1594-96**; tr. by W. Phillip; ed. by C. T. Beke. London, 1853. 8°. (Hakluyt Soc., v. 13.)

— – *Same, abridged.* (*In* **Purchas.** Pilgrimes, v. 3. 1625; — **Collection** of voy., 1793; — *and in* **Harris, J.** Col., v. 1. 1705.)

— GOEZ, B. Travels from Lahor to China, **1602.** (*In* **Pinkerton, J.** Col. of voy., v. 7. 1811; — *and in* **Green, J.** Col., v. 4. 1847.)

— – *Germ.* Reisen in des Mongols Reiche nach China. (*In* **Allgemeine Hist.**, v. 7. 1750.)

— OLEARIUS, A. Voyage en Moscovie, Tartarie, et Perse, **[1634-36]**. Nouv. éd. Par., 1659. 2 v. 4°.

— MARTINI, M. Relation de la Tartarie orientale, [1654]. (*In* **Bernard, J. F.** Rec. de voy., v. 3. 1716.)
— PEREIRA, T. Narrative of [his] journey into Tartary, [168-]. (*In* **Orléans, P. J. d'.** Hist. of the Tartar conquerors, 1854. Hakluyt Soc., v. 16.)
— VERBIEST, F. Voyage de l'empereur de la Chine dans la Tartarie, **1682–83.** (*In* **Bernard, J. F.** Recueil de voy., v. 3. 1716.)
— - *Eng.* Journey of the Emperour of China into Tartary. (*In* **Soto, F. de.** Relation. 1686; — *and in* **Orléans, P. J. d'.** Hist. of the two Tartar conquerors. 1854. Hakluyt Soc., v. 16.)
— - *Germ.* Reise in die ostliche Tartarey, 1682. (*In* **Allgemeine** Hist., v. 7. 1750.)
— GERBILLON, J. F. Voyage dans la Tartarie occidentale, **1688–98.** (*In* **Prévost d' Exiles, A. F.,** *etc.*, Hist. des voy., v. 7, 8. 1749, 50.)
— - *Eng.* Travels into W. Tartary. (*In* **Green, J.** Col. v. 4. 1747.)
— - *Germ.* Reisen in dis westliche Tartarey. (*In* **Allgemeine** Hist., v. 7. 1750.)
— IDES, E. Y. Trav. through the countries of the Mongol Tartars, [1692–93]. (*In* **Harris, J.** Col., v. 2. 1705.)
— - *Same, abridged.* (*In* **Bruin, C. de.** Travels into Muscovy. 1737.)
— TU-LI-SHIN. Narrative of the Chinese embassy to the Khan of the Tartars, **1712–15**; tr. [with] app. by Sir G. T. Staunton. London, 1821. 8°.
— STRAHLENBERG, P. J. v. Historico-geog. description of the N. and E. parts of Europe and Asia, Great Tartary, *etc.*; in their anc. and mod. state, [1730]; with dialects of 32 Tartarian nations; and vocab. of the Kalmuckmungalian tongue; tr. Lond., 1738. 4°.
— TOTT, F., *baron* de. Manners and customs of the Tartars, [1767–69]. (*In his* Memoirs, v. 1, 2. 1786.)
— CLARKE, E. D. Tartary, *etc.*, [**1800**]. (Vol. 1, 2 *of his* Travels in Europe. 1816.)
— - *Same.* Phila., 1811. 8°.
— COCHRANE, J. D. Pedestrian journey in Russia and Tartary, [1820–23]. 4th ed. London, 1825. 2 v. 12°.
— TIMKOWSKI, G. Travels of the Russian mission through Mongolia to China, **1820–21.** London, 1827. 2 v. 8°.
— ZWICK, H. A. Journey from Sarepta to several Calmuc hordes, **1823.** London, 1831. 12°.
— DAVIS, J. F. Notices of western Tartary, [1827]. (*In* **Royal Asiatic Soc.** Trans., v. 2. 1830.)
— FERRARIO, G. (*In his* Costume, v. 4. 1829.)
— ZIMMERMANN, C. Denkschrift über den untern Lauf des Oxus zum Karabugas-Haff des Caspischen Meeres, *etc.*, [1841]. Berl., 1845. 4°.
— HUC, E. R., *l'abbé.* Souvenirs d'un voy. dans la Tartarie, *etc.*, **1844–46.** 2e éd. Paris, 1853. 2 v. 12°.
— - *Eng.* Travels in T., *etc.*; tr. by W. Hazlitt. London, [1852]. 2 v. 12°.
— ATKINSON, *Mrs.* T. W. Recollections of Tartar steppes, *etc.*, [1848–53]. Lond., 1863. 8°.
— ATKINSON, T. W. Explorations in Chinese Tartary, 1848–53. (*In his* Oriental and W. Siberia. 1858.)
— DUBEUX, L., *and* VALMONT, V. Tartarie, Beloutchistan, *etc.* Paris, **1848.** 8°. (Univers.)
— TRONSON, J. M. A voyage to Japan, Tartary, *etc.*, [**1854–56**]. London, 1859. 8°.
— FLEMING, G. Travels on horseback in Mantchu Tartary, [1861]. London, 1863. 8°.
— TORRENS, H. D. Travels in Ladâk, Tartary, and Kashmir, [1861]. London, 1862. 8°.
— MICHIE, A. Siberian overland route from Pekin to Petersburg, [1863]. London, 1864. 8°.
— *Map.* TARTARIA sive Magni Chami imperium. *n.p.*, [16–]. (E 78, no. 275)

See also **Amoor river**; — **Bokhara**; — **Corea**; — **Kazan**; — **Khiva**; — **Mantchu Tartars**; — **Mantchuria**; — **Mogul Empire**; — **Mongolia**; — **Oxus**; — **Siberia**; — **Taurida**; — **Turkestan.**

Ethnology.

— SCHOTT, W. Aelteste Nachrichten von Mongolen und Tataren. (*In* **Berlin. Ak. d. Wiss.** Abh., 1845.)
See also **Kirghiz.**

History.

— GUIGNES, J. de. Histoire des Tartares occidentales, [**209** av. J. C. – **1754** apr. J. C.]. Paris, 1756–58. 5 v. 4°.
— ACCOUNT of Independent Tartary, [1186–1658]. (*In* **Pinkerton, J.** Col. of voy., v. 9. 1811.)
— SKETCH of revolutions in Tartary, **1200–1405.** (*In* **Kerr, R.** Col. of voy., v. 1. 1824.)

See also **Altai**; — **Corea**; — **Mongolia**; — **Timour**; — *also Description.* 1730 (STRAHLENBERG).

Language and Literature.

See **Mantchu language and literature** (p. 1857).

Missions.

— HISTOIRE très-véritable de la cruauté exercée par les Tartares envers trois pères capucins et plusieurs Chrestiens, **1608.** (*In* **Ternaux-Compans, H.** Archives des voy., v. 2. 1841.)
— HUC, E. R., *l'abbé.* Christianity in China, Tartary, *etc.* London, 1857–58. 3 v. 8°.

Tartini, Giuseppe Maria. Rerum Italicarum scriptores. Florentiæ, 1748–70. 2 v. f°.
Contents. Vol. 1. **Sozzomeno** *pistojese.* Excerpta ex historia, 1001–1284. — **Palmieri, M.** Excerpta ex libro de temporibus, 1294–1448. — **Palmieri, M.,** *of Pisa.* Opus de temporibus suis, 1449–83. — **Gregory VII.,** *Pope.* Epistolæ. — **Marangone, B.** Croniche della città de Pisa, al 1406. — **Benevenuti, B.,** *and* **Unctis, P.** de. Fragmenta Fulginatis hist., 1188–1440. — **Gori, J.** Istoria della città di Chiusa, 936–1595. 2. **Piero, P.** di. Cronica, 1080–1305. — **Minerbetti, P.** di G. Cronica, 1385–1409. — **Manni, D. M.** Commentaria della vita del famoso capt. Giovanni Aguto. — **Ursus, R.** De obsidione Tiphernatum, 1474. — **Ricordi** di Firenze, 1459. — **Rucellai, B.** De urbe Roma.
— LYSER, J. P. (*In his* Neue Kunst-Novellen. 1837.)

Tartt, W. M. Summary convictions under the criminal justice act of 1855. (*In* **Nat. Assoc. Prom. Soc. Sci.** Trans., 1859.)

Tartuffe, Le; comédie. *See* **Molière, J. B. P.** de.

Taruffi, Cesare. GELLI, A. (*In* **Amato, G. d'.** Panteon, v. 2. 1851.)

Tarugi, Domenico. SIMONI, N. de. (*In* **Crescimbeni, G. M.** Vite degli Arcadi illustri, v. 2. 1710.)

Tarver, John Charles. The royal phraseological English-French, French-English dictionary. 4th ed. London, 1862–67. 2 v. 8°.

Tarvisium. *See* **Treviso.**

Tasborough, John. TRYAL and conviction of J. Tasborovgh and Ann Price for subornation in endeavouring to perswade S. Dugdale to retract his evidence about the horrid Popish Plot. London, 1680. f°. (A 50)

Taschenbuch, Das; von A. v. **Kotzebue.** (*In his* Theater, v. 38. 1841.)

Taschereau, Jules Antoine. Histoire de la vie et des ouvrages de P. Corneille. 2e éd., augm. Paris, 1855. 12°.
— Histoire de la vie et des ouvrages de Molière. Paris, 1825. 8°.
— *Same.* 3e éd. Paris, 1844. 12°.

Taschereau de Fargues, Paul Augustin Jacques. Plan de finances pour percevoir les tributs en un seul jour. [Paris, 1794.] 8°. (B 1892)

Tasistro, Louis Fitzgerald. Random shots and southern breezes. N. Y., 1842. 2 v. 12°.

Tasman, Abel Janssen. Journal of a voy. from Batavia for making disc. of the unknown South land in 1642. (*In* **Burney, J.** Discovery in the South Sea, v. 3. 1813.)
Note. For other accounts *see* **Harris, J.** Col., v. 1. 1705, 1764; — **Callander, J.** Terra Australis, v. 2. 1768; — **Dalrymple, A.** Col. of voy., v. 2. 1770; — **Pinkerton, J.** Col., v. 11. 1812; — **Montémont, A.** Biblioth., v. 1. 1833; — *and, Germ.*, **Allgemeine** Hist., v. 12. 1754.
— Second voyage of discovery. (*In* **Burney, J.** Discov. in the South Sea, v. 3. 1813.)

Tasmania. *See* **Van Dieman's Land.**

Tasmanian royal kalendar, colonial register, and almanac; compiled by J. Wood. Hobart-Town, 1849. 12°.

Tassi, Tassis, *or* **Taxis** (*Lat.* **Tassius**), Jan Baptiste de. Commentariorum de tumultibus Belgicis sui temp. libri VIII. (*In* **Hoynck van Papendrecht,** C. P. Vita, v. 2, pt. 2. 1743.)

Tassin, J. B. Map of upper Assam, showing the tea tracts discovered by C. A. Bruce. *n.p.*, 1839.

Tassis, Juan de, *conde de Villamedina.* *See* **Villamedina,** *conde* de.

Tasso, Bernardo. L'amadigi; colla vita dell' autore e illustrazione, [da P. Serassi]. Bergamo, 1755. 4 v. 12°.

— Lettere; con la vita dell' autore [da] A. F. Seghezzi. Padova, 1733. 2 v. 8°.

— Sonetti. — Canzone. (*In* **Gironi,** R. Rac. di lir. ital. 1808.)

Tasso, Faustino. Agostini, G. degli. (*In his* Notizie degli scrit. viniz., v. 2. 1754.)

Tasso, Torquato. Opere; con le controversie sopra la Gerusalemme, e con le annotazioni intere di varii autori. Venezia, 1735–42. 12 v. 4°.

Contents. Vol. 1. Il Gofredo ovvero la Gerusalemme liberata. 2, 3. Critiche e apologie uscite per impugnazione e per disesa di T. int. il Goffredo. 4. La Gerusalemme conquistata. — Del giudizio sopra la Gerusalemme riformata dall' autore. — Il Rinaldo. 5. Le sette giornate del mondo creato. — Il re Torrismondo; tragedia. — Tragedia non finita. — L'Aminta; favola boschereccia. — Intrighi d'amore; commedia. — Discorsi del poema eroico. — Discorsi dell' arte poetica, e in particolare sopra il poema eroico. 6. Rime, amorose eroiche, sacra e morali. — Varie lezioni. — Opposizioni d' incerto al 'Spino', *ec.* — Risposta del Tasso. — Della fortuna; interpretazione del sonetto 'quella che nome aver di dea non merta'. — Considerazioni sopra tre canzoni di G. B. Pigna. — Lezione sopra il sonetto del casa, 'Questa vita mortal che in una o in due'. — La cavalletta, ovvero della poesia toscana; dialogo. 7, 8. Dialoghi. 8. Discorsi e orazioni. — Comparazione di Omero, Virgilio, e Tasso di P. Beni. 9. Lettere. — Lettere familiari, pte. 1a. 10. Lettre familiari, pte. 2a. — Lettere poetiche scritte da T. e da altri. — Lettere inedite, rac. da L. A. Muratori. — Esposizioni di T. d'alcune sue rime. 11. Orazione in morte di Barbara d'Austria. — Orazione nella morte del Santino. — Rime inedite da' mss. del L. A. Muratori. — La bilancia critica di Mario Zito. — Discorso di F. Pigafetta in materia de' due titoli del poema della Gerusalemme. — Discorsi e annot. di G. Guastavini sopra la Gerusalemme liberata. — Risposta di G. Guastavini ad alcune opposizioni fatte alla proposizione e invocazione usata dal Tasso nella Gerusalemme liberata. — Della comparazione d'Omero, Virgilio, e T. Tasso, dialoghi tre di P. Beni estratti dall' impressione di Padova di Battista Martini del 1612. — Lettera di Diomede Borghesi tratta della terza parte delle sue lettere discorsive. 12. Annot. di Scipione Gentili e di G. Guastavini. — Allegoria del poema. — Notizie istoriche di L. Pignoria. — Annotazioni del card. Bonifazio Martinelli sopra la Gerusalemme liberata. — Il farnetico savio, ovvero il Tasso, dialogo di A. Guarini. — Indice generale.

— Opere; ricor. ed illust. dal prof. G. Rosini. Pisa, 1821–32. 33 v. 8°.

Contents. Vol. 1. Il Rinaldo; poema. 2. Aminta. — Il rogo di Corinna. — Il re Torrismondo. 3-6. Rime. 7-9. Dialoghi. 7. Il padre di famiglia. — Il messaggiero. — Il Gonzaga, ovvero del piacere onesto. — Il Nifo, ovvero del piacere. — Il cavaliere amante e la gentildonna amata. — Il Ficino, ovvero dell' arte. — La cavaletta, ovvero della poesie toscana. 8. I bagni, ovvero della pietà. — Il forno, ovvero della nobiltà. — Della dignità. — Il Malpiglio, o della corte. — Il Malpiglio secondo, o del fuggir la moltitudine. — La molza, o dell' amore. — Il Cataneo o delle conclusioni. — Conclusioni amorose. — Il Romeo, ovvero del giuoco. 9. Il Gonzaga seconda, o del giuoco. — Il Beltramo, o della cortesia. — Il Rangone, o della pace. — Il Ghirlinzone, o l'epitaffio. — Il forrestiero napoletano. — Il Gianluca, o delle maschere. — Il Minturno, o della bellezza. — Il Costantino, o della clemenza. — Il Porzio, o delle virtu. — Il Cataneo, o degli idoli. — Il Manso, o dell' amicizia. — Il conte, o dell' imprese. 10. Prose varie. 11, 12. Discorsi. 13-17. Lettere. 18-23. Controversie sulla Gerusalemme liberata. 24-26. La Gerusalemme liberata, con illustrazioni. 27. Il mondo creato. 28, 29. La Gerusalemme conquistata. 30. Postille alla Divina commedia di Dante. — Intrighi d' amore. 31. Rimario della Gerusalemme liberata. 32. Rime inedite o disperse. 33. Vita di T. Tasso. — Indice gen.

— Aminta, [e canzone amorose]. Lond., 1780. 12°.

— Aminta. Nuova ed. Parigi, 1781. 12°.

— *Same.* Ed. ster. Parigi, 1800. 18°.

— *Same.* Firenze, 1804. f°.

— *Same.* *See, below,* Gerusaleme. 1823.

— *Same.* (*In* **Bachi,** P. Teatro scelto ital., 1829.)

— *Eng.* Amyntas; tr. by L. Hunt. London, 1820. 12°.

— *Span.* Aminta; tr. by J. de Jauregui. (*In* **Sedano,** J. J. L. de. Parnaso español, v. 1. 1768; — **Fernandez,** R. Poetas españoles. v. 6. 1786; — *and in* **Quintana,** M. J. Poesias castellanas, v. 3. 1807.)

— Canzone amorose. *See, above,* Aminta. 1780; *and, below,* Sonetti.

— Gerusalemme liberata. Londra, 1778. 2 v. 12°.

— *Same.* Pisa, 1807. 2 v. f°.

— *Same.* La Gerusalemme e Aminta; con note per studio di A. Buttura. Parigi, 1823. 2 v. 8°.

— *Same.* Gerusalemme liberata; con discorso critico di U. Foscolo. 3a ed. Firenze, 1850. 12°.

— *Eng.* Godfrey of Boulogne; or, The recoverie of Jerusalem; done into Eng. verse by E. Fairfax; with the life of Godfrey. London, 1624. f°.

— *Same.* London, 1687. 8°.

— *Same.* Jerusalem delivered; tr. by J. Hoole. 8th ed. London, 1803. 2 v. 8°.

— *Same.* 1st Amer. from 8th London ed. Newburyport, 1810. 2 v. 8°.

— *Same.* (*In* **Chalmers,** A. Eng. poets, v. 21. 1810.)

— *Same.* Tr. with life of the author by J. H. Wiffen. 2d ed. London, 1826. 3 v. 8°.

— *Same.* N. Y., 1846. 12°.

— *Germ.* Befreites Jerusalem; übers. von K. Streckfuss. 2e verb. Aufl. Lpz., 1835. 2 v. 12°.

— *Same, extract.* Armida. (*In* **Heinse,** W. Sämmt. Schr., v. 10. 1838.)

— Lettere; illustrate da C. Guasti. Firenze, 1852–55. 5 v. 12°.

— Lezione sopra il sonnetto LIX. de G. Della Casa. (*In* **Rac.** di prose ital., v. 2. 1809.)

— Madrigale. (*In* **Trucchi,** F. Poesie ital., v. 4. 1847.)

— Il re Torrismondo. (*In* **Teatro** ital. ant., v. 7.)

— Le sette giornate del mondo creato. Londra, 1780. 18°.

— Sonetti. — Canzoni. (*In* **Gironi,** R. Rac. di lir. ital. 1808.)

— Stories and life. (*In* **Hunt,** J. H. L. Stories from Ital. poets. 1846.)

— Alberti, M. Manoscritti ined. di T. ed altri documenti, per servire alla biografia del medesimo. Lucca, 1837. f°.

— Bernardi, A. E. F. de. Un arrêt du parlement de Paris qui ordonne la suppression de quelques vers d'un poème de Tasse. (*In* **Paris. Inst.** *Ac. d. Inscr.* Mém., v. 5. 1821.)

— Black, J. Life of T. Edin., 1810. 2 v. 4°.

— Drake, N. The frenzy of T. (*In his* Literary hours, v. 1. 1804.)

— Fabroni, A. Elogi di Dante. Parma, 1800. 8°.

— Galilei, G. Considerazione alla Gerusalemme liberata. (*In his* Opere, v. 15. 1856.)

— Gladstone, W. C. Homer and some of his successors in epic poetry. (*In his* Studies on Homer, v. 3. 1858.)

— Heinse, W. Leben des T. (*In his* Sämmtliche Schriften, v. 10. 1838.)

— Malden, H. (*In his* Disting. men, v. 1. 1838; v. 37 of Lib. ent. knowl.; *and* v. 1. 1840; v. 123 of Harper's fam. lib.)

— Malespini, L. G. T. Orazione in lode di T. (*In* **Dati,** C. Prose fior., pt. 1, v. 1. 1751.)

— Milman, R. Life of T. Lond., 1850. 2 v. 12°.

— MONTÉGUT, E. (*In* Revue d. D. Mondes, sept. 1864.)
— MONTGOMERY, J. (*In his* Lives of the lit. and sci. men, v. 2. 1835. Lardner. Cab. cyc.)
— NICERON, J. P. (*In his* Mém., v. 25. 1734; — *and, Germ.*, v. 23. 1771.)
— VOIGHT, G. Tasso am Hofe von Ferrara. (*In* Historische Zeitschrift, v. 20. 1868.)
— WILDE, R. H. Conjectures conc. the love, madness, *etc.*, of T. N.Y., 1842. 2 v. 12°.

Tasso and Leonora; by [E. Manning]. London, 1856. 12°.

Tassoni, Alessandro. Manifesto intorno le relazioni passate tra. esso e i principi di Savoia. — Estratti di lettere al canonico Sassi a Modina. (*In* Archivio stor. ital., app., v. 7. 1849.)
— La secchia rapita, con la dichiarazzioni del G. Salviani. In Osford, 1737. 2 v. 8°.
— *Same.* Londra, 1779. 12°.
— *Same.* Pisa, 1811. f°.
— MONTGOMERY, J. (*In his* Lives of lit. and sci. men, v. 2. 1835. Lardner. Cab. cyc.)

Taste, Timothy, *pseud.* The freaks of Columbia; a farce. Wash., 1808. 8°. (B 474)

Taste. *See* Æsthetics.

Taste, Sense of. FOLSOM, N. Essay on the senses of smell and taste. From the Boston med. and surg. journ., v. 68. Boston, 1863. 8°. (B 1553)
— ON the senses; tr. by C. A. Alexander from the 'Aus der Natur'. (*In* Smithsonian Inst. Report, 1866.)

Taste; a comedy. *See* Foote, S.

Tastu, Joseph. Notice d'un atlas en langue catalane, ms. (*In* Paris. Inst. *Ac. d. Inscr.* Not., v. 14, 2e pte. 1841.)

Tastu, *Mme.* Sabine Casimia Amable Voïart. L'écho de la harpe. *See* Muse française, La.
— Eloge de Mme. de Sévigné. (*In* Sévigné, M. de R. C. Lettres choises. 1844.)
— Prose. Brux., 1837. 2 v. 16°.
Contents. Vol. 1. Fabien le rêveur. — Rouget-de-l'-Isle. — Le souhait. — Susanne Centlivre. — La protegée. — La belle Cauchoise. — La bonne idée de Norah Clary. — La guirlande. 2. Esther à Saint-Cyr. — Trop tard. — Une journée de dupe. — Le bracelet maure. — Deux visites à la Malmaison. — Les expériences.
— SAINTE BEUVE, C. A. (*In* Revue d. D. Mondes, fév. 1835; — *and in his* Portraits contemp., v. 1. 1852.)

Taswell, Wm., *D.D.* Autobiography and anecdotes, 1651-82; ed. by G. P. Elliott. London, 1853. 4°. (Camden Soc., v. 55.)

Tate. *See also* Tait.

Tate, James, *Canon of St. Paul's.* Introduction to Greek tragic and comic metres. 2d ed. London, 1829. 8°.

Tate, James. Major est veritas et prævalebit. Modern vindication of infant baptism. Savannah, 1790. 8°. (B 255)

Tate, Nahum. Elegy on Tillotson. Lond., 1695. f°. (A 45)
— New version of the Psalms. [1757.] *See* Bible. *Psalms* (p. 279).
— AUSTIN, W. S., *Jr.* (*In his* Lives of the poets-laureate. 1853.)

Tate, Ralph. Report of Zetland anthropolog. exped. (*In* Anthropolog. Soc. Mem., v. 2. 1866.)

Tate, Thomas. Strength of materials. London, 1850. 8°.

Tate, Wm. Elements of commercial calculations. London, 1819. 2 pt. 8°.
— Modern cambist. 10th ed. London, 1861. 8°.

Tatham, Charles Heathcote. Etchings of Grecian and Roman architectural ornament. London, 1806. f°.
— Gallery at Castle Howard. London, 1811. f°.

Tatham, Edward, *D.D.* Observations on the scarcity of money. 3d ed. (*In* Pamphleteer, 1816; v. 7 of B 838)

Tatham, Sandford. Observations on the Glasgow, Paisley, and Ardrossan canal and the harbour at Ardrossan. Glasgow, 1807. 8°. (B 1744)

Tatham, Wm. Comparative view of the four canals supposed to be in competition between Norfolk and No. Carolina. Norfolk, 1808. 8°. (B 426)
— Culture and commerce of tobacco. London, 1800. 8°.
— Traité général de l'irrigation; trad. de l'Angl. par de R. Paris, 1803. 8°.

Tatianus. Writings. Edin., 1867. 8°. (Ante Nicene Chr. lib., v. 3.)
Contents. Tatianus; tr. by B. P. Pratten. Address to the Greeks; — Fragments of lost works. — Theophilus. The III books to Autolycus; tr. by M. Dods. — Clemens *Romanus.* Recognitions; tr. by T. Smith.
— Harmonia evangelica, e Latina Victoris Capuani vers. translata in ling. Theotiscam antiquiss.; accedit Christi cum Samaritana muliere colloquium. (*In* Schilter, J. Thes. antiq., v. 2. 1727.)
— Oratio contra Græcos. (*In* Justinus *martyr.* Opera. 1686.)
— DONALDSON, J. [Memoir of] Tatian. (*In his* Critical hist. of Chr. lit., v. 3. 1866.)

Tatius. *See* Achilles Tatius.

Tatler, The; a journal of literature and the stage; ed. by L. Hunt. Vol. 1-4. London, 1830-32. 4 v. f°.

Tatler, The; or, Lucubrations of I. Bickerstaff, Esq. [Sir R. Steele]. Lond., 1710-11. 4 v. 8°.
— *Same.* [No. 1-271, April 1709 - Jan. 1710.] London, 1785. 8°. (Harrison's Brit. classics, v. 3.)
— *Same.* (Vols. 1-5 *of* Chalmers, A. Brit. essayists. 1803.)
— DRAKE, N. Essays, biog., crit., and hist., illustrative of the Tatler, Spectator, and Guardian. London, 1805. 3 v. 12°.
Note. For Addison's contributions *see his* Works, v. 2. 1811.

Tatler in Cambridge, The; May term. London, 1871. 4°.

Tatnall, Edward. Catalogue of phænogamous and filicoid plants of Newcastle Co., Delaware. Wilmington, 1860. 8°.

Tatton, John. Account of the voyage of S. Castleton to Priaman, 1612. (*In* Green, J. Col. of voy., v. 1. 1745.)

Tattuva Kattalei, law of the Tattuvam; a synopsis of the mystical philosophy of the Hindus, tr. from the Tamil, by H. R. Hoisington. (*In* Amer. Orient. Soc. Journ., v. 4. 1854.)

Tatum, Thomas. Affections of the muscular system. (*In* Holmes, T. Syst. of surg., v. 3. 1862.)

Taubert, *Capt.* Use of field artillery on service; tr. from the German by H. H. Maxwell. London, *Weale*, 1856. 12°.

Taubmann, Friedrich. NICERON, J. P. (*In his* Mém., v. 16. 1731; *and, Germ.*, v. 12. 1755.)

Taubstumme, Der, oder Der Abbé de l'Epée; von A. v. Kotzebue. (*In his* Theater, v. 10. 1840.)

Tauler, Johann. HISTORY and life of T.; with 25 sermons; tr. from the German, with additional notices of his life by S. Winkworth. London, 1857. 4°.
— BÖHRINGER, F. (*In his* Die Kirche Christi, Bd. 2, Abth. 3. 1855.)
— KINGSLEY, C. (*In his* New miscellanies. 1860.)

Taunton, *Mass.* EMERY, S. H. Ministry of Taunton; with incidental notices of other professions; with introd. notice by F. Baylies. Boston, 1853. 2 v. 12°.

Taunton directory, 1850, 57, 59, 66. Taunton, 1850-66. 4 v. 16° *and* 8°.
Note. 1850, by G. H. Babbitt; 1857, by G. Adams; 1859, by Adams, Sampson, & Co.; 1866, by Sampson, Davenport, & Co.

Taureau blanc, Le. *See* Voltaire, F. M. A. de.

Taurica. *See* Euripides.

Taurida. HERMANN, C. T. De l'état actuel de la population tatare en Tauride. (*In* St. Petersburg. Ac. Sci. Mém., 6e sér., v. 1. 1832.)

Taurinus, *St., Bp. of Evreux.* DEODATUS. (*In* Acta sanct., v. 36. 1867.)

Taurinus, Titus Cæsius. Votum fortunæ Prænestinæ. (*In* Lemaire. Poetæ Lat. min., v. 3. 1824. Bibl. class. Lat.)

Tauris. CRAMPON, E. (*In* Paris. Soc. de Géog. Bul., 5e sér., v. 16. 1868.)

Taurobolia. Boze, C. G. de. Explication d'une inscription antique trouvée depuis peu à Lyon. Paris, 1705. 8°.

Tauroentum. Giraud, M., *abbé*. Sur Tauroentum ou recherches archéol. topograph. et hist. crit. sur cette colonie phocéenne. (*In* **Paris. Inst.** *Ac. d. Inscr.* Div. sav., 2e sér., v. 3. 1854.)

Tautphoeus, Jemima (Montgomery), *Freiherrinn* von. At odds. Phila., 1863. 12°.

— Cyrilla; a tale. Lpz., *Tauchnitz*, 1853. 2 v. 12°.

— Quits. Phila., 1857. 2 v. in 1. 12°.

Tavannes, Charles Nicolas Saulx de, *Abp. of Rouen*. Catalogue [de ses] livres, la vente 25 mai 1759. Paris, 1759. 8°. (B 891)

Tavannes, Gaspard de Saulx, *seigneur* de. *See* **Tavannes,** Jean de Saulx.

Tavannes, Guillaume de Saulx, *seigneur* de. Mémoires. (*In* **Perrin,** A. Col. de mém., v. 49. 1789; — *in* **Petitot,** C. B. Col. des mém., 1e sér., v. 35. 1824; — *and in* **Michaud,** J. F. Col. des mém., v. 8. 1854.)

Tavannes, Jean de Saulx, *vicomte* de. Mémoires de Gaspard de Saulx, seigneur de Tavannes. (*In* **Perrin,** A. Col. univ. des mém., v. 26–28. 1787; — *in* **Petitot.** Col. des mém., 1e sér., v. 23–25. 1822; — *and in* **Michaud.** Col. des mém., v. 8. 1854.)

— Brantôme, P. de B. de. (*In his* Œuvres complètes, v. 2. 1823.)

Tavarone, Lazzaro. Bixio, C. L. (*In* **Grillo,** L. Elogi di Lig., v. 2. 1846.)

Tavel, George Frederic. Catalogue of the classical and theological library of G. F. T., sold. London, 1829. 8°. (B 1618)

Taverne, La; comédie. *See* **Sardou,** V.

Taverner, Richard. Postils on the epistles and gospels; ed. by E. Cardwell. Oxf., 1841. 8°.

Tavernier, Jean Baptiste, *baron d'Aubonne*. Six voyages en Turquie, en Perse, et aux Indes. Nouv. éd. Rouen, 1713. 5 v. 12°.

Note. Vol. 5 has the title-page, 'Recueil de plusieurs relations qui n'ont point été mis dans ses six premiers voyages, t. 5'.

Contents. Vol. 1, 2. Voy. de Perse. 3. Voy. des Indes. 4. Suite des voyages des Indes. 5. Relation du Japon. — Rel. de ce qui s'est passé dans la négociation des députez qui ont été en Perse. — Obs. sur le commerce des Indes Orientales, *etc.* — Rel. du royaume du Tunquin. — Hist. de la conduite des Hollandais en Asie.

— *Same, vol. 5.* Recueil, *etc.*, avec Relation de l'intérieur du serrail du Grand Seigneur. Paris, 1692. 12°.

— *Eng.* Col. of travels through Turky into Persia, *etc.* London, 1684. 2 v. f°.

Contents. Vol. 1. Persian travels. — Indian travels. 2. Hist. of the rev. of the dominions of the Great Mogul. — Rel. of Japon, *etc.* — Rel. of what passed in the negociation of the deputies to Persia and the Indies. — Obs. upon the trade of the E. Indies. — Relation of the kingdom of Tunquin. — Island of Formosa, *etc.* — New rel. of the Grand Seignor's seraglio.

— *Same, extracts.* (*In* **Harris,** J. Col. of voy., v. 2. 1705; v. 1. 1764; — *and in* **Pinkerton,** J. Col. of voy., v. 8. 1811.)

— Voyage dans l'Indoustan. (*In* **Montémont,** A. Biblioth. des voy., v. 31. 1836.)

— *Germ.* Reisen im Indostanischen. (*In* **Allgemeine** Hist., v. 11. 1723.)

— St. John, J. A. (*In his* Lives of cel. travellers, v. 1. 1844.)

Taverns. Letters on the errors of the present system of licensing taverns. (*In* **Pamphleteer,** 1815; v. 7 of B 838) — Beaumont, J. T. B. Injustice of the present system of licensing taverns. (*In* 1817; v. 9 of B 838)

Tavigliano, Giam Piero Baroni, *conte* di. Modello della chiesa di S. Filippo di Torino, inventato da F. Ivvaro. Torino, 1758. f°.

Tax-collectors. Dickinson, R. Digest of the powers and duties of sheriffs, coroners, constables, and collectors of taxes. Springfield, 1810. 8°.

Tax-payer's manual, *etc.* N. Y., 1862–63. 8°. (E 90)

Tax-payers and assessor's guide. N. Y., 1867. 8°.

Taxation. Mirabeau, V. R., *marq.* de. Théorie de l'impôt. *n.p.*, 1761. 12°.

— Petty, *Sir* W. Treatise of taxes and contributions. (*In his* Tracts. 1769.)

— Historical remarks on the taxation of free states. London, 1778. 4°. (A 27)

— Hamilton, A. Enquiry into the principles of taxation, chiefly applic. to articles of immediate consumption. Dublin, 1791. 8°.

— Thoughts on taxation; with some suggestions rel. to the means of raising supplies for the present year; by a commissioner of taxes. Newark, 1799. 8°. (B 763)

— Ricardo, D. Principles of political economy and taxation. [1817.] London, 1819. 8°.

— — *Same.* (*In his* Works, v. 1. 1852.)

— Jones, R. Essay on the distribution of wealth and sources of taxation. London, 1831. 8°.

— Taxation and taxes. [From the Penny cyclopædia.] London, *C. Knight*, 1843. 18°.

— McCulloch, J. R. Principles and practical influence of taxation and the funding system. London, 1845. 8°.

— — *Same.* 3d ed. London, 1863. 8°.

— Farr, W. Income and property tax; [or, on the equitable taxation of property]. London, 1853. 8°. (B 1536)

— — *Same.* (*In* **Statist.** Soc. Journ., v. 16. 1853.)

— Parieu, M. L. P. F. E. de. Taxes upon enjoyments. (*In* **Statistical** Soc. Journ., v. 24. 1861.)

— Royer, C. A. Théorie de l'impôt. Paris, 1862. 2 v. 8°.

See also **Excise;** — **Glass;** — **Political economy;** — **Tariff;** —
also **Gr. Brit.** *Finance* (pp. 1233–35); — **India** *Statistics;* — **U. S.** *Finance.*
also **Nat. Assoc.** for **Prom.** of **Soc. Sci. Trans.**

Taxation no tyranny; [by S. Johnson]. London, 1775. 8°. (B 381, 706)

— *Same.* 3d ed. London, 1775. 8°. (B 361, 1719)

Taxidermy. Lee, *Mrs.* S. Art of collecting, preparing, and mounting objects of natural history. 13th ed. London, 1823. 12°.

— Swainson, W. Taxidermy; with the biog. of zoölogists and notices of their works. London, 1840. 16°. (Lardner. Cab. cyc., v. 119.)

— Baird, S. F. Directions for collecting, preserving, *etc.*, specimens of nat. hist. (*In* **Smithsonian Inst.** Report, 1856.)

Tay, Waren. Report on surgery. (*In* **Sydenham** Soc. Biennial retrospect, 1869–70.)

Tayler. *See also* **Tailer;** — **Tailor;** — **Taylour;** — **Tayleure;** — **Taylour.**

Tayler, Charles Benjamin. Social evils, and their remedy. London, 1833–35. 4 v. 16°.

Contents. Vol. 1. Mechanic. 2. Pastor of Dronfells. — Labourer and his wife. 3. Country town. — Live and let live; or, Manchester weavers. 4. The soldier. — Leaside farm.

— Preface. (*In* **Vulliemin,** L. *and* C. Some acc. of the life of Gonthier. 1837.)

Tayler, John. Report of the trial of S. Van Rensselaer *vs.* J. T. (*In* **Jenkins,** E., *vs.* **Van Rensselaer,** S. Report. 1808. B 408)

Tayler, John James. [Address.] (*In* **Robberds,** J. G. Services. 1841.)

— Attempt to ascertain the character of the fourth gospel. London, 1867. 8°.

— A Catholic Christian church the want of our time. London, 1867. 16°. (B 1964)

— Christian aspect of faith and duty. 2d ed. London, 1855. 8°.

— Sermon; the humility of Christ. (*In* **Beard,** J. R. Sermons. 1832.)

Tayler, Joseph Needham. Plans for the formation of harbours of refuge, improvement of rivers and sea-ports. Plymouth, Eng., 1840. 4°.

Tayleur, Edward. Specifications for the passenger engines on the Caledonian railway. (*In* **Tredgold,** T. Principles, *etc.*, of steam engines, v. 1. 1850.)

Tayleur, Wm., *Funeral sermon on.* 1796. *See* **Houlbrooke,** T.

Tayleure, Clifton W. The boy martyrs; a drama. (*In* **Sargent,** E. Mod. stand. dr., v. 32.) — Horseshoe Robinson; a drama. (*In* v. 27.)

Tayloe, John. Virginia husbandry. — Remarks. (*In* Phil. Agric. Soc. Mem., v. 2. 1811.)

Taylor, —. Catalogue of books, sold by [him], Dec. 7, 8, 1829. *n.t.p.* [London, 1829.] 8°. (B 1618)

Taylor, Abraham. Insufficience of natural religion; disc. at lecture in London; reprinted on occasion of Dr. Mayhew's sermons; preface by A. Croswell. Boston, 1755. 8°. (B 476)

— Letter to a friend, occas. by a rhapsody delivered in the Old Jewry by a reverend bookseller in London. London, 1729. 8°. (D 60)

— - Postscript. London, 1729. 8°. (D 60)

Taylor, Alexander S. Account of the grasshoppers and locusts of America. (*In* Smithsonian Inst. Report, 1858.)

— Bibliografa Californica; or, Notes and materials to aid in forming a bibliography of California. 1863. (Cutting from the Sacramento daily union of June 25, 1863.)

Taylor, Alfred Swaine. Elements of medical jurisprudence. London, 1843. 8°.

— *Same.* 6th ed. London, 1858. 12°.

— *Same, revised.* Principles and practice of medical jurisprudence. London, 1865. 8°.

— Observations and experiments on the lungs of new-born children in relation to medical jurisprudence. (*In* Dunglison, R. Med. and surg. mon., v. 1. 1838.) — Perforations of the stomach from poisoning. (*In* v. 3. 1840.)

— Poisons, in rel. to medical jurisprudence and medicine. 2d ed. London, 1859. 12°.

Taylor, *Mrs.* Ann (Hinton). Itinerary of a traveller in the wilderness. Boston, 1825. 18°.

— Retrospection. Boston, 1822. 18°.

Taylor, Arthur. The glory of regality; an historical treatise on the anointing and crowning of the kings and queens of England. London, 1820. 8°.

Taylor, B. B. Address before the Keystone Assoc. of Pittsburgh, on the principles, duties, *etc.*, of the Amer. statesman. Pittsburgh, 1842. 8°. (B 1499)

Taylor, Bayard. At home and abroad. 1st, 2d ser. N. Y., 1860–62. 2 v. 12°.

— By-ways of Europe. N. Y., 1869. 8°.
Note. Reprinted from 'Atlantic monthly', v. 20–22. 1867–68.

— Colorado; a summer trip. N. Y., 1867. 16°.

— Cyclopædia of modern travel. Cincinnati, 1856. 8°.

— Hannah Thurston; a story of American life. N. Y., 1863. 12°.

— Japan in our day. N. Y., 1872 [1871]. 8°.

— John Godfrey's fortunes; a story of American life. N. Y., 1865. 12°.

— Joseph and his friends; a story of Pennsylvania. N. Y., London, 1870. 12°.
Note. Repub. from 'Atlantic monthly', v. 25, 26, 1870.

— Journey to Central Africa. N. Y., 1854. 12°.

— Lands of the Saracen; or, Pictures of Palestine, Asia Minor, Sicily, and Spain. N. Y., 1855. 12°.

— Life, travels, and books of A. von Humboldt. N. Y., 1859. 12°.

— Northern travel; pictures of Sweden, Denmark, *etc.* N. Y., 1858. 12°.

— Picture of St. John. Boston, 1866. 12°.

— Poems of the Orient. Boston, 1855. 8°.

— *Same.* 6th ed. Boston, 1863. 16°.

— Poet's journal. Boston, 1863. 12°.

— Recollections of Mendelssohn. (*In* Lampadius, W. A. Life of Mendelssohn. 1865.)

— Story of Kennett. N. Y., 1866. 16°.

— Views a-foot; with pref. by N. P. Willis. N. Y., 1847. 12°.

— Visit to India, China, and Japan in 1853. N. Y., 1855. 12°.

Taylor, Benjamin Cook. Annals of the classis and township of Bergen. 2d ed. N. Y., [1857]. 12°.

— The school of the prophets; sermon, New Brunswick, N. J., July 11. N. Y., 1839. 8°. (B 1383)

Taylor, Brook. Kirby, J. Perspective of architecture from the principles of T. London, 1761. f°.

— Malton, T. Compleat treatise on perspective on the principles of T. 2d ed. London, 1779. f°.

Taylor, C. B. A fireside book; or, Christmas at Old Court. 2d ed. London, 1829. 8°.

Taylor, Charles, *d.* 1821 *or* 1823. Scripture illustrated by means of natural science. London, 1803. 4°.

Taylor, Charles. Should the contagious diseases act be extended to the civil population? (*In* Nat. Assoc. Prom. Soc. Sci. Trans., 1869.)

Taylor, Christopher. Probable causes and consequences of the American War. Lond., 1864. 8°.

Taylor, Daniel T. Voice of the church on the coming and kingdom of the Redeemer; ed. by H. L. Hastings. 2d ed. Peace Dale, 1855. 12°.

Taylor, Edward J. Böhme's Theosophick philosophy unfolded; also Principal treatises of the author abridged. London, 1691. 4°.

Taylor, Edward T. (Father Taylor). Breckenridge, W. L. Speech, June 1, against the aspersions of Rev. Mr. T., May 29. Louisville, 1841. 8°. (B 1183)

Taylor, Fanny. Irish homes and Irish hearts. London, 1867. 16°.

Taylor, Fitch Waterman. The flagship; or, Voyage round the world in the U. S. frigate Columbia. N. Y., 1840. 2 v. 12°.

Taylor, Francis. Exposition of the first three chapters of Proverbs. London, 1655. 4°.

Taylor, George, *d.* 1781. Sanderson, J. (*In his* Biography of the signers, v. 9. 1827.)

Taylor, George, *d.* 1851. Memoir of R. Surtees; ed. by J. Raine. London, 1852. 8°. (Surtees Soc., v. 24.)

Taylor, George, *of Brooklyn, N. Y.* Martyrs to the revolution in British prison ships in Wallabout Bay. N. Y., 1855. 8°.

Taylor, George Keith. Substance of a speech on the bill to amend the penal laws of [Va.]. Richmond, 1796. 4°. (W 33, 58)

Taylor, George L., *and* Cresy, E. Architectural antiquities of Rome. Lond., 1821–22. 2 v. f°.

— Architecture of the Middle Ages. 1829. *See* Cresy, E.

Taylor, *Rev.* H. B. Comprehensive view of the evidences of revelation; annexed some of the results of paganism and Christianity. Phila., 1848. 12°. (D 29)

Taylor, *Sir* Henry. Poetical works. London, 1864. 3 v. 16°.
Contents. Vol. 1. Philip van Artevelde. 2. Edwin the fair. — Isaac Comnenus. 3. Sicilian summer. — St. Clement's eve. — Minor poems.

— Edwin the fair. London, 1842. 16°.

— Notes from books. London, 1849. 8°.
Contents. Poet. works of Wordsworth. — Wordsworth's sonnets. — De Vere's poems. — The ways of the rich and great.

— Notes from life. 3d ed. London, 1849. 8°.
Contents. Money. — Humility and independence. — Choice in marriage. — Wisdom. — Children. — The life poetic.

— Philip van Artevelde. Camb., 1835. 2 v. 16°.

— St. Clement's Eve; a play. Lond., 1862. 12°.

— The statesman. London, 1836. 12°.

— Horne, R. H. (*In his* New Spirit, v. 2. 1844.)

— Milsand, J. (*In* Revue d. D. Mondes, jan. 1852.)

Taylor, *Sir* Herbert. Correspondence of Earl Grey with William IV. and T. London, 1867. 2 v. 8°.

— Memorandum of the illness and decease of the Duke of York. (*In* Pamphleteer, 1826; v. 27 of B 838)

Taylor, Isaac, *b.* 1787, *d.* 1865. Antient Christianity and the doctrines of the Oxford tracts for the times. London, 1844. 2 v. 8°.
— Fanaticism. London, 1833. 8°.
— History of the transmission of ancient books to modern times; together with the process of historical proof. New ed. enl. London, 1859. 8°.
— Logic in theology, and other essays. London, 1859. 16°.
Contents. Logic in theology. — State of Unitarianism in England. — Nilus. — Paula. — Theodosius. — Julian. — Without controversy. — Supplementary to the fifth essay.
— Loyola; and Jesuitism in its rudiments. London, 1849. 12°.
— Memoirs of Jane Taylor. Lowell, 1829. 12°.
— Natural history of enthusiasm. N. Y., 1831. 12°.
— Personal recollections. (*In* Good words, v. 5. 1864.)
— Physical theory of another life. N. Y., 1836. 12°.
— Restoration of belief. Camb., Eng., 1855. 12°.
— *Same.* New ed. with add. section. Boston, 1867. 12°.
— Spirit of the Hebrew poetry. London, 1861. 8°.
— Spiritual despotism. N. Y., 1835. 12°.
— Wesley and Methodism. London, 1851. 12°.
— Beaver, J. Exposure of the unfairness of the 'General reply to all objections' of the author of 'Ancient Christianity'. London, 1840. 8°. (B 1230)
— Stephen, J. The historian of enthusiasm. From the Edin. rev., v. 71. (*In his* Essays in eccl. biog., v. 2. 1850.)

Taylor, *Rev.* Isaac. Words and places; or, Etymological illust. of history, ethnology, and geography. London, 1864. 8°.

Taylor, J. Decorations for parks and gardens. London, [182-?]. 8°.

Taylor, J. On coal. (*In* Armstrong, *Sir* W. G., *and others.* Industrial resources. 1864.)

Taylor, *Rev.* James. Sermon, Northampton, Aug. 20. Northampton, 1818. 8°. (B 1010)

Taylor, James. View of the money system of England, from the Conquest. Lond., 1828. 8°.

Taylor, James, *Quartermaster Gen. U.S.A.* Memorial and statement in rel. to his claim against the U. S. *n.t.p.* [183-.] 8°. (B 1460)

Taylor, *Rev.* James, *of Wakefield.* True doctrine of the eucharist, in refutation of Wilberforce's book. London, 1855. 8°.

Taylor, James B. Lives of Virginia Baptist ministers. 2d ed. enl. Richmond, 1838. 12°.

Taylor, James W. History of the State of Ohio, 1650-1787. Cincin., 1854. 8°.
— Report upon the gold and silver mining east of the Rocky Mountains. Wash., 1867. 8°.
— *and* Browne, J. R. Reports upon the mineral resources of the U. S. Wash., 1867. 8°.

Taylor, Jane. Display; a tale. Boston, 1815. 18°.
— Poetical remains of T., with extracts from her corresp.; [ed.] by I. Taylor. Lowell, 1829. 12°.
— Taylor, I. Memoirs of T. Lowell, 1829. 12°.

Taylor, Jeremy, *Bp.* Works; with life, *etc.*, by R. Heber. London, 1822. 15 v. 8°.
Contents. Vol. 1. Life. — Funeral sermon, by Bp. Rust. — Corresp. with Mr. H. Jeanes. — Christian consolations. 2. The life of Christ. — 2, 3. The history of Jesus. 3. Contemplations of the state of man in this life and in that which is to come. 4. The rule and exercises of holy living. — The rule and exercises of holy dying. 5, 6. Sermons. 7. Of the sacred order and offices of episcopacy. — Apology for authorized and set forms of liturgy. — 7, 8. Θεολογία ἐκλεκτική; or, A discourse of the liberty of prophesying. 8, 9. The doctrine and practice of repentance. 9. Deus justificatus. — 10. On the real presence of Christ in the holy sacrament. 10, 11. A dissuasive from popery. 11. Letters. — Χρίσις τελειωτική, a discourse of confirmation. — A discourse of the nature, offices, and measures of friendship, *etc.* — 11-14. Ductor dubitantium; or, The rule of conscience. 14. Rules and advices to the clergy of the diocess of Down and Connor. 15. The golden grove; or, A manual of daily prayers and litanies fitted to the days of the week. — The psalter of David, with titles and collects, *etc.* — A collection of offices, or forms of prayer. — The worthy communicant; or, A discourse of the nature, effects, and blessings consequent to the wor thy receiving of the Lord's supper. — Prayers.
— Works; rev. and corr. by C. P. Eden. (Vol. 2, 3, 4, new ed.) London, 1854, 50, 49-52, 50-52. 10 v. 8°.
Note. Vol. 9, 10, ed. by A. Taylor.
Contents. Vol. 1. Clerus domini. — Dedication of grammar. — Prayers before and after sermon. — Friendship. — Rules and advices to the clergy of the diocese of Down and Connor. — Sermon, the gate to Heaven a strait gate. — Life of J. T. — Funeral sermon on T. by G. Rust. — Indexes. 2. Life of Christ. 3. Holy living and dying. 4. Sermons. 5. Episcopacy. — Apology for set forms. — Reverence due to the altar. — Liberty of prophesying. — Confirmation. 6. Real presence of Christ in the sacrament. — Dissuasive from Popery. — Five letters to persons tempted to a change in their religion. 7. Unum necessarium. — Deus justificatus. — Correspondence with Warner and Jeanes. — Golden grove. — Hymns. 8. Worthy communicant. — Supplement of sermons. — Coll. of offices. 9, 10. Ductor dubitantium.
— Collection of polemical and moral discourses. London, 1657. f°.
Contents. The golden-grove; or, A manuall of daily prayers and litanies. — An apology for authorized and set forms of liturgy. — The sacred order and office of episcopacy. — The real presence and spirituall of Christ in the blessed sacrament proved against the doctrine of transubstantiation. — A discourse of the liberty of prophesying. — Deus justificatus; or, A vindication of the glory of the divine attributes in the question of original sin. — A discourse, nature and offices of friendship. — Sermon, St. Maries Church, Oxford. — Discourse; nature, offices, and measures of friendship; added, two letters to persons changed in their religion.
— Contemplations of the state of man. *See* Nieremberg, J. E. *Note.*
— Discourses on various subjects. Boston, 1816. 3 v. 8°.
— Dissuasive from popery.— Real presence and spiritual of Christ in the blessed sacrament. (*In* Cardwell, E. Tracts on points at issue, v. 1. 1836.)
— Ductor dubitantium; or, the rule of conscience. London, 1660. f°.
— The great exemplar; life and death of Jesus. London, 1653. f°.
— *Same.* London, 1667. f°.
— *Same, abridged.* Life of Christ. Newburyport, 1796. 12°.
— Poems. (*In* Grosart, A. B. Miscel., v. 1. 1871. Fuller worthies' lib., v. 9.)
— Selections from the works of T.; with life. (*In* Young, A. Lib. of old Eng. prose writers, v. 8. 1833.)
— Selections from the works of T. (*In* Montagu, B. Selections. 1853.)
— Malden, H. (*In his* Disting. men, v. 2. 1838; v. 38 of Lib. ent. knl.)

Taylor, John, *the water poet*, *b.* 1580, *d.* 1654. Works; comprised in the folio ed. of 1630. [Manchester,] 1869. f°. (Spencer Soc.)
Contents. Urania. — First part of the troubles and destruction of Jerusalem. — Second part and finall destruction of Jerusalem by Titus and Vespasian. — Life and death of the Virgin Mary. — Superbiæ flagellum. — Against cursing and swearing. — The fearefull summer. — The travels of twelvepence. — The Armado, or navy of ships that faile as well by land as by sea. — The begger. — Taylor's goose. — Jacke a Lent. — Pennilesse pilgrimage. — Acts and exploits of Wood, the great eater in Kent. — Sir Gregory Nonsence. — A very merry wherry voyage from London to Yorke. — A new disc. by sea with a wherry, from London to Salisbury. — A kicksie winsie, or a lerry cum twang. — Taylor's motto. — An epicedium. — The eight wonder of the world. — Laugh and be fat. — Coriat's newes and letter with the authour's paraphrasing verses. — A bawd very modest. — A whore very honest. — A thiefe very true. — A

hangman very necessary. — The unnatural father. — Taylor's revenge against Fenner. — Fenner's defence. — A cast over the water to Fenner. — The water-man's suite conc. players. — Wit and mirth. — A dogge of warre. — The worlde runs on wheeles. — The nipping or snipping of abuses. — A briefe of the chronicle from Brute to this present in verse. — A briefe of the chronicle from the Norman conquest to this present. — A farewell to the Towre bottles. — The marriage of the Princess Elisabeth. — Funerall elegie for King James, — Earl of Nottingham, — Earl of Holdernesse, — Bp. of Winchester, — Duke of Richmond and Linox, — John Moray. — The summe of the Bible in verse. — The summe of the book of martyrs in verse. — Archie, his making peace with France. — Praise of hempseed. — Pastorall. — Three weekes and three days travells from London into Germany. — Taylor's travell to Bohemia. — An Englishman's love to Bohemia. — The dolphin's danger and deliverance. — The cormorant. — A brave sea-fight by Captaine J. Weddell in the gulfe of Persia. — The sculler. — Christian admonitions. — The great O Toole. — The churches deliverances. — Prince Chales, his welcome from Spaine. — The praise of clean linnin.

— Works not incl. in the folio vol. of 1630. [Manchester,] 1870–78. (Spencer Soc., v. 7, 14, 19, 21, 25.)

Contents. Vol. 1. Thame Isis. — The old, old, very old man; the life of T. Par. — Part of this summer's travels. — Praise of the needle. — Differing worships. — A swarme of sectaries and schismatiques. — Religion's enemies. — The liar. — A pedlar and a Romish priest. — Tale in a tub. — Answer against the writer of A tale in a tub. — Plea for prerogative. — Life and progresse of H. Walker, the ironmonger. — Mad fashions, od fashions, *etc.* — Apology for private preaching. — Cluster of coxcombes. — Aqua-musæ. — Complaint of Christmas. — Kings most excellent Majesties wellcome to his own house. — Ἱππ-ἀνθρωπος; an ironicall expostulation with death and fate, for the losse of the late Lord Mayor of London. — Wandering to see the wonders of the west. — Number and names of all the kings of Eng. and Scotland. — Christmas in and out. — Short rel. of a long journey. 2. Suddaine turne of ffortunes wheele. — The fearefull summer. — Carriers cosmographie. — Drinke and welcome. — J. Taylor's last voyage and adventure. — Irish footman's poetry. — Devil turn'd Round-head. — Heads of all fashions. — Crop-eare curried; or, Tom Nash, his ghost. — Mad verse, sad verse, glad verse, and bad verse. — No Mercurius aulicus. — J. Taylor to J. Booker. — Rebells anathematized and anatomized. — Causes of the diseases and distempers of this kingdom. — Ale ale-vated into the ale-titude. — Epigrammes, written on purpose to be read. — Certain travailes of an uncertain journey. 3. A bawd. — Taylor's travels. — Bull, beare, and horse, cut, curtaile, and longtaile. — Taylor's feast. — Sad and deplorable elegy. — Taylor's manifestation. — Truth's triumph. — Oxford besiedged. 4. Taylor's Arithmeticke. — The generall complaint. — A most learned and eloquent speech. — Honorable and memorable foundations. — A valorous and perillous sea-fight. — Complaint of M. Tenter-hooke. — England's comfort and London's joy. — A reply as true as steele. — The hellish parliament. — A delicate, dainty, damnable dialogue. — To the Right Hon. Assembly. — An humble desired union. — Mercurius infernalis. — Travels from London to the Isle of Wight. — Ranters of both sexes. — The essence, quintessence, *etc.*, of nonsence upon sence. 5. Faire and fowle weather. — Mercurius Aquaticus; or, The water-poets answer to all that hath or shall be writ by Mercurius Britanicus. — The conversion, *etc.*, of a mis-led, ill-bred, rebellious Round-head. — A letter sent to London from a spie at Oxford. — An honest answer to the late published 'Apologie for private preaching'. — The noble cavalier caracterised, and a rebellious caviller cauterised.

— Extracts rel. to T. Coryate. (*In* **Coryat**, T. Crudities, v. 3. 1776.)

— Prince Charles; his welcome from Spaine. (*In* **Somers**, J. Col. of tracts, v. 2. 1809.) — Heaven's blessing and earth's joy; or, A relation of the supposed sea-fights and fireworks at the marriage of Frederick and Elizabeth. (*In* v. 3. 1810.)

— Wit and mirth. (*In* **Hazlitt**, W. C. Shakespeare jest books, v. 3. 1864.)

Taylor, John, *of Norwich*, *b.* 1694, *d.* 1761. Advertisement [of] an Hebrew concordance. London, *n.d.* 8°. (B 53)

— Paraphrase with notes on the epistles to the Romans. 2d ed. London, 1847. 4°.

— Scheme of scripture divinity. (*In* **Watson**, R. Col. of theol. tracts, v. 1. 1791.) — Key to the apostolic writings. (*In* v. 3. 1791.)

— Scripture doctrine of original sin proposed to free and candid examination; with a supplement. 2d ed. London, 1741. 8°.

— Edwards, J. The great Christian doctrine of original sin defended in reply to T. Boston, 1758. 8°.

— — *Same.* (*In his* Works, v. 6. 1809.)

Taylor, John, *Archdeacon of Buckingham*, *b.* 1704, *d.* 1766. Annotationes ad Demosthenem. (*In* **Schaefer**, G. H. Apparatus crit. ad Demosthenem. 1824–33.)

— Commentarius ad L. Decemviralem de inope debitore in partis dissecando. Cantab., 1742. 4°.

Note. Contains also Notæ ad Marmor Bosporanum Ioui Vrio sacrum. Dissertatio de voce Yonane; explicatio inscriptionis in antiquo marmore Oxon. [a T. Barlow]; De historicis Anglicanis commentatio [T. Barlow].

— Ad Dinarchum et Andocidem annotatiunculæ. — Prolegomena ad Demosthenem. (*In* **Reiske**, J. J. Orat. Gr., v. 8. 1773.)

— Sermon at Bishop-Stortford, Aug. 22, 1749; anniversary of the school feast. Camb., 1749. 4°. (B 1348)

— Sermon before the Ho. of Com., Feb. 11th. London, 1757. 4°. (B 1256)

Taylor, John, *LL.D.*, *Prebendary of Westminster*, *d.* 1788. L tter to S. Johnson on a future state. London, 1787. 8°. (A 32)

— Sermons; also S. Johnson's sermon for the funeral of [Mrs. Taylor]. (Vol. 1, 3d ed.) London, 1795, 92. 2 v. 8°.

Taylor, John, *of Deerfield, Mass.* Account of the mischief done by the enemy in Deerfield from the death of Mr. Williams to the conclusion of the French war. (*In* **Williams**, J. Redeemed captive. 1793.)

— Century sermon, Deerfield, Feb. 29; commemoration of the destruction of the town by the French and Indians. Greenfield, 1804. 8°. (B 163, 333, 842)

Taylor, John, *Lieut. Col.* Letters on India. London, 1800. 4°.

Taylor, John, *of Caroline Co., Va.*, *d.* 1824. Construction construed and constitutions vindicated. Richmond, 1820. 8°.

— Defence of the measures of the administration of T. Jefferson; by Curtius. Wash., 1804. 8°. (B 424)

— Enquiry into the principles and tendency of certain public measures. Phila., 1794. 8°. (B 640)

— Live fences. — Clearing-ground. — Gypsum. (*In* **Phila. Soc. Prom. Agric.** Mem., v. 1. 1808.)

Taylor, John, *d.* 1832. Records of my life. London, 1832. 2 v. 8°.

Taylor, John, *vs.* **Delevan**, E. C. Report of trial. Albany, 1840. 8°. (B 1435)

Taylor, John, *Master of the Free School at Wakefield.* True doctrine of the eucharist; refutation of Wilberforce's book. London, 1855. 8°.

Taylor, John. Drunkenness as an indirect cause of crime. (*In* **Nat. Assoc. Prom. Soc. Sci.** Trans., 1859.)

Taylor, John, *d.* 1864. The battle of the standards. London, 1864. 8°.

— Catechism of foreign exchanges and the effects of an abasement of bullion. Lond., 1835. 12°.

— Catechism of the currency. London, 1835. 16°.

— Discovery of the author of the letters of Junius. London, 1813. 8°. (B 690)

— The Great Pyramid. London, 1859. 8°.

— Identity of Junius with a distinguished living character [Sir P. Francis] established. 1st Amer. ed. N. Y., 1818. 8°.

Taylor, John Glanville. United States and Cuba. London, 1851. 12°.

Taylor, John James. Moral education of the people; discourse, Dec. London, 1833. 8°. (B 1346)

— Sketch of the life and character of J. E. Bowman. (*In* **Lit. and Phil. Soc. of Manchester.** Mem., v. 12. 1846.)

Taylor, John L., *of Ohio*, *d.* 1870. Speech on the Mexican indemnity bill, Jan. 20. Wash., 1852. 8°. (B 1510)

Taylor, John Lord, *D.D.* How shall we provide the ministry that we need? address at his inaug. as professor in the Andover Theol. Seminary, Aug. 6. Andover, 1868. 8°. (E 75)

— Memoir of S. Phillips. Boston, 1856. 8°.
— PARK, E. A. Taylor's memoir of Judge Phillips. [Pp. 853-891 of Bibliotheca sacra, Oct., 1856.] (B 1459)
Taylor, John Pitt. Expediency of passing an act to permit defendants in criminal courts to testify. (*In* **Nat. Assoc. Prom. Soc. Sci.** Trans., 1860.)
Taylor, John Sydney. Selections from the writings of T. London, 1843. 8°.
Taylor, Joseph. COLLIER, J. P. (*In his* Memoirs of the actors in the plays of Shakespeare. 1846. Shakespeare Soc., v. 39.)
Taylor, Joseph. Oratio funebris in obitum E. Wigglesworth. *n.p.*, 1765. 8°. (B 17, 212, 471, 850)
Taylor, Joseph W. Plea for the University of Alabama; address before the Erosophic and Philomathic Societies, Aug. 9. Tuskaloosa, 1847. 8°. (B 1581)
Taylor, *Rev.* Joseph W. Sermons; the mortality of man and the eternity of the Word of God. (*In* **Free** church pulpit. 1855.)
Taylor, Joshua. Oration, Portland, July 4th. Portland, 1805. 8°. (B 342)
Taylor, *Col.* Meadows. Descriptions of cairns, *etc.*, in the Dekhan. — Cairns on Twizell Moor. (*In* **Royal Irish Acad.** Antiq., v. 24. 1865.)
— Native literature of India. (*In* **Afternoon** lectures, v. 2. 1864.)
Taylor, Michael. Sexagesimal table exhibiting the result of any proportion, *etc.*; also tables of equation, *etc.* London, 1780. 4°.
— Tables of logarithms of numbers from 1 to 101,000. London 1792. 4°.
Taylor, Michael Angelo. Speech. (*In* **Speeches** of the managers in the trial of W. Hastings, v. 4. 1861.)
Taylor, Nathaniel. Discourse on the nature and necessity of faith in Christ with an answer to the plans of Unitarians for the sufficiency of bare morality. London, 1700. 8°.
Taylor, Nathaniel Wm., *D.D.* WOODS, L. Letters to N. W. Taylor. (*In his* Works, v. 4. 1851.)
Taylor, Nellie M. BROCKETT, L. P. (*In his* Woman's work in the civil war. 1867.)
Taylor, Oliver Alden. Catalogue of the library of the Theological Seminary in Andover, Mass. Andover, 1838. 8°.
— *Same.* 1st supplement. Andover, 1849. 8°.
Taylor, Peter. RITCHIE, J. E. (*In his* British senators. 1869.)
Taylor, *Rev.* Richard. Te Ika a Maui; or, New Zealand and its inhabitants. Lond., 1855. 8°.
Taylor, Richard Cowling. Notice of a model of the western portion of the Schuylkill coal field of Penn., *etc.* (*In* **Assoc. of Amer. Geol.** Reports, 1843.)
— *and* **Clemson,** T. G. Notice of a vein of bituminous coal, recently explored in the vicinity of the Havana, in Cuba. (*In* **Amer. Phil. Soc.** Trans., n. s., v. 6. 1839.)
Taylor, Robert. Oratio anniversaria in theatro Collegii Regalis Medicorum Lond. ex Harveii instituto festo divi Lucæ habita 1755. London, 1756. 4°. (A 63)
Taylor, Rowland. FOX, J. Life of T. (*In* **Wordsworth,** C. Eccl. biog., v. 2. 1839.)
Taylor, Samuel. Literary and musical entertainments for the people. (*In* **Nat. Assoc. Prom. Soc. Sci.** Trans., 1858.)
Taylor, Samuel Harvey, *D.D.* Address. (*In* **Pinkerton Academy.** Commemorative services at the semicent. anniv. 1866.)
— Memoir of E. L. Parker. (*In* **Parker, E. L.** Hist. of Londonderry. 1851.)
Taylor, Stephen. Wisconsin; its rise and progress; with notices of Mineral Point and Richland Co. (*In* **Wisconsin Hist. Soc.** Col., v. 2. 1856.)
Taylor, T. P. The bottle; a drama. (*In* **Minor** drama, v. 3.)
Taylor, Theodore, *pseud.* *See* **Hotten,** J. C.
Taylor, Thomas, *the Puritan, d.* 1632. Christ revealed; or, The types and shadows of our Saviour in the Old Testament explained. London, 1635. 4°.
— Commentary upon the epistle to Titus. Camb., 1612. 4°.
— Der geistliche Bau; übersetzet von J. Nicolai. Helmstad, 1682. 12°.

Taylor, Thomas, *of Cambridge.* Jacob wrestling with God; a treatise conc. faith in prayer. London, 1692. 12°.
Taylor, Thomas. Observation of the Lord's day recommended. Boston, 1792. 8°. (B 1303)
Taylor, Thomas, *'the Platonist', d.* 1835. Dissertation on the Eleusinian and Bacchic mysteries. 2d ed. (*In* **Pamphleteer,** 1816; v. 8 *of* B 838)
— Elements of a new arithmetical notation, and new arithmetic of infinities. Lond., 1823. 8°.
— Five hymns. (*In* **Sallustius** *philosophus.* The gods and the world. 1793.)
— Theoretic arithmetic; cont. the substance of all that has been written by Theo, Nicomachus, Iamblichus, and Boetius. London, 1816. 8°.
Taylor, Thomas, *of Manningtree.* Life of W. Cowper. London, 1833. 8°.
— *Same.* Phila., 1833. 12°.
Taylor, Timothy. Defence of sundry positions. 1646. *See* **Eaton,** S. (B 1)
Taylor, Tom. The babes in the wood; a comedy. (No. 56 *of* **Spencer's** univ. stage.)
— The fool's revenge; a drama. (*In* **Sargent,** E. Mod. stand. dr., v. 42.) — Helping hands; a drama. (*In* v. 34.)
— Henry Dunbar; or, A daughter's trials; drama. (No. 8 *of* **De Witt's** acting plays.) — The hidden hand; or, The gray lady of Porth Vennon; a drama. (No. 60.)
— Life and times of Sir J. Reynolds. *See* **Leslie,** C. R.
— Life of B. R. Haydon; from his autobiog. and journals. London, 1853. 3 v. 12°.
— *Same.* N. Y., 1853. 2 v. 12°.
— New men and old acres; a comedy. (No. 115 *of* **De Witt's** acting plays.)
— Nine points of the law; a comedy. (No. 21 *of* **Spencer's** univ. stage.) — Payable on demand; a drama. (No. 70.)
— Plot and passion; a drama. (No. 61 *of* **De Witt's** acting plays.)
— Retribution; a domestic drama. (*In* **Sargent,** E. Mod. stand. drama, v. 19.)
— A sheep in wolf's clothing; drama. (No. 79 *of* **De Witt's** acting plays.)
— Still water runs deep; comedy. (*In* **Sargent,** E. Mod. stand. dr., v. 34.) — Ticket-of-leave man; a drama. (*In* v. 42.) — Victims; comedy. (*In* v. 24.) — *and* **Reade,** C. Masks and faces; comedy. (*In* v. 30.) — Two loves and a life; drama. (*In* v. 35.)
Taylor, W. F. Guide to Windsor, Eton, and Virginia water. London, [18—]. 16°.
Taylor, *Rev.* W. R. Sermon, Christ the propitiation for the sins of the whole world. (*In* **Free Church** pulpit. 1853.)
— Sermon, The sword of the Spirit. (*In* **Suddards,** W. British pulpit, v. 1. 1837.)
Taylor, Whately Cooke. Indirect sources of advanced female education. (*In* **Nat. Assoc. Prom. Soc. Sci.** Trans., 1868.)
Taylor, Wm. Reply, *etc.* *See* **Sterns,** J. (A 20)
Taylor, *Rev.* Wm., *of Glasgow.* The education of the children of the poor; sermon, May 29. Edin., 1796. 8°. (B 1860)
— Trust in God, *etc.*; sermon, Mar. 8, national fast. Glasgow, 1798. 8°. (B 1860)
Taylor, *Capt.* Wm. LA GRANGE, J. M. de. Mémoire pour W. T. capitaine du navire américain la Calliope. Paris, [180-]. 4°. (A 3, 7)
Taylor, Wm. A vision seen by N. Barlow, of Freetown. *n.t.p.* [1801.] 8°. (B 432)
Taylor, *Rev.* Wm. Sermon; festival of St. Patrick, Mar. 21. N. Y., 1819. 8°. (B 956)
Taylor, Wm., *of Norwich, b.* 1765, *d.* 1836. Historic survey of German poetry; with translations. London, 1829-30. 3 v. (v. 1 w.). 8°.
— ROBBERDS, J. W. Memoir of life and writings of T. London, 1843. 2 v. 8°.
Taylor, Wm., *of California.* Cause and probable results of civil war in America. London, 1862. 8°.
Taylor, Wm. Benj. Sarsfield. History of the University of Dublin. London, 1845. 8°.

— Origin, progress, *etc.*, of fine arts in Gr. Brit. and Ireland. London, 1841. 2 v. 12°.

Taylor, Wm. Cooke. Factories and the factory system. London, 1844. 8°.

— Hand book of silk, cotton, and woolen manufactures. London, 1843. 16°.

— History of Ireland; with add. by W. Sampson. N. Y., 1847. 2 v. 18°. (Harper's fam lib., v. 51–52.)

— Life and times of Sir R. Peel. London, [1846–50]. 4 v. 8°.

— Manual of ancient and modern history; rev. with a chapter on the hist. of the U. S. by C. S. Henry. 2d ed. N. Y., 1845. 8°.

— Natural history of society. London, 1840. 2 v. 12°.

— Notes of a tour in the manufacturing districts of Lancashire. London, 1842. 16°.

— Occult sciences. *See* **Smedley, E.**

Taylor, Wm. Cooper. The seasons in England; descr. poems. Boston, 1807. 16°.

Taylor, Zachary. The slavery question. *See* **Cass, L.**

— COALITION of the democracy and the abolitionists in opposition to the administration of T. *n.p.*, 1849. 8°. (B 1502)

— GEN. Taylor and the Wilmot proviso. Boston, 1848. 8°. (B 1502)

— GEN. Taylor's moral, intellectual, and professional character, as drawn by J. J. Crittenden, *etc.* Wash., 1848. 8°. (B 1502)

— GEN. Taylor's two faces; published by the National and Jackson Democratic Assoc. Com. Wash., 1848. 8°. (B 1502)

— LESTER, C. E. Memoir. (*In his* Gallery of Americans. 1850.)

— LIFE and public services of T.; by an officer of the U.S.A. N. Y., 1846. 8°. (B 1460)

— POORE, B. P. Life of T. [Boston, 18—.] 8°. (B 1502)

— REASONS good and true for supporting the nomination of T. Wash., 1848. 8°. (B 1460, 1502)

— REVIEW of the life, character, and political opinions of T. Boston, 1848. 8°. (B 1502)

— SKETCH of the life and character of T.; with Hist. of the Mexican war. Boston, 1847. 8°. (B 1502)

— SKETCH of the life and public services of T.; with considerations in favor of his election. *n.t.p.* [Wash., 1848.] 8°. (B 1460, 1502)

— STEARNS, C. Facts in the life of T. Boston, 1848. 12°. (C 256)

For addresses on his death see **Anderson, T. D.**; — **Baldwin, O. P.**; — **Bell, L. V.**; — **Ely, A. B.**; — **Fiske, J. O.**; — **Flint, J.**; — **Hopkins, J. H.**; — **Krebs, J. M.**; — **Mason, E. N.**; — **Pope, L.**; — **Potter, H.**; — **Prentiss, G. L.**; — **Quincy, J.**; — **Slafter, E. F.**; — **Thompson, B.**; — **U. S.** *Cong.*; — **Upham, C. W.**; — **Ware, J. F. W.**

Taylour, Thomas, 1st *Marquis of Headfort.* *See* **Massy, C.**, *vs.* **Taylour, T.**

Tazewell, Littleton Waller. GRIGSBY, H. B. Discourse on the life and character of T. Norfolk, 1860. 8°.

Tchao-chi-kou-eul; l'orphelin de la Chine, drame; tr. du chinois par S. Julien. Paris, 1834. 8°.

Tchavtchavadze, Anne. VEDEREVSKI, —. Captivité de deux princesses russes dans le sérail de Chamyl. (*In* **Revue d. D. Mondes**, mai 1856.)

Tcheou-li. RITES des Tcheou; tr. par E. Biot. Paris, 1851. 2 v. 8°.

— BIOT, J. B. Communication sur le Tcheou-li. (*In* **Paris. Inst.** *Ac. d. Sci. Mor.* Comte rendu, v. 19. 1851.)

Tchinovnicks; sketches of provincial life, from the mem. of Saltikow; tr., with notes, from the Russian by F. Aston. London, 1861. 12°.

Tchong-yong, ou Le juste milieu. (*In* **Mémoires** conc. les Chinois, v. 1. 1797.)

Tchudic race. *See* **Savoloks**; — **Yemen.**

Tea. SHORT, T. Discourses on tea, milk, and punch. London, 1750. 8°.

— LETTSOM, J. C. Diss. inaug. med. sistens observationes ad vires theæ pertinentes. Lugd. Bat., 1769. 8°. (B 968)

— TWINING, R. Answer to the report of the East India directors resp. the sale and prices of tea. London, 1785. 8°. (B 1682)

— GRIFFITH, W. Report on the tea plant of Upper Assam. *n.t.p.* [18—.] 8°. (B 1141)

— MARTIN, R. M. Past and present state of the tea-trade of England. London, 1832. 8°. (B 1060)

— ALCOTT, W. A. Tea and coffee. Boston, 1839. 18°.

— SIGMOND, G. G. Tea; its effects, medicinal and moral. London, 1839. 16°.

— BALL, S. Cultivation and manufacture of tea in China. London, 1848. 8°.

— FORTUNE, R. Journey to the tea countries of China. London, 1852. 8°.

— SIEBOLD, P. F. Landwirthschaft, Kunstfleiss, und Handel. (*In his* Nippon, 5. Bd., 5. Abth. 1852.)

— PAYEN, A. (*In* **Revue d. D. Mondes**, jan. 1860.)

Teach, Edward. WILKINSON, S. Voyages and adventures of Teach, called Black Beard the pirate. Boston, 1808. 12°. (C 158)

Teacher, The; or, Moral influences in the instruction of the young. *See* **Abbott, J.**

Teachers. *See* **Education.**

Teacher's assistant, The. *See* **Trimmer, S.**

Teacher's gift, The; by M. B. L. Boston, 1837. 18°. (N. E. S. S. Union.)

Teacher's offering. London, 1846–47. 2 v. 18°.

Tears of the foot guards upon their departure for America; by an ensign of the provincial army. 2d ed. London, 1776. 4°.

Teate, *city.* *See* **Chieti.**

Teatra Warszawska. Warszawa, 1834–40. 27 v. 16°.

Contents. Pt. 1, v. 1. **Duveyrier, A. H. J.**, *and* **Leroux, H.** Zachód słońca, komedyo-opera; tłum. przez Fr. Szymanowski. 2, 3. *Wanting.* 4. **Ben-Dawid**, czyli żyd i chrześcianin; tłum. przez B. Halperta. 6. **Duveyrier, A. H. J.** Zampa, opera komiczna; przeł. przez J. Jasinski. 7. **Scribe, A. E.** Ona go nienawidzi; przeł. przez S. Boguslawski. 8. **Skarbka, F. H.** Bióraliści, komedyo-opera. 9. **Sewrin, C. A.** Komornik poeta, komedyo-opera; przeł. przez Fr. Szymanowski. 10. **Dla czego?** tłom. przez B. H. 11. **Dawne grzechy**, komedyo-opera; przeł. przez S. Kassyanowicz. 12. **Drugi rok**, czyli i kióż winny, komedyo-opera; przeł. przez J. P. i J. P. Pt. 2, v. 1. **Xieżna i paź**; przeł. przez L. Zuczkows. 2. *Wanting.* 3. Malwina; tłum. przez L. Zuczkows. 4. **Pigault Lebrun, G. C. A.** Miłość i rozsądek; tłum. na polskie. 5. **Wolff, A.** Precjosa, drama liryczne; przeł. przez J. D. Minasowicz. 6. **Siedm** dziewcząt pod bronia; przeł. przez J. N. Kamiński. 7. **Scribe, A. E.**, *and* **Terrier, T.** Dziesieć lat życia kobiety. 8. **Scribe, A. E.** Estella; przeł. przez A. R. 9. **Planard, F. A. E. de**, *and* **Saint Georges, H. de.** Błyskawica, opera komiczna; tłum. przez J. S. Jasinski. 10. **Chavanges, A. de**, *baron.* Nawet w chatce byle z nim. 11. **Mallian, J. de**, *and* **Cormon.** Włóczęga; przeł. przez A. Riedla. 12. **Scribe, A. E.**, *and* **Dumanoir, P.** Bydż kochanym lub umrzeć; przetł. przez A. Riedla. Pt. 3, v. 1. **Prawda** i Klamstwo, tłom. przez I. Milakowski. 2. **Duveyrier, A. H. J.**, *and* **Carmouche, P. F. A.** Dwa Pojedynki; tłum. przez L. z D. Z. 3. *Wanting.* 4. **Ancelot, J. A. P. F.** Marya, czyli trzy epoki; przeł. przez S. Kassyanowicz. 5. **Scribe, A. E.**, *and* **Duveyrier, A. H. J.** Zoe; pzetł. przez S. Lasocki. 6. Colomb, — Biedny Rybak, komedyo opera; przeł. przez S. Kassyanowicz. 7, 8. **Desnoyers, C.** Rita Hiszpanka; przeł. przez M. Pawlowski. 9. **Boguslawski, A.** Krewni.

Teatro comico, Il; commedia. *See* **Goldoni, C.**

Teatro critico universal. *See* **Feyjoo y Montenegro, F. B. G.**

Teatro español. *See* **Huerta, V. G. de la.**

Teatro italiano antico. Milano, *Soc. Tip. Class. Ital.*, 1808–12. 10 v. 8°.

Contents. Vol. 1. **Origine** e progresso del teatro italiano. — **Trissino, G. G.** La Sofonisba. — **Rucellai, G.** La Rosmunda. — **Divizio da Bibbiena, B.** La calandria. — **Ariosto, L.** La Cassaria. 2. **Rucellai, G.** L'Oreste. — **Alamanni, L.** L'Antigone. — **Ariosto, L.** I suppositi. 3. **Martelli, L.** La Tullia. — **Ariosto, L.** Il negromante; — La Lena. 4. **Speroni, S.** La Canace. — **Giraldi, G. B.** Orbecche. — **Alamanni, L.** La Flora. 5. **Giraldi, G. B.** Arrenopia. — **Dolce, L.** Marianna. 6. **Dolce, L.** Giocasta. — **Aretino, P.** Il marescalco; — La cortigiana. 7. **Tasso, T.** Il re Torrismondo. — **Aretino, P.** Lo ipocrito. 8. **Anguil-**

lara, G. A. dell'. Edippo. — Aretino, P. La talanta. — Rinuccini, O. La Dafne. 9. Horte, A. D. da. Acripanda. — Chiabrera, G. Angelica in Ebuda. — Aretino, P. Il filosofo. 10. Berni, F. La Catrina; — Il mogliazzo. — Buonarroti, M. A. La tancia. — Mariani, F. Assetta. — Cartajo, S. Capotondo. — Campani, N. Coltellino. — Baldovini, F. Canzone per maggio. — Mariani, F. Le nozze di Maca.

Teatro nuevo español. Madrid, 1800-01. 6 v. 12°.
Contents. Vol. 1. Plano, J. F. del. Gombela y Suni-Ada. — Arellano, V. R. de. Cecilia y Dorsan. — Pastor, J. F. Pablo y Virginia. — Bouilly, J. N. El abate de l'Epee; tr. por J. de Estrada. 2. Molière, J. B. P. de. El avaro; tr. por D. de Isusquiza. — Kotzbue, A. F. F. v. La reconciliacion ó los dos hermanos; tr. por V. R. de Arellano. — La Acelina. — El preso, ó el parecido. — Lemercier, L. J. N. Agamemnon; tr. por D. E. T. 3. Destouches, P. N. La orgullosa; tr. por F. del Plano. — Schiller, F. El amor y la intriga. — Meseguer, F. El chismoso. — Harleville, C. d'. El solteron y su criada. 4. Quintana, M. J. El duque de Viseo. — Arellano, V. R. de. La Fulgencia; — Clementina y Desormes; nouv. tr. — Rochon *de Chambannes*, M. A. J. Los amantes generosos. 5. La Virtud en la indigencia. — Galvez, M. R. de. Ali - Bek. — Arellano, V. R. de. La ópera cómica; tr. — Galvez, M. R. de. Catalina; — Un loco hace ciento. — El califa de Bagdad. 6. El conde de Olsbach. — La prueba caprichosa; tr. por F. de P. Naranjo. — Adolfo y Clara, ó los dos presos. — El padre de familia. — Desforges, P. J. B. C. La muger zelosa; tr. por J. de Velasco.

Tebaldeo, Antonio. Menalca, e Melibes. (*In* Ferrario, G. Poesie past. 1808.)

Tebaldo e Isolina; dramma per musica. *See* Morlacchi, F.

Tebalducci, Antonio Giacomini. Pitti, J. Vita. (*In* Archivio stor. ital., v. 4, pt. 2. 1853.)

Tebalducci, Lorenzo Giacomini. *See* Malespini, L. G. T.

Tebbets, Ezra Martin. Batchelder, J. (*In* Higginson, T. W. Harvard memorial biog., v. 2. 1866.)

Tebbets, *Rev.* Theodore. Memoir of W. Gibbons. N. Y., *priv. printed* [1861]. 8°.
— Towne, E. C. Memorial of T. Tebbets; sermon, Medford. Boston, 1863. 8°. (B 1594)

Techener, Jacques Joseph. Considérations sérieuses à propos de diverses publications sur la Bibliothèque Royale; suivies du plan pour en faire le catalogue en trois ans. Paris, 1847. 8°.

Techener, Léon. Répertoire univ. de bibliog.; catalogue de livres composant la librairie de T. Vol. 1. Paris, 1869. 8°.
See also Bulletin du bibliothécaire.

Technical dictionary. *See* Arts, Useful. *Dictionaries* (p. 149).

Technical education. Mass. *Commissioners to Prepare a System for an Institution for Instruction in the Practical Arts and Sciences.* Report. *n.t.p.* [1825.] 8°.
— Yorke, G. Some account of the Birmingham Free Industrial School. (*In* Nat. Assoc. Prom. Soc. Sci. Trans., 1868.)
— Russell, J. S. Systematic technical education for the English people. London, 1869. 8°.

Technical repository; by T. Gill. Vol. 1-11. London, 1822-27. 11 v. 8°.
Continued as
— Gill's technical repository; by T. Gill. Vol. 1-6. London, 1827-30. 6 v. 8°.

Technology. *See* Arts, Useful.

Techo, Nicolas del. *See* Du Toict, N.

Tecumseh. Speech at Vincennes, 1810. — Speech to Gen. Proctor. (*In* Moore, F. Amer. eloquence, v. 2. 1864.)
— Brunson, A. Death of Tecumseh at the battle of the Thames, 1813. — Kingston, J. T. Death of Tecumseh. (*In* Wisconsin State Hist. Soc. Col., v. 4. 1859.)
— Drake, B. Life of Tecumseh and his brother the prophet, *etc.* Cincin., 1856. 12°.

Tedaldi, Pieraccio di Maffeo. Sonetti. (*In* Trucchi, F. Poesie ital., v. 2. 1846.)

Tedaldi Fores, Carlo. Lucia. (*In* Poeti ital. contemp. 1843.)

Tees, River. Armstrong, *Sir* W. G., *and others.* Industrial resources, *etc.*, of the Tyne, Wear, and Tees. 2d ed. London, 1864. 8°.

Teeth. Ruspini, B. Treatise on the teeth. London, 1784. 8°.
— Cummings, J. A. Self-denistry. Bost., [18—]. 32°. (D 38)
— Skinner, R. C. Treatise on the human teeth. N. Y., 1801. 8°. (B 393)
— Fox, J. Natural hist. of the human teeth; added, account of diseases which affect children during the first dentition. London, 1803. 4°.
— Hunter, J. Natural history of the human teeth; added, practical treatise on diseases of the teeth. 3d ed. London, 1803. 4°.
— Baumes, J. B. T. Traité de la première dentition. Paris, 1806. 8°.
— James, B. Management of the teeth. Boston, 1814. 12°.
— White, C. Remarks on the preservation of the teeth with directions for using [his] absorbent tooth powder. [Boston, 1816.] 12°. (D 38)
— Bew, C. Diseases in the teeth and gums. London, 1819. 8°.
— Delabarre, C. F. Traité de la seconde dentition. Paris, 1819. 8°.
— Parmly, L. S. Natural history and management of teeth. London, 1820. 8°.
— Peabody, N. The art of preserving teeth. [1824.] 2d ed. Salem, 1828. 8°. (C 270)
— Hertz, J. P. Popular treatise on the causes, prevention, and treatment of the diseases of the teeth. London, 1829. 8°. (B 1053)
— Scott, J. Art of preventing the loss of teeth. London, 1831. 8°.
— Mann, D. Treatise on the preservation of the teeth. [Newburyport, 1838.] 12°. (C 269)
— Owen, R. Odontography; comparative anatomy of the teeth. London, 1840-45. 2 v. 4°.
— Gray, J. Preservation of the teeth. London, 1842. 12°. (D 38)
— Dillingham, J. R. Explanation on the use and abuse of dental surgery. Lynn, 1844. 8°. (B 1552)
— Snell, I. Five minutes conversation, *etc.*, on the preservation of the teeth. Wash., 1845. 8°. (C 271)
— Brown, W. S. Treatise on the human teeth. Lowell, 1847. 8°. (B 1549)
— Morton, W. T. G. On the loss of the teeth and modern way of restoring them. 2d ed. Boston, 1848. 32°. (D 39)
— Salter, S. J. A. Surgical disease connected with the teeth. (*In* Holmes, T. System of surgery, v. 4. 1864.)
— Arthur, R. Treatment and prevention of decay of the teeth. Phila., 1871. 16°.
— Holmes, O. W. Claims of dentistry; address at the commencement exercises of the Dental Dept. in Harv. Univ., Feb. 14. Boston, 1872. 8°. (H 8)

Teeth, Artificial. Fabre, —. Rapport sur les dents artificielles de la composition de M. Fonzi. *n.p.*, [18—]. 4°. (A 8)
— Dubois de Chermant, N. Artificial teeth. London, 1804. 8°.
— Morton, W. T. G. The loss of the teeth, and modern way of restoring them. 2d ed. Boston, 1848. 32°. (D 39)

Tefft, Benjamin Franklin, *D.D.* Daniel Webster; his life and character. Rochester, 1852. 8°. (B 1727)
— Inaug. address as President of Genesee Coll., July 10. Cincin., 1851. 8°. (B 1580)
— Webster and his master pieces. Auburn, 1854. 2v. 12°.

Tegahkouita, Catharine. McGee, T. D. (*In his* Cath. hist. of N. A. 1855.)

Tegetmeier, Wm. B. The poultry book. London, 1867. 8°.

Tegg, Thomas. Young man's book of knowledge; added, epitome of Amer. hist. 1st Amer. from 20th London ed. N. Y., [18—]. 12°.

Tegnér, Esaias, *Bp. of Wexiö.* Axel, poëme; tr. [par L. Enault]. (*In* **Chatillon, A. de,** *and* **Enault, L.** Frantz Müller. 1862. C 392)

— Children of the Lord's supper; tr. by H. W. Longfellow. (*In* **Longfellow, H. W.** Ballads. 1848; — *and* Seaside and the fireside. 1850.)

— Frithiof's saga; a legend of the north; tr. from the Swedish by G. S.; revised with an introd. letter by the author; [also Sketch of the life of T., by F. M. Franzén]. Stockholm, London, 1839. 8°.

— *Same.* Tr. by W. L. Bleekley. 1st Amer. ed. N. Y., 1867. 12°.

— *French.* Frithiof. (*In* **Revue d. D. Mondes,** jan. 1833.)

— *Germ.* Frithiof-Sage; übertragen von M. A. Windorf. Berlin, 1854. 12°.

— Smärre samlade dikter. 1a Bd. 2a Uppl. Stockholm, 1832. 8°.

Tegoborski, Louis de. Commentaries on the productive forces of Russia. London, 1855–56. 2 v. 8°.

— Present state of finances and currency in Austria. Lpz., 1853. 8°.

Tegrimò, Nicolo. Vita Castruccii Antelominelli, Lucensis ducis, 1301–28. (*In* **Muratori, L. A.** Rer. Ital. script., v. 11. 1727.)

Tegue-o-Divelly, the Irish priest; a comedy. *See* **Shadwell, T.**

Tehuantepec, Isthmus of. RAMIREZ, J. F. Memorial setting forth the reasons which Mexico has for not recognizing the validity of the privilege granted to D. Jose Garay, for opening a way of communication by the Isthmus of T. N. Y., 1852. 8°. (B 1600)

— - Memorias, negoc., y doc. para servir a la hist. de las diferencias que han suscitado entre Mexico y los Estados-Unidos los tenedores del antiquo privilegio, por el istmo de Tehuantepec, [1841–53]. Mexico, 1853. 8°.

— GARAY, J. de. Survey of T. Lond., 1844. 8°.

— WILLIAMS, J. J. Isthmus of Tehuantepec; with maps. N. Y., 1852. 2 v. 8°.

— TEHUANTEPEC RAILROAD COMPANY. Maps [8] illustr. the Isthmus of T. N. Y., 1852.

Tehuantepec Railroad Company. *See previous entry.*

Tehuantepec Railway. STEVENS, S. Tehuantepec Railway; its location, features, and advantages under the La Sera grant of 1869. N. Y., 1869. 8°.

Teignmouth, *Lord.* *See* **Shore, C. J.**

Teinturier parfait, ou L'art de teindre les soyes, laines, *etc.* Paris, 1716. 2 v. 12°.

Teios. CHISHULL, E. Monumenta Teia. (*In his* Antiq. 1728.)

Teissier, Antoine. NICERON, J. P. (*In his* Mém., v. 5. 1728; *and, Germ.*, v. 5. 1751.)

Teissonnière, —. Vins. (*In* **France.** *Com. Imp. de l'Expos.* de 1867. Rapports, v. 11.)

Tejada Paez, Agustin de. Canciones. (*In* **Sedano, J. J. L. de.** Parnaso esp., v. 1, 5, 7. 1768–82.)

Tejedor de Segovia, El. 1a, 2a pte.; por J. R. Alarcon. (*In* **Ochoa, E. de.** Tesoro del teatro esp., v. 4. 1838.)

Tejo River. CABRAL, E. D. Sobre os damnos causados pelo Téjo nas suas ribanceiras. (*In* **Lisbon. Ac. d. Sci.** Mem. econ., v. 2. 1790.)

Telecleides. Fragm. (*In* **Meineke, A.** Fragm. com. Gr., v. 2, pt. 1. 1839.)

Telegraph. U. S. *27th Cong. 3d sess. Ho. of Reps.* (Report 17.) Electro-magnetic telegraphs. Wash., 1842. 8°. (B 1186)

— VAIL, A. American electro-magnetic telegraph; reports of Congress; description of all telegraphs. Phila., 1845. 8°.

— FIGUIER, G. L. La télégraphie en Amérique, en Angleterre, et en France. (*In* **Revue d. D. Mondes,** août 1849.)

— HEAD, *Sir* F. B. Stokers and pokers; or, the London and N. W. R. R., the electric telegraph, *etc.* London, 1849. 16°.

— JOHNSON, W. R. Recent improvements in recording magnetic telegraphs. (*In* **Amer. Assoc. for Adv. of Sci.** Proc., v. 1. 1849.) — WALKER, S. C. Substance of a report on the experience of the U. S. coast survey in regard to telegraph operations. (*In* v. 2. 1850.)

— BABINET, J. La télégraphie électrique. (*In* **Revue d. D. Mondes,** juin 1853.)

— MACY, W. A. Remarks on the mode of applying the electric telegraph in connection with the Chinese language. (*In* **Amer. Orient. Soc.** Journ., v. 3. 1853.)

— FARMER, M. G. Improvements in the electric telegraph. (*In* **Amer. Assoc.** Proc., v. 9. 1856.)

— HEAD, *Sir* F. B. The electric telegraph. (*In his* Descriptive essays, v. 2. 1857.)

— LEFFERTS, M. The electric telegraph. (*In* **Amer. Geog. Statist. Soc.** Bul., v. 2. 1857.)

— REPORT of the dinner given by the Americans in Paris, Aug. 17, to S. F. B. Morse, in honor of his invention of the telegraph. Paris, 1858. 8°. (B 1597)

— SMITHSONIAN INST. Extract from the proceedings of the regents in relation to the electro-magnetic telegraph. (*In their* Miscel. col., v. 2. 1862.)

— SEWARD, W. H. Communication upon the subject of an intercontinental telegraph, by way of Behring's Strait. Wash., 1864. 8°.

— BLAVIER, E. E. Nouveau traité de télégraphie électrique. Paris, 1865–67. 2 v. 8°.

— VAN CHOATE, S. F. Ocean telegraphing. Cambridge, 1865. 4°.

— FRANCE. *Com. Imp. de l'Expos. de* 1867. Matériel et procédés de la télégraphie. (*In their* Rapports du jury, v. 10.)

— MORSE, S. F. B. Examination of the telegraphic apparatus, and the processes in telegraphy. (*In* **U. S.** *Commiss. for Paris Expos.*, 1867. Reports, v. 4.)

— SABINE, R. The electric telegraph. London, 1867. 8°.

Hand books and vocabularies.

— PARKER, J. R. U. S. telegraph vocabulary. Boston, 1832. 8°.

— SMITH, F. O. J. Secret vocabulary for Morse's telegraph. Portland, 1845. 4°.

— JONES, A. System for condensing communications for transmission by magnetic telegraph. N. Y., 1848. 18°.

— BOND, R. Handbook of the telegraph. London, *Weale,* 1862. 12°.

— CAUDERAY, H. Manuel pratique de télégraphie électrique. 2d éd. augm. Lausanne, 1863. 16°.

— CULLEY, R. S. Handbook of practical telegraphy. 2d ed. enl. London, 1867. 8°.

— CLARKE, L., *and* SABINE, R. Electrical tables and formulæ, for the use of telegraph inspectors and operators. London, 1871. 8°.

History.

— MONGEZ, A. Les signaux des anciens. (*In* **Paris. Inst.** *Ac. d. Inscr.* Mém., v. 5. 1821.)

— HIGHTON, E. The electric telegraph; its hist. and progress. London, *Weale,* 1852. 12°.

— WILSON, G. Progress of the telegraph. Camb., 1859. 8°.

— PRESCOTT, G. B. History, theory, and practice of the electric telegraph. Boston, 1860. 12°.

See also **Atlantic telegraph; — Electricity; — Fire alarm telegraph; — French Atlantic cable; — Magnetism; — Postal telegraph.**

Telegraph, The; Jan. 27, 1795 - June 9, 1796. London, 1795–96. f°.

Telegraph, Daily; 1868–71; July - Dec. 1872. London, 1868–72. 9 v. f°.

Telemachus, *pseud.* Wonderful narr. of two families, in five letters. *n.t.p.* [18—.] 8°. (B 534)

Télémaque, Aventures de; par F. de S. de la M. Fénelon. Nouv. éd. Londres, 1767. 12°.

— *Same.* Paris, 1785. 2 v. f°.

— *Same*. Paris, 1846. 12°.
— *Same*. (*In his* Œuvres, v. 3. 1845.)
— *Eng*. Adventures of Telemachus; from the Fr. by J. Hawkesworth. London, 1826. 24°.
Telephanes. Fragm. (*In* Mueller, C. Fr. hist. Gr., v. 4. 1851.)
Telephus *Pergamenus*. Fragm. (*In* **Mueller, C.** Fr. hist. Gr., v. 3. 1849.)
Telesarchus. Fragm. (*In* **Mueller,** C. Fr. hist. Gr., v. 4. 1851.)
Telescope. EULER, L. Dioptrica; de constructione telescopiorum. Petropoli, 1769-71. 3 v. 4°.
— TWINING, A. C. Experimental researches tending towards an improvement in the telescope. (*In* **Amer. Assoc.** Proc., v. 6. 1852.)
Telesilla. Fragm. (*In* **Bergk, T.** Poetæ lyr. Gr. 1853.)
Telesio, Bernardino. Delle cose naturali; volgarizzamento di F. Martelli. (*In* **Palermo, F.** Manoscritti palat., v. 3. 1868.)
— NICERON, J. P. (*In his* Mém., v. 30. 1734.)
Telestes. Fragm. (*In* **Bergk, T.** Poet. lyr. Gr. 1853.)
Telestri regina della Amazzoni. (*In* **Maria Antonie Walpurgis,** *Electress of Saxony*. Varj componimenti. 1772.)
Telfair, Alexander. Oration, Savannah, July 4. Savannah, 1813. 8°. (B 457)
Telford, Thomas. Charts, *etc.*, to the report on communication between England and Ireland. London, 1809. f°.
— Life of T., written by himself; descriptive narr. of his professional labours; ed. by J. Rickman, with a preface, supplement, annot., and index. London, 1838. 4° *and* Atlas f°.
— SMILES, S. Life of T. (*In his* Lives of the engineers, v. 2. 1861.)
Tell, Wilhelm. BORDIER, H. L. Le Gruetli et Guillaume Tell, ou Défense de la tradition vulgaire sur les origines de la Confédération Suisse. Genève, Bâle, 1869. 8°.
— DELEPIERRE, O. (*In his* Historical difficulties. 1868.)
— FLORIAN, J. P. C. de. (*In his* Œuvres, v. 4. 1805.)
— LAMARTINE, A. de. (*In his* Memoirs of celebrated characters, v. 3. 1856.)
— MONNIER, M. Tell et les trois Suisses; la legénde et l'histoire. (*In* **Revue** d. D. Mondes, jan. 1870.) — OLIVIER, J. De l'hist. de la Suisse et des nouv. recherches sur T. (*In* mai 1844.)
— RILLIET, A. Lettre à H. Bordier à propos de sa Défense de la tradition vulgaire sur les origines de la Confédération Suisse. Genève, Bâle, 1869. 8°.
— SCHILLER, J. C. F. von. Wilhelm Tell; Schauspiel. (*In his* Werke, v. 6. 1865.)
Tell-Troth, Tim, *pseud.* Knavery of astrology discover'd. London, 1680. 4°. (B 12)
Tell-Truth, Robert, *pseud.* Advice to the nobility, *etc.*, of this nation in the qualifications and election of their knights and burgesses. *n.p.*, [168-?]. f°. (A 54)
— COUNTRIES vindication, The, from the aspersions of R. Tell-Truth's 'Advice', *etc.* *n.t.p.* [16—.] f° (A 54)
Teller, Abraham, *b.* 1609. *See* **Weller, J.** Grammatica Græca nova.
Teller, Wilhelm Abraham, *b.* 1734. Ueber das Entstehen der Reue in der menschlichen Seele. — Ueber die lange Weile. (*In* **Berlin. Ac. d. Wiss.** Abh., 1792-97.)
Tellez, Balthasar. Travels of Jesuites in Ethopia; Arabia, *etc.* London, 1710. 4°.
— Extrait de l'histoire d'Ethiopie. (*In* **Recueil** de divers voy. 1674.)
Tellez, Gabriel (*pseud.* Tirso de **Molina**). La beata enamorada, Marta la piadosa. (*In* **Ochoa,** E. de. Tesoro del teatro esp., v. 4. 1838; *and* Col. de piezas escog. 1840.)
— El burlador de Sevilla, y combidado de piedra. *n.t.p.* [Barcelona, 17—.] 4°.
— *Same*. (*In* **Ochoa,** E. de. Tesoro del teatro esp., v. 4. 1838; *and* Col. de piezas escog. 1840.)
— Cigarrales de Toledo. 1a pte. *t.p.w.* [Madrid, 1630.] 4°.
— Comedias escogidas; ilustr. por J. E. Hartzenbush. 2a ed. Madrid, 1850. 8°. (Aribau. Bibl., v. 5.)
Contents. Prologo del colector. — Articulos biog. y crit. acerca de Tellez, de A. Duran, R. de Mesonero Romanos, A. Lista, F. J. de Burgos, F. Martinez de la Rosa, y A. G. de Zarate. — Catalogo razonado de las obras dramaticas de Tellez. — *Comedias*. Palabras y plumas. — El pretendiente al reves. — La villana de Vallecas. — El castigo del penséque. — Quien calla otorga: 2a pte. de El castigo del penséque. — La Gallega Mari-Hernandez. — La celosa de si misma. — Amor y celos hacen discretos. Amar por razon de estado. — El condenado por desconfiado. — El vergonzoso en palacio. — Por el sotano y el torno. — Esto si que es negociar. — No hay peor sordo. — La prudencia en la mujer. — La villana de la Sagra. — El amor y el amistad. — Privar contra su gusto. — Celos con celos se curan. — El amor médico. — Don Gil de las calzas verdes. — Amar por arte mayor. — Marta la piadosa. — Amar por señas. — Desde Toledo á Madrid. — Cautela contra cautela. — La ventura con el nombre. — En Madrid y en una casa. — Las balcones de Madrid. — El burlador de Sevilla y convidado de piedra. — El Rey don Pedro en Madrid y el Infanzon de Illescas. — El celoso prudente. — La huerta de Juan Fernandez. — Del enemigo el primer consejo. — Averigüelo Vargas. — Los Amantes de Teruel. — *Apéndices*. Jornada tercera de la comedia titulada Lo que hace un manto en Madrid. — Fragmentos 1, 2, y 3 de la comedia titulada El rey don Pedro en Madrid, incluida en una quinta parte de Comedias de Calderon, impresa en Barcelona año de 1677. — Observaciones acerca de la comedia titulada La prudencia en la mujer, por A. Duran. — Examen de El condenado por desconfiado, por A. Duran.
— Deleytar aprovechando. Madrid, 1677. 4°.
— En Madrid y en una casa. *See Note under* **Rojas.**
— No le arriendo la ganancia. — El colmenero divino. (*In* **Pedroso,** E. G. Autos sacramentales. 1865.)
— El pretendiente al revès. *n.t.p.* [Madrid, 17—.] 4°.
— La prudencia en la muger. — Don Gil de las calzas verdes. (*In* **Ochoa,** E. de. Tesoro del teatro esp., v. 4. 1838.)
— Los tres maridos burlados. (*In* **Rosell,** C. Nov. post. a Cervantes, v. 1. 1851.)
— El vergonzoso en palacio. Madrid, 1817. 4°.
Telliamed. *See* **Maillet, B.**
Tellier. *See* **Le Tellier.**
Tello, Antonio. Fragmentos de una historia de la Nueva Galicia. (*In* **Icazbalceta,** P. G. Col. de doc., v. 2. 1866.)
Tellurium. BRADLEY, L. Tellurium. (*In* **Amer. Assoc.** Proc., v. 16. 1868.)
Temestitán, *Mexico*. CONQUISTADOR anónimo, El; relacion de algunas cosas de la Nueva España, y de la gran ciudad de Temestitán, México. (*In* **Icazbalceta,** J. G. Col. de doc., v. 1. 1858.)
Temistocle; da P. **Metastasio.** (*In his* Opere, v. 5. 1782.)
Temistokles; tragedya; przez F. D. Kniaznin. (*In his* Dzieła, v. 5. 1837; v. 36 of Bobrowicz, J. N. Bibl. klass. Polskich.)
Temminck, Koenraad Jacob. Manuel d'ornithologie ou Tableau systématique des oiseaux d'Europe. 2e éd. Paris, 1820-35. 3 v. 8°.
Tempelhof, *Col.* Georg Friedrich von. Extract from Tempelhoffe's History of the seven years' war. (*In* **Lindsay,** C. Military miscel. 1793.)
Temper. CHAPONE, *Mrs.* H. (Mulso). Government of temper. (*In* **Ladies'** pocket library. 1797.)
See also **Passions.**
Temper; by R. Bell. (*In* **Sargent,** E. Mod. stand. dr., v. 7.)
Temper; a tale by A. Opie. Bost., 1812. 2 v. 18°.
— *Same*. Boston, 1827. 2 v. 12°.
Temperament. PERNETY, A. J., *l'abbé*. Sur les différens tempéramens, et sur leur effets. — De l'influence des causes physiques sur le tempérament. (*In* **Berlin.** Ak. d. **Wiss.** Abh., 1777.)
See also **Nervous system** (p. 2097).
Temperance. MATHER, I. Wo to drunkards; two sermons against drunkenness. [1673.] 2d ed. Boston, 1712. 8°. (C 14)
— IMPORTANCE of sobriety. London, [17—?]. 12°. (C 203)
— INDICTMENT and trial of Sir R. Rum, *etc.* 8th ed. N. Y., [176-]. 8°. (B 517)
— *Same*. Boston, 1835. 16°. (D 24)
— BADGER, S. Nature and effects of drunkenness considered; two disc., Natick, Oct. 1773. Boston, 1774. 8°. (B 213)

— BENEZET, A. Mighty destroyer displayed; account of the havock made by the use of distilled spirituous liquors; by a lover of mankind. (*In his* Potent enemies of America laid open. 1774.)
— LETTSOM, J. C. History of some of the effects of hard drinking. [1789.] 6th ed. London, 1791. 4°. (B 650)
— - *Same.* Hints resp. the effects of hard drinking. London, 1798. 8°. (B 822)
— FOTHERGILL, A. Essay on the abuse of spirituous liquors, *etc.* Bath, 1796. 8°. (B 822)
— AMER. TRACT SOC., *New York.* Rewards of drunkenness. N. Y., [18—]. 12°. (C 204)
— EVENTFUL twelve hours, The; or, The wretchedness of a drunkard. *n.t.p.* [18—.] 16°. (C 246)
— KENTUCKY. *Gen. Assembly.* Report on the petitions for the repeal of laws for the sale of liquors. *n.p.*, [18—]. 8°. (B 1280)
— PORTER, E. Fatal effects of ardent spirits; sermon, [1805]. Hartford, 1811. 8°. (B 549)
— - *Same.* Morristown, 1812. 8°. (B 915)
— RUSH, B. Effects of ardent spirits upon the body and mind. (*In* Concise miscel. 1809. C 220)
— - *Same.* 4th ed. Phila., [18—]. 8°. (C 85)
— - *Same.* 8th ed. Boston, 1823. 12°. (C 119)
— BADGER, S. Two discourses on temperance. Boston, 1811. 12°. (C 203)
— FORSTER, T. Physiological reflections on the destructive operation of spirituous liquors on the animal system. London, 1812. 8°. (B 814)
— FAIRFIELD CO., (WESTERN DISTRICT) CONSOCIATION. Intemperance; address to the churches and congregations. Hartford, 1813. 8°. (B 459)
— TROTTER, T. Essay on drunkenness. Boston, 1813. 12°.
— ABBOT, A. Addresses before Mass. Soc. for Suppressing Intemperance. Camb., 1815. 12°. (C 203)
— SANDARS, D. C. Sermon, Mar. 14, before the Wrentham Auxiliary Soc. for the Suppression of Intemperance. Dedham, 1815. 8°. (B 330)
— APPLETON, J. Address before Mass. Soc. for Suppressing Intemperance. Boston, 1816. 8°. (B 938)
— LETTERS on public-house licensing; showing the errors of the present system. (*In* Pamphleteer, 1816; v. 7 of B 838)
— SHORT letter on the dangerous competition of the distilleries with the breweries. (*In* Pamphleteer, 1816; v. 7 of B 838)
— BEAUMONT, J. T. B. Letter showing the extreme injustice of the present system of public house licensing. (*In* Pamphleteer, 1817; v. 9 of B 838)
— TORREY, J. Essays on the use of distilled spirits. (*In his* Intellectual torch. 1817. C 83)
— OBSERVATIONS on the evil effects produced by spirituous liquors. 2d ed. (*In* Pampheleteer, 1818; v. 12 of B 838)
— ADDRESS to the citizens of the U. S. on ardent spirits. N. Y., 1819. 12°. (C 65)
— DIMMICK, L. F. Intemperance; sermon, fast-day. Newburyport, 1819. 8°. (B 549)
— HERTTELL, T. Expose of the causes of intemperate drinking. N. Y., 1819. 8°. (B 549, 1108)
— - *Same.* N. Y., *printed*, Haverhill, *repr.* 1820. 8°. (B 1278)
— NICHOLS, A. Address, Danvers, before the Soc. for Suppressing Intemperance, April 27. Salem, 1819. 8°. (B 565)
— SEWALL, T. Address on the effects of intemperance on the intellectual, moral, and physical powers. *n.p.*, [182-?]. 12°. (D 24, W 13)
— BOUND, J. J. The means of curing, and preventing intemperance. N. Y., 1820. 12°. (C 147)
— ADVANTAGES and disadvantages of drunkenness. Camb., 1821. 12°. (C 203)
— WARREN, H. Address, Roxbury, before the Society for Suppressing Intemperance. Boston, 1821. 8°. (B 565)
— ABBOTT, W. Address to Danvers Auxiliary Soc. for Suppressing Intemperance. Salem, 1822. 8°. (B 565)
— PROCTOR, J. W. Address to Danvers Auxiliary Soc. for Suppressing Intemperance. Salem, 1822. 8°. (B 565)
— BEECHER, L. Six essays on the nature, *etc.*, of intemperance. [1825.] New ed. Bradford, 1830. 12°. (D 24)
— - *Same.* Six lectures. (*In his* Works, v. 1. 1852.)
— KITTREDGE, J. Address, effects of ardent spirits, Lyme, N. H., Jan. 8. Conc., 1827. 8°. (B 1278, 1881)
— - *Same.* N. Y., 1828. 12°. (C 204)
— PALFREY, J. G. Discourses on intemperance, April 5, 8. Boston, 1827. 24°. (D 13)
— PUTNAM, R. A. The causes, evils, and the remedy of intemperance. Boston, 1827. 8°. (B 1237)
— SPRAGUE, C. Address before the Mass. Soc. for the Suppression of Intemperance. Boston, 1827. 8°. (B 565, 1759, 1793)
— SPRAGUE, W. B. Intemperance a just cause for alarm and exertion; sermon, West Springfield, April 5, fast-day. N. Y., 1827. 8°. (B 1278, W 3)
— GREGG, D. H. Address before the Newton Temperance Society, July 4. Boston, 1828. 8°. (B 1278, 1755)
— HUMPHREY, H. Parallel between intemperance and the slave trade; address, Amherst Coll., July 4. Amherst, 1828. 8°. (B 938, 1203, 1237)
— MACNISH, R. Anatomy of drunkenness. Phila., 1828. 24°.
— - *Same.* From 5th Glasgow ed. N. Y., 1835. 12°.
— NICHOLS, I. Address before the Portland Assoc. for the Promotion of Temperance, Feb. 22. Portland, 1828. 8°. (B 938, 1759)
— NOTT, S. Appeal to the temperate. Hartford, 1828. 18°.
— O'FLAHERTY, T. J. Medical essay on drinking. Hartford, 1828. 8°. (B 969)
— EVILS of intemperance exemplified in prose and poetry. Boston, 1829. 12°. (D 24)
— SWEETSER, W. Dissertation on intemperance. (*In* Mass. Med. Soc. Med. comm., 1829.)
— DICKINSON, A. Appeal to American youth. *n.t.p.*, [183-?]. 12°. (B 203)
— JEFFREYS, H. Temperance tract; an appeal, *etc.* *n.t.p.* [183-?] 12°. (B 203)
— TILLY, T. The temperance catechism. London, [183-?]. 8°. (B 1280)
— AUSTIN, J. T. Address before the Mass. Soc. for the Suppression of Intemperance, May 27. Boston, 1830. 8°. (B 938, 1662, 1761, 1793, 2014)
— HITCHCOCK, E. Essay on alcoholic and narcotic substances. Amherst, 1830. 12°. (C 203)
— KIMBALL, C. O. Address, 2d anniv. of the Haverhill Temperance Soc. Haverhill, 1830. 12°. (B 1278)
— KITTREDGE, J. Address to the Temperance Soc. of Plymouth, N. H. Boston, 1830. 12°. (C 204)
— LYMAN, H. Address before the Temperance Soc. of Frankinville. N. Y., 1830. 8°. (B 1278)
— PARKER, J. Address. Keene, N. H., 1830. 12°. (C 204)
— STUART, M. Essay on the prize-question, whether the use of distilled liquors or traffic in them is compatible with making a profession of Christianity. N. Y., 1830. 8°. (B 1278, C 199)
— AMER. TEMP. UNION. Permanent T. documents. [1831-52.] N. Y., 1851-52. 3 v. 8°.
— BARBOUR, I. R. Statistical table, showing the influence of intemperance on the church. [Boston, 1831.] 12°. (C 203)
— BROWN, S. F. Address before the Livermore Temp. Soc. Portland, 1831. 12°. (C 203)
— DRAKE, D. Oration on the causes, evils, and preventives of intemperance, Columbus, Feb. 12. Columbus, 1831. 8°. (B 1064)
— FESSENDEN, T. G. Address before the Charlestown Temperance Society, Jan. 31. Charlestown, 1831. 8°. (B 1021)
— GILLPATRICK, *Rev.* J. Nature and remedy of intemperance; address to Mt. Desert Temp. Soc. Boston, 1832. 12°. (C 203)
— ONE hundred and thirty questions. Boston, 1832. 12°. (C 204)
— SCHOOLCRAFT, H. R. Address on the influence of ardent spirits on the condition of the Indians. Detroit, 1832. 8°. (B 1278)
— SPEECHES at a meeting at Washington for promotion of temperance. *n.p.*, [1832]. 12°. (C 204)
— V., M. L. Licensed houses; examination of the license law of Mass. [1832.] Boston, 1833. 8°. (B 1074, 1768, 1783, 1802, 2014)
— WARE, H. Combination against intemperance explained and justified; address before Cambridge Temperance Soc., Mar. 27. Camb., 1832, 8°. (B 1278)
— - *Same.* 3d ed. Boston, 1832. 8°. (C 301)
— SARGENT, L. M. [Temperance tales.] No. 1-4. Boston, 1833-34. 4 pams. 24°. (D 18)
— - *Same.* No. 1; My mother's gold ring. 22d ed. Boston, 1834. 24°. (D 24)
— - *Same.* No. 1. *n.t.p.* [183-.] 8°. (C 204)
— - *Same.* No. 6-10. Boston, 1835. 24°.
— - *Same.* No. 8: What a curse! or Johnny Hodges the blacksmith. Boston, 1835. 24°. (D 24)
— FOX, T. B. Argument against the manufacture and sale of ardent spirits. Dover, 1833. 12°. (C 204)
— HALL, E. Address in behalf of the Temperance Soc., Norwalk, Feb. 26. Norwalk, 1833. 8°. (B 1278)

— NOYES, G. R. Address on the temperance reformation. Brookfield, 1833. 12°. (B 1278)
— PROCEEDINGS and speeches at a meeting for the prom. of the cause of temperance in the U. S., Wash., Feb. 24. Wash., 1833. 8°. (B 1783)
— SARGENT, L. M. Address at Worcester before the Worcester Temp. Soc. Boston, 1833. 8°. (B 1085)
— - Address before the Mass. Soc. for the Suppression of Intemperance, May 27. 2d ed. Boston, 1833. 8°. (B 2014)
— - *Same.* 5th ed. Boston, 1833. 8°. (B 1072)
— - Address before the Seaman's Bethel Temperance Soc. Boston, 1833. 8°. (B 1085, 2014)
— SIGOURNEY, L. H. The intemperate; and The reformed [by G. Smith]. Boston, 1833. 12°. (C 204)
— SMITH, G. Letter to E. C. Delavan, reformation of the intemperate. *n.t.p.* [1833.] 8°. (B 1760)
— SNOW, A. B. Address, formation of Seamen's Bethel Temp. Soc., Boston. Boston, 1833. 8°. (B 1278, 2014)
— WOOD, H. Address before the Salisbury Temp. Soc. Concord, 1833. 8°. (B 1278)
— CHANNING, W. Thoughts on the origin, *etc.*, of the temperance reform. Boston, 1834. 8°. (B 1095, 1882, 2014)
— DESULTORY notes on the origin, uses, and effects of ardent spirit. Phila., 1834. 8°.
— GRIMKÉ, T. S. Temperance reformation the cause of Christian morals; address before the Charleston Temp. Soc. Charleston, 1834. 8°. (B 1116)
— MASS. TEMP. SOC. Making money by selling rum. Boston, 1834. 12°. (C 171, 204)
— - Solemn appeal to citizens of Boston, on the city expenses for pauperism, vice, and crime. Boston, 1834. 12°. (C 204)
— SARGENT, L. M. Address before the Temperance Soc. of Harvard Univ., Nov. 20. Camb., 1834. 8°. (B 1279, 1723)
— - Hymn for the simultaneous celebration of the Suffolk Co. Temp. Soc., Feb. 1834. [Boston, 1834.] Broadside. (B 1280)
— STEWART, A. Prize addr. for N. Y. City Temperance Soc. on licenses to retail ardent spirits. Utica, [1834]. 8°. (B 1280)
— TENNY, E. Address before the Temperance Soc. in Lyme, July 4. Hanover, N. H., 1834. 8°. (B 1888)
— TRACY, O. Address before the Female Temperance Soc. at Newport, Feb. 2d ed. Concord, 1834. 12°. (D 24)
— DELAVAN, E. C., *and* SPRAGUE, *Rev. Dr.* Correspondence. [1835-36.] Albany, 1837. 8°. (B 1279)
— BARTLETT, E. The laws of sobriety; address before the Young Men's Temp. Soc., Mar. 8. Lowell, [1835]. 8°. (B 1239, 1279)
— DISCOURSE on the pernicious effects of drunkenness. Penrith, 1835. 8°. (B 1279)
— JOE Anderson and old Jim Bayley. Boston, 1835. 16°. (D 24)
— JUSTITIÆ AMICUS, *pseud.* Utility of ardent spirits; address for an Anti-Temperance Soc. Boston, 1835. 8°. (B 1768)
— MASS. TEMP. SOC. Cranberry meadow. Boston, 1835. 12°. (C 203)
— YOUNG MEN'S LEAGUE. Address. Boston, [1835]. 12°. (C 203)
— AMERICAN TEMPERANCE SOCIETY. The temperance manual. Boston, 1836. 8°. (B 1279, 1888)
— BOSTON IRISH TEMPERANCE SOCIETY. Address to their countrymen in Amer. Boston, 1836. 8°. (B 1279)
— CROCKETT, S. L. Voice from Leverett St. prison. Boston, 1836. 12°. (C 203, 253)
— EDWARDS, J. Letter to the friends of temperance in Mass. Boston, 1836. 8°. (B 1116, 1812, 1880, 2014)
— - *Same.* 2d ed. enl. Boston, 1836. 8°. (B 1120, 1806, 1872)
— - *Same.* 3d ed. enl. Boston, 1836. 8°. (B 1880)
— FACTS and estimates for the people. *n.t.p.* [1836.] 8°. (B 1278)
— HOPKINS, S. M. Correspondence on temperance, with G. Smith, J. Edwards, and S. H. Cox. Pt. 1. Geneva, 1836. 8°. (B 1279)
— SARGENT, L. M. Letter on the 'State of the temperance reform' to Rev. C. Stetson. Boston, 1836. 8°. (B 1239, 1279)
— CHANNING, W. E. Address on T. Boston, 1837. 12°.
— HITCHCOCK, E. An argument for early temperance. Boston, 1837. 16°. (D 24)
— NAZARITE, The; or, The letter and spirit of the Bible, on the use of wine. Boston, 1837. 12°. (D 24)
— ABBOTT, J. S. C. Lecture on the license law. Boston, 1838. 12°. (C 203)
— BACON, L. Discourse on the traffic in spirituous liquors. New Haven, 1838. 8°. (B 1280)
— CLARK, T. M. Annual address before the Mass. Temperance Soc., May 27. Boston, 1838. 8°. (B 1732, 1880)
— GOODRICH, S. G. Five letters to neighbor Smith, touching the fifteen gallon jug; added, a 6th letter. 5th ed. Boston, 1838. 12°. (B 1279)
— HISTORY of the striped pig. 3d ed. Boston, 1838. 12°. (D 24)
— LETTER to the Legislature on the repeal of the license laws. [Boston, 1838.] 8°. (B 1770)
— MOREWOOD, S. Hist. of inventions and customs in the manufacture and use of inebriating liquors. Dublin, 1838. 8°.
— PHILLIPS, J., *and others.* Address to the people of Mass., by the friends of T. Bost., 1838. 8°. (B 1280)
— - Reply to the report of a committee of those opposed to the license law. [Boston, 1838.] 8°. (B 1279, 1748)
— SOUTHWICK, S. Oration before the Albany Co. Temp. Soc., July 4. Albany, 1838. 8°. (B 1280)
— THAYER, M. Remarks on the license law. [Boston, 1838.] 12°. (C 204)
— WILLIAMS, M. Cracked jug; or, Five ans. to neighbor Parley's Five letters, cracking his 'Fifteen gallon jug'; by 'Neighbor Smith'. Boston, 1838. 12°. (B 1279)
— WOODWARD, S. B. Essay on asylums for inebriates. [Worcester, 1838.] 8°. (B 1748)
— BOLLES, J. A. Oration, July 4, Medfield, Mass., at a temperance celebration. Boston, 1839. 8°. (B 1143)
— DAMON, N. Remarks on the importance of obedience to law and the duty of sustaining it, Dec. 30, 1839. Boston, 1840. 8°. (B 1280)
— ELEMENTS of medical philosophy; compr. a cure for intemperance; [by H. Sternberg ?]. Albany, 1839. 8°. (B 1552)
— HEWIT, N. The wine question. Bridgeport, 1839. 8°. (B 1280)
— INVESTIGATION into the 15 gallon law of Mass.; with arguments of F. Dexter and B. F. Hallett. Boston, 1839. 8°. (B 1142, 1279)
— JEWETT, C. The rum-seller's and rum-drinker's lamentation. Boston, 1839. Broadside. (B 1280)
— LETTERS to H. G. Otis on the repeal of the license law. Boston, 1839. 12°. (C 204)
— OTIS, H. G., *and others.* Memorial on the license law. [Boston, 1839.] 8°. (B 1279)
— SPRAGUE, P. Argument, upon the memorial of H. G. Otis and others. Boston, 1839. 8°. (B 1748)
— BEACON, The. *n.t.p.* [184-?] 18°. (C 246)
— CLAPP, H. Address from the mass meeting of Suffolk, Norfolk, Plymouth, and Bristol Co. Washingtonians, to the public. Lynn, [184-]. 8°. (B 1280)
— DELAVAN, E. C. Adulteration of liquors. [N. Y., 184-.] 12°. (C 203)
— GREEN, S. G. The Christian aspect of teetotalism. [London, 184-?] 16°. (D 24)
— BATHER, E. The awful case of drunkards, *etc.* London, 1840. 12°. (C 203)
— HALL, E. B. Temperance reform; a review of Rosanna; or, Scenes in Boston. From the Christian Examiner for March. 3d ed. Boston, 1840. 8°. (B 1280)
— HISTOIRE de l'eau-de-vie en Canada. (*In* Lit. and Hist. Soc. of Quebec. Col., v. 1. 1840.)
— JEFFREYS, H. Religious objection to tetotalism. London, 1840. 8°. (B 1280)
— PURKITT, J. H. Address on man's likeness to God. Boston, 1840. 8°. (B 1280)
— NEW impulse, The; life and reformation of J. H. W. Hawkins. Boston, 1841. 12°. (C 203)
— PARSONS, *Rev.* B. The wine question settled. London, 1841. 12°. (C 204)
— DEAD child, The. Boston, 1842. 4°. (D 24)
— GROSVENOR, G. J. Address on the importance of female influence to temperance reformation. Geneva, 1842. 8°. (B 1280)
— MARSHALL, T. F. Address before the City Hose Co., no. 33, May 16. N. Y., 1842. 8°. (B 1280)
— STREIT, P. B. Address, 4th of July, at the request of the Hampshire Co. Temperance Soc. Romney, 1842. 8°. (B 1280)
— TEMPERANCE tract, in Cherokee. Park Hill,] 1842. 24°. (E 132)
— HOLMES, S. L. Address on the temperance pledge. Albany, 1843. 8°. (B 1280)
— RHETT, A. Address before the temperance societies of Charleston, July 4. Charleston, 1843. 8°. (B 1280)
— TORREY, W. Address at the Temperance Conven., Morristown, Dec. 13; with proceedings, *etc.*, of the Convention and also that at Hackettstown, Sept. 26. Newark, 1843. 8°. (B 1280)

— BOARDMAN, G. S. Address, Waterville, before the Oneida County Temperance Soc., Feb. 22. Rome, 1844. 8°. (B 1281)
— EASY Nat; or, Boston bars and Boston boys; a tale of home trials. Boston, 1844. 8°. (B 1280)
— ELLIS, S. Address. Boston, 1844. 12°. (C 203)
— EVIL, The, of intoxicating liquor and the remedy; [in Cherokee]. 2d ed. Park Hill, 1844. 24°. (E 132)
— MISCELLANEOUS pieces [on temperance; in the Cherokee language]. Park Hill, 1844. 24°. (E 132)
— ROOT, J. Horrors of delirium tremens. N. Y., 1844. 8°.
— TUCKER, E. Address before the Tuckerton Temperance Soc., July 4. Phila., 1844. 8°. (B 1280)
— CHAPIN, E. H. Present exigencies of the temperance cause; address, Nov. 23, 1845. Boston, 1846. 12°. (D 24)
— FOWLER, O. S. Temperance founded on phrenology and physiology. [1845.] 24th ed. N. Y., 1846. 8°. (B 1281)
— LEVIN, L. C. Intemperance the prelude to gambling and suicide, illust. in the life of C. C. Colton. Phila., 1845. 8°. (B 1281)
— WHITNEY, F. A. Address on temperance, Town Hall, Brighton, Dec. 21, 1845. Boston, 1846. 8°. (B 1281)
— ELLIS, G. E. Lecture on temperance, Charlestown. Boston, 1846. 8°. (B 1281)
— MY own experience. Boston, 1846. 12°. (D 24)
— NOYES, G. F. Temperance essays. No. 1: On the duties of influential classes. Bost., 1846. 12°. (C 204)
— TONCEY, I. Review of the message before the General Assem., Connecticut, May 6. *n.p.*, [1846]. 8°. (B 1281)
— VAN LOON, C. Sons of Temperance defended; address, Poughkeepsie. Poughkeepsie, 1846. 8°. (B 1281)
— WHITAKER, E. K. Address, Medfield, before Norfolk Co. Washington Total Abs. Soc., July 4. Boston, 1846. 8°. (B 1281)
— ARTHUR, T. S. Christmas box for sons and daughters of temperance. Phila., 1847. 12°.
— — *Another copy.* (C 203)
— CLARK, J. H. Present position and claims of the temperance enterprise; prize essay. N. Y., 1847. 8°. (B 1281)
— SARGENT, L. M. Letter to Rev. J. Marsh. Boston, 1847. 8°. (B 1281)
— BRITISH spirits; comments upon the evidence affecting the spirit trade; by a Scotchman. London, 1848. 8°. (B 1536)
— FORBES, J. Physiological effects of alcoholic drinks; with documents of the Mass. Temp. Soc. Boston, 1848. 12°.
— OTIS, H. G. Letter from an aged and retired citizen of Boston, on coercive measures in aid of temperance. Boston, 1848. 8°. (B 1281)
— FEW practical reflections, A, on the grog ration in the United States navy; by an old officer. *n.p.*, 1849. 8°. (B 1281)
— HOSMER, C. L. Aldermanic wisdom and aldermanic virtue on the question of license and no license. Boston, 1849. 8°. (B 1279)
— JUSTICE, *pseud.* Temperance at entertainments. *n.p.*, [1849]. 4°. (A 65)
— LAMAS, M. The glass; or, Trials of Helen More. Phila., 1849. 8°. (B 1281)
— REMARKS on the use of alcohol for the preparation of medicines. Boston, 1849. 12°. (C 204, 271)
— To the clergy and Christian professors in the U. S. *n.p.*, [1849]. 8°. (C 203)
— CARPENTER, W. B. Use and abuses of liquors. Boston, 1851. 12°.
— — *Same.* (*In* Mass. Temp. Soc. When will the day come? 1857.)
— MASS. TEMP. SOC. Alcohol in the British navy. Boston, 1851. 12°. (C 203)
— ALGER, W. R. Facts of intemperance, and their claims on the public action of the people. Boston, 1852. 8°. (B 1281)
— BARNES, A. Discourse in behalf of a law prohibiting traffic in intoxicating drinks. Philadelphia, 1852. 8°. (B 1283)
— BUCKINGHAM, S. Bible temperance against ultra teetotalism. N. Y., 1852. 8°.
— LEVY, M. E. Address before the Temperance Society of Micanopy. Jacksonville, 1852. 8°. (B 1281)
— LICENSE question, and the liquor traffic. Boston, [1852]. 16°. (C 204)
— LOVEJOY, J. C. The law and the offence; lecture on prohibitory laws. Boston, 1852. 8°. (B 1281)
— MASSACHUSETTS anti-liquor law; also, Proceedings of the temperance convention at Worcester. Boston, 1852. 8°. (B 1281)
— AMER. TEMP. UNION. Appeal to the public from 'Results of the Maine law'. N. Y., 1853. 8°. (B 1281)
— BEECHER, L., *and others.* Address and memorial. Boston, 1853. 12°. (C 203)
— BREWER, W. A. On the liquor law. Boston, 1853. 12°. (C 203)
— CHARACTERISTICS and claims of a prohibitory law. — Practical working of the Maine law. [Pp. 137-161 of some work on temperance. 1853?] 12°. (C 203)
— DE QUINCEY, T. Temperance movement. (*In his* Narrative papers, v. 2. 1853.)
— GOUGH, J. B. Habit; a lecture before the Young Men's Christian Assoc., Nov. 22. [London,] 1853. 8°. (B 1281)
— LOVEJOY, J. C. Speech on the repeal of the liquor law. Boston, [1853]. 12°. (C 204)
— MINOR, L. Reasons for abolishing the liquor traffic. Richmond, 1853. 12°. (D 24)
— BUCKINGHAM, J. S. History and progress of the T. reformation. Lond., 1854. 8°.
— WARREN, J. C. Effect of stimulating drinks. (*In his* Preservation of health. 1854.)
— BEGGS, T. Dear bread and wasted grain; a lecture, Dec. 20, 1855. London, 1856. 8°. (B 1536)
— POTTER, A. The drinking usages of society. Boston, 1855. 12°. (C 204)
— DELAVAN, E. C. Letter to Gov. King; appeal for co-operation in T. reform. Albany, 1857. 8°. (B 1281)
— MASS. TEMP. SOC. When will the day come? Boston, [1857]. 12°.
— NOTT, E. Lectures on T.; with an introd. by by T. Lewis, ed. by A. McCoy. N. Y., 1857. 12°.
— MARSH, J. The temperance battle not man's but God's. N. Y., 1858. 8°. (B 1281)
— PLUMMER, C. H. Oration. 2d ed. Lawrence, 1858. 16°. (C 204)
— CHEEVER, G. B. The dream; or, True history of Deacon Giles's distillery and Deacon Jones's brewery. N. Y., 1859. 8°. (B 1281)
— HARRISSON, D. A voice from the Washingtonian Home, being a hist. of the Inst. in Boston for the Reformation of Inebriates. Boston, 1860. 8°.
— LALLEMAND, L., *and others.* Du rôle de l'alcool et des anesthésiques dans l'organisme. Paris, 1860. 8°.
— MACLEOD, A. Repression and drunkenness. (*In* Nat. Assoc. Prom. Soc. Sci. Trans., 1860.)
— BAYLY, *Mrs.* M. Mended homes and what repaired them. London, 1861. 16°.
— MAIR, J. Nephaleia; or, Total abstinence the doctrine of the Bible. N. Y., 1861. 12°.
— MASSACHUSETTS TEMPERANCE SOCIETY. Addresses by A. Potter and others. Boston, 1861. 12°.
— THOUGHTS on the moral physiology and pathology of the disease liquor drinking. Bost., 1862. 8°. (B 1281)
— KIRK, J. State of parishes in Scotland in rel. to the traffic in strong drink. (*In* Nat. Assoc. Prom. Soc. Sci. Trans., 1863.)
— DELAVAN, E. C. Temperance essays and selections. Albany, 1865. 12°.
— HUTTON, *Rev.* T. The licensing system and its needed reforms. (*In* Nat. Assoc. Prom. Soc. Sci. Trans., 1865.)
— ANDREW, J. A. Errors of prohibition; argument before a comm. of the Gen. Court, Apr. 3. Boston, 1867. 8°. (B 1928)
— FRANCE. *Com. Imp. de l'Expos. de* 1867. Boissons fermentées. (*In their* Rapports, v. 11.)
— SONS OF TEMPERANCE, *N. A.* Directory, 1868. Boston, 1868. 12°.
— BEGGS, T. On the remedies which lie within the scope of voluntary effort. — NEWMAN, F. W. On the drink traffic. (*In* Nat. Assoc. Prom. Soc. Sci. Trans., 1869.)

Periodicals.

— AMERICAN quarterly T. magazine. Vol. 1-2. Albany, 1833-34. 2 v. 8°.

— TEMPERANCE advocate; Jan.-Dec. Honolulu, 1843. 4°. (E 168)

See also **Alcohol; — Delirium tremens; — Distilling; — Liquors; — Maine.** *Liquor law.* **— Narcotics; — Spirituous liquors; — Still; — Stimulants; — Tobacco; — Wine;** — *also* **Mathew, T.**

Note. For Proceedings, addresses, *etc.*, of temperance societies *see* the list under **Temperance societies.**

Temperance Convention, 4th National, *Saratoga*, Aug. 20, 1851. Proc., speeches, and addresses. N. Y., 1851. 8°. (Permanent T. doc., v. 3.)

Temperance Convention *of Mass.*, Boston, Sept. 23, 1835. Proc.; with address. Boston, 1836. 8°. (B 1124, 1279, 1812)

Temperance Convention *of Mass.*, Boston, Feb. 12, 1840. Proc. Boston, 1840. 8°. (B 1280)

Temperance Convention *of Mass.*, Worcester, June 23, 24, 1852. Mass. anti-liquor law; also proc. Boston, 1852. 8°. (B 1281)

Temperance Convention *of Mass.*, Worcester, Sept. 18, 1833. Journal of proc. Boston, 1833. 8°. (B 1768)

Temperance Convention *of N. Jersey*, Hackettstown, Sept. 26, 1843. Proc. (*In* **Torrey, W.** Speech. 1843. B 1280)

Temperance Convention *of N. Jersey*, Morrisstown, Dec. 13, 1843. Proc. (*In* **Torrey, W.** Speech. 1843. B 1280)

Temperance Convention *of Penn.*, Harrisburg. Jan., 12, 13, 1842. Proc. Shiremanstown, 1842. 8°. (B 1280)

Temperance Convention of the Young Men of Mass., Worcester, July 1, 2, 1834. Proc. Boston, 1834. 8°. (B 1278)

Temperance Societies. For proceedings, *etc.*, of temperance societies, *see* the name of the Society as **Albany. Young Men's Temp. Soc.; — Amer. Temp. Soc.; — Amer. Temp. Union; — Bombay Temp. Soc.; — Boston. Irish Temp. Soc.; — Boston. Young Men's Temp. Soc.; — Boston Young Men's Tot. Abst. Soc.; — Cambridge Temp. Soc.; — Congressional Temp. Soc.; — Congressional Tot. Abst. Soc.; — Hampshire Co. Temp. Soc.; — Haverhill. Soc. Prom. Temp. in H.; — Mass. Div. No. 71 of the Sons of Temp.; — Mass. Soc. for the Suppression of Intemp.; — Mass. Temp. Soc.; — Mass. Temp. Union; — Nat. Temp. Soc.,** *London*; **— N. Y. City Temp. Soc.; — N. Y. State Soc. Prom. Temp.; — Penn. Soc. for Discouraging the Use of Ardent Spirits; — Rhode Island State Temp. Soc.; — Sons of Temp.; — Tuckerton Temp. Soc.; — Watertown Washington Abst. Soc.**

Temperate discussion of the causes which have led to the present high price of bread; [by C. Long]. London, 1800. 8°. (B 1535)

— *Same.* (*In* **Pamphleteer,** 1817; v. 10 of B 838)

Temperature in diseases. WUNDERLICH, C. A. On the temperature in diseases; tr. from 2d German ed. by W. B. Woodman. London, 1871. 8°. (Sydenham Soc. Pub., v. 49.)

Temperature of the air. KIRWAN, R. Estimate of the temperature of the different latitudes. London, 1787. 8°.

— WEBSTER, N. Dissertation on the supposed change in the temperature of winter. (*In* **Conn. Acad.** Mem., v. 1, pt. 1. 1810.)

— SCHOTT, C. A. Abstract of the results of obs. for temperature made by the 2d Grinnell exped., 1853-55. (*In* **Amer. Assoc.** Proc., v. 13. 1860.)

— DOVE, H. W. Darstellung der Wärme-Erscheinungen durch fünftägige Mittel, 1782-1855, mit besonderen Berücksichtigung strenger Winter. Berlin, 1856. f°. (Berlin. Ak. d. Wiss. Abh., 1r suppl. Band.)

— JOHNSTON, A. K. Distribution of heat over the globe. (*In his* Physical atlas. 1856.)

— DEWEY, C. Best hours of daily observation to find the mean temperature of the year. (*In* **Smithsonian Inst.** Report, 1857.)

Temperature of the Earth. CORDIER, P. L. A. Temperature of the interior of the Earth; tr. by the junior class of Amherst College. Amherst, 1828. 12°.

Tempest, The. *See* **Shakespeare, W.**

Tempest, The; or, The enchanted island; comedy, by J. **Dryden.** (*In his* Works, v. 3. 1808.)

Tempest in a tea-pot, A; comedy, by **F. Picton.** (No. 120 *of* **De Witt's** acting plays.)

Tempio dell' eternità, Il; da P. **Metastasio.** (*In his* Opere, v. 4. 1782.)

Templar, Benjamin. Importance of teaching soc. econ. in elementary schools, *etc.* (*In* **Nat. Assoc. Prom. Soc. Sci.** Trans., 1858.) — Religion of secular schools. (*In* 1859.) — Ten years' experience of the Manchester Free School. (*In* 1866.)

Templars, Knights. RAYNOUARD, F. J. M. Monumens rel. à la condamnation des Chev. du Temple et à l'abolition de leur Ordre. Paris, 1813. 8°.

— GALEANI NAPIONE, G. F. Dei Templarj e dell' abolizione dell' ordine loro. (*In* **Turin. Ac. d. Sci.** Mem., v. 27. 1823.)

— MICHELET, J. Procès des Templiers. Paris, 1841-51. 2 v. 4°. (Doc. inéd.)

— ADDISON, C. G. Hist. of the Knights Templars. London, 1842. 8°.

— SOLDAN, W. G. Ueber den Process der Templer und die gegen ihren Orden erhobenen Beschuldigungen. (*In* **Historisches** Taschenbuch, 1845.)

See also **Garway,** *Herefordshire*; **— Knighthood.**

Temple, *Earl. See* **Grenville, R.**

Temple, Anthony. The written word the only rule of Chr. faith; three discourses. 2d ed. Newcastle upon Tyne, 1772. 8°. (B 1346)

Temple, Daniel. Sermon, Boston, Dec. 16, just before his departure as a missionary to Western Asia. Boston, 1821. 8°. (B 278, 301, 1353)

Temple, Ebenezer, *Funeral sermon on, and address.* 1841. *See* **Fletcher, A.**

Temple, Edmond. Travels in Peru. London, 1830. 2 v. 8°.

Temple, Elizabeth, *Lady, Funeral sermon on.* 1809. *See* **Gardiner, J. S. J.**

Temple, Frederick, *D.D.* Education of the world. (*In* **Essays** and reviews. 1860.)

— National education. (*In* **Oxford** essays, 1856.)

— Sermons in Rugby School Chapel, 1858-60. New ed. London, 1870. 16°.

Temple, *Sir* Grenville Temple. Excursions in the Mediterranean: Algiers and Tunis. London, 1835. 2 v. 12°.

— Excursions in the Mediterranean: Greece and Turkey. London, 1836. 2 v. 12°.

Temple, Henry John, 3*d Viscount Palmerston.* Selections from private journals of tours in France in 1815-18. London, 1871. 8°.

— Speech, May 19, on Lord Sandon's resolution [for the reduction of duties on foreign sugar]. London, 1841. 12°. (C 257)

— Speech on the treaty of Washington. London, 1843. 8°. (B 1187)

— CONINGHAM, W. Lord Palmerston and Prince Albert; with the 'Suppressed pamphlet', entitled 'Palmerston, what has he done'. London, 1854. 8°. (B 1534)

— LA GUÉRONNIÈRE, A. de. (*In his* Les hommes d'état de l'Angleterre. 1855.)

— MARTINEAU, H. (*In her* Biog. sketches. 1869.)

— MONTEITH, R. Reasons for demanding investigation into charges against Lord P. London, *reprinted* 1840. 8°. (B 1164, 1530)

— RITCHIE, J. E. (*In his* British senators. 1869.)

Temple, Isaac. Two sermons, Halifax, Apr. 16, death of George III. and accession of George IV. Halifax, 1820. 8°. (B 283)

Temple, Josiah Howard. Early ecclesiastical hist. of Whately; discourse, Jan. 7. Northampton, 1849. 8°.

Temple, Launcelot, *pseud.* Sketches. *See* **Armstrong, J.,** *M.D.*

Temple, Neville, *pseud. See* **Fane, J. C. H.**

Temple, Samuel. Concise introduction to practical arithmetic. 7th ed. Boston, 1813. 12°.

Temple, *Sir* Thomas. Apology for the coinage in **Mass.** (*In* **Mass. Hist.** Soc. Col., v. 7. 1801.)

Temple, *Sir* Wm. Works. London, 1740. 2 v. f°.

Contents. Vol. 1. Life and character of Sir W. Temple. — Observations upon United Provinces of the Netherlands. — Miscellanea. — Memoirs. 2. Letters. — Introduction to the Hist. of England.

— Mémoires, 1672-79; tr. de l'anglois. (*In* **Petitot, A.** Col. des mém., 2e sér., v. 64. 1828; — *and in* **Michaud** *and* **Poujoulat.** Nouv. col. des mém., v. 32. 1854.)

— Remarques sur l'estat des Provinces Unies des Pais-Bas, 1672; tr. de l'anglois. La Hague, 1674. 8°.
— COURTENAY, T. P. Memoirs of the life and correspondence of T. Lond., 1836. 2 v. 8°.
— NICERON, J. P. (*In his* Mém., v. 13. 1730.)
Temple, Wm. James. SWAN, W. H. (*In* **Higginson**, T. W. Harvard mem. biog., v. 2. 1866.)
Temple, *N. H.* BLOOD, H. A. History of Temple. Boston, 1860. 8°.
Temple. MIDDLE Temple; memoir of the Hall, [1562-1759]. (*In* **Weale**, J. Quarterly papers on archit., v. 2. 1844.)
Temple at Jerusalem. *See* **Jerusalem.**
Temple Bar. London, 1860–80. 60 v. 8°.
Temple beau; a comedy; by H. **Fielding.** (*In his* Works, v. 1. 1813.)
Temple Church. *See* **London. Temple Church** (p. 1778).
Temple de Gnide, Le; par C. de S. de **Montesquieu.** (*In his* Œuvres, v. 7. 1799.)
Temple de la gloire, Le; opéra. *See* **Voltaire, F. M. A.** de.
Temple de mémoire; en un acte. *See* **Le Sage, A. R.**
Temple du destin, Le; en un acte. *See* **Le Sage, A. R.**
Temple family, *Amer.* WHITMORE, W. H. Account of the Temple family; with pedigree of family of Bowdoin. Boston, 1855. 8°.
Temple family, *Eng.* HANNAY, J. (*In his* Three hundred years. 1867.)
Temple of nature; a poem. *See* **Darwin, E.**
Templeman, Peter, *M.D.* Antiquities of Egypt. (*In* **Norden**, F. L. Travels in Egypt. 1757.)
Templer, John, *D.D.* Idea theologiæ Leviathanis. Londini, 1673. 8°.
Temples. ADAMS, W. H. D. Temples, tombs, and monuments of ancient Greece and Rome. Boston, 1871. 8°.
— MONTANO, G. B. [Scelta di varii tempietti antiche: date in luce da G. B. Soria. Roma, 1624.] f°.
— OWEN, J. History of the consecration of altars, temples, and churches. *t.p.w.* [1706.] 4°. (B 95)
— PIRANESI, G. B. *and* F. Raccolta de tempj antichi. Parigi, 1836. 2 v. f°. (v. 3.)
See also **Athens.** *Art*; — **Greece.** *Architecture*; — **India.** *Architecture*; — **Pæstum**; — **Rome.** *Architecture* (p. 2546); — **Rome.** *Description* (p. 2548); — *also* **Ellora** (*and add. a ref. to v. 2 of the* **Royal Asiatic Soc.** Trans.).
Templeton, *Mass.* **1st Congregational Church.** ADAMS, E. G. Hist. disc. in commem. of the 100th anniversary. Boston, 1857. 8°.
Templi carmina; Bridgewater collection of sacred music. 15th ed. Boston, 1825. obl. 8°.
Tempsky, Gustav Ferdinand. Mitla; a journey in Mexico, Guatemala, *etc.*, 1853–55; ed. by J. S. Bell. London, 1858. 8°.
Temptation. CÆSARIUS *Heisterbacensis.* De tentatione. [122–.] (*In his* Dial. mirac, v. 1. 1851.)
— OWEN, J. Temptation; nature and power of it. Oxford, 1658. 16°.
Temptation and atonement; by C. G. Gore. Boston, 1847. 8°.
— *Same.* (*In* **Littell's** living age, v. 11. 1846.)
Ten Eyck, Philip. Observations on the eclipse of the sun, July 28, 1851. (*In* **Amer. Assoc.** Proc., v. 6. 1852.)
Ten Have, Nicolas. Transisalania provincia. *n.p.*, [16—]. (E 78, no. 63a)
Ten nights in a bar room; by W. W. Pratt. (*In* **Sargent**, E. Mod. stand. dr., v. 43.)
Ten Rhyne, Willem. *See* **Rhyne, W. ten.**
Ten thousand a year; [by S. Warren]. Phila., 1840. 6 v. 12°.
— *Same.* (*In* **Blackwood's** mag., v. 46–50. 1839–41.)
Ten times one is ten; the possible reformation, by [E. E. Hale]. Boston, 1871. 16°.
Note. From Old and new, v. 1. 1870.
Ten tribes of Israel. *See* **Jews.**
Ten years of imperialism in France. Edin., London, 1862. 8°.

Tena, Ludovic. Commentaria et disputationes in epistolam Pauli ad Hebraeos. Lond., 1661. f°.
Contents. **Tena, L.** Commentaria. — **Spanheim, F.** De authore epistolæ ad Hebræos. — **Catharinus, A.** Dissertatio de Epistola ad Hebræos. — **Schlegel, C.** Quæstiones de persona Melchisedeci. — **Guisard, H.** Vindiciæ Testamentariæ in IX ad Hebræos. — **Hopkinson, J.** Descriptio Paradisi. — **Helwich, C.** De libris Thargumicis, Thalmudicis, et Chaldaicis Bibliorum paraphrasibus adversus Judæos. — **More, A.** Ad quædam loca Novi Fœderis notæ nunc primum editæ. — Index.
Tenampua, *Honduras.* SQUIER, E. G. Ruins of T. *n.t.p.* [1853.] 8°. (B 1601)
Tenant of Wildfell Hall; by A. **Brontë.** N. Y., 1857. 12°.
Tenant right. FANE, C. Tenant right; its necessity as a means of promoting good farming. From the Law review, v. 9. [London, 1849.] 8°. (B 1531)
Tenants of Malory; by J. S. Le Fanu. (*In* **Dublin** univ. mag., v. 69–70. 1867; — *and in* **Littell's** living age, v. 94–95. 1867–68.)
Tenby. LEWES, G. H. Sea-side studies at Tenby. Edin., London, 1858. 8°.
Tench, *Gen.* Watkin. REDDING, C. (*In his* Personal reminiscences, v. 3. 1867.)
Tencin, *Mme.* Claudine Alexandrine Guérin de. Mémoires du comte de Comminges. — Le siége de Calais; nouv. hist. — Les malheurs de l'amour. (*In* **La Fayette**, M. M. P. de la V., *comtesse* de. Œuvres, v. 3. 1820.) — Anecdotes de la cour et du règne d'Edouard II., roi d'Angleterre. — Lettres de Mme. de Tencin à M. de Richelieu. — Extrait d'une lettre de Mme. de Tencin à M. de Fontenelle. (*In* v. 4.)
— Les malheurs de l'amour. — Histoire d'Eugénie. (*In* **Biblioth.** univ. des romans, Nouv., v. 1. 1798.)
— KAVANAGH, J. (*In her* French women of letters, v. 1. 1862.)
— MUSSET, P. de. (*In his* Femme de la Régence. 1858.)
Tender husband. *See* **Steele**, *Sir* **R.**
Tender, Legal. *See* **Legal tender.**
Tenébreuse affaire, Une; par H. de Balzac. Paris, 1865. 16°.
Tenedos. Island of. LACROIX, P. L. Histoire et description. (*In his* Iles de la Grèce. 1853. Univers.)
Teneriffe. SMYTH, C. P. An astronomer's experiment; illustrated with photo-stereographs. London, 1858. 8°.
— ZURCHER, F., *and* MARGOLLÉ, E. (*In their* Les ascension célèbres. 1867. Bibl. des merv.)
Tengborg, Jona C. Hortus culinaris. (*In* **Linné**, C. Amœn. acad., v. 7. 1769.)
Tenhove, Nicholas. Memoirs of the House of Medici; [tr.] with notes and obs. by R. Clayton. Bath, 1797. 2 v. 4°.
Teniers, David. MICHIELS, A. (*In* **Gazette** des beaux-arts, v. 27. 1869.)
Teniers family. MICHIELS, A. (*In his* Hist. de la peinture flamande, v. 7, 8. 1869.)
Tenison. *See also* **Tennyson.**
Tenison, Thomas, *Abp. of Canterbury.* Argument for union. London, 1683. 4°. (B 1396)
— Last will and testament. London, 1716. 8°. (B 100)
Tenivelli, Carlo. AMATO, G. d'. (*In his* Panteon, v. 2. 1851.)
Tennant. *See also* **Tennent.**
Tennant, Charles. Letter to Sir G. Murray, on systematic colonization. London, 1830. 8°. (B 935)
— Letters to N. W. Senior conc. systematic colonization. London, 1831. 8°. (B 933)
Tennant, James. Gems and precious stones. (*In* **Soc. of Arts.** Lectures. 1851, 52.)
Tennant, James Francis, *Maj.* Report on the total eclipse of the sun, Aug. 17–18, 1868. (Vol. 37, pt. 1 *of* **Roy. Astron. Soc.** Mem. 1869.)
Tennant, Wm. Thane of Fife. Phila., 1822. 12°.
Tennemann, Wilhelm Gottlieb. Geschichte der Philosophie. Leipzig, 1798–1814. 9 v. in 10 pts. 8°.
— Grundriss der Geschichte der Philosophe *in Eng.* Manual of the history of philosophy; tr. by A. Johnson. Oxford, 1832. 8°.
— *Same.* Enl. by Morell. Lond., *Bohn*, 1852. 8°.
— *French.* Manuel de l'histoire de la philosophie; tr. par V. Cousin. Paris, 1829. 2 v. 8°.

— Lehren und Meinungen der Sokratiker über Unsterblichkeit. Jena, 1791. 12°.
— Life of Plato. (*In* **Edwards**, B. B., *and* **Park**, E. A. Selections. 1839.)
— HAMILTON, *Sir* W. Johnson's translation of Tennemann's Manual. (*In his* Discussions. 1852.)
Tennnet, G. R. The jury system. (*In* **Nat. Assoc. Prom. Soc. Sci.** Trans., 1867.)
Tennent. *See also* **Tennant.**
Tennent, *Rev.* Gilbert. The danger of an unconverted ministry; sermon. Boston, 1742. 4°. (B 45)
— The espousals; a sermon. Boston, 1741. 8°. (C 5)
— The 'Examiner' examined; with some remarks upon the querist's third part. [Phila., 1743.] 8°. (D 4)
— Late assoc. for defence encouraged, *etc.*; sermon, Phila., Dec. 24, 1747. Phila., [1748]. 8°. (B 862)
— Remarks on a protestation to the synod of Philadelphia, June 1. Phila., 1741. 8°. (C 59)
— The righteousness of the scribes and Pharisees. Boston, 1741. 8°. (B 63)
— HANCOCK, J. The examiner; or, Gilbert against Tennent; confutation of Tennent and his adherents, with strictures on the preface to [his] Five sermons. Boston, 1743. 8°. (C 43)
Tennent, *Sir* James Emerson. Ceylon; an account of the island. London, 1859. 2 v. 8°.
— History of modern Greece from B.C. 146. London, 1830. 2 v. 8°.
— Letters from the Ægean. London, 1829. 2 v. 12°.
— Sketches of the natural history of Ceylon. London, 1861. 16°.
— Social economy. (*In* **Nat. Assoc. Prom. Soc. Sci.** Trans., 1860.)
— Story of the guns. London, 1864. 8°.
— *and others.* A picture of Greece in 1825; with sketches of the principal military, *etc.*, chiefs. N. Y., 1826. 2 v. 12°.
— ANOTHER story of the guns; or, Sir J. E. T. and the Whitworth gun; by the Fraser reviewer. London, Camb., 1864. 8°.
— PALMA, *Conte* A. Greece vindicated; critical remarks on works recently published. London, 1826. 8°.
Tennent, *Rev.* Wm., *d. Apr.* 1777. FIELD, R. S. Review of the trial of T. (*In* **New Jersey Hist. Soc.** Proc., v. 6. 1853.)
Tennent, *Rev.* Wm., *d. Aug.* 1777. Speech, Jan. 11, 1777. (*In* **Ramsay**, D. History of the Independent Ch. in Charleston. 1815.)
Tennent, *Rev.* Wm. Mackay. Sermon; love of money. (*In* **Austin**, D. Amer. preacher, v. 3. 1791.)
Tenner, Adolf, *M.D.* Nature and origin of epileptiform convulsions. *See* **Kussmaul**, A.
Tennessean, The; by A. Royall. New Haven, 1827. 12°.

Tennessee.
— *Bank.* *See* **Bank of Tennessee** (p. 199).
— *Courts.* CROSS, N. D. Schedule of the courts of Tennessee. Nashville, 1860. 16°. (C 277)
— *Legislature.* Remonstrance and petition [to the U. S. conc. the Cherokee boundary. Phila.,] 1797. 8°. (U. S. 5th Cong. 2d sess. B 495)
— *State Geologist.* Geological reconnoissance of Tenn.; 1st biennial report to the 31st Gen. Assembly, Dec. 1855. Nashville, 1856. 8°.
— - 2d biennial report. Nashville, 1857. 8°.
— *State Library.* Catalogue. Nashville, 1855. 8°.

Antiquities.

— TROOST, G. Account of ancient remains in Tennessee. (*In* **Amer. Ethnological Soc.** Trans., v. 1. 1845.)
See also, next column, Natural history.

Description.

— SHORT descr. of the Tennessee gov., or the territory of the U. S. south of the Ohio. Phila., 1793. 8°. (B 420)
— *Same.* [With] the Constitution. Phila., 1796. 12°. (C 61)
— BRENTS, J. A. Patriots and guerillas of East T. and Kentucky. N. Y., 1863. 12°.
— GILMORE, J. R. Down in T. and back by way of Richmond. N. Y., 1864. 12°.
— BOKUM, H. Tennessee handbook and immigrant's guide. Phila., 1868. 12°.

Geology.

— SAFFORD, J. M. Geological map of T. [185—.] 1 sheet.
— TROOST, G. List of the fossil crinoids of Tennessee. (*In* **Amer. Assoc.** Proc., v. 2. 1850.) — HALL, J. Comparison of the geological features of Tennessee and New York. (*In* v. 6. 1852.)
See also Natural history, below.

History.

— HAYWOOD, J. Civil and political history of T., [1606]-1796. Knoxville, 1823. 8°.
— PUTNAM, A. W. History of Middle T., [1742-1814]. Nashville, 1859. 8°.
— NOTICE of the first settlements, [1768-83]. (*In* **Mass. Hist. Soc.** Col., v. 17. 1818.)
— RAMSEY, J. G. M. Annals of T., [1769-1800]. Charleston, 1853. 8°.
— STEVENSON, C. S. Report of exped. into East Tennessee, [1863]. (*In* **Holmes**, T. H. Report. 1864.)
— WILLIAMS, J. S. Report of operations in East T., Sept. 27 - Oct. 15, 1863. Richmond, 1864. 8°.
— MISCELLANEOUS newspapers; Sept. 1865 - June 1866. *n.p.*, 1865-66. 2 v. f°.
See also **Murfreesboro**; — **Nashville University**; — **Paris**, *Tenn.*; — **Pillow, Fort.**

Natural history.

— HAYWOOD, J. Natural aboriginal hist. of T., to 1768. Nashville, 1823. 8°.
Tennessee Evangelical Lutheran Church. *See* **Evangelical Lutheran Church**, *Tenn.*
Tennessee. Prot. Episc. Church. *See* **Prot. Episc. Church, Diocese of Tenn.**
Tennessee River. BEENE, J., *and others.* Memorial to the legislature of Alabama on connecting the Tenn. and Alabama rivers; with the act. Cahawba, 1824. 8°. (B 1108, 1605)
Tenney, Caleb Jewett. New England distinguished; discourse, Wethersfield, Nov. 29, 1827, thanksgiving. Wethersfield, 1828. 8°. (B 1145)
Tenney, Edward Payson. Jubilee essays; a plea for the unselfish life. Boston, 1862. 12°.
Contents. The constitution of nature. — Covetousness. — The retributions. — The luxurious life. — God comes to the rescue. — Covetousness in the church. — Luxurious life in the church. — Church discipline. — Constitution of the church. — Doing business for God. — The rewards. — The coming fifty years. — The argument. — What Baxter says about it.
Tenney, Horace Addison. Early times in Wisconsin. (*In* **Wisconsin Hist. Soc.** Col., v. 1. 1855.)
Tenney, Samuel, *M.D.* Account of a number of medicinal springs at Saratoga, N. Y. — Observations on prismatick colors. (*In* **Amer. Acad. of Arts and Sci.** Mem., v. 2.) — Account of an earthquake in New Eng. (*In* v. 3. 1809.)
— Letter on the dark day, May 19, 1780. (*In* **Mass. Hist. Soc.** Col., v. 1. 1792.) — Topog. descript. of Exeter, N. H. (*In* v. 4. 1795.)
Tenney, Sanborn. Manual of zoölogy. N. Y., 1865. 12°.
— *and* **Tenney**, A. A. Natural history of animals. N. Y., 1866. 12°.
Tenny, Erdix. Address before the Temperance Soc. in Lyme, July 4. Hanover, N. H., 1834. 8°. (B 1888)
— Self-denial; sermon before the Cong. Soc. in Lyme, N. H., June 23. Hanover, 1833. 8°. (B 1888)
Tennyson. *See also* **Tenison.**
Tennyson, Alfred. Enoch Arden. London, 1864. 12°.
Contents. Enoch Arden. — Aylmer's field. — Sea dreams. — The grandmother. — Northern farmer. — Tithonus. — The voyage. — In the Valley of Cauteritz. — The flower. — Requiescat. — The sailor boy. — The islet. — The ringlet. — A welcome to Alexandra. — A dedication. — Experiments.

— *Same.* Boston, 1864. 12°.
Contents. Same as above, with the add. of Ode sung at the opening of the Internat. Exhib. — Boädicea. — In quantity. — Specimen of a tr. of the Iliad in blank verse.

— The holy grail and other poems. Bost.,1870. 12°.
Contents. The coming of Arthur. — The holy grail. — Pelleas and Ettarre. — The passing of Arthur. — The northern farmer; new style. — The victim. — Wages. — The higher pantheism. — Flower in the crannied wall. — Lucretius. — The golden supper.

— Idyls of the King. Boston, 1860. 16°.
Contents. Enid. — Vivien. — Elaine. — Guinevere.

— In memoriam. Boston, 1860. 16°.

— The last tournament. Boston, 1871. 12°.

— Maud and other poems. Boston, 1855. 16°.
Contents. Maud. — The brook; an idyl. — The letters. — Ode on the death of the Duke of Wellington. — The daisy. — To the Rev. F. D. Maurice. — Will. — The charge of the light brigade.

— Poems. New ed. Boston, 1859. 2 v. 16°.

— The princess; a medley. Boston, 1848. 16°.

— Timbuctoo; poem which obtained the chancellor's medal, at Cambridge, 1829. (*In* **Cambridge Univ.** Prolusiones. 1829. **B 1236**)

— *and* Tennyson, C. Poems by two brothers. London, 1827. 8°.

— Austin, A. (*In his* Poetry of the period. 1870.)

— Bayne, P. Tennyson and his teachers. (*In his* Essays. 1871.)

— Brightwell, D. B. Concordance of the works of Tennyson. London, 1869. 8°.

— Brimley, G. A. Tennyson's poems. (*In his* **Essays.** 1860; — *and in* **Cambridge** essays, 1855.)

— Fischer, H. (*In* **Archiv** f. d. Stud. d. n. Sprachen, v. 15. 1854.) — Doellen, —. (*In* v. 17. 1855.)

— Dowden, E. Mr. Tennyson and Mr. Browning. (*In* **Afternoon** lectures, 5th ser. 1869.)

— Dudley, A. (*In* **Revue** d. D. Mondes, fév. 1856.) — Forgues, P. E. D. (*In* mai 1847.)

— Hallam, A. H. (*In his* Remains. 1862.)

— Horne, R. H. (*In his* New Spirit of the age, v. 2. 1844.)

— Ingram, J. K. Tennyson's works. (*In* **Afternoon** lectures, 4th ser. 1866.)

— Milsand, J. (*In* **Revue** d. D. Mondes, juil. 1851.) — Montégut, E. (*In* nov. 1859, mars 1866.)

— Shepherd, R. H. Tennysoniana; notes bibliog. and crit. London, 1866. 16°.

— Sterling, J. Tennyson's poems. (*In his* **Essays** and tales, v. 1. 1868.)

— Stirling, J. H. (*In his* Jerrold. 1868.)

— Tainsh, E. C. A study of the works of T. London, 1868. 16°.

— Wilson, J. Tennyson's poems. (*In his* **Essays**, v. 2. 1856.)

Tennyson, Charles. Poems. *See* **Tennyson, A.** Poems by two brothers.

Tennyson, Frederick. [Ægyptus;] carmen Græcum numismate annuo dignatum. 1828. (*In* **Cambridge Univ.** Prolusiones. 1828. **B 1236**)

Tennysoniana. *See, above,* **Shepherd, R. H.**

Tenon, Jacques. **Cuvier, G. L. C. F. D.** (*In his* **Eloges** hist., v. 2. 1819.)

Ténot, Pierre Paul Eugène. Paris en déc. 1851; étude hist. sur le coup d'état. 6e éd. Paris, 1868. 8°.

— *Eng.* Paris in December 1851; tr. by S. W. Adams and A. H. Brandon. N. Y., 1870. 8°.

— La Province en déc. 1851; étude hist. sur le coup d'état. 8e éd. Paris, 1868. 8°.

Tenotomy. **Richardson, S. B.,** *M.D.* Observations on T. Louisville, Ky., 1840. 8°. (**B 1186**)

Tension. **Tredgold, T.** Principles of tension. (*In* **Instit. of Civil Engin.** Trans., v. 1. 1842.)

Tent on the beach. *See* **Whittier, J. G.**

Tenterden, *Lord.* *See* **Abbott, C.**

Tents. Rhodes, G. Tents and tent life from the earliest ages to the present time. New ed.; with suppl. London, 1859. 8°.
See also **Camp.**

Tentzel (*Lat.* **Tentzelius**), Wilhelm Ernst. **Niceron, J. P.** (*In his* **Mém.**, v. 3. 1727; *and, Germ.*, v. 8. 1753.)

Tenure in capite. Madox, T. Baronia Anglica; an history of T. London, 1741. f°.

Teonge, Henry. Diary, 1675–79. Lond., 1825. 8°.

Teplitz. *See also* **Franzensbad.**

Tercero de su afrenta, El; comedia. *See* **Martinez de Meneses, A.**

Tercier, Jean Pierre. Mémoire sur l'origine de la dynastie des Sophis en Perse. (*In* **Sérieys, A.** Bibl. acad., v. 7. 1811.)

Térée; tragédie, par A. M. **Lemierre.** (*In his* **Œuvres,** v. 1. 1810.)

Terence. *See* **Terentius Afer, P.**

Terentianus *Maurus.* De literis, syllabis, pedibus, et metris; N. Brissæo Montiuillario commentatore et emendatore. Paris, 1531. 8°.

— Dawes, R. Emendationes selectæ in Terentianum Maurum. (*In his* Misc. crit. 1800.)

Terentius Afer, Publius. Terentius; cum commentariis Donato, Guidone, Ascensio, *etc. t.p.w.* [Colophon:] Argent., *J. Grüninger*, 1499. f°.

— *Same.* [Cum argumentis P. Melanchthonis, notis Donati, Calphurnii, *etc.*] Venetiis, *ap. H. Scotum*, 1545. f°.

— Comédies; tr. en franç. avec le latin à costé, [par *Le Maistre de Sacy*]. Paris, 1647. 12°.
Contents. L'Andrienne. — Les Adelphes. — Le Phormion.

— *Same, by the same editor.* 9e éd. Paris, 1682. 16°.

— *Same.* Nouvellement trad., avec le latin à costé, par M. de *Martignac.* Paris, 1686. 16°.
Contents. L'eunuque. — Le fâcheux à soi-mesme. — L'hecyre.

— Comœdiæ; com. perpet. illust.; acc. interpr. vet. Donatus, Eugraphius, Calphurnius, cur. A. H. *Westerhovius.* Hagæ Com., 1726. 2 v. 4°.
Contents. Vol. 1. Præfatio, *etc.* — Terentii vita. — D. Heinsii diss. ad Horatii de Plauto et Terentio judicium. — Variorum de comœdia, de fabularum, theatrorum, scenarum, ac scenicorum antiqua consuetudine. — Andria. — Eunuchus. — Heautontimoroumenos. — Adelphi. 2. Hecyra. — Phormio. — Eugraphii comm. — Lindenbruchii obs. — Indices.

— *Same.* Interp. et notis illust. N. *Camus*; in usum Delphini. Londini, 1758. 8°.

— *Same.* Ex rec. D. *Heinsii*; cum Ital. vers. [auctore N. Fortiguerra]; recens. notasque add. C. *Cocquelines.* Rome, 1767. 2 v. f°.
Contents. Vol. 1. Vita. — Andria. — Eunuchus. — Heautontimorumenos. 2. Adelphi. — Hecyra. — Phormio.

— *Same.* Ad fidem ed. *Westerhovianæ.* Londini, 1818. 12°.

— *Same.* Ex optimarum ed. textu recensitæ illust. N. E. *Lemaire.* Paris, 1827–28. 2 v. 8°. (Lemaire. Bibl. class. Lat.)
Contents. Vol. 1. Vita. — Andria. — Eunuchus. — Heautontimorumenos. 2. Adelphi. — Hecyra. — Phormio. — Exempla imitationis e comœdia quam Molière inscripsit Les fourberies de Scapin. — Index.

— *Same.* Ex recens. *Bentleii.* Nova ed. ster. Lipsiæ, 1829. 16°.

— *Same.* Rec. A. *Fleckeisen.* Lips., 1857. 16°.

— *Same.* With a commentary by E. St. J. *Parry.* London, 1857. 8°. (Long's Bibl. class.)

— *Same.* With notes by W. *Wagner.* Camb., 1869. 8°.

— *Eng.* Comedies; translated into blank verse by G. *Colman.* 2d ed. London, 1768. 2 v. 8°.
Contents. Vol. 1. Life of Terence. — The Andrian. — The eunuch. — The self-tormentor. 2. The brothers. — The step-mother. — Phormio. — The merchant.

— - *Same, by the same editor.* New ed. London, 1810. 8°.

— - *Same.* Tr. by H. T. *Riley*; added, trans. of Phædrus by C. Smart. Lond., *Bohn*, 1853. 8°.

— *French.* Comédies; trad. de *Le Monnier.* Paris, 1820. 3 v. 8°. (Levée and Le Monnier. Théâtre des Latins, v. 9-11.)

Contents. Vol. 1. L'Andrienne. — L'eunuque. 2. L'heautontimorumenos. — Les Adelphes. 3. L'hecyre. — Le Phormion.

— - *Same.* *See, above,* Comédies. 1647; 1682; 1686.

— *Ital.* Commedie; tr. da V. *Alfieri.* Italia, 1815. 2 v. 8°. (Alfieri. Opere, v. 18, 19.)

Contents. Vol. 1. L'Andria. — L'eunuco. — L'uspreggia se stesso. 2. Gli adelfi. — Formione. — L'ecira.

— - *Same.* Tr. da V. *Alfieri.* (*In his* Opere, v. 8. 1821.)

— Floures for Latine speakyng sel. oute of Terence and tr. into Eng. by N. Udall. *n.p.*, 1560. 8°.

— Andria Adelphique; ex ed. Westerhoviana cura C. K. *Dillaway.* Boston, 1839. 18°.

— Andria; notulis Anglicis illust. C. *Wallace.* Bostoniæ, 1830. 12°.

— *Ital.* Tradotta in toscano [da N. *Macchiavelli*]. (*In* **Macchiavelli, N.** Opere, v. 5. 1813.)

— MELANCHTHON, P. Enarratio comœdiarum. (*In his* Opera, v. 19. 1853.)

— RUHNKEN, D. In Terentii comœdias dictata; cura L. Schopeni. Bonnæ, 1825. 8°.

Terenzi, Luca. Sonetti. (*In* **Trucchi, F.** Poesie ital., v. 4. 1847.)

Terenzio, Il; commedia di carattere antico romano; da C. **Goldoni.** (*In his* Opere, v. 8. 1789.)

Terésa, *St.* (*originally* **Teresa Sanchez Cepeda Davila y Ahumada**). Escritos, añididos por V. de la Fuente. Madrid, 1861-62. 2 v. 8°. (Aribau. Bibl., v. 53, 55.)

Contents. Vol. 1. Preliminares. — Vida de Santa Teresa de Jesus. — Libro de las relaciones. — Libro de las fundaciones.— Libro de los constituciones. — A visos de Santa Teresa. — Modo de visitar los conventos de religiosas. — Camino de perfeccion. — Conceptos del amor de Dios. — Las Moradas. — Exclamaciones del alma á su Dios. — Escritos breves de Santa Teresa. — Escritos sueltos. — Obras atribuidas á Santa Teresa. — Documentos relativos á Santa Teresa y sus obras. 2. Preliminares. — Cartas de Santa Teresa de Jesus. — Apéndices.

— COLLET, P. La vie de S. Jean de La Croix confesseur de Sainte-Thérese. Turin, 1769. 12°.

Teresa, *of Portugal.* DISSERTAÇÃO historica-juridica sobre a ligitimidade de D. Teresa, mulher do conde D. Henrique, e mãi do rei Affonso Henriques. (*In* **Lisbon. Ac. d. Sci.** Mem. lit., v. 8. 1812.)

Térèsa; drame, par **A. Dumas.** (*In his* Théâtre, v. 2. 1863.)

Terhune, Mary Virginia (Hawes), *pseud.* **Marion Harland.** Beechdale. (*In* **Galaxy,** v. 5-6. 1868.)

— Miriam. N. Y., 1862. 12°.

— Sunnybank. N. Y., 1866. 12°.

Terino, —. Canzone. (*In* **Trucchi, F.** Poesie ital., v. 1. 1846.)

Terminus. BOZE, C. G. de. Du dieu Terme, son culte ches les Romains. (*In* **Sérieys, A.** Bibl. acad., v. 2. 1810.)

Ternaux, Louis Mortimer-. Histoire de la Terreur, 1792-94. (v. 1, 3, 3é ed., v. 2, 4, 5, 2e éd.) Paris, 1868, 63-69. 7 v. 8°.

— Le 20 juin 1792. Paris, 1863. 18°.

Ternaux-Compans, Henri. Archives des voyages. Paris, [1840-41]. 2 v. 8°.

Contents. Vol. 1. **Loarca,** M. de. Relation des Iles Philippines. 1583. — **Espinosa,** G. de. Rel. de l'expéd. dans l'Isthme de Panama. 1517. — **Roman,** J. B. Rel. de la Chine. 1584. — **Lettre** d'un capitaine de la garnison d'Oran, [1623?]. — **Barré,** N. Lettres sur la navigation du Chevalier de Villegaignon es Terres de l'Amérique oultre l'aequinoctial, jusque soubz le Tropique de Capricorne. — **Cartier,** J. Discours du voy. aux terres-neufues dites Nouvelle France. — **Relation** du voy. et prinse, faite par les galères de Malte, sous F. de Cremeaux; tr. d'ital. par Haberat. 1629. — **L'arrivée** et l'entrée publique de l'ambassadeur du roy du Jappon dans Rome, 2 nov. 1615. — **Histoire** de quatre pères capucins, cruellement tyrannisez et mis à mort par le grand baschal de Damas, *etc.* — **N.,** P. Nouvelle de la venue de la royne d'Algier à Rome, et du baptesme d'icelle, et [des autres] de sa compagnie, *etc.* — **Histoire** de la prise des vaisseaux de plusieurs corsaires et pirattes turcs, et sont prisonniers à Vallongue. — **Conversion** du roy des Indes orientales à la foy catholique, *etc.* — **Michel,** *roi des Jolphes.* Lettre au roy d'Espagne, sur sa conversion. — **Les plaintes** et justifications du Grand Turc au Roy sur tout ce qui s'est passé en Turquie entre les François et les Anglois, juil. 1620. — **Relation** du combat et prise de deux galions du roy de Thunis, oct. 1628, par les galères de Malte, commandées par Cremeaulx. — **Advis** moderne de l'estat et grand royaume de Mogor. — **Marque-d'Or,** *capt.* Furieuse bataille donnée entre les Portugais et les Hollandois. 1621. — **Extraict** des lettres d'un gentilhomme de la suitte de M. de Rambouillet, ambassadeur au royaume de Pologne, 1573. — **Lettre** escrite de Constantinople, cont. la trahison du bascha Nassouf, sa mort estrange, *etc.* — **La prise** de plusieurs vaisseaux de guerre, *etc.*, sur les Portugais, par la flotte hollandoise. — **Foucques,** *capt.* Mémoires présentés au roy, après estre delivré de la captivité des Turcs. 1612. — **Victoire** obtenue par des galères de France sur les corsaires du Turc. 1620. — **Gedouyn,** *consul d'Alep.* Lettre escrite de Belgrade le 26 jan. 1624, avec un récit des desordres, *etc.*, qui sont en l'Empire des Turcs. — **Jaque de los Rios de Mancaned,** C. de. Voy. aux Indes orientales et occidentales, [1599]. — **Récit** des événements de Mindanao, dans les Iles Philippines avant l'année 1734. — **Mastrili,** M. F. Lettre, dans laquelle il rend comte de la conquête de Mindanao. — **Emanuel,** *King of Portugal.* Lettre[sur] la conquête de Malaca, *etc.*, 1513. — **Récit** de la conquête de l'ile de Tercère et des autres îles Açores, faites par Alvai de Baçan, 1583. — **Discours** au vray de la conversion de la royne de Bandas par le moyen des pères religieux de l'Ordre des Carmes, *etc.* — **Relation** de la prinse de la Baya de todos los Santos, et de la ville de S.-Sauveur au Brésil, par la flotte hollandoise. 1624. — **Pacifique,** *le père de Provin.* Lettre sur l'estrange mort du Grand Turc, emp. de Konstantinople. — **Récit** de ce qui s'est passé entre les Hollandois et les Portuguais. 1616.

2. **Cartier,** J. Seconde navigation faicte au parachèvement de la descouverture des terres occidentales, *etc.* — **Knight,** F. Récit de sept années d'esclavage chez les Turcs d'Alger. — **Arsène,** *père capucin.* Dernière lettre au R. P. Provincial des Capucins de la province de Paris, 1612. — **Bartolotti,** J. Victoire des galères de Malte, obtenuë contre les corsaires turcs de Tripoly, 19 juil. 1634. — **Relation** des particularitez de la rebellion de Stenko-razin contre le grand Duc de Moscovie; tr. de l'anglois par C. Des Mares. — **Croyance** populaire à l'égard des escarboucles. — **Relation** de la Nouvelle France. — **Relation** de la reprise du Sénégal et de Gorée. — **Lettre** d'un religieux minime de la Martinique, datée du fort St.-Pierre le 6 mars 1695. — **Relation** de l'expédition de M. de Pointis contre Carthagène. — **Moriset,** P. Lettre écrite de Chandernagor, le 3 jan. 1697. — **Lettre** écrite de Jérusalem le 11 juin 1698, au sujet du rétablissement de l'église du Saint-Sépulcre. — **Lettre** datée du Grand Caire le 30 oct. 1697. — **Lavanha,** J. B. Naufrage du vaisseau le Saint-Albert. — **Pardo de Figueroa,** B. Mémoire présenté à Louis XIV, pour l'engager à entreprendre la conquête du Pérou. — **Sierra,** L. de. Rapport sur les richesses qui ont été tirées de la montagne de Potosi. 1784. — **Relation** de l'expéd. de la Tercère; tr. du ms. espagnol. — **Nouvelles** du pays de Brésil; tr. de l'allemand. — **Naufrage** sur la côte de Sumatra, commerce de cette île et de Bencoolen, par un voyageur hollandois. — **Relation** d'un voyage d'un Hollandois. — **Victoire** obtenue par les galions de Malte, sur les vaisseaux turcs de Thunis. — **L'entrée** solemnelle faicte à Rome aux ambassadeurs du roy de Perse, le 5 avril 1601. — **C.,** L. S. Lettre d'un gentilhomme de M. le baron de Cesi, touchant la prise de cinq galères turques, *etc.* — **Histoire** très-véritable de la cruauté exercée par les Tartares envers trois pères capucins et plusieurs chrestiens, *etc.* — **Discours** au vray de la deffaitte de quarante mille Arabes, par le sophy de Perse, 1607, *etc.* — **Séjour** des ambassadeurs moscovites à Paris. — **La grande** sédition arrivé depuis peu en la ville de Constantinople, touchant l'élection d'un nouveau empereur, *etc.* — **Claude,** *d'Abbeville.* Lettre d'un père capucin, estant de présent en l'Inde nouvelle appellée Maragnon. 1612. — **La déffaicte** de cinq cens hommes et de quatre vaisseaux de guerre, *etc.* — **Beaulaigue,** — de. Discours véritable de le prinse de l'Ango en l'Archipellago par les Chevalliers de Malte. — **La cruelle** mort soufferte par Bernardin Deguisiany. — **Relation** de la découverte des mines de Puno au Pérou. 1679. — **Relation** de la Nouvelle France. 1691. — **Histoire** véritable de ce qui s'est passé en Turquie, pour la délivrance et redemption des Chrestiens captifs depuis l'année 1600. — **Sebastian,** P. C.

Voyage dans la plus grande partie du monde, *etc.* — Morales, B. de. Dialogue des guerres d'Oran.

— Bibliothèque américaine; catalogue des ouvrages rel. à l'Amérique. Paris, 1837. 8°.

— Bibliothèque asiatique et africaine; catalogue des ouvrages rel. à l'Asie et à l'Afrique. Paris, 1841. 8°.

— Voyages, relations, et mémoires pour servir à l'hist. de la découverte de l'Amérique. Paris, 1837-41. 20 v. 8°.

Contents. Vol. 1. **Federmann,** *le jeune*, N. Narration du premier voy. de F. 2. **Magalhanes de Gandavo,** P. de. Hist. de Sancta-Cruz. 3. **Staden,** H. Hist. du pays nommé Amérique. 4. **Xérès,** F. Conquête du Pérou et du Cuzco. 5. **Schmidel,** H. Hist. d'un voy. fait dans l'Amér. 6. **Nuñez Cabeça de Vaca,** A. Commentaires. 7. **Nuñez Cabeça de Vaca,** A. Relation et naufrages. 8. **Ixtlilxochitl,** F. d'A. Cruautés des conquérants du Mexique. 9. **Castañeda de Nagera,** P. de. Relation du voyage de Cibola, 1540. 10. **Recueil** de pièces rel. à la conquête du Mexique. 11. **Zurita,** A. de. Rapport sur les classes de chefs de la Nouv.-Espagne. 12, 13. **Ixtlilxochitl,** F. d'A. Histoire des Chichimèques. 14. **Oviedo y Valdés,** G. H. de. Histoire du Nicaragua. 15. **Balboa,** M. C. Histoire du Pérou. 16. **Second** recueil de pièces sur le Mexique. 17. **Montesinos,** F. Mém. historiques sur l'ancien Pérou. 18, 19. **Velasco,** J. de. Histoire du Royaume de Quito. 20. **Recueil** de pièces sur la Floride.

Ternay, Charles Gabriel d'Arsac, *marq.* de. Traité de tactique; aug. par F. Koch. Nouv. éd. Brux., 1840. 8° *and* Atlas 4°.

Terni. MAP. Amst., [17—]. (E 60)

Ternite, Wilhelm. Wandgemälde aus Pompeji und Herculanum; mit e. erläuternden Text von Müller [und] Welcker. Berl., [1839-60?]. f°.

Terpander. Fragm. (*In* **Bergk,** T. Poetæ lyr. Gr. 1853.)

Terra-cotta. COMBE, T. Description of the terra-cottas in the Brit. Museum. Lond., 1810. 4°.

— GRUNER, L. The terra-cotta architecture of North Italy, 12th-15th cent., from drawings and restorations by F. Lose; engraved, *etc.*, with descriptive text by V. Ottolini and F. Lose. London, 1867. 4°.

Terra del Fuego. COUTO, D. do. Naufragio da nao S. Thomè na Terra dos Fumos, 1589. (*In* **Gomes de Brito,** B. Hist. trag. marit., v. 2. 1736.)

— WEDDELL, J. Visit to T., 1824. (*In his* Voyage towards the South Pole. 1825.)

— FERRARIO, G. Descrizione de la T. del F. (*In his* Costume ant. e mod., v. 17. 1829.)

— LACROIX, F. Patagonie, Terre du Feu, et Archipel des Malouines. (*In* **Famin,** C. Chili, *etc.* 1840.)

— SNOW, W. P. A two years' cruise off Terra del Fuego, [1855-57]. London, 1857. 2 v. 8°.

— *Map.* TABULA Magellenica qua Tierræ del Fuego descriptio. *n.p.*, [16—]. (E 78, no. 324)

See also **Magellan, Strait of;** — **Patagonia;** — *also* **Voyages round the world.**

Terra Firma. ANDAGOYA, P. de. Narrative of the proceedings of P. Davila in Tierra Firme or Castilla del Oro, *etc.*, [1514-36]. London, 1865. 8°. (Hakluyt Soc., v. 34.)

— PELLEPRAT, P. Relation des missions de la Comp. de Jésus dans la Terre Ferme de l'Amérique Méridionale, [1651-55]; avec une introd. à la langue des Galibis. Paris, 1655. 8°.

— — *Same.* (*In* **Voyages** et travaux des missionnaires de la Compagnie de Jésus, v. 1. 1857.)

Terraces. AGASSIZ, L. Terraces and ancient river bars, *etc.*, of Lake Superior. (*In* **Amer. Assoc.** Proc., v. 1. 1849.) — HITCHCOCK, E. River terraces of the Connecticut Valley, *etc.* (*In* v. 2. 1850.) — Terraces and sea beaches formed since the drift period. (*In* v. 6. 1852.)

Terracina, Laura. Sonetto. — Ode. — Per l'Italia. (*In* **Poeti** ital. contemp. 1843.)

Terræ-Filius. *See* **Amhurst,** N.

Terrai, Joseph Marie, *l'abbé.* *See* **Terray,** J. M.

Terras, J. P. Traité practique de la maladie vénérienne. Paris, 1810. 8°.

Terrasson, Jean, *l'abbé.* Life of Sethos; [tr.] by T. Lediard. London, 1732. 2 v. 8°.

— ALEMBERT, J. le R. d'. (*In his* Œuvres, v. 6. 1805.)

Terray, Joseph Marie, *l'abbé.* Compte rendu au roi. *n.t.p.* [1773?] 12°. (C 165)

— COQUEREAU, J. B. L. Mémoires de T. London, 1776. 12°.

Terrible tractorations by C. Caustic. *See* **Fessenden,** T. G.

Terrick, Richard, *Bp. of Peterborough.* Sermon before the Ho. of Lords, Jan. 30. London, 1758. 4°. (B 1466)

— Sermon before the Soc. for the Prop. of the Gospel in For. Parts; in the parish church of St. Mary-le-Bow, Feb. 17. London, 1764. 8°. (B 333)

— Sermon, Dec. 18, general fast on occasion of the rebellion. London, 1745. 4°. (B 1256)

Terrick, Samuel. Sermon, June 27, 1706, thanksgiving for victory over the French in Brabant. York, [1706]. 4°. (B 1251)

Terrier, Thomas. Dziesięć lat życia kobiety. 1837. *See* **Scribe,** A. E.

Territories. MANN, H. Speech on the right of Congress to legislate for the territories, June 30. Wash., 1848. 8°. (B 1477, 1700)

Terror, The reign of. *See* **France.** *Hist.* (*Rev.*) p. 1044-47.

Terrot, Charles Hughes, *Bp.*, *and* **Drummond,** D. T. K. Correspondence. Edin., 1842. 8°. (B 1720)

Terry, Adrian R. Travels in the equatorial regions of South America, 1832. Hartford, 1834. 12°.

Terry, Charles. New Zealand, its advantages and prospects as a British colony; with a full acc. of the land claims, sales of crown lands, *etc.* London, 1842. 8°.

— Financial condition of New Zealand. (*In* **Chapman,** H. S. The New Zealand portfolio. 1843.)

Terry, Daniel. Guy Mannering. (*In* **Sargent,** E. Mod. stand. dr., v. 10.)

Terry, Edward. Relation of a voy. to India in 1616. (*In* Kerr, R. Col. of voy., v. 9. 1824.)

Terson, —. Lettre sur le Polybe de Folard. (*In* **Polybius.** Histoire, v. 7. 1774.)

Terson, —. Un St-Simonien au peuple de Lyon, à l'occasion des événemens d'avril 1834. Lyon, 1834. 8°. (B 1660)

Tertre, Jean Baptiste du. *See* **Du Tertre,** J. B.

Tertulias de Madrid, Las, ó El por que de las tertulias; por R. de la **Cruz y Cano.** (*In his* Teatro, v. 8. 1789.)

Tertullianus, Quintus Septimius Florens. Opera, N. Rigaltii notis illustrata. Lutetiæ, 1634. f°.

Contents. Apologeticus. — Ad nationes. — De testimonio animæ. — Ad Scapulam. — De spectaculis. — De idololatria. — De corona. — De pallio. — De pœnitentia. — De oratione. — Ad martyras. — De patientia. — De cultu feminarum. — Ad uxorem. — De virginibus velandis. — Adversus Judæos. — De præscriptione hæreticorum. — De baptismo. — Adversus Hermogenem. — Adversus Valentinianos. — De anima. — De carne Christi. — De resurrectione carnis. — Adversus Marcionem. — Scopiace. — Adversus Praxeam. — De exhortatione castitatis. — De monogamia. — De fuga in persecutione. — De jejuniis. — De pudicitia. — Index Sacrarum Scripturarum. — Incerti auctoris versus. — Adversus Marcionem. — De judicio Domini. — Genesis. — Sodoma. — Index rerum. — Index scriptorum veterum. — N. Rigaltii Observationes et notæ. — Index glossarum stili Africani.

— Opera; curante E. F. Leopold. Lps., 1839-41. 4 v. 16°. (Gersdorf, E. G. Biblioth. patrum, v. 4-7.)

Contents. Vol. 1. Libri apologetici. 2. Libri ad ritus et mores Christianorum pertinentes. 3, 4. Libri polemici et dogmatici.

— *Eng.* Writings; tr. by S. Thelwall and P. Holmes. Edin., 1869-70. 3 v. 8°. (Roberts. Ante-Nicene lib., v. 11, 15, 18.)

Contents. Vol. 1. To the martyrs. — On the spectacles. — On the testimony of the soul. — To Scapula. — Apology. — On idolatry. — On prayer. — Of patience. — On baptism. — On repentance. — To his wife. — On female dress. — On the soldier's chaplet. — On flight in persecution. — The antidote to the scorpion's bite. — To the nation. 2. De præscriptione hæreticorum. — Adversus Hermogenem. — Adversus Valentinianos. — De carne Christi. — De resurrectione carnis. — Adversus Praxean. — De anima. 3. Introduction. — Exhortation to chastity. — Monogamy. — Modesty. — Fasting. — Veiling of virgins. — The ascetics' mantle. — — Answer to the Jews. — Against all heresies. —

Fragment concerning the cursing of the heathen's gods. — A strain of Jonah the prophet. — A strain of Sodom. — Genesis. — A strain of the judgment of the Lord. — Five books in reply to Marcion. — Fragment of an epistle of Dionysius, against the Sabellians. — Fragment on the creation of the world, by Victorinus. — Commentary on the Apocalypse of John, by St. Victorinus. — Instructions of Commodianus in favour of Christian discipline, against the gods of the heathens. — Indices.

— The five books against Marcion; tr. by P. Holmes. Edin., 1868. 8°. (Roberts, A. Ante-Nicene lib., v. 7.)

— De præscriptionibus; Uebersetzung. (*In* **Lessing, G. E.** Sämmtl. Schriften, v. 17. 1793.)

— The rule of faith. (*In* **Tracts** for the times, v. 1. 1840.) — Baptism. (*In* v. 2. 1840.)

— Böhringer, F. (*In his* Die Kirche Christi, v. 1, Abth. 1. 1842.)

— Neander, J. A. W. Antignostikus; or, The spirit of Tertullian. (*In his* Hist. of the planting of the Christian Ch., v. 2. 1851.)

Terzi, Franz. Andresen, A. (*In his* Der deutsche Peintre-Graveur, v. 2. 1865.)

Tesauro, Emmanuel. Patriarchæ, sive Christi servatoris genealogia; acc. Cæsarum elogia. London, 1657. 8°.

Teschemacher, James E. Address at annual meeting of the Boston Nat. Hist. Soc., May 5. Boston, 1841. 8°. (B 1583)

— Concise application of structural botany to horticulture. Boston, 1840. 12°.

— Description of the oxide of tin found at the tourmaline locality, Chesterfield, Mass. (*In* **Assoc. of Amer. Geol.** Reports, 1843.)

Teseide, La; da **G. Boccaccio**. (*In his* Opere, v. 9. 1731.)

Tesoretto, Il. *See* **Latini, B.**

Tesoro, Emmanuel. *See* **Tesauro, E.**

Tesoro de historiadores españoles. *See* **Ochoa, E. de.**

Tesoro de los poemas españoles. *See* **Ochoa, E. de.**

Tesoro de los prosadores españoles. *See* **Ochoa, E. de.**

Tesoro de los romanceros españoles. *See* **Ochoa, E. de.**

Tesoro del teatro españoia. *See* **Ochoa, E. de.**

Tesoro español. *See* **Josse, A. L.**

Tessier, Alexandre Henri, *l'abbé*. Complete treatise on merinos and other sheep; tr. from the Fr. N. Y., 1811. 8°.

— Instructions sur la manière de cultiver la betterave; et 'Sur les procédés à suivre pour l'extraction du sucre', par Deyeux. Paris, 1811. 8°. (B 528)

— *and others*. Agriculture. Paris, 1787–1821. 7 v. 4°. (Encyc. méthod., v. 1–7.)

Note. Vol. 1, par Tessier, Thouin, et Fougeroux de Bondaroy; 2–4, par Tessier et Thouin; 5–7, par Tessier, Thouin, et Bosc; 7, Dictionnaire de la culture des arbres et de l'aménagement des forêts, par Bosc et Baudrillard.

See also **Annales** de l'agriculture françoise.

Tessillo, Santiago de. Guerra de Chile, causas de su duracion, medios para su fin, exemplificado en el govierno de Don F. Lasso de la Vega. Madrid, 1647. 8°.

Test laws.

Note. In the following works * added to the title means that the works are in favor of the test laws.

— Cooper, A. A., *Earl of Shaftesbury*. Letter from a person of quality to his friend in the country. [London,] 1675. 4°. (B 1921)

— Discourse for taking off the tests and penal laws about religion. London, 1687. 4°. (B 91)

— Penn, W. Good advice to the Church of Eng., Roman Catholic, and Protestant Dissenter. Lond., 1687. 4°. (B 91)

— — *Same*. (*In his* Select works, v. 4. 1782.)

— Public documents declaratory of the principles of the Protestant Dissenters, [1688-1727]; and proving that the repeal of the corporation and test-acts was desired by William III., *etc.* Birmingham, London, 1790. 8°. (B 126)

— Answer to the Bp. of Oxford's reasons for abrogating the test. London, 1688. 4°. * (B 92)

— Seven papers. London, 1689. 4°. (B 8)

— Removal of the sacramental test considered. London, [17—]. 8°. (B 94)

— Review of our present tests and subscriptions. London, [17—]. 8°. (B 122)

— Sherlock, T. Arguments against a repeal of the corporation and test acts. [171–.] (*In* **Churchman** armed, v. 1. 1814.)

— Gray, J. Reasons for abrogating the corporation and test acts; [against] Sherlock. London, 1718. 8°. (B 1378)

— Hoadly, B., *Bp.* Dr. Sherlock's 'Vindication of the test act' examined, and the false foundations exposed; in answer to so much of his book against the Bp. of Bangor, as rel. to the Protestant Dissenters. London, 1718. 8°. (B 103)

— Sherlock, T. Vindication of the corporation and test acts; in answer to the Bishop of Bangor's reasons for the repeal of them; [with] a 2d part conc. the religion of oaths. London, 1718. 8°. * (B 103)

Note. For the subsequent tracts in this controversy *see* **Sherlock, T.**

— Some considerations offer'd touching the administration of the lord's supper as directed by the test act. [1726.] 2d ed. London, 1733. 8°. (B 122)

— Answer to some queries in 'Reasons against pushing for the repeal of the corporation and test acts'. London, 1732. 8°. (B 122)

— Chandler, J. Reflections upon the corporation and test-acts as they relate to the Protestant Dissenters. London, 1732. 8°. (B 1378)

— Danger, The, of a rash application for the repeal of the corporation and test acts. London, 1732. 8°. (B 122)

— Gibson, E. The dispute adjusted about the proper time of applying for a repeal of the corporation and test-acts. London, 1732. 8°. * (B 122)

— Hoadly, B. True churchman's reasons for repealing the corporation and test laws. 1732. (*In* **Baron, R.** Pillars of priestcraft, *etc.*, v. 3. 1768.)

— Humble representation to the gentlemen who met in Silver St., Nov. 29; by a citizen of London. London, 1732. 8°. (B 122)

— Letter to S. Holden [on] his speech, Nov. 29. London, 1732. 8°. * (B 122)

— Swift, J. The advantages proposed by repealing the sacramental test impartially considered; added, remarks on a pamphlet entitled 'The nature and consequences of the sacramental test considered'. Dublin, London, *reprinted* 1732. 8°. * (B 122)

— Address to the gentlemen, deputed from the several congregations of Protestant Dissenters, to attend the report of the comm. [on] the repeal of the corporation and test acts. London, 1733. 8°. (B 122, 135)

— Animadversions on a paper, 'An answer to some queries'. London, 1733. 8°. (C 272)

— Barrington, J. Reflexions on the 12th query in a paper entitled 'Reasons against pushing for the repeal of the corporation and test acts'. London, 1733. 8°. * (B 122)

— Church, The, in perils among false brethren. London, 1733. 8°. (B 122)

— Harris, W. Remarks on the history of the test act. London, 1733. 8°. (B 122)

— Neal, D. Letter from a Dissenter to the author of 'The Craftsman'. London, 1733. 8°. (B 122)

— Narrative of the proc. of the Protestant Dissenters of the three denominations rel. to the repeals of the corporation and test-acts. London, 1734. 8°. (B 122)

— Ellis, A. Plea for the sacramental tests. London, 1736. 4°. *

— Harris, W. Short remarks upon [Ellys'] 'Plea for the sacramental test'. London, 1736. 8°. (B 123)

— Warburton, W. Necessity of a test law demonstrated. [1736.] (*In his* Works, v. 7. 1811; — *and in* **Churchman** armed, v. 1. 1814.) *

— Case of the Dissenters, as it stands upon the corporation and toleration acts. London, 1739. 8°. (B 122)

— Fleming, C. Delays dangerous; no tomorrow for the repeal of the test and corporation acts. London, 1739. 8°. (B 122)

— Philochristus, *pseud.* Letter to S. Chandler [upon] his 'Case of subscription to articles of faith'. London, 1748. 8°. (B 1378)

— Palmer, J. Free thoughts on the inconsistency of conforming to any religious test as a condition of toleration. London, 1779. 8°.

— — *Another copy.* (B 238)

— Horsley, S., *Bp.* Review of the case of the Protestant Dissenters with ref. to the corporation and test acts. [1786.] (*In* **Churchman** armed, v. 1. 1814.) *

— Beaufoy, H. Substance of [his] speech, Mar. 28, on the repeal of the test and corporation acts. London, 1787. 8°. (B 127)

— Berington, J. Address to the Protestant Dissenters who have petitioned for a repeal of the corporation and test acts. London, 1787. 8°. (B 126)

— DEBATE on the repeal of the test and corporation act, in the Ho. of Commons, Mar. London, 1787. 8°. (B 127)
— RIGHT of Protestant Dissenters to toleration asserted; [with] an historical acc. of the test laws; by a layman. [1787.] 2d ed. corr. London, 1789. 8°. (B 126, 750, 772, 1964)
— BRADBERRY, D. Letter to the bishops on the application of the Protestant Dissenters to Parliament. London, 1789. 8°. (B 750)
— BRIEF state of the controversy resp. the corporation and test acts. [London, 1789.] 8°. (B 126)
— DEBATE in the House of Commons on Meaufoy's motion, for the repeal of such parts of the test and corporation acts as effect the Protestant Dissenters. London, 1789. 8°. (B 127)
— ADDRESS to the bishops upon a late letter from one of their lordships to certain clergy in his diocese; with letter prefixed. London, 1790. 8°. (B 240)
— BARBAULD, A. L. Address to the opposers of the repeal of the corporation and test acts. [1790.] (*In her* Works, v. 2. 1826.)
— - *Same.* 4th ed. London, 1790. 8°. (B 746)
— CHURCH OF SCOTLAND. *Gen. Assembly.* Debates on taking into consideration an overture from Jedburgh, resp. the test act, 1790; add., Speech of Ld. Lansdown, 1719. London, 1791. 8°. (B 127)
— COUNTRY curates' obs. on the advertisement from the Leeds clergy rel. to the test act, *etc.* New ed. London, [1790]. 8°. (B 1379)
— DEBATE in the Ho. of Com. on the repeal of the corporation and test acts, Mar. 2. 2d ed. London, 1790. 8°. (B 127)
— FOX, C. J. Speech in the Ho. of Commons, Mar. 2, 1790, upon his motion for the repeal of the corporation and test acts. London, 1790. 8°. (B 127)
— - Two speeches in the Ho. of Com. Mar. 2, in support of repeal of test acts. London, 1790. 8°. (B 636, 1241)
— HOADLY, B. Refutation of Bp. Sherlock's arguments against a repeal of the corporation and test acts. London, 1790. 8°. (B 126)
— HOBHOUSE, B. Address to the public, in answer to the objections urged in the Ho. of Com. by Lord North and Wm. Pitt against the repeal of the test laws. Bath, London, 1790. 8°. (B 126)
— SHARP, R. Letter to the public meeting of the friends to the repeal of the test acts, *etc.* London, 1790. 8°. (B 1379)
— CASSAN, S. H. Considerations against the repeal of test and corporations acts. London, 1828. 8°. * (B 1363)
— - *Same.* 2d ed. London, 1828. 8°.
See also **Corporation acts.**

Test and protest against Popery, from the Quakers. London, 1680. 4°. (C 284)
Test for the times, A; or, The treachery and inconsistency of democratic politics manifested, in the case espec. of Somers *vs.* Somers. 2d ed. Dublin, 1795. 8°. (B 1842)
Testa de Nevill. *See* **Great Britain.** *Record Commission* (p. 1202).
Testacea. BORN, I. E. von. Testacea musei Cæsarei Vindobonensis. Vindobonæ, 1780. f°.
— DUBOIS, C. Epitome of Lamarck's arrangement of testacea. London, 1824. 8°.
Testament, Old and New. *See* **Bible** (pp. 268-291).
Testament de la comtesse, Le. *See* **Bréhat**, A. de.
Testament de M. Chauvelin, Le; par A. Dumas. Nouv. éd. Paris, 1861. 18°.
Testi, Fulvio. Canzoni. (*In* **Gironi**, R. Rac. di lirici ital. 1808.)
— Canzoni. (*In* **Poesie** di diversi autori. 1783.)
Testimonials on behalf of G. Combe, as a candidate for the chair of logic in the Univ. of Edinburgh. Edin., 1836. 8°.
Testimony for the truth, A; Christ and his light. *See* Cobbet, R. Word to the upright. 1668. (C 284)
Testimony of a number of New Eng. ministers at Boston, Sept. 25, professing the ancient faith of these churches, *etc.* Boston, 1745. 8°. (B 42, 247)
Testimony of an association of laymen, at Boston, resp. the present times. Boston, 1745. 4°. (B 583)
Testimony of Christ's second coming. *See* **Youngs**, B. S.
Testis, *pseud.* Expose and review of The vindication [of Gelston & Haff]. N. Y., 1817. 8°. (B 1448)
Testis. SPAULDING, M. Schirrous testis cured by electricity. (*In* **Mass. Med. Soc.** Med. com., v. 1. 1808.)
— COOPER, *Sir* A. Structure and diseases of testis. 2d ed., by B. B. Cooper. Lond., **1841.** 4°.
— CURLING, T. B. Diseases of the testis, spermatic chord, and scrotum. Phila., **1856.** 8°.
— WARREN, J. M. Supposed encephaloid testicle; hermaphrodism. From the Amer. Journ. Med. Sci., July. *n.p.*, **1859.** 8°. (**B 1564, E 70**)
See also **Generative organs; — Hydrocele; — Urethra.**

Teston, —. Articles de voyage et de campement. (*In* **France.** *Com. Imp. de l'Expos. de* 1867. Rapports du jury, v. 4. 1868.)
Testu, Jacques. ALEMBERT, J. le R. d'. (*In his* Œuvres, v. 10. 1805.)
Testu, Romain le. *See* **Le Testu**, R.
Testu de Mauroy, Jean. ALEMBERT, J. le R. d'. (*In his* Œuvres, v. 9. 1805.)
Testudinata. AGASSIZ, L. T. of North Amer. (*In his* Contrib. to the nat. hist. of U. S., v. 1. 1857.)
Tetanus. MAY, F. Inaug. diss. on the animating principle, or anima mundi, in lock-jaw. Boston, 1795. 8°. (B 814, 969)
— WARD, M. Hydrophobia and tetanus. [**1804.**] (*In his* Opiate friction. 1809.)
— BARTLETT, J. Case of tetanus, cured by amputation. (*In* **Mass. Med. Soc.** Med. com., v. **1. 1808.**)
— BABBITT, T. Application of hot iron in cases of lockjaw. (*In* **Mass. Med. Soc.** Med. com., v. 2. 1813.)
— PARRY, C. H. Cases of tetanus and rabies contagiosa. Bath, **1814.** 8°.
— MORRISON, J. Treatise on tetanus. Newry, **1816.** 8°.
— REID, R. Nature and treatment of tetanus and hydrophobia, *etc.* Dublin, **1817.** 8°.
— POLAND, A. Tetanus. (*In* **Holmes**, T. Syst. of surgery, v. 1. **1860.**)
See also **Hydrophobia.**

Tête de Boule Indians. ADAMS, J. Sketches. (*In* **Lit. and Hist. Soc. of Quebec.** Trans., v. 2. 1831.)
Tête noire, La. *See* **Le Sage**, A. R.
Tétot, —. Bibliothèque diplomatique; répertoire des traités. Paris, 1866-[67]. 2 v. 8°.
Contents. Vol. 1. Partie chronologique, 1493-1866. 2. Partie alphabétique, 1493-1867.
Tetrachordon; by J. M[ilton]. London, 1645. 4°.
Tetrapolitan confession. SCHELHORN, J. G. Analecta ad historiam confessionis Tetrapolitanæ. (*In his* Amœn. lit., v. 6. 1727.)
Tetten Hall Regis, The Costomary of the mannor of T. (*In* **Smith**, J. T. English gilds. 1870. E. E. Text Soc.)
Teucer *Cyzicenus.* Fragm. (*In* **Mueller**, C. Fr. hist. Gr., v. 4. 1851.)
Teufels Lustschloss, Des; von A. v. **Kotzebue.** (*In his* Theater, v. 14. 1841.)
Teules chichimecas. SAMANO, J. de. Relacion de la conquista de los Teules chichimecas. (*In* **Icazbalceta**, J. G. Col. de doc., v. 2. 1866.)
Teulet, A. François. Les codes de l'Empire Français. 8e éd. Paris, 1858. 8°.
Teulet, Jean Baptiste Alexandre Théodore. Relations politiques de la France et de l'Espagne avec l'Ecosse au 16e siècle. Paris, 1862. 5 v. 8°.
Teulié, Pietro. LOMBROSO, R. Vita. (*In* **Amato**, G. d'. Panteon, v. 1. 1851.)
Teupalus, *Andriensis.* Fragm. (*In* **Mueller**, C. Fr. hist. Gr., v. 4. 1851.)
Teutonic languages. CHASLES, V. E. P. Essai sur les destineés et les sources des langues teutoniques et latines. (*In his* Etudes sur l'antiquité. 1847.)
— HELFENSTEIN, J. Comparative grammar of the Teutonic languages. London, 1870. 8°.
Teutonic Order. TERRA Pomerania quomodo subjecta est Ordini Frat. Theuton. (*In* **Hirsh**, T. Script. rerum Pruss., v. 1. 1861.) — BLUMENAU, L. Historia de Ordine Theutonicorum cruciferorum. — HISTORIA brevis magistrorum Ordinis Theutonici generalium, *etc.* (*In* v. 4. 1870.)
Teutsch, G. D., *and* Firnhaber, F. Urkundenbuch zur Geschichte Siebenbürgens. 1 Theil. Wien, 1857. 8°. (Fontes rerum Austr., 2. Abth., 15. Bd.)

Teuzzone; dramma. *See* Zeno, A.

Teverino; par George Sand. Paris, 1856. 16°.

Teverone River. DELRIO, M. A. Brevis defensio pro fluvio Aniene vocato Teverone. (*In* Grævius. Thes. antiq. Ital., v. 8, pt. 4. 1723.)

Teviotdale. LIZARS, W. H. Views of the abbeys of T.; with descriptions from the 'Monastic annals of Teviotdale, by J. Morton'. Edin., 1832. 4°.

Tew, Edmund. Resignation no proof; letter to J. Jebb. London, 1776. 8°. (B 1379)

Tewkesbury. VERY antient trusses of timber supporting arches at Tewkesbury. [18—. *Engr.*] (E 55)

Tewkesbury, Abbey of. ANNALES monasterii de Theokesberia, 1066–1263. (*In* Annales monastici, v. 1. 1864.)

Texada Paez, Agustin de. Canciones. (*In* Sedano, J. J. L. de. Parnaso español, v. 1, 5, 7; — *and in* Quintana, M. J. Poesias, v. 3. 1807.)

Texas.

STATE OF COAHUILA AND TEXAS, 1824–36.

— Laws and decrees of the State of Coahuila and Texas; in Span. and Eng.; [with] the constitution; tr. by J. P. Kimball. Houston, 1839. 8°.

PROVISIONAL GOVERNMENT, 1835.

— Journals of the consultation held at San Felipe de Austin [*sic*], Oct. 16, 1835. Houston, 1838. 8°. (E 11)

— Journal of the proc. of the general council of the republic of Texas, held Nov. 14th 1835. Houston, 1839. 8°. (E 11)

— Ordinances and decrees of the consultation, provisional gov., and the convention, March 1836. *t.p. mut.* Houston, 1838. 8°.

REPUBLIC, 1836–45.

Congress.

— Laws [passed by the 1st] – 9th Congress [1836–45]. Houston, 1838–45. 12 v. 8°.
Note. Laws of the 6th Cong. publ. at Austin; of the 7th and 9th at Washington.

— *Another ed.* Laws passed at 2d sess. of 2d Cong., Apr., May, 1838. *n.t.p.* [Houston, 1838.] 8°.

— U. S. *Ho. of Representatives.* Report of the committee on foreign relations, with documents. *n.d.*, [1840]. 8°. (E 11)

House of Representatives.

— Journals, Nov. 14, 1842. Wash., 1843. 8°.

STATE.

Constitutional Convention, 1845.

— Constitution. Austin, 1845. 8°.

Constitutional Convention, 1861.

— Constitution, as amended in 1861; ordinances of state convention, and address to the people, and constitution of Confed. States. Austin, 1861. 8°.

— Declaration of the causes which impel the state to secede. *n.p.*, 1861. 8°.

Governor.

— Message of Gov. H. R. Runnels. Austin, 1859. 8°.

— Message of Gov. S. Houston. Austin, 1860. 8°.

Legislature.

— Laws, 1st legislature. Austin, 1846. 8°.

— *Same.* 2d legislature. Houston, 1848. 8°.

— General laws of extra sess., 9th legislature; 10th legislature, 2d extra sess. Austin, 1863–65. 2 v. 8°.

— HARTLEY, O. C. Digest of the laws of Texas. Phila., 1850. 8°.

See also Moore, *Commodore* E.

Botany.

— GRAY, A. Plantæ Wrightianæ Texano-Neo-Mexicanæ. (*In* Smithsonian Inst. Contrib., v. 3, 5. 1852–53.)

Description.

— F—N, G. L'héroine du Texas, ou Voyage de Mme. *** aux Etats-Unis et au Mexique. Paris, 1819. 8°.

— HOLLEY, *Mrs.* M. A. Observations, hist., *etc.*, in letters written during a visit to Austin's colony in 1831; with app. Balt., 1833. 12°.

— PARKER, A. A. Trip to the West and Texas, 1834–35. 2d ed. Concord, 1836. 12°.

— BONNELL, G. W. Topographical description of T.; added, an account of the Indian tribes. Austin, 1840. 16°.

— BELLEMARRE, E. L. G. de F. (*pseud.* G. Ferry). Une expéd. amér. au T., [1841–42]. (*In* Revue d. D. Mondes, juin 1849.)

— KENDALL, G. W. Narrative of the Texan Santa Fé exped., [1841–42]. 6th ed. N.Y., 1855. 2 v. 12°.

— KENNEDY, W. Texas; its geography, natural history, *etc.* N. Y., 1844. 8°.

— PRAIRIEDOM; Rambles in Texas or New Estrémadura; by a Suthron. N. Y., 1845. 12°.

— DOMENECH, E., *l'abbé.* Journal d'un missionnaire au T., [1846–52]. (*In* Revue d. D. Mondes, juin, nov. 1856.)

— — *Eng.* Missionary adventures in T. and Mexico; tr. London, 1858. 8°.

— BARTLETT, J. R. Explorations and incidents in T., *etc.*, 1850–53. N. Y., 1854. 2 v. 8°.

— OLMSTED, F. L. Journey through T., [1856]. N.Y., 1857. 8°.

Maps.

— MAP of Texas. Phila., *Williams*, 1845.

— NEW map of Texas, *etc.* Phila., *Mitchell*, 1846.

— U. S. *Bureau of Topog. Engineers.* Reconnoissances of routes from San Antonio de Bexar, el Paso del Norte, *etc.* Phila., 1849. (31st Cong., 1st sess. Senate. Ex. doc., no. 64.)
See also Samar.

Ecclesiastical affairs.

— GILLETTE, C. A few historic records of the church in the diocese of Texas during the rebellion; with corresp. [with Bp.] Gregg. N. Y., 1865. 8°.

Finance.

— GOUGE, W. M. Fiscal history of Texas, 1834–52. Phila., 1852. 8°.

— HUNT, M. The public debt and lands of T. [From De Bow's Commercial review. N. Orleans, 1848.] 8°. (B 1510)

History.

— FOOTE, H. S. Texas and the Texans, [1519–1837]. Phila., 1841. 2 v. 12°.

— MAILLARD, N. D. Hist. of the republic of Texas, [1527–1842]. London, 1842. 8°.

— KENNEDY, W. Rise and progress of the republic, [1600–1839]. London, 1841. 2 v. 8°.

— YOAKUM, H. History of Texas, 1685–1846; with app. N. Y., 1856. 2 v. 8°.

— HARTMANN, —, *and* MILLARD, —. Texas, ou notice hist. sur le Champ d'Asile, [1817–19]. Paris, 1819. 16°.

— DEWEES, W. B. Letters from an early settler, [1819–50]. Louisville, Ky., 1852. 12°.

— TRANSLATION of the laws, orders, and contracts on colonization, 1821–29, in virtue of which, Col. S. F. Austin introduced and settled foreign emigrants in Texas. Columbia, 1837. 8°. (E 11)

— FILISOLA, V. Mem. para la hist. de la guerra de Tejas, [1836-37]. Mexico, 1849. 2 v. 8°.
— LECLERC, F. Le T. et sa revolution, [1836-37]. (*In* Revue d. D. Mondes, mars, avril 1840.)
— DOCUMENTS connected with the late controversy between Gen. T. J. Chambers of Texas, and Messrs. Wilson and Postlethwaite of Kentucky. Louisville, 1836. 8°. (E 11)
— FILISOLA, V. Translation of the representation to the supreme government, in defence of his honor, [1836]. Columbia, 1837. 8°. (E 11)
— HOUSTON, *Maj.-Gen.* S. Documents to D. G. Burnet, president of Texas; containing account of the battle of San Jacinto. New Orleans, [1836]. 8°. (E 11)
— PHILLIPS, E. D. Texas and its late military occupation and evacuation, [1845-46]. N. Y., 1862. 8°.

See also Houston, *Gen.* S.; — *also* Cattle. *Diseases.*

Politics.

— AUSTIN, S. F. Address, Louisville, Mar. 7. Lexington, 1836. 12°. (C 266)
— - *Same.* N. Y., 1836. 8°. (E 11)
— LUNDY, B. The war in Texas, [1836]. [2d ed. enl.] Phila., 1837. 8°. (B 1510, 1655)
— OPINION on the four hundred leagues' grant of Texas land. N. Orleans, 1836. 8°. (E 11)
— WHARTON, W. H. Address, N. Y., Apr. 26; also, address of S. F. Austin, Louisville, Ky., Mar. 7; with other docs. explanatory of the contest in which Texas is engaged. N. Y., 1836. 8°. (E 11)
— CHANNING, W. E. Letter to H. Clay on the annexation of Texas to the U. S. Boston, 1837. 8°. (C 266)
— - *Same.* (*In his* Works, v. 2. 1847.)
— - *Same.* 2d ed. Boston, 1837. 8°. (B 1120, C 199, D 58)
— SIDNEY, *pseud.* Letters to Channing [on] his letter to H. Clay. Charleston, 1837. 12°. (C 266)
— ADAMS, J. Q. Speech on the annexation of Texas. Wash., 1838. 8°. (B 1655, 2008)
— COLMAN, H. Remarks, Jan. 25, on the annexation of Texas to the U. S. *n.p.*, [1838]. 12°. (C 226)
— CUCHEVAL-CLARIGNY, P. A. Le T. et les Etats-Unis. (*In* Revue d. D. Mondes, mars, av. 1840.)
— CHILD, D. L. The Texan revolution; also, a letter from Washington on the annexation of Texas, *etc.* Wash., 1842. 8°. (B 1510)
— ADAMS, C. F. Texas and the Mass. resolutions. Boston, 1844. 8°. (B 1510, 1733)
— APPEAL to the people of Mass. on the Texas question. Boston, 1844. 8°. (B 1199, 1510)
— BENTON, T. H. Speech, annexation of Texas, May 16, 18, 20. Wash., 1844. 8°. (B 1510)
— - Speech, Saint Louis, Oct. 14. St. Louis, 1844. 8°. (B 1500)
— DEWEY, O. Discourse; slavery and the annexation of Texas. N. Y., 1844. 8°. (B 1476)
— GIDDINGS, J. R. Speech, annexation of Texas, May 21. Wash., 1844. 8°. (B 1510)
— McDUFFIE, G. Speech on the treaty for the reannexation of Texas. Wash., 1844. 8°. (B 1174)
— PROPOSED treaty with Texas a great usurpation of power. Phila., 1844. 8°. (B 1510)
— SANTANGELO, O. de A. Texas question rev. by an adopted citizen of the U. S. N. Y., 1844. 8°. (B 1510)
— - Circular to members of Congress, [accompanying his Texas question]. N. Y., 1844. 8°. (B 1510)
— SEDGWICK, T. Thoughts on the proposed annexation of Texas. 2d ed. N. Y., 1844. 8°. (B 1510)
— WALKER, R. J. Letter rel. to the annexation of Texas. Phila., 1844. 8°. (B 1174)
— - *Same.* Wash., 1844. 8°. (B 1510)
— BARNARD, D. D. Speech, annexation of Texas. Wash., 1845. 8°. (B 1197)
— COLLAMER, J. Speech, annexation of Texas. Wash., 1845. 8°. (B 1197)
— HAYES, J. L. Remarks made at Democratic meeting, Portsmouth, Jan. 7, in defence of J. P. Hale in relation to the annexation of Texas. *n.p.*, [1845]. 8°. (B 1501)
— HUDSON, C. Speech on the annexation of Texas, Jan. 20. Wash., 1845. 8°. (B 1510)
— KENNEDY, J. P. Speech on the annexation of Texas, Jan. 11. Wash., 1845. 8°. (B 1510)
— LISLE, *pseud.* Letters upon the annexation of Texas, to J. Q. Adams. Boston, 1845. 8°. (B 1510, 2544)
— PROCEEDINGS of a convention at Fanueil Hall, Jan. 29, 1845, to consider the annexation of Texas. Boston, 1845. 8°. (B 1510)
— SAMPLE, S. C. Speech on the annexation of Texas, Jan. 10. Wash., 1845. 8°. (B 1510)
— SUMNER, C. Speech against the admission of Texas as a slave state, 1845. (*In his* Orations, v. 2. 1850.)
— TRACT for the day; how to conquer Texas before Texas conquers us. Bost., 1845. 8°. (B 1199, 1510)
— WINTHROP, R. C. Speech on the annexation of Texas, Jan. 6. Wash., 1845. 8°. (B 1174, 1510)
— WETMORE, W. S. Memorial of the revenue bondholders of the late repub. of Texas. *n.t.p.* [1850.] 8°. (B 1516)

See also Houston, *Gen.* S.

Texas almanac. Galveston, 1867. 8°.

Texas Indians. BONNELL, G. W. Account of the Indian tribes. (*In his* Topogr. description. 1840.)

Texas state register. Galveston, 1867. 8°.

Texas Western R. R. Co. GRAY, A. B. Southern Pacific R. R.; survey of a route for the S. P. R. R. on the 32d parallel for the Texas Western R. R. Co. Cincinnati, 1856. 8°.

Texeira, Jozé de. NICERON, J. P. (*In his* Mémoires, v. 5. 1728; *and*, *Germ.*, v. 6. 1752.)

Texier, Charles Félix Marie. La ville et le port de Fréjus. (*In* Paris. Inst. *Ac. d. Inscr.* Mém. div. sav., 2e sér., v. 2. 1849.)
— *and* Pullan, R. P. Byzantine architecture; illustrated by examples of edifices erected in the east; with descriptions. Lond., 1864. f°.

Texier, Edmond. La Grèce et ses insurrections. Nouv. éd. Paris, [1854]. 12°.
— Les petites industries. (*In* Paris guide, v. 2. 1867.)

Texier de la Pommeraye, A. Abridgment of French and English grammar. Phila., 1822. 8°.

Textile fabrics. ADDA, G. d'. Essai bibliographique sur les anciens modèles de lingeries, de dentelles, et de tapisseries. (*In* Gazette des beaux-arts, v. 15, 17. 1863-64.)
— MICHEL, F. Recherches sur le commerce, la fabrication, *etc.*, des étoffes de soie, d'or, et d'argent pendant le Moyen Age. Paris, 1852-54. 2 v. 4°.
— MONGEZ, A. Notice sur les tissus des anciens asiatiques. (*In* Paris. Inst. *Ac. d. Inscr.* Mém., v. 9. 1831.)
— TAYLOR, W. C. Handbook of the silk, cotton, and woolen manufactures. Lond., 1843. 16°.
— ROYLE, J. F. Fibrous plants of India fitted for cordage, clothing, *etc.* London, 1855. 8°.
— TOUSTAIN, F. Fabrication des tissus de toute espèce. Paris, 1859. 2 v. 18° *and* Atlas 4°. (Manuel-Roret.)
— PHIN, J. The structure of textile fibers. (*In* Moore, D. D. T. Manual of flax culture. 1863.)
— WOODCROFT, B. Brief biographies of inventors of textile fabrics. London, 1863. 8°.
— ALCAN, M. Fabrication des étoffes: Les arts textiles à l'Exposition de 1867. Paris, 1868. 2 v. 8° *and* Atlas 4°.
— STEVENS, P. Report on clothing and woven fabrics. (*In* U. S. *Commissioners for Paris Expos.*, 1867. Reports, v. 6.)
— MAXWELL, S. D. History of the exposition of textile fabrics held in Cincinnati. Cincinnati, [1869]. 12°.
— ROCK, D. South Kensington Museum: Textile fabrics; a descriptive catalogue of the col. of church-vestments, dresses, *etc.*, forming that section of the museum. London, 1870. 8°.

See also Framework knitters.

Textuarius, *pseud.* Scripture its own interpreter in relation to Christ. Providence, 1818. 8°. (B 964)

Texugo, F. Torres. Letter on the slave trade still carried on along the eastern coast of Africa called Mozambique. London, 1839. 8°. (B 1163)

Teynham, *Ld.* *See* Roper-Curson, H. F.

Tezcoco. BOTURINI BENADUCI, L. Tezcoco en los ultimos tiempos de sus antiguos reyes; redactados por M. Veytia; publicalos con notas y adiciones C. M. de Bustamante. Mexico, 1826. 8°.

— IXTILXOCHITL, F. d' A. Historia chichimeca. (*In* King, R., *Earl of Kingston.* Antiq. of Mexico., v. 9. 1848.)
— — *French.* Histoire des Chichimèques ou des anciens rois de Tezcuco. (Vol. 12-13 *of* Ternaux-Campans, H. Voyages. 1840.)
— SAMANO, J. de. Relacion de la conquista de los Teules chicimecas, [1530-31]. — ACAZLITLI, F. de S. Relacion de la conquista y pacificacion de los Indios chichimecas de Xuchipila, [1541]. (*In* Icazbalceta, J. G. Col. de doc., v. 2. 1866.)
Tezel, Johann. Epistola. (*In* Schelhorn, J. G. Amœn. lit., v. 3. 1730.)
Tezozomoc, Fernando de Alvarado. Cronica mexicana. (*In* King, R., *Earl of Kingston.* Antiq. of Mexico, v. 9. 1848.)
— *French.* Histoire du Mexique; tr. par H. Ternaux-Compans. Paris, 1853. 2 v. 8°.
Thaarup, Frederik, *and* Martensen, H. A. The latest revis'd Sound-tariff; with the Christianopel tariff in the Dutch. Copenhagen, 1821. 8°. (C 152)
Thacher. *See also* Thatcher.
Thacher, Anthony. Narr. of his shipwreck. (*In* Young, A. Chronicles of Mass. 1841.)
Thacher, George H. Key to the 'Trustees' statement; letters to the majority of the trustees of the Dudley Observatory, showing the misrepresentation, *etc.*, of their mis-statement. From the Atlas and Argus, Oct. *n.p.*, 1858. 8°. (B 1644)
Thacher, James, *M.D.* American medical biography. Boston, 1828. 2 v. 8°.
— American modern practice. Ed. impr. Boston, 1826. 8°.
— American New dispensatory; with app. Boston, 1810. 8°.
— *Same.* 3d ed. Boston, 1817. 8°.
— American orchardist. Boston, 1822. 8°.
— Case of preternatural retention of the urine. (*In* Mass. Med. Soc. Med. comm., v. 1. 1808.)
— Essay on demonology, ghosts, *etc.* Boston, 1831. 12°.
— History of Plymouth, 1620-1832. Boston, 1832. 12°.
— On hydrophobia. Plymouth, 1812. 8°.
— Military journal during the American revolutionary war; with app. cont. biographical sketches. Boston, 1823. 8°.
— Observations upon iron ores. (*In* Mass. Hist. Soc. Col., v. 9. 1804.)
— Observations relative to the execution of Major André. From N. E. mag., May 1834. *n.t.p.* [18—.] 8°.
— BIOGRAPHICAL notice of T. (*In* Mass. Med. Soc. Med. com., v. 7. 1848.)
— DAVIS, N. S. Life of T. (*In* Gross, S. D. Lives of eminent Amer. physicians. 1861.)
Thacher, Jonathan, *Funeral sermon on.* 1808. *See* Hyde, A. (B 1247)
Thacher, *Rev.* Moses. Address before the Montgomery Lodge, Medway, Mass., Apr. 22, and St. Albans Lodge, Wrentham, May 13th. Boston, 1829. 12°. (B 1271)
— Masonic oaths neither morally nor legally binding; address, Weymouth, June 21, Worcester, July 5, Reading, July 12. Boston, [1830]. 8°. (B 1794)
— Sermon, Foxborough, funeral of S. Pratt. Dedham, 1822. 8°. (B 1127)
— REPORT of the case of Thatcher *vs.* Gen. P. Pond, for slander. *n.p.*, 1838. 8°. (B 1436)
— WRENTHAM, *North Parish.* Report of committee on the reply of M. Thacher, to their request to administer to them the Lord's supper; also facts exhibited to the eccl. council, Dec. 14, 1830. Boston, 1831. 16°. (C 236)
Thacher, Oxenbridge. The sentiments of a British American. Boston, 1764. 8°. (C 70)
Thacher, *Rev.* Peter, *b.* 1651, *d.* 1727. MATHER, C. Comfortable chambers opened and visited, upon the departure of T. Boston, 1796. 8°. (B 853)
Thacher, *Rev.* Peter, *b.* 1677, *d.* 1738. Man's frailty practically exhibited in his life and death; sermon, death of Mrs. S. Gee, July 17. Boston, 1730. 8°. (B 86)
— Wise rulers; sermon, election, May 25. Boston, 1726. 8°. (B 63, C 40)
— ACCOUNT of the reasons [against] P. Thacher's ordination. Boston, 1720. 8°. (C 4)
— LYMAN, C., *and others.* Vindications of the New-North-Church from falsehoods in Account of the reasons [against] P. Thacher's ordination. Boston, 1720. 8°. (C 4)
— *Funeral sermon on.* 1739. *See* Colman, B. (B 308); — Cooper, W. (B 281)
Thacher, *Rev.* Peter, *b.* 1688, *d.* 1744. The fear of God restraining men from iniquity in commerce; sermon, Middleborough, Nov. 17, 1718. Boston, 1720. 8°. (B 233, 867)
— PRINCE, T. Memorial of T. (*In* Christian hist., v. 2. 1744; — *and in* Middleborough. Account of the great revival. 1842.)
Thacher, *Rev.* Peter, *b.* 1748, *d.* 1785. Prayer the breath of a good man, as long as he breathes; sermon, May 19, 1782. *Reprinted* Providence, 1820. 8°. (B 963)
Thacher, Peter, *D.D.*, *b.* 1752, *d.* 1802. Nature and effects of Christian sympathy considered; sermon, Jan. 19, death of S. Stillman, Jun. Boston, 1794. 8°. (B 333)
— Observations upon the present state of the clergy of New England. Boston, 1783. 8°. (B 34, 233)
— Oration, Watertown, Mar. 5, 1776. (*In* Orations at Boston. 1785; — 1807; — *n.d.* B 614)
— Reply to the strictures of J. S. on [T.'s] 'Observations on the present state of the clergy in New Eng.' Boston, [17—]. 8°. (B 34)
— The rest which remaineth to the people of God; sermon, Boston, Sept. 13, death of A. Eliot. Boston, [1778]. 8°. (B 233, 281)
— Sermon, Apr. 17, death of T. Russell. Boston, 1796. 8°. (B 151, 233, 867, D 2, W 81)
— Sermon, Apr. 6, interment of J. Clarke. Boston, 1798. 8°. (B 172, 233, 281, 867)
— Sermon, artillery election. Boston, 1793. 8°. (B 179)
— Sermon, Aug. 13, ordination of T. C. Thacher. Boston, [1794]. 8°. (B 168, 233, 855)
— Sermon, death of G. Washington, Feb. 22. Boston, [1800]. 8°. (B 173, 233, 867, E 162, W 50)
— Sermon, Dorchester, before the Anc. and Hon. Soc. of Freemasons. Boston, 1797. 8°. (B 844)
— Sermon, Feb. 12, before the Mass. Cong. Charit. Soc. Boston, 1795. 8°. (B 233, 844, 855)
— Sermon, Feb. 29, interment of J. Paine, Jr. Boston, 1788. 8°. (B 233)
— Sermon, June 9, death of N. Gorham. Boston, 1796. 8°. (B 233)
— Sermon, June 2, ordination of W. F. Rowland. Exeter, 1790. 8°. (B 233)
— Sermon, June 12, interment of I. Sumner. Boston, 1799. 8°. (B 151, 172, 233, 867)
— Sermon, Mar. 25, the death of R. Gill. Boston, 1798. 8°. (B 333)
— Sermon, Nov. 14, 1790, death of J. Bowdoin. Boston, 1791. 8°. (B 233, 867, W 25)
— Sermon, Oct., ordination of E. Kellogg. *n.p.*, [1788]. 8°. (B 233)
— Sermon, Oct. 20, death of J. Hancock. Boston, 1793. 8°. (B 233, 1218)
— Sermon to the Church and Soc. in Brattle St., Bost., Dec. 29, 1799, on completion of a century. Boston, 1800. 8°. (B 148, 233, 275, 867)
— That the punishment of the finally impenitent shall be eternal; three sermons, Oct. 1782. Salem, 1783. 8°. (B 42, 233)
— ELIOT, J. Memoirs of P. Thacher. (*In* Mass. Hist. Soc. Col., v. 8. 1802.)
— LORING, J. S. (*In his* Hundred Boston orators. 1852.)
— *Funeral sermon on.* 1802. *See* Emerson, W. (B 87, 174, 220, 872)
Thacher, Peter Oxenbridge. Address, March 1831, before the bar of Suffolk Co., Mass. Boston, 1831. 8°. (B 936, 1021, 1804, 1828)
— Address to the Mass. Char. Fire Soc., Boston, May 31. Boston, 1805. 8°. (B 669)
— Charge to the grand jury of Suffolk, Dec. 1831. Boston, 1832. 8°. (B 1052)
— Charge, *etc.* Boston, 1832. 8°. (B 1110, 1802)
— Charge, *etc.*, Dec. Boston, 1834. 8°. (B 1099, 1110)
— Charge, *etc.*, Dec. Boston, 1835. 8°. (B 1435, 1812)
— Observations on some of the methods known in the law of Mass. to secure an impartial jury. Boston, 1834. 8°. (B 1110, 1756, 1809)
— Oration, Boston, July 4. Boston, 1807. 8°. (B 1839)
— *Same.* 2d ed. Boston, 1807. 8°. (B 394)
— Two charges, *etc.*, Dec. 1836, and Mar. Boston, 1837. 8°. (B 1824)
— LORING, J. S. (*In his* Hundred Boston orators. 1852.)
— QUINCY, J. (*In his* Hist. of the Boston Athenæum. 1851.)
— *Funeral sermon on.* 1843. *See* Lothrop, S. K. (B 1226, 1963); — Williams, J. M. (B 1226)
Thacher, Samuel. Oration, Concord, July 4. Boston, 1796. 8°. (B 1006)

Thacher, *Rev.* Samuel Cooper. Apology for rational and evangelical Christianity; discourse, dedication of a new church on Church Green, Boston. Boston, 1815. 8°. (B 333, 1310)
— Elements of religion and morality, *etc.* *See* Channing, W. E. (B 662)
— Evidence necessary to establish the doctrine of the Trinity. 2d ed. Boston, 1828. 12°. (A. U. A. 1st ser., 18. C 168, v. 2)
— Memoir of J. S. Buckminster. (*In* Buckminster, J. S. Sermons. 1814.)
— Memoir of W. Emerson. (*In* Mass. Hist. Soc. Col., v. 11. 1814.)
— Sermons; with memoir by F. W. P. Greenwood. Boston, 1824. 8°.
— Unity of God; sermon, delivered in America, Sept. 1816 [1815]. Liverpool, 1816. 8°. (B 334)
— *Same.* 2d Amer. ed. Worcester, 1817. 8°. (B 1591)
— CATALOGUE of the Library of T., sold. Boston, 1818. 8°. (B 1617, 1620)
— QUINCY, J. (*In his* Hist. of Boston Athenæum. 1851.)

Thacher, Stephen. Oration, Kennebunk, 4th of July. Boston, 1803. 8°. (B 944)

Thacher, *Rev.* Thomas, *b.* 1620, *d.* 1678. A fast of God's chusing: fast [serm.], 1674. Bost., 1678. 12°. (B 233)

Thacher, *Rev.* Thomas, *b.* 1756, *d.* 1812. Biographical memoir of Dr. West. [Boston,] 1808. 8°. (B 209, 282, 867, 908)
— Danger of despising the divine counsel; disc., Sept. 13, 1801, execution of J. Fairbanks. Dedham, 1802. 8°. (B 195, 233)
— Discourse, April 9, [fast day]. Dedham, 1812. 8°. (B 333)
— Discourse before the Humane Soc. of Mass., June 10. Boston, 1800. 8°. (B 770, 1694, 1914, 1923)
— Discourse, Dedham, Feb. 19, [thanksgiving-day]. Boston, 1795. 8°. (B 843, 857)
— Discourse, errors of popery, May 8, [Dudleian lecture]. Camb., 1805. 8°. (B 203)
— Discourse, Mar. 16, funeral of J. Chickering. Dedham, 1812. 8°. (B 333)
— Discourse, Milton, Sept. 9, dedication of the academy. Dedham, 1807. 8°. (B 296, 333, 864, 867)
— Discourse, Peterborough, Oct. 23, 1799, ordination of E. Dunbar. Amherst, 1800. 8°. (B 1313, 1007)
— Eulogy on Washington, Dedham, Feb. 22. Dedham, 1800. 8°. (E 162)
— Principles and maxims on which the security of a republic depends; sermon, election day, May 29. Boston, [1811]. 8°. (B 333, 1830, 1875)
— Sermon, Dedham, Apr. 7, a day of humiliation and prayer. Dedham, 1808. 8°. (B 209, 333)
— Sermon, Dedham, Dec. 25, 1797. Dedham, 1798. 8°. (B 333, 844)
— Sermon, Dedham, Jan. 11. Dedham, 1801. 8°. (B 961)
— Sermon, Milton, after the interment of N. Robbins, 1795. Boston, 1796. 8°. (B 233)
— Sermon, ordination of J. Tuckerman, Chelsea, Nov. 4. Boston, 1801. 8°. (B 166, 167, 233, 1313)
— Sermon, Peterborough, Oct. 27. Dedham, 1799. 8°. (B 1127)
— Tribute of respect to the memory of [Gov.] S. Adams, who died Oct. 2, 1803. Dedham, 1804. 8°. (B 203, 623)
— Two discourses; 1st, on taking leave of the old meeting house, and 2d, at the dedication of the new house, in Dedham. Dedham, 1809. 8°. (B 333, 868)

Thacher, *Rev.* Thomas Cushing. Eulogy on Washington, Jan. 13. Boston, [1800]. 8°. (E 61)
— Sermon, death of Mrs. Carnes, Oct. 5, 1800. Boston, 1801. 8°. (B 87)
— Sermon, Lynn, Nov. 20. Boston, 1794. 8°. (B 333)

Thacher, Tyler. Arminianism examined; a review of 'A discourse on predestination and election', by W. Fisk. Boston, 1833. 8°. (B 1239)

Thacher, W. S. CATALOGUE of library, sold Dec. 13. Boston, 1859. 8°. (B 1690)

Thacher, *Rev.* Wm. Sermon on Christian perfection. *n.t.p.* (B 1285)

Thackeray, Anne Isabella, *afterwards Mrs.* Ritchie. Abigail. (*In* Fraser's magazine, v. 72. 1865.)
— Bluebeard's keys. (*In* Cornhill mag., v. 23. 1871.)
— Fisherman of Auge. (*In* St. Paul's magazine, v. 6-7. 1870.)
— Five old friends and a young prince. London, 1868. 8°.
Contents. The sleeping beauty in the wood. — Cinderella. — Beauty and the beast. — Little Red Riding Hood. — Jack the giant-killer. — A young prince.
— From an island. (*In* Cornhill mag., v. 18-19. 1868-69.)
— Jack the giant killer. (*In* Cornhill mag., v. 16-17. 1867-68.)
— Sola. (*In* Cornhill mag., v. 20. 1869; — *and in* Littell's living age, v. 102. 1869.)
— Story of Elizabeth. N. Y., 1863. 18°.
Note. From Fraser's mag., v. 6-7. 1862-63.
— Village on the cliff. 2d ed. London, 1867. 8°.
— *Same.* (*In* Cornhill mag., v. 13-15. 1866-67; — *and in* Littell's living age, v. 90-92. 1866-67.)

Thackeray, *Rev.* Francis. History of W. Pitt, Earl of Chatham. London, 1827. 2 v. 4°.
— Researches into the eccl. and polit. state of anc. Britain under the Roman emperors. London, 1843. 2 v. 8°.

Thackeray, Wm. Makepeace. Adventures of Philip. N. Y., 1862. 8°.
— *Same.* (*In* Cornhill mag., v. 3-6. 1861-62; — *and in* Harper's mag., v. 22-25. 1861-62.)
— Ballads. Boston, 1856. 16°.
— Barry Lyndon. *See, below,* Luck.
— Book of snobs. N. Y., 1864. 12°.
— Catharine. (*In* Fraser's mag., v. 19-21. 1839-40.)
— Christmas books. New ed. London, 1866. 16°.
Contents. Mrs. Perkins's ball. — Our street. — Dr. Birch; with illustrations.
— Confessions of Fitz-Boodle; and Passages in the life of Maj. Gahagan. N. Y., 1864. 12°.
Note. From Fraser's mag., v. 25-27. 1842-43.
— Denis Duval. N. Y., 1869. 8°.
— *Same.* (*In* Cornhill mag., v. 9. 1864; — *and in* Harper's mag., v. 28-29. 1863-64.)
— Doctor Birch and his young friends; by M. A. Titmarsh. London, 1849. 8°.
— Early and late papers; hitherto uncollected; [gathered by J. E. Babson]. Bost., 1867. 16°.
Contents. Memorials of gormandizing. — Men and coats. — Bluebeard's ghost. — Dickens in France. — John Leech's pictures of life and character. — Little travels and roadside sketches. — On men and pictures. — Picture gossip. — The anonymous in periodical literature. — Goethe. — A leaf out of a sketch book. — The last sketch. — Strange to say, on club paper. — Autour de mon chapeau. — On a peal of bells. — On some carp at Sans Souci. — Dessein's. — On a pear-tree. — On a medal of George IV. — On Alexandrines. — The notch on the axe. — De finibus.
— English humorists of the 18th century; a series of letters. London, 1853. 8°.
Contents. Swift. — Congreve and Addison. — Steele. — Prior, Gay, and Pope. — Hogarth, Smollett, and Fielding. — Sterne and Goldsmith.
— *Same.* [With a lecture on humour and charity.] N. Y., 1853. 8°.
— Fitz-Boodle's confessions. *See, above,* Confessions.
— The four Georges. N. Y., 1860. 12°.
— *Same.* (*In* Cornhill mag., v. 2. 1860; — *and in* Harper's mag. v. 21. 1860.)
— The great Hoggarty diamond. N. Y., [1848]. 8°.
Note. From Fraser's mag., v. 24. 1841.
— History of Henry Esmond. London, 1852. 3 v. 8°.
— *Same.* Lpz., *Tauchnitz,* 1852. 2 v. 12°.
— *Same.* N. Y., 1854. 8°.
— History of Pendennis. N. Y., 1850. 2 v. 8°.
— *Same.* Illust. by the author. N. Y., 1863. 2 v. 8°.
— Jeames's diary; Legend of the Rhine; Rebecca and Rowena. N. Y., 1864. 12°.
— Kickleburys on the Rhine. N. Y., 1851. 12°.
— Lovel the widower; a novel. N. Y., 1860. 8°.
— *Same.* (*In* Cornhill mag., v. 1. 1860; — *and in* Harper's mag., v. 20-21. 1860.)
— Luck of Barry Lyndon. N. Y., 1864. 12°.
Note. From Fraser's mag., v. 29-30. 1844.
— Men's wives. N. Y., 1864. 12°.
Note. From Fraser's mag., v. 26-28. 1842-43.
— Miscellanies. London, 1856. 3 v. 12°.
Contents. Vol. 1. Ballads. — Book of snobs. — The tremendous adventures of Major Gahagan. — The fatal boots. — Cox's diary. 2. Memoirs of Mr. C. J. Yellowplush. — Diary of C. Jeames de la Pluche, Esq. —

Sketches and travels in London. — Novels by eminent hands. — Character sketches. 3. The memoirs of Barry Lyndon, Esq. — A legend of the Rhine. — Rebecca and Rowena. — A little dinner at Timmins's. — The Bedford-Row conspiracy.

— *Same.* Vol. 4, 5. Boston, 1869-70. 8°.

Contents. Vol. 4. The four Georges. — The English humorists of the 18th century. — Charity and humor; lecture. — Roundabout papers. — The second funeral of Napoleon. — Little travels and roadside sketches. — The Fitz-Boodle papers. — Critical reviews. — The wolves and the lamb. 5. Catherine; a story. — Titmarsh among pictures and books. — Fraser miscellanies. — The Christmas books: Mrs. Perkins's ball; — Our street; — Doctor Birch; — The Kickleburys on the Rhine; — The rose and the ring. — The anonymous in periodical literature. — Goethe. — The leaf out of a sketch-book. — Selections from Punch. — Ballads, *etc.*

— The Newcomes; ed. by A. Pendennis. London, 1854. 2 v. 8°.

— *Same.* N. Y., 1855. 2 v. in 1. 8°.

— *Same.* N. Y., 1859. 2 v. 8°.

Note. From **Harper's** mag., v. 7-11. 1853-55.

— Notes of a journey from Cornhill to Grand Cairo. N. Y., 1846. 12°.

— Novels by eminent hands. (*In* **Punch**, v. 12, 13. 1847.)

Note. Also called 'Punch's prize novelists'.

Namely. George de Barnwell (Bulwer). — Lords and liveries (Mrs. Gore). — Codlingsby (Disraeli). (*In* v. 12.) — Phil. Fogarty (Lever). — Barbazure (G. P. R. James). — Stars and stripes (Cooper). (*In* v. 13.)

— Our street; by M. A. Titmarsh. 2d ed. London, 1848. 8°.

— Pendennis. *See, above,* History.

— Punch's prize novelists. *See, above,* Novels.

— Rebecca and Rowena; by M. A. Titmarsh. London, 1850. 8°.

Note. From **Fraser's** mag., v. 34. 1846.

— The rose and the ring. N. Y., 1855. 16°.

— Roundabout papers. N. Y., 1863. 12°.

Contents. On a lazy, idle boy. — On two children in black. — Ribbons. — On some late great victories. — Thorns in the cushion. — On screens in the dining-rooms. — Tunbridge toys. — De juventute. — On a joke I once heard from T. Hood. — Round about the Christmas tree. — On a chalk-mark on the door. — On being found out. — One hundred years hence. — Small-beer chronicle. — Ogres. — Two roundabout papers I intended to write. — A Mississippi bubble. — On Lett's diary. — Notes of a week's holiday. — Nil nisi bonum.

Note. From **Cornhill** mag., v. 21-22. 1849.

— Shabby genteel stories, and other tales. N.Y., 1864. 12°.

Contents. Shabby genteel story. — Professor. — Bedford row conspiracy. — Little dinner at Timmins's.

— Sketches in Ireland. Phila., [1843?]. 2 v. 8°.

— Speeches. (*In* **Hotten**, J. C. Thackeray. 1864.)

— Vanity fair. London, 1848. 8°.

— *Same.* N. Y., [1850]. 8°.

— *Same.* With illust. by the author. N. Y., 1864. 8°.

— *Same.* N. Y., 1865. 3 v. 12°.

— *Same.* N. Y., 1869. 8°.

— The Virginians; a tale of the last century. N. Y., 1859. 8°.

Note. From **Harper's** mag., v. 16-19. 1857-59.

— Yellowplush correspondence. Phila., 1838. 8°.

— Yellowplush papers. N. Y., 1864. 12°.

Note. From **Fraser's** mag., v. 16-21. 1837-40.

— *French.* Mémoires d'un valet de pied; tr. par W. L. Hughes. Paris, 1859. 12°.

— **Brown**, J. Thackeray's literary career and death. (*In his* Spare hours, 2d ser. 1866.)

— **Forgues**, E. (*In* **Revue** d. D. Mondes, oct. 1843, sept. 1854, juin 1864.) — **Chasles**, V. E. P. (*In* fév., mars 1849.)

— **Hannay**, J. Brief memoir of Thackeray. Edin., 1864. 12°.

— - Studies on Thackeray. London, 1869. 18°.

Note. From Every Saturday, v. 6, 7. 1868, 69.

— **Hodder**, G. (*In his* Memories of my time. 1870.)

— **Hotten**, J. C. Thackeray the humorist and the man of letters. London, 1864. 8°.

— - *Same.* N. Y., 1864. 8°.

— **Senior**, N. W. (*In his* Essays on fiction. 1864.)

— **Taine**, H. A. (*In his* Essais de critique et d'histoire. 1858; — Hist. de la littérature anglaise, v. 4. 1864; — *and in* **Revue** d. D. Mondes, fév. 1857.)

Thackham, Thomas. Defence of his conduct towards J. Palmer. (*In* **Nichols**, J. G. Narratives of the Reformation. 1859. Camden Soc., v. 77.)

Thackwell, Edward Joseph. Narrative of the second Sikh war, 1848-49. 2d ed., rev. with add. London, 1851. 12°.

Thaddeus of Warsaw; a novel, by J. Porter. Hartford, 1851. 2 v. 16°.

Thaer, Albrecht Daniel. Principles of agriculture; tr. by W. Shaw and C. W. Johnson. (*In* **Skinner**, J. S. Farmer's library, v. 1. 1846.)

Thal von Almeria, Das; von A. v. **Kotzebue**. (*In his* Theater, v. 27. 1841.)

Thalaba the destroyer. *See* **Southey**, R.

Thalaba the destroyer; a melo-drama. *See* **Ball**, E.

Thalatta; a book for the sea side; [ed., by S. Longfellow and T. W. Higginson]. Boston, 1853. 12°.

Thalatta! Thalatta! (*In* **Fraser's** mag., v. 65. 1862.)

Thales *or* **Thalelas**. Fragm. (*In* **Bergk**, T. Poetæ lyrici Græci. 1853.)

— **Figuier**, L. (*In his* Vies des savants. 1866.)

Thallus. Fragm. (*In* **Mueller**, C. Fragm. hist. Græc., v. 3. 1849.)

Thame, Philip de. Knights Hospitallers in England; being a report to the Grand Master E. de Villanova, 1338; ed. by L. B. Larking; with an introd. by J. M. Kemble. London, 1857. 4°. (Camden Soc., v. 65.)

Thames Navigation Commissioners. *See* **Great Britain.** *Thames Navig. Commissioners* (p. 1204).

Thames River. **Ireland**, S. Picturesque views on the T. London, 1792. 2 v. 8°.

— **Coombe**, W. History of the T. London, *J. and J. Boydell*, 1794-96. 2 v. f°.

— **Colquhoun**, P. Treatise on the commerce and police of the T. London, 1800. 8°.

— **Murray**, J. F. Picturesque tour of the T. London, 1849. 8°.

— **Gr. Britain.** *Commissioners Appointed to Enquire into Plans for Embanking the T.* Report. London, [1861]. f°.

— *Maps.* **Bellin**, J. N. Carte reduite de la rade des dunes avec une partie des entreés de la T. *n.p.*, 1757. (E 87, no. 10.)

— - Carte des entrées de la T. *n.p.*, 1759. (E 87, no. 9)

— - **Heather**, W. Chart of the entrances to the T. London, 1794. (E 65)

See also **London.** *Bridges* (p. 1774); — **London.** *Commerce*; — **Middlesex**; — **Surrey.**

Thames tunnel. **Brunel**, *Sir* M. I. The tunnel under the Thames. *n.t.p.* [1833.] 8°. (B 1744)

— **Explication** des travaux entrepris pour la construction de la tonnelle sous la Tamise. Londres, 1836. ob. 12°.

— **Law**, H. (*In* **Weale**, J. Quar. papers, v. 3, 5. 1845-46.)

Thane of Fife. *See* **Tennant**, W.

Thanet, Isle of. **Brayley**, E. W. Delineations hist. and topog. of the Isle of Thanet and Cinque Ports. London, 1817-18. 8°.

Tharin, Robert S. Arbitrary arrests in the South. N. Y., 1863. 12°.

Thasos, Island of. **Lacroix**, P. D. Histoire et descrip tion. (*In his* Iles de la Grèce. 1853. Univers.)

That boy of Norcott's; by C. Lever. Lond[illegible] 1869. 8°.

Note. From **Cornhill** mag., v. 18, 19. 1868-[illegible]

Thatcher. *See also* **Thacher.**

Thatcher, Benjamin Bussey. Church-yard s[illegible]

(*In* **Boston** book, 3d col. 1841.)

— Indian biography. N. Y., 1848. (Harper's fam. lib., v. 45, 46.)

— Memoir of Phillis Wheatley. Boston, 1834. 16°.

— Memoir of S. O. Wright. Boston, 1834. 16°.

— Traits of the tea party; memoir of G. R. T. Hewes; by a Bostonian. N. Y., 1835. 16°.

Thatcher, Henry Knox. HEADLEY, J. T. (*In his* Farragut. 1867.)

Thaumur de la Source, —. Lettre. (*In* **Shea, J. M.** Relation de la mission du Missisipi. 1861.)

Thaun, Philippe de. La livre des creatures. — The bestiary. (*In* **Wright, T.** Pop. treatises. 1841.)

Thaxter, Adams Wallace. A poem before the Iadma of Harv. Coll. Camb., 1850. 16°. **(C 190)**

Thaxter, *Mrs.* Celia (Laighton). Among the Isles of Shoals. (*In* **Atlantic** monthly, v. 24-25. 1870.)

— Poems. N. Y., 1872 [1871]. 16°.

Thaxter, Robert, *M.D.* On the excessive use of ardent spirits. (*In* **Mass. Med. Soc.** Med. comm., v. 4. 1829.)

Thaxter, Samuel, *Eulogy on.* 1842. *See* **Huntoon, B. (B 1218)**

Thaxter, Thomas. Narrative of the proceedings in the North-Parish of Hingham. Salem, 1807. 8°. **(B 139, 431)**

Thayendanegea. *See* **Brant, J.**

Thayer, *Rev.* Christopher Toppan. Address, dedication of Memorial Hall, Lancaster, July 17; ode by H. F. Buswell. Boston, 1868. 8°.

— Address, 1st parish, Beverly, Oct. 2, 1867, 200th anniversary. Boston, 1868. 8°.

— Discourse, Beverly, at the fast in Mass. on account of the prevailing cholera, Aug. 9. Salem, 1832. 8°. **(B 1069)**

— Our faith; sermon, Beverly, May 7. Boston, 1843. 8°. **(B 1303)**

— Valedictory discourse, Beverly, July 4. Boston, 1858. 8°. **(B 1303)**

Thayer, Cornelius, *Funeral sermon on.* 1745. *See* **Chauncy, C. (B 68, 912)**

Thayer, David. Address as president, 1863. — (*In* **Mass. Homœop. Med. Soc.** Pub., 1862-63.) — Bromine in disease of the heart. (*In* 1863-64.) — Gall-stones and other biliary obstructions radically cured by China officinalis. (*In* 1865-66.)

Thayer, *Rev.* Ebenezer, *of Roxbury.* Christ the great subject of Gospel preaching; twelve sermons; [added, Practical reflections on the first and last days of the year; two sermons]. *t.p.w.* [Boston, 1722.] 12°.

Note. The 'Practical reflections' has a separate title page and paging.

— Jerusalem instructed and warned; sermon, election. Boston, 1725. 8°. **(B 63)**

— Ministers of the Gospel Christ's ambassadours; sermon, at Wookstock, May 24, ordination of A. Throop. Boston, 1727. 12°. **(C 5)**

Thayer, Eli. The Central American question; speech, Jan. 7. Wash., 1858. 8°. **(B 1508)**

— Fair play; speech, Feb. 24. Wash., 1859. 8°. **(B 1508)**

— The suicide of slavery; speech, March 25. Wash., 1858. 8°. **(B 1481)**

Thayer, Elihu. Funeral discourse at the interment of J. Bartlett. Exeter, 1795. 8°. **(B 1090)**

Thayer, Gideon French. Spelling words and teaching meaning. (*In* **Amer. Inst. Instr.** Lect., 1830.) — Courtesy and school instruction. (*In* 1840.)

Thayer, James Bradley. Biography of E. Ripley. (*In* **Higginson, T. W.** Harvard mem. biog., v. 1. 1866.)

Thayer, *Rev.* John. Account of [his] conversion [to] the Roman Catholic religion. 5th ed. London, 1788. 12°. **(C 46, 58)**

— *Same.* Baltimore, 1788. 8°. **(C 46)**

— *French.* Relation de [sa] conversion. Paris, 1788. 12°. **(C 28)**

— Controversy [with] G. Lesslie. [Boston, 1793.] 8°. **(B 149)**

— Discourse, Boston, May 9, [national fast]. Boston, 1798. 8°. **(B 170, 232, 856, W 53)**

Thayer, *Rev.* Joseph Henry. Criticism confirmatory of the Gospels. (*In* **Boston** lectures. 1871.)

ayer, Martin Russell. Reciprocal influence of the physical and intellectual world; oration before the Zelosophic Soc. of the Univ. of Penn., Oct. 29. Phila., 1842. 8°. **(B 1579)**

eply to C. Ingersoll's 'Letter to a friend in a slave state'. Phila., 1862. 8°. **(B 1481)**

Minott. Remarks in the Ho. of Rep., April 1838, the license law. [Boston, 1838.] 12°. **(C 204)**

thaniel, *D.D.* Account of an uncommon frost, 17, 1794. (*In* **Mass. Hist. Soc.** Col., v. 4. 1795.)

— Character of St. John the Baptist; discourse. Leominster, 5797 [1797]. 8°. **(B 196)**

— Character of St. Paul; sermon, ordination of Rev. S. Willard, Deerfield, Sept. 23. Greenfield, 1807. 8°. **(B 334)**

— Christian doctrine; sermon, installation of W. B. Greenfield, Oct. 12. Greenfield, 1825. 8°. **(B 1323)**

— Discourse, [election,] May 28. Boston, 1823. 8°. **(B 958, 1830)**

— Discourse, ordination of J. S. Fitzwilliam, Mar. 6. Keene, 1805. 8°. **(B 205)**

— Means by which Unitarians may refute misrepresentations of their faith; discourse, Townsend, Feb. 10. Lancaster, 1828. 8°. **(B 1303)**

— Revivals of religion. (*In* **Liberal** preacher, v. 1. 1828.)

— The preaching of the apostles; sermon, ordination of E. Whitcomb, Pepperellborough, July 3. Portland, 1799. 8°. **(B 166)**

— Sermon, Aug. 20. Worcester, 1812. 8°. **(B 1194)**

— Sermon before the Anc. and Hon. Artil. Co., Boston, June 4. Boston, 1798. 8°. **(B 177, 334)**

— Sermon, Dec. 23, funeral of T. Harrington. Amherst, N. H., 1796. 8°. **(B 87, 1218)**

— Sermon, fast day, Apr. 2. Boston, 1795. 8°. **(B 856)**

— Sermon, installation of W. Emerson, Oct. 16. Boston, 1799. 8°. **(B 165, 232)**

— Sermon. Lancaster, Dec. 29, 1816. Worcester, 1817. 8°. **(B 1194, 1303)**

— Sermon, Lancaster, Jan. 1, dedication of the new house of worship. Lancaster, 1817. 8°. **(B 1303)**

— *Funeral sermon on.* 1840. *See* **Hill, A. (B 1226)**

Thayer, *Mrs.* Sarah, *Funeral sermon on.* 1857. *See* **Bartol, G. (B 1594)**

Thayer, *Capt.* Simeon. Invasion of Canada in 1775; journal of the march to Quebec; with notes by E. M. Stone. (*In* **R. I. Hist. Soc.** Col., v. 6. 1867.)

Thayer, *Rev.* Thomas Baldwin. The Christian man in politics; discourse, Boston, Oct. 7. Boston, 1860. 8°. **(B 1303)**

— Origin and history of endless punishment. Boston, 1856. 8°.

— Why are you a Universalist? (*In* **Pitts-Street Chapel.** Lectures. 1858.)

Thayer, *Rev.* Wm. Makepeace. Pioneer boy, and how he became president. Boston, 1865. 12°.

— *Greek.* 'Ο ἀποικος παίς. 'Εκ τοῦ 'Αγγλικοῦ ὑπὸ Γ. Κωνσταντίνου. 'Εν 'Αθήναις, 1865. 8°.

— Sermon on Moses' fugitive slave bill, Ashland, Mass., Nov. 3. Boston, 1850. 8°. **(B 1303)**

Theagenes *Macedo.* Fragm. (*In* **Mueller, C.** Fr. hist. Gr., v. 4. 1851.)

Theatre. *History.*

— *Ancient.* DUBOS, J. B. Inquiry into the rise and progress of the theatrical entertainments of the ancients. (*In his* Crit. reflections, v. 3. 1748.)

— - MAGNIN, C. Etudes sur les origines du théâtre antique. (*In* **Revue** d. D. Mondes, mars 1838.)

— - PASQUALI, G. Del teatro, [origine, *ec.*]. Venezia, 1773. 4°. **(E 40)**

— *Eng.* MALONE, E. Historical acc. of the Eng. stage, [1110-1741]. (*In* **Shakespeare, W.** Works, v. 3. 1821.)

— - COLLIER, J. P. History of English dramatic poetry and annals of the stage, [1182-1656]. London, 1831. 3 v. 8°.

— - JONES, S. Brief view of the rise and progress of the Eng. stage, [1378-1809]. (*In* **Baker, D. E.,** *and others.* Biog. dram., v. 1. 1812.)

— - WRIGHT, J. Historia histrionica; hist. acc. of the Eng. stage, [1391-1662]. (*In* **Dodsley, R.** Col. of old plays, v. 1. 1825.)

— - SKOTTOWE, A. Ancient theatres and theatrical usages [in Shakespeare's time]. (*In his* Life of S., v. 1. 1824.)

— - HAZLITT, W. C. The English drama under the Tudor and Stuart princes, 1543-1664. [London,] 1869. 4°. (Roxb. lib.)

— - ALLEYN, E. The Alleyn papers; illust. of the early Eng. stage, [1580-1626; ed.] by J. P. Collier. Lond., 1843. 8°. (Shakespeare Soc.)

— - DORAN, J. Annals of the English stage from Betterton to Kean, [1587-1833]. N. Y., 1865. 2 v. 12°.

— - GENEST, J. Account of the English stage, 1660-1830. Bath, 1832. 10 v. 8°.

— - GILLILAND, T. Dramatic mirror, cont. the history of the stage, of dramatic writers and performers, 1660-1807. Lond., 1808. 2 v. 8°.
— - BETTERTON, T. History of the Eng. stage, [1662-1736]; revised with add. notes, by C. L. Coles. Boston, 1814. 8°.
— - BOADEN, J. History of the stage from the time of Garrick to the present period, [1740-1825]. (*In his* Mem. of J. P. Kemble. 1825.)
— - COWELL, J. Thirty years among the players in England and America, [1812-42]. N. Y., 1844. 8°.
— *European.* MAGNIN, C. Des origines du théâtre en Europe. (*In* Revue d. D. Mondes, juin 1835.)
— - RICCOBONI, L. Historical and crit. acc. of the theatres of Europe; with notes by the author and tr., [1198-1735]. London, 1741. 8°.
— *French.* FONTENELLE, J. de. Vie de P. Corneille, avec l'histoire du théâtre français jusqu'à lui. (*In his* Œuvres, v. 4. 1825.)
— - DU CASSE, A. Histoire anecdotique de l'ancien théâtre en France, [1402-1747]. Paris, 1864. 2 v. 8°.
— - PLANCHE, G. Le théâtre et l'esprit public en France, [1636-1856]. (*In* Revue d. D. Mondes, sept. 1856.)
— *German.* JUNKER, G. A., *and* LIÉBAULT, —. Dissertation sur l'origine, les progrès, et l'etat actuel du théâtre allemand. (*In their* Théâtre allemand, v. 1. 1785.)
See also Germany. *Drama* (p. 1140).
— *Greek.* EVANTHIUS. De theatrorum antiqua consuetudine. — FABRICIUS, J. L. De ludis scenicis. (*In* Gronovius, J. Thes. Gr. antiq., v. 8. 1699.)
See also Greece. *Drama* (p. 1266).
— *Irish.* WALKER, J. C. Historical essay on the Irish stage. (*In* Roy. Irish Ac. Trans., v. 2. 1788.)
— *Jewish.* EICHHORN, J. G. De Judæorum re scenica. (*In* Goettingen. Ges. d. Wiss. Comm., 1811-13.)
— *Mexican.* BRASSEUR DE BOURBOURG, C. E. Essai sur la poésie, la musique, la dance, et l'art dramatique chez les Mexicains avant la conquête. (*In his* Col. de documens, v. 2. 1862.)
— *Portuguese.* TRIGOZO D' ARAGÃO MORATO, F. M. Sobre o theatro portuguez. (*In* Lisbon. Ac. d. Sci. Mem., v. 5. 1817.)
— *Roman.* BERNARDI, J. E. D. L'origine des jeux sceniques chez les Romains. (*In* Paris. Inst. *Ac. d. Inscr.* Mém., v. 8. 1827.)
See also Rome. *Amphitheatres* (p. 2546); — Rome. Teatro di Tor di Nona (p. 2549).
— - LIPSIUS, J. De amphitheatro liber. (*In his* Opera, v. 3. 1675; — *and in* Græevius, J. Thes. antiq. Rom., v. 9. 1699.)
— *United States.* BROWN, T. A. History of the American stage, biog. sketches, 1733-1870. N. Y., [1870]. 8°.
— - DUNLAP, W. History of the Amer. theatre, [1752-1821]. N. Y., 1832. 8°.
— - ATTEMPT to establish a play-house in New Hampshire, [1762]. (*In* New Hampshire Hist. Soc. Col., v. 5. 1837.)
— - CLAPP, W. W. Record of the Boston stage, [1792-1849]. Boston, 1853. 16°.
— - WOOD, W. B. Personal recollections of the stage, [1798-1854]. Phila., 1855. 8°.
— - COWELL, J. Thirty years among the players in Eng. and Amer., [1812-42]. N. Y., 1844. 8°.

Mechanism.

— FRANCHI DE PONT, G. Sopra le scene stabili e mobili degli antichi, e sopra altri teatrali ornamenti. (*In* Turin. Ac. d. Sci. Mem., v. 19. 1811.)
— BORGNIS, J. A. Traité de mécanique appliquée aux arts; des machines imitatives et des machines théâtrales. Paris, 1818-20. 8 v. 4°.

Morality and miscellaneous works.

— GOSSON, P. The school of abuse; a pleasant invective against poets, players, *etc.*. [1579]. London, 1841. 8°. (Shakespeare Soc.)
— - *Same.* Apologie of the schoole of abuse, 1579. London, 1868. 12°. (Arber's Eng. reprints, v. 1.)
— - *Same.* (*In* Somers, J. Col., v. 3. 1810.)
— NORTHBROOKE, J. Treatise against dicing, dancing, plays, and interludes. [1579.] London, 1843. 8°. (Shakespeare Soc.)
— STAGE players complaint, 1641. — MR. Prynne his defence of stage plays. 1649. (*In* Hazlitt, W. C. English drama. 1869.)
— NICOLE, P. de. De la comédie, [1659]. (*In his* Œuvres philosophiques. 1845.)
— COLLIER, J. Second defence of the 'Short view', *etc.* London, 1700. 8°.
— - Dissuasive from the play-house. London, 1704. 8°.
— - Defence of the 'Short view of the profaneness of the English stage'. London, 1705. 8°.
— - Reply to Dr. Filmer's 'Defence of plays'. *t.p.w.* [1707.] 8°.
— LAW, W. Absolute unlawfulness of the stage entertainment fully demonstrated. London, 1726. 8°. (B 129)
— BEDFORD, A. Sermon, London, Nov. 30, 1729, on the erecting of a play-house. London, 1730. 8°. (B 1861)
— PORÉE, C. Oration, the stage a school for virtue, 1733. London, 1734. 8°. (C 71)
— DORAT, C. J. La déclamation théâtrale; poëme didactique. [1766.] 4e éd. Paris, 1771. 18°.
— MILIZIA, F. Trattato del teatro. [1771.] (*In his* Opere, v. 1. 1826.)
— MARMONTEL, J. F. Apologie du théâtre; analyse de la lettre de M. Rousseau au sujet des spectacles. (*In his* Œuvres, v. 16. 1787.)
— GARDINER, J. Speech on the law against theatrical exhibitions, *etc.* Boston, 1792. 8°.
— - *Another copy.* (B 397)
— HALIBURTON, W. Effects of the stage on the manners of a people. Boston, 1792. 8°. (W 26)
— LIGNE, C. J. de. Lettres à Eulalie. (*In his* Mélanges mil., v. 11. 1796.)
— MILLER, S. Sermon on the late dispensation of Providence in [Richmond]. N. Y., 1812. 8°. (B 284, 909)
— LAWRENCE, J. Dramatic emancipation; strictures on the state of the theatres and degeneration of the drama. (*In* Pamphleteer, 1813, v. 2 of B 838) — DELPLA, A. French drama; or, Best means of making the theatres [promote] taste and morals. (*In* 1818; v. 12 of B 838) — P., I. The plagiary warned; vindication of the drama, the stage, and public morals, from the plagiarisms of J. A. James. [1824.] 2d ed. (*In* 1825; v. 25 of B 838)
— REMARKS on the theatre and the late fire at Richmond. 2d ed. York, 1814. 12°. (C 246)
— LETTERS on the new theatre. [Boston, 1827.] 8°. (B 942)
— HEINE, H. Ueber die französische Bühne. [1837.] (*In his* Sämmt. Werke, v. 3. 1856.)
— BUNN, A. The stage; before and behind the curtain. London, 1840. 3 v. 8°.
— VIVIEN, A. F. Les théâtres. (*In* Revue d. D. Mondes, mai 1844.)
— BENNETT, J. B. Theatrical amusements; lecture, Jan. 19. London, 1847. 8°. (B 1332)
— DESCHANEL, E. La tragédie antique, la tragédie du 17e siècle, et la drame moderne. (*In* Revue d. D. Mondes, av. 1847.) — QUINET, E. Du drame moderne. (*In* juin 1853.)
— RIGAULT, A. H. Questions des spectacles. (*In his* Œuvres, v. 4. 1859.)
— MONTÉGUT, E. Le théâtre contemporain de 1862. (*In* Revue d. D. Mondes, jan. 1862.) — PONTMARTIN, A. de. (*In* mai 1862.) — PREVOST PARADOL, L. A. L'art théâtral et le théâtre contemp. (*In* déc. 1862.) — FRANK. F. Le théâtre en 1863. (*In* sept. 1863.)
— NEWHALL, F. H. Discourse, March 15. Boston, 1863. 8°. (B 1591)
— REDE, L. T. Guide to the stage: added, list of the London theatres; ed. by F. C. Wemyss. (*In* Sargent, E. Mod. stand. dr., v. 28. 1864.)
— SARCEY, F. Le théâtre. (*In* Alcan, M. Almanach de l'encyclopédie générale. 1869.)
— FITZGERALD, P. Principles of comedy and dramatic effect. London, 1870. 8°.

See also **Actors**; — **Covent Garden Theatre**; — **Drama**; — **Dramatic authors**; — **London stage**; — **Masques**; — **Mimetic arts**; — **Miracle plays**; — **Mysteries, Dramatic**; — **Tremont Theatre**; — *and the division Literature (Drama), under various countries*; — *also* **English literature**; — **Latin literature**.

Periodicals.

— THEATRICAL censor and critical miscellany; by G. Gryphon, Sept. - Dec. No. 1 - 13. Phila., 1806. 8°.

— *Same.* No. 12. Phila., 1806. 8°. (B 979)

Théâtre de Nohant; par George Sand [A. A. L. Dudevant]. Paris, 1856. 12°.

Théâtre des Grecs. *See* **Brumoy, P.**

Théâtre français, Repertoire du. *See* **Petitot, P. C. B.**

Théatre français au Moyen Age. *See* **Monmerqué, L. J. N.**, *and* **Michel, F.**

Theatres, a poetical dissection. *See* **Nipclose, N.** (A 40)

Theatrical candidates, The; a musical prelude. *See* **Garrick, D.**

Theatrical censor and critical miscellany; by G. Gryphon, Sept. - Dec. No. 1 - 13. Phila., 1806. 8°.

— *Same.* No. 12. Phila., 1806. 8°. (B 979)

Theatrical management in the West and South. *See* **Smith, S. F.**

Thébaïde, La; tragédie; par J. **Racine**. (*In his* Œuvres, v. 1. 1816.)

Thebais. *See* **Statius.**

Thebais. IRWIN, E. Series of adventures, in a voyage up the Red-Sea, and of a route through the desarts of Thebais, **1777.** 3d ed. London, 1787. 2 v. 8°.

— CAILLIAUD, F. Voyage à l'Oasis de Thèbes, *etc.*, **1815-18**; réd. par Jomard. Paris, 1821. f°.

— - *Eng.* Travels in the Oasis of Thebes, *etc.* London, 1822. 8°.

Thebes, *Egypt.* MOMGEZ, A. La psychostasie, et Thèbes d'Egypte. (*In* **Paris. Inst.** *Ac. d. Inscr.* Mém., v. 5. 1821.)

— WILKINSON, *Sir* J. G. Topography of Thebes and view of Egypt. London, **1835.** 8°.

— - Modern Egypt and T. Lond., **1843.** 2 v. 8°.

— GREENE, J. B. Fouilles exécutées à Thèbes, **1855.** Paris, 1855. f°.

Thebes, *Greece.* Cox, G. W. Tale of Thebes and Argos. London, **1864.** 12°.

— CURTIUS, E. Theben als griechische Grossmacht. (*In his* Gr. Gesch., v. 3. 1867.)

Thedel Unverfährt von Walmoden. (*In* **Simrock, K.** Deutschen Volksbücher, v. 9. 1856.)

Theganus, *Suffragan Bp. of Treves.* Vita Hludowici imp. (*In* **Pertz**, G. H. Mon. Germ., Scr., v. 2. 1829.)

— *French.* Vie de Louis-le-débonnaire. (*In* **Guizot**, F. T. G. Col. des mém., v. 3. 1824.)

Theiner, Augustin. Annales ecclesiastici. *See* **Baronio, C.**, *and others.*

— Storia del pontificato di Clemente XIV.; tr. [da] F. Longhena. Firenze, 1854. 4 v. 12°.

Note. Vol. 4, Epistolæ et brevia.

— Vetera monumenta Hibernorum et Scotorum hist. illustrantia ex Vaticani, *etc.*, tabulariis, 1216-1547. Romæ, 1864. f°.

— Vicissitudes de l'Eglise Catholique des deux rites en Pologne et en Russie; préc. d'un avant-propos par le comte de Montalembert. Paris, 1843. 2 v. 8°.

Their present majestie's government proved to be throughly settled, *etc.* London, 1691. 4°. (B 7)

Their wedding journey; by W. D. Howells. Boston, 1872 [1871]. 16°.

Note. From The **Atlantic** monthly, v. 28. 1871.

Théis, Alexandre Etienne Guillaume, *baron* de. Glossaire de botanique. Paris, 1810. 8°.

Theism. THOMPSON, R. A. Christian theism. N. Y., **1855.** 12°.

— NEWMAN, F. W. Doctrinal and practical theism. London, **1858.** 4°.

— WHARTON, F. Treatise on theism. Phila., **1859.** 12°.

See also **God**; — **Infidelity**; — **Religion of the universe.**

Theller, Edward Alexander. Canada in 1837-38. Phila., 1841. 2 v. 12°.

Thelwall, Algernon Sydney. The iniquities of the opium trade with China. London, 1839. 8°.

Thelwall, John. Rights of nature against the usurpations of establishments. London, 1796. 8°. (B 777)

Themis. Θέμις, ἡ ἐπιθεώρησις τῆς Ἑλληνικῆς νομοθεσίας, ἐκδιδ. παρὰ Λ. Λ. Σγουτα. Τόμ. ά, β',γ',ζ'. Ἐν Ἀθήναις, 1846-56. 4 v. 8°.

Thémis, ou Bibliothèque du jurisconsulte, 1819-31; [pub. par Blondeau et autres]. Paris, 1819-31. 10 v. 8°.

Themiso. Fragm. (*In* **Mueller, C.** Fr. hist. Gr., v. 4. 1851.)

Themistagoras *Ephesius.* Fragm. (*In* **Mueller, C.** Fr. hist. Gr., v. 4. 1851.)

Themistius. Orationes [Græce; cum emend. H. Stephani]. Augsb., *H. Stephanus*, 1562. 8°.

— Oratio de præfectura sua. (*In* **Mai, A.** Class. auct., v. 4. 1831.)

Themistocle. *See* **Zeno, A.**

Themistocles. KOUTORGA, —. Le parti persan dans la Grèce ancienne, et le procès de T. (*In* **Paris. Inst.** *Ac. d. Inscr.* Div. sav., 1e sér., v. 6. 1860.)

— NEPOS, C. Vita. (*In his* Vitæ; *and, Eng.*, Lives.)

— PLUTARCHUS. (*In his* Vitæ; *and, Eng.*, Lives.)

Themistogenes *Syracusanus.* Fragm. (*In* **Mueller, C.** Fr. hist. Græc., v. 2. 1848.)

Themmen, Phœbus Hitzer. Diss. physiol. med. inaug. de mensibus ex materia quadam peculiari ovariis secreta oriundis. Lugd. Bat., 1781. 8°. (B 1563)

Thénard, Louis Jacques, *baron.* Essay on chemical analysis; tr. from the 4th vol. of the Chem. élément. with add. by J. G. Children. London, 1819. 8°.

— Outillage pour la fabrication du sucre de betterave. (*In* **France.** *Com. Imp. de l'Expos. de* 1867. Rapports, v. 8.)

— Traité de chimie élémentaire. 4e éd., corr. et aug. Paris, 1824. 5 v. 8°.

— FLOURENS, M. J. P. Memoir of T. (*In* **Smithsonian Inst.** Report. 1862.)

Theobald I., *King of Navarre, previously comte de Champagne et de Brie.* Chansons. (*In* **Auguis, P. R.** Poëtes françois, v. 2. 1824.)

— CARY, H. F. (*In his* Early French poets. 1846.)

— LETRONNE, J. A. L'authenticité de la lettre de Thibaud à l'évêque de Tusculum. (*In* **Paris. Inst.** *Ac. d. Inscr.* Mém., v. 16, pt. 2. 1846.)

Theobald, John, *M.D.* Every man his own physician. 10th ed. London, Boston, 1767. 8°. (B 1563)

Theobald, Wm. Advancement of law reform. (*In* **Nat. Assoc. Prom. Soc. Sci.** Trans., 1857.)

Theobald; or, The fanatic; by H. Jung-Stilling; tr. by S. Schæffer. Phila., 1846. 12°.

Théobald; ou, L'enfant charitable; par M. E. W. 3e éd. Tours, 1846. 18°. (Bibl. de la jeunesse chrétienne.)

Theocles. Fragm. (*In* **Mueller, C.** Fr. hist. Gr., v. 3, 4. 1849-51.)

Theocrenus, Benedictus. *See* **Tagliacarne, B.**

Theocritus. Quæ extant; cum Græcis scholiis, indicibus, et Scaligeri, Casauboni, et Heinsii annot.; [ed. R. *West*]. Oxon., 1699. 8°.

— Decem idyllia; Latinis pleraque numeris a Wetstenio reddita adnot. instruxit L. C. Valcknaer. Lips., 1810. 8°.

— Quæ supersunt; Gr. et Lat.]. (*In* **Briggs, T.** Poetæ bucolici Gr. 1821.)

— Idillion. — Epigrammata; rec. C. F. *Ameis*; [Gr. et Lat.]. (*In* **Poetæ** bucol. 1851.)

— Theocritus, Bion, Moschus. 3um ed. A. *Meinike* Berolini, 1856. 8°.

— Reliquiæ. (*In* **Ahrens, F. L. H.** Bucolicorum Gr. rel., v. 1. 1855.) — Scholia. (*In* v. 2. 1859.)

— *Eng.* Works; tr. by F. *Fawkes.* (*In* **Anderson, R.** Brit. poets, v. 13. 1795; — *and in* **Chalmers, A.** Eng. poets, v. 20. 1810.)

— - Idylls [and Epigrams] of Theocritus; tr. into prose by J. *Banks*; with metrical versions by J. M. Chapman. Lond., *Bohn*, 1853. 8°.

— Idylliums; with Rapin's 'Discourse of pastorals'; [tr. by T. *Creech*]. Oxf., 1684. 12°.

— Amaryllis. — Epithalamium of Helen and Menelaus. — The despairing lover. — Daphnis and Chloris. (*In* **Dryden, J.** Works, v. 12. 1808.)

— El Bucoliastai; tr. por E. M. de Villegas. (*In* **Sedana, J. J. L. de.** Parnaso español, v. 2. 1770.)

— Encomium of Ptolemy; tr. by Dodd. (*In* **Callimachus.** Hymns. 1755.)

— Epithalamium Helenæ; ex rec. Valkenarii animadv. illust. et disputationem de carminibus nuptialibus præmisit C. G. Siebdrat. Lips., 1796. 8°.

— Idyl XIX; Cupid and the bee. — Dead Adonis. — Epitaph of Anacreon. — Offerings to the Muses and Phœbus. — Epitaph of Eurymedon, — of Hipponax. — Thyrsis mourns his dead kid. (*In* **Fisher, R. S.** Trans. 1838.)

— DUEBNER, F. Scholia in Theocritum; [acc.] Scholia et paraphrases in Nicandrum et Oppianum; ed. U. C. Bussemaker Græce. Parisiis, *Didot*, 1849. 8°.

— WELCKER, F. G. Theokrits vierte Idylle. (*In his* Kleine Schriften, v. 4. 1861.)

Theocritus *Chius*. Fragm. (*In* **Bergk, T.** Poet. lyr. Gr. 1853; — *and in* **Mueller, C.** Fr. hist. Gr., v. 2. 1848.)

Théodat; tragédie. *See* **Corneille, T.**

Theodebert I., *King of the Franks*. EXCERPTA ex vitis sanctorum de Theodeberto I. (*In* **Bouquet, M.** Recueil des hist., v. 3. 1869.)

— VIE de Théodebert I. (*In* **Hist. lit. de la France**, v. 3. 1735.)

Theodebert II., *King of the Franks*. EXCERPTA ex vitis sanctorum de Theodeberto II. et Theoderico II. (*In* **Bouquet, M.** Rec. des hist., v. 3. 1869.)

Theodectes. Fragm. (*In* **Nauck, J. A.** Tr. Gr. fragmen. 1856; — *and in* **Wagner, F. W.** Frag. Eurip. 1846.)

Theodectes *Phaselita*. Fragm. (*In* **Mueller, C.** Fr. hist. Gr., v. 2. 1848.)

Theodericus, *St., d.* 523. VITA. (*In* **Acta** sanct., v. 28. 1867.)

Theodericus, *Abb. Andaginensis*. VITA. (*In* **Acta** sanct., v. 38. 1867.)

— VITA. (*In* **Pertz, G. H.** Mon. Germ., Scr., v. 12. 1856.)

Theodicy. PLUTARCHUS. Concerning such whom God is slow to punish. (*In his* Morals, v. 4. 1870.)

— LEIBNITZ, G. W. Essais de théodicée. [1710.] (*In his* Opera philosoph. 1840.)

— ZOELLNER, J. F. Ueber den Versuch einer Theodicee. (*In* **Berlin. Ak. d. Wiss.** Abh., 1790-91.)

— SMITH, T. S. Divine government. [1816.] 2d ed. Boston, 1834. 12°.

— - *Same*. 5th ed. Phila., 1866. 8°.

— MAISTRE, J. M. de. Les soirées de Saint Pétersbourg ou Entretiens sur le gouvernement temporel de la Providence. [1821.] 6e éd. Lyon, Paris, 1850. 2 v. 8°.

— DAMIRON, J. P. Rapport sur l'examen critique des principaux systèmes modernes de théodicée. (*In* **Paris. Inst.** *Ac. d. Sci. Mor.* Mém., v. 10. 1860.)

— LÉVÊQUE, C. La science de l'invisible; études de psychologie et de théodicée. Paris, 1865. 18°.

See also **Natural religion.**

Theodolphus, *Bp. of Orléans*. HAURÉAU, J. B. (*In his* Singularités hist. et lit. 1861.)

Theodora. BOYLE, R. Martyrdom of Theodora and Didymus. (*In his* Works, v. 5. 1772.)

Théodora; tr. de l'allemand de C. Schmid par L. Friedel. (*In his* Œufs de pâques. 1846.)

Theodore, *St., Abp. of Canterbury*. BEDA *venerabilis*. Vita S. Theodori. (*In* **Acta** sanct., v. 46. 1867.)

Theodore, *King of Abyssinia*. BLANC, H. A narrative of captivity in Abyssinia; with some acc. of the late emperor Theodore, his country and people. London, 1868. 8°.

— GAGE, W. L. Abyssinia and the emperor Theodore; supplementary pages to Baker's 'Nile tributaries'. Hartford, 1868. 8°.

— LEJEAN, G. Théodore II et le nouvel Empire d'Abyssinie. (*In* **Revue d. D. Mondes**, nov., déc. 1864, mars 1868.)

— STERN, H. A. The captive missionary; an acc. of Abyssinia; embracing a narr. of King Theodore's life. London, [1869]. 8°.

Theodore I., *styled King of Corsica*. *See* **Neuhoff, T. S.,** *Freiherr* von.

Théodore, vierge et martyre; tragédie chrétienne. *See* **Corneille, P.**

Theodoretus. Commentarius in canticum Salomonis. (*In* **Mai, A.** Class. auct., v. 9. 1837.)

— Theodoriti et Evagrii scholastici historia ecclesiastica; item excerpta ex hist. Philostorgii et Theodori; H. Valesius Græca emendavit, Lat. vertit, et annotationibus illustravit. Moguntiæ, 1679. f°.

— *Eng.* History of the Church; tr. from the Greek. London, *Bohn*, 1854. 8°.

— *French.* Histoire de l'Eglise. (*In* **Cousin, L.** Histoire, v. 4. 1676.)

Theodoric I., II., III., *King of the Franks*. *See* **Thierry.**

Theodoric, *the Ostrogoth, King of Italy*. Epistolæ. (*In* **Bouquet, M.** Recueil, v. 4. 1869.)

— DU ROURE, L. M. Histoire de T. Paris, 1846. 2 v. 8°.

— RASPONI, R. Ravenna liberata dai Goti, o sia opuscolo sulla Rotunda di Ravenna provata edifizio romano, ne mai sepolcro di Teodorico re de' Goti. Ravenna, 1766. 4°.

Theodoricus, *monk of Tholey*. Vita et passio Conradi archiep. Treverensi. (*In* **Pertz, G. H.** Mon. Germ., Scr., v. 8. 1848.)

Theodorus, *monk*. Annales Palidenses. (*In* **Pertz, G. H.** Mon. Germ., Scr., v. 16. 1859.)

Theodoricus, *monk of Treves*. Ex translatione S. Celsi. (*In* **Pertz, G. H.** Mon. Germ., Scr., v. 8. 1848.)

Theodorus *anagnostes*. Abrégé de l'histoire de T. par Nicephorus Callistus. (*In* **Cousin, L.** Hist. de l'Eglise, v. 4. 1676.)

— Excerpta ex historia eccles. Theodori. (*In* **Theodoretus.** Historia. 1679.)

Theodorus *Gadarenus*. Fragm. (*In* **Mueller, C.** Fr. hist. Gr., v. 3. 1849.)

Theodorus *Gazinus*. NICERON, J. P. (*In his* Mém., v. 29. 1734.)

Theodorus *Hierapolita*. Fragm. (*In* **Mueller, C.** Fr. hist. Gr., v. 4. 1851.)

Theodorus *Hyrtacenus*. LA PORTE DU THEIL, F. J. G. de. D'un volume de la Bibl. Nat., conten. les opuscules et lettres anec. de T. l'Hyrtacènien. (*In* **Paris. Inst.** *Ac. d. Inscr.* Not., v. 6. 1801.)

Theodorus *Iliensis*. Fragm. (*In* **Mueller, C.** Fr. hist. Gr., v. 4. 1851.)

Theodorus *Rhodius*. Fragm. (*In* **Mueller, C.** Fr. hist. Gr., v. 4. 1851.)

Theodorus *Samothrax*. Fragm. (*In* **Mueller, C.** Fr. hist. Gr., v. 4. 1851.)

Theodorus *Siceota, St., Ep. Anastatiopolitanus*. ELEUSIUS. Vita T. (*In* **Acta** sanct., v. 12. 1866.)

Theodorus *Tabernæmontanus*, Jacob. Neuw Kreuterbuch. Franckf. a. M., 1588-91. 2 v. f°.

Theodorus *verax, pseud*. *See* **Walker, C.**

Theodorus, Flavius Mallius. *See* **Mallius Theodorus, F.**

Theodorus Prodromus. Amicitia exulans. (*In* **Wagner, F. W.** Fragm. Eurip. 1846; — *and in* **Stobæus, J.** Sententiæ. 1559.)

— Τῶν κατὰ Ῥοδάνθην καὶ Δοσικλέα βιβλία θ'. (*In* **Erotici** script. Gr., v. 2. 1859.)

— *French.* Les amours de Rhodante et Dosiclès; tr. par P. F. G. de Beauchamps. Paris, 1797. 8°. (Bibl. d. romans grecs., v. 11.)

Theodosius. Argumentum collectionis de Romanorum legationibus ad ethnicos. (*In* **Byzant.** hist., v. 1. 1729.)

Theodosius II., *Emperor, and* **Valentinianus** III. Novellæ leges; ex Ottoboniano ms. cod.; ed. A. Zirardinus. Faventiæ, 1766. 8°.

— BAUDI DI VESME, C. In difficiliora duo loca e fragmentis cod. Theodosiani a Blossio repertis. (*In* **Turin. Ac. d. Sci.** Mem., ser. 2, v. 2. 1840.)

— FLECHIER, E. Histoire de T. (*In his* Œuvres complètes, v. 1, pt. 1. 1782.)

— PEYRON, A. Codicis Theodosiani frag. ined. (*In* **Turin. Ac. d. Sci.** Mem., v. 28. 1824.)

Theodosius *Alexandrinus.* Canones. (*In* **Bekker,** A. I. Anecdota Gr., v. 3. 1821.)
— Grammatica; ed. C. G. Gœttling. Lps., 1822. 8°.
— PEYRON, A. In Theodosii tractatum de prosodia commentatio. (*In* **Turin. Ac. d. Sci.** Mem., v. 23. 1818.)
Theodosius *cœnobiarcha, St.* VITA. (*In* **Acta** sanct., v. 1. 1863.)
Theodosius *diaconus.* Acroases de Creta capta. (*In* **Niebuhr.** Byzant. hist., v. 5. 1828.)
Theodosius, *monk of Syracuse.* Epistola de Syracusanæ urbis expugnatione. (*In* **Muratori,** L. A. Rer. Ital. scr., v. 1, pt. 2. 1725.)
Theodosius and Constantine, Correspondence of. *See* **Langhorne,** J.
Theodosius; or, The force of love; a tragedy, by N. Lee. (*In* **Bell,** J. Brit. theatre, v. 10. 1797.)
Theogerus *Metensis* (*Germ.* **Dietger** *von Metz*). VITA. (*In* **Pertz,** G. H. Mon. Germ., Scr., v. 14. 1851.)
Theognetus. Fragm. (*In* **Meineke,** A. Fr. com. Gr., v. 4. 1841.)
Theognis *Atheniensis.* Fragm. (*In* **Nauck,** A. Trag. Gr. fr., 1856; — *and in* **Wagner,** F. W. Frag. Eurip. 1846.)
Theognis *Chius.* Fragm. (*In* **Mueller,** C. Fr. hist. Gr. v. 4. 1851.)
Theognis *Megarensis.* Sententiæ elegiacæ; [Gr.]. (*In* **Bergk,** T. Poet. lyr. Gr. 1853.)
— Sententiæ; versio Lat. P. Melanchthone interp. (*In* **Melanchthon,** P. Opera, v. 19. 1853.)
— *Eng.* Works; tr. by J. Banks; with a metrical version by J. H. Frere. (*In* **Hesiod.** Works. 1856.)
Theognis restitutus. *See* **Frere,** J. H.
Theognostus *Alexandrinus.* Fragments of his seven books of Hypotyposes or Outlines; tr. by S. D. Salmond. — BIOG. notice. (*In* **Methodius.** Writings. 1869.)

Theologia deutsch; hrsg. von Dr. F. Pfeiffer. 2e verm. Aufl. Stuttgart, 1855. 16°.
— *Eng.* Theologia Germanica; tr. by S. Winkworth. 2d ed. London, 1854. 16°.

Theologians. LEIGH, E. Treatise of religion and learning, and of religious and learned men. London, 1656. f°.

Theological and biblical magazine. Vol. 5. London, 1805. 8°.

Theological and literary journal; ed. by D. N. Lord. Vol. 5-11; July 1852 - April 1859. N. Y., 1853-59. 7 v. 8°.

Theological education. APPEAL from the condemnatory sentence of man, to the testimony of Christ and his apostles. Hartford, 1815. 16°. (B 659)
— SOC. FOR PROM. THEOLOGICAL EDUCATION IN HARVARD COLL. Address of the directors. Boston, 1832. 8°. (B 1662, 1695, 1739, H 3)

Theological magazine; or, Synopsis of mod. religious sentiment. Vol. 1-3; July 1795 - Feb. 1799. N. Y., 1796-99. 3 v. 8°.
— *Same.* Oct., 1797 - May, 1798. *n.t.p.* [1797.] 3 nos. 8°. (B 198)
Theological magazine. *See* **Quarterly** theol. mag. 1813-14.
Theological repository. *See* New Theol. repos., v. 6. 1803.

Theological repository; [ed. by J. Priestley]. (Vol. 1, 2, 3d ed., 3, 2d ed.) Vol. 1-3, London, v. 4 - 6, Birmingham, 1795, 84-88. 6 v. 8°.

Theological School of the Ref. Dutch Ch. TAYLOR, B. C. School of the prophets; sermon, July 11. N. Y., 1839. 8°. (B 1303)
Theological Seminaries. *See* **Bangor Theol. Seminary**; — **Princeton Theol. Seminary**; — **Harvard College.** *Divinity School* (p. 1351, 1352).
Theological system of government, A, adapted to the immediate final salvation of mankind. Boston, 1784. 8°. (B 663)

Theology. *Bibliography.*
— DUPIN, L. E. Nouvelle bibliothèque des auteurs eccles. Paris, **1693-1715.** 19 v. 4°.
— *Eng.* History of eccles. writers. 2d ed. London, 1693-95. 7 v. f°.
— BRAY, T. Bibliotheca parochialis, Pt. 1. London, **1697.** 4°.
— - *Another copy.* (B 1398)
— - *Same.* 2d ed., with large add. Vol. 1. London, 1707. 8°.
— - Bibliotheca catechetica; or, Country curates library. London, **1699.** 4°.
— DODD, C. Certamen utriusque ecclesiæ; or, List of all the eminent writers of controversy, Catholics and Protestants, since the Reformation, [**1724**]. (*In* **Somers,** J. Col. of tracts, v. 13. 1815.)
— CLEAVER, W. List of books recommended to the younger clergy; with H. Dodwell's catalogue. [**1791.**] 2d ed. Oxford, 1792. 8°.
— - *Same.* 3d ed. Oxford, 1808. 8°.
— ROESSELT, J. A. Anweisung zur Kenntniss der besten allgemeinern Bücher in allen Theilen der Theologie. 4e Aufl. Lpz., **1800.** 8°.
— EICHHORN, J. G. *See, History, on the next page.*
— ERSCH, J. S. Theologie. (*In his* Handbuch der Deutschen Lit., v. 1. **1822.**)
— NODIER, C. Bibliothèque sacrée grecque-latine; comprenant le tableau chronol., biog., et bibliog. des auteurs inspirés et des auteurs ecclés. depuis Moïse jusqu'à St. Thomas d'Aquin; réd. d'après Mauro et B. Gamba. [**1826.**] 2e éd. Brux., 1828. 8°.
— ZUCHOLD, E. A. Bibliotheca theologica, **1830-62,** in Deutschland erschienenen Schriften. Göttingen, 1864. 2 v. 8°.
— ENSLIN, T. C. F. Bibliotheca theologica bis **1831**; fortgesetzt von C. W. Loeflund. Stuttg., 1833. 8°.
— TALBOYS, D. A. Bibliotheca theologica; catalogue of theolog. books. Oxford, **1835.** 12°.
— NUTT, D. Catalogue of foreign theology. London, **1837,** 45. 4 v. 8°.
— WINER, G. B. Handbuch der theologischen Literatur. Lips., **1838-42.** 3 v. 8°.
— LOWNDES, W. T. British librarian. London, [**1839-43**]. 8°.
— STRAKER, W. Catalogue of books in Eng. and foreign theology. London, [**184-**]. 8°.
— LESLIE, J. Catalogue of Eng. and foreign theology, **1843, 44, 50, 56.** London, 1843-56. 4 v. 8°.
— STRONG, W. Catalogue of English and foreign theology. Bristol, **1845.** 8°.
— DARLING, J. Cyclopædia bibliographica. London, **1854-59.** 3 v. 8°.
— NUTT, D. Catalogue of theological books in foreign languages; on sale. Lond., **1857.** 8°.
— - - Appendix. London, 1857. 8°.
— DARLING, J. Cyclopædia bibliographica; subjects: Holy Scriptures. London, **1859.** 8°.
— MALCOM, H. Theological index; references to the principal works in religious literature. Boston, **1868.** 8°.

See also **Books condemned to be burnt.**

Bibliography. (*Periodicals.*)
— BIBLIOTHECA theologica oder geordnete Uebersicht aller auf dem Gebiete der evangelischen Theologie in Deutschland neu erschienenen Bücher; hrsg. von C. J. Ruprecht. Gött., [1859-66]. 16 pts. 8°.

Common-place books.
— ARETIUS, B. Loci communes Christianæ religionis. Ed. nova. *t.p.mut.* Genevæ, 1617. f°.
— CHEMNITZ, M. Locorum theologicorum, quibus et loci com. Melanchthonis explicantur, tres partes ed. P. Leysero. Witeb., 1610. 3 v. f°.
— MUSCULUS, A. Loci communes ex patribus ac orthodoxis ecclesiæ doctoribus. 2a ed. Erphordiæ, 1568. f°.

History.

— EICHHORN, J. G. Geschichte der theologischen Wissenschaften, 1450-1810. (*In his* Gesch. der Litter., v. 6, pt. 1, 2. 1810-11.)
— VOSSIUS, G. J. Theses theologicæ et hist. de variis doctrinæ Christianæ capitibus. (*In his* Opera, v. 6. 1701.)
— JEFFERIES, —. Five several schemes of Christian religion. London, 1738. 8°. (B 22)
— CLAP, T. Brief history and vindication of the doctrines received in the churches of New England. 2d ed. Boston, 1757. 8°. (C 25, 127)
— PRIESTLEY, J. History of the corruptions of Christianity. Boston, 1797. 2 v. 12°.
— BECK, C. D. Commentarii historici decretorum religionis Christianæ et formulæ Lutheriæ. Lips., 1801. 8°.
— NEWMAN, J. H. Essay on the development of Christian doctrine. N. Y., [1845?]. 8°.
— - *Same.* (*In* Milman, H. H. Savonarola, *etc.* 1870.)
— BAUR, F. C. Lehrbuch der christl. Dogmengeschichte. [1847.] 2e Ausg. Tüb., 1858. 8°.
— HAGENBACH, K. R. Compendium of the history of doctrines; tr. by C. W. Buch. 3d ed. Edin., 1858-59. 2 v. 8°.
— NEANDER, J. A. W. Lectures on the history of Christian dogmas; ed. by J. L. Jacobi; tr. by J. E. Ryland. London, *Bohn*, 1858. 2 v. 8°.
— SHEDD, W. G. T. History of Christian doctrine. N. Y., 1863. 2 v. 8°.
— DONALDSON, J. Critical hist. of Christian literature and doctrine to the Nicene Council. London, 1864-66. 3 v. 8°.

Miscellaneous and collected works.

— BIBLE. *See* Bible (p. 268-291).
— FATHERS OF THE CHURCH. *See* Fathers (p. 965, 966).
— PETRUS *Lombardus, Bp. of Paris, d.* 1164. Sententiarum libri IV. Lugd., 1618. 8°.
— WYCLIF, J., *d.* 1384. Select English works; ed. by T. Arnold. Oxford, 1869-71. 3 v. 8°.
— CUSA, N. de, *Card., d.* 1464. Opera. Basileæ, [1565]. 3 v. f°.
— ZWINGLE, U. Werke, [1522-31; hrsg. von] M. Schuler und J. Schulthess. Zürich, 1828-42. 8 v. 8°.
— TYNDALE, W., *d.* 1536. Doctrinal treatises and introd. to different portions of the Scriptures. Camb., 1843. 8°. (Parker Soc.)
— BULLINGER, H. The old faith. [154-.] (*In* Coverdale, M. Writings. 1844.)
— LUTHER, M., *d.* 1546. Sämmtliche Werke; hrsg. (1-20) von J. G. Plochmann, (21-27) v. J. C. Irmischer. Erlang., 1826-57. 67 v. 8°.
— - The table talk of L.; tr. and ed. by W. Hazlitt. New ed. London, 1857. 8°.
— WILD, J., *d.* 1554. Opuscula varia. Lugd., 1567. 16°.
— HUTCHINSON, R., *d.* 1555. Works. Camb., 1842. 8°. (Parker Soc.)
— PHILPOT, J., *d.* 1555. Examinations and writings; ed. by R. Eden. Camb., 1842. 8°. (Parker Soc.)
— RIDLEY, N., *d.* 1555. Works. Camb., 1841. 8°. (Parker Soc.)
— CRANMER, T., *d.* 1556. Miscel. writings and letters. Camb., 1846. 8°. (Parker Soc.)
— MELANCHTHON, P., *d.* 1560. Opera; ed. (v. 1-15) C. G. Bretschneider, (v. 16-28) K. E. Bindseil. Hal. Sax., 1834-60. 28 v. 4°. (Corpus reformatorum, v. 1-28.)
— TERESA, *St.* Escritos [1561-81]; añididos por V. de la Fuente. Madrid, 1861-62. 2 v. 8°. (Aribau. Bibl., v. 53, 55.)
— BALE, J., *Bp., d.*, 1563. Select works; ed. for the Parker Soc., by H. Christmas. Camb., 1849. 8°. (Parker Soc.)
— COVERDALE, M., *d.* 1569. Remains; ed. by J. Pearson. Camb., 1846. 8°. (Parker Soc.)
— - Writings and translations. Camb., 1844. 8°. (Parker Soc.)
— GRINDAL, E., *d.* 1583. Remains; ed. by W. Nicholson. Camb., 1843. 8°. (Parker Soc.)
— GRANADA, L. de, *d.* 1588. Obras. Madrid, 1850-63. 3 v. 8°. (Aribau. Bibl., v. 6, 8, 11.)
— ZANCHI, G., *d.* 1590. Operum theologicorum tom. VII, VIII. *n.p., excudebat S. Gamonetus,* 1605. 2 v. in 1. f°.
— RAMUS (*French* LA RAMÉE), P. Commentariorum de religione Christiana libri IV. Francof., 1594. 16°.
— PALLANTIERI, G. P. Lectiones aureæ in IV libros Mag. sentent. Venetijs, 1599. 2 v. 4°.
— HOOKER, R., *d.*, 1600. Works. Lond., 1676. f°.
— - *Same.* 2d ed. Oxford, 1841. 3 v. 8°.
— PERKINS, W., *d.* 1602. Workes. Camb., 1608-13. 3 v. f°.
— ARMINIUS, J., *d.* 1609. Works; tr. by J. Nichols and W. R. Bagnall. Auburn, 1853. 8°.
— RENECCIUS, J. Panoplia, i. e., armatura theologica II libris quorum I. originem, II. ordinem Dei cognitionis aperit, ita ut R. Bellarmini mendacia refutentur. Witeb., 1609. f°.
— BOEHME, J. Aurora. [1612.] (*In his* Theosophia revelata, v. 1. 1730; — Sämmtliche Werke, v. 2. 1831.)
— - *Eng.* Aurora. London, 1656. 4°.
— - The remainder of [his] books; Englished by J. Sparrow. London, 1662. 4°.
— SUAREZ, F., *d.* 1617. Opera. Vol. 4, 5. *t.p.w.* [Mogunt., Lugd., 1630.] f°.
— AMES, W. Ad responsum N. Grevinchovii rescriptio contracta. Lugd. Bat., 1617. 24°.
— FULLER, N. Miscellaneorum theologicorum libri IV. Heidelbergæ, 1618. 16°.
— FREWEN, J. Choice grounds and principles of the Christian religion. London, 1621. 16°.
— ARNDT, J. De vero Christianismo. Lunæburgi, [1625]. 12°.
— PARATITLA theologica. *t.p.w.* [Herbornæ, 1625.] 4°.
— VOSSIUS, G. J. Theses de variis doctrinæ Christianæ capitibus. Ed. emend. Oxonii, 1631. 4°.
— POLYANDER, J., *and others.* Synopsis purioris theologiæ. Ed. 2a. Lugd. Bat., 1632. 8°.
— DOWNE, J. Certain treatises. Oxford, 1633. 4°.
— WEEMSE, J. Treatise of the foure degenerate sonnes. London, 1636. 4°.
— JACKSON, T., *d.* 1640. Works. London, 1673. 3 v. f°.
— OWEN, J. Works. [1642-79.] Lond., 1721. f°.
— GROTIUS (*or* DE GROOT), H. In consultationem G. Cassandri annot. cum animadversionibus A. Riveti. Lugd. Bat., 1642. 16°.
— MACCOVIUS (*Polish* MAKOWSKI), J., *d.* 1644. J. Maccovius redivivus op. N. Arnoldi. Ed. alt. Franeq., 1654. 4°.
— WATSON, R. Collection of theol. tracts. [1656-1779.] 2d ed. London, 1791. 6 v. 8°.
— HAMMOND, H., *d.* 1660. Works. (Vol. 1, 2, 2d ed.; 3, 3d ed.) London, 1684, 71-84. 4 v. f°.
— PASCAL, B., *d.* 1662. Pensées. Paris, 1803. 2 v. 12°.

— - Pensées, fragmens, et lettres; pub. par P. Faugère. Paris, 1844. 2 v. 8°.
— - *Same*. Pub. par E. Havet. Paris, 1852. 8°.
— - *Eng*. Thoughts on religion; tr. by D. Kennet. 3d ed. London, 1731. 8°.
— Le Blanc, L. Theses theologicæ, in Acad. Sedanensi editæ. [1663.] Ed. 3a. Londini, 1683. f°.
— Guthrie, W., *d.* 1665. Christian's great interest. Boston, 1728. 12°.
— - *Same*. Andover, 1815. 12°.
— Tillotson, J. The rule of faith; an answer to the treatise of J. Sergeant, 'Sure-footing,' *etc.*; adj., Reply to J. S., his 3d appendix, *etc.*, by Edw. Stillingfleet. [1666.] 2d ed. London, 1676. 8°.
— Taylor, J., *d.* 1667. Whole works. London, 1822. 15 v. 8°.
— Brown *or* Broun, J. Libri duo [contra] Wolzogium [et Welthusium]. Amst., 1670. 12°.
— Leibnitz, G. W., *Freiherr* von. Opera theologica. [1671-1716.] (Vol. 1 *of his* Opera omnia. 1768.)
— Fowler, E. Design of Christianity. [1671.] London, 1676. 8°.
— - *Same*. (*In* Watson, R. Col. of theol. tracts, v. 6. 1791.)
— Templer, J. Idea theologiæ Leviathanis. Londini, 1673. 8°.
— Milton, J., *d.* 1674. Treatise on Christian doctrine; tr. by C. R. Sumner. From London ed. Boston, 1825. 2 v. 8°.
— More, H. Opera theologica; Opera omnia; Script. philos. tom. alter. Londini, 1675-79. 3 v. f°.
— - *Eng*. Theological works. London, 1708. f°.
— Reynolds, E., *d.* 1676. Works. London, 1679. f°.
— Bull, G. Examen censuræ; sive Responsio ad quasdam animad. in librum 'Harmonia apostolica'. Londini, 1676. 4°.
— Glanvill, J. Essays on subjects in philosophy and religion. London, 1676. 4°.
— Owen, J. Σύνεσις πνευματική, causes, waies, and means of understanding the mind of God as revealed in his word. Lond., 1678. 8°.
— Vitringa, K. Observationum sacrarum libri vi. [1683-1708.] Ed. noviss. Jenæ, 1723. 4°.
— Leighton, R., *d.* 1684. Select works. London, 1823. 2 v. 8°.
— - Whole works. New ed. Lond., 1828. 2 v. 8°.
— Hale, *Sir* M. Discourse of religion. (*In his* Several tracts. 1684.)
— Pearson, J., *Bp.*, *d.* 1686. Minor theological works; col., with mem., by E. Churton. Oxford, 1844. 2 v. 8°.
— Rapin, R., *d.* 1687. Use of philosophy in religion. (*In his* Crit. works, v. 2. 1731.)
— Bunyan, J., *d.* 1688. Works; ed. by G. Offor. Glasgow, 1853. 3 v. 8°.
— Hopkins, E., *d.* 1690. Works. London, 1809. 4 v. 8°.
— Flavel, J., *d.* 1691. Works. London, 1701. 2 v. f°.
- - - Πλανηλογία; disc. of mental errors. London, 1691. 16°.
— Polhill, E. The divine will considered in its decrees and holy execution of them. 2d ed. London, 1695. 16°.
— Bates, W., *d.* 1699. Works. 2d ed. London, 1723. f°.
— Religious Tr. Soc. Casgliadau allan ór Ysgrythyrau sanctaidd, yn gosod allan athrawiaethau a dyled swyddau y grefydd Gristionogol. Chelsea, [17—?]. 12°. (C 220)
— Bossuet, J. B., *d.* 1704. Œuvres. Paris, 1841. 4 v. 8°.
— Howe, J., *d.* 1705. Works. N. Y., 1835. 2 v. 8°.
— Beveridge, W., *Bp.*, *d.* 1708. Theological works. Oxford, 1844-47. 10 v. 8°.
— - Short view of B.'s writings. Lond., 1711. 8°.
— Cockburn, J. Answer to queries on some important points of religion occasioned by the late sermon of the Bp. of Bangor. London, 1717. 8°. (C 231)
— Peirce, J. Plain Christianity defended. London, 1719, 20. 4 pts. 8°. (B 108)
— - The security of truth, without the assistance of persecution or scurrility. London, 1721. 8°. (B 108)
— Turretin, J. A. On fundamentals in religion. [1719.] (*In* Sparks, J. Col. of essays, v. 1. 1823.)
— Bulstrode, W. Essays. London, 1724. 8°.
— Clarke, S., *d.* 1729. Works. London, 1738. 4 v. f°.
— Chubb, T. Collection of tracts on various subjects. London, 1730. 4°.
— Waterland, D. Remarks upon Dr. Clarke's Exposition of the Church catechism. 2d ed. London, 1730. 8°. (C 232)
— Gill, J. Doctrines of God's love to his elect; with other truths. London, 1732. 8°.
— - Answer to the Birmingham dialogue writer, *etc.* London, 1737. 8°.
— Wightwick, G. Remarks on Chubbs' 'True Gospel of Jesus'. London, 1740. 8°. (B 117)
— Wilson, T., *Bp.* The knowledge and practice of Christianity made easy, *etc.* [1740.] 2d ed., with add. London, 1741. 12°.
— - *Same*. 1st Amer. from the 8th London ed. Camb., 1815. 12°.
— Dickinson, J. Letters upon subjects in religion. Boston, 1745. 8°.
— Taylor, J. Key to the apostolic writings. [1745.] (*In* Watson, R. Col. of tracts, v. 3. 1791.)
— Watts, I., *d.* 1748. Works; ed. by D. Jennings and P. Doddridge. Lond., 1753. 6 v. 8°.
— Seaton, T., *ed.* Cambridge prize poems; collection of such English poems as have obtained the premium in the Univ. of Cambridge, 1750-1806. Camb., 1817. 2 v. 8°.
— Hodges, W. Christian plan. [1752.] 2d ed. with add. London, 1755. 8°.
— Middleton, C. Miscellaneous works. [1752.] 2d ed. London, 1755. 5 v. 8°.
— Jones, T. Works. [1754-61.] 3d ed. London, 1764. 8°.
— Burton, J. De fundamentalibus diss. theol. Oxonii, 1756. 8°. (E 136)
— Prémontval, A. P. Le G., *dit* de. La théologie de l'être, ou chaine d'idées de l'être jusqu'à Dieu. (*In* Berlin. Ak. d. Wiss. Abh., 1757.)
— Edwards, J., *d.* 1758. Works. 1st Amer. ed. Worcester, 1808-09. 8 v. 8°.
— Hervey, J., *d.* 1758. Whole works. London, 1825. 6 v. 8°.
— Protestant system; containing disc. on the doctrines of natural and revealed religion. London, 1758. 8°.
— Specimen of true theology, or Bible divinity. London, 1758. 8°. (B 132)
— Allen, T. Answer to Pilate's question, What is truth? Prov., 1765. 8°. (B 1713)
— Carpov, J. Œconomia salutis Novi Testamenti. Tomus 4. Rudolstadtii, 1765. 4°.
— Erskine, J. Theological dissertations. London, 1765. 12°.
— M'Ewen, W. Select essays, doctrinal and practical. [1767.] 5th ed. Glasgow, 1790. 12°.
— Riccaltoun, R., *d.* 1769. Works. Edin., 1771-72. 3 v. 8°.

— WHITEFIELD, G., *d.* 1770. Works. London, 1771. 4 v. 8°.
— BLAIR, J. Essays on the sacraments, regeneration, the means of grace. N. Y., 1771. 8°. (B 251)
— PRIESTLEY, J. Institutes of natural and revealed religion. [1772-74.] Vol. 1. 3d ed. London, 1794. 12°. (C 139)
— - *Same.* Vol. 2. London, 1794. 12°. (Unit. Soc. Prom. Christ. Knowl. Tracts. C 140)
— GLAS, J., *d.* 1773. Works. 2d ed. Perth, 1782-83. 5 v. and index 1796. 8°.
— BERRIDGE, J. Christian world unmasked. London, 1773. 8°.
— - *Same.* London, 1805. 12°.
— WARBURTON, W., *d.* 1779. Works. New ed. London, 1811. 12 v. 8°.
— MACGOWAN, J., *d.* 1780. Works. London, 1825. 2 v. 8°.
— PRIESTLEY, J. Appeal to professors of Christianity; added, account of the trial of Elwall. London, 1783. 12°. (C 69)
Note. For other eds. *see* Priestley, J. (p. 2416).
— LOMÉNIE, P. F. M. de. Theses theologico-Hebraicæ, Samaritanæ, et Græcæ. Parisiis, [1785]. 4°. (B 1399)
— NEWTON, T. Twenty six letters on religious subjects, by Omicron. London, 1785. 12°.
— WATSON, R. Collection of theological tracts. [1785.] 2d ed. London, 1791. 6 v. 8°.
— JEBB, J., *d.* 1786. Works. Lond., 1787. 3 v. 8°.
— BROWN, J., *d.* 1787. Posthumous works. Perth, 1797. 12°.
— SKELTON, P., *d.* 1787. Works. London, 1824. 6 v. 8°.
— LE COURAYER, P. F. Déclaration de mes derniers sentimens sur les differens dogmes de la religion ; pub. par G. Bell. Lond., 1787. 8°.
— PRICE, R. Sermons on the Christian doctrine. [1787.] Boston, 1815. 8°. (B 1649)
— - *Same.* With appendix. Boston, 1815. 8°. (B 1008)
— GIB, A. Sacred contemplations. Phila., 1788. 8°.
— WARBURTON, W. Nature and genius of the Christian religion. [1788.] (*In his* Works, v. 6. 1811.)
— LINDSEY, T. The catechist; or, Inquiry into the doctrine of the Scriptures, *etc.* London, 1792. 12°.
— HALL, R. Polemical and other essays. [1793.] From 7th London ed. Boston, 1827. 12°.
— BEVERIDGE, J. Private thoughts upon religion. London, 1795. 12°.
— PRIESTLEY, J. Continuation of the letters to the philosophers and politicians of France on religion, and letters in answer to Paine's 'Age of reason'. Northumberland, 1795. 8°. (B 159, 236, 772)
— WILBERFORCE, W. Practical view of the prevailing religious system of professed Christians in the higher and middle classes, contrasted with real Christianity. [1797.] 3d Amer. ed. Boston, 1803. 16°.
— - *Same.* 4th Amer. ed. Boston, 1815. 8°.
— THEOPHILANTHROPY; or, Spirit of religion in the thirty-nine articles. Lancaster, 1799. 8°. (C 232)
— WORCESTER, N. Remedy for schism as matured in a conference between Abiel and Clement. Brooklyn, [18—]. 8°. (C 226)
— EATON, D. Scripture the only guide to religious truth. London, 1823. 12°.
— - *Same.* York, 1800. 8°. (B 131, 136)
— FREND, W. Animadversions on [Tomline's?] 'Elements of theology. London, 1800. 8°.
— - *Another copy.* (D 131)
— SCOTT, T. Essays on the most important subjects of religion. London, 1800. 8°.
— LUC, J. A. de. Lettres sur le christianisme. Berlin, 1801. 8°. (B 732)
— BEREAN, The; appeal to the Scriptures on questions of utmost importance to the human race. No. 1. Boston, *Berean Soc.*, 1802. 8°. (C 149, 199)
— *Same.* No. 2. Boston, 1802. 12°. (C 160)
— HERDER, J. G. von, *d.* 1803. Vom Geist des Christenthums. (*In his* Sämmtliche Werke, v. 11. 1852.)
— FESSENDEN, T. Theoretic explanation of the science of sanctity. Brattleboro', 1804. 8°.
— PIRIE, A., *d.* 1804. Miscellaneous and posthumous works. Edin., 1805-06. 6 v. (v. 1, 2, 6 w.). 12°.
— PROUDFIT, A. M. Discourses on the doctrines of Christianity. 3d ed. Salem, N. Y., 1806. 12°.
— PAINE, T., *d.* 1809. Theological works; with other pieces. Boston, 1840. 12°.
— SEDGWICK, J. Hints on the nature and effects of evangelical preaching. Pt. 2. *n.t.p.* [London, 1809.] 8°. (B 1357)
— WEBSTER, N. The peculiar doctrines of the Gospel explained and defended, in a letter. [1809.] 3d ed. Portland, 1811. 12°.
— FIVE interesting dialogues between a number of Epis., Presbyt., and Baptist divines, in which the principal doctrines of the Gospel are discussed. New Haven, 1810. 8°. (B 1356)
— WATEROUS, T. T., *Jr.*, *and* Z. Battle-axe, *etc.* [1811.] 2d ed. Groton, 1841. 8°.
— APPLETON, J., *d.* 1814. Lectures and occas. sermons. Brunswick, 1822. 8°.
— SCOTT, T. Treatises on theological subjects. Middletown, Conn., 1815-17. 6 v. 12°.
— FULLER, A., *d.* 1815. Principal works. London, *Bohn*, 1852. 8°.
— FOX, W. J. Sermon on free enquiry in matters of religion. 1815. (*In his* Col. works, v. 1. 1865.)
— SCHELLING, F. W. J. von. Philosophie der Offenbarung. [1815.] Stuttg. und Augsb., 1858. 2 v. 8°. (Werke, pt. 2, v. 3, 4.)
— WILSON, T. Knowledge and practice of Christianity made easy. Camb., 1815. 12°.
— - Maxims of piety and of Christianity. London, 1815. 12°.
— SCHLEIERMACHER, F. E. D. Zur Theologie. [1817.] Berlin, 1836. 8°. (Sämmt. Werke, 2. Bd., 1. Abth.)
— SINCLAIR, H. Letter on the principles of the Christian faith. [1817.] From 2d Lond. ed. Boston, 1820. 8°. (C 232)
— Two heavenly memorialists. Manchester, 1818. 8°.
— BUTLER, T. Faint ray of glorious liberty, *etc.* London, 1819. 8°.
— NORTON, A. Thoughts on true and false religion. Boston, 1820. 8°. (B 964)
— - *Same.* 2d ed. Camb., 1823. 8°.
— SYNOPSIS of theology; examination of the leading doctrines of divinity; two dialogues between Doceo, Studio, and Rationalis. Boston, 1821. 8°. (C 226)
— CLARK, S. Essays. *t.p.w.* [1822.] 12°. (C 220)
— SPARKS, J. Collection of theological essays. Boston, 1823-24. 4 v. 12°.
— COOK, E. B. Testimony of God on the Christian revelation. 2d ed. Hartford, 1823. 12°. (C 221)
— COLERIDGE, S. T. Aids to reflection. [1825.] 1st Amer. ed. from 1st London ed.; with prelim. essay and notes by J. Marsh. Burlington, 1829. 8°.
— WHATELY, R. Essays on the Christian religion. [1st ser. 1825.] 2d ed. Oxford, 1827. 8°.
— HEBEL, J. P., *d.* 18 6. Biblische Erzählungen. — Liturgische Beiträge. — Vermischte Aufsätze. (*In his* Sämmt. Werke, v. 4, 7, 8. 1838.)
— ANDREWS, W. S. Treatise on theological subjects. Camb., 1829. 12°.
— DOCTRINAL TRACT AND BOOK SOC. Publications. No. 1-34. Boston, [1829?]. 12°. (D 69)
— FEARN, J. First principles of physical theology. (*In his* Manual of physiology of mind. 1829.)
— COOKE, J., *d.* 183-. Select remains. London, 1841. 2 v. 12°.

— Bickersteth, E. The Christian student. Boston, 1830. 12°.
— Hall, R., *d.* 1831. Works; with mem. by Dr. Gregory. N. Y., 1833. 3 v. 8°.
— Irving, E., *d.* 1834. Collected writings. London, 1864–65. 5 v. 8°.
— Hase, K. Theologische Streitschriften. Lpz., 1834. 8°.
— Beecher, L. Views in theology. [1835.] 2d ed. Cincin., 1836. 12°.
— - *Same.* (Vol. 3 *of his* Works. 1853.)
— Janney, S. M. Conversations on religious subject and familiar dialogues. [1835.] 4th ed. enl. Phila., 1860. 2 v. in 1. 12°.
— Muzzey, A. B. Doctrinal distinctions not always doctrinal differences. Boston, *A. U. A.*, 1835. 12°. (C 168, v. 9)
— Francis, C. Christianity as a purely internal principle. Boston, *A. U. A.*, 1836. 12°. (C 168, v. 9)
— Marshall, H. Rise of man; or, Christianity unvailed. *n.t.p.* [1837.] 8°. (B 1358)
— De Quincey, T. Theological essays. [1839–52.] Boston, 1854. 2 v. 16°.
— Edwards, B. B., *and* Park, E. A. Selections from German literature. Andover, 1839. 8°.
— Whately, R. Essays on dangers to Christian faith, *etc.* London, 1839. 8°.
— Emmons, N., *d.* 1840. Works; ed. by J. Ide. Boston, 1861–63. 6 v. 8°.
— Blachowicz, P. Nauka chrzescijanska dla uzytku instytutowplci zenskiej. Wydanie 3e. Warszawa, 1840. 12°.
— Inquiry, what is the one true faith? London, 1840. 8°.
— Manahan, A. Theses ex universa theologia. Romæ, 1841. 4°. (A 61)
— Parker, T. Discourse on the transient and permanent in Christianity. 2d ed. Boston, 1841. 8°. (B 1778, 1878)
— - *Same.* (*In his* Critical writings. 1843.)
— Channing, W. E., *d.* 1842. Works. 7th ed. Boston, 1847. 6 v. 12°.
— Parker, T. Discourse of matters pertaining to religion. [1842.] 3d ed. Boston, 1847. 12°.
— Adams, F. W. Theological criticisms, *etc.* Montpelier, 1843. 8°.
— Paulus, H. E. G. Die endlich offenbar gewordene positive Philosophie der Offenbarung. Darmst., 1843. 8°.
— Robinson, E. Bibliotheca sacra; or, Tracts and essays on topics connected with theology. N. Y., London, 1843. 8°.
— Chateaubriand, F. A. R. de. Le génie du christianisme; suivi de la défense du génie du christianisme et de la lettre à M. de Fontanes. Vol. 1. Paris, 1844. 12°.
— Peabody, A. P. Lectures on Christian doctrine. [1844.] New ed., with an introd. lecture on the Scriptures. Bost., Camb., 1857. 16°.
— Matter, A. J. Schelling ou la philosophie de la nature et la philosophie de révélation. Nouv. éd. Paris, 1845. 8°.
— Smyth, T. Fundamental doctrines of Christianity, *etc.*; disc. Phila., 1846. 8°. (C 210)
— Stuart, M. Miscellanies. [1846.] N. Y., 1851. 12°.
— Mountford, W. Christianity; deliverance of the soul and its life, with introd. by F. D. Huntington. Boston, 1847. 16°.
— Muench, F. Treatise on religion and Christianity, orthodoxy and rationalism. Boston, 1847. 12°.
— - *Another copy.* (C 224)
— Feuerbach, L. Das Wesen des Christenthums. 3e Aufl. Lpz., 1849. 8°.
— Newman, F. W. Phases of faith; or, Passages from the history of my creed. [1850.] London, 1865. 8°.
— Bellows, H. W. Re-statements of Christian doctrine. [1851–59.] Boston, *Amer. Unitarian Assoc.*, 1869. 8°.
— Gioberti, V., *d.* 1851. Della filosofia della rivelazione. Torino, 1856. 8°. (Opere ined., v. 2.)
— Woods, L. Works. Boston, 1851. 5 v. 8°.
— Brownson, O. A. Essays and reviews on theology, *etc.* N. Y., 1852. 8°.
— Huntington, F. D., *Bp.* Doctrines of Scripture. Boston, 1852. 16°.
— Maurice, J. F. D. Theological essays. [1853.] From the 2d London ed., with a new preface, *etc.* N. Y., 1854. 12°.
— Wiseman, N., *Card.* Essays on various subjects. London, 1853. 3 v. 8°.
— Noyes, G. R. Collection of theological essays from various authors; with an introd. [1856.] 5th ed. Boston, *Amer. Unitarian Assoc.*, 1867. 12°.
— Schedel, H. E., *d.* 1857. Emancipation of faith; ed. by G. Schedel. N. Y., 1858. 2 v. 8°.
— Adams, N. Evenings with the doctrines. [1858–59.] Boston, 1861. 12°.
— Mansel, H. L. Limits of religious thought; Bampton lectures for 1858. 3d ed. London, 1859. 8°.
— Parker, T. Sermon on false and true theology. Boston, 1858. 8°. (B 1968)
— Views in New England theology; New Eng. theol. contrasted with new Arminianism; The new apostacy; or, A word to the Laodiceans. Boston, 1859–60. 2 nos. 8°. (C 224)
— Hitchcock, E. A. Christ the spirit; the primitive view of Christianity. [1859.] 2d ed. N. Y., 1861. 12°.
— Taylor, I. Logic in theology, and other essays. London, 1859. 16°.
— Essays and reviews. London, 1860. 8°.
— Recent inquiries in theol.; being 'Essays and reviews', ed. with an introd. by F. H. Hedge. 2d Amer. ed., with app. Boston, 1861. 8°.
— Replies to 'Essays and reviews'. Oxford, 1862. 8°.
— Hennell, S. S. Thoughts in aid of faith, gathered chiefly from recent works in theology and philosophy. London, 1860. 8°.
— Tracts for priests and people. London, 1861–62. 2 v. 12°.
— - *Same.* [Vol. 1.] Boston, 1862. 12°.
— Denison, G. A. Analysis of 'Essays and reviews'. London, 1861. 8°.
— Macleod, N. Parish papers. Lond., 1862. 8°.
— Boyd, A. K. H. Graver thoughts of a country parson. Boston, 1863-65. 2 v. 12°.
— Hasted, F. [Coll. of tracts by him. Buffalo, 1863.] 8°.
— James, H. Substance and shadow; morality and religion in their relation to life. Boston, 1863. 8°.
— Frothingham, E. L. *and* A. L. Philosophy as absolute science, including ontology, theology, and psychology made one. Vol. 1. Boston, 1864. 8°.
— Guizot, F. P. G. Méditations sur l'essence de la religion chrétienne. Paris, 1864. 8°.
— - *Eng.* Meditations on the essence of Christianity. London, 1864. 8°.

— Mc Whorter, G. C. Church essays. N. Y., 1864. 8°.
— Rémusat, F. M. C., *comte* de. Philosophie religieuse. Paris, 1864. 18°.
— Manning, H. E., *Card.* Essays on religion and literature. London, 1865. 8°.
— Reville, A. Quatre conférences sur le christianisme. Paris, 1865. 8°.
— Child, A. B. Christ and the people. Boston, 1866. 16°.
— Guizot, F. P. G. Méditations sur l'état actuel de la religion Chrétienne. [2e sér.] Paris, 1866. 8°.
— Martineau, J. Theology in its rel. to progressive knowledge; address. (*In his* Essays, philos. and theolog., v. 1. 1866.)
— Martineau, J. Studies of Christianity; or, Timely thoughts for religious thinkers; a series of papers, ed. by W. R. Alger. Boston, *A.U.A.*, 1867. 12°.
— Bremen lectures, The, on fundamental, living, religious questions [1869]; tr. from the German by Rev. D. Heagle, with introd. by A. Hovey. Boston, 1871. 8°.
— Newman, J. H. Essay in aid of a grammar of assent. 2d ed. London, 1870. 8°.
— Brown, J. B. First principles of ecclesiastical truth; essays on the Church and society. London, 1871. 8°.
— Hutton, R. H. Essays, theological and literary. London, 1871. 2 v. 8°.
— Smith, G. V. The Bible and popular theology. 2d ed. augm. London, 1871. 8°.
— Weiss, J. American religion. Bost., 1871. 12°.
— Woolsey, T. D. The religion of the present and of the future. N. Y., 1871. 8°.

Study.

— Herder, J. G. von. Vom Studium der Theologie und dem christlichen Predigtamt. (*In his* Sämmt. Werke, v. 9. 1852.) — Briefe das Studium der Theologie betreffend. (*In* v. 11, 12. 1852.)

Systematic works.

— Thomas *Aquinas, St., d.* 1274. Summa totius theologiæ. Ed. novis. Paris, 1607. f°.
— - *French.* Somme théologique; tr. par F. Lachat. Paris, 1854–61. 16 v. 8°.
— Calvin, J., *d.* 1564. Institutio Christianæ religionis. (*In his* Opera, v. 6. 1617.) — Tractatus theologici. (*In* v. 7.)
— - *Eng.* Institution of Christian religion; tr. by T. Norton. *t.p.w.* [London, 1587.] 4°.
— - *Same.* London, 1599. 4°.
— Dens, P., *d.* 1577. Theologia moralis et dogmatica. Ed. nova. Dublinii, 1832. 8 v. 12°.
— Pareus *or* Waengler, D. Corpus doctrinæ orthodoxæ, sive Catecheticarum explicationum Z. Ursini opus absolutum D. Parei; adj. sunt Miscellanea catechetica. [1598.] Ed. nova. Heidelbergæ, 1616. 8°.
— Willard, S., *d.* 1607. Body of divinity. Boston, 1726. f°.
— Polanus, A. Syntagma theologiæ Christianæ. Ed. absolutissima. Genevæ, 1617. f°.
— - *Same.* Ed. postrema absolutissima. Francof., Hanov., 1655. f°.
— Yates, J. Modell of divinitie. Lond., 1622. 4°.
— Ames, W. Medulla theologica. [1623.] Ed. noviss. Amstel., 1652. 24°.
— - *Eng.* The marrow of sacred divinity; translated out of the Latine. *t.p.mut.* London, [1642]. 4°.
— Bucan, G. Institutiones theologicæ. Ed. postr. Genevæ, 1625. 16°.
— Polyander, J., *and others.* Synopsis theologiæ. [1625.] Ed. 2a. Lugd. Bat., 1632. 16°.
— Chamier, D. Panstratiæ catholicæ. Genevæ, 1626. 4 v. f°.
— Wolleben, J., *d.* 1629. Compendium theologiæ Christianæ. Ed. 2a. Amst., 1637. 24°.
— - *Same.* Ed. nov. Amstel., 1642. 24°.
— - *Same.* *t.p.w.* [17—.] 12°.
— Colonius, D. Analysis paraphrastica 'Institutionum theologicarum J. Calvini'; disputationibus xli contexta. Lugd. Bat., *ex officina Elzeviriana*, 1636. 12°.
— Fisher, E. Marrow of modern divinity. [1644.] 18th ed., notes by T. Boston. Berwick, 1781. 2 v. 12°.
— Heylyn, P. Theologia veterum; or, The summe of Christian theologie cont. in the Apostles' creed, *etc.* London, 1654. 8°.
— Jeanes, H. Second part of the mixture of scholasticall divinity. Oxford, 1660. 4°.
— Baxter, R. Methodus theologiæ Christianæ. London, 1681. f°.
— Turretin, F., *d.* 1687. Compendium theologiæ didactico-elencticæ auct. et illust. a L. Rissenio. Amstel., 1695. 4°.
— Limborch, P. van. Theologia Christiana. Ed. altera. Amstel., 1695. f°.
— Craig, J. Theologiæ Christianæ principia mathematica. Londini, 1699. 4°.
— Mastricht, P. van, *d.* 1706. Theoretico-practico-theologia. Vol. 1. Amst., 1724. 4°.
— Gastrell, F., *Bp. of Chester.* Christian institutes. [1707.] 10th ed. London, 1771. 12°.
— - *Same.* 14th ed. London, 1808. 24°.
— Beveridge, W., *d.* 1708. Thesaurus theologicus; complete system of divinity. (*In his* Theol. works, v. 9, 10. 1847.)
— Stackhouse, T. Body of divinity. [1729.] 4th ed. London, 1760. f°.
— Dickson, D. True principles of the Christian religion. Glasgow, 1749. 12°.
— Blackwell, T., *d.* 1757. Forma sacra; or, Sacred platform of natural and revealed religion; [with] introd. by S. Williams. Boston, 1774. 16°.
— Doddridge, P. Lectures on pneumatology, ethics, and divinity; [ed. with add.] by A. Kippis. [1763.] London, 1794. 2 v. 8°.
— Bulkley, C. The œconomy of the gospel; in four books. London, 1764. 4°.
— Gill, J. Complete body of divinity. [1769–70.] London, 1796. 3 v. 8°.
— Important truths rel. to Christianity, selected from spiritual writers; with extracts from 'The way to Christ', by J. Behmen. London, 1769. 12°.
— Bielefeld, J. J. F. (*In his* Elements of univ. erudition, v. 1. 1770.)
— Valla, J. Institutiones theologicæ ad usum scholarum. Lugd., 1780. 6 v. 12°.
— Bergier, N. S. Théologie. Paris, 1788–90. 3 v. 4°. (Vol. 157–159 of Encyl. méthod.)
— Hopkins, S. System of doctrines. [1793.] 2d ed. Boston, 1811. 2 v. 8°.
— Tomline, G., *Bp. of Lincoln.* Elements of Christian theology. Vol. 1. 2d ed. London, 1799. 8°.
— - *Same.* *t.p.w.* [London, 1799.] 8°.
— Freylinghausen, J. A. Abstract of the Christian religion. London, 1804. 8°.

— CONN. MISSIONARY Soc. Summary of Christian doctrine and practice; by trustees of the Miss. Soc. of Conn. Hartford, 1804. 8°.
— MARSH, H. Course of lectures cont. a descrip. and systematic arrangement of the several branches of divinity. Pt. 1, 4. [1809-16.] (Pt. 1, 2d ed.) Camb., 1810-19. 2 v. 8°. (B 1016)
— GENERAL view of the doctrines of Christianity. Boston, 1809. 12°.
— CAMPBELL, G. Lectures on systematic theology and pulpit eloquence. Boston, 1810. 8°.
— NEW HAMPSHIRE MISSIONARY Soc. Summary of Christian doctrines. Exeter, 1813. 12°. (C 69, 226)
— DWIGHT, T., *d.* 1817. Theology explained and defended; sermons. Lond., 1827. 6 v. 12°.
— CATLIN, J. Compendium of the system of divine truth. Hartford, 1818. 12°.
— SCHLEIERMACHER, F. E. D. Der christliche Glaube nach den Grundsäzen der evangelischen Kirche. [182–.] 3e Ausg. Berlin, 1835-36. 2 v. 8°. (Sämmtl. Werke, v. 3, 4.)
— ELY, E. S. Synopsis of didactic theology. Phila., 1822. 12°.
— COQUEREL, A. L. C. Cours de religion chrétienne. Paris, 1833. 12°.
— - *Eng.* Treatise on the Christian religion; ed. by J. I. T. Coolidge. Boston, 1851. 18°.
— HOPKINS, J. The Christian's instructer. 2d ed. Auburn, 1833. 12°.
— CONYBEARE, W. D. Elementary course of theological lectures, 1834. 2d ed. London, 1836. 12°.
— WORDSWORTH, C. Christian institutes. [1836.] 2d ed. London, 1842. 4 v. 8°.
— KENRICK, F. P., *Bp.* Theologia dogmatica. Phila., 1839-40. 4 v. 8°.
— PERRONE, J. Prælectiones theologicæ. Romæ, 1840-44. 8 v. in 9 pts. 8°.
— FINNEY, C. G. Lectures on systematic theology; ed. with introd. by G. Redford. London, 1851. 8°.
— RÉVILLE, A. Manuel d'instruction religieuse. Paris, 1863. 8°.

Dictionaries or Encyclopedias.

— LANGE, J. Novissima polyanthea. Francof., 1616. f°.
— - *Same.* Ed. nov. Lugd., 1669. f°.
— ALPHABETICAL explication of some terms in Scriptures, *etc.* *n.p.*, 1786. 12°. (C 227)
— STURM, C. C. Handlexicon für Prediger und theologische Schriftsteller. Göthen, 1790. 2 v. 8°.
— BUCK, C. Theological dictionary. Woodward's 6th Amer. ed., with add.; also acc. of the Cumberland Presbyterians of the U. S. Phila., 1821. 2 v. in 1. 8°.
— VOCABULARY of religious terms. 2d ed. London, 1825. 32°. (D 31)
— BROWN, J. N. Encyclopedia of religious knowledge. Brattleboro, 1836. 2 v. 8°.
— CORRIE, G. E. — ROSE, H. J. (*In* Smedley, E., *and others.* Encycl. metrop., v. 2. 1845.)
— HOOK, W. F. Church dictionary. 5th ed. London, 1846. 12°.
— HERZOG, J. J. Real-Encyklopädie für protestantische Theologie und Kirche. 1.-23. Heft. Hamburg, 1854. 3 v. 8°.
— - 19.-21. Band, oder 1.-3. Supplement-Band. Gotha, 1865-66. 3 v. 8°.
— - Generalregisterband. Gotha, 1868. 8°.
— M'CLINTOCK, J., *and* STRONG, J. Cyclopædia of biblical, theolog., and eccles. literature. N. Y., 1867-80. 9 v. 8°.

Periodicals.

— ADVOCATE of revealed truth and inspector of the religious world. Dublin, 1804. 2 v. 12°.
— AMERICAN and foreign Christian union. N. Y., 1850-60. 11 v. 8°.
— AMERICAN Presbyterian and theol. rev.; ed. by H. B. Smith and J. M. Sherwood. N. s., v. 1. N. Y., 1863. 8°.
— BIBLICAL repertory; a col. of tracts in Biblical lit.; by C. Hodge. Vol. 1-3; 1825-28. Vol. 1 Princeton, v. 2, 3 N. Y., 1825-28. 3 v. 8°.
— *Same.* Biblical repertory; a journal of Bibl. lit. and theol. sci. Vol. 4, n.s. v. 1. Princeton, 1829. 8°.
— *Same.* Biblical repertory and theol. review. Vol. 5. Phila., 1833. 8°.
— *Same.* Biblical repertory and Princeton review. Vol. 13 no. 1, 22, 23 no. 2-4, 24-55. Phila. (v. 41, 42 N. Y.), 1841-80. 35 v. 8°.
— BIBLICAL repository. Andover, 1831-38. 12 v. (v. 10 w.). 8°.
— *Same.* 2d ser. N. Y., 1839-44. 12 v. 8°.
— *Same.* 3d ser. N. Y., 1845-49. 5 v. (v. 4, pt. 3, 4 w.). 8°.
— BIBLIOTHECA sacra. Andover, 1844-80. 37 v. 8°.
— BOSTON quarterly review; [ed. by O. A. Brownson]. Boston, 1838-42. 5 v. 8°.
— BRITISH critic; quarterly theol. review and eccles. record, Jan. 1827 - Apr. 1843. London, 1827-43. 33 v. (v. 28 w.). 8°.
— BROWNSON'S quarterly review. Boston, 1844-46. 3 v. 8°.
— *Same.* 2d ser. Boston, 1847-52. 6 v. 8°.
— *Same.* 3d ser. Boston, 1853-55. 3 v. 8°.
— *Same.* N. Y. ser. N. Y., 1856-63. 8 v. 8°.
— *Same.* National ser. N. Y., [1864]. 8°.
— *Same.* Last ser. N. Y., 1873-75. 3 v. 8°.
— CHRISTIAN disciple; [ed. by N. Worcester]. Boston, 1813-18. 6 v. 8°.
— *Same.* New ser. Christian disciple and Theol. review. Boston, 1819-23. 5 v. 8°.
— CHRISTIAN examiner. Bost., 1824-69. 87 v. 8°.
— CHRISTIAN guardian and Church of Eng. mag. for 1823-24. London, 1823-24. 2 v. 8°.
— CHRISTIAN magazine; by the members of the Mendon Assoc. Vol. 3. Boston, 1826. 8°.
— CHRISTIAN monitor; by Soc. Prom. Christian Knowl. 2d ed. Boston, 1806-10. 8 v. 12°.
— CHRISTIAN observatory. Bost., 1847-48. 4 v. 8°.
Note. Vol. 1, 2 ed. by N. W. McClure; 3, 4 by N. Adams and others.
— CHRISTIAN observer. Vol. 1-20, 22-66. London, 1802-67. 66 v. 8°.
— CHRISTIAN remembrancer; monthly [afterwards quarterly]. Lond., 1841-68. 56 v. 8°.
— CHRISTIAN review. N. Y., 1836-63. 28 v. 8°.
— CHRISTIAN spectator; [pub.] by an assoc. of gentlemen, Jan. 1819 - Nov. 1838. New Haven, 1819-38. 20 v. 8°
— CHRISTIAN visitant; or, Religious miscellany. Boston, 1827-28. 2 v. 12°.
— CHRISTIAN'S magazine; [ed. by J. M. Mason]. N. Y., 1806-11. 4 v. 8°.
— CHRISTLICHE Monatschrift; hrsg. von J. L. Ewald. 2r Bd., 7s-12s Stük. Nürnberg, 1800. 8°.
— CHURCH review and ecclesiastical register; Apr. 1848 - Jan. 1869. Vol. 1-16 New Haven, v. 16-20 N. Y., 1848-69. 20 v. 8°.
Note. After v. 10 called American quarterly review and ecclesiastical register.

— Churchman's magazine. Vol. 6–8. N. Y., 1809–11. 3 v. 8°.
— *Same.* N.s., vol. 1. Elizabethtown, 1813. 8°.
— *Same.* Conducted by the Bp. and clergy of Conn. Vol. 2, 3. Hartford, 1822–23. 2 v. 8°.
— Churchman's repository for the Eastern Diocese. Vol. 1, no. 1–6. Newburyport, 1820. 8°.
— Congregational quarterly; Jan. 1859 – Oct. 1878. Boston, 1859–78. 20 v. 8°.
— Congregational review; devoted to theology and literature. Vol. 7–9. Boston, 1867–70. 3 v. 8°.
— *Same.* 2d ser. Chicago, [1870–71]. 2 v. 8°.
— Congregational visitor; 1850, 53; cont. the proceedings of the Congregational Union of Eng. and Wales. London, 1850–53. 2 v. 8°.
— Connecticut evangelical magazine; July 1800–June 1803. Hartford, 1800–03. 3 v. 8°.
— Cottager's monthly visitant for 1835. Vol. 15, n.s. London, 1835. 12°.
— Edinburgh evangelical magazine. Vol. 1 – 3. Edin., 1803–05. 3 v. 8°.
— Evangelical guardian and review; May 1817 – Apr. 1819. N. Y., 1817–19. 2 v. 8°.
— Evangelical magazine; July 1793 – Dec. 1796; Jan. 1802 – Dec. 1812. London, 1793–1812. 20 v. (v. 5–9, 11 w.). 8°.
— Freewill Baptist quarterly. Vol. 5, 7, 8, 9. Dover, 1857–61. 4 v. 8°.
— Gospel advocate. Vol. 1–6. Boston, 1821–26. 6 v. 8°.
— Gospel magazine; or, Spiritual treasury. Vol. 2. London, 1767. 8°.
— Guardian and monitor. Vol. 8, 9. New Haven, 1826–27. 2 v. 12°.
— Journal of sacred literature; ed. by B. H. Cowper. Vol. 1, 5th ser. London, 1867. 8°.
— Journal of the ministry at large; ed. by C. F. Barnard; Feb. – Dec. Boston, 1841. 8°.
— Latter day luminary; by a committee of the Baptist Board of Foreign Missions. Vol. 1. Boston, 1818. 8°.
— Literary and theological review; [ed.] by L. Wood. N. Y., Boston, 1834–38. 5 v. 8°.
— Menschenfreund, Der; eine Zeitschrift, red. von J. P. Lange. 10r Jahrg. Düsselthal, 1834. 12°.
— Methodist magazine and quarterly review. New ser. [2d], v. 7–11 (whole no., v. 17 – 21). N. Y., 1836–40. 5 v. 8°.
— Methodist quarterly review. 3d ser., v. 1 – 8, (whole no. 23 – 30); ed. by G. Peck. N. Y., 1841–48. 8 v. 8°.
— *Same.* 4th ser., v. 1 – 26, 28, (whole no. 31 – 58). N. Y., 1849–76. 28 v. 8°.
— Monthly magazine of religion and literature; ed. by W. M. Reynolds. Vol. 1; Feb. 1840 – Jan. 1841. Gettysburg, 1840–41. 8°.
— Monthly miscellany of religion and letters. Boston, 1839–43. 9 v. 12°.
— Monthly religious magazine. Boston, 1844–74. 51 v. 8°.
— Monthly repository of theology and general literature. Vol. 1, 2, 4. London, 1806–09. 3 v. 8°.
— *Same.* New ser. Vol. 1 – 5. London, 1827–31. 5 v. 8°.
— New Jerusalem magazine. Vol. 1 – 44. Boston, 1828–72. 44 v. 8°.
— New theological repository. Liverpool, 1800–03. 6 v. 12°.
Note. Vol. 6 called 'Theological review'.

— Olive branch and Christian inquirer; ed. by A. Kneeland. Vol. 1; May 17 – Dec. 27, 1828. N. Y., 1828. 8°.
— Piscataqua evangelical magazine. Vol. 1. Portsmouth, [1805]. 8°.
— *Same.* Vol. 1–3; 1805–07. Portsmouth, [1805–07]. 3 v. 8°. (B 208)
— *Same.* Nov., Dec. 1807. *n.p.*, [1807]. 8°. (B 209)
— Prospective review; a quarterly journal of theol. and literature. Vol. 7 – 10. London, 1851–54. 4 v. 8°.
— Quarterly theological magazine and religious repository. Vols. 1, 2, Burlington, N. J.; v. 3, 4, Phila., 1813–14. 4 v. 8°.
— Radical, The. Boston, 1866–72. 10 v. 8°.
— Religious magazine; ed. by G. D. and J. Abbott; Oct. 1833 – Dec. 1836. Boston, [1833 – 36]. 3 v. 8°.
— Religious magazine and family miscellany; ed. by E. A. Andrews. Boston, [1837–38]. 2 v. 8°.
— Religious monitor; or, Scots Presbyterian magazine. Vol. 2. Edin., 1804. 8°.
— Sabbath at home, The; an illust. magazine. Boston, *Amer. Tract Soc.*, 1867–69. 3 v. 8°.
— Surplice, The; Nov. 29, 1845 – Nov. 27, 1846. [London, 1845–46.] 8°.
— Theological and Biblical magazine for 1805. Vol. 5. London, 1805. 8°.
— Theological and literary journal; ed. by D. N. Lord. Vol. 5–11; July 1852 – Apr. 1859. N. Y., 1853–59. 7 v. 8°.
— Theological magazine.' Vol. 1–3. N.Y., 1796–99. 3 v. 8°.
— Tract magazine and Christian miscellany, 1842, 43, 45–48. London, [1842–48]. 5 v. 12°.
— Unitarian, The; cond. by B. Whitman. Camb., 1834. 8°.
— United States Catholic magazine. Vol. 2–8. Balt., 1843. 7 v. 8°.
— Universalist expositor, The. Vol. 1. Boston, 1831. 8°.
— *Same.* New ser., called The expositor and universalist review. Vol. 1 – 4. Boston, 1834–40. 4 v. 8°.
Note. Vol. 1, ed. by H. Ballou and H. Ballou 2d; v. 1–4, n.s., by H. Ballou 2d.
— Universalist magazine. Vol. 1. Boston, 1819/20. 4°.
— Universalist quarterly and general review. Vol. 1 – 12. Boston, 1844–55. 12 v. 8°.
— Witness, The. Vol. 1, Jan. – June. Boston, [1809]. 12°.

See also **Angels; — Anti-Christ; — Assurance; — Atonement; — Baptism; — Bible; — Catechism; — Children; — Christianity, Evidences of; — Confessions of faith; — Confirmation; — Covenant; — Creation; — Creeds; — Cross, The; — Depravity; — Development; — Devil; — Election; — Eschatology; — Faith; — Fall, The; — Free grace; — God; — Grace; — Grace (before meat); — Half-way covenant; — Heaven; — Heresy; — Holiness; — Holy Spirit; — Immortality; — Infallibility; — Jesus Christ; — Judgment; — Liberty of the will; — Millennium; — Miracles; — Mysticism; — Original sin; — Orthodoxy; — Pelagianism; — Penance; — Perfection; — Plurality of worlds; — Predestination; — Prescience; — Private judgment; — Promises, Divine; — Prophecies; — Providence; — Rationalism; — Reconciliation; — Redemption; — Regeneration; — Religion; — Repentance; — Reprobation; — Retribution; — Revelation; — Righteousness; — Sacraments; — Sacrifice; — Salvation; — Sanctification; — Sin; — Spirits; — Spiritualism; — Tractarianism; — Tradition; — Transubstantiation; — Trinity; — Unregenerate, The.**

For the doctrines of the various sects *see* the names of the sects, a list of which is on p. 2684.

Theology, Natural. *See* Atheism; — Free religion; — God; — Natural religion; — Unbelievers.

Theology, Practical. CLEMENT *Alexandrinus*, *d.* 220. The instructor. (*In his* Writings, v. 1. 1867.)

— BONAVENTURA, *St.*, *d.* 1274. Stimulus divini amoris. Parisius, *D. Rosse*, [151-?]. 8°.

— THOMAS *a Kempis*. De imitatione Christi. [1441?] Londini, 1827. 18°.
Note. For other eds. and translations *see* Thomas *a Kempis*.

— - Soliloquy of the soul; added, meditations and prayers for sick persons, by G. Stanhope. Bennington, 1816. 12°.

— HEROLT, J. Liber discipuli de eruditione χpistifidelium. [Ruotlingiæ, 148-?] f°.

— MAGNUS, J. Sophologium. Paris, 1516. 4°.

— THEOLOGIA deutsch [1516]; hrsg. von F. Pfeiffer. 2e verm. Aufl. Stuttg., 1855. 16°.

— - *Eng.* Theologia Germanica; tr. by S. Winkworth. 2d ed. London, 1854. 16°.

— VALDÉS, J. de. Hundred and ten considerations [1550]; tr. by J. T. Betts. (*In* Wiffen, B. B. Life of V. 1865.)

— BRADFORD, J. Godly meditations. [1553.] London, 1614. 24°.

— GOLDEN words. Pt. 1: The rich jewel of God's word. Pt. 2: Prayer. [1554-1684.] London, 1862. 12°.

— HUTCHINSON, R., *d.* 1555. Works. Camb., 1842. 8°. (Parker Soc.)

— BECON, T., *d.* 1570. Catechism, with other pieces. Camb., 1844. 8°. (Parker Soc.)

— - Early works. Camb., 1843. 8°. (Parker Soc.)

— WALTHER, G. Regulæ vitæ Christianæ. Viteb., 1572. 16°.

— DERING, E., *d.* 1576. Works. Lond., 1614. 4°.

— WOOLTON, J., *Bp.* The Christian manual. [1576.] Camb., 1851. 16°. (Parker Soc.)

— GRANADA, L. de, *d.* 1588. Contemptus mundi, *etc.* Madrid, 1596. 24°.

— CRUZ, S. J. de la, *d.* 1591. Obras. (*In* Escritores del siglo XVI., v. 1. 1853; v. 27 of Aribau. Bibl.)

— NORDEN, J. A progress of piety, *etc.* [1596.] Camb., 1847. 16°. (Parker Soc.)

— CABRERA, A. Tratado de los escrupulos y de sus remedios. Valencia, 1599. 16°.

— LEIGH, *Mrs.* D. The mother's blessing. *t.p.w.* [16—.] 12°

— ARNDT, J. De vero Christianismo libri IV. [1608.] Lunæburgi, [1625]. 24°.

— SUTTON, C. Learn to live. [1608.] 2d Amer. ed. N. Y., 1844. 12°.

— COWPER, W. Holy alphabet for Sion's scholars. London, 1613. 4°.

— HALL, J. Contemplations on the hist. of the N. Testament; rev. by W. Dodd. [1617.] 2d ed. London, 1765. 12°.

— BAYLY, L. Practice of piety, [1619.] 71st ed. Perth, 1792. 12°.

— FRANÇOIS DE SALES, *d.* 1622. Introduccion a la vida devota; tr. por F. de Quevedo Villegas. (*In* Quevedo y Villegas, F. G. de. Obras, v. 2. 1859.)

— - Lettres à des gens du monde. Paris, 1865. 8°.

— DONNE, J. Devotions [1624]; pref., Life by I. Walton. London, 1840. 16°.

— - Works. London, 1839. 6 v. 8°.

— DOWNAME, J. Christian warfare. London, 1634. f°.

— SCUDDER, H. The Christian's daily walk in security and peace. [1637.] 12th ed. rev. London, 1761. 12°.

— LA SERRE, — de. The mirrour which flatters not, *etc.*; tr. by T. Cary. *t.p.w.* [London, 1639.] 12°.

— BROWNE, T. Religio medici. [1642.] 8th ed. corr.; also Obs. by Sir K. Digby. London, 1682. 16°.
Note. For other eds. *see* Browne, T. (p. 401).

— FULLER, T. Holy and profane states; [1642.] Boston, 1831. 16°. (Young's lib. of old Eng. prose writers.)

— - *Same.* New ed. with notes by J. Nichols. London, 1841. 8°.

— - *Same.* [Ed. by E. Abbot.] Bost., 1864. 16°.

— QUARLES, F. Judgment and mercy for afflicted souls. [1644.] New ed., with introd. by B. Wolfe. London, 1807. 16°.

— FULLER, T. Good thoughts in bad times; and other papers. [1645.] Boston, 1863. 16°.

— BURROUGHS *or* BURROUGHES, J. Irenicum; to the lovers of truth and peace. London, 1653. 4°.

— DELL, W. The trial of spirits in teachers and hearers. [1653.] Charlestown, 1809. 12°.

— QUARLES, F. Enchiridion. [1654.] London, 1856. 16°.

— HALL, J., *Bp.*, *d.* 1656. Works. London, 1628. f°.

— WHOLE duty of man, Works by the author of the. [1657.] London, 1687. 2 pts. f°.
Note. For other editions *see* Whole duty of man.

— BOYLE, R. Motives and incentives to the love of God. [1660.] 6th ed. corr. [London,] 1678. 16°.

— BROOKS, T. The silent soul, *etc.* [1660.] Boston, 1728. 12°.

— - *Same, entitled,* The mute Christian under the smarting rod. 13th ed. Glasgow, 1738. 24°.

— JEANES, H. Second part of the mixture of scholasticall divinity with practical. Oxford, 1660. 4°.

— MEAD, M. The almost Christian discovered. 1661. 16th ed. Boston, 1742. 12°.

— - *Same.* 2d Amer. ed. Phila., 1827. 12°.

— DYER, W. Christ's famous titles; The cabinet of jewels; Christ's voice to London. [1663-83.] *t.p.w.* Lond., [16— *or* 17—]. 18°.

— - *Same.* *t.p. and end wanting.* [16— *or* 17—.] 12°.

— AMBROSE, I., *d.* 1664. Christian warrior, *etc.*; abr. by T. Jones. London, 1837. 16°.

— BRINSLEY, J., *d.* 1665. Third part of the true watch, taken out of Ezekiel IX. *t.p.w.* 4°.

— GUTHRIE, W., *d.* 1665. Short treatise of the Christian's great interest. Boston, 1728. 12°.

— - *Same.* Pref., mem. and preface by R. Traill. Andover, 1815. 12°.

— TAYLOR, J., *d.* 1667. Contemplations of the state of man in this life and that which is to come. 9th ed. Boston, 1723. 16°.

— - Rules and exercises of holy living and dying. (*In his* Works, v. 4. 1822; v. 3. 1850.)

— BAXTER, R. Call to the unconverted. [1669.] London, 1767. 12°.

— - *Same.* With introd. by T. Chalmers. N. Y., *Amer. Tr. Soc.*, *n.d.* 18°.

— - *Germ.* Zuruf an Unbekehrte. N. Y., [18—]. 12°.

— RANEW, N. Solitude improved by divine meditation. [1670.] Lond., *Religious Tract Soc.*, [1847]. 12°.

— GALE, T. Theophilie; or, Discourse of the saints amitie with God. *t.p.w.* [London, 1671.] 8°.

— BOUTON, N. Plain scriptural directions to sinners. [1673.] Portsmouth, N. H., 1830. 12°.

— Espinola, F. Directorio de religiosas. Lisboa, 1676. 16°.
— Hale, *Sir* M. Contemplations, moral and divine. [1676.] (Vol. 2, 4th ed.) Glasgow, 1763, 46. 2 v. 12°.
— Janeway, J. Heaven upon earth, *etc.* [1677.] From 3d ed. corr. Boston, 1760. 8°.
— Vincent, T. True Christian's love of the unseen Christ. *t.p.w.* [1677?] 12°.
— Nesse, C. A Christian's walk and work on earth. London, 1678. 16°.
— Flavel, J. Touchstone of sincerity. [1679.] N. Haven, 1809. 12°.
— West, E. Mr. E. West's legacy, *etc.* London, 1679. 16°.
— Corbet, J., *d.* 1680. Self-employment in secret. New ed., by W. Unwin. Charlestown, 1807. 32°.
— Scott, J. Christian life. [1681-86.] 6th ed. London, 1694-96. 4 v. 8°.
— - *Same.* Vol. 1, 2. 12th ed; 3, 4, 6th ed., 5, 8th ed. London, 1757. 5 v. 8°.
— Kettlewell, J. Measures of Christian obedience. [1681.] 3d ed. with add. London, 1696. 8°.
— Keach, B. The progress of Sin; or, The travels of ungodliness. [1683.] 5th ed. corr. with add. London, 1736. 12°.
— Dorney, H. Contemplations. [1684.] 3d ed. Bath, [1773]. 12°.
— Falkner, W. Treatises [and] sermons. London, 1684. 4°.
— Bunyan, J., *d.* 1688. Grace abounding to the chief of sinners, *etc.* 14th ed., with his character. London, 1791. 12°.
— - The Jerusalem sinner saved. Glasgow, 1792. 24°. (D 10)
— - Pilgrim's progress; ed. with introd. by G. Offor. London, 1847. 8°. (Hanserd Knollys Soc.)
Note. For other editions and translations *see* Bunyan, J. (p. 417).
— Borstius, J. Geestlicke genees-konst. Amst., 1689. 2 v. 8°.
— Rawlet, J. The Christian monitor. [1689.] 20th ed. London, 1696. 16°.
— Baxter, R., *d.* 1691. Works; with life by W. Orme. London, 1830. 23 v. 8°.
— Flavel, J., *d.* 1691. A saint indeed; work of a Christian explained. London, 1832. 32°.
— - Treatise on keeping the heart; selected from the works of J. Flavel. 3d ed. Boston, 1819. 24°.
— Ramus, P. Commentarium de religione Christiana libri iv. Francof., 1694. 8°.
— Shaw, S., *d.* 1696. Works. 1st Amer. ed. Boston, 1821. 2 v. 16°.
— Spinckes, N. Of trust in God, *etc.* London, 1696. 8°.
— Lucas, R. Religious perfection, *etc.* [1697.] 3d ed. London, 1704. 8°.
— - Practical Christianity. [1700.] 6th ed. London, 1708. 8°.
— Steele, *Sir* R. The Christian hero; or, No principles but those of religion sufficient to make a great man. 1701. Worcester, 1802. 12°. (B 63)
— Gastrell, F., *Bp. of Chester.* Christian institutes. [1707.] 10th ed. London, 1771. 12°.
— - *Same.* 14th ed. London, 1808. 24°.
— Beveridge, W., *Bp.* Private thoughts upon religion. [1709.] London, 1795. 2 pts. 12°.
— Mather, C. Bonifacius; essay upon the good, *etc.* Boston, 1710. 8°.
— - *Same.* Essays to do good. New ed., improved by G. Burder. Boston, 1808. 12°.
— - *Same.* Johnstown, 1815. 12°.
— - *Same.* Glasgow, 1825. 12°.
— - *Same.* Dover, 1826. 16°.
— Ladies library; pub. by [R.] Steele. Vol. 3: Religion. London, 1714. 3 v. 12°.
— Fénelon, F. de S. de la M., *d.* 1715. Letter upon the truth of religion and its practice. Dublin, 1758. 8°. (D 30)
— - Pious reflections for every day of the month; tr. from the French. Boston, 1818. 24°.
— Wadsworth, B. Sermons on subjects to promote godliness. *t.p.mut.* Bost., 1717. 24°.
— Browne, S. Collection of occasional papers. Vol. 3. London, 1719. 8°.
— La Salle, J. B. de, *d.* 1719. Les devoirs d'un chrétien envers Dieu, *etc.* Nouv. éd. rev. et corr. Montauban, [179-?]. 12°.
— Boston, T. Human nature in its fourfold state. [1720.] 4th ed. Edin., 1744. 16°.
— Cardoso, P. Escada mystica de Jacob. Lisboa, 1721. 16°.
— Walter, N. Disc. on vain thoughts which are hindrances of men's being saved. Boston, 1721. 12°.
— Vitringa, C., *d.* 1722. Korte schets van de Christelyke zeden-leere. Amst., 1724. 16°.
— Bennet, B. Christian oratory; or, Devotion of the closet displayed. [1725.] 3d ed. London, 1732. 8°.
— Law, W. Practical treatise upon Christian perfection. 2d ed. London, 1728. 8°.
— - *Same.* Portsmouth, 1822. 8°.
— Vincent, N. The day of grace, *etc.* Boston, 1728. 16°.
— Great concern of human life. Lond., 1729. 8°.
— Wright, S. Human virtues; or, Collection of the rules of Scripture. London, 1730. 8°. (B 1864)
— Burkitt, W. The poor man's help, and young man's guide. Boston, 1731. 12°.
— Bentley, W. The Lord the helper of his people, *etc.* [1733.] London, 1848. 12°.
— Hayward, J. Hell's flames avoided, *etc.* 35th ed. London, 1733. 24°.
— Danes, P. L. Tractatus de fide, spe, et charitate; de scriptura, traditione, ecclesia, pontifice, et conciliis. [1734.] Ed. nova. Lovanii, 1770. 8°.
— Rowe, *Mrs.* E. Devout exercises of the heart, *etc.* [1737.] 4th ed. Boston, 1742. 12°.
— - *Same.* Walpole, N. H., 1802. 12°.
— Wilson, T., *Bp.* The knowledge and practice of Christianity made easy, *etc.* [1740.] 2d ed., with add. London, 1741. 12°.
— - *Same.* 1st Amer. from 8th London ed. Camb., 1815. 12°.
— Shaw, S. Immanuel; or, A discovery of true religion. Boston, 1741. 16°.
— - *Same.* 3d ed. Boston, 1744. 12°.
— Melmoth, W., *d.* 1743. Importance of a religious life; memoir and app. by C. P. Cooper. London, 1849. 8°.
— Welwood, A. Meditations representing a glimpse of glory, *etc.* Boston, 1744. 12°.
— Hervey, J. Meditations and contemplations. [1746-47.] Brattleborough, 1814. 2 v. in 1. 12°.
— - Meditations among the tombs. [1746.] New ed. Exeter, 1824. 12°.
— Jones, T. Works. [1754-61.] 3d ed. London, 1764. 8°.

— MASON, J. Self-knowledge. [1754.] 5th ed. London, 1755. 8°.
— - *Same.* Wilmington, 1801. 12°.
— - *Same.* Boston, 1821. 18°.
— MOSHEIM, J. L. von, *d.* 1755. Vollständiger Kern aus Mosheim Sitten-Lehre heiliger Schrift; hrsg. von G. F. Sommerau. Neue Aufl. Quedlinburg, 1763. 16°.
— WILLIAMS, J., *d.* 1755. Extracts from the diary of J. W.; [ed. by B. Fawcett]. New ed. London, 1825. 24°.
— YOUNG, E. The centaur not fabulous. [1755.] 1st Boston from 3d London ed. Boston, 1805. 12°.
— HERVEY, J., *d.* 1758. The beauties of Hervey, selected from [his] works. Phila., 1796. 12°.
— MORRICE, M. Social religion exemplified. London, 1759. 8°.
— HERVEY, J. Collection of letters. [1760.] Glasgow, 1792. 12°.
— LAW, W., *d.* 1761. Serious call to a devout and holy life. 17th ed. Boston, 1818. 12°.
— - *Same.* New ed., abr. by H. Malcolm. Boston, 1835. 12°.
— BELLAMY, J. Essay on the nature and glory of the gospel of Jesus. Boston, 1762. 12°.
— GREATEST concern in the world, The; essay to answer, What must I do to be saved? 4th ed. New Haven, 1765. 8°. (B 259)
— WALKER, S. Practical Christianity; illust. in nine tracts. London, 1766. 12°.
— M'EWEN, W. Select essays doctrinal and practical. [1767.] 5th ed. Glasgow, 1790. 12°.
— ALARUM, The; thoughts on Christianity. Pt. 1. London, 1768. 8°. (C 227)
— LANGDON, S. Summary of Christian faith and practice. Boston, 1768. 8°. (B 60, 227, 250)
— - *Same.* *n.t.p.* [17—.] 8°. (B 860)
— STRATTON, T. Aureæ sententiæ; select sentences from eminent divines, *etc.* London, 1768. 16°.
— BERRIDGE, J. Christian world unmasked. London, 1773. 8°.
— - *Same.* New ed., added, Chearful piety. London, 1805. 12°.
— BOSTON, T. Distinguishing characters of true believers. [1773.] Falkirk, 1791. 12°.
— CHAPONE, *Mrs.* A. M. Letters on the improvement of the mind. [1773.] Boston, [17—]. 2 v. 12°.
— - *Same.* N. Y., 1819. 32°.
— - *Same.* Boston, 1834. 18°.
— - *Same.* Also The father's legacy, by J. Gregory; [and] Mother's advice, by Lady Pennington. Boston, 1822. 18°.
— HASENKAMP, J. H. Christliche Schriften [1778-1814]; hrsg. von C. H. G. Hasenkamp. 2e Aufl. 1s Bdchen. Münster, 1818. 8°.
— SCOTT, T. Treatises on theological subjects. [1779-1803.] From the Phila. ed. Middletown, Conn., 1815-17. 6 v. 12°.
— GENLIS, S. F. D. de St. A. La religion considérée comme base du bonheur. [1781.] Paris, 1826. 12°. (Œuvres, v. 83.)
— SPRING, S. Friendly dialogue upon duty. Newbury-Port, 1784. 12°.
— ALMEYDA, T. de. El hombre feliz. [1785.] T. 1, tr. por B. E. de Riol. 6a impr.; t. 2, 3, tr. por J. F. Monserrate y Urbina. Madrid, 1788, 85. 3 v. 16°.
— NEWTON, J. Twenty-six letters on religious subjects, by Omicron. London, 1785. 12°.
— BURN, *Gen.* A. Who fares best, the Christian, or the man of the world? [1789.] 1st Amer. from 3d London ed. Boston, 1816. 18°.
— SMITH, S. S. Discourse; guilt and folly of being ashamed of religion, Oct. 17, 1790. Boston, 1791. 8°. (B 231, 854, 2508)
— MORE, H. Estimate of the religion of the fashionable world. [1791.] (*In her* Works, v. 3. 1818.)
— CHRISTIAN economy; tr. from the Greek of an old ms. found in Patmos. Phil., 1792. 12°. (C 149)
— THOMSON, J. Nature of true religion, *etc.*; sermon, Nov. 25, 1792. Edin., 1793. 8°. (B 1860)
— ARVISINET, C. Mémorial des vierges chrétiennes; trad. libre du 'Memoriale vitæ sacerdotalis'. [1794.] Troyes, 1829. 12°.
— TOWNSEND, S. Gospel news divided into eleven sections. Boston, 1794. 8°.
— GOBINET, C. Instruccion de la juventud en la piedad christiana; tr. por J. A. Turbique. Barcelona, 1795. 4°.
— MURRAY, L. Power of religion on the mind. Trenton, 1795. 12°.
— - *Same.* 15th ed. York, 1810. 8°.
— - *Same.* New ed. London, 1845. 12°.
— SCOTT, T. Treatise on growth in grace, with ref. to St. Paul's prayer for the Philippians. London, 1795. 8°. (C 193)
— SPALDING, J. J. Religion eine Angelegenheit des Menschen. [1797.] 3e Aufl. Berlin, 1799. 12°.
— WILBERFORCE, W. View of the religious system of professed Christians. 5th ed. London, 1797. 12°.
— - *Same.* 4th Amer. ed. Boston, 1815. 12°.
— STEARNS, C. Principles of religion and morality. [1798.] 3d ed. Portsmouth, N. H., 1807. 12°.
— DISNEY, J. Superiority of religious duties to worldly considerations; sermon. Lond., 1800. 8°. (B 1916)
— HILL, R. Village dialogues. [1801.] From 18th London ed. N. Y., 1825. 3 v. 12°.
— GROU, J. N., *d.* 1803. The hidden life of the soul; [tr.] from the French. Phila., 1871. 16°.
— NEALE, *Miss* H. Experimental religion delineated; with pref. by J. Ryland, and mem. by S. Greatheed. 2d ed. 1803. 12°.
— ALLINE, H. Two mites cast into the offering of God, *etc.* Dover, N. H., 1804. 12°.
— DOBSON, T. Letters on the Deity, and on the moral state of man. Phila., 1804. 2 v. 12°.
— DODDRIDGE, P. Rise and progress of religion in the soul. Northampton, 1804. 12°.
— - *Same.* 3d ed. N. Y., 1817. 12°.
— - *Gaelic.* [Tr. by] P. Macpharlain. Edin., 1811. 12°.
— KNEELAND, A. Columbian miscellany for the followers of Christ. Keene, 1804. 12°.
— PRIESTLEY, J., *d.* 1804. Views of Christian truth, piety, and morality; with mem. by H. Ware, Jr. Camb., 1834. 12°.
— REFUGE, The. 1st Amer. ed. Phila., 1804. 12°.
— BUCK, C. Treatise on religious experience. [1805.] From the 2d London ed. Boston, 1810. 12°.
— DIVINE breathings, *etc.* 2d Amer. ed. Boston, 1805. 12°.
— SCOUGAL, H. The life of God in the soul of man; with pref. by Bp. Burnet and others. Phila., 1805. 12°.
— - *Same.* [With] mem. of the author. Boston, 1806. 8°. (D 29)
— CONSIDERATIONS on the alliance between Christianity and commerce, applied to the present state of this country. London, 1806. 8°. (B 779)

— INNES, W. Sketches of human nature. [1807.] 3d ed. Edin., 1823. 12°.
— MASON, W. Spiritual treasury. Boston, 1809. 2 v. 12°.
— ZSCHOKKE, J. H. D. Meditations on death and eternity [1809?]; tr. by F. Rowan. London, 1862. 8°.
— - Meditations on life and its religious duties [1809?]; tr. by F. Rowan. Lond., 1863. 8°.
— COLLIER, W. Gospel treasury; comp. chiefly from London evang. mag. Charlestown, 1810-11. 4 v. 12°.
— CECIL, R., *d.* 1810. Remains; ed. with mem. by J. Pratt. Armstrong's ed. Boston, 1817. 12°.
— TRUMBULL, B. Treatise on covenanting with God. N. Y., 1810. 12°.
— WEEKLY monitor, The; essays [contrib. to Charleston Courier] by a lay-man. Phila., 1810. 8°.
— MORE, H. Practical piety. Boston, 1811. 2 v. 12°.
— - *Same.* Balt., 1812. 2 v. in 1. 12°.
— - *Same.* (*In her* Works, v. 5. 1818.)
— GRIFFIN, J. Decline of religion; inquiry into [its] causes; sermon. 2d ed. London, 1812. 8°. (B 284)
— FELTON, J. The pleasures of religion; letters to his son. Pt. 1. [1813.] 2d ed. London, 1814. 12°. (C 160)
— FOSTER, *Miss* R. Miscellaneous writings. Boston, 1813. 12°.
— MANAGEMENT of the tongue; tr. from the French. Boston, 1813. 12°.
— MORE, H. Christian morals. 1st Amer. from 4th London ed. N. Y., 1813. 12°.
— - *Same.* (*In her* Works, v. 7. 1818.)
— SPRING, G. Essays on traits of Christian character. N. Y., 1813. 8°.
— - *Same.* Boston, 1819. 12°.
— PENN, G. The bioscope; added, a trans. of St. Paulinus's epistle to Celantia on the rule of Christian life. 2d ed. London, 1814. 12°.
— BIDDULPH, T. T. Inconsistency of conformity to the world with a profession of Christianity. [1815.] 1st Amer. ed. Boston, 1816. 12°.
— GOSSNER, J. E. The heart of man the temple of the Lord or the Devil's workshop. [1815. In Armenian.] Calcutta, 1839. 16°.
— STRAUSS, G. F. A. The chime of the bells [1815; tr.] by H. Bokum. Boston, 1836. 12°.
— WILSON, T. Maxims of piety and of Christianity. Bath, 1815. 12°.
— WOODBURY, *Miss* F. Writings; selected and ed. by J. Emerson. Boston, 1815. 12°.
— CROWTHER, P. W. Christian's manual; compiled from the 'Enchiridion militis Christiani' of Erasmus. London, [1816]. 8°.
— KEBLE, J. Letters of spiritual counsel and guidance, [1817-65]; ed. by R. F. Wilson. 2d ed. Oxford, London, 1870. 8°.
— WILKS, S. C. Christian essays. [1817.] From 2d London ed. Boston, 1829. 12°.
— THOUGHTS on vital religion. [182-.] 2d ed. Boston, *A.U.A.*, 1830. 12°. (C 168, v. 3.)
— RAMMOHUN ROY. Appeal in defence of the 'Precepts of Jesus'. Calcutta, 1820. 8°.
— - *Another copy.* Calcutta, 1820. 8°. (B 1469)
— CHALMERS, T. Application of Christianity to the commercial and ordinary affairs of life. N. Y., 1821. 8°.
— DICKINSON, R. Christian and miscellaneous portfolio. Phila., 1823. 12°.
— ORIGINAL memorials; by a clergyman of the Church of England. 2d ed. Lond., 1823. 12°.
— WILKS, S. C. Essay on the influence of a moral life, *etc.*, on our judgment in matters of faith. Boston, 1823. 8°. (B 273)
— COLERIDGE, S. T. Aids to reflection. [1825.] 1st Amer. from 1st London ed.; with prelim. essay and notes by J. Marsh. Burlington, 1829. 8°.
— TAYLOR, *Mrs.* The itinerary of a traveller in the wilderness. Boston, 1825. 12°.
— EXPERIMENTAL religion. Boston, *A.U.A.*, 1827. 12°. (C 168, v. 2.)
— BROOKS, C. Daily monitor; or, Reflections for each day in the year. Boston, 1828. 8°.
— LINSEY, J. H. Lectures on the relations and duties of the middle-aged. Hartford, 1828. 12°.
— BICKERSTETH, E. The Christian student. [1829.] From 2d London ed. Boston, 1830. 12°.
— BULLARD, A. Select memoirs of pious individuals. Vol. 2. Boston, *Mass. S. S. Union*, 1829. 18°.
— EVANGELICAL spectator. 2d ed. London, 1829. 12°.
— NEW year. *n.t.p.* [183-?] 12°. (C 204)
— WRIGHT, T. A good life, ex. from 'The true plan of a living temple'; with introd. essay by J. Brazer. [1830.] Boston, 1836. 12°.
— FURNESS, W. H. The genius of Christianity. Manchester, 1830. 12°. (C 246)
— - *Same.* 2d ed. London, 1832. 8°. (C 207)
— - *Same.* 2d ed. Boston, *A.U.A.*, 1830. 12°. (C 168, v. 3.)
— CARTER, J. Old things and new things, *etc.* Sleaford, 1831. 8°.
— HINTS for reflection; comp. from various authors. London, 1831. 32°.
— WARE, H., *Jr.* Formation of the Christian character. 2d ed. London, 1831. 12°.
— - *Same.* 12th ed. Boston, 1845. 12°.
— COGSWELL, W. Harbinger of the millenium. Boston, 1833. 12°.
— SHERMAN, J. A help to acquaintance with God. From 8th London ed. Boston, 1833. 16°.
— STEVENS, *Mrs.* M. Progressive experience of the heart. Phila., 1833. 12°.
— COBBETT, W. Thirteen sermons on hypocrisy, *etc.* N. Y., 1834. 12°.
— LAMENNAIS, H. F. R. de. Words of a believer; tr. from the French. New York, 1834. 12°.
— THORNTON, J. The preciousness of Christ to all who believe. Boston, 1834. 12°.
— ABERCROMBIE, J. Essays and tracts. [1835.] Edin., [1842]. 12°.
— FITCH, C. Inquirer's guide, *etc.* Hartford, 1835. 12°.
— PIKE, J. G. Religion and eternal life, *etc.* N. Y., 1835. 12°.
— CHARLES, T. Essays, letters, and papers; ed. by E. Morgan. London, 1836. 12°.
— WAY of escape, The, from temporal evils and eternal death. Boston, 1836. 12°.
— INNES, W. Food for meditation. Edin., 1837. 32°.
— HALSEY, J. F. Union; or, The destinies of the world in the hands of the Church. N. Y., 1838. 12°.
— BAD effects of speculative theology on the morals of mankind. 3d ed. Phila., [1839?]. 8°. (B 1354)
— BAIN, W. T. Letters and meditations. Raleigh, 1839. 12°.
— PALMER, R. Spiritual improvement; aid to growth in grace. Boston, 1839. 12°.

— Park, E. A. Duties of a theologian; anniv. address before the Theolog. Soc. of Dartmouth Coll., July 24. N. Y., 1839. 8°. (B 1840)
— James, J. A. The anxious inquirer after salvation. N. Y., *Amer. Tract Soc.*, [184-?]. 18°.
— Hedge, F. H. Practical goodness the true religion; sermon. Bangor, 1840. 8°. (B 1878)
— Merritt, T. The Christian's manual, *etc.* N. Y., 1840. 32°.
— Serious thoughts on the two tables of the law. Boston, 1840. 12°. (C 225)
— Kenrick, F. P., *Bp.* Theologia moralis. Phila., 1841-43. 3 v. 8°.
— Hints for daily meditation and examination, *etc.* 3d ed. Bath, [1842]. 16°.
— Waterson, R. C. Thoughts on moral and spiritual culture. Boston, 1842. 16°.
— White, H. The gospel promotive of true happiness. Dublin, 1843. 8°.
— Goldolphin, G. The unique; cont. hints for ministers, churches, and Christians. Boston, 1844. 12°.
— Smith, J. The book that will suit you. N. Y., 1844. 24°.
— Hamilton, J. Life in earnest; or, Christian activity and ardour, *etc.* Phila., *Amer. S. S. Union*, [1845]. 12°.
— Robbins, C. Our pastors' offering. Boston, 1845. 16°.
— Bushnell, H. Views of Christian nurture. Hartford, 1847. 12°.
— - *Same.* Christian nurture. [New ed. enl.] N. Y., 1861. 12°.
— Mountford, W. Christianity the deliverance of the soul and its life. Boston, 1847. 16°.
— Ware, H., *Jr.* Progress of the Christian life. 2d ed. 1847. 12°.
— Magoon, E. L. Proverbs for the people. Boston, 1849. 12°.
— Weethee, J. P. The battle of Armageddon, *etc.* 2d ed. rev. and enl. Boston, 1849. 12°.
— Education for God. London, 1851. 16°.
— Mountford, W. Euthanasy; or, Happy talk towards the end of life. 3d ed. with add. Boston, 1851. 16°.
— Briggs, G. W. Lessons upon religious duties. Boston, 1852. 16°.
— Brownson, O. A. Essays and reviews on theology, *etc.* N. Y., 1852. 8°.
— Mayo, A. D. Graces and powers of the Christian life. Boston, 1852. 12°.
— Abbott, J. The corner stone. N. Y., 1855. 8°. (Young Christian ser., v. 2.)
— Bartol, C. A. Grains of gold, *etc.* 3d thous. Boston, 1855. 24°.
— Haven, *Miss* C. M. Beginning and growth of Christian life. [1855.] 4th ed. Boston, *A.U.A.*, 1867. 16°.
— - The homeward path. [1856.] 4th ed. Boston, 1868. 16°.
— Cumming, J. The daily life, *etc.* Boston, 1857. 12°.
— Swetchin, *Mme.* A. S. S., *d.* 1857. Writings of Mme. Swetchine; ed. by Count de Falloux; tr. by H. W. Preston. Bost., 1869. 12°.
— Peabody, E. Christian days and thoughts. Boston, 1858. 16°.
— Beecher, H. W. New star papers. N. Y., 1859. 12°.
— Phelps, A. The still hour. Bost., 1860. 16°.
— Goulburn, E. M. Thoughts on personal religion. [1861.] 4th Amer. ed.; with a pref. note by G. H. Houghton. N. Y., 1869. 12°.
— Greenwell, D. A present heaven. Boston, 1863. 12°.
— Reville, A. Manuel d'instruction religieuse. Paris, 1863. 8°.
— Cobbe, F. P. Religious duty. Boston, 1865 [1864]. 12°.
— Dodge, M. A. Stumbling-blocks. Boston, 1864. 12°.
— Maurice, J. F. D. The conflict of good and evil in our day. London, 1865. 8°.
— Branks, W. Meet for heaven, *etc.* 31st thousand. Edin., 1866. 16°.
— Friswell, J. H. The silent hour. 2d ed. [London,] 1868. 16°.
— Child, A. B. Better views of living. Boston, 1869. 16°.
— Hitchcock, A. Organic and parallel rel. of some of the practical truths and errors of Christianity and medical science. (*In* Mass. Med. Soc. Med. com., v. 11. 1869.)
— Spurgeon, C. H. John Ploughman's talk, *etc.* N. Y., [1869]. 16°.
— Beecher, H. W. Lecture-room talks; disc. on themes of general Christian experience. N. Y., 1870. 8°.
— Goulburn, E. M. The pursuit of holiness; sequel to 'Thoughts on personal religion'. N. Y., 1870. 12°.

See also **Afflicted; — Bible; — Blasphemy; — Camp-meeting; — Catechising; — Charity; — Christian character; — Christian hero; — Christian life; — Christian gentleman; — Conferences; — Conscience; — Conversion; — Cross, The; — Devotion; — Doubt; — Family worship; — Fanaticism; — Fasting; — Fasts; — Festivals; — Forgiveness; — Grace** (*before meat*)**; — Holiness; — Indifference; — Kisses; — Mourning; — Penitence; — Perfection; — Perjury; — Perseverance of saints; — Piety; — Prayer; — Private judgment; — Religious affections; — Religious education; — Repentance; — Responsibility; — Revivals; — Righteousness; — Sabbatarians; — Sanctification; — Self-knowledge; — Silent worship; — Temptation.**

Theolytus. Fragm. (*In* **Mueller,** C. Fr. hist. Gr., v. 4. 1851.)
Theon *Alexandrinus.* Scholia. (*In* **Aratus** *Solensis.* Diosemea. 1815.)
Theon, Aelius. Προγυμνάσματα. (*In* **Spengel,** L. Rhetores Gr., v. 2. 1854.)
Theon Utazása Görögorszagban, 1835. Posonyban, 1836. 12°.
Theonas, *Bishop of Alexandria.* Epistle to Lucianus, the chief chamberlain; tr. by S. D. Salmond. — Biog. notice. (*In* **Methodius.** Writings. 1869.)
Theophanes *Byzantius.* Excerpta. (*In* **Byzantinæ** hist. scr., v. 1. 1729; — *and in* **Niebuhr.** Byzant. hist. script., v. 14. 1829.)
— Fragm. (*In* **Mueller,** C. Fr. hist. Gr., v. 4. 1851.)
Theophanes *Isaurus.* Chronographia. (*In* **Byzantinæ** hist. scr., v. 6. 1729; — *and in* **Niebuhr.** Byzant. hist. script., v. 39, 40. 1839-41.)
Note. For continuation *see* **Byzant.** hist. scr., v. 16, *and* **Niebuhr.** Byzant. hist., v. 33.
Theophanes, Cneius Pompeius. Fragm. (*In* **Mueller,** C. Fr. hist. Gr., v. 3. 1849.)
Theophilanthropist, The; containing crit., moral, theolog., and lit. essays; by a society. N. Y., 1810. 8°.
Theophilanthroy; or Spirit of religion, in thirty-nine ar-h ticles. Lancaster, 1799. 8°. (C 84, 232)
Théophile, Le miracle de; par Rutebeuf. (*In* **Monmerqué,** L. J. N., *and* **Michel,** F. Théâtre franç. 1842.)
Theophilus. Comment in Canticum canticorum. (*In* **Mai,** A. Class. auct., v. 9. 1837.)
Theophilus *or* **Rugerus.** De diversis artibus; with Eng. tr. by R. Hendrie. London, 1847. 8°.
Theophilus *Aletheus.* *See* **Lyser,** J.
Theophilus *Anglicanus.* *See* **Wordsworth,** C.
Theophilus *antecessor.* Institutiones [Gr., ed.] D. Gothofredo; acc. Theophili benedictorum et perperam ab eodem admissorum libri IV, auct. Gothofredo. [Genevæ,] 1620. 4°.

— Paraphrase der Institutionen Justinian's; übersetzt von R. Wüstmann. Berlin, 1823. 2 v. 8°.
— Paraphasis Græca institutionum Cæsarearum; cum notis P. Nannii, J. Curtii, et al.; ed. G. O. Reitz. Hagæ Com., 1751. 2 v. 4°.
Theophilus *comicus*. Fragm. (*In* **Meineke, A.** Fr. com. Gr., v. 3. 1840; Poet. com. Græc. fragm. 1855.)
Theophilus *historicus*. Fragm. (*In* **Mueller, C.** Fr. hist. Gr., v. 4. 1851.)
Theophilus *Patriarcha Antiochenus*. Contra Christ. relig. calumniatores ad Autolycum. (*In* **Justinus.** Opera. 1686.)
— - *Eng.* Three books to Autolycus; tr. by M. Dods. (*In* **Tatianus.** Writings. 1867. Ante-Nicene lib., v. 3.)
— Donaldson, J. [Memoir of] Theophilus. (*In his* Critical history of Chr. lit., v. 3. 1866.)
Theophilus, *pseud.* Defence, *etc.* 1787. *See* **O'Leary, A.** (B 341)
Theophilus, *pseud.* [S. Spring?]. Essay on the discipline of Christ's house; [with] remarks on the 'Plan of eccl. order', which the Gen. Assoc. has presented for publick consideration. Newburyport, 1816. 8°. (B 260, 263)
Theophilus, *pseud.*, *and* **Eugenio**, *pseud.* Letters on the moral pravity of man. Phila., 1747. 4°. (A 2)
Theophrastus. Opera quæ supersunt omnia; [Gr.] ex recog. F. *Wimmer*. Vol. 1, 2. Lips., *typis Teubnerii*, 1854. 2 v. 16°.
Contents. Vol. 1. Historia plantarum. 2. De causis plantarum ll. vi.
— Characteres; [Gr.] (*In* **Siebenkees, J. P.** Anecdota Græca. 1798.)
— Characters; tr. and illust. by physiognomical sketches; subjoined the Greek text with notes and hints on the varieties of human nature, by F. Howell. London, 1824. 4°.
— The moral characters in Græca majora; tr., [with] notes, [by C. D. Cleveland]. Andover, 1826. 8°.
— Characteres, Marci Antonini commentarii, *etc.*, Gr. et Lat.; emend. F. Dübner. Parisiis, *Didot*, 1840. 8°.
— *Eng.* The moral characters; tr. with notes; prefixed, a critical essay on characteristic writings by H. Gally. London, 1725. 8°.
— - Characters; illustrated by physiognomical sketches [by F. Howell]. Boston, 1831. 12°.
See also, above, Characters, 1824; Moral characters. 1826.
— *French.* Les caractères; tr. par La Bruyère; avec add. et notes par J. G. Schweighæuser. Paris, 1813. 12°.
— - *Same.* (*In* **La Bruyère, J. de.** Caractères, v. 2. 1822.)
— - *Same.* Tr. avec les caractères ou les mœurs de ce siècle par La Bruyère. Nouv. éd., par A. Destailleur. Paris, 1861. 2 v. 18°.
Contents. Vol. 1. Les caractères de La Bruyère. 2. Les caractères de T.
— Περὶ τῶν λίθων; with Eng. vers. and notes. 2d ed., enl. by the add. of a Greek index of all the words in T., *etc.*, by J. Hill. London, 1774. 8°.
— Figuier, G. L. (*In his* Vies des savants illustres. 1866.)
Theophylactus, *Bishop of Bulgaria.* In quatuor Evangelia enarrationes [J. Œcolampadio interprete]. Basil., 1527. f°.
Theophylactus *Simocatta*. Ex ejus Historia de legatis Romanorum ad gentes. (*In* **Byzant.** hist. scr., v. 1, 1729.) — Historiarum libri viii. (*In* v. 3. 1729; — *and in* **Niebuhr.** Byzant. hist. scr., v. 22. 1834.)
— Histoire de l'empereur Maurice. (*In* **Cousin, L.** Hist. de Constantinople, v. 3. 1772.)
Theopompus *Chius*. Hellenica. — Philippica, *etc.* (*In* **Mueller, C.** Fr. hist. Gr., v. 1. 1841.)
Theopompus *comicus*. Fragm. (*In* **Meineke, A.** Fr. com. Gr., v. 2. 1840.)
Theoptes, *pseud.* *See* **Durfee J.**

Théorie de l'impôt; [par V. R. de Mirabeau]. *n.p.*, 1761. 12°.
Theory of agency; or, Essay on moral freedom; [by a well-wisher to mankind]. Boston, 1771. 8°. (B 251)
Theory of agreeable sensations; the laws obs. by nature in the distribution of pleasure investigated, *etc.*, incl. a diss. upon harmony of style; [by L. J. Levesque de Pouilly]. Boston, 1812. 32°.
Theory of human progression; [by P. E. Dove]. London, 1850. 8°.
Theory of practice; an ethical enquiry. *See* **Hodgson, S. H.**
Theory of teaching; by [Mrs. A. C. Lowell]. Boston, 1841. 12°.
Theosebes, *pseud.* Letters on the worship of Christ, addressed to G. Horne. London, 1786. 8°. (B 238)
Theosebes, Bereanus, *pseud.* Discourse on Paul's mystery of godliness. Falmouth, 1786. 4°. (A 30, B 69)
Theotimus. Fragm. (*In* **Mueller, C.** Fr. hist. Gr., v. 4. 1851.)
Thera, *Island.* Böckh, A. Ueber die von Herrn v. Prokesch in Thera entdeckten Inschriften. (*In* **Berlin. Ak.** d. Wiss. Abh., 1836.)
Theramenes. M., F. (*In his* Stemmata Atheniensia. 1837.)
Therapeutics. Salmon, W. Medicina practica; also, Philos. works of Hermes Trismegistus, Kalid Persicus, Geber Arabs, Artefius longævus, Nicholas Flammel, R. Bachon, and G. Ripley; tr. into Eng. Lond., 1692. 8°.
— General obs. and prescriptions in the practice of physick; by an eminent London physician. London, 1715. 8°.
— Boerhaave, H. Consultationes medicæ. London, 1744. 8°.
— - *Eng.* Med. correspondence. Lond., 1745. 8°.
— Theobald, J. Every man his own physician. [1764.] 10th ed. London, Boston, 1767. 8°. (B 1563)
— Graham, J. General state of medical and chirurgical practice. Bath, 1778. 4°.
— Brown, J. Observations on the principles of the old system of physic; compendium of the new doctrine of physic. Edin., 1787. 8°.
— Jackson, H. Inaug. diss. on the efficacy of certain external applications, 1802. (*In* **Caldwell, C.** Med. theses, v. 2. 1806.)
— Townsend, J. Elements of therapeutics. Boston, 1802. 8°.
— Jadelot, J. F. N. De l'art d'employer les médicamens. Paris, 1805. 12°.
— Bardsley, S. A. Med. reports, cases, and experiments. London, 1807. 8°.
— Watt, R. Treatment of disease in general. (*In his* Cases, *etc.* 1808.)
— Sylvan, *pseud.* Formula of prescriptions. Prov., 1812. 8°.
— - *Another copy.* (B 814)
— - Confidential communication of the enemy of human diseases. Hartford, 1814. 8°. (B 814)
— - *Same.* Prov., 1815. 8°.
— - *Same.* *n.p.*, 1815. 8°. (B 830)
— - - Continuation. Prov., 1815. 8°.
— Instructions for the relief of the sick poor in some diseases of frequent occurrence. [1819.] 2d ed. Gloucester, 1820. 12°. (C 147)
— Chapman, N. Therapeutics and materia medica. Phila., 1821–22. 2 v. 8°.
— Sutleffe, E. Medical and surgical cases. London, 1824–25. 2 v. 8°.
— Begin, L. J. Traité de thérapeutique. Paris, 1825. 2 v. 8°
— Thomsonian and botanic medical adviser. Baltimore, 1831. 8°. (B 1854)
— Thomson, A. T. Elements of materia medica and therapeutics. London, 1832–33. 2 v. 8°.
— Chabert, J. X. Medical notice of diseases reputed incurable; [with] certificates from persons cured by C. N. Y., 1834. 8°. (B 1716)

— PEREIRA, J. Elements of materia medica and therapeutics. [1838-40.] 2d ed. London, 1842. 2 v. 8°.
— GIACOMINI, G. A. Traité philosophique et expérimental de matière médicale et de thérapeutique; trad. de l'ital. par Mojon et Rognetta. [Paris, 1842.] 8°.
— HALL, M. Relation between anatomy, physiol., pathol., and therapeutics. London, 1842. 8°.
— PAINE, M. Materia medica and therapeutics. N. Y., 1848. 8°.
— HOOKER, W. Rational therapeutics. (*In* **Mass. Med. Soc.** Pub., v. 1. 1856.)
— TULLY, W. Materia medica; or, Pharmacology and therapeutics. Vol. 1. Springfield, 1857. 2 pt. 8°.
— STILLÉ, A. Therapeutics and materia medica. Phila., 1860. 2 v. 8°.
— FLAGGE, C. H. Report on materia medica and general therapeutics. (*In* **New Sydenham Soc.** Biennial retrospect for 1865-66.) — STEVENSON, T. Report on materia medica and general therapeutics. (*In* 1867-68.)
— JONES, H. B. Lectures on some applications of chemistry and mechanics to T. London, 1867. 8°.
— HOPE, G. H. Till the doctor comes, and how to help him. London, [187-]. 32°.
— PAPILLON, J. H. F. Les derniers progrès de la thérapeutique. (*In* **Revue d. D. Mondes**, juin 1872.)

See also **Acholic diseases**; — **Astringents**; — **Baths and Bathing**; — **Blood-letting**; — **Counter-irritation**; — **Electricity**; — **Heat cure**; — **Inhalation**; — **Medicine**; — **Nursing**; — **Pathology and Therapeutics**; — **Pharmacopœias**; — **Rest**; — **Temperature in disease**.

Theremin, Charles. De l'état présent de l'Europe. Paris, 1816. 8°.
Theresa, *St.* *See* **Teresa**, *St.*
Theresa, *St.*, *Queen of Portugal.* VIDA da T. (*In* **Bayam**, J. P. Portugal glorioso. 1727.)
Theresa, *pseudon.* The breechiad; a poem. Boston, 1807. 12°. (C 112, 188)

Thermometer. LUC, J. A. de. Hist. critique du baromètre et du thermomètre. (*In his* **Recherches**. 1784.)
— LESLIE, J. Experiments and instruments depending on the relations of air to heat and moisture. Edin., 1813. 8°.
— BIDONE, G., *and* PLANA, G. Comparaison avec le mètre de l'ancienne coudée trouvée à Memphis. (*In* **Turin. Ac. d. Sci.** Mem., v. 30. 1826.)
— LEWIS, J. Registering thermometer. (*In* **Amer. Assoc.** Proc., v. 14. 1861.)

Thermopylæ. GORDON, *Maj. Gen. Sir* C. Account of two visits to the Anopæa or highlands above Thermopylæ. Athens, 1838. 8. (B 1164)
Théroigne de Méricourt *or* **Marcourt**, Anne Josephe. GONCOURT, L. A. H. de *and* A. H. de. (*In their* Portraits intimes du 18e siècle. 1857.)
Theron and Aspasio. *See* **Hervey, J.**
Theron, Paulinus, and Aspasio. *See* **Bellamy, J.**

Théroulde. La chanson de Roland; acc. d'une tr., d'une introd., et de notes par F. Génin. Paris, 1850. 8°.

Therry, Roger. Memoir of G. Canning. (*In* **Canning, G.** Speeches, v. 1. 1828.)
— Reminiscences of thirty years' residence in New South Wales and Victoria. London, 1863. 8°.

Thersytes. (*In* **Child, F. J.** Four old plays. 1848.)
Thesaurus, Emmanuel. *See* **Tesauro, E.**
Thesaurus antiq. et hist. Sicil., *etc.* *See* **Grævius, J. G.**
Thesaurus elocutionis oratoriæ Gr.-Lat. *See* **Benz., J.**
Thesaurus hymnologicus. *See* **Daniel, H. A.**
Thesaurus phrasium poeticarum. *See* **Buchler, J.**
Thesaurus. *See* **Dictionary.**
Theseus. Fragm. (*In* **Mueller, C.** Fr. hist. Gr., v. 4. 1851.)
— PLUTARCHUS. (*In his* Vitæ; *and*, *Eng.*, Lives.)
Thesiger, *Sir* Frederick, *and others.* Convocation; opinions upon a case submitted by the Soc. for the revival of Convocation. London, 1853. 8°. (B 1376)

Thespis. Fragm. (*In* **Nauck, A.** Trag. Græc. fr. 1856; — *and in* **Wagner, F. W.** Frag. Eurip. 1846.)
Thessalonians, Epistle of Paul to the. *See* **Bible** (p. 290).
Thessalonica. JOANNES *Cameniata, and* DEMETRIUS *Cydonius.* De excidio Thessalonicæ. (*In* **Byzant.** hist., v. 16. 1729.) — ANAGNOSTA, J. De excidio urbis Thessalonicensis; — Monodia de excidio urbis Thessalonicensis. (*In* v. 23. 1733; — *and in* **Niebuhr.** Corpus Byzant., v. 36. 1838.)
— EUSTATHIUS *Thessalonicensis.* De Thessalonica urbe a Normannis capta narratio. (*In his* Opuscula. 1832.)

Thessaly. BOWEN, G. F. Mt. Athos, Thessaly, and Epirus. London, 1852. 12°.
See also **Aleuadæ**; — **Pharsalia.**

Thétis et Pélée; tragédie. *See* **Fontenelle, B. le B. de.**
Theuriet, André. L'abbé Daniel; étude de la vie de campagne. (*In* **Revue** d. D. Mondes, nov. 1863.) — Lucile Desenclos. (*In* oct. 1866.) — Les souffrances de Claude Blouet. (*In* oct. 1869.) — L'Ondine; scènes de la vie provinciale. (*In* mars 1873.) — Mlle. Guignon. (*In* nov., déc. 1873.) — [Various articles.] (*In* août 1857 - oct. 1873.)

Theux, X. de. Bibliographie liégeoise. Brux., 1867. 2 v. 8°.

Théveneau, Charles Marie Simon. Elémens d'arithmétique. (*In* **Clairaut, A. C.** Elémens d'algèbre, v. 1. 1801.)

Théveneau de Morande, Charles. Gazette noir; par un homme qui n'est pas blanc, ou Œuvres posthumes du gazetier cuirassé. [Londres,] 1784. 8°.

Thévenin, —, *Dr.* Du climat de Mogador sous le rapport des affections pulmonaires. (*In* **Paris. Soc. de Géog.** Bul., 5e sér., v. 15. 1868.)

Thévenin, Evariste. Association polytechnique; cours d'économie industrielle. 4e série. Paris, 1866. 4 v. 12°.
Contents. 1e sér. **Garnier, J. C.** Qu'est ce que l'économie industrielle? — **Baudrillart, H. J. L.** Le capital. — **Horn, I. E.** Les machines. 2e sér. **Batbie, A. P.** Du travail et du salaire. — **Levasseur, P. E.** Les corporations et la liberté du travail. 3e sér. **Duval, J.** Les sociétés co-opératives. — **Wolowski, L. F. M. R.** Echange et monnaie. 4e sér. **Courcelle-Seneuil, J. G.** Intéret et usure. — **Coq, P.** Le crédit. — **Passy, F.** La liberté commerciale.

Thévenot, Jean de. Travels into Levant. (*In* **Harris, J.** Col. of voy., v. 2. 1705; 1764.)
— *Same, extract.* (*In* **Knox, J.** Col. v. 6. 1767.)
— Travels through Thibet, *etc.* (*In* **Moore, J. H.** New col. of voy., v. 2. 1778.)
— Voyage en Asie, 1655. (*In* **Montémont, H.** Biblioth. univ., v. 31. 1836.)

Thévenot, Nicolas Melchisédec. Relations de divers voyages curieux. Paris, 1696. 2 v. f°.
Contents. Vol. 1. **Greaves, J.** Descr. des pyramides d'Egypte. — **Relation** des Cosaques. — **Luca, J. de.** Rel. des Tartares de Crim, *etc.* — **Lamberti, A.** Rel. de la Colchide. — **Valle, P. della.** Informatione della Georgia. — **Jenkinson, A.** Voy. au Cathay. — **Relation** de l'ambassade que les Hollandais envoyèrent en 1656, 57, au Tartare. — **Hawkins, —.** Rel. de la cour du Mogol. — **Roe,** *Sir* **T.** Mémoires. — **Terry, E.** Voy. aux états du Mogol. — **Kosmas** *monachus.* Descr. des plantes et des animaux des Indes Orientales. — **Abu-l-Feda, I.,** *King of Hammah.* Les climats alhend et alsend. — **Commencement** d'un livre des Caldéens de Bassora. — **Methold, W.** Rel. de Golconda, Tannassari, *etc.* — **Floris, P. W.** Rel. du golfe de Bengale. — **Schouten, J.** Relation de Siam. — **Bontekoe, W. I.** Voy. aux Indes Orientales. — **Découverte** de la terre australe. — **Avis** sur le commerce des Indes et du Japon. — **Pelsart, F.** Autre avis sur le commerce des Indes. — **Motta, A. da.** Routier pour la navigation des Indes. — **Carte** portugaise de la Carrera. — **Vues** des côtes des Indes; 4 feuilles. — **Beaulieu, F.** Mém. du voyage aux Indes. — **Bañvelos y Carrillo, H. de.** Rel. des Isles Philippines. — **Rios Coronel, F.** di los. Rel. et mém. de l'estat des Isles Philippines. — **Grau y Montfalcon, J.** Mém. pour le commerce des Isles Philippines. — **Relation** des Isles Philippines, par un réligieux. — **Relation** de Mindanao. — **Caron, F.** Rel. du Japon. — **Gysbertz, R.** Rel. des martyrs du Japon. — **Relation** de la découverte de la terre d'Jeso. — **Boym, M.** Rel. de la Chine; — Flora Sinensis. 2. **Route** du voy. des ambassadeurs hollandais à Pekin. — **Ambassade** des Hollandais à la Chine. — **Martini, M.** Atlas chinoise avec une carte qui convient à sa description, et une addition au royaume du Japon. —

Rapport de la Compagnie Hollandaise des Indes Orientales, 1661. — Palafox, J. de. L'Indien. — Acarete, —. Voy. sur la rivière de la Platte. — Voyage à la Chine des PP. Grueber et d'Orville. — La même, en italien. — Science morale des Chinois. — Almeida, M. d'. Hist. de la haute Ethiopie. — Remarques sur les relations d'Ethiopie des PP. Lobo et Tellez. — Lobo, J. Rel. des Abyssins, des sources du Nil, *etc.* — Découverte de quelques païs qui sont entre l'empire des Abyssins et la côte de Melinde. — Protais, —. Rel. du voyage du Zaid, ou de la Thébaïde, 1668. — Histoire de l'Empire Mexicain representé par figures, avec leur explication. — Gages, T. Rel. du Mexique, avec l'hist. de la Nouv. Espagne. — Route d'A. Tasman autour de la terre australe, *etc.* — Instruction sur la route et les vents qui se rencontrent dans les voy. des Païs-Bas jusqu'à Battavie, *etc.* — L'Ambassade de Schahrok fils de Tamerlam à l'empéreur du Katay. — Autre rel. d'une ambassade à l'empéreur du Katay, 1633. — Synopsis chronologique de la monarchie chinoise, *etc.* — L'Asie de Barros, *etc.* — Ignace *de Jésus.* Rel. des chrestiens de S. Jean. — Voyage de la Tercera, fait par le commandeur de Chaste. — Elémens de la langue tartare.

— Camus, A. G. Mémoire sur la Collection de T. (*In his* Mémoire. 1802.)

Thevet, André. Portraits et vies des hommes illustres. Paris, 1584. f°.

— Niceron, J. P. (*In his* Mém., v. 23. 1733.)

Thian-Tchu. *See* India.

Thiard *or* **Tyard,** Pontus de, *marquis de Bissy.* Niceron, J. P. (*In his* Mém., v. 21. 1733; *and, Germ.*, v. 16. 1758.)

Thibaud, *King of Navarre. See* Theobald I.

Thibaudeau, Antoine Claire. Le Consulat et l'Empire, ou Histoire de la France et de Napoléon, 1799-1815: Consulat. Paris, 1834. 3 v. 8°.

— *Same.* Empire. Paris, 1834-35. 7 v. 8°.

— Mémoires sur la Convention et le Directoire. Paris, 1824. 2 v. 8°. (Berville and Barrière. Col. des mém.)

Thibault, Girard. Académie de l'espée, où se demonstrent la théorie et pratique du maniement des armes à pied et à cheval; grav. par A. Bolswert, *etc.* [Anvers.] 1628. f°.

Thibault, Jean Thomas. Application de la perspective linéaire aux arts du dessin. Paris, 1827. 4°.

Thibaut I., *King of Navarre. See* Theobald I.

Thibaut, Antoine Frédéric Just. Ueber Besitz und Verjährung. Jena, 1802. 12°.

— Civilistische Abhandlungen. Heidelb., 1814. 8°.
Contents. Ueber das interdictum de glande legenda. — Ueber die Römische habitatio, und den partus ancillæ. — Ueber das Zurückbehalten unnützer Real-Servituten. — Ueber die Verpflichtung des Schenkers zur Evictions-Leistung. — Ueber den Grundsatz, nemo pro parte testatus, pro parte intestatus decedere potest. — Ueber das Verhältniss der einzelnen Theile des römischen Rechts. — Ueber das Verhältniss besonderer Sätze des älteren Rechts zu neuen Regeln. — Ueber die Aedilen und das ädilitische Edict. — Grundzüge einer vollständigen Darstellung der Lehre von der Concurrenz der Civil-Klagen. — Ueber die Arten das Corpus juris romani zu allegiren. — Ueber die Natur der Rechte des Emphyteuta. — Ueber die Beschaffenheit und den heutigen Gebrauch der fiduciana tutela. — Ueber Pfand-Separatisten. — Ueber die Zulässigkeit der Rückforderung eines für eine Nichtschuld bestellten Pfandes. — Ueber die possessio des beschenkten Ehegatten. — Ueber das Verhältniss und die Rechte neuer und alter Gläubiger bey einer abermaligen Verarmung des Gemeinschuldners. — Beyträge zur der Lehre von den Bedingungen. — Ueber die rechtlichen Grundsätze bey Vertheilung der Gemeindesachen. — Ueber die Nothwendigkeit eines allgemeinen bürgerlichen Rechts. — Ueber die Vereinbarlichkeit der actio negotiorum gestorum des Geschäftsführers mit einem demselben von einem Dritten gegebenen Auftrage.

— System des Pandekten-Rechts. 6e Ausg. Jena, 1823. 3 v. 8°.

— Theorie der logischen Auslegung des römischen Rechts. 5e Ausg. Altona, 1806. 12°.

— Versuche über einzelne Theile der Theorie des Rechts. 2e Aufl. Jena, 1817. 2 v. 8°.

Thibet. Goez, B. de. Description of Tibet, [1602]. (*In* Green, J. Col. of voy., v. 4. 1747; — *and in* Pinkerton, J. Col. of voy., v. 7. 1811; — *and, Germ., in* Allgemeine Hist., v. 7. 1750.)

— Travels through Tibet by several missioners, [1661-1741]. (*In* Pinkerton, J. Col. of voy., v. 7. 1811.)

— Neueste Nachrichten von Tibet und Butan, [1773]. (*In* Sprengel, M. C., *and* Forster, G. Neue Beiträge, v. 3. 1790.)

— Saunders, R. Some account of the vegetable and mineral productions of Bootan and Tibet, [1783]. (*In* Turner, S. Account of embassy, *etc.*, 1800; 1806.)

— - *Germ.* Bemerkung über die vegetab. und mineral. Produkte. (*In* Sprengel, M. C., *and* Forster, G. Neue Beiträge, v. 3. 1790.)

— Turner, S. An account of an embassy to the court of Teshoo Lama in Tibet, [1783]. London, 1800. 4°.

— - *Same.* 2d ed. London, 1806. 4°.

— Jacquemont, V. Letters from India describing a journey in Thibet, *etc.*, 1828-31. London, 1834. 2 v. 8°.

— Ferrario, G. (*In his* Costume antico e moderno, v. 4. 1829.)

— Huc, E. R., *l'abbé.* Souvenirs d'un voyage dans la Tartarie, le Thibet, et la Chine, 1844-46. 2e éd. Paris, 1853. 2 v. 12°.

— - *Eng.* Travels in Tartary, *etc.*; tr. by W. Hazlitt. London, 1852. 2 v. 12°.

— Knight, H. W. Diary of a pedestrian in Cashmere and Thibet, [1860]. London, 1863. 8°.

— Desgodins, A., *missionnaire au Tibet.* Extraits de [ses] lettres, 1864. (*In* Paris. Soc. de Géog. Bul., 5e sér., v. 18. 1869.)

See also Himalaya Mts.

Language.

— Schmidt, I. J. Ueber den Ursprung der tibetischen Schrift. (*In* St. Petersburg. Ac. Sci. Mém., 6e sér., v. 1. 1832.)

— Lepsius, K. R. Ueber die Umschrift und Lautverhältnisse einiger hinterasiatischer Sprachen namentlich der chinesischen und der tibetischen. (*In* Berlin. Ak. d. Wiss. Abh., 1860.)

Religion.

— Schlagintweit, E. Buddhism in Tibet. Lpz., London, 1863. 8°.

Thiboust, Lambert. Les femmes qui pleurent. 1859. *See* Siraudin, P. (E 21)

— *and* Barrière, T. Les filles de marble; drame. Nouv. éd. Paris, 1862. 4°. (E 8)

Thiébault, Paul. Journal des opérations militaires du siège et du blocus de Gênes, *etc.* Paris, 1801. 4°.

— Manuel général du service des états-mayors géneraux et divisionnaires dans les armées. Paris, 1813. 8°.

Thiébault, Paul Charles François Adrien Henri Dieudonné. Mémoire sur cette question, La langue d'un peuple quelqu'il soit est-elle plutôt propre à la poésie qu'à la prose. (*In* Sérieys, A. Bibl. acad., v. 11. 1811.)

— Souvenirs de vingt ans de séjour à Berlin. (*In* Barrière, F. Bibl. des mém., v. 23, 24. 1860.)

— De l'usage considéré comme maître absolu des langues. (*In* Berlin. Ak. d. Wiss. Abh., 1781.)

Thiébaut de Berneaud, Arsène. Annuaire de l'industrie française. 1811. *See* Sonnini de Manoncourt, C.N.S.

Thiebland *or* **Thieblin,** Nicholas L. A little book about Gr. Britain; by Azamat-Batuk. London, 1870. 16°.

Thiele, F. The mysteries of Berlin; tr. by C. B. Burkhardt. N. Y., 1845. 8°.

Thiele, Just Matthias. Thorwaldsen and his works; tr. by P. C. Sinding. N. Y., 1869. 4 v. 4°.

Thieme, Veit. Andresen, A. (*In his* Der deutsches Peintre-Graveur, v. 3. 1866.)

Thiénot, J. Rapports sur les études hist.: Temps modernes. (*In* Geffroy, M. A. Rapports. 1861. Rec. de rapports.)

Thierry I., *King of the Franks.* EXCERPTA ex vitis sanctorum de Theoderico I. (*In* **Bouquet, M.** Rec. des hist., v. 3. 1869.)

Thierry II., *King of the Franks.* EXCERPTA ex vitis sanctorum de Theodeberto II. et Theoderico II. (*In* **Bouquet, M.** Rec. des. hist., v. 3. 1869.)

Thierry III., *King of the Franks.* EXCERPTA ex vitis sanctorum de Theoderico III. (*In* **Bouquet, M.** Rec. des hist., v. 3. 1869.)

Thierry, Amédée Simon Dominique. Arles et le tyran Constantin. (*In* **Revue d. D. Mondes**, mars 1857.)

— Histoire d'Attila et de ses successeurs. Paris, 1856. 2 v. 8°.

— Histoire de la Gaule sous l'administration romaine. Paris, 1840-47. 3 v. 8°.
Contents. Vol. 1. Introd. — B.C. 98 - A.D. 197. 2. 197-286. 3. 286-394.

— *Same.* Nouv. éd. 1e pte. Paris, 1866. 2 v. 8°.

— Histoire des Gaulois, jusqu'à l'entière soumission à la domination romaine. 3e éd., rev. et aug. Paris, 1844. 3 v. 8°.

— Nouveaux récits de l'histoire romaine: 4e, 5e siècles. Paris, 1865. 8°.

— Rapport sur les Etats Géneraux. (*In* **Paris. Inst.** *Ac. d. Sci. Mor.* Mém., v. 5. 1847.)

— Récits de l'histoire romaine: Derniers temps de l'Empire d'Occident. Paris, 1860. 8°.

— *Same.* St. Jérome; la société chrétienne à Rome, et l'émigration romaine en Terre Sainte. Paris, 1867. 2 v. 8°.

— Tableau de l'Empire Romaine jusqu'à la fin du gouvernement impérial en Occident. Paris, 1862. 8°.

— Numerous articles.] (*In* **Revue d. D. Mondes**, jan. 1840 - juin 1873.)

Thierry, Edouard. Rapport sur les progrès de la littérature française: Théâtre. (*In* **Silvestre de Sacy, S. U.**, *and others.* Rapport sur le progrès des lettres. 1868.)

Thierry, J., *and* **Mensing, C.** Twee catalogussen van boeken. s' Graavenhaage, [1796]. 8°. (B 893)

Thierry, Jacques Nicolas Augustin. Histoire de la conquête de l'Angleterre par les Normands. 2e éd., rev., corr., et aug. Paris, 1826. 4 v. 8°.
Contents. Vol. 1. Jusqu'à 1066. 2. 1066-1137. 3. 1137-1189. 4. 1189-1485.

— *Eng.* History of the conquest of England. London, 1841. 8°.

— Histoire du Tiers Etat. 3e éd. Paris, 1856. 2 v. 12°.
Contents. Vol. 1. 1302-1685. 2. 1685-1789.

— *Eng.* Formation and prog. of the Third Estate in France; tr. by F. B. Wells. London, *Bohn*, 1859. 2 v. 8°.

— Recueil des monuments inédits de l'hist. du Tiers Etat. 1e série: Chartes, coutumes, actes municipaux, statuts des corporations. Paris, 1850-70. 4 v. 4°. (Docs. inéd.)
Contents. *Région du Nord.* Vol. 1. Amiens, 1057-15e siècle. 2. 15e - 17e siècle. 3. Amiens, 18e siècle - 1789, et l'Amienois. 4. Abbeville et la Basse Picardie.

— - Rapport sur cet collection. (*In* **France.** *Minist. de l'Instruc. Pub.* Collection de doc. inéd. Rapports. 1839.)

— Several articles.] (*In* **Revue d. D. Mondes**, août 1833 - mai 1850.)

— MAGNIN, C. (*In* **Revue d. D. Mondes**, mai 1841.) — GUERLE, E. de. (*In* sept. 1858.)

— RENAN, J. E. (*In his* Essais de morale et de critique. 1860.)

— - Le Tiers Etat. (*In* **Revue d. D. Mondes**, juil. 1852.)

Thierry, Jacques Pierre François. LAMOUROUX, J. V. F. Notice hist. sur T. Caen, 1824. 8°. (B 1155)

Thierry de Menonville, Nicolas Joseph. Travels to Guaxaca. (*In* **Pinkerton, J.** Col. of voy., v. 13. 1812.)

Thierry and Theodoret. *See* **Beaumont, F.**, *and* **Fletcher, J.**

Thiers, Jean Baptiste. NICERON, J. P. (*In his* Mém., v. 4. 1728; *and, Germ.*, v. 5. 1751.)

Thiers, Marie Joseph Louis Adolphe. Discours. (*In* **Paris. Inst.** *Acad. Fr.* Recueil des discours, 1830-39.)

— Du droit du propriété. (*In* **Paris. Inst.** *Ac. d. Sci.* Petits traités, v. 1. 1848; — *and in Ac. d. Sci. Mor.* Mém., v. 7. 1850.)

— L'Espagne et l'Orient. — Négociations de Londres, question d'Orient. (*In* **Revue d. D. Mondes**, août 1840.)

— Histoire de la Révolution Française. 2e éd. Paris, 1828-29. 10 v. 8°.
Contents. Vol. 1. Août 1787 - sept. 1791. 2. Sept. 1791 - août 1792. 3. Août 1792 - jan. 1793. 4. Jan - mai 1793. 5. Mai - nov. 1793. 6. Nov. 1793 - juillet 1794. 7. Juillet 1794 - sept. 1795. 8. Sept. 1795 - fév. 1797. 9. Fév. - déc. 1797. 10. Déc. 1797 - nov. 1799.

— *Eng.* Hist. of the French Rev.; tr. with notes by F. Shoberl. London, 1838. 5 v. 8°.

— Histoire du Consulat et de l'Empire. Paris, 1845-62. 20 v. 8° *and* Atlas 1859. f°.
Contents. Vol. 1. Nov. 1799 - juillet 1800. 2. Août 1799 - avr. 1801. 3. Avr. 1801 - août 1802. 4. Août 1802 - mars 1804. 5. Avr. 1804 - août 1805. 6. Août 1805 - sept. 1806. 7. Sept. 1806 - juillet 1807. 8. Juillet 1807 - juillet 1808. 9. Mai 1808 - fév. 1809. 10. Jan. - juillet 1809. 11. Fév. 1809 - avr. 1810. 12. Avr. 1810 - mai 1811. 13. Mars 1811 - juin 1812. 14. Juin - déc. 1812. 15. Mai 1812 - juin 1813. 16. Juin 1813 - nov. 1814. 17. Nov. - mai 1814. 18. Avr. 1814 - mars 1815. 19. Jan. - juin 1815. 20. Juin 1815-21.

— - Vignettes et portraits pour l'Hist. du Consulat et de l'Empire. Paris, 1856-62. 15 liv. 8°.

— *Eng.* History of the Consulate and Empire of France; tr. by D. F. Campbell. London, 1845-62. 20 v. 8°.

— The Mississippi bubble; a mem. of J. Law; tr. and ed. by F. S. Fiske; added, the Darien expedition and South Sea scheme. N. Y., 1859. 12°.

— Notice sur la vie et les lettres de la marquise Du Deffand. (*In* **Du Deffand, M. de V. C.,** *marquise de.* Lettres, v. 1. 1864.)

— Rapport; précédé de la proposition [de P. J.] Proudhon, rel. à l'impôt sur le revenu, et son discours 31 juil. Paris, 1848. 8°.

— *and* Bodin, F. History of the French Revolution; tr. from the French. London, 1825. 3 v. 8°.

— BARNI, J. Napoléon I et son historien, Thiers. Paris, 1869. 18°.

— BLANC, C. Le cabinet de Thiers. (*In* **Gazette des beaux-arts**, v. 12. 1862.)

— CUVILLIER-FLEURY, A. A. Thiers historien de l'Empire. (*In his* Historiens, v. 1. 1863.)

— LERMINIER, J. L. E. (*In* **Revue d. D. Mondes**, mars 1845; jan. 1847.)

— LOMÉNIE, L. L. de. (*In his* Sketches of living characters of France. 1841.)

— MEISSNER, F. Die Reaction gegen seine Geschichtschreibung. (*In* **Archiv f. d. Stud. d. n. Spr.**, v. 38. 1865.)

— PLANCHE, G. Reception de M. Thiers à l'Acad. Fr. (*In* **Revue d. D. Mondes**, déc. 1834.) — LOÈVE-VEIMARS, A. (*In* déc. 1835.)

— SAINTE-BEUVE, C. A. (*In* **Revue d. D. Mondes**, jan. 1845; — *and in his* Portraits contemp., v. 2. 1852.)

Thiers. BARANTE, A. G. P. B. de. Notice sur la ville de T. (*In his* Etudes histor., *etc.*, v. 2. 1857.)

Thiersch, Bernhardt. Urgestalt der Odyssee. Königsb., 1821. 8°.

Thiersch, Friedrich Wilhelm von. Ueber die Epochen der bildenden Kunst unter der Griechen. 2e Aufl. München, 1829. 8°.

— De l'état actuel de la Grèce. Lpz., 1833. 2 v. 8°.

— Griechische Grammatik. 3e verm. Aufl. Lpz., 1826. 8°.

— Ueber die neugriechische Poesie. München, 1828. 4°.

— *and others.* Reise in Italien seit 1822. 1r Thiel. Lpz., 1826. 8°.

Thies, Louis. Catalogue of the collection of engravings bequeathed to Harvard College by F. C. Gray. Camb., 1869. 8°.

Thietmarus, Dithmarus, *or* **Ditmarus,** *Bp.* Chronicon, 919-1018. (*In* **Pertz, G. H.** Mon. Germ. hist., Scr., v. 5. 1849.)

Thigh. COALE, W. E. Essay to describe the best mode of treating fractures of the thigh. Boston, 1845. 8°. (B 1692)

— MUSSEY, R. D. Fractures of the neck of the thigh bone. [From the Amer. journal of med. sci., Apr. 1857.] *n.p.*, [1857]. 8°. (B 1558)

Thillaye, L. J. S. Nouveau manuel du teinturier. *See* **Riffault des Hêtres, J. R. D.**

Thilo, Valentin. Topologia oratoria. Amst., 1653. 12°.

Things as they are. 3d ed. London, 1758. 8°. (B 790)

Things by their right names. Boston, 1812. 12°.

Things not generally known; ed. by D. A. Wells. N. Y., 1857. 12°.

Thinking. BURDON, W. Materials for thinking. London, 1820. 2 v. 8°.

— MARTINEAU, H. Essays on the art of thinking. (*In her* Miscel., v. 1. 1836.)

Thinking bayonet, The; by J. K. Hosmer. N. Y., 1865. 12°.

Thinks-I-to-myself; [by E. Nares]. Bost., 1812. 12°.

Thiollet, François. Choix de maisons, édifices, *etc.*, de Paris et ses environs. Paris, 1829. 4°.

Thionville. MAP. Amst., [17—]. (E 60)

Third leaf, A, omitted out of the Record report; remarks on the evidence adverse to the Commission. London, 1837. 8°. (E 107)

Third letter to the people of England on liberty, taxes, *etc.* London, 1756. 8°. (B 1520)

Thirlwall, Connop, *Bp.* Charge delivered to the clergy of the diocese of St. David's, Oct. 1863. 2d ed. London, Oxford, 1864. 8°.

— History of Greece. London, 1835-44. 8 v. 16°. (Lardner. Cab. cyc.)

Contents. Vol. 1. Geog. outlines of Greece. — To B. C. 582. 2. 624-471. 3. 476-413. 4. 413-387. 5. 387-346. 6. 346-327. 7. 327-318. 8. 301-106. — Modern Greece.

Thiroux de Mondesir, —. Manuel du dragon. Nouv. éd. Paris, 1781. 12°.

Thirteen months in the rebel army; by an impressed New Yorker [W. G. Stevenson]. N. Y., 1862. 12°.

Thirteen years' war. LINDAU, J. Geschichte des 13jahrigen Krieges. [1454-66]. (*In* **Hirsch, T.** Scr. rer. Prus., v. 4. 1870.)

Thirty. HOMEYER, K. T. Der Dreissigste. (*In* **Berlin. Ak. d. Wiss.** Abh., 1864.)

Thirty nine articles. *See* **Church of England** (p. 576); — **Subscription** (p. 2879, 2880); — **Test-laws** (p. 2939, 2940).

Thirty years' war. *Biography.* CUST, *Sir* E. Lives of the warriors of the thirty years' war. London, 1865. 2 pts. 8°.

— - LIGNE, C. J., *prince* de. Grands généraux de la guerre de trente ans. (*In his* Œuvres, v. 1. 1809; v. 3. 1860; — *and in his* Mélanges mil., v. 19. 1797.)

— *History.* SCHILLER, F. v. Geschichte des 30jahrigen Krieges. Lpz., 1802. 2 v. 16°.

— - - *Same.* (*In his* Sämmtl. Werke, v. 14. 1820; v. 9. 1867.)

— - - *Eng.* History of the thirty years' war; tr. by Blaguière. Dublin, 1800. 2 v. 8°.

— - - *Same.* (*In his* Hist. works, v. 2. 1828; — *and in his* Works, v. 1. 1851.)

— - CHAPMAN, B. History of Gustavus Adolphus and the thirty years' war. Lond., 1856. 8°.

— - BIEDERMANN, K. Deutschlands trübste Zeit. Berlin, [1862]. 8°. (Schmidt, F. Deutsche Nat. Bibl., v. 3.)

— - ERDMANNSDÖRFFER, B. Zur Geschichte und Geschichtschreibung des dreissigjahrigen Krieges. (*In* **Historische Zeitschrift, v. 14. 1865.**)

— - GARDINER, S. R. Letters, *etc.*, illust. the rel. between Eng. and Germany at the commencement of the thirty years' war. Lond., 1865-68. 2 ser. 4°. (Camden Soc., v. 90, 98.)

— - WARD, A. W. The House of Austria in the thirty years' war. London, 1869. 8°.

See also **Gustavus Adolphus**; — **Munster**; — **Prague, Peace of.**

This war; a satire for the times. N. Y., 1863. 12°.

Thistle, The; by R. Rover and others. No. [1]-3. *n.t.p.* [1807.] 18°. (D 15)

— *Same.* No. [1], 2. [Boston,] 1807. 2 nos. 8°. (B 242)

Thistlethwaite, James. The consultation; a mock heroic, in three cantos. Bristol, 1774. 8°. (B 1468)

Thistlethwaite, Wm. Sermon. (*In* **London Soc. for Prom. Christianity among the Jews.** 15th report. 1823. B 1034)

Thistlewood, A. PROCÈS de T. (*In* **Causes politiques** célèbres, v. 3. 1827.)

Thocus, Guilielmus. *See* **Tocco, G.**

Tholen. HOYNCK VAN PAPENDRECHT, C. P. Reliquiæ actorum exstincti capituli ecclesiæ collegiatæ B. M. V. Tholensis. (*In his* Vita Viglii, v. 3, pt. 2. 1743.)

Tholuck, Friedrich August Gotttreu. Blüthensammlung aus der morgenländischen Mystik. Berlin, 1825. 8°.

— Credibility of evangelical hist. illustrated. (*In* **Beard, J. R.** Voices of the Church, *etc.* 1845.)

— The doctrine of inspiration. (*In* **Noyes, G. R.** Col. of theological essays. 1867.)

— Guido and Julius; or, Sin and the propitiation exhibited in the true consecration of the sceptic; tr. by J. E. Ryland. Bost., 1854. 12°.

— Kommentar zum Briefe Pauli an die Römer. Neue Ausarb. Halle, 1842. 8°.

— Life, character, *etc.*, of St. Paul. — Sermons. (*In* **Edwards, B. B.,** *and* **Park, E. A.** Selections, *etc.* 1839.)

— Vermischte Schriften grosstentheils apologetischen Inhalts. Hamburg, 1839. 2 v. 8°.

Contents. Vol. 1. Die Wunder Muhammed's und der Character dieses Religionsstifters. — Ueber die Wunder der Katholischen Kirche und insbesondere über das Verhältniss dieser und der biblischen Wunder zu den Erscheinungen des Magnetismus und Somnambulismus. — Ueber Apologetik und ihre Litteratur. — Ueber die Hypothese des Ursprunges des Namens Jehovah aus Aegypten, Phönicien, oder Indien. — Die Geschichte Bileams. — Graf Zinzendorf. 2. Abriss einer Geschichte der Umwälzung, seit 1750, auf dem Gebiete der Theologie in Deutschland. — Was ist das Resultat der Wissenschaft in Bezug auf die Urwelt? Zugleich eine litterarische Nachweisung der wichtigsten Schriften über diesen Gegenstand. — Einleitende Bemerkungen in das Studium der paulinischen Briefe, die Lebensumstände, den Charakter, und die Sprache des Apostels betreffend. — Die Verdienste Calvin's als Ausleger der heiligen Schrift. — Anzeigen. — Ueber die Natur der Sünde wider den heiligen Geist. — Nachtrag zu dem Aufsatze über die Katharina von Emmerich im 1. Bande der Vermischten Schriften.

Thom, Alexander. Statistics of Ireland. Dublin, 1853. 8°.

Thom, David. Dialogues on universal salvation. 2d ed. London, 1847. 16°.

— Memorial regarding the theological points of his case. 2d ed. [Liverpool, 1825.] 8°. (B 1277)

— Miracles of the Irving school shewn to be unworthy of serious examination. London, 1832. 8°. (B 1277)

— Number and names of Apocalyptic beasts. Pt. 1. London, 1848. 8°.

— Preface. (*In* **Barclay, J.** Without faith. 1836.)

— Remarks on a series of charges against him. Liverpool, 1825. 8°. (B 1277)

— Three questions proposed and answered; the life forfeited by Adam, the resurrection, and eternal punishment. Liverpool, 1828. 8°. (B 1277)

— Why is Popery progressing? London, 1835. 8°. (B 1277)

Thom, *Rev.* John Hamilton. Life of J. B. White. *See* **White, J. B.**

— The religious spirit that befits this crisis, *etc.*; sermon, Liverpool. London, 1854. 8°. (C 218)

— St. Paul's Epistles to the Corinthians; an attempt to convey their spirit and significance. Boston, 1852. 12°.

Thom, Nath. Catalogue of books to be sold, Dec. 5. [London, 1738.] 8°. (B 874)

Thom, Wm., *d.* 1850. Rhymes and recollections of a hand-loom weaver. London, 1845. 12°.

— KENNEDY, J. P. Some passages in the life of T. *n.p.*, 1846. 12°. (C 256)

Thomar. DESCRIPÇÃO de certa porção de comarca de Thomar. (*In* **Lisbon. Ac. d. Sci.** Mem., v. 8, pt. 2. 1823.)

Thomas, *the Apostle, pseud.* Gospel of the infancy of Jesus Christ. (*In* **Apocryphal** gospels. 1867.)

Thomas, —. Notice sur les principales productions du Mexique. (*In* **France.** *Com. Imp. de l'Expos. de* 1867. Rapports, v. 11.)

Thomas [Becket], *St., Archbp.* Epistolæ; ed. J. A. Giles. Oxonii, 1845. 2 v. 8°.

— BERINGTON, J. Thomas à Beckett vindicated against Ld. Lyttelton. (*In his* History of the reign of Henry II. 1790.)

— BRIAL, J. J. D'un ms. latin cont. l'histoire de la vie et du martyre de St. T. (*In* **Paris. Inst.** *Ac. d. Inscr.* Not., v. 9. 1813.)

— FLÉCHIER, E. (*In his* Œuvres, v. 3, pt. 1. 1782.)

— FOLLIOT, G. Epistolæ; ed. J. A. Giles. Oxoniæ, 1845. 2 v. 8°.

— FREEMAN, E. A. Saint Thomas of Canterbury and his biographers. (*In his* Hist. essays. 1871.)

— GILES, J. A. Life and letters of Thomas à Becket. London, 1846. 2 v. 8°.

— - Vita S. Thomæ Cantuariensis; ab auctoribus contemporaneis. Oxoniæ, 1845. 2 v. 8°.

— HERBERT *of Boseham.* Opera quæ extant omnia; ed. I. A. Giles. Oxonii, 1845-46. 2 v. 8°.

— JOHN *of Salisbury.* Vita S. Thomæ. (*In* **Joannes** *Saresberiensis.* Opera, v. 5. 1848.)

— PAULI, R. Canterbury and the worship of St. Thomas. (*In his* Pictures. 1861.)

— ROBERT *of Gloucester.* Life and martyrdom of Thomas à Becket; ed. by J. H. Black. London, 1845. 8°. (Percy Soc., v. 19.)

— ROBERTSON, J. C. Thomas à Becket; a biography. London, 1859. 8°.

— STANLEY, A. P. Murder of T. à Becket. (*In his* Memoirs of Canterbury. 1855.)

— VIE St. Thomas le martir; altfranzösisches Gedicht; hrsg. v. Bekker. (*In* **Berlin. Ak. d. Wiss.** Abh., 1838.) — La VIE St. Thomas le martir; aus der Hdschr. des Brit. Mus. ergänzt v. Bekker. (*In* 1844.)

Thomas [Hæmmerlein, *Lat.* Malleolus] *à Kempis.* De imitatione Christi. Londini, 1827. 18°.

Note. The authorship is also ascribed to Jean Charlier de Gerson, and to Giovanni Gerson or Gesson of Vercelli. *See* **Oettinger.** Bibliog. biog.; **Graesse.** Allgemeine Lit., v. 3, p. 35, 168, 350-352; **Larousse.** Dict. univ., v. 9, p. 583, 584.

— *Eng.* The Christian's pattern; or, A treatise of the imitation of Christ; add., Meditations and prayers for sick persons, by G. Stanhope. 2d ed. London, 1700. 16°.

— *Same.* New ed. Charlestown, 1812. 8°.

— *French.* L'imitation de Christ; tr. nouv. avec réflexions par l'abbé F. de Lamennais. Nouv. éd. Paris, 1864. 12°.

— *Same.* Tr. et paraphrasée par P. Corneille. (*In* **Corneille, P.** Œuvres complètes, v. 3. 1838.)

— *Spanish.* Comtemptus mundi, ó menosprecio del mundo y imitacion de Chisto; tr. por L. de Granada. (*In* **Granada, L. de.** Obras, v. 3. 1863; v. 11 of Aribau. Bibl.)

— Soliloquy of the soul; added, Meditations and prayers for sick persons by G. Stanhope. Bennington, 1816. 12°.

— BOEHRINGER, F. (*In his* Kirche Christi, Bd. 2, Abth. 3. 1855.)

— GALEANI NAPIONE, G. F. Del manoscritto de imitatione Christi detto il codice di Arona. (*In* **Turin. Ac. d. Sci.** Mem., v. 19, 33. 1811-29.)

— MEZLER, T. Epistola dedicatoria quam præfixit libris de imitatione Christi. (*In* **Schelhorn, J. G.** Amœn. lit., v. 13. 1730.) — P., C. R. Epistola critica de punctis controversiæ Kempisianæ præcipuis. (*In* v. 8. 1726.)

— TAMIZEY DE LARROQUE, P. Preuves que T. a K. n'a pas composé l'Imitation de N. S. J.-C. Paris, 1862. 8°.

Thomas *a Villanova, St.* *See* **Tomas** *de Villanueva.*

Thomas *Aquinas, St.* Comment. in Epist. Pauli; [acc. sermones pro dominicis et festibus diebus; add. opusculum de venerabili sacramento altaris. Parisiis ?, 1654?] f°.

— Summa totius theologiæ. Paris., 1607. f°.

— *French.* Somme théologique; tr. et annot. par F. Lachat. Paris, 1854-61. 16 v. 8°.

— Secreta alchemiæ magnalia. — Thesaurus alchemiæ secretissimus. (*In* **Zetzner, L.** Theatrum chem., v. 3. 1613.) — Tractatus sextus de esse et essentia mineralium. (*In* v. 5. 1622.)

— FIGUIER, G. L. (*In his* Vies des savants illustres du Moyen Age. 1867.)

— MONTET, L. Mémoire sur St. Thomas d'Aquin. (*In* **Paris. Inst.** *Ac. d. Sci. Mor.* Sav. étr., v. 2. 1847.)

— NEANDER, J. A. W. Ueber die Eintheilung der Tugenden bei Thomas Aquinas und das Verhältniss dieser ethischen Begriffsbestimmung zu den dabei zu Grunde liegenden philosophischen Standpunkten des Alterthums. (*In* **Berlin. Ak. d. Wiss.** Abh., 1846.)

— TOCCO, G. Vita S. T. — BERNARDUS *Guidonis.* Vita S. T. (*In* **Acta** sanct., v. 7. 1865.)

Thomas, *Bishop of Strengnäs.* Carmen de Engelbrecto. — Carmen de violata fide Erico Puke publice data. 1437. (*In* **Fant, E. M.** Scriptores rer. Svecicarum, v. 2. 1828.)

Thomas *Cantimpratensis.* Vita S. Lutgardis. (*In* **Acta** sanct., v. 24. 1867.)

Thomas *Cantuariensis.* *See* **Thomas [Becket].**

Thomas *de Burton.* Chronica monasterii de Melsa, ad 1396; acc. contin. ad 1406, a monacho quodam; ed. by E. A. Bond. London, 1866-68. 3 v. 8°. (Chron. and mem.)

Thomas *de Cantilupe, St., Bp. of Hereford.* VITA S. Thomæ. (*In* **Acta** sanct., v. 49. 1866.)

Thomas *de Celano.* Dies iræ [Lat. et Angl.]. Camb., 1863. 12°.

Thomas *de Eccleston.* De adventu Fratrum Minorum in Angliam. (*In* **Brewer, J. S.** Monumenta Francis. 1858.)

Thomas *de Elmham.* Historia monasterii S. Augustini Cantuariensis. London, 1858. 8°. (Chron. and mem.)

Thomas *Magister.* Ὀνομάτων Ἀττικῶν ἐκλογαί. N. Blancardus emend., animadv. adj. L. Bos. Franeq., 1698. 12°.

— *Same.* [Cum var. animadv. ed.] N. Blancardus. Lugd. Bat., 1757. 8°.

— *Same.* Ex. rec. F. Ritschelii. Hal. Sax., 1832. 8°.

Thomas *of Erceldoune, called the rhymer.* Sir Tristrem; ed. by W. Scott. Edin., 1811. 8°.

— *Same.* (*In* **Scott, W.** Poetical works, v. 5. 1833; — *and in* **Gottfried** *von Strassburg.* Werke, v. 2. 1823.)

— IRVING, D. Life. (*In his* Lives of Scottish poets, v. 1. 1804.)

— LIFE. (*In* **Soc. of Ancient Scots.** Lives of Scottish poets, v. 1, pt. 1. 1822.)

Thomas *of Marlborough, Abbot of Evesham.* *See* **Dominicus** *Eveshamensis.*

Thomas *of Reading.* DELONEY, T. (*In* **Thoms, W. J.** Early Eng. prose romances, v. 1. 1858.)

Thomas *of Woodstock, Duke of Glocester.* Voy. into Prussia, 1391. (*In* **Hakluyt, R.** Col. of voy., v. 1. 1809.)

Thomas *the rhymer.* *See* **Thomas** *of Erceldoune.*

Thomas, A. Considérations sur l'avenir de la culture du coton et sur les conditions de l'agriculture en Algérie. Alger, 1870. 16°.

Thomas, A. C. COOPER, J. T. Answers to 'Questions without answers' [by A. C. Thomas]. Phila., 1844. 8°. (B 1387)

Thomas, Abel. Account of a journey in the southern states in 1781. (*In* **New Jersey Hist. Soc.** Proc., v. 1. 1845-46.)

Thomas, Alexandre Gérard. [Several articles.] (*In* **Revue** d. D. Mondes, mars 1845 - déc. 1851.)

Thomas, André. Pascal et Charlotte. (*In* **Semaine** lit., v. 4.)

Thomas, Annie. *See* **Cudlip,** *Mrs.* Annie.

Thomas, Antoine Léonard. Œuvres complètes. Paris, 1802. 7 v. 8°.

Contents. Vol. 1. Notice sur la vie et les ouvrages de T. — Eloge de Maurice, comte de Saxe. — Eloge de H. F. d'Aguesseau, chancelier de France. — Eloge de René Duguay-Trouin, lieutenant-gén. des armées navales. — Eloge de Maximilien de Béthune, duc de Sully. 2. Eloge de Marc-Aurèle. — Eloge de René Descartes. — Lettre de M. de Voltaire à l'auteur de l'éloge de Descartes. — Eloge de Louis, dauphin de France. — Petit commentaire de Voltaire sur l'éloge du Dauphin. — Discours prononcé à l'Académie Françoise le 22 jan. 1767. — Réponse du président de l'Académie, au discours de M. Thomas. 3, 4. Essai sur les éloges. 4. Essai sur le caractère, les mœurs, et l'ésprit des femmes, dans les différens siècles. 5. Préface du poëme de Jumonville. — Jumonville. — Poëmes. — Réflexions philosophiques et littéraires sur le poëme de la religion naturelle. — A la mémoire de Mme. Geoffrin. 6. Le czar Pierre I; poëme. — Traduction de la 10e satire de Juvénal, sur les vœux des hommes. — Poésies diverses. 7. Discours prononcé à la réception de l'archevêque de Toulouse, le 6 sept. 1770. — Traité de la langue poëtique. — Correspondance avec Mme. Necker, 1781-85. — Correspondance avec Mlle. —, 1766-82. — Correspondance avec Ducis, 1778-85. — Lettre à Barthe. — Extraits de quelques lettres à M. —. — Lettre au Baron —, sur l'épitre au peuple. — Lettre au président Bonnier d'Alcoff. — Morceaux retranchés à la censure dans l'essai sur les éloges. — Relation de la captivité du Frédéric dans les prisons de Custrin, et du supplice du jeune Katt, son favori.

— Œuvres diverses. Amst., 1768. 2 v. (v. 1 w.). 12°.

Contents. Vol. 1. *Wanting.* 2. Eloge de René Descartes. — Lettre de M. de Voltaire à M. Thomas. — Extrait des affiches de Paris, no. 43. — Eloge de Louis, dauphin de France. — Discours à l'Acad.

— Eloge de Descartes. (*In* **Descartes,** R. Œuvres, v. 1. 1824.)

— Eulogium on Marcus Aurelius; tr. from the French [by D. B. Warden]. N. Y., 1808. 8°. **(B 809)**

— Jumonville; poëme. *n.p.*, 1759. 8°.

Thomas, Artus. L'histoire de la décadence de l'Empire Grèc, contin. par T. *See* **Chalcocondyles,** L.

Thomas, Benjamin. Letter to the Bp. of Landaff. Marlborough, 1774. 8°. **(B 906)**

Thomas, Benjamin Franklin. Sketch of the life of Chief Justice Shaw. (*In* **Mass. Hist.** Soc. Proceedings, 1867-69.)

Thomas, Charles Grandison. Hereditary property justified; reply to Brownson's article on the laboring classes. Camb., 1841. 8°. **(B 1702)**

Thomas, Charles Louis Ambroise. Le caïd; opéra-bouffon; [paroles] de T. Sauvage. Paris, 1849. 16°. **(E 17)**

— Le Conservatoire de Musique et de Déclamation. (*In* **Paris** guide, v. 1. 1867.)

Thomas, Charles W. Adventures and obs. on the west coast of Africa. N. Y., 1860. 12°.

Thomas, Dalby. Historical account of the rise and growth of the West India collonies, and of the great advantages they are to Eng. in resp. to trade. London, 1690. 8°.

Thomas, *Rev.* Daniel. Oration, Abington, July 4, 1810. Boston, 1810. 8°. **(B 415)**

— Oration, Bridgewater, Sept. 12, 1804, anniv. election of the Philandrian Soc. Prov., [1804]. 8°. **(B 435)**

— Sermon, funeral of D. Sawin, Apr. 29. Boston, 1822. 8°. **(B 283)**

— Norton, J. Things as they are; or, Trinitarianism developed; answer to a letter of D. Thomas, with strictures on the sentiments of S. Hopkins, *etc.*, in rel. to the Trinity. Boston, 1815. 2 pts. 8°. **(B 264)**

Thomas, David. Travels through the western country in 1816. Auburn, N. Y., 1819. 12°.

Thomas, *Mrs.* E. Brockett, L. P. (*In his* Woman's work in the civil war. 1867.)

Thomas, Ebenezer Smith. Reminiscences of the last sixty-five years. Hartford, 1840. 2 v. 8°.

Thomas, *Sir* Edmund. Short view of the conduct of the English clergy. London, 1737. 8°. **(B 580)**

— *Same.* (*In* **Baron,** R. Pillars of priestcraft. 1768.)

Thomas, Edward. Chronicles of the Pathán kings of Dehli. London, 1871. 8°.

Thomas, Francis. Annual message. *See* **Maryland.** *Governor.*

Thomas, Francis Sheppard. Handbook to the public records. London, 1853. 8°.

— Historical notes, 1509-1714. London, 1856. 3 v. 8°.

Contents. Vol. 1. Henry VIII.-Elizabeth. 2. James I.-Anne. 3. Notes. rel. to Scotland and Ireland, and lists of treaties with all countries.

Thomas, Frédéric. Le Palais de Justice. (*In* **Paris** guide, v. 2. 1867.)

Thomas, Gabriel. Hist. and geog. acc. of the province and country of Pensilvania and of West New Jersey in Amer. Lond., 1698. 8°.

— *Same.* London, 1698, N. Y., *lithographed,* 1848. 8°.

Thomas, George. Davenport, R. A. (*In his* Lives of individuals who have raised themselves to eminence. 1841. Fam. lib., v. 79.)

Thomas, *Gen.* George Henry. Shanks, W. F. G. Thomas as a tactician. (*In his* Personal recollections of distinguished generals. 1866.)

Thomas, Gustave Fréderic Maximilien. Guerre de 1870: Metz. Poitiers, 1871. 8°.

Thomas, Isaiah. Communications to members of the Amer. Antiq. Soc., 1814. (*In* **Amer. Antiq.** Soc. Addresses, v. 1. 1814.)

— History of printing in America; with biog. of printers, *etc.* Worcester, 1810. 2 v. 8°.

— Mass., Ct., R. I., N. H., Vt. almanach for 1800. Worcester, [1799]. 8°. **(E 28)**

— Oration, Lancaster, June 24, 1779 to Trinity Lodge. Worcester, 1781. 8°. **(B 555)**

— Burnside, S. M. Memoir. (*In* **Amer. Antiq.** Soc. Archæologia, v. 2. 1836.)

Thomas, James. Second voyage to Barbary, 1552, by Capt. T. Windham. (*In* **Green,** J. Col. of voy., v. 1. 1745.)

Thomas, Jesse B. Report of the statistics conc. Chicago. Chicago, 1847. 8°. **(B 1605)**

Thomas, John, *Maj. Gen.*, *b.* 1725, *d.* 1766. Coffin, C. The lives and services of Maj. Gen. J. T., Col. T. Knowlton, *etc.* N. Y., 1845. 12°.

— - Life and services of T. N. Y., 1844. 8°. **(B 1460)**

— Headley, J. T. (*In his* Washington, v. 2. 1847.)

Thomas, John, *Bp.*, *d.* 1781. Sermon before the Soc. for the Prop. of Gosp. in Foreign Parts. London, 1751. 4°. **(A 29)**

— Sermon, Feb. 6, a day of general fast on occasion of the late earthquake. London, 1756. 4°. **(B 1256)**

— Sermon, Feb. 17, 1747, fast [day]. London, 1748. 4°. **(B 1256)**

— Sermon, Feb. 17, 1758, fast. London, 1758. 4°. **(B 1257)**

— Sermon, Northampton [Eng.] before the Pres. and governors of the county infirmary, Sept. 22, 1748. Northampton, 1748. 8°. **(B 1346)**

Thomas, *Rev.* John. Blair, W. Pastor and deacon examined; candid remarks on T.'s appeal in vindication of W. Hale. London, 1810. 8°. **(B 785)**

Thomas, John, *M. D.* Chronic affections of the digestive organs; remarks on mineral waters. 2d ed. Cheltenham, 1821. 8°.

Thomas, John Hanson. Oration, July 4, request of the Washington Soc. of Alexandria. Alexandria, [1807]. 8°. **(B 243, C 104)**

Thomas, John J. American fruit culturist. Auburn, 1849. 12°.

— - *Same.* New ed. N. Y., 1871. 8°.

Thomas, Joseph, *M.D.* Universal pronouncing dictionary of biog. and mythology. Phila., 1870. 2 v. 8°.

— *and* Baldwin, T. Lippincott's pronouncing gazetteer. Phila., 1855. 8°.

— - *Same.* Phila., 1856. 8°.

Thomas, Joshua, *and others.* To the electors of the County of Plymouth, Mass. *n.p.*, 1811. 8°. **(B 440)**

— Bradford, A. Memoir of T. (*In* **Mass. Hist.** Soc. Col., v. 20. 1823.)

Thomas, *Rev.* Josiah. Address to a meeting holden for the purpose of forming a Ch. Missionary Soc. 5th ed. (*In* **Pamphleteer,** 1818; v. 11 of **B 838**)

Thomas, Lynall. Rifled ordnance; application of the principle of the rifle to guns and mortars. 1st Amer. from 5th Eng. ed. New York, 1864. 8°.

Thomas, Marcia Abiah. Memorials of Marshfield, and guide book to its localities at Green Harbor. Boston, 1854. 12°.

Thomas, *Mrs.* Mary, *Funeral sermon on.* 1818. *See* Bancroft, A. (B 304)

Thomas, Moses. History of facts; also the dealings of some of the 2d Baptist Ch. in Middleborough with Elder Hinds. Middleborough, 1787. 8°. (C 172)

Thomas, Moses G. Sermon; associations awakened by the Lord's table. — Sermon; we cannot be converted till we will. (*In* Liberal preacher, n.s., v. 4. 1834.)

Thomas, Nathaniel. Letter on the exped. against Philip, to Gov. Winslow, 1675. (*In* Mass. Hist. Soc. Col., v. 6. 1800.)

Thomas, P. Mémoires pour servir à l'hist. naturel des sangsues. Paris, 1806. 8°.

Thomas, Pascoe. A true and impartial journal of a voy. to the South Seas and round the globe, under the command of Com. G. Anson. London, 1745. 8°.

Thomas, R., *A.M.* Authentic acc. of the most remarkable events; containing the lives of the most noted pirates and piracies, shipwrecks, *etc.* N. Y., 1837. 2 v. 12°.

Thomas, Ralph, (*pseud.* Olphar Hamst). Handbook of fictitious names. London, 1868. 8°.

— A martyr to bibliography; a notice of the life and works of J. M. Quérard. Lond., 1867. 8°.

Thomas, Robert, *M.D.* Modern practice of physic. From 2d London ed.; corr. and enl., with app. by E. Miller. N. Y., 1811. 8°.

— Treatise on domestic medicine. 1st Amer. ed., revised by D. Hosack. N. Y., 1822. 8°.

Thomas, Robert Baily, *ed.* *See* Farmer's almanack.

Thomas, S. F. Tulles et dentelles. (*In* Lacroix, E. Etudes sur l'Exposition de 1867, v. 1.)

Thomas, Seth James. Address before the Democratic citizens of Plymouth Co., Mass., East Abington, July 4. Boston, 1839. 8°. (B 1143)

Thomas, *Rev.* Thomas. Virtues of hazel; or, Blessings of government. London, 1794. 8°. (B 776)

Thomas, Thomas E. Covenant breaking and its consequences; two discourses, Hamilton, Ohio, July 4 and 11. Rossville, 1847. 8°. (B 1303)

Thomas, W. H. B. Indications of weather as shown by animals and plants. (*In* Amer. Assoc. Proc., v. 7. 1856.)

Thomas, W. Cave. Mural or monumental decoration. London, [1869]. 8°.

Thomas, Wm., *d.* 1554. The pilgrim; a dialogue on the life and actions of Henry VIII.; ed. by J. A. Froude. London, 1861. 8°.

Thomas, Wm. Commentaries on the treatment of schirri and cancers. London, 1805. 8°.

Thomas Agni *de Lentino.* Vita S. Petri Martyris. (*In* Acta sanct., v. 12. 1866.)

Thomas and James; a dialogue. *n.t.p.* [N. Y., 18–?] 8°. (C 246)

Thomas and Sally; a musical entertainment. *See* Bickerstaff, I.

Thomas du Fosse, Pierre. Mémoires du sieur de Pontis. (*In* Michaud. Col. des mém., v. 20. 1854.)

— NICERON, J. P. (*In his* Mém., v. 41. 1740.)

Thomasis, Lucia de. RANIERI, A. Necrologia di T. (*In* Archivio stor. ital., n.s., v. 9. 1859.)

Thomason, *Rev.* Thomas T. Sermon. (*In* Church Missionary Soc. for Africa and the East. 2d report. 1819.)

Thomason's medallic illustration of the Scriptures. 60 medals in 5 cases. 1833.

Thomassin, Louis. NICERON, J. P. (*In his* Mém., v. 3. 1727; *and, Germ.*, v. 3. 1750.)

Thomassy, Marie Joseph Raymond. Géologie pratique de la Louisiane. Nouvelle Orléans, 1860. 4°.

— Les papes géographes et la cartographie du Vatican. (*In* Paris. Soc. Géog. Bul., 4e sér., v. 5. 1853.)

Thomaston, *Me.* EATON, C. History of T., *etc.* Hallowell, 1865. 2 v. 12°.

— SULLIVAN, J. Topog. descrip. of T. (*In* Mass. Hist. Soc. Col., v. 4. 1795.)

Thome, James A., *and* Kimball, J. H. Emancipation in the West Indies. N. Y., 1838. 12°.

— *Same.* N. Y., 1838. 8°. (B 1475, 1814, 2015. Anti-slavery examiner, no. 7.)

— Speech. (*In* Stanton, H. B. Debate at Lane Seminary. Cincin., 1834. 8°. B 1474)

Thomes, Wm. H. The gold hunter's adventures; or, Life in Australia. Boston, 1866. 12°.

Thomlinson, *Capt.* John. Correspondence [on] the settlement of the boundary lines between Mass. Bay and New Hampshire. (*In* New Hamp. *Legislature.* Provincial papers, v. 4. 1870.)

Thompson, —. Voyages en Afrique. (*In* Montémont, A. Biblioth. univ., v. 29. 1835.)

Thompson, *Capt.* Survey of the entrance of Sierra Leone River. London, 1794. (E 67)

Thompson, Alfred. The happy despatch. (*In* Scott, C. W. Drawing-room plays. 1870.)

Thompson, Ambrose W. Letter to W. M. Gwin [on trade with China]. *n.t.p.* [Wash., 1851.] 8°. (B 1505)

Thompson, Augustus Charles, *D.D.* Address, April 7, funeral of M. Codman; sermon, by J. H. Means. Boston, 1857. 8°. (B 1244)

— Marriage supper of the Lamb; a New Year's sermon. Boston, 1859. 8°. (B 1303)

— Military success from God; sermon, Roxbury, fast day, Apr. 3. Boston, 1862. 8°. (B 1593)

— Sermons; pastor's joy, and the first duty to a pastor. Boston, 1852. 8°.

Thompson, Benjamin, *d.* 1714. New England's crisis; [a poem]. *n.t.p.* [1676.] 16°. (C 62)

Thompson, *Sir* Benjamin, *Count Rumford*, *b.* 1753, *d.* 1814. Essays, political, economical, and philosophical. (Vol. 3 new ed.) Boston, 1798, 89, 1804. 3 v. 8°.

Contents. Vol. 1. Acc. of an establishment for the poor at Munich. — Fundamental principles on which establishments for the poor may be formed. — Food and feeding the poor. — Chimney fire-places. — Acc. of several public institutions in Bavaria; with app. to 1st vol. 2. Management of fire and economy of fuel. — Of the manner in which heat is propagated in fluids; with conj. resp. the final cause of the saltness of the sea. — Propagation of heat in various substances. — Inquiry conc. the source of heat excited by friction. 3. Construction of kitchen fire-places and kitchen utensils, with rem. rel. to cookery. — Obs. conc. the salubrity of warm rooms in cold weather. — Salubrity of warm bathing, and principles on which warm baths should be constructed. — Suppl. obs. rel. to the management of fires in closed fire-places. — Of the use of steam for transporting heat.

— Essay x., on the construction of kitchen fire places, and kitchen utensils; with observ. rel. to the processes of cookery. *n.t.p.* [1799?] 8°. (B 1741)

— Philosophical papers. Vol. 1. Lond., 1802. 8°.

— Proposals for forming a public institution for diffusing knowledge of mechanical inventions, *etc.* [London, 1799.] 8°. (B 696, 1741)

— BIGELOW, J. Life and works of Count Rumford. (*In his* Modern inquiries. 1867.)

— CUVIER, G. L. C. F. D. (*In his* Eloges hist., v. 2. 1819.)

— ELLIS, G. E. Memoir of T.; with notices of his daughter. Boston, 1871. 8°.

— RENWICK, J. Life of Count Rumford. (*In* Sparks, J. Amer. biog., v. 15. 1845.)

— YOUNG, T. Life of T. (*In his* Miscellaneous works, v. 2. 1855.)

Thompson, Benjamin, *of Kingston-upon-Hull, tr.* The stranger. *See* Kotzebue, A. F. F. de.

Thompson, Benjamin, *b.* 1798, *d.* 1852. Funeral oration on the death of Z. Taylor, July 31. Charlestown, 1850. 8°. (B 1225)

— *Funeral sermon on.* 1852. *See* Ellis, G. E. (B 1226)

Thompson, Benjamin F. History of Long Island. 2d ed. rev. and enl. N. Y., 1843. 2 v. 8°.

Thompson, Charles. Travels through Turkey, the Holy Land, Egypt, *etc.* Lond., 1754. 2 v. 12°.

Thompson, Daniel Pierce. The Green Mountain boys. Rev. ed. Boston, 1857. 2 v. 12°.

— History of Montpelier, Vt. Montpelier, 1860. 8°.

— The rangers; or, The Tory's daughter. Boston, 1851. 2 v. in 1. 12°.

Thompson, D'Arcy Wentworth. Day dreams of a schoolmaster. 2d ed. Edin., 1864. 16°.

— History and progress. (*In* **Afternoon** lectures, 3d ser. 1866.) — History and philosophy of story-telling. (*In* 4th ser.)

— Sales Attici; or, Maxims of the Athenian tragic drama. Edin., 1867. 12°.

— Status of teachers. (*In* **Nat. Assoc. Prom. Soc. Sci.** Trans., 1867.)

— Wayside thoughts; a series of desultory essays on education. N. Y., 1868. 12°.

Thompson, Edmund Symes, *M.D.* Influence of occupation on health and life. (*In* **Nat. Assoc. Prom. Soc. Sci.** Trans., 1862.)

Thompson, *Capt.* Edward. Poems. (*In* **Campbell**, T. Spec. of Brit. poets, v. 7. 1819.)

Thompson, George. Travels in Southern Africa. London, 1827. 2 v. 8°.

Thompson, George. Discussion on Amer. slavery, between G. T. and R. J. Breckinridge. 2d Amer. ed., with notes by [W. L.] Garrison. Boston, 1836. 8°.

— Letters and addresses in the United States. Boston, 1837. 12°.

— Prison life and reflections; narrative of the arrest, imprisonment, *etc.*, of [Alanson] Work, [James E.] Burr, and [George] Thompson in Missouri penitentiary for attempting to aid some slaves to liberty. 3d ed. Hartford, 1849. 12°.

— Burleigh, C. C. Reception of T. in Great Britain. Boston, 1836. 18°.

Thompson, George, *Lieut. Col. of Engineers.* The war in Paraguay; with a hist. sketch of the country and its people. London, 1869. 8°.

Thompson, George Alexander. Narrative of an official visit to Guatemala from Mexico. London, 1829. 12°.

— New theory of the two hemispheres; the time and manner in which America was peopled. (*In* **Pamphleteer**, 1815; v. 5 of B 838)

Thompson, *Rev.* Henry, *St. Johns Coll., Camb.* Heraldry. (*In* **Smedley**, E., *and others.* Encyc. metrop., v. 5. 1845.)

— Occult sciences. 1855. *See* **Smedley**, E.

Thompson, Henry, *surgeon.* Practical lithotomy and lithotrity. London, 1863. 8°.

— Surgery of the male urinary organs. (*In* **Holmes**, T. System of surg., v. 4. 1864.)

Thompson, Isaac. Bills of mortality for Middleborough, Mass., 1799-1813. (*In* **Mass. Hist.** Soc. Col., v. 8-10, 12. 1802-14.)

Thompson, J. Radford. Symbols of Christendom. London, 1867. 16°.

Thompson, James, *D.D.* [Half-century] discourse, Barre, Jan. 11; with app. Boston, 1854. 8°.

Thompson, James. Essay on English municipal history. London, 1867. 12°.

Thompson, James Wm. The claims of free-masonry stated; address, Leicester, on the anniv. of John the Baptist, June 24, A. L. 5831. Cambridge, 1831. 8°. **(B 1064)**

— Discourse, Sept. 9, as a tribute to the memory of H. Colman. Boston, 1849. 8°. **(B 1244)**

— Sermon, by request of the Female Char. Soc. in Salem, June 24. Salem, 1832. 8°. **(B 1328)**

Thompson, John, *Baron Haversham.* Account of the late Scotch invasion, 1708/9. (*In* **Somers**, J. Col. of tracts, v. 13. 1815; — *and in* **Harleian** misc., v. 11. 1810.)

Thompson, John, *d.* 1840. Smith, A. The minister-painter. (*In his* Last leaves. 1868.)

Thompson, John Hanson. Thompson, J. P. (*In his* Sergeant's memorial. 1863.)

Thompson, John Samuel. Christian guide to a right understanding of the Scriptures; commentary on the evangelists. New translation; pref., a mem. of the author and an introd. Utica, N. Y., 1826. 8°.

Note. All but the 'memoir and introd.' wanting.

Thompson, Joseph. Considerations resp. the trade with China. London, 1835. 12°.

Thompson, Joseph Parrish, *D.D.* Christianity and emancipation; or, The teachings and influence of the Bible against slavery. N. Y., 1863. 8°. **(B 1472)**

— Duties of the Christian citizen; a discourse. N. Y., 1848. 8°. **(B 1303)**

— Man in Genesis and in geology; or, The Biblical account of man's creation tested by scientific theories of his origin and antiquity. N. Y., 1870. 12°.

— Memoir of D. Hale; with selections from his writings. 2d ed. Hartford, 1850. 8°.

— Memoir of D. T. Stoddard. N. Y., 1858. 12°.

— Moses. (*In* **Boston** lectures. 1871.)

— Photographic views of Egypt, past and present. Boston, 1854. 12°.

— The sergeant's memorial; by his father. N. Y., *1863. 12°.

— Sermon, death of A. Lincoln. (*In* **Lincoln**, A. Our martyr president. 1865.)

— Vice progressive; sermon to young men, Aug. 2. 2d ed. N. Y., 1846. 8°. **(B 1303)**

Thompson, Justus. *See* **Berry**, J., *vs.* **Thompson**, J. **(B 340)**

Thompson, Leslie A. Manual or digest of statute law of Florida. Boston, 1847. 8°.

Thompson, *Mrs.* Margaret. Phrenological character of R. Dunbar. Albany, 1851. 8°. **(B 1444)**

Thompson, Matthew La Rue Perrine, *D.D.* Sermon at Canandaigua, Aug. 28. Rochester, 1842. 8°. **(B 1184)**

— Two discourses at Canandaigua, June 23, 1839, on the death of E. M. and G. R. Hubbell. Canandaigua, 1841. 8°. **(B 1218)**

Thompson, Murray, *D.D.* Contamination of water by manufactories. (*In* **Nat. Assoc. Prom. Soc. Sci.** Trans., 1863.)

Thompson, *Rev.* Otis. Address before the Bristol Co. Agric. Soc. Taunton, 1837. 8°. **(B 1129)**

— Sermon, installation of S. W. Colbourn, Abbington, Oct. 27. Boston, 1813. 8°. **(B 333)**

— Sermon, national thanksgiving for the restoration of peace, April 13. Prov., 1815. 8°. **(B 1253)**

— Signs of the times; sermon, Attleborough, fast day, April 9. Prov., 1812. 8°. **(B 1259)**

Thompson, Pishey. Collections for a topog. and historical account of Boston and Skirbeck. London, 1820. 4°.

— History and antiquities of Boston [England]. Boston, 1856. 8°.

Thompson, Richard W. Speech on the tariff bills. Wash., 1842. 8°. **(B 1174)**

Thompson, Robert. Patent uterine truss. Columbus, 1843. 8°. **(C 271)**

Thompson, Robert Anchor. Christian theism; the testimony of reason and revelation to the existence and character of the Supreme Being. N. Y., 1855. 12°.

Thompson, Samuel. Universal restoration vindicated; a reply to a disc. by J. Horton, Weymouth, Dec. 18, 1808. Charlestown, 1809. 8°. **(B 136, 1713)**

Thompson, Theophilus, *M.D.* Annals of influenza in Gr. Brit., 1510-1837. London, 1852. 8°. (Sydenham Soc.)

Thompson, Thomas, *Funeral sermon on.* 1808. *See* **Spring**, S. **(B 282)**

Thompson, Thomas Perronet. Catechism on the corn laws. 3d ed. (*In* **Pamphleteer**, 1826; v. 27 of **B 838**)

— *Same.* 10th ed. London, 1829. 8°. **(B 927)**

— *Same.* 13th ed. London, 1829. 8°.

— Exercises, political and others; from Westminster review. London, 1842. 6 v. 12°.

— Extracts from the works of T. *n.t.p.* [Manchester, 1841.] 8°. **(B 1187)**

— Theory and practice of just intonation. 2d ed. London, 1857. 12°.

— Blanchard, L. (*In his* Saunders' portraits, v. 1. 1838.)

Thompson, Waddy. Recollections of Mexico. N. Y., London, 1846. 8°.

Thompson, Wm., *d.* 1766. Poems. (*In* **Anderson**, R. Brit. poets, v. 10. 1795; — *and in* **Chalmers**, A. Eng. poets, v. 15. 1810.)

Thompson, Wm., *b.* 1805, *d.* 1852. Natural history of Ireland: Birds. London, 1849–51. 3 v. 8°.

Thompson, Wm. To the committee on elections [of Iowa respecting election of member of Congress]. *n.t.p.* [1850.] 8°. (**B 1504**)

Thompson, Wm. Theodore. Major Jones's courtship. 2d ed. illust. by Darley. Phila., 1844. 12°.

— Major Jones's scenes in Georgia. Phila., [1858]. 12°.

— Major Jones's sketches of travel. Phila., 1848. 12°.

Thompson, Zadock. Hist. of Vermont, natural civil, and statistical. Burlington, 1842. 8°.

Thompson. *See also* **Thomsen**; — **Thomson**; — **Tomson**.

Thoms, Peter Perring, *tr.* *See* **Hwa-tsëen**.

Thoms, Wm. Book of the court; history, duties, and privileges of the English nobility and gentry. 2d ed. London, 1844. 8°.

Thoms, Wm. John (*pseud.* Ambrose **Merton**). Anecdotes and traditions illustr. of early Eng. history and literature. London, 1839. 8°. (Camden Soc.)

— Early English prose romances. 2d ed. enl. London, 1858. 3 v. 8°.

Contents. Vol. 1. **Robert** the deuyll. — **Thomas** a Reading. — **Frier** Bacon. — **Frier** Rush. 2. **Virgilius**. Robin Hood. — **George** a Green. — **Tom** a Lincolne. 3. **Helyas**. Doctor Faustus. — **Second** report of Doctor Faustus.

— Gammer Gurton's famous histories. N. Y., 1846. 4°.

— Gammer Gurton's pleasant stories. N .Y., 1849. 4°..

Thomsen, Christian Jürgensen. Færoeske Oldsager. (*In* **Copenhagen. K. Com. f. Olds. Opb.** Antiq. Ann., v. 3, pt. 2. 1820.)

— *and* Devegge, O. Catalogus numorum veterum Gr. et Rom. quos possidebat olim G. F. Timm; acc. recensio numorum orientalium a J. C. Lindberg. Havniæ, 1832. 16°.

— - Fortegnelse over G. F. Timmes Mynt- og Medaille Sammlung. 3. deel: Skandinavien Lande. Kiöb., 1834. 16°.

Thomson. *See also* **Thompson**; — **Thomsen**; — **Tomson**.

Thomson, —. La Perse; sa population, *etc*; avec notes par N. de Khanikof. (*In* **Paris. Soc. de Géog.** Bul., 5e sér., v. 18. 1869.)

Thomson, Adam, *D.D.* Bible emancipation; or, The extraordinary results of unfettered Bible printing. Edin., 1846. 8°. (**B 1373**)

Thomson, Alexander. Aberdeen industrial feeding schools. — History of preventive and reformatory work in Aberdeen. (*In* **Nat. Assoc. Prom. Soc. Sci.** Trans., 1860.)

— Our treatment of the lower and lowest classes of society. — Prevention is better than cure. (*In* **Talbot**, C., *Viscount Ingestre*. Meliora, 2d ser. 1843.)

Thomson, Andrew, *D.D.* Life of J. Owen. Edin., 1853. 12°.

— Introductory essay. (*In* **Mather**, C. **Essays** to do good. 1825.)

— The Sabbath. Glasgow, [184-]. 8°. (**B 1374**)

— Sermon, the character of religious zeal. (*In* **Suddards**, W. Brit. pulpit, v. 1. 1837.)

— Ultimate and universal prevalence of the Chr. religion; sermon before the Society in Scotland for Propagating Christian Knowledge, June 5. Edin., 1817. 8°. (**B 1642**)

Thomson, Antony Todd, *M.D.* Conspectus of the pharmacopœias of London, Edinburgh, and Dublin. 10th ed. London, 1838. 18°.

— Domestic management of the sick room. London, 1841. 12°.

— Elements of materia medica and therapeutics. London, 1832–33. 2 v. 8°.

— Lectures on the elements of botany. Vol. 1. London, 1822. 8°.

— The London dispensatory. 2d ed. London, 1818. 8°.

Thomson, *Mrs.* Anthony Todd. *See* **Thomson, K.**

Thomson, Charles. Letters rel. to Dr. Kippis. (*In* **Mass. Hist. Soc.** Col., v. 4. 1795.)

— The Holy Bible, trans. *See* **Bible** (p. 269).

Thomson, Charles Edward Poulett, *Lord Sydenham.* Scrope, G. P. Memoir of the life of Lord Sydenham. London, 1843. 8°.

— Blanchard, L. (*In his* Saunders portraits, v. 1. 1838.)

Thomson, Charles West. Notices of the life and character of R. Proud. (*In* **Penn. Hist. Soc.** Mem., v. 1. 1826.)

Thomson, E. H. The emigrant's guide to Michigan; [in Germ. and Eng.]. N. Y., 1849. 8°.

Thomson, George. Memorandum of the engineer operations at the taking of Ghuznee. (*In* **Gr. Brit.** *Corps of Roy. Engin.* Papers, v. 4. 1840.)

Thomson, John Cockburn. Almæ matres; by Megathym Splene. London, [1849]. 16°.

Thomson, James, *d.* 1748. Works; with the life of the author by P. Murdoch. London, 1802. 3 v. 8°.

Contents. Vol. 1. Life; by P. Murdoch. — The seasons. — A hymn. — The castle of indolence. — Poem to the memory of Sir I. Newton. — Poem to the memory of Lord Talbot. — Verses occasioned by the death of Mr. Aikman. — Ode. — Epitaph on Miss Stanley. — To the Rev. Mr. Murdoch. — Paraphrase on the latter part of the sixth chapter of Matthew. — Songs. — Odes. — Hymn on solitude. 2. Britannia. — Liberty. — Sophonisba. — Edward and Eleonora. 3. Agamemnon. — Alfred. — Tancred and Sigismunda. — Coriolanus.

— Edward and Eleonora; adapted to the stage by T. Hull. London, 1775. 8°.

— *Same.* (*In* Bell, J. Brit. theatre, v. 32. 1797.)

— Liberty; a poem. Pts. 1–3. London, 1735. 3 pts. 4°.

Contents. Pt. 1. Ancient and modern Italy compared. 2. Greece. 3. Rome.

— *Same.* Pt. 1–5. Glasgow, 1776. 24°.

Contents. Pt. 1-3 *same as above.* 4. Britain. 5. The prospect.

— Poem to the memory of Wm. Congreve; with preface and notes by P. Cunningham. London, 1843. 8°. (Percy Soc., v. 9.)

— Poems. (*In* **Campbell**, T. Spec. of Brit. poets, v. 5. 1819.)

— Poems. (*In* **Chalmers**, A. Eng. poets, v. 12. 1810.)

— Poetical works. (*In* **Anderson**, R. Brit. poets, v. 9. 1795.)

— Poetical works; [ed. by F. J. Child with life by Sir H. Nicolas]. Boston, 1854. 2 v. 16°.

Contents. Vol. 1. Poems. — Songs. — Prologues. — Epilogues. — Britannia. — Liberty. 2. The seasons. — The castle of indolence.

— Preface. (*In* **Milton**, J. Areopagitica. 1738. **B 582**)

— The seasons; a poem; [also a poem to the memory of Sir I. Newton, and Britannia]. London, 1730. 8°.

— Tancred and Sigismunda. (*In* **Bell**, J. Brit. theatre, v. 14. 1797; — *in* **Scott**, W. Brit. dr., v. 1, pt. 2. 1804; — *and in* **London** stage, v. 4.)

— Barante, A. G. P. B. de. (*In his* Mélanges hist. et lit., v. 3. 1836.)

— Johnson, S. (*In his* Works, v. 11. 1806; Lives of Eng. poets, v. 2. 1810.)

— Life. (*In* **Society of Anc. Scots.** Lives of Scottish poets, v. 1, pt. 2. 1822.)

— Wilson, J. (*In his* Recreations of C. North, v. 2. 1857.)

Thomson, James, *D.D.* Letters on the moral and religious state of S. America. London, 1827. 12°.

— Address to the citizens of the U. S. on behalf of the new nations lately subject to the Spanish government. N. Y., 1830. 12°. (**C 266**)

Thomson, *Rev.* John. Grounds of faith; sermon, Edin., June 2. Edin., 1785. 8°. (**B 169**)

— The nature of true religion; sermon, Nov. 25, 1792. Edin., 1793. 8°. (**B 1860**)

Thomson, John. Tables of interest. 6th ed. London, 1794. 16°.

Thomson, John. Letters of Curtius; [with] speech on the British treaty, and sketch of his life. Richmond, 1804. 12°. (B 616)

Thomson, John, *M.D.* Lectures on inflammation. Edin., 1813. 8°.

— Varioloid epidemic in Edinburgh, *etc.* London, 1820. 8°.

Thomson, *Mrs.* Katharine (Byerley), *wife of* A. T. Thomson. Life and times of George Villiers Duke of Buckingham. London, 1860. 3 v. 8°.

— Life of Wolsey. (*In* **Soc. Dif. Usef. Knl.** Lib. usef. knl. Lives of eminent persons. 1833.)

— Memoirs of Sarah Duchess of Marlborough. London, 1839. 2 v. 8°.

— Memoirs of the Court of Henry VIII. London, 1826. 2 v. 8°.

— Memoirs of Viscountess Sundon. London, 1847. 2 v. 12°.

— Recollections of literary characters and celebrated places. London, 1854. 2 v. 8°.
Contents. Vol. 1. Dr. Maginn. — Ham House. — Hampton Court. — Holland House. — Mrs. Montagu and her friends. — Whitehall; Palace of Westminster; York House. — Anc. Palace of Greenwich and the days of the Tudors. — Kenilworth. — Siege of Raglan Castle, and the Somerset family. 2. Basing House. — Latham House, and the Stanley family. — Coleridge; Sir James Hall; Leslie; Mackintosh; Blanco White. — Mrs. Serres; Charles Mills; L. E. L. — John Galt. — T. Campbell, Mrs. Siddons. — Wilkie, Chantrey. — Hatton Rectory. — Allan Cunningham. — Publishers and authors. — Chartley Castle and the Ferrers family, Laurence, Earl Ferrers; Whitefield; Lady Huntingdon.

— *and* **Thomson, J. C.** Queens of society; by G. and P. Wharton. N. Y., 1861. 12°.
Contents. Sarah, Duchess of Marlborough. — Mme. Roland. — Lady Mary Wortley Montagu. — Georgiana, Duchess of Devonshire. — L. E. Landon. — Mme. de Sévigné. — Sydney Lady Morgan. — Jane, Duchess of Gordon. — Mme. Récamier. — Lady Hervey. — Mme. de Staël. — Mrs. Thrale-Piozzi. — Lady Caroline Lamb. — Anne Seymour Damer. — La marquise du Deffand. — Mrs. Elizabeth Montague. — Mary, Countess of Pembroke. — La marquise de Maintenon.

— - Wits and beaux of society; by G. and P. Wharton. N. Y., 1861. 12°.
Contents. George Villiers, 2d Duke of Buckingham. — Count de Grammont, St. Evremond, Ld. Rochester. — Beau Fielding. — Clubs and club-wits under Anne. — Wm. Congreve. — Beau Nash. — Philip, Duke of Wharton. — Ld. Hervey. — Philip Dormer Stanhope, 4th Earl of Chesterfield. — Abbé Scarron. — François, duc de la Rochefoucault and the duc de St. Simon. — Horace Walpole. — George Selwyn. — Sheridan. — Beau Brummell. — T. E. Hook. — Sydney Smith. — G. B. Dodington, Ld. Melcombe.

Thomson, *Capt.* Mowbray. The story of Cawnpore. London, 1859. 12°.

Thomson, Richard. Chronicles of London Bridge; by an antiquary. 2d ed. London, 1839. 16°. (Fam. lib., v. 66.)

— Illustrations of the history of Gr. Britain. Edin., 1828. 2 v. 18°. (Constable's miscel., v. 20, 21.)

Thomson, Robert. Divine authority of the Bible; a refutation of Paine's 'Age of reason'. 1st Amer. ed. Boston, 1807. 12°.

Thomson, Robert. Furnaces for heating shot. (*In* **Gr. Brit.** *Corps of Royal Engin.* Papers, v. 3. 1839.) — Experiments on condensation of gravel and sand. — Failure of a floor in Edin. (*In* v. 7.) — Failure of masonry at Corfu. (*In* v. 8. 1845.)

Thomson, Robert Dundas, *M.D.* Proper source of waters for domestic supply. (*In* **Nat. Assoc. Prom. Soc. Sci.** Trans., 1862.)
See also **British** annual.

Thomson, Samuel. Brief sketch of the causes and treatment of disease. Boston, 1821. 12°. (C 147)
See also **Boston** Thomsonial manual and lady's companion; — **Thomsonian** and botanic medical adviser. 1831.

— BROWN, J. A. Quackery exposed; a few remarks on the Thomsonian system of medicine. Boston, 1833. 8°. (B 1549)

Thomson, Spencer, *M.D.* Wayside weeds; botanical lessons from lanes and hedgerows. London, 1864. 8°.

Thomson, T. R. Narrative of the exped. to the Niger. *See* **Allen, W.,** *R. N.*

Thomson, Thomas, *M.D.* Chemistry of animal bodies. Edin., 1843. 8°.

— First principles of chemistry. London, 1825. 2 v. 8°.

— Outline of the sciences of heat and electricity. London, 1830. 8°.

— Sketch of the progress of physical science; also lect. on astronomy by D. Lardner. 3d ed. N. Y., 1843. 8°.

— System of chemistry. Edin,, 1802. 4 v. 8°.

— *Same.* 4th ed. Edin., 1810. 5 v. 8°.

— System of chemistry of inorganic bodies. 7th ed. London, Edin., 1831. 2 v. 8°.

— Travels in Sweden, 1812. London, 1813. 4°.
See also **Annals** of philosophy.

Thomson, *Rev.* Thomas. Biographical dict. of eminent Scotsmen, suppl. vol. *See* **Chambers, R.**

Thomson, Wm. Poems. (*In* **Chalmers, A.** English poets, v. 15. 1810.)

Thomson, Wm. Two journeys through Italy and Switzerland. London, 1835. 12°.

Thomson, Wm., *Archbishop of York.* Address on education, 1864. (*In* **Nat. Assoc. Prom. Soc. Sci.** Trans., 1864.)

— Aids to faith; reply to 'Essays and reviews'. N. Y., 1862. 12°.
Contents. **Mansel, H. L.** Miracles as evidences of Christianity. — **Fitzgerald, W.** Study of evidences of Christianity. — **McCaul, A.** Prophecy. — **Cook, F. C.** Ideology and subscription. — **McCaul, A.** Mosaic record of creation. — **Rawlinson, G.** Genuineness and authenticity of the Pentateuch. — **Browne, E. H.** Inspiration. — **Thomson, W.** Death of Christ. — **Ellicott, C. J.** Scripture and its interpretation.

— Crime and its excuses. (*In* **Oxford** essays, 1855.)

— Death of Christ. (*In* **Thomson, F.** Aids to faith. 1862.)

— Outline of the necessary laws of thought; a treatise on logic. 4th ed. London, 1857. 16°.

Thomson, *Sir* **Wm.,** *and* **Tait, P. G.** Treatise on natural philosphy. Vol. 1. Oxford, 1867. 8°.

Thomson, *Rev.* Wm. Aird. Sermon; necessity of testifying repentance toward Christ. (*In* **Free** church pulpit. 1853.)

— Sermon before the Society in Scotland for Propagating Christian Knowledge, June 6, 1822. Edin., 1823. 8°. (B 1642)

Thomson, Wm. M., *D.D.* The land and the book; or, Biblical illustrations from scenes, *etc.*, in the Holy Land. N. Y., 1859. 2 v. 12°.

Thomsonian, The, and botanic medical adviser, published monthly. No. 1. Baltimore, 1831. 8°. (B 1854)

Thomsonian manual and lady's companion. *See* **Boston** Thomsonian manual, *etc.*

Thomsonian system. *See* **Thomson, S.** (B 1594)

Thon, Sixt Arnim. ANDRESEN, A. (*In his* Die deutschen Maler-Radirer, v. 4. 1870.)

Thor, Land of. *See* **Browne, J. R.**

Thorburn, Grant. Forty years residence in America. Boston, 1834. 12°.

— Gentleman and gardener's calendar. N. Y., 1807. 18°.

— Men and manners in Britain. N. Y., 1834. 12°.

Thorburn, Joseph. Sermon; sanctified affliction. (*In* **Free** church pulpit. 1853.)

Thoré, Etienne Joseph Théophile (*pseud.* Willem Bürger). Les collections particulières. (*In* **Paris** guide, v. 1. 1867.)

— Nouvelles études sur la galerie Suermondt à Aix-la-Chapelle. (*In* **Gazette** des beaux-arts, v. 26. 1869.)

Thoreau, Henry David. Excursions. Boston, 1863. 16°.

Contents. Biog. sketch by R. W. Emerson. — Nat. hist. of Mass. — A walk to Wachusett. — The landlord. — A winter walk. — Succession of forest trees. — Walking. — Autumnal-tints. — Wild apples. — Night and moonlight.

— Letters [and poems]. Boston, 1865. 12°.

— Maine woods. Boston, 1866. 12°.

— Walden; or, Life in the woods. Boston, 1854. 12°.

— Week on the Concord and Merrimack rivers. Boston, Camb., 1849. 12°.

— Yankee in Canada; with anti-slavery and reform papers. Boston, 1866. 12°.

Contents. A Yankee in Canada. — Anti-slavery and reform papers. — Slavery in Massachusetts. — Prayers. — Civil disobedience. — A plea for Capt. J. Brown. — Paradise (to be) regained. — Herald of freedom. — T. Carlyle and his works. — Life without principle. — Wendell Phillips before the Concord Lyceum. — The last days of J. Brown.

— EMERSON, R. W. *See, above,* 'Excursions'.

— LOWELL, J. R. (*In his* My study windows. 1871.)

Thoresby, Ralph. Diary, 1677-1724; ed. by J. Hunter. London, 1830. 2 v. 8°.

— Ducatus Leodiensis; or, Topography of Leeds; added, a catalogue of his musæum, *etc.* 2d ed., with notes and add. by T. D. Whitaker. Leeds, 1816. f°.

— LETTERS of eminent men, addressed to R. Thoresby. London, 1832. 2 v. 8°.

Contents. Vol. 1. 1679-1703. 2. 1703-23. — *Appendix.* Acc. of a tour in Scotland.

Thoresen, Magdalene. Old Olaf. (*In* **Goldschmidt, M.** The flying mail. 1870.)

Thorfinn Karlsefne, *and* **Snorre Thorbrandson.** Sagaen. (*In* **Copenhagen. K. Nord. Oldsk.** Antiq. Amer. 1837.)

Thorius, Raphael. Cheimonopegnion; or, A winter song; newly tr. London, 1651. 16°.

— Epistola de I. Casauboni morbi mortisque causa. — De morbo et morte I. C. (*In* **Casaubon, I.** Epistolæ. 1638.)

— Hymnus tabaci; a poem in honour of tabaco; tr. by P. Hausted. London, 1651. 16°.

Thorkelin, Grim Johnson, *LL.D., tr. See* **Danorum rebus** gestis secul. 3 et 4, De.

Thorlacius, Børge (*Lat.* Birgerus). [Several papers.] (*In* **Copenhagen. K. Com. f. Olds. Opb.** Antiq. Ann., v. 1, pt. 1; 2, pt. 1; 3, pt. 1; 4, pt. 1, 2. 1812.)

Thorlacius, Skule Thordsen. [Several papers.] (*In* **Copenhagen. K. Com. f. Olds. Opb.** Antiq. Ann., v. 1, pt. 1, 2; 2, pt. 1, 2. 1812.)

Thorn, N. Catalogue of books to be sold 5th Dec. 1738. [London, 1738.] 8°. (B 874)

Thorn, *Prussia.* FAITHFUL narrative of the horrid tragedy lately acted at Thorn. London, [1725]. 8°. (B 602)

Thornbury, George Walter. British artists from Hogarth to Turner. London, 1861. 2 v. 8°.

Contents. Vol. 1. Gainesborough in green lanes. — Wilson in Tottenham-court Road. — Lawrence in London drawing rooms. — Nolekins in Mortimer Street. — Two fop artists: Sherwin and Cosway. — Fuseli in Somerset House. — Barry in the Adelphi. — Reynolds at his easel in Leicester Square. — Brauwer in the Antwerp hospital. — Fra Angelico in the chapel of the Vatican. — A pupil of the school of Watteau. — The day after Hogarth's death. — The flower painter's death. 2. A ship full of nobodies. — The prophet in Carnaby Market. — Blake the visionary. — The English caricaturists. — Men of promise: Proctor and Deare. — West, the monarch of mediocrity in Newman St. — Stothard the graceful. — Morland in the sponging house. — David Scott. — Epochs of painting. — Greek art. — Moorish art. — Gothic art.

— Life in Spain; past and present. Re-arranged from Household words, v. 18, 19. London, 1859. 2 v. 12°.

— Life of J. M. W. Turner. Lond., 1862. 2 v. 8°.

— Old stories retold. London, 1870. 8°.

Contents. Life of a Methodist preacher, 1715. — A gambler's life in the last century, 1725. — Sarah Malcolm, 1733. — The duel between Ld. Byron and Mr. Chaworth, 1765. — Old Patch, the forger, 1784. — The Battle of Vinegar Hill, 1798. — Emmet's insurrection, 1803. — Trafalgar, 1805. — The O. P. riots. — The two great murders in Ratcliff Highway, 1811. — The Luddites, 1812. — Assassination of Mr. Perceval, 1812. — Burning of Wildgoose Lodge, 1816. — Bombardment of Algiers, 1816. — Wreck of the Medusa, 1816. — Wager of battle, Murder of Mary Ashford, 1817. — Cato st. conspiracy, 1820. — T. G. Wainewright, the poisoner, 1830. — Murder of Wm. Weare, 1823. — Trial and execution of Fauntleroy, 1824. — Loss of the Kent, East Indiaman, by fire, 1825. — The red barn, 1827. — Resurrection men, Burke and Hare, 1829. — Bristol riots, 1831. — Fieschi and the infernal machine, 1835.

— Shakspeare's England; sketches of social history in the reign of Elizabeth. London, 1856. 2 v. 8°.

— A tour round England. London, 1870. 2 v. 8°.

Thorndale; or, The conflict of opinions. *See* **Smith, W.**

Thorndike, Augustus. CATALOGUE of the library of A. Thorndike, sold May, 1860. [ms. prices.] Boston, 1860. 8°.

Thorndike, Israel, *and others.* Report of merchants and manufacturers of Boston on the proposed tariff, 1824. Boston, [1824]. 8°. (B 533)

Thorndike, Samuel Lothrop. Biography of W. S. Hooper. (*In* **Higginson, T. W.** Harvard mem. biog., v. 1. 1866.)

Thorne, Robert. Brief notice of the discovery of Newfoundland. (*In* **Kerr, R.** Col. of voy., v. 6. 1824.)

— Declaration of the Indies and landes discovered and subdued into the emperour and king of Portugal, 1527. (*In* **Hakluyt Soc.** Pub., v. 7: Divers voy. 1850.)

Thornes, Vincent. Discorso della fisica sublimatione. Venetia, 1582. 4°. (A 44)

Thornton, Bonnell. The battle of the wigs; an additional canto to Dr. Garth's 'Dispensary'. London, 1768. 8°. (A 46)

— Connoisseur. *See* **Colman, G.,** *the elder.*

Thornton, Edward. Observations on the report of the committee of the Ho. of Com. [on] the high price of gold bullion; with remarks on the work of Blake, 'Observations', *etc.* London, 1811. 8°. (B 727)

Thornton, Edward. Gazetteer of the territories under the government of the East India Co., and the native states. Lond., 1854. 4 v. 8°.

Contents. Vol. 1. Abo-Coc. 2. Cog-Jyt. 3. Kab-Oog. 4. Ooj-Zyn.

Thornton, Henry. BOURNE, H. R. F. (*In his* Famous London merchants. 1869.)

Thornton, J. Quinn. Oregon and California in 1848. N. Y., 1849. 2 v. 12°.

Thornton, *Rev.* John. Preciousness of Christ to all who believe. Boston, 1834. 12°.

— Repentance explained and enforced. Boston, 1818. 18°.

Thornton, John Wingate. Colonial schemes of Popham and Gorges; speech at the Fort Popham celebration, Aug. 29, 1862. Boston, 1863. 8°.

— Genealogical mem. of the Gilbert family. Boston, 1850. 8°.

— First records of Anglo-American colonization. Boston, 1859. 8°.

— Mementos of the Swett family. Roxbury, *privately printed* 1851. 8°.

— Note to the history of Scarborough. (*In* **Maine Hist. Soc.** Col., v. 3. 1853.) — Ancient Pemaquid; an historical review. (*In* v. 5. 1857.)

— Peter Oliver's 'Puritan commonwealth' reviewed. Boston, 1857. 8°.

— Pulpit of the Amer. Revolution; political sermons of the period of 1776. Boston, 1860. 8°.

Contents. **Thornton, J. T.** Hist. introd. — **Mayhew, J.** Sermon, Jan. 30, 1750, death of Charles I. — **Chauncy, C.** Thanksgiving sermon on the repeal of the stamp act, 1766. — **Cooke, S.** Election sermon, 1770. — **Gordon, W.** Thanksgiving sermon, 1774. — **Langdon, S.** Election sermon, Watertown, 1775. — **West, S.** Election sermon, 1776. — **Payson, P.** Election sermon, 1778. — **Howard, S.** Election sermon, 1780. — **Stiles, E.** Election sermon, 1783.

Thornton, Matthew. Letter, 1775. (*In* **New Hampshire Hist. Soc.** Col., v. 6. 1850.)

— SANDERSON, J. (*In his* Biog. of the signers, v. 5. 1824.)

Thornton, Robert John, *M.D.* Defence of vaccination. London, 1806. 8°.
— Grammar of botany; [incl. J. Lee's Dictionary of botanical terms]. N. Y., 1818. 12°.
— The Lord's prayer. *See* **Bible** (p. 287. A 61)
— Pastorals of Virgil; with a course of Eng. reading. London, 1821. 2 v. 12°.
— Philosophy of botany; incl. a new illustration of the sexual system of Linnæus. London, 1799–1809. 2 v. f°.

Thornton, Thomas. Present state of Turkey. London, 1809. 2 v. 8°.

Thornton, Wm., *M.D.* Cadmus; or, The elements of written language; with an essay on teaching the deaf and dumb to speak. Phila., 1793. 8°. (B 737)

Thornton, Wm. [Mode of obtaining] patents. *n.t.p.* Wash., 1811. 8°. (C 81)
— Speech.] Wash., 1805. 8°. (B 1106)

Thornton, Wm. Thomas. On labour. London, 1869. 8°.

Thornton (*Eng.*), **Manor of.** COURT leet, 19 Oct. 1773–81. MS.

Thornton romances. *See* **Halliwell**, O.

Thornwell, James Henry, *D.D.* Our national sins. (*In* Fast day sermons. 1861.)
— The sacrifice of Christ; sermon before the Gen. Assembly of the Presbyterian Ch., N. Y., May 18. N. Y., 1856. 8°. (B 1330)

Thorogood, B. His opinion of the succession, to a brother of the blade in Scotland. *n.t.p.* [1679.] 8°. (A 52)

Thorowgood, Thomas. Digitus Dei; new discoveryes; with sure arguments to prove that the Jews inhabite now in America; added, a disc. of J. Dury with the history of Ant. Monterinos. London, 1652. 4°.

Thorp, Robert. Establishments in religion, and religious liberty; sermon before the Univ., Cambridge, July 1. Camb., 1792. 4°. (B 1263)

Thorpe, Benjamin. Ancient laws and institutes of England, to Henry I.; also, 7th–10th cent. *n.p.*, 1840. f°.

Note. The Anglo-Saxon laws have an Eng. and the ancient Latin version.

— Codex Exoniensis, Anglo-Saxon poetry with an English translation. London, 1842. 8°.

Contents. To Jesus Christ. — To the Virgin Mary. — The Nativity. — To the Trinity. — The Nativity and Ascension. — The Ascension and the harrowing of hell. — Hymn of praise and thanksgiving. — Day of judgment. — Crucifixion. — Of souls after death, *etc.* — Poem, moral and religious. — The legend of St. Guthlac. — The story of Hananiah, Mishael, and Azariah paraphrased. — The phœnix. — The legend of St. Juliana. — The wanderer. — Endowments and pursuits of men. — A father's instruction to his son. — The seafarer. — Monitory poem. — The scōp or scald's tale. — Various fortunes of men. — Gnomic verses. — Wonders of creation. — Riming poem. — The panther. — The whale. — A fragment. — A departed soul's address to the body: a condemned soul; a blessed soul. — Deor the scald's complaint. — Riddles. — The exile's complaint. — Day of judgment. — A supplication. — Resurrection and the harrowing of hell. — Religious poem. — A fragment. — The Lord's prayer paraphrased. — Maxims. — Riddles. — A fragment. — The ruin. — Riddles. — Notes. — Index of persons. — Index of countries and folks. — Verbal index.

— Northern mythology; popular traditions of Scandinavia, *etc.* London, 1851–52. 3 v. 8°.
— Outline of Anglo-Saxon grammar. (*In* **Pauli**, R. Life of Alfred the Great. 1833.)
— Yule-tide stories; a collection of Scandinavian and North German popular tales and traditions. London, *Bohn*, 1853. 8°.

See also **Anglo Saxon** chronicle.

Thorpe, Markham John. Calendar of state papers rel. to Scotland. London, 1858. 2 v. 8°.

Contents. Vol. 1. 1509–89. 2. 1589–1603. — *Appendix*, 1543–92. — Mary, Queen of Scots, 1568–87.

Thorpe, Robert, *LL.D.* Commentary on the treaties between [Gr. Brit., Spain, and Netherlands on the slave trade]. (*In* **Pamphleteer**, 1819; v. 14 of B 838)
— AFRICAN INSTITUTION. Special report of the directors resp. allegations by T. London, 1815. 8°. (B 673)

Thorpe, Thomas. Pt. 3 for 1829; a catalogue. [London,] *n.d.* 8°.
— Ancient seals, a catalogue of impressions collected by J. Caley. [London, 183–?] 8°.
— Drawings from ancient British seals [by Howlett for J. Caley]; a catalogue. [London, 183–?] 8°.
— State papers; catalogue lib. mss. biblioth. Southwellianæ. [Pt. 4 for 1834. London,] *n.d.* 8°.
— Catalogue. [Pt. 5, 7 for 1834. Lond.,] *n.d.* 8°.
— Catalogue of early plays, pageants, *etc.* [London, 1834?] 8°.
— Bibliotheca Heberiana; catalogue of some 1000 vols. from the library of R. Heber. [Pt. 3 for 1834. London, *n.d.*] 8°.
— Bibliotheca selecta. [London, 1835?] 8°.
— Catalogue of ancient mss. [London, 1835.] 8°.
— - Supplement to catalogue of anc. mss. [London,] 1836. 8°.
— Catalogue of mss. and autographs. [London, 1835.] 8°.
— Abingdon papers; catal. of royal and noble autograph letters, papers rel. to America, *etc.* [London, 1835.] 8°.
— Catalogue of books from the libraries of Ld. H. Fitzroy, Alex. Chalmers, *etc.* [Pt. 4 for 1835. London, 1835.] 8°.
— Catalogue of books from the libraries of Ch. Matthews, *etc.* [Pt. 8 for 1835. London, 1835.] 8°.
— Descriptive catalogue of the muniments of Battle Abbey, on sale. [London,] 1835. 8°.
— Topographical drawings and engravings. [London, 1835?] 8°.
— Bibliotheca selecta. [London,] *n.d.* 8°.
— Catalogue of upwards of 1400 mss. [London, 1836.] 8°.
— General catalogue for 1836. [Lond., 1836.] 8°.
— - 1836, pt. 3. [London,] *n.d.* 8°.
— Catalogue. [Pt. 5 for 1836. London,] 1836. 8°.
— Catalogue. [Pt. 6 for 1836. London,] 1836. 8°.
— Catalogue of autograph letters, corresp. of the Earl of Buchan. [Pt. 9 for 1836. London,] *n.d.* 8°.
— Upwards of 1000 autograph letters of the 16th–18th cent. [London, 1836.] 8°.
— Pt. 2 for 1837. [London,] *n.d.* 8°.
— Catalogue of autograph letters. [London, 1837.] 8°.
— Part 2 for 1840. [London,] *n.d.* 8°.
— Part 3 for 1840. [London,] *n.d.* 8°.
— Catal. of mss. [Pt. 4 for 1840. Lond.,] *n.d.* 8°.
— 1843. Catal. of books. [Lond.,] *n.d.* 8°.
— Suppl. to catal. for 1843. [London,] *n.d.* 8°.
— 2d suppl. to catal. for 1843. [Lond.,] *n.d.* 8°.
— 1843, pt. 4. [London,] *n.d.* 8°.
— 1843, pt. 5. [London,] *n.d.* 8°.
— 1843. Catal. of 5500 autograph letters, *etc.* [London,] *n.d.* 8°.
— Manuscripts. [London,] 1843. 8°.
— Autograph letters. [London,] 1844. 8°.
— Bibliotheca Sussexiana; catal. of theological books from the library of the late Duke of Sussex. [Pt. 3, 1844. London,] *n.d.* 8°.
— 1844. General catal. [London,] *n.d.* 8°.
— Catalogue. [London,] 1845. 8°.
— Part 2 of a general catalogue. [Lond.,] 1845. 8°.
— Pt. 3 of a gen. catal. [London,] 1845. 8°.
— 1851. General catalogue. [London,] *n.d.* 8°.

— Catal. of books selected. *n.t.p.* 1851. 8°.
— Bibliotheca manuscripta; mss. of the late Duke of Sussex, R. Southey, *etc.* [Lond.,] 1854. 8°.
Thorpe, W., *of Bristol.* Sermon; The prevalence of infidelity and the signs of the times. (*In* **Suddards**, W. British pulpit, v. 1. 1837.)
Thorpe, William. Examination of W. T.; [by himself]. (*In* Fox, J. Acts. 1641; — *in* **Wordsworth**, C. Eccles. biog., v. 1. 1839; — *and in* **Bale**, J. Select works. 1849.)
Thorpe; a quiet English town, and life therein; by W. Mountford. Boston, 1852. 16°.
Thortsen, Karl Adolph. Historisk Udsigt over den danske Litteratur indtil Aar 1814. 5e Oplag. Kjöb., 1858. 8°.
Thorwaldsen, Albert *or* Bertel. [Christ and ten of the Apostles; also the Kneeling angel of baptism. Rome, 1845?] f°.
Contents. Christ; engraved by G. Folo. — Kneeling angel of baptism. — Paul; engr. by P. Folo. — James, P. Bettelini. — James, minor, P. Fontana. — Bartholomew, P. Folo. — Thomas, P. Fontana. — John, P. Bettelini. — Simon, P. Bettelini. — Philip, Dom Marchetti. — Matthew, P. Folo. — Peter, P. Folo.
— Trionfo di Alessandro; inciso da F. Garzoli, colle illustrazioni del abate Misserini. Roma, 1829. f°.
— Delaborde, H. (*In* **Revue** d. D. Mondes, juin 1868.)
— Oehlenschläger, A. G. Tale i Anledning af Thorvaldsens Hiemkomst til Fædrelandet. Kiöb., [1819]. 16°.
— Plon, E. Thorvaldsen, sa vie et son œuvre; grav. par F. Gaillard. Paris, 1867. 8°.
— Thiele, J. M. Thorwaldsen and his works; tr. by Prof. P. C. Sinding. N. Y., 1869. 4 v. 4°.
— Reumont, A. von. (*In his* Zeitgenossen, v. 2. 1862.)
Thothmes III. Birch, S. Annals of Thothmes III as derived from the hieroglyphic inscriptions. (*In* **Archæologia**, v. 35. 1853.)
Thou (*Lat.* Thuanus), Jacques Auguste de. Hist. sui temporis, 1543–1607, libri CXXXVIII. Vol. 1–3, 5, Genevæ, v. 4, Aurelianæ, 1630, 1626–30. 5 v. f°.
Contents. Vol. 1. 1543–60. 2. 1560–74. 3. 1574–84. 4. 1585–89. 5. 1589–1607.
Note. Vol. 4 has the title page 'Continuatio', *etc.*
— *Same, called* Tom. 4. Continuatio, 1608–18. Francof., 1628. f°.
— *French.* Histoire universelle, 1543–1607; tr. sur l'éd. latine. London, 1734. 16 v. 4°.
Contents. Vol. 1. Mém. de la vie de J. A. de T. — 1543–50. 2. 1550–55. 3. 1556–60. 4. 1560–64. 5. 1564–70. 6. 1570–73. 7. 1573–78. 8. 1578–82. 9. 1582–87. 10. 1587–89. 11. 1589–93. 12. 1593–96. 13. 1596–1601. 14. 1601–07. 15. 1607–10. 16. Table.
— Mémoires. (*In* **Perrin**. Col. des mém., v. 53. 54, 1789; — **Petitot**. Col. des mém., 1e sér., v. 37. 1823; — *and in* **Michaud**. Col. des mém., v. 11. 1854.)
— Thuana, sive Excerpta ex ore J. A. Thuani. *n.p.*, 1669. 8°.
— Collinson, J. Life of Thuanus. London, 1807. 8°.
— Niceron, J. P. (*In his* Mém., v. 9. 1729; *and, Germ.*, v. 10. 1754.)
— Weguelin, J. Sur J. A. de Thou. (*In* **Berlin. Ak. d. Wiss.** Abh., 1783, 85; — *and in* **Serieys**, A. Bibl. acad., v. 6. 1811.)
Thouar, Pietro. L., L. Necrologia di T. (*In* **Archivio** stor. ital., n.s., v. 13. 1861.)
Thought. *See* **Intellect**; — **Psychology**; — **Philosophy**.
Thought, Laws of, Science of. *See* **Logic** (p. 1770, 1771).
Thought, Mechanism in. *See* **Holmes**, O. W. (p. 1435).
Thought and study in Europe from the foundation of Universities to the Reformation. London, 1857. 16°.
Thoughts and feelings in verse. *See* **Stagg**, E.
Thoughts conc. the origin of power. Bristol, 1772. 12°. (B 390)
Thoughts in a series of letters, in answer to a question resp. the division of the states. *n.t.p.* [1813.] 8°. (B 453)
Thoughts in my garden. *See* **Ware**, M. G.
Thoughts in past years; [by I. Williams]. 6th ed. Oxford, 1852. 32°.
Thoughts of a layman conc. patronage and presentations. Edin., 1769. 8°. (B 256)
Thoughts of a private person about the justice of the gentlemen's undertaking at York, Nov., 1688. *n.p.*, 1689. 4°. (B 6)
Thoughts of a traveller upon our Amer. disputes. London, 1774. 8°. (B 674)
Thoughts of an honest Tory upon the present proc. of that party. London, 1710. 8°. (B 590)
Thoughts on American slavery; by a northerner. Hartford, 1838. 12°.
Thoughts on continental connections by marriage. London, 1761. 8°. (B 746)
Thoughts on education. Boston, 1749. 8°. (B 744)
Thoughts on executive justice, Observations on. London, 1786. 8°. (C 114)
Thoughts on government, occasioned by Mr. Burke's 'Reflections', *etc.* London, 1790. 8°. (B 634)
Thoughts on happiness. *n.t.p.* [18—.] 16°. (C 190)
Thoughts on labor, capital, currency, *etc.* Balt., 1864. 8°. (B 1545)
Thoughts on men and things; essays. *See* **Gushington**, A.
Thoughts on slavery. *n.t.p.* [182–.] 12°. (C 258)
Thoughts on taxation; with some suggestions rel. to the means for raising supplies for the present year. Newark, 1799. 8°. (B 763)
Thoughts on the cause of the present discontents; [by E. Burke]. 2d ed. London, 1770. 8°. (B 591)
— *Same.* 5th ed. London, 1775. 8°. (B 1706)
Thoughts on the causes of the present distresses, in a letter to the citizens of the U. S. Albany, 1837. 8°. (B 1536)
Thoughts on the colonization of free blacks. *n.t.p.* [1815.] 8°. (W 8)
Thoughts on the Eng. government, addressed to the quiet good sense of the people of Eng.; a series of letters. London, 1795. 8°. (B 777)
Thoughts on the importance of the manners of the great to general society. 8th ed. Phila., [17— ?]. 12°. (B 658)
Thoughts on the increasing wealth and national economy of the U. S. Wash., 1801. 8°. (B 401)
Thoughts on the laws, government, and morals. Boston, 1840. 8°. (B 1162, 1360)
Thoughts on the moral physiology and pathology of the disease, liquor drinking. Bost., 1862. 8°. (B 1281)
Thoughts on the national defence. London, 1804. 8°. (B 1412)
Thoughts on the old and new administrations. London, 1804. 8°. (B 782)
Thoughts on the practical advantages of those who hold doctrines of peace, *etc.* N. Y., 1816. 8°. (B 1274)
Thoughts on the present condition of the stage and upon the construction of a new theatre. London, 1809. 8°. (B 726)
Thoughts on the probable influence of the French Revolution on Gr. Britain. Dublin, 1790. 8°. (B 1842)
— *Same.* *t.p.w.* [1790?] 8°. (B 634)
Thoughts on the slavery of the negroes. London, 1784. 8°. (B 764)
Thoughts on the subject of naval power in the U. S. Phila., 1806. 8°. (B 426)
Thoughts upon liberty; by an Englishman. London, 1772. 12°. (B 390)
Thoughts upon our present situation; with remarks upon the policy of a war with France. Dublin, 1793. 8°. (B 1524)
— *Same.* 2d ed., with a postscript. London, 1793. 8°. (B 1407)
Thoughts upon the conduct of our administration in rel. to Gr. Brit. and France, in reference to the late negotiation conc. the attack on the Chesapeake; by [J. Lowell]. Boston, 1808. 8°. (B 971, 2520)
Thoughts upon the political situation of the U. S., *etc.*; by a native of Boston [J. Jackson]. Worcester, 1788. 8°.
— *Other copies.* (B 632, 1117)
Thoüin, André. Agriculture. *See* **Tesser**, H. A.
— Cours de culture et de naturalization des végétaux. Paris, 1827. 3 v. 8°.
— Hist. de l'agric. dans l'anc. et dans le nouv. monde et en Europe. (*In* **Paris. Ecoles Normales.** Séances, v. 9. 1800.)
Thouret, Jacques Guillaume. Abrégé des revolutions de l'ancien gouvernement françois; extrait de l'abbé Dubos and l'abbé Mably. 2e éd. Paris, 1819. 8°

Thoyras, Paul de Rapin. *See* **Rapin Thoyras**, P. de.
Thrace. GATTERER, J. C. De Herodoti ac Thucydidis Thracia. (*In* Goettingen. Ges. d. Wiss. Comm., 1782-84.)
Thracian wonder; a comical history. *See* **Webster, J.,** *and* **Rowley,** W.
Thrale. *See* **Piozzi.**
Thrasher, John S. Notes and a preliminary essay. (*In* **Humboldt,** F. H. A. von. Island of Cuba. 1856.)
Thrasybulus. NEPOS, C. (*In his* Vitæ; — *and, Eng.,* Lives.)
Thrasyllus *Mendesius.* Fragm. (*In* **Mueller,** C. Fr. hist. Gr., v. 3. 1849.)
Three ages, The; by H. Martineau. London, 1833. 18°.
Three articles on modern spiritualism; by [T. B. Hall]. Boston, 1863. 12°.
Three bodies. CONDORCET, J. A. N. C., *marquis* de. Du problème des trois corps. (*In his* Essais d'analyse. 1768.)
— LA GRANGE, J. L., *comte* de. Essai sur le problème des trois corps. [Paris,] 1772. 4°.
Three brothers, The; a novel; by Mrs. Oliphant. N. Y., 1870. 8°.
Note. From St. Paul's mag., v. 4-6. 1869-70.
Three clerks; by Anthony Trollope. N. Y., 1860. 12°.
Three courses and a dessert; by G. Cruikshank. London, *Bohn,* 1850. 8°.
Three crowns; by the author of 'Christus Victor'. Boston, 1866. 12°.
Three curious pieces. *See* **A.,** P.
Three degrees of banking; or, The romance of trade. Boston, 1838. 12°.
Three experiments of living; [by Mrs. H. F. Lee]. 2d ed. Boston, 1837. 18°.
Three fingered Jack. *See* **Obi**; or, The history of three-fingered Jack.
Three guardsmen, The; a drama; by C. Rice. (*In* **Sargent,** E. Mod. stand. dr., v. 18.)
Three heavenly witnesses. *See* **Bible.** *N.T.* (p. 291).
Three knights, The, and the smock; by J. Basin. (*In* **Le Grand d'Aussy,** P. Fabliaux, v. 2. 1815.)
Three letters to Burke, on the state of public affairs; and particularly on the outrageous attacks on his pension. London, 1796. 8°. (**B 1538**)
Three letters to Dr. Price; cont. remarks on his 'Observations on the nature of civil liberty', *etc.,* by a member of Lincoln's Inn, F. R. S., F. S. A. London, 1776. 8°.
— *Another copy.* (**B 681**)
Three marriages; by Mrs. J. Hubback. Phila., 1856. 12°.
Three months in Ireland; by an English Protestant. London, 1827. 12°.
Three months leave. *See* **Rose,** W. G.
Three patriots; addressed to voters of Maryland. Balt., 1811. 8°. (**B 440**)
Three political letters to a noble lord. *See* **Gordon,** T.
Three questions, with a postscript on Hume's 'Natural history of religion'; [by C. Fleming]. London, 1757. 8°. (**B 576, 580**)
Three scouts, The; by J. T. Trowbridge. Boston, 1865. 12°.
Three successful girls; by J. Crouch. N. Y., 1871. 8°.
Three weeks after marriage; a comedy. *See* **Murphy,** A.
Three weeks in Palestine and Lebanon. N. Y., *Prot. Episc. S. S. Union,* [183-]. 18°.
Threlkeld, L. E. Australian grammar. Sydney, 1834. 8°.
Thrice married; by H. Paul. (No. 83 *of* **De Witt's** acting plays.)
Throat. FITCH, J. An account of the numbers that have died ofthe distemper in the throat, [in] New Hampshire. Boston, 1736. 8°. (**C 19, 50**)
— HUXAM, J. Dissertation on malignant ulcerous sore-throat. [1750.] (*In his* Essay on fevers. 1772.)
— BAYLIES, W. Ulcerated sore throat at Dighton, 1785-86. (*In* **Mass. Med. Soc.** Med. com., v. 1. 1808.)
— JACKSON, H. Observations on the putrid malignant sore throat. Portsmouth, 1786. 8°. (**B 665**)
— SIMS, J. Observations on the scarlatina anginosa, [or] ulcerated sore throat. Boston, 1796. 8°. (**B 643, 813, 822**)
See also **Bronchitis.**
Throop, Enos Thompson. JENKINS, J. S. (*In his* Lives of the governors of N. Y. 1851.)
Throop, Wm. Sermon, funeral of B. Sylvester, 1752. Boston, 1753. 4°. (**B 69**)
Through night to light; novel by F. Spielhagen; from the German by Schele de Vere. N. Y., 1870. 12°.
Through the looking-glass, and what Alice found there; by L. Carroll [C. L. Dodgson]. Boston, 1872 [1871]. 8°.
Thrown away; by Mrs. A. M. Münster. (*In* **Bentley's** miscel., v. 59-61. 1866-67.)
Thrupp, John. Anglo-Saxon home; history of the domestic institutions and customs of Eng., 5th to 11th cent. London, 1862. 8°.
Thrush, Thomas. Letter to the editor of the Monthly mag. on the unlawfulness of war. York, 1826. 8°. (**B 542**)
— Observations on the causes and evils of war. Pt. 2. N. Y., 1826. 8°. (**B 542**)
— ANDERSON, W. Answer to a letter to the King, by T. Thrush. Portsea, 1825. 8°. (**B 542**)
Thuanus, Jacques Auguste. *See* **Thou,** J. A. de.
Thucydides. Historiæ lib. I., II. Parisiis, *ex officina Wechelli,* 1535. 2 v. 4°.
Contents. Vol. 1. Lib. I. 2. II.
— Thucydides; cum scholiis; acc. I. *Camerarii* comm. cum annot. Basileæ, 1540. f°.
— De bello Peloponnesiaco; cum adnot. H. Stephani et J. Hudsoni; rec. et not. add. J. Wasse; ed. cur., animad. adj. C. A. *Dukerus.* Amst., 1731. f°.
Note. Also contains 'Annales, præmittitur apparatus, cum vitæ T. synopsi chron. ab H. Dodwello'.
— *Same.* Gr. et Lat. ad ed. J. Wasse et C. A. *Dukeri,* cum var. lect. et adnot. Biponti, 1788-89. 6 v. 8°.
Contents Vol. 1. Marcellini de T. vita. — Hist. lib. I. 2. II-III. 3. IV-V. 4. VI-VII. 5. VIII. — Σχολια. 6. Annotationes in scholia Gr. — Indices.
— *Same.* Ex rec. I. *Bekkeri.* Hilpertohusæ, Nov. Yorici, 1831. 8°.
— *Same.* Recens. et adnot. illust. F. *Goeller.* Londini, 1835. 2 v. 8°.
Contents. Vol. 1. Præf. — Vita. — Lib. I-IV. 2. V-VIII. — Tab. topog. Syracusarum. — Indices.
— Historia belli Peloponnesiaci; cum tr. Lat. F. *Haasii*; acc. Marcellini vita, scholia Gr., et indices. Parisiis, *Didot,* 1842. 8°.
— De bello Peloponnesiaco; explan. E. F. *Poppo.* Gothæ, 1843-51. 4 v. 8°.
Contents. Vol. 1. I-II. 2. III-IV. 3. V-VII. 4. VIII.
— Ξυγγραφή, mit Anm. hrsg. v. K. W. *Krüger.* Berlin, 1860, 58, 46-47. 2 v. in 4 pt. 8°.
Contents. Vol. 1, pt. 1. 1es, 2es Buch. 3e Aufl. 1, 2. 3es, 4es Buch. 2e Aufl. 2, 1. 5es, 6es Buch. 2, 2. 7es, 8es Buch. — Namenverzeichniss, *etc.*
— History of the Peloponnesian war; [Gr.;] with notes by T. *Arnold.* 4th ed., with indexes by R. P. G. Tiddeman. Oxford, London, 1857. 3 v. 8°.
Contents. Vol 1. I-III. 2. IV-VI. 3. VII-VIII.
— *Eng.* History of the Peloponnesian war; tr. [with] life, *etc.,* by W. *Smith.* 4th ed. London, 1805. 2 v. 8°.
Contents. Vol. 1. Book I-IV. 2. V-VIII.
— The hist. of T.; tr. with annot. [and] life by S. T. *Bloomfield.* Lond., 1829. 3 v. (v. 1 w.). 8°.
Contents. Vol. 1. *Wanting.* 2. Book III-V. 3. VI-VIII. — State of Greece at the beginning of the war.
— *Same.* Tr. by T. Hobbes. (*In* **Hobbes,** T. Works, v. 8, 9. 1843.)

— History of the Peloponnesian war; [tr.] by H. *Dale.* London, *Bohn*, 1848. 2 v. 8°.
Contents. Vol. 1. Book I-IV. 2. V-VIII.

— Selections.] Conciones [Græce]. Paris., 1531. 4°.

— Ἐκ τῆς γ' ξυγγραφῆς Κλέωνός τε καὶ Διοδότου περὶ τῶν Μιτυλυναίων δημηγορίαι. *n.t.p.* [15—.] 4°.

— Illustres loci. (*In* **Wyttenbach, D.** Selecta principum hist. 1808.)

— Fragm. (*In* **Bergk, T.** Poet. lyr. 1853.)

— *Eng.* Account of the plague of Athens. (*In* **Hippocrates.** Air, water, and situation. 1734.)

— *French.* Extraits de T. Paris, 1807. 8°.
Contents. Oraison funébre de Péricles. — Obs. sur la description de la peste. — Factions dans la Grèce. — Siége de Platée.

— *Germ.* Die Belagerung, Eroberung, und Zerstorung von Platäa; aus Thucydides Geschichte des peloponnesischen Krieges. (*In* **Seume, J. G.** Spaziergang nach Syrakus. 1802.)

— DIONYSIUS *Halicarnassensis.* De Thucydide judicium. — De iis quæ Thucyd. propria sunt. (*In his* Historiographica. 1823.)

— GATTERER, J. C. De Herodoti ac Thucydidis Thracia. (*In* **Goettingen. Ges. d. Wiss.** Comm., 1782-84.)

— GIRARD, J. A. Essai sur Thucydide. Paris, 1860. 18°.

— LERMINIER, E. (*In* **Revue** d. D. Mondes, mars 1834.)

— M., F. (*In his* Stemmata Atheniensia. 1837.)

— MEIEROTTO, J. H. L. Mémoire sur Thucydide. — Ueber den Thucydides. (*In* **Berlin. Ak. d. Wiss.** Abh., 1790-91.)

— MELANCHTHON, P. Interpretatio Lat. orationum lib. I-IV, VI, VII. (*In his* Opera, v. 17. 1851.)

— PEYRON, A. Del territorio piraico, illustrazione del luogo di Tucidide lib. III. (*In* **Turin. Ac. d. Sci.** Mem., v. 26. 1821.)

— POPPO, E. F. Peculiarities of Thucydidean phraseology; tr. [with suppl.] by G. Burges. Camb., [1837]. 8°.

— RAPIN, R. Comparison of Thucydides and Livy. (*In his* Crit. works, v. 1. 1731.)

— SELLAR, W. Y. Characteristics of Thucydides. (*In* **Oxford** essays, 1857.)

— WHEELER, J. T. Analysis and summary of Thucydides. London, *Bohn*, 1855. 8°.

— ZENO, A. In concionem Periclis et Lepidi ex Historiis Thucydidis et Sallustii. Comment. Venet., 1569. 4°.

Thudichum, John Louis Wm. Treatise on gallstones. London, 1863. 8°.

— Treatise on the pathology of the urine. London, 1858. 8°.

Thuemmel, Moritz August von. Sämmtliche Werke; hrsg. von J. E. von Grüner. Lpz., 1812-19. 7 v. 16°.
Contents. Vol. 1. Vermischte Gedichte. 2-6. Reise in die mittäglichen Provinzen von Frankreich. 7. Leben T.'s; von J. E. v. Grüner.

Thugenides. Fragm. (*In* **Meineke, A.** Fragm. com. Gr., v. 4. 1841.)

Thugs. RAMASSEEANA, or a vocabulary of the lang. used by the Thugs; with introd. and app. Calcutta, 1836. 8°.

— SLEEMAN, W. H. The Thugs or Phansigars of India; comprising a history of [their] rise and progress. Phila., 1839. 2 v. 12°.

Thulia; a poem. *See* **Palmer, J. C.**

Thuillier, Vincent. Historia dissidii litterarii circa hæc studia. (*In* **Mabillon, J.** Tractatus de studiis monast. 1745.)

Thumb, *Judge.* Answer to 'Cursory strictures' on a charge deliv. by Lord Chief Justice Eyre. London, 1794. 8°. **(B 1433)**

Thumb, Thomas, *pseud.* The monster of monsters. Boston, 1754. 8°. **(B 135, 149, C 70)**

Thumb, Thomas, *pseud.* Proposals for printing the life of Sir T. Brazen. *n.p.*, 1760. 8°. (B 462)
Note. Supposed authors, B. Brandon, of Boston, and J. Mayhew.

Thumb, Tom. *See* **Stratton, C. S.**

Thunberg, Carl Pehr. Acc. of the Cape of Good Hope. (*In* **Pinkerton, J.** Col. of voy., v. 16. 1814.)

— Families of plants. (*In* **Linné, C.** Families of plants, *etc.* 1787.)

— Travels in Europe, Africa, and Asia, 1770-79. London, 1795-96. 4 v. 8°.

— Voyages au Japon; tr., red., et aug. de notes par L. Langles; rev. quant à la partie d'hist. nat. par J. B. Lamarck. Paris, 1796. 4 v. 8°.

Thunder. GRIMM, J. Ueber die Namen des Donners. (*In* **Berlin. Ak. d. Wiss.** Abh., 1854.)

Thunder storms. HARRIS, W. S. Nature o thunder storms; and protection against lightning. London, **1843.** 8°.

— HARE, R. On J. Wise's observations, *etc.* resp. the phenomena of a thunder storm to which he was exposed during an aerial voyage, June 3, 1852, from Portsmouth, Ohio. (*In* **Smithsonian Inst.** Report, 1854.)

— FONVIELLE, W. de. Eclairs et tonnerre; illustré par E. Bayard et H. Clerget. Paris, **1867.** 16°. (Bibl. des merv.)

See also **Meteorology; — Lightning; — Storms.**

Thurber, George, *M.D.* American weeds and useful plants; rev. with add. by T. *See* **Darlington, W.**

Thuringia. LIMMER, C. Entwurf einer urkundl.-pragmat. Geschichte von Thüringen. Ronneburg, 1837-39. 8°.

— *Maps.* ERICH, A. Thuringia. [Amst., 16—.] **(E 78,** no. 164)

— - HOMANN, J. B. Landgraviæ Thuringiæ tabula. Norb., [17—]. **(E 94)**

Thurloe, John. Collection of the state papers of T., cont. memorials of the Eng. affairs, 1638 to the restoration; prefixed, life of T., by T. Birch. London, 1742. 7 v. f°.
Contents. Vol. 1. 1638-53. 2. 1653-54. 3. 1654-55. 4. 1655-56. 5. 1655. 6. 1657-58. 7. 1658-60.

— CAMPBELL, J. Letter to a friend in the country on, the publication of Thurloe's State papers. 2d ed. London, 1742. 8°. **(B 581)**

Thurlow, Edward, *baron.* BROUGHAM, H., *Ld.* (*In his* Statesmen, ser. 1. 1839.)

— ROSCOE, H. Life of E. Thurlow. (*In his* Lives of British lawyers, v. 2. 1841. Lardner. Cab. cyc.)

Thurlow, Thomas John Hovell. The [East India] Company and the crown. Edin., London, 1866. 8°.

— Trade unions abroad and hints for home legislation. London, 1870. 8°.

Thurm, Johann Jacob. Selecta ex itinere literario J. Thurmii. (*In* **Schelhorn, J. G.** Amœn. lit., v. 11. 1729.)

Thurnam, John. Two principal forms of ancient British and Gaulish skulls. (*In* **Anthrop. Soc.** Mem., v. 1. 1865.)

Thurneisser zum Thurn, Leonhard. Impletio, oder Erfüllung der Verheissung L. Thurneissers. Nürnberg, 1581. 4°.

Thurnmayer (*Lat.* **Aventinus**), Johannes. *See* **Aventinus.**

Thurócz, J. de. *See* **Thwrocz, J. de.**

Thurot, Charles. Notices et extraits de divers mss. latins pour servir à l'hist. des doctrines grammaticales au Moyen Age. (*In* **Paris. Inst.** *Ac. d. Inscr.* Not., v. 22, 2e pte. 1868.)

Thurot, Jean François. SILVESTRE DE SACY, A. I. La vie et les ouvrages de T. (*In* **Paris. Inst.** *Ac. d. Inscr.* Mém., v. 12. 1836.)

Thurston, Anson Grandcelo. RICHARDSON, W. L. (*In* **Higginson, T. W.** Harvard mem. biog., v. 2. 1866.)

Thurston, *Rev.* Asa. [Obituary notice.] (*In* **Hawaiian Club.** Papers. 1868.)

Thurston, *Rev.* Benjamin. Discourse, Northampton, May 30, death of his consort. Portsmouth, 1789. 8°. **(B 133)**

— Two sermons, Northampton. Newburyport, 1793. 8°. **(B 1303)**

Thurston, *Rev.* David. Brief history of Winthrop, Me., 1764-1855. Portland, 1855. 12°.

— Sermon, ordination of D. Smith, Temple, Me., Feb. 21, 1810. Hallowell, 1811. 8°. **(B 1007, 1849)**

— Sermon, Saco, June 26, 1816, before the Maine Miss. Soc. Hallowell, 1816. 8°. **(B 334)**

Thurston, George H. Directory of Pittsburgh and Alleghany cities, 1864-65. [Pittsb.,] 1864. 4°.

— Pittsburgh as it is. Pittsburgh, 1857. 12°.

— Route book from Philadelphia to Chicago. Pittsburgh, [18—]. 12°. (C 277)

Thurston, James. CANDID enquiries rel. to the difficulties which existed in Manchester, 1816, [reply to Parsons]; by a friend to truth. *n.p.*, [1825]. 8°. (B 1128)

— PARSONS, T. Truth espoused rel. to the difficulties that existed in Manchester, between T. and a number of the inhabitants, *etc.* Dedham, 1823. 8°. (B 1128)

Thurston, Louise Meliscent. Forrest mills; a peep at child life from within. Boston, 1868. 16°. (S. S. Soc.)

Thurston, Thomas, *Funeral sermon on.* 1806. *See* Barton, T. T. (B 87)

Thury. *See* Hericart de Thury.

Thury, César François Cassini de. *See* Cassini de Thury.

Thust, Thomas, *Jr.*, *and* Kühn, C. M. Biographisches Künstler-Album. Lpz., [186-]. f°.

Contents. L. Barnay. — B. Blume-Santer. — F. Bognar. — B. Dawison. — R. Dreyschoch. — G. Gunz. — F. Haase. — A. Haizinger. — Neuman. — H. Hendrichs. — L. Harriers. — Wippern. — C. Laroche. — O. Lehfeld. — F. J. Nachbaur. — C. Patti. — H. Raabe. — E. Scaria. — C. Scherbarth. — B. Scherbarth-Flies. — A. Ubrich. — P. Ulrich. — T. Wachtel. — A. Wallner. — C. Ziegler.

Thwackius, Herman, *pseud.* Fragments of the hist. of Bawlfredonia. 1819. *See* Clopper, J.

Thwing, Thomas. Address before the Assoc. of Delegates from the Benevolent Societies of Boston. *n.p.*, 1843. 12°. (C 183, 274)

Thwrócz, János de. Chronica Hungarorum. *n.t.p.* [Aug. Vind., 1483.] 4°.

Thyades. PANOFKA, T. Dionysos und die Thyaden. (*In* Berlin. Ak. d. Wiss. Abh., 1852.)

Thyatira. STOSCH, F. Thyatirenæ antiquitates. Zwollæ, 1763. 8°.

Thylesius, Antonius. De coloribus. (*In* Gronovius, J. Thes. Græc. antiq., v. 9. 1701.)

Thymus, The. HAUGSTED, F. C. Thymi in homine, *etc.*, descriptio. Hafniæ, 1832. 8°.

Thynn, Thomas. BURNET, G. Confession of J. Stern, *etc.*, [who] had murthered T. London, 1683. f°. (A 51)

Thynne, Francis. Chaucer; animadversions uppon the annotacions and corrections of some imperfections of impressions of Chaucer's workes reprinted in 1598; ed. by G. H. Kingsley. London, 1865. 8°. (Early English Text Soc.)

— Debate between pride and lowliness; ed. by J. P. Collier. Lond., 1841. 8°. (Shakspeare Soc.)

Thynne, *Rev. Lord* John, *Prebendary of Westminster.* Sermon at the festival of the Sons of the Clergy, May 2. London, 1839. 4°. (B 1270)

Thyræus, Petrus. De apparitionibus. Colon. Agrip., 1600. 4°

Thyroid gland. COOTE, H. Diseases of the thyroid gland. (*In* Holmes, T. Syst. of surg., v. 4. 1864.)

Thyrsis, *pseud.* De veldgezangen van Thyrsis. Leyden, 1702. 4°.

Thys (*Lat.* Thysius), Antonius. Roma illustrata; acc. G. Fabricii veteris Romæ cum nova collatio. Amst., *Elziviriana*, 1657. 24°.

— De repub. Atheniensium discursus politicus. — Collatio legum Atheniensium et Rom. (*In* Gronovius, J. Thes. Gr. antiq., v. 5. 1699.)

— Synopsis purioris theologiæ. *See* Polyander, J.

Thys, Pauline. Le roman d'un curé. Paris, 1867. 12°.

Contents. Le professeur de bon sens. — Ma mie Fanchette. — L'homme au grand nez. — Le talisman. — Le roman d'un curé.

Tiaden, Enno Johann Heinrich. Das gelehrte Ost Friesland. Aurich, 1785. 3 v. 8°.

Tiarks, John Gerhard. A practical grammar of the German language. Boston, 1834. 12°.

Tiarks, John Lewis. Results of Capt. Foster's chronometrical observations. *n.t.p.* [183-?] 8°. (B 1741)

Tibbits, George. Essay on the expediency of creating home markets for agricultural productions and raw materials by the introd. of artizans and manufacturers. Phila., 1827. 8°. (B 1512, 1884)

— *Same.* Phila., 1829. 8°. (B 1115)

— Receipt for sprouting thorn plants. (*In* Soc. Prom. Useful Arts in N. Y. Trans., v. 4, pt. 2. 1819.)

Tiber. BAXTER, W. E. The Tagus and the Tiber. London, 1852. 2 v. 12°.

Tiberius, *Emperor.* BEULÉ, C. E. Tibère et l'héritage d'Auguste. Paris, 1868. 8°.

— VILLEMAIN, A. F. (*In his* Etudes de lit. anc. et étrangère. 1852.)

Tiberius *rhetor.* De figuris, una cum Rufi arte rhetorica; ed. J. F. Boissonade. Londini, 1815. 8°.

— *Same.* (*In* Spengel, L. Rhetores Gr., v. 3. 1856.)

Tiberius in Capreæ. *See* Cumberland, R.

Tibesti. NACHTIGAL, —, *Dr.* Voyage au Tibesti. (*In* Paris. Soc. de Géog. Bul., 5e sér., v. 19. 1870.)

Tibet. *See* Thibet.

Tibetan literature. *See* Mahajana.

Tibia. HAZELTINE, R. Compound dislocation of the tibia. (*In* Mass. Med. Soc. Med. com., v. 1. 1808.)

Tibullus, Albius. [Elegiæ, cum comment. *Bernardini* Veronensis. Colophon:] Brixiæ, 1486. f°.

— Equitis Rom. lib. I-IV. (*In* Catullus. Excerpta, 1534; Opera. 1772; 1776.)

— Elégies, [en latin et en français, avec un essai]. (*In* Guys, P. A. Voy. lit., v. 4. 1783.)

— Tibullus und Lygdamus; berichtiget nach Handschriften von J. H. *Voss.* Heidelberg, 1811. 8°.

Note. With ms. German translation and notes.

— Quæ supersunt omnia opera; var. lect., nov. comm., imitationibus Gallicis, *etc.*, instruxit P. A. de *Golbéry.* Parisiis, 1826. 8°. (Lemaire. Bibl. class. Lat.)

Note. The French imitations are by La Harpe, Lebrun, Loyson, and Andrieux. There is also a Greek imitation by Morellus.

— Albii Tibulli libri IV; recog. A. *Rossbach.* Lips., 1855. 16°.

— Electa ex Ovidio et Tibullo in usum scholæ Etonensis. Ed. nov. Etonæ, 1818. 12°.

— *Eng.* Works; tr. by J. Grainger. (*In* Anderson, R. Brit. poets, v. 13. 1795; — *and in* Chalmers, A. Eng. poets, v. 20. 1810.)

— - Elegies, Books I-IV, in prose and verse. (*In* Catullus. Poems. 1854.)

— *French.* *See, above,* 'Elégies'.

— *Germ.* *See, above,* 'Tibullus'.

— GUYS, P. A. *See, above,* 'Elégies'.

— PRESTON, W. On the hist. of antient amatory writers, and the comparative merits of Ovid, Tibullus, and Propertius. (*In* Royal Irish Acad. Trans., v. 9. 1803.)

— SOURY, J. La Délia de Tibulle. (*In* Revue d. D. Mondes, sept. 1872.)

Tibur. *See* Tivoli.

Tic douloureux. HUTCHINSON, B. Cases of neuralgia spasmodica, [or] tic douloureux. 2d ed. London, 1822. 8°.

Tichborne *vs.* Lushington. The Tichborne romance; full account of the trial. 2d ed. Manchester, London, 1871. 8°.

Tichtel, Johann. Tagebuch, 1477-95. (*In* Vienna. K. Acad. d. Wiss. Fontes rerum Austr. 1e Abth., B. 1. 1850.)

Ticida, Caius. Fragm. (*In* Estienne, R. Frag. Poet. vet. Lat. 1564.)

Tickell, Richard. Anticipation; substance of His M—y's speech to both Houses. London, 1778. 8°.

— *Same.* 3d ed. London, 1778. 8°. (B 365)

— *Same.* (*In* Pamphleteer, 1822; v. 19 of B 838)

— Anticipation; for the year 1779, *etc.* London, 1779. 8°.

— The green box of M. De Sartine, found at Mlle. Du Thé's lodgings. 4th ed. London, 1779. 8°. (B 365)

— *French.* La cassette verte de M. Sartine. La Haye, 1779. 12°.

Tickell, Thomas. Poetical works; with life by Dr. [S.] Johnson. Boston, 1854. 16°.
— Poems. (*In* **Anderson,** R. Brit. poets, v. 8. 1795.) — Poems. (*In* **Campbell,** T. Spec. of Brit. poets, v. 5. 1819.) — Poems. (*In* **Chalmers,** A. Eng. poets, v. 11. 1810.)
— JOHNSON, S. (*In his* Works, v. 10. 1806; Lives of eminent Eng. poets, v. 2. 1810.)

Ticket of leave man, The; by T. Taylor. (*In* **Sargent,** E. Mod. stand. dr., v. 42.)

Ticknor, Caleb B., *M.D.* Philosophy of living. [2d ed.] N. Y., [1836]. 16°. (Harper's fam. lib., v. 77.)
– Letter to the Hon. — —; with reasons for examining and believing homœopathy. N. Y., 1840. 8°. (B 1563)

Ticknor, George. History of Spanish literature, N. Y., 1849. 3 v. 8°.

Contents. Vol. 1. Introduction. — Early national literature. — Alfonso the Wise. — Lorenzo Segura and Juan Manuel. — Alfonso XI. — Archpriest of Hita. — Anon. poems. — Chancellor Ayala. — Old ballads. — Chronicles. — Romances of chivalry. — Early drama. — Provençal literature in Spain. — Catalonian and Valencian poetry. — Courtly school in Castile. — The Manriques, the Urreas, and Juan de Padilla. — Prose writers of the latter part of the 15th cent. — The Cancioneros and the courtly school concluded. — Discouragements of Spanish culture at the end of this period, and its general condition. — Condition of Spain during the 16th and 17th centuries. — Italian school of Boscan and Garcilasso. — Contest conc. the Italian school. — Diego Hurtado de Mendoza. — Didactic poetry and prose. — Castilian language. — Hist. literature. 2. Theatre in the time of Charles V., and first part of the reign of Philip II. — Luis de Leon. — Miguel de Cervantes Saavedra. — Lope Felix de Vega Carpio. — Francisco de Quevedo y Villegas. — The drama of Lope's school. — Pedro Calderon de la Barca. — Drama of Calderon's school. — Old theatres. — Hist. and narrative poems. — Lyric poetry. 3. Satirical poetry, epistolary, elegiac, pastoral, epigrammatic, didactic, and descriptive. — Ballad poetry. — Romantic fiction. — Prose pastorals. — Stories in the gusto picaresco; Serious and hist. romances; Tales. — Eloquence. — Epistolary correspondence. — Hist. composition. — Didactic prose. — Concluding remarks on the period. —Reign of Philip V. — Reigns of Philip V. and Ferdinand VI. — Reign of Charles III. — School of Salamanca and other poets. — Reign of Charles IV. — Theatre in the 18th cent. — Reigns of Charles IV. and Ferdinand VII. — Conclusion. — *Appendices:* Origin of the Spanish language. — The romanceros. — Fernan Gomez de Cibdareal, and the Centon epistolario. — The Buscapié. — Eds., trans., and imitations of the Don Quixote. — Early collections of old Spanish plays. — On the origin of cultismo. — Inedita. — Index.

— *Same.* London, 1849. 3 v. 8°.
— *Same.* 3d Amer. ed. Boston, 1863. 3 v. 12°.
— Lecture on the best methods of teaching the living lang.; deliv. before the Amer. Inst., Aug. 24, 1832. Boston, 1833. 8°. (B 1072, 1802)
— Life of Wm. H. Prescott. Boston, 1864. 4°.
— Memoir of N. A. Haven. (*In* **Haven,** N. A. Remains. 1827.)
— Papers discussing the merits of Prescott's and Wilson's histories. *n.p.*, 1861. 8°. (B 1601)
— Remarks on 'A new history of the conquest of Mexico' by R. A. Wilson. (*In* **Mass. Hist. Soc.** Proc., 1858-60.)
— Remarks on changes lately proposed or adopted in Harv. Univ. [Boston,] 1825. 8°. (B 1759, E 42, H 12)
— *Same.* 2d ed. [Boston,] 1825. 8°. (B 918)
— Review of [Mrs. Lee's] 'Memoirs of J. Buckminster and J. S. Buckminster'. Camb., 1849. 8°. (B 1454)
— Union of the Boston Athenæum and the Public Library. Boston, 1853. 8°. (E 20)
— CATALOGUE of his books, sold, Boston, 1814; [partly priced]. Boston, 1814. 8°. (B 1617)
— MÉRIMÉE, P. (*In* **Revue** d. D. Mondes, av. 1851.)

Ticknor, Luther. Address to candidates for degrees, *etc.*, in the Med. Institution of Yale Coll., Jan. 20. New Haven, 1841. 8°. (B 1563)

Ticknor & Fields. DODGE, M. A. A battle of the books. Camb., 1870. 8°.

Ticonderoga. WINSLOW, *Gen.* J. Letter to the Earl of Halifax, rel. to his conduct, and that of the troops under his command on the Ticonderoga exped. in 1756. (*In* **Mass. Hist. Soc.** Col., v. 6. 1800.)
— WATSON, W. C. Military annals of the fortresses of Crown Point and Ticonderoga, 1758-77. (*In his* Mil. and civil hist. of Essex Co. 1869.)
— WILSON, *Commissary.* Orderly book; expedition of the British and Provincial army under Maj.-Gen. Amherst against Ticonderoga and Crown Point, 1759. Albany, 1857. 4°.
— ALLEN, E. Narrative of the capture of Ticonderoga, [1775]. 6th ed. Burlington, 1852. 8°.
— PAPERS rel. to the Ticonderoga exped., 1775. (*In* **Conn. Hist. Soc.** Col., v. 1. 1860.)
— PAPERS rel. to the Ticonderoga and Crown Point, [1775]. (*In* **Mass.** *Provincial Cong. at Cambridge.* Journals. 1838.)

Ticozzi, Stefano. Dizionario degli architetti, scultori, pittori, intagliatori, *ec.* Milano, 1830-33. 4 v. 8°.
— Raccolta di lettere sulla pittura, scultura, *ec. See* **Bottari,** G.
— Storia cronol. di quaranta avvenimenti della vita di Gesu Cristo e di Maria Vergine. Milano, 1826. f°. (E 278)
— Vita dei pittori Vecellj di Cadore. Milano, 1817. 8°.

Tidd, Betsy, *Funeral sermon on.* 1816. *See* **Long,** D. (B 322)

Tidd, Jacob. Discourse, primitive and present state of man, *etc.* Boston, 1832. 8°. (B 1303)
— Woe unto the wicked; correspondence [with] H. Ballou. Boston, 1823. 8°. (B 538, 1713)

Tidd, Wm. Practice of the Court of Kings Bench in personal actions. 1st Amer. from London ed. Phila., 1807. 2 v. 8°.
— - Suppl. London, 1830. 8°.

Tides. LALANDE, J. J. le F. de. Traité du flux et du réflux de la mer. Paris, 1781. 4°.
— ROMME, C. Tableaux des vents, des marées, et des courans. Paris, 1806. 2 v. 8°.
— YOUNG, A. Theory of the tides. [1813.] (*In his* Miscel. works, v. 2. 1855.)
— BENNETT, S. New explanation of the ebbing and flowing of the sea. N. Y., 1816. 12°.
— SAINTE-PIERRE, J. H. B. de. Mémoire sur les marées. (*In his* Œuvres, v. 11. 1826.)
— AIRY, G. B. Tides and waves. (*In* **Smedley,** E., *and others.* Encyc. metrop., v. 5. 1845.)
— DAVIS, C. H. Theory of the geol. action of the tides. (*In* **Amer. Assoc.** Proc., v. 1. 1849.)
— - Geol. action of the tidal and other currents of the ocean. (*In* **Amer. Acad.** Mem., n. s., v. 4. 1850.)
— - Law of the deposit of the flood tide. (*In* **Amer. Assoc.** Proc., v. 5. 1851; — *and in* **Smithsonian Inst.** Contrib., v. 3. 1852.)
— SCHOTT, C. A. Results of an investigation of the tidal currents in Long Island Sound. — Abstract of the principal results of the obs. of the tides, made by the 2d Grinnell exped., 1853-55. (*In* **Amer. Assoc.** Proc., v. 8, 14. 1855-61.)
— BACHE, A. D. Tides at Key West, Florida. — Tides on the western coast of the U. S. (*In* **Amer. Assoc.** Proc., v. 7. 1856.) — Preliminary determination of co-tidal lines on the Atlantic coast of the U. S. (*In* v. 8. 1855.) — Approximate co-tidal lines of diurnal and semi-diurnal tides of the coast of the U. S. — Notes on the progress made in the coast survey in prediction tables for the tides of the U. S. coast. (*In* v. 10. 1857.) — Heights of the tides of the Atlantic coast of the U. S. (*In* v. 11. 1858.) — GRAHAM, J. D. Investigation of the problem regarding the existence of a lunar tidal wave on the great fresh-water lakes of N. America. (*In* v. 14. 1861.)
— RUSSELL, J. S. Notes illust. of the tidal charts, of the world. and the British seas. (*In* **Johnston,** A. K. Physical atlas. 1856.)

Tidsskrift for Phrenologien; udg. af C. Otto. Suppl.-Hefte, 1829. Kiöb., [1829]. 12°.

Tieck, Johann Ludwig. Gesammelte Novellen. Berlin, 1852-54. 12 v. 16°.

Contents. Vol. 1. Die Gemälde. — Die Verlobung. — Die Reisenden. — Musikalische Leiden und Freuden. — Der Geheimnissvolle. 2. Das Fest zu Kenelworth. — Dichterleben. — Dichterleben, 2r Theil (der Dichter und sein Freund). 3. Glück giebt Verstand. — Der funfzehnte November. — Tod des Dichters. 4. Der Jahrmarkt. — Der Hexen-Sabbath. 5. Der Wassermensch. — Der Mondsüchtige. — Weihnacht-Abend. — Das Zauberschloss. — Uebereilung. 6. Der Gelehrte. — Die Ahnenprobe. — Der Wiederkehrende griechische Kaiser. 7. Eine Sommerreise. — Die Wundersuchtigen. — Pietro von Abano. 8. Das alte Buch und die Reise ins Blaue hinein. — Der Alte vom Berge. — Eigensinn und Laune. — Die Gesellschaft auf dem Lande. 9. Der Schutzgeist. — Die Klausenburg. — Abendgespräche. — Wunderlichkeiten. — Die Clocke von Aragon. 10. Des Lebens Ueberfluss. — Der Aufruhr in den Cevennen. — Liebeswerben. — Waldeinsamkeit. 11. Die Vogelscheuche. 12. Der junge Tischlermeister.

— Kritische Schriften. Lpz., 1848–52. 4 v. 12°.
Contents. Vol. 1. Die Kupferstiche nach der Shakspeare-Galerie in London. — Shakspeare's Behandlung des Wunderbaren. — Die neüesten Musenalmanache und Taschenbücher. — Briefe über Shakspeare. — Die altdeutschen Minnelieder. — Das altenglische Theater. — Die Anfänge des deutschen Theaters. 2. Heinrich von Kleist. — Der spanische Dichter Vicente Espinel. — Bücherschau. — Die neue Volkspoesie. — Kritik und deutsches Bücherwesen. — Göthe und seine Zeit. — Die geschichtliche Entwickelung der neueren Bühne und F. L. Schröder. — Zur Geschichte der Novelle. — Adelheid Reinbold (Franz Berthold). — Ein Brief an Friedrich Laun. — Ueber nordische Volksmärchen. — Ein Brief an den Uebersetzer der Electra. 3, 4. Dramaturgische Blätter.

— The elves. (*In* **Carlyle**, T. Germ. romances, v. 2. 1827; — *and in* **Hedge**, F. H. Prose writers of Germany. 1848.)

— Fair-haired Eckbert. — Trusty Eckart. — Runenberg. — The goblet. (*In* **Carlyle**, T. German romance, v. 2. 1827.)

— The lover of nature; tr. by J. Smith [H. S. McKean]. Camb., 1833. 18°.

— Phantasus; eine Sammlung von Märchen, Erzahlungen, u. Schauspielen. Berlin, 1844–45. 3 v. 16°.
Contents. Vol. 1. Einleitung. — Phantasus. — Der blonde Eckbert. — Der getreue Eckart. — Der Runenberg. — Liebeszauber. — Liebesgeschichte der schönen Magelone und des Gräfen Peter von Provence. 2. Die Elfen. — Der Pokal. — Leben und Tod des kleinen Rothkäppchens. — Der Blaubart. — Der gestiefelte Kater. 3. Die verkehrte Welt. — Leben und Thaten des kleinen Thomas, genannt Däumchen.

— Reisebrief. (*In* **Varnhagen von Ense, K. A.** Aus dem Nachlass, v. 1. 1867.)

— Spring. (*In* **Brooks**, C. T. Songs and ballads. 1842.)

— CARUES, C. G. Zur Geschichte seiner Vorlesungen in Dresden. (*In* **Historisches** Taschenbuch, 1845.)

— CATALOGUE de la bibliothèque de T. Berlin, 1849. 8°.

— HOLTEI, K. v. Briefe an T. Breslau, 1864. 4 v. 8°.

Tiedemann, Friedrich. Anatomy of the fœtal brain; tr. from the French of A. J. L. Jourdan by W. Bennett. Edin., 1826. 8°.

Tiele, P. A. Mémoire bibliographique sur les journaux des navigateurs néerlandais réimprimés dans les collections de De Bry et de Hulsius, *etc.*, la plupart en la possession de F. Muller. Amst., 1867. 8°.

Tielke, Johann Gottlieb. Account of the war, 1756–63, with a treatise of the military art; tr. by C. and R. Craufurd. London, 1787–88. 2 v. 8°.

Tienhoven, Cornelis van. Brief statement. (*In* **Donck**, A. van der. Remonstrance of New Netherland. 1856.)

Tiepolo, Antonio. Relazione di T. tornato ambasciatore straordinario dalle corti di Spagna e di Portogallo, 1572. — Relazioni di T., 1567. (*In* **Venice**. Relazioni degli ambasciatori veneti, ser. 1, v. 5. 1861.)

Tiepolo, Niccolò. Relation de T. après le congrès de Nice; [en ital. et en franç.]. (*In* **Tommaseo**, N. Relations des ambas. vén., v. 1. 1838.)

— Relazione di T. ritornato ambasciatore da Carlo v., 1532. (*In* **Venice**. Rel. degli ambas. ven., ser. 1, v. 1. 1839.) — Relazione del clarissimo messer T. ritornato ambasciatore dal convento di Nizza dove fu fatta la tregua fra Carlo v. e Francesco I. con l'intervento di papa Paolo III. letta in Pregadi il dí 12 giugno 1538. (*In* v. 2. 1840.)

Tiepolo, Paolo. Relazione di Ferdinando re dei Romani, 1557. (*In* **Venice**. Rel. degli ambas. ven., ser. 1, v. 3. 1853.) — Relazione di T. letta in senato il 19 gennajo 1563. (*In* v. 5. 1861.)

Tiepolo *di Venezia*, Famiglia di. (*In* **Litta**, P. Fam., v. 14.)

ierney, George. BROUGHAM, H., *Ld.* (*In his* Statesmen of times of George III., v. 2. 1839.)

Tierra del Fuego. *See* **Terra del Fuego**.

Tiers Etat. *See* **France**: *Tiers Etat* (p. 1032).

Tietjens, Teresa. CLAYTON, E. C. (*In her* Queens of song. 1865.)

Tiffany, George A., *and others*. **Harbor** at Milwaukee, W. T. *n.t.p.* [Milwaukee, 1840.] 8°. (**B 1605**)

Tiffany, Osborn. Sketch of the life of Gen. O. R. Williams. Balt., 1851. 8°. (**B 1608**)

Tiffin, Walter F. Gossip about portraits. London, 1867. 16°.

Tiger at large, The; comic burletta. *See* **Blink**, **G**.

Tighe, *Mrs.* Mary Blachford. Psyche; a poem. (*In* **Apuleius**, L. Works. 1853.)

Tighe, Robert Richard, *and* **Davis**, J. E. Annals of Windsor; a history of the castle and town with some account of Eton. London, 1858. 2 v. 8°.

Tighe, Wm. The plants; and occasional poems. London, 1808. 8°.

Tight lacing. FOWLER, O. S. Tight lacing. N. Y., 1847. 8°. (**B 1700**)

Tigranes; ein heroisch-tragisches Singspiel. *See* **Filistri**, A. de'.

Tigri, Giuseppe. Canti popolari toscani. 2a ed. Firenze, 1860. 12°.

Tigrini, Francesco. FABRONI, A. (*In his* Mem. di illustri Pisani, v. 1. 1790.)

Tigurum. *See* **Zurich**.

Tilden, Joseph. Account of a singular property of lamprey eels. (*In* **Amer. Acad.** Mem., v. 3. 1809.)

Tilden, Samuel Jones. Address on the constitution at the organization of the Society for the Diffusion of Political Knowledge. (*In* **Hand-book** of the democracy. 1864.)

Tilden, Wm. Phillips. Discourse on the evangelical alliance. Concord, 1846. 8°. (B 1303)

— Shall the sword devour forever? disc., death of E. Eastman. Concord, 1847. 8°. (B 1214)

— Temperance; sermon, Fitchburg, April 13. Fitchburg, 1856. 8°. (B 1303)

Tilden & Co. Catalogue of medicinal extracts prepared in vacuo. N. Y., 1855. 8°. (**B 1563**)

Tildesley, J. E. Locks and lockmaking. — Wolverhampton trades. (*In* **Timmins**, S. Resources. 1866.)

Tiles. WITHERS, R. I. Examples of encaustic tiles from Beaulieu Abbey. (*In* **Weale**, J. Quarterly papers on archit., v. 4. **1845**.)

— JEWITT, L. Some encaustic paving tiles recently discovered in Derby. (*In* **Reliquary**, v. 3. 1862–63.) — A tile-kiln and some paving and other tiles discovered at Repton, Derbyshire. (*In* v. 8. 1867–68.)
See also **Pottery**.
Note. For patterns *see* **Mosaic pavement**.

Tileston, Edward Griffin. Handbook of the administrations of the U. S. Boston, 1871. 16°.

Tilghman, Wm. Address before the Phila. Soc. for Prom. Agric. Phila., 1820. 8°. (**B 540**)

— Eulogium in commemoration of C. Wistar, Mar. 11. Phila., 1818. 8°. (**B 357, 1828, W 4**)

— *Eulogium on*. 1827. *See* **Binney**, H. (**W 4**) ; — **Du Ponceau**, P. S. (**B 1226, 1828, W 4**)

Till, Salomon van. RAMBACH, F. E.? (*In* **Niceron, J. P.** Nachrichten, v. 17. 1758.)

Till, Wm. Spooner. Report on the sewers and sewerage of Birmingham. (*In* **Nat. Assoc. Prom. Soc. Sci.** Trans., 1862.)

Till Eulenspiegel. (*In* **Simrock, K.** Deutschen Volksbucher, v. 10. 1864.)

Till the doctor comes, and how to help him. London, [187–]. 32°.

Tilladet, Jean Marie de la Marque de. NICERON, J. P. (*In his* Mém., v. 8. 1729; *and*, *Germ.*, v. 8. 1753.)

Tillæus, Petrus C. Potus theæ. (*In* **Linné**, C. Amœn. acad., v. 7. 1769.)

Tillard, I. WARBURTON, W. Remarks on T.'s 'Future rewards and punishments'. (*In his* Works, v. 11. 1811.)

Tillard, Richard. Thoughts conc. the safety of granting relief in the matter of subscription to the clergy of the Ch. of Eng. London, 1773. 8°. (**B 1379**)

Tillaux, —. Modèles d'anatomie. (*In* **France.** *Com. Imp. de l'Expos. de* 1867. Rapports, v. 2. 1868.)

Tilleard, James. On elementary school books. (*In* **Nat. Assoc. Prom. Soc. Sci.** Trans., 1859.)

Tillemont, Louis Sébastien Lenain de. Hist. des empereurs durant les six premiers siècles de l'église. (Vol. 1–4, 2e éd.) Brux., 1732, 10. 5 v. f°.

Contents. Vol. 1. 40 B.C. - 72 A.D. 2. 69–193. 3. 193–284. 4. 284–364. 5. 364–423.

— Mémoires pour servir à l'hist. ecclesiastique des six premiers siècles. (Vol. 7, 2e éd.) Brux., 1732. 10 v. f°.

Contents. Vol. 1. 20 B.C. -100 A.D. 2. 33 A.D. - 177. 3. 177–253. 4. 253–300. 5. 284–324. 6. 303–392. 7. 328–375. 8. 375–394. 9. 329–380. 10. 300–420.

Note. There should be 6 volumes more, as in the Paris edition, to perform the promise of the title-page. Vol. 10 stops at the beginning of the 5th century.

— Vie de Saint Louis. Paris, 1847–51. 6 v. 8°. (Soc. de l'Hist. de France.)

— NICERON, J. P. (*In his* Mém., v. 15. 1731; *and, Germ.*, v. 11. 1754.)

Tillet, Evrard Titon du. *See* **Titon du Tillet, E.**

Tilli (*Lat.* Tillius), Michel Angelo. **FABRONI, A.** (*In his* Vitæ Ital., v. 4. 1779.)

Tillinghast, Allen. *See* **Pinniger, D.** Trial. 1808. (**B 474**)

Tilliot, Jean Bénigne Lucotte du. *See* **Du Tilliot, J. B. L.**

Tillman, Samuel D. Chemical diagrams and derivative symbols, illustrating the prominent characteristics of chemical elements. — A new chemical nomenclature. — On a method of measuring musical intervals upon a spiral projection. (*In* **Amer. Assoc.** Proc., v. 16.) — On the combining power of chemical elements. (*In* v. 17.) — New musical notation. — Improvements for common roads and inland navigation. (*In* v. 19. 1870.)

Tillotson, John, *Archbp. of Canterbury.* Works; containing 54 sermons, with the 'Rule of faith'. 6th ed. London, 1710. f°.

— Discourse against transubstantiation. London, 1728. 12°. (**C 1**)

— Hazard of being saved in the Church of Rome. (*In* **Cardwell, E.** Tracts on points, *etc.*, v. 3. 1837.)

— The rule of faith; or, Answer to the treatise of J. S[ergeant], 'Sure-footing,' *etc.*; adj. a reply to J. S. his 3d app., *etc.*, by E. Stillingfleet. 2d ed. London, 1676. 16°.

— A seasonable vindication of the trinity. (*In* **Seasonable vindication**, *etc.* 1697.)

— Sermons, Cripplegate. London, 1709. 8°.

— Sermons conc. the divinity and incarnation of our Saviour. 2d ed. London, 1695. 8°.

— Sermons upon several occas. (Vol. 1, 8th ed., 2, 6th ed., 3, 4th ed.) Lond., 1694–95. 4 v. 8°.

Note. Vol. 3. has the title 'Sermons and discourses upon several occasions'.

— Six sermons in Church of St. Lawrence, Jury. London, 1694. 8°.

— Sixteen sermons on several occasions; ed. by R. Barker. Vol. 2–4. Lond., 1696–97. 3 v. 8°.

Note. Vol. 2, 3 have the title 'Sixteen sermons on several occasions'; v. 4 has the title 'Several discourses'.

— NICERON, J. P. (*In his* Mém., v. 38. 1737; *and, Germ.*, v. 17. 1758.)

— SHORT animadversions on a sermon preached by [T.]. London, 1680. 4°. (**B 1904**)

— WILLIAMS, J., *Bp. of Chichester.* Vindication of J. [T.'s] sermons [on] the divinity of our Saviour, from [T. Firmin's] 'Considerations on the explications of the trinity'. London, 1695. 4°. (**B 96**)

— WORDSWORTH, C. (*In his* Ecclesiastical biography, v. 4. 1839.)

— *Elegy on.* 1695. *See* **Tate, N.** (**A 45**)

Tillotson, Margaret, *Funeral sermon on.* 1823. *See* **Parker, D.** (**B 1226**)

Tilly, Jacques Pierre Alexandre, *comte* de. Mémoires. (*In* **Barrière, J. F.** Bibl. des mém., v. 25. 1862.)

Tilly, Jean Tserclaes, *comte* de. **BENEDEY, J.** Tilly und Gustav Adolf nach Onno Klopp. (*In* **Historische Zeitschrift**, v. 7. 1862.)

— CUST, E. (*In his* Lives of the warriors of the 30 years' war, v. 1. 1865.)

Tilly, *Rev.* Thomas. Temperance catechism; Brit. and For. Temperance Soc. *n.t.p.* [Lond., 183–.] 8°. (**B 1280**)

Tilsley, Hugh. Digest of the stamp acts. 9th ed., rev. by E. H. Tilsley. London, 1865. 8°.

Tilt, Edward John, *M.D.* Diseases of women. 2d ed. London, 1853. 8°.

Tilton, James, *M.D.* Peach trees. (*In* **Phil. Soc. Prom. Agric.** Mem., v. 1. 1808.) — Observations on the propriety of a farmer living on the produce of his own land. (*In* v. 3. 1814.)

— Species of curculio, destructive to fruit. (*In* **Soc. Prom. Useful Arts in N. Y.** Trans., v. 4, pt. 1. 1816.)

Tilton, Theodore. The American Board and American slavery; speech, Jan. 25, 1860. 2d ed. N. Y., 1860. 18°. (**D 37**)

Timæus. Fragm. (*In* **Mueller, C.** Fragmenta hist. Gr., v. 1. 1841.)

Timæus *Locrus.* Treatise on the soul of the world and nature. (*In* **Plato.** Works, v. 6. 1848.)

Timagenes *Alexandrinus.* Fragm. (*In* **Mueller, C.** Fr. hist. Gr., v. 3. 1849.)

Timagetus. Fragm. (*In* **Mueller, C.** Fr. hist. Gr., v. 4. 1851.)

Timagoras. Fragm. (*In* **Mueller, C.** Fr. hist. Gr., v. 4. 1851.)

Timanthes. *See* **Hoole, J.**

Timavus. RAPICIO, G. Balneorum quæ ad Timavi ostia sunt descriptio. (*In* **Grævius.** Thes. antiq. Ital., v. 6, pt. 4. 1722.)

Timber. HILL, J. Construction of timber explained by the microscope. Lond., 1770. 8°.

— DUNDAS, H., *Visc. Melville.* Letter to S. Percival on naval timber. London, 1810. 8°. (**B 1418**)

— BARLOW, P. Essay on strength and stress of timber, *etc.* London, 1817. 8°.

— - *Same.* 3d ed. London, 1826. 8°.

— CHAPMAN, W. Preservation of timber. London, 1817. 8°.

— LINGARD, J. Philosophic and practical inquiry into the nature and constitution of timber. (*In* **Pamphleteer**, 1820; v. 16 of **B 838**)

— VEGETABLE substances; timber trees. London, 1829. 12°. (Lib. ent. knowl., v. 10.)

— NELSON, R. Mode of bending timber used in Prussia. (*In* **Gr. Brit.** *Corps of Roy. Engin.* Papers, v. 3. 1839.) — On various kinds of timber. (*In* v. 5. 1842.) — ALDERSON, R. Preservation of timber from dry rot. (*In* v. 1. 1844.)

— DENISON, W. Experiments on different kinds of American timber. (*In* **Inst. of Civil Engin.** Trans., v. 2. 1842.)

— SILLOWAY, T. W. Text book of modern carpentry; comprising treatise on building timber, *etc.* Boston, 1858. 12°.

See also **Dry rot.**

Timber trade. MARRYAT, J. Speech, June 5, 1820, upon the petition of the ship owners of the Port of London against any alteration in the duties on timber. 2d ed. (*In* **Pamphleteer**, 1820; v. 17 of **B 838**) — DUNSKY, H. D. Statement on the present timber and deal trade, as regards Europe and the Brit. Amer. colonies. (*In* 1821; v. 18.)

— REMARKS on the impolicy of restrictions on commerce; with particular application to the present state of the timber trade. London, 1821. 8°. (**B 1847**)

Timbrel, Wm. Hall. Management of ruptures. From last London ed. Boston, 1809. 12°.

Timbs, John. Club life of London. London, 1866. 2 v. 12°.

— Curiosities of London. New ed. enl. London, 1868. 8°.

— Curiosities of science. London, 1859–60. 2 ser. 16°.

— Laconics; or, Best words from best authors. 3d ed. London, 1829. 3 v. 18°.

— Nooks and corners of Eng. life. Lond., 1867. 8°.

— Popular errors explained. London, 1841. 16°.

— Romance of London. London, 1865. 3 v. 8°.

Contents. Vol. 1. Historic sketches. — Remarkable duels. — Notorious highwaymen. — Rogueries, crimes, and punishments. 2. Rogueries, *etc.*, *contin.* — Love and marriage. — Supernatural stories. — Sights and shows and public amusements. 3. Sights, *etc.*, *contin.* — Strange adventures and catastrophes. — Remarkable persons. — Miscellaneous.

— School-days of eminent men. Columbus, 1860. 8°.
— Something for everybody. London, 1861. 12°.
— Things not generally known. 2d ser. London, 1859. 16°.
— Year-book of facts in the international exhibition, 1862. London, 1862. 16°.
— Zoology: Birds. London, 1831. 18°.
— *and* Gullick, T. J. Painting popularly explained. London, 1859. 16°.
See also Year-book of facts in science and art, 1840-80.

Timbuctoo. Jackson, J. G. Account of Timbuctoo and Housa; notes, *etc.*, [1787-1820]. London, 1820. 8°.
— - Account of Marocco and Suse; added, acc. of Timbuctoo. London, 1809. 4°.
— - *Same, with omissions.* Phila., 1801. 12°.
— Adams, R. Narrative of R. A., wrecked on the coast of Africa 1810, resided several months in Tombuctoo. London, 1816. 4°.
— Caillie, R. Travels through Central Africa to Timbuctoo, 1824-28. Lond., 1830. 2 v. 8°.
— Hoefer, J. C. F. Afrique australe. Paris, 1848. 8°. (Univers.)
— Beaumier, A. Prémier établissement des Israëlites à Timbouktou. (*In* Paris. Soc. de Géog. Bul., 5e sér., v. 19. 1870.)

Time. Euler, L. Sur l'espace et le tems. (*In* Berlin. Ak. de Wiss. Abh., v. 4. 1748.)

Time and the hour; a drama. *See* Simpson, J. P., *and* Dale, F.

Time and tide; drama. *See* Leslie, H.

Time of the end, The; illustrated by the history of prophetic interpretation, *etc.*; by a congregationalist. Boston, 1856. 8°.
Contains also 'Our present position in the prophetic callendar', with his 'Apocalyptic seven-sealed scroll', by E. B. Elliott; lectures on the nature and nearness of the advent, by J. Cumming; lectures on the new heavens and new earth by Dr. Chalmers, Dr. Hitchcock, and J. Wesley. Testimony of more than one hundred witnesses against the mod. Whitlyan theory of a millennium before the advent.

Time table, showing the number of months and days from any day in one month to the same day in any other month. (*In* Brooks, L. Short and easy method of obtaining the average time. 1851.)

Time the avenger; by [Mrs. A. C. Marsh]. London, 1851. 3 v. 16°.

Time tries all; by J. Courtney. (*In* Sargent, E. Mod. stand. dr., v. 37.)

Time works wonders. *See* Jerrold, D.

Time-keepers. Morgan, G. Observations on the history and progress of the art of watch-making, from the earliest period to modern times. (*In* Archæologia, v. 33. 1849.)
— Cumming, A. Elements of clock and watch-work. London, 1766. 4°.
— Account kept during thirteen months of the going of a pocket chronometer, made by J. Arnold. London, 1780. 4°. (A 21)
— Mayer, C. Letter on the going of a new pendulum clock made by J. Arnold; tr. from the German. London, 1781. 4°. (A 21)
— Mudge, T., *Jr.* Narrative of facts rel. to some time-keepers constr. by T. Mudge [Sen.]. London, 1792. (B 899) 8°.
— Maskelyne, N. Answer to 'A narrative of facts', pub. by T. Mudge, rel. to time-keepers. London, 1792. 8°.
— Mudge, T., *Jr.* Reply to the 'Answer' of Maskelyne to 'A narrative'; added, explan. of the methods of calculting a mean daily rate, by Count de Bruhl. Lond., 1792. 8°.
— Grafton, E. Horology; or, Sketch of clock and watch making. 3d ed. Lond., [18—]12°.
— Berthoud, F. Histoire de la mesure du temps par les horloges. Paris, 1802. 2 v. 4°.
— Earnshaw, T., *and* Arnold, J. Explanation of time-keepers constructed by [them]. London, 1806. 4°.
— Mouxy Deloche, F. Antiquités d'Aix-les-Bains: horloge antique. (*In* Turin. Ac. d. Sci. Mem., v. 17. 1809.)
— Chardin, *Le* P. —. Diss. sur les échappemens d'horloges. (*In* Sérieys, A. Bibl. acad., v. 12. 1811.)
— Parkinson *and* Frodsham. Brief account of the chronometer; with remarks on those furnished by them. London, [1832]. 8°.
— Reid, T. Treatise in clock and watch-making. [1832.] 7th ed. Glasgow, 1859. 8°.
— Smyth, W. H. Description of an astrological clock belonging to the Soc. of Antiquaries of London. (*In* Archæologia, v. 33, 34. 1849-52.)
— Denison, E. B. Rudimentary treatise on clock and watch making. Lond., *Weale*, 1850. 12°.
— Schwilgué, C. Descr. abrégée de l'horloge astronomique de la Cathédrale de Strasbourg. 6e éd. Strasb., 1856. 16°.
— Belgrano, L. T. Degli antichi orologi pubblici d'Italia con aggiunta di notizie della posta in Genova. (*In* Archivio stor. ital., ser. 3, v. 7, pt. 1. 1868.)
— Breguet, —. Horlogerie. (*In* France. *Com. Imp. de l'Expos. de* 1867. Rapports, v. 3. 1868.)
— Kemlo, F. Watch repairer's hand-book. Boston, 1869. 8°.
See also Chronometers; — Pendulum.

Timely retreat; or, Year in Bengal before the mutinies; by [Misses M. and R. W. Dunlop]. London, 1858. 2 v. 8°.

Times, The; June 29, 30, July 1, 2, 3, Sept. 3, 4, 6-11, 13-18, 20-25, Oct. 27-30, Nov. 1-6, 8-13, 15, 17-20, Dec. 2, 1790; Feb. 13, 1793, Oct. 30, 1795. London, 1790-95. f°. (E 179)
— *Same.* June 21. London, 1799. f°. (E 179)
— *Same.* Mar. 25 - Apr. 10. London, 1807. f°. (E 172)
— *Same.* July - Dec. 1824, Jan. 1830-80. London, 1824, 1830-80. f°.
— Index, 1862, 63; by J. Giddings. London, 1863-64. 2 v. 8°.
— *Same.* April 1, 1863 - Sept. 30, 1880; by S. Palmer. London, 1880, 79, 78, 77, 76, 75, 68-80. 69 v. 4°.

Times, Pictorial. *See* Pictorial times.

Times; a poem. *See* Markoe, P.

Times and seasons, The. Vol. 5. Nauvoo, 1844. 8°.

Time's telescope; guide to the almanack, 1814, 15, 19, 20, 23, 27. (1814 3d ed., 1815, 1823 2d ed.) London, 1822, 21, 19-27. 6 v. 12°.

Times' whistle; or, A newe daunce of seven satires; and other poems; compiled by R. C., gent.; with introd., notes, and glossary, by J. M. Cowper. London, 1871. 8°. (Early Eng. Text Soc.)

Timesitheus. Fragm. (*In* Wagner, F. W. Fragm. Eurip. 1846.)

Timkowski, George. Travels of the Russia mission to China. London, 1827. 2 v. 8°.
— Voy. à Pekin par la Mongolie. (*In* Montémont, A. Biblioth. univ., v. 33. 1836.)

Timm, Georg Friedrich. Thomsen, C., *and* Devegge, O. Catalogus numorum Græcorum quos possidebat olim T. Hafniæ, 1832. 12°.

Timmins, Samuel. Resources, products, and industrial hist. of Birmingham and the Midland hardware district; reports col. by the local industries committee of the British Assoc. at Birmingham, 1865. Lond., 1866. 8°.
Contents. Jukes, J. B. Geol. structure of the South Staffordshire coalfield. — Johnson, H. So. Staffordshire coalfield. — Bailey, S. The economic value of various measures of coal and ironstone in the So. Staffordshire coalfield. — Drainage of the South Staffordshire coalfield. — Statistics of the marketable products of the

coalfield. — **Myers**, E. The limestones of So. Staffordshire. — **Jones**, J. Report on the iron trade of South Staffordshire, 1865. — **Tildesley**, J. E. Locks and lock-making. — **Piggott**, G. Boiler plate working. — **Jones**, J. Staffordshire manufactures. — **Kenrick**, W. Cast-iron hollow-ware, tinned and enamelled, and cast-iron mongery. — **Ball**, E. The hand-made nail trade. — **Loveridge**, H. Wolverhampton trades; addenda by J. E. Tildesley. — **Franklin**, W. The Walsall trades; addenda by J. E. Tildesley. — **Harrison**, G. The Stourbridge fire clay; with a table of analysis, by D. Forbes, *etc.* — **Midland** salt works. — **Coghill**, H. Ceramic manufactures of Staffordshire. — **Chance**, H. Manufacture of plate, crown, and sheet glass. — **Madeley**, W. Report on glass works at Wordsley, Amblecote, Stourbridge, and Dudley. — **Kenword**, J. Light-house illumination, and the dioptric apparatus. — **Basaltic** stone manufacture. — **Chance**, H. Manufacture of alkali and acids in Birmingham and the neighborhood. — **Adkins**, H. Manufacture of soap; — Manufacture of red lead. — **Coventry** ribbon and watch trades. — **Bartleet**, R. S., *and* **Woodward**, J. M. Manufacture of needles and fish-hooks. — **Timmins**, R. The industrial hist. of Birmingham. — **Aitken**, W. C. Brass, and brass manufactures. — **Goodman**, J. D. Birmingham gun trade. — **Turner**, J. P. Birmingham button trade. — **Wright**, J. S. Jewellery and gilt-toy trades. — **Middlemore**, T. Birmingham saddlery trade. — **Ryland**, W. Plated wares and electro-plating trades. — **Ryland**, A. The Birmingham assay office. — **Aitken**, W. C. Cast and electro-deposit statuary, in bronze and copper. — **Powell**, J. H. The art of stained glass in Birmingham. — **Birmingham** flint-glass manufacture. — **Optical** and mathematical instruments. — **Aitken**, W. C. The revived art of metal-working in the precious metals, brass, and iron, on mediæval principles. — **Heaton**, R. Birmingham coinage; — Die-sinking. — **Aitken**, W. C. Papier-mâché manufacture. — **Gansby**, J. B. Block-paper and its uses. — **Wright**, J. T. Rope-making; hemp and twine. — **Lean**, C. Wire-drawing and steel wire. — **Gansby**, J. B. Wire-working. — **Phipson**, T. The pin trade. — **Chamberlain**, J. Manufacture of iron wood-screws. — **Martineau**, F. E. Patent wrought-iron hinges. — **Martineau**, R. F. Cut nails. — **Yates**, T. Pewter and britannia metal trade. — **Peyton**, E. Manufacture of iron and brass bedsteads. — **Rabone**, J., *Jr.* Measuring rules. — **Timmins**, S. The Birmingham steel-pen trade. — **Browett**, J. B., *and others.* Miscel. trades. — **Barker**, S., *and others.* Chemical trades. — **Bunce**, J. T. Social and economical aspects of Birmingham. — **Heslop**, T. P. The medical aspects of Birmingham. — **Aitken**, W. C. Coffin-furniture manufacture.

Timocles. Fragm. (*In* **Meineke**, J. A. Fr. com. Gr., v. 3. 1840; — *and in* **Wagner**, F. W. Fr. Eurip. 1846.)

Timocrate; tragédie. *See* **Corneille**, T.

Timocreon. Fragm. (*In* **Bergk**, T. Poet. lyr. Gr. 1853.)

Timolaus. Fragm. (*In* **Mueller**, C. Fr. hist. Gr., v. 4. 1851.)

Timoleon. Nepos, C. Vita. (*In his* Vitæ.)

— Plutarchus. Vita T. (*In his* Vitæ; — *and, Eng.,* Lives.)

Timoleon, *pseud.* Epistle to all electors. London, 1768. 4°. (A 12, 19)

Timoleone; tragedia. *See* **Alfieri**, V.

Timomachus. Fragm. (*In* **Mueller**, C. Fr. hist. Gr., v. 4. 1851.)

Timon; ed. by A. Dyce. London, 1842. 8°. (Shakespeare Soc.)

Timon, The new. *See* **Lytton**, *Sir* E. G. E. L. B., *Baron.*

Timon of Athens; a play. *See* **Shadwell**, T.; — **Shakespeare**, W.

Timonax. Fragm. (*In* **Mueller**, C. Fr. hist. Gr., v. 4. 1861.)

Timoneda, Juan de. Aucto de la Oveja perdida. — Aucto de la Fee. — Aucto de la Fuente de los siete sacramentos. — Farsa del Sacramento de la fuente de San Juan. — Obra llamada los Desposorios de Christo. (*In* **Pedroso**, E. G. Autos sacramentales. 1865.)

— Los ciegos y el mozo. (*In* **Ochoa**, E. de. Tes. del teatro esp., v. 1. 1838; — *and in* **Moratin**, N. F. *and* L. F. de. Obras. 1857; Aribau. Bibl., v. 2.)

— El patrañuelo. — El sobremesa y alivio de caminantes. (*In* **Aribau**, B. C. Nov. ant. á Cervantes. 1850; Bibl., v. 3)

Timonides *Leucadius.* Fragm. (*In* **Mueller**, C. Fr. hist. Gr., v. 2. 1848.)

Timorcus, Theophilus, *pseud.* The covenanters plea against absolvers; discourse [in answer to] Dr. Featly and Dr. Gauden. London, 1661. 4°. (B 2)

Timostratus. Fragm. (*In* **Meineke**, A. Fr. com. Gr., v. 4. 1841.)

Timoteo *da Ferrara.* Sonetti. (*In* **Trucchi**, F. Poesie ital., v. 3. 1847.)

Timotheus. Fragm. Argolicorum, *etc.* (*In* **Mueller**, C. Fr. hist. Gr., v. 4. 1851.)

Timotheus *Atheniensis.* Fragm. (*In* **Meineke**, A. Fr. com. Gr., v. 3. 1840.)

Timotheus, *the general, son of Conon.* Nepos, C. (*In his* Vitæ.)

Timotheus *Hierosolymitanus.* Sermo in Simeonem justum. (*In* **Mai**, A. Class. auct., v. 10. 1838.)

Timotheus *Milesius.* Fragm. (*In* **Bergk**, T. Poet. lyr. Gr. 1853.)

Timothy, *pseud.* Letter to the moderator. 1812. *See* **Worcester**, T.

Timothy, *pseud.* Fifty-five reasons for not being a Baptist. New England, 1830. 12°. (C 238)

Timothy, Epistle of Paul to. *See* **Bible** (p. 290).

Timothy and Philatheus, Dialogue between. 1709. *See* **Oldisworth**, W.

Timothy to the rescue; a farce; by H. J. Byron. (No. 133 *of* **De Witt's** acting plays.)

Timour. *See* **Timur.**

Timperley, —. Acc. of harbour and docks at Kingston-upon-Hull. (*In* **Inst. Civil Engin.** Trans., v. 1. 1842.)

Timperley, C. H. Dictionary of printers and printing; with the prog. of literature anc. and modern, *etc.* London, 1839. 8°.

Timpson, *Rev.* Thomas. What have I to do with missions? London, 1841. 18°.

Timson, John. The bar to free admission to the Lord's supper removed; a vindication of Mr. Humfrey's 'Free admission'. London, 1654. 12°.

Timur, Tamerlane, Timur-lenc, *or* **Timur bec,** *Emperor of the Moguls.* Institutes political and military; [in Persian with an Eng. tr.] by W. Davy, ed. by J. White. Oxford, 1783. 8°.

— The mulfuzat Timūry; or, Autobiographical mem. of the Moghul Emperor Timur; tr. by C. Stewart. [London,] *Orient. Trans. Fund,* 1830. 8°.

— Account of the grand festival, after his defeat of Bajazet; tr. by Col. Francklin. (*In* **Oriental Trans. Fund.** Misc. trans., v. 2. 1834.)

— Charmoy, M. Expédition de Timoûr-i-lenk ou Tamerlan contre Toqtamiche, khân de l'Ouloûs de Djoûtchy, en 795 de l' Hégire ou 1391 de notre ère. (*In* **St. Petersburg. Ac. Sci.** Mém., 6e sér., v. 3. 1836.)

— Clavijo, R. G. de. Narrative of embassy to the court of Timour, 1403–06. London, 1859. 8°.

— Sharaf-ad-Din Ali *al Yerdi.* Histoire de Timur-Bec; tr. par F. Petis de la Croix. Delf, 1823. 4 v. 12°.

— Silvestre de Sacy, A. I. Une correspondance inédite de Tamerlan avec Charles vi. (*In* **Paris. Inst.** *Ac. d. Inscr.* Mém., v. 6. 1822.)

Timur Bec. *See* **Timur.**

Tin. Coste, L., *and* Perdonnet, A. Mém. sur le traitement des minérais, *etc.*, en Angleterre. Paris, 1830. 8°.

Tin trade. Hawkins, C. Observations on the tin trade of the ancients in Cornwall. London, 1811. 8°.

Tindal, Matthew. Address to the inhabitants of Lond. and Westminster in rel. to [Gibson's] pastoral letter [on] infidelity. Lond., 1729. 8°. (B 114, E 169)

— *Same.* 2d ed. with notes and add. London, 1730. 8°. (E 169)

— 2d address to the inhabitants of London and Westminster; with rem. on 'Scripture vindicated', *etc.* London, 1730. 8°. (B 114, E 169)

— Christianity as old as the creation. 2d ed. London, 1732. 8°.

— *Same.* Newburgh, 1798. 8°.

— Defection considered and the designs of those who divided the friends of the government set in a true light. 5th ed. London, 1717. 8°. (B 756)

— Defence of 'The rights of the Christian Church' against a late visitation sermon by W. Wotton. London, 1707. 12°. (B 83)

— Essay conc. obedience to the supreme powers. — Essay conc. the law of nations. (*In* Col. of state tracts, v. 2. 1706.)
— Jacobitism, perjury, and popery of high church priests. London, 1710. 8°. (B 99)
— Letter conc. the trinity and Athanasian creed. *n.p.*, 1694. 4°. (B 96)
— Priestcraft in perfection [with Reflections by A. Collins]. 3d ed. London, 1710. 8°. (B 113)
Note. Both pamphlets are attributed by the ed. of Somers' tracts to A. Collins.
— *Same, without Reflections.* (*In* Somers, J. Col. of tracts, v. 12. 1814.)
— Reasons against restraining the press. (*In* **Baron, R.** Pillars of priestcraft, v. 4. 1768.)
— Rights of the Church asserted. Pt. 1. 2d ed. London, 1706. 8°.
— BALGUY, J. Second letter to a deist. London, 1731. 8°. (B 116)
— BROUGHTON, T. Christianity distinct from the religion of nature. London, 1732. 8°.
— - *Same.* Part 2. London, 1732. 8°. (B 116)
— BROWNE, S. Defence of the religion of nature, *etc.*, against 'Christianity as old as the creation'. London, 1732. 8°.
— - Close of the Defense of the religion of nature, *etc.* London, 1733. 8°. (B 1371)
— BULLOCK, T. The Gospel a reinforcement of the law of nature; sermon, Nov. 24, 1728. London, 1730. 8°. (B 35)
— BURNET, T. Argument in 'Christianity as old as the creation' reviewed and confuted. Conference 3. London, 1732. 8°. (B 1371)
— COLLINS, A. Reflections on [Tindal's] 'Priestcraft in perfection'. *n.t.p.* [London, 1710.] 8°. (B 99)
— CONYBEARE, J. Defence of revealed religion against the exceptions in 'Christianity as old as the creation'. London, 1732. 8°.
— CRAWFORD, W. Short manual against the infidelity of the age. Edin., 1734. 12°.
— DEFENCE of the most essential articles of Christian belief, against C-ll-ns, and Tindal. London, 1733. 8°. (E 154)
— FOSTER, J. Usefulness, truth, and excellency of the Chr. revelation defended. London, 1731. 8°.
— HALLET, J. Essay on the nature and use of miracles. London, [17—]. 8°. (B 40)
— JACKSON, J. Remarks on T.'s 'Christianity as old as the creation' with regard to ecclesiastical antiquity. Camb., 1733. 8°. (B 116)
— JUDGMENT and opinion of H. Grotius conc. the principles and notions of the 'Rights'. London, [17—]. 8°.
— *Same.* (*In* **Oldisworth, W.** Dialogue, v. 3. 1711.)
— LELAND, J. Answer to 'Christianity as old as the creation'. Dublin, 1733. 2 v. 8°.
— LETTER to Dr. Waterland containing remarks on his vindication of Scripture in answer to 'Christianity as old as the creation', *etc.* London, 1731. 8°. (B 119)
— MIDDLETON, C. Letter to D. Waterland; remarks on his 'Vindication of Scripture'; in answer to [T.'s 'Christianity as old as the creation', *etc.* London, 1731. 8°. (B 119)
— OLDISWORTH, W. Dialogue between Timothy and Philatheus in which the principles of 'The rights of the Christian Church', *etc.*, are answered; added, seven tracts rel. to the same subject. London, 1709–11. 3 v. 8°.
— REMARKS on a book intituled 'Christianity as old as the creation', with regard to ecclesiastical antiquity. Pt. 1 continued. Cambridge, 1733. 8°. (B 116)
— S., T. Christianity as old as the creation, vol. 2; rectifying some mistakes in Dr. T.'s vol. 1. London, 1749. 8°.
— STEBBING, H. Defence of Dr. Clarke's 'Evidences of natural and revealed religion'; answer to the 14th chapter of 'Christianity as old', *etc.* London, 1731. 8°. (B 116)
— WATERLAND, D. Scripture vindicated; in answer to 'Christianity as old as the creation'. Pt. 1. London, 1730. 8°. (B 116)

Tindal, Nicholas. Guide to classical learning; or, [Spence's] Polymetis abridged. 2d ed. London, 1765. 12°.
— *Continuator. See* **Rapin de Thoyras, P.** History of Eng. 1785–89.
Tindale *or* **Tyndall.** *See* **Tyndale.**
Tindall, Wm. FOX, J. Life of T. (*In* **Wordsworth, C.** Eccles. biog., v. 2. 1839.)
Tinea. COOKE, W. Tinea capitis contagiosa. London, 1810. 8°.
Tinker, Edward. TRIAL for the murder of a youth called Edward, Sept. Newbern, 1811. 8°. (B 477)
Tinkham, A. W. [Various reports on a R.R. to the Pacific, and letters to I. I. Stevens.] (*In* **U. S.** *War Dep't.* Reports of explorations in 1853, 54, v. 1.)
Tinne, *Mlle.* Alexina. CORTAMBERT, R. (*In his* Les illustres voyageuses. 1866.)
— NACHTIGAL, *Le docteur.* Relation de la mort de T. (*In* **Paris. Soc. de Géog.** Bul., 5e sér., v. 19. 1870.)
Tinneh. Ross, B. R. The eastern Tinneh. (*In* **Smithsonian Inst.** Reports, 1866.)
Tinnevally Mission of the Missionary Soc. *See* **Pettitt, G.**
Tinseau d'Amoudans, Charles Marie Therèse Léon. Apologie des émigrés françois. London, 1803. 8°. (B 1411)
— L'empire germanique réduit en départements, sous la préfecture de l'Electeur de [Brandenbourg]; tr. de l'allemand. Hambourg, 1802. 8°. (B 1411)
— *Eng.* The Empire of Germany; tr. by W. Cobbett. London, 1803. 8°. (B 1411)
— Examen de l'état polit. et milit. où la paix continentale mettra l'Europe par rapport à la France. Hambourg, 1803. 8°. (B 1411)
— Statistical view of France. London, 1803. 8°.
Tintium. Rupertus de incendio Tintiensi. (*In* **Pertz, G.** Mon. Germ. hist., v. 14. 1861.)
Tintoretto, Jacopo **Robusti,** *called.* Christ before Pilate, and Christ bearing the cross; photographs of paintings by T. in the Scuolo di San Socco, Venice. London, [1857]. (Arundel Soc.)
Tio, El, y la tia; zarzuela. *See* **Cruz y Cano, R.** de la.
Ti-ping revolution. LIN-LE. History of the Ti-ping revolution. London, 1866. 2 v. 8°.
Tippecanoe; a legend of the border. [Prov.?] 1840. 8°. (B 1498)
Tippecanoe text book. *See* **Niles, W. O.**
Tippoo *Sultan.* OFFICIAL documents rel. to the negotiation of Tippoo with the Fr. and other for. states against the British, *&c.* Calcutta, *Company's Press*, 1799. 4°.
— *Same, without the original French documents.* Calcutta, *Mirror Press*, 1799. 4°.
— STEWART, C. Catalogue of the Oriental library of Tippoo Sultan; with memoirs. Camb., 1809. 4°.
Tiraboschi, Girolamo. Biblioteca modenese; notizie degli scrittori di Modena. Modena, 1781–86. 6 v. 4°.
Contents. Vol. 1. A - Caste. 2. Castr - Gi. 3. Gr - Pal. 4. Pan - Sad. 5. Sal - Z. 6. Suplemento e notizie.
— Notizie biografiche in continuazione della Biblioteca modenese. Raggio, 1833–37. 5 v. 4°.
Contents. Vol. 1. L. Cerretti. — F. Cassoli. — V. Cattelani. — G. M. Soli. — F. Fontanese. — F. Re. — D. Gentili. — G. Jacopetti. — C. Frassoni. — G. Olio, dall'. — G. Castiglioni. — P. Ruffini. — D. Pacchi. — L. Campi. 2. B. Asioli. — L. Asioli. — G. Asioli. — P. A. Guglielmi. — C. Vecchi. — L. Bolognini. — L. A. Vincenzi. — B. Corti. — G. Venturi. — G. Mussini. — G. A. Lotti. — F. Ciardi. — G. Bosi. — Gioachino Salvioni. — Girolamo Salvioni. — S. Salvioni. 3. G. Lusverti. — G. B. Tomaselli. — P. Pozzetti. — G. Venturi. — P. E. Campi. — F. A. Camuncoli. — G. M. Savani. — G. Gabardi. — C. D. Fossa. 4. L. Lamberti. — B. Valdrighi. — F. Valdrighi. — L. Valdrighi. — L. Spallanzani. — G. M. Taschini. — P. A. Zanoni. — D. V. Junìore. — I. Valdastri. — G. A. Rangone-Terzi. 5. D. A. Pacchioni. — L. Rossi. — G. Fassi-Vicini. — F. L. Mazzali. — C. Antonioli. — P. Cerretti.
— Vita di Dante Alighieri. (*In* **Dante, A.** Opere, v. 5. 1830.)
— FABRONI, A. (*In his* Vitæ Ital., v. 16. 1795.)

Tirésias; opéra-comique. *See* **Piron, A.**
Tireuse de cartes, La; drame. 2e éd. Paris, 1860. 12°. (E 8)
Tiridate, ou Comédie et tragédie; par N. Fournier. *n.p.*, [1836]. 12°. (E 22)
Tirso de Molina, *pseud.* *See* **Tellez, G.**
'Tis pity she's a whore; a tragedy. *See* **Ford, J.**
Tischbein, Johann Heinrich Wilhelm. ANDRESEN, A. (*In his* Die deutschen Maler-Radirer, v. 2. 1867.)
Tischendorf, Lobegott (*Lat.* Ænotheus) Friedrich Constantin von. Authenticity of our Gospels. (*In* **Bremen lectures**, 1871.)
— Notitia editionis codicis Bibliorum Sinaitici, auspiciis imperatoris Alexandri II. susceptæ; ac. catalogus codicum nuper ex oriente Petropolin perlatorum; item, Origenis scholia in Proverbia Salomonis. Lips., 1860. 4°.
— Novum Testamentum Sinaiticum. *See* **Bible** (p. 282).
— Novum Testamentum Vaticanum. *See* **Bible** (p. 282).
— Origin of the four Gospels; tr. by W. L. Gage from the 4th Germ. ed. Boston, *Amer. Tract Soc.*, [1867]. 16°.
— SAINT RENÉ TAILLANDIER. (*In* **Revue d. D. Mondes**, juil. 1885.)
Tison, Thomas. Briefe note of a voyage made before 1526 to the West Indies. (*In* **Hakluyt**, R. Col. of voy., v. 3. 1810; — *and in* **Kerr**, R. Col. of voy., v. 6. 1824.)
Tissandier, Gaston. L'eau. 2d éd., illust. de vignettes, *etc.* Paris, 1869. 12°. (Bibl. des merveilles.)
— *Eng.* The wonders of water; tr. with add. by S. de Vere. N. Y., 1872 [1871]. 8°.
— Travels in the air. 1871. *See* **Glaisher, J.**
Tissandier, J. B. Des sciences occultes et du spiritisme. Paris, 1866. 18°.
Tissanier, Joseph. Relation de son voyage de France au Tonkin, 1654–58. — Son séjour au Tonkin; description de ce royaume. — Evénements mémorables de la mission du Tonkin, 1558–60. (*In* **Voyages** et travaux des missionnaires de la Compagnie de Jesus, v. 2. 1858.)
Tissington, Silvester. Collection of epitaphs, *etc.* London, 1857. 8°.
Tissot, Claude Joseph. L'animisme et ses adversaires. (*In* **Stahl**, G. E. Œuvres, v. 6. 1864.)
Tissot, Pierre François. Discours. — Discours, pour la tr. des restes de la Harpe. (*In* **Paris. Inst.** *Acad. Fr.* Recueil des disc., 1830–39.)
— Notice sur Carnot. (*In* **Carnot**, L. N. M. Mémoires. 1824.)
Tissot, Simon André. Avis au peuple sur sa santé. 2e éd. Paris, 1765, 64. 2 v. 12°.
— *Eng.* Advice to people in general with regard to health; tr. by J. Kirkpatrick; also art of preserving health, by J. Mackenzie. London, 1767. 2 v. 12°.
— Traité des nerfs et de leurs maladies. Lausanne, 1784. 4 v. 12°.
Tissues of animals. *See* **Anatomy**. *General.*
Titan; von J. P. F. Richter. (*In his* Sämmt. Werke, v. 15–16. 1841.)
Titan; a monthly magazine. Vol. 24, Jan.–June 1857. Edin., London, 1857. 8°.
Note. This is a continuation of Hogg's instructor.
Titcomb, *Col.* Moses, *Funeral sermon on.* 1755. *See* Lowell, J. (B 227, 282)
Titcomb, Timothy, *pseud.* *See* **Holland, J. G.**
Tithes. CHRIST's order, and the disciples practice; whereby claiming tithes appeares to be contrary to to the Gospel. *n.t.p.* [16—.] 4°. (B 1)
— CARTER, J. Vindiciæ decimarum; of tithes, a plea for the jus divinum. London, 1640. 4°.
— SPELMAN, *Sir* H., *d.* 1641. English works; with his posthumous works. 2d ed. London, 1721. f°.
— GR. BRITAIN. *Parl.* Ordinance for the true payment of tythes. London, 1644. 4°. (B 647)
— MAR-PRIEST, *Young* M., *pseud.* The ordinance for tythes dismounted from all Mosaicall and true magesteriall right. Europe, 1646. 4°. (C 284)
— K., E. That neither temporallities nor tythes is due to the bishops nor clergy by any gospel rule. *n.p.*, 1672. 4°. (C 284)
— MATHER, I. Discourse [on] the maintenance due to those that preach the gospel; tithes [not] by divine law the ministers' due. Boston, 1706. 8°. (C 14)
— LESLIE, C. Essay conc. the divine right of tithes. (*In his* Theol. works, v. 2. 1721.)
— PAPERS rel. to the Quakers' tythe bill. 3d ed. London, 1736. 8°. (B 123)
— GRATTAN, H. Speech on tythe [*sic*], Feb. 14. Dublin, 1788. 8°. (W 29)
— SALES, A. Respuesta a la pregunta de D. Ximeno [sobre diezmos]. (*In* **Valladares**, A. Seman. erud., v. 16. 1788.)
— COVE, M. Inquiry into the necessity, justice, and policy of a commutation of thithes. Hereford, 1800. 8°. (B 1409)
— BENETT, J. Essay on the commutation of tithes. (*In* **Pamphleteer**, 1815; v. 6 of B 838)
— - Reply to the letter of Wm. Coxe, on commutation of tithes; also a prize essay. Salisbury, [1815 ?]. 8°. (B 680)
— DUDLEY, *Sir* H. B. Short address recommendatory of some commutation of the tythes of Ireland. (*In* **Pamphleteer**, 1815; v. 6 of B 838) — EDMEADS, W. National establishment national security; or, Thoughts on the consequences of commuting the tithes. (*In* 1816; v. 7.) — WILLIS, J. Prize essay on the commutation of tithes. (*In* 1816; v. 8.)
— FISHER, *Rev.* J. Letter to F. Lewis on the commutation of tithes. London, 1817. 8°. (B 1376)
— TADMAN, L., *pseud.*? To the editor of the Brit. review, in answer to his remarks on the consequences of commuting the tithes. (*In* **Pamphleteer**, 1818; v. 12 of B 838) — FRY, J. S. Concise history of tithes, *etc.* (*In* 1819; v. 15.)
— ESSAY on the tithe system; its advantages and disadvantages. Oxford, 1822. 8°. (B 1376)
— BALDWIN, W. J. The Catholic question and on tythes. London, 1823. 8°.
— WILLICH, C. M. Annual supplement to the tithe commutation tables. London, 1846. 4°. (A 65)
Titi. History of Prince T.; [by St. Hyacinthe;] tr. by a lady. London, 1736. 16°.
Titi, Roberto. NICERON, J. P. (*In his* Mém., v. 13. 1730.)
Titian. *See* **Tiziano Vecellio.**
Titinius. Fragm. (*In* **Estienne**, R. Fr. poet. vet. Lat. 1564; — *and in* **Ribbeck**, O. Scen. Rom. poesis fr., v. 2. 1855.)
Titius, Gerhardus, *d.* 1681. NICERON, J. P. (*In his* Mém., v. 41. 1740.)
Titius, Johann Peter. Manuductio ad excerpendum. Gedani, 1676. 12°.
Titles. LOWELL, J. Essay on hereditary titles and university degrees; by a New Eng. farmer. Boston, 1798. 8°. (B 423)
— HAMPSON, R. T. Origines patriciæ; a deduction of European titles of nobility from their sources. London, 1846. 8°.
Titmarsh, Michael Angelo, *pseud.* *See* **Thackeray, W. M.**
Tito, Il; ovvero Gerusalemme desolata. *See* **Lalli, G. B.**
Titon du Tillet, Everard. Description du Parnasse françois. 1e pte. Paris, 1760. f°.
Titres de la dynastie napoléonienne. Paris, 1868. 8°.
Titsingh, Isaac. Illustrations of Japan; memoirs of the sovereigns, tr. by F. Shoberl. London, 1822. 4°.
Titus, Epistle of Paul to. *See* **Bible.** *N.T.* (p. 290).
Titus, *Emperor.* BEULÉ, C. E. Titus et sa dynastie. Paris, 1870. 8°.
Titus, *Col.* Silas. Killing no murder. *See* **Allen, Wm.**, *pseud.*
Titus; tragédie. *See* **Belloy**, P. L. B. de; — **Engel, J. J.**
Titus and Berenice; a tragedy. *See* **Otway, T.**
Titus Andronicus. *See* **Shakespeare, W.**
Tiverton, *County of Devon.* HARDING, Wm., *Lieut.-Col.* History of Tiverton. Tiverton, 1845–47. 2 v. 8°.
Tiverton, *R.I.* MAP of the town of T.; surveyed by W. G. Borden. 1854.
— FOWLER, O. History of Fall River, with notice of Freetown and Tiverton. Fall River, 18[illegible]2. 8°.

Tivoli. DELRIO, A. Antiquitates Tiburtinæ. — MARZO, F. Historia Tiburtina amplificata. (*In* Grævius. Thes. antiq. Ital., v. 8, pt. 4. 1723.)
— LIGORIO, P. Descriptio villæ Tiburtinæ Hadrianeæ; Latine vertit S. Havercampus; acc. Italus contextus. (*In* Grævius. Thes. antiq. Ital., v. 8, pt. 4. 1723.)
— - *and* CONTINI, F. Ichnographia villæ Tiburtinæ Hadriani. *n.t.p.* [Romæ, 1751.] f°.
— PALMUCCI, D. Villa da Adriano in Tivoli. [Rome, 17—.] f°. (E 99)
— SEBASTIANI, F. A. Viaggio a Tivoli, 1825; lettere. Fuligno, 1828. 8°.

Tixier de Ravisi (*Lat.* Ravisius Textor), Jean. De memorabilibus et claris mulieribus; diversorum scriptorum opera. Parisiis, *S. Colinæus*, 1521. f°.
Contents. Plutarchus. De claris mulieribus. — Foresti, G. De virtutibus præditis, scelestisque mulieribus. — Pins, J. de. Opusculum in quo Divæ Catharinæ Senensis vitam narrat. — Opusculum aliud historiarum varietate copiosum. — Vita Sanctæ Monegundis. — Fregoso, G. B. De fœminis quæ doctrina excelluerunt. — Maffei, R. De moribus mulierum. — Blanchæ Francorum reginæ vita. — Joannæ Francorum reginæ vita. — Tixier de Ravisi, J. De mulieribus quibusdam illustribus. — Meretrices quædam. — Mulieres doctæ. — Nomina quarundum fœminarum illustrium. — Mulieres bellicosæ et masculæ virtutis. — Bella et alia quædam mala a mulieribus orta. — Varannes, V. de. De gestis Joannæ virginis Francę. — Vita dé S. Clotilde. — Vita de S. Genovefa.

Tiziano Vecellio, *di Cadore.* Œuvre du T.; [avec] une description. (*In* Toulongeon, F. E. Man. du Mus. Fr., v. 8. 1805.)
— Lettere. (*In* Ticozzi, S. Vite dei Vecelli. 1817.)
— DUMAS, A. (*In his* Trois maîtres. 1861.)
— GILBERT, J. Cadore or Titian's country. London, 1869. 4°.
— MENGS, A. G. Riflessioni sopra i tre gran pittori Raffaello, il Coreggio, e Tiziano e sopra gli antichi. (*In his* Opere. 1787.)
— NORTHCOTE, J. Life of Titian. London, 1830. 2 v. 8°.
— PLANCHE, G. (*In* Revue d. D. Mondes, fév. 1857.)
— TICOZZI, S. (*In his* Vite dei Vecelli. 1817.)
— TOULONGEON, —. (*In his* Manuel du Muséum Français, v. 8. 1805.)
— VASARI, G. (*In his* Vite dei pittori, v. 13. 1857.)

Tizzoni, *Counts of Desana.* GAZZERA, C. Memorie storiche dei Tizzoni conti di Desana e notizia delle loro monete. (*In* Turin. Ac. d. Sci. Mem., ser. 2, v. 4. 1842.)

To be or not to be; tr. from Danish of H. C. Andersen by Mrs. Bushby. London, 1857. 12°.

To Daimonion; or, The Spiritual medium. *See* Samson, G. W.

To parents and guardians. (*In* Sargent, E. Mod. stand. dr., v. 16.)

To those born on the soil, who know nothing but the advancement of their country's good. N. Y., 1854. 8°. (B 1506)

Toadstools. *See* Mushrooms.

Toaldo, Giuseppe. Della vera influenza degli astri sulle stazioni e mutazioni di tempe. Padua, 1781. 4°.
— Tavole trigonometriche. Padua, 1794. 4°.
— FABRONI, A. (*In his* Vitæ Ital., v. 17. 1798.)

Tobacco. METAMORPHOSIS of tobacco. 1602. (*In* Collier, J. P. Illust. of early Eng. lit., v. 1. 1863.)
— JAMES I., *of England.* Counterblaste to tobacco. 1604. (*In his* Essays of a prentise. 1869.)
— MAGNEN, J. C. De tobaco exercitationes. Hagæ Com., 1658. 12°.
— VIRGINIA. *Gen. Assembly.* Case of the planters of tobacco in Virginia, *etc.* London, 1733. 8°.
— - *Another copy.* (B 1743)
— KNOX, T. Letter to W. Nelson [on the tobacco-duty]. Bristol, 1759. 8°. (W 32)
— FOWLER, T. Effects of tobacco in dropsies and dysuries. [1785.] 2d ed. rev. with add. London, 1788. 8°.
— CLARKE, A. Dissertations on the use and abuse of tobacco. [1797.] 3d ed. Liverpool, 1805. 8°. (B 822, 1550)
— - *Same.* 1st Amer. ed. Burlington, N. J., 1812. 8°. (B 822)
— TATHAM, W. Culture and commerce of tobacco. London, 1800. 8°.
— WATERHOUSE, B. Cautions to young persons conc. health. *n.p.*, 1805. 8°. (B 427)
— - *Same.* 5th ed. Camb., 1822. 8°. (B 1353, 1565)
— - *Germ.* Vorsichtsregeln zur Erhaltung der Gesundheit der Junglinge. Wien, 1808. 8°. (B 813)
— MCALLISTER, A. Diss. on the medical properties and injurious effects of tobacco. [1830.] 2d ed. Boston, 1832. 12°. (C 269)
— MUSSEY, R. D. Essay on the influence of tobacco upon life and health. Boston, 1836. 16°. (C 175)
— ADAMS, C. S. Poem on tobacco, before the Temperance Soc. of Orleans, Dec. 25, 1837. Boston, 1838. 12°. (C 80)
— FOWLER, O. Disquisition on the evils of using tobacco. 1841. 3d ed. Boston, 1842. 8°. (B 1553)
— BARRAL, J. A. L'industrie et le monopole des tabacs en France et à l'étranger. (*In* Revue d. D. Mondes, av. 1843.)
— LANE, B. I. Mysteries of tobacco; introd. letter by S. H. Cox. N. Y., 1846. 12°.
— BURDELL, J. Tobacco; its use and abuse. N. Y., 1848. 12°. (C 267)
— TRASK, G. Thoughts and stories on tobacco for American lads. Boston, 1852. 24°.
— PRESCOTT, H. P. Tobacco and its adulterations. London, 1858. 8°.
— WARREN, J. C. Use of tobacco. (*In* Mass. Temp. Soc. Addresses. 1861.)
— TURGAN, J. Manufacture impériale des tabacs. (*In his* Les grandes usines de France, v. 2. 1863.)
— DE COIN, R. L. History and cultivation of cotton and tobacco. London, 1864. 8°.
— COCKE, J. H. Treatise on tobacco. (*In* Delavan, E. C. Temperance essays. 1865.)
— BARRAL, —. Tabacs. (*In* France. *Com. Imp. de l'Expos. de* 1867. Rapports, v. 6. 1868.) — CAVARÉ, —. Préparation des tabacs. (*In* v. 8. 1868.)
— DU CAMP, M. Les manufactures de tabac à Paris. (*In* Revue d. D. Mondes, août 1868.)
— FISKE, J. Tobacco and alcohol. N. Y., 1869. 12°.
— PRESCOTT, H. P. Strong drink and tobacco smoke; structure, growth, and uses of tobacco. London, 1869. 8°.
— MURRAY, J. C. Smoking; when injurious, when innocuous, when beneficial. London, 1871. 12°.

Tobacconist, The; a farce. *See* Gentleman, F.

Tobago Island. P., J. C. Tobago insulæ Caraibicæ in America sitæ fatum. Groningæ, 1727. 4°.
— YOUNG, *Sir* W. Tour through the Islands of Barbadoes, Tobago, *etc.*, 1791-92. (*In* Edwards, B. Hist. survey of the Is. of St. Domingo. 1801.)
— DAUXION LAVAYSSE, J. F. Statistical, commercial, and political descr. of Venezuela, Trinidad, Margarita, and Tobago; from the French; with a preface and explanatory notes, by E. Blaquière. 2d ed. London, 1821. 8°.
— BYRES, J. Map. London, 1794. (E 67)

Tobey, Alvan. Christianity from God. Boston, *Amer. Tract Soc.*, *n.d.* 16°.

Tobey, Gerard Curtis. Biography of H. Richardson. (*In* Higginson, T. W. Harvard mem. biog., v. 1. 1866.)

Tobia. *See* Zeno, A.

Tobias Wilson; a tale, by J. Clemens. 1st ser. Phila., 1865. 16°.

Tobiesen, Henry A. Nauta. 1855. *See* Soden, C. T. von.

Tobin, John. The curfew; a play. *n.t.p.* [18—.] 12°. (D 44)
— *Same.* (*In* London stage, v. 4.)
— Honey-moon. (*In* Sargent, E. Mod. stand. dr., v. 1.)

Tobitt, John H. What I heard in Europe during the American excitement. N. Y., 1864. 8°.

Tobler, Titus. Beitrag zur medizinischen Topographie von Jerusalem. Berlin, 1855. 8°.
— Bethlehem in Palästina. St. Gallen, Bern, 1849. 8°.
— Bibliographica geographica Palæstinæ. Lipz., 1867. 8°.
— Denkblätter aus Jerusalem. 2e Ausg. Constanz, 1856. 8°.
— Golgatha; seine Kirchen und Klöster. St. Gallen, 1851. 8°.
— Die Siloahquelle und der Oelberg. St. Gallen, 1852. 8°.
— Topographie von Jerusalem. Berlin, 1853-54. 2 v. 8°.

Toby, *pseud.* Character of R. St—le; with remarks. London, 1713. 8°. (D 54)

Toby, Uncle. *See* **Trask**, G.

Tocci, Pier Francesco. Vita di V. Viviani. (*In* **Crescimbeni**, G. M. Vite degli Arcadi illustri, v. 1. 1708.)
— **Fabroni**, A. (*In his* Vitæ Ital., v. 17. 1798.)

Tocco (*Lat.* **Thocus**), Guglielmo. Vita S. Thomæ Aquinatis. (*In* **Acta** sanct., v. 7. 1865.)

Tochman, *Major* Gaspar. Petition to Congress. *n.p.*, 1847. 8°. (B 1450, 1460)
— To the Senate and Ho. of Rep.; supplementary petition. *n.p.*, 1848. 8°. (B 1460)
— Report of the committee on claims. *See* **Confederate States of Amer.** *Congress* (p. 645).

Tochon, Joseph François. **Dacier**, B. J. La vie et les ouvrages de T. (*In* **Paris. Inst.** *Ac. d. Inscr.* Mém., v. 8. 1827.)

Tochter Pharaonis, Die; von A. v. **Kotzebue**. (*In his* Theater, v. 16. 1841.)

Tocqueville, Alexis Charles Henri Clérel de. Œuvres; pub. par M. de Tocqueville. Paris, 1864. 9 v. 8°.

Contents. Vol. 1-3. La démocratie en Amérique. 4. L'ancien régime et la révolution. 5. Correspondance et œuvres posthumes. 6. Correspondance. 7. Nouvelle correspondance. 8. Mélanges. — Fragments historiques. — Notes sur l'ancien régime, la révolution, et l'empire. — Voyages. — Pensées. 9. Etudes économiques, politiques, et littéraires.

— Œuvres et correspondance inédites, préc. d'une notice par G. de Beaumont. Paris, 1861. 2 v. 8°.

Contents. Vol. 1. Notice sur A. de T. — Œuvres inédites. — Frag. de l'ouvrage qui devait faire suite à 'L'ancien régime et la révolution'. — Corr. inédite. 2. Corr. inédite, 1829-59.

— *Eng.* Memoirs, letters, and remains. Camb., London, 1861. 2 v. 8°.
— *Same.* Boston, 1862. 2 v. 16°.

Contents. Vol. 1. Memoir; by G. A. de la B. de Beaumont. — Unpublished works of A. de T. — France before the Consulate. — Letters to L. de Kergolay. — Letters to E. and A. Stoffels. — Letters, 1829-35. 2. Correspondence, *etc.*, 1835-59.

— L'ancien régime et la révolution. 2e éd. Paris, 1856. 8°.
— *Eng.* On the state of society in France before the Revolution; tr. by H. Reeve. London, 1856. 8°.
— Coup d'œil sur le règne de Louis XVI. Paris, [184-]. 8°.
— Démocratie en Amérique. 5e éd. Paris, 1836. 2 v. 12°.
— *Same.* 4e éd. Brux., 1837. 3 v. 12°.
— *Eng.* Democracy in America; tr. by H. Reeve. London, 1835. 4 v. 8°.

Note. Vol. 3 has the title 'Democracy in America; part the second'.

— *Same.* Tr. by H. Reeve; ed. with notes by F. Bowen. Camb., 1862. 2 v. 8°.
— Discours. (*In* **Paris. Inst.** *Acad. Fr.* Recueil des disc., 1840-49, pt. 1, 2.)
— Report to the chamber of deputies on the abolition of slavery in the French colonies, July 23, 1839; trans. Boston, 1840. 8°. (B 1471)
— Systeme pénitentiaire. *See* **Beaumont**, G. A. de la B. de.
— Several articles.] (*In* **Revue** d. D. Mondes, avr. 1840-déc. 1860.)
— **Greg**, W. R. (*In his* Literary and social judgments. 1869.)
— **Loménie**, L. de. (*In* **Revue** d. D. Mondes, mai 1859.) — **Janet**, P. (*In* juil. 1861.)
— **Review** of [his] 'Democracy in America'. From the London review, no. 3, Oct. 1835. N. Y., 1836. 12°. (C 297)
— **Towle**, G. M. (*In* **North** Amer. rev., v. 95. 1862; *and in his* Glimpses of history. 1866.)
— **Wegele**, F. X. A. von T. (*In* **Historische** Zeitscrift, v. 20. 1868.)

Tocsin, The; a solemn warning against the dangerous doctrine of nullification; [by M. Carey]. 4th ed. corr. Phila., 1832. 8°. (B 1636, 1790)

Tocsin, The; or, The call to arms; an essay; enquiry into the late proc. of Great Britain, in her attack upon the liberty of the United States. Charleston, 1807. 8°. (B 432)

Tod, Isabella M. S. Advanced education for girls of the upper and middle classes. (*In* **Nat. Assoc. Prom.** Soc. Sci. Trans., 1867.)

Tod, James, *Lieut.-Col.* Annals and antiquities of Rajast'han. London, 1829-32. 2 v. 4°.

Tod, Thomas. Consolatory thoughts on Amer. independence; by a merchant. Edin., 1782. 8°.
— *Another copy.* (W 32)

Tod Abels, Der; von S. **Gessner**. (*In his* Schriften, v. 1. 1762.)

Tod Adams, Der; von F. G. **Klopstock**. (*In his* Sämmt. Werke, v. 8. 1821.)

Tod des Dichters; von L. **Tieck**. (*In his* Gesam. Novellen, v. 3. 1853.)

Tod des Empedokles, Der. *See* **Hölderlin, J. C. F.**

To-day; a Boston literary journal, ed. by C. Hale. Vol. 1, 2. Boston, 1852: 2 v. 8°.

Todd, Alpheus. Parliamentary government in Eng. London, 1867-69. 2 v. 8°.

Todd, *Rev.* B., *and* **Lake**, E. H. The Middleborough discussion; a debate on universal salvation and endless punishment. Boston, 1850. 12°. (C 243)

Todd, Francis. Brief sketch of the trial of W. L. Garrison, for libel on F. Todd. *n.p.*, 1830. 8°. (B 1717)
— *Same.* Boston, 1834. 8°. (B 1435)

Todd, Henry John. Illustrations of the lives and writings of Gower and Chaucer. London, 1810. 8°.
— Memoirs of the life and writings of B. Walton. London, 1821. 2 v. 8°.
— Some acc. of the life and writings of J. Milton. 2d ed., with verbal index to the whole of M.'s poetry. London, 1809. 8°.
— *Same.* (*In* **Milton**, J. Poetical works, v. 1. 1801; v. 7. 1809.)
— Some account of the life of Spenser. (*In* **Spenser**, E. Works, v. 1. 1805.)

Todd, James Henthorn, *D.D.* The books of the Vaudois; Waldensian mss. in the Library of Trinity Coll., Dublin. London, 1865. 8°.
— Introduction and notes. (*In* **Wicliff**, J. Apology for Lollard doctrines. 1842. Camden Soc., v. 20.)
— On some fragments of an ancient waxed table-book found in a bog at Maghera. (*In* **Roy. Irish Acad.** Trans., v. 21. 1848.) — On an ancient Irish missal, and its silver box, described by Dr. O'Coner in his catalogue of the Stowe mss. (*In* v. 23. 1856.) — Descriptive catalogue of the contents of the Irish ms. commonly called 'The book of Fermoy'. — Some account of the Irish ms. deposited by the president De Robien in the public library of Rennes. (*In* Proc., Irish mss. ser., v. 1, pt. 1. 1870.)
— St. Patrick; a memoir. Dublin, 1864. 8°.
— The war of the Gaedhil with the Gaill; Irish text with tr. and introd. London, 1867. 8°. (Chron. and mem.)

Todd, John, *D.D.* Address, at Amherst Coll., Aug. 25, before the Society of Inquiry. Amherst, 1833. 8°. (B 1239)
— The foundations of success; oration before the Philomathæan and Phrenakosmian Societies of Pa. College, Sept. 19. Northampton, 1843. 12°. (C 273)
— Lectures to children; illustrating important truth. 2d ed. Northampton, 1834. 16°.

— *Same.* 6th ed. Northampton, 1835. 16°.
— Principles and results of congregationalism; sermon, dedication of the 1st. Cong. Church in Phila. Phila., 1837. 8°. (B 1310)
— The pulpit, its influence upon society; sermon, dedication of the Edwards Church in Northampton, Dec. 25, 1833; with the address at laying the corner stone, and statistics of the 1st Church in N. Northampton, 1834. 12°.
— Questions on the lives of the patriarchs, embracing the book of Genesis. Southampton, 1856. 16°.
— Religious teachers tested; sermon, dedication of Union Church in Groton, Mass. Camb., 1827. 8°. (B 1310)
— *and* Childs, H. H. Address. (*In* **Addresses** at the dedication of the new college building of the Berkshire Medical Inst. 1852. B 1587)
Todd, *Rev.* John E. Death in the palace; a sermon in memory of Everett, Jan. 22. Boston, 1865. 8°. (B 1961)
— Sketch of life and character of Hon. W. J. Hubbard, delivered at his funeral; with proc. of the Suffolk Bar, and remarks of Chief Justice Bigelow and H. W. Paine. Boston, 1864. 8°. (B 1639)
Todd, *Rev.* Jonathan. Faithful narrative of the proc. of the First Soc. in Wallingford; with a vindication of J. Dana, *etc.*, by W. Hart; [also] an app. New Haven, 1759. 8°. (B 155, 248)
— Reply to E. Eell's "Serious remarks upon the 'Faithful narrative'"; with supplement to the Narrative; [also] an answer to Hobart's Principles, *etc.*, by W. Hart. New Haven, 1760. 8°. (B 248)
Todd, Robert Bentley, *M.D.* Clinical lectures on certain diseases of the urinary organs, and of dropsies. Phila., 1857. 8°.
— Clinical lectures on paralysis and diseases of the brain. 2d ed. London, 1856. 16°.
— Cyclopædia of anatomy and physiology. London, 1835–59. 5 v. 8°.
— *and* Bowman, W. Physiological anatomy and physiology of man. Phila., 1857. 8°.
Todd, Sereno Edwards. Essay. (*In* **Judd,** O. Manual of flax culture. 1865.)
Todd, *Mrs.* Susan Hill. Occasional poems. Boston, 1851. 12°.
Todd, Tweedy John. Book of analysis; or induction applied to medicine, *etc.* London, 1831. 8°.
Todd, Wm. Oration before the Society of Free and Accepted Masons, in Keene, Dec. 27, 5789. Keene, N.H., [1789]. 4°. (B 1271)
Todd, Wm. C. Letter on Fort Venango. (*In* **Mass. Hist.** Soc. Proc., 1866-67.)
Toderini, Giovanni Battista, *il abate.* De la littérature des Turcs; tr. de l'ital. par A. de Cournand. Paris, 1789. 3 v. 8°.
Todhunter, Isaac. Algebra for the use of colleges. 4th ed. London and Camb., 1866. 8°.
Todi. LEONII, L. Documenti tratti dall' archivio segreto del comune di Todi. (*In* **Archivio** stor. ital., ser. 3, v. 2, pt. 2. 1865.)
Todi, Jacopone da. *See* **Jacopone** *da Todi.*
Todleben, *Gen.* Franziska Eduard. Défense de Sebastopol. Vol. 1. St. Pétersbourg, 1863, *and* Atlas. f°.
— RUSSELL, W. H. Review of T.'s History of the defence of Sebastopol. Lond., 1865. 8°.
Todte Neffe, Der; von A. v. **Kotzebue.** (*In his* Theater, v. 17. 1841.)
Toe. ASHTON, T. J. Ingrowing of toe-nails, corns, and bunions. London, 1852. 12°.
Toepfer, Karl. Dichter und Page; Lustspiel in einem Auszuge. Lond., Edin., [1860?]. 8°.
Toepffer, Rodolphe. Gesammelte Schriften. Lpz., 1847–52. 7 v. 16°.
Contents. Vol. 1. Die beiden Gefangenen. — Die Bibliothek. — Henriette. 2. Die beiden Scheldegg. — Die Erbschaft. — Col d'Auterne. 3. Elisa und Widmer. — Die See von Gers. — Jenzeit des Ozeans. — Das Thal von Trient. — Der grosse St. Bernhard. — Die Furcht. 4-7. Das Pfarrhaus.

— Nouveaux voyages en zigzag; avec notice par Sainte-Beuve. Paris, 1854. 8°.
— Nouvelles génévoises. 3e éd. illustrée. Paris, 1851. 8°.
— Premiers voyages en zigzag. 4e éd. Paris, 1855. 8°.
— Rosa et Gertrude; préc. de notices par Sainte-Beuve et de la Rive. Paris, 1855. 16°.
— SAINTE-BEUVE, C. A. (*In his* Portraits contemp., v. 2. 1852; — *and in* **Revue** d. D. Mondes, mars 1841.)
Toeppen, Max. Zur Geschichte der ständischen Verhältnisse in Preussen. (*In* **Historisches** Taschenbuch, 1847.) — Der lange königsberger Landtag. (*In* 1849.)
— Scriptores rerum Prussicarum. 1861–74. *See* **Hirsch,** T
Tofanelli, Agostino. Descrizione delle sculture e pitture che si trovano al Campidoglio. Ed. 4a. Roma, 1820. 16°.
— *French.* Descr. des objets de sculpture et de peinture qui se trouvent au Musée du Capitole. Rome, 1835. 12°.
Tofino de San Miguel, Vicente. Plan of the town and fortifications of Gibraltar; from the Spanish. [18—.] (E 232)
Tofts, Katherine. CLAYTON, E. C. (*In her* Queens of song. 1865.)
Togno, Joseph, *M.D.* Annual medical statistical report of [his] infirmary for the cure of deafness. Phila., 1835. 8°. (B 1111)
— Popular essay on acoustics, *etc.*; and anat. and physiology of the ear. Phila., 1834. 8°. (B 1563)
Tohfut-ul-Mujahideen. *See* **Zin-ud-din.**
Toilers of the sea; a novel, [by V. Hugo]. N. Y., 1866. 8°.
Toilet. *See* **Cosmetics.**
Toiras, Jean du Caylar de St. Bonnet, *mareschal* de. BAUDIER, M. Histoire du mareschal de T. Paris, 1644. f°.
Toison d'Or, Ordre de la. *See* **Order of the Golden Fleece.**
Token, The; a Christmas and new year's present. *See* **Goodrich,** S. C.
Token for children. *See* **Janeway,** J.
Tokens. *See* **Numismatics;** for London tokens *see* **London.** *Trades*(p. 1777).
Tola Efisio. AMATO, G. d'. (*In his* Panteon, v. 2. 1851.)
Toland, John. Danger of mercenary parliaments. *t.p.mut.* London, 172-. 8°. (B 1517)
— Funeral elogy and character of Princess Sophia. London, 1714. 8°. (D 54)
— Life of J. Harrington. (*In* **Harrington,** J. Oceana, 1700; 1747; 1871.)
— Remarks on the state anatomy of Gr. Brit. London, 1707. 8°. (B 756)
— *Same.* 9th ed. London, [171-]. 8°. (B 756)
— *Same.* 2d part. 2d ed. London, 1717. 8°. (B 756)
— Tetradymus, containing Hodegus, Clidophorus, Hypatia, Mangoneutes. London, 1720. 8°. (B 32)
See also **Political** classics.
— BLACKALL, O. Reasons for not replying to [T.'s 'Amyntor'. London, 1699. 8°. (C 227)
— CLARKE, S. Some reflections on that part of Amyntor which relates to the writings of the primitive Fathers and the New Testament. (*In his* Works, v. 3. 1738.)
— D'ISRAELI, I. (*In his* Calamities of authors, v. 2. 1812.)
— NICERON, J. P. (*In his* Mém., v. 1. 1729; *and Germ.*, v. 2. 1749.)
— NYE, S. Historical acct. of the canon of the New Testament; answer to Amyntor. London, 1700. 8°. (B 117)
Toldervy, Wm. Select epitaphs. London, 1755. 2 v. 12°.
Toldy, Franz. (*In* **Ungarns** Männer. 1862.)
Toledo, Francisco. Commentaria et quæstiones in Aristotles libros de anima. *t.p.w.* [Colon. Agrip., 1576.] 4°.
Toledo, Gabriel Alvarez de. Noticias biográficas. — Poesias. (*In* **Cueto,** L. A. de. Poetas liricos del siglo 18. 1869; v. 61 of Aribau. Bibl.)
Toledo, *Ohio.* WALES, C. T. Statement of trade and commerce for 1862–63, 65; prepared for the Toledo blade. Toledo, 1864–66. 2 v. 8°.

Toledo, *Spain*. Articles of agreement between Toledo and R. Jones for supplying the inhabitants with water. London, 1723. 8°. (B 899)
— JONES, R. Articles of agreement between Jones [and others, forming a joint-stock company or the Toledo Water Works]. London, 1723. 8°. (B 899)
— ANALES Toledanos. (*In* **Florez, H.** España sagrada, v. 23. 1767.)
— FLORINI, M. Toledo. *n.p.*, [16—]. (**E 78**, no. 21)
Toledo, *Spain*. **Cathedral.** FLOREZ, H. De la iglesia de Toledo. (*In his* España sagrada, v. 5, 6. 1750–51.)
— MADRID. AC. D. L. HIST. Memoria sobre la inscripcion hebrea de la iglesia de Nuestra Señora del Tránsito de Toledo, que publicò J. J. Heydeck. (*In its* Mem., v. 3. 1799.)
Toleration. *See* **Comprehension**; — **Dissenters**; — **Liberty, Religious**; — **Liberty of conscience.**
Tolet, François. Traité de la lithotomie. Paris, 1682. 12°.
Toll, Thomas. Dipper dipped; answer to Anabaptists. London, 1661. 8°.
— Female duel; between a Rom. Catholic lady and the wife of a dignitary of the Church of England. London, 1661. 8°.
Tolla; par E. About. Paris, 1856. 12°.
Tolland, *Conn.* WALDO, L. P. Early history of T. Hartford, 1861. 8°.
Tolland Co. Assoc. Reply to Mr. Abbot's statement of proceedings in the First Society, Coventry, Conn. Hartford, 1812. 8°. (**B 260**)
Tolommei, Claudio. Madrigali. (*In* **Trucchi, F.** Poesie ital., v. 3. 1847.)
— Orazione contra Leone Secretario. (*In* **Raccolta di** prose ital., v. 2. 1809.)
— Sonetti. (*In* **Gironi, R.** Rac. di lir. ital. 1808.)
Tolommeo dei Fiadoni. Historia ecclesiastica ad 1312, cum add. (*In* **Muratori, L. A.** Rerum Ital. scr., v. 11. 1727.)
— Roberti Guiscardi ac aliorum regum Siciliæ genealogia. (*In* **Grævius.** Thes. antiq. Sicil., v. 5. 1723.)
Tolondron. *See* **Baretti, G.**
Tolosanus, Joannes Pinus. *See* **Pins, J. de.**
Tolrà, Juan José. Compendio hist. de la vida, *etc.*, de J. F. de Isla. *t.p.w.* [Madrid, 1803?] 16°.
Tolson, F. Hermathenæ; or, Moral emblems and ethnick tales. *n.t.p.* [London? 17—.] 8°.
Tolstoï, Nicola. Nicolinka; [autobiographie juvenile] tr. de la trad. anglaise de Meysenberg par P. E. D. Forgues. (*In* **Revue** d. D. Mondes, fév. 1863.)
Tolynus. Fragm. (*In* **Meineke, A.** Poet. com. fr. 1855.)
Tom *o'Bedlam*, *pseud.* The great Jesuit swallows the less; defence of Tom o'Bedlam's first letter to F. de la Pillonniere. London, [17—]. 8°. (**B 31**)
— Letter to the B - - - [Bishop] of B - - - r's [Bangor's] Jesuit. London, 1717. 8°. (**B 31**)
Tom *the joyner*, *pseud.* The ripping up of Sir John Presbyter's garment, or The ground-work of schism, *etc.* *n.t.p.* [167–.] f°. (**A 54**)
Tom a Lincolne. (*In* **Thoms, W. J.** Early Eng. prose romances, v. 2. 1858.)
Tom Brown at Oxford; by [T. Hughes]. Boston, 1861. 2 v. 12°.
— *Same.* Boston, 1869. 2 pt. 12°.
Note. From **Macmillan's** mag., v. 1–4. 1860–61.
Tom Brown's school days; by [T. Hughes]. Camb., 1857. 12°.
Tom Burke of Ours; by C. Lever. Vol. 1 Phila., v. 2 Boston, 1844. 2 v. 8°.
Tom Cringle; a drama, by E. **Fitzball.** (*In* **Sargent, E.** Mod. stand. dr., v. 18.)
Tom Cringle's log; by M. Scott. New ed. Edin., London, 1854. 12°.
— *Same.* 2d ser. Phila., 1833. 2 v. 12°.
Note. First published with various titles, 'Scene off Bermuda', *etc.*, in Blackwood's mag., v. 29–34. 1831–33.
Tom Jones, History of. (*In* **Fielding, H.** Works, v. 7–9. 1815; v. 6–7. 1821.)
Tom Jones à Londres. *See* **Desforges.**
Tom Noddy's secret; a farce. *See* **Bayly, T. H.**
Tom Pippin's wedding; a novel; [by H. W. Pullen]. Phila., 1871. 16°.
Tom Thumb; a burlesque opera. *See* **O'Hara, K.**
Tom Thumb the little, Metrical hist. of, as issued early in the 18th cent.; ed. by J. O. Halliwell. London, 1860. 16°.

Tom Tiddler's ground; a Christmas budget, by C. Dickens and others. N. Y., 1861. 8°.
Tomas [**Garcias**] *de Villanova*, *St.* MUGNATONIUS, J. — SALON, M. (*In* **Acta** sanct., v. 45. 1868.)
Tomas. *See also* **Thomas**; — **Tommas.**
Tomasini, Jacopo Filippo. NICERON, J. P. (*In his* Mém., v. 29. 1734.)
Tomb, Samuel. Oration on the auspicious birth, sublime virtues, and triumphant death of Washington, Feb. 22, Newbury 2d parish; [with] 2 odes and an acrostic. Newburyport, 1800. 8°. (**E 48**)
— Sermon, March 31, [fast day]. Newburyport, 1803. 8°. (**B 171**)
Tomb of James Molai; or, The secret of the conspirators. Boston, 1797. 8°. (**B 1096**)
Tombeau de Nostradamus, Le; en un acte. *See* **Le Sage, A. R.**
Tombeau sur la colline, Le; tr. de l'allemand de A. F. F. Kotzebue. (*In* **Biblioth.** univ. des romans, Nouv., v. 39. 1801.)
Tombleson, W. Views of the Rhine; ed. by W. G. Fearnside. London, 1852. 2 v. 8°.
Tombs. *See* **Burial**; — **Funerals**; — **Sepulchres.**
Tombuctoo. *See* **Timbuctoo.**
Tomes, Charles Sissmore. Address at the commencement of the Dental Dept. in Harv. Univ., Feb. 12. St. Louis, 1873. 8°. (**H 8**)
Tomes, Robert. Americans in Japan; abridgment of the narrative of the Com. Perry exped. N. Y., 1857. 12°.
— The champagne country. N. Y., 1867. 8°.
— Panama in 1855. N. Y., 1855. 16°.
Tomkins. *See also* **Tompkins.**
Tomkins, Martin. Case of M. Tomkins; an account of the proc. of the dissenting congregation at Stoke-Newington, upon occasion of a sermon by him, July 13, 1718. London, 1719. 8°. (**B 110**)
— Jesus Christ the mediator. 2d ed. London, 1761. 8°. (**B 1917**)
Tomkins, *Rev.* Martin. HERVEY, J. Three letters on Tomkins' 'Calm inquiry'. (*In* **Amana.** Catholic question. 1815. **B 266**)
Tomkins the troubadour; a farce, by Messrs. Lockroy and Marc Michel. (No. 134 *of* **De Witt's** acting plays.)
Tomkinson, *Rev.* Joseph, *Funeral sermon on.* 1837. *See* **Mattison, S.** (**B 1226**)
Tomkis, —. Albumazar. (*In* **Dodsley, R.** Col. of plays, v. 7. 1825: — *and in* **Scott,** *Sir* **W.** Anc. Brit. dr., v. 2. 1810.)
Tomline, George Pretyman, *Bp.* Charge to the the clergy of the diocese of Lincoln. (*In* **Pamphleteer,** 1813; v. 1 of **B 838**)
— Elements of Christian theology. Vol. 1. London, 1799. 8°.
— Introduction to the study of the Bible. Phila., 1806. 12°.
— Memoirs of the life of Wm. Pitt. Phila., 1821. 2 v. 8°.
— Refutation of Calvinism. 6th ed. London, 1812. 8°.
— Sermon, Dec. 19, 1797, thanksgiving. London, 1798. 4°. (**B 1252**)
— ADAIR, *Sir* R. Letters in answer to a charge made in the 'Life of W. Pitt'. Lond., 1821. 8°.
— EUSTACE, J. C. Answer to the charge delivered by the Bp. of Lincoln. (*In* **Pamphleteer,** 1813; v. 2 of **B 838**)
— FREND, W. Animadversions on the 'Elements of Christian theology'. London, 1800. 8°.
— - *Another copy.* (**B 131**)
Tomlins, *Sir* Thomas Edlyne. Proc. of the Court of Enquiry upon the conduct of Sir H. Dalrymple in Portugal, 1808; with his life, *etc.* London, 1808. 8°.
Note. The initials in the book are W. E.
Tomlinson, Charles. Experimental essays. London, *Weale*, 1863. 12°.
Contents. On motions of camphor on water. — Motion of camphor towards light. — History of the modern theory of dew.
— Introd. to the study of natural philosophy. 3d ed. London, *Weale*, 1853. 12°.

— Pneumatics. 3d ed. London, *Weale*, 1854. 12°.
— Pottery and porcelain. (*In* C., W. T. Hist. of proc. of manuf. and uses of printing, *etc.* 1864.)
— Rudimentary mechanics. 4th ed. London, *Weale*, 1855. 12°.
— Rudimentary treatise on the construction of locks. London, *Weale*, 1853. 12°.
— Rudimentary treatise on warming and ventilation. London, *Weale*, 1850. 12°.
— Winter in the Arctic Regions. Lond., [1860]. 16°.
Tomlinson, Daniel, *Jr.*, *Funeral sermon on.* 1810. *See* **Snell,** T. (B 332)
Tomlinson, John C. Science of phrenology consistent with the doctrine of Christianity. (*In* **Pamphleteer,** 1826; v. 26 of B 838)
Tommas. *See also* **Thomas**; — **Tomas.**
Tommas, John. Oration at the grave of J. Newton; and sermon at the interment, by C. Evans. Bristol, [1790]. 8°. (B 1221)
Tommaseo, Niccolò. Canti popolari, toscani, corsi, illirici, greci. Venezia, 1841-42. 4 v. 8°.
Contents. Vol. 1. Toscani. 2. Corsi. 3. Greci. 4. Illirici.
— Intorno ad un passo disputato di Paolo diacono. (*In* **Archivio** stor. ital., app., v. 7. 1849.) — Sopra gli studi storici e le pubblicazioni dei monumenti. (*In* n.s., v. 1, pt. 1.) — Della civiltà italiana nelle Isole Ionie e di N. Delviniotti. (*In* v. 2, pt. 1.) — Della Corsica di P. de Paoli e M. Buttafuoco. (*In* v. 11, pt. 2.) — Moti fiorentini del 1378 de' quali ebbe Caterina da Sienna. (*In* v. 12, pt. 1.) — Andrea Mustoxidi. (*In* v. 12, pt. 2.) — Pensieri sulla storia di Firenze. (*In* v. 13, pt. 2.) — Salvatore Viale e la Corsica. (*In* v. 15, pt. 2.) — D'una sconfitta nel Vicentino rammentata nel IX. canto del Paradiso di Dante. (*In* v. 12, pt. 2.) — Concetto storico, civile, e morale della poesia di Virgilio. (*In* ser. 3a, v. 13, pt. 3. 1871.) — Batracomiomachia, esperimento di recensione critica, con traduzione letterale. (*In* 3a ser., v. 14. 1871.)
— Nuovo dizionario dei sinonimi della lingua italiana. 4a ed. Milano, 1858-59. 2 v. 8°.
Contents. Vol. 1. A-L. 2. W-Z.
— Scintille. [Venezia, 1841.] 8°.
— L'universo. — Natura ed arte. — Solitudine. — Ad una. — Ad altra. (*In* Poeti ital. contem. 1843.)
Tommasi, Antonio. Sonetti. (*In* **Gironi,** R. Rac. di lir. ital. 1808.)
Tommasi, Donato. Elogio storico del G. Filangieri. (*In* **Filangieri,** G. La scienza della legislazione, v. 1. 1807.)
Tommasi, Francesco. Continuatio historiæ Senensis J. Bandini de Bartholomæis. (*In* **Muratori,** L. A. Rer. Ital. scr., v. 20. 1731.)
Tommasi, Girolamo. Sommario della storia di Lucca, 1004-1700, contin. all anno 1799 per curo di C. Minutoli. (*In* **Archivio** stor. ital., v. 10. 1847.)
Tommasi, Giuseppe Maria. BORROMEO, A. M. Vita. (*In* **Crescimbeni,** G. M. Vite degli Arcadi illustri, v. 3. 1714.)
— NICERON, J. P. (*In his* Mém., v. 3. 1727; *and, Germ.*, v. 4. 1751.)
Tommassini, Jacopo Filippo, *Bp.* De donariis ac tabellis votivis. (*In* **Grævius,** J. G. Thes. antiq. Rom., v. 12. 1699.)
— Laurentii Pignorii vita, bibliotheca, et museum. (*In* **Grævius,** J. G. Thes. antiq. Ital., v. 6, pt. 3. 1722.)
— De tesseris hospitalitatis. — Manus æneæ Cecropii votum referentis dilucidatio. (*In* **Gronovius.** Thes. Gr. antiq., v. 9, 10. 1701.)
— NICERON, J. P. (*In his* Mém., v. 29. 1734.)
Tommasini-Paruta, Tommaso. AGOSTINI, G. (*In his* Notizie degli scr. viniz., v. 1. 1752.)
Tommaso I, *conte di Savoja.* SCLOPIS DI SALERANO, F. P. Considerazioni storiche intorno a T.; con aggiunta di documenti inediti. (*In* **Turin.** Ac. d. Sci. Mem., v. 34. 1830.)
Tommaso, Alvise Contarini di. Compendio dei dispacci, 1630-32. (*In* **Barozzi,** N., *and* **Berchet,** G. Relazioni degli stati europei, ser. 2, v. 2. 1859.)
Tommasuccio. Profezia. (*In* **Trucchi,** F. Poesie ital., v. 2. 1846.)
Tommy Try and what he did in science. *See* **Napier,** C. O. G.
Tomo Chi-Chi, *Mico of the Yamacraws.* JONES, C. C., *Jr.* Historical sketch of Albany. N. Y., 1868. 8°.
Tompkins. *See also* **Tomkins.**
Tompkins, Cornelia M. FORMAN, *Rev.* J. G. (*In* **Brockett,** L. P. Woman's work in the civil war. 1867.)
Tompkins, *Gov.* Daniel D. Letter to A. M'Intyre. *n.p.*, 1819. 8°. (B 997)
— Message. 1812. *See* **N. Y.** *Governor.* (B 444)
— EDMONDS, J. W. Some passages in the life of Gov. Tompkins. (*In* **New York Hist. Soc.** Proceedings. 1844.)
— M'INTYRE, A. Letter. Albany, 1820. 8°. (B 1418)
— GRANGER, G. Reason for voting against the grant of $11,875.50 to Gov. T. Albany, [1829]. 8°. (B 1457)
— SKETCH.] (*In* **Longacre,** J. B., *and* **Herring,** J. Nat. portr. gal., v. 1. 1837.)
Tompkins, Edward. Speech. (*In* **Litchfield Co.,** *Conn.* Centennial celebration. 1851.)
Tompkins, Isaac. The character and future blessedness of the righteous; sermon at the funeral of Mrs. M. C. Burnham. Concord, 1814. 8°. (B 1785)
Tompkins County, *N. Y.* TROWBRIDGE, D. Account of ancient fort and burial-ground in Tomkins Co. (*In* **Smithsonian Inst.** Report, 1863.)
Toms, John. The great mission of the Son of God, *etc.*; sermon, decease of W. Tucker; address at the interment, and memoir of W. Tucker. Chard, 1814. 8°. (B 1226)
Tomson, Robert. Voy. into New Spaine, *etc.*, 1555. (*In* **Hakluyt,** R. Col. of voy., v. 3. 1810.)
Tone, John F. On railways and locomotives. (*In* **Armstrong,** *Sir* W. G., *and others.* Industrial res. of the Tyne. *etc.* 1864.)
Tone, Theobald Wolfe. Argument in behalf of the Catholics of Ireland. 5th ed. Dublin, 1792. 8°.
— *Another copy.* (C 155)
— Life of T.; by himself; ed. by W. T. W. Tone. Wash., 1826, 2 v. 8°.
Contents. Vol. 1. Life previous to his mission to France. — App. to Life, 1789-95. — Political works. 2. Life and journals during his mission to France, and acc. of his family after his death. — App. to Life, 1799-1816.
Tone, Wm. Theobald Wolfe. Essay on the necessity of improving our national forces. N. Y., 1819. 8°. (B 545)
— School of cavalry; system of organization, *etc.*, proposed for the cavalry of the U. S. Georgetown, 1824. 8°.
Tonelli, Giovanni. Poesie. (*In* **Gamba,** B. Rac. di poesie in dial. venez. 1845.)
Toner, Joseph M., *M.D.* History of inoculation in Massachusetts. (*In* **Mass. Med. Soc.** Pub., v. 2. 1867.)
— Maternal instinct or love. Balt., 1864. 18°.
Tong, *Rev.* Wm. Account of the life and death of M. Henry. Berwick, 1794. 12°.
— EMLYN, T. Remarks on 'The doctrine of the trinity defended by four London ministers', *etc.* London, 1719. 8°. (B 112)
— LETTER to [him on] the late differences amongst the Dissenters; by a layman. 2d ed. London, 1719. 8°. (B 1865)
— LETTER to Mr. Tong, Robinson, and others. *t.p.w.* [1719.] 8°. (B 110)
Tonga Islands. AUTHENTIC narrative of a four years' residence at Tongataboo, 1796. London, 1810. 8°.
— MARTIN, J. Account of the natives of the Tonga Islands, from the com. of W. Mariner, 1805. 1st Amer. ed. Boston, 1820. 8°.
— — *Same.* 3d ed. Edin., 1827. 2 v. 12°. (Constable's miscel., v. 13, 14.)
Tonge, Thomas. Heraldic visitation of the northern counties, 1530; ed. by W. H. D. Longstaffe. London, 1862. 8°. (Surtees Soc., v. 41.)
Tongiorgi, Salvatore. Institutions philosophicæ. Ed. alt. Paderbornæ, 1863. 3 v. 12°.
Contents. Vol. 1. Logica. 2. Ontologia. — Cosmologia. 3. Psychologia. — Theologia.
Tong-kien-kang-mou; histoire gén. de la Chine; tr. par J. A. M. M. de Mailla; pub. par Grosier. Paris, 1777. 4 v. 4°.
Contents. Vol. 1. B.C. 2953-967. 2. B.C. 966-141. 3. B.C. 140 - A.D. 194. 4. 194-420.

Tongue, James. Inaug. diss.; attempt to prove that the the lues venerea was not introduced into Europe from America; experimental inquiry into the modus operandi of mercury; experimental proof that lues venerea and gonorrhea are distinct forms of disease. 1801. (*In* **Caldwell, C.** Medical theses, v. 2. 1806.)

Tongue. MALLE, P. F. N. On swelling of the tongue. (*In* **Paris. Acad. de Chirurg.** Sel. mem. **1848.**)

— COOK, H. Diseases of the tongue. (*In* **Holmes,** T. Syst. of surg., v. 3. **1862.**)

Toni; ein Drama, von C. T. **Körner.** (*In his* Sämmt. Werke. 1801; Dramatische Beyträge, v. 1. 1821.)

Tonna, *Mrs.* Charlotte Elizabeth (Browne Phelan), *pseud.* **Charlotte Elizabeth.** Works; with introd. by **H. B. Stowe.** N. Y., 1844-47. 2 v. 8°.

Contents. Vol. 1. Personal recollections. — Osric. — The rockite. — Helen. — Fleetwood. — Siege of Derry. — Letters from Ireland. — Miscel. poems. — Flower garden. — War with the saints. 2. Judæa capta. — Deserter. — Falsehood and truth. — Judah's lion. — Conformity. — Wrongs of women. — Passing thoughts. — Izram. — Principalities and powers. — Second causes. — Poems.

— Floral biography. 4th Amer. from 2d Lond. ed. N. Y., 1844. 12°.

— Judæa capta. N. Y., 1845. 8°.

Tonnage. *See* **Gauging.**

Tonneaux, Les deux; opéra comique. *See* **Voltaire, F. M. A. de.**

Tonning, Henricus. Rariora Norvegiæ. (*In* **Linné,** C. Amœn. acad., v. 7. 1769.)

Tonquin. MISSION du Tonquin, **1630-65.** (*In* **Voy.** et trav. des missionnaires de la Comp. de Jésus, v. 2. 1858.)

— BESCHREIBUNG von Tunkin, **[1685].** (*In* **Allgemeine** Hist., v. 10. 1752.)

— TAVERNIER, J. B. Relation du royaume de Tunquin. (*In his* Rec. de plusieurs relations. **1692.**)

— BARON, S. Description of the kingdom of T., [17—]. (*In* **Churchill,** O. *and* J. Col. of voy., v. 6. 1746; — *and in* **Pinkerton,** J. Col. of voy., v. 9. 1811.)

— RICHARD, J. History of Tonquin, [1778?]. (*In* **Pinkerton,** J. Col. of voy., v. 9. 1811.)

Tonti, *le chevalier.* Dernières découvertes dans l'Amérique Septentrionale de M. de la Sale. Paris, 1697. 16°.

— *Eng.* Account of M. de La Salle's last expedition and discoveries in North America. (*In* **New York Hist. Soc.** Col., v. 2. 1814.)

Note. 'The book bearing Tonty's name is a compilation full of error. He disowned its authorship'. — *Parkman.* La Salle, p. 129. — The 'Memoir' mentioned below forms the basis of the 'Découvertes.'

— Memoir sent in 1693, on the discovery of the Mississippi by M. de La Salle from the year 1678 to the time of his death, and by the Sieur de Tonty to 1691. (*In* **French,** B. F. Hist. col. of Louisiana, v. 1. 1846.)

— Petition to the King. — Account of the route from the Illinois by the River Mississippi to the Gulf of Mexico. (*In* **French,** B. F. Hist. col. of Louisiana, v. 1. 1846.)

Tontine, La; comédie. *See* **Le Sage, A. R.**

Tony Butler; by C. Lever. (*In* **Blackwood's** mag., v. 94-97. 1863-65; — *and in* **Littell's** living age, v. 79-84. 1863-65.)

Tony Lumpkin in town. *See* **O'Keeffe, J.**

Too bright to last; a novel; [by A. Fisher]. Boston, 1869. 8°.

Too true; a story of to-day. (*In* **Putnam's** mag., n.s., v. 1, 2. 1868.)

Toogood, John, *D.D.* The book of nature; a discourse on the power, *etc.*, of God; [with] the duty of mercy, from Primatt's dissertation. Bost., 1802. 12°. (**C 145**)

Toohey, Martin. Trial for murder. *See* **Strobel, M.**

Tooke, Andrew. The Pantheon. *See* **Pomey, F. A.**

Tooke, John Horne. Ἔπεα πτερόεντα; or, The diversions of Purley. 1st Amer. from 2d Lond. ed. Phila., 1806-07. 2 v. 8°.

— Letter to a friend on the reported marriage of the Prince of Wales. 2d ed. London, 1787. 8°. (**B 595**)

— Letter to Ld. Ashburton [on] the debate in the Ho. of Commons, on Mr. Pitt's motion. London, *n.d.* 8°. (**B 767**)

— Warning to the electors of Westminster; [reply to J. Paull]. London, 1807. 8°. (**B 1416, 1673**)

— BARCLAY, J. A sequel to the Diversions of Purley. London, 1826. 8°.

— BEDDOES, T. Spirit and tendency of the doctrines of nature of demonstrative evid. 1793.)

— BLANCHARD, —. Trial for libel, July 4, 1777. London, 1767 [1777]. 4°. (**A 14**)

— BROUGHAM, H., *Ld.* (*In his* Statesmen of times of George III., ser. 2. 1839.)
the Ἔπεα πτερόεντα· (*In his* Observations on the

— CATALOGUE of his library sold, 1813; [with ms. prices and names]. London, *n.d.* 8°.

— FEARN, J. Anti-Tooke; an analysis of principles, *etc.*, of language. London, 1824. 8°.

— HAZLITT, W. Tooke's 'Diversions of Purley'. (*In his* Literary remains, v. 1. 1836.)

— PAULL, J. Refutation of his calumnies. London, 1807. 8°. (**B 1419**)

— ROGERS, S. (*In his* Recollctions. 1859.)

— STEPHENS, A. Memoirs of J. H. Tooke. London, 1813. 2 v. 8°.

— - Sketch of T. (*In* **Junius.** Post. works. 1829.)

— TUCKERMAN, H. T. The philologist. (*In his* Characteristics of lit., 2d ser. 1851.)

— YOUNG, A. (*In his* Miscel. works, v. 3. 1855.)

Tooke, Thomas. History of prices, 1792-1856. London, 1823-57. 6 v. 8°.

Note. Vol. 1, 2 are entitled Thoughts and details of the high and low prices of the last 30 years; 3, History of prices and of the circulation in 1838 and 39, with remarks on the corn laws and on alterations proposed in the banking system; 4, History of prices, 1839-47, with a review of the currency question; 5, 6, History of prices, 1848-56; by T. Tooke and W. Newmarch.

Tooke, Wm., *b.* 1744. History of Russia to the accession of Catharine II. London, 1800. 2 v. 8°.

Contents. Vol. 1. Introd.: Of the Slaves. — Hist. 862-1613. — Obs. on the state of civilization in the Russian nation to 1613. — Hist. inquiry conc. the situation of Tmutarakan; by A. I. M. Paschkin. — St. Petersburg. — Narva. — Dorpat. — Reval. — Riga. — Cronstadt. — Archangel. 2. Hist. 1613-1762. — Sketch of Mosco.

— Life of Catharine II. 4th ed. London, 1800. 3 v. 8°.

— View of the Russian Empire during the reign of Catharine II. and to the close of 18th cent. 3d ed. Dublin, 1801. 3 v. 8°.

Tooke, Wm., *b.* 1777. Life of C. Churchill. (*In* **Churchill,** J. Poet. works. 1854.)

Toole, *Rev. Canon.* Religion an essential element in the school education of the poor. (*In* **Nat. Assoc.** Prom. Soc. Sci. Trans., 1866.)

Tooley, Nicholas. COLLIER, J. P. (*In his* Mem. of the principal actors in the plays of Shakespeare. 1846. Shakespeare Soc., v. 39.)

Toomer, Joshua W. Oration at the 1st centennial of the South Carolina Soc. Charleston, 1837. 8°. (**B 1129, 1696**)

Tootle, Hugh. Church hist. of England, 1500-1688, chiefly with regard to the Catholics. Brussels [Sherborne], 1737-42. 3 v. f°.

Contents. Vol. 1. 1500-58. 2. 1558-1622. 3. 1622-88.

Topham, Edward. Address to E. Burke on his late letter, rel. to the affairs of America. Lond., 1777. 4°. (**A 20**)

— Life of J. Elwes. 2d ed. (*In* **Pamphleteer,** 1825; v. 25 of **B 838**)

Topham, John. Some account of the collegiate chapel of St. Stephen's; [with descr. of add. plates by Sir H. C. Englefield. London, *Soc. of Antiq.*, 1795.] f°.

Topics of the time. *See* **Parton, J.**

Topin, Marius. The man with the iron mask; tr. and ed. by H. Vizetelly. London, 1870. 8°.

Topinard, Paul. L'ataxie locomotrice progressive. Paris, 1864. 8°.

Toplady, Augustus Montagu. Church of England vindicated from the charge of Arminianism; letter to Nowell. London. 1769. 8°. (**B 21**)

— Clerical subscription no grievance; the doctrines of the Church of Eng. proved to be the doctrines of Christ; sermon. London, 1772. 8°. (**B 904**)

— Free thoughts on the projected application to Parl. for the abolition of ecclesiastical subscription. London, 1771. 8°. (**B 904**)

— Letter to J. Wesley [on] his pretended abridgment of Zanchius on predestination. 2d ed. London, 1771. 8°. (B 1371)
— Two letters to Dr. Priestley. (*In* **Amana.** Remarks on American Unitarianism. 1815. B 266)
— FLETCHER, J. Answer to Toplady's 'Vindication of the decrees'. — Reply to the principal arguments by which the Calvinists support the doctrine of absolute necessity; being remarks on T.'s 'Scheme'. (*In his* Works. v. 7. 1802.)
— MEMOIRS of T. Boston, 1817. 8°. (B 263)

Topliff, Nathaniel. Poems. Boston, 1809. 12°.
— *Funeral sermon on.* 1819. *See* **Harris,** T. M. (B 283)

Topographical drawing. EASTMAN, S. Treatise on topographical drawing. New York, 1837. 8°.
— MAHAN, D. H. (*In his* Industrial drawing. 1858.)

Topography. *See* **Geography**; — **Surveying.**

Topography, Military. *See* **Military Topography.**

Toppan, David. Duty of private Christians to pray for their ministers; two sermons, Apr. 24, 1774. Newbury-port, 1778. 8°. (C 42)

Toppi, Nicolò. Biblioteca napoletana, et apparato a gli huomini illustri in lettere di Napoli, ec. Napoli, 1678. f°.

Topsfield, *Mass.* CLEAVELAND, N. Address, 200th anniv. of the incorporation of Topsfield, Mass., 1850. N. Y., 1851. 8°.

Topsham, *Ga.* LECTURES on the recent relig. excitements in Brunswick and T. Brunswick, 1834. 8°. (B 1358)

Topsham, *Me.* ELLIS, J. Description of Topsham, Me. (*In* **Mass. Hist. Soc.** Col., v. 3. 1794.)

Toquera vizcaina, La; por J. P. de Montalvan. (*In* **Ochoa,** E. de. Tesoro del teatro esp., v. 4. 1838; — *and in* **Mesonero Romanos,** R. de. Dram. contemp. **à** Lope de Vega, v. 2. 1858; v. 45 of Aribau. Bibl.)

Tor di Nona. GIORGI, F. Descrizione del teatro. Roma, 1795. 4°.

Tor Hill; [by H. Smith]. Phila., 1826. 2 v. 12°.

Torcy, *marquis* de. *See* **Colbert,** J. B., *marq. de Torcy.*

Tordenskiold, Peder Wessel. DAVENPORT, R. A. (*In his* Lives of individuals who have raised themselves to eminence. 1841. Fam. lib., v. 79.)

Tordenskiold; Syngespil, af Öhlenschläger. Kiöb., 1821. 8°.

Tordo, Giuseppe. GIRARDI, L. A. (*In* **Amato,** G. d'. Panteon, v. 1. 1851.)

Toreen, Olof. Voyage à Suratte, à la Chine, *etc.*, 1750–52; tr. par D. Blackford. Milan, 1771. 12°.
— *Eng.* Voyage to Suratte, China, *etc.*; tr. by J. R. Forster. (*In* **Osbeck,** P. Voy. 1771.)

Torelli, Lelio. Lettere. (*In* **Dati,** C. Prose fior., pt. 4, v. 4. 1751.)

Torelli *di Ferrara*, Famiglia di. (*In* **Litta,** P. Fam., v. 4.)

Torelli Strozzi, Barbara. In morte del marito. (*In* **Poeti** ital. contemp. 1843.)

Toreno, José Maria Queypo de Llano Ruiz de Saravia, *conde* de. Histoire du soulèvement de la guerre de la révolution d'Espagne; tr. Paris, 1836–38. 5 v. 8°.
— Information on the principal events in the government of Spain, from the insurrection in 1808, to the dissolution of the Cortes in 1814; tr. by W. Walton. (*In* **Pamphleteer,** 1820; v. 17 of B 838)

Toribio *de Benavente called* **Motolinia,** *Fray.* RAMIREZ, J. F. Noticias de la vida y escritos de T. (*In* **Icazbalceta,** J. G. Col. de doc., v. 1. 1858.)

Tories, American. *See* **American loyalists.**

Tories, English. CHARACTER of a Tory, The. London, 1681. f°. (A 54)
— THOUGHTS of an honest Tory upon the present proceedings of that party. London, 1710. 8°. (B 590)
— STATE and prospects of T., Jan. 1834. From Fraser's mag. [London, 1834.] 8°. (B 1529)
See also **Whigs.**

Torlonia, Giovanni. Discorso critico int. alla vita di F. Orioli. (*In* **Archiv.** stor. ital., n.s., v. 7, pt. 2. 1858.)
— GORI, A. de'. Necrologia di T. (*In* v. 8. 1858.)

Torments of hell; [by S. Richardson]. (*In* **Phenix,** v. 2. 1708.)

Tornabuoni *di Firenze*, Famiglia di. (*In* **Litta,** P. Fam., v. 14.)

Tornabuoni de' Medici, Lucrezia. Cristo al limbo. (*In* **Poeti** ital. contemp. 1843.)
— Lauda. (*In* **Trucchi,** F. Poesie ital., v. 2. 1846.)

Tornadoes. ACCOUNT of the great whirlwind in New Hampshire, Sept. 9, 1821. (*In* **New Hampshire Hist.** Soc. Col., v. 1. 1824.)
— REDFIELD, W. C. Remarks on the tornado which visited N. Brunswick, in N. Jersey, June 19, 1835. *n.t.p.* [N. Y., 1841.] 8°. (B 1186)
— HARE, R. Causes of the tornado or water spout. (*In* **Amer. Phil. Soc.** Trans., n.s., v. 5. 1837.)
— BROCKLESBY, J. Tornado which passed over Connecticut, Aug. 9, 1851. (*In* **Amer. Assoc.** Proc., v. 8. 1855.)
— BROOKS, C. The tornado of 1851, in Medford, W. Cambridge, and Waltham. Boston, 1852. 24°.
— EUSTIS, H. L. The tornado of Aug. 22, 1851, in Waltham, W. Cambridge, and Medford, Mass. (*In* **Amer. Acad.** Mem., n.s., v. 5, pt. 1. 1855.)
— STODDARD, O. N. Brandon tornado of Jan. 20, 1854. (*In* **Amer. Assoc.** Proc., v. 8. 1855.) — REDFIELD, W. C. Spirality of motion in whirlwinds and tornadoes. (*In* v. 10. 1857.)

Torner, Erik. Centuria II. plantarum. (*In* **Linné,** C. Amœn. acad., v. 4. 1759.)

Tornielli, Agostino. NICERON, J. P. (*In his* Mém., v. 11. 1730; *and, Germ.*, v. 9. 1754.)

Torniello Boromeo, Livia. Sonetto. (*In* **Poeti** ital. cont. 1843.)

Toro, Honoré Jean (*or* Joseph) Bernard. LAGRANGE, L. (*In* **Gazette** des beaux-arts, v. 25. 1868.) — Catalogue de l'œuvre de Toro. (*In* v. 26. 1869.)

Toronto. Magnetical and Meteorological Observatory. Observations made at the Observatory; printed under the superintendence of Lieut.-Col. E. Sabine. Vol. 1, 1840–42. London, 1845. 4°.

Torpedo. CLOQUET, H. De torpedinis vi electrica. (*In* **Plinius Secundus,** C. Historia naturalis, v. 8. 1829. Lemaire. Biblioth. class. Lat.)

Torquato Tasso; commedia. *See* **Goldoni,** C.

Torquato Tasso; ein Schauspiel. *See* **Goethe,** J. W. von.

Torquatus, Antonius. Predictions wherein the downfall of France and Rome is delineated. (*In* **Atwood,** W. Wonderful predictions. 1689. A 52)

Torquemada *or* **Turrecremata,** Juan de. PUSEY, E. B. Analysis of Turrecremata's 'Treatise on the truth of the conception of the most blessed Virgin'. (*In his* First letter to J. H. Newman. 1869.)

Torre, Alfonso de la. Vision delectable de la filosofia y artes liberales, metafisica, y filosofia moral. (*In* **Castro,** A. de. Curiosidades bibliog. 1855; v. 36 of Aribau. Bibl.)

Torre, Bachiller Francisco de la, *pseud.* *See* **Quevedo Villegas,** F. G. de.

Torre, Bertrand della. Voyage to Polynesia. (*In* **Callander,** J. Terra Australis cognita, v. 1. 1766.)

Torre, Federico. Vite dei martiri di Roma. (*In* **Amato,** G. d'. Panteon, v. 2. 1851.)

Torre (*Lat.* **Turre**), Filippo del. Diss. de Beleno, et aliis quibusdam Aquilejensium diis, ac de colonia Foro Juliensi. (*In* **Grævius,** J. G. Thes. antiq. Ital., v. 6, pt. 4. 1722.) — Monumenta veteris Antii. (*In* v. 8, pt. 4. 1723.)
— Explicatio inscriptionis taurobolii Lugdunensis. (*In* **Sallengre,** H. H. Novus thes. antiq. Rom., v. 3. 1719.)
— FABRONI, A. (*In his* Vitæ Ital., v. 6. 1780.)
— NICERON, J. P. (*In his* Mém., v. 1. 1729; *and, Germ.*, v. 1. 1749.)

Torre, Francisco de la. Agudezas de J. Owen; tr. en metro castellano con adiciones. *See* **Owen,** J.
— Odas. (*In* **Sedano,** J. J. L. de. Parnaso esp., v. 1. 1768.) — Cancion. — Odas. (*In* v. 2. 1770.)
— Tirsi. — Egloga. — Canciones. — Odas. — Sonetos. (*In* **Quintana,** M. J. Poesias sel. castel., v. 1. 1807.)

Torre, Gian Raffaele della. Congiura di Giulio Cesare Vacchero descritta. (*In* **Archiv.** stor. ital., app., v. 3. 1846.)

Torre, Giovanni Maria della. BORGOGNO, T. Elogio di T. (*In* **Grillo,** L. Elogi di Liguri, v. 3. 1846.)

Torre, José Maria de la. Elementos de cronologia universal. 2a ed. Habana, 1845. 16°.

Torre, Miguel de la. Manifiesto para satisfacer al mundo entero de la conducta franca y generosa tenida por el gobierno español con el gefe de los disdentes de Venezuela. Madrid, 1821. 4°. (B 396)
— DIAZ, J. D. Manifiestos de la correspondencia entre T. con S. Bolivar. Madrid, 1821. 4°. (B 396)

Torre Espada. ACCOUNT of the Royal Portuguese military order of the Tower and the Sword. London, 1813. 8°. (B 690)

Torre di Rezzonico, Carl Gastone di. *See* **Rezzonico della Torre,** C. G.

Torrehermosa, *conde* de. Papel sobre restablecer la junta de comercio. (*In* **Valladares,** A. Seman. erud., v. 30. 1790.)

Torrendel; a tragedy. *See* **Cumberland, R.**

Torrens, Henry D'Oyley. Travels in Ladak, Tartary, and Kashmir. London, 1862. 8°.

Torrens, Robert. Letter on the petition against Ld. Binning's return being declared frivolous and vexatious. (*In* **Pamphleteer,** 1819; v. 14 of **B 838**)

— Letters on commercial policy. London, 1833. 8°. (**B 1070**)

— Paper on the means of reducing the poor's rates, and affording relief to the labouring classes. (*In* **Pamphleteer,** 1817; v. 10 of **B 838**)

— On wages and combination. London, 1834. 8°.

Torrens, Robert R. On the relations between Great Britain and her possessions abroad. — System of conveyancing by registration of titles. (*In* **Nat. Assoc. Prom. Soc. Sci.** Trans., 1863.) — Is it desirable that state aid should be given to emigration, and, if so, in what form? (*In* 1869.)

Torrentino, Lorenzo. Annali della tipografia fiorentina. Firenze, 1811. 8°.

Torrepalma, Alonso Verdugo Castilla, *conde* de. El Deucalion. (*In* **Sedana,** J. J. L. de. Parnaso esp., v. 3. 1782.)

Torres, *Conde* de las. Informe en punto de terremoto. (*In* **Valladares,** A. Seman. erud., v. 16. 1788.)

Torres (*Lat.* **Turrianus**), Francisco de. Niceron, J. P. (*In his* Mém., v. 29. 1734; *and, Germ.*, v. 18. 1758.)

Torres, Luis Vaez de. Letter describing his voyage through the Torres Straits. (*In* **Morga,** A. de. The Philippine Islands. 1868.)

— Relation conc. the discoveries of Quiros; tr. by A. Dalrymple. (*In* **Burney,** J. Discoveries in the South sea, v. 2. 1806; — *and in* **Major,** R. H. Early voy. to Terra Australis. 1859.)

— Voyage de P. F. de Quiros et L. V. de Torres en 1606. (*In* **Fleurieu,** C. P. C. de. Découvertes des François en 1768-69. 1790.)

Torres, Manuel de, *and* **Hargous,** L. Nature displayed in her mode of teaching language; adapted to the Spanish by T. *See* **Dufief,** N. G.

Torres, Simon Perez de. Viage del mundo. (*In* **Barcia,** A. G. Hist. prim., v. 3. 1749.)

Torres de Mendoza, Luis. Coleccion de documentos ined. rel. al descubrimiento, conquista, y colonization de las posesiones españoles en América y Occeania, sacados del Real Archivo de Indias. Madrid, 1864-74. 21 v. 8°.

Torres Naharro, Bartolomé de. Comedia himenea. (*In* **Ochoa,** E. de. Tesoro del teatro esp., v. 1. 1838.)

Torres Vedras. Jones, *Sir* J. T. Memoranda relative to the lines [of T. V.] thrown up to cover Lisbon in 1810. (*In* **Jones,** *Sir* J. T. Journal of sieges carried on in Spain. 1846.)

— Madeira Torres, M. A. Descripção da villa e termo de Torres Vedras. (*In* **Lisbon. Ac. d. Sci.** Mem., v. 6. 1819.)

Torres y Villarroel, Diego de. Noticias biográficas. — Poesias. (*In* **Cueto,** L. A. de. Poetas liricos del siglo 18. 1869; v. 61 of Aribau Bibl.)

Torrescano, Pablo M. The other side. 1850. *See* **Alcarez, R.**

Torrey, F. P. Cruise of the U. S. ship Ohio, 1839-41, in the Mediterranean. Boston, 1841. 18°.

Torrey, Henry Warren. Some topics in criminal law. (*In* **Amer. Soc. Sci. Assoc.** Trans., v. 1. 1869.)

Torrey, Jesse, *Jr.* The intellectual torch; a plan for the dissemination of knowledge by free public libraries; with essays on the use of distilled spirits. 2d ed. Ballston Spa, 1817. 12°. (**C 83**)

— Portraiture of domestic slavery in the U. S. Phila., 1817. 8°. (**B 977**)

Torrey, John D. Botany of the boundary. (*In* **U. S.** *Dept. of the Interior.* U. S. and Mexican boundary survey under Emery, v. 2. 1859.)

— Catalogue of plants col. by the expedition. (*In* **U. S.** *War Dept.* Exploration of the Great Salt Lake, under H. Stansbury. 1852.)

— Compendium of the flora of the northern and middle U. S. N. Y., 1826. 12°.

— Description of the plants col. during the exploration. (*In* **U. S.** *War Dept.* Exploration of the Red River of Louisiana, by J. B. Marcy and G. B. McClellan. 1854.)

— Flora of the northern and middle sections of the U. S. Vol. 1. N. Y., 1824. 8°.

— Flora of the State of New York. (*In* **New York,** State. Natural history, pt. 2. 1843.)

— List of the plants collected by W. H. Emery. (*In* **U. S.** *War Dept.* Notes of a military reconnoissance from Fort Leavenworth to San Diego, Cal. 1848.)

— New plants discovered by Col. Fremont in California. (*In* **Amer. Assoc.** Proc., v. 4. 1851.)

— Plantæ Fremontianæ; a description of plants collected by J. C. Fremont in California. — Observations on the batis maritima. — On the darlingtonia Californica; a new pitcher plant from N. California. (*In* **Smithsonian Inst.** Contrib., v. 6. 1854.)

— Reports on the botany of the expedition. (*In* **U. S.** *War Dept.* Reports of explorations for a R. R. to the Pacific, 1853-54, v. 2, 4, 5, 6, 7. 1855-57.)

— Structure and affinities of the genus batis of Linnæus. (*In* **Amer. Assoc.** Proc., v. 4. 1851.)

— *and* **Fremont,** J. Description of some new plants, collected in the exploring expedition to Oregon in 1843-44. (*In* **U. S.** *War Dept.* Report. 1845.)

Torrey, Joseph. Biog. notice of T. (*In* **Mass. Med. Soc.** Med. comm., v. 8. 1854.)

Torrey, Rufus. History of Fitchburg, Mass.; comprising also Lunenburg, to 1764. [2d ed.] Fitchburg, 1865. 8°.

Torrey, Susanna, *vs.* **Field,** R. M. Trial for libel. *n.t.p.* [Woodstock? 1835.] 8°. (**B 1813**)

Torrey, *Capt.* Wm. Brief discourse conc. futurities; with a preface by Prince. Boston, 1757. 8°. (**B 254, 1713, C 22**)

Torrey, *Rev.* Wm. Address at the Temperance Convention, Morristown, Dec. 13, 1843; with the proc. *etc.*, of the convention, and also of that at Hackettstown, Sept. 26. Newark, 1843. 8°. (**B 1280**)

Torrey, *Rev.* Wm. Turner. Sermon, Plymouth, Dec. 28, 1821. Boston, 1822. 8°. (**B 275**)

Torri, Alessandro. Su i comenti a due passi della Divina commedia, l'uno astronomico, l'altro filologico. — Su l'inedito comento di F. da Buti alla Divina commedia. (*In* **Centofanti** S., *and others.* Studi su Dante. 1846.)

Torriani *di Valsassina,* Famiglia di. (*In* **Litta,** P. Fam., v. 14.)

Torriano, Giovanni. Vocabolario italiano et inglese; a dictionary compiled by J. Florio enriched with additions; added, a dictionary Eng. and Ital.; rev. by J. D. Lond., 1688. f°.

Torricelli, Evangelista. De sphæra et solidis sphæralibus. Florentiæ, 1644. 4°.

Contents. De solidis sphæralibus. — De motu. — De dimensione parabolæ. — De solido hyperbolico; cum app. de cycloide et cochlea.

— Fabroni, A. (*In his* Vitæ Ital., v. 1. 1778.)

— Niceron, J. P. (*In his* Mém., v. 15. 1731; *and, Germ.*, v. 11. 1754.)

— Ricci-Poggi, D. Biografia di T. (*In* **Hercolani,** A. Biog. illustri Romag., v. 1. 1834.)

Torrigiano. Sonnet. (*In* **Trucchi,** F. Poesie ital., v. 1. 1846.)

Torrigio, Francesco Maria. *See* **Turrigi,** F. M.

Torrismondo, Il re; tragedia. *See* **Tasso,** T.

Torsellino, H. *See* **Tursellinus,** H.

Torshell, Samuel. Design to harmonize the Bible. (*In* **Phenix,** v. 1. 1707.)

Torstenson, Leonard. Cust, E. (*In his* Lives of the warriors of the thirty years' war, v. 2. 1865.)

Tortajada, Damian Lopez de, *compiler.* Flower of the ballads of the twelve peers of France with metrical versions by T. Rodd. (*In* **Rodd,** T. History of Charles the Great, v. 1, 2. 1812.)

Tortelli, Giovanni. Niceron, J. P. (*In his* Mém., v. 25. 1734.)

Torti, Francisco. Therapeutice specialis ad febres quasdam perniciosas. Mutinæ, 1712. 4°.

Torti, G. Carme sulla passione di Gesù Cristo. (*In* **Poeti** ital. contem. 1843.)

Torti, Girolamo. Maino, G. Oratio de vita H. Torti. (*In* **Schelhorn,** J. G. Amœn. lit., v. 4. 1730.)

Tortola. Wilkinson, R. Map. London, 1798. (**E 67**)

Tortoli, Giovanni. G. Bardelli. (*In* **Archivio** stor. ital., ser. 3 a, v. 3, pt. 2. 1866.)

Tortosa. Vinayma, V. Hydrologia; o, Tratado de las aguas ferrugineas de Tortosa. Valencia, 1738. 16°.

Tortugas. Chart. London, 1790. (**E 67**)

Torture. Lea, H. C. (*In his* Superstition and force. 1866.)

Torunxa. Brief accounts of Harmuz or Ormuz. (*In his* Hist. of Persia. 1715.)

Toryism. *See* **Tories.**

Toscano, Giam Matteo. Carmina illustrium poetarum Italorum. Lutetiæ, 1576. 2 v. 24°.

Contents. Vol. 1. J. Carga. — J. F. Bonhomus. — H. Amaltheus. — C. Amaltheus. — J. B. Amaltheus. — J. B. Possevinus. — F. M. Molsa. — P. Pansa de Molsa. — B. Castalio. — J. Cotta. — B. Lampridius. — P. Bembus. — Varii autores in Bembi obitum. — A. Naugerius. — M. A. Casanova. — A. Tebaldeus. — A. Marius. — L. Bonamicus. — J. Casa. — H. Fasitellus. — J. M. Aurelius. — P. Vicecomes. — J. Etruscus. — T. Porcatius. — H. Aleander. — B. Naugerius. — H. Malevoltus. — H. Ulpius. — H. Salina. — N. Archius. — J. Vitalis. — M. Silvius. — M. Faetanus. — T. Frangipanis. — A. Fumanus. — J. Parlistanus. — J. M. Toscanus. — Antiq. inscriptiones. 2. H. Frascatorius. — A. Politianus. — J. Sadolerus. — A. Palearius. — J. Camillus. — H. Capilupus. — J. Bonfadius. — P. Manutius. — P. Myrteus. — B. Palladius. — F. Panigerola. — C. Paleotus. — C. Tolomeus. — A. Caracciolus. — A. Coccejanus. — B. Zanchus. — P. Zanchus. — G. Altilius. — J. A. Vulpa. — L. Fenarolus. — A. Colotius. — P. Cursius. — J. F. Binus. — T. Bentius. — A. Priulus. — J. Chrysostomus. — F. Bellinus. — B. Parthenius. — U. Genuensis. — J. B. Sanga. — B. Baldinus. — J. B. Pius. — J. Lascaris. — P. Gauricus. — O. Maninus. — Frizolius. — J. Tonsus. — H. Vicecomes. — J. A. Tuccius. — A. S. Minturnus. — A. Dactius. — F. Franchinus. — L. Areostus. — M. Molsa. — J. Caspareus. — J. Antonius Taygetus. — D. Ceretus. — J. Angelus Taygetus. — J. B. Pigna. — G. Faernus. — G. Posthumus. — L. Capilupus. — H. Stroza. — T. Stroza. — C. Boba. — A. Vacca.

Tosini, Eutropia. Ode. (*In* **Poeti** ital. contemp. 1843.)

Tossanus, Daniel, *d.* 1602. Niceron, J. P. (*In his* Mém., v. 36. 1736; *and*, *Germ.*, v. 19. 1759.)

Tossanus, Paul. Niceron, J. P. (*In his* Mém., v. 36. 1736; *and*, *Germ.*, v. 10. 1754.)

Tosti *or* **Torti.** Antonio di Pietro. Diarium Romanum, 1404–17. (*In* **Muratori,** L. A. Rer. Ital. scr., v. 24. 1738.)

Tosti, Luigi. Storia del Concilio di Constanza. Napoli, 1853. 2 v. 8°.

— Storia della lega lombarda. Monte-Cassino, 1848. 8°.

— Storia di Abelardo e dei suoi tempi. Napoli, 1851. 8°.

— Storia di Bonifazio VIII. e dei suoi tempi. Monte Cassino, 1846. 2 v. 8°.

— Renan, E. (*In his* Essais de morale et de critique. 1860.)

Total abstinence. *See* **Temperance.**

Total abstinence societies, *see* the name of the society, as **Boston Young Men's Total Abstinence Society**; — **Congressional Young Men's Total Abstinence Society**; — **Massachusetts Washington Young Men's Total Abstinence Society**; — **Norfolk County Washington Young Men's Total Abstinence Society**; — **Watertown Young Men's Total Abstinence Society.**

Total depravity. *See* **Depravity**; — *also* **Sin.**

Tothill, Edward. Principles and practice of steam navigation in sea and river service. (*In* **Tredgold,** T. Principles, *etc.*, of steam engines, v. 2. 1851.)

Toti, Torquato. Marescotti, N. Vita di T. (*In* **Amato,** G. d'. Panteon, v. 2. 1851.)

Tott, François, *baron* de. Memoirs of the Turkish Empire and the Crimea. London, 1786. 2 v. 8°.

Tottel, Richard, *ed.* Songes and sonettes by H. Howard Earl of Surrey, Sir T. Wyatt, N. Grimald, *etc.*, 1557; [ed.] by E. Arber. London, 1870. 16°. (Eng. reprints, v. 11.)

Totten, Benjamin J. Naval text book and dictionary. Boston, 1841. 8°.

— *Same.* New ed. rev. N. Y., 1862. 16°.

Totten, Joseph Gilbert. Report on the effects of firing with heavy ordnance from casemate embrasures and against the same embrasures with various kinds of missiles. Wash., 1857. 8°. (Papers on practical engineering, 6.)

— Sudden disappearance of the ice of our northern lakes in the spring. (*In* **Amer. Assoc.** Proc., v. 14. 1861.)

— Barnard, J. G. Eulogy on T. Wash., 1866. 8°. (**B 1639**)

— — *Same.* (*In* **Smithsonian Inst.** Report, 1865.)

Note. Reprinted from **National Acad. of Sci.** Annual, 1865.

Tottenham, *Rev.* Edward. Sermon, May 1, 1834, in behalf of the British Soc. for Prom. the Religious Principles of the Reformation. *n.p.*, [1834]. 8°. (**B 1346**)

Tottenham. *See* **Bruce Castle.**

Tottie, John. Charge rel. to the articles of the Ch. of Eng. to the clergy of the archdeanery of Worcester. Oxford, 1772. 8°. (**B 905**)

— Sermons. (*In* **Family** lectures. 1791.)

Totze, Eobald. *See* **Toze,** E.

Toucey, Isaac. Review of [his] message before the General Assembly [Conn.], May 6, 1846. *n.p.*, [1846]. 8°. (**B 1281**)

Touch. Engel, J. Ueber einige Eigenheiten des Gefühlssinnes. (*In* **Berlin. Ak. d. Wiss.** Abh., 1788–89.)

Touchard-Lafosse, G. Chroniques des Tuileries et du Luxembourg. Paris, 1837, 41, 38. 4 v. 8°.

— *and* **Roberge,** F. Dictionnaire des découvertes, inventions, *etc.*, en France, 1789–1820. Paris, 1826. 17 v. 8°.

Contents. Vol. 1. A–Basc. 2. Basi–Champignons. (anal.) 3. Champignons (Traitm.) — Corps célestes. 4. Corps colorés–Dia. 5. Dic–Electi. 6. Electa–Fer. 7. Fer–Galèn. 8. Gales–Hepa. 9. Hept.–I. 10. J–Mach. 11. Mact–Mousses. 12. Moussel–Parc. 13. Pari–Poli. 14. Poli–Science. 15. Sciences–Thé. 16. Thea–Z. 17. Tables.

Touch'em, Timothy, *pseud.* The age of frivolity; a poem. London, 1806. 12°. (**C 146**)

Touchet, James, *Earl of Castlehaven.* Memoirs; or, Review of the civil wars in Ireland, pref. hist. notices of the author's family and life. Dublin, 1815. 8°.

Touchet, Samuel. Letter to a merchant at Bristol, [on] a petition of T.— to the King for an exclusive grant to the trade of the Senegal. Lond., 1762. 8°. (**W 29**)

Touchstone, Geoffry, *pseud.* He wou'd be a poet; or 'Nature will be nature still'; an heroic poem. Phila., 1796. 8°. (**B 423**)

Touchstone, Timothy, *pseud.* His reply to Mr. Christian's letter, in vindication of the innocence of the Earl of Danby. *n.t.p.* [16—.] f°. (**A 51**)

— Reply to Sir Anonymous, at Mr. Christian's lodging, between Hambden and Danby houses. *n.t.p.* [1682?] f°. (**A 51**)

Touchstone to the people of the U. S. on the choice of a president. N. Y., 1812. 8°. (**B 442**)

Tough yarns; by M. H. Barker. *t.p.w.* [London, 1858.] 12°.

Toujours; comédie. *See* **Scribe,** A. E.

Toul, *France.* Journal de Metz, pour 1765, avec une notice sur Toul. Metz, 1765. 16°.

Toulmin, H. Short view of the life, sentiments, and character of J. Mort; address to the Dissenters of Atherton, and in a sermon in New Bent Chapel, Jan. 20, 1788. London, 1793. 12°. (Unit. Soc. Prom. Christ. Knowl. Tracts. **B 158, C 138**)

Toulmin, Joshua. American war lamented; sermon, Taunton, Feb. 18, 25. London, 1776. 8°. (**B 392**)

— Exhortation to all Christian people to refrain from Trinitarian worship. *n.p.*, [1789]. 12°. (Unit. Soc. Prom. Christ. Knowl. Tracts. **C 132**)

— Memoir of F. Socinus. London, 1777. 8°.

— The promise of Christ's presence with his disciples; sermon, Bridwell Chapel, Jan. 4; with address by J. Williams. Taunton, 1792. 8°. (**B 961**)

— Review of the life, *etc.*, of J. Biddle. London, 1791. 12°. (Unit. Soc. Prom. Christ. Knowl. Tracts. **C 134**)

— Review of the preaching of the Apostles; efficacy of the Unitarian doctrine. Utica, 1817. 8°. (**C 82, 85**)

— Sermon, opening of Bridwell Chapel, near Ufculine, Devon, Jan. 4, 1792. Taunton, [1792]. 8°. (**B 961**)

— Two letters on the applications to Parliament by the dissenting ministers. London, 1774. 8°. (**B 907**)

— Watchfulness incumbent on ministers; charge at the ordination of I. Smith, June 24. Taunton, [1778]. 8°. (**B 334, 1312**)

Toulon. *History.* Letter rel. to the exped. into Provence and siege of Thoulon [by] Prince Eugene; done from a French copy from the Hague. *t.p.mut.* London, [1707]. 4°.

— - LETTER to Admiral Hood on the cruelties exercised during his command at Toulon. Paris, [1792]. 8°. (B 715)
— - MARMONT, A. F. L. V. de. Prise de T., 1793. (*In his* Mém., v. 1. 1857.)
— - NAPOLEON I. Siége de Toulon, 1793. (*In his* Commentaries, v. 1. 1867.)
— *Maps.* PLAN de Toulon, la veüe de sa rade et situation de ses tours, celles des hauteurs de St. Anne où sont campées les troupes du roi; le camp des alliez, avec les deffences de la place. Amst., [17—]. (E 60)
— - MAP. [London,] 1794. (E 65)

Toulongeon, François Emmanuel, *comte* de. Histoire de France depuis la révolution de 1789. Paris, 1801-10. 7 v. 8°.

Contents. Vol. 1. 1787-21 juin 1791. 2. 21 juin-25 oct. 1792. 3. 2 sept. 1792-2 juin 1793. 4. 1 av.-27 juil. 1793. 5. 27 juil. 1793-24 nov. 1795. 6. 28 oct. 1795-4 sept. 1796. 7. App.: 4 sept. 1796-99.

— Manuel du Muséum Français. Paris, 1802-08. 10 v. 8°.

Contents. Vol. 1. Œuvre du Poussin. 2. Dominiquin et Spada. 3. Rubens. 4. Raphael. 5. Le Brun. 6. Van Ostade. — Gerard Dow. — Van Dyck. 7. Vernet. 8. Titian. 9. Paul Veronese. 10. F., M. L. R. Galerie de Saint-Bruno, par Lesueur.

— DACIER, B. J. La vie et les ouvrages de T. (*In* **Paris. Inst.** *Ac. d. Inscr.* Mém., v. 5. 1821.)
— QUATREMÈRE DE QUINCY, A. C. [Discours aux funérailles de T. Paris, 1812.] 4°. (E 71)

Toulouse. MAGI, —. Mémoire hist. sur l'inquisition de Toulouse. — SERMET, A. P. H. Recherches hist. sur l'inquisition de Toulouse. (*In* **Sérieys, A.** Bibl. acad., v. 6. 1811.)

Tour de Nesle, La; drame. *See* **Hugo, V.**

Tour de Nesle, La; drame; par A. **Dumas.** (*In his* Théâtre, v. 3. 1864.)

Tour in quest of genealogy through Wales, *etc.*; by R. Fenton. London, 1811. 8°.

Tour of Holland, Dutch Brabant, the Austrian Netherland, *etc.* London, 1772. 12°.

Tour round my garden; by J. B. A. Karr, ed. by J. G. Wood. 5th thous. Lond., 1856. 16°.

Tour Saint Jacques, La; drame; par **H. Dumas.** (*In his* Théâtre, v. 13. 1865.)

Tour through the whole island of Gr. Brit.; by [D. Defoe]. 4th ed. London, 1748. 4 v. 16°.

Tour through Upper and Lower Canada; by [Ogden]. Litchfield, 1799. 12°.

Touraine. CHEVALIER, C. Promenades pittoresques en Touraine; histoire, *etc.* Tours, 1869. 8°.

Tourist, The; pocket manual for travellers on the Hudson River, *etc.* 2d ed. N. Y., 1831. 24°.

Tourist in Europe; by [G. P. Putnam]. N. Y., 1838. 12°.

Tournachon, Félix. *See* **Nadar, F. T.**

Tournaisis. DINAUX, A. Les trouvères de la Flandre et du Tournaisis. Paris, 1839. 8°. (Trouvères, v. 2.)

Tournament, The; a ballad; illustr. by a Crowquill. London, Edin., 1839. 24°. (D 20)

Tournay, Wm., *D.D.* Sermon, consecration of J. Parsons, Bp. of Peterborough. Oxford, 1813. 4°. (A 60)

Tournay. MAP. Paris, 1708. (E 60)
— MAP. Paris, 1745. (E 60)
— MAP. [Amst., 17—.] (E 60)
— PLAN de Tournay avec les attaques de Schulenborg. Amsterdam, [17—]. (E 60)
— PLAN de Tournay investie par les allies. 1709. Amst., [1700]. (E 60)

Tournefort, Joseph Pitton de. Elémens de botanique; éd. augm. par N. Jolyclerc. Lyon, 1797. 6 v. 8°.

— Voyage into the Levant; prefixed [his] life [by Lauthier]; also Elogium by Fontenelle. London, 1708. 2 v. 4°.
— NICERON, J. P. (*In his* Mém., v. 4. 1728; *and, Germ.*, v. 5. 1751.)
— ST. JOHN, J. A. (*In his* Lives of cel. travellers, v. 2. 1847.)

Tournemine, René Joseph. NICERON, J. P. (*In his* Mém., v. 42. 1741.)

Tourneur, Tournour, *or* **Turner,** Cyril. The atheist's tragedy. (*In* **Lamb, C.** Spec. of dram. poets. 1808; 1854.)
— Revenger's tragedy. (*In* **Dodsley, R.** Col. of old plays, v. 4. 1825; — *in* **Lamb, C.** Spec. of dram. poets. 1808; 1854; — *and in* **Scott,** *Sir* **W.** Anc. Brit. dr., v. 2. 1810.)

Tourneys. DU CANGE, C. du F. L'origine et l'usage des tournois. (*In his* Gloss. med. et infim. Lat., v. 7. 1850; — **Perrin.** Col. des mém., v. 2. 1785; — *and in* **Petitot.** Col. des mém., 1e sér., v. 3. 1819.)

Tournon, Carlo Tommaso Maillard di, *Card.* CRESCIMBENI, G. M. (*In his* Vite degli Arcadi, v. 3. 1714.)

Tournour. *See* **Tourneur.**

Touro, Judah. WALKER, A. Life of J. Touro. (*In* **Hunt, F.** Lives of Amer. merchants, v. 2. 1858.)

Touron, Antoine de. Histoire générale de l'Amérique. Paris, 1768-70. 14 v. 12°.

Tourreil, Jacques de. NICERON, J. P. (*In his* Mém., v. 27. 1734; *and, Germ.*, v. 22. 1762.)

Tours. TILTRES de l'establissement du cours de ville de Tours. Tours, 1661. 4°. (A 3)

Tourson, Wm. *See* **Towrson, W.**

Tourte-Cherbuliez, *Mme.* Comédies de société; récréations dramatiques pour la jeunesse. Genève, Paris, 1861. 18°.

Contents. Le petit chaperon rouge. — La belle au bois dormant. — Ali Cogia. — Alfred le grand. — Cendrillon. — Une après-midi de vacances.

Tourtechot-Granger. Journey through Egypt; tr. by J. R. Forster. (*In* **Riedesel, J. H.** Travels through Sicily. 1773.)

Tourville, Hilarion de, *maréchal.* CUST, *Sir* E. (*In his* Lives of the warriors who have commanded fleets, v. 2. 1869.)

Tousard, Louis. Justification of T.; address to the National Convention of France, Jan. 24; by himself. Phila., 1793. 8°. (B 641)

Tousard, Louis de. American artillerist's companion; or, Elements of artillery. Phila., 1809. 2 v. 8° *and* Plates. 4°.

Toussain, Paul. Index in Sacra Biblia ex Latina I. Tremellii et F. Junii versione quoad Vetus, et T. Bezæ quoad Novum Testamentum. Hanoviæ, 1624. f°.

Toussaint, Anna Luiza Geertruide. *See* **Bosboom, A. L. G. T.**

Toussaint, François Vincent. Les mœurs. 5e éd. *n.p.*, 1752. 12°.

Toussaint, Jacques. Plan d'éducation publique. Paris, [an] x, 1802. 12°. (C 302)

Toussaint-Louverture, François Dominique. *See* **Louverture, F. D. T.**

Toustain, Félix. Nouveau manuel de la fabrication des tissus de toute espèce. Paris, 1859. 2 v. 18° *and* Atlas 4°. (Manuels-Roret.)

Tower, David Bates. The gradual reader. 5th ed. Boston, 1842. 12°.
— Intellectual algebra. N. Y., [1845]. 16°.
— Progressive speaker and common school reader. Boston, 1858. 12°.
— *and* **Tweed, B. F.** First lessons in language; elements of Eng. grammar. N. Y., 1855. 12°.

Tower, *Col.* R. Appeal to the people of N. York, in favor of the construction of the Chenango canal. Utica, 1830. 8°. (B 1063)

Tower and the Sword, Order of the. *See* **Torre e Espada.**

Tower Hamlets. EPISODES in an obscure life; being experiences in the Tower Hamlets, by a curate. Phila., 1870. 8°.

Tower menagerie; comprising the nat. hist. of the animals, with anecdotes of their character and history; [by E. T. Bennett;] illust. by portraits of each taken from life by W Harvey. London, 1829. 8°.

Tower of London. *See* **London, Tower of** (p. 1781).

Tower of London; historical romance; by W. H. Ainsworth. London, 1845. 8°.

Towers, Joseph. Observations on the rights and duty of juries in trials for libel. London, 1784. 8°. (B 707)

— Oration. (*In* **Palmer**, J. Sermon, death of C. Fleming. 1779. **B 1851**)
— Oration, London Tavern, Nov. 4, commemoration of the Revolution. London, 1788. 8°. (B 399)
— Thoughts on the commencement of a new Parliament; with remarks on the letter of E. Burke on the revolution in France. London, 1790. 8°.
— *Same.* Dublin, 1791. 8°. (**B 634**)
— Tracts on polit. and other subjects. London, 1796. 3 v. 8°.
Contents. Vol. 1. Vindication of the political principles of Locke. — Letter to S. Johnson. — Obs. on Hume's Hist. of England. 2. Obs. on the rights and duty of juries in trials for libels, *etc.* — Letter to Dr. Nowell. — Exam. into the charges against Ld. Russel and A. Sydney. — Dialogue conc. the application to Parliament for relief in subscription to the 39 articles, *etc.* — Rev. of the genuine doctrines of Christianity. — Oration at the interment of C. Fleming. 3. Thoughts on the commencement of a new Parliament. — Dialogue on the grounds of the late associations and commencement of war with France. — Rem. on the conduct, *etc.*, of the assoc. at the Crown & Anchor. — Essay on S. Johnson.

Towerson, Gabriel. Explication of the catechism of the Church of England. London, 1685. f°.

Towerson, Wm. Voyages to the coast of Guinea, 1555–57. (*In* **Green**, J. Col. of voy., v. 1. 1745; — **Hakluyt**, R. Col. of voy., v. 2. 1810; — *and in* **Kerr**, R. Col. of voy., v. 7. 1824; — **Moore**, J. H. New col. of voy., v. 1; — *and*, *Germ.*, *in* **Allgemeine Hist.**, v. 1. 1748.)

Towgood, *Rev.* Micaiah. The baptism of infants a reasonable service. London, 1765. 8°. (**B 16**)
— *Same.* Boston, 1765. 8°. (**B 52, 255, C 125**)
— Calm answer to Why are you a Dissenter? London, 1772. 8°. (**B 906, 1964**)
— *Same.* Boston, 1773. 8°. (**C 37, 185**)
— Church-power by our constitution, *etc.*; the dissenting gentleman's postscript to his 'Three letters to J. White'. London, 1750. 8°. (**B 124**)
— Dissent from the Ch. of England, fully justified; added, letter to a bishop. 3d ed. London, 1765. 12°.
— *Same.* 4th ed. Boston, 1768. 12°. (**C 185**)
— Dissenting gentleman's answer to Mr. White's 'Three letters'. 5th ed. Boston, 1748. 8°.
— *Another copy.* (**B 1897, C 305**)
— The dissenting gentleman's 2d letter to White in answer to his 'Three letters'; with postscript cont. remarks on White's "Defence of his 'Three letters'", *etc.* London, 1747. 8°. (**B 124**)
— The Englishman directed in the choice of his religion; with pref. address vindic. the King's supremacy accord. to the concession of the dissent. gentleman's answer to the Rev. Mr. White's letters; [by J. Wetmore]. Boston, 1748. 8°. (**B 1906**)
— High-flown Episcopal and priestly claims freely exam-in'd; dialogue betwixt a country gentleman and a country vicar. London, 1737. 8°. (**B 123**)
— Manning, J. Life and writings of T. Exeter, 1792. 8°.
— White, J. Defence of the 'Three letters' against the 'Dissenting gentleman's answer to White's letters', *etc.* London, 1746. 8°. (**B 124**)
— - *Same.* 2d ed. London, 1748. 8°. (**B 1897**)

Towle, George B. Criticism criticized! inquiry into the circumstances attending the termination of the services of G. B. Towle; by a disinterested citizen. [Athol?] 1861. 8°. (**B 1460**)

Towle, George Makepeace. Glimpses of history. Boston, 1866. 12°.
Contents. Memorable assassinations. — J. Bright. — Opening scenes of the rebellion. — The last of the Stuarts. — Lord Chancellor Campbell. — Count Cavour. — Last days of Chatham. — Leigh Hunt. — Alexis de Tocqueville. — The cardinal. — Kings. — A century of Eng. history, 1760–1860.

Towle, Nathaniel Carter. History and analysis of the Constitution of the U. S. Bost., 1860. 12°.

Towle, Thomas. Address at the interment of N. Trotman. (*In* **Barber**, J. Sermon; death of N. Trotman. 1793. **B 1226**)
— Oration, interment of E. Hitchin. (*In* **Brewer**, S. Sermon. **B 1218**)

Town, Ithiel. Atlantic steamships, pub. 1832; also description of the Sirius and Great Western. N. Y., 1838. 12°. (**C 180**)
— Description of [his] improvement in the construction of bridges. New Haven, 1821. 8°. (**B 526**)
— *Same.* N. Y., 1839. 4°.
— *Another copy.* (**A 44**)
— Outlines of a plan for an Academy of Fine Arts. Y. N., 1835. 8°. (**B 1166**)

Town, Salem, *LL.D.* County teacher's institutes. (*In* **Amer. Inst. Instr.** Lectures, 1845.)
— Town's speller and definer. Rev. ed. Boston, 1856. 12°.
— *and* Holbrook, N. M. 1st–4th progressive reader. Boston, [1856–58]. 4 v. 12°.

Town and country; by T. Morton. (*In* **Sargent**, E. Mod. stand. dr., v. 9.)

Town and country magazine. Vol. 15. London, [1783]. 8°. (**B 1749**)

Town and forest; by A. Manning. (*In* **Littell's living age**, v. 60–63. 1858–59.)

Towne, Benjamin. Goddard, W. Conduct of T. delineated. (*In his* Partnership. 1770. **B 618**)

Towne, *Rev.* Edward C. Memorial of T. Tebbets; sermon, Medford. Boston, 1863. 8°. (**B 1594**)

Towne, George W. Candid inquiry into the divine properties and character of God. Salem, 1816. 8°. (**B 1360**)

Towne, *Rev.* Joseph H. Colleges and free institutions; discourse, Worcester, Oct. 23, 1853. N. Y., 1854. 8°. (**B 1329**)
— Hints on baptism. 1842. *See* **Cooke**, P. (**D 32**)
— Manual for the use of members of the Ch. of Christ in Leyden Chapel. Boston, 1846. 8°.
— Sermon before the Boston City Miss. Soc. Boston, 1843. 8°. (**B 1303**)

Towneley, J., *and* **Harley**, A. Catalogue of books incl. the libraries of T. and H.; [sold 1817]. London, [1817]. 8°.

Towneley Gallery. *See* **British Museum** (p. 388).

Towneley mysteries; [ed. by J. Raine and J. Gordon]. London, 1836. 8°. (Surtees Soc., v. 3.)

Townley, —. Buccaneer adventures. (*In* **Burney**, J. Discoveries in the South Sea, v. 4. 1816.)

Townley, Henry. Sermon; influence of the love of Christ. (*In* **Suddards**, W. British pulpit, v. 2. 1836.)

Townley, James, *d.* 1778. High life below stairs. (*In* London stage, v. 1.)

Townley, James, *D.D.* Illustrations of Biblical literature; hist. of the sacred writings. London, 1821. 3 v. 8°.

Townley, Robert. Modern knowledge and ancient belief; lecture, Charlestown, Jan. 9. Boston, 1853. 8°. (**B 1303**)

Towns. Bridge, T. Jethro's advice to the inhabitants of Boston to chuse well-qualified men and haters of covetousness for town officers. Boston, 1710. 16°. (**D 47**)
— - *Same.* 2d ed. Boston, 1733. 8°. (**C 34, 51**)
— Sharp, G. Plan for laying out towns and townships. *n.p.*, 1794. 8°. (**B 997**)
— Parker, *Prof.* J. Paper on the origin, organization, and influence of the towns of New England. (*In* **Mass. Hist. Soc.** Proc., 1866–67.)

Laws.

— County and town officer; an abridgment of the laws of Mass. Bay, rel. to county and town officers; by a gentleman. Boston, 1768. 8°.
— *Another copy.* (**B 706**)
— Freeman, S. The town officer; power and duty of town officers in Massachusetts; added, the power of towns. [2d ed.] Boston, 1793. 12°.
— Dickinson, R. Laws of Massachusetts [relative to towns and town officers]; with an app. cont. legal forms. Boston, 1811. 8°.
— Goodwin, I. Laws of Massachusetts relating to town officers. Worcester, 1824. 12°.
— - *Same, entitled* Town officer. 2d ed. rev. and enl. Worcester, 1829. 12°.

— Richardson, W. M. New Hampshire town officer. Concord, 1829. 12°.
— Goodwin, I. New England sheriff; or, Digest of the duties of civil officers. Worcester, 1830. 12°.
— Herrick, W. A. The powers, duties, and liabilities of town and parish officers in Massachusetts. Boston, 1870. 8°.
See also **Villages.**

Townsend, Alexander. Address to the Charitable Fire Society on the principles of their institution. [Boston,] 1809. 8°. (**B 138, 669**)
— Oration, July 4, at the request of the Selectmen of Boston on the feelings, manners, and principles that introduced the Amer. independence. The orig. ms. 25 × 16.5cm.
— *Same.* Boston, 1810. 8°. (**B 394, 1839**)
— Loring, J. S. (*In his* Hundred Boston orators. 1852.)

Townsend, David. Principles and obs. applied to the manufacture of pot and pearl ashes. Boston, 1793. 8°. (**B 526, 835**)

Townsend, Francis. Calendar of knights, 1760–[1828]. London, 1828. 8°.

Townsend, George, *Funeral sermon on.* 1784. *See* **Fawcett, J.** (**B 1226**)

Townsend, George, *prebendary of Durham.* Infidelity not an involuntary error but a wilful sin; sermon, death of W. Van Mildert, Feb. 28. Durham, 1836. 4°. (**B 1243**)
— Butler, C. Vindication of 'The Book of the Roman Catholic Church' against G. Townsend's 'Accusations of history against the Church of Rome'. 2d ed. London, 1826. 8°.
— Corless, G. Reply to a pamphlet, by G. Townsend. London, 1827. 8°. (**B 1382**)

Townsend, George. Summary of Persian history. *See* **Hunt, G. H.**

Townsend, George Alfred. The new world compared with the old; government, institutions, and enterprises. Hartford, Conn., 1870. 8°.

Townsend, George H. Manual of dates; a dict. of reference to events. Lond., N. Y., 1862. 16°.
— *Same.* 2d ed. enl. London, 1867. 8°.

Townsend, *Rev.* Horatio. Statistical survey of the County of Cork; with observations on the means of improvement. Dublin, 1810. 8°.

Townsend, *Rev.* John, *d.* 1826. Memoirs of T. Boston, 1831. 12°.

Townsend, John. The doom of slavery in the union; its safety out of it; [address before the Edisto Island Vigilant Assoc.]. Charleston, 1860. 8°.
— The South alone should govern the South. 3d ed. Charleston, 1860. 12°.
— *Another copy.* (**B 1481**)

Townsend, John K. Narrative of a journey across the Rocky Mts. to Columbia River, *etc.* Phila., 1839. 8°.

Townsend, Jonathan. Caveat against strife; sermon, Medfield, Nov. 13, 1748. Boston, 1749. 8°. (**B 42, 584**)
— Sermon, at the desire of the ministers of Mass. Bay, in Boston, June 1. Boston, 1758. 8°. (**B 334**)

Townsend, *Rev.* Joseph. Dissertation on the poor-laws, by a well-wisher to mankind, 1786. London, 1817. 8°. (**B 693**)
— Elements of therapeutics. Boston, 1802. 8°.
— Journey through Spain, 1786–87. 2d ed. London, 1792. 3 v. 8°.
— Physician's vade mecum, a compendium of nosology and therapeutics. From the 6th London ed. Boston, 1805. 16°.

Townsend, Joseph Phipps. Rambles and observations in New South Wales. London, 1849. 8°.

Townsend, Meredith. The poor. (*In* **Questions for a reformed Parliament.** 1867.)
— **Sanford, J. L.** (*In his* Great governing families of Eng. 1865.)

Townsend, Penn, *Funeral sermon on.* 1727. *See* **Foxcroft, T.** (**B 314**)

Townsend, Peter S., *M.D.* Diss. on the influence of the passions in the production of disease. N. Y., 1816. 8°. (**B 814**)

Townsend, Robert. Catalogue of the library of Capt. R. T., sold June 9. N. Y., [186–]. 8°.

Townsend, Shearjashub Bourne. Oration on the aids of genius, Prov., Sept. 3. Prov., 1822. 8°. (**B 1714**)
— Oration on the means of preserving our civil and religious liberties, Sherburn, July 4. Boston, 1821. 8°. (**B 557**)

Townsend, Shippie. Attention to the Scriptures for an answer to the inquiry whether unbelievers are under the law and curse. Boston, 1795. 12°. (**B 659**)
— The gospel considered and the manner in which it should be preached. Boston, 1792. 8°. (**B 998**)
— Gospel news. Boston, 1794. 8°.
— Peace and joy; a brief attempt to consider the blessings of peace between Great Britain and America. Boston, 1788. 8°. (**B 250**)

Townsend, Thompson. The lost ship; drama. (*In* **Sargent, E.** Mod. stand. dr., v. 39.)

Townsend, Wm. Charles. Lives of twelve eminent judges. London, 1846. 2 v. 8°.
Contents. Vol. 1. F. Buller. — Lord Kenyon. — Lord Alvanley. — Lord Loughborough. — Sir Vicary Gibbs. — Lord Ellenborough. — Lord Erskine. 2. Lord Erskine, contin. — Lord Redesdale. — Sir W. Grant. — Lord Tenterden. — Lord Stowell. — Lord Eldon.
— Modern state trials. London, 1850. 2 v. 8°.
Contents. Vol. 1. J. Frost. — E. Oxford. — J. Stuart. — J. Thomas, Earl of Cardigan. — F. B. Courvoisier. — D. M'Naughton. — A. Alexander. — S. O'Brien. 2. Lord Cochrane and others. — The Wakefields. — Hunter, and others. — J. A. Williams. — C. Pinney. — Moxon. — O'Connell.

Townsend, Wm. E., *M.D.* Notice of T. (*In* **Mass. Med. Soc.** Med. com., v. 11. 1867.)

Townshend, Charles. Defence of the minority on general warrants. (*In* **Coll.** of scarce tracts, v. 1. 1763. **B 604**)
— Fitzgerald, P. C. Townsend, wit and statesman. London, 1866. 8°.

Townshend, *Rev.* Chauncy Hare. Facts in mesmerism; ed. by R. H. Collyer. 1st Amer. ed. Boston, 1841. 12°.
— The three gates. London, 1859. 8°.

Townshend, Frederick Trench. Ten thousand miles of travel, sport, and adventures. London, 1869. 8°.

Townshend, George, 1*st Marquis Townshend.* Baratariana; political pieces pub. during [his] administration in Ireland. 3d ed. Dublin, 1777. 12°.
— Letter to an Hon. Brig.-Gen., com. in chief of the forces in Canada. London, 1760. 8°.

Townshend, N. S. Speech on the present position of the Democratic party, June 23. Washington, 1852. 8°. (**B 1506**)

Townson, Robert. Travels in Hungary, 1793. London, 1797. 4°.
— Voyage en Turquie. (*In* **Montémont, A.** Biblioth. univ., v. 46. 1836.)

Townson, Thomas, *D.D.* Sermon, visitation of the Bp. of Chester, Aug. 13, 1778. Chester, [1778]. 4°. (**A 58**)
— **Blunt, J. J.** T.'s discources. (*In his* Essays. 1860.)

Towrson, Wm. *See* **Towerson, W.**

Toxicology. *See* **Poisons.**

Toxophilus. *See* **Ascham, R.**

Toy, The; or, The lie of the day. *See* **O'Keefe, J.**

Toynbee, *Capt.* The condition of sea men. (*In* **Nat. Assoc. Prom. Soc. Sci.** Trans., 1866.)

Toy-shop, The; a farce. *See* **Dodsley, R.**

Toze, Eobald. Present state of Europe; pref., a discourse on polity and government; tr. by T. Nugent. London, 1770. 3 v. 8°.

Tozer, *Rev.* Henry Fanshawe. Researches in the highlands of Turkey; with notes on the ballads, tales, and classical superstitions of the modern Greeks. London, 1869. 2 v. 8°
— Monks of Mt. Athos. — Norway. (*In* **Galton, F.** Vacation tourists. 1860.)

Tozzetti, Giovanni Targioni. *See* Targioni-Tozzetti, G.
Tozzi, Luca. NICERON, J. P. (*In his* Mém., v. 17. 1732, *and*, *Germ.*, v. 13. 1756.)
Trabea. Fragm. (*In* Estienne, R. Fr. poet. vet. Lat. 1564; — *and in* Ribbeck, O. Scen. Rom. poesis frag., v. 2. 1855.)
Tracer, T., *and others*. G. C. Smith unmasked. *n.t.p.* [1836?] 8°. (B 1395)
Trachalus, Galerius. BERNARDI, A. E. F. Recherches sur T., orateur et consul romain. (*In* Paris. Inst. *Ac. d. Inscr.* Mem., v. 7. 1824.)
Tracheotomy. TALBOT, I. T. Tracheotomy in croup. (*In* Mass. Homœop. Med. Soc. Pub. 1862.)
Tract for the day; how to conquer Texas before Texas conquers us. Boston, 1845. 8°. (B 1510)
Tract magazine and Christian miscellany, 1842, 43, 45–48. London, 1842–48. 5 v. 12°.
Tract on the arrogant pretensions of the Orthodox Clergy. *n.p.*, [18—]. 4°. (B 1354, 1754)
Tract Societies. *See* the name of the society, as American Tract Society; — Christian Tract Soc.; — New Eng. Tract Soc.; — Religious Tract Soc.
Tractarianism. *See* Tracts for the times.
Tractatus de contractibus juri hodierno Galliæ accommodatus, ad usum seminarii Cenomanensis. Ed. 2a Mechlin. Mechliniæ, 1822. 12°.
Tractatus varii Latini a Crevier, Brotier, Auger. Londini, 1788. 8°.
Tractors. PERKINS, E. Evidences of the efficacy of Dr. Perkins' patent metallic instruments. Phila., [1797]. 12°. (C 159)
— LANGWORTHY, C. C. Enquiry into the influence of metallic tractors. 2d ed. Bath, 1798. 8°. (B 816)
— PERKINS, B. D. Experiments with metallic tractors as pub. by Herholdt and Rafn. London, 1799. 8°.
Tracts, Religious. ADDRESS to Christians, recommending the distribution of cheap religious tracts. Charlestown, 1802. 8°. (B 657)

Collections.

— WATSON, R. Collection of theological tracts. London, 1791. 6 v. 8°.
— ENTERTAINING, moral, and religious repository. Vol. 1. Elizabeth-Town, 1798. 12°.
— AMER. TRACT SOC. Elegant narratives. N. Y., [18—]. 12°.
— - Pictorial narratives. N. Y., [18—]. 12°.
— CHEAP repository tracts. [Vol. 1, pp. 265–380, v. 2, pp. 1–112.] 1st Boston from latest Eng. ed. Boston, 1802. 2 v. 8°. (C 163)
— COTTAGE LIBRARY OF CHRISTIAN KNOWLEDGE. Religious tracts. Vol. 2. London, 1806. 12°.
— CHRISTIAN TRACT SOCIETY. Tracts to inculcate moral conduct on Christian principles. London, 1812–15. 3 v. 12°.
— NEW ENGLAND TRACT SOCIETY. Tracts. Andover, 1814. 2 v. 12°.
— TRACTS, moral and religious. Boston, 1848. 8°.
— PERRY, N. Experimental knowledge. Nos. 1–23. 2d ed. Boston, 1850. 2 v. 12°.
— - *Same.* Nos. 29, 33. *n.t.p.* [18—.] 12°.
Tracts conc. the ancient means of national defence by free militia; [by G. Sharp]. London, 1781. 8°. (B 767)
Tracts for priests and people. London, 1861–62. 2 v. 12°.
Namely. Vol. 1. **Hughes,** T. Religio laici. — **Maurice,** F. D. The mote and the beam. — **Garden,** F. Atonement as a fact and as a theory. **Davies,** J. L. The signs of the kingdom of Heaven. — **P.,** C. K. Boundaries of the Church. — **Langley,** J. N. The message of the Church. — **Ludlow,** J. M. A dialogue on doubt; — On laws of nature, and the faith therein; — On positive philosophy. — **Maurice,** J. F. D. Morality and divinity. **2. Chretien,** C. P. Evidences for those who think and feel more than they can read. — **Ludlow,** J. M. Dissent from and dissent in the Church. — **Garden,** F. The creeds. — **Strachey,** *Sir* E. The prophets of the Old Testament. — **Maurice,** J. F. D. Do kings reign by the grace of God? — **Davies,** J. L. The Spirit giveth life; — The death of Christ. — **Lyttleton,** W. H., Testimony of Scripture to the authority of conscience and reason. — **Garden,** F. Doctrine of sacrifice vindicated. — **Hutton,** R. H. Incarnation and principles of evidence; with a letter to the writer by F. D. Maurice. — **Langley,** J. N. English voluntaryism. — **Voluntary** principle in America; by an Eng. clergyman.
— *Same.* Vol. 1. Boston, 1862. 12°.
Tracts for the new times. N. Y., 1847. 8°. (B 1470)
Namely. **Letter** to a Swedenborgian. — **Wilkinson,** J. J. G. Science for all; — Popular sketch of Swedenborg's philosophical works.
Tracts for the times; by members of the University of Oxford, [18—]. London, 1833–40. 5 v. 8°.
Contents. Vol. 1. No. 1. **Newman,** J. H. Thoughts on the ministerial commission. 2. **Newman,** J. H. The Catholic Church. 3. **Thoughts** on alterations in the liturgy. 4. **Keble,** J. Adherence to the apostolical succession the safest course. 5. **Williams,** I. Short address on the nature and const. of the ch. of Christ, and on the branch of it in Eng. 6. **Newman,** J. H. The present obligation of primitive practice. 7. **Newman,** J. H. Episcopal Church apostolical. 8. **Newman,** J. H. The gospel a law of liberty. 9. **Froude,** R. H. Shortening the church service. 10. **Newman,** J. H. Heads of a week-day lecture. 11, 20, 47. **Newman,** J. H. The visible church. 12. **Keble,** T. Richard Nelson: Bishops, priests, and deacons. 13. **Keble,** J. Sunday lessons; The principles of selection. 14. The ember days. 15. **Newman,** J. H. Apostolical succession of the English church. 16. **Advent.** 17. The **ministerial** commission a trust from Christ for the benefit of his people. 18. **Pusey,** E. B. Thoughts on the benefits of the system of fasting. 19. **Newman,** J. H. On arguing conc. the apostolical succession. 20. *See* 11. 21. **Newman,** J. H. Mortification of the flesh a Scripture duty. 22. **Keble,** T. Richard Nelson: The Athanasian creed. 23. The **faith** and obedience of churchmen, the strength of the church. 24. The **Scripture** view of the apostolic commission. 25. **Beveridge,** W., *Bp.* Public prayer. 26. **Beveridge,** W., *Bp.* Frequent communion. 27, 28. **Cosin,** J., *Bp.* History of popish transubstantiation. 29, 30. **Williams,** I. Christian liberty. 31. **Reformed** church. 32. **Standing** ordinances of religion. 33. **Primitive** episcopacy. 34. **Newman,** J. H. Rites and customs of the church. 35. The people's interest in their minister's commission. 36. **Account** of religious sects at present in England. 37. **Wilson,** *Bp.* T. Form of excommunication. 38, 41. **Newman,** J. H. Via media. 39. **Wilson,** *Bp.* T. Form of receiving penitents. 40. **Keble,** J. Richard Nelson: Baptism. 41. *See* 38. 42, 44, 46, 48, 50, 53, 55, 62, 65. **Wilson,** *Bp.* T. Meditations on his sacred office. 43. **Keble,** J. Richard Nelson: Length of the public service. 44. *See* 42. 45. **Newman,** J. H. The grounds of our faith. 46. *See* 42. *Records of the Church.* I. **Ignatius** *Antiochenus, Bp.* Epistle to the Ephesians. — II. **Ignatius** *Antiochenus, Bp.* Epistle to the Magnesians. — III. **Eusebius** *Cæsariensis.* The apostle St. John and the robber. — IV. **Ignatius** *Antiochenus, Bp.* Epistle to Polycarp. — V. **Ignatius** *Antiochenus, Bp.* Epistle to the Trallians. — VI. **Eusebius** *Cæsariensis.* Account of the martyrs of Lyons and Vienne. — VII. **Ignatius** *Antiochenus, Bp.* Epistle to the Smyrneans. — VII. **Ignatius** *Antiochenus, Bp.* Epistle to the Romans. — IX. **Martyrdom** of Ignatius at Rome. — X. **Ignatius** *Antiochenus, Bp.* Epistle to the Philadelphians. — XI. **Eusebius** *Cæsariensis, Bp.* Account of the martyrdom of St. James the apostle. — XII. **Irenæus,** *St.* The martyrdom of Polycarp. — XIII. **Justinus** *martyr.* Primitive Christian worship. — XIV. **Irenæus,** *St.* Rule of faith. — XV. **Justinus** *martyr.* The temporal condition, and the principles of Christians; from the epistle to Diognetus. — XVI. **Clemens** *Alexandrinus.* Address of Clement of Alexandria to the heathen. — XVII, XVIII. **Tertullianus,** O. S. F. Rule of faith.
2, pt. 1. 47. *See* 11. 48. *See* 42. 49. The **kingdom** of heaven. 50. *See* 42. 51. On **dissent** without reason in conscience. 52. **Keble,** J. Sermon for St. Matthias' day. 53. *See* 42. 54. **Keble,** J. Sermon for the annunciation. 55. *See* 42. 56. Holydays observed in the English church. 57. **Keble,** J. Sermon for St. Mark's day. 58. On the **church,** as viewed by faith and by the world. 59. **Palmer,** W. The position of the church of Christ in England relatively to the state of the nation. 60. **Keble,** J. Sermon for St. Philip's and St. James' day. 61. The Catholic church a witness against illiberality. 62. *See* 42. 63. **Froude,** R. H. The antiquity of the existing liturgies. 64. **Bull,** G., *Bp.* Ancient liturgies. 65. *See* 42. 66. **Pusey,** E. B. Thoughts on fasting.
2, pt. 2. 67. **Pusey,** E. B. Scriptural views of holy baptism. 68–70. Same, contin. *Wanting.* *Records of the Church.* XIX, XX, XXI. **Cyprianus,** *St.* Unity of the Church. — XXII. **Tertullianus,** Q. S. F.

Baptism. — XXIII. Martyrdom of St. Felix and St. Lawrence. — XXIV, XXV. Vincentius *Lirinensis*. Tests of heresy.

3. 71. **Newman**, J. H. On the controversy with the Romanists. 72. **Usher**, J., *Abp.* Prayers for the dead. 73. Newman, J. H. On the introduction of rationalistic principles into religion. 74. Catena patrum, no. 1: Apostolical succession. 75. **Newman**, J. H. On the Roman breviary as embodying the substance of the devotional services of the Catholic Church. 76. Catena patrum, no. 4: Baptismal regeneration. 77. **Pusey**, E. B. Earnest remonstrance to the author of the 'Pope's letter'.

4. 78. Catena patrum, no. 2: Testimony of writers in the later Eng. Church to the duty of mantaining quod semper, quod ubique, quod ab omnibus traditum est. 79. Newman, J. H. On purgatory. 80. **Williams**, I. On reserve in communicating religious knowledge. 81. Catena patrum, no. 4: Eucharistic sacrifice. 82. Newman, J. H. Letter to a magazine on Dr. Pusey's tracton baptism.

5. 83. Newman, J. H. Advent sermons on Antichrist. 84. **Whether** a clergyman of the Church of England is bound to have morning and evening prayers daily in his parish church? 85. **Newman**, J. H. Lectures on the Scripture proofs of the doctrines of the church. 86. **Williams**, I. Indications of a superintending Providence in the preservation of the prayer book and in the changes which it has undergone. 87. **Williams**, I. On reserve in communicating religious knowledge. 88. **Andrews**, L., *Bp.* The Greek devotions of A., tr. and arr. by J. H. Newman.

Note. No. 68-70 were not reprinted for this set.

— *Same.* No. 80. **Williams**, I. Oxford theology: Reserve in communicating religious knowledge. N. Y., 1843. 8°. (B 1377)

— *Same.* Tract no. 90. Newman, J. H. Remarks on passages in the 39 articles. N. Y., 1865. 12°.

— *Same.* Tract no. 90. With preface by E. B. Pusey; also, Catholic subscription to 39 articles by J. Keble. London, 1865. 8°.

— EXTRACTS from the 'Tr. for the times', Lyra Apostolica, *etc.*, showing that to oppose Ultra-Protestantism is not to favor Popery. *n.p.*, [1839 or 40]. 8°. (B 1148)

— BARTER, W. B. Remarks made by Lord Morpeth on the authors of 'The tracts for the times' and the University of Oxford, considered. London, 1841. 8°. (B 1361)

— BIRD, C. S. Plea for a reformed church; observations on a declaration of the Tractarians, in the British critic, July. London, 1841. 8°.

— BRICKNELL, W. S. Resignation and lay communion; Keble's view of the position and duties of the Tractarians in his 'Letter to Coleridge'. London, 1841. 8°. (B 1230)

— WILLIAMS, I. A few remarks on the charge of the Ld. Bp. of Glocester on No. 80 and 87. Oxford, 1841. 8°. (B 1377)

— BEASLEY, *Rev.* F. Examination of No. 90 of the Oxford tracts for the times. New York, 1842. 8°. (B 1377)

— LIFE and defence of Bp. E. Bonner; by a Tractarian Brit. critic. London, 1842. 8°.

— ROGERS, H. Anglicanism; or, The Oxford tractarian school. [1843.] — Recent developments of tractarianism. [1844.] (*In his* Essays, v. 3. 1860.)

— ANTHON, *Rev.* H. The churchman warned against the errors of the times. N. Y., 1843. 8°. (B 1377)

— BRICKNELL, W. S. Oxford tract no. 90 and Ward's 'Ideal of a Christian church'. Oxford, 1844. 8°.

— TAYLOR, I. Ancient Christianity and doctrines of Oxford tracts. Lond., 1844. 2 v. 8°.

— GOODE, W. Tract 90 historically refuted. London, 1845. 8°.

— ATKINSON, G. Appeal to the Church of Eng. pointing out the dangers to which the Church is exposed from the tractarian movement. London, 1848. 8°. (B 1377)

— CAUTIONS for the times. No. 9-25. London, [1851-53]. 8°. (B 1377)

— GRESLEY, W. Letter to the Dean of Bristol [Gilbert Elliot] on what he considers the 'Fundamental error' of Tractarianism. London, 1851 8°. (B 1377)

— — A second word of remonstrance, *etc.* London, 1851. 8°. (B 1377)

— — A word of remonstrance with the Evangelicals, *etc.* 3d ed. Lond., 1851. 8°. (B 1377)

— NEWMAN, J. H. (*In his* Apologia. **1864**; 1865.)

— OAKELEY, F. History of the tractarian movement, 1833-45. London, **1865**. 12°.

— BENNETT, W. J. E. Some results of the tractarian movement of 1833. (*In* **Shipley**, O. The Church and the world. **1867**.)

Tracts for to-day. *See* **Conway**, M. D.

Tracts illustrative of the traditionary and hist. antiquities of Scotland. Edin., 1836. 8°.

Namely. **Hay**, R. Vindication of E. More and her children. — **Gordon**, J. Dissertation conc. the marriage of Robert II. with E. More. — **Waddel**, A. Remarks on Innes's 'Crit. essay on ancient inhabitants of Scotland'. — **Cunningham**, J. Essay on inscrip. of Macduff's Crosse in Fyfe. — **Memoirs** rel. to the restoration of James I. of Scotland. — **Taitt**, A. Roman acc. of Britain and Ireland, in ans. to Innes. — **Ruthven**, *Ld.* P. Relation of the death of D. Rizzio. — **Johnston**, R. Historie of Scotland during the minority of James VI.; tr. by T. Middleton. — **True** acc. of the baptism of Prince Henry Frederick.

Tracts on constitutional subjects. *See* **Northcote**, T.

Tracts on health. No. 15. *n.t.p.* [18—.] 8°. (C 271)

Tracts on liberty of conscience and persecution, 1614-1661. *See* **Underhill**, E. B.

Tracts rel. to military proc. in Lancashire during the great civil war. [Manchester,] 1844. 4°. (Chetham Soc., v. 2.)

Tracy, *Mrs.* Ann (Bromfield). Reminiscences of J. Bromfield. Salem, 1852. 8°.

Tracy, Antoine Louis Claude Destutt de. *See* **Destutt de Tracy**, A. L. C., *comte*.

Tracy, Henry R. Memoir of the pilgrimage to Va. of the Knight Templars. *See* **Freemasons**. *De Molay Encampment.*

Tracy, Joseph, *D.D.* Address before the Soc. for Religious Inquiry in the Univ. of Vt., Aug. 6. Boston, 1839. 8°. (B 1145)

— Christian liberty; sermon, ordination of D. Weld, Brookfield, Vt., July 1. Windsor, 1830. 8°. (B 1145)

— Colonization and missions; historical examination of the state of society in Western Africa. Boston, 1844. 8°. (B 1484, 2541)

— *Same.* 4th ed. Boston, 1845. 8°. (B 1881)

— *Same.* 5th ed. enl. Boston, 1846. 8°. (B 1484)

— Idolatry misrepresents the deity; sermon, ordination of I. Tracy, Hartford, Oct. 28, 1832. Windsor, 1833. 8°. (B 1145)

— Natural equality; sermon before the Vt. Colonization Soc., Montpelier, Oct. 17. Windsor, 1833. 8°. (B 1145)

Tracy, Nathaniel. Letter respecting the posterity of D. Gookin. (*In* **Mass. Hist. Soc.** Col., v. 2. 1870.)

Tracy, *Rev.* Oren. Address [to] the Female Temperance Soc., Newport, N. H. [2d ed.] Concord, 1834. 12°. (D 24)

Tracy, *Rev.* Thomas. Sermon; death of Belshazzar. (*In* Liberal preacher, v. 3. 1830.) — **Striving** to enter at the strait gate. (*In* n.s., v. 4. 1834.) — The Christian panoply. — Salvation come to the house of Zaccheus. (*In* n.s., v. 5. 1836.)

Tracy, Uriah. Scipio's reflections on Monroe's 'View of the conduct of the executive', 1794-96. Boston, 1798. 12°.

— *Other copies.* (B 133, 597, 741, 1080, C 73)

— *Same.* Reflections, *etc.*, under the signature of Scipio; [with add.]. *n.p.*, *n.d.* 8°. (B 597)

Note. Falsely attributed at one time to Alexander Hamilton.

— Speech in the Senate, Dec. 2, [on the 12th amendment to the Constitution]. Wash., 1803. 8°. (B 623)

— Speech on a proposed amendment of the Constitution, 1802. — Remarks on the judiciary system. (*In* **Moore**, F. Amer. eloquence, v. 1. 1864.)

— To the freemen of Conn., [Sept. 6]. *n.p.*, 1803. 8°. (B 405, 609)

Tracy, Wm. TYNDALE, W. T.'s testament expounded. (*In his* Answer to Sir T. More, *etc.* 1850.)

Tracy, Wm. S. Oration, July 4, before the Republicans of Norwich, Franklin, and Bozrah. Norwich, 1820. 8°. (B 1097)

Trade. *See* **Commerce**; — *also* the names of the different trades.

Trade, Boards of. *See* **Boston. Board of Trade**; — **National Board of Trade**; — **New York. Chamber of Commerce**; — **Philadelphia. Chamber of Commerce.**

Trade circular annual for 1871. N. Y., 1871. 8°.

Trade unions. NATIONAL ASSOC. FOR THE PROMOTION OF SOC. SCIENCE. Trades societies and strikes; report of the committee. London, 1860. 8°.

— GR. BRIT. *Commissioners on the Organization and Rules of Trades Unions.* 1st-4th reports. London, 1867. 4 v. f°.

— - *Parl.* Correspondence with Her Majesty's missions abroad, regarding industrial questions and trades unions. London, 1867. 8°.

— LUSHINGTON, G. Workmen and trade unions. (*In* Questions for a reformed parliament. 1867.)

— PARIS, L. P. A. d'O., *comte* de. Les associations ouvrières en Angleterre. Paris, 1869. 18°.

— - *Eng.* The trades' unions of Eng.; tr. by N. J. Senior; ed. by T. Hughes. London, 1869. 8°.

— BRENTANO, L. On the history and developement of gilds, and the origin of trade unions. (*In* Smith, J. T. English gilds. 1870.)

— GREG, W. R. Intrinsic vice of trade unions. (*In his* Political problems. 1870.)

— STIRLING, J. Mr. Mill on trades unions; a criticism. (*In* Grant, *Sir* A. Recess studies. 1870.)

— THURLOW, T. J. H. Trade unions abroad and hints for home legislation. London, 1870. 8°.

See also Shoemakers.

Tradescant, John. Voyage to Russia. (*In* Hamel, J. Eng. and Russia. 1854.)

Tradesman; or, Commercial mag. Vol. 1-8; July 1808-June 1812. London, 1808-12. 8 v. 8°.

Tradition. WRIGHT, S. Scripture and tradition considered; sermon, Feb. 6. London, 1735. 8°. (B 33)

— WIGGLESWORTH, E. The authority of tradition considered; [Dudleian] lecture, Nov. 5, 1777. Boston, 1778. 8°. (B 67, 152, 200, 234)

— SALISBURY, E. E. Contribution to the science of Muslim tradition. (*In* Amer. Orient. Soc. Journ., v. 7. 1862.)

Traditions tératologiques. *See* Berger de Xivrey, J.

Trafford, F. G., *pseud.* *See* Riddell, *Mrs.* J. H.

Tragédies du foyer, Les; par P. Deltuf. Paris, 1868. 18°.

Tragedies of the wilderness. *See* Drake, S. G.

Tragedy. QUADRIO, F. S. Storia e ragione della tragica poesia. (Vol. 3 *of his* Storia d' ogni poesia. 1743.)

— SCHILLER, J. C. F. von. Ueber den Grund Vergnügens an tragischen Gegenständen. — Die tragische Kunst. [1792.] (*In his* Werke, v. 11. 1867.)

— PRESTON, W. On the choice of subjects for tragedy. (*In* Roy. Irish Acad. Trans., v. 8. 1802.)

— BAVA DI SAN PAOLO, E. Dialogo tra morti, cioè tra Cornelio e Maffei sopra la tragedia. (*In* Turin. Ac. d. Sci. Mem., v. 15. 1805.)

— SUEVERN, J. W. Ueber einige historische und politische Anspielungen in der alten Tragödie. (*In* Berlin. Ak. d. Wiss. Abh., 1824.)

Tragedy of errors; [by Mrs. M. L. Putnam]. Boston, 1862. 16°.

Tragedy of success; [by Mrs. M. L. Putnam]. Boston, 1862. 12°.

Tragedy of tragedies; or, The life and death of Tom Thumb the Great. *See* Fielding, H.

Traggia, Joaquin. Ilustracion del reynado de Ramiro II de Aragon. (*In* Madrid. Ac. d. l. Hist. Mem., v. 3. 1799.) — Sobre el origen y succesion del reyno pirenaico hasta Don Sancho el Mayor. (*In* v. 4. 1805.) — Sobre el origen del condado de Ribagorza. (*In* v. 5. 1817.)

Tragicorum Græcorum fragmenta. *See* Nauck, A.

Tragicorum Latinorum reliquiæ. *See* Ribbeck, O.

Trail, James. Sermon, parish church of Lisburn, June 28, 1767, death of R. Archbold. Dublin, 1768. 8°. (B 1208)

Trail, Wm. Sermon before the synod of Angus and Mearns, Dundee, Apr. 19, 1748. Edin., 1749. 8°. (B 1902)

Traill, *Mrs.* Catherine Parr. The backwoods of Canada; letters from the wife of an emigrant officer. London, 1836. 12°. (Lib. ent. knowl., v. 33.)

Traill, Robert. Letter to his wife. Edin., 1762. 8°. (B 655)

Traill, *Rev.* Robert. Life of W. Guthrie. (*In* Guthrie, W. Christian's great interest. 1815.)

Traill, *Prof.* Thomas Stewart. The thermometer and pyrometer. (*In* Soc. Diff. Usef. Knowl. Lib. U. K., Nat. phil., v. 2. 1832.)

Train, *Rev.* Charles. Discourse, Medway, festival of St. John the Baptist, June 24, A. L. 5817. Dedham, 1817. 8°. (B 334)

— Oration, Hopkinton, Mass., July 4. Worcester, 1823. 8°. (B 1202)

— Sermon, Littleton, dedication of the Baptist meeting-house, and ordination of A. Sanderson. Boston, 1823. 8°. (B 296)

Train, George Francis. American merchant in Europe, Asia, and Australia; with introd. by F. Hunt. N. Y., 1857. 12°.

— Union speeches delivered in England. Phila., 1862. 8°.

Training. *See* Gymnastics.

Traité de la formation mécanique des langues; [par C. de Brosses]. Paris, 1765. 2 v. 12°.

— *Same.* [Nouv. éd.] Paris, 1801. 2 v. 12°.

Traité de Londres, 1852, 1863. *See* Gr. Brit. *King* (p. 1215).

Traité des finances et de la fausse monnaie des Romains; [par Chassipol]. Paris, 1740. 12°.

Traité sur l'amour; par Ibn Ebi Hagelet. (*In* Biblioth. univ. des romans, Nouv., v. 1. 1798.)

Traitor, The; a tragedy. *See* Shirley, J.

Traitre puni, Le; comédie. *See* Le Sage, A. R.

Traits and stories of the Irish peasantry. 1869. *See* Carleton, W.

Traits and trials of early life; by L. E. L. Maclean. (*In her* Works, v. 1. 1850.)

Trajan's column. PIRANESI, G. B. Trofeo o sia magnifica colonna fatte da Traiano. *n.p.*, *n.d.* f°. (v. 8.)

Trajanus, Marcus Ulpius, *afterwards* Cæsar Nerva Trajanus Augustus, *emperor.* Epistolæ. (*In* Plinius Cæcilius Secundus, C. Epistolarum lib. 1853.)

Note. For other eds. and trans. *see* Plinius (p. 2360).

— AMPÈRE, J. J. A. L'histoire romaine à Rome: Trajan. (*In* Revue d. D. Mondes, mars 1857.)

— ARNOLD, T. Life of T. (*In his* History of the Roman commonwealth, v. 2. 1849.)

— PLINIUS CÆCILIUS SECUNDUS, C. Epistolæ ad T. — Panegyricus. (*In his* Epistolarum lib. 1853.)

Note. For other eds. and trans. *see* Plinius (p. 2360).

Trampa adelante. *See* Moreto y Cabaña, A.

Tramps. *See* Vagabonds.

Tramways. PALMER, H. R. Description of a railway on a new principle. London, 1824. 8°.

Tranaltos, F. de. Histoire de la guerre civile amér. 1867. *See* Cortambert, L.

Tranca, *El caballero de la, pseud.* Discursos de la viuda de veinte y cuatro maridos. (*In* Castro, A. de. Curios. bibliogr. 1855.)

Tranchant de Laverne, Léger Marie Philippe. L'art militaire chez les nations de l'antiquité et de temps moderne analysé et comparé. Paris, 1805. 8°.

— Life of Field Marshal Souvarof. Balt., 1814. 8°.

Tranchepain de St. Augustin, Marie. Relation du voyage des premières Ursulines à la Nouvelle Orléans et de leur établissement. N. Y., 1859. 4°.

Trancoso. CAMPOS DE MESQUITA, J. M. de. Sobre a cultura e utilidade dos nobos na comarca de Trancoso. (*In* Lisbon. Ac. d. Sci. Mem. econ., v. 5. 1815.)

Tranquility. ALBERTI, L. B. Della tranquillità dell' animo. (*In his* Opere volgari, v. 1. 1843.)

Transactions. HUNT, E. B. Systematizing the abbreviations of titles of periodicals, trans., *etc.* (*In* Amer. Assoc. Proc., v. 10, pt. 2. 1857.)

Transactions. For Transactions of any society *see* the name of the society.

Transactions in India, 1756-83; a history of the British interests. London, 1786. 8°.

Transcaucasia. HAXTHAUSEN, A. v. Nations between the Black Sea and Caspian. London, 1854. 8°.

— BJOERKLUND, —. Esquisses de voyage en Trans-Caucasie. (*In* Paris. Soc. de Géog. Bulletin, 5e sér., v. 16. 1868.)

Transcendentalism. ALEXANDER, J. W., *and* DOD, A. B. Transcendentalism of the Germans and of Cousin. Camb., 1840. 8°.

— BRADFORD, A. Human learning favourable to true religion; address before the Φ. B. K. of Bowdoin Coll., Sept. 2. Boston, 1841. 8°. (B 1181)

— GREENE, W. B. Transcendentalism. West Brookfield, 1849. 8°. (B 1356)

See also **Kant. I.** (p. 1611, 1612).

Trans-continental, published daily on the Pullman hotel express between Boston and San Francisco, May 24 – June 30. *n.p.*, 1870. 4°.

Transcript, Daily evening; July 24,–Dec. 31, 1830; 1831-34; June 8, 1835 – June 1880. Boston, 1830 – 80. 53 v. f°.

Note. From Jan. 1854, called 'Boston evening transcript'.

Transit. HOUGH, G. W. Remarks on personal equation in transit obs. (*In* Amer. Assoc. Proc., v. 16. 1868.)

Translation. BITAUBÉ, P. J. Du goût national, considéré par rapport à la traduction. (*In* Berlin. Ak. d. Wiss. Abh., 1779.)

— TYTLER, A. F. Principles of T. London, 1797. 8°.

— GÉDOYN, N., *l'abbé*. Des traductions. (*In* Sérieys, A. Bibl. acad., v. 11. 1811.)

— SCHLEIERMACHER, F. E. D. Ueber die verschiedenen Methoden des Uebersetzens. (*In* Berlin. Ak. d. Wiss. Abh., 1812–13.)

Translations and sketches of biog.; by a lady. London, 1839. 12°.

Contents. German. Amelia, Duchess of Saxe Weimar. — J. C. F. von Schiller. — J. W. von Goethe. — A. W. von Schlegel. — J. G. von Herder. — K. S. Körner. — F. von Matthisson. — J. L. Uhland. — J. J. Hottinger. — C. A. Tiedge. — *Italian.* F. Petrarch. — P. Metastasio. — V. Colonna. — T. Molsa. — L. Ammanati. — V. Gambara. — L. Clasio. — A. de G. Bertola. — G. Roberti. — *Spanish and Portuguese.* M. Cervantes Saavedra. — L. de Vega. — P. Calderon de la Barca. — M. Valdez. — T. de Yriarte. — L. Camoens. — *French.* A. L. G. de Stael Holstein. — F. de Malherbe. — J. B. P. de Molière. — J. Racine. — J. B. Massillon. — F. T. B. d'Arnaud. — J. B. L. Gresset.

Translations from the Chinese and Armenian. *See* **Neumann, C. F.**

Transmission. *See* **Heredity.**

Transmission of disease. *See* **Hereditary diseases.**

Transmutation of metals. *See* **Alchemy.**

Transon, Abel Louis Etienne. Affranchissement des femmes; prédication du 1er janvier. Paris, 1832. 8°. (B 1660)

— De la religion saint simonienne; aux élèves de l'Ecole Polytechnique. Brux., 1831. 8°. (B 1659)

— Prédication du 11 décembre; vue générale sur le nouv. caractère de l'apostolat saint simonien; Morale individuelle; Allocution par P. M. Laurent. Paris, 1831. 8°. (B 1660)

Transplanted flowers; memoirs of Mrs. Rumpff, *etc.* *See* **Baird, R.**

Transplanting. LOUREIRO, J. de. Da trasplantaçaõ das arvores. (*In* Lisbon. Ac. d. Sci. Mem. econ., v. 1. 1789.)

Transport ships. DUNDAS, H., *Visc. Melville.* Speech on troop-ships. London, 1810. 8°. (B 1418)

— GREAT BRIT. *House of Com.* Report from the select committee on transport service. [London, 1861.] f°.

See also **Military transportation.**

Transport voyage to Mauritius and back. London, 1857. 12°.

Transportation. DUPIN, C. Des nouvelles forces motrices, et des nouveaux moyens de transport. (*In* Paris. Inst. *Ac. d. Sci. Mor.* Mém., v. 2. 1839.)

— POTTS, J. D. The science of transportation. (*In* Amer. Soc. Sci. Assoc. Trans., v. 2. 1870.)

See also **Carriages; — Ferries; — Steamboats; — Steam navigation.**

Transportation, Military. *See* **Military transportation.**

Transportation (*punishment*). BENTHAM, J. Panopticon *vs.* New South Wales. [1802.] (*In his* Works, v. 4. 1843.)

— GR. BRITAIN. *Ho. of Commons.* Report on transportation. [London, 1812.] 8°.

— - Report on secondary punishments. [London, 1831.] f°.

— - Report, 1832. [London, 1832.] f°.

— WHATELY, K. Thoughts on secondary punishment. London, 1832. 8°.

— THERRY, R. Chapter on transportation and the ticket-of-leave system. (*In his* Reminiscences. 1863.)

Transubstantiation.

Works in favor of transubstantiation.

— LANFRANC, *Arbp.*, *d.* 1089. Liber de corpore et sanguine Domini nostra adversus Berengarium. (*In his* Opera, v. 2. 1844.)

— ENGLAND, J., *Bp. of Charleston.* Explanation of a passage from Tertullian against transubstantiation, 1824. — Letter on obs. of Rev. Mr. Bedell [on] transubstantiation, 1827. — Letters on transubstantiation to J. Bachman, 1838. (*In his* Works, v. 1. 1849.)

Works against transubstantiation.

— FRITH, J. Book answering M. More's letter conc. the sacrament of the body and blood of Christ. [153–.] (*In his* Works. 1831.)

— HOOPER, J., *Bp.* Answer to the Bp. of Winchester's book. 1546. (*In his* Early writings. 1843. Parker Soc.)

— LUKE, *physician.* The enterlude of John Bon and Mast Person; a dialogue on the festival of Corpus Christi and on transubstantiation [1548]; ed. by W. H. Black. London, 1852. 8°. (Percy Soc., v. 30.)

— RIDLEY, N. Determination conc. the sacrament. 1549. — Brief declaration of the Lord's supper; or, Treatise against the error of transubstantiation. 1555. (*In his* Works. 1841.)

— GRINDAL, E., *Abp.* A fruitful dialogue between custom and verity, declaring these words of Christ 'This is my body'. [1551.] (*In his* Remains. 1843. Parker Soc.)

— TUKE, T. Concerning the Holy Eucharist and the popish breaden God. 1625. (*In* Grosart, A. B. Fuller Worthies' lib. Miscel., v. 3. 1871.)

— DOWNE, J. The reall presence by transubstantiation unknown to ancient fathers. (*In his* Certain treatises. 1633.)

— TAYLOR, J., *d.* 1667. Real presence of Christ in the holy sacrament. (*In his* Works, v. 9. 1822; v. 6. 1852.)

— C., J. Short discourse against transubstanciation. London, 1675. 16°. (D 68)

— ROMAN tradition examined; answer to Rational disc. of transubstantiation. *n.p.*, 1676. 4°. (B 1396)

— CLAGETT, W. Paraphrase with notes upon the sixth chapter of John. London, 1686. 4°.

— BURNET, G. Discourse conc. transubstantiation and idolatry, an answer to the Bp. of Oxford's plea. London, 1688. 4°. (B 92)

— TILLOTSON, J., *Abp. of Canterbury, d.* 1694. Discourse against transubstantiation. London, 1728. 12°. (C 1)

— HARRIS, W. Discourse conc. transubstantiation. London, 1735. 8°. (B 33)

— BIRD, C. S. Transubstantiation tried by Scripture and reason. 2d ed. London, 1839. 8°. (B 1381)

— CROPP, J. Popery and its priesthood condemned; transubstantiation unreasonable and idolatrous; lecture. London, 1850. 8°. (B 1383)

See also **Lord's supper** (p. 1785–87).

Transvaal. CHESSON, F. W. Dutch republics of S. Africa. London, 1871. 8°.

Transversals. CARNOT, L. N. M. Mémoire sur la relation entre les distances respectives de cinq points; théorie des transversales. Paris, 1806. 4°.

Transylvania. *Description and travels.*

— PAGET, J. Hungary and Transylvania, [1839]. New ed. London, 1850. 2 v. 8°.

— ANSTED, D. T. Short trip in Hungary and Transylvania, 1862. London, 1862. 8°.

— BONER, C. Transylvania; its products and its people. London, 1865. 8°.
— *Maps.* SCHOLLENBERGER, J. Transylvania. *n.p.*, [16—]. (E 78, no. 260)
— - TRANSYLVANIA. *n.p.*, [16—]. (E 78, no. 259)

History.

— TEUTSCH, G. D., *and* FIRNHABER, F. Urkundenbuch zur Geschichte Siebenbürgens, 1075-1301. 1. Theil. Wien, 1857. 8°. (Fontes rerum Austr., 2. Abth., 15. Bd.)
— KRAUS, G. Siebenbürgische Chronik des Schässburger Stadtschreibers. Wien, 1862-64. 2 v. 8°. (Fontes rer. Austr., 1. Abth., 3, 4. Bd.)
— NIKLOS, B., *Gróf.* Mémoires sur les affaires de Transylvania, [1659-79]. (*In* Brenner, *L'abbé.* Hist. des révolutions. 1739.)
See also Hungary; — Slavic nations; — Slavonia.

Transylvania University. Catalogue of the officers and students. Lexington, 1830. 8°. (B 946)
— CROSS, J. E. Present condition of the medical department of the Univ. Lexington, Ky., 1834. 8°. (B 1551)

Trant, T. Abercromby; narrative of a journey through Greece, 1830; with remarks upon the actual state of the naval and military power of the Ottoman Empire. London, 1830. 8°.

Trap to catch a sunbeam, A.; by Mrs. M. A. P. Mackarness. (*In her* Sunbeam stories, v. 1. 1868.)

Trapany, Domingo Gian. *See* Gian-Trapany, D.

Trap'em, Tristram, *pseud.* Boston assemblage, The; a peep at Caucus-hall. Boston, 1812. 8°. (B 443)

Trapezuntium. *See* Trebizond.

Trapier, *Rev.* Paul. Plan for giving the Gospel to our servants; a sermon in Charleston, on Sundays in February. Charleston, 1848. 8°.
— RELIGIOUS instruction of the black population; [review of T.'s sermon from the Southern Presbyterian review]. *n.t.p.* [1847.] 8°.

Trapp, Joseph, *D.D.* Prælectiones poeticæ. Ed. 3a. Londini, 1736. 2 v. 12°.
— Preservative against unsettled notions in religion; in several discourses. Lond., 1715. 8°.
— Real nature of the church or kingdom of Christ; sermon June 2. London, 1717. 8°. (B 31)
— Sermon before the Lord Mayor, Jan. 30. London, 1729. 4°. (B 1465)
— BURNET, G. Letter to Trapp [on] his sermon on the real nature of the Church. Lond., 1717. 8°. (B 32)
— LAW, W. Earnest and serious answer to T.'s discourse, *etc.* *t.p.w.* [London, 1740.] 8°. (B 141)
— SINGLE combat or personal dispute between J. T. and his anonymous antagonist. Antwerp, 1728. 8°. (B 149)

Trapp, S. Clement. The pollution of rivers. (*In* Nat. Assoc. Prom. Soc. Sci. Trans., 1866.)

Trappe, John. Brief commentary or exposition upon the Gospel of St. John. London, 1646. 4°. (B 1904)

Trasenter, S. Abolition of octrois in Belgium. (*In* Nat. Assoc. Prom. Soc. Sci. Trans., 1862.)

Trask, *Rev.* George. Thoughts and stories on tobacco for American lads; by Uncle Toby. Boston, 1852. 24°.

Trask, John B. Report on geology. *See* California. *Geological Survey.*

Trask, Wm. Blake. Genealogy of the Sumner family. (*In* Sumner, W. H. Memoir. 1854.)

Trato de Argel, El. *See* Cervantes Saavedra, M.

Trato muda costumbre, El; comedia. *See* Mendoza, A. H. de. (E 112)

Traun, Otto Ferdinand, *Graf von Abensberg.* CUST, *Sir* E. (*In his* Lives of the warriors who have commanded fleets, v. 1. 1869.)

Trauter Herd und fremde Woge; von M. Solitaire [W. Nürnberger]. Lpz., 1856. 8°.

Trautwine, John C. Rough notes of an exploration for a canal route in New Granada. Phila., 1854. 8°.

Travailleurs de la mer, Les; par V. Hugo. Brux., 1866. 3 v. 8°.

Travancore. DRURY, H. Account of T. (*In* Visscher, J. C. Letters from Malabar. 1862.)

Travel. *History.* SMILES, S. Early roads and modes of travelling. (*In his* Lives of the engineers, v. 1. 1861.)
— - RANTOUL, R. S. Some notes on old modes of travel. (*In* Essex Inst. Hist. col., v. 11. 1871.)
— HOWELL, J. Instructions for forreine travell. 1642. London, 1869. 12°. (Arber, E. Eng. reprints, v. 8.)
— ART de voyager utilement. Amst., 1698. 12°.
— BLANCHARD, E. Religion des voyageurs. [1714.] (*In* Sérieys, A. Bibl. acad., v. 2. 1810.)
— ESSAI d'instructions pour voyager utilement. (*In* Bernard, J. F. Rec. de voy., v. 1. 1716.)
— LINNÉ, C. von. Oration [on] travelling in one's own countrey. 1741. (*In* Stillingfleet, B. Miscel. tracts. 1769.)
— HURD, R. Uses of foreign travel. [1764.] (*In his* Moral and pol. dialogues. 1759; v. 3. 1776.)
— BERCHTOLD, L. Essay to direct the inquiries of travellers with obs. on the means of preserving life, *etc.* [1789.] (Vol. 2, 2d ed.) London, 1793, 89. 2 v. 8°.
— QUESTIONS de statistique à l'usage des voyageurs; par ***. Paris, 1813. 8°. (B 795)
— SCHLEIERMACHER, F. E. D. Ueber die Auswanderungsverbote. (*In* Berlin. Ak. d. Wiss. Abh., 1816-17.)
— CUNNINGHAM, J. W. Cautions to continental travellers. (*In* Pamphleteer, 1822; v. 21 of B 838)
— GALTON, F. Art of travel. London, 1855. 12°.
— LORD, J. K. At home in the wilderness. 2d ed. London, 1867. 12°.
— TESTON, —. Articles de voyage et de campement. (*In* France. *Com. Imp. de l'Expos. de* 1867. Rapports, v. 4. 1868.)
— LORD, W. B., *and* BAINES, B. Shifts and expedients of camp-life. London, 1871. 8°.

Travel through Belgium and along the Rhine, 1814. Amst., 1815. 12°.

Traveller, The; Oct. 11. London, 1806. f°. (E 198)

Traveller, The; Apr. 2-11. London, 1807. f°. (E 172)

Traveller, Daily evening; Sept. 1846 - Dec. 1876. Vol. 2-33. Boston, 1846-76. 32 v. f°.
Note. For previous vols., *see* American traveller. In 1846 there were two editions, the morning, called American traveller' and the 'Daily evening traveller'.

Traveller, The. *See* Goldsmith, O.

Travellers. ST. JOHN, J. A. Lives of celebrated travellers. N. Y., 1844-47. 3 v. 16°. (Harper's fam. lib., v. 38-40.)
— GUÉRIN, L. Les navigateurs français. Paris, 1847. 8°.
— CORTAMBERT, R. Les illustres voyageuses. Paris, 1866. 8°.
See also the names of noted travellers, as Bell, J.; — Benjamin *of Tudela*; — Bernier, F.; — Bruce, J.; — Buckingham, J. S.; — Burckhardt, J. L.; — Burton, J. — Cabot, S.; — Champlain, S. de; — Chardin, J.; — Clarke, E. D.; — Colombo, C.; — Cook, *Capt.* W.; — Dampier, *Capt.* W.; — Denon, D. E.; — Drake, *Sir* F.; — Forster, G.; — Gama, V. de; — Hanney, J.; — Hasselquist, F.; — Heber, R.; — Herodotus; — Humboldt, F. H. A. von; — Ibn Batuta; — Kaempfer, E.; — La Salle, R. C. de; — Ledyard, J.; — Leo, J.; — Livingstone, D.; — Magalhaens, F. de; — Markham, C. R.; — Maundrell, H.; — Montagu, *Lady* M. P. W.; — Niebuhr, K.; — Pallas, P. S.; — Park, M.; — Pococke, R.; — Polo, M.; — Rubruquis, W.; — Shaw, *Dr.* T.; — Stanley, H. M.; — Tavernier, J. B.; — Taylor, B.; — Ulloa, A. *and* F. de; — Valle, P. della; — Volney, C. F. C. de; — Zeno, N. *and* A.; — *also* Voyages and travels (*Collections*).

Travellers, The; by [Miss C. M. Sedgwick]. N. Y., 1825. 18°.

Travels. *See* Voyages and travels.

Travels in Bohemia; by an old traveller. London, 1857. 2 v. 12°.

Travels in the Crimea, 1793; by a secretary to the Russian embassy. London, 1802. 8°.

Travels of Cyrus. *See* **Ramsay, A.**
Travels of ungodliness. *See* **Keach, B.**
Travels through Spain and part of Portugal. 1st Amer. ed. Boston, 1808. 12°.
Travers, Benjamin. On constitutional irritation. London, 1826. 8°.
— Pathology of venereal affections. London, 1830. 8°.
— Process of nature in repairing injuries of the intestines. London, 1812. 8°.
— Synopsis of diseases of the eye. 2d ed. London, 1821. 8°.
— *and* Cooper, A. P. Surgical essays. (Pt. 1, 3d ed.; pt. 2, 2d ed.) London, 1818–20. 2 pt. 8°.
Travers, George. Trial for the murder of J. McKim and T. Hasey. Boston, 1815. 8°. (B 344)
Travers, Walter. Supplication to the Council. (*In* **Hooker, R.** Works, v. 3. 1841.)
Traversari, Ambrogio (*Lat.* **Ambrosius** *Camaldulensis*). Traversarii aliorumque ad ipsum et ad alios de Ambrosio Latinæ epistolæ, a P. Canneto observ. illustratæ; [cum orationibus VI et] Ambrosii vita in qua historia litteraria Florentina ab a. 1192 ad 1440 deducta est a L. Mehus. Florentiæ, 1759. 2 v. f°.
— Niceron, J. P. (*In his* Mém., v. 19. 1732.)
Traverse, Jean Victor, *baron* de. Etude militaire; extract du traité de l'art de la guerre du maréchal de Puysegur; extraits des commentaires de M. de Folard, *etc.* Paris, 1758. 3 v. 12°.
Traverso, Nicolò. Cevasco, G. (*In* **Grillo, L.** Elogi di Liguri, v. 3. 1846.)
Travesuras de Pantoja, Las; comedia. *See* **Moreto y Cabana, A.**
Travesuras son valor; comedia. *See* **Moreto y Cabana, A.**
Travis, G. Porson, R. Letters to T. in answer to his 'Defence of the Three heavenly witnesses'. London, 1790. 8°.
Traydor contra su sangre, El; comedia. *See* **Matos Fragoso, A.** (E 112)
Treadwell, Daniel. On the construction of improved ordnance. Camb., 1862. 8°.
— Description of a machine, called a gypsey, for spinning hemp and flax. (*In* **Amer. Acad.** Mem., n.s., v. 1. 1833.) — Practicability of constructing cannon of great caliber capable of enduring long-continued use under full charges. (*In* v. 6. 1857.) — Measure of the forces of bodies moving with different velocities. (*In* v. 8. 1861.) — Construction of hooped cannon; sequel to a memoir 'On the practicability of constructing cannon of great caliber', *etc.* (*In* v. 9, pt. 1. 1867.)
— Relation of science to the useful arts; lecture before the Amer. Acad. of Arts, *etc.* Camb., 1855. 8°. (B 1583)
— Report to the mayor of Boston, on supplying the inhabitants with water. Boston, 1825. 8°. (B 285, 942, 2533, E 62)
— Short account of an improved cannon. Camb., 1845. 12°.
Treadwheel. Good, J. M. Letter on the mischiefs incidental to the tread-wheel. 2d ed. (*In* **Pamphleteer,** 1824; v. 23 of B 838)
Treason. Bacon, F., *Baron*, *d.* 1626. Cases of treason. (*In his* Works, v. 7. 1859.)
Note. For other eds. *see* **Bacon** (p. 181–183).
— Discourse concerning high treason. London, 1683. f°. (A 54)
— Eyre, J. Charge; in a special commission to enquire of certain high treasons and misprisons of treason, within the County of Middlesex. [London,] 1794. 4°. (B 1433, 1434)
See also **Trials for treason.**
Treason's master piece; or, Conference between Oliver [Cromwell] and a com. of Parliament. London, 1680. 8°.
Treasure trove; a tale, by S. Lover. N. Y., 1850. 8°.
Treasury, Biographical, *etc.* *See* **Maunder, S.**
Treasury Department. *See* **France.** *Ministère des Finances*; — **Great Britain.** *Treasury*; — **United States.** *Treasury Dept.*
Treasury notes. Calhoun, J. C. Speech on a bill authorizing an issue of treasury notes, Sept. 19. Wash., 1837. 8°. (B 1496)
— Barnard, D. D. Speech on the treasury note bill, Mar. 25. Wash., 1840. 8°. (B 1497)
— Duncan, A. Speech on the bill to authorize the issue of treasury notes, Mar. 26. Wash., 1840. 8°. (B 1817)
— King, T. B. Speech on the bill add. to the act on treasury notes, Mar. 18. *n.t.p.* [1840.] 8°. (B 1497, 1817)
— Evans, G. Speech on the bill to authorize an issue of treasury notes, January 19. Wash., 1841. 8°. (B 1497)
— Wise, H. A. Speech on the treasury note bill, Jan. 27, 28, 29. Wash., 1841. 8°. (B 1497)
Treat, *Capt.* Joseph. Vindication against Maj. Gen. J. Brown; report of the battle of Chippeway. Phila., 1815. 8°. (A 1)
Treat, Samuel. Address. (*In* **Washington Univ.** Inauguration. 1857.)
Treaties. Bernard, M. The obligation of treaties. (*In his* Four lectures. 1868.)
— Egger, E. Les traités publics dans l'antiquité. (*In* **Paris. Inst.** *Ac. d. Inscr.* Mém., v. 24, 1e pte. 1861.)

Lists.

— Thomas, F. S. Lists of treaties, leagues, covenants, congresses, *etc.*, mentioned in history, [1153–1856]. (*In his* Hist. notes, v. 3. 1856.)
— Tétot, —. Répertoire des traités; table générale des recueils. Paris, 1866–[67]. 2 v. 8°.
Contents. Vol. 1. Partie chronologique, 1493–1866. 2. Partie alphabétique, 1493–1867.

Collections.

— Dumont, J., *and others.* Corps diplomatique du droit des gens, avec suppléments, [800–1738]. Amst., 1726–39. 13 v. f°.
— Chalmers, G. Collection of treaties between Gr. Brit. and other powers, **1259–1787.** London, 1790. 2 v. 8°.
— Recueil des traitez entre les couronnes d'Espagne et de France, **1526–1611.** 2e éd. Anvers, 1645. 12°.
— Koch, C. G. de. Histoire abrégé des traités de paix, **1648–1815**; ouvrage refondu par M. Schoell. Paris, 1817–18. 15 v. 8°.
— General collection of treatys, declarations of war, manifestos, and other public papers, relating to peace and war, among the potentates of Europe, from 1648 to the present time. London, 1710. 8°.
— Collection of all the treaties between Gr. Brit. and other powers, **1688–[1771].** London, 1772. 2 v. 8°.
Contents. Vol. 1. 1688–1727. 2. 1727–71.
— Lamberty, G. de. Mémoires, traités, *etc.*, **1690–1731.** La Haye, 1731–40. 4 v. 4°.
— Recueil des traités, *etc.*, conc. l'Autriche et l'Italie, **[1703–1859].** Paris, 1859. 8°.
— Clercq, A. de. Recueil des traités de la France, **1713–1872.** Paris, 1864–72. 10 v. 8°.
— Recueil des traitez de paix, *etc.*, **1713–68.** Lyon, [176–]. 12°.
— Martens, G. F. Recueil des principaux traités depuis **1761.** Gott., 1791. 7 v. 8°.
— - Suppl., préc. de traités du 18e siècle. Gott., 1802–20. 8 v. (v. 5 w.). 8°.
— Rousset De Misset, J. Recueil d'actes, négotiations, *etc.*, depuis la paix d'Utrecht, **[1714–44].** La Haye, 1728–45. 18 v. 12°.
— All the treaties between the U. S. and Gr. Brit., 1783–1814. Boston, 1815. 8°. (A 1, B 1602)
— Burch, S. General index to the laws of the U. S., Mar. 4., **1789** - Mar. 3, **1827,** [with] all [the] treaties. Wash., 1828. 8°.
— British and foreign state papers. **1812–67.** Vol. 1–57. London, 1825–71. 57 v. 8°.

— Archives diplomatiques, 1861-74. Paris, *F. Amyot*, 1861-74. 45 v. 8°.
— Oettinger, E. M. Moniteur des faits, *etc.* (*In his* Moniteur des dates. 1866.)
See also France (p. 1026); — Great Britain. *King* (p. 1214, 1215); — Munster; — Nimeguen; — Osnaburg; — Seville, Treaty of; — Utrecht; — Vienna, Congress of; — Westphalia, Congress of; — *also* U. S.
Treatise intended for the good of mankind, setting forth wherein true happiness of king and subject consists. Canterbury, [17—]. 8. (B 368)
Treatise on happiness. London, 1833. 2 v. 12°.
Treatise on practical husbandry; by an experienced farmer. Dublin, 1792. 8°.
Treatise on the advantages and necessity of frequent communion. Dublin, 1793. 18°.
Treatise on the currency and the exchanges; proposing a general exchange office. N. Y., 1841. 8°. (B 544)
Treatise on the first principles of Christianity. Halifax, 1808. 8°. (B 273)
Treatise on the law of contracts. Boston, 1840. 12°.
Treatise on the millennium. Boston, 1838. 12°.
Treatise on the ministry of the Church. Dublin, 1817. 8°.
Treatise on the nature and constitution of the Christian Church. London, 1773. 8°. (B 904)
Treatise on the police and crimes of the metropolis. London, 1829. 8°.
Treatise on the principles, practice, and history of commerce; [by J. R. M'Culloch]. (*In* Soc. Diff. of Knowledge. Lib. usef. knowl. 1831.)
Treatise on the proceedings of a camp-meeting held in Bern, N. Y., Sept. 1810. Albany, [1810]. 8°. (B 666)
Treatise on the progress of literature, and its effects on society; incl. a sketch of the progress of Eng. and Scottish literature. Edin., 1834. 8°.
Treaty, The, its merits and demerits fairly discussed and displayed. *n.p.*, [179-]. 8°. (B 619)
Trebeck, George. Travels in the Himalayan provinces, 1841. *See* Moorcroft, W.
Trebeck, *Rev.* James. Letter to J. Hollis on his reasons for scepticism. London, 1796. 8°. (B 1408)
Trebizond. Finlay, G. Hist. of Greece and of the Empire of Trebizond, 1204-1461. Edin., 1851. 8°.
— Panaretus Chronicon Trapezuntinum, [1204-1426]. — Eugenicus. Laus Trapezuntis, [14—]. (*In* Eustathius *Thessalonicensis*. Opusc. 1832.)
Trechsel, F. Die protestantischen Antitrinitarier vor Faustus Socin. Heidelb., 1839-44. 2 v. 8°.
Contents. Vol. 1. Michael Servet und seine Vorgänger. 2. Lelio Sozini und die Antitrinitarier seiner Zeit.
Tredgold, Thomas. Elementary principles of carpentry. London, 1820. 4°.
— Experiments on the expansion of water by heat. — Principles of tension. (*In* Instit. of Civil Engineers. Trans., v. 1. 1842.)
— Joinery and stone-masonry. (*In* Ashpitel, A. Treatise on archictecture, *etc.* 1867.)
— Notes and additions to R. Buchanan's 'Practical essays on mill work', *etc.* London, 1823. 2 v. 8°.
— Practical essay on the strength of cast iron and other metals. 2d ed. London, 1824. 8°.
— Practical treatise on railroads and carriages. London, 1825. 8°.
— *Same.* 2d ed. with add. London, 1831. 8°.
— Principles of warming and ventilating public buildings. London, 1824. 8°.
— Rudimentary treatise on the principles of construction in carpentry. *See* Robison, J.
— On the steam engine. London, 1827. 4°.
Trediakovski, Wassili Kirilovitch. Ode sur là reddition de Dantzick, 1734. (*In* Pappadopoulo, M. L., *and* Gallet, P. D. Choix des meilleurs morceaux. 1800.)
Tree of legal knowledge. Raleigh, 1838. f°.
Trees. Parkinson, J. Paradisi in sole Paradisus terrestris. London, 1629. f°.

— - Theatrum botanicum; the theater of plantes; an herball of large extent. London, 1640. f°.
— Barck, H. Vernatio arborum. (*In* Linné. Amœn. acad., v. 3. 1764.)
— - *Eng.* The foliation of trees. 1753. (*In* Stillingfleet, B. Miscellaneous tracts. 1769; *also* B 1913)
— Duhamel du Monceau, H. L. Traité des arbres fruitiers. Paris, 1768. 2 v. 8°.
— Weston, R. Method of raising timber trees, fruit-trees, *etc.* (*In his* Gardener's and planter's calendar. 1778.)
— Marshall, H. Arbustrum Americanum; catalogue of forest trees, *etc.* Phila., 1785. 8°.
— - *Another copy.* (W 43)
— Marshall, W. Planting and rural ornaments. 2d ed. London, 1796. 2 v. 8°.
— Few minutes advice to gentlemen of landed property, *etc.* Chester, [18—]. 8°. (B 519)
— Michaux, F. A. Histoire des arbres forestiers de l'Amér. Septent., pins et sapins. Paris, 1810. 8°.
— Nicol, W. The planter's kalender; nursery, forest, and grove. Edin., 1812. 8°.
— Michaud, F. A. North Amer. sylva. Phila., 1817-19. 3 v. 8°.
— Bosc, L. A. G., *and* Baudrillard, J. J. Dictionnaire de la culture des arbres. (Vol. 7 *of* Encyclopédie méthodique. 1821.)
— Phillips, H. Sylva florifera. London, 1823. 2 v. 8°.
— Sylvan sketches; or, Companion to the park and the shrubbery. London, 1825. 8°.
— Big black walnut tree, The, in Chatauque County, N. Y., and other trees. Phila., 1827. 8°. (B 1743)
— Browne, D. J. Sylva Americana; description of forest trees of the U. States. Boston, 1832. 8°.
— Steuart, H. The planter's guide. 1st Amer. from 2d London ed. N. Y., 1832. 8°.
— London, J. C. Arboretum et fruticetum Britannicum, [1834-38]. 2d ed. London, 1854. 8 v. 8°.
— Browne, D. J. Trees of America, native and foreign, pictorially and botanically delineated. N. Y., 1846. 8°.
— Emerson, G. B. Trees and shrubs growing naturally in Mass. Boston, 1846. 8°.
— Nuttall, T. Continuation of Michaux's North Amer. sylva. Phila., 1853. 3 v. 8°.
— Pappe, L. Silva Capensis; descrip. of South African forest trees. Cape Town, 1854. 8°.
— Piper, R. U. Trees of America. No. 1-4. Boston, 1855-[58]. 4°.
— Harvey, A. Trees and their nature. London, 1856. 16°.
— Cooper, J. G. Distributions of the forest trees of N. America. (*In* Smithsonian Inst. Report, 1858.)
— Coultas, H. What may be learned from a tree. N. Y., 1860. 8°.
— Turgan, J. Les pépinières d'A. Leroy, à Angers. (*In his* Les grandes usines de France, v. 3. 1863.)
— Daubeny, C. Trees and shrubs of the ancients. Oxford, 1865. 8°.
See also Forests; — Fruit trees; — Landscape gardening; — Oak; — Olive; — Pine trees.
Tregelles, Samuel Prideaux. Account of the printed text of the Greek New Testament. London, 1854. 8°.
Treille (*Lat.* Trelæus), Nicolas Clement de. Austrasiæ reges et duces epigrammatis descripti. Coloniæ, 1591. 4°.
Trelawny, Edward John. Adventures of a younger son. London, [18—]. 12°.
— Recollections of the last days of Shelley and Byron. Boston, 1858. 16°.

Trelawny, *Sir* Jonathan, *Bp.* STRICKLAND, A. (*In her* Lives of the seven bishops. 1866.)

Trelawny of Trelawne; by [A. E.] Bray. London, 1845. 16°. (Novels, v. 7.)

Trelawny papers. (*In* Camden miscel., v. 2. 1835. Camden Soc., v. 55.)

Trelier, Etienne. Coutumes et statuts de la ville de Bergerac. Bergerac, 1779. 12°.

— De jure jurando. (*In* Grævius, J. G. Thes. antiq. Rom., v. 5. 1696.)

Trellon, Claude de. Poésie. (*In* Annales poét., v. 12. 1779.)

— Sonnets, *etc.* (*In* Auguis, P. R. Poètes françois, v. 5. 1824.)

Tremain, Frederick Lyman. TREMAIN, J[...] rial of T. Albany, 1865. 8°.

Tremain, Lyman. Memorial of F. T., late Lieut.-Col. of the 10th N. Y. Cavalry. Albany, 1865. 8°.

Tremaine; or, The man of refinement; by R. P. Ward. Phila., 1825. 2 v. 12°.

Note. From Blackwood's mag., v. 17. 1825.

Trembecki, Stanislaw. Poezye. W Lipsku, 1836. 2 v. 18°. (Bobrowicz, J. N. Bibl. klass. pol.)

Contents. Vol. 1. Krótka wiadomość o życiu S. Trembecki. — Bajki. — Wiersze rozmaite. — Listy. — Wiersze pod imieniem Bielawskiego. 2. Zofijówka. — Polanka i Powązki. — Początek księgi IV Eneidy Wirgiliusza. — — Sierota Chiński. — Syn marnotrawny.

Trembles. DRAKE, D. Memoir on the trembles or milk-sickness. Louisville, Ky., 1841. 8°. (B 1186)

Trembley, Jean. Essai sur 'Quelles sont les lumières qu'il importe le plus aux hommes d'acquérir, et quels sont les sentimens qu'on doit surtout chercher à leur inspirer'. (*In* Berlin. Ak. d. Wiss. Abh., 1795–97.) — Examen d'un passage de Macrobe. (*In* 1796.) — Sur une discussion relative à la chronologie ancienne. (*In* 1797.) — Observations sur un passage du dialogue de Platon, intitulé Menon. (*In* 1799–1800.) — Sur la philosophie des poëtes. (*In* 1801–02.) — Observations sur quelques points de la chronologie grecque. (*In* 1804.)

Tremella. VAUCHER, J. P. Histoire des trémelles. (*In his* Hist. des conferves. 1803.)

Tremellius, Emmanuel. NICERON, J. P. E. Fremellius [*sic*]. (*In his* Mém., v. 40. 1739.)

Tremenhere, Hugh Seymour. Constitution of the U. S. compared with our own. London, 1854. 8°.

— On examination of boys about to leave elementary day schools. (*In* Nat. Assoc. Prom. Soc. Sci. Trans., 1857.) — Factory schools and education under the print-works' act. — Children's employment commission. (*In* 1865.)

— Paper to the education commission. *n.t.p.* [London, 1861.] f°.

Tremiti Isles. COCHORELLA, B. Tremitanæ olim Diomedeæ insulæ descriptio. (*In* Grævius. Thes. antiq. Sicil., v. 14. 1725.)

Tremlett, *Rev.* F. W. Letter to the parish of St. Botolph, on his resignation. Boston, 1851. 8°. (B 1392)

Tremoille *or* Tremouille. *See* La Tremouille.

Tremont theatre. PELBY, W. Letters to the primitive subscribers. Boston, 1830. 8°. (B 942, 1794)

Trémouille, Charlotte de la. *See* Stanley, C. de la T.

Trench, Francis. A few notes from past life, 1818–32; ed. from correspondence. Oxford, 1862. 8°.

— Lecture at Reading, Eng., Dec. 19, 1854. (*In* Peabody, A. P. Conversation. 1867.)

Trench, *Mrs.* Melesina Chenevix. Correspondence. (*In* Leadbeater, M. Papers, v. 2. 1862.)

— Remains; [journals, letters, *etc.*, 1768–1827;] ed. by R. C. Trench. London, 1862. 8°.

Trench, Richard Chenevix, *Abp. of Dublin.* On the authorized version of the New Testament. 2d ed. London, 1859. 8°.

— Calderon; his life and genius; with specimens. N. Y., 1856. 12°.

— English past and present. N. Y., 1855. 12°.

— Five sermons before the University of Cambridge, Nov. 1856. London, 1857. 16°.

— History of the English sonnet. (*In* Afternoon lectures, v. 4. 1866; 1867.)

— The lessons in proverbs. From 2d Lond. ed. rev. and enl. N. Y., 1853. 12°.

— Notes on the miracles of our Lord. 4th ed. London, 1854. 8°.

— Poems. N. Y., 1856. 12°.

— Sacred Latin poetry, chiefly lyrical. London, 1864. 12°.

Contents. Adam of St. Victor. — St. Ambrose. — Pistor. — Peter the venerable. — Alanus. — Hildebert. — Mauburn. — Prudentius. — Fortunatus. — St. Bernard. — Bonaventura. — Robert II., King of France. Bede. — Alard. — Abelard. — Buttmann. — Jacobus de Benedictis. — Balde. — Marbod. — Damiani. — Thomas of Celano. — Bernard of Clugny. — Thomas of Kempen.

— Sermons preached in Westminster Abbey. N. Y., 1860. 12°.

— Some deficiencies in our English dictionaries. London, 1857. 8°.

— *Same.* 2d ed. (*In* Philolog. Soc. Trans., 1857.)

— Studies in the Gospels. London, 1867. 8°.

— The study of words. From 2d London ed. enl. N. Y., 1854. 12°.

— Synonyms of the New Testament. Camb., 1854, 63. 2 pt. 16°.

Trench, W. Steuart. Realities of Irish life; illustrations by J. T. Trench. London, 1868. 8°.

Trench, Wm. Stewart, *M.D.* On excessive infant mortality. (*In* Nat. Assoc. Prom. Soc. Sci. Trans., 1864.)

Trenchard, *Sir* John, *d.* 1695. WOOLRYCH, H. W. (*In his* Lives of serjeants-at-law, v. 1. 1869.)

Trenchard, John, *d.* 1723. History of standing armies in England. London, 1739. 8°. (B 578)

— *Same, abridgment.* With preface upon government. *n.p.*, [1780]. 8°. (B 767)

— The independent Whig. 1735. *See* Gordon, T., *and* Trenchard, J.

— Letter on the duty of the representatives of the Commons in Parliament, *etc.*, from Cato's letters. *n.t.p.* [London, 1789.] 8°. (B 767)

— *and* Gordon, T. Cato's letters; essays on liberty, civil and religious. 6th ed. London, 1755. 4 v. 12°.

Contents. Vol. 1. 1720–21. 2. 1721. 3. 1721–22. 4. 1722–23.

Trenck, Friedrich, *Freiherr* von der. Examen de l''Histoire secrète de la cour de Berlin'; [attribué à Mirabeau]. Berlin, [1789?]. 8°.

— Life; containing his adventures and his excessive sufferings during 10 years imprisonment at the fortress of Magdeburg, by command of Frederick the Great. Albany, 1853. 8°. (B 1460)

— Life of Baron Trenck; [by himself; tr. by T. Holcroft]. *t.p.mut.* [London, 1826.] 24°.

— DAVENPORT, R. A. Adventures of Baron Trenck. (*In his* Narratives, v. 1. 1840. Fam. lib., v. 74.)

Trendall, E. W. Original designs for cottages and villas. London, [1831]. 4°.

Trendelenburg, Friedrich Adolf. Ueber den letzten Unterschied der philosophischen Systeme. (*In* Berlin. Ak. d. Wiss. Abh., 1847.) — Ueber Spinoza's Grundgedankan und dessen Erfolg. (*In* 1849.) — Friedrich der Grosse und sein Grosskanzler Samuel von Cocceji. (*In* 1863.)

Trenor, John, *M.D.* Observations on neuralgia; with cases. *n.t.p.* [1823?] 8°. (B 1716)

Trent. WANGEN, F. von. Codex Wangianus; Urkundenbuch des Hochstiftes Trient, hrsg. von R. Kink. Wien, 1852. 8°. (Fontes rerum Austr., 2. Abth., 5. Bd.)

Trent, Council of. Canones et decreta; acc. annotationes. Valentiæ, 1639. 12°.

— Canones et decreta Concilii Tridentini ex ed. Romana 1834; ed. A. L. Richter. Lips., 1853. 8°.

— *Eng.* Canons and decrees; tr. into English by J. Waterworth, with essays on the history of the Council. London, 1848. 8°.

— BUNGENER, L. F. History of the Council of Trent. N. Y., 1855. 12°.
— CHEMNITZ, M. Concilii Tridentini decretorum examen. Francof., 1574. f°.
— NEW popish creed, The, decreed by the Council of Trent. London, 1714. 8°. (B 261)
— PALLAVICINO, P. S. Istoria del Concilio di Trento. Faenza, 1792. 6 v. 4°.
— - *Same.* (*In his* Opere, v. 1, 2. 1761, 63.)
— SARPI, P. Istoria del Concilio Tridentino, 1615. 2a ed. Geneva, 1629. 4°.
— - *Eng.* Historie of the Council of Trent; tr. by N. Brent. London, 1620. f°.
— - *Same.* Geneva, 1629. 4°.
— STILLINGFLEET, E., *Bp.* Council of Trent examined and disproved by Catholic traditions. (*In* **Cardwell, E.** Tracts, v. 3. 1837.)
— - *Same.* (*In his* Opere, v. 2-4. 1845, 46.)

Trent, *ship.* CASE of the Trent examined. London, 1862. 8°.
— GASPARIN, A. C., *comte* de. Une parole de paix sur le différend entre l'Angleterre et les Etats-Unis. Paris, 1862. 8°.
— GR. BRITAIN. *Parl.* Correspondence resp. the seizure of Messrs. Mason, Slidell, McFarland, and Eustis, from on board the 'Trent' by the commander of the U. S. ship of war 'San Jacinto'. London, 1862. f°.
— HAUTEFEUILLE, L. B. Affaire du T. (*In his* Questions de droit. 1868.)
— SMITH, P. A. Seizure of the southern commissioners considered with ref. to international law. London, 1862. 8°.

Trenton, *N. J.* **Convention,** 1812. Proceedings and address. *n.p.* [1812]. 8°. **(B 441)**

Trenton, *N. J.* **Convention,** 1828. Proceedings and address in favor of the present administration. Trenton, 1828. 8°. **(B 1494)**

Trepanning. PLA, J. D. C. Diss. de trepanatione sterni. Lugd. Bat., 1781. 4°. **(A 63)**

Trepka, X. Rozmyslania religijne i polityczne. W Paryzu, 1840. 16°. **(E 81)**

Tres portentos de Dios, Los. *See* **Guevara, L. V. de.**

Trescot, Wm. Henry. American view of the eastern question. Charleston, 1854. 12°. (C 264)
— Diplomacy of the revolution. N. Y., 1852. 12°.
— Diplomatic hist. of the administration of Washington and Adams. Boston, 1857. 8°.
— Letter to A. P. Butler, on the diplomatic system of the U. S. Charleston, 1853. 8°. **(B 1506)**
— Position and course of the South. Charleston, 1850. 8°. **(B 1504)**

Trescott, Samuel. Speech. (*In* **Doane,** G. H. Fourth of July at Burlington College. 1850. **B 1573)**

Tresham, Henry. Britannicus to Buonaparte. London, 1803. 4°.

Trésor, Le; comédie. *See* **Andrieux.** F. G. J. S.

Tresor, Li livres dou. *See* **Latini,** B.

Tressan, Louis Elizabeth de la Vergne, *marquis de Broussin, comte* de. Œuvres choisies. Paris, 1787-91. 12 v. 8°.

Contents. Vol. 1-3. Amadis de Gaule. **4-6.** Roland furieux. **7-10.** Romans de chevalerie. **7.** Tristan de Lénois. — Artus de Bretagne. — Flores et Blanche Fleur. — Cléomades et Claremonde. — Roman de la Rose. — Pierre de Provence. **8.** La fleur de batailles. — Huon de Bordeaux. — Guérin de Montglave. **9.** Dom Ursino le Navarin. — Le petit Jehan de Saintré. — Gerald de Nevers. **10.** Regner Lodbrog. — Zélie ou l'ingénue. **11, 12.** Œuvres posthumes. **11.** Vie. — Pièces fugitives. **12.** Réflexions sommaires sur l'esprit.

— Histoire du petit Jehan de Saintré et de la dame des belles-cousines; éd. ornée de figures dessinées par Moreau le jeune. Paris, 1791. 12°.
— Sur les progrès des arts et des sciences. (*In* **Sérieys,** A. Bibl. acad., v. 12. 1811.)
— **CONDORCET,** J. A. N. C., *marq.* de. (*In his* Œuvres, v. 3. 1847.)

Treswell, Robert. Relation of the journey of Charles, Earl of Nottingham, ambassador to Spain, 1604; printed 1605. (*In* **Somers,** J. Col. of tracts, v. 2. 1809.

Trethill farm; by L. Parr. (*In her* Blue bell of Red-neap. 1871.)

Trevelyan, Arthur. To the people; the moral lunacy of our class legislators, *etc.*, demonstrated. London, 1749. 8°. (B 1277)

Trevelyan, *Sir* Charles. GR. BRIT. *Parl.* East India; correspondence on proposed financial measures in India and despatches on the recal of Sir C. Trevelyan. [London, 1860.] f°.

Trevelyan, *Sir* Charles Edward. Application of the Roman alphabet to the Oriental languages; series of papers by Trevelyan, J. Prinsep, Tytler, A. Duff, and H. T. Prinsep. Serampore press, 1834. 8°.
— From Pesth to Brindisi in the autumn of 1869. (*In* **Grant,** *Sir* A. Recess studies. 1870.)

Trevelyan, George Otto. The competition wallah. London, 1864. 8°.
— *Same.* (*In* **Macmillan's** mag., v. 8-10. 1863-64.)
— Ladies in parliament and other pieces. Camb., 1869. 8°.

Trevelyan papers. Pts. 1-3. [London,] 1857-72. 3 v. 4°. (Camden Soc., v. 67, 84.)

Note. Vols. 1, 2, ed. by J. P. Collier, v. 3, by W. C. and C. E. Trevelyan.

Contents. Vol. 1. 670-1551. **2.** 1446-1643. **3.** 1477-1776.

Trevern, Jean François Marie. *See* **Le Pappe Trevern,** J. F. M.

Treves. PERROT, G. La ville de Trèves; étude d'archéologie et d'histoire, [-1865 A. D.]. (*In* **Revue** d. D. Mondes, avr. 1865.)
— **GESTA** Treverorum, -1629. (*In* **Pertz,** G. H. Mon. Germ., Scr., v. 8. 1848.)
— **HANSSEN,** G. Die Gehöferschaften, Erbgenossenschaften, im Regiersingsbezirk Trier. (*In* **Berlin. Ak. d. Wiss.** Abh., **1863.**)
— *Maps.* ARCHIEPISCOPATUS Trevirensis. *n.p.*, [16—]. **(E 78,** no. 91)
— - VISSCHER, J. N. Amst. Bat., [17—]. 2 maps. f°. **(E 64)**

Treves. Cathédrale. ROISIN, F. de. Cathédrale de Trèves. (*In* v. 12, 13. 1852-53.)

Treves. *See also* **St. Elizabeth's Hospital.**

Treves. Notre Dame. DIDRON, A. N. Notre-Dame de Trèves. (*In* **Annales** archéol., v. 11. 1851.)

Treves. S. Eucharius. ANNALES, 1015-1092. (*In* **Pertz,** G. H. Mon. Germ. hist., Scr., v. 5. 1849.)

Treves. S. Maximin. ANNALES. 708-987. (*In* **Pertz,** G. H. Mon. Germ., Scr., v. 2. 1829.)

Treves, Holy coat of. MARX, J. Geschichte des heil. Rockes zu Trier. Trier, **1844.** 12°.
— VOLLSTÄNDIGE Geschichte des heiligen Rockes in der Domkirche zu Trier. 3. Aufl. Coblenz, 1844. 12°.
— HEIL.-ROCK-Album; Aktenstücke, Berichte, *etc.* Lpz., [**1845**?] 12°.
— JOHN Ronge and the holy coat of Treves. N. Y., 1845. 12°.

See also **Ronge,** J.

Trevett, John, *vs.* **Weeden.** VARNUM, J. M. Case for refusing paper bills at par, Newport, Sept. 1786. Prov., 1787. 8°. (B 626)

Trevisano *or* **Trevigiano** (*Lat.* **Bernardus** *Trevisanus*). De chemico miraculo, quod lapidem philosophiæ appellant. (*In* **Zetzner,** L. Theatrum chem., v. 1. 1613.)
— *Eng.* Treatise on the philosophers-stone. (*In* **Cooper,** W. Col. chymica. 1684.)
— NICERON, J. P. (*In his* Mém., v. 13. 1730.)

Treviso. REDUSIO DE QUERO, A. Chronicon Tarvisinum, **1368-1428.** (*In* **Muratori,** L. A. Rer. Ital. scr., v. 19. 1731.)
— **MAURISIO,** G. Dominorum de Romano et Marchiæ Tarvisinæ historia, [1183-1238]. — **ROLANDINUS,** *grammaticus.* Libri chronicorum de factis in Marchia et prope ad Marchiam Tarvisinam, [1188-1262]. — MONACHI Paduani chronicorum libri tres, de rebus in Insubribus et Euganeis, [1207-1270]. (*In* **Grævius.** Thes. antiq. Ital., v. 6, pt. 1. 1722.)

Trevor, Arthur Hill, *Viscount Dungannon.* Life and times of William III. London, 1835. 2 v. 8°.
— Letter to the Bp. of Bangor on the proposed Paris testimonial. Osevestry, 1847. 8°. (B 1231)

Trevor, Edward, *pseud.* *See* **Lytton, E. R. B.**

Trevor, *Rev.* George. The conscience clause. (*In* **Shipley, O.** The church and the world. 1866.)

— Elementary education. — On mental competence. (*In* **Nat. Assoc. Prom. Soc. Sci.** Trans., 1864.)

Trévoux, Dictionnaire de. *See* **Dictionnaire** universel françois et latin. 1704.

Trévoux, Mémoires de. *See* **Mémoires** pour l'hist. des sciences et des beaux arts. 1701-04 (p. 1950).

Trew, Christoph Jacob. Plantæ selectæ quarum imagines pinxit G. D. Ehret, collegit notisque illust. C. J. Trew, et vivis coloribus repræs. J. J. Haid. Decuriæ I-X. Norimbergæ, 1750-73. f°.

Note. The description of plates 1-71 is by C. J. Trew, 72-100 by B. C. Vogel.

Trewendt, Eduard. Volks-Kalender, 1870. Breslau, [1869]. 16°. (**E 19**)

Trial. *See also* **Tryal.**

Trial, The; Calvin and Hopkins *vs.* the Bible and common sense; by a lover of the truth. 2d ed. enl.; add., some remarks on the Andover Institution. Boston, 1819. 8°.

Trial, The; King *vs.* Hurdy Gurdy. *n.t.p.* [179-?] 8°. (**B 429**)

Trial, The; more links of the 'Daisy chain'; by [C. M. Yonge]. N. Y., 1864. 2 v. in 1. 12°.

Trial by jury. *See* **Jury.**

Trial of Antichrist; [by W. Gregory]. 1st Amer. ed. Boston, 1810. 12°.

Trial of J. Allen. Boston, 1773. 8°. (**C 27**)

Trial of J. P. Zenger; added, the trial of W. Owen. London, 1765. 8°. (**B 1632**)

Trial of Mr. Whitefield's spirit; remarks upon his fourth journal. London, 1741. 8°. (**B 34**)

Trial of persons charged with burning the convent in Charlestown. *n.t.p.* [1834.] 8°. (**B 1441**)

Trial of the alleged assassins and conspirators, Washington, May and June, 1865, for the murder of Pres. Lincoln. Phila., 1865. 8°.

Trial of W. Wemms, *etc.*, for the murder of C. Attucks [and others]. Boston, 1770. 12°. (**C 77**)

— *Same.* Boston, 1807. 8°.

— *Another copy.* (**B 948**)

— *Same.* (*In* **Chandler, P. W.** Amer. criminal trials, v. 1. 1841; — *and in* **Kidder, F.** History of the Boston massacre. 1870.)

Trial of Wm. Brodie and G. Smith for robbery. Edin., 1788. 4°. (**A 15**)

Triall of treasure, Enterlude of the; ed. J. O. Halliwell. Lond., 1850. 8°. (Percy Soc., v. 28.)

Trials. Prévost-Paradol, L. A. Sur la procédure criminelle en Angleterre et aux Etats-Unis. (*In his* Essais de pol. 1861.)

Collections.

— Burke, P. Romance of the forum, [1125-1846]. London, [1861]. 8°.

— Howell, T. B. Complete collection of state trials to the year 1783, contin. to the present time by T. J. Howell, [1163-1820]. London, 1816-28. 34 v. 8°.

— Gayot de Pitaval, F. Causes célèbres; contin. par J. C. de La Ville, [1431-1740]. Amster., 1775. 26 v. 12°.

— Collection of the most remarkable and interesting trials, [1535-1776]. London, 1775-76. 2 v. 4°.

— Burke, P. Celebrated trials connected with the aristocracy, [1541-1846]. London, 1849. 8°.

— Jardine, D. Criminal trials, [1554-1605] London, 1832-35. 2 v. 12°. (Lib. ent. kn., v. 16, 17.)

— Craik, G. L. English causes célèbres; or, Reports of remarkable trials, [1628-1797]. London, 1844. 16°.

— Chandler, P. W. American criminal trials, [1637-1798]. Boston, 1841-44. 2 v. 12°.

— Goss, A. Account of the tryalls at Manchester, Oct. 1694. Manchester, 1864. 4°. (Chetham Soc., v. 61.)

— Méjan, M. Recueil des causes célèbres, [1757-1810]. 2e éd. Paris, 1808-11. 10 v. 8°.

— Feuerbach, P. J. A. Merkwürdige Criminal-Rechtsfälle, [1770-1824]. (1r Bd., 2e Aufl.) Giessen, 1821, 11. 2 v. 8°.

— - *Eng.* Narratives of remarkable criminal trials; tr. by Lady D. Gordon. Lond., 1846. 8°.

— Causes politiques célèbres du 19e siécle. Paris, 1826-28. 4 v. 8°.

— Townsend, W. C. Modern state trials, [1814-48]. London, 1850. 2 v. 8°.

— Warren, S. Modern state trials, [1814-48]. (*In his* Miscellanies, *etc.* 1855.)

Trials, Civil. *See* **American Print Works** *vs.* C. W. Lawrence. 1852; — **Amistad,** *Schooner.* 1841; — **Annesley,** J. 1743; — **Assoc. Ref. Ch. in N. Amer. Synod** *vs.* Proprietors of Meeting House in Federal St. 1854; — **Atkins,** J., *vs.* Sanger. 1822; — **Bacon,** S. T. *vs.* Chambers. 1859; — **Baker,** J., *vs.* Draper. 1860; — **Bank of the United States** *vs.* **Hammond,** C. 1823; — **Barnes,** T., *vs.* 1st Parish in Falmouth. 1810; — **Berry,** J., *vs.* Thomson. 1818; — **Blanchard,** L., *vs.* Smith. 1833; — **Boston Gas Light Co.,** *vs.* Gault. 1848; — **Bourne,** E. A., *vs.* City of Boston. 1853; — **Bradstreet,** *Mrs.* M., *vs.* Cooper. 1834; — **Brooks,** A. L., *vs.* Fisk and Norcross. 1854; — **Brooks,** W., *vs.* Byam. 1842; — **Burnett,** J., *vs.* Wadsworth. 1870; — **California** *vs.* Butler and McGlynn. 1861; — **Capell** *and* **Burton** *vs.* The overseers of Aston. 1849; — **Carr,** *Sir* J., *vs.* Hood and Sharpe. 1808; — **Chapman,** E., *vs.* Shaw. 1790; — **Charles River Bridge.** 1837; — **Cherokee Indians** *vs.* **Peters,** R. 1831; — **Chisholm** *vs.* Georgia. 1793; — **Clarke,** F., *vs.* Rochester City. 1857; — **Clason,** I., *vs.* Bailey and Voorhees. 181-; — **Cohens** *vs.* Virginia. 1821; — **Cooper,** J. F., *vs.* Greeley. 1843; — **Corn** factors. 1783; — **Cox,** R. A., *vs.* Kean. 1825; — **Cricklade** case. 1781; — **Day & Martin** *vs.* Brown. 1821; — **Desor,** E., *vs.* Davis. 1851; — **Dey,** A., *vs.* Dunham. 181-; — **Dodge,** J., *vs.* Perkins. 1830; — **Doty,** J. D., *vs.* Mason. 1840; — **Dunham,** D., *vs.* Bailey. 181-; — **Edwin,** *barque vs.* Naumkeag Steam Cotton Co. 1860; — **Farmer,** M., *vs.* Storer. 1830; — **Fay,** J., *vs.* Bissell. 1816; — **Fink,** F. H. *vs.* Fink's executor. 1857; — **Fletcher,** R., *vs.* Peck. 1807; — **Forsey,** T., *vs.* Cunningham. 1764; — **Franklin,** T., *vs.* Clinton, 1816; — **Gaines,** M. C. 1850, 1858; — **Gardiner,** S., *vs.* Flagg. 1767; — **Gelston,** D., *and* **Schenck** *vs.* Hoyt. 1813; — **Gouverneur,** I., *vs.* Le Guen. 1798; — **Grattan,** T. C., *vs.* Appleton. 1844; — **Gray,** J., *vs.* Hawaiian gov't. 1845; — **Greene,** W. H., *vs.* Briggs. 1852; — **Griswold,** N. L., *vs.* Waddington. 181-; — **Groves,** M., *vs.* Slaughter. 1841; — **Hall,** W. L., *vs.* Barrow. 1820; — **Hallett,** A. S., *vs.* Novion. 181-; — **Hauteville.** 1840; — **Hayden,** J., *vs.* Suffolk Manuf. Co. 1863; — **Hendricks,** H., *vs.* Walden. 1818; — **Hickey** *vs.* Eggleston. 1806; — **Hinchman** *vs.* Ritchie. 1849; — **Hope,** *brig.* 1794; — **Hoyt,** G., *vs.* Gelston and Schenck. 1816; — **Irving** *vs.* Manning. 1847; — **Ives,** R. H., *vs.* Hazard. 1852; — **Jackson,** J., *vs.* Delancy. 1815; — *vs.* Robins. 1819; — *vs.* Sebring. 1819; — **Jeffers,** W., *vs.* Tyson. 1808; — **Jeune Eugénie,** *vessel.* 1821; — **Johnson,** E., *vs.* Low. 1848; — **Joy,** G., *vs.* Birch. 183-; — **Kamper,** P., *vs.* Hawkins. 1793; — **Kittredge** *vs.* Emerson. 1844; — **Kittredge** *vs.* Warren. 1844; — **Lawrence,** W. B., *vs.* Dana. 1866; — **Lyman,** J., *vs.* United Ins. Co., N. York. 1818; — **Lyon,** M., *and* Brockway *vs.* Richmond. 1816; — **M'Neven,** W. J., *vs.* Livingston. 181-; — **Mann,** M., *vs.* Mann. 181-; — **Marsh,** J. F., *vs.* Prall. 1818; — **Massachusetts** *vs.* Aves. 1836; — **Maurice,** J., *vs.* Judd. 1818; — **Meteor,** *steamship.* 1867; — **Metropolitan Bank** *vs.* H. H. Van Dyck. 1863; — **Miller,** S., *vs.* Noah. 1823; — **Murray,** J. B., *vs.* Riggs. 1816; — **Olive Branch,** *ship.* 1798; — **Olmsted,** G., *vs.* Rittenhouses executrices. 1778; — **Parish,** H. 1857; — **Parker,** G., *vs.* M'Dougall. 1808; — **Parker,** J. A., *vs.* Winnipiseogee Lake Cotton and Woolen Manuf. Co. 1859; — **Pelly,** G., *vs.* Charlton. 1844; — **Pennsylvania, State of,** *vs.* Smith. 1809; — **Phillips,** D., *and wife.* 1813; — **Poultney,** J., **Heirs of,** *vs.* W. Cecil's executor. 1835; — **Prigg** *vs.* Pennsylvania. 1842; — **Raspail,** F. V. 1846; — **Richardson,** T., *vs.* City of Boston 1855; — **Russell,** S., *vs.* Howe. 1831; — **Sands,** R., *vs.* Hildreth. 181-; — **Saunders,** R., *vs.*

Smith. 1839; — Scott, D. 1856; — Seaman, E., *vs.* Waddington. 1818; — Shultz, H., *vs.* Bank of Georgia. 1843; — Sims, T. 1851; — Simson, J., *vs. the snow* St. Joseph and St. Helena. 1752; — Slater, H. N., *vs.* Emerson. 1855; — Stockton, R. F., *vs. ship* Mariana Flora. 1822; — Taylor, J., *vs.* Delevan. 1840; — Tichborne *vs.* Lushington. 1871; — Torrey, S., *vs.* Field. 1835; — U. S. *vs. Brigantine* William. 1808; — U. S. *vs.* Davis, C. G. 1851; — U. S. *vs.* Hertz. 1855; — U. S. *vs. Schr.* Crenshaw. 1861; — U. S. *vs.* Smith. 1865; — Van Cortlandt *vs.* Underhill. 1818; — Vans *vs.* Codman. 1824; — Vidal *vs.* City of Phila. 1844; — Walden *vs.* Hendricks. 1818; — Wheeler *vs.* Williamson. 1855; — White, J., *vs.* Cahoone. 1825; — White, M., *and* J., *vs.* Skinner. 1818; — Wildes, G., *vs.* Parker. 1840; — Winans, *vs.* Eaton, Gilbert & Co. 1850.

Trials at large held upon H. Page, C. Davids, W. Griffiths and C. Smelt, also upon Capt. G. Burrish, from Sept. to Oct. 1745; enquiry into the conduct of the said gentleman in the late engagement of Feb. 1743. London, 1745. 8°. (E 86)

Trials at nisi prius, Law rel. to. *See* Nisi prius.

See also Conspiracies; — Habeas Corpus; — Jacobite trials; — Military trials.

Trials by Court-Martial. *See* Abbot, J. 1822; — Ambrose, J. 1745; — Arnold, B. 1779-80; — Barron, J. 1808; — Binney, A. 1810; — Brown, J. H. 1810; — Burbank, C. 1818; — Burrish, G. 1743; — Byng, J. 1757; — Calder, *Sir* R. 1806; — Cushing, T. H. 1812; — Davids, C. 1743; — Devlin, J. S. 1852; — Dillon, R. 1809; — Gardner, C. K. 1816; — Germain, G., *Vsct. Sackville.* 1760; — Goodale, E. 1812; — Gordon, C. 1808; — Griffin, T. 1750; — Hall, J. 1792; — Hanson, A. C. 1809; — Henley, D. 1778; — Hook, W. 1808; — Houston, R. 1817; — Howe, R. 1781; — Howe, T. 1810; — Hull, *Capt.* I. 1822; — Hull, W. 1814; — Keppel, A. 1778; — Knowles, C. 1749; — Learned, J. D. 1814; — Loring, J. 1812; — Mackenzie, A. S. 1843; — Marston, M. 1818; — Maxwell, W. P. 1808; — Mordaunt, *Sir* J. 1757; — Norris, R. 1743; — Page, H. 1743; — Palliser, *Sir* H. 1779; — Pinniger, D. 1808; — Porter, F. J. 1863; — Powell, R. 1792; — Quentin, G. 1814; — Ratford, J. 1807; — Schuyler, P. 1778; — Shaw, J. 1822; — Smith, J. 1823; — Tillinghast, A. 1808; — Whitelock, J. 1808; — Whiting, N. 1808; — Williams, E. 1745; — Winthrop, G. T. 1832.

Trials for adultery. *See* Barrow, G. 1808; — Caroline, *Queen.* 1820; — Cochrane, J. 1819; — Forrest, C. A. 1852; — Kean, E. 1825; — McDougall, A. 1808; — Mordaunt, *Sir* C. 1870; — Tyson, J. 1807.

Trials for arson. *See* Buzzell, J. R. 1834; — Clark, S. M. 1821; — Crockett, S. L. 1836; — Wade, J. 1735.

Trials for assault and battery. *See* Bethell, S. 1681; — Broad, A. 1809; — Coke, A. 1721; — Dennie, J. 1841; — Disney, D. 1767; — Hogan, W. 1821; — Little, W. 1808; — Parkinson, W. 1811; — Scot, W., *of Mossphennan.* 1712; — Sirr, C. H. 1802; — Van Rensselaer, S. 1808; — Woodburne, J. 1721.

Trials for bastardy. *See* Whistelo, A. 1808.

Trials for bigamy. *See* Feilding, R. 1708.

Trials for blasphemy. *See* Carlile, R. 1797; — Elwall, E. 1726; — Kneeland, A. 1834; — Williams, T. 1797.

Trials for burglary. *See* McGlochlin, J. [1787.]

Trials for conspiracy. *See* Georges *et al.* 1804; — O'Connell, D. 1843; — Parkins, *Sir* W. 1696; — Phila. boot and shoemakers. 1806; — Walker, T. 1794; — Wilson, R. T. 1816.

Trials for contempt of court. *See* Irvine, B. 1808; — Workman, J. 1808.

Trials for embracery. *See* Clough, E. 1833.

Trials for extortion. *See* Bell, B. 1797.

Trials for forgery. *See* Harten, G. von. 1807; — Huntington, C. B. 1856.

Trials for heresy. *See* Elwall, E. 1726; — Hill, J. 1793; — Prescott, O. S. 1851.

Trials for high crimes and misdemeanors. *See* Blount, W. 1797; — Chase, S. 1804; — Dundas, H., *Visc. Melville.* 1806; — Eyre, E. J. 1868; — Hampden, J. 1683; — Lafayette, M. J. P. R. Y. G. de M., *marquis* de. 1793; — Sacheverell, H. 1709; — Shippen, E. 1805.

Trials for libel. *See* Almon, J. 1770; — Arcularius, P. I. 1807; — Baldwin, C. N. 1818; — Buckingham, J. T. 1822; — Carlile, R.; — Cheetham, J. 1810; — Cheetham, S. 1807; — Child, D. L. 1829; — Cobbett, W. 1800; — Croswell, *Rev.* H. 1804; — Delavan, E. C. 1840; — Eaton, D. I. 1794; — Field, R. M. 1835; — Ford, J. 1838; — Garrison, W. L. 1830; — Greeley, H. 1843; — Hone, W. 1817; — Hood, T., *and* Sharpe, C. 1808; — Horne, J. 1777; — Lehre, *Col.* T. 1811; — Livingston, M. 1807; — Loomis, H. N. 1850; — Lyman, T., *Jr.* 1828; — Noah, M. M. 1823; — Owen, W. 1765; — Paine, T. 1792; — Shipley, W. D. 1784; — Stockdale, J. 1804; — Tooke, J. H. 1777; — Verren, A. 1841; — Whitmarsh, J. A. 1838; — Wright, A. 1806; — Zenger, J. P. 1735.

Trials for misdeameanor. *See* Braynard, S. 1826; — Bright, M. 1809; — Cochrane, T., 10*th Earl of Dundonald.* 1816; — Kerr, *Col.* L. 1807; — Niven, G. W. 1822; — O'Connell, D. 1844; — Prescott, J. 1821; — Reading, N. 1679; — Renshaw, J. 1809; — Smith, W. S. 1806; — Workman, J. 1807.

Trials for murder. *See* Acton, W. 1789; — Adams, M. 1815; — Aram, E. 1759; — Arnold, S. 1865; — Atzerodt, G. A. 1865; — Avery, E. K. 1833; — Ball, E. 1811; — Bellingham, J. 1812; — Bevans, W. 1816; — Boorn, S. *and* J. 1819; — Bories, J. 1829; — Bowen, G. 1816; — Broadfoot, A. 1743; — Campbell, H. A. 1808; — Chapman, L. 1832; — Clifton, A. 1787; — Clough, J. 1833; — Coolidge, V. P. 1848; — Coombs, G. 1816; — Corey, D. H. 1830; — Cornwallis, C. 1679; — Cox, G. 1849; — Curtis, W. 1826; — Daley, D. 1806; — Darnes, W. P. 1840; — Dean, C. B. 1808; — Dennis, R. 1804; — DeWolf, O. 1845; — Dunbar, R. 1850; — Fairbanks, J. 1801; — Freeman, W. 1846; — Fualdès, (murderers of), 1818; — Giles, J. 1681; — Godfrey, S. E. 1818; — Goodwin, R. M. 1820; — Gordon, J. *and* W. 1844; — Hackman, J. 1779; — Hardy, W. 1807; — Haunt, W. 1711; — Herold, D. E. 1865; — Hersey, G. C. 1861; — Hitchcock, A. 1807; — Hodge, A. 1811; — Jennings, R. 1819; — Kinney, *Mrs.* H. 1840; — Knapp, J. F. 1830; — Knowlton, W. E. 1849; — Livermore, A. 1813; — Lynn, D. 1809; — M'Adams, T. 1737; — M'Donnough, W. 1817; — M'Lellan, A. 1841; — McLeod, A. 1818; — McManus, C. 1798; — McPherson, D. 1712; — Mayo, S. M. 1807; — Mohun, C. *Ld.* 1693; — Mudd, S. A. 1865; — Nelson, T. L. K. 1867; — O'Laughlin, M. 1865; — Parker, M. 1825; — Patch, R. 1806; — Payne, L. 1865; — Phillips, H. 1817; — Porteous, J. 1736; — Raspail, F. V. 1846; — Regicides, The, 1660; — Rheinhard, C. de. 1818; — Rogers, A. 1844; — Scot, W. 1712; — Selfridge, E. 1827; — Selfridge, T. O. 1806; — Shaftsbury, G. L. 1851; — Spangler, E. 1865; — Standsfield, P. 1688; — Strang, J. 1827; — Surratt, J. H. 1867; — Surratt, M. E. 1865; — Tinker, E. 1811; — Toohey, M. *and* M. 1819; — Travers, G. 1814; — Van Alstine, J. 1819; — Webster, J. W. 1850; — Wemms, W. 1770; — White, J. D. 1826; — Williams, J. 1818.

Trials for perjury. *See* Chippindall, —. 1817.

Trials for piracy. *See* Collins, D. 1864; — Delano, C. C. 1820; — Gibert, P. 1834; — Green, T. 1705; — Hibbert, P. 183–; — Holmes, W. 1819; — Savannah. *privateer.* 1862; — Tulley, S. 1812.

Trials for rape. *See* Conelly, J. 18—; — Joice, J. 1849, — Murphy, S., *and* Doyle, J. 1817; — Riley, J. 1849; — Wakely, C. 1810; — Wheeler, E. 1805.

Trials for receiving stolen goods. *See* Cook, C. L. 1835.

Trials for riot. *See* Cordwainers of N. Y. 1810; — Lincoln, W. S. Gilman, *etc.* for riot at Alton; — Phila. Boot and shoe makers. 1805; — Shaw, B. 1822.

Trials for robbery. *See* Hare, J. 1818; — Kenniston, L. 1817; — Lyon, P. 1798; — Martin, M. 1821; — Mellon, M. 1830; — Porter, J. 1830; — Wilson, G. 1830; — Wyman, W. 1844.

Trials for sedition. *See* Crandall, R. 1836; — Gerrald, J. 1794; — Muir, T. 1793; — Palmer, T. F. 1793; — Skirving, W. 1794; — Vallandigham, C. L. 1863; — Walker, T. 1794; — Winterbotham, W. 1793.

Trials for seduction. *See* Fairchild, J. H. 1844.

Trials for subornation of perjury. *See* Lyon, E. 1804; — Tasborough, J., *and* Price, A. 1680.

Trials for treason. Historical account of all the tryals and attainders of high-treason, from the beginning of the reign of Charles I., chronologically digested, **[1636-84]**. London, 1716. 16°.

— Pitman, B. Trials for treason at Indianapolis. Cincinnati, **1865.** 8°.

See also Burr, A. 1807; — Coleman, E. 1678; — Cooper, A. A., 1*st Earl of Shaftesbury.* 1681; — Cornish, H. 1685; — Despard, E. M. 1803; — Dorr, T. W. 1844; — Fitz Harris, E. 1681; — Friend, *Sir* J. 1696; — Fries, J. 1800; — Garnet, H. 1606; — Hodges, J. 1815; — Hone, W. 1683; — Howard, *Sir* W. 1680; — Ireland, W. 1678; — Langhorn, R. 1679; — Layer, C. 1722; — McLane, D. 1797; — Osborne, T. 1678; — Paine, T. 1792; — Parkins, *Sir* W. 1696; — Plunket, O. 1681; — Radclyffe, J. 1716; — Rosewell, T. 1684; — Rous, J. 1683; — Russell, W., *Ld.* 1683; — Scroggs, W. 1680; — Seton, G., *Earl of Winton.* 1716; — Sidney, A. 1683; —

Smith, J. 1794; — Vaughan, T. 1696; — Wakeman, *Sir* G. 1679; — Walcot, T. 1683; — Wentworth, T., *Earl Strafford*. 1640.

Trials of Charles I., and of some of the regicides; with notes. London, 1832. 16°. (Fam. lib., v. 39.)

Contents. Trial of Charles I.; his execution. — Remarks on the trial. — Memoir of H. Ireton. — J. Bradshaw. — T. Harrison. — Memoirs of the regicides. — Introd. to the trials of the regicides. — Trial of T. Harrison. — Trial of H. Peters. — Execution of the regicides.

Trials of Margaret Lindsay; by [J. Wilson]. Boston, 1823. 12°.

Trials of the heart; by [A. E.] Bray. London, 1845. 16°. (Novels, v. 8.)

Trials of the Tredgolds. (*In* **Temple** Bar, v. 7-10. 1863-64.)

Trials on impeachment. *See* **Addison**, A. 1803; — **Blount**, W. 1797; — **Chase**, S. 1805; — **Dundas**, H., 1*st Vsct. Melville*. 1806; — **Hopkinson**, F. 1780; — **Howard**, *Sir* W. 1680; — **Johnson**, A. 1868; — **Lafayette**, M. J. P. R. Y. G. de M., *marquis* de. 1792; — **Prescott**, J. 1821; — **Sacheverell**, H. 1810; — **Suratt**, J. H. 1867.

Triangle, The. *See* **Investigator.**

Tribe of Issachar; or the asse couchant; [in verse]. *n.t.p.* [London, 1691.] 4°. (B 651)

Tribulation. RIBADENEYRA, P. de. Tractado de la T. (*In his* Obras escogidas. 1868; **Aribau.** Biblioteca, v. 60.)

Tribune almanac for 1838-68; comprehending the Politician's register and the Whig almanac. *Reprint*, N. Y., 1868. 2 v. 8°.

— *Same.* 1869-81. N. Y., [1868]-81. 8°.

Tribune Club. Proceedings, presentation, anniversary dinner. N. Y., 1855. 8°. (B 1597)

Tribune essays. *See* **Congdon, T.**

Tribur. SCHAEFER, A. D. Der Fürstentag zu Tribur im Jahre 1076. (*In* **Histor.** Zeitschrift, v. 8. 1862.)

Trichet Dufresne, Raphael. Epistola de Charondæ effigie in Catanensi nummo expressa. (*In* **Gronovius**, J. Thes. Gr. antiq., v. 10. 1701.)

Trichina. BOWDITCH, H. I. Trichina spiralis. *n.t.p.* [Boston, 1842.] 8°. (B 1548)

— CALKINS, M. Cases of trichina spiralis in Springfield. (*In* **Mass. Med. Soc.** Pub., v. 2. 1867.)

Trick to catch the old one. *See* **Middleton**, T.

Trick upon trick. (*In* **Col.** of most esteemed farces, v. 5. 1792.)

Tricotel, Edouard. Variétés bibliographiques. Paris, 1863. 12°.

Triebner, *Rev.* Christopher Frederick. The Christian's Scriptural guide; one hundred and four hist. of the O. and N. Testament. Lond., [179-?]. 8°. (B 1017)

Triennial Baptist register, 1836; by I. M. Allen. Phila., 1836. 8°.

Triest. CHMEL, J. (*In his* Urkunden zur Geschichte von Osterreich, *etc.* 1849. Fontes rer. Austr., 2. Abth., 1. Bd.)

Trifler; or, Ramble among wilds of fancy and works of nature. Dublin, 1779. 12°.

Trifling mistake in Ld. Erskine's recent preface; by the author of 'Defence of the people'. London, 1819. 8°. (B 1528, 1673)

Trigault (*Lat.* **Trigautius**), Nicolas. De Christianis apud Japonios triumphis. Monachii, 1623. 4°.

Trigge, Thomas. Calendarium astrologicum, 1744. *See* **Almanacs.** CALENDARIUM.

Trigland (*Lat.* **Triglandius**), Jakob. Conjectanea de Dodone. (*In* **Gronovius**, J. Thes. Gr. antiq., v. 7. 1699.)

Trigonometer. WALL, G., *Jr.* Description of the trigonometer. Phila., 1788. 8°. (W 31)

Trigonometrical surveying. *See* **Geodesy.**

Trigonometry. BLUNDEVILLE, T. Exercises. [**1594.**] 6th ed. London, 1622. 4°.

— WALLIS, J. De sectionibus angularibus tractatus. **1685.** (*In his* Opera math., v. 2. 1693.)

— MANESSON MALLET, A. La trigonométrie. (*In his* Géométrie pratique, v. 2. **1702.**)

— KEILL, J. Elements of plane and spherical trigonometry. [**1715.**] (*In* **Euclides.** Elements. 1728; 1745; 1762.)

— WELLS, E., *d.* **1727.** Young gentleman's trigonometry. 2d ed. London, 1731. 8°.

— WARD, J. Compendium of plain trigonometry. (*In his* Posthumous works. **1730.**)

— SIMPSON, T. Trigonometry plane and spherical; with construction, *etc.*, of logarithms. [**1748.**] 2d ed. London, 1765. 8°.

— EMERSON, W. Elements of trigonometry. [**1749.** 2d ed.] *t.p.w.* [London, 1764.] 8°.

— SIMSON, R. Elements of plane and spherical trigonometry. [**1756.**] (*Appended to his* Elements of Euclid. 1791.)

— ABEL, T. Subtensial plain trigonometry wrought with a sliding-rule, with Gunter's lines; and also arithmetically. Phila., 1761. 8°. (**D 14**)

— BEZOUT, E. La trigonométrie rectiligne et sphérique. [**1764.**] (*In his* Cours de math. 1812.)

— MAUDUIT, A. R. New and complete treatise of spherical trigonometry; tr. by W. Crakelt. [**1765.**] London, 1791. 8°.

— CAGNOLI, A. Trigonométrie rectiligne et sphérique; tr. par N. M. Chompré. [**1786.**] 2e éd. aug. Paris, 1808. 4°.

— PLAYFAIR, J. Elements of plain and spherical trigonometry. [**1794.**] (*In his* Elements of geometry. 1814; 1819; 1833.)

— KEITH, T. Introd. to the theory and practice of plane and spherical trigonometry. 5th ed. corr. [**1796.**] London, 1826. 8°.

— LACROIX, S. F. Traité élém. de trigonom. rectil. et sphér., et d'applic. de l'algèbre à la géométrie. [**1798.**] 6e éd. rev. et corr. Paris, 1813. 8°.

— - *Eng.* Elementary treatise on trigonometry; tr. [by J. Farrar]. Camb., 1820. 8°.

— - *Same.* 4th ed. Boston, 1837. 8°.

— VINCE, S. Treatise on plane and spherical trigonometry. [**1800.**] 2d ed. Cambridge, 1805. 8°.

— BONNYCASTLE, J. Treatise on plane and spherical trigonometry. [**1806.**] 3d ed. London, 1818. 8°.

— LESLIE, J. Elements of geometry, and plane trigonometry; with an app. and notes. [**1809.**] 2d ed. enl. Edin., 1811. 8°.

— - *Same, without* Geom. anal. 3d ed. enl. Edin., 1817. 8°.

— WOODHOUSE, R. Treatise on plane and spherical trigonometry. [1809.] 2d ed. corr. and enl. Camb., 1813. 8°.

— BRIDGE, B. Comp. treatise on elements of plane trigonometry. [**1811.**] 3d ed. London, 1822. 8°.

— NICHOLS, F. Treatise of plane and spherical trigonometry. Phila., 1811. 8°.

— SNIADECKI, J. Trygonometrya kulista analitycznie wyłożona. [**1817.**] Wydanie 2e. Wilmie i Warszawie, 1820. 8°.

— WILSON, R. System of plane and spherical trigonometry. Camb., **1831.** 8°.

— DEMORGAN, A. Elements of spherical trigonometry. *n.t.p.* [London, **1833**?] 8°. (Lib. useful knowl.)

— HOPKINS, W. Elements of trigonometry. London, **1833.** 8°. (Lib. usef. knowl.)

— RUEMKER, C. Ueber die Oerter sphärischer Dreiecke. Hamburg, **1834.** 4°. (**A 40**)

— AIRY, G. B. (*In* **Smedley**, E., *and others.* Encyclopædia metropolitana, v. 1. **1845.**)

— CHAUVENET, W. Treatise on plane and spherical trigonometry. [**1850.**] 5th ed. Phila., 1860. 8°.

— KIRKMAN, T. P. First mnemonical lessons on geometry and trigonometry. London, *Weale*, **1852.** 12°.

— HANN, J. Elements of plane trigonometry. 2d ed. corr. London, *Weale*, **1854.** 12°.

— DAVIES, C., *LL.D.* Elements of geometry and trigonometry; with applications in mensuration. N. Y., 1855. 12°.

Tables.

— TOALDO, G. Tavole trigonometriche. [1769.] Ed. 3a. corr. ed accr. Padova, 1794. 4°.

— BORDA, C. Tables trigonométriques décimales; rev., *etc.*, par J. B. J. Delambre. Paris, 1801. 4°.

See also **Geometry**; — **Mathematical tables**; — **Mathematics**; — **Navigation**; — **Spherics**; — **Surveying.**

Trigoso *or* **Trigozo d'Aragão Morato,** Francisco Manoel. Elogio [de] M. do Cenaculo, Arbo. d'Evora; de J. G. C. Müller. (*In* **Lisbon. Ac. d. Sci.** Mem., v. 4. 1815.) — Sobre o teatro portuguez. (*In* v. 5. 1817.) — Sobre o estabelecimento da Arcadia de Lisboa, *etc.* (*In* v. 6. 1819.) — Que até ao tempo d'el rei Diniz naõ existio lei alguma em Portugal que prohibisse as igrejas e mosteiros a aquisição de bens de raiz. (*In* v. 7. 1821.) — Sobre a lei das sesmarias. (*In* v. 8. 1823.)

Triqueros, Candido Maria. El sacrificio de Efigenia. (*In* **Calderon de la Barca,** P. Comedias, v. 4. 1848; Aribau. Bibl., v. 14.)

Triller, Daniel Wilhelm. Observationes criticæ in varios Græcos et Latinos auctores. Francof., 1742. 8°.

Trillo y Figueroa, Francesco de. Poesias. (*In* **Castro,** A. de. Poetas liricos de los siglos 16 y 17, v. 2. 1857; Aribau. Bibl., v. 42.)

Trilobite. BRADLEY, F. H. Description of a new trilobite from the Potsdam sandstone. (*In* **Amer. Assoc.** Proc., v. 14. 1861.)

Trimble, David. Address cont. proof that he did not make statements attributed to him, in rel. to the charges against the president and H. Clay. Frankfort, 1828. 8°. (B 1102)

— Reply to Mr. McDuffie on the amendment of the Constitution, Apr. 1. *n.t.p.* [1826.] 8°. (B 1493)

Trimble, Isaac R. PHILA., WILMINGTON, AND BALTIMORE R. R. Co. Investigation into the alleged misconduct of [T.] the late superintendent; phonographically reported by A. Cannon. Phila., 1854–55. 2 v. 8°.

Trimble, Robert. Slavery in the U. S. of N. America; lect., deliv. in Liverpool, 1861. London, Liverpool, Manch., 1863. 8°.

Trimble, Wm. A. CAMPBELL, J. W. (*In his* Biog. sketches. 1838.)

Trimmer, Joshua. Practical chemistry for farmers and land owners. London, 1842. 12°.

Trimmer, *Mrs.* Mary. Natural history of quadrupeds, birds, fishes, *etc.* Boston, 1836. 12°.

Trimmer, *Mrs.* Sarah Kirby, *d.* 1810. Teacher's assistant. London, 1815. 2 v. 12°.

Trimmer. COVENTRY, W. Character of a trimmer. London, 1688. 4°

Trimnell, Charles, *Bp.* Sermon before the Sons of the Clergy, the day of their annual feast, Dec. 2, 1707. London, 1708. 4°. (B 1269)

— Speech. (*In* **Fisher,** J. Speeches on the impeachment of H. Sacheverell. 1710.)

— Speech at the opening of the 2d article of the impeachments against Dr. Sacheverell. (*Appended to* **Wake,** W. Speeches, *etc.* 1710. B 99)

Trincavelli, Vettore. AGOSTINI, G. degli. (*In his* Notizie degli scrittori vinz., 1754.)

Trinci, Cosimo. L'agricoltore sperimentato; con il Manuale de' giardinieri di A. Mandirola. Roveredo, 1733. 8°.

Trinci, Ugolino. FABRETTI, A. (*In his* Biog. dei capitani venturieri dell' Umbria, v. 1. 1842.)

Trinci *di Foligno,* **Famiglia di.** (*In* **Litta,** P. Fam., v. 14.)

Trinidad. *Description and Travels.*

— DUDDELEY, *Sir* R. Voyage to Trinidad, *etc.*, 1594–95. (*In* **Hakluyt,** R. Col. of voy., v. 4. 1811.)

— ANDERSON, A. Nachricht von dem Asphaltsee auf der Insel Trinidad, [1784]. (*In* **Sprengel,** M. C., *and* **Forster,** G. Neue Beiträge, v. 3. 1790.)

— M'CALLUM, P. F. Travels in Trinidad, 1803. Liverpool, 1805. 8°.

— DAUXION-LAVAYSSE, J. F. Statistical description of Venezuela, Trinidad, *etc.*; with notes by E. Blaquiere, [1820]. 2d ed. London, 1821. 8°.

— WALL, G. P., *and* SAWKINS, J. G. Report of the survey of the economic geology of Trinidad. (*In* **Smithsonian Inst.** Report, 1856.)

— VERTEUIL, L. A. A. de. Trinidad; its geography, natural resources, present condition, and prospects. London, 1858. 8°.

— *Map.* CHART. London, 1798. (E 67)

History and Politics.

— JOSEPH, E. L. History of Trinidad, [1498–1837]. Trinidad, [1838]. 12°.

— CRISIS of the sugar colonies; an inquiry into the objects and probable effects of the French exped. to the West Indies; subjoined, Sketches of a plan for settling the vacant lands of Trinidad. London, 1802. 8°. (B 685, 782)

— PECK, N., *and* PRICE, T. S. Report on the advantages to be derived by colored people migrating to Guiana and Trinidad. Balt., 1840. 8°. (B 1484)

See also **West Indies.**

Trinitarians. WORCESTER, N. Address to the trinitarian clergy rel. to their manner of treating opponents. Boston, 1812. 12°. (D 63)

Trinitatis et Redemptionis Captivorum Ordo. *See* Ordo.

Trinity. *History.*

— ALLIX, P. The Fathers vindicated; animad. on "The judgment of the Fathers touching the trinity against Dr. Bull's 'Defence of the Nicene faith' ". London, 1697. 8°.

— WHISTON, W. An account of the primitive faith conc. the trinity and incarnation. (*In his* Primitive Christianity revived, v. 4. 1711.)

— CLAYTON, R., *Bp.* Essay on spirit; the doctrine of the trinity considered, with an inquiry into the sentiments of the Fathers, and the doctrine as maintained by the Egyptians, Pythagoreans, and Platonists. London, 1751. 8°.

— - Sequel. London, 1752. 8°.

— MAURICE, *Rev.* T. Hebrew trinity and Oriental triads of Deity investigated. (Vol. 4, 5 *of his* Indian antiq. 1794.)

— - *Same.* London, 1801. 8°.

— FORREST, J. Origin and progress of trinitarian theol. in the 2d and succeeding centuries. Glasgow, 1836. 8°.

— GREENE, W. B. Doctrine of the trinity briefly examined in the light of hist. and philosophy. West Brookfield, 1847. 8°. (B 1388)

— CORDNER, J. Philosophic origin and hist. progress of the doctrine of the trinity; lecture. Montreal, 1851. 8°. (B 1688)

— LAMSON, A. Church of the first three centuries, with special ref. to the doct. of the trinity. Boston, 1860. 8°.

Controversial works.

Note. For a list of pamphlets occasioned by proceedings of dissenting ministers at Salters-Hall in 1719, *see* **Dissenters** (p. 790).

— HAYGATE, W. E., *and* APPLETON, N. Doctrines of original sin and the trinity. Boston, 1859. 8°. (B 1388)

Note. In the following works * added to the title means that the works are against the doctrine of the Trinity.

— NOVATIANUS, *fl. abt.* 250. Concerning the trinity. (*In* **Cyprianus.** Writings, v. 2. 1869.)

— HILARIUS, *St.*, *d. abt.* 370. De trinitate. (*In his* Opera. 1652.)

— ATHANASIUS, *St.*, *d.* 372. Opera omnia. Parisiis, 1627. 2 v. f°.

— EPIPHANIUS, *d.* 402. Ancoratus. (*In his* Opera, v. 2. 1682.)

— AUGUSTINUS, *St.*, *d.* 430. De trinitate. (*In his* Opera, v. 3. 1635.)

— OWEN, J. Declaration and vindication of the doctrine of the trinity. [1668.] 3d impr. London, 1676. 8°.
— GARDINER, S. Catholicæ circa trinitatem fidei delineatio; annexa est responsio ad [Sandium]. Londini, 1677. 8°.
— SHERLOCK, W. Vindication of the doctrine of the trinity. London, 1690. 4°.
— HOWE, J. Calm and sober inquiry conc. the possibility of a trinity in the godhead. [1691.] (*In his* Works, v. 1. 1835.)
— BUNYAN, J. Of the trinity and a Christian. [1692.] (*In his* Works, v. 2. 1835.)
— BOYS, J. Doctrine of Fathers and schools conc. a trinity. Pt. 1. London, 1695. 4°.
— CLARK, G. The judgment of the Fathers [on] the trinity. Pt. 1. London, 1695. 4°. (B 96)
— BARROW, I. Defence of the trinity. London, 1697. 16°.
— SEASONABLE vindication of the trinity; col. from the works of J. Tillotson and E. Stillingfleet. Lond., 1697. 16°.
— STILLINGFLEET, E. Vindication of the doctrine of the trinity, with answer to late Socinian objections. 2d ed. London, 1697. 8°.
— DIFFERENCE between Mr. E— and the Protestant dissenting ministers of D— truly represented. *t.p.w.* [17—.] 4°. (B 1398)
— HOLY thoughts on a God made man; or, Mysterious trinity proved. London, 1704. 8°.
— LESLIE, C. Socinian controversy discussed in six dialogues, *etc.* [1705.] (*In his* Works, v. 1. 1721.)
— CLARKE, S. Scripture-doctrine of the trinity. [1712.] 3d ed. London, 1732. 8°.
— - *Same.* (*In his* Works, v. 4. 1738.)
— WELLS, E. Remarks on Clarke's introd. to his 'Scripture-doctrin of the trinity'. Oxford, 1713. 8°. (B 28)
— EMLYN, T. Full inquiry into the original authority of 1 John v. 7. London, 1715. 8°. *
— JACKSON, J. Queries, wherein objections against Clarke's 'Scripture doctrine of the trinity' are answered; with an appendix. London, 1716. 8°.
— EMLYN, T. Dr. Bennett's new theory of the trinity examined, and his examination of Clarke's 'Scripture-doctrine of the trinity'. London, 1718. 8°. * (B 111)
— - Remarks on the 'Doctrine of the trinity defended by four London ministers, Tong, [and others]. London, 1719. 8°. * (B 112)
— FINCH, D. Answer to Whiston's letter on the eternity of the Son of God and of the Holy Ghost. [1719.] 9th ed. London, 1721. 8°. (B 28)
— LAYMAN'S letters, The, to the dissenting ministers of London; cont. thanks to those who subscribed the declaration for the trinity, *etc.* London, 1719. 8°. (B 32)
— PEIRCE, J. Remarks upon the account of what was transacted in the assembly at Exon. London, 1719. 8°. * (B 107)
— R. E. Letter to a Dissenter in Exeter, occasioned by the late heats in those parts. London, 1719. 8°. * (B 107)
— TOMKINS, M. Case of T.; proceedings of the dissenting congregation at Stoke-Newington, upon occasion of a sermon by him, July 13, 1718. London, 1719. 8°. * (B 110)
— TRUE relation of some proceedings at Salters' Hall by those ministers who signed first article of the Church of England. London, [1719]. 8°. (B 107, 110, 1865)
— WHISTON, W. Letter to the Earl of Nottingham [on] the eternity of the Son of God and of the Holy Spirit. London, 1719. 8°. * (B 28)
— FOSTER, J. Essay on fundamentals; with partic. regard to the doct. of the trinity. [1720.] 2d ed. London, 1754. 4°. *
— - *Other copies.* (B 136, 189)
— SOBER reply to Higge's 'Merry arguments', *etc.* London, 1720. 8°. * (B 32)
— ANSWER to the anon. pamphlet, by one of the Exeter advisers 'Texts compared rel. to the deity of the Son and Holy Ghost'. London, 1721. 8°. * (B 110)
— PYKE, J. Impartial view of the difficulties [of] the Trinitarian [and] Arian scheme. London, 1721. 8°. (B 256)
— BENNET, B. Irenicum; a review of some controversies about the trinity, private judgment, *etc.* London, 1722. 8°. (B 111)
— BROWNE, S. Letter to T. Reynolds, on his funeral sermon for the late S. Pomfret. London, 1722. 8°. (B 39, 110)
— FANCOURT, S. Enthusiasm retorted; or, Remarks on Morgan's 2d letter to the four London ministers; and on [his] invectives against the doctrine of the trinity. London, 1722. 8°. (B 110)
— MONIS, *Rabbi* J. Nothing but the truth; essay, [proving] the doctrine of the trinity. (*In* Colman, B. Disc. before the baptism of M. 1722. D 3)
— MORGAN, T. Letter to Dr. Waterland [on] his late writings in defence of the Athanasian hypothesis. London, 1722. 8°. * (B 114)
— - Letter to R. Blackmore, [on] his 'Modern Arian unmasked'. London, 1722. 8°. * (B 114)
— - Refutation of the false principles assumed and applyed by J. Pyke, *etc.*; added, remarks on R. Blackmore's prejudices against the Arian hypothesis. London, 1722. 8°. * (B 114)
— HALLETT, J., *Jr.* The reconciler; that Christians are more agreed conc. the trinity than represented; with reply to Ball's answer to some objections. London, 1727. 8°. (B 39)
— E., H. Answer to Clark and Whiston conc. the divinity of the Son and Holy Spirit; with account of the writers of the three first ages. London, 1729. 8°. (B 149)
— BROWNE, S. Sober and charitable disquisition conc. the importance of the doctrine of the trinity. London, 1732. 8°. (B 39)
— CHARITY and sincerity defended; reply to P. C.'s letter to the author of the 'Vindication of Nation's sermons at Exon'; added a 2d letter to P. C. from Mr. Nation. [Arian]. London, 1732. 8°. * (B 121)
— SANTINELLI, S. Orationes de sanctissima trinitate. (*In his* Diss. 1734.)
— TRYAL of W. Whiston, for defaming and denying the trinity. 3d ed. London, 1740. 8°. * (B 576)
— LARDNER, N. Two schemes of a trinity considered. [1747. London,] 1784. 8°. * (B 249, 1917)
— - *Same.* London, 1793. 12°. (C 137)
— WATTS, I. Christian doctrine of the trinity. — Seven diss. on the trinity. (*In his* Works, v. 6. 1753.)
— - *Same, extracts.* Boston, [18—]. 8°. (C 242)
— JONES, W. The catholic doctrine of a trinity proved by Scripture. [1756.] London, 1802. 12°.
— - *Same.* 10th ed. London, 1820. 12°.
— ELLIOT, R. Divine revelation the only test of sound doctrine; the doctrine of the trinity not revealed in the Scriptures. London, 1773. 8°. *
— LESSING, G. E. Des A. Wissowatius Einwürfe wider die Dreieinigkeit. 1773. (*In his* Sammt. Schr., v. 7. 1822.) *
— MACGOWAN, J. Socinianism brought to the test. [1773.] (*In his* Works, v. 2. 1825.)
— BURGH, W. Scriptural confutation of the arguments against the one Godhead of the Father, Son, and Holy Ghost by Lindsey in his 'Apology'. London, 1774. 8°.
— LINDSEY, T. Apology on resigning the vicarage of Catterick. London, 1774. 8°.
— - *Same.* 3d ed. London, 1774. 8°. (B 1917)
— - *Same.* 4th ed. London, 1782. 8°.
— - - Sequel. London, 1776. 8°.
— TUCKER, J. Brief view of the difficulties attending the Trinitarian, Arian, and Socinian systems. Glocester, 1774. 8°. (B 1371)
— FREE and serious address to the Christian laity, esp. such as embracing Unitarian sentiments conform to Trinitarian worship. Lond., 1781. 8°. * (B 53, 750)
— FRIENDLY dialogue between a Unitarian and an Athanasian. London, 1784. 12°. * (C 242)
— PURVES, J. Humble attempt to investigate the Scripture doct. conc. Father, Son, and Holy Spirit. Edin., 1784. 12°.
— FREND, W. Address to the members of the Ch. of Eng. exhorting them to turn from the false worship of three persons. 2d ed. Lond., 1788. 8°. * (B 53, 158, 290)

— PRIESTLEY, J. General view of the arguments for the unity of God against the divinity and pre-existence of Christ. 3d ed. Birmingham, 1788. 8°. * (C 69, 241)
— - *Same.* (*In his* Appeal. 1791. C 131)
— - *Same. t.p.w.* 12°. (C 241)
— BAILLIE, J. Vindication of the divinity of Christ; sermon. Newcastle, 1789. 12°. (C 242)
— FREND, W. Second address to the members of the Church of Eng. and to Prot. Trinitarians. 2d ed. London, 1789. 8°. * (B 53, 142)
— TOULMIN, J. Exhortation to all Christian people to refrain from Trinitarian worship. *n.p.*, [1789]. 12°. * (C 132)
— CHRISTIE, W. Discourses on the Divine unity, with a confutation of a trinity. 2d ed. Montrose, 1790. 12°. *
— EVELEIGH, J. The doctrine of the trinity. Oxford, 1791. 8°. (B 1703)
— LINDSEY, T. Catechist; an inquiry into the doctrine of the Scriptures conc. the only true God. London, 1792. 12°. *
— - *Other copies.* (B 158, C 136)
— JONES, B., *ed.* Athrawiaeth y drindod mewn tair pregeth. Machynlleth, 1793. 12°. (C 300)
— STONE, J. H. Lettre à Du F*****. Paris, 1806. 8°. (B 740)
— APPEAL to the candid. No. 1-3: [Unitarian controversy]. *n.t.p.* [181-?] 8°. * (B 264)
— PEARSON, E. Sermon, doctrine of the trinity. (*In his* Essay on the pre-existence of Christ. 1810.)
— WORCESTER, N. Bible news of the Father, Son, and Holy Spirit. Concord, 1810. 8°.
— - *Other copies.* (B 141, 261)
— GARDINER, J. S. J. Preservative against Unitarianism; sermon, Trinity Church, June 9. Boston, 1811. 8°. (B 314)
— CEPHAS, *pseud.* Inquiries occas. by the address of the Gen. Assoc. of New Hampshire on the doctrine of the trinity. Boston, 1812. 8°. * (B 664, C 118)
— WORCESTER, N. Respectful address to the Trinitarian clergy. Boston, 1812. 12°. * (C 84)
— TIMOTHY, *pseud.* Letter to the moderator of the N. Hampshire Association. Bost., 1812. 12°. * (C 236)
— NORTON, J. Things set in a proper light; answer to a letter from T. A. to a friend. Boston, 1814. 8°. * (B 264)
— WARDLAW, R. Discourses on the principal points of the Socinian controversy. [1814.] Andover, 1815. 8°. *
— CRITIQUE upon Kidd's 'Essay on the trinity'. *n.p.*, [1815]. 8°. * (B 666)
— KIDD, J. Doctrine of the trinity [proved] by demonstration founded upon duration and space, some of the divine perfections, powers of the soul, language of Scripture, and tradition. London, 1815. 8°.
— NORTON, J. Things as they are, or Trinitarianism developed; answer to D. Thomas, *etc.* Bost., 1815. 2 pts. 8°. * (B 264)
— PRIESTLEY, J. Tracts in controversy with Bp. Horsley; with notes by [T. Belsham, and] four letters to the bishops. London, 1815. 8°. *
— YATES, *Rev.* J. Vindication of Unitarianism. [1815.] Boston, 1816. 8°. *
— THACHER, *Rev.* S. C. The evidence necessary to establish the doctrine of the trinity. [1816?] 2d ed. Boston, 1828. 12°. * (A.U.A., 1st ser., 18. C 168, v. 2.)
— WARDLAW, R. Unitarianism incapable of vindication; reply to Rev. J. Yates. [1816.] Andover, 1817. 8°.
— WELLS, W. Some communications, first pub. in the Brattleborough paper. Brattleboro, 1816. 8°. * (B 265)
— WRIGHT, R. Answer to 'Why are you not a Trinitarian?' 1st Amer. fr. 2d Liverpool ed. *n.p.*, 1816. 12°. * (C 82)
— CLARKE, G. General obs. on the common mode of defending the trinity, and the union of the two natures in Jesus Christ. Boston, 1817. 8°. * (B 263, 271)
— NORTON, J. Review of the correspondence of Dr. Worcester with W. E. Channing on Unitarianism. Boston, 1817. 8°. * (B 266)

— TOULMIN, J. Review of the preaching of the Apostles; or, The efficacy of the Unitarian doctrine. Utica, 1817. 8°. * (C 82, 85)
— WORCESTER, T. A new chain of plain argument against Trinitarianism. Bost., 1817. 8°. * (B 265)
— YATES, *Rev.* J. Sequel to 'Vindication of Unitarianism'. Liverpool, 1817. 8°. *
— - *Another copy.* (B 1017)
— COMPARATIVE view of the Scriptural evidence for Unitarianism and Trinitarianism. [1818?] 2d ed. London, 1819. 12°. * (C 242)
— EDDY, S. Reasons offered for his opinions to the 1st Baptist Ch. in Providence, from which he was compelled to withdraw for heterodoxy. 2d ed. *n.p.*, 1818. 8°. * (B 272)
— GARBETT, *Rev.* J. Unitarianism indefensible. London, 1818. 8°. (B 1389)
— BROWN, J. Letter to W. E. Channing [on the trinity]. *n.t.p.* [1819.] 8°. (B 298)
— LETTER to Rev. Mr. Channing, in favor of the doctrine of the trinity, and in opposition to the sentiments in his Baltimore sermon; [by a layman]. *n.t.p.* [1819.] 8°. (B 298)
— LAYMAN, *Jr.*, *pseud.* Letter to 'A layman', in reply to his letter to Channing. *n.t.p.* [1819.] 8°. * (B 298)
— IN consequence of some remarks on the Layman, he offers the following arguments in addition to the former observations on the trinity. *n.t.p.* [1819.] 8°. (B 298)
— NORTON, J. Humble attempt to ascertain the Scripture doctrine of the Father, Son, and Holy Spirit; added, 'The awakener'. Bost., 1819. 8°. * (B 273)
— NORTON, A. Statement of reasons for not believing the doctrines of Trinitarians respecting the nature of God and the person of Christ. Boston, 1819. 8°. * (B 298)
— - *Same.* Cambridge, 1833. 12°.
— STUART, M. Letters to W. E. Channing, on his sermon at Baltimore. 2d ed., corr. and enl. Andover, 1819. 8°. (B 298, 1874)
— FEW remarks, A, on Prof. Stuart's reply to Mr. Channing's sermon; by a layman. *n.t.p.* [1819.] 8°. (B 298)
— REVIEW of [Stuart's Letters to W. E. Channing, containing remarks on his sermon at Baltimore, from the Christ. disciple, no. 11, n.s. Boston, 1819. 8°. (B 298)
— WATERMAN, —. The wren and eagle in contest; or, A short method with the Unitarian nobility; by Aquæ Homo. Boston, 1819. 8°. * (B 272)
— RAMMOHUN ROY. [1st,] 2d appeal to the Christian public in defence of the 'Precepts of Jesus'. Calcutta, 1820-21. 2 v. 8°. *
— - *Another copy.* (B 1469)
— - Precepts of Jesus extracted from the four Evangelists; added the 1st and 2d appeal in reply to Marshman. [1820-21.] N. Y., 1825. 8°. *
— - Final appeal. Calcutta, 1823. 8°. *
— - *Same.* Boston, 1828. 8°. *
— HUMPHREYS, —. Impartial review; general view of the controversy between Unitarians and the Orthodox, as it appears in a review in 'The Christian disciple' of Stuart's letters, *etc.* Portsmouth, 1820. 8°. (B 298)
— WARE, H., *Jr.* Two letters on the genuineness of I John v. 7, and on the Scriptural argument for Unitarians. [1820.] 3d ed. rev. Bost., 1823. 12°. (C 242)
— WARFIELD, C. Essay on the trinity; added, remarks on the character of Christ. Balt., 1820. 8°. (B 272)
— FLINT, J. Discourse [on] the doctrine of the trinity, 1823. Boston, 1824. 12°. * (C 207)
— HOLMES, D. Letter to the Church in Amherst, N. H. Boston, 1823. 8°. * (B 272)
— SPARKS, J. Inquiry into the comparative moral tendency of Trinitarian and Unitarian doctrines. Boston, 1823. 8°. *
— CATHOLICUS, VERUS, *pseud.* Letter to the Roman Cath. clergy of Ireland on the primary doctrine of revealed religion, and the purity of the early Irish church. London, 1824. 8°. *
— MOORE, H. Treatise on the divine nature, exhibiting the distinction of the Father, Son, and Holy Spirit. Boston, 1824. 8°.
— REMARKS on a late article in the Wesleyan journal. Charleston, S. C., 1825. 8°. * (B 1388)

— AMERICAN UNITARIAN ASSOCIATION. One hundred Scriptural arguments for the Unitarian faith. Boston, 1826. 12°. * (C 168, v. 1, 214)
— CORNELIUS, E. Sermon, doctrine of the trinity. 2d ed. Salem, 1826. 8°. (B 1286)
— NOBLE, S. True object of Christian worship demonstrated, and the doctrine of the trinity elucidated. Boston, 1828. 8°. (C 224)
Note. *Maintains* 'that the whole divine trinity centres in the one undivided person of Christ'.
— DRUMMOND, W. H. Unitarianism no feeble and conceited heresy. London, 1829. 8°. * (B 1389)
— HOBART, J. H. Duty of the clergy with respect to inculcating the doctrine of the trinity; a charge. N. Y., 1829. 8°. (B 1814)
— CARPENTER, L. Proofs from Scripture, that God even the Father is the only true God. 3d ed. Bristol, 1829. 12°. *
— CLERICUS, *pseud.* The doctrine of the trinity. *n.t.p.* [183-?] 8°. (B 1888)
— CORNELIUS, E. Plain and practical view of the doctrine of the trinity. N.Y., *Am. Tract Soc.*, [183- or 4-?]. 12°. (C 272)
— ADAMS, N. Remarks on the Unitarian belief. Boston, 1832. 18°.
— WARE, H., *Jr.* Outline of the testimony of Scripture against the trinity. Liverpool, 1832. 12°. * (C 242)
— LOWRIE, J. W. One Father; the unrivalled grandeur of the paternity of God. Bost.. 1833. 8°. * (B 1388)
— SHAW, E. Bible truth rel. to God, Christ, and the Holy Spirit. Portland, 1833. 18°. * (C 225)
— CARSON, A. Review of the discussion of the Unitarian controversy between J. S. Porter and D. Bagot. Belfast, 1834. 8°. (B 1389)
— BULFINCH, S. G. Argument from Scripture hist. against the trinity. Boston, *A.U.A.*, 104, 1836. 12°. * (C 168, v. 9)
— CLARKE, W. B. 'Paul' no Unitarian, *etc.* London, 1836. 8°. * (B 1389)
— WARE, H., *Jr.* Letter to N. Adams on his 'Injuries done to Christ'. Boston, 1841. 8°. * (D 29)
— CHADWICK, J. Trinitarianism examined and refuted. Auburn, 1842. 8°. (C 241)
— CHRISTIAN layman, The; or, The doctrine of the trinity fully considered. 2d ed. Mobile, 1842. 12°. *
— BAKEWELL, W. J. Unitarianism untenable; letter to the Unitarians of Chester, *etc.*; with app. Reprint fr. Amer. ed. London, 1843. 12°. (C 242)
— BEARD, J. R. Historical and artistic illustrations of the trinity. London, 1846. 8°. *
— SIMMONS, G. F. The trinity; its Scripture foundation, *etc.* Springfield, 1849. 8°. (B 1301)
— WILSON, J. Unitarian princip. confirmed by Trinitarian testimony. Boston, 1855. 12°. *
— BICKERSTETH, E. H. Rock of ages; with introd. by F. D. Huntington. Boston, 1860. 8°.
— ELLIS, G. E. The Christian trinity; discourse, Feb. 5. Charlestown, 1860. 8°. * (B 1289)
— KING, T. S. Trinitarianism not the doctrine of the New Testament; two lectures. Boston, 1860. 8°. * (B 1388)
— WALKER, J. P. New discussion of the trinity. Boston, 1860. 16°. *
— ADAMS, J. Search the Scriptures; against the Unitarian doctrine. Roxbury, 1864. 8°. (B 1282)

See also **Athanasian creed**; — **Arians**; — **Dissenters**; — **Jesus** *Christ.* (*Deity*); — **Logos**; — **Socinianism**; — **Unitarianism**; — *also* **Brandt, G.**; — **Hill, J.** Trial for heresy.

Trinity Church, *Boston.* *See* **Boston. Trinity Church** (p. 348).

Trinity Church, *N. Y.* *See* **New York. Trinity Church** (p. 2125).

Trinity College, *Dublin.* O'CONNOR, M. Pastoral in imitation of the first eclogue of Virgil; inscribed to the Provost, Fellows, and Scholars of Trinity College. Dublin, 1719. 8°. (Percy Soc., v. 7.)

Trinity of Italy, The; or the Pope, the Bourbon, and the victor; being hist. revelations of the past, present, and future of Italy; by an Eng. civilian. London, 1867. 8°.

Trinuzia, La; commedia. *See* **Firenzuola, A.**

Triomphe de l'amour, Le; comédie. *See* **Marivaux, P. C. de C. de.**

Triomphe de Plutus, Le; comédie. *See* **Marivaux, P. C. de C. de.**

Triomphe du nouveau monde, Le; par l'ami du corps social [J. A. Brun]. Paris, 1785. 2 v. 8°.

Triomphe hermétique; par A. T. Limojon de Saint Didier. Amst., 1689. 12°.

Trionfo d'amore, Il. *See* **Metastasio, P. A. D. B. T.**

Trionfo della fedeltà, Il. *See* **Baviera, M. A. W.**

Trionfo di Clelia, Il. *See* **Metastasio, P. A. D. B. T.**

Trionfo di Melibeo, Il. *See* **Baldwin, G.**

Trip, A, made by a small man; answer to the Baltimore millers' memorial, and T. Jefferson's letter. *n.p.*, [181-]. 8°. (B 664)

Trip of the steamer Oceanus to Fort Sumpter and Charleston, Apr. 14. Brooklyn, 1865. 8°.

Trip to Calais, A; a comedy. *See* **Foote, S.**

Trip to Scarborough, A; comedy. *See* **Sheridan, R. B. B.**

Trip to Scotland, A. *See* **Whitehead, W.**

Tripier, Louis. Les constitutions françaises, 1789–1848; suivies de la constit. des Etats-Unis. Paris, 1848. 12°.

Triple mariage, Le; comédie. *See* **Destouches, P. N.**

Tripler, Charles Stuart. Manual of the medical officer: Pt. 1: Recruiting and inspection of recruits. Cincin., 1858. 12°.

Tripod, The; or, New satirist; July, 1814. London, *n.d.* 8°.

Tripods. BARUCCHI, P. Dei tripodi in generale ed in particolare di quello d'industria. (*In* **Turin. Ac. d. Sci.** Mem., v. 33. 1829.)

Tripoli, *Africa.* *Description.*

— VOYAGE of the ship Jesus to Tripolis in Barbary, 1583. (*In* **Hakluyt, R.** Voyages, v. 2. 1810.)
— EWALD, C. F. Reise von Tunis nach Tripolisim, 1835; hrsg. von P. Ewald. Nurnberg, 1837. 8°.
— HOEFER, J. C. F. Etats tripolitains. (*In* **Rozet, C. A.** Algérie. 1850. Univers.)
— ROHLFS, G. Voyage de Tripoli à Lagos, [1865–67]. (*In* **Paris. Soc. de Géog.** Bul., 5e sér., v. 14. 1867.)

History.

— HISTORY of T., [to 1750]. (*In* **Compleat** hist. of the piratical states of Barbary. 1750.)
— BARTOLOTTI, J. La mémorable victorie des galères de Malte contre les Turcs de Tripoli, 19 juil. 1634. (*In* **Ternaux-Compans, H.** Archives, v. 2. 1841.)
— HISTORY of the war between U. S. and Tripoli, [1784–1806]. Salem, 1806. 12°.
— MESSAGE from the President of the U. S. communicating a letter from R. O'Brien [on] transactions before Tripoli. Wash., 1802. 8°. (B 504)
— COWDERY, *Dr.* American captives in Tripoli; or, Dr. Cowdery's journal in miniature, [1804–05]. Boston, 1806. 8°. (B 65)
— E., W. Interesting detail of the operations of the American fleet in the Mediterranean, [1805]. Springfield, [1805?]. 8°. (B 427, 609)
— PREBLE, E. Message from the Pres. of the U. S. transm. a letter from Commodore Preble, giving an account of the transactions of the vessels under his command from July 9 to Sept. 10. *n.p.*, [1805]. 8°. (W 10)

Tripoli, *Syria.* ALDERSEY, L. Voyage to Jerusalem and Tripolis, 1581. — ELDRED, J. Voyage to Tripolis, 1583. (*In* **Hakluyt, R.** Col. of voy., v. 2. 1810.)

Trippings of Tom Pepper; by H. Franco [C. F. Briggs]. N. Y., 1847. 12°.

Trismegistus, Hermes. *See* **Hermes Trismegistus.**

Trissino, Giovan Giorgio. Tutte le opere. Verona, 1729. 2 v. f°.

Contents. Vol. 1. Vita del Trissino. — Prefazione. — Italia liberata dai Gotti. — Sofonisba; tragedia. — I simillimi, commedia. — Rime. — Sonetti' da altri eccellentissimi poeti scritti al Trissino. — Encomium Maximiliani Cæsaris. — Pharmaceutria, seu de morte Batti. — Epigrammata duo. 2. Della poetica. — Dante della volgar eloquenza, col testo latino a colonna. — Epistola delle lettere nuovamente aggiunte. — Dubbj grammaticali. — Il castelano. — La grammatichetta. — I ritratti.

— Epistola della vita che dee tenere una donna vedova. — Orazione al Doge Gritti. — Grammatices introductionis liber primus. — Risposta di Lodovico di Lorenzo Martelli all' Epistola delle lettere. — Di Adriano Franzi da Siena. — Ragionamento di Angelo Firenzuola. — Dialogo di Nicolo Liburnio. — Vincentii Oreadini Perusini opusculum.

— Italia liberata; [vita da P. C. Vicentino]. Londra, 1779. 3 v. 12°.

— Madrigali. (*In* **Trucchi, F.** Poesie ital., v. 3. 1847.)

— La Sofonisba. (*In* **Teatro** ital. ant., v. 1. 1802.)

— NICERON, J. P. (*In his* Mém., v. 29. 1734.)

Trissmosinus, Salomon. Aureum vellus; oder, Gulden Schatz und Kunst-Kammer. Hamburg, 1708. 4°.

Trist, Nicholas P. Reply to the resolutions adopted by the meeting of ship masters and owners. *n.p.*, [1840?]. 8°. (B 1166)

— CLARK, F. American captives in Havana; a reply to T. Boston, 1841. 8°. (B 1498)

— DOCUMENTS A - F rel. to Consul Trist.] *n.p.*, [1839-40]. 8°. (E 256) — [Doc. A.] (B 1448) — [Doc. A, B, C.] (B 1159) — [Doc. D, E, F.] (B 1166) *Namely*. Doc. **A**. Case of Capt. A. Wendell, Jr., of the Brig Kremlin of N. Y., arising from an outrage perpetrated by him upon Wm. Bell, first officer of said brig, in Havana, July, 1838. **B**. Commander Babbit and Consul Trist at Havana. **C**. Reply of N. P. Trist to the resolutions at a meeting in Boston, on the subject of the cases of Capt. A. Wendell, Jr., and the crew of the ship Wm. Engs. — **D**. Case of the crew of the ship Wm. Engs, embracing the inquiry, Who is R. R. Maddon? **E**. Condition of Amer. seaman at Havana, with illustr. of the nature of consular duties. — **F**. Reply of N. P. Trist to the preamble and resolutions adopted by the meeting of ship-masters and owners, convened Aug. 8 and 14, 1839.

— MADDEN, R. R. Letter to W. E. Channing on the abuse of the flag of U. S. in the Island of Cuba. Boston, 1839. 8°. (B 1172)

— REMARKS upon a letter by L. C. Vanuxem, in regard to the conduct of N. P. Trist towards N. Cross. Boston, 1841. 8°. (B 1449)

— U. S. *26th Cong. 1st sess. House*. Report [of] committee on commerce rel. to the conduct of N. P. Trist, consul at Havana. *n.t.p.* [Wash., 1840.] 8°. (Rep. no. 707. B 1159, E 256)

Tristan. GOTTFRIED *von Strassburg*. Werke: Tristan und Isolde; mit [Forsetzungen, und Tristan und Isolde nach Thomas von Ercel-doune]. Breslau, 1823. 2 v. 8°.

— - Tristan; hrsg. von R. Bechstein. Lpz., 1869. 2 v. 16°. (Deutsche Class. des Mittelalters, v. 7, 8.)

— MICHEL, F. Recueil des poëmes relatifs à ses aventures; en françois, en anglo-normand, et en grec. Londres, 1835. 2 v. 16°.

— TRISTAN und Isalde. (*In* **Simrock, K. J.** Deutschen Volksbücher, v. 4. 1846.)

— THOMAS *of Erceldoune*. Sir Tristrem; ed. by W. Scott. Edin., 1811. 8°.

— - *Same*. (*In* Scott, W. Poetical works, v. 5. 1833; — *and in* **Gottfried** *von Strassburg*. Werke, v. 2. 1823.)

Tristan d'Acunha, *Island*. SEAVER, B. F. Letter conc. the islands, 1811. (*In* **Mass. Hist. Soc.** Col., v. 12. 1814.)

— EARLE, A. Journal of a resience in T., 1827. (*In his* Narrative. 1832.)

Tristan de Nanteuil. MEYER, P. Notice sur le roman de T. (*In* **Jahrb.** f. rom. und eng. Lit., v. 9. 1868.)

Tristan le voyageur; ou, La France au 14e siècle; par L. A. F. de Marchangy. 2e éd. Paris, 1825-26. 6 v. 8°.

Tristan l'Hermite, François. Mariamne; tragédie. (*In* **Rousseau, J. B.** Œuvres, v. 4. 1820; — *and in* **Annales** poét., v. 20. 1782.)

— Le page disgracié. (*In* **Biblioth.** univ. des romans, Nouv., v. 22. 1799.)

Tristram, *Rev.* Henry Baker. Great Sahara; wanderings south of the Atlas Mts. London, 1860. 8°.

— Land of Israel; a journal of travels in Palestine. London, 1865. 8°.

— Natural history of the Bible. London, *Soc. Prom. Chr. Knowl.*, 1867. 12°.

— Winter ride in Palestine. (*In* **Galton, F.** Vacation tourists, 1862-63.)

Tristram Shandy, gent, Life and opinions of; by **L. Sterne**. (Vol. 1-3 *of his* Works, 1795; 1803.)

Tristrem. *See* **Tristan.**

Trithemius (*Germ.* **Tritheim** *or* **Trittenheim**, *properly* von **Heidenberg**), Johannes. Tractatus chemicus nobilis. (*In* **Zetzner, L.** Theatrum chem., v. 4. 1613.)

— NICERON, J. P. (*In his* Mém., v. 38. 1737; *and, Germ.*, v. 18. 1758.)

Trithen, F. H. On the structure of the Russian verb. — Formation of the past tense in certain European languages. (*In* **Philolog. Soc.** Proc., 1842-44.) — Origin of the Greek Hermes. (*In* 1846-48.) — On the position occupied by the Slavonic dialects among the other languages of the Indo-European family. (*In* 1848-50, 1850-52.)

Tritogenea; synopsis of universal philosophy. *See* **Field, G.**

Triumph of beauty, The. *See* **Shirley, J.**

Triumph of love, The. *See* **Beaumont, F.**

Triumph of peace, The; a masque. *See* **Shirley, J.**

Triumphale, The; a poetical hist. of the triumphs of the Recorder over the Free Press. Halifax, 1820. 18°. (D 20)

Triumphs of health and prosperity, The; by **T. Middleton**. (*In his* Works, v. 5. 1840.)

Triumphs of honour and industry; by **T. Middleton**. (*In his* Works, v. 5. 1840.)

Triumphs of integrity, The; by **T. Middleton**. (*In his* Works, v. 5. 1840.)

Triumphs of love and antiquity; by **T. Middleton**. (*In his* Works, v. 5. 1840.)

Triumphs of time; by [A. C. Marsh-Caldwell]. N. Y., 1844. 8°.

Triumphs of truth, The; by **T. Middleton**. (*In his* Works, v. 5. 1840.)

Triumvirat, Le; tragédie. *See* **Voltaire, F. M. A. de.**

Triumvirat, Le, ou La mort de Cicéron; tragédie. *See* **Crébillon**, P. J.

Triunfo de Ave Maria, comedia; de un ingenio de esta corte. (*In* **Mesonero Romanos**, R. de. Dramaticos posteriores a Lope de Vega, v. 2. 1859; v. 49 of Aribau. Bibl.)

Triunfo del interés, El; saynete. *See* **Cruz y Cano**, R. de la.

Triunfo dell' amicizia, Il; tragicommedia. *See* **Gozzi, C.**

Trivet *or* **Treveth** (*Lat.* **Trivetus** *or* **Tripos**), Nicolas. Annales sex regum Angliæ; rec. T. Hog. Londini, 1845. 8°. (Eng. Hist. Soc.)

— Commentaria.] (*In* **Augustinus**, *St.* De ciuitate Dei. 1473.)

— JOURDAIN, C. M. G. B. Des commentaires inéd. de G. de Conches et de N. Triveth sur la 'Consolation de la philosophie' de Boèce. (*In* **Paris. Inst.** *Ac. d. Inscr.* Not., v. 20, pte. 2. 1862.)

Trivisano, Zaccaria, *b.* 1370. AGOSTINI, G. degli. (*In his* Notizie degli scrittori viniz, v. 1. 1752.)

Trivisano, Zaccaria, *b.* 1413. AGOSTINI, G. degli. (*In his* Notizie degli scrittori viniz., v. 1. 1752.)

Trivulzio *di Milano*, Famiglia di. (*In* **Litta**, P. Fam., v. 14.)

Troade. *See* **Troy.**

Troades. *See* **Euripides.**

Trochu, *Gen.* Louis Jules. L'armée française en 1867. 18e éd. Paris, 1867. 8°.

— Une page d'hist. contemporaine devant l'Assemblée Nationale. Paris, 1871. 8°.

Troemel, Paul Friedrich. Cat. d'une collection de livres sur l'Amérique, en vente chez F. A. Brockhaus. Lpz., 1861. 8°.

See also **Allgemeine** Bibliographie.

Trognianus, Guilielmus. Scripta de lapide. (*In* **Zetzner**, L. Theatrum chem., v. 6. 1661.)

Trognon, A., *pseud.* *See* **Joinville, F. F. P. L. M.** d'O., *prince* de.

Trognon, Auguste. Fragment sur l'hist. de France. (*In* **Guizot, F. P. G.** Col. des mém., v. 31. 1826.)

Trogus Pompeius. *See* **Justinus.**

Troil, Uno von. Letters on Iceland. (*In* **Pinkerton**, J. Col. of voy., v. 1. 1808.)

Troilus and Cressida. *See* **Shakespeare**, W.

Troilus and Cressida; or, Truth found to late; tragedy, by **J. Dryden**. (*In his* Works, v. 6. 1808.)

365, Les; annuaire de la littérature et des auteurs contemporains; par le dernier d'entre eux. Paris, 1858. 12°.

Trois commères, Les; comédie. *See* **Le Sage, A. R.**
Trois cousines, Les; comédie. *See* **Dancourt, F. C.**
Trois frères rivaux, Les; comédie. *See* **Lafont, J. de.**
Trois Maupin, Les, ou La veille de la régence; par [E.] Scribe et H. Boisseaux. Berlin, 1859. 8°. (E 21)
Trois mousquetaires, Les; par A. Dumas. Paris, 1853. 2 v. 8°.
— *Same.* Nouv. éd. Paris, 1862. 2 v. 18°.
Note. Contin. as 'Vingt ans après'.
Trois sermons sous Louis xv; par F. Bungener. 3e éd. Paris, 1854. 3 v. 8°.
Trois regnes, Les. *See* **Delille, J.**
Trois sultanes, Les; comédie. *See* **Favart, C. S.**
Trois-Etoiles, *pseud.* *See* **Murray, E. C. G.**
Trojani, Filippo. Pianta di Roma incisa nel Dicastero Gen. del Censo. Roma, 1832. (E 278)
— Pianta. Roma, 1835. (E 278)
Trokelowe, Johannes de, *and* **Blaneforde, H. de.** Chronica et annales, 1259–96; 1307–24; 1392–1406. London, 1866. 8°. (Chron. and mem.)
Trollope, Anthony. Barchester towers. Lpz., *Tauchnitz,* 1859. 2 v. 16°.
— *Same.* London, 1866. 8°.
Note. The order of the Barchester novels: Warden, Barchester Towers, Doctor Thorne, Framley Parsonage, Small House at Allington, Can you forgive her, Last chronicle, Phineas Finn, Phineas Redux, Prime minister, The Duke's children. The last three are on the supplementary catalogue.
— Belton estate. Phila., 1866. 12°.
— *Same.* Lpz., *Tauchnitz,* 1866. 2 v. 16°.
— *Same.* (*In* **Fortnightly** review, v. 1-3. 1865-66; — *and in* **Littell's** living age, v. 86-88. 1865-66.)
— Bertrams, The; a novel. Lpz., *Tauchnitz,* 1859. 2 v. 16°.
— *Same.* N. Y., 1867. 12°.
— Best means of extending and securing an international law of copyright. (*In* **Nat. Assoc. Prom. Soc. Sci.** Trans., 1866.)
— British sports and pastimes. London, 1868. 8°.
— Can you forgive her? London, 1864. 2 v. 8°.
— *Same.* N. Y., 1865. 8°.
— *Same.* Lpz., *Tauchnitz,* 1865. 3 v. 16°.
— Castle Richmond. N. Y., 1860. 12°.
— *Same.* Lpz., *Tauchnitz,* 1860. 2 v. 16°.
— Claverings, The. London, 1867. 2 v. 8°
— *Same.* Lpz., *Tauchnitz,* 1867. 2 v. 16°.
— *Same.* (*In* **Cornhill** mag., v. 13-15. 1866-67; — *and in* **Littell's** living age, v. 88-92. 1866-67.)
— Clergymen of the Ch. of England. From the Pall Mall gazette. London, 1866. 16°.
— Doctor Thorne. Lpz., *Tauchnitz,* 1858. 2 v. 16°.
— *Same.* N. Y., 1860. 12°.
— An editor's tales. London, 1870. 8°.
Note. From **St. Paul's** mag., v. 5-6. 1870.
Contents. The Turkish bath. — Mary Gresley. — Josephine de Montmorenci. — The Panjandrum. — The spotted dog. — Mrs. Brumby.
— Eustace diamonds. (*In* **Galaxy,** v. 12-15. 1871-73.)
— Framley Parsonage. N. Y., 1861. 12°.
— *Same.* Lpz., *Tauchnitz,* 1861. 2 v. 16°.
— *Same.* (*In* **Cornhill** mag., v. 1-3. 1860-61.)
— He knew he was right. London, 1869. 2 v. 8°.
— *Same.* Lpz., *Tauchnitz,* 1869. 3 v. 16°.
Note. From **Every Saturday,** v. 6-7. 1868-69.
— Last chronicle of Barset. N. Y., 1867. 8°.
— *Same.* Lpz., 1867. 3 v. 16°.
— Linda Tressel. London, Edin., 1868. 2 v. 16°.
— *Same.* (*In* **Blackwood's** mag., v. 102-103. 1867-68; — *and in* **Littell's** living age, v. 95-97. 1868.)
— Lotta Schmidt. London, 1867. 8°.
— Miss Mackenzie. N. Y., 1865. 8°.
— Nina Balatka. Edin. and Lond., 1867. 2 v. 8°.
— North America. London, 1862. 2 v. 8°.
— *Same.* N. Y., 1862. 12°.
— *Same.* Phila., 1862. 12°.
— Orley farm. N. Y., 1862. 8°.
— *Same.* Lpz., *Tauchnitz,* 1862. 3 v. 16°.
— *Same.* (*In* **Harper's** mag., v. 23-25. 1861-62.)
— Phineas Finn, the Irish member; illust. by J. E. Millais. London, 1869. 2 v. 8°.
— *Same.* Lpz., *Tauchnitz,* 1869. 3 v. 16°.
— *Same.* (*In* **St. Paul's** mag., v. 1-4. 1868-69; — *and in* **Littell's** living age, v. 95-101. 1868-69.)
— Rachel Ray; a novel. Lpz., *Tauchnitz,* 1863. 2 v. 16°.
— Ralph the heir. London, 1871. 8°.
— Sir Harry Hotspur, of Humblethwaite. N. Y., 1871. 8°.
— Small house at Allington. London., 1864. 2 v. 8°.
— *Same.* N. Y., 1864. 8°.
— *Same.* Lpz., *Tauchnitz,* 1864. 3 v. 16°.
— *Same.* (*In* **Cornhill** mag., v. 6-9. 1862-64; — *and in* **Harper's** mag., v. 25-29. 1862-64.)
— Struggles of Brown, Jones, and Robinson. (*In* **Cornhill** mag., v. 4-5. 1861-62.)
— Tales of all countries. London, 1864. 12°.
Contents. La mère Bauche. — The O'Conors of Castle Conor. — John Bull on the Guadalquiver. — Miss Sarah Jack. — The courtship of Susan Bell. — Relics of Gen. Chassé. — An unprotected female at the Pyramids. — The chateau of Prince Polignac. — Aaron Trow. — Mrs. General Talboys. — The parson's daughter of Oxney Colne. — George Walker at Suez. — The mistletoe bough. — Returning home. — A ride across Palestine. — The House of Heine Brothers. — The man who kept his money in a box.
— Three clerks, The. N. Y., 1860. 12°.
— Vicar of Bullhampton; a novel. New York, 1870. 8°.
— *Same.* Lpz., *Tauchnitz,* 1870. 2 v. 8°.
— W. M. Thackeray. (*In* **Hotten, J. C.** Thackeray. 1864.)
— The warden. Lpz., *Tauchnitz,* 1859. 16°.
— West Indies and Spanish Main. 4th ed. Lond., 1860. 8°.
— Montégut, E. (*In* **Revue** d. D. Mondes, oct. 1858.) — Forgues, E. (*In* sept. 1860, juin 1867.)
Trollope, *Mrs.* **Frances Eleanor (Milton).** Belgium and West Germany, 1833. London, 1834. 2 v. 12°.
— Charles Chesterfield. N. Y., 1858. 8°.
— Domestic manners of the Americans. 2d ed. London, 1832. 2 v. 12°.
— Jessie Phillips. London, 1844. 8°.
— Life, *etc.,* of Jonathan Jefferson Whitlaw. London, 1836. 3 v. 12°.
— Life and adventures of Michael Armstrong, the factory boy. London, 1840. 8°.
— *Same.* N. Y., 1840. 2 v. 12°.
— Mœurs américaines des Etats Unis. (*In* **Montémont,** A. Biblioth., v. 39. 1835.)
— Mother's manual. London, 1833. 8°.
— Second love. London, 1851. 3 v. 12°.
— Vienna and the Austrians. London, 1838. 2 v. 8°.
— Visit to Italy. London, 1842. 2 v. 8°.
— American criticisms on [her] 'Domestic manners of the Americans'. London, 1833. 8°. (B 1070, 1073)
— Cortambert, R. (*In his* Illustres voyageuses. 1866.)
— Horne, R. H. (*In his* A new Spirit of the age, v. 1. 1844.)
— Johnston, D. C. Trollopania: sketches to be referred to in perusing 'Domestic manners of the Americans'. (*In his* Scraps. 1833.)
Trollope, Theodosia (Garrow), *wife of* Thomas Adolphus, *d.* 1865. Social aspects of the Italian revolution. London, 1861. 12°.
Trollope, Thomas Adolphus. Artingale Castle. London, 1867. 3 v. 16°.
— La beata. London, 1861. 2 v. 16°.
— Beppo the conscript; a novel. London, 1864. 2 v. 8°.

— A decade of Italian women. Lond., 1859. 2 v. 8°.
Contents. Vol. 1. St. Catherine of Siena. — Caterina Sforza. — Vittoria Colonna. 2. Tullia d'Aragona. — Olympia Morata. — Isabella Andreini. — Biana Cappello. — Olympia Pamfili. — Elisabetta Sirani. — La Corilla.
— Dream numbers; a novel. Lond., 1868. 3 v. 16°.
— Durnton Abbey; a novel. N. Y., 1871. 8°.
— Filippo Strozzi; last days of Italian liberty. London, 1860. 8°.
— Garstang Grange; a novel. Phila., 1870. 8°.
— Gemma; a novel. Phila., 1868. 12°.
— Girlhood of Catherine de Medicis. London, 1856. 8°.
— Giulio Malatesta; a novel. Lond., 1863. 3 v. 8°.
— *Same.* Sealed packet. Phila., [1871]. 8°.
— History of the Commonwealth of Florence. London, 1865. 4 v. 8°.
— Lenten journey in Umbria and the Marches. London, 1862. 8°.
Contents. Vol. 1. 1107-1328. 2. 1328-1428. 3. 1428-92. 4. 1492-1530.
— Leonora Casaloni; or, The marriage secret. Phila., [1869]. 16°.
— *Same.* (*In* **Fortnightly rev.**, v. 9-10. 1868.)
— Lindisfarn Chase. N. Y., 1864. 8°.
— *Same.* (*In* **Littell's** liv. age, v. 81-82. 1864.)
— Marietta; novel. London, 1862. 2 v. 8°.
— Paul the Pope and Paul the friar. London, 1861. 8°.
— Sealed packet. *See, above,* 'Giulio'.
— A siren. London, 1870. 3 v. 8°.
— Summer in Brittany. London, 1840. 2 v. 8°.
— Tuscany in 1849, 1859. London, 1859. 8°.
— Forgues, E. (*In* **Revue** d. D. Mondes, juin 1867.)

Trollope, *Mrs.* Thomas Adolphus (Ternan). Anne Furness. N. Y., 1871. 8°.
— *Same.* (*In* **Fortnightly rev.**, v. 14-16. 1870-72; — *and in* **Harper's** mag., v. 41-42. 1871.)
— Mabel's progress. (*In* **All** the year round, v. 17-18. 1867.)
— The sacristan's household. N. Y., 1869. 8°.
— *Same.* (*In* **Littell's** liv. age, v. 94-95. 1867-68; — *and in* **St. Paul's** mag., v. 2-4. 1868-69.)

Trollope, *Rev.* Wm. Analecta theologica. New ed. London, 1842. 2 v. 8°.
— Belgium since the revolution of 1830. Lond., 1842. 12°.
— Essay on the connexion between the Jewish and Christian dispensations. Lond., 1822. 8°.
— Notæ philol. et grammat. in Euripidis tragedias selectæ. Londini, 1828. 2 v. 8°.

Tromelin, Legoarant (de?). Voyage autour du monde. (*In* **Montémont, A.** Biblioth. univ., v. 18. 1834.)

Tromm, Abraham. Concordantiæ Gr. versionis LXX. Amst., Traj. ad R., 1718. 2 v. f°.

Tromp, Cornelis, *Admiral General.* Cust, *Sir* E. (*In his* Lives of the warriors, *etc.* v. 2. 1869.)

Tromp, Martin, *Admiral.* Cust, *Sir* E. (*In his* Lives of the warriors who have commanded fleets, *etc.*, v. 2. 1869.)

Tromsöe, *Norway.* Marmier, X. Tromsöe. (*In* **Revue** d. D. Mondes, déc. 1838.)

Tron, Vincenzo. Sommario della relazione di Germania, 1576. (*In* **Venice.** Rel. deg. ambasc. veneti, ser. 1, v. 6. 1862.)

Tronchet, François Denis. Delamalle, G. G. W. Eloge. Paris, 1806. 4°. (A 9)

Tronchin, Théodore. Condorcet, J. A. N. C., *marq.* de. (*In his* Œuvres, v. 2. 1847.)

Tronson, John M. Voyage to Japan, Kamtschatka, Siberia, Tartary, and various parts of the the coast of China, in H. M. S. Barracouta. London, 1859. 8°.

Troost, Gerard. An account of ancient remains in Tennessee. (*In* **Amer. Ethnolog. Soc.** Trans., v. 1. 1845.)
— Description and chem. anal. of the retinasphalt disc. at Cape Sable, Magothy River, Ann Arundel Co., Md. — Notice of a new crystalline form of the yenite of R. I. (*In* **Amer. Phil. Soc.** Trans., n.s., v. 2. 1825.)
— Geological survey of the environs of Philadelphia. Phila., 1826. 8°. (B 526)
— List of the fossil crinoids of Tennessee. (*In* **Amer. Assoc.** Proc., v. 2. 1850.)
— Various articles.] (*In* **Academy of Nat. Sci. of Phila.** Journ., v. 2-5. 1821-27.)

Troost, L. Chimie. (*In* **Baccalauréat ès sciences, Le,** v. 3. 1864.)

Trop heureuse, ou Un jeune ménage; comédie, par [H.] Leroux. Berlin, 1838. 12°. (E 22)

Tropes. Mansart, E. A. Du sublime et des tropes. Londres, 1833. 12°.

Trophonius. Panofka, T. Trophonioskultus in Rhegium. (*In* **Berlin. Ak. d. Wiss.** Abh., 1848.)

Tropical medicine. Annals of tropical medicine. (*In* **Annals** of military and naval surgery. 1864.)

Tropical plants. U. S. *25th Cong. 2d sess. Senate. Committee on Agriculture.* Report to encourage the introd. and cultivation of tropical plants. [Wash., 1838.] 8°. (No. 300.)

Tropics. Friedmann, S. Ueber Arzneikunde aus Kriegschiffen, Akklimatisation in den Tropenländern und der Tropenkrankheiten. Erlang., 1850. 8°.
— Burmeister, H. Der tropische Urwald. (*In* **Geologische** Bilder. 1855.)
— Hartwig, G. The tropical world; a popular scientific account of the nat. hist. of the animal and vegetable kingdoms in the equatorial regions. London, 1863. 8°.

Tropics, In the, by a settler in Santo Domingo [J. W. Fabens]; with introd. by R. B. Kimball. 2d ed. N. Y., London, 1863. 12°.

Troplong, Raymond Théodore. De l'influence du christianisme sur le droit civil des Romains. 3e éd. Paris, 1868. 16°.
— *Same.* (*In* **Paris. Inst.** *Ac. d. Sci. Mor.* Mém., v. 4. 1844.)
— De la propriété d'après le code civil. (*In* **Paris. Inst.** *Ac. d. Sci.* Petits traités, v. 2. 1848; — Mém., v. 7. 1850.)
— Républiques d'Athènes et de Sparte. (*In* **Paris. Inst.** *Ac. d. Sci. Mor.* Mém., v. 8. 1852; — *and in* Séances. 2e sér., v. 10; 3e sér., v. 9. 1851.)
— Taine, H. A. (*In his* Essais de critique. 1859.)

Troppi, I; commedia. *See* **Alfieri,** V.

Trosse, George, *D.D.* Eveleigh, J. Vindication of T. from the charge of uncharitableness, *etc.* London, 1719. 8°. (B 112)
— Humphrey, H. Memoir of T. (*In his* Christian memoirs. 1836.)

Trot, John, *yeoman.* The craftsman extraordinary; cont. an answer to the "Defence of the 'Enquiry into the reasons of the conduct of Gr. Brit.'" London, 1729. 8°. (B 757)

Trotman, Nathaniel. Letter to his church. (*In* **Barber,** J. Sermon, death of T. 1793. B 1226)

Trotter, Alexander. Observations on the financial position and credit of such of the states as have contracted public debts. London, 1839. 8°.

Trotter, James. General view of the agriculture of the County of West Lothian. Edin., 1794. 4°. (W 77)

Trotter, John Bernard. Memoirs of the latter years of C. J. Fox. London, 1811. 8°.

Trotter, Thomas. Essay on drunkenness. 1st Phila. ed. corr. and enl. Boston, Phila., 1813. 12°.
— Observations on the scurvy; Dr. Milman refuted. Phila., 1793. 8°. (C 271)
— View of the nervous temperament. London, 1807. 18°.
— *Same.* Troy, 1808. 12°.

Trotter, Wm. Brief report. [1841?] *See* **Barker.** J.

Trou de l'Enfer, Le; par A. Dumas. Nouv. éd. Paris, 1862. 18°.

Troubadours. *See* **Provençal language** *and* **Provençal literature** (p. 2432); — **Trouvères**; — **Trovatori.**

Troughton, John. Charge to W. Moss, M. Leeson, and W. Willets, at their ordination, June 11. London, 1724. 8°. (B 120)

Troughton, Richard. MADDEN, F. Petition of T. to the privy council in the reign of Queen Mary, rel. to the share taken by him in the Duke of Northumberland's plot. (*In* **Archæologia**, v. 23. 1831.)

Troup, George McIntosh, *Gov. of Georgia*. Message. 1825. *See* **Georgia.** *Governor* (p. 1128. **B 1102**)

Troup, Robert. Letter to B. Livingston on the lake canal policy of N. Y. Albany, 1822. 8°. (**B 900**)

Trousseau, Armand. Lectures on clinical medicine, delivered at the Hotel-Dieu, Paris. Vol. 3, 4, 5; tr. and ed. by J. R. Cormack. Lond., 1868-72. 5 v. 8°. (New Sydenham Soc., v. 35, 42, 51, 55.)

Note. Vol. 1; tr. and ed. with notes and app. by P. V. Bazire; v. 2-5; tr. from ed. of 1868, being the 3d rev. and enl. ed. by J. R. Cormack.

— On diphtherite. (*In* **Semple, R. H.** Memoirs on diphtheria. 1859. New Syd. Soc., v. 3.)

— *and* **Belloc**, H. Practical treatise on laryngeal phthysis, chronic laryngitis, and diseases of the voice; tr. by J. A. Warder. Phila., 1839. 8°.

Troussel-Delvincourt, Jean François Alfred. Mémoire sur le croup. 2e éd. Paris, 1821. 8°.

Trouvères. AUGUIS, P. R. Langue d'oil, trouvères, 13e siècle. (*In his* Poètes franç., v. 1. 1824.)

— LA RUE, G., *abbé* de. Essais hist. sur les bardes et les trouvères normands et anglonormands. Caen, 1834. 3 v. 8°.

— SIMONDE DI SISMONDI, J. C. L. (*In his* De la lit. du Midi de l'Europe, v. 1. 1829; — *and, Eng.*, v. 1. 1823.)

— LAUBEN, B. F. A. J. D., *Freiherr* zur. Sur un ms. contenant les chansons des trouvères de la Souabe ou de l'Allem. (*In* **Sérieys**, A. Bibl. acad., v. 9. 1811.)

See also **Cuvelier**; — **Benoist.**

Trovador, El; drama caballeresco. *See* **Gutierrez**, A. G.

Trovatori. (*In* **Trucchi**, F. Poesie ital., v. 1. 1846.)

Note. For Provençal troubadours *see* **Provençal literature.**

Trow's New York city directory. *See* **Wilson**, H.

Troward, Richard. Collection of statutes, *etc.*, rel. to elections; with an index and app. 2d ed. London, 1796. 8°.

Trowbridge, David. Account of ancient fort and burial ground in Tompkins Co., N. Y. (*In* **Smithsonian Inst.** Report, 1863.)

Trowbridge, John, *ed.* *See* **Annual** of sci. discov. 1870, 71.

Trowbridge, John Townsend. Cudjo's cave. Boston, 1864. 12°.

— Jack Hazard and his fortunes. Boston, 1871. 8°.

— Martin Merivale. Boston, 1854. 12°.

— Neighbor Jackwood. (*In* **Sargent**, E. Mod. stand. dr., v. 37.)

— Neighbors' wives. Boston, 1867. 12°.

— Three scouts. Boston, 1865. 12°.

— The vagabonds, and other poems. Boston, 1869. 12°.

Trowbridge, Thomas R. Hist. of Long Wharf, New Haven. (*In* **New Haven Col. Hist. Soc.** Papers, v. 1. 1865.)

Trowbridge, Wm. P. Deep-sea soundings. (*In* **Amer. Assoc.** Proc., v. 12. 1859.)

Trowel, *Adjutant* (*pseud.* for Thomas Dawes). PROPOSALS for printing by subscription the history of Adj. T. and Bluster [James Otis]. *n.t.p.* [Boston, 1761.] 12°. (**B 659**)

Troy. COLONNE, G. delle. Gest hystoriale of the destruction of Troy; ed. by G. A. Panton, and D. Donaldson. [1287.] Pt. 1. Lond., 1869. 8°. (E. E. Text Soc.)

— LE CHEVALLIER, J. B. Voyage de la Troade. 1785-86. Paris, 1802. 3 v. 8°.

— MACLAURIN, J. Diss. to prove that Troy was not taken by the Greeks. (*In his* Works, v. 1. 1798; — *and in* **Roy. Soc. of Edin.** Trans., v. 1. 1788.)

— LE CHEVALIER, J. B. Tableau de la Plaine de Troye. (*In* **Roy. Soc. of Edin.** Trans., v. 3. 1794.) — DALZEL, A. Chevalier's Tableau de la Plaine de Troye illustrated. (*In* v. 4. 1798.)

— CHANDLER, R. History of Ilium or Troy, and the adjacent country. London, 1802. 4°.

— GELL, *Sir* W. Topography of Troy. London, 1804. f°.

— GREG, R. H. Remarks on the site of Troy and the Trojan plain. (*In* **Literary and Phil. Soc. of Manchester.** Mem., 2d ser., v. 4. 1824.)

— FERRARIO, G. (*In his* Costume ant. e mod., v. 3. 1829.)

— WELCKER, F. G. Ueber die Lage des homerischen Ilion. 1843. (*In his* Kleine Schriften, v. 2. 1845.) — Alte Autoren in Bezug auf die Lage Ilions. 1857. (*In* v. 4. 1861.)

Troy, *N. H.* CAVERLY, A. M. Historical sketch of T., 1764-1855. Keene, 1859. 12°.

Troy, *N. Y.* Ordinances of the trustees of the village of Troy. Troy, 1806. 8°. (**B 1000**)

— WOODWORTH, J. Reminiscences of Troy, N. Y., 1790-1807. Albany, 1853. 8°.

— WRIGHT, J., *and* HALL, J. Catalogue of plants growing without cultivation in the vicinity of Troy. Troy, 1836. 8°. (**B 1138**)

See also **Rensselaer Polytechnic Institute.**

Troy, *N. Y.* **Episcopal Institute.** Annual catalogue. Troy, 1839. 8°. (**B 1144**)

Troy, *N. Y.* **1st Presbyterian Church.** ACCOUNT of the origin and progress of the divisions. Troy, 1827. 8°. (**B 952**)

Troy. Young Men's Association. Catalogue of the library. Troy, 1859. 8°.

Troy and Greenfield R. R. *Mass. Commissioners.* Report upon the R. R. and Hoosac Tunnel. N. Y., 1863. 8°.

Troya, Carlo. Della condizione de Romani vinti da' Longobardi. Ed. 2a, con observ. di F. Rezzonico. Milano, 1844. 8°.

— X***. Necrologia di Troya. (*In* **Archivio** stor. ital., n. s., v. 7. 1858.) — MAMIANI, T. Elogio. (*In* v. 12, pt. 2. 1860.)

Troyennes, Les; tragédie. *See* **Chateaubrun**, J. B. V. de.

Troyes, Chrestien. *See* **Chrestien** *de Troyes.*

Troyes, Jean de. *See* **Jean** *de Troyes.*

Troyes. DU FRESNE DE FRANCHEVILLE, J. Sur une expédition faite par les troupes de l'empereur Othon le Grand, devant Troyes, [959]. (*In* **Berlin. Ak. d. Wiss.** Abh., 1776.)

— *Same.* (*In* **Sérieys**, A. Bibl. acad., v. 7. 1811.)

— DARCEL, A. Troyes et ses expositions d'art. (*In* **Gazette** des beaux-arts, v. 17. 1864.)

Troyes. St. Etienne. COFFINET, J. B. Trésor de St. Etienne. (*In* **Annales** archéol., v. 20. 1860.)

Troyon, Constant. LA FORGE, A. (*In his* Peinture contemporaine en France. 1856.)

— MANTZ, P. (*In* **Gazette** des beaux arts, v. 18. 1865.)

Troyon, Frederick. Habitations lacustres des temps anciens et modernes. Lausanne, 1860. 8°.

— On the crania Helvetica. (*In* **Smithsonian Inst.** Report, 1864.)

Truair, *Rev.* John. Sacred music; address, Westhampton, May 23. Northampton, 1827. 8°. (**B 1237**)

Trublet, Nicolas Charles Joseph. ALEMBERT, J. le R. d'. (*In his* Œuvres, v. 11. 1805.)

— SKETCH. (*In* **Men** and women of France, v. 3. 1852.)

Trucchi, Francesco. Poesie italiane inedite dall' origine della lingua infino al sec. XVII. Prato, 1846-47. 4 v. 8°.

Contents. Vol. 1. Antico anonimo siciliano. — Re Giovanni. — Rinaldo d'Aquino. — J. Mostacci. — Jacopo d'Aquino. — Folco di Calabria. — Ruggieri Pugliese. — Sonetto per incerta donna dugentista. — Jacopo da Lentino. — Ciuncio Fiorentino. — Polo di Lombardia. — Ciacco dell' Anguillara. — Arrigo re de Sicilia. — Re Manfredi. — P. Doria. — Ubertino d'Arezzo. — C. Ghiberti. — Terino. — B. Dietaiuti. — Baldo da Passignano. — N. Visdomini. — P. Angiolieri. — Monte di Firenze. — Rinuccino. — Monaldo da Soffena. — Noffo Bonaguidi. — Piero Asino. — Torrigiano. — C. Donzella. — Ubertino Giovanni del Bianco. — Lapo del Rosso. — M. di Naldo da Colle. — Migliore degli Abati. — Sonetto per incerto dugentista. — B. Palmieri. — Jacopo da Leona. — C. Davanzati. — B. Urbiciani. — B. Latini. — Dante da Maiano. — Rustico di Filippo. — O. Orafo. — Berardo. — Cione. — Monte da Firenze. — Pallamidesse. — Sonetto per incerto dugentista. — Albizzo de' Pallavillani. — Chiaro Davanzati. — Sonetti per incerti dugentisti diversi. — B. Dietaiuti. — Sonetti per incerti dugentisti diversi. — Rustico di Filippo. — G. Orlandi. —

Onesto da Bologna. — Federigo dell' Ambra. — Rustico di Filippo. — G. Orlandi. — A. Lancia. — A. di Guido Donati. — D. Frescobaldi. — D. Compagni. — C. d'Ascoli. — C. Angiolieri. — G. Cavalcanti. — Cino da Pistoia. — Dante Allighieri.

2. Giotto dipintore. — Cane della Scala. — Serventese per incerto trecentista. — Simone dall' Antella. — Rinaldo da Cepperello. — A. Orcagna. — Ballata per incerto donna trecentista. — Pieraccio di Maffeo Tedaldi. — Ballata per incerto trecentista. — Canzone per incerto trecentista lucchese. — B. Bonichi da Siena. — Sennuccio del Bene. — M. Frescobaldi. — Fazio degli Uberti. — Betrico d'Arezzo. — Stoppa de' Bostichi. — Giannozzo da Firenze. — B. Visconti. — R. degli Albizzi. — Sonetti per incerti trecentisti diversi. — Serventese per incerto trecentista da Cesena. — Tommasuccio. — Poesie musicale di autori trecentisti. — Gherardo da Castel Fiorentino. — C. di F. Rinuccini. — Ballata per incerto trecentista. — M. di L. degli Albizzi. — S. di Cino. — G. Calonista. — P. Strozzi. — F. degli Organi. — Ballati per incerti trecentisti diversi. — F. Sacchetti. — N. Soldanieri. — F. Petrarca. — G. Sacchetti. — Bartolommeo da Castel della Pieve. — A. de' Bardi. — F. degli Albizzi. — Bonaccorso da Montemagno. — Bosone da Gubbio. — Sinibaldo Perugino. — G. dal Palagio. — F. de' Brunelleschi. — Antonio di Meglio. — G. M. di Antoniodi Meglio. — Federigo di Messer Geri d'Arezzo. — G. de' Conti da Valmontone F. degli Alberti. — F. Alfani. — R. Rosselli. — Ballata per incerta donna quattrocentista. — L. B. Alberti. — A degli Alberti. — Lucrezia Tornabuoni nei Medici. — Domenico da Prato. — B. Cambini. — R. Orsato. — Felice da Bologna. — Sonetto per incerto quatrocentista.

3. A. Forteguerri. — C. Coletta. — F. Spinello. — F. Galeotto. — P. J. de' Gennari. — J. da Bientina. — G. P. dalla Mirandola. — A. Diotallevi. — T. da Ferrara. — J. Sannazzaro. — B. da Urbino. — Sonetti per incerto quattrocentista. — Canti di guerra. — G. della Rovere. — D. Bonifazio. — Egidio. — F. Strozzi. — M. Cavallo. — F. Scambrilla. — C. Gonzaga. — Alfonso Marchese del Vasto. — G. Cittadino. — Gradito. — C. Agnello. — F. Riva. — T. Castellani. — N. Amanio. — N. Macchiavelli. — L. Ariosto. — G. Trissino. — Pietro Bembo. — A. Navagero. — F. Berni. — A. de' Pazzi. — V. Colonna. — V. Gambara. — A. Caro. — F. M. Molza. — I. de' Medici. — G. della Casa. — B. Castiglione. — L. Domenichi. — G. Muzzarelli. — M. Aversa. — S. Piccolomini. — P. Aretino. — G. Verita. — L. Alamanni. — L. Gonzaga. — M. A. Buonarotti. — D. Giannotti. — Ballata per incerto cinquecentista. — Sonetto per incerto Napolitano. — Madrigali per S. M. C. — Madrigali per incerti cinquecentisti. — S., G., P. e A. Petrei. — G. B. Gelli. — Il Brevio. — A. Bino. — N. Antico. — Satiro. — Madrigale per incerto cinquecentista. — Orazio. — L. Fessen. — F. Frillo. — F. Ciprio. — P. Egidio. — Florio. — Pamfilo. — Madrigale per incerto cinquecentista. — Giraldi. — Beatrice del Sera. — Emilia Angiusciola. — G. Molino. — G. dalla Pieve. — A. F. Grazzini. — Silvia. — Madrigali per incerto cinquecentista. — Laura Battiferri negli Ammannati. — L. Fiamminghi. — M. Bandini. — C. Tolomei. — L. Benucci. — F. Contrini.

4. T. Tasso. — M. Veniero. — C. Romano. — V. Salvi. — L. Salviati. — G. B. Strozzi. — M. A. Serafini. — A. Bonaguidi. — P. del Nero. — P. Rucellai. — M. A. Gondi. — B. Antinori. — M. Menadori. — Madrigali per incerto cinquecentista. — T. Malaspina e D. Gherardi. — O. Rinuccini. — A. Ginori. — F. Rovai. — G. A. Capponi. — V. Orsino. — M. A. Buonarroti. — J. Peri. — C. di Persia. — Maria Guicciardini nei Filicaia. — Lucrezia della Rena Punta. — Margherita Bargellini ne' Capponi. — Delle Befanate. — A. Petrei. — A. Malatesti. — Il Lasca [A. F. Grazzini]. — L. Salviati. — Maria Guicciardini. — S. Porcellotti. —Orazio Persiani. — C. da Marignolle. — S. Vai. — A. Salvadori. — G. Cicognini. — J. Salviati. — L. Migliorucci. — F. Baldovini. — L. Giraldi. — Anna Capponi ne' Felicaia. — Luca Terenzi. — Baragalli. — G. B. Marino.

Truce of God. SEMICHON, E. Le paix et le trève de Dieu; hist. des développements du tiers-état par l'Eglise et les associations de la fin du 10e siècle à la fin du 13e. 2e éd. augm. Paris, 1869. 2 v. 16°.

Truck system. GR. BRITAIN. *Commissioners on the Truck System.* Report. London, 1871. 2 v. f°.

Trudaine, Charles Louis? CATALOGUE [de ses] livres; la vente an XII 16 jan. 1804. Paris, an XII, 1803. 8°. **(B 886)**

Trudaine de Montigny, Jean Charles Philibert. CONDORCET, J. A. N. C., *marq.* de. (*In his* **Œuvres,** v. 2. 1847.)

Trudelle, Charles, *l'abbé.* Hoc erat in votis. (*In* **Littérature** canadienne, v. 2. 1864.)

True, Charles H. Maine in the war for the Union. *See* **Whitman,** W. E.

True, The, the beautiful, and the good. *See* **Cousin,** V.

True account of the baptism of Prince Henry Frederick. (*In* **Tracts** illust. of antiq. of Scotland. 1836.)

True account of the author of Εἰκὼν Εασιλικὴ (*sic*); or, The pourtraiture of his majesty in his sufferings; with an answer to all objections by Hollingworth *etc.*; [by A. Walker]. London, 1692. 4°. **(B 8)**

True account of the entertainment of the D. of Y., by the artillery men, Oct. 21. [London, 1679.] f°. **(A 54)**

True account of the occurrences that have happened in the warre between the Eng. and the Indians in New England, May-Aug. 1676. (*In* **Drake,** S. G. Old Indian chronicle. 1836.)

True American; May 25. Trenton, 1822. f°. **(E 181)**

True American. 1840. *See* **Coe,** J.

True and impartial state of the Province of Pennsylvania; answer to 'A brief state' and 'A brief view'. Phila., 1759. 8°.

True and particular relation of the dreadful earthquake at Lima, 28 Oct. 1746. 2d ed. London, 1848. 8°.

True Briton; Aug. 19. London, 1803. f°. **(E 198)**

True Christian faith in Christ asserted. Phila., 1822. 12°. **(C 198)**

True churchman warned against the errors of the time; [by H. Hughes]; ed. with notes by H. Anthon. N. Y., 1843. 8°. **(B 1377)**

True constitutional means for putting an end to the dispute between Gr. Britain and the American colonies. London, 1769. 8°. **(B 463)**

True coppie of a discourse by a gentleman employed in the voyage of Spaine and Portugale, 1589. (*In* **Hakluyt,** R. Col. of voy., v. 5. 1812; — *and in* **Selection** of curious, rare, and early voyages. 1812.)

True delta, Daily, 1865. New Orleans, 1865. 2 v. f°.

True estimate of the value of leasehold estates and of annuities, *etc.* London, 1731. 8°. **(B 1535)**

True flower of brimstone, extracted from the Briton, No. Briton, and Auditor. [London,] 1763. 8°. **B 698)**

True grounds and reasons of the Christian religion, in opposition to [Collins'] 'Grounds and reasons'. London, 1725. 8°. **(E 154)**

True history of a late short administration; [by C. Lloyd]. London, 1766. 8°. **(B 591, 1634)**

— *Same.* (*In* **Collection** of scarce tracts. 1787. **B 605)**

True history of a late short administration. London, 1807. 8°. **(B 1416)**

Note. This is an imitation of the previous entry.

True interest of America impartially stated, in "Strictures on a pamphlet intitled 'Common sense'," Phila., 1776. 8°. **(B 362)**

— *Same.* 2d ed. Phila., 1776. 8°. **(B 703, B 990)**

True interest of the land-owners of Gr. Brit.; cont. a short view of the impediments to inclosing our common fields. London, 1734. 8°. **(B 1518)**

True interests of the provinces of Europe in the present state of affairs; or, Reflections upon 'A letter from Monsieur to Monsieur'. London, 1689. 4°. **(B 8)**

True interpretation of the American civil war. *See* **Onesimus** *Secundus.*

True merits of [Paine's] treatise intitled, 'Common sense' clearly pointed out. London, 1776. 8°. **(B 381, 615)**

True narrative of the late design of the Papists to charge their horrid plot upon the Protestants. London, 1679. f°. **(A 51, 53)**

True narrative of the late success of the fleet against the King of Spain's West India fleets, *etc.* London, 1656. f°.

True narrative of the proceedings at Guild-Hall, 4th Feb., election of four members to serve in Parliament. *n.t.p.* [London, 1681.] f°. **(A 50)**

True notion of passive obedience stated. London, 1690. 4°. **(B 6)**

True patriot, The. Nos. 1, 3, 4, 7, 9-11, 13, 23-24. (*In* **Fielding,** H. Works, v. 13. 1816; v. 8. 1821.)

True plan of a living temple. *See* **Good** life.

True portraiture of the kings of England; drawn from their titles, successions, raigns, and ends. London, 1688. 4°. **(B 5)**

True Protestants' appeal to the city and country. London, 1681. f°. **(A 54)**

True relation of some proceedings at Salters' Hall by those ministers who signed the 1st article of the Ch. of Eng. London, [1719]. 8°. **(B 107, 110, 1865)**

— LETTER to J. Peirce. London, 1719. 8°. **(B 1865)**

— PEIRCE, J. Animadversions on 'A true relation'. London, 1719. f°. **(B 107, 1865)**

— - Letter in defence, *etc.* London, 1719. f°. **(B 1865)**

True relation of the cruelties [of] the rebels in Scotland. London, 1679. 4°. (B 12)

True report of the voyage to Java by a fleete of 8 ships of Amsterdam, 1598-99. (*In* Hakluyt, R. Col. of voy., v. 5. 1812; — *and in* Selection of curious voy. 1812.)

True sentiments of America, [drawn up in part by S. Adams,] with diss. on the canon and feudal law; by J. Adams. Lond., 1768. 8°.

— *Other copies.* (B 374, 462)

True state of the difference between the Reformed Presbytere, and some who lately deserted them. Edin., 1753. 8°. (B 256)

True story about the fight at Dame Europa's school; showing how the French boy began the fight, boasting was punished, and justice done. London, 1871. 12°. (E 158)

True tragedy of Richard III.; appended, the Latin play of Richardus Tertius by T. Legge; with an introd. and notes by B. Field. London, 1844. 8°. (Shakespeare Soc., v. 21.)

True unto death; a drama. *See* Knowles, J. S.

True version of the fight at Dame Europa's school; by an Englishman. London, [18—]. 16°. (E 158)

True vindication of Sherlock; reply to the pretended Answers of his 'Case of allegiance due to sovereign powers'. London, 1690. 4°. (B 7)

True Whig sentiment of Mass.; resolutions of the Whig convention in Boston, Sept. 23, and speeches of C. Hudson, D. Webster, and R. C. Winthrop. [Boston, 1846.] 8°. (B 1502)

True widow, A; comedy. *See* Shadwell, T.

Trueba y Cosio, Joaquin Telesforo des. Romance of history: Spain. London, 1830. 3 v. 12°.

Trueba y la Quintana, Antonio de. El libro de los cantares. (*In* Coleccion de autores esp., v. 6. 1868.)

Truebner, Charles. Current gold and silver coins of all countries. 1863. *See* Martin, L. C.

Truebner, Nicholas. Bibliographical guide to American literature. London, 1859. 8°.

— Bibliotheca scacceriana; catalogue d'ouvrages sur le jeu des échecs. [Londres, 1861.] 12°.

Truebner & Co. Catalogue of books chiefly in Oriental languages. London, 1853. 8°.

— Catalogue of linguistic literature. Pt. 4. London, 1864. 8°.

Truebner's American and Oriental literary record. No. 1-12, Mar. 16, 1865 - Feb. 26, 1866. London, *n.d.* 1. 8°.

Trueman, Abraham, *pseud.* Letter to James, the scribe. London, *reprint.* 1760. 8°. (B 1520)

Trueman, Robert. CATALOGUE of [his] library, sold Nov. 30 and Dec. 1. Boston, 1859. 8°. (B 1690)

Truhelka, A. V. Praktischer Leitfaden zur Selbsterlernung der kroatisch-serbischen Sprache. Pest, 1867. 8°.

— - Aufgabenschlüssel. Pest, 1867. 8°.

Trumbull, Benjamin, *D.D., of North Haven.* Address on prayer and family religion. (*In* Vincent, T. Explicatory catechism. 1805.)

— Appeal to the public rel. to the unlawfulness of marrying a wife's sister. *n.p.*, 1810. 8°. (B 286)

— Appeal to the public with respect to the unlawfulness of divorces. New Haven, 1788. 8°. (B 523)

— Century sermon, North Haven, Jan. 1. New Haven, 1801. 8°. (B 163, 334)

— Complete hist. of Connecticut, civil and ecclesiastical, to 1764. Vol. 1, Hartford; vol. 2, New Haven, 1797-1818. 2 v. 8°.

Contents. Vol. 1. 1630-1712. 2. 1711-64.

— Discourse, anniversary meeting of the freemen of New Haven, Apr. 12. New Haven, 1773. 8°. (B 477)

— General history of the U. S., 1492-1792. Boston, 1810. 3 v. (v. 2, 3 w.). 8°.

Contents. Vol. 1. 1492-1765.

— God to be praised; sermon at North Haven, Dec. 11. 1783, thanksgiving [for] peace with Gr. Britain New Haven, 1784. 8°. (B 1903)

— *Same.* 2d ed. New Haven, [178-]. 12°. (W 44)

— Majesty and mortality of created gods illust. and improved; funeral disc., North Haven, Dec. 20, 1799, death of Washington. New Haven, 1800. 8°. (W 50)

— Plea in vindication of the Conn. title to contested lands west of N. Y. New Haven, 1774. 8°. (B 517, 585)

— FREE remarks on [his] appeal to the public rel. to the unlawfulness of marrying a wife's sister. Norwich, 1810. 8°. (B 469)

Trumbull, David. Letter to J. Belknap [rel. to Gov. Trumbull's papers], 1794. (*In* Mass. Hist. Soc. Col., v. 32. 1854.)

Trumbull, Henry. History of the discovery of Amer., of the landing of our forefathers, and of their most remarkable engagements with the Indians; annexed, the defeat of Generals Braddock, Harmer, and St. Clair; by a citizen of Connecticut. Norwich, 1811. 8°.

— *Same.* Boston, 1813. 8°.

— Life and adventures of Robert, the hermit of Mass. Prov., 1829. 8°. (B 1722)

Trumbull, Henry Clay. The knightly soldier; biog. of Maj. H. W. Camp, 10th Conn. Vols. Boston, 1865. 16°.

Trumbull, James Hammond. Introd. and notes. (*In* Lechford, T. Plain dealing. 1867; — *and in* Mass. Hist. Soc. Col., v. 23. 1833.)

— Letter on the Indian name 'Shawmut'. (*In* Mass. Hist. Soc. Proc., 1866-67.)

Trumbull, John, *LL.D., d.* 1831. The anarchiad. *See* Anarchiad.

— Biography of Jonathan Trumbull. *n.t.p.* [1809.] 8°. B 312)

— Elegy on the times. First printed at Boston, Sept. 20, 1774. New Haven, 1775. 8°. (B 355)

— M'Fingal. Canto first. Phila., 1775, 8°. (B 362)

— *Same.* In four cantos. Hartford, 1782. 8°. (C 76)

— *Same.* 6th ed. with explanatory notes. London, 1793. 8°. (B 632)

— *Same.* With explanatory notes. Boston, 1799. 16°.

— *Same.* With explanatory notes. Hallowell, 1813. 18°.

— *Same.* Rev. and corr. with copious and explan. notes and mem. of author. Hartford, 1856. 8°.

— *Same.* With introd. and notes by B. J. Lossing. N. Y., 1864. 16°.

— Poetical works. Hartford, 1820. 2 v. 8°.

Contents. Vol. 1. McFingal. 2. Progress of dulness. — Genius of America. — Lines to Dwight & Barlow. — Ode to sleep. — To a young lady. — Speech of Proteus; a trans. — Prophecy of Balaam. — Owl and sparrow. — Prospect of the future glory of America. — Vanity of youthful expectations. — Advice to ladies of a certain age. — Characters. — Elegy on the death of St. John. — Destruction of Babylon. — Elegy on the times. — App.

— Progress of dullness, The. Pt. 3; sometimes called, the progress of coquetry; or, Adventures of Miss H. Simper. New Haven, 1773. 8°. (B 661)

Trumbull, *Col.* John, *d.* 1843. Autobiography, reminiscences, and letters. N. Y., London, 1841. 8°.

— CATALOGUE of his paintings in the gallery of Yale College. New Haven, 1852. 8°.

— SKETCH.] (*In* Longacre, J. B., *and* Herring, J. Nat. portr. gal., v. 1. 1837.)

Trumbull, Jonathan, *Gov. of Conn., d.* 1785. Address to the Gen. Assem. and freemen of Conn. declining further election to public office. N. London, 1783. 4°.

— *Another copy.* (A 42)

— Brief aan J. D. van der Capellen den 31 Aug. 1779. (*In* Verzameling van stukken tot dertien Vereenigde Staaten, *etc.* 1781.)

— *Eng.* Letter to Baron J. D. Van der Capellan (*sic*) giving a hist. of the U. S., its resources, *etc.* (*In* Mass. Hist. Soc. Col., v. 6. 1799.)

— *and* Livingstone, W. Lettres à J. D. baron van der Capellen. *n.p.*, [177-]. 8°. (B 631)

— SKETCH. (*In* Longacre, J. B., *and* Herring, J. Nat. portr. gal., v. 7. 1839.)

— STUART, I. W. Life of J. Trumbull. Boston, 1859. 8°.

— *Funeral sermon on* 1785. *See* Ely, Z. (C 8, W 39)

Trumbull, Jonathan, *Gov. of Conn., d.* 1809. TRUMBULL, J. Biography of J. Trumbull. *n.t.p.* 8°. (B 312)

— *Funeral sermon on.* 1809. *See* Dwight, T. (B 282, 311, 869); — Ely, Z. (B 286, 312)

Trumps; a novel, by G. W. Curtis; illust. by A. Hoppin. N. Y., 1861. 12°.

Trunkenbold, Der; von A. v. **Kotzebue**. (*In his* Theater, v. 18. 1841.)

Truran, Wm. Iron manufacture of Gr. Brit. 2d ed., rev. by J. A. Phillips and W. H. Dorman. London, 1862. 4°.

Truro. DAMON, J. Indian places in T. (*In* **Mass. Hist. Soc.** Col., v. 1. 1792.) — FREEMAN, J. Topographical description of T., 1794. (*In* v. 3.)

Trusler, John. The accomplished gentleman; or, The principles of politeness; extracted from the letters of the late Earl of Chesterfield to his son; added, Moral maxims and reflections, by the late Duke de la Rochefoucauld; tr. from the French. Phila., 1789. 12°.

— *Same.* Boston, 1806. 16°.

— Chronology; or, The historian's vade-mecum. 7th ed. London, 1774. 18°.

— Summary of the constitutional laws of Eng. London, 1788. 12°.

Trusses. THOMPSON, R. Patent uterine truss. Columbus, 1843. 8°. (C 271)

Trustees of Donations to the Prot. Episc. Ch. Diocese of Mass. Abstract of records. Boston, 1870. 8°.

Trusty Eckart, The; [by] L. Tieck. (*In* **Carlyle**, T. German romance, v. 2. 1827.)

Truth. BEATTIE, J. Essay on the nature and immutability of truth in opposition to sophistry and scepticism. [1770.] 3d ed. London, 1772. 8°.

— - *Same.* 3d ed. Dublin, 1773. 8°.

— - *Same.* 6th ed. Edin., 1777. 8°.

— - *Same.* (*In his* Works, v. 4, 5. 1809.)

— FORMEY, J. H. S. Examen de 'Si toutes les vérités sont bonnes à dire?' (*In* **Berlin. Ak. d. Wiss.** Abh., 1777.)

— FULLER, A. Essay on truth. Boston, 1806. 8°. (B 1356)

— HALL, E. B. Spirit of truth; disc., June 28. Camb., 1854. 8°. (B 1308)

Truth; a romantic drama. *See* **Mathews, C. J.**

Truth and honesty. *n.t.p.* [18—.] 12°. (C 246)

Truth revealed; statement and review of the case of the Rev. J. H. Fairchild; by a member of the Suffolk Bar. Boston, 1845. 8°.

Truth, The, resp. the revolution in Paris, 1830; tr. from the French. London, 1831. 8°. (B 976)

Truth unveiled; or, A calm and impartial expos. of the origin, *etc.*, of the riots in Phila., May. Phila., 1844. 8°. (B 1500)

Truth-finder, The; or, The story of inquisitive Jack; by [S. G. Goodrich]. Phila., 1845. 18°.

Truthteller, The; [ed.] by W. E. Andrews. Vol. 7; Apr. - June 1827. London, *n.d.* 8°.

Truxtun, Thomas. Remarks, *etc.*, rel. to latitude and longitude; variations of the compass, *etc.* Phila., 1794. f°.

— WILSON, T. (*In his* Biog. of Amer. military and naval heroes, v. 1. 1817.)

Tryal, The; a comedy. *See* **Baillie, J.**

Tryal of the witnesses of the resurrection of Jesus; [in which] T. Woolston's 'Objections' are considered. 4th ed. London. 1729. 8°. (B 1864)

— *Same.* Trial, *etc.* From 12th London ed. Boston, 1809. 8°.

— *Another copy.* (B 189)

Tryal, *etc.*, of twenty-one regicides, murtherers of Charles I. London, 1739. 4°.

Tryamour. *See* **Syr Triamoure.**

Trye, Charles Brandon. Case of rupture of the corpora penis. — Injury of the internal table of the scull successfully treated. (*In* **Soc. Prom. Med. Knowl.** Med. com., v. 2. 1790.)

Trye *vs.* **The Corporation of Gloucester.** DARLING, J. Validity of a bequest of money [for] erecting buildings for a charity, with ref. to the case of T. London, 1856. 8°. (B 1433)

380. (6. 4. 81.)

Tryon County, *N.Y.* CAMPBELL, W. W. Annals of T. N. Y., 1831. 12°.

— - *Same.* New ed. N. Y., 1849. 12°.

Tryphiodorus. Ilii excidium; [Gr. cum. Lat.] vers. N. Frischlini; cum annot. J. Merrick. Oxonii, [1741]. 8°.

— *Same.* Gr. et Lat.; ed. F. S. Lehrs. (*In* **Hesiodus.** Carmina. 1841.)

— *Eng.* The destruction of Troy; tr. by J. Merrick. Oxford, [1739]. 8°.

Tryphon. De tropis. (*In* **Spengel, L.** Rhet. Gr., v. 3. 1856.)

— De passionibus dictionum. (*In* **Varennius, J.** Syntaxis, *etc.* 1564.)

Trzy gody; sielanka; przez F. D. **Kniaźnin**. (*In his* Dzieła, v. 4. 1837. Bobrowicz, J. N. Bibl. kieszonkowa klass. Polsk., v. 35.)

Tscherning, Andreas. Gedichte. (*In* **Mueller, W.** Bibl. deutscher Dichter, v. 7. 1825.)

Tschirnhaus, Ehenfried Walther von. Briefwechsel zwischen Leibniz und Tschirnhaus. (*In* **Leibnitz**, G. W. von. Gesam. Werke, 3e Folge, 4r Bd. 1859.)

— RAMBACH, F. E. (*In* **Niceron, J. P.** Nachrichten, v. 17. 1758.)

Tschudi, Ægidius. Chronicon Helveticum oder eigentliche Beschreibung der sowohl im H. Röm. Reich als besonders in einer löbl. Eydgenossschaft vorgeloffenen Begegnussen; hrsg. v. J. R. Iselin. Basel, 1734–36. 2 v. f°.

Contents. Vol. 1. 1000–1415. 2. 1415–70.

Tschudi, Friedrich von. Sketches of nature in the Alps; from the German of F. von T. London, 1856. 12°.

Tschudi *or* **Schudi**, Johann Jakob von. Reisen durch Südamerika. Lpz., 1866–69. 5 v. 8°.

— Travels in Peru, 1838–42; tr. by T. Ross. N. Y., 1847. 12°.

Tseën Tsze Wăn; or, The thousand character classic. (*In* **Chinese** repository, v. 4. 1835.)

Tsonnonthouan, *a king of the Indian nation called Roundhead.* MEMOIRS of the life and adventures of T. Vol. 2. London, 1763. 12°.

Tu et toi, Les, ou La parfaite égalité; comédie. *t.p.w.* [18—.] (B 1626)

Tu-li-shin. Narrative of the Chinese embassy to the khan of the Tourgouth Tartars in 1712–15 by the Chinese ambassador; tr. with app. by Sir G. T. Staunton. London, 1821. 8°.

Tuberculous diseases. CLARK, *Sir* J. (*In his* Treatise on pulmonary consumption. 1837.)

Tubular bridges. *See* **Iron bridges.**

Tucher, Endres. Memorial, 1421–40. (*In* **Munich. K. Ak. d. Wiss.** *Hist. Comm.* Chroniken d. deutschen Städte: Nürnberg, v. 2, 4, 5. 1864, 72, 74.)

Tuck, Amos. Payment for slaves; speech. (*In* **United States.** *30th Cong. 1st sess.* Debates in Congress on slavery. 1848. B 1477)

Tucker, Abraham. Light of nature pursued. 2d ed., with his life by Sir H. P. St. J. Mildmay. London, 1805. 7 v. 8°.

— *Same.* [Abridged by W. Hazlitt.] London, 1807. 8°.

Tucker, Benjamin, *sec. to the Earl of St. Vincent.* Observations on A concise statement of facts and the treatment [of] Sir H. Popham, *etc.* 3d ed. London, [180–]. 8°. (B 1413)

Tucker, Benjamin, *Surveyor General of the Duchy of Cornwall.* Report conc. the obstacles, *etc.*, attending the formation of a safe roadstead within the Islands of Scilly. London, 1810. 8°. (B 1744)

Tucker, Beverley. *See* **Tucker, N. B.**

Tucker, Ebenezer. Address before the Tuckerton Temperance Soc., July 4. Phila., 1844. 8°. (B 1280)

Tucker, George. Description of the U. States of N. Amer. (*In* **Long, G.**, *and others.* Geog. of America. 1841. Lib. usef. knowl.)

— Discourse on the progress of philosophy, *etc.*, before the Va. Hist. and Philosoph. Soc. Richmond, 1835. 8°. (B 1584)

— History of the U. S. Phila., 1856–57. 4 v. 8°.

Contents. Vol. 1. 1607–1797. 2. 1797–1813 3. 1813–29. 4. 1829–41.

— Life of T. Jefferson. Phila., 1837. 2 v. 8°.
— Progress of the U. S. in population and wealth, in fifty years. N. Y., 1843. 8°.
Tucker, H. TURGAN, J. Literie Tucker. (*In his* Les grandes usines de France, v. 2. 1863.)
Tucker, Henry. When this cruel war is over; words by C. G. Sawyer. Macon, [186-]. 4°. (E 171)
Tucker, Isaac Miller. In memoriam; sermon by E. R. Craven, July 20, 1862, oration by J. T. Foster, July 29, 1862, Newark, death of I. M. Tucker, 2d Regt. N. J. Vols. Newark, 1862. 8°. (B 1639)
Tucker, J. W. Thoughts on truth as applied to practical Christianity; address, Unionville, S. C., June. Mobile, 1864. 8°.
Tucker, Jedidiah Stephens. Memoirs of the Earl of St. Vincent. London, 1844. 2 v. 8°.
Tucker, John, *D.D.* A. Hutchinson's reply to the 'Remarks' on his sermon 'Valour for the truth' considered. Boston, 1768. 8°. (B 60, 156)
— Brief account of an ecclesiastical council in Newbury, Mar. 31, and Apr. 21, 1767 [with] discourse. Boston, [1767]. 8°. (B 72, 156, 257)
— Four sermons: Danger of sinners; God's special care; Scripture doctrine of reconciliation; Being born of God. Boston, 1756. 12°.
— *Another copy.* (B 43)
— God's goodness; discourse, thanksgiving, Nov. 25, 1756. Boston, 1757. 8°. (B 146)
— Letter to J. Chandler rel. to [notes] in his sermon at Newburport, June 25. Bost., 1767. 8°. (B 72, 156)
— Ministers considered as fellow-workers, *etc.*; sermon before the ministers of Mass.-Bay at their convention in Boston, May 26. Boston, 1768. 8°. (B 54, 60, 1311)
— Ministers of the Gospel as Spiritual guides, *etc.*; two discourses, death of J. Lowell, May 15. Boston, 1767. 8°. (B 72)
— Observations on the doctrines of J. Parsons. Boston, 1757. 8°. (B 16, C 123)
— Remarks on a discourse of J. Parsons, 'Freedom from civil and eccl. slavery the purchase of Christ'. Boston, 1774. 8°. (B 16, 156, C 123)
— Remarks on a sermon of A. Hutchinson, 'Valour for the truth'. Boston, 1767. 8°. (B 72, 156)
— Remarks on J. Chandler's 'Serious address'. Boston, 1768. 8°. (B 60, 156)
— Reply to J. Chandler's 'Answer' in a second letter to J. C. Boston, 1768. 8°. (B 60, 156, 232)
— Sermon, Cambridge, anniv. election. Boston, 1771. 8°. (B 178, 181, 185)
— Sermon, choice of a colleague with T. Cary. Newburyport, 1788. 8°. (B 202, 232, 841)
— Sermon, ordination of A. Moody, Pelham, Nov. 20, 1765. Boston, 1766. 8°. (B 232, 1311)
— Two sermons in Newburyport, Apr. 9. Boston, 1769. 8°. (B 147)
— Validity of Presbyterian ordination argued, *etc.*; Dudleian lect. Boston, 1778. 8°. (B 67, 232)
— CHANDLER, J. Answer to J. Tucker's Letter rel. to [notes] in [J. C.'s] sermon at Newburyport, June 25. Boston, 1767. 8°. (B 60, 156)
— - Serious address in Newburyport, [on] two letters by J. T. to make void a sermon preached June 25, 1767. Boston, 1768. 8°. (B 60, 156)
— HUTCHINSON, A. Reply to the 'Remarks' of J. T. on [A. H.'s] 'Valour for the truth'. Boston, 1768. 8°. (B 60, 156)
— SHANGAR, M. Letter to J. Tucker, upon his 'Remarks' on a discourse of J. Parsons. *n.p.*, 1775. 8°. (B 16, 156)
— *Funeral sermon on.* 1792. *See* **Eames, J.** (B 917); — **Webster, S.** (B 334)
Tucker, John Henry. COTTON, J. W. Biog. of T. (*In* **Higginson, T. W.** Harvard mem. biog., v. 2. 1866.)
Tucker, *Rev.* Joshua Thomas. The Christian's day and night; discourse in memory of A. Hawes. Holliston, 1854. 8°. (B 1245)
— Revolutions to be accomplished; disc., Holliston, July 4. Holliston, 1858. 8°. (B 1303)
— Young men; disc., Holliston, Sept. 25. Holliston, 1853. 8°. (B 1303)
Tucker, Josiah, *D.D.*, *Dean of Gloucester.* Apology for the present Ch. of Eng. 2d ed. Glocester, 1772. 8°. (B 905)
— Brief essay on the advantages and disadvantages [of] France and Gr. Brit. with regard to trade. London, 1787. 8°. (B 644)
— Brief view of the difficulties attending the Trinitarian, Arian, and Socinian systems. Glocester, 1774. 8°. (B 1371)
— Cui bono? an inquiry what benefits can arise to Eng., Amer., French, Spaniards, or Dutch in the present war; letters to Necker. Glocester, 1781. 8°. (B 629)
— *Same.* 2d ed., with plan for general pacification. Glocester, 1782. 8°.
— *Another copy.* (B 348)
— *French.* Cui bono, ou Examen quels avantages les Anglois, ou les Américains, *etc.*, retireront-ils des plus grandes victoires ou des plus grandes succès dans la guerre actuelle? Londres, 1782. 8°. (C 165)
— Four letters on important national subjects. 2d ed. London, 1773. 8°. (B 633)
— Four tracts, together with two sermons on political and commercial subjects. Glocester, 1774. 8°. (B 752)
— *Same.* 3d ed. Glocester, 1776. 8°. (B 380)
— Humble address and earnest appeal [on] separation from the colonies of America. Glocester, 1775. 8°.
— *Same.* 2d ed. Glocester, 1775. 8°. (B 1719)
— *Germ.* Demüthige Vorstellung und ernstliche Appellation an Personen in Grossbrittannien und Irrland. (*In* **Remer, J. A.** Amerikanisches Archiv, v. 2. 1777.)
— Letter to E. Burke, in ans. to his printed speech, March 22. Glocester, 1775. 8°. (B 369)
— Letter to Kippis [on] his 'Vindication of the Protestant dissenting ministers'. London, 1773. 8°. (B 125, 905)
— Reflections on matters in dispute between Gr. Brit. and Ireland. London, 1785. 8°. (B 1522)
— Religious intolerance no part of Mosaic or Christian dispensation, *etc.* Glocester, 1774. 8°. (B 1379)
— Tract V: Pleas and arguments of the mother country and colonies distinctly set forth. Glocester, 1776. 8°. (B 380)
— True interest of Britain, in regard to the colonies. Phila., 1776. 8°. (B 363, 703, 990)
— ESTWICK, S. Letter to J. T. in ans. to his humble address. London, 1776. 8°. (B 380)
— LETTER to J. Tucker, occasioned by his 'Apology for the present Church of Eng., by a petitioning clergyman. London, 1773. 8°. (B 1379)
— SCRIPTURE the only test as well as the only rule of Christian faith, maintained in a letter to J. Tucker. London, 1772. 8°. (B 1379)
Tucker, Mark, *D.D.* Discourse. thanksgiving, July 21. Providence, 1842. 8°. (B 1254)
— STATEMENT of facts rel. to the call and installation of T. over the Soc. at Northampton. Northampton, 1824. 8°. (B 1393)
Tucker, Nathaniel. Tentamen med. inaug. de corporis humani singulis vitæ stadiis mutationibus. Lugd. Bat., 1777. 8°. (B 1563)
Tucker, Nathaniel Beverly. Lecture; the last of a course on the philosophy of government and constitutional law. *n.t.p.* [1839.] 8°. (B 1430)
— The partisan leader. N. Y., 1861. 2 v. 12°.
Tucker, Pomeroy. Origin and progress of Mormonism. N. Y., 1867. 12°.
Tucker, St. George. Dissertation on slavery; with a proposal for the abolition of it in Va. Phila., 1796. 8°. (B 764)
— Examination of the question, How far the common law of England is the law of the U. S. Richmond, [18—]. 4°. (B 651, W 80)
— Letter to J. Morse. Richmond, 1795. 8°. (C 73)
— Queries resp. the slavery and emancipation of negroes in Mass., answered by Rev. Dr. Belknap. (*In* **Mass. Hist. Soc.** Col., v. 4. 1795.)
Tucker, *Com.* Samuel. To the surviving officers and soldiers of the Revolution. From the Wiscasset Yankee. *n.t.p.* [1832.] 8°. (B 1494)
— SHEPPARD, J. H. Life of Tucker. Boston, 1868. 12°.
Tucker, Thomas, *Bp. of Bangor.* Sermon before the Ho. of Lords, Jan. 30. London, 1740. 4°. (B 1465)
Tucker, Wm., *Funeral sermon on.* 1814. *See* **Toms, J.** (B 1226)
Tucker, Wm. Predestination considered, from principles of reason. From 3d Lond. ed. with introd. essay by L. I. Hoadley. Boston, 1835. 12°.
Tuckerman, Edward. Catalogue of lichens [on the route from the Sacramento Valley to the Columbia River]. (*In* **U. S.** *War Dept.* Reports of explorations for a R. R. to the Pacific, 1853–54, v. 6.)
— Introduction and notes. (*In* **Josselyn, J.** New England rarities. 1865.)

Tuckerman, Frederick Goddard. Poems. Bost., 1864. 16°.

Tuckerman, Henry Theodore. America and her commentators. N. Y., 1864. 8°.

— Artist-life; or, Sketches of American painters. N. Y., 1847. 12°.
Contents. B. West. — Copley. — Stuart. — Trumbull. — Allston. — Malbone. — Vanderlyn. — Morse. — Durand. — W. E. West. — Sully. — Inman. — Cole. — Leslie. — Weir. — Chapman. — Edmonds. — Freeman. — Leutze. — Huntington. — Deas. — Flagg. — G. L. Brown.

— Book of the artists; American artist life. N. Y., 1867. 8°.
Contents. Introd. — Early portrait painters. — Portraiture, genre, and historical painters. — Landscape painters. — Sculptors. — Appendix.

— Character and portraits of Washington. N. Y., 1859. 4°.

— Characteristics of literature. Phila., 1849. 12°.
Contents. The philosopher, Browne. — The dilettante, Shenstone. — The moralist, Canning. — The wit, Swift. — The philanthropist, Roscoe. — The humorist, Lamb. — The historian, Macaulay. — The idealist, Sterling. — The rhetorician, Burke. — The scholar, Akenside. — The biographer, final memorials of Lamb and Keats.

— *Same.* 2d ser. Phila., 1851. 12°.
Contents. The novelist, Manzoni. — The censor, Steele. — The naturalist, Humboldt. — The correspondent, Madame de Sévigné. — The philologist, Tooke. — The magazine writer, Wilson. — The dramatist, Talfourd. — The traveller, Beckford. — The critic, Hazlitt. — The orator, Everett. — The reformer, Godwin.

— The collector. London, [1868]. 8°.
Contents. Introduction by Dr. Doran. — Inns. — Authors. — Pictures. — Doctors. — Holidays. — Lawyers. — Sepulchres. — Actors. — Newspapers. — Preachers. — Statues. — Bridges.

— Essays, biographical and critical. Bost., 1857. 8°.
Contents. Washington, the patriot. — Lord Chesterfield, the man of the world. — Boone, the pioneer. — Southey, the man of letters. — Digby, the modern knight. — Lafitte, the financier. — Kean, the actor. — Körner, the youthful hero. — Fulton, the mechanician. — Constable, the landscape painter. — Chateaubriand, the poet of the old regime. — Jeffrey, the reviewer. — Williams, the tolerant colonist. — Savage, the literary adventurer. — Clinton, the national economist. — Jenny Lind, the vocalist. — Berkeley, the Christian philosopher. — Leopardi, the sceptical genius. — De Foe, the writer for the people. — Audubon, the ornithologist. — Sterne, the sentimentalist. — D'Azeglio, the literary statesman. — Smith, the genial churchman. — Brown, the supernaturalist. — Wilkie, the painter of character. — Addison, the lay preacher. — Morris, the American statesman. — Pellico, the Italian martyr. — Campbell, the popular poet. — Franklin, the American philosopher.

— Isabel; or, Sicily, a pilgrimage. Phila., 1839. 12°.

— Italian sketch-book. Phila., 1835. 12°.

— *Same.* 2d ed. Boston, 1837. 12°.

— *Same.* 3d ed. N. Y., 1848. 12°.

— Life of J. P. Kennedy. N. Y., 1871. 8°.

— Life of S. Talbot. N. Y., 1850. 18°.

— Memorial of H. Greenough. N. Y., 1853. 12°.

— Month in England. N. Y., 1853. 12°.

— The optimist. N. Y., 1850. 12°.

— Poems. Boston, 1851. 16°.

— Rambles and reveries. N. Y., 1841. 12°.
Contents. Sketches. — Thoughts on the poets. — Miscellany.

— Ravenna. (*In* **Boston** book, 3d col. 1841.) — Mary. (*In* 4th col. 1850.)

— Sketch of Amer. literature. (*In* **Shaw**, T. T. Manual of Eng. lit. 1867.)

— Thoughts on the poets. New ed. N. Y., 1851. 8°.

Tuckerman, Joseph, *D.D.* Discourse before the Soc. for Prop. the Gospel in N. Amer., Nov. 1. Camb., 1821. 8°. (**B 287, 1150**)

— Distinctive character and claims of Christianity; sermon, ordination of O. Dewey, Dec. 17, 1823. New Bedford, 1824. 8°. (**B 280**)

— Essay on the wages paid to females for their labour. Phila., 1830. 12°. (**C 311**)

— Funeral oration, death of Washington. 22 Feb. Boston, 1800. 8°. (**B 61, 87, 872, E 61, W 55**)

— Introduction. (*In* **Gerando**, J. M. de. Visitor of the poor. 1832.)

— Letter on the principles of the missionary enterprise. 2d ed. Boston, *A. U. A.*, 1827. 12°. (**C 168**)

— Letter to the committee of the Benevolent Fraternity of Churches respecting their organization for the support of the ministry at large in Boston, Sept. 1834. *n.t.p.* 8°. (**C 311**)

— Report. *See* **Boston. Benevolent Fraternity of Churches** (p. 346), **Ministry at Large**, (p. 348).

— Reports. *See* **American Unitarian Assoc.**

— Sermon, artillery election. Boston, 1804. 8°. (**B 202**)

— Sermon on the 20th anniv. of his ordination. Boston, 1821. 8°. (**B 287, 1651**)

— Sermon, ordination of C. F. Barnard and F. T. Gray as ministers at large in Boston; with the charge by W. E. Channing. Bost., 1834. 8°. (**B 262, 1112, 1695**)

— Sermon, ordination of S. Gilman, Charleston, Dec. 1, 1819. Charleston, S. C., 1820. 8°. (**B 1323**)

— Sermon; religion a practical principle. (*In* **Liberal** preacher, v. 1. 1828.)

— Sermon; the gospel a blessing to the poor. (*In* **Beard**, J. R. Sermons. 1832.)

— Two sermons, Marblehead, May 14. Salem, 1820. 8°. (**B 1303**)

— Channing, W. E. Discourse on the life and character of T. (*In his* Works, v. 6. 1847.)

Tuckett, F. F. Col de la Reuse de l'Arolla. (*In* **Ball**, J. Peaks, passes, *etc.*, 2d ser., v. 1. 1862.) — Ascent of Aletschhorn. — Contrib. to Alpine hypsometry. — Tables of Alpine peaks and passes. — Hunting grounds of Victor Emmanuel. — Night bivouac on the Grivola. — Phenomena observed on peaks, passes, *etc.* (*In* 2d ser., v. 2. 1859.)

Tuckett, Harvey Garnett Phipps. Where to go, and what to pay; hand-book to the World's Fair, May. Phila., 1851. 12°. (**C 277**)

Tuckett, John. Devonshire pedigrees. London, [1859]. 2 v. 4°.

Tuckey, James Kingston. Maritime geography and statistics. London, 1815. 4 v. 8°.

— Narrative of an exped. under him to the River Zaire; with Journal of Prof. Smith. London, 1818. 4°.

Tuckey, *Miss* Mary B. The wrongs of Africa. Glasgow, 1838. 16°. (**C 190**)

Tuckniss, *Rev.* Wm. Essay on the agencies in operation in the metropolis for the suppression of vice and crime. (*In* **Mayhew**, H. London labour. 1862.)

Tucuman. Funes, G. Historia civil del T., *etc.* Buenos Ayres, 1816. 3 v. 4°.

Tudehope, A. Attachment to the house of God; sermon, dedication of the 9th Pres. Ch., Phila. Phila., 1841. 8°. (**B 1310**)

Tudela, Benjamin of. *See* **Benjamin** *of Tudela.*

Tudela, *Spain.* Piedrafita y Albis, J. A. Por la provision del apellido criminal que suplica la ciudad de Tudela. *n.t.p.* [1662.] f°. (**A 68**)

Tudor, Frederic. Letter on the ice trade. (*In* **Mass. Hist.** Soc. Proc., 1855-58.)

— Havana ice-house controversy. 1846. *See* **Damon**, J. W.

Tudor, Henry. Narrative of a tour in N. America, with excursion to Cuba, 1831-32. London, 1834. 2 v. 8°.

Tudor, *Col.* Wm., *b.* 1750, *d.* 1819. Discourse, request of the Mass. Char. Fire Soc., June 1. Boston, 1798. 8°. (**B 669**)

— Gratulatory address before the Soc. of the Cincinnati of Mass. Boston, 1790. 8°. (**B 774, W 30**)

— Oration, Mar. 5, 1779, to commem. the tragedy, Mar. 5, 1770. Boston, 1779. 4°. (**A 6**)

— *Same.* (*In* **Orations**. 1785. **B 614**)

— Loring, J. S. (*In his* Hundred Boston orators. 1852.)

— Tudor, W., *Jr.* (*In* **Mass. Hist.** Soc. Col., v. 18. 1819; *also* **B 570**)

Tudor, Wm., *b.* 1779, *d.* 1830. Character of S. Adams. (*In* **Boston** book, 3d col. 1841.)

— Discourse before the Humane Society, May. Boston, 1817. 8°. (**B 357, 1694, 1923**)

— Letter on propriety, *etc.*, of an appropriate national name. (*In* **Mass. Hist.** Soc. Col., v. 6. 1800.)

— Letters on the Eastern States. N. Y., 1820. 12°.

— *Same.* 2d ed. Boston, 1821. 8°.

— Life of J. Otis. Boston, 1823. 8°.

— Memoir of W. Tudor. *n.t.p.* [1819.] 8°. (**B 570**)
Note. From **Mass. Hist.** Soc. Col., v. 18. 1819.

— Miscellanies. Boston, 1821. 12°.
Contents. Monthly anthology. — Obs. on Mme. de Staël's Corinna. — Cranberry sauce. — Toast. — Purring of cats. — Things in general. — N. A. review. — Geological systems. — Antiquity of the U. S. — Miseries of human life. — Epigram. — On hearing of the death of a friend. — Letter from a country gentleman. — Tour to Landwich. — Secret causes of the Amer. and Fr. revolutions. — The prince of the power of the air. — A ballad.
— Oration, July 4. Boston, 1809. 8°. (B 394)
— CAREY, M. Addr. to W. Tudor, intended to prove the calumny and slander of his Remarks on the Olive branch. Phila., 1821. 12°.
— LORING, J. S. (*In his* Hundred Boston orators. 1852.)
— QUINCY, J. Biog. notice. (*In his* History of the Boston Athenæum. 1851.)
Tudor, Wm. Ode. (*In* **Harvard College.** *Class of* 1871. Baccalaureate. B 1927, H 2)
Tudors. THOMSON, *Mrs.* A. T. The days of the Tudors. (*In her* Recollections of lit. char., v. 1. 1854.)
Tuebingen. KLUEPFEL, C. Geschichte und Beschreibung der Universität Tübingen. Tübin., 1849. 8°.
— TUEBINGER historische Schule. (*In* **Historische** Zeitschrift, v. 4. 1860.)
— MACKAY, R. W. The Tuebingen school and its antecedents; review of the history and condition of modern theology. London, Edin., 1863. 8°.
Tuerk, Karl. Forschungen auf dem Gebiete der Geschichte. Rostock, 1829–35. 5 v. 8°.
Contents. Vol. 1. Ueber das westgothische Gesetzbuch. 2. Altburgund und sein Volksrecht. — Studium und Quellen der deutschen Geschichte. — Sechs Briefe aus meinem Leben. 3. Kritische Geschichte der Franken, bis zu Chlodwigs Tode, 511. — Das salfränkische Volksrecht. 4. Geschichte des langobardischen Volks, bis auf Desiderius, 774. — Das langobardische Volksrecht. 5. Altfrisland und sein Volksrecht. — Die dänischen Geschichtsquellen.
Tufnell, E. Carleton. Education of pauper children. (*In* **Nat. Assoc. Prom. Soc. Sci.** Trans., 1862.)
Tufts, Cotton, *M.D.* Account of the horn distemper in cattle. (*In* **Amer. Acad.** Mem., v. 1. 1785.)
— Oration in honour of Washington, 22d of Feb. Boston, 1800. 8°. (B 87, E 48, W 55)
— *Funeral sermon on.* 1815. *See* **Norton, J.**
Tufts, John. Anti-ministerial objections. Boston, 1725. 8°. (C 52)
Tufts, Marshall. Book of philosophy. Camb., 1830. 8°.
Tufts College. Addresses at the inaug. of A. A. Miner as President, July 9. Boston, 1862. 8°. (B 1576)
Tugnot de Lanoye, Ferdinand. The sublime in nature; comp. from the description of travellers, *etc.*; with add. N. Y., 1870. 12°.
Tuilleries. MILLIN, A. L. Description des statues des Tuilleries. Paris, an VI, 1798. 8°. (C 108)
— BALTARD, L. P. Mém. sur la réunion des palaces des T. et du Louvre. Paris, 1811. f°.
Tuke, Daniel Hack, *M.D.* *See* **Bucknill, J. C.**
Tuke, Henry. Principles of religion professed by the Friends. N. Y., 1819. 12°.
Tuke, John. General view of the agriculture of the North Riding of Yorkshire. London, 1794. 4°. (W 75)
Tuke, *Sir* Samuel, *d.* 1673. Adventures of five hours. (*In* **Dodsley, R.** Col. of old plays, v. 12; — *and in* **Scott,** *Sir* W. Anc. Brit. dr., v. 3. 1810.)
Tuke, Samuel, *d.* 1857. Description of the Retreat, an institution near York for insane persons of the Soc. of Friends. (*In* **Phila. Asylum for the Relief of Persons Deprived of their Reason.** Account. 1814. C 144)
— Introd. (*In* **Jacobi, M.** Hospitals for insane. 1841.)
— Letter on pauper lunatic asylums. N. Y., 1815. 12°. (C 65)
— Practical hints on the construction and economy of pauper lunatic asylums. (*In* **Watson** *and* **Pritchett.** Plans, *etc.* 1819.)
Tuke, Thomas. Concerning the Holy Eucharist and the popish breaden God. 1625. (*In* **Grosart, A. B.** Fuller worthies lib., Miscel., v. 3. 1871.)
Tulipe noire, La; par Alex. Dumas. Nouv. éd. Paris, 1862. 18°.
— *Same.* (*In* **Semaine** lit., v. 2.)

Tulk, Alfred, *and* **Henfrey**, A. Anatomical manipulation. London, 1845. 16°.
Tulle. GESTA episcoporum Tullensium ad 1107. (*In* **Pertz, G. H.** Mon. Germ., Scr., v. 8. 1848.)
— SCHERER, H. Der Raub der drei Bisthümer Metz, Tull, und Verdun im 1552 bis zu ihrer förmlichen Abtretung an Frankreich im westfälischen Frieden, [1552–1648]. (*In* **Historisches** Taschenbuch, 1842.)
Tullia, La; tragedia. *See* **Martelli, L.**
Tullius, Servius. MAURY, L. F. A. Le véritable caractère des événements qui portèrent Servius Tullius au trône. (*In* **Paris. Inst.** *Ac. d. Inscr.* Mém., v. 25, 2e pt. 1866.)
Tulloch, John. English Puritanism and its leaders Cromwell, Milton, Baxter, Bunyan. Edin., 1861. 8°.
— Leaders of the Reformation, Luther, Calvin, Latimer, Knox. 2d ed. Edin., 1860. 8°.
— Parish schools of Scotland. (*In* **Nat. Assoc. Prom. Soc. Sci.** Trans., 1860.)
Tully. *See* **Cicero, Marcus Tullius.**
Tully, Samuel. LIFE of S. Tully, who was executed at South Boston, Dec. 10, for piracy. Boston, 1812. 8°. (B 344, 1693)
— TRIAL of S. Tully and J. Dalton, on an indictment for piracy and murder, committed Jan. 21. 2d ed. Boston, 1812. 8°. (B 443)
Tully, Thomas. BULL, G. Apologia pro Harmonia contra declamationem [T.]. (*In his* Opera. 1703; *and* Examen censuræ. 1676.)
Tully, Wm., *M.D.* Materia medica; or, Pharmacology and therapeutics. Springfield, 1857. 2 v. 8°.
— Examination of the strictures on 'Essays on fevers'. 1823. *See* **Miner, T.**
Tumali. TUTSHEK, *Dr.* L. On the Tumali language. (*In* **Philological Soc.** Proc., v. 3. 1846–48.)
Tumba Semiramidis. (*In* **Cooper, W.** Collectanea chymica. 1684.)
Tumble-down Dick; or Phaeton in the suds; a dramatic entertainment. *See* **Fielding, H.**
Tumors. RUFF, J. Tractaet van de phlegmatijke geswellen. 2e druck. Amst., 1662. 8°.
— ABERNETHY, J. Surgical observations. Vol. 1: Classification of tumours, *etc.* London, 1804. 8°.
— NOOTH, J. Schirrous tumours of the breast. 2d ed. with add. London, 1806. 8°.
— EARLE, J. Obs. on hæmorrhoidal excrescences. 2d ed. London, 1807. 8°. (B 828)
— KIRBY, J. Obs. on the treatment of certain severe forms of hemorrhoidal excrescence. London, 1817. 8°. (B 827)
— WARREN, J. C. Surgical obs. on tumours. Boston, 1837. 8°.
— WARREN, J. M. Amputation at the hip-joint for a large osteo-sarcomatous tumor of the femur. *n.t.p.* [Boston, 1859.] 8°. (E 70)
— PAGET, J. Innocent tumours. (*In* **Holmes, T.** System of surg., v. 1. 1860.)
— WARREN, J. M., *M.D.* Cystic tumors of the jaw. *n.t.p.* [1866.] 8°. (B 1692)
See also **Cancer**; — **Ulcer.**
Tumultibus Americanis, De, deque eorum concitatoribus; [ab E. Bentham]. Oxonii, 1776. 8°.
— *Another copy.* (B 347)
Tumults. SKETCHES of popular tumults. Lond., 1837. 12°.
Tunbridge-Wells. BURR, T. B. History of T. London, 1766. 8°.
Tungusic language and literature. BAYER, G. S. Elementa litteraturæ Brahmanicæ, Tangutanæ, Mungalicæ. (*In* **St. Petersburg.** **Acad. Scient.** Commentarii, v. 3. 1728.) — MUELLER, G. F. De scriptis Tanguticis in Sibiria repertis commentatio. (*In* v. 10. 1747.)
— SCHOTT, W. Die fürwörtlichen Anhänge in den tungusischen Sprachen und im mongolischen. (*In* **Berlin. Ak. d. Wiss.** Abh., 1869.)
Tunis. Convention between the governments of Gr. Brit. and Tunis, rel. to the holding of real property by British subjects in Tunis, Oct. 10, 1863. London, [1864]. f°.

Description.

— VERGIL, P. Voyage of Henric, Earle of Derbie [Henry IV.] to Tunis, [1390]. (*In* Hakluyt, R. Col. of voy., v. 2. 1810.)

— ILLESCAS, G. de. Jornada de Carlos V á Tunez, [1535]. (*In* Rosell, C. Hist. de sucesos particulares, v. 1. 1858; v. 21 of Aribau. Bibl.)

— READ, P. Voyage to Tunis, 1538. (*In* Hakluyt, R. Col. of voy., v. 2. 1810.)

— MCGILL, T. Account of Tunis. Glasgow, 1811. 8°.

— EWALD, C. F. Reise von Tunis nach Tripolis, im 1835; hrsg. von P. Ewald. Nürnberg, 1837. 8°.

— KENNEDY, J. C. Algeria and Tunis in 1845. London, 1846. 2 v. 12°.

— DUMAS, A. Impressions de voyage; le véloce, ou Tanger, Alger, et Tunis, [1846]. Paris, 1855. 2 v. 8°.

— FRANK, L., *and* MARCEL, J. Tunis. Paris, 1850. 8°. (Univers.)

— *Map.* THUNIS. *n.p.*, [16–]. (E 78, no. 301b.)

History.

— SILVESTRE DE SACY, A. I. Le traité fait entre le roi de Tunis et Philippe-le-hardi, en 1270. (*In* Paris. Inst. *Ac. d. Inscr.* Mém., v. 9. 1831.)

— FOUCQUES, —. Mémoires presentés au roy, après estre delivré de la captivité des Turcs de Thunes, [1612]. (*In* Ternaux-Compans, H. Archives des voy., v. 1. 1840.) — VICTOIRE obtenue par les galions de Malte, sur les vaisseaux turcs de Thunis, [1621]. (*In* v. 2. 1841.) — RELATION véritable du combat et prise de deux galions du roy de Thunis, oct. 1628, par les galères de Malte. (*In* v. 1. 1840.)

— BRICARD, —. Voyages faits à Thunis. (*In* Recueil hist. 1666.)

— HISTORY of T., [to 1750]. (*In* Compleat history of the piratical states of Barbary, Tripoli, and Morocco. 1750.)

Tunnels. WALKER, J. On ventilating and lighting tunnels. (*In* Instit. of Civil Eng. Trans., v. 1. 1842.)

— STORROW, C. S. Report on European tunnels. (*In* Mass. *Commissioners upon the Greenfield R. R. and Hoosac Tunnel.* Report. 1863.)

See also Cenis, Mont; — Forth River; — Hoosac tunnel; — Thames tunnel.

Tunquin *or* Tunkin. *See* Tonquin.

Tuomey, Michael. On the results of obs. in the tertiary region of S. Carolina. (*In* Amer. Assoc. Proc., v. 1. 1849.) — Palæozoic rocks of Alabama. — Exhibition of a fossil reptile belonging to the genus leiodon. — Alleged subsidence of the coast of S. Carolina. — Cretaceous formation of Alabama, and the artesian wells in that state. (*In* v. 3. 1850.)

— Report. *See* Alabama. *Geol. Survey.*

Tupper, Martin Farquhar. Crock of gold. N. Y., 1845. 16°.

— Heart. N. Y., 1845. 8°.

— Homes of the poor. (*In* Talbot, C. J., *Visc. Ingestre.* Meliora, ser. 1. 1852.)

— Hymn for all nations; tr. into 30 languages, [by various persons], music by S. S. Wesley. [2d ed.] London, [1851]. 8°.

— Poetical works. N. Y., 1849. 24°.

— Proverbial philosophy. 2d ed. Boston, 1840. 12°.

— Rides and reveries of A. Smith. London, 1858. 12°.

— A third series of proverbial philosophy. London, 1867. 12°.

— A thousand lines. Phila., 1846. 8°. (B 1468)

— The twins. N. Y., 1845. 12°.

— WILSON, J. Tupper's Geraldine. (*In his* Essays, v. 3. 1857.)

Tura, A. Chronicon Senensis. (*In* Muratori, L. A. Rer. Ital. scr., v. 15. 1729.)

Turandot; fiaba. *See* Gozzi, C.

Turba philosophorum. — In Turbam philosophorum sermo. — Allegoriæ sapientum, et distinctiones XXIX supra librum Turbæ. (*In* Zetzner, L. Theatrum chem., v. 5. 1622.)

Turbervill, Edward. Information [conc. the Popish plot], 9th Nov. London, 1680. f°. (A 53)

Turbervile, George. Epitaphes, epigrams, songs, and sonets. Corr. with add. London, 1567 [*reprinted, J. P. Collier,* 1867]. 4°.

— Poems. (*In* Chalmers, A. Eng. poets, v. 2. 1810.)

Turbolo, Gian-Donato. Discorsi e relaz. sulle monete del regno di Napoli. (*In* Economisti class. ital., pte. ant., v. 1. 1803.)

Turcaret; comédie. *See* Le Sage, A. R.

Turcici Imperii status; seu Discursus varii de rebus Turcarum. Lugd. Bat., *Elzevir,* 1630. 32°.

Turco, The; by E. About. (*In* Every Saturday, v. 2. 1866.)

Turell, *Rev.* Ebenezer. Brief exhortation to his people, fast [day], Jan. 28. Boston, 1748. 8°. (B 68, 232, 257)

— Detection of witchcraft. (*In* Mass. Hist. Soc. Col., v. 20. 1823.)

— Dialogue between a minister and his neighbor about the times; with an answer to J. Lee's remarks on the Directions to his people. 2d ed. Boston, 1742. 8°. (C 51)

— Directions to his people with rel. to the present times. Boston, 1742. 8°. (C 51)

— *Same.* 2d ed. Boston, 1742. 16°. (C 52)

— Life and character of B. Colman. Boston, 1749. 8°.

— *Another copy.* (B 218)

— Memoirs of Mrs. J. Turell. (*In* Colman, B. Reliquiæ Turellæ. 1735. C 5)

— Ministers should carefully avoid giving offence in anything; sermon, Camb., Sept. 12, 1739; ordination of S. Cooke. Boston, 1740. 8°. (B 144, 232, 1315)

— BLANCHARD, J. Sober reply to a mad answer; letter to A. Croswell occasioned by his letter to E. T. Boston, 1742. 16°. (C 51)

— CROSWELL, A. Letter to T. in answer to his direction to his people. Boston, 1742. 8°. (B 243)

Turell, *Mrs.* Jane. COLMAN, B. Reliquiæ Turellæ; two sermons, Medford, Apr. 6, after the funeral of Mrs. T.; added, memoirs by E. Turell. Boston, 1735. 8°. (C 5)

Turenne, Henri de la Tour d'Auvergne, *duc de Bouillon, vct. de Turenne,* 1555–91. *See* Bouillon.

Turenne, Henri de la Tour d'Auvergne, *vicomte* de, *maréchal de France, b.* 1611, *d.* 1675. De bello Turcico; oratio. (*In* Conring, H. De bello contra Turcas. 1664.)

— Mémoires. (*In* Michaud *and* Poujoulat. Col. des mém., v. 27. 1854.)

— Mémoires sur la guerre; avec mémoires conc. les hôpitaux militaires par Monsieur *** [La Marie d'Oldinville]. Paris, 1739. 2 v. 12°.

— COCKAYNE, T. O. Life of Turenne. London, 1853. 12°.

— CUST, E. (*In his* Lives of the warriors of the civil wars, pt. 1. 1867.)

— FLÉCHIER, E. Oraison funèbre. (*In his* Œuvres, v. 2, pt. 2. 1782.)

— GUIBERT, J. A. H. de. Invitation à la nation franç. sur l'année séculaire de la mort de Turenne. (*In his* Œuvres, v. 5. 1803.)

— MALDEN, H. (*In his* Distinguished men of mod. times, v. 2. 1838; v. 38 of Lib. of ent. kn.)

— NAPOLEON I. Précis des guerres du maréchal de Turenne. (*In his* Commentaires, v. 6. 1867.)

— RAGUENET, F. Histoire du vict. de Turenne. Paris, 1744. 2 v. 12°.

— RAMSAY, A. M. Histoire du vicomte T. Paris, 1735. 2 v. 4°.

Turgan, Julien. Les grandes usines de France. Paris, 1861–65. 8 v. 8°.

Contents. Vol. 1. Les Gobelins. — Les moulins de Saint-Maur. — L'imprimerie impériale. — Usines des bougies de Clichy. — Papeterie d'Essonne. — Sèvres. — Orfévrerie Christofle. 2. Les établissements Derosne et Cail. — La savonnerie Arnavon. — La monnaie. — Manufacture impériale des tabacs: — Literie Tucker. — Fabrique de pianos de MM. Pleyel, Wolff, et Cie. — Filature de laine de M. Davin. 3. La manufacture de glaces de Saint-Gobain. — Les omnibus de Paris. — Les charbonnages des Bouches-du-Rhone. — Usine électro-métallurgique d'Auteuil. — Boulangerie centrale des hôpitaux de Paris. — La foudre: filature de coton. — Pépiniéres d'André Leroy, à Angers. — Usines à gaz de la Compagnie Parisienne. — Usine à gaz portatif de Paris. — Manufacture d'impression sur étoffes. — Aciéries Jackson et Cie. — Cristallerie de Baccarat. 4. Les établissements Dollfus-Mieg. — Manufacture de tapis de

Requillart, Roussel, et Chocquecl. — Fabrique d'or en feuilles de Goguel et Cie. — Manufacture de papiers peints de Defossé et Karth. — Parfumerie L. T. Piver. — Orgues expressifs. — Fabrique de coutellerie de Mermilliod frères. — Etablissement thermal de Vichy. — Hauts-fournaux, forges, et aciéries de Petin, Gaudet, et Cie.—Mines et fonderies de zinc de la Vieille-Montagne.— Faiencerie de Signoret. — Teinturerie de soie de Guinon, Marnas, et Bonnet. — Fabrique de boutons céramiques de Bapterosses. — Imprimerie administrative de P. Dupont. 5. Fabrique de sucre de betteraves. — Etablissement mercier. — Etablissements C. Flavigny. — Etablissements R. Renault. — Taillerie de diamants de Coster. — Fabrique d'ameublements en bois massif de Mazaroz-Rebaillier. — Fabrique de dentelles, O. de Vergnies et sœurs. — Brasserie Peters. — Platrières de Vaux. — Fabrique de rubans de Gérentet et Coignet. — Fabrique d'armes de l'état. — Manufacture impériale d'armes de Chatellerault. 6. Le Creusot. — Etablissement J. Hennessy. — Filature de soie de L. Blanchon. — Ardoisières d'Angers. — Tuilerie de Montchanin. — Fabrique d'acier fondu de F. Krupp. — Forges impériales de la Chaussade. — Dentelles du Puy. — Fabrique d'aiguilles de Schuhmacher. — Caves de Roquefort. — Fabriques d'aluminium. 7. Fonderie de canons de la marine impériale. — Usine de Noisiel. — Exploitation agricole distillerie et sucrerie de la Briche. — Joaillerie Rouvenat. — Etablissement I. Leroy. — Etablissement Bonnet. Compagnie générale des verreries de la Loire et du Rhone. — Faiencerie de Gien. — Etablissements Japy. — Forges et chantiers de la Méditerranée. 8. Indret. — Reims: tissus de laine. — Fabrique de caoutchouc de Guibal. — Fabrique d'amorces et de cartouches de chasse et de guerre. — Fabrique d'armes de Lefaucheux. — Fabrique de toiles cirées de A. Baudoin. — Fabrique de machines agricoles de Pinet.

— La monnaie. — La manufacture des tabacs. (*In* **Paris** guide, v. 2. 1867.)

Turgenef, Ivan Sergeïevitch. Fathers and sons; a novel, tr. from the Russian, by E. Schuyler. N. Y., 1867. 12°.

— Moumounia. (*In* **Revue** d. D. Mondes, mars 1856.) — Faust; récit en neuf lettres. (*In* déc. 1856.) — Anouchka; souvenirs des bords du Rhin. (*In* oct. 1858.) — Les trois rencontres; souvenirs de chasse et de voyage. (*In* oct. 1859.) — Le journal d'un homme de trop. (*In* déc. 1861.) — L'aventure du lieutenant Yergounof. (*In* avr. 1868.) — Etrange histoire. (*In* mars 1870.) — Le roi Lear de la Steppe. (*In* mars 1872.) — Le gentilhomme de la Steppe. (*In* déc. 1872.) — Trop menu le fil casse; scènes de la vie russe. (*In* juil. 1861.)

Turgenef, Nicolai. Economic results of the emancipation of serfs in Russia. (*In* **Amer. Soc. Sci. Assoc.** Journ., v. 1. 1869.)

Turgot, *Monk of Durham*. Vita S. Margaretæ. — Excerpta e scriptis. (*In* **Symeon** *of Durham*. Opera, v. 1. 1868.)

Turgot, Anne Robert Jacques, *baron d'Aulne*. Œuvres. Vol. 1, 2e éd. Paris, 1811, 08–10. 9 v. 8°.

Contents. Vol. 1. Mémoires sur la vie, l'administration, et les ouvrages de T. 2. Lettre à l'abbé de Cicé sur le papier supplée à la monnoie. — Discours sur les avantages que l'établissement du Christianisme a procurés au genre humain. — Discours sur les progrès successifs de l'esprit humain. — Lettre à Buffon. — Réflexions philosophiques sur l'origine des langues par Maupertuis. — Remarques critiques sur les 'Réflexions'. — Plans et projets d'ouvrages qui ont occupé T. lorsque'il étoit en Sorbonne, *etc.* — Géographie politique. — Mappemondes politiques, 1e - 7e. — Histoire universelle. — Lettres sur la tolérance. — Le conciliateur, ou Lettres d'un ecclesiastique à un magistrat sur le droit des citoyens, *etc.* 3. Articles dans l'Encyclopédie: Etymologie; — Existence; — Expansibilitie; — Foires et marchés; — Fondation et fondations; — Réflexions sur les langues; — Réfutation du système de Berkeley. — Valeurs et monnoies. — Pensées diverses. — Sur les économistes. — Lettre à Marmontel. — Eloge de Gournay. — Observations géologiques. — Lettre à Voltaire. 4. Déclarations conc. la taille tarifée dans la généralité de Limoges. — Lettre aux commissaires des tailles. — L'état de Limoges rel. à l'imposition de la taille pour 1762. — Lettre au contrôleur-général pour refuser l'intendance de Lyon. — Mémoire sur les doubles emplois des tailles entre Limoges et de la Rochelle. — Projet d'arrêt du conseil. — Projet d'une imposition territoriale. — Projet du roi portant abonnement des vingtièmes, *etc.* — Obs. sur ce project. — Plan d'un mémoire sur les impositions en général. — Lettre à Laverdy. — Avis sur l'imposition de la taille de Limoges pour 1763–66. — Mém. sur la surcharge des impositions qu'éprouvait la gén. de Limoges dans lequel l'auteur traite de la grand et de la petite culture. — Programmes de la Soc. d'Agric. de Limoges. — Obs. sur le mém. couronné rel. aux effets de l'impôt indirect. — Obs. sur le mém. dont l'auteur croyait l'impôt indirect préférable à l'impôt direct. — Suppression des corvées. — Commerce des grains. — Mémoire sur la législation rel. à l'exploitation des mines et des carrières. 5. Reflexions sur la formation et la distribution des richesses. — Obs. sur les points dans lesquels Smith est d'accord avec la théorie de T., et sur ceux dans lesquels il s'en est écarté. — Questions sur la Chine. — Encouragemens demandés pour l'établissement de quelques manufactures. — Lettre à Trudaine. — Réponse de Trudaine. — Réplique de Turgot. — Projet d'arrêt du conseil. — Avis sur l'imposition de la taille de Limoges in 1769. — Lettre au contrôleur-gén. — L'imposition de la taille de Limoges en 1770. — Mém. sur les prêts d'argent. — Lettres circulaire sur les pertes de bestiaux. — Travaux rel. à la disette de 1770. — Arrêt du conseil d'état pour maintenir la liberté du commerce des grains. — Assemblées et bureaux de charité. — Les moyens les plus convenables de soulager les pauvres, *etc.* — Lettre circulaire aux curés. — Lettre circulaire aux subdélégués. — le délibération de l'Assemblée de Limoges. 6. Supplément aux instructions conc. la suppression de la mendacité. — Obligation de nourir leur métayers imposée aux propriétaires. — Ordonnance qui enjoint aux propriétaires de pourvoir à la subsistance de leur colons. — Ordonnance qui charge les propriétaires et habitans des paroisses de Limoges de pouvoir à la subsistance des pauvres jusqu'à la récolte. — Lettre aux subdélégués accomp. l'ordonnance préc. — Ordonnance pour faciliter les opérations des bureaux de charité. — Ordonnance contre les attroupemens, *etc.* — Ordonnance qui en annuelle une des officiers municipaux de Turenne, et leur enjoint d'exécuter la déclaration du 25 mai 1763 et l'édit de juil. 1764. — Ordonnance qui enjoint l'exécution de ces mêmes lois, *etc.* — Arrêt du conseil d'état, *etc.* — Atteliers de charité. — Mesures prises pour empêcher que le paiement des rentes en grains pendant la disette ne renfermât une injustice. — Lettre au chancellier sur ce sujet. — Avis sur l'imposition de la taille dans Limoges. — Obs. sur l'état des récoltes de 1770. — Effets de ces obs. — Lettre à Terray. — Liberté du commerce des grains. — Lettres à M. le Contrôleur-général; 1e - 7e. — Extension de la liberté du commerce des colonies. — Lettre à Rochefort. — Lettre à M. le Contrôleur-gén. — Avis sur l'impôsition de la taille en 1772. — Suite des opérations rel. à la disette de 1770, 71. — Avis sur l'imposition de la taille pour 1773. — Lettre à Ormesson. — Lettre à Monteynard. — Avis sur l'imposition de la taille pour 1774. — Lettre à Ormesson sur ce que la province au lieu d'être soulagée était surchargée. — Lettre à Terray. 7, 8. Ministère de T. 7. Août 1774 - juil. 1775. 8. Août 1775 - mai 1776. 9. Traductions en vers: La prière univ. de Pope. — Prière de Cléanthe. — Virgille. — Prosodie de la langue fr. et versification métrique. — Invocation à la muse d'Homère. — Tr. du 4e livre de l'Enéide, *etc.* — Horace. — Elégie de Tibulle. — Pope. — Vers au bas du portrait de Franklin. — Lettre sur les poësies erses. — Poésie allemande. — A Mme. de Graffigny sur les lettres péruviennes. — A M. de C. sur le livre de l'esprit. — Les 37 vérités opposées aux 37 impiétés de Bélisaire. — Commencement de l'hist. du Jansénisme et du Molinisme. — Premières opérations tendantes à regler les mesures et les poids par un étalon physique. — Lettres. — Mém. à Franklin. — Mém. sur la gomme élastique. — Mém. sur le voy. du capitaine Cook. — Suppl. au tome 4.

— Œuvres. Nouv. éd. avec notes de Dupont de Nemours; aug. de lettres inédites et notes nouvelles par Daire et Dussard. Paris, 1844. 2 v. 8°.

Contents. Vol. 1. Notice sur la vie et les œuvres de Turgot. — Economie politique. — Industrie manufacturière et commerciale. — Impôt. — Lettres au curés de Limoges. 2. Travaux rel. à la disette de 1770, 71, dans le généralité de Limoges. — Lettres au Contrôleur-général. — Actes du ministère de Turgot. — Œuvres diverses.

— Lettre à M. le docteur Price. (*In* **Mirabeau**, H. G. R. Considérations sur l'ordre de Cincinnatus. 1784.)

— *Same, with trans.* (*In* **Price**, R. Observations on the importance of the Amer. Rev. 1784.)

— Reflections on the formation and distribution of wealth. London, 1795. 8°.

— Baudrillart, H. J. L. (*In* **Revue** d. D. Mondes, sept. 1846.)

— Condorcet, J. A. N. C., *marq.* de. (*In his* Œuvres, v. 5. 1847.)

— Du Puynode, M. G. P. (*In his* Etudes sur les principaux économistes. 1868.)
— Malden, H. (*In his* Distinguished men of mod. times, v. 3. 1838; v. 39 of Lib. of ent. kn.)
— Passy, H. P. Rapport sur le concours Léon Faucher rel. à la vie et aux œuvres de Turgot. (*In* **Paris. Inst.** *Ac. d. Sci. Mor.* Mém., v. 11. 1862.)

Turgot, Etienne François, *marquis*. Correspondance entre Turgot et Condorcet. (*In* **Condorcet, J. A. N. C.** Œuvres, v. 1. 1847. — Condorcet, J. A. N. C. Eloge de Turgot. (*In* v. 3. 1847.)

Turia, Ricardo del. La burladoro burlada. (*In* **Mesonero Romanos, R.** de. Dramaticos contemporaneos a Lopé de Vega, v. 1. 1857; v. 43 of Aribau. Bibl.)

Turin. Statuta ac privilegia, [1341–1472]. (*In* **Sardinia.** Mon. hist. pat., Leges mun., v. 2. 1838.)

Antiquities.

— Paroletti, M. Notice sur une inscription consulaire trouvée dans les décombres du donjon d'une des portes de Turin. (*In* **Turin. Ac. d. Sci.** Mem., v. 15. 1805.) — Cordero di S. Quintino, G. Ricerche intorno ad alcune cose antiche dissotterrate in Torino negli 1830 e 31. (*In* v. 36. 1833.)

Description.

— Casalis, G. Torino, provincia e città. (*In his* Diz. geog. di Sardegna, v. 21, 22. 1851-52.)
— Sewell, E. M. Impressions of Rome, Florence, Turin, [1861]. London, 1862. 16°.

Maps.

— Imperial cittá d'Augusta, La. Venetia, [17—]. (**E 60**)
— Map. Amst. 1706. (**E 60**)
— Plan de Turin tel qu'il a esté assiégee en 1706. Amst., [17—]. (**E 60**)

Ecclesiastical affairs.

— Meyranesio, G. F. De episcopis et archiepiscopis Taurinensibus, 312–1778. (*In* **Sardinia.** Mon. hist. pat., Scr., v. 11. 1863.)
— Necrologium Prioratus S. Andreæ Taurinensis. — Necrologium Monasterii S. Solutoris, Adventoris, et Octavii Taurinensis. — Summariæ constitutiones Monasterii B. Mariæ de Abundantia. — Necrologium insignis collegii canonicorum S. Petri et Ursi Augustæ Prætoriæ. (*In* **Sardinia.** Mon. hist. pat., Scr., v. 5. 1848.)

History.

— Pingone, E. F. Augustæ Taurinorum chronica, [b. c. 1529 - a. d. 1577]. (*In* **Grævius.** Thes. antiq. Ital., v. 9, pt. 6. 1699.)

Prisons.

— Pellico, S. Life of the marchesa Giulia Falletti di Barolo, reformer of the Turin prisons; from the orig. by Lady G. Fullerton. London, 1866. 8°.

Social distinctions.

— Balbo, C. Dei titoli e della potenza dei conti, *ec.*, dell' Italia settentr. e in partic. dei conti di Torino. (*In his* Regno. 1862, *where it is reprinted, with the add. of an appendix, from* **Turin. Ac. d. Sci.** Mem., v. 38. 1835.)

Turin. Accademia Reale delle Scienze. Memorie. Turin, 1759–1838. 40 v. 4°.

Note. The title varies as follows: Vol. 1. Miscellanea philosophico-mathematica Societatis Privatæ Taurinensis. 2-5. Mélanges de philosophie et de mathématique de la Société Royale de Turin, 1760–73. [6–10.] Mémoires de l'Académie Royale des Sciences, 1784–91. [11.] Mémoires de l'Acad. des Sci. de Turin, 1792–1800. [12, 13.] Mémoires de l'Acad. des Sci., Lit., et Beaux-Arts de Turin, années 10 et 11. [14-21.] Mémoires de l'Acad. Imp. des Sci., Lit., et Beaux-Arts de Turin, [1804]-12. 22. Mémoires de l'Acad. Roy. des Sci. de Turin, 1813–14. 23–40. Memorie della Reale Accad. delle Sci. di Torino.

☞ There are indexes in v. 22 to v. 1-21; in v. 32 to v. 22-32; in v. 40 to v. 33-40.

Contents. Vol. 1. **Cigna, J. F.** Commentarii. — **Saluzzo, C.** Sur la nature du fluide élastique qui se développe de la poudre à canon. — **La Grange, J. L.** de. Sur la méthode de maximis et minimis; — L'intégration d'une équation différentielle à différences finies. — **Cigna, J. F.** De analogia magnetismi, et electricitatis; — De colore sanguinis experimenta non nulla. — **Gaber, J. B.** Exper. circa putrefactionem humorum animalium. — **Piazza, M. A.** Fasciculus stirpium Sardiniæ in diœcesi Calaris lectarum. — **Bertrandi, A.** De glanduloso ovarii corpore, de utero gravido, *etc.* — **Saluzzo, C.** Suite des recherches sur la fluide élastique de la poudre à canon. — **La Grange, J. L.** de. Sur la nature et la propagation du son. — **Daviet de Foncenex, F.** Sur les quantités imaginaires. — **Richeri, L.** Philosophia primæ realis characteristica specimen.

2. **Haller, A.** Emendationes et auctaria ad stirpium Helveticarum historiam. — **Allioni, C.** Synopsis methodica stirpium horti Taurinensis. — **Cigna, J. F.** De motibus electricis experimentum. — **Gaber, J. B.** Exper. de putrefactione humorum animalium. — **Saluzzo, C.** Réfléxions sur le fluide élastique de la poudre à canon. — **Cigna, J. F.** De frigore ex evaporatione, et affinibus phænomenis nonnullis; — De caussa extinctionis flammæ, et animalium in aere interclusorum. — **Valle, F.** Taurinensis florula Corsicæ. — **Saluzzo, C.** Addition aux réflexions sur le fluide élastique. — **Euler, L.** Lettre à M. de La Grange sur la propagation des ébranlemens dans un milieu élastique. — **La Grange, J. L.** de. Nouvelles recherches sur la nature et propagation du son; — Essai d'une nouv. méthode pour déterminer les maxima et les minima des formules intégrales indéfinies; — Application de la méthode précédente à la solution de différens problèmes de dynamique. — **Daviet de Foncenex, F.** Sur les principes fondamentaux de la méchanique. — **La Grange, J. L.** de. Addition à la 1e pte. des recherches sur la nature et la propagation du son. — **Daviet de Foncenex, F.** Eclaircissemens pour le mémoire sur les quantités imaginaires. — **Gerdil, G. S.**, *père*. De l'infini absolu considéré dans la grandeur. — **Richeri, L.** Algebræ philosophicæ in usum artis inveniendi. — **Carena, G.** Obs. sur le cours du Pô, avec des recherches sur les changemens qu'il a souffert.

3. **Macquer, P. J.** Mémoire sur la dissolubilité des sels neutres dans l'esprit de vin, *etc.* — **Cigna, J. F.** De novis quibusdam experimentis electricis. — **Saluzzo, C.** De l'action de la chaux vive sur différentes substances; — Expériences pour chercher les causes des changemens qui arrivent au sirop violat par le mélange de différentes substances. — **Gaber, J. B.** De humoribus animalibus. — **Allioni, C.** Stirpium aliquot descriptiones cum duorum novorum generum constitutione; — Manipulus insectorum Taurinensium. — **Dana, J. P. M.** De hirudinis nova specie, noxa, remediisque adhibendis; — De quibusdam urticæ marinæ vulgo dictæ differentiis. — **Euler, L.** Eclaircissemens sur le mouvement des cordes vibrantes; — Recherches sur le mouvement des cordes inégalement grosses; — Recherches sur l'integration de l'équation $\left(\frac{ddz}{dt^2}\right) = aa\left(\frac{ddz}{dx^2}\right) + \frac{b}{x}\left(\frac{dz}{dx}\right) + \frac{c}{x^2}z$; — Recherches sur la construction des lunettes à 5 et 6 verres, *etc.* — **La Grange, J. L.** de. Formules de dioptrique nécessaires pour l'intelligence du mémoire précédent. — **Euler, L.** Observationes circa integralia formularum $sx^{p-1}dx\left(1-x^n\right)^{\frac{q}{n}-1}$, posito post integrationem $x=1$. — **La Grange, J. L.** de. Solution de différens problèmes de calcul intégral. — **Alembert, J. le R. d'.** Extrait de différentes lettres à M. de La Grange.

4. **Roffredi, M.** Sur la trompe du cousin, et sur celle du taon. — **Monnet, A. G.** Recherches sur la décomposition du nitre, et du sel marin par les intermèdes terreux. — **Haller, A.** von. Ad agrostographiam Scheuzeri supplementum. — **Monnet, A. G.** Lettre au sujet du minium; — Mém. sur la rectification et purification de l'alkali volatil obtenu des substances animales. — **Marini, J. A.** Thermarum Vinadiensium encheireticæ syntaxis. — **Monnet, A. G.** Mém. sur la combination du mercure avec le tartre. — **Roffredi, M.** Lettres sur les nouvelles obs. microscopiques de M. Néedham, et ses notes sur les recherches de M. Spallanzani. — **Dana, J. P. M.** Descriptio et usus agarici seu boleti pellicei. — **Saluzzo, C.** Obs. chimiques. — **Condorcet, M. J. A. N. C.**, *marq.* de. Solution de ce probléme: une équation différentielle aux différences infiniment petites, et qui admet une solution générale, étant donnée, trouver l'intégrale: — Obs. sur la théorie des équations différentielles. — **La Grange, J. L.** de. Solution d'un probléme d'arithmétique; — Sur l'intégration de quelques équations différentielles, dont les indéterminées sont séparées, mais dont chaque membre en particulier n'est point intégrable. — **Alembert, J. le R. d'.** Recherches mathématiques. — **La Grange, J. L.** de. Sur la méthode des variations; — Sur le mouvement d'un corps qui est attiré vers deux centres fixes. — **Condorcet, M. J. A. N. C.**, *marq.* de. Add. au premier mémoire sur le calcul intégral. — **Gianella, P.** De integratione indefinitomii. — **Laplace, P. S.**, *marq.* de. Recherches sur le calcul intégral aux différences infiniment petites, et aux différences finies.

5. *Classe philos.* **Gerdil, G. S.** L'ordre. — **Mouroux,** *Comte.* Exam. phys.-chim. sur la couleur des fleurs et quelques autres substances végétales. — **Allioni,** C. Auctarium ad synopsim methodicam stirpium Horti Reg. Taurinensis. — **Cigna, J. F.** De electricitate; — De respiratione. — **Dana, J. P. M.** De solano melanoceraso H. R. Taur. — **Macquer, P. J.** Sur la différente dissolubilité des sels neutres dans l'esprit de vin, cont. obs. partic. sur plusieurs de ces sels. — **Saluzzo, C.** Sur un essai de chimie comparée. — *Cl. math.* **Condorcet, M. J. A. N. C.,** *marq.* de. Sur différentes questions d'analyse; — Addition, ou Mém. sur les solutions partic. des équations différentielles. — **Monge, G.,** *comte* de. Sur la détermin. de fonctions arbitraires dans les intégrales de quelques équations aux différences partielles; — 2d mém. sur le calcul intégral de quelques équations aux diff. partielles. — **La Grange, J. L.** de. Sur la figure des colonnes; — Sur l'utilité de la méthode de prendre le milieu entre le resultat de plusieurs obs., dans lequel on examine les avantages de cette méthode par le calcul des probabilités, et où l'on resoud différens problêmes relatifs à cette matière. — **Condorcet, M. J. A. N. C.,** *marq.* de. Theorème pour servir de suite au mém. sur différentes questions d'analyse; — Sur les équations déterminées, *etc.*

6. Mém. historiques. — **Saluzzo, C.,** *comte* de. De l'action des acides sur diff. substances métalliques et salino-terreuses de nature vitriolique. — **Monge, G.,** *comte* de. Sur l'expression anal. de la génération des surfaces courbes. — **Brugnone, J.** Sur la nature et causes d'une épizootie à Fossan parmi les chevaux des dragons du roi, 1783. — **Saluzzo, C.,** *comte* de. Expér. et obs. sur le gaz déphlogistiqué. 1e pte. — **La Grange, J. L.** de. Sur la percussion des fluides. — **Caluso,** *l'abbé* T. V. de. Sur la mesure de la hauteur des montagnes par le baromètre. — **Penchienati, A.** Recherches anat.-pathol. sur les anévrismes des artères crurale et poplitée; — Des divisions, ramifications, *etc.* — **Nicolis de Robilant, E. B.** *or* J. B. Essai géog. suivi d'une topog. souterraine minéralogique et d'une docimasie des états de S. M. en Terre-Ferme. — **Morozzo, C. L.,** *comte* de. Sur la rosée, *etc.*; — Expér. eudiométriques sur l'air pur, vicié par la respiration animale. — **Bonvoisin, B.** Mém. sur la dépuration de l'acide phosphorique tirés des os, *etc.*, 1e, 2e pts. — **Galeani Napione, C. A.** Desc. minéralogique des montagnes du Canovois. — **Reyneri, —.** Desc. d'un fœtus pétrifié. — **Bonvoisin, B.** Anal. du même fœtus. — **Penchienati, A.** Obs. anat. sur une fille qui avoit passé pour être née sans nombril. — **Gianella, P.** Sur quelques series. — **Bonvoisin, B.** De la pierre hydrophane du Piémont.

7. **St. Martin de la Motte,** *comte* F. de. Sur la fontaine verte de S. Marcel. — **Brugnone, J.** De testium in fœtu positu, de eorum in scrotum descensu, *etc.* — **Michelotti, J. T.** Mém. physico-math. cont. les résultats des expér. hydrauliques faites à Turin, 1783. — **Fontana, G. M. U.** Anal. des eaux thermales de Vinay, *etc.* — **Nicolis de Robilant, E. B.** *or* J. B. Expériences sur la platine. — **Saluzzo, C.,** *comte* de. Continuation d'expériences et d'obs. sur le gaz déphlogistiqué, 2e, 3e pts. — **La Grange, J. L.** de. Sur une nouv. méthode de calcul intégral pour les différentielles affectées d'un radical carré, sous lequel la variable ne passe pas le 4e deg. — **Caluso,** *l'abbé* T. V. de. De l'utilité des projections orthographiques en général, *etc.* — **Morozzo, C. L.,** *comte.* Sur une aurore boréale extraordinaire obs. à Turin, 1780. — **Perenotti, —.** Sur la construction et l'accroissement des os. — **Balbe, P.,** *comte* de. Sur le sable aurifère de l'Orco et des environs. — **Bonvoisin, B.** Anal. des principales eaux de la Savoie. — **Tingry, —.** Recherches anal. sur les schistes de Sallenche. — **Senebier, J.** Expér. propres à faire connoître les procédés les plus convenable pour fabriquer le savon. — **Van Swinden, —.** Obs. sur quelques partic. météorol. de 1783. — **Bernoulli, D.** Essai d'une nouv. manière d'envisager les diff. ou les fluxions des quantités variables. — **Caluso, T. V.** de, *l'abbé.* Addition.

8. **Morozzo, C. L.,** *comte.* Sur la couleur noire des feuilles exposées à l'air inflam. des marais. — **Brezé,** *marq.* de. Anal. des eaux médicinales de Casteletto Adorno et de S. Genis, *etc.* — **Penchienati, A.** Desc. d'un monstre humain à double tête de sept mois. — **Fontana, G. M. U.** Méthode très sure de préparer un excellent kermès minéral. — **Penchienati, A.** Sur les effets de l'eau de laurier-cerise sur les cadavres de deux personnes mortes à Turin, 1785. — **Caluso, T. V.** de, *l'abbé.* De l'orbite d'Herschel ou Uranus. — **Saluzzo, C.,** *comte* de. Examen des phénomènes que présente la réduction de quelques chaux métalliques; — Examen de la prétendue absorption du charbon dans les vases clos. — **Lorgna, A. M.** Méthode pour sommer les séries réciproques de sinus ou co-sinus d'arcs en progression arith. — **Nicolis de Robilant, E. B.** *or* J. B. Desc. partic. du duché d'Aoste, *etc.* — **Morozzo, C. L.,** *comte.* Examen physico.-chim. des couleurs animales. — **Dana, J. P. M.** Fœtus octimestris in quo maxilla inferior immobilis, uvula exerta, lingulata, osque necessario apertum cum lingua bifida inclusa inveniebantur; — Desc. fœtus absque pene et vulva ultra biennium viventis, obscurique sexus ideo habiti. — **Monnet, A. G.** Sur la nature de la terre du spath fusible. — **Saluzzo, C.,** *comte* de. Addition. Extrait des mém. de Monnet, *etc.* — **Monnet, A. G.** Sur la formation des minéraux; — Sur les mines de plomb antimoniées, *etc.*; — Sur une nouv. substance minérale trouvée dans les mines de Braunsdorff près de Freyberg en Saxe, 1770. — **Berthollet, C. L.,** *comte.* Sur quelques combinaisons de l'acide muriatique oxygené. — **Fontana, G. M. U.** Expér. chimiques sur la bile de bœuf. — **Lorgna, A. M.** Théorie d'une nouv. espèce de calcul fini et infinitésimal. — **Morozzo, C. L.,** *comte.* Expér. sur la fiole de Bologne. — **Scopoli, —.** Examen de quelques espèces de bois de pins; de la térébenthine, *etc.* — **Morozzo, C. L.,** *comte.* Relation d'un violente détonnation arrivée à Turin 1785 dans un magasin de farine, *etc.* — **Caluso,** *l'abbé* T. V. de. Des diff. manières de traiter cette partie des math. que les uns appellent calcul différentiel et les autres méthode des fluxions. — **Penchienati, A.** Moyens d'augmenter la récolte des olives. — **Brugnone, J.** Obs. anat. sur les vésicules séminales. — **Bonvoisin, B.** Anal. chim. et comparée de la plupart des sels marins qu'on distribue dans l'états de S. M. — **Perolle, E.** Expér. phys.-chim. rel. à la propagation du son dans quelques fluides aériformes. — **Retzio, A. G.** Venus lithophaga descripta.

9. Mém. hist. — **Morozzo, C. L.,** *comte.* Sur la mesure des principaux points des états du roi, *etc.* — **Guyton-Gorveau, L. B.** Sur la saturation des sels, et l'affinité d'un composé avec un de ses principes par excès. — **Giobert, G. A.** Expér. chim. sur différens corps marins fossiles, *etc.*; — Obs. phys. sur le phosphorisme du tartre vitriolé. — **Saluzzo, C.,** *comte* de. Obs. prélim. sur les imperfections des milieux coërcitifs, *etc.* — **Morozzo, C. L.,** *comte.* Desc. d'une cygne sauvage pris en Piémont, 1788, *etc.* — **Brugnone, J.** Obs. et expér. sur la qualité vénéneuse et même meutrière de la renoncule des champs. — **Penchienati, A.** Sur un fœtus humain monstreux. — **Monnet, A. G.** Diss. et expér. rel. aux principes de la chimie pneumatique. — **Vasco, G. B.,** *l'abate.* Obs. sur l'insecte qui ronge les cocons des vers à soie. — **Brezé,** *marq.* de. Anal. de l'eau sulfureuse de Lu en Montferrat. — **Saluzzo, C.,** *comte* de. Expér. sur des liqueurs gaseuses artificielles. — **Perenotti, —.** Sur une nouv. espèce d'insecte trouvé dans l'eau d'un puits d'Alexandrie. — **St. Real, —.** Mém. sur cette question: trouver le moyen de rendre le cuir imperméable à l'eau, *etc.* — **Galeani Napione, C. A.** Anal. de la mine de manganèse rouge du Piémont. — **Morozzo, C. L.,** *comte.* Sur la température de l'eau de quelques lacs et rivières. — **Galeani Napione, C. A.** Sur une nouv. méthode pour tirer parti des scories de l'affinage du fer. — **Caluso, T. V.,** *l'abbé.* De la navigation sur le sphéroide elliptique, *etc.* — **Marini, J. A.** Desc. anat. præternaturalis dimensionis ventriculi humani. — **Bonvoisin, B.** Du vinaigre radical et glacial tiré des cristaux de vénus, *etc.*; — Sur l'acali phlogistiqué. — **Brugnoni, J.** De ovariis, eorumque corpore luteo. — **Saussure, H. B.** Desc. d'un cyanomètre; — Descr. d'un diphanomètre; — Effets chimiques de la lumière sur une haute montagne, *etc.* — **Michaud, —.** Obs. sur les trombes de mer vues de Nice 1789. — **Bacounin, A.** de. Sur les gordius d'eau douce des environs de Turin. — **Actis,** *L'abbé.* Sur l'écho de l'église cathédrale de Girgenti. — **Malfatti, G. F.** Essai anal. sur l'intégration de deux formules différentielles, *etc.* — **Lambre, —** de. Réduction à l'ecliptique. — **Michelotti, I.** Obs. et expér. sur la mesure du choc d'une veine fluide. — **Balbe, P.,** *comte* de. Extrait des mém. de M. Belly sur la minéralogie de la Sardaigne.

10. Mém. hist. — **St. Martin de la Motte, F.,** *comte.* Sur le moyen d'obtenir un alkali phlogistiqué extemporané. — **Eandi, G. A. F. J.,** *l'abbé.* Sur l'électricité dans le vide. — **Penchienati, A.** Sur quelques prétendus hermaphrodites. — **Giobert, G. A.** Essai sur la combinaison de l'oxigène avec l'acide sulphurique, *etc.* — **Senebier, J.** Sur divers phénomènes produits par des feuilles de plantes exposées sous l'eau à l'action de la pompe pneumatique. — **Vassali Eandi, A. M.** Expér. électrométriques. — **Fontana, G. M. U.** Expér. anal. sur l'Osmonda regalis. — **Caluso, T. V.,** *l'abbé.* Applications des formules du plus court chemin sur le sphéroïde elliptique. — **Vasco, G. B.,** *l'abate.* Sur le décreusement de la soie. — **Morozzo, C. L.,** *comte.* Sur la variolite du Piémont. — **Galeani Napione, C. A.** Sur les principes constituans de la mine d'argent grise. — **Vassali Eandi, A. M.** Parallèle de la lumière solaire avec celle du feu commun. — **Morozzo, C. L.,** *comte.* De l'action du fer et du zinc incandescens sur l'air, *etc.* — **Bellardi, C. A. L.** Appendix ad floram Pedemontanam. — **Vassali Eandi, A. M.** Supplément au parallèle de la

lumière du soleil, *etc.* — **Giobert**, G. A. Examen chimique de la doctrine du phlogistique, *etc.* — **Balbe**, P., *comte* de. Essais d'arithmétique politique. — **Bonvoisin**, B. Sur quelques propriétés irrégulières de la teinture violette des fleurs de mauve, *etc.*; — Essai d'expér. propres à découvrir dans les végétaux la nature de quelques substances qui ne sont pas encore assez connues. — **Smith**, J. E. Tentamen botanicum de filicum generibus dorsiferarum. — **Trembley**, J. Sur les équations différentielles du premier deg.; — Sur les intégrales particulières des équations diff. — **Pezzi**, —. Formules d'intégration pour les équations aux différences infiniment petites. — **Lambre**, —. De l'usage du calcul diff. dans la construction des tables astron. — **Maraldi**, J. P. Obs. des éclipses des satellites de Jupiter à l'Périnaldo, 1789, 90, 91. — **Teghil**, —. Desc. d'une hydro-céphale. — **Rossi**, F. Expér. [sur] la manière dont la bile cystique se sépare, *etc.* — **Perolle**, E. Mém. phys., 1e, 2e pte. — **Comparetti**, A. Sur la structure organique, *etc.*

11. *Math. et phys.* **Eandi**, G. A. F. J. Résolution de quelques questions sur l'électricité, *etc.*; — Théories de la respiration, *etc.* — **Rossi**, F. Hist. monstri anatomica. — **Giulio**, G. C., *and* **Rossi**, F. De excitabilitate contractionum in partibus musculosis involuntariis ope animalis electricitatis. — **Vassali Eandi**, A. M. de. Sur l'utilité des conducteurs électriques, *etc.* — **Amoretti**, C. Sur le trap du mont Simmolo. — **Michelotti**, V. J. Sur les moyens les plus convenables pour la division et subdivision pratique des arcs circulaires. — **St. Real**, —, *and* **Maistre**, P., *comte* de. Sur quelques expér. dans lesquelles le soufre, quoique dans des vaisseaux privés d'air, et l'acide sulfurique se former sans inflammation du soufre. — **Bellardi**, C. A. L. Sur une nouv. espèce d'agaric. — **Morozzo**, C. L., *comte*. De la lumière phosphorique que quelques pierres donnent, *etc.*; — Examen d'un gaz hidrogène. — **Dana**, J. P. M. Sur la prépara tion du carthame. — **Caluso**, T. V., *l'abbé*. De la résolution des équations numériques de tous les dégrés; — Examen d'un problême dont la résolution anal. ne seroit pas facile. — **Galeani Napione**, C. A. Obs. lithologiques et chim. sur une espèce de marbre primitif; — Nouv. méthode pour séparer l'argent qui se trouve allié au cuivre dans la monnoie de billon. — **Saorgio**, *le père*. Un nombre entier étant donné pour l'un des côtés d'un triangle rectangle, trouver toutes les couples des nombres aussi entiers qui avec le côté donné forment ce triangle. — **Rossi**, F. Obs., dissect., et expér. sur la morsure d'animaux enragés; — Sur la génération des animaux ovipares et surtout des poules. — **Brugnone**, J. Descr. d'un monstre humain, *etc.* — **Penchienati**, A. Desc. anat. d'un vagin double, *etc.* — **Bonvoisin**, B. Sur la véritable nature de la turquoise, *etc.* — **Barletti**, —. Des mouvemens obs. par M. Mariotte dans les corps flottants sur la surface des liquides. — **Torraca**, G. Des étoiles et des hérissons de mer. — **Marabelli**, F. Sur la nature de quelques matières animales altérées par des maladies, *etc.* — **Canali**, L. Questions sur la loi découverte par Volta rél. à l'électricité des vapeurs, *etc* — **Franchini**, —. Sur la résolution des équations d'un degré quelconque. — **Mouxy de Loches**, *comte*. Obs. sur les insectes, *etc.*; — Entomologie. — **Borson**, S. Ad oryctographiam Pedemontanam auctarium. — **Maistre**, X., *comte* de. Exper. sur les huiles. — **Buniva**, M. F. Obs. et exper. quæ B. instituit ad recognoscenda bubulæ speciei potissimum in subalpina regione infesta animalia, horumque nocendi modum detegendum. — **Amoretti**, C., *l'abbé*. Lettre au citoyen Giobert.

12. *Sci. math. et phys.* **Vassali Eandi**, A. M. de. Sur la vie et les ouvrages d'Eandi. — *Mém. de math. et phys.* **Brugnone**, J. Sur l'origine de la membrane du tympan, *etc.* — **Balbis**, G. B. Obs. sur les œillets. — **Giulio**, G. C. Hist. d'un tétanos avec symptômes d'hydrophobie. — **Bellardi**, C. A. L. Sur la revivification d'une petite fougère desséchée. — **Giulio**, G. C., *and* **Rossi**, F. Desc. d'un monstre, *etc.* — **Balbis**, G. B. Sur trois nouv. espèces d'hépatique. — **Buniva**, M. F. Sur la phys. et pathol. des poissons. — **Vassali Eandi**, A. M. de. Sur le fluide de l'electro-moteur de Volta. — **Brugnone**, J. Obs. myologiques. — **Botta**, C. Sur la nature des tons et sons. — **Giorna**, E. Mém. d'entomologie. — **Bonvoisin**, B. Sur [les] produits du règne minéral en Piémont. — **Fontana**, G. M. L. Sopra il solido generato dalla rivoluzione dell' ellisse attorno ad uno de' suoi diametri; — Sopra il centro di gravità della logaritmica, *etc.*; — Problema statica; — Probl. idraulico; — Probl. di ottica. — **Giobert**, G. A. Anal. de la magnésie de Baudissero en Canavais; — Addit. au mém. précédent. — **Balbis**, G. B. Miscell. botanica, *etc.* — **Rossi**, F. De l'électricité animale. — **Vassali Eandi**, A. M. de. Notice d'un météorographe. — **Bellardi**, C. A. L. Stirpes novæ vel minus notæ Pedemontii desc., *etc.* — **Giorna**, E. Sur un zèbre métis. — **Michelotti**, J. T. Sur la détermination des vîtesses de l'eau par la grandeur des jets.

13. *Lit. et beaux arts.* **Bava di San Paolo**, E. Sur la littérature. — **Galleani Napione di Cocconato**, G. F., *conte*. Osserv. intorno all' ode XXVII del libro III d'Orazio. — **Regis**, F. De animalculis microscopicis carmen. — **Tarin**, V. Desc. d'un ancien ouvrage en mosaïque. — **Fallette-Barol**, O. A. Sur plusieurs points concernans la théorie des opérations et facultés intellectuelles. — **Bava de San Paolo**, E. Disc. prelim. o proemiale al prospetto istor. de' progressi delle scienze, *ec.*, dal secolo XI sino al secolo XVIII. — **Caluso**, T. V., *l'abbé*. Di Livia Colonna. — **Marenco**, P. Della natura poetica. — **Vigo**, G. B. Servandus est in lit. studiis excolendis laborum, atque animi contentionum modus; — Docti homines cum aliis morbis, *etc.*, elegia. — **Roero di Rovello**, D. Versi. — **Pécheux**, L. De la beauté rel. aux arts de peint. et sculpt. — **Dépéret**, G. Sur le langage des sons articulés. — **Grassi**, G. Prespetto dell' istor. polit. dell' uomo dalla creazione sino a G. Cesare. — **Bava de San Paolo**, E. Sur la palingénésie de toutes espèces. — **Tarin**, *Conte*. Sur l'utilité des grandes col. de médailles antiques, *etc.* — **Regis**, F. Mitologia consid. come maestra di morale e di politica. — **Roero di Rovello**, D. La fortuna. — **Bava de San Paolo**, E. Coup d'œil sur le règne de Charlesmagne. — **Pécheux**, L. Sur l'harmonie en peinture. — **Galeani Napione di Cocconato**, G. F., *conte*. Notizia de' principale scrittori di arte militare italiani. — **Roero di Rovella**, D. La capanna, poemetto per nozzo a T. V. Caluso. — **Caluso**, T. V., *l'abbé*. Risposata a D. Roero di Rovella. — **Bava de San Paolo**, E. Dialogo tra morti. — **Saluzzo**, C. Varie poesie. — **Charron**, J. Fable.

14. *Sci. phys. et math.* **Vassali Eandi**, A. M. de. Desc. et usage d'un nouv. baromètre portatif, *etc.*; — D'une trombe de terre obs. dans Revel, 1798. — **Sénébier**, J. Sur la différente conducibilité de la chaleur. — **Balbis**, G. B. De crepedis nova specie, *etc.* — **Rossi**, F. Sur les effets des acides nitrique et muriatique oxigéné, employés localement dans le traitement de diff. maladies. — **Vassali Eandi**, A. M. Obs. mét. pendant l'éclipse du soleil an XII à Turin. — **Bellardi**, C. A. L. Sur une espèce de cassia, *etc.* — **Vassali Eandi**, A. M. Sur la nature du fluide galvanique. — **Bonvoisin**, B. Sur les mines de plombagnie des départemens de la Sture et du Pô; — Essais entrepris pour arriver à améliorer l'huile de noix. — **Giobert**, G. A. Sur l'action que le fluide galvanique exerce sur diff. fluides aériformes. — **Rossi**, F. Mém. anat. et phys. — **Balbo**, P. Probl. dipendente dalla teoria delle permutazioni e delle combinazioni. — **Giorna**, E. Sur un poisson accidentellement épineux. — **Rizzetti**, G. G. De phthisi pulmonali specimen chem.-med. — **Brunacci**, V. Sull' uso della variazione delle constanti nell' integrazione a coefficienti variabili. — **Ponza**, L. Coleoptera salutiensia, *etc.* — **De Suffren**, P. Sur le mouvement des cils de l'hyphnum adiantoides. — **Mouxy de Loches**, F., *comte*. D'une résine employée par l'abeille á la construction de ses gâteaux. — **Disderi**, —. Fasciculus entomol. obs., pars 1, 2. — **Cumino**, U. Fungorum vallis Pisii specimen. — **Bossi**, C. L. Sur l'or natif en paillettes que l'on trouve dans les sables.

15. *Lit. et beaux arts.* **Tarin**, V. L'utilité des sci. lit. *etc.*; — Explic. d'un bas-relief ant. — **Bava de San Paolo**, E. Sur les causes de la chûte des lettres aux siècles de l'ère vulgaire, appelés de fer. — **Dépéret**, G. Sur les divers systêmes de versification. — **Pécheux**, L. Du goût en peinture. — **Revel**, —. Sur l'art de bien draper les figures. — **Bava de San Paolo**, E. Dialogo tra morti, cioè tra P. Cornelio e 'l marchese Maffei sopra la tragedia; — Dialogo tra Paracelso, F. Pizarro, e L. Sozzese. — **Regis**, F. Sulla natura dell' eloquenza. — **Galeani Napione di Cocconato**, G. F. Della patria C. Colombo. — **Paroletti**, M. Sur une inscription consulaire trouvée dans la ville de Turin. — **Balbo**, P. Vita di A. V. Papacino d'Antoni. — **Revelli**, V. A. Sulla necessità che corre di rettificare la vista agli allievi disegnatori. — **Galeani Napione di Cocconato**, G. F. Dell' origine delle stampe delle figure in legno. — **Morardo**, G. La luna abitata. — **Franchi-Pont**, G. De' torsi secusini. — **Gerando**, J. M. de. De l'influence de l'esprit de méditation sur les lettres. — **Galeani Napione di Cocconato**, G. F. Della traduzione degli amori di Dafni e Cloe di Longo, *ec.* — **Franchi-Pont**, G. Aggiunta alla dissertazione sui torsi secusini.

16. *Sci. phys. et math.* **Giorna**, E. Des poissons d'espèces nouv. — **Vassali-Eandi**, A. M. de. Obs. mét. faites à l'Obs. de l'Acad. 1787-1807. — **Rizzetti**, G. G. De phthisi pulmonali specimen chem.-med. fasc. secundus. — **Rossi**, F., *and* **Michelotti**, I. Anal. 1e de pus. — **Buniva**, M. F. Résultats d'expér. sur les phénomènes de l'infection, *etc.* — **Paroletti**, M. Sur l'influence que la lumière exerce sur la propagation du son. — **Vassali Eandi**, A. M. de, *and others*. Précis de nouv. expériences galvaniques. — **Brugnone**, J. Obs. anat.-phys. sur le labyrinthe de l'oreille. — **Giorna**, E. Suite du mém. sur les poissons. — **Michelotti**, I. Essai sur la détermination des vîtesses, *etc.* — **Balbis**, G.

B. Miscell. altera botanica. — **Caluso, T. V.**, *l'abbé*. Projet de tables du soleil et de la lune pour d'ancien tems; — De la courbe élastique. — **Brugnone, J.** Sur la digestion dans les oiseaux. — **Giorna, E.** Desc. du Flammant, phænicopterus de Linn. tué en Piémont, 1806. — **Caire-Morand, —.** Sur l'astérie des anciens, *etc.* — **Bidone, G.** Sur la nature de la transcendante $\int \frac{dz}{log.\ z}$; — Méthode pour reconnaître le nombre de solutions qu'admet une équation transcendante à une seule inconnue. — **Rolando, L.** Sur la structure du sphinx Nerii et d'autres insectes. — **Disderi, —.** Obs. variæ entomologicæ. — **Souza Coutinho, R.** de. Sur les problèmes 32 et 34 du tom. III du calcul intégral de M. Euler.

17. *Lit. et beaux-arts.* **Durandi, J.** Sopra alcune recenti scoperte geog. fatte nell' Africa setten. e singolarmente sopra il paese de Garamanti. — **Galeani Napione di Cocconato, G.** Dell' origine dell' Ordine di S. Giovanni di Gerusalemme. — **Dépéret, G.** Du principe de l'harmonie des langues, *etc.* — **Franchi-Pont, G.** Delle antichità di Pollenza, *ec.* — **Galeani Napione di Cocconato G.** Osserv. riguardanti l'origine delle stampe delle figure in legno. — **Regis, F.** Sopra il passaggio di Annibale per le Alpi. — **Morardo, G.** Dell' origine, *ec.*, delle anime umane. — **Corte, A.** Esame delle cagioni per cui molti suppongono non abbia potuto fiorire la tragedia appo gli antichi Romani. — **Roero di Rovello, D.** Scherzo; — La poezia; — Le rovine. — **Bava de San Paolo, E.** Dialogo tra morti, Dante, e Milton; — Dialogo tra Alcibiade e G. Boccacio. — **Galeani Napione di Cocconato, G. F.** Giunte e correzioni all' origine dell' Ordine di S. Giovanni di Gerusalemme. — **Franchi-Pont, G.** Avvertimento circa la diss. delle antichità di Pollenza. — **Mouxy de Loches, F.**, *comte*. Antiquité d'Aix-les-bains. — **Barucchi, P. I.** Discorso delle monete d'Ateen.

18. *Sci. phys. et math.* **Vassali-Eandi, A. M.** de. Mém. hist.; — Eloge hist. de M. Reineri, — de M. Marini, — de M. Giorna. — **Brugnone, J.** Des animaux ruminans, *etc.* — **Rossi, F.**, *and* **Michelotti, V.** Sur la décomposition de l'eau par le moyen de la pile de Volta. — **Rossi, F.** Sur l'asphyxie. — **Bonvoisin, B.** Sur le titane oxidé de la vallée d'Aoste. — **Saluzzo, C.** de. Sur l'extraction et la purification du nitre par la filtration à travers les pores des utensils d'argile ordinaires. — **Bidone, G.** Descr. d'une nouv. boussole propre à obs. les mouvemens de rotation et de translation de l'aiguille aimantée, *etc.* — **Caluso, T. V.**, *l'abbé*. De la trigonométrie rationnelle. — **Bidone, G.** Sur la chaleur du soleil comp. à celle de l'ombre. — **Vassali-Eandi, A. M.** de. Hist. météorol. des années 1807 et 1808, *etc.* — **Brugnone, J.** Des animaux ruminans. 2e mém. — **Balbis, G. B.** Horti Acad. Taurinensis stirpium minus cognitarum, *etc.* — **Buniva, M. F.** Partic. les plus remarquables de deux corné-cailleux anglais nommés J. et R. Lambert, obs. à Turin 1809. — **Bellardi, C. A. L.** Addit. novi generis ad floram Pedemontano-Gallicam. — **Michelotti, V.** Sur la méthode de dernière anal. du gluten. — **Bonelli, F. A.** Obs. entomol. — **Dubois Aymé, —.** De quelques propriétés des rayons de courbure et des développées planes des courbes planes. — **Garneri, H.** Obs. duorum fœtuum uno ovo inclusorum, *etc.* — **Carena, G.** Desc. d'un instrument propre à indiquer et mesurer l'inclinaison des vents à l'horizon, *etc.* — **Rossi-Amatis, G.** Mesure géom. des corps réduite dans la méthode la plus simple et gén. — **Borsarelli, A. E.** Anal. de la plante tagetes lucida de Cavanilles. — **Plana, G. A. A.** Equation de la courbure formée par une lame élastique quelles que soient les forces qui agissent sur la lame; — Sur l'intégration des équations linéaires aux diff. partielles du 2e et 3e ordre. — **Servois, J. F.** De principio velocitatum virtualium commentatio in responsum quæstioni ab illust. Acad. Taurinensi pro 1810 propositæ conscripta.

19. *Lit. et beaux-arts.* **Durandi, J.** Della popolazione d'Italia in circa l'anno di Roma 526; — Sopra l'età in cui la sede ed il culto delle Muse si trasportò dal Monte Olimpo in su quelli del Parnaso, dell' Elicona, Pindo, *ec.*; — Dell' origine dell' diritto regale della caccia. — **Galeani Napione di Cocconato, G. F.**, *conte*. Int. agli antichi terremoti del Piemonte. — **Vernazza, G.** Prima parlata nell' Acad. Imp. di Tor. 1810. — **Bava di San Paolo, E.** Dei progressi e vicende dell' arte della danza o ballo. — **Durandi, J.** Delle antiche contese de' Pastori di Val di Tanaro e di Val d'Arozia e de' politici accidenti sopravenuti. — **Galeani Napione di Cocconato, G. F.**, *conte*. Del manoscritto di Imitatione Christi, detto il Codice di Arona, *etc.* — **Pécheux, L.** Sur l'hist. de l'éponge de Protogène; — Concernant l'anecdote de la ligne d'Apelle sur le tableau de Protogène, citée par Pline livre 35. — **Galeani Napione di Cocconato, G. F.**, *conte*. Intorno alla interpretazione data dal L. Pecheux ad un luogo di Plinio. — **Regis, F.** Intorno alle cagioni della decadenza delle lettere; — Sopra il soggiorno di Annibale a Capoa. — **Galeani Napione di Cocconato, G. F.**, *conte*. Esame critico del primo viaggio di Amerigo Vespucci. — **Paroletti, E.** Sur le caractère et l'étude des deux langues l'italienne et française. — **Corte, A.** Intorno all' interesse personale. — **Franchi Pont, G.** Sopra le scene stabili e mobili degli antichi, *ec.* — **Vernazza, G.** Sur un manuscrit du Romuleon. — **Marenco, V.** Il fonte del Valentino. — **Galeani Napione di Cocconato, G. F.**, *conte*. Delle prime ed. e di un manoscritto delle memorie del Gen. Montecuccoli, *ec.* — **Durandi, J.** Memoria sopra Errico conte d'Asti, e della occidental Liguria; — Schiarimenti sopra la carta del Piemonte antico, e de' secoli mezzani; — Giunta alle Contese de' Pastori di Va di Tanaro. — **Galeani Napione di Cocconato, G. F.**, *conte*. Giunta e correzioni intorno al manoscritto di I. C. detto il Codice di Arona, *ec.*; — Giunte e correz. all' esame crit. del primo viaggio di A. Vespucci. — **Franchi Pont, G.** Aggiunte alla crit. sopra le scene stabili e mobili degli antichi, *ec.* — **Pullini, C. A.**, *abate*. Saggio di antiche gemme incise, *ec.*

20. *Sci. phys. et math.* **Vassali-Eandi, A. M.** Mém. historique; — Obs. météorologiques faites sur la mer Atlantique, *etc.*, par Garola; — Rapport sur la descr. d'un tourbillon à Viguzzolo, 1804, par Mme. M. Garimberti Leardi. — **Objets** d'hist. nat. presentés à l'Acad. — **Machines**, instrumens, et ouvrages d'arts présentés à l'Acad. — **Rossi, F.**, *and* **Balbis, G. B.** Rap. sur un fœtus monstrueux. — **Bidone, G.** La cause des ricochets que font les pierres, *etc.*, lancés obliquement sur la surface de l'eau. — **Zach, F.** de. Le degré du méridien mesuré en Piémont par G. Beccaria. — **Michelotti, V.** La préparation de l'indigo. — **Bidone, G.** Mém. sur diverses intégrales définies. — **Carena, G.** Descr. d'un nouveau baromètre pour les aëronautes. — **Plana, G. A. A.** Sur divers problèmes de probabilité; — Obs. de l'opposition de Jupiter, 1813. — **Vassali-Eandi, A. M.**, *and others*. Expériences et obs. conc. les effets de divers poisons sur les animaux. — **Bonelli, F. A.** Obs. entomologiques. — **Plana, G. A. A.** Mém. sur le mouvement d'une ligne d'air, *etc.* — **Saissy, J. A.** Obs. sur quelques mammifères hibernans. — **Vagnon, A.** Sur le corindon rougejaunâtre de Traverselle, *etc.* — **Lavini, G.** Mém. sur le poison du laurier-cerise. — **Ravina, F.** Spec. de motu cerebri.

21. *Lit. et beaux-arts.* **Saluzzo, C.** Not. intorno alla vita di G. B. Vigo. — **Bava di San Paolo, E.** Progressi dell' economia pubblica e polit. dal mille sino a tutto il secolo 18o. — **Paroletti, M.** Sur la mort du surintendant Foucquet. — **Marenco, V.** Rifless. sopra la prosodia metrica italiana. — **Roero di Rovello, D.** La navigazione; ode ad A. Etrusca. — **Galeani Napione di Cocconato, G. F.** Osserv. intorno ad alcune antiche monete del Piemonte. — **Valpera, T.** In luctu egregii adolescentis F. Balbi. — **Roero di Rovello, D.** Elegia in morte del padre. — **Vernazza, G.** Recensio nummorum qui Secusii anno 1812 sunt reperti. — **Bava di San Paolo, E.** Progressi dell' arte poetica. — **Vernazza, G.** Not. di lettere ined. del conte B. Castiglione; — Vita di Giambatista di Savoja, e not. delle sue monete. — **Roero di Rovello, D.** Canzone ad Apollo. — **Botta, C.** La Camilleide, *ec.* — **Vernazza, G.** Inscr. Caietana emendata. — **Grassi, F.** In comitem Salutium Acad. Taurinensis Scientiarum et Artium nedum præsidem, *etc.* — **Vernazza, G.** Lapida romana. — **Millin, L. A.** Mém. sur quelques pierres gravées qui représentent l'enlèvement du Palladium. — **Gråberg af Hemsö, J.** Doutes et conjectures sur les Bohémiens et leur première apparition en Europe.

22. **Vassali-Eandi, A. M.** Mém. historique. — **Extrait** des procès-verbaux de la classe des sci. phys. et mathématiques. — **Saluzzo, C.** Atti compendiati della classe di letteratura, 1809–14. — **Livres** et autres imprimés presentés à l'Acad., 1813–14. — **Objets** d'hist. naturelle, machines, instrumens, et ouvrages d'arts présentés à l'Acad., 1813–14. — **Plana, G. A. A.** Mém. sur la latitude et la longitude de l'observatoire de Turin. — **Carena, G.** Sur le givre figuré dont se couvrent les vitres, *etc.* — **Disderi, S.** Vespæ Gallicæ historia. — **Gergonne, J. D.** Mém. sur le cercle tangent à trois cercles données, *etc.* — **Bava di San Paolo, E.** Contin. de progressi della poesia. — **Galeani Napione di Cocconato, G. F.** Vita di F. Asinari. — Indice degli autori, 1759–1814. — Indice degli autori i lavori de quali sono nella parte storica dei volumi accademici. — Indice generale, 1759–1814.

23. **Vassali-Eandi, A. M.** Annali della R. Accad. d. Sci., 1815–18. — **Stato** del R. Accad., 1818. — Libri presentati alla R. Accad., 1815–18. — **Macchine,** stromenti, *ec.*, presentate alla R. Accad. — **Carena, G.** Not. intorno ai lavori della classe di sci. mat. e fis., 1815–17. — Sci. mat. — Sci. fis. — *Sci. fis. e mat.* **Maistre, X.** de. Mém. sur l'oxidation de l'or par le frottement. — **Plana, G. A. A.** Mém. sur les intégrales définies. — **Jurine, L.** Obs. sur le xenos vesparum. — **Giraudo, H.** Disquisitiones in veram testium e lumbis in scrotum descen-

sus caussam. — **Rossi, F.** Sur les miasmes, *etc.* — **Balbis, G. B.** Elenchus recentiorum stirpium quas Pedemontanæ floræ addendas censet B. — **Carena, G.** Elogio di V. A. Gioanetti. — **Bellingeri, C. F.** Esper. ed osserv. sul galvinismo. — **Vieillot, L. P.** Mém. pour servir à l'hist. des oiseaux d'Europe. — **Bonelli, F. A.** Mém. sur l'eurychile, *etc.* — **Cisa di Gresi, T. A.** Consid. sur l'équilibre des surfaces flexibles et inextensibles. — **Bidone, G.** Mém. sur les transcendantes elliptiques. — **Biroli, G.** De nova phyteumatis specie. — **Vassali-Eandi, A. M.** Osserv. meteorol. fatte alla specola della R. Accad., 1817. — **Plana, G. A. A.** Obs. astron. faites à l'observatoire de l'Acad. Roy. d. Sci. — **Maistre, X. de.** Procédé pour composer avec l'oxide d'or une couleur pourpre, *etc.* — **Vassali-Eandi, A. M.** Sopra il tremuoto, 1818. — *Sci., mor. stor., e filol.* **Franchi di Pont, G.** Illustr. di un vaso di bronzo nel R. Museo d'antichita di Torino. — **Giobert, G. A.** Dell' aratro degli antichi paragonato coll' aratro piemontese. — **Vernazza, G.** Diploma di Adriano; — App. 1. Diplomata imperatorum, *etc.*; — App. 2. Classiariæ inscriptiones selectæ. — **Corte di Bonvicino, G. A.** Dissert. sulle sibille. — **Galeani Napione di Cocconato, G. F.** Paragone tra la caduta dell' Impero Romano e gli evenimenti del fine dello scorso secolo 18; — Di un antico diploma del secolo 11. — **Peyron, V. A.** In Theodosii Alexandrini tractatum de prosodia. — **Vernazza, G.** Anulus illustratus postridie calendas Junii, 1816; — Della città d'Industria. — **Galeani Napione di Cocconato, G. F.** Osserv. intorno al 'Pensieri sulla istoria', *ec.*, di M. Delfico. — **Vernazza, G.** Lapida romana in Cagliari inedita. — Indice, v. 1–22.

24. Elenco degli accademici. — Doni fatti alla R. Accad. d. Sci., 1818–20. — *Sci. fis. e mat.* **Damoiseau, M. C. T.** Mém. sur l'époque du retour au périhélie de la comète de 1759. — **Cisa de Grési, T. A.** Demonstr. des formules de Gauss pour déterminer le jour de Pâque suivant les deux calendriers Julien et Grégorien. — **Bellingeri, C. F.** Sull' elettricità del sangue nelle malattie; — Sulla elettricità dei liquidi minerali. — **Borson, S.** Mém. sur des mâchoires et des dents du mastodonte trouvées fossiles en Piémont. — **Jurine, L.** Obs. sur les ailes des hyménoptères. — **Rolando, L.** Osserv. sul peritoneo e sulla pleura. — **Vassali-Eandi, A. M.** La meteorologia torinese. — **Bidone, G.** Mém. sur les transcendantes elliptiques, 2e pte. — **Gravenhorst, J. L. C.** Monographia ichneumonum Pedemontanæ regionis. — **Plana, G. A. A.** Solution de problèmes relatifs à la loi de l'attraction exercée sur un point matériel par le cercle, *etc.* — **Carena, G.** Elogio di C. G. Brugnone. — **Bellingeri, C. F.** Mém. sull' elettricità dell' orina. — **Lavini, G.** Contin. sopra le ricerche fisico-chimiche de' prodotti del prunus lauro-cerasus di Linneo, *ec.* — **Bonelli, F. A.** Descr. d'une nouvelle espèce de poisson de la Méditerranée, *etc.* — **Cisa de Gresi, T. A.** Mém. sur le mouvement de rotation d'un corps autour de son centre de gravité. — **Biroli, G.** Phyteuma charmelioides descriptum et icone illustratum. — *Sci. mor., stor., e filol.* **Galeani Napione di Cocconato, G. F.** App. all' esame crit. del primo viaggio di A. Vespucci al nuovo mondo. — **Balbo, P.** Disc. intorno alla fertilità del Piemonte. — **Grassi, G.** Not. intorno ad un operetta ined. del principe R. Montecuccoli, *ec.*

5. Elenco degli accademici. — **Vassali-Eandi, A. M.** Ragguaglio di efemeridi medico-meteorologiche. — Doni fatti alla R. Accad., 1820-21. — **Carena, G.** Not. dei lavori della classe di sci. fis. e mat. — *Sci. fis. e mat.* **Bellingeri, C. F.** Sulla proprietà elettrica dei solidi animali. — **Lavini, G.** Ricerche chim. e med. sul crithmum maritimum. — **Bidone, G.** Expériences sur le remou et la propagation des ondes. — **Plana, G. A. A.** Note sur la théorie des ondes donnée par Poisson. — **Balbo, P.**, *and* **Vasco, A.** Rel. sopra un nuovo pestatojo da canapa. — **Mouxy Deloche, F.** Des causes qui déterminent les abeilles à construire leurs gateaux parallèlement en ligne droit, *etc.* — **Borson, S.** Saggio di orittografia piemontese. — **Zumstein, J.** Voy. sur le Mont-Rose, et première ascension sur le sommet mérid. confinant avec le Piémont. — **Ferrero della Marmora, A.** Mém. sur deux oiseaux, *etc.* — **Risso, A.** Mém. sur deux nouvelles espèces de poissons, *etc.*; — Mém. sur une nouveau genre de poisson. — **Carena, H.** Monographie du genre hirudo. — Elogio de F. Sammartino della Motta. — **Colla, L.** Mém. sul genere musa e monografia. — **Plana, G. A. A.** Note sur une nouvelle expression analytique des nombres Bernouilliens, *etc.* — **Balbo, P.** Parere della R. Accad. d. Sci. intorno alle misure e ai pesi distese dal P. B. 1816. — *Sci. mor., stor., e filol. Wanting.*

26. Elenco degli accademici. — **Vassali-Eandi, A. M.** Mem. istor. intorno alla vita ed. agli studi di G. Cigna. — *Sci. fis. e mat.* **Avogadro di Quaregna, A.** Nouv. consid. sur la théorie des proportions déterminées dans les combinaisons, *etc.* — **Borella, B.** Cenni d'ortopedia. — **Cisa di Gresi, T. A.** Mém. sur les intégrales définies. — **Borson, S.** Contin. del saggio di orittografia piemontese. — **Michelotti, V.** Saggio intorno ad alcuni fenomeni elettromagnetici e chimici. — **Canobbio, G. B.** Mem. sulla composizione chimica di diverse specie di borace brutto di Levante. — **Gravenhorst, J. L. C.** De natura vegetabili gorgoniarum. — **Michelotti, V.** Descr. di una particolare batteria Voltiana. — **Avogadro di Quaregna, A.** Mém. sur la manière de ramener les composés organiques aux lois ordinaires des proportions déterminées. — **Colla, A.** Ad vebascum Cisalpinum a J. Biroli Novariensi descriptum. — **Plana, G. A. A.** Note sur l'intégrale équation $\frac{d^2 y}{dx^2} + gx^m . y = 0$. — **Rolando, L.** Descr. d'un animal nouveau qui appartient à la classe des echinodermes. — **Plana, G. A. A.** Add. à la note sur l'intégrale de l'équation $\frac{d^2 y}{dx^2} + gx^m . y = 0$. — *Sci. mor., stor., e. filol.* **Peyron, V. A.** Del territorio Piraico: illustr. del luogo di Tucidide lib. 3. no. 91. — **Boucheroni, C.** De J. Vernazza Albensi.

27. Elenco degli accademici. — Doni fatti all' Accad. Reale d. Sci., 1822 - 23. — **Carena, G.** Not. intorno ai lavori della classe di sci. fis. e mat., 1822. — Indice degli articoli della precedente notizia. — *Sci. fis. e. mat.* **Michelotti, V.** Contin. del saggio intorno ad alcuni fenomeni elettromagnetici, *ec.* — **Borson, S.** Note sur des dents du grand mastodonte trouvées en Piémont, *etc.* — **Avogadro di Quaregna, A.** Mém. sur la construction d'un voltimètre multiplicateur, *etc.* — **Bidone, G.** Expériences sur divers cas de la contraction de la veine fluide, *etc.* — **Rossi, F.** Osserv. intorno a due porzione di sanguisuga. — **Plana, G. A. A.** Recherches analytiques sur la densité des conches de l'atmosphère, *etc.* — **Colla, A.** Illustr. generis dysodii, *etc.* — *Sci., mor., stor., e filol.* **Sauli d'Igliano, L.** Del Cavaliere errante, romanza di Tommaso III., marchese di Saluzzo. — **Galeani Napione di Cocconato, G.** Della patria di C. Colombo. — **Raymond, G. M.** Eloge de J. de Maistre. — **Peyron, V. A.** Del comando militare θέσθε τὰ ὅπλα. — **Cordero de' Conti Sanquintino, G.** De' marmi lunensi. — **Galeani Napione di Cocconato, G.** Not. di un opera poetica pastorale di G. Britonio; — Dei templarj e dell' abolizione dell' ordine loro.

28. Elenco degli Accademici. — Doni fatti all' Accad., 1823–24. — *Sci. fis. e mat.* **Carena, G.** Not. intorno ai lavori della classe di sci. fis. e. mat., 1823. — *Mem.* **Avogadro di Quaregna, A.** Sur l'affinité des corps pour le calorique, *etc.* — **Bellingeri, C. F.** De medulla spinali nervisque ex ea prodeuntibus. — **Libri, G.** Mém. sur divers points d'analyse. — **Bidone, G.** Expériences sur la dépense de reversoirs, *etc.* — **Carena, G.** Suppl. à la monographie du genre hirudo. — *Sci. mor., stor., e filol.* **Grassi, G.** Elogia di G. B. Piacenza. — *Mem.* **Galeani Napione di Cocconato, G.** Della scienza militare di E. Colonna, *ec.* — **Omodei, F.** Del petardo di guerra. — **Peyron, V. A.** Codicis Theodosiani fragm. ined. — **Gazzera, C.** Osserv. bibliog. letterarie intorno ad un' operetto falsamente ascritta al Petrarca.

29. Elenco degli accademici. — Doni fatti all' Accad., 1824-25. — *Sci. fis. e mat.* **Carena, G.** Not. intorno ai lavori della classe di sci. fis. e mat., 1824. — *Mem.* **Rolando, L.** Recherches anat. sur la moelle alongée. — **Avogadro di Quaregna, A.** Deuxième mém. sur l'affinité des corps pour le calorique, *etc.* — **Rolando, L.** Osserv. sul cervelletto. — **Losana, M.** De animalculis infusoriis. — **Cantù, G. L.** Essai de l'existence du iode dans les eaux minérales sulfureuses, *etc.*; — Specimen chemico-medicum de mercurii præsentia in urinis syphyliticorum, mercurialem curationem potientium. — **Canobio, G.** Sperienze analitiche sopra un fluido latteo reso dalle vie urinarie. — **Bonelli, F. A.** Sopra un ippopotamo del Museo di Torino. — **Borson, S.** Contin. del saggio di orittografia piemontese. — *Sci. mor., stor., e filol.* **Cordero de' Conte Sanquintino, G.** De' più antichi marmi statuari adoperati per la scultura in Italia. — **Balbo, P.** Del metro sessagesimale antica misura Egizia rinnovata in Piemonte. — **Randoni, C.** Sulla prospettiva degli antichi. — **Vernazza, G.** Not. d'un pittore a servizio della corte di Savoja. — **Barucchi, P. I.** Sopra una medaglia greca in bronzo di Caracalla. — **Gazzera, C.** Not. di una sconosciuta edizione piemontese delle 'Eroidi' di Ovidio del secolo 15. — **Peyron, V. A.** Saggio di studi sopra papiri, codici cofti, *ec.* — **Gazzera, C.** Applicazione delle dottrine di Champollion minore ad alcuni monumenti geroglifici del Museo Egizio. — **Cordero de' Conte Sanquintino, G.** Sopra alcune iscrizioni antichi fra le ruine di Libarna, *ec.*; — Descr. delle medaglie imperiali alessandrine ined., *ec.* — **Balbo, P.** Lezioni intorno alla storia della Università di Torino. — **Galeani Napione di Cocconato, G.** Not. di un manoscritto miniato già appartenente a Francesco I., Re di Francia. — **Cordero de' Conte Sanquintino, G.**

Osserv. intorno all' età, ed alla persona rappresentata dal maggiore colosso del R. Museo Egiziano di Torino; — Interp. e confronto di una bilingue iscrizione sopra una mummia egiziana nel R. Museo di Torino.

30. Elenco degli accad. — Doni fatti all' Accad., 1825–26. — *Sci. fis. e mat.* **Carena, G.** Intorno ai lavori della classe di scienze fisiche e mathemat. nel corso dell' anno 1825; — Notizie biog. del A. M. de Vassalli Eandi. — *Mem.* **Rossi, F.** Osserv. anatomico patol. con esperienze sopra l'idrofobia e sobra la rabbia. — **Bellingeri, C. F.** Exper. in nervorum antagonismum. — **Michelotti, V.** Sur le plomb carbonaté de la mine de Monteponi dans la Sardaigne. — **Poletti, G.** Nuovo metodo per determinare le radici immaginarie delle equazioni numeriche. — **Avogadro de Quaregna,** Sur la densité des corps solides et liquides, *etc.* — **Rossi, F.** De nonnullis monstruositatibus in internis humani corporis partibus. — **Bonelli, F. A.** Desc. di sei nuove specie d'insetti dell' ordine dei lepidoteri diurni. — **Michelotti, V.,** *and* **Giobert, G. A.** Sopra qualche fenomeno elettrico. — **Bidone, G.** Sur la propagation du remous. — **Bellingeri, C. F.** Exper. phys. in medullam spinalem. — *Sci. mor. stor. e fil.* **Raymond, G. M.** Des principaux systêmes de notation musicale. — **Galeani Napione di Cocconato, G. F.,** *conte.* Della iscrizione e dei bassi rilieve dell' arco di Susa; — Giunta alle mem. intorno al luogo di Plinio in cui narra la contesa tra Apollo e Protogene. — **Balbo, P.** Del metro sessagesimale, lezione III. — **Bidone, G.,** *and* **Plana, G. A. A.** Rapport, priés par le prés. de comparer avec le mètre l'ancienne coudée trouvée à Memphis. — **Datta, P.** Di Abbone fondatore del monastero novalicense, e del preteso suo patriziato. — **Barucci, P. I.** Sopra una moneta d'oro di Odoacre Re d'Italia. — **Omodei, F.** Delle spingarde; — Delle Colubrine. — **Hammer Purgstall, J.** Notizia di diciotto codici persiani della biblioteca della Regia Univ. di Torino.

31. *Mat. e fis.* Elenco degli accad. — Doni fatti all' Accad., 1826–27. — **Carena, G.** Intorno ai lavori della classe di scienze mat. e fisiche, nell' anno 1826. — *Mem.* **Avogadro de Quaregna, A.** Sur la densité des corps solides et liquides. 2e mém. — **Rossi, F.** 2e essai sur les miasmes. — **Colla, I.** Illust. et icones rariorum stirpium quæ in ejus horto Ripulis florebant, 1824. — **Losana, M.** Sopra la milza, *ec.* — **Poletti, G.** Sopra il movimento di un corpo considerato come un punto, *ec.* — **Re, G. F.** Ad floram Pedemontanam appendix altera. — **Cisa de Gresi, T. A.** Sur la décomposition des fractions exponentielles en fractions partielles à l'infini. **Borson, S.** Intorno alle sostanze di cui sono formati i monumenti del Reg. Museo Egizio, *ec.* — **Bellingeri, C. F.** In electricitatem sanguinis, urinæ, et bilis animalium experimenta habita. — **Colla, A.** Illust. et icones rariorum stirpium, *etc.*, addita ad Hortum Ripulensem append. II. — **Plana, G. A. A.** Note sur un mém. de M. de la Place 'Sur les deux grandes inégalités de Jupiter et Saturne', *etc.*; — Sur l'intégration de l'équation linéaire ..... dans le cas particulier où le polynome .... renferme un nombre quelconque de racines égales; — Addit. rel. à première partie de l'écrit intitulé, Note sur un mém., *etc.* — **Poletti, G.** Risoluzione gen. di qualunque probl. indeterm. di secondo grado a tre incognite. — *Mor. stor. e fil.* **Barucci, P. I.** Sopra un quinaro d'oro di Pertinace, ed un chiodo di bronzo, trovati in Acqui. — **Peyron, V. A.,** *l'abbé.* Papyri Græci Reg. Musei Ægyptii Taurinensis. — **Balbo, P.** Del metro sessagesimale, lezione IV. — **Galeani Napione di Cocconato, G. F.,** *conte.* Notizia ed. illust. di una carta dell' anna MXXXVI, da cui resulta, che Unberto I., *ec.*; — Interpretazione di un luogo del primo canto dell' Inferno di Dante.

32. Elenco degli accad. — Doni fatti alla Accad., 1827–28. — **Plana, G. A. A.** Obs. astron. faites en 1822-25 à l'Obs. Roy. de Turin. — **Indice,** v. 23–32.

33. Elenco degli accad. — Doni fatti alla Accad. — *Sci. fis. e mat.* **Carena, G.** Notiz. stor. dei lavori della cl. di scienza fisiche e mat. negli 1827, 28; — Elogio storico dell' acad. dottore L. Bellardi. — *Mem.* **Losana, M.** De animalculis microscopicis seu infusoriis. — **Avogadro de Quaregna, A.** Compar. des obs. de Mr. Dulong sur les pouvoirs réfringens des corps gaseux, avec les formules de relation entre ces pouvoirs et les affinités pour le calorique, déduites des chaleurs spécifiques. — **Colla, A.** Illust. et icones rariorum stirpium, *etc.* Append. III. — **Cantu, G. L.** Sur une nouv. mine de manganèse trouv. dans. la vallée de Lanzo, commune d'Ala. — **Borson, S.** Sur quelques fossiles de la Tarantaise en Savoye. — **Lavini, G.** Anal. de la cendre du Vésuve de l'éruption de 1822. — **Bellingeri, C. F.** In electricitatem salivæ, muci, et puris simplicis, *etc.* — **Re, J. F.** Reliquiæ Bellardianæ. — **Avogadro de Quaregna, A.** Sur la loi de la force élastique de l'air par rapport à sa densité dans le cas de compression sans perte de calorique, *etc.* — **Cisa de Gresi, T. A.** Sur le probl. de la perturbation des planètes. — **Plana, G. A. A.** Méthode élémentaire pour découvrir et démontrer la possibilité des nouv. théorèmes sur la théorie des transcendantes elliptiques publiés par Mr. Jacobi. — **Cisa di Gresi, T. A.** Addit. au précéd. mém. sur la problème de la perturbation des planètes. — *Sci. mor., stor., e. fil.* **Peyron, V. A.,** *l'abbé.* Papyri Græci Regii musei Ægyptii Taurinensis. — **Sclopis de Salerano, F. P.,** *conte.* De' Longobardi in Italia. — **Galeani Napione di Cocconato, G. F.,** *conte.* Del regale della zecca in Italia nei secoli X e XI. — **Barucci, P. I.** Dei tripodi in generale, ed in partic. di quello d' industria. — **Peyron, V. A.,** *l'abbé.* Illust. di due papiri greco egizi dell' Imp. R. Museo di Vienna. — **Gazzera, C.** Iscrizione metrica vercellese. — **Galeani Napione di Cocconato, G. F.,** *conte.* Dissertazione seconda intorno al codice De imitatione Christi.

34. Elenco degli accad. — Doni fatti all' Accad. — Mutazioni nel corps Accad., *etc.* — *Sci. mat. e fis.* **Programme** del premio proposto dalla cl. delle scienze fisiche mat. nel mese di giugno, 1829. — **Carena, G.** Notizia storica intorno ai lavori della cl. di scienze mat. e fisiche nel corso dell' anno 1829. — *Mem.* **Plana, G. A. A.** Sur la partie du coëfficient de la grande inégalité de Jupiter et Saturne qui dépend du carré de la force perturbatrice. — **Balbo, P.** Saggi di aritmetica politica e di pubblica economia. — **Lavini, G.** Sur un sel double d'argent et de fer. — **Avogadro de Quaregna, A.** Sur les pouvoirs neutralisans des différens corps simples, *etc.* — **Rossi, F.** Osserv. anat. e patol. sull' organo della vista, *etc.* — **Bidone, G.** Sur la forme et la direction des veines et des courans d'eau, lancés par diverses ouvertures; — Sur la détérmination théorique de la section contractée des veines liquides. — *Sci. mor., stor., e fil.* **Sclopis de Salerana, F. P.,** *comte.* Rapport sulla 'Dell' industria delle sete ne' Regii Stati'. — **Peyron, V. A.,** *l'abbé.* Illust. d'una stele greca del Reg. Museo Egizio di Torino. — **Gazzera, C.** Il Castello di Bodincomago diverso dalla città d' Industria. — **Sclopis de Salerana, F. P.,** *comte.* Consid. storiche intorno a Tommaso I., conte di Savoja; con aggiunta di documenti inediti. — **Lencisa, F.** Sopra l'industria delle sete nei Reg. Stati. — **Vernazza, G.** Consid. sopra la salvaguardia di Talloires, del 1397. — **Manno, G.,** *barone.* Saggio sull' indifferenza, *ec.*

35. Elenco degli accad. — Doni fatti all' Accad. — Mutazioni accadute nel corps accad. dopo la pub. del prec. vol. — *Sci. nat. e fis.* **Plana, G. A. A.** Sur le calcul de la partie du coëff. de la grande inégalité de Jupiter et Saturne, *etc.* — **Poletti, G.** Exposizione di un altro metodo per determ. le radici immaginarie delle equazioni numeriche, *ec.* — **Hildebrandt, F.** Esper. fatti allo scopo di ritrovare un metodo più opportuno per conservare alcune preparazioni anat. e patolog. e vantaggi ottenuti dal H. — **Rolando, L.** Della struttura degli emisferi cerebrali. — **Colla, A.** Addita ad Hortum Ripulensem appendice IV. — **Michelotti, V.** Sur la composition de l'or natif de Piémont. — **Bonino, G. G.** Essai statistique sur la mortalité dans les anciens troupes de S. M. le Roi de Sardaigne en temps de paix. — **Rolando, L.** Del passagio dei fluidi allo stato di solidi organici, *ec.* — **Cisa de Gresi, T. A.** Sur quelques formules dans le mém. sur le probl. de la perturbation des planètes. — **Plana, G. A. A.** Addit. à la note sur la partie du coëff. de la grande inégalité de Jupiter et Saturne qui dépend du carré de la force perturbatrice. — *Sci. mor., stor., e fil.* **Gazzera, C.** Di un decreto di patronato e clientela della C. G. A. Usellis, *ec.* — **Galeani Napioni di Cocconato, G.** Consid. intorno alla ristaurazione delle scienze di stato seguita in Italia, circa la metà del sec. XIV. — **Ferrero della Marmora, A.** Desc. e spiegazione di tre idoletti di bronzo ritrovati in Sardegna. — **Carena, G.** Pensieri sull' istinto tanto negli animali che nell' uomo. — **Baille, L.** Lezione intorne ad un diploma di demissione militare dell' Imp. Nerva, ritrovato in Sardegna. — **Gazzera, C.** Notizia di alcuni nuovi diplomi imp. di congedo militare, e ricerche int. al consolato di Tiberio Catio Frontone.

36. Elenco degli accad. — Mutazioni accadute nel corpo accad., *ec.* — Doni fatti alla Accad. — *Sci. mat. e fis.* **Carena, G.** Notizia storico intorno ai lavori della cl. di scienze fis. e mat. dal 1830 a tutto il 1831. — **Colla, L.** Elogio storico dell' accad. prof. G. B. Balbis. — *Mem.* **Sismonda. A.** Essai géognostique dans les deux vallées voisines de Stura et de Vinay. — **Lavini, G.** Sur deux nouv. sels doubles d'argent et de fer; — Anal. de l'eau de St. Genis dans le but partic. de déterm. la proportion de l'jode. — **Borson, S.** Sur quelques ossemens fossiles trouvés en Piémont. — **Plana, G. A. A.** Sur le développement des termes du cinquième ordre qui font partie du coëff. de la grande inégalité de Jupiter et Saturne. — **Moris, G.** Illust. rariorum stirpium horti botanici R. Univ. Taurin. — **Lavini, G.** Sur les altérations de la bile extraite du

cadavre d'une femme qui était affectée de manie. — **Rio, N. da.** Sur le gissement des trachytes en gén., *etc.* — **Avogadro de Quaregna, A.** Sur la force élastique de la vapeur du mercure à diff. températures. — **Gené, G.** Mem. per servire alla storia naturale di una specie di cecidomia che vive sugli iperici. — **Cantù, G. L.** Saggio chim.-med. sulla presenza simultanea del prussiato di ferro, *ec.* — **Gené, G.** Intorno alla tiliguerta o caliscertula di Cetti. — *Sci. mor., stor., e fil.* Programmi, *ec.* — **Manno, G.**, *barone.* Delle politico e delle lettere. — **Galeani Napione di Cocconato, G. F.**, *conte.* Notizia delle antiche biblioteche della Real Casa di Savoia. — **Cibrario, G. A. L.** Delle finanze della monarchia di Savoia nei secoli XIII e XIV. — **Cordero de' Conti San-quintino, G.** Intorno ad alcune cose antiche dissotterate in Torino, 1830–31. — **Cibrario, G. A. L.** Delle finanze delle monarchia di Savoia; discorso 2o.

37. Elenco degli accad. — Mutazioni accadute nel corpo accad., *ec.* — Adunanza gen. onorata dalla Maesta del Re, 31 ottobre, 1833. — Doni fatti alla Accad. — *Sci. fis. e mat.* **Carena, G.** Notizia intorno ai lavori della cl. di scienze fis. e mat. 1832–33; — Notizie biog. dell' accad. cav. Vichard di Sanreal; — Dell' accad. prof. S. Borson; — Dell' accad. conte A. Vagnone. — *Mem.* **Losana, M.** Sur l'os hyoïde de quelques reptiles. — **Lavini, G.** Sur divers produits des vers-à-soie. — **Colla, A.** Plantæ rariores in regionibus Chilensibus. — **Lavini, G.** Esame fis.-chim. delle sostanze trovate nell' interno d'alcune urne negli scavi attorno a Torino, 1830, 31. — **Sismonda, A.** Anal. d'une idiocrase violette de la vallée d'Ala. — **Moris, G.** Plantæ Chilensis novæ minusve cognitæ. — **La Marmora, A. de.** Déterm. et descr. des diff. d'âge de l'Aigle Bonelli. — **Gené, G.** Elogio storico di F. A. Bonelli. — **Bellingeri, C. F.** Elogio storico del L. Rolando. — **Gené, G.** Sur quelques particularités organiques du chamois et des moutons. — **Lavini. G.** Anal.-chim. della farina di fromento, *ec.* — **Capelli, P.** Alcune riflessione sul circolo-meridiano dell' osserv. di Torino. — **Gené, G.** Descr. di una singolare varietà di pecora a coda adiposa e della femmina del becco selvatico dell' Alto Egitto; — Descr. de quelques espèces de la collection zoologique de Turin. — **Losana, M.** Saggio sopra le formiche indigene del Piemonte. — — *Sci. mor., stor., e fil.* Programma, *ec.* — **Cordero di Conti Sanquinto, G.** Desc. della medaglie dei nómi ossia delle antiche province e città dell' Egitto. — **Dureau de Lamalle, A. J. C. A.** Examen des causes gén. qui, chez les Grecs et Romains, dûrent s'opposer au développement de la population, *etc.* — **Gazzera, C.** Intorno alle zecche e ad alcune rare monete degli antichi marchesi de Ceva, d'Incisa, e del Carretto. — **Manno, G.**, *barone.* Saggio di alcune espressione figurate, e maniere di dire vivaci della barbara latinità. — **Cibrario, G. A. L.** Delle finanze della monarchiadi Savoja, *ec.*; discorso terzo.

38. Elenco degli accad. — Mutazioni accadute nel corpo accad., *ec.* — Doni fatti alla Accad. — *Sci. fis. e. mat.* **Carena, G.** Notizia intorno ai lavori della cl. della sci. fis. e mat., 1834–35. — **Barbanti, C.** Livello a cannochiale. — **Giobert, G. A.** Cenni biog. — **Lavini, G.** Découverte du sulfate de magnésie dans la chaux sulfatée de Piobesi. — **Sobrero, C.** Nuova sostanza minerale che accompagna il manganese di San Marcello. — **Moris, G.** Plantæ novæ aut minus cognitæ. — **Colla, A.** Plantæ rariores in regionibus Chilensibus. Fasc. IV et V. — **Moris, G.** Plantæ Chilensis novæ aut minus cognitæ. Fasc. III. — **La Marmora, A. de.** Obs. géol. sur les deux iles Baléares; Majorque et Minorque. — **Sobrero, C.** Sur les méthodes suivies dans les fonderies de bronze pour l'artillerie, *ec.* — **De Michelis, F.** Intorno la natura mucosa della membrana interna del sistema vasale. — **Lavini, G.** Sur le byssus de la 'pinna nobilis'. — **Colla, A.** Plantæ rariores, *etc.* Fasc. VI. — **Sismonda, A.** Osserv. geologiche sulla valle di Susa. — **Savi, G.** Sull' 'origanum Majorana, Creticum', *etc.* — **Rossi, F.** 3e essai sur les miasmes. — **Savi, P.** Osserv. sugli organi sessuali del genere 'stapelia'. — **Plana, G. A. A.** Sur le mouvement d'un pendule dans un milieu résistant. — *Sci. mor., stor., e fil.* **Borghese, B.** Dichiarazione d'una lapida Gruteriana per cui si determina il tempo della prefettura urbana di Pasifilo, *ec.* — **Arri, G. A.** Lapide fenicia di Nora in Sardegna. — **La Marmora, A. de.** Sopra alcune monete fenicie delle isole Baleari. — **Omodei, F.** Dell' origine della polvere da guerra, *ec.* — **Gazzera, C.** Dichiarazione di un dittico consolare ined. della chiesa cattedrale della città di Aosta. — **Balbo, C.** Dei titoli e della potenza dei conti, *ec.*, dell' Italia settentrionale. — **Cibrario, G. A. L.** Appendice. Dei conti d'Asti ne' secoli IX, X, XI. — **Manno, G.**, *barone.* Della libertà dei giudizi storici sopra i morti. — **Sclopis de Salerana, F. P.**, *conte.* Della legislazione civile.

39. Elenco degli accad. — Mutazioni accadute nel corpo accad., *ec.* — Doni fatti alla Accad., 1835–36. — *Sci. fis. e mat.* **Carena, G.** Notizia intorno ai lavori della cl. della scienze fis. e mat., 1835–36. *Mem.* **Colla, A.** Plantæ rariores in regionibus Chilensibus, Fasc. VII. — **Avogadro de Quaregna, A.** Sur le pouvoir neutralisant de quelques corps simples. — **Botto, G. D.** Sur une machine locomotive, mise en mouvement par l'électro-magnétisme. — **Gené, G.** De quibusdam insectis Sardiniæ, *etc.* — **Lavini, G.** Examen chim. de l'eau contenue dans un puits de Gaurène. — **De Notaris, G.** Mantissa muscorum ad floram Pedemontanam. — **Sismonda, A.** Intorno ad alcune valli delle Alpi del Piemonte. — *Sci. mor., stor., e fil.* — **Baïlle, L.** Not. di un nuovo congedo militare. — **Barucchi, P. I.** Sopra una moneta greco-egizia del R. Museo d'Antichità, *ec.* — **Arri, G. A.** In quosdam Abbasidarum numos atque in alia monumenta arabico-cufica. — **Promis, D. C.** Monete ossidionali del Piemonte. — **Omodei, F.** Intorno all' istoria de' razzi. — **Cavedoni, C.** Sul tipo rappresentante gli orti di Alcinoo nelle monete di Corcira, *ec.* — **Baudi di Vesme, C.**, *and* **Fossati, S.** Vicende della proprietà in Italia dalla caduta dell' Imperio Romano fino allo stabilimento dei feudi.

40. Elenco degli accad. — Mutazioni accadute nel corpo accad. — Doni fatti alla Accad., 1838. — *Sci. fis. e mat.* **Carena, G.** Notizia intorno ai lavori della cl. di sci. fis. e mat., 1836–37. — *Mem.* **Bidone, G.** Sur les contractions partielles des veines d'eau, *etc.*; — Sur la percussion des veines d'eau. — **Avogadro de Quaregna, A.** Sur quelques points douteux relatifs à l'action capillaire. — **De Notaris, G.** Specimen de tortulis italicis. — **Balsamo, J.**, *and others.* Pugillus muscorum Italiæ. — *Sci. mor., stor., e fil.* **Durandi, J.** Saggio sulla Lega Lombarda, *ec.* — **Gingens la Sarraz, F. de.** Sur l'établissement des Burgenden dans la Gaule. — Indice degli autore delle mem. contenute negli otto vol. accad. posteriori al 32. — Indice degli autore i lavori dei quali sono soltanto ramentati nella notizia storica dei vol. accad. — Indice gen. delle materie contenute negli otto vol. posteriori al 32.

— Serie 2a. Memorie. Torino, 1839–49. 10 v. 4°.

Note. In v. 10 are indexes to v. 1–10.

Contents. Vol. 1. *Sci. fis. e mat.* Elenco degli accademici. — Mutazione nel corpo accademico. — Doni fatti alla Reale Accad. d. Sci., 1838–39. — **Gené, G.** Not. stor. intorno ai lavori della classe delle sci. fis. e mat., 1838. — Programma di fisica con assegnamento di premio. — Programma di botanica, *ec.* — **Sismonda, A.** Osserv. geol. e mineral. sopra i monti tra Aosta e Susa. — **Gené, G.** De quibusdam insectis Sardiniæ. — **Sismonda, A.** Due fossili trovati nei colli di Santo Stefano Roero. — **Vérany, J. B.** Mém. sur six nouvelles espèces de céphalopodes trouvés dans la Méditerranée à Nice; — Deux nouvelles espèces de céphalopodes trouvés dans l'océan. — **Bellingeri, C. F.** Sulla struttura e posizione degli organi dell' udito e della vista nei principali generi dei mammiferi. — **Colla, L.** Elogio di C. Bertero. — **Bruno, G. D.** Illustr. di un nuova cetaceo fossile. — **Billiet, A.** Obs. thermométriques faites à St. Jean de Maurienne, 1826–38. — **Botto, G. D.**, *and* **Avogadro di Quaregna, A.** Mém. sur les rapports entre le pouvoir conducteur des liquides pour les courans électriques, *etc.* — **Porro, C.** Talune variazioni offerte da molluschi fluviatili e terrestri a conchiglia univalve. — **Gené, G.** Synopsis reptilium Sardiniæ indigenorum. — **Notaris, G. de.** Primitiæ hepaticologiæ Italicæ. — **Pagani, G. M.** L'équilibre des colonnes. — **Griseri, V.** Applicazione del carbone animale per estrarre il principio amaro del camepiteos e sull' azione del medesimo sul solfato di chinina, *ec.* — *Sci. mor., stor., e filol.* Programmi per premii. — **Galeani Napione di Cocconato, G.** Osserv. intorno alla discesa ed. irruzione de' Cimbri in Italia. — **Sauli d'Igliano, L.** Rapporto della giunta incaricata di esaminare lo scritto inviato al concorso del premio proposto dalla classe, 1836. — **Pinelli, A.** Mem. ragguardanti alla storia civile del Piemonte nel secolo 17. — **Gazzera, C.** Congetture intorno ad una statuina del gabinetto del re C. Alberto. — **Sclopis di Salerano, F. P.** Doc. che servono alla storia della reggenza di Christina di Francia e de' principi Maurizio e Tommaso, *ec.* — **Promis, C.** Dell' antica città di Luni e suo stato presente. — **Peyron, V. A.** Orig. dei tre illustri dialetti greci paragonata con quella dell' eloquio italiano. — **Arri, G. A.** De lingua Phœnicum. — **Cibrario, G. A. D.** Cronol. de' principi di Savoia.

2. Elenco degli accademici. — Mutazioni nel corpo accademico. — Doni fatti alla R. Accad. d. Sci., 1839–40. — *Sci. fis. e mat.* **Gené, G.** Not. storica intorno ai lavori della classe delle sci. fis. e mat., 1839. — **Billiet, A.** Les tremblemens de terre dans la prov. de Maurienne, 1838–40. — **Sismonda, A.** Osserv. mineral. e geol. per servire alla formazione della car a geol. del Piemonte. — **Gené, G.** Descr. di un nuovo falcone di Sardegna. — **Savi, P.** Osserv. sulla struttura ed esistenza degli s.omi in alcune

piante. — **Moris, G.,** *and* **Notaris, G.** de. Florula Caprariæ. — **Menabrea, L. F.** Calcul de la densité de la terre; — Mouvement d'un pendule composé lorsqu'on tient compte du rayon du cylindre qui lui sert d'axe, *etc.* — **Carlini, F.** La détermination de la densité moyenne de la terre, déduite de l'obs. du pendule faite à Mont Cenis. — **Bonaparte, C. L.,** *principe de Canino.* Amphibia Europæa ad systema nostrum vertebratorum ordinata. — **Botto, G. D.** Obs. microscopiques sur les mouvements des globules végétaux suspendus dans un menstrue. — *Sci. mor., stor., e filol.* **Manno, G.** Della vita e opere di G. Grassi. — **Cibrario, G. A. L.** Dei governatori, maestri, e biblioteche de' principi di Savoia fino ad Emanuele Filiberto, *ec.* — **Ricotti, E.** Milizie merenarie in Italia sino alla pace di Costanza. — **Baudi di Vesme, C.** In difficiliora duo loca e fragmentis codicis Theodosiani a Clossio repertis. — **Provana del Sabbione, L. G.** Scrittori del monastero Benedittino di S. Michele della Chiusa ne' secoli 11 e 12, *ec.* — **Pallavicini, F.** Alcuni passi del codice arabo-sicolo paragonati ad avvenimenti nello stato di Genova. — **Ricotti, E.** Milizia dei comuni italiani nel medio evo. — **Gazzera, C.** Narr. contemp. delle avventure e imprese di una flotta di crociati partita dalle foci della Schelda, 1189.

3. Elenco degli accademici. — Mutazioni nel corp accademico. — Doni fatti alla R. Accad. d. Sci., 1840-41. — *Sci. fis. e mat.* **Gené, G.** Not. stor. intorno ai lavori della classe delle sci. fis. e mat., 1840. — **Sobrero, A.** Les épidotes et spécialement celle de St. Marcel en Piémont. — **Bonjean, J.** Mém. sur la pulpe du fruit du Baobad. — **Sismonda, A.** Mem. sui terreni stratificati delle Alpi. — **Notaris, G.** de. Micromycetes Italici novi vel minus cogniti. — **Savi, P.** La microscopica composizone degli strobili di alcune conifere. — **Bellardi, L.,** *and* **Michelotti, G.** Saggio orittografico sulle classe dei gasteropodi fossili dei terreni terziarii del Piemonte. — **Giulio, C. I.** La resistance des fers forgés dont on fait le plus d'usage en Piémont. — **Bellardi, L.** Descr. des cancellaires fossiles des terrains tertiaires du Piémont. — **Lavini, G.** Anal. chim. esplorativa di un météorolite à Cereseto. — **Giulio, C. I.** Expériences sur la force e sur l'élasticité des fils de fer. — *Sci. mor., stor., e filol.* **Peyron, B.** Papiri greci del Museo Britannici della biblioteca Vaticana. — **Carmignani, G.** Nuovo programma di completo insegnamento del dritto. — **Balbo, C.** Sulla divisione e suddivisione della storia d'Italia. — **Aldini, P. V.** Sul tipo primario delle antiche monete della Romana repubblica. — **Petitti di Roreto, C. I.** Del lavora de' fanciulli nelle manifatture.

4. Elenco degli accademici. — Mutazioni nel corpo accademico. — Doni fatti alla R. Accad. d. Sci., 1841-42. — *Sci. fis. e mat.* **Gené, G.** Not. stor. dei lavori della classe delle sci. fis. e mat., 1841. — **Pillet-Will, F.** Programme de la classe des sciences phys. et math. — **Question de physique proposée par la même classe.** — **Ménebréa, N. L. F.** Disc. sur la vie et les ouvrages de G. Bidone. — **Sismonda, E.** Monografia degli echinidi fossili del Piemonte. — **Sismonda, A.** Osserv. geol. sulle Alpi marittime e sugli Appenini Liguri. — **Zanardinio, G.** Synopsis algarum in mari Adriatico, *etc.* — **Visiani, R.** de. Sopra la gastonia palmata. — **Lavini, G.** Ricerche sopra una polvere depositata da una neve di color rosso nelle vallate de Vegezzo. — **Notaris, G.** de. Algologiæ maris Ligustici specimen. — **Abbene, A.,** *and* **Borsarelli, P. A.** Del gaz idrogeno antimoniato, antimoniuro d'idrogeno. — **Giulio, C. I.** Sur la torsion des fils métalliques et l'élasticité des ressorts en hélices. — **Sismonda, E.** App. alla monografia degli echinidi fossili del Piemonte. — *Sci. mor., stor., e filol.* **Gazzera, C.** Mem. dei Tizzoni, conti di Desana. — **Aldini, P. V.** Intorno al tipo ordinario delle antiche monete librali romane.

5. Elenco degli accademici. — Mutazioni nel corpo accademico. — Doni fatti alla R. Accad. d. Sci., 1843. — *Sci. fis. e mat.* **Gené, G.** Not. stor. dei lavori della classe delle sci. fis. e mat., 1842. — **Meneghinio, G.** Monographia nostochinearum Ital., *etc.* — **Vittadinio, C.** Monographia lycoperdineorum. — **Botto, G. D.** Les rapports entre l'induction électromagnétique et l'action électrochimique, *etc.* — **Baldassini, F.** Sulla emissione di un liquido colorante dei molluschi, *ec.* — **Plana, G. A. A.** La chaleur des gaz permanens. — **Colla, L.** Illustr. della portulaca Gilliesii corredata dell' analisi chimica compar. colla oleracea. — **Spinola, M.** Dei prioniti et coleotteri ad essi più affini. — **Sismonda, A.** Osserv. geol. sui terreni della formazioni terziaria e cretacea in Piemonte. — **Colla, L.** Obs. sur la famille des rutacées, sur le genre correa, et formation du nouveau genre antommarchia. — *Sci. mor., stor., e filol.* **Boncampagni, C.** Not. sulla vita di S. Boezio e sulla storia de' suoi tempi. — **Fossati, S.** De ratione nummorum, ponderum, et mensurarum in Galliis sub primæ et secundæ stirpis regibus. — **Spitalieri di Cessole, G. A. I.** Not. sul monumento dei trofei d' A. di Torbia e sulla via Giulia Augusta. — **Cordero de' Conti Sanquintino, G.** Not. sopra alcune monete battute in Pavia da Ardoino, marchese d'Ivrea e re d'Italia, *ec.*; — Della parte dovuta agl' Italiani nello studio delle monete battute nel corso dei secoli 13 e 14, nelle prov. merid. dell' impero greco in Europa, *ec.*

6. Elenco degli accademici. — Mutazioni nel corpo accademico. — Doni fatti alla R. Accad. d. Sci., 1843-44. — *Sci. fis. e mat.* **Gené, G.** Not. stor. dei lavori della classe della sci. fis. e mat., 1843. — **Plana, G. A. A.** Mém. sur la découverte de la loi du choc direct des corps durs; pub. par A. Borelli, *etc.* — **Solier, A. J. J.** Essai sur les collaptérides de la tribu des molurites. — **Sismonda, E.** Mem. geo-zoöl. sugli echinidi fossili di Nizza. — **Notaris, G.** de. Isias orchideum genus. — *Sci. mor., stor., e filol.* **Sauli d'Igliano, L.** Sulla condizione degli studi nella monarchia di Savoia sino all' età di E. Filiberto. — **Cibrario, L.** Della qualità e dell' uso degli schioppi nel 1347, *ec.*; — Storia di Genevra, *ec.* — **Gazzera, C.** Alcune carte antiche concernenti al Piemontese che furono alla quinta crociata. — **Eandi, G.** Sulle casse di risparmio nei reggii stati di Terra-Ferma, *ec.* — **Provana de Sabbione, L. G.** Not. di un ined. doc. dell' archivio vescov. d'Ivrea, 1094, *ec.*

7. Elenco degli accademici. — Mutazioni nel corpo accademico. — Doni fatti alla R. Accad. d. Sci., 1844-45. — *Sci. fis. e mat.* **Gené, G.** Not. stor. dei lavori della classe delle sci. fis. e mat., 1844. — **Chamousset, —.** Lettera sulla temperatura media di Sciamberi. — **Sobrero, A.** Sull' acido eugenico; — Nota sui prodotti della decompozione dell' etere nitroso sotto l'influenza del calore. — **Cigalla, G.** de. Sunto di una statistica ined. dell' isola di Santorino. — **Notaris, G.** de. Mycromycetes Italici novi vel minus cogniti. — **Despine, C. M. J.** Obs. sur les grêles tombées en 1840, dans les états de Terre-Ferme de S. M. le roi de Sardaigne. — **Plana, G. A. A.** Mém. sur la distribution de l'électricité à la surface de deux sphères conductrices complètement isolées. — *Sci. mor., stor., e fil.* **Barucchi, F.** Disc. crit. sopra la cronologia egizia. — **Provana del Sabbione, L. G.** Studi crit. sovra la storia d'Italia a' tempi del re Ardoino. — Parere della giunta accad. intorno agli scritti inviati al concorso di premio, *ec.*

8. Elenco degli accademici. — Mutazioni nel corpo accademico. — Doni fatti alla R. accad. d. Sci., 1845-46. — *Sci. fis. e mat.* **Gené, G.** Not. stor. dei lavori della classe delle sci. fis. e mat., 1845. — **Notaris, G.** de. Repertorium floræ Ligusticæ. — **Menabrea, L. F.** Mém. sur la série de Lagrange. — **Avogadro di Quaregna, A.** Mém. sur les volumes atomiques, *etc.* — **Ménabréa, L. F.** Mém. sur les quadratures. — **Sobrero, A.** Sur la résine del' olivile, *etc.* — **Colla, A.** Gesneriæ zebrinæ illustratio. — **Sobrero, A.** Faits pour servir à l'hist. de l'action del' acide nitrique sur les corps organiques non azotés. — **Botto, G. D.** Les lois de la chaleur degagée par le courant voltaïque, *etc.* — **Avogadro di Quaregna, A.** Mém. sur les volumes atomiques des corps composés. — *Sci. mor., stor., e filol.* **Cibrario, L.** Not. d'Ursicino vescovo di Torino. — **Cordero de' Conti Sanquintino, E.** Delle monete dell' imperatore Giustiniano II. — **Peyron, V. A.** Legum barbarorum fragm. ined., *etc.* — **Baudi di Vesme, C.** Frammenti di orazione panegir. di M. A. Cassiodoro. — **Barucchi, F.** Disc. sopra la cronologia egizia.

9. Elenco degli accademici. — Mutazioni nel corpo accademico. — Doni fatti alla R. Accad. d. Sci., 1846-47. — *Sci. fis. e mat.* **Sismonda, E.** Not. stor. dei lavori della classe delle sci. fis. e mat., 1846. — Programme de concours à quatre prix fondés par **F. Pillet-Will.** — **Sismonda, A.** Not. sulla costituzione delle Alpi Piemontese. — **Notaris, G.** de. Repertorium floræ Ligusticæ. — **Bellardi, C. A. L.** Monografia delle pleurotome fossili del Piemonte. — **Bellingeri, C. F.** Anatomia di una foca vitulina. — **Plana, G. A. A.** La découverte de la loi de la pésanteur des planètes vers le soleil, *etc.* — **Gené, G.** Mem. per servire alla storia nat. degli issodi. — **Cantù, G, L.** L'influence du carbone sur la stabilité des iodures métalliques lorsqu'ils se trouvent soumis à l'action du calorique, *etc.*

10. Elenco degli accademici. — Mutazioni nel corpo accademico. — Doni fatta alla R. Accad. d. Sci., 1848-49. — *Sci. fis. e mat.* **Sismonda, E.** Not. stor. dei lavori fatti dalla classe delle sci. fis. e mat., 1847; — Descr. dei pesci e dei crostacei fossili nel Piemonte. — **Lavini, G.** Il principio epispastico dei meloe paragonato a quello della cantaride officinale. — **Selmi, F.** Intorno alla solubilità dell' ammoniuro d'oro in cianuri. — **Ménabréa, L. F.** Obs. sur la véritable interprétation de la série de Lagrange. — **Notaris, G.** de. Monografia delle escipule della flora italica. — **Peyrone, M.** Sopra alcuni isomeri del sal verde di Magnus. — **Sobrero, A.** Alcuni nuovi composti fulminanti ottenuti col mezzo dell' azione dell' acido nitrico sulle sostanze organiche vegetali. — **Colla, A.** Archimenæ: Gesneriacearum tribus nova, *etc.*; — Ad Gesneriaceas addit., *etc.* — **Bel-**

lardi, C. A. L. Monografia delle columbelle fossili del Piemonte. — **Plana, G. A. A.** La découverte de la loi de la pesanteur des planètes vers le soleil, *etc.* — **Notaris, G. de.** Micromycetes Italici novi vel minus cogniti; — Abrothallus, novum lichenum genus; — Monografia del genere discosia della famiglia dei pirenomiceti basidiospori; — Nuovi caratteri di alcuni generi della tribù delle parmeliacee, *ec.* — **Filippi, F. de.** Nuovo genere di anellidi della famiglia di sanguisughe. — **Indice** degli autore, t. 1-10. — **Indice** delle materie. — *Sci. mor., stor., e filol.* **Cordero de Conte Sanquintino, G.** Monete del 10o e 11o secolo scoperte nei dintorni di Roma, 1843. — **Peyron, V. A.** De loco geometrico in Platonis Menone. — **Gingins la Sarra, F. de.** Doc. pour servir à l'hist. des comtes de Biandrate, *etc.* — **Cordero de Conti Sanquintino, G.** Sopra argomenti spettanti a monete coniate in Italia nei secoli 14 e 17. — **Matile, G. A.** Etudes sur la gombette. — **Avogadro di Valdenga, G.** Illustr. di due carte vercellesi, *ec.* — **Parere** della giunta accad. sopra la dissert. di F. de Gingins la Sarraz, 'Recherches sur la donation', *etc.* — **Gingins la Sarra, F.** Recherches sur la donation faite au monastère de Fruttuaria, *etc.* — **Cordero de' Conti Sanquintino, G.** Osserv. intorno all' origine ed antichità della moneta veneziana. — Parere della giunta accad. intorno alla dissert., 'Quali furono le cause per le quali la repub. d'Atene andò da Pericle in poi decadendo, sinchè venne in potere dei Romani?' — Programme della classe delle sci. mor., stor., e filol. sull' influenza dell' educazione, *ec.* — Indice degli autore, t. 1-10. — Indice delle materie.

— Rotondi, P. Memorie della Accad. della Scienze di Torino, ser. 2, v. 1-10. (*In* **Archivio** stor. ital., n. s., v. 10, pt. 2. 1859.)

— Vassali-Eandi, A. M. Mémoire historique. (*In* **Turin. Ac. d. Sci.** Memorie, v. 22. 1813-14.) — Annali della Accademia, 1815-18. (*In* v. 23. 1818.)

Turin. San Filippo. Tavigliano, G. P. B., *conte* di. Modello di chiesa disegnato da F. Ivvara. Torino, 1758. f°.

Turkestan *or* **Bukharia.** Travels through Tartary, Tibet, and Bukharia, [1246-1741]. (*In* **Green, J.** Col. of voy., v. 4. 1747; — *and, Germ., in* **Allgemeine** Hist., v. 7. 1750.)

— Ferrier, J. P. Caravan journeys in Persia, Turkistan, *etc.*, [1845-52]; tr. by W. Jesse; ed. by H. D. Seymour. 2d ed. Lond., 1857. 8°.

See also **Khiva.**

Turkey. *Sultan.* Translation of the firmân of 'Abd-ul-Megîd granted to his Protestant subjects, Nov. 1850 and June 1853. (*In* **Amer. Orient. Soc.** Journal, v. 3, 4. 1853, 54.)

Biography.

— Boissard, J. J. Vitæ et icones sultanorum. Frankf. a. M., 1596. 4°.

— Ducange, C. du F. Familiæ Turcicæ. (*In* **Byzant.** hist., v. 21. 1729.)

— Notice sur la cour du Grand Seigneur. *n.t.p.* [181-?] 8°. (B 734)

— Sansovino, F. T. Gl' annali turcheschi overo vite de principi della casa othomana. Venitia, 1573. 4°.

Christians in Turkey.

— Cooper, A. A., *Earl of Shaftsbury.* Religious liberty in Turkey; speech on the manifesto of the Emperor of Russia. 2d ed. Lond., 1854. 8°. (B 1534)

— Gr. Brit. *Consular Corps.* Reports received from H. M.'s consuls rel. to the condition of the Christians in Turkey. Lond., 1860. 8°.

— Denton, W. The Christians in Turkey. London, 1863. 8°.

— Clarke, H. Supposed extinction of the Turks and increase of the Christians in Turkey. (*In* **Statist. Soc.** Journ., v. 28. 1865.)

Commerce.

— Dearborn, H. A. S. Memoir on the commerce and navigation of the Black Sea, and the trade and maritime geography of Turkey and Egypt. Boston, 1819. 2 v. *and Atlas* 8°.

— Urquhart, D. 1833. *See Politics* (p. 3038).

— Colin, A. Relations commerciales de la Turquie. (*In* **Revue** d. D. Mondes, jan. 1839.) — Relations, *etc.* (*In* av. 1847.)

Description and Travels.

— Morell, J. R. 1234-1854. *See History.*

— Geuffre, A. Aulæ Turcicæ descrip.; in Lat. ling. convers. per W. Godelevæum; acc. P. Bizarus De bello Cyprio, *etc.* Basiliæ, [1573]. 16°.

— Voyage of five marchant ships of London to Turkie, *etc.*, 1586. (*In* **Hakluyt, R.** Col., v. 2. 1810.)

— Wratislaw, W., *Baron.* Adventures, 1599; tr. by A. H. Wratislaw. London, 1862. 8°.

— Sandys, G. Relation of a journey begun 1610. *t.p.w.* [London, 1615.] f°.

— Valle, P. della. Viaggi, cioè la Turchia, *ec.*, [1614-16]. Venetia, 1661-63. 4 v. 12°.

— Turcici Imperii status, seu Discursus de rebus Turcarum. Lug. Bat., *ex. of. Elzev.*, 1630. 32°.

— Evliya. Narrative of travels in Europe, Asia, *etc.*, [1631-70]; tr. by J. von Hammer. Lond., *Orient. Tr. Fund*, 1834-50, 44. 3 v. 4°.

— Tavernier, J. B. Six voyages en Turquie, *etc.*, [1638-75]. Nouv. éd. Rouen, 1713. 5 v. 12°.

— - *Eng.* Collections of travels through Turky, *etc.* London, 1684. 2 v. f°.

— Thevenot, J. Travels to Constantinople, abridged, 1655-56. (*In* **Knox, J.** Col. of voy., v. 6. 1767.)

— Gemelli Careri, G. F. Of Turkey, 1693-94. (*In* **Churchill,** O. *and* J. Col. of voy., v. 4. 1745.)

— Hill, A. Present state of the Ottoman Empire, [1708]. 2d ed. London, 1710. f°.

— Montagu, *Lady* M. P. W. Letters during Mr. Wortley's embassy, [1716-18]. (*In her* Works, v. 2, 3. 1803; v. 1. 1837.)

— Tott, F., *baron* de. Memoirs of the Turkish Empire and the Crimea, [1755]. London, 1786. 2 v. 8°.

— Accurate account of Turkey in Europe. (*In* **Moore, J. H.** New col. of voy., v. 2. 1778.)

— Habesci, E. Present state of the Ottoman Empire; tr. from the French. Lond., 1784. 8°.

— Moreno, J. Viage á Constantinopla, 1784. Madrid, 1790. 4°.

— Mouradja d'Ohsson, I. Tableau général de l'Empire Othoman. Paris, 1787-90. 2 v. f°.

— Olivier, G. A. Travels in the Ottoman Empire, *etc.*, 1792-98; tr. from the French. 2d ed. London, 1801. 2 v. 8°.

— - Atlas. 2d ed. London, 1802. 4°.

— Eton, W. Survey of the Turkish Empire, [1798]. 2d ed. London, 1799. 8°.

— Clarke, E. D. Russia, Turkey, *etc.*, [1800]. Phila., 1811. 8°.

— - *Same.* (*In his* Travels in Europe, v. 1-3. 1816-17.)

— Thornton, T. Present state of Turkey, [1808]. 2d ed. with corr. and add. London, 1809. 2 v. 8°.

— Galt, J. Voyages and travels, 1809-11; obs. on Gibraltar, Turkey, *etc.* London, 1812. 4°.

— Hobhouse, J. C. Journey through Albania and other Provinces of Turkey, 1809-10. London, 1813. 4°.

— - *Same.* 2d ed. London, 1813. 2 v. 4°.

— - *Same.* Phila., 1817. 2 v. 8°.

— Walpole, R. Memoirs relating to Turkey. London, 1817. 4°.

— Fuller, J. Tour through some parts of the Turkish Empire, [1818-19]. London, 1830. 8°.

— Laurent, P. E. Tour through Greece, Turkey, and Italy, 1818-19. 2d ed. London, 1822. 2 v. 8°.

— Madden, R. R. Travels in Turkey, *etc.*, 1824-27. London, 1829. 2 v. 8°.

— Webster, J. Travels through the Crimea, Turkey, *etc.*, 1825-28. London, 1830. 2 v. 8°.

— CARNE, J. Letters during a tour through Turkey, *etc.* 2d ed. London, 1826. 2 v. 16°.
— URQUHART, D. 1827-37. *See History.*
— FRANKLAND, C. C. Travels to and from Constantinople, 1827-28. London, 1829. 2 v. 8°.
— ARMSTRONG, T. B. Travels in Russia, Turkey, *etc.*, [1828-29]. London, 1831. 8°.
— SLADE, A. Records of travels in Turkey, Greece, *etc.*, and of a cruise in the Black Sea, 1829-31. London, 1832. 2 v. 8°.
— MAGNETTI, C. Costume dell' Impero Ottomano. (*In* **Ferrario, G.** Costume ant. e mod., v. 7. 1829.)
— DEKAY, J. E. Sketches of Turkey, 1831-32. N. Y., 1833. 8°
— MY travels in France, Italy, Malta, Turkey, [1831-32]. London, 1837. 16°.
— SKETCHES in Greece and Turkey, [1832]. London, 1833. 8°.
— TEMPLE, *Sir* G. Excursions in the Mediterranean, [1834]. London, 1836. 2 v. 12°.
— ELLIOTT, C. B. Travels in Austria, Russia, and Turkey, [1835-36]. London, 1838. 2 v. 8°.
— ROSE, W. G. Three months' leave. London, 1838. 12°.
— BOUÉ, A. La Turquie d'Europe. Paris, 1840. 4 v. 8°.
— HAHN-HAHN, I. M. L. G. Letters of a German countess in Turkey, *etc.*, 1843-44. London, 1845. 3 v. 12°.
— SCHOTT, W. Chinesische Nachrichten über die Kang-gar und das osmanische Reich. (*In* **Berlin. Ak. d. Wiss.** Abh., 1844.)
— BOWEN, G. F. Mount Athos; from Constantinople to Corfu, [1849]. London, 1852. 12°.
— DEVERE, A. T. Picturesque sketches of Greece and Turkey. Lond., 1850. 2 v. 12°.
— SPENCER, E. Travels in European Turkey in 1850. London, 1851. 2 v. 8°.
— SMITH, J. V. C. Turkey and the Turks, [1851]. Boston, 1852. 8°. (B 1604)
— - *Same.* Boston, 1854. 12°.
— BELGIOJOSO, C. T., *princesse* de. Oriental harems and scenery, 1852; tr. N. Y., 1862. 12°.
— - Scènes de la vie turque. Paris, 1858. 18°.
— TOZER, H. F. Researches in the highlands of Turkey, *etc.*, [1853-65]. Lond., 1869. 2 v. 8°.
— BESSÉ, A. de. Turkish Empire; its hist, statist., and relig. condition; tr. and revised by E. J. Morris. Phila., 1854. 12°.
— HANDBOOK for travellers in Turkey. 3d ed. London, *Murray*, 1854. 12°.
— HORTON, T. G. Turkey; the people, country, and government. London, 1854. 8°.
— KAZINSKI, L., *count.* Two lectures: Turkey and Russia; The exile in a foreign land. Manchester, N. H., 1854. 8°. (B 1604)
— SMYTH, W. W. A year with the Turks. N. Y., 1854. 12°.
— SPENCER, E. Turkey, *etc.*, [1854]. 6th thous. London, 1855. 12°.
— YOUNG, *Mrs.* M. Our camp in Turkey and the way to it. London, 1854. 8°.
— MORONI, G. (*In his* Diz. di erud. stor. eccl., v. 81. 1856.)
— SENIOR, N. W. Journal kept in Turkey and Greece, 1857-58. London, 1859. 12°.
— NICOLAÏDY, B. Les Turcs et la Turquie contemporaine. Paris, 1859. 2 v. 16°.
— SMYTHE, E. A. B., *Viscountess Strangford.* The eastern shores of the Adriatic in 1863. London, 1864. 8°.
— MACKENZIE, *Miss* G. M. M., *and* IRBY, *Miss* A. P. Travels in the Slavonic provinces of Turkey-in-Europe, [1863]. Lond., 1867. 8°.
— COLLAS, B. C. La Turquie en 1864. Paris, 1864. 8°.
— FARLEY, J. L. Turkey. London, 1866. 8°.
— BRADSHAW'S through route and overland guide to India, Turkey, *etc.* London, 1867. 16°.
— TREVELYAN, *Sir* C. E. From Pesth to Brindisi in the autumn of 1869. (*In* **Grant,** *Sir* **A.** Recess studies. 1870.)

See also **Balcan; — Bosphorus; — Constantinople; — Danube; — Danubian Principalities; — Kars; — Levant; — Montenegro; — Palestine; — Scutari; — Seraglio.**

Maps.

— ANVILLE, J. B. B. de. Map. Lond., 1794. f°. (E 66)
— BLAEU, W. *and* J. Turcicum imperium. [Amst., 16—.] (E 78, no. 296)
— FADEN, W. Turkey in Europe. London, 1795. (E 66)
— LEJEAN, G. Les cartes de la Turquie d' Europe. (*In* **Paris. Soc. de Géog.** Bul., 5e sér., v. 17. 1869.)
— SEUTTER, M. Theatrum belli sive novissima tabula qua maxima pars Danubii et Hungaria cum aliis adjacentibus regnis, *etc.* Aug. Vind., [17—]. (E 93)

Education.

— DUPPA, B. F. Education in Turkey. (*In* **Cent. Soc. of Educ.** Pub., v. 1. 1837.)

Finances.

— COR, J. M. Le budget de la Turquie. (*In* **Revue d. D. Mondes**, sept. 1850.) — GIRARDIN, M. De la moralité des finances turques. (*In* jan. 1861.)

History.

— GAZA, T. De origine Turcarum. (*In* **Byzant.** hist. scr., v. 23. 1733.)
— LAMARTINE, M. L. de P. de. Histoire de la Turquie, [500-1839]. Paris, 1855. 8 v. 8°.
— ENAULT, L. Constantinople et la Turquie; tableau historique, pittoresque, statistique, et moral, [500-1833]. Paris, 1855. 12°.
— GUIGNES, J. de. Histoire des Huns, des Turcs, *etc.*, [545-1453]. Paris, 1756-58. 5 v. 4°.
— UPHAM, E. History of the Ottoman Empire, [570]-1828. Edin., 1829. 2 v. 12°. (Constable's miscel., v. 40, 41.)
— NEU-eröffnetes Amphitheatrum Turcicum worinnen der Kern türckischer Geschichten kurtz versehen, [570-1724]. Erffurth, 1724. f°.
— SAGREDO, G. Memorie istoriche de' monarchi ottomani, 570-1644. 4a impr. Venetia, 1688. 4°.
— ABU-L-FEDA, I. Annales Moslemici, [570-1015]; tr. J. J. Reiske. Lps., 1778. 4°.
— JOUANNIN, J. M., *and* GAVER, J. van. Turquie, [635-1839]. Paris, 1843. 8°. (Univers.)
— KNOLLES, R. General hist. of the Turkes, [755-1610]. 2d ed. [London,] 1610. f°.
— - *Same.* Turkish history; contin. to 1687 by Sir P. Rycaut. 6th ed., with effigies of all the kings and emperors. London, 1687-1700. 3 v. f°.
— MUENCH, E. H. J. von. Heerzüge des christlichen Europas wider die Osmanen, [1097]-1822. Basil, 1823-26. 5 v. (v. 1 w.). 8°.
— CONRING, H. De bello contra Turcas [1145-1663] libri varii selecti. Helmest., 1664. 4°.
— ZINKEISEN, J. W. Geschichte des Osmanischen Reiches in Europa, [v.c. 1200]-1774. Hamburg, Gotha, 1850-63. 7 v. *and* Register 8°. (Heeren u. U. Europ. Staat.)
— CANTIMIR, D. Histoire de l'Empire Othoman, [1214-1711]; tr. par De Joncquières. Paris, 1743. 2 v. 4°.
— MORELL, J. R. Turkey, past and present, [1234-1854]. 20th thousand. London, 1854. 16°.

— CREASY, E. S. History of the Ottoman Turks, [1250-1839]. London, 1854. 2 v. 8°.
— LÖWENKLAU, J. Annales Sultanorum Othmanidarum, 1289-1588. (*In* Byzantinæ hist. scr., v. 16. 1729.)
— HAMMER-PURGSTALL, J. de. Histoire de l'Empire Ottoman, 1300-1774; tr. par J. J. Hellert. Paris, 1835-43. 18 v. 8° *and* Atlas f°.
— MIGNOT, V. History of the Turkish or Ottoman Empire, 1300-1740; tr. by A. Hawkins. Exeter, 1787. 4 v. 8°.
— CHALCOCONDYLAS, L. Historiarum libri x. interp. G. Clausero cum annalibus sultanorum ex interpretatione J. Leunclavii, [1300-1464]. (*In* Byzantinæ hist. scr., v. 16. 1729; — *and in* Niebuhr. Byzant. hist., v. 42. 1843.)
— - *French.* Histoire de la décadence de l'Empire Grec, *etc.*; contin. jusqu' à 1632 par A. Thomas. Paris, 1632. f°.
— ROBERT, C. Slave provinces of T., [1400-1851]. (*In* Ranke, L. History of Servia. 1853.)
— LÖWENKLAU, J. Pandectes Historiæ Turcicæ, ad illustrandos Annales, 1444-1552. (*In* Byzant. hist. scr., v. 16. 1729.)
— RUSSELL, J., 1*st Earl.* Establishment of the Turks in Europe; an hist. disc., [1453-1828]. London, 1828. 12°.
— - *French.* De l'établissement des Turcs en Europe; tr. par A. B. Paris, 1828. 8°.
— HADJI KHALFA. History of the maritime wars of the Turks, [1459-1557]; tr. by J. Mitchell. London, *Oriental Tr. Fund*, 1831. 4°.
— BUONACCORSI, F. De bello Turcis inferendo oratio, [1486]. — De his quæ a Venetis tentata sunt contra Turcos historia, [148-]. (*In* Bizari, P. Rerum Persic. hist. 1601.)
— RANKE, L. Osmanen u. die spanische Monarchie im 16ten u. 17ten Jahrhundert. (Vol. 1 *of his* Fürsten und Völker von Süd-Europa. 1857.)
— BUSBEQUIUS, A. G. Epistles conc. his embassy into T., [1554-62]; tr. fr. Lat. Lond., 1694. 12°.
— BEHRNAUER, W. F. A. Kogabeg's Abhandlung über den Verfall des osmanischen Staatsgebäudes seit Sultan Suleiman dem Grossen, [1566-1620]. (*In* Zeitschr. d. D. morg. Ges., v. 15. 1861.)
— REIMANN, E. Beiträge zur türkischen Geschichte, [1566-90]. (*In* Historische Zeitschrift, v. 8. 1862.)
— MINADOUS, J. T. Historia de bello inter Turcas et Persas, [1576-87]. — PORSIUS, H. De bello inter Murathem III. Turcarum et Mehemetem Hodabende, Persarum regem gesto narratio, [1577-78]. — DE belli Persici successu, [1580-87]. (*In* Bizari, P. Rer. Pers. hist. 1601.)
— NAIMA. Annals of the Turkish Empire, 1591-1659; tr. by C. Fraser. London, *Orient Tr. Fund*, 1832. 4°.
— SOPRA una missione di Gaspare Scioppio a Lucca come ambasciatore del sultano Iachia, 1609-34. (*In* Giornale storico degli archivi toscani, v. 4. 1860.)
— HISTOIRE véritable de ce qui s'est passé en Turquie, pour la délivrance et redemption des chrestiens captifs, 1609-13. — LETTRE d'un gentilhomme de M. le baron de Cesi touchant la prise de cinq galères turques, et autres exploicts, 1620. (*In* Ternaux-Compans, H. Archives des voy., v. 2. 1841.)
— MONCADA, F. de, *conde de Osuna.* Espedicion de los Catalanes y Aragoneses contra Turcos y Griegos, [1620]. (*In* Ochoa, E. de. Tes. de hist. esp., 1840; — *and in* Rosell, C. Hist. de sucesos partic., v. 1. 1858; v. 21 of Aribau. Bibl.)
— - *French.* Expédition des Catalans et des Arragonais contre les Turcs et les Grecs; tr. par de Champfeu. Paris, 1828. 8°.
— PLAINTES et justifications du Grand Turc au Roy sur tout ce qui s'est passé en Turquie entre les François et les Anglois le mois de juil. 1620. — PACIFIQUE *de Provin.* Lettre sur l'estrange mort du Grand Turc, 1622. — GEDOUYN, *consul d'Alep.* Copple d'une lettre escrite de Belgrade le 26 jan. 1624; avec un recit des desordres, *etc.*, qui sont en l'Empire des Turcs. (*In* Ternaux-Compans, H. Archives des voyages, v. 1. 1840.) — DÉFAICTE de cinq cens hommes et de quatre vaisseaux de guerre, 1621, par le S. de Beaulieu. — GRANDE et estrange sédition arrivée depuis peu en Constantinople touchant l'élection d'un Empereur, 1622. (*In* v. 2. 1841.)

— MONTECUCCULI, R., *comte* de. De la guerre contre le Turc. — Relation de la campagne de 1664. (*In his* Mém. 1760.)
— LUEDEKE, J. W. Beschreibung des turkischen Reiches, 1750-1800. Lpz., 1771-89. 3 v. 8°.
— VALENTINI, G. W. Précis des dernières guerres des Russes contre les Turcs, [1769-1812]; tr. par E. de la Coste. Paris, 1828. 8°.
— LIGNE, C. J. Lettres sur la dernière guerre des Turcs, [1787-89]. (*In his* Œuvres, v. 2. 1860; — *and in* Mélanges mil., v. 7. 1796.)
— - Campagne de 1788 et 1789 contre les Turcs. (*In his* Mélanges mil., v. 24. 1801.)
— SHORT history of the stratagems employed by Alemdár Mustafá Páshá and others to depose Sultan Mustafá, 1807. (*In* Orient. Tr. Fund. Misc. tr., v. 2. 1834.)
— ADAIR, *Sir* R. Negotiations for the peace of the Dardanelles, 1808-09. London, 1845. 2 v. 8°.
— ROSEN, G. Geschichte der Türkei, 1826-56. Lpz., 1866-67. 2 v. 8°. (Staatengeschichte der neuesten Zeit.)
— URQUHART, D. The spirit of the East, [1827-37]. London, 1838. 2 v. 8°.
— CHESNEY, F. R. Russo-Turkish campaigns in 1828-29. N. Y., 1854, 12°.
— U. S. *President.* Message; [with] copies of the corresp. rel. to the negotiation of the treaty with the Sublime Porte, *etc.* Wash., 1832. 8°. (22d Cong. 1st sess. B 1057)
— GIRARDIN, M. La question d'Orient, 1840, 62. (*In* Revue d. D. Mondes, sept., oct. 1862.) — Controverse sur la question d'Orient. (*In* nov. 1863.) — La question d'Orient. (*In* mai 1864 - déc. 1865.)

See also Ali *Pasha*; — Crimean war; — Huns; — Montenegro; — Omer *Pasha*; — Scanderbeg; — Syria.

Language.

— KOELLE, S. W. Ueber türkische Verbal-Wurzeln. (*In* Zeitschrift d. D. morg. Ges., v. 24. 1870.)
— VOLNEY, C. F. C. de. Simplification des langues orientales, ou Méthode nouvelle d'apprendre, *etc.* Paris, 1795. 8°.

Dictionaries.

— KIEFFER, J. D., *and* BIANCHI, T. X. Dictionnaire turc-français. Paris, 1835-37. 2 v. 8°.
— REDHOUSE, J. W. English and Turkish and Turkish and English [dictionary]. London, 1856-57. 2 v. 12°.

Grammars.

— HOLDERMANN, J. P. Grammaire turque. Constantinople, 1730. 4°.
— JAUBERT, P. A. E. P. Eléments de la grammaire turke. 2e éd. Paris, 1833. 8°.
— BARKER, W. B. Turkish grammar. London, 1854. 18°.

Literature.

— TODERINI, G. B. De la littérature des Turcs; tr. par A. de Cournand. Paris, 1789. 3 v. 8°.
— *Poetry.* HAMMER-PURGSTALL, J. Geschichte der osmanischen Dichtkunst. Pesth, 1836-38. 4 v. 8°.
— *Proverbs.* AGNELLINI, T. Proverbii in lingua araba, persiana, e turca. Padova, 1688. 8°.
— *Specimen.* ANNA Ros. [Turkish, in the Armenian character.] Malta, 1829. 12°.

See also Bible (p. 284).

Military and Naval affairs.

— MARSIGLI, L. F. L'état militaire de l'Empire Ottoman. La Haye, 1732. f°.
— TRANT, *Capt.* T. A. Remarks on the actual state of the naval and military power of the Ottoman Empire. (*In his* Narrative. 1830.)
— POUJADE, E. Scènes et souvenirs de la vie politique et militaire en Turquie. (*In* Revue d. D. Mondes, déc. 1855; av., sept. 1856.)

Missions.

— AMER. BOARD OF COMM. FOR FOR. MISSIONS. Historical sketch of [their] missions in European Turkey, *etc.* N. Y., 1866. 8°. (E 10)

— MUEFFLING, F. K. F. Narrative of missions to Constantinople and St. Petersburg, 1829, 30. London, 1855. 12°.

— TARILLON, F. Mission de Constantinople. (*In* Lettres édifiantes, v. 1. 1810.)

Names.

— ORTHOGRAPHY of the Armenian and Turkish proper names. (*In* **Amer. Orient. Soc.** Journ., v. 4. 1854.)

National character and Social life.

— GEORGIEVICZ, B. De Turcicarum moribus epitome. Geneva, **1629**. 32°.

— PORTER, *Sir* J. Observations on the religion, laws, and manners of the Turks. Dublin, **1768**. 2 v. 12°.

— NOTICE sur la cour, *etc.* 181–. *See Biog.* (p. 3035).

— PARDOE, J. City of the Sultan and domestic manners of the Turks, **1836**. Phila., 1837. 2 v. 12°.

— ALLOM, T. Character and costume in Turkey and Italy. London, [184–]. f°.

— MAC FARLANE, C. Kismet; or, The doom of Turkey. London, **1853**. 12°.

— OSCANYAN, C. The Sultan and his people. N. Y., **1857**. 12°.

Politics.

— BALBI, G. De rebus Turcicis, [1526]. (*In his* Opera, v. 2. 1792.)

— DU MAY, L. Discours sur le traité de paix entre Léopold I. et Mahomet, empereur des Turcs, **1664**. — BRÈVES, —. Discours des moyens d'anéantir la monarchie des princes ottomans. (*In* **Recueil** hist. 1666.)

— GUYS, P. A. Lettres sur les Turcs, [1776]. (*In his* Voyage lit. de la Grèce, v. 3. 1783.)

— GENTZ, F. von. Essai sur les rapports entre la Porte Ottomane et les principales puissances de l'Europe, **1815, 16**. — Mémoire sur l'insurrection des Grecs considérée dans ses rapports avec les puissances européennes, **1823**. (*In his* Nachlasse, v. 2. 1868.)

— REMARKS on the present state of Turkey considered in its commercial and political rel. with Eng. London, **1821**. 8°. (B 791)

— CONSIDÉRATIONS sur la guerre actuelle entre les Grecs et les Turcs. (*In* **Pamphleteer, 1824**; v. 24 of B 838)

— GRASSI, A. Charte turque, ou Organisation religieuse, civile, et militaire de l'Emp. Ottoman. Paris, **1825**. 2 v. 8°.

— RUSSELL, J., *Earl*. **1828**. *See History.* **1453-1828.**

— URQUHART, D. The spirit of the East, [**1830**]. London, 1838. 2 v. 8°.

— - Turkey and its resources. London, **1833**. 8°.

— ENGLAND, France, Russia, and Turkey. 2d ed. London, **1834**. 8°. (B 1109)

— SULTAN Mahmoud, The, and Mehemet Ali Pasha, [**1834**]. London, 1835. 8°. (B 1109)

— SLADE, A. The Sultan and Mehemet Ali; or, The present crisis in Turkey. London, **1839**. 8°. (B 1153)

— URQUHART, D. The crisis; France in face of the four powers. 2d ed. Paris, **1840**. 8°.

— DESPREZ, H. Les questions sociales dans la Turquie d'Europe. (*In* **Revue** d. D. Mondes, juin **1848**.) — La Turquie et l'alliance austro-russe. (*In* nov. **1849**.)

— APPEAL on the Eastern question to the Senatus Academicus of the Royal Coll. of Edinburgh; by a Russian. Edin., **1854**. 8°. (B 1534)

— ENGLISH government and the Eastern question; by a looker-on. London, 1854. 8°. (B 1534)

— GOLOVIN, I. Nations of Russia and Turkey and their destiny. London, 1854. 8°.

— LAYARD, A. H. Turkish question; speeches in the Ho. of Com. 2d ed. London, 1854. 8°. (B 1534)

— RANKE, L. von. Zur orientalischen Frage; Gutachten im Juli 1854 Sr. Majestät König Friedrich Wilhelm IV. (*In* **Historische Zeitschrift**, v. 13. 1865.)

— SPECULATIONS on the Eastern question; by a soldier. London, 1854. 8°. (B 1534)

— TRESCOT, W. H. American view of the Eastern question. Charleston, 1854. 12°. (C 264)

— URQUHART, D. War of ignorance; a prognostication. London, 1854. 8°. (B 1534)

— WHY are we at war with Russia? or, Englishmen sacrificed to Mahomet; letter by an East Anglian. London, 1854. 8°. (B 1534)

— ZINKEISEN, J. W. Die orientalische Frage in ihrer Kindheit; eine geschichtliche Studie zur vergleichenden Politik. (*In* **Historisches** Taschenbuch, **1855-56**.) — Der Westen und der Norden im dritten Stadium der orientalischen Frage. (*In* **1858**.)

— GR. BRITAIN. *Parl.* Papers rel. to administrative and financial reforms in Turkey, **1858–61**. London, [1861]. f°.

— ZINKEISEN, J. W. Das vierte Stadium oder das jüngste Jahrhundert und die Zukunft der orientalischen Frage. (*In* **Historisches** Taschenbuch, **1859**.)

— SMYTH, P. E. F. W. Chaos, [**1863**]. (*In his* Selection, v. 1. 1869.)

— SAINT-AMAND, I. de. Les reformes et la Turquie en **1865**. (*In* **Revue** d. D. Mondes, mai 1865.)

— SMYTHE, P. E. F. W. Occasional notes on Turkey, [**1866-68**]. (*In his* Selection, v. 1. 1869.)

— MENDELSSOHN BARTHOLDY, K. Ali Pascha von Janina; ein Beitrag zur Geschichte der orientalischen Frage. (*In* **Historisches** Taschenbuch, **1867**.)

— BURNOUF, E. La Turquie à la fin de **1869**. (*In* **Revue** d. D. Mondes, déc. 1869.)

— ETUDES pratiques sur la question de l'Orient. Paris, 1869. 8°.

— ST. CLAIR, S. G. B., *and* BROPHY, C. A. Residence in Bulgaria; notes on the resources and administration of Turkey. London, 1869. 8°.

— FROUDE, J. A. The Eastern question. (*In his* Short studies. 2d ser. **1871**.)

— DIE TUERKEI und ihre letzten Conflicte. (*In* **Unsere** Zeit, 1871, 1r H.)

Religion.

See **Mohammedans.**

Turkish bath, The; a farce. *See* **Williams, M.**, *and* Burnand, F. C.

Turkish evening entertainments; by A. I. H. Suhiali, tr. by J. P. Brown. N. Y., 1850. 8°.

Turle, James, *M.D.* What are proper situations for metropolitan hospitals? (*In* **Nat. Assoc. Prom. Soc. Sci.** Trans., 1862.)

Turler, Hieronymus. Remarks on England, 1574; tr. from the Latin. (*In* **Rye, W. B.** England as seen by foreigners. 1865.)

Turnbuch. *See* **Gymnastics.**

Turnbull, —. Review of the anti-government-scheme; with app. Edin., 1783. 8°. (B 256)

— NEWTON, A. A voice to seceders; a letter to Mr. T. supposed author of 'A review of the anti-government scheme'; also The seceder's catechism. Edin., 1783. 8°. (B 256)

Turnbull, Alexander, *M.D.* Investigation into the external application of veratria. Wash., 1834. 8°. (E 35)

— Treatment of the diseases of the eye by means of prussic acid vapour, *etc.* London, 1843. 8°.

Turnbull, David. French Revolution of 1830. London, 1830. 8°.

— Travels in the West; Cuba, Porto Rico, and the slave trade. London, 1840. 8°.

Turnbull, George, *LL.D.* Connexion between the doctrines and miracles of Christ. 2d ed. London, 1732. 8°.

Turnbull, John D. Rudolph; [a play]. *n.t.p.* [Boston, 1807.] 16°. (D 42)

Turnbull, Robert, *D.D.* Genius of Italy; sketches of Italian life, *etc.* 3d ed. N. Y., 1852. 12°.

— Hearing the word; circular letter to the Boston Baptist Assoc., 1842. *n.t.p.* [1842.] 8°. (B 1360)

— Sermon; the thoughts of God. (*In* **American** nat. preacher, v. 22. 1848.)

Turnbull, Robert James. The crisis; essays on the usurpations of the federal government; by Brutus. Charleston, 1827. 8°. (B 1066)

— Oration, July 4. Charleston, 1832. 8°. (B 1067)
— Visit to the Phila. prison. Phila., 1796. 8°. (B 343)
— HAMILTON, *pseud.* Review of ['The crisis']. Charleston, 1828. 8°.
— - *Other copies.* (B 971, 1063)
— *Eulogium on.* 1833. *See* **Hamilton, J.** (B 1226)

Turnbull, Wm., *M.D.* Medical works. Vol. 1: Treatise on health. London, 1805. 12°.
— Naval surgeon. London, 1806. 8°.
— Rules and instructions for those afflicted with ruptures. London, 1806. 12°.

Turnbull, *Col.* Wm., *U.S. Engineer.* Description of the coffer-dam for the pier of the Potomac aqueduct. (*In* **Gr. Brit.** *Corps of Roy. Engin.* Papers, v. 3. 1839.)

Turnbull, Wm. Principles of calculation in ref. to the strength of cast iron beams. (*In* **Gr. Brit.** *Corps of Roy. Engin.* Papers, v. 6. 1843.)

Turnbull, Wm. Barclay David Donald. Calendar of state papers, foreign ser., reign of Edward VI., 1547-53. London, 1861. 8°
— Calendar of state papers, foreign series, reign of Mary, 1553-58. London, 1861. 8°.

Turnebus (*French* **Turnèbe**), Adrianus. Adagia. (*In* **Erasmus,** D. E. Adagiorum chil. quat. 1574.)
— De vino ac ejus usu et abusu. (*In* **Gronovius,** J. Thes. Gr. antiq., v. 9. 1701.)
— NICERON, J. P. (*In his* Mém., v. 39. 1738.)

Turneham, Robert. Voy. under Prince Edward, into Syria, 1270. (*In* **Hakluyt,** R. Col. of voy., v. 2. 1810.)

Turner. *See also* **Turnor.**

Turner, *Rev.* Charles. Due glory to be given to God; discourse, [fast day,] May 15. Boston, 1783. 8°. (B 232, C 74)
— General directions for fulfilling the gospel ministry; sermon, ordination of G. Daman, Tisbury, Oct. 1, 1760. Newport, 1762. 8°. (B 334)
— Gospel ministers considered as the servants of Christ; sermon, ordination of T. Haven, Nov. 7, 1770, Reading. Boston, 1776. 8°. (B 334, 1311)
— Sermon, election. Boston, 1773. 8°. (B 180, 185)
— Sermon, thanksgiving day, Plymouth, Dec. 22, 1773. Boston, 1774. 8°. (B 65, 232)

Turner, Charles. Description of Natardin or Catardin Mountain. (*In* **Mass. Hist. Soc.** Col., v. 18. 1819.)

Turner, Daniel. Treatise on the diseases incident to the skin. 5th ed. London, 1736. 8°.

Turner, Dawson. Memoir of Rev. R. Forby. (*In* **Forby,** R. Vocabulary of East Anglia. 1830.)

Turner, *Rev.* Dawson Wm. Notes on Herodotus. 2d ed. London, *Bohn,* 1853. 8°.

Turner, *Rev.* Edward. Discourse, Charlestown, May 20. Boston, 1821. 8°. (B 1303)
— Substance of a disc. at the public recognition of the 1st Universalist Church in Roxbury, Jan. 4. Charlestown, 1822. 8°.

Turner, Edward, *M.D.* Elements of chemistry; incl. recent discoveries and doctrines. 2d ed. enl. and rev. London, 1828. 8°.

Turner, Edward, *M.A.* College and priory of Hastings, and the priory of Warbleton. (*In* **Sussex Archæological Soc.** Col., v. 13. 1861.) — Decorative tiles found at Keymer. (*In* v. 16. 1864.)

Turner, Elizabeth. *Funeral sermon on.* 1755. *See* **Brine,** J. (B 1242)

Turner, Francis, *Bp. of Ely.* Animadversions [on Bp. Croft's] 'Naked truth; or, The true state of the primitive church'. London, 1676. 4°. (B 1921)
— STRICKLAND, A. (*In her* Lives of the seven bishops. 1866.)

Turner, George. General view of the agriculture of the County of Gloucester. London, 1794. 4°. (W 73)

Turner, *Rev.* George. Nineteen years in Polynesia. London, 1861. 8°.

Turner, *Dr.* Henry E. Oration, East-Greenwich, July 4, 1809. Providence, [1809]. 8°. (B 457)

Turner, J. B. The three great races of men. Springfield, 1861. 8°.

Turner, *Sir* James. Memoirs of his own life and times, 1632-70. Edin., 1829. 4°.

Turner, *Col.* James, *and others.* TRIAL for felony and burglary. 1664. (*In* **Craik,** G. L. Eng. causes célèbres. 1844.)

Turner, John. The wisdom of God in the redemption of man. (*In* **Boyle** lecture sermons, v. 2. 1739.)

Turner, John P. The Birmingham button trade. (*In* **Timmins,** S. Resources of Birmingham. 1866.)

Turner, John W. Report. (*In* **Gillmore,** Q. A. Engineer operations against Charleston. 1865.)

Turner, Joseph Mallord Wm. Liber studiorum; photographs from his drawings. Series 1, 2. London, 1861-62. 2 v. f°.
— Will. [London,] 1861. f°.
— GR. BRIT. *Ho. of Lords.* Report from the select committee on the Turner and Vernon pictures. 1861. [London,] 1861. f°.
— RUSKIN, I. Notes on the Turner gallery at Marlborough House. 3d ed. London, 1857. 8°.
— - Turner and his works. (*In his* **Lectures** on architecture and painting. 1854.)
— THORNBURY, W. Life of T. London, 1862. 2 v. 8°.
— TURNER gallery; with catalogue of Vernon collection. London, [1857]. 16°.

Note. For works illustrated by him *see* **Byron,** G. G. W.; — **Hakewill,** J.; — **Rogers,** S.; — **Scott,** *Sir* W.; — *also* **Keepsake,** The.

Turner, O. History of the pioneer settlement of Phelps & Gorham's Purchase, and Morris' Reserve; added, hist. of Munroe County. Rochester, 1851. 8°.
— Pioneer hist. of the Holland Purchase of western N. Y. Buffalo, 1849. 8°.

Turner, *Capt.* Samuel. Account of an embassy to the court of the Teshoo Lama in Tibet; added, views taken by S. Davis, and obs. botan., mineralog., and med., by R. Saunders. London, 1800. 4°.
— *Same.* 2d ed. London, 1806. 4°.
— Voyage au Thibet. (*In* **Montémont,** A. Biblioth. des voy., v. 31. 1836.)

Turner, *Rev.* Samuel. Sermon; the matriculation of a new class. (*In* **Prot. Episc.** pulpit, v. 2. 1832.)

Turner, Samuel Hulbeart, *D.D.* Address before the General Theological Seminary of the Prot. Episc. Ch. N. Y., 1823. 8°. (B 291)
— Appeal to Episcopalians in behalf of clerical education; sermon, Hartford, Aug. 5. N. Y., 1829. 8°. (B 1776)
— Introductory discourse, opening of the Theological Seminary of the Prot. Episc. Ch. in U. S. Hartford, 1820. 8°. (B 290, W 3)
— Remarks on a late editorial article in the Churchman. N. Y., 1845. 8°. (B 1360)

Turner, Sharon. Affinities and diversities in the languages of the world, and their primeval cause. (*In* **Royal Soc. of Lit.** Trans., v. 1. 1827.)
— History of England. London, 1814-23. 3 v. 4°.

Note. Vol. 1. has the title-page, Hist. of Eng. from the Norman conquest to Edward I.; v. 2. Hist., *etc.,* from Edward I. to the death of Henry V.; v. 3. Hist., *etc.,* during the Middle Ages; Henry VI. - Henry VII.

— History of the Anglo-Saxons. 2d ed. London, 1807. 2 v. 4°.

Contents. Vol. 1. To 1066. 2. Manners of the Saxons. — Landed property. — Government. — Laws. Literature. — Religion. — Language.

— History of the reign of Henry VIII.; with the commencement of the Eng. reformation. London, 1826. 4°.
— History of the reigns of Edward VI., Mary, and Elizabeth. London, 1829. 4°.
— Sacred history of the world. Lond., 1832-37. 3 v. 8°.
— *Same.* N. Y., 1842. 3 v. 18°. (Harper's fam. lib., v. 32, 72, 84.)
— Vindication of the genuineness of the anc. Brit. poems of Aneurin, Taliesin, Llywarch-Hen, and Merdhin. London, 1803. 8°.

Turner, Sydney. Responsibility in alms and means. (*In* **Nat. Assoc. Prom. Soc. Sci.** Trans., 1857.)

Turner, Thomas. Epitome of book-keeping by double entry. Portland, 1804. 12°.

Turner, Thomas Hudson. Some account of domestic architecture in England from the conquest to the end of the 13th century. Oxford, 1851. 8°.

Note. For continuation *see* **Parker**, J. H.

Turner, Wm., *vicar of Walberton.* Compleat hist. of the most remarkable Providences; added, whatever is curious in the works of nature and art. London, 1697. f°.

Turner, *Rev.* Wm. Essay on crimes and punishments. (*In* **Literary and Philos. Soc. of Manchester.** Mem., v. 2. 1789.)

Turner, Wm., *of the Foreign Office.* Journal of a tour in the Levant. London, 1820. 3 v. 8°.

Turner, *Rev.* Wm., *Jr., of Newcastle.* Address, laying the foundation stone of a new chapel at Sunderland. [Newcastle, 183–.] 12°. (C 274)

— English Unitarian writers. — Unitarian general Baptists. — Unitarianism in Eng. (*In* **Beard, J. R.** Unitarianism exhibited. 1846.)

— The ground of Paul's confidence, *etc.*; sermon. Newcastle, 1834. 8°. (C 218)

— Memoir of T. Bewick. (*In* **Jardine**, *Sir* **W.** Naturalist's lib., Orn., v. 6. 1836.)

— The power of Christianity to deliver from the fear of death. *n.t.p.* [Newcastle, 183–?] 12°. (C 248)

— Sermon; the connexion of the resurrection of Christ with a general resurrection. (*In* **Beard, J. R.** Sermons. 1832.)

Turner, Wm. Petition against blood-letting, to the Legislature of N. York. *n.t.p.* [N. Y., 1851.] 8°. (B 1563)

— Triumphs of young physic; or, Chromo-thermal facts. N. Y., [1847]. 8°. (B 1563)

Turner, Wm. Wadden. Additions to the lit. of Amer. aboriginal languages. (*In* **Ludewig, H. E.** Lit. of Amer. abor. lang. 1858.)

— Letter on Indian philology. (*In* **Smithsonian Inst.** Report, 1851.)

— On the recent discoveries of Himyaritic inscriptions, and the attempts made to decipher them. (*In* **Amer. Ethnolog. Soc.** Trans., v. 1. 1845.)

— Report upon the Indian tribes near the 35th parallel. (*In* **U. S.** *War Dept.* Reports of explorations for a R. R. to the Pacific, 1853–54, v. 3.)

— The Sidon inscription; with a tr. (*In* **Amer. Orient. Soc.** Journ., v. 5. 1856.) — Remarks on the Phœnician inscription of Sidon. (*In* v. 7. 1862.)

— Catalogue of the library of W. W. T., sold May. N. Y., 1860. 8°.

Turnerelli, Edward Tracy. Kazan the ancient capital of the Tartar Khans; with an acc. of the province and the tribes which form its population, *etc.* London, 1854. 2 v. 12°.

Turning. Moxon, J. 1694. (*In his* Mechanick exercises, v. 1. 17—.)

— Handbook of turning; cont. concentric, elliptic, and eccentric turning, *etc.* London, 1859. 16°.

Turning the tables; a farce. *See* **Poole, J.**

Turnips. Broussonnet, P. M. A. Instruction sur la culture des navets, les différentes manières de les conserver, *etc.* *n.t.p.* [Paris, 1803.] 8°. (B 528)

— Campos de Mesquita, J. M. de. Sobre a cultura e utilidade dos nobos na comarca de Trancoso. (*In* **Lisbon. Ac. d. Sci.** Mem. econ., v. 5. 1815.)

Turnor. *See also* **Turner.**

Turnor, *Sir* Edmund. Adamson, J. Sermon, funeral of T., Apr. 14; with an account of his charity. London, 1707. 8°. (B 1242)

Turnor, Edmund. Short view of the proceedings of several committees [on] the intended petition for a limited exportation of wool in 1781, 82; with R. Glover's letter. (*In* **Pamphleteer**, 1824; v. 23 of **B 838**)

Turnor, Thomas. Case of the bankers and their creditors stated and examined. 3d impression, with add. *t.p.mut.* London, 1675. 8°.

Turnour, George. Essay on Páli Buddhistical literature. (*In* **Mahawanso**, v. 1. 1837.)

Turnpike. *See* **Proprietors of the Second Turnpike Road in New Hampshire.** 1804. (D 57)

Turnus. Satira. (*In* **Lemaire, N. E.** Poetæ Lat. min., v. 2. 1824. Bibl. class. Lat.)

Turocz, J. de. *See* **Thwrocz, J. de.**

Turpie, D. Speech in the Senate of the U. S., Feb. 7, 1863. (*In* **Hand-book** of the democracy. 1864.)

Turpilius, Sextus. Fragm. (*In* **Estienne, R.** Fr. poet. Lat. 1564.)

— Fragm.; [Lat. and Fr.]. (*In* **Levée, J. B.**, *and* **Le Monnier, G. A.** Théâtre des Latins, v. 15. 1823.)

— Fragm. (*In* **Ribbeck, J. K. O.** Scenicæ Rom. poesis fr., v. 2. 1855.)

Turpin, François Henri. History of Siam. (*In* **Pinkerton, J.** Col. of voy., v. 9. 1811.)

Turpin, Joannes, *Bp. of Rheims, pseud.* *See* **Turpinus, J.**

Turpin de Crissé, Lancelot, *comte.* Commentaires sur les Institutions militaires de Végèce. Montargis, 1779. 3 v. 4°.

— Commentaires sur les Mémoires de Montecuculi. Paris, 1769. 3 v. 4°.

— Essai sur l'art de la guerre. Paris, 1754. 2 v. 8°.

— *Eng.* Essay on the art of war; tr. by J. Otway. London, 1761. 2 v. 4°.

Turpinus, *or* **Tilpinus**, Joannes, *Arbp.* History of Charles the Great and Orlando; ascribed to T. (*In* **Rodd, T.** Hist. of Charles, v. 1. 1812.)

Turre, Philippus a. *See* **Torre, F. della.**

Turreau de Garambouville, Louis Marie, *baron.* Aperçu sur la situation politique des Etats-Unis d'Amérique. Paris, 1815. 8°. (C 91)

— Mémoires sur l'histoire de la guerre de la Vendée. Paris, 1824. 8°. (Berville and Barrière. Col. de mém.)

Turreff, Gavin. Antiquarian gleanings from Aberdeenshire records. Aberdeen, 1859. 12°.

Turretin, François. Theologiæ didactico-elencticæ compend. a L. Riissenio. Amst., 1695. 4°.

Turretin, Jean Alphonse. Fundamentals in religion. (*In* **Sparks, J.** Col. of essays, v. 1. 1823.)

— Traité de la vérité de la religion chrétienne; tiré du lat. par J. Vernet. Paris, 1753. 2 v. 12°.

— University oration conc. the different fates of the Christian religion. 1709. (*In* **Somers, J.** Col. of tracts, v. 12. 1814.)

Turrianus, Franciscus. *See* **Torres, F. de.**

Turrigi, Francisco Maria. Notæad ursi togati inscriptionem. (*In* **Grævius, J. G.** Thes. antiq. Rom., v. 12. 1699.)

Turris, Raphael de. Dissidentis desciscentis receptæque Neapolis lib. vi. (*In* **Gravier, C.** Rac., v. 8. 1770.)

Turrisi Colonna, Giuseppina. Giuditta. — Alle donne siciliane. (*In* **Poeti** ital. contem. 1843.)

Tursellinus (*Lat.* **Torsellino**), Horatius. Histoire de Nostre Dame de Lorette. Douay, 1600. 8°.

— De particulis Latinæ orationis libellum. (*In* **Forcellini, E.** Totius Latinitatis lexicon. 1828.)

Tursen, Erland Zach. Anandria. (*In* **Linné, C.** Amœn. acad., v. 1. 1749.)

Turton, *Sir* Thomas, *Bart.* Address to the people in behalf of dealers in corn. 2d ed. London, 1800. 8°. (B 1682)

Turton, Wm., *M.D.* Conchological dictionary of the British Islands. London, 1819. 12°.

— Manual of the land and fresh-water shells of the British Islands. London, 1831. 16°.

— Medical glossary. 2d ed. London, 1802. 4°.

— System of nature of Linnæus; tr. from Gmelin, Fabricius, Wildenow, *etc.*; with a life of Linnæus by T. London, 1806. 7 v. 8°.

Turton. Church of St. Ann. French, G. J. Bibliographical notices of the church libraries at T. and Gorton. [Manchester,] 1855. 4°. (Chetham Soc., v. 38.)

Tuscaloosa, *ship.* Gr. Brit. *Parl.* Correspondence resp. the Tuscaloosa. London, 1864. f°. (N. A. papers, no. 6.)

Tuscany. Milanesi, C. Istituzione dell' Archivio Centrale di Stato in Firenze. (*In* **Archiv.** stor. ital., app., v. 9. 1853.) — Galeotti, L. Dell' Archivio Centrale di Stato nuova menti instituito in Toscana. (*In* n.s., v. 2. 1855.

Agriculture.

— Leroy-Beaulieu, P. P. Les populations agricoles de la Toscane. (*In* **Revue d. D. Mondes**, jan. 1870.)

Art.

— LASTRI, M. L'Eturia pittrice; storia della pittura toscana. Firenze, 1791-95. 2 v. f°.

— PERKINS, C. C. Tuscan sculptors, their lives, works, and times. London, 1864. 2 v. 4°.

Biography.

— AMATO, G. d'. Bersaglieri toscani. (*In his* Panteon, v. 2. 1851.)

See also **Ferdinand II.**, *of Tuscany*; — **Matilda,** *of Tuscany*; — *also, above, Art.*

Botany.

See Description and Travels. SANTI, G.

Commerce.

— SASSETTI, F. Sul commercio tra la Toscana e le nazioni levantine, 1577. (*In* Archiv. stor. ital., app., v. 9. 1853.)

Description and Travels.

— TARGIONI TOZZETTI, G. Viaggi in diverse parti della Toscana, [1742-45]. Firenze, 1768-79. 12 v. 8°.

— - *French, in part.* Voyage en Toscane, 1742. Paris, 1792. 2 v. 8°.

— SANTI, G. Viaggio 1o-3o per la Toscana, [1789-93]. Pisa, 1695-1806. 3 v. 8°.

Note. This half title covers the works 'Viaggio al Montamiata' and 'Viaggio 2o', 'Viaggio 3o per le due provincie senesi'.

— FONTANI, F. Viaggio pittorico della Toscana. Firenze, 1801-03. 3 v. f°.

— FERRARIO, G. (*In his* Costume, v. 10. 1829.)

— REPETTI, E. Dizionario geog., fisico, storico della Toscana. Firenze, 1833-46. 6 v. 8°.

— TROLLOPE, T. A. Tuscany in 1849 and in 1859. London, 1859. 8°.

— CRAWFORD, M. S. Life in Tuscany, [1849]. London, 1859. 8°.

— *Map.* BLAEU, W. Stato della Chiesa con la Toscana. [Amst., 16–.] (E 78, no. 216)

See also **Leghorn**; — **Massa**; — **Pistoria.**

History.

— *Bibliography.* MORENI, D. Bibliografia storica ragionata della Toscana. Firenze, 1805. 2 v. 4°.

— PIGNOTTI, L. Storia della Toscana, [B.C. 724-1743]. Livorno, 1820-21. 12 v. 12°.

— - *Eng.* History of Tuscany; tr. by J. Browning. London, 1826. 4 v. 8°.

— ISTORIE pistolesi; ovvero delle cose avvenute in Toscana, e diario del Monaldi, 1300-48. Firenze, 1733. 4°.

— CANESTRINI, G. Négociations diplomatiques de la France avec la Toscane; pub. par A. Desjardins. Tome 1: 1311-1498. Paris, 1859. 4°. (Doc. inéd.)

— GIORNALE degli archivi toscani, [1335-1862]. Firenze, 1857-62. 6 v. 8°.

— GUASTI, C. Delle relazioni diplomatiche tra la Toscana e la Francia, 1483-98. (*In* Archivio stor. ital., n.s., v. 14, pt. 2. 1861.)

— GALLUZZI, R. Storia del granducato di T., [1537-1737]. Nuova ed. Fir., 1822. 11 v. 8°.

— ZOBI, H. Memorie economico-politiche, 1737-1859. Firenze, 1860. 2 v. 8°.

— - Storia civile della Toscana, 1737-1848. Firenze, 1850-52. 5 v. 8°.

— BINAUT, L. La Toscane sous la maison de Lorraine, [1747-1848]. (*In* Revue d. D. Mondes, mars 1857.)

— MAZADE, C. de. Le marq. de Lajatico et la Toscane, [1847-60]. (*In* Revue d. D. Mondes, jan. 1860.) — PERRENS, F. T. Souvenirs de la révolution toscane, [1847-48]. (*In* mai 1856.)

See also **Pistoria.**

Literature.

— ILDEFONSO DI SAN LUIGI. Delizie degli eruditi toscani. Firenze, 1770-89. 24 v. in 25 pts. 8°.

— TOMMASEO, N. Canti popolari toscani. (Vol. 1 *of his* Canti popolari. 1841.)

— MARCOALDI, O. Canti popolari. (*In his* Canti pop. umbri. 1855.)

— TIGRI, G. Canti popolari toscani. 2a ed. Firenze, 1860. 12°.

Periodicals.

— GIORNALE storica degli archivi toscani. Firenze, 1857-62. 6 v. 8°.

Monuments.

— GONNELLI, G. Monumenti sepolcrali della Toscana. Firenze, 1819. f°.

— - *French.* Monumens sépulcraux de la Toscane. Nouv. éd. Florence, 1821. f°.

Ornithology.

— SAVI, P. Ornitologia toscana. Vol. 1. Pisa, 1827. 8°.

Proverbs.

— FIACCCI, L. Dei proverbi toscani, lezione, 1813; con la Dichiarazione de' proverbi di G. M. Cecchi. 2a ed. Firenze, 1820. 8°.

— GIUSTI, G. Raccolta di proverbi toscani. Firenze, 1853. 12°.

Tuscarora. GR. BRITAIN. *Parl.* Correspondence rel. to the steamers Nashville and Tuscarora at Southampton. London, 1862. f°. (N. Amer. papers, no. 6.)

Tusculum (*Ital.* **Frascati**). MATTEI, D. B. Memoriæ antiqui Tusculi, [ad a. 1191]. (*In* Grævius. Thes. antiq. Ital., v. 8, pt. 4. 1723.)

— GUASCO, F. E. Dissertazione tusculana, sopra un' antica inscrizione appartenente ad una ornatrice. Roma, 1771. 8°.

— CANINA, L. Descrizione dell' antico Tusculo. Roma, 1841. f°.

Tuski. HOOPER, W. H. Ten months among the tents of the T.; exped. in search of Sir J. Franklin. London, 1853. 8°.

Tuson, E. W. A. British consul's manual. London, 1856. 8°.

Tuson, Edward Wm. Myology illustrated. London, 1825. f°.

— Suppl. to Myol., cont. arteries, veins, nerves, brain, *etc.* London, 1828. f°.

Tussaud, *Mme.* Marie (Grosholtz). Memoirs of the French Revolution; ed. by F. Hervé. Phila., 1839. 2 v. 12°.

Tusser, Thomas. Five hundred points of good husbandrie, besides the book of huswifery, 1599. (*In* **Somers,** J. Col. of tracts, v. 3. 1810.)

— *Same.* Ed. by W. Mavor. London, 1812. 8°.

— A hundreth good pointes of husbandrie. From 1st ed. 1557. (*In* **Brydges,** *Sir* S. E. British bibliog., v. 4. 1814.)

Tustin, *Rev.* Josiah P. Discourse; dedication of the Baptist Church in Warren, R. I., May 8. Prov., 1845. 18°.

Tustin, Septimus, *D.D.* Closing address. (*In* **Lafayette** College. Addresses. 1858. B 1578)

Tutchin, John, *ed. See* **Observator,** The.

Tuteur, Le; comédie. *See* **Dancourt,** F. C. (C 289)

Tuthill, *Mrs.* Louisa Caroline (Huggins). I will be a gentleman. Boston, 1844. 18°.

— Onward! Right onward. Boston, 1845. 18°.

Tutore, Il; commedia. *See* **Goldoni,** C.

Tutore novizio, Il, ossia Gl' inconvenienti del non parlar chiaro. *See* **Giraud,** G.

Tutor's assistant modernized. *See* **Peacock,** T.

Tutshek, Lorentz. On the Tumali language. — Tumali alphabet. (*In* **Philolog. Soc.** Proc., 1846-50.)

Tuttell, Thomas. Description of mathematical instruments. London, 1701. 8°. (C 68)

Tuttle, Henry. Historical catechism of important items in the history of the U. S. 8th ed. Utica, 1835. 8°. (C 278)

— *Same, called* Historical collection. Lowell, 1855. 8°. (C 278)

Tuttle, Hudson. The origin and antiquity of physical man scientifically considered. Boston, 1866. 12°.

Tuttle, Joseph Farrand. Biographical sketch of Gen. W. Winds. (*In* **New Jersey Hist.** Soc. Proc., v. 7. 1853-55.)

— Happiness in being with Christ. (*In* **Amer.** nat. preacher, v. 22. 1848.)

Tuy, *Spain*. FLOREZ, H. De la iglesia de Tuy. (*In his* España sagrada, v. 22, 23. 1767.)

Twain, Mark, *pseud*. *See* **Clemens**, S. L.

Twait, *Miss* Matilda, *Funeral address on*. 1785. *See* **Cottingham**, J. (B 1858)

Tweddell, John. Remains; [ed.] by R. Tweddell. 2d ed. London, 1816. 4°.

Contents. Biog. mem. — Correspondence. — Appendix. — Addenda. — Prolusiones juveniles.

— HUNT, P. Narrative of what is known resp. his lit. remains. London, 1816. 8°. (B 692)

Tweed, Benjamin Franklin. Claims of teaching to the rank of a district profession. (*In* **Amer. Inst. of Instruction.** Lect., 1855.)

— First lessons in language. *See* **Tower**, D. B.

Tweedale County, *Scotland*. JOHNSTON, T. General view of the agriculture of the County of T. London, 1794. 4°. (W 77)

Tweedie, Alexander. Clinical illustrations of fever. Boston, 1831. 8°.

— Library of medicine. London, 1840-41. 8 v. 8°.

Contents. Vol. 1-5. Practical med. 6. **Rigby**, E. Midwifery. 7, 8. **Cruveilhier**, J. Descr. anatomy.

Tweedie, Wm. King, *D.D.* The heart established by the grace of God. (*In* **Sermons** for Sabbath evenings. 185-.)

— Select biographies. Edin., 1845-47. 2 v. 8°. (Wodrow Soc.)

Contents. Vol. 1. **Kirkton**, J. Hist. of J. Welsh. — **Simsone**, A. True record of the life and death of P. Simsone; with sermon on his death. — Life of J. Livingstone by himself; — Discourse, Oct. 13, 1662. — J. Livingstone before the council, Dec. 11, 1662; — Letter to his paroch before his departure; — Letter dated Rotterdam, Oct. 7, 1671; — Letters of J. Livingstone rel. to public events of his time; — Remarks on preaching and praying in public; — Observ. previous to his death; — Memorable characteristics, and remarkable passages of divine Providence exemplified in the lives of eminent ministers, *etc*. — **Colvill**, *Lady* E. Letters to J. Livingstone. — **Gordon**, J., *Viscount Kenmure*. Last speeches. — **Pringle**, W. Memoirs. — **Hamilton**, *Mrs*. J. Account of the particular soliloquies and covenant engagements of Mrs. J. H. 2. **Wodrow**, R. Life of Rev. D. Dickson. — **Dunlop**, W. Life of W. Guthrie. — **Guthrie**, W. Sermon on sympathy. — **Fraser**, J. Memoirs. — Life and sufferings of J. **Nisbet** in Hardhill. — **Stevenson**, J. Rare soul-strengthening and comforting cordial for old and young Christians. — **Goodal**, *Mrs*. Memoir of Mrs. Goodal, by herself. — Last words of Lady **Coltness**, who died June 8, 1675. — A rel. of my Lady A. **Elcho** about her being burnt Feb. 17, 1700.

Twelfth night; or, What you will. *See* **Shakespeare**, W.

Twells, Leonard. Answer to the 'Enquiry into the meaning of demoniacks'. London, 1737. 8°. (E 122)

— Answer to the 'Further enquiry into the meaning of demoniacks'. *t.p.mut.* [London, 1738.] 8°. (E 122)

Twelve mery jests of the wydow Edyth. (*In* **Hazlitt**, W. C. Shakespeare jest-books, v. 3. 1864.)

Twelve peers of France, Ballads of. *See* **Tortajada**, D. L. de.

Twenger, Johann. ANDRESEN, A. (*In his* Der deutsche Peintre-Graveur, v. 2. 1865.)

Twenty five sermons; anniv. meetings of the charity schools in London and Westminster, 1704-28. London, 1729. 8°.

Contents. 1704, **Willis**, R. — 1705, **Stanhope**, G. — 1706, **Kennet**, W. — 1707, **Gastrell**, F. — 1708, **Moss**, R. — 1709, **Bradford**, S. — 1710, **Smalbridge**, G. — 1711, **Snape**, A. — 1712, **Willoughby de Broke**, *Ld*. — 1713, **Dawes**, W. — 1714, **Robinson**, J. — 1715, **Wake**, W. — 1716, **Gibson**, E. — 1717, **Talbot**, W. — 1718, **Lupton**, W. — 1719, **Sherlock**, T. — 1720, **Knight**, J. — 1721, **Marshal**, N. — 1722, **Boulter**, H. — 1723, **Waterland**, D. — 1724, **Wilson**, T. — 1725, **Berriman**, W. — 1726, **Mangey**, T. — 1727, **Watson**, J. — 1728, **Talden**, T.

Twenty-ninth Congress, its men and its measures, *etc*.; a review of the 1st sess. of 29th Cong.; [by E. Brooks. Wash., 1846.] 8°. (B 1502)

Twenty-second of Dec., Landing of the Pilgrims on the. *See* **Plymouth, Landing of the Pilgrims at.**

Twice married. (*In* **Putnam's** mag., v. 5, 6. 1855.)

Twice-told tales; by N. Hawthorne. New ed. Boston, 1853. 2 v. 8°.

Twilight; a poem, at Litchfield, July 4, 1812, [by F. Knight]. N. Y., 1813. 12°. (C 84)

Twin brothers. New York, 1843. 18°.

Twin brothers, The; or, Good luck and good conduct; by M. Hughes. London, 1810. 12°. (C 149)

Twin rivals, The; a comedy. *See* **Farquhar**, G.

Twin roses; by A. C. Ritchie. Boston, 1857. 12°.

Twin sisters; by Miss [Elizabeth] Sandham. Boston, 1813. 18°.

Twining, —. Voy. en Norwège. (*In* **Montémont**, A. Biblioth., v. 46. 1836.)

Twining, Alexander Catlin. Experimental researches tending towards an improvement of the telescope. (*In* **Amer. Assoc.** Proc., v. 6. 1852.) — A demonstration of Euclid's assumed axiom relative to parallel lines. (*In* v. 18. 1869.)

Twining, Henry. Elements of picturesque scenery. London, 1853-56. 2 v. 8°.

Twining, Louisa. Symbols and emblems of early and mediæval Christian art. London, 1852. 4°.

— Workhouses. (*In* **Nat. Assoc. Prom. Soc. Sci.** Trans., 1857.) — Objects and aims of workhouse visiting society. (*In* 1858.) — Training and supervision of workhouse girls. (*In* 1859.) — Workhouse inmates. (*In* 1860.) — Workhouse education. (*In* 1861.)

Twining, Richard. Answer to the 2d report of the East India directors, resp. the sale and prices of tea. London, 1785. 8°. (B 1682)

Twining, Thomas, *d*. 1804. Two dissertations on poetical and musical imitation. (*In* **Aristoteles.** Treatise on poetry. 1815.)

Twining, Thomas. Letter to the chairman of the East India Co. on the danger of interfering in the religious opinions of the natives of India. 2d ed. London, 1807. 8°. (B 1844)

— FULLER, A. Answer to T. (*In his* Apology, pt. 1. 1808. B 1846)

— OWEN, J. Address to the chairman of the East India Co. occasioned by Twining's 'Letter', *etc*. 3d ed. London, 1807. 8°. (B 679, 1844)

Twins. FRESNE DE FRANCHEVILLE, J. Recherches hist. sur les jumeaux de tous les temps. (*In* **Sérieys**, A. Bibl. acad., v. 3. 1810.)

Twins, The; by M. F. Tupper. N. Y., 1845. 16°.

Twins, The. *See* **Woods**, W.

Twisleton, Edward Turner Boyd. Evidences as to the religious working of common schools in Massachusetts. 2d ed. London, 1854. 8°.

— Preface, and collateral evidence. (*In* **Chabot**, C. Handwriting of Junius. 1871.)

Twiss, Horace. Public and private life of Lord Eldon. London, 1844. 3 v. 8°.

Twiss, Richard. Chess. London, 1787-89. 2 v. 8°.

— Travels through Portugal and Spain, 1772-73. London, 1775. 4°.

Twiss, *Sir* Travers. Law of nations; rights and duties in time of peace. Oxford, Lond., 1861. 8°.

— *Same*. Pt. 2: Rights and duties in time of war. Oxford, 1863. 8°.

— The Oregon question examined. London, 1846. 8°.

— The relations of Schleswig and Holstein to Denmark and the Germanic Confederation. London, 1848. 8°.

— Trade and international law. (*In* **Nat. Assoc. Prom. Soc. Sci.** Trans., 1862.)

— View of the progress of political economy in Europe since the 16th century. London, 1847. 8°.

Twiss, Wm.(?) Preface. (*In* **Mede**, J. Key of Revelation. 1643.)

Twitchell, Amos, *M.D.* BOWDITCH, H. I. Memoir of T. Boston, 1851. 12°.
— BIOGRAPHICAL notices of T. (*In* **Mass. Med. Soc.** Med. com., v. 8. 1854.)

Twitt, John. True report of a voyage for the West Indies by C. Newport. (*In* **Hakluyt**, R. Col. of voy., v. 4. 1811.)

Two admirals, The; by [J. F. Cooper]. Phila., 1842. 2 v. 12°.
— *Same.* Rev. ed. N. Y., 1851. 12°.
— *Same.* Illust. by Darley. N. Y., 1861. 8°.

Two angry women of Abingdon. *See* **Porter**, H.

Two associations, The; one subscribed by CLVI members of the Ho. of Com. in 1643, the other seized in the closet of the Earl of Shaftsbury [1681]. London, 1681. f°. (**A 51**)

Two baronesses; by H. C. Andersen. N. Y., 1869. 12°.

Two Bonnycastles. *See* **Morton**, J. M.

Two college friends; by F. W. Loring. Boston, 1871. 16°.
— *Same.* (*In* **Old and new**, v. 3. 1871.)

Two connoisseurs. *See* **Hayley**, W.

Two defaulters, The; by Mrs. M. Griffiths. N. Y., 1842. 18°.

Two discourses; on the creation by Christ; and on the resurrection through the man Christ. 3d ed. Camb., 1787. 8°. (**B 1371**)

Two elegies. London, 1767. f°. (**A 45**)

Two Figaros, The; a musical comedy. *See* **Planché**, J. R.

Two friends. *See* **Lacy**, R.

Two gay deceivers; or, Black, White, and Grey; farce. **Robertson**, T. W.

Two gentlemen in a fix; an interlude. *See* **Suter**, W. E.

Two gentlemen of Verona. *See* **Shakespeare**, W.

Two guardians, The; a drama. *n.p.*, [18—]. 16°. (**D 42**)

Two guardians, The; or, Home in this world; by C. M. Yonge. N. Y., 1866. 12°.

Two heads better than one; a farce. *See* **Horne**, L.

Two idle apprentices. (*In* **Household words**, v. 16. 1857.)

Two legacies; [by G. L. Putnam]. Camb., 1863. 12°.

Two letters on the present conjuncture of affairs in N. Amer. London, *reprinted* 1755. 8°. (**B 742**)

Two letters to 'a barrister', cont. strictures on 'Hints to the public', *etc.*; by a looker-on. Oxford, 1809. 8°. (**B 726**)

Two loves and a life; by T. Taylor and C. Reade. (*In* **Sargent**, E. Mod. stand. dr., v. 35.)

Two marriages; by [Mrs. D. M. Mulock Craik]. N.Y., 1867. 12°.

Two mentors, The; by C. Reeve. Lond., 1803. 12°.

Two misers, The. *See* **O'Hara**, K.

Two noble kinsmen, The. (*In* **Beaumont**, F., *and* **Fletcher**, J. Dramatick works, v. 10. 1778; v. 11. 1846; — *and in* **Lamb**, C. Spec. of dram. poets. 1854.)

Two old men's tales; by [Mrs. Marsh-Caldwell]. London, 1850. 16°.

Two plunges for a pearl; by M. Collins. (*In* **London society**, v. 19. 1871.)

Two Puddifoots, The; a farce. *See* **Morton**, J. M.

Two schemes of a Trinity considered. [London,] 1784. 8°. (**B 249**)

Two sermons on a fast-day during the late war with France. London, 1778. 8°. (**B 240**)

Two Sicilies. *See* **Naples.**

Two sisters, The; a tale for the 'Good Shepherd'; by Lady Herbert. Boston, 1870. 16°.

Two strings to your bow. *See* **Jephson**, R.

Two tariffs compared and both found wanting in the element of protection for American labor; [by J. Mann]. With app. Boston, 1846. 8°. (**B 1514**)

Two vacations; or, The sisters of mercy at home, by [Mrs. E. R. Charles]. N. Y., 1865. 12°.

Two words of counsel, and one of comfort, addressed to the Prince of Wales. London, 1795. 8°. (**B 1406**)

Two years before the mast; [by R. H. Dana]. N. Y., [1840]. 18°. (Harper's fam. lib., v. 106.)
— *Same.* London, 1841. 8°.
— *Same.* New ed., with subsequent matter. Boston, 1869. 12°.
— *Same.* (*In* **Perils of the ocean.** 183–. **A 67**)

'Twould puzzle a conjuror. *See* **Poole**, J.

Twyne, John. De rebus Albionicis, Britannicis, atque Anglicis libri II. Londini, 1590. 8°.

Twysden, *Sir* Roger, *Bart.* Certaine considerations upon the government of England; ed. [with an introd.] by J. M. Kemble. London, 1849. 4°. (Camden Soc., v. 45.)

Tyard, Pontus de. *See* **Thiard**, P. de.

Tycho Brahe. *See* **Brahe**, Tygo *or* Tycho.

Tychsen, Thomas Christian. De numis Cuficis in bibliotheca regia Goettingensi adservatis. (*In* **Goettingen. Ges. d. Wiss.** Comm., 1787–88, 90.) — De numis Cuficis. — De numis orientalibus in Bibliotheca Regia Gottingensi adservatis. (*In* 1789–90.) — De numis Hasmonæorum paralipomena. (*In* 1791–92.) — De religionum Zoroastricarum apud exteras gentes vestigiis. (*In* 1791–93.) — De numis Arabico-Hispanicis bibliothecæ Götting. Acad. cum epimetro ad superiores commentationes. — De numis Indicis, maxime in Bibliotheca Göttin. Acad. asservatis. (*In* 1798–99.) — Quatenus Muhammedes aliorum religionum sectatores toleraverit. — De rei numariæ apud Arabes origine et progressu, cum examine critico historiæ monetæ Arabicæ Macrizii nuper editæ. (*In* 1800–03.) — De Afganorum origine et historia. — De commerciis et navigationibus Hebræorum ante exilium Babylonicum. (*In* 1804–08.) — De numis veterum Persarum. (*In* 1808–11, 1811–13.) — De numis veterum Persarum, qua inprimis tetradrachma Arsacidarum recensentur. — De numis Orientalibus in bibliotheca regia Gottingensi adservatis inprimis Selgiucidarum et Gengiscanidarum. — De poeseos Arabum origine et indole antiquissima. (*In* 1814–15.) — De chartæ papyraceæ in Europa per Medium Ævum usu. (*In* 1816–18.) — De defectibus rei numariæ Muhammedanorum. — De inscriptionibus Indicis et privilegiis Judæorum et Christianorum S. Thomæ in ora Malabarica cum explicatione inscriptionis trilinguis a Buchanano adlatæ. — De numo Atheniensi tetradrachma antiquissima in thesauris biblioth. Universitatis Regiæ adservato. (*In* 1819–22.) — De numis Græcis et barbaris in Bochara nuper repertis imprimis numo Demetrii Indiæ regis. — De origine ac fide antiquæ Persarum historiæ qualis a scriptoribus Orientalibus traditur. (*In* 1823–27.) — Memoria J. G. Eichhorn. (*In* 1823–28.) — In chartam donationis librorum Ecclesiæ Hildesiensi seculo XII. a Brunone episc. factæ. — De inscriptionibus Arabicis in Hispania repertis. (*In* 1828–32.)

Tyde, The, taryeth no man; by G. Wapull, 1576. (*In* **Collier**, J. P. Illust. of early Eng. lit., v. 2. 1864.)

Tydeman, H. W. CATALOGUE de la bibliothèque de T., la vente 24 oct. - 8 nov. 1864. La Haye, 1864. 8°.

Tyder, James. Bonaparte à Sainte-Hélène; tr. de l'Anglais. Paris, 1816. 8°.

Tyerman, *Rev.* Daniel, *and* **Bennet**, G. Journal of voyages and travels in the South Sea Islands, *etc.*, comp. by J. Montgomery. London, 1831. 2 v. 8°.

Tyler, *Lieut.* The battle of Waterloo taken on the spot after the action, 18th June 1815. London, 1815. MAP.

Tyler, Adaline. BROCKETT, L. P. (*In his* Woman's work in the civil war. 1867.)

Tyler, Benjamin Owen. Declaration of independence; answer to J. Binns. Wash., 1818. 8°. (**C 81, 119**)

Tyler, Bennet, *D.D.* Letter to Dr. Bushnell on Christian nurture. *n.t.p.* [1847.] 8°. (**B 1354**)
— Memoirs of the life and character of A. Nettleton. 2d ed. Hartford, 1845. 12°.
— Serious call to those who are without the pale of the Episcopal Church. *n.t.p.* [18—?] 8°. (**C 198**)
— Sermon; free salvation. (*In* **National** preacher, v. 2. 1827–28.)
— Sermon, Litchfield, before the Foreign Mission Society, Feb. 10. New Haven, 1813. 8°. (**B 1010**)
— RAYNER, M. Observations on Tyler's sermon on the 'saints' perseverance. New Haven, 1817. 8°. (**B 273**)

Tyler, Comfort. Correspondence developing the purposes of those engaged in the Wilkinson and Burr revolution. (*In* **Safford**, W. H. Blennerhasset. 1841.)

Tyler, Daniel P. Statistics of certain branches of industry in Conn. for the year ending Oct. 1, 1845. Hartford, 1846. 8°.

Tyler, E. R. Slaveholding a malum in se, or invariably sinful. Hartford, 1839. 8°. (B 1471)
Tyler, George Palmer. Our nationality; discourse before the Cong. Soc., Brattleborough, Vt., thanksgiving day, Nov. 4. Boston, 1862. 8°. (B 1592)
Tyler, George W. Address before the Mercantile Lib. Assoc. of Boston, Mar. 11. Bost., 1836. 8°. (B 1582)
Tyler, James Endell. Henry of Monmouth; or, Memoirs of Henry v. London, 1838. 2 v. 8°.
— On oaths; their history, *etc.* London, 1834. 8°.
— Sermon, consecration of E. [Copleston], Bp. of Llandaff. London, 1828. 4°. (A 60)
— Sermon, consecration of E. [Denison], Bp. of Salisbury. London, 1837. 4°. (A 60)
Tyler, John. Speech on Mr. Tazewell's motion to amend the general appropriation bill, Feb. 24. Wash., 1831. 8°. (B 1801)
— CONFEDERATE STATES. *Congress.* Proceedings on the death of J. Tyler, Jan. 20. Richmond, 1862. 8°. (B 1639)
— CUMMING, H. Secret history of the perfidies, intrigues, and corruptions of the Tyler dynasty. Wash., 1845. 8°. (B 1501)
— JOHN Tyler; his history, character, and position. N. Y., 1843. 8°. (B 1460)
— WISE, H. A. Seven decades of the Union; Memoir of J. T. Phila., 1872 [1871]. 8°.
Tyler, Royall. The Algerine captive. Walpole, 1797. 2 v. 12°.
Tyler, Samuel. Argument of the State in the case of Maryland *vs.* board of commis. for the Frederick Female Seminary. *n.p.*, 1851. 8°. (B 1439)
Tyler, Sarah. Mad's Christmas adventure. (*In* Parr, L. The Blue Bell. 1871.)
Tyler, Wm. Seymour, *D.D.* Colleges, their place among Amer. instit.; address before the Soc. for the Prom. of Collegiate and Theol. Educ. at the West. N. Y., 1857. 8°. (B 1609)
— Joshua and Judges; or, Heroic age of Israel. (*In* **Boston** lectures. 1871.)
Tyll Owlglass, The marvellous adventures of; [by T. Murner; tr.] by R. R. H. Mackenzie. Boston, 1860. 8°.
Tylney Hall; by T. Hood. (*In his* Works, v. 3, 4. 1862.)
Tylor, Edward Burnett. Anahuac; or, Mexico and the Mexicans, ancient and modern. London, 1861. 8°.
— Condition of pre-historic races as inferred from observation of modern tribes. (*In* **International Congress of Pre-Historic Archæology.** Trans., 1868.)
— Primitive culture; researches into mythology, *etc.* London, 1871. 2 v. 8°.
— Researches into the early hist. of mankind and the development of civilization. London, 1865. 8°.
Tymms, Samuel. The family topographer; acc. of the antient and present state of the counties of England. London, 1832–43. 7 v. 16°.
Contents. Vol. 1. *Home circuit.* Essex. — Hertfordshire. — Kent. — Surrey. — Sussex. 2. *Western circuit.* Cornwall. — Devonshire. — Dorsetshire. — Hampshire. — Somersetshire. — Wiltshire. 3. *Norfolk circuit.* Bedfordshire. — Buckinghamshire. — Cambridgeshire. — Huntingdonshire. — Norfolk. — Suffolk. 4. *Oxford circuit.* Berkshire. — Gloucestershire. — Herefordshire. — Monmouthshire. — Oxfordshire. — Shropshire. — Staffordshire. — Worcestershire. 5. *Midland circuit.* Derbyshire. — Leicestershire. — Lincolnshire. — Northamptonshire. — Nottinghamshire. — Rutlandshire. — Warwickshire. 6. *Northern circuit.* Cumberland. — Durham. — Lancashire. — Northumberland. — Westmorland. — Yorkshire. 7. Middlesex. — London and Westminster.
— Wills and inventories from the registers of the commissary of Bury St. Edmund's and the archdeacon of Sudbury. London, 1850. 4°. (Camden Soc., v. 49.)
Tymms, W. R. The art of illuminating illustrated by borders, initial letters, *etc.*, chromolithographed. (*In* Wyatt, M. D. Art of illuminating, *etc.* 18—.)
Tympius, Matthæus. Mensæ theolophilosophicæ, h.e., Quæstiones symposiacæ. Monast. Westphal., 1629. 2 v. 12°.
Tyndale. *See also* **Tindal**; — **Tyndall.**
Tyndale, John Warre. The island of Sardinia. London, 1849. 3 v. 12°.
Tyndale, Wm. Answer to Sir T. More's Dialogue; Supper of the Lord; W. Tracy's Testament expounded; ed. by H. Walter. Camb., 1850. 8°. (Parker Soc.)
— Doctrinal treatises and introductions to the Scriptures; ed. by H. Walter. Camb., 1848. 8°. (Parker Soc.)
— Expositions and notes on Scripture; [with] practice of prelates; ed. by H. Walter. Camb., 1849. 8°. (Parker Soc.)
— Several tracts, being parts of vols. 2, 3, 4 of some work unknown.]
Namely. Obedience of a Christian man. — Practice of prelates. — Answer to Sir T. More's dialogue. — Pathway into the Scripture. — Testament of master W. Tracy expounded. — Supper of the Lord.
— ANDERSON, C. (*In his* Annals of the English Bible, v. 1. 1845.)
Tyndall, John. Day among the séracs of the Glacier du Géant. (*In* Ball, J. Peaks, *etc.* 1859.)
— Faraday as a discoverer. Lond., 1868. 8°.
— Fragments of science for unscientific people. London, 1871. 8°.
Contents. The constitution of nature. — Thoughts on prayer and natural law. — Miracles and special providences. — Matter and force. — An address to students. — Scope and limit of scientific materialism. — Scientific use of the imagination. — On radiation. — On radiant heat in relation to the colour and chemical constitution of bodies. — On chemical rays and the structure and light of the sky. — Dust and disease. — Life and letters of Faraday. — Elementary lecture on magnetism. — Slates. — Death by lightning. — Science and spirits. — Vitality. — Additional remarks on miracles.
— From Lauterbrunnen to the Aeggishhorn. (*In* Galton, F. Vacation tourists. 1860.)
— Glaciers of the Alps. London, 1860. 8°.
— Heat considered as a mode of motion. London, 1863. 8°.
— Hours of exercise in the Alps. Lond., 1871. 16°.
— Importance of the study of physics by all classes. (*In* Roy. Inst. Lect., 1855.)
— Mountaineering in 1861. London, 1862. 8°.
— Notes of lectures on electrical phenomena and theories. London, 1870. 16°.
— Notes of nine lectures on light, 1869. London, 1870. 16°.
— On radiation; 'Rede' lecture before the Univ. of Cambridge, Eng., May 16. N. Y., 1865. 12°.
— *Same.* (*In his* Fragments of sci. 1871; — *and in* Smithsonian Inst. Reports. 1868.)
— Researches on diamagnetism and magne-crystallic action, incl. diamagnetic polarity. London, 1870. 8°.
— Sound; eight lectures. London, 1867. 8°.
— Use and limit of the imagination in science. London, 1870. 8°.
— BASTIAN, H. C. (*In his* Modes of origin. 1871.)
— FORBES, J. D. Reply to T.'s remarks [in 'Glaciers of the Alps'] rel. to Rendu's 'Théorie des glaciers'. Edin., 1860. 8°.
Tyne *River.* ARMSTRONG, *Sir* W. G., *and others.* (*In his* Indust. resources. 1864.)
Tyng, Dudley Atkins. Address to the Anc. and Hon. Soc. of Masons, Newburyport on the feast of St. John the Evangelist, 5786. Newburyport, 5787. 4°. (A 70, B 14, 69)
— Obituary notice of W. D. Peck. (*In* **Mass. Hist. Soc.** Col., v. 20. 1823.)
— Reports of cases argued and determined in the Supreme Court of Mass., 1806–22. (Vol. 1, 2d ed.) Boston, 1816, 11, 08–23. 17 v. 8°.
Note. Vol. 1 is ed. by E. Williams.
— LOWELL, J. Biog. notice of D. A. Tyng. (*In* Mass. Hist. Soc. Col., v. 22. 1830.)
Tyng, Edward. ALDEN, T. Memoir of E. and W. Tyng. Boston, 1808. 8°. (B 268)
— *Same.* (*In* **Mass. Hist. Soc.** Col., v. 10. 1809.)

Tyng, Stephen Higginson, *D.D.* The connexion between early religious instruction and mature piety; sermon. Phila., 1837. 12°. (C 210)
— Four Gospels arranged as a practical family commentary. N. Y., 1853. 8°.
— Guide to confirmation. Phila., 1846. 32°.
— *Same.* N. Y., 1858. 32°. (D 31)
— Letter sustaining the ordination of A. Carey. N. Y., 1843. 8°. (B 1392)
— The path of the just. (*In* **Amer. pulpit.** 1831; — *and in* **Protestant** Episcopal pulpit, v. 1. 1831. B 1779)
— Sermon, death of A. Lincoln. (*In* **Lincoln, A.** Our martyr president. 1865.)

Tyng, Wm. Alden, T. Memoir of W. and E. Tyng. Boston, 1808. 8°. (B 268)
— - *Same.* (*In* **Mass. Hist. Soc.** Col., v. 10. 1809.)

Tyngsborough, *Mass.* Fox, C. J. (*In his* History of Dunstable. 1846.)
— Lawrence, N. Historical sketch of T. (*In* **Mass. Hist. Soc.** Col., v. 14. 1816.)

Tynnichus. Fragm. (*In* **Bergk, T.** Poetæ lyr. Gr. 1853.)

Typee. *See* **Melville, H.**

Types. *See* **Jesus.** *Christology of the Old Testament* (p. 1576).

Types (*in printing*). *See* **Printing** (p. 2421).

Types of mankind. *See* **Ethnology** (p. 932).

Typhoid fever. Jackson, J. Cases of typhoid fever, Mass. Gen. Hospital, 1821-35. (*In* **Mass. Med. Soc.** Med. comm., v. 6. 1841.)
— Louis, P. C. A. Examen de l'Examen de Broussais relativement à la phthisie, et à l'affection typhoide. Paris, **1834.** 8°.
— Andral, G. Observations on the treatment of typhoid fever by purgatives by M. de Larroque. (*In* **Dunglison, R.** Med. monographs, v. 1. 1838.)
— Hale, E. Typhoid fever of New England. Boston, 1839. 8°.
— - *Same.* (*In* **Mass. Med. Soc.** Med. comm., v. 6. 1841.)
— Huss, M. Observations sur l fièvre typhoide qui a regné **1841-42.** *n.t.p.* Paris, 1845.] 8°.
— Ramsay, H. A. Necrological appearances of southern typhoid fever in the negro. *n.p.*, 1852. 8°. (B 1561)

See also **Typhus fever.**

Typhon, Le, ou la Gigantomachie; poème burlesque. *See* Scarron, P.

Typhus fever. Buchanan, G. Treatise upon the typhus fever. Balt., 1789. 16°. (W 45)
— Jackson, R. History of the cure of epidemic and contagious fever. Edin., **1798.** 8°.
— Armstrong, J. Practical illustrations of typhus, *etc.* London, **1816.** 8°.
— Mills, T. Morbid anatomy of the brain in typhous or brain fever. 2d ed. Dublin, 1818. 8°. (C 147)
— Percival, E. Practical observations on typhous fever. [1818.] London, 1819. 8°.
— Clutterbuck, H. Observations on the prevention and treatment of the epidemic fever. London, **1819.** 8°.
— Jackson, R. Sketch of the history and cure of contagious fever. London, 1819. 8°.
— Louis, P. C. A. Disease known under the name of gastro-enterite, *etc.*, fever, [**1828**]; tr. by H. I. Bowditch. Boston, 1836. 2 v. 8°.
— Saint Anthoine, D. Quels sont les rapports qui existent entre le typhus et les affections typhoïdes? Paris, 1835. 4°. (A 44)
— Roupell, G. L. Short treatise on typhus fever. [**1839.**] Phila., 1840. 8°.
— Stokes, W. Researches on the state of the heart and the use of wine in typhus fever. (*In* **Dunglison, R.** Med. and surg. monographs, v. 3. **1840.**)
— Upham, J. B. Records of maculated typhus, **1847-48.** N. Y., 1852. 8°.
— - *Another copy.* (B 1692)
— Ingalls, W. Case of typhus or ship-fever with remarks. Boston, 1848. 8°. (B 1555)
— Wynne, J. Typhus fever, at Baltimore almshouse, 1850-51. (Pages 417-425 *of* **Amer.** journal of medical sci., n.s., v. 23. 1852. B 1565)
— Smith, J. L. Essay on the sudden coma of typhus and typhoid fevers. N. Y., 1853. 8°. (B 1562)
— Upham, J. B. Illustrations of typhus fever in Great Britain; with account of the reappearance of typhus in Boston, **1857-58.** Boston, 1858. 8°.
— - *Another copy.* (B 1563)
— Murchison, C. Typhus fever. (*In his* Treatise on the continued fevers of Great Britain. 1862.)
— Virchow, R. Du typhus famélique et de quelques maladies voisines; tr. de l'allemand. Paris, 1868. 8°. (E 26)

See also **Epidemics; — Fever; — Malaria; — Ship fever; — Spotted fever; — Typhoid fever.**

Typography. *See* **Electrotype; — Elzevirs; — Printing.**

Tyræus, Petrus. *See* **Thyræus, P.**

Tyrannic love; or, The royal martyr; tragedy, by J. **Dryden.** (*In his* Works, v. 3. 1808.)

Tyrannical liberty men; discourse upon negro slavery in the U. S. Hanover, N. H., 1795. 8°. (B 523)

Tyrannicide. Titus, *Col.* Killing no murder. London, **1656,** *reprinted* 1775. 8°. (B 681)
— Baxter, S. Tyrannicide proved lawful; discourse, Symsbury, Conn. London, **1782.** 8°. (B 681)

Tyranny. Alfieri, V. Della tirannide. (*In his* Opere, v. 3. 1806; *and* Opere filosofiche, v. 2. 1822.)

Tyranny and Popery lording it, *etc.*; being a further acc. of the growth of knavery; [by R. L'Estrange]. London, 1678. 4°. (B 9)

Tyranny unmasked; answer to [S. Johnson's] 'Taxation no tyranny'. London, 1775. 8°. (B 363)

Tyrans de village, Les; par Meurice. Par., 1857. 18°.

Tyrant king of Crete, The; tragedy, by Sir C. Sedley. (*In his* Works, v. 9. 1722.)

Tyrants. Lucianus *Samosatensis.* Declamatio D. Erasmi Roterodami L. tyrannicidæ respondens. (*In his* Opera, v. 1. 1687.)

Tyre. Recherches sur la fondation de la ville de Tyr. (*In* **Sérieys, A.** Bibl. acad., v. 1. 1810.)

Tyrie, James. Knox, J. An answer to a letter of a Jesuit named Tyrie. (*In* **Knox, J.** Works, v. 6, pt. 2. 1864.)

Tyringham. Brewer, E. History of T. (*In* **Field, D. D.** History of the County of Berkshire, pt. 2. 1829.)

Tyrol, *King of Scotland.* Paræneses ad filium Friderbrantum. (*In* **Schilter, J.** Thes. antiq. Teut., v. 2. 1727.)

Tyrol, The. *Description.*

— Alison, *Sir* A. The Tyrol. (*In* **Blackwood's mag.,** v. 5. 1819; — *and in his* Misc. essays. 1845.)
— Allom, T. Views in the Tyrol after sketches by J. V. Isser; with descriptions by a companion of Hofer. London, [182-?]. 8°.
— Inglis, H. D. The Tyrol, [1834]. 2d ed. Frankfort o. M., 1839. 18°.
— Golbéry, P. de. [1838.] *See History* (p. **1234-1814**).
— Barrow, J. Tour in Austrian Lombardy, the northern Tyrol, *etc.*, **1840.** Lond., 1841. 12°.
— White, W. On foot through Tyrol in the summer of **1855.** London, 1856. 8°.
— Baedeker, K. (*In his* Switzerland. 1863; *and, Germ.,* Schweiz. 1869.)
— How we spent the summer; or, A 'voyage en zigzag', *etc.*, [1865 ?]. 3d ed. London, 1866. obl. 4°.
— Pictures in Tyrol and elsewhere, [1866]; from a family sketch book, by the author of 'A voyage en zigzag'. London, 1867. 4°.
— Knapsack guide for travellers in Tyrol and the eastern Alps. Lond., *Murray,* **1867.** 12°.

Maps.

— Jansson, J. Comitatus Tirolensis. [Amst., 16—.] (E 78, no. 120)
— Seutter, M. Principali dignitate gaudens comitat. Tirolis. Aug. Vindel., [17—]. (E 93)
— Spergs, J. de. Tyrolis pars meridionalis. Vienna, 1762. (E 66)

See also **Alps; — Dolomite Mountains.**

History.

— Golbery, P. de. Histoire et description de la Suisse et du Tyrol, [**1234-1814**]. Paris, 1838. 8°. (Univers.)
— Chmel, J. Urkunden zur Geschichte von Oesterreich, Tirol, *etc.*, [**1246-1300**]. Wien, 1849. 8°. (Fontes rer. Aust., 2. Abth., 1. Bd.)

— STREITER, J. Der tiroler Befreiungskampf von 1813. (*In* **Historische** Zeitschrift, v. 15. 1866.)
— BELGIOJOSO. C. T., *princesse* de. L'insurrection du Tyrol italien, [1848]. (*In* **Revue** d. D. Mondes, jan. 1849.)

Literature.

— MEYER, M. Sagen-Kränzlein aus Tirol. Pest, Wien, und Lpz., 1856. 8°.

Tyrolese minstrels, The; or, The romance of every day life, by a lady. Boston, 1841. 18°.

Tyrrell, Edward. CATALOGUE of the lib. of T., sold April. London, 1864. 8°.

Tyrrell, *Sir* James. General history of England. London, 1700–04. 5 v. f°.
Contents. Vol. 1. 52 B.C.–1066 A.D. 2. 1031–1199. 3. 1199–1272. 4. 1272–1377. 5. 1377–99.

Tyrtæus. Fragm. (*In* **Bergk,** T. Poet. lyr. Gr. 1853.)
— War songs; tr. by J. Banks; with a metrical version by J. M. Chapman. (*In* **Theocritus.** Idylls. 1853.)

Tyrwhitt, *Rev.* Richard St. John. Handbook of pictorial art; perspective by A. Macdonald. Oxford, 1868. 8°.
— The religious use of taste. (*In* **Weir,** A. The Church and the age. 1870.)
— Sinai. (*In* **Galton,** F. Vacation tourists. 1862–63.)

Tyrwhitt, Thomas. Appendix, *etc.* (*In* **Gr. Brit.** *Ho. of Com.* Proceedings, 1620, 21, v. 2. 1766.)
— Dissertatio de Babrio. Londini, 1776. 8°.
— Essay on the language and versification of Chaucer. (*In* **Chaucer,** G. Canterbury tales, v. 1. 1822.)
— Translations in verse; Pope's Messiah, Philips's Splendid shilling in Latin, The Eighth Isthmian of Pindar in English. Oxford, 1752. 4°. **(A 69)**

Tyscovecius, Johannes. BREVIS relatio de Tyscovicii martyrio. (*In* **Sand,** C. von der. Bibliotheca Anti-trinitariorum. 1684.)

Tyson, Bryan. The institution of slavery considered in connection with our sectional troubles. Wash., 1863. 8°.

Tyson, Henry. Report. *See* **Baltimore.** Report on Jones's Falls. 1870; — **Baltimore.** *Sewerage Commission.*

Tyson, James. Brief hist. view of the causes of the decline of the commerce of nations. London, 1813. 8°. **(B 239)**

Tyson, Job Roberts. Discourse before the Young Men's Colonization Soc. of Penn., Oct 24. Phila., 1834. 8°. **(B 1483)**
— Discourse, colonial history of the eastern and some of the southern states. Phila.. 1842. 8°. **(B 1607)**
— Discourse, integrity of the legal character, before the Law Academy of Phila. Phila., 1839. 8°. **(B 1143)**
— Discourse, surviving remnants of the Indian race in the U. S., Oct. 24, 1836, before the Soc. for Commem. the Landing of W. Penn. Phila., 1836. 8°. **(B 1171)**
— Lecture, social and moral influences of the Amer. Revolution. Phila., 1838. 8°. **(B 1585)**
— Lottery system in the U. S. Phila., 1837. 12°.
— Memoir of T. C. James. (*In* **Penn. Hist. Soc.** Mem., v. 3, pt. 2. 1836.)
— Social and intellectual state of Penn. prior to 1743. Phila., 1843. 8°. **(B 1188, 1611)**

Tyson, John. *See* **Jeffers,** W., *vs.* **Tyson.** 1808. **(B 408)**

Tyson, John S. Speech on the Jew bill, in the House of Delegates, Md. (*In* **Brackenridge,** H. M. Speeches. 1829.)

Tyson, Wm. Some transactions in Bristol in the reigns of Henry VI. and Edward IV. — St Nicholas of the tower. (*In* **Archæol. Inst.** of **Gr. Brit.** Memoirs illust. hist. of Bristol. 1853.)

Tyssen, Amherst Daniel. Church bells of Sussex. (*In* **Sussex Archæological** Soc. Col., v. 16. 1864.)

Tyssot de Patot, Simon. Voyages et avantures de Jaques Massé [pseud.]. L'Utopie, 1760. 8°.

Tytler, Alexander Fraser, *Lord Woodhouselee.* Essay on military law and the practice of courts martial. 3d ed., by C. James. London, 1814. 8°.
— Essay on the principles of translation. 2d ed. London, 1797. 8°.
— Memoirs of H. Home of Kames; sketches of the progress of literature, *etc.*, in Scotland during the 18th cent. Edin., 1807. 2 v. 4°.
— Universal history to the end of the 18th cent. Lond., 1834. 6 v. 16°. (Fam. lib., v. 45–50.)
Contents. Vol. 1. Greece, to 336 B.C. 2. 336–168 B.C. — Rome, to 343 B.C. 3. 343 B.C. – 392 A.D. 4. 392–1270. 5. 1250–1760. 6. 1357–1724.
— *Same.* Continued to 1820, by E. Nares. N.Y., 1848. 6 v. 18°. (Harper's fam. lib., v. 86–91.)
Contents. Vol. 1. Greece, to 168. 2. Greece, 168. Rome, to 30 B.C. 3. 30 B.C. – 1066. 4. 1066–1763. 5. 1513–1724. 6. 1715–1820.
— ALISON, A. Memoir of T. (*In* **Roy. Soc. of Edin.** Trans., v. 8. 1818.)

Tytler, James. Paine's 2d part of the 'Age of reason' answered. Salem, 1796. 8°.
— Proposals for publishing a new system of geography, ancient and modern. Salem, 1802. 8°. **(B 398)**
— Treatise on plague and yellow fever. Salem, 1799. 8°.

Tytler, John. Application of the Roman alphabet to Oriental languages. 1834. *See* **Trevelyan,** C. E.

Tytler, Patrick Fraser. Account of the life and writings of Sir T. Craig; incl. biog. sketches of legal characters since the institution of the court of session till the union. Edin., 1823. 12°.
— England under Edward VI. and Mary, with the contemporary hist. of Europe; illust. in a ser. of original letters. London, 1839. 2 v. 8°.
Contents. Vol. 1. 1546–51. 2. 1551–58.
— Historical view of the progress of discovery on the more northern coasts of Amer.; with sketches of nat. hist. of the N. American regions, by J. Wilson; add., app. cont. remarks on a late memoir of S. Cabot, with a vindication of R. Hakluyt. Edin., 1832. 16°.
— *Same.* N. Y., 1846. 16°. (Harper's fam. lib. v. 53.)
— History of Scotland. Edin., 1828–50. 9 v. *and* Index 8°.
Contents. Vol. 1. 1249–1329. 2. 1329–71. 3. 1371–1437. 4. 1437–97. 5. 1497–1546. 6. 1546–65. 7. 1565–74. 8. 1573–87. 9. 1586–1603.
— Life of Henry VIII. Edin., 1837. 16°. (Edin. cab. lib., v. 22.)
— Life of Sir W. Raleigh. Edin., 1833. 16°. (Edin. cab. lib., v. 11.)
— Life of the Admirable Crichton. 2d ed. Edin., 1823. 12°.
— Lives of Scottish worthies. London, 1831–33. 3 v. 16°. (Fam. lib., v. 29–31.)
Contents. Vol. 1. Alexander III. — M. Scott. — Sir W. Wallace. 1, 2. Robert Bruce. 2. J. Barbour. — A. Wynton. — J. de Fordun. 2, 3. James I. 3. R. Henryson. — W. Dunbar. — G. Douglas. — Sir D. Lindsay.
— AMYOT, T. Reply to Tyler's Historical remarks on the death of Richard II. (*In* **Archæologia,** v. 23. 1831.)
— REMARKS on 'Historical view of the progress of discovery', *etc.* *n.p.*, 1833. 8°. **(B 1070)**

Tytler, Robert, *M.D.* Inquiry into the origin, *etc.*, of Budaic Sabism. Calcutta, 1817. 4°.

Tytler, Sarah, *pseud.* *See* **Keddie,** *Miss.*

Tytler, Wm. MACKENZIE, H. Short account of the life and writings of W. T. (*In his* Works, v. 7. 1808; — *and in* **Roy. Soc. of Edin.** Trans., v. 4. 1798.)

Tzetzes, Johannes. Ante-Homerica, Homerica, et Post-Homerica; ed. et comment. instr. F. Jacobs. Lps., 1793. 8°.
— *Same.* Gr. and Lat.; ed. F. S. Lehrs. (*In* **Hesiodus.** Carmina. 1841.)
— Die Theogonie des Tzetzes aus der Bibliotheca Casanatensis; hrsg. von Bekker. (*In* **Berlin. Ak. d. Wiss.** Abh., 1840.)

Tzimiscis, Joannes. Excerpta ex historiis Arabum de expeditionibus Syriacis Nicephori Phocæ et J. T. (*In* **Niebuhr.** Byzant. hist. scr., v. 5. 1828.)

Tzschirner, Heinrich Gottlieb. Sermons; on the end of the world. — The world purified by the judgments of God. (*In* **German** pulpit. 1829.)

u. A. w. g., oder: Die Einladungskarte; von A. v. Kotzebue. (*In his* Theater, v. 36. 1841.)

Ubaldo, Marco di. Sonnet. (*In* Rosetti, D. G. Early Ital. poets. 1861.)

Ubaldo; von A. v. Kotzebue. (*In his* Theater, v. 23. 1841.)

Ubaldus *Eugubinus*, *St.*, *Bp.* THEOBALDUS, *Bp.* (*In* Acta sanct., v. 16. 1866.)

Ubeda, Francisco Lopez de, *pseud.* See Perez, A.

Uberti, Bonifacio *or* Fazio degli. Ditta mundi. [Colophon:] Venetia, 1501. 8°.

— *Same.* Il dittamondo; pub. dal cav. V. Monti. Milano, 1826. 8°.

— *Eng.*, *extracts.* (*In* Rossetti, D. G. Early Ital. poets. 1860.)

— Serventesi. (*In* Trucchi, F. Poesie ital., v. 2. 1846.)

Uberti, Lapo Farinata degli. Ein Spruchgedicht. (*In* Jahrbuch f. rom. u. eng. Lit., v. 10. 1869.)

Ubertino, *frate, d'Arezzo.* Canzoni. (*In* Trucchi, F. Poesie italiane, v. 1. 1846.)

Ubertino, Giovanni del Bianco, *d'Arezzo, giudice.* Sonetti. (*In* Trucchi, F. Poesie ital., v. 1. 1846.)

Ubique, *pseud.* See Gillmore, P.

Uchard, Mario. La comtesse Diane. (*In* Revue d. D. Mondes, sept., oct. 1863.) — Jean de Chazol. (*In* juin, juil., août 1868.)

Udall (*Lat.* Odovallus), Nicholas. Flowers for Latine speakyng gathered oute of Terence. [London,] 1560. 8°.

— Ralph Roister Doister, a comedy; and The tragedie of Gorboduc, by T. Norton and T. Sackville; ed. by W. D. Cooper. London, 1847. 8°. (Shakespeare Soc.)

Udalricus (*Germ.* Ulric) *Bambergensis.* Codex. (*In* Jaffé, P. Bibliotheca rer. Germ., v. 5. 1869.)

Udalricus *Cellensis.* Ex vita St. Udalrici; ed. R. Wilmans. (*In* Pertz, G. H. Mon. Germ. hist., Scr., v. 12. 1856.)

Udalricus, Oudalricus, Ulricus, *or* Dethelrecus, *St., episc. Augustanus.* VITA. (*In* Acta sanct., v. 29. 1867.)

Uddman, Isaac Lepra. (*In* Linné, C. Amœn. acad., v. 7. 1769.)

Ude, Louis Eustache. The French cook; a system of cookery adapted to the use of English families. 13th ed.; with an app. London, 1835. 8°.

Uebel Laune; von A. v. Kotzebue. (*In his* Theater, v. 9. 1840.)

Uebereilung; von L. Tieck. (*In his* Gesam. Novellen, v. 5. 1853.)

Ueberlacher, Gregor. Nachricht über die Wirksamkeit und Nützlichkeit der Kuhpocken-Impfung mit dem Schorfe. Wien., 1809. 8°. (C 271)

Ueberweg, Friedrich. System of logic and history of logical doctrines. London, 1871. 8°.

Uffenbach, Peter. Thesaurus chirurgicus; continens præstantissimorum autorum opera chirurgica. Francof., 1610. f°.

Contents. Pareus, A. Opuscula. — Tagault, J. Institutiones chirurgicæ. — Houlier, J. De materia chirurgica; liber sextus institutionum chirurgicarum. — Sanctis, M. de. Compendium chirurgicum. — Bolognini, A. De cura ulcerum. — De unguentis. — Angelo, M. De partibus ictu sectis citissime sanandis, *etc.*; — De origine morbi Gallici deque ligni Indici ancipiti proprietate. — Ferri, A. De sclopetorum sive archibusorum vulneribus. — De caruncula sive callo, quæ cervici vesicæ innascuntur. — Dondi, J. Enumeratio remediorum simplicium et compositorum, *etc.* — Examen leprosorum. — Fabricius, W. Observationum et curationum chirurgicarum centuria; — De combustionibus libellus.

Uffingus *Werthimensis.* Vita S. Idæ. (*In* Pertz, G. H. Mon. Germ. hist., Scr., v. 2. 1829.)

Uffizio della B. Vergine Maria. *See* Catholic Church (p. 496).

Ughelli, Ferdinando. NICERON, J. P. (*In his* Mém., v. 41. 1740.)

Ughi, Giuliano. Cronica di Firenze, 1501-46. (*In* Archivio stor. ital., app., v. 7. 1849.)

Ugly customer, An; a farce, by T. J. Williams. (No. 58 *of* Spencer's univ. stage.)

Ugolin; tragédie; par C. H. Millevoye. (*In his* Œuvres, v. 5. 1823.)

Ugolini, Filippo. Necrologia di G. Arcangeli. (*In* Archivio stor. ital., n.s., v. 2. 1855.) — Della vita e dei tempi di G. S. F. Ponziglione. (*In* v. 5, pt. 2.)

— GELLI, A. Necrologia di Ugolini. (*In* Archivio stor. ital., ser. 3, v. 1. 1865.)

Ugolino. *See* Booth, J. B.

Ugolino; von H. W. Gerstenberg. (*In his* Verm. Schriften, v. 1. 1815.)

Uguccione, *Bp. of Ferrara.* FABRONI, A. (*In his* Mem. di più illustri Pisani, v. 1. 1790.)

Uhden, Johann Daniel Wilhelm Otto von. Ueber ein altes Vasengemälde. (*In* Berlin. Ak. d. Wiss. Abh., 1804-11.) — Ueber Iphigenia in Aulis [und] in Tauris nach alten Werken der bildenden Kunst. (*In* 1812-13.) — Ueber die Todtenkisten der alten Etrusker, besonders über die an denselben gebildeten Reliefs. (*In* 1816-17.) — Ueber die Todtenkisten der Etrusker. — Virbius und Hippolytus in antiken Werken der bildenden Kunst. (*In* 1818-19.) — Ueber einen antiken geschnittenen Ringstein. (*In* 1820-21.) — Ueber drei antike Musiv-Gemälde im Königlich-Preussischen Museum. (*In* 1825.) — Ueber die etruskischen Todten-Kisten im hiesigen Königlichen Museum. (*In* 1827, 1830.) — Ueber die etruskischen Todten-Kisten. (*In* 1828, 1831.) — Ueber die thönernen Todtenkisten der Etrusker. (*In* 1829.) — Ueber die unter dem Namen der farnesischen bekannte antike Onyxchale im K. Bourbonischen Museum zu Neapel. (*In* 1835.)

Uhland, Johann Ludwig. Beitrag zur Geschichte der Freischiessen. (*In* Fischart, J. Glückhaftes Schiff. 1828.)

— Gedichte. 2e Aufl. Stuttg. u. Tüb., 1853. 16°.

Contents. Lieder. — Vaterländische Gedichte. — Sinngedichte. — Sonette, Octaven, Glossen. — Dramatische Dichtungen. — Balladen und Romanzen. — Altfranzösische Gedichte. — Fortunat und seine Söhne.

— Songs. (*In* Brooks, C. T. Songs and ballads. 1842.)

— Walther von der Vogelweide. Stuttg. u. Tüb., 1822. 8°.

— NOTTER, F. Ludwig Uhland, sein Leben und seine Dichtungen. Stuttg., 1863. 12°.

Uhle, Paul Johann, *and* Wagner, E. Handbuch der allemeinen Pathologie. Lpz., 1862. f°.

Uhlhorn, Johann Gerhard Wilhelm. Modern representation of the life of Jesus; tr. from 3d Germ. ed. by C. E. Grinnell. Bost., 1868. 16°.

— Resurrection of Christ as a soteriological fact. (*In* Bremen lectures. 1871.)

Uhr, Die, und die Mandeltorte; von A. v. Kotzebue. (*In his* Theater, v. 16. 1841.)

Ukek. FRAEHN, C. M. Ueber die ehemalige mongolische Stadt Ukek im Süden von Saratow und einen dort unlängst gemachten Fund. (*In* St. Petersburg. Ac. Sci. Mém., 6e sér., v. 3. 1836.)

Ukert, Friedrich August. Geographie der Griechen und Römer von den frühesten Zeiten bis auf Ptolemäus. Weimar, 1816-48. 3 v. in 6 pts. 8°.

Contents. Vol. 1, pt. 1. Geschichte der geographischen Entdeckungen und der Geographen. 2, pt. 2. Mathematische Geographie der Griechen und Römer. 2, pt. 1. Physische Geographie. 2, pt. 2. Ueber den Norden von Europa nach den Ansichten der Alten. 3, pt. 1. Germania. 3, pt. 2. Skythien und das Land der Geten oder Daker.

Ukraine. ACCOUNT of U. (*In* Harris, J. Col. of voy., v. 2. 1764.)

— BEAUPLAN, G. le V., *sieur* de. Description of Ukraine. (*In* Churchill, O. *and* J. Col. of voy., v. 1. 1744.)

— JAWORSKI, J. Przypomnienia Ukrainskie. [Paryż,] 1846. 8°. (E 83)

— *Map.* TYPUS generalis Ukrainæ. *n.p.*, [16—]. (E 78, no. 266.)

Ukrainki; [przez] M. Czaykowski. Paryż, 1841. 8°.

Contents. Termolama. — Czerwona sukienka. — Kto z Bogiem, to Bóg z nim. — Konstanty Horodeński. — Do Pani Konstancji L. — Trech-tymirów. — Złoty krzyżyk. — Słobodyszcze.

Ulbach, Louis. Monsieur et Madame Fernel. 7e éd. Paris, 1864. 18°.

— La politique au Palais Bourbon. (*In* Paris guide, v. 2. 1867.)

— Le prince Bonifacio. 2e éd. Paris, 1864. 18°.

— Les roués, sans le savoir. Paris, 1857. 18°.

— Les sécrets du diable. Paris, 1858. 18°.

Ulcers. COL DE VILARS, E., *d.* 1747. Traité des ulcères. (*In his* Cour de chirurgie, v. 4. 1757.)

— BAYLIES, W. Ulcerated sore throat at Dighton, 1785-86. (*In* Mass. Med. Soc. Med. com., v. 1. 1808.)

— HOME, *Sir* E. Practical observations on the treatment of ulcers on the legs. [1797.] 2d ed. enl. London, 1801. 8°.
— KIRKLAND, T. Ulcers. [1812.] (*In his* Appendix to an enquiry. 1813.)
— EVANS, J. Ulcerations of the genital organs. London, 1819. 8°.
— DAHLERUP, E. A. Dissert. de ulcere ventriculi perforante. Havniæ, 1840. 16°.
— BRINTON, W. Ulcer of the stomach. Lond., 1857. 12°.
— PAGET, J. Ulcers. (*In* **Holmes, T.** Syst. of surg., v. 1. 1860.)
See also **Stomach.**

Ulfilas, Ulfila, *or* **Wulfilas.** Die heiligen Schriften in gothischer Sprache; mit gr. und lat. Texte, Anmerk., Wörterbuch, Sprachlehre, u. Einleit. von H. F. Massmann. Stuttg., 1857. 8°.

Uli der Knecht; von A. **Bitzius.** (*In his* Gesam. Schriften, v. 2. 1861.)

Uli der Pächter; von A. **Bitzius.** (*In his* Gesam. Schrift., v. 3. 1861.)

Ulisse il giovane; tragédie. *See* **Lazzarini, D.**

Ulliac Trémadeure, *Mlle.* Sophie. Souvenirs d'une vieille femme. Paris, 1861. 18°.

Ullman, Carl. Sinless character of Christ. (*In* **Edwards, B. B.** Selections from Germ. lit. 1839.)

Ullmann, Daniel. Address before the Tippecanoe and other Harrison associations of N. York, Feb. 22. N. Y., 1841. 8°. (B 1572)

Ullmark, Hinricus. Prolepsis plantarum. (*In* **Linné, C.** Amœn. acad., v. 6. 1763.)

Ulloa, Alfonso. Vita dell' imperator Carlo v.; di nuovo ristampata and ricorretta. Venetia, *Aldo,* 1575. 4°.

Ulloa, Antonio de. Noticias americanas; entretenimientos fisico-historicos sobre la América meridional, y la septentrional oriental. Madrid, 1792. 4°.
— *French.* Mémoires philosophiques, historiques, physiques, conc. la découverte de l'Amérique, ses anciens habitans, *etc.*; avec des obs. et add. de J. G. Schneider; par [Lefebvre de Villebrune]. Paris, 1787. 2 v. 8°.
— Noticias secretas de America. *See* **Juan y Santacilia, J.**
— ST. JOHN, J. A. (*In his* Lives of celebrated travellers, v. 2. 1847.)

Ulloa, Francisco de. Navigatione per discoprire l'isole delle speciere. (*In* **Ramusio.** Nav., v. 3. 1565.)
— Voyage to California. (*In* **Callander, J.** Terra austr. cogn., v. 1. 1766; — **Burney, J.** Discoveries in the South Sea, v. 1. 1803; — *and in* **Hakluyt,** R. Col. of voy., v. 3. 1810.)

Ulloa, Martin de. Disertacion sobre el origen de los duelos, desafios e leyes de su observancia. — Sobre el origen y patria de los Godos. — Sobre el principio de la monarquia goda en España. (*In* **Madrid. Ac. d. l'Hist.** Mem., v. 1.) — Tratado de cronologia para la hist. de España. (*In* v. 2. 1796.)

Ulloa y Pereira, Luis de. Epistola. — Romance. — Soneto del Señor Rey Carlos II. (*In* **Sedano, J. J. L. de.** Parnaso español, v. 2. 1782.)
— **Raquel;** poema. (*In* **Sedano, J. J. L. de.** Parnaso esp., v. 1. 1768; — **Quintana, M. J.** Poesias selectas castel., v. 3. 1807; — **Rosell,** C. Poemas epicos, v. 2. 1854; v. 29 of Aribau. Bibl.)

Ulm. WEYERMANN, A. Nachrichten von Gelehrten, Künstlern, und andern merkwürdigen Personen aus Ulm. Ulm, 1798. 8°.
— BARING, *Lieut.* E. (*In his* Staff college essays. 1870.)

Ulmann, Heinrich. Ernst Graf zu Münster. (*In* **Historische** Zeitschrift, v. 20. 1868.)

Ulpius, Joannes. Adagia. (*In* **Erasmus,** D. E. Adagiorum chiliades quatuor, v. 2. 1574.)

Ulrich *von Turheim.* Tristan und Isolde; Fortsetzung. (*In* **Gottfried** *von Strassburg.* Werke, v. 2. 1823; *and* Tristan, v. 2. 1869.)

Ulrich, Louis. Nouveau manuel du teinturier, 2e pte. Paris, *Roret,* 1861. 18°.
— *Eng.* Complete treatise on dyeing cotton and wool; added, receipts for dyeing wool, by Prof. A. Dussauce. Phila., 1863. 12°.

Ulrich; a tale, by Countess Hahn-Hahn; tr. by J. B. S. London, 1854. 18°.

Ulrichs, Ludwig. Beschreibung der Stadt Rom. *See* **Platner,** E. 1830–42.

Ulster County gazette; Jan. 14, 1800 [cont. an account of the death of Washington]. Kingston, [N. Y.,] 1800, [*reprinted* 185–?]. f°. (W 49)

Ulster (*N.Y.*) **Historical Society.** Collections. Vol. 1, pts. 1, 2, 3. Kingston, 1860–62. 8°.
Contents. Vol. 1, pt. 1. Constitution. — Proceedings of meetings at New Paltz and Kingston, 1859. — Circular of the executive committee. — **Hasbrouck,** A. B. Address. — **Eltinge,** E. On the New Paltz settlement. — **Brodhead,** J. R. Early history of Kingston, Hurley, and Marbletown. — **Brant,** J. Letters. — **Jay,** J. Letter to sheriff Dumond. — **Petition** of inhabitants of Rochester to Gov. Clinton. — Treaty between Col. **Nicolls** and the **Esopus Indians.** — **Proclamation** of the election of Gov. G. Clinton. — **Bill** of sale and warranty of a negro boy in 1707. — **Inscriptions** in 1st Dutch churchyard, at Kingston. — **Hasbrouck,** J. W. The 'New Dorp'. — **Special** meeting, Mar. 20, 1860. **1,** 2. Proceedings of June meeting, 1860. — **Jones,** N. W. Notes upon the Esopus Indians. — **Brodhead,** J. R. Note upon the Esopus treaty. — **Ulster** sheriffs. — **Colonial** statutes relating to Ulster Co. — **Clinton** papers relating to Ulster Co. — **Pratt,** G. W. Vaughan's expedition up the Hudson in 1777. — Letters of denization for A. **DuBois.** — Jan **Eltinge's** certificate of church membership. 1, 3. Proceedings of October meeting, 1861. — **Stitt,** C. H. The Huguenots of New Paltz. — **Lounsbery,** W. The Ulster regiment in the great rebellion. — **Scott,** C. Origin and meaning of the word Shawangunk; — The Indian forts of 1663. — Concerning **Ulster** Co. records.

Ultramontanism. AVIS fraternels aux ultramontains concordatistes. Londres, 1809. 8°. (C 89)
— MONTLOSIER, F. D. R., *comte* de. Mémoire à consulter sur un système religieux et politique, tendant à renverser la religion, la société, et le trône. 5e éd. Paris, 1826. 8°.
— QUINET, E. L'ultramontanisme; ou, L'église romaine et la société moderne. [1842–44.] (*In his* Œuvres complètes, v. 2. 1857.)
— ROCHELLE, P. L'ultramontanisme dévoilé et combattu dans ses tendences anti-chrétiennes, antirationelles, antisociales, et anti-libérales. Paris, 1861. 16°.

Ulug *Bey.* Tabulæ long. ac. lat. stellarum fixarum. (*In* **Hyde,** T. Syntagma, v. 1. 1767.)

Ulvæ. VAUCHER, J. P. Histoire des ulves. (*In his* Hist. des conferves. 1803.)

Ulysses. *See* **Rowe,** N.

Ulysses, Adventures of; by C. Lamb. London, 1839. 16°.

Umbria. *Antiquities.* DINI, F. Antiquitates Umbrorum, *etc.* (*In* **Grævius.** Thes. antiq. Ital., v. 8, pt. 1. 1723.)
— *Biography.* FABRETTI, A. Biografie dei capitani venturieri dell' Umbria. Montepulciano, 1842–46. 5 v. 12°.
— *Description.* TROLLOPE, T. A. Lenten journey into Umbria and the Marches. London, 1862. 8°.
— *Language.* NEWMAN, F. W. On the Umbrian language. (*In* **Philological Soc.** Trans., 1862–63.)
— *Literature.* MARCOALDI, O. Canti popolari. (*In his* Canti popolari. 1855.)
See also **Tigri,** G. Canti popolari toscani, 1860.

Umfreville, Eduard. Gegenwärtiger Zustand der Hudsons Bay. (*In* **Sprengel,** M. C., *and* **Forster,** G. Neue Beiträge, v. 6. 1791.)
— *Eng.* Present state of Hudson's Bay and of the fur trade. London, 1790. 8°.
— – Selections from the 'Present state of Hudson's Bay', rel. to the Indians of Hudson's Bay and their language; by W. Willis. (*In* **Maine Hist. Soc.** Col., v. 6. 1859.)

Una, The; devoted to the elevation of woman; February 1853 – October 1855. Prov., 1853–55. 3 v. 4°.

Una delle due ultime sere di carnovale; commedia veneziana. *See* **Goldoni,** C.

Unanue, José Hipólito. Observaciones sobre el clima de Lima. Lima, 1806. 8°.

Unbelievers under the law and curse. *See* **Townsend**, S. (B 659)

Uncas, *Sachem of the Mohegans.* Agreement between Uncas and the colony of Connecticut. (*In* **Mass. Hist. Soc.** Proc., 1867-69.) — HOLMES, A. Mem. of the Moheagans and of Uncas. (*In* Col., v. 9. 1804.)

— STONE, W. L. Uncas and Miantonomoh; disc., Norwich, July 4, 1842, on the erection of a monument to Uncas. N. Y., 1842. 18°.

Uncle Peter's fairy tales. N. Y., 1845. 18°.

Uncle Philip, *pseud.* *See* **Hawks**, F. L.

Uncle Richard's relation of W. E. Parry's voyages for the discovery of a North West passage. Boston, [1826]. 8°.

Uncle Sam, adventures of, in search after his lost honor. *See* **Fidfaddy**, F. A.

Uncle Tom at home; rev. of reviewers of Mrs. Stowe's 'Uncle Tom'. *See* **Adams**, F. C.

Uncle Tom in England; an echo of the Amer. 'Uncle Tom'. N. Y., [1852]. 8°.

Uncle Tom's cabin; by H. B. Stowe. Boston, 1852. 2 v. 12°.

— *Same.* With key. Boston, 1853. 8°.

— *Welsh.* Caban F'Ewyrth Tum; cyfieitrad H. Williams. Llundaia, 1853. 8°.

— *Armenian.* [Venice,] 1854. 2 v. 12°.

Uncle Tom's cabin; by G. Aiken. (*In* **Sargent**, E. Mod. stand. dr., v. 28.)

Uncommercial traveler. (*In* **Dickens**, C. Message from the sea. 1861; — *in* All the year round, v. 9-10, 1863; — *and in his* Works, v. 1. 1869.)

Unconnected Whigs address, An, to the public upon the present civil war and state of public affairs. London, 1777. 8°. (B 681)

Unctis, Petruccio de. Fragmenta Fulginatis historiæ. (*In* **Muratori**, L. A. Antiq. Ital., v. 4. 1741; — *and in* **Tartini**, G. M. Rer. Ital. scr., v. 1. 1748.)

Under one roof; Christmas extra number of Chambers's journal. *n.t.p.* [Edin., 1867.] 8°.

Under the red cross. (*In* **Blackwood's** mag., v. 109. 1871.)

Under the willows. *See* **Lowell**, J. R.

Undercurrents of Wall street. *See* **Kimball**, R. B.

Underhill, Abraham I. *See* **Van Cortlandt**, P. Case. 1818. (B 340)

Underhill, Edward. Autobiographical anecdotes. (*In* **Nichols**, J. G. Narratives of the Reformation. 1859. Camden Soc., v. 77.)

Underhill, Edward Bean. Confessions of faith, illustrative of the hist. of the Baptist churches of Eng. in the 17th cent. London, 1854. 8°. (Hanserd Knollys Soc.)

Contents. Introd. notice. — Confession of **Amsterdam**, 1611. — Confession of 7 **churches**, 1646. — Appendix to Confession, 1646. — Confession of **Somersets**, 1656. — **London** confession, 1660. — An **Orthodox** creed, 1678. — **Confession** of assembly, 1688. — **Baptist** catechism. — **Public** documents; illust. of the history of the Baptist churches of Eng., 1647-61. — **Declaration** by cong. societies in and about London, 1647. — **Petition** and representation of Anabaptists, 1649. — **Heart-bleedings** for professors' abominations, 1650. — **Patient**, T. Letter to the Ld. Lieut. of Ireland. — **Harrison**, *Col.* T. Letter to Cromwell. — **Chamberlen**, P. Letter to Cromwell. — **Letter** from the people of Bedfordshire to Cromwell, and the council of the army. — **Kiffin**, W., *and others.* Letter. — **Representation** and vindication of the messengers, elders, and brethren of the churches in this nation, of their opinions and resolutions touching the civil government, and of their deportment. — **Address** from the Baptist churches in Northumberland, *etc.*, to the Ld. Protector. — **Address** of the Anabaptist ministers in London to the Ld. Protector. — **Address** of the baptized Christians in Dublin to the Ld. Protector. — **Apology** of the Anabaptists. — **Second** address of Anabaptists, in the Co. of Lincoln, to Charles II. — To the King, the representation of the Anabaptists, where they declare their innocency, sufferings, desires, and resolutions.

— Historical introduction. (*In* **Bristol**, *Eng.* Records of a church, 1640-87.)

— Letter to E. Cardwell; with documents on the condition of Jamaica. London, 1865. 8°.

— Records of the churches at Fenstanton, Warboys, and Hexham, 1644-1720. London, 1854. 8°. (Hanserd Knollys Soc.)

— Tracts on liberty of conscience and persecution, 1614-61. London, 1846. 8°. (Hanserd Knollys Soc.)

Contents. Vol. 1. **Underhill**, E. B. Historical introduction. — **Busher**, L. Religious peace; or, A plea for liberty of conscience. — **Persecution** for religion judged and condemned, in a discourse between an antichristian and a Christian. — **Murton**, J., *and others?* A most humble supplication of many of the king's majesty's loyal subjects, ready to testify all civil obedience, who are persecuted only for differing in religion, contrary to divine and human testimonies. — **Richardson**, S. The necessity of toleration in matters of religion; or, Certain questions propounded to the Synod, to prove that in matters of religion men ought to have liberty and freedom; also the edict of Constantinus and Licinius, to grant unto all men liberty to choose and follow what religion they thought best. — **Jeffries**, W., *and others.* An humble petition and representation of the sufferings of subjects called Anabaptists, inhabitants in the County of Kent, and now prisoners in the gaol of Maidstone. — **Sturgion**, J. A plea for toleration of opinions and persuasions in matters of religion, differing from the Church of England. — **Monck**, J., *and others.* Sion's groans for her distressed, or endeavours to prevent innocent blood, *etc.* — Addenda. — Index.

— West Indies; their social and religious condition. London, 1862. 8°.

Underhill, *Capt.* John. History of the Pequot war. (*In* **Mass. Hist. Soc.** Col., v. 26. 1837.)

Understanding. *See* **Intellect**; — **Psychology**.

Underwood, Alvan. Life of man on earth; disc., West Woodstock, Conn., 50th anniversary of [his] ordination. Boston, 1851. 8°. (B 1326)

Underwood, Francis Henry. Cloud pictures. Boston, 1872 [1871]. 16°.

Contents. The exile of Von Adelstein's soul. — Topankalon. — Herr Regenbogen's concert. — A great-organ concert.

Underwood, John. COLLIER, J. P. (*In his* Mem. of the actors in the plays of Shakespeare. 1846. Shakespeare Soc.)

Underwood, Joseph Rogers. Speech on the amendment to bill for the support of the army appropriating $300,000 to carry on military operations in Florida, July 13. Wash., 1840. 8°. (B 1497)

— Speech on the resolution to censure J. Q. Adams for presenting a petition for the dissolution of the Union, Jan. 27. Wash., 1842. 8°. (B 1174, 1499)

Underwood, Michael. Diseases of children. New ed. Phila., 1802. 2 pts. 12°.

— *Same.* From 6th London ed. Boston, 1806. 3 pts. in 2 v. 8°.

Underwoods. *See* **Jonson**, B.

Undine; von F. H. C. de La Motte Fouqué. 3e Aufl. Berlin, 1820. 16°.

Note. For other eds. and trans. *see* **La Motte Fouqué**, F. H. C. (p. 1661).

Undine; by G. Soane. (*In* **Sargent**, E. Mod. stand. dr., v. 26.)

Unfortunate female, To the. Brunswick, 1824. 16°. (C 246)

Ungarns erster Wohlthäter; von A. v. **Kotzebue**. (*In his* Theater, v. 29. 1841.)

Ungarns Männer der Zeit; Biografien und Karakteristiken; erzählender Skizzen aus der Feder eines Unabhängigen. Lpz., 1862. 16°.

Contents. Toldy. — Deák. — Eötvös. — Horn. — Pulssky. — Markó. — Jókay. — Arany. — Kertbeny. — Klapka.

Unger, Carl Richard. Oldnorsk Læsebog. 1847. *See* **Munch**, P. A.

Unger, Franz. Fossile Pflanzenreste. (*In* **Hochstetter**, F. von, *and others.* Novara; geol. Th., v. 1, pt. 2. 1864.)

Ungewitter, Franz Heinrich. Europe, past and present; a manual of geography and history. N. Y., 1850. 8°.

Note. The name on the title page is **Francis**; Graesse gives Friedrich Heinrich.

Ungluecklichen, Die; von A. v. **Kotzebue**. (*In his* Theater, v. 7. 1840.)

Unhappy favourite; or, The Earl of Essex. *See* **Banks**, J.

Uniacke, Crofton. Letter to the Lord Chancellor, on a code of the laws of Eng.; annexed, the new bankrupt law. Boston, 1827. 8°. (B 975, 1798)

Unicorn. Bartholin, T. De unicornu observationes novæ. Patavii, 1644. 8°.

Uniform des Feldmarschalls Wellington, Die; von A. v. **Kotzebue.** (*In his* Theater, v. 33. 1841.)

Uniformity. *See* **Nonconformity.**

Uniforms of the Confederate States navy. [Plates.] *n.t.p.* 4°.

Unigenitus, The bull *or* **constitution.** Boursier, J. L. Explication des principales questions qui ont rapport aux affaires présentes. *n.p.*, 1731. 12°.

— Le Gros, N. Abrégé des principaux événemens qui ont précédé la constitution unigenitus. *n.p.*, 1732. 12°.

Uninterrupted succession of the eccl. mission asserted. London, 1717. 8°. (B 31)

Unio. Lea, I. Descr. of eleven new species of the genus unio. — Descr. of six new species of the genus unio. (*In* **Amer. Phil. Soc.** Trans., n.s., v. 3. 1830.)

— - Observations on the genus unio. Vol. 6-13. Phila., [1858?-74?]. 8 v. 4°.

— - - Index to vol. 1-13. Phila., 1867-74. 3 v. 4°.

Union, *Me.* Sibley, J. L. History of U. Boston, 1851. 12°.

Union (of England and Ireland, 1800). *See* **Great Britain.** *History and Politics*; — **Ireland.**

Union (of England and Scotland, 1603). *See* **Great Britain.** *History and Politics*; — **Scotland.**

Union (of the U. S.). *See* **United States.**

Union, The; [a poem]. Boston, 1860. 12°.

Union, Semi-weekly; May 5 - Dec. 29, 1845. Wash., 1845. f°.

Union and liberty; powers of Cong. in rel. to the slaves; with a form of enactment. *n.t.p.* [186-?] 8°. (B 1481)

Union and patriotic album; illustrated envelope holder. Boston, 1861. 12°.

Union and State Rights Meeting, *St. Johns.* Proceedings, Sept. 24. *n.t.p.* [1831.] 8°. (B 1067)

Union Brigade. Proceedings on the death of Washington; also Mr. Austin's prayer, and Capt. S. White's oration. New Jersey, 1800. 8°. (E 61)

Union Canal Company. Paleske, C. G. Observations on the application for a law to incorporate the company. *n.t.p.* [1808.] 8°. (B 469)

Union College, *Schenectady.* General catalogue of officers, graduates, and students, 1795-1854. Schenectady, 1854. 8°.

— Laws. Albany, 1802. 8°. (B 946)

— Supplement to the laws. Albany, 1805. 8°. (B 699)

— Nott, E. Addresses delivered to the candidates for the baccalaureate. Schenectady, 1814. 12°.

Union, The; condemnation of Mr. Helper's scheme. N. Y., [1856?]. 8°. (B 1477)

Union County, *N. J.* Boyd, W. H. Business directory of Essex, N. J. N. Y., 1859. 12°.

Union Insurance Co. Constitution. Boston, 1804. 32°. (D 57)

Union League Club of N. Y. Proceedings in reference to the death of J. A. Andrew, Nov. 11. [N. Y.,] 1867. 16°. (E 91)

Union of churches, The, in the spirit of charity, *etc.*, Oct. 1, 1858. Boston, 1860. 8°. (B 1390)

Union of the northern and southern Democracy upon Cass & Butler. Wash., 1848. 8°. (B 1503)

Union, The, or Scotch and English poems. *n.p.*, *n.d.* [18—.] 8°. (C 307)

Contents. The thistle and the rose. — **Shipley,** —. Verses on the death of Queen Caroline. — **Lowthe,** —. Genealogy of Christ repr. on the east window of Winchester Coll. chapel. — **Mallet,** D. A fragment. — **Scott,** A. The eagle and the robin-redbreast. — **Warton,** J. Ode to fancy; — Ode to evening. — **Collins,** W. Ode to evening. — **Mason,** W. Isis. — **Warton,** T. Triumph of Isis. — **Hammond,** J. A love elegy. — The **tears** of Scotland. — **Gray,** T. Elegy in a country churchyard. — **Murray,** D., *Visc. Stormont.* On the death of Frederic, Prince of Wales. — **Clitherow,** J. On the same. — **Ode** on the approach of summer. — **Pastoral** in the manner of Spenser. — **Inscribed** on a grotto. — **Smallet,** —. Love elegy. — **Mason,** W. Choruses from Elfrida. — **Collins,** W. Ode on the death of Thomson. — The **child-birth.** — **Hammond,** J. On a lady's presenting a sprig of myrtle to a gentleman. — **To** a young lady, with Fontenelle's Plurality of worlds. — A **song.** — Part of the prologue to Sir David Lyndesay's dream. — **Hardyknute.** — **Akenside,** M. Ode on lyric poetry.

Union, The, past and future, how it works and how to save it; by a citizen of Virginia. Wash., 1850. 8°. (B 1504)

— Derby, E. H. Reality *vs.* fiction; a review of 'The union, *etc.*' Boston, 1850. 8°. (B 1504)

Union questions. *See* **American Sunday School Union.**

Union; treatise of the consanguinity between Christ and his Church. *See* **Kelly,** J. (B 53)

Unionidæ. Lea, I. Synopsis. 4th ed. enl. Phila., 1870. 8°.

Unique, The. *See* **Godolphin,** G.

Unitarian, The; ed. by B. Whitman. Camb., 1834. 8°.

Unitarian advocate; ed. by E. Q. Sewall. Boston, 1828-29. 4 v. 12°.

Unitarian advocate and religious miscel. Boston, 1830-32. 6 v. 12°.

Unitarian, The, and foreign religious miscellany; ed. by G. E. Ellis. Vol. 1. Boston, 1847. 12°.

Unitarian annual register, 1846-47. Boston, [1846-47]. 12 v. 12°.

Unitarian Association. *See* **American Unitarian Assoc.**

Unitarian congregational register, 1848-55. Boston, *n.d.* 8 v. 12°.

Unitarian controversy, a half century of the. *See* **Ellis,** G. E.

Unitarian miscellany and Christian monitor. Balt., 1821-24. 6 v. 12°.

Note. Vol. 1-3, ed. by J. Sparks; 4-6, by F. G. S. Greenwood.

Unitarian Society for Promoting Christian Knowledge and the Practice of Virtue. Rules, *etc.* *n.t.p.* [London, 1791.] 8°. (B 131)

— Tracts. Vol. 1, 2, 4-12. London, 1791-1800. 11 v. 16°. (C 131, 132, 134-142)

Contents. Vol. 1. (C 131) **Priestley,** J. Appeal to the serious and candid professors of Christianity; — Familiar illustration of certain passages of Scripture; — General view of the arguments for the unity of God. 2. (C 132) **Disney,** J. Friendly dialogue between a common Unitarian Christian and an Athanasian. — Reasons for resigning the rectory of Panton. — **Letter** to the Rev. Mr. D—; by a layman. — **Toulmin,** J. Exhortation to all Christian people to refrain from Trinitarian worship. — **Frend,** W. 1st, 2d address to the members of the Church of Eng. 3. *Wanting.* 4. (C 134) **Toulmin,** J. Review of the life, character, and writings of J. Biddle. — **Cornish,** J. Life of T. Firmin. 5. (C 135) **Hanway,** —. Advice from farmer Trueman to his daughter Mary. 6. (C 136) Serious address to unlearned Christians of Trinitarian and Calvinistic sentiments. — Representation of the nature of true religion. — **Lindsey,** T. The catechist. — **Rogers,** G. Five sermons. 7. (C 137) **Lardner,** N. Letter written in 1730, concerning the question whether the Logos supplied the place of an human soul in the person of Jesus Christ; — Two schemes of a Trinity considered. 8. (C 138) **Smith,** J. A designed end to the Socinian controversy. — **Toulmin,** H. Life of J. Mort. — **Hartley,** D. Of the truth of the Christian religion. 9, 10. (C 139, 140) **Priestley,** J. Institutes of natural and revealed religion. 11. (C 141) **Haynes,** H. Scripture-account of the attributes and worship of God. 12. (C 142) Sermon preached in the chapel of Trinity College, Camb., Dec. 19, 1793. — **Belsham,** T. Review of Wilberforce's 'Practical view of professed Christians'.

Unitarian Society for the Diffusion of Christian Knowledge. Debates in the Soc. respecting the election of a committee and office-bearers for 1859-60. Belfast, 1859. 12°. (C 236)

Unitarianism vindicated against the charge of not going far enough; [by J. Walker]. (*In* **Amer. Unit. Assoc.** Tracts, v. 1. 1827. C 168, v. 1.)

Unitarians, Unitarianism. *Bibliography.*

— Sand, C. von der. Bibliotheca anti-trinitariorum sive catalogus scriptorum, *etc.* Freistad., 1684. 12°.

Biography.

— Scrutator; *pseud.* A letter; [biog. sketches of Unitarians]. *t.p.w.* [182-.] 12°. (C 241)

— Sprague, W. B. Unitarian congregational. (Vol. 8 *of his* Annals of the Amer. pulpit. 1865.)

See also **Belsham, T.; — Buckminster, J. S.; — Channing, W. E.; — Greenwood, F. W. P.; — Lindsey, T.; — White, J. B.**

Book of common prayer.

— D., J. Book of common prayer for the use of Unitarian congregations. London, **1792.** 8°.

— Martineau, J. Common prayer for Christian worship; in ten services for morning and evening. Boston, **1863.** 12°.

Hymn books, etc.

— Hymn, tune, and service book for Sunday schools. Boston, *A.U.A.*, 1869. 16°.

— Livermore, L. J. Hymn and tune book, for the church and the home; and services for congregational worship. Boston, *A.U.A.*, 1868. 16°.

— - Social hymns and tunes for the conference and prayer meeting and home; with services and prayers. Boston, *A.U.A.*, 1868. 16°.

Registers.

— Unitarian annual register, 1846-47. Boston, [1846-47]. 2 v. 12°.

— Unitarian congregational register, 1848-55. Boston, *n.d.* 8 v. 12°.

— Year-book of the Unitarian churches. Boston, *A.U.A.*, 1856-58, 67-78. 15 v. 12°.

History.

— Lindsey, T. Historical view of the state of the Unitarian doctrine and worship. London, **1783.** 8°.

— Trechsel, F. Die protestantischen Antitrinitarier vor Faustus Socin. Heidelb., **1839-44.** 2 v. 8°.

— History and prospects of Unitarianism. Camb., 1842. 8°. (B 1388)

— Beard, J. R. Unitarianism exhibited in its actual condition; essays illust. of the rise, progress, and principles of Christian anti-trinitarianism. London, **1846.** 8°.

See also **Unitarians in the United States.**

General and miscellaneous works.

Note. For works in defence of Unitarianism which discuss chiefly the doctrine of the trinity *see* **Trinity.** Works which are not confined to that doctrine but relate to the other doctrines held by Unitarians have been put here.

☞ In the following works * added to the title means that the work is against Unitarianism.

— Bibliotheca fratrum Polonorum quos Unitarios vocant. Irenop. [Amst.], **1656-92.** 9 v. in 6. f°.

— Taylor, N. Disc. on the nature and necessity of faith in Jesus; with answer to the pleas of Unitarians. London, **1700.** 8°.

— Emlyn, T., *d.* **1741.** Works. 4th ed. London, 1746. 3 v. 8°.

— Fleming, C. Another defence of the unity. London, **1766.** 8°.

— Priestley, J. Appeal to the serious and candid professors of Christianity; [with] acc. of the trial of Mr. Elwall. Lond., **1783.** 12°.

— - *Another copy.* (C 69)

— - *Same.* Phila., 1784. 8°. (B 158)

— - *Same.* Birmingham, 1784. 12°. (C 69)

— - *Same.* London, 1791. 8°. (C 131)

— - *Same.* Phila., 1794. 12°. (C 83, 224)

— Hopkins, W. Friendly dialogue between a Unitarian and an Athanasian. London, 1784. 12°. (D 30)

— Priestley, J. Defences of Unitarianism for 1788, 89; letters to Horsley, *etc.* Birm., [179-]. 8°. (B 236)

— Elwall, E. The triumph of truth; trial of E. for heresy and blasphemy; [with add. by Priestley]. Birmingham, 1788. 12°. (C 253)

Note. For other eds., *see* **Priestley, J. Appeal.**

— Frend, W. Address to the inhabitants of Cambridge. St. Ives, 1788. 8°. (B 1389)

— Christie, W. Discourses on the divine unity. 2d ed. corr. Montrose, **1790.** 12°.

— Priestley, J. Familiar letters in refutation of several charges advanced against the Dissenters and Unitarians, by Madan. 2d ed., with add. and corr. Birmingham, 1790. 8°. (B 773)

— Vindication of speaking openly in favour of the divine unity. Taunton, 1790. 12°. (C 82)

— Dialogue between a clergyman of the Ch. of Eng. and a lay-gentleman [on] the late application to Parliament for the repeal of penal laws against Anti-Trinitarians. London, 1792. 8°. (B 240, 1916)

— Serious address to unlearned Christians of Trinitarian and Calvinistic sentiments; by a Unitarian Christian. London, 1792. 4°. (B 207, 243, C 154)

— Kentish, J. Vindication of the principles upon which several Unitarian Christians have formed themselves into societies for avowing their views of religious doctrines. [1794.] 2d ed. London, 1800. 12°. (C 242)

— Priestley, J. Unitarianism explained and defended; discourse. Phila., 1796. 8°. (B 236, W 59)

— Carpenter, L. Errors resp. Unitarianism. *etc.*; disc. Bristol, June 22, before the Soc. of Unitarian Christians. Exeter, 1808. 8°. (C 215)

— - Unitarianism the doctrine of the Gospel. [1809.] 2d ed. London, 1811. 12°.

— Smith, J. P. Letters to T. Belsham on subjects referred to in his disc. on the death of Priestley. 1st Amer. from 2d London ed. Boston, 1809. 12°. *

— Phila. 1st Unitarian Society. Coll. of tracts illust. of the faith of those Christians who hold the principles of the unity of God, *etc.* Phila., **1810.** 8°.

— Fox, W. J. Memorial edition of collected works. [1813-33.] London, 1865. 3 v. 8°.

— Aspland, R. A plea for Unitarian Dissenters; in a letter to H. H. Norris. [1813.] 2d ed. Hackney, 1815. 12°. (C 118)

— Examination of Mr. Cobbett's objections to the bill for the relief of the Unitarians. (*In* **Pamphleteer,** 1813; v. 2 of **B 838**)

— Fox, W. J. The comparative tendency of Unitarianism and Calvinism; discourse, June 30. London, 1813. 8°. (C 217)

— - *Same.* 2d ed. London, 1816. 12°. (C 118)

— Belsham, T. Disc. in commem. of the repeal of the laws against [Anti-trinitarians]. London, **1814.** 8°.

— - Amer. Unitarianism; compiled from docs. communicated by J. Freeman and W. Wells, *etc.* 3d ed. Boston, 1815. 8°. (B 266)

— Amana, *pseud.* Catholick question, containing remarks on T. Belsham's 'American Unitarianism'. Boston, 1815. 8°. (B 266)

— Belsham, T. Letters to [W. Howley] in vindication of Unitarians. London, 1815. 8°.

— - *Same.* 2d ed. London, 1815. 8°. (B 241, 272)

— Channing, W. E. Letter to S. C. Thacher, on the aspersions in a late number of the Panoplist, on the ministers of Boston. 2d ed. Boston, 1815. 8°. (B 266, 298, 2537)

— - Obs. on the proposition for increasing the means of theological education at the University in Cambridge. Camb., 1815. 8°. (B 266)

— Daubeny, C. Remarks on the Unitarian method of interpreting the Scriptures. London, 1815. 8°. * (B 1338)

— Language of Scripture resp. the Savior in rel. to God the Father; by a layman. Boston, 1815. 8°. (B 266)

— Lowell, J. Are you a Christian or a Calvinist? by a layman. Boston, 1815. 8°. (B 266, 1388, 2537)

— - Inquiry into the right to change the ecclesiastical constitution of the Congregational churches of Mass., [with] Morse's report to the Gen. Assoc. of Mass.; 1815. Boston, 1816. 8°. (B 266, 2537)

— REVIEW of 'Amer. Unitarianism'. From the Panoplist. [Boston, 1815.] 8°. * (B 266)
— WORCESTER, S. Letter to W. E. Channing, on his letter to S. C. Thatcher, rel. to the review in the Panoplist of Amer. Unitarianism. Boston, 1815. 8°. * (B 298, 2537)
— - *Same*. 3d ed. Boston, 1815. 8°. (B 266)
— CHANNING, W. E. Remarks on Dr. Worcester's Letter to C. on the 'Review of Amer. Unitarianism'. Boston, 1815. 8°. (B 266, 298, 2537)
— WORCESTER, S. 2d letter to W. E. Channing, on Unitarianism. 2d ed. Boston, 1815. 8°. * (B 298, 2537)
— - *Same*. 3d ed. Boston, 1815. 8°. (B 266)
— CHANNING, W. E. Remarks on Dr. Worcester's 2d letter to C. on Amer. Unitarianism, Bost., 1815. 8°. (B 266, 298, 2537)
— CURSORY remarks on Dr. Worcester's 2d letter on the trinity; by a layman. Boston, 1815. 8°. (B 266)
— WORCESTER, S. 3d letter to W. E. Channing on Unitarianism. Boston, 1815. 8°. (B 266)
— BROADBENT, W. An open and fearless avowal of the Unitarian doctrine; sermon, London, June 5, before the friends and supporters of the Unitarian fund. London, 1816. 8°. (C 215)
— WRIGHT, R. Answer to the question. 'Why are you not a Trinitarian?' 1st Amer. fr. 2d Liverpool ed. *n.p.*, 1816. 8°. (B 665)
— GIFFORD, J. The remonstrance of a Unitarian. London, 1818. 8°. (B 1389)
— CHANNING, W. E. Objections to Unitarian Christianity considered. *n.t.p.* [Boston, *A.U.A.*, 1819.] 12°. (B 270)
— - Sermon; ordination of J. Sparks, in Baltimore. Boston, 1819. 8°. (B 298)
— - *Same*. 2d ed. Balt., 1819. 8°. (B 297)
— HUNTER, J. The Deist, the Christian, the Unitarian; sermon, Nov. 28. London, 1819. 12°. (C 218)
— LETTER to Prof. Stuart, in answer to his letters to W. E. Channing and in vindication of the New Eng. clergy. Bost., 1819. 8°. (B 298)
— DEFENCE of Dr. Woods; cont. remarks illustrative of his letters to Unitarians. Boston, 1820. 8°. * (B 337)
— HUMPHREYS, —. Impartial review; general view of the controversy between Unitarians and the Orthodox, as it appears in a review in 'The Christian disciple' of Stuart's letters, *etc*. Portsmouth, 1820. 8°. * (B 298)
— LETTER to Dr. Woods [on] his address to Unitarians; by a layman. Boston, 1820. 8°. (B 338)
— REMARKS on charges made against the religion and morals of Boston by G. Spring in a sermon, Dec. 22. N. Y., 1820. 8°. (B 272, 2537)
— WARE, H. Letters to Trinitarians and Calvinists, occasioned by Dr. Woods' letter to Unitarians. Cambridge, 1820. 8°. (B 338)
— WARE, H., *Jr*. Two letters to A. M'Leod, cont. rem. upon the texts from which he preached, Apr. 30 and May 7. N. Y., 1820. 8°. (B 338)
— - *Same, entitled*, Two letters on 1 John v. 7, and John xvii. 3. 3d ed. Boston, 1823. 12°. (C 111, 210)
— WOODS, L. Letters to Unitarians, occas. by [W. E. Channing's] sermon. Andover, 1820. 8°. * (B 337)
— - Reply to Dr. Ware's letters to Unitarians and Calvinists. [1820.] (*In his* Works, v. 4. 1851.) *
— LETTERS [1-5, 8-10] to Rev. S. Miller on his charges against Unitarianism. Balt., 1821-22. 12°. (C 111)
— MILLER, S. Letter to the ed. of the Unitarian miscel. in reply to an attack by an anon. writer on a late ordination sermon. Balt., 1821. 8°. * (B 520)
— - *Same*. 2d ed. Boston, 1821. 12°. (C 111, D 63)
— KOHLMANN, A. Unitarianism philosoph. and theolog. examined. [No. 1.] Wash., 1821. 8°. * (B 964)
— - *Same*. Vol. 2 [*i.e.* nos. 8 – 12]. Wash., 1822. 8°. *
— WOODS, L. Reply to Dr. Ware's 'Letters to Trinitarians and Calvinists'. Andover, 1821. 8°. * (B 337)
— POMEROY, J. L. Reply to 'Objections to Unitarian Christianity considered'. Bost., 1822. 12°. * (C 111)
— WARE, H. Answer to Dr. Woods' reply, in a second series of letters to Trinitarians and Calvanists. Camb., 1822. 8°. (B 338)
— FOX, W. J. The apostle John an Unitarian; letter to C. J. Blomfield. *n.t.p.* [Lond., 1823.] 12°. (C 248)
— SPARKS, J. Inquiry into the comparative moral tendency of Trinitarian and Unitarian doctrines. Boston, 1823. 8°.
— WARE, H. Postscript to the second series of letters to Trinitarians and Calvinists, in reply to the remarks of Dr. Woods. Cambridge, 1823. 8°. (B 338)
— EXHIBITION of Unitarianism with Scriptural extracts. Greenfield, 1824. 8°. * (C 111)
— FRENCH, D. Letter to Ld. Gifford; with an apology for the author's creed. Lond., 1824. 8°. * (B 1380)
— HINTS to Unitarians. 2d ed. Liverpool, 1824. 8°. * (B 1388)
— CHANNING, W. E. Discourse, dedication of the 2d Cong. Unitarian church, N. Y. N. Y., 1826. 8°. (B 298)
— - *Same*. 2d ed. N. Y., 1827. 8°. (B 1650, 1963)
— DEWEY, O. The Unitarian's answer. 3d ed. Boston, 1826. 12°. (C 241)
— - *Same*. 4th ed. No. 7. Boston, *A.U.A.*, 1826. 12°. (C 168, v. 1.)
— REVIEW of Channing's disc. at the dedication of the 2d Cong. Unit. Ch., N. Y., Dec. 7, 1826. Boston, 1827. 8°. * (B 1779)
— WALKER, J. Causes of the progress of liberal Christianity in New England. Boston, 1826. 8°. (C 210)
— WHITMAN, N. Unitarianism sound doctrine; sermon, Waltham, ordination of Rev. B. Whitman, Feb. 15. Cambridge, 1826. 8°. (B 1324)
— GILCHRIST, J. Unitarianism abandoned. London, 1827. 8°. * (B 1389)
— TAPPAN, L. Letter from a gentleman in Boston to a Unitarian clergyman [H. Ware, Jr. 1827]. 2d ed. Boston, 1828. 8°. * (D 63, C 184)
— - *Same*. 3d ed. Boston, 1828. 8°. * (C 226)
— - *Same*. 4th ed. Boston, 1828. 8°. * (D 61)
— WALKER, J. Unitarianism vindicated against the charge of not going far enough. (*In* Amer. Unit. Assoc. Tracts, v. 1. 1827. C 168, v. 1.)
— COOKE, P. Unitarianism an exclusive system, *etc.*; sermon, Apr. 3, 1828. *t.p.w.* 12°. * (C 145)
— REMARKS on the Letter from a gentleman in Boston, [L. Tappan] to a Unit. clergyman, and the 'Reply' and 'Review'. Boston, 1828. 12°. (C 242)
— REVIEW of a 'Letter from a gentleman in Boston, *etc.* 2d ed. Boston, 1828. 12°. (C 184, 242)
— - *Same*. 3d ed. Boston, 1828. 8°. (C 226)
— WARE, H. Reply of a Unitarian clergyman to the 'Letter of a gentleman in Boston'. Boston, 1828. 8°. (C 226, D 63)
— - *Same*. 2d ed. Boston, 1828. 8°. (C 242)
— THAYER, N. Means by which Unitarian Christians may refute misrepresentations of their faith; disc. Lancaster, 1828. 8°. (B 1303)
— CANDOR, *pseud.* Address to the Unitarian ministers in Boston and vicinity in three letters. [Boston,] 1829. 8°. * (B 1388, 1688)
— COOKE, P. Reply to a letter in the 'Christian examiner'. Boston, 1829. 12°. * (C 150, D 63)
— KIMBALL, D. Thoughts on Unit. Christianity; sermon, Milton, Sept. 27. Dedham, 1829. 8°. (B 1295)
— HARRIS, G. Christian worship; reply to the Expostulation of G. Struthers. 2d ed. Glasgow, 1830. 12°. (C 230)
— - Letter to G. Struthers on his refusal to meet H. at a funeral. [6th Sept. 1830]. 7th ed. Glasgow, 1830. 12°. (C 230)
— MARTINEAU, H. The essential faith of the universal Church. [1830.] Boston, 1833. 12°.
— YOUNG, A. Evangelical Unitarianism adapted to the poor. Boston, 1830. 12°. (C 145)
— HARRIS, G. Antichrist, what it is and what it is not. Glasgow, 1831. 12°. (C 230)
— HUTTON, J. Unitarians entitled to the name of Christians; sermon. London, 1831. 8°. (B 1344)
— MAY, S. J. Letters to J. Hawes, in review of his tribute to the memory of the Pilgrims. Hartford, 1831. 8°. (B 1358)
— WHITMAN, B. Reply to the Review of W.'s letters to Prof. Stuart, in the 'Spirit of the times' for March. Boston, 1831. 8°. (E 277)
— - Two letters to M. Stuart on religious liberty. 2d ed. Boston, 1831. 8°. (E 277)
— ADAMS, N. Remarks on the Unitarian belief. Boston, 1832. 12°. *
— KELL, E. Unitarians not Socinians; appeal to the good sense of Christians against the improper use of the term 'Socinian'. 3d ed. London, [1832]. 12°. (C 242)
— WHITMAN, B. Answer to E. Pearson's 'Letter to the candid. Boston, 1832. 8°. (E 277)
— CHARITY supported by Orthodoxy; Mr. Cheever convicted of ignorance and misrepresentation, and the Unitarian faith vindicated. [1833-34.] Salem, 1834. 8°. (B 1388, 1688)
— GANNETT, E. S. Unitarianism not a negative system; discourse. Boston, 1833. 8°. (B 1308)
— WILSON, J. Scripture proofs and Scriptural illustrations of Unitarianism. [1833.] 3d ed., rev. London, 1846. 8°.

— AFFECTIONATE appeal to Unitarians. Salem, 1834. 12°. * (D 63)

— BEARD, J. R. The question 'What is Unitarianism' answered. 2d ed. London, 1834. 8°. (C 213, D 62)

— CHEEVER, G. B. The course and system of the Unitarians surveyed; letter to the Christian examiner. Boston, 1834. 8°. * (B 1388, 1688)

— DEWEY, O. Brief statement and explanation of the U. belief. Boston, *A.U.A.*, 1835. 12°. (C 168, v. 19.)

— - On the Unitarian belief. N. Y., 1835. 8°. (B 1878)

— SOBER thoughts on the state of the times, addressed to the Unitarian community. Boston, 1835. 12°. (C 168, v. 9; 241)

— DEWEY, O. Discourses in explanation and defence of Unitarianism. Boston, 1840. 12°.

— CINCINNATI UNITARIAN SOC. Correspondence and remarks rel. to the recent attempt to exclude Unitarians from the Young Men's Bible Soc. Cincin., 1841. 8°. (B 1388)

— BUTLER, P. E. Essential passages of a letter to the Unitarians of Ipswich, Eng., on J. Ketley's renunciation of Unitarianism. Boston, 1842. 12°. * (C 241)

— CHANNING, W. E., *d.* 1842. Works. 7th ed. Boston, 1847. 6 v. 8°.

— EYRE, *Rev.* C. Second series of remarks on P. E. Butler's letter to the Unitarians of Ipswich, and J. Ketley's discourse. London, [1842]. 8°. (B 1389)

— WILSON, J. Concessions of Trinitarians. Manchester, 1842. 8°.

— THAYER, C. F. Our faith. Boston, 1843. 8°. (B 1303)

— LAMSON, A. What is Unitarianism? or, Statement of the views of the Unitarian Congregationalists of the U. S. Boston, 1844. 8°. (E 41, 231)

— PEABODY, A. P. Lectures on Christian doctrine. [1844.] New ed. Boston, 1857. 12°.

— GANNETT, E. S. Faith of the Unit. Christian explained, *etc.*; disc. Bost., 1845. 8°. (B 1308, 1649)

— BEARD, J. R. Unitarianism exhibited in its natural conditions; essays by Unitarian ministers and others. London, 1846. 8°.

— DUNN, S. Socinianism as contained in 21 publications of G. Harris investigated and confuted. [Newcastle-on-Tyne, 1846.] 12°. * (C 242)

— HARRIS, G. Christian Unitarianism, what it really is; reply to Dunn. Newcastle-on-Tyne, 1846. 12°. (C 242)

— WARE, H., *Jr.* Works; ed. by C. Robbins. Boston, London, 1846. 4 v. 8°.

— BRIEF statement of the Unitarian belief. Boston, 1847. 8°. (B 1388, 1688)

— BURNAP, G. W. Position of Unitarianism defined. Balt., 1848. 8°. (B 1284)

— FULLER, A. B. Discourse in vindication of Unitarianism. Manchester, 1848. 8°. (B 1291)

— HIGGINSON, T. W. The Unitarian autumnal convention; sermon. Boston, 1853. 8°. (B 1293)

— ANDREWS, W. S. Unitarianism in reference to the trinity, atonement, and future punishment. Boston, 1854. 12°. (C 241)

— WILSON, J. Unitarian principles confirmed by Trinitarian testimonies. Boston, 1855. 12°.

— MCFARLAND, J. R. Relations of Unitarianism to the age; two disc. Charleston, 1858. 8°. (B 1296)

— HEYWOOD, J. H. Discourse on the evangelical character of Unitarian Christianity, Louisville, Ky., July 3. 2d ed. Balt., 1859. 8°. (B 1293)

— AMER. UNITARIAN ASSOC. Tracts; army series. Boston, 1865. 8°.

Periodicals.

— CHRISTIAN examiner. Bost., 1824-69. 87 v. 8°.

— MONTHLY journal of the Amer. Unit. Association. Boston, 1860-69. 10 v. 12°.

— MONTHLY religious magazine. Boston, 1844-74. 51 v. 8°.

— QUARTERLY journal of the Amer. Unit. Association. Boston, 1854-59. 6 v. 12°.

— UNITARIAN, The; cond. by B. Whitman. Camb., 1834. 8°.

— UNITARIAN advocate; ed. by E. Q. Sewall. Boston, 1828-29. 4 v. 12°.

— - *Same, entitled* Unitarian advocate and religious miscellany. N.s., conducted by an assoc. of gentlemen. Boston, 1830-32. 6 v. 12°.

— UNITARIAN and foreign religious miscellany; sel. by G. E. Ellis. Boston, 1847. 12°.

— UNITARIAN miscellany and Christian monitor. Balt., 1821-24. 6 v. 12°.

Note. Vol. 1-3, ed. by J. Sparks, 4-6, by F. G. S. Greenwood.

See also **Jesus Christ**; — **Socinianism**; — **Trinity**; — *also* **Society of Unitarian Christians in the West of England.**

Unitarians in England. Report of the proceedings of a meeting of Unitarians at Essex St. Chapel, London, 1838, convened to [consider] the present state of the denomination and its future welfare. London, 1838. 8°. (C 1389)

— American slavery; report of a meeting of [Unitarians], to deliberate on the duty of Eng. Unitarians, in reference to slavery in the U. S. London, 1851. 12°. (C 257)

Unitarians in the U. S. *National Conference of Unitarian and other Christian Churches.* Report of 4th meeting, N. Y., Oct. 1869. Boston, 1870. 8°.

— BELSHAM, T. American Unitarianism; a brief hist. of the progress of the Unitarian churches in America. [1812.] 3d ed. Boston, 1815. 8°. (B 266, 271)

— ELLIS, *Rev.* G. E. A half century of the Unitarian controversy. Boston, 1857. 8°.

United Brethren. Principles and discipline of the societies of United brethren in Gnadenhuetten, Sharon, and Dover. New Phila., 1844. 12°. (C 235)

— SPANGENBERG, A. G. Nachricht von der Verfassung der Brüder-Unität. 3e Aufl. Barby, 1793. 12°.

Doctrine.

— DAILY words and doctrinal texts of the Brethren's congregation for 1828. Lond., 1827. 18°.

— SPANGENBERG, A. G. Exposition of Christian doctrine as taught in the Protestant Church of the United Brethren. London, 1784. 8°.

History.

— HENRY, J. Sketches of Moravian life and character; gen. view of the hist., *etc.*, of the Unitas Fratrum, [1457-1855]. Phila., 1859. 12°.

— CRANZ, D. Ancient and modern hist. of the Brethren, [1457-1769]; tr. by B. La Trobe. London, 1780. 8°.

— GINDELY, A. Quellen zur Geschichte der böhmischen Brüder, [1457-1577]. (*In* **Vienna. Ak. d. Wiss.** Fontes rer. Aust., 2e Abth, 19r Bd. 1859.)

— OGDEN, J. C. Excursion into Bethlehem and Nazareth, Penn., 1799; with hist. of the Soc. of United Brethren. Phila., 1800. 12°.

Missions.

— LOSKIEL, G. H. Geschichte der Mission der evangelischen Brüder in Nordamerika, [1727-87]. Barby, 1789. 8°.

— - *Eng.* Hist. of the mission of the United Brethren in N. America, tr. by C. P. La Trobe. London, 1794. 8°.

— HECKEWELDER, J. Moravian mission among the Indians, [1732-1808]. Phila., 1820. 8°.

— OLDENDORP, C. G. A. Geschichte der Mission auf den Caraibischen Inseln, [1732-68]; hrsg. von J. J. Bossart. Barby, 1777. 2 v. 8°.

— HOLMES, J. Missions of the United Brethren, [1733-1816]. Dublin, 1818. 8°.

— SPANGENBERG, A. G. An account of the manner in which the Protestant Church of the Unitas Fratrum preach the Gospel and carry on their missions. [1780.] London, 1788. 8°.

Necrology.

— TODTENBUCH der Geistlichkeit der Böhmischen Brüder. (*In* **Vienna. Ak. d. Wiss.** Fontes rer. Austr., 1. Abth., 5. Bd.)

United Colonies of New England. Articles of confederation. (*In* **Mass.** *Gen. Court.* The Compact. 1836; — *and in* Bowen, F. Doc .1854.)
— Records. (*In* Hazard, E. Hist. col., v. 2. 1794.)
— Resolve conc. Quakers. (*In* **New Hamp. Hist. Soc.** Col., v. 1. 1824.)
— ADAMS, J. Q. N. E. confederacy of 1643. Boston, 1843. 8°. (B 1428)
— - *Same.* (*In* **Mass. Hist. Soc.** Col., v. 29. 1846.)
United Foreign Missionary Soc. 1st, 2d an. report. N. Y., 1818-19. 2 v. 8°. (B 1043)
United Insurance Co. of N. Y. N. Y. *Assembly.* An act to incorporate the company. N. Y:. [1798]. 8°. (D 57)
— LYMAN, J., *vs.* United Insurance Co. of N. Y. N. Y., 1818. 8°. (B 340)
United Irishmen. GR. BRIT. *Ho. of Com.* Report on the United Irishmen. *n.t.p.* [1798?] f°. (A 25)
— GR. BRIT. *Ho. of Lords.* Rapport du comité secret. [sur les Irlandois Unis]. *n.p.*, [1798]. f°. (A 66)
See also **Soc. of United Irishmen.** (C 155)
United Kingdom. *See* **Great Britain** (p. 1197-1257).
United Kingdom Alliance. Licenses for the sale of alcoholic liquors. (*In* **Nat. Assoc. Prom. Soc. Sci.** Trans., 1866.)
United Kingdom, The, tributary to France. (*In* **Pamphleteer,** 1820; v. 17 of **B 838**)
United Netherlands, United Provinces. *See* **Netherlands.**
United St. Bartholomew Committee. Documents rel. to the settlement of the Ch. of Eng. by the act of uniformity, 1662; with hist. introd. [by P. Bayne]. London, 1862. 8°.
United Secession Church. VOLUNTARY 'Church Association', and their manifesto against establishments considered; with an exposure of the abandonment of their principles by the U. S. C. 2d ed. [enl.]. Edin., [183-]. 12°. (B 1966)
United service journal and naval and military magazine. London, 1829-68. 117 v. 8°.
Note. Vols. 38-41 are called 'United service magazine'; vols. 42-46 'Colburn's united service magazine'.

United States.

Arrangement. A. Works of which the United States must be considered the author, and works published by the government:

I. In general.

II. Under the Confederation, *namely:*

III. Under the Constitution: 1st, general works (especially Registers, Constitution, Convention, Treaties); 2d, publications of the various branches of the government, and works about these branches, *namely:*

* *With the subdivisions:* Acts, laws, *etc.*; — Contested elections; — Debates and proceedings; — Obituary addresses; — Petitions, *etc.*; — Publications; — Reports of committees; — State papers: — Whig members of Congress; — History; — Dictionaries.

B. Works about the U. S. under the heads: —

☞ This is followed by **United States (separate states).**

A. WORKS AND PUBLICATIONS OF THE GOVERNMENT.

I. IN GENERAL.

— American's guide. Phila., 1844. 12°.
Contents. Constitution of the U. S. — American constitutions. — Dec. of independence. — Art. of confederation.
— AMERICAN keepsake, cont. the Declaration of independence; Constitution, Washington's Inaugural address, 1st message and Farewell address, date of formation of state constitutions, *etc.*, [and] postage law of 1845. Boston, 1845. 12°. (C 265)
— BOWEN, F. Documents, from Magna charta to 1789. Camb., 1854. 8°.
Contents for America. Massachusetts Body of liberties. — Confederacy of the N. E. Colonies. — Franklin's Plan of union. — Declaration of independence. — Va. Bill of rights. — Articles of confederation. — Mass. Declaration of rights. — Constitution.
— COE, J. The true American. Concord, 1840. 12°.
Contents. Dec. of independence. — Constitution. — First annual addresses and messages of the presidents, 1789-1839. — Maysville road veto. — Bank veto. — Washington's, — Jackson's farewell address. — **Address** to the young men and to the people of Amer. — The **currency.** — **Hamilton, A.** Opinions. — **Morton, M.** Perfection of government. — **Democracy** and reform. — **Prospects** of the democracy. — **Washington, G.** Opinion of paper money.

— FREEMAN'S guide. Charlestown, 1812. 12°.
Contents. Declaration of Independence. — Washington's farewell address. — Federal constitutions. — Constitutions of the states, with the latest amendments.

— GOODELL, W. Our national charters; with notes. N. Y., 1861. 12°.
Contents. Legal rules of interpretation. — Federal Constitution. — Articles of confederation, Declaration of independence. — Articles of association. — App.
Note. The documents contained in the collections above are also added to several of the works containing the collected constitutions of the several states: *see* **United States (Separate States)** p. 3162-63.

— HOUGH, F. B. Proclamations for thanksgiving issued by the Continental Congress, Washington, *etc.* Albany, 1858. 8°.

II. UNDER THE CONFEDERATION.

Treaties.

— Journal of treaty, Albany, Aug. 1775, with the Six Nations. (*In* **Mass. Hist. Soc.** Col., v. 25. 1836.)
— Treaty of commerce [with] France, Jan. 30, 1778; — of alliance [with] France, Jan. 30, 1778; — of commerce [with] the Netherlands, Oct. 8, 1782; — Provisional articles,[or, Definitive treaty with Gr. Brit.], Paris, Nov. 30, 1782. *See* **U. S. (Separate states).** Constitutions, 1783, 178–, and 1797 (p. 3162–63).
— Convention [with] the Netherlands conc. vessels, Oct. 8, 1782. *See* p. 30—. Constitutions, 1783.
— Articles of definitive treaty between Gr. Brit. and the U. S., [1783]. (*In* **U. S.** *Cont. Cong.* Articles of confederation. 1784. **C 265, W 69**)
See also **U. S. (Separate states).** Constitutions. 1797 (p. 3163).
— Treaty of amity and commerce between the U. S. and the King of Prussia. *n.p.*, 1786. 8°. (**B 1488**)
— *Same.* [Fr. and Eng.] *n.t.p.* [1786.] 8°. (**B 986**)

Army.

— MANUAL exercise as ordered by His Majesty in **1764.** Boston, [1774]. 4°. (**W 58, 70**)
— KAPP, F. Die Soldatenhandel deutscher Fürsten nach Amerika, 1775–83. Berlin,1864. 8°.
— U.S. *Census Office.* Census of pensioners for revolutionary or mil. services. Wash., 1841. f°.

Committee of the States.

— Journal of proceedings, June [4] - Aug. [9,] 1784; pub. by Congress. [Phila.,] 1784. 8°.
— *Same. See, below, Continental Cong.* Journals. 1823.

Continental Congress.

Note. From 1781 to 1788 Congress met annually on the 1st Monday in Nov.

— Journal. Phila., v. 3 N. Y., 1777-[89]. 13 v. 8°.
Contents. Vol. 1. Sept. 5, 1774 - Dec. 30, 1775. 2. Jan. 1 - Dec. 31, 1776. 3. 1777. 4. 1778. 5. 1779. 6. 1780. 7. Jan. 1, 1781 - Nov. 2, 1782. 8. Nov. 4, 1782 - Nov. 1, 1783. 9. Nov. 3, 1783 - June 3, 1784. [10.] Nov. 1, 1784 - Nov. 4, 1785. [11, misnumbered 12.] Nov. 7, 1785 - Nov. 3, 1786. 12. Nov. 6, 1786 - Oct. 30, 1787. 13. Nov. 5, 1787 - Oct. 21 ,1788. — App.: Nov. 3, 1788 - Mar. 2, 1789.
Note. Vol. 6 has the title 'Resolutions, acts, and orders'.
— *Same.* Phila., *Folwell,* 1800-01. 13 v. 8°.
— *Same.* [Vol. 6.] Phila., [1781]. 8°.
— *Same.* Vol. 7. N. Y., 1787. 8°.
— Journals, Sept. 5, 1774 - Nov. 1, 1788. Wash., 1823. 4 v. 8°.
Contents. Vol. 1. Sept. 5, 1774 - Dec. 31, 1776. 2. Jan. 1, 1777 - July 31, 1778. 3. Aug. 1, 1778 - Mar. 30, 1782. 4. Apr. 1, 1782 - Nov. 1, 1788. — Journal of the Committee of the States, 1st Friday in June to 1st Friday in Aug. 1784.
— Secret journals of the acts and proceedings, [May 10, 1775 - Sept. 16, 1788]; pub. under direction of the Pres. conformably to resolution of Cong., Mar. 27, 1818, and Apr. 21, 1820. Boston, 1821, 20-21. 4 v. 8°.
Contents. Vol. 1. Domestic affairs. — History of the Confederation. 2. Foreign affairs, Nov. 29, 1775 - Aug. 24, 1781. 3. July 27, 1781 - May 15, 1786. 4. May 17, 1786 - Sept. 16, 1788.

Sess. at Phila., Sept. 5 - Oct. 26, 1774.

— The association, with addresses to the people of Great Britain, and to the inhabitants of the Colonies.] *t.p.w.* [1774.] 8°. (**W 59**)
— Journal. Phila., 1774. 8°. (**B 992**)
— *Same.* With Petition to the King and Gen. Gage's letter. Phila. 1774 - [75]. 8°. (**B 359**)
Note. The Petition, *etc.*, has a separate title-page 'Phila., 1775'.
— *Same.* London, *E. and C. Dilley,* 1775. 8°.
Note. This is a reprint of only such parts of the 'Journal' as were omitted in the London ed. of the 'Extracts' (*see below*); it also contains the 'Petition', but not the 'Letter'.
— *Same.* London, *J. Almon,* 1775. 8°. (**B 387**)
— *Same as preceding, without the 'Petition'.* London, *J. Almon,* 1775. 8°. (**B 387**)
— Extracts from the votes and proceedings. Phila., *printed,* Hartford, *reprinted* 1774. 8°.
Contents. Extracts. — Bill of rights. — List of grievances. — Occasional resolves. — The association. — Address to the people of Gr. Brit. — Memorial to the inhabitants of the British Amer. Colonies. — Address to the inhabitants of Quebec.
— *Same.* New London, 1774. 4°. (**A 64**)
— *Same.* London, 1774. 8°. (**B 388**)
— *Same, without the* Address to the inhabitants of Quebec. Boston, 1774. 8°. (**B 1092**)
— Address to the inhabitants of Quebec, Oct. 26. (*In* **Dickinson, J.** Political writings, v. 2. 1801.)
— LETTER from the Connecticut delegates, Oct. 1774. (*In* **Mass. Hist. Soc.** Col., v. 12. 1816.)
— CHANDLER, T. B. What think ye of the Congress now? enquiry, how far are Americans bound to abide by and execute the decisions of the late Congress. N. Y., **1775.** 8°. (**B 343, W 21**)

Sess. at Phila., May 10, 1775 - Dec. 12, 1776.

— Journal, May 10 [- Aug. 1, omitting some resolutions rel. to military operations]. N. Y., *reprinted* 1775. 8°. (**B 361**)
— *Same.* London, *reprinted* 1776. 8°. (**B 384**)
— - Extracts from the journals. Nov. 25, 1775 - Apr. 3, 1776, rel. to the capture and condemnation of prizes and fitting out privateers; with rules of the navy, *etc.* Phila., 1776. 8°. (**W 68**)
— De Acte van onafhanglijkheid, de Artijkelen van confederatie, *enz.* (*In* **Verzameling.** 1781.)
— Rules and articles for the better government of the troops, June 30. Phila., Watertown, *reprinted* 1775. 8°. (**B 515**)
— Declaration, July 6, setting forth the causes of their taking up arms. Phila., 1775. 8°. (**W 23**)
— Humble petition of the twelve United Colonies to the King; July 8. Phila., 1775. 8°. (**B 360**)
— Address of the United Colonies of N. Amer. by their representatives in Cong. to the people of Ireland; July 28. Phila., 1775. 8°. (**B 360, 1092, W 21**)
— Several methods of making salt-petre; recommended to the inhabitants of the Colonies by their representatives in Cong.; July 28. Phila..1775. 8°. (**W 23**)
— *Same.* With app. by W. Whiting. Watertown, 1775. 8°. (**C 84**)
— Rules and articles for the better government of the troops; Nov. 7. Phila., 1775. 8°. (**W 68**)
— Declaration of independence, [July 4, 1776]. (*In* **American's guide.** 1844; — *in* **U. S.** Constitution. 1846; 1851; — *and in* **Bowen, F.** Documents. 1854.)
— *Same.* With a counter-declaration published at New York in 1781. (*In* **Deane, S.** Paris papers.)
— *Same. See Acts, laws, etc.* (p. 3059), where two editions of the 'Laws' and the 'Public statutes at large' contain the Declaration; — *also* **U. S. (Separate states)** p. 3162-63.
— Rules and articles for the better government of the troops; Sept. 20. Phila., 1776. 8°. (**B 615, W 4, 68**)
— *Same.* [With resolution of Cong., Apr., 14, 1777.] Boston, 1777. 12°. (**C 102**)
— *Same.* [With appendix.] Phila., 1794. 12°. (**W 68**)

Sess. at New York, Sept. 30, 1777 - June 27, 1778.

— Articles of confed. and perpetual union Nov. 15, Lancaster, Penn.] Boston, *reprinted* **1777.** f°. (**A 25**)
— *Same.* [With] the [Va.] Declaration of rights and Constitution and the Articles of definitive treaty between Gr. Brit. and the U. S.; pub. by [Va.] Gen. Assemb. Richmond, [1784]. 8°. (**C 265, W 69**)
— *Same.* (*In* **American's** guide. 1844; — *and in* **Bowen, F.** Documents. 1854.)
— *Same. See Acts, laws, etc.* (p. 3059), where the 'Laws' and the 'Public statutes at large' contain in v. 1 the articles of confederation.

Sess. at Phila., July 2, 1778 – June 21, 1783.

— Observations on the Amer. revolution. Phila., 1779. 8°. (B 635)
— *Same.* Providence, *reprinted* 1780. 8°. (C 76)
— Regulations for the order and discipline of the troops, 29th March. Phila., 1779. 8°.
— *Same.* [With] the U. S. militia act [of] May 1792, and [that] of Mass. [of] June 22, 1793. New ed. by F. W. A. Steuben. Bost., 1794. 12°.
— *Same, without the acts.* Phila., 1800. 12°.
— *Same.* Boston, 1802. 12°.
— *Same.* With exercises and evolutions of the cavalry. Bennington, 1803. 12°.
— Circular letter from the Congress of Amer. to their constituents; Sept. 13. Phila., *printed*, Boston, *reprinted* 1779. 8°. (B 515)
— *Same.* Phila., *printed*, New London, *reprinted* [1779]. 12°. (C 265)
— Address and recommendations to the states by the U. S.; Apr. 24. Phila., 1783. 8°. (B 1488, W 21)
— *Same.* Boston, *reprinted* 1783. 8°. (B 516, 972, 2501, C 308, D 53)
— *Same, entitled* Addresses, *etc.* London, *reprinted* 1783. 8°. (B 682, 1638)
— Constitutions of the states, declaration of independence, *etc.*; pub. by order of Cong. Phila., *printed*, London, *reprinted* 1783. 8°.

Sess. at N. York, Jan. 11, 1785 – Nov. 1. 1788.

— Plan for the general arrangement of the militia of the U. S.; [by the Secretary, H. Knox]; 18th March. *n.p.*, 1786. 8°. (W 68)
— Resolve of Congress, Sept. 28, and resolutions of the Gen. Court of Mass. *n.p.*, [1787]. 8°. (C 265)

Superintendant of Finance.

— Statement of accounts; 20th Feb. 1781 – 1st Nov. 1784. Phila., 1785. f°.

Board of the Treasury.

— Report on the establishment of a mint; Apr. 8, 1786. *n.t.p.* [1786.] 4°. (B 649)
— Statement of the Dr. and Cr. states, in account with U. S.] *n.t.p.* [Phila., 1786?] f°. (A 25)

III. UNDER THE CONSTITUTION.

Constitutional Convention and Constitution.

— Journal, acts, and proceedings of the convention. Boston, 1819. 8°.
— Secret proceedings and debates of the convention; from notes taken by R. Yates; including the genuine information laid before the Legislature of Maryland, by L. Martin; also other historical documents. Albany, 1821. 8°.
— *Same.* Wash., 1836. 8°.
— *Same.* Richmond, 1839. 8°.
— Debates in the state conventions on the adoption of a Federal constitution; with Journal of the Federal Convention, L. Martin's letter, Yates's letter, Congressional opinions, Virginia and Kentucky resolutions, *etc.*; rev. by J. Elliot. 2d ed. Phila., 1861. 5 v. 8°.

Constitution.

— Constitution of the U. S. as proposed by the convention at Phila., Sept. 17, 1787, and since ratified with amendments. *n.t.p.* [Phila., 1787.] 8°.
— Constitution, The; or, Frame of government for the U. S. Boston, 1787. 8°. (B 527)
— *Same.* [Another ed.] *n.t.p.* [1787.] 8°. (C 265)
— Constitution. (*In* **Mass.** *Constitution.* 179–.)
— *Same.* *See Acts and laws* (p. 3059), where two editions of the 'Laws' and the 'Public statutes at large' have the Constitution.
— Constitution of Mass. and that of the U. S., *etc.* Brookfield, 1807. 12°.
— *Same.* (*In* **View** of the whole ground. **1809**; — **Freeman's** guide. **1812**; — **Coe, J.** True American. **1840**; — *and in* **American's** guide. **1844.**)
— The constitution; causes of its adoption; Declaration of independence, *etc.* Wash., 1846. 12°.
— The constitution; with alphabetical analysis, the Declaration of independance, *etc.*; by W. Hickey. 4th ed. Phila., 1851. 12°.
— Constitution. (*In* **Bowen, F.** Documents. **1854**; — *and in* **Goodell, W.** Our nat. charters. **1861.**)
— – *French.* Constitution. (*In* **Tripier, L.** Les constitutions. 1848; — **Bigelow, J.** Les Etats-Unis. 1863; — *and in* **Lecomte, F.** Guerre. 1863.)

See also Constitution (p. 3113–15); — *also* (p. 3162–63) **U. S. Separate States,** (where the 'Constitutions' also contain the U. S. Constitution).

Conventions.

— Convention between the French Republic and the U. S. Wash., 1801. 4°. (B 649)
— Convention between H. M. and the U. S., additional to the treaty Apr. 7, 1862, for the suppression of the African slave trade. London, [1870]. f°. (E 76)
— Convention between H. M. and the U. S. rel. to naturalization; signed, London, May 13, 1870. London, [1870]. f°. (E 76)

Treaties.

— Treaties and conventions since July 4, 1776. Wash., 1871. 8°. (41st C. 3d. s. Sen. Doc. 36.)
— *Same.* Rev. ed. Wash., 1873. 8°.
— All the treaties between the U. S. and Gr. Brit., 1783–1814. Boston, 1815. 8°. (A 1)

See also Congress (Acts, laws, *etc.*) p. 3059.

(*Single treaties.*)

— Treaty of amity, commerce, and navigation between [Gr. Brit.] and the U. S., June 24; [Jay's treaty, with] app. Phila., [1795]. 8°. (B 1119)
— Treaty of limits between the U. S. and the Choctaw Indians, Mt. Dexter, Nov. 16, 1805; Jan. 15, 1808. Wash., 1808. 8°. (Sen. B 489)
— Articles of a treaty between the U. S. and the Ottaway, Chippeway, Wyandot, and Pottawatamie Indians, Detroit, 17 Nov. 1807; Jan. 15, 1808. Wash., 1808. 8°. (Sen. B 489)
— *Same.* Jan. 30, 1808. Wash., 1808. 8°. (Ho. B 489)
— *Same.* 2d ed. Phila., 1795. 8°. (B 790, W 63)
— *Same.* (*In* **Treaty,** The, its merits, *etc.*, 179–. B 619)
— Treaty of amity and commerce between Prussia and the U. S. *n.t.p.* [Wash., 1799.] 8°. (B 986)
— Treaty between the U. S. and the Piankeshaw Indians, Apr. 15. 1806. (*In* **U. S.** *Pres.* Message. 1806. B 485)
— Articles of a treaty between the U. S. and the Ottaway, Chippeway, Wyandot, and Pottawatamie Indians, Detroit, Nov. 17, 1807; Jan. 15. Wash., 1808. 8°. (B 489)
— Treaty between the U. S. and Mexico, Feb. 2, 1848; including art. I., V. of the unratified convention of Nov. 20, 1843, convention Apr. 11, 1839. Wash., 1849. 8°. (Commiss. on Claims ag. Mexico. B 1510)
— Traité conclu entre les Etats-Unis d'Amérique et l'Empire du Japon. (*In* **Paris. Soc. de Géog.** Bull., 4e sér., v. 8. 1854.)

ADMINISTRATION, DEPARTMENTS, OFFICES, *etc.*

— BIGELOW, J. Forme du gouvernement. (*In his* Les Etats-Unis. 1863.)
— TILESTON, E. S. Handbook of the administrations, [1789–1871]. Boston, 1871. 16°.
— U. S. *36th Cong. 1st sess. Ho.* The Covode investigation; [report] from the select committee. *n.t.p.* [1860.] 8°. (No. 648)

Registers.

— U. S. *Dept. of State.* Registers of officers and agents, civil, military, and naval, in the service of the U. S., 1816, 21, 25, 27, 37-47, 55, 61-67, 79. Wash., 1816-79. 20 v. 8°.

Note. In 1861 and after published under the direction of the *Department of the Interior.*

— HUNTER, A. Register of officers and agents. Wash., 1860–61. 8°.
— – United States register or blue book for 1861, 62, 69; pub. by J. Disturnell. N. Y., [1861–69]. 3 v. 12°.

See also, Adjutant General (p. 3157); — *Army* (p. 3157–58); — *Navy* (p. 3093); — *Registers* (p. 3160).

Adjutant General.
(Subordinate to the *War Department.*)

— Military laws, rules, *etc.*, for the army, 1813, 14, 16. [Wash., 1813-16.] 3 v. 12°.
Note. 1814 printed for the War Department.
— Proceedings of the court martial, in the case of W. Hull. Wash., 1814. 12°. (B 658)
— Army register, 1815-44, 47-68, 70-72. Phila., [1815-16, Wash., 1817-72.] 57 v. 8°.
Note. From 1818-72 called Official army register; For 1848 there is a register for Jan. and also for Oct., and for 1861 for Jan. and Sept.
— *Same.* 1845-47. [Wash., 1845-47.] 3 v. 4°.
— General orders, 1861-63; chronol. arr. by T. M. O'Brien and O. Diefendorf. N.Y., 1864. 8°.
— General orders, no. 1-400. [Wash., 1863.] 400 nos. 16°.
— Instructions for the government of the armies of the U. S. in the field; by F. Lieber. N. Y., 1863. 8°. (Gen. order, 100.)
See also War Dept. Reports (p. 3107).

Adjutant General's Office. Northern Division.

— Official digest of the orders received since the organization of the peace establishment. Sacket's Harbor, 1818. 8°. (B 456)

Agent General on Claims of British Subjects.

— Observations on the part of the U. S. to the reply of D. Dulany. *n.p.*, [1798]. 4°. (A 26)

Agents for Exchange of Prisoners.

— Official correspondence between the agents, with Mr. Ould's report. Richmond, 1864. 8°.

Board of Agriculture.

— Report, 1862-70, 73-76. Wash., 1863-77. 13 v. 8°.
Note. For reports 1847-61 *see Patent Office* (p. 3094); the missing reports and duplicates of those here given are contained in the full set of Congressional doc.; *see House* (p. 3064-92); — *Senate* (p. 3096-3106).
— Monthly report of the condition of the crops, July 1863 - Dec. 1864. Wash., [1863] - 64. 12 v. 8°.
Note. For Nov. - Dec. 1863 the title reads 'Monthly report of the Dept. of Agriculture'; and Jan. - Dec. 1864, 'Bimonthly report', *etc.*
— Letter of the Commiss. transmitting the report of the commission [on] the practicability of cultivating and preparing flax or hemp as a substitute for cotton. *n.t.p.* [1865.] 8°.

Naval Academy at Annapolis.
(Subordinate to the *Navy Dept.*)

— U. S. *Navy Dept.* Rules and regulations for the Acad. Wash., 1850. 8°.
— Marshall, E. C. History of the U. S. Naval Academy. N. Y., 1862. 12°.

Army.

See also Army, under the Confederation (p. 3055).
— Army regulations, 1775, *etc.* *See Continental Cong.* (p. 3055-56); — *Adjutant Gen.* (*above*); — *President* (p. 3095); — — *War Department* (p. 3107-09).
— Collection of papers rel. to half-pay and commutation, [1778 - June 7, 1783]. Bost., 1783. 8°. (B 518)
— *Same.* (*In* Washington, G. Last official addr. 1783.)
— *Same.* [1778 - Mar. 22, 1783.] Fishkill, 1783. 8°. (B 1095)
— Washington, G. Revolutionary orders 1778, 80-82; ed. by H. Whiting. N. Y., London, 1844. 8°.
— - *Same.* N. Y., 1844. 8°.
— Steuben, F. W. A. H. F., *Baron.* Letter on an established militia and military arrangements; addr. to the inhabitants of the U. S. N. Y., 1784. 4°. (A 27, W 58, 70)
— U. S. *2d Cong. 1st sess.* Bill establishing an uniform militia. *n.t.p.* [1792.] f°. (A 66)
— Harper, R. G. Speech in the House on the reduction of the army. Phila., 1800. 12°. (C 104)
— Fisher, D. Rules and regulations designed for the forces. (*In his* System of military tactics. 1805.)
— Military Philosophical Society. Extracts from the minutes, Oct. 6, 1806. *n.t.p.* [1806.] 4°. (A 5)
— - *Same.* Jan. 30, 1808. Wash., 1808. 4°. (A 5)
— - *Same.* Dec. 28, 1809. N. Y., 1809. 4°. (A 5)
— U. S. *9th Cong. 1st sess.* An act for establishing rules and articles for the armies [1806; with rules and regulations of the War Dept., 1812]. Wash., 1812. 16°.
— Max[an] ***. Military reflections on four modes of defence for the U. S.; tr. by E. Anderson. Balt., 1807. 8°. (B 432)
— Eppes, J. W. Speech on the proposition for raising 50,000 volunteers, Dec. 30. *n.p.*, [1808]. 8°. (B 410)
— U. S. *Congress.* Laws rel. to the military establishment in force 12th Apr., 1808. Wash., 1812. 16°.
— - *9th Cong. 1st sess.* Act for establishing rules and articles for the government of armies; with regulations. Wash., 1808. 16°.
— Tallmadge, B. Speech, Jan. 27, 1809, on providing an additional military force. *n.p.*, [1809]. 8°. (B 410, 553)
— Bird's eye sketch of the military concerns of the U. S. *n.t.p.* [1812.] 8°. (B 451)
— Sheffey, D. Speech, bill to raise additional military force, Ho., Jan. 3. *n.t.p.* [1812.] 8°. (B 450, C 61)
— Regulations for the field exercise and conduct of the infantry of the U. S.; by an officer; with plates. Phila., 1812. 8°.
— Stanford, R. Speech, bill to raise an additional mil. force, Jan. 6, 1812. *n.t.p.* 8°. (B 450, 2530, C 61)
— U. S. *Census Office. 6th census,* 1840. Census of pensioners for revolutionary or military services. Wash., 1841. f°.
— - *12th Cong. 1st sess.* Acts increasing the military establishment. Wash., 1812. 16°.
— - Acts rel. to the military establishment. *n.t.p.* [1812.] 16°.
— - Acts [rel.] to the militia. *n.t.p.* [1812.] 16°.
— - Act authorizing the Pres. to accept and organize certain voluntary military corps. *n.t.p.* [1812.] 16°.
— Clay, H. Speech, Jan. 8, bill for raising an additional military force. Balt., [1813]. 8°. (B 669)
— Emott, J. Speech, Jan. 12, on the bill in add. to 'An act to raise an additional military force'. Alexandria, [1813]. 8°. (B 669)
— - *Same.* Boston, 1813. 8°. (B 1491)
— Quincy, J. Speech, Jan. 5, on the bill in addition to 'An act to raise an add. military force. Boston, 1813. 8°. (B 669, 1491)
— Miller, M. S. Speech, army bill, Jan. Georgetown, 1814. 8°. (B 669, 2530)
— Sheffey, D. Speech, bill to authorize the President to call upon the states for their respective quotas of 80,000 men, Dec. 10. Wash., [1814]. 8°. (B 669)
— Stockton, R. Speech, Dec. 10, bill to authorize the president to call upon the several states for their respective quotas of 80,000 men. Georgetown, 1814. 8°. (B 669, 2531)
— Ward, A. Speech, bill to authorize the President to call upon the states for their respective quotas of 80,000 men, Dec. 14. Wash., [1814]. 8°. (B 669)
— - Speech, Mar. 5, bill for making appropriations for the support of the military estab. of the U. S. for 1814. Boston, 1814. 8°. (B 669)
— Webster, D. Speech, Jan. 14, bill making further provisions for filling the ranks of the regular army, *etc.* Alexandria, [1814]. 8°. (B 669, 2530)
— Tone, W. T. W. Essay on the necessity of improving our national forces. N. Y., 1819. 8°. (B 545)
— Hill, M. L. Narrative shewing the promises made to officers of the continental army and how far [they] have been fulfilled. Elizabethtown, 1826. 8°. (B 1106)
— Memoir on the organization of the army of the U. S. Georgetown, 1826. 8°. (B 1105, 1107)
— Officers of the late war. To the, [on] an application to Cong. for lands. N. Y., 1826. 12°. (C 194)
— Law and the facts submitted to the militia of the U. S.; case of the six militia men and Gen. Jackson's vindication. From the 'Democratic press'. *n.t.p.* [1827.] 8°. (B 1493)

— WOODBURY, L. Remarks on the bill for relief of surviving officers of the Revolution. Wash., 1828. 8°. (B 971)

— ADAMS, J. Q., *and others*. Correspondence between A. and several citizens of Mass. conc. the charge of a design to dissolve the union. Boston, 1829. 8°. (B 978, 1648, 1702, 1761, 1796)

— - *Same*. 2d ed. Boston, 1829. 8°. (B 1770)

— MILITIA of the U. S. *n.t.p.* [183–.] 8°. (B 1807)

— HARDIN, B. Speech, Adams's resolutions conc. the loss of the fortification bill of the last session. Wash., 1836. 8°. (B 1791)

— REED, J. Speech in rel. to the failure of the fortification bill, Jan. 27. Wash., 1836. 8°. (B 1791)

— WEBSTER, D. Speech, on the 3,000,000 appropriation, and the loss of the appropriation bill for fortifications, Jan. 14. Wash., 1836. 8°. (B 1721)

— WISE, H. A. Speech on the causes of the loss of the fortification bill, Jan. 22. Wash., 1836. 8°. (B 1777, 1791)

— U. S. *34th Cong. 2d sess. Senate.* Statistical report on the sickness and mortality in the army, 1839–55. (*In its* Executive documents, v. 18. 1856. Doc. 96.) — *36th Cong. 1st sess. Senate.* 1855–60. (*In* v. 13. 1860. Doc. 52.)

— - *26th Cong. 1st sess.* Report of the committee on the militia, on so much of the report of the Sec. of War as relates to the reorganization of the militia, June 3. [Wash., 1840.] 8°. (B 1823)

— NEFF, J. K. The army and navy of America. Lancaster, 1857. 8°.

— MAYO, C. Medical service of the Federal army. (*In* Galton, F. Vacation tourists. 1862, 63.)

— SMITH, G. B. Official army list of the volunteers of Illinois, Indiana, Wisconsin, *etc.*; comp. by S. Chicago, 1862. 12°.

— STEFFEN, W. Digest of U. S. tactics. Boston, 1862. 16°.

— ELLIOTT, E. B. Military statistics of the U. S. Berlin, 1863. 4°. (International Statistical Cong. at Berlin.)

— LA FRUSTON, F. de. Constitution et organization de l'armée de terre des Etats-Unis. Paris, 1863. 8°.

— KAUTZ, A. V. Customs of service for non-commissioned officers and soldiers. Phila., 1864. 16°.

— HAUROWITZ, H. v. Das Militärsanitätswesen der Vereinigten Staaten des letzten Krieges. Stuttgart, 1866. 8°.

— MICKLEY, J. M. 43d regiment U. S. colored troops. Gettysburg, 1866. 8°.

— U. S. SANITARY COMMISSION. *Statistical Bureau.* Ages of the U. S. vol. soldiery. N. Y., 1866. 8°.

— VIGO ROUSSILLON, F. P. Puissance militaire des Etats-Unis d'après la guerre de la sécession. Paris, 1866. 8°.

Dictionary and Registers.

— GARDNER, C. K. Dictionary of all officers in the army of the U. S., 1789–1853; with supplement [to 1859]. 2d ed. New York, 1860. 12°.

— REGISTER of the army and navy; by P. Force. Wash., 1830. 12°.

Note. For army registers *see also Adjutant General* (p. 3057).

See also Adjutant General (p. 3057); — *Surgeon General* (p. 3107); — *War Department* (p. 3107–09); — *Military Acad. at West Point* (p. 3109); — *also Military biography* (p. 3111); — *History* (p. 3122–31).

Periodicals.

— MILITARY and naval magazine of the U. S. [Wash., 1833–36.] 6 v. 8°.

— UNITED STATES army and navy journal. N. Y., [1864–80]. 17 v. f°.

— UNITED STATES service magazine. N. Y., 1864–66. 5 v. 8°.

Army Medical Museum.

— U. S. *Surgeon General.* Catalogue of the surgical section; prepared under the direction of the Surg. Gen.; by A. A. Woodhull. Wash., 1866. 4°.

— - Catalogue of the medical section; prepared under the direction of the Surg. Gen. [J. K. Barnes]; by J. J. Woodward. Wash., 1867. 4°.

Attorney General.

Various reports of the Attorney General may be found, by means of the indexes, in the Congressional documents (*House*, p. 3064–92; *Senate*, p. 3096–3106).

National Banks.

— U. S. *38th Cong. 1st sess.* National bank act. N. Y., 1864. 8°. (B 1545)

See also Fiscal Bank (p. 3064); — **Bank notes** (p. 198); — **Bank of the U. S.** (p. 199;) — **Banks** (p. 201–202).

Census Office.

(Subordinate to the *Dept. of the Interior.*)

(The census was taken by the Department of State till the establishment of the Department of the Interior in 1869.)

— Statistical view of the population of the U. S., 1790–1830. Wash., 1835. f°.

— GARFIELD, J. A. The American census. (*In* Amer. Soc. Sci. Assoc. Trans., v. 2. 1870.)

— *1st Census*, 1790. Return of the number of persons within the U. S. Phila., 1791. 8°. (B 563, W 17, 68)

— - *Same.* Wash., 1802. 8°. (B 354, 1699)

— *2d census*, 1800. Return of the whole number of persons within the U. S. *n.p.*, [1801]. f°.

Note. Has no schedule for Tennessee.

— - *Same, with schedule of Tennessee.* Wash., 1802. 8°. (B 354)

— *3d census*, 1810. 3d census of inhabitants of the U. S. within Mass.; [and manufactures in all the states]. *n.p.*, [1813]. 4°.

— - Aggregate amount of persons within the U. S. 1810.] *n.t.p.* 1810. obl. f°.

— - Series of tables of the several branches of American manufactures so far as returned in 1810. *n.p.*, [18–]. 4°. (A 19)

— *4th census*, 1820. Census. Wash., 1821. f°.

— - Digest of accounts of manufacturing establishments in the U.S. and of their manufactures. Wash., 1823. f°.

— *5th census*, 1830. 5th census; enumeration of persons within the U. S., 1830; [with] a schedule of the number of persons taken in 1790, 1800, 10, 20. Wash., 1832. f°.

— - Abstract of the returns of the 5th census, showing the number of free people, the number of slaves, *etc.* Wash., 1832. 8°. (B 1058)

— *6th census*, 1840. 6th census. Wash., 1841. f°.

— - Compendium of the enumeration of the inhabitants and statistics of the U. S., from the returns of the 6th census; added, abstract of each preceding census. [Wash.,] *T. Allen*, 1841. f°.

— - *Same.* Wash., *Blair and Rives*, 1841. f°.

— - Census of pensioners for revolutionary or military services. Wash., 1841. f°.

— RUSSELL, A. Principles of statistical inquiry, in ref. to the U. S. census of 1840. N. Y., 1839. 8°.

— *7th census*, 1850. History and statistics of Maryland according to the returns of the 7th census of the U. S. Wash., 1852. f°.

— - Report of the superintendent of the census, [J. C. G. Kennedy,] Dec. 1, 1852; with the report of Dec. 1, 1851. Wash., 1853. 8°.

— - DeBow, J. D. B. Statistical view of the U. S.; compendium of the 7th census. Wash., 1854. 8°.
— - *Same.* Wash., 1853. 4°.
— - Smith, T. Speech on printing the returns of the 7th census, Jan. 12. Wash., 1852. 8°. (B 1505)
— *8th census*, 1860. Agriculture in 1860. Wash., 1862. 4°.
— - Manufactures. Wash., 1865. 4°.
— - Population. Wash., 1864. 4°.
— - Preliminary report; by J. C. G. Kennedy. Wash., 1862. 8°.
— - Statistics. Wash., 1866. 4°.
— - Jay, J. Statistical view of Amer. agric., with suggestions for the schedules of the census in 1860. N. Y., 1859. 8°.
— *9th census*, 1870. Wash., 1872. 3 v. 4°.
Contents. Vol. 1. Population. 2. Vital statistics. 3. Wealth and industry.
— - A compendium of the 9th census; by F. A. Walker. Wash., 1872. 8°.

Christian Commission.

See **United States Christian Commission** (p. 3163).

Circuit Court.

— Bassett, R. Protest against two acts of Congress of Mar. 8 and Apr. 29, 1802, to abolish the offices of the judges of the circuit courts of the U. S. Phila., 1802. 8°. (B 402)
— Bill of indictment for treason against A. Burr, with examinations, evidence, *etc.*; 22 May 1807. *n.t.p.* [Wash., 1808.] 8°. (B 490)
— Rules for the first circuit. Bost., 1812. 8°. (B 452, 469)
— Rules in civil causes of admiralty and maritime jurisdiction. *n.t.p.* [1812?] 8°. (B 1430)
— Opinion in and for the eastern district of Penn., on the will of S. Zane. Phila., 1834. 8°. (B 1439)
— Notice of the death of Chief Justice Taney. Boston, 1864. 8°. (B 1540)

Claims.

See Court of Claims (p. 3062); — *Claims* (p. 3112).

Coast Survey.

(Subordinate to the *Treasury Department.*)

— Annual reports, 1851-77. Wash., 1852-80. 27 v. 8° *and* 4°.
☞ Duplicate volumes of those here enumerated are contained in the full set of Congressional doc., *see House* (p. 3064-92); — *Senate* (p. 3096-3106).
Note. The maps for 1841 and 1851 were issued in separate volumes. In the other years they are included in the report.
— Report on the hist. and progress of the Amer. coast survey up to 1858. *n.p.*, 1858. 8°.
— Hassler, F. R. Papers on various subjects connected with the survey of the coast of the U. S. (*In* Amer. Phil. Soc. Trans., n.s., v. 2. 1825.)
— - Corrections to the papers on the coast survey in the Philosoph. trans. of Phila. N. Y., 1826. 8°. (B 1108)
— Pearce, J. A. Speech, coast survey of the U. S., Feb. 17. 2d ed. Wash., 1849. 8°. (B 1503)
— Bache, A. D. Progress of the survey of the coast of the U. S. (*In* Amer. Assoc. Proc., v. 2. 1850.)

Commissioners for Exchange of Prisoners.
See Agents for Exchange of Prisoners.

Commissioner on the Boundary between the U.S. and the Possessions of his Catholic Majesty in America.

— Ellicott, A. Journal of E., late commissioner, 1796-1800. Phila., 1803. 4°.

Commissioners Appointed to Confer with the Insurgents in the western Counties of Penn.

— Report. Phila., 1794. 8°. (B 1000)

Commissioners at Paris under the Convention, Apr. 1803.

— People of the U. S., To the. Phila., 1807. 8°.

Commissioners of the City of Washington.
See 6th Cong. 1st sess. Ex docs. (p. 3071) and *7th C. 1st s.* Ex. doc. 'Also' (p. 3071).

Commissioners of the District of Columbia.
See 43d Cong. 2d sess. Ex. doc., v. 8. (p. 3091).

Commissioners of the Land Board for the District of Detroit.
See 10th Cong. 1st sess. (p. 3078).

Commissioners of the Navy Pension Fund.
See 9th Cong. 1st sess. Ex. doc. (p. 3075).

Commissioners of the Sinking Fund.
See House. Ex. doc. (p. 3064, and foll.).

Commissioners on the Georgia Mississippi Territory.
See 7th Cong. 2d sess. (p. 3074).

Commissioners on the 6th article of the treaty between [Gr. Brit.] and the U. S.

— Sundry resolutions and proceedings in cases before the Board. Phila., 1799. 4°.
— *Another copy.* (A 26)

Congress.

I. PUBLICATIONS OF CONGRESS.

☞ For all publications of the House of Representatives *see House* (p. 3064-92); for publications of the Senate *see Senate* (p. 3096-3196).

Acts, laws, etc. (Collections.)

— Laws. Vol. 1 - 4, Phila., 5 - 20, Wash., 1796-[1823]. 20 v. (v. 18, 19 w.). 8°.
Note. Vol. 9-11 printed for the Department of State; v. 12-17 have only the half-title 'Acts passed', *etc.*; v. 12, 15-17 have the separate sessions paged separately.
Contents. Vol. 1. Constitution. — Acts and treaties, 1st Cong. 1st - 3d sess. 2. 2d Cong. — Declaration of independence. — Articles of confederation. — Ordinance for the government of the territory north-west of the River Ohio. 3. Acts, 3d - 4th Cong. [4.] 5th Cong. — Treaty between the U. S. and the Cherokee Indians, Oct. 2, 1798. 5. Acts and treaties, 6th Cong. 6. Acts, treaties, and proclamations, 7th Cong. 7. 8th Cong. 8. 9th Cong. 9. 10th Cong. 10. 11th Cong. [11.] 12th Cong. [12.] 13th Cong. [14.] 14th Cong. [15.] 15th Cong. [16.] 16th Cong. [17.] 17th Cong. 18, 19. *Wanting.* 20. 20th Cong.
— Laws. Vol. 1. N. Y., [17—?]. 8°.
Contents. Constitution. — Acts, 1st Cong. 1st - 3d sess. — Treaties between the U. S. and foreign nations and the several Indian tribes. — Declaration of independence. — Resolves and ordinances.
— Public statutes at large, 1789-1875. Vol. 1 - 15, 17, 18, pt. 3. Boston, 1861, 60, 62, 61, 62, 57, 55 - 78, 77. 19 v. in 21 pts. f°.
Note. Vol. 1-8, ed. by R. Peters; 9, 10, by G. Minot; 11 by G. Minot and G. P. Sanger; 12-17, by G. P. Sanger, 18, 19, pub. under the direction of the Sec. of State. In v. 9 the title changes to 'Statutes at large and treaties'; in v. 11, 'Statutes', *etc.*, 'and proclamations'; in v. 16'Statutes at large and proclamations; and treaties and postal conventions'; v. 18, pt. 1, 2d ed, 'Revised statutes'; 18, pt. 2, 'Revised statutes rel. to the District of Columbia'; in v. 18, pt. 3, 19, 'Statutes at large and recent treaties, postal conventions, and executive proclamations'. Vol. 5 has an index to v. 1-5; v. 8 to v. 1-8; v. 6, 7, 9-18, for their respective vols.
Contents. Vol. 1. Tables of acts, 1789-1845. — Declaration of independence. — Articles of confederation. — Constitution. — Amendments to the Constitution. — Public acts, 1st - 5th Cong. 2. 6th - 12th Cong. 3. 13th - 17th Cong. — App.: Proclamations, *etc.* 4. 18th - 23d Cong. — App. 5. 24th - 28th Cong. — App. 6. Private acts, 1st-28th Cong. 7. Indian treaties concluded Sept. 17, 1778 - Oct. 11, 1842. — App. 8. Foreign treaties, Feb. 6, 1778 - Nov. 10, 1845. — App. 9. Public and private acts, 29th - 31st Cong. — Treaties, March 17, 1841 - April 17, 1850. — App. 10. Public and private acts, 32d - 33d Cong. — Treaties, March 3, 1849 - Feb. 27, 1855. — App. 11. Public and private acts, 34th - 35th Cong. — Treaties, Jan. 17, 1837 - Apr. 19, 1858. — App.: Proclamations, Jan. 24, 1791 - Feb. 26, 1859 (omitting those published in the appendices to the previous vols.). 12. Public and private acts, 36-37th Cong. — Treaties,

Apr. 11, 1859 - March 19, 1863. — App.: Proclamations, June 25, 1860 - March 30, 1863. 13. Public and private acts, 38th Cong. — Treaties, July 11, 1861 - Nov. 3, 1864. — App.: Proclamations, Sept. 24, 1862 - Nov. 24, 1865. 14. Public and private acts, 39th Cong. — Treaties, June 9, 1863 - July 19, 1866. — App.: Proclamations, Apr. 2, 1863 - March 30, 1867. 15. Public and private acts, 40th Cong. — Treaties, Oct. 1, 1859 - Aug. 13, 1868. — App.: Proclamations, Apr. 16, 1863 - Dec. 25, 1868. 16. Public and private acts, 41st Cong. — Treaties, Oct. 14, 1864 - Oct 5, 1870. — App.: Proclamations, Apr. 8, 1869 - March 24, 1871. 17. Public and private acts, 42d Cong. — Treaties, Feb. 6, 1778 - Jan. 18, 1873. — App.: Proclamations, Apr. 20, 1871 - Feb. 21, 1873. [18, pt. 1.] Revised statutes, 1st sess. 43 Cong. [18, pt. 2.] Revised statutes rel. to the District of Columbia and post roads, 1st sess. 43d Cong., with treaties in force Dec. 1, 1873. 18, pt. 3. Public and private acts, 43d Cong. — Treaties and postal conventions, July 2, 1863 - Feb. 1, 1875. — Proclamations, May 22, 1873 - Feb. 17, 1875. 19. Public and private acts, 44th Cong. — Treaties, *etc.*, Aug. 6, 1873 - Jan. 12, 1877. — Proclamations, June 2, 1875 - Mar. 2, 1877.

— U. S. *Senate.* Synoptical index to the laws and treaties, Mar. 4, 1789 - Mar. 3, 1851. Boston, 1860. 8°.

— Acts and resolutions, 37th Cong. 1st, 3d sess., 38th–43d C. 1st s. Wash., 1861–74. 11 v. 8°.

— Herty, T. Digest of laws of the U. S. to and of the 5th Cong. Balt., 1800. 8°.

— Graydon, W. Abridgment of laws of the U. S.; with app. Harrisb., 1803. 8°.

— Burch, S. General index to laws of the U. S., 1789–1827. Wash., 1828. 8°.

— Gordon, T. F. Digest of laws of the U. S.; abstract of judic. decisions. Phila., [1841]. 8°.

— Dunlop, J. Digest of general laws of the U. S. Phila., 1856. 8°.

Acts, laws, etc. (*Single sessions.*)

— 1*st Cong.* Acts. N. Y., [1789–90]. f°.

— *Same.* [1st sess. Another ed.] N. Y., [1789]. f°.

— - Acts. Hartford, 1791. 8°.

— - Acts, 1st [-3d sess.]. Phila., 1793. 8°.

— 2*d Cong.* Acts. Phila., [1791–93]. 8°.

— - *Same.* 1st sess. Phila., [1791]. 8°.

— 5*th Cong.* Acts. Phila., [1780]. 8°.

— 6*th Cong.*, 1*st sess.* Acts. [Phila., 1780.] 8°.

— 22*d Cong.*, 1*st sess.* List of acts passed. *n.t.p.* [Wash., 1831-32.] 8°. (B 1057)

Acts, laws, etc. (*Special subjects.*)

— *Army.* 9*th Cong.* 1*st sess.* Act for establishing rules and articles for the government of the armies. Wash., 1808. 16°.

— - - *Same.* [With add.] Wash., 1812. 8°.

— - - Laws rel. to the military establishment, in force 12 Apr. 1808. Wash., 1812. 16°.

— - 12*th Cong.* 1*st sess.* Acts increasing the military establishment. Wash., 1812. 16°.

— *Bankrupt law.* 6*th Cong.* 1*st sess.* National bankrupt law. *n.t.p.* [1800?] 8°.

— - Chandler, P. W. N.Y., 1842. 16°.

— *Commerce.* Montefiore, J. Compendium of laws, customs, *etc.*, of the U. S. rel. to commerce. Phila., 1811. 8°.

— *Corps of Engineers.* U. S. 12*th Cong.* 1*st sess.* Act making further provision for the Corps. *n.t.p.* [1812.] 12°.

— *Embargo.* 9*th Cong.*, 1*st sess.* An act to enforce an act laying an embargo on all ships and vessels in the ports of the U. S. *n.p.*, [1809]. 8°. (B 412)

— *Judges and Justices of the Peace.* Bayard, S. Abstract of the laws of the U. S., which relate to duties, *etc.*, of the judges of inferior state courts and justices of the peace. N.Y., 1804. 8°.

— *Militia.* 12*th Cong.* 1*st sess.* Acts rel. to the militia. *n.t.p.* [1812.] 16°.

— - Dearborn, H. A. Militia laws. Boston, 1840. 12°.

— - Sumner, W. H. Militia laws of the U. S. and of Mass. Boston, 1846. 18°.

— *Mint.* 24*th Cong.* 2*d sess.* Act, Jan. 18, rel. to the mint and coinage; [with other legal provisions still in force]. Phila., 1864. 8°. (B 1644)

— *National banks.* U. S. 38*th Cong.* 1*st sess.* National bank act of 1864. N. Y., 1864. 8°. (B 1545)

— *North West Territory.* 1*st Cong.* 1*st sess.* Edit pour les terres dependantes situées au Nord Ouest de l'Ohio [tr. de l'anglois]. [Paris,] 1789. 8°. (C 87)

— *Naturalization laws.* 14*th Cong.* 1*st sess.* Laws of the U. S. rel. to naturalization. Wash., 1816. 8°.

— *Pension laws.* *See Pension Office* (p. 3094).

— *Public lands.* *See Public lands* (p. 3159–60).

— *Revenue laws.* (*Tariff, etc.*) Addington, L. Digest of the revenue laws. Phila., 1804. 12°.
See also Tariff (p. 3161–62).

— *Taxes.* Redfield, A. A. Hand-book of the U. S. tax law, July 1, 1862; with the amendments and notes. 2d ed. N. Y., 1863. 16°.

— - - *Same.* 3d ed. N. Y., 1863. 16°.

— - Tax-payers' manual; acts of Cong. imposing taxes. N. Y., 1862. 8°. (E 90)

— - 37*th Cong.* 1*st*, 2*d sess.* Laws rel. to direct and excise taxes. Wash., 1862. 8°.

— - Boutwell, G. S. Direct and excise tax system of the U. S.; with the forms and regulations. Boston, 1863. 8°.

— - - *Same.* 4th ed., [with application to the act of 1864]. Boston, 1864. 8°.

— - Estee, C. F. Excise tax law approved July 1. 1862; with amendments and with forms, *etc.* N. Y., 1863. 8°.

— - New and complete taxpayer's manual. N. Y., 1863. 8°. (E 90)

— - U. S. 38*th Cong.* 1*st sess.* Act to provide internal revenue; with the Senate's amendments. Wash., 1864. 8°.

— - - The new internal revenue law approved June 30, 1864; comp. by H. E. Dresser. N. Y., 1864. 8°. (E 90)

— - U. S. *Commissioner of Internal Revenue.* Laws in force Aug. 1. Wash., 1866. 8°. (E 90)

— - Taxpayers' and assessors' guide; amendments to the internal revenue law. N. Y., 1867. 8°. (E 90)

— - U. S. 41*st Cong.* 2*d sess.* Internal revenue law passed July 13; with such other acts rel. to internal revenue as are now in effect; comp. by H. E. Dresser. N.Y., 1870. 8°. (E 90)

— *Volunteer Military Corps.* U. S. 12*th Cong.* 1*st sess.* Act authorising the President to accept and organize certain corps. *n.t.p.* [1812.] 12°.

Contested elections.

— Duponceau, P. S., *and* Davezac, A. Case and opinion on the contested seat of D. Levy, delegate from Florida. Alexandria, 1842. 8°. (B 1499)

— Bartlett, D. W. Cases of contested elections, 1834–65. Wash., 1865. 8°.

Debates and proceedings.

— Benton, T. H. Abridgment of the debates of Congress, 1789–1856. N. Y., 1857–61. 16 v. 8°.

— Debates and proceedings, 1789–1824. Wash., *Gales and Seaton*, 1834–56. 42 v. 8°.
Note. Has the half-title 'Annals of Congress'. Vol. 1-2 compiled by J. Gales, Sen.

— Debates on the bill for repealing the law for the organization of the Courts of the U. S.; 4 Jan. - 3 March 1802. Albany, 1802. 8°.

— Debates in 3d sess. of the 11th Cong. [Wash.,] 1811. 8°.

— Register of debates in Congress, Dec. 6, 1824–37. Wash., *Gales and Seaton*, 1825–37. 14 v. in 29 pts. 8°.

— CONGRESSIONAL globe, 23d – 38th Cong. 1st sess.; 38th Cong. 2d sess., pt. 2 – 41st Cong. 2d sess., pt. 1; 41st – 42d Cong. Wash., 1834–73. Bd. in 103 v. 4°

Note. 1833–49 ed. by Blair and Rives; 1850–64, by J. C. Rives; 1865–67, by F. and J. Rives; 1867–73, by F. and J. Rives and G. A. Bailey. The suppl. of the 40th Cong., 2d sess. contains the trial of A. Johnson.

Directory.

— Congressional directory, 34th Cong. 1st sess., 35th Cong. 2d sess., 36th Cong. 1st sess., 37th Cong. 2d, 3d sess., 38, 39th Cong., 40th Cong. 1st – 3d sess., 41st – 45th Cong. Wash., 1856–77. 23 v. 8°.

Note. 34th–38th Congress compiled by the postmaster of the House; 39th–44th by B. P. Poore. 35th Cong. 2d sess., 39th C. 1st s., 40th C. 2d, 3d. s., 41st C. 1st s., all 2d ed; 41st Cong. 2d s., 42d C. 2d s., 1st and 2d eds; 43d C. 1st s., 3d ed.; 43d C. 2d s., 1st and 3d eds.; 44th C. 1st sess., 1st, 2d, and 3d ed.; 44th C. 2d s., 1st and 2d ed.

House of Representatives.
See House (p. 3064–92).

Obituary addresses.

— *30th Cong. 1st sess.* Addresses and funeral solemnities, death of J. Q. Adams, Feb. 23. Wash., 1848. 8°. (B 1207)

— *31st Cong. 1st sess.* Obituary addresses, death of Z. Taylor, July 10; with funeral sermon by S. Pyne, July 13. Wash., 1850. 8°. (B 1225)

— — – Obituary addresses, death of D. P. King, July 27. Wash., 1850. 8°. (B 1219)

— *32d Cong. 1st sess.* Obituary addresses, death of H. Clay, June 30, 1852, and funeral sermon of Rev. C. M. Butler, in the Senate, July 1. Wash., 1852. 8°.

— — – *2d sess.* Obituary addresses, death of D. Webster, Dec. 14 and 15, 1852. Wash., 1853. 8°.

— — – Obituary addresses, death of A. H. Buell, Jan. 31. *n.t.p.* [Wash., 1853.] 8°. (B 1209, 1506)

— *33d Cong. 1st sess.* Obituary addresses, death of W. R. King, Dec. 8, '53. Wash., 1854. 8°.

— *37th Cong. 1st sess.* Addresses, death of S. A. Douglas, July 9. Wash., 1861. 8°.

— — – *Another copy.* (B 1451)

— – *2d sess.* Addresses, death of E. D. Baker, Dec. 11, 1861. Wash., 1862. 8°.

— *38th Cong. 2d sess.* Addresses, death of T. H. Hicks, Feb. 15. Wash., 1865. 8°. (B 1639)

— *39th Cong. 1st sess.* Proceedings on the death of Hon. Solomon Foot, April 1866. Wash., 1866. 8°.

— – Addresses, death of J. Collamer, Dec. 14, 1865. Wash., 1866. 8°. (B 1639)

— — – Memorial address on the life of A. Lincoln, at the request of Congress, Feb. 12, by G. Bancroft. Wash., 1866. 8°.

— — – Oration on the life of H. W. Davis, by J. A. J. Creswell, Feb. 22. Wash., 1866. 8°.

— — – Proceedings on the death of S. Foot, including addresses, April 12. Wash., 1866. 8°.

— *41st Cong. 2d sess.* Memorial addresses on the life and character of W. P. Fessenden, Dec. 14, 1869. Wash., 1870. 8°.

— – *3d sess.* Memorial addresses on the life and character of J. Covode, Feb. 9, 10. Wash., 1871. 8°.

Petitions, etc.

— PETITION to the Congress of the U. S. [Frankfort, 1824.] 8°. (B 1431)

— NORTHAMPTON, *Mass.* Memorial to the 27th Congress, Mar. 1842. *n.p.*, 1842. 8°. (B 1499)

Publications.

— *16th Cong. 1st sess.* Secret journals of the Continental Cong. *See* p. 3055.

385. (13. 7. 81.)

— *28th Cong. 2d sess.* Magnetical and meteorological observations at Wash., by J. M. Gilliss. Wash., 1845. 8°.

— *31st Cong. 1st sess.* Letter from the Secretary of the Interior transmitting the report on the copper lands of Lake Superior. *n.t.p.* [Wash., 1850.] 8°. (Ex. doc. 69.)

Note. The Report has a titlepage.

Reports from Committees.

— *37th Cong. 3d sess. Joint Committee on the Conduct of the War.* Report. Wash., 1863. 3 v. 8°.

— *38th Cong. 1st sess. Joint Select Committee on the Conduct of the War.* Report. *n.t.p.* [1864.] 8°. (Report no. 65.)

— *38th Cong. 2d sess. Joint Committee on the Conduct of the War.* Report. Wash., 1865. 3 v. 8°.

— – Suppl. report. Wash., 1866. 2 v. 8°.

— *39th Cong. 2d sess. Joint Special Committee [on] the Condition of the Indian Tribes.* Condition of the Indian tribes; report, with app. Wash., 1867. 8°.

— *40th Cong. 3d sess. Joint Committee on Ordnance.* Report. *n.t.p.* [Wash., 1869.] 8°. (No. 266.)

— *41st Cong. 2d sess. Sel. Com [on] the Causes of the Reduction of American Tonnage.* Causes, *etc.*; report. Wash., 1870. 8°. (No. 28.)

Rules.

— Rules of the Senate [and] the joint rules of the two Houses. Wash., 1862. 8°.

Senate.
See Senate (p. 3096–3106).

State papers.

— American state papers; docs. from the 1st to the 35th [25th] Cong. Wash., *Gales and Seaton*, 1832–60. 38 v. f°.

Contents. Class **1.** Foreign relations. 6 v. Vol. 1. 1st – 4th Cong., Apr. 30, 1789 – Feb. 28, 1797. 2. 5th – 9th Cong., 19 May 1797 – 19 Feb. 1807. 3. 10th – 13th Cong., Oct. 27, 1807 – March 3, 1815. 4. 14th – 17th Cong. 1st sess., Dec. 5, 1815 – May 3, 1822. 5. 15th – 19th Cong. 1st sess., Feb. 9, 1818 – Apr. 15, 1826. 6. 19th – 20th Cong. 1st sess., Apr. 22, 1826 – May 24, 1828. **2.** Indian affairs. 2 v. Vol. 1. 1st – 13th Cong., May 25, 1789 – Nov. 18, 1814. 2. 14th – 19th Cong., Dec. 6, 1815 – March 1, 1827. **3.** Finance. 5 v. Vol. 1. 1st – 7th Cong. 1st sess., Apr. 11, 1789 – Apr. 29, 1802. 2. 7th Cong. 2d sess. – 13th Cong., Dec. 20, 1802 – March 2, 1815. 3. 14th – 17th Cong. 1st sess., Dec. 8, 1815 – March 12, 1822. 4. 17th Cong., 2d sess. – 18th Cong. 1st sess., Dec. 3, 1822 – March 22, 1824. 5. 18th – 20th Cong. 1st sess., Apr. 19, 1824 – May 16, 1828. **4.** Commerce and navigation. 2 v. Vol. 1. 1st – 13th Cong., Apr. 13, 1789 – Feb. 9, 1815. 2. 14th – 17th Cong., Dec. 18, 1815 – Feb. 25, 1823. **5.** Military affairs. 7 v. Vol. 1. 1st – 15th Cong., 10 Aug. 1789 – Feb. 25, 1819. 2. 16th – 18th Cong., Dec. 27, 1819 – Feb. 28, 1825. 3. 18th – 20th Cong. 1st sess., Dec. 3, 1823 – May 10, 1828. 4. 20th Cong., 2d sess. – 22d Cong., 1st sess., Dec. 2, 1828 – March 8, 1832. 5. 22d – 24th Cong. 1st sess., Mar. 15, 1832 – Jan. 5, 1836. 6. 24th Cong., Jan. 12, 1836 – Feb. 25, 1837. 7. 24th Cong. 2d sess. – 25th Cong. 2d sess., March 1, 1837 – March 1, 1838. **6.** Naval affairs. 4 v. Vol. 1. 3d – 18th Cong. 1st sess., Jan. 20, 1794 – Dec. 2, 1823. 2. 18th – 19th Cong., May 13, 1824 – Jan. 10, 1827. 3. 19th Cong. 2d sess. – 21st Cong., Jan. 12, 1827 – March 1, 1831. 4. 21st Cong. 2d sess. – 24th Cong. 1st sess., March 1, 1831 – June 15, 1836. **7.** Post Office. 1 v. 1st Cong. 2d sess. – 22d Cong., Jan. 22, 1790 – Feb. 21, 1833. Appendix: 14th Cong. 2d sess. – 18th Cong., March 1, 1817 – Dec. 2, 1823. **8.** Public lands. 8 v. Vol. 1. 1st – 10th Cong., July 31, 1789 – Feb. 27, 1809. 2. 11th – 13th Cong., June 12, 1809 – Feb. 14, 1815. 3. 14th – 18th Cong. 1st sess., Dec. 22, 1815 – May 26, 1824. 4. 18th – 19th Cong., Dec. 8, 1823 – March 3, 1827. 5. 20th Cong., Dec. 4, 1827 – Feb. 25, 1829. 6. 21st – 23d Cong. 1st sess., Apr. 11, 1834. 7. 23d Cong., Apr. 11, 1834 –

March 3, 1835. 8. 24th Cong., Dec. 8, 1835 - Feb. 28, 1837. 9. Claims. 1 v. 1st Cong. 2d sess. - 17th Cong., Feb. 5, 1790 - March 3, 1823. 10. Miscellaneous. 2 v. Vol. 1. 1st - 10th Cong., Apr. 18, 1789 - Feb. 16, 1809. 2. 11th - 17th Cong., June 8, 1809 - March 3, 1823.

— American state papers; authentic documents [Dec. 3, 1805-07]. Boston, 1808. 8°.
Note. From the 'Monthly anthology', v. 3, 4, app.

— State papers, 1789-1814. Boston, 1815, 14-15. 8 v. 8°.
Contents. [Vol. 1.] 1789-96. [2.] Jan. 9 - June 22, 1797. [3.] June 21, 1797 - Feb. 7, 1801. — App.: Jan. 14, 1813. [1 of the series beginning with Jefferson's accession.] March 4, 1801 - Jan. 17, 1806. [2.] Dec. 6, 1805 - July 1807. [3.] Mar. 22, 1808 - Aug. 15, 1809. [4.] Nov. 29, 1809 - July 15, 1811. [5.] Nov. 7, 1811 - June 29, 1814.

— *Same.* 2d ed. Vol. 1-3, 10. Bost., 1817. 4 v. 8°.
Contents. Vol. 1. Apr. 30, 1789 - Apr. 4. 1794. 2. Apr. 4, 1794 - Jan. 16, 1797. 3. Jan. 19, 1797 - Apr. 3, 1798. 4-9. *Wanting.* 10. Confidential state papers, Feb. 9, 1790 - Feb. 18, 1813.

— *Same.* 3d ed. Vol. 3, 11, 12. Boston, 1819. 3 v. 8°.
Contents. Vol. 3. Jan. 19, 1797 - Apr. 3, 1798. 11. Dec. 5, 1815 - Feb. 28, 1818. 12. Mar. 14 - Aug. 1, 1818. — Inaugural of Pres. Adams, Mar. 4, 1797. — Proclamation, Sept. 1, 1815.

Southern delegates.

— Address to their constituents. *n.t.p.* [1849?] 8°. (B 1499)

Whig members of Congress.

— Proceedings and address at a meeting of the Whig members of the 27th Congress., Sept. 11. Wash., 1841. 8°. (B 1498)

II. WORKS ABOUT CONGRESS.

History.

— HISTORY of Cong.; [1789-93]. Phila., 1843. 8°.
— LIST of members of Senate and House of Reps., [4th Cong.]. *n.p.*, [179-]. Broadside. (E 181)
— HISTORY of the last session of Congress commenced Dec. 7, 1801. [1801-02.] Wash., 1802. 8°. (B 402)
— MARCH, C. W. Reminiscences of Congress, [1813-34]. N.Y., 1850. 12°.
— WHEELER, H. G. History of Congress; biog. and polit., [1839-47]. N.Y., 1848. 2 v. 8°.
— REID, H. Acc. of C. (*In his* Sketches in N. Amer. 1859.)
— BARNES, W. H. History of the 39th Congress, [1865-67]. N.Y., 1868. 8°.

Dictionaries.

— LANMAN, C. Dictionary of Congress. Phila., 1859. 8°.
— - *Same.* 2d ed. Wash., 1864. 8°.
— - *Same.* 3d ed. Wash., 1867. 8°.

Directory.
See Directory (p. 3061).

Miscellaneous.

— SPROAT, P. W. General welfare; investigation of the powers vested in Cong. Phila., 1828. 8°. (B 1494)
— ANTI-slavery examiner, no. 5: The power of Congress over the District of Columbia. 4th ed. N. Y., 1838. 8°. (B 1654)
— PARTON, J. Congressional peccadilloes. — How Congress wastes its time. — Log-rolling at Washington. (*In his* Topics of the times. 1871.)
— VERPLANCK, G. C. Letter in assertion of the constitutional power of Congress to impose protecting duties. N. Y., 1831. 8°.

Library of Congress.

— Catalogue. [Wash.,] 1804. 8°. (B 881)
— *Same.* Wash., 1808. 8°. (B 881)
— *Same.* Wash., 1812. 8°. (B 881)
— *Same.* Annexed a copious index. Wash., 1815. 4°.
Note. Comprises the private library of Jefferson. It is arranged upon a system of classification prepared by him, and based upon Bacon's division of knowledge.

— - Supplement. Wash., 1827. 8°.
— *Same.* Dec. 30. Wash., 1830. 8°.
— *Same.* Wash., 1835. 4°.
— - Supplement, Dec. 1840, 42-48. [Wash., 1840-48.] 8 v. 8°.
— *Same.* Chapter 1: Anc. hist. Wash., 1854. f°.
— *Same.* Wash., 1861. 8°.
— Alphabetical catalogue: Authors. Wash., 1864. 8°.
— Catalogue: Index of subjects. Wash., 1869. 2 v. 18°.
— Catalogue of additions, Dec. 1, 1862-75. Wash., 1863-76. 11 v. 8° *and* l. 8°.
Note. From 1866 to 1872 the title reads 'Catalogue of books added to the Library'. The last vol. has the title 'Catalogue of recently added books, 1873-75'.

Court of Claims.

— Reports. *See House.* 34th *Cong.* 1*st and* 2*d sess.* (p. 3088); — 37*th Cong.* 3*d sess.* (p. 3089).

Court of Equity.

— Rules of practice. Boston, 1827. 12°. (C 252)

Courts.

— BAYARD, J. A. Speech on the bill resp. the organization of courts in the U. S., Feb. 19, 20. Worcester, 1802. 8°. (C 158)
— - *Same.* Hartford, 1802. 8°. (B 926, 1489)
— - *Same.* Boston, 1802. 8°. (B 553, 621)
— DEBATES on the bill for repealing the law for the organization of the courts of the U. S. Albany, 1802. 8°.
— DEBATES in the Senate on the judiciary, 1st sess. 7th Cong. Phila., 1802. 8°.
— *Another copy.* (B 402)
— GILES, W. B. Speech in the Ho. of Reps., on courts, Feb. 18, 1802. *n.p.*, [1802]. 8°.
— - *and* BAYARD, J. A. Speeches, Feb., on An act to repeal certain acts resp. the organization of the courts of the U. S. Boston, 1802. 8°. (B 553, 621, 2525)
— BIBB, G. M., *and others.* Petition to Cong. [urging the reorganization of the judiciary]. *n.t.p.* [1824.] 8°. (W 5)
— DUPONCEAU, P. S. Diss. on the nature of the jurisdiction of the courts of the U. S. Phila., 1824. 8°.
— WOODBURY, Q. Speech. judiciary bill, in the Senate, April 11. *n.t.p.* [1826.] 8°. (W 13a)
— GIBBS, G. List of judges in Eng. and Amer. Camb., 1834. 8°.
— BILL conc. the judicial system of the U. S. for the relief of the Supreme Court and some of the Circuit Courts; with remarks. *n.p.*, [184-]. 8°. (B 1498)
— CHOATE, R. Speech, bill to provide further remedial justice in the courts of U. States, May. Wash., 1842. 8°. (B 1499, 1871)
— TAPPAN, B. Speech, resolution to limit the term of office of the judges of the Supreme and inferior courts, Jan. 16. Steubenville, 1843. 8°. (B 1499)
— U. S. *Ho. of Reps.* Report of the committee on the judiciary on the costs and expenses of the federal courts, *etc.*, Jan. 29. Wash., 1852. 8°. (B 1505)
See also Circuit Court (p. 3059); — *Court of Claims* (*above*); — *Court of Equity* (*above*); — *Supreme Court* (p. 3107).

Diplomatic, Consular, and other Officers in Foreign Countries.
(Subordinate to the *Department of State.*)

— U. S. *Department of State.* Instructions to the envoys extraordinary and ministers plenipotentiary to the French Republic; [with] dispatches, *etc.* Phila., 1798. 8°.
Note. For the so-called 'Diplomatic correspondence', *see Department of State.* Papers relating to foreign relations (p. 3106).
— - List of diplomatic and consular officers, May 1, 1862, Dec. 1, 1863. Wash., 1862-63. 2 v. 8°.

— ABBOT, G. J. United States consular system. Wash., 1856. 8°.

— - *Same.* U. S. consul's manual. 2d ed. Wash., 1863. 8°.

District-Attorney.

— Evidence furnished by District Attorney [at the trial of A. Burr]. *n.t.p.* Wash., [1808]. 8°. (B 490)

Bureau of Education.

(Subordinate to the *Dept. of the Interior.* Established in 1867.)

☞ Duplicates of the reports here enumerated are contained in the full set of Congressional docs. *see House* (p. 3064-92); — *Senate* (*p.* 3096-3106).

— Reports of the Commissioner, 1867/68, 70-78. Wash., 1867-80. 10 v. 8°.

Note. No report was published in 1869; its place was taken by a special report on the District of Columbia.

Corps of Engineers.

(Subordinate to the *War Department.*)

— Papers on practical engineering. Nos. 3, 6, 8, 9. Wash., N. Y., 1854-64. 4 v. 8°.

Namely. No. 3. **Poncelet, J. V.** Sustaining walls. **6. Totten, J. C.** Report on the effects of firing with heavy ordnance from casemate embrasures and against the same with various missiles. **8. Gillmore, Q. A.** Official report of the siege and reduction of Fort Pulaski, Georgia, 1862. **9. Gillmore, Q. A.** Practical treatise on limes, hydraulic cements, and mortars.

— Professional papers. Nos. 4, 7, 12, 14-20. *n.p.*, 1853-77. 15 v. 4° *and* 8° *and* Atlases obl. f°.

Namely. No. **4. Humphreys, A. A.,** *and* **Abbot, H. L.** Report upon the physics and hydraulics of the Mississippi River. Phila., 1861. 4°. **7. Woodbury,** *Capt.* D. P. Treatise on the various elements of stability in the well-proportioned arch. N. Y., 1858. 8°. **12. Lee,** *Capt.* T. J. Tables and formulæ useful in surveying, geodesy, and practical astronomy. 2d ed. Wash., 1853. 8°. **14. Abbot, H. L.** Siege artillery in the campaigns against Richmond; with notes on the 15 inch gun. Wash., 1867. 8°. **15. Williamson, R. S.** On the use of the barometer, and surveys and reconnaissance; with app. N. Y., 1868. 4°. **16. Gillmore, Q. A.** Engineer and artillery operations against the defences of Charleston Harbor in 1863; with suppl. N. Y., 1868. 8°. **17. King, W. R.** Report on experimental and theoretical investigations rel. to quality, form, *etc.*, of materials for defensive armor. Wash., 1870. 4°. **18. King, C.** Report of the geological exploration of the 40th parallel. Wash., 1870-77. 6 v. 8° *and* 2 Atlases f°. (Vol. 1. Systematic geology. 2. Descriptive geology. 3. Mining industry; with Atlas. 4. Ornithology and paleontology. 5. Botany. 6. Microscopical petrography.) **19. Gillmore, Q. A.** Report on béton aggloméré or coignet béton. Wash., 1871. 8°. **20. Barnard, J. G.** Report on the defences of Wash. Wash., 1871. 4°.

— U. S. *12th Cong. 1st sess.* Act making further provision for the Corps. *n.t.p.* [1812.] 12°.

Office of the Bureau of Topographical Engineers.

(Subordinate to the *War Department.*)

— Report to illustrate a map of the hydrographical basin of the upper Mississippi; by I. N. Nicollet, Feb. 16, 1841. Wash., **1843.** 8°. (26th Cong. 2d sess. Sen. Doc. 237.)

— Report of the exploring exped. to the Rocky Mountains, 1842, and to Oregon and N. California, 1843-44; by J. C. Frémont. Wash., **1845.** 8°. (28th Cong. 2d sess. Sen. Doc. 174.)

— *Same.* Wash., 1845. 8°. (28th Cong. 2d sess. Ho. Doc. 166.)

— Observations at the magnetic and meteorological observatory, Girard Coll., under the direction of A. D. Bache, 1840-45. Wash., **1847.** 3 v. 8°.

— Determination of the latitude with zenith and equal altitude telescope; [by T. J. Lee]. Wash., [**1848**]. 4°.

— Notes of a military reconnoissance from Fort Leavenworth to San Diego; by W. H. Emory. Wash., 1848. 8°. (30th Cong. 1st sess. Sen. Doc. 7.)

— *Same.* [With report of J. W. Abert of his examination of Mexico.] Wash., 1848. 8°. (30th Cong. 1st sess. Ex. doc. 41.)

— Reconnoissances of routes from San Antonio de Bexar, el Paso del Norte, *etc.* Phila., **1849.** (31st Cong. 1st. s. Sen. Ex. doc. 64.)

— Exploration and survey of the valley of the Great Salt Lake of Utah; by H. Stansbury. Phila., **1852.** 8°. (32d Cong. Spec. sess. Sen. Doc. 3.)

— Report of Lieut. Col. Graham on the boundary line between U. S. and Mexico. *n.t.p.* [Wash., 1852.] 8°. (32d Cong. 1st sess. Sen. Doc. 121.)

— Report of a reconnaissance and survey in California from the Mississippi River to the Pacific Ocean, 1853; by R. S. Williamson. *n.p.*, [**1853**]. 8°. (33d C. 1st s. Ex. doc. 129.)

— Report of exploration of a route for the Pacific R.R. near the 32d parallel, from Red River to the Rio Grande; by J. Pope. [Wash., **1854.**] 8°. (33d Cong. 1st sess. Ho. Ex. doc. 129.)

— Report of exploration of a route for the Pacific railroad near the 47th and 49th parallels from St. Paul to Puget Sound; by I. I. Stevens. Wash., 1854. 8°. (33d Cong. 1st sess. Ho. Ex. doc. 129.)

— Report of explorations for a railway route near the 35th parallel from the Mississippi to the Pacific; by A. W. Whipple. [Wash., 1854.] 8°. (33d C. 1st s. Ho. Ex. doc. 129.)

— Report of explorations for that portion of a railway route, near the 32d parallel, between Dona Ana and Pimas villages; by J. G. Parke. [Wash., 1854.] 8°. (33d Cong. 1st sess. Ho. Ex. doc. 129.)

— Report of the Sec.; transm. a map illust. the surveys from a canal in Florida. *n.t.p.* [Wash., **1856.**] 8°. (34th Cong. 1st sess. Sen., no. 89.)

Office of the Chief of Engineers.

(Subordinate to the *War Department.*)

— Annual report to the Secretary of War, 1868-79. Wash., 1869-79. 15 v. in 20 pts. 8°.

For the reports from 1863-67 *see War Department.* Report (p. 3107).

☞ Duplicates of the reports here given are contained in the full Congressional set of documents, *see House* (p. 3064-92); — *Senate* (p. 3096-3106).

— Report of the engineer and artillery operations of the army of the Potomac; by J. G. Barnard and W. F. Barry. N. Y., **1863.** 8°.

— Military maps illustrating the operations of the armies of the Potomac and James, May 4, **1864** - April 9, **1865.** Wash., 1869. f°.

— Report on the exploration of the Yellowstone River; by W. F. Raynolds. Wash., **1868.** 8°. (40th Cong. 1st sess. Ex. doc. 77.)

Exploring Expedition, 1838-42.

— REYNOLDS, J. N. Address on the exploring exped. to the South Seas; with corresp. and doc. N. Y., **1836.** 8°.

— U. S. *24th Cong. 1st sess. Sen.* Report of committee on naval affairs, to whom was referred a memorial from Conn. praying that an exploring expedition be fitted out to the Pacific and South seas. Wash., 1836. 8°. (Doc. 262. B 1111)

— REYNOLDS, J. N., *and* DICKESON, M. Correspondence touching the South Sea exploring expedition. N. Y., 1837-38. 8°.

— WILKES, C. Narrative of the U. S. exploring expedition, 1838-42. *n.p.*, 1845-58. 23 v. (v. 7, 8, pt. 1, 11, 13, 14, 16-19, 21-23 w.). f° *and* 4° *and* 10 (4 w.) Atlases f°.

Contents. Vol. 1-5. **Wilkes, C.** Narrative of the U. S. exploring exped. Phila., 1845. 5 v. *and* Atlas 4°. 6. **Hale, H.** Ethnography and philology. Phila., 1846. 4°. 7. *Wanting.* (**Dana, J. D.** Zoophytes, with Atlas.) 8, pt. 1. *Wanting.* (**Peale, T. R.** Mammalia and ornithology.) 8, pt. 2. **Cassin, J.** Mammalogy and ornithology. Phila., 1858. 4° *and* Atlas f°. 9. **Pickering, C.** Races of men. Phila., 1848. 4°. 10. **Dana, J. D.** Geology. N. Y., *n.d.* 4° *and* Atlas f°. 11. *Wanting.* (**Wilkes, C.** Meteorology.) 12. **Gould, A. A.** Mollusca and shells. Boston, 1852. 4° *and* Atlas f°. 13, 14. *Wanting.* (**Dana, J. D.** Crustacea. 2 v. *and* Atlas.) 15. **Gray, A.** Botany: Phanerogamia. Vol. 1. N. Y., 1854. 4° *and* Atlas. 1857. f°. 16. *Wanting.* (**Brackenridge, W. D.** Botany: Cryptogamia, with an Atlas.) 17-19. *Wanting.* 20. **Girard, C.** Herpetology. Phila., 1858. 4° *and* Atlas f°. 21, 22. *Wanting.* 23. *Wanting.* (**Wilkes, C.** Hydrography, with Atlases.)

— - *Another ed. of* Vol. 1-5. Phila., 1850. 5 v. 4°.

— - - *Same.* London, 1852. 2 v. 8°.

— - *Another ed. of* Vol. 9. New ed., by J. C. Hall. London, *Bohn*, 1851. 8°.

— WILKES, C. Synopsis of the exped.; added, list of officers and scientific corps. Wash., 1842. 8°.

Exploring Expedition to the China Seas and Japan, 1852-54.

— Narrative of the expedition, of an Amer. squadron to the China Seas and Japan, 1852-54, under Com. Perry; by F. S. Hawks. Wash., 1856. 3 v. 8°.

Note. Vol. 1 was compiled from the orig. notes and journals of P. and his officers, by F. L. Hawks; v. 2 is Natural history by D. S. Green and others, with illustrations; v. 3 has the title page U. S. Japan Expedition; obs. on the zodiacal light, by G. Jones.

Exploring Expedition to the Dead Sea, 1848.

— Narrative of the expedition to the Jordan and Dead Sea; by W. F. Lynch. New ed. Phila., 1849. 8°.

— - Official report. Balt., 1852. 4°. (30th Cong. 2d sess. Sen. Doc. 34.)

☞ For other exploring expeditions *see Bureau of Topographical Engineers* (p. 3062); — *Office of Chief of Engineers* (p. 3063); — *Naval Astronomical Expedition* (p. 3093); — *Navy Department* (p. 3093); — *Department of State* (p. 3106); — *War Department* (p. 3108).

Bureau of Refugees, Freedmen, and Abandoned Lands.

(Surbordinate to the *War Department.*)

— Circulars; *etc.*, to [Dec. 31, 1867; with acts, *etc.*, rel. to said Bureau. Wash., 1867. 12°.

— School-houses and cottages for the south; prepared by C. T. Chase. Wash., 1868. 8°.

Fiscal Bank.

— ALLEN, W. Speech, Feb. 11. *n.t.p.* [Wash., 1840.] 8°. (B 1663)

— BIDLACK, B. Speech on the U. S. Fiscal Bank bill. Wash., 1841. 8°. (B 1663)

— BROWN, A. V. Speech, Aug. 4. Wash., 1841. 8°. (B 1664)

— BUCHANAN, J. Speech, Sept. 2. *n.t.p.* [Wash., 1841.] 8°. (B 1664)

— HUBARD, E. W. Speech, Aug. 4. Wash., 1841. 8°. (B 1664)

— KENNEDY, A. Speech, Aug. 2. *n.t.p.* [Wash., 1841.] 8°. (B 1664)

— MCCLELLAN, R. Speech on the U. S. Fiscal Bank bill. Wash., 1841. 8°. (B 1663)

— MASON, J. T. Speech, Aug. 3. *n.t.p.* [Wash., 1841.] 8°. (B 1664)

— SAUNDERS, R. M. Speech, Aug. 2. Wash., 1841. 8°. (B 1664)

— TAPPAN, B. Speech, July 14. Wash., 1841. 8°. (B 1664)

— U. S. *Pres.* Message; with objections to the bill to incorporate the Fiscal Bank, Aug. 16. *n.t.p.* [Wash., 1841.] 8°. (B 1664)

— WELLER, J. B. Speech, Aug. 4. *n.t.p.* [Wash., 1841.] 8°. (B 1664)

— WOOD, F. Speech, Aug. 3. Wash., 1841. 8°. (B 1664)

— WOODBURY, L. Speech, July 10. Wash., 1841. 8°. (B 1664)

Flag.

— HAMILTON, S. History of the national flag. Phila., 1852. 12°.

General in Chief.

— Reports. (*In* U. S. *War Dept.* An. report.)

Geological Survey.

(Subordinate to the *Department of the Interior.*)

— Geological report of an examination, 1834, of the elevated country between the Missouri and Red Rivers; by G. W. Featherstonhaugh. Wash., 1835. 8°.

— Report of a geological reconnoissance, 1835, by the way of Green Bay and the Wisconsin Territory to the Coteau de Prairie; by G. W. Featherstonhaugh. Wash., 1836. 8°. (Sen. Doc. 333.)

— Report on the geology and topography of a portion of the Lake Superior district in Michigan; by J. W. Forster and J. D. Whitney. Wash., 1850-51. 2 v. 8° *and* Atlas 8°.

Note. In v. 1 the title-page is preceded by a 'Letter from the Secretary of the Interior transmitting the report. 31st Cong., 1st sess. Ex. doc. 69'.

— Report of a geological survey of Wisconsin, Iowa, Minnesota, and a portion of Nebraska; by D. D. Owen. Phila., 1852. 2 v. 4°.

— Preliminary field report of Colorado and New Mexico; by F. V. Hayden. Wash., 1869. 8°.

House of Representatives.

I. PUBLICATIONS OF THE HOUSE.

Indexes.

Note. There are full indexes to public documents prior to 1823 in the American state papers (p. 3061).

— 18*th Cong.* 1*st sess.* Index to executive communications until the end of the 14th Cong., inclusive; also, index to all printed committee reports. Wash., 1824. 8°. (House. Doc. 163.)

Note. Contains references not only to printed but to ms. documents.

— - 2*d* (?) *sess.* Index to executive communications and reports of committees, Dec. 3, 1817 to Mar. 3, 1823, 15th Cong. - 18th Cong. 1st sess. Wash., 1823. 8°.

— BOSTON PUBLIC LIBRARY. Alphabetical index to all papers of public interest from 18th Cong. 1st sess. to 35th Cong. 2d sess. (*In its* Index, Bates Hall. 1865.) 36th, 37th Cong. (*In* 1st supplement. 1866.)

— 22*d Cong.* 2*d sess.* Digested index to executive documents and reports of committees, 18th-21st Cong. Wash., 1832. 8°. (Ho. Doc.)

— 25*th Cong.* 2*d sess.* Index, 22d-25th Cong., Dec., 1831 - Mar. 1839. Wash., [1840]. 8°.

— 40*th Cong.* 3*d sess.* Consolidated index of executive documents, 26th - 40th Cong. Wash., 1870. 8°. (Ho. Doc.)

— - Consolidated index of reports of com. 26th-40th Cong. Wash., 1869. 8°. (Ho. Doc.)

— 46*th Cong.* 2*d sess.* General index of the Journals of Congress, 1st-10th incl., with refs. to the Debates, Docs., and Statutes; by A. Ordway. Wash., 1880. 4°. (Ho. report, 1776.)

☞ The greater part of the following documents as far as the 1st sess. of the 6th Congress were issued without note of place of publication, but probably at Philadelphia. The place is mentioned in the list below only when it is upon the title-page. As the succeeding documents were generally published at Washington, sometimes with and sometimes without imprints, we give the place of publication in the entries in the smaller type only when it is not Washington.

The sign w.* is put in parentheses after the numbers of documents that are not in our set but are not referred to in the indexes, and therefore were probably never published; w. (without a *) is put after numbers of documents that are wanting in the set and are referred to in the indexes; this therefore indicates a real gap in the set.

With the set of Congressional documents are furnished the publications of the Census Bureau, but without indication whether they belong to the House or Senate. (*See Census Office*: p. 3058, 56.)

1st Cong. 1st sess., March 4 - *Sept.* 29, 1789.

— Journal. N. Y., [1789]. f°.

— State paper.] *Treas. Dept.* Report of the Sec. concerning expenditures, *etc.*; Sept. 19, 1789.] *n.t.p.* [1789.] f°.

1st Cong. 2d sess., Jan. 4 - *Aug.* 12, 1790.

— Journal. N. Y., 1790. f°.

— State papers. *n.t.p.* [1790-91.] f°.

Namely: *Treas. Dept.* Report rel. to a provision for the support of the public credit; Jan. 14. — *Attorney Gen.* Report [on such matters rel. to the administration of justice as may require to be remedied, *etc.*]; Dec. 31, 1790. — *Treas. Dept.* Report relative to appropriations of money for purposes therein mentioned; Jan. 6, 1791.

Also: *Dept. of State.* Report on establishing uniformity in the weights, measures, and coins; [July 4, 1790]. N. Y. 8°. **(B 478, W 17)** — Return of the whole number of persons within the several districts of the U. S., Oct. 24, 1791. Phila. 8°. **(B 492)**

— Ex. doc., no. 2.] *War Dept.* Plan for the general arrangement of the militia; Jan. 18. N. Y., 1790. f°.

— - *Treas. Dept.* Report of Sec. pursuant to the act for establishing the Treasury Dept.; March 1, 1790. *n.p.*, [1790]. f°.

1st Cong. 3d sess., Dec. 6, 1790 - *March* 3, 1791.

— Journal. Phila., 1791. f°.

— Ex. docs. *n.t.p.* [1790-91.] f°.

Namely: *Treas. Dept.* Report on such further provision as may be necessary for establishing the public credit; Dec. 13, 1790; — Report rel. to appropriations of money for certain purposes therein mentioned; Jan. 6, 1791. — [Report on] the establishment of a Mint; Jan. 28. — Amendments to the constitution of the U. S.; 3d March.

— Ex. docs. *n.t.p.* [1791.] f°.

Namely: *Treas. Dept.* Letter transm. a general abstract of the duties on the tonnage employed in the U. S. for one year; Jan. 6, 1791; — Two abstracts of the duties on imports; Jan. 7.

Also: *Dept. of State.* Rept. of Sec. on the cod and whale fisheries; Feb. 1, 1791. Phila. **(B 478)** — Report on privileges and restrictions on the commerce of U. S., in foreign countries; [14 Feb.]. Phila. **(B 478)**

— Ex. doc.] *Attorney Gen.* Report [on the judiciary system], Dec. 31, 1790. *n.t.p.* [1790.] f°.

2d Cong. 1st sess., Oct. 24, 1791 - *May* 8, 1792.

— Journal. Phila., 1792. f°.

— Ex. docs. *n.t.p.* [1791-92.] f°.

Namely: *Treas. Dept.* Account of payments and receipts of public monies, 1 Oct. 1790 - 30 June 1791; 26 Oct. 1791; — Estimates of the expenditures for the Civil list, *etc.*, for 1792; Nov. 4; — Report on manufactures; Dec. 5; — Report on the act for laying duties on spirits, *etc.*; March 6, 1792; — Report on the best mode of raising the additional supplies for the ensuing year; Mar. 16; — Report on farther compensation to the officers employed in the collection of the revenue; Apr. 5; — Report accompanying an estimate of sums necessary to be appropriated in addition to those provided for by the act passed 23d of Dec. 1791; Apr. 16; — Report on the petitions, A, B, and C; Apr. 16; — Report [on] petitions praying the renewal of certificates alledged to have been destroyed or lost; Apr. 18.

— Ex. docs. *n.t.p.* [1791-92.] f°.

Namely: *Treas. Dept.* Account of payments and receipts of public monies, 1 Oct. 1790 - 30 June 1791; 26 Oct. 1791. — *Dept. of State.* Report of the quantity and situation of the lands not claimed by the Indians, nor granted to, nor claimed by any citizens within the U. S.; Nov. 10. — *Treas. Dept.* Specie account of the Treas., 1 July - 30 Sept.; Dec. 5; — Specie account ending 31 Dec. 1791; Feb. 28, 1792.

— Ex. docs. *n.t.p.* [1791-92.] f°.

Namely: *Treas. Dept.* Report on manufactures; Dec. 5, 1791; — Report on the public debt; Dec. 7, 1792. — *War Dept.* [Statement of the causes of the hostilities between the U. S. and tribes of Indians northwest of the Ohio;] Jan. 26.

— Ex. docs. *n.t.p.* [1791-92.] f°.

Namely; *Treas. Dept.* Accounts and receipts of public monies Oct. 1, 1790 - June 30, 1791; Oct. 26, 1791; — Report of Sec. Jan. 23, 1792; — Report accomp. an estimate of sums to be appropriated in addition to those provided by the act passed December 23, 1791; April 16; — Report on the petitions marked A, B, and C; Apr. 16.

— Ex. doc.] *Treas. Dept.* Report on manufactures [by the] Sec.; 5 Dec. 1791. 6th ed. Phila., 1827. 8°.

— PROCEEDINGS resp. the contested election for the Eastern District of Georgia; Dec. 13, 1791. Phila., 1792. 8°. **(B 516, 774, 1488)**

2d Cong. 2d sess., Nov. 5, 1792 - *March* 2, 1793.

— Journal. Phila., 1793. f°.

— Ex. docs. *n.t.p.* [1792-93.] f°.

Namely: *Treas. Dept.* Acc. of payments and receipts of public monies, 1 Jan. - 30 Sept.; Nov. 6, 1792. — *Commissioners for Purchasing the Public Debt.* Report; Nov. 17. — *Pres.* Arrangement made by the Pres. for raising a revenue upon foreign and domestic distilled spirits; Nov. 22. — *Dept. of State.* Rept. of the assays and experiments on the gold and silver coins of France, Spain, England, and Portugal; Jan. 8, 1793. — *Treas. Dept.* Acc. of payments and receipts of public monies, 1st Oct. - 31st Dec. 1792; Feb. 27. — *War Dept.* Report on 35 petitions; Feb. 27.

— Ex. docs. *n.t.p.* [1792-93.] f°.

Namely: *Treas. Dept.* Estimate of the expenditure of the Civil list for 1793; Nov. 14, 1792 — *Commissioners for Purchasing the Public Debt.* Report; Nov. 17. — *Treas. Dept.* Report of the Sec. respecting the redemption of the public debt, *etc.*; Nov. 30; — Statements respecting foreign loans, *etc.*; Jan. 3, 1793; — Statements in conformity with the resolution of the Ho., 23 Jan. 1793; Feb. 4. — *War Dept.* Report on 47 petitions; Feb. 8. — *Treas. Dept.* [Letter conc. foreign loans, *etc.*]; Feb. 13; — Report rel. to the loans negotiated 4 and 12 Aug. 1790; Feb. 13; — [Letter conc. foreign loans, bills, *etc.*]; Feb. 19.

— Ex. docs. *n.t.p.* [1792-93.] f°.

Namely: *Treas. Dept.* Rept. resp. the redemption of the public debt and the re-imbursement of the loan made of the Bank of the U. S.; Nov. 30, 1792; — Letter transm. sundry statements resp. foreign loans; Jan. 3, 1793; — Communications to the House; 2 March.

— Ex. docs. *n.t.p.* [1793.] f°.

Namely: *Treas. Dept.* Statements respecting the foreign loans; [Jan. 11, 1793]; — Statements by the Sec. in conformity with the resolution of the House, 23 Jan. 1793; [Feb. 4]; — Report of the Sec. rel. to the loans negotiated under the acts of the 4 and 12 of August, 1790; [Feb. 13]; — Statements made by the Sec. pursuant to an order of the Senate, 23 Jan. 1793; [Feb. 14]; — Letter conc. foreign loans; [Feb. 19].

— Ex. docs. *n.t.p.* [1793.] f°.

Namely: *Treas. Dept.* Abstract of goods, *etc.*, exported 1 Oct. 1791 - 30 Sept. 1792, also an abstract of the duties on goods, *etc.*, imported 1 Oct. - 31 Dec. 1791; with an abstract of duties on the tonnage of vessels, 1st Oct. - 31st Dec. 1791; Feb. 27, 1793; — Treas. account of payments and receipts of public monies, 1 Oct. - 31 Dec. 1792; Feb. 27.

— Ex. doc.] *Treas. Dept.* Account of receipts and expenditures of the U. S. [from] the establishment of the Treas. Dept. under the present government [to] the 31 of Dec. 1791; Nov. 10, 1792. Philadelphia, 1793. f°.

— - - Letter transm. statements rel. to the disbursements made by the Dept. of War; also copy of a letter from the Comptroller of the Treas. on the subject, Dec. 7, 1792.] Phila., 1792. f°.

3d Cong. 1st sess. Dec. 2, 1793 - June 9, 1794.

— Journal. Phila., 1793, [94?]. 8°.

— Ex. docs. *n.t.p.* [1793-94.] f°.

Namely: *Commissioners to Execute Acts of Congress to Provide for the Settlement of Accounts between the United States and the Individual States.* Report; [Dec. 5, 1793]. — *Treas. Dept.* Treas. account of payments and receipts of public monies, 1 Jan. - 30 June, also the War Dept. accounts 1 Jan. - 31 Dec.; Dec. 7, 1793; — Estimates and statements rel. to appropriations for the service of 1794; Dec. 23. — *Committee on the Naval Force Necessary for the Protection of the Commerce of the U. S. against the Algerine Corsairs.* Report; Jan. 2, 1794. — *Committee on Standing Rules and Orders of the House.* Report; Jan. 7. — *Treas. Dept.* Report of Sec. respecting the tonnage of vessels; Jan. 7. — *Committee* [*on*] *the Petitions of the Quakers of New England, the Providence Soc. for the Abolition of the Slave Trade, etc.* Report; Feb. 11. — *Committee on such of the Ports and Harbors as Require to be Put in a State of Defence.* Report; Feb. 28. — *War Dept.* Report of Sec. on 60 petitions; 12 March. — *Treas. Dept.* Abstract of exports for year ending 30 Sept. 1793, *etc.*; June 2.

— Ex. docs. *n.t.p.* [1793.] f°.

Namely: *Treas. Dept.* Account of the receipts and expenditures of the U. S. for 1792; [with appendix;] Dec. 18, 1793; — Statements rel. to the foreign and domestic debt, and the funds for the reduction of the domestic debt; [undated, possibly later Cong.].

— Ex. docs. *n.t.p.* [1783-94.] f°.

Namely: *Treas. Dept.* Estimates and statements rel. to appropriations for 1794; [Dec. 23, 1793]; — Summary statement of receipts and expenditures from the commencement of the present government to the end of 1793; [Jan.? 1794]; — Statement [of] receipts from domestic resources, also expenditures other than the re-payment of domestic loans, or out of the proceeds of bills drawn on Amsterdam, *etc.*; [Jan.?]; — Report of Sec. respecting the tonnage of vessels; [Jan. 13]. — *Committee* [*on*] *a Petition of Inhabitants from the County of Washington, Md., and Petitions from the Counties of Chester and Lancaster in Penn.* Report; [May 16]. — *Treas. Dept.* Letter transmitting an abstract of goods, *etc.*, exported 1st Oct. 1792 - 30th Sept. 1793; [June 3].

— Ex. docs. *n.t.p.* [1794.] f°.

Namely: *War Dept.* Report on 60 petitions; 17th March. — *Treas. Dept.* Statements rel. to the foreign and domestic debt, *etc.*, pursuant to a resolution of the Ho., 24th Feb., 1794; May 22, 1794.

— Ex. docs. *n.t.p.* [1794.] f°.

Namely: *Committee* [*on*] *the Naval Force Necessary for the Protection of Commerce against the Algerine Corsairs.* Report; [Jan. 2. 1794]. — *War Dept.* Report of Sec. on 60 petitions, 1764; [17 March]. — *Dept. of State.* Letter from Sec. accomp. an address from the Committee of Public Safety, [French Republic; April 24]. — *Committee to whom was Re-committed a Report on the Memorial of A. St. Clair.* Report; [May 14].

Also: **Genet, E. C.** Correspondance of the minister plenipotentiary of France, 29 Oct., 1793; French originals. Phila. (B 478) — Papers rel. to Gr. Britain; 4th Dec. 1793. *n.t.p.* [Phila.] (B 478) — *Pres.* Message to Congress rel. to France and Gr. Brit., Dec. 5.; with papers referred to, [and] the French originals; Dec. 5. 1793. Phila. (B 478, W 57, 67, 83) — *Dept. of State.* Report of Sec., on the privileges and restrictions on the commerce of the U. S. in foreign countries; Dec. 16. 1793. Phila. (B 478, W 67) — *Dept. of State.* Message, from the Pres. transm. report of Sec. of State of laws, decrees, and ordinances respecting commerce; [Dec. 30, 1793]. Phila. (B 478) — *Pres.* Motion for commercial restrictions, Jan. 3, 1794. Wash., 1806. (B 485) — *Pres.* Message transm. copy of letter of the minister plenipotentiary of the French republic; 25th Dec. 1793; proceedings of the Legislature of South Carolina; 15th Jan. (Sen. doc.?) (B 478, W 57) — *Pres.* Message transm. extracts from last advices from Minister in London; 22d Jan. (B 478) — *Dept. of State.* Message, from the Pres. transm. report of Sec. of State upon complaints against spoliations on commerce, since commencement of European war; 5th March. (B 478) — *Pres.* Message, enclosing three letters from the minister plenipotentiary of the U. S. in London; also from minister of French republic to Sec. of State, and his answer; 4th April. Phila. (B 478, W 57, 67) — *Pres.* Message, trans. docs. rel. to threats against territories of Spain [near] the U. S.; [20th May]. Phila. (B 478, W 57, 67) — *Com. to Examine into the State of the Treas. Dept.* Report; May 22. Phila. (B 479, W 10, 57) — *Pres.* Message transm. a copy of a letter from the minister plenipotentiary of his Britannic Majesty, in answer to a letter from the Sec. of State; also a letter from the Sec.; May 23.] Phila. (Sen. doc.? W 67) — *Pres.* Message; with comm.; May 23. Phila. (B 478) — *Pres.* Message transm. a letter from the Sec. of State to the minister plenipotentiary of His Britannic Majesty, with an enclosure, in answer to a letter from the minister dated 22 May; June 4. Phila. (B 478, W 67) — *Dept. of State.* Letter from Sec. to the minister plenipotentiary of His Brit. Maj.; [4th June]. Phila. (B 478)

— Ex. doc.] *Pres.* Message rel. to France and Gr. Brit.; Dec. 5, 1793. Phila., 1795. 8°.

— — *Treasury Dep't.* Summary statement of the receipts and expenditures of the U. S. from the commencement of the present government to the end of 1793; Jan.? 1794. *n.t.p.* [Phila., 1794.] f°.

— — *War Dept.* Rept. on 60 petitions, 1794; 12th March, 1794. *n.t.p.* [Phila., 1794.] f°.

3d Cong. 2d sess., Nov. 3, 1794 - March 3, 1795.

— Journal. Phila., 1794, [95?]. 8°.

— Ex. doc.] *Treas. Dept.* Account of the Treas. of payments and receipts of public monies, 1 Apr. - 30 June, 1794; also payments and receipts of the War Dept., 1st Apr. - 30 Sept.; Nov. 12, 1794. *n.t.p.* [Phila., 1794.] f°.

Also: **Papers** rel. to Gr. Britain: 4 Dec. 1793. (W 67) — *Com. Appointed to Examine the State of the Treasury Dept.* Report; May 23, 1794. (W 67) — *Commissioners to confer with the Insurgents in the Counties of Penn.* Report; Oct. 7. Phila. (Sen. doc.? W 59) — *Dept. of State.* Message of the Pres. transm. a report of the Sec. of State of such laws, *etc.*, resp. commerce in the countries with which the U. S. have commercial intercourse; Dec. 30. Phila. (W 67) — *Treas. Dept.* Report of the Sec., Jan. 19, 1795, [with] a plan for the further support of public credit; Jan. 19, 1795. (B 479) — *Treas. Dept.* Report of the Sec. for the improvement of the revenues of the U. S.; 2 Feb. Phila. (B 493, W 57, 67) — **Hillhouse, J.** Motion, Feb. 16, committed to a committee of the whole house on Thursday next. (B 493) — *House.* Bill to provide for organizing, arming, and disciplining the militia of the U. S., Feb. 18. Phila. (W 57, 67) — *Com. on the State of the Mint.* Report; Feb. 23. Phila. (W 67) — *Treas. Dept.* Abstract of goods, wares, and merchandize exported from the U. S., 1 Oct. 1793 - 30 Sept. 1794; Feb 26. Phila. (B 493)

4th Cong. 1st sess., Dec. 7, 1795 - June 1, 1796.

— Journal. Phila., 1795, [96]. 8°.

— Ex. docs. *n.t.p.* [1795-96.] f°.

Namely: *Treas. Dept.* Letter from the Sec. to the chairman of the comm. of ways and means, accomp. a statement of the debts of the U. S., with a view of the sums annually requisite for discharging them; Jan. 4. 1795; — Statement shewing the final liquidation of the French loans and their full reimbursement at the Treas.; 19th Jan. 1796; — Letter from Sec. accomp. a report and statements made in pursuance of two resolutions of the Ho.; Jan. 25; — Letter from Sec. accomp. a return of exports, 1 Oct. 1790 - 30 Sept. 1795, also letter from Commissioner of Revenue; Jan. 25; — Letter from Sec. rel. to additional provisions for the execution of the act making farther provision for the support of public credit and redemption of the public debt; 3 Feb. — *War Dept.* Letter and reports of the Sec. to the committee [on] the naval equipment; 2 March. — *Treas. Dept.* Letter from Sec. accomp. an abstract of the emoluments and expenditures of the officers of the Customs for 1795, also letter from the Comptroller of the Treas.; Apr. 4.

— Ex. docs. *n.t.p.* [1796.] f°.

Namely: *Treas. Dept.* Letter accomp. a statement of the debts of the U. S., with a view of the sums annually requisite for discharging them; 4 Jan. 1796; — Statement shewing a final liquidation of the French loans, and their re-imbursement at the Treasury; 19 Jan.; — Letter accomp. a return of the exports of the U. S., 1 Oct. 1790 - 30 Sept. 1795 [25 Jan.]; — Letter accomp. an estimate of the receipts and expenditures for 1796; 18 May.

— Ex. docs. *n.t.p.* [1796.] f°.

Namely: *Treas. Dept.* Letter from Sec. accomp. statements in pursuance of the resolutions of the 2 March 1795, and 26 Feb. 1796; also a report thereon by the Commissioner of the Revenue; 7 March 1796; — Letter from Sec. to the chairman of the committee of ways and means; 12 March; — Letter rel. to an inaccuracy in the printed statement of receipts and expenditures for 1794; 18 April; — Letter accomp. estimate of the receipts and expenditures for 1796; May 18.

Also: *Pres.* Speech; 8 Dec. 1795. (Sen. doc.? B 493) — *Committee on such Standing Rules and Orders of Proceeding as are Proper to be Observed in this House.* Report; 11 Dec. (B 493) — *Committee appointed to Prepare and Report an Address to the President in Answer to his Speech to Both Houses of Congress.* Report; 14 Dec. 1795. (B 493) — *Mint.* Letter from the Sec. of State enclosing the reports of late and present director of the Mint; 14 Dec. (B 492) — *Treas. Dept.* Estimate for an appropriation for the services of the year 1796; accompanying a letter and report; 14 Dec. (B 493) — *Treas. Dept.* Sundry estimates and statements rel. to appropriations for the year 1796, and to the expenditures of certain sums heretofore appropriated; 14 Dec. (B 493, W 66) — *War Dept.* Letter from the Sec. accomp. statements rel. to the present state of the military force, *etc.*; 14 Dec. (B 493, W 67) — *Treas. Dept.* Accounts of payments and receipts of public monies, Jan. 1 - Dec. 31, 1795; [17 Dec. 1795]. (B 479) — *Commissioners of the Sinking Fund.* Report; Dec. 18. (W 67) — *Treas. Dept.* Proceedings of the accounting officers upon certain claims not admitted to be valid; accompanying a letter from the Sec. of the Treas.; 24 Dec. (B 493, W 57, 67) — *Com.* [*on*] *the Reports on the Memorial of Parker, Hopkins, and Meers.* Report; 29 Dec. (B 493) — **Harper, R. G.** Motion; 31 Dec. 1795. (B 493) — *Com. of Claims.* Report on the petition of J. B. Dumon; 4 Jan. 1796. (B 493) — **Smith, S.** Motion conc. unlawfulness of foreign vessels landing in the U. S. any goods not the production of the nation to which the vessel belongs; 4 Jan. (B 493) — *Pres.* Message; 4 Jan. (B 493) — *Com. on Commerce and Manufactures.* Report on the petitions of J. Devereux, [and others]; 11 Jan. (B 493) — *Com. of Elections to whom was Recommitted their Report on the Memorial of J. Richards.* Report; 13 Jan. (B 493) — *House.* Proceedings in the case of R. Randall and C. Whitney; 13 Jan. (B 493) — *Treas. Dept.* Message from the Pres., accompanying an official statement of the expenditure to the end of the year 1795; 13 Jan. (B 493) — *War Dept.* Report rel. to the fortifications of the ports and harbours of the U. S.; 20 Jan. (B 493, W 67) — *Pres.* Message accompanying a memorial of the commis. [on] establishing the temporary and permanent seat of the government of the U. S.; Jan. 8, 1796, referred to J. Smith, *etc.*; 25 Jan., report made. (Sen. doc.? B 493) — *Attorney-General.* Letter and report [on] the petition of J. Mackey; 26 Jan. (B 493) — *Com. of Claims.* Report on the petition of J. Griffin; 26 Jan. (B 493) — *Com. of Claims.* Report on the petition of S. Clark; 26 Jan. (B 493) — *Com.* [*on*] *the Actual State of the Naval Equipment Ordered by a Former Law of the U. S.* Report [on] further provision necessary; 29 Jan. (B 493, W 66) — *Com. of Elections.* Report [on] the petition of M. Lyon, of Vt., complaining of an undue election and return of I. Smith as a member of the House; 4 Feb. (B 493, 494) — *Com. of Ways and Means.* Report [on] further measures necessary to reinforce the existing provisions for the public debt; 4 Feb. (B 493) — *Com. of Commerce and Manufactures.* Report on the petitions of I. Loring, sundry merchants of Phila. and N. Y., J. R. Silva, N. Somes, and J. Strange; 8 Feb. (B 493) — **Papers** rel. to an application to Cong. for an exclusive right of searching for and working mines in the N. West and S. West territory; by N. I. Roosevelt, J. Mark, and [others]; Feb. 10. (B 493) — *Coms. on the Petitions of Sundry Refugees from Canada and Nova Scotia.* Reports; 17 Feb. (B 493) — *Com. of Ways and Means.* Report on the provisions requisite for improving the internal revenues of the U. S., and for more effectually securing the collection of the same; 23 Feb. (B 493) — *Com.* [*on*] *the Legislative Provision for the Relief of American Seamen Impressed into the Service of Foreign Powers, etc.* Report; 25 Feb. — *Treas. Dept.* Accounts of payments and receipts of public monies; also account of receipts and expenditures for War Dept., 1 Jan. - 31 Dec. 1795; Feb. 26, 1796. (B 479) — *Pres.* Proclamation [conc.] a treaty between the U. S. and H. B. M.; [with the treaty in full]; 29 Feb. (Sen. doc.? **B 493, W 66**) — *Com.* [*on*] *the Message from the President Accompanying the Copy of a Letter from the Governor of the Territory South of the River Ohio to the Sec. of War.* Report; 10 Mar. (B 493) — *Com. of Elections.* Report [on] the memorials and petitions of sundry citizens and electors of the 2d middle district of Mass., complaining of an undue election and return of J. B. Varnum; 15 March. (B 493) — *Treas. Dept.* Letter and report of the Sec. on the memorial of sundry merchants of the city of Phila.; 16 Mar. (B 493) — *Sec. of the Treas.* Letter and report on the petitions of H. Yeaton, G. House, J. Greenman, and E. Perkins; 16 March. (B 493) — *Com. of Ways and Means.* Report on the state of the receipts and expenditures of the U. S., and the existing and approaching exigences for which provision will be requisite; 17 March. (B 493) — *Com.* [*on*] *Alterations to be Made in the Present Military Establishment of the U. S.* Report; 25 March. (B 493) — *Pres.* Message accomp. the translation of a letter from the minister of the French Republic to the Sec. of State; 25 March. (B 493) — *Pres.* Message accomp. a copy of the treaty of friendship, limits, and navigation between the U. S. and the King of Spain; 29 March. (B 493) — *Pres.* Message assigning the reasons which forbid his compliance with the resolution requesting 'a copy of the instructions, correspondence, and other documents, relative to the treaty lately concluded between the U. S. and Great Britain' 30 March. (B 493) — **Kitchell, A.** Motion; 1 Apr. (B 493) — *Com.* [*on*] *Alterations in the Act to Establish the Post-Office and Post-Roads within the U. S.* Report; 4 April. (B 493) — *Dept. of State.* Letter from Sec. inclosing the estimates referred to in the President's Message of the 29th ult., rel. to the treaty with Spain and other for. nations and with the Indian tribes; 7 Apr. (B 493) — **Blount, W.** Motion in the committee of the whole House, on the message from the Pres. of the U. S. of the 30th ult.; 6 Apr. (B 493) — *Com.* [*on*] *so much of the Report of the Sec. of State, July 13, 1790, and the Message from the President. Jan. 8, 1795, as Relates to Weights and Measures.* Report; 12 Apr. (B 493) — *Com.* [*on*] *the Message from the President Relative to the Territory of the U. S. South of the River Ohio.* Report; 12 April. (B 493) — **Maclay, S.** Motion, 14 Apr. (B 493) — *Com. to Enquire into the Truth of the Information that a Son of Gen. Lafayette is in the U. S.* Report; 26 April. (B 494) — *Com. of Ways and Means.* Report [conc.] the Bank of the U. S., loans to government, *etc.*; 3 May. (B 494) — *Attorney Gen.* Letter accompanying his report rel. to the contract between U. S. and J. C. Symmes; 5 May. (B 494) — *Com. of Claims.* Report on the memorial of S. G. and C. Fowler, administrators of S. Fowler; 7 May. (B 494) — **Smith, S.** Motion, [conc. selling within the U. S. any vessel or goods captured]; 7 May. (B 494) — *Com.* [*on*] *the State of the Fortifications of our Harbours.* Report; 9 May. (B 494) — *Attorney Gen.* Letter accompanying his report on the petition of sundry inhabitants of the County of St. Clair; 10 May. (B 494) — *Com. of Ways and Means.* Report rel. to appropriations for the military and naval establishments, and for the payment of military pensions; 10 May. (B 494) — *Treas. Dept.* Letter from the Sec. accompanying a statement of goods, wares, and merchandize imported from the U. S., Oct. 1, 1794 - Sept. 30, 1795; 12 May, 1796. (B 494) — *Com. of Claims.* Report on the petition of C. Greene; 13 May. (B 494) — *Com. on the Petition of Sundry Inhabitants of the Counties of St. Clair and Randolph, Northwest of the River Ohio.* Report; 13 May. (B 494) — *Com. of Claims.* Report [on] An act making an extra allowance to certain clerks in the public offices, and to the widows of certain deceased clerks; 17 May. (B 494) — *Com. of Claims.* Report on the petition of A. Fowler; 17 May. (B 494) — *Com. of Claims.* Report on the petition of O. Pollock; 26 May. (B 494)

— Ex. doc.] *Treas. Dept.* Letter accompanying an abstract of the emoluments and expenditures of the officers of the customs for 1795; 4 Apr. *n.p.*, [1796]. f°

— Debates. Pt. 1: The constitutional powers of the House, with resp. to treaties. Pt. 2: The British treaty. Phila., 1796. 2 v. 8°.

— *Same, with single titlepage.* Phila., 1796. 2 v. 8°.

— *Same.* Debates upon questions involved in the British treaty of 1794. 2d ed. Phila., 1808. 2 v. 8°.

— Cobbett, W. Prospect from the Congress gallery during the session begun Dec. 7, 1795. Phila., 1796. 8°. (B 984)

4th Cong. 2d sess., Dec. 5th 1796 - *March 3d*, 1797.

— Journal. Phila., 1796-[97]. 8°.

— Ex. docs. *n.t.p.* [1796-97.] f°.

Namely: *Treas. Dept.* Account of the receipts and expenditures for 1795; Nov. 28, 1796; — Appendix, cont. statements shewing the operation of the funds for reducing the domestic debt to the close of 1795; also statements of the foreign and domestic debts and expenditure of the proceeds of foreign loans; — Letter from the Sec. accomp. a plan for laying and collecting direct taxes, *etc.*; 14 Dec. — *Com. of Claims.* Report on the petition of J. Gibbons; 22 Dec. — *Treas. Dept.* Letter from the Sec. accomp. an abstract of the official emoluments and expenditures of the officers of the Customs for 1796, *etc.*; 17 Feb. 1797.

Also: *Com. of Claims*. Report on the petition of H. Hill; 9 Dec. 1796. (B 494) — *Com. of Revisal and Unfinished Business*. Report on bills and reports depending at the last session of Congress; 9 Dec. (B 495) — *Committee* [*on*] *an Address to the Pres. in Answer to his Speech to Both Houses of Congress*. Report; 12 Dec. (B 495) — *Treasury Department*. Letter accompanying sundry statements in rel. to the annual expenditure of the War Dept., from the commencement of the present government to 31 Dec., 1795; 12 Dec. 1796. (B 494, W 66) — *Treasury Dept*. Statement of the monies expended for the military establishment from the commencement of the present government to Jan. 1, 1796; 12 Dec. (Sen. doc.? B 494) — *War Dept*. Statement by the accountant of the expenditure at the war office for the military establishment from the commencement of the present government to 1 Jan. 1796; 12 Dec. (B 494) — *Commis. of the Sinking Fund*. Report stating the amount of their purchases, *etc.*; 16 Dec. (B 494) — *Treas. Dept.* — Letter accomp. a report and estimates of the sums necessary to be appropriated for 1797; also statement of the receipts and expenditures for one year preceding Oct. 1, 1796; 16 Dec. (B 495, W 66) — *Treas. Dept*. Letter accompanying a statement exhibiting the amount of drawbacks paid upon the dutiable articles exported from the U. S. in 1793–95; 16 Dec. (B 494, W 57, 66) — *Treasury Dept*. Aggregate of the appropriations made by law, to 1 Jan. 1796; [16 Dec.]. (Sen. doc? B 494) — *Mint*. Letter from the Sec. of State incl. a report of the Director of the Mint; 20 Dec. (B 494, W 66) — *Committee on the Memorial of the Commissioners Appointed under the Act for Establishing the Temporary and Permanent Seat of the Gov. of the U. S., and on so much of the Pres. Speech as rel. to the Estab. of a Nat. University*. Report; 21 Dec. (B 494, W 57, 66) — *Com. of Ways and Means*. Report on the measures to be taken rel. to the balances found by commis. for settling accounts between the U. S. and the individual states to be due from certain states to the U. S.; 26 Dec. (B 494) — *War Dept*. Letter from the Sec. incl. his report on the petition of H. L. White; 26 Dec. (B 494) — *Com. of Claims*. Report on the petition of W. Parsons; 27 Dec. (B 494) — *Com. of Com. and Manufactures*. Report on the petition of S. Legaré, J. Theus, and S. Prioleau; 27 Dec. (B 494) — *Com. of Claims*. Report on copies of the proceedings of the Accounting officers of the Treas. upon certain claims not admitted to be valid, 29 Dec. (B 494) — *Treas. Dept*. Letter from the Sec. transm. a report and statements exhibiting a view of the debts of the U. S., Jan. 1, 1790, 91, 96; 29 Dec. (B 494, W 66) — *Treas. Dept*. Letter from the Sec. transmitting the copy of a letter from the commis. [on] the seat of the government of the U. S.; with documents marked A, B, C, D, E, and F.; 29 Dec. (B 494) — *Navy Dept*. Letter rel. to expense of building and equipping certain vessels of war; 2 Jan. 1797. (B 492) — *Com. of Ways and Means*. Reports [on] further revenues and the provisions requisite for improving and more effectually securing the internal revenues; 3 Jan. (B 495) — *Com. of Claims*. Report on the petition of G. Dench, 4 Jan. (B 495) — *Com. on the Petition of J. Car*. Report; 5 Jan. (B 495) — *War Dept*. Report of the Sec. on the petition of M. Poirey; Jan. 5. (B 495) — Smith, W. Motion to amend the constitution of the U. S.; 6 Jan. (B 495) — *Com.* [*on*] *Alterations in the Compensations Allowed by Law to the Officers of the U. S.* Report; 9 Jan. (B 495) — *Com. of Claims*. Report on the petition of J. Ore; 12 Jan. (B 495) — *Com. of Claims*. Report on the petition of O. Pollock; 12 Jan. (B 495) — *Attorney Gen*. Letter accompanying his report on the petition of F. Forsyth; 13 Jan. (B 495) — *Com. of Claims*. Report [on] the petition of H. Hill, and several reports thereon, 13 Jan. (B 495) — *Com.* [*on*] *Amendments Necessary in the Act 'to Ascertain and Fix the Military Establishment of the U. S.'* Report; 13 Jan. (B 495) — *Illinois and Wabash Land Co*. Memorial; 13 Jan. (B 495) — *Com. of Claims*. Report on the petition of the widow of Scolacuttaw or Hanging Maw, one of the chiefs of the Cherokee nation; 17 Jan. (B 495, W 57, 65) — *Com.* [*on*] *the Petition of H. L. White*. Report, and the report of the Sec. of War thereon; 17 Jan. (B 495, W 65) — *Pres*. Message rel. to the French Republic, with papers therein referred to; Jan. 19. [Eng. and French.] (B 480) — *Pres*. App. [to the Message of the Pres. rel. to the French Republic; Jan. 19]. (W 64) — *Treas. Dept*. Letter from the Sec. accompanying his report and two estimates of the Sec. of War of the of the sums required for the use of the naval department; 19 Jan. (B 495, W 65) — *Com. of Ways and Means*. Report [conc.] a tax upon all theatrical exhibitions; also, additional duties on articles of foreign growth or manufacture, *etc.*; 23 Jan. (B 495, W 57, 65) — *Com. of Claims*. Report on the petition of E. St. S. Livermore; 24 Jan. (B 495, W 65) — *Com. on the State of the Naval Equipment ordered by Former Acts of Cong., etc.* Report; 25 Jan. (B 495, W 65) — *War Dept*. Letter from the Sec. to the chairman of the com. on the naval equipment; inclosing statements rel. to the subject; 25 Jan. (B 495, W 57, 65) — *Commis. of the Sinking Fund*. Report rel. to the sale of a part of the capital stock of the Bank of the U. S.; 26 Jan. (B 495) — *Com.* [*on*] *the Progress made in Carrying into effect the Act, 'Providing for the Sale of the Lands of the U. S. in the Territory northwest of the Ohio and above the Mouth of the Kentucky*. Report; 30 Jan. (B 495, W 65) — *Com. on the Memorial of the Illinois and Wabash Land Co.* Report; 3 Feb. (B 495, W 65) — *Com. of Claims*. Report on the petition of A. Welsh; 7 Feb. (B 495) — *Com.* [*on*] *the Memorial of A. de Neufville*. Report; 7 Feb., 1797. (B 495) — *Com. of Commerce and Manuf*. Report on the memorials of sundry manufacturers of chocolate; 8 Feb. Phila. (B 495) — *Com. of Claims*. Report on the petition of C. Sands and others; 9 Feb. (B 492) — *Com. on a Report of the Attorney Gen. rel. to the Contract between the U. S. and J. C. Symmes*. Report with documents; 9 Feb. (B 495, W 65) — Harper, R. G. Motion [conc. contested elections]; 9 Feb. (B 495) — *Treas. Dept*. Letter from the Sec. accompanying a statement of goods, wares, and merchandise exported from the U. S. during one year prior to Sept. 30, 1796; 9 Feb. 1797. Phila. (B 495) — *Com. of Claims*. Report on the petition of the corporation of Rhode Island College; 11 Feb. (B 495) — *Com.* [*on*] *the State of the Fortifications of the Forts and Harbours of the U. S.* Report; 11 Feb. (B 495) — *Com. on a Letter from the Sec. of State*. Report incl. a report of the Director of the Mint; 13 Feb. (B 495) — *Treas. Dept*. Letter from the Sec. accompanying his report, with an estimate of the Sec. at War of the sums necessary to make good deficiencies in the appropriations for the service of the military department in the year 1796; 15 Feb. 1797. (B 495) — *Treas. Dept*. Letter from the Sec. accompanying a report, statements, and papers rel. to the application and expenditure of the sums appropriated for expenses attending the intercourse between the U. S. and foreign nations; 16 Feb. (B 495) — *Treas. Dept*. Message accompanying an official statement of the expenditure to the end of 1796; 16 Feb. (B 495) — *War Dept*. Letter from the Sec. transm. an explanatory letter from the Sec. of the Treas.; also statements rel. to the expenditures in the military department for the year 1796; 20 Feb. (B 495) — *Com. of Claims*. Report on the petitions of S. Abbot and others; 21 Feb. (B 495) — *Com. on a Resolution of the Senate for Obtaining Information rel. to the Amendment Proposed by Cong. to the Constitution, conc. the Suability of States*. Report, re-committed; 21 Feb. Phila. (B 495) — *Treas. Dept*. Accounts of the Treasurer of payments and receipts of public monies, 1 Jan.-Dec. 1796; also receipts and expenditures of the War Dept., 1 Jan. - 31 Dec. 1796; Feb. 22. (B 495) — *Com. of Commerce and Manuf*. Report on the memorials of sundry manufacturers of soap and candles in Phila., N. Y., Boston, and Baltimore; of manufacturers of cordage in Newport; and of S. Addington, callico printer, Germantown; 23 Feb. (B 495) — *Com. of Commerce and Manuf*. Report on the petition of North and Vezey; 23 Feb. (B 495) — *Dept. of State*. Report of the Sec. on the memorial of A. Carmichael; 23 Feb. (B 495) — *Com. of Claims*. Report on the expediency of designating certain claims against the U. S. to be excepted from the operation of the acts of limitation; 24 Feb. (B 495) — *Attorney Gen*. Letter inclosing his report on the memorial of J. Hobby; 27 Feb. (B 495) — *Dept. of State*. Report of the Sec. on the memorial of sundry citizens in Phila.; 27 Feb. (B 492) — *Com.* [*on*] *the Operation of the Act for the Relief and Protection of American Seamen*. Report; 28 Ferurary. (B 495) — *Committee to whom was referred the Resolutions of the Senate respecting the Southern and Western Boundary of Georgia*. Report; 2 Mar. (B 495)

— Ex. doc.] *Treas. Dept*. Letter from the Sec. accomp. a plan for laying and collecting direct taxes, *etc.*; Dec. 14, 1796. *n.p.*, [1796]. f°.

— - *Treas. Dept*. Accounts of payments and receipts of public monies, 1st Jan. - 31st Dec.; also account of receipts and expenditures of the War Dept. *n.t.p.* [1796.] 8°.

— - *Pres*. Message to Cong. rel. to the French Republic; with papers therein referred to; Jan. 19, 1797. Phila., [1797]. 8°.

5th Cong. 1st sess., May 15 - *July* 10, 1797.

— Journal. Phila., 1797. 8°.

— Ex. doc.] *Com. of Ways and Means*. Report on additional revenue for the public service; 2 May, 1798. *n.t.p.* [1798.] f°.

Also: *House*. Standing rules and order. (B 495) — *Pres*. Speech to both Houses of Cong.; 16 May. (Sen. doc.? B 495) — Documents referred to in the Pres. speech 16 May; 19 May. (B 432, W 65) — *Treas. Dept*. Letter from the Sec. transm. a letter from the commis. of Wash., excluding documents marked A, B, C, D, and E, exhibiting a view of the receipts and expenditures of all monies entrusted to them from 18 Nov. 1796-18 May 1797; 3 June. (B 495) — *Com.* [*on*] *Further Provision for the Fortification of the Ports and Harbours of the U. S.* Report; June 10. (B 495) — *Dept. of State*. *Pres*. Message transm. report and docs. from Sec. of State rel. to the boundary line between U. S. and East and West Florida; June 12. (B 481, W 65) — *Treas. Dept*. Accounts of receipts and expenditures of the U. S., 1 April, 1796-31 March, 1797; June 14. (B 495) — *War Dept*. Letter from the Sec. transm. statements rel. to the frigates United States, Constitution, and Constellation; June 17. (B 495) — *War Dept*. Report of the Sec. [resp. the corps of artillerists and engineers in the service of the U. S.; 19 June.] (B 495) — *Dept. of State*. Message from the Pres. transm. a report and documents from the Sec. of the depredations on the commerce of the U. S. since 1 Oct. 1796; June 22. Phila. (B 432) — *Pres*. Confidential message; [with] docs. from the Depts. of State and War rel. to the intercourse of the U. S. with foreign nations; July 3. Phila. (B 481, W 65)

5th Cong. 2d sess., Nov. 13, 1797 - July 16, 1798.

— Journal. Phila., 1797-[98]. 8°.

— Ex. docs. *n.t.p.* [1797-98.] 8°.

— Ex. docs. *n.t.p.* [1798.] f°.

Namely: *Com. of Revisal and Unfinished Business*. Report on bills, *etc*., reports, 2d sess. of 4th Cong. and at last session; 20 Nov. 1797. — *Com.* [*on*] *the Operation of the Act for the Relief and Protection of Amer. Seamen*. Report; 22 Nov. (*Also* B 492) — *Commis. of the Sinking Fund*. Report, enclosing a report to them from the Sec. Treas., *etc*.; 5 Dec. (*Also* B 495) — *Com. on a Letter from the Sec. State*. Report, enclosing a report of the Director of the Mint; 8 Dec. *Dept. of State*. Letter enclosing report of the Director of the Mint; 8 Dec. (*Also* B 492) — *Com. on the Petition of J. Carr*. Report; 8 Dec. — *Com. of Revisal and Unfinished Business*. Report in part on such laws as are near expiring; 11 Dec. — *Com. of Ways and Means*. Report [on] alterations in the Act laying duties on stamped vellum, parchment, and paper; 11 Dec. (*Also* B 495) — *Com.* [*on*] *Alterations in the Law Intituled Act for regulating Foreign Coins, etc.*; 11 Dec. (*Also* B 495) — *Treas. Dept*. Letter from Sec. accom. report and estimates of sums necessary for the service of 1798; also statement of receipts and expenditures for year preceding 1 Oct. 1797; 11 Dec. (*also* B 495); — Letter from Sec. accomp. report from the commis. of Wash., and statements A, B, C, D, and E, 18th May - 18 Nov. 1797; 14 Dec. (*Also* B 495) — *Com. on the Motion rel. to the Method of Taking Evidence to be Adduced in the Trial of Contested Elections of the Members of this House*. Report; 15 Dec. — *Com. of Ways and Means*. Report on the petition of W. Tomlinson and others; 18 Dec. (*Also* B 495) — *Mint*. Letter from the Director, accomp. report and statements 1-4; Dec. 19. (*Also* B 495) — **Tennessee.** *Legislature*. Remonstrance and petition; 20 Dec. (*Also* B 495) — *Com. on the Remonstrance and Petition of the Legislature of Tenn*. Report; 20 Dec. (*Also* B 495) — *Com. on so much of the President's Speech as Rel. to Protection of Commerce and Defence of the Country*. Report; 26 Dec. (*Also* B 495) — *Com. on the Memorial of* [*the*] *Daughters of the Compte de Grasse*. Report; Dec. 27. (*Also* B 495) — *Treas. Dept*. Report rel. to the claim of Kosciusko; Dec. 28. (*Also* B 495) — *Com. on establishing a Uniform Militia throughout the U. S.* A bill; Jan. 1, 1798. — *War Dept*. Report rel. to the running of a line of experiment from Clinch River to Chilhowee Mountain; Jan. 5. (*Also* B 496) — *Treas. Dept*. Report in pursuance of a resolution of the Ho. 14 Dec. [1797]; Jan. 8. (*Also* B 496) — *Com. on President's Speech Rel. to Protection of Commerce, etc*. Report; 16 Jan. (*Also* B 492) — *Dept. of State*. Message accomp. report of Sec. and copies of acts of legislatures of Conn., Md., and Va., ratifying the amendment proposed by Cong. conc. the suability of States; 17 Jan. (*Also* B 492) — *Treas. Dept*. Letter accomp. report on the petitions of inhabitants of Newport, *etc*.; 6 Feb. (*also* B 496); — Message trans. statement of the expenditure to the end of 1797 from sums heretofore granted to defray the charges of government; 13 Feb. (*Also* B 496) — *Com. of Ways and Means*. Further report [on] alterations in the Act laying duties on stamped vellum, parchment, *etc*.; 14 Feb. (*also* B 492); — Report on alterations in acts imposing duties on spirits distilled within the U. S.; 14 Feb. (*Also* B 492) — *Dept. of State*. Message accomp. report by Sec. exhibiting a statement of losses recovered by citizens of the U. S. under the treaty with Gr. Brit.; 19 Feb. (*Also* B 482) — *Com. on the President's Speech rel. to Protection of Commerce, etc*. Report in part; 8 Mar. (*Also* B 492) — *War Dept*. Letter from the Sec. inclosing his report on the petition of S. Cantrill; 5 April (*also* B 492); — Letter from Sec. on the President's speech rel. to the protection of commerce and defence of the country; 11 Apr.; — Letter from Sec. enclosing a statement of the number of cannon purchased for the use of the frigates, *etc*., since Jan. 1794, with prices for each size; 12 Apr. (*Also* B 496) — *Treas. Dept*. Letter from Sec. enclosing his report on the petition of J. Jackson, and the mem. of A. Whitney; 18 Apr. (*Also* B 496) — *Treas. Dept*. Accs. of payments and receipts of public monies 1 Jan.-31 Dec. 1798; also account of receipts and expenditures for the War Dept.; May 14. (*Also* B 496) — *Com. on the President's Speech rel. to Protection of Commerce, etc*. Report; 22 May. — *Treas. Dept*. Letter [on] a calculation of the quotas of the respective states in a tax of two millions, *etc*.; 25 May. (*Also* B 496) — *Treas. Dept*. Report and estimate of appropriation of monies for the compensation of clerks in the offices of the Commis. of Loans, *etc*.; 28 May; — Letter trans. copy of a letter from the commis. app. under the 'Act for establishing the temporary and permanent seat of government, with docs. A, B, C, and D; 29 May. (*Also* B 496) — *Senate*. Amendments to an 'Act to authorize the defence of the merchant vessels against French depredations'; 20 June. — *Com.* [*on*] *Alterations in the Acts Establishing the Executive Departments*. Report; 5 July.

— Ex. docs. *n.t.p.* [1798.] f°.

Namely: *Treas. Dept*. Letter from Sec. transm. statements of goods, *etc*., imported for two years, one commencing 1 Oct. 1794, and the other, 1 Oct. 1795; 8 Jan. 1798; — Letter from the Sec. accomp. a statement [of] the drawbacks paid upon dutiable articles exported during 1794-96 compared with duties on similar articles during the same period; Feb. 9; — Letter from the Sec. accomp. report of the Commis. of the Revenue, *etc*.; 23 Feb. — *Dept. of State*. Letter from the Sec. accomp. report and abstract of all the returns of registered Amer. seamen and of the protests and returns respecting impressed seamen since the 17 Feb. 1797, *etc*.; 1 March. — *Treas. Dept*. Letter from the Sec. transm. a statement of goods, *etc*., exported during the year prior to 1 Oct. 1797; 6 March; — Letter from the Sec. accomp. a letter from the Comptroller of the Treas., also an abstract of the official emoluments and expenditures of the officers of the customs; 20 March. — *War Dept*. Letter from Sec. to the chairman of the com. [on] the expenditures of the monies heretofore appropriated for a naval armament, *etc*.; 1 May.

— Ex. docs. *n.t.p.* [1798.] f°.

Namely: *Dept. of State*. Letter from the Sec. accomp. report and abstract of all the returns of registered Amer. seamen, and protests and returns of impressed seamen since 17 Feb. 1797; 1 March, 1798. — *Com. of Ways and Means*. Report [on] what additional revenues will be wanted for the public service; 2 May.

— Ex. docs. *n.t.p.* [1798.] f°.

Namely: *Dept. of State*. Letter from the Sec. accomp. report of the returns of registered seamen and protests respecting impressed seamen; March 1, 1798.— *War Dept*. Letter from the Sec. to the chairman of the com. to enquire into the expenditure of monies appropriated for a naval armament, *etc*; May 1.

— Ex. docs. *n.t.p.* [1798.] f°.

Namely: *Treas. Dept*. Letter and report of the Sec., accomp. with statements rel. to the military and naval establishments and to the fortification of ports and harbours; Feb. 7, 1798. — **Cunningham, W., and Co.** *vs*. U. S. Claim and answer; Apr. 3. — *Treas. Dept*. Letter from the Sec. accomp. two statements exhibiting the tonnage of shipping belonging to the U. S., 1796, also view of the tonnage of all vessels which paid duties in the ports of the U. S., 1790-96; 6 Apr. — **U. S.** *Agent*. Obs. on the reply of D. Dulany; April 17.

Also: *Com. of Claims*. Report [on] the petition of H. Hill and several reports thereon; 22 Nov. (B 495) — *Com. of Commerce and Manufactures*. Report on the petition of North and Vesey, Charleston, S. C.; 22 Nov. (B 492) — *Pres*. Speech to both Houses of Cong.; Nov. 23. (B 495) — U. S. *Cong. House*. Address in answer to the speech of the Pres.; Nov. 27. (B 495) — *Com.* [*on*] *Articles of Impeachment against W. Blount* [*for*] *High Crimes, etc*. Report; [Dec. 5]. (B 481, 2505) — *Com. of Claims*. Report on the expediency or inexpediency of designating certain claims against the U. S. to be excepted from the acts of limitation; 6 Dec. (B 492)

— *Com. of Commerce and Manufactures.* Report on the petition of P. J. Flamend in behalf of L. Le Guen; 8 Dec. (B 495) — *Com. on a Report of the Director of the Mint.* Report; 8 Dec. (B 492) — *Com. of Claims.* Report on the petition of the corporation of R. I. College; 12 Dec. (B 495) — *Com. of Claims.* Report on the petition of C. Sands; 20 Dec. (B 495) — *Com. of Com. and Manufactures.* Report on the petitions of O. Cook, A. Wood, Jr., and R. Hooper; 29 Dec. (B 495) — *Com. of Impeachment against Wm. Blount*; Further report; [deposition of A. Holden, Jr.]; 30 Dec. Phila. (Sen. doc.? B 481) — *Com. of Ways and Means.* Report, in part, on a letter and rep. from the Sec. of the Treas. with estimates of the sums necessary to be appropriated for 1798; 1 Jan. 1798. (B 496) — *Com. of Claims.* Report on the petition of S. Alexander, widow of the late Maj.-Gen., Earl of Stirling; 2 Jan. (B 496) — *Com. of Com. and Manufactures.* Report on the petition of P. Aupoix; 2d Jan. (B 496) — *Com. of Commerce and Manuf.* Report on the petition of W. Bell; 4 Jan. (B 496) — *Com. of Claims.* Report on the memorial of W. Alexander; 4 Jan. (B 496) — *Com. of Claims.* Report on the petition of J. Frank; 8 Jan. (B 496) — *Com. of Commerce and Manufactures.* Report on the petition of N. Cutter; 10 Jan. (B 496) — *Treas. Dept.* Letter from the Sec. accomp. his report respecting the execution of the third section of the act regulating foreign coins, *etc.*; 11 Jan. (B 496) — *Com. of Claims.* Report on the petition of J. Carr; 17 Jan. (B 496) — *Com. of Claims.* Report on the petition of L. Clark; 18 Jan. (B 496) — *Pres.* Message accompanying a representation from the judge of the district of Penn., and a report of the Attorney Gen. rel. to inconveniences which have occurred in the execution of the act intituled 'An act for the relief of persons imprisoned for debt; Jan. 18. (B 496) — **Yrujo,** *Chev. d'*, *and* **Ripley,** J. P. Letters to chairman of com. of impeachment against W. Blount; 19 Jan. (Sen. doc.? B 481) — *Com. of Claims.* Report on the petitions of J. Nelson and S. Russell; 23 Jan. (B 496) — *Dept. of State.* Message of the Pres. accomp. report from Sec. rel. to affairs on the Mississippi, *etc.*; 23 Jan. (B 481) — *Com. of Impeachment against W. Blount.* Further report. [Articles of impeachment; 25 Jan.] (B 481) — *Treas. Dept.* Letter and report of the Sec. accomp. a plan for regulating the collection of duties on imports and tonnage; 25 Jan. (B 496) — *Com. of Claims.* Report on the expediency of extending the provisions of the Act in addition to the act for making farther provision for the protection of the frontier; 29 Jan. (B 496) — *Com. of Claims.* Report [on] the memorial of A. Macomb and W. Edgar; 30 Jan. (B 496) — *Com. of Revisal and Unfinished Business.* Report [on] the message of the Pres., with representation of the Sec. of War on the subject of clerks in his office; 31 Jan. (B 492) — *Com. of Privileges.* Report rel. to the expulsion from [the] House of M. Lyon, for a violent attack on R. Griswold; 2 Feb. (B 492) — *Pres.* Message accomp. copies of two acts of the Parl. of Gr. Brit. rel. to the carrying into execution the treaty of amity, commerce, and navigation, between H. M. and the U. S.; 2 Feb. (B 482) — *Pres.* Message inclosing a letter from the Gov. of So. Carolina [with] depositions of witnesses to captures and outrages committed within the limits of the U. S. by a French privateer, the Vertitude or Fortitude; Feb. 5. (B 492) — *Com. of Commerce and Manufactures.* Report on the petition of J. Heron, and others; 9 Feb. (B 496) — *Com. of the Whole House.* Testimony before a committee of the whole Ho. rel. to a report of [the] committee of privileges; [Feb. 12]. (B 492) — *Com. of Claims.* Report on the petition of H. Hill; 14 Feb. (B 492) — *Com. on so much of the Pres.'s Speech as rel. to the Reimbursement of certain Advances Made by the Consuls of the U. S. in Foreign Countries.* Report; 14 Feb. Phila. (B 492) — *Com. of the Whole House.* Amendment to the bill in addition to the act for the relief of American seaman; 15 Feb. (B 492) — *Com. of Privileges.* Report on a motion for the expulsion of R. Griswold and M. Lyon, for riotous and disorderly behaviour, in the House; 20 Feb. (B 492) — *Pres.* Message inclosing a memorial of the commissioners representing the situation and circumstances of the city of Wash.; 23 Feb. Phila. (B 496) — *Com. of Claims.* Report [on] the memorials of J. Ball; 26 Feb. (B 492) — *Com. on the Message from the Pres. rel. to the Execution of the Act for the Relief of Persons Imprisoned for Debt.* Report; 26 Feb. Phila. (B 496) — *Com* [on] *Amendments to the Bill for the Relief of the Refugees from the British Provinces.* Report; 27 Feb. Phila. (B 492) — *Com. on the Message from the Pres. Inclosing a Memorial from the Commis.* Report; 8 March. (B 496) — *Com. of Claims.* Report on the memorials and petitions of G. P. Frost, C. Jackson, and others; 19 March. (B 496) — *President.* Message conc. the dispatches from the envoys extraordinary of the U. S. to the French Republic, March 19. (B 482) — *Treas. Dept.* Accounts of payments and receipts of public monies, Jan. 1 - Dec. 31, 1797; also, receipts and expenditures for the War Dept., Jan. 1 - Dec. 31, 1797; March 21. (B 493) — *Com. of Claims.* Report on the memorial of J. Perry; 22 March. (B 496) — *Post Office Dept.* Letter from the Assistant Post-Master Gen. accompanying a specification of the various post-offices and the compensations allowed the Deputy Post-Masters, 1 April - 30 Sept. 1797; 26 March. Phila. (B 496) — *Com. of Claims.* Report on a motion rel. to the amendments in the acts resp. invalid pensioners; 26 March. (B 492) — *Com. of Claims.* Report on the petition of T. Elliot; 2 April. (B 496) — *Com. on the Pres. Speech rel. to the Protection of Commerce and the Defence of the Country.* Report; 9 April. (B 496) — *War Dept.* Letter from the Sec. on so much of the Pres. speech as rel. to the protection of commerce and defence of the country; 11 April. (B 496) — *Treas. Dept.* Letter from the Sec. accompanying his report on the memorial of sundry merchants and traders of Phila.; 13 April. (B 496) — *Com. of Claims.* Report on the petition of J. Haskell; 16 April. (B 496) — *Com. of Commerce and Manufactures.* Report on the petition of G. and H. Colhoun; 18 April. (B 496) — *War Dept.* Letter from the Sec. accomp. a report and sundry statements supplementary to his report; 23 April. Phila. (B 496) — *Com.* [on] *The Act for the Relief of Persons Imprisoned for Debt, and An Act Mitigating or Remitting the Forfeitures, Penalties, etc.* Report, also the petition of J. Greenleaf; 25 April. (B 496) — *Com. of Claims.* Report on the petition of T. Lewis; 25 April. (B 496) — **Clark,** *Gen.* E. Deposition resp. letter to D. Morphy, consul at Charleston, S. C.; 27 April. (Sen. doc.? B 481) — *Com. of Claims.* Report on the petition of B. Wells; 2 May. (B 496) — *Com. on a Representation and Remonstrance of the Legislature of Georgia.* Report; 3 May. (B 496) — *Pres.* Message to both Houses, May 4. (Sen. doc.? B 482, 593) — *Com. of Revisal and Unfinished Business.* Report on the memorial of W. Simmons; 7 May. (B 496) — *Com. of Claims.* Report on the petition of J. Vaughan; 19 May. (B 496) — **Harper,** R. G. Motion [conc. volunteers; 5 June]. (B 496) — *Pres.* Message accomp. the communications from the envoys extraordinary to the French Republic; 5 June. Phila. (B 482, 593, W 57) — **Foster,** D. Motion; June 6. (B 496) — *Com.* [on] *the Act Providing for the Sale of the Lands North-West of the Ohio.* Report; 13 June. (B 496) — *Com. on the Letters from R. Putnam.* Report; 13 June. (B 496) — *Pres.* Message accomp. communication no 8 from the envoys extraordinary to the French Republic; 18 June. Phila. (B 482, W 65) — *Pres.* Message to both Houses; June 21. (Sen. doc.? B 482) — *Pres.* Message inclosing letter and documents from the Gov. of Penn. respecting the arrival in the ports of the U. S. of sundry French inhabitants of the West Indies; 27 June. Phila. (B 482)

— Ex. doc.] *Treas. Dept.* Account of the receipts and expenditures for 1796; [with appendix]; [26 March, 1798]. Phila., [1797]. f°.

— - *Dept. of State.* Instructions to the envoys extraordinary, *etc.*, from the U. S. to the French Republic; 22 June, 1798. Phila., [1798]. 8°.

5th Cong. 3d sess., Dec. 3, 1798 - *March* 4, 1799.

— Journal. Phila., 1798-[99]. 8°.

— Ex. doc.] *Treas. Dept.* Letter from the Sec. accomp. copy of a letter from the Commiss. of Washington and statements A, B, C, D, and E, *etc.*; 11 Dec., 1798. Phila., 1798. f°.

Also: *Pres.* Speech to both Houses; 8 Dec. 1798. Phila. (B 481) — *Com. appointed to prepare Address to the Pres.* Report; 12 Dec. (B 481) — **Harper,** R. G. [Motion conc. settlement of accounts between the U. S. and the several states; 12 Dec.] (B 481) — *Commis. of the Sinking Fund.* Report, [with] report from the Sec. of Treas.; 17 Dec. Phila. (B 492) — *Com. on a Representation and Remonstrance of the Legislature of Georgia.* Report; 24 Dec. (B 481) — *Com. of Claims.* Report on the petition of J. Haskell; 24 Dec. (B 481) — *Treas. Dept.* Letter, inclosing report and estimates of sums necessary for the service of 1799; also, statement of receipts and expenditures at the Treas. of the U. S. for year preceding Oct. 1, 1788; 24 Dec. Phila. (B 496) — *Navy Dept.* Letter from the Sec. accomp. statements rel. to the vessels of war employed in and preparing for the service of the U. S.; 26 Dec. Phila. (B 496) — *Senate.* Message from the Senate, communicating copy of plea in behalf of W. Blount; 26 Dec. (Sen. doc? B 481) — *War Dept.* Message from the Pres. accompanying a report from the Sec. rel. to the military establishment; 31 Dec. (B 496) — *Navy Dept.* Letter from the Sec. with estimates rel. to the expense of building and equipping certain vessels of war; 2 Jan. 1799. (B 492) — *Treas. Dept.* Letter, to the chairman of the committee of ways and means, accomp. a plan for amending acts rel. to duties on spirits distilled within the U. S. and on stills; Jan. 7. (B 497) — *Com. of the Whole House.* Amendments to the bill for establishing an uniform system of bankruptcy throughout the U. S.; [8 Jan.?]. (B 497) — *Post Office Dept.* Letter, accomp. draughts of two bills with explan. remarks, rel. to the Post Office and post roads within the U. S.; 8 Jan. (B 497) — *Pres.* Message accomp. his annual account of the application of grants made by Congress for the contingent charges of government, 1 Jan. - 31 Dec. 1798; 8 Jan. Phila. (B 497) — *Pres.* Message accomp. papers rel. to the impressment of American seamen from public armed vessels of the U. S. by vessels of war belonging to the King of Gr. Brit.; 8 Jan. Phila. (B 497) — *Com. [on] the Pres. Speech rel. to the 'Naval Establishment, the Augmentation of the Navy, and the Adoption of Systematic Measures for Procuring Timber and other Supplies'.* Report, [in part]; 17 Jan. (B 497) — *Pres.* Message accomp. papers rel. to the affairs of the U. S. with the French Republic; 18 Jan. (B 482, W 65) — **French originals of all the documents, translations of which accompanied the message of the Pres. 18 Jan. 1799, rel. to the affairs of the U. S. with the French Republic; 18 Jan. Phila. (B 482) — *Com. of Ways and Means.* Report [on] the probable annual amount of the duties on stamped vellum, parchment, and paper in the respective districts, *etc.*; 21 Jan. (B 497) — *Com. of Ways and Means.* Report [on] amendments [to] the act to provide for the valuation of lands and dwelling houses, *etc.*; 21 Jan. (B 497) — *Dept. of State.* Message from the Pres. accomp. a report of the Sec. cont. obs. on some of the docs. communicated by the Pres. on the 18th; 21 Jan. Phila. (B 482, W 60, 63) — *Navy Dept.* Bill for the government of the Navy of the U. S.; 23 Jan. (B 497) — *Treas. Dept.* Abstract of cases transmitted to the Sec. pursuant to the sixth section of the act entitled An act further to suspend the commercial intercourse between the U. S. and France and the dependencies thereof; Jan. 23. (Sen. doc.? B 49.) — *Com. of Claims.* Report on the petition of S. Sayre; 25 Jan. (B 497) — *Pres.* Message accomp. extract of a letter from the minister plenipotentiary of the U. S. at London to the Sec. of State, and an edict of the Executive Directory of the French Republic, of Oct. 29, 1798; 28 Jan. Phila. (Sen. doc.? B 482) — *Com. of Claims.* Report on the petition of M. White with the report of the former Sec. of the Treas.; 4 Feb. (B 497) — *Post Office Dept.* Alterations to be made in the bill reported by the Post-master Gen. 'To establish the Post Office of the U. S.'; 7 Feb. (B 497) — *Com. of Claims.* Report [on] the petition of C. Sands and others, with several reports thereon; 12 Feb. (B 497) — *Navy Dept.* Letter from the Sec. to the chairman of the committee on so much of the Pres. speech as rel. to the naval establishment, *etc.*; 12 Feb. (B 497) — **Foster, A.** Motion for an amendment to the Constitution of the U. S.; 16 Feb. (B 497) — *Com. on Memorials Complaining of the Act concerning Aliens.* Report; 21 Feb. (B 492) — *Com. on a Resolution for Causing a Publ. of the Constitution of the U. S., with the Amendments, etc.* Report; 21 Feb. (B 497) — *Dept. of State.* Letter from the Sec. accomp. his report on the claim of J. B. Cutting; 27 Feb. (B 497)

6th Cong. 1st sess., Dec. 2, 1799 - *March* 14, 1800.

— Journal. Phila., [1800]. 8°.

— Ex. docs. *n.t.p.* [1799-1800.] 8°.

Namely: *Commis. of the City of Washington.* Letter to the Pres. with account of the present state of the public buildings; 5 Dec. 1799 (*also* B 497); — Two letters, with docs. 1-10 [on] the receipts and expenditures of monies entrusted to them; 5 Dec. (*Also* B 497) — *Pres.* Message transm. docs. on the insurrection in Penn., the renewal of commerce with St Domingo, and the Mission to France; 5 Dec. (*Also* B 482, 497) — *Com. to Prepare an Address to Congress.* Report; 6 Dec. (*Also* B 497) — *Com. of Revisal and Unfinished Business.* Report on bills and reports depending at the last sess. of Cong.; 10 Dec. (*Also* B 497) — *Dept. of State.* Letter from Sec. inclosing abstracts of returns of registered and impressed seamen; 10 Dec. (*Also* B 497) — *Commis. of the Sinking Fund.* Report enclosing a report to them from Sec. Treas., *etc.*; 11 Dec. (*Also* B 497) — *Treas. Dept.* Letter from the Sec. accomp. with report and estimates of sums for the service of 1800; also a statement of receipts and expenditures for year preceding 1 Oct.; 18 Dec. (*Also* B 497) — *Com. of Revisal and Unfinished Business.* Further report on laws which have expired or are near expiring; 24 Dec. (*Also* B 497) — *Navy Dept.* Report on the petition of French officers in the prison of Burlington, N. J.; 27 Dec. — *War Dept.* Letter from Sec. accomp. a report [on] the expenses of the Armory at Springfield, Mass.; 7 Jan. 1800. (*Also* B 498) — *Pres.* Message transmitting an original letter from Mrs. Washington [conc.] the interment of Gen. W. in the Capitol; 8 Jan. (*Also* B 493) — *Mint.* Message from the Pres. transmitting statements rel. to the Mint; 8 Jan. (*Also* B 493) — **Mississippi Territory.** Petition of C. West and others; 13 Jan. (*Also* B 498) — *War Dept.* Message from Pres. transmitting a report of the Sec. on the improvement of our military system; 13 Jan. (*Also* B 498) — *Com. of Claims.* Report on the petition of M. White; 15 Jan. (*Also* B 498) — *Com. on the Message of the President, with a Letter from J. Randolph.* Report; 20 Jan. (*Also* B 498) — *Treas. Dept.* Message from the Pres. accomp. an account of the application of grants for the contingent expenses of government, 1 Jan. - 5 Dec. 1799; 20 Jan. (*Also* B 498) — *Com. of Revisal and Unfinished Business.* Report on the amendments of the Senate to the bill intituled, 'An act for mitigating or remitting the forfeitures, *etc.*, accruing in cases therein mentioned'; 23 Jan. (*Also* B 498) — *Dept. of State.* Message from the Pres. accomp. a report of the Sec., with a letter from M. Clarkson, and a list of the claims adjusted by the commissioners under the 21st article of our treaty with Spain; 23 Jan. (*Also* B 498) — *Dept. of State.* Message from Pres. transmitting a report of the Sec. and docs. rel. to the [case] of J. Robbins; 7 Feb. (*Also* B 498, W 10) — *Com. of Commerce and Manufactures.* Report on the Petition of H. Stouffer and A. Wallace; 10 Feb. (*Also* B 498) — *Treas. Dept.* Letter from the Sec. transmitting two statements [on] the duties and drawbacks on goods, *etc.*, imported and exported 1795-98; Feb. 10. — *Com. of Commerce and Manufactures.* Report on the amendments by the Senate to the bill intituled 'An act providing for salvage in cases of re-capture'; 11 Feb. (*Also* B 498)

— Ex. docs. *n.t.p.* [1800.] f°.

Namely: *Treas. Dept.* Letter from Sec. transmitting report with two statements rel. to the internal revenue; Feb. 5, 1800. — *Com. to Examine the Accounts of the United States rel. to the Public Debt.* Report; May 8.

Also: *Pres.* Speech to both Ho. of Cong.; 3 Dec. (Sen. doc.? B 497) — *Dept. of State.* Report on the communications from the agents employed under the act for the relief and protection of American seamen; [Dec. 10]. (B 497) — *Com. of Claims.* Report on the petition of J. Vaughan; 17 Dec. (B 497) — *Com. [on] the Bill Intituled An Act for the Relief of Persons Imprisoned for Debt.* Report; 23 Dec. (B 497) — *Com. [on] so much of the Pres. Speech as rel. to a System of National Defence.* Report; 13 Jan. 1800. (B 498) — *Com. of Claims.* Report [on] the petitions of T. Elliot, S. Sommers, and W. Boyce; 25 Jan. (B 493) — **Foster, A.** Motion for an amendment to the Constitution of the U. S.; 4 Feb. (B 493) — *Treas. Dept.* Letter from the Sec. transm. a statement of goods, *etc.*, exported from the U. S., 1799; Feb. 10. Phila. (B 498) — *Navy Dept.* Letter to the chairman of the com. on so much of the Pres. speech as rel. to the naval establishment, inclosing a bill fixing the pay of the capt. and commanders of vessels of the U. S.; 12 Feb. (B 497) — **Livingston, E.** Motion [that no judge of any court of the U. S. shall during his continuance in office, or within six months after he may have resigned the same, be appointed to any other than a judiciary office under the U. S.]; 13 Feb. (B 498) — *War Dept.* Letter from the Sec. to the com. on so much of the speech of the Pres. as relates to A system of nat. defence; 13 Feb. (Sen. doc.? B 493) — *Com. of Commerce and Manufactures.* Report [conc.] the act suspending commercial intercourse with France; 14 Feb. (B 498) — *Com. of Claims.* Report on the petition of the corporation of Rhode Island College; 17 Feb]. — **Bayard.** Motion [conc. the delivery to justice of T. Nash, otherwise called J. Robbins; 17 Feb.]. (B 498) — *War Dept.* Letter from the Sec. and the Sec. of the Treas. transmitting a report of the claim of S. Harding; 17 Feb. (B 498) — *Com. on Alterations in the Laws Authorizing the Sale of the Lands of the U. S. North-West of the Ohio.* Report, in part; 18 Feb. (B 492) — *Com. on a Petition of C. West and Others in behalf of Themselves and the Other Inhabitants of Mississippi Territory.* Report, in part; 18 Feb. (B 498) — *Com. of Claims.* Report on the petition of M. Gill; 19 Feb. (B 498) — **Livingston, E.** Motion [conc. delivery of J. Robbins]; 20 Feb. (B 498) — *Com. of Claims.* Report [on] the petition of C. Smith; 21 Feb. (B 498) — *Com. of Ways and Means.* Report on a loan; 21 Feb. (B 498) — *Com. on the Petition of I. Zane.* Report; 21 Feb. (B 498) — *Com. on the Petition of J. Mountjoy.* Report; 21 Feb. (B 492, 498) — *Com. of Claims.* Report on the petition of A. Elliot; 23 Feb. (B 499) — *Com. [on] Alterations in the Judicial Establishment of the Territory North-West of* *the Ohio, etc.* Report; 3 March. (B 498) — *Com. of Claims.* Report [on] the petition of S. Sayre; 4 March. (B 498) — *Com. of Claims.* Report [on] the petition of T. Rudolph; 6 March. (B 498) — *Com. of Claims.* Report [on] the memorial of D. Jones and W. Rogers; 10 March. (B 498) — **Harper, R. G.** Motion [on post roads]; 10 March. (B 498) — **Lee, H.** Motion [on communication by post-roads]; 10 March. (B 498) — *Treas. Dept.* Letter from the Sec. transm. a letter from the Comptroller, with an abstract of the compensations of the officers of the customs, 1799; 10 March. (B 498) — *Com. of Claims.* Report [on] the petitions of T. Frothingham [and] citizens of Washington and Allegany, *etc.*; 11 March. (B 498) — *Com. on so much of the Pres. Speech as rel. to a Revision and Amendment of the Judiciary System.* Report, in part; 11 Mar. (B 498) — *Com. on the Petition of C. West and others.* Report with a motion; 13 March. (B 493) — *Com. of Claims.* Report on the memorial of J. Somervell and H. T. Compton; 14 March. (B 498) — *Com. [on] the Petition of Sundry Inhabitants of Mount Pleasant, N. Y.* Report; 14 March. (B 498) — **St. Clair, A.** Letter on a division of the [North western] territory; and the petition of G. Tevebaugh and others; 14 March. (B 498) — *War Dept.* Letter from the Sec. accomp. his report on the petitions of W. Milton and others, exhibiting claims for militia services in Georgia; 14 March. (B 498) — *Com. [on] the Expediency of Authorizing the Pres. to Appoint an Agent to Purchase of the Indians a Tract of Land on the South Side of Lake Superior, which shall Include the Great Copper Bed.* Report; 17 March. (B 498) — *Com. of Claims.* Report [on] the petition of A. Dardin; 18 March. (B 498) — *Navy Dept.* Letter and report of the Sec.; 20 March. (B 492) — *Com. of Claims.* Report [on] the petition of G. Dench; 21 March. (B 498) — *Com. on the Bill Authorizing the Acceptance from Connecticut of a Cession of the Jurisdiction of the Territory West of Penn.* Report; [21 March?]. (B 497) — *Com. on the Consideration of the Expediency of Accepting from Connecticut a Cession of Jurisdiction of the Territory West of Penn. Called the Western Reserve of Connecticut.* Report; 21 March. (B 498) — *War Dept.* Letter from the Sec. accompanying his report on the petition of J. Armstrong; 21 March. (B 492, 498) — *Treas. Dept.* Letter from the Sec. accomp. his reports on the memorial of D. Jones, and the petitions of O. Scott, and of G. and J. Gilbert; 25 March. (499) — *Com. of Claims.* Report of the Com. instructed to inquire whether any alterations ought to be made in the law passed June 12, 1798; 28 March. (B 499) — *Com. on the Petitions of T. Burling, J. Collier, C. West, and Others.* Report; 2 April. (B 499) — *Com. on the Petition of A. Bell and Others.* Report; 2 Apr. (B 499) — *Treas. Dept.* Letter from the Sec. accompanying his report on the petition of B. Wells, *etc.*; 2 Apr. (B 499) — *Com. on the Petition of W. Hill and Others.* Report; 4 April. (B 499) — *Com. on the Memorial of M. Patterson and Other Persons Residing on the Western Borders of N. and S. Carolina.* Report; 8 April. (B 499) — *Com. of Claims.* Report on the petition of W. Nichols; 9 April. (B 499) — *Com. [on] the Expediency of Making Further Provision for the Relief for the Widow and Children of Col. J. Harding, and for the Orphan Daughter of Major A. Trueman.* Report; 9 April. (B 499) — *Com. on the Petition of W. Tazewell.* Report; 9 April. (B 499) — *Treas. Dept.* Letter from the Sec. to the chairman of the committee of ways and means, transm. a letter from the commis. of valuation of houses and lands in N. Y.; 10 April. (B 499) — *Com. of Claims.* Report on the petition of T. Johnson; 16 April. (B 499) — *Com. [on] Petitions of Persons Residing in the North-Western Territory, on Judge Symme's Purchase.* Report; 16 April. (B 499) — *Com. of Claims.* Report on the petition of O. Pollock; 18 April. (Sen. doc.? B 499) — *Treas. Dept.* [Report] accompanying the report of the com. of claims on the petition of O. Pollock; 18 April. (B 499) — **Hornblower, J.** Letter to Mr. Kitchell on Schuyler's copper mine in N. J.; April, 18 (B 499) — *Com. of Claims.* Report on petition of B. Wells; 21 April. (B 499) — *Com. of Claims.* Report on the petitions of B. Bird, E. Sudler, [and others] and the bill intituled An act for the relief of the legal representatives of S. Lapsley; 22 April. (B 499) — *Com. [on] the Operation of Acts making Provision for the Establishment of Trading Houses with the Indian Tribes.* Report; 22 April. (B 492) — *Treas. Dept.* Report from the Sec. accompanying an estimate for an appropriation of monies to carry into effect The act respect. quarantines and health-laws; [24 Apr.]. (B 499) — *Com. of Claims.* Report on the petition of J. B. Verdier; [25 April]. — *Com. [on the Bill sent from the Senate An Act Prescribing the Mode of Deciding Disputed Elections of Pres. and Vice-Pres.* Report; 25 April. (B 499) — *Treas. Dept.* Letter from the Sec. transm. letter from the Comptroller of the Treas. with sundry statements prepared in obedience to An act establishing a mint, and regulating the coins of the U. S.; 25 April. (B 499) — *Com. of Claims.* Report on the petition of J. Lynch; 26 April. (B 499) — *Com. of Claims.* Report on the petition of M. Wooster; 28 April. (B 499) — *Com. of Claims.* Report on the mem. of C. Pettit with report of the Sec. of the Treas.; 29 April. (B 500) — *Com. of Ways and Means.* Report on further revenue; 30 April. (B 499) — *Com. on so much of the President's Speech as rel to a Revision and Amendment of the Judiciary System.* Report; 1 May. (B 499) — *Com. of Ways and Means.* Report on appropriations for the diplomatic department; 5 May. (B 499) — *Com. of Ways and Means.* Report on appropriations for the Indian Department; 5 May. (B 499) — **Latrobe, B. H.** [Letters to the chairman of the com. of commerce and manufactures, on the petition of N. I. Roosevelt and his associates, praying for an act of incorporation of a mine and metal company. Undated; possibly belongs to a later Congress.] (B 499) — **Nicholas, J.** Motion for amending the bill to provide for the execution of the twenty-seventh article of the treaty of amity, commerce, and navigation with Gr. Brit. [Undated; possibly belongs to a later Cong.] (B 498)

— Ex. doc.] *Treas. Dept.* Letter from the Secretary transmitting report with two statements relative to the internal revenue; February 5. *n.p.*, [1800]. f°.

6th Cong. 2d sess., Nov. 17, 1800 - March 3, 1801.

— Journal. Wash., [1800–01]. 8°.

— Ex. docs. *n.p.*, [1800–01]. 8°.

Namely: **Nicholas, J.** Motion [conc. articles proposed as amendments to the Constitution; Nov. 21. (B 499) — *Pres.* Speech to both Houses of Cong.; 22 Nov. (B 500) — *Com. Appointed to Prepare an Address in Answer to the Speech of the Pres. to Both Houses of Cong.* Report; 25 Nov. (B 499) — *Com. of Elections Appointed to Examine the Credentials of Members Returned to Serve in this House.* Report, in part; Nov. 26. (B 499) — *Com. of Revisal and Unfinished Business.* Report, in part; Nov. 26. (B 499) — *Com of the Sinking Fund.* Report inclosing a report from the Sec. of the Treas; 28 Nov. (B 499) — *Navy Dept.* Letter from the Sec. transm. a report of the commis. of the fund for navy pensions and half pay pursuant to the act for the better government of the Navy of the U. S.; 2 Dec. (B 499) — *Com. of Commerce and Manufactures.* Report on the petition of R. Hooper; 9 Dec. (B 500) — *Com. of Commerce and Manufactures.* Report on the petition of T. Jenkins and sons; 9 Dec. (B 500) — *Treas. Dept.* Letter from the Sec. with a report and estimates of the sums to be appropriated for 1801; also a statement of the receipts and expenditures at the Treas. for one year preceding 1 Oct. 1800; 11 Dec. (B 499) — *Dept. of State.* Letter from Sec. inclosing abstracts of all the returns made by the collectors of the different ports of registered and impressed seamen; 12 Dec. (B 499) — *Com. on so much of the Speech of the Pres. as Respects the District of Columbia.* Report, in part; 17 Dec. (B 499) — *Com. of Revisal and Unfinished Business.* Further report; 19 Dec. (B 499) — *Com. on the Bill Directing the Erection of a Mausoleum to G. Washington.* Further report, in part; 19 Dec. (B 499) — *Com. of Ways and Means.* Report [conc.] An act to provide for the valuation of lands and dwelling houses, and the enumeration of slaves, within the U. S.; 31 Dec. (B 499) — **Wayne Co.** Petition of sundry citizens; 2 Jan. 1801. (B 500) — *Navy Dept.* Report of the Sec. accompanying sundry docs. rel. to the naval establishment of the U. S.; 15 Jan. (B 500) — *Pres.* Message transmitting statements relative to the Mint; Jan. 21. (B 500) — *Com. [on] a Motion for Amending the Constitution of the U. S.* Report; 22 Jan. (B 500) — *Com. on the Letter from the Sec. of the Treas. Announcing his Resignation.* Report; 28 Jan. (B 500) — *Com. on the Representation of the Ho. of Rep. of the Mississippi Territory.* Report; 19 Feb. 1801. (B 500) — *Treas. Dept.* Letter from the Sec. in rel. to the destruction of official books and papers by the fire; inclosing sundry reports from the principals in the offices of that department; 24 Feb. (B 500)

— Ex. doc.] *Treas. Dept.* Account of the receipts and expenditure for 1800. Wash., [1801]. f°.

7th Cong. 1st sess., Dec. 7, 1801 - May 3, 1802.

— Journal. Wash., [1801–02]. 8°.

— Ex. docs. *n.t.p.* [1801–02.] f°.

Namely: *Treas. Dept.* Account of the receipts and expenditures for 1800; Nov. 23, 1801. — *Dept. of State.*

Return of the whole number of persons within the U. S.; 8 Dec. — *Commis. of the Sinking Fund.* Rept. accomp. a statement of the proceedings authorised by the Board since 28 Nov. 1800; 17 Dec. — *Treas. Dept.* Letter from Sec. accomp. statements of the importations in Amer. and foreign vessels, 1 Oct.-30 Sept. 1800; 17 Dec.; — Letter from Sec. accomp. a rept. and statements [on] the Act supplementary to an act to establish the Treas. Dept.; 21 Dec.; — Letter from Sec. transm. two statements rel. to the internal revenues, also letter from the Commis. of the Revenue; 21 Dec. — *Dept. of State.* Letter from Sec. enclosing a table shewing the comparative duties paid in the ports of Gr. Brit. on goods imported in Amer., foreign, and Brit. bottoms since 5 Jan. 1798; 7 Jan. 1802. — *Treas. Dept.* Letter from Sec. accomp. annual statements of the district tonnage of the U. S., 31 Dec. 1800; 2 March; — Letter from Sec. accomp. statement of the emoluments of the officers employed in the Customs, 1801, with letter from the Comptroller of the Treas.; 2 March.

— Ex. docs. *n.t.p.* [1801-02.] f°.

Namely: *Treas. Dept.* Letter from Sec. accomp. statements of the importations in Amer. and foreign vessels, 1 Oct. 1798-30 Sept. 1800; 17 Dec. 1801; — Letter from Sec. accomp. report and statements [on] An act to establish the Treas. Dept.; [21 Dec.]; — Letter transm. two statements rel. to the internal revenues; 21 Dec.; — Letter enclosing a table shewing the comparative duties paid in the ports of Gr. Brit. on goods imported into Gr. Brit. in Amer., foreign, and Brit. bottoms since 5 Jan. 1798; 7 Jan. 1802; — Letter accomp. a statement of the emoluments of the officers of the Customs, 1801; 2 March; — Letter accomp. a statement of the emoluments of the officers of the Customs, 1801; 2 March; — Letter accomp. annual statements of the district tonnage, 31 Dec. 1800; 2 March.

Also: *Pres.* Message and communication to the Senate and House, with accomp. documents; 8 Dec. (B 500) — *Treas. Dept.* Letter from the Sec. covering two letters from the city commis., with documents, *etc.*; 21 Dec. (B 500) — *Pres.* No. 1: Papers rel. to the trans. of the U. S. with the Barbary powers, accompanying a message from the Pres.; Dec. 22, 1801. (B 500) — *Com. [on] Indian Affairs.* Memorial; 7th Jan. (Sen. doc.? B 500) — *Treas. Dept.* Letter from the Sec. accompanying a statement exhibiting the amount of duties and drawbacks on goods imported and exported, 1798-1800; 7 Jan. (B 500) — *Pres.* Message, transm. a letter to him from the Sec. of State; 12 Jan. (B 500) — *Treas. Dept.* Communication from the Sec. to the chairman of the com. appointed to investigate the state of the Treas.; Jan. 21. (Sen. doc.? B 500) — *Navy Dept.* Letter from the Sec. inclosing 'Copies of Instructions to the commanders of vessels in the public service, authorizing the capture of vessels belonging to the French Republic'; 25 Jan. (B 500) — *Navy Dept.* Letter from the Sec. to S. L. Mitchell, chairman of the select committee appointed to consider so much of the message of the Pres. as rel. to naval preparations, *etc.*; 30 Jan. (B 500) — *Treas. Dept.* Letter from the Sec. accomp. statement of goods, wares, *etc.*, exported, Oct. 1, 1800-Sept. 30, 1801; 11 Feb. (B 501) — **Indiana Territory.** Message from the Pres., transm. laws of the Indiana Territory, Jan. 1801 - Feb. 1802; 14 Feb. (B 501, 503) — *Pres.* Message, transm. docs. rel. to trans. with the Barbary powers; Feb. 17. (B 501) — *Treas. Dept.* Message from the Pres., accomp. report of the Sec., and two statements, A and B, on subject of marine hospitals; also docs. resp the situation of seamen and boatmen of U. S. frequenting the port of New Orleans; 24 Feb. (Sen. doc.? B 501) — *Dept. of State.* Message from the Pres. inclosing a report of the Sec. to him, and statements [on] the statement no 8 accomp. the message of the 8 Dec.; 26 Feb. 1802. (Sen. doc.? B 500) — *Com. of Ways and Means.* Documents accompanying a bill making an appropriation defraying the expenses which may arise from carrying into effect the convention made between the U. S. and the French Republic; [12 March]. (Sen. doc.? B 500) — *Treas. Dept.* Letter from the Sec., accomp. letter from Comptroller of Treas., and statements, A, B, C, D, E, in pursuance of 'Act establishing a mint, and regulating coins'; 24 March. (B 501) — *Com. on Motion Resp. Adjustment of Disputes Between Commis. of Wash. and Others [conc.] Plan of Said City.* Report; 8 April. (B 501) — *Pres.* Message, transm. docs. resp. French corvette Berceau; 16 April. (B 501) — *Mint.* Message from the Pres., inclosing letter from the Director of Mint resp. compensations of officers [in] that establishment; 20 April. (Sen. doc.? B 501) — *Pres.* Message, transm. report from Sec. of State, and [other] docs.; 20 April. (B 501) — *Treas. Dept.* Estimate for the contingent expences of the House, 1802; also, statement of disbursements for contingent expences, 1798; 24 April. (B 501) — *Com. on the Message of the Pres. rel. to 'Naval Preparations and Establishment of Sites for Naval Purposes'*; Further report; 27 April. (Sen. doc.? B 501)

— Ex-doc.] *Dept. of State.* Return of the whole number of persons within the U. S.; 8 Dec. 1801. *n.p.*, *n.d.* [1802.] f°.

— Debates in the Senate on the repeal of the internal taxes; March 31-April 24. Georgetown, 1802. 8°. (B 622)

7th Cong. 2d sess., Dec. 6, 1802 - *March* 3, 1803.

— Journal. Wash., [1802-03]. 8°.

— Ex. docs. *n.t.p.* [1803.] f°.

Namely.: *Treas. Dept.* Letter from Sec. transm. two statements rel. to the internal revenues; 6 Jan. 1803; — Letter from Sec. transm. a statement of goods, *etc.*, exported during the year prior to the 1 Oct. 1802; Jan. 17; — Letter transm. two statements of the importations in Amer. and foreign vessels, 1 Oct. 1800-30 Sept. 1801; 9 Feb.; — Letter transm. a letter from the Comptroller of the Treas., and statements A, B, C, and D; 3 March; — Report of the Sec. [on] the finances; Oct. 25; — Report of Sec. [on the direct tax]; 17 Dec.

Also: *Com. of Revisal and Unfinished Business.* Report, in part; 13 Dec. (Sen. doc.? B 501) — *Pres.* Message to both Houses of Cong. [with docs.]; 15 Dec. (B 502) — *Com. of Commerce and Manufactures.* Report on the petition of S. Corp; 16 Dec. (B 502) — *Com. of Commerce and Manufactures.* Report on the petition of J. Holland, Jr.; 22 Dec. (B 502) — *Dept. of State.* Message transm. a report from the Sec., with information rel. to the violation on the part of Spain of the 22d article of the treaty between U. S. and Spain; 22 Dec. (Sen. doc.? B 502) — **Worthington, T.** Letter, inclosing an ordinance passed by the Convention of Ohio; with the constitution formed for the State; 23 Dec. (B 502) — *Com. of Claims.* Report on the memorial of P. C. L'Enfant; 24 Dec. (B 502) — **M'Henry, J.** Letter to the Speaker of the House of Representatives; read in that House, 28 Dec. Balt. (W 10) — *Navy Dept.* Message from the Pres. transm. plans and estimates of a dry dock for the preservation of our ships of war; 28 Dec. (Sen. doc.? B 502) — *Com. of Claims.* Report on the petition of C. Hyde; 29 Dec. (B 502) — *Dept. of State.* Letter from the Sec. transm. documents rel. to the claim of P. C. L'Enfant for planning and laying out Washington; 3 Jan. 1803. (B 502) — **Dawson, J.** Motion [conc. establishment of post-roads]; 4 Jan. (B 502) — *Com. of Commerce and Manufactures.* Report on the memorial of H. Messonier; 6th Jan. (B 502) — *Com. of Revisal and Unfinished Business.* Further report on such laws of the U. S. as have expired; 7 Jan. (B 502) — *Navy Dept.* Letter from the Sec., enclosing information resp. timber deposited in navy yards of the U. S. for building ships of war; 7 Jan. (B 502) — *Com. of Ways and Means.* Report on the petition of H. Alexander; 10 Jan. (B 502) — *Com. on so much of the President's Message as Rel. to our Navy Yards and the Building of Docks.* Report; 10 Jan. (B 502) — *Mint.* Message from the Pres. transm. a report from the Director of the Mint on that institution; 11 Jan. (B 500, 502) — *Com. [conc.] Alterations in the Military Establishment of U. S.* Report; 17 Jan. (B 502) — *War Dept.* Message from the Pres. transm. a report by the Sec.; 17 Jan. (B 502) — *Treas. Dept.* Message from the Pres. accomp. the annual account of the fund for defraying the contingent charges of government in 1802; 19 Jan. (Sen. doc.? B 502) — *Com. of Claims.* Report on the petition of W. Ray and J. Follawell; 20 Jan. (B 502) — **New York. Chamber of Commerce.** Memorial; 24 Jan. (B 502) — *Com. of Ways and Means.* Report [on] alterations [in] 'An act to amend An act to lay and collect a direct tax within the U. S.'; 24 Jan. (B 502) — *Com. on 'An Act to Carry into effect several Resolutions of Cong. for Erecting Monuments to the Memories of Generals Wooster, Harkemer, Davidson, and Scriven'.* Report; 24 Jan. — *Com. of Revisal and Unfinished Business.* Report on the probable amount for which the property occupied by the Mint in Phila could be sold; 25 Jan. (B 502) — *Com. on so much of the Pres. Message as Refers to the Warfare with Tripoli, and to the Relation with the other Barbary Powers.* Report; 25 Jan. (B 502) — *Dept. of State.* Letter from Sec. enclosing his report on the memorial of T. Lear; 25 Jan. (B 502) — *Pres.* Message transm. documents rel to the affairs of Washington; 25 Jan. (Sen. doc.? B 502) — *Dept. of State.* Letter from the Sec. enclosing his report on the mem. of T. Lear; 25 Jan. (B 502) — **Mississippi Territory.** Proceedings of a meeting of citizens; 25 Jan. (B 500, 502) — *Com. of Claims.* Report on the petition of G. Abeel and others; 26 Jan. (B 502) —

Com. of Commerce and Manufactures. Report on the petition of J. Holland, Jr.; 26 Jan. (B 502) — *Com. of Commerce and Manufactures.* Report on the petition of S. Corp; 23 Jan. (B 502) — *Com. on the Memorial of the Town of Wilmington, N. C.* Report; 26 Jan. (B 502) — *Com. of Commerce and Manufactures.* Abstract of the exportation to European ports of Gr. Brit. and France, 1800–01, of sundry articles; 27 Jan. (B 502) — *Com. of Claims.* Report on the petition of M. White; 27 Jan. (B 502) — *Com. of Claims.* Report on the petition of the mayor and commonalty of the town of Alexandria, Dist. of Columbia; 27 Jan. (B 502) — *Com. of Commerce and Manufactures.* Report on the petition of J. and H. M'Lellan; 27 Jan. (B 502) — **New York.** Memorial of mechanics; 27 Jan. (B 500, 502) — *Com. of Claims.* Report on the petition of G. Mason; 28 Jan. (B 502) — *Com.* [*on*] *the Usefulness of Constructing Docks at Either of the Public Navy Yards within the U. S., for the Building and Repair of Ships of War.* Report; 28 Jan. (B 502) — **Newburyport,** *Mass.* Memorial of merchants; 28 Jan. (Sen. doc.? B 502) — *Com. on so much of the Pres. Message as Rel. to our Concerns with the Indian Tribes, and the Establishment of a New Settlement.* Report; 31 Jan. (B 500, 502) — *Com. of Claims.* Report on the petition of B. Wells, with report of the Sec. of the Treas. thereon, Apr. 2, 1800; 1 Feb. (B 502) — *Com. of the Norfolk Chamber of Commerce, in Virginia.* Report; 1 Feb. (B 502) — *Com. on Letter*[*s*] *from E. Tiffin and T. Worthington of* [*Ohio*], *Enclosing a Copy of the Constitution thereof, etc.* Report; 2 Feb. (B 502) — *Com.* [*on*] *Memorials and Petitions of Citizens of U. S. Praying Relief in Case of Spoliations by Cruisers of the French Republic during the Late European War.* Report; 2 Feb. (Sen. doc.? B 501, 502) — **Bayard,** J. A. Motion; 2 Feb. (B 502) — **Dardin,** A. Petition; 3 Feb. (Sen. doc.? B 502, 503) — *Com. of Claims.* Report on the petition of L. Jarvis; 4 Feb. (B 502, 503) — **Lancaster,** *Penn.* Memorial of gun manufacturers; 4 Feb. (B 502, 503) — *War Dept.* Letter from the Sec., transm. a report on the claims to lands for military services; 4 Feb. (B 503) — *War Dept.* Letter from the Sec., accomp. report and documents respecting claims against the U. S. for services of the militia of Georgia; 4 Feb. (B 502, 503) — *Com. on so much of the Pres. Message as Rel. to the Military Institution of the U. S.* Report; 7 Feb. (B 503) — *Com. of Claims.* Report on the petition of A. Elliott; 8 Feb. (B 503) — **Indiana Territory.** Letter from W. H. Harrison, enclosing a memorial for a suspension of the 6th art. of the compact with the U. States; 8 Feb. (Sen. doc.? B 1489) — *Commis.* [*on*] *the Amicable Settlement of Limits with Georgia, and Establishment of a Government in the Mississippi Territory.* Report; 10 Feb. (B 503) — *Commis. on the Georgia Mississippi Territory.* Documents accomp. the report; Feb. 10. (B 503) — *Com. on the Report of the Sec. of War.* Report, with documents resp. claims against the U. S. for services of the militia of Georgia; 10 Feb. (B 503) — **Mississippi Territory.** *Gen. Assembly.* Resolutions and a memorial to the Pres., Senate, and House; 10 Feb. (B 503, C 265) — *Com. of Claims.* Report on the petition of B. Glenn; 11 Feb. (B 503) — *Com. of Ways and Means.* Report on a memorial of sugar refiners of Balt., Maryland; 11 Feb. (B 503) — *Com. of Commerce and Manufactures.* Report on the petition of T. Storm, and others, sugar refiners of the city of N. Y.; 12 Feb. (B 503) — *Com. on so much of the Pres. Message as Rel. to the Fostering of the Fisheries of the U. S.* Report; 12 Feb. (B 503) — *Navy Dept.* Letter from the Sec. to J. H. Nicholson, transm. a statement of the distribution and employment of the officers and privates of the marine corps; 14 Feb. (Sen. doc.? B 503) — *Com.* [*on*] *Pensions to Persons under Disabilities in consequence of Known Wounds Received in the Actual Service of the U. S. not heretofore Provided for.* Report; 15 Feb. (B 503) — *Com. of Claims.* Report on the memorial of P. Coulon, a French citizen; 16 Feb. (B 503) — *Com. of Claims.* Report on a report of a com. of claims on the petition of P. C. L'Enfant; also a letter from the Sec. of State enclosing docs. rel. to [his] claim; 17 Feb. (B 503) — *Com. of Claims.* Report on the memorial of T. Lear, with the report of the Sec. of State; 18 Feb. (B 503) — *Pres.* Message enclosing docs. rel. to J. Pickering, district judge of the district court of New Hampshire; 18 Feb. (B 505) — *Com. on a Message from the Pres. Enclosing Docs. rel. to J. Pickering, District Judge of the District of New Hampshire.* Report; 18 Feb. (B 503) — *Com. of Commerce and Manufactures.* Report on the several memorials and petitions of the Franklin Assoc. and other journeymen printers, of comb-makers, *etc.*; 21 Feb. (B 503) — **Payne,** W., *and others.* Letter; 22 Feb. (B 503) — *Dept. of State.* Message from the Pres. transm. a report from the Sec. and documents in the case of the Danish brigantine Henrick; 24 Feb. (B 503) — *Com. on the Provision which Ought to be Made by Law for the Regulation of Quarantine within the District of Columbia.* Report; 25 Feb. (B 503) — *Treas. Dept.* Letter from the Sec. inclosing his report on the state of the collection of the direct tax, with a letter rel. thereto; 1 March. (B 503) — *Com. on a Letter from W. H. Harrison, Pres. of the Convention Held at Vincennes in the Indiana Territory.* Report; 2 Mar. (B 503)

— Ex. doc.] *Treas. Dept.* Letter from Sec. accomp. his report [on] An act to establish the Treas. Dept.; 20 Dec. Wash., 1802. f°.

8th Cong. 1st sess., Oct. 17, 1803 - March 27, 1804.

— Journal. Wash., [1803–04]. 8°

— Ex. docs. *n.t.p.* [1804.] f°.

Namely: *Treas. Dept.* Letter from Sec. to chairman of committee appointed to enquire whether any, and if any, what claims against the U. S. are barred by the statutes of limitation, enclosing report of the Register of the Treas.; 6 Dec. 1804; — Letter from Sec. transmitting the annual statement of the district tonnage, 31 Dec. 1802; 15 Feb. — Letter transmitting two statements of the importations in Amer. and foreign vessels, 1 Oct. 1801 - 30 Sept. 1802; 18 Feb. — *Post Office Dept.* Letter from Post-Master General transmitting a report of the amount of postage in each state for three years, 1 Oct. 1800 - 30 Sept. 1803, and statements A, B, C, and D, *etc.*; 22 March. — *Treas. Dept.* Letter from Sec. transmitting a letter from the Comptroller; 3 March. — *War Dept.* Message transmitting the last returns of the militia; 22 March.

Also: **Philadelphia. Artisans and Manufacturers.** Memorial; 9 Dec. 1803. (Sen. doc.? C 265) — *Com. on the Report of a Select Com. on the Fisheries of the U. S.* Report; 3 Jan., 1804. (B 505) — *Mint.* Message from the Pres. enclosing a report of the Director of the Mint of the trans. of that institution for 1803; 13 Jan. (Sen. doc.? B 505) — *Navy Dept.* Letter from the Sec. accomp. a statement of monies advanced for the pay, clothing, *etc.*, of the corps of marines from the time of [its] organization and establishment to the close of the last year; 13 Jan. (B 505) — *Treas. Dept.* Letter from the Sec. accomp. his report and marked A, B, and C docs. exhibiting an acc. of the money received for the support of sick and disabled seamen; 13 Jan. (B 505) — *Pres.* Message accomp. documents rel. to a delivery of possession, by the commissary of the French Republic, to the commis. of the U. S., of the Territory of Louisiana; 16 Jan. (Sen. doc.? B 505) — *Com. on the Petitions of Residents and Purchasers of Land in Ohio.* Report, in part; 23 Jan. (B 500) — *Com. of Commerce and Manufactures.* Report on the petitions and memorials of manufacturers of corks, calico printers, dyers, and manufacturers of paper within the U. S.; 25 Jan. (B 505) — *Treas. Dept.* Letter transm. a statement of goods, *etc.*, exported from the U. S., for one year prior to 1 Oct. 1803; 25 Jan. (B 505) — *Com.* [*on*] *the Expediency of Amending the several Acts Providing for the Sale of the Public Lands of the U. S.* Further report in part; 27 Jan. (B 505) — *Com. of Claims.* Supplementary report on the petition of D. Valenzin; 1 Feb. (B 505) — *Com. of the Sinking Fund.* Report accomp. statements exhibiting the proceedings authorized by the board since their report of Feb. 5, 1803; Feb. 6. (Sen. doc.? B 505) — *Com. of Commerce and Manufacturers.* Report [on] the expediency of laying and collecting a tonnage duty on ships and vessels entering the ports and harbours of the U. S.; 18 Feb. (B 505) — *Com. of Claims.* Report on the petition of W. Eaton; 29 Feb. (Sen. doc.? B 505) — *Com. on the Message from the Pres.* Report [with] a report of the surveyor of the public buildings at Washington; 6 March. (B 505) — *Com. of Commerce and Manufactures.* Report on the expediency of authorizing the Pres. to employ persons to explore such parts of Louisiana as he may deem proper; 8 March. (B 505) — *Pres.* Message communicating extract of a letter from Gov. Claiborne to the Secretary of State; 8 March. (Sen. doc.? B 505) — *Com. on the Memorials of Merchants of the City and State of New York, and of Merchants and Ship Owners of the City of Hudson.* Report, 12 March. (B 505) — **Connecticut.** Representation of merchants and others; 15 March. (Sen. doc.? B 505) — *Treas. Dept.* Letter transm. a letter from the Comptroller of the Treas.; with statements prepared in obedience to the act establishing a Mint and regulating the coins of the U. S.; 21 March. (B 505) — *Treas. Dept.* Letter from the Sec. accomp. a report and two statements respect. the monies which since the establishment of the present government have been paid as fees to assistant counsel and for legal advice in the business of the U. S.; 24 March. (B 505)

— Ex. doc.] *Treas. Dept.* Account of the receipts and expenditures of the United States for 1803. Wash., 1804. f°.

8th Cong. 2d sess., Nov. 8, 1804 - *March* 1, 1805.

— Journal. Wash., 1804-[05]. 8°.

— Ex. docs. *n.t.p.* [1804.] f°.

Namely: *Treas. Dept.* Letter from the Sec. enclosing report and docs. [on] An act to establish the Treas. Dept.; 21 Nov., 1804; — Letter transm. two statements of the importations in Amer. and foreign vessels, 1 Oct. 1802 - 30 Sept. 1803; 13 Dec.

— Ex. docs. *n.t.p.* [1805.] f°.

Namely: *Post Office Dept.* Letter from the Post Master General inclosing a list of the persons with whom contracts have been made for carrying the mail 1 Dec. 1801 - [31] Dec. 1804, *etc.*; 2 Jan. 1805. — *Dept. of State.* Letter from Sec. accomp. statements and abstracts rel. to the number of Amer. seamen impressed, *etc.*; 23 Jan. — *Commis. of the Sinking Fund.* Report accomp. with statements exhibiting proc. which have been authorized by the Board since 4 Feb. 1804; 5 Feb. — *Dept. of State.* Letter from the Sec. accomp. abstract of evidences of title to lands claimed under any act or pretended act of the state of Georgia; 14 Feb — *Treas. Dept.* Letter from Sec. accomp. statements of the emoluments of the officers of the Customs, 1804; 26 Feb. — *War Dept.* Message from the President transm. a statement of the militia of the several states; 28 Feb.

Also Pres Message to both Houses of Cong.; 8 Nov. 1804. (**B 504**) — *Treas. Dept.* Letter from the Sec. transm. report and estimates of the appropriations for 1805; 19 Nov. (**B 504**) — *Pres.* Message accompanying copies of treaties concluded with the Delaware and Piankeshaw Indians for the extinguishment of their title to the lands therein described; 30 Nov. (Sen. doc.? **B 504**) — *Com. Appointed to Enquire into the Expediency of Making Provision, by Law, for the Completion of the Public Buildings Belonging to the U. S. near Phila.*; Report; 24 Dec. (**B 504**) — **Louisiana.** Representation and petition of the reps. elected by the freemen of Louisiana; Jan. 4, 1805.. (Sen. doc.? **B 483**) — *Com. of Claims.* Report on the memorial of A. Murray; 8 Jan. (**B 483**) — *Treas. Dept.* Letter from the Sec. transm. a statement of fees paid to assistant counsel, and for legal advices in the business of the U. S.; 15 Jan. (**B 483**) — **Indiana Territory.** Translation of a memorial in French of citizens of the County of Wayne, Indiana; Jan. 17. (Sen. doc. **B 483**) — **Dist. Columbia.** Memorial of delegates; 22 Jan. (Sen. doc.? **B 483**) — *Treas. Dept.* Letter from Sec. accomp. his accounts of receipts and expenditures; 22 Jan. (**B 483**) — *Com. on so much of the Message of the Pres. as Rel. to an Amelioration of the Form of Government of Louisiana, etc.* Report; 25 Jan. (**B 483**) — *Mint.* Report of the Director of the operations of that institution during the last year; 25 Jan. (Sen. doc. **B 483**) — *Mint.* Message from the Pres. communicating the report of the Director of the Mint; 25 Jan. (Sen. doc.? **B 483**) — *Treas. Dept.* Letter from the Sec. accomp. a rept. and two statements exhib. the tonnage of vessels paying foreign duties collected in the ports of the U. S., 1 July - 30 Sept. 1804; 25 Jan. (**B 483**) — *Com. of Commerce and Manuf.* Report [on] the petitions and memorials of a number of merchants, *etc.*, on the waters of the Roanoke and Cashie Rivers; 28 Jan. (**B 483**) — *Post Office Dept.* Message from the Pres. communicating information, in part, on a post road from Wash. to New Orleans; 1 Feb. (**B 483**) — *Com. on the Memorials and Petitions of the Board of Trustees of Jefferson College and of W. Dunbar.* Report; 7 Feb. (**B 483**) — *Com. on the Memorial of the Legislative Council and the House of Mississippi.* Report, in part; 9 Feb. (**B 483**) — *Com. of Claims.* Report on the memorial of R. Taylor; Feb. 13. (**B 483**) — *Treas. Dept.* Letter from the Sec. [with] his report on the petitions of J. M. Fadon, and of J. M. Fadon and F. Johonnot; 15 Feb. (**B 483**) — *Com. of Claims.* Report on the petition of F. Mentges; 16 Feb. (**B 483**) — *Com. of Claims.* Report on the memorial of R. J. Meigs, Jr.; 18 Feb. (**B 483**) — *Com. of Claims.* Report on a message from the Pres. and the documents; 20 Feb. (**B 483**) — *Com. of Claims.* Report [on] the petition of G. Little; 20 Feb. (**B 483**) — *Pres.* Message, transm. a letter from Com. Preble giving a detailed account of the trans. of the vessels under his command, 9 July - 10 Sept. last; 20 Feb. (Sen. doc.? **B 483**) — *Dept. of State.* Letter from the Sec. with a list of the persons who have invented any new and useful art, machine, *etc.*; 22 Feb. (**B 483**) — *Treas. Dept.* Account of the appropriation of 20,000 dollars for contingent charges of government, 1804; 28 Feb. (Sen. doc.? **B 483**) — *Treas. Dept.* Message from the Pres. transm. the annual account of the fund for defraying the contingent charges of government for 1804; 28 Feb. (Sen. doc.? **B 483**) — *Treas. Dept.* Letter from the Comptroller to the Sec. of the Treas. with statements prepared in obedience to An act establishing a Mint, and regulating the coins of the U. S.; 1 March. (Sen. doc.? **B 483**) — *Treas. Dept.* Letter from the Sec. with statements prepared in obedience to An act establishing a Mint and regulating the coins of the U. S.; 1 March. (**B 483**) — **New Eng. Mississippi Land Co.** Memorial of the agents, with a vindication of their title at law annexed. [Undated; possibly belongs to a later Congress]. (Sen. doc.? **B 483**) — **Fromentin, E.** Observations on a bill for ascertaining and adjusting the titles and claims to land in Orleans and Louisiana. [Undated; possibly belongs to later Congress.] (Sen. doc.? **B 483**)

9th Cong. 1st sess., Dec. 2, 1805 - *Apr.* 21, 1806.

— Journal. Wash., 1805-[06]. 8°.

— Ex. docs. *n.t.p.* [1805-06.] f°.

Namely: *Treas. Dept.* Letter from Sec. transm. report [on] An act to establish a Treas. Dept.; Dec. 10, 1805; — Letter from Sec. transm. a statement of goods, *etc.*, exported during the year prior to 1 Oct. 1805; Apr. 9, 1806.

— Ex. docs. *n.t.p.* [1805-06.] f°.

Namely: *Commis. of the Fund for Navy Pensioners.* Report; Dec. 31, 1805. — *Commis. of the Sinking Fund.* Report accomp. statements [of] the proceedings authorized by the Board since 5 Feb. 1805; Feb. 5, 1806. — *War Dept.* Message from Pres. transm. a report by Sec. rel. to fortifications at ports and harbours of the U. S., and money disbursed on account of the Navy since the establishment of the Navy Dept.; Feb. 18. — *Treas. Dept.* Letter from Sec. transm. the annual statement of the district tonnage, 31 Dec. 1804; Feb. 21. — *Department of State.* Letter from Secretary accompanying statements of applications to the British government in cases of impressments; March 8. — *War Dept.* Message from the Pres. transmitting a statement of the militia; Apr. 11.

Also: *Pres.* Message; Dec. 3. (Sen. doc.? **B 484**) — [Another ed.] (**B 430**) — Documents accomp. message from the Pres.; Dec. 6. (Sen. doc.? **B 484**) — *Com. of Ways and Means.* Report [on] the petition of A. Benezet and others; Dec. 9. (**B 485**) — **Phila. Manufacturers of Hats.** Memorial; Dec. 10. (Sen. doc.? **B 485, 1511**) — *Pres.* Message, supplementary to [that] of the 6th communicating docs. resp. Louisiana; Dec. 10. (Sen. doc.? **B 484**) — *Treas. Dept.* Letter from the Sec. accomp. with report and estimates of appropriation for 1806; Dec. 13. (**B 506**) — *Com. of Commerce and Manufactures.* Report for the relief of T. Armstead; Dec. 16. (**B 485**) — *Com. of Claims.* Report on the petition of the crew of the U. S. frigate Philadelphia; Dec. 17. (**B 485**) — *Com. of Elections.* Report on the petition of T. Spalding, Georgia; Dec. 18. (**B 485**) — *Com. on a resolution Resp. W. Eaton.* Report; Dec. 23. (**B 485**) — *Com. on so much of the Message of the President as Rel. to the Aggressions on our Coasts, Defence of Ports and Harbors, etc.* Report; Dec. 23. (**B 485**) — *Pres.* Message, transm. a report from the Governor and presiding Judge of Michigan rel. to the state of that Territory; Dec. 23. (Senate doc.? **B 485**) — *Surveyor of Public Buildings.* Message from the Pres. communicating a report of the Surveyor; Dec. 27. (Sen. doc.? **B 485**) — *Treas. Dept.* Communication from Sec. on transm. a letter on the operation of the law of public debt; Dec. 28. (**B 506**) — *Com.* [*on*] *so far Amending an Act to Provide for Mitigating or Remitting the Forfeitures, etc., as to Extend the Powers* [*of*] *the District Judges to the Judges of the Judicial Courts.* Report; Jan. 2. 1806. (**B 485**) — *Com. on so much of the Message of the President as rel. to the Militia.* Report; Jan. 2. (**B 485**) — *Dept. of State.* Report of the Secretary on the memorial of P. Landais; Jan. 2. (**B 485**) — *Treas. Dept.* Letter from the Sec. accomp. bill declaring consent of Congress to an act of So. Carolina, Dec. 1804; 2 Jan. (Sen. doc.? **B 506**) — **Georgia.** *Legislature.* Memorial; Jan. 13. (**B 484**) — *Pres.* Message respecting application of H. Caramalli, ex-bashaw of Tripoli; Jan. 13. (Sen. doc.? **B 485**) — **Philadelphia. Merchants and Traders.** Memorial; Jan. 16. (**B 484**) — **Indiana Territory.** Memorial of inhabitants of the Counties of Randolph and St. Clair, Indiana Territory; Jan. 17. (Sen. doc.? **B 485**) — *Pres.* Message resp. violation of neutral rights, *etc.*; [docs. only]; Jan. 17. (Sen. doc.? **B 484**) — **Gray, E.** Motion, that any member of this House who shall accept of, solicit, or enter into any contract for expenditures of any monies appropriated for the service of the U. S. shall be disqualified from a seat in this House; Jan. 24. (Sen. doc.? **B 485**) — *Navy Dept.* Letter and report of the Sec. on condition of the frigates and other public armed vessels;

30 Jan. (B 506) — *Pres.* Message transmitting an act of the State of So. Carolina ceding various forts and fortifications and sites for the erection of forts; Feb. 3. (B 485) — *President.* Message, transm. additional docs. resp. application of H. Caramalli; Feb. 4. (B 484) — **Clay, J.** Motion conc. the commerce of the U. S.; Feb. 5. (B 485) — **Penn. 11th Congressional District.** Petition; Feb. 6. (B 485) — **Randolph, J.** Motion conc. the removal of judges; Feb. 7. (B 485) — **Nicholson, J. H.** Motion conc. prohibition of certain imported articles; Feb. 10. (B 485) — **Sloan, J.** Motion conc. impressment of Amer. seamen; Feb. 12. (B 485) — *Com. on the Report of a Select Com. on the Letter of W. H. Harrison.* Report; Feb. 14. (B 485) — *Com. on Public Lands.* Report [conc.] expediency of providing by law for the legal adjudication of claims, in virtue of purchases or transfers from purchasers of lands of the U. S. previous to the emanation of grants under their authority; Feb. 19. (B 485) — *Com. on the Motion of W. Lewis and H. Maxwell.* Report; Feb. 19. (B 485) — *Pres.* Message communicating disc. made in exploring the Missouri by Lewis, Clark, and others; Feb. 19. (Sen. doc.? B 485) — *Com. of Commerce and Manufactures.* Report on the memorial of sundry inhabitants of Charlestown, Virginia; Feb. 20. (B 485) — **Norfolk and Portsmouth,** *Va.* **Citizens.** Resolutions; Feb. 20. (B 484) — *Com. of Commerce and Manufactures.* Report on the expediency of authorizing the Sec. of the Treas. to cause a survey of the shoals of Cape Hatteras, Cape Lookout, and the Frying Pan; Feb. 27. (B 485) — *Com. on the Petition of the Legislative Council of the Territory of Orleans, etc.* Report in part; Feb. 27. (B 485) — *Com. of Commerce and Manufactures.* Report on the petition of sundry merchants of Newburyport, Mass.; March 4. (B 485) — *Com. on Public Lands.* Report on the petitions of the Mayor, Aldermen, *etc.*, of Natchez, of the board of trustees of Jefferson Coll., Miss., and of W. Dunbar; March 4. (B 485) — *Com. of Commerce and Manufactures.* Report on several petitions of merchants, traders, and farmers on the waters of Roanoke and Cashie Rivers in Edenton, No. Carolina, with a report made at the last session; March 5. (B 485) — *Com. on the Petition of the Pres. and Directors of the Chesapeake and Delaware Canal Co.* Report; March 5. (B 485) — *Navy Dept.* Letter communicating services rendered to captive crew of the late frigate Philadelphia by the Danish consul at Tripoli; Mar. 5. (B 506) — *Com. of Claims.* Report on the petition of A. E. de Beaumarchais; March 10. (B 485) — *Com. on Public Lands.* Report [on] two petitions of E. Lewis, and two petitions of sundry inhab. of Miss. Territory, also, mem. of the legis. council, *etc.*, of the Territory; March 11. (B 485) — *Committee on the Petition of A. J. Villard.* Report; March 17. (B 485) — *Com. on the Message of the Pres.* Report transm. a report from the Gov. of Michigan; March 18. (Sen. doc.? B 485) — *Pres.* Message, transm. docs. in rel. to the incursions by the Spanish troops into Louisiana; March 20. (Sen. doc.? B 485) — **New York. Citizens.** Memorial; March 21. (B 485) — *Post Office Dept.* Letter from the Post-master Gen. transm. report shewing obstructions to the transmission of the mail from Athens, Ga., to New Orleans, *etc.*; March 21. (B 485) — *Com. of Ways and Means.* Report on petitions of purchasers of public lands in Ohio and Indiana; March 22. (B 485) — *Com. on a Memorial of the Legislative Council and Ho. of Rep. of the Mississippi Territory, and on a Petition of Sundry Inhabitants.* Report in part; March 26. (B 485) — *Com. on the Letter of W. Tatham to the Speaker.* Report; April 1. (B 485) — *Treas. Dept.* Letter from the Secretary with statements, A, B, C, and D, in obedience to Act estab. a Mint and regulating coins; also, letter from Comptroller of the Treas.; Apr. 1. (B 506) — *Treas. Dept.* Letter from the Sec. rel. to the redemption within a fixed period of the whole of the public debt; Apr. 2. (Sen. doc.? B 506) — *Com. on Public Lands.* Report [on] the expediency of repealing all such parts of the acts for sale of lands of the U. S. as authorize a credit on any part of the purchase money of said lands; Apr. 5. (B 485) — *Navy Dept.* Letter from the Sec. transm. estimate of sums necessary for repairs of vessels, *etc.*, and contingent expenses for 1806; Apr. 11. (B 506) — *Pres.* Message, transm. a treaty between the U. S. and the Piankeshaw Indians; April 15. (Sen. doc.? B 485) — **Dana, S. W.** Motion concerning protection of commerce and seamen; April 17. (B 507) — *Committee on so much of the President's Message as Relates to the Organization of the Militia and to the Augmentation of our Land Forces.* Report; April 18. (B 507) — **Documents** accompanying Act in addition to act supplementary to act providing for naval peace establishment, *etc.*; April 19. (Senate documents? B 486)

9th Cong. 2d sess., Dec. 1, 1806 - *March* 3, 1807.

— Journal. Wash., 1806-[07]. 8°.

— Ex. docs. *n.t.p.* [1806.] f°.

Namely: *Treas. Dept.* Letter from the Sec. enclosing a report in obedience to the act supplementary to the act intituled An act to establish the Treas. Dept.; Dec. 5, 1806; — Letter from Sec. transm. a statement of deposits of public money in the U. S. and other banks for the last three years, *etc.*; Dec. 23.

— Ex. docs. *n.t.p.* [1807.] 8°. (Sen. docs.?)

Namely: *Pres.* Message transm. information touching an illegal combination of private individuals against the union, *etc.*; Jan. 22, 1807; — Message transm. further information [on the same subject]; Jan. 26; — Message transm. further information [on the same subject]; Jan. 28; — Message transm. further information [on the same subject]; Feb. 10.

Also: *Pres.* Message recommending the suspension of the act to prohibit the importation of certain goods, *etc.*; Dec. 3. (Senate doc.? B 507) — **Clopton, J.** Motion on an amendment to the Constitution; Dec. 11. (B 507) — *Surveyor of Public Buildings at Wash.* Message from the Pres. communicating a report of the Surveyor; Dec. 15. (B 507) — *Com. on that Part of the President's Message [rel.] to an Invasion of our Territory by Spain.* Report, in part; Dec. 18. (B 507) — **Crowninshield, J.** Motion [to reduce the duties on foreign refined sugar, sugar candy, *etc.*]; Dec. 19. (B 507) — *Com. of Claims.* Report [conc. capture of the brig Flying Fish] on the petition of G. Little, Mass.; Dec. 22. (B 507) — *Committee on the Message of the Pres. rel. to the Exploring of the Western Waters.* Report; Dec. 22. (B 507) — *Pres.* Message transm. accounts stating the several sums which have been expended on the Capitol, the President's house, the public offices, *etc.*; Dec. 23. (B 507) — *Com. on Commerce and Manufactures.* Report on the petition of S. Kingston, Philadelphia; 30 Dec. (Senate doc.? B 507) — *Com. on the Bill to Revive and Make Permanent an Act to prescribe the Mode of Making Evidence in Cases of Contested Elections for Members of the House.* Report; Dec. 30. (B 507) — **Documents** accomp. a bill making appropriations for support of government, 1807; Dec. 30. (Sen. doc.? B 486) — **Dana,** S. W. Motion [for the encouragement and security of seamen of the U. States]; Dec. 30. (B 507) — *Com. of Ways and Means.* Report on the petition of A. Benezet and others; Dec. 31. (B 507) — *Treasury Department.* Letter from Sec. transm. report rel. to the direct tax, specifying quotas assigned to each state, *etc.*; Dec. 31. (B 486) — *Com. of Revisal and Unfinished Business.* Report, in part, on such matters of business as were depending and undetermined at the last session; Jan. 2, 1807. (B 507) — **Dana,** S. W. Motion on prosecutions at law for libellous publications, or defamatory words touching persons holding offices under the U. S.; Jan. 2. (B 507) — **Dana,** S. W. Motion that a com. be appointed to inquire whether prosecutions at common law should be sustained in the courts of the U. S.; Jan. 2. (B 507) — *Com. of Revisal and Unfinished Business.* Further report on such laws of the U. S. as are near expiring; Jan. 5. (Sen. doc.? B 507) — *Committee [on] the Petition and Memorial of the Pres. and Directors of the Highland Turnpike Co.* Report; Jan. 5. (B 507) — *Com. on the Petition of A. J. Villard conc. Improvement in the Mode of Mounting Cannon.* Report; Jan. 5. (B 507) — *Navy Dept.* Message from the Pres. transm. report by Sec. of Navy rel. to state of the frigates; Jan. 5. (B 486) — *Treas. Dept.* Letter from the Treasurer, accomp. general acc'ts of receipts and expenditures; also, acc'ts for War and Navy Dep'ts, Oct. 1, 1805 - Sept. 30, 1806; Jan. 5. (B 486) — *Com. Appointed to Inquire what Description of Claims against the U. S. are Barred by the Statutes of Limitation.* Report; Jan. 6. (B 507) — *Post Office.* Letter from the Post Master Gen. transm. a report of the persons employed as clerks in his office, 1806, specifying the amount which they receive as yearly salaries; Jan. 6. (B 507) — *Treas. Dept.* Documents accomp. bill repealing acts laying duties on salt, and continuing in force the first section of Act further to protect commerce and seamen against the Barbary powers; Jan. 7. (B 486) — *Treas. Dept.* Letter from Secretary transmitting statement of amount of duties and drawbacks on goods, *etc.*, imported into U. S. and exported, 1803-05; Jan. 8. (B 486) — *Com. of Claims.* Report on the petition of S. Sayre; Jan. 12. (B 507) — *Com. of Commerce and Manufactures.* Report [on] a petition of the Rensselaer glass factory in N. Y., and of a window glass manufactory in the same State; Jan. 12. (B 507) — *Com. of Commerce and Manufactures.* Report [on] petitions on the Roanoke and Cashie Rivers, Edenton, N. C.; Jan. 12. (B 507) — *Com. on so much of the [President's Message]* *as Relates to Fortifications, etc.* Report; Jan. 12. (B 507) — *Dept. of State.* Report of Sec. inclosing list of clerks, 1806; [and] amount [of] salaries; Jan. 14. (Sen. doc.? B 486) — *War Department.* Letter from Sec. transm. report rel. to invalid pensioners; Jan. 14. (B 486) — **Documents** accomp. bill for defence of the mouth of the Mississippi, and for protection of N. Orleans; 15 Jan. (Sen. doc.? B 486) — *War Department.* Letter from Sec. transm. report of clerks in his office, and [that] of accountant of War Dept., 1806; specifying amount [of] salaries; Jan. 15. (B 486) — *Com. of Claims.* Report [on] the petition of J. Snowden; Jan. 19. (B 507) — *Post Office.* Letter from the Post Master Gen. transm. a statement of the expenses and net proceeds of the Dept. for one year ending June 30, 1806; Jan. 19. (Sen. doc.? B 507) — **Indiana Territory.** Letter from W. H. Harrison inclosing certain resolutions by the legislative council and House of [Indiana] Territory rel. to a suspension for a certain period of the sixth article of the compact between the U. S. and the territories and states north-west of the Ohio, made July 13, 1787; Jan. 21. (B 507) — *Pres.* Message transm. information touching an illegal combination against the Union, *etc.*; Jan. 22. (Sen. doc.? B 507) — *Post Office Dept.* Letter from the Postmaster Gen. accomp. with a report rel. to post roads; Jan. 22. (B 507) — *Pres.* Message transm. information touching an illegal combination of private individuals against the peace and safety of the Union, and a military exped. planned by them against the territories of a power in amity with the U. S.; Jan. 22. (Sen. doc.? B 507) — *Treas. Dept.* Letter transm. report of clerks, 1806; specifying amount [of] salaries; Jan. 22. (B 486) — *Com. of Claims.* Report on the petition of O. Pollock, Penn.; Jan. 23. (B 507) — **Documents** accomp. bill making compensation to Lewis, Clarke, and [others]; 23 Jan. (Sen. doc.? B 486) — *Pres.* Message transm further information touching an illegal combination of private individuals against the peace and safety of the Union, *etc.*; Jan. 26. (Sen. doc.? B 507) — *Treas. Dept.* Letter from the Sec. transm. report in obedience to an Act directing the Sec. to cause the coast of No. Carolina between Cape Fear and Cape Hatteras to be surveyed; Jan. 27. (B 486) — U. S. treaty accompanying a bill making appropriations for carrying into effect a treaty between the U. S. and the Chickasaw Indians; 27 Jan. (Sen. doc.? B 486) — *Mint.* Message from the Pres. communicating the report of the director; Jan. 28. (Sen. doc.? B 507) — *Treasury Department.* Letter from the Sec. inclosing copies of acc'ts of expenses in pub. prosecutions bef. the Circuit Court for Conn., Apr. and Sept. 1806; Jan. 28. (B 507) — *Pres.* Message transm. the annual account of the fund for defraying the contingent charges of government, 1806; Jan. 28. (Sen. doc.? B 486) — *Committee of Commerce and Manufactures.* Report [on] the memorial of E. Toppan [and others] of Mass.; 31 Feb. (B 507) — *Com. of Public Lands.* Report [on] the petition of officers who served in Amer. during the war between France and Gr. Brit.; Feb. 3. (B 507) — *Com. [on] an Act Establishing Circuit Courts in Ky., Tenn., and Ohio.* Report; Feb. 4. (B 507) — **Documents** accomp. a bill resp. seizures made under the authority of the U. S.; 4 Feb. (B 507) — *Pres.* Message transm. further information touching an illegal combination of private individuals against the peace and safety of the Union, and a military expedition planned by them against the territories of a power in amity with the U. S.; Feb. 10. (Sen. doc.? B 507) — *Com. on the Letter from W. H. Harrison, Gov. of Indiana Territory.* Report; Feb. 12. (B 507) — *Com. on the Report of the Sec. of State on the Petition of J. Jay.* Report; Feb. 17. (B 507) — **Clay, J.** Motion [that rules be added to the standing rules and orders of the House]; Feb. 19. (B 507) — *Pres.* Message communicating information of a treaty with Gr. Britain, *etc.*; Feb. 19. (Sen. doc.? B 507)

10th Cong. 1st sess., Oct. 26, 1807 - Apr. 2, 1808.

— Journal. Wash., 1807-[08]. 8°.

— - Supplemental journal of such proc. of Cong. as were ordered to be kept secret. [Wash., 1808.] 8°. (B 488)

— Ex. docs. *n.t.p.* [1807-08.] 8°.

Namely: **Papers** rel. to French affairs; 17 Dec. 1807. — *Pres.* Message transm. letter from Sec. of State to Mr. Monroe on the attack on the Chesapeake; corresp. of Mr. Monroe with the Brit. government, also Mr. Madison's corresp. with Mr. Rose on the same subject; March 23, 1808.

Also: *Surveyor of Public Buildings.* Letter and report on the [public] buildings; 28 Oct. 1807. (B 489) — **New York.** *Legislature.* Letter from the Pres. of the Senate, incl. resolutions of the legislature rel. to the protection of the port of N. Y.; Oct. 29. (B 489) — *Treas. Dept.* Letter from the Sec. transm. an estimate of extraordinary expenses incurred by the Navy Dept., 1807; 29 Oct. (B 487) — **Rhea, J.** Motion; Oct. 30. (Sen. doc.? B 489) — **Eaton, W.** Letter to the Speaker covering a communication from H. Caramelli, ex-Bashaw of Tripoli; Nov. 3. (B 489) — **Documents** accompanying the bill making further appropriations for the support of the Navy during 1807; 5 Nov. (Sen. doc.? B 487, 489) — *Committee of Elections.* Report on the petition of J. Barney; Nov. 9. (B 489) — *Com. of Revisal and Unfinished Business.* Report in part on such laws of the U. S. as have expired, *etc.*; Nov. 10. (Sen. doc.? B 489) — *Com. [on] the Petition of J. Jay.* Report; Nov. 13. (B 489) — *Com. of Claims.* Report [on] the petition of D. Buck; Nov. 16. (B 489) — *Com. on so Much of the Message of the Pres. as rel. to Aggressions Committed within our Ports and Waters by Foreign Armed Vessels.* Report, in part; Nov. 17. (B 488, 489) — *Com. Appointed to Prepare and Report such Standing Rules and Orders as are Proper to be Observed in this House.* Report; Nov. 19. (B 489) — *Com. on the Petition of A. J. Villard.* Report; Nov. 19. (B 489) — *Com. on the Petition of W. Levis, and H. Maxwell.* Report and bill; Nov. 19. (B 489) — *Pres.* Message transm. a copy of his proclamation interdicting the harbours and waters of the U. S. to British armed vessels; Nov. 19. (B 488, 489) — *Com. on so much of the Message of the Pres. as rel. to our Military and Naval Establishments.* Report, in part; Nov. 19. (B 489) — *Com. of Revisal and Unfinished Business.* Further report, in part; Nov. 21. (Sen. doc.? B 489) — *Com. of Ways and Means.* Report on the petitions of S. Beebee and E. Weld; Nov. 23. (B 489) — *Com. of Ways and Means.* Report [on] the petitions of the inspectors of the customs for the ports of Balt., N. Y., and Boston; with a report of the Sec. of the Treas.; Nov. 23. (B 489) — *Com. on so much of the Message of the Pres. as rel. to Aggressions Committed within our Ports and Waters by Foreign Armed Vessels.* Further report, in part; Nov. 24. (B 488) — *Com. on the Erection of a Bridge over the Potomac.* Report; Nov. 24. (B 489) — *Navy Dept.* Letter from the Sec. on so much of the message of the Pres. as rel. to aggressions committed within our ports and waters by foreign armed vessels; Nov. 24. (Sen. doc.? B 487, 488) — *Navy Dept.* Letters from the Sec. to the com. on so much of the Pres. message as relates to aggressions committed within our ports and waters by foreign armed vessels, *etc.*; Nov. 30. (Sen. doc.? B 489) — **Bassett, B.** Motion on standing rules and orders of the House; Dec. 1. (B 489) — **Randolph, J.** Motion [conc. support of officers and soldiers of the Revolution, arming and equipping the militia. *etc.*]; Dec. 1. (B 489) — *War Dept.* Letter from the Sec. inclosing three statements of the amount of merchandise and supplies purchased on behalf of the U. S., by the supt. of Indian trade, *etc.*; Dec. 1. (B 487) — *Com. on so much of the Message of the Pres. as rel. to the Military and Naval Establishments.* Report, in part; Dec. 2. (B 479) — *Com. on the Petition of O. Evans.* Report; Dec. 2. (B 489) — *Navy Dept.* Letter from the Sec. transm. a statement of the amount of merchandise and supplies purchased on behalf of the U. S. by the navy-agents in the different ports, *etc.*; Dec. 2. (B 487) — *War Dept.* Letter from the Sec. transm. a statement of the respective numbers of officers and soldiers comp. the army of the U. S.; Dec. 3. (B 487) — *Com. of Revisal and Unfinished Business.* Further report; Dec. 4. (Sen. doc.? B 489) — *Treas. Dept.* Letter from the Sec. accompanying a report and estimates of appropriations for 1808, *etc.*; Dec. 4. (B 487) — *Com. of Elections.* Amendatory report on the memorial of J. Barney; Dec. 7. (B 489) — *War Dept.* Letter from the Sec. on so much of the message of the Pres. as rel. to the military and naval establishments; Dec. 9. (B 487) — *Dept. of State.* Report of the Sec. on a message of the Pres., 6 Feb., transm. a memorial of the French minister on the claim of A. E. De Beaumarchais; Dec. 14. (Sen. doc.? B 487, 489) — *Com. of Elections.* Report on a letter and memorial from D. McFarland complaining of the undue election and return of J. Culpepper as a member of the House of N. C.; Dec. 17. (B 489) — *Com. on a Letter from W. Eaton Covering a Communication from H. Caramelli.* Report; Dec. 18. (B 489) — **Dana, S. W.** Motion [conc. conduct of merchant vessels]; Dec. 18. (B 489) — **Boucherie, A.** Petition; Dec. 18. (Sen. doc.? B 489) — *Com. on the Letters and Reports from the Commissioners under the Act for the Relief of the Refugees from the British Provinces.* Report; Dec. 22. (B 489) — **Crowninshield, J.** Motion [conc. establishment of telegraph]; Dec. 22. (B 489) — **Bassett, B.** Motion [that provision ought to be made to prohibit officers of the government from making contracts, on behalf of the U. S., with any member of either House, or with any other person for his or their use, *etc.*]; Dec. 29. (B 489) — *Treas. Dept.* Letter from the Sec. accompanying a bill intituled Act to protect the commerce and seamen of the U. S. against the Barbary powers; Dec. 29. (Sen. doc.? B 487) — *Pres.* Message communicating letters from Gov. Hull resp. the Indians in the vicinity of Detroit residing within our lines; Dec. 30. (Sen. doc.? B 489) — *Committee Appointed to Inquire into Facts rel. to the Conduct of J. Smith.* Report; Dec. 31. (B 1196) — *Post Office Dept.* Letter from the Post-Master General, with a report rel. to post roads within the U. S.; Jan. 7, 1808. (B 489) — *Com. of Claims.* Report on the petition of M. Barclay; Jan. 8. (B 489) — *Mint.* Message from the Pres. communicating the report of the Director of the Mint of the operations during the last year; Jan. 8. (Sen. doc.? B 489) — *Treas. Dept.* Message from the Pres. transm. the annual acc. of the fund for defraying the contingent charges of government for 1807; Jan. 8. (Sen. doc.? B 489) — *Com. of Commerce and Manufactures.* Report on the petition of sundry merchants and traders of Phila.; Jan. 11. (B 489) — **Clark, D.** Deposition rel. to the conduct of Gen. J. Wilkinson; Jan. 13. (B 489, 490) — *Treas. Dept.* Letter from the Sec. transm. a report referring the memorial of sundry merchants of Phila. praying the benefit of drawback on certain articles exported; Jan. 13. (Sen. document? B 487) — **Morrow, J.** Motion [that the Pres. be authorized to loan Ohio for seven years seven thousand stand of arms, *etc.*, for the purpose of arming, in part, the militia of said State]; Jan. 14. (B 489) — *Treas. Dept.* Letter from the Sec. transm. a report of the clerks in the Treasury Department, 1807; specifying the amount which they respectively receive as yearly salaries; Jan. 18. (B 487) — *War Dept.* Letter from the Sec. transm. a report in rel. to invalid pensioners; Jan. 18. (B 487) — *Treas. Dept.* Letter from the Treas. accomp. his general accounts of receipts and expenditures, [with] his accounts for the War and Navy Departments from Oct. 1, 1806 - Sept. 30, 1807; Jan. 18. (B 787) — *Treas. Dept.* Letter from the Sec. transm. a report prepared in obedience to An act regulating the currency of the foreign coins in the U. S.; Jan. 19. (B 487) — *Treas. Dept.* Letter from the Sec. transm. a statement of the amount of duties and drawbacks on goods, wares, and merchandise imported and exported, 1804–06; Jan. 19. (B 487, 489) — *Pres.* Message, [with] docs. and information [conc.] official conduct of Gen. J. Wilkinson; Jan. 20. (B 490) — *Treas. Dept.* Letter and report from the Sec. on the amount of tonnage employed in the exportation of articles the produce or manufacture of the U. S.; Jan. 20. (B 487) — *Com. of Commerce and Manufactures.* Report on the petitions and memorial of P. and J. W. Revere, [and others]; Jan. 21. (Sen. doc.? B 489) — *Navy Dept.* Letter from the Sec. on so much of the Pres. message as relates to our military and naval establishments; Jan. 25. (Sen. doc.? B 487) — *Dept. of State.* Letter from the Sec. transm. a list of the clerks in the Department of State, with the amount of salary allowed to each; Jan. 25. (B 487) — *Treas. Dept.* Letter from the Sec. accompanying a bill authorizing the raising of an additional number of seamen for the service of the U. S.; Jan. 25. (Sen. doc.? B 487) — *War Dept.* Letter from the Sec. transm. a list of the clerks in his office and in the office of the accountant of the War Department, with amount of salary; Jan. 25. (B 487) — **Campbell, G. W.** Motion proposing an amendment to the Constitution of the U. S. rel. to the judges of the Supreme Court and other courts of the U. S.; Jan. 30. (B 489) — *Com. of Claims.* Report on the memorial of C. Minifie; Jan. 30. (B 489) — *Pres.* Message transm. treaty at Detroit Nov. 17, 1807, between the U. S. and the Ottaway, Chippeway, Wyandot, and Pottawatomie Indians; Jan. 30. (B 489) — *Pres.* Message transm. a treaty of limits between the U. S. and the Choctaw Indians; Jan. 30. (B 489) — *Post Office Dept.* Report of the Post-Master General on the petition of S. Whiting; Feb. 3. (Sen. documents? B 489) — *Pres.* Message transmitting an official communication against the maritime rights of neutrals; Feb. 3. (B 488) — *Pres.* Message, communicating farther information in pursuance of two resolutions of the House, 13 Jan.; Feb. 4. (B 489) — *Com. of Commerce and Manufactures.* Resolution [on] the disposition of certain charts of the coast of North Carolina; Feb. 5. (B 487) — *Com. of Commerce and Manufactures.* Resolution, in the form of a concurrent resolution of the two Houses of Cong., to authorize the disposition of certain charts of the coast of N. C.; Feb. 5. (B 489) — *Treas. Dept.* Letter from the Sec. to J. O. Mosely, on the claim of M. Smith and D. Gates jointly, and D. Gates separately; Feb. 5. (Sen. doc.? B 487) — *War Dept.* Letter from the Sec. inclosing his report on the petition of A. Delozcair; Feb. 6. (B 487) — **Burwell, W. A.** Motion [conc. the expediency of authorizing the Pres. to procure arms for the U. S.]; Feb. 8. (Sen. doc.? B 489) — *Pres.* Message communicating information rel. to the commencement of war by the Dey of Algiers against the U. S.; Feb. 9. (Sen. doc.? B 489) — *Navy Dept.* Letter from the Sec. on so much of the message of the Pres. as relates to our military and naval establishments, respect. the number of seamen employed; Feb. 10. (Sen. doc.? B 487) — *Treas. Dept.* Letter from the Sec. accompanying the bill in addition to An act supplementary to the act intituled An act laying an embargo on all ships and vessels in the ports and harbors of the U. S.; Feb. 11. (Sen. doc.? B 487) — *Treas. Dept.* Letter from the Sec. to the chairman of the committee of commerce and manufactures; Feb. 11. (Sen. doc.? B 489) — *Pres.* Message communicating information that the late differences between the U. S. and the Dey of Algiers have been amicably adjusted; Feb. 15. (Sen. doc.? B 489) — *Com. of Claims.* Report on the petition of J. Shattuck; Feb. 17. (B 489) — *Pres.* Message communicating an additional report of the proc. of the commis. appointed to regulate the laying out a road from Cumberland, Maryland, to Ohio; Feb. 19. (Sen. doc.? B 489) — *Treas. Dept.* Document accompanying the bill extending the terms of credit on revenue bonds in certain cases, and for other purposes; Feb. 23. (B 487) — *Com. of Elections.* Amendatory report in relation to the contested election of P. B. Key; Feb. 24. (B 489) — **Penn.** *General Assemb.* Resolutions proposing an amendment to the Constitution of the U. S.; Feb. 24. (B 489) — **Smilie, J.** Motion [conc. violation of decorum and order in the House]; Feb. 24. (Sen. doc.? B 489) — *Post Office Dept.* Letter from the Assistant Post-Master Gen. inclosing a report in rel. to the mail route from Alexandria to Fredericksburg; Feb. 26. (B 489) — *War Dept.* Message inclosing a letter from the Sec. in rel. to an increase of the army, and authorizing the raising of twenty-four thousand volunteers; Feb. 26. (Sen. doc.? B 487) — **Clopton, J.** Motion proposing an amendment to the Constitution of the U. S.; Feb. 29. (Sen. doc.? B 489) — **Virginia.** *Legislature.* Resolution proposing an amendment to the Constitution of the U. S.; Feb. 29. (B 489, 1489) — **Document** accompanying the bill to punish conspiracies to commit treason against the U. S.; 2 March. (Sen. doc.? B 487) — *Com. of Claims.* Report on the petition of D. Cotton; March 7. (B 489) — *Pres.* Message communicating information of the situation of parcels of ground in and adjacent to New Orleans; March 7. (Sen. doc.? B 489) — *Commissioners of the Land Board for the District of Detroit in the Territory of Michigan.* Letter from the Sec. of the Treas. enclosing a copy of a representation from the Commissioners to investigate land titles in Michigan; March 7. (Sen. doc.? B 487) — *War Dept.* Letter from the Sec. transm. an additional report in rel. to invalid pensioners; March 7. (B 487) — **Document** accompanying the bill in addition to the Act to regulate the laying out and making a road from Cumberland, Maryland, to Ohio; 8 March. (Sen. doc.? B 489) — *Com. Appointed to Enquire if any Compensation ought to be made to Capt. Pike and his Companions, for their Services in Exploring the Mississippi River, etc.* Report; Mar. 9. (B 489) — *War Dept.* Letter from the Sec. transm. a further report in rel. to invalid pensioners; March 10. (B 489) — *War Dept.* Report of the Sec. on the petition of G. Hunter; Mar. 10. (B 487) — *Pres.* Message transm. two decrees, of the Emperor of the French, [and] of the King of Spain; March 17. (B 488) — *Com. on so much of the Message of the Pres. as rel. to the Military and Naval Establishments.* Report; March 18. (B 489) — **Documents** accompanying the bill for the relief of I. Briggs; 18 March. (B 489) — **Rowan, J.** Motion for inquiry into the conduct of A. Innis, district judge of Kentucky; March 21. (Sen. doc.? B 490) — *Dept. of State.* Message from the Pres. transm. a letter from the Sec. of State to Mr. Monroe on the attack of the Chesapeake, *etc.*; March 22. (B 488) — **Monroe, —.** Letter to the Sec. of State, Feb. 28; March 23. (B 488) — **Papers** rel. to French affairs communicated by Gen. Armstrong to Mr. Monroe; March 23. (B 488) — *Dept. of State.* Letters from the Sec. to Mr. Monroe on the impressments, *etc.*; March 23. (B 488) — *Dept. of State.* Letters from the Sec. to Monroe and Pinkney on subjects committed to their joint negotiation, with their communications to the Sec. of State; March 23. (B 488, 1490) — *Pres.* Message resp. the execution of the act for fortifying the ports and harbours of the U. S.; March 25. (Sen. doc.? B 489) — *Com. Appointed to Inquire what Compensation should be Allowed for issuing Commissions, rel. to Claims under the Act to Provide for Persons who were Disabled by Wounds Received in the War.* Report; March 28. (B 489) — **Champagny, J. B. N. de.** Letter to Gen. Armstrong; Apr. 2. (B 488) — *Committee on so much* *of Pres. Message as respects Foreign Relations.* Report, in part; Nov. 22. (B 491) — *Pres.* Message, communicating proclamation, in consequence of opposition, in the neighborhood of Lake Champlain, to laws laying an embargo; Nov. 30. (B 491) — *Pres.* Message, transm. copies of all acts, decrees, *etc.*, affecting commercial rights of neutral nations, since 1791; Dec. 23. (B 491, W 86) — *Com. on Military and Naval Establishments.* Report, in part, on resolution for placing the nation in a more complete state of defence; Dec. 26. (B 491) — **Erskine, D. M.** Letter to the Sec. of State on the British orders in council, 11 Nov. 1807; April 2. (B 488) — **Campbell, G. W.** Motion [conc. embargo]; Apr. 8. (B 489) — *Treas. Dept.* Documents accompanying the bill making a farther appropriation for the support of government, 1808; April 13. (Sen. doc.? B 487) — *Com. [on] a Bill to make good a Deficit in the Appropriation of 1807, and to make a farther Appropriation for Completing the South Wing of the Capitol.* Report; April 21. (B 489)

10th Cong. 2d sess., Nov. 7, 1808 - March 3, 1809.

— Journal. Wash., 1808-[09]. 8°.

— - Supplemental journal of the House, Nov. 8 - 25, 1808. *n.t.p.* [Wash., 1808.] 8°. (B 491)

— Ex. docs. *n.t.p.* [1808.] 8°. (Sen. docs.?)

Namely: *Pres.* Message; Nov. 8, 1808; — Docs. accomp. message; Nov. 9. — *Com. on so much of the Pres. Message as Respects our Foreign Relations.* Report in part; Nov. 22.

— Ex. docs. *n.t.p.* [1808-09.] 8°.

Namely: *Com. on the Pres. Message as Respects our For. Relations.* Report in part; Nov. 22, 1808. — *Pres.* Message communicating further information rel. to the affairs of the U. S. with Gr. Brit.; Jan. 17, 1809. (*Also* B 491)

— Ex. docs. *n.t.p.* [1809.] f°.

Namely: *Treas. Dept.* Letter from Sec. transm. two statements of the importations in Amer. and foreign vessels, 1 Oct. 1806 - 30 Sept. 1807; Feb. 22, 1809; — Report of Sec. of the official emoluments of the officers of the Customs, 1 Jan. - 30 Sept. 1808; Feb. 27; — Letter from Sec. transm. a statement of the balances charged on the books of the Treas. for advances made prior to the 30 June, 1808; March 3.

Also: *Mint.* Message, transm. report of the Director of the Mint; Jan. 7, 1809. (Sen. doc.? B 491) — *Com. on Public Lands.* Report [on] petitions from inhab. of Ohio, and resolution to inquire into the expediency of abolishing credit on pub. lands; Jan. 19. (B 491) — *War Dept.* Letter from Sec. transm. report in rel. to invalid pensioners; Jan. 19. (B 491) — *Pres.* Message communicating further inform. rel. to affairs with Gr. Brit.; Jan. 30. (Sen. doc.? B 491) — **Durrell, D. M.** Motion, considering capture, *etc.*, of a vessel of the U. S. as a declaration of war; Feb. 4. (Sen. doc.? B 491)

— FURTHER and still more important suppressed documents, [1807-08]. [Flatbush, N. Y., 1809.] (B 531)

— *Same.* [Boston, 1809.] 8°. (B 1117)

— Ex. doc.] *Pres.* Message to both Houses of Congress; Nov. 8, 1808. Wash., 1808. 8°. (Senate doc.?)

— - Docs. accomp. the message from the Pres. at the commencement of the 2d sess. of the 10th Cong.; Nov. 9, 1808. *n.t.p.* [Wash., 1808.] 8°. (Senate doc.?)

— - *Treas. Dept.* Report of the Sec. [on] 'An act to establish the Treas. Dept.'; [Dec. 10, 1808]. *n.t.p.* [1808.] f°.

11th Cong. 1st sess., May 22 - June 28, 1809.

— Journal. Wash., 1809. 8°.

— Ex. docs. *n.t.p.* [1809.] f°.

Namely: *Treas. Dept.* Letter from Sec. transm. his annual report; June 2, 1809. — *Navy Dept.* Letter from Sec. transm. a statement of the number of gun boats built, *etc.*; June 8. — *War Dept.* Letter from the Sec. transm. three statements, A, B, C, of contracts made by the Sec. and the Purveyor of Public Supplies, 1808; June 17; — Report of the Sec. [on] Act making further provision for the support of public credit and redemption of the public debt; June 23. — *Com. to inquire whether Monies drawn from the Treasury have been faithfully Applied to the Object for which they were Appropriated, etc.* Report in part; June 27, 1809. — *Committee of Investigation.* Supplemental report; June 28.

— BAYLIES, W. View of the proceedings of the Ho. of Rep. in the Plymouth election. Boston, **1809**. 8°. (B 1838)

11th Cong. 2d sess., Nov. 27, 1809 - May 1, 1810.

— Journal. Wash., 1809. 8°.

— Ex. docs. *n.t.p.* [1809.] 8°.

Namely: *Pres.* Message at the commencement of 2d sess., 11th Cong.; Nov. 29, 1809; — Docs. accomp. the message of the Pres.; Nov. 29, 1809.

— Ex. docs. *n.t.p.* [1809-10.] f°.

Namely: *Treas. Dept.* Letter from the Comptroller transm. a statement of the accounts in the Treas., War, and Navy Depts. which have remained more than three years unsettled, *etc.*; Dec. 1, 1809. — *Navy Dept.* Message transm. report of Sec. cont. statements referred to in the message of the 29th ult.; Dec. 5. — *Treas. Dept.* Letter from Sec. transm. his annual report, *etc.*; Dec. 8. — *Navy Dept.* Letter from the Sec. transm. a report on the Navy Pension Fund; Jan. 6, 1810. — *Treas. Dept.* Message transm. report of Sec. on disbursements in the intercourse with the Barbary powers; Jan. 22. — Letter from Sec. transm. annual statement of the emoluments of the officers employed in the collection of the Customs for 1809; March 16. — *Dept. of State.* Message transm. report of Sec. State in compliance with a resolution of the Ho. of the 23d inst.; April 27.

Also: *Pres.* Important state papers; documents accompanying the president's message; Nov. 29, 1809. (Sen. doc.? **B 474, C 190, 194**) — *Same.* [Another ed.] [Boston.] (**B 1490, 1885**) — **Documents** accompanying bill for relief of H. Caldwell and A. Jackson; 22 Dec. (Sen. doc.? **B 1490**) — *Treas. Dept.* Report of the Sec. resp. the direct tax; Dec. 28. (**B 1000**) — *Pres.* Message resp. our for. relations; Jan. 3, 1810. (Sen. doc.? B 509) — *Com. on the Naval Establishment.* Further report, in part, on navy hospitals; Jan. 4. (Sen. doc.? B 509) — *Navy Dept.* Letter from the Sec. trans. a statement of the expenditure and application of the monies drawn from the Treas.; 4 March - 30 Sept.; Jan. 5. (B 509) — *Com. on so much of the Message of the Pres. as rel. to the Naval Establishment of the U. S.*; Report in part; Jan. 6. (B 509) — *Treas. Dept.* Letter from the Sec. accomp. report and estimates of appropriations for 1810, *etc.*; Jan. 6. (B 509) — *Com. on so much of the Message of the Pres. as rel. to the Military Establishment of the U. S.* Report, in part; Jan. 8. (B 509) — *Com. on the Public Lands.* Report on the petition of J. Garret; Jan. 8. (Sen. doc.? B 509) — *Navy Dept.* Letter from the Sec. transm. a report in obedience to the act regulating and fixing the compensation of clerks, *etc.*; Jan. 9. (B 509) — *Com. of Claims.* Report on the petition of E. Hamilton; Jan. 11. (B 509) — *Com. of Claims.* Report on the petition of R. Taylor; Jan. 11. (Sen. doc.? B 509) — *Com. on the Pres. Message Communicating a Report of the Surveyor of the Public Buildings.* Report; Jan. 11. (Sen. doc.? B 509) — *Mint.* Message from the Pres. communicating a report of the Director of the Mint, 1809; Jan. 11. (Sen. doc.? (B 509) — *Treas. Dept.* Letter from the Sec. transm. a report on the petition of A. Buck; Jan. 11. (B 509) — *Dept. of State.* Message communicating a report of the Sec. of State requesting information rel. to the blockade of the ports of the Baltic by France; Jan. 12. (B 509) — *Dept. of State.* Message from the Pres. communicating a report of the Sec. requesting information resp. seizures, *etc.*, of the ships and merchandise of the citizens of the U. S. under the authority of Denmark; Jan. 12. (B 509) — *Com. of Claims.* Report on the petition of M. Lapsly; Jan. 17. (B 509) — **Documents** accompanying the bill for the relief of I. Briggs; Jan. 17. (Sen. doc.? B 509) — *War Dept.* Letter from the Sec. transm. a report of the names of the clerks employed in that department, 1809; Jan. 18. (B 509) — *War Dept.* Letter from the Sec. transm. an account of sales of public arms; Jan. 20. (B 509) — *Com. of Claims.* Report on the petition of J. Thomson; Jan. 23. (B 509) — *Treas. Dept.* Message from the Pres. transm. an account of the contingent expenses of government, 1809; Jan. 23. (Sen. doc.? B 509) — *Treas. Dept.* Letter from the Sec. transm. copies of instructions to the collectors of the customs; Jan. 24. (B 509) — *Com. [on] the Expediency of Allowing an Additional Judge to the Mississippi Territory.* Report; Jan. 25. (Sen. doc.? B 509) — *Treas. Dept.* Letter from the Sec. transm. a statement of the monies expended during 1809; Jan. 25. (B 509) — **Documents** accompanying the appropriation bill for 1810; Jan. 30. (Sen. doc.? B 509) — *Com. of Claims.* Report on the petition of R. Elwell; Jan. 31. (B 509) — *Com. [on] the Petitions of Sundry Surviving Officers of the late Revolutionary Army.* Report; Jan. 31. (B 509) — *Com. on the Petition of D. Boon.* Report; Feb. 1. (B 509) — *Navy Dept.* Message from the Pres. transm. copies of the orders issued under the present or any former administration, with resp. to foreign armed ships in waters of the U. S.; Feb. 1. (B 509) — *Com.*

for the District of Columbia. Report on the several petitions rel. to the Bank of Alexandria, of Potomac, of Wash., and of the Union Bank of Georgetown; Feb. 2. (Sen. doc.? B 509) — *Com. of Claims.* Report on the petition of P. Landais; Feb. 5. (B 509) — *Dept of State.* Message from the Pres. transm. a report of the Sec. [conc.] free navigation of the Mobile, *etc.*; Feb. 9. (B 509) — *Treas. Dept.* Letter from the Sec. to the chairman of the com. of claims [in rel. to the claim of P. Audrain]; Feb. 14. (Sen. doc.? B 509) — *Com.* [*on*] *the Memorial of the Stockholders of the Bank of the U. S.* Report; Feb. 19. (B 509) — *Pres.* Message transm. copies of communications to France and Gr. Brit. with resp. to orders and decrees of either violating the lawful commerce and neutral rights of the U. S. also communicating information touching the forgery of papers purporting to be those of Amer. vessels; Feb. 19. (B 509) — *Com. of Commerce and Manufactures.* Report on the petition of G. Armroyd & Co.; Feb. 21. (B 509) — **Papers** rel. to the ship Jane, accomp. a message from the Pres.; Feb. 21. (Sen. doc.? B 509) — *Post Office Dept.* Letter from the Post Master General; incl. a report and bill to establish post roads; Feb. 22. (B 509) — *Com. of Claims.* Report on the petition of A. St. Clair; Feb. 23. (B 509) — *Com.* [*on*] *the Petition of T. Campbell.* Report; Feb. 27. (B 509) — *Com. on the Petition of A. Dardin.* Report; Feb. 28. (B 509) — *Treas. Dept.* Letter from the Sec. to the chairman of the Com. of Commerce and Manuf. accompanying a bill for the relief of the collectors of Phila. and Norfolk; 28 Feb. (Sen. doc.? B 509) — **Poindexter, G.** Motion for the institution of an action in the District Court of New Orleans to try the right to the batture; March 1. (Sen. doc.? B 509) — *Post Office Dept.* Letter from the Post Master Gen. transm. a report of the names of clerks, and salaries; March 6. (B 510) — *Pres.* Message transm. treaties concluded with sundry tribes of Indians; March 6. (Sen. doc.? B 510) — *Dept. of State.* Letter from the Sec. on the subject of foreigners naturalized as citizens of the U. S. and who have been registered as Amer. seamen; Mar. 9. (Sen. doc.? B 510) — *Com. on Public Lands.* Report on the petition of M. Piercy; Mar. 13. (B 510) — *Treas. Dept.* Letter from the Sec. transm. a statement of the emoluments and expenditures of the collector of Balt., 1808–09; Mar. 13. (B 510) — *Com. of Claims.* Report on the petition of M. Young; Mar. 14. (B 510) — *Com. on the Petition of A. Scott, of So. Carolina.* Report; 14 March. (B 510) — **Poydras, J.** Speech in support of the right of the public to the batture in front of St. Mary; March 14. (Sen. doc.? B 510) — *Com. of Conference.* Report on the disagreeing vote of the two Houses on the amendments to the bill respect. the commercial intercourse between the U. S. and Gr. Brit. and France; Mar. 15. (B 510) — *Com. on Public Lands.* Report on the petition of S. C. Young; March 17. (B 510) — *Pres.* Message transm. a copy of a treaty concluded with the Kickapoo Indians; March 17. (Sen. doc.? B 510) — *Treas. Dept.* Letter from the Sec. in answer to a letter of the chairman of the Com. of Ways and Means, requesting information as to the most eligible method of obtaining loans; March 21. (B 510) — *Com. of Commerce and Manuf.* Report on the petition of A. Buck; March 23. (B 510) — *Com. on the Comptroller's Report of Unsettled Balances.* Report; March 23. (B 510) — *Com. on the Petition of A. Whipple.* Report; March 26. (Senate doc.? B 510) — *Com. to Inquire into the State of the ancient Public Records and Archives of the U. S.* Report; Mar. 27. (B 510) — *Pres.* Message, requesting a copy of any letters or despatches from Mr. Pinkney since his receipt of the letter of Nov. 23, 1809, from the Sec. of State; Mar. 28. (B 510) — *Post Office Dept.* Letter from the Post Master Gen. transm. two reports prepared in obedience to the resolutions of the House; March 29. (B 510) — *Treas. Dept.* Letter from the Sec. to the chairman of the Com. of Claims; March 31. (Sen. doc.? B 510) — *Com. on a Resolution rel. to the Establishment of a National Bank.* Report; April 2. (B 510) — **Documents** accompanying a bill for the relief of A. Buck; April 3. (B 510) — *Com. of Claims.* Report on the petition of C. Bean; April 9. (Sen. doc.? B 510) — *Committee of Claims.* Report on the petition of L. and C. Garanger, French officers in the Revolutionary war; April 9. (Sen. doc.? B 510) — *Treas. Dept.* Letter from the Sec. transm. a report, in part, on Amer. manufactures; April 19. (B 510) — *Treas. Dept.* Letter from the Sec. transm. his report rel. to advances of public money to W. Short; April 26. (B 510) — *Com. on Causes of the great Mortality in that Detachment of the Army ordered for Defence of New Orleans.* Report; Apr. 27. (B 508) — *Com.* [*on*] *Conduct of Brig. Gen. J. Wilkinson.* Report; May 1. (B 508) — **Macon, N.** Motion proposing an amendment to the Constitution of the U. S.; May 1. (B 510) — *Pres.* Message transm. [report of Sec. of State, *etc.*,] rel. to our relations with Gr. Brit. and France; May 1. (B 510)

— — Ex. doc.] **Important** state paper; docs. accompanying the Pres. message to Congress, Nov. 29, 1809. *n.t.p.* [Boston, *Boston Gazette office*,] 1809. 8°.

11th Cong. 3d sess., Dec. 3, 1810 – *March* 3, 1811.

— Ex. docs. *n.t.p.* [1810–11.] f°.

Namely: *Treas. Dept.* Letter from Sec. transm. annual statement of duties and drawbacks on goods, *etc.*, imported and exported, 1807–09; Dec. 17, 1810; — Report of Sec. accomp. statement of merchandise exported during year ending 30 Sept. last [1810]; Feb. 7, 1811.

Also: *Pres.* Message to Cong.; Dec. 5. (Sen. doc.? B 510) — **Documents** accompanying the message of the Pres. to Cong.; Dec. 5. (Sen. doc.? B 510) — **United Illinois and Wabash Land Companies.** Memorial; Dec. 10. (Sen. doc.? B 508) — *Dept. of State.* Message from the Pres. enclosing a report of the Sec. of State rel. to funds for the relief and protection of destitute Amer. seamen in foreign countries; Dec. 12. (Sen. doc.? B 510) — *Com. of Revisal and Unfinished Business.* Report, in part; Dec. 14. (Sen. doc.? B 510) — *Bank of the U. S.* Mem. of the stockholders; Dec. 18. (Sen. Doc.? B 510) — *Dept. of State.* Letter from the Sec. enclosing a statement of the public expenditures for the relief of Amer. seamen in Europe, *etc.*; Dec. 19. (Sen. doc.? B 510) — *Com. on Public Lands.* Report on the petition of sundry officers and soldiers who served in the British army in Amer. in the war between Eng. and France; Dec. 24. (B 510) — **Phila. Merchants.** Petition praying exemption from the provisions of the non-intercourse law; Dec. 24. (Sen. doc.? B 510) — **Swoope, I.** Resolutions [concerning bills of exchange on Degen, Purviance, & Co.]; Dec. 24. (B 510) — *Com. of Claims.* Report on the petition of A. Dardin; Dec. 27. (B 510) — *Com. of Claims.* Report on the petition of A. Dardin; Dec. 27. (B 510) — *Com. of Claims.* Report on the petition of J. Shattuck; Dec. 27. (B 510) — *Com. of Claims.* Report on the petition of R. Taylor; Dec. 27. (Sen. doc.? B 510) — *Com.* [*on*] *the Bill from the Senate to suspend the Second Section of the Act, entituled An Act regulating Foreign Coins and for Other Purposes.* Report; Dec. 27. (B 510) — *Com. on Public Lands.* Report respect. the location of Virginia land warrants; Dec. 28. (B 510) — *Pres.* Message transm. further information rel. to the duties imposed by the Emperor of France on all articles [imported] in Amer. vessels, *etc.*; Dec. 31. (B 508, 510) — *Treas. Dept.* Letter from Sec. transm. estimates of appropriations for 1811; also receipts and expend., Oct. 1, 1809 – Sept. 30, 1810; a statement of balances unexpended; Dec. 31. (B 508) — *Com. on the Public Lands.* Report on the petition of W. Coleman; Jan. 3, 1811. (Sen. doc.? B 512) — *Com.* [*on*] *Mr. Macon's Resolution proposing an Amendment to the Constitution.* Report; Jan. 4. (B 512) — *War Dept.* Letter from the Sec. transm. an account of the sale of public arms to the State of Maryland; Jan. 4. (B 512) — *Treas. Dept.* Letter from the Sec. [with] report and estimates of appropriations for 1810; Jan. 6. (B 509) — *Com. of Claims.* Report on the petition of J. Calhoun; Jan. 7. (B 512) — *Com. of Public Lands.* Report on the petitions of R. Tervin, S. Mims, E. Lewis, J. Wilson and the Baptist Church at Salem of the Mississippi Territory; Jan. 7. (B 512) — *Navy Department.* Report of the Sec. resp. several bills of exchange drawn on Degen, Purviance, & Co.; Jan. 7. (B 512) — *Select Committee on the Petition of Capt. T. Campbell.* Report; Jan. 7. (B 512) — *Committee* [*on*] *Admitting Mississippi into the Union as a State* Report; Jan. 9. (B 512) — *Treas. Dept.* Letter from Sec. transm. information rel. to the claim of the Board of Commissioners west of Pearl River, Miss., to additional compensation; Jan. 9. (B 512) — *Pres.* Message transm. a copy of a letter from the minister of the U. S. at London to the Sec. of State and another to the Brit. Secretary for Foreign Affairs; Jan. 14. (Sen. doc.? B 512) — *Navy Dept.* Letter from the Sec. transm. his annual report of the names and salaries of the clerks in the Navy Department; Jan. 14. (B 512) — *Pres.* Message transm. a copy of his proclamation, 2d Nov. 1810, and also a copy of the circular letter of the Sec. of the Treas. to the collectors of the customs; Jan. 15. (B 512) — *Surveyor of Public Buildings.* Message from the Pres. transm. a report of the Surveyor of public buildings rel. to the progress and present state; Jan. 15. (Sen. doc? B 512) — *Treas. Dept.* Message from the Pres. transm. an account of the contingent expenses of government, 1810; Jan. 15. (Sen. doc.? B 512) — *Pres.* Message transm. reports of the superintendent of the city, and of the Surveyor of the Public Buildings, of the expenditure of the money appropriated May 1, 1810, for completing the Capitol; Jan. 15. (B 512) — *Navy Dept.*

Letter from Sec. transm. statement of contracts made by the Dept., 1810; Jan. 15. (B 512) — *War Dept.* Letter from the Sec. transm. his ann. report of the names and salaries of the clerks in the dept., 1810; Jan. 15. (B 512) — *Com. on Opening a Road from Vincennes in Indiana towards Dayton, Ohio.* Report; Jan. 17. (B 512) — *Com. on Public Lands.* Report on the petition of commis. to fix a site for Pulaski in Tenn.; Jan. 18. (Sen. doc.? B 512) — **New Haven. Merchants.** Memorial; Jan. 18. (B 512) — *War Dept.* Letter from the Sec. to the com. on that part of the message of the Pres. rel. to land forces and fortifications transm. estimate of monies required for 1811; Jan. 18. (B 512) — *Com. of Claims.* Report on the petition of E. Brooke; Jan. 19. (B 512) — *Select Com. [on] the Petition of J. Brumback and Others.* Report; Jan. 19. (B 512) — **Mississippi Territory.** *Legislative Council, and House of Representatives.* Memorial praying admission as a State in the Union; Jan. 21. (B 512) — *Treas. Dept.* Letter from the Treas. transm. his general accounts of receipts and expenditures; also his accounts for the War and Navy Dept.; 1 Oct. 1809-1 Oct., 1810; Jan. 22. (B 512) — *Com. on Public Lands.* Report on the memorial of the Legislative Council and House of Indiana Territory; Jan. 23. (Sen. doc.? B 512) — *Select Committee [on] the Memorial of J. Bioren, W. J. Duane, and R. C. Weightman.* Report; Jan. 23. (B 512) — *Select Committee on the Petition of J. Craig.* Report; Jan. 24. (B 512) — *Select Com. on the Memorial of Gen. A. St. Clair.* Report; Jan. 24. (B 512) — *Treas. Dept.* Additional estimates of appropriations for 1811; Jan. 26. (B 512) — *Treas. Dept.* Message from the Pres. transm. a report of the superintendent of Wash. of the expenditures under the act for the better accommodation of the general Post-Office and Patent Office; Jan. 26. (B 512) — *Select Com. on the Memorial of B. Tyler, Jr., and J. Tyler.* Report; Jan. 28. (B 512) — *Com. on Public Lands.* Report on the memorial of the United Illinois and Wabash Land Companies; Jan. 30. (B 512) — **Macon, N.** Motion [as amended] proposing an amendment to the Constitution of the U. S.; with the amendment offered by Mr. Quincy in com. of the whole on the state of the Union; Jan. 30. (B 512) — *Navy Dept.* Letter from the Sec. to the Com. on the Naval Establishment; Jan. 30. (Sen. doc.? B 512) — *Post Office Dept.* Letter from the Post Master Gen. transm. report on the petitions of the Synod of Pittsburg, [and others]; Jan. 31. (B 512) — *Com. of Claims.* Report on the petition of J. Nelson; Feb. 1. (512) — *Com. of Commerce and Manufactures.* Report on so much of the message of the Pres. as rel. to the encouragement of Amer. manufactures and navigation; Feb. 5. (512) — *Com. on so much of the Message of the Pres. as rel. to the Encouragement of American Manufactures and Navigation.* Report; Feb. 5. (B 512) — *Select Com. to whom was referred sundry Bills from the Senate, to Incorporate sundry Banks in the District of Columbia.* Report; Feb. 5. (B 512) — *Treas. Dept.* Letter from the Sec. in reply to a letter from the chairman of the Com. of Ways and Means, respecting the imposition of additional duties on importations; Feb. 6. (B 512) — *Com. of Claims.* Report on repealing acts of limitation; Feb. 7. (B 513) — *Treas. Dept.* Letter from the Sec. enclosing his report on the petition of the inspectors of the customs for Philadelphia; Feb. 7. (B 512) — *Select Com. [on] Letter of W. Lambert rel. to precedents of Order in the House.* Report; Feb. 11. (B 513) — *Navy Dept.* Letter from Sec. transm. docs. exhibiting experiments in the city and harbor of N. Y., [under] Act making appropriation for the practical use of the torpedo; Feb. 14. (B 513) — *Com. on Public Lands.* Report on reports and decisions of the commis. appointed to settle claims to land in Kaskaskia; Feb. 15. (B 513) — *Com. [on] that Part of the President's Message which rel. to Establishment of a Seminary by the National Legislature.* Report; Feb. 11. (Sen. doc.? B 511) — *Dept. of State.* Message from the Pres. transm. report of the Sec. requesting information rel. to legal repeal or modification of orders and decress [*sic*] affect. nuetral [*sic*]. commerce since Nov. 1, 1810; Feb. 19. (B 511) — *Treas. Dept.* Letter from the Sec. to the com. of com. and manuf. on the propriety of encouraging culture of hemp by protecting impost duties or by prohibiting importation; Feb. 21. (B 511) — *Pres.* Message accomp. by return of the bill entitled Act incorp. the Prot. Epis. Ch. in Alexandria, D. C.; Feb. 21. (B 511) — *Com. [on] the Conduct of Gen. Wilkinson.* Report; Feb. 26. (Sen. doc.? B 511) — *Pres.* Message transm. reports from superintendent of the city and Surveyor of Pub. Buildings, exhib. the sum already expended on the capitol, sum necessary to finish each wing, and sum now due for labor and materials; Feb. 26. (B 511) — *Pres.* Message, returning bill entitled Act for relief of R. Tervin and others and Baptist Ch. at Salem Meeting House, Miss. Territory; Feb. 28. (B 511) — **Barlow, J.** Letter to the Speaker of the House [with] letter of the comptroller of the Treas. stating settlement of accs. with Barbary; Mar. 1. (B 511) — *War Dept.* Letter from the Sec. transm. acc. of expenses of the national armories at Springfield and Harper's Ferry; Mar. 2. (B 513) — *War Dept.* Report of Sec. on petition of T. Simpson; Mar. 2. (B 513)

— Ex. doc.] *Treas. Dept.* Report from Sec. on Amer. manufactures; Apr. 19, 1810. Boston, 1810. 8°.

12th Cong. 1st sess., Nov. 4, 1811 - *July* 6, 1812.

— Journal. Wash., 1811. 2 v. (v. 2 w.). 8°.

— Ex. docs. *n.t.p.* [1811-12.] 2 v. 8°.

Contents. Vol. 1. *Pres.* Message; Nov. 5, 1811; — Docs. accomp. the message of the President; Nov. 6. (*Also* B 513) — *Navy Dept.* Proceedings of a court of inquiry on board the U. S. frigate President; 30 Aug. — *Dept. of State.* Message communicating copies of a correspondence between the Brit. minister and the Sec. State rel. to the agression committed by a Brit. ship of war on the U. S. frigate Chesapeake; Nov. 14. — **West Florida.** Petition of inhabitants; Nov. 20. — *Com. of Elections.* Report on the petition of J. Taliaferro contesting the election of J. P. Hungerford; Nov. 21. — *Com. of Revisal and Unfinished Business.* Report; Nov. 21. — *Com. on the Public Lands.* Report [on the] provision to be made respecting the location of Virginia military land warrants, *etc.*; Nov. 26. — *Treas. Dept.* Annual report of the Sec. in obedience to the Act regulating the currency of foreign coins in the U. S., 10 Apr. 1806; Nov. 28. — *Com. on the Expediency of Laying out and Making the Roads contemplated by the Treaty of Brownstown*, 25 Nov., 1808. Report; Nov. 28. — *Com. on so much of the Message of the Pres. as rel. to our Foreign Relations.* Report; Nov. 29. (*Also* B 513) — *Com. to Prepare Standing Rules and Orders [of] the House.* Report; Dec. 2. — *Treas. Dept.* Letter from the Sec. rel. to the evasions of the non-importation act; Dec. 2. — *Com. on the Public Lands.* Report on the petition of the Legislative Council and Ho. of Reps. of Indiana Territory; Dec. 5; — Report on the petition of the Mayor and Aldermen of N. Orleans; Dec. 5. — *Com. on the President's Message rel. to the Spanish American Colonies.* Report; Dec. 10. — *Com. of Claims.* Report on the petition of J. Shattuck; Dec. 10. — *Treas. Dept.* Docs. accomp. a bill to authorize the refunding of the duties of importation of certain copper articles; Dec. 11. — *Com. on the Message of the Pres. rel. to the Manufacture of Cannon, etc.* Report; Dec. 16. — **Mississippi Territory.** *Ho.* Letter from the Speaker enclosing a copy of a presentment against H. Toulmin; Dec. 16. — *War Dept.* Docs. accomp. the bill providing ordnance and other military stores; 16 Dec. — *Com. of Claims.* Report on the petition of J. Murray; Dec. 17. — *Com. [on] a Memorial of the Legislative Council and Ho. of Reps. of Mississippi Territory, etc.* Report; Dec. 17. — *Com. [on] the Message of the Pres. rel. to the Defence of our Maritime Frontier.* Report in part; Dec. 17. — *Com. [on] the President's Message rel. to the Naval Establishment.* Report; Dec. 17. — *Com. on the Public Lands.* Report [on] the reports and decisions of the Commis. for settling claims to land in the district of Kaskaskia; Dec. 17. — **Indiana Territory.** *Gov.* Message from the President transmitting two letters from Gov. Harrison [conc.] the expedition against the hostile Indians on the Wabash, Dec. 19. — **Washington.** Petition of inhabitants; Dec. 19; — [Another] petition; Dec. 19. — *Com. of Claims.* Report [on] the expediency of repealing or suspending the statutes of limitation; Dec. 21. — **New York.** *Legislature.* Message from the President transm. the copy of an act of the Legislature of N. Y. rel. to a canal navigation from the Great Lakes to Hudson River; Dec. 23. — *Post Office Dept.* Report of the Postmaster General on the petitions of the Synod of Presbyters, *etc.*; Dec. 27. — *Com. of Com. and Manuf.* Report on the petition of E. Hubbel; Dec. 30. — *Com. of Ways and Means.* Report on the petitions of the Collectors of the Ports of Phila., Norfolk, *etc.*, and of the Naval officer of the Port of Phila.; Dec. 30. — *Treas. Dept.* Letter from the Sec. transm. estimates of appropriations for service of 1812; Dec. 31. — *Com. of Claims.* Report on the petition of J. Connell; Jan. 1, 1812. — *Com. on Post Offices and Post Roads.* Report [on] the petitions of the Synod of Presbyters, *etc.*, and the report of the Postmaster Gen.; Jan. 3.

2. Documents accompanying a bill to authorize the Secretary to purchase of W. Lewis his patent-right to the new method of lighting light-houses, *etc.*; 3 Jan. 1812. — *Com. of Ways and Means.* Supplementary report on the petitions of the Collectors of the Ports of Phila., Norfolk, *etc.*; Jan. 6. — *Com. [on] the Message of the Pres. transm. Letters from Gov. Harrison [on]

the Expedition against the Indians, etc. Report; Jan. 8. — *Navy Dept.* Statement of the clerks employed during 1811, with the salary of each; Jan. 8. — *Treas. Dept.* Letter, transm. statement of the banks in which the public monies are deposited; Jan. 13. — *Dept. of State.* Pres. message transm. copies of a correspondence between the Brit. minister and Sec. State.; Jan. 16; — Message communicating a letter from the Brit. minister to the Sec. State disavowing any agency of the Brit. government in the hostile measures of the Indian tribes; Jan. 17. — *Com. of Ways and Means.* Letter from chairman to the Sec. Treas. rel. to the revenue for the service of the U. S. for present and future years, *etc.*; Jan. 20. (*Also* **B 1491**) — *Dept. of State.* Letter transm. report of the names of the clerks employed in the Dept. of State during 1811; Jan. 21, 1812. — *War Dept.* Letter transm. the annual report of the names of the clerks in the War Dept. during 1811; Jan. 21. — *Navy Dept.* Letter enclosing report on the petitions of P. Mills, ordered to be printed Jan. 1, 1812, and J. Connell; Jan. 22. — Docs. accomp. a bill making appropriations for the support of the military establishment for 1812; Jan. 31. *Com. of Claims.* Report on the petition of Capt. S. Benton; Jan. 31. — *Com. on the Petition of C. Miller.* Report; Feb. 3. — *Com. of Claims.* Report on the petition of Lieut.-Col. W. D. Beal; Feb. 7. — *Com. [on] the Memorial of the Canal Companies therein Mentioned.* Report; Feb. 20. — *Dept. of State.* Message transmitting copies of docs. obtained from a secret agent of the Brit. government employed in fomenting disaffection to the authorities, *etc.*; March 9. — *Com. of Claims.* Report on the petition of the heirs of C. de Beaumarchais; March 23. — *Com. of Accounts.* Report on the nature of the contingent expenses and application of the contingent fund of the Ho. of Reps.; March 30. — *Com. [on] the Petition of the Legislative Council, etc., of Indiana Territory, Praying to be Admitted into the Union, etc.* Report; March 31. — *Com. of Claims.* Report on the petition of A. Greeley; March 31. — *Com. on a Resolution touching the Claims of the Officers and Soldiers of the Virginia Line of the Revolutionary Army to Military Boundary Lands.* Report; April 2. — *Com. of Claims.* Report on the petition of T. F. Reddick; Apr. 3. — *Com. of Ways and Means.* Report on the petition of L. Fagan; Apr. 3. — *Treas. Dept.* Docs. accomp. a bill authorizing the Sec. Treas. to suspend the payment of bills drawn by J. Armstrong, late Minister at the Court of France, upon the Treas. of the U. S.; Apr. 6. — *Com. of Claims.* Report on the petition of A. Dardin; Apr. 10. — *Com. on the Petition of E. Clark rel. to his Floating Battery;* Apr. 13. — *Com. on a Message from the President transmitting a Report and Letter rel. to a Road from Cumberland, Md., to Ohio.* Report; Apr. 14. — *Com. [on] the Petition of W. and J. G. Ladd.* Report; April 22. — *Com. on the Bill for Improving the Navigation of the Potomac opposite Washington, etc.* Report; May 7. — *Treas. Dept.* Letter from Sec. to the chairman of the Com. of Ways and Means rel. to the loan authorized by an act of March 14, 1812; May 18. — *Navy Dept.* Letter from Sec. transm. a report cont. regulations for the government of navy hospitals; May 26. — *Dept. of State.* Message from the Pres. transm. the correspondence between the Sec. and Minister Plenipotentiary of the U. S. at Paris; May 26. — *Com. on Public Lands.* Report on the bill from the Senate entitled 'An act to authorize the state of Tenn. to issue grants and perfect titles on entries and locations of lands therein decribed' (*sic*); May 28; — Report on a resolution to inquire into the expediency of confirming claims to land in the Mississippi Territory founded on Spanish warrants of survey; May 29; — Report on a resolution to inquire what provision ought to be made resp. lands granted by the Brit. government of W. Florida; May 29. — *Dept. of State.* Correspondence between Mr. Foster and Mr. Monroe, and between the Sec. of State and Mr. Russell; June 1. — *Pres.* Message recommending an immediate declaration of war against Gr. Brit.; June 1. — *Com. of For. Relations.* Report of the causes of war with Gr. Brit.; June 3. — *Dept. of State.* Message transmitting copies of a correspondence between the Brit. Minister and the Sec. State on the Orders in Council; June 4; — Message communicating letters which have passed between the Sec. State and the Envoy Extraordinary and Minister Plenipotentiary of Gr. Brit. on the Orders in Council and impressed seamen; June 9. — *War Dept.* Report of the Sec. on the petition of D. Henley; June 9. — *Com. [on] the Report of the Sec. Navy Containing Rules and Regulations for the Government of the Navy Hospitals.* Report; June 11. — *Dept. of State.* Message transm. correspondence between Mr. Monroe and Mr. Foster rel. to the alleged encouragement by the Brit. government of the Indians to commit depredations, and to a seaman claimed by the Brit. gov.; June 11. — *Com. of Claims.* Amendatory report on the petition of J. Shattuck; June 12. — *Com. to Ascertain the Number of Persons employed in, and to Inquire into the State and Condition of the Patent Office.* Report in part; June 12. — *Com. on Indian Affairs.* Report rel. to excitements on the part of Brit. subjects of the Indians to commit hostility against the U. S., *etc.*; June 13. — *Dept. of State.* Message transm. copies of a corresp. between the Brit. Minister and the Sec. State on the Orders in Council; June 15. — *Pres.* Message transm. [letters] on the Orders in Council; June 16. — *Treas. Dept.* Letter from the Sec. in reply to a letter of the chairman of the Com. of Ways and Means, accomp. a bill 'partially to suspend for a limited time acts prohibiting importations from Gr. Brit., *etc.*'; June 19; — Letter from the Sec. accomp. a bill supplementary to an act authorizing a loan for a sum not exceeding eleven millions; June 29. — *Pres.* Message recommending the expediency of making provision for commissioning the officers of the volunteer force, *etc.*; June 30.

— Ex. docs. [1811.] 8°. (Sen: docs.?)

Namely: *Pres.* Message; Nov. 6, 1811; — Docs. accomp. message of the President; November 6; — Message transmitting letters from the late and present plenipotentiaries of France to the Department of State; Nov. 8, 1811.

— Ex. docs. *n.t.p.* [1811-12.] f°.

Namely: *Treas. Dept.* Letter from Sec. transm. annual statement of the duties and drawbacks on goods, *etc.*, imported and exported, 1808-10; Nov. 27, 1811; — Letter from Sec. transm. two statements of the importation of goods, *etc.*, in Amer. and foreign vessels, 1 Oct. 1809 - 30 Sept. 1810; Feb. 4, 1812.

— Ex. doc.] *Dept. of State.* Aggregate amount of each description of persons within the U. S. and Territories, 1810; June 1, 1811. *n.t.p.* [1811.] obl. f°.

— — - Message from Pres. transmitting a report of the Sec. with a list of captures made by the belligerents of Europe during the present European war, July 6, 1812. Wash., 1812. f°.

— ADDRESS of members of the Ho. of Reps. of the U. S. to their constituents, on the subject of the war with Gr. Britain. Alexandria, 1812. 8°. (**B 1193, 1491, W 13 a**)

— *Same.* Boston, 1812. 8°. (**B 1491**)

12th Cong. 2d sess., Nov. 2, 1812 - *March* 3, 1813.

— Journal. Wash., 1812-[13]. 8°.

— Ex. docs. *n.t.p.* [1813.] f°.

Namely. *Treas. Dept.* Letter from Sec. transm. a statement of the emoluments of the officers of the Customs for 1812; Feb. 25, 1813. — *Pres.* Message transm. rolls of persons having office or emolument under the U. S.; March 3, 1813.

— Ex. doc.] *Treas. Dept.* Letter from the Sec. transm. annual report on the finances; Dec. 5, 1812. Wash., 1812. f°.

Ex. doc.] *Com. on For. Relations.* Report in part, accomp. with bills for the regulation of seamen on public vessels and in the merchant service; Jan. 29, 1813. *n.t.p.* 8°. (Sen. doc.?)

— - *Com. on Impressed Seamen.* Report with the evidence and docs. accompanying it; [26 Feb.]. Boston, 1813. 8°.

13th Cong. 1st sess., May 24 - *Aug.* 2, 1813.

— Journal. Wash., 1813. 8°.

— Ex. docs. *n.t.p.* [1813.] 8°. (Sen. docs.?)

Namely: *Pres.* Message transm. information [conc.] the French decree purporting to be a repeal of the Berlin and Milan decrees; July 12. (*Also* **B 1491**) — *Com. of For. Relations.* Report on a message from the Pres. [conc.] the decree purporting to be a repeal of the Berlin and Milan decrees; July 13.

— Ex. doc.] *Treas. Dept.* Letter from the Sec. transm. his annual rept. on the finances; June 3, 1813. Wash., 1813. f°.

— - *Com. on so much of the Message of the Pres. as relates to the Spirit and Manner in which the War has been waged by the Enemy.* Report; July 13, 1813. Wash., 1813. 8°. (Sen. doc.?)

— *Same, with supplementary docs.* Worcester, 1814. 12°.

13th Cong. 2d sess., Dec. 6, 1813 - *Apr.* 18, 1814.

— Journal. Wash., 1813-[14]. 8°.

— Ex. docs. *n.t.p.* [Wash., 1813-14.] 2 v. 8°.

Contents. Vol. 1. No. 1-48. 2. 49-97 (93 w.). *Also* no. 54. Albany, 1814. 2 pt. 12°.

— Ex. docs. *n.t.p.* [1814.] 2 v. f°. (Sen. doc.?)
Contents. Vol. 1. *Treasury Department.* Letter from acting Secretary transm. a statement of unsettled accounts; Dec. 10, 1813. — *Navy Dept.* Letter from Sec. transm. a statement of unsettled accounts in the office of the accountant of the Navy Dept.; Dec. 14. — *War Dept.* Letter from the Sec. transm. statements [of] the application of monies transferred from several appropriations for the use of the military dept.; Dec. 28. — *Navy Dept.* Letter from Sec. transm. an exhibit of the expenditures of monies drawn on account of the Navy, 1 Oct. 1812 - 30 Sept. 1813, and of unexpended balances, 1 Oct. 1812; Jan. 3, 1814. — *War Dept.* Letter from Secretary transmitting a statement of the expenditure of money drawn from the Treasury for the military dept., 1 Oct. 1812 - 30 Sept. 1813; Jan. 3. — *Mint.* Message transm. the report of the Director of the Mint of the operations of that establishment during the last year; Jan. 6. — *War Dept.* Letter from the Sec. transm. a statement of the expenditure of monies for the military establishment for 1813; Jan. 7. — *Treas. Dept.* Letter from Sec. transm. his annual report; Jan. 10; — Letter from Sec. transm. two statements of the importations of goods, *etc.*, in Amer. and foreign vessels, with an aggregate view of both from Oct. 1, 1811, to Sept. 30, 1812; Jan. 10; — Message transm. an account of the contingent expenses of the government for 1813; Jan. 14. — *Commis. of the Navy Pension Fund.* Letter from Sec. Navy transm. the annual report of the commissioners; Jan. 17. — *Treas. Dept.* Letter from acting Sec. transm. the annual statement of duties and drawbacks on goods imported and exported for the years 1810-12; Jan. 17. — *War Dept.* Letter from Sec. transm. a report on the claims of the states and territories for monies advanced in calling into service detachments of militia, *etc.*; Jan. 25. — *Dept. of State.* Letter from Sec. transm. the names of persons to whom patents have been issued for any new or useful art, *etc.*, Jan. 1, 1813 - Jan. 1, 1814; Jan. 31. — *Treas. Dept.* Letter from acting Sec. transm. his annual statements of moneys paid during 1813 for miscellaneous claims; of contracts made for the same year, and of payments made by collectors in 1812 for the relief of sick and disabled seamen; Feb. 4.
2. *Treas. Dept.* Letter from the acting Secretary transm. a report of the names of clerks in the offices of the Treas. Dept. during 1813, with the sums paid to each; Feb. 4, 1814; — Letter transm. a statement of the exports, 1813; Feb. 5, 1814. — *Commis. of the Sinking Fund.* Report, accomp. statements [of] the proceedings authorized by the Board subsequent to 6 Feb. 1813; Feb. 7, 1814. — *Post Office Dept.* Letter from the Post-Master General transm. reports rel. to public contracts and the names and salaries of the clerks in 1813; Feb. 10, 1814. — *Treas. Dept.* Letter from Sec. transm. the annual statement of district tonnage, 31 Dec. 1812; Feb. 22, 1814. — *War Dept.* Letter from Sec. transm. a statement [of] the names of the clerks in the War Dept. during the last year, with salary allowed to each; Feb. 26, 1814. — *Treas. Dept.* Letter from the Sec. transm. a statement of the emoluments of the officers of the Customs, 1813; Mar. 2, 1814; — Letter transm. a statement of monies disbursed for expenses of intercourse with the Barbary powers, 1813; March 4, 1814. — *War Dept.* Letter from Sec. transm. a statement of contracts for the supply of rations to the army; Apr. 2, 1814. — *Treas. Dept.* Letter from the Comptroller transm. the annual list of unsettled balances; Apr. 5, 1814; — Letter from Sec. transm. a letter from the Comptroller accomp. statements [on] the Act establishing a Mint and regulating the coins of the U. S.; Apr. 9, 1814; — Letter, transmitting a statement of the debt of the U. S., 1 January 1813; April 14, 1814.

— Ex. doc.] *Pres.* Message; Dec. 7. Wash., 1813. 8°. (Sen. doc.?)

— - *Treas. Dept.* Account of the receipts and expenditures for 1813. Wash., 1814. f°.

— - - Letter from the Sec. transm. annual report [on] An act to establish the Treas. Dept.; Jan. 10. Wash., 1814. f°.

— - *Post Office Dept.* Message from the Pres. transm. report of the Postmaster General; Feb. 28, 1814. Wash., 1815. f°.

13th Cong. 3d sess., Sept. 19, 1814 - *March* 3, 1815.

— Journal. Wash., 1814-[15]. 8°.

— Ex. docs. *n.t.p.* [1814-15.] 2 v. 8°.
Contents. Vol. 1. No. 1-24. 2. 25-73.
Also no. 6, 8, 10, 25, 66. *n.t.p.* [1814.] 8°.
Also no. 24. Wash., 1814. 8°.
Also the following unnumbered f° docs.: *Treas. Dept.* Sec. Treas., annual report; Sept. 26, 1814; — Letter from Sec. transm. statements of the revenue; Oct. 15. — *War Dept.* Letter from Paymaster General giving account of moneys disbursed for bounties and premiums; Oct. 27; — Letter from Sec. transm. statement of the men recruited for the army during the present year; Nov. 10. — *Navy Dept.* Letter from Sec. transm. a statement of contracts made during 1813, 14; Dec. 2; — Letter from Sec. transm. an exhibit of the expenditure of moneys, 1 Oct. 1813 - 30 Sept. 1814; Jan. 6, 1815. — *Treas. Dept.* Letter from Sec. transm. a statement of goods, *etc.*, imported in Amer. and foreign bottoms, 1 Oct. 1812 - 30 Sept. 1813; Jan. 9. — *Mint.* Message from the Pres. transm. a report of the Director, 1814; Jan. 11. — *Navy Dept.* Letter from Sec. accomp. statements of the salaries paid the clerks in the offices of the Sec. and Accountant, 1814; Jan. 20. — *Treas. Dept.* Letter from Sec. accomp. statement [of] sums paid to each clerk in the Treas. Dept., 1814; Jan. 20; — Letter from Sec. transm. annual statement of the district tonnage, 31 Dec. 1813; Jan. 20, 1815. — *Navy Dept.* Letter from Sec. transm. a report on the Navy Pension Fund; Jan. 24, 1815. — *Dept. of State.* Letter from Sec. transm. a list of persons who have made any new and useful invention for which patents have been obtained, 31 Dec. 1813 - 1 Jan. 1815; Jan. 30. — *Treas. Dept.* Letter from Sec. transm. a statement of drawbacks on goods, *etc.*, imported and exported, 1811-13; Feb. 3; — Letter from Sec. transm. statements accomp. report on the finances 23 Sept.]1814]; Feb. 4; — Letter from Sec. transm. a statement of moneys paid at the Treas., 1814, for miscel. claims, and statement of contracts for supplies or services; Feb. 6. — *Commis. of the Sinking Fund.* Report; Feb. 7. — *Treas. Dept.* Letter from Sec. transm. a statement of the exports during year ending 30 Sept. 1814; Feb. 9. — *War Dept.* Letter from Sec. transm. statements of contracts made by the War Dept. during 1814, and by the Commissary General of Purchases 1 Jan. - 1 Nov. 1814; Feb. 9. — *Post Office Dept.* Letter from Postmaster General transm. a report of unproductive post roads and a list of contracts, 1814; Feb. 11. — *War Dept.* Letter from Sec. transm. a statement of the expenditure of the money appropriated for the contingent expenses of the military establishment, 1814; Feb. 21. — *Mint.* Letter from Sec. Treas. transm. statements rel. to the Mint establishment; Feb. 23. — *Treas. Dept.* Letter from acting Comptroller transm. statements of accounts in Treas. and Navy Depts., which have remained unsettled more than three years, *etc.*; Feb. 27. — *Post Office Dept.* Letter from the Postmaster General transm. a list of the clerks and salary received by each; Feb. 28.

— Ex doc.] *Treas. Dept.* Account of receipts and expenses for 1813. Wash., 1814. f°.

— - *Committee* [on] *the Causes and Particulars of the Invasion of Washington by the British Forces, Aug.* 1814. Report; Nov. 29. Wash., 1814. 8°.

— House bills, 1-90. *n.t.p.* [1815.] f°.

14th Cong. 1*st sess., Dec.* 4, 1815 - *Apr.* 30, 1816.

— Journal. Wash., 1815-[16]. 8°.

— Ex. docs.] *n.t.p.* [1815-16.] 2 v. 8°.
Contents. Vol. 1. No. 1-36. 2. 37-90.

— Ex. docs. *n.t.p.* [Wash., 1815-1816.] 3 v. f°.
Contents. Vol. 1. *Treas. Dept.* Letter from Sec. transm. his ann. rep. upon the finances; Dec. 7, 1815. — *War Dept.* Letter from Sec. transm. statements showing the application of moneys transferred from several appropriations to other appropriations for the support of the military establishment since the last sess. of Congress; Dec. 11. — *Treas. Dept.* Letter from the Comptroller transm. a list of balances due more than three years prior to 30 September [1814]; also a list of balances due more than three years prior to 1 Jan. 1815; Dec. 12. — *Navy Dept.* Letter from Sec. transm. a statement of the expenditures and application of moneys drawn from the Treas. on account of the Navy Dept., 1 Oct. 1814 - 30 Sept. 1815, and of the unexpended balances remaining, 1 Oct. 1815; Dec. 15. — *Treas. Dept.* Letter from Sec. transm. two statements of the importation of goods, *etc.*, in Amer. and foreign vessels, 1 Oct. 1813 - 30 Sept. 1814; [Dec. 19]. — *Navy Dept.* Letter from Sec. transm. statements of moneys transferred from certain appropriations for particular branches of expenditure to other branches in the Navy Dept.; Dec. 21. — *Treas. Dept.* Letter from Sec. transm. the annual statement of the duties of Customs for 1814, and the sales of public lands for the year ending 30 Sept. 1815; also statements rel. to the internal duties and direct tax for 1814; Dec. 21; — Abstract of the emoluments and expenditures of the collectors of internal duties and direct tax for 1814; [Dec. 21]; — Statement of the amounts of the direct tax, 1814; [Dec. 21]; — Statement resp. the internal duties for 1814; [Dec. 21]; — Letter from Sec. transm. a statement of the amount of duties

and drawbacks on goods, *etc.*, imported and exported, 1812-14; Dec. 28. — *Navy Dept.* Letter from the Sec. transm. a statement of contracts made in 1815; Jan. 3, 1816. — *Treas. Dept.* Letter from Sec. transmitting the estimates of appropriations for the service of 1816; Jan. 3.

2. *Navy Dept.* Letter from Sec. transm. statement of contracts made in 1815; Jan. 3, 1816. — *Treas. Dept.* Letter from Sec. transm. the estimates of appropriations for the service of 1816; Jan. 3. — *War Dept.* Letter from Sec. transm. statements of the expenditure and application of money drawn from the Treas. for the use of the military dept., 1 Oct. 1814-30 Sept. 1815; Jan. 4. — *Post Office Dept.* Letter from the Post Master General, transm. a list of contracts made in 1815; Jan. 17. — *Treas. Dept.* Letter from the Comptroller transm. a statement of the balances due more than three years prior to the 30 Sept. [1815]; Jan. 20; — Letter from Sec. transm. the annual statement of the district tonnage, 31 Dec. 1814; Jan. 22; — Letter from Sec. transm. a statement of the valuation of lands, lots, and dwelling houses, and of slaves, 1813; Jan. 25. — *War Dept.* Letter from the Sec. transm. the annual statement of contracts for 1815; Jan. 25. — *Treas. Dept.* Letter from Sec. transm. statements of receipts and expenditures, 3 March 1789-31 March 1815; Jan. 26. — *Dept. of State.* Letter from Sec. transm. a list of names of persons to whom patents have been granted for the invention of any new or useful art, *etc.*, 1 Jan. 1815-1 Jan. 1816; Feb. 3. — *War Dept.* Letter from Sec. to the chairman of committee of ways and means transm. a detailed estimate of sums necessary for the Ordnance Dept. for 1816; Feb. 5. — *Treas. Dept.* Letter from the Sec. transm. comparative statements between the annual amount of the expenditures of the military and naval establishments; Feb. 6. — *Commissioners of the Sinking Fund.* Report showing the measures authorized by the Board subsequent to their report, 6 Feb. 1816; Feb. 8. — *Treas. Dept.* Letter from Sec. presenting a statement of the valuation of lands, *etc.*; Feb. 15; — Letter transm. a statement of the exports during the year ending 30 Sept. 1815; Feb. 15; — Letter transm. a statement of the emoluments of the officers of the Customs for 1815; Feb. 24; — Letter transm. a statement of additions to the funded public debt, and to the floating public debt since 30 Dec. [1815]; March 2; — Message transm. a report of the Sec. of expenses incurred for public edifices and improvements in Washington; March 11. — *War Dept.* Message from the Pres. transm. a statement of the militia; March 11. — *Treas. Dept.* Letter transm. an abstract of the valuation of lands, *etc.*, in Maryland; March 18; — Letter from the Comptroller transm. abstracts of the accounts which were unsettled 30 Sept. 1812, and still remain unsettled; March 19; — Report of Sec. resp. the valuation of lands, *etc.*, in Penn.; March 22; — Report of Sec. rel. to expenses in the prosecution of offences against the U. S. in Conn., Mass., N. H., Vt., and N. Y., 1808-15; Apr. 1. — *Mint.* Letter from Sec. transm. statements rel. to the Mint for 1815; Apr. 8. — *War Dept.* Letter from Sec. transm. statements [of] the names of the clerks and the sums given to each; April 11.

3. *Treas. Dept.* Letter from the Sec. transm. statements [of] the bounty paid on the exportation of pickled fish, *etc.*, from the commencement of the present government to Dec. 31, 1814, with the quantity of salt imported into each state for the year ending Sept. 30, 1805; Feb. 2, 1816. — *War Dept.* Letter from Sec. transmitting docs. exhibiting the expenses of the Indian Dept.; March 14, 1816. — *Treas. Dept.* Message from President transm. report of Sec. rel. to measures to complete an accurate survey of the coast; April 4, 1816.

— Ex. doc.] *Treas. Dept.* Account of the receipts and expenditures for 1814; Nov. 27, 1815. Wash., 1815. f°.

— Reports of com. *n.t.p.* [Wash., 1816.] 8°.

Contents. No. 1-90 (1, 4-6, 8, 12, 18, 20, 22-28, 32-34, 36, 42, 50, 53, 58-60, 65, 67, 68, 70-74, 78-81, 84-87 w.*).

14*th Cong.* 2*d sess., Dec.* 2, 1816-*March* 3, 1817.

— Journal. Wash., 1816-[17]. 8°.

— Ex. docs.] *n.t.p.* [1816-17.] 2 v. 8°.

Contents. Vol. 1. No. 1-39. 2. 40-102.

Contents. Vol. 1. *War Dept.* Letter from acting Secretary transmitting statements showing the application of moneys transferred from several appropriations to [others] for the support of the military establishment; Dec. 18, 1816. — *Treas. Dept.* Letter from the Sec. transmitting annual report on the finances; Dec. 20, 1816; — Letter from Sec. transm. statements of the duties on merchandise imported from the British W. I. and their Amer. colonies, Oct. 1801-Sept. 1814; Dec. 23, 1816. — *War Dept.* Letter from the acting Sec. transmitting a statement of the expenditure and application of money drawn from the Treas., 1 Oct. 1815-30 Sept. 1816. — *Navy Dept.* Letter from Sec. transm. a statement of moneys transferred from sundry appropriations to [others]; Jan. 3, 1817. — *Dept. of State.* Letter from Sec. transm. a list of persons to whom patents have been issued, Jan. 1, 1816-Jan. 1, 1817; Jan. 6, 1817. — *Treas. Dept.* Letter from Sec. transm. an estimate of the appropriations for the service of 1817; Jan. 6, 1817. — *Navy Dept.* Letter from Sec. transm. a statement of moneys drawn from the Treas. on account of the Navy, Oct. 1, 1816-Sept. 30, 1816; Jan. 7, 1817. — *Treas. Dept.* Letter from the Sec. transm. a statement of the names of the clerks in the Treas. Dept. during 1816; Jan. 7, 1817. — *War Dept.* Letter from the acting Sec. transm. statements of contracts made at the War Dept., 1816; Jan. 11, 1817; — Letter from acting Sec. transmitting a statement of the officers and privates comprising the military establishment; Jan. 13, 1817. — *Commis. of the Navy Pension Fund.* Report, cont. statements rel. to that fund; Jan. 17, 1817. — *Treas. Dept.* Letter from the Sec. transmitting the annual statement of the district tonnage, 1815; Jan. 17, 1817. — *War Dept.* Letter from the acting Sec. transm. a statement showing the actual number of the army, and stations of each corps; Jan. 23, 1817. — *Treas. Dept.* Letter from Sec. transm. statements of moneys paid at the Treas. during 1816; Jan. 27, 1817. — *War Dept.* Correspondence between the chairman of committee of ways and means and the acting Sec. of War rel. to the expenditures and appropriations for the Ordnance and Quarter-Master General's Depts.; Jan. 31, 1817. — *Treas. Dept.* Letter from Sec. transm. a statement of goods, *etc.*, exported during year ending Sept. 30, 1816; Feb. 3, 1817.

2. *Treas. Dept.* Letter from Comptroller of the Treas. transm. a statement of balances due more than three years prior to Sept. 30, 1816; Feb. 5, 1817. — *Commis. of the Sinking Fund.* Annual report; Feb. 7. — *Treas. Dept.* Letter from Sec. transm. statements of the internal duties, 1815, of the amount of direct tax, *etc.*; Feb. 11; — Letter from Sec. transm. a statement showing the quantity of public lands sold and the receipts therefor in Ohio and Indiana and the Illinois and Mississippi Territories during the year ending 30 Sept. 1816; Feb. 14. — *Post Office Dept.* Letter from the Postmaster Gen. transm. a list of contracts made in the year 1816 for transporting the mails; Feb. 15. — *Treas. Dept.* Letter from the Comptroller of the Treas. transm. a statement of balances due for more than three years prior to Sept. 30, 1816, on the books of the Accountant of the Navy; Feb. 19. — *Post Office Dept.* Letter from the Postmaster General transm. a list of unproductive post roads for 1817; Feb. 20. — *War Dept.* Letter from acting Sec. War transm. a statement showing the expenditure of moneys for the contingent expenses of the military establishment for 1816; Feb. 24. — *Treas. Dept.* Letter from Sec. transm. a statement of the emoluments and expenditures of the officers of the customs in 1816; Feb. 25; — Letter from the Sec. transm. statements rel. to the Mint; Feb. 28.

3. *Treas. Dept.* Letter from Sec. transm. his accounts for 1816; Feb. 25, 1817; — Letter from Sec. transm. statements of the importations of goods, *etc.*, in Amer. and foreign vessels from 1 Oct.-30 Sept. 1815; Feb. 28.

— Ex. doc.] *Treas. Dept.* Account of the receipts and expenditures for 1815; November 27, 1816. Wash., 1816. f°.

— Reports of committees. *n.t.p.* [Wash., 1816-17.] 8°.

Contents. No. 1-202 (1-3, 8, 10, 15, 21. 24-26, 31, 32, 39, 40, 45, 47, 53, 54, 59, 63-65, 82, 83, 87, 91, 94, 97 w.*; 85 w.).

15*th Cong.* 1*st sess., Dec.* 1, 1817-*Apr.* 20, 1818.

— Journal. Wash., 1817. 8°.

— Ex. docs. *n.t.p.* [Wash., 1817-18.] 8 v. 8°.

Contents. Vol. 1. No. 1-4. 2. 5-37 (29 w.). 3. 38-69. 4. 70-95 (78 w.). 5. 96-124 (106, 112 w.). 6. 125-149, 155 (146, 148, 149 w.). 7. 150-154, 156-194 (188 w.). 8. 195-702.

Also no. 187 (B 1536).

— Ex doc.] Account of the receipts and expenditures for 1816; Nov. 27, 1817. Wash., 1817. f°.

15*th Cong.* 2*d sess., Nov.* 16, 1818-*March* 3, 1819.

— Journal. Wash., 1818. 8°.

— Ex. docs. *n.t.p.* [Wash., 1818-19.] 8 v. 8°.

Contents. Vol. 1. No. 1-30 (26 w.). 2. 31-46, 48. 3. 47. 4. 49-85. 5. 92. 6. 86-91, 94-123 (93 w.). 7. 124-136. 8. 137-150.

— Ex doc.] Account of receipts and expenditures for 1817. Wash., 1818. f°.

— Debate in the House on the Seminole war, Jan., Feb. 1819. Wash., 1819. 12°.

16th Cong. 1st sess., Dec. 6, 1819 - *May* 15, 1820.

— Journal. Wash., 1819. 8°.

— Ex. docs. *n.t.p.* [Wash., 1819-20.] 9 v. 8°.
Contents. Vol. 1. No. 1-11. 2. 12-33. 3. 34-54. 4. 55. 5. 56-75. 6. 76-92. 7. 93-108. 8. 109-122. 9. 123.

— Reports of committees. *n.t.p.* [Wash., 1819-20.] 8°.
Contents. No. 1-98 (3 w.*; 42, 88 w.).

— Account of receipts and expenditures for 1818. Wash., 1819. f°.

16th Cong. 2d sess., Nov. 13, 1820 - *March* 3, 1821.

— Journal. Wash., 1820. 8°.

— Ex. docs. *n.t.p.* [Wash., 1820-21.] 9 v. 8°.
Contents. Vol. 1. No. 1-9, 11-34. 2. 35-44. 3. 10. 4. 45-55. 5. 56-80. 6. 81-96. 7. 97-108. 8. 109, 110. 9. 111, 112.
Also No. 109. Wash., 1821. 8°.

— Reports of com. *n.t.p.* [Wash., 1820-21.] 8°.
Contents. No. 1-70.

— Account of receipts and expenditures for 1819. Wash., 1820. f°.

17th Cong. 1st sess., Dec. 3, 1821-*May* 8, 1822.

— Journal. Wash., 1821. 8°.

— Ex. docs. *n.t.p.* [Wash., 1821-22.] 9 v. 8°.
Contents. Vol. 1. No. 1-10. 2. 11-33. 3. 34-39. 4. 40-47. 5. 48-56. 6. 57-66. 7. 67-93. 8. 94-115. 9. 116-134.

— Reports of committees. *n.t.p.* [Wash., 1821-22.] 2 v. 8°.
Contents. Vol. 1. No. 1-69, 94, 105, 107. 2. 70-93, 95-104, 106, 108-111.

— Account of receipts and expenditures for 1820. Wash., 1821. f°.

— Digest of account of manufacturing establishments. Wash., 1823. f°.

17th Cong. 2d sess., Dec. 2, 1822 - *March* 3, 1823.

— Journal. Wash., 1822. 8°.

— Ex. docs. *n.t.p.* [Wash., 1822-23.] 9 v. in 10 pts. 8°.
Contents. Vol. 1. No. 1-27. 2. 28-31, 33-53. 3. 32. 4. 54-67. 5. 68-85. 6. 86-98. 7. 99-104. 8. 105-110. 9. 111, pts. 1, 2.

— Reports of committees. *n.t.p.* [Wash., 1822-23.] 2 v. 8°.
Contents. Vol. 1. No. 1-55. 2. 56-105.

— Account of receipts and expenditures for 1821. Wash., 1822. f°.

18th Cong. 1st sess., Dec. 1, 1823 - *May* 27, 1824.

— Journal. Wash., 1823. 8°.

— Ex. docs. *n.t.p.* [Wash., 1823-24.] 12 v. 8°.
Contents. Vol. 1. No. 1-16. 2. 17-39, 41-51. 3. 40. 4. 52-76. 5. 77-103. 6. 104-128. 7. 130. 8, 9. 140. 10. 129, 131-139, 141-150. 11. 151-161 (155 w.). 12. 162, 163.
Note. No. 163 is an index to 1st-14th Cong.
Also no. 130. Wash., 1824. 8°.

— Reports of committees. *n.t.p.* [Wash., 1823-24.] 2 v. 8°.
Contents. Vol. 1. No. 1-80. 2. 81-133.

— Account of receipts and expenditures for 1822. Wash., 1823. f°.

18th Cong. 2d sess., Dec. 6, 1824 - *March* 3, 1825.

— Journal. Wash., 1824. 8°.

— Ex. docs. *n.t.p.* [Wash., 1824-25.] 9 v. 8°.
Contents. Vol. 1. No. 1-5. 2. 6-39. 3. 40-58. 4. 59-81. 5. 82-90. 6. 91-108. 7. 109. 8. 110. 9. 111.

— Reports of committees. *n.t.p.* [Wash., 1824-25.] 2 v. 8°.
Contents. Vol. 1. No. 1-78. 2. 79-90.
Note. This sess. probably published the 'Index to exec. communications and reports of committees, 15th-17th Cong.'; *see Indexes* (p. 3064).

— Account of receipts and expenditures for 1823. Wash., 1824. f°.

19th Cong. 1st sess., Dec. 5, 1825 - *May* 22, 1826.

— Journal. Wash., 1825. 8°.

— Ex. docs. *n.t.p.* [Wash., 1825-26.] 10 v. 8°.
Contents. Vol. 1. No. 1-19. 2. 20. 3. 21-49. 4. 50-80. 5. 81-105. 6. 106-111, 113-122. 7. 112. 8. 123-147. 9. 148-165. 10. 166-184.

— Ex. doc.]. List of reports to be made to the House at the 1st sess. 19th Cong. Wash., 1825. 8°. (An unnumbered document at the end of v. 1 of Ho. docs.)

— Reports of committees. *n.t.p.* [Wash., 1825-26.] 2 v. 8°.
Contents. Vol. 1. No. 1-130 (10 w.*). 2. 131-232 (205 w.*).
Also no. 228 (B 902).

— Account of receipts and expenditures for 1824. Wash., 1825. f°.

19th Cong. 2d sess., Dec. 4, 1826 - *March* 3, 1827.

— Journal. Wash., 1826. 8°.

— Ex. docs. *n.t.p.* [Wash., 1826-27.] 12 v. 8°.
Contents. Vol. 1. No. 1-2. 2. 3-34. 3. 35-56 (45 w.). 4. 57-67, 69-72. 5. 73-111, 113-119 (76, 77, 88, 90 w.). 6. 120-131. 7. 132-140, 142, 143, 145, 146 (132, 134 w.). 8. 112. 9, 10. 68: Claims of France, Naples, Holland, and Denmark. 11. 141. 12. 144.
Also no. 57. Wash., 1827. 8°.
Also no. 103 (B 1493).

— Reports of committees. *n.t.p.* [Wash., 1826-27.] 3 v. 8°.
Contents. Vol. 1. No. 1-78 (52, 54 w.). 2. 79, 97, 99-102 (101 w.). 3. 98.

— Account of receipts and expenditures for 1825. Wash., 1826. f°.

20th Cong. 1st sess., Dec. 3, 1827 - *May* 26, 1828.

— Journal. Wash., 1827. 8°.

— Ex. docs. *n.t.p.* [Wash., 1827-28.] 7 v. 8°.
Contents. Vol. 1. No. 1-9. 2. 10-60. 3. 61-129. 4. 130-178, 226. 5. 179-222. 6. 223-225, 227-267. 7. 268-288.
Also no. 7, 107 (B 1798).

— Reports of committees. *n.t.p.* [Wash., 1827-28.] 4 v. 8°.

— Account of the receipts and expenditures of the U. S. for 1826. Wash., 1827. f°.
Contents. Vol. 1. No. 1-59. 2. 60-140. 3. 141-227 (143 w.). 4. 228-270.
Note. There is a 149A and 149B but no 150.

20th Cong. 2d sess., Dec. 1, 1828 - *March* 3, 1829.

— Journal. Wash., 1828. 8°.

— Ex. docs. *n.t.p.* [Wash., 1828-29.] 6 v. 8°.
Contents. Vol. 1. No. 1-19. 2. 20-88. 3. 89-120, 122-133. 4. 134-145, 147. 5. 121. 6. 146.
Also no. 102 (B 1058, 1887).

— Reports of committees. *n.t.p.* [Wash., 1828.] 8°.
Contents. No. 1-104.

— Account of the receipts and expenditures for 1827. Wash., 1827. f°.

21st Cong. 1st sess., Dec. 7, 1829 - *May* 31, 1830.

— Journal. Wash., 1829. 8°.

— Ex. docs. *n.t.p.* [Wash., 1829-30.] 4 v. 8°.
Contents. Vol. 1. No. 1-23. 2. 24-52. 3. 53-89. 4. 90-126. — Rep. com., no. 380, 381.

— Reports of committees. *n.t.p.* [Wash., 1829-30.] 3 v. 8°.
Contents. Vol. 1. No. 1-175 (128-130, 152 w.*; 89, 106, 148, w.). 2. 176-298 (193, 230 w.). 3. 299-379, 382-419 (400 w.*; 328, 417 w.).
Note. No. 380, 381 are bound at the end of v. 4 of the Ex. docs.
Also no. 165 (B 1512) — 271 (B 1717, 1884); — 289 (B 1743); — 358 (B 1064, 1541, 1792, 1805).

21st Cong. 2d sess., Dec. 6, 1830 - *March* 3, 1831.

— Journal. Wash., 1830. 8°.

— Ex. docs. Wash., 1830-31. 4 v. 8°.
Contents. Vol. 1. No. 1-30. 2. 31-50 (39 w.). 3. 51-104 (65 w.). 4. 105-150.

— Reports of committees. *n.t.p.* [Wash., 1830–31.] 8°.
Contents. No. 1–119.

22d Cong. 1st sess., Dec. 5, 1831 – *July* 16, 1832.

— Journal. Wash., 1831. 8°.
— Ex. docs. Wash., 1830–31. 8 v. 8°.
Contents. Vol. 1. No. 1–18 (1 w.*). 2. 19–82. 3. 83–103. 4. 104–185. 5. 186–234. 6. 235–307 (235 w.). 7, 8. 308.
Note. No. 308 has the separate title-page, 'Document rel. to the manufactures in the U. S.' Wash., 1832. 2 v. 8°.
Also No. 2 without docs. (**B 1057**); — *Same*, docs. only not incl. those accomp. rept. of Sec. Navy. (**B 1058**); — 3 (**B 1057, 1805**); — 82 (**B 1056**); — 186 (**B 1056**); — 99 (**1057**); — 222 (**B 1056**); — 230 (**B 1062**); — 249 (**B 1057**); — 250 (**B 1057**); — 262 (**B 1062**); — 263 (**B 1058**); — 301 (**E 95**).
— Reports of committees. Wash., 1831–32. 5 v. 8°.
Contents. Vol. 1. No. 1–223. 2. 224–325. 3. 326–459. 4. 460–463. 5. 464–513.
Also 101 (**B 1058, 1801**); — 226 (**B 1053**); — 279 (**B 1056**); — 283 (**B 1059**); — 420 (**B 1058**); — 448 (**B 1057**); — 460 (**E 95**); — *Same*. Report of minority [only] (**B 1062**); — 478 (**B 1089**); — 481 (**B 1056**); — 496 (**B 1655**).
Also 460. [Without docs.] (*Appended to* **Amer.** quart. rev., v. 11. 1832; *also* **B 1062**)

22d Cong. 2d sess., Dec. 3, 1832 – *March* 2, 1833.

— Journal. Wash., 1832. 8°.
— Ex. docs. Wash., 1832–33. 3 v. 8°.
Contents. Vol. 1. No. 1–45. 2. 46–109. (89, 107 w.*). 3. 110–148.
Also no. 2 (**B 1790**); — 8 (**B 1515**); — 9 (**B 1790**).
— Reports of committees. Wash., 1832–33. 8°.
Contents. No. 1–128 (98 w.).
Also no. 5 (**B 1801**); — 85 (**B 1790**); — 121 (**B 1541**); — 122: Tariff report of J. Q. Adams. Boston, 1833. 8°. (**B 1427**); — 112: Report of the minority of the committee on manufactures. Boston, 1833. 8°. (**B 1427**).
— Digested index to Ex. docs. and Reports of committees. Wash., 1832. 8°.

23d Cong. 1st sess., Dec. 2, 1833 – *June* 30, 1834.

— Journal. Wash., 1833. 8°.
— Ex. docs. *n.t.p.* [Wash., 1833–34.] 6 v. 8°.
Contents. Vol. 1. No. 1–49. 2. 50–79. 3. 80–203 (81 w.). 4. 204–349 (269 w.*). 5. 350–440 (408 w.*). 6. 441–523 (507 w.*).
Also no. 2 (**B 1541**); — 15 (**B 1087**); — 175 (**B 1088**); — 355, 467 (**B 1087**).
Also no. 175. *n.t.p.* [1834.] 8°.
Also no. 498. Wash., 1834. 8°.
— Reports of committees. *n.t.p.* [Wash., 1833–34.] 5 v. 8°.
Contents. Vol. 1. No. 1–200. 2. 201–313. 3. 314–445 (370 w.*). 4. 447–560. 5. 446.
Also no. 312 (**B 1810**); — 313 (**B 1515, 1810**); — 474 (**B 1089**); — 481 (**B 1541, 1810**).
Also no. 414. *n.t.p.* [Wash., 1834.] 8°.

23d Cong. 2d sess., Dec. 1, 1834 – *March* 3, 1835.

— Journal. Wash., 1835. 8°.
— Ex. docs. *n.t.p.* [Wash., 1833–35.] 5 v. 8°.
Contents. Vol. 1. No. 1–20. 2. 21–77. 3. 78–133. 4. 134–177. 5. 178–198.
Also no. 2, 3 (**B 1087**); — 25 (**B 1811**); — 103 (**B 1768**); — 187, 230 (**B 1818**).
Also no. 151. Wash., 1835. 8°.
— Reports of committees. *n.t.p.* [Wash., 1833–34.] 2 v. 8°.
Contents. Vol. 1. No. 1–102, 104–142. 2. 103.
Also no. 1 (**B 1811**); — 103 (**B 1768**).

24th Cong. 1st sess., Dec. 7, 1835 – *July* 4, 1836.

— Journal. Wash., 1835. 8°.
— Ex. docs. *n.t.p.* [Wash., 1835–36.] 7 v. 8°.
Contents. Vol. 1. No. 1–16 (1 w.*). 2. 17–58. 3. 59–113 (105 w.). 4. 114–197 (186 w.). 5. 198–214. 6. 215–269. 7. 270–998.
Also no. 2 (**B 1829**); — 3, 5 (**E 43**); — 256 (**B 1655**).
Also no. 146. Wash., 1836. 8°.

— Reports of committees. *n.t.p.* [Wash., 1835–36.] 3 v. 8°.
Contents. Vol. 1. No. 1–349 (61, 200 w.*). 2. 350–540. 3. 541–857 (773 w.).
Also no. 663 (**B 1817**).

24th Cong. 2d sess., Dec 5, 1836 – *March* 3, 1837.

— Journal. Wash., 1837. 8°.
— Ex. docs. *n.t.p.* [Wash., 1836-37.] 4 v. 8°.
Contents. Vol. 1. No. 1–19. 2. 20–79. 3. 80–143. 4. 144–189.
— Reports of committees. *n.t.p.* [Wash., 1836–37.] 3 v. 8°.
Contents. Vol. 1. No. 1–192, 195–229 (128, 209 w.*). 2. 230–327. 3. 193, 194.

25th Cong. 1st sess., Sept. 4 – *Oct.* 16, 1837.

— Journal. Wash., 1838. 8°.
— Docs. of the House. Wash., 1837. 8°.
Contents. No. 1–54.
Also no. 1 (**B 1871**).

25th Cong. 2d sess., Dec. 4, 1837 – *July* 9, 1838.

— Journal. Wash., 1838. 8°.
— Ex. docs. *n.t.p.* [Wash., 1837–38.] 12 v. 8°.
Contents. Vol. 1. No. 1–8. 2. 9–70 (49 w.*). 3. 71–78. 4. 79. 5. 80–125. 6. 126–146 (142 w.*). 7. 147–200. 8. 201–296 (212 w.*). 9. 297–329 (301 w.). 10. 330–350, 352–422. 11. 351. 12. 423–467.
Also no. 3 (**B 1751**); — 23 (**E 43**); — 121 (**B 1128, 1147**); — 372 (**B 1273**).
— Reports of committees. *n.t.p.* [Wash., 1837–38.] 4 v. 8°.
Contents. Vol. 1. No. 1–330. 2. 331–350. 3. 351–819, (448, 631 w.*; 353, 615, 617 w.). 4. 820–1068, (929 w.*; 907, 980, 983 w.).
Also no. 737. (**B 1128**)
— Index to Ex. docs. and Reports of committees, 1831–39. Wash., [1839]. 8°.

25th Cong. 3d sess., Dec. 3, 1838 – *March* 3, 1839.

— Journal. Wash., 1839. 8°.
— Ex. docs. Wash., 1838–39. 6 v. 8°.
Contents. Vol. 1. No. 1–9. 2. 10–29. 3. 30–120. 4. 121–210. 5. 211–227. 6. 228–253.
Also no. 164 (**E 43**); — 181, 183 (**B 1817**); — 253 (**B 1818**).
— Reports of committees. *n.t.p.* [Wash., 1838–39.] 2 v. 8°.
Contents. Vol. 1. No. 1–273 (120, 121 w.*; 189 w.). 2. 274–325 (312 w.*).
Also no. 101 (**B 1147, E 43**); — 313 (**B 1817**).

26th Cong. 1st sess., Dec. 2, 1839 – *July* 21, 1840.

— Journal. Wash., 1840. 8°.
— Ex. docs. *n.t.p.* [Wash., 1839–40.] 7 v. 8°.
Contents. Vol. 1. No. 1–11. 2. 12–58. 3. 59–149. (66, 79, 98 w.*). 4. 150–171, 173–205. 5. 172. 6. 206–239. 7. 240–265 (243 w.*).
Also no. 2 (**B 1663, 1818, E 43**); — 43 (**B 1147**); — 127, 129, 162, 188, 205, 222 (**E 249**).
— Reports of committees. *n.t.p.* [Wash., 1839–40.] 4 v. 8°.
Contents. Vol. 1. No. 1–299 (1, 14, 242 w.*; 283 w.). 2. 300–506. 3. 507–587. 4. 588–716.
Also no. 277. *n.t.p.* [Wash., 1840.] 8°. (*Also* **E 123**)
Also no. 707. *n.t.p.* [1840.] 8°. (*Also* **B 1147, 1159**)

26th Cong. 2d sess., Dec. 7, 1840 – *March* 3, 1841.

— Journal. Wash., 1841. 8°.
— Ex. docs. *n.t.p.* [Wash., 1840–41.] 6 v. 8°.
Contents. Vol. 1. No. 1–20. 2. 21–84 (81, 83 w.*). 3. 85–110. 4. 111. 5. 112–122, 124. 6. 123.
Also no. 2 (**B 1167**); — 33 (**B 1823**); — 38 (**B 1164**); — 173 (**B 1167**).
— Reports of committees. *n.t.p.* [Wash., 1840–41.] 8°.
Contents. No. 1–249.
Also no. 186, 187 (**E 249**).

27th Cong. 1st sess., May 31 - Sept. 13, 1841.

— Journal. Wash., 1841. 8°.

— Ex. docs. and Reports of committees. *n.t.p.* [Wash., 1841.] 8°.
Contents. Ex. docs., no. 1-63. — Rep. of comm., no. 1-11.

27th Cong. 2d sess., Dec. 6, 1841 - Aug. 31, 1842.

— Journal. Wash., 1841. 8°.

— Ex. docs. *n.t.p.* [Wash., 1841-42.] 6 v. 8°.
Contents. Vol. 1. No. 1-25. 2. 26-120 (75 w.*). 3. 121-164. 4. 165-211, 213-240 (211 w.*). 5. 241-293. 6. 212.
Also no. 209 (B 1513).

— Reports of committees. *n.t.p.* [Wash., 1841-42.] 5 v. 8°.
Contents. Vol. 1. No. 1-322. 2. 323-552. 3. 553-740. 4. 741-945. 5. 946-1106.
Note. There are two documents numbered 641, one bd. with no. 141 in v. 2.
Also no. 461 (B 1513, 1871); — 835 (B 1173); — 1098 (E 249).

27th Cong. 3d sess., Dec. 5, 1842 - March 3, 1843.

— Journal. Wash., 1843. 8°.

— Ex. docs. *n.t.p.* [Wash., 1841-43.] 8 v. 8°.
Contents. Vol. 1. No. 1-11. 2. 12-29 (19 w.*). 3. 30-109. 4. 110-148. 5. 149-197. 6. 198-205. 7. 206-215. 8. 216-220.

— Reports of com. *n.t.p.* [Wash., 1842-43.] 4 v. 8°.
Contents. Vol. 1. No. 1-146 (124 w.*; 60 w.) 2. 147-270. 3. 271-283. 4. 284-296.
Also no. 17 (B 1186).

— Proceedings in Ho. of Rep. on presentation of the sword of Washington and staff of Franklin; Feb. 7, 1843; [with app.]. Wash., 1843. 8°. (B 1499)

28th Cong. 1st sess., Dec. 4, 1843 - June 17, 1844.

— Journal. Wash., 1844. 8°.

— Ex. docs. *n.t.p.* [Wash., 1843-44.] 6 v. 8°.
Contents. Vol. 1. No. 1-14. 2. 15. 3. 16-70. 4. 71-177 (98 w.*). 5. 178-249. 6. 250-280 (250 w.*).
Also no. 276. Wash., 1844. 8°.

— Reports of com. *n.t.p.* [Wash., 1843-44.] 3 v. 8°.
Contents. Vol. 1. No. 1-352. 2. 353-515 (397 w.*). 3. 516-582.
Also no. 114 (B 1566); — 306 (B 1513); — 406 (B 1174); — 581 (B 1199).

28th Cong. 2d sess., Dec. 2, 1844 - March 3, 1845.

— Journal. Wash., 1844-45. 8°.

— Ex. docs. *n.t.p.* [Wash., 1844-45.] 4 v. in 5 pts. 8°.
Contents. Vol. 1. No. 1-23. 2. 24-72. 3. 73-139. 4, pt. 1. 140-165. 4, pt. 2. 166-168.
Note. Vol. 4, pt. 2 has the separate titlepage 'Report of the exploring exped. to the Rocky Mts., 1842, and to Oregon and N. California, 1843, 44, by Capt. J. C. Frémont'.
Also no. 166. Wash., 1845. 8°.

— Reports of committees. Wash., 1844-45. 8°.
Contents. No. 1-200, 438.

29th Cong. 1st sess., Dec. 1, 1845 - Aug. 10, 1846.

— Journal. Wash., 1845-46. 8°.

— Ex. docs. *n.t.p.* [Wash., 1845-46.] 8 v. 8°.
Contents. Vol. 1. No. 1-5. 2. 6-12. 3. 13-56. 4. 57-139 (132 w.*). 5. 140-161. 6. 162-208. 7. 209-225, 227, 228. 8. 226.

— Reports of committees. *n.t.p.* [Wash., 1846-47.] 4 v. 8°.
Contents. Vol. 1. No. 1-210 (163 w.*). 2. 211-497 (381-389 w.*). 3. 498-686. 4. 687-846.

29th Cong. 2d sess., Dec. 7, 1846 - March 3, 1847.

— Journal. Wash., 1846-47. 8°.

— Ex. docs. *n.t.p.* [Wash., 1846-47.] 4 v. 8°.
Contents. Vol. 1. No. 1-4. 2. 5-11. 3. 12-59. 4. 60-124.
Note. Nos. 13, 22, 74-95, 96, 102-116 were printed by the Senate and can be found in the Senate docs. only.

— Reports of com. *n.t.p.* [Wash., 1846-47.] 8°.
Contents. No. 1-90.

30th Cong. 1st sess., Dec. 6, 1847 - Aug. 14, 1848.

— Journal. Wash., 1847-48. 8°.

— Ex. docs. *n.t.p.* [Wash., 1847-48.] 9 v. (v.2 w.). 8°.
Contents. Vol. 1. No. 1-7. 2. *Wanting.* 3. 9-40. 4. 41. 5. 42-53, 55-59. 6. 54. 7. 60. 8. 61-77. 9. 78-86.

— Misc. docs. Wash., 1848. 8°.
Contents. No. 1-101.
Also no. 23. (E 123)
Also no. 26. Wash., 1848. 8°.

— Reports of committees. *n.t.p.* [Wash., 1847-48.] 4 v. 8°.
Contents. Vol. 1. No. 1-199. 2. 200-479. 3. 480-739. 4. 740-841.

30th Cong. 2d sess., Dec. 4, 1848 - March 3, 1849.

— Journal. Wash., 1848-49. 8°.

— Ex. docs. *n.t.p.* [Wash., 1848-49.] 7 v. 8°.
Contents. Vol. 1. No. 1. 2. 2-10. 3. 12. 4. 11, 13-41. 5. 42-51. 6. 59. 7. 52-58, 60-69.

— Misc. docs. Wash., 1849. 8°.
Contents. No. 1-62.

— Reports of committees. *n.t.p.* [Wash., 1844.] 2 v. 8°.
Contents. Vol. 1. No. 1-144. 2. 145.

31st Cong. 1st sess., Dec. 3, 1849 - Sept. 30, 1850.

— Journal. Wash., 1849-50. 8°.

— Ex. docs. *n.t.p.* [Wash., 1849-50.] 11 v. in 14 pts. 8°.
Contents. Vol. 1. No. 1-3. 2. 4. 3. 5, pts. 1-3. 4. 6-14. 5. 17. 6. 20, pts. 1, 2. 7. 15, 16, 18, 19, 21-39. 8. 40-67. 9. 68-73. 10. 74-87. 11. 88-90.
Also no. 17. *n.t.p.* [1850.] 8°.
Also no. 69. Wash., 1850. 8°.

— Misc. docs. Wash., 1850. 2 v. 8°.
Contents. Vol. 1. No. 1-49. 2. 50-57.

— Reports of committees. *n.t.p.* [Wash., 1849-50.] 3 v. 8°.
Contents. Vol. 1. No. 1-199. 2. 200-399. 3. 400-503.

31st Cong. 2d sess., Dec. 2, 1850 - March 3, 1851.

— Journal. Wash., 1850-51. 8°.

— Digested summary and alphabetical list of private claims presented to the House, from the 1st - 31st Cong. Wash., 1853. 3 v. 8°.
Contents. Vol. 1. A-G. 2. H-O. 3. P-Z.

— Ex. docs. *n.t.p.* [Wash., 1850-51.] 8 v. in 10 pts. 8°.
Contents. Vol. 1. No. 1. 2. 2-5. 3. 6-11. 4. 12-22. 5. 23-31, 33-52, 54. 6. 32, pt. 1, 2. 7. 53, pt. 1, 2. 8. Extra vol. cont. unnumb. doc.: Comm. and navig.

— Misc. docs. Wash., 1851. 8°.
Contents. No. 1-21.

— Reports of committees. *n.t.p.* [Wash., 1850-51.] 8°.
Contents. No. 1-109 (36 w.).

32d Cong. 1st sess. Dec. 1, 1851 - Aug. 31, 1852.

— Journal. Wash., 1851-52. 8°.

— Ex. docs. *n.t.p.* [Wash., 1851-52.] 15 v. in 19 pts. 8°.
Contents. Vol. 1. No. 1, 3. 2. 2, pts. 1-3. 3. 4-22. 4. 26. 5, 23-25, 27-52. 6. 53, 54, 57-87. 7. 55. 8. 56. 9. 88-101. 10. 102, pts. 1, 2. 11. 103. 12. 104-122. 13. 123-135 (126 w.*). 14. Comm. and nav. [Unnumb. doc.] 15. 136.

— Misc. docs. Wash., 1852. 8°.
Contents. No. 1-71 (3 w.* ; 45 w.).

— Reports of committees. Wash., 1852. 8°.
Contents. No. 1-176.

32d Cong. 2d sess., Dec. 6, 1852 - March 3, 1853.

— Journal. Wash., 1852. 8°.

— Ex. docs. *n.t.p.* [Wash., 1852-53.] 11 v. in 13 pts. 8°.
Contents. Vol. 1. No. 1, pts. 1, 2. 2. 2-6. 3. 7-23. 4. 24-42. 5. 43: Explor. of the Valley of the Amazon;

pt. 1, by L. Herndon. 6. 44-61, 63. 7. 62. 8. 64. 9. 65, pt. 1, 2. 10. 66-69. 11. Com. and nav. [Unn. doc.]
Note. Vol. 8 has a separate title page.
Also no. 43; with maps. Wash., 1854. 8°.

— Misc. docs. Wash., 1853. 8°.
Contents. No. 1-24 (1 w.*).

— Reports of committees. *n.t.p.* [Wash., 1852-53.] 8°.
Contents. No. 1-7.

33*d Cong.* 1*st sess., Dec.* 5, 1853 - *Aug.* 7, 1854.

— Journal. Wash., 1853. 8°.

— Ex. docs. Wash., 1854-55. 19 v. in 27 pts. 8° *and* 4°.
Contents. Vol. 1. No. 1, pts. 1-3. 2. 2-3. 3. 4-11, 4. 12. 5. 13-36. 6. 37, 38. 7. 39, pts. 1, 2: Patents. 8. 40-52, 54-65. 9. 53: Explor. of the Valley of the Amazon; pt. 2; by L. Gibbon. 10. 66-85. 11. 86-96. 12. 97-106. 13. 107-111. 14. 112-120. 15, pts. 1-3. 6. 121: U. S. Naval Astron. Exped. to the Southern Hemisphere. 16. 122-124, 126-128. 17. 125. 18, pts. 1-4. 129: Pacific R. R. explor. 19. Com. and nav. [Unnumb. doc.]
Note. Vol. 4 has the sep. t. p. 'Rept. of the Supt. of the Coast Survey, 1853.' Pts. 4, 5 of 15 are wanting in this set, and no mention is made in the index or elsewhere of their having been published.
Also no. 53; with maps. Wash., 1854. 8°.
Also the following separate parts of no. 129: —
STEVENS, I. I. Report of exploration of a route for the Pacific R. R. near the 47th and 49th parallels. *n.p., n.d.* [1854.] 8°.
WHIPPLE, A. W. Report of explorations for a railway route near the 45th parallel. *n.p., n.d.* [1854.] 8°.
POPE, J. Report of exploration of a route near the 32d parallel. *n.p., n.d.* [1854.] 8°.
PARKE, J. G. Report of explorations for a railway route near the 32d parallel. *n.p., n.d.* [1854.] 8°.
WILLIAMSON, R. S. Report of a reconnaissance and survey in California in connexion with explorations for a route from the Mississippi River to the Pacific. *n.p., n.d.* [1853.] 8°.

— Misc. docs. Wash., 1854. 8°.
Contents. No. 1-98 (11, 15, 25, 36, 37, 43, 66, 67, 68, 81, 88-91; w. 17, 74 w.*).
Also no 97: Smithsonian Inst. 8th ann. rept., 1853. Wash., 1854. 8°.

— Reports of committees. Wash., 1854. 3 v. 8°.
Contents. Vol. 1. No. 1-121 (21, 106 w.). 2. 122-266 (192 w.*). 3. 267-372.
Also no. 347. Wash., 1854. 8°.

33*d Cong.* 2*d sess., Dec.* 4, 1854 - *March* 3, 1855.

— Journal. Wash., 1854. 8°.

— Ex. docs. Wash., 1855. 14 v. in 30 pts. 8° *and* 4°.
Contents. Vol. 1. No. 1, pts. 1-3. 2. 2, 3. 3. 4-9. 4. 10-16. 5. 17-19, 21-58. 6. 20. 7. 59, pts. 1-3. 8. 60-85. 9. 86. 10. 87-90, 92-96. 11. 91, pts. 1-11: Explor. and survey for a R. R. to the Pacific. 12. 97, pts. 1-3: Nav. of an Amer. squadron to the China Seas and Japan, 1852-54 under Com. Perry. 13. 98. 14. Comm. and nav. [Unnumb. doc.]
Note. Vol. 6 has the separate titlepage 'Rept. of the Supt. of the Coast Survey'.
Also no. 97: Vol. 1, 3. Wash., 1856. 2 v. 8°.

— Misc. docs. Wash., 1855. 8°.
Contents. No. 1-38.
Also no. 37: Smithsonian Inst. 9th ann. rept., 1854. Wash., 1855. 8°.

— Reports of committees. Wash., 1855. 8°.
Contents. No. 1-151.
Also no. 141. *n.t.p.* [1855.] 8°. (*Also* E 123)

34*th Cong.* 1*st and* 2*d sess., Dec.* 3, 1855 - *Aug.* 30, 1856.

Note. The documents of the 2d sess. are bound with those of the 1st sess.

— Journal. Wash., 1855. 1 v. in 2 pts. 8°.

— Ex. docs. Wash., 1856-59. 16 v. in 26 pts. 8° *and* 4°.
Contents. Vol. 1, pts. 1-4. No. 1. 2, 2-5, 7-9. 3. 6: Coast survey. 4. 10. 5. 11, 13. 6. 12, pts. 1-3. 7. 14-39. 8. 40. 9. 41-46, 48-92 (72 w.). 10. 47, pts. 1-4: Commercial rel. with for. nations. 11. 93-103. 12. 104-121, 123-134, 136, 137. 13. 122. 14. 135, pts. 1-3; U. S. Mexican Boundary survey. 15. 138-146. — 2d sess., no. 1. 16. Commerce and nav. [Unnumb. doc.]

— Reports from the Court of Claims. Wash., 1856. 2 v. 8°.
Contents. Vol. 1. No. 1-26. 2. 27-41.

— Reports of committees. Wash., 1856. 3 v. 8°.
Contents. Vol. 1. No. 1-199 (161 w.). 2. 200. Kansas affairs. 3. 201-359 (205, 346 w.). — 2d sess. No. 1.
Also no. 200. Wash., 1856. 8°.

— Misc. docs. Wash., 1856. 2 v. 8°.
Contents. Vol. 1. No. 1-79. 2. 80-142. — 2d sess. No. 1, 2.

34*th Cong.* 3*d sess., Dec.* 1, 1856 - *March* 3, 1857.

— Journal. Wash., 1856. 8°.

— Ex. docs. Wash., 1857. 13 v. in 17 pts. 8°.
Contents. Vol. 1. No. 1, pts. 1-3. 2. 2. 3. 3-17, 19-30. 4. 18: Coast survey. 5. 31-39. 6. 40-59, 61-64. 7. 60: Com. rel. 8. 65, pts. 1-4. 9. 66-81. 10. 82-85. 11. 86. 12. 87-88. 13. Com. and nav. [Unnumb. doc.]

— Misc. docs. Wash., 1857. 8°.
Contents. No. 1-73 (2 w.).

— Reports from the Court of Claims. Wash., 1857. 8°.
Contents. No. 43-80.

— Reports of committees. Wash., 1857. 3 v. 8°.
Contents. Vol. 1. No. 1-174. 2. 175. 3. 176-269 (208 w.).

35*th Cong.* 1*st sess., Dec.* 7, 1857 - *June* 14, 1858.

— Journal. Wash., 1857. 8°.

— Ex. docs. Wash., 1858. 14 v. in 20 pts. 8°, 4°.
Contents. Vol. 1. No. 1, 3-10. 2. 2, pts. 1-3 [also a vol. of maps]. 3. 11, 12, 14-16, 18-20. 4. 13. 5. 17: Com. rel. 6. 21: Coast survey. 7. 22-31. 8. 32, pts. 1-4. 9. 33-70. 10. 71-88. 11. 89-96. 12. 97-118. 13. 119-140 (126 w.). 14: Com. and nav. [Unnumb. doc.]

— Misc. docs. Wash., 1858. 3 v. 8°.
Contents. Vol. 1. No. 1-67. 2. 68. 3. 69-137.
Also no 135: Smithsonian Inst. [12th] ann. rept., 1857. Wash., 1858. 8°.

— Reports fr. Ct. of Claims. Wash., 1858. 3 v. 8°.
Contents. Vol. 1. No. 82-126. 2. 127-151. 3. 152-175.

— Reports of committees. Wash., 1858. 6 v. 8°.
Contents. Vol. 1. No. 1-200. 2. 201-351. 3. 352-411. 4. 412-457. 5. 458-551.

35*th Cong.* 2*d sess., Dec.* 6, 1858 - *March* 4, 1859.

— Journal. Wash., 1858. 8°.

— Ex. docs. Wash., 1859. 13 v. in 20 pts. 8°, 4°.
Contents. Vol. 1. No. 1, 3. 2. 2, pts. 1-5. 3. 4-13. 4. 14-22. 5. 23-32, 34-49. 6. 33: Coast survey. 7. 50-84. 8. 85: Com. rel. 9. 86-104, 106-108. 10. 105, pts. 1-4. 11. 109. 12. 110-114. 13. Com. and nav. [Unnumb. doc.]

— Misc. docs. Wash., 1859. 2 v. 8°.
Contents. Vol. 1. No. 1-42, 44-61. 2. 43.

— Reports fr. Ct. of Claims. Wash., 1859. 8°.
Contents. No. 176-199.

— Reports of committees. Wash., 1859. 3 v. 8°.
Contents. Vol. 1. No. 1-183, 185-187, 190-255. 2. 184. 3. 188, 189.

36*th Cong.* 1*st sess., Dec.* 5, 1859 - *June* 25, 1860.

— Journal. Wash., 1859. 2 pts. 8°.

— Ex. docs. Wash., 1860-61. 15 v. in 17 pts. 8° *and* 4°.
Contents. Vol. 1. No. 1-3, 5, 6, 8, 9. 2. 4: Com. rel. 3. 7. 4. 10-13. 5. 14-22. 6. 23-40, 42-43. 7. 41: Coast survey. 8. 44-52. 9. 53-54, 57-70. 10, pts. 1, 2. 55: Results of meteorol. survey [by] the Smithsonian Inst., 1854-59. — Rept. of the Commis. of Patents. 11, pts. 1, 2. 56: Reports of explorations for a R. R. to the Pacific. Vol. 12. book 1, 2. 12. 71-85. 13. 86-89, 91-102. 14. 90: Report upon the Colorado River of the West, explor., 1857, 58. 15. Com. and nav. [Unnumb. doc.]
Also no. 56. Vol. 12, bk. 2. Wash., 1860. 4°.

— Misc. docs. Wash., 1860. 7 v. 8°.
Contents. Vol. 1. No. 1-2, 4-7. 2. 3. 3. 8. 4. 9-11. 5. 12-42. 6. 43-89. 7. 90-100.
Also no. 90: Smithsonian Inst. [14th] ann. rept., 1859. Wash., 1860. 8°.

— Reports from the Court of Claims. Wash., 1860. 5 v. 8°.
Contents. Vol. 1. No. 199-208. 2. 209-225. 3. 226. 4. 227-240. 5. 241-255.

— Reports of committees. Wash., 1860. 5 v. 8°.
Contents. Vol. 1. No. 1-200. 2. 201-321. 3. 322-510. 4. 511-647, 649-667. 5. 648: The Covode investigation.
Also no. 78. *n.t.p.* [1861.] 8°.
Also no. 648. *n.t.p.* [1868.] 8°.

36*th Cong.* 2*d sess., Dec.* 3, 1860 - *March* 4, 1861.

— Journal. Wash., 1860. 8°.
— Ex. docs. Wash., 1861. 11 v. (v. 11 w.). 8°.
Contents. Vol. 1. No. 1. 2. 2. 3. 3-6, 8, 9. 4. 7. 5. 10-12. 6. 13, 15-41. 7. 14. 8. 42-48. 9. 49-72. 10. 73-82 (74 w.*, 'was lost in the Committee of Ways and Means'). 11. *Wanting.* Com. and nav.

— Misc. docs. Wash., 1860. 8°.
Contents. No. 1-44.

— Reports from the Court of Claims. Wash., 1861. 3 v. 8°.
Contents. Vol. 1. No. 256-258. 2. 259-269. 3. 270-276.

— Reports of committees. Wash., 1860, 61. 3 v. in 4 pts. 8°.
Contents. Vol. 1. No. 1-77. 2. 78-103, 105-107. 3. 104, pts. 1, 2.
Also no. 59, 79, 87, 88, 91. Wash., 1861. 8°.
Also no. 78. *n.t.p.* [1861.] 8°.

37*th Cong.* 1*st sess., July* 4 - *Aug.* 6, 1861.

— Journal. Wash., 1861. 8°.
— Ex. docs. and Reports of committees. Wash., 1861. 8°.
Contents. Ex. docs. No. 1-20. — Rep. of com. 1-4.

— Misc. docs. Wash., 1861. 8°.
Contents. No. 1-24.

37*th Cong.* 2*d sess., Dec.* 2, 1861 - *July* 17, 1862.

— Journal. Wash., 1862. 8°.
— Ex. docs. Wash., 1862. 12 v. in 13 pts. 8° *and* 4°.
Contents. Vol. 1. No. 1-27. 2. 28-34. 3. 35-44, 46-52. 4. 45: For. rel. 5. 53-69, 71-79. 6. 70: Coast survey. 7. 80-99. 8. 100-104. 9. 105-124. 10. 125-136, 138-151. 11. 137. 12. Com. and nav. [Unnumb. doc.]
Also no. 100. *n.t.p.* [1862.] 8°.

— Misc. docs. Wash., 1862. 8°.
Contents. No. 1-91.
Also no. 77: Smithsonian Inst. [16th] ann. rept., 1861. Wash., 1862. 8°.

— Reports from the Court of Claims. Wash., 1862. 2 v. 8°.
Contents. Vol. 1. No. 277-290. 2. 291-293.

— Reports of committees. Wash., 1862. 4 v. 8°.
Contents. Vol. 1. No. 1, 2, pt. 1. 2. 2, pt. 2, 3-85. 4. 86-148.
Also no. 2. Wash., 1861. 8°.
Also no. 86. *n.t.p.* [1862.] 8°.

37*th Cong.* 3*d sess., Dec.* 1, 1862 - *March* 4, 1863.

— Journal. Wash., 1862. 8°.
— Ex. docs. Wash., 1863-64. 12 v. in 14 pts. 8° *and* 4°.
Contents. Vol. 1-4. No. 1. 4. 2-21. 5. 23-51. [Extra v. 5. Maps for doc. no. 1.] 6. 53-62. 7. 64-77. 8. 79-85. 9. 22: Coast survey. 10, pts. 1, 2. 52: Patent reports. 11. 78. 12. 63: Com. and nav.

— Misc. docs. Wash., 1863. 2 v. 8°.
Contents. Vol. 1. No. 1-24, 26, 27. 2. 25.
Also no. 25: Smithsonian Inst. [7th] ann. rept. 1862. Wash., 1863. 8°.

— Reports of committees and Court of Claims. Wash., 1862. 8°.
Contents. Com., no. 1-64. — Court, 294-296.

38*th Cong.* 1*st sess., Dec.* 7, 1863 - *July* 4, 1864.

— Journal. Wash., 1863. 8°.
— Ex. docs. Wash., 1864. 16 [17] v. 8° *and* 4°.
Contents. Vol. 1, 2. No. 1: Diplomatic. 3. 1: Interior. 4. 1: Navy. 5. 1: War and Postmaster-General. 6. 2-3. 7. 4-26 (6 w.*). 8. 11: Coast survey. 9. 27-40, 42-59 (37, 51 w.*). 10. 41: Commercial relations. 11, 12. 60: Patent reports. 13. 61-73 (60, 68 w.*). 14. 74: Prize cases in N. Y. 15. 75-90, 92-104 (101 w.*). 16. 91: Agric. [17. Com. and nav.]
Note. A vol. of maps accompanies doc. 1.
Also no. 11. Wash., 1865. 8°.
Also no. 69. Wash., 1864. 8°.
Also no. 405. *n.t.p.* [1864.] f°.
Also another ed. of no. 405. *n.t.p.* 8°.

— Misc. docs. Wash., 1864. 4 v. 8°.
Contents. Vol. 1. No. 1-15. 2. 16-27. 3. 28-82, 84, 85. 4. 83.
Also no. 83: Smithsonian Inst. [18th] ann. rept. 1863. Wash., 1864. 8°.

— Reports of committees. Wash., 1864. 2 v. 8°.
Contents. Vol. 1. No. 1-111. 2. 112-144.

38*th Cong.* 2*d sess., Dec.* 5, 1864 - *March* 4, 1865.

— Journal. Wash., 1865. 8°.
— Ex. docs. Wash., 1865-66. 15 v. in 16 pts. 8° *and* 4°.
Contents. Vol. 1-4. No. 1: Dipl. 5. 1: Int. and Postm.-General. 6. 1: Navy. 7. 2, 3: Finance. 8. 4-14, 16-50. 9. 15: Coast survey. 10, pt. 1, 2. 51: Patent rept. 11. 60: Comm. rel. 12. 68: Agriculture. 13. 52-59, 61-67, 69-82. 14. 83-85. 15. Com. and nav. [Unnumb. doc.]

— Misc. docs. Wash., 1865. 3 v. 8°.
Contents. Vol. 1. No. 1-54, 56, 58. 2. 55: Smithsonian Inst. report, 1864. 3. 57: Contested elections, 1834-65.
Also no. 55: Smithsonian Inst. [19th] ann. rept., 1864. Wash., 1865. 8°.
Also no. 57. Wash., 1865. 8°.

— Reports of committees. Wash., 1865. 8°.
Contents. No. 1-30.

39*th Cong.* 1*st sess., Dec.* 4, 1865 - *July* 28, 1866.

— Journal. Wash., 1866. 8°.
— Ex. docs. Wash., 1866-67. 16 [17] v. in 25 pts. 8° *and* 4°.
Contents. Vol. 1. No. 1: Dipl., pts. 1-4. 2. 1: Int. 3, 4. 1: War, pts. 1, 2, and app., pts. 1, 2. 5. 1: Navy. 6. 1: Postm.-Gen. — 2-4. 7. 5-49. 8. 50, 51, 53, 55, 57-72. 9. 52, pts. 1-3: Patent reports. 10. 56: Commer. rel. 11. 73, pts. 1, 2: Mexican affairs. 12. 73, 74, 76-101, 103-133. 13. 75: Coast survey. 14. 102: Smithsonian Inst. rept. 15. 136: Agric. 16. 134, 135, 137-156. [17.] Com. and navig. [Unnumb. doc.]
Also no. 12. *n.t.p.* [1865.] 8°.
Also no. 34, 34 pt. 2, 51, 62, 68 (all with additions and omissions), and with additional reports. Wash., 1866. 8°.
Also no. 102: Smithsonian Inst. [20th] ann. rept., 1865. Wash., 1866. 8°.

— Misc. docs. Wash., 1866. 3 v. 8°.
Contents. Vol. 1. No. 1-7. 2. 8-55. 3. 56-130.

— Reports of committees. Wash., 1866. 3 v. 8°.
Contents. Vol. 1. No. 1-29, 32-100, 102-117 (31, 94 w.*). 2. 30. 3. 101.

39*th Cong.* 2*d sess., Dec.* 3, 1866 - *March* 4, 1867.

— Journal. Wash., 1867. 8°.
— Ex. docs. Wash., 1867, 69. 16 [17] v. in 21 pts. 8° *and* 4°.
Contents. Vol. 1. No. 1: Dipl., pts. 1-3. 2. 1: Int. 3. 1: War. 4. 1: Navy, Postm.-Gen. and no. 2. 5. 3-8. 6. 9-24. 7. 25-49. 8. 50-54. 9. 55-56. 10. 57-70. 11. 71-75, 77-80, 82-86, 88-106, 108, 110-116. 12: 76: Mexican aff. 13. 81: Commer. rel. 14. 87: Coast survey. 15. 107: Agric. 16. 109: Patents, pts. 1, 2. [17]: Com. and nav. [Unnumb. doc.]
Also no. 2. *n.t.p.* [1867.] 8°.
Also no. 58. *n.t.p.* [Wash., 1867.] 8°.

— Misc. docs. Wash., 1867. 8°.
Contents. No. 1-82.
Also no. 83: Smithsonian Inst. [21st ann. rept., 1866. Wash., 1867. 8°.

— Reports of committees. Wash., 1867. 4 v. 8°.
Contents. Vol. 1. No. 1-15 (9 w.*). 2. 16. 3. 17-33. 4. 34.
Also no. 16. Wash., 1867. 8°.

40th Cong. 1st sess., March 4 - Dec. 2, 1867.

— Journal. Wash., 1867. 8°.

— Ex. docs. Wash., 1868. 8°.
Contents. No. 1-36.

— Misc. docs. Wash., 1868. 2 v. 8°.
Contents. Vol. 1. No. 1-37, 39-55. 2. 38.

— Reports of committees. Wash., 1868. 8°.
Contents. No. 1-7.

40th Cong. 2d sess., Dec. 2, 1867 - Nov. 10, 1868.

— Journal. Wash., 1868. 8°.

— Ex. docs. Wash., 1868. 20 [22] v. in 27 pts. 8° *and* 4°.
Contents. Vol. 1. No. 1: Dipl., pt. 1, 2. 2. 1: War, pts. 1, 2. 3. 1: Int. 4. 1: Navy and Postm.-Gen. 5. 2, 3. 6. 4, 5. 7. 6-22, 24-57. 8. 23: Wirz trial. 9. 58-95. 10. 96, pts. 1-4: Patent Office. 11. 97-98, 100-156. 12. 99: Ordnance. 13. 157-159, 161-180. 14. 160: Commer. rel. 15. 181-201, 203-252 (206 w.). 16. 202: Mineral res. W. of the Rocky Mts. 17. 253-274, 276-295. 18. 275: Coast survey. 19. 296-311. 20. 312-343. [21. Dept. of Agric. Unnumb. doc.] [22. Com. and nav. Unnumb. doc.]

— Misc. docs. Wash., 1868. 2 v. 8°.
Contents. Vol. 1. No. 1-84. 2. 85-168.

— Reports of committees. Wash., 1868. 2 v. 8°.
Contents. Vol. 1. No. 1-46. 2. 47-84.

40th Cong. 3d sess., Dec. 7, 1868 - Mar. 4, 1869.

— Journal. Wash., 1869. 8°.

— Ex. docs. Wash., 1869-71. 14 [16] v. in 21 pts. 8° *and* 4°.
Contents. Vol. 1. No. 1: Dipl., pts. 1, 2. 2. 1: Int. 3. 1: War, pts. 1, 2. 4. 1: Navy and Postm.-Gen. 5. 2, 3. 6. 4, 5. 7. 6-28, 30-49 (7, 8 w.*). 8. 29: Claims against China. 9. 50, 51, 53-70, 72-82. 10. 52: Patents, pts. 1-4]. 11. 71: Coast survey. 12. 83: Smithsonian Inst. rep. 13. 84-86, 88-102. 14. 87: Commer. rel. [15.] Agric. [16.] Commerce and nav.
Also no. 83: Smithsonian Inst. [23d] ann. rept., 1868. Wash., 1869. 8°.

— Consolidated index of the Ex. docs., 26th - 40th Cong.; [by] E. McPherson. Wash., 1870. 8°.

— Misc. docs. Wash., 1869. 8°.
Contents. No. 1-57.

— Reports of committees. Wash., 1869. 4 v. 8°.
Contents. Vol. 1. No. 1-30, 32-40, 42-44. 2, 3. 31, 41: Election frauds in N. Y. 4. 45: Treatment of prisoners of war by Rebel authorities.

— Consolidated index to Reports of committees, 26th - 40th Cong. Wash., 1869. 8°.

41st Cong. 1st sess., March 4 - Apr. 10, 1869.

— Journal. Wash., 1869. 8°.

— Ex. docs. Wash., 1869. 8°.
Contents. No. 1-6.

— Misc. docs. Wash., 1869. 8°.
Contents. No. 1-36.

— Reports of committees. Wash., 1869. 8°.
Contents. No. 1-12.

41st Cong. 2d sess., Dec. 6, 1869 - July 15, 1870.

— Journal. Wash., 1870. 8°.

— Ex. docs. Wash., 1870-72. 13 [15] v. in 18 pts. 8° *and* 4°.
Contents. Vol. 1. No. 1: Navy and Postm.-Gen. 2. 1: War, pts. 1, 2. 3. 1: Int. 4. 2, 3. 5. 4-48. 6. 49-101, 103-142 (76 w. *). 7. 143-205, 208-215. 8. 206. Coast survey. 9. 102, pts. 1-4: Patents. 10. 207: Mines. 11. 216-256 (232, 254 w.*). 12. 257-307 (273 w.*). 13. 308-315. [14.] Com. and nav. [15.] Agric.
Note. Agric., com., and nav. are not no.
Also no. 27. *n.t.p.* [1870.] 8°.
Also no. 240. Wash., 1870. 8°.

— Misc. docs. Wash., 1870. 5 v. 8°.
Contents. Vol. 1. No. 1-25. 2. 13: Barns *vs.* Adams. — 14: Switzler *vs.* Dyer. — 15: Reid *vs.* Julian. 3. 26-151, 153. 4. 152: Contested elections. 5. 154, pts. 1, 2: Contested elections in Louisiana.

— Reports of committees. Wash., 1870. 3 v. 8°.
Contents. Vol. 1. No. 1-32. 2. 33-72. 3. 73-122 (76 w.).

Also no. 28. Wash., 1870. 8°.
Also no. 65. *n.t.p.* [1870.] 8°.
Also no. 114. *n.t.p.* [1870.] 8°.

— Report of the Commis. of Agriculture on the diseases of cattle in the United States. Wash., 1871. 8°.

41st Cong. 3d sess., Dec. 5, 1870 - March 4, 1871.

— Journal. Wash., 1871. 8°.

— Ex. docs. Wash., 1871-73. 12 [13] v. in 16 pts. 8° *and* 4°.
Contents. Vol. 1. No. 1: For. rel. 2. 1: War, pts. 1, 2. 3. 1: Navy and Postm.-Gen. 4. 1: Int., pts. 1, 2. 5. 2, 3. 6. 4-18. 7. 19-60. 8. 61-88, 90-94. 9. 89, pts. 1-4: Patent Office. 10. 95-110. 11. 112: Coast survey. 12. 111, 113-153. [13.] Agric.
Also no. 153: Smithsonian Inst. [24th] ann. rept., 1869. Wash., 1871. 8°.

— Misc. docs. Wash., 1871. 2 v. 8°.
Contents. Vol. 1. No. 1-65. 2. 66-107.

— Reports of committees. Wash., 1871. 8°.
Contents. No. 1-53.

42d Cong. 1st sess., March 4 - Apr. 20, 1871.

— Journal. Wash., 1871. 8°.

— Ex. docs. Wash., 1871. 2 v. 8°.
Contents. Vol. 1. No. 1-10. 2. 11-20.
Also no. 19. Wash., 1872. 8°.
Also no. 20: Smithsonian Inst. [25th] ann. rept., 1871. Wash., 1872. 8°.

— Misc. docs. Wash., 1871. 8°.
Contents. No. 1-43.

42d Cong. 2d sess., Dec. 4, 1871 - June 10, 1872.

— Journal. Wash., 1872. 8°.

— Ex. docs. Wash., 1872-74. 18 [19] v. in 23 pts. 8° *and* 4°.
Contents. Vol. 1. No. 1, pt. 1: For. rel. 2. 1, pt. 2: War, pts. 1, 2. 3. 1, pt. 5: Int., pts. 1, 2. 4. 1, pts. 3, 4: Navy, no. 2. 5. 3: Currency. 4: Int. rev. 6 5-20. 7. 21-84. 8. 85-106. 9. 107-109. 10. 110-120, 122-212. 11. 121: Coast survey. 12. 213-219, 221-277. 13. 278-281, 283, 290, 294, 322. 14. 282: Case of Gr. Brit: Geneva Conference, pts. 1, 2, 3. 15. 284-289, 291-293, 295-321, 323, 325, 326. 16. 324. Counter-case of Gr. Brit. 17. 327: Agric., 1871. 18. 220: Com. rel. [19.] Agric., 1872.
Note. Vol. 19 has a sep. t.p. and is not numbered.
Also no. 282. Wash., 1872. 3 v. 8°.
Also no. 324. Wash., 1872. 8°.

— Misc. docs. Wash., 1872. 4 v. 8°.
Contents. Vol. 1. No. 1-33. 2. 34-110. 3. 111-200. 4. 201-230.

— Reports of committees. Wash., 1872. 4 v. in 16 pts. 8°.
Contents. Vol. 1. No. 1-21, 23-71. 2. 22, pts. 1-13: Affairs in the late insurrectionary states; Ku-Klux conspiracy (pt. 1. Rep. of com., *etc.* 2. N. Carolina. 3-5. S. Carolina. 6-7. Georgia. 8-10. Alabama. 11-12. Miss. 13. Florida). 3. 72-83. 4. 84-99.

42d Cong., 3d sess., Dec. 2, 1872 - March 4, 1873.

— Ex. docs. Wash., 1873, 72, 75. 12 [13] v. in 20 pts. 8°

— Journal. Wash., 1873. 8°, 4°.
Contents. Vol. 1. No. 1, pt. 1: For. rel., pts. 1-6: (1-4. Geneva arbitration. 5. Berlin. 6. Gen.) 2. 1, pt. 2.: War, pts. 1, 2. 3. 1, pt. 5: Int., pts. 1, 2 (pt. 2. Education). 4. 1, pts. 3, 4, 6, 7, and No. 2. 5. 3-4, 6-19. 6. 5, 190, *also* Misc. doc. 44. 7. 20-91. 8. 92-150. 9. 151-159, 161-210. 10. 160: Com. rel. 11. 211-239, 241, 242. 12. 240: Coast Survey. [13.] Agric.
Also no. 185. Wash., 1873. 8°.

— Misc. docs. Wash., 1873-74. 5 v. 8°.
Contents. Vol. 1. No. 1-25. 2. 26-43, 45-99. 3. 100-112. 4. 109: Index to private claims, 32d - 41st Cong. 5. 113: Darien survey.
Note. No. 44 is bound in v. 6 of Ex. docs.
Also no. 107: Smithsonian Inst. [27th] annual rept., 1869. Wash., 1871. 8°.

— Reports of committees. Wash., 1873. 3 v. 8°.
Contents. Vol. 1. No. 1-76, 79, 80, 83-94, 96, 97, 2. 77, 78, pts. 1, 2. 81, 82, 95. 3. 98: Indian frauds.

43d Cong. 1st sess., Dec. 1, 1873 - *June* 23, 1874.

— Journal. Wash., 1873. 8°.
— Ex. docs. Wash., 1874. 73, 75. 17 v. in 22 pts. 8° *and* 4°.
Contents. Vol. 1. No. 1, pt. 1: For. rel., pts. 1-3. 2. 1, pt. 2: War, pts. 1-3. 3. 1, pt. 3, 4: Navy and Postm.-Gen. 4. 1, pt. 5: Int., pt. 1, 2. 5. 1, pt. 6 and No. 2. 6. 3, 4. 7. 5, 36, 124, 187. 8. 6-35, 37-57. 9. 58-122. 10. 123, 125-132, 134-141. 11. 133: Coast survey. 12. 142, 144-182, 184-186, 188-210. 13. 143: Com. rel. 14. 183: Com. and nav. 15. 211-219. 16. 220-255. 17. 256-290.
Also no. 127. *n.t.p.* [1875.] 8°.
Also no. 193. Wash., 1874. 8°.
Also no. 220. *n.t.p.* [1874.] 8°.
Also no. 221. Wash., 1874. 8°.
Also no. 285. Wash., 1875. 8°.
— Misc. docs. Wash., 1874, 75. 6 v. 8° *and* 4°.
Contents. Vol. 1. No. 1-52. 2. 53-125. 3. 126-264. 4. 174. 5. 265-301. 6. 300: Explor. of the Colorado River of the West; by J. W. Powell.
Note. Vol. 6 has a separate title page.
— Reports of committees. Wash., 1874. 5 v. 8°.
Contents. Vol. 1. No. 1-262. 2. 263-434. 3. 435-611. 4. 612-770. 5. 771-843.

43d Cong. 2d sess., Dec. 7, 1874 - *March* 4, 1875.

— Journal. Wash., 1875. 8°.
— Ex. docs. Wash., 1875, 74, 77. 18 [19] v. 8° *and* 4°.
Contents. Vol. 1, pt. 1: For. rel. 2-4. 1, pt. 2: War. 5. 1, pt. 3: Navy. Pt. 4: Postm.-Gen. — No. 7: Attorney-Gen. 6. 1, pt. 5: Int., pt. 1. 7. 1, pt. 5. Int., pt. 2: Education. 8. 1, pt. 6: Commis. of D. C. — No. 2: Finance. 9. 3: Currency. — 4. Int. rev. 10. 5, 6, 150. 11. 8-44. 12 45-78. 13. 79-99. 14. 100: Coast survey. 15. 101-149, 151, 156, 158-170. 16. 157: Com. rel. 17. 171: Com. and nav. 18. 172-180. [19]: Dept. of Agric. [Unnumb. doc.]
Note. Vol. 19 has a sep. title-page.
— Misc. docs. Wash., 1875. 3 v. 8°.
Contents. Vol. 1. No. 1-36. 2. 37-95. 3. 96-100.
Also no. 56: Smithsonian Inst. [29th] ann. rept., 1874. Wash., 1875. 8°.
— Reports of committees. Wash., 1875. 7 v. 8°.
Contents. Vol. 1. No. 1-100. 2. 101-133, 135-149. 3. 134. 4. 150-260, 263-265. 5. 261, pts. 1, 2. 6. 262. 7. 266-345.

44th Cong. 1st sess., Dec. 6, 1875 - *Aug.* 15, 1876.

— Journal. Wash., 1875. 8°.
— Ex. docs. Wash., 1876-78. 17 v. in 26 pts. 8° *and* 4°.
Contents. Vol. 1. No. 1, pt. 1: For. rel., pts. 1, 2. 2. 1, pt. 2: War, pts. 1, 3, 4, and no. 2, v. 1, 2. 3. No. 1, pts. 3, 4: Navy and Postm.-Gen. 4. 1, pt. 5: Int., pts. 1, 2. 5. 1, pts. 6-9, and no. 7-13. 6. 2: Treasury. 7. 3, 4. 8. 5, 6, 107. 9. 14-21. 10. 22-80, 82, 83. 11. 81: Coast survey. 12. 84-106, 108-123, 125-158. 13. 124: Com. and nav. 14. 159-165, 167-190, 192-195. 15. 166: Com. rel. 16. 191: Mail contracts. 17. 196: Vienna Expos., pts. 1-4.
— Misc. docs. Wash., 1876. 10 v. 8°.
Contents. Vol. 1. No. 1-49. 2. 50-60, 62-64, 66-82. 3. 61, 65. 4. 83-103. 5. 104-169, 171-174. 6-8. 170, pts. 1-9: Investigation of the Navy Department: (6, pt. 1-3; 7, pt. 5; 8, pt. 4, 6-9). 9. 175-186. 10. 187-194.
— Reports of committees. Wash., 1876. 9 v. 8°.
Contents. Vol. 1. No. 1-342 (4 w.*). 2. 343-440 (353, 394 w.*). 3. 441-578, 580-622. 4. 579: Emma mine. 5. 623-784. 6. 785-793. 7. 794-798, 801-814. 8. 799, 800. 9. 815-842.

44th Cong. 2d sess., Dec. 4, 1876 - *March* 4, 1877.

— Journal. Wash., 1876. 8°
— Ex. docs. Wash., 1877, 76. 13 v. in 21 pts. (v. 10, pts. 1, 2 w.). 8° *and* 4°.
Contents. Vol. 1. No. 1, pt. 1: For. rel. 2. 1, pt. 2: War, pts. 1, 3, 4 and no. 2, v. 1-3. 3. No. 1, pts. 3, 4: Postm. and Navy. 4. 1, pt. 5: Int., pts. 1, 2. 5. 1, pts. 6-8: Commis. of the D. C. — 7-20. 6. 2: Finance. 7, 3: Currency. — 4: Int. rev. 8. 5: Appropriations. 6: Indian disbursements. 36: Patents. 9. 21-35, 37-39, 41-42, 44. 10. *Wanting.* (40, pts. 1, 2: Centen. Exhib. gov. col.) 11. 43: Mail contracts. 12. 45: Com. rel. 13. 46, pts. 1, 2: Com. and nav.
— Miscellaneous documents. Wash., 1877. 7 v. 8°.
Contents. Vol. 1. No. 1-12, 14-30, 32, 33, 36-45. 2. 13: Counting electoral votes. 3. 31, pts. 1-3: Election in So. Carolina. 4-6. 34, pts. 1-6: Election in Louisiana. 7. 35, pts. 1-3. Election in Florida.
— Reports of committees. Wash., 1877. 2 v. 8°.
Contents. Vol. 1. No. 1-156. 2. 157-219.

45th Cong. 1st sess., Oct. 15 - *Dec.* 3, 1877.

— Journal. Wash., 1877. 8°.
— Ex. docs. Wash., 1877. 8°.
Contents. No. 1-4, 6-21.
Note. No 5 is bound in v. 13 of the Ex. docs. (Ho.) 2d sess.
— Miscellaneous documents. Wash., 1877. 5 v. 8°.
Contents. Vol. 1-5: Contested elections. 1. No. 1-5, 9, 12-15, 17-20. 2. 6: Dean *vs.* Field. — 7: Richardson *vs.* Rainey. 3. 8: Haralson *vs.* Shelley. — 11: Tellmar *vs.* Smalls. 4. 10: Finley *vs.* Bisbee. 5. Nutting *vs.* Reilly.
Note. The Reports of com. for this sess. are bound with those of the 2d sess.

45th Cong. 2d sess., Dec. 3, 1877 - June 20, 1878.

— Journal. Wash., 1878. 8°.
— Ex. docs. Wash., 1878. 22 v. in 23 pts. 8° *and* 4°.
Contents. Vol. 1. No. 1, pt. 1: For. rel. 2-6. 1, pt. 2, v. 1-4: War Dept. (v. 1: Rept. of the Sec. of War. — 2, pt. 1, 2: Engineers. — 3: Ordnance. — 4: Signal Office). 7. 1, pts. 3, 4: Navy and Postm. 8, 9. 1, pt. 5, v. 1, 2: Int. (v. 1 Rep. of Sec. of Int. — 2. Education). 10. 1, pts. 6-8. — No. 7-33. 11. 2: Rept. of Sec. of Treas. 12. 3: Currency. — 4: Int. rev. 13. No. 5 of 1st sess. — 5, 6, 61, 73. 14. 34, 36-38, 40-50, 52-60, 62-72. 15. 35, 39. 16. 51: Mail contracts. 17. 74-88, 100, 101. 18-20. 89: Fishery awards, v. 1-3. 21. 90: Com. and nav. 22. 102: Com. rel.
— Misc. docs. Wash., 1878. 7 v. 8°.
Contents. Vol. 1. No. 1-30, 32-35. 2. 31. 3. 36-50. 4. 51, 53-56. 5. 52. 6. 57-62, 64-66. 7. 63.
— Reports of committees. Wash., 1878. 5 v. 8°.
Contents. Vol. 1. 1st sess. no. 1-4. — 2d sess. 1-245. 2. 246-588. 3. 589-701. 4. 702-833. 5. 834-898, 900-1017.
Note. 'No. 899 was never printed'. No. 1018 is bound in v. 1 of the Reports of com. 3d sess.

45th Cong. 3d sess., Dec. 2, 1878 - *March* 3, 1879.

— Journal. Wash., 1878. 8°.
— Ex. docs. Wash., 1879. 18 v. (v. 10 w.). 8°.
Contents. Vol. 1. No. 1, pt. 1: For. rel. 2-7. 1, pt. 2, v. 1-4: War Dept. (v. 1: Rept. of the Sec. of War. — 2, pt. 1-3: Engineers. — 3: Ordnance. — 4: Signal Officer). 8. 1, pts. 3, 4. Navy and Postm. 9, 10. (v. 10 *wanting.*) 1, pt. 5, v. 1, 2: Int. (v. 1: Rept. of the Sec. of Int. — 2: Education). 11. 1, pts. 6, 7. — No. 7-31. 12. 2: Sec. of Treas. 13. 3: Currency. — 4: Int. rev. 14. 5: Appropriations. — 6: Disbursements for Indian Dept. — 48: Patents. — Reports of com. no. 52: Index to Journals of Cong. 15. 32, pts. 1, 2: Com. and nav. 16. 33-47, 49-87, 89-107. 17. 88: Mail contracts. 18. 108: Com. rel.
— Misc. docs. Wash., 1879. 5 v. 8°.
Contents. Vol. 1. No. 1-21. 2. 22: Investigation of Judge Blodgett. — 23: Investigation of J. I. Davenport. 3. 24-30, 32-34. 4, 5. 31, pts. 1-5: Presidential election. (4. 31, pt. 1: Testimony taken at Washington. 5. 31, pt. 2: Florida. — 3: Louisiana. — 4: Cipher telegrams. — 5: Anal. index.)
— Reports of committees. Wash., 1879. 2 v. 8°.
Contents. Vol. 1. 2d sess. no. 1018. — 3d sess. 1-51, 53-118, 120-168. 2. 119, 169-291.
Note. No. 52 is bound in v. 14 of the Ex. docs. 3d sess.

46th Cong., 2d sess., Dec. 1, 1879 - *June* 16, 1880.

— Reports of committees. Wash., 1880. 4°.
Namely. No. 1776: General index of the Journals of Congress, 1st - 10th Cong. incl.; by A. Ordway.

WORKS ABOUT THE HOUSE.

— Lloyd, T. Congressional register; history of the proc. and debates of the 1st Ho. of Rep. of the U. S. Vol. 1-3, no. 1-3. N. Y., 1789-90. 4 v. 8°.

— Debates in the House during the 1st sess. of the 4th Cong., pt. 1: The constitutional powers of the House with respect to treaties. Phila., 1796. 8°.

— Gaston, W. Speech in support of the proposition to expunge from the rules of the House the 'previous question'. Georgetown, 1816. 8°. (B 669)

— Everett, E. Remarks on the apportionment bill, May 17, 1832. Wash., 1832. 8°. (B 1056)

— Huntington, J. W. Speech in favor of electing representatives by districts, May 31. Wash., 1842. 8°. (B 1499)

— Russell, A. Remarks on the apportionment of the Ho. of Rep. according to the 6th census. N. Y., 1842. 8°. (B 1499)

— Collamer, J. Speech on the constitutional validity of Cong. requiring the election of representatives to be by districts. Wash., 1844. 8°. (B 1174)

Office of Indian Affairs.

(Subordinate to the *Department of the Interior.*)

— Report [of commissioner]. Wash., 1837. 8°. (25th Cong. 2d sess., Ex. Doc., no. 3. B 1160)

— *Same.* 1869, 1872-75. Wash., 1869-75. 5 v. 8°.

Note. 1872-75 have the title 'Annual report'.

☞ The missing volumes and duplicates of those enumerated here are contained in the full set of Congressional documents, *see House* (p. 3064-92); — *Senate* (p. 3096-3106).

— Cushing, C. Speech on the bill making appropriations for the expenses of the Indian Dept., Feb. 1. Wash., 1837. 8°. (B 1718)

Board of Indian Commissioners.

(Subordinate to the *Department of the Interior.*)

— 1st] - 3d report, 1869-71. Wash., 1870-72. 3 v. 8°.

Note. The 2d and 3d reports have the title 'Annual report'.

☞ The succeeding reports are contained in the full set of Congressional documents, *see House* (p. 3064-92); — *Senate* (p. 3096-3106).

Department of the Interior.

— Register of officers and agents, civil, military, and naval, 1861-67, 79. Wash., 1862-79. 5 v. 8°.

Note. 1879 is in two vols.; vol. 1, Legislative, executive, judicial; v. 2, Post Office Dept. For previous years, *see Department of State* (p. 3106).

— Report on the U. S. and Mexican boundary survey, by W. H. Emory. Wash., 1857-58. 2 v. 4°. (34th Cong. 1st sess. Sen. Doc., no. 108.)

Contents. Vol. 1, pt. 1. **Emory, W. H.** Report. 1, pt. 2. **Parry, C. C.,** *and* **Schott, A.** Geological reports. — **Hall, J.** Palæontology and geology. — **Conrad, T. A.** Description of cretaceous and tertiary fossils. 2, pt. 1. *Botany:* **Parry, C. C.** Introduction. — **Torrey, J.** General botany. — **Engelmann, G.** Cactaceæ. 2, 2. *Zoology:* **Baird, S. F.** Mammals, birds, and reptiles. — **Girard, C.** Fishes.

See also Census Office (p. 3058); — *Bureau of Education* (p. 3063); — *Geological Survey* (p. 3064); — *Board of Indian Commis. (above)*; — *Office of Indian Affairs (above)*; — *General Land Office (next col.)*; — *Patent Office* (p. 3094); — *Pension Office* (p. 3094).

Office of Internal Revenue.

(Subordinate to the *Treasury Department.*)

— Report of the Commissioner, 1863-67. Wash., 1864-67. 5 v. 8°.

☞ The missing vols. and duplicates of those here enumerated are contained in the set of Congressional docs. *see House* (p. 3064-92); — *Senate* (p. 3096-3106).

— Laws rel. to internal revenue in force Aug. 1, 1866; prepared under the direction of the Commissioner. Wash., 1866. 8°. (E 90)

General Land Office.

(Subordinate to the *Department of the Interior.*)

— Operations of land offices; statements, 1834/35. *n.t.p.* Wash., 1835.] 8°. (24th Cong. 1st sess. Ho. doc. 5. E 43)

— Report from the Secretary of the Treasury with the annual report of the Commissioner, 1835/36. *n.t.p.* [Wash., 1836.] 8°. (24th Cong. 1st sess. Sen. Doc., 3. E 43)

— Affairs of Land Office; report, 1836/37. [Wash., 1837.] 8°. (25th Cong. 2d sess. Ho. Doc. 23. E 43)

— Report from the Secretary of the Treasury transmitting report of the Commissioner, 1837/38. *n.t.p.* [Wash., 1838-39.] 2 pts. 8°. (25th Cong. 3d sess. Sen. Doc. 17.)

— Annual report, 1839/40. Wash., 1841. 8°. (26th Cong. 2d sess. Ho. Doc. 38. B 1164)

— Report, 1866-69, 71. Wash., 1867-75. 5 v. 8°.

☞ The missing vols. and duplicates of those here enumerated are contained in the full set of Congressional documents, *see House* (p. 3064-92); — *Senate* (p. 3096-3106).

Light House Board.

(Subordinate to the *Treasury Department.*)

— List of lighthouses, lighted beacons, *etc.*, Jan. 1. Wash., 1858. 8°.

☞ The reports are contained in the Congressional documents, *see House* (p. 3064-92); — *see Senate* (p. 3096-3106).

Marine Corps.

— Reynolds, J. G. Exculpation of the marine corps in Mexico; with record of the general court martial, Brooklyn, 1852. N. Y., 1853. 8°.

Medical Department.

(Subordinate to the *War Department.*)

See Surgeon General's Office (p. 3107).

Commission on Claims against Mexico.

— Treaty between the U. S. and Mexico, Feb. 2, 1848; including art. I, V. of the unratified convention of Nov. 20, 1843, convention of Apr. 11, 1839, act of Congress, Mar. 3, 1849, creating a commission, rules, and orders of commissioners. Wash., 1849. 8°. (B 1510)

Military Commission to Europe.

(Subordinate to the *War Office.*)

— Delafield, R. Report on the art of war in Europe, 1854-56. Wash., 1861. 4°. (36th Cong. 2d sess. Ho. Ex. doc.)

— McClellan, G. B. Report. Wash., 1857. 4°. (34th Cong. Spec. sess. Sen. Doc. 1.)

— Mordecai, A. Report. Wash., 1860. 4°. (36th Cong. 1st sess. Sen. Doc. 60.)

Commissioner of Mining Statistics.

(Subordinate to the *Treasury Department.*)

— Statistics of mines and mining west of the Rocky Mts., [1st, 2d,] 4th, 6th report; by R. W. Raymond.' Wash., 1869-74. 4 v. 8°.

Note. The 1st report is by the Special Commissioner, and has the title 'Mineral resources west of the Rocky Mts.'

☞ The missing vols. and duplicates of those here enumerated are contained in the full set of Congressional documents, *see House* (p. 3064-92); — *Senate* (p. 3096-3106).

Mint.

☞ For reports of the Director *see* the set of Congressional documents, *House* (p. 3064-92); — *Senate* (p. 3096-3106).

National Observatory.

See Naval Observatory (p. 3093).

Naval Academy at Annapolis.

See Naval Academy at Annapolis (p. 3057).

Naval Astronomical Expedition, 1849-52.

— Naval Astronomical Exped. to the southern hemisphere, 1849-52. Wash., 1855-56. 6 v. (v. 4, 5 w.). 4°. (33d Cong. 1st sess. Ho. Doc. 121.)

Contents. Vol. 1. **Gilliss, J. M.** Chile: its geography, climate, earthquakes, *etc.* 2. **MacRae, A.** The Andes and Pampas. — **Smith, J. L.** Minerals. — **Ewbank, T.** Indian remains. — **Baird, S. F.** Mammals. — **Cassin, J.** Birds. — **Girard, C.** Reptiles, fishes, and crustacea. — **Gould, A. A.** Shells. — **Gray, A.** Dried plants. — **Brackenridge, W. D.** Living plants and seeds. — **Wyman, J.** Fossil mammals. — **Conrad, T. A.** Fossil shells. 3. **Gilliss, J. M.** Observations to determine the solar parallax. 4, 5. *Wanting.* 6. **Gilliss, J. M.** Magnetical and meteorological observations.

Naval Observatory (formerly *National Observatory*).

(Subordinate to the *Navy Department.*)

— Sands, B. F., *and others.* Report on obs. of the total eclipse of the Sun, Aug. 7, 1869. Wash., 1870. 4°.

Note. The official report of the expedition to the Dead Sea was published at the Observatory.

Navy.

— *History.* Emmons, G. F. Statistical hist. of the navy, **1775-1853.** Wash., 1853. 4°.

— - Boynton, C. B. History of the navy during the rebellion. N. Y., 1867-68. 2 v. 8°.

— Gallatin, A. Substance of two speeches on the bill for augm. the navy establishment of U. S. Phila., **1799.** 8°. (B 628)

— Harper, R. G. Speech on the navy. Phila., **1799.** 8°. (B 628)

— U. S. *President.* Marine rules and regulations. Boston, 1799. 8°.

— Barry, J., *Senior Officer.* Signals presented to the navy of the U. S. Norfolk, **1800.** 8°.

— Mercer, — (?) Address on maintaining a permanent navy. Phila., **1802.** 8°. (B 621)

— U. S. *President.* Naval regulations, Jan. 25. *n.p.*, [1802]. 12°. (C 116)

— Thoughts on the subject of naval power in the U. S. Phila., **1806.** 8°. (B 426)

— Lloyd, J. Speech, on the bill conc. the naval establishment, Feb. 28. *n.p.,n.d.* [1812.] 8°. (B 443)

— Quincy, J. Speech, Jan. 25, in rel. to maritime protection. Alexandria, 1812. 12°. (B 443, W 4)

— Policy of the nation as it respects a navy in the present crisis. N. Y., **1814.** 8°. (B 454)

— U. S. *14th Cong. 1st sess.* Document exhibiting the naval force, Jan. 1, **1816.** Wash., 1816. 8°. (Doc. 15. B 1492)

— Letters on the establishment of a navy yard for the Southern Dept. Norfolk, 1816. 8°. (B 997)

— Sertorius, *pseud.* Letter on the naval depot. *n.p.*, [182-]. 8°. (A 1)

— Goldsborough, C. W. United States naval chronicle. Vol. 1. Wash., **1824.** 8°.

— U. S. *Navy Dept.* Rules regulating the civil administration of the navy. Wash., **1832.** 12°.

— Bell, J. Speech on the naval appropriation bill, Mar. 17 [16], 22, and 23. Wash., **1836.** 8°. (B 1777, 2009)

— Cushing, C. Speech, on clauses in the navy appropriation bill rel. to navy yards, Feb. 11, 1836. *n.t.p.* [1836.] 8°. (B 1721)

— Evans, G. Speech, bill making appropriations for the naval service, Mar. 15. Wash., 1836. 8°. (B 1113, 1777)

— Jarvis, L. Speech on the navy appropriation bill, April 4. Wash., 1836. 8°. (B 1496)

— McNally, W. Evils and abuses in the naval and merchant service exposed, *etc.* Boston, **1839.** 12°.

— Adams, J. Q. Speech in rel. to the navy pension fund, Dec. 28. [Wash., 1840.] 8°. (B 1428, 1823)

— Ward, A. Speech, navy appropriation bill. Wash., **1841.** 8°. (B 1664)

— Few practical reflections on the grog ration of the U. S. navy; by an old officer. *n.p.*, **1849.** 8°. (B 1281)

— U. S. *Navy Dept.* Uniform for officers of the navy. N. Y., **[1863]**. 4°.

— Dickerson, E. N. The navy of the U. S.; speech. N. Y., **1864.** 8°.

— U. S. *War Dept.* Regulations for the government of the navy. Wash., **1865.** 16°.

— Dislère, P. Note sur la marine des Etats-Unis. *n.t.p.* [Paris, **1868.**] 8°.

Registers.

— U. S. *Navy Dept.* Register of the navy, Dec. **1815,** 21, 23-26, 28, 30, 32-37, 39-40, 43-56, 58, 61-73, **80.** Wash., 1814 [misprint for 1815] - 80. 45 v. 8°.

— Naval register. (*In* **Bowen, A.** Naval monument. **1816.**)

— Register of the army and navy; by P. Force. Wash., **1830.** 12°.

— Homans, B. Register of the navy of the U. S., corr. to 1st April 1843; added, laws passed 3d sess., 27th Cong. Balt., **1843.** 8°.

Periodicals.

— Military and naval magazine of the U. S. [Wash., 1833-36.] 6 v. 8°.

— Naval magazine. N. Y., 1836-37. 2 v. 8°.

— United States army and navy journal. N. Y., [1864-80]. 17 v. f°.

— United States naval chronicle. Vol. 1. Wash., 1824. 8°.

— United States service magazine. N. Y., 1864-66. 5 v. 8°.

See also Exploring Expeditions (p. 3063-64); — *Naval Astronomical Expedition* (*previous column*); — *Naval Biog.* (p. 3111); — *Naval history* (p. 3141, 42).

Navy Department.

— Report, 1862-68, 72-76. Wash., 1863-76. 12 v. 8°.

Note. The title for 1864 reads 'Message of the Pres. and accomp. docs'.

☞ The missing volumes and duplicates of those here enumerated are contained in the full set of Congressional docs.; *see House* (p. 3064-92); — *Senate* (p. 3096-3106).

— Register of the navy, Dec. **1815,** 21, 23-26, 28. 30, 32-37, 39-40, 43-56, **58,** 61-73, **80.** Wash., 1814 [mispr. for 1815] - 80. 45 v. 8°.

— Official letters to the Secretary of the Navy, [rel. to the war of **1812, 13**; copies]. MS.

Note. Vols. 4, 5, 10 of some collection.

— Documents accompanying the report of the Sec. of the Navy. Wash., **1832.** 8°. (22d Cong. 1st sess. Doc. 2. B 1058)

— Rules regulating the civil administration. Wash., 1832. 12°.

— Johnson, W. R. Report to the Navy Dept. on American coals. Wash., **1844.** 8°. (28th Cong. 1st sess. Ho. Doc. 276.)

— Magnetical and meteorological obs. made under orders of the Sec., at Wash.; by J. M. Gilliss. Wash., **1845.** 8°. (28th Cong. 2d sess. Sen. Doc. 172.)

— Rules and regulations for the Naval Acad. at Annapolis. Wash., **1850.** 8°.

— Exploration of the Valley of the Amazon; by W. L. Herndon and L. Gibbon. Wash., **1854.** 2 v. 8° *and* Maps. (Pt. 1, 32d Cong. 2d sess. Ho. Doc. 43. Pt. 2, 33d Cong. 1st sess. Ho. Doc. 53.)

— Report and charts of the cruise of the brig Dolphin; by S. P. Lee. Wash., 1854. 8° *and* Map. (33d Cong. 1st sess. Sen. Doc. 59.)

— Uniforms for officers of the navy. N. Y., [1863]. 4°.

— Report in relation to armored vessels. Wash., 1864. 8°. (38th Cong. 1st sess. Ho. Doc. 69.)

— BOSTON BOARD OF TRADE. Report of the special committee [on] the prosecution of F. W. Smith by the United States Navy Department. Boston, 1865. 8°. (E 127)

— Regulations for the government of the navy. Wash., 1866. 16°.

Note. Luce's 'Instructions for naval light artillery afloat and ashore. 2d ed., N. Y. 1862' have been adopted by the Navy Dept.

See also Naval Acad. at Annapolis (p. 3057); — *Naval Observatory* (p. 3093); — *Exploring Expeditions* (p. 3063-64); — *Naval Astronomical Expedition* (p. 3093); — *Navy* (p. 3093); — *Naval biog.* (p. 3111); — *Naval hist.* (p. 3141, 42).

Commission [on] the site for a Navy Yard on the Mississippi.

— Letter of the Sec. of the Navy communicating the report. [Wash., 1865.] 8°. (38th Cong. 2d sess. Sen. Doc. 19.)

Commissioners for the Exploration and Survey of the Northern Boundary.

— Message from the President transmitting the report. [Wash., 1841.] 8°. (26th Cong. 2d sess. Doc. 173. B 1167)

National Observatory.

See Naval Observatory (p. 3093).

Ordnance Department.

(Subordinate to the *War Department.*)

— Reports of experiments on the strength and other properties of metals for cannon; [by H. K. Craig]. Phila., 1856. 4°.

— Reports of experiments on the properties of metals for cannon and the qualities of cannon powder; by T. J. Rodman. Boston, 1861. 4°.

Commissioners for the Paris Exposition, 1867.

(Subordinate to the *Department of State.*)

— Reports, 1867; ed. by W. P. Blake. Wash., 1867. 6 v. 8°. (40th Cong. 2d sess. Sen. Doc.)

Contents. Vol. 1. **Seward, W.** Introd. — **Beckwith, N. M.**, *and others.* Selections from corresp. showing the organization and administration of the U. S. section. — **Seymour, C. B.**, *and others.* General survey of the Expos.; with report on the U. S. section. — **Leslie, F.** Report on the fine arts. — **Leslie, F.**, *and others.* Fine arts app. to the useful arts. — **Blake, W. P.** Extract from the report of the internat. committee on weights, measures, and coins; — Bibliog. of the Expos. — Index. 2. **Hewitt, A. S.** Iron and steel. — **Blake, W. P.** Precious metals. — **Smith, J. L.** Industrial chemistry. 3. **Barnard, F. A. P.** Machinery. 4. **Morse, S. F. B.** Telegraphic apparatus, *etc.* — **Auchincloss, W. S.** Steam engineering. — **Blake, W. P.** Engineering and public works. — **Beckwith, L. F.** Béton-coigné. — **Beckwith, A.** Asphalt and bitumen. — **Bowen, J. H.** Buildings, building materials, *etc.* — **Aligny, H. F. Q. d'.** Mining. **Ruggles, S. B.** Cereals produced in different countries compared. — **Hazard, G. S.** Quality, *etc.*, of the cereals exhibited. — **Johnstone, W. E.** Preparation of food. — **Aligny, H. F. Q. d'.** Beet-root sugar and alcohol; — Pressed coal; — Photographs and photog. apparatus; — Outline of the hist. of the Atlantic cables. — **Wilder, M. P.**, *and others.* Culture and products of the vine; with app. on the production of wine in California. — **Freese, J. R.** School-houses, *etc.* — **Norton, C. B.**, *and* **Valentine, W. J.** Munitions of war. — **Evans, T. W.** Instruments and apparatus of medicine, surgery, *etc.* — **Stevens, P.** Musical instruments. 6. **Mudge, E. R.**, *and* **Hayes, J. L.** Wool and manufactures of wool. — **Mudge, E. R.**, *and* **Nourse, B. F.** Cotton. — **Cowdin, E. C.** Silk and silk manufactures. — **Stevens, P.** Clothing and woven fabrics. — **Hoyt, J. W.** Education. — List of the reports.

Patent Office.

(Subordinate to the *Department of the Interior.*)

— Report [of superintendent] on the state of the Patent Office. Wash., 1831. 8°. (22d Cong. 1st session, Doc. 2. B 1058)

— Annual report of the commissioner, 1847-71, 76-78. Wash., 1848-79. 67 v. 8°.

Note. The first report was made in 1837. 1847-48 are for arts, manufactures, and agriculture in 1 v. for each year; 1849-61 have the report on agriculture in a separate vol.; 1854, 55, 59-64 have the arts and manufactures in 2 v.; 1856-58, 66 in 3 v; 67-70 in 4 v.; 1871 has a 2d v. not given in the Ex. doc. of the House; 1876-77 are in 1 v. Vol. 3 of 1858, v. 4 of 1869, v. 3, 4 of 1870 are wanting. In 1862 and after the report on agriculture was made by the Board of Agriculture. 1849-64, and v. 1 of 1868 have the title 'Report of commissioner'.

— Report for 1849; with introd. by H. Greeley. N. Y., 1850. 8°.

— Results of investigation into causes of explosion of steam boilers. [Wash., 1849.] 8°. (32d Cong. 1st sess. Sen. Misc. doc. 32.)

— Results of meteorological obs. under direction of U. S. Patent Office and Smithsonian Institution, 1854-59; report by the Commissioner [W. D. Bishop]. Vol. 1. Wash., 1861. 4°. (36th Cong. 1st sess. Sen. Ex. doc.)

— Report of J. Claiborne on the consumption of cotton in Europe, March. Wash., 1858. 8°. (35th Cong. 1st sess. Sen. Doc. 35.)

— AMERICAN journal of improvements in the useful arts, and mirror of the Patent Office; ed. by J. L. Skinner. Vol. 1. Wash., 1828. 8°.

Pension Office.

(Subordinate to the *Department of the Interior.*)

☞ For the reports of the pension office *see House* (p. 3064-92); — *Senate* (p. 3096-3106).

— Pension laws now in force, Jan. 19, 1838. *n.t.p.* 8°. (25th Cong. 2d sess. Ho. Doc. 118. B 1756)

— *Same.* Mar. 3, 1849. Wash., 1849. 8°.

Post Office Department.

— Annual report, [1867, 68, 70-73, 76-78]. Wash., 1867-78. 9 v. 8°.

☞ The missing vols. and duplicates of those here enumerated are contained in the Congressional documents; *see House* (p. 3064-92); — *Senate* (p. 3096-3106); — *see also State papers* (p. 3061).

— Post-office law, with instructions and forms for the regulation of post-offices. Wash., 1804. 8°. (W 10, 11)

— STEVENS, C. F. List of the post offices in the U. S.; with the laws and regulations. N. Y., 1808. 8°. (B 1119)

— Letter from the Postmaster General [R. J. Meigs] transmitting a list of contracts made by the Dept. during 1817. Wash., 1818. 8°. (B 1000)

— U. S. 21th *Cong. 1st sess. House.* Report of committee on post-offices and post-roads on Sunday mails, Mar. 5, 1830. *n.p.*, [1830]. 8°. (Ho. Doc. 27. B 1884)

— CLAYTON, J. M. Speech on the resolution of Mr. Grundy [on] the removals from the Dept. Wash., 1831. 8°. (B 1805)

— Table of post-offices in the U. S. Wash., 1842. 12°.

— MILES, P. Post-office in the U. S. and England. (*In* Amer. Geog. and Statist. Soc. Bul., v. 1. 1854.)

— - Postal reform; its urgent necessity and practicability. N. Y., 1855. 8°.

— - *Another copy.* (B 1758)

— LEECH, D. D. T. Post office directory; guide to post offices in the U. S. N. Y., 1856. 8°.

— NATIONAL BOARD OF TRADE. Report on the ocean postal service of the U. S. *n.t.p.* [1870.] 8°. (E 77)

President.

— WILLIAMS, E. Addresses and messages, 1789-1846; with a memoir of each and a history of their administrations, *etc.* N. Y., 1846. 2 v. 8°.

— Speeches, addresses, and messages, [1789-1825]; also Declaration of Independence, Constitution and Washington's farewell address. Phila., 1825. 8°.
— *George Washington*, 1789-97. Collection of speeches to Congress, 1789-96, with addresses, *etc.*; with app. cont. the Circular letter to the governors of the several states. Boston, July, 1776. 12°.
— - *Same, with a correction*. Bost., July, 1796. 12°.
— - Inaugural address, 1789. — Farewell address. (*In* Moore, F. Amer. eloquence, v. 1. 1864.)
— - Proceedings of the executive of the U. S. resp. the insurgents, 1794. Phila., 1795. 8°. (B 479)
— - Farewell address to the people of the U. S., Sept. 17, 1796. N. Y., 1850. 4°.
Note. For other eds. *see* Washington, G.
— - Message [on] the French republic, Jan. 19, 1797. Phila., [1797]. 8°.
— - *Another copy*. (W 65)
See also Washington, G.
— *John Adams*, 1797-1801. Rules and regulations resp. the recruiting service. *n.p.*, [1798]. 8°. (W 68)
— - Marine rules and regulations. Bost., 1799. 8°.
See also Adams, J. (pp. 13, 14).
— *Thomas Jefferson*, 1801-1809. Naval regulations, Jan. 1802. *n.p.*, [1802]. 12°. (C 116)
— - Inaugural speeches and messages. Boston, 1809. 12°. (C 103)
See also Jefferson, T. (p. 1568).
— *James Madison*, 1809-17. Important state papers; doc. accompanying the President's message, Nov. 29, 1809. *n.t.p.* [1809.] 8°. (B 474, C 109, 194)
— - *Same.* [Another ed.] *n.t.p.* [Boston, 1809.] 8°. (B 1490, 1885)
— - Three messages, Nov. 1811; with doc. Wash., *printed*, London, *reprinted* 1812. 8°.
— - Message, with documents on the failure of the arms on the northern frontier. . Albany, 1814. 8°. (13th Cong. 2d sess. Ho. Doc. 54.)
See also Madison, J. (p. 1832, 1833).
— *James Monroe*, 1817-25. Commercial regulations of foreign countries. Wash., 1819. 8°.
— - Message transmitting a digest of the commercial regulations. Wash., 1824. 8°. (18th Cong. 1st sess. Ho. Doc. 130.)
See also Monroe, J. (p. 2019).
— *John Quincy Adams*, 1825-29. Address at his inauguration. (*In* Speeches of the Presidents. 1825.)
— - Message in rel. to survey of a canal between the Gulf of Mexico and the Atlantic, Feb. 28, 1829. [Wash., 1829.] 8°. (20th Cong. 2d sess. Doc. 102. B 1887)
See also Adams, J. Q. (p. 14, 15).
— *Andrew Jackson*, 1829-37. Message. Wash., 1831. 8°. (22d Cong. 1st sess. Ho. Doc. 2. B 1057)
— - Message with docs. [on the arbitration of the King of the Netherlands on the north-eastern boundary, Dec. 7, 1831]. *n.p.*, [1831]. 8°. (E 317)
— - Message and docs. [on the northeastern boundary], Feb. 3, 1832. *n.p.*, 1832. 8°. (E 317)
— - Message, Apr. 2, 1832, [rel. to the northeastern bounary]. *n.p.*, [1832]. 8°. (E 317)
— - Message, Dec. 4. *n.t.p.* [Wash., 1832.] 8°. (U. S. 22d Cong. 2d sess. Ho. Doc. 2. B 1790)
— - Message returning the bank bill, with his objections. Wash., 1832. 8°. (22d Cong. 1st sess. Sen. Doc. 180. B 1057)
— - Proclamation against nullification. Louisville, 1833. 12°. (C 182)
— - Message at the commencement of the first sess. of the 24th Cong., Dec. 8, 1835. Wash., 1835. 8°. (24th Cong. 1st sess. Ho. Doc. 2. B 1829)
— - Messages. Concord, 1837. 12°.
See also Jackson, A. (p. 1551).
— *Martin Van Buren*, 1837-41. Message, 1st session, 25th Cong. [on the sub-treasury bill]. Wash., 1837. 8°. (25th Cong. 1st sess. Ho. Doc. 1. B 1663)
— - Message. [Dec. 2.] 1839. Wash., 1839. 8°. (26th Cong. 1st sess. Ho. Doc. 2. B 1663, 1881, E 43)
— - Message, Dec. 5, 1840. *n.t.p.* [Wash., 1841.] 8°. (26th Cong. 2d sess. Ho. Doc. 2. B 1167)
— - *Same.* *n.t.p.* [Wash., 1841.] 8°. (26th Cong. 2d sess., Sen. Doc. 1. B 1663)
— - *Same.* [With accompanying doc.] Wash., 1840. 8°. (26th Cong. 2d sess. Sen. Doc. 1. B 1823)
See also Van Buren, M.
— *Wm. Henry Harrison*, 1841-45. *See* Harrison, W. H.
— *James Knox Polk*, 1845-49. *See* Polk, J. K.
— *Zachary Taylor*, 1849, 50. California and New Mexico; message trans. information. [Wash., 1850.] 8°. (31st C. 1st sess. Ho. Ex. doc. 17.)
See also Taylor, Z.
— *Franklin Pierce*, 1853-57. *See* Pierce, F. (p. 2343).
— *James Buchanan*, 1857-61. Messages communicating information rel. to the compulsory enlistment of American citizens in the army of Prussia, *etc.* Wash., 1860. 8°. (36th Cong. 1st sess. Sen. Ex. doc. 38.)
— - Message communicating the instructions to and dispatches from the late and present ministers in China. [Wash., 1860.] 8°. (36th Cong. 1st sess. Sen. Ex. doc. 30.)
See also Buchanan, J. (p. 408).
— *Abraham Lincoln*, 1861-65. The martyr's monument; speeches, messages, *etc.*, 1860-65. N.Y., [1865]. 12°.
— - Emancipation proclamations, Sept. 22, 1862, Jan. 1, 1863. (*In* McPherson, E. Polit. hist. of U. S. 1864.)
— - *French.* (*In* Lecomte, F. Guerre. 1863.)
See also Lincoln, A. (p. 1740).
— *Andrew Johnson, Apr.* 15, 1865-69. Message com. information in rel. to the states lately in rebellion, *etc.* [Wash., 1865.] 8°. (39th Cong. 1st sess. Sen. Doc. 2.)
— Speeches. Boston, 1865. 12°.
See also Johnson, A.
— *Ulysses Simpson Grant*, 1869-77. *See* Grant, U. S.
☞ Other documents by or relating to the President may be found in the Congressional documents; *see House* (p. 3064-92); — *Senate* (p. 3096-3106).

WORKS ABOUT THE PRESIDENT.

— WILLIAMS, E. Memoirs, 1789-1846. *See, back*, WILLIAMS (p. 3094).
— LUDLOW, J. M. Gallery of Amer. pres. (*In* Macmillan's mag., v. 12-13. 1865-66.)
— BYSTANDER, The; letters on legislative choice in which the constitutional right, *etc.*, are considered. Balt., 1800. 8°. (B 613)
— ELECTION of President of the U. S.; by a citizen. Bost., 1823. 8°. (B 532)
— SOMERVILLE, W. C. Extracts of a letter on the mode of choosing the Pres. Balt., 1825. 8°. (B 532)
— SUGGESTIONS on presidential elections, with ref. to a letter of W. C. Somerville. Boston, 1825. 8°. (B 532)
— STORRS, H. R. Speech, proposition to amend the Constitution resp. the election of president and vice-president, Feb. 17. Wash., 1826. 8°. (B 554)
— CONKLING, A. Powers of the executive department. Albany, 1866. 12°.
— ADAMS, C. F., *Jr.* The election of presidents. (*In* Amer. Soc. Sci. Assoc. Trans., v. 2. 1870.)

Proclamations.

— HOUGH, F. B. Proclamations for thanksgiving issued by the Continental Congress, Washington, the national and state govs. on the peace of 1815, *etc.* Albany, 1858. 8°.
— U. S. *Pres.* (Lincoln). Emancipation proclamations, Sept. 22, 1862, Jan. 1, 1863. (*In* McPherson, E. Polit. hist. of U. S. 1864.)
— - *French.* (*In* Lecomte, F. Guerre. 1863.)
See also Congress. Acts, laws, etc. (p. 3059, 60).

Bureau of the Provost Marshall General.

(Subordinate to the *War Dept.* Established March 17, 1863, abolished Aug. 28, 1866.)

— Final report; operations, 1863-66. [Wash., 1866.] 2 v. 8°. (Pt. 3, 4 of the Report of the War Dept. for 1865-66.)
— U. S. *War Department.* Rules and regulations. Wash., 1864. 8°.

Quartermaster General.

— *Quartermaster Gen.* Roll of honor, 1-27; names of soldiers interred in the national cemeteries. Wash., 1865-72, 27 pam. 8°.

Note. No. 1-10 are in Tr. **B 1954**; 11-15 in **B 1955**; 16-19 in **B 1956**; 20-23 in **B 1957**; 24-27 in **B 1958**. The title varies slightly in the different nos.

Contents. No. 1. Washington. 2. Battlefields of the Wilderness and of Spottsylvania Court House, Va. 3. Andersonville, Ga. 4. Alexandria, Va. 5. Fortress Monroe and Hampton, Va. 6. Eastern and Central District of Texas, Rio Grande District, Texas, Camp Ford, Tyler, Texas, and Corpus Christi, Texas. 7. Maine, Minnesota, Maryland, Penn., R. I., Arkansas, Miss., Florida, La., and Colorado Territory. 8. Arkansas, California, Indiana, Michigan, Minnesota, and Nevada, and the territories of Arizona, Colorado, Idaho, New Mexico, and Washington. 9. N. H., Mass., Conn., N. J., O., Ill., Wisconsin, Oregon, Maryland, S. C., Florida, La., Miss., Texas, Missouri, military division of Miss., and the Territory of Dakota. 10. Wisconsin, N. Y., Tenn., Iowa, Maryland, Mo., N. C., Arkansas, Kansas, and Dakota Territory. 11. Chattanooga (*see also* no. 23), Stone's River (*see also* no. 23), Knoxville (*see also* no. 23). 12. N. Y., N. J., Penn., Md., Va., Ill., Missouri, Iowa, Arkansas, Texas, Utah Territory, and the Pacific Coast. 13. N. Y., Ill., Va., W. Va., Missouri, and the territories of Colorado and Utah. 14. Prisons at the South. 15. Antietam, Arlington (add.), Culpepper Court House, Cold Harbor, Winchester (*see also* no. 26), Staunton, and various scattered localities in Va. 16. Brookline, Cambridge, and Worcester, Mass.; Buffalo, Chautauqua, Cypress Hill (add.), Fort Niagara, Lockport, Lodi, Madison Barracks, Plattsburg Barracks, and Rochester, N. Y.; Gettysburg, Mercersburg, Reading, Phila., Tamaqua, and Upton, Penn.; Brattleboro and Montpelier, Vt.; City Point (add.), Danville (add.), Glendale, Richmond, and Yorktown (add.), Va. 17. Kentucky; and New Albany, Jeffersonville, and Madison, Indiana; Lawton (Millen) and Andersonville, Ga. (suppl.). 18. Fort Harrison, Va.; Wilmington and Raleigh, N. C.; Port Hudson, La.; Brownsville, San Antonio, Galveston, Texas; Little Rock, Fayetteville, and Fort Smith, Ark. (*see also* no. 26); Indianapolis, Ind.; Mound City, Ill.; Cincinnati, Ohio; Springfield, Mo.; Forts Scott and Leavenworth, Kansas (*see also* no. 26); and in local cemeteries and at posts in Texas, Indiana, Ill., Ohio, Wisc., Mich., Iowa, and Kansas. 19. Baltimore, Md.; Petersburg, Va. (*see also* no. 26); New Berne, N. C.; Florence, S. C. (add.); Baton Rouge, Fort St. Philip, La.; Jefferson City, Mo.; and various posts in Minn., New Mexico, Arizona, Colorado, Dakota, Indian Territory, Montana, Utah, and Washington Territory. 20. Corinth, Miss.; Pittsburg Landing, Tenn. (*see also* no. 26); Jefferson Barracks, Mo. 21. Memphis, Tenn.; Chalmette, La. 22. Nashville, Tenn. 23. Marietta, Ga.; Fort Donalson, Tenn.; Chattanooga, Tenn. (add. to no. 11); Murfreesboro, Tenn. (add. to no. 11); Knoxville, Tenn. (add. to no 11). 24. Vicksburg, Va. (*see also* no. 27); New Albany, Ind. 25. Fredericksburg, Va.; Mobile, Ala.; Fort Gibson, I. T.; and names not heretofore published at Hampton, Va.; Barrancas, Florida; Alexandria, La. 26. Mound City, Ill.; Cincin., Columbus, Gallipolis, Cleveland, Sandusky, and Drayton, Ohio; Little Rock, Fayetteville, and Fort Smith, Ark. (add. to no. 18); Fort Leavenworth, Kansas (add. to no. 18); Petersburg, Va. (add. to no. 19), Hampton, Va. (add. to no. 25); Winchester, Cold Harbor, and Culpepper Court House, Va. (add. to no. 15). 27. Beaufort, S. C.; Natchez, Miss., Vicksburg, Miss. (add. to no. 24); Pittsburg Landing, Tenn. (add. to no. 20).

— Alphabetical index to nos. 1-13. Wash., 1868. 8°. (B 1954)

— RESPECTFUL observations on the bill rel. to the establishment of a Quartermaster's Department. *n.t.p.* [Wash., 1811.] 8°. (B 513)

See also (p. 3107) *War Department.* Report.

Register's Office.

(Subordinate to the *Treasury Dept.*)

— Letter from the Secretary of the Treasury transmitting statements shewing the commerce and navigation, Sept. 1833, 37, 39, 41, 42, June 1843, 45, 49, 50-65. Wash., [1833-] 66. 24 v. 8°.

Note. For the reports for 1821, 1825, *see Treasury Dept.* (p. 3107). The title varies slightly for the different years.

— *Same.* 1831. [Wash., 1832.] 8°. (**B 1062**) — 1833. [Wash., 1834.] 8°. (**B 1087**) — 1834. [Wash., 1835.] 8°. (B 1818) — 1835. [Wash., 1836.] 8°. (**B 1871**) — 1837. [Wash., 1838.] 8°. (**B 1160**) — 1838. [Wash., 1839.] 8°. (B 1818)

Deputy Special Commissioner of the Revenue.
See Bureau of Statistics (p. 3161).

Special Commissioner of the Revenue.

— Letter from the Sec. of the Treasury transmitting a report from D. A. Wells, 1866. *n.t.p.* [Wash., 1867.] 8°. (39th Cong. 2d sess. Ho. doc. 2.)

— Report; Letter from the Sec. of the Treasury transmitting the report, 1869. [Wash., 1870.] 8°. (Ho. Doc. 27.)

Commission [on] the Revision of the Revenue System.

— Reports, 1865/66. Wash., 1866. 8°.

— *Same.* App. to special report no. 3; selections from the testimony in respect to cotton as a source of national revenue. Wash., 1866. 8°. (39th Cong. 1st sess. Ho. Doc. 34, pt. 2.)

Seal.

— REMARKS on the device of the seal. (*In* **Mass. Hist.** Soc. Proc., 1866-67.)

Sanitary Commission.
See **U. S. Sanitary Commission.**

Senate.

— Rules. Wash., 1862. 8°.

— BILBO, W. N. Dissertation on the abuse of the right of instructions as they affect the Senate; senators as national representatives, and the representative system the most beautiful flower of modern civilization. Nashville, 1845. 8°. (**B 1501**)

Indexes.

Note. There are full indexes to public documents prior to 1823 in the American state papers, *see* p. 3061.

— BOSTON PUBLIC LIBRARY. Alphabetical index to all papers of public interest from 18th Cong. 1st sess. to 35th Cong. 2d sess. (*In its* Index, Bates Hall. 1875.) — 36th, 37th Cong. (*In* 1st supplement. 1866.)

— Synoptical index to the laws and treaties, Mar. 4, 1789 - Mar. 3, 1851. Boston, 1860. 8°.

— *46th Cong. 2d sess. House.* General index of the Journals of Congress, 1st-10th Cong. incl., with ref. to the debates, docs., and statutes connected therewith; by A. Ordway. Wash., 1880. 4°. (Ho. Reps. 1776.)

☞ The greater part of the following documents as far as the 1st session of the 6th Congress were issued without note of place of publication, but probably at Philadelphia. The place is mentioned in the list below only when it is upon the title place. As the succeeding documents were generally published at Washington, sometimes with and sometimes without imprints, we give the place of publication only when it is not Washington.

The sign w.* is put in parentheses after the numbers of documents that are not in our set but are not referred to in the indexes, and therefore were probably never published; w. (without a *) is put after numbers of documents that are wanting in the set and are referred to in the indexes; they therefore indicate a real gap in the set.

With the set of Congressional documents are furnished the publications of the Census Office, but without indication whether they belong to the House or Senate. (*See Census Office*, p. 3058.) A number of other documents of doubtful origin have been included in the list of House documents, with a query.

1st Cong. 1st sess., March 4 - Sept. 29, 1789.

— Journal. N. Y., 1789. f°.

— *Same.* Wash., 1820. 8°.

1st Cong. 2d sess., Jan. 4–Aug. 12, 1790.

— Journal. N. Y., 1790. f°.

1st Cong. 3d sess., Dec. 6, 1790–*March* 3, 1791.

— Journal. Phila., 1791. f°.

— Reports.] *Dept. of State.* Rept. of the Sec. on the cod and whale fisheries; Feb. 1, 1791. Phila., 1791. f°.

2d Cong. 1st sess., Oct. 24, 1791–*May* 8, 1792.

— Journal. Phila., 1791–[92]. f°.

— *Same.* Wash., 1820. 8°.

2d Cong. 2d sess., Nov. 5, 1792–*March* 2, 1793.

— Journal. Phila., 1792–[93]. f°.

— *Same.* Wash., 1820. 8°.

3d Cong. 1st sess., Dec. 2, 1793–*June* 9, 1794.

— Journal. Phila., 1793–[94]. f°.

— Docs. *n.t.p.* [1794.] 8°.

Namely: *Commis. of the Sinking Fund.* Report, Dec. 16; May 29. (B 478) — Pinckney, T. Memorial; answer of T. Hammond and letter rel. to British instructions; June 8. (B 478, W 67)

3d Cong. 2d sess., Nov. 3, 1794–*March* 3, 1795.

— Journal. Phila., 1774–[95]. f°.

— *Same.* Wash., 1820. 8°.

— Doc.] Proceedings of the executive of the U. S. respecting the insurgents, 1794; Feb. 21. (W 83)

4th Cong. 1st sess., Dec. 7, 1795–*June* 1, 1796.

— Journal. Phila., 1795–[96]. 8°.

— *Same.* Wash., 1820. 8°.

— Doc.] *Attorney General* Report containing a col. of charters, *etc.*, rel. to the land situate in the south-western parts of the U. S.; April 26. Phila., 1796. 8°. (B 598, W 63)

4th Cong. 2d sess., Dec. 5, 1796–*March* 3, 1797.

— Journal. Phila., 1796–[97]. 8°.

— *Same.* Wash., 1820. 8°.

5th Cong. 1st sess., May 15–*July* 10, 1797.

— Journal. Phila., 1797. 8°.

— *Same.* Wash., 1820. 8°.

— Doc.] *Com. of Impeachment against Wm. Blount.* Further report; enclosing his letter, July 6, 1797. *n.t.p.* [Phila., 1797.] 8°. (B 481)

5th Cong. 2d sess., Nov. 13, 1797–*July* 16, 1798.

— Journal. Phila., 1797–98. 8°.

— *Same.* Wash., 1820. 8°.

— Docs. *n.t.p.* [1798.] 8°.

Namely: *Com. [on] Proper Measures to be Adopted rel. to Articles of Impeachment against W. Blount.* Report; Feb. 22. (B 481) — *Com. resp. the Territory of the U. S. Southward and Westward of Georgia.* Report; Feb. 23. (B 496) — *Pres.* Message; with a letter from Envoys Extraordinary at Paris, with other documents; 5 March. (B 482) — *Com. [on] the Memorial and Petition of M. Lapsley.* Report; March 19. (B 496) — Pinckney, C. C., *and others.* Authentic copies of corresp.; Apr. 3. London, 1798. 8°. (B 1488) — *Pres.* Message [with corresp. of C. C. Pinckney, *etc.*]. (B 482, 593, C 73, W 57, 65) — *Dept. of State.* Instructions to C. C. Pinckney, J. Marshall, and E. Gerry, Envoys Extraordinary and Ministers Plenipotentiary to the French Republic; April 9. (B 482)

— Doc.] Tennessee. *Legislature.* Remonstrance and petition to the Senate; Oct. 20. [Wash.,] 1797. 8°.

5th Cong. 3d sess., Dec. 3, 1798–*Mar.* 4, 1799.

— Journal. Phila., 1799. 8°.

— *Same.* Wash., 1820. 8°.

— Doc.] *Pres.* Message accomp. papers rel. to the affairs of the U. S. with the French Republic; 22 Jan. *n.p.*, 1799. 8°. (W 63)

6th Cong. 1st sess., Dec. 2, 1799–*March* 14, 1800.

— Journal. Phila., 1799–[1800]. 8°.

— *Same.* Wash., 1821. 8°.

— Reports. *n.t.p.* [1800.] 8°.

Namely: *Com. [on] the Memorial of D. Smith.* Report; [Jan. 23, 1800]. (*Also* B 498) — *Com. [on] the Petition of S. Glass and Others.* Report; [Jan. 23.] (*Also* B 498) — Conn. Acad. of Arts and Sciences. Memorial [with] Memorial of the Amer. Philosophical Society; Jan. 23. (*Also* B 498) — *Com. on the Bill entitled 'An Act to suspend in Part an Act to Augment the Army of the U. S.' etc.* Report; Feb. 7.

Also: *Com. of Privileges.* Report on the measures it will be proper to adopt rel. to a publ. in the General advertiser or Aurora; 19 Feb. (B 498) — *Com. on the Message of the Pres. with the Report of the Direct ofor the Mint.* Report. (B 498) — *Com. [on] the Petitions of J. Russell, Jr., M. Jackson, and others.* Report; [March 17]. (B 492) — *Com. of Privileges.* Report, in part, on the form of proc. in the case of Wm. Duane; [March 22]. (B 498) — *Com. of Privileges.* Further report, in part, no the form of proc. in the case of W. Duane; March 25. (B 499) — *Treas. Dept.* Letter from the Sec. transm. a statement of duty on salt; allowances made to vessels employed in the fisheries, and bounties on fish and salted provisions exported, 1793–98; April 3. (B 499) — *Com. [on] the Letter of J. Henderson to W. Serjeant, and the Extract of a Letter from Gov. Serjeant.* Report; April 7. (B 499) — *Dept. of War.* Message, transm. a report from the Sec., *etc.*: April 17. (B 499) — Georgia. *Legislature.* Address and remonstrance; 29 Nov. (B 500)

6th Cong. 2d sess., Nov. 17, 1800–*March* 3, 1801.

— Journal. Wash., 1800–[01]. 8°.

— *Same.* Wash., 1821. 8°.

7th Cong. 1st sess., Dec. 7, 1801–*May* 3, 1802.

— Journal. Wash., 1801–[02]. 8°.

— *Same.* Wash., 1821. 8°.

— Docs. *n.t.p.* [Wash., 1801–02.] 8°.

Namely; *Treas. Dept.* Message transm. a roll of the persons having office or employment under the U. S.; Feb. 16. (B 354) — *Pres.* Message; 29 March. (B 501) — *Com. on Petition of J. C. Symmes.* Report; Apr. 29. (B 501)

— Debates on the judiciary. Phila., 1802. 8°.

— *Another copy.* (B 402)

7th Cong. 2d sess., Dec. 6, 1802–*March* 3, 1803.

— Journal. Wash., 1802–[03]. 8°.

— *Same.* Wash., 1821. 8°.

— Doc.] *Dept. of State.* Report by the Sec. rel. to the privileges and restrictions of the commerce of the U. S.; Jan. 26. Wash., 1803. 8°. (B 502)

— Duane, W. Mississippi question; report of a debate 23–25 Feb. 1803. Phila., 1803. 8°.

8th Cong. 1st sess., Oct. 17, 1803–*March* 27, 1804.

— Journal. Wash., 1803–[04]. 8°.

— *Same.* Wash, 1821. 8°.

— Docs. *n.t.p.* [1804.] 8°.

Namely: *Navy Dept.* Letter from the Sec. [with his report]; 22 Feb. (B 505) — *Com. Appointed to Examine Precedents, and to Prepare Forms Necessary in the Trial of J. Pickering, impeached of High Crimes and Misdemeanors.* Report; March 2. *n.t.p.* (B 505)

8th Cong. 2d sess., Nov. 5, 1804–*March* 3, 1805.

— Journal. Wash., 1804. 8°.

— *Same.* Wash., 1821. 8°.

— Journal in cases of impeachments: [Blount, Pickering, and Chase]. Wash., 1805. 8°. (B 483)

— Docs. *n.t.p.* [1805.] 8°.

Namely: U. S. *vs.* Chase. Trial for high crimes and misdemeanors; Jan. 2. (B 483) — Hovey, B. Communication rel. to opening a canal navigation near the rapids of Ohio River, with docs.; Jan. 25. (B 483) — *House.* Replication to the Answer of S. Chase, to the articles of impeachment exhibited against him by the House; Feb. 7. (B 504)

9th Cong. 1st sess., Dec. 2, 1805–*Apr.* 21, 1806.

— Journal. Wash., 1805–[06]. 8°.

— *Same.* Wash., 1821. 8°.

— Ex. docs. *n.t.p.* [1806.] 8°.

Namely: *Pres.* Message, communicating discoveries in the Missouri, Red River, and Washita, by Capts. Lewis, Clark [and others]; with a statistical account of the countries adjacent; Feb. 19, 1806. — U. S. Articles of a treaty between the U. S. and the Piankeshaws, 30 Dec. 1805; Apr. 15. — *War Dept.* Letter and report of the Sec. War, the Sec. Treas., and the Comptroller, commissioners under the Act for the relief of the refugees from Canada and Nova Scotia; Apr. 21.

Also: *Navy Dept.* Report of Sec. conc. appro. for support of the navy; Dec. 6. (B 506) — *Treas. Dept.* Letter and rep. from Sec.; Dec. 27. (B 506) — **Orleans Terri. tory.** *House of Repr.* Memorial [for] alteration in the law resp. titles to lands, and encouragement to the culture of sugar; Dec. 31. (B 485) — **New York. Merchants.** Memorial conc. laws of neutral commerce; Jan. 6. (B 484) — *Pres.* Message, transm. docs. and papers rel. to complaints by the gov. of France against the commerce carried on by American citizens to the French island of Saint Domingo; Jan. 10. (B 485) — *Com. on a Further Appropriation for the Augmentation of the Congressional Library.* Report, in part; Jan. 20. (B 485) — *Dept. of State.* [Report of Sec. conc. neutrality laws; Jan. 25]. (B 484) — *Dept. of State.* [Report from Sec. on such laws of Great Britain as impose higher duties on exportation of goods, *etc.*, to U. S. than to those exported to Europe; Jan. 28.] (B 484) — **Baltimore. Merchants.** Message of Pres. transm. memorial on violation of neutral rights; Jan. 29. (B 484) — *Com. on that Part of the Pres. Message which Relates to Spoliation of our Commerce on the High Seas.* Resolutions; Feb. 5. (B 484) — *Dept. of State.* Extract of letter from Sec. rel. to impressments; 5 Feb. (B 484) — **Documents** resp. application of Hamet Caramalli, ex-bashaw of Tripoli; Feb. 15. (B 484) — **New Haven.** *Chamber of Commerce.* Memorial; Feb. 17. (B 484) — *Com.* [*on*] *Message of Pres. on Application of Hamet Caramalli.* Report; 17 March. (B 484) — *Treas. Dept.* Report of Sec. conc. memorial of J. Chester, former supervisor of internal revenues, *etc.*, with letters referred to in report; Mar. 26. (B 506) — *Treas. Dept.* Letter from the Treas. [with] general acc'ts of receipts and expenditures, and acc'ts for War and Navy Depts., Oct. 1, 1804 - Oct. 1, 1805; Apr. 10. (B 506) — **Allen, I.** Memorial to the government of the U. S.; [with report of the Sec. of State]; 17 Apr. (B 507)

— Report.] *Treas. Dept.* Letter from the Sec. transm. a report [on] 'An act to establish the Treas. Dept.'; Dec. 10, 1805. Wash., 1805. f°.

9th Cong. 2d sess. Dec. 1, 1806 - *March* 3, 1807.

— Journal. Wash., 1806-[07]. 8°.

— *Same.* Wash., 1821. 8°.

— State papers. *n.t.p.* 1806-[07.] 8°.

Namely: *Pres.* Message, 2 Dec. 1806 (*also* B 507); — Docs. accomp. message from the Pres.; Dec. 2 (*also* B 507); — Message transm. a letter from the ministers of the U. S. at London, and from the minister at Paris, rel to the late imperial decree; also a letter from C. Mead, acting Gov. of Mississippi Territory, resp. the surrender of A. Burr; Feb. 19. (*Also* B 507)

Also: *Com.* [*on*] *that Part of Message of the Pres. rel. to the Protection of Seaports, Harbors, etc., of the U. S.* Report; Dec. 15. (B 486) — **Clay, H.** Motion [that a committee be appointed to bring in a bill to extend to the districts of Kentucky, Tennessee, and Ohio the circuit courts of the U. S.]; Jan. 2. (B 507) — *Com. to Examine the Papers rel. to the Contemplated Bridge across the Potomac. and Direct such as they May Think Proper to be Printed.* [Papers; 6 Jan.] (B 507) — *War Dept.* Estimates of the Sec. on the military establishment; Jan. 12. (B 486) — **Georgetown. Citizens.** Additional documents on bridges [no. 4-7]; Jan. 14. (B 507) — *Com.* [*on*] *the Memorial of the Chesapeake and Delaware Canal Company.* Report; Jan. 15. (B 507) — *Pres.* Message transm. further information touching an illegal combination against the peace and safety of the Union, *etc.*; Jan. 28. (B 507) — **Adams, J. Q.** Resolution, *etc.*; Jan. 30. (B 507) — **Mitchill, S. L.** Report; Feb. 11. (B 507) — *Com.* [*on*] *An Act to Authorisethe State of Tennessee to Issue Grants, Titles, etc.* Report; Feb. 17. (B 507) — *Treas. Dept.* Queries resp. canals; March 2. (A 64)

10th Cong. 1st sess., Oct. 26, 1807 - *Apr.* 25, 1808.

— Journal. Wash., 1807. 8°.

— *Same.* Wash., 1821. 8°.

— State papers. *n.t.p.* [1807-08.] 8°.

Namely: *Pres.* Message; 27 Oct. 1807 (*also* B 488, 489); — Docs. accomp. message; Oct. 27. (*Also* B 488, 489) — *Com.* [*on*] *the Conduct of J. Smith, Senator from Ohio.* Evidence reported; Dec. 21. (*Also* B 1460) — **Erskine, D. M.** Letter to Sec. State and a note from E. Champagny; Apr. 2, 1808. — *Treas. Dept.* Report of Sec. on the public roads and canals; Apr. 2, 1808.

— State papers. *n.t.p.* [1808.] 8°.

Namely: *Pres.* Message transm. a letter from the Sec. State to Mr. Monroe on the attack on the Chesapeake; also Mr. Monroe's correspondence with the Brit. government, and Mr. Madison's correspondence with Mr. Rose on the same subject; March 22, 1808. — *Dept. of State.* Letters from the Sec. to Mr. Monroe on impressments, colonial trade, *etc.*: also extracts from and enclosures in the letters of Mr. Monroe to the Sec. prior to the mission of him and Mr. Pinckney; March 22; — Letters from Mr. Madison to Messrs. Monroe and Pinkney, with communications rel. to the treaty, with the treaty, and a subsequent letter from Mr. Monroe, *etc.*; 22 March. — **Papers** rel. to French affairs; [March 30].

Also *Com.* [*on*] *the Representation and Resolution of the Legislative Council of the Indiana Territory.* Report; Nov. 13. (B 489) — *Com.* [*on*] *the Bill Making Further Appropriations for the Support of the Navy during* 1807. Report; Nov. 16. (B 487) — **Tiffin, E.** Motion [conc. Act to establish circuit courts]; Nov. 17. (B 489) — *Com. on that Part of the Message of the Pres. which Rel. to the Defence of our Sea-port Towns and Harbors.* Report, in part; Nov. 20. (B 487) — **Adams, J. Q.** Motion [conc. the return of impressed Amer. seamen]; Nov. 25. (B 489) — *Com. on that Part of the Message of the Pres. which Relates to the Defence of our Sea-port Towns and Harbors.* Further report; Dec. 3. (B 487) — **Gilman, —.** Motion [to engage an additional engrossing clerk]; Dec. 4. (B 487) — **Georgetown,** *D. C.* Memorial of the citizens to the Senate of the U. S. on the Act authorizing the erection of a bridge over the Potomac, within the District of Columbia; Dec. 7. (B 489) — U. S. Articles of agreement and cession, April 24, 1802, between the commissioners of the U. S. and those of Georgia; Dec. 16. (B 489) — *Com. on the Message of the Pres. Recommending an Embargo on the Vessels of the U. S.* Report, in part; Dec. 22. (B 488, 489) — *Com* [*on*] *the Conduct of J. Smith, as Alleged Associate of A. Burr.* Report; Dec. 31. (B 490) — **Adams, J. Q.** Motion [conc. the present embargo]; Jan. 11, 1808. (B 489) — **Smith, J.** Application for time to procure testimony, *etc.*; Jan. 13. (B 490) — **Tiffin, E.** Motion [on the expediency of authorising a loan for seven years of seven thousand stand of arms, *etc.*, to Ohio, for the purpose of assisting to arm the militia of said State]; Jan. 13. (B 489) — *Com. on the Expediency of Extinguishing the Claims of the U. S. to certain Balances Reported to be Due from Several of the States to the U. S.* Report; Jan. 15. (B 489) — U. S. Articles of a treaty between the U. S. and the Ottaway, Chippeway, Wyandot, and Pottawatamie Indians, Detriot, 17 Nov. 1807; Jan. 15. (B 489) — U. S. A treaty of limits bet. the U. S. and the Choctaw Indians, Mt. Dexter, Nov. 16, 1805; Jan. 15. (B 489) — **Giles, W. B.** Motion [that the message of the Pres. rel. to the penal laws of the U. S. be referred to a comm.]; Jan. 16. (B 489) — *Com. on the Memorial of J. Chase and J. Gardner.* Report; Feb. 10. (B 489) — **Maclay, S.** Motion [that the constitution be so altered and amended as to prevent the Congress of the U. S., and the legislatures of any state, from authorizing the importation of slaves]; Feb. 23. (B 489) — **Mitchill, S. L.** Motion [on the application of the money appropriated by the Act making a further appropriation for the support of a library]; Feb. 23. (B 489) — **Giles, W. B.** Motion [conc. writ of habeas corpus act in criminal cases]; Feb. 16. (B 489) — *Com. on the Petition of P. Turner.* Report; March 7. (B 489) — **Bradley, S. R.** Motion [that a comm. be appointed to report what business is necessary to be done by Congress in the present session, and when to close the same]; March 17. (B 489) — *Com. on the Petition of Gen. A. St. Clair.* Report; March 29. (B 489) — *Senate.* Motion submitted for consideration; April 1. (B 489) — *Joint Com.* Report [conc.] what business is necessary to be done by Cong. in the present session; April 7. (B 489) — *Library Com. of the Two Houses of Congress.* Annual report; Apr. 11. (B 489) — **Hillhouse, J.** Amendments to the Constitution of the U. S. submitted for consideration; Apr. 12. (B 489) — *Com.* [*on*] *the Correspondence between Monroe and Canning, and Madison and Rose, rel. to the Attack on the Chesapeake, etc.* Report; April 16. (B 488) — *Com.* [*on*] *the Petition of Sundry Inhabitants of Boston, Praying Liberty to Export a Quantity of Dry and Pickled Fish.* Report; Apr. 21. (B 489) — **Reed, P.** Motion [that the Sec. of the Senate be authorized to pay, out of the contingent fund, J. Mathers, F. Durity, and T. Simpson]; Apr. 22. (B 489)

10th Cong. 2d sess., Nov. 7, 1808 - *March* 3, 1809.

— Journal. Wash., 1808. 8°.

— *Same.* Wash., 1821. 8°.

— Docs. *n.t.p.* [1808-09.] 8°.
Namely: **Documents** accomp. the message of the President, Nov. 8, 1808. — *Pres.* Message transmitting copies of all orders and decrees of the belligerent powers of Europe affecting the commercial rights of the U. S. passed since 1791; Dec. 28; — Message communicating letters between Mr. Canning and Mr. Pinkney; Jan. 17, 1809; — Message transm. letter from Mr. Pinkney covering one to him from the Brit. Sec. State, with his reply; Jan. 30. — *Dept. of State.* Message of Pres. transm. information resp. the execution of the act of 21 Feb. 1806, appropriating two millions for extraordinary expenses attending the intercourse between the U. S. and foreign nations; Jan 24. (*Also* **B 491**)
Also: *Pres.* Message; 8 Nov. 1808. (**B 491**) — *Com. on Part of the Message of the President which Relates to the Embargo Laws.* Report; Dec. 8. (**B 491**) — **Boston, Salem, N. Y., etc. Merchants.** Memorials rel. to the infringements of our neutral trade, with resolutions of the Senate; Nov. 18. (**B 491**) — **Chesapeake and Delaware Canal Co.** Memorial and petition of pres. and directors; Jan. 24, 1809. (**B 491**) — **Mass.** *Legislature.* Memorial and remonstrance against certain acts of the General gov.; Feb. 27. (**B 491**) — *Treas. Dept.* Report of Sec. [on] memorial of stockholders of the Bank of the U. S., praying a renewal of their charter; Mar. 2. (**B 491**) — *Pres.* Message, communicating letters between Brit. Sec. of State, Mr. Canning, and Mr. Pinkney; Jan. 17. (**B 491**)

11*th Cong.* 1*st sess., May* 22 - *June* 28, 1809.

— Journal. Wash., 1821. 8°.

11*th Cong.* 2*d sess., Nov.* 27, 1809 - *May* 1, 1810.

— Journal. Wash., 1809. 8°.
— *Same.* Wash., 1821. 8°.
— Ex. docs. *n.t.p.* [1809.] f°.
Namely: *Pres.* Message to both Houses; Nov. 29, 1809; — Docs. accomp. message; Nov. 29; — Message transm. papers called for by a resolution of Mr. Quincy; Dec. 15; — Message transm. extracts from the correspondence of Mr. Pinkney; Dec. 18.
Also: *Com.* [*on*] *the Petition of D. Boon.* Report; with the bill for his relief; Jan. 12, 1810. (**B 509**) — *Navy Department.* Letter from the Sec. [conc.] the number of midshipmen, able seamen, *etc.*, necessary to carry into effect the provisions of a special bill; Jan. 19. (**B 509**) — *Attorney General.* Report; Feb. 9. (**B 509**) — **Documents** accompanying the report of the committee [on] the bill to prevent the issuing of sea-letters except to certain vessels; Feb. 22. (**B 509**) — *Dept. of State.* Letter from the Sec. transm. a report made in obedience to an order of the Senate; Feb. 22. (**B 509**) — *Treas. Dept.* Message from the Pres. transm. report of the Sec. resp. instructions to collectors of customs under non-intercourse act; Feb. 23. (**B 509**) — *Com.* [*on*] *the Expediency of Employing the Torpedo or Submarine Explosions.* Report; Feb. 26. (**B 509**) — *Com.* [*on*] *so much of the Message of the Pres. as Rel. to an Effectual Organization of the Militia of the U. S.* Report; March 6. (**B 509**) — **Leib, M.** Motion; March 8. (**B 509**) — **Orleans.** *House of Representatives and Legislative Council.* Memorial in behalf of the inhabitants thereof; Mar. 12. (**B 510**) — *War Dept.* Letter from the Sec. rel. to the establishment of a Quarter Master's Department; March 12. (**B 510**) — *Dept. of State.* Report of the Sec. on the petition of J. Shattuck; Mar. 21. (**B 510**) — *Com. on the Petition of R. B. Lee.* Report, and the report of the Sec. of War thereupon; Mar. 28. (**B 510**) — *Joint Com. App. to Inquire what Business is Necessary to be Acted on during the Present Sess., and when it may be Expedient to Close the same.* Report; March 29. (**B 510**) — *Com.* [*on*] *the Petition of Father U. Guillet.* Report; April 2. (**B 510**) — *Dept. of State.* Message from the Pres. transm. a report of the Sec. of State; April 2. (**B 510**) — *Select Com. on the Petition of S. Easton and D. Jones.* Report; April 9. (**B 510**) — *Com. on the Petition of E. Winters.* Report; April 17. (**B 510**)

11*th Cong.* 3*d sess., Dec.* 3, 1810 - *March* 3, 1811.

— Journal. Wash., 1810. 8°.
— *Same.* Wash., 1821. 8°.
— Ex. docs. *n.t.p.* [1810-11.] 8°.
Namely: **Documents** accomp. message of the Pres.; Dec. 5, 1810. — *Pres.* Message transm. a letter from the charge d'affaires of the U. S. at Paris to the Sec. State; another from the same to the French minister of foreign relations; also two letters from the agent of the Amer. consul at Bordeaux to the Sec. State; Jan. 31, 1811. (*Also* **B 512**)
Also: **Phila. Chamber of Commerce.** Memorial of the members rel. to the Bank of U. S.; Dec. 24, 1810. (**B 510**) — *Com. on the Report of the Sec. of War on Improving the Discipline of the Militia.* Compendious exercise for the garrison and field ordnance as practised in the U. S.; Dec. 31. (**B 510**) — *Com. on the Memorial of I. Wayne.* Report; Jan. 10, 1811. (**B 512**) — *Pres.* Message transm. copies of a letter from the minister plenipotentiary of U. S. to the Secretary of State, and of another from the same to the Brit. Secretary for Foreign Affairs; Jan. 12. (**B 512**) — **Lloyd, —.** Motion [conc. property confiscated under act of March 1, 1809, *etc.*]; Jan. 18. (**B 512**) — *Treas. Dept.* Message from the Pres. transm. a report of the Sec. of the Treas. on the resolutions of the 21st; Jan. 28. (**B 512**) — *Treas. Dept.* Message from the Pres. transm. a report of the Sec. on the execution of an act providing for the survey of the coast of the U. S.; Feb. 4. (**B 512**) — *Dept. of State.* Message from the Pres. transm. a report of the Sec.; Feb. 5. (**B 512**) — *Treas. Dept.* Letter from the Sec. in reply to a letter from the chairman of the Com. on the Memorial of the Pres. and Directors of the Bank of the U. S.; Feb. 5. (**B 512**) — *Treas. Dept.* Message, transm. report of the Sec. of Treas. [rel. to awards under the 7th article of the Brit. treaty]; Feb. 11. (**B 513**) — *Dept. of State.* Letter from the Sec. transm. statement of persons born in for. countries, naturalized, and registered as Amer. seamen, annually; Feb. 12. (**B 513**) — *Com.* [*on*] *the Memorial of Gen. Wilkinson, Praying to be Remunerated for Monies Disbursed in the Service of the U. S.* Report; Mar. 2. (**B 513**) — *Com.* [*on*] *the Memorial of the Stockholders of the Bank of the U. S.* Report; Mar. 2. (**B 513**)

12*th Cong.* 1*st sess., Nov.* 4, 1811 - *July* 6, 1812.

— Journal. *t.p.w.* [Wash., 1811?] 8°.
— *Same.* Wash., 1821. 8°.
— Ex. docs. *n.t.p.* [1811-12.] 8°.
Namely: *Pres.* Message, at commencement of the 12th Congress; Nov. 5, 1811. (**B 513, 1490**) — *Pres.* Message, transm. letters from the late and present plenipotentiaries of France; Nov. 8. (**B 513**) — *Pres.* Message transm. copies of docs. obtained from a secret agent of the Brit. government; March 9, 1812. (**W 13a**)

12*th Cong.* 2*d sess., Nov.* 2, 1812 - *March* 3, 1813.

— Journal. Wash., 1812. 8°.
— *Same.* Wash., 1821. 8°.
— Ex. docs. *n.t.p.* [1813.] 8°.
Namely: *Pres.* Message transm. docs. rel. to a declaration and order in council of the Brit. government; July 13. — *Dept. of State.* Message from Pres. transm. report of Sec. with papers marked A and B; March 3.

13*th Cong.* 1*st sess., May* 24 - *Aug.* 2, 1813.

— Journal. Wash., 1813. 8°.
— *Same.* Wash., 1821. 8°.
— Houston, J. A. Proceedings and debates of the Senate. Wash., 1848. 4°.

13*th Cong.* 2*d sess., Dec.* 6, 1813 - *Apr.* 18, 1814.

— Journal. Wash., 1813-[14]. 8°.
— *Same.* Wash., 1821. 8°.
— Senate papers. *n.t.p.* [1813-14.] 8°.
Namely: *Pres.* Message to both Ho. of Cong.; Dec. 7, 1813. — **Tait, C.** Motions; Dec. 8. — **Dana, S. W.** Motion; Dec. 13. — **Fromentin, E.** Motions; Dec. 17. — **Worthington, T.** Motion; Dec. 20. — *Treas. Dept.* Message transm. a rept. from the acting Sec.; Dec. 20. — *Com. on Naval Affairs.* Report in part; Dec. 29; — [Another] report in part; Dec. 29. — *Navy Dept.* Letter from the Sec. to the chairman of the naval com., with docs.; Dec. 31. — *Treas. Dept.* Message transm. a rep. from the acting Sec.; Jan. 11, 1814. — **Mason, J.** Motion; Jan. 20. — **N. E. Mississippi Land Company.** Memorial of the directors; Jan. 28. — **Dana, S. W.** Motion; Feb. 2. — **Daggett, D.** Motion; Feb. 11. — **Mason, J.** Motion; Feb. 14. — **Cunow, J. G.** Mem. and petition in behalf of the directors of the missionary concerns of the United Brethren; Feb. 18. — *Navy Dept.* Letter from Sec. transm. a list of all the commissioned officers in the navy, also of all the midshipmen; Feb. 21. — *Com.* [*on*] *the Memorial of I. M'Pherson and Others.* Report; Feb. 25. — **Gore, C.** Motion; Feb. 28. — *Joint Com. to Inquire when it may be Expedient to Adjourn the Two Ho. of Cong.* Report; March 4. — **Bibb, G. M.** Motion; March 7. — *Com. of Foreign Relations.* Report on the petition of Don R. de Lenaris Gonzales and Don R. de Colmenero; March 14. — *Com. on the Print-*

ing of the Senate. Report; March 14. *Navy Dept.* Docs. from the Sec. rel. to the navy; March 18. — **Horsey, O.** Motion; March 23. — *Com. on the Petition of S. Girard.* Report; March 24. — **Gore, C.** Motion; March 25. — *Pres.* Message transm. copies of commissions prepared in pursuance of a resolution of the 26 March; March 29. — *Pres.* Message recommending exportations and a repeal of laws [that] prohibit the importation of articles not the property of enemies; March 31. — *Com. on the Memorial of Bowie, Kurtz, and Others.* Report; Apr. 8. — *Dept. of State.* Message transm. report of Sec. rel. to individuals selected from Amer. prisoners of war and sent to Gr. Brit. for trial; also rel. to any orders for retaliation; Apr. 16.

— Ex. docs. *n.t.p.* [1814.] f°.

Namely: *Pres.* Message transmitting reports of the Sec. War and Sec. Navy; Feb. 3, 1814. — *Post Office Dept.* [Report of Postmaster Gen.]; March 22. — *Dept. of State.* Message from the Pres. transmitting lists of ministers and consuls who have been appointed since the adoption of the constitution by the Pres. in the recess of the Senate; also copies of the commissions granted to A. Gallatin [and others] to negotiate and sign [treaties] of commerce with Gr. Brit. and Russia; Apr. 9.

13th Cong. 3d sess., Sept. 19, 1814 - *March* 2, 1815.

— Journal. Wash., 1814-[15]. 8°.

— State papers. *n.t.p.* [1814-15.] 8°.

Namely: **Giles, W. B.** Motion; Sept. 21, 1814. — **Worthington, T.** Motion; Sept. 21. — *Com. to Revise the Standing Rules of the Senate.* Report; Sept. 22. — **Giles, W. B.** Motion; Sept. 22; — [Another] motion; Sept. 23. — *Dept. of State.* Message transm. report from the acting Sec. on our relations with the continental powers of Europe; Oct. 3. — **Lacock, A.** Motion; Oct. 3. — *Navy Dept.* Letter from Sec. to the chairman of the naval committee transm. docs. from Capt. Macdonough rel. to the capture of the Brit. fleet on Lake Champlain; Oct. 4. — *Naval Com.* Report [on] the gallant conduct of Capt. Macdonough, officers, seamen, *etc.*, in capturing the Brit. squadron on Lake Champlain, 11 Sept. 1814; Oct. 6. — *Navy Dept.* Letter from Sec. transm. the official account of the capture of the Epervier by the Peacock commanded by Capt. L. Warrington, 29 Apr. last; Oct. 10. — *Joint Com.* Report on the Library of Congress; Oct. 7. — *Naval Com.* Report [on] the gallant conduct of Capt. Warrington in the capture of the Brit. sloop of war Epervier; Oct. 10; — Report [on] the gallant conduct of Capt. Blakeley in the capture of the Brit. sloop of war Reindeer; Oct. 17. — *Navy Dept.* Letter from Sec. transm. account of the capture of the Reindeer by the Wasp, commanded by Capt. J. Blakeley, 28 June; Oct. 17. — **Fromentin, E.** Motion; Oct. 21. — **German, O.** Motion; Oct. 21. — **Bledsoe, J.** Motion; Nov. 3. — *Com. on the Petition of Bowie, Kurtz, and Others, Owners of the Alleghany.* Report; Nov. 4. — **Dana, S. W.** Motions; Nov. 5. — *War Dept.* Letter from chairman of military committee and reply of Sec. [with] docs. rel. to the military establishment; Nov. 5. — **Fromentin, E.** Motion; Nov. 7. — **Mason, J.** Motion; Nov. 7. — *Navy Dept.* Letter from Sec. transm. a report rel. to the better organization of the Dept. of the navy; Nov. 16. — **Horsey, O.** Motions; Nov. 19. *Com. on Naval Affairs.* Report [conc.] provision for the appointment of officers above the grade of captain; also for conferring rank by brevet; Nov. 28. — *Joint Com. to contract for the Library of Jefferson late Pres. of the U. S.*; Nov 28. — **Anderson, J.** Motion; Nov. 30. — **Horsey, O.** Motion; Dec. 6. — *Com. on Naval Affairs.* Report [conc.] the expediency of making provision by law that the officers and crews of vessels built or purchased by an act, 15 Nov. 1814, may receive the whole of the prize money from the sale of vessels and cargoes they capture; Dec. 8. — **Lacock, A.** Motion; Dec. 8. — *Com. [on] Amendments to the Bill to Authorize the President to Call upon the States and Territories for their Quotas of Militia for the Defence of the Frontier.* Report; Dec. 17. — **Hunter, W.** Motion; Dec. 21. — **Daggett, D.** Motion; Dec. 27. — **King, R.** Motion; Dec. 29. — **Varnum, J. B.** Motion; Dec. 29. — **Horsey, O.** Motion; Jan. 2, 1815. — *Treas. Dept.* Message transm. report from Sec. [conc.] proceedings under the 'Act to regulate the laying out a road from Cumberland, Md. to Ohio'; Jan. 2. — **Bledsoe, J.** Motion; Jan. 5. — **Dana, S. W.** Motion; Jan. 9. — **Mason, J.** Motion; Jan. 10. — *Com. on Military Affairs.* Report [on] the resolution of the 2d inst.; Jan. 16. — *Com. for the Relief of E. Barry and G. Hodge.* Docs. accomp. the bill reported; Jan. 18. — **Mississippi Territory.** *Legislative Council and Ho. of Reps.* Resolution rel. to the propositions of the Brit. ministers at Ghent; Jan. 21. — *Com. on the Report of Sec. Treas.* [conc.] *the Road from Cumberland, Md., to Ohio.* Report; Jan. 24. — *Com. [on] the Petitions of Citizens of N. H., Mass., Conn., N. Carolina, and Ohio praying Congress to prohibit the Transportation and Opening of the Mail on the Sabbath.* Report; Jan. 27. — *Pres.* Message returning the 'Act to incorporate the subscribers to the Bank of the U. S.' with objections for not signing the same; Jan. 30. — **Baltimore.** *Com. of Vigilance and Safety.* Memorial on the necessity of providing an adequate force for the protection of that city during the next campaign; Feb. 1. — *Com. on Military Affairs.* Report on the resolution rel. to veterinary surgeons; Feb. 9. — *Com. on the Resolution rel. to Compensation to Individuals whose Property may have been Destroyed during the War by the Authorities of the U. S.* Report; Feb. 9. — **Horsey, O.** Motion; Feb. 13. — *Military Com.* Resolutions expressive of the high sense entertained by Congress of the patriotism and good conduct of the people of Louisiana and New Orleans during the military operations before that city; Feb. 13; — *Com. on Naval Affairs.* Resolutions [expressive of the high sense entertained by Congress of the valor of Commodore D. T. Patterson and others for their co-operation with Gen. Jackson in the defence of N. Orleans]; Feb. 13. — *Military Com.* Resolutions expressive of the thanks of Congress to Maj. Gen. Jackson and troops for their gallantry in the defence of N. Orleans; Feb. 13. — **Dana, S. W.** Motion; Feb. 17. — *Treas. Dept.* Letter from Sec. transm. a report on the petition of G. Hoyt; Feb. 17. — **Barbour, J.** Motion; Feb. 18. — *Library Com.* Report on providing a library room, and transporting the library of T. Jefferson to Washington; Feb. 20. — *Joint Com.* Report on expenses of stationery, printing and binding under the authority of both Houses, *etc.*; Feb. 25. — **Brown, J.** Motion; Feb. 27. — *Com. of Foreign Relations.* Report [on] making provision by law to release claims of the U. S. to penalties under acts which have imposed prohibitions on commercial intercourse, *etc.*; Feb. 27. — *Com. [on] the Bill entitled 'An Act for the Relief of J. Doyle'.* Report; Feb. 27. — *Com. of Foreign Relations.* Report on the message of the Pres. recommending certain regulations resp. Amer. seamen; Feb. 28. — *Com. on Military Affairs.* Report on the differences between the U. S. and individual states resp. relative powers over the militia; Feb. 28. — **King, R.** Motion; March 1. — *Dept. of State.* Message transm. report from acting Sec. [conc.] traffic in the W. Indies by the sale of negroes taken from the U. S. by the Brit. forces since the present war; March 2. — *Com. on Foreign Relations.* Report on the message of Pres. resp. the unauthorized mode of warfare of the enemy, on plea of retaliation; March 3.

Also: *Com. of Sen. on Memorial of Bowie and Kurtz and Others.* Report; [Jan. 1815]. Georgetown, 1816. **(B 1492)**

— Ex. doc.] *Post Office Dept.* Message from the Pres. transm. a report of the Post-Master Gen.; Feb. 28, 1814. Wash., 1815. f°.

14th Cong. 1st sess., Dec. 2, 1815 - Mar. 3, 1816.

— Journal. Wash., 1815-[16]. 8°.

— Sen. docs. *n.t.p.* [Wash., 1815-16.] 8°.
Contents. No. 1-94 (50, 62 w*.).

Also no. 15. *Com. on Naval Affairs.* Documents exhibiting the naval force, Jan. Wash., 1816. 8°. (B 1492)

Note. This is indexed as no. 15, although it is not numbered. Another document is similarly indexed and is numbered 15.

14th Cong. 2d sess., Dec. 2, 1816 - *Mar.* 3, 1817.

— Journal. Wash., 1816-[17]. 8°.

— Sen. docs. *n.t.p.* [1816-17.] 2 v. 8°.
Contents. No. 1-123 (2, 13, 14, 68, 69 w.).

15th Cong. 1st sess., Dec. 1, 1817 - *Apr.* 20, 1818.

— Journal. Wash., 1817. 8°.

— Sen. docs. *n.t.p.* [Wash., 1817-18.] 2 v. 8°.
Contents. Vol. 1. No. 1-131 (5, 116 w*; 84 w.). 2. 132-193.

15th Cong. 2d sess., Nov. 16, 1818 - *March* 3, 1819.

— Journal. Wash., 1818. 8°.

— Sen. docs. *n.t.p.* [Wash., 1818-19.] 2 v. 8°.
Contents. Vol. 1. No. 1-63 (35 w.). 2. 64-102.

16th Cong. 1st sess., Dec. 6, 1819 - *May* 15, 1820.

— Journal. Wash., 1819. 8°.

— Sen. docs. *n.t.p.* [Wash., 1819-20.] 4 v. 8°.
Contents. Vol. 1. No. 1-73 (14 w.). 2. 74-98, 100-135 (131, 133 w.). 3, 4. 99.

16th Cong. 2d sess., Nov. 13, 1820 - *Mar.* 3, 1821.

— Journal. Wash., 1820. 8°.
— Sen. docs. *n.t.p.* [Wash., 1820-21.] 5 v. 8°.
Contents. Vol. 1. No. 1-41. 2. 42-91. 3. 92-117. 4. 118 (119 w.). 5. 120: Treas. accounts.

17th Cong. 1st sess., Dec. 3, 1821 - *May* 8, 1822.

— Journal. Wash., 1821. 8°.
— Sen. docs. *n.t.p.* [Wash., 1821-22.] 3 v. 8°.
Contents. Vol. 1. No. 1-63 (23 w.; 56 w.*). 2. 64-94. 3. 95.

17th Cong. 2d sess. Dec. 2, 1822 - *March* 3, 1823.

— Journal. Wash., 1822. 8°.
— Sen. docs. *n.t.p.* [Wash., 1822-23.] 2 v. 8°.
Contents. Vol. 1. No. 1-12. 2. 13-43.

18th Cong. 1st sess., Dec. 1, 1823 - *May* 27, 1824.

— Journal. Wash., 1823. 8°.
— Sen. docs. *n.t.p.* [Wash., 1823-24.] 3 v. 8°.
Contents. Vol. 1. No. 1-30. 2. 31-45. 3. 46-80.

18th Cong. 2d sess., Dec. 6, 1824 - *March* 3, 1825.

— Journal. Wash., 1824. 8°.
— Sen. docs. *n.t.p.* [Wash., 1824-25.] 4 v. 8°.
Contents. Vol. 1. No. 1-9. 2. 10-32 (17 w.). 3. 33-43. 4. 44-45.
Also no. 32 (B 1798).

19th Cong. 1st sess., Dec. 5, 1825 - *May* 22, 1826.

— Journal. Wash., 1825. 8°.
— Sen. docs. *n.t.p.* [Wash., 1825-26.] 5 v. 8°.
Contents. Vol. 1. No. 1-19. 2. 20-55. 3. 56-76. 4. 77-101. 5. 102.

19th *Cong. 2d sess., Dec.* 4, 1826 - *March* 3, 1827.

— Journal. Wash., 1826. 8°.
— Sen. docs. *n.t.p.* [Wash., 1826-27.] 4 v. (v. 4 w.). 8°.
Contents. Vol. 1. No. 1 (2 w.). 2. 3-49 (11, 22, 35, 44 w.). 3. 50-69. 4. 70-72. *Wanting.*
Also no. 1. *n.t.p.* [1826.] 8°.

20th Cong. 1st sess., Dec. 3, 1827 - *May* 26, 1828.

— Journal. Wash., 1827. 8°.
— Sen. docs. *n.t.p.* [Wash., 1827-28.] 5 v. 8°.
Contents. Vol. 1. No. 1-25. 2. 26-72. 3. 73-109. 4. 110-170. 5. 171-207.
Also no. 175, pt. 2. Wash., 1828. 8°.

20th Cong. 2d sess., Dec. 1, 1828 - *March* 3, 1829.

— Journal. Wash., 1828. 8°.
— Pub. docs. *n.t.p.* [Wash., 1828-29.] 2 v. 8°.
Contents. Vol. 1. No. 1-79 (14 w.*). 2. 80-106.
Also no. 46 (B 1374, 1814); — 46 [another ed.]. Balt. (B 1663).

21st Cong. 1st sess., Dec. 7, 1829 - *May* 31, 1830.

— Journal. Wash., 1829. 8°.
— Pub. docs. *n.t.p.* [Wash., 1829-30.] 2 v. 8°.
Contents. Vol. 1. No. 1-49. 2. 50-146 (140 w.).

21st Cong. 2d sess., Dec. 6, 1830 - *March* 3, 1831.

— Journal. Wash., 1830. 8°.
— Pub. docs. Wash., 1830-31. 2 v. 8°.
Contents. Vol. 1. No. 1-40. 2. 41-76.
Also no. 11, 12 (B 1801).

22d Cong. 1st sess., Dec. 5, 1831 - *July* 16, 1832.

— Journal. Wash., 1831. 8°.
— Pub. docs. Wash., 1830-31. 3 v. 8°.
Contents. Vol. 1. No. 1-55 (1 w.*). 2. 56-110. 3. 111-182.
Also no. 119 (B 1801); — 128, 145 (B 1062, 1801); — 170, 180 (B 1057); — 460 (B 1059); — 460, *the minority report only, pp.* 297-367 *repaged* (B 1059); — 460, *Report of Mr. Adams only, pp.* 369-410 *repaged* (B 1059).
390. (2. 6. 81.)

— Ex. doc., confidential.] Docs. accomp. the President's message of Jan. 27, 1832, [on the north eastern boundary]; Feb. 8, 1832. *n.t.p.* [1832.] 8°. (E 317)
— Ex. doc., confidential.] *Com. on Foreign Relations.* Report [on] the messages of the President of Dec. 7, 21, 1831, Jan. 27, Feb. 8, 1832, with [accomp.] docs. [rel. to the north eastern boundary]; Mar. 21, 1832. *n.t.p.* [1832.] 8°. (E 317)
— Debate in Senate, on the nomination of M. Van Buren to be minister of U. S. to Gr. Brit. 24, 25 Jan. *n.t.p.* [1832.] 8°. (B 1062, 1831)

22d Cong. 2d sess., Dec. 3, 1832 - *March* 2, 1833.

— Journal. Wash., 1832. 8°.
— Pub. docs. Wash., 1832-33. 8°.
Contents. No. 1-84.
Also no. 2, 30 (B 1790).

23d Cong. 1st sess., Dec. 2, 1833 - *June* 30, 1834.

— Journal. Wash., 1833. 8°.
— Pub. docs. Wash., 1834-35. 14 [15] v. 8° *and* f°.
Contents. Vol. 1. No. 1-39. 2. 40-139 (119 w.*). 3. 140-266 (254 w.). 4. 267-372 (262 w.*). 5. 373-423. 6. 424-504, 506-511, 513 (460 w.*) 7-11. 512: Indian removals. 12-14. 514: Pension roll. [15.] 505.
Note. Docs. 505, 512, 514 have separate title-pages. 505, 'Statistical view of the population of the U. S., 1790-1830. Wash., 1835'. f°. This doc. is indexed as belonging to v. 7. 514 is 'Report of the Sec. of War rel. to the pension establishment'. Wash., 1835. 8°.
Also no. 72, 92 (B 1810); — 323 (B 1495, 1810).

23d Cong., 2d sess., Dec. 1, 1834 - *March* 3, 1835.

— Journal. Wash., 1834. 8°.
— Pub. docs. Wash., 1833-34. 4 v. 8°.
Contents. Vol. 1. No. 1-8. 2. 9-39. 3. 40-139. 4. 140-154.
Also no. 17 (B 1810); — 40, 86 (B 1811); — 108 (B 1495, 1811).

24th Cong. 1st sess., Dec. 7, 1835 - *July* 4, 1836.

— Journal. Wash., 1835. 8°.
— Pub. docs. Wash., 1835-36. 6 v. 8°.
Contents. Vol. 1. No. 1-15. 2. 16-149. 3. 150-269. (209 w.). 4. 270-339. 5. 340-403. 6. 404-430.
Also no. 89 (B 1721); — 262 (B 1111).
Also no. 333. Wash., 1836. 8°.
Also no. 334 (B 1817).

24th Cong., 2d sess., Dec. 5, 1836 - *March* 3, 1837.

— Journal. Wash., 1836. 8°.
— Pub. docs. Wash., 1836-37. 3 v. 8°.
Contents. Vol. 1. No. 1-59. 2. 60-213 (188 w.*). 3. 214-226.
Also no. 224. Wash., 1837. 8°. (*Also* B 1815)

25th Cong. 1st sess., Sept. 4, 1837 - *Oct.* 16, 1837.

— Journal. Wash., 1837. 8°.
— Pub. docs. Wash., 1837. 8°.
Contents. No. 1-37.
Also no. 85 (B 1871); — 494 (B 1748); — 499 (B 1748).

25th Cong. 2d sess., Dec. 4, 1837 - *July* 9, 1838.

— Journal. Wash., 1837. 8°.
— Pub. docs. Wash., 1838. 6 v. 8°.
Contents. Vol. 1. No. 1-92 (16 w.). 2. 93-138. 3. 139-261. 4. 262-387 (324 w.*). 5. 388-470 (388 w). 6. 471-509.
Also no. 300. Wash., 1838. 8°.

25th Cong. 3d sess., Dec. 3, 1838 - *March* 3, 1839.

— Journal. Wash., 1838. 8°.
— Pub. docs. Wash., 1839. 5 v. 8°.
Contents. Vol. 1. No. 1-17. 2. 18-146. 3. 147-253. 4. 254-276. 5. 277-307.
Also no. 14, 17 (E 43); — 31 (B 1273).

26th Cong. 1st sess., Dec. 2, 1839 - *July* 21, 1840.

— Journal. Wash., 1839. 8°.
— Pub. docs. Wash., 1840. [illegible] v. 8°.
Contents. Vol. 1. No. 1-11. 2. 12-58 (14 w.). 3. 59-123. 4. 124-196. 5. 197-278. 6. 279-346. 7. 447-559. ~~8. 447-559.~~ [illegible]. 560-621.

Also no. 1 (E 43); — 2 (B 1817); — 107 (B 1147); — 198 (E 249); — 319 (B 1817); — 347 (E 249); — 368 (B 1817); — 509, 560 (B 1823).
Also no. 36. *n.t.p.* [1840.] 8°.
Also no. 174. Wash., 1840. 8°.

26th Cong. 2d sess., Dec. 7, 1840 - *March* 3, 1841.

— Journal. Wash., 1840. 8°.
— Pub. docs. Wash., 1841. 5 v. in 6 pts. 8°.
Contents. Vol. 1. No. 1-5. 2. 6-60. 3. 61-150. 4. 151-235 (232 w.*). 5, pt. 1. 236, 238. 5, pt. 2. 237.
Also no. 1 (B 1663, 1823).
Also no. 237. Wash., 1843. 8°.

27th Cong. 1st sess., May 31, 1841 - *Sept.* 13, 1841.

— Journal. Wash., 1841. 8°.
— Pub. docs. *n.t.p.* [1841.] 8°.
Contents. No. 1-124. (47 w.*).

27th Cong. 2d sess., Dec. 6, 1841 - *Aug.* 31, 1842.

— Journal. Wash., 1841. 8°.
— Pub. docs. *n.t.p.* [Wash., 1841-42.] 5 v. 8°.
Contents. Vol. 1. No. 1-8. 2. 9-109. 3. 110-240. 4. 241-335. 5. 336-444.
Also no. 1 (B 1871); — 340 (B 1513); — 835 (B 1173).

27th Cong. 3d sess., Dec. 5, 1842 - *March* 3, 1843.

— Journal. Wash., 1842. 8°.
— Pub. docs. *n.t.p.* [Wash., 1842-43.] 4 v. 8°.
Contents. Vol. 1. No. 1. 2. 2-67. 3. 68-195. 4. 196-247.
Also no. 1, 223 (E 190).

28th Cong. 1st sess., Dec. 4, 1843 - *June* 17, 1844.

— Journal. Wash., 1843. 8°.
— Pub. docs. Wash., 1844. 7 v. 8°.
Contents. Vol. 1. No. 1. 2. 2-99. 3. 100-168. 4. 169-288. 5. 289-349. 6. 350-398. 7. 399-408.
Note. The drawings belonging to doc. 243 will be found at the end of v. 7.

28th Cong. 2d sess., Dec. 2, 1844 - *March* 3, 1845.

— Journal. Wash., 1844. 8°.
— Pub. docs. Wash., 1845. 11 v. in 12 pts. 8°.
Contents. Vol. 1. No. 1-11. 2. 12-67 (18 w.*). 3. 68-96. 4, 5, 6. 97, pts. 1-3: Obs. magnetical and meteorol. at Girard Coll.; with suppl. 7. 98-135. 8. 136-149. 9. 150-171, 173. 10. 172. 11. 174-177.
Note. The 'Suppl'. to no. 97 is bound separately with sep. titlepage 'Suppl.' to Doc. 97; being plates of curves illust. the magnetic and meteorol. obs., *etc.*
Also no. 16 (B 1196); — 67 (B 1501).
Also no. 97. Wash., 1847. 3 v. 8°.
Also no. 172. Wash., 1845. 8°.
Also no. 174. Wash., 1845. 8°.

29th Cong. 1st sess., Dec. 1, 1845 - *Aug.* 10, 1846.

— Journal. Wash., 1845-46. 8°.
— Pub. docs. Wash., 1846. 9 v. 8°.
Contents. Vol. 1. No. 1. 2. 2. 3. 3-43. 4. 44-195. 5. 196-306. 6. 307. 7. 308-376. 8. 377-438. 9. 439-490.
Also no. 108 (B 1605).

29th Cong. 2d sess., Dec. 7, 1846 - *March* 3. 1847.

— Journal. Wash., 1846-47. 8°.
— Pub. docs. Wash., 1847. 3 v. 8°.
Contents. Vol. 1. No. 1-3. 2. 4-100. 3. 101-224.

30th Cong. 1st sess., Dec. 6, 1847 - *Aug.* 14, 1848.

— Journal. Wash., 1847-48. 8°.
— Ex. docs. Wash., 1847. 8 v. (v. 2 w.). 8°.
Contents. Vol. 1. 1. 2. 2-5. *Wanting.* 3. 6-11. 4. 12-31. 5. 32-40. 6. 41-50. 7. 51-64. 8. 65-73.
Also no. 7. Wash., 1848. 8°.
Also no. 26. Wash., 1848. 8°.
Also no. 41. Wash., 1848. 8°.
Also no. 50. *n.t.p.* [1848.] 8°.
— Misc. docs. Wash., 1848. 8°.
Contents. No. 1-101.
Also no. 23: Smithsonian Inst. 2d ann. rept., 1847. *n.t.p.* [Wash., 1848.] (E 123)

— Reports of committees. Wash., 1847. 8°.
Contents. No. 1-243.
Also no. 15 (B 1509)

30th Cong. 2d sess., Dec. 4, 1848 - *March* 3, 1849.

— Journal. Wash., 1849. 8°.
— Docs. *n.t.p.* [Wash., 1848-49.] 4 v. 8°.
Contents. Vol. 1. No. 1, 3-21. 2. 2. 3. 22-38. 4. 32-38.
Also no. 18. *n.t.p.* [1848.] 8°.
Also no. 34. Balt., 1852. 4°.
— Misc. docs. Wash., 1849. 2 v. 8°.
Contents. Vol. 1. No. 1-66. 2. 67.
— Reports of committees. Wash., 1849. 8°.
Contents. No. 244-331.

31st Cong. Special sess., March 5-23, 1849.

— Pub. docs. Wash., 1849. 8°.
Contents. No. 1-4.

31st Cong. 1st sess., Dec. 3, 1849 - *Sept.* 30, 1850.

— Journal. Wash., 1849-50. 8°.
— Ex. docs. Wash., 1849-50. 14 v. 8°.
Contents. Vol. 1-3. No. 1, pts. 1-3. 4. 2. 5. 3-5. 6. 6-14, 16, 17, 19-28. 7, 8. 15, pt. 1, 2. 9. 18. 10. 29-38, 40-48. 11, 12. 39, pt. 1, 2. 13. 49-63. 14. 64-82.
— Misc. docs. Wash., 1850. 2 v. 8°.
Contents. Vol. 1. 1-119, 121-128 (128 w.). 2. 120.
Also no. 120: Smithsonian Inst. 4th ann. rept., 1849. Wash., 1850. 8°.
— Reports of committees. *n.t.p.* [Wash., 1849-50.] 8°.
Contents. No. 1-216.
— Obituary addresses, death of J. C. Calhoun, April 1; with funeral sermon of Rev. C. M. Butler, April 2. Wash., 1850. 8°. (B 1210)

31st Cong. 2d sess., Dec. 2, 1850 - *March* 3, 1851.

— Journal. Wash., 1850-51. 8°.
— Ex. docs. Wash., 1851. 5 v. 8°.
Contents. Vol. 1. No. 1. 2. 2-7. 3. 8-22, 24-37. 4. 23. 5. 38-45.
— Misc. docs. Wash., 1851. 8°.
Contents. No. 1-33.
— Reports of committees. Wash., 1851. 8°.
Contents. No. 217-320 (264, 266 w.*).

32d Cong. Spec. sess., March 4 - 13, 1851.

— Docs. Wash., 1851. 3 v. 8°.
Contents. Vol. 1. Misc. docs., no. 1, 2. — Repts. of comm., no. 1. — Ex. docs., no. 1, 2. 2. Ex. docs., 3: Explor. of the Valley of the Great Salt Lake. 3. Ex. docs., 4.
Also no. 1. Wash., 1857. 4°.
Also Ex. doc. no. 3. Phila., 1852. 8°.
Also Miscel. doc. no. 1: Smithsonian Inst. 5th ann. rept. 1850. Wash., 1851. 8°.

32d Cong. 1st sess., Dec. 1, 1851 - *Aug.* 31, 1852.

— Journal. Wash., 1851-52. 8°.
— Ex. docs. Wash., 1852. 16 v. in 17 pts. 8°.
Contents. Vol. 1-3. No. 1, pts. 1-3. 4. 2, 4-17, 18-27. 5, pts. 1, 2. 3. 6. 28. 7. 29-38. 8. 39-55. 9. 56-94. 10. 95-111, 113-117. 11. 112. 12, 13. 118, pts. 1, 2: Patents. 14. 119. 15. 120-131. 16. Commerce and navigation. [Unnumbered doc.]
Also no. 112. Wash., 1853. 8 v. *and* Maps.
— Misc. docs. Wash., 1852. 8°.
Contents. No. 1-111.
Also no. 32. *n.t.p.* [1849.] 8°.
Also no. 108: Smithsonian Inst. 6th ann. rept., 1851. Wash., 1852. 8°.
— Reports of committees. Wash., 1852. 2 v. 8°.
Contents. Vol. 1. No. 1-209 (126 w.*).
Also no. 15 (B 1509).

32d Cong. 2d sess., Dec. 6, 1852 - *March* 3, 1853.

— Journal. Wash., 1852. 8°.
— Ex. docs. *n.t.p.* [Wash., 1852-53.] 11 v. in 12 pts. 8° *and* 4°.
Contents. Vol. 1, 2. No. 1, pts. 1, 2. 3. 2, 3, 5-21, 23-35, 37-40. 4. 4. 5. 22. 6, pt. 1, 2. 36: Explor. of

the Valley of the Amazon, pts. 1, 2. **7.** 41-53, 56, 57. **8.** 54. **9.** 55, pts. 1, 2: Patents. **10.** 59: Exped. down the Zuni and Colorado Rivers. **11.** 58: Explor. of the Valley of the Amazon, pt. 1, 2.

Note. Vol. 11 has a separate titlepage 'Report of the Supt. of the Coast Survey, 1852'.

— Misc. docs. Wash., 1853. 8°.
Contents. No. 1-59.
Also no. 53: Smithsonian Inst. 7th ann. rept., 1852. Wash., 1853. 8°.

— Reports of committees. Wash., 1853. 8°.
Contents. No. 358-432.

33*d Cong. Special sess., March* 4 - *Apr.* 11, 1853.

— Docs. Wash., 1853. 8°.
Contents. Misc. docs., no. 1-3. — Rept. of comm., no. 1, 2. — Ex. docs., no. 1-8.

33*d Cong.* 1*st sess., Dec.* 5, 1853 - *Aug.* 7, 1854.

— Journal. Wash., 1853. 8°.

— Ex. docs. Wash., 1854. 13 v. in 15 pts. 8°.
Contents. Vol. **1-3.** No. 1, pts. 1-3 [also a vol. of maps to accomp. doc. 1]. **4.** 2-13, 15-24. **5.** 25-26, 28, 29. **6,** 7. 27, pts. 1, 2. **8.** 30-58, 60. **9.** 59, 61. **10.** 62-66, 68. **11.** 67, 69. **12.** 70-89. **13.** 14.
Note. Vol. 13 has the sep. title-page 'Report of Supt. of Coast Survey'.
Also no. 59. Wash., 1854. 8° *and* Map.
Also no. 72 (B 1509).
Also no. 121. Wash., 1855-56. 6 v. (v. 4, 5, w.). 4°.

— Misc. docs. Wash., 1854. 8°.
Contents. No. 1-74 (54 w.*; 72 w.).
Also no. 72 (B 1509).
Also no. 73: Smithsonian Inst. 8th ann. rept., 1853. Wash., 1854. 8°.

— Reports of committees. Wash., 1854. 2 v. in 3 pts. 8°.
Contents. Vol. **1.** No. 1-181. **2,** pt. 1. 183-394 (276, 278 w.*). **2,** pt. 2. 182.
Also no. 15 (B 1509).

33*d Cong.* 2*d sess., Dec.* 4, 1854 - *March* 3, 1855.

— Journal. Wash., 1854. 8°.

— Ex. docs. Wash., 1855-56. 14 v. in 26 pts. 8° *and* 4°.
Contents. Vol. **1-3.** No. 1, pts. 1-3. **4.** 2. **5.** 3 and Com. and nav. **6.** 4-9, 11-34 (30 w.). **7.** 35-41, 43-63. **8-10.** 42, pts. 1-3. **11.** 64-77. **12.** 10. **13.** 78, pts. 1-11: Explor. and surveys for a R. R. to the Pacific. **14.** 79, pts. 1-3: Narr. of an exped. of an Amer. squadron to the China Seas and Japan under Com. Perry.
Note. Vol. 12 has the sep. t. p., 'Rept. of the Supt. of the Coast Survey'.
Also no. 34. *n.t.p.* [Wash., 1855.] 8°.
Also no. 78. Wash., 1855-59. 11 v. 4°.
Also no. 79. Wash., 1856. 3 v. 4°.

— Misc. docs. Wash., 1855. 3 v. 8°.
Contents. Vol. **1.** No. 1-24 (20 w.*). **2.** 25-26. **3.** 27.

— Reports of committees. Wash., 1855. 8°.
Contents. No. 395-551.

— Addresses on the presentation of the sword of Gen. Jackson to the Congress of the U.S., Feb. 26. Wash., 1855. 8°. (B 1611)

34*th Cong.* 1*st and* 2*d sess., Dec.* 3, 1855 - *Aug.* 30, 1856.

— Journal. Wash., 1856. 8°.

— Ex. docs. Wash., 1856-58. 20 v. in 25 pts. 8° *and* 4°.
Contents. Vol. **1-4.** No. 1, pts. 1-4. **5.** 2. **6.** 3-19. **7-9.** 20, pts. 1-3. **10.** 21, 24-43. **11.** 23. **12.** 44-65. **13.** 66-76. **14.** 77-95, 97, 98 (89 w.). **15.** 99-103. **16.** 104-106, 109. Com. and nav. — No. 1, 2 of 2d sess. **17.** 22: Coast survey. **18.** 96: Statist. rep. on the sickness and mortality in the army, 1839-55. **19.** 107, pts. 1-4: Commer. rel. **20.** 108, pts. 1-3: U. S. and Mexican boundary survey.
Also no. 108. Wash., 1857-59. 2 v. 4°.

— Misc. docs. Wash., 1856. 8°.
Contents. 1st sess. No. 1-82 (1 w.). — 2d sess. 1, 2.
Also no. 73: Smithsonian Inst. 10th ann. rept. Wash., 1856. 8°.

— Reports of committees. Wash., 1856. 2 v. 8°.
Contents. Vol. **1.** No. 1-197 (19, 31 w.). **2.** 198-290.

Note. No reports of committes were made during the 2d sess.

34*th Cong.* 3*d sess., Dec.* 1, 1856 - *March* 3, 1357.

— Journal. Wash., 1856, 57. 8°.

— Ex. docs. Wash., 1857. 16 v. 8°.
Contents. Vol. **1.** No. 1-4. **2-4.** 5, pts. 1-3. **5.** 6-11, 13-22. **6.** 23-27. **7.** 28-34, 36. **8.** 37-52, 54-63, 66-70. **9-12.** 53, pts. 1-4. **13.** Rep. on com. and nav. [Unno. doc.] **14.** 35: Rep. of Sec. of State on commer. rel. **15.** 12: Coast survey. **16.** 65: 4th Meteorol. report.
Note. 'There is no doc. no. 64'.
Also no. 62. Wash., 1857. 8°.
Also no. 65. Wash., [1857]. 4°.

— Misc. docs. Wash., 1857. 8°.
Contents. 3d sess. no. 1-56. — Spec. sess., no. 1-3.
Also no. 54: Smithsonian Inst. [11th] ann. report. Wash., 1857. 8°.

— Report of committees. Wash., 1857. 8°.
Contents. Spec. sess., no. 7. — 3d sess. 291-447.

35*th Cong. Spec. sess., March* 4 - 14, 1857.

Note. For Journal and Miscellaneous docs. of this sess. *see* 34*th Cong.* 3*d sess.*

— Ex. docs. Wash., 1857. 4°.
Contents. No. 1: Report of the Sec. of War com. the rept. of G. B. McClellan [on] war in Europe, 1855, 56.

35*th Cong.* 1*st sess., Dec.* 7, 1857 - *June* 14, 1858.

— Journal. Wash., 1857-58. 8°.

— Ex. docs. Wash., 1858. 16 v. 8° *and* 4°.
Contents. Vol. **1.** No. 1-10, 12-16 (2 w.). **2-5.** 11, pts. 1-4. **6.** 17-19. **7.** 20-29, 31, 32, 34, 35. **8-11.** 30, pts. 1-4. **12.** 36-52, 54-57. **13.** 58-73. — Spec. sess., no. 1. **14.** Com. and nav. [Unnumb.] **15.** 33: Coast survey. **16.** 53: For. rel.
Also no. 35. Wash., 1858. 8°.

— Misc. docs. Wash., 1858. 4 v. 8°.
Contents. Vol. **1.** No. 1-94 (44 w.*). **2.** 95-145 (101 w.). **3.** 146-250 (180 w.*). **4.** 251-273.

— Reports of committees. Wash., 1858. 2 v. 8°.
Contents. Vol. **1.** No. 1-160. **2.** 161-330.

35*th Cong. Spec. sess., June* 15-16, 1858.

Note. For Journal and Miscellaneous docs. of this sess. *see* 34*th Cong.* 3d sess.

35*th Cong.* 2*d sess., Dec.* 6, 1858 - *March* 3, 1859.

— Journal. Wash., 1858-59. 8°.

— Ex. docs. Wash., 1859. 18 v. in 19 pts. 8° *and* 4°.
Contents. Vol. **1-5.** No. 1, pts. 1-5. **6,** pt. 1. **2.** — Spec. sess., no. 1. **6,** pt. 2. 3-6. — Spec. sess., no. 2. **7.** 7-13, 15-21, 23-28. **8, 9.** 22, pts. 1, 2. **10.** 29-36, 38-45, 48. **11-14.** 47, pts. 1-4. **15.** Com. and nav. **16.** 14: Coast survey. **17.** 37: Com. rel. **18.** 46: Explor. and surveys for a R. R. to the Pacific; suppl. report of explor. near the 47th and 49th parallel of N. lat.

— Misc. docs. Wash., 1859. 8°.
Contents. No. 1-55. — Spec. sess., no. 1, 2.
Also no. 49: Smithsonian Inst. [13th] ann. rept. Wash., 1859. 8°.

— Reports of committees. Wash., 1859. 8°.
Contents. No. 331-396.

36*th Cong. Spec. sess., March* 4-10, 1859.

Note. For Journal, Ex. docs., and Miscellaneous docs. of this sess. *see* 35*th Cong.* 2*d sess.*

36*th Cong.* 1*st sess., Dec.* 5, 1859 - *June* 25, 1860.

— Journal. Wash., 1859, 60. 8°.

— Ex. docs. Wash., 1860. 15 v. 8° *and* 4°.
Contents. Vol. **1-4.** No. 2, pts. 1-4. **5.** 1, 3-10, 13-15. **6.** 11. **7, 8.** 12, pt. 1, 2. **9.** 16-29, 31-37. **10.** 30. **11.** 38-51, 53-58. **12.** Com. and nav. [Unnumb.] **13.** 52: Statist. report on the sickness and mortality in the army, 1855-60. **14.** 59: Report on the art of war in Europe, 1854-56; by Maj. R. Delafield. **15.** 60: Military commis. to Europe, 1855-56; report of Maj. A. Mordecai.
Also no. 30. *n.t.p.* [1860.] 8°.
Also no. 38. Wash., 1860. 8°.
Also no. 52. Wash., 1860. 4°.

Also no. 55. Vol. 1. Wash., 1861. 4°.
Also no. 56. Wash., 1860. 4°.
Also no. 60. Wash., 1860. 4°.
Also Reports of explorations for a R. R. to the Pacific. Vol. 12, bk. 1. Wash., 1860. 4°. (Unnumbered doc.)

— Misc. docs. Wash., 1860. 8°.
Contents. 1st sess., no. 1-62. — Spec. sess., no. 1.

— Reports of committees. Wash., 1860. 2 v. 8°.
Contents. Vol. 1. No. 1-204. 2. 205-284.

36*th Cong. Spec. sess., June* 26-28, 1860.
Note. For Journal and Misc. doc., *see 1st sess.*

36*th Cong.* 2*d sess., Dec.* 3, 1860 - *March* 4, 1861.

— Journal. Wash., 1860-61. 8°.
— Ex. docs. Wash., 1861. 9 v. in 11 pt. 8°, 4°.
Contents. Vol. 1-3. No. 1, pts. 1-3. 4. 2-5, 8, 10-13. — Spec. sess., no. 1, 2. 5, 6. 7, pts. 1, 2. 7. 9. 8. Com. and nav. [Unnumb. doc.] 9. 6: Com. rel.
Also no. 3. *n.t.p.* [1860.] 8°.

— Misc. docs. Wash., 1861. 8°.
Contents. 2d sess., no. 1-21. Spec. sess., no 1-4.
Also no. 21: Smithsonian Inst. [15th] ann. rept., 1860. Wash., 1861. 8°.

— Reports of committees. Wash., 1861. 8°.
Contents. No. 285-311.

37*th Cong. Spec. sess., March* 4-28, 1861.
Note. For Journal, Ex. docs., and Miscellaneous docs. of this sess. *see 36th Cong. 2d sess.*

37*th Cong.* 1*st sess., July* 4 - *Aug.* 6, 1861.

— Journal. Wash., 1861. 8°.
— Ex. and Misc. docs., and Reports of committees. Wash., 1861. 8°.
Contents. Ex. docs., no. 1-8. — Misc. docs., no. 1-12. — Rept. of com., no. 1.

37*th Cong.* 2*d sess., Dec.* 2, 1861 - *July* 17, 1862.

— Journal. Wash., 1861. 8°.
— Ex. docs. Wash., 1862. 6 [7] v. 8°.
Contents. Vol. 1-3. No. 1, pts. 1-3, [4: *Extra* maps]. 4. 2-31. 5. 32-65. 6. 66-72.
Also no. 1. Wash., 1861. 8°.

— Misc. docs. Wash., 1862. 8°.
Contents. No. 1-108.

— Reports of committees. Wash., 1862. 8°.
Contents. No. 1-69.

37*th Cong.* 3*d sess., Dec.* 1, 1862 - *March* 4, 1863.

— Journal. Wash., 1863. 8°.
— Ex. docs. Wash., 1863. 8°.
Contents. No. 1-50.

— Misc. docs. Wash., 1863. 8°.
Contents. 3d sess., no. 1-42. — Spec. sess., no. 1.

— Reports of committees. Wash., 1863. 4 v. 8°.
Contents. Vol. 1. No. 70-107. 2-4. 108, pts. 1-3: Reports on the conduct of the war.
Also no. 75. *n.t.p.* [1863.] 8°.
Also no. 89 (B 1566).

38*th Cong. Spec. sess., March* 4-14, 1863.
Note. For Journal and Miscellaneous docs. of this sess. *see 37th Cong. 3d sess.*

— Ex. docs. Wash., 1863. 8°.
Contents. No. 1, 2.
Also no. 1. *n.t.p.* [1863.] 8°.
Also no. 2. Wash., 1863. 8°.

— Report of the Sec. of Treas. on commerce and navigation. Wash., 1864. 8°.

38*th Cong.* 1*st sess., Dec.* 7, 1863 - *July* 4, 1864.

— Journal. Wash., 1863. 8°.
— Ex. docs. Wash., 1864. 8°.
Contents. No. 1-56 (39 w.).

— Misc. docs. Wash., 1864. 8°.
Contents. No. 1-136.
Also no. 98, 123 (with additions). Wash., 1864. 8°.

— Reports of committees. Wash., 1864. 8°.
Contents. No. 1-105.
Also no. 41. *n.t.p.* [1864.] 8°.

— Papers relating to Mexican affairs, [1861-64]. Wash., 1865. 8°.

38*th Cong.* 2*d sess., Dec.* 5, 1864 - *March* 4, 1865.

— Journal. Wash., 1864. 8°.
— Ex. docs. Wash., 1865. 8°.
Contents. No. 1-35.
Also no. 19. *n.t.p.* [1865.] 8°.
Also no. 35. *n.t.p.* [1865.] 8°.

— Misc. docs. Wash., 1865. 8°.
Contents. 2d sess., no. 1-48. — Spec. sess., 1-3.

— Reports of committees. Wash., 1865. 4 v. 8°.
Contents. Vol. 1. No. 106-141. — Spec. sess., no. 1. 2-4. 2d sess., 142, pts. 1-3: Conduct of the war.
Also no. 142. Wash., 1865. 8°.
Note. There are two suppl. vols. to doc. 142 in the 1st sess., 39th Cong. Sen. Reports of com.

39*th Cong. Spec. sess., March* 4 - 11, 1865.
Note. For Journal, Miscellaneous docs., and Reports of com. of this sess. *see 38th Cong. 2d sess.*

39*th Cong.* 1*st sess., Dec.* 4, 1865 - *July* 28, 1866.

— Journal. Wash., 1865. 8°.
— Ex. docs. Wash., 1866. 2 v. 8°.
Contents. Vol. 1. No. 1-26. 2. 27-65.
Also no. 2. *n.t.p.* [1865.] 8°.
Also no. 62. *n.t.p.* [1866.] 8°.

— Misc. docs. Wash., 1866. 8°.
Contents. No. 1-125.

— Reports of committees. Wash., 1866. 8°.
Contents. No. 1-140.

— - Supplemental report of the joint committee on the conduct of the war; suppl. to Sen. rept. no. 142, 38th Cong. 2d sess. Wash., 1866. 2 v. 8°.

39*th Cong.* 2*d sess., Dec.* 3, 1866 - *March* 4, 1867.

— Journal. Wash., 1867. 8°.
— Ex. docs. Wash., 1867. 2 v. 8°.
Contents. Vol. 1. No. 1-6. 2. 7-38.

— Misc. docs. Wash., 1867. 8°.
Contents. No. 1-54.

— Reports of committees. Wash., 1867. 8°.
Contents. No. 141-178.
Also no. 156. Wash., 1867. 8°.

40*th Cong.* 1*st sess., March* 4 - *Dec.* 2, 1867.

— Journal. Wash., 1867. 8°.
— Ex. docs. Wash., 1868. 8°.
Contents. No. 1-20. — Spec. sess., no. 1-9.

— Reports of com. and Misc. docs. Wash., 1868. 8°.
Contents. Rept. of com., no. 1-3. — Misc. docs., no. 1-43. — Spec. sess. Misc. docs., no. 1-5.

40*th Cong. Spec. sess.,* April 1-20, 1867.
Note. For Journal, Ex. docs., and Miscellaneous docs. of this sess. *see 1st sess.*

40*th Cong.* 2*d sess., Dec.* 2, 1867 - *Nov.* 10, 1868.

— Journal. Wash., 1868. 8°.
— Ex. docs. Wash., 1868. 2 v. 8°.
Contents. Vol. 1. No. 1-40 (8 w.). 2. 41-86 (84 w.).
Also no. 29. Wash., 1868. 8°.
Also no. 77. Wash., 1868. 8°.

— Misc. docs. Wash., 1868. 8°.
Contents. No. 1-110.
Also no. 86: Smithsonian Inst; [22d] ann. rept. Wash., 1868. 8°.

— Reports of committees. Wash., 1868. 8°.
Contents. No. 4-189.

— Reports of the U. S. commissioners to the Paris Univ. Expos., 1867; ed. by W. P. Blake. Wash., 1867. 6 v. 8°.

— Trial of Andrew Johnson, President, on impeachment for high crimes and misdemeanors. Wash., 1868. 3 v. 8°.

40th Cong. 3d sess., Dec. 7, 1868 - *Mar.* 4, 1869.

— Journal. Wash., 1869. 8°.
— Ex. docs. Wash., 1869. 8°.
Contents. No. 1-56.
— Misc. docs. Wash., 1869. 8°.
Contents. No. 1-57.
— Reports of committees. Wash., 1869. 8°.
Contents. No. 190-273.
Also no. 266. *n.t.p.* [1869.] 8°.

41st Cong. 1st sess., March 4 - *Apr.* 10, 1869.

— Journal. Wash., 1869. 8°.
— Ex. docs. Wash., 1870. 6 v. 8°.
Contents. Vol. 1. No. 1-10, 12. 2-6. 11, pts. 1-5: Alabama claims.
— Reports of committees and Misc. docs. Wash., 1870. 8°.
Contents. Rep. of com., no. 1-8. — Misc. docs., no, 1-25.

41st Cong. 2d sess., Dec. 6, 1869 - *July* 15, 1870.

— Journal. Wash., 1870. 8°.
— Ex. docs. Wash., 1870. 3 v. 8°.
Contents. Vol. 1. No. 1-39. 2. 40-90 (76 w.*). 3. 91-116.
Also no. 108. Wash., 1870. 8°.
— Misc. docs. Wash., 1870. 8°.
Contents. No. 1-164 (159 w.*).
— Reports of committees. Wash., 1870. 8°.
Contents. No. 9-265.
Also no. 47. Wash., 1870. 8°.
Also no. 114. *n.t.p.* [1870.] 8°.
Also 234. Wash., 1869. 8°.

41st Cong. 3d sess., Dec. 5, 1870 - *March* 4, 1871.

— Journal. Wash., 1871. 8°.
— Ex. docs. Wash., 1871. 2 v. 8°.
Contents. Vol. 1. No. 1-35, 37-53. 2. 36: Treaties and conventions since July 4, 1776.
Also no. 36. Wash., 1871. 8°.
— *Same.* Rev. ed. Wash., 1873. 8°.
— Misc. docs. Wash., 1871. 8°.
Contents. No. 1-90.
— Report of the Commis. of Agric. on the diseases of cattle in the U. S. Wash., 1871. 4°.
— Reports of committees. Wash., 1871. 8°.
Contents. No. 266-380.

42d Cong. 1st sess., Mar. 4 - *April* 20, 1871.

— Journal. Wash., 1871. 8°.
— Ex. docs. Wash., 1871. 8°.
Contents. 1st sess., no. 1-12. — Spec. sess., 1, 2.
— Misc. docs. Wash., 1871. 8°.
Contents. 1st sess., no. 1-53. — Spec. sess., no. 1-3.
— Reports of committees. Wash., 1871. 8°.
Contents. No. 1-5: 1-3, 1st sess.; 4, 5, spec. sess.
Also no. 1. Wash., 1871. 8°.

42d Cong. Spec. sess., May 10-27, 1871.

Note For Journal, Ex. docs., Miscellaneous docs., and Reports of com. of this sess. *see 1st sess.*

42d Cong. 2d sess., Dec. 4, 1871 - *June* 10, 1872.

— Journal. Wash., 1872. 8°.
— Ex. docs. Wash., 1872. 3 v. 8°. *and* 4°.
Contents. Vol. 1. No. 1-5, 7-35. 2. 36-87. 3. 6: Reports of explor. and surveys [for] a ship-canal between the Atlantic and Pacific by the way of the Isthmus of Tehuantepec.
Also no. 6. Wash., 1872. 4°.
Also no. 31. Wash., 1872. 8°.
Also no. 39. Wash., 1872. 8°.
— Misc. docs. Wash., 1872. 2 v. 8°.
Contents. Vol. 1. No. 1-61. 2. 62-167.
Also no. 149: Smithsonian Inst. [26th] ann. rept., 1871. Wash., 1873. 8°.

— Reports of committees. Wash., 1872. 4 v. in 18 pts. 8°.
Contents. Vol. 1. No. 6-40, 42-182, 184-226, 228-232. 2. 41, pts. 1-13: Affairs in the late insurrectionary states; the Ku-Klux conspiracy. (Pt. 1. Rep. of com., *etc.* 2. N. Carolina. 3-5. S. Carolina. 6, 7. Georgia. 8-10. Alabama. 11, 12. Mississippi. 13. Florida.) 3. 183: Sales of ordnance. 4. 227, pts. 1-3: Alleged frauds in N. Y. Custom House.

42d Cong. 3d sess., Dec. 4, 1872 - *March* 4, 1873.

— Journal. Wash., 1873. 8°.
— Ex. docs. Wash., 1873. 8°.
Contents. No. 1-52.
— Misc. docs. Wash., 1873. 2 v. 8°.
Contents. Vol. 1. No. 1-73, 75-103. — Spec. sess., no. 1-11. 2. 74: Fresh water fisheries.
— Reports of committees. Wash., 1872. 3 v. 8°.
Contents. Vol. 1. No. 233-456. 2. 457. 3. 458-523. — Spec. sess., no. 1.

43d Cong. Spec. sess., March 4-26, 1873.

Note. For Journal, Miscellaneous docs., and Reports of com. of this sess. *see 42d Cong. 3d sess.*

43d Cong. 1st sess., Dec. 1, 1873 - *June* 23, 1874.

— Journal. Wash., 1873. 8°.
— Ex. docs. Wash., 1874. 4 v. 8°. *and* 4°.
Contents. Vol. 1. No. 1-42. 2. 43-56. 3. 57: Ship-canal via Lake Nicaragua. 4. 58: Patents.
— Misc. docs. Wash., 1874. 2 v. 8°.
Contents. Vol. 1. No. 1-128. 2. 130.
Note. No. 129 was consolidated with no. 108 of the 2d sess., v. 2 Miscel. docs.
Also no. 130: Smithsonian Inst. [28th] ann. rept., 1873. Wash., 1874. 8°.
— Reports of committees. Wash., 1874. 4 v. in 7 pts. 8°.
Contents. Vol. 1. No. 1-280. 2. 281-306, 308-452, 454-478. 3. 307, pts, 1, 2: Routes to the seaboard. 4. 453, pts 1-3: Affairs in D. C.
Also no. 307, pt. 1. Wash., 1874. 8°.

43d Cong. 2d sess., Dec. 7, 1874 - *March* 4, 1875.

— Journal. Wash., 1874. 8°.
— Ex. docs. Wash., 1875. 8°.
Contents. 2d sess., no. 1-32. — Spec. sess., no. 1, 2.
— Misc. docs. Wash., 1875. 2 v. 8°.
Contents. Vol. 1. No. 1-107, 109-122. — Spec. sess., no. 1-6. 2. 108: Fish and fisheries.
— Reports of committees. Wash., 1875. 8°.
Contents. No. 479-693 (540 w.* 691 w.).

44th Cong. Spec. sess., March 5 - 24, 1875.

Note. For Journal, Ex. docs., and Miscellaneous docs. of the sess. *see 43d Cong. 2d sess.*

44th Cong. 1st sess., Dec. 6, 1875 - *Aug.* 15, 1876.

— Journal. Wash., 1875. 8°.
— Ex. docs. Wash., 1876. 8°.
Contents. No. 1-94.
— Misc. docs. Wash., 1876. 2 v. 8°.
Contents. Vol. 1. No. 1-106, 108-131. 2. 107: Propagation of food-fishes.
Also no. 115: Smithsonian Inst. 30th ann. rept., 1875. Wash., 1876. 8°.
— Reports of committees. Wash., 1876. 3 v. in 4 pts. 8°.
Contents. Vol. 1. No. 1-328. 2. 329-526, 528-534. 3. 527, pts, 1, 2: Mississippi elections.

44th Cong. 2d sess., Dec. 4, 1876 - *March* 3, 1877.

— Journal. Wash., 1876. 8°.
— Ex. docs. Wash., 1877. 4 v. (v. 4 w.). 8 *and* 4°.
Contents. Vol. 1-20. 2. 21-30, 32-36, 39-46. — Spec. sess., no. 1. 3. 31: Claims of the U. S. and Mexico. — 38: Appropriations, Mar. 4, 1789 - June 30, 1876. 4. 37: Coast survey. *Wanting.*
Also no. 27. Wash., 1877. 8°.
Also no. 41. Wash., 1878. 4°.

— Misc. docs. Wash., 1877. 6 v. in 8 pts. (v. 5 w.). 8°.

Contents. Vol. 1. No. 1-13, 15-43. 2. 14: Louisiana elections. 3. 44: Electoral votes. — 46: Smithsonian rept. 4. 45: Mississippi elections. 5. 47: Fish and fisheries. *Wanting.* 6. 48, pts. 1-3: S. Carolina in 1876.

Also no. 46: Smithsonian Inst. [31st] ann. rept., 1876. Wash., 1877. 8°.

— Reports of committees. Wash., 1877. 5 v. in 8 pts. 8°.

Contents. Vol. 1. No. 535-610, 612-688, 690-702, 704-706. 2. 611: Florida elections. 3. 689: Chinese immigration. 4. 701, pts. 1-3: Louisiana elections. 5. 703, pts. 1, 2: Monetary commission.

45*th Cong.* 1*st sess.*, *Oct.* 15 - *Dec.* 3, 1877.

— Journal. Wash., 1877. 8°.

— Ex. docs. Wash., 1877, 4 [5] v. (v. 4 w.). 8° *and* 4°.

Contents. Vol. 1. 1st sess., no. 1, 2, 5-9. — 2d sess., no. 1-11, 13-35. 2. 36-68, 70-83, 85-100. 3. 1st sess., no. 3, 4. — 2d sess., no. 84. 4. 12: Coast survey. *Wanting.* 5. 69: Bridging the Mississippi between St. Paul and St. Louis.

— Misc. docs. Wash., 1877, 3 [4] v. 8°.

Contents. Vol. 1. 1st sess., no. 1-15. — 2d sess., no. 1-35. 2. 36-48, 51-89. 3. 49: Fresh water fisheries. [4.] 50: Patents.

Also no. 45: Smithsonian Inst. [32d] ann. rept., 1877. Wash., 1878. 8°.

Also no. 50. Wash., 1878. 8°.

— Reports of committees. Wash., 1877. 3 v. 8°.

Contents. Vol. 1. 1st sess., no. 1-25. — 2d sess., no. 25, pt. 2-209. 2. 210-512. 3. 513-546.

45*th Cong.* 2*d sess.*, *Dec.* 3, 1877 - *June* 20, 1878.

— Journal. Wash., 1877. 8°.

Note. For docs. of this sess. *see* 1*st sess.*

45*th Cong.* 3*d sess.*, *Dec.* 2, 1878 - *March* 4, 1879.

— Journal. Wash., 1878. 8°.

— Ex. docs. Wash., 1879. 5 v. (v. 2, 4 w.). 8° *and* 4°.

Contents. Vol. 1. No. 1-12, 14-26, 28-48. 2. 13, 75. *Wanting.* — Misc. docs., no. 16. 3. 27: Hall's 2d Arctic explor. exped. 4. 49-57, 59-74. *Wanting.* 5. 58: Monetary commission.

Also no. 58. Wash., 1879. 4°.

— Misc. docs. Wash., 1879. 4 v. in 5 pts. (v. 2 w.). 8°.

Contents. Vol. 1. No. 1-15, 17-30, 32-52, 54-58, 60-80. 2. 31. *Wanting.* 3. 53, 59. 4. 81, pts. 1, 2: Private claims.

Note. No. 16 is bd. in v. 2 of the Senate ex. docs. 3d sess.

Also no. 59: Smithsonian Inst. [33d] ann. rept., 1878. Wash., 1879. 8°.

— Reports of committees. Wash., 1879. 4 v. 8°.

Contents. Vol. 1. No. 547-693. 2. 694-743, 745-854. 3. 744: Report on bill to estab. a U. S. Court in the Indian Territory. 4. 855: Election in Louisiana, So. Carolina, and Mississippi, 1878.

Smithsonian Institute.

See **Smithsonian Institute** (p. 2770-2776).

Department of State.

— Papers rel. to Gr. Britain. *n.p.*, [179-]. 8°. (W 57)

— Letter from Mr. Pickering to the chev. de Yrujo, Aug. 8. [Phila., 1797.] 8°. (W 65)

— Instructions to the envoys extraordinary and ministers plenipotentiary from the U. S. to the French Repub.; [with] dispatches, *etc.* Phila., **1798**. 8°.

— *Other copies.* (B 516, 593, W 64)

— Register of officers and agents, civil, military, and naval, in the service, **1816**, 21, 25, 27, 37-47, **55**. Wash., 1816-55. 6 v. 12°.

Note. For continuation, *see Department of the Interior* (p. 3092).

— Reports upon weights and measures; by J. Q. Adams, sec. Wash., **1821**. 8°. (16th Cong. 2d sess. Ho. Doc. 109.)

— Proceedings in the French Chamber of Deputies on the treaty between France and the U. S., July 4, **1831**; tr. from Paris Moniteur by order of the Sec. of State. Wash., 1834. 8°.

— Report on the commercial relations of the U. S. with foreign countries, **1841**, 56-65, 67-72, 74-75. Wash., 1842-76. 22 v. 8° *and* 4°.

Note. In 1857-59 the title reads 'Letter transmitting a statement of the com. rel.'; in 1860-68 'Letter transm. a report; in 1869-74 'Annual report'; in 1875', Report'. The report for 1856 is in 4 pts.; v. 1, Digests; 2, Comparative tariffs; 3, 4, Consular returns.

— Correspondence between Ld. Ashburton and D. Webster on McLeod's case; on the Creole case; on impressment. *n.p.*, 1842. 8°. (B 1499, 1871)

— Correspondence between the U. S. and Gr. Brit. on recruiting for the British army. Wash., 1856. 8°. (B 1508)

— *Same.* With correspondence conc. the arbitration of the Central American question. Wash., 1856. 8°. (B 1508)

— Instructions in regard to consular emoluments, *etc.*, 1856, 63. *See Diplomatic, Consular, and other Offices* (Abbot, G. J.) p. 3063.

— The Austro-Hungarian question; correspondence between Mr. Hülsemann and D. Webster. Wash., 1857. 8°. (B 1505)

— Letter [giving] information rel. to the explorations of the Amoor River. Wash., **1858**. 8°. (35th Cong. 1st sess. Ho. Ex. doc. 98.)

— Papers relating to foreign affairs. Wash., **1861-77**. 32 v. 8°.

Note. For 1861-64, 68-70, 73, v. 1, the title is 'Message of the President', *etc.*; after 1871, 'Papers relating to the foreign relations of the U. S.'; the title of vol. 4 for 1866 is 'Appendix to diplomatic correspondence of 1865. Assassination of A. Lincoln; expressions of condolence and sympathy', of which the large paper edition is mentioned below.

— List of diplomatic and consular officers, May 1, **1862**, Dec. **1863**. Wash., 1862-63. 2 v. 8°.

— Report on the present condition of Mexico. Wash., **1862**. 8°. (37th Cong. 2d sess. Ho. Ex. doc. 100.)

— French Universal Exposition for 1867; official corresp. cont. general regulations, classification of articles, *etc.* Wash., **1865**. 4°.

— Message from the Pres. transm. a report from the Sec. of State conc. the Univ. Exposition to be held at Paris in 1867. [Wash., 1865.] 8°. (39th Cong. 1st sess. Ho. Doc. 12.)

— Summary of claims of citizens of the U. S. against Great Britain for damages during our late civil war. Wash., 1866.] f°. (E 242)

— Assassination of A. Lincoln, with the attempted assass. of W. H. and F. W. Seward, Apr. 14, 1865. Wash., **1867**. 4°.

— Despatches of Mr. Seward to Mr. Adams,] Jan. 12, 1867; April 16, 1867. *n.t.p.* [Wash., 1867.] 2 pam. f°. (E 242)

— Derby, E. H. Letter to the Secretary of State as to the rel. of the U. S. with the British provinces, and the actual condition of the question of the fisheries; [appended] a preliminary report on the treaty of reciprocity with Gr. Brit., *etc.* Wash., 1867. 8°.

— Correspondence in rel. to the seizure of Amer. vessels and injuries to Amer. citizens during the hostilities in Cuba. Wash., **1870**. 8°.

See also Census Office (p. 3058); — *Commissioners for Paris Expos.*, 1867 (p. 3094); — *State papers* (p. 3061); — *Diplomatic, Consular, and other officers in Foreign Countries* (p. 3062).

Bureau of Statistics.

(Subordinate to the *Treasury Dept.*)

— Annual report of the Deputy Special Commissioner of the Revenue on commerce and navigation, 1868, 69, 71-74, 76. Wash., 1869-77. 7 v. 8°.

Note. For 1871-76 the title reads 'Annual report of the Chief of the Bureau of Statistics'.

— Monthly reports on commerce and navigation, for year ended June 30. Wash., 1870. 4°.

Supreme Court.

— Case decided in Feb. 1793; whether a state be liable to be sued by a private citizen of another state. Phila., 1793. 8°. (B 598)

— RUTLEDGE, J. Speech, Feb. 24 and 25, 1802, on 'An act to repeal certain acts of the courts of the U. S. *n.p.*, [1802]. 8°. (B 621, 2525)

— Opinion at Jan. term, 1832, deliv. by Chief Justice Marshall, together with the opinion of Justice McLean in the case of S. A. Worcester *vs.* the State of Georgia. Wash., 1832. 8°. (B 1805)

— PETERS, R., *Jr., reporter of the Supreme Court.* Correspondence upon charges of error in his reports. *n.t.p.* [Phila., 1836.] 8°. (B 1756)

— Opinions of the judges in the case of the Proprietors of Charles River Bridge *vs.* the Proprietors of Warren Bridge and others, Wash., 1837. Boston, 1837. 8°. (B 1829)

— Supreme Court, Dec. term, 1851; decision of Judge McCaleb in the case of M. G. Gaines *vs.* Relf Chew *et al.* *n.p.*, [1851]. 8°. (E 229)

See also Courts (p. 3062).

Surgeon General.

— Meteorological register, 1822-25. Wash., 1826. 8°. (A 43, B 526)

— *Same.* 1826-30, [by] T. Lawson; appended, the registers for 1822-25, [by] J. Lovell. Phila., 1840. 8°.

— *Same.* 1831-42, 1843-54, [by] T. Lawson. Wash., 1851, 55. 2 v. 8°.

— FORRY, S. Climate of the U. S. and its endemic influences, based on the records of the Med. Dept. and Adj. General's Office, U. S. Army. N. Y., 1842. 8°.

— 1st, 4th report on meteorology, by J. P. Espy. 1843, 1857. Wash., [1843-57]. 2 v. 4°.

— Statistical report on the sickness and mortality in the army, 1855-60; by T. Lawson and R. H. Coolidge. Wash., 1860. 4°. (36th Cong. 1st sess., Sen. Doc. 52.)

— Circular. No. 1, 2, 5-7. Wash., 1868-69, 67, 65-67. 4°.

Contents. No. 1. Woodward, J. J. Report on epidemic cholera and yellow fever in the army of the U. S., 1867. 2. Otis, G. A. Report on excisions of the head of the femur for gunshot injury. 5. Woodward, J. J. Report on epidemic cholera in the army of the U. S., 1866. 6. Woodward, J. J. Reports on the extent and nature of the materials available for the preparation of a medical and surgical history of the rebellion. 7. Otis, G. A. Report on amputations at the hip-joint in military surgery.

— Reports on materials available for preparation of med. and surg. history of the rebellion. Phila., 1865. 4°.

Surveyor of the Public Buildings at Washington.

— LATROBE, B. A. Private letter to the individual members of Congress on the public buildings at Washington. Wash., 1806. 8°. (B 507)

For the reports of the Surveyor *see* the Congressional documents, *House* (p. 3064-92); — *Senate* (p. 3096-3106).

Treasury Department.

— Report on the subject of manufacturers; Dec. 1791; by A. Hamilton. 6th ed. Phila., 1827. 8°.

— *Other copies.* (B 1049, 1887)

— EXAMINATION of the late proc. in Congress respecting the conduct of the Sec. *n.p.*, [1793]. 8°. (W 83)

— Abstract of cases transm. to the Secretary pursuant to the 6th section of An act further to suspend commercial intercourse between the U. S. and France. *n.t.p.* [1800.] 8°. (B 1488)

— LAW, T. Remarks on the report of the Sec., Mar. 1, 1819. Wilmington, 1820. 8°. (B 531)

— Letter from the Secretary transm. statements showing the commerce and navigation, Sept., 1821, 25. Wash., 1822-26. 2 v. 8°.

Note. For continuation *see Register's Office* (p. 3096).

— Letter from the Secretary in rel. to the amt. of continental money issued during the Rev. war, Jan. 30, 1828. Wash., 1828. 8°. (20th Cong. 1st session. House. Doc. B 1798)

— Report on the state of the finances, 1831-32, 49, 53, 56, 57, 59-61, 63-71, 73-80. Wash., [1831]-80. 26 v. 8°.

Note. For 1831-32 the title reads 'Annual report'.

— *Same.* 1831. [Wash., 1831.] 8°. (B 1057, 1805) — 1832. [Wash., 1832.] 8°. (B 1790) — 1833. [Wash., 1833.] 8°. (B 1087) — 1840. [Wash., 1840.] 8°. (B 1823)

☞ The missing vols. and duplicates of those here enumerated are contained in the set of Congressional documents, *see House* (p. 3064-92); — *Senate* (p. 3096-3106); — *see also State papers* (3061).

— Specification of the materials and mechanical execution of a custom house to be erected in N. Y. *n.t.p.* [1833?] 8°. (B 1082)

— Report on the present system of keeping and disbursing the public money. *n.t.p.* [Wash., 1834.] 8°. (23d Cong. 2d sess. Ho. Doc. 27. B 1768)

— WOODBURY, L. Tables and notes on the cultivation, *etc.*, of cotton. Wash., 1836. 8°. (24th Cong. 1st sess., Ho. Doc. 46.)

— Report of the Sec., Jan. 9, 1838, rel. to the sales of pub. lands. [Wash., 1838.] 8°. (25th Cong. 2d sess. Sen. Doc. no. 85. B 1871)

— Letter from the Sec. respecting land to which the Indian title has been extinguished, *etc.*; Feb. 7, 1839. *n.t.p.* [Wash., 1839.] 8°. (Ho. Doc. 164. E 43)

— Report of the Secretary transm. a bill to provide revenue from imports, May 9. *n.t.p.* [1842.] 8°. (27th Cong. 2d sess. Ho. Doc. 209. B 1513)

— Reports in rel. to sugar and hydrometers; by R. S. McCulloh. 1845. Revised ed. Wash., 1848. 8°. (30th Cong. 1st sess. Sen. Doc. 50.)

— Letter transm. report as to the condition of the banks [in] the U. S., 1857, 58, 1863. Wash., 1857-63. 3 v. 8°.

— Commercial intercourse with and in the states in insurrection; circulars, proclamations, and and orders. Wash., 1863. 8°.

— Statistics of the for. and domestic commerce. Wash., 1864. 8°.

— Preliminary report on the treaty of reciprocity with Gr. Brit. to regulate the trade between the U. S. and the provinces of British N. Amer., by E. H. Derby. 1866. (*Appended to* Derby, E. H. Letter to W. H. Seward. 1867.)

See also Coast Survey (p. 3059); — *Office of Internal Revenue* (p. 3092); — *Light-House Board* (p. 3092); — *Commissioner of Mining Statistics* (p. 3092); — *Register's Office* (p. 3096); — *Bureau of Statistics* (p. 3106).

War Department.

— Report, [1863-65, 67, 68, 72, 73]. Wash., 1863-73. 13 v. 8°.

Note. Includes the reports of subordinate bureaus such as Adjutant Gen., Quartermaster Gen., Surgeon Gen., Chief of Ordnance, Chief of Engineers. The title for 1863 reads 'Message of the President and accompanying docs.' The reports for 1865, 67, 68, 72 have each 2 v.; for 1873, 3 v.

☞ The missing vols. and duplicates of those here enumerated are contained in the set of Congressional documents, *see House* (p. 3064-92); — *Senate* (p. 3096-3106); — *see also State papers* (p. 3061).

— Proceedings of a court of inquiry held at the request of Gen. J. Harmar to investigate his conduct [in] the expedition against the Miami Indians, 1790. Phila., 1791. f°.

— Official letters to the Sec. of War, [rel. to the war of 1812, 13, *etc.*; copies]. MS.

Note. Vols. 8, 11, 12 of some collection.

— Regulations for the field exercise, manœuvres, and conduct of the infantry; with plates. Phila., 1812. 8°.

— Message from the Pres. transm. a letter of the Secretary; with documents to explain the causes of the failure of the arms of the U. S. on the northern frontier. Albany, **1814.** 12°.

— Organization of the military peace establishment of the U. S. in conformity to an act 3d March 1815. Wash., **1815.** 8°.

— IZARD, G. Official correspondence with the War Dept. as to military operations on the northern frontier, 1814–15. Phila., **1816.** 8°.

— General regulations for the Army of U. S. Phila., **1821.** 8°.

— Extract from rules and regulations for manœuvres of infantry. Boston, **1823.** 12°.

— Infantry tactics for the army [by a board, W. Scott president]. Wash., **1825.** 8°.

— Explanation of plates [to preceding]. Wash., 1825. 8°.

— Indian treaties; laws and regulations rel. to Indians affairs. Wash., **1826.** 8°.

— Documents, accompanying the President's message to Congress. Pt. 3. [Wash., 1826.] 8°. (19th Cong. 2d sess. Sen. Doc. 1.)

— Documents accompanying the President's message; report of a board of officers rel. to the organization of the militia; also report from the Indian Office, Pension Office, and Bounty Land Office. [Wash., 1826.] 8°.

— Letter from the Secretary, transm. a report of the survey of the Kennebec River. Wash., **1827.** 8°. (19th Cong. 2d sess. Ho. Doc. 103. B 1493)

— Letter transmitting a system of cavalry tactics for militia of U. S. Wash., 1827. 8°. (19th Cong., 2d sess. Ho. Doc. 57.)

— DAVIS, J. Report of the claim of Mass. upon the U. S. for militia services during the last war, May 30. Boston, **1831.** 8°. (B 1805)

— Letter from the Sec. [on] the Act [on] the relief of officers and soldiers of the Revolution. Wash., **1832.** 8°. (22d Cong. 1st sess. Sen. Doc. 170. B 1057)

— System of exercise and instruction of field artillery. Boston, **1833.** 12°.

— Proceedings of the military court of inquiry in the case of Maj. Gen. Scott. Wash., **1837.** 8°. (24th Cong. 2d sess. Sen. Doc. 224.)

— *Another copy.* (B 1815)

— Abstract of [Scott's] infantry tactics for use of militia. Boston, **1839.** 8°.

— Regulations for the organization and government of the Military Academy at West Point. N. Y., 1839. 8°.

— Letter from the Sec. transm. a system of reorganization of the militia of the U. S., Mar. 20, 1840. [Wash., **1840.**] 8°. (26th Cong. 1st sess. Sen. Doc. 560. B 1823)

— RUSCHENBERGER, W. S. W. Regulations for the recruiting service. (*In* **Marshall**, H. On enlisting. 1840.)

— Regulations for the pay department of the army of the U. S. Wash., **1846.** 8°.

— Exploration of the Red River of Louisiana in 1852; by R. B. Marcy and G. B. McClellan, 1852. Wash., **1854.** 8°. (33d Cong. 1st sess. Ex. doc.)

Contents. **Marcy**, R. B. Report; — Meteorological observations; — Tables of courses and distances. — **Shepard**, C. U. Report on the minerals collected. — **Hitchcock**, E. Notes upon the specimens of rocks and minerals. — **Shumard**, G. G. Remarks upon the general geology of the country traversed. — **Shumard**, B. F. Description of the species of carboniferous and cretaceous fossils. — **Marcy**, R. B. Mammals. — **Baird**, S. F., *and* **Girard**, C. Reptiles; — Fishes. — **Adams**, C. B., *and* **Shumard**, G. G. Shells. — **Girard**, C. Orthopterous insects, arachnidians, and myriapods. — **Torrey**, J. Description of the plants collected during the exped. — **Marcy**, R. B. Vocabulary of the Comanches and Witchitas; with some general remarks by W. W. Turner.

— Reports of explorations for a R.R. to the Pacific. Wash., **1855–60.** 12 v. in 13 pts. 4°. (Sen. doc.)

Contents. Vol. 1. **Davis**, J. Report. — **Humphreys**, A. A. Exam. of reports of explorations by A. A. Humphreys and G. K. Warren. — **McClellan**, G. B. Railway memoranda. — **Jesup**, T. S. Letter. — **Stevens**, I. I. Report. 2. **Beckwith**, E. G. Report upon the route near the 38th and 39th parallels explored by J. W. Gunnison; — Report upon the route near the 41st parallel. — **Lander**, F. W. Report of a reconnaissance from Puget Sound via South Pass to the Mississippi River. — **Pope**, J. Report upon the route between the Red River and Rio Grande. — **Parke**, J. G. Report upon the route between the Rio Grande and Pimas village on the Gila. — **Emory**, W. H. Ex. from report of a reconnaissance of the route between the mouths of the San Pedro and Gila Rivers. 3. **Whipple**, A. W. Ex. from the preliminary report of W. upon the route near the 35th parallel, *etc.*; — Pt. 1–4 of report upon the route near the 35th parallel. 4. **Whipple**, A. W. Pt. 5, 6, and appendices of the report upon the route near the 35th parallel. 5. **Williamson**, R. S. Report upon the routes in California to connect with the routes near the 35th and 32d parallels. 6. **Abbot**, H. L. Report upon the routes in Oregon and California explored by R. S. Williamson, 1855. 7. **Parke**, J. G. Report upon the routes in California to connect with the routes near the 35th and 32d parallels, *etc.* — **Davis**, J., *and* **Humphreys**, A. A. Conclusion of the official review of the reports upon explorations and surveys for railroad routes from the Mississippi to the Pacific. 8–10. Gen. report upon the zoology of the Pacific railroad routes. 8. **Baird**, S. F. Mammals. 9. **Baird**, S. F. Birds. 10. **Baird**, S. F. Reptiles. — **Girard**, C. Fishes. — **Beckwith**, E. G. Zoological portion of the repts. upon the route near the 38th and 39th parallels surveyed by J. W. Gunnison, and upon the route near the 41st parallel surveyed by himself. — **Whipple**, A. W. Nos. 2–5 of pt. 6 of the rept. upon the route near the 35th parallel. — **Parke**, J. G. Zoological portion of the report upon the route near the 32d parallel from the Rio Grande to the Pimas villages, 1853–54. — **Williamson**, R. S. Pt. 4 of the rept. upon routes in California to connect with routes near the 35th and 32d parallels. — **Abbot**, H. L. No. 4 of pt. 4 of the report upon the routes in Oregon and California explored by R. S. Williamson, 1855. 11. **Humphreys**, A. A. Letter, transmitting Lieut. Warren's memoir. — **Warren**, G. K. Mem. upon the material uses and methods employed in compiling the map to illustrate the reports of surveys for railroad routes from the Mississippi to the Pacific. — **Maps**, profiles, and sketches. 12, pt. 1. **Stevens**, I. I. Pt. 1 and the appendices of the narr. and final report upon the route near the 47th and 49th parallels. 12, pt. 2. **Stevens**, I. I. Pt. 2, 3, of the narr. and final report of S.

— Regulations for the army of the U. S., 1857. N. Y., [1857]. 12°.

— Report of the Sec. on the purchase of camels for purposes of military transportation. Wash., 1857. 8°. (34th Cong. 3d sess. Sen. 62.)

— Report on the dangers and defences of New York; by J. G. Barnard. N. Y., **1859.** 8°.

— Infantry tactics. Phila., **1861.** 16°.

— Instruction for field artillery. Phila., 1861. 8°.

— Revised regulations for army of the U. S., 1861. Phila., 1861. 8°.

— Cavalry tactics. Phila., **1862.** 3 v. 16°.

Contents. Vol. 1. School of the trooper, of the platoon, and of the squadron: Dismounted. 2. *Same.* Mounted. 3. Evolutions of a regiment.

— Infantry tactics; by S. Casey. N. Y., **1863, 62.** 3 v. 24°.

Contents. Vol. 1. School of the soldier and company. — Instructions for skirmishers and music. 2. School of the battalion. 3. Evolutions of a brigade and corps d'armée.

— Report on the battle of Murfreesboro'; by Gen. Rosecrans. Wash., 1863. 8°. (37th Cong. Spec. sess. Sen. Doc. 2.)

— Letter transm. report on the organization of the Army of the Potomac and its campaigns under command of Maj. Gen. Geo. B. McClellan, 1861 to Nov. 7, 1862. Wash., **1864.** 8°. (38th Cong. 1st sess. Ho. Doc. 15.)

— Revised regulations for the government of the Bureau of the Provost Marshal General of the U. S. Wash., 1864. 8°.

Note. Duane's Handbook for infantry, Phila., 1813. 8°, and Casey's Infantry tactics, N. Y., 1863, 62, 3 v. 12° were adopted by the War Dept.

See also Continental Congress (p. 3055, 56); — *Adjutant General* (p. 3057); — *Army* (p. 3057, 58); — *Army Med. Museum* (p. 3058); — *Corps of Engineers* (p. 3063); — *Office of Chief of Engineers* (p. 3063); — *Bureau of Refugees, Freedmen, etc.*, (p. 3064); — *Military Commission to Europe* (p. 3092); — *Ordnance Department* (p. 3094); — *President* (p. 3095); — *Military Acad. at West Point* (*below*); — *also* **Grant**, U. S. (Report of the armies of the U. S., 1864-65); — **Meade**, G. G. (Report, 3d military district and dept. of the South. 1868); — **Rosecrans**, W. S. (Battle of Murfreesboro'. 1863); — **Saxton**, R. (General orders, Dept. of the South. 1867).

Military Acad. at West Point.
(Subordinate to the *War Department.*)

— Register of officers and cadets, 1821, 23, 27, 32, 34-36, 38, 39, 41-50. *n.p.*, [1831-50]. 19 v. 8°.
— Cullum, G. W. Register of officers and graduates, 1802-50. N. Y., 1850. 12°.
— Register of graduates commissioned in the army, 1802-28. *n.p.*, [1828]. 4°.
— *Another copy.* (A 32)
— Exposé of facts conc. recent trans. relating to the cadets. Newburgh, 1819. 8°. (B 547)
— Memorial [of cadets] to Congress. *n.p.*, [1819]. 8°. (16th Cong. 1st sess. Ho. doc. 14. B 547)
— United States. *War Depart.* Regulations. New York, 1823. 8°. (B 525, 1715)
— Register, officers, and cadets. *n.p.*, 1828. 8°. (B 946)
— U. S. *War Dept.* Regulations. N. Y., 1832. 8°.
— - *Same.* N. Y., 1839. 8°.
— Park, R. History and topography of West Point. Phila., 1840. 12°.
— United States. *Commission [on] the Organization, etc., of the Mil. Acad. at West Point.* Report. [Wash., 1860.] 8°. (36th Cong. 2d sess., Sen. Doc. 3.)
— Marshall, E. C. Are the West Point graduates loyal? N. Y., 1862. 18°.
— Strong, G. C. Cadet life at West Point; with descriptive sketch of West Point by B. J. Lossing. Boston, 1862. 12°.
— Boynton, E. C. History of West Point. N. Y., 1863. 8°.
— West Point battle monument, history of the project; Maj. Gen. McClellan's address. N. Y., 1864. 12°.
— Cullum, G. W. Biographical register. N.Y., 1868. 2 v. 8°.

B. WORKS ABOUT THE UNITED STATES.

Agriculture.

— Observations on the agriculture, *etc.*, of the U. S.; by a citizen of the U. S. N. Y., 1789. 8°. (B 417)
— Parkinson, R. Tour in America, 1798-1800; [with] a particular acc. of the Amer. system of agriculture. London, 1805. 2 v. 8°.
— Strickland, W. Observations on the agriculture of the U. S. London, 1801. 4°. (B 519)
— Cary, M. Address to the farmers of the U. S. on the ruinous consequences to their interests of the existing policy of this country. Phila., 1821. 8°. (B 548, 1835)
— - Farmer's and planter's friend. No. 1-7. *n.t.p.* [Phila., 1821.] 8°. (B 564)
— - Address before the Phila. Soc. for Promoting Agric. Phila., 1824. 8°. (B 541, 548, 1636)
— Tibbits, G. Essay on the expediency of improving home markets. Phila., 1827. 8°. (B 1884)
— U. S. *Cong.* Report on tropical plants. *See* p. 3112.
— Jay, J. Statistical view of Amer. agric., its home resources and foreign markets. N. Y., 1859. 8°.

See also Board of Agriculture (p. 3057); — *also* **Indiana**; — **Maine**; — **Massachusetts**; — **New York**; — **North America**; — *also* **Prairies, American.**

Antiquities.

See **America.** *Antiquities* (p. 60, 61); — **Mississippi River**; — **Mississippi Valley**; — **New England**; — *also* **Georgia**; — **Illinois**; — **Kentucky**; — **New England**; — **New York**; — **Ohio**; — **Pennsylvania**; — **Tennessee**; — **Wisconsin.**

Almanacs.
See, forward, Registers.

Art (including biography of artists).

— Verplanck, G. C. Address, 10th exhib. of the Amer. Acad. of the Fine Arts. [1824.] 2d ed. N. Y., 1825. 8°.
— Lawrence, W. B. Address before the Amer. Academy. N. Y., 1825. 8°. (B 567)
— Ray, R. Address before the Amer. Acad. of the Fine Arts. N. Y., 1825. 4°.
— Morse, S. F. B. Discourse, May 3, 1827, before National Acad. of Design. N. Y., 1827. 8°. (B 954)
— - Reply to No. Amer. rev., [v. 29, on] 'Academies of arts'. N. Y., 1828. 8°. (B 954)
— Dunlap, W. History of the arts of design in the U. S. N. Y., 1834. 2 v. 8°.
— Bethune, G. W. Prospects of art in the U. S.; address before the Artist's Fund Soc. of Phila., May. Phila., 1840. 8°. (B 1171)
— Amer. Art Union for the Promotion of the Fine Arts in the U. S. Transactions for 1844. N. Y., 1844. 8°. (B 1195)
— Tuckerman, H. T. Artist life; sketches of Amer. painters. N. Y., 1847. 8°.
— - Book of the artist; American artist life. N. Y., 1867. 8°.
— Perkins, C. C. Art education in America. [1870.] (*In* Amer. Soc. Sci. Assoc. Journ., no. 3. 1871.)

Banks.

— U. S. *Treasury Dept.* Letter from the Sec. transmitting reports as to the condition of the banks, 1857, 58, 63. Wash., 1857-63. 3 v. 8°.

Bibliography.

— Norton's literary letter; catalogue of rare and valuable books rel. to Amer. N. Y., 1857-60. 6 nos. 4°.
— Sabin, J. Dictionary of books rel. to America from its discovery to the present time. Vol. 1-13. N. Y., 1868-80. 13 v. 8°.

See also **America.** *Bibliography* (p. 60); — **Rhode Island** (p. 2508).

Biography.
Bibliography.

— Whitmore, W. H. Handbook of Amer. genealogy. Albany, 1862. 4°.

General and miscel. biography.

— American Nepos; the lives of men who have contributed to the discov., settlement, and independence of America. Balt., 1805. 12°.
— Belknap, J. American biography. Boston, 1794-98. 2 v. 8°.
— - *Same.* With add. and notes by F. M. Hubbard. N. Y., 1851. 3 v. 16°. (Harper's fam. lib., v. 161-163.)
— Campbell, J. W. Biographical sketches. Columbus, 1838. 8°.
— Crosby, N. Annual obituary notices of eminent persons in the U. S. for 1857. Boston, 1858. 8°.
— Holgate, J. B. Amer. genealogy; a hist. of some of the early settlers of N. Amer. and their descendants. Albany, 1848. 4°.

— HOWE, H. Adventures and achievements of Americans. Cincin., 1865. 8°.

— HUNT, F. Lives of American merchants. N. Y., 1856–58. 2 v. 8°.

— JONES, A. D. Illustrated Amer. biog., from Columbus to the present. Vol. 1. N. Y., 1853. 8°.

— KNAPP, *Col.* S. L. Biographical sketches of eminent lawyers, statesmen, and men of letters. Boston, 1821. 8°.

— LESTER, C. E. Gallery of illustrious Americans; [12] portraits and biog. sketches. N. Y., 1850. f°.

— LIVINGSTON, J. Biographical sketches of distinguished Americans now living. N. Y., London, 1853. 8°.

— LONGACRE, J. B., *and* HERRING, J. National portrait gallery of distinguished Americans. Phila., 1837–39. 4 v. 8°.

— PARTON, J. Famous Americans of recent times. Boston, 1867. 8°.

— PORTRAIT monthly of the N. Y. illustrated news. Vol. 1, no. 4, 7, 10; Oct. 1863, Jan., Apr. 1864. N. Y., 1863-64. 3 nos. 4°. (A 67)

— SAVAGE, J. Our living representative men. Phila., 1860. 12°.

— SPARKS, J. Library of Amer. biog. Boston, 1834–48. 2 ser. in 25 v. (v. 21 w.). 12°.

— SPARKS, W. H. Memories of fifty years; brief biog. notices of distinguished Americans, *etc.* Phila., 1870. 8°.

— STOWE, *Mrs.* H. E. B. Men of our times. Hartford, 1868. 8°.

— WOODWARD, T. Columbian Plutarch; [from Columbus to Jefferson]. Phila., 1819. 12°.

Dictionaries.

— ALLEN, W. Amer. biographical and historical dictionary. Camb., 1809. 8°.

— - *Same.* 2d ed. Boston, 1832. 8°.

— - *Same.* 3d ed. Boston, 1857. 8°.

— ROGERS, T. J. New Amer. biog. dictionary. 3d ed. Easton, Penn., 1824. 8°.

Index.

— DURRIE, D. S. Bibliographia genealogica Americana; index to American pedigrees. Albany, 1868. 8°.

See also **America**; — **Boston.** *History (town and city)*; — **Chicago**; — **Dartmouth Coll.**; — **Harvard Coll.** — **Medford**; — **Mississippi Valley**; — **New England**; — **New York** (*City*) p. 2117); — **New York.** STATE (p. 2122i; — **Ohio**; — *also* **Indians.**

For individual biography *see* the following names: — **Appleton, N.**; — **Appleton, S.**; — **Appleton, W.**; — **Barnum, P. T.**; — **Bates, J.**; — **Beckwourth, J. P.**; — **Benezet, A.**; — **Bigelow, E. B.**; — **Bromfield, J.**; — **Brown, Jas.**; — **Brown, N.**; — **Browne, C. F.**; — **Burroughs, S.**; — **Carson, C.**; — **Cartwright, E.**; — **Chickering, J.**; — **Claxton, T.**; — **Colburn, Z.**; — **Crockett, D.**; — **Curtis, J.**; — **Dowse, T.**; — **Eddy, T.**; — **Foster, J. W.**; — **Garrison, W. L.**; — **Gibbons, W.**; — **Gilbert, T.**; — **Girard, S.**; — **Graydon, A.**; — **Hawkins, J. H. W.**; — **Hewes, G. R. T.**; — **Hopper, I. T.**; — **Howland, J.**; — **Jackson, P. T.**; — **Johnson, J.**; — **Lawrence, A.**; — **Lawrence, W.**; — **Ledyard, J.**; — **Lincoln, N.**; — **Livermore, G.**; — **Locke, J.**; — **Mason, F.**; — **Neal, J.**; — **Page, H.**; — **Phelps, M.**; — **Pilsbury, A.**; — **Punchard, J.**; — **Russell, T.**; — **Shaw, J. R.**; — **Shaw, W. S.**; — **Shepard, E. H.**; — **Sherwin, T.**; — **Slater, S.**; — **Smith, A.**; — **Smith, H. M.**; — **Southack, J.**; — **Stewart, V. A.**; — **Sturgis, W.**; — **Swain, R.**; — **Tappan, L.**; — **Thorburn, G.**; — **Vassa, G.**; — **Wilder, S. V. S.**; — **Wright, H. C.**

For genealogies of families *see* the following: — **Adams fam.**; — **Alden, E.**; — **Appleton, J.**; — **Baker, P.**; — **Bowdoin fam.**; — **Brainerd fam.**; — **Brigham fam.**; — **Bright, J. B.**; — **Bullard fam.**; — **Burke, R.**; — **Champney fam.**; — **Chapin, O.**; — **Chauncey fam.**; — **Clark fam.**; — **Clarke, T.**; — **Coffin fam.**; — **Crane**; — **Curwen fam.**; — **Curtis, W.**; — **Cushman, H. W.**; — **Cutler fam.**; — **Dane, J.**; — **Dudley fam.**; — **Dumaresq fam.**; — **Fairfax fam.**; — **Farrar fam.**; — **Foote fam.**; — **Frost fam.**; — **Fuller, J.**; — **Gilbert fam.**; — **Giles fam.**; — **Glover fam.**; — **Grant, U.**; — **Hall fam.**; — **Haven, R.**; — **Herrick, J.**; — **Hodges fam.**; — **Holbrook fam.**; — **Hoyt fam.**; — **Hull, R.**; — **Hunt fam.**; — **Huntington fam.**; — **Hutchinson fam.**; — **Hyde fam.**; — **Lawrence fam.**; — **Leverett, T.**; — **Litchfield fam.**; — **Mather fam.**; — **Metcalf, E. W.**; — **Moody fam.**; — **Mudge fam.**; — **Neal fam.**; — **Nichols fam.**; — **Oliver fam.**; — **Pettee fam.**; — **Plummer fam.**; — **Pool fam.**; — **Pope fam.**; — **Rantoul fam.**; — **Rawson, S. S.**; — **Redfield fam.**; — **Reed fam.**; — **Rice fam.**; — **Scranton fam.**; — **Shattuck, L.**; — **Slafter, E. F.**; — **Smith fam.**; — **Spotswood fam.**; — **Sprague fam.**; — **Steele fam.**; — **Stetson fam.**; — **Stickney fam.**; — **Stoddard, A.**; — **Swett fam.**; — **Symonds fam.**; — **Tainter, D. W.**; — **Temple fam.**; — **Upham fam.**; — **Van Brunt fam.**; — **Vinton fam.**; — **Walker fam.**; — **Ward fam.**; — **Warren, J. O.**; — **Wetmore fam.**; — **White fam.**; — **Whitmore fam.**; — **Wight fam.**; — **Willard fam.**; — **Williams fam.**; — *also* **Shrewsbury,** *Mass.*

Actors.

See **Booth, E.**; — **Cushman,** *Mrs.* **C. S.**; — **Fennell, J.**; — **Ritchie,** *Mrs.* **A. C. O. M.**; — **Wallack, J. W.**

Artists.

See Art (incl. biography of artists, p. 3109); — *also* **Allston, W.**; — **Cole, T.**; — **Greenough, H.**; — **Harding, C.**; — **Leslie, C. R.**; — **Veaux, J. de**; — **West, B.**

Ecclesiastical biography.

— SPRAGUE, W. B. Annals of the American pulpit. N. Y., 1857–69. 9 v. 8°.

See also **Allyn, J.**; — **Ashmun, J.**; — **Bacon, S.**; — **Bailey, J.**; — **Baker, D.**; — **Baldwin, T.**; — **Ballou, H.**; — **Bates, J.**; — **Beecher, L.**; — **Belknap, J.**; — **Boehm, H.**; — **Brainerd, D.**; — **Brewster, W.**; — **Buckminster, J.**; — **Buckminster, J. S.**; — **Burgess, G.**; — **Byles, M.**; — **Channing, W. E.**; — **Chase, P.**; — **Chester, J.**; — **Clapp, T.**; — **Cobbs, N. H.**; — **Codman, J.**; — **Colman, B.**; — **Cornelius, E.**; — **Croswell, W.**; — **Dwight, T.**; — **Edwards, J.**; — **Eliot,** *Rev.* **J.**; — **Finley, J. B.**; — **Finley, R.**; — **Fisk, P.**; — **Fuller, A. B.**; — **Gallaudet, T. H.**; — **Green, S.**; — **Hall, G.**; — **Hallock, J.**; — **Harrington, J.**; — **Haynes, L.**; — **Hill, J. B.**; — **Hobart, J. H.**; — **Holley, H.**; — **Hopkins, S.**; — **Jones, A.**; — **Judd, S.**; — **Judson, A.**; — **Kendrick, A.**; — **King, T. S.**; — **Knapp, J.**; — **Larned, S.**; — **Little, G. B.**; — **Lovejoy, E. P.**; — **Lunt, W. P.**; — **McVickar, J.**; — **Marsh, J.**; — **Mather, C.**; — **Mayhew, J.**; — **Mills, S. J.**; — **Moore, J.**; — **Murray, J.**; — **Murray, N.**; — **Nettleton, A.**; — **Osborn, E.**; — **Parker, T.**; — **Parsons, L.**; — **Payson, E.**; — **Popkin, J. S.**; — **Prince, T.**; — **Prince, W. R.**; — **Robinson, E.**; — **Robinson, W.**; — **Rogers, W. M.**; — **Schlatter, M.**; — **Shepard, T.**; — **Spring, G.**; — **Stiles, E.**; — **Stoddard, D. T.**; — **Stow, B.**; — **Ward, N.**; — **Ware, H., Jr.**; — **Wayland, F.**; — **Wheelock, E.**; — **Wigglesworth, M.**; — **Williams, J.**; — **Woodbridge, T.**; — **Worcester, N.**; — **Wright, S. O.**; — **Zeisberger, D.**; —
also **New England**; — **Rhode Island**; — **Virginia.**

Female biography.

— BROCKETT, L. P., *and* VAUGHAN, *Mrs.* M. C. Woman's work in the civil war. Phila., 1867. 8°.

— ELLET, E. F. Women of the American Revolution. N. Y., 1848. 2 v. 12°.

— MOORE, F. Women of the [civil] war. Hartford, 1866. 8°.

See also Literature. Collections (HART) p. 3132; — *Literature. Poetry (Collections)* GRISWOLD p. 3139; —

also **Adams,** *Mrs.* **A. (S.)**; — **Adams, H.**; — **Anthony, S.**; — **Bethune,** *Mrs.* **J. G.**; — **Bridgman, L.**; — **Coghlan,** *Mrs.* **M. (M.)**; — **Dimmick,** *Mrs.* **C. M.**; — **Dyson, J. A. P.**; — **Felt,** *Mrs.* **A. A. (S.)**; — **Fiske, F.**; — **Gannett,** *Mrs.* **D. S.**; — **Hamlin, H. A. L.**; — **Haven,** *Mrs.* **A. B.**; — **Huntington,** *Mrs.* **S. (M.)**; — **Judson,** *Mrs.* **A. H.**; — **Judson,** *Mrs.* **E. C.**; — **Lyon, M.**; — **Newell,** *Mrs.* **H.**; — **Ossoli, S. M.,** *marchesa* d'; — **Peters,** *Mrs.* **P. W.**; — **Ramsay,** *Mrs.* **M. L.**; — **Richards,** *Mrs.* **A. M.**; — **Rowson, S.**; — **Sedgwick, C. M.**; — **Seton,** *Mrs.* **E. A. (B.)**; — **Sigourney,** *Mrs.* **L. H.**; — **Slowman, J.**; — **Smith,** *Mrs.* **S. L. (H.)**; — **Ware,** *Mrs.* **M. L.**; — **Waters, A.**

Legal biography.

— Flanders, H. Lives and times of the Chief Justices of the U. S. Phila., 1858. 2 v. 8°.

— Gibbs, G. Judicial chronicle; list of judges. Camb., 1834. 8°.

— Livingston, J. Biog. sketches of eminent American lawyers now living. Pt. 1, 4. [N. Y.,] 1852. 2 v. 8°.

— Van Santvoord, G. Sketches of the lives and judicial services of the Chief Justices of the Supreme Court. N. Y., 1854. 8°.

See also Beardsley, L.; — Browne, J. W.; — Butler, B. F.; — Choate, R.; — Clinton, D. W.; — Collamer, J.; — Dallas, A. J.; — Dexter, S.; — Everett, E.; — Frelinghuysen, T.; — Hoyt, J.; — Iredell, J.; — Livingston, E.; — Otis, J.; — Parsons, T.; — Petigru, J. L.; — Phillips, S.; — Pinkney, W.; — Plumer, W.; — Prentiss, S. S.; — Quincy, J.; — Quincy, J., *Jr.*; — Rantoul, R.; — Smith, J.; — Story, J.; — Sullivan, J.; — Taney, R. B.; — Tazewell, L. W.; — Willard, J.; — Wirt, W.; — *also* Maine; — Rhode Island; — South Carolina; — *also* references under *Political biography, in the next column.*

Literary biography.

See Literature: History (p. 3132).

Medical biography.

— Gross, S. D. Lives of eminent Amer. physicians and surgeons. Phila., 1861. 8°.

— Thacher, J. American med. biography. Boston, 1828. 2 v. 8°.

See also Bartlett, E.; — Chapman, N.; — Darlington, W., — Jackson, J., *Jr.*; — Kane, E. K.; — Physick, P. S.; — Twitchell, A.; — Warren, J.; — Warren, J. C.; — *also* Rhode Island. *Biog.* (p. 2508).

Military biography.

— Garden, A. Anecdotes of the Revolutionary War with sketches of character. Charleston, 1822. 8°.

— Gardner, C. K. Dictionary of all officers of army, 1789-1859. 2d ed. N. Y., 1860. 12°.

— Hillard, E. B. The last men of the Revolution. Hartford, 1864. 12°.

— Shanks, W. F. G. Personal recollections of distinguished generals. N. Y., 1866. 12°.

— Shea, J. G. Fallen brave; a biog. memorial of Amer. officers. N. Y., 1861. 4°.

— Snow, W. P. Southern generals, who they are and what they have done. N. Y., 1865. 8°.

— - *Same.* Southern generals, their lives and campaigns. N. Y., 1866. 8°.

— Williams, *Mrs.* C. R. Biog. of revolutionary heroes; containing life of W. Barton and S. Olney. Prov., 1839. 12°.

— Wilson, T. Biography of Amer. military and naval heroes. N. Y., 1817-19. 2 v. 12°.

See also Quartermaster General (p. 3096); — *Mil. Acad. at West Point* (p. 3109); — *Female biog.* (p. 3110); *also* Adair, *Gen.* J.; — Allen, E.; — Allen, H. W.; — Arnold, B.; — Bacon, W. K.; — Bigelow, T.; — Bland, T. — Boone, D.; — Brown, J.; — Burnside, *Gen.* A. E.; — Butler, B. F.; — Camp, H. W.; — Clap, R.; — Cresap, M.; — Dahlgren, U.; — Dale, S.; — Dearborn, H.; — Dwight, W.; — Eaton, W.; — Francis, E.; — Fremont, J. C.; — Glover, J.; — Grant, U. S.; — Gray, J.; — Greene, N.; — Grout, J. W.; — Hanford, L.; — Heath, W.; — Holmes, M.; — Hull, W.; — Jackson, T. J.; — Johnson, R. M.; — Johnson, *Sir* W.; — Kilpatrick, H. J.; — Knowlton, T.; — Lamb, J.; — Lee, C.; — Lee, R. E.; — McClellan, G. B.; — Marion, F.; — Morgan, D.; — Paine, J. W.; — Pickering, T.; — Potter, I. R.; — Pulaski, C.; — Putnam, I.; — Quitman, J. A.; — Riedesel, F. A.; — Scammell, A.; — Schuyler, P.; — Scott, W.; — Sheridan, P. H.; — Smith, S.; — Standish, M.; — Stark, J.; — Stobo, R.; — Stuart, J. E. B.; — Sullivan, J.; — Thomas, J.; — Thompson, J. H.; — Tremain, F. L.; — Van Rensselaer, S.; — Warner, S.; — Warren, J.; Washington, G.; — Wayne, A.; — Wilkinson, J.; — Willett, M.; — *also* Brown University; — Harvard College; — *also* Georgia; — Illinois; — Rhode Island; — Vermont.

Naval biography.

— Hamersly, L. R. Records of living officers of the U. S. Navy and Marine Corps. Phila., 1870. 8°.

— Headley, J. T. Farragut and our naval commanders. N. Y., 1867. 8°.

See also Bainbridge, W.; — Barney, J.; — Blake, G. S.; — Decatur, S.; — Fanning, N.; — Farragut, D. G.; — Fox, E.; — Jones, J. P.; — Perry, O. H.; — Preble, E.; — Sherburne, A.; — Smith, M.; — Stringham, S. H.; — Talbot, S.; — Tucker, S.

Political biography.

— Lanman, C. Dictionary of Congress. Phila., 1859. 8°.

— - *Same.* 2d ed. Wash., 1864. 8°.

— - *Same.* 3d ed. Wash., 1866. 8°.

— Maury, S. M. Statesmen of America in 1846. London, 1847. 12°.

— Moore, J. B. Memoirs of American governors. Vol. 1. N. Y., 1846. 8°.

— Parker, T. Historic Americans. Boston, 1870. 8°.

— Sabine, L. American loyalists. Bost., 1847. 8°.

— - Biographical sketches of loyalists of the Amer. Revolution. Boston, 1864. 2 v. 8°.

— Wheeler, H. G. History of Congress, biographical and political. N. Y., 1848. 2 v. 8°.

See also Adams, J.; — Adams, J. Q.; — Adams, S.; — Andrew, J. A.; — Andros, *Sir* E.; — Baker, E. D.; — Briggs, G. N.; — Burges, T.; — Burr, A.; — Calhoun, J. C.; — Calvert, L.; — Cass, L.; — Clay, H.; — Colfax, S.; — Dallas, G. M.; — Davis, H. W.; — Davis, J.; — Dostie, A. P.; — Douglas, S. A.; — Edwards, N.; — Fessenden, W. P.; — Foot, S.; — Franklin, B.; — Frelinghuysen, T.; — Gerry, E.; — Hamilton, A.; — Hancock, J.; — Harrison, W. H.; — Henry, P.; — Houston, S.; — Izard, R.; — Jackson, A.; — Jarvis, W.; — Jay, J.; — Jefferson, T.; — Johnson, A.; — King, W. R.; — Lawrence, *Col.* T. B.; — Lee, A.; — Lee, R. H.; — Legaré, H. S.; — Lincoln, A.; — Lincoln, L.; — Linn, L. F.; — Livingston, W.; — Madison, J.; — Meade, G. G.; — Morris, G.; — Morris, R.; — Oglethorpe, J. E.; — Otis, J.; — Pepperell, *Sir* W.; — Pierce, F.; — Quincy, J, *Jr.*; — Randolph, J.; — Reed, J.; — Reed, R. R.; — Stephens, A. H.; — Strong, C.; — Taylor, Z.; — Trumbull, J.; — Tyler, J.; — Van Buren, M.; — Van Schaack, P.; — Ward, S.; — Washington, G.; — Webster, D. — Webster, F.; — Williams, R.; — Winthrop, J.; — Wolcott, C.; — Wright, S.; — *also* Boston. *History (town and city)*; — N. Y. *Biography*; — Ohio. *Legislature*; — *also* American loyalists; — Signers of the Declaration of Independence.

Scientific biography.

See Audubon, J. J. — Barton, B. S.; — Bartram, J.; — Bowditch, N.; — Fitch, J.; — Franklin, B.; — Fulton, R.; — Goodyear, C.; — Marshall, H.; — Mason, E. P.; — Rittenhouse, D.; — Silliman, B.; — Thompson, *Sir* B.; — Whitney, E.; — Willard, L.; — Wilson, A.

Botany.

— Michaux, A. Histoire des chênes de l'Amérique. Paris, 1801. f°.

— Rich, O. O. Synopsis of the genera of American plants, according to the latest improvements on the Linnæn [*sic*] system. Georgetown, 1814. 8°.

— Bigelow, J. American medical botany. Boston, 1817-20. 3 v. 4°.

— Eaton, A. Manual of botany; southern and middle states of Amer. [1817.] 3d ed. rev. Albany, 1822. 12°.

— Torrey, J. Flora of the northern and middle United States. N. Y., 1824. 8°.

— - Compendium of the flora of the northern and middle U. S. N. Y., 1826. 12°.

— BECK, L. C. Botany of the northern and middle states. Albany, 1833. 12°.

— GRAY, A. U. S. exploring exped., 1838-42, under C. Wilkes: Botany. N. Y., 1854. 4° *and* Atlas 1857. f°.

— U. S. *25th Cong. 2d sess. Senate.* Report of committee of agriculture on the memorial of Dr. H. Perrine to promote the cultivation of tropical plants in the U. S., March 12, 1838. *n.t.p.* [Wash., 1838.] 8°. (Doc. 300)

— - *Another copy.* (B 1816)

— GRAY, A. Genera of the plants of the U. S.; illust. by figures by I. Sprague. Boston, 1848-49. 2 v. 8°.

— - Manual of botany of the northern U. S. [1848.] 2d ed. enl. N. Y., 1856. 8°.

— DARLINGTON, W. American weeds and useful plants; rev. with add. by G. Thurber. N. Y., 1859. 12°.

See also **Arkansas; — Georgia; — Iowa; — Louisiana; — Massachusetts; — New Mexico; — New York; — North America; — South Carolina; — Texas; — Virginia; — Wisconsin.**

Boundary.

— AMERICAN boundary question. [No. 3.] *n.t.p.* [18—.] 8°. (B 1601)

See also Commissioner on the Boundary between the U. S. and the Possessions of his Catholic Majesty in America (p. 3059); — **North Eastern Boundary** (p. 2152); — **North West Boundary** (p. 2153); — *also* **Alaska; — Connecticut; — Delaware; — Florida; — Louisiana; — Maryland; — Mason & Dixon's Line; — Massachusetts; — Mexico; — New Jersey; — New York; — Oregon; — Pennsylvania; — Rhode Island; — San Juan, *N.A.***

Charities.

See the names of the separate States.

Chronology.

— RAMSEY, D. Chronological table of the U. S., 1607-1810. Charleston, 1811. 8°. (B 439)

See also History (*Civil war: chronology*) p. 3127.

Civilization.

— INGERSOLL, C. J. Discourse, influence of Amer. on the mind. Phila., 1823. 8°. (B 567)

Claims.

— CUTTING, J. B. Facts and obs., justifying the claims of C. against the U. S. *n.p.*, [1795]. 8°. (B 343, 2517)

— CUNNINGHAM, W., & Co. Reply to the answer of the U. S. to their claim and memorial. Phila., 1798. 8°. (A 26)

— U. S. *Agent General on Claims of Brit. Subjects.* Observations on the part of the U. S. to the reply of D. Dulaney. *n.p.*, [1798]. 4°. (A 26)

— ALLEN, A., *vs.* U. S. Claim and answer, with subsequent proc. Phila., 1799. 4°. (A 35)

— CASE of the Rt. Rev. C. Inglis. *n.t.p.* [1799.] 4°. (A 26, B 1434)

— CLAIM, answer, [and] proc. in the case of C. Inglis against the U. S. Phila., 1799. 4°. (A 31, B 1731)
Note. Said to be by S. Sitgreaves.

— MEADE, R. W. The claim of M. upon the U. S. chronologically and concisely stated. Phila., 1825. 8°. (W 12)

— FETTYPLACE, W. Memorial; case of the schooner 'Reward', before the commissioners for the settlement of claims, under the treaty with France. *n.t.p.* [Boston, 1835.] 8°. (B 1756)

— GR. BRIT. *Parl.* Correspondence with the U. S. resp. the imprisonment of Warren and Costello. London, [1868]. f°. (N. A. papers, no. 2. E 242)

— - Correspondence resp. the negotiations with the U. S. gov. on the questions of the 'Alabama' and British claims, naturalization, and San Juan water boundary. London, [1869]. f°. (North Amer. papers, no. 1. E 242)

— - Despatch from Mr. Seward to Mr. Adams resp. Brit. and Amer. claims arising out of the late civil war in the U. S. London, [1868]. f°. (N. A. papers, no. 1. E 242)

See also Congress: State papers (p. 3061); — *also* **Cathcart, J.; — Cunningham, Wm., & Co.; — *also* Massachusetts.**

Climate.

— VOLNEY, C. F. C. Tableau du climat et du sol des Etats-Unis d'Amér. Paris, 1803. 2 v. 8°.

— - *Eng.* View of the climate and soil of the U. S. London, 1804. 8°.

— ESSAY on the climate of the U. S.; or, Causes of the difference between the eastern side of North America and Europe. Phila., 1809. 8°. (B 436)

— FORRY, S. Climate of the U. S. and its endemic influences. N. Y., 1842. 8°.

— BLODGET, L. Climatology of the U. S. Phila., 1857. 8°.

See also **Florida; — New England.**

Commerce.

— '37 and '57; a brief account of the financial panics in U. S., 1690-1857; with a particular history of 1837 and '57. N. Y., 1857. 8°.

— COLUMBUS, *pseud.* Reflections on the policy and necessity of encouraging the commerce of the citizens of the U. S. Richmond, [178-]. 8°. (W 31)

— CHAMBON, —. Traité du commerce de l'Amérique, *etc.* Amst., 1783. 2 v. 4°.

— HOLROYD, J. B. Observations on the commerce of the Amer. states. 2d ed. Lond., 1783. 8°.

— - *Same.* New ed. enl. London, 1784. 8°.

— BINGHAM, W. Letter on the restraining proclamation; and strictures on Ld. Sheffield's 'Commerce of the Amer. states'. London, 1784. 8°. (B 663, 1638)

— - *Same.* Phila., 1784. 8°. (B 472, 630, 2512, W 62)

— CHAMPION, R. Considerations on the present situation of Gr. Britain and the U. S. with a view to their future commercial connections; [in reply to] Lord Sheffield. London, 1784. 8°. (B 629, 1638)

— - *Same.* 2d ed. London, 1784. 8°.

— DEANE, S. Address to the U. S. London, 1784. 8°. (B 702)

— EDWARDS, B. Thoughts on the late proc. of government resp. the trade of the West India Islands with the U. S. Lond., *reprinted* Boston, 1784. 8°. (B 702, 1638, 2517)

— - *Same.* 2d ed. London, 1784. 8°. (B 462, 1638)

— REMARKS on Ld. Sheffield's 'Observations on the commerce of the Amer. states'. London, 1784. 8°. (B 702)

— STEVENSON, J. Address to B. Edwards, on his 'Thoughts on the late proc. of government resp. the trade of West India with the U. S.'; also obs. on 'Considerations on the intercourse between H. M. sugar colonies and the U. S.' London, 1784. 8°. (B 463)

— COMMERCIAL conduct of the U. S. considered. N. Y., 1786. 8°. (B 417)

— CLAVIÈRE, E., *and* BRISSOT DE WARVILLE, J. P. De la France et des Etats-Unis. Londres, 1787. 8°.
Note. For other eds. and trans. *see* **Clavière** (p. 601).

— REFLECTIONS on the policy of encouraging the commerce of the U. S. Richmond, *printed*, N. Y., *reprinted* 1786. 8°. (B 1535)

— ENQUIRY into the principles on which a commercial system for the U. S. should be founded. London, 1787. 8°. (B 625)

— CAREY, M. Brief examination of Ld. Sheffield's 'Observations on the commerce of the U. S.' Phila., 1791. 8°.

— JEFFERSON, T. Report to Cong. on the nature of the privileges of the commercial intercourse of the U. S. with for. nations. London, 1794. 8°. (B 686)

— SMITH, W. Speeches on certain commercial regulations proposed by Madison. Phila., 1794. 8°. (B 628, 2525)

— JAY, J. Features of [his] treaty; [with] a view of the commerce of the U. S. Phila., 1795. 8°. (W 62)

— BOWDOIN, J. Opinions resp. the commercial intercourse between the U. S. and Gr. Brit. Boston, 1797. 8°. (B 594, 741)

— TALLEYRAND PÉRIGORD, C. M. Memoir conc. the commercial rel. of the U. S. with Eng., [with] an essay. [1797.] London, 1806. 8°. (B 680)

— - *Same.* Boston, 1809. 8°. (B 411, 536, 2521)

— - *Same.* (*In* Pamphleteer, 1814; v. 4 of B 838)

— INDÉPENDANCE absolue des Américains des Etats-Unis, L', prouvée par l'état actuel de leur commerce; [par Tho. W. Griffith?]. Paris, an VI, 1798. 8°. (B 423)

— ATCHESON, N. American encroachments on British rights. [1805.] London, 1808. 8°. (B 722)

— - Same. (In Pamphleteer, 1815; v. 6 of B 838)

— MOORE, C. Inquiry into the effects of our foreign carrying trade upon the agriculture, etc., of the country. N. Y., 1806. 8°. (B 430)

— AGRICOLA, pseud. Letter to the inhabitants of N. Y., on the commerce of the Western waters. N. Y., [1807]. 12°. (C 104)

— SOCIETY OF SHIP OWNERS OF GR. BRIT. Col. of reports, etc., on the trade of Gr. Brit. in the W. Indies and America. Lond., 1807. 8°.

— MANN, A. Letter to the merchants [and others] interested in trade to U. S. [Lond., 1808.] 8°. (B 722)

— SIDNEY, A., pseud. Address to the people of New Eng., Dec. 15, 1808. Wash., 1808. 8°. (B 410)

— BROWN, C. B. Address to Congress, on the utility and justice of restrictions upon foreign commerce. Phila., 1809. 8°. (B 412)

— HOLROYD, J. B. Orders in council and the Amer. embargo beneficial to Gr. Britain. London, 1809. 8°. (B 725)

— ENQUIRY into the causes of the present commercial embarrassments in the U. S. n.t.p. [181-.] 8°. (B 448, 563)

— MONTEFIORE, J. American trader's companion; laws of the U. S. rel. to commerce. Phila., 1811. 8°.

— SECOND crisis of America, The; or, View of the peace between Gr. Brit. and the U. S.; examining the manner this event will operate on the commerce of America; by a citizen of Phila. N. Y., 1815. 8°. (B 444)

— PITKIN, T. Statistical view of the commerce of the U. S., etc. Hartford, 1816. 8°.

— - Same. 2d ed. N. Y., 1817. 8°.

— - Same. New Haven, 1835. 8°.

— SPANISH America and the U. S.; views of the actual commerce of the U. S. with the Spanish colonies, etc. Phila., 1818. 8°. (B 974)

— ARISTIDES, pseud. Letter to the Secretary of the Treasury, on the commerce and currency of the U. S. N. Y., 1819. 8°. (B 536)

— U. S. Pres. Commercial regulations of the foreign countries with which the U. S. have intercourse. Wash., 1819. 8°.

— CAREY, M. View of the ruinous consequences of dependence on foreign markets. Phila., 1820. 8°. (B 985, 1887)

— MELISH, J. Letter to J. Monroe, on the state of the country. Phila., 1820. 8°. (B 563)

— PEABODY, J., and others. Memorial to Congress on the discontinuance of restrictions on commerce. Salem, 1820. 8°. (B 533)

— WOLCOTT, O. Remarks on the present state of currency, credit, commerce, and national industry. N. Y., 1820. 8°. (B 563)

— U. S. Register's Office. Letter from Sec. of the Treas. transm. statements [of] the comm. and navig., [1821]-65. Wash., 1822-66. 26 v. 8°.

— U. S. Pres. Commercial regulations of foreign nations; Feb. 2, 1824. Wash., 1824. 8°. (18th Cong. 1st sess. Ho. Doc. 130.)

— LLOYD, J. Remarks in the report of the Committee of Commerce on Brit. colonial intercourse, March 31. n.p., [1826]. 8°. (B 1512)

— DIRCKINCK-HOLMFELD, C. Englands und Nordamerikas neuere Handelspolitik. Copenhagen, 1829. 8°.

— SPRAGUE, P. Speech, arrangement of the colonial trade with Gr. Brit. Wash., 1832. 8°. (B 1056)

— BAKER, J. M. View of the commerce between U. S. and Rio de Janeiro. Wash., 1838. 8°.

— ELLET, C. Essay on the laws of trade in reference to the works of internal improvement in the U. S. [1838.] Richmond, 1839. 8°.

— U. S. Dept. of State. Report on the commercial relations of the U. S. with foreign countries, 1841, 1856-65, 67-72, 74-75. Wash., 1842-76. 22 v. 8° and 4°.

— - 27th Cong. 2d sess. Report of committee on commerce. n.t.p. [Wash., 1842.] 8°. (Ho. no. 835. B 1173)

— MACGREGOR, J. Commercial and financial legislation of Europe and America. London, 1841. 8°.

— BAYLEY, G. Tables shewing the progress of the shipping interest of the British Empire, U. S., and France. London, 1844. 8°. (E 106)

— MACGREGOR, J. Commercial statistics of the U. S. (In his Commercial statistics, v. 3. 1847.)

— GREGG, J. Commerce of the prairies. 4th ed. Phila., 1850. 2 v. 12°.

— - Same. Scenes and incidents in the western prairies. Phila., 1857. 2 v. 12°.

— WALLACE, J. W. Want of uniformity in the commercial law between the different states; disc. before the Law Acad., Nov. 26. Phila., 1851. 8°. (B 1430)

— SEWARD, W. H. Whale fishery and American commerce in the Pacific; speech, July 29. Wash., 1852. 8°. (B 1506, 1668)

— ANDREWS, I. D. Report on the trade of the British North Amer. colonies and of the great lakes and rivers. Wash., 1853. 8° and Maps.

— U. S. 33d Cong. 1st sess. House. Report of select committee on the trade between the U. S. and Peru; July 39. n.t.p. [1854.] 8°. (No. 347)

— WALLEY, S. H. Financial revulsion of 1857; an address. Boston, 1858. 8°. (B 1515)

— EDGE, F. M. Destruction of the American carrying trade. London, 1863. 8°.

— MCHENRY, G. The cotton trade in connection with the system of negro slavery in the Confederate States. London, 1863. 8°.

— U. S. Treasury Dept. Commercial intercourse with and in states declared in insurrection; circulars, proclamations, and orders. Wash., 1863. 8°.

— - Statistics of the foreign and domestic commerce of the U. S. Wash., 1864. 8°.

— - On the treaty of reciprocity with Gr. Brit. to regulate the trade between the U. S. and the provinces of Brit. N. A.; by E. H. Derby, 1866. (Appended to Derby, E. H. Letter to W. H. Seward. 1867.)

— U. S. Bureau of Statistics. Annual report of the Deputy Special Commissioner of the Revenue on commerce and navigation, 1868, 69, 71-74, 76. Wash., 1869-77. 7 v. 8°.

— HILL, H. A. American shipping; its decline and the remedies. Boston, 1869. 8°. (E 77)

— - The relations of the business men of the U. S. to the national legislation. Boston, 1870. 8°. (E 77)

— - Same. (In Amer. Soc. Sci. Assoc. Journ., no. 3. 1871.)

— U. S. Bureau of Statistics. Monthly reports on commerce and navigation for the year ended June 30. Wash., 1870. 8°.

See also State papers (p. 3061); — Tariff (forward); — also Alaska; — Massachusetts; — New England; — New York; — Prairies, American.

Conchology.

See North America (p. 2148).

Constitution.

☞ For various documents of the Constitution see p. 3056.

— WEBSTER, P. Dissertation on the political union and Constitution of the thirteen U. S. Phila., 1783. 8°. (B 515)

— ADAMS, J. Defence of the constitutions of government. London, 1787-88. 3 v. 8°.

— - Same. Phila., 1787. 12°.

— ADDRESS to the people of N. Y. on the constitution agreed upon at Phila., Sept. 17. N. Y., 1787. 8°. (A 38, B 651)

— ELLIOTT, J. Debates, resolutions, and other proceedings [of the several states] on the adoption of the Constitution, [1787]. Wash., 1827-30. 4 v. 8°.

—- *Same.* Debates in the several state conventions; with L. Martin's letter; Yates's minutes; Congressional opinions, Va. and Kentucky resolutions. 2d ed. Phila., 1861. 5 v. 6°.

— EXAMINATION into the leading principles of the federal constitution. Phila., 1787. 8°. (B 465)

— LEE, R. H. Observations leading to a fair examination of the system of gov. proposed by the late convention; letters from the Federal farmer to the Republican. *n.p.*, 1787. 12°.

Note. Appended with a continuous pagination, 'An add. number of letters from the Federal farmer. 1788'.

—- *Another copy.* (B 65, C 151)

—- *Another copy, without the additional letters.* (B 613)

— OBSERVATIONS on the new Constitution; by a Columbian patriot. *n.t.p.* [Boston? 1787?] 8°. (C 265, 615)

— *Same.* Boston, N. Y., *reprinted* 1788. 8°. (B 701)

— PINCKNEY, C. Observations on the plan of government submitted to the Federal Convention. N. Y., [1787]. 4°. (B 651)

— REMARKS on the 'Address of 16 members of the Assembly of Penn. to their constituents, Sept. 29, 1787'; with some strictures on their objections to the Constitution. Phila., 1787. 8°. (B 473)

— VIEW of the Constitution at Phila. Phila., 1787. 8°. (B 991)

— WEAKNESSES, The, of Brutus exposed; some remarks in vindication of the Constitution. Phila., 1787. 12°. (B 65, 614)

— NICHOLAS, J. Decius's letters on the opposition to the Constitution in Virginia, 1788-89. 3d ed., with introd. and notes. Richmond, 1818. 8°. (B 456)

— ADDRESS to the people of N. Y. showing the necessity of making amendments to the Constitution previous to its adoption. N. Y., 1788. 8°. (B 701)

— FEDERALIST, The; essays on the new Constitution, by J. Jay and J. Madison. N. Y., 1788. 2 v. 12°.

Note. For other eds. *see* Federalist (p. 968).

— HALL, A. Oration to celebrate the ratification of the Constitution by N. Hampshire. Keene, 1788. 8°. (B 399)

— JACKSON, J. Thoughts on the political situation of the U. S.; with obs. on the Constitution. Worcester, 1788. 8°.

—- *Other copies.* (B 632, 1117)

— MARTIN, L. Genuine information to the Legislature of Md. rel. to proceed. of the general convention at Phila. Phila., 1788. 8°. (B 701, 971)

—- *Same.* (*In* U. S. *Constitutional Convention.* Secret proc. 1821; 1836; *and* Debates. 1861.)

— MASS. *Convention*, 1788. Debates, and other proceedings of the convention of Mass., Boston, Jan. 9, 1788, for the purpose of ratifying the Constitution. Boston, 1788. 8°.

— PENN. *Convention*, Nov. 20, 1787. Debates on the Constitution for the U. S. Vol. 1. Phila., 1788. 8°.

— S. CAROLINA. *Ho. of Reps.* Debates on the Constitution of the U. S. Charleston, 1788. 4°. (B 1899)

— VIRGINIA. *Convention*, June 2, 1788. Debates and other proc.; pref. the Constitution. Petersburg, 1788. 8°.

—- *Same.* 2d ed. Richmond, 1805. 8°.

—- Journal. Richmond, 1827. 8°.

— LIVINGSTON, W. Examen du gouvernment d'Angleterre, comp. aux constitutions des Etats-Unis; tr. [par M. Gallois]. Londres, 1789. 8°.

— SULLIVAN, J. Observations upon the government of the U. S. Boston, 1791. 8°. (B 631, 1488)

— HORTENSIUS, *pseud.* Enquiry into the constitutional authority of the Supreme Federal Court, *etc.* Charleston, 1792. 8°. (B 625)

— LA CROIX, F. P. A review of the Constitutions of the states of Europe, and the U. S.; tr. with notes. London, 1792. 2 v. 8°.

— CASE decided in the Supreme Court of the U. S., Feb. 1793; whether a state be liable to be sued by a private citizen of another state. Phila., 1793. 8°. (B 598, W 56)

— REVIEW of the question, 'In whom has the Constitution vested the treaty power'? Phila., 1796. 8°. (B 400)

— ADDISON, A. Analysis of the report of the committee of the Virginia Assembly on the proceedings of other states. Phila., 1800. 12°. (C 77, W 13)

— FRIEND to the Constitution, A. *n.t.p.* [1801?] 8°. (B 621, C 194)

— BLACKSTONE, *Sir* W. Commentaries; with notes of reference to the Constitution and laws of the Federal government, by St. G. Tucker. Phila., 1803. 4 v. in 5 pts. 8°.

— DEFENCE of the Legislature of Mass.; or, Rights of N. Eng. vindicated. Bost., 1804. 8°. (B 424, 1198, 1489)

— HILLHOUSE, J. Propositions for amending the Constitution of the U. S. *n.p.*, [1808]. 8°. (B 407, 1080, W 13b)

—- *Same.* [2d ed. rev.] New Haven, 1808. 8°. (B 1489, 1885, 2520)

— MACON, —. Motion, as amended, proposing an amendment to the Constitution; with the amendment by Mr. Quincy, Jan. 30. Wash., 1811. 8°. (B 512)

— GILES, W. B. Letter to the Legislature of Va. on instructions to senators from state legislatures. [Wash., 1812.] 8°. (W 86)

— WILLARD, S. Columbian constitution an amendment to the Constitution of the U. S. Albany, 1815. 8°.

— MASS. *Gen. Assem.* [Proposed amendment of the Constitution. Boston, 1816.] 8°. (B 1768)

— VIRGINIA. *House of Delegates.* Exposition of the Constitution contained in the report called Madison's report. Richmond, 1819. 8°.

— TAYLOR, J. Construction construed and constitutions vindicated. Richmond, 1820. 8°.

— BARTLETT, I. Speech, proposition to amend the Constitution, Mar. 30. Wash., 1826. 8°. (B 554)

— EVERETT, E. Speech, proposition to amend the Constitution Mar. 9, in the Ho. of Rep. Wash., 1826. 8°. (B 926, W 13)

— MCDUFFIE, G. Speech, proposition to amend the Constitution. Wash., 1826. 8°. (B 1831)

— TRIMBLE, D. Reply to McDuffie on the amendment of the Constitution, Apr. 1. *n.t.p.* [Wash., 1826.] 8°. (B 1493)

— VANCE, I. Reply to McDuffie, Apr. 1826. Wash., 1826. 8°. (C 194)

— STANSBURY, A. J. Elementary catechism on the Constitution. Boston, 1828. 12°.

— SULLIVAN, W. Political class book intended to instruct the higher classes in schools in the origin, nature, and use of political power; with an app. by G. B. Emerson. [1830.] New ed., with add. Boston, 1839. 12°.

— ELLIOT, J. The Virginia and Kentucky resolutions, 1798-99; with Jefferson's original draught. Wash., 1832. 8°. (B 1066)

— OLIVER, B. L. Rights of an American citizen; on state rights, the Constitution, and policy of the U. S. Boston, 1832. 8°.

— BAYARD, J. Exposition of the Constitution of the U. S. Phila., 1833. 12°.

— CONSTITUTION of the U. S.; proposed alterations, *etc.*, by a Federalist of 1788 and still a Constitutionalist. *n.t.p.* [1833.] 8°. (B 1495)

— STORY, J. Commentaries on the Constitution. Boston, 1833. 3 v. 8°.

— DUPONCEAU, P. S. Brief view of the Constitution. Phila., 1834. 12°.

— STORY, J. Constitutional class-book. Boston, 1834. 8°.

— MANSFIELD, E. D. Political grammar of the U. S. N. Y., 1836. 12°.

— ADAMS, J. Q. Jubilee of the Constitution; disc., N. Y., Apr. 30. N. Y., 1839. 8°. (B 1428, 1655, 1697, 1819)

— MARSHALL, J. Writings upon the Constitution. Boston, 1839. 8°.

— RAYMOND, D. Elements of constitutional law. Balt., 1840. 12°. (C 252)

—- *Same.* 1st stereotype ed. Cincin., 1845. 16°.

— Aiken, P. F. Comparative view of the constitutions of Gr. Brit. and the U. S. London, 1842. 16°.
— Duer, W. A. Constitutional jurisprudence of the U. S. N. Y., [1843]. 16°. (Harper's fam. lib., v. 160.)
— Spooner, L. Unconstitutionality of slavery. Pt. 1. Boston, 1845. 8°.
— - *Same*. Pt. 2. Boston, 1847. 12°. (C 261)
— - *Same*. Pt. 1, 2. Boston, 1847. 12°.
— Hudson, C. Speech, constitutional power of Cong. over territories, *etc.* Wash., 1848. 8°. (B 1477)
— Smith, E. F. Commentaries on statute and constitutional law and statutory and constitutional construction. Albany, 1848. 8°.
— Curtis, G. T. Strength of the Constitution; discourse. Boston, 1850. 8°. (B 1430)
— Béchard, F. Lois municipales des républiques de la Suisse et des Etats-Unis. Paris, 1852. 12°.
— Goodrich, C. B. Science of government as exhibited in the institutions of the U. S. Boston, 1853. 8°. (Lowell lectures.)
— Curtis, G. T. History of the Constitution. N. Y., 1854-58. 2 v. 8°.
— Blake, L. Constitutional text book. N. Y., 1854. 8°.
— Bowen, F. Documents of the Constitution of England and America. Camb., 1854. 8°.
— Tremenheere, H. S. Constitution of the U. S. compared with our own. London, 1854. 8°.
— Corry, W. M. Speech, with proposed amendments to the Constitution, Mar. 11. *n.p.*, 1857. 8°. (B 1508)
— Towle, N. C. History and analysis of the Constitution of the U. S. Bost., 1860. 12°.
— Burnett, P. H. The Amer. theory of government considered with reference to the present crisis. N. Y., 1861. 8°.
— U. S. (Separate states). *Conference Convention, Wash.*, 1861. Report of debates and proceedings; by L. E. Chittenden. N. Y., 1864. 8°.
— Fisher, S. G. The trial of the Constitution. Phila., 1862. 8°.
— Whiting, W. War powers under the Constitution of the U. S. [1862.] 10th ed. Boston, 1864. 8°.
— Tract on government. Boston, 1863. 8°.
— Upshur, A. P. Nature and character of the federal government; review of Story's Commentaries. Phila., 1863. 8°.
— - *Another copy*. (B 1724)
— Burr, C. C. Notes on the Constitution. N.Y., [1864]. 12°.
— Evans, T. W. Lettres d'un oncle à son neveu sur le gouvernement des Etats-Unis. Paris, 1866. 8°.
— Farrar, T. Manual of the Constitution. Boston, 1867. 8°.
— Jameson, J. A. The constitutional convention; its history, powers, and modes of proceeding. N. Y., 1867. 8°.
— Jennings, L. J. Eighty years of republican government in the U. S. London, 1868. 8°.

See also House (Debates) p. 3064; — State rights (p. 2849); — Territories (p. 2938).

Defence.

See Army (p. 3057, 58); — *Fortification* (p. 3121, 22).

Description.

☞ The section *Description* under British Colonies in America, (p. 386) was entirely insufficient; all the titles are therefore repeated here.

— Tuckerman, H. T. America and her commentators. N. Y., 1864. 8°.
— Nuñez Cabeça de Vaca, A. Relatione. [1527.] (*In* Ramusio, G. B. Navig., v. 3. 1565.)
— - *Eng.* Narrative, [1527]; tr. by B. Smith. Wash., 1851. 4°.
— - *Same, entitled* Relation; tr. by B. Smith. [2d ed., augm.] N. Y., 1871. 8°.
— Marquette, J., *and* Joliet, —. Voyage et découverte de quelque pays de l'Amér. Sept., 1673. Paris, 1681, *reprinted* 1845. 12°.
— La Salle, R. C. de. [1678-90.] For various accounts of the voyage *see* La Salle (p. 1674).
— Gravier, J. Relation ou journal du voyage en 1700. N. Y., 1859. 4°.
— Keith, G. Journal of travels from New Hampshire to Caratuck, [N. C., 1702-04]. London, 1706. 4°.
— Knight, *Madam* S. Journal [on a journey from Boston to N. York], 1704; and [Diary of J.] Buckingham, 1710. N. Y., 1825. 12°.
— Grant, *Mrs.* A. Memoirs of an American lady, [1709-79]. Boston, 1809. 2 v. 12°.
— - *Same*. N. Y., 1846. 12°.
— Maury, A. Journal of travels in Virginia, N. Y., *etc.*, 1715, 16. (*In her* Mem. of a Huguenot fam. 1853.)
— Charlevoix, P. F. X. de. Letters to the Dutchess of Lesdiguieres; giving an account of a voy. to Canada, and travels through that country and Louisiana to the Gulf of Mexico, [1720-22]. London, 1763. 8°.
— - *Same*. Letters 28-32. (*In* French, B. F. Hist. col. of Louisiana, v. 3. 1851.)
— Evans, L. Geographical, hist., *etc.*, essays. 1: Analysis of a map of the middle British colonies in Amer., [1749]. 2d ed. Phila., 1755. 8°. (A 21)
— Mac Sparran, J. America dissected; full account of all Amer. colonies, [1752]. Dublin, 1753. 8°. (B 464)
— Account of the several provinces in North America, 1755. (*In* N. Hamp. Hist. Soc. Col., v. 5. 1837.)
— Palairet, J. Concise description of the Eng. and French possessions in N. Amer. 2d ed. Phila., 1755. 8°. (B 464)
— Burnaby, A. Travels through the middle settlements in N. America, 1759-60. London, 1775. 8°.
— - *Same*. 2d ed. London, 1775. 8°.
— - *Same*. 3d ed. London, 1798. 4°.
— - *Same*. (*In* Pinkerton, J. Col. of voy., v. 13. 1812.)
— Hutchins, T. Topographical description of Virginia, Pennsylvania, *etc.*, [1764-75]. London, 1778. 8°.
— - *Another copy*. (B 343)
— - *Same*. Boston, 1787. 12°. (C 64)
— Cluny, A. The American traveller; obs. on the British colonies in America. London, 1769. 4°.
— - *Other copies*. (A 20)
— - *French*. Le voyageur américain; tr. de l'anglois, augm. d'un précis sur l'Amérique et la république des treize Etats-Unis par J. M[andrillon]. Amst., 1783. 8°.
— Crèvecœur, J. H. St. J. de. Letters from an American farmer, [1770-84]. Lond., 1782. 8°.
— - *French, with additions*. Lettres d'un cultivateur américain à Wm. S...on, 1770-86; tr. de l'anglois. Paris, 1787. 3 v. 8°.
— Anburey, T. Travels through the interior parts of America; in a series of letters; by an officer, [1776-81]. London, 1789. 2 v. 8°.
— - *French*. Journal d'un voyage, *etc.*; tr. de l'anglois [par P. L. Lebas, avec des] notes par M. Noël. Paris, 1793. 2 v. 8°.
— Watson, E. Men and times of the Revolution; memoirs, incl. journals of travels in Europe and America, 1777-1842. N. Y., 1856. 8°.

— Chastellux, F. J., *marq.* de. Voyages dans l'Amér. Sept., 1780–82. Paris, 1786. 2 v. 8°.
Note. For other eds., trans., and remarks on the Voyages *see* **Chastellux** (p. 534).

— Robin, C. C., *l'abbé.* Nouveau voyage dans l'Amérique Septentrionale, 1781. Phila., 1782. 8°.

— - *Same.* Phila., 1783. 8°. (**B 615**)

— - *Eng.* New travels through North America in a series of letters. Boston, 1784. 8°. (**B 632, 703, 992, 2503**)

— Smyth, J. F. D. Tour in the U. S. London, 1784. 2 v. 8°.

— Crevecœur, J. H. St. J. Voyage dans la haute Pennsylvanie et dans l'état de N. Y., [1785–96?]. Paris, 1801. 3 v. 8°.

— Castiglioni, L. Viaggio negli Stati Uniti dell' America Settentrionale, 1785–87. Milano, 1790. 2 v. 8°.

— European traveller in America. Hartford, 1785. 8°. (**B 523**)

— Coxe, T. View of the U.S., in a series of papers written between 1787 and 1794. Phila., 1794. 8°.

— Brissot de Warville, J. P. Nouveau voy. dans les Etats-Unis, 1788. Par., 1791. 3 v. 8°.

— - *Eng.* New trav. in the U. S. Dublin, 1792. 8°.

— - *Same.* Incl. commerce of America with Europe. *n.p.*, [1794]. 2 v. 8°.

— - *Germ.* Neue Reise. 3r Theil. Hof, 1796. 8°.

— Morse, J. The Amer. geography; a view of the present situation of the U. S. Elizabethtown, 1789. 8°.

— Chateaubriand, F. A. R. de. Voyage en Amérique, [1791–92]. (*In his* Œuvres, v. 6. 1859.)

— Bayard, F. M. Voyage dans l'intérieur des Etats Unis, 1791. Paris, 1797. 8°.

— Bruchstücke zur Staatskunde des Nordamerikanischen Freystaats. (*In* **Sprengel, M. C.,** *and* **Forster, G.** Neue Beiträge, v. 12. 1793.)

— Janson, C. W. Stranger in America, [1793–1805]. London, 1807. 4°.

— Ebeling, C. D. Erdbeschreibung und Geschichte von America: Die Vereinigten Staaten. Hamburg, 1793–97. 4 v. 8°.

— Priest, W. Travels in the U. S., 1793–97. London, 1802. 8°.

— Cooper, T. Some information resp. America, [1793–94]. 2d ed. London, 1795. 8°.

— Drayton, J. Letters during a tour through the Northern and Eastern states. Charleston, 1794. 8°. (**W 84**)

— Letters on emigration to America. London, 1794. 8°. (**B 686**)

— Wansey, H. Journal of an excursion to the U. S., 1794. Salisbury, 1796. 8°.

— - *Same.* 2d ed. Salisbury, 1798. 12°.

— La Rochefoucauld-Liancourt, F. A. F. de. Voyage dans les Etats-Unis, 1795–97. Paris, [1799]. 8 v. 8°.

— - *Eng.* Travels through the U. S. London, 1799. 2 v. 4°.

— Jardine, L. J. Letter from Penn. to a friend in Eng. cont. valuable information in respect to America. Bath, 1795. 8°. (**B 686**)

— Pictet de Rochemont, C. Tableau de la situation actuelle des Etats-Unis. Paris, 1795. 2 v. 8°.

— Winterbotham, W. Historical, geographical, *etc.*, view of the U. S. and of the European settlements in America and the West Indies, [1795]. 1st Amer. ed. N. Y., 1796. 4 v. 8°.

— Baily, F. Journal of a tour in unsettled parts of N. A., 1796, 97. London, 1856. 8°.

— Look before you leap; hints to such artizans, *etc.*, as are desirous of emigrating to America; with app. 2d ed. [London,] 1796. 8°. (**B 686**)

— Zimmermann, E. A. W. von. Essai de comparison entre la France et les Etats Unis; tr. de l'allemand. Lpz., 1797. 2 v. in 1. 16°.

— Davis, J. Travels in the U. S., 1798–1802. London, 1803. 8°.

— Parkinson, R. Tour in America, 1798–1800; [with] a particular acc. of the Amer. system of agriculture. London, 1805. 2 v. 8°.

— Thurston, G. H. Route book from Philadelphia to Chicago. Pittsburgh, [18—]. 12°. (**C 277**)

— Beaujour, L. P. F. de. Aperçu des Etats-Unis, 1800–10. Paris, 1814. 8°.

— - *Eng.* Sketch of the U. S.; tr. by W. Walton. London, 1814. 8°.

— Michaux, F. A. Voyage à l'ouest des monts Alléghanys, [1801–03]. Paris, 1804. 8°.

— - *Eng.* Travels to the west of the Alleghany Mts. London, 1805. 8°.

— Rafinesque, C. S. A life of travels and researches in N. Amer., *etc.*, 1802–35. Phila., 1836. 12°.

— Volney, C. F. Tableau du climat et du sol des Etats-Unis. Paris, 1803. 2 v. 8°.

— - *Eng.* View of the climate and soil of the U. S. London, 1804. 8°.

— Allen, P. History of the exped. under Lewis and Clark, 1804–06. Phila., 1814. 2 v. 8°.

— - *Same.* Rev. by A. M'Vickar. N. Y., 1845–47. 2 v. 16°. (Harper's fam. lib., v. 154, 155.)

— Gass, P. Journal of travels of a corps under Capts. Lewis and Clarke in N. A., 1804–06. Pittsburgh, 1807. 12°.

— Moore, S. S., *and* Jones, T. W. Traveller's directory from Phila. to N. Y. and to Washington. 2d ed. Phila., 1804. 8°.

— Melish, J. Travels in the U. S., 1806–11. Phila., 1812. 2 v. 8°.

— Journal de l'Amérique du Nord. Nos. 1–4; pub. par H. Caritat. Paris, 1806–07. 8°.

— Ashe, T. Travels in America, 1806. London, 1808. 3 v. 16°.

— Notes on the U. S. Phila., 1806. 8°. (**B 429**)

— Kendall, E. A. Travels through the northern parts of the U. S., 1807–08. N. Y., 1809. 3 v. 8°.

— Schultz, C., *Jr.* Travels [in the U. S.], 1807–08. N. Y., 1810. 2 v. 8°.

— Ker, H. Travels through the western interior of the U. S., 1808–16. Elizabethtown, N. J., 1816. 8°.

— Bradbury, J. Travels in the interior of America, 1809–11. Liverpool, 1817. 8°.

— Knight, H. C. Letters from the south and west; by A. Singleton [pseud.]. 1814–19. Boston, 1824. 8°.

— - *Another copy.* (**B 551**)

— Melish, J. Description of roads in the U. S. Phila., 1814. 12°.

— - *Another copy.* (**C 278**)

— Hall, F. Travels in Canada and the U. S., 1816–17. Boston, 1818. 8°.

— Montlezun, *le baron* de. Voyage, 1816–17, de New-Yorck à la N. Orléans, *etc.* Paris, 1818. 2 v. 8°.

— Examen impartial d'un ouvrage intit. 'Voyage fait 1816–17, de New Yorck à la N. Orléans', *etc.* Paris, 1818. 8°. (**B 449**)

— Harris, W. T. Remarks on a tour through the U. S. in 1817–19. Liverpool, [1819]. 8°. (**B 529**)

— Birkbeck, M. Notes on a journey in America, [1817]. 2d ed. London, 1818. 8°.

— Fearon, H. B. Sketches on America, [1817]. London, 1818. 8°.

— HINTS to emigrants to the U. S.; with extracts from the journ. of T. Hulme. Liverpool, 1817. 8°. (B 692)
— WALDO, S. P. Tour of J. Monroe in 1817. Hartford, 1818. 12°.
— FLINT, J. Letters from America, [1818-20]. Edin., 1822. 8°.
— DUNCAN, J. M. Travels through the U. S. and Canada, 1818-19. N. Y., 1823. 2 v. 12°.
— BRISTED, J. Resources of the U. S. N. Y., 1818. 8°.
— DARBY, W. Tour from N. Y. to Detroit, 1818. N. Y., 1819. 8°.
— GRASSI, G. Notizie varie sullo stato presente della repubblica degli Stati Uniti, 1818. Ed. 2a. Milano, 1819. 8°.
— WORCESTER, J. E. Gazetteer of the U. S. Andover, 1818. 8°.
— HODGSON, A. Remarks during a journey through N. A., 1819-21. N. Y., 1823. 8°.
— FAUX, W. Memorable days in America; journal of a tour to the U. S., [1819-20]. London, 1823. 8°.
— GALL, L. Meine Auswanderung nach den Vereinigten-Staaten in Nord-Amerika, 1819-20. Trier, 1822. 2 v. 8°.
— MACKENZIE, E. Historical, topographical, and descriptive view of the U. S. Newcastle upon Tyne, [1819]. 8°.
— SILLIMAN, B. Remarks made on a tour between Hartford and Quebec, 1819. 2d ed. New Haven, 1824. 12°.
— WARDEN, D. B. Statistical, political, and historical acc. of the U. S. Edin., 1819. 3 v. 8°.
— MACKENZIE, W. L. Sketches of Canada and the U. S., [1821-32]. London, 1833. 12°.
— ONIS, L. de. Mem. upon the negotiations between Spain and the U. S. which led to the treaty of 1819; with a statistical notice of that country; tr. from the Spanish by T. Watkins. Wash., 1821. 8°. (B 535)
— MELISH, J. Geographical desc. of the U. S. New ed. Phila., 1822. 8°.
— ROYALL, A. Sketches of history, life, and manners in the U. S., [1823-24]; by a traveller. N. Haven, 1826. 12°.
— POLETICA, P. Aperçu de la situation intérieure des Etats-Unis d'Amérique et de leurs rapports politiques avec l'Europe, [1823]. London, 1826. 8°.
— - *Eng.* Sketch of the internal condition of the U. S., [1823]; tr. from the French. Balt., 1826. 8°.
— TALBOT, E. A. 1823. (*In his* Five years'. 1824.)
— LEVASSEUR, A. Lafayette en Amérique, 1824-25. Paris, 1829. 2 v. 8°.
— - *Eng.* Lafayette in America; tr. by J. D. Godman. Phila., 1829. 2 v. 8°.
— STAGE register; [supplement to the Amer. traveller; pub. by Badger and Porter]. Vol. [1]-7. Bost.. 1825-32. 7 v. (v. 1, no. 1 w.). 8°.
— *Same.* July and Aug. Boston, 1839. 8°. (B 1179)
— DE ROOS, F. F. Personal narrative of travels in the U. S., 1826. London, 1827. 8°.
— STUART, J. Three years in N. A., [1828-31]. Edin., 1833. 2 v. 12°.
— DARBY, W. View of the U. S.; historical, geographical, and statist. Phila., 1828. 12°.
— COBBETT, W. The emigrant's guide; in ten letters. London, 1829. 12°.
— DWIGHT, T. Sketches of scenery and manners in the U. S. N. Y., 1829. 12°.
— FASHIONABLE tour; guide to travellers visiting the middle and northern states and Canada. 4th ed. Saratoga, 1830. 12°.

392. (15. 6. 81.)

— O'FERRALL, S. A. Ramble of six thousand miles through the U. S., [1830]. London, 1832. 8°.
— TOCQUEVILLE, A. de. Voyage aux Utats-Unis, [1831-32]. (*In his* Mélanges hist. 1865.)
— FERGUSSON, A. Practical notes during a tour in Canada and the U.S., 1831. Edin., 1833. 16°.
— VIGNE, G. T. Six months in America, [1831]. London, 1832. 2 v. 12°.
— ARFWEDSON, C. D. United States and Canada, 1832-34. London, 1834. 2 v. 8°.
— MAXIMILIAN, A. P., *Prinz von Wied-Neuwied.* Travels in N. Amer., 1832-34; tr. by H. E. Lloyd. Lond., 1843. 4° *and* Atlas 1844. f°.
— KEMBLE, F. A. Journal, [1832-33]. Phila., 1835. 2 v. 12°.
— LATROBE, C. J. Rambler in N. Amer., 1832-33. 2d ed. London, 1836. 2 v. 12°.
— COKE, E. T. A subaltern's furlough in the U. S., 1832. London, 1833. 8°.
— FIDLER, I. Observations in the U. S. and Canada, 1832. London, 1833. 12°.
— HINTON, J. H. Topography of the U. S. (Vol. 2 *of his* Hist. and topography. 1832.)
— CHEVALIER, M. Lettres sur l'Amér. du Nord, [1833-35]. Brux., 1837. 2 v. 16°.
— - *Same.* Ed. spéciale. Paris, 1837. 2 v. 8°.
— - *Eng.* Society, manners, and politics in the U. S.; tr. [by T. G. Bradford]. Boston, 1839. 8°.
— POWER, T. Impressions of America, 1833-35. Phila., 1836. 2 v. 12°.
— ABDY, E. S. Journal of a residence and tour in the U. S., 1833-34. Lond., 1835. 3 v. 12°.
— DARBY, W., *and* DWIGHT, T. New gazetteer of the United States Hartford, 1833. 8°.
— FINCH, J. Travels in the U. S. and Canada. London, 1833. 8°.
— RICH, O. General view of the U. S. London, 1833. 16°.
— MITCHELL, S. A. Accompaniment to his reference and distance map of the U. S. Phila., 1834. 8°.
— LIEBER, F. The stranger in America. Phila., 1835. 8°.
— BUCKINGHAM, J. S. America, historical, statistical, and descriptive, [1837]. London, [1841]. 3 v. 8°.
— MARRYAT, F. Diary in America, [1837]. London, 1839. 3 v. (v. 3 w.). 12°.
— - *Same.* Pt. 2. London, 1839. 3 v. 12°.
— COMBE, G. Notes on the U. S., 1838-40. Phila., 1841. 2 v. 8°.
— GILMAN, *Mrs.* C. Poetry of travelling in the U. S. N. Y., 1838. 12°.
— WOOD, *Rev.* S. Letters from the U. S. *n.p.*, [1838]. 8°. (B 1603)
— GRATTAN, T. C. Civilized America, [1839-45]. London, 1859. 2 v. 8°.
— CHEVALIER, M. Histoire et description des voies de communication aux Etats-Unis. Paris, 1840-41. 2 v. 4°.
— CAMPBELL, J. Observations upon the U. S. (*In his* Brit. army as it was, *etc.* 1840.)
— HARVEY, G. Scenes of the primitive forest of America, [1840]. N. Y., 1841. f°.
— MAXWELL, A. M. Run through the U. S., 1840. London, 1841. 2 v. 12°.
— WILLIS, N. P. L'Amérique pittoresque; enrichi de gravures faites sur les dessins de W. H. Bartlett; tr. par L. de Bauclas. Londres, 1840. 8°.

— TAYLOR, J. G. The U. S. and Cuba, [1841-49]. London, 1851. 8°.
— LYELL, *Sir* C. Travels in North America, [1841-42]. London, 1845. 2 v. 12°.
— - *Same.* N. Y., 1845. 2 v. 12°.
— DWIGHT, T. Northern traveller. 6th ed. N. Y., 1841. 12°.
— BUCKINGHAM, J. S. Eastern and western states. London, [1842]. 3 v. 8°.
— DICKENS, C. American notes for general circulation. London, 1842. 2 v. 8°.
— - *Same.* N. Y., 1842. 8°.
— - *Another copy.* (B 1603)
— - *Same.* Lpz., *Tauchnitz*, 1842. 12°.
— GODLEY, J. R. Letters from America, [1842]. London, 1844. 2 v. 12°.
— GREAT western magazine, 1842: U. S. and England. *n.t.p.* [1842.] 8°. (B 1664)
— BROMME, T. Hand- und Reisebuch für Auswanderer nach Nord Amerika. 2e Aufl. Bayreuth, 1843. 12°.
— HASKELL, D., *and* SMITH, J. C. Gazetteer of the U. S. N. Y., 1843. 8°.
— MATTHIAS, B. Traveler's guide from Phila. to N. Y., by steamboats and rail-road; cont. descriptions, *etc.* Phila., 1843. 12°. (D 41)
— SILLIMAN, A. E. A gallop among American scenery. N. Y., 1843. 16°.
— WARBURTON, E. Hochelaga, or England in the New World, [1844-46]. N. Y., 1846. 2 v. 12°.
— RAUMER, F. von. America and the American people, [1844]; tr. by W. W. Turner. N. Y., 1846. 8°.
— LYELL, *Sir* C. Second visit to the U. S., [1845-46]. N. Y., 1849. 2 v. 12°.
— RUBIO, *pseud.* Rambles in U. S. and Canada; 1845; with acc. of Oregon. Lond., 1846. 12°.
— SIGOURNEY, L. H. Scenes in my native land. Boston, 1845. 12°.
— LANMAN, C. Adventures in the wilds of the U. S., [1846-56]. Phila., 1856. 2 v. 8°.
— MITCHELL, D. W. Ten years in the U. S., [1848-58]. London, 1862. 8°.
— FLEISCHMANN, C. L. Der nordamerikanische Landwirth; ein Handbuch für Ansiedler in den Vereinigten Staaten. N. Y., 1848. 8°.
— BREMER, F. The homes of the new world; impressions of America, [1849-51]; tr. by M. Howitt. N. Y., 1853. 2 v. 12°.
— MACKIE, J. M. From Cape Cod to Dixie and the tropics, [185-?]. N. Y., 1864. 12°.
— BURR, W. Descriptive view of Burr's moving mirror of the lakes; [with] the range of border scenery of the U. S. and Canadian shores, from lake Erie to the Atlantic. Boston, 1850. 8°. (B 1603)
— WILLIAMS, W. APPLETON's new and complete U. S. guide book. N. Y., 1850. 16°.
— AMPÈRE, J. J. A. Promenade en Amérique, [1851-52]. Nouv. éd. Paris, 1860. 2 v. 8°.
Note. From Revue d. D. Mondes, jan.-oct. 1853.
— BOGEN, F. W. The German in Amer.; advice for German emigrants; [in Eng. and Germ.]. 2d ed. Boston, 1851. 12°.
— HORN, H. B. Overland guide to California. N. Y., 1852. 12°.
— MONTÉGUT, E. Les Etats-Unis en 1852. (*In* Revue d. D. Mondes, juil. 1852.)
— SLEIGH, *Capt.* A. W. Impressions of the U. S., [1852]. (*In his* Pine forests. 1853.)
— BENWELL, J. An Englishman's travels in America. London, [1853]. 16°.
— BUNN, A. Old England and New England. Phila., 1853. 12°.
— CHAMBERS, W. Things as they are in America, [1853]. Phila., 1854. 12°.
— HAYWARD, J. Gazetteer of the U. S. Hartford, 1853. 8°.
— SHAW, J. Twelve years in America, [1854-66]. London, 1867. 12°.
— MURRAY, *Hon.* A. M. Letters from the U. S., Cuba, and Canada, [1854-55]. N. Y., 1856. 12°.
— ENGLISHWOMAN in America, [1854]. London, 1856. 12°.
Note. This is not the same as Mrs. Maury's 'Englishwoman in America'.
— HAMMOND, S. H. Hills, lakes, and forest streams. N. Y., 1854. 12°.
— BEAUVALLET, L. Rachel and the new world; a trip to the U. S. and Cuba, [1855-56]; tr. from the French. N. Y., 1856. 8°.
— FOSTER, V. Work and wages; emigrant's guide to the U. S. and Canada. 6th ed. London, [1855]. 8°. (C 278)
— HANDBOOK descriptive of the route to Ogdensburgh, Montreal, Quebec, White Mountains, *etc.* Buffalo, 1858. 32°. (D 41)
— REID, H. Sketches in North America; with some account of Congress and of the slavery question, [1859-61]. London, 1861. 16°.
— PUMPELLY, R. Across America and Asia, [1860-61]. N. Y., 1870. 8°.
— TALLACK, W. Friendly sketches in America, [1860]. London, 1861. 8°.
— LAUGEL, A. Les Etats-Unis pendant la guerre, 1861-65. Paris, 1866. 12°.
— - *Eng.* The U. S. during the war. N. Y., 1866. 8°.
— RUSSELL, W. H. My diary North and South, [1861-63]. London, 1863. 8°.
— - *Same.* Boston, 1863. 12°.
— WHITE, A. D. Letter to W. H. Russell on passages in his 'Diary'. From London ed. Syracuse. 1863. 8°.
— FERRI-PISANI, C. Lettres sur les Etats-Unis d'Amérique, [1861]. Paris, 1862. 12°.
— TROLLOPE, A. North America, [1861]. London, 1862. 2 v. 8°.
— - *Same.* N. Y., 1862. 12°.
— - *Same.* Phila., 1862. 2 v. 12°.
— WESTON, E. P. The pedestrian; journal of a walk from Boston to Washington, 1861. N. Y., 1862. 8°.
— LAWRENCE, G. A. Border and bastile, [1862-63]. N. Y., [1863]. 12°.
— DANIEL, L. La guerre aux Etats-Unis; topographie, mœurs, *etc.* Paris, 1862. 8°.
— DICEY, E. Six months in the Federal states, [1862]. London, 1863. 2 v. 8°.
— SALA, G. A. My diary in America in the midst of war, [1863-64]. Lond., 1865. 2 v. 8°.
— BIGELOW, J. Les Etats-Unis en 1863. Paris, 1863. 8°.
— HUNT, E. B. Union foundations; a study of Amer. nationality as a fact of science. N. Y., 1863. 8°.
— MASSIE, J. W. America; the origin of her present conflict, *etc.*; illust. by incidents of travel in 1863. London, 1864. 8°.
— DUVERGIER DE HAURANNE, E. Huit mois en Amérique, 1864-65. Paris, 1866. 2 v. 12°.
Note. From Revue d. D. Mondes, août 1865, avr. 1866.
— FERGUSON, R. America during and after the war, [1864-65]. London, 1866. 12°.
— GLOSS, A. Das Leben in den Vereinigten Staaten. Lpz., 1864. 2 v. 8°.

— Kennaway, J. H. On Sherman's track, [1865–66]. London, 1867. 8°.
— Skinner, J. E. H. After the storm, 1865–66. London, 1866. 2 v. 8°.
— Bowles, S. Across the continent; a journey to the Rocky Mts., *etc.* Springfield, 1865. 12°.
— Dilke, C. W. Greater Britain. Vol. 1: 1866–67. London, 1868. 8°.
— Latham, H. Black and white; three month's tour in the U. S., [1866–67]. Lond., 1867. 8°.
— Campbell, J. G. E. H. D. S., *Marquis of Lorne.* Trip to the tropics and home through America, [1866]. London, 1867. 8°.
— Chisholm's hand-book of travel and tourist's guide through Canada and the U. S. Montreal, 1866. 12°.
— Haurowitz, H. von. Schilderungen von Land und Leuten. (*In his* Militärsanitätswesen. 1866.)
— Dixon, W. H. New America. London, 1867. 2 v. 8°.
— - *Same.* Phila., 1867. 12°.
— Hall, E. H. Appletons' hand-book of American travel. 9th ed. N. Y., 1867. 12°.
— Maguire, J. F. The Irish in America, [1867]. London, 1868. 8°.
— Zincke, F. B. Last winter in the U. S., [1867]. London, 1868. 8°.
— Townshend, F. T. Ten thousand miles of travel, sport, and adventure, [1868]. London, 1869. 8°.
— Townsend, G. A. The new world compared with the old, government, institutions, and enterprises. Hartford, Conn., 1870. 8°.
— American Social Science Assoc. Handbook for immigrants to the U.S. N. Y., 1871. 16°.

Maps.

— American military pocket atlas; maps of the British colonies. London, [1776?]. 8°.
— Andrews, J. Map of the British N. American colonies, the seat of war. London, 1777.
— Faden, W. Map. [Lond.,] 1793. (E 68)
— Holland, N. New chart of the coast of No. America from N. Y. to Cape Hatteras. London, 1794. (E 68)
— Arrowsmith, A. London, 1796. f°. (E 68)
— Carey, M. Minor American atlas; 19 maps. Phila., 1802. 4°.
— Carleton, O. Map of the U. S. Boston, 1806.
— Melish, J. Military and topographical atlas of the U. S. incl. the British Possessions and Florida. Phila., 1815. 8°.
— Morse, S. E. Atlas of the U. S. on an improved plan. N. Haven, 1823. 4°.
— Mitchell, S. A. Traveller's guide through the U. S. Phila., 1832.
— - *Same.* Phila., 1834.
— Atlas of the U. S. printed for the use of the blind. Boston, 1837. 4°.
— Bradford, T. G. Illust. atlas of the U. S. and adjacent countries. Boston, 1837. f°.
— Burr, D. H. American atlas; [13 maps of the U. S.]. Boston, [1839]. f°.
— Colton, J. H. Maps of the U. S. N. Y., 1850.
— Fisher, R. S. Map of railroads and canals of the U. S. and Canada. N. Y., *Dinsmore & Co.*, 1856.
— Rogers, H. D., *and* Johnston, A. K. Atlas of the U. S., Canada, *etc.* London, 1857. f°.

See also **Alleghany Mts.; — Columbia River; — Confederate States of America; — Great Salt Lake; — Mississippi River; — Mississippi Valley; — Missouri River; — Mormons; — New England; — New Mexico; — Northwest, *U.S.*; — Northwest Territory; — Ohio River; — Potomac River; — Prairies, American; — Red River; — San Juan; — South, The; — South West, The; — Superior, Lake; — Washington Territory; — West, The;** — *also the division Description under the various states;* — *also* Atlases (p. 165, 166).

Directory.

— American advertising directory, 1831. N. Y., 1831. 12°.

Ecclesiastical affairs.

History.

— Rupp, I. D. History of the religious denominations in the U. S., [1492–1844]. Phila., 1844. 8°.
— Hawks, F. L. Contributions to the ecclesiastical history of the U. S., [1606–1835]. N. Y., 1836–39. 2 v. 8°.
— Baird, R. Progress and prospects of Christianity in the U. S. of America, [1607–1851]. London, [1851]. 8°.
— Spencer, E. Account of the dissenting interest in the middle states, 1759. (*In* Mass. Hist. Soc. Col., v. 11. 1814.)
— Waylen, E. Ecclesiastical reminiscences of the U. S., 1834–46. N. Y., 1846. 8°.

General and miscellaneous works.

— Critical commentary on Abp. Secker's letter conc. bishops in America. London, 1770. 8°.
— *Another copy.* (B 140)
— Garrettson, F. Letter to L. Beecher with strictures on 'An address of the Char. Soc. for the Education of Indigent Pious Young Men for the Ministry, [1816]. Boston, 1817. 8°. (B 664)
— Hobart, J. H. The U. S. compared with European countries, particularly Eng.; disc., N. Y., Oct. N. Y., 1825. 8°. (B 1293)
— - *Same.* 2d ed. with add. notes. N. Y., 1826. 8°. (B 1293)
— Reed, A., *and* Matheson, J. Visit to the American churches by the deputation from the Congregational Union of Eng. and Wales. N. Y., 1835. 2 v. 8°.
— Political action of our church members and clergy a chief cause of our present religious declension. N. Y., 1848. 8°. (B 1503)
— Baird, R. State and prospects of religion in America, 1855. N. Y., 1856. 8°.
— Stanton, R. S. The church and the rebellion, [1860–64]. N. Y., 1864. 12°.
— Laboulaye, E. L'église et l'état en Amér. (*In* Revue d. D. Mondes, oct. 1873.)

See also Description (Reed, A. 1835); — *Ecclesiastical biography* (p. 3110); — *also* **Antinomians; — Baptists; — Congregational churches; — Friends, Society of; — Methodism; — Methodist Episc. Ch.; — Mormons; — Protestant Episc. Ch.; — Reformed Dutch Churches in N. Amer.; — Sabbatarians;** — *also* **Maine; — Massachusetts; — New England; — New Hampshire; — New York; — Rhode Island; — Texas; — Vermont; — Virginia; — Westchester Co., *N. Y.***

Education.

— Coram, R. Political inquiries; [with] a plan for the general establishment of schools throughout the U. S. Wilmington, 1791. 8°. (B 741)
— Our colleges, academies, and common schools. From Colman's monthly miscellany for August. *n.t.p.* [18—.] 8°. (B 1827)
— Thoughts on the condition of popular education in the U. S.; by a citizen of Pennsylvania. *n.p.*, [18—]. 8°. (B 1718)
— Prospectus of a national institution, to be established in the U. S. Wash.-City, 1806. 8°. (B 428, 2526)
— Dupont de Nemours, P. S. Sur l'éduc. nationale dans les Etats-Unis. 2e éd. Paris, 1812. 8°. (B 648)
— Johnson, W. R. Obs. on the improvement of seminaries of learning in the U. S. Phila., 1825. 8°. (B 552)
— Siljeström, P. A. Resa i förenta staterna. 1a delen: om bildlingsmedlen och bildningen. Stockholm, 1852. 8°.

— - *Eng.* Educational institutions of the U. S., their character and organization; tr. by F. Rowan. London, 1853. 12°.
— NORTON'S literary register, 1854. Vol. 2. N. Y., [1854]. 12°.
— LAUGEL, A. Des principes de l'éducation populaire dans la société américaine. (*In* Revue d. D. Mondes, mai 1859.) — LAVELEYE, E. de. L'enseignement populaire dans les écoles américaines. (*In* nov. 1865.) — Le progrès et les resources financières de l'enseignment aux Etats-Unis. (*In* déc. 1867.)
— FRASER, J. Schools Inquiry Commissions; report on the common school system of the U. S. and Canada. London, 1866. 8°.
— PACKARD, F. A. Daily public school in the U. S. Phila., 1866. 8°.
— BLAKE, S. J. Visit to some American schools and colleges. London, 1867. 12°.

See also **California; — Connecticut; — Illinois; — Indiana; — Kentucky.** *Supr. of Public Instruction* (p. 1620); — **Maine; — Maryland; — Massachusetts; — Michigan,** *Supr. of Pub. Instruction* (p. 1972); — **New Hampshire; — New York; — Pennsylvania.**

Embargo.

See **Embargo** (p. 879).

Entomology.

— SAY, T. American entomology. Phila., 1824-28. 4 v. 8°.

See also **Massachusetts.** *Commis. of the Zoöl. and Bot. Survey* (p. 1891); — **New England.** *Nat. History*; — **New York; — North America; — Washington Territory.**

Finance.

— BRECK, S. Historical sketch of continental paper money. Phila., 1843. 8°.
— OBSERVATIONS on the peculiar case of the Whig merchants indebted to Gr. Brit. at the commencement of the war. N. Y., 1785. 8°. (B 635)
— M'CONNELL, M. Essay on the domestic debts of the U. S. Phila., 1787. 8°. (W 17)
— CONSIDERATIONS on the nature of a funded debt; [against adopting] the debts of the respective states. N. Y., 1790. 8°. (B 465)
— MEMORIAL [to Congress] of the public creditors, citizens of New Jersey. Trenton, 1790. 8°. (W 17)
— WEBSTER, P. Plea for the poor soldiers; essay to demonstrate that the soldiers must be paid. Phila., 1790. 8°. (B 625)
— FINDLEY, W. Review of the revenue system. Phila., 1794. 8°. (B 641)
— HAMILTON, A. Income and expenditure of the U. S. for 1794. London, 1794. 8°. (B 686)
— SMITH, W. Speech, subject of the reduction of the public debt, Dec. 1794. *n.p.*, [1794]. 8°. (B 420)
— SHORT history of excise laws; [with] account of the interruption to the manufactories of snuff and refined sugar. Phila., 1795. 8°. (B 397, 663, 991, W 83)
— GALLATIN, A. Sketch of the finances of the U. S. N. Y., 1796. 8°. (B 395)
— CALLENDER, J. T. Sedgwick & Co.; or, Key to the 6 per cent. cabinet. Phila., 1798. 8°. (B 420)
— GALLATIN, A. Views of the public debt, receipts, and expenditures of the U. S. N. Y., 1800. 8°. (B 620)
— BAYARD, J. A. Speech, on the bill resp. the organization of the courts of the U. S., Feb. 19, 20. Hartford, 1802. 8°. (B 926, 1489)
— DEBATES in the Senate on the repeal of the internal taxes. Georgetown, 1802. 8°. (B 622)
— WOLCOTT, O. Address to the people of the U. S. on the report of a committee 'to examine whether monies from the Treasury have been applied to the objects for which they were appropriated', Apr. 29. Boston, 1802. 8°. (B 531, 622, 1489, 2514, W 4)
— ADDINGTON, L. Digest of the revenue laws. Phila., 1804. 12°.
— FORSYTH, J. Speech, bill to authorize a loan, Ho. Reps., 22, 23 Feb. Wash., 1814. 8°. (C 61)
— GASTON, W. Speech on the [loan bill], Feb. Georgetown, 1814. 8°. (B 669, 2530)
— - *Same.* (*In* Moore, F. Amer. eloquence, v. 2. 1864.)
— HANSON, A. C. Speech, loan bill, Feb. 14. Georgetown, 1814. 8°. (B 669, 2530)
— PICKERING, T. Speech, Feb. 26, 28, on the [loan bill]. Georgetown, 1814. 8°. (B 669)
— PITKIN, T. Speech on the loan bill, Feb. 10. Alexandria, 1814. 8°. (B 669)
— SHEFFEY, D. Speech, on the [loan bill], Feb. 11. Alexandria, 1814. 8°. (B 669, 2530)
— BOLLMAN, E. Plan of an improved system of the money concerns of the union. Phila., 1816. 8°. (B 455)
— NATIONAL money: or, A simple system of finance. Georgetown, 1816. 8°. (B 455)
— PITKIN, T. Statist. view of the commerce of the U. S., *etc.*, and an account of the pub. debt revenues, *etc.* Hartford, 1816. 8°.
— - *Same.* 2d ed., with add. and corr. N. Y., 1817. 8°.
— - *Same.* N. Haven, 1835. 8°.
— SWAN, J. Address on the means of creating a national paper by loan offices. Boston, 1819. 8°. (B 531)
— PARADOX, The, solved; or, A financial secret worth knowing. Balt., 1820. 8°. (B 986)
— WOLCOTT, O. Remarks on the present state of currency, credit, *etc.* N. Y., 1820. 8°. (B 563)
— CORRESPONDENCE rel. to the proposals for five millions of five per cent. stock. Phila., 1822. 8°. (B 1000)
— PUBLIC defaulters brought to light; letters to the people of the U. S., by a native of Virginia. N. Y., 1822. 8°. (B 531, 2005)
— LAW, T. Considerations tending to render the policy questionable of plans for liquidating within the next four years the 6 per. ct. stocks of the U. S. Wash., 1826. 8°. (B 1105)
— CORRESPONDENCE [with] the Treasurer of the Western shore of Maryland upon the U. S. for interest due upon sums advanced during the late war. Annapolis, 1827. 8°. (W 13, 14)
— DICKERSON, M. Speech, distribution of revenue, Feb. 1. Wash., 1827. 8°. (B 1814)
— EVERETT, E. Speech on retrenchment, Feb. 1. Wash., 1828. 8°. (B 926, 1805)
— LAW, T. Address to the Columbian Inst., on a moneyed system. Wash., 1828. 8°. (B 1101)
— WOODBURY, L. Report, present system of keeping and disbursing the public money. [Wash., 183-.] 8°. (B 1768)
— DAVIS, J. Speech on the bill for the more effectual collection of impost duties, May 4, 1830. Wash., 1830. 8°. (B 1494)
— CLAY, H. Speech, defence of the American system, against the British colonial system, Feb.; with app. of docs. Wash., 1832. 8°. (B 1810, 1831)
— COOPER, J. F. Administration financière des Etats-Unis. (*In* Revue d. D. Mondes, jan. 1832.)
— HOLMES, J. Speech on the annual appropriation bill. Wash., 1832. 8°. (B 1056)
— U. S. 22*d Cong.* 2*d sess. House.* Correspondence with the Bank of the U. S., Dec. 13, 1832. [Wash., 1833.] 8°. (Doc. 9. B 1790)
— GOUGE, W. M. Short history of paper money and banking in the U. S. Phila., 1833. 8°.
— ADAMS, J. Q. Speech on the removal of the public deposits and its reasons. Wash., 1834. 8°. (B 1721, 1732)
— - *Same.* Suppl. to the Daily Advertiser. [Boston,] *n.d.* 8°. (B 1089, 1427, 1648, 1810)
— CORCELLE, F. de. Administration financière des Etats-Unis. (*In* Revue d. D. Mondes, mars 1834.)
— LEIGH, B. W. Speech on Benton's motion to expunge the resolution of Mar. 28, 1834, [on removal] of public deposites. Wash., 1836. 8°. (B 1721, 1791)
— WEBSTER, D. Speech on the distribution of the surplus revenue, May 31. Wash., 1836. 8°. (B 1777, 2009)
— WISE, H. A., *and* PEYTON, B. Speeches rel. to the agents of the treasury and the deposite banks, Apr. 14, 19, 1836. Wash., 1836. 8°. (B 1777)
— FINANCIAL register of the U. S., July 1837 - Dec. 1838. Phila., 1837-38. 2 v. 8°.
— BENTON, T. H. Speech, bill designating and limiting the funds receivable for the revenues of U. S. Wash., 1837. 8°. (B 1663)
— CLAY, H. On the bill imposing additional duties, as depositaries, on public officers, Sept. 25. Boston, 1837. 8°. (B 1496, 1668, 1791, 1815, 2010)
— CORWIN, T. Speech on the bill to reduce the revenue, Jan. 12. Wash., 1837. 8°. (B 1124, 1496, 1718, 1723, 2009)
— KING, J. P. Speech on the bill imposing additional duties, as depositaries, on public officers, Sept. 23. Wash., 1837. 8°. (B 1496)

— RANTOUL, R., *jr.* Oration before the Democratic citizens of Worcester Co., July 4. 2d ed. Worcester, 1837. 8°. (B 1751, 2005)
— SMITH, F. O. J. Letters in vindication of his vote against the sub-treasury bill. Portland, 1837. 8°. (B 1496)
— SMITH, O. H. Speech, sub-treasury system, Sept. 21. Wash., 1837. 8°. (B 1777)
— WALKER, R. J. Speech, on bill for collection, *etc.*, of public money, Sept. 27. *n.t.p.* [Wash., 1837.] 8°. (B 1663, 1664)
— WEBSTER, D. Speech on the currency, and on the new plan for col. the pub. moneys, Sept. 28. Wash., 1837. 8°. (B 1777, 2010)
— BOND, W. K. Speech, resolution to correct abuses in the public expenditures. [Wash., 1838.] 8°. (B 1816)
— BROWN, B. Speech, bill imposing add. duties, as depositaries, in certain cases, on pub. officers, Feb. 23. Washington, 1838. 8°. (B 1791)
— CALHOUN, J. C. Speech on the sub-treasury bill. Wash., 1838. 8°. (B 1663)
— DAVIS, J. Speech upon the sub-treasury bill, Feb. 28 and Mar. 1. Wash., 1838. 8°. (B 1129, 1791, 1815)
— LEGARE, H. S. Letter on the probable effects of the sub-treasury policy with the specie clause. Wash., 1838. 8°. (B 1814)
— REMEDY, The, in a national bank of the people, *vs.* a treasury bank and a national bank of a party. N. Y., 1838. 8°. (B 1544)
— WEBSTER, D. Speech, sub-treasury bill, Mar. 12. *n.p.*, [1838]. 8°. (B 1129, 1646, 1723, 1751, 1791, 2010)
— - *Same.* And speech in answer to Calhoun. Wash., 1838. 8°. (B 1732)
— WINTHROP, R. C. Speech on the resolutions relating to the sub-treasury system. *n.p.*, 1838. 8°. (B 1496, 1732, 1751, 1814)
— TROTTER, A. Financial position of such states as have contracted debts. London, 1839. 8°.
— ADAMS, J. Q. Speech [on] the bill rel. to the col. of duties on imports. Boston, 1840. 8°. (B 1428, 1497)
— ALLEN, W. Speech [on] the assumption of debts of the States; Feb. 18. Wash., 1840. 8°. (B 1663)
— BENTON, T. H. Speech, on assuming State debts; Jan. 6. Wash., 1840. 8°. (B 1663)
— COLTON, C. The crisis of the country; by Junius. [N. Y., 1840.] 8°. (B 1500)
— - Sequel to The crisis of the country; by Junius. [N. Y., 1840.] 8°. (B 1500)
— CALHOUN, J. C. Speech, assumption of the debts of states, Feb. 5. Wash., 1840. 8°. (B 1663, 1817)
— - *Same.* [Worcester, 1840.] 8°. (B 1497)
— COOPER, M. A. Speech, bill to establish an independent treasury, June. Wash., 1840. 8°. (B 1497)
— DAVIS, J. Speech, sub-treasury bill, Jan. 23. Boston, 1840. 8°. (B 1496)
— - *Same.* [Wash., 1840.] 8°. (B 1496, 1871)
— MONTGOMERY, W. Speech, bill to authorize the issue of treasury notes. Wash., 1840. 8°. (B 1663)
— SALTONSTALL, L. Speech, reply to Mr. Parmenter on the bill providing for the expenses of the government, Apr. 21. Wash., 1840. 8°. (B 1823)
— WEBSTER, D. Remarks upon that part of the President's message [rel.] to the revenue and finances, Dec. 16, 17. Wash., 1840. 8°. (B 1147, 1823)
— BENTON, T. H. Speech on the loan bill. *n.t.p.* [1841.] 8°. (B 1664)
— DUNCAN, A. Speech, treasury note bill, Jan. 25, 1841. Wash., 1840 [1841]. 8°. (B 1664)
— HUNTER, R. M. T. Speech on the loan bill, July 10, 1841. Wash., 1841. 8°. (B 1664)
— JONES, J. W. Speech on the loan bill, July 12. Wash., 1841. 8°. (B 1664)
— SHIELDS, B. Speech, bill to repeal the independent treasury, Aug. 7. Wash., 1841. 8°. (B 1664)
— STEENROD, L. Speech on bill no. 8. *n.t.p.* [1841.] 8°. (B 1664)
— WARD, A. Speech on the revenue bill. Wash., 1841. 8°. (B 1664)
— WELLER, J. B. Speech, loan bill. Wash., 1841. 8°. (B 1663)
— WISE, H. A. Speech, treasury note bill. Wash., 1841. 8°. (B 1167)
— HENSHAW, D. Exchequer and currency. Boston post extra, Dec. 17, 1842. (B 1544)
— PUBLIUS, *pseud.* The crisis and the remedy. N. Y., 1842. 8°. (B 1544)
— SALTONSTALL, L. Speech, tariff bills, June 17. Wash., 1842. 8°. (B 1871)
— WOODBURY, L. Speech. Wash., 1842. 8°. (B 1663)
— WINTHROP, R. C. Speech on the resolution that the exchequer plan ought to be adopted, Jan. 25. Wash., 1843. 8°. (B 1499)
— DAVIS, G. Extract from [his] speech exhibiting the expenditures of M. Van Buren, *etc.* Wash., 1844. 8°. (B 1174)
— HUDSON, C. Speech, three million appropriation bill, Feb. 13. Wash., 1847. 8°. (B 1502)
— GIDDINGS, J. R. Speech, bill to supply the deficiency of appropriations for the year ending June 30, 1848; Feb. 28. Wash., 1848. 8°. (B 1502)
— ROCKWELL, J. A. Speech, review of the report of the Sec. of the Treasury, Mar. 1. Wash., 1848. 8°. (B 1502)
— VINTON, S. F. Speech, the loan bill, Feb. 8, 1848. Wash., 1848. 8°. (B 1502)
— BROOKS, J. Speech on the deficiency bill, March 20. Wash., 1852. 8°. (B 1506)
— BOSTON BOARD OF TRADE. Report on internal taxation. Boston, 1862. 8°. (E 127)
— COCHUT, A. Les finances et les banques des Etats-Unis. (*In* Revue d. D. Mondes, sept. 1862.)
— ESTEE, C. F. Excise tax law approved July 1, 1862; with amendments and with forms, *etc.* N. Y., 1863. 8°.
— REDFIELD, A. A. Hand-book of the U. S. tax law, July 1, 1862; with the amendments and notes. 2d ed. N. Y., 1863. 16°.
— TAXPAYERS' manual; acts of Cong. imposing taxes. N. Y., 1862. 8°. (E 90)
— U. S. *37th Cong. 1st, 2d sess.* Laws rel. to direct and excise taxes. Wash., 1862. 8°.
— WALKER, R. J. American finances and resources; 5 letters. London, 1863-64. 5 v. 8°.
— BOUTWELL, G. S. Manual of the direct and excise tax system. Boston, 1863. 8°.
— - *Same.* 4th ed., [with applications to the act of 1864]. Boston, 1864. 8°.
— NEW and complete tax-payers' manual. N. Y., 1863. 8°. (E 90)
— SHERMAN, J. Speech on the taxation of bank bills, Jan. 8. Wash., 1863. 8°. (B 1515)
— STETSON, A. W. Is our prosperity a delusion? Our national debt and currency. Boston, 1864. 12°.
— HILL, H. A. Report on stamping freight receipts; made to the [Boston] Board [of Trade], Sept. 19. Boston, 1864. 8°. (E 77, 127)
— U. S. *38th Cong. 1st sess.* Act to provide internal revenue; with the Senate's amendments. Wash., 1864. 8°.
— - The new internal revenue law approved June 30, 1864; comp. by H. E. Dresser. N. Y., 1864. 8°. (E 90)
— NEWCOMB, S. Examination of our financial policy during the rebellion. N. Y., 1865. 16°.
— WALKER, J. Les finances amér. après la guerre civile. (*In* Revue d. D. Mondes, juil. 1865.)
— U. S. *Commissioner of Internal Revenue.* Laws in force Aug. 1. Wash., 1866. 8°. (E 90)
— FERRIS, J. A. Financial economy of the U. S. San Francisco, 1867. 12°.
— GIBBONS, J. S. Public debt of the U. S., its organization, liquidation, *etc.* N. Y., 1867. 12°.
— TAXPAYERS' and assessors' guide; amendments to the internal revenue law. N. Y., 1867. 8°. (E 90)
— BARROT, G. H. O. Le budget des Etats-Unis. (*In* Revue d. D. Mondes, sept. 1868, juil. 1869.)
— POOR, H. V. Analysis of the debts of the U. S. (*In his* Manual of the R. R. of the U. S. 1869.)
— U. S. *41st Cong. 2d sess.* Internal revenue law passed July 13; with such other acts rel. to internal revenue as are now in effect; comp. by H. E. Dresser. N. Y., 1870. 8°. (E 90)
— WALKER, F. A., *and* ADAMS, H. The legal-tender act. (*In* Adams, C. F., *Jr.*, *and* H. Chapters of Erie. 1871.)

See also Bureau of Statistics (p. 3107): — *Treasury Dept.* (p. 3106, 07); — *also* **Bank of the U. S.**; — **Confederate States of America**; — **Continental money**; — **Indian trust bonds**; — **Repudiation**; — **Treasury notes**; — *also* **Massachusetts**; — **New England**; — **New Hampshire**; — **New York**; — **North Carolina.** *Currency*; — **Pennsylvania**; — **Rhode Island**; — **Texas.**

Fortification.

— U. S. *Dept. of War.* Report rel. to the fortification of the ports and harbours. [Wash., 1796.] 8°. (W 67)

— QUINCY, J. Speech, Apr. 15, bill for fortifying the ports and harbours. Bost., 1806. 8°. (B 429, 2519)
— EVANS, G. Speech, rel. to the failure of the bill making appropriations for fortifications, Jan. 28. Wash., 1836. 8°. (B 1496, 1721, 1813)

Genealogy.

See Biography (p. 3109, 10).

Geology.

— MEASE, J. Geological account of the U. S. Phila., 1807. 18°.
— MACLURE, W. Suite des observations sur la géologie des Etats-Unis. *n.t.p.* [1811.] 4°. (A 6)
— EATON, A. Index to the geology of the northern states. Leicester, 1818. 8°. (B 816)
— - *Same.* 2d ed. Troy, N. Y., 1820. 12°.
— ASSOC. OF AMER. GEOLOGISTS AND NATURALISTS. Reports of the 1st–3d meetings, 1840–42. Boston, 1843. 8°.
— AGASSIZ, L. Remarks upon the unconformability of the palæozoic formation of the U. S. (*In* Amer. Assoc. Proc., v. 6. 1852.)
— EMMONS, E. American geology. Part 1. Albany, 1854. 8°.

See also Alabama; — Alleghany Mts.; — Arkansas; — California; — Colorado; — Delaware; — Illinois; — Indiana; — Iowa; — Kentucky; — Louisiana; — Maine; — Massachusetts; — Michigan; — Minnesota. *Description*; — Mississippi. *Description*; — Missouri; — Nebraska; — New Hampshire. *State Geologist*; — New Jersey. *Geol. Survey* (p. 2112); — New Mexico; — New York; — North America; — Ohio. *Nat. hist.*; — Pennsylvania; — South Carolina; — Superior, Lake; — Tennessee; — Vermont; — Wisconsin; — Washington Territory.

Herpetology.

— HOLBROOK, J. E. North American herpetology; or, Description of the reptiles inhabiting the U. S. Phila., 1842. 5 v. 4°.

See also Massachusetts. *Commis. on Zoöl. and Bot. Survey* (p. 1891); — North America.

History.

— *Bibliography.* SUPPLEMENT to the 4th part of Dr. Priestley's lectures on history. New Haven, 1801. 8°. (B 643)
— - LUDEWIG, H. E. Literature of American local history. N. Y., 1846. 8°.

See also Massachusetts. *History* (p. 1899); — New York. *Agent, etc.* (p. 2118).

Comprehensive works.

— GOODRICH, C. A. History for schools; brought down to the present by W. H. Seavey. Boston, 1867. 8°.
— CIBO, S. F. Cenni storici sugli Stati Uniti, [-1865]. Poligno, 1865. 16°.
— FAY, T. S. Die Sklavenmacht; Blicke in die Geschichte der Ver. Staaten von Amerika [zu 1865]. Berlin, 1865. 8°.
— BIGELOW, J. Les Etats-Unis, leur histoire politique, *etc.*, [-1863]. Paris, 1863. 8°.
— LOEHNIS, H. Die Vereinigten Staaten von Amerika, [-1863]. Lpz., 1864. 8°.
— HOWITT, M. Popular history of the U. S. [to 1858]. London, 1859. 2 v. 8°.
— PATTON, J. H. History of the U.S., [to 1858]. N. Y., 1860. 8°.
— FIRST lessons in the hist. of the U. S.; by a practical teacher, [to 1855]. Bost., 1856. 12°.
— ELIOT, S. Manual of U. S. history, [to] 1850. Boston, 1857. 12°.
— WILLSON, M. History of the U. S., [to 1845]. 14th thous. N. Y., 1847. 12°.
— HOLGATE, J. B. Atlas of American history, [to 1842. Boston,] 1842. f°.
— MURRAY, H. The U. S. [to 1842]. Edin., 1844. 3 v. 16°. (Edin. cab. lib., v. 35–37.)
— SPARKS, J. Remarks on American history, to 1837. Boston, 1837. 8°. (B 1119)
— VAN BUREN, M. Inquiry into the origin and course of parties in the U. S., [to 1834]; ed. by his son. N. Y., 1867. 8°.
— TUTTLE, H. Historical catechism; important items in the hist. of the U. S., [to 1831]. 8th ed. Utica, 1835. 8°. (C 278)
— - *Same, called* Historical collection. Lowell, 1855. 8°. (C 278)
— HOLMES, A. American annals, to 1806 [1805]. Camb., 1805. 2 v. 8°.
— - *Same.* To 1826. 2d ed. Camb., 1829. 2 v. 8°.
— WILLARD, E. Hist. of the U. S., [to 1826]. 4th ed. N. Y., 1831. 8°.
— DUFEY DE L'YONNE, P. J. S. Résumé de l'hist. des révolutions de l'Amérique Septentrionale, to 1825. Paris, 1826. 2 v. 12°.
— BARBAROUX, C. O. L'histoire des Etats-Unis, [to 1824]; éd. revue et corrigé. Boston, 1832. 12°.
— GRIMSHAW, W. History of the U. S. to 1821. Revised ed. Phila., 1826. 12°.
— HILDRETH, R. History of the U. S., [to 1821]. N. Y., 1849–52. 6 v. 8°.
— HALE, S. History of the U. S., [to 1815]. *t.p.w.* [Keene, N. H., 1830.] 12°.
— - *Same.* To 1817. N. Y., [1840]. 2 v. 16°. (Harper's fam. lib., v. 119, 120.)
— HISTORY of the U. S.; by a citizen of Mass., [to 1815]. Keene, 1823. 12°.
— MCCULLOCH, J. Concise history of the U. S., till 1813. 4th ed. Phila., 1813. 12°.
— ROUX DE ROCHELLE, J. B. G. Etats-Unis d'Amérique, [to 1811]. Paris, 1853. 8°. (Univers.)
— BLUNT, J. Historical sketch of the formation of the confederacy with ref. to the jurisdiction over the Indian tribes, [to 1802]. N.Y., 1825. 8°.
— CALLENDER, J. T. Sketches of the hist. of America, [to 1797]. Phila., 1798. 8°.
— - *Another copy.* (B 396)
— CASS, L. Discourse before the Amer. Hist. Soc., [to 1789]. Wash., 1836. 8°. (B 939, 1121)
— WEBSTER, N. History of the U. S., [to 1789]. New Haven, 1832. 12°.
— WINTERBOTHAM, W. Hist. of the U. S., [to 1789]. (*In his* View of the U. S., *etc.*, v. 1. 1796.)
— BANCROFT, G. History of the U. S., to 1782, (Vol. 1, 7, 12th ed.) Boston, 1845, 37–75. 60–66. 9 v. 8°.
— - *Same.* (Vol. 1, 2, 15th ed., v. 3, 14th ed.) Boston, 1855, 54. 6 v. 8°.
— - CIRCOURT, *comte* A. Histoire des Etats-Unis, par Bancroft. Genève, 1846. 8°. (B 1601)
— HILLIARD D'AUBERTUIL. Essais hist. et polit. sur les Anglo-Américains, [to 1778]. Brux., 1781–82. 4 v. 8°.
— BINAUT, L. Les origines de la République des Etats-Unis et ses historiens, [-1776]. (*In* Revue d. D. Mondes, avr. 1856.)
— CARLIER, A. Histoire du peuple américain, à 1776. Paris, 1864. 2 v. 8°.
— TRUMBULL, B. History of the U. S., to 1765. Vol. 1. Boston, 1810. 8°.
— HAZARD, E. Historical col. of state papers, *etc.*, [to 1664]. Phila., 1792–94. 2 v. 4°.
— PELET DE LA LOZÈRE, J., *comte.* Précis de l'histoire des Etats-Unis, [1512–1844]. Paris, 1845. 8°.
— WALSH, R. Appeal from the judgments of Gr. Brit. resp. the U. S.; an hist. outline of their merits and wrongs as colonies, [1578–1818]. Phila., 1819. 8°.

— LOEHNIS, H. Die Vereinigten Staaten von Amerika, [1606–1864]. Lpz., 1864. 8°.
— NEUMANN, C. F. Geschichte der Vereinigten Staaten von Amerika, [1606–1861]. Berlin, 1863–66. 3 v. 8°.
— FERGUS, H. History of the U. S., [1606–1830]. London, 1830–32. 2 v. 16°. (Larder. Cab. cyc.)
— COOPER, *Rev.* —. History of N. A.; first settlement of Brit. colonies, their rise and progress, [1606–1783]. Phila., 1797. 12°.
— TUCKER, G. History of the U. S., [1607]–1841. Phila., 1856–57. 4 v. 8°.
— RICH, O. Hist. of the U. S., [1607–1833]. (*In his* General view of the U. S. 1833.)
— WALSH, R., *Jr.* An appeal from the judgments of Gr. Brit. resp. the U. S., [1607–1819]. Phila., 1819. 8°.
— RAMSAY, D. History of the U. S., 1607–1808; contin. by S. S. Smith. 2d ed. Phila., 1818. 3 v. 8°. (Universal hist., v. 10–12.)
— EBELING, C. D. [1614–1797.] *See, back, Description* (p. 3116).
— ASTIÉ, J. F. Histoire de la république des Etats-Unis, 1620–1860; préface par E. Laboulaye. Paris, 1865. 2 v. 8°.
— LABOULAYE, E. R. L. Hist. politique des Etats-Unis, 1620–1789. Paris, 1855–66. 3 v. 8°.
— HALIBURTON, T. C. Rule and misrule of the English in America, [1620–1783]. N. Y., 1851. 8°.
— WEBSTER, N. Hist. and geog. account of the U. S., [1634–1789]. 3d ed. *n.p.*, 1809. 12°. (Elements of useful knowl., v. 2.)
— CLUSKEY, M. W. Political text book, [1643–1860]. 13th ed. Phila., 1860. 8°.
— PARTRIDGE, J. A. The making of the American nation, [1670–1860]. London, 1866. 8°.
— ADAMS, J. Q. Jubilee of the Constitution, [1775–1839]; a discourse, Apr. 30. N. Y., 1839. 8°. (B 1428, 1655, 1697, 1819)
— LUDLOW, J. M. Sketch of the history of the U. S., from independence to secession, [1776–1861]; added, The struggle for Kansas; by T. Hughes. Camb., 1862. 8°.
— GREELEY, H. History of the struggle for slavery extension or restriction in the U. S., [1776–1856]; mainly compiled from the journals of Congress and other official records. N. Y., 1856. 8°.
— MOORE, F. Materials for hist. from original mss.; with notes and illlustrations, [1776–1782]. 1st ser. N. Y., 1861. 4°.
— WILLIAMS, E. Addresses and messages of the presidents of the U. S.; and history of their administrations, *etc.*, [1777–1846]. N. Y., 1846. 2 v. 8°.
— HALL, B. F. The republican party, 1796–1832. N. Y., 1856. 12°.

See also Chronology (p. 3112); — *and. forward, Naval history*; — *also* **American Party**; — **Democratic Party**; — **Whig Party**; — *also* **Anglo-American colonization**; — **Delaware River**; — **Mississippi River**; — **Mississippi Valley**; — **Northwest Territory**; — **Ohio River**; — **Plymouth Council.**

Revolution, and previous controversy.

— RAMSAY, D. History of the American Revolution, [to 1789]. Phila., 1789. 2 v. 8°.
— PRADT, D. D. de, *l'abbé.* Des colonies et de la rév. actuelle de l'Amérique, [–1778]. Paris, 1817. 2 v. 8°.
— - *Spanish.* De las colonias y de la revolucion actual de la América. Bord., 1817. 2 v. 8°.
— GRAHAM, J. History of the U. S., till the Declaration of independence, [to 1776]. London, 1836. 4 v. 8°.
— MARSHALL, J. History of the English colonies in America till their independence, [to 1776]. Phila., 1824. 8°.
— - *Same.* (*In his* Life of Washington, v. 1. 1804.)
— ABBOTT, J. American history: Revolt of the colonies, [to 1775]. N. Y., 1864. 16°.
— IMPARTIAL sketch of the various indulgences granted by Gr. Brit. to her colonies, upon which they have founded their presumption of soaring towards independence; by an officer, [to 1778]. Lond., 1778. 8°. (B 463)
— GORDON, W. History of the rise, progress, and establishment of independence of the U. S., [1558–1784]. London, 1788. 4 v. 8°.
— LOSSING, B. J. Seventeen hundred and seventy-six; or, The war of independence, [1598–1789]. N. Y., 1847. 8°.
— CHALMERS, G. Introduction to the history of the revolt of the American colonies, [1603–1760]. Boston, 1845. 2 v. 8°.
— GREENE, G. W. Historical view of the Amer. Revolution, [1607–1783]. Boston, 1865. 16°.
— LUCAS, S. On some preparatives of the American revolt, [1643–1776]. (*In his* Secularia. 1862.)
— THORNTON, J. W. Pulpit of the American Revolution, [1750–83]. Boston, 1860. 8°.
— DRAYTON, J. Memoirs of the Amer. Revolution, [1753]–76. Charleston, 1821. 2 v. 8°.
— MAYER, C. J. de. Les ligues achéenne, suisse, et hollandoise et révolution des Etats-Unis comparées ensemble; [1754–84]. Genève, 1787. 2 v. 12°.
— GRIFFITH, W. Historical notes of the colonies and the Revolution, 1754–75. Burlington, N. J., 1843. 8°.
— ADAMS, J. History of the dispute with America from 1754–74. London, 1784. 8°. (B 637, 1638)
— - *Dutch.* Geschiedenis van het geschil tusschen Groot Britannie en Amer. Amsterdam, 1782. 8°. (B 464)
— SNOWDEN, R. The Columbiad; a poem on the Amer. war, [1755–81]. Phila., 1795. 12°. (W 46)
— - *Same.* (*In his* Amer. Revolution. 179–.)
— SEVENTY-SIX-SOCIETY. Publications, [1757–87]. Phila., 1855–57. 4 v. 8°.
— GRENVILLE, G. Conference between G. and the colony agents, 1762. (*In* **Mass. Hist. Soc.** Col., v. 9. 1804.)
— PITKIN, T. Political and civil history of the U. S., 1763–97. New Haven, 1828. 2 v. 8°.
— LENDRUM, J. History of the Amer. Revolution, [1763–89]. Boston, 1795. 2 v. 12°.
— - *Same.* Trenton, 1811. 2 v. (v. 2 w.). 12°.
— DÉMEUNIER, J. W. Essai sur les Etats-Unis, [1763–84]. Paris. 1786. 4°. (A 27)
— - *Same.* (*In his* Economie politique, v. 2. 1786.)
— ELSNER, H. Befreiungskampf der nordamerikanischen Staaten, [1763–83]. Stuttg., 1835. 8°.
— WILSON, S. F. History of the Amer. Revolution, [1763–83]. 3d ed. Balt., 1838. 12°.
— STEDMAN, C. History of the origin, *etc.*, of the American war, [1763–82]. London, 1794. 2 v. 4°.
— RAYNAL, G. T. F., *l'abbé.* Révolution de l'Amérique, [1763–81]. Londres, 1781. 8°.
— - *Same.* La Haye, 1781. 8°. (B 615)
— - *Dutch.* Staatsomwenteling van Amerika. Amst., 1781. 8°.
— - *Eng.* The Rev. of America. Lond., 1781. 12°.
— - *Same.* Edin., 1782. 12°. (C 219)
— - *Same.* Salem, 1782. 8°. (C 321)
— - *Same.* 2d ed. Phila., 1782. 8°. (B 472)
— PAINE, T. Letter to Abbé Raynal on the affairs of North America. Phila., 1782. 8°. (B 592, 2503, W 23)

— History of the war in Amer. between Gr. Brit. and her colonies, [1763]-78. Dublin, 1779-85. 3 v. 8°.

— Murray, J. Impartial history of the present war in Amer., *etc.*, 1763-78. Newcastle upon Tyne, [1781?]. 2 v. 8°.
Note. Written for him by J. Neal and Mr. Watkins.

— Chas, J., *and* Lebrun, —. Histoire politique et philosoph. de la Révolution de l'Amérique Septentrionale, [1764-83]. Paris, [1801]. 8°.

— Longchamps, P. de. Histoire des évènemens de la dernière guerre, [1764-83]. Amst., 1785. 3 v. 12°.

— - *Same.* 3e éd. Amst., 1787. 3 v. 12°.

— Warren, M. History of the Amer. Revolution, [1764-83]. Boston, 1805. 3 v. 8°.

— Shepherd, W. History of the Amer. Rev. [1764-82]. 1st Amer. ed. Bost., 1832. 12°.

— Almon, J. Collection of papers rel. to the dispute between Gr. Brit. and America, 1764-75; [the 'Prior documents']. Lond., 1777. 8°.

— History of the origin of the war between Gr. Brit. and her colonies, 1764-74. Lond., 1780. 8°. (C 180)

— Allen, P. Hist. of the Amer. Rev., [1764-83]. Balt., 1822. 2 v. 8°.

— Gentz, F. von. Origin of the Amer. Rev. compared with the French Revolution, [1765-83]; tr. [by J. Q. Adams]. Phila., 1800. 8°.

— Botta, C. Storia del guerra dell' independenza degli Stati Uniti d'America, [1765-83]. 3a ed. Milan, 1819. 4 v. 8°.

— - *Eng.* History of the war of the independence of the U. S.; tr. by G. A. Otis. Phila., 1820. 2 v. 8°.

— - *Same.* 8th ed. New Haven, 1838. 2 v. 8°.

— - *French.* Histoire de la guerre de l'indépendence des Etats-Unis; tr. par L. de Sevelinges. Paris, 1812-13. 4 v. 8°.

— Moore, F. Songs and ballads of the Amer. Revolution, [1765-83]. N. Y., 1856. 12°.

— Hutchinson, T. Representations of Gov. H. and others, *etc.*; with resolves of the two Houses, [1767-69]. Boston, 1773. 8°.

— - *Another copy.* (B 610)

— - *Same.* Copy of letters sent to Gr. Brit. by H. and others, which have been returned to Amer. and laid before the Ho. of Reps. Boston, 1773. 8°. (B 611)

— - *Same.* Letters of Gov. H. and Lieut. Gov. Oliver, *etc.* London, 1774. 8°. (B 467)

— - *Same.* Letters, *etc.* 2d ed. Lond., 1774. 8°. (B 385)

— Soulés, F. Histoire des troubles de l'Amérique anglaise, [1768-83]. Paris, 1787. 4 v. 8°.

— Eddis, W. Letters from America, 1769-77. London, 1792. 8°.

— Stansbury, J., *and* Odell, J. Loyal verses rel. to the Amer. Rev., [1771-84]; ed. by W. Sargent. Albany, 1860. 4°. (Munsell's hist. ser., v. 7.)

— Niles, H. Principles and acts of the Revolution in America, [1771-83]. Balt., 1822. 8°.

— Belknap, J. The Foresters; an American tale, [1771-76]. 2d ed. Boston, 1796. 16°.
'An historical allegory, in which the events of the Revolution are dramatized'.

— Andrews, J. Letters, 1772-76; compiled with introd. by W. Sargent. Camb., 1866. 8°.
Note. From Mass. Hist. Soc. Proc., 1864-65.

— Snowden, R. The American Revolution, [1773-83], written in scriptural or ancient historical style. Balt., [179-]. 12°.

— Hamilton, J. C. Hist. of the U. S. as traced in the writings of A. Hamilton and his cotemporaries, [1774-1804]. (Vol. 7, 2d ed.) N. Y., 1857-64. 7 v. 8°.

— Garden, A. Anecdotes of the Revolution, [1774-86]. 2d ser. Charleston, 1828. 12°.

— American archives; a documentary hist. of the colonies. 4th ser., 5th ser., vol. 1-3: [1774-76]. Wash., 1827-51. 9 v. f°.

— Washington, G. Official letters to Congress during the war between the Colonies and Gr. Brit., [1775-78]. London, 1795. 2 v. 8°.

— - *Same.* Boston, 1795. 2 v 8°.

— - *Same.* Boston, 1795. 2 v. 12°.

— Sparks, J. Correspondence of the American Revolution, [1775-97]. Boston, 1853. 4 v. 8°.

— Remembrancer, The; 1775-84. London, *J. Almon*, 1775-84. 17 v. 8°.

— Curwen, S. Journal and letters, 1775-84; added, biog. notices of loyalists by H. A. Ward. N.Y., 1842. 8°.

— Andrews, J. History of the war with America, France, Spain, and Holland, 1775-83. London, 1785-86. 4 v. 8°.

— Boucher, —. Hist. de la dernière guerre entre la Grande-Bretagne et les Etats-Unis, 1775-83. Paris, 1787. 4°.

— Continental and militia troops on the American war, 1775-83. (*In* New Hamp. Hist. Soc. Col., v. 1. 1824.)

— Kapp, F. Der Soldatenhandel deutscher Fürsten nach Amerika, 1775-83. Berlin, 1864. 8°.

— Lossing, B. J. Field book of the Amer. Revolution, [1775-83]. N. Y., 1851-52. 2 v. 8°.

— Moultrie, W. Memoirs of the Amer. Revolution, [1775-83]. N. Y., 1802. 2 v. 8°.

— Joly de St. Valier, —. Histoire raisonnée de la dernière guerre, [1775-83]. Liège, 1783. 8°.

— Judd, *Rev.* S. Moral review of the Revolutionary war, [1775-83]; discourse. Hallowell, 1842. 8°. (B 1184)

— Saffell, W. T. R. Records of the Revolutionary War, [1775-83]. N. Y., 1858. 12°.

— Smith, C. American war, 1775-83. N. Y., 1797. 8°.

— Curtis, G. T. Report of committee on exchange of prisoners during the Amer. Revolution, [1775-82]. (*In* Mass. Hist. Soc. Proc., 1860-62.)

— Revolutionary correspondence, 1775-82. (*In* Rhode Island Hist. Soc. Col., v. 6. 1867.)

— American historical and literary curiosities, [1775-81]; fac-similes of documents rel. to the Revolution, *etc.*; col. and ed. by J. J. Smith and J. F. Watson. No. 1, 2. Phila., 1847. 2 v. 4°.

— Moore, F. Diary of the Amer. Revolution from newspapers, *etc.*, [1775-81]. N. Y., 1860. 2 v. 8°.

— Detail and conduct of the Amer. war under Gens. Gage, Howe, and Burgoyne, [1775-80]. 3d ed. London, 1780. 8°. (B 462)

— Howe, W. Narrative rel. to his conduct during command of the king's troops in North America, [1775-78]. 3d ed. London, 1781. 4°. (A 27)

— Hall, *Capt.* History of the civil war in America, 1775-77. Vol. 1. 2d ed. London, 1780. 8°.

— Allen, T. Inquiry into the views, principles, *etc.*, of the leading men in the origination of our Union. [No. 1: 1774-75.] Boston, 1845. 8°. (B 1501)

— - *Same.* No. 3. [1775-76.] Bost., 1846. 8°. (B 1601)

— Carter, W. Genuine detail of the several engagements, *etc.* of the royal and American armies, 1775-76. London, 1784. 4°. (A 20)

— Remer, J. A. Amerikanisches Archiv, [1775-76]. Braunschweig, 1777-78. 3 v. 8°.

— D'Bernicre, H. Gen. Gage's instructions of 22 Feb. 1775. Boston, 1779. 8°. (B 466)

— Henshaw, *Col.* W. Orderly book, Apr. 20 - Sept. 26, 1775. Reprint from the Mass. Hist. Soc., Oct. 1876. Boston, 1877. 8°.

— VOYAGE to Boston, A; poem. Phila., 1775. 8°. (B 469)
— WITT, C. de. La Rév. Amér. et la Rév. Française, [1776-89]. (*In* Revue d. D. Mondes, avr. 1857.)
— SPARKS, J. Diplomatic correspondence of the Amer. Revolution, [1776-84]. Boston, 1829-30. 12 v. 8°.
— TRESCOT, W. H. Diplomacy of the Revolution, [1776-84]. N. Y., 1852. 12°.
— EELKING, M. von. Die deutschen Hülfstruppen im nordamerikanischen Befreiungskriege, 1776-83. Hannover, 1863. 2 v. 8°.
— STOKES, A. View of the constitution of the British colonies in N. A. and the W. I. at the time of the civil war [with] such alterations as have happened since that time, [1776-83]. London, 1783. 8°.
— TAMMANY SOC. Account of the interment of the remains of 11,500 American seamen, soldiers, and citizens, victims to the cruelties of the British on board prison ships, [1776-82]. N. Y., 1808. 8°. (B 407)
— ANBUREY, T. [1776-81.] *See, back, Description* (p. 3115).
— PFISTER, F. Der nordamerikanische Unabhängigkeits-Krieg, [1776-79]. 1r Bd. Kassel, 1864. 8°.
— GALLOWAY, J. Letters on the conduct of the war in the middle colonies, [1776-78]. 2d ed. London, 1779. 8°. (B 638, 1635)
— - Reply to the observations of Sir W. Howe on 'Letters to a nobleman', [1776-78]. London, 1780. 8°. (B 702)
— - *Same*. Phila., 1787. 8°. (B 700)
Note. The latter has two title pages; the first reading: 'A short history of the war in America during the command of Sir W. Howe', *etc*.
— EXAMINATION of J. Galloway before the Ho. of Commons [rel. to events, 1776-78]. 2d ed. London, 1780. 8°. (B 1635)
— *Same*. Ed. by E. Balch. Phila., 1855. 8°. (Seventy-Six Soc.)
— AMERICAN military pocket atlas. London, [1776]. 8°.
— LIST of the minority in the Ho. of Com. who voted against the bill to repeal the stamp act. Paris, 1766. 8°.
— *Another copy*. (B 371)
— STEELE, J. Account of a late conference on occurrences in America. London, 1766. 8°. (B 371, 373)
— ANDREWS, J. Map of the seat of war. London, 1777.
— BURGOYNE, J. Orderly book, 1777; ed. by E. B. O'Callaghan. Albany, *Munsell*, 1860. 4°.
— - State of the exped. from Canada, [1777]. London, 1780. 4°.
— - *Another copy*. (A 21)
— REMARKS on Gen. Burgoyne's state of the expedition from Canada, [1777]. London, 1780. 8°. (B 632)
— LYMAN, T., *Jr*. The diplomacy of the U. S.; acc. of for. relations, 1778-1814. Boston, 1826. 8°.
— - *Same*. 1778-[1828]. 2d ed. Boston, 1828. 2 v. 8°.
— WASHINGTON, G. Revolutionary orders, 1778-82; from the mss. of J. Whiting. N. Y., London, 1844. 8°.
— HISTORY of the war in America between Gr. Brit. and her colonies, [1778-79]. Vol. 2. London, *printed*, Boston, *reprinted* 1780. 16°. (C 152)
— HARTLEY, D. Letters on the American war, [1778.] 8th ed. London, 1779. 8°. (B 348)
— LETTER to Ld. G. Germaine, giving an account of the origin of the dispute between Great Britain and her colonies. London, 1778. 8°. (B 388)
— VIEW of the evidence rel. to the war under Sir W. Howe, Lord Howe, and Gen. Burgoyne. London, [1779]. 8°. (B 366)
— GALLOWAY, J. [1780.] *See, forward, Politics*.
— HOUGH, F. B. Northern invasion of Oct. 1780; expeditions from Canada. N. Y., 1866. 8°. (Bradford Club, no. 6.)

— BRIEF review of the campaign in North America, 1781; to justify Sir H. Clinton, and to place the character of Cornwallis in a fair light; by a gentleman in Nova Scotia. Nova Scotia, 1789. 12°. (C 158)
— CLINTON, *Sir* H. Narrative rel. to his conduct in N. America, 1781. 5th ed. London, 1783. 8°. (B 392)
— DWIGHT, T. Sermon, Northampton, 28 Nov. 1781; capture of the Brit. army under Cornwallis. Hartford, [1781]. 8°. (B 914, C 43)
— LOOSJES, A. Gedenkzuil ter gelegenheid der vry-verklaaring van Noord-America. Amst., 1782. 8°.

Personal narratives.

— HOW, D. Diary in the American Revolution, [1775-77]. Morrisania, 1865. 8°. (Dawson's gleanings, v. 4.)
— PRICE, E. Diary, May 23, 1775 - Aug. 16, 1776. MS.
— - *Same*. (*In* Mass. Hist. Soc. Proc., 1863-64.)
— BLOODGOOD, S. DeW. The sexagenary; or, Reminiscences of the Amer. Revolution, [1776-83]. Albany, 1866. 8°.
— RIEDESEL, F. C. L. Berufs-Reise nach America, 1776-83. 2e Aufl. Berlin, 1801. 12°.
— - *Eng*. Letters and mem. rel. to the war of American Independence; tr. [by J. Wallenstein]. N. Y., 1827. 12°.
— - *Same*. Tr. by W. L. Stone. Albany, 1867. 8°.
— LETTER from an officer at N. Y., to a friend in London. London, 1777. 8°. (B 674)
— DEUX-PONTS, *Count* G. de. My campaigns in Amer., 1780-82; tr. from the Fr., with introd. and notes by S. A. Green. Bost., 1868. 8°.

See also Barnstable Co.; — Boston. *Massacre* (p. 343); — Concord, *Mass.*; — Connecticut (HINMAN, p. 634); — Georgia (MOULTRIE) p. 1129; — Illinois (CLARKE) p. 1495; — Maine (KIDDER) p. 1840; — Maryland (BALCH) p. 1883; — Massachusetts. *Convention of* 1779-80 (p. 1891); — Mecklenburg Co.; — New Hampshire. *Legislature* (KIDDER) p. 2108, 2109; — New Jersey. *Governor* (HAVEN) p. 2112; — New York (NEW YORK) p. 2117; — North Carolina (MACKENZIE) p. 2152; — Pennsylvania (WESTCOTT) p. 2286; — Penobscot; — Quebec (MELVIN) p. 2451; — Queen's Co., *N. Y.*; — Rhode Island (COWELL) p. 2508; — Savannah; — South Carolina. *Provincial Cong.* (DRAYTON, GIBBES) p. 2812; — Suffolk Co., N. Y.; — Vermont. *Constitution of* 1775; — Virginia, *Convention*, 1775, *Convention*, 1776, *Gen. Assembly*, *Senate* (GILPIN); — Wallabout Bay; — Williamsburg; —
also Adams, J.; — Allen, E.; — André, *Maj*. J.; — Andros, T.; — Arnold, B.; — Barton, *Brig. Gen.* W.; — Bigelow, *Col.* T.; — Bland, T.; — Burgoyne, *Sir* J.; — Cornwallis, C., 1*st Marquis*; — Everheart, L.; — Franklin, B.; — Graham, S.; — Graves, W.; — Greene, *Maj. Gen.* N.; — Heath, W.; — Henry, P.; — Howe, R., 1*st Earl Howe*; — Howe, *Maj. Gen.* R.; — Howland, J.; — Jones, J. P.; — Lafayette, M. J. P. R. Y. G. de M., *marq.* de; — Landais, P.; — Lee, A.; — Lee, *Maj. Gen.* C.; — Lee, R. H.; — Leslie, *Gen.* A.; — Morgan, J., *M.D.*; — North, F., 2*d Earl of Guilford*; — Putnam, P.; — Steuben, T. W. A. H. F., *Baron*; — Washington, G.; — Woodhull, N.; — *also* American loyalists; — Bunker Hill battle; — Lexington, *Mass.*, Battle of; — Martyrs to the Rev.; — Olive Branch, *ship*; — Rainbow, *ship*; — Stamp act; — *also* Authentic narrative of facts rel. to the exchange of prisoners taken at the Cedars, [1776]; — Carroll, C. (Journal during his visit to Canada, 1776); — Livermore, D. (Journal of the march of Gen. Poor's brigade on the western exped., 1779); — Mauduit, I. (Remarks upon Gen. Howe's acct. of the proc. on Long Island, 1776); — Simcoe, J. G. (History of the operations of the Queen's Rangers, 1777-83).
also the following fictitious works: Alfieri, V. (America libera); — G., L. C. D. L. (L'Amér. délivrée); — Campbell, T. (Gertrude of Wyoming); — Child, L. M. (The rebels); — Cooper, J. F.; — Dunlap, W. (André); — Emmons, L. (Battle of Bunker's Hill); — Freneau, P. (Poems); — Hopkinson, F. (Battle of the kegs); — Kennedy, J. P. (Horseshoe Robinson); — Kotzebue, A. F. F. v. (Die Quäker); — Lord, W. W. (André); — Moore, F. (Songs and ballads of the Rev.); — Postel, K. (Der Legitime et die Republikaner); — Read, T. B. (Wagoner of the Alleghanies); — Sedgwick, C. M. (The Linwoods); — Thompson, D. P. (The rangers); — Trumbull, J. (McFingal).

For accounts of the action of the Indians in the Revolution *see* **Indians** (p. 1511).

1783, *etc.*

— SULLIVAN, W. Familiar letters on public characters and public events, **1783-1815**. Boston, 1834. 12°.

— TRUE picture of the U. S.; brief statement of [its] conduct towards Gr. Britain, 1783-[1807]. London, 1807. 8°. (B 671)

— COBBETT, W. Porcupine's works, [1783-1801]. *See, forward, Politics.*

— BRADFORD, A. History of the Federal government, **1789-1839**. Boston, 1840. 8°.

— GIBBS, G. Memoir of the administration of Washington and Adams; ed. from papers of O. Wolcott, [**1789-1801**]. N. Y., 1846. 2 v. 8°.

— TRESCOT, W. H. Diplomatic hist. of the administration of Washington and Adams, 1789-1801. Boston, 1857. 8°.

— WISE, H. A. Seven decades of union, **1790-1862**; memoir of J. Tyler. Phila., 1872 [1871]. 8°.

— LEE, W. Les Etats Unis et L'Angleterre, [**1791-1814**]. Bordeaux, 1814. 8°.

— HAMILTON, J. A. Reminiscences; or, Men and events during three quarters of a century, [**1793-1866**]. N. Y., 1869. 8°.

— GEBHARDT, A. G. Actes et mém. conc. les négotiations entre la France et les Etats-Unis, **1793-1800**. Londres, 1807. 3 v. 12°.

— PICKERING, T., *and* ADET, P. A. Review of the administration, 1793-[97]. Bost., 1797. 8°. (B 525)

— MONROE, J. View of the conduct of the executive in affairs with France, **1794-96**. Phila., 1797. 8°.

— - *Another copy.* (B 1079)

— TRACY, U. Scipio's Reflections on Munroe's 'View of the conduct of the executive'. Boston, 1798. 12°.

— - *Other copies.* (B 133, 741)

— - *Same.* Reflections, *etc.*, under the signature of Scipio; [with add.]. *n. p.*, *n. d.* 8°. (B 597)

— CALLENDER, J. T. American annual register; hist. memoirs of the U. S. for **1796**. Phila., 1797. 8°.

— - *Another copy.* (B 395)

— - History of the United States for 1796. Phila., 1797. 8°.

Note. Continuation of Amer. annual register.

— HAMILTON, A. Observations on certain documents in nos. 5, 6 of the history of U. S. for 1796 [by J. T. Callender]. Phila., 1800. 8°. (B 640, 1842)

— - *Same.* Phila., 1800. 8°. (B 354)

— - *Same.* N. Y., 1865. 8°. (Hamilton Club ser., no. 2.)

— WOOD, J. History of the administration of J. Adams, [**1797-1801**]. N. Y., 1802. 8°.

— HALL, B. F. The republican party and its presidential candidates, [**1800-51**]. N. Y., 1856. 12°.

— CHEETHAM, J. Narrative of the suppression by Col. Burr of [Wood's] 'History of the administration of J. Adams'; added, biography of Jefferson and Hamilton, with strictures on J. Adams and C. C. Pinckney, by a citizen of N. Y. N. Y., **1802**. 8°.

— - *Another copy.* (B 1885)

— - *Same.* 2d ed. N. Y., 1802. 8°. (B 622)

— LIFE of J. C. Calhoun, presenting a condensed history of pol. events, 1811-43. N. Y., 1843. 8°. (B 1666)

— REGNAULT, E. G. S. O., *and* LABAUME, J. Suite des Etats-Unis [par Roux de Rochelle, 1812-46]. (*In* Regnault, C. Histoire des Antilles. 1849.)

See also Naval history (p. 3141); — *also* **Burr, A.**; — **Safford, W. H.** (Blennerhassett papers); — *also* **Shay's Rebellion**; — *also* **Chesapeake,** *U. S. frigate.*

War of 1812-15.

— ARMSTRONG, J. Notices of the war of 1812. N. Y., 1840. 2 v. 12°.

— ATHERTON, W. Narrative of the suffering and defeat of the N. W. army under Gen. Winchester, 1842-44. Frankfort, Ky., 1842. 12°.

— BAINES, E. History of the late war; with app. by E. H. Cummins. Balt., 1820. 12°.

— BRANNAN, J. Official letters of military and naval officers of U. States, 1812-15. Wash., 1823. 8°.

— COBBETT, W. Letters on the late war between the U. S. and Gr. Brit., *etc.*, [1811-15]. N. Y., 1815. 8°.

— - Glimpse of the Amer. victories on land, on the lakes, and on the ocean. (*In his* Britannia. 1815.)

— DAVIS, P. M. Authentic hist. of the late war, [1812-15]. N. Y., 1836. 12°.

— DWIGHT, T. History of the Hartford Convention; with review of the policy which led to the war of 1812, [1804-14]. N. Y., 1833. 8°.

— EXPOSITION of the causes and character of the late war with Gr. Britain. Balt., 1815. 8°. (B 1492)

Note. Attributed to Secretary Dallas. — *Stevens.*

— FAY, H. A. Official accounts of all the battles by sea and land of the war of 1812-15. N. Y., 1817. 8°.

— GILLELAND, J. C. History of the late war between the U. S. and Gr. Brit. 2d ed. Balt., 1817. 12°.

— - *Same.* Abridged ed. Balt., 1817. 8°. (C 58)

— GLEIG, G. R. Campaigns of the British army at Washington and New Orleans, 1814-15. London, 1821. 8°.

— GRIMSHAW, W. Original history of the late war between the U. S. and Gr. Brit. (*In* Baines, E. Hist. of the wars of the French Revolution, v. 2. 1835.)

— HISTORY of the American war of 1812. 2d ed. Phila., 1816. 12°.

— HULL, W. Memoirs of the campaigns of the north western army of the U. S., 1812. Boston, 1824. 8°.

— - *Another copy.* (W 3)

— INGERSOLL, C. J. Historical sketch of the 2d war between the U. S. and Gr. Brit. Phila., 1845-53. 2 ser. in 4 v. 8°.

— INGRAHAM, E. D. Sketch of the events which preceded the capture of Washington by the British, 1814. Phila., 1849. 8°.

— IZARD, G. Official corresp. rel. to operations of the army under Gen. I., 1814-15. Phila., 1816. 8°.

— JAMES, W. Full and correct acc. of the military occurrences of the late war. London, 1818. 2 v. 8°.

— JAY, W. Table of killed and wounded in the war of 1812. (*In* **New York Hist. Soc.** Col., ser. 2, v. 2. 1849.)

— LATHROP, J. Compendious history of the late war, 1811-15. Boston, 1815. 8°.

— - *Another copy.* (A 1)

— LATOUR, A. L. Historical mem. of the war in West Florida and Louisiana, 1814-15. Phila., 1816. 8°.

— LOSSING, B. J. Pictorial field-book of the war of 1812. N. Y., 1869. 8°.

— MCAFEE, R. B. History of the late war in the western country. Lexington, 1816. 8°.

— PALMER, T. H. Historical register of the U. S., 1812-14. (Vol. 1, 2, 2d ed.) Phila., 1814-16. 4 v. (v. 3 w.). 8°.

— POETICAL account of the American campaigns of 1812, 1813; with sketches of party politics [of] the U. S. Halifax, 1815. 8°.

— Stuart, J. Refutation of aspersions on Stuart's 'Three years in N. Amer.' London, 1834. 8°. (B 1082)

— U. S. *War Dept.* Message from the President transm. a letter from the Sec. of War [on] the failure of the arms of the U. S. on the northern frontier, [1813-14]. Albany, 1814. 2 pt. 18°.

— U. S. *13th Cong. 1st sess.* Barbarities of the enemy exposed, a report of the committee appointed to inquire into the manner in which the war has been waged; and the docs. Worcester, 1814. 12°.

See also Canada (Veritas) p. 465; — Conn. *Gen. Assem.* (p. 655); — Dartmoor Prison; — Erie, Lake, Battle of; — Ghent; — Kentucky (Darnell), p. 1621; — McHenry, Fort; — New Hampshire. *Governor* (p. 2108); — New Jersey, (Alden) p. 2112; — New Orleans; — Niagara Falls; — Washington; — *also* Hartford Convention; — *also* Boyd, J. P.; — Hull, *Brig. Gen.* W; — *also* Detroit, *brig.*; — *also* the following fictitious works: Emmons, R. (Fredoniad); — Fidfaddy, F. A. (Adventures of Uncle Sam in search after his lost honor); — Hildreth, R. (White slave); — Wars of the Gulls.

1815-61.

— Onis. L. de. Memoir upon the negotiations between Spain and the U. S. which led to the treaty of 1819, [1815-19]; tr. by T. Watkins. Wash., 1821. 8°. (B 535)

— Benton, T. H. Thirty years in the U. S. Senate, 1820-50. N. Y., 1854-56. 2 v. 8°.

— Political mirror; or, Review of Jacksonism, [1824-35]. N. Y., 1835. 12°.

— Chevalier, M. De la présidence du gén. Jackson et du choix de son successeur, [1828-36]. (*In* Revue d. D. Mondes, oct. 1836.)

— Mayo, R. Political sketches of eight years in Washington, [1829-37]. [Pt. 1.] Balt., 1839. 8°.

— Ramirez, J. F. Memorias, negoc., y doc. para servir a la historia de las diferencias que han suscitado entre Mexico y los Estados-Unidos los tenedores del antiguo privilegio por el istmo de Tehuantepec, [1841-53]. Mexico, 1853. 8°.

— Palfrey, J. G. A chapter of Amer. history; five years' progress of the slave power, [1845-50]. Boston, 1852. 8°. (B 1479, 1504)

Chase, L. B. History of the Polk administration, [1845-49]. N. Y., 1850. 8°.

— Hughes, T. The struggle for Kansas, [1853-61]. (*In* Ludlow, J. M. Sketch of the history of the U. S. 1862.)

— Laugel, A. Une campagne des Amér. contre les Mormons, [1857-58]. (*In* Revue d. D. Mondes, sept. 1859.)

See also Florida (Florida) p. 1003.

☞ For the Mexican war *see* Mexico (p. 1968).

Civil war (and previous controversy), 1860-65.

— *Bibliography.* Bartlett, J. R. Literature of the rebellion; with works on American slavery. Boston, 1866. 8°.

— - Kelly, J. List of pamphlets, sermons, and addresses on the civil war in the U. S., 1861-66. (*In his* American catal. 1866.)

— *Chronology.* Dresser, H. E. The battle record of the American rebellion, [1860-62]. N. Y., [1863]. 8°.

— Eyma, X. Les trente-quatre étoiles de l'Union Américaine, [-1861]. Paris, 1862. 2 v. 8°.

— Milliroux, J. F. Conféderation Américaine, [-1861]. Paris, 1861. 8°.

— Shaffner, T. P. War in America, the origin and cause, [to 1861]. London, [1862]. 8°.

— Massie, J. W. *See, back, Description* (p. 3118).

— Dye, J. S. History of the plots and crimes of the great conspiracy, [1776-1865]. N. Y., [1866]. 8°.

— Greeley, H. The American conflict; a hist. of the rebellion, [1776-1865]. Hartford, 1864-66. 2 v. 8°.

— Giddings, J. R. History of the rebellion; its authors and causes, [1776-1862]. N. Y., 1864. 8°.

— Anneke, F. Der zweite Freiheitskampf der Vereinigten Staaten von Amerika. 1r Band: [1776-1861]. Frankfurt a. M., 1861. 16°.

— Ellison, T. Slavery and secession in America; historical and economical, [1776-1861]. London, [1861]. 8°.

— Fowler, W. C. The sectional controversy, [1776-1861]. N. Y., 1863. 8°.

— Lunt, G. Origin of the late war, [1776-1861]. N. Y., 1866. 8°.

— Cluskey, M. W. Political text-book for politicians, *etc.*, [1776-1860]. 13th ed. Phila., 1860. 8°.

— Foote, H. S. War of the rebellion, [1784-1865]. N. Y., 1866. 12°.

— Noel, B. W. The rebellion in America, [1787-1863]. London, 1863. 8°.

— Jones, W. D. Mirror of modern democracy, 1825-61. N. Y., 1864. 12°.

— Whitney, L. H. History of the war for the preservation of the Federal Union. Vol. 1: [1830-61]. Phila., 1863. 8°.

— Botts, J. M. The great rebellion, [1832-65]. N. Y., 1866. 12°.

— Buchanan, J. Mr. Buchanan's administration, [1857-61]. N. Y., 1866. 8°.

— Hopkins, J. B. The fall of the confederacy, [1860-67]. London, 1867. 16°.

— Guernsey, A. H., *and* Alden, H. M. Harper's pictorial history of the great rebellion, [1860-66]. Pt. 1, [2. N. Y., 1866-67.] 2 v. f°.

— Balme, J. R. Synopsis of the Amer. war, [1860-65]. London, 1865. 16°.

— Cortambert, L., *and* Tranaltos, F. de. Histoire de la guerre civile américaine, 1860-65. Paris, 1867. 2 v. 8°.

— Fay, T. S. Die Sklavenmacht; Blicke in die Geschichte der Vereinigten Staaten von Amerika zur Erklärung der Rebellion, 1860-65. Berlin, 1865. 8°.

— Goddard, S. A. American rebellion; letters, 1860-65. London, 1870. 8°.

— Kettell, T. P. History of the great rebellion, [1860-65]. Hartford, 1866. 8°.

— Lossing, B. J. Pictorial history of the civil war, [1860-65]. Phila., 1866-68. 3 v. 8°.

— Moore, F. Anecdotes, poetry, and incidents of the war, 1860-65. N. Y., 1867. 8°.

— - Rebellion record; a diary of American events, [1860-65]. N. Y., 1861-68. 11 v. 8°.

— - *Same.* Supplementary vol., pt. 1: Spirit of the pulpit. N.Y., 1861. 8°.

— - *Same.* Supplement. Vol. 1. N. Y., 1869. 8°.

— Pollard, E. The lost cause; a southern history, [1860-65]. N. Y., 1866. 8°.

— McPherson, E. Political history of the U. S., 1860-64. Wash., 1864. 8°.

— - *Same.* 2d ed. Wash., 1865. 8°.

— Brownlow, W. G. Sketches of the rise, progress, and decline of secession, [1860-62]. Phila., 1862. 12°.

— Headley, J. T. The great rebellion. Vol. 1: [1860-62]. Hartford, 1863. 8°.

— Halstead, M. Caucuses of 1860; history of the conventions of the presidential campaign. Columbus, 1860. 8°.

— Abbott, J. S. C. Heroic deeds, [1861-65]. (*In* Harper's mag., v. 30-34. 1864-67.)
— Bernard, M. Historical acc. of the neutrality of Gr. Brit. during the Amer. civil war, [1861-65]. London, 1870. 8°.
— Bowman, S. M., *and* Irwin, R. B. Sherman and his campaigns, [1861-65]. N. Y., 1865. 8°.
— Cooke, J. E. Wearing of the gray, [1861-65]. N. Y., 1867. 8°.
— Coynart, R. de. Précis de la guerre des Etats-Unis, [1861-65]. Paris, 1867. 8°.
— Crawford, J. M. Mosby and his men, [1861-65]. N. Y., 1867. 12°.
— Draper, J. W. History of the Amer. civil war, [1861-65]. N. Y., 1867-70. 3 v. 8°.
— Harrison, W. Pickett's men; a fragment of war history, [1861-65]. N. Y., 1870. 12°.
— Kratz, A. La guerre d'Amérique; résumé des opérations, [1861-65]. Paris, 1866. 8°.
— Laugel, A. Les Etats-Unis pendant la guerre, 1861-65. Paris, 1866. 12°.
— - *Eng.* The U. S. during the war. N. Y., 1866. 8°.
— Lecomte, F. Guerre de la sécession; evénements militaires et politiques, 1861-65. Paris, 1866-67. 3 v. 8°.
— Monitors, 1861-65; 9 lithographs.] N. Y., 1864-65. Plates.
— Peyton, J. L. The Amer. crisis; pages from the note-book of a state agent during the civil war, [1861-65]. London, 1867. 2 v. 8°.
— Post, L. M. Soldiers' letters, [1861-65]; pub. for the U. S. Sanitary Commission. N. Y., 1865. 12°.
— Stacke, H. Story of the American war, 1861-65. London, 1866. 8°.
— Stephens, A. H. Constitutional view of the late war between the states, [1861-65]. Phila., [1868-70]. 2 v. 8°.
— Swinton, W. Campaigns of the Army of the Potomac, [1861-65]. N. Y., 1866. 8°.
— - The twelve decisive battles of the war, [1861-65]. N. Y., 1867. 8°.
— U. S. 37*th Cong.* 3*d sess.* Report of joint committee on the conduct of the war, [1861-63]. Wash., 1863. 3 v. 8°. (Ho. Rep. 108.)
Contents. Vol. 1. Army of the Potomac. 2. Bull Run. — Ball's Bluff. 3. Western Department. — Miscellaneous.
— - Franklin, W. B. Reply to the report of the joint committee. N. Y., 1863. 8°.
— - 38*th Cong.* 2*d sess.* Report of the joint committee, *etc.*, [1864-65]. Wash., 1865. 3 v. 8°. (Sen. Rep. 142.)
Contents. Vol. 1. Army of the Potomac. — Battle of Petersburg. 2. Red River expedition. — Fort Fisher expedition. — Heavy ordnance. 3. Sherman, Johnston. — Light-draught monitors. — Massacre of the Cheyenne Indians. — Ice contracts. — Rosecrans's campaigns. — Misc.
— - 39*th Cong.* 1*st sess.* Supplemental report. Wash., 1866. 2 v. 8°. (Sen. Rep.)
Contents. Vol. 1. Report by Maj. Gen. Sherman. — Thomas. 2. Pope. — Foster. — Pleasanton. — Hitchcock. — Sheridan. — Ricketts. — Communication of Wiard. — Memorial of Wiard.
— White, R. G. Poetry of the civil war, [1861-65]. N. Y., 1866. 12°.
— Woodbury, A. Maj. Gen. Burnside and the 9th army corps, [1861-65]. Prov., 1867. 8°.
— Youth's history of the civil war, 1861-65. N. Y., 1866. 16°.
— Aschmann, R. Drei Jahre in der Potomac-Armee, [1861-64]. Richtersweil, 1865. 16°.
— Confederate States of Amer. Official reports, [1861-64]. *See* Confederate States (p. 646, 647).
— Fletcher, H. C. History of the American war, 1861-64. London, 1865-66. 3 v. 8°.
— Hackett, H. B. Christian memorials of the war, [1861-64]. Boston, 1864. 12°.
— Personne, *pseud.* Gleanings from an army note-book, [1861-64]. Columbia, S. C., 1864. 8°.
— Moreau, H. La politique française en Amérique, 1861-64. Paris, 1864. 8°.
— Pollard, E. A. Southern history of the war, [1861-64]. N. Y., 1863-65. 3 v. 8°.
— Raymond, H. J. History of the administration of President Lincoln, [1861-64]. N. Y., 1864. 12°.
— Stanton, R. L. The Church and the rebellion, [1861-64]. N. Y., 1864. 12°.
— Wilson, H. History of the anti-slavery measures of the 37th and 38th Congress, 1861-64. Boston, 1864. 12°.
— Wolff, A. Den nordamerikanske Borgerkrig, [1861-64]. Kjöbenhavn, 1867. 8°.
— Bishop, A. W. Loyalty on the frontier; sketches of union men of the South-West, [1861-63]. St. Louis, 1863. 8°.
— Dodge, W. S. History of the old 2d division, Army of the Cumberland, [1861-63]. Chicago, 1864. 8°.
— Pollard, E. A. 1st, 2d year of the war, [1861-63]. Richmond, 1862-63. 2 v. 8°.
— - *Same.* [Vol. 1.] Improved ed. Richmond, 1862. 8°.
— Tharin, R. S. Arbitrary arrests in the South, [1861-63]. N. Y., 1863. 12°.
— Webster, B. F. Annals of the Army of the Cumberland, [1861-63]. Phila., 1863. 8°.
— Abbott, J. S. C. History of the civil war in America. Vol. 1: [1861-62]. Springfield, 1863. 8°.
— Barnard, J. G., *and* Barry, W. F. Report of the engineer and artillery operations of the Army of the Potomac, [1861-62]. N. Y., 1863. 8°.
— Brents, J. A. Patriots and guerillas of East Tennessee and Kentucky, [1861-62]. N. Y., 1863. 12°.
— C., T. E. Battlefields of the South from Bull Run to Fredericksburg; by an English combatant, [1861-62]. London, 1863. 2 v. 8°.
— Clarke, H. C. Diary of the war for separation, from the inauguration of Lincoln to the Battle of Shiloh, [1861-62]. Vicksburg, 1862. 8°.
— Elliott, E. B. Military statistics of the U. S., [1861-62]. Berlin, 1863. 4°.
— Fuller, H. North and South, [1861-62]; by the White Republican. London, 1863. 8°.
— Joinville, F. J. P. L. M. d'O., *prince* de. Campagne de l'Armée du Potomac, [1861-62]. N. Y., 1862. 8°.
— - *Eng.* The Army of the Potomac; tr. by W. H. Hurlbert. N. Y., 1862. 8°.
— Laugel, A. La guerre civile aux Etats-Unis, 1861-62. — Le gouvernement fédéral; les armées et les partis. (*In* Revue d. D. Mondes, oct. 1863.)
— Lecomte, *Lieut. Col.* F. Guerre des Etats-Unis d'Amérique, [1861-62]; rapport au département militaire suisse. Paris, 1863. 8°.
— - *Eng.* The war in the U. S. N. Y., 1863. 8°.
— McClellan, G. B. Report on the organization and campaigns of the Army of the Potomac, [1861-62]. Wash., 1864. 8°. (35th Cong. 1st sess. Ex. doc. 15.)

— - *Same.* (*In* **Handbook** of the Democracy. 1864.)
— - *Same.* Added, account of the campaign in Western Va. N. Y., 1864. 8°.
— MARKS, J. J. Peninsula campaign in Virginia, [1861-62]. Phila., 1864. 12°.
— STARS and stripes in rebeldom, [1861-62]; ed. by W. C. Bates. Boston, 1862. 12°.
— LAUGEL, A. Les causes et le caractère de la guerre civile aux Etats-Unis. (*In* **Revue** d. D. Mondes, nov. 1861.)
— LOUNSBERY, W. The Ulster regiment in the great rebellion, [1861]. (*In* **Ulster Hist. Soc.** Col., v. 1, pt. 3. 1862.)
— MONK, J. Map of the seat of war; Virginia and Maryland; [with ms. notes]. Phila., 1861.
— U. S. *36th Cong. 2d sess.* Reports of the select committee of five on collection of duties on imports, hostile organization against the government in the D. C., naval force of the U. S., corresp. between the Pres. and the commis. of S. C., seizure of forts, *etc.*, of the U. S. Wash., 1861. 8°. (Ho. Committee reports.)
— - *37th Cong. 2d sess.* Government contracts; report [of] special committee on the contracts growing out of operations in suppressing the rebellion. *n.t.p.* [1861.] 8°. (Ho. Rep. 2.)
— VIGO ROUSSILLON, F. P. Exemples d'opérations stratégiques et administratives tirés de l'histoire de la guerre, [1862-65]. (*In his* Puissance militaire des Etats-Unis. 1866.)
— RECLUS, J. J. E. La guerre civile aux Etats-Unis; les deux dernières années de la lutte, [1862-64]. (*In* **Revue** d. D. Mondes, oct. 1864.)
— BISHOP, A. W. Loyalty on the frontier; [1862-63]. St. Louis, 1863. 16°.
— SCHALK, E. Campaigns of 1862-63. Phila., 1863. 12°.
— WILKES, G. McClellan; from Ball's Bluff to Antietam, [1862-63]. N. Y., 1863. 8°.
— BARNARD, J. G. Peninsular campaign and its antecedents, [1862]. N. Y., 1864. 12°.
— HOUGH, F. B. History of Duryée's brigade during the campaign of 1862. Albany, 1864. 8°.
— JOINVILLE, F. F. P. L. M. d'O., *prince* de. Quatre mois à l'Armée du Potomac. (*In his* Etudes, v. 2. 1870.)
— PETERSEN, F. A. Military review of the campaign in Virginia and Maryland, 1862. Pt. [1,] 2. N. Y., [1862-63]. 2 v. 8°.
— SCOTT, J. Partisan life with Mosby, [1863-65]. N. Y., 1867. 8°.
— CROSS, J. Camp and field; papers of an army chaplain. Book 2: [1863]. Macon, 1864. 16°.
— - *Same.* Books 3, 4: [1863-64]. Columbia, 1864. 8°.
— GILMORE, J. R. Patriot boys and prison pictures, [1863-64]. Boston, 1866. 12°.
— GR. BRITAIN *and* LAIRD BROTHERS. Correspondence resp. the iron clads building at Birkenhead, 1863-64. London, 1864. 8°.
— GR. BRITAIN. *Parl.* Return of American vessels sold to British subjects, in 1863. [London, 1864.] f°.
— NOEL, B. W. The rebellion in America. London, 1863. 8°.
— SCOTT, *Rev.* A. M. Chronicles of the great rebellion. [Ch. 1-10: 1863.] 14th ed. Cincin., 1864. 8°.
— U. S. *37th Cong. 3d sess.* Report in part [of] the select comm. [on] the chartering of transport vessels for the Banks exped., *etc.* *n.t.p.* [Wash., 1863.] 8°. (Sen. Rep. 75.)
— AYER, I. W., *M.D.* The great north-western conspiracy; plot to plunder and burn Chicago, *etc.*, [1864-65]. Chicago, 1865. 8°.
— BARNARD, G. N. Photographic views of Sherman's campaign, [1864-65]. N. Y., [1866?]. Obl. 4°.
— EARLY, J. A. Memoir of the last year of the war, 1864-65. Lynchburg, 1867. 8°.
— GRANT, U. S. Report of the armies of the U. S., 1864-65. N. Y., 1865. 8°.
— LAUGEL, A. Les Etats-Unis pendant la guerre, 1864-65. (*In* **Revue** d. D. Mondes, déc. 1864, av., juil. 1865.)
— MICKLEY, J. M. The 43d regiment U. S. colored troops, [1864-65]. Gettysb., 1866. 8°.
— NICHOLS, G. W. Story of the great march, [1864-65]. N. Y., 1865. 12°.
— U. S. *Office of the Chief of Engineers.* Military maps illust. the operations of the armies of the Potomac and James, May 4, 1864 – Apr. 9, 1865. Wash., 1869. f°.
— ADAMS, F. C. Siege of Washington, D. C., [1864]. N. Y., [1867]. 18°.
— PITMAN, B., *rep.* Trials for treason at Indianapolis; plans for a north-western confederacy, 1864. Cincin., 1865. 8°.
— SHERMAN, W. T. Official account of his march, *etc.*, [1864]. N. Y., 1865. 12°.
— G., J. C. Lee's last campaign, [1865]. Raleigh, 1866. 16°.

(*Hospitals and Charities.*)

— GOODRICH, F. B. The tribute book; a record of the munificence, patriotism, *etc.*, of the American people during the war for the Union, 1861-65. N. Y., 1865. 8°.
— BROCKETT, L. P., *and* VAUGHAN, M. C. Woman's work in the Southern rebellion, [1861-65]. Phila., 1867. 8°.
— MOORE, F. Women of the war, [1861-65]. Hartford, 1866. 8°.
— BROCKETT, L. P. Philanthropic results of the war, [1861-64]. N. Y., 1864. 12°.
— NOTES of hospital life, Nov. 1861 - Aug. 1863. Phila., 1864. 12°.
— ELLIS, T. T. Leaves from the diary of an army surgeon, [1861-62]. N. Y., 1863. 12°.
— H., *Mrs.* Three years in the field hospitals of the Army of the Potomac, [1862-65]. Phila., 1867. 12°.
— LETTERMAN, J. Med. recollections of the Army of the Potomac, [1862-63]. N. Y., 1866. 8°.
— OLMSTED, F. L. Hospital transports, [1862]. Boston, 1863. 16°.
— HOSPITAL scenes after the Battle of Gettysburg, 1863; by the Patriot Daughters of Lancaster. Phila., 1864. 12°.

See also Alcott, L. M. (Hospital sketches. 1863.)

Personal narratives.

— ESTVAN, B. War pictures from the South, [1861-62]. London, 1863. 2 v. 8°.
— - *Same.* N. Y., 1863. 12°.
— BROWNE, J. H. Four years in Secessia, [1861-65]. Hartford, 1865. 8°.
— COFFIN, C. C. Four years of fighting, [1861-65]. Boston, 1866. 8°.
— ELLIS, D. Thrilling adventures, [1861-65]. N. Y., 1867. 12°.
— FONTANE, M. La guerre d'Amérique, [1861-65]. Paris, [1866]. 2 v. 12°.
— GILMOR, H. Four years in the saddle, [1861-65. N. Y., 1866. 12°.
— - *Same.* London, 1866. 8°.

— Gurowski, A. G. de. Diary, 1861-65. Boston, 1862-66. 3 v. 12°.

— Hairbreadth escapes and humorous adventures of a volunteer in the cavalry service, [1861-65]. Cincin., 1865. 8°.

— Hardinge, *Mrs.* B. B. . Belle Boyd in camp and prison, [1861-65]. Lond., 1865. 2 v. 8°.

— Jones, J. B. Rebel war clerk's diary, [1861-65]. Phila.,1866. 2 v. 8°.

— Richardson, A. D. The secret service; the field, the dungeon, the escape, 1861-65. Hartford, 1865. 8°

— Stevens, G. T. Three years in the 6th corps, 1861-65. Albany, 1866. 8°.

— Blake, H. N. Three years in the Army of the Potomac, [1861-64]. Boston, 1865. 8°.

— Locke, E. W. Three years in camp and hospital, [1861-64]. Boston, 1870. 8°.

— Macnamara, M. H. The Irish Ninth, Virginia and Maryland campaigns, [1861-64]. Boston, 1867. 8°.

— Stewart, A. M. Three years and a half with the Army of the Potomac, [1861-64]. Phila., 1865. 12°.

— Edmonds, S. E. E. Nurse and spy in the Union army, [1861-63]. Hartford, 1865. 8°.

— Quint, A. H. Potomac and Rapidan; army notes, 1861-63. Boston, 1864. 12°.

— Reminisco, P. Q., *pseud.* Life in the union army; a rhythmical hist. of the 15th N. Y. Engineers, 1861-63. N. Y., 1864. 8°.

— Strother, D. H. Personal recollections of the war, [1861-63]. (*In* Harper's mag., v. 33-35. 1866-67.)

— Adams, F. C. Story of a trooper; campaign on the Peninsula, [1861-62]. N. Y., 1865. 12°.

— Aughey, J. H. The iron furnace; or, Slavery and secession, [1861-62]. Phila., 1863. 12°.

— Castleman, A. L. Army of the Potomac; behind the scenes, [1861-62]. Milwaukee, 1863. 12°.

— Coffin, C. C. Following the flag; from Aug. 1861 to Nov. 1862. Boston, 1865. 16°.

— - My days and nights on the battle-field, [1861-62]; by Carleton. Boston, 1864. 16°.

— Ellis, T. T. Leaves from the diary of an army surgeon, [1861-62]. N. Y., 1863. 12°.

— Fisher, G. A. A Yankee conscript; or, Eighteen months in Dixie, [1861-62]. Phila., 1864. 16°.

— Stevenson, W. G. Thirteen months in the rebel army; by an impressed New Yorker, [1861-62]. N. Y., 1862. 16°.

— Day, S. P. Down South; or, An Englishman's experience at the seat of war, 1861. London, 1862. 2 v. 8°.

— Frémont, J. B. Story of the guard, [1861]. Boston, 1863. 12°.

— Borcke, H. von. Memoirs of the confederate war for independence, [1812-15]. Edin., 1866. 2 v. 8°.
Note. From Blackwood's mag., v. 98-99. 1865-66.

— Houghton, E. B. Campaigns of the 17th Maine, [1862-65]. Portland, 1866. 12°.

— Fiske, S. Mr. Dunn Browne's experiences in the army, [1862-64]. Boston, 1866. 8°.

— Higginson, T. W. Army life in a black regiment, [1862-64]. Boston, 1870 [1869]. 12°.

— Lyle, W. W. Lights and shadows of army life, [1862-64]. 2d ed. Cincin., 1865. 12°.

— Bickham, W. D. Rosecrans' campaign with the 14th army corps, [1862-63]. Cincin., 1863. 12°.

— Geer, J. J. Beyond the lines; a Yankee prisoner loose in Dixie, [1862-63]. Phila., 1864. 16°.

— Grant, J. W. The flying regiment; journal of the campaigns of 12th Regt., R. I. Vol., [1862-63]. Prov., 1865. 18°.

— Haines, Z. T. Letters from the 44th reg. M. U. M., 1862-63; by 'Corporal'. Boston, 1863. 8°.

— Hosmer, J. K. The color-guard; notes of military service in the 19th army corps, [1862-63]. Boston, 1864. 8°.

— Johns, H. T. Life with the 49th Mass. Vol., [1862-63]. Pittsfield, 1864. 12°.

— Red-tape and pigeon-hole generals, 1862-63. N. Y., 1864. 12°.

— Nott, C. C. Sketches of the war, [1862]. N. Y., 1863. 12°.

— Noyes, G. F. The bivouac and the battle-field; campaign sketches in Va. and Maryland, 1862. N. Y., 1863. 12°.

— Pittenger, W. Daring and suffering; history of the great railroad adventure, [1862]. Phila., 1863. 12°.

— Bradley, G. S. The Star Corps; or, Notes during Sherman's march to the sea, [1863-65]. Milwaukee, 1865. 8°.

— Duganne, A. J. H. Camps and prisons; twenty months in the department of the Gulf, [1863-64]. N. Y., 1865. 12°.

— Sala, G. A. H. Diary in America in the midst of the war, [1863-64]. London, 1865. 2 v. 8°.

— Fremantle, A. J. Three months in the Southern states, Apr. - June. London, 1863. 8°.

— - *Same.* Mobile, 1864. 8°.

— Hepworth, G. H. The whip, hoe, and sword; or, The Gulf department in '63. Boston, 1864. 12°.

— Nichols, G. W. Story of the great march, [1864]. N. Y., 1865. 12°.

— Estabrooks, H. L. Adrift in Dixie; or, A Yankee officer among the rebels, [1865]. N. Y., 1866. 16°.

— With Gen. Sheridan in Lee's last campaign, [1865]. Phila., 1866. 12°.

(Personal vindications.)

— Copeland, R. M. Statement. Boston, 1864. 8°.

— Franklin, *Maj. Gen.* W. B. Reply to the report of the committee on the conduct of the war. N. Y., 1863. 8°.

— Hudson, H. N. A chaplain's campaign with Gen. Butler. N. Y., 1865. 8°.

— McDowell, I. Statement in review of the evidence before the court of inquiry. Wash., 1863. 8°.

— Sanderson, J. M. My record in rebeldom. N. Y., 1865. 8°.

Prison life.

— Greenhow, *Mrs.* R. O'N. My imprisonment and the first year of abolition rule at Washington, [1861-62]. London, 1863. 8°.

— Howard, F. K. Fourteen months in American bastiles, [1861-62]. Balt., 1863. 8°.

— Goss, W. L. The soldier's story of his captivity at Andersonville, Belle Isle, *etc.*, [1862-64]. Boston, 1867. 8°.

— Sabre, G. E. Nineteen months a prisoner of war; experience in the prisons and stockades of Morton, Mobile, Atlanta, Libby, *etc.*, [1863-65]. N. Y., 1865. 12°.

— GLAZIER, W. W. The capture, prison pen, and escape, [1863-64]. Albany, 1866. 12°.
— POLLARD, E. A. Observations in the North; eight months in prison and on parole, [1864]. Richmond, 1865. 8°.
— ABBOTT, A. O. Prison life at Richmond, Macon, Savannah, *etc.*, 1864-65. N. Y., 1865. 8°.
— KELLOGG, R. H. Life and death in rebel prisons, [1864-65]. Hartford, 1865. 12°.

See also **Andersonville; — Belle Isle; — Libby.**

See also Quartermaster Gen. (p. 3096); — *Literature* (*Ballads, etc.*, p. 3132; — *Poetry*, p. 3139); — *Politics* (p. 3142, *etc.*); — *also* **Foreign enlistment; — Freedmen; — Negroes; — Secession; — Slavery; — South; — United States Christian Commission; — U. S. Sanitary Commission.**

also **Alabama.** *Convention, Gen. Assembly, Governor,* (MISCELLANEOUS newspapers) p. 35; — **Alexandria; — Arkansas.** (BAXTER) p. 138; — **Baltimore; — Charleston,** *S. C.*; — **Confederate States of Amer.; — Connecticut.** *Adjutant Gen.* (p. 654); — **East Tennessee; — Exeter,** *N. H.*; — **Florida.** *Gen. Assembly* (p. 1002); — **Georgia.** *Adjutant Gen., Comptroller Gen., Gen. Assembly, Governor, Treasurer* (p. 1128); — **Indiana.** *Adjutant Gen.* (p. 1509); — **Iowa.** *Adjutant Gen.*, (INGERSOLL) p. 1527; — **Kansas** (ARMY list) p. 1610; — **Kentucky.** (BRENTS, HISTORY of the election in K.) p. 1621; — **Louisiana.** *Convention, Governor,* (p. 1794); — **Maine.** *Adjutant Gen., History and politics* (p. 1840, 1841); — **Mass.** *Adjutant Gen., Governor, Master of Ordnance, History* (p. 1889, 1895, 1896, 1899, 1900); — **Melrose,** *Mass.*; — **Michigan.** *Adjutant Gen.* (LANMAN) p. 1971, 1972; — **Minnesota.** *Adjutant Gen., Army, Legislature* (p. 1996); — **Mississippi.** *Legislature* (p. 2003); — **Missouri.** *Adjutant Gen., Convention* (KELSO) p. 2004; — **Mobile; — Nebraska.** (ARMY list) p. 2092; — **New Hampshire.** *Adjutant Gen.* (p. 2108); — **New Jersey.** *Adjutant Gen.* (FOSTER) p. 2112; — **New Orleans; — New York.** *Adjutant Gen., Volunteers* (p. 2118, 2121; — **N. Y.** *County. Board of Supervisors* (p. 2118); — **North Carolina.** *Comptroller, Convention, Gen. Assembly, Governor, Treasurer, History* (p. 2151, 2152); — **Ohio.** *Adjutant Gen.* (REID) p. 2174, 2175; — **Oregon.** *Adjutant Gen.* (p. 2188); — **Pennsylvania.** *Adjutant Gen., Military Dept.*, (SYPHER) p. 2285, 2286; — **Rhode Island.** *Adjutant Gen.*, (STONE, GRANT) p. 2507, 2508; — **Richmond; — St. Albans; — San Juan; — Savannah Chatham Artillery; — South Carolina.** *Convention of* 1860-61, *Convention of* 1862, *Governor*, (STEVENSON, WILLIAMS) p. 2935; — **Texas.** *Constitutional Convention,* 1861, *Legislature* (p. 2941); — **Vermont.** *Adjutant and Inspector Gen., Volunteers,* (WALKER); — **Virginia.** *Adjutant Gen., Auditor of Accts., Convention between V. and C. S. A., Convention* 1861, *Legislature, Senate, Governor. Military Institute, Paymaster Gen., Quartermaster Gen., Sec. War, Treasurer, Volunteers* (MARKS); — **W. Virginia.** *Adjutant Gen.*; — **Wisconsin.** *Adjutant Gen.* (LOVE); —

also **Baker's Creek; — Bristoe's Station; — Chancellorsville; — Droop Mt.; — Five Forks; — Fortress Monroe; — Gettysburg; — Helena; — Kelleysville; — Lafayette, Fort; — Manassas; — Murfreesboro'; — Pea Ridge; — Pillow, Fort; — Pulaski, Fort; — Shenandoah Valley; — Spottsylvania,** *Va.*; — **Staunton River; — Sumpter, Fort; — Vicksburg; — Warren, Fort; — Wilderness; — Williamsburgh,** *Va.*; —

also **Alabama,** *steamer*; — **Cassius,** *ship*; — **Chesapeake,** *steamship*; — **Florida,** *ship, C. S. A.*; — **Kearsarge,** *U. S. ship of war*; — **Meteor,** *steamship*; — **Nashville,** *steamer*; — **Savannah,** *privateer*; — **Saxon,** *ship*; — **Sumpter,** *steamer*; — **Trent,** *ship*; —

also **Brown,** *Capt.* **J.**, *of Ossawattomie*; — **Buchanan, J.; — Davis, J.; — Johnson, A.; — Lincoln, A.;** —

also **Banks, N. P.; — Burnside, A. E.; — Butler, B. F.; — Dahlgren, U.; — Dupont, S. F.; — Farragut, D. G.; — Grant, U. S.; — Hindman, T. C.; — Hooker, J.; — Jackson, T. J.: — Kilpatrick, H. J.; — Lee, R. E.; — McClellan, G. B.; — Meade, G. G.; — Morgan, J. H.; — Porter, F. J.; — Rosecrans, W. S.; — Scott, W.; — Sheridan, P. H.; — Sherman, W. T.;** —

also the following fictitious works: **Aughey, J. H.;** (The iron furnace); — **Child, L. M.** (A romance of the republic); — **Clemens, J.** (Tobias Wilson); — **Cooke, J. E.;** (Surry of Eagle's nest, Wearing of the gray); — **Copperheads,** Ye book of; — **Davis, R. B. H.** (Waiting fo the verdict); — **Gilmore, J. R.** (Down in Tennseee); — **Halpine, C. G.** (Baked meats of the funeral, Life and adventures of Miles O'Reilly); — **Hosmer, J. K.** (The thinking bayonet); — **Kadmus, K.,** *pseud.* (Hist. of Magnus Maharba and the black dragon); — **Kelso, I.** (Stars and bars); — **Loring, F. W.** (Two college friends); — **Terhune, M. V.** (Sunnybank); — **Trowbridge, J. T.** (Cudjo's cave, Three scouts); — **Tucker, N. B.** (The partizan leader); — *also* **Murdoch, J.** (Patriotism in poetry and prose. 1865.)

Ichthyology.

See also **Illinois; — Massachusetts; — New Jersey.** *Descr. and Nat. hist.*; — **New York; — North America; — Ohio River.**

Immigration.

— CHICKERING, J. Immigration into the U. S. Boston, 1848. 8°.
— BROMWELL, W. J. History of immigration to the U. S. N. Y., 1856. 8°.

See also Description (LETTERS. 1794, LOOK. 1796, HINTS. 1817, COBBETT. 1829, BOGEN. 1851, FOSTER. 1855, AMER. SOC. SCI. ASSOC. 1871); — *also* **Minnesota.** *Description.*

Indians.

See **Indians; — New Mexico.**

Internal improvements.

— WHEELER, H. G. History of internal improvements. (*In his* Hist. of Cong., v. 2. 1848.)
— PORTER, P. B. Speech on internal improvements, Feb. 8, 1810. *n.t.p.* [1810.] 8°. (B 436. 2521)
— MERCER, C. F. Speech on internal improvement, Ho. of Reps., March 12. Phila., 1818. 8°. (W 13a)
— M'DUFFIE. G. Defence of a liberal construction of the powers of Congress as regards internal improvement, written, 1821. Phila., 1831. 8°. (B 1768)
— - *Same.* 3d ed. Phila., 1832. 8°. (B 1790)
— FACILITATED carrying; short statement of the proc. on June 3, on internal improvement. Boston, 1825. 8°. (B 1798)
— UNITED STATES. *18th Cong. 2d sess.* Report of an examination by the Board of Engineers for Int. Improvement, Feb. 14. Wash., 1825. 8°. (Senate. Doc. 32. B 1698.)
— STRICKLAND, W., *and others, ed.* Reports, specifications and estimates of public works in the U. S. London, *Weale*, 1841. 8°.

See also **Chicago; — Cincinnati; — Clinton River; — Cod, Cape; — Georgetown; — Georgian Bay Canal; — Hudson River; — Maine; — Massachusetts; — Memphis, Convention; — Michigan; — Milwaukee; — Mississippi; — Montreal; — New York; — North Carolina; — Ohio; — Pennsylvania; — Philadelphia; — Saint John River; — S. Carolina; — Virginia.**

Language.

See **California; — English language; — Indians.**

Law.

— REVIEW of the laws of the U. S. London, 1790. 8°.
— TUCKER, ST. G. Examination of the question, How far the common law of Eng. is the law of the federal gov. of the U. S.?? Richmond, *n.d.* 4°. (W 80)
— HAMPDEN, *pseud.* Letter to the President of the U. S. touching the prosecutions under his patronage, in Conn. New Haven, 1808. 8°. (B 408)
— GOODENOW, J. M. Principles and maxims of Amer. jurisprudence in contrast with the doctrines of the Eng. common law. Steubenville, 1819. 8°.
— KENT, J. Commentaries on American law. New York, 1826. 4 v. 8°.
— - *Same.* 11th ed.; ed. by G. F. Comstock. Boston, 1866. 4 v. 8°.
— SMITH, E. F. Commentaries on statute and constitutional law. Albany, 1848. 8°.

See also Congress (*Acts and laws*) p. 3059, 60; — *Courts* (p. 3062); — *Commerce* (p. 3112, 13); — *also* **Aliens; — Bankruptcy; — Embargo; — Fugitive slaves; — Inhertance; — Insolvency; — Sedition;** — *also* **Florida; — Louisiana; — Maine; — Massachusetts; — Michigan; — New Hampshire; — New York; — Pennsylvania; Rhode Island; — Virginia.**

Libraries.

— SPOFFORD, A. R. Public libraries of the U. S. (*In* Amer. Soc. Sci. Assoc. Trans., no. 2. 1870.)

Literature.

Bibliography.

— CATALOGUE of all the books printed in the U. S. Boston, 1804. 12°. (B 898)

— TRUEBNER, N. Bibliographical guide to Amer. lit.; books pub. during the last forty years. London, 1859. 8°.

— ROORBACH, O. A. Bibliotheca Americana; catalogue of Amer. publications, 1820-48. N. Y., 1849. 8°.

— - Supplement. N. Y., 1850. 8°.

— - *Same.* 1820-52. N. Y., 1852. 8°.

— - Supplement, 1852-55. N. Y., 1855. 8°.

— - Addenda, 1855-58. N. Y., 1858. 8°.

— NORTON'S literary advertiser. Vols. 1-3, 1851-53; n.s., vol. 1, 1854. N. Y., 1851-55. 4 v. f°.
Note. In v. 2 the title is changed to 'Norton's literary gazette and publisher's circular'.

— NORTON'S literary register, 1853; Norton literary and educ. reg., 1854; Norton's lit. reg. or annual book list, 1856, [prepared by R. A. Guild]. N. Y., 1853-56. 3 v. 12°.

— AMERICAN publishers' circular and literary gazette; [ed.] by C. R. Rode. Vol. 2-7, Jan. 1856 - Nov. 15, 1861. N. Y., [1856-61]. 6 v. (v. 1 w.; 6, 7, incomplete). 4°.

— *Same.* May 1863 - Jan. 15, 1872. N. Y., 1863-72. 18 v. 8°.

— KELLY, J. The American catalogue of books published in the U. S., 1861-71. N. Y., 1866-71. 2 v. 8°.

— AMERICAN catalogue of books for 1869, 71. N. Y., *Leypoldt and Holt*, 1870-72. 2 v. 8°.

— TRADE circular annual for 1871. N. Y., 1871. 8°.
See also California; — Minnesota; — New York; — North America; — Vermont.

History (incl. biography of American authors).

— POE, E. A. The literati. (Vol. 3 *of his* Works. 1853.)

— TUCKERMAN, H. T. Sketch of Amer. lit. (*In* Shaw, T. B. Complete manual. 1867.)
See also Collections, below (DUYCKINCK, CLEVELAND); — *also Female biog.* (p. 3110); — Connecticut. *Literature*; — South. *Biog.*
Note. The library has lives of the following authors besides those contained in their works: Allston, W.; — Brown, C. B.; — Buckingham, J. T.; — Burk, J. D.; — Chauncy, C.; — Colburn, W.; — Fairfield, S. L.; — Follen, C. T. C.; — Goodrich, S. G.; — Greeley, H.; — Hale, D.; — Halleck, F. G.; — Ingalls, H. A.; — Irving, W.; — Kennedy, J. P.; — Mann, H.; — Paine, T.; — Percival, J. G.; — Person, W.; — Porter, W. T.; — Prescott, W. H.; — Seaton, W. W.; — Sparks, J.; — Wheaton, R.; — Young, A. J.

Miscellaneous works about the literature.

— MITCHILL, S. L. Discourse, state and prospects of Amer. literature. Albany, 1821. 8°. (B 936)

— DU PONCEAU, P. S. Necessity and means of making our national literature independent of that of Gr. Britain. Phila., 1834. 8°. (B 1084, 2539)

— CHASLES, P. De la littérature dans l'Amérique du Nord. (*In* Revue d. D. Mondes, juil. 1835.) — Des tendances littéraire en Amérique et en Angleterre. (*In* août 1844.) — De la littérature pseudo-populaire en Amérique. (*In* sept. 1847.)

Collections and Selections.

— SPIRIT of the public journals, 1805. Balt., 1816. 12°.

— CHEEVER, G. B. Amer. common-place book of prose. Cooperstown, 1842. 12°.

— HART, J. S. Female prose writers of America, with specimens. Phila., 1852. 8°.

— GRISWOLD, R. W. Prose writers of America. 4th ed. Phila., 1853. 8°.

— DUYCKINCK, E. A. *and* G. L. Cyclopædia of Amer. literature. N. Y., 1855. 2 v. 8°.

— - Supplement. N. Y., 1866. 8°.

— CLEVELAND, C. D. Compendium of American literature. Phila., 1858. 8°.
See also Boston book; — Charleston book; — New Hampshire book; — West Point scrap book; — *also* Maryland. *Literature.*
Note. The Library has also the collected works of the following authors: Adams, J.; — Ames, F.; — Calhoun, J. C.; — Duché, J.; — Franklin, B.; — Genin, T. H.; — Hamilton, A.; — Haven, N. A.; — Hopkinson, F.; — Humphreys, D.; — Irving, W.; — Jefferson, T.; — Paine, R. T., *Jr.*; — Poe, E. A.; — Rush, R.; — Sands, R. C.; — Seward, W. H.; — Willis, N. P.; — Woodbury, L.

Ballads and Songs. (Collections.)

— MOORE, F. Songs and ballads of the American Revolution. N. Y., 1856. 12°.

— DREW, T. The campaign of 1856; Fremont songs, orig. and selected. Boston, 1856. 16°.

— CAMPAIGN songs. (*In* Handbook of the Democracy for 1863-64.)

— HEWES, G. W. Ballads of the war. N. Y., 1862. 12°.

— SHEPPERSON, W. G. War songs of the South. *n.t.p.* [Richmond, 1862.] 12°.

— SONGS of the South. Richmond, Va., 1862. 18°.

— SONGS of the South. Richmond, 1813. 18°.

— MOORE, F. Personal and political ballads. N. Y., 1864. 16°.

— JACK Morgan songster; by a captain in Lee's army. Raleigh, 1865. 18°.

— MOORE, F. Songs of the soldiers. N. Y., 1864. 32°.

— SONGS of love and liberty; by a North Carolina lady. Raleigh, 1864. 18°.

— NEW and popular songs. Phila., 1865. 12°.

— SCHREINER, H. L. The Gen. Lee songster. Macon, 1865. 18°.

— LELAND, C. G. Hans Breitmann's ballads. Phila., 1869. 8°.

— HAY, J. Pike County ballads and other pieces. Boston, 1871. 12°.

Drama.

Note. The library has the collected plays of the following authors: Baker, G. M.; — Boker, G. H.; — — and separate plays (some of them in the Works of the authors) by Bannister, N. H.; — Bernard, W. B.; — Booth, J. B.; — Bradbury, *Mrs.* S. L. A.; — Curtis, *Mrs.* A. W.; — Deering, N.; — Dimond, W. H.; — Dunlap, W.; — English, T. D.; — Gayler, C.; — Goodrich, F. B.; — Hill, F. S.; — Hillhouse, J. A.; — Holland, E. G.; — Howe, J. W.; — Huff, H. W.; — Huntington, G.; — Johnson, S. D.; — Jones, J. S.; — Leland, O. S.; — Lord, W. W.; — Miles, G. H.; — Mowatt, A. C.; — Neal, J.; — Payne, J. H.; — Phillips, J. B.; — Pratt, W. W.; — Pray, I. C.; — Rice, G. E.; — Saunders, C. H.; — Smith, W. H.; — Stevens, G. L.; — Tayleure, C. W.; — Trowbridge, J. T.; — Warren, M.; — Watterston, G.; — Wilkins, E. G. P.; — Willis, N. P.; — Woodworth, S.
See also Theatre (p. 2947).

Essays.

The chief essayists whose works the library contains are: Adams, C. F., *Jr.*; — Alcott, A. B.; — Atkinson, W. P.; — Bancroft, G.; — Beecher, H. W.; — — Calvert, G. H.; — Carey, M.; — Child, *Mrs.* L. M.; — Clark, W. G.; — Congdon, C. T.; — Cozzens, F. S.; — Crafts, W.; — Crane, W. C.; — Curtis, G. W.; — Dana, R. H.; — Dodge, M. A.; — Emerson, R. W.; — Everett, A. H. — Fairbanks, C. B.; — Farley, H.; — Fields, J. T.; — Franklin, B.; — Garrison, W. L.; — Giles, H.; — Gilman, S.; — Goddard, W. G.; — Godwin, P.; — Gray, J. C.; — Greene, G. W.; — Greenwood, F. W. P.; — Hazard, R. G.; — Higginson, T. W.; — Hoffman, D.; — Holland, E. G.; — Holland, J. G.; — Holmes, O. W.; — Hopkins, M.; — Hyde, N. M.; — Johnston, D. C.; — King, T. S.; — Lackland, T.; — Lippincott, *Mrs.* S. J.; — Littell, W.; — Lowell, J. R.; — Ludlow, F.; — Lunt, G.; — Milburn, W. H.; — Mitchell, D. G.; — Morton, S. W.; — Nichols, W.; — Parton, J.; — Peabody, E. P.; — Phillips, W.; — Rogers, N. P.; — Rush, B.; — Saunders, F.; — Sawyer, F. W.; — Sigourney, *Mrs.* L. H.; — Theophilanthropist, *ps.*; — Thoreau, H. D.; — Tuckerman, H. T.; — Tudor,

W.; — Van Santvoord, C.; — Wallace, H. B.; — Walsh, R.; — Ware, M. G.; — Warner, C. D.; — Watmough, E. C.; — Webster, N.; — Westman, H. O.; — Whipple, E. P.; — White, C. — Winthrop, T.; — Whittier, J. G.; — Willis, N. P.

Fables.

See **Æsopus** (p. 22).

Fiction.

The library has works of fiction by the following authors: **Abbott, A. W.; — Abbott, J.; — Adams, N.; — Alcott, L. M.; — Alden, J.; — Aldrich, T. B.; — Allston, W.; — Arthur, T. S.; — Austin, J. G.; — Avery, S. P.; — Bache,** *Mrs.* **A.; — Baker, W. M.; — Barnard, C.; — Barrell,** *Miss*; **— Beecher, H. W.; — Belknap, J.; — Benjamin, S. G. W.; — Bird, R. M.; — Brackenridge, H. H.; — Briggs, C. F.; — Brown, C. B.; — Brown, W. H.; — Browne, C. F.; — Brownson, O. A.; — Bulfinch, T.; — Cary, A.; — Chamberlain, J. E.; — Chamberlain, N. H.; — Chesboro', C.; — Child, L. M.; — Clark, T. M.; — Clemens, J.; — Clemens, S. L.; — Coffin, R. B.; — Comins, L. B.; — Cooper, J. F.; — Cozzens, F. S.; — Crouch, J.; — Cummins, M. S.; — Curtis, G. W.; — Dana, M. S. B.; — Darling, M. G.; — Davis, J.; — Davis, R. B. H.; — Dawes, R.; — Derby, G. H.; — Devereux, G. H.; — Diaz,** *Mrs.* **A. M.; — Dix, D. L.; — Dixon,** *Rev.* **—.; — Dodge, M. A.; — Douglas, A. M.; — Embury, E. C.; — Everett, W.; — Fay, T. S.; — Finch, J.; — Flint, T.; — Follen, E. L.; — Ford, S. R.; — Foster,** *Mrs.* **H. W.; — Foster,** *Miss* **S. H.; — Fry, C. W. T.; — Gilman,** *Mrs.* **C. H.; — Gilman, S.; — Gilmore, J. R.; — Goodrich, S. G.; — Greene, A.; — Greenough, H.; — Greenough,** *Mrs.* **R. H.; — Griffiths,** *Mrs.* **M.; — Hale, E. E.; — Haliburton, T. C.; — Hall, B. R.; — Hall, J.; — Hall,** *Mrs.* **L. J.; — Halpine, C. G.; — Hamilton, C. V.; — Harris,** *Mrs.* **M. C.; — Harris, S. S.; — Harte, B.; — Hawthorne, N.; — Hentz,** *Mrs.* **C. H.; — Hentz, N. M.; — Herbert, H. W.; — Higginson, T. W.; — Hildreth, R.; — Hilliard, H. W.; — Hills, A. C.; — Holland, J. G.; — Holmes, O. W.; — Hooper, J. J.; — Hosmer, J. K.; — Howells, W. D.; — Hughs,** *Mrs.* **M.; — Hunt, T. P.; — Huntington, J. V.; — Ingraham, J. H.; — Irving, W.; — Irving, Wm.; — James, H.,** *Jr.*; **— Jarves, J. J.; — Joliffe, J.; — Jones, J. S.; — Judd, S.; — Kadmus, K.,** *ps.*; **— Kellogg, E.; — Kennedy, J. P.; — Kirkland,** *Mrs.* **C. M.; — Lee,** *Mrs.* **E. B.; — Lee,** *Mrs.* **H. F.; — Leslie, E.; — Locke, D. R.; — Longfellow, H. W.; — Longstreet, A. B.; — Loring, F. W.; — Lowell, R. T. S.; — Macduff, J. R.; — McIntosh, M. J.; — Mannering, G.,** *ps.*; **— Mayo, W. S.; — Melville, H.; — Mitchell, D. G.; — Moore,** *Mrs.* **H. G.; — Motley, J. L.; — Mountford, W.; — Myers, P. H.; — Neal, J.; — Newell, R. H.; — Nordhoff, C.; — Nowell,** *Mrs.* **S. A.; — Otis,** *Mrs.* **H. G.; — Palfrey, S. H.; — Parkman, F.,** *Jr.*; **— Parton,** *Mrs.* **S. P.; — Paul, H. H.,** *ps.*; **— Paulding, J. K.; — Peabody,** *Mrs.*; **— Perch, P.; — Phelps, E. S.; — Phlogobombos, T.,** *ps.*; **— Poe, E. A.; — Porter,** *Mrs.* **A. E.; — Powers, S.; — Prentiss, E.; — Preston, H. W.; — Putnam, G. L.; — Putnam,** *Mrs.* **M. L.; — Pye, H. J.; — Read, H. T.; — Read, T. B.; — Requier, A. J.; — Ritchie, A. C. M.; — Robinson, S.; — Roe, A. S.; — Royall, A.; — Sabin, E. R.; — Sargent, E.; — Sargent, L. M.; — Schoolcraft, H. R.; — Schuyler, M.; — Scudder, H. E.; — Sedgwick, C. M.; — Sedgwick,** *Mrs.* **S. R.; — Seemuller, A. M. C.; — Sherburne, H.; — Shillaber, B. P.; — Shindler, M. S. B.; — Sigourney, L. H.; — Simms, W. J.; — Smith, J. P.; — Snelling, W. J.; — Spofford,** *Mrs.* **H. E. P.; — Stevens, A.; — Stowe, H. E. B.; — Symmes, J. C.; — Taylor, J. H. B.; — Terhune,** *Mrs.* **M. V.; — Thomes, W. H.; — Thompson, D. P.; — Thompson, W. T.; — Thurston, L. M.; — Trowbridge, J. T.; — Tucker, N. B.; — Tuckerman, H. T.; — Tuthill,** *Mrs.*; **— Tyler, R.; — Underwood, F. H.; — W., S. R.; — Ware, H.; — Ware, W.; — Warner, A. B.; — Warner, S.; — Washburn, W. T.; — Watson, H. C.; — Weld, H. H.; — White, R. G.; — Whitney,** *Mrs.* **A. D. T.; — Whittier, J. G.; — Willis, N. P.; — Winthrop, T.; — Wise, H. A.; — Wood, G.; — Woodruff,** *Mrs.* **J. L. M.; — Wormeley, G.; — Wright, S. A.; — Vingut, G. F. de;** —

also the following anonymous works: **Aunt Mary's** tales for little boys; — **Beauties** of Brother Bull-us; — **Christian Indian**, The; — **Commonplace** book of romantic tales; — **Convert** of Massachusetts, The; — **Cooper's** son; — **Family** story book; — **Filial** affection; — **Happiness**; — **Henry** Wallace; — **Home** and the world; — **Howard** Erwin; — **Looking-glass** for the mind; — **My** boy's first book; — **Mysterious** messenger, The; — **Narina** and other tales; — **Original** tales; — **Pebblebrook** and the Harding family; — **Saratoga**; — **Three** degrees of banking; — **Twin** brothers; — **Tyrolese** minstrels, The; — **Yorktown**; — **Young** man's offering.

Legends.

See **Indians.**

Letters.

— Sparks, J. Correspondence of the American Revolution; being letters of eminent men G. Washington. Boston, 1853. 4 v. 8°.

— - Diplomatic correspondence of the American Revolution. Boston, 1829-30. 12 v. 8°.

See also **Adams,** *Mrs.* **A.; — Adams, J.; — Adams, J. Q.; — Adams, J.; — Franklin, B.; — Hamilton, A.; — Jefferson, T.; — Madison, J.; — Washington, G.; — Webster, D.** Many letters are to be found in the Lives of their authors.

Oratory.

— Grimké, T. S. Oration on the comparativ [*sic*] elements and dutys [*sic*] of Gr. and Am. eloquence. Cincin., **1834.** 8°. (**B 1116, 2545, E 221**)

— Parker, E. G. Golden age of Amer. oratory. Boston, 1857. 12°.

Oratory. (Collections.)

— Cooke, J. American orator; extracts in prose and poetry; pref. diss., on delivery and gesture. New Haven, **1819.** 12°.

— - American oratory; selections from speeches of Americans. Phila., **1845.** 8°.

— Moore, F. American eloquence; a col. of speeches and addresses. **N. Y., 1864.** 2 v. 8°

Note. The library has also orations by the following authors: **Adams, J.; — Adams, J. Q.; — Adams, S.; — Bayard, J. A.; — Boudinot, E.; — Brown, A. G.; — Burges, T.; — Calhoun, J. C.; — Choate, R.; — Clay, C. M.; — Clay, H.; — Clinton, De Witt; — Crafts, W.; — Davis, H. W.; — Dix, J. A.; — Drayton, W. H.; — Ellsworth, O.; — Emmet, T. A.; — Everett, E.; — Gallatin, A.; — Garrison, W. L.; — Gaston, W.; — Giles, W. B.; — Gore, C.; — Grimké, T. S.; — Hamilton, A.; — Hancock, J.; — Harper, R. G.; — Hayne, R. Y.; — Henry, P.; — Hillhouse, J.; — Hilliard, J. W.; — Jay, J.; — Johnson, A.; — King, R.; — Lee, H.; — Lee, R. H.; — Lincoln, A.; — Livingston, A.; — Livingston, R. R.; — Livingston, W.; — Madison, J.; — Marshall, J.; — Martin, L.; — Minot, G. R.; — Morris, G.; — Otis, H. G.; — Otis, J.; — Phillips, W.; — Pinckney, C.; — Pinkney, W.; — Prentiss, S. S.; — Quincy, J.,** *Jr.*; **— Randolph, J.,** *of Roanoke*; **— Red Jacket; — Rush, B.; — Rutledge, R.; — Sergeant, J.; — Seward, W. H.; — Schurz, C.; — Sprague, P.; — Story, J.; — Strong, C.; — Sumner, C.; — Tecumseh; — Tracy, U.; — Winthrop, R. C.; — Woodbury, L.;** — besides many single speeches and addresses.

Periodical literature. (Bibliography, History, etc.)

— Buckingham, J. T. Specimens of newspaper literature; with personal memoirs, *etc.* Boston, **1852.** 2 v. 12°.

— Roorbach, O. A. List of periodicals pub. in Amer. (*In his* Bibl., Suppl. 1850; *and* Bibl. 1852.)

— Cucheval-Clarigny, P. A. Origines de la presse amér. et son rôle dans la rév. (*In* **Revue** d. D. Mondes, août **1853.**) — La presse en Amér. depuis l'indépendence jusqu'à nos jours. (*In* mai **1857.**)

— Montégut, E. La presse aux Etats-Unis, mœurs et caractère du journalisme amér. (*In* **Revue** d. D. Mondes, juin **1856.**)

— Rowell, G. P., & Co. American newspaper directory; lists of all newspapers and periodicals pub. in the U. S. and Brit. Colonies. **N. Y., 1860, 70, 73, 76.** 4 v. 8°.

— - The men who advertise; [with newspaper rate-book and directory]. **N. Y., 1870.** 8°.

— Sketches of writers in the Princeton review.] (*In* **Biblical** repertory, Index vol. **1871.**)

Periodicals, including newspapers.

Academician. Vol. 1. 1818-20. *m.* N. Y., 1820. 8°.

Advertiser, Daily; Apr. 29, 1799 - Aug. 30, 1806. N. Y., 1799-1806. 8 v. f°.

Advocate of peace. Vol. 1-7, 15, 16. *b.m.* B., Wor., [1837-68]. 9 v. 8°.

African observer. Vol. 1, no. 1-10, 12. *m.* P., 1827-28. 8°.

African repository; 1825-60. *m.* W., 1826-60. 36 v. 8°.

Alabama. [Miscel. newspapers. 1863-68.] *v.p.*, 1863-68. 9 v. f°.

Albion. *w.* N. Y., 1822-76. 54 v. f°.

American advocate of peace. *q.* H., [1834-36]. 2 v. 8°.
Am. and commercial advertiser. *d.* Balt., 1863-76. 26 v. f°.
Am. annals of educ.; 1830-38. *m.* B., 1831-38. 8 v. 8°.
Am. annual cyclopædia; 1861-73. N. Y., 1862-74. 13 v. 8°.
Am. Apollo. Vol. 2, 3. *w.* B., 1792-94. 2 v. f°.
Am. Baptist mag. N. s., v. 1-4, *b. m.*; v. 5-9, *m.* B., 1817-29. 9 v. 8°.
Am. eclectic. *b. m.* N. Y., B., 1841-42. 4 v. 8°.
Am. educational year-book. *a.* B., *etc.* 1857-58. 2 v. 12°.
Am. gardener's magazine. *m.* B., 1835-36. 2 v. 8°.
Note. For contin. *see* **Magazine** of horticulture.
Am. herald. Vol. 3-5. *w.* B., 1784-86. 3 v. f°.
Am. journ. of educ. *m.* B., 1826-[30]. 5 v. 8°.
Note. For contin. *see* **Amer.** annals of educ.
Am. journ. of educ. Vol. 1-15, 24. *q.* H., 1856-73. 16 v. 8°.
Am. journ. of for. medicine. Vol. 1, no. 1; June, 1827. *n.p.*, 1827. 8°.
Am. journ. of homœopathia. Vol. 1, no. 4; Aug., 1835. [N. Y., 1835 ?] 8°.
Am. journ. of horticulture. *m.* B., 1867-71. 9 v. 8°.
Am. journ. of improvements in the useful arts. *q.* W., 1828, 1846. 2 v. 8° *and* 4°.
Am. journ. of insanity. Vol. 1-7, 16-25, 32-36. *q.* U., 1844-80. 22 v. 8°.
Am. journ. of numismatics. *q.* N. Y., B., 1866-76. 10 v. 8°.
Am. journ. of science and arts. 1st-3d ser. *q.*, *m.* N. Y., N. H., 1818-79. 108 v. 8°.
Am. journ. of the med. sciences. *q.* P., 1827-80. 105 v. 8°.
Note. A continuation of the 'Phila. journal'.
Am. jurist and law mag. *q.* B., 1829-43. 28 v. 8°.
Am. laborer. Vol. 1. *m.* N. Y., 1842-43. 8°.
Am. law journal. *q.* P., B., 1808-13. 4 v. 8°.
Am. law magazine. *q.* P., 1843-45. 4 v. 8°.
Am. magazine. Vol. 1. *m.* N. Y., [1787-88]. 8°.
Am. mag. and hist. chronicle; 1743-46. *m.* B., 1744-46. 3 v. 8°.
Am. med. and philosoph. register; 1810-14. *q.* N. Y., 1811-14. 4 v. 8°.
Am. medical intelligencer; 1837-41. *f.* P., 1838-41. 4 v. 8°.
Am. medical recorder. Vol. 1, 2, 4-14, 16. *q.* P., 1818-29. 14 v. 8°.
Am. mercury. Vol. 18-20. H., 1802-04. 3 v. f°.
Am. messenger. Vol. 4-6. *m.* N. Y., 1846-48. 3 v. f°.
Am. mineralogical journ. Vol. 1. [1810.] *q.* N. Y., 1814. 8°.
Am. Minerva. *d.* N. Y., 1794-97. 4 v. f°.
Am. monthly advertiser; Feb. 1838. *n.t.p.* [1838.] 8°.
Am. monthly magazine. Vol. 1, 2, n. s., v. 1-5. B., N. Y., 1829-38. 7 v. 8°.
Am. monthly mag. and crit. review. N. Y., 1817-[18]. 2 v. 8°.
Am. monthly review. C., B., 1832-33. 4 v. 8°.
Am. museum; 1787-92. *m.* P., 1790-92. 12 v. 8°.
Am. museum, or annual register; 1798. P., 1799. 8°.
Am. musical journal. *m.* N. Y., 1834-35. 4°.
Am. naturalist; 1867-79. *m.* S., 1868-79. 13 v. 8°.
Am. phrenological journ. Vol. 17-20. *m.* N. Y., 1853-54. 4 v. 4°.
Am. Presbyterian review. N. ser., v. 1. *q.* N. Y., P., 1863. 8°.
Am. publishers' circular. Vol. 2-7, n. ser., v. 1-18. *w.*, *f.* N. Y., P., 1856-72. 23 v. 8° *and* 4°.
Note. From Jan. 18, 1872, called 'The publishers' and stationers' weekly trade circular'.
Am. quarterly observer. B., 1833-34. 3 v. 8°.
Note. United with 'Biblical repository', 1835.
Am. quarterly register and mag. P., N. Y., [1848-51]. 6 v. 8°.
Note. After v. 3, called 'Stryker's Am. register'.
Am. quarterly review. P., [1827]-37. 22 v. 8°.
Am. quarterly temperance mag. A., 1833-[34]. 2 v. 8°.
Am. railroad journal. Vol. 1, pt. 1; 2, pt. 2; 3, 6, 7, 12, 13, 16-18. [4 ser.] *w.*, *f.* N. Y., 1832-[45]. 10 v. 8° *and* 4°.
Am. register; gen. repository of hist., *etc.*, 1806-10. *a.* P., 1807-11. 7 v. 8°.
Am. register; summary review of hist., *etc.* *a.* P., 1817. 2 v. 8°
Am. review; a Whig journal. *m.* N. Y., 1845-52. 16 v. 8°.
Note. After v. 11, entitled 'Am. Whig review'.
Am. review and literary journal. *q.* N. Y., 1801-02. 2 v. 8°.
Am. review of hist. and politics. *q.* P., 1811-12. 4 v. 8°.
Am. statesman. *s.w.* B., 1821-25. 5 v. f°.
Note. Continued as **Boston** d. Am. statesman.
Am. Sunday school mag. Vol. 4, 5. *m.* P., 1827-28. 2 v. 8°.
Am. traveller. Vol. 1-11, 13-21. *s.w.* B., 1826-45. 20 v. f°.
Note. For later vols. *see* **Traveller.**
Analectic magazine. Vol. 1-14; n. s., v. 1, 2. *m.* P., 1813-20. 16 v. 8°.
Annual of scientific discovery. B., 1850-71. 21 v. 12°.
See also **Annual registers**; — **Annuals.**
Anti-Masonic Christian herald. *w.* B., 1829. f°.
Appletons' journal. Vol. 5-15. *w.*; *n. s.*, v. 1-7. *m.* N. Y., [1871-79]. 18 v. 4°.
Appleton's mechanics' magazine. Vol. 1, 3. 1851-53. *m.* N. Y., 1851, 54. 2 v. 8° *and* 4°.
Archives of useful knowledge; 1810-13. *q.* P., 1811-13. 3 v. 8°.
Arcturus; 1840-41. *m.* N. Y., 1841. 2 v. 8°.
Arminian magazine. *m.* P., 1789-90. 2 v. 8°.
Army Argus and crisis; Dec. 3, 1864-Apr. 1, 1865. *w.* Mobile, 1864-65. f°.
Astronomical journal; 1849-54. *f.* C., 1851-54. 3 v. 4°.
Athenæum; spirit of Eng. magazines. Ser. 1-4. *f.* B., [1817]-32. 30 v. 8°.
Aurora; 1805-14, 17, 18. *d.* P., 1805-18. 15 v. f°.
Balance; 1802-06. *w.* Hudson, [1802-06]. 5 v. 4°.
Balloon post. No. 1-6. *d.* B., 1871. 4°.
Baltimore med. and philosoph. lycæum. Vol. 1, no. 1-3. *q.* Balt., [1811]. 8°.
Baltimore med. and phys. recorder. *q.* Balt., 1809. 8°.
Baltimore med. and surg. journal. *q.* Balt., 1833-34. 2 v. 8°.
Note. Continued as 'North American archives', *etc.*
Baltimore patriot. (Wanting July-Dec. of 1817, 27, and 28.) *d.* Balt., 1814-60. 91 v. f°.
Baltimore weekly patriot. Vol. 5, 6, 8. Balt., 1854-58. 3 v. f°.
Banker's magazine. Vol. 5-7, 13-23. [1st-3d ser.] *m.* B., N. Y., [1850-68]. 14 v. 8°.
Banner of light. Vol. 22-26. *w.* B., 1867-69. f°.
Bay state Democrat. *d.* B., 1842-44. 5 v. f°.
Belles-lettres repos. and monthly mag. Vol. 2. 1819-20. N. Y., 1820. 8°.
Biblical repertory. Vol. 1-3; n. s., vol. 1, 5, 13, pt. 1, 22-53. *q.* Princeton, P., N. Y., 1825-79. 37 v. 8°.
Biblical repository. 1st-3d ser. *q.* And., *etc.*, 1831-[49]. 28 v. 8°.
Bibliotheca sacra. *q.* And., 1844-79. 36 v. 8°.
Boatswain's whistle. *d.* B., 1864. f°.
Bohemian. Christmas no. 1. Rich., 1863. 8°.
Boston courier. *d.* B., 1824-55. 36 v. f°. (Incomplete.)
Same. *w.* 1841, 42-47, 53, 54. B., 1841-54. 5 v. f°.
Same. *s.w.* 1827, 32, 35-37, 40, 44-49, 51-54, 56. B., 1827-56. 17 v. f°.
Bost. cultivator; 1846-48, 61-71. *w.* B., 1846-71. 6 v. f°.
Bost. daily advertiser. B., 1813-80. 122 v. f°.
Bost. daily advocate. B., 1832-35. 8 v. f°.
Bost. daily Amer. statesman; 1825-32, 34. B., 1825-34. 9 v. f°.
Bost. daily atlas. B., 1832-60. 32 v. f°.
Bost. daily bee. B., 1855-57. 3 v. f°.
Bost. daily courier. B 1856-65. 20 v. f°.
Bost. daily journal. B., 1846-80. 70 v. f°.
Bost. daily mail. B., 1847-49. 2 v. f°.
Bost. daily times. B., 1836-57. 47 v. f°.
Bost. daily Whig. B., 1847-48. 3 v. f°.
Bost. evening bulletin. *d.* B., 1827-29. 4 v. f°.
Bost. evening post; 1741-60, 65-74, 81-83. *d.* B., 1741-83. 7 v. f°.
Bost. guide to health. Vol. 1843-45. *m.* B., 1845. 8°.
Bost. herald; 1852-56, 61-80. *d.* B., 1852-80. 43 v. f°.
Bost. journal of philos. and the arts; 1823-26. *b.m.* B., 1824-26. 3 v. 8°.
Bost. literary magazine. Vol. 1. *m.* B., 1833. 8°.
Bost. lyceum. Vol. 1. *m.* B., [1827]. 8°.
Bost. magazine. Vol. 1. *f.* [B., 1805-06.] 4°.
Bost. medical and surgical journal. Vol. 1-4, 7, 8, 10, 12, 14-16, 19-27, 29-97. *w.* B., 1829-77. 89 v. 8°.
Bost. medical intelligencer. *w.* B., 1823-28. 5 v. 8°, 4°.
Bost. mercantile journal; 1833, 35, 40-45. *d.* B., 1833-45. 15 v. f°.
Bost. mirror. *w.* B., 1808-09. f°.
Bost. miscellany. *m.* B., N. Y., [1842]. 2 v. 8°.
Bost. observer. Vol. 1 (no. 1-3 w.). *w.* B., 1835. f°.
Bost. patriot; 1809-31, 41-42. *s.w.* B., 1809-42. 30 v. f°.
Bost. pearl. Vol. 5. *w.* B., 1836. 4°.
Bost. quarterly review. B., 1838-42. 5 v. 8°.
Bost. recorder; 1816-23, 26-35, 37-48. *w.* B., 1816-48. 30 v. f°.
Bost. republican. *d.* B., 1848-49. 3 v. f°.
Bost. review. *b.m.*, *q.* B., *etc.*, 1861-66. 6 v. 8°.
Note. Continued as the Congregational review.
Bost. shipping list; 1854-55, 69-70. *s.w.* B., 1854-70. 3 v. f°.
Bost. spectator. *w.* B., 1814. f°.
Bost. Sunday courier. *w.* B., 1869-75. 5 v. f°.
Bost. telegraph. *w.* B., 1824. f°.
Bost. weekly magazine. 1802-05. B., 1803-05. 3 v. 4°.
Note. Continued as the Boston magazine.
Bost. weekly magazine. B., 1816-18. 2 v. 4°.
Bost. weekly magazine. Vol. 1. B., 1838-39. 4°.
Bost. weekly messenger; 1811-15, 26-29, 31-34. B., 1811-34. 8 v. f°.
Bost. weekly report. B., 1819-27. 17 v. f°.
Brownson's quarterly review. [6 ser.] B., N. Y., 1844-75. 24 v. 8°.

Buffalo medical journal and monthly review. Vol. 2. *m.* [Buf., 1846-47.] 8°.
Cabinet. *w.* [B., 1811.] 8°.
Calumet. Vol. 1. *b.m.* N. Y., [1831-34]. 8°.
Campbell's foreign semi-monthly mag. Vol. 4-6. P., 1843-44. 3 v. 8°.
Casket; 1828-30, 32, 36, 38, 39. *m.* P., [1828]-39. 7 v. 8°.
Censor. Vol. 1, 2. *w.* B., 1771-72. f°.
Charleston daily courier. Charl., 1832-68. 22 v. f°. (Incomplete.)
Same. July 26 - Dec. 31, 1861, 63. Charl., 1861-63. 2 v. f°.
Charleston tri-weekly courier; 1870-71. Charl., 1870-71. 2 v. f°.
Charleston Mercury. *d.* Charl., 1857-61. 6 v. f°.
Same. 1861; 1863. Charl., 1861-63. 2 v. f°.
Same. Apr. 21, June 21, 1862; Apr. 5, 1864. 3 nos. f°.
Charleston weekly courier; Oct. 1838 - Sept. 1840. Charl., 1838-40. f°.
Charlestown chronicle; 1868-71. Charl., 1869-71. 3 v. f°.
Cherokee phœnix; Feb. 28, 1828 - Apr. 14, 1830; Apr. 21, 1830 - Aug. 11, 1832. New Echota, 1828-32. 2 v. f°.
Chicago daily republican; May 1865 - Dec. 1870. Chic., 1865-70. 12 v. f°.
Chicago record; 1857-58. *m.* Chic., [1858]. 4°.
Chicago tribune. *d.* and *w.* Chic., 1861-76. 31 v. f°.
Children's magazine. Vol. 3, 8. *m.* N. Y., 1831-36. 2 v. 18°.
Child's friend. Vol. 9-19. *m.* B., 1848-52. 11 v. 12°.
Child's paper; Jan. 1852 - Feb. 1853. *m.* N. Y., *etc.*, 1852-53. 4°.
Christian disciple. [2 ser.] *m.*, *b.m.* B., 1813-23. 11 v. 8°.
Note. Continued as '**Christian** examiner'.
Christian examiner. *b.m.* B., N. Y., 1824-69. 87 v. 8°.
Christian library; 1834-35. *w.* N. Y., 1835. 2 v. 8°.
Christian magazine. Vol. 3. *m.* B., 1826. 8°.
Christian mirror. *w.* Portl., 1865-73. 9 v. f°.
Christian monitor. *q.* B., 1806-10. 8 v. 12°.
Christian register. Vol. 1-16, 18-59. *w.* B., 1821-80. 58 v. f°.
Christian review. *q.* B., *etc.*, 1836-63. 28 v. 8°.
Christian spectator. Vol. 1-10, *m.*; 11-20, *q.* N. H., N. Y., [1819-38]. 20 v. 8°.
Christian visitant. *b.m.* B., 1827-28. 2 v. 12°
Christian watchman; Dec. 1820 - Dec. 1821; 1832; 1836-1842; 1865-74. *w.* B., 1820-74. 17 v. f°.
Note. From Jan. 1867, called 'Watchman and reflector'.
Christian witness. Feb. 1835-44; 1866-71. *w.* B., 1835-71. 11 v. f°.
Christian's magazine. Vol. 1, 2, *q.*; 3, 4, *m.* N. Y., [1807]-11. 4 v. 8°.
Chronicle, Daily, and sentinel; June, 1862-65. Aug., 1862-65. 5 v. f°.
Chronotype. *d.* B., 1846-49. 8 v. f°. (Incomplete.)
Church review. *q.* N. H., *etc.*, [1848]-69. 20 v. 8°.
Note. From v. 20, called 'Amer. quarterly church review'.
Churchman. Vol. 5-28. *w.* N. Y., 1835-59. 25 v. f°.
Churchman's magazine; 1809-11, 13, 22, 23. [3 ser.] *b.m.* N. Y., *etc.*, 1809-23. 6 v. 8°.
Churchman's repository. Vol. 1, no. 1-6. *m.* [Newburyp., 1820.] 8°.
Churchman's year book. *a.* H., 1871. 12°.
Cincinnati daily commercial; 1863, 65, 66, 68-76. Cin., 1863-76. 24 v. f°.
Classical journ. and scholar's rev. *m.* B., 1830-31. 2 v. 8°.
Claypoole's advertiser. *d.* P., 1799-1800. 2 v. f°. (Incomplete.)
Collegian. *m.* C., 1830. 8°.
Collegian. No. 1-3. *f.* [C., 1866.] 4°.
Colonizationist; 1833-34. *m.* B., 1834. 8°.
Columbian centinel; June, 1790 - Dec., 1839. *s.w.* B., 1790-1839. 45 v. f°.
Columbian chronicle; Aug., 1809 - Dec. 1810. *s.w.* P., 1809-10. f°.
Columbian gazette; Apr. 6 - June 22, 1799. N. Y., 1799. f°.
Columbian magazine; 1786-91. *m.* P., [1787-91]. 5 v. 8°.
Columbian Minerva. *w.* D., 1799-1803. 3 v. f°.
Columbian phenix; Jan. - July, 1800. *m.* B., 1800. 8°.
Commentator; Dec. 12, 1829 - Feb. 20, 1831. *w.* B., 1829-31. 2 v. f°.
Commercial advertiser; Oct. 1797 - Dec. 1803. *d.* N. Y., 1797-1803. 12 v. f°.
Commercial advertiser; April, 1832 - April, 1833. *s.w.* Salem, 1832-33. f°.
Commercial and financial chronicle. *w.* N. Y., [1865]-80. 30 v. 4°.
Commercial gazette. *d.* B., 1829. 2 v. f°.
Commercial review. *m.* N. O., *etc.*, 1846-50. 8 v. 8°.
Note. Continued as 'De Bow's review'.
Common school journal. *b.m.* B., 1839-48. 10 v. 8°.
Commonwealth; Jan. 1851 - June 1854; 1862-73. *w.* B., 1851-73. 18 v. f°.

Confederate newspapers. *See* **Confederate States of America.** *Periodicals* (p. 648).
Congregational quarterly. B., N. Y., 1859-78. 20 v. 8°.
Congregational review. Vol. 7-11. *q.* B., *etc.*, 1867-[71]. 5 v. 8°.
Congregational visiter. *m.* B., 1844-48. 5 v. 8°.
Congregationalist. *w.* B., 1868-74. 7 v. f°.
Congressional globe, 23d - 38th Cong., 1st sess.; 38th Cong., 2d sess., pt. 2 - 41st Cong., 2d sess., pt. 1; 41st Cong., 3d sess. - 42d Cong. W., 1834-73. 4°.
Connecticut courant. *w.* H., 1802-23. 10 v. f°.
Same. July 29 - Nov. 4, 1799; Mar. 10 - Dec. 29, 1800; Mar. 16 - July 20, 1801.
Connecticut evangelical magazine. *m.* H., [1800]-09. 9 v. 8°.
Connecticut mirror; July 10, 1809 - July 1, 1811. *w.* H., 1809-11. f°.
Connecticut observer; Jan. - Oct. 1839. *w.* H., 1839. f°.
Constitutional telegraph; Oct. 1799 - Dec. 1800; Jan. - May 19, 1802. *s.w.* B., 1799-1802. 3 v. f°.
Constitutionalist. *w.* [Exeter, 1810-12.] 2 v. f°.
Constitutionalist, Daily; [odd nos.]. Aug., Ga., 1862-64. f°.
Continental journal; May 30, 1776 - April 28, 1785. *w.* B., 1776-85. 3 v. f°.
Corrector; Mar. 28 - Apr. 26, 1804. *s.w.* N. Y., 1804. f°.
Countersign, Daily; May 17 - June 4, 1864. St. L., 1864. f°.
Country Porcupine; Mar. 5 - May 7, Nov. 1, 1798 - Aug., 1799. *t.w.* P., 1798-99. 2 v. f°.
Courier de Boston; 23 avril - 15 oct. 1789. *w.* B., 1789. f°.
Courrier de la France et des colonies; 15 oct. 1795 - 14 mars. 1796. *d.* P., 1795-96. f°.
Courrier de la Louisiane; fév. 22, 1822. N. O., 1822. f°.
Courrier des Etats Unis. *s.w.* N. Y., 1829-55. f°. (Incomplete.)
Covenant and official magazine of the Grand Lodge of the U. S. Vol. 1, 3. *m.* *n.p.*, 1842-44. 2 v. 8°.
Crayon. *w.* N. Y., 1855-60. 7 v. 4°.
Cultivator. [1st - 3d ser.] *m.* A., [1834]-54. 21 v. 8°.
Dartmouth, The. Vol. 5. 1843-44. *m.* Hanover, 1844. 8°.
De Bow's review. Vol. 9-19, 22-30. *m.* N. O., *etc.*, 1850-61. 20 v. 8°.
Note. For previous vols. *see* **Commercial** review.
Same. Aug. 1861 - Aug. 1862; July, Aug., 1864. N. O., *etc.*, 1862-64. 8 nos. 8°.
Same. After the war series. Nashville, 1866-70. 7 v. 8°.
Dedham gazette. Vol. 51-57. *w.* D., 1865-70. 7 v. f°.
Note. Continued, with Hyde Park journal, as the Norfolk Co. journal.
Democrat; Jan. 4, 1804, May 25, 1809. *s.w.* B., 1804-09. 6 v. f°.
Democratic press; Jan. - June, 1813. *d.* P., 1813. f°.
Democratic review. Vol. 1-24, 26-29, 31, 40. *q.* W., N. Y., 1838-57. 30 v. 8°.
Deseret news; Mar. 14, 1855 - Mar. 4, 1857. *w.* Gt. Salt L. City, 1855-57. f°.
Dial; 1840-44. *q.* B., 1841-44. 4 v. 8°.
Dispatch, Daily. Richm., 1863-64. 2 v. f°.
Dwight's journal of music. Vol. 1-38. *w.* B., 1853-78. 38 v. 4°.
Eastern Argus. *w.* Port., 1803-11. 8 v. f°.
Eclectic journal of medicine. Vol. 1, no. 1, 2. *m.* *n.p.*, 1836. 8°.
Eclectic magazine. *m.* N. Y., P., 1844-63. 60 v. 8°.
Eclectic museum. *m.* N. Y., 1843. 3 v. 8°.
Eclectic repertory. 1810-20. *q.* P., 1811-20. 10 v. 8°.
Emporium of arts and sciences. [2 ser.] *m.* P., 1812-14. 5 v. 8°.
Essayist. Vol. 1, n. s. 1831-33. *irreg.* B., 1833. 8°.
Essex gazette; Aug. 1769 - Nov. 1776; Aug. 1782 - July 1784. *w.* S., 1769-84. 7 v. f°.
Note. For succeeding vols. *see* **Independent** chronicle.
Essex patriot; 1817-21. *w.* Hav., 1818-21. f°.
Essex register, April 3. S., 1822. f°.
Evangelical guardian; 1817-19. *m.* N. Y., 1817-18. 2 v. 8°.
Every Saturday; Jan. 1866 - Oct. 1874. Boston, 1866-69, 72-74. 14 v. *and* 1870-71. 3 v. f°.
Examiner. *b.m.* N. Y., [1813-15]. 4 v. 8°.
Exchange, Daily; July - Dec. 1858; July - Dec. 1859; July 1860 - June 1861. Balt., 1858-61. 4 v. f°.
Expositor and Univ. review; 1833-40. *b.m.* B., 1834-40. 4 v. 8°.
Note. A contin. of the Universalist expositor.
Family magazine. Vol. 7. 1839-40. *m.* N. Y., *etc.*, 1840. 4°.
Farmer and gardener. Vol. 1. 1834-35. *w.* Balt., 1835. 4°.
Farmer's monthly visitor. Con., 1839-[48]. 10 v. 4°.
Farmer's weekly museum. Walpole, 1797-98. f°.
Federal gazette and Balt. daily advertiser. Balt., 1806-08. 3 v. f°.
Same. Feb. 8, 1822. Balt., 1822. f°.

Federal gazette and daily advertiser; Jan. 1 - Feb. 22. B., 1798. f°.
Same. Jan. 1 - March 26. B., 1798. f°.
Federal observer; Nov. 22, 1798 - May 29, 1800. *w.* Ports., 1798-1800. f°.
Federal orrery. *s.w.* B., 1794-96. 2 v. f°.
Federal republican and Balt. telegraph. *s.w.* Balt., 1817-18. 2 v. f°.
Same. May 25. Balt., 1822. f°.
Federal republican and com. gazette. *d.* Balt., 1808-10. 2 v. f°.
Financial register of the U. S.; 1837-38. *f.* P., 1838. 2 v. 8°.
Frank Leslie's illustrated newspaper. Vol. 13-35. N. Y., 1862-73. 12 v. f°.
Franklin journal. *m.* P., 1826-28. 6 v. 8°.
Note. Continued as 'Journal of the Franklin Institute'.
Free trade advocate. *w.* P., 1829. 2 v. 8°.
Freeman's journal; Columbian chron. *w.* P., 1809-10. f°.
Freeman's journal; or, N. Am. intelligencer. *w.* P., 1781-83. f°.
Friend of peace. *irreg.* B., C., [1815]-27. 4 v. 8°.
Friend of progress; Nov. 1864 - Aug. 1865. *m.* N. Y., 1864-65. 8°.
Friend of virtue. Vol. 9. *b.m.* B., 1846. 8°.
Same. Vol. 12, no. 2, June 1849. [B., 1849.] 8°.
Galaxy. Vol. 3-24. *m.* N. Y., 1867-77. 22 v. 8°.
Gardener's monthly. Vol. 2-21. P., 1860-79. 20 v. 8°.
Gazette, The; May 6, 1865 - May 19, 1866. *w.* Yonkers, 1865-66. f°.
Gazette of the U. S. *d.* P., 1789-1810. 20 v. f°. (Incomplete.)
General Assembly's missionary mag.; 1805-09. *m.* P., 1806-09. 5 v. 8°.
General repository and review. *q.* C., 1812-13. 4 v. 8°.
Genesee farmer; Monthly. R., 1836-39. 4 v. 4°.
— New Genesee farmer. Vol. 3, 4, 6-9. *m.* R., 1842-48. 6 v. 4°.
Gentleman's mag. and monthly Amer. rev. Vol. 4, 5. P., 1839. 2 v. 8°.
Georgia journal; Nov. 27. Milledgeville, 1821. f°.
— [Miscel. newspapers.] *v.p.*, 1865-66. 4 v. f°.
Georgian, The; May 7. Savannah, 1822. f°.
Globe. *d.* and *s.w.* W., 1833-45. 12 v. f°. (Incomplete.)
Gospel advocate. *m.* B., 1821-26. 6 v. 8°.
Graham journal. *w.* B., 1837-38. 2 v. 8°.
Harbinger. *w.* N. Y., B., 1845-49. 8 v. 8°.
Harper's bazar. Vol. 5. *w.* N. Y., [1872]. f°.
Harper's new monthly magazine. N. Y., 1850-80. 60 v. 8°.
Harper's weekly. Vol. 5-23. N. Y., 1861-80. 20 v. 4°.
Harvard advocate; 1866-77. *f.* [C., 1866-77.] 22 v. 4°.
Harvard lyceum; July 1810 - March 1811. *f.* C., 1811. 8°.
Harvard magazine; 1854-61. *m.* C., 1855-61. 7 v. 8°.
Harvard register; 1827-28. *m.* C., 1828. 8°.
Harvardiana. *m.* C., B., 1835-38. 4 v. 8°.
Hierophant; 1842-43. *m.* N. Y., 1844. 8°.
Historical magazine. 1st - 3d ser. 1857-73. *m.* B., Morrisania, 1859-73. 19 v. 4° *and* 8°. (Incomplete.)
Home missionary. Vol. 1-34. *m.* N. Y., 1829-62. 34 v. 8°.
Horticultural register. *m.* B., 1835-39. 4 v. 8°.
Horticulturist. Vol. 1, 2.; 14-23. *m.* A., 1847-68. 12 v. 4° *and* 8°.
Hunt's merchant's magazine. *m.* N. Y., 1839-70. 63 v. 8°.
Note. After 1870 included in the 'Commercial and financial chronicle'.
Hygienic monitor; 1859. *m.* B., 1860. 8°.
Illinois and Indiana med. and surg. journ. 1846-48. *b.m.* Chic., [1847]-48. 2 v. 8°.
Illinois gazette, March 2. Shawnee-town, 1822. f°.
Illinois teacher. Vol. 11, 12. *m.* Peoria, 1865-66. 2 v. 8°.
Impartial register. Vol. 1. *s.w.* S., 1800. f°.
Independent The. *w.* N. Y., 1855-76. 23 v. f° *and* 4°.
Independent American; July 11 - Dec. 30. *t.w.* Georgetown, 1809. f°.
Independent chronicle. *w.* B., 1776-1815. 29 v. f°. (Incomplete.)
Independent ledger. *w.* B., 1778-85. f°. (Incomplete.)
Independent reflector. No. 2-52. *w.* [N. Y., 1752-53.] f°.
Independent statesman and Maine republican; Apr. 12, 1822.
Index. *w.* Toledo, 1870-80. 11 v. 4°.
Jenks' Portland gazette; 1799, 1801-06. *w.* Port., 1799-1806. 2 v. f°.
Journal of foreign med. science. Vol. 2, 3. *q.* P., N. Y., [1822-23]. 2 v. 8°.
Journal of health and recreation. P., 1830-[33]. 4 v. 8°.
Journal of speculative philosophy. *q.* St. L., 1867-79. 13 v. 8°.
Journal of the American Inst.; 1835-39. *m.* N. Y., 1836-40. 4 v. 8°.
Journal of the Amer. Temp. Union. N. Y., 1837-40. 4 v. 4°.
Journal of the Franklin Inst. *m.* P., 1829-80. 101 v. 8°.
Note. For preceding vols. *see* **Franklin** journal.
Journal of the ministry at large. *m.* [B., 1841.] 8°.
Juvenile rambler. *w.* B., 1833. 4°.
Juvenile reformer. *w.* Port., 1835-37. f°.
Juvenile watchman. *w.* B., 1833-34. f°.
Knickerbocker. Vol. 1, 2; 4-9; 11-65. *m.* N. Y., 1833-65. 63 v. 8°.
Ladies' companion. Vol. 18. 1842-43. *m.* N. Y., 1843. 8°.
Ladies' garland. Vol. 2-14. *m.* P., 1839-48. 13 v. 8°.
Ladies' magazine. *m.* B., 1828-34. 7 v. 8°.
Lady's monthly journal of fashion; 1832. No. 1-6. B., [1832]. 8°.
Lady's pearl. Vol. 3. 1842-43. *m.* L., 1843. 8°.
Latter day luminary. Vol. 1. 1818-19. *q.* P., 1818. 8°.
Law reporter; 1838-48. *m.* B., 1839-48. 10 v. 8°.
Note. For continuation *see* **Monthly** law reporter.
Liberator. *w.* B., 1831-65. 35 v. f°.
Library of health. *m.* B., 1837. 12°.
Literary and philosophical repertory. Vol. 2. 1814-17. Middlebury, [1817]. 8°.
Literary and theol. review. *q.* N. Y., B., 1834-38. 5 v. 8°.
Literary companion. *w.* [N. Y., 1821.] 8°.
Literary journal. Vol. 1, no. 4, 6, 11. *w.* Latin school, B., 1829. 8°.
Literary magazine and American register. *m.* P., *etc.*, 1803-08. 8 v. 8°.
Literary miscellany. *q.* C., 1805-06. 2 v. 8°.
Literary world. N. Y., 1847-53. 13 v. 4°.
Littell's living age. [5 ser.] *f.* B., 1844-80. 146 v. 8°.
Livingston's law register for 1852-[54]. *a.* N. Y., 1852-54. 2 v. 8°.
Louisiana. [Miscel. newspapers.] 1865-66. 9 v.
Louisville daily journal; 1863 - June 1864; 1865-69. Louisv., 1863-69. f°.
Same. [Courier journal.] *w.* Louisv., 1870-77. f°.
Louisville journal of med. and surgery. *q.* Louisv., 1838. 8°.
Lowell offering. *m.* L., [1840]-43. 3 v. 8°.
Lowell weekly journ. L., 1850-59. 3 v. f°.
Magazine of horticulture. *m.* B., 1837-47. 11 v. 8°.
Note. A continuation of the 'Amer. gardener's mag.'
Magnolia weekly; a Southern home journ. Rich., 1862-65. 2 v. f°.
Massachusetts gazette; Dec. 5, 1785 - Oct. 12, 1787. *w.* B., 1785-87. f°. (Incomplete.)
Massachusetts gazette and Boston news-letter. B., 1710-75. 11 v. f°. (Incomplete.)
Massachusetts gazette and The post boy, *etc.* B., 1765-73. f°. (Incomplete.)
Massachusetts magazine. *m.* B., 1789 96. 8 v. 8°.
Massachusetts mercury. *s.w.* B., 1793-1800. 6 v. f°.
Massachusetts missionary mag. *m.* S., B., [1803-08]. 5 v. 8°.
Massachusetts quarterly review. B., 1848-50. 3 v. 8°.
Massachusetts spy. *w.* B., Wor., 1770-1809. f°. (Incomplete.)
Massachusetts teacher. Vol. 1-3, 9, 12, 13, 19-22. *b.m.* B., [1848-69]. 10 v. 8°.
Mathematical diary. No. 1-6. *q.* N. Y., 1825. 12°.
Mathematical monthly; 1858-61. C., N. Y., 1859-61. 3 v. 4°.
Medical and agric. register; 1806-07. *m.* B., [1807]. 8°.
Medical examiner. Vol. 4, n.s., v. 1. *f.* P., 1841-42. 2 v. 8°.
Medical expositor. Vol. 1, no. 9. L., 1852. 4°.
Medical investigator. Vol. 7-10. *m.* Chic., 1870-73. 4 v. 8°.
Medical magazine; 1832-35. *m.* B., 1833-[35]. 3 v. 8°.
Medical news and library. Vol. 6, 8, 10, 23-34, 36, 37. *m.* P., 1848-79. 17 v. 8°.
Medical repository. *q.* N. Y., 1798-1822. 22 v. 8°.
Medical review. *q.* P., 1824-26. 3 v. 8°.
Medical world; 1856-57. *f.* B., 1857. 2 v. 8°.
Mentor and fireside review. *m.* N. Y., 1839. 2 v. 12°.
Mercantile advertiser; March 28, 1799 - 1800. *d.* N. Y., 1799-1800. f°.
Same. April 24. N. Y., 1822. f°.
Mercantile journal, Evening; Feb. 5, 1833, 35, 40-45. *d.* B., 1833-45. 15 v. f°.
Note. For succeeding vols. *see* **Boston** daily journ.
Mercury and N. Eng. palladium. *s.w.* B., 1801-03. 3 v. f°.
Note. For succeeding vols. *see* **New England** palladium.
Merrimack intelligencer; July 20, 1816 - Feb. 8, 1817. *w.* Hav., 1816-17. f°.
Methodist magazine and quarterly review. 2d ser., v. 7-11. N. Y., 1836-40. 5 v. 8°.
Methodist quarterly review. 3d, 4th ser. N. Y., 1841-76. 36 v. 8°.
Military and naval mag. of U. S. *m.* [W., 1833-36.] 6 v. 8°.
Mining magazine; July 1853 - Dec. 1856. *m.* N. Y., 1853-56. 7 v. 8°.

Mirror of taste. Vol. 1, 3, 4. *m.* P., 1810–11. 3 v. 8°.
Missionary herald. Vol. 17–75. B., [1821]–79. 59 v. 8°.
Note. For vols. 1–16 *see* **Panoplist.**
Missouri Democrat, Daily. St. L., 1863–72. 19 v. f°.
Missouri Republican, Daily. St. L., 1861–64. 7 v. f°.
Mobile commercial register; April 15, May 6. Mobile, 1822. f°.
Mobile daily news; 1865. Mobile, 1865. f°.
Mobile daily register and advertiser; Feb. - Dec. 1863; 1864; Jan. - April 26, 1865. Mobile, 1863–65. 3 v. f°.
Same. 1868. Mobile, 1868. 2 v. f°.
Same. Weekly; 1870–71. Mobile, 1870–71. 2 v. f°.
Modern thinker. No. 1, 2. N. Y., 1870–73. 2 v. 8°.
Monitor. *m.* B., 1823–24. 2 v. 12°.
Monthly anthology. B., 1804–11. 10 v. 8°.
Monthly chronicle of events, *etc.* B., 1840–42. 3 v. 8°.
Monthly chronicle of original lit. Vol. 1, no. 1. [N. Y., 1839.] 8°.
Monthly journal of agriculture; 1845–48. N. Y., 1846–48. 3 v. 8°.
Monthly journal of for. medicine. Vol. 2, 3. P., 1528–29. 2 v. 8°.
Monthly law reporter. N. s., v. 1–12. B., 1848–59. 12 v. 8°.
Note. This is v. 11–22 of the 'Law reporter'.
Monthly magazine and Amer. review; 1799–1800. N. Y., 1800. 3 v. 8°.
Monthly magazine of religion and lit.; 1840–41. Gettysburg, 1840. 8°.
Monthly miscellany. B., *etc.*, 1839–43. 9 v. 12°.
Monthly register and review of the U. S. Charleston, N. Y., 1806–07. 3 v. 8°.
Monthly religious magazine. B., 1844–74. 51 v. 8°.
Note. Continued as 'The Unitarian review'.
Monthly traveller. Vol. 5. [B., 1834.] 8°.
Mother's magazine. Vol. 6, 7. *m.* N. Y., 1838–39. 2 v. 8°.
Mrs. A. S. Colvin's weekly messenger. 2d ser., v. 2. 1827–28. W., 1828. 8°.
Museum of foreign lit. and science. Vol. 1–20, 23, 24, 28–45. P., N. Y., [1822–42]. 38 v. 8°.
Nashville daily union; Mar. 1863 - June 1864; 1865; Jan. - June 1866. N., 1863–66. 5 v. f°.
Nashville despatch; Sept. 16, 1863 - June 30, 1864; Jan. - June 1865. N., 1863–65. 2 v. f°.
Nation, The. *w.* N. Y., 1865–80. 31 v. 4°.
National advocate. *s.w.* and *d.* N. Y., 1820. f°.
National ægis; Dec. 1801 - Nov. 1803. *w.* Wor., 1801–03. 2 v. f°.
Same. April 3. Wor., 1822. f°.
National anti-slavery standard. *w.* N. Y., 1869–70. f°.
Note. For succeeding vols. *see* **National** standard.
National freedman. *m.* N. Y., 1865–66. 2 v. 8°.
National gazette; by P. Freneau. *s.w.* [P.,] 1792–93. f°.
National gazette and lit. register. *t.w.* P., 1821–41. 21 v. f°.
National intelligencer, Tri-weekly; Nov. 28, 1800 - Dec., 1804; 1807–68. W., 1800–68. f°.
National magazine; 1845–46. *m.* N. Y., 1846. 3 v. 8°.
National philanthropist. *w.* B., 1826–29. 2 v. f°.
National preacher. Vol. 1–11, 15, 16, 22, 27, 28. *m.* N. Y., 1826–54. 16 v. 8°.
National preacher and village pulpit. N. s., v. 1, 3. *m.* N. Y., 1858–60. 2 v. 8°.
National quarterly review. N. Y., 1860–62. 4 v. 8°.
National republican. *d.* W., 1862–68. 5 v. f°. (Incomplete.)
National standard. *w.* N. Y., 1870–71. 2 v. f°.
Naturalist, The; 1830–32. *m.* B., 1831–32. 2 v. 8°.
Naval magazine. *b.m.* N. Y., 1836–37. 2 v. 8°.
New England Baptist register. *w.* B., 1831. f°.
N. E. farmer. *w.* B., 1823–46. 24 v. 4°.
N. E. farmer. *f.* B., 1849–71. 19 v. 8°.
N. E. farmer. *w.* B., 1865–74. f°.
N. E. galaxy. *w.* B., 1817–31. 7 v. f°.
N. E. hist. and geneal. register. *q.* B., 1847–80. 34 v. 8°.
N. E. journ. of med. and surgery. *q.* B., 1812–27. 16 v. 8°.
Note. For continuation *see* **Boston** med. and surg. journal.
N. E. magazine. *m.* [B., 1831–35.] 9 v. 8°.
Note. Continued as 'American monthly mag.'
N. E. palladium. *s.w.* B., 1804–31. 27 v. f°.
Note. For previous vols. *see* **Mercury** and N. E. palladium.
N. E. puritan. B., 1841–45. 2 v. f°. (Incomplete.)
N. E. quar. journ. of med. and surg.; 1842–43. B., 1843. 8°.
N. E. quarterly magazine. No. 1–3. B., 1802. 8°.
N. E. spectator. *w.* B., 1836–37. f°.
N. E. telegraph. Vol. 2. No. Wrentham, 1836. 8°.
N. E. weekly journal. B., 1727–30. f°.
New Englander. *q.* N. H., [1843–80]. 39 v. 8°.
New Hampshire and Vt. journal. *w.* Walpole, 1797–99. f°.
New Hampshire gazette; 1788; 89; 1795–99; 1803–04; 1807–55. *w.* Ports., 1788–1855. 56 v. f°.
New Hampshire patriot. *w.* Concord, 1811–15. f°.
New Hampshire repository. *q.* Gilmanton, 1846. 8°.
New Jerusalem magazine. *m.* B., 1828–72. 44 v. 8°.
Note. Continued as 'New Church magazine'.
New nation. *w.* N. Y., 1864. 2 v. f°.
New world. *w.* N. Y., 1841–42. f°.
New York American. *s. w.* N. Y., 1824–29. 6 v. f°.
N. Y. daily gazette. N. Y., 1788–1808. 12 v. f°. (Incomplete.)
Same. Apr. 18 - May 14. N. Y., 1799. f°.
Same. Apr. 10. N. Y., 1822. f°.
N. Y. daily tribune. N. Y., 1845–80. 43 v. f°.
N. Y. evening post; 1802–10, 12, 18–32. *d.* N. Y., 1802–32. f°.
N. Y. gazette and weekly mercury, Sept. 7. N. Y., 1778. f°.
N. Y. herald; July 28, 1804–06; 1809; July 1861–80. *d.* N. Y., 1804–80. 39 v. f°.
N. Y. journal of commerce; 1831–33, 35. *d.* N. Y., 1831–35. 8 v. f°.
N. Y. ledger. *w.* N. Y., 1859–73. f°.
N. Y. legal observer. Vol. 5. *m.* N. Y., 1847. 8°.
N. Y. literary gazette. *w.* N. Y., 1825–26. 8°. (Incomplete.)
N. Y. magazine. Vol. 2–5. *m.* N. Y., 1791–94. 4 v. 8°.
N. Y. medical and philosoph. journ. *q.* N. Y., 1809–11. 3 v. 8°.
N. Y. medical and physical journ. *q.* N. Y., 1822–[30]. 9 v. 8°.
N. Y. medical magazine. 1814–15. *a.* N. Y., 1815. 8°.
N. Y. military magazine. *w.* N. Y., 1841. 4°.
N. Y. mirror. *w.* N. Y., 1833–38. 3 v. f°. (Incomplete.)
N. Y. missionary magazine. 1800–01. *q.* N. Y., 1801. 2 v. 8°.
N. Y. observer; Mar. - Dec. 1841; 1844–59. *w.* N. Y., 1841–59. 9 v. f°.
N. Y. price current; Aug. 16, 1800 - Aug. 15, 1801. *w.* N. Y., [1800–01]. 4°.
N. Y. quarterly magazine; Oct., 1836. Vol. 1, no. 1. N. Y., 1836. 8°.
N. Y. review. *m.* and *q.* N. Y., 1837–42. 10 v. 8°.
N. Y. review and athenæum magazine. N. Y., 1825–26. 2 v. 8°.
N. Y. spectator; 1808–10; 1820; Oct. 10, 1828 - Oct. 28, 1831. *s.w.* N. Y., 1808–31. f°.
Same. Jan. 15. N. Y., 1822. f°.
N. Y. statesman; May 13. N. Y., 1822. f°.
N. Y. teacher. Vol. 15. 1865–66. *m.* A., 1866. 8°.
N. Y. times. *d.* N. Y., 1861–77. 25 v. f°.
Niles' weekly register. Balt., P., 1811–48. 75 v. 8°.
Norfolk county journal. *w.* D., 1871. f°.
Note. For preceding vols. *see* **Dedham** gazette.
North American and mercantile daily advertiser. Balt., 1808–09. 2 v. f°.
North American archives of med. and surg. science; 1834–35. *m.* Balt., 1835. 2 v. 8°.
North American magazine; 1832–35. *m.* P., 1833–35. 5 v. 8°.
North American review. *b.m.* and *q.* B., 1815–80. 130 v. 8°.
North Carolina. [Miscel. newspapers.] *v.p.*, 1865–66. 3 v. f°.
Norton's literary advertiser. *m.* N. Y., 1851–55. 4 v. f°.
Norton's literary letter. *irreg.* N. Y., 1857–60. 6 nos. 4°.
Norton's litetary register, *etc.* *a.* N. Y., 1853–56. 3 v. 12°.
Occasional reverberator. No. 1, 2. *w.* N. Y., 1753. f°.
Ohio educational monthly. Vol. 14. Columbus, 1865. 8°.
Old and new. *m.* B., 1870–[75]. 11 v. 8°.
Old Colony memorial. *w.* Plymouth, 1822–23. f°.
Olive branch and Christian inquirer. Vol. 1. *w.* N. Y., 1828. 8°.
Omnium gatherum. [Vol. 1.] B., 1810. 8°.
Opal. Vol. 4. *m.* Utica, 1854. 8°.
Ordeal. *w.* B., 1809. 8°.
Orphans' advocate; June 11 - July 7. *d.* W., 1866. 8°.
Our daily fare; June 8–21. *d.* P., 1864. 4°.
Overland monthly. *m.* S. F., 1868–75. 15 v. 8°.
Panoplist; 1805–20. *m.* B., 1806–20. 16 v. 8°.
Panoplist and Missionary mag. Vol. 1, no. 7, 10. (**B 211**); no. 9. (**B 210**).
Parent's gift; or, Youth's magazine. *m.* P., 1830–31. 2 v. 16°.
Parley's magazine. *m.* N. Y., B., [1838]. 16°.
Patriarch; or, Family library magazine. *irreg.* N. Y., 1841–[42]. 2 v. 8°.
Penn monthly magazine. P., [1870]–78. 9 v. 8°.
Pennsylvania chronicle; Jan. 30, 1769 - Jan. 22, 1770. *w.* P., 1769–70. f°.
Pennsylvania inquirer; Feb. 1845 - Dec. 1848; Jan. 1850 - Mar. 1860. *t.w.* P., 1845–60. f°.
Note. For succeeding vols. *see* **Phila.** inquirer.
Pennsylvania journ. of prison discipline. *q.* P., 1845–55. 10 v. 8°.
People's friend and daily advertiser. *d.* N. Y., 1806–07. f°.
People's magazine. *f.* B., [1833–35]. 2 v. f°.

Phila. gazette and daily advertiser. P., 1801-08. 6 v. f°. (Incomplete.)
Same. June 12, 13. P., 1822. f°.
Phila. inquirer. *d.* P., 1860-76. f°.
Note. For preceding vols. *see* **Pennsylvania** inquirer.
Phila. journal of med. and phys. sciences. *q.* P., 1820-27. 14 v. 8°.
Note. For previous nos. *see* **American** journal of med. sci.
Phila. literary gazette. *w.* [P., 1821.] 4°.
Phila. magazine and review. *m.* P., [1799]. 8°.
Phila. med. and phys. journal. P., 1804-08. 3 v. 8°.
Phila. med. museum. *q.* P., 1805-08. 5 v. 8°.
Phila. monthly magazine. Vol. 1. P., 1798. 8°.
Phila. visitor. Vol. 1-4, 6. *f.* P., 1835-40. 5 v. 8°.
Philobiblion. *m.* N. Y., 1861-63. 4°.
Pictorial national library. *m.* B., 1848-49. 2 v. 8°.
Pilot; Sept. 25, 1812 - Jan. 16, 1813. *s.w.* B., 1812-13. f°.
Pilot. *w.* Vol. 28-36. B., 1865-73. 9 v. f°.
Pioneer. Vol. 2, 4. *m.* S. F., 1854-55. 2 v. 8°.
Piscataqua evangelical magazine. Vol. 1. *b.m.* Ports., [1805]. 8°.
Same. Vol. 1-3. Ports., [1805-07]. 3 v. 8°.
Plaindealer; Dec. 3, 1836 - Sept. 30, 1837. *w.* N. Y., 1836-37. 8°.
Plough, loom, and anvil. Vol. 3, 4, 7. 1850-55. *m.* P., N. Y., 1851-55. 3 v. 8°.
Polar star and Boston daily advertiser. B., 1796-97. f°.
Political and commercial register; July 2, 1804-1808. *d.* P., 1804-08. 5 v. f°.
Same. March 20. Vol. 16, no. 68. P., 1812. f°.
Political gazette; Sept. 10, 1795 - Aug. 4, 1796. *w.* Newburyport, 1795-96. f°. (Incomplete.)
Political observatory. *w.* Walpole, 1805. f°.
Political register; Nov. 3, 1794 - Mar. 3. 1795. P., 1795. 8°.
Polyanthos; 1805-07; 1812-14. [2 ser.] *m.* B., 1805-14. 9 v. 12°.
Porcupine's gazette. *d.* P., Bustletown, 1797-99. f°. (Incomplete.)
Portfolio. [5 ser.] *w.* P., [1801]-20. 34 v. 8°.
Portico. Vol. 3. *m.* [Balt., 1817.] 8°.
Portsmouth journal of literature and politics. *w.* Ports., 1822-38. 4 v. f°. (Incomplete.)
Portsmouth oracle; Oct. 5, 1811 - Aug. 9, 1817. *w.* Ports., 1811-17. f°.
Post, Daily morning. B., 1831-76. 93 v. f°.
Post, Evening. *d.* N. Y., 1853-80. 27 v. f°.
Poulson's Amer. advertiser; 1801-05, 1808. *d.* P., 1801-08. 6 v. f°.
Present, The. *m.* [N. Y., 1843-44.] 8°.
Prisoners' friend. Vol. 1-5, 7. *m.* B., 1849-55. 6 v. 8°.
Providence journal. *w.* Prov., 1799-1801. f°.
Providence patriot; Mar. 16. Prov., 1822. f°.
Providence theol. mag. Vol. 1, no. 1. Sept. 1821. Prov., 1821. 8°.
Putnam's monthly magazine. N. Y., 1853-57. 10 v. 8°.
— New ser. N. Y., 1868-70. 6 v. 8°.
Quarterly homœopathic journal. B., 1849-50. 2 v. 8°.
Quarterly journ. of psychol. med., *etc.* Vol. 3. N. Y., 1869. 8°.
Quarterly theological magazine. Burl., N.J., 1813. 2 v. 8°.
Radical, The. *m.* B., 1866-72. 10 v. 8°.
Railway times. Vol. 12-17. *w.* [B., 1860-65.] 6 v. 4°.
Record of news, history, *etc.*; June 18 - Dec. 10. *w.* Rich., 1863. 4°.
Religious magazine; 1833-36. *m.* B., N. Y., P., [1834]-36. 3 v. 8°.
Religious mag. and family miscellany. *m.* B., 1837-38. 2 v. 8°.
Repertory, The. *s.w.* B., 1803-12. 8 v. f°.
Republic, The; May 10 - Dec. 30. *d.* Rich., 1865. 8°.
Republic of letters. Vol. 1. *w.* N. Y., 1834. 8°.
Republican gazetteer. *s.w.* B., 1803. f°.
Restorationist. Vol. 1. *m.* B., 1837. 8°.
Rhode Island American. *s.w.* Prov., 1808-31. 6 v. f°.
R. I. educational mag. Vol. 2. 1853. *m.* Prov., 1854. 8°.
R. I. schoolmaster. Vol. 11. *m.* *n.p.*, [1865]. 8°.
Richmond age. Vol. 1, no. 5. *m.* Rich., 1865. 8°.
Richm. commercial compiler; Mar. 30. Rich., 1822. f°.
Richm. dispatch; Feb. 7 - Dec. 31. *d.* Rich., 1861. f°.
Richm. enquirer; 1817; 18; 1828-29. *s.w.* Rich., 1817-29. 3 v. f°. (Incomplete.)
Same. Dec. 4. Rich., 1821. f°.
Richm. enquirer, Daily. Rich., 1861-64. 3 v. f°.
Richm. examiner, Daily; 1861 - Mar. 1865. Rich., 1861-65. f°.
Richm. Whig; 1861 - Mar. 1865. *s.w.* Rich., 1861-65. f°.
Roberts' semi-monthly. *f.* B., 1841-42. 2 v. 8°.
Round table. *w.* N. Y., 1863-71. 11 v. f° *and* 4°.
Rural magazine. *m.* Rutland, [1795]-96. 2 v. 8°.
Sabbath at home. *m.* B., 1867-69. 3 v. 8°.
Sabbath school herald; 1829-30. *m.* New Haven, 1830. 2 v. 12°.
Sabbath school record. Vol. 2. *m.* N. Haven, 1833. 12°.
Sabbath school treasury. Vol. 1-4, 7. *m.* B., 1828-34. 5 v. 12°.
Same. New ser. Vol. 1, 4. B., 1837-40. 2 v. 12°.
Sailor's magazine. Vol. 1, 3, 6-39, 41. 1828-69. *m.* N. Y., 1829-[69]. 37 v. 8°.
Salem courier; May 16, 1818 - May 6, 1820; Sept. 17, 1828 - Sept. 9, 1829. *w.* S., 1818-29. 2 v. f°.
Salem gazette. *w.* S., 1781-1833. f°. (Incomplete.)
Same. Jan. 2, 1801. S., 1801. f°.
Salem mercury. *w.* S., 1786-90. f°. (Incomplete.)
Salem register. *s.w.* S., 1800-71. 38 v. f°. (Incomplete.)
Same. Feb. 2-26. S., 1801. f°.
Saturday evening express. *w.* B., 1865-71. 5 v. f°.
Saturday evening gazette; 1822-39; 56-61, 65, 66, 69-76. *w.* B., 1822-76. f°.
Saturday magazine. *w.* P., N. Y., [1821-22]. 2 v. 8°.
Savannah daily republican; May 17. Sav., 1822. f°.
Same. 1861-64. Sav., 1861-64. f°. (Incomplete.)
Same. July - Dec. 1866; Jan., Dec. 1868. Sav., 1866-68. 3 v. f°.
Savannah weekly republican; 1870 - May 1873. Sav., 1870-73. 3 v. f°.
Scientific American. Vol. 5-7, 9-14. *w.* [N. Y., 1849-59.] 9 v. f°.
Same. New ser. [N. Y., 1859-80.] 42 v. f°.
Same. Supplement. Vol. 1-10. N. Y., 1876-80. 10 v. f°.
Scribner's monthly; 1870-80. N. Y., [1871-80]. 19 v. 8°.
Select journ. of foreign period. lit. *q.* B., 1833-34. 4 v. 8°.
Select reviews, *etc.* *m.* P., 1809-12. 8 v. 8°.
Shrine, The. Vol. 1, 2. *m.* Amherst, B., 1832-33. 2 v. 8°.
Something. *w.* [B., 1809-10.] 8°.
Something new. Vol. 1, no. 1, 2. *w.* B., 1830. 8°.
South Carolina. [Miscel. newspapers.] *v.p.* 1865-66. 2 v. f°.
Southern Episcopalian. Vol. 8, no. 1. *m.* Charleston, [1861]. 8°.
Southern field and fireside. Vol. 2. *w.* Augusta, 1864. 4°.
Southern illust. news. *w.* Rich., 1862-64. 3 v. 4°.
Southern literary gazette; Feb. *n.p.* 1829. 8°.
Southern literary messenger; Aug. 1834 - June 1864. *m.* Rich., 1835-64. 36 v. 8°.
Southern monthly. Vol. 1, no. 1. Memphis, 1861-62. 8°.
Southern patriot and comm. adv.; Jan. 21, March 30, April 4. Charleston, 1822. f°.
Southern planter. Vol. 1. 1841. *m.* Rich., 1842. 8°.
Southern Punch; Aug. 15, 1863 - Oct. 2, 1864. *w.* Rich., 1863-64. 2 v. 4°.
Southern quarterly review. [3 ser.] N. O., *etc.*, 1842-56. 28 v. 8°.
Southern review. *q.* Charleston, 1828-32. 8 v. 8°.
Southern review. *q.* Balt., *etc.*, 1867-77. 22 v. (v. 19, 20, w.) 8°.
Southern rose. Vol. 7, no. 2. Charleston, 1838. 8°.
Spirit of missions. Vol. 9, 11-14, 37, 38. *m.* N. Y., 1844-[73]. 7 v. 8°.
Spirit of seventy-six. *s.w.* W., 1810-11. f°.
Spirit of the Pilgrims. *m.* B., 1828-33. 6 v. 8°.
Spiritual philosopher. *w.* B., 1850-51. 2 v. 4°.
Spiritualist register. *a.* Auburn, 1857-61. 5 v. 16°.
Springfield daily republican. Sp., 1863-80. f°.
Student's magazine. Vol. 1, no. 2; Feb. 1838. *n.p.*, 1838. obl. f°.
Students' repository. Vol. 1, 2. 1863-64. *q.* Spartanburg, *etc.*, 1864. 2 v. 8°.
Sunday times. *w.* B., 1868-71. 3 v. f°.
Symbol, The. *m.* B., 1843-44. 3 v. 8°.
Tennessee. [Miscel. newspapers.] *v.p.*, 1865-66. 2 v. f°.
Theatrical censor. No. 1-13. *w.* P., 1806. 8°.
Theological and literary journal. Vol. 5-11. *q.* N. Y., 1853-59. 7 v. 8°.
Theological magazine; 1795-99. *b.m.*, *q.* N. Y., 1796-99. 3 v. 8°.
Theophilanthropist. *m.* N. Y., 1810. 8°.
To-day; a Boston literary journal. B., 1852. 2 v. 8°.
Transcript, Daily evening; July 24 - Dec. 31, 1830; 1831-1834; June 8, 1835-1880. B., 1830-80. 53 v. f°.
Traveller, Daily evening. Vol. 2-33. B., 1846-76. 32 v. f°.
Note. For previous vols. *see* **American** traveller.
True delta, Daily. N. O., 1865. 2 v. f°.
Una, The; 1853-55. *m.* [Prov., B., 1853-55.] 3 v. 4°.
Unitarian. Vol. 1. *m.* C., B., 1834. 8°.
Unitarian advocate. *m.* B., 1828-29. 4 v. 12°.
Unitarian advocate and relig. miscel. *m.* B., 1830-32. 6 v. 12°.
Unitarian, The, and for. relig. miscel. *m.* B., 1847. 12°.
Unitarian annual register; 1846-47. B., [1846-47]. 12 v. 12°.
Unitarian congregational register; 1848-55. B., [1848-55]. 8 v. 12°.
Unitarian miscellany and Christian monitor. *m.* B., 1821-24. 6 v. 12°.
United States army and navy journ.; 1863-80. *w.* N. Y., [1864-80]. 17 v. f°.

U. S. Catholic magazine. Vol. 2-7. *m.* Balt., 1843-48. 6 v. 8°.
U. S. law intelligencer. *m.* Prov., P., 1829-31. 3 v. 8°.
U. S. literary gazette; 1824-25. *f.* B, 1825-26. 3 v. 8° *and* 4°.
U. S. magazine of science, *etc.*; 1854-57. *m.* N. Y., [1856]-57. 5 v. 8°. *and* 4°.
U. S. monthly law magazine. Vol. 4. N. Y., 1851. 8°.
U. S. naval chronicle. Vol. 1. W., 1824. 8°.
U. S. review; 1826-27, *m.* B., N. Y., 1827. 2 v. 8°.
U. S. service magazine. *m.* N. Y., 1864-66. 5 v. 8°.
U. S. statistical register. *w.* P., 1840-42. 6 v. 4°.
Univercœlum. Vol. 1-4. 1847-49. *w.* N. Y., 1848-[49]. 4 v. 4°.
Universal gazette. *w.* P., W., 1797-1800. f°.
Universalist, The. *w.* B., 1865-74. 10 v. f°.
Universalist and ladies' repository. Vol. 4-10. 1835-42. B., 1836-42. 7 v. 4°.
Universalist expositor. [2 ser.] *b. m.* B., 1831-40. 6 v. 8°.
Universalist magazine. *w.* B., 1819-21. 2 v. 4°.
Universalist quarterly. Vol. 1-9, 11, 12. B., 1844-55. 11 v. 8°.
Virginia. [Miscel. newspapers.] *v. p.*, 1865-66. 10 v. f°.
Voice, Daily evening. B., 1864-67. 3 v. 8°.
Voice of the fair. *w.* and *d.* Chic., 1865. 1 v. f°.
Volunteer, The; 1831-33. *m.* B., L., 1832-23. 2 v. 8°.
Washington federalist. *t. w.* Georgetown, 1809. f°.
Washington gazette. *d.* W., 1822. f°.
Waverley magazine; illustrated. Vol. 14-17. *w.* B., [1857-58]. 4 v. 4°.
Weekly monitor. P., Charleston, 1810. 8°.
Weekly visitant. [S., 1806.] 8°.
Western herald and Steubenville gazette; May 11. Steubenv., 1822. f°.
Western messenger. Vol. 2-8. 1836-41. *m.* Louisv., Cin., 1837-41. 7 v. 8°.
Western monthly review; 1827-30. Cin., 1828-30. 3 v. 8°.
Western review; 1819-21. *m.* Lex., 1820-21. 3 v. 8°.
Wilkes' spirit of the times. Vol. 7-11. *w.* N. Y., 1862-64. 5 v. 4°.
Wilmington daily commercial. Wilmington, 1867-71. 10 v. f°.
Witness, The. [Vol. 1.] 1809. *m.* B., [1809]. 12°.
Worcester magazine. *w.* Wor., 1786-88. 4 v. 8°.
Worcester mag. and hist. journal; 1825-26. *f.* Wor., 1826. 2 v. 8°.
Working farmer; 1849-54. *m.* N. Y., 1850-54. 6 v. 4°.
World. *d.* N. Y., 1860-76. 33 v. f°.
Yankee. *w.* B., 1812-19. 5 v. f°.
Yankee and Boston lit. gazette. N. s., v. 1. *m.* [B., 1829.] 8°.
Young mechanic. Vol. 1-4, 1832-36. *m.* B., 1832-35. 4 v. 8°.
Youth's cabinet. *m.* N. Y., 1846-[48]. 3 v. 8°.
Youth's companion. *w.* B., 1840-58. 16 v. 4°.
Youth's friend. *m.* P., 1838-39. 2 v. 18°.

A., Albany; And., Andover; Aug., Augusta; B., Boston; C., Cambridge; Chic., Chicago; Con., Concord; D., Dedham; H., Hartford; Hav., Haverhill; L., Lowell; N., Nashville; N. O., New Orleans; P., Philadelphia; Port., Portland; Ports., Portsmouth; R., Rochester; Rich., Richmond; S., Salem; S. F., San Francisco; Sav., Savannah; Sp., Springfield; St. L., St. Louis; U., Utica; W., Washington; Wor., Worcester; *a.*, annually; *b. m.*, bimonthly; *d.*, daily; *f.*, fortnightly; *m.*, monthly; *q.*, quarterly; *s. m.*, semi-monthly; *t. w.*, tri-weekly; *w.*, weekly.

Poetry. (*Bibliography, etc.*)

— EVERETT, E. American poets; a poem before the Φ.B.K. *n. t. p.* [Camb., 1812.] 8°. (B 469)
— *Same, on large paper.*
— KETTELL, S. Catalogue of Amer. poetry. (*In his* Specimens, v. 3. 1829.)

Poetry. (*Collections.*)

— COLLECTION of poems; by several hands. Boston, 1744. 4°. (B 654)
— COLUMBIAN muse; a selection of American poetry. N. Y., 1794. 12°.
— BRYANT, W. C. Selections from the American poets. N. Y., [18—]. 18°. (Harper's fam. lib., v. 111.)
— SPECIMENS of the American poets; with critical notices, *etc.* London, 1822. 12°.
— KETTELL, S. Specimens of Amer. poetry. Boston, 1829. 3 v. 12°.
— KEESE, J. Poets of America. N. Y., 1840. 16°.
— GRISWOLD, R. W. Poets and poetry of America. Phila., 1842. 8°.
— CHEEVER, G. B. American commonplace-book of poetry. Phila., 1843. 12°.
— WHIPPLE, E. P. Poets and poetry of America. (*In his* Essays, v. 1. 1848.)
— READ, T. B. Female poets of America; with biog. notices and specimens. Phila., 1849. 8°.
— GRISWOLD, R. W. Female poets of America. 2d ed. Phila., 1853. 8°.
— MOORE, F. Rebel rhymes and rhapsodies. N. Y., 1864. 16°.
— READ, T. B., *and others.* Poems commemorative of our defenders on land and sea. (*In* Murdoch, J. Patriotism. 1865.)
— WHITE, R. G. Poetry of the civil war. N. Y., 1866. 8°.

See also **Bowdoin poets**; — **Connecticut**; — **Maine**; — **Portsmouth**; — **West, The.**

Note The Library has also poems by the following authors: **Adams, J.**; — **Adams, J. Q.**; — **Aldrich, T. B.**; — **Allen, P.**; — **Allston, W.**; — **Alsop, R.**; — **Ames, N.**; — **Arnold, G.**; — **Bacon, W. T.**; — **Ballou, H.**; — **Bancroft, G.**; — **Barlow, J.**; — **Bartlett, S. R.**; — **Batchelder, E.**; — **Bennison,** *Mrs.* **D. M.**; — **Bethune, G. W.**; — **Bishop, P. P.**; — **Boker, G. H.**; — **Bolles, J. R.**; — **Bradstreet,** *Mrs.* **A. D.**; — **Brainerd, J. G. C.**; — **Branagan, T.**; — **Brooks, J. G.**; — **Brooks, M. E.**; — **Brooks,** *Mrs.* **M. G.**; — **Brownell, H. H.**; — **Bryan, D.**; — **Bryant, W. C.**; — **Bulfinch, S. G.**; — **Burke, J.**; — **Butler, W. A.**; — **Carter,** *Mrs.* **A. A.**; — **Cary, A.**; — **Channing, W. E.**; — **Clifton, W.**; — **Clinch, J. H.**; — **Colcraft, H. R.**; — **Colgan, W. J.**; — **Cooke, P. P.**; — **Coxe, A. C.**; — **Crafts, W.**; — **Dana, R. H.**; — **Davidson, L. M.**; — **Davidson,** *Mrs.* **M. M.**; — **Dinsmoor, R.**; — **Dix, W. G.**; — **Drake, J. R.**; — **Dwight, T.**; — **Dyer, S.**; — **Eastburn, J. W.**; — **Eaton, B. A.**; — **Everett, A. H.**; — **Elliot, J.**; — **Emerson, R. W.**; — **Emmons, R.**; — **Eustaphieve, A.**; — **Evans, N.**; — **Fairfield, S. L.**; — **Farmer, H. T.**; — **Felton, J. B.**; — **Fenner, C. G.**; — **Fessenden, T. G.**; — **Fields, J. T.**; — **Flint, M. P.**; — **Freneau, P.**; — **Frothingham, N. L.**; — **Fuller, R. F.**; — **G., A. S.**; — **Genin, T. H.**; — **Gilman,** *Mrs.* **C.**; — **Gilman, S.**; — **Godfrey, T.**; — **Gould, H. F.**; — **Hale, S. J.**; — **Hall,** *Mrs.* **L. J.**; — **Halleck, F. G.**; — **Harte, F. B.**; — **Hawser, H.** *ps.*; — **Head, J.**; — **Heywood, J. C.**; — **Hill, F. S.**; — **Hill, G.**; — **Hiller, T. O. P.**; — **Hillhouse, J. A.**; — **Hine, E. C.**; — **Hirst, H. B.**; — **Hitchcock, D.**; — **Holland, J. G.**; — **Holmes, O. W.**; — **Hooper, L.**; — **Hopkins, L.**; — **Hopper, E.**; — **Horton, G. M.**; — **Hosmer, B. G.**; — **Hosmer, W. H. C.**; — **Humphreys, D.**; — **Hunt, J.**; — **Judd, S.**; — **Key, F. S.**; — **Keyes, F. J.**; — **Knight, H. C.**; — **Law, T.**; — **Leland, C. J.**; — **Lewis, A.**; — **Linn, J. B.**; — **Lippincott,** *Mrs.* **S. J.**; — **Longfellow, H. W.**; — **Lyde, A. F.**; — **McDonald,** *Mrs.* **M. N.**; — **Markoe, P.**; — **Marston, P. B.**; — **Mayo,** *Mrs.* — **Meditatus,** *ps.*; — **Mellen, G.**; — **Melville, H.**; — **Miller, C. H.**; — **Morris, G. P.**; — **Morton,** *Mrs.* **S. W.**; — **Newell, R. H.**; — **Norton, A.**; — **Odiorne, T.**; — **Osander,** *ps.*; — **Osborn, S.**; — **Osgood, F. S.**; — **Pabodie, W. J.**; — **Packard, H. J.**; — **Palmer, J. C.**; — **Parks, J.**; — **Parsons, T. W.**; — **Paulding, J. K.**; — **Peirson,** *Mrs.* **L. J.**; — **Percival, J. G.**; — **Peters,** *Mrs.* **P. W.**; — **Pickering, H.**; — **Pierpont, J.**; — **Plumer, W.,** *Jr.*; — **Power, T.**; — **Pray, I. C.**; — **Putnam,** *Mrs.* **M.**; — **Rand, E. S.,** *Jr.*; — **Randall, J. W.**; — **Read, T. B.**; — **Redden, L. C.**; — **Rich, I. B.**; — **Ricord,** *Mrs.* **E.**; — **Rogers, J. H.**; **Rowson,** *Mrs.* **S.**; — **Sands, R. C.**; — **Sargent, E.**; — **Sargent, L. M.**; — **Saxe, J. G.**; — **Schaad, J. C.**; — **Scott, J. M.**; — **Sears, R.**; — **Sewall, J. M.**; — **Sigourney, L. H.**; — **Simms, W. G.**; — **Smith,** *Mrs.* **E. O.**; — **Smith, S.**; — **Smith,** *Mrs.* **S. L. P.**; — **Southwick, S.**; — **Sprague, C.**; — **Stagg, E.**; — **Stearns, C.**; — **Stoddard, R. H.**; — **Story, I.**; — **Story, J.**; — **Story, W. W.**; — **Street, A. B.**; — **Tappan, W. B.**; — **Taylor, B.**; — **Thaxter, C.**; — **Thoreau, H. D.**; — **Todd, S. H.**; — **Topliff, N.**; — **Trowbridge, J. T.**; — **Trumbull, J.**; — **Tuckerman, F. G.**; — **Tuckerman, H. T.**; — **Walker, J.**; — **Walter, W. B.**; — **Warren,** *Mrs.* **M.**; — **Webster,** *Mrs.* **M. M.**; — **White, W. A.**; — **Whiting, H.**; — **Whitney, A.**; — **Whitney, A. D. T.**; — **Whittier, J. G.**; — **Wigglesworth, M.**; — **Wilde, R. H.**; — **Willis, N. P.**; — **Willson, F.**; — **Wolcott, R.**; — **Woodman, H. J.**; — **Wright, N. H.**; — **Wright, R. W.**; — **Very, J.**; —
also the following anonymous poems: **Déese, La**; — **Dove** and eagle; — **Fudge** family in Washington; — **Harbinger**, The; — **Horace** in New York; — **New** Diogenes; — **One** week at Amer.; — **Poems**, by a S. Carolinian; — **Poetical** acc. of Amer. campaigns of

1812; — Poetical picture of America; — State triumvirate; — This war; — Union, The.

Sonnets.

— Hunt, J. H. L., *and* Lee, S. A. The book of the sonnet. Boston, 1867. 2 v. 12°.

Wit and Humor.

See Browne, C. F.; — Clemens, S. L.; — Davis, C. A.; — Derby, G. H.; — Halpine, C. G.; — Harte, F. B.; — Holmes, O. W.; — Irving, W.; — Leland, C. G.; — Locke, R. A.; — Lowell, J. R.; — Paige, E. F.; — Poe, E. A.; — Saxe, J. G.

Manufactures.

— Bishop, J. L. History of Amer. manufactures, 1608–1860. Vol. 1, 2. Phila., 1861–64. 2 v. 8°.

— Batchelder, S. Introd. and early progress of the cotton manufactures in the U. S., [1768–1862]. Boston, 1863. 16°.

— Coxe, T. Address to an assembly of the friends of Amer. manufactures. Phila., 1787. 8°. (W 31)

— U. S. *Treasury.* Report [of Alex. Hamilton, Sec.] on manufactures, Dec. 5, 1791. 6th ed.; pref., by [M. Carey]. Phila., 1827. 8°.

— - *Other copies.* (B 1049, 1887)

— Essay on the manufacturing interest of the U. S.; also the Memorial of the Soc. of Artists and Manufactures of Philadelphia. Phila., 1804. 8°. (B 1511)

— Coxe, T. Arts and manufactures of the U. S., 1810. Phila., 1814. 4°.

— U. S. *Census.* Series of tables of the several branches of Amer. manufacturers so far as returned in reports in 1810. *n.p.*, [18—]. 4°. (A 19)

— - Manufactures in all the states. (*In its* 3d census. 1313.)

— - Digest of accounts of manufacturing establishments in the U. S. Wash., 1823. f°.

— Harrisburg. General Convention of Agriculturists, Manufacturers, and Others Friendly to the Support of the Domestic Industry of the U. S., July 30. [Proceedings.] *n.t.p.* [1827.] 8°. (B 1717)

— Hastings, S., *and* Pickering, T. Remarks upon the manufacturing bill. [Wash., 1830.] 8°. (B 1792)

— Industrie de la soie aux Etats-Unis. (*In* Revue d. D. Mondes, août 1840.)

— Montgomery, J. Practical detail of the cotton manufacture of U. S. contrasted and compared with that of Gr. Brit. Glasgow, 1840. 8°.

— Fleischmann, C. L. Erwerbszweige, Fabrikwesen, und Handel der Vereinigten Staaten von Nordamerika. Stuttg., 1850. 8°.

— De Bow, J. D. B. Industrial resources of the southern and western states. New Orleans, 1852–53. 3 v. 8°.

— Lesley, J. P. Iron manufacturer's guide to the furnaces, forges, *etc.* N. Y., 1859. 8°.

— U. S. *Census.* Manufactures, 1860. Wash., 1865. 4°.

— De Coin, R. L. History and cultivation of cotton and tobacco. London, 1864. 8°.

— Reybaud, M. R. L. L'industrie et les ouvriers du coton aux Etats-Unis depuis la guerre de la sécession. (*In* Revue d. D. Mondes, nov. 1870.)

See also Census (p. 3058); — *also* Textile fabrics; — *also* Virginia.

Medicine.

— Currie, W. Hist. account of the climates and diseases of the U. S. Phila., 1792. 8°.

— Stearns, S. American herbal or materia medica. Walpole, 1801. 12°.

— Barton, B. S. Collections for an essay towards the materia medica of the U. S. Phila., 1801. 2 pts. 8°.

— Currie, W. View of the diseases prevalent in the U. S. Phila., 1811. 8°.

— Barton, W. P. C. Vegetable materia medica, [1818]. (Vol. 1, 2d ed.) Phila., 1825, 18. 2 v. 4°.

— Paine, M. Defence of the med. profession in the U.S.; address. 7th ed. N. Y., 1846. 8°. (B 1559)

— Mitchell, T. D. Past, present, and future of the med. profession in the U. S. Louisville, 1852. 8°. (B 1558)

— Moorman, J. J. The mineral waters of the U. S. and Canada. Balt., 1867. 12°.

— Laboulaye, E. R. L. La médicine militaire aux Etats-Unis. (*In* Revue d. D. Mondes, déc. 1869.)

Mineralogy and Mines.

— Henfrey, B. Plan with proposals for forming a company to work mines in the U. S., *etc.* Phila., 1797. 8°. (B 418)

— Chevalier, M. Les mines d'argent et d'or du Nouveau Monde. (*In* Revue d. D. Mondes, déc. 1846, av. 1847.)

— Shepard, C. U. New localities of Amer. minerals. (*In* Amer. Assoc. Proc., v. 4. 1851.) — Smith, J. L. Re-examination of Amer. minerals. (*In* v. 9. 1856.)

— Whitney, J. D. Metallic wealth of the U. S. Phila., 1854. 8°.

— Head, *Sir* F. B. Cornish miners in America. (*In his* Desc. essays, v. 1. 1857.)

— Piggot, A. S. Description of the principal copper mines of the U. S. (*In his* Chemistry. 1858.)

— Hittell, J. S. Mining in the Pacific states of N. America. San Francisco, 1861. 24°.

— Daddow, S. H., *and* Bannan, B. Coal, iron, and oil, our mines and mineral resources. Pottsville, Pa., 1866. 8°.

— Browne, J. R., *and* Taylor, J. W. Reports on the mineral resources of the U. S. Wash., 1867. 8°.

— Browne, J. R. On the mineral resources of the states and territories west of the Rocky Mts. Wash., 1868. 8°.

— U. S. *Commissioner of Mining Statistics.* Statistics of mines and mining west of the Rocky Mts., [1st, 2d,] 4th, 6th repts.; by R. W. Raymond. Wash., 1869–74. 4 v. 8°.

See also Arkansas; — California; — Colorado; — Illinois; — Massachusetts; — Missouri; — New York; — North America; — Wisconsin; — *also* American mineralogical journal; — Mining magazine.

Missions.

— Congregational Churches in Conn. *Gen. Association.* Narrative of the missions to the new settlements. New Haven, 1794. 8°. (B 247)

See also Indians; — Missions. *Home Missions. also* Maine; — Mississippi Territory.

Music.

See also Boston. *History* (Gilmore. National peace jubilee) p. 343; — New England. *Music*; — Slave songs of the U. S.

Name.

— N. Y. Historical Soc. Report of the committee on a national name. *n.t.p.* [1845.] 8°. (B 1196)

National character.

— Algerine spy in Pennsylvania, 1783–[87]. Phila., 1787. 18°.

— Poetical picture of America; obs. made at Alexandria and Norfolk, 1799–1807. London, 1809. 12°.

— Shahcoolen, *pseud.* Letters of a Hindu philosopher in Phila., to his friend El Hassan, of Delhi. Boston, 1802. 12°. (C 167)

— Ingersol, C. J. Inchiquin the Jesuit's letters. N. Y., 1810. 8°.

— - *Another copy.* (B 434)

— Dwight, T. Remarks on the review of Inchiquin's letters pub. in the Quarterly review. Boston, 1815. 8°.

— PAULDING, J. K. United States and Eng.; reply to criticism on Inchiquin's letters, in the Quarterly review. N. Y., 1815. 8°.
— - *Another copy*. (A 1)
— NICHOLS, T. L. Forty years of American life, [1815-64]. London, 1864. 2 v. 8°.
— REVIEWERS reviewed; or, British falsehoods detected by Amer. truths. N. Y., 1815. 8°. (B 666)
— WRIGHT, F. Views of society and manners in Amer.; in letters, 1818-20. Lond., 1821. 8°.
— HARE, R. Defence of the American character; essay on wealth. Phila., 1819. 8°. (B 448, 534)
— EUROPEAN delineation of Amer. character. From the Lit. and scientific repository. N. Y., 1820. 8°. (B 534)
— COOPER, J. F. Notions of the Americans, [1824]. Phila., 1828. 2 v. 12°.
— MURAT, N. A., *prince*. Esquisse morale et politique des Etats-Unis; [10 lettres, 1821-32]. Paris, 1832. 16°.
— - *Eng*. Sketch of the United States. London, 1833. 12°.
— - Lettres sur les Etats-Unis, [1821-27]. Paris, 1830. 16°.
Note. The first four of the letters of the 'Esquisse'.
— TROLLOPE, *Mrs*. F. Domestic manners of the Americans, [1827-30]. 2d ed. London, 1832. 2 v. 12°.
— AMERICAN criticisms on Mrs. Trollope's 'Domestic manners of the Americans'. London, 1833. 8°. (B 1073)
— JOHNSTON, D. C. Trollopania; sketches to be referred to in perusing 'Domestic manners of the Americans'. (*In his* Scraps. 1833.)
— JOUFFROY, T. S. Mœurs des Américains d'après mistress Trollope. (*In* Revue d. D. Mondes, juin, juil., oct. 1832.)
— UNITED STATES, The, as they are. London, 1828. 8°.
— AMERICA and the Americans, [1829-31]; by a citizen of the world. London, 1833. 8°.
— HAMILTON, *Capt*. T. Men and manners in America, [1830-31]. Edin., 1833. 2 v. 8°.
— DUHRING, H. Remarks on the U. S. with regard to the state of Europe, [1832]. London, 1833. 12°.
— COLTON, C. The Americans; by an American in London. London, 1833. 12°.
— GRUND, F. J. Americans in their naval, social, and political relations, [1831]. London, 1837. 2 v. 8°.
— MARTINEAU, H. Society in America. N. Y., 1837. 2 v. 12°.
— GRUND, F. J. Aristocracy in America. London, 1839. 2 v. 12°.
— PUTNAM, G. P. American facts; notes and statistics. London, 1845. 8°.
— BREMER, F. Homes of the New World. N.Y., 1853. 2 v. 8°.
— MONTÉGUT, E. Scènes de la vie amér.; études de mœurs et de caractères par un médecin. (*In* Revue d. D. Mondes, jan. 1855.) — Le capitaine Négrier. (*In* fév. 1855.)
— MACKAY, C. Life and liberty in America, 1857-58. London, 1859. 2 v. 8°.
— GUROWSKI, A. G. de. America and Europe. N. Y., 1857. 12°.
— CARLIER, A. Le mariage aux Etats-Unis. Paris, 1861. 16°.
— FISCH, G. Les Etats-Unis en 1861. Paris, 1862. 16°.
— LABOULAYE, E. R. L. Paris en Amérique, par le docteur R. Lefebvre, [1862]. 4e éd. Paris, 1863. 12°.
— - *Eng*. Paris in America; tr. by M. L. Booth. N. Y., 1863. 12°.

— MILLIROUX, J. F. Aperçus sur les institutions et les mœurs des Américains. Paris, 1862. 8°.
See also Bundling.
also the following fictitious works: Aimard, G.; — Beecher, H. W. (Norwood); — Briggs, C. F. (Trippings of Tom Pepper); — Bristed, C. A. (The upper ten thousand); — Cary, A. (Clovernook); — Cooper, J. F.; — Cummins, M. (The lamplighter); — Curtis, G. W. (Potiphar papers, Trumps); — DeForest, J. W. (Overland); — Derby, G. H. (Phœnixiana, Squibob papers); — Dickens, C. (Martin Chuzzlewit); — Fay, T. S. (Norman Leslie); — Haliburton, T. C. (Sam Slick); — Hall, B. R. (New purchase); — Harte, F. B.; — Hawthorne, N. (Blithedale romance, House of the seven gables, Scarlet letter); — Holmes, O. W. (Elsie Venner, Guardian angel); — Huntington, J. V. (Alban); — Judd, S. (Margaret); — Kimball, R. B. (Undercurrents of Wall street); — Kirkland, C. M. (Forest life, Western clearings); — Longfellow, H. W. (Kavanagh); — Lowell, R. T. S. (The new priest in Conception Bay); — Marryat, F. (Valerie, Narrative of the travels, *etc*., of Monsieur Violet); — Melville, H.; — Phelps, E. S. (The silent partner); — Postel, K. (Lebensbilder aus der Westlichen Hemisphäre, Morton oder die grosse Tour, Süden und Norden); — Quincy, E. W. (Wensley); — Sedgwick, C. M.; — Stowe, H. B.; — Taylor, B. (John Godfrey's fortune); — Trowbridge, J. T. (Neighbor Jackwood); — Tyler, R. (Algerine captive); — Warner, A. B. *and* S.; — Wetherell, E. (The wide, wide world); — Whitney, A. D. T.; — Whittier, J. G. (Snow bound); — Wraxall, *Sir* C. F. L. (The backwoodsman).

Natural history.

— DESCOURTILZ, M. E. Voyages d'un naturaliste; détails sur l'expédition du gén. Leclerc. Paris, 1809. 3 v. 8°.
— AGASSIZ, L. J. R. Contributions to the natural hist. of the U. S. Boston, 1857. 4°.
See also Botany (p. 3111); — *Geology* (p. 3122); — *Ichthyology* (p. 3131); — *Mineralogy* (p. 3140); — *Ornithology* (p. 3142); — *Zoology* (p. 3162); — *also* Alabama; — California; — Florida; — Illinois; — Indiana; — Iowa; — Kansas; — Minnesota. *Description*; — Nebraska; — N. England; — N. America; — Ohio; — Red River; — Rhode Island; — South, The; — Tennessee; — Washington Territory.

Naval history.

— COOPER, J. F. History of the navy of the U. S., [1613-1815]. Phila., 1839. 2 v. 8°.
— - *Same*. Contin. to 1851. N. Y., 1856. 3 v. in 1. 8°.
— NEFF, J. K. Army and navy of America; warlike operations on land and sea, [1753-1848]. Lancaster, 1857. 8°.
— DAWSON, H. B. Battles of the U. S., by sea and land, [1775-1847]. N. Y., [1858]. 2 v. 4°.
— CLARK, T. Sketches of the naval hist. of the U. S., [1775-1813]. Phila., 1813. 12°.
— GALLOWAY, J. Letter to Ld. H[owe] on his naval conduct during the war, [1776-78]. London, 1779. 8°. (B 1635)
— CANDID and impartial narrative of the transactions of the fleet under Lord Howe, [1778]. 2d ed. London, [1779]. 8°. (B 463)
— AMERICAN naval battles, 1794-1831; [by H. Kimball?]. Boston, 1831. 8°.
— BADGER, B. Naval temple; a hist. of battles fought by the navy of the U. S., [1794-1816]. Boston, 1816. 8°.
— JAMES, W. Inquiry into the merits of the principal naval actions between Gr. Brit. and U. S., 1812-[16]. Halifax, N. S., 1816. 4°. (B 653)
— BOWEN, A. Naval monument; account of battles during the late war, [1812-15]. Boston, 1816. 8°.
— JAMES, W. Full and correct account of the naval occurrences of the late war, [1812-15]. London, 1817. 8°.
— COGGESHALL, G. History of American privateers and letters of marque, 1812-14. N. Y., 1856. 8°.

— LETTERS to the Secretary of the Navy, [rel. to the war of 1812-13; copies]. MS.
Note. Vols. 4, 5, 10 of some collection.

— WATERHOUSE, B. Journal of a young man of Mass., captured at sea by the British, May 1813; [1813-15]. 2d ed. Boston, 1816. 12°.

— INQUIRY into the present state of the British navy, together with reflections on the late war with America; by an Englishman. London, 1815. 8°.

— BOYNTON, C. B. History of the navy during the rebellion, [1861-65]. N. Y., 1867-68. 2 v. 8°.

— HAMERSLY, L. R. Records of living officers of the U. S. Navy and Marine Corps; with a hist. of naval operations, 1861-65. Phila., 1870. 8°.

— ROBERTS, A. Never caught; blockade-running, 1863-64. London, 1867. 16°.

See also *Navy* (p. 3093); — *Navy Department* (p. 3093-94); — *also* **Erie, Lake**; — **Tripoli.**

Navigation.

See **Mississippi River**; — **Ohio River.**

Numismatics.

— HART, C. H. Historical sketch of the national medals issued [by] Congress, 1776-1815. Phila., 1867. 8°.

— MEASE, J. Description of medals rel. to important events in N. A. (*In* **N. Y. Hist. Soc.** Col., v. 3. 1821; — *and in* **Mass. Hist. Soc.** Col., v. 24. 1834.)

— FISHER, J. F. Description of American medals. (*In* **Mass. Hist. Soc.** Col., v. 26. 1837.) — MEASE, J. Old American coins. (*In* v. 27. 1838.)

— UNITED STATES. 32*d Cong.* 1*st sess. Sen.* Report by Hunter rel. to the change in the coinage, March 8. Wash., [1852]. 8°. (B 1544)

— WYATT, T. Medals of the U. S. N. Y., 1854. 12°.

— HICKCOX, J. H. Historical account of Amer. coinage. Albany, 1858. 8°.

— STICKNEY, M. A. Notes on the American currency. (*In* **Essex Institute.** Hist. col., v. 1-3. 1859-64.)

— DICKESON, M. W. American numismatical manual. Phila., 1859. 4°.

— PAINE, N. Report upon American coins and tokens. (*In* **Amer. Antiq. Soc.** Proc., v. 2. 1860.)

— SATTERLEE, A. H. Arrangement of medals and tokens in honor of the Presidents of the U. S., *etc.* N. Y., 1862. 8°.

— APPLETON, W. S. Description of a selection of coins and medals rel. to America, exhibited to the Mass. Hist. Soc., April 28. Camb., 1870. 8°.

See also **New England**; — **Vermont.**

Ornithology.

— WILSON, A. American ornithology; or, The natural hist. of the birds of the U. S. Phila., 1808-14. 9 v. 4°.

— BONAPARTE, C. L. J. L., *prince.* American ornithology; birds in the U. S. not given by Wilson. Phila., 1825-33. 4 v. 4°.

— - Observations on the the nomenclature of Wilson's 'Ornithology'. Phila., 1826. 8°.

— WILSON, A., *and* BONAPARTE, C. L. J. L., *prince.* Amer. ornithology; the nat. hist. of the birds of the U. S.; ed. by R. Jameson. Edin., 1831. 4 v. 16°. (Constable's misc., v. 68-71.)

— AUDUBON, J. J. Birds of America. London, 1828-39. 4 v. f°.

— - Ornithological biography; or, Habits of birds of the United States. Edin., 1831-49, [39]. 5 v. 8°.

— - *Same.* Vol. 1. Phila., 1831. 8°.

— NUTTALL, T. Manual of the ornithology of the U. S.: Land birds. Camb., 1832. 12°.

— - *Same.* 2d ed., with add. Boston, 1840. 12°.

— - *Same.* Water birds. 2d ed. Bost., 1834. 12°.

See also **Illinois**; — **Indiana**; — **Iowa**; — **Mass.** *Commis. on Zool. and Bot. Survey* (p. 1891); — **N. England.** *Nat. history*; — **N. America**; — **Wisconsin.**

Paleontology.

— HITCHCOCK, E. Attempt to discriminate and describe the animals that made the fossil footmarks of the U. S., especially of New Eng. (*In* **Amer. Acad.** Mem., n.s., v. 3. 1848.)

Physical geography.

— ELLET, C. Contributions to the physical geog. of the U. S. (*In* **Smithsonian Inst.** Contrib., v. 2. 1851.)

See also **Mississippi.** *Description*; — **North America.**

Political economy.

— THOUGHTS on the increasing wealth and national economy of the U. S. Wash., 1801. 8°. (B 401)

— BALDWIN, L. Thoughts on the study of pol. econ. as connected with the U. S. Camb., 1809. 8°. (B 409, 754)

— MELISH, J. Views on political economy. *n.p.*, 1822. 8°. (B 564)

— POLITICAL economist, The. No. 1-13; Jan.-May 1824. Phila., 1824. 8°. (B 1887)

— - *Same.* Nos. 1-6, Jan., Feb. Phila., 1824. 8°. (B 564)

— DEW, T. R. Lectures on the restrictive system. Richmond, 1829. 8°.

— COLTON, C. Junius tracts, no. 7: Labor and capital; by Junius. N. Y., 1844. 8°. (B 1500)

— PETO, *Sir* S. M. Resources and prospects of America, in 1865. London, 1866. 8°.

— - *Same.* N. Y., 1866. 12°.

— MCINTOSH, L. Class despotism during the struggle for freedom, and the evils of individual wealth considered as affecting the well-being of the mass of a people. London, 1867. 16°.

Politics.

General works.

— MABLY, G. B. de, *l'abbé.* Observations sur le gouvernement et les loix des Etats-Unis d'Amérique. Amst., 1784. 12°. (C 98)

— - *Same.* Nouv. éd. Amst., 1790. 12°.

— - *Same.* (Vol. 7 *of his* Col., 1794; — *and in his* Œuvres, v. 8. 1797.)

— - *Eng.* Remarks conc. the government and the laws of the U. S.; with an app. Lond., 1784. 8°. (B 625)

— MAZZEI, P. Recherches sur les Etats-Unis par un citoyen de Virginie, avec quatre lettres d'un bourgeois de New Heaven [Condorcet]. Colle, 1788. 4 v. 8°.

— POLITICAL reformer; a proposed plan of reformations in the laws and governments of the U. S.; added, Strictures on J. Adams' defence of the Constitutions of the U. S. Phila., 1797. 8°.

— *Another copy.* (B 397)

— DUANE, W. Politics for Amer. farmers; series of tracts exhibiting the blessings of free government, as in the U. S. Wash., 1807. 8°.

— - *Other copies.* (B 433, 1750)

— ADAMS, T. Democracy unveiled, a letter to Sir F. Burdett. London, 1811. 8°.

— BARBÉ-MARBOIS, F. de. Discours sur la constitution et le gouvernement des Etats-Unis. (*In his* Histoire de la Louisiane. 1829.)

— WAKEFIELD, E. G. England and America; comparison of the social and political state of both nations. London, 1833. 2 v. 8°.

— TOCQUEVILLE, A. C. H. C. de. Démocratie en Amérique. 5e éd. Paris, 1836. 2 v. 12°.

— - *Same.* 4e éd. Brux., 1837. 3 v. 12°.

— - *Same.* (*In his* Œuvres, v. 1-3. 1864.)

— - *Eng.* Democracy in America; tr. by H. Reeve. London, 1835. 4 v. 8°.
Note. Vol. 3 has the title 'Democracy in America; part the second'.

— - *Same.* Tr. by H. Reeve; ed. with notes by F. Bowen. Camb., 1862. 2 v. 8°.

— Review of Democracy in America'. From the London review, no. 3, Oct. 1835. N. Y., 1836. 12°. (C 297)

— Mercer, C. F. Exposition of the weakness of the government of the U. S. *n.p.*, 1845. 12°.

— Poussin, G. T. De la puissance américaine, origine, institutions, esprit politique, ressources militaires, *etc.*, des Etats-Unis. 3e éd., augm. Paris, 1848. 2 v. 8°.

— Mohl, R. von. Staatsrecht der Ver. Staaten von Nordamerika. (*In his* Staatswissenschaften, v. 1. 1855.)

— Scott, J. The lost principle; or, Sectional equilibrium. Richmond, 1860. 8°.

— Weakness and inefficiency of the government of the U. S.; by a late Amer. statesman. London, 1863. 8°.

— Johnson, S. M. Free government in England and America. N. Y., 1864. 8°.

— Cutts, J. M. Origin, history, and state of parties. (*In his* Constitutional and party questions. 1866.)

— Monroe, J. The people the sovereigns; a comparison of the gov. of the U. S. with previous republics; ed. by S. L. Gouverneur. Phila., 1867. 12°.

— Van Buren, M. Inquiry into the origin and course of parties in the U. S.; ed. by his sons. N. Y., 1867. 8°.

— Mulford, E. The nation; the foundations of civil order and political life in the U. S. N. Y., 1870. 8°.

1. *The Revolution and previous controversy.*

— Franklin, B. American politics, 1754-77. (*In his* Political pieces. 1779.)

— - *Same, enl.* (*In his* Complete works, v. 3. 1806; *and* Works, v. 3-5. 1836-37.)

— - Plan of union of the colonies. [1754.] (*In* Bowen, F. Documents. 1854.)

— Gr. Brit. *Parl.* Bill for better regulating of charter and proprietary governments in America, [176-?]. (*In* Mass. Hist. Soc. Col., v. 7. 1801.)

— Bernard, *Sir* F. Letters on the trade and government of Amer., 1763-68; added, the petition of the Assembly of Mass. Bay against the Gov., his answer, and the order of the King. Boston, 1769. 8°. (B 616)

— - *Same.* 2d ed. London, 1774. 8°.

— - *Another copy.* (B 467)

— Boucher, J. View of the causes and consequences of the Amer. Revolution; 13 discourses, 1763-65. London, 1797. 8°.

— Essay in vindication of the continental colonies from the censure of A. Smith. London, 1764. 8°.

— Fitch, T. Reasons why the British colonies in America should not be charged with internal taxes. New Haven, 1764. 8°. (B 473, 517)

— Otis, J. Rights of the British colonies asserted and proved. Boston, 1764. 8°. (B 515)

— - *Same.* 3d ed. corr. London, *reprinted* 1766. 8°. (B 370, 515)

— Pownall, T. Administration of the colonies. London, 1764. 8°. (B 391)

— - *Same.* 2d ed. London, 1765. 8°.

— - *Same.* 4th ed. London, 1765. 8°.

— - *Same.* 5th ed. London, 1774. 2 v. 8°.

— Dickinson, J. Late regulations resp. the Brit. colonies considered. Phila., 1765. 8°.

— - *Same.* London, *reprinted* 1765. 8°. (B 370, 592)

— - *Same.* London, *reprinted* 1766. 8°. (B 373)

— Dulaney, D. Considerations on the propriety of imposing taxes in the Brit. colonies. North Amer., [1765]. 8°. (B 348, 592, 2503)

— - *Same.* 2d ed. Annapolis, 1765. 4°.

— - *Same.* 2d ed. London, 1766. 8°.

— - *Other copies.* (B 370, 373, 378)

— Fothergill, J. Considerations rel. to the North American colonies. [1765.] (*In his* Works, v. 2. 1783.)

— Grenville, G. The regulations conc. the colonies and the taxes imposed on them considered. London, 1765. 8°. (B 377)

— Hopkins, S. The rights of colonies examined. Prov., 1765. 4°. (B 14, 652)

— Letter from a gentleman at Halifax to his friend in R. Island cont. remarks upon [Hopkins's] 'Rights of colonies examined'. Newport, 1765. 4°. (A 42, B 652, 1117)

— Defence of the 'Letter from a gentleman at Halifax'. Newport, 1765. 4°. (B 652, 1117)

— Otis, J. Brief remarks on the defence of the Halifax libel on the British-Amer. colonies. Boston, 1765. 8°. (B 626, 1117)

— - Considerations on behalf of the colonists. 2d ed. London, 1765. 8°. (B 391)

— - Vindication of the British colonies, against the aspersions of the Halifax gentleman. Boston, 1765. 8°. (B 626)

— Knox, W. Claim of the colonies to an exemption from internal taxes. London, 1765. 8°. (B 391)

— Letter to a member of Parl. wherein the power of the British legislature and the case of the colonists are considered. London, 1765. 8°. (B 391)

— Rights of the British colonies considered. London, [1765?]. 8°.

— Appleton, N. Thanksgiving sermon on the total repeal of the stamp act; May 20, 1766. Boston, 1766. 8°. (B 47, 163, 212)

— Application of general political rules to the present state of Gr. Brit., Ireland, and America. London, 1766. 8°.

— *Other copies.* (B 371, 375)

— Chauncy, C. Discourse, the good news from a far country, July 24, thanksgiving [for] the repeal of the stamp act. Boston, 1766. 8°. (B 47)

— Correct copies of two protests against the bill to repeal the stamp act; with lists of speakers and voters. Paris, 1766. 8°.

— *Other copies.* (B 371, 375, 379, 467)

— Cumings, H. Thanksgiving sermon, Billerica, 1766. Boston, 1767. 8°. (B 67, E 167)

— Emerson, J., *of Pepperell.* Thanksgiving sermon, July 24, repeal of stamp-act. Boston, 1766. 8°. (B 220, 871)

— Examiner examined, The; letter [on] the colonies [and] taxes imposed by Parl. New London, 1766. 4°. (B 652)

— Free and candid remarks on a late oration [by W. Pitt]. London, 1766. 8°.

— Hopkins, S. Grievances of the Amer. colonies candidly examined. London, *reprinted* 1766. 8°. (B 391, 467)

— Justice and necessity of taxing the Amer. colonies demonstrated. London, 1766. 8°. (B 375)

— Late occurrences in N. Amer. and the policy of Gr. Brit. considered. London, 1766. 8°. (B 370, 373)

— Mayhew, J. The snare broken; thanksgiving disc. on repeal of stamp act. Boston, 1766. 8°. (B 47, 853, 2506)

— Necessity of repealing the American stamp act demonstrated. Boston, *reprinted* 1766. 8°. (B 466)

— Observations on the perpetual union of the colonies with [Gr. Brit.]. (*In* Succinct view. 1766.)

— Ray, N. Importance of the colonies and the interest of Gr. Brit. with regard to them considered; with remarks on the stamp duty, by W. Bollan. London, 1766. 4°. (A 12, 18)

— Stillman, S. Good news; sermon, May 17, repeal of the stamp act. Boston, 1766. 12°. (C 22)

— Dickinson, J. Letters from a farmer; [also The monitor, 1767]. *n.t.p.* 4°. (B 651)

— - *Same, without* The monitor. Boston, 1768. 8°.

— - *Another copy.* (B 632)

— - *Same.* London, 1768. 8°. (B 374)

— American gazette of addresses, *etc.*, rel. to the disputes between Gr. Brit. and her colonies. Nos. 1, 5. London, 1768-69. 8°. (B 346)

— Adams, J. Letters [to Dr. Calkoen on the U. S. London, *printed not pub.*, 1768.] 8°.

— - *Another copy.* (W 23)

— - *Same.* *n.t.p.* [1786.] 8°. (B 594)

— - *Same.* Twenty-six letters resp. the Revolution of America. N. Y., 1789. 12°. (C 74)

— BOLLAN, W. Continued corruption, standing armies, and popular discontents considered; and the establishment of the English colonies in America. London, 1768. 4°. (A 12)
— BRADBURY, T. The ass or the serpent: a comparison between the tribes of Issachar and Dan in their regard for civil liberty. London, [1712]. 12°. (E 125)
— - *Same.* Boston, 1768. 8°. (B 161, C 72)
— CANNING, G. Letter to the Earl of Hillsborough on the connection between Gr. Brit. and her Amer. colonies. London, 1768. 8°. (B 389)
— ENGLISHMAN deceived, The; a political piece. London *printed*, Salem *reprinted* 1768. 8°. (B 610)
— LIVINGSTON, W. Letter to J. [Ewer], Bp. of Landaff; occasioned by his sermon, Feb. 20, 1767, in which the Amer. colonies are loaded with great and undeserved reproach. Boston, 1768. 8°. (B 16, 22, 141, 2502)
— POWER and grandeur of Gr. Britain founded on the liberty of her colonies. N. Y., 1768. 8°.
— TRUE sentiments of America [drawn up in part by S. Adams,] with diss. on the canon and feudal law; by J. Adams. London, *Almon*, 1768. 8°.
— *Other copies.* (B 374, 462)
— ADAMS, S. Appeal to the world; or, Vindication of Boston. Boston, 1769. 8°. (B 610, 1005, 1081, 1091, 2502)
— - *Same.* London, *reprinted* 1770. 8°.
— - *Another copy.* (B 389)
— BERNARD, *Sir* F., *and others.* Letters to the Earl of Hillsborough. Boston, *printed*, Lond., *reprinted* 1769. 8°. (B 462)
— - Letters to the ministry. Boston, 1769. 8°. (B 462, 992)
— CASE of Gr. Britain and America, addressed to the King and both Ho. of Parliament. 2d ed. London, 1769. 8°.
— *Another copy.* (B 346)
— *Same.* 3d ed. Boston, *n.d.* 8°. (B 626, 1094)
— LETTERS to the Earl of Hilsborough on the present situation of affairs in America; also app. in answer to Constitutional right of Gr. Brit. to tax the colonies. Boston, *repr.* 1769. 8°. (B 610, 1081, 2502)
— MORRIS, A. Reflections on the Amer. contest; address to E. Burke, [1769]. London, 1776. 8°. (B 379, 706)
— OBSERVATIONS on several acts of Parliament passed in the 4th, 6th, and 7th years of his present Majesty's reign; and also, on the conduct of the officers of the customs, since those acts were passed. Boston, 1769. 8°. (B 610, 1094)
— TRUE constitutional means for putting an end to the disputes between Gr. Brit. and the Amer. colonies. London, 1769. 8°. (B 463)
— CHAUNCY, C. Trust in God; sermon, May 30. Boston, 1770. 8°. (B 146, 1092)
— MASERES, F. Considerations on the expediency of admitting representatives from the Amer. colonies into the Brit. Ho. of Commons. London, 1770. 8°. (B 380)
— WITHERSPOON, J. Ignorance of the British with respect to America; [and other tracts and speeches, 1771-80]. (*In his* Works, v. 4. 1802.)
— NEWELL, T. Extracts from an original diary, 1773-74. (*In* Mass. Hist. Soc. Proc., 1858-60.)
— AMERICAN alarm; the Bostonian plea for the rights and liberties of the people; by a British Bostonian. Bost., 1773. 8°. (B 663)
— ORATION on the beauties of liberty; or, Essential rights of Americans; by a British Bostonian. Boston, 1773. 8°. (B 744)
— *Same.* 3d ed. New London, 1773. 8°. (B 399)
— EXAMINATION into the conduct of the present administration, 1774-78; and a plan of accommodation with America. 2d ed. London, 1779. 8°. (B 46)
— ADAMS, J. Novanglus and Massachusettensis; or, Political essays, 1774-75. Bost., 1819. 8°.
— ALLEN, W. The American crisis; letter to Earl Gower, *etc.* London, 1774. 8°. (B 662)
— ANSWER to 'Considerations on certain political trans. in S. Carolina'. *n.t.p.* [1774.] 8°. (B 635)
— APPEAL to the justice and interests of the people of Gr. Brit. London, 1774. 8°.
Note. For authorship and other editions, and a translation, *see* Appeal.
— ARGUMENT in defence of the exclusive right claimed by the colonies to tax themselves. London, 1774. 8°. (B 379)
— BERNARD, *Sir* F. Causes of the present distractions in Amer. explained. [Boston,] 1774. 8°. (B 992, 2503)
— BOLLAN, W. Petition to the King, Jan. 26, 1774; with illustrations. London, 1774. 4°. (A 12)
— - Petition to Parliament; with [an] introd. London, 1774. 4°. (A 12, 27, 76)
— - Rights of the English colonies in America. London, 1774. 4°. (A 5)
— BURKE, E. Speech, American taxation, Apr. 19, 1774. 3d ed. London, 1775. 8°. (B 1706)
— - *Same.* 3d ed. London, 1775. 8°. (B 381)
— - *Same.* 3d ed. N. Y., 1775. 8°. (B 592)
— CONG. CHURCHES IN CONN. *Gen. Assoc.* Letter to the clergymen in Boston, [1774]. — CONG. CHURCHES IN MASS. *Gen. Assoc.* Copy of an answer to a letter from the Gen. Assoc. in Conn. to the Assoc. pastors in Boston, [1774]. (*In* Mass. Hist. Soc. Col., v. 12. 1814.)
— COOPER, M. American querist, The; or, Questions proposed rel. to the disputes between Gr. Brit. and her American colonies. Boston, 1774. 8°. (B 359, 467)
— - Friendly address to Americans on our political confusions, in which the consequences of opposing the King's troops and a general non-importation are stated. N. Y., 1774. 8°. (W 32)
— - *Same.* London, 1774. 8°. (B 381)
— - *Same.* America, 1774. 8°. (B 1081)
— - The other side of the question; defence of the liberties of N. America; by a citizen. N. Y., 1774. 8°. (B 378, 629)
— DIALOGUE between a southern delegate and his spouse on his return from the grand Continental Congress. *n.p.*, 1774. 8°. (B 378)
— DICKINSON, J. Essay on the constitutional power of Gr. Brit. over the colonies in Amer.; with the resolves of the comm. of the Province of Penn. Phila., 1774. 8°. (B 359, 377, C 157)
— - *Same.* A new essay. London, *reprinted* 1774. 8°. (B 348)
— DRAYTON, W. H. Letter to the deputies of N. Amer. in Congress at Phila. Charlestown, S. C., 1774. 4°. (A 27)
— FREE consideration of the misunderstandings between Gr. Brit. and the Amer. colonies. Salem, 1774. 8°. (B 1005)
— GRAY, H. Few remarks upon some of the votes and resolutions of the Continental Congress at Phila., [1774], *etc.* *n.p.*, [1775]. 8°. (B 657, 1081)
— INTEREST of the merchants and manufacturers of Gr. Brit. in the contest with the colonies. London, 1774. 8°. (B 377)
— *Same.* Dublin, 1775. 8°. (B 515)
— JEFFERSON, T. Summary view of the rights of British America. Williamsburg, *printed*, London, *reprinted* 1774. 8°. (B 629)
— - *Same.* Williamsburg, *printed*, Phila., *reprinted* 1774. 8°. (B 515)
— JINGLE, Bob, *pseud.* The association, *etc.*, of delegates of the colonies at the grand Congress at Phila. versified and adapted to music. *n.p.*, 1774. 8°. (B 378, W 26)
— LETTER from a veteran to the officers of the army encamped at Boston. Amer., 1774. 8°. (B 467)
— LETTER from a Virginian to members of the Congress to be held at Phila., Sept. 1, 1774. London, *reprinted* 1774. 8°. (B 386)
— *Same.* Boston, *reprint.* 1774. 8°. (B 65, 972, 1081)
— POOR man's advice, The, to his poor neighbors; a ballad. N. Y., 1774. 8°. (W 26)
— PRESCOTT, B. Free and calm consideration of the misunderstandings between the Parl. of Gr. Brit. and Amer. colonies. Salem, [1774]. 8°. (B 475)
— QUINCY, J., *Jr.* Observations on the Boston port-bill; with thoughts on civil society and standing armies. Bost., 1774. 8°. (B 348, 350, 389, 1693, 2503)
— - *Same.* London, *reprinted* 1774. 8°. (B 389)
— RIGHT of the British legislature to tax the American colonies vindicated. Lond., 1774. 8°.
— *Another copy.* (B 380)
— RIGHT of the British legislature to tax the colonies considered. London, [1774]. 8°. (B 662)
— ROBINSON, M. Considerations on the measures carrying on with respect to the colonies. London, [1774]. 8°. (B 682)
— SERIOUS address to the inhabitants of N. Y. [on the] Boston port act. N. Y., 1774. 4°. (A 14)
— SHIPLEY, J. Speech intended to have been spoken on the bill for altering the charter of Mass. Bay. London, 1774. 8°.
Note. For other eds. *see* Shipley, J. (p. 2722).

— LEE, A. Speech never intended to be spoken; in answer to [Shipley's] 'Speech intended to have been spoken'. London, 1774. 8°.
— SHORT advice to the counties of New York; by a country gentleman. New York, 1774. 8°. (B 703, 990)
— THOUGHTS of a traveller upon our American disputes. London, 1774. 8°. (B 674)
— TUCKER, J. Four tracts; with two sermons on political and commercial subjects. Glocester, 1774. 8°. (B 752)
— VERY short and candid appeal to free-born Britons; by an American. London, 1774. 8°. (B 386)
— W., A., *farmer*. Congress canvassed; or, An examination into the conduct of delegates at the grand convention, Sept. 1, 1774; by [S. Seabury?]. London, *reprinted* 1775. 8°. (B 387)
— - Free thoughts on the proc. of the Congress; by a farmer [I. Wilkins or S. Seabury?]. *n.p.*, 1774. 8°. (C 112, 265, W 21)
— - *Same*. London, 1775. 8°.
— - View of the controversy between Gr. Britain and her colonies. N. Y., 1774. 8°.
— - *Other copies*. (B 377, 702)
— - *Same*. London, 1775. 8°.
— WILSON, J. Considerations on the nature and extent of the legislative authority of the British Parl. Phila., 1774. 8°. (B 359, 377)
— WONDERFUL appearance of an angel, devil, and ghost in Boston, Oct. 14-16. Bost., 1774. 8°. (B 655)
— TRUMBULL, J., *and* LIVINGSTON, W. Lettres à Johan-Derk baron van der Capellen, [1775-78]. *n p.*, [177-]. 8°. (B 631)
— AMERICA'S appeal to the impartial world. Hartford, 1775. 8°. (B 517, 655)
— BRIEF extract of arguments in support of the supremacy of the British legislature. London, 1775. 8°. (B 384)
— BURKE, E. Speech on American taxation, Apr. 19. 2d ed. London, 1775. 8°. (B 1706)
— - Speech on moving his resolutions for conciliation with the colonies, Mar. 22. London, 1775. 8°. (A 28, B 703)
— - *Same*. 3d ed. London, 1775. 8°. (B 369)
— - *Same*. N. Y., 1775. 8°. (B 360)
— CHANDLER, T. B. What think ye of Congress now,' *etc.*; [with 'A plan of a proposed union between Gr. Brit. and the colonies'; by J. Galloway]. *n.p.*, [1775]. 8°. (B 343, W 21)
— CONSIDERATIONS on the commencement of the civil war in America. London, 1775. 8°. (B 386)
— DALRYMPLE, *Sir* J. Address of the people of Gr. Brit. to the inhabitants of America. London, 1775. 8°. (B 360, 592, 618, 1080, 1094, 1521, 1719)
— ENGLAND'S tears; a poem. London, 1775. 4°. (A 28)
— ENGLISHMAN'S answer, An, to the address from the delegates to the people of Gr. Britain. N. Y., 1775. 8°. (B 378)
— EVIDENCE of the laws, usage, *etc.*, in proof of the rights of Britons. London, 1775. 8°. (B 635)
— EXTRACTS from a letter by a London merchant to his friend in Virginia, 1775. (*In* Mass. Hist. Soc. Col., v. 9. 1804.)
— GALLOWAY, J. Candid examination of the mutual claims of Gr. Brit. and the colonies. N. Y., 1775. 8°. (B 359, 363, 381, 611, 1635)
— - Reply to Address to the author of 'Candid examination', *etc.* N. Y., *printed* 1775, London, *republished* 1780. 8°. (B 363)
— HAMILTON, A. The farmer refuted; in answer to a letter from A. W. farmer. N.Y., 1775. 8°. (B 992) (B 515, W 33)
— HEWES, J. Collection of occurrences and facts which illustrate the truth of James III. 5, 6. *n.p.*, 1775. 8°.
— HUNT, I. The political family; adventures of an union between Gr. Brit. and her colonies. No. 1. Phila., 1775. 8°. (B 359)
— HUNTINGTON, E. Sermon, Middletown, July 20, 1775; [fast] day appointed by the Continental Congress. Hartford, [1775]. 8°. (C 60)
— J., C. Letter to Rev. Dr. Auchmuty. America, 1775. 8°. (B 517)
— JOHNSON, S. Taxation no tyranny. London, 1775. 8°. (B 381, 706)
— - *Same*. 3d ed. London, 1775. 8°. (B 361, 1719)
— - *Germ*. Schatzung keine Tiranney; nach der 4n Ausg. (*In* Remer, J. A. Amer. Archiv, v. 2. 1777. E 32)
— ANSWER to 'Taxation no tyranny'. London, 1775. 8°. (B 1719)
— DEFENCE of the resolutions and address of the Americans. London, [1775]. 8°. (B 632)
— PAMPHLET, The, entitled, 'Taxation no tyranny', considered. London, [1775]. 8°. (B 635)
— RESISTANCE no rebellion; answer to 'Taxation no tyranny'. London, 1775. 8°. (B 632)
— JOHNSTONE, G. Speech on the address declaring the colony of Mass. Bay in rebellion, also two letters of Junius in favor of the Americans. London, [1775]. 8°. (B 386)
— LEE, C. Strictures on a pamphlet entitled 'Friendly address', *etc.*, [by M. Cooper]. Boston, *reprinted* 1775. 8°. (B 635, 1081)
— BARRY, H. "Strictures [by C. Lee] on M. Cooper's 'Friendly address'" examined. *n.p.*, 1775. 8°. (B 611, 991, 1081)
— LETTER to Ld. Camden, on the bill for restraining the trade and fishery of the four provinces of New Eng. London, 1775. 8°. (B 1719)
— LIND, J. Remarks on the principal acts of the 13th Parl. of Gr. Britain. Vol. 1, cont. rem. on the acts rel. to the colonies, with a plan of reconciliation. London, 1775. 8°.
— PITT, W. The plan offered to the Ho. of Lords, for settling the troubles in America, rejected. London, 1775. 4°. (A 28)
— - Speech in the Ho. of Lords, Jan. 20. New ed. London, 1775. 4°. (A 28)
— PLAIN state of the argument between Gr. Brit. and her colonies. London, 1775. 8°. (B 389)
— PLAN for conciliating the jarring political interests of Gr. Brit. and her colonies. London, 1775. 8°. (B 390)
— PRESENT crisis with respect to America considered. London, 1775. 8°. (B 381)
— PROPOSITION for the present peace and future government of the British colonies in North America. London, [1775]. 8°. (B 681)
— REMARKS on the new essay of the Pennsylvania farmer [J. Dickinson]; by the author of the 'Rights of the British legislature vindicated'. London, 1775. 8°.
— REMARKS on the 'Patriot' [by S. Johnson], including hints respspecting Americans. London, 1775. 8°. (B 384)
— REPLY of a gentleman in select society upon the contest between Gr. Britain and America. London, 1775. 8°. (B 386)
— SAGITTARIUS, *pseud*. Letters and political speculations from the Public ledger. Boston, 1775. 8°. (B 475, 2501)
— SECOND appeal to the justice and interests of the people of Gr. Britain in the present disputes with Amer. London, 1775. 8°.
— *Another copy*. (W 27)
— SENTIMENTS of a foreigner on the disputes of Gr. Brit. with America; tr. from the French. Phila., 1775. 8°. (B 360)
— SHORT address to the government and colonists in America, on the present state of affairs. London, 1775. 8°.
— SPEECH in support of the petition from the general Congress at Phila. London, *E. and C. Dilly*, 1775. 8°. (B 635)
— *Same*. London, *J. Almon*, 1775. 8°. (W 15)
— SPEECHES in the last session of Parliament by Gov. Johnstone [and others]. N. Y., 1775. 8°. (B 360)
— STEARNS, W. A view of the controversy subsisting between Gr. Brit. and the Amer. colonies; sermon. Watertown, 1775. 8°. (C 25)
— SUPREMACY of the British legislature over the colonies candidly discussed. London, 1775. 8°. (B 347)
— TRUMBULL, J. Elegy on the times; first printed at Boston, Sept. 20, 1774. New Haven, 1775. 8°. (B 355)
— TUCKER, J. Address and appeal on the question of separation from the colonies. Glocester, 1775. 8°.
— - *Same*. 2d ed. Glocester, 1775. 8°. (B 1719)
— - *Germ*. Demüthige Vorstellung und ernstliche Appellation an Personen in Grossbrittannien und Irrland. (*In* Remer, J. A. Amer. Archiv, v. 2. 1777.)
— WARREN, *Mrs.* M. The group; a farce, [with a ms. list of characters]. Boston, 1775. 8°. (C 190)
— WESLEY, J. Calm address to our Amer. colonies. London, [1775]. 12°. (B 390)
— CONSTITUTIONAL answer to J. Wesley's 'Calm address to the American colonies'. London, 1775. 12°. (B 390)
— YANKIES' war-hoop, The; or, Ld. North's Te-Deum for the victorious defeat at Boston, 17 June; [verses] by an American. London, 1775. 4°. (A 28)

— ZUBLY, J. J. Law of liberty; sermon at the opening of the Congress of Georgia. Phila., 1775. 8°. (B 47, 362)

— WEBSTER, P. Political essays on the nature and operation of public finances, [1776-91]. Phila., 1791. 8°.

— NORTHCOTE, T. Tracts on constitutional subjects, with a discourse on 'the powers that be'; written on various occasions, 1776-86. London, 1786. 8°. (B 767)

— MURDIN, C. Three sermons on fast days on account of the American rebellion, [1776-79]. Southampton, [1779]. 8°. (B 366)

— ABSTRACT of speeches in the Ho. of Lords on [suspending] hostilities against the Americans. N. Y., 1776. 8°. (B 363)

— ANSWER to the declaration of the Amer. Congress. 2d ed. London, 1776. 8°. (B 364)

— *Same.* 5th ed. London, 1776. 8°. (B 706)

— BENTHAM, E. De tumultibus Americanis deque eorum concitatoribus. Oxonii, 1776. 8°.

— - *Another copy.* (B 347)

— CARTWRIGHT, J. American independence the interest and glory of Great Britain. Phila., 1776. 8°. (B 703, 990)

— DALRYMPLE, *Sir* J. Rights of Gr. Britain asserted against the claims of America. 3d ed, with add. London, 1776. 8°. (B 347)

— - *Same.* 9th ed. Added, a further refutation of Price's 'State of the national debt'. London, 1776. 8°.

— - *Other copies.* (B 363, 367)

— DEMOPHILUS, *pseud.* Genuine principles of the anc. Saxon or Eng. constitution. Phila., 1776. 8°. (B 703, 990)

— DRAYTON, W. H. Charge on the rise of the Amer. Empire. Charlestown, [S. C.,] 1776. 8°. (B 635)

— ESTWICK, S. Letter to J. Tucker, in answer to his 'Humble address and earnest appeal'. London, 1776. 8°. (B 380)

— ERSKINE, J. Equity, *etc.*, of measures that have occasioned the American revolt tried by the sacred oracles. Edin., 1776. 8°. (B 611)

— - Reflections on the rise, progress, *etc.*, of the present contentions with the colonies. Edin., 1776. 8°. (B 611)

— EVANS, C. Reply to Fletcher's "Vindication of Wesley's 'Calm address'". Bristol, [1776]. 12°. (C 112)

— EXAMINATION of the rights of the colonies upon principles of law; by a gentleman at the bar. London, 1776. 8°. (B 678)

— FALL of British tyranny, The; [a play]. Phila., 1776. 8°. B 363)

— *Same.* *n.t.p.* [177-.] (C 115)

— FLETCHER, J. W. American patriotism farther confronted with reason, Scripture, and the Constitution; with a Scriptural plea. Shrewsbury, 1776. 8°. (B 662)

— GERMAIN, G., 1*st Viscount Sackville.* The rights of Gr. Brit. asserted against the claims of America. Phila., 1776. 8°. (B 472, 630, 2512)

— BAILLIE, H. Observations on 'The rights of Gr. Britain asserted', *etc.* London, 1776. 8°. (B 384)

— H., I. Faction, a sketch; or, Summary of the cause of the present most unnatural of all rebellions, the very first excepted; written 1776 [in verse]. N. Y., 1777. 8°. (B 364)

— HARTLEY, D. Substance of a speech in Parl. upon the state of the nation and the war with America. London, 1776. 4°. (A 28)

— INDEPENDENCE the object of the Congress in America. London, 1776. 8°. (B 382)

— LETTER to Ld. Chatham conc. the war with America; by a gentleman of the Inner Temple. London, [1776]. 8°. (B 383)

— LETTER to Ld. G. Germain, [conc. the military and naval force of the colonies]. London, 1776. 8°. (B 683)

— LORD Chatham's prophecy; an ode. New ed. London, 1776. 4°. (A 28, W 51)

— MORGAN, J. Vindication of his public character [as] director general of the military hospitals and physician in chief to the Amer. army, 1776. Boston, 1777. 8°. (B 1906, C 102)

— PAINE, T. Common sense; addressed to the inhabitants of America. 2d ed. Phila., 1776. 8°. (B 361, 990, 2502, W 23)

Note. For other editions *see* Paine, T. (p. 2208-2209).

— ADDITIONS to 'Plain truth'; cont. remarks on [T. Paine's] 'Common sense' wherein are clearly shown that American independence is illusory. Phila., 1776. 8°. (C 265)

— TRUE interest of America impartially stated in strictures on 'Common sense'. Phila., 1776. 8°. (B 362)

— *Same.* 2d ed. Phila., 1776. 8°. (B 703, 990)

— TRUE merits of 'Common sense' clearly pointed out. London, 1776. 8°. (B 381, 615)

— PINTO, I. Letters on the Amer. troubles, [1776]; tr. from the French. London, 1776. 8°. (B 385)

— PLAIN questions upon the dispute with our Amer. colonies. 3d ed. London, 1776. 12°. (B 390)

— PLEA of the colonies on the charges brought against them by Lord M—d, and others. London, 1776. 8°. (B 678)

— PRICE, R. Observations on the nature of civil liberty, principles of government, and the justice and policy of the war with America; added, an app. 4th ed. London, 1776. 8°.

Note. For other eds. and trans. *see* Price, R.

— CURSORY remarks on Price's 'Observations on the nature of civil liberty'; in a letter to a friend; by a merchant. London, 1776. 8°.

— D., T. Letter to R. Price on his 'Observations on civil liberty'. London, [1776]. 8°. (B 386)

— EXPERIENCE preferable to theory; answer to Dr. Price's 'Observations on the nature of civil liberty'. London, 1776. 8°. (B 681)

— FERGUSON, A. Remarks on a pamphlet lately published by Dr. Price, 'Observ. on the nature of civil liberty', *etc.*; in a letter from a gentleman in the country to a member of Parliament. London, 1776. 8°.

— STEWART, J. Total refutation and political overthrow of Dr. Price; or, Gr. Brit. vindicated against American rebels. London, 1776. 8°. (B 681)

— RICHARDS, G. Declaration of independence: poem, [1776]. Boston, 1793. 8°. (B 89)

— SHEBBEARE, J. Essay on the origin of national society; in which the principles of government, *etc.*, contained in Dr. Price's 'Observations', *etc.*, are fairly examined, and fully refuted, *etc.* London, 1776. 8°. (B 383)

— THREE letters to Dr. Price, cont. remarks on his 'Observations', *etc.*; by a member of Lincoln's Inn, F.R.S., F.S.A. London, 1776. 8°.

— *Another copy.* (B 681)

— PROSPECT of the consequences of the present conduct of Gr. Brit. towards Amer. London, 1776. 8°. (B 467)

— WESLEY, J. Some observations on liberty; occasioned by a late tract. London, 1776. 12°. (B 390)

— ROBINSON, M. Further examination of our present Amer. measures. Bath, 1776. 8°.

— ROEBUCK, J. Enquiry whether the guilt of civil war in Amer. ought to be imputed to Great Britain or America. New ed. London, 1776. 8°. (B 384)

— SHERWOOD, S. The Church's flight into the wilderness; observations on Scripture prophecies, shewing that [they] relate to Gr. Britain and the American colonies, Jan. 17. N. Y., 1776. 8°. (B 362, 465)

— POLITICAL mirror, The; by a student of the Inner Temple. London, 1776. 8°. (B 681)

— To their excellencies R. and W. Howe; [signed] A Carolinian; [dated] Charleston, Oct. 22, 1776. *n.t.p.* [1776.] 8°. (B 635)

— TUCKER, J. Tract v.: Pleas and arguments of the mother country and colonies distinctly set forth. Glocester, 1776. 8°. (B 380)

— - True interest of Britain, in regard to the colonies. Phila., 1776. 8°. (B 363, 703)

— WASHINGTON, G. Letters in June and July, 1776; view of American politics. Phila., 1795. 8°. (B 356)

— WINCHESTER, E. Thirteen hymns suited to the present times. 2d ed. Balt., 1776. 8°. (W 46)

— BERTIE, W. Thoughts on the letter of E. Burke, [1777]. 7th ed. Oxford, 1780. 8°. (B 638)

— BURKE, E. Letter to J. Farr and J. Harris, sheriffs, on the affairs of America. Bristol, 1777. 8°. (B 1537, E 163)

— C., H. Answer to the letter from E. Burke. 2d ed. London, 1777. 8°. (B 463)

— DOUBLE delusion; a joco-serious review of our American embroilment. London, 1777. 8°. (B 368)

— LETTER to the English nation, on war with America, by an officer returned from that service. London, 1777. 8°. (B 379)

— PEMBERTON, I., *and others.* Address to the inhabitants of Penn. Phila., *reprinted* London, 1777. 8°. (B 390, 667)

— - *Same.* Phila., *printed*, N. Y., *reprinted* 1777. 8°. (B 364)

— PRICE, R. Additional obs. on the nature and value of civil liberty, and the war with America, *etc.* London, 1777. 8°. (B 383)
— DODD, A. C. The contrast; or, Strictures on Price's 'Additional observations'. Lond., 1777. 8°. (B 384)
— GRAY, J. Doctor Price's notions of civil liberty shewn to be contradictory to reason and Scripture. London, 1777. 8°. (B 383)
— LETTER to Dr. Price on his 'Additional observations', *etc.* London, 1777. 8°. (B 383)
— REFLECTIONS on the present combination of the Amer. colonies against the British legislature and their claim to independency; with remarks on the character and trial of John the painter. London, 1777. 8°. (B 364, 463)
— ROBINSON, M. Peace the best policy. London, 1777. 8°. (B 382)
— TURGOT, A. R. J. Sur la guerre d'Amérique, [1777]. (*In his* Œuvres, v. 8. 1809.)
— UNCONNECTED Whig's address, An, upon the present civil war, *etc.* London, 1777. 8°. (B 681)
— WESLEY, J. Calm address to the inhabitants of England. London, 1777. 12°. (B 390)
— APPEAL, An, to reason and justice in behalf of the British Constitution and the subjects of the British Empire; added, remarks on 'Thoughts on the present state of affairs with America, by Wm. Pulteney'. London, 1778. 8°. (B 678)
— COLLECTION of papers rel. to the proc. of His Majesty's commissioners, *etc.* N. Y., 1778. 8°. (B 366)
— COMMON SENSE, *pseud.* Memorial upon the present crisis between Gr. Brit. and America. London, 1778. 8°. (B 674, 1488)
— CONCILIATORY bills considered. London, 1778. 8°. (B 368)
— CONSIDERATIONS on the mode and terms of a treaty of peace with America. London, 1778, *reprinted* Hartford, 1779. 12°. (B 476)
— *Same.* Phila., 1779. 12°. (B 616)
— DRAYTON, W. H. Speech, Jan. 20, 1778, in the General Assembly upon the Articles of confederation of the U. S. Charlestown, 1778. 12°. (B 616)
— HISTORICAL remarks on the taxation of free states. London, 1778. 4°. (A 27)
— LETTER to Ld. G. Germaine on the dispute between Gr. Brit. and the colonies. London, 1778. 8°. (B 388)
— LETTER to the people of America; with a postcript, by the ed. to Sir W****** H***. London, 1778. 8°. (B 463)
— PROPOSALS for a plan towards reconciliation and reunion with the thirteen provinces of America. London, 1788. 8°. (B 388)
— PULTENEY, W. Thoughts on the present state of affairs with America. London, 1778. 8°. (B 388)
— SERIOUS address to such Quakers as profess scruples rel. to the present government. 2d ed. Phila., 1778. 8°. (B 465)
— STEVENSON, J. Letters in answer to Price's two pamphlets on civil liberty, *etc.* London, 1778. 8°. (B 365)
— TICKELL, R. Anticipation; containing the substance of His Majesty's speech. London, 1778. 8°.
— - *Same.* 3d ed. corr. London, 1778. 8°. (B 365)
— - *Same.* (*In* Pamphleteer, 1822; v. 19 of B 838)
— ZERO, *pseud.* Succinct review of the American contest, 1778. London, [1782]. 8°.
— BRACKENRIDGE, H. H. Eulogium delivered at Philadelphia, July 5, 1779. (*In* Moore, F. Amer. eloq., v. 1. 1864; *also* B 937)
— BURGOYNE, *Sir* J. Letter upon his late resignation. 6th ed. London, 1779. 8°. (B 635)
— CONSIDERATIONS upon the French and American war. London, 1779. 8°. (W 27)
— DALLAS, R., *Jr.* Considerations upon the American inquiry. London, 1779. 8°. (B 678)
— GR. BRITAIN. *King's Advocate* (J. Marriott). Mémoire justicatif de la conduite de la Grande Bretagne en arrêtant les navires étrangers et les munitions de guerre, destinées aux insurgens de l'Amérique. London, 1779. 4°.
— MCFARLANE, J. Britain's victory over the fleets of France and Spain insured, *etc.* Glasgow, 1779. 8°.
— PITT, W. Genuine abstracts from two speeches, and reply to the Earl of Suffolk. London, 1779. 8°. (B 462)
— PULTENEY, W. Considerations on the present state of public affairs. Edin., 1779. 8°. (B 365, 1704)
— REED, J. Remarks on Gov. Johnstone's speech in Parliament. Phila., 1779. 8°. (W 30)
— - *Same.* Phila., 1783. 8°. (B 417)
— REMARKS on the rescript of the Court of Madrid, and on the manifesto of the Court of Versailles; [with] the rescript, the manifesto, and a memorial of Dr. Franklyn to the Court of Versailles. London, 1779. 4°. (B 463)
— REPLY to Lieut.-Gen. Burgoyne's letter to his constituents. 2d ed. London, 1779. 8°.
— TICKELL, R. Anticipation; for the year 1779. London, 1779. 8°.
— U. S. *Cont. Cong.* Observations on the American Revolution. Phila., 1779. 8°. (B 635)
— POWNALL, T. Three memorials to the sovereigns of Europe, of Gr. Brit., and of Amer. ica, [1780–83]. London, 1784. 8°.
— VERGENNES, C. G. Projet de méditation de la Russie entre la France et l'Angleterre à l'occasion de l'independence américaine, 1780–82. (*In* Paris. Soc. de l'Hist. de France. Bul., v. 2. 1835.)
— ADAMS, J. Letters to Dr. Calkoen on the U. S., [1780]. *n.t.p.* [London, *printed not published* 1786.] 8°.
— - *Another copy.* (W 23)
— - *Same.* *n.t.p.* [1786.] 8°. (B 594)
— - *Same.* Twenty-six letters resp. the Revolution of America, 1780. N. Y., 1789. 12°. (C 74)
— ALARM, The; or, Plan of pacification with America; [and] The New York freeholder, nos. 1–7. N. Y., [1780]. 16°. (C 81)
— CANDID retrospect, The; or, The American war examined by Whig principles. Charlestown, *printed*, N. Y., *reprinted* 1780. 8°. (C 121)
— CÉRISIER, A. M. Le destin de l'Amérique. ou Dialogues pittoresques, [1780]; tr. de l'anglois. London, [1782]. 8°. (B 806)
— CONWAY, *Gen.* H. S. Speech, 5th May 1780, that leave be given to bring in a bill for quieting troubles in the British colonies of America. London, 1781. 8°.
— DISPASSIONATE thoughts on the American war. London, 1780. 8°. (B 348)
— GALLOWAY, J. Plain truth; or, A letter to the author of 'Dispassionate thoughts'. London, 1780. 8°. (B 417, 1635)
— FOTHERGILL, J. An English freeholder's address to his countrymen, [1780]. (*In his* Works, v. 3. 1784.)
— GALLOWAY, J. Cool thoughts on the consequences to Gr. Brit. of Amer. independence. Lond., 1780. 8°. (B 638, 1635)
— - Letters to a nobleman on the conduct of the war in the middle colonies. 3d ed. London, 1780. 8°. (B 638)
— - Historical and political reflections on the rise and progress of the Amer. rebellion. London, 1780. 8°. (B 638, 1635)
— HUMPHREYS, D. Poem addressed to the armies of the U. S. New Haven, 1780. 8°. (B 355, W 21)
— - *French.* Discours en vers aux officiers et aux soldats des différentes armies américaines. Paris, 1786. 8°. (W 47)
— POWNALL, T. Memorial on the present state of affairs. London, 1780. 8°.
— QUERNO, C. The American times; a satire. London, 1780. 4°. (A 20)
— COLLECTION of state papers rel. to the first acknowledgment of the sovereignty of the U. S. A. and the reception of their minister [J. Adams] by the United Netherlands, [1781–82]; by an American. London, 1782. 8°. (B 596)
— ADAMS, J. Memorie aan Hunne Hoog-Mogenden de Staaten-Generaal der Vereënigde Nederlanden. *n.t.p.* [1781.] 12°. (C 265)
— ALMON, J. Letter to C. Jenkinson. 2d ed. London, 1781. 4°. (A 27)
— BAXTER, S. Tyrannicide proved lawful; discourse, Symsbury, Conn., 1781. London, 1782. 8°. (B 681)
— CICERO, *pseud.* Letter to Lord H—e, occasioned by his speech in the H—e of C—ns. London, 1781. 8°. (B 463)
— DEANE, S. Paris papers, [1781]. N. Y., [17—]. 16°.
— JENNINGS, E. Translation of [T. Pownall's] Memorial to the sovereigns of Europe on the present state of affairs between the Old and the New World. London, 1781. 8°. (B 595)

— MEIGS, J. Oration, New Haven, Nov. 5, 1781. New Haven, 1782. 4°. (B 650)
— TUCKER, J. Cui bono? Glocester, 1781. 8°. (B 629)
— - *Same.* 2d ed., with plan for a general pacification. Glocester, 1782. 8°.
— - *Another copy.* (B 348)
— - *French.* Cui bono, ou Examen quels avantages les Anglois ou les Américains, *etc.*, retireront-ils des plus grandes victoires dans la guerre actuelle? trad. de l'angl. London, 1782. 8°. (C 165)
— KNOX, W. Extra official state papers; by a late under secretary of state, [1782–87]. London, 1789. 2 v. 8°.
— CONSIDERATIONS on the Attorney General's proposition for a bill for the establishment of peace with America. London, 1782. 8°. (B 633)
— VERMONT. *Council.* Copy of the remonstrance against the resolutions of Congress of Dec. 5, [1782]. Hartford, 1783. 8°. (B 476)
— DAY, T. Reflections upon the present state of England, and the independence of America, [1782]. 4th ed., with add. London, 1783. 8°. (B 637)
— PAINE, T. Letter to Abbé Raynal on the affairs of N. Amer.; in which the mistakes in the Abbé's account of the Revolution of America are corrected. Phila., 1782. 8°. (B 592, 2503, C 321, W 23)
— - *Same.* London, *reprinted* 1782. 8°. (B 637)
— - *Same.* London, 1793. 8°. (B 600)
— PLAN of reconciliation with America. London, 1782. 8°. (B 678, 702)
— RETROSPECTIVE view of the causes of difference between Gr. Brit. and the colonies. London, [1782]. 8°.
— TOD, T. Consolatory thoughts on American independence; the great advantages that will arise from it. Edin., 1782. 8°.
— - *Other copies.* (B 1704, W 32)
— WILLIAMS, J. Considerations on the American war. London, 1782. 4°. (A 20)
— COBBETT, W. Porcupine's works; exhibiting a faithful picture of the U. S., 1783–1801. London, 1801. 12 v. 8°.
— CANDID and impartial considerations on the preliminary articles of peace with France and Spain and the provisional treaty with the U. S. London, 1783. 8°. (B 678)
— DEFENSIVE arms vindicated; and the lawfulness of the Amer. war made manifest. *n.p.*, 1783. 12°. (W 46)
— FRISBIE, L. Oration, Ipswich, Apr. 29, restoration of peace. Boston, 1783. 4°. (B 14, 654)
— G., L. C. D. L. L'Amérique délivrée; esquisse d'un poëme sur l'indépendance de l'Amérique. Amst., 1783. 2 v. 8°.
— KIPPIS, A. Considerations on the provisional treaty with America and the preliminary articles of peace with France and Spain. London, 1783. 8°.
— - *Other copies.* (B 1705, W 27)
— MAGAPICA, M., *pseud.* British and American liturgy. London, 1783. 8°. (B 678)
— POWNALL, T. Memorial addressed to the sovereigns of America. London, 1783. 8°. (B 638)
— WASHINGTON, G. Resignation and address; circular letter to the President of N. H. Exeter, 1783. 4°.
— - *Another copy.* (B 14)
— - *Same, entitled* Last official address; annexed, papers rel. to half-pay and commutation of half-pay granted by Congress to the officers of the army. Hartford, 1783. 8°. (B 1005, 1092)
— - *Same, entitled* Col. of papers, *etc.* Boston, 1783. 4°. (B 518)
— CHALMERS, G. Opinions on interesting subjects of public law and commercial policy arising from Amer. independence. London, 1784. 8°. (B 701)
— CHAMPION, R. Considerations on the present situation of Gr. Britain and the United States. London, 1784. 8°. (B 629)
— - *Same.* 2d ed. London, 1784. 8°.
— HAMILTON, A. Letter from Phocion to citizens of N. Y. on the politics of the day. Boston, 1784. 8°. (B 626, 992, 2503)
— - *Same.* Phila., 1784. 8°. (B 472, 630, 2512)
— - 2d letter from Phocion to the citizens of N. Y. on politics. Phila., 1784. 8°. (B 630, 2512)
— MAILHE, J. B. Discours sur la grandeur et importance de la révolution qui vient de s'opérer dans l'Amérique Septentrionale. Toulouse, 1784. 8°. (W 47)
— PRICE, R. Observations on the importance of the Amer. Revolution. London, 1784. 8°. (B 619, W 18, 64)
Note. For other eds. and trans. *see* **Price, R.**
— MIRABEAU, H. G. R. de. Reflections on [R. Price's] 'Observations on the importance of the Amer. Revolution'. Phila., 1786. 8°. (B 472)
— REMARKS on 'A dissertation on the political union of the 13 U. S., by a citizen of Philadelphia'; by a Connecticut farmer. *n.p.*, 1784. 8°. (B 466)
— OBSERVATIONS on the peculiar case of the Whig merchants indebted to Gr. Brit. at the commencement of the late war. N. Y., 1785. 8°. (B 635)
— PROSPECT, The; or, Reunion of Gr. Brit. and America; a poem. London, 1785. 4°. (A 14)
— WEBSTER, N. Sketches of American policy under [different] heads. Hartford, 1785. 8°. (A 2)
— HONESTY shewed to be true policy; or, A general impost defended by a plain politician. N. Y., 1786. 8°. (B 517)
— HUNT, I. Discourse on the late attempt to assassinate His Majesty; with remarks on the miserable situation of the U. S., Aug. 20, 1786. 3d ed. *n.p.*, [1786]. 8°. (B 319)
— CLAVIÈRE, E., *and* BRISSOT DE WARVILLE, J. P. De la France et des Etats-Unis. Londres, 1787. 8°. (B 793)
Note. For other editions *see* **Clavière, E.,** *and* **Brissot de Warville, J. P.**
— EXAMINATION into the leading principles of the federal Constitution proposed by the late convention at Phila. Phila., 1787. 8°. (W 17)
— MARTIN, L. Genuine information laid before the Legislature of Maryland. (*In* U. S. *Constitutional Convention,* 1787. Secret proc. 1821; 1836.)
— - *Same.* With remarks relative to a standing army and bill of rights. Phila., 1788. 8°. (B 701, 971)
— GALLOWAY, J. Claim of Amer. loyalists reviewed and maintained. London, 1788. 8°. (B 617)
— JACKSON, J. Thoughts upon the political situation of the U. S. Worcester, 1788. 8°.
— - *Other copies.* (B 632, 1117)
— LEE, R. H. Additional letters to the Republican, leading to a fair examination of the system of government proposed by the Convention. *n.p.*, 1788. 8°. (B 65, 151)
— - *Same.* (*Appended to his* Observations. 1787.)
— LIBERTY; a poem on the independence of America. Richmond, 1788. f°.
— AMERICAN independent catechism adapted to the liberal spirit of the U. S. Boston, 1789. 8°. (B 658)
— ESSAY on the seat of the federal government and the exclusive jurisdiction of Cong. over a ten-miles district. Phila., 1789. 8°. (B 625)
— HILLHOUSE, W. Diss., in answer to a late lecture on the political state of America, Jan. 12; [with] a poem. New Haven, [1789]. 8°. (B 355)
— POLITICAL passing bell, The; an elegy parodized from Gray. Boston, 1789. 8°. (B 355)
— HOPKINSON, J., *Jr.* What is our situation and what our prospects? *n.t.p.* [179–.] 8°. (B 631)
— SULLIVAN, J. Observations on the government of the U. S. Boston, 1791. 8°. (B 631, 1488)
— REFLEXIONS on the state of the union. Phila., 1792. 8°. (B 465)
— POLITICKS and views, The, of a certain party displayed. *n.p.*, 1792. 8°. (B 593, 631, 2517, 2526, W 28)
Note. Said to be written by Wm. Smith of So. Carolina.
— GEBHARDT, A. G., *ed.* Actes et mém. conc. les négociations entre la France et les Etats-Unis de l'Amérique, 1793–1800. Londres, 1807. 3 v. 12°.
— GENET, E. C. Correspondence between G. and the Federal Government; prefixed, [his] instructions. Phila., 1793. 4°. (A 16, 27, W 58)
— CALLENDER, J. T. Political register; or, Proceedings in Congress, Nov. 3, 1794 – Mar. 3, 1795. Vol. 1. Phila., 1795. 8°.
— ENQUIRY into the principles and tendency of certain public measures. Phila., 1794. 8°. (B 400, 983)
— GORE, C. Manlius; with notes and references. No. 1–7. *n.p.*, [1794]. 8°. (B 594, 984)

— Marcellus, nos. 1-6; publ. in the Virginia gazette, Nov. and Dec. 1794. *n.p.*, [1794]. 8°. (B 631, (2521)
— Randolph, E. Germanicus. *n.p.*, [1794]. 8°. (B 594)
— Smith, W. Address, in defence of his opposition to Madison's resolutions]. Phila., 1794. 8°. (B 597)
— Taylor, J. Enquiry into the principles and tendency of certain public measures. Phila., 1794. 8°. (B 640)
— American remembrancer; essays, speeches, *etc.*, rel. to the treaty with Gr. Britain. Phila., *M. Carey*, 1795. 3 v. 8°.
— Candid examination of the objections to the treaty between the U. S. and Gr. Brit. N. Y., *reprinted* 1795. 8°. (B 625, W 28)
— Carey, M. Features of Jay's treaty; [with] a view of the commerce of the U. S. Phila., 1795. 8°. (B 986, W 62)
— Cobbett, W. A little plain English on the treaty with [Gr. Brit.] and the conduct of the President rel. thereto. London, 1795. 8°. (B 625)
— - *Same.* Phila., 1795. 8°. (W 28)
— Jay, J. Features of [his] treaty. Phila., 1795. 8°. (B 986)
— Puglia, J. P. The federal politician. Phila., 1795. 8°.
— Randolph, E. Vindication of [his] resignation. Phila., 1795. 8°. (B 479, 741, 1850, 2526, W 28)
— Treaty, The, its merits and demerits, [1784-95]. *n.p.*, [1795.] 8°. (B 619)
— Address to the Ho. of Rep. of the U. S. on Lord Grenville's treaty. Phila., 1796. 8°. (B 420, W 63)
— Ames, F. Speech in support of the treaty [with] Gr. Brit. Phila., 1796. 8°. (B 640, W 62)
— - *Same.* (*In* Moore, F. Amer. eloquence, v. 1. 1864.)
— British honour and humanity; or, Wonders of Amer. patience. Phila., 1796. 8°. (W 56)
— Cobbett, W. New-year's gift to the Democrats; or Observations on 'A vindication of E. Randolph's resignation'. Phila., 1796. 8°. (B 479, 2518, W 28)
— Duane, W. Letter to G. Washington, cont. strictures on his address, 17 Sept. 1796. Phila., 1796. 8°. (B 356, 628)
— Harper, R. G. Address to his constituents; [with] his reasons for approving the treaty with Gr. Brit. Boston, 1796. 8°. (B 527, 614, 1906)
— Page, J. Address to the citizens of York, Va. *n.p.*, 1786. 8°. (B 343)
— Paine, T. Letter to G. Washington on affairs public and private. Phila., 1796. 8°. (356, 641, W 60)
— Political truth; or, Animadversions on the past and present state of pub. affairs, with an inquiry into the truth of the charges against E. Randolph. Phila., 1796. 8°. (B 479)
— U. S. *4th Cong. 1st sess. House.* Debates upon questions involved in the Brit. treaty of 1794. [1796.] 2d ed. Phila., 1808. 2 v. 8°.
— Washington, G. Address to the people of the U. S. *n.t.p.* [1796.] 8°. (B 741)
Note. For other eds. *see* Washington, G.
— Wilmer, J. J. Address to the citizens of the U. S. on national representation. Balt., [1796]. 8°. (W 60)
— Examination of the conduct of the executive of the U. S. towards the French Republic. Phila., 1797. 8°. (B 423, W 56)
— Fauchet, J. Sketch of the present state of our political rel. with the U. S. Phila., 1797. 8°. (B 2508, W 59, 68)
— Harper, R. G. Observations on the dispute between U. S. and France. Phila., 1797. 8°. (W 68)
— - *Same.* 3d Amer. ed. Phila., 1798. 8°. (W 59)
— - *Same.* 4th Amer. ed. Boston, 1798. 8°. (B 597, 1701)
— - *French.* Tr. de l'angl. Londres, 1798. 8°. (B 804)
— Kennedy, P. Answer to Paine's letter to Gen. Washington; including counsel to Mr. Erskine. London, 1797. 8°. (B 525)
— - *Same.* 3d ed. London, 1797. 8°. (B 619)
— - *Same.* Phila., 1798. 8°. (W 60)
— Monroe, J. View of the conduct of the executive in the foreign affairs of the U. S. Phila., 1797. 8°.
— - *Same.* London, 1798. 8°. (B 1079)
— Observations on some late public transactions in and out of Congress. Charleston, 1797. 8°. (B 628)
— Pickering, T. Letters of Verus to the Native American. Phila., 1797. 8°. (B 465, 2525)
— Tanguy de la Boissière, C. C. Observations sur la dépêche écrite par M. Pickering, le 16 jan. Phila., 1797. 8°. (B 634)

— - *Eng.* Observations on the dispatch, Jan. 16; tr. by S. Chandler. Phila., 1797. 8°. (B 423, 1699)
— Address to the people of Virginia [on] the alien and sedition laws. Richmond, 1798. 8°. (C 116, W 69)
— Address to the voters of Anne Arundel and Prince George's Counties and city of Annapolis. Annapolis, 1798. 8°.
— Allen, J. Speech, rel. to employing the armed vessels as convoys. Phila., 1798. 8°. (B 631)
— Coup d'œil sur la situation des affaires entre la France et les Etats-Unis. *n.p.*, 1798. 8°. (B 615)
— Dennis, J. Address on the origin, progress, and present state of French aggression. Phila., 1798. 8°. (B 640)
— Gallatin, A. Speech on the amendment to the foreign intercourse bill. *n.t.p.* [1798.] 8°. (B 423)
— - *Same.* Phila., 1798. 8°. (B 631)
— Addison, A. Observations on the speech of A. Gallatin on the foreign intercourse bill. Wash., 1798. 8°. (B 428, W 63)
— Harper, R. G. Short account of the proc. of Cong. in the late session, and a sketch of the state of affairs between the U. S. and France, in July 1798. Phila., 1798. 8°. (B 397)
— Infallible cure for political blindness. *n.p.*, 1798. 8°. (W 54)
— Kirkland, J. T. Oration, July 19. Boston, 1798. 8°. (B 1193)
— Nicholas, G. Letter justifying the conduct of the citizens of Kentucky as to some of the late measures of the general gov. Lexington, 1798. 8°. (W 68)
— Selection of the patriotic addresses to the President [J. Adams]; with [his] answers. Boston, 1798. 12°.
— What is our situation and what our prospects? by an American. *n.p.*, [1798]. 8°. (W 10)
— Cobbett, W. Selections from Porcupine's Gazette, [1799-1800]. *n.p.*, *n.d.* 8°.
— Fenno, J. W. Desultory reflections on the political aspects of public affairs in the U. S., 1799. N. Y., 1800. 8°. (B 641)
— Barlow, J. Letter on certain political measures. *n.t.p.* [1799.] 8°. (B 631, 1750)
— - To his fellow-citizens of the U. S. *n.t.p.* [1799.] 8°. (B 631)
— Cary, J. View of the New England illuminati. Phila., 1799. 8°. (W 62)
— Livermore, E. S. Oration, dissolution of the political union between U. S. and France. Portsmouth, 1799. 8°. (B 651)
— Nicholas, G. Letter justifying the conduct of the citizens of Kentucky as to some of the late measures of the general government. Lexington, *printed*, Phila., *reprinted* 1799. 8°. (B 628)
— Packard, H. Federal republicanism; two discourses. Boston, 1799. 8°. (B 89, 170, 229, 857)
— Pendleton, E. Address, present state of our country. Boston, 1799. 8°. (B 614, 1701)
— Pinckney, C. Three letters: On the case of J. Robbins; On the recent capture of Amer. vessels by Brit. cruisers; On the right of expatriation. Phila., 1799. 8°. (B 356, 423)
— Slender, R., *pseud.* Letters [mostly from the] Aurora. Phila., 1799. 8°. (B 397)
— Callender, J. T. The prospect before us. Richmond, 1800-01. 2 v. 8°.
— - *Same.* Vol. 1. Richmond, 1800. 8°. (B 983, 2514)
— American independence; in vindication of the President's nomination of a new embassy to France. Boston, [18—]. 12°. (B 613)
— Answer to a dialogue between a federalist and a republican. Charleston, [18—]. 12°. (B 613)
— Circular to the electors of the County of York. *n.t.p.* [180-?] 8°. (B 424)
— Addison, A. Analysis of the report of the committee of the Va. Assembly, in answer to their resolutions. Phila., 1800. 12°. (C 77, W 13)
— Bishop, A. Connecticut republicanism; oration on political delusion. Phila., 1800. 8°. (B 620)
— Desaussure, H. W. Address to the citizens of S. C. on the approaching election of president and vice president of U. S. Charleston, 1800. 8°. (B 640)
— Fenno, J. W. Desultory reflections on the new political aspects of affairs in the U. S. N. Y. *printed*, Phila. *reprinted* 1800. 8°. (B 984)
— Gr. Brit. *Board of Commissioners.* Brief statement of opinions given in the Board under the 6th article of the treaty with Gr. Britain. Phila., 1800. 8°. (B 597)

— LETHERBURY, P., *and others.* Address to the citizens of Kent [County, Del.], on the election. *n.p.*, [1800]. 8°. (B 397)
— OUTWATER, J., *and others.* Address to the Federal Republicans of N. J., recommending A. Ogden and others for representatives in the 7th Cong. of the U. S. Trenton, 1800. 8°. (B 401)
— SOLEMN address to Christians and patriots upon the approaching election of a President of the U. S., in answer to 'Serious considerations', *etc.* N. Y., 1800. 8°. (B 401)
— WEBSTER, N. Ten letters to J. Priestley in answer to his letters to the inhabitants of Northumberland. New Haven, 1800. 12°. (B 613)
— BISHOP, A. Oration, Wallingford, Mar. 11. New Haven, 1801. 8°. (B 609, 620)
— CRANCH, W. Examination of the President's reply to the New Haven remonstrance. N. Y., 1801. 8°. (B 535, 620, 984)
— HAMILTON, A. Address to the electors of N. York. Albany, [1801?]. 12°. (C 69)
— HARPER, R. G. Letter to his constituents. *n.p.*, 1801. 8°. (B 154, 535, 597)
— AGE of enquiry; a clue to the present political controversy, [1802]. Hartford, 1804. 8°.
— AUSTIN, D. The national 'barley cake' or the 'rock of offence' into a 'glorious holy mountain'; in discourses and letters. Wash., 1802. 8°. (B 303)
— BLACK list; list of Tories who took part with Gr. Brit. in the Revolutionary war, and were attainted of high treason. Phila., 1802. 8°. (B 1000)
— CALLENDER, J. T. Letters to A. Hamilton, King of the Feds. N. Y., 1802. 8°. (B 422)
— - *Same.* N. Y., 1866. 8°. (Hamilton Club, no. 4.)
— LINCOLN, L. A farmer's letters to the people. Phila., 1802. 8°. (B 621)
— WEBSTER, N. Miscellaneous papers on political and commercial subjects. N. Y., 1802. 8°. (B 403)
— ADAMS, J. Correspondence [with] W. Cunningham, 1803-12. Boston, 1823. 8°.
— - *Another copy.* (B 1654)
— PICKERING, T. Review of corresp. between J. Adams and W. Cunningham, 1803-12. Salem, 1824. 8°.
— - *Other copies.* (B 1493, 1761, W 13)
— AUSTIN, B., *Jr.* Constitutional republicanism in opposition to fallacious federalism. Boston, 1803. 8°.
— GR. BRIT. *Parl.* Correspondence between Gr. Brit. and France on the late negotiation [at Amiens]. London, 1803. 8°. (B 1811)
— REPUBLICAN address to the freemen of Conn. *n.p.*, 1803. 8°. (B 623, 986)
— SIDNEY, A., *pseud.* Vindication of the measures of the present administration. Wash., 1803. 8°. (B 623)
— ADDRESS to the people of Mass. *n.p.*, [1804]. 8°. (B 424)
— BISHOP, A. Oration in honor of the election of Pres. Jefferson, *etc.*, at Hartford, May 11. [Hartford,] 1804. 8°. (B 424)
— IMPARTIALIS, *pseud.* Address to the electors of New Hampshire. *n.p.*, [1804]. 8°. (B 424, 971)
— TAYLOR, J. Defence of the measures of the administration of T. Jefferson, by Curtius. Wash., 1804. 8°. (B 424)
— WOLCOTT, O. British influence on the affairs of the U. S. proved and explained. Boston, 1804. 8°. (B 424)
— AMERICAN state papers; authentic documents rel. to the history, politics, statistics, *etc.*, of the U. S., [1805-07]. Boston, 1808. 8°.
Note. From the 'Monthly anthology,' v. 3, 4. app.
— ADDRESS to the people of Mass. on the choice of electors of president and vice-president. *n.p.*, [1805]. 8°. (B 427)
— CHASE, S. Answer and pleas to the articles of impeachment exhibited against him by the Ho. of Representatives. Albany, 1805. 8°. (B 458)
— - *Same.* Salem, 1805. 8°. (B 1431)
— - *Same.* Wash., 1805. 8°. (B 139)
— STEPHEN, J. War in disguise; or, Frauds of neutral flags. London, 1805. 8°. (B 715)
Note. For other editions, *see* Stephen, J. (2856).
— MORRIS, G. Answer to [J. Stephen's] 'War in disguise'. N. Y., 1806. 8°.
— - *Other copies.* (B 430, 754, 1417, 2523)
— INQUIRY into the present state of the foreign relations of the Union. Boston, 1806. 8°. (B 430)
— MORRIS, G. British treaty. *n.p.*, [1806]. 8°. (B 432, 1117)
— - *Same.* With appendix of state papers. 2d ed. London, 1808. 8°. (B 685)
— RANDOLPH, J. Speech, Mar. 5, 1806, on Gregg's resolution for a non-importation of Brit. goods. *n.p.*, 1806. 8°. (C 265)
— - *Same.* [Another ed.] *n.t.p.* [1806.] 8°. (B 430, 1838)
— - *Same.* (*In* Moore, F. Amer. eloquence, v. 2. 1861.)
— - *Same.* With an introd. by the author of 'War in disguise'. London, 1806. 8°. (B 783)
— - 2d speech on the non-importation resolution of Mr. Gregg. *n.t.p.* [1806.] 8°. (B 430)
— EPAMINONDAS, *pseud.* Vindication of the doctrine advocated by J. Randolph. N. Y., 1806. 8°. (B 430)
— STEPHEN, J. Observations on the speech of J. Randolph. London *printed*, N. Y. *reprinted* 1806. 8°. (B 430, 2519)
— NEW YORK. CITIZENS. Memorial. Wash., 1806. 8°. (B 485)
— SIXTH of Aug.; or, The Litchfield festival; address to the people of Conn. *n.t.p.* [1806.] 8°. (B 429, 1838)
— WHITE, S. Speech, bill interdicting all intercourse between the U. S. and St. Domingo, Feb. 20. *n.p.*, 1806. 8°. (B 429)
— B., A. Six letters on the differences between Gr. Brit. and the U. S. London, 1807. 8°. (B 671)
— CHEETHAM, J. Peace or war? Thoughts on our affairs with England. N. Y., 1807. 8°. (B 432)
— DAVEISS, J. H. View of the President's conduct, conc. the conspiracy of 1806. Frankfort, 1807. 8°. (B 433)
— EMANCIPATION in disguise; or, The true crisis of the colonies. London, 1807. 8°. (B 72, 671)
— HORNET, *pseud.* The go-between or two-edged sword. N. Y., 1807. 8°. (B 432)
— LOWELL, J. Peace without dishonor, war without hope; enquiry into the question of the Chesapeake. Boston, 1807. 8°. (B 432, 532, 1879, 2019, 2520, 2525)
— LYCURGUS, *pseud.* War or no war? with a view of our national decline and present embarrassments. N. Y., 1807. 8°. (B 432)
— MIHIR, B., *pseud.* Considerations in answer to the pamphlet containing Madison's instructions to Munroe. Albany, 1807. 8°. (B 432)
— PATRIOTICUS, *pseud.* Solid reasons for continuance of war. [London,] 1807. 8°. (B 783)
— REMARKS on the British treaty with the U. S. Liverpool, 1807. 8°. (B 986, 2007)
— TOCSIN, The; or, The call to arms! enquiry into the late proceedings of Gr. Brit. Charleston, 1807. 8°. (B 432)
— WILSON, J. The lie direct! refutation of the charges in the proclamation of Pres. Jefferson. London, 1807. 8°. (B 671)
— ADAMS, J. Q. Letter to H. G. Otis on our national affairs. Boston, 1808. 8°. (B 1427, 1837, 2520)
— - *Same.* 2d ed. Boston, 1808. 8°. (B 1761, 2019)
— - *Same.* Salem, 1808. 8°. (B 1489)
— - *Same.* London, 1808. 8°. (B 532)
— - *Same.* With app. Balt., 1824. 8°. (B 1427)
— ADDRESS to the citizens of Mass. on the causes of our national distresses. Boston, 1808. 8°. (B 406, C 151)
— ADDRESS to the people of the U. S.; [with] a letter from T. Pickering exhib. a view of the danger of an unnecessary war. Northampton, 1808. 8°. (B 406)
— COX, P., *chairman.* The new crisis of Amer. independence. *n.t.p.* [1808.] 8°. (B 452)
— BARING, A. Causes and consequences of the orders in Council; conduct of Gr. Britain towards America. London, 1808. 8°.
— ESSEX CO. Resolutions [at a meeting to consider the alarming condition of pub. affairs]. *n.p.*, [1808]. 8°. (B 406)
— GARDINIER, B. Speech on foreign relations, Dec. 1808. [Boston, 1808.] 8°. (B 410, 553, 1489, 1837)
— GENET, E. C. Communications on the next election for president of the U. S. *n.p.*, 1808. 8°. (B 406, 1489)
— HANCOCK, *pseud.* The whole truth; to the freemen of N. Eng. *n.p.*, [1808]. 8°. (B 407)
— INGERSOLL, C. J. A view of the rights and wrongs, power and policy of the U. S. Phila., 1808. 8°. (B 983)
— KETELTAS, W. Political hipocrites unmasked. N. Y., 1808. 8°. (B 426)
— LOWELL, J. Analysis of the late correspondence between our administration and Gr. Brit. and France, [1808]. Boston, [1809]. 8°. (B 1837)
— - *Same.* *n.p.*, *n.d.* 8°. (B 531)

— - Supplement to the late 'Analysis of the corresp. between our cabinet and that of France and Gr. Brit.' *n.p.*, [1808]. 8°. (B 410, 531, 535)
— PICKERING, T. Letter exhibiting the imminent danger of our unnecessary and ruinous war. Boston, 1808. 8°. (B 1489, 1837, 2520)
— POLITICAL sermon, addr. to the electors of Middlesex. *n.p.*, [1808]. 8°. (B 406)
— POLITICAL sketch of America. Edin., 1808. 8°. (B 724)
— QUINCY, J. Speech on the 1st resolution reported by the committee on foreign relations. Boston, 1808. 8°. (B 410, 553)
— - 2d speech, *etc.* *n.p.*, [1808]. 8°. (B 410)
— SERMON; the question of war with Gr. Brit. examined upon moral and Christian principles. Boston, 1808. 8°. (B 247, 976)
— UNITED STATES. *Dept. of State.* Letters from Madison to Monroe and Pinkney, with their communications rel. to the treaty with [Gr. Brit.], *etc.* Wash., 1808. 8°. (B 535)
— - *Same.* With additional letters. Wash., 1808. 8°. (B 1490)
— VINDEX, *pseud.* The honest politician. Pt. 1. Balt., 1808. 8°. (B 406)
— WILLIAMS, D. R. Speech, 9th Dec., in the House, on [submission to the late edicts of Gr. Brit.]. *n.t.p.* [1808.] 8°. (C 83)
— ADAMS, J. Q. American principles; review of works of F. Ames. Boston, 1809. 8°. (B 137, 411, 534, 1427, 1837)
— ADAMS, J. Correspondence; originally pub. in the Boston patriot. Boston, 1809. 8°.
— AMER. candour in 'Analysis of the late corresp. between our administration, Gr. Brit., and France'. Boston, 1809. 8°. (B 783)
— BLISS, G., *and others.* Address to the people of the County of Hampshire. Northampton, 1809. 8°. (B 398)
— BRISTOLL, W. Address intended to have been delivered in New Haven, on public affairs. New Haven, 1809. 8°. (B 976, 986)
— DUANE, W. J. Law of nations investigated in a popular manner. Phila., 1809. 8°.
— - *Another copy.* (B 1750)
— DWIGHT, T. Remarks on the documents accompanying the message of Pres. Madison, Nov. 29, 1809. *n.t.p.* [1809.] 8°. (B 1490)
— IMPORTANT state papers; documents accompanying the Pres. message, Nov. 29, 1809. *n.t.p.* [Boston, 1809.] 8°. (B 1490, 1885)
— *Same.* *n.t.p.* [1809?] 12°. (B 474, C 109, 194)
— LOWELL, J. Diplomatick policy of Madison unveiled; strictures on the correspondence of Smith and Jackson. *n.t.p.* [1809.] 8°. (B 409)
— - *Same.* London, 1810. 8°. (B 1420, 1838)
— QUINCY, J. Speech, Jan. 19, on the bill for holding an extra session of Congress. *n.p.*, [1809]. 8°. (B 553)
— SENEX. Letters [signed] Senex, and a farmer, comprehending an examination of the conduct of our executive towards France and Gr. Brit. Balt., 1809. 8°. (B 411, 2521)
— VIEW of the question between Spain and U. S. resp. Louisiana and Florida. (*In* Political, *etc.*, sketches of the Spanish Empire. 1809)
— WOODWARD, A. B. Considerations on the executive gov. of the U. S. Flatbush, 1809. 8°. (B 411)

☞ For correspondence relating to the dismissal of Mr. Jackson (1809) *see* **Jackson, F. J.**

— ARGUMENTS proving the inconsistency and impolicy of granting to foreigners the right of voting; from a pamphlet pub. in 1810. Phila., 1844. 8°. (B 1500)
— GOLDSMITH, L. Exposition of the conduct of France towards America; illust. by cases decided in the council of prizes in Paris. 3d ed. London, 1810. 8°. (B 753)
— HANSON, A. C. Reflections upon the corresp. between Sec. Smith and F. J. Jackson. Balt., 1810. 8°. (B 437, 1490, 2521)
— HARE, R. Brief view of the policy and resources of the U. S., *etc.* Phila., 1810. 8°.
— - *Another copy.* (B 414)
— NEW England patriot, The; a comparison of the Washington and Jefferson administrations. Boston, 1810. 8°. (B 142, 437, 525)
— POTTER, E. R. Address to the freemen of R. I. Newport, [1810]. 8°. (B 436)
— REAL American; true state of the rel. between Gr. Brit. and the U. S. London, 1810. 8°. (B 689)
— SULLY, *pseud.* Remarks on the report of the Legislature on our foreign relations. Boston, 1810. 8°. (B 437)
— WORD to Federalist and to those who love the memory of Washington. *n.p.*, [1810]. 8°. (B 436, 971)
— APPEAL to the people on the causes and consequences of a war with Gr. Brit. Boston, 1811. 8°. (B 532)
— AUSTIN, J. T. Resistance to the laws of the U. S. considered; in four letters to H. G. Otis. Boston, 1811. 8°. (B 440, 1792)
— EMOTT, J. Speech in relation to the non-intercourse. Wash., 1811. f°. (B 439, 553)
— RANDOLPH, J. Sketch of [his] 1st speech on the report of the committee of foreign relations. *n.t.p.* [Georgetown, 1811.] 8°. (B 450, C 83)
— - Sketch of [his] 2d speech on the report of the committee on foreign relations, Dec. 16. *n.t.p.* [Georgetown, 1811.] 12°. (B 450, C 61)
— TAGGART, S. Address to electors of Hampshire North District. Greenfield, 1811. 8°. (B 440)
— GILES, W. B. Political miscellanies; [1812–29. Richmond, 1830?] 8°.
— SECOND crisis of America, The; or, View of the peace between Gr. Brit. and the U. S., [1812–15]; by a citizen of Philadelphia. N. Y., 1815. 8°. (B 444)
— ADDRESS to the citizens of Norfolk County exposing the absurdity of the present war; by a republican of Norfolk. *n.p.*, [1812?]. 8°. (B 441, 1491)
— AMERICAN view of American affairs. Phila., 1812. 8°. (B 452)
— BIBLE and the sword; or, The appointment of the general fast indicated; propriety of opposing British piracy and outrage. Balt., 1812. 8°. (W 9)
— BOREAS, *pseud.* Slave representation. *n.p.*, 1812. 8°. (B 452)
— DISPUTE with Amer. considered in letters from a cosmopolite to a clergyman. London, [1812]. 8°. (B 689)
— DWIGHT, T. History of the Hartford Convention; [and the causes of] the war of 1812. N. Y., 1833. 8°.
— JEFFERSON against Madison's war. *n.p.*, [1812]. 8°. (B 441)
— KETELTAS, W. The crisis; an appeal to a candid world on the war against Gr. Britain. Poughkeepsie, 1812. 8°. (B 441, 452)
— LETTER to a member of Congress, on a British war. Prov., 1812. 8°. (B 450)
— LOWELL, J. Madison's war; a dispassionate inquiry into the reasons for declaring war against Gr. Britain. Boston, 1812. 8°. (B 441, 2537)
— - *Same.* 2d ed. Boston, 1812. 8°. (B 532)
— - Perpetual war the policy of Mr. Madison. Boston, 1812. 8°. (B 441)
— MASS. *Gen. Court.* Speech of Gov. C. Strong, Oct. 16, 1812, with docs.; added, the answer of the Ho. of Reps. Boston, 1812. 8°. (B 1193, 1490)
— OSGOOD, D. Solemn protest against the late declaration of war; discourse. Camb., 1812. 8°. (B 1876)
— - *Same.* 2d ed. Exeter, 1812. 8°. (B 286, 915)
— PITTSBURGH DEMOCRATIC REPUBLICAN COMMITTEE. Address favourable to the election of De Witt Clinton. Pittsburgh, 1812. 8°. (B 986, 1491)
— ROAD to peace, commerce, wealth, and happiness; by an old farmer. *n.t.p.* [1812.] 8°. (B 452)
— REPUBLICAN PARTY, *Penn.* Address of the general committee of corresp. on the presidential election. Phila., 1812. 8°. (B 452)
— REPUBLICAN PARTY, *North Convention, Rockingham Co., Sept.* 10, 1812. [Proceedings; Portsmouth, 1812.] 8°. (B 1491)
— SHEFFEY, D. Speech, bill for raising an additional military force, Jan. 3, 1812. *n.t.p.* [1812.] 8°. (B 450, C 61)
— SLOAN, J. Address to the citizens of the U. S. particularly those of the middle and eastern states. Phila., 1812. 8°. (B 441)
— SULLIVAN, G. Speech at the Rockingham Convention. Exeter, 1812. 8°. (B 441)
— - *and others.* Address of members of the House on the war with Gr. Britain. Alexandria, 1812. 8°. (B 441, 1491, W 13)
— - *Same.* Boston, 1812. 8°. (B 452, 532, 1491)
— - *Same.* Suppl. to the Boston weekly messenger. [Boston, 1812.] 8°. (B 1492)
— TOUCHSTONE to the people of the U. S. on the choice of a president. N. Y., 1812. 8°. (B 442)
— WASHINGTON to the people on the choice of a president. Boston, 1812. 8°. (B 442)

See also, for the proceedings of conventions in 1812, **Buckstown; — Dedham; — Gray, *Me.*; — Ipswich; — Northampton; — Trenton; — Worcester.**

— AIKEN, S. Address to federal clergyman, on the war proclaimed by Congress against Gr. Brit. and Ireland. Boston, 1813. 8°. (B 453)

— ANTICIPATION of marginal notes on the declaration of government of 9 Jan. London, 1813. 8°. (B 239)
— *Same.* (*In* Pamphleteer, 1813; v. 1 of B 838)
— CORRESPONDENCE with the ed. of the 'Times' rel. to the American question. (*In* Pamphleteer, 1813; v. 2 of B 838)
— FACTS and documents rel. to the state of the controversy between America and Gr. Britain. Boston, 1813. 8°. (B 453, 1000)
— MASS. *Gen. Court.* Public documents containing the speech of Gov. Strong, *etc.* Boston, 1813. 8°. (B 1000, 1193)
— MONROE, J. Letter on the rejected treaty between the U. S. and Gr. Brit. Portland, 1813. 8°. (B 1491)
— ROMAINE, B. Tammany Society; 24th anniv. address. N. Y., 1813. 8°. (B 444)
— TAGGART, S. Address on impressments. *n.t.p.* [1813.] 8°. (B 453, 2530)
— THOUGHTS; in a series of letters in answer to a question respecting the division of the States; by a Mass. farmer. *n.p.*, [1813]. 8°. (B 453)
— VAN CORTLANDT, P., *and others.* Address to the Republican citizens of N. Y. Albany, 1813. 8°. (B 453)
— WHITE, W. C. Avowals of a Republican. Worcester, 1813. 8°. (B 453)
— ADDRESS to the clergy of N. E. on their opposition to the rulers of the U. S. Concord, 1814. 8°. (C 194)
— APPEAL to the good sense of the Democrats and the public spirit of the Federalists. Boston, 1814. 8°. (B 454)
— BIGELOW, T. Address on the 3d anniv. of the Washington Benev. Soc., Apr. 30. Boston, 1814. 8°. (W 49)
— CAREY, M. Calm address to the people of the eastern states, on the representation of slaves, *etc.* Boston, 1814. 8°. (C 194)
— - The olive branch; or, Faults on both sides. [1814.] 3d ed. Boston, 1815. 12°.
— - *Same.* 10th ed. Phila., 1818. 8°.
— - An address to W. Tudor, intended to prove the calumny and slander of his remarks on 'The olive branch'. Phila., 1821. 12°.
— ANSWER to certain parts of 'The olive branch'; by a Federalist. [Phila., 1816.] 12°.
— COMPRESSED view of the points to be discussed in treating with the U. S. London, 1814. 8°. (B 791)
— *Same.* (*In* Pamphleteer, 1815; v. 5 of B 838)
— CONCILIATOR, *pseud.* Why are we still at war? the American question considered. (*In* Pamphleteer, 1814; v. 5 of B 838)
— HARPER, R. G. Speech at the celebration of the recent triumphs of the cause of mankind in Germany, Annapolis, Jan. 20. Alexandria, [1814]. 8°. (B 554)
— - *Same.* Boston, 1814. 8°. (B 454)
— LOWELL, J. To the electors of a representative in Cong. in the district of Norfolk. *n.t.p.* [1814.] 8°. (B 469)
— NORTHERN grievances; a letter to J. Madison. N. Y., 1814. 8°. (B 454)
— COBBETT, W. The pride of Brittannia humbled; added, a glimpse of the American victories. New ed. Phila., 1815. 12°.
— SHEFFEY, D. Address [on the state of public affairs]. Wash., 1815. 8°. (B 1491, 2531)
— TURREAU DE GARAMBOUVILLE, L. M. Aperçu sur la situation polit. des Etats-Unis d'Amérique. Paris, 1815. 8°. (C 91)
— EVENS, J. New mode of government by laws in the form of bills, *etc.* 4th ed. revised from the orig. Essays of 1816, 31, and 43. Warren Co., 1847. 8°. (B 1500)
— - New mode of petitioning, instructing our representatives, *etc.*; revised from the original essays of 1816, 31. Warren Co., O., 1843. 8°. (B 1500)
— BRIGGS, I. Statements addressed to T. Newton on agriculture, manufactures, and commerce. Wash., 1816. 8°. (B 455)
— MEMORIAL of the inhabitants on the Niagara frontier, to the Senate and Ho. of Rep. Wash., 1817. 8°. (B 445, 1602)
— SWAN, J. Address to the Senate and House on an inquiry into the state of agriculture, *etc.* Boston, 1817. 8°. (B 445)
— VERUS, *pseud.* Observations on the existing differences between Spain and the U. S. No. 3. Phila., 1817. 8°. (B 445)
— TYLER, B. O. Declaration of independence; answer to J. Binn. Wash., 1818. 8°. (C 119)
— DEBATES in the Ho. of Reps. of the U. S. on the Seminole war, 1819. Wash., 1819. 12°.

— TAMMANY SOC. Address to its absent members and members of its branches throughout the U. S. N. Y., 1819. 8°. (B 568)
— CAVEAT, A; or, Considerations against the admission of Missouri with slavery. New Haven, 1820. 8°. (B 984)
— NATIONAL dangers and means of escape. [Boston, [1821?] 8°. (B 991, 1492, W 6)
— CAREY, M. Address to the citizens of the U. S. on the tendency of our system of intercourse with foreign nations. Phila., 1822. 8°. (B 977)
— DEFENCE of the exposition of the middling interest, *etc.* Boston, 1822. 8°. (B 978)
— PUBLIC defaulters brought to light; letters to the people of the U. S., by a native of Virginia. N. Y., 1822. 8°. (B 531, 2005)
— REMARKS on the censures of the government in Europe; by a citizen of the U. S. [A. H. Hill]. Boston, 1822. 8°. (B 1492)
— RHEA, J. To his constituents, May 8. [Wash., 1822.] 8°. (B 1492)
— INGERSOLL, C. J. Discourse; influence of Amer. on the mind. Phila., 1823. 8°. (B 567, 1828)
— PHILO-JACKSON, *pseud.* The presidential election. Frankfort, 1823. 8°. (B 532)
— - *Same.* 2d ser. Louisville, 1823. 8°. (B 1105)
— - *Same.* 6th ser. Frankfort, 1824. 8°. (B 1105)
— POLITICAL thoughts. No. 1: Idea of a patriot president. Wash., 1823. 8°. (B 1492)
— BENTON, J. Address on the presidential election. Nashville, 1824. 8°. (C 194)
— DISCLOSURE no. 1: Documents rel. to violations of the law during the late war with Gr. Brit. Bath, 1824. 8°. (B 300, 932, 1106)
— TALLMADGE, J. Speech, giving the choice of presidential electors to the people, Aug. 5. Albany, [1824]. 8°. (B 1805)
— PRADT, D. D. de. Vrai système de l'Europe rel. à l'Amérique et à la Grèce. (*In* Pamphleteer, 1825, 26, v. 25, 26 of B 838)
— NEWMAN, *Sir* J. The Tennessee administration advocate. *n.p.*, [1825]. 8°. (B 976)
— EVERETT, E. Claims of citizens of the U. S. on Naples, Holland, and France. Camb., 1826. 8°.
— - *Another copy.* (B 1148)
— ADDRESS of the administration convention at Raleigh, Dec. 20, 1827, to the freemen of N. Carolina. *n.p.*, [1828]. 8°. (B 971)
— GREENSBURGH, *Pa.* MEETING OF THE FRIENDS OF THE GENERAL ADMINISTRATION. Proceedings, Nov. 20. *n.p.*, 1827. 8°. (B 1494)
— LEA, P. Circular to voters in the 2d district of Tenn. *n.p.*, 1827. 8°. (B 1106)
— SNYDER, S. Letters upon the subject of the presidential election. Phila., 1827. 8°. (B 1106)
— ADAMS, J. Q. Correspondence between A. and citizens of Mass. conc. the charge of a design to dissolve the Union, [1828]. Boston, 1829. 8°. (B 978, 1648, 1702, 1761, 1796)
— - *Same.* 2d ed. Boston, 1829. 8°. (B 1770)
— FRANKLIN, *pseud.* [Address to the citizens of Penn.] *n.p.*, [1828]. 8°. (B 1106)
— HALE, M., *and others.* Address to the electors of the 9th ward. N. Y., 1828. 8°. (B 1106)
— HAMILTON, *pseud.* Review of a pamphlet under the signature of Brutus; from the Charleston courier. Charleston, 1828. 8°.
— - *Other copies.* (B 971, 1066)
— PRINCIPLES and acts of Adams's administration vindicated against the address of the Jackson convention at Concord. Concord, 1828. 8°. (B 1494)
— RANDOLPH, J. Speech, retrenchment resolutions, Feb. 1. Boston, 1828. 8°. (B 1494)
— - *Same.* Speech, retrenchment and reform. 2d ed. Wash., 1828. 8°. (B 1494)
— - *Same.* Extract. (*In* Moore, F. Amer. eloquence, v. 2. 1864.)
— REPUBLICAN PARTY, *N. Y. State Convention.* Proceedings and address of the young men of N. Y., Aug. N. Y., 1828. 8°. (B 1106)
— TRENTON, *N. J.* CONVENTION, 1828. Proceedings and address of N. J. Convention in favor of the present administration. Trenton, 1828. 8°. (B 1494)
— UNITED STATES, The, as they are. London, 1828. 8°.
— WEBSTER, E. Defence of the national administration; address to the people of N. H.; by Cato. Concord, 1828. 8°. (B 1494)
— WETHERILL, S., *and others.* Address to the people of Penn. *n.p.*, [1828]. 8°. (B 1106)

— APOLOGY for the United States of America. Liverpool, [*reprinted at* Boston,] 1829. 8°. (B 1494)
— DIX, J. A. Speeches and addresses, [1830-63]. N. Y., 1864. 2 v. 8°.
— HOLMES, J. Speech on his resolutions calling upon the President for the reasons of removing from office and filling the vacancies in the recess of the Senate. Wash., 1830. 8°. (B 1494)
— REIGN of reform. *n.t.p.* [Preface dated Wheeling, 1830.] 18°. (C 194)
— RICHARDSON, J. S. To the people; address, with [a] speech in opposition to disunion, convention, and nullification. Charleston, 1830. 8°. (B 1066)
— U. S. ANTI-MASONIC CONVENTION. Proceedings. Phila., 1830. 8°.
— BALTIMORE NATIONAL REPUBLICAN CONVENTION. Journal. Wash., 1831. 8°. (B 1064, 1494, 1814)
— BEAUMONT, A. J. An American's defence of his government. [London,] 1831. 8°. (B 933)
— EATON, J. H. Candid appeal in reply to Messrs. Ingham, Branch, and Berrien on the dissolution of the late cabinet. Wash., 1831. 8°. (B 1099)
— CAREY, M. Dissolution of the union; by a citizen of Phila. Phila., 1832. 8°. (B 1790)
— - *Same*. 2d pt. 3d ed. Phila., 1832. 8°. (B 1068)
— - The olive branch. No. 3. Phila., 1832. 8°. (B 1115)
— CONDUCT of the administration. Boston, 1832. 8°. (B 1060, 1790)
— OLIVER, B. L. Rights of an American citizen. Boston, 1832. 8°.
— OUSELEY, W. G. Remarks on the statistics and political institutions of the U. S.; added, statistical tables. London, 1832. 8°.
— WEBSTER, D. Speech at the national republican convention, Worcester, Oct. 12. Boston, 1832. 8°. (B 1646, 1882)
— WORCESTER NATIONAL REPUBLICAN CONVENTION, Oct. 11. Journal. Boston, 1832. 8°. (B 1064)
— DAVIS, C. A. Letters of J. Downing, [1833-34]. N. Y., 1834. 12°.
— FRANCE. *Chambre des Députés*. Proceedings on the treaty with the U. S., 1833-34. Wash., 1834. 8°.
— CAREY, M. The olive branch once more. No. 1-4. *n.t.p.* [1833.] 8°. (B 1115)
— GRIMKÉ, T. S. Oration, principal duties of Americans, before the Wash. Soc., July 4. Charleston, 1833. 8°. (B 1203, 2545, E 221)
— REMARKS on the ordinance of nullification, the President's proclamation and last message; by a South Carolinian. Charleston, 1833. 8°. (B 1067, 1665)
— WAKEFIELD, E. G. England and America. London, 1833. 2 v. 8°.
— BINNEY, H. Speech, contested election of Letcher and Moore. Wash., 1834. 8°. (B 1085)
— CUSHING, C. Reply to the letter of J. F. Cooper. Boston, 1834. 8°. (B 1025, 1085)
— REMARKS on article IX, [by A. H. Everett], in no. 84 of the N. Amer. review, entitled 'Origin and character of the old parties'. Boston, 1834. 8°. (B 1495)
— COBDEN, R. England, Ireland, and America. London, 1835. 8°. (B 1109)
— - *Same*. (*In his* Political writings, v. 1. 1867.)
— EVERETT, E. Remarks on the French question, Feb. 7 and Mar. 2. Boston, 1835. 8°. (B 1495, 1813)
— EVANS, G. Speech in rel. to the failure of the bill making appropriations for fortifications, Jan. 28. Wash., 1836. 8°. (B 1496, 1721, 1813)
— GUARDIAN genius of the federal union. *n.t.p.* [1836.] 12°. (C 195)
— HALL, H. Speech on the fortification bill, May 24. Wash., 1836. 8°. (B 1496)
— MASSACHUSETTS. Constitution or form of government; with [13 articles of amendment, the last ratified 1836]. *n.t.p.* [1841.] 8°. (C 195)
— PLAIN facts for plain people. Balt., 1836. 8°. (B 1663)
— CARTER, —. Speech, Feb. 2, 1837. Boston, 1837. 8°. (C 195)
— ROGERS, G. Address on our destiny. N. Y., [1837]. 8°. (C 195)
— VAIL, E. A. Réponse à quelques imputations contre les Etats-Unis. Paris, 1837. 8°. (B 1134)
— WHIG STATE CENTRAL COMMITTEE, *Mass.* To the electors of Mass. *n.p.*, [1837]. 8°. (B 1496)
— APPEAL to the citizens of Boston before voting. *n.p.*, *n.d.* [1838.] 12°. (C 195)
— WAR with England; the case fairly stated; with an address to Pres. Van Buren. N. Y., 1838. 8°. (B 1496)
— BROTHERS, T. The United States as they are, [1839]. London, 1840. 8°.
— LOUISIANA NATIVE AMER. ASSOCIATION. Address. N. Orleans, 1839. 8°. (B 1497)
— THOMAS, S. J. Address before the Democratic citizens of Plymouth Co., Mass., at East Abington, July 4. Boston, 1839. 8°. (B 1143)
— BANCROFT, G. Address before the Democratic Convention of the Young Men of Connecticut, Feb. 18. Boston, 1840. 8°. (B 1498)
— BUCHANAN, J. Answer to the misrepresentations of Mr. Davis's speech, in Senate, March 6. Worcester, [1840]. 8°. (B 1544)
— COLTON, C. American Jacobinism. [N. Y., 1840.] 8°. (B 1500)
— CONCIVIS, *pseud.* Letters to the people of the U. S. N. Y., 1840. 8°. (B 1167)
— CUSHING, C. Outlines of the life and public services of W. H. Harrison. Boston, 1840. 12°. (C 195)
— ELLIS, P. Address before the Missouri Native American Assoc. Dec. 11, 1840. St. Louis, 1841. 8°. (C 265)
— FACTS for the laboring man. Newport, 1840. 8°. (B 1187)
— FAUQUIER COUNTY WHIG CENTRAL COMMITTEE. 1st, 2d address on the army bill. Wash., 1840. 8°. (B 1498)
— FINE, J. Letter to his constituents, Aug. 1840. *n.t.p.* [1840.] 8°. (C 265)
— GAINES, E. P. Memorial to Congress [on a system of national defence]. Memphis, 1840. 8°. (B 1820)
— HARTFORD CONVENTION. Identity of the Hartford Convention Federalists with the modern Whig Harrison party. Boston, 1840. 8°. (B 1167)
— HILDRETH, R. The contrast; or, W. H. Harrison *vs.* M. Van Buren. Boston, 1840. 12°. (C 195)
— HOPKINS, G. W. Letter to J. H. Piper. Wash., 1840. 8°. (B 1663)
— JOSSELYN, L. Appeal to the people; proof of an alliance between American Whigs and British Tories. Boston, 1840. 8°. (B 1498)
— LETTERS on the presidency; by a Kentucky Democrat. *n.t.p.* [1840.] 8°. (B 1494, 1498)
— LOG cabin and hard cider melodies; dedicated to the friends of Harrison and Tyler. Boston, 1840. 12°. (D 21)
— MCVICKAR, J. American finances. [Pages from the N. Y. review, July, 1840.] 8°. (B 1543)
— PARMENTER, W. Speech, civil and diplomatic appropriation bill, Apr. 20. Wash., 1840. 8°. (B 1497)
— PAYNE, J. A., *and others*. Address to the working-men of the U. S. [Wash., 1840.] 8°. (B 1663)
— PROCEEDINGS of the opponents of the present administration, at public meetings, Feb. 15, 18, 1840. *n.t.p.* [Wash., 1840.] 8°. (B 1497)
— RITTENHOUSE, D. Der Spiegel oder einige Nägel zur Ausbesserung unserer Constitution. *n.p.*, 1840. 12°. (C 265)
— STEARNS, I. To the public, especially to the friends of liberty in N. England. *n.p.*, 1840. 8°. (B 1498)
— TAYLOR, J. D. Log-cabin song book. Cincin., 1840. 24°. (D 21)
— WARNING to the Democracy. *n.p.*, [1840 ?]. 8°. (B 1498)
— CLARK, J. C. To the electors of Chenango County, N. Y. *n.p.*, 1841. 8°. (B 1498)
— HAWES, R. To his constituents of Clarke, Fayette, Woodford, and Franklin Counties. Wash., 1841. 8°. (B 1498)
— HAZARD, R. G. Lecture on the causes of the decline of political and national morality. Prov., 1841. 8°. (B 1775)
— To the electors of the city of New York. *n.t.p.* [1841.] 8°. (C 195)
— WAYNE, A. To the Democratic party of Virginia, on the next presidential election. Phila., 1841. 8°. (B 1498)
— ADAMS, J. Q. Address to his constituents, Braintree, Sept. 17. Boston, 1842. 8°. (B 1428)
— ALLEN, W. Letter to the Young Men's Democratic Convention. Wash., 1842. 8°. (B 1663)
— BERRIEN, J. M. Address to the people of the U. S.; reported by the Committee of Fifteen. [Wash., 1842.] 8°. (B 1499)
— BLUNT, J. Report to the national convention of the Home League, N. Y., Oct. 13. *n.p.*, 1842. 8°. (B 1513)
— DUPONCEAU, P. S., *and* DAVEZAC, A. Case and opinion on the contested seat of D. Levi. Alexandria, 1842. 8°. (B 1499)
— JUDD, *Rev.* S. Discourse; moral review of the Rev. war. Hallowell, 1842. 8°. (B 1184, 1295)
— OUR relations with England, *etc.* From June no. of the Southern literary messenger. *n.t.p.* [1842.] 8°. (B 1475)

— SANTANGELO, O. de A. The honor of the U. S. under the administration of Tyler, Webster, & Co. N. Y., 1842. 8°. (B 1499)
— ANSWER to the speech of the great agitator [D. O'Connell] before the Repeal Assoc., *etc.*; by an Amer. citizen. N. Y., 1843. 8°. (C 195)
— AYDELOTT, B. P. Our country's evils and their remedy. Cincin., 1843. 12°. (C 195)
— COLTON, C. The test; or, Parties tried by their acts; [Junius tract]. N. Y., 1843. 8°. (B 1500)
— COMPLAINT of Mexico, and conspiracy against liberty; with an app. by D. Webster. Boston, 1843. 8°. (B 1510)
— COMPROMISES of the Constitution considered in the organization of a national convention. *n.p.*, [1843?]. 8°. (B 1497)
— KENDALL'S expositor. Vol. 3, no. 18: Address to the Democracy. Wash., 1843. 8°. (B 1664)
— QUINTUS, *pseud.* Conservatives and reformers; a pamphlet for the times. Boston, 1843. 8°. (B 1499)
— STANLY, E. To the people of Tyrrell, Washington, Hyde, [and other] counties, N. Carolina. [Wash., 1843.] 8°. (B 1499)
— WHITE, A. S. Speech, reply to Mr. Holmes, on the principles which divide the two parties, Feb. 8, 1843. [Wash., 1843.] 8°. (B 1499)
— APPEAL to the Democratic party on the principles of a national convention for the nomination of president and vice-president. *n.p.*, [1844?]. 8°. (B 1500)
— BACON, D. F. Progressive democracy; discourse on Amer. politics. N. Y., 1844. 8°. (B 1500)
— BARNARD, D. D. Review of the report of the committee of ways and means. Wash., 1844. 8°. (B 1498)
— BUCKINGHAM, J. T. Golden sentiments; address to the native Americans of N. Y., with the declaration of sentiments of native Americans of Boston. Boston, 1844. 12°. (C 195)
— CRISIS, The; appeal to our countrymen on foreign influence in the U. S. N. Y., 1844. 8°. (B 1500)
— GROUARD, G. M. A practical printer's answer to Mr. Kendall's tract No. 5 on public printing. [Wash.,] 1844. 8°. (B 1500)
— KENNEDY, J. P. Defence of the Whigs; by a member of the 27th Congress. N. Y., 1844. 12°.
— WHIG CONGRESSIONAL EXECUTIVE COMMITTEE. Prospect before us; or, Locofoco impositions exposed. *n.t.p.* [Wash., 1844.] 8°. (B 1500)
— WHIG text book; or, Democracy unmasked. Wash., 1844. 8°. (B 1500)
— CHILDE, E. V. Letters, 1845-56. (*In his* Letters. 1857.)
— SUMNER, C. Orations and speeches, [1845-50]. Boston, 1850. 2 v. 8°.
— CLINGMAN, T. L. Speech, late presidential election. Wash., 1845. 8°. (B 1174)
— CUMMING, H. Secret hist. of the perfidies, intrigues, *etc.*, of the Tyler dynasty. Wash., N. Y., 1845. 8°. (B 1501)
— EXPOSITION of the weakness and insufficiency of the government of the U. S. *n.p.*, 1845. 12°.
Note. This is supposed to be by C. F. Mercer.
— FEW hasty reasons, A, why the mission of the U. S. at the court of Vienna should be restored. Wash., [1845]. 8°. (B 1501)
— SOUTH WESTERN CONVENTION, *Memphis, Nov.* 12. Proceedings. Memphis, 1845. 8°.
— LOWELL, J. R. The Biglow papers, [1846-47]. Camb., 1848. 12°.
— BROOKS, E. The 29th Congress, its men and its measures. Wash., 1846. 8°. (B 1502)
— COXE, R. S. Review of the relations between the U. S. and Mexico. N. Y., 1846. 8°.
— PALFREY, J. G. Papers on the slave power first published in the 'Boston Whig'. Boston, [1846]. 8°. (B 1502, 1504, 1653)
— — Correspondence between N. Appleton and J. G. Palfrey, supplement to 'Papers on the slave power'. Boston, 1846. 8°. (B 1502, 1698, 1736)
— SITUATION des partis aux Etats-Unis. (*In* Revue d. Mondes, déc. 1846.)
— FIELD, D. D. Speech, Chicago Convention. N. Y., 1847. 8°. (B 1502)
— VOICE from the South; letters from Georgia to Massachusetts, *etc.* Balt., 1847. 8°. (B 1477)
— BOTTS, J. M. To the whole Whig party of the U. S. Wash., 1848. 8°. (B 1502)
— CABELL, E. C. Letter on election of speaker, Jan. 13. Wash., 1848. 8°. (B 1503)
— CHARLES F. Adams' platform; or Looking-glass for the worthies of the Buffalo Convention. Wash., [1848]. 8°. (B 1503)
— GARDINER, O. C. The great issue; or, The three presidential candidates. N. Y., 1848. 8°. (B 1503)
— HALL, W. Letter to the Whigs. Boston, 1848. 8°. (B 1502)
— LINCOLN, A. Speech, reference of the president's message, Jan. 14. Wash., 1848. 8°. (B 1502)
— MARVIN, D. Letter rel. to supporting the nominees of the Buffalo Convention. Wash., 1848. 8°. (B 1503)
— NORTHERN no, A; address to the delegates from the free states to the Whig National Convention at Philadelphia. *n.p.*, 1848. 8°. (B 1503)
— POLITICAL action of our church members and clergy a chief cause of our present religious declension. N. Y., 1848. 8°. (B 1503)
— REPUBLICANUS, *pseud.* Restoration of the Constitution. N. Y., 1848. 8°. (C 196)
— STEWART, A. Speech, presidential question, June 26. Wash., 1848. 8°. (B 1502)
— CHEVALIER, M. La liberté aux Etats-Unis. (*In* Revue d. D. Mondes, juil. 1849.)
— HUNT, M. Letter to Senator Sam Houston. [Austin, 1849.] 8°. (B 1503)
— MATHIESON, A. Appeal to the Democracy of Wisconsin. *n.t.p.* [Milwaukee, 1849.] 8°. (C 265)
— MONTGOMERY, C. The King of Rivers; with a chart of our slave and free soil territory, [1849.] N. Y., 1850. 8°. (B 1477)
— MUSSEY, O. Review of E. Fisher's lecture on the North and South. Cincin., 1849. 8°. (B 1503)
— PROTOCOL question, originally published in the National intelligencer, Aug. 18. *n.t.p.* [1849.] 8°. (B 1503)
— SCHENCK, R. C. Speech, reply to Giddings, Dec. 27, 1849. Wash., 1850. 8°. (B 1504)
— UNITED STATES government, The, has injured the liberty of the people of Cuba; the people of Cuba demand justice of the people of America. *n.p.*, [1849?]. 12°. (C 266)
— DOCUMENT for the people; Fugitive slave law of 1850; Democratic platform, 1852, *etc.* Wash., 1853. 8°. (B 1485)
— APPEAL to the whole country for an union of parties; by a republican of the school of 1800. U. S., 1850. 8°. (B 1504)
— BOTTS, J. M. Speech at Powhatan Court-house, Va., June 15. [Richmond? 1850.] 8°. (B 1504)
— BROWN, A. G. Letter to his constituents. Wash., 1850. 8°. (B 1504)
— CLAY, H. Speech on the diplomatic rel. with Austria, Jan. 7. Wash., 1850. 8°. (B 1504)
— CLINGMAN, T. L. Letter in reply to a speech by Mr. Stanly. Wash., 1850. 8°. (B 1504)
— CUCHEVAL-CLARIGNY, P. A. Les partis de l'Union en 1850, la crise entre les Etats du Sud et les Etats du Nord. (*In* Revue d. D. Mondes, jan. 1850.)
— DERBY, E. H. Reality *vs.* fiction; a review of 'The Union, past and future'. Boston, 1850. 8°. (B 1504)
— FACTION and treachery exposed; [course of the Connecticut representatives in the ballot for speaker]. *n.p.*, [1850]. 8°. (B 1504)
— CINCINNATI NATIONAL REFORM ASSOCIATION. Friend of man; the principles of national or land reform. Cincin., 1850. 8°. (B 1504)
— GRAYSON, W. J. Letter on the dissolution of the Union. Charleston, S. C., *reprinted* Savannah, Ga., 1850. 8°.
— NEW HAVEN UNION MEETING, BREWSTER HALL. Proceedings, Oct. 24, 1850. New Haven, 1851. 8°. (B 1505)
— PALFREY, J. G. Letter to a friend. Camb., 1850. 8°. (B 1504)
— PARKER, T. The state of the nation considered; sermon, thanksgiving day, Nov. 28, 1850. Boston, 1851. 8°. (B 1968)
— PROCEEDINGS of the constitutional meeting at Faneuil Hall, Nov. 26. Boston, 1850. 8°. (B 1504)
— RUSH, R. Speech at the meeting of friends of the Constitution in Phila., Nov. 21, 1850. Phila., 1850. 8°. (B 1504)
— SMOLNIKAR, A. B. Important disclosures; also, an invitation to a convention of the republican Protestants against Papists. [Eng. and Germ.] Pittsburgh, 1850. 8°. (B 1504)
— STANLY, E. Speech exposing the causes of the slavery agitation, Mar. 6. Wash., 1850. 8°. (B 1504)
— UNION past and future, The; how it works and how to save it; by a citizen of Virginia. Wash., 1850. 8°. (B 1504)
— WELLBORN, M. J. To the voters of the 2d Congress. district of Georgia. [Wash.? 1850.] 8°. (B 1507)

— Parker, T. Additional speeches, addresses, and occasional sermons, [1851-54]. Boston, 1855. 2 v. 12°.
— Aspinwall, W., *and others*. Address to the people of Mass. [on the coalition. Boston, 1851.] 8°. (B 1507)
— Ewing, T. Speech, Bradbury's resolutions on removals from office, Jan. 7. Wash., 1851. 8°. (B 1505)
— Grayson, W. J. Letters of Curtius; pub. originally in the Charleston courier. Charleston, 1851. 8°. (B 1505)
— King, J. A. Letter to his constituents. Jamaica, L. I., 1851. 8°. (B 1505)
— Parker, T. The chief sins of the people; sermon at the Melodeon, Boston, Apr. 10. Boston, 1851. 8°. (B 1968)
— Past, The, the present, and the future. [From the National intelligencer.] *n.p.*, 1851. 8°. (B 1505)
— Rush, R. The 22d of Feb. From the Pennsylvania inquirer, Feb. 22. Phila., 1851. 8°. (B 1505)
— Soulé, P. Speech, Opelousas, Louisiana, Sept. 6. New Orleans, 1851. 8°. (B 1505)
— Curtis, G. T. Speech on the presidential election, Faneuil Hall. Oct. 6. Boston, 1852. 8°. (B 1506)
— Giddings, J. R. Baltimore platforms: slavery question; speech, June 23. Wash., 1852. 8°. (B 1479)
— Platforms of 1852. The; also J. R. Hale's letter of acceptance. *n.p.*, [1852]. 8°. (B 1506)
— Stanly, E. Remarks in reply to Mr. Giddings, Feb. 11. Wash., 1852. 8°. (B 1506)
— Stephens, A. H. Homestead bill, state of parties, and the presidency; speech on the state of the country, Apr. 27. Wash., 1852. 8°. (B 1506)
— Townshend, N. S. Speech, on the present position of the Democratic Party, June 23. Wash., 1852. 8°. (B 1506)
— Godwin, P. Political essays, [1853-55]; from contributions to Putnam's magazine. N.Y., 1856. 12°.
— Ampère, J. J. Les partis politiques à Washington. (*In* Revue d. D. Mondes, juin 1853.)
— Chapman, C. Speech, on the prosecution of claims against the government by members of Congress, Jan. 11. Wash., 1853. 8°. (B 1506)
— Raymond, X. Diplomatie anglo-amér., les Amér. et les Anglais au Mexique et dans l'Amér.-Centrale. (*In* Revue d. D. Mondes, av. 1853.)
— Smith, G. Speech on the reference of the president's message, Dec. 20. Wash., 1853. 8°. (B 1506)
— Warner, H. W. The liberties of America. N. Y., 1853. 12°.
— Cass, L. Speech, Clayton-Bulwer treaty, Jan. 11. Wash., 1854. 8°. (B 1506)
— Clayton, J. M. Speech in reply to Mr. Cass on the treaty of Washington, Jan. 12-16. Wash., 1854. 8°. (B 1504, 1506)
— Giddings, J. R. Speech on the message of the President on our rel. with Spain, Mar. 16. [Wash., 1854.] 8°. (B 1506)
— Meacham, J. Defence of the clergy; speech, May 17. Wash., 1854. 8°. (B 1506)
— Right of petition; New England clergyman; remarks of Everett, Mason, *etc.*, on the memorial from 3,050 clergymen, against the Nebraska bill, Mar. 14. Wash., 1854. 8°. (B 1506)
— Smith, G. Letter to his constituents. Wash., 1854. 8°. (B 1479)
— To those born on the soil who know nothing but their country's good; written by nobody knows who, and dedicated to all who like it. N. Y., 1854. 8°. (B 1506)
— Davis, H. W. Speeches and addresses, 1855-65; preceded by an oration by J. A. J. Cresswell. N. Y., 1867. 8°.
— Blanchard, J. P. Principles of the Revolution. Boston, 1855. 8°. (B 1507)
— Capen, N. Letter to N. Hall, conc. politics and the pulpit. Boston, Camb., 1855. 8°. (B 1506)
— Houston, S. Speeches on the increase of the army and the Indian policy, Jan. 29, 31. Wash., 1855. 8°. (B 1507)
— Banks, N. P. Address from the steps of the Merchants exchange, N.Y., Sept. 25. N. Y., 1856. 8°. (B 1508)
— - American republican politics; remarks, Jan. 13. Wash., 1856. 8°. (B 1507)
— Broom, J. Defense of Americanism; speech, Aug. 4. Wash., 1856. 8°. (B 1508)
— Brown, A. V. Address before the Democratic Assoc. of Nashville, June 24. Nashville, 1856. 8°. (B 1508)
— Burlingame, A. Defence of Massachusetts; speech, June 2. Wash., 1856. 8°. (B 1507)
— Campbell, L. D. Americanism; speech at the American mass meeting, Feb. 29. Wash., 1856. 8°. (B 1508)
— Carroll, A. E. Union of the states. Boston, 1856. 12°. (C 196)
— Cincinnati National Democratic Convention. Proceedings, June 26. Cincin., 1856. 8°. (B 1508)
— Cucheval-Clarigny, P. A. L'abolitionisme et l'élection de M. Buchanan à la présidence des Etats-Unis. (*In* Revue d. D. Mondes, déc. 1856.)
— Day, T. C. Democratic party as it was and as it is; speech, Apr. 23. Wash., 1856. 8°. (B 1508)
— Duty of conservative Whigs in the present crisis; letter to R. Choate. Boston, 1856. 8°. (B 1507)
— Fearful issue to be decided in Nov. next! Shall the Union stand or fall? *n.p.*, [1856]. 8°. (B 1507)
— Fessenden, W. P. Speech on the President's message, Dec. 4. Wash., 1856. 8°. (B 1507)
— Fish, H., *and* Hamilton, J. A. Fremont the conservative candidate; correspondence. *n.p.*, 1856. 8°. (B 1508)
— Freedley, E. T. The issue and its consequences; an address. Phila., 1856. 8°. (B 1480)
— Pearce, J. A. Letter on the politics of the day, July 31. [Wash., 1856.] 8°. (B 1508)
— Pearson, H. B. Freedom *vs.* Slavery; letters to R. Choate. Portland, 1856. 8°. (B 1480)
— Quincy, J. Whig policy analyzed and illustrated. Boston, 1856. 8°. (B 1508)
— Republican scrap book. Boston, 1856. 8°. (B 1507)
— Wilson, H. Defence of the Republican party; speech on the President's message, Dec. 19, 1856. Wash., 1856. 8°. (B 1507)
— Words of counsel to men of business; by a man of business. *n.p.*, [1856]. 8°. (B 1507)
— Carey, H. C. Letters to the President, on the foreign and domestic policy of the Union, [1857-68]. Phila., 1858. 8°.
— Banks, N. P. The great questions of national and state politics; speech, Worcester, Sept. 8. Boston, 1857. 8°. (C 265)
— Clark, B. C. Speech, petition of L. Baker and others, Apr. 2. [Wash.,] 1857. 8°. (B 135, 1508)
— Etheridge, E. Speech. revival of the slave trade, and the President's message, Feb. 21. Wash., 1857. 8°. (B 1508)
— Grattan, P. R. Speech, General Assembly at Cleveland, June 2. Richmond, 1857. 8°. (B 1508)
— Higginson, T. W. The new revolution; speech before the American Anti-slavery Soc., May 12. Boston, 1857. 8°. (B 1480)
— Hopkins, J. H. American citizen. N. Y., 1857. 12°.
— Hutcheson, —. Speech on the Swiss resolutions, Mar. 16. Columbus, 1857. 8°. (B 1508)
— Manifest destiny of the American union. N. Y., 1857. 8°. (C 196)
— Worcester State Disunion Conventions. Proceedings, Jan. 15. Boston, 1857. 8°. (B 1480)
— Burlingame, A. Appeal to the patriots against fraud and disunion; speech, March 31. Wash., 1858. 8°. (B 1508)
— Lincoln, A., *and* Douglas, S. A. Political debates in 1858 in Illinois. Columbus, 1860. 8°.
— Richardson, J. W. Speech upon the Bell resolutions, Feb. 8. Wash., 1858. 8°. (B 1508)
— Davis, T. Address to the electors of the eastern congressional district of R. Island. *n.p.*, 1859. 8°. (B 1508)
— Haskin, J. B. Remarks in reply to attack by 'The Constitution' upon Anti-Lecompton Democrats, Dec. Wash., 1859. 8°. (B 1508)
— Hickman, J. Who have violated compromises? speech, Dec. 12. Wash., 1859. 8°. (B 1508)
— Thayer, E. Fair play; speech, Feb. 24. Wash., 1859. 8°. (B 1508)
— Washburn, I. The Republican Party; speech, Jan. 10. Wash., 1859. 8°. (B 1508)
— Witt, C. de. Le partie démocratique aux affaires. (*In* Revue d. D. Mondes, juil. 1859.)

Civil war.

Note. In the following works * added to the title means that the writer is in favor of the South.

— Smith, G. Sermons and speeches, 1858-61. N.Y., 1861. 8°.
— Train, G. F. Union speeches delivered in England, [1859-62]. Phila., 1862. 8°.
— Goddard, S. A. Letters on the Rebellion, 1860-65. London, 1870. 8°.

— Moore, F. Personal and political ballads, [1860-62]. N. Y., 1864. 16°.
— Cucheval-Clarigny, P. A. La nouv. élection présidentielle et les partis aux Etats-Unis en 1860. (*In* Revue d. D. Mondes, déc. 1860.)
— Halstead, M. History of the national political conventions of the present presidential campaign. Columbus, 1860. 8°.
— Hour and the man; [in favor of S. A. Douglas as president. Boston, 1860.] f°. (B 1508)
— Macon, N. Letters [Aug. - Oct. 1860] to C. O'Conor; the destruction of the Union is emancipation. Phila., 1862. 8°. * (B 1724)
— Spooner, L. Address of the Free Constitutionalists to the people of the U. S. Boston, 1860. 8°. (B 1481).
— Townsend, J. The South alone should govern the South, *etc.* Charleston, 1860. 8°. * (B 1481)
— - *Same.* 3d ed. Charleston, 1860. 8°.
— Wilson, H. Aggressions of the slave power; speech, Jan. 26. Wash., 1860. 8°. (B 1481)
— Lowell, J. R. The Biglow papers. 2d ser., [1861-66]. Boston, 1867. 12°.
— Balme, *Rev.* J. R. Synopsis of the American war [1861-65]. London, 1865. 12°. *
— Bright, J. Speeches on the Amer. question, [1861-65]; with introd. by F. Moore. Boston, 1865. 8°.
— Drake, C. D. Union and anti-slavery speeches, [1861-64]. Cincin., 1864. 8°.
— Assollant, J. B. A. Canonniers à vos piéces! Paris, 1861. 8°.
— Bellot des Minières, E. La question amèricaine. Paris, 1861. 4°. *
— Bernard, M. Two lectures on the present American war. Oxford, London, [1861]. 8°.
— Breckinridge, R. J. Four articles on the state of the country and the civil war. Cincin., 1861. 8°.
— Burnett, P. H. American theory of government with ref. to the present crisis. N. Y., 1861. 8°.
— C., F. La guerre civile en Amérique et l'esclavage. Paris, 1861. 8°. *
— Chimes of freedom and union; by various authors. Boston, 1861. 16°. (D 35)
— Conway, M. F. Shall the war be for union and freedom or union and slavery; speech, Dec. 12. Wash., 1861. 8°. (B 1481)
— Des Essarts, A. S. L. La guerre des frères. Paris, 1861. 8°.
— Gasparin, A. E. de. Les Etats Unis en 1861; un grand peuple qui se relève. Paris, 1861. 8°.
— - *Eng.* The uprising of a great people; the U. S. in 1861; from the Fr. by M. L. Booth. N. Y., 1861. 12°.
— - *Same.* Abridged from the French; with app. London, 1861. 16°.
— Gr. Brit. *Parl.* Correspondence with the U. S. government resp. blockade. London, [1861]. f°.
— Hautefeuille, L. B. Quelques questions du droit international maritime, à propos de la guerre d'Amérique. Paris, 1861. 8°. *
— Jay, J. The American rebellion; address, at Mt. Kisco, N. Y., July 4. London, 1861. 8°.
— - *Same.* N. Y., 1861. 12°. (B 1573)
— Lemprière, C. The American crisis considered. London, 1861. 8°. *
— Letters of the Southern spy in Washington and elsewhere. *n.p.*, 1861. 12°. *
— MacMahon, T. W. Cause and contrast; essay on the American crisis, [1861]. Richmond, 1862. 8°. *
— Motley, J. L. Causes of the American civil war; letter to the London Times. N. Y., 1861. 12°.
— Pecquet, P. La révolution américaine dévoilée. Paris, 1861. 8°. *
— Peissner, E. The American question in its national aspect. N. Y., 1861. 12°.
— Pickett, C. E. The existing revolution; its causes and results. Sacramento, 1861. 8°. *
— Prevost, F., *and* Pecquet, P. Le blocus américain. Paris, 1861. 8°.
— Renouf, S. L'union américaine et l'Europe. Paris, 1861. 8°. *
— Sécession aux Etats-Unis, La, et son origine; par un journaliste américain. Paris, 1861. 8°.
— Smith, P. A. The seizure of the Southern commissioners, [1861]. London, 1862. 8°.
— Spence, J. American union; secession as a constitutional right, *etc.* Lond., 1861. 8°. *
— - *Same.* 1st Amer. from the 4th Eng. ed. Richmond, 1863. 8°.
— Stiles, J. C. The national controversy. N. Y., 1861. 12°. *
— Tobitt, J. H. What I heard in Europe during the American excitement, [1861]. N. Y., 1864. 8°.
— Trimble, R. Slavery in the U. S., [1861]. London, 1863. 8°.
— U. S. *36th Cong., 2d sess. Ho.* Abstracted Indian trust bonds; [report] from select committee. *n.t.p.* [1861.] 8°. (No. 78.)
— Great Britain. *Parl.* North American papers, 1862-69. London, [1862-69]. 8 v. f°.
Note. For complete list *see* Great Britain. *Parl.* (North Amer.) p. 1219, 20.
— Nye, C. Portion of original papers upon the Amer. question in 1862-63. *n.t.p.* [1863.] f°. (A 66)
— American question: secession, tariff, slavery. Brighton, [Eng.,] 1862. 16°.
— Anent the U. S. and Confederate States of N. America. London, 1862. 8°. *
— Boislecomte, A. O. E. S., *comte* de. De la crise américaine et de celle des nationalités en Europe. Paris, 1862. 8°. *
— Bright, J. Speech in the Town Hall, Birmingham, Dec. 18. Birmingham, [1862]. 8°.
— Cairnes, J. E. The revolution in America; a lecture. Dublin, [1862]. 16°.
See also his Slave power. 1862.
— Carlier, A. Considérations sur la situation actuelle de l'Union. (*In his* L'esclavage. 1862.)
— Conway, M. D. The golden hour. Boston, 1862. 8°.
— - The rejected stone. Boston, 1862. 8°.
— D***, A. La guerre civile aux Etats-Unis; impuissance du Nord, l'indépendance du Sud inévitable. Paris, 1862. 8°. *
— Fresnel, R. F. Que l'Europe soit attentive aux événements possibles en Amérique. Paris, 1862. 8°.
— Gasparin, A. E. de. L'Amérique devant l'Europe. Paris, 1862. 8°.
— - *Eng.* America before Europe; tr. by M. L. Booth. 3d ed. N. Y., 1862. 8°.
— - Une parole de paix sur le différend entre l'Angleterre et les Etats Unis. Paris, 1862. 8°.
— Grandguillot, A. La reconnaissance du Sud. Paris, 1862. 8°. *
— Gr. Brit. *Parl.* Extract of a despatch from Lord Lyons resp. political arrests in the U. S. London, 1862. f°.
— Hall, N. The American war; a lecture to working men, London, Oct. 20, 1862. London, [1862]. 16°.
— Haut, M. de. La crise américaine, ses causes, ses résultats, *etc.* Paris, 1862. 8°. *

— Hope, A. J. B. American disruption; three lectures. 6th ed. London, 1862. 8°. *
— Ingersoll, C. Letter to a friend in a slave state. Phila., 1862. 8°. (B 1724)
— Kirkland, C. P. Letter to B. R. Curtis, in review of his pamphlet on the 'Emancipation proclamation', [1862]. 3d ed. N. Y., 1863. 8°.
— Laboulaye, E. R. L. Les Etats Unis et la France. Paris, 1862. 8°.
— Lacouture, E. La vérité sur la guerre d'Amérique. Paris, 1862. 8°. *
— Lettre à Napoléon III sur l'esclavage aux Etats du Sud. Paris, 1862. 8°.
— Loring, C. G., *and* Field, E. W. Correspondence on the present relations between Great Britain and the United States. Boston, 1862. 8°.
— Massie, J. W. The American crisis in rel. to the anti-slavery cause. London, 1862. 12°.
— Merson, E. La guerre d'Amérique et la médiation. Paris, 1862. 8°. *
— Mill, J. S. The contest in America, 1862. (*In his* Dissertations and discussions, v. 3. 1867.)
— - Slave power. [1862.] (*In his* Dissertations, v. 3. 1865.)
— O'Sullivan, J. L. Union, disunion, and reunion. London, 1862. 8°. *
— Palmer, *Sir* R. Speech, North American blockade. London, 1862. 8°.
— Philo-Americanus, *pseud.* The American struggle; appeal to the people of the North. London, 1862. 8°. *
— Picard, A. Les blancs et les noirs en Amérique, et le coton dans les Deux Mondes. Paris, 1862. 8°.
— - Le conflit américain et sa solution probable. Paris, 1862. 8°.
— Rawlins, C. E. American disunion constitutional or unconstitutional? London, 1862. 16°.
— Reynolds, E. W. The true story of the barons of the South; or, The rationale of the Amer. conflict. Boston, 1862. 8°.
— Rush, B. Letter on the rebellion. Phila., 1862. 8°. (B 1724)
— Sayve, *Le comte* de. Etude sur la révolution des Etats-Unis, [1862]. Paris, 1863. 8°.
— Schobert, *Le baron.* Paix à l'Amérique. Paris, 1862. 8°. *
— Sinclair, P. Freedom or slavery in the U. S. 2d ed. London, [1862]. 8°.
— Spence, J. On the recognition of the Southern Confederation. 3d ed. Lond., 1862. 8°. *
— Story, W. W. The American question. London, 1862. 8°.
— Taylor, W. Cause and probable results of civil war in America. London, 1862. 8°.
— Wilks, W. English criticism on Pres. Lincoln's anti-slavery proclamation and message. *n.t.p.* [London, 1862.] 8°.
— Williams, J. The South vindicated. London, 1862. 8°. *
— Kennedy, J. P. Mr. Ambrose's letters on the rebellion, [1863–65]. N. Y., 1865. 16°.
— Hand book of the democracy for 1863–64. *n.t.p.* [N.Y., 1864.] 8°.
— Adams, W. E. The slaveholders' war; an argument for the North and the negro. London, 1863. 8°.
— American thanksgiving dinner at St. James Hall, London, November 26. London, 1863. 8°.

— Bacon, L. Reply to J. Parker's letters. From the New Englander, April 1863. *n.p.*, [1863]. 8°.
— Ballot box, The, the palladium of our liberties. N. Orleans, 1863. 8°. *
— Beecher, H. W. American rebellion; speeches delivered in [Gr. Britain, 1863]. Manchester, 1864. 8°.
— Bernard, M. Lecture on the alleged violations of neutrality by Eng. in the present war. London, 1863. 8°.
— Bishop, J. P. Thoughts for the times. Boston, 1863. 8°.
— Brown, G. American war and slavery. Manchester, 1863. 16°.
— Campbell, W. F., *Ld. Campbell.* Speech on the right of the neutral powers to acknowledge the Southern Confederacy. London, 1863. 8°. *
— Carrey, E. Grandeur et avenir des Etats-Unis. Paris, 1863. 8°.
— Clergy of the Confederate States of America. Address to Christians. London, 1863. 8°. *
— Cobbe, F. P. The red flag in John Bull's eyes. London, 1863. 16°.
— Cobden, R. American war, [1863]. (*In his* Speeches on questions of public policy, v. 2. 1870.)
— D., B. Federals and confederates; for what do they fight? 3d ed. London, [1863]. 16°.
— Edge, F. M. Destruction of the American carrying trade. London, 1863. 8°.
— Fairbanks, C. The American conflict from a European point of view. Boston, 1863. 8°.
— Gibbs, F. W. Foreign enlistment act. 2d ed. London, 1863. 8°. *
— - Recognition. London, 1863. 8°. *
— Hope, A. J. B. B. Social and political bearings of the American disruption. 3d ed. London, 1863. 8°. *
— Hughes, T. The cause of freedom; which is its champion in America? London, [1863]. 16°.
— Ingersoll, J. R. The diplomatic year; being a review of Seward's foreign correspondence of 1862; by a northern man. 2d ed., with a postscript. Phila., 1863. 8°. (B 1724)
— Lawrence, G. G. Three months in America, 1863; two lectures. Huddersfield, [1863.] 16°.
— Letter on the American war, by a northern sympathiser. Ryde, London, 1863. 16°.
— Loring, C. G. Neutral rel. of England and the U. S. Boston, 1863. 8°.
— Moody, L. Destruction of the republic the object of the rebellion. London, 1863. 16°.
— Nation's sin and punishment, The; by a chaplain of the U. S. A. [S. A. Hodgman? 1863.] N. Y., 1864. 12°.
— Nemo, *pseud.* Policy of recognizing the independence of the Southern States. London, 1863. 8°. *
— Newman, F. W. Character of the Southern States. Manchester, 1863. 8°.
— - The good cause of President Lincoln. [London, 1863.] 16°.
— Noel, B. W. The rebellion in America. London, 1863. 8°.
— Nouette-Delorme, E. Les Etats-Unis et l'Europe. Paris, 1863. 8°. *
— - Un Européen au President A. Lincoln; réponse à son dernier message. Paris, 1863. 8°. *

— Nye, G. Papers upon the Amer. question and upon the relations of the U. S. with England and France. *n.t.p.* [Hong Kong, 1863.] f°. (A 66)
— Onesimus *Secundus, pseud.* True interpretation of the American civil war. 2d ed. London, 1863. 8°. *
— Pelletan, P. C. E. Adresse au roi coton. Paris, 1863. 8°
— Pollard, E. A. Rival administrations; Richmond and Wash. in Dec. 1863. Richmond, 1864. 8°. *
— Refutation of fallacious arguments anent the American question. 2d ed. London, 1863. 8°. *
— S., C. The crisis. N. Y., 1863. 8°. *
— Smith, G. Does the Bible sanction American slavery? Oxford, 1863. 12°.
— Spence, J. Southern independence; address, 26th Nov. London, 1863. 8°. *
— Stock, J. Duties of British Christians in rel. to the struggle in America. London, [1863]. 16°.
— Sumner, C. Our foreign relations; speech, Sept. 10. N. Y., 1863. 8°.
— Tyson, B. The institution of slavery considered in connection with our sectional troubles. Wash., 1863. 8°. *
— Walker, R. J. Jefferson Davis; repudiation, recognition, and slavery. London, 1863. 16°.
— War ships for the Southern Confederacy; report of a meeting in Manchester, *etc.*; with letter from Prof. G. Smith to the 'Daily news'. Manchester, 1863. 8°.
— Anent the North American continent. London, 1864. 8°.
— Bemis, G. Precedents of American neutrality; in reply to Sir Roundell Palmer. Boston, 1864. 8°.
— Bishop, J. P. Secession and slavery considered as a question of constitutional law. Boston, 1864. 8°.
— Edge, F. M. England's danger and her safety. London, 1864. 8°.
— - President Lincoln's successor. Lond., 1864. 8°.
— Farrar, C. C. S. The war; its causes and consequences. Cairo, *etc.*, 1864. 12°.
— Gilmore, J. R. Down in Tennessee and back by way of Richmond. N. Y., 1864. 12°.
— Goodwin, T. S. The natural history of secession. N. Y., 1864. 12°.
— Kerr, W. S. R. The confederate secession. Edin., 1864. 16°. *
— Laugel, H. Les corsaires confédérés et le droit des gens. (*In* Revue d. D. Mondes, juil. 1864.)
— Lewis, T. State rights; a photograph from the ruins of anc. Greece. Albany, 1864. 12°.
— Loehnis, H. Die Vereinigten Staaten von Amerika. Lpz., 1864. 8°.
— Nye, G. Some casual papers upon the Alabama and her commander. *n.t.p.* [Hong Kong, 1864.] f°. (A 66)
— - Some casual papers upon the American question and national amenities. *n.t.p.* [Hongkong, 1864.] f°. (A 66)
— Partridge, J. A. The false nation and its 'basis'; or, Why the South can't stand. London, 1864. 8°.
— Phelps, *Mrs.* A. H. L. Our country; original articles by American writers. Balt., 1864. 12°.
— Pollard, E. A. Letter on the state of the war. *n.t.p.* [1864.] 8°. *
— - The two nations; key to the history of the American war. Richmond, 1864. 8°. *
— Sargent, F. W. England, the U. S., and the Southern Confederacy. 2d ed. London, 1864. 8°.
— - Les Etats Confédérés et l'esclavage. Paris, 1864. 8°.
— Shirreff, E. Chivalry of the South. London, 1864. 16°.
— Smith, G. Letter to a Whig member of the Southern Independence Assoc. London, 1864. 16°.
— - *Same.* Boston, 1864. 16°.
— Taylor, C. The probable causes and consequence of the American war. London, 1864. 8°. *
— Andrew, J. A. Address on dedicating the monument to Ladd and Whitney, Lowell, June 17, 1865. Boston, 1865. 8°. (B 1611, 1928)
— Draper, J. W. Thoughts on the future civil policy of America. N. Y., 1865. 8°.
— Senior, N. W. (*In his* Hist. and philos. essays, v. 1. 1865.)
— U. S. *President.* Message in rel. to the states lately in rebellion; [with] report of Carl Shurz, also report of Lieut. Gen. Grant. [Wash., 1865.] 8°. (39th Cong. 1st sess. Sen. Ex. doc. 2.)

☞ For works on the trial of the conspiracy against Lincoln *see* Lincoln, A.

— Bemis, G. American neutrality; its honorable past, its expedient future; a protest against the repeal of the neutrality laws. Boston, 1866. 8°.
— Davidson, J. Oration before the Legislature of N. Jersey upon 'Our sleeping heroes', Feb. 22. Trenton, 1866. 8°. (B 1639)
— Evans, T. W. Lettres d'un oncle sur le gouvernement des Etats-Unis. Paris, 1866. 8°.
— Goedel, C. Sklaverei und Emancipation in den Vereinigten Staaten von Nordamerika. Zürich, 1866. 8°.
— Locke, D. R. Swingin round the cirkle; by Petroleum V. Nasby; his ideas of men, politics, and things, 1866. Boston, 1867. 16°.
— Oliphant, L. Present state of political parties in America. Edin., London, 1866. 8°.
— Partridge, J. A. The making of the American nation. London, 1866. 8°.
— Polignac, C., *prince* de. L'union américaine après la guerre. Paris, 1866. 8°.
— Smith, G. The civil war in America. London, 1866. 8°.
— White, R. G. The new gospel of peace. N. Y., 1866. 12°.

☞ For works on reconstruction *see* Reconstruction (p. 2477).

— Dabney, R. L. A defence of Virginia, and through her of the South. N. Y., 1867. 12°. *
— Duvergier de Hauranne, E. Les Etats-Unis en 1867. — Johnson et Congrès. (*In* Revue d. D. Mondes, nov. 1867.)
— Oil on the waters; [rights and wrongs of the North and South]. Boston, 1867. 8°.
— Peabody, A. P. Lessons from our late rebellion; address, anniv. of the Amer. Peace Soc., May 19. Boston, 1867. 8°. (B 1927)
— Sumner, C. Speech on the cession of Russian America to the United States. Wash., 1867. 8°.
— Chicago. National Union Repub. Convention. Proceedings, May 20, 21. Chicago, [1868]. 8°.
— Duvergier de Hauranne, E. L'élection présidentielle; le gén. Grant et les partis aux Etats-Unis. (*In* Revue d. D. Mondes, déc. 1868.)

— HAUTEFEUILLE, L. B. Questions de droit maritime international. Paris, 1868. 8°.

For works on the impeachment of Pres. Johnson, see Johnson, A. (p. 1586, 87).

— MOTLEY, J. L. Historic progress and American democracy; address. N. Y., 1869. 8°.

— PARTON, J. The Danish islands; are we bound in honor to pay for them? Boston, 1869. 8°.

— LAUGEL, A. Le traité de Washington entre l'Angleterre et les Etats-Unis, 1871. (*In* Revue d. D. Mondes, août 1871.) — DUVERGIER DE HAURANNE, E. L'election présidentielle, 1872. (*In* déc. 1872.)

— HILL, H. A. Relations of business men to national legislation. (*In* Amer. Soc. Sci. Assoc. Journ., no. 3. 1871.)

— JONES, J. H. The kingdom of heaven; what it is, where it is, and the duty of Amer. Christians conc. it. Boston, 1871. 8°.

Note. 'The U. S. of America is the Kingdom of Heaven which Christ came to establish'.

See also Alaska; — California; — Confederate States of America; — Connecticut; — Dist. of Columbia; — Georgia; — Iowa; — Kansas; — Kentucky; — Louisiana; — Maryland; — Massachusetts; — Mexico; — Mississippi; — Missouri; — Nebraska; — New Hampshire; — New Jersey; — New Mexico; — New York; — Nicaragua; — Oregon; — Pennsylvania; — Rhode Island; — South, The; — S. Carolina; — Texas; — Vermont; — Virginia; — West Indies; — *also* American Party; — Calhoun doctrine; — Central America; — Chesapeake, *U. S. Frigate*; — Commerce; — Compromise; — Debts of the States; — Democratic Party; — Embargo; — Federal Party, *U. S.*; — Fisheries; — Fortification; — Free trade; — Hartford Convention; — Impressment; — Indians; — Intervention; — Knights of the Golden Circle; — Naturalization; — North Eastern Boundary; — Orders in Council; — Reconstruction; — Republican Party, *U. S.*; — Reciprocity; — River and harbor improvements; — Seminole war; — Slave trade; — Slavery; — State rights; — Tariff; — Territories.

For debates in Congress *see Congress* (p. 3060, 61); — *House* (p. 3064-92); — *Senate* (p. 3096-3106); — *also* Clay, H.; — Jackson, A.; — Adams, J. Q., *etc.*, for pamphlets recommending or opposing their election.

Population.

— WIGGLESWORTH, E. Calculations on American population. Boston, 1775. 8°. (B 350)

— STATISTICAL view of the population of the U. S., 1790-1830. Wash., 1835. f°.

— BARTON, W. On the progress of population, *etc.*, in the U. S. *n.p.*, 1791. 4°. (W 71)

— TUCKER, G. Progress of the United States in population and wealth in 50 yrs. N. Y., 1843. 8°.

See also Census Office (p. 3058, 59).

Prisons and Prison discipline.

— BEAUMONT, G. A. de la B. de, *and* TOCQUEVILLE, A. de. Système pénitentiare aux Etats-Unis, *etc.*, [1833]. 2e éd. Paris, 1834. 2 v. 8°.

— - *Eng.* Penitentiary system, *etc.*; tr. by F. Lieber. Phila., 1833. 8°.

— CRAWFORD, W. Report on the penitentiaries of the U. S. [London,] 1835. f°.

— DIX, D. L. Remarks on prisons and prison discipline in the U. S. Boston, 1845. 8°.

— - *Same.* 2d ed. Phila., 1845. 8°.

— GRAY, F. C. Prison discipline in America. Boston, 1847. 8°.

— - *Same.* London, 1848. 8°.

— REFORMATORY CONVENTION. Proc. of the 2d convention of managers and superintendents of houses of refuge, *etc.*, in the U. S., 1859. N. Y., 1860. 8°.

— WINES, E. C., *and* DWIGHT, T. W. Report on the prisons and reformatories of the U. S. and Canada. Albany, 1867. 8°.

See also Connecticut; — Georgia; — Kentucky. *Penitentiary* (p. 1620); — Mass. *State Prison* (p. 1897); — New York. *State Prisons* (p. 2121); — Pennsylvania; — *also* Prisons, Prison discipline; — Reform schools; — Reformatory education.

Public buildings.

See Surveyor of Public Buildings (p. 3107).

Public lands.

— *Laws.* U. S. 11*th Cong.* 2*d sess.* Laws, treaties, *etc.*, [rel.] to public lands; col. pursuant to an act passed Apr. 27. Wash., [1810]. 8°.

— - - *Another copy.* [Introduction only.] (B 510)

— - - 19*th Cong.* 1*st sess.* Laws, resolutions, treaties, *etc.*, resp. public lands; comp. in obedience to a resolution of the House, 1st March, 1826. Wash., 1828. 8°.

— PAINE, T. Public good; an examination into the claim of Va. to the vacant western territory, *etc.* Phila., 1780. 8°. (B 702, W 21)

— U. S. *Attorney-General.* Report; containing a col. of charters, *etc.*, rel. to the land situate in the south-west parts of the U. S. Phila., 1796. 8°. (B 598, W 63)

— 9*th Cong.* 2*d sess.* Report of the comm. of public lands on the petition of sundry officers who served in Amer. during the war between France and Gr. Brit. Wash., 1807. 8°. (B 507)

— - 11*th Cong.*, 3*d sess.* Report of committee on the memorial of the Legislative Council and House of the Indiana Territory; Jan. 23. Wash., 1811. 8°. (B 512)

— - - Report of committee on public lands on the memorial of the United Illinois and Wabash Land Companies. Wash., 1811. 8°. (B 512)

— - - Report of committee on public lands on the petition of commissioners to fix a site for Pulaski in Tenn. Wash., 1810 [1811]. 8°. (B 512)

— - - Report of the comm. on the public lands on the petition of W. Coleman. Wash., 1810 [1811]. 8°. (B 512)

— - - Report of comm. on the public lands on the petitions of R. Tervin, S. Mims, E. Lewis, J. Wilson, and the Baptist Church at Salem, of the Mississippi Territory. Wash., 1811. 8°. (B 512)

— NOTES on the bill supplementary to the act for the final adjustment of land titles in Louisiana and Missouri. Wash., 1816. 8°. (B 1602)

— SPARKS, J. Review of the Md. report on the appropriation of public lands for schools, Jan. 30, 1821. From the N. Amer. review, Oct. Balt., 1821. 8°. (B 552)

— MAXCY, V. The Maryland resolutions, and the objections to them considered. Balt., 1822. 8°. (B 535, 976)

— RECTOR, W. Answer to charges against him by D. Barton. St. Louis, 1824. 8°. (B 1101)

— GRUNDY, F. Speech on Mr. Foot's resolution relative to the public lands, *etc.*, Feb. 29. Wash., 1830. 8°. (B 1494)

— JOHNSTON, J. S. Speech, on the resolution of Foot rel. to public lauds, Mar. 30. Wash., 1830. 8°. (B 1494, 1792)

— LIVINGSTON, E. Speech on Mr. Foot's resolution rel. to the public lands, Feb. 29. Wash., 1830. 8°. (B 1494)

— WEBSTER, D. Speech on the public lands, Jan. 20. Wash., 1830. 8°. (B 1792, 1831)

— - Speech in reply to Hayne, on Foot's resolution rel. to public lands, Jan. 26. Wash., 1830. 8°. (B 1792)

— - 2d speech in the Senate, Jan. 26, with sketch of debate on resolution of Mr. Foot respecting the sale of public lands. Boston, 1830. 8°. (B 1836)

— U. S. 22*d Cong.* 1*st sess.* Report of committee on public lands. May 18, 1832. *n.t.p.* [Wash., 1832.] 8°. (Sen. Doc. 145. B 1062)

— - Report of comm. on manufactures on reducing the price of pub. lands; Apr. 16, 1832. *n.t.p.* [Wash., 1832.] 8°. (Sen. Doc. 128. B 1062)

— - Reports of committees on the propriety of disposing of the public lands to those states in which they lie. [Wash., 1832.] 8°. (Ho. Doc. 448. B 1057)

— U. S. 23*d Cong.* 1*st sess.* Report of committee on public lands, on the president's message of Dec. 4, 1833, returning, with his objections, the bill relating to the proceeds of the sales of public lands. *n.t.p.* [Wash., 1834.] 8°. (Sen. Doc. 323. B 1495)

— CUSHING, C. Speech, resolutions of Kentucky and Mass. recommending the distribution of the proceeds of the public lands among the states. Wash., 1836. 8°. (B 1113, 1718)

— CRITTENDEN, J. J. Speech upon the resolution of Ewing to rescind the order requiring specie in payment for public lands, Dec. 20. Wash., 1836. 8°. (B 1496)

— EWING, G. Speech, bill to appropriate the proceeds of the sales of pub. lands, Mar. 15, 16. Wash., 1836. 8°. (B 1777)

— U. S. *24th Cong. 1st sess.* Report of committee on public lands, Jan. 27. *n.t.p.* [1836.] 8°. (Sen. Doc. 89. B 1721)

— WEBSTER, D. Speech [on the resolutions of Ewing to rescind the order requiring specie in payment for public lands,] Dec. 21. Wash., 1836. 8°. (B 1496)

— KING, J. P. On the land bill, Jan. 31. Wash., 1837. 8°. (B 1496)

— U. S. *25th Cong. 3d sess.* Report of the committee on finance [on] the reduction and graduation of pub. lands, Dec. 17, 1838. [Washington, 1839.] 8°. (Sen. Doc. 14. E 43)

— - *Treasury.* Report of the Sec., Jan. 9, 1838, rel. to the sales of pub. lands. [Wash., 1838.] 8°. (25th Cong. 2d sess. Sen. 85. B 1871)

— - Letter from the Sec. resp. land to which the Indian title has been extinguished, *etc.*, Feb. 7, 1839. [Wash., 1839.] 8°. (House. Doc. 164. E 43)

— CALHOUN, J. C. Speech, prospective pre-emption bill. *n.t.p.* [Wash., 1841.] 8°. (B 1663)

— LINN, L. F. Speech on Mr. Crittendon's amendment to distribute the proceeds of the sales of the public lands among the states, Jan. 29. Wash., 1841. 8°. (B 1823)

— MCKEON, J. Speech on the bill to distribute the proceeds of the public lands. Wash., 1841. 8°. (B 1664)

— RAYNER, K. Speech on the bill proposing to distribute annually among the several states the proceeds of the sales of the public lands. Wash., 1841. 8°. (B 1167)

— MARYLAND. *Governor.* Message in rel. to the report of the committee on the public lands. *n.t.p.* [1841.] 8°. (B 1663)

— WINTHROP, R. Remarks on the distribution bill; July 2, 1841. [Wash., 1841.] 8°. (B 1167, 1498)

— COLTON, C. Junius tracts, no. 8. The public lands, by Junius. N. Y.. 1844. 8°. (B 1199)

— FELCH, A. Speech on ceding public lands to the states in which they are situated, Jan. 13. Wash., 1851. 8°. (B 1505)

— STEVENS, T. Speech on the public lands; June 11. Wash., 1852. 8°. (B 1506)

— CUTTS, J. M. The public land system of the U. S. (*In his* Brief treatise upon constitutional and party questions. 1866.)

See also State papers (p. 3061); — *also* **Georgia.** *Miscellaneous* (p. 1129); — **Massachusetts.** *Com. on Pub. Lands* (p. 1895); — **Wisconsin**; — *also* **Pre-emption.**

Public works.

See Internal improvements (p. 3131).

Railroads.

— DISTURNELL, J. Railroad and steamboat book, July 1848, Jan. 1850, Jan. 1854. N. Y., *n.d.* 3 v. 16°.

— DODGETT's railroad guide and gazeteer for 1848. N. Y., 1848. 16°.

— DINSMORE's railroad and steam navigation guide; Sept. 1850; Apr. 1851; May, Sept. 1853; Apr., July 1854; Apr. 1858. N. Y., 1850–58. 7 v. 16°.

— APPLETON's railway and steam navigation guide, July 1856; Oct. 1857; July 1859; Jan., Feb., June 1860; June 1862. N. Y., 1856–62. 7 v. 16°.

— HOMANS, B. U. S. railroad directory, 1856. N. Y., 1856. 8°.

— RHODES, C. C. Railroad and steamboat directory. Phila., 1857. 8°.

— POOR, H. V. Manual of the railroads of the U. S., 1868 69, 69/70, 74/75, 78/79, 79; with an analysis of the debts of the United States and of the several states. N. Y.. 1868–79. 5 v. 8°.

See also **California**; — **Maryland**; — **Massachusetts**; — **New York**; — **Pennsylvania.**
See also Maps (p. 3119).

Registers.

— GAINE's universal register or Columbian kalendar. N. Y., 1793. 24°.

— UNITED STATES register, 1794–95. Phila., 1794. 2 v. 12°.

— HISTORICAL register of the U. S.; ed. by T. H. Palmer. Phila., 1814. 4 v. (v. 3 w.). 8°.

— NATIONAL calendar, 1820–36; by P. Force. Wash., [1820–36]. 14 v. 12°.
Note. Vol. 9, 2d ed. No vols. pub. for 1825–27.

— UNITED STATES national almanac, 1825–27. Phila., *Desilver*, 1825–27. 3 v. 8°.

— AMERICAN almanac, 1830–62. Boston, *n.d.* 33 v. 12°.

— DESILVER's U. S. register and almanac, 1833. Phila., 1833. 8°.

— UNITED STATES' almanac; or, Complete ephemeris, 1844–45; also statistics. Phila., 1844–45. 2 v. 12°.

— DISTURNELL's United States national register, 1852. N. Y., *n.d.* 12°.

— NATIONAL almanac and annual record, 1863–64. Phila., 1863–64. 2 v. 16°.

— AMERICAN year book and national register for 1869; ed. by D. N. Camp. Vol. 1. Hartford, 1869. 8°.

See also **Massachusetts**; — **New Jersey**; — **New York**; — *also* **Registers** (p. 2484).

Slavery.

See **Slavery** (p. 2747–56).

Social life.

See National character and Social life (*p.* 3140–41).

Sports.

— HERBERT, H. W. Frank Forester's field sports of the U. S. 6th ed. N. Y., [1848]. 2 v. 8°.

— LEWIS, E. J. American sportsman. Phila., 1855. 8°.

— HERBERT, H. W. Frank Forester's fish and fishing of the U. S. and British provinces. New ed., with a treatise on fly-fishing by 'Dinks'. N. Y., 1859. 8°.

— RÉVOIL, B. H. Shooting and fishing in North America; tr. London, 1865. 2 v. 8°.

Statistics.

— DONNANT, D. F. Statistical account of the U. S.; tr. by W. Playfair. London, 1805. 8°. (B 712)

— BLODGETT, S., *Jr.* Economica; a statistical manual for the U. S. Wash., 1806. 8°.

— - *Another copy.* (B 428)

— PITKIN, T. Statistical view of the commerce of the U. S.; its connection with agriculture, *etc.*, and an acc. of the pub. debt, revenues, and expenditures, *etc.* Hartford, 1816. 8°.

— - *Same.* 2d ed., with add. and corr. N. Y., 1817. 8°.

— - *Same.* N. Haven, 1835. 8°.

— SEYBERT, A. Statistical annals of the U. S. Phila., 1818. 4°.

— OUSELEY, W. G. Remarks on the statistics and political institutions of the U. S.; added, statistical tables. London, 1832. 8°.

— FACTS and calculations resp. the population and territory of the U. S. *n.p.*, [1835?]. 4°. (A 5)

— DIETERICI, K. F. W. Ueber die Vertheilung der Bevölkerung nach Geschlecht und Alter in den nordamerikanischen Freistaaten. (*In* **Berlin. Ak. d. Wiss.** Abth., 1848.)

— KETTELL, T. P. Southern wealth and northern profits, exhibited in statistical facts and official figures. N. Y., 1861. 8°.

See also **Massachusetts**; — **New Hampshire**; — **Oregon.** *Description and history.*

Tariff.

Note. In the following works * added to the title means that the works are more or less in favor of free trade, † that they are in favor of protection.

— NEW YORK MECHANICS. Memorial. Wash., 1803. 8°. † (B 502)

— CORRECT list of duties payable on goods imported. N. Y., 1806. 12°. (C 266)

— TARIFF; or, Rates of duties after June 30. Boston, 1816. 8°.

— PERKINS, J., *and others.* Report of the committee of merchants of Boston, on the tariff. Boston, 1820. 8°. * (B 536, 1076, 1511, 1787)

— WINSLOW, I. Old and new tariffs compared; with obs. on the effect of high duties on revenue and consumption. Boston, 1820. 4°. † (A 35)

— CAMBRELENG, C. C. Examination of the tariff proposed by H. Baldwin. N. Y., 1821. 8°. *

— CAREY, M. Address to the farmers of the U. S. on the existing policy of this country. Phila., 1821. 8°. † (B 548, 1835)

— U. S. 16*th Cong.* 2*d sess.* Report of committee on manufactures on memorials for and against an increase of duties on imports. *n.t.p.* [1821.] 8°. (Ho. Doc. 34) † (B 1835)

— CAREY, M. Address to the citizens of the U. S. on the tendency of our system of intercourse with foreign nations. Phila., 1822. 8°. † (B 977)

— - Appeal to common sense and justice; [against] the tariff. 2d ed. Phila., 1822. 8°. † (B 548)

— - *Same.* 3d ed. Phila., 1822. 8°. † (B 1887)

— - Facts and obs. illustrative of the past and present situation, and future prospects of the U. S. 2d ed. Phila., 1822. 8°. † (B 548)

— - *Same.* Extracts. *n.t.p.* 8°. (B 564)

— - The crisis; a solemn appeal to the President and citizens of the U. S. on its agriculture, manufactures, commerce, and finances. Phila., 1823. 8°. † (B 548)

— - *Same.* Extracts. 2d ed. Phila., 1823. 8°. (B 548)

— GR. BRIT. *Parl.* American tariffs; papers rel. to tariffs published in the U. S. in 1824, 28. London, [1828]. f°.

— CAREY, M. Fifty-one substantial reasons against any modification of the existing tariff. Phila., 1824. 8°. † (B 548, 1511)

— - Warning voice to the cotton and tobacco planters, farmers, and merchants of the U. S. Phila., 1824. 8°. † (B 548)

— CLAY, H. Speech, support of an Amer. system for the protection of Amer. industry, Mar. 30, 31. Wash., 1824. 8°. † (B 554)

— COOPER, T. Tract on the proposed alteration of the tariff, submitted to the consideration of the members of So. Carolina. Phila., 1824. 8°. * (B 548)

— CAREY, M. Examination of a tract on the alteration of the tariff, by T. Cooper; [with] the tract. Phila., 1824. 8°. † (B 548, 1636, C 266)

— HAYNE, R. Y. Speech against the tariff bill, Apr. Charleston, 1824. 8°. * (B 1066)

— NEW YORK CHAMBER OF COMMERCE. Memorial, with statements [of] the present rate of duties, *etc.* N. Y., 1824. 8°. * (B 536)

— TARIFF or rates of duty, after June 30. N. Y., 1824. 12°.

— THORNDIKE, I., *and others.* Report of the committee of merchants and others of Boston on the tariff. Boston, 1824. 8°. * (B 533, 1076, 1511)

— WEBSTER, D. Speech upon the tariff, Apr. Boston, 1824. 8°. * (B 1702)

— - *Same.* Wash., 1824. 8°. (B 554, 1787, 1804, 2010)

— CAREY, M. Essays tending to prove the ruinous effects of the policy of the U. S. on the farmers, planters, and merchants. Phila., 1826. 8°. † (B 1068, 1637)

— - Examination of the Charleston memorial. No. 1-5. Phila., 1827. 8°. † (B 1637)

— LEE, H. Report of a committee of citizens of Boston opposed to a further increase of duties on importations. Boston, 1827. 8°. *

— - *Other copies.* (B 551, 1511, 1797)

— CAREY, M. Examination of the report of a committee of the citizens of Boston [written by H. Lee] opposed to an increase of duties on importation. Phila., 1828. 8°. † (B 1511, 1884)

— OBSERVATIONS upon the memorial and report of the citizens of Boston opposed to a further increase of duties, *etc.* Providence, 1828. 8°. † (B 1511)

— REVIEW of the report of a comm. of citizens of Boston opposed to a further increase of duties. Phila., 1828. 8°. † (B 1511)

— MCCORD, D. J. Speech [against] the proposed woollens bill. Columbia, 1827. 8°. * (B 1066)

— MEMORIAL to Cong. against a further increase of duties; by citizens of Boston and vicinity. Boston, 1827. 8°. * (B 1511)

— GRIMKE, T. S. Speech, Dec. 1828, resp. the tariff. Charleston, 1829. 8°. † (B 1075, 2545, E 221)

— SMITH, R. B. Address of citizens of Colleton district to the people of S. Carolina [on the late tariff bill; advocating a state convention]. *n.p.*, 1828. 8°. * (B 1066)

— CAREY, M. The protecting system. No. 1-9. Phila., 1829.] 8°. † (B 1512)

— HILL, I. Speech on Clay's resolutions on the tariff. *n.p.*, [183-]. 8°. * (B 1495)

— CAMBRELENG, C. C. Merchant's 2d ed. of C.'s Report on commerce and navigation, Feb. 8. N. Y., 1830. 8°. * (B 1512)

— CALHOUN, J. C. Sentiments on state rights and the tariff; with Va. and Ky. resolutions of 1798, 99, *etc.* Boston, 1831. 8°. * (B 1494)

— HAMBDEN, *pseud.* First reflections on reading the president's message to Cong., Dec. 7, 1830. Wash., 1831. 8°. † (B 1831)

— OGDEN, E. D. Tariff on and after Jan. 1840–30 June 1842; also tariff law of 1832, *etc.* N. Y., 1840. 8°.

— - Tariff from and after 1846. New York, 1846. 8°.

— CAREY, M. The crisis; an appeal to the good sense of the nation, *etc.* No. 1, 2. 3d ed. corr. Phila., 1832. 8°. † (B 1636)

— - The dissolution of the union. Phila., 1832. 8°. (B 1790)

— - *Same.* 2d pt. 3d ed. Phila., 1832. 8°. † (B 1068)

— CLAY, H. Speech, in defence of the American system against the British colonial system, Feb. 2, 3, 6; with app. of documents. Wash., 1832. 8°. † (B 1056, 1721, 1805, 1810, 1831, 2009)

— DRAYTON, W. Address to the people of S. C. [Charleston, 1832?] f°. * (B 1067)

— EVANS, G. Speech, support of the protective system. Wash., 1832. 8°. † (B 1056)

— EVERETT, E. Speech, proposed adjustment of the tariff, June 25. Wash., 1832. 8°. † (B 1495, 1790, 1961)

— HAMBDEN, *pseud.* Strictures on Lee's Exposition of evidence on sugar duty in behalf of the Free Trade Convention. *n.p.*, [1832]. 8°. † (B 1056, 1512)

— HAYNE, R. Y. Speech, reduction of the tariff, Jan. 9, 1832. Wash., [1832]. 8°. * (B 1067, 1810)

— ERRORS in fact advanced by Hayne in his anti-tariff speech. Phila., 1832. 8°. † (B 1512)

— IMPORT duties in rel. to the happiness of the people and prosperity of the Union. Phila., 1832. 8°. † (B 1512)

— LINCOLN, L. R., *and* EVELETH, S. Tariff payable from and after Mar. 3, 1833. Boston, 1832. 12°.

— MCDUFFIE, G. Speech on the bill proposing a reduction of the duties on imports, May 28. Wash., 1832. 8°. * (B 1056, 1067)

— - *Same.* Charleston, 1832. 8°. (B 1067)

— - Speech on the 3d reading of the tariff bill, in the Ho. of Rep. June 28, 1832. *n.t.p.* [Wash., 1832.] 8°. * (B 1067)

— SPRAGUE, P. Speech on the tariff, Mar. 22. Wash., 1832. 8°. * (B 1790)

— STEWART, A. Speech in support of the tariff policy and in reply to McDuffie. Wash., 1832. 8°. † (B 1056, 1831)

— U. S. 22*d Cong.* 1*st sess.* Tariff, manufactures; report of com. on manufactures. Wash., 1832. 8°. † (Ho. Doc. 481. B 1056, 1790)

— - *Treasury Dept.* TARIFF of duties; report of the Sec. Wash., 1832. 8°. † (Ho. Doc. 222. B 1056)

— - 22*d Cong.* 1*st sess.* Reduce the duties on imports; views of the minority of the committee on ways and means. Wash., 1832. 8°. † (Ho. Rep. 279. B 1056)

— APPLETON, H. Speech on the bill to reduce the duties on imports, Jan. 23. Wash., 1833. 8°. † (B 1069, 1790, 1831)

— CAREY, M. To the manufacturers of the U. S. [Phila., 1833.] f°. † (A 66)

— REED, J. Speech, tariff bill, Jan. 22. Wash., 1833. 8°. † (B 1790)

— U. S. 22*d Cong.* 2*d sess. House.* Report of the minority of the committee on manufactures; by J. Q. Adams and L. Condict,] Feb. 28. Boston, 1833. 8°. † (Ho. Doc. 122. B 1427, 1648)

— - *Same.* Tariff report of J. Q. Adams. Boston, 1833. 8°. (B 1427)

— CORWIN, T. Speech on bill to reduce the revenue of U. S., Jan. 12, 1837. Wash., 1837. 8°. * (B 1124, 1496, 1718, 1723)
— HASTINGS, J. Speech on the tariff bill. *n.t.p.* [Wash., 1841.] 8°. * (B 1664)
— LOUISIANA and the tariff; by a native of Louisiana. New Orleans, 1841. 8°. † (B 1513)
— SLADE, W. Speech in favor of a protecting tariff. [Wash., 1841.] 8°. (B 1174)
— WINTHROP, R. C. Remarks on the revenue bill, July 28. Wash., 1841. 8°. † (B 1498)
— - Speech on the resolution to refer that part of the President's message relating to the tariff to the com. on manufactures, Dec. 30, 1841. Wash., 1842. 8°. † (B 1513)
— CALHOUN, J. C. Speech on the passage of the bill. Wash., 1842. 8°. * (B 1664)
— CHOATE, R. Speech, power, and duty of Cong. to continue the policy of protecting Amer. labor, Mar. 14. Wash., 1842. 8°. † (B 1871)
— FRIENDS OF A PROTECTIVE TARIFF IN THE CO. OF WINDSOR, WOODSTOCK, VT. Memorial and resolutions. *n.p.*, [1842]. 8°. † (B 1513)
— HUDSON, C. Speech on discriminating duties. Wash., 1842. 8°. † (B 1174)
— HUNTINGTON, J. W. Speech upon the resolutions of Clay, Mar. 21. Wash., 1842. 8°. † (B 1499)
— KENNEDY, J. P. Letter on the principles and value of the protective system. [Wash., 1842.] 8°. † (B 1174)
— MANSFIELD, E. D., *and others*. Memorial, in rel. to the promotion and protection of national industry. Cincin., 1842. 8°. † (B 1188)
— SALTONSTALL, L. Speech upon the tariff bills, June 17. Wash., 1842. 8°. (B 1513, 1871)
— STUART, A. H. H. Speech. [Wash., 1842.] 8°. * (B 1174)
— THOMPSON, R. W. Speech on the tariff bill. Wash., 1842. 8°. † (B 1174)
— U. S. 27*th Cong.* 2*d sess.* Report of L. Saltonstall of the com. of manufactures upon the tariff, *etc.*, Mar. 31, 1842. *n.t.p.* [Wash., 1842.] 8°. † (Ho. Rep. 461. B 1513, 1871)
— - - Report of Simmons of the committee on manufactures, July 1, 1842. *n.t.p.* [Wash., 1842.] 8°. † (Sen. Rep. 340. B 1513)
— - - Report of the minority of the committee on manufactures; [by] Mr. Habersham. [Wash.,] 1842. 8°. * (Ho. Rep. 641. B 1513)
— - *Treas. Dept.* Revised tariff; report of Sec., May 9, 1842. *n.t.p.* [Wash., 1842.] 8°. † (Ho. Doc. 209 B 1513)
— U. S. 27*th Cong.* 2*d sess.* Act to provide revenue from imports and to change existing laws imposing duties on imports. Boston, 1842. 12°. † (C 266)
— WASHINGTON, W. H. Speech on the tariff bill. [Wash., 1842.] 8°. † (B 1174)
— WINTHROP, R. C. Speech on the resolution offered by Mr. Filmore to refer that part of the President's message rel. to the tariff to the comm. of manufactures. Wash., 1842. 8°. † (B 1174)
— RODET, D. L. Tariff et tendances du commerce des Etats-Unis. (*In* Revue d. D. Mondes, juil. 1843.) †
— CHAMBERS, T., *and others*. Letter to G. Evans against the repeal of duty on railway iron, by the tariff of 1842. Phila., 1844. 8°. † (B 1513)
— CHOATE, R. Speech upon protecting American labor by duties on imports. Washington, 1844. 8°. † (B 1174)
— COLTON, C. Junius tracts, no. 10: The tariff triumphant; by Junius. N. Y., 1844. 8°. † (B 1500)
— GRINNELL, J. Speech on the tariff, with statistical tables of the whale fisheries of the U. S. Wash., 1844. 8°. † (B 1174)
— McDUFFIE, G. Speech on the tariff in reply to Messrs. Evans and Huntington. Wash., 1844. 8°. * (B 1174)
— PLEBEIAN tracts. No. 2: Injustice of the tariff on protective principles. N. Y., 1844. 8°. * (B 1513)
— ROCKWELL, J. Speech on the tariff bill. Wash., [1844]. 8°. † (B 1174)
— TARIFF doctrine; [pub. by order of the 'Whig Congressional Executive Committee']. Wash., 1844. 8°. † (B 1513)
— *U. S.* 28*th Cong.*, 1*st sess.* Revenue minority report; [by] D. L. Seymour. Wash., 1844. 8°. † (Ho. Rep. 406. B 1174)
— CHARLESTON. CHAMBER OF COMMERCE. Report of M. C. Mordecai, from the committee on the questions proposed by the Secretary of the Treasury respecting the tariff; Nov. 13. Charleston, 1845. 8°. * (B 1514)
— KENNEDY, J. P. To the mechanics, manufacturers, and working men of Baltimore. Balt., 1845. 8°. † (B 1514)
— BURKE, E., *of N. H.* The protective system in connection with the present tariff. Wash., 1846. 8°. * (B 1514)
— DAVIS, J. Speech on the bill to reduce duties and for other purposes, July 16, 17. Wash., 1846. 8°. † (B 1502)
— HUDSON, C. Speech on the tariff, June 29. Wash., 1846. 8°. † (B 1514)
— MANN, J. Two tariffs compared and both found wanting in the element of protection for American labor. Boston, 1846. 8°. (B 1514)
— ROCKWELL, J. A. Speech, bill to reduce the duties on imports, June 26. Wash., 1846. 8°. † (B 1514)
— WEBSTER, D. Speech on the tariff bill, July 25. Wash., 1846. 8°. † (B 1514)
— COMPARATIVE statement of the tariffs of 1842 and 1846. Phila., 1847. 8°. (B 1514)
— MEACHAM, J. Speech, modification of the tariff, June 9, 10. Wash., 1852. 8°. (B 1506)
— STEVENS, T. Speech on public lands; the tariff, June 11. Wash., 1852. 8°. † (B 1506)
— BAKER, J. L. Hard times; important suggestions to laborers, *etc.* Boston, 1855. 8°. † (B 1514)
— DEWITT, A. Speech on the tariff, Feb. 12. Wash., 1857. 8°. * (B 1514)
— U. S. tariff on and after 1 July 1857; with the tariff of 1846 in parallel lines. N. Y., 1857. 8°.
— RICE, A. H. Legislative protection to the industry of the people; speech, Apr. 26, Wash., 1860. 8°. * (B 1514)
— CAREY, H. C. French and American tariffs compared, in letters to Chevalier. Phila., 1861. 8°. † (B 1514)
— U. S. 36*th Cong.* 2*d sess.* U. S. tariff of [Feb.] 1861; with an hist. sketch showing changes in the tariffs, 1789–1861. N. Y., 1861. 8°.
— U. S. 37*th Cong.* 1*st sess.* Act to provide increased revenue from imports, *etc.*, Aug. Wash., 1861. 8°. (B 1514)
— - *Same.* U. S. tariff of [Aug.] 1861, with an hist. sketch showing changes, 1789–1861. N. Y., 1861. 8°.
— U. S. 42*d Cong.* 2*d sess.* Tariff and internal revenue law, approved June 6; with acts of which it is amendatory, *etc.*; comp. by H. E. Dresser. N. Y., 1872. 8°.

Note. For many other discussions on the tariff *see* the *Congressional* globe, especially for 1841, 42, 46, 57, 61, 72.

See also **Political economy; — State rights.**

Taxes.

See Congress (p. 3060).

Theatre.

See **Theatre** (p. 2946–48).

Trees.

— MARSHALL, H. Arbustrum Americanum. Phila., 1785. 8°.
— - *Another copy.* (W 43)
— BROWNE, D. J. Sylva Americana; description of the forest trees of the U. S. Boston, 1832. 8°.
— - Trees of America, native and foreign. N. Y., 1846. 8°.
— PIPER, R. U. The trees of America. No. 1–4. Boston, 1855. 4°.

See also **Massachusetts.** *Commis. on Zoöl. and Bot. Survey* (p. 1891); — **North America.** *Botany.*

Zoölogy.

See **California; — Georgia; — Illinois; — Massachusetts; — New England.** *Nat. hist.*; — **New York; — North America; — Wisconsin.**

United States (Separate States). Constitutions, *etc.*; pub. by Congress. Phila., London, *repr.*, 1783. 8°.

Contents. Decl. of independence. — Arts. of confederation. — Constitutions of the thirteen states. — Treaty of amity and commerce between France and the thirteen states, Jan. 30, 1778. — Treaty of alliance betw. France and the states, Jan. 30, 1778. — Treaty of amity and commerce between the United Netherlands and the U. S., Oct. 8, 1782. — Provisional arts., signed at Paris Nov. 30, 1782, by the commissioners of Gr. Brit. and of the U. S. — List of the presidents of Cong., 1774-81.

— Constitutions, *etc.*; [ed. by W. Jackson]. London, 1783. 8°.
Contents. Decl. of rights. — Non-importation agreement. — Last petition to the King. — Dec. of independence. — Arts. of confederation. — Constitutions. — Treaty of amity and commerce between France and the U. S., Jan. 30, 1778. — Treaty of alliance betw. France and the U. S., Jan. 30, 1778. — Treaty of amity and commerc betw. the United Netherlands and the U. S., Oct. 8, 1782. — Convention betw. the United Netherlands and the U. S. conc. vessels, Oct. 8, 1782. — Provisional articles signed at Paris, Nov. 30, 1782. — List of pres. of Cong., 1774-81.

— Constitutions, *etc.* *t.p.m.* [178-.] 8°.
Contents. Constitutions of the thirteen states. — Decl. of independence. — Arts. of confederation. — Treaty of amity and commerce betw. France and the U. S., Jan. 30, 1778. — Treaty of alliance betw. France and the U. S., Jan. 30, 1778. — Treaty of amity and commerce between the United Netherlands and the U. S., Oct. 8, 1782. — Definitive treaty betw. Gr. Brit. and America, Nov. 30, 1782.

— Constitutions, *etc.* Phila., 1791. 12°.
Contents. Constitutions. — Decl. of independence. — Federal constitution. — Amendments.

— Constitutions, *etc.* Boston, 1797. 12°.
Contents. Declaration of Independence. — Articles of confederation. — Definitive treaty with Gr. Brit., 3 Sept. 1783. — Constitution of the U. S., — of the separate states.

— Constitutions of the different states. (*In* **Freeman's** guide. 1812; — *and in* **American's** guide. 1844.

— AMERICAN's own book; or, The constitutions, *etc.*; by J. R. Bigelow. N. Y., 1849. 8°.
Contents. Declaration of independence. — Constitution of the U. S., — of the several states.

— Constitutions, *etc.* N. Y., 1852. 8°.
Contents. Decl. of independence. — Arts. of confederation. — Constitution of the U. S., — of the several states.

— *Dutch.* Verzameling van de constitutiën der Vereenigde onafhanglijke Staaten van Amerika, benevens de acte van onafhanglijkheid, de artijkelen van confederatie, *enz.* 1e stuk. Dordrecht, 1781. 8°.

— *French.* Constitutions des treize Etats-Unis de l'Amérique. Phila., 1783. 8°.

— SMITH, W. Comparative view of the constitutions of the several states with each other, and with that of the United States. Phila., 1796. 4°.

— PACIFICUS, *pseud.* Essays on the rights and privileges of the several states in regard to slavery. [Wash.,] 1842. 8°. (B 1174, 1499)

— SMITH, S. Letters on Amer. debts. London, 1843. 8°. (B 1188)

— WAYLAND, F. Article on the debts of the states. Boston, 1844. 8°. (B 1647)

— WALLACE, J. W. Want of uniformity in the commercial law between the different states of our union. Phila., 1851. 8°. (B 1430)

— WRIGHT, C. J. Official journal of the Conference Convention, at Washington City, Feb. 1861. Wash., 1861. 8°.

— CHITTENDEN, L. E. Debates and proc. in secret sessions at the Conference Convention, Wash., Feb. 1861. N. Y., 1864. 8°.

See also State rights; — United States. *Politics* (*Civil War*) p. 3155-58.

United States *vs.* Brigantine William. BLAKE, F. Examination of the embargo laws. Worcester, 1808. 8°.

— - *Other copies.* (B 984, 1438)

United States *vs.* T. Fillebrown, *Jr.* THOMPSON, S., *Justice.* [Opinion of the Supreme Court of the U. S.] *n.t.p.* [1833.] 8°. (B 1440)

United States *vs.* H. Hertz *et al.*, charged with hiring persons to go beyond the jurisdiction of the U. S. with the intent to enlist in the British foreign legion for the Crimea. Phila., 1855. 8°.

— *Another copy.* (B 1438)

United States *vs.* The property of Thomas, Griswold, & Co. DAY, L. M. Argument for plaintiffs. [*n.t.p.*] 8°. (B 1438)

United States *vs.* S. R. Wood. Important case of alleged fraud upon the revenue. *n.t.p.* [1839.] 8°. (B 1438)

United States, *war steamer.* FABER, C., *and* BIERWIRTH, L. Petition, *etc.* Wash., 1849. 8°. (B 1503)

United States Academy and Institution of the Fine Arts. TOWN, I. Outlines of a plan for establishing in N. Y. an academy of fine arts. N. Y., 1835. 8°. (B 1166)

United States Agricultural Society. Journal. Vol. 1, pts. 3 and 4, v. 2 and 3. Boston, 1854-56. 3 v. 8°.

United States almanac, 1844, 45; by J. Downes. Phila., 1844-45. 2 v. 12°.

United States army and navy journal and gazette of the regular and volunteer forces. Vol. 1-17; Aug. 1863 - July, 1880. N. Y., 1863-80. 17 v. f°.

United States calendar, 1801-47. *See* Massachusetts register (p. 1913).

United States catholic magazine and monthly; ed. by C. I. White. Vol. 2-7. Balt., 1843-48. 6 v. 8°.

United States Christian Commission. 1st, 2d, 4th annual report. Phila., 1863, 66. 3 v. 8°.

— Record of the federal dead buried from Libby, Belle Isle, Danville, and Camp Lawton prisons, and at City Point, and in the field before Petersburg and Richmond. Phila., 1865. 8°. (B 1959)

— MOSS, *Rev.* L. Annals of the Commission. Phila., 1868. 8°.

United States Christian magazine. Vol. 1, no. 1. *n.t.p.* 8°. (B 200)

United States gazette for the country; Jan. 5 - Dec. 31, 1814. [Phila.], 1814. 4°.

United States law intelligencer and review. Vol. 1-3; 1829-31. Prov., 1829, Phila., 1830-31. 3 v. 8°.

United States literary gazette. Vol. 1-3; April 1824 - April 1826. Boston, 1825-26. 3 v. 4° *and* 8°.
Note. For continuation *see* United States review and literary gazette.

United States Loan Fund Assoc. BLAKE, A. P. Articles of the United States Loan Fund Association; also the design and practical operation. Boston, 1855. 16°. (C 197)

United States magazine of science, art, *etc.*, May 1854 - Dec. 1857. N. Y., [1854-57]. 5 v. 4° *and* 8°.
Note. Vol. 5 is entitled Emerson's mag. and Putnam's monthly.

United States monthly law magazine; ed. by J. Livingston. Vol. 4; July - Dec. 1851. N. Y., 1851. 8°.

United States monthly review, Nov. 1842. Vol. 1, no. 1. *n.t.p.* 8°. (B 1775)

United States national almanac, 1825-27. Phila., *Desilver*, [1825-27]. 3 v. 8°.
Note. For 1825; by D. M'Clure; for 1826, 27, by S. Smith.

United States national register, 1852. *See Registers*, p. 3160 (DISTURNELL's).

United States naval chronicle. Vol. 1. Wash., 1824. 8°.

United States Protestant Episc. Church. *See* Prot. Episc. Church in the U. S.

United States railroad directory, 1856; comp. by B. Homans. N. Y., 1856. 8°.

United States register, 1794-95. Phila., 1794. 2 v. 18°.

United States register or blue book, 1861–62, 69; pub. by J. Disturnell. N. Y., [1861–69]. 3 v. 8°.

United States review and literary gazette. Vols. 1, 2; Oct. 1826 - Oct. 1827. Boston, N. Y., 1827. 2 v. 8°.

Note. This is a continuation of the U. S. literary gazette.

— *Another copy of* vol. 1. (B 1873)

United States Sanitary Commission. Ages of the U. S. volunteer soldiery; by B. A. Gould. N. Y., 1866. 8°.

— Bulletin. Vol. 1, 2; Nov. 1863 - Aug. 1865. N. Y., 1863–64. 2 v. 8°.

— Contributions rel. to the causation and prevention of disease; ed. by A. Flint. N. Y., 1867. 8°.

— Documents of the U. S. Sanitary Commission. No. 1–95. N. Y., 1866. 2 v. 8°.

Contents. Vol. 1. Nos. 1–60; May 18, 1861 - Feb. 14, 1863. 2. Nos. 61–95; Jan. 21, 1863 - Dec. 15, 1865.

— History of the U. S. Sanitary Commission; by C. J. Stillé. Phila., 1866. 8°.

— Hospital transports; [by F. L. Olmsted]. Boston, 1863. 8°.

— Sanitary Commission of the U. S. army; a narrative of its works and purposes. N. Y., 1864. 8°.

— Sanitary memoirs of the war of the rebellion; investigations in the military and anthropological statistics of the American soldiers; by B. A. Gould. N. Y., 1869. 8°.

— To the people of the U. S.; [appeal for aid]. [N. Y., Nov. 8, 1864.] 4° (A 64)

Works about the Commission.

— Wormeley, K. P. U. S. Sanitary Commis-
1863. 12°.

— Forman, J. G. The Western Sanitary Com-
sion; its purposes and its work. Boston,
mission; its origin, history, *etc.* St. Louis,
1864. 8°.

— Evans, T. W. La Commission Sanitaire des Etats-Unis. Paris, 1865. 8°.

— Brockett, L. P. Northwestern Sanitary Commission. — Pittsburgh Branch U. S. Sanitary Commission. — Women's Pennsylvania Branch of U. S. Sanitary Commission. (*In his* Woman's work in the civil war. 1867.)

See also **Chicago. Northwestern Soldiers' Fair**; — *also* **Post, L. M.** Soldiers' letters.

United States service magazine. Vol. 1–5. N. Y., 1864–66. 5 v. 8°.

Unity of the Church. *See* **Christian union** (p. 654).

Unity of God. *See* **Trinity** (p. 3011–14).

Unity of worlds and of nature; three essays, by B. Powell. 2d ed. rev. and enl. London, 1856. 16°.

Univercœlum, The, and spiritual philosopher; Dec. 4, 1847 - June 30, 1849. N. Y., 1848–49. 4 v. 4°.

Note. The Univercœlum ends with no. 5 of v. 4, and is continued under the title of 'Spirit of the age'.

Univers, L'; histoire et description de tous les peuples. Paris, *Didot*, 1835–53. 63 v. 8°.

Note. The set should contain 67 vols. 'Provinces danubiennes', 'Grèce depuis la conquête des Romans jusqu'à nos jours', and 'Asie Mineure' (2 v.) are wanting.

Namely. **1835.** **Pouqueville,** F. C. H. L. Grèce [ancienne]. **1836–38.** **Domeny de Rienzi,** G. L. Océanie. 3 v. **1838–42.** **Chopin,** J. Russie. — **Famin,** C. La Crimée; — Circassie et Géorgie. — **Bové,** E. Arménie. 2 v. 1838. **Golbéry,** M. P. A. de. Histoire et descr. de la Suisse et du Tyrol. **1839, 38.** **Le Bas,** P. L'Allemagne. 2 v. **1839.** **Denis,** J. F. Brésil. — — **Famin,** C. Colombie et Guyanes. 1839. **Le Bas,** P. Suède et Norwége. **1840–45.** **Le Bas,** P. France; dictionnaire encyclopédique. 12 v. **1840, 43.** **Le Bas,** P. France; annales historiques. 2 v. **1840.** **Famin,** C. Chili, Paraguay, Buenos-Ayres. — **Lacroix,** F. Patagonie, Terre-du-Feu, et Archipel des Malouines; — **Bory de Saint Vincent,** J. B. G. M. Iles diverses des trois océans et régions circompolaires. — **Forster,** C. Pologne. **1841.** **Dubeux,** L. La Perse. **1842–44.** **Galibert,** L., *and* **Pellé,** C. Angleterre. 4 v. (v. 4, Angleterre, Ecosse, et Irlande). **1842.** **Le Bas,** P. Etats de la Confédération Germanique. **1843.** **Jouannin,** J. M., *and* **Van Gaver,** J. Turquie. — **Larenaudière,** P. de. Mexique et Guatemala; — **Lacroix,** F. Pérou et Bolivie. **1844.** **Avezac-Macaya,** M. A. P. d'. Afrique; esquisse générale de l'Afrique et Afrique ancienne; — **Dureau de la Malle,** A. J. C. A., *and* **Yanoski,** J. Carthage; — **Lacroix,** P. L. Numidie et Mauritanie; — **Yanoski,** J. L'Afrique chrétienne, et domination des Vandales en Afrique. — **Hasselt,** A. van. Belgique et Holland. — **Lavallée,** J. A. F., *and* **Gueroult,** A. Espagne. — **Roux de Rochelle,** J. B. G. Villes anséatiques. **1845.** **Dubois de Jancigny,** A. P., *and* **Raymond,** L. A. X. Inde. — **Munk,** S. Palestine; description géog., hist. et archéol. **1846.** **Denis,** J. F. Portugal. — **Eyriès,** J. B. B., *and* Chopin, J. M. Danemark. **1847.** **Champollion-Figeac,** J. J. Egypte ancienne. — **Noel Desvergers,** J. M. A. Arabie; avec une carte par E. F. Jomard. — **Tardieu,** E. A. Senegambie et Guinée; — **Chérubini,** S. Nubie; — **Noel Desvergers,** J. M. A. Abyssinie. **1848.** **Avezac-Macaya,** A. Iles de l'Afrique; avec la collaboration de E. de Froberville, F. Lacroix, F. **Hoefer,** O. Maccarthy, V. Charlier. — **Hoefer,** J. C. F. Afrique australe, orientale, centrale; Empire de Maroc. — **Marcel,** J. J. Egypte depuis la conquête des Arabs jusqu'à la domination française; — **Ryme,** A. Sous la domination française; — **P.,** —, *and* **H.,** —. Sous Méhémet Aly. — **Dubeux,** L., *and* **Valmont,** V. Tartarie, Bélouchistan, Boutan, et Népal; — **Raymond,** L. A. X. Afghanistan. — **Yanoski,** J., *and* **David,** J. A. Syrie ancienne et moderne. **1849.** **Regnault,** E. G. S. O. Histoire des Antilles, *etc.* — **Regnault,** E. G. S. O., *and* **Labaume,** J. Suite des Etats Unis; — **Lacroix,** F. Possessions anglaises dans l'Amér. du Nord; — **Denis,** J. F. Les Californies, l'Orégon, et les possessions russes en Amérique, *etc.* **1850.** **Dubois de Jancigny,** A. P. Japon, Indo-Chine, Ceylan. — **Lavallée,** J. A. F. Espagne, depuis l'expulsion des Maures jusqu'à 1847; — **Lacroix,** F. Isles Baléares et Pithyuses; — **Grégory,** G. de. Sardaigne; — **Friess de Colonna,** C. Hist. de la Corse. — **Rozet,** C. A., *and* **Carette,** E. Algérie; — **Hoefer,** J. C. F. Etats tripolitains; — **Frank,** L. Tunis; rev. par J. Marcel. **1851.** **Duruy,** V., *and others.* Italie ancienne. 2 v. **1852.** **Artaud de Montor,** A. F. Italie; — **La Salle,** A. E. G. de. Sicile. — **Hoefer,** J. C. F. Chaldée, Assyrie, Médie, Babylonie, Mesopotamie, Phénicie, Palmyrène. **1853.** **Lacroix,** P. L. Iles de la Grèce. — **Pauthier,** J. P. G., *and* **Bazin,** A. Chine. 2 v. — **Roux de Rochelle,** J. B. G. Etats Unis d'Amérique.

Universal, El. Mexico. (*City*) *Comision de la Junta Civica.* Refutacion en la parte historica del articulo de fondo, pub. en num 305 del 'Universal'. Mexico, 1849. 8°.

Universal American register. 1775. *n.t.p.* 32°.

Universal British directory. *See* **Barfoot,** P., *and* **Wilkes,** J.

Universal Church, The; its faith, doctrine, and constitution. London, 1866. 8°.

Universal gallant, The, or, The different husbands; a comedy. *See* **Fielding,** H.

Universal gazette; Nov. 16, 1797 - Nov. 27, 1800. Phila. (Nov. 13-27, 1800, Wash.), 1797–1800. f°.

Universal history, from the earliest account of time; compiled from original authors, illust. with maps, *etc.* [Antient part.] London, 1747–54. 21 v. (v. 5, 16 w.). 8°.

Contents. Vol. **1.** Cosmogony; or, Creation of the world. — History of the world till the flood. — From the deluge to the birth of Abraham. — Egypt to the time of Alexander. **2.** Egyptian chronology to the time of Alexander. — History of the Moabites, Ammonites, Midianites, Edomites, Amalekites, Canaanites, Philistines. — Antient Syrians. — Phœnicians. — History of the Jews to the Babylonish captivity. **3.** *Same, contin.* to 1426 B.C. — App. **4.** to 588 B.C. — Assyrians. — Babylonians. — Antient Phrygians. Trojans, Lycians, Lydians, *etc.* **5.** *Wanting.* **6.** Celtes. — Scythians. — Lydians. — Lycians. — Cicilians. — Fabulous and heroic times: Argos, Attica, Bœotia and Thebes, Arcadia, Thessaly, Phocis, Corinth, Lacedæmon, Elis. — Athenians. **7.** Lacedæmonians. — Thebes. — Achaia. — Ætolia.

— Athens, from the Achæan league to the present time (A.D. 1747). — Ionia. — Xenophon's retreat. — Sicily. — Syracuse, 483-06 B.C. 8. Syracuse, 406-198 B.C. — Rhodes. — Crete. — Cyprus. — Samos. — Other Greek islands. — Macedonians, to 324 B.C. 9. Macedonians, 323-148 B.C. — Seleucidæ in Syria. — Ptolemies of Egypt. — Armenians. — Pontus. 10. Cappadocians. — Pergamus. — Thrace. — Epirus. — Bithynia. — Colchis, Iberia, Albania, Bosporus, Media, Bactria, Edessa, Emesa, Adiabene, Characene, Elymais, Comagene, and Chalcidene. — History of the Jews, from their return from the Babylonish captivity to the destruction of Jerusalem by Titus Vespasian. 11. Parthians, from Arsaces to the recovery of the kingdom by the Persians. — Persians. — Roman history, to the burning of the city by the Gauls. 12. Roman history, to the perpetual dictatorship of Sylla, 379-104 B.C. 13. Roman history, 104-1 B.C. 14. 1-69 A.D. 15. Roman history, to the removal of the imperial seat to Constantinople by Constantine the Great, 69-330. 16. *Wanting.* 17. Constantinopolitan history to 1453. — Hist. of the Carthaginians to the destruction of Carthage by the Romans. 18. To 698. — Numidians. — Mauritanians. — Gætulians. — The Melanogætuli, *etc.* — The Libyans of Marmarica, Cyrenaica, and of the Regio Syrtica. — Ethiopians. — Arabs to Mohammed. — Nice and Trapezond. — Spain. — Antient state of the Gauls, to the irruption of the Franks. 19. Germans. — Britain, to the invasion of the Angles and Saxons. — Hunns. — Goths. — Antient state of the Vandals. — Franks, till their settling in Gaul. — Antient state of the Burgundians. — Alemans. — Gepidæ. — Heruli. — Marcomans. — Quadians. — Sarmatians. — Dacians. — Lombards. — Bulgarians. — Ostrogoths in Italy. — Lombards from the death of Clephis to Desiderius. 20. Preface. — Turks, Tartars, and Moguls. — Indians. — Chinese. — Diss. upon the peopling of America. — Independency of the Arabs. — Index. 21. Chronological tables.

— Modern part of An universal history; by the authors of the antient part. London, 1759-82, 61-82, 61-83, 62-64. 41 v. (v. 32, 33, 35 w.). 8°.

Note. Vol. 9, 19-24, 26, 27, 31, 34 belong apparently to another edition.

Contents. Vol. 1. Life of Mohammed. — History of the Arabs, to 655. 2. 655-940. 3. 940-1401. 4. General hist. of the Turks, and the empires founded by them in Tartary and the lower Asia. — The Seljûkians of Persia, Kermân, and of Rûm. — History of the Moguls and Tartars from the time of Jenghiz Khan. — Mogul Empire to 1294. 5. Mogul Empire, 1294-1505. — History of the Shâh's reigning in Persia, to 1666. 6. 1667-1747. — Arab kings of Ormuz to 1514. — History of the Turkmâns and Usbeks. — Kingdom of Karazm. — History of the Uzbek Khâns of Karazm. — Description of Hindûstân, or the Empire of the Great Mogol. — Description of the countries in the hither peninsula of India. — Religion of the Hindûs. 7. Description of the countries contained in the farther peninsula of India. — History of the eastern Tartars. 8. History of China, with an app. containing the descr. and hist. of Korea. 9. Conquests, settlements, and discoveries of the Dutch, — Danes, — [and] French in the East Indies. — Historical acc. of the Ostend East India Company. — East India Company estab. in Sweden. — Othmân Empire, to 1481. 10. History of the English East-India Company. — Conquests, settlements, and discoveries of the Dutch in the East Indies. 11. Conquests, settlements, and discoveries of the Danes [and] French in the East Indies. — Histor. acc. of the Ostend East India Co. — East India Co. estab. in Sweden. — Terra Australis; or, A history of the Southern Continent. 12. History of the Othman Empire, 1214-1687. 13. 1687-99. — History of the dispersion of the Jews. 14. History of Africa, and of all the principal nations and states which inhabit it. — Modern history of Egypt, to 1250. — African islands. 15. History of Abyssinia. — History of Dancali, Adel, and Magadoxa, *etc.*; with an account of the fabulous kingdom of Adea. — Zanguebar. — Melinda. — Kingdom and islands of Mombaso and Quiloa. — Mosambico. — Sosala. — Monomotapa. — Monoemugi. — History of the Hottentots. 16. West coast of Africa. — The Giagas. — Kongo. — Amgola. — Loango. — Incursions of a new tribe of Giagas into Kongo, *etc.* — Benin. — The slave coast. 17. History of the gold coast. — The ivory coast. — The grain coast. — Sierra Leona. — Interior countries of Africa. 18. History of Barbary. — Tremecen. — Morocco. — Algiers. — Tunis. — Tripoli. 19. Portugal. — Navarre. — History of France, to 1180. 20. 1180-1574. 21. 1574-1715. 22. History of Italy, to 1428. 23. 1428-1700. — Republic of Venice, to 1381. 24. History of Venice, to 1700. — Naples, to 1269. 25. History of France, 1643-1715. — Italy, to 1304. 26. German Empire, 1115-1619. 27. 1619-1797. — Republic of Holland. 28. Naples, 774-1722. — Genoa, to 1684. 29. Germany, 911-1519. 30. 1519-1797. — The Golden bull; or, Constitution of Charles IV. 31. Poland, 1669-1715. — Prussia. — Russia. 32, 33. *Wanting.* 34. Milan. — House of Savoy. — America, to the execution of Pizarro, 1548. 35. *Wanting.* 36. Tuscan states: Florence, to 1277. 37. Bologna. — Parma and Piacenza. — Geneva. — Milan. — Modena and Ferraca. — Mantua. — Savoy, Piedmont, *etc.* 38. History of America: Mexico, Peru. 39. The Incas. — Spanish and Portuguese settlements [in] America. — Terra Firma, Peru, Chili, Buenos Ayres, Paraguay, Brazil, *etc.* — Terra Magellanica, Brasil, the country of the Amazons, and the European settlements in Guiana. — First establishment and progress of the British settlements in N. America. — Virginia, Newfoundland, Nova Scotia, New England, New York, New Jersey, Canada to 1668. 40. 1668-1760. — Louisiana and Florida. — Carolina. — Georgia. — Maryland. 41. Pennsylvania. — Hudson's Bay. — The American West Indies. — Sequel to the history of Virginia.

Note. Vol. 25 contains a duplicate of Bk. XIX, ch. 4, sec. XIII. in v. 21.

Universal-Lexikon. *See* **Pierer, H. A.; — Zedler, J. H.**

Universal magazine. Vol. 33, 52, 58, 64, 65, 70, 71, 88, 89, 92-100, 102-105, 109; 1763-1801. London, 1763-1801. 23 v. 8°.

— New series. Vol. 2, 9-14; 1804-10. London, 1804-10. 7 v. 8°.

— *Same.* April, 1795. [London, 1795.] 8°. (B 1275)

Universal register, Daily; Jan. 14, 1785. London, 1785. f°. (E 199)

Universal salvation. *See* **Future life; — Future punishment; — Redemption; — Salvation.**

Universalist, The, 1865-71. *w.* Boston, 1865-71. 5 v. f°.

Universalist, The, and ladies' repository. Vol. 4-10. Boston, 1836-42. 7 v. 8°.

Note. Vol. 4 ed. by D. D. Smith; 5-7 by H. Bacon; 8-10 by H. Bacon and Miss S. C. Edgarton.

Universalist expositor, The. Boston, 1831-32. 2 v. 8°.

— *Same.* New ser. The expositor and Universalist review. Vol. 1-4. Boston, 1834-40. 4 v. 8°.

Note. Vol. 1 ed. by H. Ballou and H. Ballou 2d; v. 1-4 n.s. by H. Ballou 2d.

Universalist magazine; ed. by H. Ballou. Vol. 1, 2. Boston, 1819-21. 2 v. 4°.

Universalist Missionary Soc. [Tracts] 1-5, 10, 11. N. Y., [18—]. 16°. (C 243)

Namely. No. 1. What is Universalism? 2. The new birth. 3. Repentance. 4. Punishment and forgiveness. 5. Good and evil. 10. Some reasons for rejecting the doctrine of endless misery. 11. Scripture evidences of the world's salvation.

Universalist quarterly and general review; [ed. by H. Ballou]. Vol. 1-12. Boston, 1844-52. 12 v. 8°.

Universalist S. School Union. 5th annual report, Oct. 15, 1856; with charter and by-laws. Boston, 1856. 8°. (B 1758)

Universalists, Universalism. Articles of faith, and plan of church government, adopted by churches believing in the salvation of all men, with recommendations and letter. Phila., 1790. 8°. (C 74)

Bibliography.

— ABBOT, E. A. Duration of future punishment. (*In his* Literature of the doctrine of a future life; *also in* Alger, W. R. Critical history of the doctrine of a future life. 1864.)

History.

— WHITTEMORE, T. Modern history of Universalism, from the era of the Reformation to the present time. Boston, 1830. 8°.

General works.

— HERALD of life and immortality; by E. Smith. Vol. 1, no. 1. *n.t.p.* [Boston. 1819.] 8°. (B 477)

— RIGHT of Universalists to testify in a court of justice vindicated. Boston, 1828. 8°. (B 1759)

— KNEELAND, A. Appeal to Universalists on excommunication [for] diversity of opinion. N. Y., 1829. 8°. (B 964, 1884)

— WHITTEMORE, T. The plain guide to Universalism. Boston, 1840. 8°.

— UNIVERSALIST Anti-trinitarians in the U. S. (*In* Beard, J. R. Unitarianism exhibited, *etc.* 1846.)

— BROWNE, L. C. Vindication of the moral tendency of Universalism and the moral character of Universalists. (*In his* Review of the life of Smith. 1847.)

— BALLOU, H. A voice to Universalists. Boston, Cincin., 1851. 12°.

See also Ballou, *Rev.* H.; — *also* Future punishment; — Hell; — Western Assoc. of Universalists, *N. Y.*

Universality and efficiency of divine grace, On the. Phila., 1818. 8°. (C 198)

Universe. FISHBOUGH, W. The macrocosm and microcosm; or, The universe without and the universe within; an unfolding of the plan of creation and the correspondence of truths in the world of sense and the world of soul. Pt. 1: Macrocosm. N. Y., 1852. 12°.

See also Astronomy; — Cosmogony.

Université de la France. *See* France (p. 1032).

Universities. *See* Colleges and Universities (p. 624).

University College, *London.* Proceedings at the annual meeting of proprietors, Feb. 28. London, 1838. 8°. (E 56)

University extension. ROGERS, J. E. T. (*In* Shipley, O. The church and the world. 1866.)

University of Alabama. Military department. Tuscaloosa, [1860?]. 8°.

— BRIEF hist. notice of the literary affairs, during the 1st 7 yrs. of its operation. (*In* Woods, A. Valedictory address. 1837.)

— RICHARDSON, W. G. Catalogue of the library. Tuscaloosa, 1848. 8°.

— TAYLOR, J. W. Plea for the Univ. of Alabama; an address before the Erosophic and Philomathic Societies, Aug. 9. Tuskaloosa, 1847. 8°. (B 1581)

University of Edinburgh. STEWART, D. Short statement of facts rel. to the late election of a mathematical professor. 3d ed. Edin., 1805. 8°. (B 1782)

— - Postscript to [D.] Stewart's Short statement, *etc.* Edin., 1806. 8°. (B 1782)

— INGLIS, J. Exam. of Stewart's pamphlet rel. to the election of a mathematical professor in the University of E. Edin., London, 1805. 8°. (B 1782)

— PLAYFAIR, J. Letter to the author of the exam. of Stewart's 'Short statement of facts'; with an app. Edin., London, 1806. 8°. (B 1782)

— LETTER to Rev. Principal Hill, on the case of J. Leslie. Edin., 1805. 8°. (B 1782)

— EXAMINATION of the letter addressed to Principal Hill, with rem. on Stewart's 'Postscript' and Playfair's pamphlet. Edin., 1806. 8°. (B 1782)

University of London. Deed of settlement. London, 1826. 8°.

— Description of the building for the Univ. London, 1828. 8°.

— Examinations for the degree of bachelor of medicine. London, 1839. 8°. (B 1557)

— Proprietors of shares. London, 1827. 8°.

— Statement by the council explanatory of the nature and objects of the Institution. London, 1827. 8°.

— 2d statement by the council explanatory of the plan of instruction. London, 1828. 8°.

— Resolutions of the Senate with ref. to the analysis of reports rec. from foreign Universities. *n.t.p.* [18—.] 8°. (B 1742)

— FOSTER, C. J. The University of London a parliamentary constituency. London, [1851]. 8°. (B 1532)

Note. For lectures delivered in the Univ. *see* Conolly, J.; — Grant, R. E.; — Lardner, D.; — Muehlenfels, L. von; — Long, G.; — Hurwitz, H.

University of New York. *See* New York. *University* (p. 2121).

University of Pennsylvania. COXE, J. R. Appeal to the public from the proc. of the trustees of the Univ. of Pa., vacating the chair of materia medica and pharmacy. Phila., 1835. 8°. (B 1551)

— SMITH, W. Account of the College, Academy, and Charitable School of Phila. (*In his* Disc. 1763.)

University of Virginia. Proceedings and report of the commissioners for the Univ. of Richmond, 1818. 8°. (B 446)

— Report of the rector and visitors, Oct. 4. Richmond, 1864. 8°.

— JEFFERSON, T., *and* CABELL, J. C. Early history of the Univ. Richmond, 1856. 8°.

— JOHNSON, J. L. The University memorial; sketches of the alumni of the Univ. who fell in the Confederate war. Balt., 1871. 5 v. in 1. 8°.

Unkind word, The, and other stories; by [D. M. Craik]. N. Y., 1870. 12°.

Note. From Harper's mag., v. 29–31. 1864–65.

Unknown river, The; by P. G. Hamerton. *See* Arroux.

Unnatural combat, The. *See* Massinger, P.

Uno, L'; commedia. *See* Alfieri, V.

Unprotected females in Norway, passing through Denmark and Sweden. London, 1857. 12°.

Unprotected females in Sicily, Calabria, and on the top of Mt. Ætna. London, N. Y., 1859. 12°.

Unreasonableness of Romanists in requiring our communion with the present Romish Church. London, 1670. 12°.

Unregenerate. HOPKINS, S. Enquiry concerning an unregenerate state; containing remarks on two sermons by Dr. Mayhew. Boston, 1765. 8°.

— - *Other copies.* Boston, 1772. 8°. (B 252, C 305)

— HEMMENWAY, M. Seven sermons on the obligation of the unregenerate, *etc.* Boston, 1767. 8°.

— - *Other copies.* (B 246, 252)

— MILLS, J. Inquiry conc. the state of the unregenerate under the gospel; cont. remarks on S. Hopkins's answer to Dr. Mayhew's sermon. N. Haven, 1767. 8°. (B 253)

— HOPKINS, S. True state and character of the unregenerate. New Haven, 1769. 8°.

— HEMMENWAY, M. Vindication of the power of the unregenerate, against S. Hopkins in his reply to Mills [on] the unregenerate. Boston, 1772. 8°.

— - *Another copy.* (B 252)

— - Remarks on Mr. Hopkins's answer to 'Vindication of the power of the unregenerate', *etc.* Boston, 1774. 8°.

— - *Same.* Boston, 1774. 8°. (B 252)

— TAPPAN, D. Two friendly letters from Toletus to Philalethes, or from D. Tappan to S. Spring. Newburyport, 1785. 8°. (B 150)

Uns, Les, et les autres. *See* Méry, J.

Unser Fritz; von A. v. Kotzebue. (*In his* Theater, v. 14. 1841.)

Unsere Zeit; Jahrbuch zum Conversations-Lexicon. Lpz., 1857–64. 8 v. 8°.

— Neue Folge, Deutsche Revue der Gegenwart. Lpz., 1865–80. 30 v. 8°.

Unsichtbare Loge, Die; von J. P. v. Richter. (*In his* Sammtliche Werke, v. 1, 2. 1840.)

Unsichtbare Mädchen, Das; von A. v. Kotzebue. (*In his* Theater, v. 27. 1841.)

Untersdorf. ANNALES Undersdorfenses, 1173–1483. (*In* Pertz, G. H. Mon. Germ. hist., Scr., v. 17. 1861.)

Unum, E Pluribus, *pseud.* *See* Nye, G., *Jr.*

Unvermaehlte, Die; von A. v. Kotzebue. (*In his* Theater, v. 22. 1841.)

Unwin, *Rev.* Wm. J. Early removal of children from school. (*In* Nat. Assoc. Prom. Soc. Sci. Trans., 1857.)

Unzer, Johann August. Principles of physiology; also dissertation on the functions of the nervous system by G. Prochaska; tr. and ed. by T. Laycock. London, 1851. 8°. (Sydenham Soc.)

Uodalscalcus *Augustensis*, *St.* De Eginone et Herimanno. (*In* Pertz, G. H. Mon. Germ., Scr., v. 12. 1861.)

Uomini illustri di Urbino, Degli; comentario. Urbino, 1819. 4°.
Note. 'Il raccoglitore di queste memorie si protesta debitore di moltissima parte delle notizie che qui sono contenute alla erudizone del Dott. Antonio Rosa'.
Uomo di mondo, L'; commedia. *See* Goldoni, C.
Uomo prudente, L'; commedia. *See* Goldoni, C.
Up and down the world. (*In* Dublin univ. mag., v. 72-73. 1868-69.)
Up for the cattle show; a farce, by H. Lemon. (No. 106 *of* De Witt's acting plays.)
Upanishad. Brihad Aranyaka upanishad, and the commentary of Sankara Acharya on its first chapter; tr. by E. Röer. Calcutta, 1856. 8°. (Bibliotheca Indica, v. 2, pt. 3, nos. 27, 38, 135.)
— Cena upanishad, one of the chapters of the Sama veda; [tr.] by Rammohun Roy. Calcutta, 1816. 8°. (B 679, 1469)
— The Chhandogya upanishad of the Sama veda, with extracts from the commentary of Sankara Acharya; tr. by Rajendralala Mitra. Calcutta, 1862. 8°. (Bibliotheca Indica, nos. 78, 181.)
— Ishopanishad, one of the chapters of the Yajur veda; [tr.] by Rammohun Roy. Calcutta, 1816. 8°. (B 679)
— Kuth-opunishud of the Ujoor-ved, accord. to gloss of Sunkuracharya; [tr.] by Rammohun Roy. *n.p.*, [181-]. 8°. (B 1469)
— Moonduk-opunishud of the Uthurvu-ved, accord. to gloss of Shunkura-Charyu; [tr.] by Rammohun Roy. Calcutta, 1819. 8°. (B 1469)
— The Taittariya, Aitareya, Svetasvatara, Kena, Isakatha, Prasna, Mundaka, and Mandukya upanishads; translated by E. Röer. Calcutta, 1853. 8°. (Bibliotheca Indica, v. 15, nos. 41, 50.)
— Müller, F. M. Alphabetisches Verzeichniss der upanishads. (*In* Zeitschrift d. D. morg. Ges., v. 19. 1865.)
— Weber, A. Die Rama-Tâpanîya-upanishad. (*In* Berlin. Ak. d. Wiss. Abh., 1864.)
Upcott, Wm. Bibliographical account of works rel. to English topography. London, 1818. 5 v. 8°.
Contents. Vol. 1. General topography.—Bedfordshire-Hampshire. 2. Herefordshire-Lincolnshire. — Suppl. to v. 1, 2. 3. Middlesex. — London. 4. Monmouthshire-Sussex. 5. Warwickshire-Yorkshire. — Bibliotheca topographica Britannica. — Suppl. to v. 3-5. — Index of places. — Index of names.
Note. The 5 vols. are paged continuously.
— Catalogue of the library of W. U. London, 1846. 8°.
— Catalogue of the coll. of mss. and autograph letters. London, 1846. 8°.
— Catalogue of prints, pictures, *etc.* [London,] 1846. 8°.
— Catalogue of prints, drawings, miniatures, *etc.* London, 1846. 8°.
— *and* Shoberl, F. Biog. dictionary of living authors of Gr. Brit. and Ireland. London, 1816. 8°.
Up-country letters; ed. by Prof. B—. N. Y., 1852. 12°.
Updike, Wilkins. Memoirs of the Rhode Island bar. Boston, 1842. 8°.
Upham, Albert Gallatin. Notices of the life of J. Upham and his descendants. Concord, 1845. 12°.
Upham, Caleb, *Fun. serm. on. See* Whitman, L. (B 1090)
Upham, Charles Wentworth. Address at the rededication of the 4th meeting-house of the 1st church, Dec. 8. Salem, 1867. 8°.
— Conclusion of the Salem controversy. Salem, 1834. 8°. (B 1394)
— Discourse on prophecy as an evidence of Christianity. Salem, 1835. 8°.
— Discourse on the anniversary of the Association of the First Parish. Hingham, 1832. 8°. (B 1126)
— Discourse on the death of W. H. Harrison, May 14. Boston, 1841. 8°. (B 1217)
— Discourse on the Sabbath after the decease of Hon. T. Pickering. Salem, 1829. 8°. (B 960)
— E. Everett. (*In* Longacre, J. B. Nat. portr. gal., v. 4. 1839.)
— Eulogy on the life and character of Z. Taylor, and address by N. Silsbee. Salem, 1850. 8°. (B 1225)
— J. Q. Adams. (*In* Longacre, J. B. Nat. port. gal., v. 4. 1839.)
— Lectures on witchcraft. Boston, 1832. 12°.
— Letters on the logos. Boston, 1828. 12°.
— Life, explorations, and public services of J. C. Fremont. 45th thous. Boston, 1856. 12°.
— Life of Sir H. Vane. (*In* Sparks, J. American biog., v. 4. 1835.)
— Life of Washington, in the form of an autobiography. Boston, 1840. 2 v. 8°.
— Memoir of G. A. Ward. (*In* Essex Inst. Hist. col., v. 7. 1865.) — Mem. of F. Peabody. (*In* v. 9. 1868.) — Mem. of D. P. King. (*In* v. 10. 1869.)
— Memoirs of J. Prince. (*In* Mass. Hist. Soc. Col., v. 25. 1836.)
— Nebraska and Kansas; speech, May 10. [Wash., 1854.] 8°. (B 1509)
— Oration at the request of the city authorities of Salem, July 4. Salem, 1842. 8°. (B 1204)
— Oration before the New Eng. Soc. in New York, Dec. 22, 1846. 2d ed. Boston, 1847. 8°. (B 1736)
— Principles of congregationalism; the 2d century lecture of the 1st Church. Salem, 1829. 8°.
— *Another copy.* (B 952)
— Principles of the Reformation; sermon at the dedication of the 1st Cong. Ch. in Salem. Salem, 1826. 8°. (B 296, 1310)
— Records of Mass. under the first charter. (*In* Mass. Hist. Soc. Lect., 1869.)
— Salem witchcraft; with account of Salem village and hist. of witchcraft. Boston, 1867. 2 v. 8°.
— Goddard, D. A. The Mathers weighed in the balances and found not wanting. Boston, 1870. 12°.
— Poole, W. F. Cotton Mather and Salem witchcraft. Boston, 1869. 8°.
Note. Reprinted from the N. Amer. review.
— - Cotton Mather and witchcraft, two notices of Mr. Upham his reply. Boston, London, 1870. 16°.
— - Mather papers. Cotton Mather and Salem witchcraft. Boston, 1868. 12°.
Note. Repr. from the Boston daily advertiser.
Upham, Edward. History and doctrine of Buddhism. London, 1829. f°.
— History of the Ottoman Empire. Edin., 1829. 2 v. 18°. (Constable's miscel., v. 40, 41.)
Contents. Vol. 1. To 1529. 2. 1529-1828.
— The Mahávansi; Rájá-Ratnácari, and the Rájá-Vali; sacred books of Ceylon; with tracts illust. of Buddhism. London, 1833. 3 v. 8°.
Upham, Jabez Baxter. Acoustic architecture. New Haven, 1853. 8°.
Note. Repub. from Amer. journ. of sci., v. 15, 16. 1853.
— Account of experiments made in connection with the case of M. Groux. [Boston, 1859.] 8°. (B 1563)
— Address before the Handel and Haydn Soc., May 30. Boston, 1864. 8°. (B 1589)
— Hospital notes and memoranda; in illust. of congestive fever or epidemic cerebro-spinal meningitis, in camps, Newbern, [N. C.,] 1862-63. Boston, 1863. 8°.
— Illustrations of typhus fever in Great Britain, 1853; app., Brief acc. of typhus in Boston, 1857-58. Boston, 1858. 8°.
— *Another copy.* (B 1563)

— Inaug. address at the festival of the Handel and Haydn Society, 50th anniversary, May 23. Boston, 1865. 8°. (B 1611)
— Records of maculated typhus or ship fever. N. Y., 1852. 8°.
— *Another copy*. (B 1692)
— Tabular history and analysis of all undoubted cases of typhoid and typhus fever treated at the Boston City Hospital from 1864. Boston, 1870. 8°.

Upham, John. UPHAM, **A. G.** Notices of the life of J. Upham, the first inhabitant of N. England who bore that name. Concord, 1845. 12°.

Upham, Nathaniel Gookin. Eulogy on Lafayette, Concord, June 17. Concord, 1835. 8°. (B 1220)
— Opinion in case of the barque Jones. London, 1854. 8°. (B 1437)

Upham, *Prof.* Thomas Cogswell, *D. D.* Account of the destruction of the Willey family in the notch of the White Mts., 1826. (*In* **New Hamp. Hist. Soc.** Col., v. 3. 1832.)
— Elements of mental philosophy. Boston, 1831. 2 v. 8°.
— *Same*. Elements of mental philosophy, embracing the intellect and the sensibilities. 3d ed. Portland, 1839. 2 v. 8°.
— Essays on a congress of nations. (*In* **Amer. Peace Soc.** Prize essays. 1840.)
— Life of Madame Catharine Adorna. 3d ed. N. Y., 1855. 16°.
— Life of Mme. Guyon with some account of Fénelon. N. Y., 1847. 2 v. 12°.
— Manual of peace. N. Y., 1836. 8°.
— *Same*. Boston, *Mass. Peace Soc.*, 1842. 16°.
— Outlines of imperfect and disordered mental action. N. Y., 1848. 18°. (Harper's fam. lib., v. 100.)
— Ratio disciplinæ; or, The constitution of Congregational churches. Portland, 1829. 2 pts. 12°.
— *tr.* *See* **Jahn, J.** Biblical archæology. 1832.

Upham, Wm. Phineas. Memoir of Gen. J. Glover of Marblehead. (*In* **Essex Inst.** Hist. col., v. 5. 1863.)

Upholsterer, The; or What news? a comedy. *See* **Murphy, A.**

Upland. Record of the court at Upland, 1676–81. (*In* **Penn. Hist. Soc.** Mem., v. 7. 1860.)

Upper Canada. *See* **Canada** (p. 452–465).

Upper Canadian Convention of Friends to Enquiry. Trans.; with addresses. Niagara, 1818. 8°. (B 456)

Upper Sandusky, *O.* FINLEY, **J. B.** History of the Wyandott mission at U. S., under the direction of the Methodist Episcopal Church. Cincin., 1840. 12°.

Ups and downs on land and water. *See* **Hoppin, A.**

Upsala. NAUCLERUS, S. Descriptio horti Upsaliensis. (*In* **Linnæus, C.** Amœn. acad., v. 1. 1749.)

Upshur, Abel Parker. Enquiry into the nature and character of the Federal government; review of Judge Story's Commentaries. Phila., 1863. 8°.
— BUTLER, C. M. Address on the occasion of the funeral of A. B. Upshur and others, Feb. 28. Wash., 1844. 8°. (B 1194)

Upton, Emory. New system of infantry tactics, double and single rank. N. Y., 1867. 18°.

Upton, James. Ποικίλη ἱστορία, sive novus historiarum fabellarumque delectus ex Æliano, *etc.* Etonæ. 1785–89. 2 v. 12°.

Upton, John? Remarks on the Faerie Queen. (*In* **Spenser, E.** Works, v. 2. 1805.)

Upton, *Mass.* WOOD, B. Centennial address, June 25. Boston, 1835. 8°. (B 1882)

Uranius. Fragm. (*In* **Mueller, C.** Fr. hist. Gr., v. 4. 1851.)

Uranus, *planet.* ADAMS, J. C. Explanation of irregularities in the motion of U. London, 1846. 8°.
— BOUVARD, A. Tables astronomiques pub. par le Bureau de Longitude, contenant les tables de Jupiter, Saturne, et d' Uranus, construites d'après la théorie de la Méchanique céleste. Paris, 1821. 4°.
— LOOMIS, E. Satellites of Uranus. (*In* **Amer. Assoc.** Proc., v. 8. 1855.)

Urbain Grandier; drame, par **A. Dumas.** (*In his* Théâtre, v. 11. 1865.)

Urban VIII. [Maffeo **Barberino**], *Pope.* Poemata. Antwerp., *ex offic. Plantiniana*, 1634. 4°.
— Carta al conde de Olivares. (*In* **Valladares, A.** Seman. erud., v. 2. 1787.)
— GIANNONE, P. Ragioni sopra la successione della casa Barberini derivanti dalle disposizioni del pontefice Urbano VIII. (*In his* Opere posthume, v. 3. 1824.)

Urbano, L'. *See* **Boccaccio, G.**

Urbicciani, Bonagiunta. Rime. (*In* **Ozanam, A. F.** Doc. 1850.)
— Sonetti. (*In* **Trucchi, F.** Poesie ital., v. 1. 1846.)
— Sonnets. (*In* **Rossetti, D. G.** Early Ital. poets. 1861.)

Urbino. DENNISTOUN, J. Memoirs of the Dukes of U., 1440–1630; illustrating the arms, arts, and literature of Italy. London, 1851. 3 v. 8°.
— DIARIO della ribellione d' Urbino, 1572. (*In* **Archivio stor. ital.**, n. s., v. 3, pt. 1. 1856.)
— UOMINI illustri di Urbino. Urbino, 1819. 4°.
— VETERANO, F. Inventario della libreria urbinate compilato nel secolo XV. (*In* **Giornale degli archivi toscani**, v. 6. 1862.)

Urceo, *surnamed* **Codrus,** Antonio. NICERON, J. P. (*In his* Mém., v. 4. 1728; *and, Germ.*, v. 5. 1751.)

Urda; et norsk antiqvarisk-historisk Tidsskrift, udgivet af Directionen for det Bergenske Museum. Bergen, 1837–42. 2 v. 4°.

Urdu language. *See* **Hindustani.**

Ure, Alexander. Diseases of the nose. (*In* **Holmes, T.** Syst. of surg., v. 3. 1862.)

Ure, Andrew, *M.D.* Cotton manufacture of Great Britain investigated. London, 1836. 2 v. 8°.
— Dictionary of arts, manufactures, and mines. London, 1839. 2 v. 8°.
Contents. Vol. 1. A–Go. 2. Gr.–Z.
— *Same.* 4th ed. Boston, 1853. 2 v. 8°.
Contents. A–I. 2. K–Z.
— *Same.* 5th ed.; by R. Hunt. London, 1860. 3 v. and suppl. 1878. 8°.
Contents. Vol. 1. A–C. 2. D–L. 3. M–Z. 4. Supplement.
— Dictionary of chemistry on the basis of Nicholson's, with instructions for converting the alphabetical arrangement into a systematic order of study; with notes by R. Hare and F. Bache. 1st Amer. ed. Phila., 1821. 2 v. 8°.
Contents. Vol. 1. A–D. 2. E–W.—Plates.
— New system of geology. London, 1829. 8°.
— Philosophy of manufactures; or, Exposition of the factory system of Gr. Britain. London, 1835. 8°.
— *Same.* 3d ed., contin. by P. L. Simmonds. London, *Bohn*, 1861. 12°.
— Recent improvements in arts, manufactures, and mines; a supplement to his Dictionary. London, 1844. 8°.

Ure, Andrew, *M.D.*, *vs.* **Ure, C.** Case of divorce. *n.t.p.* [1819.] 8°. (B 1561)

Ure, *Rev.* David. General view of the agriculture of the County of Dumbarton. London, 1794. 4°. (W 76)
— General view of the agriculture of the County of Kinross. Edinburgh, 1797. 4°. (W 77)
— General view of the agriculture of the County of Roxburgh. London, 1794. 4°. (W 77)

Ure, John Francis. Improvements in the Tyne. (*In* **Armstrong,** *Sir* **W. G.** Indust. resources. 1864.)

Urea. FLINT, A. Physiological effects of severe and protracted muscular exercise. N. Y., 1871. 8°.

Urethra. FOOT, J. Antient and modern method of curing diseases in the urethra, *etc.* [1774.] 7th ed. London, 1822. 8°.

— HOME, *Sir* E. Practical observations on the treatment of strictures in the urethra, *etc.* [1795.] 3d ed. London, 1805-21. 3 v. 8°.

— ABERNETHY, J. Diseases of the urethra. (*In his* Surg. observ., v. 2. 1806; *and* Surg. and physiol. works, v. 1. 1825.)

— ANDREWS, M. W. Application of lunar caustic to strictures in the urethra, *etc.* London, 1807. 8°.

— LUXMOORE, T. Observations on strictures of the urethra. London, 1809. 8°.

— WADD, W. On the best mode of curing strictures in the urethra; with rem. on caustic applications. [1809.] 2d ed. enl. London, 1812. 8°.

— BELL, *Sir* C. Letters conc. diseases of the urethra. Boston, 1811. 8°.

— ARNOTT, J. Stricture of the urethra; with an app. noticing the application of a new instrument, *etc.* London, 1819. 8°.

— - *Same.* With app. on dilatation by fluid pressure. 2d ed. London, 1840. 8°.

— BINGHAM, R. Strictures of the urethra and diseases of the testicle. London, 1820. 8°.

— MACILWAIN, G. Stricture of the urethra. London, 1824. 8°.

— SLADE, D. D. Observations on the treatment of narrow and irritable stricture of the urethra. Boston, 1858. 8°. (B 1532)

See also **Urinary organs.**

Urfé, Honoré d'. NICERON, J. P. (*In his* Mém., v. 6. 1728; *and, Germ.*, v. 6. 1752.)

Uri. ZSCHOKKE, H. Der Aufruhr von Stans und der Urkantone im Sommer, 1799. (*In his* Ausgewählte hist. Schr., v. 2. 1830.)

Uriarte y Herrera, Miguel de. Representacione al Rey sobre los adelantamientos de aquellos vastos paises y opulencia que pueden producir á España. (*In* Valladares, A. Seman. erud., v. 24. 1739.)

Uricoechea, Ezequiel. Mapoteca colombiana; titulos de los mapas, planos, *etc.*, rel. á la America Española, Brasil, é islas adyacentes. Londres, 1860. 8°.

Urinary organs. JOHNSTON, H. Practical observations on gravel and stone; diseases of the bladder and prostate gland. Edin., 1806. 16°.

— HOWSHIP, J. Observations on diseases of the urinary organs. London, 1816. 8°.

— HALE, E. Boylston medical prize dissertations for 1819, 21: Experiments on the communication between the stomach and urinary organs. Boston, 1821. 8°. (B 830)

— WILSON, J. Lectures on the male urinary and genital organs. London, 1821. 8°.

— BRODIE, *Sir* B. C. Lectures on the diseases of the urinary organs. London, 1832. 8°.

— - *Same.* 3d ed. with alterations and additions. London, 1842. 8°.

— PROUT, W. Gravel, calculus, and other diseases of the urinary organs. Lond., 1832. 8°.

— TODD, R. B. Diseases of the urinary organs and dropsies. Phila., 1857. 8°.

— MORLAND, W. W. Diseases of the urinary organs. Phila., 1858. 8°.

— THOMPSON, H. Surgery of the male urinary organs. (*In* Holmes, T. Syst. of surg., v. 4. 1864.)

See also **Bladder; — Calculus; — Diabetes; — Generative organs; — Kidney; — Lithotomy; — Lithotrity; — Prostate gland; — Stone; — Urethra.**

Urine. MANNING, H. Incontinence of urine. — THACHER, J. Case of retention of urine. (*In* **Mass. Med. Soc.** Med. com. v. 1. 1808.)

— OSBORNE, J. Sketch of the physiology and pathology of urine. London, 1820. 8°. (B 827)

— BECQUEREL, A. Séméiotique des urines; suiv. d'un traité de la maladie de Bright. Paris, 1841. 8°.

— THUDICHUM, J. L. W. Pathology of the urine. London, 1858. 8°.

— PARKES, E. A. Composition of urine. London, 1860. 8°.

— NEUBAUER, C. T. L., *and* VOGEL, J. Guide to the analysis of the urine; tr. by W. O. Markham. London, 1863. 8°. (New Sydenham Soc., v. 20.)

— BERGERET DE ST. LÉGER, A. De l'urine. Paris, [1868]. 8°.

Uring, *Capt.* Nathaniel. Notices of New England. 1709. (*In* **New Hamp. Hist. Soc.** Col., v. 3. 1832.)

Uriya, *or* **Oriya,** *or* **Orissa,** *or* **Autkali lang.** *See* **Bible** (p. 270, 284).

Urlin, R. Denny. Conflict between the laws of England and Ireland. — Present position of the landed Estates Court, Dublin. — (*In* **Nat. Assoc. Prom. Soc. Sci.** Trans., 1862.) — Present state of real property law. (*In* 1864.)

Urlsperger, Johann August. De præstantia coloniæ Georgico-Anglicanæ præ coloniis aliis. Aug. Vind., 1747. 4°.

Urlsperger, Samuel. Ausführliche Nachricht von den saltzburgischen Emigranten, die sich in America niedergelassen haben. Halle, 1744. 4°.

Contents. Umständlicher Vorbericht. — **Boltzius,** J. M., *and* **Gronau,** I. C. Reise-Diarium, von Halle aus bis nach Georgien. — **Boltzius,** J. M. Das Reise-Diarium von Eben-Ezer bis Charles-Toun und wieder zurück. — **Reck,** P. G. F. von. Reise-Diaria; — Kurtze Nachricht von Georgien und denen dasigen Indianern. — **Merckwürdige** hieher gehörige Briefe.

— Continuation, 1e-18e. Halle, 1738-52. 3 v. in in 18 pts. 4°.

Contents. Vol. 1, pt. 1. **Boltzius,** J. M., *and others.* Tage-Register der Prediger zu Eben-Ezer in Georgien, 17 Jul. 1734-1735. (*Also for* 1736 *in* pt. 2, Jan. - Jun. 1737 *in* pt. 3, Jul. 1737 - Mar. 1738 *in* pt. 4, Apr. - Dec. 1738 *in* pt. 5, 1739 *in* pt. 6, 1740 *in* pt. 7, Jan. - Jun. 1741 *in* pt. 8, Jul. - 12 Nov. 1741 *in* pt. 9, 13 Nov. 1741 - Mar. 1742 *in* pt. 10, Apr. - Dec. 1742 *in* pt. 11, 1743 *in* pt. 12, Jan. - Jun. 1747 *in* pt. 13, Jul. 1747 - Apr. 1748 *in* pt. 14, May - Dec. 1748 *in* pt. 15, Jan. - Jun. 1749 *in* pt. 16, Jul. 1749 - Aug. 1750 *in* pt. 17, Sept. 1750 - Mar. 1751 *in* pt. 18.) — **Belcher,** J. Zwischen B. und einigen indianischen Nationen zu Deerfield gehaltenen Conferentz. — **Appleton, N.** Ein bey der Ordination des Herrn J. Sargent, Aug. 1735, gehaltenen Predigt. Pt. 2. **Reck,** P. G. F. von. Diarium, von seiner Reise nach Georgien, mit dem dritten Transport evangelischer Emigranten, 1735. — **Belcher,** J., — **Colman,** B. Briefe aus Neu-England. — **Briefe,** 1735-38. 3. **Briefe,** 1737-39. — Eine kurtze **Aufmunterung** zu einer christlichen und freywilligen Liebes-Steuer von Eben Ezer, *etc.* 4. **Briefe,** 1739. — **Sanftleben,** G. Ein Extract aus S.'s kleinem Reise-Diario, als derselbe zu Ende des Jan. 1739, mit etlichen Colonisten wieder nach Georgien gegangen. — Ein **Verzeichniss** aller Personen, die theils den 19 May 1739, in Eben Ezer gelebet, theils von Anno 1734, bis dahin gestorben. 5. **Briefe,** 1739, 40. — Ein **Dancksagungs**-Schreiben der saltzburgischen Colonisten in Eben Ezer an alle ihre bisherige Wohlthäter in und ausser Teutschland. — **Ermahnungs**-Schreiben an ihre, sonderlich mit ihnen bekannte und verwandte Landsleute in und ausser dem Reich. 2, pt. 6. **Briefe,** 1740. 7. **Briefe,** Jahr 1740, 41. 8. **Briefe,** 1741. — **Nachricht** von dem Zustand der in Preussen und Litthauen etablirten saltzburgischen Emigranten, und derselben Schreiben an die ebenezerische Gemeine. 9. **Muellern,** J. G. von. Reise-Diarium von Augspurg bis London. — **Vigera,** —. Diarium von London bis Eben Ezer. — **Briefe,** 1742. — Nachricht vom Einfall der Spanier, in Georgien. 10. **Briefe,** 1741. — **Extracte** einiger Schreiben so wol der Herren Prediger, als auch etlicher Glieder der Gemeine zu Eben Ezer. 11. **Boltzius,** J. M. Ein kleines Reise-Journal des Herrn Bolzius nach und von Charlestown. 3, pt. 12. Inhalt 6en - 12en Continuation. 13. **Briefe,** 1744-48. — **Beschreibung** des in Eben Ezer, den 10. Merz 1744 gefeyerten jährlichen Dankfestes. — **Urlsperger,** S. Copien von den respective Vocationen und Instructionen der Prediger in Eben Ezer Bolzius und Gronau. 14. **Briefe,** 1748, 49. — **Briefe** von London des Jahres 1749. — **Boltzius, J. M.** Probe einiger aus dem Reiche der Natur, August 1748, auf besonderes Verlangen von Bolzius gemachten Anmerkungen. 15. **Boltzius, J. M.** Fernere Probe einiger aus dem Reiche der Natur im Sept. 1748 auf besonderes Verlangen gemachten Anmerkungen. — **Briefe**, 1749. 16. **Urlsperger, S.** Ein schriftmässige Ermunterungsrede an die ebenezerische Gemeine. — **Briefe**, 1749–50. — **Verzeichniss** der vom May 1749 bis Ende des Sept. 1750 für Ebenezer eingelaufenen Liebesgaben. 17. Eine **Erinnerung** für die alte und neue Welt, sonderlich in Ebenezer, an die vor 20 Jahren geschribene grosse salzburgische Emigration. — **Briefe**, 1750–51. 18. **Gewisse** an Bolzius aus Europa gethane Fragen und seine darauf gegebene Antworten von Carolina und Georgien. — **Urlsperger, S.** Trauungsrede. — **Nachricht** von dem evangelischen Armenhause in Augsburg.

Note. 1e–6e Continuation are paged continuously with the Nachricht; 7–12, and 13–18 form two other volumes. Continuation 17 is imperfect. Many of the 'Briefe' are by Boltzius and Gronau. Each Continuation has a Vorrede by Urlsperger.

Urmston, *Sir* James Brabazon. Observations on the China trade and on the importance and advantages of removing it from Canton to some other part of the coast of the empire. London, 1834. 8°. **(B 1084)**

Urquhart, David. Appeal against faction in respect to the concurrence of the present and the late administrations to prevent the House of Commons from performing its highest duties; added, an analysis of Count Nesselrode's despatch, 20 Oct. 1838. London, 1843. 8°. **(B 1531)**

— The crisis; France in face of the four powers. 2d ed. Paris, 1840. 8°.

— The Edinburgh review and the Affghan war. London, 1843. 8°.

— Exposition of transactions in Central Asia, through which the independence of states and the affections of people, barriers to the British possessions in India, have been sacrificed to Russia by Viscount Palmerston, constituting grounds for the impeachment of that minister. London, 1841. 4°.

— Pillars of Hercules; a narrative of travels in Spain and Morocco, 1848. London, 1850. 2 v. 8°.

— Progress of Russia in the west, north, and south by opening the sources of opinion and appropriating the channels of wealth and power. 3d ed. London, 1853. 12°.

— The spirit of the East; illustrated in a journal of travels through Roumeli during an eventful period. London, 1838. 2 v. 8°.

— Turkey and its resources, its municipal organization and free trade, the state and prospects of English commerce in the East, the new administration of Greece, its revenue and natural possessions. London, 1833. 8°.

— The war of ignorance; a prognostication. London, 1854. 8°. **(B 1534)**

Urquhart, David Henry, *prebendary of Lincoln.* Commentaries on classical learning. London, 1803. 8°.

Urquhart, Thomas. Letter to W. Wilberforce on impressment. — Substance of a letter, with plan to raise British seamen, do away with impressments, *etc.* (*In* **Pamphleteer**, 1824; v. 24 of **B 838**)

Urquhart, Wm. Pollard. Taxation. (*In* **Nat. Assoc. Prom. Soc. Sci.** Trans., 1864.)

Urquidi, Francisco. The other side. 1850. *See* **Alcaraz, R.**

Ursatus, Sertorius. *See* **Orsato, S.**

Ursicino, *Bp. of Turin.* CIBRARIO, L. Notizie d'Ursicino vescovo di Torino nel secolo VI. (*In* **Turin. Ac. d. Sci.** Mem., ser. 2, v. 8. 1846.)

Ursins, Jean Juvénal des. Histoire de Charles VI. (*In* **Michaud.** Col. des mém., v. 2. 1854.)

Ursins, Marie Anne de La Trémoille, *princesse* des. Lettres inédites de Madame de Maintenon et de la princesse des Ursins. Paris, 1826. 4 v. 8°.

Contents. Vol. 1. A Mme. la princesse des Ursins, 1706–09. 2. 1709–11. — A Mme. la duchesse d'Albe, 1711. — A Mme. la princesse des Ursins, 1711–13. — Mme. d'Aumale à la même, 1713. 3. A Mme. Maintenon, 1705–07. — A M. le marq. de Torcy, 1705. 4. 1707–11. — A diverses, 1714.

— *Eng.* Correspondence. London, 1827. 3 v. 8°.

— COMBES, F. La princesse des Ursins, sa vie. Paris, 1858. 8°.

Ursinus, Fulvius. *See* **Orsini, F.**

Ursinus, Zacharias. PAREUS, D. Corpus doctrinæ orthodoxæ, sive Catecheticarum explicationum Ursini opus absolutum. Ed. nova. Heidelb., 1616. 8°

— Heidelberg catechism. *See* **Palatinate** (p. 2213).

Ursius, Josephus Augustinus. *See* **Orsi, G. A.**

Urso *Genuensis.* De victoria quam Genuenses ex Frederico II. retulerunt, 1242; carmen. (*In* **Sardinia.** Mon. hist. pat., v. 6.)

Ursua, Pedro de. *See* **Orsua, P. de.**

Ursula, *St.* WISEMAN, H. E. The truth of supposed legends and fables. (*In* **Manning, H. E.** Essays on religion and literature. 1865.)

Ursula; a tale of country life; by [E. M. Sewell]. N. Y., 1858. 2 v. 12°.

Ursule Mirouët; par H. de Balzac. Paris, 1865. 16°. (Œuvres complètes, v. 43.)

Ursuline Convent, *Charlestown.* AUSTIN, J. T. Argument in the case of J. Buzzell, charged with being concerned in destroying the Ursuline Convent. Boston, 1834. 8°. **(B 1085, 1110)**

— CHARLESTOWN convent; its destruction, Aug. 11, 1834, with the trials of the rioters. Boston, 1870. 8°.

— FAY, R. S. Argument on the petition of B. Fenwick and others. [Ursuline Convent indemnity.] Boston, 1835. 8°.

— MARY EDMOND ST. GEORGE, *Sister.* Answer to [R. T. Reed's] 'Six months in a convent'. Boston, 1835. 8°.

— — *Other copies.* **(B 1384, 1798, 1843)**

— REED, R. T. Six months in a convent. Boston, 1835. 12°.

— REVIEW of the Lady Superior's reply; a vindication of Miss Reed. Boston, 1835. 8°.

— *Same.* *n.t.p.* 8°. **(B 2017)**

— TRIAL of persons charged with burning [it]. *n.t.p.* [1834.] 8°. **(B 1441)**

Ursuline Convent, The; a poem, by P. Scank. Louisville, 1835. 12°.

Ursuline Nuns. ENGLAND, J., *Bp.* Substance of a disc. in Charleston, S. C.; [with] an abstract of the Hist. of the [Ursuline] order, the rules of St. Augustin, *etc.* Charleston, 1835. 8°. **(B 1112)**

— TRANCHEPAIN DE ST. AUGUSTIN, M. Relation du voyage des premières Ursulines à la Nouv. Orléans et de leur établissement. N. Y., 1859. 4°.

Ursus, Robertus. *See* **Orso, R.**

Urtheil des Midas, Das; ein komisches Singspiel. (*In* **Wieland, C. M.** Sämmt. Werke, v. 26. 1825.)

Urtheil des Paris, Das; von A. v. Kotzebue. (*In his* Theater, v. 16. 1841.)

Uruguay. FAMIN, C. Chili, Uruguay, *etc.* Paris, 1840. 8°. (Univers.)

— HORNER, G. R. B. Medical topography of U. Phila., 1845. 8°.

— RECLUS, J. J. E. La guerre de l'Uruguay, [1862–64]. (*In* **Revue** d. D. Mondes, fév. 1865.)

Urville, Dumont d'. *See* **Dumont d'Urville.**

Uscocchi. MINUCCI, M. Storia degli Uscocchi. (*In* **Sarpi,** P. Opere, v. 4. 1763.)

Use. SPENCER, H. Use and beauty. (*In his* **Universal** progress. 1864.)

Used up; a petit comedy. *See* **Mathews, C. J.**

Useful cabinet, The. Vol. 1, no. 1. Boston, 1808. 8°. **(B 976)**

Useful knowledge, Handy helps to. *See* **Handy** helps.

Useful suggestions favourable to the comfort of the labouring people and of decent housekeepers. London, 1795. 8°. **(B 747)**

Uses. Bacon, *Sir* F. Learned reading upon the statute of uses. London, 1642. 4°.

Usher, Bridget, *Funeral sermon on.* *See* **Foxcroft,** T. 1723. (C 36)

Usher, Freeman L. The signal, proposing a Society for the Improvement of the Clergy. Boston, 1815. 12°. (C 84)

Usher (*or* **Ussher**), James, *Abp.* Annales Veteris Testamenti a prima mundi origine deducti, una cum rerum Asiaticarum et Ægyptiacarum chronico a temporis historici principio usque ad Maccabaicorum initia producto. Londini, 1650-54. 2 v. f°.

Contents. Vol. 1. Ad annum a. Chr. 176. 2. In qua præter Maccabaicam et Novi Testamenti historiam Imperii Romanorum Cæsarum ortus rerumque in Asia et Ægypto chronicon usque ad Vespasiani initia atque extremum Templi et Reipublicæ Judaicæ excidium, deductum.

— *Eng.* Annals of the world, cont. the historie of the Old and New Testament, *etc.* London, 1658. f°.

— De Macedonum et Asianorum anno solari. (*In* **Gronovius,** J. Thesaurus Græcarum antiquitatum, v. 9. 1701.)

— Prayers for the dead. (*In* **Tracts** for the times, v. 3. 1840.)

— Aikin, J. Lives of J. Selden and Abp. Usher. London, 1812. 8°.

— Niceron, J. P. (*In his* Mém., v. 5. 1872; *and, Germ.*, v. 1. 1749.)

Usher, John. Deed to the colony of Massachusetts Bay. — Gorges, *Sir* F. Deed to J. Usher. (*In* **Maine Hist. Soc.** Col., v. 2. 1847.)

Usher, Rebecca R. Moore, F. (*In his* Women of the war. 1866.)

Usher, Wm. Geology and palæontology, in connection with human origins. (*In* Nott, J. G., *and* **Gliddon,** G. R. Types of mankind. 1854.)

Usher family. Whitmore, W. H. Brief genealogy of the Usher family of New Eng. Boston, 1869. 8°. (B 1962)

Usiglio, Angelo. La donna. Brus., 1838. 12°.

Usinger, Rudolf. Zur Beurtheilung Heinrich des Zweiten. (*In* **Historische** Zeitschrift, v. 8. 1862.) — Die Zerstörung Magdeburgs. (*In* v. 13.) — Gneisenau. (*In* v. 14.) — Thomas Buckle. (*In* v. 19.) Der Haushalt der Stadt Hamburg im 14. Jahr. (*In* v. 24. 1870.)

Usnach, *Sons of.* *See* **Deirdri.**

Ussel, — *vicomte* de. Ventilation du palais de l'Exposition. (*In* **France.** *Com. Imp. de l'Expos.* de 1867. Rapports, v. 8.)

Usserius, Jacobus. *See* **Ussher,** J.

Ussher, George Neville. Elements of English grammar; added, a concise treatise on rhetoric. 2d Amer. ed. Exeter, 1796. 8°.

Ussher, James. *See* **Usher,** J.

Ustariz, Geronymo de. Théorie et pratique du commerce et de la marine; tr. libre sur l'espagnol sur la 2e éd. de ce livre à Madrid en 1742, par F. Veron de Forbonnais. Paris, 1753. 4°.

Ustrialof, N. [Istoritcheskoe ovozrenie Nikolaia I. St. Petersburg,] 1847. 8°.

— O monastuirskik, *etc.*: Monastic property in Russia.] (*In* **St. Petersburg.** Ac. Sci. Mém., 6e sér., Sci. pol., v. 4. 1840.)

Usufruct. Pellat, C. A. Traduction du livre VII des Pandectes, accompagnée d'un commentaire; précédée d'un exposé des principes générales du droit de propriété, et particulièrement de l'usufruit. Paris, 1837. 8°. (B 1859)

Note. The 'traduction' is wanting.

Usumare, Martino, *continuator.* *See* **Caffaro,** Annales Genuenses.

Usuri River. Budichtchef, —. La région de l'Oussouri. (*In* **Paris.** Soc. de Géographie. Bulletin, 5e sér., v. 15. 1868.)

Usurier, L'; comédie. *See* **Sumarocof,** A.

Usury. *History.* Murray, J. B. C. History of usury. Phila., 1866. 8°.

— Saumaise, C. De modo usurarum. Lugd. Bat., *ex officina Elseviriorum*, 1639. 8°.

— Formey, J. H. S. Examen de l'usure suivant les principes du droit naturel. (*In* **Berlin.** Ak. d. Wiss. Abh., 1749.)

— Smith, H. Examination of usury; sermon. [London,] 1751. 8°. (C 18)

— Onslow, A. Substance of [his] speech, 23d of May, 1816, on the bill to repeal the laws which regulate or restrain the rate of interest. (*In* **Pamphleteer,** 1816; v. 8 *of* B 838)

— Hay, G. Speech in support of a bill to repeal all the laws concerning usury. Richmond, 1817. 8°. (B 1545)

— Savigny, F. K. von. Ueber den Zinswucher des M. Brutus. (*In* **Berlin.** Ak. d. Wiss. Abh., 1818-19.)

— Bentham, J. Defence of usury, showing the impolicy of the present legal restraints on the terms of pecuniary bargains; added, a letter to Adam Smith on the discouragement opposed by the above restraints to the progress of inventive industry. 4th ed., added, 3d ed., Protest against law-taxes. London, 1818. 12°.

— - *Same.* (*In his* Works, v. 3. 1843.)

— - *Same.* Added, a letter to A. Smith on discouragements opposed by above restraints to inventive industry. N. Y., 1837. 12°. (C 297)

— Dormer, J. Usury explained; or, Conscience quieted in the case of putting out money at interest; by Philopenes [pseudon.]. (*In* **Pamphleteer,** 1818; v. 11 of B 838)

— Cooke, E. Thoughts on the expediency of repealing the usury laws. (*In* **Pamphleteer,** 1819; v. 13 of B 838)

— Vindication of the laws limiting the rate of interest from the objections of J. Bentham. Richmond, 1820. 12°.

— Maugham, R. Treatise on the principles of the usury laws. (*In* **Pamphleteer,** 1824; v. 23 of B 838)

— McCulloch, J. R. Interest made equity. N. Y., 1826. 8°. (B 1545)

— Blazy, A. Questions sur le prêt à usure, les intérets du prêt, et les décisions romaines du 18 août 1830. Paris, 1837. 12°.

— Dew, T. R. Essay on the interest of money and the policy of laws against usury. Shellbanks, Va., 1834. 4°. (A 40)

— Mass. *General Court.* Report of committee rel. to banks and to the law against usury, Mar. 6. Boston, 1834. 8°. (B 1545)

— Whipple, J. Importance of usury laws. [1836. Boston, 1850.] 8°. (B 1545)

— - *Same.* Free trade in money; or, Note-shaving the cause of fraud, poverty, and ruin. Boston, 1855. 8°. (B 1515)

— Bolles, J. A. Treatise on usury and usury laws. Boston, 1837. 8°.

— - *Other copies.* (B 1142, 1545, 1652)

— Proudhon, P. J., *and* Bastiat, F. Intérêt et principal. Paris, 1850. 18°.

— Brooks, L. Short and easy method for obtaining the average time upon bills, notes, *etc.*, based upon interest at 6 per cent. *n.p.*, 1851. 8°.

— Courcelle Seneuil, J. G. Intérêt et usure. (*In* **Thévenin,** E. Cours d'économie industrielle, v. 4. 1866.)

Tables.

— Tables of interest. *t.p.w.* [17—.] 8°.

— Webb, B. Complete annuitant; tables of interest. London, 1762. 16°.

— Thomson, J. Tables of interest. 6th ed. London, 1794. 16°.

— Rowlett, J. Rowlett's tables of discount or interest. Phila., 1802. 4°.

— Hartshorn, J. Commercial tables. Boston, 1852. f°.

See also **Genoa.**

Ut de poitrine, L'; par A. de Lavergne. Paris, 1866. 18°.

Utah. *See* **Great Salt Lake**; — **Mormons.**

Uterus. Hunter, W. Anatomia uteri humani gravidi, tabulis illustrata. [1774.] London, 1851. f°. (Sydenham Soc.)
— Rigby, E. Essay on the uterine hemorrhage, *etc.* [1775.] 3d ed. Phila., 1786. 8°. (B 822)
— - *Same, extract.* (*In* Mass. Med. Soc. Med. comm., v. 1. 1808.)
— - Essay on uterine hæmorrhage. 5th ed. London, 1811. 8°.
— Pasta, A. Traité des pertes de sang chez les femmes enceintes et des accidens rel. aux flux de l' utérus qui succèdent à l'accouchement; tr., avec notes, par J. L. Alibert. Paris, an VIII [1800]. 2 v. 8°.
— Burns, J. Uterine hæmorrhage. London, 1807. 8°.
— - *Same.* (*In his* Obstetrical works. 1809.)
— Holyoke, E. A. History of the retroverted uterus. (*In* Mass. Med. Soc. Med. comm., v. 1. 1808.)
— Prescott, O. Case of ruptured uterus. (*In* Mass. Med. Soc. Med. comm., v. 1. 1108.)
— Drayton, C. Essay on the partial and concealed inversion of the uterus. Phila., 1809. 8°. (B 736)
— Leroux, L. C. P. Observations sur les pertes de sang des femmes en couche. 2e éd. Dijon, 1810. 8°.
— Merriman, S. Retroversion of the womb. London, 1810. 8°.
— Fisher, J. Use of sulphate of copper in uterine hæmorrhage. (*In* Mass. Med. Soc. Med. comm., v. 2. 1813.)
— Stewart, D. Uterine hæmorrhage. London, 1816. 8°.
— King, J. Analysis of extra-uterine fœtation, and of the retroversion of gravid uterus. *n.p.*, 1818. 8°. (E 59)
— Boivin, M. A. V. G., *and* Dugès, A. Maladies de l'utérus. Paris, 1833. 2 v. 8° *and* Atlas f°.
— - *Eng.* Diseases of the uterus; tr. by G. O. Heming. London, 1834. 8° *and* Atlas f°.
— Lisfranc, J. Diseases of the uterus [1833], ed. by H. Pauly; tr. by G. H. Lodge. Boston, 1839. 8°.
— Channing, W. Discourse on irritable uterus. (*In* Mass. Med. Soc. Med. comm., v. 5. 1836.)
— - *Another copy.* (B 1550)
— Hull, A. G. Brief account of the application and use of the utero-abdominal supporter. N. Y., 1836. 8°. (B 1555)
— Duparcque, F. Traité sur les altérations de la matrice. 2e éd. Paris, 1839. 8°.
— Ashwell, S. On incision in cases of occlusion and rigidity of the uterus. (*In* Dunglison, R. Med. and surg. monog., v. 3. 1840.)
— Lee, R. Anatomy of the nerves of the uterus. London, 1841. f°.
— Lever, J. C. W. Organic diseases of the uterus. Newburg, N. Y., 1845. 8°.
— Simpson, J. Y. Diagnosis and treatment of retroversion of the unimpregnated uterus. Dublin, 1848. 8°. (B 1562)
— Coale, W. E. Treatise on uterine displacements. Boston, 1852. 8°.
— - *Another copy.* (B 1551)
— Lee, R. Clinical reports of ovarian and uterine diseases. London, 1853. 12°.
— Lyman, G. H. Non-malignant diseases of the uterus; Boylston prize essay. Boston, 1854. 8°. (B 1557)
— Storer, H. R. Elm tents for the dilation of the cervix uteri. Boston Med. and surg. journal, Nov. 8. *n.t.p.* [1855.] 8°. (B 1562)
— Read, W. Influence of the placenta upon the development of the uterus during pregnancy. From the American journal of medical science, April 1858. *n.t.p.* 8°. (B 1561)
— Priestley, W. O. Development of the gravid uterus. London, 1860. 8°.
— Sims, J. M. Clinical notes on uterine surgery. N. Y., 1866. 8°.

See also Fecundity; — Fœtus; — Generative organs; — Midwifery; — Placenta; — Ovariotomy; — Woman (*Medicine*).

Uterine supporter. Betts, *Mrs.* J. Utility of the uterine supporter. 5th ed. Phila., 1847. 8°. (B 1547)

Uti possidetis and status quo; political satire. London, 1807. 8°. (B 721)

Utica, *N. Y.* Map. 1835.

Utica Insane Asylum. Chase, *Rev.* H. Two years and four months in a lunatic asylum. Saratoga Springs, 1868. 16°.

Utica Republican State Convention. Two speeches, [by C. G. Haines]; with Proceedings of the Convention. and an app. [in favor of De Witt Clinton]. N. Y., 1824. 8°. (B 1492)

Utile giornale per l'anno bisestil 1832. Milano, *n.d.* 16°.

Utilitarianism. Mill, J. S. Utilitarianism. London, 1863. 8°.
— *Same.* (*In his* Dissertations and discussions, v. 3. 1865.)
Note. Reprinted from Fraser's magazine, v. 64. 1861.
— Grote, J. Examination of the utilitarian philosophy; ed. by J. B. Mayor. Camb., 1870. 8°.

Utility, The, of country banks considered. London, 1802. 8°. (B 782)

Utino, Leonardus de. *See* **Leonardus.**

Utopia. *See* **More,** *Sir* T.

Utopie, ou règne du grand Selrahcengil par C. J. de Ligne. (*In his* Œuvres, v. 1. 1809; 1860.)

Utrecht. Blondeel, V. J. Beschryving der stad Utrecht. Utrecht, 1757. 8°.
— Hoynck van Papendrecht, C. P. Catalogus historico-chronologicus præpositorum et decanorum quinque ecclesiarum Ultrajectensium. — Catalogus abbatum Sancti Pauli in civitate Ultrajectina. (*In his* Vita Viglii ab Aytta Zuichemi, v. 3, pt. 1. 1743.)
— *Maps.* Blaeu, W. Ultrajectum dominium. [Amst., 16—.] (E 78, no. 54)
— - Map. *n.p.*, [17—]. f°. (E 65)

Utrecht. Provinciaal Utrechtsche Genootschap. [Verhandelingen.] Utrecht, 1827. 8°.
Namely. Bennet, R. G., *and* Wijk, J. van. Verhandeling over de Nederlandsche ontdekkingen in Amerika, Australië, de Indiën, en de Poollanden.

Utrecht, Treaties of. Tractatus translationis seu cessionis et ditiones Ultrajectinæ. (*In* Hoynck van Papendrecht, C. P. Vita Viglii ab Aytta Zuichemi, v. 3, pt. 1. 1743.)
— Colbert, J. B., *marq. de Torcy.* Mémoires pour servir à l'hist. des négociations depuis le traité de Riswick jusqu'à la paix d'Utrecht. La Haye, 1756. 3 v. 12°.
— Recueil des traitez de paix, de commerce, navigation, et marine, conclus à Utrecht le 11 avril 1713. Lyons, [176-]. 12°.
— Sevelinges, L. de. Précis de la paix d'Utrecht. (*In* Dubois, G., *card.* Mém., v. 1. 1815.)
— Giraud, C. La bataille de Denain et la paix d'Utrecht. (*In* Revue d. D. Mondes, oct. 1870.)

Utrecht University. Cousin, V. Visite à l'Université d'Utrecht. (*In* Revue d. D. Mondes, fév. 1837.)

Utterson, Edward Vernon. Catalogue of [his] library sold March, 1857. [London,] 1857. 8°.

Uvarof, Sergei Semenovitch. Mémoire sur les tragiques grecs. (*In* St. Petersburg. Ac. Sci. Mém., v. 10. 1821-22.)

Uwins, Daniel, *M. D.* Modern maladies, and present state of medicine; anniv. oration before the Medical Soc. of London. (*In* Pamphleteer, 1819; v. 13 of B 838)

Uxbridge. Dugdale, *Sir* W. Narrative of the treaty at U. in 1644. (*In his* View of late troubles. 1644.)

Uz, Johann Peter. Poetische Werke; hrsg. von C. F. Weisse. Wien, 1804. 2 v. 8°.
Contents. Vol. 1. Vorbericht. — Biographie, hrsg. von Schlichtegroll. — Versuch über die Kunst stäts fröhlich zu seyn. — Der Sieg des Liebesgottes. — Briefe. 2. Lyrische Gedichte.

Uz de Velasco, Alfonso. *See* **Velazquez de Velasco, A.**

Uztariz, Geronymo de. *See* **Ustariz,** G. de.

Uzzano, Niccolò da. Versi predicendo la mutazione dello stato. (*In* Archivio storico italiano, v. 4, pt. 1. 1843.)

V., J. Letter to Lord Viscount Althorp. London, 1831. 8°. (B 930)

V., J. M. D. Manuel moral. (*In* Elémens de politesse, *etc.* 1781.)

V., L. S. CATALOGUE [de ses] livres, la vente 22 déc. Paris, an XIII, 1804. 8°. (B 890)

V., M. L. Licensed houses, *etc.* *See* Sargent, L. M. (B 1074, 1763, 1783, 1802, 2014)

V., P. Campagne du roy, 1667. *See* Visconti, P.

V., R. On the interests of the Church of England. 2d ed. (*In* Pamphleteer, 1822; v, 19 of B 838)

Vaca de Guzman y Manrique, José María. Las naves de Cortes destruidas. (*In* Rosell, C. Poemas epicos, v. 2. 1854; v. 29 of Aribau. Bibl.)

Vacances, Les; comédie. *See* Dancourt, F. C.

Vacances de Camille, Les; par H. Murger. Nouv. éd. Paris, 1862. 18°.

Vacances de la comtesse, Les; par E. About. Paris, 1865. 8°. (La Vieille Roche.)

Vacation tourists. *See* Galton, F.

Vacchero, Giulio Cesare. TORRE, G. R. della. Congiúra di V. (*In* Archivio stor. ital., app., v. 3. 1846.)

Vaccination.

Note. In the following works * added to the title means that the work is opposed to vaccination.

— JURIN, J., *M.D.* Account of success of inoculating small pox in Gr. Brit. 2d ed. London, 1724. 8°. (B 476)

— BOLAINE, N. Remarks on Delafaye's vindication of his sermon, 'Inoculation an indefensible practice'. London, 1754. 8°.

— ADAMS, J. Acute contagions, partic. the variolous and vaccine. [1795.] (*In his* Morbid poisons. 1807.)

— JENNER, E. Further observations on the variolæ vaccinæ or cowpox. London, 1799. 4°. (E 272)

— - Instructions for vaccine inoculation. *n.p.*, [1799]. 4°. (B 1563)

— CUMING, R. Address on the cow-pox inoculation; advantages over the small-pox inoculation. Romsey, [18—]. 8°. (B 821)

— COMPARATIVE statements of facts rel. to the cow-pox; published by Drs. Jenner and Woodville. London, 1800. 4°. (E 272)

— DUNNING, R. Some obs. on vaccination. London, 1800. 8°.

— FERMOR, W. Reflections on cow pox. Oxford, 1800. 8°.

— - *Another copy.* (E 119)

— RUSSELL, W. T. Diss. med. inaug. de vaccina. Edin., 1800. 8°. (B 823)

— WATERHOUSE, B. Prospect of exterminating the small-pox; hist. of the variolæ vaccinæ or kine-pox, commonly called cow-pox. Camb., 1800. 8°. (B 736, 821)

— - *Same.* Pt. 2. Camb., 1802. 8°. (B 812)

— WOODVILLE, W. Obs. on the cow-pox. London, 1800. 8°. (B 821)

— AIKIN, C. R. Concise view of facts conc. cow-pox. London, 1801. 16°.

— CARRO, J. de. Obs. sur la vaccination. [1801.] 2e éd. corr. et augm. Vienne, 1802. 8°.

— CREASER, T. Evidences of the utility of vaccine inoculation. Bath, 1801. 18°. (C 267)

— LETTSOM, J. C. Obs. on the cow pock. [London,] 1801. 4°.

— - *Same.* [London,] 1801. 8°. (B 782, 821)

— LOY, J. G. Expériences sur l'origine de la vaccine [1801]; tr. de l'anglois par J. de Carro. Vienne, 1802. 12°. (D 38)

— PARIS. SOC. DE MÉDECINE. Primer informe sobre la inoculacion de la vacuna; tr. del fr. Madrid, 1801. 8°. (D 39)

— MURRAY, C. Debates in Parliament resp. the Jennerian discovery, [1802–07]; with report of the Roy. Coll. of Physicians. London, 1808. 8°. (B 717)

— BRYCE, J. Practical obs. on the inoculation of cow pox. [1802.] 2d ed. Edin., 1809. 8°.

— DENNEY, T. G. Diss. med. inaug. de vaccina. Edin., 1802. 8°. (B 823)

— LETTSOM, J. C. Address on variolous and vaccine inoculations. [From the Gentleman's mag., Nov. 1802.] London, 1803. 8°. (B 812, 821)

— DESPORTES, F. Précis des travaux des comités de vaccine du département du Haut-Rhin, [1803–04]. Colmar, [1804]. 4°. (A 10)

— INSTITUTION for the extermination of the small-pox. *n.t.p.* [1803.] 8°. (B 813)

— LETTSOM, J. C. Apology for differing in opinion from the authors of the Monthly and Critical reviews. London, 1803. 8°. (B 812, 826)

— - *Same.* 2d ed. London, 1804. 8°. (B 821)

— - Appeal to the calm reflection of the authors of the Critical review, on abusive language, *etc.* London, 1803. 8°. (B 814, 821, 826)

— PARIS. SOCIÉTÉ CENTRALE DE VACCINE. Rapport. Paris, 1803. 8°.

— ROYAL JENNERIAN SOCIETY. Acc. of the first festival of the Soc. for the extermination of the small-pox. [London, 1803.] 8°. (B 812, 821)

— - Address; with instructions for vaccine inoculation, *etc.* London, 1803. 8°. (B 969)

— WARREN, T. A. Address on cow-pox or vaccine inoculation. London, 1803. 8°. (B 812, D 59)

— CARRO, J. de. Histoire de la vaccination en Turquie, Grèce, *etc.* Vienne, 1804. 8°.

— HUME, G. Obs. on angina pectoris, cow pox, and gout. Dublin, 1804. 8°.

— JENNER, E. On the varieties and modifications of the vaccine pustule, occasioned by an herpetic skin. [1804.] Cheltenham, 1806. 4°. (E 272)

— LETTSOM, J. C. Memoir of E. Jenner; from oration, 1804. *n.t.p.* [London, 1804.] 8°. (B 821)

— - *Same.* London, 1805. 8°. (B 813)

— MOSELEY, B. Treatise on lues bovilla or cow-pox. [1804.] 2d ed. London, 1805. 8°. *

— RING, J. Answer [to W.] Goldson, proving that vaccination is a permanent security against small-pox. London, 1804. 8°. (B 821)

— JENNER, G. C. Evidence resp. Dr. Jenner's discovery of vaccination. London, 1805. 8°.

— LETTSOM, J. C. Expositions on the inoculation of small pox and of the cow pock. London, 1805. 8°. (B 813, 814, 821)

— MERRIMAN, S. Obs. on some late attempts to depreciate the value and efficacy of vaccine inocculation. London, 1805. 8°.

— PARIS. SOCIÉTÉ CENTRALE DE VACCINE. Disc. par [J. I.] Guillotin; [avec] rapport par [H. M.] Husson. *n.t.p.* [Paris, 1805.] 8°

— RING, J. Answer to Dr. Moseley, cont. a defence of vaccination. London, 1805. 8°.

— ROGERS, W. R. Examination of evidence rel. to cow-pox, [before] the House of Commons; added, a letter to the author from J. Birch. 2d ed. London, 1805. 8°. *

— SQUIRRELL, R. Observations on cow-pox and small-pox inoculation. London, 1805. 8°. *

— PARIS. SOCIÉTÉ CENTRALE DE VACCINE. Rapport sur les vaccinations en France en 1806–07; [par H. M. Husson]. Paris, 1809. 8°.

— BIRCH, J. Serious reasons for objecting to the practice of vaccination. Lond., 1806. 8°. *

— BLAIR, W. The vaccine contest; or facts and arguments resp. vaccine inoculation. London, 1806. 8°.

— MOSELEY, B. Commentaries on lues bovilla or cow-pox. 2d ed. London, 1806. 8°. *

— RING, J. Letter to Birch in answer to his late pamphlet against vaccination. London, 1806. 8°. (E 119)

— THORNTON, R. J. Defence of vaccination. London, 1806. 8°.

— WILLAN, R. On vaccine inoculation. London, 1806. 4°.

— - Answers to all objections against cow pox. 5th ed., with add. London, 1807. 8°. (B 828)

— ADAMS, J. Popular view of vaccine inoculation. London, 1807. 16°.

— BELL, G. Treatise on cow-pox. 2d ed. Edin., London, 1807. 16°.

— RING, J. A Rowland for an Oliver; answer to Dr. Mosely, and Mr. Birch; cont. a defence of vaccination. London, 1807. 8°. (B 717)

— BOWEN, P. Facts rel. to small-pox and cow pock, 1808. (*In* Mass. Med. Soc. Med. comm., v. 2. 1813.)

— MASS. MED. SOC. Report on vaccination. (*In their* Med. comm., v. 1. 1808.)

— MURRAY, C. Answer to Highmore's objections to the bill to prevent the spreading of the small-pox, *etc.* London, 1808. 8°. (B 717)
— VACCINE phantasmagoria, The. London, 1808. 4°. (A 48)
— MILTON, *Mass.* Collection of papers rel. to the transactions of Milton to promote inoculation. Boston, 1809. 8°. (B 139, 436, 1558)
— UEBERLACHER, G. Nachricht über die Wirksamkeit und Nutzlichkeit der Kuhpocken-Impfung mit dem Schorfe. Wien, 1809. 16°. (C 271)
— VACCINE scourge. No. 2. Lond., 1809. 8°. (B 1563)
— BATEMAN, T. Progress and present state of vaccination. [1811.] York, 1812. 12°. (C 267)
— NATIONAL VACCINE ESTABLISHMENT. Report. [London, 1811.] 8°. (B 787)
— FANCHER, —, *M.D.* Progress of vaccination in America. (*In* **Mass. Hist. Soc.** Col., v. 14. 1816.)
— MED. SOC. OF THE CITY AND CO. OF N. Y. Report on the epidemic small pox and chicken pox, explanatory of causes of supposed failures of vaccine disease. N. Y., 1816. 8°. (B 814, 826, 831)
— JENNER, E. Letter on the effects of vaccination, in preserving from the small-pox. Phila., 1818. 8°. (B 833, E 59)
— MALDEN, J., *M.D.* Remarks on the cow-pox. London, 1820. 8°. (B 827)
— SOARES, J. M. Sobre os trabalhos da Instituição Vaccinica, 1820. (*In* **Lisbon. Ac. d. Sci.** Mem., v. 7. 1821.)
— JENNER, E. Letter to C. H. Parry on the influence of artificial eruptions in certain diseases, [1821]. London, 1822. 4°. (A 63, E 272)
— RODRIGUES DA SILVEIRA, F. E. Acerca dos trabalhos da Inst. Vaccinica, 1821. (*In* **Lisbon. Ac. d. Sci.** Mem., v. 8. 1823.)
— SALLION, B. Examen comparatif de la petite-vérole et de la vaccine. Nantes, 1822. 16°.
— FISHER, J. D. Description of small pox, varioloid, cow pox, chicken pox. Bost., 1829. 4°.
— — *Same.* 2d ed. Boston, 1834. 4°.
— VACCINATION and revaccination; the result of five years' experience in the kingdom of Wirtemberg. Repr. from no. 13 of the Brit. and for. med. rev. London, 1839. 8°. (B 1153)
— CEELY, R. Obs. on the variolæ vaccinæ; with an acc. of experiments in the vaccination, utro-vaccination, *etc.*, of cows. Worcester, *Eng.*, 1840. 8°.
— GIBBS, J. Copy of a letter, June 30, 1855, to the Board of Health, entitled 'Compulsory vaccination'. [London, 1856.] f°. * (A 66)
— — More words on vaccination. London, 1856. 12°. * (C 268)
— ADAMS, H. Vaccination, 1858. (*In* **Mass. Med. Soc.** Med. comm., v. 9. 1860.)
— CLARK, H. G. Letter enclosing a descr. of the vaccine vesicle and instructions rel. to vaccination from the National vaccine establishment, London. *n.t.p.* [Boston, 1859.] 8°. (B 1548)
— N. Y. EASTERN DISPENSARY OF THE CITY OF N. Y. Vaccine; information on vaccination. N. Y., 1859. 8°. (B 1563)
— SEATON, E. C. Handbook of vaccination. London, 1868. 16°.
— BACON, F., *and others.* Vaccination; a report, 1869. (*In* **Amer. Soc. Sci. Assoc.** Trans., v. 2. 1870.)
— SMITH, E. The value of vaccination. (*In* **Nat. Assoc. Prom. Soc. Sci.** Trans., 1869.)

See also **Epidemics**; — **Inoculation**; — **Small-pox**; — **Varioloid**; — *also* **Jenner, E.**; — **Montagu,** *Lady* **M. W.** (Letters and works.)

Vaccine phantasmagoria, The. London, 1808. 4°. (A 48)
Vaccine scourge. No. 2: cont. a new song, The blacksmith's progress, or, I and my partner Joe. London, 1809. 8°. (B 1563)
Vaccolini, Domenico. Biografia di G. Melandri. (*In* **Hercolani, A.** Biog. rom., v. 1. 1834.) — Biografia di M. Attendoli. (*In* v. 3. 1836.)
Vacherot, Etienne. La démocratie. 2e éd., augm. Brux., 1860. 8°.
— La Sorbonne. (*In* **Paris guide**, v. 1. 1867.)
— Several articles.] (*In* **Revue d. D. Mondes**, juin 1868–jan. 1875.)
— JANET, P. La philosophie de Vacherot. (*In his* La crise philos. 1865.)
Vacquerie, Auguste. Profils et grimaces. Paris, 1856. 18°.

Vadianus, Joachim. *See* **Watt, J.** von.
Vadimonium. ZENGER, F. X. Ueber das vadimonium der Römer. Landshut, 1826. 12°.
Vadis, Egidius de (**Du Wés** *or* **Du Guez**, Giles de). Dialogus inter naturam et filium philosophiæ. (*In* **Zetzner, L.** Theat. chem., v. 2. 1613; — *and in* **Manget, J. J.** Bibl. chem., v. 2. 1702.)
— Tabula, diversorum metallorum vocabula quibus usi sunt veteres ad artem celandam, explicans. (*In* **Zetzner, L.** Theat. chem., v. 2. 1613.)
Væ *or* **ve.** WILLIAMS, J. Force of the Latin prefix væ or ve in the composition of nouns and adjectives. (*In* **Roy. Soc. of Edin.** Trans., v. 13. 1836.)
Vænius, Otho. *See* **Veen, O.** van.
Vaez, Jean Nicolas Gustave van **Nieuwenhuysen**, *called.* Le capitaine Henriot. 1866. *See* **Sardou, V.**
— Mosquita la sorcière. *See* **Scribe, A. E.** (E 9)
Vagabond adventures; by R. Keeler. Bost., 1870. 12°.
Vagabonds. AWDELEY, J. The fraternitye of vacabondes; [with] Caveat or warening for vagabones, by T. Harman; ed. by E. Viles and F. J. Furnivall. London, 1869. 8°. (Early Eng. Text Soc. Ex. ser., v. 9.)
— LIBER vagatorum;] book of vagabonds and beggars; ed. by M. Luther in 1528; tr., with introd. and notes, by J. C. Hotten. London, 1860. 16°.
Vagabonds, The, and other poems; by J. T. Trowbridge. Boston, 1869. 12°.
Vagina. OSGOOD, J. Preternatural obstructions of the vagina. (*In* **Mass. Med. Soc.** Med. comm., v. 1. 1808.)
— WARREN, J. M. Cases of occlusion of the vagina. Boston, 1853. 8°.
— — *Another copy.* (E 70)
— HOMANS, J., *Jr.* The pathology and treatment of vaginal cystocele. (*In* **Mass. Med. Soc.** Pub., v. 2. 1867.)
Vagnone, *conte* Antonio. CARENA, G. Notizie dell' accademico A. V. (*In* **Turin. Ac. d. Sci.** Mem., v. 37. 1834.)
Vahram. Chronicle of the Armenian kingdom in Cilicia during the Crusades. (*In* **Neumann, K. F.** Trans., 1831.)
Vai, Stefano. Lamento di Cecco da Montui. (*In* **Trucchi, F.** Poesie ital., v. 4. 1847.)
Vai language. ROLA, —. Narrative in the Vai language. London, 1851. 12°.
Vaiasseida; poema heroico. *See* **Cortese, G. C.**
Vaiden, Thomas J. Commencement of a practical syst. of medicine. Mobile, 1845. 8°. (B 1563)
— Domestic practice; medical tract to illustrate preceding publications. Gainesville, 1844. 8°. (B 1563)
— Treatise on domestic practice. Gainesville, 1844. 8°. (B 1563)
Vail, Alfred. The American electro-magnetic telegraph; and a desc. of all telegraphs. Phila., 1845. 8°.
— Memorial to the Senate, *etc.* *See* **MORSE, S. F. B.**, *and others.* (B 1503)
Vail, Eugène A. Réponse à quelques imputations contre les États-Unis. Paris, 1837. 8°. (B 1134)
Vail, Stephen M., *D.D.* The Bible against slavery; with replies to J. H. Hopkins, N. Lord, *etc.* Concord, N. H., 1864. 8°. (B 1472)
Vaillance et Richard; par J. Sandeau. Paris, N. Y., 1846. 16°.
Note. From **Revue d. D. Mondes**, sept., oct., déc. 1849, jan. 1850.
Vaillant, François le. *See* **Le Vaillant, F.**
Vaillant, Jean Baptiste Philibert. Extrait d'un rapport à l'empereur, 16 juin 1854, au sujet de la création de plusieurs communes de plein exercice dans l'Algérie. — Rapport présenté à l'empereur sur la situation de l'Algérie, 1853. (*In* **Paris. Soc. de Géog.** Bul., 4e sér., v. 8. 1854.)
— Horary variations for the barometer; [tr. from the Archives de la Commission Scientifique du Mexique, 1865;] with notes by Prof. Henry. (*In* **Smithsonian Inst.** Reports, 1866.)
Vaillant, Jean Foy, *b.* 1632, *d.* 1706. Numismata imperatorum Romanorum. Lut. Paris., 1692. 2 v. 4°.
— NICERON, J. P. (*In his* Mém., 1727; *and, Germ.*, v. 4. 1751.)

Vaillant, Jean François Foy, *b.* 1665, *d.* 1708. NICERON, J. P. (*In his* Mém., v. 22. 1733; *and, Germ.*, v. 16. 1758.)

Vaillant, Sébastien. Sermo de structura florum; [Lat. et Gallice]. Lugd. Bat., 1718. 4°.
— NICERON, J. P. (*In his* Mém., v. 8. 1729; *and, Germ.*, v. 8. 1753.)

Vaiseshika. KANÂDA. Die Lehrspruche der Vaiçeshika-Philosophie; aus dem Sanskrit übers. und erläut. von E. Röer. (*In* **Zeitschrift** d. D. morg. Ges., v. 21, 22. 1867, 68.)

Vaisse, Jean Louis. Une voix sortie des cieux. Paris, 1852. 8°.

Valacrius, Joannes. *See* **Walker, J.**

Valadier, André. *See* **Valladier, A.**

Valadier, Giuseppe. Opere di architettura e di ornamento. Roma, 1833. f°.
Note. Includes 'Nuova facciata della chiesa de San Rocco' separately paged.

Valadier, Luigi M. Raccolta di ornati antichi. Roma, 1829. f°.

Valaresso, Fantino. AGOSTINI, G. degli. (*In his* Notizie degli scrittori viniz., v. 1. 1754.)

Valaresso, Zaccaria. Rutzvanscad il giovine. (*In* **Raccolta** di trag. scr. nel. secolo 18, v. 2. 1825.)

Valbezen, A. de (*pseud. le major* Fridolin). Récits d'hier et d'aujourd'hui. Paris, 1855. 18°.
Contents. La queue du chien d'Alcibiade. — La retraite des dix milles. — La veillée au chateau.
— Various articles.] (*In* **Revue** d. D. Mondes, juil. 1851–jan. 1861.)

Valbonnays, Jean Pierre Moret de Bourchenu, *marquis* de. NICERON, J. P. (*In his* Mém., v. 19. 1732; *and, Germ.*, v. 15. 1757.)

Valbuena, Bernardo de. *See* **Balbuena, B. de.**

Valbuena, Manuel. Diccionario latino-español. 7a ed., aum. por V. Salvá. Paris, 1832. 8°.

Valckenaer, Jan. Oratio de schola Cuiaciana, XXII Martii MDCCLXXXII. Franequeræ, 1782. 4°. (**A 6**)

Valckenaer, Lodewijk Kaspar. Animadversionum ad Ammonium libri; acc. specimen scholiorum ad Homerum ineditorum. Lugd. Bat., 1739. 4°.
— Diatribe de Aristobulo Judæo; acc. P. Wesselingii lectio publica; ed. J. Luzac. Lugd. Bat., 1806. 8°.
— Epistola ad M. Roverum. — Dissertatio de codice Leidensi. (*In* **Orsini, F.** Virgilius. 1747.)
— Observationes ad origines Græcas; et J. D. a Lennep De analogia linguæ Græcæ; recens. E. Scheidius. Traj. a. R., 1790. 8°.
— *Same.* Ed. alt. Traj. a. R., 1805. 8°.

Valckenburch, Lucas van. Linsum Austriæ, vulgo Lintz. *n.p.*, 1594. (**E 78**, no. 125)

Valcour, *pseud.* *See* **Plancher-Valcour, P. A. L. P.**

Valdengo, Gustavo Avogadro di. *See* **Avogadro di Valdengo, G.**

Valdenses. *See* **Waldenses.**

Valdepeiras; par [H. E. F. A.] Reybaud. Paris, 1864. 16°.

Valdepeñas, Rodrigo de. Glosa de las coplas de J. Manrique hechas a la muerte de R. Manrique. (*In* **Manrique, J.** Coplas. 1779.)

Valderrabaño, Manuel Perez. La angelomaquia, ó cayda de Luzbel. Valencia, 1786. 8°. (**D 36**)

Valdés, Juan de, *d.* 1540. Dos dialogos. *n.p.*, 1850. 8°.
— WIFFEN, B. B. Life and writings; with a tr. of his 110 considerations, by J. T. Betts. London, 1865. 8°.

Valdesso, Juan de. *See* **Valdés, J. de.**

Valdez, Francisco Travassos. Six years in Westtern Africa. London, 1861. 2 v. 8°.

Valdivia, Luis de. Relacion de lo que sucedio en la jornada que hicimos el gobernador deste reyno y yo desde Arauco á Paycavi á conducir las paces de Ilicura ultima regua de Tucapel y las de Puren y la Imperial. — CERDA, C. de la. Informe sobre el padre L. de V. (*In* **Gay, C.** Hist. de Chile, v. 2. 1852.)

Valdivia, Pedro de. Cartas a Carlos V. — CARTAS sobre V. (*In* **Gay, C.** Hist. de Chile, v. 1. 1846.)

Valdivielso, José de. El peregrino, acto sacramental. — Del hijo pródigo, acto sacramental. — La amistad en el peligro, acto sacramental. — De la Serrana de Plasencia, acto sacramental. — El hospital de los locos, acto sacramental. (*In* **Pedroso, E. G.** Autos sacramentales. 1865; v. 58 of Aribau. Bibl.)
— Vida y muerta de San Josef, esposo de nuestra Señora. (*In* **Rosell, C.** Poemas epicos, v. 2. 1854; v. 29 of Aribau. Bibl.)

Vale of false lovers. The. (*In* **Le Grand d'Aussy, P. J.** Fabliaux, v. 2. 1815.)

Valedictory address to the young gentlemen who commenced bachelor of arts at Yale Col., July 25. New Haven, 1776. 8°. (**B 655**)

Valedictory oration, commencement in New Jersey, Sept. 26. New York, 1759. 8°. (**B 994**)

Valencia, Martin de, *and others.* Carta al emperador. (*In* **Icazbalceta, J. G.** Col. de doc., v. 2. 1866.)

Valencia, *Spain.* ESCLAPÉS DE GIULLI, P. Resumen historial de la fundacion de Valencia; sus progressos, *etc.*, to 1738. Valencia, 1805. 4°.
— VILLARROYA, J. Disertacion sobre el origen del arte tipografico, y su introduccion en Valencia. Valencia, 1796. 8°.
— COLOMER, V. M. Sucesos de Valencia; desde 23 de mayo hasta 28 de junio 1808. Valencia, 1810. 8°.

Valencia. Real Sociedad Economica. Consideraciones sobre el hilado y torcido de la seda; memoria por J. Lapayese. Valencia, 1794. 4°.

Valenciennes, Achille. Histoire naturelle des poissons. *See* **Cuvier, G. L. C. F. D.**

Valenciennes, Henri de. Fondation de l'emp. latin de Constantinople. (*In* **Michaud** *and* **Poujoulat.** Col. des mém., v. 1. 1854.)

Valenciennes, Pierre Henri. Elémens de perspective pratique. Paris, 1820. 1 v. *and* plates 4°.

Valenciennes, *France.* MOSKOWA, J. N. N., *prince* de la. Le siége de V., [1677]. (*In* **Revue** d. D. Mondes, mai 1855.)
— MAP. Amst., [17—]. (**E 60**)

Valens, *Emp. of the West.* BROGLIE, A., *prince* de. (*In his* L'église et l'empire romain, v. 3. 1856.)

Valens, Petrus. NICERON, J. P. (*In his* Mém., v. 36. 1736.)

Valentia, *Viscount.* *See* **Annesly, G.**

Valentin, Basil. *See* **Valentinus, B.**

Valentin, Louis. Mémoire sur les fluxions de poitrine. Nancy, 1815. 8°.
— Notice biog. sur le docteur Jenner. Montpellier, 1805. 8°. (**B 1457**)
— *Same.* Notice hist. sur J. 2e éd. Nancy, 1824. 8°. (**B 1457**)
— Voyage médical en Italie, 1820; préc. d'une excursion au volcan du Mont-Vésuve, et aux ruines d'Herculanum et de Pompeia. Nancy, 1822. 8°.

Valentine, David Thomas. History of the city of New York. N. Y., 1853. 8°.
— Manual of the corporation of N. Y., 1842–45, 47, 49–54, 56–61, 63–65. N. Y., [1842]–65. 16° *and* 12°.

Valentine, James. Means of elementary education in Aberdeen. — Ancient music or song schools of Scotland. (*In* **Nat. Assoc.** Prom. Soc. Sci. Trans., 1863.)

Valentine, T. W. Words fitly spoken. (*In* **Amer. Inst.** of Instr. Lect., 1858.)

Valentine, Wm. J. Report on the munitions of war. (*In* **U. S.** *Commissioners for Paris Expos.* 1867. Reports, v. 7.)

Valentine; par George Sand [Mme. Dudevant]. Paris, 1856. 12°.

Valentinelli, Giuseppe, *il abate.* Bibliografia dalmata, tratta da' codici dalla Marciana. Venezia, 1845. 8°.
— Diplomatarium Portusnaonense; series documentorum, 1276–1514. Wien, 1865. 8°. (Fontes rerum Austr., 2. Abth., 24. Bd.)

Valentine's eve; by Mrs. A. Opie. Boston, 1827. 12°.

Valentini, Decio. Biog. di G. Morgagni. (*In* **Hercolani**, A. Biografie di Rom. illustri, v. 1. 1834.) — Biog. di G. Mercuriali. (*In* v. 2. 1835.)

Valentini, Georg Wilhelm, *Freiherr* von. Précis des dernières guerres des Russes contre les Turcs; tr. par E. de la Côste. Paris, 1828. 8°.

Valentini, Michael Bernhard. Amphitheatrum zootomicum, exhibens historiam animalium anatomicam. Francof. a. M., 1720. f°.

— Constitutio epidemica Hassiaca, 1693-95. (*In* **Sydenham**, T. Opera, v. 1. 1723.)

Valentinian; tragedy. *See* **Beaumont**, F., *and* **Fletcher**, J.

Valentinians. Tertullianus, Q. S. F. Treatise against the V.s; concise account of the theology of that sect. (*In his* Writings, v. 2. 1870.)

Valentinianus I., *Emp. of Rome*. Broglie, A., *prince* de. (*In his* L'église et l'empire rom., v. 3. 1856.)

Valentinianus III. Novellæ leges. 1766. *See* **Theodosius** II.

Valentinus, *d. abt.* 161. Frag. apud Hippolytum servata. (*In* **Bunsen**, C. C. J. Christianity, v. 5. 1854.)

Valentinus, Basilius. Last will and testament. London, 1670. 16°.

Contents. Last will. — Practick treatise, with twelve keys of the great stone of the ancient philosophers. — Treatise of the sulphur, vitriol, and magnet of the philosophers. — Treatise conc. the microcosme, or the little world which is man's body. — Treatise [of] his manual operations. — Treatise of things natural and supernatural.

— Opus præclarum quod dedit filio. (*In* **Zetzner**, L. Theatr. chem., v. 4. 1613.)

— Practica, cum duodecim clavibus et app. de magno lapide antiquorum sapientum. (*In* **Musæum** hermeticum, 1677; — *and in* **Manget**, J. J. Bibl. chem., v. 2. 1702.)

— — *Eng*. Practick treatise. *See his* 'Last will', *above*.

— — *French*. Les douze clefs de philosophie; plus l'Azoth, ou le moyen de faire l'or caché des philosophes. Paris, 1659. 16°.

Note. 'Azoth' has a separate title-page and paging.

Valenzuela, Fernando de. Poesias. (*In* **Castro**, A. de. Poetas lir. de los siglos 16 y 17, v. 2. 1857; v. 42 of Aribau. Bibl.)

Valerian, *Emp. of Rome*. Montégut, J. F. de. Essai hist. sur la famille de l'empereur Valérien. (*In* **Sérieys**, A. Bibl. acad., v. 4. 1811.)

Valeriani, Luca. In lode de' calzoni. (*In* **Berni**, F. Opere burlesche, v. 2. 1824.)

Valeriani Molinari, Luigi. Montanari, I. (*In* **Hercolani**, A. Biog. de rom., v. 1. 1834.)

— Papotti, T. Elogio di V. (*In his* Elogi d'illust. Imolesi. 1841.)

Valeriano Bolzani, Giovanni Pierio, *orig.* Pietro. Antiquitatum Bellunensium sermones quatuor. (*In* **Grævius**. Thes. antiq. Ital., v. 6, pt. 4. 1722.)

— Commentaires hiéroglyphiques, ou, Images des choses; aug. de deux livres de C. Curio. Lyon, 1576. 2 v. f°.

— Compendium in sphæram. (*In* **Sacro Bosco**, J. de. De sphæra. 1577.)

— De fulminum significationibus. (*In* **Grævius**, J. G. Thes. antiq. Rom. v. 5. 1696.)

— Niceron, J. P. (*In his* Mém., v. 26. 1734.)

Valerie; an autobiography; by F. Marryat. Lpz., *Tauchnitz*, 1849. 16°.

Valerie; comédie. *See* **Scribe**, A. E.

Valerine de Monsabran, ou La victime de la confiance; par L. F. G. B. de la Rochelle. (*In* **Biblioth**. univ. des romans, Nouv., v. 20. 1799.)

Valerio, Agostino. *See* **Valieri**, A.

Valerius, *St., Abbot of S. Pedro de Montes*. Opuscula anecdota. (*In* **Florez**, H. España sagrada, v. 16. 1762.)

Valerius, Julius. Res gestæ Alexandri; tr. ex Æsopo Græco. (*In* **Mai**, A. Class. auct., v. 7. 1835; — *and in* **Curtius Rufus**, Q. De rebus gestis, v. 3. 1824.)

Valerius; a Roman story. *See* **Lockhart**, J. G.

Valerius Æditµus. Fragm. (*In* **Estienne**, R. Fragm. poet. vet. Lat. 1564; — *and in* **Ribbeck**, J. K. O. Scenicæ Rom. poesis fragm., v. 2. 1855.)

Valerius Cato. *See* **Cato**, V.

Valerius Flaccus, Caius. Argonauticon; not. var. cur. P. Burmanno. Leidæ, 1724. 4°.

— *Same*. Recens. a J. A. Wagner. Gott., 1805. 8°.

— *Same*. Paris, 1824-25. 2 v. 8°. (Lemaire. Bibl. class. Lat.)

— Mérian, J. B. Sur un passage de V. F. (*In* **Berlin**. Ak. d. Wiss. Abh., 1799-1800.)

Valerius Maximus. *See* **Maximus**, V. (p. 1929).

Valery, Antoine Claude Pasquin. Voyages hist. et lit. en Italie, 1826-28; ou L'indicateur italien. Paris, 1831-33. 5 v. 8°.

— *Same*. 2e éd. Paris, 1838. 3 v. 8°.

— *Eng*. Historical, literary, and artistical travels in Italy, *etc.*; tr. from the 2d ed., by C. E. Clifton. Paris, 1839. 8°.

Valesius. *See* **Valois**.

Valet de pied, Mémoires d'un; [par] W. M. Thackeray; tr. par W. L. Hughes. Paris, 1859. 12°.

Valet de sham, The; a farce. *See* **Selby**, C.

Valetta, Joannes N. 'Ομήρου βίος καὶ ποιήματα; πραγματεια. 'Εν Λονδίνῳ, 1867. 4°.

Valgius, Titus. Fragm. (*In* **Estienne**, R. Frag. poet. vet. Lat. 1564.)

Valguarnera, Mariano. De origine et antiquitate Panormi, primisque Siciliæ et Italiæ incolis. (*In* **Grævius**. Thes. antiq. Sicil., v. 13. 1725.)

— Anacreonte tradotto di V. — Gregorio, R. di. Vita di V. (*In his* Disc. int. alla Sicilia, v. 1. 1821.)

Valiente justiciero, El, y rico hombre de Alcala. *See* **Moreto y Cabaña**, A. de.

Valière, *Chevalier* de la. *See* **La Valière**, *Chev.* de.

Valieri, Agostino. Niceron, J. P. (*In his* Mém., v. 5. 1728; *and, Germ.*, v. 5. 1751.)

Valin, René Josué. Nouveau commentaire sur l'ordonnance de la marine du mois d'août 1681. Nouv. éd. Rochelle, 1776. 2 v. 4°.

— *Same*. Commentaire, *etc.*, avec des notes par V. Becane. Poitiers, 1829. 4°.

Valincourt, Jean Baptiste Henri du Trousset, *sieur* de. Niceron, J. P. (*In his* Mém., v. 24. 1733.)

Valise trouvée, La. *See* **Le Sage**, A. R.

Valisneria; [by] E. Pfeiffer. *t.p.w.* [London, 1857.] 16°.

Valla, Joseph. Institutiones theologicæ, ad usum scholarum. Lugd., 1780. 6 v. 12°.

Vallabhacharyas. *See* **Mahárájas**.

Valladares de Sotomayor, Antonio. Semanario erudito. Madrid, 1787-91. 34 v. 4°.

'*Note*. This book, ill arranged and worse selected, contains yet many curious docs. for the hist. of Spain, but was suppressed by the influence of Godoy, in the time of Charles IV. as a dangerous publication. — *Ticknor*.

Contents. Vol. 1. **Quevedo y Villegas**, F. G. de. Harpa; — Soneto; — Cartas; — Anales de quince dias; — Discurso de las privanzas; — El zurriago. — **Ferdinand** V., *of Spain*. Carta al conde de Rivagorza; commentos por F. de Quevedo. — **Lerma**, F. de X. de S., *marq. de Denia, duca de*. Carta al rey D. Felipe IV. — **Ponze**, M. Oracion funebre en la muerte de R. Calderon, marques de Siete Iglesias. 2. **Burriel**, A. M. Cartas. — **Salazar y Castro**, L. de. Discurso sobre la Flagueza de la monarquia española en el reynado de D. Carlos II., y valimiento del conde de Oropesa, 1687. — **Vera**, J. A. de. Fragmentos historicos de la vida de Gaspar de Guzman. — **Urbano** VIII. Carta al conde de Olivares. 3. **Quevedo y Villegas**, F. G. de. Caida de su privanza y muerte del conde-duque de Olivares. — **Alvarez**, G. Carta al conde-duque de Olivares sobre lo que se decia de su conducta. — **Riol**, S. A. Informe sobre la creacion, *ec.*, de los consejos y tribunales. — **Cangas Inclan**, V. de. Carta sobre el origen y serie de las Cortes. — **San Felipe**, marq. de. El arte del reynar. — Indice, t. 1-3. 4. **Grandes** ruidosas controversias entre la reyna madre, Juan de Austria y Juan Everardo, sobre la direccion y gobierno de estos reynos. 5. Visita de la Esperanza y el Tiempo; Dialogo sobre las operaciones de D. **Juan** de Austria. — Paz de **Castilla** y Portugal, 1668. — **Respuesta** al rey Felipe IV. sobre las cosas de Portugal. — **Sarmiento**, M. Catalogo para una libreria de 3 ó 4000 libros; — Sobre el origen de los Maragatos. — **Macanaz**, M. R. de. Auxilios para bien gobernar una monarquia catolica. 6. **Saavedra Fajardo**, D. de. Locuras de Europa; dialogo entre Mercurio y Luciano. — **Palafox y Mendoza**, J. de. Juicio interior y secreto de la monarquia para mi solo. — **Riol**, S. Representacion sobre el patronato real, *etc.*, 1735. — **Ruiz de Alarcon**, L. M. de V. Disertacion critico historica sobre la causa de la alevosa muerte de Garci-Sanchez, ultimo conde de Castilla. — **Sarmiento, M.** El porque si, y porque no; — Origen de los Villanos; — Cartas al duque de Medina Sidonia. — **Villegas, S. B.** de. Papel al rey Felipe II., 1574, sobre la venta de los vasallos de las Iglesias, y otras cosas. — **Quevedo y Villegas, F.** de. Carta á A. de Mendoza; — Declamacion de Jésu-Christo. — **Laureles, J. A.** Venganza de la lengua española contra el autor del 'Cuento de cuentos'. — Indice, t. 4–6. 7–9. **Macanaz, M. R.** de. Papeles y obras. — Indice, tomo 7–9. 10. **Quevedo y Villegas, F. G.** de. Tres coronas en el ayre; conferencias entre Richelieu, Mazarini, y O. Cromuel, sobre los negocios del otro mundo. — **Discurso** politico economico sobre la influencia de los gremios. — **Roda, M.** de. Carta á J. Martin, para la educacion de sus sobrinos. — **Varias** obras correspondientes à la regencia en la menor edad de Carlos II. 11. **Academia** politica del año de 1679. — **Abusos** que se cometen en el manejo y direccion de todas las rentas reales. — **Adame, N. J.** de. Nuevo reglamento para las fabricas de seda y de lana. — **Instruccion** que se dió al Señor Felipe IV. sobre materias de gobierno de estros reynos. — **Somoza y Quiroga, A.** Unico desengaño y perfecto remedio de los menoscabos de la corona de Castilla. — **Philip V.** Carta, 14 de Enero de 1624 à su hijo el principe del Asturias Don Luis. 12. **Gandara, M. A.** de. Informe reservado relativo á varios puntos del Concordato. — **Purgar, H.** del. Tratado de los reyes de Granada y su origen. — **Conquista** del reyno de Portugal por Felipe II. — **Rubio, A.** Dictamen sobre deudas antiguas de la real hacienda. — **Mina,** *marques* de la. Dictamen sobre la reformacion del exercito de España en la retirada de Italia. — **Sandoval Moscoso, B.,** *Cardinal.* Carta sobre la contribucion de millones del estado eclesiástico. — **Ensanada,** *marq.* de la. Representacion proponiendo medios para el adelantamiento da la monarquia. — Indices, tomo 10–12. 13. **Macanaz, M. R.** de. Disertacion historica; — Noticias particulares para la historia politica de España. — **Sagarzazu, L.** Reglas y documentos dados al Rey Fernando VI. — **Discurso** de la grandeza de España. — **Ponce de Leon, P.** Censura sobre los anales é historias de C. C. Tácito. 14. **Memorias** historicas de la monarquia de España, de Enrique IV. hasta Carlos II. — **Charles V.** Carta á su hijo Felipe II., desde Palamos. — **Morales, A.** de. Sobre la Santa Iglesia de Santiago. — **Philip IV.** Carta á G. Albanél, arzobispo de Granada, sobre el breve en razon de residencia de los obispos. — **Representacion** hecha al excelentisimo Señor marques de la Ensenada, sobre la politica exterior é interior de España. 15. **Macanaz, M. R.** de. Disertacion historica, 3a parte. — **Haro de San Clemente, J.** Memorial á Felipe V. — **El compas,** que ofrece su autor á Felipe IV. — **Salucio, A.** Discurso acerca los estatutos de limpieza de sangre. — **Quevedo, F.** Memorial contra el conde-duque de Olivares, dado al rey Felipe IV. — **Respuesta** al Memorial del conde de Oropesa á Carlos II. — Indice, t. 13–15. 16. **Burriel.** Carta á Juan de Amaya. — **Ximeno,** *Don.* Pregunta [sobre los diezmos]. — **Sales, A.** Respuesta. — **Torres,** *conde* de las. Informe en punto de terremoto. — **Obando,** *marq.* de. Carta sobre la inundacion del Calleo, y terremotos, *etc.*, de Lima. — **Isla, J. F.** de. Carta sobre el terremoto de Portugal. — **Oracion** sobre la utilidad de la filosofia. 17. **Mayans y Siscar, G.** Cartas eruditas y criticas. — **Burriel, A. M.** Representacion á M. Quintano y Bonifaz. — **Philip IV.** Carta al cardenal Sandoval, sobre contribucion de millones del estado eclesiastico; — Otra sobre el mismo asunto al Dean y Cabildo de dicha Santa Iglesia. — **Sandoval,** —. Carta al presidente de Castilla. — **Cadahalso, J.** de. Anales de cinco dias en Madrid. — **Guia** de hijos de vecinos y forasteros, porque el ingenio va á Guias. — **Carta** de una señora andaluza á su marido en la corte. 18. **Chacon, P.** Historia de la Universidad de Salamanca. — **Reparos** criticos contra varios pasages del marq. de San Felipe, por un Valenciano. — **Representacion** que a nombra del duque de Mantua hizo el principe de Auli al emperador Carlos V. — **Mendoza, D.** de. Papel de los Catarriberas. — **Trulloz y Esconinimberg, F.** de. Papel satirico que se dió al Almirante de Castilla, haciéndole presentes sus procedimientos en el gobierno. — **Enriquez, F.** Carta á Carlos V. — Indice, t. 16–18. 19. **Vazquez de Acuña, J.** Vida del cardinal-duque de Richelieu. — **Sarmiento, M.** Discurso sobre la primera educacion de la juventud. — **Representacion** y decreto al sujeto del conde de Olivares. — **Arte** de lo bueno y de lo justo, para la causa que motivó la prision del marques del Carpio. 20. **Sarmiento, M.** Sobre buenos caminos en España. — **Pinuer, I.** Extracto de su relacion sobre una ciudad grande de Españoles en India. — **Carta** que escribió el cura del Llano de Olmedo sobre la labranza y ganado, 1609. — **Ximenes de Cisneros, F.,** *card.* Instruccion al arzobispo Tortoza, al sujeto de la llegada de Carlos V. á España. — **Lison, M.** Voto y proposicion del reyno. — **Isla, J. F.** de. Carta del barbero de Corpa. 21. **Retes, J. F.** Conveniencia y concordia de ambas jurisdicciones en materia de inmunidad local, o derecho de asilo. — **Sarmiento, M.** Reflexiones literarias para una biblioteca real. — **Respuesta** a la Junta de Agricultura. — Indice, t. 19–21. 22. **Seguier, A. L.** Discurso en el Parlamento de Paris contra 'La historia', *etc.*, del comercio, *etc.*, en las dos Indias, por G. T. Raynal'; tr. G. de Homar. — **Betancurt y Figueroa, L.** de. Derecho de las iglesias metropolitanas y catedrales de India. — **El Tordo Viscayno,** en que el autor defiende á Viscaya. — **Quevedo y Villegas, F.** de. Impugnacion á un memorial contra el conde-duque de Olivares. — **Carvajal y Lancaster, J.** de. Representacion al rey sobre un decreto que abolia las exênciones exclusivas, 1752. 23. **Villarreal, J.** de. Informe al rey Fernando VI. sobre contener y reducir los Indios de Chile. — **Quiroga, G.** de. Compendio hist. de la conquista de Chile, hasta 1656. — **Breve** discurso de un antiguo oficial de caballeria. — **Perez, V.** Ultima enfermedad de la reyna. 24. **Discursos** politicos y económicos para que la España se restablezca, *etc.* — Carta á **Feyjoo,** refutando su paralelo entre Luis XIV. de Francia, y Pedro I., czar de Moscovia. — **Salazar y Castro, L.** de. Representacion que hizo el duque de Arcos á Felipe V., 1701, sobre querer S. M. igualar á los duques pares de Francia con los grandes de España. — **Ubilla, A.** de. Papel que de órden del rey escribió al duque de Arcos, en respuesta de la Representacion antecedente. — **Arcos,** *duque* de. Respuesta á la Real Orden anterior. — **Campillo, J.** del. Cartas á A. G. de Mier. — **Mendoza, D.** de. Carta al capitan Salazar sobre el libro que escribió de la derrota de los Saxones. — **Lucuce, P.** de. Carta á J. Finestres y Monsalvo, sobre la legua española. — **Ocampo, F.** de. Respuesta, satisfaciendo á ciertas preguntas. — **Uriarte y Herrera, M.** de. Representacion al rey sobre los adelantamientos de aquellos vastos paises y opulencia que pueden producir á España. — **Ovando,** *marq.* de. Carta á F. Pignateli. 25. Concordato entre **Fernando VI.** y **Benedicto XIV.** — **Mayans y Siscar, G.** Observaciones sobre el Concordato. 26. **Sarmiento de Sotomayor, A. A.** Documentos é instruciones en las operaciones de todos estados. — **Heros, J. A.** de los. Discursos sobre el comercio y sus utilidades. 27. **Representacion** al rey sobre el comercio clandestino de America. — **Representacion** al sujeto de los cinco gremios de Madrid. — **Freyle, F.,** *and others.* Dictamen sobre los gremios y el interes que pueden llevar. — Indice, t. 25–27. 28. **Montufar y Frasco, J. P.** de. Sobre el estado y gobernacion de la Audiencia de Quito. — **Caresmar, J.** Autenticidad de los archivos, en especial de las iglesias. — **Fragmentos** historicos de la vida de J. **Patiño,** secretario, *etc.*, de Felipe V. — **Lanz de Casafonda, M.** Estado presente de la literatura en España. — **Ferdinand V.** Carta á su embaxador en Roma, mandandole que hablase sobre su contenido al Papa. — **Palavicino, O. F.** Proposicion al rey Felipe IV., 1526. — **Philip II.** Respuesta á archiduque Cárlos, sobre los Paises Baxos; — Carta al principe de Melitó, su virrey y capitan general en Cataluña, sobre la defensa de Cataluña; — Carta al embaxador de Roma. 28, 29. **Historia** del rey Don Pedro. — **Causa** de la decadencia de la Monarquia Española, y sus remedios. — **Cartas** sobre la muerte de Felipe III. — **Sobrecasas, F.** Consulta al rey. — **Utilisima** instruccion para un privado, 1612. — **Olivares, G.** de G., *conde de Olivares.* Quatro papeles sobre la educacion de los señores infantes. — **Velasco, J. F.** de. Carta al papa Clemente VIII. 30. **Philip II.** Instruccion á D. Covarrubias, obispo de Segovia; — Instruccion al consejo de la Cámara en 6 de Enero de 1588. — Memorial á el duque de **Jovenazo,** 1691. — **Aponte, P. G.** de. Carta sobre los reyes de Navarra. — **Torrehermosa,** *conde* de. Papel sobre restablicer la Junta de Comercio. — **Benedict XIV.** Carta al Inquisidor General de España, sobre las obras del cardenal de Noris. — Tratado sobre la Monarquia **Columbina.** — Resumen en dialogo de la historia **romana.** — **Solsona,** *Bp. of.* Representacion al rey Carlos II., 1694. — Indice, t. 28–30. 31–33. **Pellicer y Tobar, J.** Avisos historicos de España desde 1639. 33. **Hancourt,** *conde* de. Representacion al rey de Francia. — Dos **memoriales** de los diputados de Aragon al rey Felipe IV. — **Guillen,** —. Carta al rey Fernando, hallandose cercado de sus vasallos, 1492. — **Haro, L.** de. Carta y avisos desde el otro mundo al marques de Caracena. — Indice, t. 31–33. 34. **Gran Puente y Guadalevin, M.** Carta apologetica del 'Atlante español'. — Papel presentado al rey **Felipe IV.** sobre crecer el valor de la moneda, 1620. — **Isla, J.** de. Representacion al rey. — **Manefiesto,** *etc.*, sobre las operaciones de **Montemar,** en Italia, en la campaña de 1742. — **Vvinkel, F. G.** Reflexiones sobre el comercio del trigo, 1761. — **Oropesa,** *conde* de. Representacion rey Carlos II. — **Método** de estudiar la jurisprudencia. — **Ferrante Brancia.** Sobre la alternativa en lo eclesiástico. — **Isla, J. F.** de. Conversaciones entre

Fabio, y Silvio, sobre cierto sermon, 1740. — Representacion al conde de **Oropesa**, [por un buen vasallo]. — **Discurso** fisico sobre la abundancia y igualacion de monedas, de oro, plata, y vellon. — **Villegas**, D. E. de. Advertencias eruditas para principes y ministros.

Valladier, André. Labyrinth royal de l'Hercule gaulois triomphant; sur le suject des faicts héroiques de Henry IV representé à l'entrée triomphante de la royne, nov. 19. Avignon, 1600. 4°.

— NICERON, J. P. (*In his* Mém., v. 18. 1732; *and*, *Germ.*, v. 14. 1756.)

Valladolid. CERVANTES SAAVEDRA, M. Relacion de las fiestas de V. en 1605. (*In his* Obras, v. 2. 1863.)

Valladolid. *Monte Pio.* Reglamento del Monte Pio, aprobado por el Real consejo de Castilla; para socorro de las viudas é hijos de los dependientes de todas rentas reales de Valladolid. Valladolid, 1784. 4°. (B 1896)

Vallancey, *Col.* Charles. Description of an ancient monument in the church of Lusk, in the Co. of Dublin. — Language, *etc.*, of an Anglo-Saxon colony in the baronies of Forth and Bargie Co., Wexford, Ireland, 1167-69. (*In* **Royal Irish Academy.** Trans., v. 2. 1788.)

Vallandigham, Clement L. TRIAL of [V.] by a military commission and proceedings under his application for writ of habeas corpus in the circuit court of U. S. for the southern dist. of Ohio. Cincin., 1863. 8°.

Vallauri, Tommaso. Storia della poesia in Piemonte. Torino, 1841. 2 v. 8°.

Valle, *marques* del. Relacion de los servicios del marques. (*In* **Icazbalceta**, J. G. Coleccion de doc., v. 2. 1866.)

Valle, Gulielmo della. Lettere senesi sopra le belle arti. Venezia, 1782-86. 3 v. 4°.

— Storia del Duomo di Orvieto. Roma, 1791. 4°.

Valle, Pietro della. Viaggi; divisi in tre parti, cioé la Turchia, la Persia, e l'India. Venetia, 1661-63. 4 v. 12°.

— *Eng.* Pt. 2. Travels in Persia. (*In* **Pinkerton**, J. Col. of voy., v. 9. 1811.)

— ST. JOHN, J. A. (*In his* Lives of cel. travellers, v. 1. 1844. Harpers' fam. lib.)

Vallée, Geoffroi. NICERON, J. P. (*In his* Mém., v. 29. 1734.)

Vallée, Louis Léger. Traité de la géométrie descriptive. Paris, 1819. 4° *and* Planches.

Vallée, Louis René Oscar de. Les manieurs d'argent; études hist. et morales, 1720-1857. 5e éd. Paris, 1858. 18°.

Vallée noire, La; [par A. A. L. Dudevant]. (*In her* Le secrétaire intime. 1857.)

Valleix, François Louis Isidore. Clinique des maladies des enfants. Paris, 1838. 8°.

— Fréquence du pouls, *etc.* *n.t.p.* [184-.] 8°.

— Guide du médecin praticien. Paris, 1842-47. 10 v. 8°.

Vallensis, Robertus. *See* **Vaux**, R. de.

Vallet, —. Recit des principaux faits qui se sont passés dans la salle de l'ordre du clergé depuis le commencement des Etats-généraux jusqu' à la réunion des trois ordres. Paris, 1790. 8°.

Vallet de Viriville, Auguste. L'Ecole des Chartes. (*In* **Paris** guide, v. 1. 1867.)

— Obs. sur la chronique de Cousinot. (*In* **Paris. Inst.** *Ac. d. Inscr.* Div. sav., 1e sér., v. 5. 1857.) — La vie et les écrits de R. Blondel. (*In* Not., v. 17, 2e pt. 1851.) — Du ms. 'Geste des nobles françoys descendus du roy Pryam'. (*In* v. 19, 2e pt. 1858.)

Valletta (*Lat.* **Valeta**), Giovanni. Epistola. (*In* **Graevius**. Thes. antiq. Sicil., v. 15. 1725.)

Valley Forge. REPORT of the harvest home, July 26, 1828, at Valley Forge encampment ground. *n.t.p.* [1828.] 8°. (B 1099)

— VALLEY FORGE letters. (*In* **Smith, H. W.** Nuts for historians to crack. 1856.)

Valley of a hundred fires; by [J. Stretton]. London, [1861?]. 8°.

Vallier, H. La musique. (*In* **Almanach** de l'encyclopédie. 1869.)

Vaillière. *See* **La Vallière.**

Vallière, Joseph Florent, *marquis* de. Défence des places par les contre-mines, avec principes de l'artillerie. Paris, 1768. 8°.

Vallisnieri, Antonio. De corpi marini che su monti si trovano; agg. Lettere contra le opere del Sig. Andry. 2a ed. Venezia, 1728. 4°.

— Raccolta di varie osservazioni spettanti all' istoria medica e naturale; comp. da G. J. Danielli. Venezia, 1728. 4°.

— FABRONI, A. (*In his* Vitae Ital., v. 7. 1781.)

— NICERON, J. P. (*In his* Mém., v. 16. 1731; *and*, *Germ.*, v. 12. 1755.)

Vallory, *Mme.* Louise. Madame Hilaire. 3e éd. Paris, 1859. 18°.

Válmiki. Le Ramayana; poème sanscrit; tr. en fr. par H. Fauche. Paris, 1864. 2 v. 16°.

— *Eng.* Tr. by R. T. H. Griffith. London, 1870-72. 3 v. 8°.

— AMPÈRE, J. J. A. Le Ramayana. (*In* **Revue** d. D. Mondes, sept. 1847.)

Valmout, V. Tartarie, Béloutchistan, Boutan, *etc.* *See* **Dubeux**, L.

Valois (*Lat.* **Valesius**), Adrien de. Epistolæ quædam ined. ad J. A. Portnerum. (*In* **Schelhorn**, J. G. Amœn. lit., v. 6. 1727.)

— NICERON, J. P. (*In his* Mém., v. 3. 1727; *and*, *Germ.*, v. 4. 1751.)

Valois, Charles de. *See* **Angoulême**, Charles de Valois, *duc* d'.

Valois (*Lat.* **Valesius**), Henri de. Epistolæ quædam ineditæ ad J. A. Portnerum. (*In* **Schelhorn**, J. G. Amœn. lit., v. 6. 1727.)

— De populis fundis. (*In* **Graevius**, J. G. Thes. antiq., v. 2. 1694.)

— De schismate Donatistarum. — De Anastasi et martyrio Hierosolymitano. — De versione LXX interpretum. — De martyrologio Romano. (*In* **Eusebius** *Cæsariensis.* Historia. 1672.)

— NICERON, J. P. (*In his* Mém., v. 5. 1728; *and*, *Germ.*, v. 5. 1751.)

Valois, Marguerite de. *See* **Margaret.**

Valois *or* **Vallensis**, Thomas. Comment. J. Valois et N. Triveth in Augustinum. (*In* **Augustinus**, A. De Civitate Dei. 1743.)

Valois de Forville —. Le comte de Saint Pol. Paris, 1860. 18°.

— Le conscrit de l'an VIII. Paris, 1860. 18°.

— Marquis de Pazaval. Paris, 1858. 18°.

Valon, Alexis de. [Numerous articles.] (*In* **Revue** d. D. Mondes, juin 1843-juil 1851.)

— MÉRIMÉE, P. (*In* **Revue** d. D. Mondes, sept. 1851.)

Valon, Jacques-Louis. ALEMBERT, J. C. R. d'. (*In his* Œuvres, juin 1843-juil. 1851.)

Valori, Baccio. Lettera. (*In* **Dati**, C. Prose fior., pt. 4, v. 4. 1751.)

Valori, Bartolommeo. ROBBIA, L. della. (*In* **Archivio** stor. ital., v. 4, pt. 1. 1843.)

Valori, François Florent, *comte* de. Précis histor. du voyage enterpris par Louis XVI le 21 juin 1791. Paris, 1815. 8°. (B 800)

— *Same.* (*In* **Mémoire** sur l'affaire de 1823. Berville *and* **Barrière.** Col. des mém., v. 54.)

Valori, Louis Gui Henri, *marquis* de. Mémoires des négociations du marquis de V. Paris, 1820. 2 v. 8°.

Valori, Niccolò. Vita [di] L. de' Medici. (*In* **Buonaccorsi**, B. Diario. 1568.)

Valori *di Firenze*, Famiglia di. (*In* **Litta**, P. Fam., v. 15.)

Valparaiso. RADIGUET, M. R. (*In* **Revue** d. D. Mondes, juill. 1847.)

Valperga; or, Life and adventures of Castruccio; by [Mrs. M. W. Shelley]. London, 1823. 3 v. 12°.

Valperga de Caluso, Tommaso (**Massino**), *il abate.* Di Livia Colonna. — Risposta a Glaucilla. (*In* **Turin.** Ac. d. Sci. Mem., v. 13. 1803.) — In luctu F. Balbi elegia. (*In* v. 21. 1813.)

Valpy, Abraham John. Valpy's national gallery of painting and sculpture. Lond., [1828]. 8°.

Valpy, Richard, *D.D.* Address to his parishioners. 3d ed. London, 1811. 8°.

— Anniversary sermon of the Royal Humane Soc. 4th ed. London, 1804. 8°. (B 823)

— Elements of Greek grammar. Lond., 1807. 8°.
— Same. 2d Amer. ed., with add. Boston, 1817. 12°.
— Same. With add. by C. Anthon. 9th ed. N. Y., 1834. 12°.
— Importance of local statistics. (*In* **Nat. Assoc. Prom. Soc. Sci.** Trans., 1862.)
— Poetical chronology of ancient and English hist.; added, Amer. chronology. Boston, [1816]. 12°.
— Sermon, Aug. 13, 1798, consecration of the colors of the Reading Assoc. Reading, 1798. 8°. (B 1857)
— Short sketch of a short trip to Paris, 1788. (*In* **Pamphleteer**, 1814; v. 3 of B 838)

Valrey, Max. Les confidences d'une puritaine. Paris, 1865. 18°.
— Les filles sans dot; Marcelle-Léonie. Paris, 1859. 18°.
— Marthe et Montbrun. Paris, 1857. 18°.

Valsalva, Antonio Maria. FABRONI, A. (*In his* Vitæ Ital., v. 5. 1779.)
— FARINI, L. C. Biografia di A. M. Valsalva. (*In* **Hercolani, A.** Biog. rom., v. 2. 1835.)
— PAPOTTI, T. (*In his* Elogi d'illust. Imolesi. 1841.)

Valsecchi (*Lat.* **Valsechius**), Virginio. FABRONI, A. (*In his* Vitæ Ital., v. 6. 1780.)

Valsha; a drama. *See* **Coyne, J. S.**

Valstain, Alberto. *See* **Wallenstein, A. W. E.**

Value. STORCH, H. Des choses qui sont susceptibles d'avoir de la valeur. — Analyse des différentes espèces de biens. (*In* **St. Petersburg. Ac. Sci.** Mém., v. 3. 1811.)
— JOHNSON, A. B. Inquiry into the nature of value and of capital. N. Y., 1813. 8°.
— BAILEY, S. Letter to a political economist, on value. London, 1826. 8°.

Value, Standard of. *See* **Money.**

Valvasone, Erasmo di. La Caccia; poema. Milano, *Soc. Tip. de Clas. Ital.*, 1808. 8°.
— Sonetto. (*In* **Gironi, R.** Raccolta di lir. ital. 1808.)

Valvèdre; par G. Sand [Mme. Dudevant]. Paris, 1861. 12°.

Valvidares y Longo, Ramon. La Iberiada; poema épico. Cadiz, 1813. 2 v. (v. 2. w.). 4°.

Vámbéry, Arminius. The dervishes and hadjis of the East. (*In* **Anthropol. Soc.** Mem., v. 2. 1866.)
— Sketches of Central Asia; additional chapters of my travels, *etc.* Phila., 1868. 8°.
— Travels in Central Asia; from Teheran to Samarcand. London, 1864. 8°.

Vampire, Le; drame. *See* **Dumas, A.**

Van. ☞ For names of Dutchmen beginning with this prefix *see* the following part of the name; English names so compounded are put under Van.

VanAlstine, John. Life and dying confession of V., executed for the murder of Wm. Huddleton. Schoharie, 1819 8°. (B 458)

Vanbrugh, *Sir* **John.** Plays. London, 1776. 2 v. (v. 1 w.). 12°.
Contents. Vol. 1. *Wanting.* 2. The confederacy. — The mistake. — The country house. — Journey to London. — The provok'd husband.
— City wives' confederacy. (*In* **Bell, J.** Brit. theatre, v. 22. 1797; — *and in* **London** stage, v. 3.)
— Country house. (*In* **Scott,** *Sir* **W.** Brit. dr., v. 3. 1804.)
— Mistake. (*In* **Bell, J.** Brit. theatre, v. 25. 1797.)
— Poems. (*In* **Campbell, T.** Spec., v. 5. 1819.)
— Provoked wife. (*In* **Bell, J.** Brit. theatre, v. 27. 1797; — **London** stage, v. 3; — *and in* **Scott,** *Sir* **W.** Brit. dr., v. 2, pt. 1. 1804.)
— The relapse. (*In* **Bell, J.** Brit. theatre, v. 26. 1797.)
— *and* **Cibber, C.** Provoked husband; a comedy. (*In* **Bell, J.** Brit. theatre, v. 18. 1797; — **London** stage, v. 2; — *and in* **Scott,** *Sir* **W.** Brit. dr., v. 2, pt. 2. 1804.)
— CUNNINGHAM, A. (*In his* Lives of Brit. painters, v. 4. 1831. Fam. lib.)
— DUNHAM, S. A. (*In his* Lives, *etc.*, v. 3. 1838.)

Van Brunt family. BERGEN, T. G. Genealogy, 1653–1867. Albany, 1867. 8°.

Van Bruyssel, Ernest. The population of an old pear tree; from the Fr. of Van B.; ed. by [Miss C. M. Yonge]. London, 1870. 16°.

Van Buren, Martin. Considerations in favour of the appointment of R. King to the Senate. *n.p.*, [1819]. 8°. (B 533)
— Inquiry into the origin and course of political parties in the U. S.; ed. by his sons. N. Y., 1867. 8°.
See also **United States.** *President.*
— ADDRESS to the democracy of the U. S. Wash., 1843. 8°. (B 1664)
— BUTLER, W. A. M. Van Buren; lawyer, statesman, and man. N. Y., 1862. 24°.
— CROCKETT, D. Life of M. Van Buren. Phila., 1835. 12°.
— EVERETT, A. H. Character of Gen. Jackson and Mr. Van Buren, in 1832. [Boston,] 1836. 8°. (B 1495)
— G., H. D. (*In* **Longacre, J. B.,** *and* **Herring, J.** Nat. portr. gal., v. 3. 1836.)
— GRUND, F. J. Martin Van Buren als Staatsmann und kunftiger Präsident der Vereinigten Staaten. *n.p.*, 1835. 8°. (B 1495)
— HILDRETH, R. The contrast, or Harrison versus Van Buren. Boston, 1840. 8°. (C 195)
— INCONSISTENCY and hypocrisy of M. Van Buren on the question of slavery. *n.p.*, 1848. 8°. (B 1477, 1503)
— JENKINS, J. S. Lives of governors of New York. Auburn, 1851. 8°.
— KENNEY, L. Pamphlet showing how easily the wand of a magician may be broken, *etc.* *n.t.p.* [1838.] 8° (B 1497)
— MACKENZIE, W. L. Life and times of Martin Van Buren. Boston, 1846. 8°.
— — Another copy. (B 1461)
— MAURY, S. M. Statesmen of America in 1846. London, 1847. 12°.
— MR. Van Buren and the war. From the Albany Argus extra. 8°. (B 1495)
— OGLE, C. The pretended democracy of Martin Van Buren; speech, Apr. 14. Bost., 1840. 8°. (B 1497)
— REASONS for voting for M. Van Buren. Boston, 1848. 8°. (C 196)
— U. S. CONG. Debate in the Senate on the nomination of M. Van Buren to be minister of U. S. to Gr. Britain. *n.t.p.* [Wash., 1832.] 8°. (B 1062, 1805, 1831)
— VAN BUREN platform; or, Facts for the present supporters of M. Van Buren. *n.t.p.* [1848.] 18°. (B 1496, 1500)
— VOICE of the people and facts in rel. to the rejection of Mr. Van Buren by the U. S. Senate. N. Y., 1832. 8°. (B 1495)

Van Buren platform; or, Facts for the present supporters of Martin Van Buren. *n.t.p.* [1848.] 8°. (B 1496, 1500)

Van Butchell, S. J. Facts and obs. rel. to a new and successful mode of treating piles, fistula, hœmorrhoidal excrescences, tumours, and strictures. 3d ed. London, 1838. 8°.

Van Bynkershoek, Cornelius. *See* **Bynkershoek, C. van.**

Vance, Joseph. Reply to McDuffie, on the amendment of the Constitution, April 1826. [Wash., 1826.] 8°. (C 194)

Vance, Mary. HUSBAND, M. M. (*In* **Brockett, L. P.** Woman's work in the civil war. 1867.)

Van Choate, S. F. Ocean telegraphing; adaptation of new principles for working of submarine cables, *etc.* Camb., 1865. 4°.

Van Cleve, John W. Fossil zoöphytes of western Ohio. (*In* **Amer. Assoc.** Proc., v. 1. 1849.)

Van Cortlandt, Philip, *and others.* Address to the Republican citizens of New York. Albany, 1813. 8°. (B 453)

Van Cortlandt, Philip, *et al. vs.* A. I. **Underhill.** CASE on the part of the appellants. N. Y., 1818. 8°. (B 340)

Vancouver, Charles. General compendium of chemical, experimental, and natural philosophy; [with] a complete system of commerce. Vol. 1, [pp. 48 only]. Phila., 1785. 8°. (W 64)
— General view of the agriculture in the County of Cambridge. London, 1794. 4°. (W 73)
— — Appendix. [London, 1794.] 4°. (W 73)
— General view of the agriculture in the County of Essex. London, 1795. 4°. (W 73)

Vancouver, George. Voyage of discovery to the N. Pacific Ocean and round the world, 1790–95. Lond., 1798. 3 v. 4° *and* Plates f°.
— *French.* Voyage autour du monde. (*In* **Montémont**, A. Biblioth. univ., v. 14. 1834.)
Vancouver's Island. Martin, R. M. Hudson's Bay Company's territories and Vancouver Island. London, **1849.** 8°.
— Mayne, R. C. Four years in British Columbia and V. Is., [**1857–61**]. London, 1862. 8°.
— Lennard, C. E. B. Travels in British Columbia, with a yacht voyage round Vancouver's Island, [**1859–60**]. London, 1862. 8°.
— Lord, J. K. The naturalist in V. Isl, and Brit. Columbia, [**1859–65**]. Lond., 1866. 2 v. 8°.
— Macfie, M. Vancouver Island and British Columbia. London, **1865.** 8°.
— Gr. Brit. *Parl.* Further papers rel. to the union of British Columbia and Vancouver Island; in continuation of papers presented 15th June 1866. London, **1867.** 8°.
Vandamme, Dominique René. Du Casse, A. Le général Vandamme et sa correspondance. Paris, 1870. 2 v. 8°.
Vandeburgh, C. F. Mother's medical guardian. London, 1820. 8°.
Vandeleur, John Ormsby. Duty of officers commanding detachments in the field. London, 1801. 8°.
Vandelli, Alexandre Antonio. Sobre a gravidade especifica das agoas de Lisboa e seus arredores. (*In* **Lisbon.** Ac. d. Sci. Mem. econ., v. 4. 1812.)
Vandelli, Domingos. Sobre a ferrugem das oliveiras. — Sobre a agricultura destereino, e das suas conquistas. — Sobre algumas producçoes naturaes das conquistas, as quaes ou saõ pouco conhecidas, ou nao se aproveitaõ. — Sobre as producçoes naturaes do reino, e das conquistas, primeiras materias de differentes fabricas. — Sobre a preferencia que em Portugal se deve dar à agricultura sobre as fábricas. (*In* **Lisbon.** Ac. d. Sci. Mem. econ., v. 1. 1789.) — Sobre varias misturas de materias vegetaes na factura dos chapéos. — Sobre o modo de aproveitar o carvaõ de pedra, e os paos bituminosos deste reino. (*In* v. 2.) — Sobre o encanamento do Rio Mondego. — Sobre as aguas-livres. (*In* v. 3.) — Sobre o sal gemma das Ilhas de Cabo Verde. (*In* v. 4. 1812.)
Vandenhoff, George. The art of elocution. London, 1855. 16°.
Vanderbilt, *Com.* Cornelius. Choules, J. O. Cruise of the steam yacht North-Star; excursion of Mr. V.'s party. Bost., 1854. 12°.
— Parton, J. (*In his* Famous Americans. 1867.)
Vanderbilt, John. Oration before Trinity and Benevolent Lodges, N. Y., *etc.*, Dec. 28, 5807; with address, Jan. 11, 1808, by W. Burrill. N. Y., 1808. 8°. (B 1271)
Vanderbilt, *ship.* Gr. Britain, *Parl.* Correspondence respecting the capture of the Saxon by the U. S. ship Vanderbilt. London, [1864]. f°. (N. A. papers, no. 2.)
Vanderbourgh, Martin Marie Charles de Boudens, *vicomte* de. Observations sur les fables publ. à Naples, et attrib. à Phèdre. (*In* **Paris. Inst.** *Ac. d. Inscr.* Mém., v. 8. 1827.)
Van der Brugghen. *See* **Brugghen**, —, van der.
Vander-Burck, Louis Emile. L'artiste en plein vent. (*In* **Echo** des feuilletons, 3e année. 1843.)
Vanderburgh, F. Letter to V. Mott in reply to his valedictory address at N. Y. Acad. of Medicine. N. Y., 1850. 8°. (B 1563)
— Similia similibus curantur; addr. before the Acad. of Medicine of the State of N. Y., Feb. 19. N. Y., 1851. 8°. (B 1563)
Van der Does, Janus George. *See* **Does**, J. G. van der.
Vanderhaeghen, Ferdinand. Bibliographie gantoise, 1483–1850. Gand, 1858–69. 7 v. (v. 6 w.). 8°.
Contents. Vol. 1. 1483–1627. 2. 1610–1713. 3. 1704–1829. 4. 1753–1832. 5. 1803–62. 6. *Wanting.* 7. Additions: 1531–1848. — Tables.

Van der Hoeven, Jan. *See* **Hoeven**, J. van der.
Van der Kemp, Francis Adrian. Oration, Mar. 11, 1814. Utica, [1814]. 8°. (B 937, 994)
— Speech, June 1, for the institution of a Society of Agriculture. Whitestown, 1795. 4°. (B 654)
— Catalogue of his library, sold, Boston 1830. Camb., 1830. 8°. (B 1611)
Van der Kolk, Jakoba Lodewick Konraad Schroeder. *See* **Schroeder van der Kolk**, J. L. K.
Van der Maeren, Corr. Brussels tribunal of commerce. (*In* **Nat. Assoc. Prom. Soc. Sci.** Trans., 1862.)
Vandermonde, Charles Augustin. Economie polit. (*In* **Paris. Ecoles Normales.** Séance, v. 2-5, 11. 1800.)
Van der Noot. *See* **Noot**, M. A. van der.
Vanderput. *See* **Martineau**, H. Messrs. Vanderput, *etc.*
Van der Velde, C. W. M. *See* **Velde**, C. W. M. van der.
Van Deusen, Edwin M. Christianity in the republic briefly considered in seven sermons. Pittsburgh, 1856. 12°.
Van de Weyer, Sylvain. *See* **Weyer**, S. van de.
Van Diemen's Land. Bonwick, J. Last of the Tasmanians; or, The black war of Van Diemen's land, [**1642–1869**]. London, 1870. 8°.
— Jeffreys, C. Van Dieman's Land; geographical and descriptive delineations of the island. London, **1820.** 8°.
— Roberts, J. Two years at sea; narr. of a voyage to Van Dieman's Land, **1829–31.** London, 1834. 8°.
— Gr. Britain. *Ho. of Com.* Aboriginal tribes, North America, New South Wales, Van Dieman's Land, and British Guiana; return to addresses. [London,] **1834.** 4°.
— Meredith, L. A. My home in Tasmania, [**1844–52**]. London, 1852. 2 v. 12°.
— Tasmanian royal kalendar, colonial register, and almanac for **1849**; compiled by J. Wood. Hobart-Town, 1849. 12°.
— Dilke, C. W. Greater Britain; a record of travel in English speaking countries, **1866–67.** London, 1868. 2 v. 8°.
See also **Australia**; — **New South Wales.**
Van Dyck, Anthonie. *See* **Dyck**, A. van.
Van Dyck, C. V. A. On the present condition of the medical profession in Syria. (*In* **Amer. Orient. Soc.** Journ., v. 1. 1847.)
Vandyck, a play of Genoa. *See* **Richards**, A. B.
Van Dycke, Henry J. The character and influence of abolitionism; sermon, Brooklyn, Dec. 9. N. Y., 1860. 8°. (B 1591)
— *Same.* (*In* **Fast** day sermons. 1861.)
Van Dyke, Nicholas. Speech on the Missouri bill, Jan. 28. *n.t.p.* [1820.] 12°. (B 527)
Vandyke Brown; a farce, by A. C. Troughton. (No. 81 *of* **De Witt's** acting plays.)
Vane, *Lady* Anne (Hawes), *successively wife of Ld.* Wm. Hamilton *and of* Wm., *2d Visc. Vane.* Smollett, T. G. Memoirs of a lady of quality. (*In his* Peregrine Pickle, v. 2. 1751.)
Vane, Charles Wm. Stewart, *1st Earl Vane and 3rd Marquis of Londonderry.* Memoir of Viscount Castlereagh. (*In* **Stewart**, R. Memoirs, v. 1. 1850.)
— Narrative of the Peninsular war. 2d ed. London, 1828. 4°.
— Narrative of the war in Germany and France, 1813–14. London, 1830. 4°.
— Recollections of a tour in the north of Europe, 1836–37. London, 1838. 2 v. 8°.
— Steam voyage to Constantinople, *etc.* London, 1842. 2 v. 8°.
— Alison, *Sir* A. Lives of Ld. Castlereagh and Sir C. Stewart. Edin., 1861. 3 v. 8°.
— Martineau, H. (*In her* Biographical sketches. 1869.)
Vane, *Sir* Henry, *the younger.* The healing question. — Forster, J. Life of V. (*In his* lives of British statesmen, v. 4. 1837.)
— Moore, J. B. Memoir of V. (*In his* Mem. of Amer. governors, v. 1. 1846.)
— Upham, C. W. Life of V. (*In* **Sparks**, J. Amer. biog. v. 4. 1835.)

Vane (*or* **Fane**) **family.** SANFORD, J. L., *and* TOWNSEND, M. (*In their* Great governing families, v. 1. 1865.)
Van-Ess, Willem Lodewyk. *See* **Ess**, W. L. van.
Van-Evrie, John H., *M.D.* Negroes and negro slavery; the first, an inferior race; the latter, its normal condition. N. Y., 1861. 12°.
Van Eyck, J. *and* H. *See* **Eyck**, J. *and* H. van.
Van Gaver, Jules. *See* **Jouannin**, J. M. Histoire et description de la Turquie. 1843.
Vanglas, ou Les anciens amis; comédie. *See* **Picard**, L. B.
Van Halen, Juan. *See* **Halen**, J. van.
Van Hasselt, Andreas. *See* **Hasselt**, A. van.
Van Helmont, Jan Baptiste. *See* **Helmont**, J. B. van.
Van Herring, *ship*. FROM aboard the Van Herring; letter from Legorn [*sic*], Dec. 1, 1679. *n.t.p.* [1680.] f°. (**A 54**)
— FROM aboard the Van Herring; a new letter from Legorn, *etc.* *n.t.p.* [1680.] f°. (**A 54**)
— S., J. New letter from Leghorn, from aboard the Van Herring, fully discovering the present state of that ship. *n.t.p.* [London, 1681.] f°. (**A 54**)
Van Hoey, Abraham. *See* **Hoey**, A. van.
Vanière, Jacques. Dictionarium poeticum. 2a ed. Lugd., 1722. 4°.
Vanini, Lucilio. COUSIN, V. Vanini, sa vie et ses œuvres. (*In* **Revue** d. D. Mondes, déc. 1843.)
— NICERON, J. P. (*In his* Mém., v. 26. 1734.)
Vanity. RAMOS DA SILVA DE ELA, M. A. Reflexios sobre a vaidade dos homens. Lisboa, 1761. 4°.
Vanity fair. N. Y., 1860–62. 6 v. 4°.
Vanity fair; by W. M. Thackeray; illust. by the author. London, 1848. 8°.
— *Same.* N. Y., [1850]. 8°.
— *Same.* With illust. by the author. N. Y., 1864. 8°.
— *Same.* Illust. N. Y., 1865. 3 v. 16°.
— *Same.* N. Y., 1869. 8°.
Van Lennep, Henry J. Travels in little-known parts of Asia-Minor. London, 1870. 2 v. 8°.
Van Lennep, Jan. *See* **Lennep**, Jan van.
Van Lennep, Mary E., *Funeral sermon on.* 1844. *See* **Hawes**, J.
Van Loon, Charles. Sons of Temperance defended; address. Poughkeepsie, 1846. 8°. (**B 1281**)
Vanloos, The. HOUSSAYE, A. (*In* **Revue** d. D. Mondes, août 1842; — *and in* **Men** and women of France, v. 3. 1852.)
Van Male, Guillaume. *See* **Male**, G. van.
Van Mander, Carel. *See* **Mander**, C. van.
Van Merle, Paul. *See* **Merula**, P.
Van Mildert, Wm., *Bp. successively of Llandaff and Durham.* Charge to the clergy of the diocese of Llandaff. (*In* **Pamphleteer**, 1822; v. 19 of **B 838**)
— Sermon at the assizes. Durham, 1834. 4°. (**A 60**)
— *Funeral sermon on.* 1836. *See* **Townsend**, G. (**B 1243**)
Van Name, Addison. Contributions to Creole grammar. [From the Trans. of the Amer. Phil. Assoc. 1869, 70.] *n.t.p.* [1870.] 8°.
Vannes. CHAUMEREIX, — de. Relation de C., échappé aux massacres d'Aurai et de Vannes. Londres, 1795. 8°.
Vannes, *M.* de. Extrait d'un mémoire sur la nature du nitre, *etc.* (*In* **Paris. Inst.** *Ac. d. Sci.* Rec. des mém. sur la formation du salpêtre. 1776.)
Van Ness, *Mrs.* Marcia. [SKETCH.] (*In* **Longacre**, J. B., *and* **Herring**, J. Nat. portr. gal., v. 2. 1835.)
Van Ness, Wm. P. Examination of the various charges against A. Burr; by Aristides. N. Y., 1803. 8°. (**B 624, 1885**)
— Reports of two cases in the prize court for the N. Y. district. N. Y., 1814. 8°. (**B 1437**)
— APPENDIX to Aristides's vindication of the Vice-president of the U. S.; by a gentleman of N. Carolina. Virginia, [1804]. 8°. (**B 398**)
— CHEETHAM, J. Reply to Aristides. N. Y., 1804. 8°. (**B 425**)
Van Ness, Wm. W., *and others.* Speeches in the cause of the people against H. Croswell for libel on T. Jefferson. N. Y., 1804. 8°.
— *Other copies.* (**B 425, 2009**)
— PROCEEDINGS of the committee to inquire into the official conduct of W. W. V. N. Y., 1820. 8°. (**B 546**)

400. (9. 8. 81.)

Vannetti, Clementino. Lettere. (*In* **Raccolta** di prose e lettere, v. 2. 1830.)
Van Nideck, A. *See* **Nideck**, A. van.
Van Noort, Olivier. *See* **Noort**, O. van.
Vannozzo, Francesco. Poema in otto sonetti. (*In* **Archivio** stor. ital., n.s., v. 15, pt. 2. 1862.)
Vannucchi, Andrea. *See* **Sarto**, A. del.
Vannucci, Atto. Della letteratura italiana. (*In* **Archiv.** stor. ital., n.s., v. 2, pt. 2. 1855.) — Dei recenti studj sulla antica civiltà arabica e della storia dei Musulmani in Sicilia di M. Amari. (*In* v. 3, pt. 2. 1856.) — Tito Livio e la critica storica a proposito del saggio di E. Taine. (*In* v. 5, pt. 1. 1857.) — Le pubblicazioni dell Istituto di Corrispondenza Archeologica. (*In* v. 8, pt. 2. 1858.) — I giornali presso gli antichi Romani. (*In* v. 9, pt. 1. 1859.) — Le antichitá dell isola di Sardegna. (*In* v. 12, pt. 1. 1860.)
— Vite de C. Menotti e V. Borelli. (*In* **Amato**, G. d'. Panteon, v. 1. 1851.)
Vannucci, Pietro, *of Perugia.* *See* **Perugino.**
Van Ostade, Adrian. Œuvre de Van O., avec une description. (*In* **Toulongeon**, F. E. Manuel du Mus. fr., v. 6. 1804.)
Van Praet. *See* **Praet.**
Van Reenen, Jacob. *See* **Reenen**, J. van.
Van Rensselaer, Cornelia, *Funeral sermon on.* 1844. *See* **Vermilye**, F. E. (**B 1226**)
Van Rensselaer, Cortlandt. New Jersey's tribute, *etc.*; eulogy on D. Webster. Burlington, N. J., Nov. 4. Burlington, 1852. 8°. (**B 1726**)
Van Rensselaer, Maunsell. Memoir of the French and Indian exped. against the province of New York, which surprised and burned Schenectady, Feb. 9, 1689–90. (*In* **N. Y. Hist. Soc.** Proc., 1846.)
Van Rensselaer, Solomon. REPORT of the trials of E. Jenkins *vs.* Van R., Van R. *vs.* J. Tayler, *vs.* C. D. Cooper, and *vs.* F. Bloodgood. *n.p.*, 1808. 8°. (**B 408**)
Van Rensselaer, Stephen. B., N. B. (*In* **Longacre**, J. B., *and* **Herring**, J. Nat. portr. gal., v. 3. 1836.)
— BARNARD, D. D. Discourse on the life and death of V. Albany, 1829. 8°.
— *Funeral sermon on.* 1839. *See* **Sprague**, W. B. (**B 1226**); — **Vermilye**, F. E. (**B 1226**)
Van Rensselaer family. HOLGATE, J. B. (*In his* Amer. genealogy. 1848.)
Vans, Wm. Claim on the heirs of J. and R. Codman. Boston, 1824. 8°. (**B 1447**)
— Life, [by himself]. Boston, 1832. 8°. (**B 1769**)
— New ed. of the demand of W. Vans on S. Codman, and heirs of J. and R. Codman. Boston, 1824. 8°. (**B 1447**)
— Statement of facts confirmed by records of the Legislature. Boston, 1837. 8°. (**B 1718**)
— Statement of facts, in answer to S. Codman. Boston, 1838. 8°. (**B 1770**)
— Statement of facts rel. to [his] demand on estates of J. and R. Codman. *n.t.p.* [Boston, 1814.] 8°. (**B 469**)
— Statement of his case dated Jan. 1832.] *n.t.p.* [Boston, 1832.] 8°. (**B 1052, 1804**)
— True statement of the demand of W. Vans against the heirs and executors of J. Codman. *n.t.p.* [1811?] 8°. (**B 1447**)
— CHILD, D. L. Review of a report to the House of Reps., Mass., on the case of Vans. Boston, 1833. 8°. (**B 1049, 1447, 1756, 1769**)
— CODMAN, J., *and others.* Exposition of the pretended claims of W. Vans on the estate of J. Codman, with an app. Boston, 1837. 2 v. 8°.
— MASS. *Gen. Court.* *Committee on Petition of W. V.* Reports, 1812–35. *n.t.p.* [Boston, 1836?] 8°. (**B 1447**)
— POWER of the legislature to suspend a law for the benefit of an individual in Mass.; pub. by the friends of Vans. Boston, 1835. 8°. (**B 1756, 1768, 1769**)
Van Santvoord, Cornelius, *D.D.* Disc. on special occasions, and miscel. papers. N.Y., 1856. 8°.
Contents. On J. Q. Adams. — Worth of the Scriptures. — Hall and Chalmers. — Refuge from the pestilence. — Intemperance and war. — Foundation of the Church. — English diction. — H. Clay. — D. Webster. — S. Johnson and D. Webster. — C. Dickens and his philosophy. — Uncle Tom's cabin and colonization. — Pitcairn's islanders. — Cannon's Pastoral theology. — Loss of the Arctic. — Rev. Dr. Brodhead.
Van Santvoord, George. Sketches of the lives and judicial services of the Chief Justices of the Supreme Court of the U.S. N. Y., 1854. 8°.
Contents. J. Jay. — J. Rutledge. — O. Ellsworth. — J. Marshall. — R. B. Taney.

Van Santvoord, *Rev.* Staats. Discourse, dedication of the Ref. Dutch Ch. of Salem, N. Y., Jan. 30. N. Y., 1845. 8°. (B 1304)
— Discourse, sacrifice of Isaac; Albany, Oct. 30, 1842. N. Y., 1843. 8°. (B 1304)

Van Schaack, Henry C. Life of P. Van Schaack. N. Y., 1842. 8°.

Van Schaack, Peter. *See the previous entry.*

Van Schaick, G. W., *and* **Low**, G. Observations on the worm so destructive to bees. (*In* **Soc. Prom. Useful Arts in N. Y.** Trans., v. 4, pt. 1. 1816.)

Van Schaick family. Holgate, J. B. (*In his* Amer. genealogy. 1848.)

Vansittart, Nicholas, *Lord Bexley*. First letter on the Brit. and For. Bible Soc., addressed to Dr. Marsh. — Letter to J. Coker in answer to his letter to V. — Outlines of a plan of finance proposed to be submitted to Parl. — 2d letter to Dr. Marsh. (*In* **Pamphleteer**, 1813; v. 1 of B 838) — The budget for 1815. — Speech, Feb. 20, 1815. (*In* 1815; v. 6) — Substance of the speech on proposing a grant of one million for providing additional places of worship in England, Mar. 16, 1818. (*In* 1818; v. 12) — Substance of [his] speech on finance. — Substance of [his] speech on the budget. (*In* 1819; v. 15) — Letters. (*In* 1828; v. 29)
— Inquiry into the state of the finances of Gr. Brit. in answer to Morgan's 'Facts'. London, 1796. 8°.
— *Another copy.* (B 763)
— Reflections on the propriety of an immediate conclusion of peace. London, 1794. 8°. (B 776)
— Dunn, W. The Vansittart plan of finance. (*In* **Pamphleteer**, 1820; v. 16 of B 838)
— Hinton, J. H. Baptists and the Bible Soc.; letter to Lord Bexley. 2d ed. London, 1838. 8°. (B 1133)
— Letter to [him], on the revenue and public morals, as connected with restoring the wine trade, *etc.*, to its proper channels. London, 1817. 8°. (B 693)
— Marsh, H. Letter to V.; answer to his second letter on the Brit. and For. Bible Soc. (*In* **Pamphleteer**, 1813; v. 1 of B 838)
— Silver, F. Observations on V's. plan of finance. (*In* **Pamphleteer**, 1813; v. 2 of B 838)

Van Tromp, *pseud.* No. 1 of the New milk cheese; or, The comi-heroick thunderclap. Boston, 1807. 8°. (B 998)

Vanufel, Charles, *and* **Champion de Villeneuve**, A. Code des colons de Sainte Domingue, *etc.* Paris, 1826. 8°.

Vanuxem, Lardner. Analysis of blue iron earth of N. J. — Two veins of pyroxene or augite in granite. — Analysis of table spar. — New locality of the automalite. (*In* **Acad. of Nat. Sci. of Phila.** Journ., v. 2. 1821.) — Zirconite of Buncombe Co., N. C. — Lamellar pyroxene. — Exam. of fused charcoal. (*In* v. 3.) — Experiments on anthracite, plumbago, *etc.* (*In* v. 5.) — Analysis of cyanite and fibrolite. (*In* v. 6. 1829.)
— Geology of N. Y. (*In* **N. Y. State.** Natural history, geology, pt. 3. 1842.)
— Origin of mineral springs. (*In* **Assoc. of Amer. Geol.** Reports, 1843.)

Vanuxem, Luis C. Remarks on a letter of L. V. in regard to the conduct of N. P. Trist towards N. Cross. Boston, 1841. 8°. (B 1449)

Van Vechten, Abraham. Speech on encreasing the number of banks in New York. Albany, 1811. 8°. (B 444)

Van Vechten, Philip. Oration. Albany, 1813. 8°. (B 457)

Van Veen, Octavio. *See* **Veen**, O. van.

Vanves, *France.* Voisin, F., *and* Falret, J. P. Notice sur l'établissement pour le traitement des aliénés des deux sexes fondé, 1822, à Vanves prés Paris. *n.t.p.* [Paris, 18—.] 8°. (B 1568)
— — *Eng.* Establishment for the treatment of both sexes affected with insanity. *n.t.p.* [Paris, 18-.] 8°. (B 1568)

Van Wagenen, John H. Discourse in different churches within the bounds of the classes of Poughkeepsie. Hudson, 1839. 8°. (B 1304)

Van Zandt, Charles C. *See* **Zandt**, C. C. van.

Van Zandt, Tobias. Eulogy, life, and character of J. H. Livingston, N. Y., 1825. 8°. (B 1102)

Vapereau, Louis Gustave. Dictionnaire universel des contemporains. Paris, 1858. 8°.
— *Same.* 2e éd. Paris, 1861. 8°.
— *Same.* Supplément. Paris, 1863. 8°.
— *Same.* 4e éd. Paris, 1870. 8°.
— *Same.* Supplément, par L. Garnier. Paris, 1873. 8°.

See also **Année** littéraire et dramatique.

Vapor. Wright, E. Dissertation on the production of vapor. (*In* **Connecticut Acad.** Mem., v. 1, pt. 1. 1810.)

Vaporeux, Le; comédie; par B. J. Marsollier des Vivetières. (*In* **Le Texier.** Recueil de théâtre, v. 2. 1785.)

Vaqueros de Aranjuez, Los. *See* **Cruz y Cano**, R. de la.

Varaggia, Giacomo da. *See* **Voragine**, J. da.

Varagine, Jacques a. *See* **Voragine**, J. da.

Varana, Giulia, *Duchess of Urbino.* Speroni, S. Orazione in morte della Duchessa di Urbino. (*In his* Opere, v. 3. 1840.)

Varannes, Valeran de, *dit* **Valarandus** *ou* **Varanus.** De gestis Joannæ virginis Francæ. (*In* **Tixier de Ravisi**, J. De memorabilibus. 1521.)

Varano *di Camerino*, Famiglia di. (*In* **Litta**, P. Fam. v. 15.)

Varanus. *See* **Varannes.**

Varbeck; par F. F. M. de B. d'Arnaud. (*In* **Biblioth.** univ. des romans, Nouv., v. 56. 1802.)

Varchi, Benedetto. Opere. Milano, *Soc. Tipog. Class. Ital.*, 1803-04. 7 v. 8°.

Contents. Vol. 1. Vita da S. Razzi. — Dedica. — Proemio. 1-5. Storia fiorentina. 6, 7. Lettera dedicatoria di G. Bottari. — Prefazione di Bottari. — L'Ercolano dialogo nel quale si ragiona delle lingue ed in particolare della toscana e della fiorentina.

— Le terze rime. (*In* **Berni**, F. Libro dell' opere burlesche, v. 1. 1823.) Orazione nella cena di signore. (*In* **Dati**, C. Prose flor., pt. 1, v. 5. 1751.) — Lezione sopra il sonetto per Petrarca La gola il sonno e l'oziose piumet. — Sopra i sonetti 33-35 del Petrarca. (*In* pt. 2, v. 5.) — Orazione delle lodi di G. B. Savello. (*In* pt. 2, v. 6.) — Lettera. (*In* pt. 4, v. 1. 1751.)
— Historia delle guerre della Republica fiorentina; colla vita da S. Razzi, e discorso di Lorenzo di Medici, sopra la nascità et morte A. de Medici. (*In* **Grævius**, J. G.. Thes. antiq. Ital., v. 8, pt. 2. 1723.)
— Egloga. — Amarylli. (*In* **Ferrario**, G. Poesie pastorali. 1808.)
— Lezioni sul Dante e prose varie. Firenze, 1841. 2 v. 8°.

Contents. Vol. 1. Prefazione. — Vita di V. — Catalogo delle opere. — Note alla vita. — Lezioni sul Dante. 2. Frammento di una lezione sopra il sonetto del Petrarca. — Lezione sopra quei versi del Trionfo d'amore del Petrarca. — Lezione nella quale si dechiarano sette Dubbi d'amore. — Parole nel rendere il consolato in nome di Mess. Guido Guidi a Mess. Agnolo Borghini. — Lettera a Luca Martini sul verbo farneticare, preceduta da una del Martini a Mess. Lodovico ***. — Parere e lettere sopra un caso cavalleresco. — Esortazione alla caccia; frammento. — Volgarizzamenti dal greco. — Trattati filosofici e letterari. — Lettere. — Note alle prose varie. — Tavola de versi citati in questo vol. — Spoglio di voci e maniere di dire.

— Sonetti. (*In* **Gironi**, R. Raccolta di lirici italiani. 1808.)
— Niceron, J. P. (*In his* Mém., v. 36. 1736.)

Varenius, Bernhard. Compleat system of geography; improved by J. Newton and Dr. Jurin, tr. [from the Latin] by Dugdale, corr. by P. Shaw. London, 1733. 2 v. 8°.
— Geographia generalis. *n.t.p.* [Amst., 1650.] 12°.

See also **Blome**, R. Cosmography; a tr. from Sanson and V. 1693.

Varennes. Mémoires sur l'affaire de Varennes, comprenant le mémoire inédit de M. le marquis de Bouillé, deux relations également inédites de MM. les comte de Raigecourt et de Damas: celle de M. le capitaine Deslon, et le précis historique de M. le comte de Valory. Paris, 1823. 8°. (Berville and Barrière. Col. des mém.)

Varennius, Joannes. Syntaxis lingæ Græcæ; repurg. R. Guillonius. Parisiis, 1564. 8°.

Varet, Alexandre. Niceron, J. P. (*In his* Mém., v. 37. 1737.)

Varflora, Fermin Arana de. *See* **Arana de Varflora**, F.

Vargas, Alphonso de, *pseud.* Relatio de stratagematis societatis Jesu. 1641. *See* **Schoppe**, C.

Varignon, Pierre. Briefwechsel zwischen Leibniz [und] V. (*In* **Leibnitz**, G. W. von. Gesam. Werke, 3e Folge, 4r Bd. 1859.)
— Nouvelle mécanique ou statique. Paris, 1725. 2 v. 4°.
— NICERON, J. P. (*In his* Mém., v. 11. 1730; *and*, *Germ.*, v. 9. 1754.)
Varillas, Antoine de. KING, W. Reflection upon Varillas's History of heresy. (*In his* Original works, v. 1. 1776.)
— NICERON, J. P. (*In his* Mém., v. 5. 1728; *and*, *Germ.*, v. 5. 1751.)
Varin, Charles Voirin, *called*, *and* **Michel**, M. A. A. Le massacre d'un innocent; vaudeville. Paris, 1855. 16°. (E 17)
Varin, Pierre Joseph. Archives administratives de Reims. Paris, 1839-48. 3 v. in 5 pts. 4°. (Doc. inéd.)
Contents. Vol. 1, pt. 1. 314-1199. 1, 2. 1200-1299. 2, pt. 1. 1300-1330. 2, 2. 1331-49. 3. 1350-99.
— Archives législatives de Reims. Paris, 1840-52. 4 v. 4°. (Doc. inéd.)
Contents. Vol. 1. Coutumes, 1269-1557. 2. Statuts, 1190-1467. 3. 1514-1699. 4. 1701-91.
— - Archives administratives et législatives de Reims: Table par L. Amiel. Paris, 1853. 4°. (Doc. inéd.)
— Des altérations de la liturgie grégorienne en France avant le 13e siécle. (*In* **Paris. Inst.** *Ac. d. Inscr.* Div. sav., 1e sér., v. 2. 1852.) — Etudes rel. à l'état politique et religieux des Iles Britanniques au moment de l'invasion saxonne. — Les causes de la dissidence entre l'église bretonne et l'église romaine, rel. à la célébration de la fête de Pâques. (*In* v. 5. 1857.)
Varinus *Phavorinus*. *See* **Guarino**, F.
Varioloid. CROSS, J. History of the variolous epidemic, Norwich, 1819; protection of vaccination. London, 1820. 8°.
— THOMSON, J. Account of the varioloid epidemic in Edinburgh, [1819]. London, Edin., 1820. 8°.
— FISHER, J. D. (*In his* Small-pox. 1829; 1834.)
See also **Small pox**; — **Vaccination.**
Varius. Fragm. (*In* **Estienne**, R. Fr. poet. Lat. 1555.)
Varius Rufus, Lucius. Fragm. (*In* **Ribbeck**, O. Scen. Rom. poesis fr., v. 1. 1852.)
Varle, Charles. Candid considerations resp. the canal between the Chesapeake and Delaware Bays. Balt., 1827. 12°. (C 173)
Varley, *Mrs.* D. Rudimentary treatise on mineralogy. 3d ed.; added, Treatise on rocks, by J. D. Dana. London, *Weale*, 1856. 12°.
Varlo, Charles. A new system of husbandry. Boston, 1785. 2 v. 8°.
— Papers rel. to New Albion.] *n.t.p.* [1784.] 8°.
Note. The papers, which are probably forgeries (*see* an article by J. Penington in Penn. Hist. Soc. Mem., v. 4, pt. 1), are: Grant of Charles I to Sir E. Plowden, Earl Palatine of Albion [apparently a tr., with alterations, of the grant to Lord Baltimore]; — Lease from the Earl Palatine to Sir T. Danby; — Release of the cograntees to the Earl Palatine; — Address of the Earl Palatine to the public. The first three are reprinted in **Hazard's** Col. of state papers, v. 1; the last in the **Penn. Hist. Soc.** Mem., v. 4, pt. 1. *See also* **N. Jersey Hist. Soc.** Col. v. 1, pp. 8-10.
Varnhagen, Francisco Adolpho de. Amerigo Vespucci. Lima, 1865. f°.
Varnhagen von Ense, Karl August Ludwig Philipp. Aus dem Nachlass Varnhagen von Ense. Lpz., 1867. 2 v. 8°.
Contents. Vol. 1. **Humboldt**, K. W. Briefe an H. Herz. — **Chamisso**, L. C. A. von. Briefwechsel zwischen A. C. und C. Duvernay. — **Tieck**, J. L. Reisebrief. 1, 2. **Louis Ferdinand**, *Prince of Prussia*. Briefe an Pauline Wiesel, und an Rahel, nebst Briefen von Paulinen und Rahel, und Aufzeichnungen von Varnhagen. 2. **Staegemann**, F. A. von. Briefe an Dr. F. Cramer in Halberstadt. — **Beyme**, K. F. von. Briefe. — **Gneisenau**, A. N., *Graf* von. Briefe. — **Haugwitz**, C. H. K., *Graf* von. Brief. — **Pahlen**, P. von. Brief. — **Pajon**, L. E. Briefe. — **Saint-Germain**, *comte* de. Brief. — **Ruckert**, F. Briefe.
— *Same.* Tagebücher von F. von Gentz; mit einem Vor- und Nachwort von V. Lpz., 1861. 8°.
— *Same.* Tagebücher von Varnhagen von Ense; [hrsg. von L. Assing]. Leipzig, 1861-70. 14 v. 8°.
— *Same.* Blätter aus der preussischen Geschichte von Varnhagen von Ense. Lpz., 1868-69. 5 v. 8°.
— Briefwechsel zwischen Varnhagen von Ense und Oelsner; nebst Briefen von Rahel; hrsg. von L. Assing. Stuttgart, 1865. 3 v. 8°.
— Denkwürdigkeiten und vermischte Schriften. 2e Aufl. Lpz., 1843-59. 9 v. 12°.
Contents. Vol. 1-3. Denkwürdigkeiten des eignen Lebens. 1. 1785-90. 2. 1808-13. 3. 1813-17. 4-6. Vermischte Schriften. 4, 5. Biographisches. 5. Kritiken. 6. Goethe. — Erzählungen. — Gedichte. — Politisches. 7. Denkwürdigkeiten des eignen Lebens, 1810-16. — Erzählungen. — Kritiken. 8. Denkwürdigkeiten, 1809-10, 1834. — Personen: Voltaire; — A. F. Bernhardi; — K. Müller; — K. G. Von Brinckmann; — L. Tieck; — Goethe. — Kritiken. — Rahel. 9. Denkwürdigkeiten, 1816-19.
— Graf Schlabrendorf, amtlos Staatsmann, heimathfremd Bürger, begütert Arm; Züge zu seinem Bilde. (*In* **Historisches** Taschenbuch, 1832.) — Das Fest des Fürsten von Schwarzenberg zu Paris, 1810. (*In* 1833.) — Die Schlacht von Deutsch-Wagram, am 5en und 6en Juli, 1809. (*In* 1836.) — Aufenthalt in Paris, 1810. (*In* 1845.)
— AUFSAETZE verschiedener Verfasser. (*In* **Varnhagen von Ense**, K. A. Denkwürd. und vermischte Schriften, v. 8. 1859.)
— CARLYLE, T. (*In his* Critical essays, v. 4. 1860.)
— COQUEREL, A. J. Varnhagen de Ense et le parti piétiste. (*In* **Revue** d. D. Mondes, féb. 1871.)
— HUMBOLDT, A. von. Briefe an V., 1827-58; nebst Auszügen aus Varnhagen's Tagebüchern, und Briefen von Varnhagen und Andern an Humboldt; [hrsg. von L. Assing]. N. Y., [1860]. 12°.
— - *Eng.* Letters to V., 1827-58; tr. by F. Kapp. N. Y., 1860. 12°.
— TAILLANDIER, R. G. E. (*In* **Revue** d. D. Mondes, juin 1854.)
— VERZEICHNISS [seiner] Bibliothek versteig. 30 Oct. Lpz., 1859. 8°.
Varnhagen von Ense, Rahel Antonie Friederike Levin Markus. Briefe. (*In* **Varnhagen von Ense**, R. A. L. P. Aus dem Nachlass, v. 2. 1867.)
Varnish. ACCOUNT of and directions for using the different kinds of coal tar and varnish. N. Y., 1788. 8°. (B 747)
— VIOLETTE, H. Guide pratique de la fabrication des vernis. Paris, [18—]. 18°.
Varnum, James Mitchell. Case, Trevett against Weeden; for refusing paper bills at par, Newport, Sept. 1786. Prov., 1787. 8°. (B 626)
— Oration, July 4; speech of A. St. Clair, *etc.* Newport, 1788. 8°. (B 651)
Varnum, *Gen.* Joseph Bradley. Address to the 3d division of Mass. militia, Concord, Aug. 27. Camb., 1800. 8°. (B 421)
— *and others.* Reply of the majority of the representatives from Mass. to the resolutions on the embargo laws. Wash., 1808. 8°. (B 553)
Varnum, Joseph Bradley, *Jr.* Seat of government of the U. S.; notice of the Smithsonian Institution. N. Y., 1848. 8°.
— *Same.* 2d ed. Wash., 1854. 8°.
— Washington sketch book; by Viator. N. Y., 1864. 12°.
Varrentrapp, Conrad. Historische Zeitschrift; Register zu Band 1-20. München, 1869. 8°.
Varrerius, Gasparus. *See* **Barreiros**, C.
Varro, Marcus Terentius. De lingua Latina; annotata a C. O. Muellero. Lps., 1833. 8°.
— *Same.* Avec la trad. en français. (*In* **Macrobius.** Opera. 1845.)
— De re rustica. (*In* **Gesner**, J. M. Scriptores rei rus., v. 1. 1787.)

— *Eng.* Three books conc. agriculture; tr. by T. Owen, with a life of the author. Oxford, 1800. 8°.

— Fragm. (*In* **Estienne, R.** Fragm. poet. Lat. 1564.)

— Hirt, A. Ueber das Vogelhaus des M. Terentius Varro zu Casinum. (*In* **Berlin. Ak. d. Wiss.** Abh., 1792-97.) — Sur la volière de M. Terentius Varron à Casinum. (*In* 1797.)

— Labitte, C. Varron et les 'Satires ménippées'. (*In* **Revue d. D. Mondes**, août 1845.)

Varro, Publius Terentius, *Atacinus*. Fragm. (*In* **Lemaire.** Poet. Lat. min., v. 4. 1825. Bibl. class. Lat.; — *and in* **Estienne, R.** Fragm. poet. Lat. 1564.)

Varronianus. *See* **Donaldson, J. W.**

Varros, Alonzo de. Proverbios morales. (*In* **Castro, A. de.** Poetas liricos de los siglos 16 y 17, v. 2. 1857; v. 42 of Aribau. Bibl.)

Vartema *or* **Varthema** (*Lat.* **Vartomanus**), Lodovico di. Itinerario. (*In* **Ramusio.** Nav., v. 1. 1563.)

— Navigation and voyages to the regions of Arabia, Egypt, Persia, Syria, Ethiopia, and East India in 1503; tr. out of the Latin by R. Eden. (*In* **Eden, R.** History of travayle. 1577; — **Hakluyt, R.** Col. of voy., v. 4. 1810; — **Selection of curious voyages.** 1812; — *and in* **Kerr, R.** Col. of voy., v. 7.)

— Travels, 1503-08; tr. from the orig. Italian ed. of 1510 by J. W. Jones; ed. by G. P. Badger. London, 1863. 8°. (Hakluyt Society, v. 32.)

Vasari, Giorgio. Life of Giovanni Angelico da Fiesole; tr. by G. A. Bezzi. London, *Arundel Soc.*, 1850. 8°.

— Ritratti de' pittori, *ec.*, cavati [dalla sua] opera; intagliati da F. Bartolozzi e A. Cappellani. Roma, 1760. 4°.

— Vite dei pittori, scultori, e architetti. Firenze, 1846-57. 13 v. 12°.

Contents. Vol. 1. Commentarj di L. Ghiberti. — Descrizione delle opere di G. Vasari. — Proemio di tutta l'opera. — Introduzione alle tre arti del disegno. — Proemio delle Vite. — G. Cimabue. — Arnolfo di Lapo. — Niccolo e Giovanni. — A. Tafi. — G. Gaddi. — Margaritone. — Giotto. 2. Agostino e Agnolo. — Stefano e Ugolino. — P. Laurati. — A. Pisano. — B. Buffalmacco. — A. Lorenzetti. — P. Cavallini. — S. e L. Memmi. — T. Gaddi. — A. Orgagna. — Tommaso detto Giottino. — Giovanni dal Ponte. — A. Gaddi. — Berna. — Duccio. — A. Viniziano. — Jacopo di Casentino. — S. Aretino. — G. Starnina. — Lippo. — Don Lorenzo. — T. Bartoli. — Lorenzo di Bicci. 3. Jacopo dalla Quercia. — Niccolo di Piero. — Dello. — Nanni d'Antonio di Barco. — Luca della Robbia. — P. Uccello. — L. Ghiberti. — Masolino da Panicale. — P. Spinelli. — Masaccio. — F. Brunelleschi. — Donato. — M. Michellozzi. — A. Filarete e Simone. 4. Giuliano da Maiano. — Piero della Francèsca. — Giovanni da Fiesole. — L. B. Alberti. — L. Vasari. — Antonello da Messina. — A. Baldovinetti. — Vellano da Padova. — F. Lippi. — P. Romano e Maestro Mino, Chimenti Camicia e Baccio Pintelli. — Andrea dal Castagno e D. Viniziano. — Gentile da Fabriano e V. Pisanello. — P. e F. Peselli. — B. Gozzoli. — Francesco di Giorgio e L. Vecchietto. — G. Galassi. — A. Rossellino e Bernardo suo fratello. — Desiderio da Settignano. — Mino da Fiesole. — L. Costa. — E. Ferrarese. 5. J., Giovanni, e Gentile Bellini. — C. Rosselli. — Cecca. — Bartolommeo. — Gherardo. — D. Guirlandaio. — A. e P. Pollaioli. — S. Botticelli. — Benedetto da Maiano. — Andrea del Verocchio. — A. Mantegna. — F. Lippi. — B. Pinturicchio. 6. F. Francia. — P. Perugino. — V. Scarpaccia, ed altri pittori viniziani e lombardi. — Jacopo detto l'Inacdo. — L. Signorelli. — Nuove indagini con documenti inediti per servire alla storia della miniatura italiana. — Tavola dei miniatori nominati nel commentario. 7. L. da Vinci. — Giorgione da Castelfranco. — A. da Corregio. — P. di Cosimo. — Bramante da Urbino. — Bartolommeo di San Marco. — M. Albertinelli. — Raffaellino del Garbo. — Torrigiano. — Giuliano e Antonio da San Gallo. 8. Raffaello. — Guglielmo da Marcilla. — Simone detto il Cronaca. — D. Puligo. — Andrea da Fiesole ed altri Fiesolani. — Vincenzio da San Gimignano e Timoteo da Urbino. — Andrea dal monte Sansovino. — Benedetto da Rovezzano. — Baccio da Montelupo e Raffaello suo figliulo. — Lorenzo di Credi. — Lorenzetto e Boccaccino. — B. Peruzzi. — G. Francesco detto il Fattore, e Pellegrino da Modana. — Andrea del Sarto. 9. Madonna Properzia de' Rossi. — A. Lombardi, Michelagnolo da Siena, Girolamo Santa-Croce, Dosso, e Battista. — G. A. Licinio da Pordenone e altri pittori del Friuli. — G. A. Sogliani. — Girolamo da Trevigi. — Pulidoro da Caravaggio, e Maturino. — Rosso. — Bartolomeo da Bagnacavallo, e di altri pittori romagnoli. — F. Bigio. — Morto da Feltro e Andrea di Cosimo Feltrini. — Marco Calavrese. — F. Mazzuoli. — Jacomo di Palma e L. Lotto. — Giocondo e Liberale ed altri Veronesi. — F. Granacci. — Baccio d'Agnolo. — V. Vicentino, Giovanni da Castel Bolognese, Matteo dal Nasaro, ed altri eccelenti intagliatori di camei e di gioie. — M. Bolognese ed altri intagliatori di stampe. 10. Antonio da Sangallo. — G. Romano. — S. Viniziano Perino del Vaga. — D. Beccafumi. — G. A. Lappoli. — Niccolò Soggi. — Niccolo detto el Tribolo. — P. da Vinci. — B. Bandinelli. — G. Bugiardini. 11. C. Gherardi detto Doceno. — Jacopo da Puntormo. — S. Mosca. — G. e B. Genga, e G. San Marino. — M. Sanmichele. — Giovannantonio detto il Soddoma, e suoi scolari. — G. Pacchiarotti. — Girolamo del Pacchia. — Bastiano detto Aristotile. — B. Garofolo, Girolamo da Carpi, e altri Lombardi. — R., D., e B. Grillandai. — Giovanni da Udine. — B. Franco. 12. G. F. Rustici. — G. A. Montorsoli. — Francesco detto de Salviati. — D. Ricciarelli. — T. Zucchero. — Michelagnolo Buonarroti. 13. F. Primaticcio. — Tiziano da Cador. — J. Sansavino. — L. L. Aretino e d'altri scultori ed architetti. — Don Giulio Clovio. — Diversi artefici italiani, — fiamminghi. — Accademici del disegno. — G. Bologna. — Apparato fatto in Firenze per le nozze di Don Francesco de' Medici con la regina Giovanna d'Austria. — L'autore agli artefici del disegno.

— *Eng.* Lives of painters, sculptors, and architects; tr., with notes by Mrs. J. Foster. London, *Bohn*, 1850-52. 5 v. 8°.

Contents the same as in the Italian edition, v. 1 of this corresponding to v. 1, 2, and 3 of the Italian as far as Michellozzi; v. 2 ending with v. 7 of the Italian; v. 3 ending with v. 9; v. 4 ending in v. 11 with the 'altri Lombardi'; v. 5 finishing the work.

— Vite di alcuni artefici fiorentini: B. di Lorenzo. — D. Delli. — P. e F. di Pesello. — G. Toscani. — M. da Panicale e Masaccio. (*In* **Giornale** degli archiv. toscani, v. 4. 1860.) — A. del Castagno e D. Veneziano. — P. della Francesca. — D. da Settingano. — Pietro e Polito del Donzello. (*In* v. 6. 1862.)

— Wyatt, A. Le 'Libro dei disegni' du Vasari. (*In* **Gazette** des beaux-arts, v. 4. 1859.)

Vasco, GianBattista. Della moneta. — Delle Università delle Arti e Mestieri. — Mém. sur les causes de la mendicité et sur les moyens de la supprimer. (*In* **Econ.** class. ital., pt. mod., v. 33. 1804.) — La felicità pubblica considerata nei coltivatori di terre proprie. — L'usura libera. (*In* v. 34.) — Del setificio. — Annunzii ed estratti sopra diversi oggetti di economia polit. — Nuove tavole dei vitalizii. (*In* v. 35. 1804.)

Vasco Nunez de Balboa. *See* **Balboa, V. N. de.**

Vasconcellos, Agostinho Manoel de. Niceron, J. P. (*In his* Mém., v. 42. 1741.)

Vasconcellos, Diogo Mendes de. Vida do licenciado A. de Rezende. — O livro do municipio eborense. (*In* **Souza Farinha, B. J. de.** Col. das antiquidades de Evora. 1785.)

Vascular system. Dupuytren, G. Lesions; tr. by F. L. G. Clark. London, 1847. 8°. (Sydenham Soc.)

Vaselli, Crescenzio. Vita di P. M. Gabbrielli. (*In* **Crescimbeni, G. M.** Vite degli Arcadi illustri, v. 2. 1710.)

Vases. [Designs of vases.] *n.p.*, [16—]. f°. (E 118)

— Petitot, E. A. Suite des vases tirée du cabinet de Du Tillot et gravée par B. Bossi. Milan, *n.d.* [*engr.* Parme, 1764.] f°. (**E 104**)

— Piranesi, G. B. Vasi, candelabri, cippi, tripodi, lucerne, ed ornamenti antichi. *n.p.*, 1779. 2 v. f°. (v. 7.)

— - *Same.* [115 plates.] *n.p.*, 1779. 2 v. f°.

— Hamilton, *Sir* W. Col. of engravings from ancient vases. Naples, 1791-95. 3 v. f°.

— Uhden, W. Ueber ein altes Vasengemälde. (*In* **Berlin. Ak. d. Wiss.** Abh., 1804-11.)

— Heyne, C. G. Vasorum fictilium litteratorum et ectyporum genus superstes. (*In* **Goettingen.** Ges. d. Wiss. Comm., 1808-11.)

— Nicolas, F. Illustrazioni di due vasi fittile ed altri monumenti in Pesto. Roma, 1809. f°.

— Boardman, J. General account of vases. (*In his* Museum Etruriæ. 1817.)

— FRANCHI DI PONT, G., *conte.* Illustrazione di un vaso di bronzo ornato di scolture. (*In* **Turin. Ac. d. Sci.** Mem., v. 23. 1818.)
— ENGLEFIELD, *Sir* H. Vases from the col. of E. drawn and eng. by H. Moses. London, [1820]. 8°.
— ANTONINI, C. Manuale di varj ornamenti componenti la serie de' vasi antichi in Roma. Roma, 1821. 3 v. 4°.
— MÜLLER, C. O. De origine pictorum vasorum quæ per hos annos in Etruriæ agris, quos olim Volcientes tenuere, effossa sunt. (*In* **Goettingen. Ges. d. Wiss.** Comm., 1828–32.)
— INGHIRAMI, F. Pitture di vasi etrusche, [1831–37]. 2a ed. Firenze, 1852–56. 4 v. 4°.
— CAMPANARI, S. Antichi vasi dipinti della collezione Feoli. Roma, [1837]. 8°.
— GERHARD, E. Ueber die Vase des Midias. (*In* **Berlin. Ak. d. Wiss.** Abh., 1839.)
— GERHARD, E. Auserlesene griechische Vasenbilder. Berlin, 1840–58. 4 v. *and* Plates 4°.
— FALBE, C. T. Vases antiques du Pérou. [1841.] (*In* **Copenhagen. R. Nord. Oldsk. Selsk.** Mém., 1840–44.)
— GERHARD, E. Etruskische und kampanische Vasenbilder des König. Museum zu Berlin. Berlin, 1843. f°.
— – Apulische Vasenbilder des König. Mus. zu Berlin. Berlin, 1845. f°.
— PANOFKA, T. Der Vasenbildner Panphaios. — Die Vasenmaler Euthymides und Euphronios. — Von den Namen der Vasenbildner in Beziehung zu ihren bildlichen Darstellungen. (*In* **Berlin. Ak. d. Wiss.** Abh., 1848.)
— DISNEY, J. Discr. of marbles, vases, *etc.*, in the Fitzwilliam Museum. London, 1849. 4°.
— GERHARD, E. Ueber eine cista mystica des brittischen Museums. (*In* **Berlin. Ak. d. Wiss.** Abh., 1849.)
— WELCKER, F. G. Griechische Vasengemälde. (*In his* Alte Denkmäler, v. 3. 1851.)
— JACQUEMART, A. De la forme et de la nomenclature des vases. (*In* **Gazette** des beaux-arts, v. 11, 12. 1861–62.)
— WELCKER, F. G. Statuen, Basreliefe, und Vasengemälde. (*In his* Alte Denkmaler, v. 5, 1864.)
— JACQUEMART, A. Les merveilles de la céramique, ou l'art de façonner et de décorer les vases en terre cuite, *etc.* (Vol. 1, 3, 2e éd.) Paris, 1868–71. 3 v. 16°.
See also **Panthenaïc vases**; — **Portland vase**; — **Pottery**; — **Winged figures**; — *also various articles in* **Archæologia.**

Vasi, Giuseppo. Itinerario di Roma. Roma, 1763. 12°.
— Narrazione delle feste fatte celebrare la nascità de Filippo princ. delle Due Sicile. Napoli, 1749. f°.

Vasi, Mariano. [Thirty views in and near Naples; probably from his 'New picture of Naples'.] *Mounted in* 4°.

Vasquez de Coronado, Francisco. Relatione del viaggio al città di Cevola. (*In* **Ramusio, G. B.** Navig., v. 3. 1565.)
— *Eng.* Expedition, *etc.* (*In* **Burney, J.** Discoveries in South Sea, v. 1. 1803; — *and in* **Hakluyt, R.** Col. of voy., v. 3. 1810.)
— Sommario di due sue lettere del viag. fatto da M. da Nizza al città di Cevola. (*In* **Ramusio, G. B.** Navig., v. 3. 1565.)

Vassa, Gustavus. Life of V.; by himself. Boston, 1837. 12°.

Vassal family. PAIGE, L. R. Reminiscences of the Vassal family. (*In* **Mass. Hist. Soc.** Proc., 1858–60.)

Vassall, Henry Richard Fox, *3d Ld. Holland.* Foreign reminiscences. London, 1850. 8°.
— *Same.* N. Y., 1851. 12°.
— Life and writings of Lope Felix de Vega. London, 1806. 8°.
— Memoirs of the Whig Party; ed. by his son. London, 1852. 2 v. 8°.
— BROUGHAM, H., *Ld.* (*In his* Statesmen of the times of George III., v. 3. 1843.)
— MACAULAY, T. B. (*In his* Crit. and Miscel. essays, v. 4. 1843.)

Vassall Morton; a novel, by F. Parkman. Boston, 1856. 12°.

Vassalli Eandi, Anton Maria. Mémoire historique. (*In* **Turin. Ac. d. Sci.** Mem., v. 2. 1816.) — Annali della Accademia, 1815–18. (*In* v. 23.) — Memorie int. alla vita ed agli studi di G. F. Cigna. (*In* v. 26.) — CARENA, G. Notizie del prof. V. (*In* v. 30. 1826.)

Vassallo, Cesare. On Maltese antiquities. (*In* **Amer. Orient. Soc.** Journ., v. 3. 1853.)

Vassar, J. J. Copies of a corresp. with Mr. Huskisson and Mr. Perceval on the waste and abuses in the military establishments and expenditures. London, 1810. 8°. (B 1678)

Vassar College. LOSSING, B. J. Vassar Coll. and its founder. N. Y., 1867. 8°.

Vassilief, V. Der Buddhismus, seine Dogmen, Geschichte, und Literatur; aus dem russischen, 1r Theil. St. Petersburg, 1860. 8°.

Vastey, Pompée Valentin, *baron* de. A mes concitoyens, Haytiens! Cap Henry, [1815]. 4°. (A 17)
Note. Quérard gives the author's names as Pompée Valentin, but in 'Notes à Malouet', it is given as J. L.
— Le cri de la conscience; réponse à 'Le peuple de la république d'Hayti'. Cap Henry, 1815. 4°. (A 17)
— Le cri de la patrie ou les intérêts de tous les Haytiens. Cap Henry, [18—]. 4°. (A 17)
— Essai sur les causes de la révolution et des guerres civile d'Hayti. Sans-Souci, 1819. 12°.
— Notes à Malouet, en réfutation du 4e vol. de son ouvrage, 'Collection de mém. sur les colonies, *etc.* Cap-Henry, 1814. 8°. (B 795)
— Political remarks on some French works and newspapers conc. Hayti. (*In* **Pamphleteer**, 1818; v. 13 of B 838)
— Reflections sur une lettre de Mazères sur les noirs et les blancs, le royaume d'Hayti, *etc.* , Cap Henry, 1816. 8°. (B 793, 795)
— *Eng.* Reflections on the blacks and whites; remarks upon a letter, *etc.* London, 1817. 12°. (C 67)
— Système colonial dévoilé. Cap-Henry, 1814. 8°. (B 795)

Vasto, Alfonzo, *marchese* del. Sonetto. (*In* **Trucchi, F.** Poesie ital., v. 3. 1847.)

Vatabli, François. *See* **Bible** (p. 268).

Vatel, ou Le petit fils d'un grand homme; comédie-vaudeville par E. Scribe. Berlin, 1842. 12°. (E 22)

Vater, Johann Severin. Tables of eccles. hist. from the origin of Christianity; abstracted from Vater's 'Synchronistische Tafeln', by F. Cunningham. Boston, 1831. 8°.
— Litteratur der Grammatiken, Lexica, und Wörtersammlungen aller Sprachen der Erde. Berlin, 1815. 8°.
— *Same.* 2e Ausg., von Jülg. Berlin, 1847. 8°.
— *tr.* Mithridates; fortg. von V. *See* **Adelung, J. C.**

Vater von Ungefähr, Der; von A. v. **Kotzebue.** (*In his* Theater, v. 18. 1841.)

Vaterfreude; von A. W. Iffland. (*In his* Theat. Werke, v. 9. 1860.)

Vathek; [by W. Beckford]; tr. from the original French. From the 3d London ed. Phila., 1816. 18°.

Vatican. *See* **Rome. Vatican** (p. 2549, 50); — **Popes** (p. 2388, 89); — **States of the Church** (p. 2850).

Vatican Council, 1870. HERGENRÖTHER, J. A. Anti-Janus; criticism on [Huber's] 'Pope and the Council'; tr. by J. R. Robertson. Dublin, 1870. 8°.
— HUBER, V. A. The Pope and the council; by Janus; tr. from the German. Boston, 1870. 12°.
— LEGGE, A. O. (*In his* Growth of the temporal power. 1870.)
— MANNING, H. E. The Vatican Council and its definitions. London, 1870. 8°.
— OEKUMENISCHE Concil, Das, im Jahre 1870. 1er–3r Artikel. (*In* **Unsere Zeit**, 6r Jahr., 2e Hälfte, 1870.)
Note. The 3d article is by A. von Volpi.
— PRESSENSÉ, E. Le concile du Vatican. (*In* **Révue d. D. Mondes**, mars 1870.)

— QUIRINUS, *pseud.* Letters from Rome on the Council. Repr. from the Allgemeine Zeitung. London, 1870. 16°.

— VATICAN; a weekly record of the Council. [Supplement to the Tablet.] Dec. 1869 – June 25, 1870. London, 1869–70. f°.

Vaticination. DU MOULIN, P. Vates; de præcognitione futurorum. Lugd. Bat., 1640. 8°.

Vatout, Jean. Le chateau de Compiègne; souvenirs historiques. Paris, 1852. 8°.

— Le palais de Saint Cloud; souvenirs historiques. Paris, 1852. 8°.

Vatry, J., *l'abbé.* Discours sur la fable épique. (*In* Sérieys, A. Bibl. acad., pt. 10. 1811.)

Vattel, Emmerich de. Le droit des gens; accomp. des notes de Pinheiro-Ferreira et du baron de Chambrier d'Oleires; augm. du discours par Sir J. Mackintosh; complétée par l'exposition des doctrines des publicistes contemporains, *etc.*, par P. Pradier-Fodéré. Nouv. éd. Paris, 1863. 3 v. 12°.

— *Eng.* Law of nations. London, 1760, 59. 2 v. 4°.

— *Same.* New ed., corr. London, 1793. 8°.

— *Same.* New ed. London, 1797. 8°.

Vattemare, Alexandre. International literary exchanges; proceedings of a meeting of the citizens of the U. S.; with an address. Paris, 1845. 8°. (B 1187)

Vauban, Sébastien Le Prestre, *marquis* de. Œuvres militaires; rev. et augm. par P. F. Foissæ. Paris, [1795]. 3 v. 8°.

Contents. Vol. 1. Traité de l'attaque des places. 2. Traité de la défense des places. 3. Traité des mines.

— Attaque et défense des places. Tome 2: Traité des mines par [Vauban] et un autre de la guerre par un officier de distinction. Nouv. éd. La Haye, 1743. 8°.

— KIMBER, T. First system of fortification; with a life of Vauban. 3d ed. London, 1861. 8°.

— MALDEN, H. (*In his* Distinguished men of modern times, v. 2. 1838; v. 38 of Lib. ent. knl.)

Vaublanc, Vincent Marie Viénot, *comte* de. Defence of Lafayette. (*In* Lafayette, M. J. P. R. T. G. de M. IMPEACHMENT. 1793.)

— Mémoires. Paris, 1857. 8°. (Barrière, F. Bibliothèque des mém.)

Vaucanson, Jacques de. Tratado del arte de hilar, *etc.*, las sedas, segun el metodo de V. *See* Lapayese.

— CONDORCET, J. A. N. C. Eloge de Vaucanson. (*In his* Œuvres, v. 2 1847.)

Vaucelles, A. de. Le nid de loriots. (*In* Semaine lit., v. 2.)

Vaucher, Jean Pierre Etienne. Histoire des conferves d'eau douce; suivie de l'hist. des trémellis et des ulves. Genève, 1803. 4°.

Vaucher-Crémier. Plans et devis de prisons, *etc.* (*In* Aubanel, C. Mémoire, *etc.*, 1837.)

Vauchopius. *See* Wauchope.

Vaucluse. GUERIN, J. Description de la fontaine de Vaucluse. Avignon, 1804. 16°.

Vaud. VERDEIL, A. Guerre des Suisses contre le duc de Bourgogne dans le pays de Vaud, 1475–76; fragm. de la 2e éd. de 'L'histoire du canton de Vaud'. Lausanne, 1854. 16°.

— CART, J. J. Lettres sur le droit public [du pays de Vaud] et sur les événemens actuels. Paris, 1793. 8°.

Vaudemont, *Mme. la princesse* de. BASSANVILLE, A. L., *comtesse* de. (*In her* Les salons d'autrefois, 1er sér. 1862.)

Vaudois. *See* Waldenses.

Vaudoncourt, Frédéric François Guillaume de. *See* Guillaume *de Vaudoncourt*, F. F.

Vaudreuil, Louis Philippe de Rigaud, *marquis* de. 'Observations addressés au Conseil de Guerre à l'Orient. *n.p.*, [1782]. 4°. (W 71)

— GRASSE-TILLY, F. J. P. de. Réponse aux 'Observations'. *n.p.*, [1782]. 4°. (W 71)

Vaudrocques Diel d'Enambuc, Pierre. GUÉRIN, L. (*In his* Les navigateurs français. 1847.)

Vaugelas, Claude Favre de. Remarques sur la langue françoise. Nouv. éd., avec des notes de T. Corneille. Tome 1. Paris, 1787. 12°.

— NICERON, J. P. (*In his* Mém., v. 19. 1732; *and Germ.*, v. 15. 1757.)

— PATRU, O. Remarques sur les 'Remarques' de V. (*In his* Œuvres, v. 2. 1732.)

Vaughan, Benjamin. Remarks on a dangerous mistake made as to the eastern boundary of Louisiana. Boston, 1814. 8°. (B 454, 2531)

— The rural Socrates; account of a celebrated philosophical farmer lately living in Switzerland and known by the name of Kliyogg. Hallowell, 1800. 8°.

— Ten hints addressed to wise men conc. the dispute, Nov. 8, 1809, in the dismission of Mr. Jackson. *n.t.p.* [1810.] 8°. (B 437)

— GARDINER, R. H. Memoir of V. (*In* Maine Hist. Soc. Col., v. 6. 1859.)

Vaughan, Charles John, *D.D.* Plain words on Christian living. (*In* Good words, v. 5. 1864.) — Christ the light of the world. (*In* v. 6.) — Half hours in the Temple Church. (*In* v. 11. 1870.)

Vaughan, Charles Richard. Narrative of the siege of Zaragoza. 2d ed. London, 1809. 8°. (B 1420)

— *Same.* 5th ed., with add. London, 1809. 8°. (B 680)

Vaughan, Daniel. Chemical action of feeble currents of electricity. (*In* Amer. Assoc. Proc., v. 5. 1857.) — On the influence of terrestrial electricity on climate. (*In* v. 6.) — Stability of satellites revolving in small orbits. (*In* v. 10. 1857.)

— Popular physical astronomy. Cincin., 1858. 8°

Vaughan, Edward Thomas. Dissertatio Latina præmio annuo dignata Cantab. 1833. (*In* Cambridge Univ. Prolusiones. 1833. B 1236)

Vaughan, Henry. Works complete; edited with memorial introduction, essay, and notes by A. B. Grosart. Vol. 1–4. Blackburn, 1871. 4 v. 16°. (Fuller worthies lib.)

Contents. Vol. 1. Dedication to Sir J. D. Coleridge. — Preface. — Memorial-introduction. — Note. — Authoris de se emblema. — The author's preface. — Texts of Scripture. — Verse dedication to Christ. — Vain wits, *etc.* — Silex scintillans. — Thalia rediviva. — Folia Silvulæ, 1650–1678. 2. Essay on life and writings of V. — Secular poetry: Poems of 1646; — Olor Iscanus, 1651; — Thalia rediviva, 1678; — Aurea grana, 1640–61. — Verse remains of T. Vaughan, twin brother. 3. Mount of Olives. — Of the benefit we may get from our enemies, after Plutarch and M. Tyrius. — The diseases of the mind and bodie, from Plutarch. — Praise and happinesse of the countrie life. — Hermetical physick. — Epistle dedicatory to R. Vaughan's 'Coin and coinage', 1675. 4. Flores solitudinis: Temperance and patience; — Life and death, by Nierembergius; — The world contemned, by Eucherius; — Life of Paulinus, Bp. of Nola. — Additional notes and illustrations. — Indices.

— Sacred poems; with mem. by H. F. Lyte. Boston, 1854. 16°.

— Poems. (*In* Campbell, T. Brit. poets, v. 4. 1819.)

— WILLMOTT, R. A. (*In his* Lives of the English sacred poets, v. 1. 1839.)

Vaughan, Henry Halford. The effects of a national taste for general and diffusive reading. (*In* Oxford prize essays, v. 5. 1836.)

Vaughan, *Gen.* John. Expedition up the Hudson, 1777. (*In* Ulster Historical Society. Col., v. 1, pt. 2. 1861.)

Vaughan, John, *M.D.*, *d.* 1807. Chemical syllabus. [Wilmington, 1799?] 12°. (C 63)

— Valedictory lecture before the Philosophical Soc., Delaware. Wilmington, 1800. 8°. (C 63)

Vaughan, John. Abstracts from eight annual statements, 1809–16, of the deaths in Phila. (*In* Amer. Phil. Soc. Trans., n.s., v. 1. 1818.)

Vaughan, John Champion. BRADBURN, G. A statement of his connection with the 'True Democrat' and V. Cleveland, 1853. 8°. (B 1450)

Vaughan, *Mrs.* Mary C. Woman's work in the civil war. 1866. *See* Brockett, L. P.

Vaughan, Robert, *D.D.* Age of great cities. London, 1843. 8°.

— English nonconformity. London, 1862. 8°.

— History of England under the Stuarts and the Commonwealth. London, 1840. 2 v. 8°. Lib. Usef. Knowl.)

— Life and opinions of J. de Wycliffe. London, 1828. 2 v. 8°.
— Memorials of the Stuart Dynasty. London, 1831. 2 v. 8°.
— Protectorate of Cromwell, and state of Europe, during the early part of the reign of Louis XIV. London. 1838. 2 v. 8°.
— Revolutions in English history. London, 1859-63. 3 v. 8°.
Contents. Vol. 1. Celts and Romans. — Saxons and Danes. — Normans and English. — English and Normans. — Lancaster and York. 2. Nationalists and Romanists. — Protestants and Nationalists. — Romanists and Protestants. — Anglicans and Romanists. — Anglicans and Puritans. — England under Elisabeth. 3. Parliamentarians and Royalists. — Republicans and Royalists. — Court and country. — National progress since 1688.
See also the next entry.

Vaughan, Robert Alfred. Essays and remains; ed. with mem. by R. Vaughan. London, 1858. 2 v. 16°.
Contents. Vol. 1. Memoir. — Origen. — Schleiermacher. — Savonarola and his times. — Mackay's Religious development in Greece. 2. Hypatia. — Life of Sydney Smith. — The Christ of history. — Lewes's Life and works of Goethe. — The German courts. — French romances of the 13th cent. — Miscel. papers. — Fragm. of criticism. — Thoughts on religion. — Poetry.
— Hours with the mystics. London, 1856. 2 v. 16°.
Contents. Vol. 1. Introd. — Early oriental mysticism. — The mysticism of the Neo-Platonists. — Mysticism in the Greek Church, — Latin Church. — German mysticism in the 14th century. — Persian mysticism in the Middle Age. 2. Theosophy in the age of the Reformation. — The Spanish mystics. — Quietism. — Mysticism in England. — Swedenborg.

Vaughan, Thomas (*pseud.* Eugenius Philalethes), *d.* 1665. English and Latin verse-remains. (*In* **Vaughan, H.** Works, v. 2. 1871.)

Vaughan, Thomas. TRYAL and condemnation for high treason, Nov. 6, 1696. London, 1697. f°. (A 55)

Vaughan, Walter, *M.D.* Anatomy and physiology, including Prælectiones anatomicæ of F. Leber. London, 1791. 2 v. 8°.
— Essay on headaches and their cure. London, 1825. 8°.

Vaughan, Wm., *b.* 1577. Fifteen directions to preserve health; from his Naturall and artificial directions for health. (*In* **Furnivall, F. J.** The babee's book. 1868.)

Vaughan, Wm., *Councilor of N. H.* GR. BRIT. *Privy Council.* Order in council upon his petition, 1685. (*In* **New Hampshire Hist. Soc.** Col., v. 1. 1824.) — BELL, S. D. Brief notice of V. (*In* v. 8. 1866.)

Vaughan, Wm. Answer to objections against the London docks. London, 1796. 8°. (B 748)
— Comparative statement of the advantages and disadvantages of the docks in Wapping and in the Isle of Dogs, *etc.* 2d ed. London, 1799. 8°. (B 748)
— Examination of W. Vaughan in a committee of the Ho. of Com., Apr. 22, 1796, on the commerce of London and the accommodations for shipping, *etc.* London, 1796. 8°. (B 748)
— Letter to a friend on commerce and free ports, and London docks. London, 1796. 8°. (B 748)
— Narrative of D. Woodard and four seamen; cont. an account of the sufferings in the islands of Celebes; ed. by W. Vaughan. London, 1804. 8°.
— On wet docks, quays, and warehouses for the trade of London; with hints resp. trade. London, 1793. 8°. (B 748)
— Plan of the London dock, with observations resp. the river. London, 1794. 8°. (B 748)
— Reasons in favour of the London docks. London, 1796. 8°. (B 748)
— *Same.* London, 1797. 8°. (B 748)

Vaugondy. *See* **Robert de Vaugondy.**

Vaulabelle, Achille Tenaille de. Histoire des deux restaurations. 3e éd. Paris, 1855-57. 8 v. 8°.
Contents. Vol. 1. 1793-1814. 2. 1814-15. 3. 1815. 4. 1815-18. 5. 1819-21. 6. 1822-25. 7. 1824-28. 8. 1829-30.

Vault, François Eugène de. Mém. militaires rel. à la succession d'Espagne sous Louis XIV, [1701-13]; rev., *etc.*, par Pelet. Paris, 1835-62. 11 v. 4° *and* Atlas f°. (Doc. inéd.)

Vaults (*in architecture*). WARE, S. Observations on vaults. (*In* **Archæologia**, v. 17. 1814.)
— - Tracts on vaults and bridges. London, 1822. 8°.

Vaulx-Cernay, Pierre de. *See* **Pierre** *de Vaulx Cernay.*

Vaumorière, Pierre d'Ortigue de. *See* **Ortigue, P. d'.**

Vauquelin, Nicolas, *sieur des Yvetaux.* Poésies. (*In* **Annales** poétiques, v. 14. 1780.)

Vauquelin, Nicolas Louis. Chimie. (*In* **Encyclopédie** méthod., v. 53. 1815.)
— Observations. (*In* **Izarn, J.** Des pierres tombées du ciel. 1803.)

Vauquelin de la Fresnaye, Jean. Satires, epigrammes, *etc.* (*In* **Annales** poétiques, v. 9. 1779.)
— Satires, *etc.* (*In* **Auguis**, P. R. Poètes françois, v. 5. 1824.)
— Satires, *etc.* (*In* **Cary**, H. F. Early French poets. 1846.)

Vauréal, Louis Gui de Guerapin de, *évêque de Rennes.* ALEMBERT, J. le R. d'. Eloge. (*In his* Œuvres, v. 9. 1805.)

Vautrin. *See* **Balzac, H. de.**

Vauvenargues, Luc de Clapiers, *marquis* de. Œuvres complètes. Nouv. éd. Paris, 1821. 3 v. 8°.
Contents. Vol. 1. Notice de la vie et les écrits de V., par Suard. — Fragm. sur V. — Epîtres de Marmontel à Voltaire. — Extrait des mélanges littéraires. — Disc. prelim. — Introd. à la connaissance de l'esprit humain. — Réflexions sur divers sujets. — Réflexions critiques sur quelques poétes. — Les orateurs. — Caractères. 2. Réflexions et maximes. — Disc. sur la gloire. — Sur les plaisirs. — Sur le caractère des différens siècles. — Fragm. sur les effets de l'art et du savoir, *etc.* — Sur les mœurs du siècle. — Sur l'inégalité des richesses. — Eloge de P. H. E. de Seytres. — Méditation sur la foi. — Traité sur le libre arbitre. — Réponse à quelques objections. — Sur la liberté. — Réponse aux consequences de la nécessité. — Sur la justice. — Sur la Providence. — Sur l'économie de l'univers. — Imitation de Pascal. — Du stoïcisme et du Christianisme. — Illusions de l'impie. — Vanité des philosophes. — Lettres. 3. Dialogues. — Réflexions sur divers sujets. — Caractères. — Variantes. — Réflexions et maximes. — Eloge de Louis XV. — Réflexions sur le caractère des différens siècles. — Lettres inéd. de Voltaire à V.
— PERRENS, F. T. (*In* **Revue** d. D. Mondes, nov. 1857.)

Vauvilliers, Jean François. Account of the manuscript of Eschylus in the King's library. (*In* **Paris. Inst.** *Ac. d. Inscr.* Accounts of mss., v. 1. 1789.)

Vaux, Calvert. Designs for villas and cottages. N. Y., 1857. 8°.

Vaux, James Edward. Clerical celibacy. (*In* **Shipley, O.** The church and the world. 1866.) — Missions and preaching orders. (*In* 1868.)

Vaux, Robert de. De veritate et antiquitate artis chemicæ. (*In* **Zetzner, L.** Theat., v. 1. 1613.)

Vaux, Roberts. Address before Phila. Soc. for Prom. Agric. Phila., 1825. 8°. (B 541)
— Memoirs of the life of A. Benezet. Phila., *pr.*, York, *repr.* 1817. 12°.
— *French.* Mémoires sur la vie d'A. Bénezet. Paris, 1824. 16°.
— *and* **McEuen, T.** Notice of the fall of a meteoric stone at Deal, N. J. (*In* **Acad. of Nat. Sci. Phila.** Journ., v. 6. 1829.)
— PETTIT, T. M. Memoir of R. Vaux; read Mar. 18, 1840. (*In* **Penn. Hist. Soc.** Mem., v. 4, pt. 1. 1840.

Vaux, Thomas, *Ld.* Upon his white hairs; from The aged lover's renunciation of love. (*In* **Campbell, T.** Spec. of Brit. poets, v. 2. 1819.)

Vaux, Wm. Sandys Wright. Handbook to the antiquities in the British Museum. London, *Murray*, 1851. 12°.

Vaux de St. Cyr, Odet Jos. ALEMBERT, J. le R. d'. (*In his* Œuvres, v. 9. 1805.)

Vavasseur, François. De epigrammate liber, et epigrammata. Parisiis, 1669. 8°.
— NICERON, J. P. (*In his* Mém., v. 27. 1734; *and Germ.*, v. 22. 1762.)

Vawdrey, *Rev.* Daniel. Plain advice to rich and poor, *etc.* with a pastor's apology, in three sermons, Cheshire, 1839. Liverpool, 1840. 12°. (C 218)

Vayer, François de la Mothe le. *See* **La Mothe le Vayer**, F. de.

Vayraõ. RIBEIRO, J. P. Acerca da inscrip. lapidar que se acha no mosteiro do Salvador de Vayraõ, de religiosas Benedictinas, no bispado do Porto. (*In* **Lisbon. Ac. d. Sci.** Mem. lit., v. 5. 1793.)

Vayringe, Philippe. DAVENPORT, R. A. (*In his* Lives of individuals who have raised themselves to eminence, 1841. Fam. lib., v. 79.)

Vaz, Lopez. Discourse of the West Indies and South Sea; wherein certaine voyages of our Englishmen are truly reported. (*In* **Hakluyt**, R. Col. of voy., v. 4. 1811.)

— *Same, abridged.* (*In* **Purchas.** Pilgrimes, v. 4. 1625.)

— *Same, in part.* Account of Drake's voyage to Magellanica. (*In* **Callander**, J. Terra Austr., v. 1. 1766.)

Vaz, Tristrano. Viagem. (*In* **Barros**, J. de. Da Asia, v. 1. 1778.)

— *Eng.* Voyages. (*In* **General** col. of voy. by the Portuguese, *etc.* 1789.)

Vaz de Velasco, Alfonso. *See* **Velazquez de Velasco**, A.

Vazie, Wm. Observations on tunnels, 1807. *See* **Millar**, J. (B 1744)

Vazquez de Acuña, Juan. Vida del cardenal duque de Richelieu. (*In* **Valladares**, A. Seman. erud., v. 19. 1789.)

Ve. *See* **Væ.**

Veaux. *See* **De Veaux.**

Veazie, *Rev.* Samuel, *Funeral sermon on.* 1809. *See* **Jenks**, W. (B 319)

Vecchiani, Girolamo. FABRONI, A. (*In his* Mem. di pisani, v. 4. 1792.)

Vecchio bizzarro, Il; commedia. *See* **Goldoni**, C.

Vecchj, Augusto, *Il colonello.* Garibaldi at Caprera; tr. by **Mrs. Gaskell.** Camb., London, 1862. 16°.

— La leggenda della famiglia Cantelina. (*In* **Brofferio**, A. Tradiz. ital., v. 1. 1847.)

Vecellio, Tiziano. *See* **Tiziano Vecellio.**

Vecelli family. TICOZZI, S. Vite dei pittori Vecellj di Cadore. Milano, 1817. 8°.

Vecerius, Conrad. Historia de duabus seditionibus Siciliæ, 1517. (*In* **Grævius.** Thes. antiq. Sicil., v. 5. 1723.)

Vechner, Georg, *and* **Scultetus**, J. Ducatus Breslanus. Amst., *J. Jansson*, [16—]. (E 78, no. 132)

Veck, Toby, *pseud.* Facts and figures. No. 1: Ten tables telling tales of my landlord and the church, *etc.* London, 1846. 8°. (B 1536)

Vedâla Cadai; the Tamul version of a collection of tales in the Sanscrit; tr. by B. G. Babington. (*In* **Oriental Translation Fund.** Misc. trans., v. 1. 1831.)

Vedanta. The Vedant; or, Resolutions of the Vedas; abridgement of Eng. tr. by Rammohun Roy. Calcutta, 1816. 8°.

— Selections; tr. by Rammohun Roy. Calcutta, 1844. 12°. (E 133)

— Translation of an abridgment of the Vedant; by Rammohun Roy. Calcutta, 1818. 8°. (B 1469)

— COLEBROOKE, H. T. On the Védánta. (*In his* miscel. essays, v. 1. 1837.)

Vedas. Extracts. (*In* **Jones**, *Sir* W. Works, v. 6. 1799.)

— Atharva veda Prâtiçâkhya, or Çâunakîyâ caturâdhyâyikâ; translated by Wm. D. Whitney. (*In* **Amer. Orient. Soc.** Journ., v. 7. 1862.)

— Rig-vedæ specimen ed. F. Rosen. [Sanskrite et Latine.] Londini, 1830. 4°.

— Rigveda sanhita, liber I; sanskrite et Latine; ed. F. Rosen. London, *Oriental Tr. Fund*, 1838. 4°.

— *Eng.* Rig-veda-sanhita; translated and explained by F. Max Mueller. Vol. 1. London, 1869. 8°.

— - *Same.* Tr. by H. H. Wilson. London, 1850–57. 3 v. 8°.

— - Aitareya brahmanam of the Rigveda; ed. and tr. by M. M. Haug; [Sanskrit and Eng.]. Bombay, 1863. 2 v. 12°.

— - MUELLER, F. M. The Aitareya-brâhmana, 1864. (*In his* Chips from a Germ. workshop, v. 1. 1867.)

— Sanhitá of the Sáma-veda; tr. by J. Stevenson. Lond., *Oriental Trans. Fund*, 1842. 8°.

— COLEBROOKE, H. T. On the Vedas or sacred writings of the Hindus, [1805]. (*In* **Asiatic researches**, v. 8. 1808.)

— - *Same.* (*In his* Misc. essays, v. 1. 1837.)

— RAMMOHUN ROY. 2d defence of the monotheistical system of the Veds, in reply to an apology for the present state of Hindoo worship. Calcutta, 1817. 8°. (B 679, 1469)

— - *Same.* Calcutta, 1844. 12°. (E 133)

— ROTH, R. von. Morality of the Veda; tr. by Wm. D. Whitney. [1852.] (*In* **Amer. Orient. Soc. Journ.**, v. 3. 1853.)

— MUELLER, F. M. The Veda and Zend-Avesta, 1853. (*In his* Chips from a Germ. workshop, v. 1. 1867.)

— WHITNEY, W. D. On the main results of the later Vedic researches in Germany. (*In* **Amer. Orient. Soc. Journ.**, v. 3. 1853.) — On the history of the Vedic texts. (*In* v. 4. 1854.)

— WEBER, A. Zwei vedische Texte über Omina und Portenta. (*In* **Berlin. Ak. d. Wiss.** Abh., 1858.) — Die vedischen Nachrichten von den naxatra, Mondstationen. (*In* 1860.)

— BANERJEA, *Rev.* K. M. Dialogues on the Hindu philosophy, comprising the Nyaya, the Sankhya, the Vedant; added, a discussion of the authority of the Vedas. London, 1861. 8°.

— BURNOUF, E. L. Essai sur le Vêda. Paris, 1863. 8°.

— MUELLER, F. M. Lecture on the Vedas, 1865. (*In his* Chips from a Germ. workshop, v. 1. 1867.)

— WHEELER, J. T. The Vedic period. (*In his* History of India, v. 1. 1867.)

— MUIR, J. T. The Vedas; opinions of their authors and of later Indian writers on their origin, inspiration, *etc.* (Vol. 3. *of his* Orig. Sanskrit, texts. 1868.)

See also **Jyotisham**; — **Upanishads.**

Vedastus, *episc. Atrebatensis, St.* VITA. (*In* **Acta sanct.**, v. 4. 1863.)

Vedel (*Lat.* **Vedelius**), Nicolaus. NICERON, J. P. (*In his* Mém., v. 33. 1736.)

Vedia, Enrique de. Historiadores primitivos de Indias. Madrid, 1858, 62. 2 v. 8°. (Aribau. Bibl., v. 22, 26.)

Contents. Vol. 1. **Vedia**, E. de. Noticia de la vida y escritos de Francisco Lopez de Gómara; — De Cortes y sus cartas; — Apuntes sobre la vida [de] Alvar Nuñez Cabeza de Vaca. — **Cortez**, H. Cartas de relacion. — **Gomara**, F. L. de. Hispania victrix; 1a y 2a parte de la historia de las Indias, hasta 1551; con la conquista de Mejico y de la Nueva-España. — **Albarado**, P. de. [Dos relaciones.] — **Godoy**, D. Relacion hecha á Hernando Cortes en que trata del descubrimiento de diversas ciudades; de la provincia de Chamula, *etc.* — **Oviedo y Valdés**, G. H. de. Sumario de la natural historia de las Indias. — **Nuñez Cabeça de Vaca**, A. Naufragios y relacion de la jornada que hizo á la Florida con Panfilo de Narvaez; — Comentarios. 2. **Vedia**, E. de. Noticias biograficas de los autores comprendidos en este tomo. — **Diaz del Castillo**, B. Verdadera historia de los sucesos de la conquista de la Nueva-España. — **Jerez**, F. de. Verdadera relacion de la conquista del Peru y provincia del Cuzco, llamada la Nueva-Castilla, conquistada por Francisco Pizarro. — **Cieça** *de Leon*, P. La cronica del Peru. — **Zarate**, A. de. Historia del descubrimiento y conquista del Peru.

Vedova, Giuseppe. Biografia degli scrittori padovani. Padova, 1832–36. 2 v. 8°.

Contents. Vol. 1.. A-N. 2. O-Z.

Vedova in solitudine, La; commedia. *See* **Nota** A.

Vedova scaltra, La; commedia. *See* **Goldoni**, C.

Vedova spiritosa, La; commedia. *See* **Goldoni**, C.

Vée, Amédée. Matériel de la pharmacie. (*In* **France.** *Com. Imp. de l'Expos. de* 1867. Rapports, v. 8.)

Veen, Cornelis van. Kort verhaelt vande twee-jaerige voyagie ghedaen naer de Oost-Indien. (*In* **Commelin**, I. Begin, v. 1. 1646.)

Veen (*Lat.* **Vænius**), Octavio van. Horatii Flacci emblemata. Antverp., 1612. 4°.

— *French.* Théâtre de la vie humaine; expliquée par Gomberville; avec la Table du philosophe Cebes. Brux., 1678. f°.

Veer, Gerrit de. Schipvaerde der Hollandsche ende Zeeusche schepen by noorden Noorwegen, Moscovien, ende Tartarien. (*In* **Commelin**, I. Begin, v. 1. 1646.)

— *Same, abridged.* (*In* **Purchas.** Pilgrimes, v. 3. 1625; — Collection of voy. 1793; — *and in* **Harris**, J. Col., v. 1. 1705.)

— *Eng.* True description of three voyages by the north-east towards Cathay and China by the Dutch [under W. Barendsz], 1594-96; tr. by W. Phillip; ed. by C. T. Beke. London, 1853. 8°. (Hakluyt Soc., v. 13.)

Veer. MAP. *n.p.*, [17—]. (E 60)

Vega, Alonso de la. Amor vengado. (*In* Ochoa, E. de. Tesoro del teatro esp., v. 1. 1838; — *and in* Moratin, N. F. *and* L. F. de. Obras. 1857; v. 2 of Aribau. Bibl.)

Vega, Garcilaso de la, *d.* 1536. Obras. 2a ed. Madrid, 1817. 12°.
Contents. Eglogas. — Elegias. — Canciones. — Sonetos.

— *Eng.* Works; tr. into English verse by J. H. Wiffen. London, 1823. 12°.
Contents. Eclogues. — Elegies. — Odes. — Sonnets.

— Algunos obras. (*In* Boscan Almogaver, J. Obras. 1553.)

— Eclogas, oda, soneti. (*In* Quintana, M. J. Poesias sel. castel., v. 1. 1807.)

— Oda. (*In* Sedano, J. J. L. de. Parnaso español, v. 1. 1768.) — Eglogas. Soneto. (*In* v. 2. 1772.)

— Poesias. (*In* Castro, A. de. Poetas liricos de los siglos 16 y 17, v. 1. 1854; v. 32 of Aribau. Bibl.)

— MONTGOMERY, J. (*In his* Lives of lit. and sci. men of Italy, *etc.*, v. 3. 1837. Lardner. Cab. cyc.)

— NICERON, J. P. (*In his* Mém., v. 13. 1730.)

Vega, Garcilaso de la, *el Inca, d.* 1620. 1a parte de los commentarios reales. Lisbon, 1609. f°.

— *Same.* Madrid, 1723. f°.

— Historia general del Peru. [2a parte de los commentarios.] Cordova, 1617. f°.

— *Same.* 2a imp. Madrid, 1722. f°.

— *Same.* Hist., *etc.*, ó Commentarios reales de los Yncas. [1a e 2a pte.] Nueva ed. Madrid, 1800-01. 13 v. (v. 1 w.). 18°.

— *Eng.* First part of the Royal commentaries of the Yncas; tr. and ed. by C. B. Markham. Vol. 1. London, 1869. 8°. (Hakluyt Soc., v. 41, 45.)

— *Same.* Pt. 2, books 6, 7, 8, [abridged]; History of Peru, 1549, to the death of Inca Tupac Amuar. (*In* Kerr, R. Col. of voy., v. 5. 1824.)

— *French.* Le commentaire royal; tr. par I. Baudom. [1e pte.] Paris, 1633. 4°.

— Expedition of G. Pizarro, 1539-42; from the 2d part of [his] 'Royal commentaries of Peru' (*In* Markham, C. R. Expeditions into the Valley of the Amazons. 1859.)

— La Florida del Inca; historia del adelantado Hernando de Soto y de otros heroicos caballeros. Madrid, 1723. f°.

— *Same.* Historia de la Florida. Madrid, 1803. 4 v. 12°.

— *French.* Hist. de la conquête de la Floride; tr. par S. P. Richelet. Nouv. éd. Leide, 1731. 2 v. 12°.

— *Germ., abridged.* (*In* Allgemeine Hist., v. 16. 1758.)

Vega, Torquato. Lezione sopra il sonetto 59 di G. dalla Casa. (*In* Casa, G. dalla. Opere, v. 3. 1806.)

Vega Carpio, Lope Felix de. Coleccion de las obras sueltas de V. Madrid, 1776. 21 v. 8°.
Contents. Vol. 1. Laurel de Apolo. — La selva sin amor. — Silva al retrato de su Majestad. — Epistola a M. de Solis. — Sonetos. — Epistolas. 2. Angelica. — Philomena. — Descr. de la Tapada. — Andromeda. 3. Circe. — Mañana de San Juan. — La rosa blanca. — Dragontea. — Fiestas de Denia. — Poesias varias. 4. Corona tragica. — Rimas humanas. — Arte nuevo de hacer comedias en este tiempo. — Poesias varias. — Discurso en prosa sobre la nueva poesia. — Otras poesias varias. — Question sobre el honor debido a la poesia. 5. El peregrino en su patria. 6. Arcadia. 7. Dorothea. 8. Las fortunas de Diana. — El desdichado por la honra. — La mas prudente venganza. — Guzman el bravo. — Las dos venturas sin pensar. — El pronostico cumplido. — La quinta de Laura. — El zeloso hasta morir. — El castigo sin venganza. 9, 10. La Vega del Parnasso. 11, 12. El Isidro. — La justa poetica. 13. Triumphos divinos. — Rimas sacras. — Otras rimas sacras. — Contemplativos discursos. — Quatro soliloquios. — Forma de rezar el rosario. 14, 15. Jerusalem conquistada. — La virgen de la Almudena. — Romancero espiritual. 16. Pastores de Belen. 17. Soliloquios amorosos de un alma. — Triumpho de la fè en los reynos del Japon. — Varios versos y prosas. — Dos sonetos y dos cartas. — Romances. 18. Los autos, loas, y entremeses. 19. Rimas divinas y humanas de T. de Burgillos. — Oracion eclesiastica funeral de L. de V. por F. de Peralta. — Sermon funebre, por F. de Quintana. — Oracion funeral por I. de Vitoria. — Oracion, por F. Cardoso. — Egloga a la fama de L. de V. del J. A. de la Pena. 20. Fama postuma de L. de V., por J. P. de Montalvan. — Elogios. — Honras a L. de V. en el Parnasso. 21. Essequie poetiche. — Suplemento a los varios versos y prosas de L. de V. — Indices.

— Obras no dramaticas, coleccion escogida por Cayetano Rosell. Madrid, 1856. 8°. (Aribau. Bibl., v. 38.)
Contents. Dedicatoria. — Prologo. — Novelas dirigidas á la señora Marcia Leonarda. — La Arcadia. — Repuesta de Lope de Vega á un papel qué escribió un señor de estos reinos en razon de la nueva poesia. — Justa poetica al bienaventurado san Isidro. — Relacion de las fiestas que la insigne villa de Madrid hizo en la canonizacion de su bienaventurado hijo y patron, san Isidro. — Triunfo de la fè en los reinos del Japon. 1614-15. — Cien jaculatorias á Cristo nuestra Señor. — Laurel de Apolo. — Arte nuevo de hacer comedias en este tiempo. — Letrillas, glosas, romances, eglogas, canciones, odas, elegias, sonetos, epistolas. — La gatomaquia. — La Filomena. — La Andromeda. — La Circe. — La rosa blanca.

— Circe. — Canciones. — Hymno; al Amor. — Romances. — Odas. — Sonetos. — Epistola. — Silva moral. — Sonetos burlescos. (*In* Quintana, M. J. Poesias sel., v. 2. 1807.)

— Comedias escogidas; juntas en coleccion y ordenadas por J. E. Hartzenbusch. Madrid, 1853-60. 4 v. 8°. (Aribau. Bibl. de aut. españ., v. 24, 34, 41, 52.)
Contents. Vol. 1. Prologo de este ed. — Fama póstuma á la vida y muerte [de] L. F. de Vega Carpio, por J. P. de Montalban. — Adiciones á la Fama póstuma. — Juicio general de los escritos de Lope, por A. G. de Zárate. — Relacion entre las custumbres y los escritos de Lope, por A. de Castro. — El verdadero amante. — El molino. — El domine Lucas. — La viuda valenciana. — Los embustes de Celauro. — Los locos de Valencia. — La estrella de Sevilla. — La discreta enamorada. — El bobo del colegio. — La noche toledana. — La corona merecida. — El ausente en el lugar. — La niña de plata. — La dama boba. — Los melindres de Belisa. — El perro del hortelano. — El acero de Madrid. — Al pasar del arroyo. — Las flores de don Juan. — Quien ama no haga fieros. — Lo cierto por lo dudoso. — El mejor alcalde el rey. — El premio del bien hablar. — Los Tellos de Menéses, primera parte, secunda parte. — La moza de cántaro. — El castigo sin venganza. — Apéndices. 2. La Dorotea. — El maestro de danzar. — La hermosura aborrecida. — La llave de la honra. — El villano en su rincon. — La portuguesa y dicha del forastero. — Mas pueden celos que amor. — Santiago el Verde. — El hijo de los leones. — Los milagros del desprecio. — El desprecio agradecido. — Querar la propia desdicha. — La mal casada. — La porfío hasta el temor. — La despreciada querida. — La hermosa fea. — El caballero de Olmedo. — Guardar y guardarse. — Los peligros de la ausencia. — Servir á buenos. — Amar sin saber á quién. — El mayor imposible. — La esclava de su galan. — Lo que ha de ser. — La boba para los otros y discreta para sí. — Por la puente, Juana. — Las bizarrías de Belisa. — Si no vieran las mujeres! — Advertencias. 3. Contra valor no hay desdicha. — El guante de doña Blanca. — La campana de Aragon. — Dineros son calidad. — La mayor virtud de un rey. — Porfiar hasta morir. — El saber puede dañar. — El remedio en la desdicha. — La Arcadia. — La ley ejecutada. — De cuando aco nos vino? — La mayor vitoria. — Porfiando vence amor. — La fuerza lastimosa. — Peribañiz y el comendador de Ocaña. — La discreta venganza. — La buena guarda. — El despertar, á quien duerme. — El anzuelo de Fenisa. — Los novios de Hornachuelos. — El testimonio vengado. — El duque de Viseo. — El cuerdo en su casa. — Las famosas asturianas. — De cosario á cosario. — La vengadora de las mujeres. — El arenal de Sevilla. — El piadoso veneciano. — Las paces de los reyes, y judía de Toledo. — El cardenal de Belen. — El mejor mozo de España. — Fuente Ovejuna. 4. Prologo. — Advertencias y correcciones. — Prologos de ocho tomos de comedias de Lope. — Lista de comedias viejas. — Castelvines y Monteses. — El Alcalde Mayor. — El servir con mala estrella. — Servir á señor discreto. — El principe perfecto,

la, 2a parte. — La pobreza estimada. — La obediencia laureada y primer Carlos de Hungría. — El hombre de bien. — Virtud, pobreza, y mujer. — Pobreza no es vileza. — El gran duque de Moscovia y empérador perseguido. — Roma abrasada. — Los ramilletes de Madrid. — El amigo hasta la muerte. — La inocente sangre. — Don Juan de Castro, 1a, 2a parte. — Adónis y Venus. — Los prados de Leon. — Mirad á quién alabais. — La inocente Laura. — El marqués de la las Navas. — San Diego de Alcalá. — Catalogo de las comedias y autos de Vega. — El mejor amigo el muerto. — Elogio descriptivo á las fiestas a los conciertos entre el Principe de Inglaterra y la Infanta de Castilla.

— La creacion del mundo. *n.t.p.* [Sevilla, 17—?] 4°.

— La esclava de su galan. *n.t.p.* [16—?] 4°.

— Estrella de Sevilla; comedia. (*In* **Sales**, F. Sel. de obras. 1828.)

— El exemplo mayor de la desdicha y capitan Belisario. *n.t.p.* [Madrid, 1796.] 4°.

— La fianza satisfecha. *n.t.p.* [Barcelona, 1773.] 4°.

— La gatomachia; poema epico burlesco. (*In* **Sedano**, J. J. L. de. Parnasso esp., v. 2. 1770; — **Fernandez**, R. Col., v. 11. 1792; — *and in* **Quintana**, M. J. Poesias sel., v. 2. 1807.)

— *Germ.* Die Kater; aus dem spanischen übersetzt von A. Herrmann. (*In* **Archiv für** das Stud. d. neueren Spr., v. 24. 1858.)

— Jerusalen conquistada. (*In* **Ochoa**, E. de. Tes. de los poemas esp. 1840.)

— Los milagros del desprecio. — Por la puenta, Juana. — El perro del hortelano. — Si no vieran las mugeres! (*In* **Ochoa**, E. de. Coll. de piezas escogidas. 1840.)

— Odas. — Romance. — Cancion de Thomé de Burguillos. (*In* **Sedana**, J. J. L. de. Parnaso esp., v. 1. 1768.) — Soneto. (*In* v. 2.) — El siglo de oro. — Madrigal. — Estancias. — Amarilis. — Canciones. — Elegia. — La pulga. — Soneto. (*In* v. 3.) — Soneto. — Cancion. — Filas, egloga. — Soneto, por T. de Burguillos. (*In* v. 4.) — Egloga. — Canciones. — Oda. (*In* v. 7.) — Canciones. — Egloga. — Sonetos, por T. de Burguillos. (*In* v. 8.) — Elegia. (*In* v. 9. 1778.)

— Representacion moral del viaje del alma. — Del pan y del palo, auto sacramental. — La siega, auto sacramental. — De los cantares, auto sacramental. — El pastor lobo y cabaña celestial, auto sacramental. (*In* **Pedroso**, E. G. Autos sacramentales. 1865.)

— Rimas humanas y divinas, por T. de Burguillos. (Vol. 11 of **Fernandez**, R. Col. de poetas esp. 1792.)
Namely. Sonetos. — La gatomaquia. — Eclogas, *etc.*

— Romances, coplas, y canciones. (*In* **Ochoa**, E. de. Tes. de los romanceros. 1838.)

— Teatro escogido. Paris, 1838. 8°. (Ochoa. Tes. del teatro, v. 2.)
Contents. Advertencia del editor. — Noticia de L. F. de Vega Carpio. — Los milagros del desprecio. — La esclava de su galan. — El premio del bien hablar. — El mayor imposible. — La hermosa fea. — Por la puente, Juana. — Al pasar del arroyo. — El perro del hortelano. — Las flores de don Juan, y rico y pobre trocados. — Si no vieran las mugeres! — La boba para los otros, y discreta para sí. — Las bizarrias de Belisa. — Lo que ha de ser. — El molino. — La dama melindrosa. — Los locos de Valencia. — El honrado hermano, tragi-comedia famosa. — El acero de Madrid. — El nuevo mundo descubiérto por Cristóval Colon. — Los enredos de Celauro.

— Fox, H. R., *Lord Holland.* Life and writings of Lopez de Vega. London, 1806. 8°.

— Montgomery, J., *and others.* (*In their* Lives of lit. and scientif. men of Italy, v. 3. 1837. Lardner. Cab. cyc.)

Vegas, Damian de. Poesias trasladadas de su libro, Poesia cristiana, moral y divina. (*In* **Sancha**, J. de. Romancero sagr. 1855; v. 35 of Aribau. Bibl.)

Vegetable chemistry. *See* **Chemistry.**

Vegetable diet. Newton, J. F. Return to nature; defence of the vegetable regimen. (*In* **Pamphleteer**, **1822**; v. 19, 20 of B 838)

— Smith, J. Fruits and farinacea the proper food of man. London, **1845**. 8°.

— Marchand, E. De l'influence compar. du régime végétal et du régime animal sur le physique et le moral de l'homme. Paris, Bordeaux, **1849**. 8°.

Vegetable materials for manufactures. London, 1833. 12°. (Lib. ent. kn.)

Vegetable substances; timber trees; fruits. London, 1829. 12°. (Lib. ent. kn., v. 10.)

Vegetable substances used as food for man; [by E. Lankester]. London, 1832. 12°. (Lib. ent. kn., v. 11.)

— *Same.* N. Y., [1840]. 18°. (Harper's fam. lib., v. 169.)

Vegetables. Thouin, A. Cours de culture, *etc.*, des végétaux; pub. par O. Leclerc. Paris, **1827**. 3 v. 8°.

— Burr, F. Field and garden vegetables of America. Boston, **1863**. 8°.

— Quinn, P. T. Money in the garden; a vegetatable manual. N.Y., **1871**. 12°.
See also **Cabbages**; — **Cucumber**; — **Mangel wurzel**; — **Vegetable diet.**

Vegetable world. *See* **Figuier**, G. L.

Vegetius, Publius. Artis veterinariæ, sive, mulomedicinæ libri IV. (*In* **Gesner**, J. M. Scriptores rei rusticæ, v. 3. 1787.)

Vegetius Renatus, Flavius. Institutions militaires; [tr. par Bourbon de Sigrais]. Paris, 1758. 18°.

— Military institutions; tr. by J. Clarke. London, 1767. 8°.

— Vier bücher der Ritterschaft. Augsb., 1534. f°.

— Turpin de Crissé, L., *comte.* Commentaires sur les 'Institutions militaires'. Montargis, 1779. 3 v. 4°.

Vegius, Maphæus (*Ital.* Maffeo Vegio). Carmen, vel liber additus duodecim Æneidos libris. (*In* **Virgilius Maro**, P. Qualem, v. 4. 1820.)

— Niceron, J. P. (*In his* Mém., v. 26. 1734.)

Vehse, Karl Eduard. Geschichte der deutschen Höfe seit der Reformation. Hamburg, 1851–60. 48 v. 8°.
Contents. Vol. 1. Preussen, 1535–1688. 2. 1688–1713. 2, 3. 1713–40. 3, 4. 1740–86. 5. 1786–97. 5, 6. 1797–1840. 7. Oestreich, 1493–1519. 7, 8. 1519–56. 8. 1556–76. 9. 1576–1619. 9, 10. 1619–37. 10. 1637–57. 11, 12. 1657–1705. 12. 1705–11. 12, 13. 1711–40. 13, 14. 1740–80. 14, 15. 1780–90. 15. 1790–92. 15, 16. 1792–1835. 16, 17. 1835–48. 17. 1848–52. 18. Braunschweig-Hannover, 1592–1727. 18, 19. 1727–60. 19. 1760–1820. 20. 1820–51. 21, 22. Die englishe nobility, 1154–1850. 22. Braunschweig, 1514–1850. 23. Bavaria, 1598–1745. 24, 25. 1745–1850. 25, 26. Würtemburg, 1503–1850. 26. Baden, 1500–1852. 27. Hessen, 1509–1853. 28. Sachsen, 1598–1854. 29. 1553–1854. 30. 1586–1646. 31. 1656–1733. 32, 33. 1694–1733. 34. 1733–1854. 35–48. Kleine deutschen Höfe. 35–40. *Souveraine Höfe.* 35–37. Mecklenburg. 37, 38. Oldenburg. 38. Nassau. — Anhalt. 39. Lippe. — Waldeck. — Schwarzburg. — Reuss. 40. Lichtenstein. *Preussische Mediatisirte.* 40. Arenberg und Ligne. — Bentheim. 41. Salm. — Solms. — Stolberg. — Wied. — Sayn-Wittgenstein. 42. Croy-Dülmen. — Rheina-Wolbeck. — Fürstenberg. — Taxis. — *Oestreichische Mediatisirte.* Dietrichstein. — Lobkowitz. — Auersperg. — Schwarzenberg. — Esterhazy. — Windishgrätz. — Colloredo. — Khevenhüller. — Metternich. — Rosenberg. — Salm-Reifferscheid-Raitz. — Starhemberg. — Trautmannsdorf. — Harrach. — Königseck. — Kuefstein. — Schönborn. — Stadion. — Wurm brand. 43. *Baierische Mediatisirte.* Esterhazy. — Fugger. — Hohenlohe. — Leiningen. — Löwenstein. — Oettingen. — Schwarzenberg. — Thurn und Taxis. — Waldenburg. — Castell. — Erbach-Erbach. — Fugger. Giech. — Ortenburg. — Pappenheim. — Pückler-Limpurg. — Rechberg. — Rechteren. — Schönborn-Wiesentheid. — Stadion. — Törring-Gutenzell. — Waldbott-Bassenheim. — *Würtembergishe Mediatisirte.* Fürstenberg. — Hohenlohe. — Löwenstein. 44. Oettingen. — Solms-Braunfels. — Thurn und Taxis. — Truchsess-Waldburg. — Windishgrätz. — Königseck-Aulendorf. — Pückler-Limpurg. — Quadt-Wykradt. — Schäsberg-Thannheim. — Torring. — Gutenzell. — Waldbott-Bassenheim. — Waldeck-Pyrmont-Limpurg. — Isenburg-Büdingen-Meerholtz. — Neipperg. — Rechberg. — Fugger-Kirchberg-Weissenhorn. — Salm-Reifferscheidt-Dyck. — Stadion-Stadion-Thannhausen. — *Badnishe Mediatisirte.* Esterhazy. — Fürstenberg. — Leiningen. — Leien. — Löwenstein-Wertheim-Rochefort. — Salm-

Reifferscheidt-Krautheim. — Leiningen-Billigheim und Neudenau. — *Nassauische Mediatisirte.* Weid-Solms-Leien. — Metternich. — Neuleiningen-Westerburg. — Giech. — Schönborn-Wiesentheid. — Waldbott-Bassenheim. — *Hessische Mediatisirte.* Isenburg. — Leiningen. — Löwenstein-Wertheim-Rochefort. — Solms-Braunfels und Lich. — Erbach. — Görtz. — Isenburg-Wächtersbach. — Altleiningen-Westerburg. — Schönborn-Wiesentheid. — Solms-Laubach und Rödelheim. — Stolberg-Wernigerode und Rosla. — *Hannoverishe Mediatisirte.* Arenberg. — Bentheim-Bentheim und Bentheim-Steinfurt. — Platen-Hallermund. — Rheina-Wolbeck. — Stolberg-Wernigerode und Stolberg. — Wallmoden. — *Sächsische Mediatisirte.* Schonburg. — Solms-Sonnenwald. — *Bentinck.* 45-48. *Geistlichen Höfe.* 45. Mainz. — Cöln. 46. Trier. — Salzburg. — Deutschordensmeister zu Mergentheim. — Würzburg. — Bamberg. — Eichstadt. — Münster. 47. Paderborn. — Osnabrück. — Hildesheim. — Lüttich. — Speyer und Bruchsal. — Worms. — Basel. — Strasburg. — Passau. Regensburg. — Freisingen. 48. Augsburg. — Constanz. — Trident. — Brixen. — Chur. — Lübeck. — Gefürsteten Aebte und Pröbste. — Unmittelbare Reichs-Prälaten und Aebtissenen.

— Geschichte des östreichischen Hofs. *See previous entry,* v. 7-17.

— *Eng.* Memoirs of the court of Austria ; tr. by F. Demmler. London, 1856. 2 v. 8°.

Veii. Corsi, P. Civitatem Castellanam Faliscorum non Vejentum oppidum esse; poëma, cum Julii Roscii Hortini additamentis. — Mazzocchi, G. D. Veii defensi Vejorum defensoris epistola apologetica. — Nardini, F. Veii antiqui. (*In* **Grævius.** Thes. antiq. Ital., v. 8, pt. 3. 1723.)

— Botta, C. La Camilleide ossia la distruzione di Vejo; poemo eroico. (*In* **Turin. Ac. d. Sci.** Mem., v. 21. 1813.)

Veille de distribution des prix, Une; proverbe par l'abbé Lebardin. Nouv. éd. Paris, Lyon, 1863. 8°. **(E 16)**

Veillées du chateau, Les; par S. F. D. de **Genlis.** (Vol. 79-82 *of her* Œuvres. 1826.)

Veillodter, Valentin Karl. Sermons: On belief in immortality; — On the sanctity of an oath and the crime of perjury. (*In* **German** pulpit. 1829.)

Veins. Bartholin, T. Anatomical hist. conc. the lacteal veins of the thorax. Lond., 1653. 12°.

— Home, E. Practical obs. on the treatment of ulcers in the legs; on varicose veins, *etc.* 1797. 2d ed. London, 1801. 8°.

— Hodgson, J. Treatise on the diseases of arteries and veins. London, 1815. 8°.

— Channing, W. Cases of inflammation of veins, *etc.* (*In* **Mass. Med. Soc.** Med. comm., v. 5. 1836.)

— Callender, G. W. Diseases of the veins. (*In* **Holmes,** T. System of surgery, v. 3. 1862.)

Veitch, John. Memoir of Sir Wm. Hamilton. Edin., 1869. 8°.

— Memoir of D. Stewart. (*In* **Stewart,** D. Col. works, v. 10. 1858.)

Veith, Franz von Paula Anton. Diatribe de origine et incrementis artis typographicæ in Aug. Vind. (*In* **Zapf,** G. W. Annal. typog. August. 1778.)

Veith, Johann Emmanuel. Instruments of the passion of Christ; tr. from the German by T. Noethen. Boston, 1869. 12°.

Velasco, Juan de. Hist. du royaume de Quito. (*In* **Ternaux-Compans,** H. Voyages, v. 18-19. 1849.)

Velasco, Juan Fernandez de. Carta al papa Clemente viii. (*In* **Valladares,** A. Seman. erud., v. 29. 1790.)

— Banquet and entertainment given by James i. to the Constable of Castile, Aug. 19, 1604. (*In* **Rye,** W. B. England as seen by foreigners. 1865.)

Velasco, Manuel Pellicer de. Soneto. (*In* **Sedano,** J. J. L. de. Parnaso esp., v. 3. 1782.)

Velasquez, Pedro. Memoir of an exped. in Central America; discov. of Iximaya and possession of the Aztec children. N. Y., 1850. 8°.

Velazquez, Baltasar Mateo. Nadie crea de ligero. (*In* **Rosell,** C. Nov. post. à Cervantes, v. 2. 1854.)

Velazquez, Diego, *Gov. of Yucatan,* d. 1523. Carta al licenciado Figueroa, de lo que le habia fecho Cortes. (*In* **Icazbalceta,** J. G. Col. de doc., v. 1. 1858.)

Velazquez, Diego Rodriguez de Silva y. Beulé, C. E. (*In* **Revue** d. D. Mondes, juil. 1861.)

— Blanc, A. A. P. C. Vélasquez à Madrid. (*In* **Gazette** des beaux-arts, v. 15. 1863.)

— Stirling, W. Velasquez and his works. London, 1855. 16°.

— - Catalogue of the works executed by and ascribed to Velasquez. (*In his* Annals of the Artists of Spain, v. 3. 1848.)

Velazquez de la Cadena, Mariano. Dictionary of the Spanish and English lang. on the basis of Seoane's Neuman and Baretti. N. Y., 1852. 8°.

— Elementos de la lengua castellana. 3a ed. N. Y., 1827. 18°.

— *and* Simonne, T. Ollendorf's new method of learning the Spanish language; with elements of the Spanish language, *etc.,* by V. N. Y., 1848. 12°.

— - Key to the exercises [in the preceding work]. N. Y., 1850. 12°.

Velazquez de Velasco, Alfonso. El zeloso. (*In* **Ochoa,** E. de. Tesoro del teatro esp. 1838.)

Note. This name is found in various editions in the contracted forms Vz., or Uz., Vaz. and Vazquez de Velasco.

Velazquez de Velasco, Luis José, *marqués de Valdeflores.* Origines de la poesia castellana. Malaga, 1754. 4°.

Velde, C. W. M. van de. Journey through Syria and Palestine. London, 1854. 2 v. 8°.

— Map of the Holy Land. Gotha, 1858. f°.

— Memoir to accompany the map of the Holy Land. Gotha, 1858. 8°.

Velde, Karl Franz van der. Tales from the German; tr. by N. Greene. Boston, 1837. 2 v. 12°.

Contents. Vol. 1. Arwed Gyllenstierna. 2. The Lichtensteins. — The sorceress. — The Anabaptist.

Veldgezangen van Thyrsis. Leyden, 1702. 4°.

Velez, Juan. El mancebon de los palacios, ó agraviar para alcanzar. (*In* **Mesonero Romanos,** R. de. Dram. post. a Lope de Vega, v. 1. 1858. Aribau. Bibl., v. 47.)

Velez de Guevara, Luis. *See* **Guevara,** L. V. de.

Vella, Giuseppe. Codex diplomaticus Siciliæ sub Saracenorum imperio, 827-1072; ex mss Mauro-Occidentalibus, cura A. Airoldi. Tom. 1. Panormi, 1788. f°.

Note. No more of this ed. was published, but there is an Italian ed. 'Codice', *etc.,* in 3 vols. f°. The collection purports to be made by Mustafa Ben Hani ; but the whole work is a forgery and Airoldi is a pseudonym. *See* Brunet, art. Airoldi, and Biog. gén., art. Vella.

Villeius, Paterculus. *See* **Paterculus.**

Vellosillo, Fernandez. Advertentiæ sive animadversiones in S. Augustini opera. (*In* **Augustinus,** St. Opera, v. 11. 1637.)

Vellum, Books printed on. Praet, J. B. B. v. Catalogue des livres imprimés sur vélin de la Bibliothèque du Roi. Paris, 1822. 5 v. 8°.

— - Catalogue des livres imprimés sur velin qui se trouvent dans bibliothèques tant publiques que particulières. Paris, 1824-28. 4 v. 8°.

— Cotton, H. Books printed on vellum, in the Bodleian Library ; arranged [chronologically]. (*In his* Typographical gaz. 1831.)

Velly, Paul François, *and others.* Histoire de France depuis le commencement de la monarchie jusqu'au commencement du regne de Charles ix. Paris, 1775-99. 33 v. 12°.

Contents. Vol. 1. 419-814. 2. 814-1109. 3. 1108-1223. 4. 1223-50. 5. 1250-66. 6. 1266-85. 7. 1286-1315. 8. 1314-50. 9. 1350-64. 10. 1364-78. 11. 1378-87. 12. 1388-1407. 13. 1407-18. 14. 1418-30. 15. 1430-50. 16. 1450-63. 17. 1463-72. 18. 1472-80. 19. 1480-87. 20. 1487-98. 21. 1498-1504. 22. 1505-14. 23. 1515-23. 24. 1523-35. 25. 1535-47. 26. 1547-54. 27. 1555-59. 28. 1559-60. 29. 1560-62. 30. 1562-64. 31-33. Tables.

Note. Vol. 1-7 by Velly, 8-17, p. 348 by Villaret, v. 17, p. 348 - v. 30. by J. J. Garnier.

— - *Eng.* History of France ; tr. by T. Nugent. Vol. 1 : [427-888]. London, 1769. 8°.

Velocipede, The. VELOCIPEDE, The, its history, varieties, and practice. N. Y., 1869. 16°.

Velpeau, Alfred Armand Louis Marie. Diseases of the breast; tr. by S. Parkman. Phila., 1840. 8°.
— Embryologie ou ovologie humaine. Paris, 1833. f°.
— Rapport sur les progrès de la chirurgie. 1867. *See* Denonvilliers, C. P.
— Remarques sur les positions vicieuses et la version du fœtus. Paris, 1830. 8°. (B 1564)
— Traité complet d'anatomie chirurgicale. 3e éd. Paris, 1837. 2 v. 8° *and* Atlas 4°.
— Treatise on cancer of the breast and of the mammary regions; tr. by W. Marsden. London, 1856. 8°.
— Treatise on the diseases of the breast, and of the mammary regions; tr. by M. Henry. London, *Sydenham Soc.*, 1856. 8°.

Velsch, Georg Hieronymus. *See* **Welsch, G. H.**

Velser, Markus. *See* **Welser, M.**

Velthuysen, Lambert. BROWN, J. Libri duo [contra] Wolzogium [et V.]. Amst., 1670. 12°.

Velvet cushion, New covering for the. *See* **Cox, F. A.**

Vembergue, F. E. Analogies and affinities between the anc. and mod. languages of the north and south of Europe. (*In* **Lit. and Phil. Soc. of Manchester.** Mem., n. s., v. 7. 1846.)

Venables, George Stovin. The attempts made to find a North West passage; [prize] poem at Cambridge, 1831. (*In* **Cambridge Univ.** Prolusiones. 1831. B 1236)
— Biog. preface. (*In* **Lushington, H.** The Italian war. 1859.)

Venables, Robert. Practical treatise on diabetes. London, 1825. 8°.

Venæsection. ABERNETHY, J. Ill consequences of V. (*In his* Surg. essays. pt. 2. 1793.)

Venango, Fort, *Ala.* TODD, W. C. Letter on Fort Venango. (*In* **Mass. Historical Society.** Proceedings, 1866–67.)

Venango County, *Penn.* EATON, S. J. M. Petroleum; a hist. of the oil region of V. Co. Phila., 1866. 12°.

Venault de Chamilly, *Col.* Letter to Lieut. Gen. B. Tarleton. London, 1810. 8°. (B 1420)
— Narrative of his transactions in Spain. London, 1810. 8°.
— TARLETON, B. Reply to Colonel de Chamilly. London, 1810. 8°. (B 1420)

Vence, Claude Alexandre Villeneuve, *comte* de. CATALOGUE [de ses] livres, tableaux, *etc.* Paris, 1760. 8°. (B 884)
Note. Catalogue raisonné des tableaux, *etc.* par P. Remy.

Venceslao. *See* **Zeno, A.**

Venceslas; tragédie. *See* **Rotrou.**

Vendanges de Surêne, Les; comédie. *See* **Dancourt, F. C.**

Vendanges, Les, ou Le bailli d'Anières; comédie. *See* **Regnard, J. F.**

Vendangeurs, Les, ou Les deux baillis; divertissement. Paris, 1780. 12°. (C 166)

Vendée, War in the. BEAUCHAMP, A. Histoire de la guerre de la Vendée et des Chouans, [1806]. 2e éd. Paris, 1807. 3 v. 8°.
— NAPOLEON I. Pacification de la Vendée, [181-]. (*In his* Commentaires, v. 4. 1867.)
— AUBERTIN, D. Mémoires sur la guerre de la Vendée, [1819]. (*In* **Hugo, J. L. S.** Mém. v. 1. 1823.)
— LA ROCHEJAQUELEIN, M. L. V. de D., *marquise* de. Mémoires. Paris, 1823. 8°. (Berville and Barrière. Mem., v. 8.)
— - *Eng.* Memoirs. Edin., 1817. 8°.
— - *Same.* With an introduction by Sir W. Scott. Edin., 1827. 12°. (Constable's miscel., v. 5.)
— SAPINAUD, *Mme.* L. de C. de. Mémoire sur la Vendée. Paris, 1823. 8°. (Berville and Barrière. Mém., v. 55.)
— TURREAU DE GARAMBOUVILLE, L. M., *baron.* Mémoire sur l'hist. de la guerre de la V. Paris, 1824. 8°. (Berville and Barrière. Mém., v. 53.)
— SAVARY, J. J. M. Guerres des Vendéens et des Chouans contre la République Française. Paris, 1824–27. 6 v. 8°. (Berville and Barrière. Mém., v. 33–38.)
— CRÉTINEAU-JOLY, J. Histoire de la Vendée militaire, [1841]. 2e éd., augm. Paris, 1843. 4 v. 12°.
Note. A number of lives of Vendeans originally contributed by Barante to the 'Nouv. biog. gén.' may be found in his Mélanges hist. et lit., v. 1. 1836.

Vendors. SUGDEN, E. B., *Lord St. Leonard.* Treatise on the law of vendors and purchasers. 1st Amer. from 2d London ed. Phila., 1807. 8°.

Vendramin, Francesco. Relazione di Francia. 1600. (*In* **Venice.** Relazioni degli ambasciatori veneti, ser. 1, v. 4. 1860.) — Relazione di F. Vendramino. 1595. (*In* v. 5. 1861.)

Venedey, Jacob. Georg Washington; ein Lebensbild. Freib. im Breisgau, 1861. 12°.
— Hans Lorenz Küchler; ein Lebensbild. (*In* **Album von Combe-Varin.** Zur Erinnerung. 1847.)

Venedi. BAYER, G. S. De Venedis et Eridano fluvio. (*In* **St. Petersburg. Ac. Sci.** Comm., v. 7. 1840.)

Venegas, Miguel. Noticia de la California, sacada de V. y otras relaciones [por A. M. Burriel]. Madrid, 1757. 3 v. 4°.
— *Eng.* Natural and civil history of California. London, 1759. 2 v. 8°.
— *French.* Histoire nat. et civile de la Californie; tr. de l'Anglois par M. E[idous]. Paris, 1767. 3 v. 12°.

Venereal diseases. HARRIS, W. De lue venerea. [16—.] (*In* **Sydenham, T.** Opera med., v. 1. 1723.)
— FALCK, N. D. Treatise on venereal diseases. London, 1772. 8°.
— SWEDIAUR, F. X. Practical obs. on venereal complaints. [1784.] 3d ed. N. Y., 1788. 8°.
— HOWARD, J. Practical obs. on the venereal disease. [1787.] 2d ed. Lond., 1806. 2 v. 8°.
— BUCHAN, W. Treatment and cure of venereal disease. London, 1796. 8°.
— ROLLO, J. Cases of diabetes mellitus; trial of acids in lues venerea. [1797.] 2d ed. London, 1806. 8°.
— SWEDIAUR, F. X. Traité sur les maladies syphilitiques. [1798.] 4e éd. Paris, 1801. 2 v. (v. 1 w.). 8°.
— PEARSON, J. Obs. on the effects of various articles in the cure of lues venerea. [1800.] 2d ed. London, 1807. 8°.
— TONGUE, J. Inaug. diss. on lues venerea, 1801. (*In* **Caldwell, C.** Med. theses, v. 2. 1806.)
— MAHON, P. A. O. Important researches upon the nature, *etc.*, of venereal infection in pregnant women, new born infants, *etc.* London, 1808. 8°. (B 819)
— HUNTER, J. Treatise on the venereal diseases; with introd. by J. Adams. London, 1810. 8°.
— MATHIAS, A. Mercurial disease [and] its connexion with lues venerea, [1810]. Phila., 1811. 8°.
— TERRAS, J. P. Traité de la maladie vénérienne. Paris, 1810. 8°.
— CARMICHAEL, R. Essay on the venereal diseases confounded with syphilis. [1814.] 1st Amer. ed. Phila., 1817. 8°.
— EVANS, J. Pathological and practical remarks on ulceration of the genital organs. London, 1819. 8°.
— FOOT, J. Complete treatise on the nature, symptoms, and cure of lues venerea. [1819.] New ed. London, 1820. 8°.

— DUBLED, A. Exposition de la nouvelle doctrine sur la maladie vénérienne. Paris, 1829. 8°. (B 1053)
— LAWRENCE, W. Treatise on the venereal diseases of the eye. London, 1830. 8°.
— TRAVERS, B. Observations on the pathology of venereal affections. London, 1830. 8°.
— COLLES, A. Practical obs. on the venereal disease and the use of mercury. London, 1837. 8°.
— - *Same.* App. [with obs. by R. Carmichiel]. Phila., 1837. 8°.
— RICORD, P. Traité des maladies vénériennes. Paris, 1838. 8°.
— HARDWICKE, W. Can government beneficially further interfere to limit the spread of infectious diseases? — HILL, B., *and others.* Should the contagious diseases act be extended to the civil population? (*In* Nat. Assoc. Prom. Soc. Sci. Trans., 1869.)
See also Gonorrhea; — Syphilis.

Venerio (*Lat.* Venerius), Giovan Antonio. De oraculis et divinationibus antiquorum. (*In* Gronovius, J. Thes. Gr. antiq., v. 7. 1699.)

Veneroni, *dit* Vigneron, Jean. Le maître italien. Nouv. éd. Paris, 1745. 12°.

Venerosi, Brandaligio. FABRONI, A. (*In his* Mem. di più illustre Pisani, v. 3. 1792.)

Venetia; by B. Disraeli. (*In his* Works, v. 2. 1845.)

Venetia edificata, La; poema eroico. *See* Strozzi, G.

Venetia libera; poema heroico. *See* Pancetti, C.

Venetian history, literature, *etc.* *See* Venice.

Venezuela. Manfesto de la provincias de V. a todas las naciones de la Europe. *n.t.p.* [Madrid, 1820.] 8°. (B 396)
— Continuacion del cuerpo de léyes de V., año de 1834. Caracas, [1834]. 8°.

Botany.

— EATON, D. C. Felices Wrightianæ et Fendlerianæ, nempe in insula Cuba a C. Wright et in Venezuela ab A. Fendler enumeratæ 1854-60. (*In* Amer. Acad. Mem., n.s., v. 8, pt. 1. 1861.)

Description and History.

— FERRARIO, G. (*In his* Costume, v. 17. 1829.)
— DAUXION LAVAYSSE, J. F. Statistical, commercial, and political description of V., [1813]; with preface and notes by E. Blaguière. 2d ed. London, 1821. 8°.
— CAMPAIGNS and cruises in Venezuela and New Grenada, 1817-30; also Tales of Venezuela. London, 1831. 3 v. 12°.
Note. The 'Tales' fill the last two volumes, and have separate title pages and pagination.
— HIPPISLEY, G. Narrative of the exped. to the Orinoco and Apuré in South America, [1817-18]. London, 1819. 8°.
— CHESTERTON, G. L. Narrative of proceedings in V., 1819-20. London, 1820. 8°.
— TORRE, M. de la. Manifiesto para satisfacer al mundo entero de la conducta franca y generosa tenida por el gobierno español con el gefe de los disidentes de Venezuela. Madrid, 1821. 4°. (B 396)
— HAWKSHAW, J. Reminiscences of S. America from a residence in Venezuela, [1832-34]. London, 1838. 12°.
— EASTWICK, E. B. Venezuela; with the history of the loan of 1864. 2d ed. Lond., 1868. 8°.
See also Caracas; — Margarita Island; — Terra Firma; — *also* Méranda, F. de.

Venganza de Agamenon, La; tragedia de Sofocles, tr. por F. P. de Oliva. (*In* Sedano, J. J. L. de. Parnaso esp., v. 6. 1772.)

Vengeur, *ship.* CARLYLE, T. On the sinking of the Vengeur. (*In his* Crit. essays, v. 4. 1860.)

Venice. *Ambassadors.*

— Relationen venetianischer Botschafter über Deutschland und Osterreich im 6en Jahrhundert; hrsg. von J. Fiedler. Wien, 1870. 8°. (Font. rer. Austr., 2. Abth., 30. B.)
— BROWN, R. Calendar of state papers and mss. rel. to English affairs, in the archives of Venice and other libraries of Northern Italy, 1202-1556. London, 1864-77. 6 v. 8°.
Contents. Vol. 1. Oct. 1202 - May 18, 1509. 2. May 25, 1509-1519. 3. 1520-26. 4. 1527-33. 5. 1534-54. 6. 1555-56.
— Relation of the island of England, [about 1500]. London, 1867. 4°. (Camden Soc., v. 37.)
— Relazioni degli ambasciatori veneti al senato; rac., annot., e pub. da E. Albèri. Firenze, 1839-62. 3 ser. in 14 v. 8°.
— - Appendice [alla series 1a-3a]. Firenze, 1863. 8°.
Contents. 1a ser., v. 1. 1506-48. 2. 1525-58. 3. 1531-61. 4. 1492-1600. 5. 1563-98. 6. 1507-74. 2a ser., v. 1. 1527-61. 2. 1540-76. 3. 1500-58. 4. 1530-98. 5. 1566-74. 3a ser., v. 1. 1534-79. 2. 1564-92. 3. 1503-94.
— Four years at the court of Henry VIII.; selection of despatches by S. Giustinian, 1515-19. London, 1854. 2 v. 8°.
Contents. Vol. 1. Jan. 12, 1515 - Nov. 1, 1516. 2. Nov. 13, 1516 - July 26, 1619.
— Relation des ambassadeurs vénitiens sur les affaires de France en le 16e siècle; rec. et tr. par M. N. Tommaseo. Paris, 1838. 2 v. 4°. (Doc. inéd.)
Contents. Vol. 1. 1528-61. 2. 1563-77.
— Relazioni degli stati europei dagli ambasciatori veneti nel sec. 17; rac. ed. annot. da N. Barozzi e G. Berchet. Venezia, 1856-63. 4 ser. in 7 v. 8°.
Contents. 1a ser., v. 1. 1602-32. 2. 1635-1702. 2a ser., v. 1. 1603-16. 2. 1617-56. 3a ser., v. 1. 1601-1743. 4a ser., v. 1. 1607-96.
— Relationen der Botschafter Venedigs über Deutschland und Osterreich im 17en Jahrhundert; hrsg. von J. Fiedler. Wien, 1866-67. 2 v. 8°. (Fontes rer. Austr., 2e Abth., 26, 27. Bd.)
Contents. Vol. 1. 1614-54. 2. 1658-93.
— Relationen der Botschafter Venedigs über Osterreich im 18en Jahrhundert, 1708-93. Wien, 1863. 8°. (Fontes rer. Austr., 2e Abth., 22. Bd.)
— RELAZIONI degli ambasciatori veneti. (*In* Archivio stor ital., n.s., v. 9. 1859.)

Architecture.

— X., —. Sulle consorterie delle arti edificative in Venezia. (*In* Archiv. stor. ital., n.s., v. 6. pt. 1. 1867.)
— MOTHES, O. Geschichte der Baukunst und Bildhauerei Venedigs. Leipzig, 1859-60. 2 v. 8°.

Art.

— ZANETTI, A. M. Varie pitture a fresco de' principali maestri veneziani. Venezia, 1760. f°.
— - Della pittura veneziana, [1771]. Ed. 2a. Venezia, 1792. 2 v. 18°.
— LANZI, L. La scuola veneziana. (*In his* Storia pitt. della ital., v. 3. 1809; *and Eng.*, v. 3. 1828.)
— RIDOLFI, C. Maraviglie dell' arte, vite degli illustri pittori veneti, *ec.* 2a ed. Padova, 1835-37. 2 v. 8°.
— RUSKIN, J. Stones of Venice. London, 1851-53. 3 v. 8° *and* Plates f°.
— DIDRON, A. N., *and* BURGER, W. Iconographie du palais ducal de Venise. (*In* Annales archéol., v. 17. 1857.)
— TAINE, H. A. La peinture vénitienne, [1864]. (*In his* Voy. en Italie, v. 1. 1866; *and biog.* 1869.)
— DRAKE, W. R. Notes on Venetian ceramics. London, 1868. 8°.

Biography.

— SANUTO, M. Vitæ ducum Venetorum, 421-1493. — Vite de' duchi di Venezia. (*In* Muratori, L. A. Rer. ital. scr., v. 22. 1733.)

— STELLA, A. Elogia Venetorum navali pugna illustrium, [1557]. (*In* Grævius. Thes. antiq. Ital.; v. 5, pt. 4. 1722.)

— CRASSO, N., *the younger*. Elogia patritiorum Venetorum belli pacisque artibus illustrium, [1612]. (*In* Grævius. Thes. antiq. Ital., v. 5, pt. 4. 1722.)

— GIRARDI, L. A. Vite dei martiri di Venezia. (*In* Amato, G. d'. Panteon, v. 2. 1851.)

Botany.

— ZANNICHELLI, G. G. Istoria delle piante che nascono ne lidi intorno a Venezia. Venezia, 1735. f°.

Commerce.

— CANESTRINI, G. Documenti spettanti al commercio dei Veneziani con l'Armenia e Trebisonda, *ec.*, 1201-1321; prec. da un discorso. (*In* Archivio stor. ital., app., v. 9. 1853.)

Description.

— FERRARIO, G. (*In his* Costume, v. 10. 1829.)

— SABELLICO, M. A. C. De situ urbis Venetæ, magistratibus, *etc.*, [1484]. (*In* Grævius. Thes. antiq. Ital., v. 5, pt. 1. 1722.)

— SANSOVINO, F. T. Venetia descritta; ampl. da G. Stringa. Venetia, 1604. 4°.

— SPLENDOR urbis Venetiarum e figuris et descriptione emicans. (*In* Grævius. Thes. antiq. Ital., v. 5, pt. 2, 3. 1722.)

— QUADRI, A. Huit jours à Venise. Venise, 1823. 16°.

— COSTELLO, L. S. Tour to and from Venice, [1845]. 2d ed. London, 1846. 8°.

— TAINE, H. A. Venise, [1864]. (*In his* Voyage en Italie, v. 2. 1866; *and, Eng.* 1869.)

— HOWELLS, W. D. Venetian life. N. Y., 1866. 12°.

See also P. E. de Musset's La pagota. (*In* Revue d. D. Mondes, août 1852.)

Maps.

— DOMINIO Veneto nell' Italia. *n.p.*, [16—]. (E 78, no. 194)

— DOMUS Germanorum emporica Venetia. *n.p.*, [16—]. (E 78, no. 196.)

— PIACE S. Marco in Venetia. *n.p.*, [16—]. (E 78, no. 195 b)

— VENETIA. *n.p.*, [16—]. (E 78, no. 195a)

Ecclesiastical affairs.

— SAGREDO, A. Leggi ecclesiastiche dei Veneziani spettanti alla pubblica economia, [1232-1767]. (*In* Archivio stor. ital., ser. 3, v. 6, pt. 1. 1867.)

Government.

— GIANNOTTI, D., *d.* 1572. Dialogus de republica Venetorum. (*In* Grævius. Thes. antiq. Ital., v. 5, pt. 1 1722.)

History.

— *Bibliography.* CANALE, M. G. Degli archivi di Venezia, di Vienna, di Firenze, e di Genova. *In* Archivio stor. ital., *n.s.*, v. 4, pt. 2. 1856.)

— FLAVIO, B. De origine e gestis Venetorum. (*In* Grævius, J. G. Thes. antiq. Ital., v. 5, pt. 1. 1722.)

— KELSALL, C. Remarks on the Venetian Republic, [to 1816]. (*In* Pamphleteer, 1818; v. 12. of B 838.)

— HOPF, C. Venedig; der Rath, der Zehn, und die Staatsinquisition, [-1798]. (*In* Historisches Taschenbuch, 1865.)

— ROMANIN, S. Storia documentata di Venezia, [-1796]. Venezia, 1853-61. 10 v. 8°.

— SABELLICO, M. A. C. Deche de l'origine de Veneti fin a tempi nostri, [-1507]. [Venez., *cir.* 1507.] f°.

— NAVAGERO, A. Historia Veneta ad a. 1498. (*In* Muratori. Rer. Ital. scr., v. 23. 1733.)

— DANDOLO, A. Chronicon Venetum ad a. 1339. (*In* Muratori. Rer. Ital. scr., v. 12. 1728.)

— JOHANNES *diaconus*. Chronicon Venetum, ad a. 1008. (*In* Pertz, G. H. Mon. Germ. hist., Scr., v. 9. 1851.)

— GIUSTINIANI, B. De origine urbis Venetiarum, [ad an. 809]. (*In* Grævius. Thes. antiq. Ital., v. 5, pt. 1. 1722.)

— HAZLITT, W. C. History of the origin and rise of the Republic of Venice, [337-1289]. London, 1858. 2 v. 8°.

— SMEDLEY, E. Sketches from Venetian history, [400-1798]. London, 1831-32. 2 v. 16°. (Fam. lib., v. 26, 27.)

— - *Same.* N.Y., 1846, 43. 2 v. 16°. (Harper's fam. lib., v. 43, 44.)

— SANSOVINI, F. T. Cronico, [400-1603]. *n.t.p.* [1604.] 4°.

— HAZLITT, W. C. History of the Venetian Republic, [409-1457]. London, 1860. 4 v. 8°.

— DARU, P. A. N. B. Histoire de la République de Venise, [421-1798]. 2e éd. Paris, 1821. 8 v. 8°.

— ISTORICI delle cose veneziane, [421-1690]. Venezia, 1718-22. 10 v. 4°.

— FOUGASSES, T. de. General historie of the magnificent state of Venice, [421-1607; tr. by] W. Shute. London, 1612. 2 v. f°.

— WELSER, M. Examen de la liberté originaire de Venise, [421-1310]; tr. [par A. de la Houssaye]. Ratisbonne, 1677. 16°.

— AMELOT DE LA HOUSSAYE, A. N. Hist. of the government of Venice, 452-1675. London, 1677. 8°.

— PASOLINI, P. D. Delle antiche relazioni fra Venezia e Ravenna, [528-1253]. (*In* Archiv. stor. ital., ser. 3, v. 12, 13. 1870-71.)

— HOWELL, J. Survey of the Signorie of Venice, [697-1651]. London, 1651. f°.

— CRONACA veneta detta Altinate [697-1229] di autore anonimo in Latino; prec. da un commentario del Prof. A. Rossi. (*In* Archivio stor. ital., v. 8. 1845.)

— BASCHET, A. Les archives de Venise; histoire de la chancellerie secrète dans leurs rapports avec la France, [883-1797]. Paris, 1870. 8°.

— CANALE, M. Cronaca dei Veneziani, [1102-1303], nell' antico francese colla versione ital. del conte G. Galvani, e con. annot. (*In* Archivio stor. ital., v. 8. 1845.)

— URKUNDEN zur älteren Handels und Staatsgeschichte der Republik Venedig. 3r Theil, 1256-99. Wien, 1857. 8°. (Fontes rer. Austr., 2. Abth., Bd. 14.)

— FAZIO, B. De bello Veneto Clodiano, [1377]. (*In* Grævius. Thes. antiq. Ital., v. 5, pt. 4. 1722.)

— WILKEN, F. Ueber die venetianischen Consuln zu Alexandrien im 15en und 16en Jahrhunderte. (*In* Berlin. Ak. d. Wiss. Abh., 1831.)

— MALIPIERO, D. Annali veneti, 1457-1500. (*In* Archivio stor. ital., v. 7, pt. 1, 2. 1843, 44.)

— BUONACCORSI (*Lat.* Callimachus), F. De bello Turcis inferendo oratio, [1486]; De his quæ a Venetis tentata sunt contra Turcos historia, [148-]. (*In* Bizari, P. Rer. Persic. hist. 1601.)

— BEMBO, P. Historia veneta, [1487-1513]. Venezia, 1718. 4°. (Istorici delle cose ven., v. 2.)

— - *Same.* (*In his* Opere, v. 3, 4. 1809; — *and in* Grævius. Thes. antiq. Ital., v. 5, pt. 1. 1722.)

— BASCHET, A. La diplomatie vénitienne; les princes de l'Europe au 16e siècle, d'après les rapports des ambassadeurs vénitiens, [1492-1588]. Paris, 1862. 8°.

— FOSCARI, F., *and others*. Dispacci al senato veneto presso Massimiliano I. nel 1496. (*In* Archivio stor. ital., v. 7, pt. 2. 1844.)

— CASA, G. della. Della lodi di Venezia. — Per muovere i Veneziani alla lega, [15—]. (*In his* Opere, v. 2. 1806.)

— CRASSO, N. De forma republicæ Venetæ, [15—]. (*In* Grævius. Thes. antiq. Ital., v. 5, pt. 1. 1722.) — ARLUNO, B. De bello sæcolo 16 a Germanis et all. adversus Venetos [1508-16]. — MOCENIGO, A. Belli Cameracensis adversus Venetos historia [1508-16]. (*In* pt. 4. 1722.)

— DUBOS, J. B. Hist. de la ligue faite à Cambrai contre Venise, [1508-16]. 5e éd. Paris, 1785. 2 v. 12°.
— HÉLIAN, L. Harangue contre les Vénetiens, 1510; tr. du latin [par A. de la Houssaye]. (*In* **Welser, M.** Examen. 1677.)
— BARBARO, D. Storia veneziana, 1512-15. (*In* **Archivio** stor. ital., v. 7, pt. 2. 1844.)
— BAZZONI, A. Le annotazione degli Inquisitori di Stato di Venezia, [1539-1797]. (*In* **Archiv.** stor. ital., ser. 3, v. 11, pt. 1, 2. 1870.) — Appendice. (*In* v. 12, pt. 1. 1870.)
— CONTARINI, G., *d.* 1542. De republica Venetorum, *etc.* Lugd. Bat., *ex offic. Elzeviriana*, 1628. 16°.
— - *Same, extract.* (*In* **Grævius.** Thes., v. 5, pt. 1. 1722.)
— SAVORGNANO, G. Lettera alla Signoria di Venezia sui confini del Friuli, 1583. (*In* **Archivio** stor. ital., n.s., v. 14, pt. 1. 1861.)
— SARPI, P. [16—.] (*In his* Opere, v. 3-8. 1763-68.)
— - Storia partic. delle cose passate tra il pontefice Paolo v., e la republica di Venezia, 1605-07. (*In his* Opere, v. 3. 1763). *See also* the following volumes.)
— NANI, G. B. F. G. Istoria della Repubblica Veneta, [1613-71]. Venezia, 1720. 2 v. 8°. (Istorici delle cose ven., v. 8, 9.)
— - *Eng.* History of the affairs of Europe, particularly of the republic of Venice; [tr.] by Sir R. Honywood. London, 1673. f°.
— CHAMBRIER D'OLEIRES, *baron* d'. De la conjuration des Espagnols contre la république de Venise, [1618]. (*In* **Berlin. Ak. d. Wiss.** Abh., 1798-1800.)
— RANKE, F. T. von. Ueber die Verschwörung gegen Venedig, 1618. Berlin, 1831. 8°.
— ST. RÉAL, C. V. Conjurations des Espagnols contre Venise, [1618]. Ed. stér. Paris, an XI, 1803. 12°.
— - *Eng.* Conspiracy of the Spaniards against Venice, and of J. L. Fiesco against Genoa. Boston, 1828. 12°.
— ISTRUZIONE al vescovo di Montefiascone [L. Zacchia], che nel 1621 recavasi nunzio a Venezia; [parole preliminari per Achille Gennarelli]. (*In* **Archivio** stor. ital., n.s., v. 7, pt. 1. 1843.)
— BONIFACIO, B. De majoribus comitiis et judiciis capitalibus Venetorum, [1628]. (*In* **Grævius.** Thes. antiq. Ital., v. 5, pt. 1. 1772.)
— GARZONI, P. Istoria della repubblica di Venezia, [1661-1714]. Venezia, 1705-16. 2 v. 4°.
— - *Same.* (Pte. 1, 3a impr.; pte. 2, 2a impr.) Venezia, 1712-17. 2 v. 4°.
— FOSCARINI, M. Franchigie concesse agli ambasciatori residenti in Venezia, 1725. (*In* **Archivio** stor. ital., app., v. 9. 1853.)
— NAPOLEON I. Insurrection des états de Venise, [1796-97]. (*In his* Commentaires, v. 2. 1867.)
— FLAGG, E. Venice the city of the sea, 1797-1849. N. Y., 1853. 2 v. 12°.
— MAZADE, C. de. Venise, 1848-[66]. (*In* **Revue** d. D. Mondes, sept. 1866.)
— MANIN, D. Documents et piéces authentiques; tr. par F. Planat de la Faye, [1848-49]. Paris, 1860. 2 v. 8°.
— BELGIOJOSO, C. T., *princesse* de. La révolution et la répub. de Venise, 1848. (*In* **Revue** d. D. Mondes, déc. 1848.)
— PÉPÉ, G. Revolution in V., 1848. (*In his* Scenes in Italy, v. 1. 1850.)
— PROBYN, J. W. Milan et Venise, 1859-[65]. (*In* **Revue** d. D. Mondes, oct. 1865.)

Language.

See **Bada, G.** Scaramuzza; poema in vernacolo famillar veniziano; — *also* **Caravia, A.** Naspo bizaro; — *also, in the next column, Literature (Collections).*

Literature.

— *Bibliography.* AGOSTINI, G. degli. Notizie int. la vita e le opere degli scrittori viniziani. Venezia, 1752-54. 2 v. 4°.
— - CICOGNA, E. A. Saggio di bibliografia veneziana. Venezia, 1847. 8°.
— *History.* FOSCARINI, M. Della letteratura veneziana. Vol. 1. Padova, 1752. f°.
— - MOSCHINI, G. Della letteratura veneziana del secolo 18. Venezia, 1806-08. 4 v. f°.
— *Collections.* GAMBA, B. Raccolta di poesie in dialetto veneziano. Venezia, 1845. 8°.
— - WIDTER, G., *and others.* Volksmärchen aus Venetien. (*In* **Jahrbuch** für rom. u. eng. Lit., v. 7. 1866.)

Numismatics.

— CORDERO DE' CONTI SANQUINTINO, G. Origine ed antichità della moneta veneziana. (*In* **Turin. Ac. d. Sci.** Mem., ser. 2, v. 10. 1849.)

Social life.

— DEVILLE, A. Pyctomachia Veneta. — LORENZO, G. De desponsatione maris Adriatici. — WALKER, J. Spectacula Veneta, epigrammatibus celebrata. (*In* **Grævius.** Thes. antiq. Ital., v. 5., pt. 4. 1722.)

Venice, San Marco. DURAND, J. Inconographie de St. Marc de Venise. (*In* **Annales** archéol., v. 14, 15. 1854-55.)
— - Trésor de l'église St. Marc. de Venise. (*In* **Annales** archéol., v. 20, 21. 1860-61.)
Venice. Fraternità e Compagnia dei Fiorentini. Statuti, 1556. (*In* **Archivio** stor. ital., app., v. 9. 1853.)
Venice preserved; tragedy. *See* **Otway, T.**
Venier, Girolamo. Relazione di Francia di G. V. ambasciatore ordinario Luigi XIV., 1682-88. (*In* **Barozzi, N.,** *and* **Berchet, G.** Rel. degli stati europei, ser. 2, v. 3. 1863.)
Venier, Pietro. Relazione di Francia di P. V. ambasciatore ordinario a Luigi XIV., 1688-95. (*In* **Barozzi, N.,** *and* **Berchet, G.** Rel. degli. stati europei, ser. 2, v. 3. 1863.)
Venieri, Demetrio. Compendio di grammatica in dialetto grego volgare con la traduzione ital. Trieste, 1799. 4°.
Veniero, Maffeo. Madrigale. (*In* **Trucchi, F.** Poesie ital., v. 4. 1847.)
— Poesie. (*In* **Gamba, B.** Rac. di poesie in dial. venez. 1845.)
Venilia. RIVINUS, A. Dissertationes duæ de venilia et salacia, nec non malacia. (*In* **Grævius, J. G.** Syntagma. 1702.)
Venius, Otto. *See* **Veen, O. van.**
Venn, Henry, *d.* 1797. Duty of a parish priest, *etc.*; sermon, visitation of the clergy, Wakefield, July 2, 1760. 3d ed. London, 1761. 8°. (B 1922.)
Venn, Henry. Missionary life and labours of F. Xavier. London, 1862. 8°.
Venn, John, *Rector of Clapham, d.* 1813. Sermon, June 4, before the Soc. for Missions to Africa. London, 1805. 8°. (B 1194)
Venn, John. Logic of chance; essay on the province of the theory of probability with especial ref. to moral and social science. London, Camb., 1866. 16°.
— On some of the characteristics of belief, scientific and religious. London, Camb., 1870. 8°.
Vennar, Richard. Apology for England's joy. (*In* **Collier,** J. P. Illust. of old English lit., v. 3. 1866.)
Venomous insects and reptiles. BUSK, G. (*In* **Holmes,** T. Syst. of surgery, v. 4. 1864.)
Ventaglio, Il; commedia. *See* **Goldoni, C.**
Ventenat, Etienne Pierre. CUVIER, G. L. C. F. D. (*In his* Eloges hist., v. 1. 1819.)
Ventignano, Cesare della Valle, *duca* di. Medea. (*In* **Poeti** ital. contemp. 1843.)
Ventilation. BERNAN, W. History and art of warming and ventilating rooms and buildings. London, 1845. 2 v. 16°.
— WHITEHURST, J. Observations on ventilation, *etc.*; [ed. by R. Willan]. London, 1794. 4°.
— WOLTMANN, R. Theory and description of a ventilator for airing vessels, vaults, mines, *etc.* [In English and German.] Hamburgh, 1805. 8°.
— SYLVESTER, C. Mode of ventilation adopted in the Derbyshire infirmary. Nottingham, 1819. 4°.

— TREDGOLD, T. Principles of warming and ventilating public buildings, *etc.* 2d ed. London, 1824. 8°.
— HARLEY, W. New mode of ventilating stables. (*In his* Harleian dairy system. 1829.)
— HAWTHORNE, G. New mode of ventilating hospitals, *etc.* Belfast, 1830. 12°.
— HOOD, C. Practical treatise on warming buildings by hot water; added, remarks on ventilation. London, 1837. 8°.
— ARNOTT, N. Warming and ventilation. London, 1838. 8°.
— SPENCER, G. On combining mechanical ventilation with warming by steam. (*In* Gr. Brit. *Corps of Roy. Engin.* Papers, v. 6. 1843.)
— REID, D. B. Illustrations of the theory and practice of ventilation, *etc.* Lond., 1844. 8°.
— BOSTON. *School Committee.* Reports on the ventilation of school houses, 1846–47. Boston, 1847–48. 2 v. 8°.
— - *Same.* Boston, 1848. 4°.
— WYMAN, M. Practical treatise on ventilation. Camb., 1846. 8°.
— BELL, L. V. Practical methods of ventilating buildings. Boston, 1848. 8°.
— - *Same.* (*In* **Mass. Med. Soc.** Med. comm., v. 7. 1848.)
— TOMLINSON, C. Rudimentary treatise on warming and ventilation. Lond., *Weale*, 1850. 12°.
— DOWNING, A. J. Warming and ventilating. (*In his* Archit. of country houses. 1854.)
— REID, D. B. Progress of architecture in relation to ventilation, *etc.* (*In* **Smithsonian Inst.** Report, 1856.)
— FORBES, *Sir* J. S. Ventilation and heating. (*In* **Nat. Assoc. Prom. Soc. Sci.** Trans., 1860.)
— MORIN, A. Mécanique pratique; études sur la ventilation. Paris, 1863. 2 v. 8°.
— SHEDD, J. H., *and* EDSON, W. Suggestions on ventilation. *n.t.p.* [1865.] 8°. (Mass. Ho. Doc. 5.)
— BLERZY, H. (*In* **Revue d. D. Mondes**, fév. 1867.)
— SER, L. Chauffage et ventilation. (*In* **France.** *Com. Imp. de l'Expos. de* 1867. Rapports, v. 3.) — USSEL, —, *vcte.* d'. Ventilation du palais de l'Eposition. (*In* v. 8.)
— LEEDS, L. W. Treatise on ventilation. [2d ed.] N. Y., 1871. 8°.

See also **Nat. Assoc. Prom. Soc. Sci.** Trans., *passim.*

Ventouillac, L. T. French librarian; or, Literary guide. London, 1829. 8°.

Ventoux, Mont. MARTINS, C. F. (*In* **Revue d. D. Mondes**, avr. 1863.)

Ventris, *Sir* Peyton. Argument in the exchequer chamber upon a writ of error out of the Kings-bench. *n.t.p.* [1690?] 4°. (B 1434)

Ventura, Gioachimo. RÉMUSAT, F. M. C., *comte* de. Le père Ventura et la philosophie. (*In* **Revue** d. D. Mondes, mars 1853.)

Ventura, Guglielmo. Memoriale de gestis civium Astensium. (*In* **Muratori,** L. A. Rer. Ital. scr., v. 11. 1727; — *and in* **Sardinia.** Mon. hist. patr., Scr., v. 3. 1848.)

Ventura, Lorenzo. Liber de conficiendi lapidis philosophici ratione. (*In* **Zetzner,** L. Theatr. chem., v. 2. 1613.)

Ventura, Secondino. Historica quædam ab a. 1419 ad a. 1457. (*In* **Muratori,** L. A. Rer. Ital. scr., v. 11. 1727.)

Venturi, GiamBattista. Esperimenti int. i galleggianti. (*In* **Galilei,** G. Opere, v. 12. 1854.)

Venturini, Giovanni Francesco, *engraver.* Le fontane di Roma, [1691]. *See* **Falda,** G. B.

Venturoli, Giuseppe. Elements of the theory of mechanics; tr. by D. Creswell. Camb., 1822. 8°.

Venus, Mount of. REUMONT, A. Del monte di Venere ossia labirinto d' amore. (*In* **Archivio** stor. ital., 3a ser., v. 13, pt. 3. 1871.)

Venus, *planet.* ENCKE, J. F. Die Entfernung der Sonne von der Erde aus dem Venusdurchgange von 1761 hergeleitet. Gotha, 1822. 8°.
— WINTHROP, J. Relation of a voyage to Newfoundland for the observation of the transit of Venus, June 6. Boston, 1761. 8°. (B 393)
— LAGRANGE, J. L. Mémoire sur le passage de Vénus du 3 juin 1769. (*In his* Œuvres, v. 2. 1868.)
— CHAPPE D'AUTEROCHE, J. Voyage en Californie pour l'observation du passage de Vénus sur le disque du soleil, 1769; tr., éd., et pub. par C. F. de Cassini. Paris, 1772. 4°.
— WINTHROP, J. Two lectures on the parallax and distance of the sun as deducible from the transit of Venus. Boston, 1769. 8°. (B 393)
— SCHRÖTER, J. H. Aphroditographische Fragmente zur genauern Kenntniss des Planeten Venus. Helmstedt, 1796. 4°.
— LINDENAU, B. A. von. Tabulæ Veneris novæ et correctæ. Gotha, 1810. 4°.
— ALEXANDER, S. Atmospheric envelopes of Venus and other planets. (*In* **Amer. Assoc.** Proc., v. 6. 1852.) — LYMAN, C. S. Observations of Venus near inferior conjunction. (*In* v. 16. 1868.)

Venus and Adonis; a masque. *See* **Cibber, C.**

Venus and Adonis. *See* **Shakespeare, W.**

Vénus d'Arles, La; par J. Méry. Paris, 1866. 18°.

Venus di Milo. ÉMÉRIC-DAVID, T. B. La statue antique de femme découverte en 1820 dans l'île de Milo. (*In* **Paris. Inst.** *Ac. d. Inscr.* Mém., v. 12. 1836.)
— GERHARD, E. Ueber Venusidole. (*In* **Berlin. Ak.** d. Wiss. Abh., 1843.)
— GRIMM, H. Venus of Milo, from the German; tr. by A. M. Hawes. Boston, 1868. 32°.
— RAVAISSON, F. La Venus de Milo au Musée d'Antiques. (*In* **Revue** d. D. Mondes, sept. 1871.)

Vénus et Adonis; tragédie. *See* **Rousseau, J. B.**

Venuti, Niccolò Marcello, *marchese.* Description of the first disc. of the antient city of Heraclea; [tr.] by Wickes Skurray; [with] letters between J. M. Gesner, Card. Quirini, and H. S. Reimarus. London, 1750. 8°. (B 645)

Venuti, Ridolfino. Descrizione topog. delle antichitá di Roma. Ed. 3a; agg. note, *ec.*, di S. Piale. Roma, 1824. 2 v. 4°.

Vêpres siciliennes, Les; par J. F. C. **Delavigne.** (*In his* Théâtre, v. 1. 1826.)

Véra; or, The Russian princess and the English earl [by C. L. H. Dempster]. N. Y., 1871. 8°.

Vera Cruz. LONDAIZ, P. Defensa por L. B. de Cordova y Zuñiga, corrigedor de Veracruz, en la causa criminal que contra el se sigue; sobre dezir, que fue culpado en el saco executado por los pirates que infestan las costas de Tierra Firma, *etc.* *n.p.*, [168-?]. f°. (A 68)
— SUMICHRAST, F. Geographical distribution of native birds of the department of V. C.; tr. by T. M. Brewer. (*In* **Boston** Soc. Nat. Hist. Mem., v. 1. 1866–69.)

Vera Figueroa y Zuñiga, Juan Antonio, *conde de la Roca.* De la vida de G. de Guzman. (*In* **Valladares,** A. Seman. erud., v. 2. 1787.)

Veranzio, Antonio. Iter Buda Hadrianopolim. anno 1553; exaratum ab A. Varantio. (*Appended to* **Fortis,** A. Travels into Dalmatia. 1778.)

Verardi, Carlo. NICERON, J. P. (*In his* Mém., v. 8. 1729; *and, Germ.*, v. 8. 1753.)

Veratrina. TURNBULL, A. An investigation into the external application of veratria. Wash., 1834. 8°. (E 35)
— NORWOOD, W. C. Therapeutical powers, *etc.*, of veratrum viride. 2d ed. N. Y., 1856. 8°. (B 1559)

Verax, Theodorus, *pseud.* *See* **Walker, C.**

Verbannte Amor, Der, oder: Die argwöhnischen Eheleute; von A. v. **Kotzebue.** (*In his* Theater, v. 25. 1841.)

Verbanus, *Lake.* *See* **Lago Maggiore.**

Verbiest, Ferdinand. Voyage de l'empereur de la Chine dans la Tartarie. (*In* **Bernard,** J. F. Recueil de voy., v. 3. 1716.)
— *Eng.* Journey of the emperor of China into East Tartary, 1682, — West Tartary, 1683. (*In* **Relation** of the invasion of Florida. 1686.)
— *Same.* Two journeys. (*In* **Orleans,** P. J. d'. Hist. of the Tartar conquerors of China, 1854. Hakluyt Soc., v. 17.)
— - *Germ.* Reise in die östliche Tartary. 1682. (*In* **Allgemeine Hist.**, v. 7. 1750.)

Verbrechen aus Ehrsucht; von A. W. **Iffland.** (*In his* Theat. Werke, v. 5. 1859.)

Verbs. *See* **Moods**; — *also* **Greece.** *Language* (p. 1265).

Verbum sapienti; or, One word for the charter, reputation, and honour of London; address to the Mayor, *etc.* *n.t.p.* [London, 1682.] f°. (A 50)

Vercelli. Berardo, A. Relazione dell' assedio della città di V., 1617, dall' esercito di Spagna; illustrata da C. Promis. — Caluso, *marchese* de. Defesa del marchese di Caluso governatore di V., per la dedizione di questa città nel 1617. (*In* **Archivio** stor. ital., v. 13. 1847.)

— Gregory, G. G. de. Istoria della vercellese letteratura ed arti. Torino, 1819-24. 4 v. 4°.

— Gazzera, C. Iscrizione metrica vercellese. (*In* **Turin. Ac. d. Sci.** Mem., v. 33. 1829.)

— Casalis, G. Vercelli, provincia e città. (*In his* Diz. geog. di Sardegna, v. 25. 1853.)

— Map. *n.p.*, [16—]. (E 78, no. 199)

Verdad sospechosa, La; por J. R. de Alarcon. (*In* **Ochoa,** E. de. Col. de piezas escogidas, 1840; *and* Tes. del teatro esp., v. 4. 1838.)

Verdeil, Auguste. Guerre des Suisses contre le duc de Burgogne dans le Pays de Vaud, 1475-76. Lausanne, 1854. 16°.

— Réclusion dans le Canton de Vaud et du Pénitencier de Lausanne. Lausanne, 1842. 8°.

Verdeil, F. Traité de chimie anatomique et physiologique. 1853. *See* **Robin,** C. P.

Verdi, Giuseppe. Atila. [Ital. and Span.] Habana, 1848. 12°. (E 6)

— Hernani. [English.] Boston, 1847. 16°. (C 286)

— *Same.* [Ital. and Eng.] Ernani. N. Y., 1848. 12°. (E 6)

— Los Lombardos. [Ital., Span.] Habana. 1846. 12°. (E 6)

— Macbeth. [Ital. and Eng.] N. Y., 1848. 12°. (E 6)

— Nabucodonozor. [Ital. and Eng. N. Y., 1848.] 12°. (C 286, E 6)

Note. None of the librettos above have the music.

Verdier, Antoine du. *See* **Du Verdier,** A.

Verdier, Aymar. Cattois, F. Architecture civile et domestique au Moyen Age et à la Renaissance. Paris, 1858. 2 v. 4°.

Verdier, César. Abrégé de l'anatomie du corps humain. 3e éd. augm. Paris, 1761. 2 v. 12°.

Verdizzotti, G. Mario. Favole. (*In* **Raccolta** di fav. ital. 1833.)

Verdoni, —. Traité, *etc.* 1775. *See* **Léger,** —.

Verdugo de Castilla, Alfonso, *conde de Torrepalma.* El Deucalion. (*In* **Quintana,** M. J. Poesias sel. castell., v. 3. 1807.)

— Noticias biogràficas. Poesias. (*In* **Cueto,** L. A. de. Poetas lir. del sig. XVIII. 1869; v. 61 of Aribau. Bibl.)

Verdun. Scherer, H. Der Raub der drei Bisthümer Metz, Tull, und Verdun im 1552 bis zu ihrer formlichen Abtretung an Frankreich im westfälischen Frieden, [1552-1648]. (*In* **Historisches** Taschenbuch, 1842.)

— Journal de Metz, 1765; avec une notice sur Verdun. Metz, 1765. 8°.

Verdun, Bishopric of. Laurentius *de Leodio.* Gesta episc. Virdunensium et abb. S. Vitoni. (*In* **Pertz,** G. H. Mon. Germ. hist., Scr., v. 10. 1852.)

Verdun. S. Paul. Annales, 908-1215, 1249, 1419. (*In* **Pertz,** G. H. Mon. Germ., Scr., v. 16. 1859.)

Verdun. S. Vitonus. Annales sancti Vitoni Virdunensis. (*In* **Pertz,** G. H. Mon. Germ., Scr., v. 12. 1856.)

Verdy du Vernois, *le chev.* Adrien Marie François de. Sur l'origine du bailliage de l'ordre de St. Jean de Jérusalem dans l'électorat de Brandebourg. (*In* **Berlin. Ak. d. Wiss.** Abh., 1788-89.) — Essai sur la manière de rédiger l'histoire du règne de Fréderic II., de Prusse. — Sur la vente de la baronie d'Herstal, à l'évêque de Liége. (*In* 1790-91.) — Sur les possessions de la maison royale de Prusse, électorale de Brandebourg, *etc.* (*In* 1794/95, 96.) — De l'origine de la maison landgraviale de Hesse. (*In* 1797.) — Généalogie de la maison des anc. comtes de Hohen-Zollern; et en particulier, de la branche qui a formé celle des bourgraves de Nuremberg, devenue électorale de Brandebourg et royale de Prusse. (*In* 1798.) — Maison des premiers comtes de Hohen-Zollern. — Maison des premiers bourgraves de Nuremberg. (*In* 1799-1800.) — Sur l'ancienneté et les illustrations de la maison de Hesse. (*In* 1801-02.) — Remarques sur Levin de Schulenbourg. — De la constitution des troupes chez les Gaulois, et des armes qui leur étoient propres. (*In* 1802.)

Vere, Edward, *Earl of Oxford.* Poems. (*In* **Campbell,** T. Brit. poets, v. 2. 1819.)

Vere, Maximilian Schele de. *See* **De Vere,** M. S.

Vereenighde Nederlandtsche Geoctroyeerde Oost-Indische Compagnie. *See* **Oost-Indische Compagnie.**

Vergangene Tage; von Karl Gutzkow. Frankf. a. M., 1852. 8°.

Vergennes, Charles Gravier, *comte* de. Mémoire histor. et pol. sur la Louisiane; acc. d'un précis de [sa] vie, et suivi [de] mémoires sur l'Indostan, Saint Domingue, la Corse, et la Guyane. Paris, 1802. 8°.

— Projet de médiation de la Russie entre la France et l'Angleterre, 1780-82. (*In* **Soc. de l'Hist. de France.** Bul., v. 2. 1835.)

— Vicq d'Azyr, F. (*In his* Œuvres, v. 2. 1805.)

Vergerio, Pietro Paolo, *d.* 1420. De Carrariensium familia, et de illustrium ejus principum rebus gestis historia. (*In* **Grævius,** J. G. Thes. antiq. Ital., v. 6, pt. 3. 1722.)

— *Same.* Ejusdem orationes et epistolæ. (*In* **Muratori,** L. A. Rer. Ital. scr., v. 16. 1730.)

— Niceron, J. P. (*In his* Mém., v. 38. 1737.)

Vergerio (*Lat.* **Vergerius**), Pietro Paolo, *d.* 1565. Niceron, J. P. (*In his* Mém., v. 38. 1737.)

Vergilio (*Lat.* Vergilius), Polidoro. Adagia (*In* **Erasmus,** D. E. Adagiorum Chiliades quatuor, *etc.* 1574.)

— Anglicæ historiæ libri, [ad a. 1538]. Basileæ, 1556. f°.

— *Eng.* Three books of English hist.; ed. by Sir H. Ellis. London, 1844-46. 2 v. 4°. (Camden Soc., v. 29, 36.)

— De rerum inventoribus. Lugd., 1597. 8°.

— *Same.* [Genevæ,] *J. Stoer,* 1604. 8°.

Vergnaud, A. D. Nouveau manuel du peintre en batimens, *etc.* *See* **Riffault des Hêtres,** J. R. D.

— Nouveau manuel du teinturier. *See* **Riffault des Hêtres,** J. R. D.

Vergulde Draeck, De, *ship.* Account of wreck of the ship. (*In* **Major,** R. H. Early voy. to Terra Austr. 1859. Hakluyt Soc., v. 25.)

Verheyen, Philippe. Niceron, J. P. (*In his* Mém., v. 4. 1728; *and*, *Germ.*, v. 4. 1751.)

Verhoeven, Peter Wilhelms. Reise nach Ostindien, 1607-08. (*In* **Allgemeine** Hist., v. 8. 1751.)

Véricour, L. Raymond de. *See* **De Véricour,** L. R.

Verita, Girolamo. Canzone. (*In* **Trucchi,** F. Poesie ital., v. 3. 1847.)

Véritable esprit militaire, ou 'art de rendre les guerres moins funestes. Vol. 1, pt. 1. Liége, 1774. 8°.

Véritable politique, La, à l'usage des émigrés françois. Londres, 1795. 8°. (C 87)

Veritas, *pseud.* Letters from the Montreal herald; mil. administration of Sir G. Prevost. Montreal, 1815. 8°.

Veritas, *pseud.* Letter to the Ld. Chancellor, resp. the proposed St. Catharine's dock. [London, 1824.] 8°. (B 1747)

Veritas, *pseud.* Observations on a sermon at Newark by J. E. Latta. 2d ed. rev. Wilmington, 1823. 8°. (B 1040)

Verity, R. Subject and object as connected with our double brain, and a new theory of causation. London, 1870. 8°.

Verjus, Louis. Alembert, J. le R. d'. (*In his* Œuvres, v. 9. 1805.)

Verkleidungen, Die; von A. F. F. v. **Kotzebue.** (*In his* Theater, v. 37. 1841.)

Verlegenheit und List; Lustpiel frei bearbeitet nach Contretems sur contretems, von Pigault le Brun; von A. F. F. v. **Kotzebue.** (*In his* Almanach, v. 18. 1820; — *and in* Theater, v. 40. 1841.)

Verleumder, Die; von A. F. F. v. **Kotzebue.** (*In his* Theater, v. 5. 1840.)

Verlobung, Die; von J. L. **Tieck.** (*In his* Gesam. Novellen, v. 1. 1852.)

Verlorene Handschrift; Roman, von G. Freytag. Lpz., 1865. 3 v. 8°.

Verlorene Sohn, Der; Lustspiel, von F. W. Hackländer. Stuttgart, 1865. 8°.

Verlorne Kind, Das; von A. v. Kotzebue. (*In his* Theater, v. 20. 1841.)

Vermaehlungstag, Der; ein Schauspiel, von J. J. **Engel.** (*In his* Schriften, v. 5. 1803.)

Vermigli, Caterina, *wife of the following.* HUBERT, C. (*In his* Historia vera. 1562.)

Vermigli (*Lat.* Vermilius), Pietro Martire. Most fruitfull and learned commentarie on the Book of Judges. London, [1560]. f°.

— NICERON, J. P. (*In his* Mém., v. 23. 1733.)

Vermiglioli, Giovan-Battista. Bibliografia storico-perugina. Perugia, 1823. 4°.

— Biografia degli scrittori perugini. Perugia, 1828-29. 2 v. 4°.

Contents. Vol. 1. A-D. 2. E-V.

— Principj della stampa in Perugia e suoi progressi per secolo 15. 2a ed. Perugia, 1820. 8°.

— FABRETTI, A. Di G. B Vermiglioli, *etc.* (*In* Archiv. stor. ital., n.s., v. 2, pt 2. 1857.)

Vermilye, *Rev.* Ashbel G. Memoir of J. Murray. (*In* Maine Hist. Soc. Col., v 6. 1859.)

Vermilye, *Rev.* Thomas E. Farewell discourse, West Springfield, May 3. Springfield, 1835. 8°. (B 1304)

— Funeral discourse, death of Mrs. C. Van Rensselaer, Sept. 1. N. Y., 1844. 8°. (B 1226)

— Funeral discourse, death of S. Van Rensselaer, Feb. 3. Albany, 1839. 8°. (B 1226)

— Introductory address to a course of lectures before the Young Men's Assoc. in Albany, Dec. 19. Albany, 1837. 8°. (B 1588)

— Zion the city of solemnities; sermon dedication of the 3d Ref. Prot. Dutch Church. Albany, 1838. 8°. (B 1310)

Vermont. *Adjutant and Inspector General.* Register of commissioned officers of the Vermont Volunteers. *n.p.*, 1863. 8°.

— - Report, 1862-66. Montpelier, 1862-66. 5 v. 8°.

— *Board of Education.* 1st-12th report of the secretary. Ludlow, *etc.*, 1857-68. 12 v. 8°.

— *Constitutional Convention*, 1777. Constitution. Hartford. [1778]. 8°. (B 1005)

— *Council.* Copy of the remonstrance against the resolutions of Congress of 5th Dec. [1782]. Hartford, 1783. 12°. (B 476, C 106)

— *Council of Censors.* Address to the people. Bennington, 1800. 8°. (B 401)

— - Amendments of the Constitution proposed by the Council. (*In* Constitutionalist, 1814. B 1491)

— - Proceedings of 1st, 2d Council. (*In* Vermont. *Sec. of State.* State papers. 1823.)

— *General Assembly.* Laws to 1824; comp. by W. Slade. Windsor, 1825. 8°.

— - Laws; digested and compiled [by T. Tolman]. Vol. 1, 2, to 1807. Randolph, 1808. 2 v. 8°.

— - Laws, 1779-86. (*In* Vermont. *Sec. of State.* State papers. 1823.)

— - Laws, revised and passed, 1797. Rutland, 1798. 8°.

— - Acts and laws, 1798-1801. Windsor, 1801. 8°.

— - Laws, 1803, 1814-1869. *v.p.*, 1803-69. 57 v. 8°.

— - Public defence of the right of the N. H. Grants to form an independent state. Dresden, 1779. 8°. (C 121)

— - VERMONT. *Sec. of State.* Annual directory for the use of the Assembly. Montpelier, 1867. 12°.

— *Geological Surveyor.* Report on the geology of Vermont, by E. Hitchcock and others. Claremont, 1861. 2 v. 4°.

— *Secretary of State.* 1st, 2d, 4th-10th report to the Legislature rel. to the registry of births, marriages, and deaths, 1857, 58, 60-66. *v.p.*, 1859-68. 9 v. 8°.

— - Annual directory for the use of the Assembly, by G. Nichols; manual of parliamentary practice by H. Clark. Montpelier, 1867. 12°.

— - State papers; a collection of records and documents; journal of the Council of Safety, the first constitution, early journals of the Assembly, laws, 1779-1786, *etc.*; comp. by W. Slade. Middlebury, 1823. 8°.

— *State Geologist.* 1st annual report; by C. B. Adams. Burlington, 1845. 8°.

See also Geological Surveyor.

— *Volunteers.* HAYNES, E. M. History of the 10th Reg. Vermont Vol.; with biog. sketches, [1862-65]. *n p.*, 1870. 8°.

— - VERMONT. *Adjutant and Inspector General.* Register of commissioned officers of the Vermont Volunteers in service of the U. S. Montpelier, 1863. 8°.

— - WALKER, A. F. The Vermont brigade in the Shenandoah Valley, 1864. Burlington, 1869. 8°.

Bibliography.

— HALL, B. H. Bibliography of V. (*In* Norton's literary letter, n.s., no. 2. 1857.)

Biography.

— DEMING, L. Catalogue of the principal officers of Vermont, 1778-1851; with biog. notices. Middlebury, 1851. 8°.

Description.

— GRAHAM, J. A. Descriptive sketch of the present state of Vermont. London, 1797. 8°.

— DEAN, J. Alphabetical atlas; or, Gazetteer of Vermont. Montpelier, 1808. 8°.

— - *Other copies.* (B 140, 966)

— *Maps.* MAP of Maine, New Hampshire, and Vermont. Phila., *S. A. Mitchell*, 1843.

— - WALLING, H. F. Map. N. Y., [186-].

See also Addison Co.; — Bennington; — Brattleboro; — Champlain, Lake; — Chittenden Co.; — Franklin Co.; — Grand Isle Co.

Ecclesiastical history.

See Congregational Churches in Vermont.

Geology.

— HITCHCOCK, C. H. On the so-called talcose schist of Vermont. — On the marks of ancient glaciers on the Green Mountain range. — Lake ramparts in Vermont. (*In* Amer. Assoc. Proc., v. 13. 1860.) — The geology of Vermont. — PERRY, J. P. The red sandstone of Vermont and its relations, v. 16. 1868.)

See also Geological Surveyor; — *State Geologist*; — *also* Colchester; — Connecticut Valley; — Shelburne.

History.

— HEMENWAY, A. M. Vermont historical gazetteer; a magazine, embracing a history of each town. Vol. 1, 2. Burlington, Vt., v. 3, Claremont, 1867-73. 3 v. 8°.

— CHASE, F. Gathered sketches from the early history of New Hampshire and Vt., [to 1780]. Claremont, 1856. 12°.

— THOMPSON, Z. History of Vermont, natural, civil, and statistical, [1609-1841]. Burlington, 1842. 3 pts. 8°.

— HALL, H. History of Vt., [1609]-1791. Albany, 1868. 8°.

— HALL, B. H. History of eastern Vermont, [1672-1799]. N. Y., 1858. 8°.

— WILLIAMS, S. Natural and civil history of Vermont, [1724-91]. Walpole, 1794. 8°.

— - *Same, enlarged.* [To 1806.] 3d ed. Burlington, 1809. 2 v. 8°.

— ALLEN, I. Natural and political hist. of Vermont, [1741-98]. London, 1798. 8°.

— HOUGHTON, G. F. An outline of the controversy of the N. H. Grants, [1760-84]; address before the legislature. Burlington, 1849. 8°. (B 1610)

See also Addison Co; — Bennington; — Champlain, Lake; — Champlain Valley; — Cornwall; — Fair Haven; — Middlebury; — Middletown; — Montpelier; — Pomfret; — Rutland; — Salisbury; — Westminster; — Woodstock; — *also* Amer. Lit. Sci. and Mil. Acad.

Medicine.

— Gallup, J. A. Sketches of epidemic diseases in Vermont. Boston, 1815. 8°.

Numismatics.

— Slafter, E. F. The Vermont coinage. Montpelier, 1870. 8°.

— - *Same.* (*In* **Vermont Hist. Soc.** Col., v. 1. 1870.)

Politics.

— Bradley, S. R. Vermont's appeal to the world, cont. the claims of Mass., N. H., and N. Y., [and] the right Vermont has to independence. Hartford, [177-]. 8°.

— - *Another copy.* (C 102)

— **Allen, E.** Animadversary address to the inhabitants of Vermont. Hartford, 1778. 8°. (B 682)

— - Vindication of the opposition of Vermont to the government of New York. *n.p., A. Spooner*, 1779. 8°. (C 102)

— - *and* Fay, J. Concise refutation of the claims of N. Hampshire and Mass. to Vermont. Hartford, 1780. 8°. (B 585)

See also Council; — Gen. Assembly.

Vermont, University of. Alphabetical and analytical catalogue of the library. Burlington, 1854. 8°.

— Catalogus senatus academici. Burlingtoniæ, 1812. 8°. (B 648)

— Wheeler, J. Historical discourse, an address by J. R. Spalding and a poem by O. G. Wheeler, on the semi-centennial anniv. of the University. Burlington, 1854. 8°.

Vermont and Mass. R. R. Co. 1st ann. report. Boston, 1845. 8°. (B 1197)

Vermont Annual Conference of the Methodist Episcopal Church. *See* **Methodist Episcopal Church in Vermont.**

Vermont Bible Soc. 5th report, Oct. 15, 1817. Montpelier, Vt., 1817. 8°. (B 460)

Vermont Colonization Society. 14th ann. report, Oct. 18. Montpelier, 1833. 8°. (B 1276)

Note. For discourses before the Society *see* **Fowler, W. C.** (B 1483); — **Hough, J.** (B 288)

Vermont directory and Commercial almanac, 1856-59, 63; by W. W. Atwater. Burlington, Rutland, [1856-63]. 5 v. 16°.

Vermont General Convention of Congregational and Presbyterian Ministers. Address to Christian parents of the churches in Vermont. Rutland, [1833?] 12°. (C 272)

— Extracts from the minutes, Sept. Middlebury, 1813. 8°. (B 459)

Vermont historical gazetteer. *See* **Hemenway, A. M.**

Vermont Historical Society. Collections. Montpelier, 1870, 71. 2 v. 8°.

Contents. Vol. 1. Constitution, by-laws, *etc.* — **Conventions** of the inhabitants of the New Hampshire Grants in opposition to the claims of New York, 1765-77. — **Hutchinson, A.** Sermon, Windsor, July 2, 1777. — The **vision** of Janus the Benningtonite, 1777. — **Allen, I.** Miscellaneous remarks on proc. of New York against Vermont, *etc.*, May - Oct., 1777. — **Hall, H.** New York land grants in Vermont, 1765-76. — **Documents** in relation to the part taken by Vermont in resisting the invasion of Burgoyne, 1777. — **Celebration** in 1778 of the Bennington victory of 1777. — **Smith, N.** Speech, 1778. — **Jacob, S.** A poetical essay, 1778. — **Petitions** to the King, 1766. — **Slafter,** *Rev.* E. F. The Vermont coinage. — **Allen, I.** Natural and political history of Vermont. — **General index.** 2. **List** of pamphlets, publications, *etc.* — **Officers**, 1870-72. — **Additions** and corrections to vols. 1 and 2. — **Haldimand papers**, with contemporaneous history. — **Opinions** of the Haldimand negotiation. — **Completeness** of the Haldimand papers on the negotiation. — **Vermont** as a sovereign and independent state, 1783-91. — N.Y. *Council.* Early eastern boundary of N. Y. a twenty mile line from the Hudson.

Note. For address before the Society *see* **Butler, J. D.**

Vermont Medical Society. Constitution, by-laws, and proceedings. Montpelier, 1852. 8°. (B 1564)

Vermont Prot. Episc. Church. *See* **Prot. Episc. Church in U. S. Diocese of Vermont** (p. 2430).

Vermont register and almanac, 1805-06, 08-09, 11-15, 20-58, 60-63, 66-67, 71-73. Middlebury, Burlington, Montpelier, 1805-73. 58 v. in 26. 24°.

Note. There are two eds. of 1812, one having the title 'Swift's Vt. register', *etc.*; 1820-73 is called 'Walton's register and farmers' almanac'.

Vermont repository; or, Rural magazine. Vol. 1, 2, Rutland, 1795-96. 2 v. 8°.

Vermont Union of Boston and Vicinity, The. Constitution and members. Boston, 1860. 16°. (C 277)

Vermudez de Pedraza, Francisco. *See* **Bermudez de Pedraza, F.**

Vernaccia, Lodovico della. Sonnet. (*In* **Rossetti, D. G.** Early Italian poets. 1861.)

Vernazza, Batista. Ronco, G. (*In* **Grillo, L.** Elogi di Lig., v. 2. 1846.)

Vernazza, Ettore. Banchero, G. B. Elogio de V. (*In* **Grillo, L.** Elogi, v. 1. 1846.)

Vernazza, Giuseppe, *barone di Freney.* Prima parlata nell' Accademia. — Observations sur un manuscrit du Romuleon. (*In* **Turin. Ac. d. Sci.** Mem., v. 19. 1811.) — Recensio nummorum qui Secusii anno 1812 sunt reperti. — Notizia di lettere inedite del conte Castiglione. — Vita di Giambatista di Savoja. — Inscriptio Caietana. — Lapida romana spiegata. (*In* v. 21.) — Diploma di Adriano. — Diplomata imperatorum et fragmenta diplomatum quæcumque sunt edita in diem xv Martii anni 1817. — Classiariæ inscriptiones selectæ. — Anulus illustratus postridie calendas Junii 1816. — Della città d'Industria. — Lapida Romana in Cagliari inedita. (*In* v. 23.) — Notizia d'un pittore a servizio della corte di Savoja. (*In* v. 29.) Considerazioni sopra la salvaguardia di Talliores. (*In* v. 34.) — Boucheroni, C. De J. Vernazza. (*In* v. 26. 1821.)

Verne, Jules. Le désert de glace; aventures du capitaine Hatteras. Paris, [186-]. 12°.

Vernet, Antoine Charles Horace, *called* Carl. Tableaux historiques des campagnes d'Italie, d'après les dessins de C. Vernet. Paris, 1806. f°.

Vernet, Claude Joseph. Œuvre de V., [avec] une description. (*In* **Toulongeon, F. E.** Man. du Mus. fr., v. 7. 1805.)

— Delaborde, H. (*In* **Revue d. D. Mondes,** av. 1852.)

— H., M. C. (*In* **Fine arts** q. rev., v. 2. 1864.)

Vernet, Jacob. De la verité de la religion chrétienne tiré en partie du latin de J. A. Turrettin. Paris, 1753. 2 v. 12°.

Vernet, Jean Emile Horace. **Delaborde, H.** (*In* **Revue d. D. Mondes,** mars 1868.)

— H., M. C. Vernet, his life and works. (*In* **Fine arts** quart. rev., v. 2. 1864.)

— La Forge, A. (*In his* Peinture contemp. en France. 1856.)

— Lagrange, L. (*In* **Gazette des beaux-arts,** v. 15. 1863.)

— Sainte-Beuve, C. A. (*In his* Nouveaux lundis, v. 5. 1866.)

Vernevill, John. Catalogue of our Eng. writers on the Old and New Testament. 2d impress. London, 1668. 12°.

Verney, *Lady.* Stone Edge. (*In* **Cornhill** mag., v. 15-16. 1867.)

Verney, *Sir* Ralph. Notes of proceedings in the Long Parliament, temp. Charles I.; ed. by J. Bruce. Lond.,1845. 4°. (Camden Soc., v. 31.)

Verney family. Letters and papers to 1639; ed. by J. Bruce. London, 1853. 4°. (Camden Soc., v. 56.)

Vernier, Théodore, *comte de Mont-Orient.* Caractère des passions au physique et au moral. Paris, 1807. 2 v. 8°.

Vernon, Edward, *Vice-Admiral*, d. 1757. Opinion upon the present state of the British navy. London, 1744. 8°. (B 1707)

— Original papers rel. to the exped. to Carthagena. London, 1744. 8°.

— Original papers rel. to the exped. to Cuba. London 1744. 8°. (B 1707)

— Original papers rel. to the exped. to Panama. London 1744. 8°. (B 1707)

— CATHCART, J. Letter to V. conc. some misrepresentations in 'Original papers rel. to the exped. to Cuba' [under Gen. Wentworth]. London, 1744. 8°.
— - *Another copy.* (B 1707)
Vernon, Edward, *D.D.* Sermon before the Royal Coll. of Physicians, Sept. 26, 1753, according to the institution of Dr. Croun. 2d ed. London, 1756. 4°. (B 1348)
Vernon, Edward Johnston. Guide to the Anglo-Saxon tongue. London, 1846. 12°.
Vernon, Edward Venables, *Bp. of York.* Sermon, before the House of Lords, Jan. 30. London, 1794. 4°. (B 1466)
— Sermon, coronation of King George IV., July 19. London, 1821. 4°. (B 1272)
— *Same.* (*In* **Pamphleteer**, 1821; v. 19 of **B 838**)
Vernon, George John Warren, *Lord.* *See* **Warren, G. J.**
Vernon, James. Letters, illustrative of the reign of William III., addressed to the Duke of Shrewsbury; ed. by G. P. R. James. London, 1841. 3 v. 8°.
Vernon, Wm. H. Treatise on the cultivation of the mulberry tree. *See* **La Brousse, —.**
Vernon Harcourt, Wm. George. *See* **Harcourt, W. V. G.**
Vernon, Mount. *See* **Mount Vernon.**
Vernon Gallery. CATLOGUE. (*In* **Turner, J. M. W.** Turner gallery. 1857.)
— GR. BRIT. *House of Lords. Sel. Com. on the Turner and Vernon Pictures.* Report. London, 1861. f°.
Vernulz (*Lat.* **Vernulæus**), Nicolas de. NICERON, J. P. (*In his* Mém., v. 33. 1736.)
Vero amico, Il; commedia. *See* **Goldoni, C.**
Vero omaggio, Il. *See* **Metastasio, P.**
Véron, Louis Désiré. Mémoires d'un bourgeois de Paris. Paris, [1853-55]. 6 v. 8°.
— Nouveaux mémoires d'un bourgeois de Paris; le Second Empire. 2e éd. Paris, 1866. 8°.
— ARÇAY, J. d'. La salle à manger du docteur Véron. Paris, 1868. 18°.
Véron, Pierre. Boutique à treize. Paris, [186-]. 12°.
— Les mairies. (*In* **Paris guide**, v. 2. 1867.)
Veron de Forbonnais, François. *See* **Forbonnais, F. V.**
Verona, Agostino. La torre della brava figlia. — Il salto del camoscio. — Dante Pellegrino. — L'Orto d'Alessio. — Il frate dell' eremo. — I cacciatori dei Monti di S. Pellegrino. — La zampa del lupo manaro. (*In* **Brofferio, A.** Tradiz. ital., v. 4. 1850.)
— Vita di G. Pacchiarotti. (*In* **Amato, G. d'.** Panteon, v. 2. 1851.)

Verona. *Antiquities.*

— PANVINI, O. Antiquitates Veronenses. [Patavii,] 1648. f°.
— MAFFEI, F. S. De gli anfiteatri e singolarménte del Veronese. Verona, 1728. 2 v. 12°.
— - Descrizione dell' anfiteatro di Verona tratta dalla 'Verona illustrata'. [1732.] Verona, 1841. 8°.
— - Museum Veronense; hoc est antiquarum inscriptionum atque anaglyphorum collectio. Veronæ, 1749. f°.

Description and History.

— VERONÆ rythmica descriptio, circiter 790. (*In* **Muratori, L. A.** Rer. Ital. scr., v. 2, pt. 2. 1726.)
— SARAINA, T. De civitatis Veronæ origine, [-1517]. (*In* **Grævius.** Thes. antiq. Ital., v. 9, pt. 7. 1723.) — Historiarum et gestorum Veronensium libri III, [966-1400]. (*In* v. 9, pt. 8. 1723.)
— PARISIUS *de Cereta.* Cronicon Veronense, 1117-1375. (*In* **Muratori, L. A.** Rer. Ital. scr., v. 8. 1726.)
— FERRARIO, G. Governo di V., 1277-1388. (*In his* Costume ant. e mod., v. 9. 1829.)
— CHIOCCO, A. De Collegii Veronensis illustribus medicis et philosophis, [1623]. (*In* **Grævius.** Thes. antiq. Ital., v. 9, pt. 8. 1823.)
— MAFFEI, F. S. Verona illustrata. [1732.] Milano, 1825-26. 5 v. 8°.
— BLAZE DE BURY, A. H. Verone et le maréchal Radetzky. (*In* **Revue** d. D. Mondes, nov. 1850.)

Verona, Congress of, 1822. GOERRES, J. von. Die heilige Allianz und die Völker auf dem Congresse von Verona, 1822. (*In his* Gesam. Schriften, v. 5. 1859.)
— CARNÉ, L. M., *comte* de. Le Congrès de Véronne. (*In* **Revue** d. D. Mondes, mai 1838.)
— CHATEAUBRIAND, F. A. R., *vicomte* de. Congrès de Vérone. [1838.] (*In his* Œuvres, v. 12. 1860; — *and in* **Revue** d. D. Mondes, av. 1838.)
— - *Eng.* Congress of Verona; comprising a portion of Memoirs of his own times. London, 1838. 2 v. 8°.
— SCHAUMANN, A. F. H. Geschichte des Congresses von Verona. (*In* **Historisches** Taschenbuch, 1855.)
Verona. San Bernardino. GIULIARI, B., *conte.* Cappella della fam. Pellegrini nella chiesa di S. Bernardino; architettura di M. Sanmicheli. Verona, 1816. f°.
Veronese, Paolo Cagliari, *called* Paolo. Œuvre de V., avec une description. (*In* **Toulongeon, F. E.** Man. du Mus. Fr., v. 9. 1806.)
— BASCHET, A. De l'hommage d'un tableau de P. Veronèse que fit à Louis XIV. la république de Venise, 1664. (*In* **Gazette des beaux-arts**, v. 24. 1868.)
Veronese Mantovani, Angela. La rimembranza dell guiramento. — In morte di Marietta Bizzano Tarma. — I due contadinelli. — Le due gobbe. (*In* **Poeti** ital. contem. 1843.)
Veronica, *St.* MAURY, L. F. A. La Véronique. (*In his* Croyances. 1863.)
Veronica *de Binasco, St.* ISIDORUS *de Isolanis.* (*In* **Acta** sanct., v. 2. 1863.)
Verplanck, Gulian Crommelin, *LL.D.* Address, Columbia College, Aug. 2. N. Y., 1830. 8°. (B 936)
— Address, opening of the 10th exhib. of the Amer. Acad. of Fine Arts. 2d ed. N. Y., 1825. 8°.
— Anniversary discourse before the N. York Hist. Soc. N. Y., 1818. 8°. (B 446, 567)
— *Same.* (*In* **New York Hist. Soc.** Col., v. 3. 1821.)
— Essay on the doctrine of contracts. N. Y., [1825]. 8°.
— Finances and policy of N. York; speech. *n.t.p.* 8°. (B 1167)
— Garrick; his portrait in New York. N. Y., 1857. 8°.
— Importance of scientific knowledge to the manufacturer and practical mechanic. (*In* **Discourses** on the objects and uses of sci. and lit. 1840. Harper's fam. lib., v. 179.)
— Influence of moral causes upon opinion, science, and literature; discourse, Amherst College, Aug. 27. N. Y., 1834. 12°. (C 171)
— *Same.* (*In* **Discourses** on the objects and uses of science and literature. 1840. Harper's fam. lib., v. 179.)
— Letter to W. Drayton, in assertion of the constitutional power of Cong. to impose protecting duties. N. Y., 1831. 8°. (B 1020, 1062)
— Oration, July 4, before the Washington Benevolent Society of N. Y. N. Y., 1809. 8°. (B 421)
— Right moral influence, *etc.*, of liberal studies; discourse at Commencement of Geneva College, Aug. 7. N. Y., 1833. 8°. (B 1577)
— Speech, bills for the amendment of the law and the reform of the judiciary system. Albany, 1839. 8°. (B 1143, 1431, 1764)
Verrazzano, Giovanni da. Lettera sulla scoperta di nuove terre; con altra lettera di F. Carli. (*In* **Archivio** stor. ital., App., v. 9. 1853.)
— Relatione della terra per lui scoperta. (*In* **Ramusio, G. B.** Raccolta, v. 3. 1565.)
— *Eng.* Relation of the lande by him discovered. (*In* **Hakluyt, R.** Divers voyages. 1850; — *and in* **N. Y. Hist. Soc.** Col., v. 1. 1811.)
— Voyage along the coast of N. Amer., 1524; tr. by J. G. Cogswell. (*In* **N. Y. Hist. Soc.** Col., ser. 2, v. 1. 1811.)
— Voyage to the coast of Florida, 1524. (*In* **Hakluyt, R.** Col. of voy., v. 3. 1810.)
— GREENE, G. W. (*In his* Historical studies. 1850.)
— SMITH, B. An inquiry into the authenticity of documents conc. a discovery in N. Amer. claimed to have been made by Verrazzano. N. Y., 1864. 8°.

Verre d'eau, Le; comédie. *See* **Scribe, A. E.**

Verren, Antoine. CONSPIRACY and libel against A. Verren. 1841. *See* **Barthélemy, P.,** *and* **De Bullion, L.** (B 1435)

Verri, Alessandro. Opere scelte. Milano, *Soc. Tip. de Class. Ital.,* 1822. 2 v. 8°.
Contents. Vol. 1. Vita di Verri, da G. A. M. — Le avventure de Saffo. — La vita di Erostrato. 2. Le notti romane.

— Roman nights at the tomb of the Scipios; tr. Edin., London, 1825. 2 v. 12°.

Verri, Pietro, *conte.* Meditazioni sulla economia politica; con annot. di G. R. Carli. (*In* **Economisti** class. ital., pte. mod., v. 15. 1804.) — Sulle leggi vincolanti. — Sul disordine e su la riforma delle monete dello Stato di Milano. — Del progetto di una tariffa della mercanzia. (*In* v. 16. 1804.) — Mem. storiche sulla economia pubblica. — Osserv. sulla tortura. — Lettera del conte B. Gorani intorno alle Osserv. precedenti. — Varii opuscoli di econ. pub. (*In* v. 17. 1804.)

Verrill, Addison Emory. Revision of the polypi of the eastern coast of the U. S. (*In* **Boston Soc. of Nat. Hist.** Mem., v. 1. 1866-69.)

— Zoological affinities of the tabulate corals. (*In* **Amer. Assoc.** Proc., v. 16. 1868.) — Observations on phyllopod crustacea of the family branchipidæ, with description of some new genera and species, from America. (*In* v. 18. 1869.)

Verrou de la reine, Le; comédie; par **A. Dumas.** (*In his* Théatre, v. 13. 1865.)

Verrue, *Madame* de. MUSSET, P. de. (*In his* Femmes de la Régence. 1858.)

Versailles. ZINKEISEN, J. W. Versailles, [1057–1836]. (*In* **Historisches** Taschenbuch, 1837.)

— MONICART, J. B. de. Versailles immortalisé. Paris, 1720. 2 v. 4°. (All that was published.)

— ALMANACH de V, 1782. Versailles, *n.d.* 12°.

— JACOB, J. P. Le cicerone de Versailles, ou L'indicateur des curiosités de cette ville. Versailles, 1808. 24°.

— RITCHIE, L. Versailles. London, 1839. 8°. (Heath's picturesque annual.)

— VOYAGE de Paris à Versailles. Paris, [184-]. 16°. (D 70)

— NOUVEAU guide aux Musée et Chateau de Versailles. Versailles, 1843. 18°. (D 70)

Versailles, Treaty of commerce at. DUPONT DE NEMOURS, P. S. Lettre rel. au traité de commerce avec l'Angleterre. Rouen, 1788. 8°.

Verschwiegene wider Willen, Der, oder Die Fahrt von Berlin nach Potsdam; von **A. v. Kotzebue.** (*In his* Theater, v. 33. 1841.)

Verschwörung, Die, des Fiesko zu Genua; von **F. von Schiller.** (*In his* Sämmtl. Werke, v. 3. 1819; v. 2. 1865.)

Versi e canti popolari di un Fiorentino. Firenze, 1859. 12°.

Versification. EVERETT, E. A system of English versification. N. Y., Phila., 1848. 12°.

Versoehnung, Die; von **A. v. Kotzebue.** (*In his* Theater, v. 7. 1840.)

Versteeg, Wilhelmus Hubartus. Specimen literarium inaug. quo oratio Phillipica quarta Demostheni abjudicatur. Groningæ, [1818]. 8°.

Verstegan *or* **Verstegen,** Richard. Restitution of decayed intelligence conc. the English nation. London, 1634. 4°.

Vert, Claude de. NICERON, J. P. (*In his* Mém., v. 11. 1730; *and, Germ.,* v. 9. 1754.)

Vertebrates. BENNETT, E. T. The tower menagerie; natural hist. of the animals in that establishment. London, 1829. 8°.

— SWAINSON, W. Animals in menageries. London, 1838. 16°. (Lardner. Cab. cyc., v. 108.)

— OWEN, R. Odontography; comparative anatomy of the teeth of vertebrate animals. London, 1840-45. 2 v. 4°.

— LONGET, F. A. Anatomie et phys. du système nerveux des animaux vertébrés. Paris, 1842. 2 v. 8°.

— MACLISE, J. Comparative osteology; morphological studies to demonstrate the archetype skeleton of vertebrated animals. London, 1847. f°.

— BLASIUS, J. H. Fauna der Wirbelthiere Deutschlands. B. 1: Säugethiere. Braunschweig, 1857. 8°.

— OWEN, R. Anatomy of the vertebrates. London, 1866-68. 3 v. 8°.

Verteuil, L. A. A. de. Trinidad; its geography, *etc.* London, 1858. 8°.

Verthema, Ludovico de. *See* **Varthema, L. de.**

Vertoogh van Nieu Nederland. *See* **Donck, A. v. d.**

Vertot d'Aubeuf, René Aubert, *l'abbé* de. Dissertation sur l'origine des loix saliques. (*In* **Mayer,** C. J. Etats-Gén., v. 2. 1778.)

— Histoire de l'ordre des Chevaliers de Malte. Paris, 1819. 7 v. 8°.

— *Eng.* History of the Knights of Malta. London, 1728. 2 v. f°.

— Histoire des révolutions arrivées dans le gouvernment de la République Romaine. Paris, 1719. 3 v. 12°.

— *Eng.* History of the revolutions in the government of the Roman Republic; [tr.] by J. Ozell. 5th ed., pref., Memorial by Earl Stanhope to the Abbé Vertot rel. to the Roman Senate, with answer. London, 1740. 2 v. 8°.

— *Same.* 6th ed. London, 1770. 2 v. 8°.

— Histoire des révolutions de Portugal. Ed. stér. de F. Didot. Paris, 1816. 16°.

— *Eng.* The revolutions of P.; [tr.] by G. Roussillon. London, 1721. 8°.

— *Same.* Tr. from the French. Glasgow, 1750. 8°.

— Histoire des révolutions de Suède. Nouv. éd. Amst., 1777. 2 v. 12°.

— *Eng.* History of the revolutions in Sweden; [tr.] by J. Mitchel. 2d ed. Lond., 1696. 8°.

— *Same.* 2d ed. London, 1696. 8°.

— History of the revolutions in Spain; [tr.] with notes by J. Morgan. London, 1724. 5 v. 8°.

— Various articles.] (*In* **Sérieys, A.** Bibl. acad., v. 6. 1811.)

— RIVAL, P. Part of Vertot's 'Dissertation on the Salick laws' examined. Lond., 1722. 16°.

Vertova. ROSA, G. Degli statuti di Vertova e d'altri comuni rurale. (*In* **Archivio** stor. ital., n.s., v. 12, pt. 2. 1860.)

Vertrauten, Die; von **A. G. A. Mueller.** (*In his* Spiele für die Bühne, v. 1. 1818.)

Vertue, George. Anecdotes of painting in England. — Catalogue of engravers in England; [with] life of V. *See* **Walpole, H.**

Verulam, Francis, *Baron of.* *See* **Bacon, F.**

Verus, *pseud.* Letters to the Native American. Phila., 1797. 8°. (B 465, 2525)

Verus, *pseud.* Observations on the existing differences between Spain and the U. S. No. 3. Phila., 1817. 8°. (B 445)

Verus, *pseud.* West Florida. *n.t.p.* [1811.] 8°. (B 440)

Verus, Catholicus, *pseud.* Letter to the Roman Catholic clergy of Ireland, on the primary doctrine of religion and the purity of the early Irish church. London, 1824. 8°.

Verus, Catholicus, *pseud.* The Church forms a part of the Commonwealth. Bristol, 1828. 8°. (B 1229)

Verus, Lucius, *pseud.* Letter to Hon. F. Jeffrey. Glasgow, 1831. 8°. (B 933)

Verville, Beroalde de. *See* **Béroalde de Verville, F.**

Vervins, Treaty at. BELLIÈVRE, P. de, *and* SILLERY, F. B. de. Mémoires; cont. un journal conc. la négotiation de la paix traitée à Vervins, 1598. 2e pte. La Haye, 1696. 12°.

Verwandtschaften, Die; von **A. v. Kotzebue.** (*In his* Theater, v. 7. 1840.)

Very, Jones. Essays and poems. Bost., 1839. 16°.
Contents. Epic poetry. — Shakspeare. — Hamlet. — Poems.

— The Very family. (*In* **Essex Inst.** Hist. col., v. 1, 2. 1859, 60.)
Very family. VERY, J. *See previous entry.*
— VINTON, J. A. Genealogical sketches of the V. family. (*In his* Giles memorial. 1864.)
Very hard cash; by C. Reade. N. Y., 1864. 8°.
Note. From **All** the year round, v. 9–10. 1863.
Very pleasant evening, A; farce. *See* **Suter,** W. E.
Very short and candid appeal to free born Britons; by an American. London, 1774. 8°. (B 386)
Very woman, A; by S. M. Smedley. (*In* **Littell's** living age, v. 23. 1849.)
Very woman, A. *See* **Massinger,** P.
Veryard, Ellis. Account of divers remarks taken in a journey through the Low-Countries, France, Italy, *etc.*; as also a voyage to the Levant. Exon., 1701. f°.
Verzameling van de constitutien der Vereenigde onafhanglijke Staaten van Amerika, benevens de acte van onafhanglijkheid, *enz.* 1e stuk. Dordrecht, 1781. 8°.
Verzameling van stukken tot de dertien Vereenigde Staaten van Noord-America betrekkelijk. Leyden, 1781. 8°.
Contents. Voorrede over de al of niet gelijkheid der Vereenigde Staaten van Noord-America en die van deze gewesten. — **Trumbull,** J. Brief aen J. D. van der Capellen, den 31 Aug. 1779. — **Artikelen** van regeering gemaakt in 1638. — Eenige **getuigschriften** van de mishandelingen der Engelschen. — **Vraagpunten** tot den staat van Connecticut betrekkelijk, den 3 Julii 1773, met de antwoorden. — **United States.** Artikulen van confoederatie. — **Mass.** *Convention,* 1779–80. Aanspraak der vergadering gelast tot het vervaardigen eener nieuwe regeeringsvorm voor den staat van Massachusetts-Bay aan haare principales; — Constitutie. — **Hancock,** J. Redevoering bij 't aanvaarden van zijn ambt, als gouverneur van den staat van Massachusetts, 31 Oct. 1780. — **Cooper,** S. Leerede 26 Oct. 1780 zijnde de eerste dag van't begin der constitutie, en inwyjing van't nieuw staats bestuur.
Vésale (*or* **Wittings**), André. NICERON, J. P. (*In his* Mém., v. 5. 1728; *and, Germ.*, v. 5. 1751.)
Vesalius, Andreas. MORLEY, H. (*In his* Clement Marot and other studies, v. 2. 1871.)
Vesey, Wm. Sermon, New York, May 12, funeral of J. Ld. Lovelace, Gov. of N. Y. N. Y., 1709. 4°. (B 258)
Vésinier, Pierre. La vie du nouveau César. 1e pte. Genève, 1865. 12°.
Vesme, Carlo Baudi. *See* **Baudi di Vesme,** C.
Vespa. Judicium coci et pistoris judice Vulcano. (*In* **Lemaire.** Poetæ Lat. min., v. 1. 1824. Bibl. class Lat.)
Vespasiano da Bisticci. *See* **Bisticci,** Vespasiano da.
Vespéral romain. *See* **Catholic Church** (p. 496).
Vespers of Palermo; tragedy. *See* **Hemans,** *Mrs.* F. D.
Vespro, Il. *See* **Parin,** G.
Vespucci, Amerigo. Viaggi; con la vita e la diss. giustificativa del padre S. Canovai. Firenze, 1817. 8°.
— Lettere due di due sue navig. — Sommario di due sue navig. (*In* **Ramusio,** G. B. Rac. delle nav., v. 1. 1563.)
— *Eng.* Voyages to the new world. (*In* **Kerr,** R. Col., of voy., v. 3. 1824.)
— *Germ., extract of 3d, 4th voy.* (*In* **Allgemeine** Hist., v. 18. 1764.)
— *Lat.* Navigationes quatuor. (*In* **Grynæus,** S. Novus orbis, *etc.*, 1555; — *and in* **Novus** orbis. 1616; — *and in Lat. and Span. in* **Navarrete,** M. F. de. Coleccion de los viages, v. 3. 1829.)
— BANDINI, A. M. Vita e lettere di V. Firenze, 1745. 4°.
— BARTOLOZZI, F. Ricerche circa alle scoperte d'Amerigo Vespucci. Firenze, 1789. 8°.
— CALLANDER, J. (*In his* Terra Australis, v. 1. 1766.)
— CANOVAI, S. Elogio d'Amerigo Vespucci; con una dissert. giustificativa. Firenze, 1788. 4°.
— FIGUIER, L. (*In his* Vies des savants illustres du Moyen Age. 1867.)
— GALEANI NAPIONE DI COCCONATO, G. T., *conte.* Del primo viaggio di Vespucci al nuovo mondo. (*In* **Turin.** Ac. d. Sci. Mem., v. 19. 1811.) — Appendice all' esame critico del primo viaggio di A. V. al nuovo mondo. (*In* v. 24. 1820.)
— LIFE of V. (*In* **American** Nepos. 1805.)
— SANTAREM, M. F. de B. y S., *visconde* de. Researches resp. V. and his voyages; tr. by E. V. Childe. Boston, 1850. 12°.
— VARNHAGEN, F. A. de. A. V., ses écrits, sa vie, et ses navigations. Lima, 1865. f°.
See also **America.** *Discovery.*
Vesta. LIPSIUS, J. De Vesta et vestalibus syntagma. (*In his* Opera, v. 3. 1675.)
Vestiarium Christianum. *See* **Marriott,** W. B.
Vestiges of the natural history of creation. London, 1844. 12°.
— Explanations; a sequel to 'Vestiges of the natural history of creation'. London, 1845. 12°.
— BOSANQUET, S. R. 'Vestiges of the natural history of creation' examined and exposed London, 1845. 12°.
Vestigia veritatis; or, the controversy rel. to the act of the thirty fifth of Elizabeth. London, 1681. f°. (A 54)
Vestriad, The; a poem. *See* **Busk,** H.
Vestris, *Mme.* *See* **Mathews,** E. B. V.
Vesuvius. LEONE, A. De montibus Vesuvio et Abella. (*In* **Grævius,** J. G. Thes. antiq. Ital., v. 9, pt. 4. 1723.)
— VALENTIN, L. Voyage médical en Italie fait en l'année **1820**; préc. d'une excursion au volcan du Mont Vésuve, *etc.* Nancy, 1822. 8°.
— AULDJO, J. Sketches of Vesuvius with accounts of its principal eruptions. London, **1833.** 8°.
— SCHMIDT, J. F. J. Die Eruption des Vesuv im Mai **1855.** Wien, Olmüz, 1856. 8°.
— BEULÉ, E. Le drame du Vésuve. (*In* **Revue** d. D. Mondes, mai, juin **1870.**)
Vetch, John. Diseases of the eye. Lond., 1820. 8°.
— Ophthalmia in England after the return of the army from Egypt. London, 1807. 8°.
Veteran, The; by J. L. Wallack. (*In* **Sargent,** E. Mod. stand. dr., v. 28.)
Veterinary art. *Bibliography.* ENGELMANN, W. Bibliotheca veterinaria. 2e Aufl. Lpz., 1843. 8°.
— SWAINE, J. Every farmer his own cattle doctor. [**1776.**] 3d ed. London, 1786. 8°.
— WHITE, J. Treatise of veterinary medicine, containing a compendium of the veterinary art. [**1804.**] 8th ed. (Vol. 2, 3d ed.) London, 1807, 06. 2 v. 12°.
— BOARDMAN, T. Dictionary of the veterinary art. London, **1805.** 4°.
— RUSH, B. Introductory lecture on studying the diseases of animals, Nov. 2. *n.t.p.* [1807.] 8°. (B 1561)
— GODINE, *jeune.* Elémens d'hygiène vétérinaire. Paris, **1815.** 8°.
— GROGNIER, L. F. Compte-rendu des travaux de la Société Royale d'Agriculture, de Lyon, mars 1820, 21. Lyon, **1821.** 8°.
— PERCIVALL, W. Series of elementary lectures on the veterinary art. London, **1823.** 8°.
— LEBEAUD, —. Nouveau manuel complet du vétérinaire. [**1826.**] Nouv. éd. Paris, 1859. 18°. (Manuels-Roret.)
— SPOONER, W. C. (*In* **Smedley, E.,** *and others.* Encyc. metrop., v. 7. **1845.**)
— DADD, G. H. List of horse and cattle medicines; [with] remarks on the diseases of horses. Boston, 1848. 12°. (C 268)
— MAGNE, J. F. Rapport sur les progrès de la médecine vétérinaire depuis vingt-cinq ans. Paris, **1867.** 8°.
— FLEMING, G. Animal plagues; their history, nature, and prevention. London, **1871.** 8°.
See also **Cattle.** *Diseases*; — **Horse.**
Vethake, Henry. Principles of political economy. Phila., 1838. 8°.

— Encyclopædia Americana: Supplemental vol. 14. *See* **Lieber, F.**

Veto. OBSERVATIONS on the presidential veto; with a plan for a change of the constitution. Boston, 1842. 8°. (B 1499)

Vetromile, Eugene. The Abnaki Indians; with a memoir of E. Vetromile, by E. Ballard. (*In* **Maine Hist. Soc.** Col., v. 6. 1859.)

— Ahiamihewintuhangan; the prayer song; [in the Penobscot lang.]. N. Y., 1858. 8°.

— Indian good book, made for the Abnaki Indians. 3d ed. N. Y., 1858. 18°.

— Sande awikhigan, 1867; [Sunday almanac for the Abnaki Indians.] *n.p.*, [1866]. Broadside.

— Wewessi Ubibian; [Bible history in Penobscot and Micmac with Eng. trans.]. Manhattan, 1860. 12°.

Vetter aus Bremen, Der; ein Lustspiel von R. T. **Körner.** (*In his* Dramat. Beyträge, v. 2. 1821; — *and* Sämmt. Werke. 1861.)

Vettori, Francesco. Discorso alla riforma dello Stato di Firenze, 1531-32. (*In* **Archiv.** stor. ital., v. 1. 1842.) — Sommario della storia d'Italia, 1511-27; con notizia della vita di F. e di P. Vettori. (*In* App., v. 6. 1848.)

Vettori, Pietro. Trattato delle lodi e della coltivazione degli ulivi. Milano, *Soc. Tipog. Class. Ital.*, 1806. 8°.

— Lettere. (*In* **Dati, C.** Prose florentine, pt. 4, v. 1, 4. 1751.)

Vettori *di Firenze*, Famiglia di'. (*In* **Litta, P.** Fam., v. 15.)

Vetus, Joannes. NICERON, J. P. (*In his* Mém., v. 34. 1736.)

Vetusta monumenta. *See* **Society of Antiquaries of London.**

Veuillot, Louis François. Le lendemain de la victoire; scènes socialistes. (*In* **Revue** d. D. Mondes, juil. août 1849.) — Une Samaritaine; dialogue. (*In* nov. 1850.) — MAZADE, C. de. (*In* juil. 1863.)

Veuve, La; comédie. *See* **Corneille, P.**

Veuve malabar, La; tragédie. *See* **Lemierre, A. M.**

Vexillarii. ERNESTI, J. A. De vexillariis. (*In* **Goettingen.** Ges. d. Wiss. Comm., v. 1. 1751.)

Veyrat, J. P. Un enfant d'adoption. (*In* **Echo** des feuilletons, 2e année. 1842.)

Veytia, Mariano Fernandez d'Echeverria y. *See* **Echeverria y Veytia, M. F. de.**

Via veritatis unicæ. *See* **Musæum** hermeticum.

Viaggio sull' asino di Cassandro sposo, Il; commedia. *See* **Giraud, G.**

Vial, The, poured upon the sea. *See* **Mather, C.** 1726.

Vial-Duclairbois, Honoré Sébastien. Marine. (Vol. 123-125 *of* **Encycl.** 1783-93.)

Viale, Salvatore. Dell' uso della lingua patria in Corsica. (*In* **Archivio** stor. ital., n.s., v. 6, pt. 2. 1857.) — Delle mutazioni dei rigglmenti politici in Corsica. (*In* v. 14, pt. 1.) — TOMMASEO, N. Salvatore Viale e la Corsica. (*In* v. 15, pt. 2. 1862.)

Vialla, —. Voyage en Monténégro. (*In* **Montémont, A.** Biblioth. univ., v. 46. 1836.)

Viallet, Guillaume. Recherches sur la construction des digues. [1800.] *See* **Bossuet, C.**

Vialon, Prosper. Amour et chasse; nouvelles. Paris, 1863. 16°.

Contents. Grand-papa qui dort. — Le curé de Mondetour. — Vendredi 13.

Viana, Carlos, *el principe* de. QUINTANA, M. J. (*In his* Vidas. 1845; — *and* Obras. 1852; v. 19 of Aribau. Bibl.)

Viani, *padre.* Legation of C. A. Mezzabarba, from the Pope to the Emperor Kang Hi, 1720.' (*In* **Green, J.** Col. of voy., v. 3. 1746.)

Vianney, Jean Baptiste Marie. GAUTIER, E. T. L. Le curé d'Ars. (*In his* Etudes. 1866.)

— MOLYNEUX, G. The curé d'Ars; a memoir of V. 2d ed. London, 1869. 8°.

Viardot, Louis. Lazarille de Tormès. (*In* **Echo** des feuilletons, 2e année. 1842.)

— Les merveilles de la peinture. 1e sér.: Vignettes sur bois par Paquier. Paris, 1868. 16°. (Bibl. des merv.)

— Les musées d'Allemagne et de Russie. Paris, 1844. 12°.

— Les musées d'Italie; guide et memento de l'artiste et du voyageur. Paris, 1842. 12°.

— Pan Twardowski. (*In* **Semaine** lit., v. 2.)

— Scènes de la vie des animaux. 1842-44. *See* **Hetzel, P. J.**

— Topaze peintre de portraits. (*In* **Hetzel, P. J.** Scènes de la vie privée des animaux, v. 2. 1844.)

— Wonders of Italian art. London, 1870. 8°.

Viardot, *Mme.* Michelle Pauline Garcia. CLAYTON, E. C. (*In her* Queens of song. 1865.)

— MUSSET, L. C. A. de. Concert de M'lle G. — Débuts de M'lle G. (*In his* Œuvres complètes, v. 9. 1866.)

Viart, A. Le cuisinier royal; aug. par Fouret et Délan. 17e éd. Paris, 1840. 8°.

Viator, *pseud.* *See* **Varnum,** Joseph B., *Jr.*

Viator; or, A peep into my note book; by [D. Hoffman]. Boston, 1841. 12°.

Viau, Théophile de. Poésie. (*In* **Annales** poet., v. 17. 1780.)

— CHASLES, P. (*In* **Revue** d. D. Mondes, août 1839.)

— GAUTIER, T. (*In his* Les grotesques. 1856.)

— NICERON, J. P. (*In his* Mém., v. 36. 1736.)

Viaud, Pierre. DUBOIS-FONTANELLE, J. G. Le naufrage et les aventures de V. (*In* **Biblioth.** univ. des romans, Nouv., v. 17. 1779.)

— - *Eng.* Surprising voyages of P. V.; tr. by Mrs. Griffith. Phila., 1774. 12°.

— - - Shipwreck and adventures of P. V.; tr. by Mrs. Griffith. 1st Amer. ed. Dover, 1799. 18°.

Vibert, Victor. TRIANON, H. V. Vibert; la gravure 'Du bien et du mal' d'après le tableau de V. Orsel. (*In* **Gazette** des beaux-arts, v. 6. 1860.)

Vibration. MAGRINI, L. Continuous vibratory movement of all matter, ponderable and imponderable; tr. from the Revue des cours sci., no. 49. (*In* **Smithsonian Inst.** Reports, 1868.)

— PEIRCE, B. Communication of vibrations. (*In* **Amer. Assoc.** Proc., v. 16. 1868.)

Vicar of Bullhampton; a novel by A. Trollope. N. Y., 1870. 8°.

— *Same.* Lpz., *Tauchnitz*, 1870. 2 v. 16°.

Vicar of Wakefield; a tale supposed to be written by himself; [by O. Goldsmith]. London, 1777. 2 v. 12°.

— *Same.* N. Y., 1841. 32°.

— *Same.* (*In his* Miscel. works, v. 1. 1801.)

Vicar of Wakefield; by J. S. Coyne. (*In* **Sargent, E.** Mod. stand. dr., v. 11.)

Vicars, *Capt.* Hedley Shafto Johnstone. MARSH, *Miss* C. Memorials of V. N. Y., 1859. 16°.

— - Sketch of his life. Richmond, 1862. 18°.

Vicat, Béat Philippe. Vocabularium juris utriusque. Ed. 2a auct. Neapoli, 1760. 4 v. 8°.

Vice. HARGREAVES, J. G. The blunders of vice and folly. London, 1871. 8°.

Vice radical du projet de constitution présenté par la Commis. des Onze. Paris, an III [1794]. 8°. (C 92)

Vicente, Gil. Auto de San Martinho. (*In* **Pedroso, E. G.** Autos sacramentales. 1865.)

— Escena primera de la comedia de Rubena. — El viudo. — Auto pastoril del nacimiento. (*In* **Ochoa, E.** de. Tesoro del teatro espanõl, v. 1. 1838.)

Vicentino, Pierfilippo Castelli. Vita di G. G. Trissino. (*In* **Trissino, G. G.** L' Italia liberata. 1779.)

Vicenza. LAMPERTICO, F. Degli statuti rurali nel Vicentino. (*In* **Archivio** stor. ital., n.s., v. 12, pt. 2. 1860.)

— PULEX, C. Fragmenta historiæ Vincentinæ. (*In* **Muratori, L. A.** Rer. Ital. scr., v. 13. 1728.)

Viceroy, The. *n.p.*, [18—]. 12°. (C 280)

Vices et défectuosités de l'acte add. aux constitutions de l'empire, 22 avril 1824. Paris, 1815. 8°. (B 799)

Vich, *formerly* **Ausona,** *Spain.* FLOREZ, H. El estado antiquo de la iglesia ausonense. (*In his* España sagrada, v. 28. 1774.)

Vichard di San Real, Giacomo. CARENA, G. Notizie biog. dell' accademico G. V. di S. R. (*In* **Turin.** Ac. d. Sci. Mem., v. 37. 1834.)

Vichy. DAUMAS, C. Mineral waters of Vichy. 4th ed. Vichy, 1867. 18°.

Vicissitudes de l'Eglise Cath. des deux rites en Pologne et en Russie; par un prêtre de la Cong. de l'Oratoire; préc. d'un avant-propos par Montalambert. Paris, 1843. 2 v. 8°.

Vicissitudes of families. *See* **Burke, B.**

Vickris, Richard. Truth and innocency defended; a reply to J. Norris. London, 1693. 4°. (C 284)

Vicksburg, *Miss.* CAVE life in Vicksburg; by a lady, [1862]. N. Y., 1864. 12°.

— U. S. *Quartermaster Gen.* Roll of honor, XXIV. Names of soldiers interred in the national cemetery at Vicksburg. Wash., 1869. 8°. (B 1958)

Vicksburg daily citizen, July 2, 1863. Vicksburg, 1863. Broadside.

Vico, GiamBattista. Opere; ord. ed. illust. da G. Ferrari. 2a ed. Milano, *Soc. Tip. de' Class. Ital.*, 1854, 52–54, 52. 6 v. 8°.

Contents. Vol. 1. La mente. — De Parthenopea conjuratione oct. 1701. 2. De nostri temporis studiorum ratione oratio. — De antiquissima Italorum sapientia. — De rebus gestis Antonii Caraphæi. 3. De universi juris uno principio et fine uno. — De constantia jurisprudentis. 4. Principii di una scienza nuova. — Vici vindiciæ. — Vita di G. B. Vico scritta da se medesimo. 5. Principii di scienza nuova. 6. Scritti scientifici. — Orazioni ed iscrizioni. — Poesie.

— *French.* Œuvres choisies; préc. d'une introd. par Michelet. Paris, 1835. 2 v. 8°

Contents. Vol. 1. Avant-propos. — Discours sur le système et la vie de Vico. — Vie de Vico, par lui-même. — Appendice de la Vie. — Extraits de divers opuscules ou lettres. — De la méthode suivie de notre temps dans les études. — Discours, 1707. — Réponse à un journal d'Italie. — De l'unité du principe et de la fin du droit universal. — Jugement sur Dante. — Discours, 1700; Hostem hosti infensiorem quam stultum sibi esse neminem. — Discours, 1722, de mente heroicâ. — De Partenopea conjuratione, *ec.* — Notæ in acta eruditorum Lipsiensia. — De l'antique sagesse de l'Italie, retrouvée dans les origines de la langue latine. — Science nouvelle, ou principes de la philosophie de l'histoire, livre I. 2. Livre II–V. — Explication de la mythologie.

— Vita; da lui medesimo. *n.p.*, [18—]. 8°.

— *Same, with additions.* (*In* **Autobiografie.** 1857.)

— FABRONI, A. (*In his* Vitæ Ital., v. 12. 1785.)

— FERRARI, J. Vico et son époque. (*In* **Revue** d. D. Mondes, juil. 1838.)

Vicomte de Bragelonne, Le, [ou, Dix ans plus tard]; par A. Dumas [A. Maquet]. Paris, 1853. 18°.

— *Same.* Nouv. éd. Paris, 1860–61. 6 v. 18°.

Vicq-d'Azyr, Félix. Œuvres; recueillies par J. L. Moreau. Paris, 1805. 6 v. 8°.

Contents. Vol. 1. Discours sur la vie et les ouvrages de Vicq-d'Azyr. — Considérations générales sur les éloges historiques. — Discours sur la vie et sur les ouvrages de Buffon, à l'Acad. Franç., Déc. 11, 1788. — Réponse de M. de St. Lambert. — Notices sur la vie et les ouvrages de Buffon et de Daubenton, par l'éditeur. — Eloge de Cusson, — de Duhamel, — de Linné, — de Bergman, — de Bucquet, — de Macquer, — de Camper. 2. Eloge de Poulletier de la Salle, — de Schéele, — de Spielmann, — de Watelet, — de Vergennes. — Notice historique sur les principales académies. — Réflexions sur les sciences. — Discours prononcé devant le prince Henri de Prusse. — Eloge d'Arnaud de Nobleville, — de Barbeu Dubourg, — de Bouillet, — de Fothergill, — de Gaubius, — de Girod, — de Haller, — de Hunter, — de Lamure, — de Lefevre Deshayes, — de Le Roy. 3. Eloge de Lieutaud, — de Lobstein, — de Lorry, — de Macbride, — de Maret, — de Navier, — de Pringle, — de Sanchez, — de Serrao, — de Stoll, — de Taglioni, — de van Doevren, — de Montigny. — Notice sur la vie et les ouvrages de Bonafos et Bernard, et Planchon, — de Harmant, Butet et Vetillart du Ribert, — de A. Dianyère, Desmery, Rose et Darluc; — sur Lehoux et Bourdois de la Mothe. 4. Avertissement de l'éditeur. — Discours sur l'anatomie. 4, 5. Mémoires et fragmens sur l'anatomie, la physiologie, et la médecine. 5. Recherches anatomiques. 6. Recherches anatomiques sur le cerveau. — Essai sur les lieux et les dangers des sépultures; tr. librement de l'italien.

— Système anatomique: Quadrupeds; — Mammifères et oiseaux. (Vol. 154, 155 *of* **Encyclopédie** méthod. 1792–1819.)

— Traité d'anatomie et de physiologie. Tome 1: Du cerveau. Paris, 1786. f°.

— LÉMONTEY, P. E. Eloge hist. de Vicq d'Azyr. (*In* **Paris. Inst.** *Ac. Fr.* Recueil des disc., v. 1. 1843.)

Victim, The; in five letters to Adolphus. Hartford, 1807. 12°. (C 82)

Victimes cloîtrées, Les; drame, par J. M. B. de Monvil. Bordeaux, 1793. 12°. (C 166)

Victimes de l'amour; [par C. J. Dorat]. Paris, 1790. 16°.

Victims; by T. Taylor. (*In* **Sargent, E.** Mod. stand. dr., v. 24.)

Victoires, conquêtes, desastres, *etc.*, des Français. 2e éd. Paris, 1830–31. 34 v. 8°.

— ANNALES des faits et des sciences militaires, faisant suite aux Victoires, *etc.* Paris, 1818-19. 4 v. 8°.

Victor III. [*previously* **Desiderius**], *Pope.* LEO *Marsicanus*, and PETRUS *diaconus*. Vita B. Victoris. (*In* **Acta** sanct., v. 45. 1868.)

Victor *Burgensis, St.* CERASIANUM, A. Victoris historia. — FLOREZ, H. Vida y martirio de S. Victor. (*In* **Florez, H.** España sagrada, v. 27. 1772.)

Victor, Caius Marius. De perversis suæ ætatis moribus; epistola ad Salmonem. (*In* **Lemaire.** Poet. Lat. min., v. 2. 1824. Bibl. class. Lat.)

Victor, Orville James. The life and military and civic services of Lieut.-Gen. Scott. N. Y., 1861. 12°.

Victor, Pierre. Les élections de 1863. Nouv. éd. augm. de la vérification des pouvoirs. Paris, [1864]. 18°.

Victor, Publius. Descriptio Romæ. (*In* **Notitia** utraque cum Orientis, *etc.* 1552; — *in* **Notitia** dignitatum omnium. 1729; —*and in* **Grævius, J. G.** Thes. antiq. Rom., v. 7. 1698.)

— De regionibus Romæ. (*In* **Grævius, J. G.** Thes. antiq. Rom., v. 3. 1696; — *and in* **Tartini, G. M.** Rer. Ital. scr., v. 2. 1770.)

— RUCELLAI, B. In Victorem De regionibus urbis. (*In* **Tartini, G. M.** Rer. Ital. scr., v. 2. 1770.)

Victor, Sextus Aurelius. Historiæ Romanæ breviarium; illustratum A. Schotti, D. Machanei, J. Gruteri, et Annæ Tanaquili Fabri Filiæ commentariis; rec. S. Pitiscus. Traj. a. R., 1696. 8°.

— De origine gentis Romanæ. — De Cæsaribus historiæ abbreviatæ pars altera. (*In* **Historiæ** Rom. scr. min. 1789.)

— De viris illustribus urbis Romæ liber. (*In* **Historiæ** Rom. scr. min. 1798; — *and in* **Eutropius.** Hist. Rom. brev. 1795.)

— De vita et moribus imp. Romanorum; excerpta ex libris S. A. Victoris; illustrata A. Schotti, A. Vineli, J. Gruteri, M. Casauboni, et Annæ Tanaquili Fabri filiæ commentariis; rec. S. Pitiscus. Traj. ad R., 1696. 8°.

Victor Amadeus. REUMONT, A. von. Des Königs Victor Amadeus Sardinien Thron-Entsagung und Ende. (*In* **Historische** Zeitschrift, v. 4. 1860.)

Victor Emmanuel II., *King of Italy.* ARRIVABENE, C. Italy under V. E. London, 1862. 2 v. 8°.

— MUNDY, *Sir* R. (*In his* H. M. S. Hannibal at Palermo and Naples. 1863.)

Victoria I. (*fully* Alexandrina Victoria), *Queen of Gr. Britain.* Early years of the Prince Consort; compiled under the direction of the Queen by C. Grey. London, 1867. 8°.

— *Same.* N. Y., 1867. 8°.

— Leaves from the journal of our life in the Highlands, 1848–61; ed. by A. Helps. London, 1868. 8°.

— ETIENNE, L. La journal d'une reine. (*In* **Revue** d. D. Mondes, juil. 1868.)

— GRENVILLE, R. P. F. N. B. C., *Duke of Buckingham, etc.* Memoirs of the court and cabinets of William IV. and Victoria. London, 1861. 2 v. 8°.

— REMARKS on certain anonymous articles designed to render Queen Victoria unpopular; with an exposure of their authorship. Gloucester, 1864. 8°.

Victoria Mary Louisa, *Duchess of Kent.* MARTINEAU, H. Biographical sketch. (*In her* Biographical sketches. 1869.)

Victoria, Colony of. *Description.*
— THERRY, R. Reminiscences of 30 years' residence in New South Wales and Victoria, [1829-59]. London, 1863. 8°.
— MITCHELL, *Sir* T. L. Three expeditions into eastern Australia, [1831-35]. London, 1838. 2 v. 8°.
— FLETCHER, J. Letter to Earl Grey on emigration; with a hist. of the colony of Port Phillip. Edin., London, 1847. 8°.
— LANG, J. D. Phillipsland; its present condition, *etc.* London, 1847. 12°.
— HOWITT, W. Land, labor, and gold; or, Two years in Victoria, [1852-54]. Boston, 1855. 2 v. 12°.
— SIDNEY, S. Victoria- (*In his* Three colonies of Australia. 1852.)
— WESTGARTH, W. Victoria and the Australian gold mines in 1857. London, 1857. 8°.
— CHAPMAN, H. S. The industrial progress of Victoria. (*In* Statist. Soc. Journ., v. 26. 1863.)
— BOOTH, E. C. Another England; life, living, homes, and homemakers in Victoria. London, 1869. 8°.

History.

— WESTGARTH, W. Colony of Victoria; its history, commerce, and gold mining to the end of 1863. London, 1864. 8°.
— FLANAGAN, R. History of New South Wales, *etc.*, 1770-1860. London, 1862. 2 v. 8°.

Natural history.

— BUSH wanderings of a naturalist; or, Notes on the field sports of Australia Felix. London, 1861. 12°.
See also Australia.

Victoria regia. ALLEN, J. F. Victoria regia or great water-lily of America; with acc. of its discovery and introduction into cultivation; illust. by W. Sharp. Boston, 1854. f°.

Victories of love. *See* Patmore, C.

Victorine; by J. B. Buckstone. (*In* Sargent, E. Mod. stand. dr., v. 27.)

Victorinus *Amiternensis.* MARANGONI, J. Acta S. Victorini atque de martyrum Amiternensium aliisque sacris cœmeteriis. Romæ, 1740. 4°.

Victorinus *Massiliensis.* De nativitate, vita, passione, et resurrectione Domini; carmina. (*In* Mai, A. Class. auct., v. 5. 1833.)

Victorinus *Petavionensis.* Fragment on the creation of the world. — Commentary on the Apocalypse. (*In* Tertullianus, Q. S. F. Writings, v. 3. 1870.)

Victory of the vanquished; by [Mrs. E. R. Charles]. N. Y., 1871. 8°.

Vicuña, Pedro Felix. El porvenir del hombre, o Relacion entre la justa apreciacion del trabajo y la democracia. Valparaiso, 1858. 8°.

Vida, Marco Girolamo, *Bp.* Christiados; Lat. and Eng.; tr. by J. Cranwell. Camb., 1768. 8°.
— De arte poetica; tr. en fr. par C. Batteux. (*In* Batteux, C. Les quatre poetiques. 1771; — *and in* Poemata sel. Ital. 1808.)
— *Eng.* Art of poetry; tr. by C. Pitt. (*In* Chalmers, A. Eng. poets, v. 19. 1810.)
— Game of chess; a poem; tr. from the Scacchia. (*In* Murphy, A. Works, v. 7. 1786.)
— Poemata. Oxford, 1722-23. 2 v. 8°.
Contents. Vol. 1. De arte poetica. — Bucolica. — Epistola. 2. Bombycum lib. II. — Scacchia ludus. — Carmina.
— Poemata. (*In* Poemata sel. Ital. 1808.)
— NICERON, J. P. (*In his* Mém., v. 29. 1734.)

Vida de Don Gregorio Guadaña, La; por A. Enriquez Gomez. (*In his* Siglo pitagorico. 1727; — *and in* Rosell, C. Nov. post. Cervantes, v. 2. 1854.)

Vida, La, es sueño. *See* Calderon de la Barca, P.

Vidal (Françoise Fénélon) *et al. vs.* City of Philadelphia, Executors of S. Girard, *et al.* ARGUMENTS of defendants' counsel, judgment, *etc.* Phila., 1844. 8°.
— BINNEY, H. Argument. Phila., 1844. 8°. (B 1439)
— OUTLINE of the case and heads of argument by counsel of appellants.] *n.t.p.* [1844.] 4°. (B 1434)

Vidal, Léon. Memento sur les peines accessoires, et spécialement sur la surveillance de la police. Paris, 1869. 8°.

Vidal de Figueroa, Lorenzo. EN el pleyto [con] el dean y cabildo de la santa yglesia catedral de Mexico, sobre la ereccion de la yglesia. *n.t.p.* [16—.] f°. (A 68)

Vidaurre, Manuel Lorenzo. Answer. (*In* Columbia. Manifesto of reasons [for] war against Peru. 1828. B 932, 1848.)
— Discurso contra la modificacion que presentaron los encargados del proyecto de constitucion. Lima, 1827. 8°. (B 1848)
— Efectos de las facciones en los gobiernos nacientes. Boston, 1828. 8°.
— Proyecto de un codigo penal. Boston, 1828. 8°.
— Suplemento a las cartas americanas; correspondencia con Bolivar, *etc.* Lima, 1827. 8°.

Videl, Louis. Histoire de la vie du connestable de Lesdiguières [François de Bonne]. Paris, 1638. f°.
— NICERON, J. P. (*In his* Mém., v. 11. 1731; *and, Germ.*, v. 11. 1754.)

Vidocq, Eugène François. Memoirs, by himself. London, 1829. 4 v. (v. 1, 4 w.). 12°.
— *Same.* Phila., 1834. 8°.

Vidua, Carlo. Inscriptiones antiquæ in Turcico itinere collectæ. Lut. Par., 1826. 8°.

Vie d'artiste, Une; par A. Dumas [E. M. Mélingue]. Nouv. éd. Paris, 1860. 18°.

Vie, La, et les opinions de Sempronius Gundibert. (*In* Biblioth. univ. des romans, Nouv., v. 62. 1802.)

Vie, La, n'est qu'un songe; par F. le M. de Boisrobert. (*In* Biblioth. univ. des romans, Nouv., v. 5. 1799.)

Vie privée des ecclésiastiques, prélats, *etc.* Paris, 1791. 2 v. 8°.

Viehoff, Heinrich. Goethe's Leben. 3e Aufl. Stuttgart, 1858. 4 v. 16°.

Vieilh de Boisjolin, Claude Augustin. Biographie des contemporains. 1834. *See* Rabbe, A.

Vieillard, Le; par G. F. Desfontaines. (*In* Biblioth. univ. des romans, Nouv., v. 68. 1802.)

Vieilleville, François de Scépaux, *comte de Duretal.* CARLOIX, V. Mémoires de V. (Vol. 28-33 *of* Perrin. Col. des mém., 1787; — v. 26-28 *of* Petitot. Col. des mém., 1e sér. 1822; — *and* v. 9 *of* Michaud. Nouv. col. des mém. 1854.)
— SCHILLER, F. von. Denkwürdigkeiten aus dem Leben des V. (*In his* Sämmtl. Werke, v. 16. 1820.)

Vieillot, L. J. P. Histoire naturelle des oiseaux de l'Amér. Septentrionale. Paris, 1807. 2 v. f°.
— Histoire naturelle. 1802. *See* Ferussac, J. B. L. d'A.

Vieira, Antonio. Sermoens. Vol. 3. Lisboa, 1683. 4°.

Viejo zeloso, El; por M. de Cervantes Saavedra. (*In his* Comedias y entremeses, v. 2, 1749; — *and* Obras, v. 12. 1864.)

Viel-Castel, Charles Louis Gaspard Gabriel de Salirac, *baron* de. Histoire de la restauration. Paris, 1860-78. 20 v. 8°.
— Several articles.] (*In* Revue d. D. Mondes, mars 1840 - déc. 1865.)

Viel-Castel, Henri, *comte.* De la société et du gouvernement. Paris, 1834. 2 v. 8°.

Viele, *Gen.* Egbert L. Hand-book for active service. N. Y., 1861. 12°.
— Report on civic cleanliness and the economical disposition of the refuse of cities. N. Y., 1860. 8°. (B 1561)
— Topographical survey of New Jersey. (*In* Amer. Geog. and Statist. Soc. Bul., v. 2. 1857.)

Vielwisser, Der; von A. v. Kotzebue. (*In his* Theater, v. 36. 1841.)

Vien, Joseph Marie, *comte* de. AUBERT, F. (*In* **Gazette** des beaux-arts, v. 22, 23. 1867.)

Vienna. *Councils.* GIANNONE, P. Breve relazione dei consigli e dicasteri della città di Vienna. (*In his* Opere postume, v. 3. 1824.)

Art.

— PERGER, A. R. von. Die Kunstschätze Wien's in Stahlstich, nebst erläuterndem Text. Triest, **1854.** 4°.

— ENGERT, E. Catalogue de la galerie de tableaux impériale-royale au Belvédère à Vienne. Vienne, **1859.** 8°.

— WAAGEN, G. F. Die vornehmsten Kunstdenkmäler in Wien. Wien, **1866-67.** 2 v. 8°.

Description.

— ADAIR, *Sir* R. Historical memoir of a mission to the court of V., 1806. London, 1844. 8°.

— LAGARDE, A. de M., *comte* de. Journal of a nobleman; residence at Vienna during the Congress, [1812-14]. London, 1831. 2 v. 12°.

— REY, E. Le guide des étrangers à Vienne. Lyon, 1819. 8°.

— TROLLOPE, *Mrs.* F. E. Vienna and the Austrians, [1836-37]. London, 1838. 2 v. 8°.

— COKE, H. J. Vienna in 1848. London, 1849. 8°.

Maps.

— MAP. *n.p.*, [16—]. (E 78, no. 124)

— MAP. Amst., [17—]. (**E 60**)

History.

— CANALE, M. G. Degli archivi di Venezia, di Vienna, *ec.* (*In* **Archivio** stor. ital., n. s., v. 4. pt. 2. 1857.)

— ANNALES Vindobonenses. **1267-1327.** (*In* **Pertz, G. H.** Mon. Germ. hist., Scr., v. 1. 1851.)

— CHRONICON Viennense, **1367-1405.** (*In* **Vienna. Ak. d. Wiss.** Font. rer. Aust., 1. Abth., 2. B., 1. Th. 1856.)

— CHURFÜRST Johann Georg III. bei dem Entsatze von Wien im Jahre **1683**; nebst einem Anhang, den Antheil Sobieski's an dem Entsatze und eine Darstellung der Ereignisse bis zum Schlusse des Feldzuges enthaltend. (*In* **Historiches** Taschenbuch, 1848.)

— DUNDER, W. G. Denkschrift über die Wiener October-Revolution, [1848]. Wien, 1849. 8°.

Libraries.

— LAMBECIUS, P. Commentariorum de bibliotheca Cæsarea Vindobonensi fragm. (*In* **Schelhorn, J. G.** Amœn., v. 5. 1726.)

— BALBO, A. Essai statistique sur les bibliothèques de Vienne; préc. de la statistique de la Bibliothèque Impériale. Vienne, 1835. 8°.

Vienna, Congress of. Congrès de Vienne; recueil de pièces officielles rélatives à cette assemblée. Paris, 1816-18. 6 v. 8°.

— Congrès de Vienne; acte principal et traités additionnels. Paris, 1847. 8°.

— PRADT, D. D., *l'abbé* de. Du Congrès de Vienne. 2e éd. Paris, **1815.** 2 v. 8°.

— - *Eng.* The Congress of Vienna. Phila., 1816. 8°.

— GOERRES, *Prof.* J. J. von. Germany and the revolution. (*In* **Pamphleteer, 1819**; v. 15 of B 838)

— LAGARDE, A. de M., *comte* de. Journal of a nobleman; his travels from Moscow to Vienna, and his residence at V. during the Congress. London, **1831.** 2 v. 12°.

— VARNHAGEN VON ENSE, K. A. Der Wiener Kongress, 1814/15. (*In his* Denkwürdigkeiten, v. 3. **1843.**)

— CAPEFIGUE, J. B. H. R. Congrès de Vienne dans ses rapports avec la circonscription de l'Europe. Paris, **1847.** 8°.

— SCHAUMANN, A. F. H. Geschichte der Bildung des deutschen Bundes auf dem Wiener Congresse. (*In* **Historisches** Taschenbuch, **1850.**)

— SIRTEMA DE GROVESTINS, C. F. Le Congrès de Vienne en 1814-15, et le Congrès de Paris en 1856. Paris, **1856.** 8°.

— RAMÉE, D. Le Congrès de Vienne, 1814-15; histoire de l'origine, de l'action, et de l'anéantissement des traités de 1815. Paris, **1866.** 8°.

Vienna. K. Akademie d. Wissenschaften. Judicium de quibusdam propositionibus J. Münsingeri. (*In* **Schelhorn, J. G.** Amœn. lit., v. 11. 1728.)

— Verzeichniss bis 1868 veröffentlichen Druckschriften. Wien, 1869. 8°.

— *Hist. Comm.* Fontes rerum Austriacarum; Œsterreichische Geschichts-Quellen. 1e Abth. Bd. 1-8. Wien, 1855-75. 8 v. 8°.

Contents. Scriptores. Vol. 1. **Tichtel, J.** Tagebuch, 1477-95.—**Herberstein,** S. v. Selbstbiographie, 1486-1553. — **Cuspinian,** J. Tagebuch, 1502-27. — **Kirchmann,** G. Denkwürdigkeiten, 1519-53; hrsg. v. T. G. v. Karajan. **2, 6, 7. Hofler, K.** Geschichtschreiber der husitischen Bewegung in Böhmen. **3, 4. Kraus,** G. Siebenbürgische Chronik des schässburger Stadtschreibers, 1608-65. **4. Fabritius, K.** Die schässburger Chronisten des 17n Jahrhunderts. **5.** Codex Strahoviensis: **Ausbert.** Bericht über den Kreuzzug Kaiser Friedrich's I.; — Chroniken, 1167-98. — **Vincentius** *von Prag, and* **Gerlach** *v. Mühlhausen*; hrsg. von H. Tauschinski und M. Pangerl. — **Todtenbuch** der Geistlichkeit der böhmischen Brüder; hrsg. v. J. Fiedler. **6, 7.** *See* 2. **8. Loserth,** J. Königsaaler Geschichts-Quellen; mit den Zusätzen des Domherrn Franz von Prag.

— - 2e Abth. Bd. 1-11, 14-42. Wien, 1849-79. 42 v. 8°.

Contents. Diplomataria et acta. Vol. **1. Chmel,** J. Urkunden zur Geschichte von Œsterreich, Steiermark, Kämten, Krain, Görz, Triest, Istrien, Tirol, 1246-1300. **2. Chmel,** J. Urkunden, Briefe, und Actenstücke zur Geschichte der Fürsten Ladislaus Posth., Erzherzog Albrecht VI., und Herzog Siegmund von Œsterreich. **3. Zwetl. Cistercienser-Kloster.** Das Stiftungen-Buch; hrsg. von J. v. Frast. **4. Fischer,** M. Codex traditionum Ecclesiæ Collegiatæ Claustroneoburgensis. **5. Wangen,** F. Codex Wangianus; Urkundenbuch des Hochstiftes Trient, begonnen unter W., fortgesetzt von seinen Nachfolgern; hrsg. von R. Kink. **6. Petrus** *de Hallis.* Summa de literis missalibus; ed. F. Frinhaber. — **St. Bernhard Kloster.** Das Stiftungs-Buch; hrsg. v. H. J. Zeibig. **7. Vienna.** Copey-Buch der germainen Stat Wienn, 1454-64; hrsg. v. H. J. Zeibig. **8. Gottweig. Benedictiner-Stift.** Das Saal-Buch; [hrsg.] W. Karlin. **9. Kökenyesdi Vetes,** F. Actenstücke zur Geschichte Franz Rákóczy's und seiner Verbindungen mit dem Auslande. 1705-15; [hrsg.] v. J. Fiedler. **10, 28. Klosterneuburg Stifte.** Urkundenbuch bis zum Ende des 14n Jahrhunderts; bearb. von H. Zeibig. **11, 16. Heiligenkreuz, Cistercienser-Stift,** *Wienerwalde.* Urkunden; hrsg. von J. N. Weis. **12, 13.** *Wanting.* **14. Venice.** Urkunden zur älteren Handels- und Staatsgeschichte der Republik Venedig, mit besonderer Beziehung auf Byzanz und die Levante; hrsg. v. G. L. F. Tafel u. G. M. Thomas. **15. Teutsch,** G. D., *and* **Firnhaber,** F. Urkundenbuch zur Geschichte Siebenbürgens. **16.** *See* 11. **17. Klement,** J. M. Actenstücke zur Geschichte Franz Rákóczy's *u.s.w.* 1708-15; hrsg. von J. Fiedler. **18. Benedictiner-Abtei Unserer Lieben Frau zu den Schotten,** *Vienna.* Urkunden, 1158-1418; hrsg. v. E. Hauswirth. **19. Gindely,** A. Quellen zur Geschichte der Böhmischen Brüder. **20. Palacky,** F. Urkundliche Beiträge zur Geschichte Böhmens und seiner Nachbarländer im Zeitalter Georg's von Podiebrad, 1450-71. **21. Altenburg. Benedictiner-Abtei zum h. Lambert.** Urkunden, 1144-1522; gesammelt von H. Burger. — **St. Pölten. Augustiner-Chorherren-Stift.** Das Necrologium; mitgetheilt v. T. Wiedemann. **22. Venice.** *Ambasciatori.* Die Relationen über Œsterreich im 18en Jahrhundert; hrsg. von A. Ritter v. Arneth. **23. Hohenfurt. Cistercienserstift B. Mariæ V.** Urkundenbuch; hrsg. v. M. Pangerl. **24. Valentinelli.** Diplomatarium Portusnaonense; series documentorum ad historiam Portusnaonis spectantium, 1276-1514. **25. Das Baumgartenberger** Formelbuch; eine Quelle zur Geschichte des 13. Jahrhunderts vornehmlich der Zeiten Rudolfs von Habsburg zum ersten Male; hrsg. von H. Baerwald. **26, 27. Venice.** *Ambasciatori.* Die Relationen über Deutschland und Osterreich im 17en Jahrhundert; hrsg. von J. Fiedler. **28.** *See* **10. 29. Obersteier. Benedictinerstift St. Lambrecht.** Die beiden ältesten Todtenbücher; mitgetheilt von M. Pangerl. **30. Venice.** *Ambasciatori.* Relationen über Deutschland und Osterreich im

16n Jahrhundert; hrsg. von J. Fielder. 31, 35, 36. Zahn, J. Codex diplomaticus Austriaco-Frisingensis; Sammlung von Urkunden und Urbaren zur Geschichte der ehemals freisingischen Besitzungen in Oesterreich. 32, 38. Höfler, C. Der Congress von Soissons; nach den Instructionen des kaiserlichen Cabinetes und den Berichten des kaiserlichen Botschafters Stefan Grafen Kinsky. 33. Seitenstetten. Benedictiner-Stift. Urkundenbuch; von P. I. Raab. 34. Neustift. Augustiner Chorherren-Stift. Urkundenbuch; hrsg. v. T. Mairhofer. 35, 36. *See* 31. 37. Goldenkron. Cistercienserstift, *Bohemia*. Urkundenbuch; bearb. von M. Pangerl. 38. *See* 32. 39. St. Paul. Benedictiner Stift, *Carinthia*. Urkundenbuch; hrsg. von B. Schroll. 40. Zahn, J. von. Austro-Friulana; Geschichte des Conflictes, 1358-65. 41. Lilienfeld. Cistercienser Stift. Das Todtenbuch; mitgetheilt von H. R. Zeissberg. 42. Bachmann, A. Urkunden und Actenstücke zur österreichishen Geschichte, 1440-71.

— - Monumenta Habsburgica; Sammlung von Actenstücken und Briefen zur Geschichte des Hauses Habsburg, 1473-1576. Wien, 1854-55. 2 v. 8°.

Contents. 1. Abth. Chmel, J. Actenstücke u. Briefe zur Geschichte des Hauses Habsburg im Zeitalter Maximilian's I. 2. Abth. Lanz, K. Kaiser Karl V. und König Philipp II.

Vienna. K. K. allgemeine Krankenhause. Aerztlichen Bericht vom Civil-Jahre 1860. Wien, 1861. 8°.

Vienna. K. K. Gemäldegallerie. Catalogue des tableaux; par C. de Mechel. Basle, 1784. 8°.

Vienna. Monasterium Scotorum. ANNALES Scotorum, 1225-33. (*In* Pertz, G. H. Mon. Germ. hist., Scr., v. 9. 1851.)

Vienna. Universität. BORN, I. Testacea Musei Cæsarei Vindobonensis. Vindobonæ, 1780. f°.

Vienne, *France*. LETTER of the churches in Vienna and Lugdunum. (*In* Donaldson, J. Critical hist. of Christian lit., v. 3. 1866.)

Viennet, Jean Pons Guillaume. Discours. — Réponse. — Fragment de la tragédie des Etats de la Ligue. — Fables. (*In* Paris. Inst. *Acad. Fr.* Rec. des disc. 1830-39.) — Réponse. (*In* 1840-49, 1e pte.) — Discours. — Fables. (*In* 1840-49, 2e pt.) — Discours. — Epître à Clio. (*In* 1850-59, 1e pt.) — Epitre à Despreaux. — Epitre à de Pontmartin. — Epître à Villemain. — Epître à mes quartre-vingts ans. (*In* 1850-59, 2e pt.) — Résponse. — Fables. — Epitre à ma vieille muse. (*In* 1860-69, 1e pt.)

— Fables. 2e éd. Paris, 1855. 18°.

— Promenade philosophique au cimetière du Père La Chaise. Paris, 1824. 8°.

Viennot, —. L'horoscope. (*In* Echo des feuilletons, 3e an. 1843.)

Vier Tanten, Die; Lustspiel, von G. Döring. (*In* Kotzebue, A. F. F. von. Almanach, v. 20. 1822.)

Vierdmüller, Otto. *See* Wermüller *or* Vierdmüller, O.

Vieri, Francesco de. Sopra il sonnetto del Petrarca, In qual parte del cielo. (*In* Dati, C. Prose flor., pt. 2, v. 1. 1751.)

Vierjahrige Posten, Der; ein Singspiel. *See* Körner, C. T.

Vierundzwanzigste Februar, Der; eine Tragödie von F. L. Z. Werner. Lpz., Altenburg, 1815. 16°.

Viethen, Anton. Beschreibung und Geschichte des Landes Dithmarschen; nebst einer Vorrede J. A. Fabricii. Hamburg, 1733. 4°.

Viets, —. Sermon in Digby, Nova Scotia. Halifax, 1793. 8°. (B 962)

Vieusseux, André. History of Switzerland from the irruption of the barbarians. London, 1840. 8°. (Lib. useful knowl.)

— *Same*. London, 1846. 8°.

— Italy and the Italians in the 19th century. London, 1824. 2 v. 8°.

Vieusseux, Giovan Pietro. TABARRINI, M., *and* MILANESI, C. Necrologia di Vieusseux. (*In* Archivio stor. ital., n.s., v. 17. 1863.)

Vieux célibataire, Le. *See* Collin d' Harleville, J. F.

Vieux fat, Le; ou Les deux vieillards; comédie; par F. G. J. S. Andrieux. (*In his* Œuvres, v. 2. 1818.)

Vieux garçons, Les; comédie. *See* Sardou, V.

Vieux-neuf, Le. *See* Fournier, E.

View of Lord Bolingbroke's philosophy; [by W. Warburton]. London, 1854. 8°. (B 1712)

View of South America and Mexico; by a citizen of the U. S. N. Y., 1826. 2 v. 12°.

View of the articles of the Protestant and Popish faith. London, 1735. 8°. (C 81)

View of the Calvinistic clubs in the U. S. *n.p.*, [17—]. 12°. (C 62, W 69)

View of the Constitution of the U. S. as agreed to by the convention of delegates at Philadelphia, Sept. 17. Phila., 1787. 8°. (B 991)

View of the controversy between Gr. Britain and her colonies. *See* W., A., *farmer*.

View of the exertions for colonizing the free people of colour in the U. States in Africa, *etc.* Wash., 1817. 8°. (B 1483)

— *Same, with a slight omission*. Wash., 1817. 8°. (B 445)

View of the history of Gr. Britain during Lord North's administration. Part 2. London, 1782. 8°.

View of the N. England Illuminati; [by J. Cary]. Phila., 1799. 8°. (W 62)

View of the principles upon which the Independent Soc. for Public Worship, under the ministry of Mr. Frey, is established. N. Y., 1817. 8°. (B 1390)

View of the prophecies of the kingdom of our Lord. Boston, 1841. 8°. (B 1373)

View of the relative situations of Pitt and Addington, previous to and on the night of Mr. Patten's motion; by a M. P. London, 1804. 8°. (B 1413)

View of the relative states of Gr. Britain and France, 1796. 2d ed. London, 1796. 8°. (B 777, 790)

View of the Scripture revelations concerning a future state; by [R. Whately]. London, 1853. 12°.

View of the whole ground; Constitution of the U. S., the Declaration of rights and Constitution of Mass.; with all the embargo laws. Newbpt., 1809. 8°. (B 531)

Views in New England theology. No. 1: The N. E. theology contrasted with the New Arminianism. Boston, 1859. 8°. (B 224)

— *Same*. No. 2. The new apostacy; or, A word to the Laodiceans. Boston, 1860. 8°. (C 224)

Views of Judge Woodward and Bishop Hopkins on slavery illustrated from the journal of F. A. Kemble. Phila., 1863. 8°. (B 1481)

Views of nature. *See* Humboldt, F. H. A. von.

Views of society and manners in America; in a series of letters, 1818-20; by an Englishwoman [F. Wright d'Arusmont]. London, 1821. 8°.

Vieyra, Antonio de, *d.* 1697. NICERON, J. P. (*In his* Mém., v. 34. 1736; *and*, *Germ.*, v. 24. 1777.)

Vieyra Transtagano, Antonio, *d.* 1797. Dictionary of the Portuguese and Eng. languages. New ed. London, 1794. 2 v. 4°.

— New Portuguese grammar. 3d ed. London, 1794. 8°.

Viga Glum's saga. *See* Glum, *Viga*.

Vigée, *Mme.* Marie Louise Elizabeth. *See* Le Brun, M. L. E. V.

Vigel, Erik. Diæta acidularis. (*In* Linné, C. v. Amœn. acad., v. 6. 1763.)

Vigenère, Blaise de. De igne et sale. (*In* Zetzner, L. Theat. chem., v. 6. 1661.)

— NICERON, J. P. (*In his* Mém., v. 16. 1731; *and*, *Germ.*; v. 12. 1755.)

Viger, François. De præcipuis Græcæ dictionis idiotismis liber; cum animadversionibus H. Hoogeveeni, J. C. Zeunii, et G. Hermanni; ac. de pronomine αὐτός diss. Oxonii, 1813. 8°.

Vigera, —. Tage-Register von London nach Eben Ezer. (*In* Urlsperger, S. Nachrichten saltzburg. Emigrant, v. 2. 1839.)

Vigfusson, Gudbrand, *continuator*. *See* Cleasby, R. Icelandic English dictionary. 1869.

Vigil, The. Nos. 1-5. Charleston, 1798. 8°. (B 744)

Vigilante, *ship*. AFFAIRE de la V., bâtiment négrier de Nantes. Paris, 1823. 8°. (B 1003)

Vigilantius. GILLY, W. S. Vigilantius and his times. London, 1844. 8°.

Vigilius; or, The awakener. 1719. *See* Mather, C. (C 9)

Vigne, Godfrey T. Six months in America. London, 1832. 2 v. 12°.

— Travels in Kashmir, Ladak, Iskardo, the countries adjoining the mountain course of the Indus, and the Himalaya, north of the Panjab. 2d ed. London, 1844. 2 v. 8°.

Vigné, Jean Baptiste. De la médecine légale. Rouen, 1805. 8°.

Vigneron, Jean. *See* **Veneroni, J.**

Vignettes. *See* **Engravings.**

Vigneulles, Philippe Gérard de. REUMONT, A. Ricordi int. al soggiorno da lui fatto nel regno di Napoli. (*In* **Archivio** stor. ital., app., v. 9. 1853.)

Vignier, Jerôme. NICERON, J. P. (*In his* **Mém.**, v. 2. 1727; *and*, *Germ.*, v. 3. 1750.)

Vignier, Nicolas, *d.* 1546. NICERON, J. P. (*In his* **Mém.**, v. 42. 1741.)

Vignola, Giacomo Barozzi da. *See* **Barozzi** *da Vignola*, **G.**

Vignoles, Charles. Observations upon the Floridas. N. Y., 1823. 8°.

Vignoso, Simone. BACIGALUPO, A. (*In* **Grillo, L.** Elogi di Lig., v. 1. 1846.)

Vigny, Alfred Victor, *comte* de. Cinq-Mars, ou conjuration sous Louis XIII. 9e éd. Par., 1855. 12°.

— *Same.* 15e éd. Paris, 1865. 12°.

— *Eng.* Cinq-Mars; or, A conspiracy under Louis XIII.; tr. from 9th Paris ed. by W. Hazlitt. London, 1847. 12°.

— Les destinées; poëmes philosophiques. Paris, 1864. 8°.

— Discours. (*In* **Paris. Inst.** *Acad. Fr.* Recueil des disc. 1840–49, pt. 1.)

— Dolorida. (*In* **Muse** française, v. 1. 1823.)

— Poésies complètes. Nouv. éd. Paris, 1864. 8°.
Contents. Livre mystique, — antique, — moderne. — Les destinées; poëmes philosophiques.

— Servitude et grandeur militaires. 8e éd. Paris, 1864. 12°.

— *Eng.* Lights and shades of military life; ed. by Sir C. Napier. London, 1840. 2 v. 8°.

— Stello; Les consultations du docteur-noir. 9e éd. Paris, 1865. 12°.

— Théâtre complet. Nouv. éd. Paris, 1848. 12°.
Contents. Le more de Venise. — Le marchand de Venise. — Le maréchale d'Ancre. — Quitte pour la peur. — Chatterton.

— Several articles.] (*In* **Revue d. D. Mondes**, 1831–jan. 1864.)

— LOMÉNIE, L. L. de. (*In his* Gallerie des contemp. illust., v. 2. 1840.)

— MILL, J. S. Writings of A. de Vigny. (*In his* Dissertations, v. 1. 1859.)

— PLANCHE, G. (*In* **Revue** d. D. Mondes, août 1832.) — MONTÉGUT, E. (*In* mars 1867.)

— SAINTE-BEUVE, C. A. (*In* **Revue** d. D. Mondes, oct. 1835; av. 1864; — *and in his* Portraits contemp., v. 1. 1852.)

Vigo, GianBernardo. Servandus est in litterarum studiis excolendis laborum atque animi contentionum modus. — Docti homines cum aliis morbis, ob immodicas et graves contentiones animi, tum vertigine potissimum tentari solent, elegia. (*In* **Turin.** Ac. d. Sci. Mem., v. 13. 1803.) — SALUZZO, C. Notizie intorno alla vita di G. B. V. (*In* v. 21. 1813.)

Vigo Co., *Indiana.* WALLING, H. F. Map. N. Y., 1858.

Vigo Roussillon, F. P. Puissance militaire des Etats-Unis. Paris, 1866. 8°.

Vigornius, *pseud.*, *and others.* Essays on slavery; from the Boston recorder and telegraph, 1825. Amherst, 1826. 8°. (B 1237)

Vigors, Nicholas Aylward. Ornithology. (*In* **Beechey, F. W.** Zoology of Beechey's voyage. 1839.)

Vigreux, L., *and* RAUX, A. Moteurs hydrauliques. (*In* **Lacroix**, E. Etudes sur l'Exposition de 1867, v. 3.)

Viguet, —. Etat du monde à la venue de Jésus-Christ. (*In* **Geneva. Union Chrétienne de Jeunes Gens.** Séances hist., v. 1. 1857.)

Vijayanayar. TRANSLATION of inscriptions found among the ruins of Vijayanayar, by E. C. Ravenshaw. (*In* **Asiatic** researches, v. 20, pt. 1. 1836.)

Vikings. STRINNHOLM, A. M. Wikingszüge, Staatsverfassung, und Sitten der alten Skandinavier; aus dem schwedischen von C. F. Frisch. Hamburg, 1839–41. 2 v. 8°.

Vikram and the vampire; or, Tales of Hindu devilry; by R. F. Burton. London, 1870. 16°.

— *Same.* (*In* **Fraser's** mag., v. 77–78. 1868.)

Vikrama and Urvasi; a drama. *See* **Kalidasa.**

Vilanova, Juan. Prehistoric remains in Valencia. (*In* **Internat. Cong. of Prehist. Archæol.** Trans., 1868.)

Vilant, N. Elements of mathematical analysis; with notes and a synopsis of book v. of Euclid. Edin., 1798. 8°.

Vilate, Joachim, *called* Sempronius **Gracchus.** Causes sècretes de la journée du 9 au 10 thermidor an II. — Des mystères de la Mère de Dieu dévoilés. (*In* **Desmoulins**, C. Vieux cordelier. 1825. Berville and Barrière. Col. des mém., v. 16.)

Vilhalpandos, Os; comedia, por F. de **Sà de Miranda.** (*In his* Obras, v. 2. 1784.)

Villa Eden; the country house on the Rhine; by B. Auerbach; tr. by C. C. Shackford. Boston, 1869. 8°.

Village, The; a poem. *See* **Crabbe, G.**

Village belles; by [A. Manning]. New ed., rev. London, 1859. 16°.

Village communities in the east and west. *See* **Maine, H. S.**

Village dialogues. *See* **Hill, R.**

Village harmony, The; or, New England repository of sacred musick. 14th ed. Bost., [1817]. 8°.

— *Same.* 17th ed., rev. Exeter, 1820. 8°.

Village lawyer, The; a farce. (*In* **London** stage, v. 4.)

Village notary; a romance from the Hungarian of baron Eötvös; tr. by O. Wenckstern. London, 1850. 3 v. 12°.

Village on the cliff, The; by [A. I. Thackeray]. 2d ed. London, 1867. 8°.

— *Same.* (*In* **Cornhill** mag., v. 13–15. 1866, 67; — *and in* **Littell's** living age, v. 90–92. 1866–67.)

Village school. (*In* **Yonge, C. M.** Storehouse. 1870.)

Villain, Henri. Boulangerie et pâtisserie. (*In* **Lacroix**, E. Etudes sur l'Exposition de 1867, v. 2.)

Villaizan, Jeronimo de. Ofender con las finezas. — Sufrir mas por querer mas. (*In* **Mesonero Romanos**, R. de. Dramaticos contemporaneos a Lope de Vega, v. 2. 1858; v. 45 of Aribau. Bibl.)

Villalobos, Francisco de. Problemas. (*In* **Castro**, A. de. Curiosidades bibliog. 1856; v. 36 of Aribau. Bibl.)

Villalobos, Ruy Lopez de. Voyage to the Moluccas. (*In* **Burney**, J. Discoveries in the South Sea, v. 1. 1803.)

Villalpando, Juan Battista. In Ezechielem explanationes. 1596. *See* **Prado, J.**

Villamediana, Juan de Tassis, *conde* de. Poesias. (*In* **Castro**, A. de. Poetas liricos de los siglos 16 y 17, v. 2. 1857; v. 42. of Aribau. Bibl.)

Villanella rapita, La. [En ital. et en français.] Paris, 1789. 8°. (B 1625)

Villani, Filippo. Vite d' uomini illustri fiorentini; colle annot. di G. Mazzuchelli; ed una cronica inedita con illust. di F. G. Dragomanni. Firenze, 1847. 8°.

— *Continuator.* Istorie. *See* **Villani, M.**

Villani (*Lat.* **Villanius**), Giovanni. Historie fiorentine all' anno 1348. (*In* **Muratori.** Rer. Ital. scr., v. 13. 1728.)

— *Same.* Milano, *Soc. Tip. di Class. Ital.*, 1802–03. 8 v. 8°.
Contents. Vol. 1. To 1154. 2. 1154–1264. 3. 1265–92. 4. 1292–1310. 5. 1310–26. 6. 1326–33. 7. 1333–42. 8. 1342–48.

— *Same.* Cronica; con noti di I. Montier. Firenze, 1844–45. 4 v. 8°.
Contents. Vol. 1. To 1292. 2. 1292–1326. 3. 1326–42. 4. 1342–48. — Elogio di V. — App. di doc. e note di F. G. Dragomanni. — Indice.

— Cronica ridotta in terza rima. *See* **Pucci, A.**

— Rubicon in Cæsenam S. Claramontii. — De Rubicone antiquo Ariminensi in Pisciatellum Cæsenæ, responsa ad argumenta a L. Holstenio proposita. (*In* **Grævius**, J. G. Thes. antiq. Ital., v. 7, pt. 2. 1722.)

— MILANESI, G. Documento riguardanti G. Villani e il palazzo degli Alessie in Siena. (*In* **Archivio** stor. ital., n.s. v. 4, pt. 1. 1856.)

Villani, Matteo. Istorie, 1348-64; continuate da F. Villani. (*In* Muratori, L. A. Rer. Ital. scr., v. 14. 1729.)

— *Same.* Cronica; con appendici storico-geografiche da F. G. Dragomanni. Firenze, 1846. 2 v. 8°.
Contents. Vol. 1. 1348-56. 2. To 1364.

Villani *di Firenze*, Famiglia di. (*In* Litta, P. Fam., v. 15.).

Villanova, Arnaldo. Lumen luminum seu flos florum. (*In* Zetzner, L. Theatr. chem., v. 3. 1613; — *and in* Manget, J. J. Bibl., v. 1. 1702.)

— De sanguine humano distillato. (*In* Rupescissa, J. de. De consideratione. 1597.)

— Speculum alchymiæ. — Carmen. — Quæstiones tam essentiales quam accidentales ad Bonifacium VIII.; cum suis responsionibus. (*In* Zetzner, L. Theat. chem., v. 4. 1613; — *and in* Manget, J. J. Bibl., v. 1. 1702.)

— Thesaurus thesaurorum et rosarium philosophorum. — Novum lumen. — Perfectum magisterium et gaudium. — Epistola super alchemia ad regem Neapolitanum. — Semita semitæ. — Testamentum. (*In* Manget, J. J. Biblioth. chem., v. 1. 1702.)

— Figuier, L. (*In his* Vies des savants illustres du Moyen Age. 1867.)

Villanova, Giovanni Battista. Laudis Pompejæ sive Laudæ urbis historia. (*In* Græevius, J. G. Thes. antiq. Ital., v. 3, pt. 1. 1704.)

Villanova, Thomas a, *d.* 1555. *See* Tomas [Garcias] *de Villanova, St.*

Villanova Portugal, Thomas Antonio de. Sobre feiras. — — Sobre a cultura dos terrenos baldios da villa de Ourem. (*In* Lisbon. Ac. d. Sci. Mem. econ., v. 2. 1790.) — Sobre os juros relativamente á cultura das terras. — Descripçaõ da comarca de Setubal. — Observaçaõ sobre o mappa da povoaçaõ do termo de Azeitaõ. (*In* v. 3. 1791.) — [Various articles.] (*In* Mem. lit., v. 3, 5. 1792.)

Villard, Henry. Historical sketch of social science. — — People's banks of Germany. (*In* Amer. Soc. Sci. Assoc. Trans., 1869.)

Villareal, Joaquin de. Informe al Rey Fernando VI. sobre contener y reducir los Indios de Chile. (*In* Valladares, A. Seman. erud., v. 23. 1789.)

Villaret, Claude, *continuator.* *See* Velly, P. F. Histoire de France. 1775-99.

Villari, Pasquale. La storia di Savonarola. Firenze, 1859-61. 2 v. 12°.

— *Eng.* History of Savonarola and his times; tr. by L. Horner. London, 1863. 2 v. 8°.

— Lampertico, F. Il Gervinus e il Villari. (*In* Archivio stor. ital., ser. 3, v. 1, pt. 2. 1865.)

Villarino, J. J. Practical method of learning to speak the Castilian lang. N. Y., 1828. 8°.

Villarroel, Cristoval de. Soneto. (*In* Sedano, J. J. L. de. Parnaso esp., v. 5. 1771.)

Villarroya, José de. Disertacion sobre el origen del arte tipografico y su introduccion en Valencia. Valencia, 1796. 8°.

Villars, de, *abbé de Montfaucon.* Le comte de Gabalis. Mannheim, 1798. 24°

Villars, Claude Louis Hector, *maréchal, duc* de. Mémoires. (*In* Petitot. Col. des mém., 2e sér., v. 68-71. 1828; — *and in* Michaud. Col. des mém., v. 33. 1854.)

— Alembert, J. le R. d'. (*In his* Œuvres, v. 10. 1805.)

— Sainte-Beuve, C. A. (*In his* Causeries du lundi, v. 13. 1858.)

Villars, Emile. Le roman de la Parisienne. Paris, 1866. 16°.

Villars, François de Boivin, *baron* de. *See* Boivin, F. de.

Villault, *sieur de Bellfond.* Abstract of a voyage to the coast of Africa and Guinea, 1666. (*In* Green, J. Col. of voy., v. 2. 1745; — *and*, *Germ.*, Allgemeine Hist., v. 3. 1748.)

Villaviciosa, José de. La mosquera. (*In* Ochoa, E. de. Tesoro de los poemas esp. 1840; — *and in* Rosell, C. Poemas epicos, v. 1. 1851; v. 17. of Aribau. Bibl.)

Villaviciosa, Sebastian de, *and* Avallaneda, F. de. Cuantas veo tantas quiero. (*In* Mesonero Romanos, R. de. Dramaticos posteriores a Lope de Vega, v. 1. 1858; v. 47. of Aribau. Bibl.)

Ville, Antoine de. *See* Deville, A.

Ville, George. High farming without manure; six lectures on agriculture. Boston, 1866. 16°.

Ville noire, La; par G. Sand [Mme. Dudevant]. Paris, 1861. 16°.

Villedeuil, Charles, *comte* de. Paris à l'envers. Paris, 1853. 16°.

Villefort; 4e partie de Monte Cristo; par A. Dumas. (*In his* Théâtre complet, v. 8. 1864.)

Villegagnon, *or* Villegaignon, Nicolas Durand de. Barré, N. Lettres sur la navigation de V. ès terres de l'Amérique oultre l'aequinoctiel. (*In* Ternaux-Compans, H. Archives des voy., v. 1, pt. 1. 1840.)

— Guérin, L. (*In his* Les navigateurs français. 1847.)

— Léry, J. de. Extracts out of the historie of J. Lerius who lived in Brasill with Villagagnon, 1557-58. (*In* Purchas. Pilgrimes, v. 4. 1625; — *and in* Callander, J. Terra Austr., v. 1. 1766.)

— Niceron, J. P. (*In his* Mém., v. 22. 1733; *and Germ.*, v. 16. 1758.)

Villegas, Antonio de. Historia del Abencerraja y la hermosa Jarifa. (*In* Aribau, B. C. Nov. ant. á Cervantes. 1850. Bibl., v. 3.)

Villegas, Diego Enriquez de. Advertencias eruditas para principes y ministros. (*In* Valladares, A. Seman. erud., v. 34. 1790.)

Villegas, Estévan Manuel de. Las eroticas y traduccion de la Consolacion de Boecio. 2a ed. Madrid, 1797. 2 v. 12°.

— Las delicias. — Las Latinas. (*In* Sedana, J. J. L. de. Parnaso espan., v. 1. 1768.) — Satira. — Soneto. (*In* v. 2. 1770.) — Epigramas. (*In* v. 4. 1776.) — Los cien pasos; edilio. — Elegia. (*In* v. 7. 1782.) — Elegia. (*In* v. 8. 1784.) — Epistola. — Carta. (*In* v. 9. 1788.)

— Idilio. — Odas. — Cantilenas y anacreónticas. — Romance. (*In* Quintana, M. J. Poesias sel. castel., v. 1. 1807.)

— Montgomery, J. (*In his* lives of lit. and sci. men, v. 3. 1837. Lardner. Cab. cyc.)

Villegas, Francisco de. Dios hace justicia a todos; comedia. Salamanca, [17—]. 4°. (E 112)

Villegas, Sancho Busto de. Papel al rey Felipe II., 1574, sobre la venta de los vasalos de las eglesias, y otras cosas. (*In* Valladares, A. Seman. erud., v. 6. 1787.)

Villeggiatura, La; commedia, da C. Goldoni. (*In his* Opere, v. 25. 1791.)

Villehardouin, Geoffroi, *sire* de. La conqueste de Constantinoble; [avec continuation par] H. de Valenciennes [et] notes par P. Paris. Paris, 1838. 8°. (Soc. de l'Hist.)

— *Same.* [Avec notes par Buchon.] (*In* Buchon, J. A. C. Col. des chron., v. 3. 1828. 1840.)

— *Same, without notes and with trans. by* Du Cange. (*In* Petitot. Col., v. 1. 1819; — *and in* Michaud. Col., v. 1. 1854.)

— *Same, without the continuation.* Avec la suite jusques à 1240 [par] P. Mouskes. (*In* Byzant. hist. scr., v. 20. 1729.)

— *Eng.* The chronicle conc. the conquest of Constantinople; tr. by T. Smith. London, 1829. 8°.

Villehuet, Jacques Bourdé de. *See* Bourdé de Villehuet.

Villela Barbosa, Francisco. A primavera; cantata. (*In* Lisbon. Ac. d. Sci. Mem., v. 6. 1819.) — Discurso. (*In* v. 8. 1823.)

Villèle, Jean Baptiste Séraphim Joseph, *comte* de. Broglie, C. J. V. A., *duc* de. (*In* Revue d. D. Mondes, juin 1866.)

Villemain, Abel François. Choix d'études sur la littérature contemporaine. Paris, 1857. 12°.

— Cours de littérature française. Nouv. éd. Tableau de la lit. au 18e siècle. Paris, 1852. 4 v. 12°. (Œuvres.)

— *Same.* Nouv. éd. Moyen Age en France, en Italie, en Espagne, et en Angleterre. Paris, 1852. 2 v. 12°. (Œuvres.)

— Discours et mélanges litérature. Nouv. éd. Paris, 1852. 12°. (Œuvres.)
Contents. Eloges de Montaigne et de Montesquieu. — Discours sur la critique. — Notice sur Fénelon. — De Pascal comme écrivain et comme moraliste. — Discours d'ouverture des cours d'éloquence. — Discours académiques et rapports annuels.

— Etudes de littérature ancienne et étrangère. Nouv. éd. Paris, 1852. 12°. (Œuvres.)
Contents. Hérodote et de la manière de le traduire. — Du poëme de Lucrèce sur la nature des choses. — Notice

sur Cicéron, — Tibère, — Plutarque. — De la corruption des lettres romaines. — Essai sur les romans grecs. — Vies des principaux poëtes anglais: Shakespeare; — Milton; — Pope; — Byron.

— Etudes d'histoire moderne. Nouv. éd. Paris, 1852. 12°. (Œuvres.)

Contents. Discours sur l'état de l'Europe au 15e siècle. — Lascaris, ou les Grecs au 15e siècle. — Essai historique sur les Grecs depuis la conquète musulmane. — Vie du chancelier de l'Hôpital.

— Lascaris, ou Les Grecs du 15e siècle. Paris, 1825. 8°.

— M. de Chateaubriand, sa vie, ses écrits, son influence littéraire et politique. Paris, 1858. 8°.

— Réponse. — Discours. (*In* **Paris. Inst.** *Acad. Fr.* Rec. des disc., 1820–39.) — Rapports. (*In* 1830–69.)

— Souvenirs contemporains d'histoire et de littérature. Nouv. éd. Paris, 1858. 2 v. 18°.

Contents. Vol. 1. M. de Narbonne. — Souvenirs de la Sorbonne en 1825. — De M. de Feletz et de quelques salons de son temps. 2. Les cent jours.

— Tableau de l'éloquence chrétienne au 4e siècle. Nouv. éd. Paris, 1852. 12°. (Œuvres.)

Contents. Du polythéisme. — De la philosophie stoique. — Des Pères de l'eglise grecque: Athanase, Grégoire, Chrysostome, *etc.* — Des Pères de l'église latine: Hilaire, Ambroise, Jérome, Augustine, *etc.* — De l'empéreur Julien, de Symmaque, et de St. Ambroise.

— Several articles.] (*In* **Revue** d. D. Mondes, oct. 1833–mars 1859.)

— Loménie, L. L. de. (*In his* Gallerie des contemp. illust., v. 1. 1840.)

— Planche, G. (*In* **Revue** d. D. Mondes, mai 1854.)

— Sainte Beuve, C. A. (*In his* Portraits contemp., v. 1. 1852; — *and in* **Revue** d. D. Mondes, jan. 1836.)

Villemarest, Charles Maxime de. Life of Prince Talleyrand. London, 1834–36. 4 v. 8°.

Villemarqué, Théodore Claude Henri Hersart, *vicomte* de la. *See* **La Villemarqué**, T. C. H. H., *vicomte* de.

Villemot, Auguste. Le jardin et les galeries du Palais-Royal. (*In* **Paris** guide, v. 2. 1867.)

Villeneuve, *Mme.* Gabrielle Suzanne Barbot de. La jardinière de Vincennes. (*In* **Biblioth.** univ. des romans, Nouv., v. 23. 1799.)

Villeneuve, Guillaume de. Mémoires. (*In* **Perrin.** Col. des mém., v. 14. 1786; — *in* **Petitot.** Col. des mém., 1e sér., v. 14. 1820; — *and in* **Michaud.** Col. des mém., v. 4. 1854.)

Villeneuve, Théodore Ferdinand Vallon de, *and* **Livry**, C. de. Mademoiselle Dangeville; comédie. *n.p.*, [183–]. 12°. (**E 22**)

Villeneuve-Trans, Louis François, *marquis* de. Histoire de Saint Louis roi de France. Paris, 1839. 3 v. 8°.

Villeplaine, *Mme.* Boscari de. Bassanville, A. L., *comtesse* de. (*In her* Les salons d'autrefois; souvenirs intimes, v. 4. 1866.)

Villermé, Louis-René. Sur la distribution de la population française par sexe et par état civil, *etc.* (*In* **Paris. Inst.** *Ac. d. Sci. Mor.* Mém., v. 1. 1847.) — Sur l'état physique et moral des ouvriers employés dans les fabriques de soie, de coton, et de laine. (*In* v. 2.) — Des associations ouvrières. (*In* v. 7.) — Considérations sur les tables de mortalité. (*In* v. 9. 1855.)

— Several articles.] (*In* **Revue** d. D. Mondes, mars 1860–63.)

Villeroi, Nicholas de Neufville, *seigneur* de. Mémoires. (*In* **Michaud** *and* **Poujoulat.** Col. des mém., v. 11. 1854; — *in* **Petitot.** Col. des mém., 1e ser. v. 44. 1824; — *and in* **Perrin.** Col. des mém., v. 61–62. 1790.)

Villers, Charles François Dominique. Coup d'œil sur l'état actuel de la littérature ancienne et de l'hist. en Allemagne. Amst., 1809. 8°. (**B 730**)

— Coup d'œil sur les universités et la mode d'instruction de l'Allemagne protestante. Cassel, 1808. 8°. (**B 810**)

— Essay on the spirit and influence of the Reformation; tr. by B. Lambert. Dover, 1807. 8°.

— *Same.* Tr. by J. Mill, abr. by W. Marsh. London, 1836. 12°.

Villette, Charles, *marquis* de. Œuvres. Edinbourg, Paris, 1788. 8°.

Contents. Discours historiques sur la règne de Henri IV, roi de France. — Le soir. — Lettres diverses. — Poésies diverses.

— Lettres choisies sur les principaux évènemens de la Révolution. Paris, 1792. 8°.

Villette, Etienne Nicolas. Histoire de l'image miraculeuse de Notre Dame de Liesse. 2e éd. Laon, 1769. 8°.

Villette, Philippe le Valois, *marq.* de. Mémoires. Paris, 1844. 8°. (Soc. de l'Hist. de France.)

Villettes, Wm. Anne, *Lieut. Gen.* Bowdler, T. A short view of the life and character of V.; added, letters, *etc.* Bath, 1815. 8°.

Villiers, George, *1st Duke of Buckingham.* Fairholt, F. W. Poems and songs rel. to G. V. and his assassination. London, 1850. 8°. (Percy Soc., v. 29.)

— Menzies, S. (*In his* Royal favorites, v. 2. 1865.)

— Thomson, *Mrs.* K. Life of V. London, 1860. 3 v. 18°.

Villiers, George, *2d Duke of Buckingham.* Letter to the unknown author of 'A short answer to the Duke of Buckingham's paper concerning religion', *etc.* London, 1685. f°. (**A 54**)

— *Same.* (*In* **Phenix**, v. 2. 1708.)

— Rehearsal. 1672. (*In* **Arber, E.** English reprints, v. 5. 1868; — *and in* **Bell's** Brit. theatre, v. 29. 1797.)

— Short disc. upon the reasonableness of men's having a religion. London, 1685. 4°.

— *Same.* (*In* **Phenix**, v. 2. 1708.)

— Speech in a late conference. London, 1668. 8°. (**B 1709**)

— *Same.* (*In* **State** tracts. 1689. **B 28**)

— Speech in the Ho. of Lords, 16th Nov. 1675, — [in] Parl., 15th Feb. 1676. (*In* **State** tracts. 1689.)

— Care, G. Short answer to [his] paper conc. religion, *etc.* London, 1685. 4°.

— — *Another copy.* London, 1685. 4°. (**A 2**)

— True narrative of the design lately laid by Phillip le Mar and others against V. [London,] 1680. f°. (**A 54**)

Villiers, George Wm. Frederick, *4th Earl of Clarendon, and* **Bowring**, J. First report on the commercial relations between France and Gr. Brit.; with a supplementary report by J. Bowring. London, 1834. f°.

— Sketch.] (*In* **Gladstone** government, The; cabinet pictures. 1869.)

Villiers, Henry Montagu, *D.D.*, *Bp. of Durham.* The children of promise; sermon, Mar. 6, 1853. *n.p.*, [1853]. 8°. (**B 1346**)

Villiers, Jacques François de. Letter sur l'édition grecque et latine des œuvres d'Hippocrate et de Galien. *n.p.*, [17–]. 4°. (**A 19**)

Villiers, Pierre, *l'abbé.* Mémoires de la vie du comte D*** avant sa retraite; rédigés par St. Evremond. Nouv. éd. *n.p.*, 1753. 2 v. 12°.

Note. According to the Biographie universelle, V. denied the authorship of this work.

Villiers, family of. Sanford, J. L., *and* Townsend, M. (*In their* Great gov. families, v. 2. 1865.)

Villis, De, *an ordinance of Charlemagne.* Guérard, B. E. C. Explication du capitulaire de Villis. (*In* **Paris. Inst.** *Ac. d. Inscr.* Mém., v. 21, 1e pt. 1857.)

Villoison, Jean Baptiste Gaspard d' Ansse de. *See* **Ansse de Villoison**, J. B. G. d'.

Villon, François Gorbueil. Œuvres complètes; suivies d'un choix des poésies de ses disciples; ed. préparée par La Monnoye, mise au jour avec notes et glossaire par Pierre Jannet. Paris, 1867. 8°.

Contents. Le petit testament. — Le grand testament. — Poésies diverses. — Poésies attribuées à Villon.

— Cary, H. F. (*In his* Early French poets. 1846.)

— Gautier, T. (*In his* Les grotesques. 1856.)

— Niceron, J. P. (*In his* Mém., v. 5. 1728; *and, Germ.*, v. 5. 1751.)

Villot, Frédéric. Notice des tableaux du Musée Impérial du Louvre. (1e pte., 12e éd.; 2e pte., 6e éd.) Paris, 1849, 55. 2 v. 12°.

Vilmar, August Friedrich Christian. Geschichte der deutschen National-Literatur. 8e verm. Aufl. Marburg, 1860. 2 v. 12°.

Vilmorin-Andrieux (Pierre Philippe André Lévêque de) **et Cie.** Instructions pour les semis de fleurs de pleine terre, avec l'indication de leur couleur, culture, *etc.* 2e éd. Paris, 1851. 24°.

Viña del Señor, La; auto sacramental alegorico, por P. Calderon de la Barca. (*In* **Ochoa,** E. de. Tesoro del teatro esp., v. 3. 1838.)

Vinal, Wm. Sermon on the accursed thing that hinders success in war. Newport, 1755. 4°. (**B 653**)

Vinall, John. Preceptor's assistant; or, Student's guide; a treatise on arithmetic. Boston, 1792. 12°.

— Experiments in electricity. (*In* **Amer. Acad.** Mem., v. 2. 1793.)

Vinayma, Vicente. Hydrologia, o Tratado de las aguas ferrugineas de Tortosa. Valencia, 1738. 16°.

Vince, *Rev.* Samuel. Astronomical introduction to Pinkerton's Modern geography. London, 1802. 2 v. 4°.

— Complete system of astronomy. 2d ed. London, 1814-23. 3 v. 4°.

— Confutation of atheism, from the laws and the constitution of the heavenly bodies; four discourses. Camb., 1807. 8°. (**B 750**)

— Credibility of the Scriptural miracles vindicated, in answer to Mr. Hume; two discourses. 2d ed. Camb., 1809. 8°. (**B 750**)

— Elements of astronomy for students in the university. 2d ed. Camb., 1801. 8°.

— Elements of the conic sections; adapted to the use of students in philosophy. 3d ed. Camb., 1805. 8°.

— Plan of lectures on principles of natural philosophy. Camb., 1793. 8°.

— Principles of fluxions. 2d ed. Camb., 1800. 8°.

— Principles of hydrostatics; 3d ed. Camb., 1806. 8°.

— Treatise on plane and spherical trigonometry; with introd. on logarithms. 2d ed. Camb., 1805. 8°.

— Treatise on practical astron. Camb., 1790. 4°.

Vincens, Marie Antoine Emile. Sociétés par actions. — Des banques en France. Paris, 1837. 8°. (**B 1135**)

Vincent *Levita, St.* Resende, L. A. Vita Vincentii Levitæ et martyris. (*In his* De antiq. Lusit., v. 1. 1790.)

Vincent, Alexandre Joseph Hidulphe. Sur div. mss. grecs rel. à la musique. (Vol. 16, 2e pt. *of* **Paris. Inst.** *Ac. d. Inscr.* Not. 1847.) — Extraits des mss. rel. à la géométrie pratique des Grecs. (*In* v. 19, 2e pt.) — Le calendrier des Lagides à l'occas. de la découverte du décret de Canope. (*In* v. 26, 2e pt. 1870.)

Vincent, Benjamin. Supplement to Haydn's Dictionary of dates, 1868-70. London, 1871. 8°.

Vincent, Charles. Les dernières échoppes. (*In* **Paris** guide, v. 2. 1867.)

— Le tueur de brigands. 1859. *See* **David,** R. G.

Vincent, Francis. History of Delaware, from its settlement; with a description of its geography and geology. Vol. 1. Phila., 1870. 8°.

Vincent, Jean Claude Marie, *seigueur de Gournay.* Turgot, A. R. J. Eloge de M. de Gournay. (*In his* Œuvres, v. 3. 1808.)

Vincent, John Painter. Observations on surgical practice. London, 1847. 8°.

Vincent, Nathaniel. Day of grace. Boston, 1728. 18°.

— Spirit of prayer. Boston, 1702. 18°.

Vincent, *Admiral* Nicholas. Redding, C. (*In his* Personal reminiscences, v. 3. 1867.)

Vincent, *Rev.* Philip. History of the Pequot war. (*In* **Mass. Hist. Soc.** Col., v. 26. 1837.) — Hunter, J. Biog. notice of V. (*In* v. 31. 1852.)

Vincent, Strong. Swan, W. W. Biog. of V. (*In* **Higginson,** T. W. Harvard memorial biog., v. 2. 1866.)

Vincent, Thomas. Christ's certain appearance to judgment. Greenfield, 1816. 12°.

— A companion for communicants; with The sufferings of Christ, by T. Doolittel, and The Christian at the table of the Lord, by J. Earle. Boston, 1735. 12°. (**D 8**)

— Explicatory catechism; explanation of the Assembly's shorter catechism. Northampton, 1805. 12°.

— True Christian's love of the unseen Christ. *t.p.w.* [17—.] 12°.

Vincent, Wm., *D.D., Dean of Westminster.* Commerce and navigation of the ancients in the Indian Ocean. London, 1807. 2 v. 4°.

Contents. Vol. 1. The voyage of Nearchus from the Indus to the Euphrates; collected from Arrian, with illustrations. 2. The Periplus of the Erythrean Sea; with dissertations.

— Defence of public education. 2d ed. London, 1802. 8°. (**B 1410**)

— *Same.* 3d ed. London, 1802. 8°. (**B 1409**)

— Periplus of the Erythrean Sea. Pts. 1 and 2. London, 1800-05. 2 v. 4°.

Contents. Vol. 1. Navigation of the ancients, from the Sea of Suez to the coast of Zanguebar. 2. Navigation of the ancients from the Gulph of Elena, in the Red Sea, to the island of Ceylon.

— Sermon before the House of Commons, June 1, general thanksgiving. London, 1802. 4°. (**A 20, B 1252**)

— Sermon, Westminster, May 13, 1792. 2d ed. London, 1793. 8°. (**B 1858**)

— Remarks on [his] 'Defence of public education'. London, 1802. 8°. (**B 1862**)

Vincent, Wm., *pseud.* Plain narrative, — Trial of G. Gordon. *See* **Holcroft,** T.

Vincent de Beauvais. Figuier, L. (*In his* Vies des savants illustres du Moyen Age. 1867.)

Vincent de Paul, *St.* Abelli, L. Vie de V.; suivie de la vie de R. Alméras. Paris, 1839. 2 v. 8°.

— Feillet, A. La misère au temps de la Fronde et Saint Vincent de Paul. Nouv. éd. Paris, 1862. 12°.

Vincenti, Domenico. Amato, G. d'. (*In his* Panteon, v. 2. 1851.)

Vincentini, Girolamo. Vita di L. Mattei. (*In* **Crescimbeni,** G. M. Vite, v. 2. 1710.)

Vincentius *or* **Madelgarius,** *St.* Vita S. Vincentii. (*In* **Acta** sanct., v. 30. 1867.)

Vincentius, *archidiac. Cæsaraugustanus, St.* Aimoinus *monachus S. Germani.* Historia translationis S. V. — Stephanus *Ulyssipponensis.* Miracula S. V. (*In* **Acta** sanct., v. 3. 1863.)

Vincentius, *St., of Valentia.* Actas. — Augustinus, *St.* Sermones en su fiesta. — Vida. (*In* **Florez,** H. España sagrada, v. 8. 1752.)

Vincentius *of Cesena.* De Rubicone antiquo. (*In* **Grævius.** Thes. antiq. Ital., v. 7, pt. 2. 1722.)

Vincentius *of Prague.* Chronicon Boemorum, 1140-67. (*In* **Vienna. Ak. d. Wiss.** Font. rerum Austr., Abth. 1., B 5. 1863; — *and in* **Pertz,** G. H. Mon. Germ. hist., Scr., v. 17. 1861.)

Vincentius, Athanasius, *pseud. See* **Lyser,** J.

Vincenza. Tommaseo, N. D'una sconfitta rammentata nel IX canto del Paradiso di Dante. (*In* **Archivio** stor. ital., ser. 3, v. 12, pt. 2. 1870.)

Vincenzo; or, Sunken rocks; by J. Ruffini. London, 1863. 3 v. 8°.

— *Same.* (*In* **Macmillan's** mag., v. 6-9. 1862-64.)

Vinci, Leonardo da. Head of the Virgin. London, *Arundel Society,* 1859.

— Del moto e misura dell' acqua. Bologna, 1828. 4°.

— Trattato della pittura. Milano, 1804. 4°.

— *French.* Traitè de la peinture. Nouv. éd. Paris, 1803. 8°.

— Virgin and child, with portrait of the donor; chromolith. after the fresco in the Monastery of St. Onofrio at Rome. London, *Arundel Soc.,* 1859.

— Adda, G. d'. L. de' Vinci. (*In* **Gazette** des beaux-arts, v. 25. 1868.)

— Bossi, G. Del cenacolo di L. da Vinci. Milano, 1810. 4°.

— Brown, J. W. Life of L. da Vinci. London, 1828. 12°.
— Campori, G. Nouveaux documents biog. rel. à V. (*In* Gazette des beaux-arts, v. 20. 1866.)
— Dumas, A. (*In his* Italiens et Flamands, v. 1. 1862.)
— Imitations of orig. designs by L. da Vinci. London, 1796. f°.
— Kellogg, M. K. Documents rel. to a picture by V. entitled 'Herodias'. London, 1864. 4°.
— Knox, R. (*In his* Great artists. 1852.)
— Planche, G. (*In* Revue d. D. Mondes, sept. 1850.) — Clément, C. (*In* av. 1860.)
— Saunders, J. Christ's last supper; [description of Da Vinci's painting]. Boston, 1834. 8°. (B 1768)

Vinciguerra, Marco Antonio. Satira. (*In* **Raccolta** di poesie satiriche. 1808.)

Vincioli, Giacinto. Vita di S. Sperelli. (*In* **Crescimbeni**, G. M. Vite degli Arcadi illustri, v. 3. 1714.)

Vindex, *pseud.* The honest politician. Pt. 1. Balt., 1808. 8°. (B 406)

Vindex, *pseud.* Observations on the present national distress. (*In* **Pamphleteer**, 1820; v. 17 of B 838) — Postscript to Observations on the present agricultural and national distress. (*In* 1823; v. 21.)

Vindication of 'A brief account of many of the prosecutions of Quakers, by J. Besse'; added, Remarks on 'The poor vicar's plea'. London, 1737. 8°. (C 283)

Vindication of a disc. by [Stillingfleet on] the unreasonableness of a new separation. Lond., 1691. 4°. (B 4)

Vindication of an Association from the charge of countenancing heresy. Portsmouth, 1758. 8°. (B 45)

Vindication of an undertaking [to suppress] debauchery and profaneness; [by E. Fowler]. London, 1692. 4°. (B 1398)

Vindication of the answer [Bp. Williams] to the Popish address presented to the ministers of the Church of England. London, 1788. 4°. (B 1397)

Vindication of Christ's holy Catholic Church against the attempts of a dissenting gentleman; by a presbyter of the Ch. of England. London, 1747. 8°.

Vindication of Doctor W. Find; in answer to the misrepresentation of the author of the 'Second defense of the rights'. (*In* **Oldisworth**, W. Dialogue, v. 3. 1711.)

Vindication of E. Burke's 'Reflections on the Revolution in France'. London, 1791. 8°. (B 634, 1407)

Vindication of Gen. R. Smith; [by J. Pierce]. London, 1783. 8°.

Vindication of Mr. Adams's Oration; [by J. B. Moore]. Concord, 1821. 8°. (B 557)

Vindication of Mr. Randolph's resignation. Phila., 1795. 8°. (B 479, 741, 1850, 2526, W 28)

Vindication of natural society; [by E. Burke]. (*In* **Dodsley**, R. Fugitive pieces, v. 2. 1761.)

Vindication of Presbyterian ordination; by [J. **Hartley**]. Nottingham, 1714. 8°. (B 106)

Vindication of Sir T. Player; reply to an answer to [his] speech. *n.t.p.* [16—.] f°. (A 50)

Vindication of speaking openly in favour of the divine unity. Taunton, 1790. 12°. (C 82)

Vindication of the Bp. of Landaff's sermon from the misrepresentations in W. Livingston's letter to his lordship. N. Y., 1768. 8°. (B 269)

Vindication of the Bp. of London's pastoral letter. Lond., 1729. 8°. (B 115)

Vindication of the British colonies against the aspersions of the Halifax gentleman; [by J. Otis]. Boston, 1765. 8°. (B 626)
— *Same.* Boston, *printed*, London, *reprinted* 1769. 8°. (B 378, 391)

Vindication of the character of Adams, in reply to the letter of Hamilton. N. Y., 1800. 8°. (B 1701, 1838, 1850)

Vindication of the convention between Gr. Britain and Russia. 3d ed. London, 1801. 8°. (B 781)

Vindication of the divine authority of ruling elders. (*In* **White**, J. New England's lamentations. 1734. B 665)

Vindication of the Hindoos from the aspersions of C. Buchanan, *etc.* London, 1808. 8°. (B 679, 1845)
— *Same.* Pt. 2: In reply to the Christian observer, Mr. Fuller, *etc.* London, 1808. 8°. (B 1845)
— Fuller, A. Remarks on 'A vindication'. (*In his* Apology. 1808.)

Vindication of the laws limiting the rate of interest on loans from the objections of J. Bentham and the Edinburgh reviewers. Richmond, 1820. 12°.

Vindication of the 'Letter out of the North' conc. Bp. Lake's declaration of his dying in the belief of passive obedience; in answer to [Milner's] 'Defence'. London, 1690. 4°. (B 4)

Vindication of the ministers of Boston [for their advocacy of inoculation]. Boston, 1722. 8°. (C 70)

Vindication of the present M·····y from the clamours rais'd against them upon occasion of the new preliminaries. London, 1711. 8°. (B 589)

Vindication of the rights of men, in a letter to Burke occas. by his 'Reflections on the Revolution in France'. London, 1790. 8°.

Vindication of the subscribing ministers in answer to an 'Authentic account'. London, 1719. 8°. (B 1865)
— Reply to the 'Vindication'. London, 1719. 8°. (B 1865)
— – Second part of a 'Reply'. London, 1719. 8°. (B 1865)

Vindication of their majesties' authority to fill the sees of the deprived bishops. London, 1691. 4°. (B 4)

Vindication of those who have taken the new oath of allegiance to William and Mary. London, 1689. 4°. (B 6)

Vindicator vindicated, The; or, A sur-rejoynder on behalf of Sir T. Player, against H. B.'s Answer in defence of a 'Reply'. *n.t.p.* [16—.] f°. (A 50)

Vinding (*Lat.* **Vindingius**), Rasmus. Hellen in quo antiquæ Græciæ populorum incunabula et res præcipuæ gesta exponuntur. (*In* **Gronovius**, J. Thes. Græc. antiq., v. 11. 1701.)

Vine, Vineyards. Soderini, G. V. Trattato della coltivazione delle viti, *ec.* [1600.] Milano, *Soc. Tipog. Class. Ital.*, 1806. 8°.
— Bidet, N. Traité sur la culture de la vigne, *etc.* [1752.] 2e éd., rev. par H. L. du Hamil du Monceau. Paris, 1759. 2 v. 12°.
— St. Pierre, L. de. Art of planting the vine, making wines, *etc.* London, 1772. 12°.
— Botelho de Lacerdo Lobo, C. Sobre a cultura das vinhas de Portugal. (*In* **Lisbon. Ac. d. Sci.** Mem. econ., v. 1. 1790.)
— Johnson, S. W. Culture of the vine. (*In his* Rural economy. 1806.)
— Influence of climate on the cultivation of the vine. (*In* **Essay** on the climate of the U. S. 1809. B 436)
— Prince, W. R. *and* W. Treatise on the vine. N. Y., 1830. 8°.
— Fisher, S. I. Obs. on the European vine; added, manual of the Swiss vigneron, by Brun Chappuis, and the art of wine making by Bulos. Phila., 1834. 12°.
— Hoare, C. Practical treatise on the cultivation of the grape vine on open walls. [1834.] Boston, 1837. 8°.
— Payen, A. La viticulture et la maladie de la vigne. (*In* **Revue** d. D. Mondes, sept. 1856.)
— Swallow, G. C. Grape culture in Missouri. (*In* **Amer. Assoc.** Proc., v. 12. 1859.)
— Guyot, J. Culture de la vigne et vinification. [1860.] 2e éd. Paris, 1861. 12°.
— Payen, A. La vigne. (*In* **Revue** d. D. Mondes, juin, juil. 1860.)
— Redding, C. French wines and vineyards. London, 1860. 8°.
— Lavergne, L. G. L. G. de. La vigne en France. (*In* **Revue** d. D. Mondes, déc. 1862.)
— Shaw, T. G. Wine, the vine and the cellar. London, 1863. 8°.
— Denman, J. L. The vine and its fruit; more especially in rel. to the production of wine. London, 1864. 8°.
— Radau, R. Les maladies des vins. (*In* **Revue** d. D. Mondes, déc. 1866.)
— Mead, P. B. Elementary treatise on American grape culture. N. Y., 1867. 8°.
— Wilder, M. P., *and others.* Culture and products of the vine. (*In* **U. S.** *Commissioners for Paris Expos.*, 1867. Reports, v. 5.)
— Du Camp, M. Le pain, la viande, et la vin. (*In* **Revue** d. D. Mondes, juin 1868.)
— Flagg, W. J. Three seasons in European vineyards; vine culture, *etc.* N. Y., 1869. 8°.
— Liebert, E. Une nouvelle maladie de la vigne. (*In* **Revue** d. D. Mondes, déc. 1869.)

See also **Wine.**

Vineland weekly, July 31, 1869. Vineland, N. J., 1869. f°. (E 194)

Vines, E. C., *D.D.* Prison discipline. (*In* **Nat. Assoc. Prom. Soc. Sci.** Trans., 1863.)

Vinesalvus, de Vinosalvo (*Fr.* Vinisauf), Galfridus. *See* **Galfridus** *de Vinosalvo.*

Vinet, Alexandre Rodolphe. Chrestomathie française, ou Choix de morceaux tirés des meilleurs écrivains français. (Vol. 1, 2, 3e éd., 3, 2e éd.) Bâle, 1838, 40, 36. 3 v. 8°.

— SAINT RENÉ TAILLANDIER, G. E. (*In* **Revue** d. D. Mondes, jan. 1864.) — LIEBERT, E. (*In* mai 1868.)

— SAINTE-BEUVE, C. A. (*In his* Port. cont., v. 2. 1852; — *and in* **Revue** d. D. Mondes, sept. 1837.)

Vinet, Elie. Scholia in Sphæram Johannis de Sacro Bosco. (*In* **Sacro Busto,** J. de. De sphæra. 1577.)

— NICERON, J. P. (*In his* Mém., v. 30. 1734.)

Vingt ans après; par A. Dumas [A. Maquet]. Paris, 1853. 3 v. 8°.

— *Same.* Nouv. éd. Paris, 1863. 8°.

Note. A continuation of 'Les trois mousquetaires'; continued by 'Le vicomte de Bragelonne'.

Vingt-quatre février, Le; drame par **A. Dumas.** (*In his* Théâtre, v. 11. 1865.)

Vingtain, Léon. Vie publique de Royer-Collard. Paris, 1858. 18°.

Vingut, Gertrude (Fairfield) de. Irene; or, The autobiography of an artist's daughter. Boston, 1859. 8°.

Contents. Vice president's daughter. — Wife of two husbands. — Irene.

Vining, Ebenezer. Funeral sermon at the interment of M. Pierce, of Chesterfield. Conway, 1798. 12°. (B 1222)

Vining, John. Eulogium [on] Washington, Feb. 22. Phila., 1800. 8°. (E 61, W 52)

Vinisauf, Geoffrey de. *See* **Galfridus** *de Vinosalvo.*

Vink, —. Voyage to Australasia, 1663. (*In* **Callander, J.** Terra Austr., v. 2. 1768.)

Vinland. CARMEN Faeröicum in quo Vinlandiæ mentio fit. — ADAM *Bremensis.* Relatio de Vinlandia. (*In* **Copenhagen. K. Nord. Olds. Selsk.** Antiquitates Amer. 1837.) — RAFN, C. C. Astronomical evidences for the site of the chief settlement of the ancient Scandinavians in America. (*In* Mém., 1840-44.)

Vinné, Daniel de. The Methodist Episcopal Church and slavery. N. Y., 1857. 8°. (B 1472)

Vinnius, Arnold. In IV. libros institutionum imperialium commentarius. Ed. 3a. Amst., 1659. 4°.

Vinton, Alexander Hamilton, *D.D.* Farewell sermon, Boston, Oct. 3. Boston, 1858. 8°. (B 1304)

— Life a vapor, sermon, Boston, Jan. 2. Boston, 1853. 8°. (B 1304)

— The translation of Elijah; sermon, decease of Rev. Wm. Croswell. Boston, 1851. 8°. (B 1212)

Vinton, Francis, *D.D.* Fanaticism rebuked. (*In* **Fast** day sermons. 1861.)

— Loyalty and piety; thanksgiving discourse, Newport, R. I., July 21. Prov., 1842. 8°. (B 1254)

— Oration on the annals of R. I. and Providence plantations, and a rhyme on R. I. and the times by G. W. Curtis, before the Sons of R. I. in New York, May 29. N.Y., 1863. 8°.

— The philosophy of the war; or, The cause and cure of the rebellion; sermon, 224th anniv. of the Anc. and Hon. Artillery Co. (*In* **Boston. Anc. and Hon. Artillery.** Proc., 1862.)

Vinton, *Rev.* John Adams. Genealogical sketches of the descendants of J. Vinton of Lynn, 1648. Boston, 1858. 8°.

— Giles memorial. Boston, 1864. 8°.

Contents. Genealogical memoirs of the families of Giles, — Gould, — Holmes, — Jennison, — Leonard, — Lindall, — Curwen, — Marshall, — Robinson, — Sampson, — Webb, — Pool, — Very, — Tarr. — History of Pemaquid, ancient and modern.

Vinton, Samuel Finley. Northeastern boundary of Wisconsin. (*In* **Wisconsin Hist. Soc.** Col., v. 4. 1859.)

— Speech on the bill to admit Iowa and Florida into the Union, Feb. 11. Wash., 1845. 8°. (B 1197, 1501)

— Speech on the loan bill, Feb. 8. Wash., 1848. 8°. (B 1502)

— Speech, Sept., 17. 1832. Gallipolis, 1832. 8°. (B 1102)

Vintzenried, ou Mémoires du chevalier de Courtille; par F. A. Doppet. Paris, 1789. 12°.

404. (13. 9. 81.)

Viola, Miguel Navarro. *See* **Revista** de Buenos Aires, La.

Viola, Pietro. De veterum novaque Romanorum temporum ratione libellus. (*In* **Grævius,** J. G. Thes. antiq. Rom., v. 8. 1698.)

Viola; by E. Maturin. (*In* **Sargent,** E. Mod. stand. dr., v. 26.)

Violet, *Monsieur, pseud.* Travels and adventures in California, Sonora, *etc.* *See* **Marryat,** F.

Violette, J. M. Henri. Guide pratique de la fabrication des vernis. Paris, [18—]. 18°.

— *and* **Archambault,** P. J. Dictionnaire des analyses chimiques. 2d tir. Paris, 1860. 2 v. 8°.

Violin. COMPLEAT tutor for the violin. London, [17—]. 8°. (W 26)

— INSTRUCTION for the violin. *n.t.p.* [18—.] obl. 8°.

— SANDYS, W., *and* FOSTER, S. A. History of the violin; and of other instruments played with a bow. London, **1864.** 8°.

Viollet-le-Duc, Emmanuel Louis Nicolas. Catalogue des livres composant la bibliothèque poétique de V. Paris, 1847. 8°.

Viollet le Duc, Eugène Emmanuel. Dictionnaire de l'architecture française du 11e au 16e siècle. Paris, 1858-68. 10 v. 18°.

Contents. Vol. 1. A - Aro. 2. Arts - Chap. 3. Char - Conso. 4. Const - Cy. 5. D - F. 6. G - O. 7. P. 8. Q - S. 9. T - Z. 10. Table analytique.

— Dictionnaire raisonné du mobilier français de l'époque carlovingienne à la Renaissance. Paris, 1858-75. 6 v. 8°.

Contents. Vol. 1. Meubles. 2. Ustensils. 3. Vêtements, bijoux, *etc.*: A - H. 4. J - V. 5. Armes de guerre: A - G. 6. H - Z.

— Les églises de Paris. (*In* **Paris** guide, v. 1. 1867.)

— Entretiens sur l'architecture. Tom. 1. Paris, 1863. 8° *and* Atlas obl. f°.

— Essay on military architecture of the Middle Ages; tr. by M. Macdermott. Oxford, London, 1860. 8°.

— Matériel des travaux du génie civil et de l'architecture. (*In* **France.** *Com. Imp. de l'Expos. de* 1867. Rapport, v. 10.)

— La nouvelle sacristie. (*In* **Monographie** de Notre Dame. 1857.)

— *and* **Corroyer,** E. *See* **Gazette** des architectes et du bâtiment. 1863-67.

— SAINTE BEUVE, C. A. Catalogue de la bibliothèque de Viollet le Duc. (*In* **Revue** d. D. Mondes, juil. 1843.)

Vioux, *France.* **Eglise de St. Eugène.** LA PORTE DU THEIL, F. J. G. Notice historique. (*In* **Paris. Inst.** *Ac. d. Inscr.* Not., v. 4. 1779.)

Viperano, Giovanni Antonio. NICERON, J. P. (*In his* Mém., v. 25. 1734.)

Vipers. REDI, F. Osserv. int. alle vipere. (*In his* Opere, v. 2. 1742.)

Vique, *Spain.* *See* **Vich.**

Virbius. UHDEN. Virbius und Hippolytus in antiken Werken der bildenden Kunst. (*In* **Berlin. Ak. d. Wiss.** Abh., 1818-19.)

Virbluneau, Scalion de, *sieur d'Ofayel.* GAUTIER, T. (*In his* Les grotesques. 1856.)

Virchow, Rudolf. Cellular pathology as based upon physiol. and pathol. histology; tr. by F. Chance. London, 1860. 8°.

— Handbuch der speciellen Pathologie und Therapie. 5e Band, 1e Abth., 4e. 5e Lief, 5e Band, 2e Abth., 2e Hälfte. Erlangen, 1865, 61. 3 nos. 8°.

Contents. Vol. 5, pt. 1. **Biermer,** A. Krankheiten der Bronchien und des Lungen-Parenchyms. 5, pt. 2. **Friedreich,** N. Krankheiten des Herzens.

— Du typhus famélique et de quelques maladies voisines; tr. de l'allemand par H. Hallopeau. Paris, 1868. 8°. (E 26)

Viret, —. IVERNOIS, *Sir* F. d'. Innocence d'un magistrat accusé de vol. Londres, 1787. 8°. (B 684)

Viret, Pierre. NICERON, J. P. (*In his* Mém., v. 35. 1736.)

Virey, Julien Joseph. L'art de perfectionner l'homme. Paris, 1809. 2 v. 8°.

— Histoire naturelle du genre humain. Paris, 1824. 3 v. 8°.

Virey, Der, und die Aristokraten, oder Mexico im Jahre 1812; von C. **Sealsfield.** (*In his* Gesam. Werke, v. 4-6. 1846.)

Virgander, David Magnus. Frutetum Svecicum. (*In* **Linné,** C. Amœn. acad., v. 5. 1760.)

Virgilius. (*In* **Thoms,** W. J. Early Eng. prose romances, v. 2. 1858.)

Vigilius *Juvanensis.* Vita et miracula. (*In* **Pertz,** G. H. Mon. Germ. hist., Scr., v. 11. 1854.)

Virgilius, Polydorus. *See* **Vergilio, P.**

Virgilius (*or* **Vergilius**) **Maro, Publius.** Opera; acc. Virgilii aliorumque opuscula. *t.p.w.* [Antwerp., *Plantinus,* 1565.] 8°.

— Opera; per J. Ogilvium ed. Lond., 1663. f°.

— Opera; cum annot. J. Minellii. Roterodami, 1681. 12°.

— Opera; interp. et notis illust. C. Ruæus ad usum Delphini. Londini, 1727. 8°.

— *Same.* Ed. 3a. Phila., 1822. 8°.

— Codex antiquissimus a R. T. Aproniano distinctus, *etc.*, typis descriptus. Florentiæ, *typis Mannianis,* 1741. 4°.

— Opera; cum commentariis Servii, Philargyrii, Pierii; acc. Fulvii Ursini et al. ac præcipue N. Heinsii notæ, quibus animad. et var. in Servium lect. add. P. Burmannus junior. Amst., 1746. 4 v. 4°.

Contents. Vol. 1. Historia descripta per consules a Ruæo. — Bucolica. — Georgica. 2. Æneidos lib. I-V. 3. VI-XI. 4. XII. — Culex. — Ciris. — Catalecta. — Fragm. ex epistola quam Augustum Cæsarem super Æneide sua scripsit. — Pierii epistola. — J. P. Valeriani castigationes in Bucolica, — lib. Æneidos. — Index.

— Opera; [ed. J. Pine]. Vol. 1. Londini, 1755. 8°.

Contents. Virgilii historia descripta per consules a C. Ruæo. — Eclogæ. — Georgica.

— Opera; ex antiquis monimentis illustr. cura H. Justice. Vol. 1. [Hag. Com., 1757.] 8°.

Contents. Vol. 1. Bucolica. — Georgica.

— Bucolica, Georgica, et Æneis ab A. Ambrogi Ital. versu red. annot. atque var. lect. [Lat. et Ital.] Romæ, 1763-65. 3 v. f°.

Contents. Vol. 1. Bucolicon. — Georgicon. 2. Æneidos lib. I-VI. 3. VII-XII.

— Bucolica, Georgica, et Æneis. Birminghamiæ, *Baskerville,* 1766. 8°.

— Opera; ex recens. et cum animadv. P. Burmanni. Lps., 1774. 2 v. 8°.

Contents. Vol. 1. Vita. — Bucolica. — Georgica. — Æneidos lib. I-V. 2. VI-XII. — Culex. — Ciris. — Catalecta.

— P. Virgilius; var. lect. et adnot. illust. a C. G. Heyne. Ed. novis. auct. Lps., 1800. 6 v. 8°.

Contents. Vol. 1. Bucolica. — Georgica. 2. Æneidos lib. I-IV. 3. V-VIII. 4. IX-XII. 5. Culex. — Ciris. — Catalecta. — Copa. — Moretum. — Testimonia de V. — De vita Virgilii. — De codicibus et editionibus. 6. Index.

— Opera; cura J. Hunter. [2a ed.] Cupri Fifan., 1810. 2 v. 16°.

Contents. Vol. 1. Bucolica. — Georgicon. — Æneidos I-IV. 2. V-XII.

— P. Virgilius Maro qualem tertio publ. C. G. Heyne, cui Servium et var. not. cum suis subj. N. E. Lemaire. Parisiis, 1819-22. 8 v. 8°. (Lemaire. Bibl. class. Lat.)

Contents. Vol. 1. Præfationes. — Bucolica. — Georgica. 2. Disquisitio de carmine epico Virgiliano, — de rerum in Æneide inventione. — Æneidos lib. I-IV. 3. V-VIII. 4. IX-XII. — Dialogus inter Italianum philologum et editorem. — M. Vegii carmen. — De natura Æneidos auct. C. Ruæo. — De natura poematis epici. 5. Culex. — Ciris. — Catalecta. — Copa. — Moretum. — Comm. sel. e Servio, Donato, *etc.*, in Ecloga et Georgicon. 6. Comm., *etc.*, in Æneidos lib. I-VIII. 7. IX-XII. — Vita, editiones, et versiones. — Extrait du cours de poésie latin de Lemaire sur Virgil. 8. Indices.

— Opera; ed. by J. H. Jaeck. Vinariæ, 1826. 12°.

— Publius Virgilius Maro; var. lect. et adnot. illustratus a C. G. Heyne. Ed. 4a, cur. G. P. E. Wagner. Lps., 1830-33, 32, 31. 5 v. 8°.

Contents. Vol. 1. Præf. — Bucolica. — Georgica. 2. Disquisitio de carmine epico Virgiliano, — de rerum in Æneide inventione. — Æneidos lib. I-VI. 3. VII-XII. 4. Culex. — Ciris. — Catalecta. — P. Wagneri quæstiones Virgilianæ. — De codicibus et editionibus. 5. Carmina ad pristinam orthographiam revocata; ed. P. Wagner: Bucolica; — Georgica; — Æneis. — Orthographia Vergiliana. — Index in Heynii notas et comm. — Conspectus eorum quæ hac ed. continentur.

— Opera; works with notes, *etc.*, for students by J. G. Cooper. 9th ster. ed. N. Y., 1838. 8°.

— Gedichte; erklært von T. Ladewig. (Bd. 1, 3, 2e Aufl., 2, 3e Aufl.) Berlin, 1855-57, 55. 3 v. 8°.

Contents. Vol. 1. Bucolica. — Georgica. 2. Æneide, Buch I-VI. 3. VII-XII.

— Opera; with a commentary, by J. Conington. London, 1858-71. 3 v. 8°. (Long and Macleane's Bibl. class.)

Contents. Vol. 1. Life. — Eclogues. — On the later bucolic poets of Rome. — Georgics. — Later didactic poets of Rome. 2. Æneid I-VI. 3. VII-XII. — On Ribbeck's Prolegomena critica.

— *Eng.* Works; tr. by J. Ogilby. 3d ed. London, 1675. 8°.

— - Works; tr. by J. Trapp. 4th ed. London, 1755. 3 v. 12°.

Contents. Vol. 1. Pref. to the Æneis. — Eclogues. — Georgicks. 2. Æneis, I-VI. 3. VII-XII.

— - Works; the Æneid, tr. by C. Pitt, Eclogues, *etc.*, by J. Warton. London, 1763. 4 v. 12°.

Contents. Vol. 1. Life. — Diss. on pastoral poetry. — Eclogues. — Georgics. — Reflections on didactic poetry. 2. Æneid I-IV. — Diss. on the nature and conduct of the Æneid. 3. Diss. on the sixth book by Warburton. — V-VIII. — Obs. on the shield of Æneas, by W. Whitehead. 4. IX-XII. — Reflections on the character of Iapis, by Dr. Atterbury.

— - Works; tr. by Dryden. (*In* **Anderson,** R. Brit. poets, v. 12. 1795.)

— - *Same.* Pastorals. (*In* **Dryden,** J. Works, v. 13. 1808.) — Georgics. — Æneis, I-VII. (*In* v. 14.) — VIII-XII. (*In* 15.)

— - Works; tr. by Kennedy. London, 1849. 2 v. 8°.

Note. The first four pastorals, the Georgics, and the first four Æneids are trans. by R. Kennedy; the last six pastorals and last eight Æneids by C. R. Kennedy.

Contents. Vol. 1. Life. — On pastoral and didactic poetry; by R. Kennedy. — Pastorals. — Georgics. — Æneid I-IV. 2. V-XII. — Appendices.

— - Works; tr. with notes by Davidson. New ed., rev. by T. A. Buckley. London, *Bohn,* 1850. 8°.

— *Ital.* *See, above,* 'Bucolica'. 1763.

Commentaries, etc.

— Bruni Aretino, L. Invectiva in Carolum Malatestam propter derogationem statuæ in memoriam Maronis. (*In* **Schelhorn,** J. G. Amœn. lit., v. 3. 1730.)

— Chasles, V. E. P. Quelques mots sur Virgile. — Les loisirs de Virgile. (*In his* Etudes sur l'antiquité. 1847.)

— Collins, W. L. Virgil. Phila., 1871 [1870]. 16°.

— Gibbon, E. Remarques sur quelques endroits de Virgile. — Remarques crit. sur un passage de V. (*In his* Miscel. works, v. 3. 1815.)

— Henley, S. Observations on the subject of the fourth Eclogue, the allegory in the third Georgic and the primary design of the Æneid of Virgil, *etc.* London, 1788. 8°.

— Holdsworth, E. Remarks and dissertations on Virgil. London, 1768. 4°.

— Interpretes veteres. (*In* **Mai,** A. Class. auct., v. 7. 1835.)

— MACROBIUS. Saturnalia, lib. III–VI. (*In his* Opera. 1774; *and, French,* Œuvres. 1845.)
— MELANCHTHON, P. Enarratio operum Virgilii. (*In his* Opera, v. 19. 1834.)
— MISCELLANEA Virgiliana in scriptis erud. virorum. Camb., 1825. 8°.
Contents. Spence, J. Political character of Æneid. — Holdsworth, E. Observations on the four Georgics and first six books of the Æneid. — Warburton, W., *Bp.* Examination of Æneid VI. — Jortin, J. Obs. on V.
— ORSINI, F. Virgilius ex collatione script. Græc. illust. Leovardii., 1747. 8°.
— PERTZ, G. H. Ueber die berliner und die vaticanischen Blätter der ältesten Handschrift des Virgil. (*In* Berlin. Ak. d. Wiss. Abh., 1863.)
— SPERONI, S. Dialogi sopra Virgilio. (*In his* Opere, v. 2. 1740.) Principio del libro secondo della Eneida. — Discorsi sopra Virgilio. (*In* v. 4.)
— TOMMASEO, N. Concetto storico, civile, e morale della poesia di Virgilio. (*In* Archivio stor. ital., ser. 3, pt. 3, v. 13. 1871.)

Æneis.

— Libri Æneidos; notis, *etc.*, illust. I. L. de la Cerda. Lugd., 1612–19. 2 v. f°.
Contents. Vol. 1. I–VI. 2. VII–XII. — Indices.
— Æneidis lib. XII notis illust. studio E. de Bulgaris. [Lat. et Gr.] Petrop., 1791–92. 3 v. f°.
Contents. Vol. 1. I–IV. 2. V–VIII. 3. IX–XIII.
— L'Enéide; tr. par J. Delille. [En lat. et en français.] Paris, 1804. 4 v. 8°.
Contents. Vol. 1. I–III. 2. IV–VI. 3. VII–IX. 4. X–XII.
— *Same.* (Vol. 3–6 *of* Delille, J. Œuvres. 1824.)
— Traduction du 4e livre de l'Enéide en un poëme intit. Didon; avec le latin en regard. (*In* Turgot, A. R. J. Œuvres, v. 9. 1810.)
— *Eng.* Æneid; tr. by J. Beresford. London, 1794. 4°.
— - Æneid; tr. by C. Pitt. (*In* Anderson, R. Brit. poets, v. 12. 1795.)
— - Æneid; tr. by Dryden. (*In* Chalmers, A. Eng. poets, v. 19. 1810.)
— - 2d and 4th books of V.'s Æneid; tr. into Eng. verse by the Earl of Surrey. (*In* Howard, H., *and* Wyatt, *Sir* T. Works, v. 1. 1815.)
— - Æneid; tr. into Eng. verse by J. Conington. London, 1866. 8°.
— - First book; tr. by G. Sandys. (*In* Ovidius. Metamorphoses. 1632?)
— - Specimen of a translation of lib. VI.; by W. Alexander. (*In* Afternoon lectures, 1869.)
— *French.* *See, above,* 'L'Enéide; tr. par Delille. 1804, 1824; — 'Traduction'. 1810.
— *Greek.* *See, above,* Æneidis lib. 1791–92.
— *Ital.* L'Eneide; ridotta dal sig. E. Udine. Venetia, 1607. 4°.
— - L'Eneide; tr. dal com. A. Caro. Milano, *Soc. Tipog. de' Class. Ital.*, 1812. 8°. (Caro, A. Opere, v. 8.)
— - L'Eneide; tr. da V. Alfieri. Italia, 1815. 4°. (Opere, v. 21, 22.)
Contents. Vol. 1. I–VI. VII–XII.
— - *Same.* Italia, 1821. 12°. (Opere, v. 10.)
— *Spanish.* Los quatro primeros libros de la Eneida; tr. in verso castellano. (*In* Iriarte, T. de. Col. de obras, v. 3. 1805.)

Commentaries, etc., on the Æneid.

— BEATTIE, J. Remarks on some passages of the sixth book. (*In* Roy. Soc. of Edin. Trans., v. 2. 1790.)
— BENI, P. Comparazione di Omero, Virgilio, e Torquato. (*In* Tasso, T. Opere, v. 8, 11. 1738; 21, 22. 1828.)
— BOISSIER, G. La religion romaine et la vie future dans Virgile. (*In* Revue d. D. Mondes, mars, juin 1873.)
— COMMENTARY mythological, *etc.*, on Pope's Homer and Dryden's Æneid of Virgil. London, 1829. 8°.
— COTTON, C. Scarronnides; or, Virgile travestie; a mock poem on the 1st and 4th books of Virgil's Ænæis, in English burlesque. 10th ed. (*In his* Genuine works. 1715.)
— DAVIES, J. Observations on the poems of Homer and Virgil; out of the French. London, 1672. 12°.
— GIBBON, E. (*In his* Miscel. works, v. 2. 1796.)
— GLADSTONE, W. E. Homer and his successors [Virgil and Tasso] in epic poetry. (*In* Quarterly rev., v. 101. 1857; — *and in his* Studies on Homer, v. 3. 1858.)
— LALLI, G. B. L'Eneide travestita. Venetia, 1635. 12°.
— LEMON, G. W. Voyage of Æneas from Troy to Italy. (*In* Spelman, E. Additional obs. of the Greek accents, *etc.* 1773.)
— MONGEZ, A. La lecture du 6e livre de l'Enéide faite par Virgile devant Auguste et Octavie. (*In* Paris. Inst. *Ac. d. Inscr.* Mém., v. 7. 1824.)
— MONTIGNOT, H. Rapports de l'Enéide avec l'Iliade et l'Odyssée. (*In* Sérieys, A. Bibl. acad., v. 8. 1811.)
— POPE, A. Comparison between the games of Homer and Virgil. (*In* Homerus. Iliad, v. 5. 1806.)
— PARSING lessons to the first book of Virgil's Æneid. 5th ed. London, 1837. 12°.
— RAPIN, R. A comparison of Homer and Virgil. (*In his* Crit. works, v. 1. 1731.)
— SAINTE-BEUVE, C. A. Etude sur Virgile. Paris, 1857. 16°.
— VICAIRE, A. Plan de l'Enéide. Paris, 1787. 12°.

Bucolica.

— Bucolica] Les bucoliques; tr. par F. Didot. [En lat. et en français.] Paris, 1806. 8°.
— The pastorals; [in Latin; ed.] by R. J. Thornton. 3d ed. London, 1821. 2 v. 8°.
— *Eng.* Pastorals. (*In* Sedley, C. Works, v. 1. 1722.)
— - Pastoral songs; by J. M. Russell. Boston, 1799. 12°. (C 107)
— *French.* Les bucoliques; tr. et accomp. de notes par J. A. D[elille]. Paris, 1813. 8°.
— - Les bucoliques; tr. par C. H. Millevoye. (*In* Millevoye, C. H. Œuvres, v. 2. 1823.)
See also, above, 1st entry.
— *Spanish.* Egloga I, IV, tr. por G. H. de Velasco; III, V, VII, VIII, por L. de Leon, VI, IX, X, por C. de Mesa. (*In* Sedano, J. J. L. de. Parnaso esp., v. 1. 1768.)
— - Egloga I–X. (*In* Leon, L. P. de. Obras, v. 6. 1816.)
See also Bucolica and Georgica.

Commentaries on the Bucolica.

— GENISSET, F. J. Examen oratoire des Eclogues. Paris, 1804. 8°.
— OBSERVATIONS in illustr. of Virgil's fourth Eclogue. London, 1810. 8°.
— THORNTON, R. J. Pastorals, [imitations], *etc.* 3d ed. London, 1821. 2 v. 12°.
— WILLIAMS, J. The Virgilian cosmogony [Ecl. VI.]. (*In his* Essays. 1858.)

Bucolica and Georgica.

— Bucolica et Georgica explicat. notis illust. I. L. de la Cerda. Lugd., 1619. 4°.
— Ländliche Gedichte; übers. und erklärt von J. H. Voss. [Lat. und Deutsch.] Altona, 1797–1800. 4 v. 8°.
Contents. Vol. 1. Ecloga I–V. 2. VI–X. 3. Georgicon I–II. 4. III–IV.
— *Eng.* The Bucolics and Georgics; with notes, *etc.*, by T. Keightley. London, 1847. 8°.
— *Germ.* *See, above,* 'Ländliche'.

Culex.

— Culex, The; tr. by L. M. Sargent. Boston, 1807. 8°. (B 1234, 2543)
— Virgil's Gnat; tr. by E. Spencer. (*In* Spenser, E. Works, v. 7. 1805.)

Eclogues.
See Bucolica.

Georgica.

— Georgicorum lib. IV; with trans. and notes by J. Martyn. 2d ed. London, 1746. 8°.

— Georgicorum lib. IV notis illust. studio E. de Bulgaris. [Lat. et Gr.] Petropoli, 1786. f°.

— De plusieurs morceaux du 1r, 2d, 4e chant; avec le latin en regard. (*In* Turgot, A. J. R. Œuvres, v. 9. 1810.)

— *Eng.* The fourth book of Virgil. (*In* Sedley, C. Works, v. 1. 1722.)

See also, above, 1st entry.

— *French.* Les Géorgiques; trans. nouv. par J. Delille. 4e éd. Paris, 1770. 12°.

— - *Same.* (Vol 2. *of* Delille, J. Œuvres. 1824.)

See also, above, 'De plusieurs morceaux'.

— *Greek. See, above,* Georgicorum lib. 1786.

— *Spanish.* Libro 1o, 2o. (*In* Leon, L. P. de. Obras, v. 6. 1816.)

— Addison, J. Essay on V.'s Georgics. (*In his* Works, v. 1. 1721.)

See also Bucolica and Georgica.

The legend of Virgil.

— Zauberer Virgilius. (*In* Simrock, K. Deutschen Volksbücher, v. 6. 1847.)

Virgilius Maro *grammaticus.* Epistolæ. — Epitomæ. (*In* Mai, A. Class. auct., v. 5. 1833.)

Virgin, The. *See* Mary, *mother of Jesus.*

Virgin (*instrument of torture*). Pearsall, R. L. The kiss of the virgin. (*In* Archæologia, v. 27. 1838.)

Virgin Islands. Jeffreys, T. Map. London, 1797. (E 67)

Virgin martyr, The; by P. Massinger and T. Decker. (*In* Lamb, C. Spec. of dram. poets. 1854.)

Virgin unmasked, The; a musical farce, by H. Fielding. (*In* Collection of most esteemed farces, v. 2. 1792.)

Virginia. Colony.

— For the Colony in Virginea Britannia; Lawes divine, morall, and martiall, *etc.*; [comp. by W. Strachey]. 1612. (*In* Force, P. Col. of tracts, v. 3. 1844.)

— *Commissioners to the Catawba and Cherokee Indians.* Treaty, Catawba-Town and Broad-River, Feb., March 1756. Williamsburg, 1756. 8°.

— *General Assembly.* Proceedings of the first Assembly of Virginia, 1619. (*In* New York Hist. Soc. Col., ser. 2, v. 3. 1857.)

— - Blue laws, [1662-80]. (*In* Hinman, R. R. Blue laws, *etc.* 1838.)

— - Abridgement of laws. (*In* Abridgement of the laws in force and use in Her Majesty's plantations. 1704.)

— - Case of the planters of tobacco in Virginia. London, 1733. 8°. (B 1743)

— - Statutes at large; col. of all the laws of Virginia, 1619-1792; by W. W. Henning. Vol. 1, 2. N. Y., 3, 13, Phila., 4-12, Richmond, 1823, 20, 19-23. 8°.

Contents. Vol. 1. 1619-60. 2. 1660-85. 3. 1682-1710. 4. 1711-38. 5. 1738-48. 6. 1748-55. 7. 1756-63. 8. 1764-73. 9. 1775-78. 10. 1779-81. 11. 1782-84. 12. 1785-88. 13. 1789-92.

— - Collection of all public acts of the General Assembly and ordinances of the conventions, 1768 [-83] as now in force. Richm., 1785. f°.

— *Convention, March* 20, 1775, *Richmond.* Proceedings. Williamsburg, [1775]. 8°. (W 21)

— *Convention, July* 17, 1775, *at Richmond.* Ordinances. Williamsburg, [1775]. 4°. (W 71)

State.

A. State documents.

Adjutant General.

— Report, year ending Sept. 30, 1862. [Richmond, 1862.] 8°. (Doc. 4.)

— List of officers of the Virginia State Line, 1863. [Richmond, 1863.] 8°. (Doc. 19.)

Attorney General.

— Report, [Nov. 11,] 1864. [Richmond, 1864.] 8°. (Doc. 11.)

Auditor of Accounts.

— Special report, [Oct. 3, 1864]. [Richmond, 1864.] 8°. (Doc. 3.)

— Communication, Dec. 20, 1864. [Richmond,] 1865. 8°. (Doc. 5.)

— Report [on] the apportionment of representation, [Jan. 9, 1865. Richmond, 1865.] 8°. (Doc. 20.)

— Report [on] collection of taxes, Jan. 17, 1865. [Richmond, 1865.] 8°.

— Statement [on] the escape of slaves to the enemy, Feb. 1, 1865. [Richmond,] 1865. 8°. (Doc. 12.)

2d Auditor.

— Report relative to stocks held by the state in banks, *etc.* [Richmond, 1865.] 8°. (Doc. 33.)

— Communication, [Dec. 21, 1864. Richmond,] 1865. 8°. (Doc. 6.)

Board of Public Works.

— Annual report. Richmond, 1818. 8°. (B 456)

— Report of the geological reconnoissance of Virginia; by W. B. Rogers. Phila., 1836. 8°.

— Communication in regard to transportation charges by internal improvement companies, [January 19, 1865. Richmond,] 1865. 8°. (Doc. 9.)

— Report of the supt. of salt works on the capture of Saltville, [Jan. 7, 1865. Richmond, 1865.] 8°. (Doc. 28.)

Central Lunatic Asylum.

— Special report of the President and directors, Sept. 30, 1864. [Richmond, 1864.] 8°.

Commercial Agent.

— Report, with doc., [Dec. 9. Richmond,] 1864. 8°. (Doc. 19.)

Constitutional Conventions and Constitutions.

Convention of May 1776.

— Ordinances passed at a general convention of delegates from the counties of Virginia. Williamsburg, 1776. 4°. (B 652)

— Bill of rights of the Constitution of Va., 1776. (*In* Bowen, F. Documents. 1854.)

Convention of 1788.

— Debates and other proceedings, Richmond, June 2. Petersburg, 1788-89. 3 v. 8°.

— *Same.* 2d ed. Richmond, 1805. 8°.

— Journal. Richmond, 1827. 8°.

Convention of 1829-30.

— Proceedings and debates; [added,] the new constitution of Va. Richmond, 1830. 8°.

Convention of 1861.

— Convention between Va. and the Confederate States of America, Apr. 24, 1861. [Pp. 45, 46 probably of the Proceedings.]

— Ordinances adopted at the adjourned sess., June and July 1861. [Pp. 47-73 probably of the Proceedings.]

— Constitution proposed for adoption, by the convention, [Dec. 5, 1861. Richm., 1861.] 8°.

— Ordinances adopted at the adjourned sess., Nov., Dec. (*In* Va. *General Assembly.* Acts, extra sess. 1862.)

Deaf, Dumb, and Blind Institution.

— Report of the board of visitors for the year ending Sept. 30, 1864. [Richmond, 1864.] 8°.

General Assembly.

— Statutes at large, 1619-1792. *See* Colony (p. 3216).

— Col. of public acts, 1768-83. *See* Colony (p. 3216).

— Articles of confederation [of the U. S.]; the declaration of rights; the constitution of this commonwealth, and the articles of the treaty between Gr. Brit. and the U. S. Richmond, [1784]. 8°. (C 2?5)

— Articles of confederation; the declaration of rights; the constitution of [Va.]; and the articles of the treaty between Gr. Brit. and the U. S. Richmond, [1784]. 12°. (W 69)
— Proceedings on the answers of sundry states to their resolutions passed in December, 1793. Phila., 1800. 8°. (B 597)
— Virginia and Kentucky resolutions of 1798, 99. Wash., 1832. 8°. (B 1066)
— *Same.* (*In* Calhoun, J. C. Sentiments 1831; — *and in* Elliot, J. Debates, v. 4. 1861. B 1494)
— Resolutions proposing an amendment to the constit. of the U. S. authorizing state legis. to remove from office their senators, Feb. 29. Wash., 1808. 8°. (B 1489)
— Report in part of the com. on confed. relations on the sequestration of the property of aliens. *n.t.p.* [Richmond, 186-.] 8°. (Doc. 29.)
— Address of Hon. C. G. Memminger, commissioner from So. Carolina, before the assembled authorities of Va. Richmond, 1860. 8°.
— Acts, 1861-64. Richmond, 1862-64. 5 v. 8°.
Namely. Acts, 1861/62. — Extra sess., 1862; with Ordinances adopted by the Convention, Nov., Dec. 1862. — Called sess., 1862. — Called sess., 1863. — Sess., 1863/64.
— Sketches of acts and joint resolutions, 1863/64. [Richmond, 1864.] 8°.
— Resolution asserting the jurisdiction and sovereignty of Virginia over her ancient boundaries, Oct. 8, 1863. *n.t.p.* [Richm., 1864.] 8°.
— Act, Jan. 20, 1864, in regard to the arrest of deserters from the army.] *n.t.p.* [Richmond, 1864.] 8°.
— Address to the soldiers of Virginia, [1864]. *n.t.p.* [Richmond, 1864.] 8°.
— Circular to the district collectors and assessors, July 1, 1864. [Richmond, 1864.] 8°.
— Joint resolutions in relation to the existing war and as to negotiations for peace. *n.p.,n.d.* [Richmond, 1865?] 8°. (Doc. 15.)

Federal members.

— Address of the 58 federal members of the Virginia legis. to their fellow citizens, in Jan. 1799. Augusta, *Me.*, 1799. 8°. (C 115)

House of Delegates.

— Journal, 1777-90. Richmond, 1827. 26 v. 4°.
— Report of comm. [on] the proceed. of other states in ans. to resol. of 1798, commonly called Madison's report. Richm., 1819. 8°.
— Journal. Richmond, 1861-64. 7 v. 8°.
Namely. Sess. 1861/62. — Extra sess. 1862. — Called sess. 1862. — Adjourned sess. 1863. — Called sess. 1863. — Sess. 1863/64. — Called sess. 1864 (pp. 1-96).
— Calendar, Feb. 13, 1865. [Richm., 1865.] 8°.

Governor.

— Communication rel. to the surrender of R. F. Curry. (*In* N. Y. *Governor.* Message. 1841. B 1485)
— Message, and reports of the public officers of the state. Richmond, 1859. 8°. (Doc. 1.)
— Message, 1861-63. Richmond, 1861-63. 6 v. 8°.
Namely. Dec. 2, 1861 (with doc. 1). — May 5, 1862 (with doc. 1). — Sept. 15, 1862 (with docs. 1-7). Jan. 7, 1863 (with docs. 1-45). — Sept. 7, 1863 (with docs. 1-19). — Dec. 7, 1863 (with docs. 1-35).
— Governor's response to resolutions of the Gen. Assembly rel. to exempting state officers, [Jan. 10, 1865. Richm.,] 1865. 8°. (Doc. 7.)
— *Same.* Rel. to state exemptions, [Jan. 10, 1865. Richmond, 1865.] 8°. (Doc. 22.)

Military Institute.

— Report of board of visitors. [Richmond,] 1864. 8°. (Doc. 2.)
— Official report of the commandant of cadets of the battle at New Market. [Jan. 11. Richmond, 1865.] 8°. (Doc. 25.)
— Report of the superintendent relative to pay and state cadets. [Richmond,] 1865. 8°. (Doc. 24.)

Ordnance Department.

— Report of the chief of ordnance, [year ending] Sept. 30. [Richmond,] 1864. 8°. (Doc. 7.)

Paymaster General.

— Report. [Richmond,] 1865. 8° (Doc. 29.)

Penitentiary.

— Annual report of the Board of directors, Sept. 30. [Richmond, 1864.] 8°.

Quartermaster General.

— Report, [Nov. 30. Richmond, 1864.] 8°. (Doc. 8.)
— Report on the transactions of the executive connected with furnishing supplies to the people, [Feb. 2, 1865. Richmond, 1865.] 8°. (Doc. 32.)

Secretary of War.

— Medical regulations, Mar. 26. Richmond, 1862. 8°.

Senate.

— Journal. Williamsburg, 1779. 4°. (W 51)
— *Same.* And doc. [1-21]. Richmond, 1863-[64]. 8°.
— Bill for furnishing badges of honor to Va. officers and soldiers. *n.t.p.* [Richmond, 1865.] 8°. (No. 81.)

State Collector.

— Circular to the district collectors and assessors. *n.t.p.* [Richmond, 1864.] 8°.

Treasurer.

— Synopsis of the financial condition of the treasury, [year ending] Sept. 30. [Richmond,] 1864. 8°. (Doc. 4.)

University.
See University of Virginia.

Volunteers.

— Fourteenth Va. Infantry; resolutions passed at a meeting, Jan. 24. Richmond, 1865. 8°. (Doc. 30.)

B. WORKS ABOUT VIRGINIA.

Biography.

— Taylor, J. B. Lives of Virginia Baptist ministers. 2d ed. enl. Richmond, 1838. 12°.

Botany.

— Gronovius, J. F. Flora Virginica; plantas quas J. Clayton observavit. Lugd. Bat., 1762. 4°.

Canal.

— Appeal for the speedy completion of the water-line of V. Norfolk, 1857. 8°. (B 1605)

Description.

— Amadas, P., *and* Barlow, A. Voyage to the coast of Virginia, 1584. — Grenville, *Sir* R. Voyage to V., 1585. — Lane, *Sir* R. Extract of letter from V., 1585; — Account of the particular employments in V., 1585-86. — Voyage to V., 1586, for the relief of the colony. — Voyage, 1587. — Hariot, T. Briefe and true report of the commodities in V. — Description of the nature and maners of the people of V., *etc.*, [1588]. — White, J. Voyage to V., 1590. (*In* Hakluyt, R. Col. of voy., v. 3. 1810; — *and in* Pinkerton, J. Col. of voy., v. 12. 1812.)

— SMITH, J. True travels, adventures, *etc.*, **1593-1629**. From Lond. ed. of 1629. Richmond, 1819. 2 v. 8°.

— — *Same.* (*In* **Churchill**, O. *and* J. Col. of voy., v. 2. 1744.)

— — *Same, abr.* (*In* **Harris**, J. Col. of voy., v. 2. 1764.)

— GOSNOLD, B. Voyage to the north part of Virginia, [1602]. — WAYMOUTH, G. Voyage to Virginia, [1605]. — PERCY, G. Account of the plantation of the southern colony of V., **1606**. (*In* **Harris**, J. Col. of voy., v. 1. 1705.)

— STRACHEY, W. History of travaile into Virginia Britannia, **1606-12**; ed. by R. H. Major. London, 1849. 8°. (Hakluyt Soc., v. 6.)

— WINGFIELD, E. M. A discourse of Virginia, [**1607-08**]. Boston, 1860. 8°.

— — *Same.* (*In* **Amer. Antiq. Soc.** Archæol. Amer., v. 4. 1860.)

— NOVA Britannia; offering most excellent fruites by planting in Virginia. London, **1609**. (*In* **Force**, P. Col. of tracts, v. 1. 1836.)

— *Same.* With a prefatory note by F. L. Hawks. N. Y., 1867. 4°.

— TRUE declaration of the estate of the colonie in Virginia. London, **1610**. 4°.

— *Same.* (*In* **Force**, P. Col. of tracts, v. 3. 1844.)

— NEW life of Virginea; being the second part of Nova Britannia. London, **1612**. 4°.

— *Same.* (*In* **Mass. Hist. Soc.** Col., v. 18. 1819; — *and in* **Force**, P. Col. of tracts, v. 1. 1836.)

— HAMOR, R. A true discourse of the present estate of Virginia, till 18 of June **1614**. London, 1615, [*reprinted*, Albany, 1860]. 8°.

— DERMER, T. Letter describing his passage from Me. to Virginia, **1619**. (*In* **Purchas**. Pilgrimes. 1625; — *and* **N. Y. Hist. Soc.** Col., ser. 2, v. 1. 1841.)

— SMITH, J. Advertisements for the unexperienced planters of N. Eng., *etc.* London, **1631**, Boston, *reprinted* 1865. 4°.

— — *Same.* (*In* **Mass. Hist. Soc.** Col., v. 23. 1833.)

— NORWOOD, *Col.* Voyage to Virginia, **1649-50**.] (*In* **Churchill**, O. *and* J. Col. of voy., v. 6. 1746; — *and in* **Force**, P. Tracts, v. 3. 1844.)

— PERFECT description of Virginia; full and true rel. of the present state of the plantation. London, **1649**. 8°.

— *Another copy.* (B 995)

— *Same.* (*In* **Mass. Hist. Soc.** Col., v. 19. 1822; — *and in* **Force**, P. Col. of tracts, v. 2. 1838.)

— WILLIAMS, E. Virgo triumphans; or, Virginia in generall, but the south part in particular, richly valued. London, **1650**. 4°.

— — *Same.* Virginia, especially the south part thereof, richly and truly valued. 1650. (*In* **Force**, P. Col. of tracts, v. 3. 1844.)

— HAMMOND, J. Leah and Rachel; or, The two fruitful sisters Virginia and Maryland, **1656**. — SHRIGLEY, N. True relation of Virginia and Maryland, **1669**. (*In* **Force**, P. Col. of tracts, v. 3. 1844.)

— CLAYTON, J. Letters giving an account of several observables in Virginia, **1688**. (*In* **Royal Soc. of London.** Philosoph. trans., v. 17, 18. 1694, 95; — *in* **Miscellanea curiosa**, v. 3. 1707; — *and in* **Force**, P. Col. of tracts, v. 3. 1844.)

— BLOME, R. Description of Jamaica with other isles and territories in Amer., [**1671**]. London, 1672. 12°.

— ACCOUNT of the present state and government of Virginia, [**1696-98**?]. (*In* **Mass. Hist. Soc.** Col., v. 5. 1798.)

— FONTAINE, J. Journal of travels in Virginia, **1715-16**. (*In* **Maury**, A. Memoirs of a Huguenot family. 1853.)

— EXPEDITION, The, of Maj. Gen. Braddock to V. London, **1755**. 8°. (B 678)

— HUTCHINS, T. Topographical descript. of V., *etc.* London, **1778**. 8°.

— — *Another copy.* (B 343)

— — *Same.* Boston, 1787. 12°. (C 64)

— JEFFERSON, T. Notes on the state of V., [**1781**]. London, 1787. 8°.

— — *Same.* Boston, 1829. 12°.

— POETICAL picture of America; observations during a residence in V., **1799-1807**. London, 1809. 16°.

— TOUR through part of V. in **1808**; letters incl. an acct. of Harper's Ferry, the Natural Bridge, Weir's Cave, Monticello, *etc.* N. Y., 1809. 8°. (B 411)

— MARTIN, J. Comprehensive description of V. Richmond, [**1835**]. 8°.

— STROTHER, *Gen.* D. H. Virginia illustrated. (*In* **Harper's mag.**, v. 10, 11. 1854-55.)

— MY ride to the barbecue; by an ex-member of Congress, [**1858**]. N. Y., 1860. 8°.

See also **Accomac Co.**; — **Alexandria**; — **Chancellorsville**; — **City Point**; — **Danville**; — **Fauquier Co.**; — **Five Forks**; — **Grey Sulphur Springs**; — **Harper's Ferry**; — **Norfolk**; — **Northampton Co.**; — **Prince George Co.**; — **Richmond**; — **Rockbridge**; — **Shenandoah Valley**; — **Staunton River**; — **West Virginia**; — **Williamsburgh**; — *also* **Washington College**.

Maps.

— BLAEU, W. Virginiæ tabula. [Amst., 16—.] (E 78, no. 315)

— FRY, J., *and* JEFFERSON, P. Map. London, **1794**. (E 68)

— MONK, J. Map of the seat of war; [V. and Maryland]. Phila., **1861**.

— BECHLER, G. R. Atlas, showing battles, *etc.*, connected with the campaigns in V. Phila., **1864**. Obl. 8°.

— — Military map, compaigns of the Army of the Potomac in V. Phila., 1864.

— COLTON, J. H. Map of V., *etc.* N. Y., **1865**.

Ecclesiastical affairs.

— FOOTE, W. H. Sketches of V.; historical and biographical. Phila., 1850-55. 2 v. 8°.

— G., R. Virginia's cure; or, Advisive narrative concerning V., **1662**. (*In* **Force**, P. Tracts, v. 3. 1844.)

— MEADE, W. Old churches, ministers, and families of V. Phila., 1857. 2 v. 8°.

— PERRY, W. S., *ed.* Historical collections rel. to the American Colonial Church. Vol. 1: Virginia. [Hartford,] 1870. 4°.

See also **Biography**.

History.

General works.

— HOWISON, R. R. History of V., [**1584-1847**]. Phila., 1846-48. 2 v. 8°.

— HOWE, H. Hist. collections of V., [**1584-1832**]; with geog. and statistical description. Charleston, S. C., 1852. 8°.

— BURK, J. D. History of V., [**1584-1781**]; [v. 4] continued by S. Jones and L. H. Girardin. Petersburg, 1804-16. 4 v. 8°.

— CAMPBELL, C. Introduction to the hist. of the colony and ancient dominion of V., [**1584-1781**]. Richmond, 1847. 8°.

— CAMPBELL, J. W. Hist. of V., [1584]-1781; with biog. sketches. Phila., 1813. 12°.

— FORREST, W. S. Hist. sketches of Norfolk, *etc.*, [**1650-1852**]. Phila., 1853. 8°.

History (Colony).

— BROCKENBROUGH, W. H. History of V. to 1754; with abstract to [1775]. (*In* **Martin**, J. Comprehensive description. 1835.)

— BYRD, W. History of the dividing line [from N. Carolina]; and other tracts, [**1584-1739**]. Richmond, 1866. 2 v. 4°.

— KEITH, *Sir* W. Hist. of British plantations in America. Pt. 1: Virginia, [**1584-1723**]. London, 1738. 4°.

— BEVERLEY, R. Hist. of Virginia, **1584-1704**. London, 1705. 8°.

— — *Same.* [To **1720**.] 2d ed. London, 1722. 8°.

— - *Same.* Repr. from the 2d [London] ed.; introduction by C. Campbell. Richmond, 1855. 8°.

— - *French.* Histoire de la Virginie. Orléans, 1707. 12°.

— ROBERTSON, W. Hist. of V., to 1688. (*In his* History of America. 1800.)

— SMITH, J. Generall historie of Virginia, New England, and the Summer Isles, **1584–1626.** London, 1632. 4°.

— - *Same.* (*In his* True travels, v. 1, 2. 1819; — *in* **Pinkerton, J.** Col. of voy., v. 13. 1812; — *and, abstract, in* **Harris, J.** Col. of voy., v. 1. 1705.)

— SMITH, W. History of the first discovery and settlement of V., [1584-1624]. Williamsburg, 1747. 8°.

— GR. BRIT. *King.* Letters patents granted by the Queene's Maiestie to Sir W. Ralegh for the discovering and planting of new lands, **1584.** (*In* **Hakluyt, R.** Col. of voy., v. 3. 1810; — *and in* **Pinkerton, J.** Col. of voy., v. 12. 1812.)

— NAMES of those that remained one whole yeere in V. under R. Lane, **[1585-86].** (*In* **Hakluyt, R.** Col. of voy., v. 3. 1810; — *and in* **Pinkerton, J.** Col. of voy., v. 12. 1812.)

— NAMES of all which safely arrived in V. and remained there, **1587.** (*In* **Hakluyt, R.** Col. of voy., v. 3. 1810; — *and in* **Pinkerton, J.** Col. of voy., v. 12. 1812.)

— NEILL, E. D. History of the Virginia Company of London; with letters to and from the first colony, [1606–24]. Albany, 1869. 4°.

— HOPKINS, S. Youth of the Old Dominion, [1607–77]. Boston, 1856. 12°.

— SMITH, J. A true relation of V., [1607–08]; with introduction and notes by C. Deane. Boston, 1866. 4°.

— VIRGINIA affairs, **1610–24.** (*In* **Harris, J.** Col. of voy., v. 1. 1705.)

— NECESSARIES for going to Virginia, **1626.** Extr. from Smith's History. (*In* **Mass. Hist. Soc.** Col., v. 12. 1814.)

— EXTRACT from a manuscript collection of annals rel. to Virginia, **[1642].** (*In* **Force, P.** Col. of tracts, v. 2. 1838.)

History (Bacon's Rebellion).

— BERKELEY, *Sir* W. List of those who have been executed for the late rebellion in Virginia, **[1675].** — M., T. Beginning, progress, and conclusion of Bacon's Rebellion in V., **1675–76.** (*In* **Force, P.** Col. of tracts, v. 1. 1836.)

— COTTON, *Mrs.* A. Account of our late troubles in Virginia, **1675–76.** (*In* **Force, P.** Col. of tracts, v. 1. 1836.)

— HISTORY of Bacon's and Ingram's Rebellion, 1675–76. Camb., 1867. 8°.

— *Same.* (*In* **Mass. Hist. Soc.** Col., v. 11. 1814; — *in* **Force, P.** Col. of tracts, v. 1. 1836; — *and, corr., in* **Mass. Hist. Soc.** Proc., 1866–67; *also* **B 465**)

History (State).

— GILPIN, T. Exiles in Virginia, **1777–78.** Phila., 1848. 8°.

See also **Bacon, N.**; — **Pocahontas**; — **Smith,** *Capt.* **J.**; — *also* **Virginia** hist. register; — **Virginia** hist. reporter; — **Walpole grant on the Ohio.**

Industries.

— BONOEIL, J. Treatise on the art of making silke, *etc.*; with instructions how to plant and dresse vines, and to make wine, *etc.*, in Virginia. (*In his* H. M.'s letter. 1622.)

Law.

— BLACKSTONE, *Sir* W. Commentaries; with notes of reference to the constitution and laws of the U. S. and Va., by St. G. Tucker. Phila., 1803. 4 v. in 5 pts. 8°.

— HAMMOND, C. Review of the opinion of the Supreme Court in case of Cohens *vs.* Virginia. Steubenville, 1821. 8°. **(B 562)**

— DISTRESS for rent in Virginia. *n.t.p.* [1830.] 8°. **(B 1431)**

Newspapers.

— Miscellaneous newspapers;] Apr. 21 - Nov. 30. 1865; Jan. - June, Dec., 1866. *v.p.*, 1865–66. 10 v. f°.

Politics.

— GOOD, A. Speed to Virginia, **1609.** (*In* **Collier, J. P.** Illust. of early Eng. lit., v. 2. 1864.)

— PUBLICK good without private interest; condition of the English colonie. London, **1657,** [*republished* Paris, 1866?]. 4°.

— CASE of the planters of tobacco in Virginia as represented by themselves; signed by the president of the Council and speaker of the House of Burgesses; added, a vindication of the said representation. London, **1733.** 8°.

— *Another copy.* **(B 1743)**

— LETTER from a gentleman in Va. to the merchants trading to that colony; [on the dispute between Va. and Gov. Dinwiddie]. London, **1754.** 8°. **(W 32)**

— LETTER to a gentleman in London, from Virginia. Williamsburg, **1759.** 8°. **(W. 32)**

— BLAND, B. Letter to the clergy of Virginia, [vindicating] the General Assembly against the Bp. of London. Williamsburg, **1760.** 8°. **(W 19)**

— LETTER to the B----p of L----n [T. Sherlock on his] letter to the L— s of T— e, on the act to enable the inhabitants of this colony to discharge their publick dues, *etc.*, in money for the ensuing year. London, **1760.** 8°. **(W 19, 68)**

— CARTER, L. The rector detected; defence of the two-penny act against the misrepresentations of J. Camm. Williamsburg, **1764.** 4°. **(W 70)**

— CAMM, J. Review of 'Rector detected'. Pt. 1. Williamsburg, **1764.** 4°. **(W 70)**

— PAINE, T. Public good; examination into the claims of Va. to the vacant Western territory, and right of U. S. to the same, *etc.* Phila., **1780.** 8°. **(B 702, W 21)**

— TAYLOR, G. K. Substance of a speech on the bill to amend the penal laws. Richmond, **1796.** 4°. **(W 33, 58)**

— ELLIOT, J. The Virginia and Kentucky resolutions of **1798–99**; with Jefferson's original draught. Wash., 1832. 8°. **(B 1066)**

Note. Contains also Madison's report, Calhoun's address, resolutions of the several states in rel. to states' rights, with other documents in support of the Jeffersonian doctrines of '98.

— ADDISON, A. Analysis of the report of the committee of the Virginia Assembly on the proceedings of other states in answer to their resolutions. Phila., **1800.** 12°. **(C 77, W 13b)**

— CONSTITUTION of '76, The; by a member of the Staunton convention. Winchester, **[1825].** 8°. **(B 544)**

— MASON, G. Corresp. with J. Madison; with memorial and remonstrance of Va. against a bill establishing a provision for teachers of the Christian religion. Richmond, **1826.** 8°. **(B 1493)**

— ANTI-JACKSON CONVENTION, **Dec. 12, 1827.** Address and resolutions; with introd. address to the people of the State of N. Y. *n.t.p.* 8°. **(B 1493)**

— NEW YORK. *Governor.* Message transm. resolutions of the Legislature of Mississippi, and other papers in rel. to the controversy between V. and New York. [Albany, **1841.**] 8°. **(B 1485)**

— CRAIG, N. B. Lecture upon the controversy between Pennsylvania and V. about the boundary line. Pittsburgh, **1843.** 8°. **(B 1601)**

— NEW YORK. STATE. *Assembly.* Report on the matters of difference between N. Y. and V. [Albany,] **1843.** 8°. (Doc. no. 49. **B 1485)**

— BOTTS, J. M. To the Whigs of V. Wash., **1848.** 8°. **(B 1502)**

— PENDLETON, J. S., *and others.* To the Whig Party of V.; reply to Botts. Wash., **1848.** 8°. **(B 1502)**

— DABNEY, R. L. Defence of Virginia in recent and pending contests against the sectional party. N. Y., **1867.** 12°.

Slavery.

— TUCKER, St. G. Dissertation on slavery; with a proposal for the abolition of it in V. Phila., **1796.** 8°. **(B 764)**

Springs.

— ROUELLE, J. Complete treatise on the mineral waters of V. Phila., **1792.** 8°. **(B 393)**

— OBSERVATIONS on the mineral waters in the south-western part of V. Phila., 1834. 8°. (B 1564)

— BURKE, W. Mineral springs of western V. N. Y., 1842. 16°.

— BRIEF notice of Burke's 'Mineral springs'. Phila., 1843. 12°. (C 269)

— HAYWARD, G. Medicinal springs of Va. (*In his* Surgical reports, *etc.* 1855.)

Virginia, University of. *See* **University of Virginia.**

Virginia; tragedia. *See* **Alfieri, V.**

Virginia and Maryland; or, the Lord Baltamore's printed case uncased and answered. (*In* **Force, P.** Col. of tracts, v. 2. 1838.)

Virginia and North Carolina almanac, 1865. *See* **Warrock's** Va. and N. C. almanac.

Virginia Central Rail Road Co. Correspondence between the president of the R.R. and the Postmaster-General in relation to postal service. Richmond, 1864. 8°.

Virginia Company of London. Orders and constitutions for the better governing of the affaires of the Companie of Virginia in England residing, 1619-20. (*In* **Force, P.** Col. of tracts, v. 3. 1844.)

— NEILL, E. D. History of the Co. Albany, 1869. 4°.

Virginia gazette, The, *etc.*, Oct. 2, 1798; [cont. the Albemarle remonstrance against the alien and the sedition acts]. Richmond, 1798. f°. (W 68)

Virginia herald; Dec. 12, 1821; Apr. 6, 10, 1822. Fredericksburg, 1821-22. f°. (E 181)

Virginia Historical and Philosophical Society. *See* **Virginia Historical Society.**

Virginia historical register; ed. by W. Maxwell. Vol. 1-6; Jan. 1848 - Oct. 1853. Richmond, 1848-53. 6 v. 12°.

Note. Vol. 1 and 2 entitled 'Va. hist. reg. and literary advertiser'; 3 and 4, 'Va. hist. reg. and literary note book'; 5 and 6, 'Va. hist. reg. and literary companion'.

Virginia historical reporter; conducted by the Virginia Hist. Soc. Vol. 1. Richmond, 1854. 8°.

Virginia Historical Society. Proceedings, 1848-53. (*In* **Virginia** historical register, v. 1-6. 1848-53.)

Note. C. Robinson's 'Account of the discoveries in the West' was prepared for and published by the Society. *See also, above,* **Virginia** historical reporter.

Virginia Hot Springs. GOODE, T. Invalids' guide to the Virginia Hot Springs. Richmond, 1839. 24°. (D 38)

Virginia illustrated; by Gen. D. P. Strother. (*In* **Harper's** mag., v. 10-11. 1854-55.)

Virginia Indians. DE HAAS, W. History of the early settlement and Indian wars of Western Virginia. Wheeling, Phila., 1851. 8°.

Virginia Military District. LOFLAND, C. List of all the entries in the Va. military district. Columbus, 1821. 8°. (B 987)

Virginia primer, The. Richmond, 1864. 16°.

Virginia. Prot. Episc. Church. *See* **Prot. Episc. Church.** Diocese of Va.

Virginia richly valued, *etc.* *See* **Relaçam,** *etc.*

Virginia Soc. for Promoting the Abolition of Slavery, *etc.* Memorial. (*In* **Memorials** to Cong. of the U. S. by socs. for promot. abolition of slavery, *etc.* 1792. B 764, 1473, C 72)

Virginians, The; a tale of the last century; by W. M. Thackeray. N. Y., 1852. 8°.

Note. From **Harper's** mag., v. 16-19. 1857-59.

Virginie; a tragedy, by Latour; French, with an English trans. N. Y., 1855. 8°.

Virginiensis, *pseud.* Defence of the alien and sedition laws. Phila., 1798. 8°. (W 69)

Virginity. CLÉMENS *Romanus, fl. before* **100.** Two epistles concerning virginity. (*In* **Methodius.** Writings. 1869.)

— BASILIUS *Cæsaræensis, b.* 329, *d.* **379.** De vera atque integerrima virginitate. (*In his* Opera, v. 1. 1638.)

— AMBROSIUS, *St., b. abt.* 340, *d.* **397.** De virginis institutione. — Hortatio ad virginitatem. — De virginis forma vivendi, ad virginem devotam tractatus. — De virginis lapsu, ad virginem lapsam tractatus. — De virginibus, ad Marcellinam sororem. (*In his* Opera, v. 4. 1661.)

— ALDHELM, *St., b.* 639, *d.* **709.** De laudibus virginitatis. (*In his* Opera. 1844.)

Virginius; a tragedy. *See* **Knowles, J. S.**

Virgo triumphans. *See* **Williams, E.**

Viri Romæ. *See* **Lhomond, C. F.,** *l'abbé.*

Virtue. HUTCHESON, F. Inquiry into the original of our ideas of beauty and virtue. [1725.] 5th ed. London, 1753. 8°.

— NETTLETON, T. Treatise on virtue and happiness. [1729.] 2d ed. London, 1736. 8°.

— - *Same.* 5th ed. London, 1759. 8°.

— HART, W. Remarks on [J.] Edwards's 'Dissertations on virtue'. N. Haven, 1771. 8°. (B 1903)

See also **Moral philosophy.**

Virtues. DIDRON, A. N. Iconographie des vertus. (*In* **Annales** archéol., v. 20-21. 1860-61.)

Virtues of society, The; by the author of 'The virtues of nature' [S. W. Morton]. Boston, 1799. 4°.

— *Another copy.* (**A 13**)

Virtuoso, The; a comedy. *See* **Shadwell, T.**

Virtuoso's companion and coin collector's guide. London, 1797, 96-97. 8 v. 8°.

Virués, Cristobal de. El Monserrate. 4a impresion añadida [por A. Bonacasa]. Madr., 1805. 12°.

— *Same.* (*In* **Ochoa, E. de.** Tesoro de los poemas españ. 1840; — *and in* **Rosell, C.** Poemas epicos, v. 1. 1851; v. 17 of Aribau. Bibl.)

— MUENCH BELLINGHAUSEN, E. F. J., *Freiherr* von. Virués' Leben und Werke. (*In* **Jahrbuch f. roman.** u. eng. Lit., v. 2. 1860.)

Virunio, Luigi Pontico. *See* **Pontico Virunio, L.**

Viscart, Robert. *See* **Guiscard, R.**

Viscera. PEMBERTON, C. K. Treatise on disease of the abdominal viscera. London, 1807. 8°.

Visconti, Bruzzi. Ballata. (*In* **Trucchi, F.** Poesie ital., v. 2. 1846.)

Visconti, Ennio Quirino. Opere varie; per cura di G. Labus. Milano, 1827-31. 4 v. 8°.

Contents. Vol. 1. Monumento degli Scipioni. — Cat. dei monumenti scritti del Museo di T. Jenkins. — Lettera all' abate G. A. Guattani sopra un antico vaso appartenente al principe Chigi. — Let. al sig. T. Jenkins sopra un intaglio rappresentante Pallade sul carro di Diomede. — Let. al abate P. Angiolini sopra un ant. cammeo col. ritratto di A. Giuniore. — Let. all' abate C. Amaduzzi sopra di un ant. diaspro sanguigno colle teste di Acorat e Sileno. — Descr. di un ant. gruppo rappres. Ercole e Telefo con la cerva. — Osserv. su due musaici. — Let. al abate F. Cancellieri intorno alla statua di Patroclo. — Relaz. degli scavi fatti a Roma presso la Via Appia 1789-92. — Osserv. sopra un ant. cammeo rappres. Giove Egioco.—Let. su di una ant. argenteria scoperta in Roma. — Iscriz. greche triopee, con vers. ed osserv. 2. Le pitture di un ant. vasi trovato nella Magna Greca. — Espos. delle legende e dei tipi che osserv. nella medaglia 1794. — Descr. di un' ant. tromba idraulica. — Lettera su due monumenti ne' quali è memoria di Antonia Augusta. — Let. al sig. L. Lamberti su due iscrizioni. — Sopra le sedici colonne presso S. Lorenzo in Milano. — Espos. della rappres. d'un ant. musaico. — Osserv. sul catalogo degli ant. incisori in gemme. — Illust. di un gruppo rappres. Apollo e Giacinto. — Gruppo reppres. la Pace che allatta Pluto bambino. — Espos. dell' impronte di ant. gemme rac. per uso di A. Chigi. — Cat. delle gemme di S. Poniatowscki. — Dichiarazione del Tempio dell' Onore e della Virtù. — Illust. di una greca scultura. — Emend. ed agg. al Museo Pio-Clementino. — Reflessioni sulla maniera di tradur Pindaro. — Lezione accad. sulle parole d'Orazio. 'Nec quarta loqui persona laboret'. — Lettere. — Notizia biografiche di E. Q. Visconti scritte da lui medesimo. — Notizia biografiche dell' abate S. A. Morcelli. 3. Deux zodiaques de Tentyra. — Sculpteurs grecs qui ont porté le nom de Cléomènes. — Statue égyptienne qui se voit à St. Cloud. — Tête en bronze de Vespasien. — Costume des statues ant. — Explic. d'un bas-relief en l'honneur d'Alexandre le grand. — Ouvrages de sculpture du Parthénon. — Epigramme grecque qui servait d'épitaphe au tombeau des guerriers athéniens morts devant Potidée. — Cat. raisonné de quelques inscriptions grecques. — Monumens des peuples américains. — Not. sur la tapisserie brodée de la reine Mathilde. — Inscription trouvée à Autun en 1810. — Camée répres. la mort de Daphnis. — Obs. sur une médaille grecque inéd. — Deux inscriptions grecques trouvées à Athènes. — Vase peint apporté de Sicile. — Inscr. grecque découverte près d'Athènes. — Articoli estratti dal Journal des savans. — Biog. de Cléotas, — Cléomenès, — Fabretti, — Eglinger, — Ekhel. — Cat.

della dattiliotec del sig. barone de la Turbie. — Lettre sur un camée répres. Jupiter Capitolin. — Mém. sur une médaille de Aulares. 4. Descr. di monumenti del Museo Francese. — Vases ant. d'argile orné de peintures connus sous le nom de vases étrusques. — Statues, *etc.*, de la Galerie des Ant. du Musée Napoléon. — Lettere. — Sonetti. — Odi. — Componimenti poetici per l'arrivo in Roma di due principi illust. — Ottave sul possesso di Pio VI. — Ecuba di Euripide; tr.

— Iconografia greca; recata in ital. da G. Labus. Milano, 1823-25. 3 v. 8°.

Contents. Vol. 1. *Poeti.* Omero. — Archiloco. — Tirteo. — Alceo. — Saffo. — Anacreonte. — Stesicoro. — Eschilo. — Sofocle. — Euripide. — Menandro. — Moschione. — Arato. — *Legislatori ed ant. sapienti.* Licurgo. — Periandro. — Solone. — Biante. — Talete. — Pittaco. — Chilone. — Anassagora. — Esopo. — *Politici e guerrieri.* Milziade. — Temistocle. — Pericle. — Aspasia. — Alcibiade. — *Filosofi.* Pittagora.— Apollonio Tianeo. — Zenone Eleate. — Socrate. — *Accademici.* Platone. — Carneade. — Teone Smirneo. — *Peripatetici.* Aristotele. — Teofrasto. — Aristomaco. — Antistene. — Diogene. — *Stoici.* Zenone di Cipro. — Crisippo. — Possidonio. — Epicuro. — Metrodoro. — Ermarco. — *Filosofi megaresi.* Euclide di Megara. — Eraclito. — Ipparco. — *Istorici.* Erodoto. — Tucidide. — Teofane Mitileneo. — *Oratori e retori.* Lisia. — Isocrate. — Demostene. — Eschine. — Leodamante. — Mettio Epafrodito. — Elio Aristide il sofista. — *Medici e fisici.* Ippocrate. — Asclepiade.— Senofonte di Coo. — Asiatico. — Claudio Agatamero. — *Medici e botanici.* Chirone. — Sestio Negro. — Eraclide Tarantino. — Mantia. — Senocrate Afrodisieo. — Pamfilo. — Macaone. — Galeno. — Dioscoride. — Nicandro. — Rufo. — Andrea. — Apollonio di Memfi. — Cratevate. — Sesto Empirico. — *Donne celebir.* Laide. — Eucaride. 2. *Re, principi, e regine.* Sicilia. — Macedonia. — Epiro. — Sparta. — Tracia. — Illiria. — Ponto e Bosforo Cimmerio. — Bitinia. — Pergamo. — Principi che fondarono città nell' Asia Minore, o che ressero qualche paese di quella regione. — Cappadocia. — Armenia e alcuni regioni finitime. — Siria, or Seleucidi. 3. Cilicia. — Commagene e una parte della Cilicia. — Alcuna città della Siria. — Giudea. — Osroene. — Parti od Arsacidi. — Persia, della dinastia de' Sassanidi. — Battriana. — Caracene. — Egitto. — Principe Africani.

— Iconografia romana. Milano, 1818-19. 2 v. 8°.

Contents. Vol. 1. *Uomini illustri.* Romolo. — Tazio. — Numa. — Anco Marzio. — L. Giunio Bruto. — A. Postumio Regillense. — L. Domizio Enobarbo. — C. Servilio Ahala. — Servio Sulpicio. — M. Attilio Regolo. — M. Arrio Secondo. — C. Numonio Vala. — P. Scipione Africano l'antico. — M. Claudio Marcello. — T. Quinzio Flamminio. — Caio Mario. — C. Celio Caldo. — L. Cornelio Silla. — Q. Pompeo Rufo. — Lucio Cornelio, pretore. — Anzio Restio. — Pompeo. — Gneo e Sesto figli di Pompeo. — Azio Balbo, pretore. — Marco Bruto. — Q. Labieno Partico. — Gn. Domizio Enobarbo. — L. Munazio Planco. — Marco Antonio. — Marco Antonio il giovane detto Antillo. — Lucio Antonio. — Lepido, triumviro. 2. Agrippa. — Corbulone. — Urso Serviano. — Terenzio. — Quinto Ortensio. — Cicerone. — Salustio. — Virgilio. — Orazio. — Mecenate. — Seneca. — Giunio Rustico, il secondo. — Apuleio. — M. Nonio Balbo. — Viciria Archas. — Marco Calatorio. — L. Mammio Massimo.

— Monumenti gabini della Villa Pinciana; per cura del dottor G. Labus. Milano, 1835. 8°.

— Monumenti scelti borghesiani; illustr. per cura del dr. G. Labus. Milano, 1837. 8°.

— DACIER, B. J. La vie et les ouvrages de V. (*In* **Paris. Inst.** *Ac. d. Inscr.* Mém., v. 8. 1827.)

Visconti, Federigo, *Arbp. of Pisa.* FABIONI, A. (*In his* Memorie pisani, v. 4. 1792.)

Visconti, Filippo. Commentarius de peste, 1630, Mediolani. (*In* **Archivio** stor. ital., app., v. 1. 1842-44.)

Visconti, Filippo Aurelio, *and others.* Il Museo Chiaramonti con l'esplicazione. Roma, 1808-37. 2 v. f°.

Note. Vol. 1, by F. A. Visconti and G. A. Guattani; v. 2, by A. Nibby; the 3d vol. pub. in 1843, cont. 45 pl., is wanting. These form v. 8-10 of Il Museo Pio-Clementino *see* **Visconti**, G. B.

Visconti, Filippo Maria. DECEMBRIO, P. C. (*In* **Muratori**, L. A. Rer. Ital. scr., v. 20. 1731.) — MONTANO, G. Oratio funebris in morte V. (*In* v. 25. 1751.)

Visconti, Gaspard. Sonetto. (*In* **Gironi**, R. Rac. di. lir. ital. 1808.)

Visconti, GiamBattista, *and* **Ennio**, Q. Museo Pio-Clementino descritto. Rom., 1782-1807. 7 v. f°.

Note. For v. 8-10 of this work, *see* **Visconti**, F. A., *and others.* Museo Chiaramonti.

— SCAVIGLIA, G. Elogio di V. (*In* **Grillo**, L. Elogi di Lig., v. 3. 1846.)

Visconti, Giovanni Galeas. CASTELLUTTO, P. de. Ordo funeris J. G. Vicecomitis, 1402, et oratio in ejus laudem. (*In* **Muratori**, L. A. Rer. Ital. scr., v. 16. 1730.)

Visconti, Pietro Ercole. Gemme incise da J. Girometti, con illustrazioni. Roma, 1836. f°.

Visconti, Primi, *conte di San Majole.* La campagne du roy, 1677; [tr. de l'ital.]. Paris, 1678. 12°.

Visconti, Ugolino. FABRONI, A. (*In his* Mem. di. illust. Pisani, v. 2. 1791.)

Visconti *di Milano*, Famiglia di. (*In* **Litta**, P. Fam., v. 15.)

— GIOVIO, P. Vitæ duodecim Vicecomitum Mediolani principum. (*In* **Grævius**. Thes. antiq. Ital., v. 3, pt. 1. 1704.)

Visconti *già* Aicardi *di Milano*, Famiglia di. (*In* **Litta**, P. Fam., v. 15.)

Viscus quercinus. FRASER, H. Epilepsy and the use of viscus quercinus. London, 1806. 8°. (B 828)

Visdomini, Neri. Canzone. (*In* **Trucchi**, F. Poesie ital., v. 1. 1846.)

Visella. NETO, J. D. M. Memoria sobre antiquidades das caldas de Vizela. (*In* **Lisbon. Ac. d. Sci.** Mem. lit., v. 3. 1792.)

Visher, Albin. I cannot forget thee; a ballad. Augusta, [186-]. 4°. (E 171)

Vishnu Puráná. *See* **Puráná.**

Visible speech; the science of universal alphabetics. *See* **Bell, A. M.**

Visigoths. SAAVEDRA FAJARDO, D. de. Corona gótica, castellana, y austrica, politicamente ilustrada, [1645]. (*In his* Obras. 1853; v. 25 of Aribau. Bibl.)

— TUERK, K. Ueber das westgothische Gesetzbuch. (*In his* Forschungen, 1s Heft. 1829.)

— HELFERICH, A. Entstehung und Geschichte des Westgothen-Rechts. Berlin, 1858. 8°.

— LEX Wisigothorum. — CHRONICON regum Wisigothorum. (*In* **Bouquet**, M. Rec., v. 4. 1869.)

Vision. BERKELEY, G. Theory of vision vindicated. [1709.] London, 1733. 8°.

— - *Same.* Ed. by H. V. H. Cowell. London, 1860. 12°.

— - *Same.* (*In his* Works, v. 1. 1871.)

— PORTERFIELD, W. The eye, and manner and phenomena of vision. Edinburgh, 1759. 2 v. 8°.

— PRIESTLEY, J. History and state of discoveries in vision, light, and colors. London, 1772. 4°.

— FEARN, J. Letter to Stewart; on axitomatical laws of vision. (*In* **Pamphleteer**, 1818; v. 12 of B 838)

— WELLS, W. C. Essay on single vision with two eyes. (*In his* Two essays. 1818.)

— LLOYD, H. Treatise on light and vision. London, 1831. 8°.

— HILGARD, T. C. Contrib. to the physiology of sight. (*In* **Amer. Assoc.** Proc., v. 9. 1856.) — BROCKLESBY, J. Exper. on visual direction. (*In* v. 10. 1857.)

— NAGEL, A. Das Sehen mit zwei Augen und die Lehre von den identischen Netzhautstellen. Lpz., Heidelb., 1861. 8°.

— ROGERS, W. B. Experiments and references in regard to binocular vision; our inability from the retinal impression alone to determine which retina is impressed. (*In* **Amer. Assoc.** Proc., v. 14. 1861.)

— ABBOTT, T. K. Sight and touch; an attempt to disprove the Berkeleian theory of vision. London, 1864. 8°.

— HELMHOLTZ, H. L. F. Die neueren Fortschritte in der Theorie des Sehens. [1868.] (*In his* Populäre Wissenschaftliche Vorträge, v. 2. 1871.)

— LAUGEL, A. (*In* **Revue** d. D. Mondes, oct. 1868.)

Vision of Don Roderick. *See* **Scott**, *Sir* W.

Vision of judgment; by Quevedo Redivivus, Jr. [R. W. Wright]. N. Y., 1867. 12°.

Vision of Rubeta; an epic story; [by L. Osborne]. Boston, 1838. 8°.

Visionari; opera buffa; [nelle ling. ital. e spanuola]. Madrid, 1783. 12°. (D 49)

Visionaria, La; por J. E. Hartzenbusch. (*In his* Obras escogidas. 1850.)

Visions. *See* **Apparitions**; — **Dreams.**

Visit to my discontented cousin, A; [by H. W. Moncrieff]. Boston, 1871. 16°.

Visita de duelo, La. *See* **Cruz y Cano, R. de la.**

Visitant, The weekly. Vol. 1.; Jan.-Dec. 1806. *n.t.p.* [Salem, 1806.] 8°.

Visitation and search. SCHLEGEL, J. F. W. Neutral rights; an exam. of the right of search of neutral vessels under convoy; tr. from the Fr. Phila., 1801. 8°. (B 354, 356, 1699)

— - Visitation of neutral vessels under convoy; exam. of the judgment by the Eng. Court of Admiralty, June 11, 1799; tr. from the Danish by De Juge. London, 1801. 8°. (B 672)

— CROKE, *Sir* A. Remarks on Schlegel's work upon the visitation of neutral vessels under convoy. London, 1801. 8°. (B 672, 780, 1410.)

— ADAMS, J. The inadmissible principles of the King of England's proclamation, Oct. 16, 1807. Boston, 1809. 8°. (B 991)

— WHEATON, H. British claim to the right of visitation and search. Phila., 1842. 8°.

— GORDON, H. The right of search question. London, 1843. 12°. (C 182)

— LAWRENCE, W. B. Visitation and search; hist. sketch of the Brit. claim. Bost., 1858. 8°.

— MACQUEEN, J. F. Chief points in the laws of war and neutrality, search and blockade. London, 1862. 12°.
Note. From Fraser's mag., v. 79-80. 1869.

Visitations. GIBSON, E. Of visitations parochial and general. London, 1717. 8°. (B 100)

Visite à Bedlam, Une; comédie. *See* **Scribe, A. E.**

Visiting my relations and its results; [by Mrs. Kelty]. 3d ed. London, 1853. 16°.

Visitor, The weekly, May, 1834. Nos. 81-84, with supplement. *n.p.*, 1834. 8°. (B 1722)

Visitor and monthly instructor, 1842, 46-48. London, *Relig. Tract. Soc.*, 1842-48. 4 v. 8°.

Visits and sketches at home and abroad. *See* **Jameson, A.**

Visits from the shades; or, Dialogues serious, comical, and political. London, 1704-06. 3 nos. 8°. (B 646)

Visscher, Claes Janz. Afbeeldinge van de stercke vestinge genæmt Het Hooft, alous belegert door die van Dantzig. 1659. *n.p.*, [16—]. (E 78, no. 268b)

— Belgii veteris typus. *n.p.*, 1624. (E 64, no. 1)

— Caerte van't Scheldt ende Santvliet. Antwerp, 1638. (E 78, no. 46)

— Comitatus Hollandiæ denuo formâ leonis. *n.p.*, 1648. (E 78, no. 49)

— Ducatus Juliacensis, Cliviensis, Montensis. Amst., [16—]. (E 78, no. 88a)

— Insula Candia olim Creta. *n.p.*, [16—]. (E 78, no. 255)

— Meridies. Amst., 1650. (E 78, no. 314)
Note. Map of the middle of the world.

— Moraviæ delineatio. [Amst.,] 1664. (E 78, no. 129)

Visscher, Cornelius. SMITH, W. Catalogue of works of V. (*In* **Fine arts q. rev.**, v. 1, 2. 1863; v. 3. 1864-65.)

Visscher, Jacobus Canter. Letters from Malabar; from the Dutch; added, an account of Travancore, and Fra Bartolomeo's travels in that country; ed. by H. Drury. Madras, 1862. 8°.

Visscher, Nicolaes. [Maps: Europe. *n.p.*, *or Amst.*, 17—.] (E 64)
Namely. Portugalliæ et Algarbiæ regna. (No. 2.) — Environs de Balaguer et Lerida. (No. 3.) Environs de Bouchain et Cambray. (No. 4.) — Carte des provinces de Picardie, Normandie, et Isle de France. (No. 5.) — Carte d'une partie de l'Isle de France, des prov. de Champagne, et Picardie. (No. 6.) — Generalis Lotharingiæ ducatus tabula. Amst. (No. 7.) — Geographica Artesiæ comitatus tabula. (No. 8.) — Totius Alsatiæ novissima, *etc.*, tabula. (No. 9.) — Superioris Alsatiæ tabula. (No. 10.) — Landgraviatus Alsatiæ Inferioris tabula. (No. 11.) — Totius fluminis Rheni descriptio. (No. 12.) — Regionum Coloniense electoratu et archiepiscopatu subditarum peraccurata tabula. Amst. (No. 13.) — Tabula geog. archi-episcopatum Trevirensis et Coloniensis. Amst. (No. 14.) — Belgii pars meridionalis cum occid. Germaniæ et sept. Franciæ confiniis tabula. Amst. (No. 15.) — Flandriæ comitatus pars occidentalis, pars media, pars australis. Amst. (Nos. 16-18.) — Brabantiæ Bataviæ pars occidentalis. Amst. (No. 19.) — Tetrarchiæ Antverpiensis pars meridionalis. Amst. (No. 20.) — Nassovia principatus. Amst. (No. 21.) — Westphaliæ circulus. Amst. (No. 22.) — Tractus inter Sabim et Mosam. Amst. (No. 23.) — Comitatus Namurci delineatio. (No. 24.) — Archiepiscopatus ac electoratus Trevirensis ditio. Amst. (No. 25.) — Moguntini archiep. et electoratus, nec non comitatuum utriusque Cattimeliboci Verthemensis, et Erpachiensis descriptio. Amst. (No. 26.)—Juliacensis, Cliviensis, et Montensis ducatus. Amst. (No. 27.) — Nobilissimi Albis fluvii ostia, nec non Hamburgenense. Amst. (No. 29.) — Ducatus Bremæ et Ferdæ. (No. 30.) — Ducatus Brunsuicensis fereque Lunæburgensis. (No. 31.) — Ducatus Wurtenbergensis. Amst. (No. 32.) — Ducatus Luneburgici et comitatus Dannebergensis. Amst. (No. 33.) — Magnæ Prussiæ ducatus tabula. Amst. (No. 34.) — Electoratus Brandenburgi, Mekelenburgi, et maximæ partis Pomeraniæ tabula. (No. 35.) — Carte géog. du duché de Pomeranie et Mecklenbourg. (No. 36.) — Bavaria. Amst. (Nos. 37, 38.) — Tabula sedis belli Palatinatus ad Rhenum, *etc.* (No. 39.) — Bavariæ pars inferior. Amst. (No. 40.) — Bavariæ Palatinatus. Amst. (No. 41.) — Austriæ archiducatus pars superior, pars inferior. Amst. (No. 42, 43.) — Moscoviæ seu Russiæ Magnæ tabula. Amst. (No. 45.) — Archipelagi nec non Græciæ tabula. Amst. (No. 46.)

Vissian, Massimino. Federica. (*In* **Brofferio, A.** Tradiz. ital., v. 4. 1850.)

Vital affinity. ALISON, W. T. Defence of the doctrine of vital affinity. (*In* **Roy. Soc. of Edin.** Trans., v. 20. 1853.)

Vital functions, Vital principle. *See* **Biology**; — **Physiology.**

Vital-Roux, —. Mémoire sur les moyens de faire baisser les taux de l'intérêt. Paris, [18—?]. 8°. (C 303)

Vital statistics. BUFFON, G. L. L., *comte* de, *d.* 1788. (*In his* Hist. nat., v. 19. 1800.)

— WORCESTER, J. E. Remarks on longevity and the expectation of life in the U. S., rel. partic. to New Hampshire, with comparative views in rel. to for. countries. (*In* **Amer. Acad.** Mem., n.s., v. 1. 1833.)

— QUETELET, L. A. J. Sur l'homme, et la développement de sa faculté. Paris, 1835. 2 v. 8°.

— - *Eng.* Treatise on man and the development of his faculties. Edin., 1842. 8°.

— NEISON, F. G. P. Contributions to vital statistics. [1845.] 3d ed. London, 1857. 4°.

— UEBER die Vertheilung der Bevölkerung nach Geschlecht und Alter in verschiedenen Staaten Europa's und in den nordamerikanischen Freistaaten. (*In* **Berlin. Ak. d. Wiss.** Abh., 1848.)

— DIETERICI, K. F. W. Statistische Beobachtungen üb. die Todesarten und das Verhältniss derjenigen, welche das höchste Lebensalter erreichen, zu den Culturzuständen eines Landes. (*In* **Berlin. Ak. d. Wiss.** Abh., 1852.)

— ELLIOTT, E. B. Vital statistics. (*In* **Amer. Assoc.** Proc., v. 10. 1857.)

— DIETERICI, K. F. W. Ueber den Begriff der mittleren Lebensdauer und deren Berechnung für den preussischen Staat. (*In* **Berlin. Ak. d. Wiss.** Abh., 1858.)

— GOULD, B. A. Investigations in the military and anthropological statistics of American soldiers. N. Y., *U.S. Sanit. Com.*, 1869. 8°.

— BEDDOE, J. Stature and bulk of man in the British Isles. (*In* **Anthropological Soc.** Mem., v. 3. 1870.)
See also **Births**; — **Longevity**; — **Mortality**; — **Statistics**; — *also* **Statistical Soc.** Journ., *passim.*

Vitale, Salvatori. Annales Sardiniæ. (*In* **Grævius.** Thes. antiq. Sicil., v. 15. 1725.)

Vitaliano, Vincenzo. AMATO, G. d'. (*In his* **Panteon,** v. 1. 1851.)

Vitalienbrüder, Die; von J. Voigt. (*In* **Historisches** Taschenbuch, 1841.)

Vitalis, J. B. Manuel du teinturier. Rouen, 1810. 8°.

Vitalis Ordericus. *See* **Ordericus Vitalis.**

Vitalism. *See* **Biology.**

Vitality. PAINE, M. Essays on the philosophy of vitality as contra-distinguished from chemical and mechanical philosophy. N. Y., 1842. 8°. (B 1189)

— HIGGINS, H. H. (*In* **Smithsonian Inst.** Report, 1866.)

Vitelleschi, Muzio. Epistolæ III. (*In* **Jesuits.** Libri instituti Soc. Jesu, v. 10. 1635.)

Vitelli, Alessandro. FABRETTI, A. (*In his* Biog. dei cap. dell' Umbria, v. 4. 1846.)

Vitelli, Nicolo, *and* Vitellozzo, *and* Paolo. FABRETTI, A. (*In his* Biog. dei cap. dell' Umbria, v. 3. 1844.)

Vitelli di Città di Castello, *Famiglia di.* (*In* Litta, P. Fam., v. 15.)
Viterbi, LucAntonio. DAVENPORT, R. A. Sufferings of V. (*In his* Narratives, v. 2. 1840. Fam. lib., v. 75.)
Vitet, Ludovic. Discours. (*In* Paris. Inst. *Ac. Fr.* Recueil des disc., 1840-49, 1e pt. 1850-59.) — Réponses. (*In* 1850-59, 2e pt., 1860-69, 1e pt.)
— Monographie de l'église Notre-Dame de Noyon; plans, *etc.*, par D. Ramée. Paris, 1845. 4° *and* Atlas f°. (Doc. inéd.)
— Numerous articles.] (*In* Revue d. D. Mondes, sept. 1840 - mai 1873.)
Viti. *See* Fiji Islands.
Vitiligoidea. ADDISON, T. (*In his* Col. 1868.)
Vitre, Edward D. de. *See* De Vitre, E. D.
Vitringa, Kempe (*Lat.* Campejus). Commentarii ad librum Zachariæ; ed. H. Venema. Leovardiæ, 1734. 4°.
— Commentarius ad canticum Mosis, Deut. xxxii; ed. H. Venema. Harlingæ, 1734. 4°.
— Commentarius in Iesaiam. Leov., 1724. 2 v. f°.
— Korte schets van de Christelyke zeden-leere. Amst., 1724. 8°.
— Observationum sacrarum lib. VI. Ed. nov., acc., Geog. sacra et ejusdem vita. Jenæ, 1723. 4°.
— NICERON, J. P. (*In his* Mém., v. 35. 1736; *and, Germ.*, v. 19. 1759.)
Vitruvius Pollio, Marcus. De architectura lib. x; cum comm. D. Barbari. Venetiis, 1567. f°.
— *Same.* Rec. J. G. Schneider. Lps., 1807-08. 3 v. 8°.
— *Same.* Notis J. Poleni; stud. S. Stratico. Utini, 1825-30. 4 v. in 8 pt. 4°.
— *Eng.* Architecture; tr. by W. Newton. London, 1791. 2 v. f°.
— - Civil architecture; tr. with introd. by W. Wilkins. London, 1812. 4°.
— - Tr. by J. Gwilt. New ed. London, *Weale*, 1860. 12°.
— *French.* Architecture; tr. par J. Martin. Paris, 1547. f°.
— BALDI, B. De verborum Vitruvianorum significatione. Aug. Vindel., 1612. 4°.
Vitry, Jacques de. *See* Jacobus *de Vitriaco.*
Vittorelli, Jacopo. Anacreontiche sonetti. (*In* Poeti ital. contemp. 1843.)
Vittoria; by G. Meredith. (*In* Fortnightly, v. 3-6. 1866.)
Vittoria Colonna. *See* Colonna, Vittoria.
Vitulus aureus, the golden calf; a suppl. to Apuleius' Golden ass. *See* Philander, J.
Vitus, *St.* HISTORIA translationis S. Viti. (*In* Pertz, G. H. Mon. Germ., Scr., v. 2. 1829; — *and in* Jaffé, P. Biblioth. rer. Germ., v. 1. 1864.)
Vitus, Ricardus. *See* White, R.
Viuda hipócrita y avarienta, La; saynete. *See* Cruz y Cano, R. de la.
Vivarium naturæ. *See* Shaw, G.
Vivenot, Alfred von. Zur Geschichte des Rastatter Congresses. Wien, 1871. 8°.
Vivers, Richard. The vicar of Banbury further corrected; reply to B. Lovelings's 'Quakerism a complication of heresy'. London, 1703. 4°. (B 257)
Vives, Francisco Dionisio. [Correspondencia con Douzelot, gobern. de la Martinica, y Bergeret, comand. de las fuerzas navales de Francia.] Habana, 1823. f°. (A 34)
— Habitantes de la isla de Cuba; [proclamation]. Habana, 1823. f°. (A34)
Vives, Juan Luis. Commentaria. (*In* Augustinus, *St.* Opera, v. 5. 1636.)
— NICERON, J. P. (*In his* Mém., v. 21. 1733; *and, Germ.*, v. 23. 1771.)
Vivian, *Rev.* Thomas. Three dialogues between a minister and one of his parishioners on the true principles of religion. *n.p.*, [179-?]. 8°. (B 197)
Vivian Grey; by B. Disraeli. N. Y., 1826. 12°.
— *Same.* 3d Amer. ed. Balt., 1833. 2 v. 12°.
— *Same.* (*In his* Works, v. 1. 1845; — *and* Novels and tales, v. 2. 1866.)
Viviani, Domenico. CANOBBIO, G. B. (*In* Grillo, L. Elogi di Lig., v. 3. 1846.)
Viviani, Giuliano, *Abp.* FABRONI, A. (*In his* Mem. di Pisani, v. 3. 1792.)
Viviani, Vincenzio. Proposizioni meccaniche. (*In* Galilei, G. Opere, v. 11. 1854.) — Illustrazioni ai Dialoghi delle nuove scienze. (*In* v. 14.) — Vita di Galileo. (*In* v. 15. 1856.)
— FABRONI, A. (*In his* Vitæ Ital., v. 1. 1778.)
— NICERON, J. P. (*In his* Mém., v. 24. 1733; *and, Germ.*, v. 17. 1758.)
— TOCCI, P. F. (*In* Crescimbeni, G. M. Vite degli Arcadi illustri, v. 1. 1708.)
Vivien, Alexandre François Auguste. Numerous articles.] (*In* Revue d. D. Mondes, oct. 1841 - nov. 1844.)
Vivien de Saint Martin, Louis. *See* Année géographique, L', 1862-66.
Vivir loco y morir mas, capricho; por J. Zorrilla. (*In his* Obras, v. 2. 1852.)
Vizcaino, Sebastian. Expedition to California. (*In* Burney, J. Discoveries in the South Sea, v. 2. 1806.)
Vizcaino fingido, El; por M. de Cervantes Saavedra. (*In his* Obras completas, v. 12. 1864; *and* Comedias y entremeses, v. 1. 1749.)
Vizetelly, Henry. The story of the diamond necklace. London, 1867. 2 v. 8°.
Vlamingh, Willem de. Voy. to New Holland, 1696. (*In* Major, R. H. Early voy. to Terra Australis. 1859. Hakluyt Soc., v. 25.)
Vlandi, Spiridion. *See* Blandi, S.
Vlin de la Ponneraye, D. [Architectural designs.] *n.p.*, 17—]. f°. (E 63)
Vnezapne, *Fortress.* REBOUL, C. La forteresse de Vnézapné; souvenirs de la guerre du Caucase, [1848]. (*In* Revue d. D. Mondes, av. 1853.)
Vocabularium sacrum Græco-Latinum; by [*t. p. mut.*] J. C. Oxford, 1731. 8°.
Vocabulary of religious terms. 2d ed. London, 1825. 32°. (D 31)
Vocal poetry. *See* Aikin, J.
Vocalists. *See* Singers.
Vocations, Les; par A. Achard. Paris, 1859. 16°.
Vocke, Wilhelm. Geschichte des Steuern des britischen Reichs. Lpz., 1866. 8°.
Vockerodt, Johann Gotthelf von. Courte description des peuples et des provinces situées à l'occident de la mer Caspienne, depuis Astracan jusqu'au fleuve Kura, telles qu'elles se trouvoient en 1728. (*In* Berlin. Ak. d. Wiss. Abh., v. 12. 1756.) — ELOGE de V. (*In* v. 11. 1755.)
Voconia, Lex. SAVIGNY, F. C. von. Ueber die L. Voconia. (*In* Berlin. Ak. d. Wiss. Abh., 1820-21.)
— GIRAUD, C. J. B. Du vrai caractère de la loi Voconia chez les Romains. (*In* Paris. Inst. *Ac. d. Sci. Mor.* Sav. étr., v. 1. 1841.)
Vocontie. LONG, J. D. Recherches sur les antiquités romaines du pays das Vocontiens. (*In* Paris. Inst. *Ac. d. Inscr.* Div. sav., 2e sér., v. 2. 1849.)
Note. This country comprised part of Dauphiny and of Provence.
Voegen van Engelen, Jacobus. Theses medicæ inaugurales, *etc.* Duisburgi, [1777]. 8°. (C 271)
Voet, Jan. MAURICE, —. Table des commentaires de Voet analysés dans leurs rapports avec chacun des articles des codes français. Brux., 1841. 4°.
Vœu d'une morte, Le; par E. Zola. Paris, 1867. 18°.
Vœux d'un solitaire; par J. H. B. de Saint-Pierre. (*In his* Œuvres, v. 11. 1826.)
Vœux téméraires, Les; ou l'enthousiasme; par S. F. D. de St. A. de Genlis. (Vol. 21-23 *of her* Œuvres. 1825.)
Vogel, Charles. Le Portugal et ses colonies. Paris, 1860. 8°.
Vogel, Eduard. Lettre sur l'histoire naturelle de l'Afrique centrale. (*In* Paris. Soc. de Géog. Bul., 4e sér., v. 8. 1854.)
Vogel, Ernst Gustav. Literatur europäischer öffentl. u. corporations Biblioth. Lpz., 1840. 8°.
Vogel, Ewald. Liber de lapidis physici conditionibus. (*In* Zetzner, L. Theatr. chem., v. 3. 1613.)
Vogel, Julius. Guide to the analysis of the urine. *See* Neubauer, C. T. L.
— On the laws according to which the mixing of fluids and their penetration into permeable substances occurs, with special reference to the processes in the human and animal organism. (*In* Graham, T. Chem. reports. 1848.)
— Pathological anatomy of the human body; tr. with add. by G. E. Day. London, 1847. 8°.

Vogel, Ludwig. ANDRESEN, A. (*In his* Die deutschen Maler Radirer, v. 2. 1867.)
Vogel, Rudolph Augustin. HEYNE, C. G. Eulogium Rudolphi Augustini Vogel. (*In* **Goettingen. Ges. d. Wiss.** Comm., 1774.)
Vogel von Vogelstein, Karl. ANDRESEN, A. (*In his* deutschen Maler-Radirer, v. 2. 1867.)
Vogelscheuche; von J. L. **Tieck**. (*In his* Gesam. Novellen, v. 11. 1854.)
Vogelweide, Walther von der. *See* **Walther** *von der Vogelweide*.
Voght, Kaspar, *Freiherr* von. Account of the management of the poor in Hamburgh since 1788. Edin., 1795. 8°. (B 1901)
— *Same*. (*In* **Pamphleteer**, 1818; v. 11 of B 838)
Vogt, Carl. Lectures on man; his place in creation; ed. by J. Hunt. London, 1864. 8°. (Anthropol. Soc.)
Vogt, Johann. Catalogus historico-criticus librorum rariorum jam curis quartis recog. et adauct. Hamb., 1753. 8°.
Vogt, Nikolaus. Voyage pittoresque sur le Rhin; [tr.] par M. l'abbé Libert. Francfort sur le M., 1804-07. 3 v. 8°.
Vogüé, Charles Jean Melchior, *comte* de. The Hauran. (*In* **Morrison, W.** Recovery of Jerusalem. 1871.)
— Une nouvelle inscription phénicienne. (*In* **Paris. Inst.** *Ac. d. Inscr.* Div. sav., 1e sér., v. 6. 1860.)
Voice. ART of improving the voice and ear. London, 1825. 12°.
— RUSH, J. Philosophy of the human voice. Phila., 1827. 8°.
— BENNATI, F. Recherches sur le mécanisme de la voix humaine. [1830.] 2e éd. Paris, 1832. 8°.
— — Recherches sur les maladies qui affectent la voix humaine. Paris, 1832. 8°.
— RUSSELL, W. Orthophony; or, Cultivation of the voice in elocution; with suppl. on purity of tone, by G. J. Webb. [1845.] 5th ed. Boston, 1848. 12°.
— HUNT, J. Manual of the philosophy of voice and speech. London, 1859. 12°.
— LAUGEL, A. La voix. (*In* **Revue** d. D. Mondes, mai 1867.)
— SEILER, *Mad.* E. The voice in singing; tr. by [W. H. Furness]. N. Y., 1868. 12°.
— MUNROE, L. B. Manual of physical and oral training. Phila., 1869. 8°.
— GIBB, *Sir* G. D. The character of the voice in the nations of Asia and Africa. (*In* **Anthropological** Soc. Mem., v. 3. 1870.)
See also **Singing**.
Voice, Daily evening; devoted to the interests of workingmen; Dec. 2, 1864 - Oct. 16, 1867. Boston, 1864-67. 3 v. f°.
Voice from the South; letters from Georgia to Mass., *etc.* Balt., 1847. 8°. (B 1477, 1502, 1666.)
Voice of devotion; or, Course of prayers for use of Christians. 5th ed. Edin., 1841. 32°.
Voice of the Fair; pub. under the auspices of the North Western Sanitary Fair; Apr. 27 - June 24. Chicago, 1865. f°.
Voice of the people, and facts [on] the rejection of Van Buren by the U. S. Senate. N. Y., 1832. 8°. (B 1495)
Voice of truth; or, Thoughts on the affair between the Leopard and Chesapeake. N. Y., 1807. 8°. (B 432, 1854)
Voice to the city, A; or, A loud cry from heaven to London setting before her her sins, her sickness, her remedies. London, 1665. 2 pt. 4°. (B 1)
Voices from prison. *See* **Spear, C.**
Voices from Salisbury Plain; or, Who's to blame? a dialogue on the Franco-Prussian war. London, [187-]. 16°. (E 158)
Voices from the early Church; a series of poems. London, 1845. 12°.
Voices of the day. *See* **Cumming, J.**
Voices of the night. *See* **Cumming, J.**

Voigt, Johannes. Blicke in das kunst- und gewerbreiche Leben der Stadt Nürnberg im 16. Jahrh.; mit Autobiog. Berlin, [1861]. 8°. (Schmidt, F. Deutsche nat. Bibl., v. 4.)
— Briefwechsel der berühmtesten Gelehrten des Zeitalters der Reformation mit Herzog Albrecht von Preussen. Königsberg, 1841. 8°.
Contents. Kaspar Aquila, 1549-52. — J. Brentius, 1549-64. — J. Bugenhagen, 1543-52. — J. Camerarius, 1539-68. — J. Carion, 1527-37. — J. Crotus, 1530-32. — Veit Dietrich, 1542-49. — J. Draconites, 1550-64. — P. Eber, 1560-67. — L. Fuchs, 1537-65. — G. Hartmann, 1542-44. — K. Hedio, 1540-46. — J. Jonas, d. älter, 1545-49. — J. Jonas, d. junger, 1557-66. — G. Major, 1547-68. — A. Osiander, 1536-50. — K. Peucer, 1560-67. — E. Reinhold, 1542-52. — G. Spalatin, 1540-43. — V. Strigel, 1559-67. — M. Chemnitz, 1565-67.
— Handbuch de Geschichte Preussens bis zur Zeit der Reformation. Königsb., 1841-43. 3 v. 8°.
— Histoire du pape Grégoire VII et de son siècle, d'après les monuments originaux; tr. [avec] une introd., de notes, *etc.*, par l'abbé Jager. 3e éd. Paris, 1842. 12°.
— Das Stillleben des Hochmeisters des deutschen Ordens und sein Fürstenhof. (*In* **Historisches** Taschenbuch, 1830.) — Herzog Albrecht von Preussen und das gelehrte Wesen seiner Zeit. (*In* 1831.) — Fürstenleben und Fürstensitte im 6en Jahrhundert. (*In* 1835.) — Ueber Pasquille, Spottlieder, und Schmahschriften aus der ersten Hälfte des 16en Jahrhunderts. (*In* 1838.) — Die Vitalienbrüder. (*In* 1841.) — Der Freiherr Hans Katzianer im Turkenkrieg. (*In* 1844.) — Wilhelm von Grumbach und seine Händel. (*In* 1846-47.) — Zwölf Briefe über Sitten und sociales Fürstenleben auf den deutschen Reichstagen. (*In* 1851.) — Des Grafen Christoph des Aeltern von und zu Dohna Hof- und Gesandtschaftsleben. — Der Fürstenbund gegen Kaiser Karl V. (*In* 1853.)
— Stimmen aus Rom über den päpstlichen Hof im 15en Jahrhundert. (*In* **Historisches** Taschenbuch, 1833.)
— *Ital.* Ragguagli di Roma nel secolo 15; estratti da un articolo pub. nel Taschenbuch. (*In* **Archivio** stor. ital., app., v. 3. 1846.)
Voigt, Ludwig Georg. Enea Silvio de' Piccolomini als Papst Pius II., und sein Zeitalter. Berlin, 1856-63. 3 v. 8°.
— Die Eroberung von Constantinopel und das Abendland. (*In* **Historische** Zeitschrift, v. 3. 1860.) — Georg von Böhmen, der Hussitenkönig. (*In* v. 5.) — Johannes von Capistrano, ein Heiliger des fünfzehnten Jahrhunderts. (*In* v. 10.) — Johann Jacob Mascov; ein akad. Antrittsrede. (*In* v. 15.) — Torquato Tasso am Hofe von Ferrara. (*In* v. 20. 1868.)
— Universalhistorische Ideen über die Nothwendigkeit der Reformation. (*In* **Reformations** Almanach, 1817.)
— Die Wiederbelebung des classischen Alterthums, oder das erste Jahrhundert der Humanismus. Berlin, 1859. 8°.
Voigt von Silt, Der; von T. Mügge. 2e Aufl. Berlin, 1858. 2 v. 16°.
Voigtland, *Saxony*. JANSON, O. Terra Advocatorum, vulgo Voightland; J. Blaeu exc. Amst., [16—]. (E 78, no. 167)
Voiron, —. Histoire de l'astronomie, 1781-1811; suite de Bailly. Paris, 1811. 4°.
Voisin, Félix. Causes morales et physiques des maladies mentales et des affections nerveuses. Paris, 1826. 8°.
— **et Falret**. Notice sur l'établissement pour le traitement des aliénés à Vanves. *n.t.p.* [Paris, 183-.] 8°. (B 1568)
— *Eng.* Establishment for the treatment of both sexes afflicted with insanity at Vanves, July 1822. [Paris, 183-.] 8°. (B 1568)
Voiture, Vincent. Works. 3d ed. Lond., 1736. 2 v. 12°.
Contents. Letters and characters of the most eminent persons in the court of France; with notes by Richelet. — Alcidalis and Zelida, a romance; an entertainment for Mme. de Rambouillet. — Metamorphoses of ladies into various flowers. — Poems. — Tr. by J. Dryden and others.
— Poésie. (*In* **Annales** poétiques, v. 19. 1781.)

Voiture embourbée, La; par P. C. de **Marivaux.** (*In his* Œuvres, v. 12. 1781.)

Voituron, Paul. Recherches philosophiques sur les principes de la science du beau. Brux., 1861. 2 v. 8°.

Voix libre du citoyen, ou Observations sur le gouvernement de Pologne; [par Stanislas Lesczynski]. *n.p.*, 1749. 2 v. 12°.

Voix sortie des cieux, Une. *See* **Vaisse,** J. L.

Vol, Le; ou la famille d'Anglade. *See* **Accusation.** 1818. (D 15)

Volaterranus, Raphael. *See* **Maffei,** R.

Volaterrano, Giacopo. Diarium Romanorum, 1472-84; editum ex ms. codico. (*In* **Muratori,** L. A. Rer. Ital. scr., v. 23. 1733.)

Volcanoes. Scrope, G. P. Considerations on volcanos, leading to a new theory of the earth. London, 1825. 8°.

— - *Same.* Volcanos with a descrip. catalogue of all known volcanos and volcanic formations. 2d ed. London, 1862. 8°.

— Daubeny, C. G. B. Description of active and extinct volcanoes. London, 1826. 8°.

— Humboldt, A. Ueber den Bau und die Wirkungsart der Vulkane in den verschiedenen Erdstrichen. (*In his* Ansichten der Natur, v. 2. 1849; *and*, *Eng.*, Aspects of nature, v. 2. 1849; *and*, Views. 1850.)

— Johnston, A. K. The phenomena of volcanic action. (*In his* Physical atlas. 1856.)

— Zurcher, F., *and* Margollé, E. Volcans et tremblements de terre; illustré par E. Riou. [1866.] 2e éd. Paris, 1868. 16°. (Charton, E. Biblioth. des merv.)

— - *Eng.* Volcanoes and earthquakes. From the French by Mrs. N. Lockyer. London, 1868. 8°.

— Réclus, J. J. E. Les volcans et les tremblemens de terre. (*In* **Revue** d. D. Mondes, jan. 1867.)

See also **Etna,** *Mt.*; — **Popocatapetl**; — **Vesuvius**; — **France.** *Geology*; — **Hawaiian Islands**; — **Iceland.** *Description and Natural history*; — **Quito.**

Volder, Burkard. Niceron, J. P. (*In his* Mém., v. 22. 1733; *and*, *Germ.*, v. 17. 1758.)

Voleurs d'or, Les; par Mme. C. de Chabrillan. Paris, 1857. 18°.

Volkersen, Samuel. Description of the west coast of the South land, 1658. (*In* **Major,** R. H. Early voy. to Terra Australis. 1859. Hakluyt Soc., v. 25.)

Volkmann, Alfred Wilhelm. Physiologische Untersuchungen im Gebiete der Optik. 1e Heft. Lpz., 1863. 8°.

Volks-Kalender für 1853; hrsg. von K. Steffens. Berlin, [1852]. 16°.

Vollheim, Karl. Perlen der neuern englischen und americanischen Lyrik. Lpz., 1864. 8°.

Vollmer, Adolph. Andresen, A. (*In his* Die deutschen Maler-Radirer, v. 3. 1866.)

Vollständige cellische Gesangbuch, Das. Lüneburg, *J. Stern*, 1697. 12°.

Volney, Constantin François Chassebœuf, *comte* de. Answer to Dr. Priestley, on his pamphlet entitled 'Observations upon the increase of infidelity'. Phila., 1797. 8°. (B 1360, W 59)

— Chronologie des douze siècles antérieurs au passage de Xerxes en Grèce. (*In* **Encyclopédie** méthod., v. 11. 1790.)

— Common sense; or, Natural ideas opposed to supernatural. N. Y., 1795. 8°.

— Histoire. (*In* **Paris. Ecoles Normales.** Séances, v. 1-3, 11. 1800.)

— Les ruines, ou Méditation sur les révolutions des empires. 5e éd.; on y a joint La loi naturelle. Paris, 1817. 8°.

— - *Eng.* The ruins; or, Survey of the revolutions of empires; annexed, The law of nature. London, 1819. 8°. (B 1657)

— *Same, without the* 'Law'. N. Y., 1796. 12°.

— *Same.* [Added, controversy between Priestly and V.] Exeter, 1823. 12°.

— Simplification des langues orientales, ou Méthode d'apprendre les langues arabe, persane, et turque, avec des charactères européens. Paris, an III [1795]. 8°.

— Tableau du climat et du sol des Etats-Unis d'Amérique; suivi d'eclaircissemens sur la Floride, sur la colonie française au Scioto, sur quelques colonies canadiennes, et sur les sauvages. Paris, 1803. 2v. 8°.

— *Eng.* View of the climate and soil of the U. S., *etc.*; tr. from the French. Lond., 1804. 8°.

— Travels through Syria and Egypt, 1783-85. London, 1788. 2 v. 8°.

— Voyages en Afrique. (*In* **Montémont,** A. Biblioth. univ., v. 22. 1834.)

— Priestley, J. Letters to Volney on his 'Ruins'. Phila., 1797. 8°. (W 59.)

— - Increase of infidelity; animadversions on Volney's 'Ruins'. Phila., 1797. 8°.

— - *Another copy.* (W 59)

— Roberts, P. Christianity vindicated; answer to Volney's 'Ruins'. London, 1800. 8°.

— Rowe, R. J. Dissertation on the 'Ruins'; exam. of "Remarks on Volney's 'Ruins', by W. A. Hails.'" London, 1832. 8°.

— St. John, J. A. (*In his* Lives of celebrated travellers, v. 3. 1847. Harper's fam. lib., v. 40.)

Volpato, Giovanni, *b.* 1733, *and* Morghen, R. Principj del disegno tratti dalle statue antiche. Roma, 1786. f°.

Volpato, Giovanni Battista, *b.* 1633. Modo da tener nel dipinger. [Lat. and Eng.] (*In* **Merrifield,** M. P. Orig. treatises, v. 2. 1849.)

Volpe, Taddeo della. Papotti, T. (*In his* Elogi d'illust. Imolesi. 1841.)

Volpi (*Lat.* Vulpius), Geronimo. Epigrammata. *See* **Volpi,** G. A. Carmina.

Volpi, Giovanni Antonio, *the elder.* Carmina. *See the next entry.*

Volpi, Giovanni Antonio, *the younger*, *b.* 1686, *d.* 1766. Carmina. Patavii, 1725. 4°.

Contents. Carmina. — Opuscula. — Dedicationes et præfationes. — Eruditorum quorumdam virorum poemata. — J. A. Vulpii antiquioris carmina. — Hieronymi Vulpii epigrammata.

— Fabroni, A. (*In his* Vitæ Ital., v. 13. 1787.)

Volpone; by B. **Johnson.** (*In his* Works, v. 2. 1756.)

Volsci. Mommsen, T. Der volskische Dialekt. (*In his* Unteritalische Dial. 1850.)

See also **Vases.**

Völsunga saga; story of the Volsungs and Niblungs, with songs from the elder Edda; from the Icelandic by E. Magnùsson, and W. Morris. London, 1870. 8°.

Volta, Alessandro, *conte.* Arago, D. F. J. (*In his* Œuvres, v. 1. 1854.)

Volta River. Beschreibung der Küsten von Rio da Volta. (*In* **Allgemeine** Hist., v. 4. 1749.)

Voltaire, François Marie Arouet de. Collection complette des œuvres. Vol. 1-30, Genève, 31-45, Paris, 1768-96. 45 v. 4°.

Contents. Vol. 1. La Henriade, avec préfaces par M. L ... et Marmontel, et les variantes et notes par l'abbé Langlet. — Essai sur la poésie épique. — Discours en vers sur l'homme. — Le temple du goût. — Le poëme de Fontenoy. — Poëme sur le désastre de Lisbonne. — La loi naturelle; poëme. 2. Sur l'histoire. — Histoire de Charles XII, roi de Suède. — Histoire de l'Empire de Russie sous Pierre le Grand. 3-7. *Théâtre.* 3. Oedipe. — Marianne. — Brutus. — Le mort de César. — Zaire. — Alzire. 4. Mérope. — Le fanatisme. — Sémiramis. — Oreste. — Catilina. 5. Adélaïde du Guesclin. — Le duc de Foix. — L'orphelin de la Chine. — Tancrede. — Zulime. — Olimpie. 6. Le triumvirat. — — Les Scythes. — L'indiscret. — L'enfant prodigue. — Nanine, ou le préjuge vaincu. — La prude, ou la gardeuse de cassette. 7. Le droit du seigneur. — La femme qui a raison. — L'Ecossaise. — Pandore. — Samson. — La princesse de Navarre. — Le temple de la gloire. — Socrate. — Charlot. 8-10. Essai sur les mœurs et l'esprit des nations, et l'histoire depuis Charlemagne jusqu'à Louis XIII. 11, 12. Siècle de Louis XIV, auquel on a joint un précis du siècle de Louis XV. 13. *Ro-*

mans, contes philosophiques, etc. Zadig, ou la destinée. — Le monde comme il va. — Memnon. — Les deux consolés. — Histoire des voy. de Scarmentado. — Micromégas. — Histoire d'un bon bramin. — Le blanc et le noir. — Jeannot et Colin. — Candide, ou l'optimisme. — Pot-pourri. — L'ingénu. — L'homme aux quarante écus. — La princesse de Babilone. — Les lettres d'Amabed. — 14–17. *Mélanges philos., etc.* 14. Eléments du philosophie de Newton. — Mélanges. — Dialogues. — Vie de Molière. 15. Mélanges. 16. Mélanges. — Le philosophe ignorant. — Commentaire sur le livre des délits et des peines. — La défense de mon oncle. — Lettres. — Traité sur la tolérance. — Pièces originales conc. la mort des sieurs Calas, *etc.* 17. Des singularités de la nature. — Sermons et homélies. — Collections d'anciens évangiles. — Les adorateurs ou les louanges de Dieu. — Les droit des hommes et les usurpations des autres. — Mélanges. — Lettres. — Traité de Memmius. — Le cri des nations. — Articles de littérature très intéressans. 18–20. *Poésies mêlées, etc.* 18. Les Guèbres, ou la Tolérance. — Pièces détachées. 19. Les Pélopides, ou Altrée et Thieste, Sophonisbe, Le dépositaire, Les loix de Minos. — Jules César. — La comédie fameuse. — Contes de Guillaume Vadé, *etc.* 20. La Pucelle d'Orléans. — Fragmens sur quelques révol. dans l'Inde, et sur la mort du comte Lalli. — Fragment sur la justice. 21–24. Questions sur l'encyclopédie, par des amateurs. 21. A-Bib. 22. Bie-Eli. 23. Elo-I et J (Int). 24. Jui-Z. 25. Annales de l'empire depuis Charlemagne. 26. *Poésies.* Dom Pèdre, roi de Castille. — Saul. — La guerre civile de Genève. — Remonstrances du pays de Gex au roi. 27–30. *Mélanges philosophiques, etc.* 27. Histoire du parlement de Paris. — Histoire de Jenni, ou l'Athée et le sage. — Le taureau blanc. — Lettres chinoises et indiennes. 28. Dieu et les hommes. — Fragmens, *etc.* 29. L'épître aux Romains. — Le diner du comte de Boulainvilliers. — Profession de foi des théistes. — L'empereur de la Chine et frère Rigolet. — Lettre philosophique sur l'âme. — Les questions de Zapata. — Il faut prendre un parti, ou le principe d'action. — Les oreilles du comte de Chesterfield, et le chapelain Goudman. — Sur les Jésuites. — Les colimaçons. — Questions sur les miracles. — L'examen important de milord Bolingbroke. — Le préservatif. — De l'âme. — Action de Dieu sur l'homme. 30. Commentaire historique. — Lettres à messieurs de l'Académie Française. — Sur les prétendues lettres du pape Ganganelli. 31. *Théâtre.* Fragmens d'Artemire. — Eryphile. — Sophonisbe. — Irène. — Agatocles. — Tanis et Zélide. — Le baron d'Otrante. — Les deux tonneaux. — L'hôte et l'hôtesse. — Quelques poésies. 32. Lettres en vers et en prose. — Prix de la justice et de l'humanité. — Comment. sur l'Esprit des lois'. — Supplém. aux 'Causes celèbres'. — Défense du Newtonianisme. — Essai sur la nature du feu, et sur sa propagation. — Philosophie générale, métaphysique, morale, et théologie. — Sermons et homelies. — Dialogues d'Evhémère. — Mémoire sur la satyre. 33. Commentaires sur Corneille. 34. Mémoires de sa vie. — Différens éloges de sa personne et de ses ouvrages. — Sa correspondance avec l'impératrice de Russie et plusieurs autres souverains. — Mélanges de philosophie, *etc.* 35–42. Correspondance générale. 43. Correspondance avec M. d'Alembert. 44, 45. Correspondance avec le roi de Prusse.

— Œuvres complètes. [Kehl,] 1785–89. 92 v. 12°.

Contents. Vol. 1–9. *Théâtre.* 1. Préface. — Avertissement de l'édition de 1775. — Avertissement des éditeurs sur l'Œdipe. — Lettres à M. de Genonville. — Lettre au père Porée. — Préface de l'édition de 1729. — Œdipe. — Fragment d'Artémire. — Mariamne. — Brutus. — Eryphile. 2. Zaire. — Adélaide du Guesclin. — Amélie ou le duc de Foix. — La mort de César. — Alzire, ou les Américains. 3. Zulime. — Le fanatisme, ou Mahomet le prophète. — Mérope. — Semiramis. 4. Oreste. — Rome sauvée, ou Catilina. — L'orphelin de la Chine. — Tancrède. 5. Olimpie. — Le triumvirat. — Les Scythes. — Les Guèbres, ou la tolérance. — Sophonisbe. 6. Les lois de Minos. — Don Pedre. — Les Pélopides, ou Atrée et Thieste. — Irène. — Agathocle. 7. L'indiscret. — L'enfant prodigue. — La prude. — Nanine, ou le préjugé vaincu. — La femme qui a raison. 8. L'Ecossaise. — Le droit du seigneur. — Charlot, ou la comtesse de Givry. — Le dépositaire. — Socrate. 9. Samson. — La princesse de Navarre. — Le temple de la gloire. — Pandore. — Tanis et Zélide, ou les rois pasteurs. — Le baron d'Otrante. — Les deux tonneaux. — Jules César, tragédie de Shakespeare. — L'Héraclius espagnol, ou la comédie fameuse. 10. La Henriade. 11. La Pucelle. 12. 1r–7e discours en vers. — Le pour et le contre. — Sur la loi naturelle. — Le désastre de Lisbonne. — Le temple du goût. — Le temple de l'amitié. — Sur les événemens de 1744. — Poëme de Fontenoi. — Voyage à Berlin. — Précis de l'Ecclésiaste et du Cantique des cantiques. — La guerre civil de Genève. — La fête de Bellebat. — La Bastile. — Divertissement mis en musique. — La mort de Mlle. Le Couvreur. — La police sous Louis XIV. — Sur la campagne d'Italie. — Apologie de la fable. — Jean qui pleure et qui rit. — L'hôte et l'hôtesse. — Lettres. 13. Epitres, stances, et odes. 14. Contes de Guillaume Vadé. — Satires. — Poésies melées. 15. Lettres en vers et en prose. 16–21. Essai sur les mœurs et l'esprit des nations, et sur les principaux faits de l'histoire depuis Charlemagne jusqu'à Louis XIII. 22–25. Siècle de Louis XIV. 26. Histoire de Charles XII. 27. Histoire de l'empire de Russie sous Pierre le Grand. 28, 29. Annales de l'empire depuis Charlemagne. 28. 742–1378. 29. 1379–1740. 30. Histoire du parlement de Paris. 31. Mélanges historiques. — Le pyrrhonisme de l'histoire. — Supplement au 'Siècle de Louis XIV'. — La défense de mon oncle. 32. Un chrétien contre six Juifs, ou réfutation du Lettres de quelques Juifs. — De quelques niaiseries. — Incursion sur Nonotte ex-Jésuite. — Fragmens sur l'histoire. 33. Suite des 'Fragmens sur l'histoire'. — Examen de quelques objections contre 'Essai sur les mœurs'. — Des mensonges imprimés et du testament politique du cardinal de Richelieu. 34. La voix du sage et du peuple. — Idées de la Mothe le Vayer. — Pensées sur l'administration publique. — De la paix perpetuelle. — Les droit des hommes et les usurpations des papes. — Le tocsin des rois. — Fragment des instructions pour le prince royal de —. — Le cri des nations. — Des embellissemens de Paris. — Requête à tous les magistrats du royaume. — Idées républicaines. — Commentaire sur le livre des délits et des peines. — Prix de la justice et de l'humanité. 35. Commentaire sur l'Esprit des lois. — Diatribe à l'auteur des Ephemérides. — Ecrits pour les habitans du Mont-Jura et du pays de Gex. — Remontrances du pays de Gex au roi. — Traité sur la tolérance à l'occasion de la mort de Jean Calas. 36. Suite du 'Traité sur la tolérance'. — Pièces originales conc. la mort des sieurs Calas, et le jugement rendu à Toulouse. — Histoire d'E. Canning et des Calas. — Relation de la mort du Chevalier de la Barre. — Le cri du sang innocent. — Précis de la procédure d'Abbeville. — La méprise d'Arras. — Fragment sur le procès criminel de Montbailli. — Fragment sur la justice. — Précis du procès de Morangiés contre la famille Verron. 37. Essai sur les probabilités en fait de justice. — Supplément aux 'Causes célèbres'. — Fragmens historiques sur l'Inde, sur le gén. Lalli, et sur plusieurs autres sujets. 38. Elémens de philosophie de Newton. — Défense du Newtonianisme. 39. Essai sur la nature du feu et sur sa propagation. — Doutes sur la mesure des forces motrices. — Exposition du livre des institutions physiques, dans laquelle on examine les idées de Leibnitz. — Dissertation sur les changemens arrivés dans notre globe. — Des singularités de la nature. — Les colimaçons du père l'Escarbotier, [avec le] réponse du père Elie. 40. Traité de metaphysique. — Le philosophe ignorant. — Il faut prendre un parti, ou le principe d'action. — Tout en Dieu; commentaire sur Malebranche. — De l'âme; par Soranus, médecin de Trajan. — Lettres de Memmius à Ciceron. — Remarques sur les pensées de Pascal. 41. Profession de foi des théistes. — Sermons et homilies. — Discours de Bellequier. — Examen important de Bolingbroke. — Lettre de Cornsburi à Bolingbroke. 42. Défense de Bolingbroke. — Rémontrances des pasteurs du Gévaudan à A. J. Rustan. — Conseils raisonnables à M. Bergier, pour la défense du christianisme. — Les questions de Zapata; tr. par le sieur Tamponet. — Epître aux Romains; tr. de l'italien de Corbera. 43. La Bible enfin expliquée par plusieurs aumoniers de S. M. L. R. D. P. 44. D'Hérode. — Des monumens d'Hérode et de sa vie privée. — Des sectes des Juifs vers le temps d'Hérode. — Des autres sectes, et des Samaritains. — Sommaire historique des quatre évangiles. — Evangile de la naissance de Marie. — Protévangile attribué à Jacques. — Evangile de l'enfance du Christ. — Evangile de l'infance. — Evangile du disciple Nicodème. — Deux lettres de Pilate à l'empereur Tibère. — Relation [de] Pilate touchant notre Seigneur. — Relation de Marcel. — Histoire de l'établissement du Christianisme. 45, 46. Dialogues et entretiens philosophiques. 47–55. Dictionnaire philosophique. 47. A-Apo. 48. Apo-Bib. 49. Bie-Con. 50. Con-Emb. 51. Emp-Gaz. 52. Gen-I et J (Ign). 53. Ign-Nec. 54. New-Rome. 55. Sal-Z. 56–58. *Romans.* 56. Zadig, ou la destinée; histoire orientale. — Le monde comme il va; vision de Babouc. — Memnon, ou la sagesse humaine. — Les deux consolés. — Histoire des voyages de Scarmentado, écrite par lui-même. — Micromegas, histoire philosophique. — Histoire d'un bon bramin. — Candide ou l'optimisme. 57. L'ingénu, histoire veritable. — L'homme aux quarante écus. — La princesse de Babylonne. — Le blanc et le noir. — Jeannot et Colin. 58. Les lettres d'Amabed. — Histoire de Jenni. — Les oreilles du comte de Chesterfield et le chapelain Goudman. — Le taureau blanc. — Le crocheteur borgne. — Cosi-sancta. — Songe de Platon. — Bababec et les Fakirs. — Aventure de la memoire. — Les aveugles juges des couleurs. — Aventure indienne. — Voyage de la raison. 59, 60. Faceties. 60. Saul. — Questions sur les miracles. — Sur l'encyclopédie. 61. Avertissement. — Discours. — Panégyrique de Louis XV. — Eloge funèbre des officiers qui sont morts dans la guerre de 1741. — Eloge historique de la marquise du Chatelet. — Eloge de M. de Crébillon. — Eloge funèbre de Louis XV. — Vie de Molière. — Traductions du poëme de Jean Plokof. — Lettres chinoises, indiennes, et tartares. — Des divers changemens arrivés à l'art tragique. — De la tragédie anglaise. — Sur la comédie anglaise.—Du théâtre anglais. — Parallèle d'Horace, de Boileau, et de Pope. 62. Lettres à S. A. S. — Conseils à un journaliste. — Conseils à Racine. — Utile examen des trois dernières épîtres du sieur Rousseau. — Sur l'anti-Machiavel. — Mémoire sur la satire. — Le préservatif. — Courte réponse aux longs discours d'un docteur allemand. — Petit commentaire sur l'éloge du dauphin de France par M. Thomas. — Quelques petites hardiesses de M. Clair. — Refutation d'un écrit anonyme, contre la mémoire de feu J. Saurin. — Les honnêtetés littéraires. — Lettre à l'auteur des Honnêtetés littéraires, sur les mémoires de Mme. de Maintenon, publiés par la Beaumelle. 63. Commentaire historique sur les œuvres de l'auteur de la Henriade. — Connaissance des beautés et des défauts de la poésie et de l'éloquence dans la langue française. — Panégyrique de Saint Louis. 64. Mélanges littéraires. 65-67. Commentaires sur Corneille. 68-83. Recueil des lettres. 84-87. Lettres du prince royal de Prusse et Voltaire. 88. Lettres de l'impératrice de Russie et Voltaire. 89-91. Lettres de Voltaire et de D'Alembert. 92. Vie de Voltaire par le marquis de Condorcet. — Mémoires de Voltaire écrit par lui-même. — Tables.

— Œuvres complètes. Vol. 65, 66. Tables analytiques. Paris, 1825. 2 v. 8°.

— Additions à l'Essay sur l'Histoire générale', et sur l'Esprit et les mœurs des nations depuis Charlemagne jusqu'à nos jours. *n.p.*, 1763. 8°.

— Candide, ou l'optimisme. *n.p.*, 1759-61. 2 v. 8°.

— Commentaires sur P. et T. Corneille. Paris, 1806. 4 v. 18°.

— Correspondence entre Voltaire et Condorcet. (*In* **Condorcet.** Œuvres, v. 1. 1847-49.)

— Cuentos y satiras; tr. en versos castellanos por M. Dominguez. N. Y., 1825. 18°.

— Dissertation on taste. *See* **Girard, A.**

— La Henriade; Nouv. éd. Amst., 1770. 2 v. (v. 1 w.). 12°.
Contents. Vol. 1. *Wanting.* 2. Essai sur la poésie épique. — Diss. sur la mort d'Henri IV. — Bataille de Fontenoy. — Epître sur la bataille de Laufeldt. — Panégyrique de Louis XV. — La Henriade travestie [par Fougeret de Montleron].

— *Same.* La Henriade, *etc.*; notices par Auger. [Paris, 18—.] 18°.

— Histoire de Charles XII. Liége, 1789. 12°.

— *Same.* Ed. stér. Paris, 1817. 18°.

— *Same.* Paris, 1839. 12°.

— Histoire d'E. Canning et de J. Calas. — Mémoire de D. Calas. — Déclaration de P. Calas, *etc.* London, 1762. 8°.

— Histoire de l'empire Russe, sous Pierre-le-Grand. Paris, 1815. 2 v. 18°.
Contents. Vol. 1. 1672-1710. 2. 1710-1721.

— Histoire du Parlément de Paris. 5e éd. corr. *n.p.*, 1769. 8°.

— Lettres à Helvétius. (*In* **Helvetius, C. A.** Œuvres, v. 5. 1794; 1795.)

— The maid of Orleans; tr. Canto 1. London, 1780. 4°. **(A 47)**

— Pages inédites. (*In* **Revue** d. D. Mondes, mars 1862.)

— Le pauvre diable. — Plaidoyer de Ramponeau. — Les quand. — Requête de Jérôme Carré aux Parisiens. — Le Russe à Paris. (*In* **Recueil** de pièces intéressantes. 1760.)

— Siècles de Louis XIV et de Louis XV. Ed. stér. Paris, 1817. 5 v. 18°.

— *Eng.* Age of Louis XIV.; tr. by R. Griffith. London, 1779-81. 3 v. 8°.

— The sincere Huron. *t.p.w.* 12°.
Note. This is a translation of 'L'ingénu'; probably Fisshmore's, London, 1786.

— Théâtre complet; avec lettres, variantes, notes. Caen, 1788. 9 v. 12°.
Contents. Vol. 1. Œdipe. — Artémire. — Mariamne. — Brutus. — Eryphile. 2. Zaïre. — Adélaïde du Geusclin. — Amélie. — La mort de César. — Alzire. 3. Zulime. — Le fanastisme, ou Mahomet le prophète. — Mérope. — Sémiramis. 4. Oreste. — Catalina. — L'orphelin de le Chine. — Tancrède. 5. Olympie. — Les Scythes. — Les Guèbres. — Sophonisbe. — Traduction d'un monologue de Caton et d'un de Hamlet. — Le pauvre diable. 6. Le triumvirat. — Les lois de Minos. — Don Pedro. — Les Pélopides. — Irène. — Agathocle. 7. L'indiscret. — L'enfant prodigue. — La prude. — La femme qui a raison. — Nanine. 8. L'Ecossaise. — Le droit du seigneur. — Charlot. — Le dépositaire. — Socrate. 9. Samson. — La princesse de Navarre. — Le temple de la gloire. — Pandore. — Tanis et Zélide. — Le baron d'Otranto. — Les deux tonneaux. — Jules César. — L'Héraclius.

— *Same.* Ed. stér. Paris, 1813. 12 v. 18°.
Contents. Vol. 1. Œdipe. — Artémire. — Mariamne. — L'indiscret. 2. Brutus. — Eriphile. — Zaïre. — Samson. 3. Adélaïde du Guesclin. — Le mort de César. — Tanis et Zélide. — Alzire. — L'enfant prodigue. 4. Zulime. — Pandore. — Le fanatisme, ou Mahomet le prophète. — Mérope. 5. La princesse de Navarre. — Le temple de la gloire. — La prude. — Sémiramis. 6. Nanine. — La femme qui a raison. — Oreste. 7. Catalina. — Amélie. — Orphelin de la Chine. — Socrate. 8. L'écossaise. — Tancrède. — Le droit du seigneur. 9. Olimpie. — Le triumvirat. — Les Scythes. — Charlot. 10. Le dépositaire. — Baron d'Otranto. — Les deux tonneaux. — Les Guèbres. 11. Sophonisbe. — Les lois de Minos. — Les Pélopides. — Don Pedro. 12. Irène. — Agathocle. — Fête de Bellébat. — L'hôte et l'hôtesse. — Jules César. — L'Héraclius espagnol; tr. de Caldéron.

— Vie de Molière. (*In* **Molière.** Œuvres, v. 1. 1805.)

— Voyage de Ferney. (*In* **Suard**, J. B. A. Mélanges de litt., v. 2. 1803.)

— Barni, J. (*In his* Hist. des idées, v. 1. 1865.)

— Bersot, E. Correspondance de V. (*In his* Essais de philos. et de morale, v. 2. 1864.)

— Brougham, H., *Ld.* (*In his* Lives of men of letters, *etc.*, v. 1. 1845.)

— Carlyle, T. (*In his* Crit. essays, v. 2. 1860.)

— Chenier, M. J. Epître à Voltaire. 2e éd. Paris, 1806. 8°. **(B 809)**

— Condorcet, J. A. N. C., *marq.* de. (*In his* Œuvres, v. 4. 1847.)

— Documents inédits sur V. (*In* **Ravaisson, F.** Archives de la Bastille, v. 3. 1867.)

— Epitre de Belzébut à l'auteur de la Pucelle. (*In* **Recueil** de pièces intéressantes. 1760.)

— Espinasse, F. Life of V. Vol. 1. London, 1866. 8°.

— Frederic II., *of Prussia.* (*In his* Œuvres, v. 3. 1789.)

— Girardin, M. La Pucelle de Chapelain et la Pucelle de V. (*In* **Revue** d. D. Mondes, sept., déc. 1838.)

— Giraud, C. M. Epître du Diable à Voltaire. (*In* **Receuil** de pièces intéressantes. 1760.)

— Havard, J. A. V. et Mme. Du Chatelet; révélations d'un serviteur; pub. avec commentaries et notes historiques. Paris, 1863. 12°.

— Ligne, C. J., *prince* de. Mon séjour chez M. de Voltaire. (*In his* Œuvres, v. 4. 1860.)

— Longchamps, S. G., *and* Wagnière, J. L. Mémoires sur V. Paris, 1826. 2 v. 8°.

— Malden, H. (*In his* Disting. men of modern times, v. 3. 1838, v. 39 of Lib. ent. kn.)

— Perrot, G. Lettres inéd. de Voltaire. (*In* **Revue** d. D. Mondes, mars 1864.)

— Pindemonte, I. Discorso risguardante due lettere di Voltaire su la Merope del Maffei. (*In his* Arminio. 1819.)

— Quérard, J. M. (*In his* La France lit., v. 12. 1864.)

— Saint René Tallandier, G. C. La Suisse chrétienne et le 18e siècle. (*In* **Revue** d. D. Mondes, mars 1862.) — Une page de la vie de V. (*In* avr. 1865.) — — Saisset, E. E. Renaissance du voltairanisme. (*In* fév. 1845.) — Saveney, E. (*In* jan. 1869.)

— Shelley, M. W. (*In her* Lives of literary men of France, v. 2. 1839. Lardner. Cab. cyc.)

— Thomas, A. L. Réflexions philos. et littér. sur le poëme de la religion naturelle de Voltaire. (*In his* Œuvres complètes, v. 5. 1802.)

— VARNHAGEN VON ENSE, K. A. Voltaire in Frankfurt a. Main, 1753. (*In his* Denkwürd., v. 8. 1859.)

Volterra, Jacopo da. Lettere a papa Innocenzio VIII. (*In* **Archiv.** stor. ital., ser. 3, v. 7, 10, pt. 2. 1868, 69.)

Volterra. CRONACHE volterrane. (*In* **Archivio** stor. ital., app., v. 3. 1846.)

— IVANO, A. De bello Volaterrano anno 1472 a Florentinis gesto. (*In* **Muratori**, L. A. Rer. Ital. scr., v. 23. 1733.)

Voltchkof, Sergiii. [French dictionary with definitions in German, Latin, and Russian. St. Petersburg,] 1785–87. 3 v. 4°.

Volturno. CHRONICON Vulturnense. (*In* **Muratori**, L. A. Rer. Ital. scr., v. 1, pt. 2. 1725.)

Voluntary Church Association. CORMACK, J. Vol. Ch. Assoc. and their manifesto against establishments. 2d ed., [enl.]. Edin., [183-]. 12°. (B 1966)

Voluntary servitude. LA BOÉTIE, E. de. Discourse of vol. servitude. London, 1735. 12°.

Voluntary societies. PLEA for voluntary societies. N. Y., 1837. 12°.

Volunteer, The; devoted to the promotion of revivals, congregationalism, *etc.* Sept. 1831–July 1833; ed. by A. Rand. Vol. 1, Boston, v. 2, Lowell, 1832–33. 2 v. 8°.

Volunteers, The; a comedy. *See* **Shadwell**, T.

Voluspa. BUNSEN, C. C. J., *Baron.* The text of the Voluspa. (*In his* God in history, v. 2. 1868.)

Vomanus. De laudibus hortuli. (*In* **Lemaire.** Poet. Lat. min., v. 7. 1826. Bibl. class. Lat.)

Vonck, Cornelius Valerius. Lectionum Latinarum libri duo. Trag. Ult., 1745. 8°.

— Specimen criticum in varios auctores. Traj. ad R., 1744. 8°.

Vondel, Joost van den. Ovidius Herscheppinge in Nederduitsch dicht vertaelt. *See* **Ovidius Naso**, P.

Vondenvelden, Wm., *and* **Charland**, L. Extraits des titres des concessions de terre en fief et seineurie dans le Bas-Canada, *etc.* Quebec, 1803. 12°.

— *Another copy.* (C 278)

Vonk, L. C. Geschiedenis der landing van het Engelsch-Russisch leger in Noord-Holland, alsmede der krijsbedrijven en politieke gebeurtenissen, 1799. Haarlem, 1801. 2 v. 8°.

Von Raumer, Friedrich Ludwig Georg. *See* **Raumer**, F. L. G. von.

Vonved the Dane, Count of Elsinore. (*In* **Dublin** univ. mag., v. 55–56. 1860.)

Voorhees, Arnoldus. *See* **Clason**, I. Case. (B 340)

Voorhees, Philip F. Defence rel. to U. S. frigate Congress and the Argentine squadron, June 21. Wash., 1845. 8°. (B 1449)

Voormezele. ANNALES Formoselenses, 1–1136. (*In* **Pertz**, G. H. Mon. Germ., Scr., v. 5. 1849.)

Voorst (*Lat.* **Vorstius**), Adolf van. Epistola de obitu J. Meursii. (*In* **Gronovius**, J. Thes. Gr. antiq., v. 10. 1701.)

Voorst, Ælius Eberhard van. Oratio funebris in obitum C. Clusii. (*In* **L'Ecluse.** Curæ posteriores. 1611.)

— NICERON, J. P. (*In his* Mém., v. 22. 1733; *and* Germ., v. 16. 1758.)

Voorst, D. C. *and* J. J. van. Catalogue de la bibliothèque de littérature, sciences, et arts de V. [Tome 3.] Amst., 1859. 1 v. in 2 pt. 8°.

— Catalogue raisonné de la collection des manuscrits et d'autographes. [Tome 4.] Amst., 1859. 8°.

Voorst, Jan van. Commentariolus de adagiis N. T. Hebraicis. (*In* **Leusden**, J. De dialectis N. T. 1792.)

— Tractatus translationis seu cessionis ditionis Ultrajectinæ in Carolum V. (*In* **Hoynck van Papendrecht**, C. P. Vita, v. 3, pt. 1. 1743.)

Vopiscus, Flavius. Historiæ. (*In* **Historiæ** Augustæ scriptores, v. 2. 1671.)

Voragine *or* **Varagine**, Giacomo da Varaggio, *called* Jacobus de. La légendedorée; traduite et précédée d'une notice historique et bibliographique par [P. G. Brunet]. Paris, 1843. 2 v. 12°.

Vordoni, Teresa Albarelli. Sonnetti, *ec.* (*In* **Poeti** ital. contemp. 1843.)

Vormius, Olaus. NICERON, J. P. (*In his* Mém., v. 9. 1729; *and*, Germ., v. 10. 1754.)

Vormund, Der; von A. W. **Iffland.** (*In his* Theat. Werke, v. 9. 1860.)

Vorstius, Ælius Everardus. *See* **Voorst**, A. E. van.

Vose, George Leonard. Distortion of pebbles in conglomerates, with illust. from Rangely Lake. (*In* **Boston Soc. of Nat. History.** Mem., v. 1. 1866.)

— Orographic geology; origin and structure of mountains. Boston, 1866. 8°.

— Tracts of ancient glaciers in the White Mountains; with a few remarks upon the geological structure of that group. (*In* **Amer. Assoc.** Proc., v. 16. 1868.)

Vose, Henry. Topography of Mississippi. Natchez, 1835. 8°. (B 1603)

Vose, James. Disputatio pathologica de arteriæ carotidis aneurismate. Edin., 1809. 8°.

Vose, John. A compendium of astronomy. Ster. ed. Boston, 1832. 8°.

— Oration, Hanover, Aug. 27, 1805, before the Phi Beta Kappa Soc. Hanover, 1806. 8°. (B 435)

Vose, Thomas L. Brief remarks on liberal Christianity. Boston, 1842. 12°. (C 183)

Vosges. JOANNE, A. Itin. gén. de la France: Vosges et Ardennes. Paris, 1868. 16°.

Vosmeer, Michiel. Principes Hollandiæ et Zelandiæ, domini Frisiæ. Antv., 1578. f°.

Voss, Johann Heinrich. Briefe; nebst erläuternden Beilagen; hrsg. von A. Voss. 2e Ausg. Lpz., 1840. 3 v. 12°.

— Idyllen. Köningsb., 1801. 16°.

— Luise; ein ländliches Gedicht in drei Idyllen. Königsb., 1823. 8°.

— *Same.* [Lat. u. Germ.]; übers. von B. G. Fischer. Stuttg., 1820. 8°.

— BIPPEN, W. von. (*In his* Eutiner Skizzen. 1859.)

Vossius, Gerhard, *d.* 1609. NICERON, J. P. (*In his* Mém., v. 13. 1730.)

Vossius, Gerardus Joannis, *b.* 1577, *d.* 1649. Opera. Amst., 1685–1701. 6 v. f°.

Contents. Vol. 1. Etymologicon linguæ Latinæ. — De literarum permutatione tractatus. 2. Aristarchus, sive De arte grammatica. — De vitiis sermonis, et glossematis Latino-Barbaris. 3. Commentariorum rhetoricorum sive Oratoriarum institutionum libri. — De rhetoricæ natura et constitutione. — De artis poeticæ natura. — Poeticarum institutionum libri. — De imitatione, *etc.* — De veterum poetarum temporibus. — De artium et scientiarum natura. — De philosophorum sectis. 4. Ars historica. — De historicis Græcis. — De historicis Latinis. — Historiæ universalis epitome. — Vita Fabiani a Dhona. — Consilium Gregorio XV. exhibitum per M. Lonigum. — Aphorismi de statu ecclesiæ restaurando, *etc.*, per M. Lonigum. — In epistolam Plinii de Christianis, *etc.*, commentarius. — De cognitione sui. — De studiorum ratione. — Oratio in obitum Thomæ Erpenii. — Oratio de historiæ utilitate. — In fragm. L. Livii Andronici, Q. Ennii, C. Nævii, M. Pacuvii, et L. Attii castigationes et notæ. — Epistolæ selectiores. 5. De theologia Gentili et physiologia Christiana. 6. Chronologiæ sacræ isagoge. — Dissertatio gemina; una de Jesu Christi genealogia, altera de annis quibus natus, baptizanatus, mortuus. — Harmoniæ evangelicæ de passione, *etc.*, Jesu Christi, libri. — De baptismo disputationes, *etc.* — Theses theologicæ et historicæ. — Dissertationes de tribus symbolis. — Historiæ de controversiis quas Pelagius ejusque reliquiæ moverunt. — Frag. de Manichæis et Stoicis. — Dissertatio epistolica de jure magistratus in rebus ecclesiasticis. — Responsio ad judicium Hermanni Ravenspergeri, de libro ab H. Grotio pro Catholica fide de satisfactione Jesu Christi.

— Ars historica. Ed. 2a. Lugd. Bat., 1653. 4°.

— De arte grammatica. Amst., 1635. 4°.

— *Same, called* Aristarchus, sive De arte gram. Ed. 2a. Amst., 1662. 2 v. 4°.

— Harmoniæ Evangelicæ. Amst., 1656. 4°.

— De historicis Latinis. Ed. alt. Lugd. Bat., 1651. 4°.

— Institutiones linguæ Græcæ, olim quidem scriptæ a N. Clenardo, nunc autem ab erroribus expurgatæ atque locupletatæ opera G. J. Vossii. Amst., 1660. 12°.

— De logices et rhetoricæ natura et constitutione. Hag. Com., 1658. 4°.
— De philosophia et philosophorum sectis; ed. I. Vossius. Hag. Com., 1658. 4°.
— De quatuor artibus popularibus; de philologia et scientiis mathematicis; subj. chron. mathematicorum; ed. F. Junius. Amst., 1650. 4°.
— *Same*. Amst., 1660. 4°.
— Rhetorices contractæ sive partitionum oratoriarum lib. v. Ed. alt. Lug. Bat., 1627. 8°.
— Theses de variis doctrinæ Christianæ capitibus. Oxonii, 1631. 4°.
— De veterum poetarum temporibus. Amst., 1654. 4°.
— Horn, G. Defensio dissertationis de vera ætate mundi contra [V.]. Lugd. Bat., *ap. J. Elsevirium*, 1659. 4°
— Niceron, J. P. (*In his* Mém., v. 13. 1730; *and*, *Germ*., v. 1. 1749.)

Vossius, Isaac. De antiqua urbis Romæ magnitudine. (*In* Grævius, J. G. Thes. antiq. Rom., v. 4. 1697.) — De triremium et liburnicarum constructione dissert. (*In* v. 12. 1699.)
— Variarum observationum liber. Londini, 1685. 4°.
Contents. De Sibyllinis aliisque oraculis. — Responsio ad objecta nuperæ criticæ sacræ. — Ad iteratas patris Simonii objectiones altera responsio. — De antiquæ Romæ et aliarum quarumdam urbium magnitudine. — De artibus et scientiis Sinarum. — De origine pulveris bellici apud Europæos. — De triremium et liburnicarum constructione. — De emendatione longitudinum. — De paterfacienda per septentrionem ad Japonenses et Indas navigatione. — De apparentibus in luna circulis. — Diurna telluris conversione omnia gravia tendere ad medium.
— Niceron, J. P. (*In his* Mém., v. 13. 1730; *and*, *Germ*., v. 23. 1771.)

Votary of wealth, The; a comedy, by J. G. Holman. (*In* London stage, v. 4.)

Voting. Condorcet, J. A. N. C. de. Essai sur l'application de l'analyse à la probabilité des décisions rendues à la pluralité des voix. Paris, 1785. 4°.
See also Suffrage.

Votivæ Angliæ; the desires of England, *etc*.; by S. R. N. I. [T. Scot]. Vtrecht, 1624. 4°. (D 52)

Vougy, — *vicomte* de. Pose du cable transatlantique. (*In* France. *Com. Imp. de l'Expos. de* 1867. Rapports, v. 10.)

Voullonne, —. Mémoire sur la question proposée [par l'Académie de Dijon, 1776], Déterminer quelles sont les maladies dans lesquelle la médecine agissante est préférable à l'expectante, et celle ci à l'agissante, *etc*. Nouv. éd. Paris, 1799. 8°.

Vove, Fineins Canus, *pseud*. Zion's joy in her king. *See* Fenwick, J.

Vows. Carter, T. T. Vows and their relations to religious communities. (*In* Shipley, O. Church. 1866.)

Vox juvenilis; or, The loyal apprentices' vindication of their late humble address to His Majesty. London, 1681. f°. (A 54)

Vox militis; foreshewing perils [of living] without marshall discipline; [by G. M.]. London, 1625. 4°. (D 52)

Vox patriæ; resentments of the free-born subjects of England against any Popish successor; collections of the petitions and addresses to Parliament, Mar. 21. 1680. London, 1681. f°. (A 52)

Vox populi; newes from Spayne; [by T. Scot]. *n.p.*, 1620. 4°. (D 52)
— *Same*. 2d part; Gondomar in the likeness of Matchiauell in a Spanish parliament. [Goricom, 1624.] 4°. (D 52)

Vox populi; or, The people's claim to their Parliaments sitting to redress grievances, *etc*. London, 1681. 4°. (B 12)

Vox regni; or, The voice of the kingdom; a dialogue between city and country. *n.t.p.* [16—?] f°. (A 54)

Vox stellarum, 1737, 40-49; by F. Moore. London, *n.d.* 12°. (E 72)

Vox vera. *t.p.w.* [1620?] 4°. (D 52)

Voyage à la Louisiane, 1794-98; par B*** D*** [L. N. Baudry des Lozières]. Paris, 1802. 8°.

Voyage à travers l'Exhibition des beaux-arts; par E. About. Paris, 1855. 12°.

Voyage autour de ma bibliothèque. *See* Caillot, A.

Voyage autour de ma chambre; par X. de Maistre. (*In his* Works. 1854.)
— *Eng*. Journey round my room; tr. by H. Atwell. N. Y., 1871. 16°.

Voyage autour de mon jardin; par [J. B.] A. Karr. Paris, 1857. 12°.
— *Eng*. Tour round my garden; ed. by J. G. Wood. 15th thous. London, 1856. 16°.

Voyage de deux Français en Allemagne, *etc*., 1790-92; [par A. T. J. A. M. M. de Fortia de Piles]. Paris, 1796. 5 v. 8°.

Voyage de Falaise; par E. Lenoble. (*In* Biblioth. univ. des romans, Nouv., v. 23, 25. 1799.)

Voyage de Paris à Versailles. Paris, [184-]. 16°. (D 70)

Voyage d' un François en Italie, 1765, 66; [par J. J. le F. de Lalande]. Nouv. éd. Yverdon, 1769-70. 8 v. 8°.

Voyage du jeune Anacharsis en Grèce; [par J. J. Barthélemy]. 4e éd. Paris, an VII [1798]. 7 v. 8° *and* Atlas 4°.
— *Eng*. Travels, *etc*. London, 1796. 5 v. 8°.

Voyage en zigzag. *See* How we spent the summer.

Voyage fait, 1816, 17, de N. Yorck à la N. Orléans; par [le baron de Montlezun]. Paris, 1818. 2 v. 8°.
— Examen impartial d'un ouvrage intit. 'Voyage fait 1816, 17, de N. Yorck à la N. Orléans'. Paris, 1818. (B 449)

Voyage from the United States to South America 1821-23; [by W. Chase]. 2d ed. Newburyport, 1823. 8°.

Voyage of Captain Popanilla; by [B. Disraeli]. Phila., 1828. 12°.
— *Same*. (*In his* Novels, v. 2. 1866.)

Voyage of Gov. Phillip to Botany Bay; with the establishment of the colonies of Port Jackson and Norfolk Is. London, 1789. 4°.

Voyage of H. M. S. Blonde to the Sandwich Is., 1824-25, Capt. Lord Byron commander. London, 1826. 4°.

Voyage of St. Brendan; poem. (*In* Dublin univ. mag., v. 31. 1848.)

Voyage pittoresque de la France. *See* Laborde, J. B. de. Descr. gén. et partic. de la France. *Note*.

Voyage to Boston; a poem. Phila., 1775. 8°. (B 469)

Voyages, Imaginary. *See* Imaginary voyages (p. 1496).

Voyages, Scientific. Arago, D. F. Instructions, rapports, *etc*., sur les voyages scientifiques. (*In his* Œuvres, v. 9. 1857.)

Voyages and travels. *Bibliography*.
— Locke, J. Explanatory catalogue of voyages, *etc*. [1704.] (*In* Churchill, O. *and* J. Col. of voy., v. 6. 1746; — *in* Clarke, J. S. Prog. of mar. discov. 1803; — *and in his* Works, v. 10. 1823.)
— Camus, A. G. Mémoire sur la Collection des grands and petits voyages [de De Bry et Mérian] et sur la Collection de Thévenot. Paris, 1802. 4°.
— Beckmann, J. Litteratur der älteren Reisebeschreibungen. Göttingen, 1808. 2 v. in 8 pt. 8°.
— Boucher de la Richaderie, G. Bibliothéque univ. des voyages. Paris, 1808. 6 v. 8°.
— Pinkerton, J. Catalogue of books of voy. and travels. (*In his* Col. of voy., v. 17. 1814.)
— Ferrario, G. Indicazione delle opere più importanti sui viaggi, 1820-29. (*In his* Costume ant. e mod., v. 18. 1829.)
— Asher, A. Bibliog. essay on voyages pub. by L. Hulsius, *etc*. London, 1839. 4°.
— Tiele, P. A. Mémoire bibliog. sur les journaux des navigateurs néerlandais. Amst., 1867. 8°.

History.

Note. For single voyages, *see* the name of the person by whom they are made.

— GOODRICH, F. B. Man upon the sea; hist. of maritime adventure, *etc.*, [to 1858]. Phila., 1858. 8°.

— COOLEY, W. D. History of maritime and inland discovery, [to 1828]. London, 1830-31. 3 v. 16°. (Lardner. Cab. cyc.)

— STEVENSON, W. Historical sketch of the progress of discovery, navigation, and commerce, [to 1824]. (*In* Kerr, R. Col. of voy., v. 18. 1824.)

— DU PERIER, —. General history of all voyages and travels, from the first ages to the present time [1707]. London, 1708. 8°.

— LOCKE, J. History of navigation from its original to the year 1704. (*In* Churchill, O. *and* J. Col. of voy., v. 1. 1744; — *and in his* Works, v. 10. 1823.)

— EVELYN, J. Navigation and commerce, their original and progress, [to 1674]. (*In his* Miscel. writings. 1825.)

— RISE and progress of navigation and commerce, [to 1594]. (*In* Green, J. Col. of voy., v. 1. 1745.)

— GALVAM, A. Discoveries of the world to 1550; pub. in Eng. by R. Hakluyt, [in 1601]. New ed. by Vice-Adm. Bethune. London, 1862. 8°. (Hakluyt Soc., v. 30.)

— CLARKE, J. S. Progress of maritime discovery. Vol. 1: [to 1498]. London, 1803. 4°.

— AVEZAC MACAYA, M. A. P. d'. Notice des découvertes faites au Moyen Age dans l'Océan Atlantique. Paris, 1845. 8°.

— GUÉRIN, L. Les navigateurs français; histoire des navigations, découvertes, *etc.*, [1402-1842]. Paris, 1847. 8°.

— BENNET, R. G., *and* WIJK, J. van. Verhandeling over de Nederlandsche ontdekkingen in America, *etc.*, [1445-1805]. Utrecht, 1827. 8°.

Collections of voyages.

— RAMUSIO, G. B. Delle navigationi et viaggi raccolto con discorsi. (1o vol., 3a ed.) Venetia, 1563-74, 65. 3 v. f°.

— EDEN, R. History of travayle in the West and East Indies, *etc.* Lond., *Jugge*, 1577. 4°.

— PURCHAS, S. His pilgrimes. London, 1625-26. 5 v. f°.

— COMMELIN, I. Begin ende voortgangh van de vereenighde Nederlantsche geoctroyeerde Oost-Indische Compagnie. [Amst.,] 1646. 2 v. obl. 8°.

— - *Eng.* Collection of voyages by the Dutch East India Company for the improvement of trade and navigation. London, 1703. 8°.

— RAVENEAU DE LUSSAN. Voyage des flibustiers à la Mer de Sud, 1684. Paris, 1690. 12°.

— THÉVENOT, N. M. Relations de divers voyages curieux. Paris, 1696. 2 v. 8°.

— HACKE, W. Collection of original voyages. London, 1699. 8°.

— HARRIS, J. Compleat collection of voyages and travels. London, 1705. 2 v. f°.

— - *Same.* [2d ed.] London, 1764. 2 v. f°.

— BERNARD, J. F. Receuil de voyages au Nord. Amst., 1716. 3 v. 12°.

— COXE, D. Collection of voyages. London, 1741. 8°.

— CHURCHILL, O. *and* J. Collection of voyages and travels. 3d ed. London, 1744-46. 6 v. f°.

— GREEN, J. New general collection of voyages and travels. London, *T. Astley*, 1745-47. 4 v. 4°.

— OSBORNE, T. Collection of voyages and travels. London, 1745. 2 v. f°.

— PRÉVOST D' EXILES, A. F., *and others.* Histoire générale des voyages. Paris, 1746-70. 19 v. 4°.

— ALLGEMEINE Hist. der Reisen zu Wasser u. Lande; [aus dem Engl.] übersetzet. Lps., 1748-74. 21 v. (v. 9, 15 w.). 4°.

— CALLANDER, J. Terra Australis cognita; or, Voyages to the Terra Australis, *etc.* Edin., 1766-68. 2 v. 8°.

— SMOLLETT, T. Compendium of authentic and entertaining voyages. 2d ed. London, 1766. 7 v. 12°.

— KNOX, J. New collection of voyages and travels. London, 1767. 7 v. 8°.

— DALRYMPLE, A. Historical collection of voyages and discoveries in the S. Pacific. London, 1770. 2 v. 4°.

— HAWKESWORTH, J. Voyages in the southern hemisphere. London, 1773. 3 v. 4°.

— MOORE, J. H. New and complete collection of voyages and travels. Lond., [1778]. 2 v. f°.

— GENERAL collection of voyages and discoveries made by the Portugese and Spaniards, 15th and 16th centuries. London, 1789. f°.

— FLEURIEU, C. P. C., *comte* de. Découvertes des François, 1768-69, dans le sud-est de la Nouvelle Guinée, et reconnaissances postérieures par des navigateurs anglais; préc. de l'abrégé hist. des navigations et des découvertes des Espagnols. Paris, 1790. 4°.

— - *Eng.* Discoveries of the French, 1768-69, *etc.* London, 1791. 4°.

— PINKERTON, J. General collection of voyages and travels. London, 1808-14. 17 v. 4°.

— HAKLUYT, R. Early voyages, travels, and discoveries of the English. New ed. London, 1809-12. 5 v. 4°.

— LETTRES édifiantes et curieuses écrits des missions étrangères. Nouv. éd. Toulouse, 1810-11. 26 v. 12°.

— *Same.* Choix des lettres; avec des add., *etc.*, par J. B. Montmignon. Paris, 1808-09. 8 v. 8°.

— *Same.* Avec quelques relations nouv. et des notes, pub. [par] L. Aimé-Martin. Paris, 1838-43. 4 v. 8°.

— HAKLUYT, R. Selection of curious, rare, and early voyages. London, 1812. 4°.

— MACCARTHY, J. Choix de voyages dans les quatre parties du monde. Paris, 1821-22. 10 v. 8°.

— PARIS. Soc. DE GÉOG. Recueil de voyages et de mémoires. Paris, 1824-25. 2 v. 4°.

— KERR, R. General history and collection of voyages and travels. Edin., London, 1824. 18 v. 8°.

— NAVARRETE, M. F. de. Viages que hicieron los Espagnoles desde fines del siglo xv. Madrid, 1825-37. 5 v. 4°.

— MORRELL, B. Narrative of four voyages, 1822-31. N. Y., 1832. 8°.

— MONTÉMONT, A. Bibliothèque universelle des voyages. Paris, 1833-36. 46 v. 8°.

— TERNAUX-COMPANS, H. Archives des voyages. Paris, [1840-41]. 2 v. 8°.

— SZYMANOWSKY, W. Historya podróży i odkryć od początku xv. wieku; przeł. z francuzkiego. Warszawa, 1843. 8°.

— LACROIX, F. Annuaire des voyages et de la géographie. Paris, 1844-45. 2 v. 18°.

— HAKLUYT SOCIETY. [Publications.] London, 1847-80. 62 v. 8°.

— TAYLOR, B. Cyclopædia of modern travel; a record of exploration, *etc.*, for the past fifty years. Cincin., **1856.** 8°.

— VOYAGES. **1857-58.** *See, below,* **Voyages** et travaux des missionnaires, *etc.*

— GALTON, F. Vacation tourists, 1860-63. Camb., **1861-64.** 3 v. 8°.

See also **Voyages** around the world.

Periodicals.

— ANNALES des voyages, *etc.*; pub. par Malte-Brun. Paris, 1808-14. 24 v. 8°.

— - Table des matières dans les 20 premiers vols. Paris, 1813. 8°.

— - Nouvelles annales, 1e-6e série; dirigé par Eyriès, Malte-Brun, *etc.* Paris, 1819-70. 208 v. 8°.

— - Tables des matières, 1819-39. Paris, *n.d.* 8°.

— BULLETIN des sciences géographiques, économie publique, voyages; pub. [par] de Férussac. Paris, 1824-73. 28 v. 8°.

— ILLUSTRATED travels; ed. by H. W. Bates. Vol. 1-6. London, 1869-74. 6 v. 4°.

Voyages et travaux des missionnaires de la Compagnie de Jésus pour servir de complément aux 'Lettres édifiantes'. Paris, 1857-58. 2 v. 8°.

Contents. Vol. 1. *Mission de Cayenne et de la Guyane Française*; éd. par F. de Montézon. — **Pelleprat,** P. Relation des missions des pères de la Compagnie de Jesus dans les îles et dans la terre ferme de l'Amérique Méridionale. — **Grillet,** J. Lettre à P. de Saint-Gilles; — Voyage des PP. J. Grillet et F. Béchamel dans l'intérieur de Guyane, en 1674. — **Lombard,** A. Lettre sur la mission de Kourou; préc. et suivie de quelques détails sur les travaux des autres missionnaires jésuites de la Guyane jusqu'à la Révolution Française, 1723-90. — **Lettres** écrites de la Guyane Française par des missionnaires de la Compagnie de Jésus à des pères de la même compagnie. — **Pièces** justificatives. 2. *Mission de la Cochinchine et du Tonkin*; éd. par F. de Montézon et E. Estève. — **Rhodes,** A. de. Relation de la mission du Tonkin, 1630-48. — **Tissanier,** J. Relation; son voyage de France au Tonkin, *etc.*, 1654-60. — **Persécutions** diverses et martyres en Cochinchine, 1639-65; — **Extraits** des PP. de Rhodes, Saccano, et de mémoires portugais. — **Travaux** des pères de la Compagnie de Jésus dans les missions du Tonkin et de la Cochinchine, 1664-74. — **Principaux** événements depuis cette époque jusqu'à nos jours, 1857. — **Pièces** justificatives.

Voyages of Amasis; by J. H. B. de Saint Pierre; in French and English. Boston, 1795. 12°.

Voyages of the slavers St. John and Arms of Amsterdam, 1659, 63; with additional papers illust. of the slave trade under the Dutch; tr. with an introd. by E. B. O'Callaghan. Albany, 1867. 4°. (N. Y. colonial tracts, no. 3.)

Voyages poétiques d'Eugène et d'Antonine; par Mme. de Genlis. (Vol. 16 *of her* Œuvres. 1825.)

Voyages round the world.

Collective and general works.

— HENRY, D. Historical account of the voyages round the world by English navigators. London, **1773-74.** 4 v. 8°.

— HISTORICAL account of the circumnavigation of the globe. N. Y., [18—]. 18°. (Harpers' fam. lib., v. 82.)

— FANNING, E. Voyages round the world. N. Y., **1833.** 8°.

— DUMONT D'URVILLE, J. S. C. Voyage pittoresque autour du monde; resumé des voy. des découvertes. Paris, **1834-35.** 2 v. 8°.

— GARNIER, E. Abrégé de tous les voyages autour du monde, 1519-1832. Bruxelles, **1837.** 2 v. 12°.

— KERR, R. Early circumnavigations, [1519-1722]. (Vol. 10 *of his* Col. of voy. 1824.)

Separate voyages.

— MAGALHAENS, F. de. Voyages round the world, [1519-22]. *See* **Magalhaens,** F. de.

— PIGAFETTA, F. A. Viaggio atorno' il mondo, [1519-22]. (*In* **Ramusio,** G. B. Rac., v. 1. 1563; — *and in* **Pinkerton,** J. Col. of voy., v. 11. 1811.)

— - *French.* Premier voyage autour du monde sur l'escadre de Magellan, 1519-22; [pub., avec des notes, et tr. par C. Amoretti;] suivi d'une notice sur M. Behaim [par C. G. von Murr, tr. par H. J. Jansen]. Paris, an IX [1800]. 8°.

— NAVIG. d'un Portoghese attorno il mondo, [1519-20]. (*In* **Ramusio,** G. B. Rac., v. 1. 1563.)

— DRAKE, *Sir* F. Voyage, **1577-80.** *See* **Drake,** *Sir* F.

— NOORT, O. van. Beschrijvinge van de schipvaerd by de Hollanders ghedaen door de Straet oft Engte van Magallanes, **1598.** (*In* **Commelin,** I. Begin, v. 1. 1646.)

Note. For other accounts of this voy. *see* **Noort.**

— COOKE, J. Voyage round the world, **1683-91.** *See* **Cooke,** J.

— DAMPIER, W. New voyage round the world, 1683-91. (Vol. 1, 5th ed., 2, 3d ed.) London, 1703-09. 3 v. in 4 pts. 8°.

— - *Germ.* Reise um die Welt. (*In* **Allgemeine** Hist., v. 12. 1754.)

— GEMELLI CARERI, G. F. Voy. round the world, [1693-98]. (*In* **Churchill,** O. *and* J. Voy., v. 4. 1745; — *and in* **Smollett.** Compend, v. 6, 7. 1766.)

— - *Germ.* Reisen. (*In* **Allgemeine** Hist., v. 12. 1754.)

— FUNNELL, W. Voy. round the world, [**1703-06**]. (*In* **Harris,** J. Col. of voy., v. 1. 1764; — *and in* **Kerr,** R. Col. of voy., v. 10. 1824.)

— ROGERS, W. Cruising voyage round the world, **1708-11.** London, 1718. 8°.

Note. For other accounts *see* **Rogers,** W.

— DE FOE, D. New voyage round the world, [**1713-17**]. (Vol. 7. *of his* Works. 1840.)

— LA BARBINAIS LE GENTIL, —. Reise um die Welt, [1714-17]. (*In* **Allgemeine** Hist., v. 12. 1754.)

— SHELVOCKE, G. Voyage round the world, 1719-22. *t.p. mut.* London, 1726. 8°.

Note. For other accounts of the voy. *see* **Shelvocke,** G.

— ROGGEVEEN, J. Dagverhaal der ontdekkingsreis, **1721-22.** Middlebury, 1838. 8°.

— HOLMAN, J. Voyage round the world, **1727-32.** London, 1834-35. 4 v. 8°.

— ANSON, G., *Ld.* Voyage round the world, **1740-44**; compiled from his papers by R. Walter. 5th ed. London, 1749. 8°.

Note. For other eds. and accounts of this voy. *see* **Anson,** G., *Ld.*

— WALLIS, S. Voy. round the world, **1764-68.** (*In* **Hawkesworth,** J. Acc. of voy., v. 1. 1773.)

— BOUGAINVILLE, L. de. Voyage autour du monde, **1766-69.** Paris, 1771. 4°.

— - *Eng.* Voyage round the world; tr. by J. R. Forster. London, 1772. 4°.

Note. For other accounts *see* **Bougainville,** L. de.

— PAGES, P. M. F., *vcte.* de. Voyages autour du monde et vers les deux poles, par terre et mer, **1767-76.** Paris, 1782. 2 v. 8°.

— - *Eng. trans. of Vol.* 1. Travels round the world, **1767-71.** Dublin, 1791. 8°.

— COOK, J. Journal of a voyage round the world, **1768-71.** London, 1771. 4°.

— SPARRMAN, A. Voy. to the Cape of Good Hope and round the world, **1772-76.** Perth, 1789. 2 v. 12°.

— COOK, J. Voyage towards the South Pole and round the world, **1772-75.** 3d ed. London, 1779. v. 2. 4°.

Note. For other accounts *see* **Cook,** J.

— FORSTER, J. G. A. Reise um die Welt, 1772-75. (*In his* Schriften. v. 1, 2. 1843.)

— - *Eng.* Voyage round the world. London, 1777. 2 v. 4°.

— Forster, J. R. Observations during a voyage round the world, [1772-75]. London, 1778. 4°.

— Cook, J., *and* King, J. Voyage to the Pacific Ocean, 1776-80; for a north west passage. Dublin, 1784. 3 v. 8°.

— Dixon, G. Voyage round the world, 1785-88. London, 1789. 4°.

— La Pérouse, J. F. de G., *comte* de. Voyage autour du monde, [1785-88]; réd. par M. L. A. Milet-Mureau. Paris, *Impr. de la Répub.*, 1797. 4 v. 4°.
Note. For trans. and other accounts of this voy. *see* La Pérouse.

— Portlock, N. Voyage round the world, 1785-88. London, 1789. 4°.

— Delano, A. Three voyages round the world, *etc.*, [1790-1807]. Boston, 1817. 8°.

— Vancouver, G. Voyage of discovery to the N. Pacific and round the world, 1790-95. London, 1798. 3 v. 4° *and* Plates f°.

— Marchand, E. Voyage autour du monde, [1790-92]. (*In* Montémont, A. Bibl., v. 15. 1834.)

— Rossel, E. P. E. de. Voyage de Dentrecasteaux envoyé à la recherche de La Pérouse, [1791-93]. Paris, *Imp. impériale*, 1808. 2 v. 4° *and* Atlas f°.

— Grant, J. Narrative of a voyage of discovery to New South Wales, 1800-02. London, 1803. 4°.

— Langsdorff, G. H. von. Voyages and travels in various parts of the world, 1803-07. London, 1813-14. 2 v. 4°.

— Krusenstern, A. J. von. Voyage round the world, 1803-06; tr. by W. B. Hoppner. London, 1813. 2 v. 4°.

— - *French.* (*In* Montémont, A. Bibl., v. 17. 1834.)

— Lisiansky, U. Voyage round the world, 1803-06. London, 1814. 4°.

— Campbell, A. Voyage round the world, 1806-12. Edin., 1816. 8°.

— Arago, J. E. V. Souvenirs d'un aveugle; voyage, [1817]. Nouv. éd. Paris, [1843]. 2 v. 8°.

— - Voyage round the world, 1817-20. London, 1823. 4°.

— Kotzebue, O. von. Voyage round the world, 1823-26. London, 1830. 2 v. 12°.

— King, P. P., *and others*. Narrative of the voyages of H. M. S. Adventure and Beagle, 1826-36. London, 1839. 3 v. in 4. 8°.

— Laplace, C. P. T. Voyage autour du monde, [1830-32]. (*In* Montémont, A. Bibl., v. 18. 1834.)

— Reynolds, J. N. Voyage of U. S. frigate Potomac round the world, 1831-34. N. Y., 1835. 8°.

— Ruschenberger, W. S. W. Voyage round the world, 1835-37. Phila., 1838. 8°.

— Reynolds, J. N., *and* Dickerson, M. Correspondence conc. the South Sea Expedition. N. Y., 1837-38. 8°.

— Wilkes, C. Narrative of the U. S. Explor. Exped., 1838-42. *n.p.*, 1845-58. 23 v. (v. 7, 8, pt. 1, 11, 13, 14, 16-19, 21-23 w.). f° *and* 4° *and* 10 (4 w.) Atlases f°.
Note. For other eds. and accounts *see* Wilkes, C.

— Henshaw, J. S. Around the world; narrative of a voyage in the East Indian squadron under Com. G. C. Read, [1838-40]. N. Y., 1840. 2 v. 12°.

— Taylor, F. W. Voyage round the world in in the U. S. frigate Columbia [of the East India squadron], 1838-40. N. Y., 1840. 2 v. 12°.

— Simpson, *Sir* G. Journey round the world, 1841-42. London, 1847. 2 v. 8°.

— Seemann, B. Narrative of the voyage of H. M. S. Herald, 1845-51. London, 1853. 2 v. 8°.

— Pfeiffer, I. A woman's journey round the world, [1846-48]; tr. from the German. London, [1852]. 12°.

— Gerstaecker, F. Narrative of a journey round the world, [1850-51]. N. Y., 1854. 12°.

— Habersham, A. W. North Pacific surveying and exploring expedition, [1853-56]. Phila., 1858. 8°.

— Scoresby, W. Voy. to Australia and round the world, [1856], for magnetical researches; ed. by A. Smith. London, 1859. 8°.

— Scherzer, C. von. Circumnavigation of the globe by the Novara, 1857-59. London, 1861-63. 3 v. 8°.

— Coffin, C. C. Our new way round the world, [1866-69]. Boston, 1869. 8°.

— Beauvoir, L., *comte* de. Voyage round the world, [1866-67]. London, 1870. 2 v. 8°.

— Marguerit, H. Deux ans de navigation; exploration de l'amiral Cheretoff sur le Saint Nicolas. Paris, [1868]. 8°.

Vredeman, Johan, *of Fries* (*in French frison*). La très-noble perspective; augm. par S. Marolois. Amst., 1619. f°.

Vries, David Pieterz de. Voyages from Holland to America, 1632-44; tr. from the Dutch by H. C. Murphy. N. Y., *priv. printed* 1853. 4°.

— *Same.* (*In* New York Hist. Soc. Col., 2d ser., v. 3, pt. 1. 1857.) — Extracts [rel. to New Netherland] from the Voyages of V.; tr. by G. Troost. (*In* v. 1. 1841.)

Vries, Maertin Gerritz. de. Voyage of the ships Kastrikom and Breskens, M. G. de Vries commander, to the North of Japan. (*In* Burney, J. Discov. in the South Sea, v. 3. 1813.)

Vries, Simon de. Curieuse aenmerckingen der bysonderste Oost en West-Indische verwonderens-waerdige dingen; nevens die van China, Africa, *enz.* Utrecht, 1683. 4 v. 4°.

Vuillemin, Alexandre. Nouv. plan illustré de Paris. Paris, 1848.

Vuitry, Adolphe. Rapport sur le concours rel. à l'impôt avant et depuis 1789. (*In* Paris. Inst. *Ac. d. Sci. Mor.* Mém., v. 12. 1865.)

Vulcanius, Bonaventura. Niceron, J. P. (*In his* Mém., v. 34. 1736; *and, Germ.*, v. 18. 1758.)

Vulculdus. Vita Bardonis; ed. W. Wattenbach. (*In* Pertz, G. H. Mon. Germ. hist., Scr., v. 12. 1854.)

— *Same.* Ed. P. Jaffé. (*In* Jaffé, P. Biblioth. rer. Germ., v. 3. 1866.)

Vulgate. *See* Bible (p. 270, 282).

Vulliemin, Louis *and* C. Some account of the life of F. A. A. Gonthier; from the French with a preface by C. B. Tayler. [London,] *Religious Tract Soc.*, 1837. 16°.

Vulpius, Hieronymus. *See* Volpi, G.

Vulpius, Joannes Antonius. *See* Volpi, G. A.

Vulteius, Johannes. Inscriptionum libri II, Xeniorum libellus. [Paris,] *apud Sim. Colinæum*, 1538. 8°.

— Hendecasyllaborum libri IV. Paris, *apud Sim. Colinæum*, 1538. 8°.

Vuy, C. F. Alphons. De originibus et natura juris emphyteutici Romanorum. Heidelb., 1838. 8°.

Vyasa Veda. *See* Maha-Bharata.

Vyse, Charles. Tutor's guide to arithmetic. London, 1770. 12°.

— - Key. 2d ed. London, 1775. 12°.

Vyse, Wm. Sermon, Feb. 27, day of fasting and humiliation. London, 1778. 4°. (B 1257)

W. Campagne des Français en Italie en 1800. Lps., 1801. 4°.

W., A., *farmer* (I. Wilkins *or* S. Seabury?). The Congress canvassed; or, An examination into the conduct of the delegates at their convention, Phila., Sept. 1, 1774. N. Y., printed, *London, reprinted* 1775. 8°. (B 387)
— Free thoughts on the proceedings of the Continental Congress, Phila., Sept. 5, 1774; by a farmer. *n.p.*, 1774. 8°. (C 112, 265, W 21)
— *Same.* London, 1775. 8°.
— View of the controversy between Gr. Brit. and her colonies. N. Y., 1774. 8°.
— *Other copies.* (B 377, 702)
— *Same.* London, 1775. 8°.
— HAMILTON, A. The farmer refuted; answer to his 'View of the controversy'. N. Y., 1775. 8°. (B 992, 1079, 1094, 2503)

W., A. O. Eye witness; or, Life scenes in the old north state. Boston, 1865. 12°.

W., B. Additional discovery of R. L'Estrange, his further discovery of the Popish Plot wherein T. Oates and the King's evidences are vindicated in a letter to T. Oates. London, 1680. f°. (A 53)
— L'ESTRANGE, R. Discovery upon discovery; in defence of Oates against B. W. 2d ed. London, 1680. 4°. (B 10, 12)

W., C. The honest elector's proposal for rendering the votes of all constituents free and independent. London, 1767. 8°. (B 1634)

W., E. Short history of the life and death of the act made the 35th of Eliz., *etc.* London, 1681. f°. (A 54)

W., E. Virginia. *See* **Williams, E.**

W., E. S. *See* **Waters, E. S.**

W., G. Account of the intended rebellion of the negroes in the Barbadoes. (*In* **S., N.** Contin. of the state of New Eng. 1676.)

W., I. H. Dartmoor massacre. *n.p.*, [1815]. 8°. (B 941)

W., J. On the existence of the Devil. (*In* **Philadelphia. 1st Unitarian Society.** Col. of pieces. 1810.)

W., M. E. Théobald; ou, L'enfant charitable. 3e éd. Tours, 1846. 18°. (Bibl. de la jeunesse chrétienne.)

W., R. *See* Walton, I.

W., S. *See* **Ward, S.**

W., S. R. Rose Douglas; or, The autobiography of a minister's daughter. New York, 1851. 8°.

W., T. Letter to a friend. *See* **Chauncy, C.** (B 150)

W., T. Letter to a Dissenter. *See* Sairle, G.

W., W. Animadversions on [S. Bethel's] Vindication; in a letter to the Lord Mayor and Aldermen. *n.t.p.* [16—.] f°. (A 50)

W—, A—. Enchantments of Jannes and Jambres discovered. Edin., 1765. 8°. (C 24)

W—, J—. The mother's catechism. 8th ed. enl. Glasgow, 1725. 12°. (C 58)

Waagen, Gustav Friedrich. Galeries and cabinets of art in Gr. Britain. Lond., 1857. 8°.
— Handbook of painting, German, Flemish, and Dutch schools. London, 1860. 2 pts. 8°.
— Königliche Museen; Verzeichniss der Gemälde-Sammlung. 12e Aufl. Berlin, 1855. 16°.
— Kunstwerke und Künstler in England und Paris. Berlin, 1837–39. 3 v. 12°.
Contents. Vol. 1, 2. England. 3. Paris.
— *Eng.* Works of art and artists of England. London, 1838. 3 v. 12°.
— Treasures of art in Gr. Britain. London, 1854. 3 v. 8°.
Contents. Vol. 1. London. 2. London and environs. 3. Countries.
— Die vornehmsten Kunstdenkmäler in Wien. Wien, 1866–67. 2 v. 8°.
Contents. Vol. 1. Die K. K. Gemälde-Sammlungen im Schloss Belvedere und in der K. K. Kunst-Akademie die Privat-Sammlungen. 2. Manuscripte mit Miniaturen, Handzeichnungen, und Kupferstiche in der K. K. Hofbibliothek und Privat-Sammlungen. — K. K. Ambraser-Sammlungen. — K. K. Münz- und Antiken-Cabinet. — K. Schatzkammer. — K. K. Museum für Kunst und Industrie.
— Ueber den Maler P. P. Rubens. (*In* **Historisches** Taschenbuch. 1833.) Ueber Leben, Wirken, und Werke der Maler A. Mantegna und L. Signorelli. (*In* 1850.) — Ueber den künstlerischen Bildungsgang Rafael's und seine vornehmsten Werke. (*In* 1859.)

Waal River. JANSSON, J. Descriptio fluminum Rheni, Vahalis, et Mosæ. Amst., [16—]. (**E 78**, no. 60)

Wabash River. ASHE, T. Memoirs of mammoth bones found in the vicinity of the W., *etc.* Liverpool, 1806. 8°. (B 685)

Wabash Valley. ELLSWORTH, H. W. Valley of the U. W., advantages, *etc.* N. Y., 1838. 12°.

Wace, Robert. Extrait de la continuation du Brut d'Angleterre. (*In* **Michel, F.** Chroniques, v. 1. 1836.)
— BRÉQUIGNY, L. G. O. F. de. Du Roman du Rou, et des ducs de Normandie. (*In* **Paris. Inst.** *Ac. d. Inscr.* Not., v. 5. 1799.)
— BRINK, B. ten. Wace und Galfrid von Monmouth. (*In* **Jahrb. f. rom. u. eng. Lit.**, v. 9. 1868.)
— DELARUE, G. Diss. on the life and writings of W. (*In* **Archæologia**, v. 12. 1796.)
— DU MERIL, E. La vie et les ouvrages de W. (*In* **Jahrb. f. roman. u. eng. Lit.**, v. 1. 1859.) — KOERTING, G. Ueber die Aechtheit der einzelnen Theile des Roman du rou. (*In* v. 8. 1867.)

Wachler, Johann Friedrich Ludwig. P. L. Courier im Verhältniss zu seiner Zeit. (*In* **Historisches** Taschenbuch, 1830.) — Vorbereitung und Ausbruch des Auffstandes der Griechen gegen die osmanische Pforte. (*In* 1831.)

Wachsmuth, Curt. Die Niederlage der Kelten vor Delphi. (*In* **Historisches** Zeitschrift, v. 10. 1863.)

Wachsmuth, Ernst Wilhelm Gottlieb. Allgemeine Culturgeschichte. Lpz., 1850–52. 3 v. 8°.
Contents. Vol. 1. Der heidnische Orient. — Das klassische Alterthum. — Das Christenthum und das christliche Römerreich. — Der Islam. 2. Das Mittelalter. 3. Die neuere Zeit.
— Aufständ und Kriege der Bauern im Mittelalter. (*In* **Historisches** Taschenbuch, 1834.)
— Dissertation on the old Greek comedy. (*In* **Aristophanes.** Comedies, v. 1. 1837.)
— Geschichte Frankreichs im Revolutionszeitalter. Hamburg, 1840–44. 4 v. 8°. (Heeren. u. Ukert. Europ. Staat.)
Contents. Vol. 1. 1774–92. 2. 1792–98. 3. 1798–1812. 4. 1810–30.
— Hellenische Alterthumskunde. 2e Ausg. Halle, 1846. 2 v. 8°.
Contents. Vol. 1. Wohnsitze und Bestandtheile der hellenischen Nation. — Staatensystem und Völkerrecht. — Die Staatsverfassungen. — Beilagen. 2. Volks- und Staatswirthschaft. — Recht und Policei. — Kriegswesen. — Erziehung, öffentliche Zucht, Sitte im Privatleben. — Götterdienst. — Kunst. — Literatur und Wissenschaft. — Beilagen.
— *Eng.* Historical antiquities of the Greeks; tr. by E. Woolrych. Oxford, 1837. 2 v. 8°.
— Niedersächsische Geschichten; mit Autobiographie. Berlin, *n.d.* 8°. (Schmidt, F. Deutsche Nat. Biblioth., v. 10.)
— Weimars Musenhof, 1772–1807. Berlin, 1844. 8°.

Wackernagel, Karl Heinrich Wilhelm. Deutsches Lesebuch. 1r Theil: Poesie u. Prosa, 4.–15. Jahrh. 2e Ausg. Basel, 1839. 8°.
Note. With the 2d title, 'Altdeutsches Lesebuch'.

Wadd, Wm. On the best mode of curing stricture in the uretha. 2d ed. enl. Lond., 1812. 8°.

Waddel, Andrew *or* **George.** Remarks on G. Innes's critical essay on the ancient inhabitants of Scotland. (*In* **Tracts** illust. of the antiq. of Scotland. 1836.)

Waddell, I. H. Letter occasioned by ill treatment experienced by W. from A. Allen. *n.t.p.* [1812.] 8°. (B 452)

Waddell, John H. The theatre. [N. Y., 1819.] 8°. (B 447)

Waddilove, Alfred. Law of marriage and divorce. (*In* **Nat. Assoc. Prom. Soc. Sci.** Trans., 1861.) — On exclusion of evidence. (*In* 1864.) — Is it expedient to remove any and what of the remaining restrictions on admissibility of evidence in civil and criminal cases? (*In* 1865.)

Waddilove, *Rev.* Wm. James Darley. The Stewart missions; letters and journals; with a memoir of C. J. Stewart, Bp. of Quebec. London, 1838. 12°.

Waddington, Alfred. Overland route through British North America; or, The shortest and speediest road to the East. Lond., 1868. 8°.

Waddington, *Maj.* Charles. Account of the battle of Meeänee. (*In* **Gr. Brit.** *Corps of Roy. Engin.* Papers, v. 9. 1847.)

Waddington, Charles Tzaut. Ramus, sa vie, ses écrits, et ses opinions. Paris, 1855. 8°.

Waddington, George, *D.D.* Condition and prospect of the Greek Church. New ed. rev. London, 1854. 12°.

— History of the Church, to the Reformation. London, 1831-33. 2 v. 8°. (Lib. of usef. knowl.)

— History of the Reformation on the Continent. London, 1841. 3 v. 8°.

— Ode Latina numismate annuo dignatum, Cantab., 1811: Prœlium cum Gallis. *n.p.*, 1811. 8°. (B 1236)

— *and* **Barnard,** H. Journal of a visit to Ethiopia. London, 1822. 4°.

Waddington, Henry. *See* **Griswold, N.** Case. [18—.] (B 340)

Waddington, Horace. Carmen Græcum numismate annuo dignatum, Cantab., 1819: Reginæ epicedium. *n.p.*, 1819. 8°. (B 1236)

— Senarii Græci, præmio Porsoniano dignati, Cantab., 1819. *n.p.*, 1819. 8°. (B 1236)

Waddington, *Rev.* John. Church of the Pilgrim Fathers, Southwark. [London,] 1851. 12°. (C 272)

Waddington, Joshua. *See* **Griswold, N.** Case. [1800]; — **Seaman,** E. Case. 1818. (B 340)

Waddington, Wm. Henry. La chronologie de la vie du rhéteur Ælius Aristide. (*In* **Paris. Inst.** *Ac. d. Inscr.* Mém., v. 26, 1e pt. 1867.)

— The Protestant church and religious liberty in France. (*In* **Cambridge** essays, 1856.)

Wade, Arthur Savage, *D.D.* Letter to G. Canning; vindication of the present ministry. (*In* **Pamphleteer,** 1827; v. 28 of B 838)

Wade, Benjamin Franklin. Admission of Kansas; speech, July 2. Wash., 1856. 8°. (B 1509)

Wade, Henry. Rod-fishing in clear waters by fly, minnow, and worm. London, [1861]. 8°.

Wade, John. Report of [his] trial for arson, Oct. Dedham, 1835. 8°. (B 1125, 1813)

Wade, John, *Jr.*, *b.* 1808, *d.* 1851. LORING, J. S. (*In his* Hundred Boston orators. 1852.)

Wade, John. British history, to 1847, chronologically arranged. 5th ed. London, 1847. 8°.

— England's greatness; its rise and progress. London, 1856. 8°.

— History of the middle and working classes. London, 1833. 16°.

Wade, John Peter, *M.D.* Method of treating fever and dysentery in Bengal. London, 1791. 8°.

Wade, Joseph. TRIAL for murder. *See* **Parker,** M.

Wade, Wm., *b.* 1807, *d.* 1827. BULLARD, A. (*In his* Select mem., v. 2. 1829.)

Wade, Wm., *engraver.* Panorama of the Hudson River. N. Y., 1846.

Wadleigh, Robert, *Councilor of N. H.* **Bell,** S. D. (*In* **N. H. Hist.** Soc. Col., v. 8. 1866.)

Wadström, Carl Berns. Addresse au corps législatif et au directoire exécutif de la République Française. Paris, 1795. 4°. (A 8)

— Essay on colonization, particularly applied to the western coast of Africa. London, 1794-95. 2 v. 4°.

— Précis sur l'établissement des colonies de Sierra Léona et de Boulama. Paris, 1798. 8°. (B 765)

Wadström, Johan Adolf. Metamorphosis humana. (*In* **Linné,** C. Amœn. acad., v. 7. 1769.)

Wadsworth, Benjamin, *D.D.*, *Pres. Harv. Univ.*, *b.* 1669, *d.* 1737. Christ's fan in his hand separating the wheat from the chaff; sermon, Dec. 6. Boston, 1722. 12°. (C 3)

— The churches shall know that Christ searcheth the hearts; [fast] sermon, Jan. 8. Boston, 1716-17, 12°. (D 10)

— Essay for the charitable spreading of the Gospel into dark ignorant places; sermon, Oct. 16. Boston, 1718. 12°. (C 4)

— The faithful reprover. Boston, 1711. 12°. (C 16)

— Fraud and injustice detected and condemned; sermon, Feb. Boston, 1712. 16°. (D 47)

— Good souldiers a great blessing; being so represented in a sermon on the day for election of officers in the Honorable Artillery Co., June 3. Boston, 1700. 12°. (C 4)

— Guide for the doubting and cordial for the fainting saint. 2d ed. Boston, 1715. 12°.

— It's honourable, not shameful, to suffer for Christ; sermon, Apr. 11. Boston, 1725. 12°. (C 5)

— Journal, 1694. (*In* **Mass. Hist. Soc.** Collections, v. 31. 1852.)

— Preface. (*In* **Foxcroft,** T. Practical discourse. 1718. B 242)

— Rulers feeding and guiding their people with integrity and skilfulness; sermon, May 30, the day for election of counsellors. Boston, 1716. 12°. (C 7)

— Surviving servants of God carrying on the work of the deceased; sermon preached after the death of J. Leverett. Boston, 1724. 12°. (C 5)

— Twelve sermons, tending to promote godliness. Boston, 1717. 24°.

— *Funeral sermon on.* 1737. *See* **Appleton,** N. (B 79); — **Flynt,** H. (B 79, 234); — **Foxcroft,** T. (B 17, 71, C 39); — **Sewall,** J. (B 231); — **Wigglesworth,** E. (B 79)

Wadsworth, Benjamin, *D.D.*, *of Danvers*, *b.* 1750, *d.* 1826. America invoked to praise the Lord; discourse, Feb. 19 [thanksgiving day]. Salem, 1795. 8°. (W 38)

— Eulogy, character of G. Washington, Feb. 22. Salem, 1800. 8°. (B 627, E 48)

— Intemperance a national evil; discourse, Danvers, June 29. Salem, 1815. 8°. (B 1238)

— Sermon, installation of M. Dow, York, Me., Nov. 9, 1815. Andover, 1816. 8°. (B 1323)

— Social thanksgiving a pleasant duty; sermon, Dec. 15. Salem, 1796. 8°. (B 911)

Wadsworth, Chas. Thanksgiving sermon, Nov. 28. Phila., 1861. 8°. (B 1592)

— War a discipline; sermon, thanksgiving day, Nov. 24. San Francisco, 1864. 8°. (B 1592)

Wadsworth, George W., *appellant.* *See* **Burnett,** J., *vs.* **Wadsworth.** 1870.

Wadsworth, J. L. The flag. — A call to the centennial celebration. — Centennial ode. (*In* **Litchfield Co.** Centen. celebration. 1851.)

Wadsworth, *Gen.* James Samuel. ALLEN, L. F. Memorial of J. S. Wadsworth, before the New York. State Agricultural Society, Sept. 23. Buffalo, 1864, 8°. (B 1639)

— CENTURY ASSOCIATION. Proceedings in honor of W. N. Y., 1865. 8°. (B 1639)

— HOPPIN, W. J. (*In* **Higginson,** T. W. Harvard mem. biog., v. 1. 1866.)

Wadsworth, Lemuel. HILL, E. Notice of L. Wadsworth. (*In* **New Hamp. Hist. Soc.** Col. v. 2. 1827.)

Wadsworth, *Capt.* Samuel. BOUTWELL, G. S. Address, dedication of the monument to the memory of W., Sudbury, Nov. 23, 1852. *n.p.*, [185-]. 8°. (B 1611)

Wadsworth, Thomas. 'Αντιψυχοθανασία'; immortality of the soul proved by Scripture and reason; added, Faith's triumph over the fear of death. London, 1670. 8°.

Wadsworth, Wm. Murr[illegible]. Oration, Havre, Michigan, July 4. Manhatta[illegible] 1837. 8°. (B 1204)

Waengler. *See* **Pareus,** D.

Wafer, Lionel. New voyage and description of the Isthmus of America. London, 1699. 8°.

Note. For accounts of the same voyage abridged *see* **Smollett,** T. Compendium of voy., v. 5. 1766; — **Knox,** J. Col. of voy., v. 2. 1767; — **Callander,** J. Terra Australis, v. 2. 1768.

Waga, Theodor. Historya książąt i królów Polskich. Wilno, 1824. 8°.

Wagenaar, Jan. Extract from his 'Beschryving van Amsterdam' rel. to New Amstel. (*In* **N. Y. Hist. Soc.** Col., 2d ser., v. 3, pt. 1. 1857.)

Wagener, Zachary. Voyage thro' a great part of the world, *etc.* (*In* **Churchill,** O. *and* J. Col. of voy., v. 2. 1744.)

Wagenseil, Johann Christoph. Exercitationes sex. Altdorfi, 1687. 4°.

— Dissertatio ined. de Joanna papissa. (*In* **Schelhorn,** J. G. Amœn. lit., v. 1. 1730.)

— NICERON, J. P. (*In his* Mém., v. 2. 1727; *and, Germ.*, v. 2. 1750.)

Wager, *ship*. Loss of the W. on the coast of Patagonia, 1741. — HARDSHIPS suffered by part of the crew of the W. after their departure from Wager Island. — ADVENTURES of A. Campbell, and some of the officers of the W. — MORRIS, I. Dangers and distresses of M., and seven companions, 1742. (*In* **Shipwrecks** and disasters at sea, v. 2. 1812.)

Wages. SAMPSON, W. Trial of the cordwainers of the city of N. Y. for a conspiracy to raise their wages. N. Y., 1810. 8°.

— - *Another copy.* (**B 413**)

— GR. BRIT. ARTIZANS. Summary of the report of committee [on] remuneration for labor in Gr. Britain. (*In* **Pamphleteer, 1824**; v. 23 of B 838)

— SENIOR, N. W. Three lectures on the rate of wages. London, 1830. 8°. (B 934)

— TORRENS, R. Wages and combination. London, 1834. 8°.

— DAVIS, J. Reply to Buchanan, on the reduction of wages, Jan. 23. Wash., 1840. 8°. (B 1823)

— LEVI, L. Wages and earnings of the working classes. London, 1867. 8°.

See also **Labor.**

Waghorn, Thomas. Egypt in 1838. Lond., 1838. 8°. (**B 1141**)

Wagner, Albrecht. Process of repair after resection of bones and joints; tr. by T. Holmes. (*In* **New Sydenham Soc.** Pub., v. 5. 1859.)

Wagner, Carl. ANDRESEN, A. (*In his* Die deutschen Maler-Radirer, v. 2. 1867.)

Wagner, Ernst. Handbuch der allgem. Pathologie. 1862. *See* **Uhle, P. J.**

Wagner, Fredrich Wilhelm. Fragmenta Euripidis ed., perditorum trag. omnium col. Wagner; acc. Christus patiens, Ezechieli et Christianorum poetarum reliquiæ dramaticæ; emend. F. Dübner. Parisiis, *Didot*, 1846. 8°.

Contents. Thespis. — Chœrilus. — Pratinus. — Phrynichus. — Aristias. — Aristarchus. — Neophron. — Io. — Achæus Eretriensis. — Achæus Syracusanus. — Agatho. — Bion. — Euphorion. — Philocles. — Morsimus. — Melanthius. — Astydamas. — Meletus. — Iophon. Aristo. — Sophocles the younger. — Euripides minor. — Carcinus major. — Xenocles. — Carcinus minor. — Pythangelus. — Gnesippus. — Acestor. — Hieronymus. — Nothippus. — Morychus. — Sthenelus. — Dorillus. — Spintharus. — Theognis. — Critias. — Cleophon. — Nicomachus. — Diogenes. — Antiphon. — Polyidus. — Ischander. — Dionysius. — Mamercus. — Aphareus. — Theodectes. — Chæremon. — Crates. — Nearchus. — Pytho. — Cleænetus. — Moschio. — Dicæogenes. — Apollodorus. — Timesitheus. — Patrocles. — Alcimenes. — Apollonides. — Hippothoon. — Timocles. — Ecdorus. — Serapion. — Sositheus. — Lycophron. — Alexander Actolus. — Philiseus. — Sosiphanes. — Dionysiades. — Euphantus. — Æschylus Alexandrinus. — Ptolomæus Philopator. — Sophocles tertius.

Wagner, Johann Martin von. Bericht über die æginetischen Bildwerke im Besitz des Kronprinzen von Baiern; hrsg. von F. W. J. v. Schelling. Stuttg., 1817. 12°.

— *Same.* (*In* **Schelling, F. W. J.** von. Sämmtl. Werke, v. 9. 1861.)

— Le feste di Eleusi di F. Schiller, disegnato in forma d'un fregio da W. Roma, 1817. obl. f°.

— ANDRESEN, A. (*In his* Die deutschen Maler-Radirer, v. 1. 1866.)

Wagner, Johann Wilhelm. LA CONDAMINE, C. M. de. Eloge de W. (*In* **Berlin. Ak. d. Wiss.** Abh., 1746.)

Wagner, Richard. *See* **Wagner, W. R.**

Wagner, Rudolph. Elements of comparative anatomy; ed. by A. Tulk. Pt. 1: Mammalia. N. Y., 1844. 8°.

Wagner, Wilhelm Richard. Chorus of pilgrims; from 'Tannhäuser'. (*In* **Dwight, J. S.** Journal of music, v. 15. 1859.)

— FLEURY, J. Richard Wagner. Paris, 1860. 8°.

— LISZT, F. Lohengrin et Tannhaüser. Lpz., 1851. 8°.

— SCUDO, P. (*In* **Revue d. D. Mondes**, mars 1860.) — SCHURÉ, E. (*In* av. 1869.)

Wagnière, J. L. Mémoires sur Voltaire. *See* **Longchamp.**

Wagoner of the Alleghanies. *See* **Read, T. B.**

Wagons. ALBUM für Wagenbauer, 1861. 1. Heft. Berlin, 1861. f°.

Wagram. VARNHAGEN VON ENSE, K. A. Die Schlacht von Deutsch-Wagram, am 5n und 6n Juli 1809. (*In* **Historisches** Taschenbuch, 1836.)

Wagstaff, John. Historical reflections on the Bishop of Rome. Oxford, 1660. 4°. (B 2)

Wagstaff *or* **Wagstaffe**, Thomas. Defence of the 'Vindication of Charles I.' justifying his title to Eikon basilike in answer to Amyntor. London, 1699. 4°.

— LLOYD, W. Letter to W. Sherlock in vindication of that part of Josephus's History which gives an account of Iaddus, against [W.'s] "Answer to 'Obedience and submission to the present government'". London, 1691. 4°. (B 7)

— SHERLOCK, W. Vindication of the Case of allegiance due to sovereign powers, in reply to [W.'s] "Answer to 'Obedience and submission to the present government'", *etc.* London, 1691. 4°. (B 7)

Wahabis. MAURIZI, V., *or Shaik* MANSUR. History of Seyd Said; with an account of the Wahabees; tr. from the Italian. London, 1819. 8°.

— BURCKHARDT, J. L. Notes on the Bedouins and Wahabys. London, 1830. 4°.

— FINATI, G. Narrative of life and adventures; tr. by W. J. Bankes. Lond., 1830. 2 v. 16°.

— BRYDGES, *Sir* H. J. Brief history of the Wahauby. (Vol. 2 *of his* Account of the mission to Persia. 1834.)

Wahl, Christian Abraham. Clavis librorum Veteris Testamenti apocryphorum philologica. Lps., 1853. 8°.

Wahl des Herkules, Die; ein lyrisches Drama, in Musik gesetzt von A. Schweitzer; von C. M. **Wieland.** (*In his* Sämmtl. Werke, v. 25. 1825.)

Wahlbom, Johan Gustaf. Sponsalia plantarum. (*In* **Linné**, C. Amœn. acad., v. 1. 1749.)

Wahlen, Auguste. Mœurs, usages, et costumes; Afrique, Amérique, Asie, Europe, Océanie. Brux., 1843-44. 4 v. 8°.

Wählin, Andreas. Odores medicamentorum. (*In* **Linné**, C. Amœn. acad., v. 3. 1764.)

Wahlverwandtschaften, Die; von J. W. von **Goethe.** (*In his* Sämmtl. Werke, v. 3. 1854.)

Wahn, Der; von A. G. A. **Uellner.** (*In his* Spiele für die Bühne, v. 2. 1820.)

Wahraus, Erhard. Chronik, 1126-1445. (*In* **Munich. K. Baier. Akad.** Chroniken, v. 4. 1865.)

Wailly, Joseph Noël, *dit* Natalis de. Eléments de paléographie. Paris, 1838. 2 v. 4°. (Doc. inéd.)

— Mém. sur des fragments de papyrus écrits en Latin. (*In* **Paris. Inst.** *Ac. d. Inscr.* Mém., v. 15, 1e pt. 1842.) — Examen critique de la 'Vie de St. Louis' par Geoffroy de Beaulieu. (*In* v. 15, 2e pt.) — Examen de quelques questions rel. à l'origine des chroniques de St. Denys. (*In* v. 17, 1e pt.) — Un opuscule anonyme intit. 'Summaria brev. et compend. doctrina felic. exped.', *etc.* — Geffroi de Paris. — Les tablettes de cire conserv. au trésor des chartes. (*In* v. 18.) — Addition au mém. sur les tablettes, *etc.* (*In* v. 19, 1e pt.) — Sur le système monétaire de St. Louis. — Sur les variations de la livre tournois depuis le règne de St. Louis jusqu'à l'établissement de la monnaie décimale. (*In* v. 21, 2e pt.) — La date et le lieu de naissance de Saint Louis. (*In* v. 26, 1e pt.) — La langue de Joinville. (*In* v. 26, 2e pt. 1870.)

Wailly, Jules de, *fils*. Scènes de la vie de famille. Paris, 1860. 18°.

Wailly, Natalis de. *See* **Wailly, J. N.**

Wailly, Noël François de. Nouveau vocabulaire français; abrégé du dictionnaire de l'Académie. Paris, 1801. 8°.

— Principes de la langue française. *t.p.w.* [Paris, 1754?] 12°.

— *Same.* 10e éd, Paris, 1786. 12°.

— *Same.* 10e éd. Paris, 1786. 12°.

Note. These two 10e éds. are printed from different type.

— *Same.* 12e éd., rev. et augm. par E. A. de Wailly. Paris, 1808. 12°.

Wainewright, Latham. The literary and scientific pursuits at the Univ. of Cambridge described and vindicated. London, 1815. 8°.

Wainwright, Jonathan Mayhew. Discourse on the occasion of forming the African Mission School Soc., Aug. 10. Hartford, 1828. 8°. (B 1329)

— Inequality of individual wealth; sermon, annual election, Jan. 7. Boston, 1835. 8°. (B 1098, 1695, 1739, 1812)

— The land of bondage; a journal of a tour in Egypt. N. Y., 1852. 8°.

— A memorial volume; thirty-four sermons of W.; ed. by his widow. N. Y., 1856. 8°.

— Sermon, death of Rt. Rev. J. H. Hobart. N. Y., 1830. 8°. (B 1218)

— Sermon on the anniv. of the Bost. Female Asylum for Destitute Orphans. Boston, 1835. 8°. (B 1464)

— Sermons upon religious education and filial duty. N. Y., 1829. 8°.

— *and* Potts, G. No church without a bishop; or, The controversy between Drs. Potts and Wainwright. N. Y., 1844. 8°.

Wainwright, Thomas Griffiths. TALFOURD, T. N. (*In* Lamb, C. Literary sketches. 1848.)

Waistell, Charles. Designs for agricultural buildings; ed. by J. Jopling. London, 1827. 4°.

Wait, *Mrs.* Rebekah, *Funeral sermon on.* 1801. *See* Harris, T. M. (B 154, 174)

Waite, *Mrs.* Catharine V. The Mormon prophet and his harem. Camb., 1866. 16°.

Waite, *Rev.* Josiah Kendall. Discourse, Gloucester, interment of eleven mariners wrecked on Cape Ann, Dec. 15, 1839. Gloucester, 1840. 8°. (B 1227)

Waite, Otis F. R. [Eastman's] guide book for the Eastern coast of N. England. Concord, 1871. 18°.

Waiting for the verdict; by R. H. Davis. N. Y., 1868. 8°.
Note. From the Galaxy, v. 34. 1867.

Waitz, Georg. Das alte Recht der salischen Franken. Kiel, 1846. 8°.

— Deutsche Kaiser von Karl dem Grossen bis Maximilian; mit Autobiog. Berlin, *n.d.* 8°. (Schmidt, F. Deutsche Nat. Bibl., v. 5.)

— Deutsche Verfassungsgeschichte. Kiel, 1844–78. 8 v. 8°.
Contents. Vol. 1. Vor der Zeit der grossen Wanderungen. 2–4. Die deutsche Verfassung im fränkischen Reich. 2. Die merovingische Zeit. 3–4. Die karolingische Zeit. 5–8. Die Verfassung des deutschen Reichs bis zur vollen Herrschaft des Lehnwesens.
Note. Vols. 5–8 have the 2d title 'Die deutsche Reichsverfassung'.

— Falsche Richtungen. (*In* Historisches Zeitschrift, v. 1. 1859.) — Preussen und die polnische Theilung. (*In* v. 3.) — Wie soll man Urkunden ediren? (*In* v. 4.) — Neue Mittheilungen über die erste Theilung Polens. — Zur Würdigung von Ranke's historischer Kritik. (*In* v. 6.) — Ueber die Resultate der Beschäftigung mit den vaterländischen Alterthümern für die Geschichte. (*In* v. 9.) — Die Anfange des Lehnwesens. (*In* v. 13. 1865.)

— Schleswig-Holsteins Geschichte, in drei Büchern. Göttingen, 1851–52. 2 v. 8°.
Contents. Vol. 1. Vereinigung. 2. Selbständigkeit. 3. *Never published.*

Waitz, Theodor. Introduction to anthropology; ed. by J. F. Collingwood. Vol. 1. London, *Anthrop. Soc.*, 1863. 8°.

— Ueber die Einheit des Menschengeschlechtes. (*In* Historische Zeitschrift, v. 5.) — Zur Geschichtschreibung des alten Mexico. (*In* v. 6. 1861.)

Wajdelotka przez J. O. Warszawa, 1844. 3 v. 18°.

Wake, C. Staniland. Chapters on man. London, 1868. 8°.

Wake, Wm., *successively Bp. of Lincoln and Abp. of Canterbury.* Discourse of purgatory. — Discourse of prayers for the dead. (*In* Cardwell, E. Tracts on points at issue, *etc.*, v. 3. 1837.)

— Epistles of the Apostolic Fathers; tr. with preliminary discourse. *See* Apostolic Fathers.

— - Extracts from the 'Epistles'. (*In* Churchman armed. 1814.)

— An exposition of the doctrine of the Church of Eng. in the articles prop. by [Bossuet]. London, 1686. 4°. (B 90)

— Preparation for death. 5th ed. London, 1689. 12°.

— The present state of the controversy between the Church of England and the Church of Rome. London, 1687. 4°. (B 94)

— *Same, continued.* London, 1688. 4°. (B 94)

— Principles of the Christian religion; commentary on the church-catechism. 14th ed. London, 1814. 12°.

— Sermon, Jan. 30, the day of martyrdom of Charles I. London, 1715. 8°. (C 285)

— Sermons. London, 1716. 8°.

— Speech, opening of the 2d article of the impeachment against Sacheverell. London, 1710. 8°. (B 99)

— *Same.* (*In* Fisher, J. Speeches. 1710.)

— JOHNSON, —. Vindication of the Bishop of Condom's 'Exposition of the doctrine of the Catholic Church'; answer to [Walker's]' Exposition of the doctrine of the Church of England'. London, 1686. 4°.

Wakefield, E. T. Transfer of land. (*In* Nat. Assoc. Prom. Soc. Sci. Trans., 1857.)

Wakefield, Edward Gibbon. England and America; comparison of the social and political state of the two nations. Lond., 1833. 2 v. 8°.

— Facts rel. to the punishment of death in the metropolis. London, 1831. 16°

Wakefield, Edward Jerningham. Adventure in New Zealand, 1839–44. Lond., 1845. 2 v. 8°.

Wakefield, Gilbert. Correspondence with C. J. Fox; chiefly on classical literature. London, 1813. 8°.

— Enquiry into the expediency and propriety of public or social worship. 3d ed. London, 1792. 8°. (E 207)

— Examination of Paine's 'Age of reason', *etc.* London, 1794. 8°. (B 154)

— *Same.* Boston, 1794. 12°. (B 159)

— Internal evidences of the Christian religion. Warrington, 1789. 8°.

— Memoirs; [continued by J. T. Rutt and A. Wainwright]. London, 1804. 2 v. 8°.

— New Testament; tr. *See* Bible. N. T. (p. 283).

— On the origin of alphabetical characters. (*In* Literary and Phil. Soc. of Manchester. Mem., v. 2. 1789.)

— Silva critica; in auctores sacros profanosque commentarius philologus. Cantab., 1789–93. 2 v. 8°.

— Spirit of Christianity compared with the spirit of the times in Gr. Brit. London, 1794. 8°. (B 683)

— BARBAULD, A. L. Remarks on Wakefield's 'Enquiry'. 2d ed. London, 1792. 8°. (B 1361, E 207)

— POPE, J. Remarks on Wakefield's arguments against public worship. (*In his* Divine worship. 1792. E 207)

— PRIESTLEY, J. Letters occasioned by W.'s essay on public worship. London, 1792. 8°. (E 207)

— WILSON, J. Defence of public worship in a letter to Wakefield. London, 1792. 8°. (B 1371)

— YOUNG, T. (*In his* Miscel. works, v. 2. 1855.)

Wakefield, Horace P. Duties of the medical profession. (*In* Mass. Medical Soc. Med. comm., v. 11. 1867.)

Wakefield, Priscilla. Instinct displayed; sagacity of the animal creation. 2d ed. London, 1814. 12°.

— *Same.* 1st Amer. ed. Boston, 1816. 18°.

— Introduction to botany in familiar letters. 5th ed. London, 1807. 12°.

— *Same.* With app. 1st Amer. from 5th London ed. Boston, 1811. 12°.

— Mental improvement; or, Beauties and wonders of nature and art. 3d Amer. from 5th London ed. Phila., 1814. 12°.

Wakefield, *Eng.* WATSON, —, *and* PRITCHETT, —. Plans, *etc.*, for a lunatic asylum at Wakefield. York, 1819. f°.

Wakefield star and West Riding advertiser, Aug. 15. Wakefield, 1806. f°. (E 198)

Wakefulness. Hammond, W. A. Wakefulness; with an introd. on the physiology of sleep. Phila., 1866. 12°.
See also Sleep.

Wakely, Charles. Trial for rape on Mrs. R. Fay. N. Y., 1810. 8°. (B 345, 414)

Wakeman, *Sir* George, *Bart., and others.* Tryals of W., *etc.*, for high treason. London, 1679. f°. (A 49)

Wake-robin. *See* Burroughs, J.

Wala, *Abbas Corbeiensis.* Vita. (*In* Pertz, G. H. Mon. Germ., Scr., v. 2. 1829.)

Walachia. *See* Wallachia.

Walafridus Strabo. Versus. (*In* Bouquet, M. Recueil des hist., v. 6. 1870.)

Walbran, John Richard. Memorials of the Abbey of St. Mary of Fountains. [Vol. 1.] Durham, 1863. 8°. (Surtees Soc., v. 42.)
Contents. Vol. 1. 1132–1574.

Walburga, *Abbess of Heidenheim.* Life of W. (*In* Lives of the English saints, v. 2. 1844.)

Walch, Christian Wilhelm Franz. Decreti Nicæni de paschate. (*In* Goettingen. Ges. d. Wiss. Comm., 1769–70.) — De persequutionum Christianorum Romanarum caussis non solum politicis sed etiam religiosis. (*In* 1771.) — De Sarabaitis. (*In* 1775.) — Historia rerum in Homeritide seculo sexto cum a rege Judæo contra Christianos tum ab Habessinis ad hos ulciscendos gestarum. (*In* 1773.) — De Romanorum in tolerandis diversis religionibus disciplina publica. (*In* 1772.) — De αὐθεντία liborum Irenæi adv. hæreses. (*In* 1774.) — De Sabaitis. (*In* 1776.) — Rerum Christianorum apud Lucianum De morte Peregrini explicatio. (*In* 1777.) — De S. Materno uno. (*In* 1778.) — De Hystaspo ejusque vaticiniis apud patres. (*In* 1779.) — De mumiis Christianis. (*In* 1780.) — De Michælis Glycæ ætate. (*In* 1782.) — De τοῖς εἴσω τῆς ἐκκλησίας et τοῖς ἐκτὸς Constantini Magni. (*In* 1783–84.)

— Sur les Sarabaïtes. (*In* Sérieys, A. Bibl. acad., v. 6. 1811.)

— Heyne, C. G. Eulogium Walchii. (*In* Goettingen. Ges. d. Wiss. Comm., 1783–84.)

Walch, Georg. Reise der Kinder Israel aus Egypten in das gelobte Land Canaan. *n.p.*, 1640. (E 78, no. 300)

Walch (*Lat.* Walchius), Johann. Decas fabularum humani generis. Argent., 1609. 4°.

Walch, Johann Georg. Bibliotheca patristica. Jenæ, 1770. 8°.

Walcheren, *an island of Zealand.* St. Clair, T. S. Narrative of the expedition to W. (*In his* Residence in the W. Indies, v. 2. 1834.)
See also Zealand.

Walcheren remittent fever. Wright, T. History of Walcheren remittent fever. London, 1811. 8°.

Walckenaer, Charles Athanase, *baron.* Collection des relations des voyages en différentes parties l'Afrique. Paris, 1842. 21 v. 8°.
Contents. Vol. 1. Introduction. — Voyages en Afrique: Histoire des premières conquêtes des Portugais. — Premiers voy. des Vénitiens sur la côte occid. d'Afrique. 1, 2. Premiers voy. des Anglais en Afrique. 2, 3. Voyages depuis le cap Blanc jusqu'à Sierra-Leone. 3, 4. Voyages depuis le cap Blanc jusqu'à Sierra-Leone, cont. l'histoire de l'établissement du commerce des Anglais sur la Gambie. 5, 6. Nouv. voy. des Français depuis le cap Blanc jusqu'à Sierra Leone, cont. la suite de l'hist. de leurs établissements sur le Sénégal. 6, 7. Nouv. voy. des Anglais depuis le cap Blanc jusqu'à Sierra Leone et dans l'intérieur de la Sénégambie. 8. Premiers voy. en Guinée. 9. Résumé des observations des premiers voyageurs sur chacune des subdivisions de la Guinée. 10. Obs. des premiers voyageurs sur les nègres de la Côte d'Or. 11. Suite des premiers voyages dans le golfe de Guinée. 11, 12. Nouv. voy. en Guinée. 13. Premiers voy. dans l'océan Atlantique méridional sur toute la côte occidentale d'Afrique depuis le cap Lopez-Gonzalvo jusqu'à cap Negro. 13, 14. Obs. des premiers voyageurs sur les Loango, Congo, Angola, Benguella, *etc.* 14, 15. Nouv. voy. dans l'océan Atlantique méridional, *etc.* 15–21. Voyages au cap de Bonne-Espérance et le long des côtes occid. et mérid. d'Afrique depuis le cap Negro jusqu'au cap Corrientes.

— L'étendue et les limites du territoire des Gabali. (*In* Paris. Inst. *Ac. d. Inscr.* Mém., v. 5. 1821.) — La situation des Raudii Campi où Marius défit les Cimbres *etc.* — Les changemens dans le cours de la Loire entre Tours et Angers. (*In* v. 6.) — Mém. sur une portion de la voie appienne pour déterminer le nom ancien de Polignano. — Les dénominations de portes caspiennes, caucasiennes, *etc.* (*In* v. 7.) — Rapport, 1833. — Sur un pied romain trouvé dans la forêt de Maulerrier, 1834. — Extrait d'une mém. sur les progrès des découvertes géographiques dans le monde maritime. — Recherches sur les insectes qui nuisent à la vigne. (*In* v. 12, 1e pt.) — La vie et les ouvrages de Daunou, — du major Rennell, — de Dupuy, — du comte Miot. (*In* v. 14, 1e pt.) — Mémoire sur la chronologie de l'histoire des Javanais, et sur l'époque de la fondation de Madjapahit. (*In* v. 15.) — La vie et les ouvrages de Emeric-David, — du marquis de Pastoret, — de Mionnet. (*In* v. 16, 1e pt.) — La vie et les ouvrages de Mongez, — de Letronne, — de Raynouard. (*In* v. 18, 1e pt. 1855.)

— Mémoires touchant la vie et les écrits de Marie de Rabutin-Chantal, dame de Bourbilly, marq. de Sévigné. (T. 1–5, 3e éd.) Paris, 1856–65. 6 v. 12°.
Note. Vol. 6 by M. Aulenas.

— Tableau des aranéides, aranea de Linné. Paris, 1805. 8°.

— Cortambert, R. Notice biog. sur le baron W. (*In* Paris. Soc. de Géog. Bul., 4e sér., v. 5. 1853.)

— Naudet, J. La vie et les ouvrages du baron Walckenaer. (*In* Paris. Inst. *Ac. d. Inscr.* Mém., v. 18, 1e pt. 1855.)

Walcot, Thomas. Tryals of T. Walcot, W. Hone, W. Ld. Russell, J. Rous, and W. Blagg, for high treason for conspiring the death of the King, *etc.* London, 1683. f°. (A 55)

Walcott, Mackenzie Edward Charles. Cathedral reform. (*In* Shipley, O. The church and the world. 1866.)

— Church and conventual arrangement. London, 1861. 8°.

— Sacred archæology; a dictionary. London, 1868. 8°.

Walcott, Roger. Class-day oration. (*In* Harvard Coll. *Class of* 1870. Oration. 1870. B 1927)

Walcutt, W., *sculptor.* Sketch of W. (*In* Cleveland, *Ohio.* Inauguration of the Perry statue. 1861. B 1615)

Waldauer, Aug. Fanchon, the cricket; a drama. — Little Barefoot; a drama. (*In* Sargent, E. Mod. stand. dr., v. 42.)

Waldburg, Gebhard, *Truchsess* von. Barthold, F. W. G. Truchsess von Waldburg, Kurfürst und Erzbischof von Köln. (*In* Historisches Taschenbuch, 1840.)

Waldburga, *St., Abbess of Heidenheim.* Wolfhardus, *Presb.* Vita S. W. — Adaboldus, *Ep. Trajectinus.* Vita. — Medibardus. Vita. — Philippus, *Ep. Eystettensis.* — Gretser, J. Miracula virtute olei S. W. patrata. (*In* Acta sanct., v. 6. 1865.)

Waldeck. Le Bas, P. Principauté de Waldeck. (*In his* Etats de la Confédération Germanique. 1842. Univers.)

— Jansson, J. Waldeck. Amst., [16—]. (E 78, no. 163a)

Waldegrave, James, *2d Earl of Waldegrave.* Memoirs, 1754–58. London, 1821. 4°.

Waldeinsamkeit; von L. Tieck. (*In his* Gesam. Novellen, v. 10. 1854.)

Waldemar der Pilger, Markgraf von Brandenburg; Schauspiel, von F. La Motte Fouqué. (*In his* Vaterländ. Schauspiele. 1811.)

Walden, Jacob T. *and* T., *vs.* Hendricks, H., *in error.* Case on the part of the respondents. N. Y., 1818. 8°. (B 340)

Walden, Thomas. *See the previous entry.*

Walden. Thoreau, H. D. Walden; or, Life in the woods [of Concord]. Boston, 1854. 12°.

Waldenses. Melia, P. The origin, persecutions, and doctrines of the Waldenses, from documents, [to 1870]. London, 1870. 8°.

— Muston, A. The Israel of the Alps; a complete history of the Vaudois of Piedmont, [to 1850]; tr. by Rev. J. Montgomery. Glasgow, 1857. 2 v. 8°.

— Gilly, W. S. The Waldenses, [to 1848]. Liverpool, [1852]. 12°. (Ch. of Eng. Instit. lectures, 2d course, no. 9. C 275)

— Baird, R. Sketches of Protestantism in Italy; including a notice of the Waldenses, [to 1843]. Boston, 1845. 12°.

— Blair, *Rev.* A. History of the Waldenses, [to 1831]. Edin., 1833. 2 v. 8°.

— Acland, H. D. Brief sketch of the history and present situation of the Waldenses in in Piemont, [to 1825]. London, 1825. 8°.

— Perrin, J. P. History of the Waldenses and Albigenses, [to 1618]; tr. from the French. (*In* Bray, T. Papal usurpation. 1712.)

— Amato, G. Processus contra Valdenses in Lombardia superiori, 1387. (*In* Archivio stor. ital., ser. 3, v. 1, pt. 1, v. 2, pt. 1. 1865.)

— History of the persecution of the valleys of Piedmont, 1686. London, 1688. 4°. (B 4)

— Gilly, W. S. Narrative of an excursion to the mountains of Piedmont, in 1823. 4th ed. London, 1827. 8°.

— England, J., *Bp. of Charleston, d.* 1842. On the history and doctrines of the Waldenses; a controversy. (*In his* Works, v. 2. 1849.)

— Henderson, E. The Vaudois, observations [in] the valleys of Piedmont, 1844; with remarks [on] the history of that people. London, 1845. 12°.

— Gruezmacher, —. Die waldensische Bibel. (*In* Jahrbuch f. rom. u. eng. Lit., v. 4. 1862.)

— Todd, J. H. The books of the Vaudois; Waldensian mss. in the library of Trinity Coll., Dublin. London, 1865. 8°.

— Smiles, S. Visit to the country of the Vaudois. (*In* Good words, v. 11. 1870.)

Waldevus. Vita et passio Waldevi comitis. (*In* Michel, F. Chroniques anglo-normandes, v. 2. 1836.)

Waldhauser, Konrad. Apologia. (*In* Vienna. K. Ak. d. Wiss. Fontes rer. Austr. Abth. 1., B. 6. 1865.)

— Boehringer, F. (*In his* Die Kirche Christi, 2. Bd. 4. Abth., 2. Hälfte. 1858.)

Waldo, Francis W., *reporter.* Trial of J. Abbot by a naval court martial on allegations made against him by D. Porter. Boston, 1822. 8°. (B 1405)

Waldo, J. C. Water baptism; discourse, Lynn, Mass. Lynn, 1834. 8°. (B 1304)

Waldo, Loren P. Early history of Tolland; address before the Tolland Co. Hist. Soc., 22d Aug., 27th Sept. Hartford, 1861. 8°.

Waldo, *Gen.* Samuel. Circular in Germany, 1753; tr. by J. W. Locke. (*In* Maine Hist. Soc. Col., v. 6. 1859.)

— Defence of the title of J. Leverett to land in the eastern parts of Massachusetts. *n.p.*, 1736. f°.

— *Another copy.* (A 23)

— Eaton, C. Early history of the Waldo Patent. (*In his* Annals of Warren. 1851.)

— Map of the Waldo Patent. ms.

Waldo, Samuel Putnam. Life and character of S. Decatur. Hartford, 1821. 12°.

— Memoirs of A. Jackson. 5th ed. Hartford, 1820. 12°.

— Tour of J. Monroe, 1817; with his life, *etc.* Hartford, 1818. 12°.

Waldo, Sarah, *Funeral sermon on.* 1851. *See* Sweetser, S. (B 1227)

Waldo Patent, *district of Maine. See* Waldo, S.

Waldoborough, *Me.* Starmen, J. W. Account of the German settlement in W. (*In* Maine Hist. Soc. Col., v. 5. 1816.)

Waldron, Richard, *Sen.* Biog. notice of W. (*In* N. H. Hist. Soc. Col., v. 2. 1827.)

Waldron, Richard, *Jr., Councilor of N. H.* Certificate of grants of townships. 1739. (*In* N. H. Hist. Soc. Col., v. 6. 1850.) — Bell, S. D. (*In* v. 8. 1866.)

See also Allen, T. Allen *vs.* Waldron.

Waldron, W., *Funeral sermon on.* 1727. *See* Checkley, S. (B 83); — Foxcroft, T. (B 83, 223); — Mather, C. (B 83); — Webb, J. (B 83, 281)

Waldron, Manor of, *Sussex, Eng.* Ley, J. Waldron; its church, its mansions, and its manors. (*In* Sussex. Archæological Soc. Col., v. 13. 1861.)

Waldstein, Albrecht Wenceslaus Eusebius, *Graf* von. *See* Wallenstein, A. W. E., *Graf* von.

Wale (*Lat.* Walæus), Anton von. Synopsis purioris theologiæ. *See* Polyander, J.

Wale, Johann von. De motu chyli et sanguinis. (*In* Bartholin, T. Anatomia. 1666; — *and in* Spiegel, A. Opera, v. 1. 1645.)

Wales, Charles T. The Toledo blade's annual statement of the trade and commerce of Toledo, 1862–63, 65. Toledo, 1863–65. 3 v. 8°.

Wales, Ebenezer, *Funeral sermon on.* 1813. *See* Harris, T. M. (B 910)

Wales, Ephraim. Alden, E. Tribute to the memory of W. Boston, 1855. 8°. (C 256)

Wales, J. Discovery by H. Wells of the applicability of nitrous oxyd gas, ether, *etc.* Hartford, 1852. 8°. (B 1567)

Wales, Samuel. Dangers of our national prosperity, *etc.*; sermon, Hartford, May 12. Hartford, 1785. 8°. (B 334, 840)

Wales, Thomas Beale. Frothingham, N. L. A tribute to his memory. Boston, 1853. 8°. (B 1227, 1461)

Wales, Wm. Inquiry into the present state of the population in England and Wales. London, 1781. 8°. (B 705)

— On the acronyichal rising of the Pleiades. (*In* Vincent, W. Commerce and navigation of the ancients, v. 1. 1807.)

Wales, Princes of. *See* Albert Edward; — Charles I.; — Edward, *the Black Prince*; — George IV.; — Henry [Stuart].

Wales. Ancient laws and institutes of Wales; with an English translation; [ed. by A. Owen]. London, 1841. f°. (Record commission.)

Contents. Laws of Howel Dda; the Venedotion code; the Dimetian code; the Gwentian code. — Anomalous laws. — Leges Wallicæ. — Leges Howeli boni. — Statuta de Rothelan. — Indexes and glossary.

Antiquities.

— Boswell, H. Complete historical descriptions of a collection of views of antiquities of England and Wales. London, [1785]. f°.

— Grose, F. Antiquities of England and Wales, [1773–76]. New ed., [with supplement]. London, [178-]-97. 8 v. 4°.

See also Glamorganshire.

Architecture.

— Parkins, G. J. Monastic and baronial remains in England, Wales, and Scotland. London, 1816. 2 v. 8°.

Biography.

— Parry, J. H. Cambrian Plutarch; memoirs of eminent Welshmen. London, 1834. 8°.

See also Jones, R. R.

Charity schools.

— Welch piety; an account of the circulating Welch charity schools, 1763–64. London, 1764. 8°. (B 1190)

Description.

— *Bibliography.* Hotten, J. C. Handbook to the topography and family hist. of England and Wales; account of books on sale. London, [1863]. 8°.

— Giraldus de Barri *Cambrensis.* Itinerarium Kambriæ et descriptio Kambriæ, [1188]; ed. by J. Dimock. London, 1868. 8°. (Opera, v. 6. Chron. and mem.)

— Ogilby, J. Britannia. Vol. 1: An illustration of England and Wales. Lond., 1675. f°.

— — *Same, revised.* London, 1698. f°.

— Owen, J. Britannia depicta; a copy of Ogilby's survey, [with additions]. London, 1720. 4°.

— Gilpin, W. Observations on the Wye, and parts of South Wales, 1770. 3d ed. London, 1792. 8°.

— - *Same.* 5th ed. London, 1800. 8°.
— Pennant, T. Tour in Wales, 1770. London, 1778–81. 2 v. 4°.
— Mudge, W., *and others.* Trigonometrical survey of Eng. and Wales, 1784–96. London, 1799–1811. 3 v. 4°.
— Rees, D. L. Principality of W. (*In* Burlington, C. Modern univ. trav. 1785.)
— Boydell, J. *and* J. Collection of views in Wales; engraved by [S. Middiman and others]. London, 1792. obl. 4°.
— Pratt, S. J. Gleanings through Wales, Holland, *etc.*, [1795]. 3d ed. London, 1797. 3 v. 8°.
— Skrine, H. Tour through Wales, [1795]. (*In* Pinkerton, J. Col. of voy., v. 2. 1808.)
— Paterson, D. Roads in England and Wales. 11th ed., with add. London, 1796. 8°.
— Malkin, B. H. Tour through Wales, [1804–06]. (*In* Pinkerton, J. Col. of voy., v. 2. 1808.)
— Crosby's gazetteer of England and Wales; with a preface and introd. by J. Malham. London, 1807. 24°.
— Evans, J. N. Wales. (*In* Beauties of England and Wales, v. 17. 1812.) — Rees, T. S. Wales. (*In* v. 18. 1815.)
— Whittle and Laurie's new traveller's companion for W. London, 1818. f°.
— Paterson, D. Roads in Eng. and Wales. 18th ed., augm., *etc.*, by E. Mogg. London, [1829]. 8°.
— Sinclair, C. Hill and valley; or, Hours in England and Wales, [1833]. Edin., 1838. 12°.
— Bingley, *Rev.* W. Excursions in North Wales. 3d ed. with add. by W. R. Bingley, London, 1839. 8°.
— Black, A. *and* C. Picturesque tourist and road-book of England and Wales. Edin., 1844. 12°.
— Clarke, B. British gazetteer. London, 1852. 3 v. 8°.
— Black, A. *and* C. Picturesque guide through Wales, *etc.* Edin., 1853. 12°.
— Borrow, G. Wild Wales; its people, language, and scenery, [1854]. London, 1862. 3 v. 8°.
— Two days on the Welsh border. *n.t.p.* [1854.] 16°. (C 275)
— Black, A. *and* C. Picturesque tourist and road and railway guide through Eng. and Wales. Edin., 1857. 12°.
— Ramsay, A. C. Old glaciers of Switzerland and Wales. (*In* Ball, J. Peaks. 1859.)
— Cliffe, J. H. Notes and recollections of an angler; rambles among the mountains of Wales. London, 1860. 12°.
— Handbook for North Wales. 3d ed. London, *Murray*, 1868. 12°.

Maps.

— Andrews, J. London, 1786. f°.
— Cary, J. London, 1796. f°. (E 65)
— Ellis, G. New and correct atlas of England and Wales. London, 1819. 4°.

See also Anglesey; — Bala; — Gr. Britain; — St. David's Cathedral.

Ecclesiastical affairs.

— Dialogue between Rev. J. Evans and P. Dobson conc. bishops, partic. in the Principality of Wales. London, 1744. 8°.

History.

— Wright, T. Origin of the Welsh. (*In his* Essays on archæol., v. 1. 1861.)
— Woodward, B. B. History of Wales, [to 1689]. London, 1852. 2 v. 8°.
— Annales Cambriæ, [444–1288]; ed. by J. Williams ab-Ithel. Lond., 1860. 8°. (Chron. and mem.)
— Annales Cambriæ, [circ. 444–1066]. (*In* Petrie, H., *and* Sharpe, J. Monumenta historica Britannica, v. 1. 1848.)
— Brut y Tywysogion; chronicle of the princes, [681–1066]; ed. by J. Williams ab-Ithel. [In Welsh and Eng.] London, 1860. 8°. (Chron. and mem.)

See also Aberconway; — Anglesey.

Language.

— Evans, T. English and Welsh vocabulary; with grammar by T. Richards; also, diss. on the Welsh language, by J. Walters. Dolgellery, 1816. 8°.
— Richards, W. English and Welsh dictionary; rev., corr., and enl. Llangollen, 1847. 16°.
— S., W. Cambrica; Welsh glosses. (*In* Philological Soc. Trans., 1860–61.)
— Sparrell, W. Dictionary of the Welsh language. N. Y., 1861. 12°.

Law.

— Campbell, J. F., *Earl Cawdor.* Letter to Baron Lyndhurst on the administration of justice in Wales. Edin., 1828. 8°. (B 975)

Literature.

— *Bibliography.* Rowlands, W. Cambrian bibliography, 1546–[1799]; ed. and enlarged by D. S. Evans. Llanidloes, 1869. 8°.
— *History.* Halliwell, J. O. Connexion of Wales with the early science of England. London, 1840. 8°.
— - Price, *Rev.* T. Literary remains; ed. with memoir by J. Williams. Llandovery, 1854, 55. 2 v. 8°.
— - Turner, S. Vindication of the genuineness of the poems of Aneurin, Taliesin, Llywarc-Hên, and Merdhin. London, 1803. 8°.
— *Collections.* Mabinogion, The; from the Llyfr coch o Hergest, and other Welsh mss.; with an Eng. tr. and notes, by Lady C. Guest. London, 1849. 3 v. 8°.
— - Skene, W. F. The four ancient books of Wales, containing the Cymric poems attributed to the bards of the 6th century, in Welsh and English, with introd. and notes. Edin., 1868. 2 v. 8°.

See also Bible (p. 270); — Brut y Tywysogion.

Political geography.

— Milman, H. S. Political geography of Wales, 1858. (*In* Archæologia, v. 38. 1860.)

Walewski, Alexandre Florian Joseph Colonna, *comte.* Sainte-Beuve, C. A. (*In* Revue d. D. Mondes, fév. 1840.)

Walford, Cornelius. Education in the U. S. — Longevity in Scotland. (*In* Nat. Assoc. Prom. Soc. Sci. Trans., 1863.)

Walford, *Rev.* Edward. County families of the United Kingdom. London, 1860. 8°.
— *Same.* 6th ed. enl. London, 1871. 8°.
— Hardwicke's annual biography for 1856, 57. London, 1856–57. 2 v. 12°.

See also Men of the time. 1862.

Walford, Weston Styleman. A roll of arms of the 13th century. (*In* Soc. of Antiq. Archæologia, v. 39, pt. 2. 1863.)

Walgrave, Wm. Decimal arithmetic; added, the description of a very easy instrument for the taking of any heights or distances, *etc.*; also, Essay to gunnery. London, [167–]. 16°.

Walke, Henry. HEADLEY, J. T. (*In his* Farragut and our naval commanders. 1867.)
Walker. *See also* Warker.
Walker, Adam. Analysis of a course of lectures on natural and experimental philosophy. 6th ed. *n.p.*, [179-]. 8°. (B 899)
Walker, Aldace F. The Vermont brigade in the Shenandoah Valley, 1864. Burlington, Vt., 1869. 8°.
Walker, Alexander. Beauty; illustrated by analysis and classification of beauty in woman. 2d ed. London, 1846. 8°.
— Life of J. Touro. (*In* Hunt, F. Lives of Amer. merchants, v. 2. 1858.)
— Woman physiologically considered as to mind, morals, marriage, *etc.* N. Y., 1840. 12°.
Walker, Alexander. U. S. Circuit Court; report of the suit of Myra Gains *vs.* Chew, Relf, and others, for the recovery of the property of the late D. Clark. N. Orleans, 1850. 8°.
Walker, Amasa. Address before the young men of Boston associated for moral improvement, July 4. Boston, 1833. 8°. (B 1203)
— Cheap postage and how to get it. Boston, 1845. 8°. (B 1199)
— Nature and uses of money and mixed currency; with history of the Wickeborg bank. Boston, 1857. 8°.
— Political economy as a study in common schools. (*In* Amer. Inst. of Instr. Lectures, 1850.)
— Science of wealth; a manual of political economy. Boston, 1866. 8°.
— LORING, J. S. (*In his* Hundred Boston orators. 1852.)
Walker, Anthony. True account of the author of a book Εἰκὼν Εασιλικὴ [*sic*] or the pourtraiture of His Majesty in his solitudes and sufferings; with answer to all objections by Hollingworth and others. London, 1692. 4°. (B 8)
Walker, C. E. Warlock of the Glen, The; a melo-drama. (*In* Sargent, E. Mod. stand. dr., v. 37.)
Walker, *Rev.* Charles, *of Rutland.* Sermon, Brandon, Vt., sixth anniv. of the No. West branch of the Amer. Educational Soc., Jan. 11. Middlebury, 1826. 8°. (B 1329)
Walker, *Rev.* Charles, *of New Ipswich.* Sketch of New Ipswich. (*In* New Hamp. Hist. Soc. Col., v. 5. 1837.)
Walker, Charles M. History of Athens County, Ohio, and incidentally of the Ohio Land Company and the first settlement at Marietta, *etc.* Cincin., 1869. 8°. (Ohio Valley hist. ser., no. 2.)
Walker, Clement. History of the independency; or, Relations and observations upon this present Parliament; by Theodorus Verax. *n.p.*, 1648-49. 2 v. 4°.
Walker, Donald. Manly exercises; rev. by Craven [Capt. Carleton]. 9th ed. London, *Bohn*, 1855. 8°.
Walker, E. Art of book-binding, *etc.* N. Y., 1850. 8°.
Walker, Frederick. COLVIN, S. Criticism on W. (*In* Atkinson, J. B. English painters of the present day. 1871.)
Walker, Garret D. Speech, bill for the collection, safe-keeping, and disbursement of the public bills, Sept. 27. [Wash., 1837.] 8°. (B 1664)
Walker, *Rev.* George, *d.* 1807. Christian fortitude; sermon, Mar. 24. London, 1793. 8°. (B 842)
— Essay on tragedy, *etc.* (*In* Lit. and Phil. Soc. of Manchester. Mem., v. 5. 1802.)
— Essays on various subjects. London, 1809. 2 v. 8°.
Contents. Vol. 1. Memoir of W. — On the beautiful in the human form. — Tragedy and the interest in tragical representations. — A defence of learning and the arts against some charges of Rousseau. — Sequel to the 'Defence of learning', *etc.* 2. Hypocrisy and open profligacy, and the comparative infamy and demerit of each. — Probable arguments in favor of the immateriality of the soul. — Machinery of the ancient epic poem. — Moral influence of history. — Natural and moral philosophy, and the proper manner of philosophizing in both.
— Sermon, Dec. 13, 1776, general fast. London, 1777. 8°. (B 1851)
— Sermon, Feb. 27, general fast. London, 1778. 8°. (B 1851)
— Sermons. London, 1790. 2 v. 8°.
— Substance of speech at the meeting of the Co. of Nottingham, Mansfield, Feb. 28. *n.p.*, 1780. 8°. (B 767)
— Virtuous remembrance; sermon, [death] of J. Currie, Nov. 17, 1805. Liverpool, *n.d.* 8°. (B 868)
Walker, George. Chess made easy. New ed. London, 1850. 16°.
Walker, George Atkinson. Elementa liturgica; or, Churchman's primer. 3d ed. London, 1848. 12°.
Walker, *Rev.* George Leon. Offered national regeneration; sermon, Portland, national fast, Sept. 26. Portland, 1861. 8°. (B 1593)
Walker, *Rev.* H. D. Sermon, death of D. B. Shaw, E. Arlington. Boston, 1854. 8°. (B 1224)
Walker, J. Letter to Gov. Prince, acquainting him with Philip's answer to his letter. (*In* Mass. Hist. Soc. Col., v. 6. 1799.)
Walker, James. Picturesque representation of the manners and customs of the Russians. 1803-04. *See* Atkinson, J. A.
Walker, *Rev.* James, *of Edinburgh.* Agency of Providence considered and applied to recent events; sermon, 7th July. Edin., 1814. 8°. (B 1252)
Walker, James. On ventilating and lighting tunnels. (*In* Instit. of Civil Engin. Trans., v. 1. 1842.)
Walker, James, *D.D.*, *President of Harvard College*, *d.* 1874. Address at his inauguration. (*In* Harvard College. *President.* Addresses. 1853. (H 10)
— Causes of the progress of liberal Christianity in New Eng. Boston, 1826. 12°. (C 210)
— *Same.* 2d ed. Boston, 1827. 12°. (C 168, v. 1.)
— Discourse, Charlestown, July 14. Camb., 1839. 8°. (B 1304)
— Discourse, induction of F. D. Huntington, Sept. 4, as Prof. to the Univ. [of] Harvard. Camb., 1855. 8°. (B 1323, H 12)
— Discourse, law of the spiritual life. Boston, *A.U.A.*, 1835. 12°. (C 168, v. 9)
— Discourse, ordination of E. Peabody, Cincinnati, May 20. Cincin., 1832. 8°. (B 1133)
— On the exclusive system; discourse, Saco, 1827. Kennebunk, 1828. 12°. (D 64)
— *Same.* 2d ed. Boston, *A. U. A.*, 1830. 12°. (C 168, v. 4)
— Farewell discourse, Charlestown, June 23. Camb., 1839. 18°. (C 16)
— Introductory lecture. (*In* Amer. Inst. Instr. Lectures, 1831, 1856.)
— Remarks addressed to the conscientious of all denominations on the subject of praying for one another. Boston, 1822. 12°. (C 150)
— Remarks at various times.] (*In* Mass. Hist. Soc. Proc., 1858-70.) — Memoir of D. A. White. (*In* 1862-63.)— Memoir of J. Quincy. (*In* 1866-67.)
— Sermon; balance of character. (*In* Liberal preacher, v. 1. 1828.) — Religion disarming and destroying temptation. (*In* n.s., v. 1.) — Sermon; craft and management in religion. (*In* v. 3. 1833.)
— Sermon, Brooklyn, Conn., installation of S. J. May, Nov. 5, 1823. Boston, 1824. 8°. (B 959, 1595)
— Sermon, day of general election, May 28. Boston, 1828. 8°. (B 958)
— Sermon, dedication of the 2d Cong. Church in Leicester, Aug. 12. Worcester, 1834. 8°. (B 1309, 1310)
— Sermons preached in the Chapel of Harvard College. Boston, 1861. 8°.
— Smooth preaching. [N. Y., 182?.] 12°. (C 110)
— The spirit proper to the times; sermon. Boston, 1861. 8°. (C 210)
— Unitarianism vindicated against the charge of not going far enough. Boston, 1827. 12°. (C 168, v. 1)
— BEECHER, L. Reply to [W.'s] Review of B.'s sermon at Worcester. From the Christian spectator. *n. p.*, 1825. 8°. (B 271, 1238)
Walker, James Barr, *D.D.* Philosophy of the plan of salvation; introduction by C. E. Stowe. New ed. Boston, 1855. 12°.
Walker, James Bradford Richmond. Memorials of the Walkers of Old Plymouth Colony. Northampton, 1861. 8°.
Walker, James M. Tract on government. Boston, 1853. 8°.

Walker, James Perkins. The altar at home. 2d ser.: Selections and prayers for domestic worship. 5th ed. Boston, *A.U.A.*, 1869. 16°.

— The new discussion of the trinity. Boston, 1860. 12°.

Contents. Dr. **Huntington** on the trinity; from the Christian examiner. — Prof. **Huntington's** argument for the trinity; from the monthly journal of the A. U. A. — **King**, *Rev.* T. S. Trinitarianism not the doctrine of the New Testament. — **Sears**, *Rev.* E. H. Dr. Huntington on the trinity. — *Communications to the Christian register.* **A.**, E. Dr. Huntington's misquotations of Neander on the trinity; — Dr. Huntington's quotations from Scripture in proof of the trinity. — **S.**, R. P. Dr. Huntington and Dr. Pond. — **Huntington**, F. D. Letter. — **A.**, E. Review of Dr. Huntington's letter; — Gradual development of the doctrine of the trinity; — The doctrine of the trinity in the 4th century; — Further illustrations of Neander's views, and of Dr. Huntington's quotations, with a practical improvement of the subject. — **Dewey**, O. The primitive Christian creed.

Walker, Jesse. Poems; ed. by M. Schuyler. Buffalo, 1854. 12°.

Walker, John. Spectacula Veneta. (*In* **Grævius**. Thes. antiq. Ital., v. 5, pt. 4. 1722.)

Walker, John, *D.D.*, *b.* 1673, *d.* 1747. Attempt towards recovering an account of the numbers and sufferings of the clergy, *etc.*, in the grand rebellion. London, 1714. f°.

— Calamy, E. The Church and the Dissenters compar'd as to persecution; in remarks on Dr. Walker's 'Attempt', *etc.* London, 1719. 8°. (B 106, 1897)

Walker, John, *bailie, and* **Stuart**, J. Reasons of protest against acts of magistrates of Edinburgh [on] settling a minister; annexed, act of town council, June 6, 1750. Edin., 1762. 12°. (C 24)

Walker, John, *D.D.*, *b.* 1731, *d.* 1804. Jardine, *Sir* W. (*In his* Naturalist's lib., Orn., v. 12. 1839.)

Walker, John, *b.* 1732, *d.* 1807. Abridgment of his Elements of elocution. (*In* **Etheridge**, S. Christian orator. 1818.)

— Critical pronouncing dictionary of the English language. 4th ed. London, 1806. 4°.

— *Same.* 3d Amer. ed. from last London ed. N. Y., 1807. 8°.

— *Same.* Dictionary of the Eng. language. 5th Phila. from the 16th London ed. Phila., 1818. 8°.

— *Same.* Critical, *etc.*; added, a col. of Latin, French, *etc.*, phrases by A. Howard. London, 1826. 12°.

— *Same.* Palmetto series. Richmond, 1864. 16°.

— Key to the classical pronounciation of Latin proper names. Boston, 1808. 8°.

— Outlines of English grammar. New ed. London, 1810. 12°.

— Rhetorical grammar. 4th ed. London, 1807. 8°.

— *Same.* 1st Amer. ed. Boston, 1814. 8°.

— Rhyming dictionary. 3d ed. London, 1819. 2 v. 8°.

Contents. Vol. 1. A–O. 2. P–Z.

— *Same.* New and revised ed. London, 1851. 8°.

Walker, John, *M.D.*, *d.* 1830. Elements of geography and of nat. and civil history; ed. by T. Smith. 4th ed. London, 1805. 8°.

Walker, John, *Vicar of Hornechurch*, *d.* 1831. Letters by eminent persons. London, 1813. 2 v. in 3 pts. 8°.

Contents. Vol. 1. Letters, 1654–1715. 2, pt. 1. 1715–53. — Letters from the Ashmolean Museum. — Account of Hearne's journey to Whaddon-Hall, 1716, — to Reading and Silchester, 1713. — Lives of eminent men, by J. Aubrey, A–Fl. 2, 2. Fo–W. — Life of T. Hobbes of Malmesburie.

Walker, John M. Experimental inquiry into the similarity in virtue between the cornus florida and sericea, and the cinchona officinalis of Linnæus. (*In* **Caldwell**, C. Medical theses, v. 1. 1805.)

Walker, Jonathan. Brief view of American chattelized humanity and its supports. Boston, 1846. 12°. (C 261)

— Trial and imprisonment at Pensacola for aiding slaves to escape. Boston, 1845. 12°. (C 259)

Walker, Joseph Burbeen. Valley of the Merrimack. (*In* **New Hampshire Hist. Soc.** Col., v. 7. 1863.)

Walker, Joseph Cooper. Historical essay on the Irish stage. (*In* **Roy. Irish Acad.** Trans., v. 2. 1788.) — Rise and progress of gardening in Ireland. (*In* v. 4.) — Origin of romantic fabling in Ireland. (*In* v. 10. 1806.)

Walker, Ralph. Treatise on magnetism. London, 1794. 8°.

— Treatise on the magnet; with tables of the dip of the needle in different parts of the globe, *etc.* London, 1798. 8°.

Walker, Richard. Memoirs of medicine; [with] a sketch of medical hist. to the 18th cent. London, 1799, 8°. (B 717)

Walker, *Rev.* Robert, *b.* 1716, *d.* 1783. We have nothing which we did not receive; sermon, Aug. 7, 1775, before the governors of Orphan Hospital; annexed, an account of the Hospital from its establishment, 1733. Edin., 1776. 8°. (B 1858)

Walker, Robert, *of Wadham College.* Elements of the theory of mechanics. Oxford, 1830. 8°.

Walker, Robert Bruce Napoleon. The alleged sterility of women of savage races. (*In* **Anthropolog. Soc.** Mem., v. 2. 1866.)

Walker, Robert James. American finances and resources; letters 1–5. London, 1863–64. 5 v. 8°.

— Argument [in case Groves *et al. vs.* Slaughter]; in the Mississippi slave question. Phila., 1841. 8°.

— Introductory address before the National Institute, April, 1844. Wash., 1845. 8°. (B 1583)

— Jefferson Davis; repudiation, recognition, and slavery. London, 1863. 8°.

— Letter rel. to the annexation of Texas, in reply to the people of Carroll Co., Ky. Wash., 1844. 8°. (B 1510, 1174)

— Speech on the bill for collection, safe keeping, and disbursement of public moneys. Wash., 1837. 8°. (B 1663)

— Appleton, N. What is a revenue standard? and a review of R. J. W.'s Report on the tariff. Boston, 1846. 8°. (B 1514)

— Cook, M. W. Verses addressed to R. J. Walker. N. Y., [1857?]. 8°. (B 1233)

Walker, Samuel, *curate of Truro*, *b.* 1714, *d.* 1761. The Christian; a course of practical sermons. London, 1765. 12°.

— Practical Christianity, illustrated in nine tracts. London, 1766. 12°.

Walker, Samuel, *of Danvers, Mass.* Sermon, Danvers, fast day, Jan. 12. Salem, 1815. 8°. (B 1259)

Walker, Sears Cook. Determination of the longitude of several stations near the northern boundary of Ohio from transits of the moon and moon culminating stars observed in 1835 by A. Talcott. (*In* **Amer. Phil. Soc.** Trans., n.s., v. 6. 1839.)

— New Latin reader. Pt. 1. 4th ed. Boston, 1834. 12°.

— The opposition of Neptune of 1848. (*In* **Amer. Assoc.** Proc., v. 1. 1849.) — Substance of a report on the experience of the coast survey in regard to telegraph operations. — New analogy in the periods of rotation of the primary planets discovered by D. Kirkwood. (*In* v. 2. 1850.)

— Researches rel. to the planet Neptune. — Ephemeris of Neptune, 1795, 1846–51. (*In* **Smithsonian Inst.** Contrib., v. 2. 1851.) — Ephemeris of the planet Neptune, 1852. (*In* v. 3. 1852.)

— Gould, B. A., *Jr.* Address in commemoration of W. (*In* **Amer. Assoc.** Proc., v. 8. 1855.)

Walker, Thomas. Gurney, J. Whole proceedings on the trial of indictment against W. and others for a conspiracy to overthrow the government and to assist the French, Lancaster, Apr. 2. Phila., 1794. 8°. (B 772)

Walker, Thomas. Utilization of sewage. (*In* **Nat. Assoc. Prom. Soc. Sci.** Trans., 1864.)

Walker, Thomas Larkins. Architectural precedents, plans, specifications, *etc.* 3d ed. London, 1841. 8°.

Walker, *Rev.* Timothy, *of Rumford, N.H.* Those who have the form of godliness; discourse, May 12, 1771. Salem, 1772. 8°. (B 147)
— Way to try all pretended apostles; two sermons, Rumford, N. H., Jan. Boston, 1743. 8°. (B 42, 44, C 45)

Walker, Timothy, *LL.D., of Ohio, d.* 1856. Address before the Union Literary Soc. of Miami University. Cincin., 1832. 8°. (B 1072)
— Annual discourse, 1837. (*In* Ohio Hist. and Phil. Soc. Trans., v. 1, pt. 2. 1839.)
— Elements of geometry, with practical application. 3d ed. Boston, 1831. 12°.
— Introductory lecture on the dignity of the law as a profession, at the Cincinnati Coll., Nov. 4. Cincin., 1837. 8°. (B 1756)
— Oration, life and character of J. Q. Adams. Cincin., 1848. 8°. (B 1207)
— Oration, life and public services of D. Webster, before the bar of Cincinnati, Nov. 22. Cincin., 1852. 8°. (B 1726)
— The reform spirit of the day; oration before the Phi Beta Kappa Soc. of Harvard Univ., July 18. Boston, 1850. 8°. (B 1539)

Walker, W. S. Effect of poor-houses in checking pauperism. (*In* Nat. Assoc. Prom. Soc. Sci. Trans., 1863.)

Walker, Wm., *d.* 1684. A treatise of English particles and how to render them into Latine. 13th ed. London, 1706. 8°.

Walker, Wm. TRIAL for the murder of D. R. Lambert. *See* Parker, M. 1825.

Walker, *Gen.* Wm. The war in Nicaragua. Mobile, 1860. 12°.
— ASSOLLANT, J. B. A. Walker et les aventuriers amér. au Nicaragua. (*In* Revue d. D. Mondes, août 1856.)

Walker, Wm. Johnson. On the treatment of compound and complicated fractures. Boston, 1845. 8°.
— *Another copy.* (B 1564)
— *Same.* (*In* Mass. Med. Soc. Med. comm., v. 7. 1848.)

Walker, Wm. W. Valedictory address. (*In* Rensselaer Polytechnic Institute. Graduating exercises. 1856. B 1577)

Walking statue, The; or, The devil in the wine-cellar; a farce, by A. Hill. (*In his* Dramatic works, v. 1. 1760.)

Walking tour in Normandy, A. London, 1868. 8°.

Walkingame, Francis. Tutor's assistant; a compendium of arithmetic. New ed. by T. Crosby. York, 1836. 12°.
— *Same.* 13th ed., rev. by W. Birkin. St. John, N. B., 1838. 12°.
— - Key; by T. Hewitt. New ed. with add. London, 1816. 12°.

Walks and wanderings in the world of literature; by [J. Grant]. London, 1839. 2 v. 12°.

Wall, Charles. Grammatical spelling-book. 2d ed. London, 1837. 12°.

Wall, Charles William, *D.D.* Nature, age, and origin of the Sanscrit writing and language. (*In* Roy. Irish Acad. Trans., v. 18. 1838.) — The different kinds of cuneiform writing in the triple inscriptions of the Persians, *etc.* (*In* v. 21. 1848.)

Wall, *Col.* George, *Jr.* Description of the trigonometer. Phila., 1788. 8°. (W 31)

Wall, George. A public lecture on elocution, religious toleration, national reformation in morals and education, 16th Nov. Limerick, 1812. 12°. (C 65)

Wall, George P., *and* Sawkins, J. G. Report of the survey of the economic geology of Trinidad. (*In* Smithsonian Inst. Report, 1856.)

Wall, Henry. Emulation. (*In* Oxford prize essays, v. 5. 1836.)

Wall, John. Experiments and observations on the Malvern waters. 2d ed. London, 1757. 8°. (B 1190)

Wall, Martin. [Various articles.] (*In* Literary and Phil. Soc. of Manchester. Mem., v. 1, 2. 1789.)

Wall, Thomas. Second Christian warning-piece. [London, 168-?] 4°. (B 12)

Wall, W. L., & Co. Catalogue of rare books, [incl.] 200 volumes from the library of Gen. Washington, sold March 1863; [with ms. prices]. Wash., 1863. 8°.

Wall, Wm., *D.D.* Critical notes on the Old Testament. London, 1735. 2 v. 8°.

Wall painting. BENDEMANN, E. Die Wandgemälde, *etc.* Dresden, [1840?]. f°.

Wall street. WEEK in Wall St. N. Y., 1841. 12°.
— MEDBURY, J. M. Men and mysteries of Wall street. Boston, 1870. 12°.

Wallabout Bay. TAYLOR, G. Martyrs to the Revolution in British prison ships, [1776–82]. N. Y., 1855. 8°.

Wallabout Committee. *See* Tammany Soc.

Wallace, Alexander. The Bible and the working classes. Edin., 1857. 12°.

Wallace, Alfred Russell. Contributions to the theory of natural selection; a series of essays. London, 1870. 8°.

Contents. The law which has regulated the introduction of new species. (Annals of nat. hist., Sept. 1855.) — Tendency of varieties to depart indifferently from the original type. (Linnæan Soc. Proc., Aug. 1858.) — Mimicry and other protective resemblances among animals. (Westminster rev., July 1867.) — The Malayan papilionidæ or swallow-tailed butterflies as illust. of the theory of natural selection. (Linnæan Soc. Trans., 1867.) — Instinct in man and animals. — The philosophy of birds' nests. (Intellectual obs., July 1867.) — A theory of birds' nests. (Journ. of travel and nat. hist., no. 2, 1868.) — Creation by law. (Quar. journ. of Sci., Oct. 1867.) — Development of human races under the law of natural selection. (Anthropological rev., May 1864.) — Limits of natural selection as applied to man.

— The Malay archipelago; a narrative of travel. London, 1869. 2 v. 8°.
— Narrative of travels on the Amazon and Rio Negro. London, 1870. 8°.

Wallace, Edward James. Oregon question determined by the rules of international law. London, 1846. 8°. (B 1516)

Wallace, Horace Binney. Art and scenery in Europe; with other papers. Phila., 1857. 12°.

Contents. Art an emanation of religious affection. — Art symbolical, not imitative. — The law of the development of Gothic architecture. — The principle of beauty in works of art. — The cathedrals of the continent. — Notes of a tour in Switzerland. — The Roman forum. — Ascent of Vesuvius. — The great exhibition. — Remarks upon painters. — Art education in America. — Nature. — The drama. — Summer travel in America. — The rights of literature. — Defence of the country. — Various subjects. — Washington.

— Literary criticisms, and other papers. Phila., 1856. 12°.

Contents. Literary criticisms. — Literary portraits. — Fragmental literary disquisitions. — Miscel. pieces. — Dramatic criticisms.

— GODWIN, P. (*In his* Out of the past. 1870.)
— OBITUARY. Phila., 1853. 8°. (B 1452, 1461)

Wallace, James, *M. D.* Some of the causes of the high rate of mortality in Greenock. (*In* Nat. Assoc. Prom. Soc. Sci. Trans., 1860.)

Wallace, *Rev.* John A. Sermon; vineyards in the wilderness. (*In* Free church pulpit. 1853.)

Wallace, John H. American trotting register. N. Y., 1871. 8°.

Wallace, John Wm. Want of uniformity in the commercial law between the different states of our union; discourse before the Law Academy of Phila. Phila., 1851. 8°. (B 1430)

Wallace, Robert, *D.D.* Church tendencies in Scotland. (*In* Grant, *Sir* A. Recess studies. 1870.)
— On the Ictis of Diodorus Siculus. (*In* Literary and Phil. Soc. of Manchester. Mem., v. 12. 1846.)

Wallace, Samuel Jacob. Elasticity as a feature in physics. — Lakes and lake regions. (*In* Amer. Assoc. Proc., v. 19. 1870.)

Wallace, *Sir* Wm., *b. abt.* 1270, *d.* 1305. HENRY, *the minstrel.* Acts and deeds of W. *t.p.w.* [179-?] 12°.
— STEVENSON, J. Documents illustrative of Sir W. Wallace, his life and times. [Edin.,] 1841. 4°. (Maitland Club.)
— TYTLER, P. F. (*In his* Lives of Scottish worthies, v. 1. 1831. Fam. lib., v. 29.)

Wallace, Wm., *LL.D.*, *b.* 1768, *d.* 1843. Encyclopædia of geography. *See* Murray, H., *and others.*
— Hindoo astronomy and mathematics. (*In* Murray, H., *and others.* Brit. India. 1832.)

Wallace, Wm., *M.D., of Dublin.* Medical powers of chlorine, particularly in disease of the liver. London, 1822. 8°.
— Observations on sulphureous fumigations, *etc.* Dublin, 1820. 8°. (B 969)

Wallace, Wm., *barrister.* History of the life and reign of George IV. London, 1831-32. 3 v. 12°. (Lardner. Cab. lib.)
— History of England. *See* Mackintosh, *Sir* J.

Wallace; a Franconia story; by J. Abbott. N. Y., 1850. 16°.

Wallace; by W. Barrymore. (*In* Sargent, E. Mod. stand. dr., v. 33; *also* C 280)

Wallace; or, The fight of Falkirk; by Miss Holford. Phila., 1810. 12°.

Wallace-Dunlop, *Misses* Madeline *and* R. The timely retreat; or, Year in Bengal before the mutinies. London, 1858. 2 v. 8°.

Wallace-Dunlop, Rosalind. *See previous entry.*

Wallachia. THOUVENEL, E. Le Valachie en 1839. (*In* Revue d. D. Mondes, mai 1839.)
— MERCATOR, G. Walachia, Servia, Bulgaria, Romania. [Amst., 16—.] (E 78, no. 261)
— RUHEDORF, F. J. Map. *n.p.*, 1788. (E 66)

Wallachian proverbs. REINSBERG-DUERINGSFELD, *Freiherr* von. Die Sprichwörter der Romänen, im Vergleich zu denen anderer romanischen Völker. (*In* Jahrbuch für rom. und eng. Lit., v. 6. 1865.)

Wallack, James Wm. SKETCH of the life of J. W. Wallack, senior. N. Y., 1865. 8°.

Wallack, John Lester. The veteran; a drama. (*In* Sargent, E. Mod. stand. dr., v. 28.)

Walladmor; [by G. W. H. Haering]; tr. [by T. De Quincey]. London, 1825. 2 v. 8°.

Wallaszky, Paullus. Conspectus reipublicæ litterariæ in Hungaria. Ponsonii, Lips., 1785. 8°.

Wallenstein *or* Waldstein, Albrecht Wenzeslaus Eusebius, *Graf* von, *Herzog von Friedland.* BOLOGNESI, O. Ragguagli contemporanei delle ultime imprese della morte di A. Waldstein. (*In* Archivio stor. ital., n. s., v. 3, pt. 1. 1856.)
— CUST, C. (*In his* Lives of the warriors of the 30 years' war, v. 1. 1865.)
— EGERTON, F., *Earl of Ellesmore.* Life and letters of W. (*In his* Essays. 1858.)
— FÖRSTER, F. Wallenstein als regierender Herzog und Landesherr. (*In* Historisches Taschenbuch, 1834.)
— GUALDO-PRIORATO, G. di. Historia della vita d'A. Valstain. Lion, 1643. 4°.
— HASSEL, J. P. Die Absetzung der Herzoge von Mecklenburg und die Einsetzung Wallenstein's zum Fürsten des Landes; ein Beitrag zur Politic des Hauses Habsburg im Dreissigjährigen Kriege. (*In* Historisches Taschenbuch, 1867.)
— MITCHELL, J. Life of Wallenstien. 2d ed. London, 1840. 12°.
— ROEPELL, R. Der Verrath Wallenstein's an Kaiser Ferdinand II. (*In* Historisches Taschenbuch, 1845.)
See also Schiller, J. C. F. von. Wallenstein.

Wallenstein, Jules de. Mémoires pour accompagner le tableau des observations météorologiques faites à Washington, depuis le 17 avril 1823 jusqu'au 18 avril 1824. (*In* Amer. Phil. Soc. Trans., n.s., v. 2. 1825.)

Wallenstein's Tod; ein Trauerspiel. *See* Schiller, J. C. F. von.

Waller, Charles. Observations on the transfusion of blood. London, 1825. 8°. (B 829)

Waller, Edmund. Works; ed. by Fenton. London, 1744. 8°.
Contents. Poems upon several occasions. — Divine poems. — Epigrams, epitaphs, and fragm. — Speeches, letters, *etc.*
— Letters supposed to have passed between St. Evremond and W.; col. and pub. by Dr. Langhorne; pref. a biog. sketch. Balt., 1809. 12°.
— Poems. (*In* Campbell, T. Spec. of Brit. poets, v. 4. 1819.)
— Poems. (*In* Chalmers, A. Eng. poets, v. 8. 1810.)
— Poetical works. (*In* Anderson, R. Brit. poets, v. 5. 1795.)
— BELL, R. (*In his* Lives of lit. and sci. men of Gr. Brit., v. 1. 1839. Lard. Cab. cyc.)
— JOHNSON, S. (*In his* Works, v. 9. 1806; — *and* Lives of eminent English poets, v. 1. 1810.)

Waller, John. Treatise on incubus or night-mare. London, 1816. 12°.

Waller, John G. Painted or stained glass from west Wickham Ch., Kent. (*In* Weale, J. Quart. papers on architecture, v. 2. 1844.)

Waller, John Lightfoot, *LL. D.* Sermon; the dead speak. (*In* Akers, T. P. Col. of sermons. 1851.)

Waller, *Sir* Wm., *b.* 1597, *d.* 1668. CUST, E. (*In his* Lives of the warriors of the civil wars, pt. 2. 1867.)

Waller, *Sir* Wm., *son of preceeding.* Tragical history of Jetzer. London, 1679. f°. (A 52)

Walley, *Hon.* John, *Funeral sermon on.* 1712. *See* Pemberton, E. (A 38, B 73)

Walley, Samuel Hurd. Financial revulsion of 1857; address, Feb. 10, before the Amer. Statistical Assoc. Boston, 1858. 8°. (B 1515)
— *Same.* (*In* Amer. Statist. Assoc. Col., v. 2, pt. 1. 1858.)
— Speech on the Nebraska and Kansas territorial bill, May 9. Wash., 1854. 8°. (B 1509)

Wallich, George Charles. North-Atlantic sea-bed; voy. of the Bulldog, 1860; observ. on animal life and organic deposits at great depths in ocean. London, 1862. 4°.

Wallin, *Rev.* Edward, *Funeral sermon on.* 1733. *See* Gill, S. (C 201)

Walley, Wm. Phillips. Biography of F. W. Crowninshield. (*In* Higginson, T. W. Harvard mem. biog., v. 2. 1866.)

Walling, Henry F. Map of Addison Co., Vt. Boston, N. Y., 1857.
— Map of Andover, Mass. Boston, 1852.
— Map of Barnstable, Mass. *n.p.*, 1856.
— Map of the Cos. of Barnstable, Dukes, and Nantucket, Mass. Boston, N. Y., 1858.
— Map of Bennington Co., Vt.; from surveys by E. Rice and C. E. Harwood. N. Y., 1856.
— Map of the Co. of Berkshire, Mass. Boston, N. Y., 1858.
— Map of Billerica, Mass. Boston, 1853.
— Map of Blackstone, Mass. *n.p.*, 1854.
— Map of Boylston, Mass. *n.p.*, 1856.
— Map of Braintree, Mass. *n.p.*, 1856.
— Map of the Co. of Bristol, Mass. N. Y., 1858.
— Map of Canton, Mass. *n.p.*, 1855.
— Map of Chittenden Co., Vt. N. Y., 1857.
— Map of Clinton Co., Ohio. N. Y., 1859.
— Map of Easton, Mass. *n.p.*, 1855.
— Map of Fairhaven, Mass. *n.p.*, 1855.
— Map of the Cos. of Franklin and Grand Isle, Vt. N. Y., 1857.
— Map of Hampden Co., Mass. Boston, 1857.
— A topographical map of Hampshire Co., Mass. *n.p.*, 1856.
— Map of Hanson, Mass. *n.p.*, 1856.
— Map of Lexington, Mass. *n.p.*, 1853.
— Map of Marion, Mass. *n.p.*, 1855.
— Map of Marlborough, Mass., Boston, 1853.
— Map of Medford, Mass. Boston, 1855.
— Map of Merrimack Co., N. H. Boston, 1858.
— Map of Middleborough, Mass. *n.p.*, 1855.
— Map of Middlesex Co., Mass. Boston, 1856.
— Map of the Co. of Milwaukee, Wis. N. Y., 1858.
— Map of Monmouth Co.; from surveys by S. N. and F. W. Beers. N. Y., 1861.
— Map of Natick, Mass. Boston, 1853.
— Map of the Co. of Norfolk, Mass. Boston, N. Y., 1858.
— Map of Northbridge from survey by Cushing and Walling. *n.p.*, 1849.

— Map of Norton, Mass. Boston, 1855.
— Map of Orange Co. Vt. N. Y., 1858.
— Map of the Cos. of Orleans, Lamoille, and Essex. N. Y., 1859.
— Map of Oxford Co., Me. N. Y., 1858.
— Map of the Co. of Plymouth, Mass. Boston, N. Y., 1857.
— Map of Quincy, Mass. *n.p.*, 1857.
— Map of Raynham, Mass. *n.p.*, 1855.
— Map of the State of Rhode Island and Providence Plantations. *n.p.*, 1855.
— Map of Rochester, Mass. *n.p.*, 1856.
— Map of Sandwich, Mass. *n.p.*, 1857.
— Map of Tiverton, R. I., by W. G. Borden. *n.p.*, 1854.
— Map of Vigo Co., Ind. N. Y., 1858.
— Map of Washington County, Vermont. N. Y., 1858.
— Map of the Co. of Waukesha, Wis. N. Y., 1859.
— Map of Weymouth, Mass. Boston, 1853.
— Map of Worcester Co., Mass. Boston, N. Y., 1857.
— *and* GRAY, O. W. Official topographical atlas of Mass. Boston, 1871. f°.

Walling, *Prof.* Henry Francis. Atomic motions. (*In* **Amer. Assoc.** Proc., v. 17. 1869.) — On the assumption that matter is impenetrable. (*In* v. 19. 1870.)

Wallingford, *Conn.* DAVIS, C. H. S. History of Wallingford, 1670–[1870]. Meriden, 1870. 8°.
— DANA, J. Century discourse at W., Apr. 9, 1770. New Haven, [1770]. 8°. (B 310)

Wallingford (*Conn.*). **Council**, 1759. HART, W. A few remarks upon the ordination of J. Dana, and the doings of the Consociation respecting the same. N. Haven, 1759. 8°. (B 155, 248)
— - Remarks on a pamphlet wrote by Mr. Hobart considered and applied to the case of the late ordination at Wallingford. New Haven, 1760. 8°. (B 248)
— HOBART, H. Principles of Cong. churches rel. to the constitution of councils applied to the case of the late ordination at Wallingford. New Haven, 1759. 8°. (B 248)
— PAULINUS, *pseud.* Three questions rel. to the new way of taking persons into the church introduced at Wallingford by Dana. (*In his* Letter to Scriptiorista. 1760. B 155)
— TODD, J. Faithful narrative of the First Soc. in W.; with a vindication of Dana, *etc.*, by W. Hart. New Haven, 1759. 8°. (B 155, 248)
— - Reply to Eell's 'Serious remarks upon the Faithful narrative'; [also] an answer to Hobart's 'Principles', *etc.*, by W. Hart. New Haven, 1760. 8°. (B 248)
— WOLCOTT, R. Letter to N. Hobart. [Windsor, 1760.] 8°. (B 248)

Wallington, Nehemiah. Historical notices of events occurring chiefly in the reign of Charles I. London, 1869. 2 v. 8°.

Wallis, *Capt.* —. Australian views drawn by him and engraved by Preston, a convict. *n.t.p.* [London, 1820.] f°.

Wallis, Alfred, *and* **Bemrose**, W. The pottery and porcelain of Derbyshire. 2d ed. London, 1870. 8°.

Wallis, George, *M. D.* Art of preventing diseases and restoring health. N. Y., 1794. 8°.

Wallis, George, *of So. Kensington Museum.* Constitution and management of schools of art. (*In* **Nat. Assoc.** Prom. Soc. Sci. Trans., 1857.)

Wallis, *Rev.* James. [Several sermons.] *n.t.p.* [1748.] 8°. (B 161)

Wallis, John, *D. D.* Briefwechsel zwischen Leibniz und W. (*In* **Leibniz**, G. W. von. Gesam. Werke, 3e Folge, 4r Bd. 1859.)
— Correspondence. (*In* **Rigaud**, S. J. Correspondence of scientific men, v. 2. 1841.)
— De loquela. Ed. 7a. Lugd. Bat., 1740. 8°.
— Discourse of combinations, alterations, and aliquot parts. 1685. (*In* **Maseres**, F. Doctrine of permutations. 1795.)
— Grammatica linguæ Anglicanæ; præfigitur, De loquela. Ed. 6a acc. epistola ad T. Beverley de mutis surdisque informandis. Londini, 1765. 8°.
— Opera mathematica. Oxon., 1695–99. 3 v. f°.
Contents. Vol. 1. Oratio inauguralis; Mathesis universalis. — Adversus M. Meibomii de proportionibus dialogum. — De sectionibus conicis, nova methodo expositis. — Arithmetica infinitorum. — Eclipsis solaris observatio, Oxonii habita, 2 Aug. 1654. — De cycloide tractatus. — Tractatus epistolaris ad D. Hugenium. — Mechanica; sive de motu; tractatus geometricus. 2. De algebra tractatus. — De combinationibus, alternationibus, et partibus aliquotis. — De sectionibus angularibus. — De angulo contactus et semicirculi. — Ejusdem tractatus defensio. — De postulato quinto et quinta definitione lib. 6. Euclidis disceptatio geometrica. — Cono-cuneus; seu Corpus partim conum partim cuneum repræsentans geometrice consideratum. — De gravitate et gravitatione disquisitio geometrica. — De æstu maris hypothesis nova. — Commercium epistolicum. — Trigonometria J. Caswell. 3. Claudii Ptolemæi Harmonicorum libri tres; cum appendice, De veterum harmonica ad hodiernam comparata. — Porphyrii in Harmonica Ptolemæi commentarius. — Manuelis Bryennii harmonica. — Archimedis Syracusani arenarius. — Archimedis dimensio circuli. — Eutocii Ascalonitæ in Archimedis dimensionem circuli commentarius. — Aristarchi Samii de magnitudinibus et distantiis solis et lunæ. — Pappi Alexandrini libri secundi collectionum mathematicarum hactenus desiderati fragmentum. — Epistolarum quarundam collectio rem mathematicam spectantium.
— Opera quædam miscellanea. Oxon., 1699. f°.
Contents. De loquela, seu sonorum loquelarium formatione. — Grammatica linguæ Anglicanæ. — Praxis grammatica; institutio logicæ. — Tres theses congeneris naturæ. — Mens sobria serio commendata; in concione Latine habita in Tit. II. 6. ad baccalaureos determinantes; acc. Epistolæ ad Titum expositio et thesis theologica. — De fœdere evangelico concio Latine habita in Gal. iii. 17. — Resurrectio mortuorum comprobata concione in 1 Cor. xv. 20. — De Melchizedeco tractatus. — De Psalmorum titulis tractatus. — De trinitate, conciones tres in Job xvii. 3. — Defensio sabbati Christiani die dominico celebrati. — De pædo-baptismo dissertatio.
— NICERON, J. P. (*In his* Mém., v. 43. 1745.)
— RULE for finding Easter explained; wherein is shew'd that Dr. Wallis's exceptions are mistaken and groundless. London, 1709. 8°. (C 232)

Wallis, Samuel. Account of a voyage round the world, 1766–68. (*In* **Hawkesworth**, J. Account of voyages, v. 1. 1773; — *in* **Kerr**, R. Col. of voy., v. 12. 1824; — *in* **Henry**, D. Hist. account of voy., v. 3. 1773; — *and in* **Moore**, J. H. New col. of voy., v. 1.)
— *French.* Voyage autour du monde. (*In* **Montémont**, A. Biblioth. univ., v. 3. 1833.)

Wallis, Severn Teackle. Address before the Reading Room Society of St. Mary's College, Baltimore, July 20. Balt., 1841. 8°. (B 1579)
— Glimpses of Spain. N. Y., 1849. 12°.
— Lecture on the present political condition of Spain, before the Maryland Institute, Mar. 12. Balt., 1852. 8°. (B 1586)
— Spain; her institutions, politics, and public men. Boston, 1853. 12°.

Wallis Island. OLIVER, S. Wreck of the Glide; with recollections of the Fijiis, and of W. Island. N. Y., London, 1848. 12°.

Wallon, Henri Alexandre. Histoire de l'esclavage dans l'antiquité. Paris, 1847. 3 v. 8°.
Contents. Vol. 1. De l'esclavage en Orient et en Grèce. 2. De l'esclavage à Rome depuis les origines jusqu'à l'époque des Antonins. 3. De l'esclavage et du travail libre sous l'empire.
— Une inscription rel. à des esclaves fugitifs trouvée dans l'Acropole d'Athènes. (*In* **Paris. Inst.** *Ac. d. Inscr.* Mém., v. 19, 2e pt. 1853.) — La détermination des événements au Moyen Age par le jour de l'entrée du soleil dans les signes du zodiaque. (*In* v. 24, 2e pt.) — Les années de Jésus Christ. (*In* v. 23, 2e pt. 1868.)
— Jeanne D'Arc. 2e éd. Paris, 1867. 2 v. 8°.

Walloons, The; a comedy; by **R. Cumberland.** (*In his* Post. works, v. 1. 1813.)

Walmesley, Bartholomew. TRIAL. (*In* **Account** of the tryalls at Manchester, 1694. 1864. Chetham Soc., v. 61.)

Walmesley, Charles, *Bp. of Rama.* General history of the Christian Church; deduced from the Apocalypse. 4th ed.; by Pastorini [pseud.]. N. Y., 1807. 12°.
— *Same.* 5th Amer. ed. N. Y., 1851. 12°.
Walmsley, Hugh Mulleneux. Ruined cities of Zulu Land. London, 1869. 2 v. 8°.
Walmysley, Thomas. Expenses of the judges of assize riding the western and Oxford circuits, 1596-1601; ed. by W. D. Cooper. 1858. (*In* **Camden** miscel., v. 4. 1859. Camden Soc., v. 73.)
Waln, Robert, *Jr.* The hermit in America on a visit to Philadelphia. 2d ed., by P. Atall. Phila., 1819. 12°.
Walpole, *Lieut.* Frederick. The Ansyarii and the Assassins; with travels in the further east, in 1850-51, incl. a visit to Nineveh. Lond., 1851. 3 v. 8°.
Walpole, Horace, *4th Earl of Orford.* Ædes Walpolianæ; or, Description of pictures at Houghton Hall. 3d ed. London, 1767. 4°.
— Anecdotes of painting in Eng.; with account of the artists and notes on other arts; col. by G. Vertue and digested by H. Walpole. (Vol. 1-3, 3d ed., 4, 2d ed.) London, 1782. 5 v. 12°.
Note. The title-page of v. 5 reads 'Catalogue of engravers [of] Eng.; added, Life and Works of [Vertue]'.
Contents. Vol. 1. Painting, to Henry VIII. 2. Painters and other artists, James I. to the Interregnum. 3. Charles II. to Anne. 4. George I. and II. 5. Catalogue of engravers. — Life and works of G. Vertue.
— *Same.* With add. by J. Dallaway. London, 1828. 5 v. 8°.
— Castle of Otranto. London, 1796. 12°.
— Catalogue of engravers. *See, above,* Anecdotes of painting. *Note.*
— Catalogue of the royal and noble authors of England, Scotland, and Ireland; enl. and contin. by T. Park. Lond., 1806. 5 v. 8°.
Contents. Vol. 1. Royal authors of England, died, 1199-1399. — Noble auth. of Eng., 1361-1557. 2. 1557-1644. 3. 1645-1700. 4. 1701-1805. 5. Royal auth. of Scotland, 1437-1587. — Noble auth. of Scotland, 1566-1794, — of Ireland, 1397-1806. — Sir R. Dudley.
— Correspondence of W. and W. Mason; ed. by J. Mitford. London, 1851. 2 v. 8°.
Contents. Vol. 1. 1763-78. 2. 1778-97.
— Correspondence of W. with G. Montagu and others. London, 1837. 3 v. 8°.
Contents. Vol. 1. 1735-59. 2. 1760-69. 3. 1770-97.
— Counter address to the public on the late dismission of a general officer. (*In* **Collection** of scarce tracts, v. 1. 1787. **B 604**)
— Historic doubts on the life and reign of Richard III. London, 1768. 4°.
— Journal of the reign of George III.; ed. with notes by Dr. Doran. London, 1859. 2 v. 8°.
Contents. Vol. 1. 1772-75. 2. 1776-83.
— Letters to the Countess of Ossory, 1769-97; ed. by R. V. Smith. London, 1848. 2 v. 8°.
Contents. Vol. 1. 1769-80. 2. 1780-97.
— Letters; ed. by P. Cunningham. London, 1857-59. 9 v. 8°.
Contents. Vol. 1. 1735-46. 2. 1746-56. 3. 1756-62. 4. 1762-66. 5. 1766-73. 6. 1773-77. 7. 1777-81. 8. 1781-85. 9. 1785-97.
— Letters to Sir H. Mann; ed. by Lord Dover. London, 1833. 3 v. 8°.
Contents. Vol. 1. 1741-44. 2. 1744-50. 3. 1751-60.
— Letters to Sir H. Mann; [concluding series]. London, 1843. 2 v. 8°.
Contents. Vol. 1. 1760-68. 2. 1768-76.
— Memoires of the last ten years of the reign of George II.; [ed. by H. R. V. Fox, Baron Holland]. London, 1822. 2 v. 4°.
Contents. Vol. 1. 1751-55. 2. 1756-60.

— Memoirs of the reign of George III.; ed. with notes by Sir D. Le Marchant. London, 1845. 4 v. 8°.
Contents. Vol. 1. 1760-64. 2. 1764-67. 3. 1767-69. 4. 1769-71.
— Observations on modern gardening; added, Essay on the different natural situations of gardens. New ed. London, 1801. 4°.
— Reminiscences. London, 1818. 12°.
— Reminiscences and Walpoliana. Boston, 1820. 24°. (British prose writers, v. 1.)
— Baillon, *comte* de. Lord Walpole à la cour de France, 1723-30. Paris, 1867. 18°.
— Catalogue of books and tracts printed at the private press at Strawberry Hill, with those of his works printed by Bodoni, *etc.* London, 1813. 8°.
— Chasles, P. Les deux Walpole. (*In* **Revue** d. D. Mondes, av. 1845.)
— D'Israeli, I. (*In his* Calamities of authors, v. 1. 1812.)
— Gibbon, E. Remarques touchant les 'Doutes historiques'. (*In his* Miscel. works, v. 3. 1815.)
— Rémusat, C. de. (*In* **Revue** d. D. Mondes, juil. 1852.)
— Robbins, G. Catalogue of the classic contents of Strawberry Hill. London, 1842. 4°.
— Scott, *Sir* W. (*In his* Lives of the novelists, v. 2. 1826; — *and his* Prose works, v. 3. 1834.)
— Thomson, *Mrs.* K. B. (*In her* Wits and beaux. 1861.)
— Warburton, E. Memoir of H. Walpole and his contemporaries. Lond., 1852. 2 v. 8°.
Walpole, *Capt.* John. Description of a bridge over Kat River. (*In* **Gr. Brit.** *Corps of Roy. Engin.* Papers, v. 7. 1845.)
Walpole, *Sir* Robert, *1st Earl of Orford.* Secret history of one year. (*In* **Somers, J.** Col. of tracts, v. 13. 1815.)
— Speech. (*In* **Chapman,** N. Select speeches, v. 1. 1808.)
— Brougham, H., *Ld.* (*In his* Statesmen of the times of George III., v. 3. 1843.)
— Case of W. (*In* **Wilkes,** J. Reflections, *etc.* 1768. B 591)
— Chasles, P. Les deux Walpole. (*In* **Revue** d. D. Mondes, av. 1845.)
— Conduct of the late administration with regard to foreign affairs, 1722 to 1742, wherein that of Earl of Orford is vindicated. London, 1742. 8°. (B 759)
— Coxe, W. Memoirs of the life and administration of W. New ed. London, 1800. 3 v. 8°.
— Critical history of the administration of W.; by a gentleman of the Middle Temple. London, 1743. 8°.
— Forman, C. Protesilaus; or, The character of an evil minister. London, 1730. 8°. (B 746)
— Gr. Brit. *Ho. of Commons.* Report of the committee of secrecy on the conduct of the Earl of Orford during the last ten years of his being First Commissioner of the Treasury, *etc.* London, 1742. 8°.
— - Further report. *n.t.p.* [London, 1742.] 8°.
— - *Another copy.* (B 757)
— Oliphant, *Mrs.* M. O. W. The minister. (*In her* Hist. sketches, v. 1. 1869.)
— Ripley, T. Plans, elevations, *etc.*, of Houghton Hall, built by Sir R. Walpole; with a description of the house and pictures. London, 1760. f°.
— Rogers, J. E. T. (*In his* Hist. gleanings. 1869.)
— Walpole, H., *4th Earl of Orford.* Ædes Walpolianæ; description of pictures at Houghton Hall. 3d ed. London, 1767. 4°.
Walpole, *Rev.* Robert. Essay on the misrepresentations, ignorance, *etc.*, of certain infidel writers. *n.p.*, 1812. 8°. (B 690)
— Memoirs rel. to Turkey. London, 1817. 4°.
Contents. **Walpole,** R. Causes of the weakness and decline of the Turkish monarchy. — **Morritt,** J. B. S. Journey through Maiana in the Morea. — **Sibthorp,** J. Remarks illust. the preceding; — Parnassus, *etc.*; —

Obs. on nat. hist. rel. to Greece and Cyprus. — **Hunt,** P. Asia Minor. — **Sibthorp,** J. Attica. — **Carlyle,** J. D. Letters during his residence in Turkey. — **Hunt,** P. Mount Athos. — **Walpole,** R. Sepulchres of the Greeks; — Notice resp. Sibthorp's Journals. — **Sibthorp,** J. Medicinal and economical uses of the plants of Greece. — **Hume,** J. R. Plants collected in Cyprus. — **Sibthorp,** J. Birds, *etc.*, of Greece and Cyprus. — **Walpole,** R. Modes of fishing practised by modern Greeks. — **Sibthorp,** J. Extracts from [his] Journals; — The olives and vines of Zante, *etc.* — **Hawkins,** J. Produce of wheat in Greece. — **Raikes,** —. Bœotia and Phocis. — **Walpole,** R. The Bœotian Catabothra and Copaic Lake. — **Squire,** J. Military architecture of the ancient Greeks. — **Lusieri,** S. Excavations in the tombs of Attica. — **Squire,** J. The plain of Marathon; — The continent of Greece; — The Isthmus of Corinth. — **Davison,** N. The antiquities of Egypt. — **Walpole,** R. The catacombs of Alexandria. — **Hume,** J. R. Manners and customs of modern Egypt. — **Light,** H. Voyage up the Nile. — **Walpole,** R., *and* **Gordon,** G. H., *Earl of Aberdeen.* The mines of Laurium; — Coinage of the Athenians; — Revenue of Attica. — **Gordon,** G. H., *Earl of Aberdeen.* The Amyclæan marbles. — **Walpole,** R. On some Greek inscr. — **Hawkins,** J. The topography of Athens; — The Vale of Tempe; — The Syrinx of Strabo and the bridge over the Euripus. — **Walpole,** R. Antiquities of Athens. — **Haygarth,** W. Panoramic view of Athens. — **Walpole,** R. The thesauri of the Greeks; — The Demetrian system of the Troad. — **Morritt,** J. B. S. The Troad. — **Wilkins,** W. The architectural inscription from Athens now in the Brit. Museum.

Walpole, Spencer Horatio. RITCHIE, J. E. (*In his* Brit. senators. 1869.)

Walpole, *N. H.* ATTACK of the Indians at W., 1755. (*In* **New Hamp. Hist. Soc.** Col., v. 2. 1827.) — FESSENDEN, T. Letter rel. to Walpole, 1790. (*In* v. 4. 1834.)

— BELLOWS, A. Sketch of Walpole. (*In* **Mass. Hist. Soc.** Col., v. 17. 1818.)

Walpole Grant on the Ohio. Papers rel. to the grant. *n.p.*, [1771?]. 4°.

Walpole; or, Every man has his price; comedy in rhyme, by Lord Lytton. Edin., London, 1869. 4°.

— *Same.* (No. 91 *of* **De Witt's** acting plays.)

Walras, Léon. La bourse et le crédit. (*In* **Paris** guide, v. 2. 1867.)

Walraven, Diederik Adriaan. Oratio de hermeneutica sacra cum linguarum atque antiquitatum Orientalium studiis necessario copulanda. Amst., 1786. 4°. (B 1399)

Walsh, Edward. Expedition to Holland in 1799; map of North Holland and views. London, 1800. 4°.

Walsh, J. T. Aspects of phrenology on revelation. Richmond, 1846. 8°. (B 1665)

Walsh, *Sir* John. Poor laws in Ireland. London, 1830. 8°. (B 934)

Walsh, John Henry (*pseud.* **Stonehenge**). The horse in the stable and the field. New ed. London, 1871. 8°.

— Manual of British rural sports. London, 1856. 16°.

— Shot-gun and sporting rifle. London, 1859. 8°.

Walsh, Joseph Alexis, *vicomte.* Lettres vendéennes, ou Correspondance de trois amis en 1823. 4e éd. Paris, 1829. 2 v. 12°.

Walsh, Michael. New system of mercantile arithmetic. 4th ed. Newburyport, 1816. 12°.

— *Same.* With book-keeping. Salem, 1824. 12°.

Walsh, Peter. Mémoire pour W., consul américain à Cette. [Montpelier, 1808.] 4°. (A 7)

Walsh, Robert, *b.* 1784, *d.* 1859. Appeal from judgments of Gr. Britain resp. the U. S. Pt. 1. Phila., 1819. 8°.

— Corresp. with R. G. Harper respecting Russia; also speech of Harper, and an essay on the future state of Europe, by Correa de Serra. Phila., 1813. 8°.

— *Another copy.* (B 453)

— Didactics, social, literary, and political. Phila., 1836. 2 v. 12°.

Contents. Vol. 1. Happiness. — Female training. — Wedded love. — Friendship. — Winter. — Education. — Unthrift. — Commerce. — Social sympathies. — Imprisonment for debt. — The stage. — Underselling. — Social oppression. — Moral courage. — Female example. — Oratory. — Death and the dead. — Lord Byron and morality. — Tragic acting. — Revision and correction. — Public opinion. — Invention and execution. — Republican Italy. — Breach of promise of marriage. — Judges and juries. — Right and might. — General miscellany. — Sentences. — Lessons by quotation. 2. Manners. — Aristocracy. — The poor. — Operatives. — Religion and toleration. — Phrenology. — Breach of confidence. — Slander. — Force of imagination. — Force of fatal illusion. — The veto. — Disrespect. — Passion and selfishness. — The Fourth of July. — Treatment of the sex. — Female intellect. — Female sovereigns. — Tenure of office. — Original polity. — Wm. Pinkney. — Collegiate education. — Oxford. — Sensibility awry. — Duelling. — Gambling. — The naval service. — Shipwreck. — W. Irving. — Grattan and Curran. — Dr. Allison of Edinburgh. — Dr. Parr and scholarship. — Canning. — Dugald Stuart. — Washington. — Franklin.

— Letter on the genius and dispositions of French government. Phila., 1810. 8°.

— *Another copy.* (B 414)

— *Same.* Balt., 1810. 8°.

— *Same.* 2d ed. Boston, 1810. 8°.

— Letter with reference to Jomard and Dupin. (*In* **Mass. Hist. Soc.**, Proc., 1858-60.)

— HARE, R. Brief view of the policy, *etc.*, of the U. S.; with strictures on [W.'s] letter. Phila., 1810. 8°.

— - *Another copy.* (B 414)

Walsh, *Rev.* Robert, *LL.D.* Essay on ancient coins, medals, *etc.*, as illustrating the progress of Christianity. 2d ed., enl. Lond., 1828. 12°.

— Effects of intoxication; sermon. Dublin, 1803. 8°. (B 1346)

— History of Dublin. 1818. *See* **Warburton,** J.

— Narrative of a journey from Constantinople to England. 2d ed. London, 1828. 12°.

— *French, extracts.* (*In* **Montémont,** A. Bibl. univ., v. 44. 1836.)

— Notices of Brazil in 1828–29. London, 1830. 2 v. 8°.

— *French, extracts.* (*In* **Montémont,** A. Biblioth. univ., v. 42. 1836.)

— Observations which accompanied a Hebrew medal submitted to the inspection of the Roy. Irish Acad. (*In* **Roy. Irish Acad.** Trans., v. 14. 1818.)

Walsh, Robert M., *tr.* Sketches of conspicuous living characters of France. *See* **Lomérie,** L. de.

Walsh, Wm. Letters to and from W. (*In* **Pope,** A. Works, v. 7. 1806.)

— Poems. (*In* **Anderson,** R. Brit. poets, v. 6. 1795; — *in* **Campbell,** T. Brit. poets, v. 4. 1819; — *and in* **Chalmers,** A. Eng. poets, v. 8. 1810.)

— JOHNSON, S. (*In his* Lives of the Eng. poets. 1779; — *and in his* Works, v. 9. 1806.)

Walshe, Walter Hayle, *M.D.* Anatomy, physiology, and treatment of cancer; with add. by J. M. Warren. Boston, 1844. 12°.

— Nature and treatment of cancer. London, 1846. 12°.

— Practical treatise on the diseases of lungs, heart, and aorta. 2d ed. enl. London, 1854. 12°.

Walsingham, Edward. Maximes politiques; [tr. de l'Arcana aulica de E. Walsingham]. *See* **Walsingham,** *Sir* F. (DIGGES). *Note.*

Walsingham, *Sir* Francis. Journal, Dec. 1570 to Apr. 1583; ed. by C. T. Martin. (*In* **Camden** misc., v. 6. 1870. Camden Soc., v. 104.)

— DIGGES, *Sir* D. Mémoires et instructions pour les ambassadeurs [de la reine Elisabeth]; tr. [par L. Boulesteis de la Contie]. Amst., 1700. 4°.

Note. The first part of this work is a translation of Sir Dudley Digges' 'Compleat ambassador', containing numerous letters of and to Walsingham; the middle is a trans. of Edward Walsingham's 'Arcana aulica'; the end is a collection of 'Remarques sur la vie des ministres et des favoris de la reine Elisabeth'.

Walsingham, Thomas. Chronica Monasterii S. Albani; ed. H. T. Riley. London, 1867–69. 3 v. 8°. (Chron. and mem.)
Contents. Vol. 1. 793–1290. 2. 1290–1349. 3. 1349–1411.
— Chronica Monasterii S. Albani; Historia Anglicana, 1272–1422; ed. by H. T. Riley. London, 1863-64. 2 v. 8°. (Chron. and mem.)
Contents. Vol. 1. 1272–1381. 2. 1381–1422.
— Voyage of Henry IV. of England, 1390, into Prussia and Letto against the infidels. (*In* **Hakluyt**, R. Col. of voy., v. 1. 1809.)

Walt and Vult; or, The twins, [by] Jean Paul [Friedrich Richter]; tr. by E. B. Lee. Boston, 1846. 2 v. 8°.

Walter *de Hemingburg.* Chronicon. *See* **Galtherus** *de Hemingburg.*

Walter, Arthur Maynard. Journal, kept chiefly in Paris, July 3 – Sept. 4, [1804?]. MS.
— QUINCY, J. Biog. notice. (*In his* Hist. of the Boston Athenæum. 1851.)

Walter, Emile. What is free trade? adaptation of Bastiat's 'Sophismes économiques' for the Amer. reader. N. Y., 1867. 12°.

Walter, Ferdinand. Geschichte des römischen Rechts bis auf Justinian. 3e Aufl. Bonn, 1860-61. 2 v. 8°.

Walter, Hubert, *Bp. of Salisbury.* Voyage unto Syria, 1190. (*In* **Hakluyt**, R. Col. of voy., v. 2. 1810.)

Walter, Johann Gottlieb. Plates of thoracic and abdominal nerves. London, 1804. 4°.

Walter, John, *Funeral sermon on.* 1847. *See* **Willmott**, R. A. (B 1227)

Walter, *Rev.* Nathaniel. Character of a Christian hero; sermon, artillery election, June 2. Boston, 1746. 8°. (B 145, 334, 840)
— Character of a true patriot; sermon, Boston, Aug. 1. Boston, 1745. 8°. (B 26, 235)
— An heavenly and godlike zeal, *etc.*; discourse, Boston, Dec. 1741. Boston, 1742. 12°. (C 3)
— Thoughts of the heart evidence of spiritual state. Boston, 1741. 8°. (B 242, C 11)

Walter, *Rev.* Nehemiah. The body of death anatomyzed; essay concerning the sorrows of the regenerate. Boston, 1707. 12°. (C 3)
— Discourses; with life [by T. Prince and T. Foxcroft]. Boston, 1755. 8°.
— Faithfulness in the ministry; sermon at Convention, Boston, May 30. Boston, 1723. 8°. (C 11, 39, 42, 48)
— Plain discourse on vain thoughts. Boston, 1721. 18°.
— Sermons on the wonderfulness of Christ. Boston, 1713. 12°.

Walter, Richard. Voyage round the world in 1740–44, by G. Anson; compiled from his papers. 5th ed. London, 1749. 4°.
— *Same.* 6th ed. London, 1749. 8°.

Walter, Thomas. Essay upon that paradox infallibility may sometimes mistake; reply to [J. Checkley's] 'Disc. conc. episcopacy'; remarks on Checkley's 'Disc. showing who is a true pastor'; also remarks on Ignatius' Epistle to the Trallians. Boston, 1724. 8°. (C 41)
— Scriptures the only rule of faith; sermon at lecture, Sept. 5. Boston, 1723. 8°. (C 11)
— The sweet psalmist of Israel; sermon. Boston, 1722. 8°. (C 11)
— MATHER, C. A good reward of a good servant; with commemoration of T. Walter. Boston, 1725. 8°. (C 9, 50)

Walter, Wm., *D.D.* Discourse before the Humane Soc. of Mass., June 12. Boston, 1798. 4°. (B 770, 1898, 1923)

Walter, Wm. Bicker. Poems. Boston, 1821. 8°.
— Sukey; a poem. Boston, 1821. 8°.
— *Another copy.* (B 941)

Walters, *Rev.* John. Dissertation on the Welsh language. (*In* **Evans**, T. Engl. and Welsh vocab. 1816.)

Walterus *Tervanensis.* Vita Karoli comitis Flandriæ. (*In* **Pertz**, G. H. Mon. Germ., Scr., v. 12. 1856.)

Waltham, *Eng.* De inventione Sanctæ Crucis Walthamensis. (*In* **Michel**, F. Chron. anglo-normandes, v. 2. 1836.)

Waltham, *Mass.* RIPLEY, S. Topog. and hist. descr. of W. (*In* **Mass. Hist. Soc.** Col., v. 13. 1815.)
— BROOKS, C. The tornado of 1851 in Medford, Waltham, *etc.* Boston, 1852. 24°.
— BOND, H. Genealogies of families of Waltham. (*In his* Genealogies of families of Watertown. 1855.)

Waltham, *Mass.* **Trinitarian Cong. Church.** Letter to the Church; by a layman. Boston, 1827. 12°. (C 223)

Waltham Abbey, *Essex.* FULLER, T. History of Waltham Abbey in Essex, founded by King Harold. London, 1655. f°.

Waltharius; poema. (*In* **Sardinia.** Mon. hist. pat., Scr., v. 5. 1848.)

Waltheof, *St.*, *d.* 1076. VITA et passio Waldevi comitis. — DE Juditha uxore Waldevi comitis. — MIRACULA Sancti Waldevi. (*In* **Michel**, F. Chron. anglo-normandes, v. 2. 1836.)

Waltheof *or* **Walthen**, *St.*, *abb. of Melrose*, *d.* 1160. JORDANUS *Furnesiensis.* (*In* **Acta** sanct., v. 35. 1867.)
— LIFE. (*In* **Lives** of Eng. saints, v. 14. 1845.)

Walther *von der Vogelweide.* Lpz., 1866. 8°. (Pfeiffer. Deutsche Classiker, v. 1.)
— UHLAND, L. Stuttg. und Tüb., 1822. 8°.

Walther, Chr. Fr. Les elzevirs de la Bibliothèque Impériale de St. Pétersbourg; catalogue bibliog. et raisonné. St. Pétersb., 1864. 12°.

Walther, Gregorius. Regulæ vitæ Christianæ. Vitebergæ, 1572. 16°.

Walther, Samuel. Singularia Magdeburgica oder Merckwürdigkeiten aus der magdeburgischen Historie. Magd., Lpz., 1733–40. 12 pts. 4°.
Note. Parts 1 to 5 have each its own pagination; 6 to 12 have a continuous pagination.
Contents. Vol. 1. 15en–18en sec. 2. Die Haupt. Autores von der magd. Hist. gehandelt. — Land-Charten von Magdeburg. — Project zu einer generalen Historie vom Hertzogthum. — Die alten und neuen Gräntzen des Hertzogthums Magdeburg. — Die Gräntz-Streitigkeiten mit den Ertz-Bischöffen und Marggraffen wie auch Churfürsten von Brandenburg vorgefallen. 3. Von den alten Gräntzen zwischen dem magdeburgischen und halberstädtschen Ertz- und Bischoffthum. — Unionen, Verträgen, Acquisitis, *etc.* 4. Von den übeln Suiten des Interregni, vornehmlich in den magdeburgishen und halberstädtschen Gräntzen, sec. 13en–15en. 5. Von dem Amte Weferlingen. — Vom Flecken Weferlingen. — Von dem geistlichen und Kirchen-Zustand im Pabstthum, *etc.* — Von denen von Spiegel. — Von den Landgrafen von Hessen-Homburg. — Von der brandenburg-culmbachischen Linie. 6. Von der Stadt Oebsfeld. — Von dem geistlichen Zustand im Oebsfeldishen vor der Reformation. — Vor der Reformation und der Geistlichkeit. — Von den Amts-Dörffern. — Von einigen Huldigungs-Actibus. 7. Von der Ohra. — Vom Drömling. — Von den Streitigkeitenwegen des Drömlings, *etc.* — Von den angräntzenden Herrschaften. 8. Vom Halbgericht, *etc.* — Von dem Grantz-Streit zwischen den Herren von Alvensleben und Calförde. — Von dem Streit wegen der Feldmarck Pachwitz zwischen den Herren von Schenck und Calförde. — Von des Halbgerichts ältesten Besitzern. — Von den Gräntz-Streitigkeiten in und wegen des Halbgerichts. — Von denen wider diesen Streit gemachten Anstalten, *etc.*, und endliche Aufhebung a. 1707. — Von der Pfarre im Halbgerichte, Uhtmöden, und Zöbbenitz. 9. Vom angelegten Stadt-Regiment. — Von der Introduction Hertzogs Augusti. — Von den magdeburgischen Müntzen. — Merckwürdigkeiten von 1538 und 1738. 10. Von des Closters Alten-Haldensleben. — Verzeichniss der dem Closter geschenckten Stifftungen. — Von den Streitigkeiten mit den Nachbarn. — Von den Visitationen daran dieses Closter Theil gehabt. — Von den Dörffern Alten-Haldensleben, Wedringen, und Wahldorf. 11. Von der Grafschaft Osterburg. — Von den Predigern zu Altenhausen und Ivenrode, *etc.* — Genealogische Nachrichten von denen von Klencke, von Ertz-Bischofs Ernesti Zeiten an. 12. Von dem Closter Hillersleben.

Walther, Margraf. (*In* **Simrock**, K. Deutschen Volksbücher, v. 6. 1847.)

Walther und Hildegunde. (*In* **Simrock**, C. Heldenbuch, v. 3. 1857.)

Walton, Bryan, *Bp. of Chester.* Biblia Sacra polyglotta. *See* **Bible** (p. 268).
— The considerator considered; or, A brief view of certain considerations upon the Biblia polyglotta. (*In* **Todd**, H. J. Memoirs of B. Walton, v. 2. 1821.)
— TODD, H. J. Memoirs of W. Lond., 1821. 2 v. 8°.

Walton, Elijah. The coast of Norway, from Christiania to Hammerfest; text by T. G. Bonney. London, 1871. obl. f°.

Walton, George, *b.* 1740, *d.* 1804. SANDERSON, J. (*In his* Biog. of the signers to the Declaration of Independence, v. 4. 1823.)

Walton, George. *See* **Allen**, J., *alias* **Walton**, G.

Walton, George Augustus. First steps in numbers. 1849. *See* **Colburn**, D. P.

Walton, Izaak. Acc. of the life and death of R. Hooker. (*In* **Hooker**, R. Works. 1676.)
Note. See also, below, 'Lives'.

— The angler's wish. (*In* **Campbell**, T. Brit. poets, v. 4. 1819.)

— Life of G. Herbert. (*In* **Herbert**, G. Poems. 1809.)
Note. See also, below, 'Lives'.

— Life of J. Donne; with original notes by an antiquary. London, *n.d.* 12°.
Note. See also, below, 'Lives'.

— Life of R. Sanderson. (*In* **Sanderson**, R. Sermons. 1681.)
See also next entry.

— Lives of J. Donne, Sir H. Wotton, R. Hooker, G. Herbert, and R. Sanderson; ed. with notes and life of the author by T. Zouch. York, 1796. 4°.

— *Same.* Boston, 1832. 2 v. 12°. (Young, A. Libr. of old Eng. prose writers, v. 5, 6.)

— *Same.* (*In* **Wordsworth**, C. Eccles. biog., v. 3, 4. 1839.)

— Love and truth; two letters conc. the distempers of the present times; [signed R. W.]. London, 1680. 4°. (**B 12**)

— *and* **Cotton**, C. Compleat angler; with notes by M. Browne. London, 1750. 12°.

— *Same.* With lives and notes by J. Hawkins, *etc.* 8th ed. London, 1815. 8°.

— *Same.* Ed. by E. Jesse. London, *Bohn*, 1856. 8°.

Walton, *Rev.* Joseph. Series of letters between J. Buckminster, J. Walton, and H. Ballou. Windsor, 1811. 24°.

Walton, Thomas, *alias* Purser. To his countrymen. (*In* **Collier**, J. P. Illust. of early Eng. lit., v. 2. 1864.)

Walton, Wm., *b.* 1784, *d.* 1857. Exposé on the dissentions of Spanish America. London, 1814. 8°.

— Letter on the affairs of Portugal and Spain. 2d ed. (*In* **Pamphleteer**, 1827; v. 28 of **B 838**)

— Letter to Sir J. Mackintosh on his motion resp. the affairs of Portugal, June. Lond., 1829. 8°.

— Revolutions of Spain, 1808–36; with biog. sketches, *etc.* London, 1837. 2 v. 8°.

Walton, Wm., *of Trinity Coll., Camb.* Collection of problems in illustration of principles of hydrostatics and hydrodynamics. Camb., 1847. 8°.

Walton's register and farmer's almanac. *See* **Vermont** register and almanac.

Waltz. ORSAY, A. G. G. d'. Theory of the Rhenish or Spanish waltz and of the German waltz à deux temps. (*In his* Etiquette. 1843.)

Walworth, Maria Ketchum, *Funeral sermon on.* 1847. *See* **Chester**, A. T. (**B 1651**)

Walworth, Reuben Hyde. Hyde genealogy; or, Descendants from W. Hyde of Norwich. Albany, 1864. 2 v. 8°.

Walz, E. L. Worte am Sarge des verewigten J. E. Noltenius. N. Y., 1844. 8°. (**B 1304**)

Wamba, *King of the Visigoths in Spain.* JULIAN, *Bp. of Toledo.* Historia de expeditione Wambæ adversus Galliam. (*In* **Bouquet**, M. Recueil des hist. des Gaules, *etc.*, v. 2. 1869; — *and in* **Florez**, H. España sagrada, v. 6. 1751.)

Wandalin, Johannes. De feria passionis et triduo mortis Jesu Christi. (*In* **Grævius**, J. G. Syntagma. 1702.)

Wander, Karl Friedrich Wilhelm. Deutsches Sprichwörter Lexikon. Lpz., 1867–73. 3 v. 8°.

Wanderer, The; a colloquial poem. *See* **Channing**, W. E.

Wandering boys, The; a melo-drama. Boston, 1821. 12°. (**D 15**)

— *Same.* (*In* **Sargent**, E. Mod. stand. dr., v. 23.)

Wandering Jew; by E. Sue. N. Y., 1845. 8°.

Wandering Jew. LEGEND of the Wandering Jew illustrated by G. Doré; poem with prologue and epilogue by P. Dupont, *etc.* London, 1857. f°.

— GRAESSE, J. G. T. Der Tannhäuser und Ewige Jude; zwei deutsche Sagen erklärt. 2e Aufl. Dresden, 1861. 8°.

Wandering philanthropist; or, Letters from a Chinese during residence in U. S.; ed. by G. Fowler. Phila., 1810. 12°.

Wanderings and fortunes of some German emigrants; by F. Gerstaecker; tr. by D. Black. N. Y., 1848. 12°.

Wanderings of a journeyman tailor, 1824–40; by P. D. Holthaus; tr. from 3d German ed. by W. Howitt. N. Y., [18—]. 8°.

— *Another copy.* (**B 1171**)

Wanderings of Persiles and Sigismunda, by M. de Cervantes Saavedra; [tr. by L. D. Stanley]. London, 1854. 16°.

Wandregisilus, *St., abb. Fontanellensis.* VITA S. Wandregisili. (*In* **Acta** sanct., v. 32. 1868.)

Wandsbecker Bothe. *See* **Claudius**, M. Werke.

Wang-Kwei-shing. Revenue of China. (*In* **Hwa-tseen.** Chinese courtship. 1824.)

Wangen, Friedrich von. Urkundenbuch des Hochstiftes Trient. (*In* **Vienna. Ak. d. Wiss.** Fontes rer. Abth. II., v. 5. 1852.)

Waningen, Hendrick. Thresoor van't Italiaens boeck-houden; gecor. door J. Buingha. Rotterdam, 1652. f°.

Wanley, Humphrey. Librorum vett. Septent. qui in Angliæ bibliothecis extant, nec non vett. codd. Septent. catalogus. (*In* **Hickes**, G. Ling. vett. Sept., v. 2. 1705.)

Wanley, Nathaniel. Wonders of the little world; a general history of man. London, 1788. 4°.

Wännman, Karl H. Flora Capensis. (*In* **Linné**, C. Amœn. acad., v. 5. 1760.)

Wanostrocht, N. Grammar of the French language. 5th ed. London, 1795. 12°.

— *Same.* With additions. 8th Amer. ed.; also, treatise on French versification, by N. F. de Wailly. Boston, 1825. 12°.

— *Same.* With add. by N. F. de Wailly. Boston, 1834. 12°.

Wansey, Henry. Journal of an excursion to the U. S. in the summer of 1794. Salisbury, 1796. 8°.

— *Same.* Excursion to the U. S. 2d ed., with add. Salisbury, 1798. 12°.

— Wool encouraged without exportation; or, Practical observations on wool and the woollen manufacture. London, 1791. 8°. (**W 41**)

Wansleben, Johann Michael. NICERON, J. P. (*In his* Mém., v. 26. 1734.)

Wante, —. Mémoires sur la Louisiane et la Nouvelle Orléans; terminés par un écrit traitant cette question, est il avantageux à la France de prendre possession de la Louisiane. Paris, 1804. 8°.

Wanted, a young lady; by W. E. Suter. (No. 118 *of* **De Witt's** acting plays.)

Wanton, Enrique, *pseud.* Viages de W. al pais de las monas. *See* **Seriman**, Z.

Wappæus, Johann Eduard. Handbuch der Geographie und Statistik für die gebildeten Stande; begründet durch T. G. D. Stein und F. Hörschelmann; neu bearbeitet unter Mitwirkung mehrerer Gelehrten. 7e Aufl. Lpz., 1855–71. 4 v. in 11 pts. 8°.
Contents. Vol. 1, pt. 1. **Wappæus**, J. E. Allgemeiner Theil. — 1, 2. **Wappæus**, J. E. Allgemeine Uebersicht von Amerika. — Nord Amerika. 1, 3.

Wappæus, J. E. Das ehemalige spanische Mittel und Süd Amerika nebst den europaïschen Besitzungen. 1, 4. **Wappæus, J. E.,** *and* **Delitsch, D.** Brasilien, West-indien, und die Südpolar-Länder. 2, 2. **Gumprecht, L. C.,** *and others.* Afrika und Australien. 2, 3. **Brauer, J. H.,** *and* **Plath, J. H.** Asien. 3, 1. **Wappæus, J. E.,** *and others.* Ost- und Nord-Europa. 3, 2. **Willkom, M.,** *and others.* West- und Süd-Europa. 4, 1. **Brachelli, H. F.** Der deutsche Bund im Allgemeinen; — Kaiserthum Oesterreich. 4, 2. **Brachelli, H. F.** Das Königreich Preussen und die deutschen Mittel- und Klein-Staaten.

Wappetaw Church. CASE. *n.p.*, [18—]. 8°. (B 1439)

Wappinger Indians. GEOGRAPHIC and historical narrative of the controversy between the Wappinger tribe and the claimants [of] Philipse's Upper Patent. Hartford, 1768. 8°. (B 665)

War. *See* **International law; — Martial law; — Military art and science; — Military history; — Military law; — Peace.**

War; a poem. *See* **Webber, S.** (C 119)

War; an heroic poem. *See* **Cockings, G.** (B 743)

War as it is and as it should be. Lond., 1806. 8°. (B 1415)

War correspondence of the Daily News, 1870. 2d ed., with notes. London, 1871. 2 v. 8°.
Note. Principally by J. A. MacGahan, Archibald Forbes, and F. D. Millet.
Contents. Vol. 1. July 14-Dec. 4, 1870. 2. Dec. 5, 1870-Mar. 2, 1771.

War Department. *See* **France.** *Min. de la Guerre;* — **Great Britain.** *War Office;* — **U. S.** *War Dept.*

War in disguise; or, The frauds of the neutral flags; [by J. Stephen]. London, 1805. 8°. (B 715)
Note. For other eds. *see* **Stephen, J.** (p. 2856).

War in Florida; an exposition, *etc.*, by a retired staff officer. Balt., 1836. 12°.

War in Texas; a review of facts showing that it is a crusade against Mexico; [by B. Lundy]. 2d ed. Phila., 1837. 8°. (B 1510, 1655)

War lyrics, and other poems. Boston, 1866. 16°.

War map of Russia. London, *E. Stanford*, 1854.

War of the Gaedhil with the Gaill; the original Irish text, ed. with tr. and introd. by J. H. Todd. Lond., 1867. 8°. (Chron. and mem.)

War of women, The; tr. by S. Spring from the French of A. D. Dumas. N. Y., 1850. 8°.

War or no war? with a view of our national decline and present embarassments; [by Lycurgus]. N. Y., 1807. 8°. (B 432)

War, The; or, Voices from the ranks [during the Crimean war]. London, 1855. 16°.

War ships for the Southern Confederacy; report of a meeting in Free-trade Hall, Manchester; with a letter from G. Smith to the 'Daily news'. Manchester, 1863. 8°.

War songs of the Germans. *See* **Blackie, J. S.**

War to the knife; a comedy, by H. J. Byron. (No. 16 *of* **De Witt's** Acting plays.)

War-trail, The; by M. Reid. (*In* **Chambers'** journal, n.s., v. 7. 1857.)

War with England; the case fairly stated; with an address to Pres. Van Buren. N. Y., 1838. 8°. (B 1496)

War without disguise; or, The frauds of neutral commerce a justification of belligerent captures; with obs. on [Gouverneur Morris's] "Answer to 'War in disguise'" and Madison's "Examination". *n.p.*, 1807. 8°. (B 432)

Waræus, Jacobus. *See* **Ware,** *Sir* **James.**

Warbeck, Jacob. Examination into auricular confession. London, 1837. 8°. (B 1384)

Warbeck, Perkin. MADDEN, F. Documents rel. to Warbeck; with remarks on his history. (*In* **Archæologia**, v. 27. 1838.)

Warbleton, Priory of. TURNER, E. College and priory of Hastings and the priory of Warbleton. (*In* **Sussex Archæol. Soc.** Col., v. 13. 1861.)

Warboys, *Eng.* UNDERHILL, E. B., *ed.* Records of the churches at Warboys, *etc.* London, 1854. 8°. (Hanserd Knollys Soc.)

Warburton, A. F., *reporter.* Trial of the officers and crew of the privateer Savannah, on a charge of piracy. N. Y., 1862. 8°.

Warburton, Eliot Bartholomew George. The crescent and the cross. N. Y., 1845. 2 v. 12°.

— Darien; or, The merchant prince. Par., 1852. 8°.

— Memoirs of Prince Rupert. London, 1849. 3 v. 8°.

— Reginald Hastings. London, 1850. 3 v. 8°.

Warburton, *Maj.* George. Conquest of Canada. London, 1849. 2 v. 8°.

— Hochelaga; or, England in the new world; ed. by E. Warburton. N. Y., 1846. 2 v. 12°.

— A memoir of C. Mordaunt; with selections from his correspondence. London, 1853. 2 v. 8°.

Warburton, Henry. BLANCHARD, L. (*In his* Saunders' portraits, v. 1. 1838.)

Warburton, John, *and others.* History of the city of Dublin. London, 1818. 2 v. 4°.

Warburton, Wm., *Bp.* Works. New ed., [with] life by R. Hurd. London, 1811. 12 v. 8°.
Contents. Vol. 1-6. Life. — The divine legation of Moses demonstrated. 7. The alliance between church and state; or, The necessity and equity of an established religion and a test-law demonstrated. 8. Julian; or, A discourse conc. the earthquake and fiery eruption which defeated the Emperor's attempt to rebuild the temple at Jerusalem. — The doctrine of grace; or, The office and operations of the Holy Spirit vindicated from the insults of infidelity and the abuses of fanaticism. 9. The principles of natural and revealed religion, in a course of sermons. — Sermons. — A charge to the clergy of the diocese of Gloucester, 1761. 10. Sermons and discourses. — Directions for the study of theology. 11. Controversial tracts, pt. 1. 12. Pt. 2. — Letters between Dr. Middleton and W., 1736; and between Dr. Lowth and W., 1756.

— Commentary and notes. (*In* **Pope, A.** Works, v. 2. 1871.)

— Dissertation on the 6th Book of the Eneid. (*In* **Virgilius Maro, P.** Works, v. 3. 1763.)

— Divine legation of Moses demonstrated; [with] life of the author, by R. Hurd. New ed. London, 1837. 2 v. 8°.

— Examination of the 6th Æneid. (*In* **Virgilius Maro, P.** Miscellanea Virgiliana. 1825.)
Note. The 'Examination' and the 'Dissertation' above are from book II, sect. 4, 2d ed. of the 'Divine legation', but differ somewhat in the selection.

— Letters from an eminent prelate to one of his friends [R. Hurd]. London, 1809. 8°.

— *Same.* 3d ed. London, 1809. 8°.

— *Same.* 1st Amer. ed. N. Y., 1809. 8°.

— Miscellaneous translations. London, 1724. 12°.
Contents. Cæsar's oration from Sallust. — Tully's oration for Ligarius. — Select letters from Pliny. — The first book of Boetius's Consolations of philosophy. — Claudian's 'Panegyrick on Honorius'. — The battle of the cranes and pygmies. — Fragments from Claudian imitated.

— *Same.* — Enquiry into the causes of prodigies, *etc.*, as related by historians. (*In* **Parr, S.** Tracts. 1789.)

— Natural and civil events the instruments of God's moral government; sermon, fast day. London, 1756. 4°. (B 1256)

— Remarks on several occasional reflections, in answer to Dr. Middleton, *etc.*; added, general review of the argument of the 'Divine legation'; with app. in answer to 'An examination of W.'s second proposition', [by H. Stebbing]. London, 1744. 8°. (B 119)

— *Same.* Answer to Doctors Stebbing and Sykes conc. the command to Abraham and the nature of the Jewish theocracy. Pt. 2. London, 1745. 8°.

— 2d part of an epistolary corresp. [with Dr. Lowth]; without an imprimatur. *n.p.*, [1766]. 8°. (B 1371)

— Sermon, Apr. 30, before the London Hospital. London, 1767. 4°. (B 97)

— Sermon before the lords spiritual and temporal, Jan. 30. London, 1760. 4°. (B 1248)

— Of a test law. (*In* **Churchman** armed, v. 1. 1814.)

— View of Ld. Bolingbroke's philosophy. London, 1854. 8°. (B 1712)

— ANDREWS, J. Scripture doctrine of divine grace; answer to the Bp. of Gloucester. 2d ed. London, 1769. 12°.

— BLACKBURNE, F. Remarks on W.'s account of the sentiments of the early Jews conc. the soul. London, 1757. 8°. (B 576)

— BROWN, J. Letter to Dr. Lowth [on] his letter to the author of 'The divine legation'. Newcastle-upon-Tyne, 1766. 8°. (B 1371)

— CROSWELL, A. Observations on several passages in a sermon by W. before the Soc. Prop. Gosp. in For. Parts, Feb. 21, 1766. Boston, 1768. 8°. (B 251, 1922)

— DISSERTATION on the ancient Pagan mysteries; opinions of W. considered. London, 1766. 8°.

— EDWARDS, T. Canons of criticism. 5th ed. London, 1753. 8°.

Note. Absurd canons in ridicule of Warburton's notes to Shakespeare, from which they are drawn up.

— EPISTLE to W. Warburton, occasioned by his treatment of the author of the 'Pleasures of imagination' [M. Akenside]. London, 1744. 8°. (B 119)

— EXPOSITION of the orthodox system of civil rights and church power in the writings of Dr. Stebbing; with an examination of [Warburton's] 'Alliance between church and state'. London, 1749. 8°. (B 1378)

— FLEMING, C. Comment on Warburton's 'Alliance between church and state'. London, 1748. 8°. (B 582)

— GREY, L. A word of advice to W. Warburton, a dealer in many words; with an appendix. London, 1746. 8°. (B 119)

— LELAND, T. Answer to a letter to L. cont. an examination of the criticism on [his] 'Dissertation on eloquence' [shewing] the Ld. Bp. of Gloucester's idea of an inspired language. London, 1765. 4°. (A 61)

— 2D LETTER to R. Clayton, [with] a letter to Warburton occasioned by his sermon, 'The nature and condition of truth'. London, 1753. 8°. (B 1365)

— REMARKS on Dr. Lowth's letter to the Bp. of Gloucester. London, 1766. 8°. (B 1371)

— REMARKS on the 'Divine legation of Moses', *etc.*; by the author of the 'Miscellany'. London, [17—]. 8°. (B 119)

— WATSON, J. S. Life of W.; with remarks on his works. London, 1863. 8°.

Ward, Aaron. Speech, navy appropriation bill. Wash., 1841. 8°. (B 1664)

— Speech, revenue bill, July 26. Wash., 1841. 8°. (B 1664)

Ward, Adolphus Wm. Charles Dickens. (*In* **Science** lectures for the people, 2d ser. 1870.)

— House of Austria in the Thirty Years' War; two lectures. London, 1869. 8°.

Ward, Andrew Henshaw. Family register of the inhabitants of Shrewsbury, Mass., 1717–1829. Boston, 1847. 8°.

— Genealogical history of the Rice family, descendants of Edmund Rice, who settled at Sudbury, Mass., 1638 or 39. Bost., 1858. 8°.

— Ward family; descendants of Wm. Ward, who settled in Sudbury, Mass., in 1639. Boston, 1851. 8°.

Ward, *Maj. Gen.* Artemas, *b.* 1727, *d.* 1800. HEADLEY, J. T. (*In his* Washington, v. 1. 1847.)

Ward, Artemas, *b.* 1762, *d.* 1847. Speech, Dec. 14, bill to authorize the Pres. to call upon the states for their respective quotas of 80,000 men. Wash., [1814]. 8°. (B 669, 2531)

— Speech, Mar. 5, bill making appropriations for the support of the military estab. of the U. S. for 1814. Boston, 1814. 8°. (B 669)

Ward, Artemus, *pseud.* *See* **Browne,** C. F.

Ward, Edward. Writings of the author of the London spy. Vol. 2. London, 1706. 8°.

— The British Hudibras. London, 1710. 8°.

— Secret history of clubs. London, 1709. 8°.

— Song. (*In* **Campbell,** T. Brit. poets, v. 5. 1819.)

— Translation of Rustica academiæ Oxoniensis reformatæ descriptio, 1648. (*In* **Somers,** J. Col. of tracts, v. 5. 1813.)

Ward, Elias, *vs.* **the State of Maryland.** HILL, H. A. Decision of the Supreme Court of the U. S. in the case. Boston, 1872. 8°. (E 77)

Ward, F. O. Outlines of human osteology. London, 1838. 32°.

Ward, *Rev.* Ferdinand De Ward. Summer vacation abroad; or, Notes of a visit to England, Scotland, Ireland, France, Italy, and Belgium. Rochester, 1856. 12°.

— Life of J. Peabody. (*In* **Hunt,** F. Lives of Amer. merchants, v. 1. 1856.)

Ward, George Atkinson. UPHAM, C. W. Memoir of W. (*In* **Essex Institute.** Hist. col., v. 7. 1865.)

Ward, George Cabot. Biography of P. A. Porter. (*In* **Higginson,** T. W. Harvard mem. biog., v. 1. 1866.)

Ward, H. The centennial; a poem. (*In* **Litchfield County.** Centennial celebration. 1851.)

Ward, Henry Dana. Anti-masonic review and magazine. Vol. 1–2. N. Y., 1828–30. 2 v. 8°.

— On the millenium. (*In* **Himes,** J. V. First report of the conference. 1841.)

Ward, *Sir* Henry George. Mexico. 2d ed. enl.; with an account of mining companies and political events to 1829. Lond., 1829. 2 v. 8°.

— Peculiar burdens on land; speech, Mar. 14. London, 1843. 8°. (B 1187)

Ward, *Mrs.* Hetta Lord (Hayes). MEMOIR; [by her mother, her husband, *etc.*]; with selections from her writings. Boston, 1843. 12°.

Ward, James, *b.* 1769, *d.* 1859. MANTZ, P. Artistes anglais: J. Ward. (*In* **Gazette** des beaux-arts, v. 5. 1859.)

Ward, James. Workmen and wages at home and abroad. London, 1868. 8°.

Ward, James Harman. Manual of naval tactics. N. Y., 1859. 8°.

Ward, James Wilson. Poem. (*In* **Abington,** *Mass.* Celebration of the 150th anniv. of incorporation. 1862.)

Ward, John, *vicar of Stratford upon Avon.* Diary, 1648–79; arranged by C. Severn. London, 1839. 8°.

Ward, John, *of Chester.* Posthumous works; rev. by G. Gordon. London, 1730. 8°.

Contents. New method of navigation by parallel parts. — Compendiums of practical and speculative geometry and of plane trigonometry. — The doctrine of the sphere and the demonstrations and calculations of spherical trigonometry.

— Young mathematician's guide. 7th ed. London, 1740. 8°.

— *Same.* 9th ed. London, 1752. 8°.

— *Same.* 12th ed., corr. by S. Clarke. London, 1771. 8°.

Ward, John, *Prof. in Gresham College, b.* 1679, *d.* 1758. Four essays upon the Eng. language. London, 1758. 8°.

— System of oratory. London, 1759. 2 v. 8°.

— LARDNER, N. Remarks upon Dr. Ward's Dissertations upon several passages of the Sacred Scriptures. (*In his* Works, v. 11. 1788.)

Ward, *Rev.* John. Short discourse at the ordination of I. Smith, June 24. Taunton, 1778. 8°. (E 1312)

— *Same.* (*In* **Wright,** T. Sermon. 1778. B 66)

Ward, John D. Account of the steamboat controversy between the citizens of N. Y. and N. J. (*In* **New Jersey Hist. Soc.** Proc., v. 9. 1860–64.)

Ward, John Wm., *Earl of Dudley.* Letters to Bishop of Llandaff. London, 1840. 8°.

Ward, *Rev.* Jonathan. Sermon before the Maine Missionary Soc., Portland, June 26. Hallowell, 1811. 8°. (B 334)

— Sermon, ordination of J. Ward, Jr., in Biddeford. Portland, 1825. 8°. (B 1785)

Ward, *Rev.* Julius Hammond. Life and letters of J. G. Percival. Boston, 1866. 8°.

Ward, Luke. Voyage intended towards China, wherein E. Fenton was appointed generall, begun 1582. (*In* **Hakluyt,** R. Col. of voy., v. 4. 1811; — *and in* Callander, J. Terra Austr., v. 1. 1766.)

Ward, Malthus A. Address before the Mass. Horticult. Soc., Sept. 31. Boston, 1831. 8°. (B 1803, E 9)

Ward, Mary O. Songs for little ones at home. N. Y., *Amer. Tr. Soc.*, [1852]. 12°.

Ward, Michael. On opiate friction in spasmodic and febrile diseases; also, on hydrophobia and tetanus. Manchester, 1809. 8°.

Ward, Nathaniel. The simple cobler of Agawam; by Theodore de la Guard. London, 1647. 4°.

— *Same.* Ed. by D. Pulsifer. Boston, 1843. 12°.

— *Same.* (*In* **Force,** P. Col. of tracts, v. 3. 1844.)

— BROWNE, B. F. Memorial of W. (*In* **Essex Inst.** Hist. col., v. 2. 1860.)

— DEAN, J. W. Memoir of W.; with notices of his family. Albany, 1868. 8°.

Ward, Nathaniel Bagshaw. Growth of plants in closely glazed cases. London, 1842. 8°.

Ward, Richard R., *and others*. Memorial to the Senate and House of Representatives in regard to the ten million loan. N. Y., [18—]. 8°. (B 1461)

Ward, Robert Plumer. Chatsworth; or, The romance of a week. N. Y., 1844. 8°.

— Enquiry into the foundation and history of the law of nations in Europe. Dublin, 1795. 2 v. 8°.

— De Vere; or, The man of independence. Phila., 1827. 3 v. 12°.

— Fielding; or, Society; Atticus; St. Lawrence. Phila., 1837. 3 v. 12°.

— *Same*. Illustrations of human life. Paris, 1837. 8°.

— Historical essay on the revolution of 1688. London, 1838. 2 v. 12°.

— Sterling; Penruddock. Phila., 1839. 2 v. 12°.
Contents. Vol. 1. Sterling. 2. Penruddock.

— Treatise of the rights and duties of belligerent and neutral powers in maritime affairs. London, 1801. 8°. (B 719)

— Tremaine; or, The man of refinement. Phila., 1825. 2 v. 12°.
Note. From **Blackwood's** mag., v. 17. 1825.

— PATMORE, P. G. (*In his* My friends, v. 1, 2. 1854.)

— PHIPPS, E. Memoirs of W. London, 1850. 2 v. 8°.

Ward, Samuel, *D.D., of Cambridge, Eng., d.* 1643. Suffragium collegiale theologorum de v controversis Remonstrantium articulis; acc. Concio de gratia discriminante. Londini, 1633. 12°.

Ward, Samuel, *Gov. of R. I., b.* 1725, *d.* 1776. GAMMELL, W. Life of Ward. (*In* **Sparks**, J. Amer. biog., v. 19. 1846.)

— *Same, separately printed*. [Boston,] 1846. 16°.

— *Funeral sermon on*. 1776. *See* **Stillman**, S. (B 913)

Ward, Samuel, *b.* 1786, *d.* 1839. KING, C. (*In* **Hunt**, F. Lives of Amer. merchants, v. 1. 1856.)

Ward, Seth, *Bp. of Salisbury*. Essay towards an eviction of the being and attributes of God, the immortality of the soul, and the truth of Scripture. Oxford, 1655. 24°.

— NICERON, J. P. (*In his* Mém., v. 24. 1733.)

Ward, Stephen H. On Wardian cases for plants and their applications. London, 1854. 8°.

Ward, Thomas. England's reformation from Henry VIII. to Oates's plot; a poem. London, 1719. 12°.

Ward, Townsend. The insurrection in 1794 in the western counties of Penn.; appended, Gen. **Wilkins's** account of the gathering on Braddock's field, and a memoir on the insurrection, by J. Gallatin. (*In* **Penn. Hist. Soc.** Mem., v. 6. 1858.)

Ward, Wm. Account of the writings, religion, and manners of the Hindoos. Serampore, 1811. 4 v. 4°.
Contents. Vol. 1. Trans. of the Rajuturungu compiled by Mrityoonjuyu Vidyalunkaru. — Hist. of Raja Krishnu Chundru Rayu by Rajeevulochunu. — J. Rennel's divisions of India, abridged. — Bengal, its capital, *etc.* — The Hindoo shastrus. — The vadus. — Remarks on the preceding. — The six durshunus. — Trans. of the Vadantu-Saru. — Remarks on the preceding. — The Dhurnu shastrus.— Substance of Prayushchittu Nirnuyu. 2. The Tuntru shastrus. — Contents of the Tuntru-Saru. — Substance of the Peet'hu Mala. — The pooranus. — Contents of the Muhabharatu, — of the Ramayuna, — Shreebhaguvutu. — Substance of the Kashee Khundu, — of the Ootkulu-khundu, — of the Chundee, — of the Kaliku pooranu, — of the Kulkee Pooranu. — Extract from the Booddhu pooranu. — The other pooranus. — Trans. of passages in the Gunga Vakya Vulee. — The Jyotis shastrus. — Substance of Jyotish-Tutrou. — Part of Masu-kosht'hu or Hindoo Almanack. — The Voidyu shastrus. — Trans. of parts of Naree Prukashu, Nidanu, and Nidanu-sungruhu. — The Kavyu shastrus. — The Dhunoorvadu shastrus. — The Ganu shastrus. — The Shilpu shastrus. — The Sungskritu grammars. — The Sungskritu dictionaries. — Trans. from the Sungskritu and works written in Bengalee. — Ceremonies of the Hindoos commanded in their shastrus. 3. The Hindoo gods. — The Hindoo temples, images, times of worship, *etc.* — The holy places. 4. The castes. — The domestic manners and customs of the Hindoos. — The Hindoo system of philosophy and religion. — The Sikhs.

— Farewell letters on returning to Bengal. N. Y., 1821. 12°.

— View of the history, lit., and mythology of the Hindoos. New ed. London, 1822. 3 v. 8°.
Contents. Vol. 1. History. — Manners and customs. 2. Literature. 3. Mythology.

— View of the history, literature, and religion of the Hindoos. London, 1817. 2 v. 8°.
Contents. Vol. 1. Objects of worship. 2. The temples, images, priests, *etc.*, of the Hindoos. — Doctrines of the Hindoo religion. — Saints. — Religious sects.

— MARSHMAN, J. C. Life and times of Carey, Marshman, and Ward. Lond, 1859. 2 v. 8°.

Ward, Wm. George. Letter to the Rev. father Ryder on his recent pamphlet, [on the infallibility of the Church], *etc.* (*Appended to the* **Dublin** rev., n.s., v. 9. 1867.)

Ward of Delamere, The; by Mrs. Pinchard. Phila., 1816. 2 v. 12°.

Warden, Alexander J. Linen trade, ancient and modern. London, 1864. 8°.

Warden, David Bailie. Bibliotheca Americo-Septentrionalis; a collection of books for sale. Paris, 1820. 8°.

— Bibliotheca Americana; a collection of books rel. to North and South America and the West Indies. Paris, 1831. 8°. (B 1071)

— Chorographical and statistical description of the District of Columbia. Paris, 1816. 8°.

— Description des ruines près de Palenque, *etc.* — Recherches sur les antiquités des Etats-Unis. (*In* **Paris. Soc. de Géog.** Receuil de voyages, *etc.*, v. 2. 1825.)

— Dissertation sur l'origine de l'ancienne population des deux Amériques et sur les diverses antiquités de ce continent. (*In* **Dupaix**, G. Antiq. mex. 1834.)

— Mémoires pour quelques navires américains capturés par les Français. Paris, 1809–15.] 4°. (A 7)
Contents. The Bald eagle. — L'Ohio. — Le Roboreus. — La Jeanne-Marie. —Le Gouverneur Gore.— Le Whampoa. — L'Océan. — Le Palinare. — Le James Cook. — La Persévérance.

— Origin, nature, *etc.*, of consular establishments. Paris, 1813. 8°.

— Prospectus of a statist. and hist. account of the U. S. *n.p.*, 1817. 8°. (445)

— Statistical, political, and historical account of the U. S. Edin., 1819. 3 v. 8°.
Contents. Vol. 1. The physical features, climate, and natural productions of the country. — Description of Mass. and the district of Me. — N. H. — Vt. — R. I. — N. Y. 2. Ct. — N. J. — Penn. — Del. — Md. — Va. — O. — Ind. — Ky. — Tenn. — N. C. — S. C. — Ga. — La. 3. Miss. — Ala. Ty. — Ill. Ty. — Mich. Ty. — North-west Ty. — Mo. Ty. — Country between the Rocky Mts. and the Pacific Ocean. — District of Columbia, and City of Washington. — Florida. — The federal government and public establishments connected with it. — The population, agriculture, *etc.*, of the U. S. — The Indians.

Warden, Frank L. Romance after marriage; a comedy. *See* **Warden**, F. L.

Warden, Wm. Letters written on board the ship Northumberland and at St. Helena; in which the conversations of Napoleon and his suite are faithfully described. 6th ed. London, 1817. 8°.

— *Same*. Boston, 1817. 18°.

— REVIEW of [his] letters from St. Helena. Boston, 1817. 8°. (B 445)

Warden, The; by A. Trollope. Lpz., *Tauchnitz*, 1859. 16°.

Warder, T. B., *and* **Catlett**, J. M. Battle of Young's Branch or Manassas Plain, July 21, 1861; with Gen. Beauregarde's report. Richmond, 1862. 18°.

Wardlaw, *Rev.* Gilbert. Testimony of Scripture to the obligations and efficacy of prayer; three discourses. 2d Amer. ed. Windsor, 1830. 18°.

Wardlaw, Ralph, *D.D.* Discourses on the principal points of the Socinian controversy. From 1st Glasgow ed. Andover, 1815. 8°.
— Essay on benevolent associations. Glasgow, 1818. 8°. (B 676)
— The Sabbath. Glasgow, [184–]. 8°. (B 1374)
— Sermon, influence of the love of Christ. (*In* **Suddards**, W. Brit. pulpit, v. 1. 1837.)
— Unitarianism incapable of vindication; a reply to Yates's 'Vindication'. Andover, 1817. 8°.
— Yates, J. Vindication of Unitarianism; a reply to W.'s 'Discourses'. Bost., 1816. 8°.
— - Sequel to the 'Vindication of Unitarianism'. Liverpool, 1817. 8°.
— - *Another copy.* (B 1017)

Wardle, Gwyllym Lloyd. Brief account of [his] charges rel. to the Duke of York. (*In* **Clarke**, M. A. T. Authentic memoirs. 1809.)
— Erinaceus, *pseud.* Examination and complete refutation of observations contained in Col. Wardle's letter to Ld. Ellenborough. London, 1809. 8°. (B 785)
— Trial, F. Wright, plaintiff, and G. L. W., defendant; added, Col. Wardle's address to the people. London, [1809]. 8°. (B 667)

Wardrop, James. On blood-letting. London, 1835. 12°.
— *Same.* Phila., 1837. 8°.
— Essays on the morbid anatomy of the eye. Edin., London, 1808–18. 2 v. 8°.
— *Same.* 2d ed. London, 1819–20. 2 v. 8°.
— On fungus hæmatodes, or soft cancer. Edin., 1809. 8°.
— History of J. Mitchell, a boy born blind and deaf; with an account of the operation performed for the recovery of his sight. (*In* **Pamphleteer**, 1815; v. 6 of B 838)
— Nature and treatment of diseases of the heart; containing new views on the circulation of the blood, *etc.* New ed. London, 1860. 8°.

Wardwell, D. Biog. notice of W. (*In* **Mass. Med. Soc.** Med. comm., v. 8. 1854.)

Ware, Ashur. Oration, Boston, July 4. Boston, 1816. 8°. (B 457)
— Oration, Portland, July 4. Portland, 1817. 8°. (B 457)
— Loring, J. S. (*In his* Hundred Boston orators. 1852.)

Ware, Darwin Erastus. Biography of W. D. Russell. (*In* **Higginson**, T. W. Harv. mem. biog., v. 2. 1866.)

Ware, Henry, *D.D.*, *b.* 1764, *d.* 1845. Answer to Dr. Wood's reply in a second series of letters to Trinitarians and Calvinists. Camb., 1822. 8°. (B 338)
— Continuance of peace and increasing prosperity a source of consolation; sermon, Feb. 19 [national thanksgiving]. Boston, 1795. 8°. (B 234, 843, W 54)
— Correspondence [with W. Adams] rel. to the prospects of Christianity, and the means of promoting its reception in India, [1823]. Camb., 1824. 8°.
— Eulogy, July 20, 1810, interment of Rev. S. Webber. Camb., 1810. 8°. (B 435, 911)
— Inquiry into the foundation, evidences, and truths of religion. Camb., 1842. 2 v. 12°.
— Letters addressed to Trinitarians and Calvinists, occasioned by Dr. Woods' letters to Unitarians. Camb., 1820. 8°. (B 338, 2538)
— Postscript to the second series of letters to Trinitarians and Calvinists, in reply to Dr. Woods on those letters. Camb., 1823. 8°. (B 338)
— Sermon, anniversary election, May 30. Boston, 1821. 8°. (B 958, 1830)
— Sermon, Apr. 14, 1819, ordination of J. Pierpont. Camb., 1819. 8°. (B 1595)
— *Same.* 2d ed. Camb., 1819. 8°. (B 279)
— Sermon, convention of Congregational ministers of Mass., May 28. Boston, 1818. 8°. (B 334, 957)
— Sermon, death of Washington, Jan. 6. Boston, 1800. 8°. (B 172, 234, W 50)
— Sermon, Dec. 18, ordination of W. Ware. N. Y., 1821. 8°. (B 278)
— *Same.* 2d ed. N. Y., 1821. 12°. (C 212)
— Sermon, Hingham, May 5, 1805, dissolution of his pastoral relation to the church; with address from the church and his answer. Boston, 1805. 8°. (B 334, 849)
— Sermon, Jan. 1, ordination of Rev. H. Ware to the pastoral care of the second church in Boston. Boston, 1817. 8°. (B 334, 1595)
— Sermon, Jan. 17, ordination of C. Brooks, in Hingham. Boston, 1821. 8°. (B 278)
— Sermon, July 9, death of J. Adams. Camb., 1826. 8°. (B 1206)
— Sermon, Northborough, Oct. 30, 1816, at the ordination of J. Allen. Camb., 1817. 8°. (B 1595)
— Sermon, Oct. 29, ordination of A. Lamson. Dedham, 1818. 8°. (B 334, 1595)
— Sermon, Oct. 12, ordination of W. B. O. Peabody, Springfield. Springfield, 1820. 8°. (B 1323)
— Sermon, Sept. 1, interment of D. Shute. Boston, 1802. 8°. (B 234, 643)
— Service of God, as inculcated in the Bible, our reasonable choice; sermon, Scituate, Oct. 31. Boston, 1804. 8°. (B 202, 234, 847)
— Woods, L. Reply to Dr. Ware's letters to Trinitarians and Calvinists. Andover, 1821. 8°. (B 337)
— - *Same.* (*In his* Works, v. 4. 1851.)
— *Funeral sermon on.* 1845. *See* **Palfrey**, J. G. (B 1227, 1734)

Ware, Henry, *Jr.*, *D.D.*, *b.* 1794, *d.* 1843. Works; ed. by C. Robbins. Boston, London, 1846–47. 4 v. 12°.

Contents. Vol. 1. Recollections of J. Anderson. — How to spend holy time. — The poetry of mathematics; a lecture. — The village funeral. — A Sabbath with my friend. — How to spend a day. — R. Fowle. — Selections from his poetry. 2. Sketch of the life and character of Rev. J. E. Abbot. — Memoir of N. Parker. — Biog. notice of the Rev. T. Prentiss; sermon at his interment. — Sober thoughts on the state of the times, addressed to the Unitarian community. — Address, Kennebunk, before the York County Unitarian Association. — Connection between the duties of the pulpit and the pastoral office; introductory address to the members of the Theological School in Cambridge. — Duties of young men in respect to the dangers of the country. — The faith once delivered to the saints. — Three important questions answered, relating to the Christian name, character, and hopes. — Essays on personal religion. — Two letters on the genuineness of John v. 7, and on the Scriptural argument for Unitarianism, addressed to the Rev. Alex. M'Leod, of New York. — A letter to Rev. N. Adams, occasioned by his sermon entitled 'Injuries done to Christ'. — Hints on extemporaneous preaching. 3. Sermons. 4. Sermons on the character and offices of Christ. — Miscellaneous sermons. — Farewell address to the 2d church and society in Boston, Oct. 4, 1830. — Formation of the Christian character. — Progress of the Christian life.

— Address, Kennebunk, before the York Co. Unitarian Assoc., Oct. 24, 1827. Kennebunk, 1828. 12°. (C 274)
— Christ the head of the church; sermon, installation of E. H. Sears, Lancaster, Dec. 23, 1840. Boston, 1841. 8°. (B 1323)
— Combination against intemperance explained and justified; address before the Cambridge Temperance Society, March 27. Camb., 1832. 8°. (B 1278)
— *Same.* 3d ed. Boston, 1832. 8°. (C 301)
— Connection between the duties of the pulpit, *etc.*; introd. address to the members of the Theological School in Cambridge, Oct. 18, 25. Camb., 1830. 8°. (B 1662, 1739)
— Discourse, at the ordination of R. C. Waterston, Nov. 21, 1839. Boston, 1840. 8°. (B 1323, 1878)
— Discourse on the offices and character of Christ. Boston, 1825. 12°.
— The duty of improvement; a new year's sermon. *n.p.*, [18–]. 8°. (B 1304)
— The duty of promoting Christianity by circulation of books; discourse, May 31. Boston, 1838. 12°. (C 210)
— Education the business of life; two discourses, 16 July. Camb., 1837. 8°. (C 210)
— The faith once delivered to the saints. 3d ed. Boston, *A.U.A.*, 1827. 12°. (C 168, v. 1)
— The feast of tabernacles; an oratorio; music by C. Zeuner. [Boston, 1837.] 12°. (B 1770)

— Hints on extemporaneous preaching. Boston, 1824. 18°.
— Introduction. (*In* **Oberlin, J. F.** Memoirs. 1845.)
— The law of honor; disc. occas. by the recent duel in Washington, Mar. 4. Camb., 1838. 8°. (**B 1304, 1696**)
— Letter to N. Adams on his 'Injuries done to Christ'. Boston, 1841. 8°. (**D 29**)
— Life of the Saviour. Camb., 1833. 18°. (Sunday lib., v. 1.)
— Memoir of J. Priestley. (*In* **Priestley, J.** Views. 1834.)
— Memoirs of N. Worcester; with preface and notes by S. Worcester. Boston, 1844. 8°.
— The moral principle of the temperance movement; sermon, Oct. 17. *n.p.*, [1841]. 8°. (**B 1304**)
— Object and means of the Christian ministry; sermon, ordination of C. A. Bartol, Mar. 1. Camb., 1837. 8°. (**B 1323, 1878**)
— Formation of the Christian character. 2d ed. Camb., 1831. 18°.
— *Same.* 12th ed. Boston, 1845. 12°.
— Outline of the testimony of Scripture against the trinity. Reprint from Boston ed. Liverpool, 1832. 12°. (**C 242**)
— The personality of the Deity; sermon, Harvard Univ., Sept. 23. Boston, 1838. 8°. (**B 1304, 1696, 1748**)
— Poem, Cambridge, Feb. 23, 1815, celebration of peace. Camb., 1815. 8°. (**A 1, B 1768**)
— Progress of the Christian life. 2d ed. Boston, 1847. 12°.
— Recollections of Jotham Anderson; [fiction]. Boston, 1824. 12°.
— Reply of a Unitarian clergyman to the 'Letter of a gentleman in Boston'. Boston, 1828. 12°. (**C 226**)
— *Same.* 2d ed. Boston, 1828. 12°. (**C 242, D 61, 63**)
— Sermon, dedication of the 2d. Cong. church in Northampton, Dec. 7. Northampton, 1825. 8°. (**B 296**)
— Sermon, Dorchester, before the Evangelical Miss. Soc., June 7. Boston, 1820. 8°. (**B 301**)
— Sermon, duty of usefulness. (*In* **Liberal preacher**, v. 1. 1828.) — Sermon, promise of universal peace. (*In* v. 4. 1834.)
— Sermon, interment of Rev. T. Prentiss. Charlestown, 1817. 8°. (**B 334, 2013**)
— Sermon on small sins. Boston, 1827. 12°. (**C 210**)
— Sermon, ordination of C. Robbins, Boston, Dec. 4. Boston, 1833. 8°. (**B 1323**)
— Sermon, ordination of W. H. Furness, Phila., Jan. 12. Phila., 1825. 8°. (**B 1323, 1595**)
— Sermon; the religion of principle and the religion of the affections. (*In* **Beard, J. R.** Sermons. 1832.)
— Sketch of the life of J. E. Abbot. From the Christian disciple. [Boston, 1819.] 8°. (**B 570**)
— *Same.* (*In* **Abbot, J. E.** Extracts. 1830.)
— Sober thoughts on the state of the times. Boston, 1835. 8°. (**D 62**)
— Sunday library for young persons. Camb., 1833-36. 4 v. 8°.
Contents. Vol. 1. **Ware, H.,** *Jr.* Life of the Saviour. 2. **Farrar,** *Mrs.* J. Life of J. Howard. 3. **Bulfinch, S. G.** Holy land. 4. **Fox, T. B.** Sketch of the Reformation.
— Three important questions answered. 3d ed. Boston, 1823. 12°. (**C 111**)
— *Same.* 4th ed. Boston, 1826. 12°. (**C 210**)
— *Same.* 4th ed. Boston, 1830. 8°. (**D 62**)
— Two discourses, containing the history of the Old North and New Brick Churches united as the Second Church. Boston, 1821. 8°. (**B 275, 1696**)
— Two letters to A. M'Leod, cont. rem. upon the texts from which he preached, Apr. 30 and May 7. N. Y., 1820. 8°. (**B 338**)
— *Same.* 3d ed. Boston, 1823. 12°. (**C 111, 210, 242**)
— The vision of liberty; [ode] recited before The Phi Beta Kappa Soc. of Harvard Univ., Aug. 26. Boston, 1824. 8°. (**B 1730**)
— **Parkman, F.** Extracts from a discourse on W. [Pages from the 'Christian examiner', Nov. 1843.] 8°. (**B 1452, 1734**)
— **Remarks** on the 'Letter from a gentleman in Boston [Tappan] to a Unit. clergyman' [H. W., Jr.], and the Reply and Review. Boston, 1828. 12°. (**C 242**)
— **Tappan, L.** Letter from a gentleman in Boston to a Unitarian clergyman. 2d ed. Boston, 1828. 8°. (**C 184, D 63**)
— - *Same.* 3d ed. Boston, 1828. 8°. (**C 226**)
— - *Same.* 4th ed. Boston, 1828. 12°. (**D 61**)

409. (8. 10. 81.)

— **Ware, J.** Memoir of the life of H. Ware, Jr. Boston, 1846. 12°.
— *Funeral sermon on.* 1843. *See* **Robbins, C.** (**B 1194, 1227, 1247**)

Ware, Isaac. Complete body of architecture. London, 1756. f°.
— Design for the mansion house of the Ld. Mayor. **Engr.** (**E 55**)
— Plans and elevations of Houghton, delinated (*sic*) by W. *See* **Ripley, T.**

Ware (*Lat.* Waræus), *Sir* James, *d.* 1666. Ancient Irish histories. [2d ed.] Dublin, 1809. 2 v. 8°.
Contents. Vol. 1. **Spencer, E.** View of the state of Ireland, 1596. — **Campion, E.** Historie of Ireland, in the yeare 1571. 2. **Hanmer, M.** Chronicle of Ireland, 1571. — **Marleburrough, H.** Chronicle of Ireland.
— **Niceron, J. P.** (*In his* Mém., v. 18. 1732; *and*, *Germ.*, v. 14. 1756.)

Ware, James, *surgeon*, *d.* 1815. Chirurgical observations rel. to the epiphora, scrophulous and intermittent ophthalmy, extraction of the cataract, and introduction of the male catheter. 2d ed. London, 1800. 8°.
— Inquiry into the causes which have prevented success in the operation of extracting the cataract; observations on the dissipation of the cataract and gutta serena; also additional remarks on epiphora. Lond., 1795. 8°.
— Observations on the cataract and gutta serena. 2d ed. London, 1804. 8°.
— Ophthalmy, psorophthalmy, and purulent eyes of new born children. 5th ed. London, 1814. 8°.

Ware, John, *M.D.* Address before the Mass. Peace Soc., Dec. 25, 1824. Boston, 1825. 8°. (**B 565**)
— Animal magnetism. [Pages from the Christian examiner, Nov. 1851.] 8°. (**B 1564**)
— Condition and prospects of the medical profession. (*In* **Mass. Med. Soc.** Med. comm., v. 7. 1848.)
— Contribution to the history, diagnosis, and treatment of croup. Boston, 1850. 8°. (**B 1564**)
— Discourse on medical education, *etc.* Boston, 1847. 8°.
— *Another copy.* (**B 1564**)
— Dissertation on hemoptysis and on suppuration; Boylston prize diss. Boston, 1820. 8°.
— *Another copy.* (**B 833**)
— Farewell address to the medical graduates of Harvard Univ., Mar. 12. Boston, 1856. 8°. (**B 1564, H 8**)
— On hemoptysis as a symptom. (*In* **Mass. Med. Soc.** Pub., v. 1. 1856.)
— *Same.* Boston, 1860. 8°. (**B 1692**)
— Introduction and additions. (*In* **Smellie, W.** Philos. of nat. hist. 1824.)
— Introductory lecture before the medical class in Harvard Univ., Oct. 16. Boston, 1833. 8°. (**B 1564, 1880, 1882, H 8**)
— Memoir of H. Ware, Jr. Boston, 1846. 12°.
— Philosophy of natural history on the plan of W. Smellie. Boston, 1860. 12°.
— Poem before the Φ.B.K. Soc. of Harvard Univ., Aug. 28. Cambridge, 1817. 8°. (**B 357**)
— Remarks on the history and treatment of delirium tremens. Boston, 1831. 8°. (**B 1020, 1760, 2014**)
— *Same.* (*In* **Mass Med. Soc.** Med. comm., v. 5. 1836.) — Appendix. (*In* v. 6. 1841.)
— Success in the medical profession; introd. lecture at the Mass. Med. Coll., Nov. 6, 1850. Boston, 1851. 8°. (**B 1564, H 8**)
— True relation of the sexes. Boston, 1850. 12°.

Ware, *Rev.* John Fothergill Waterhouse. Change of base. — Few words with the convalescent. — The home to the camp. — The home to the hospital. — Mustered out. — On picket. — Rally upon the reserve. — The rebel. — The reconnoissance. — The recruit. — The reveille. — To the color. — Traitors in camp. — Wounded and in the hands of the enemy. (*In* **American Unitarian Assoc.** Tracts. 1865.)
— Discourse occasioned by the death of [Z. Taylor], July 14. Camb., 1850. 8°. (**B 1225**)
— Manhood the want of the day; sermon, Cambridgeport, Mar. 1. Boston, 1863. 8°. (**B 1591**)
— Sorrow of the sea; sermon, Cambridgeport, Jan. 22. Boston, 1854. 8°. (**B 1304**)

Ware, Martin. Reformatory and refuge union. (*In* **Nat. Assoc. Prom. Soc. Sci.** Trans., 1859.)

Ware, *Mrs.* Mary Greene (Chandler). Death and life. Boston, 1864. 16°.

— Thoughts in my garden. Boston, 1863. 16°.

Ware, *Mrs.* Mary Lovell (Pickard), *wife of Henry Ware, Jr.* HALL, E. B. Memoir of M. L. Ware. Boston, 1853. 12°.

— MARTINEAU, *Miss* H. The sickness and health of the people of Bleaburn. Boston, 1853. 12°.
Note. From **Household words**, v. 1. 1850.
Note. Founded on the life of Mrs. Ware. Published anonymously, and wrongly attributed to Mrs. Gaskell on pp. 316 and 1108 of this catalogue.

Ware, Robert. STEDMAN, C. E. (*In* **Higginson**, T. W. Harvard mem. biog., v. 1. 1866.)

Ware, Samuel. Tracts on vaults and bridges. London, 1822. 8°.

Ware, Samuel Hibbert. State of parties in Lancashire before the rebellion of 1715. [Manchester,] 1845. 8°. (Chetham Soc., v. 5.)
Contents. The events of church and state which preceded and accompanied the commencement of the rebellion of 1715. — March of the insurgents of 1715 from Scotland until they reached Penrith in Cumberland. — March of the insurgent force, 1715, from Penrith to Preston; by P. Clarke. — Preston fight; supplement appended to the journal of P. Clarke. — Lancashire events intervening between the surrender of Preston, and the abandonment of Jacobite hostilities in Scotland. — Lancashire events which followed the cessation of Jacobite hostilities. — The state of parties in Lancashire subsequent to the rebellion of 1715.

Ware, *Rev.* Wm. Address at the laying of the corner stone of the 2d Cong. Unit. Ch., N. Y., Nov. 24. N. Y., 1825. 16°. (C 274, D 29)

— Antiquity and revival of Unitarian Christianity. Bost., 1831. 12°. (A. U. A., 1st ser., no. 47. C 168, v. 4.)

— Aurelian. *See, below,* 'Probus'.

— The danger of delay. 2d ed. Boston, 1831. 12°. (A. U. A., 1st ser., no. 31. C 168, v. 3.)

— Julian; or, Scenes in Judea. N. Y., 1841. 2 v. 12°.

— Lancashire during the rebellion of 1715. [Manchester,] 1845. 8°. (Chetham Soc., v. 5.)

— Lectures on the works and genius of W. Allston. Boston, 1852. 12°.

— Life of N. Bacon. (*In* **Sparks, J.** Amer. biog., v. 13. 1844.)

— Ministry at large for the poor of cities. [N. Y., 1832.] 8°. (B 1783)

— Probus; or, Rome in the 3d century. N. Y., 1838. 2 v. 12°.
Note. This was afterwards published under the title of 'Aurelian'.

— Righteousness before doctrine; two sermons, Mar. 16. Boston, 1845. 8°. (B 1304)

— Sermon on the communion. N. Y., 1825. 12°. (C 210)

— Sermon on worldly mindedness. (*In* **Liberal preacher**, v. 2. 1829.) — Sermon, on evil. (*In* n.s., v. 6. 1836.)

— Sketches of European capitals. Boston, 1851. 12°.

— Zenobia; or, The Palmyra. N. Y., 1839. 2 v. 12°.

Ware, Wm. Robert. Application of Hare's system of voting to the nomination of Overseers of Harvard Coll. (*In* **Amer. Soc. Sci. Assoc.** Journ., no. 3. 1871.)

Wareham, *Mass.* DAVIS, S. Topography and history of W., 1815. (*In* **Mass. Hist. Soc.** Col., v. 14. 1816.)

Warée, C. B. Répertoire bibliographique des ouvrages de législation, de droit, et de jurisprudence pub. en France. 1789–1863. Nouv. éd., aug. par E. Thorin. Par., 1863. 8°.

Warens, Louise Eléonore de La Tour du Pil, *baronne* de. HOUSSAYE, A. Les charmettes; Rousseau et W. 2e éd. Paris, 1864. 12°.

Warfield, Charles. Essay on the trinity; added, remarks on the character of Christ. Balt., 1820. 8°. (B 272)

Wargentin, Pieter Willem. CONDORCET, J. A. N. C., *marq.* de. Eloge de W. (*In his* Œuvres, v. 3. 1847.)

Warin, Jean Baptiste Joseph Innocent Philadelphe Regnault de. *See* **Regnault de Warin, J. B. J. I. P.**

Waring, *Miss* Anna Lætitia. Hymns and meditations; with introd. by F. D. Huntington. From 8th London ed. Boston, 1863. 16°.

Waring, Edmund Thomas, *D.D.* Discourse before the Rhode Island Medical Society. Providence, 1812. 8°. (B 993)

Waring, Edward, *M.D.* Meditationes analyticæ. Cantab., 1776. 4°.

— Miscellanea analytica de æquationibus algebraicis et curvarum proprietatibus. Cantab., 1762. 4°.

Waring, Edward Scott. Tour to Sheeraz; added, history of Persia. London, 1807. 4°.

Waring, John Burley. Architectural, sculptural, and picturesque studies in Burgos. London, 1852. f°.

— The Byzantine and Romanesque court. — Mediæval, Renaissance, and Italian courts. *See* **Wyatt**, M. D.

— Illustrations of architecture and ornament. London, [1866?]. 4°.

— Stone monuments, tumuli, and ornament of remote ages. London, 1870. 4°.

Waring, John Scott, *formerly major* John Scott. Letter to E. Burke. London, 1783. 8°. (B 633)

— Letter to J. Owen, in reply to the "Brief strictures on the preface to 'Observations'", *etc.* 2d ed. London, 1808. 8°. (B 679, 1845)

— Letter to P. Francis [on affairs in India]. London, 1791. 8°. (B 1406)

— Observations on the present state of the East India Co., [1807]. 4th ed. London, 1808. 8°. (B 1844)

— Reply to a Letter to [him] in refutation of the unjust observations of the anon. writer of that letter. London, 1808. 8°. (B 1844)

— Seven letters to the people of Gr. Brit. London, 1789. 8°. (B 752)

— CONSIDERATIONS on the practicability, policy, *etc.*, of communicating to the natives of India the knowledge of Christianity; with obs. on 'prefatory remarks to a pamphlet by W.' London, 1808. 8°. (B 1845)

— FULLER, A. Remarks on Waring's letter to Owen. — Strictures on a pamphlet by Waring. — On Waring's 3d pamphlet. (*In his* Apology. 1808.)

— LETTER to [him] in refutation of his 'Observations on the present state of the East India Co.' London, 1808. 8°. (B 679, 1844)

Waring, Mary. Diary of the religious experience of W. London, 1809. 12°.

Warker, George. Sermon on parental example. (*In* **Zollikofer, G. J.** Sermons. 1809.)

Warker. *See also* **Walker**.

Warkworth, John, *D.D.* Chronicle of the 1st thirteen years of the reign of the Edward IV.; ed. by J. O. Halliwell. London, 1839. 4°. (Camden Soc., v. 10.)

Warleigh; by A. E. Bray. London, 1845. 16°. (Novels, v. 9.)

Warlock of the glen, The; by C. E. Walker. (*In* **Sargent, E.** Mod. stand. dr., v. 37.)

Warmholtz, Carl Gustav. Bibliotheca historica Sueo-Gothica. Vol. 1–6, Stockholm, 8–15, Upsala, 1702–1817. 15 v. 8°.
Contents. Vol. 1. Geographie. 2. Natural-historia. 3. Antiquiteter. 4. Kyrko-historia. 5. Almänna hist. och konunga hist. til år 1520. 6. Rikets historia, Gustaf I. – Carl IX. 7. Gustaf Adolph. 8. Christina. 9. Carl Gustaf och Carl XI. 10. Carl XII. och Eleonora. 11. Fredric och Adolph Fredric, samt atteländer för konunga husen. 12. Sveriges regering och stats författninger, eller Allmänna rätts historia. 13. Rikes Råd, K. Maj. och rik. Höga Collegier, samt ceremonialen. 14. Lagar och Stats-interesse i anseendi til främmande magter, samt miscellanea historia. 15. Bokeliga konssters- och lärdoms-historia i Sverige.

Warming. BUCHANAN, R. On heating by steam. (*In his* Practical essays on econ. of fuel. 1810.)

— TREDGOLD, T. Principles of warming and ventilating public buildings, *etc.* 2d ed. London, 1824. 8°.

— HOOD, C. Practical treatise on warming buildings by hot water. London, 1837. 8°.

— ARNOTT, N. Warming and ventilating. London, 1838. 8°.
— REID, D. B. Illustrations of the theory and practice of ventilation, with remarks on warming. London, 1844. 8°.
— BERNAN, W. History and art of warming and ventilating rooms and buildings. London, 1845. 2 v. 16°.
— BELL, L. V. Heating by steam and hot water. (*In his* Practical methods of ventilating. 1848.)
— TOMLINSON, C. Rudimentary treatise on warming and ventilation. London, *Weale*, 1850. 12°.
— DOWNING, A. J. Warming and ventilation. (*In his* Archit. of country houses. 1854.)
— FORBES, *Sir* J. S. Ventilation and heating. (*In* **Nat. Assoc. Prom. Soc. Sci.** Trans., 1860.)
— SER, L. Chauffage et ventilation. (*In* **France. Com.** *Imp. de l'Expos. de* 1867. Rapports, v. 3.)
See also **Heat**; — **Ventilation.**

Warne, Joseph A. Harmony between phrenology and revelation. (*In* **Combe,** G. Constitution of man. 1838.)

Warnefridi, Paulus. *See* **Paulus Warnefredi.**

Warner, *Rev.* Aaron. Memoir of Florence Kidder. Boston, 1832. 18°.
— Sermon, Wolfborough, Nov. 1, 1838, ordination of J. Blake. Gilmanton, N. H., 1839. 8°. (B 1324)

Warner, *Rev.* Abner B. The unwise inquiry; thanksgiving sermon, Milford, N. H., Dec. 22, 1842. Nashua, 1843. 8°. (B 1254)

Warner, Anna B., (*pseud.* **Amy Lothrop**). Dollars and cents. N. Y., 1852. 2 v. 12°.

Warner, Charles Dudley. My summer in a garden. Boston, 1871. 16°.

Warner, *Maj.* Charles L. Sketches of the life and adventures of W., more familiarly known as Davy Crockett, 2d. Toledo, 1843. 8°. (B 1461)

Warner, Daniel, *Funeral sermon on.* 1813. *See* **Bradford,** F. P. (C 202)

Warner, Edward. Overland Traction Engine Company; reports. *See* **Robinson,** A. P.

Warner, Ferdinando, *LL.D.* History of England as relates to religion and the Church. London, 1759. 2 v. f°.
Contents. Vol. 1. 50–1485. 2. 1485–1700.
— History of the rebellion and civil war in Ireland. London, 1767. 4°.

Warner, H. G. Winds and rains of California. (*In* **Amer. Assoc.** Proc., v. 12. 1859.)

Warner, H. W. Address before the Auxiliary N. Y. Bible Society. N. Y., 1813. 8°. (B 461)

Warner, Henry W. The liberties of America. N. Y., 1853. 12°.

Warner, Hermann Jackson. Visit to Bethlehem; a Christmas lesson. Boston, 1865. 12°. (C 275)

Warner, James F. Universal dictionary of musical terms. Boston, 1842. 8°.

Warner, John, *Bp. of Rochester.* Correspondence with J. Taylor. (*In* **Taylor,** J. Works, v. 7. 1850.)

Warner, Joseph. Cases in surgery. 4th ed. with add. London, 1784. 8°.

Warner, Richard. Literary recollections. London, 1830. 2 v. 8°.

Warner, Seth. CHIPMAN, D. Memoir of W. Middlebury, 1848. 16°.
— HOUGHTON, G. F. Sketch of the life of W. (*In his* Outline of the controversy. 1849. B 1610)

Warner, Susan (*pseudon.* **Elisabeth Wetherell**). The hills of the Shatemuc. N. Y., 1856. 12°.
— The house in town. N. Y., 1872 [1871]. 16°.
— The old helmet. N. Y., 1864. 2 v. 12°.
— Queechy; by E. Wetherell. N. Y., 1852. 2 v. 12°.
— What she could. N. Y., 1871. 8°.
— The wide, wide world; by E. Wetherell. N. Y., 1851. 2 v. 12°.
— FORGUES, P. E. D. (*In* **Revue d. D. Mondes,** août 1853.)

Warner, Thomas. Brief outline of the history of the Bible; sermon, Hudson, Sept. 10. N. Y., 1817. 8°. (B 956)

Warner, Wm. Works. (*In* **Chalmers,** A. Eng. poets, v. 4. 1810.) — [Extracts from] 'Albion's England'. (*In* **Campbell,** T. Brit. poets, v. 2. 1819.)

Warner, *N. H.* LONG, M. Historical sketches of W. (*In* **New Hamp. Hist. Soc.** Col., v. 3. 1832.)

Warning to the democracy, A. [1840?] 8°. (B 1498)

Warnings. *See* **Omens.**

Warnkoenig, Leopold August. Analyse du 'Traité de la possession' par Savigny. 3e éd. Liége, 1827. 8°. (B 1859)
— Eléments de droit romain privé; tr. du latin sur la 2e éd. Paris, 1827. 8°.

Warr in New England, The, visibly ended; [by R. H.]. 1677. (*In* **Drake,** S. G. Old Indian chronicle. 1867.)

Warr, G. Finden. Dynamics, construction of machinery, equilibrium of structures, and strength of materials. London, 1851. 8°.

Warrants. CONSIDERATIONS on the legality of general warrants. 2d ed. London, 1765. 8°. (B 361)
— LETTER [to J. Almon] concerning libels, warrants, *etc.* 5th ed. London, *J. Almon*, 1765. 8°. (B 706)

Warranty. *See* **Domestic animals** (HUZARD, LEVINAS).

Warren, *pseud.* Antidote to J. Wood's poison. N. Y., 1802. 8°. (B 622)
— WOOD, J. Remarks on W.'s pamphlet. (*In his* Full exposition, *etc.* 1802. B 622)

Warren, —. *See* **Kittredge** *vs.* **Warren.** 1844. (B 1436)

Warren, —. GR. BRITAIN. *Parl.* Correspondence with the U. S. resp. the imprisonment of Warren and Costello. London, [1868]. f°. (N. A., no. 2. E 242)

Warren, Charles. Address, Palmyra, July 4. Hallowell, 1823. 8°. (B 557)

Warren, *Capt.* Charles. Excavations at Jerusalem. (*In* **Morrison,** W. Recovery of Jerusalem. 1871.)

Warren, Charles H. Uniform of the revolutionary army. — Washington not a marshal of France. (*In* **Mass. Hist. Soc.** Proc., 1858–60.)

Warren, Cyrus Mores. Success of fractional condensation. — Researches on the volatile hydro-carbons. (*In* **Amer. Acad.** Mem., n.s., v. 9, pt. 1. 1867.)
— *and* Storer, F. H. Examination of a hydro-carbon naphtha obtained from the products of the destructive distillation of lime-soap. — Examination of naphtha obtained from Rangoon petroleum. (*In* **Amer. Acad.** Mem., n.s., v. 9, pt. 1. 1867.)

Warren, *Mrs.* E. Comfort for small incomes. 3d Amer. ed. Boston, 1866. 12°.
— How I managed my house on two hundred pounds a year. 6th Amer. ed. Bost., 1866. 12°.

Warren, Edouard, *comte* de. [Several articles.] (*In* **Revue** d. D. Mondes, fév. 1844 – mars 1847.)

Warren, Edward. Exceptions against the theory of the Earth. (*In* **Burnet,** T. Sacred theory of the Earth. 1691.)
— Geologia; or, Discourse conc. the Earth before the deluge. London, 1690. 4°.

Warren, Edward, *M.D.* Life of J. C. Warren. Boston, 1860. 2 v. 8°.
— *Same.* (*In* **Gross,** S. D. Lives of eminent Amer. physicians. 1861.)
— On scrofula, rheumatism, and erysipelatous inflammation. Phila., 1840. 8°. (Boylston prize diss., 1838–39.)
— Sketch of the progress of the malignant or epidemic cholera. Boston, 1832. 8°. (B 1569)

Warren, Edward, *of Palmyra, Me.* Some account of the letheon; or, Who is the discoverer? 3d ed. Boston, 1847. 8°. (B 1566)

Warren, Edward, *M.D., Prof. Univ. Maryland.* An epitome of practical surgery for field and hospital. Richmond, 1863. 12°.

Warren, Emory F. Sketches of the history of Chautauque Co., N. Y. Jamestown, 1846. 12°.

Warren, George John Venables Vernon, *5th Lord Vernon.* Chiose sopra Dante, testo inedito. Firenze, 1846. 8°.
— L'Inferno di Dante Alighieri disposto in ordine grammaticale corredato di brevi dischiarazioni. Londra, stampato a Firenze, 1858–65. 3 v. f°.
Note. For contents *see* **Dante.**

Warren, George Washington. Address, 1865, 68, 69. (*In* **Bunker Hill Mon. Assoc.** Proc., 1865-69.)
— Valedictory poem, July 13. Camb., 1830. 8°. (H 2)

Warren, Gouverneur Kemble, *Maj. Gen.* Account of the operations of the 5th army corps at the Battle of Five Forks, April 1, 1865., *etc.* N. Y., 1866. 8°.
— Memoir to accompany the map of the territory of the U. S. from the Mississippi to the Pacific, giving an acct. of each of the exploring exped. since 1800, *etc.* (*In* **U. S.** *War Dept.* Reports of exploration for a R. R. to the Pacific, 1853-56, v. 11. 1861.) — HUMPHREYS, A. A. Examination of the reports of explorations for railroad routes, *etc.* (*In* v. 1. 1855.)

Warren, Henry. Address before the Roxbury Auxiliary Soc. for the Suppression of Intemperance, Oct. 25. Boston, 1821. 8°. (B 565)

Warren, Ira? Review of Rev. W. Croswell's letter to the Bishop of the diocese of Mass; by Laicus. Boston, 1845. 12°. (C 236)

Warren, James. Observations on the effects of light on vegetation. (*In* **Amer. Acad.** Mem., v. 2. 1793.)

Warren, John, *D.D., prebendary of Exeter.* Duæ conciones ad clerum habitæ in Templo B. Mariæ apud Cantabrigienses; hæc pro gradu baccalaureatus illa pro gradu doctoratus in sacra theologia. [Pp. 345-412 of v. 2 of W.'s sermons. London, 1739.] 8°. (B 1262)

Warren, John, *D.D., prebendary of Ely.* Sermon, anniversary of the sons of the clergy, May 14. London, 1778. 4°. (A 3, B 1269)

Warren, John, *M.D.* Charge to the Anc. and Hon. Fraternity of Free and Accepted Masons, Boston, on the festival of St. John the Baptist. *n.p.*, [1782]. 8°. (B 842)
— Eulogy on T. Russell, May 4. Boston, 1796. 8°. (B 651, 1694, D 2, W 81)
— History of a large tumour in the region of the abdomen, containing hair. (*In* **Amer. Acad.** Mem., v. 1. 1786.)
— Oration, July 4, 1783. Boston, [1783]. 4°. (A 6)
— View of the mercurial practice in febrile diseases. Boston, 1813. 8°.
— *Same.* (*In* **Mass. Med. Soc.** Med. com., v. 2. 1813.)
— BARTLETT, J. Oration, death of W. Boston, 1815. 8°. (B 357)
— BROWN, B. Life of J. W. (*In* **Gross**, S. D. Lives of eminent Amer. physicians. 1861.)
— JACKSON, J. Eulogy on W. Boston, 1815. 8°.
— - *Another copy.* (B 1227)
— - *Same.* (*In* **Mass. Med. Soc.** Med. com., v. 3. 1822.)
— LORING, J. S. (*In his* Hundred Boston orators. 1852.)
— MCKEAN, J. Sermon after the death of J. Warren. Boston, 1815. 8°.
— - *Another copy.* (B 322)

Warren, *Rev.* John B. Address, dedication of the Amer. Academy on the banks of the Mississippi, near Donaldsonville, La., June 7. Plaquemine, 1835. 8°. (B 1587)
— Discourse in Mobile. N. Y., 1829. 8°. (B 1310)

Warren, John Collins, *M. D.* Address before the American Medical Association, May 8. Boston, 1850. 8°.
— *Another copy.* (B 1564)
— Address to the Boston Society of Natural History. Boston, 1853. 8°.
— Case of strangulated crural hernia. (*In* **Mass. Med. Soc.** Med. comm., v. 1. 1808.)
— Cases of organic diseases of the heart. Boston, 1809. 8°.
— *Another copy.* (B 436)
— *Same.* (*In* **Mass. Med. Soc.** Med. comm., v. 2. 1813.)
— Comparative view of the sensorial and nervous system of man and animals. Bost., 1822. 8°.
— *Another copy.* (B 830)
— *Same.* (*In* **Mass. Med. Soc.** Med. comm., v. 3. 1822.)
— Description of an Egyptian mummy; with an account of embalming. From the Boston journal of philosophy and the arts. Boston, [1824]. 8°.
— Effects of chloroform and ether as narcotic agents. Boston, 1849. 8°. (B 1567)
— Etherization, with surgical remarks. Boston, 1848. 12°.
— Extracts from Dr. Warren's journal [in relation to temperance]. (*In* **Mass. Temp. Soc.** When will the day come? 1857.)
— Genealogy of Warren. Boston, 1854. 4°.
— Great tree on Boston Common. Bost., 1855. 8°.
— History of a wound of the femoral artery. (*In* **Mass. Med. Soc.** Med. comm., v. 1. 1808.)
— Inhalation of ethereal vapor for the prevention of pain in surgical operations. From the Boston med. and surg. journal. *n.t.p.* [Boston, 1847.] 8°. (E 69)
— Letter to I. Parker on the dislocation of the hip joint. Camb., 1826. 8°. (B 830)
— Mastodon angustidens. (*In* **Amer. Assoc.** Proc., v. 2. 1850.)
— The mastodon giganteus of North America. Boston, 1852. 4°.
— *Same.* 2d ed. Boston, 1855. 4°.
— Operation for emphyma encystis steatoma. (*In* **Mass. Med. Soc.** Med. comm., v. 4. 1829.)
— Physical education. (*In* **American Inst. of Instr.** Lectures, 1830.)
— Physical education and the preservation of the health. Boston, 1846. 18°.
— *Same.* With remarks on constipation, old age, use of alcohol in the preparation of medicine. Boston, 1854. 16°.
— Prevention of constipation. From Amer. journal of med. sciences for April 1850. Boston, 1850. 8°. (B 1564, C 271)
— Remarks on some fossil impressions in the sandstone rocks of Connecticut River. Bost., 1854. 8°.
— Report on spotted or petechial fever. (*In* **Mass. Med. Soc.** Med. comm., v. 2. 1813.)
— Surgical observations on tumours. Boston, 1837. 8°.
— Use of tobacco. (*In* **Mass. Temp. Soc.** Addresses. 1861.)
— WARREN, E. Life of J. C. Warren. Boston, 1860. 2 v. 8°.
— - *Same.* (*In* **Gross**, S. D. Lives of Amer. physicians. 1861.)

Warren, Jonathan Mason, *M.D.* Account of two Indian dwarfs exhibited as Aztec children. From the Amer. journal of med. sci. Boston, 1851. 8°.
— Additions. (*In* **Walshe**, W. H. Anat. of cancer. 1840.)
— Amputation at the hip joint for a large asteo-sarcomatous tumor of the femur. From the Boston med. and surg. journal. *n.t.p.* [Boston, 1859.] 8°. (B 1564, E 70)
— Cases of occlusion of the vagina. From the Amer. journ. of med. sci. Boston, 1853. 8°.
— *Other copies.* (B 1564, E 70)
— Cystic tumors of the jaw. *n.t.p.* [1866.] 8°. (B 1692)
— Division of the sterno mastoid muscle for wry neck. (*In* **Boston** med. and surg. journ., v. 25, no. 8. 1841; *also* E 70) — Tumors in the parotid region. (*In* v. 56, no. 15. 1857; *also* E 70)
— Fissure of the soft and hard palate. From the Trans. of the American Med. Assoc. Phila., 1865. 8°.
— Foreign bodies in the air passages. From Bost. med. and surg. journ., Dec. 1847. *n.t.p.* [Boston, 184-.] 8°. (E 69)
— Inhalation of ether. From the Boston med. and surg. journ. *n.t.p.* [Boston, 1847.] 8°. (B 1567, E 69, 70)
— Ligature of both carotid arteries for an erectile tumour on the mouth, face, and neck. From the Amer. journ. of med. sci., April. Boston, 1846. 8°. (B 1564, E 69)
— Ligature of the left subclavian artery. From the Amer. journal of med. sci. Boston, 1849. 8°. (B 1564, E 69, 70)
— Lithotrity and lithotomy with the use of ether. From the Amer. journ. of the med. sci. Boston, 1849. 8°. (B 1567, E 70)
— Operation for artificial anus. From Amer. journ. of med. sci. *n.t.p.* [Boston, 1848.] 8°. (E 69, 70)
— Operation for fissure of the soft and hard palate, with the result of twenty-four cases. From the Amer. journ. of the med. sciences, Apr. Boston, 1848. 8°. (B 1564, E 69, 70)

— Recent progress in surgery; annual address before the Mass. Med. Soc., May 25. Boston, 1864. 8°.
— *Same.* (*In* **Mass. Med. Soc.** Med. comm., v. 10. 1866.)
— Rhinoplastic operations. From the Boston med. and surg. journ. Boston, 1840. 8°.
— *Another copy.* (B 1564)
— Supposed encephaloid testicle; hermaphrodism. From the Amer. journ. of med. sci., July. Boston, 1859. 8°. (B 1564, E 70)
— OBITUARY of W. (*In* **Mass. Med. Soc.** Med. comm., v. 1. 1867.)

Warren, *Gen.* Joseph. Oration, Mar. 6, to commemorate the 5th of Mar. 1770. N. Y., 1775. 8°. (B 517)
— *Same.* (*In* **Orations** to commemorate the 5th of Mar. 1770. 1785; 1807; — *and in* **Moore,** F. Amer. eloquence, v. 1. 1864.)
— BROWN, *Mrs.* R. Stories about Gen. Warren. Boston, 1835. 18°.
— BUNKER HILL MONUMENT Assoc. Inauguration of the statue of Warren, June 17, 1857. Boston, 1858. 8°.
— EULOGIUM on W.; by a Columbian. Boston, 1781. 8°. (B 555)
— EVERETT, A. H. Life of W. (*In* **Sparks, J.** Amer. biog., v. 10. 1838.)
— FROTHINGHAM, R. Life and times of J. Warren. Boston, 1865. 8°.
— KNAPP, S. L. (*In his* Biog. sketches. 1821.)
— LORING, J. S. (*In his* Hundred Boston orators. 1852.)
— MORTON, P. Oration, re-interment of J. Warren. (*In* **Orations** commem. of the 5th of March 1770. 1785; 1807.)
— SKETCH.] (*In* **Longacre, J. B.,** *and* **Herring, J.** Nat. portr. gal., v. 2. 1835.)
— WILSON, T. (*In his* Biog. of Amer. military heroes, v. 1. 1817.)

Warren, Josiah Fiske, *Funeral sermon on.* 1853. *See* **Kirk,** E. N. (B 1594)

Warren, *Mrs.* Mercy (Otis). The group; [a comedy]. Boston, 1775. 8°. (B 616, C 167)
— *Another copy, with a ms. list of the characters.* (C 190)
— History of the rise, progress, and termination of the American Revolution, Boston, 1775. Boston, 1805. 3 v. 8°.
— Poems, dramatic and miscellaneous. Boston, 1790. 12°.
Note. Contains two tragedies: The sack of Rome; and The ladies of Castile.

Warren, Samuel, *D.C.L.* Miscellanies, critical, imaginative, and juridical, contributed to Blackwood's magazine. Edin., 1855. 8°.
Contents. The bracelets; a tale. — My first circuit; law and facts from the North. — Sir Wm. Follett, knight, attorney-general. — Memoir of J. W. Smith, of the Inner-Temple, barrister-at-law. — Who is the murderer? a problem in the law of circumstantial evidence. — The Duke of Marlborough. — The paradise in the Pacific. — Uncle Tom's cabin. — Calais. — Pegsworth; a press-room sketch. — The mystery of murder, and its defence. — Modern state trials: The Welsh rioters; — High treason and murder; — Moral insanity; — The romance of forgery; — Duelling; and 'What's in a name?'; — The murdered Glasgow cotton-spinner, and the trials of D. O'Connell and Wm. S. O'Brien. — The martyr patriots. — Speculators among the stars. — A few personal recollections of Christopher North.
— Now and then. N. Y., 1848. 12°.
— Passages from the diary of a late physician. From 5th Lond. ed. N. Y., 1862–63. 3 v. 12°.
Note. From Blackwood's mag., v. 28–42. 1830–37.
— Suggestions for a more speedy, frequent, and economical administration of criminal law. (*In* **Nat. Assoc. Prom. Soc. Sci.** Trans., 1857.)
— Ten thousand a year. Phila., 1840. 3 v. 12°.
Note. From Blackwood's mag., v. 46–50. 1839–41.

Warren, Thomas Alston. Address on cow-pox. London, 1803. 8°. (B 812, D 59)

Warren, Wm. Wilkins. Life on the Nile, and a tour in Syria and Palestine, 1866–67. Paris, 1867. 16°.

Warren family. WARREN, J. C. Genealogy of Warren. Boston, 1854. 4°.

Warren, *Maine.* EATON, C. Annals of Warren: early settlement on the Waldo Patent. Hallowell, 1851. 8°.

Warren, *N. H.* LITTLE, W. The history of Warren. Manchester, 1870. 8°.

Warren, *R. I.* FESSENDEN, G. M. History of Warren. Prov., 1845. 18°.
Note. Pub. as a supplement to the next entry.
— TUSTIN, J. P. Discourse at the dedication of the Baptist Church. Prov., 1845. 18°.

Warren, Fort. *See* **Lafayette, Fort.**

Warren Association. Minutes of the Assoc., Wrentham, Sept. 7, 8. Boston, 1802. 8°. (B 154) — Newton, Sept. 13, 14. 1808. Boston, [1808]. 8°. (B 886) — Providence, Sept. 11th and 12th. Boston, 1810. 8°. (B 431) — Boston, Sept. 10, 11. 1811. Boston, [1811]. 8°. (B 459) — Bridgewater. Boston, 1818. 8°. (B 468)

Warren Bridge. MASS. *Attorney Gen.* Report rel. to W. Bridge. [Bost., 1835.] 8°. (Sen. Doc. 2. **A 43**)
See also **Charles River Bridge.**

Warren Co., *N. J.* WALLING, H. F. Map. N. Y., 1860.

Warren Hastings, *ship.* LARKINS, T. Statement of facts subsequent to striking the French frigate La Piémontaise. London, 1807. 8°. (C 115)

Warren Street Chapel. *See* **Boston. Warren St. Chapel** (p. 348).

Warreniana; with notes. Boston, 1851. 12°.
Note. Parodies, purporting to be puffs of Warren's blacking.
Contents. G. (Gifford), W. Introd. — I. (Irving), W. Warren. — W. (Wordsworth), W. Old Cumberland pedlar. — H. (Hogg), J. Warren in fairy land. — H. (Hunt), L. A nursery ode. — M. (Mills), C. Family of Warren at the time of the crusades. — S. (Southey), R. Carmen triumphale. — T. (Townshend), C. H. Triumph of Warren. — C., B. (Barry Cornwall). The girl of Saint Mary-Axe. — B. M. (Blackwood's mag.). The sable school of poetry. — B. (Byron), *Ld.* The Childe's pilgrimage. — C. (Coleridge), S. T. The dream, a psychological curiosity. — N. M. M. (New monthly mag.). Annus mirabilis. — R. of the T. (Reporter of the Times). Warren at Saint Stephen's. — S. (Scott), *Sir* W. Battle of Brentford Green. — J. B. (John Bull). Letter to the ed. of Warreniana; — Song. — G. (Gifford), W. Appendix; — Notes.

Warrington, Lewis, *Capt. U. S. N.* WILSON, T. (*In his* Biog. of Amer. mil. heroes, v. 2. 1819.)

Warrington, Thomas. Trial for murder on the high seas. *See* **Holmes, W.** (B 561)

Warrington, Wm. History of stained glass. London, 1848. f°.

Warrington, *Eng.* WARRINGTON in 1465 as described in a contemporary rent roll of the Legh family; ed. by W. Beamont. Manchester, 1849. 4°. (Chetham Soc., v. 17.)

Warrock's Virginia and North Carolina almanac, 1865. 50th ed. Richmond, *n.d.* 12°.

Wars. CUST, *Sir* E. Annals of the wars of the 18th cent. London, 1856–60. 5 v. 16°.
— - Annals of the wars of the 19th century. London, 1862–63. 4 v. 16°.
See also **Crimean War; — Peasants' War; — Peninsular War; — Pequot War; — Seven Years' War; — Thirty Years' War; — Vendee, War of the;** — *also* **Military history; — Sieges;** — *also* the division *History* under various countries.

Wars of the Gulls; an historical romance. N. Y., 1812. 8°. (B 450)

Warsaw. *See* **Matthiasstift; — Wola,** *fort near Warsaw.*

Warsaw, Diocese of. CATALOGUS episcoporum Wratislaviensium. (*In* **Stenzel, G. A. H.** Script. rer. Siles., v. 2. 1839.)

Warsaw, Grand Duchy of. PRADT, D. D. de. Histoire de l'ambassade en 1812. 7e éd. Paris, 1816. 8°. (B 803)
— - *Same.* 8e éd. Paris, 1817. 8°.

Wartberge, Hermannus de. *See* **Hermannus** *de Wartberge.*

Wartburg bei Eisenach, Die; eine historische Skizze. Eisenach, 1845. 8°. (C 275)

Warter, John Wood. The seaboard and the down. London, 1860. 2 v. 16°.

Wartmann, Eliè. Report on the Trans. of the Soc. of Physics and Nat. Hist. of Geneva, June 1867 to June 1868. (*In* **Smithsonian Inst.** Reports, 1868.)

Warton, —. Instructions for using ervalenta [for] constipation. 3d Eng. tr. from 10th Fr. ed. Paris, 1844. 12°. (C 268)

— Obstinate, inveterate, *etc.*, constipation overcome by the use of natural means discovered in France. 5th English tr. from 22d French ed. Paris, 1844. 12°. (C 267)

Warton, Joseph. Essay on the genius and writings of Pope. 5th ed. corrected. London, 1806. 2 v. 8°.

— Essays on pastoral, didactic, and epic poetry. (*In* **Virgilius Maro**, P. Works, v. 1, 2. 1763.)

— Poems. (*In* **Campbell**, T. Brit. poets, v. 7. 1819.)

— Poetical works. (*In* **Chalmers**, A. Eng. poets, v. 18. 1810.)

— Cary, H. F. (*In his* Lives of Eng. poets. 1846.)

Warton, Thomas, *b.* 1687, *d.* 1745. Poems. (*In* Campbell, T. Brit. poets, v. 5. 1819.)

Warton, Thomas, *b.* 1728, *d.* 1790. History and antiquities of Kiddington. 3d ed. London, 1815. 4°.

— History of English poetry. New ed. [by R. Price]. London, 1824. 4 v. 8°.

Contents. Vol. 1. Preface by R. Price. — The origin of romantic fiction in Europe. — The introd. of learning into England. — The gesta Romanorum. — History of Eng. poetry to 1250. 2. 1250–1476. 3. 1476–1550. 4. 1550–1625.

— *Same.* With pref. by R. Price, and notes variorum; ed. by W. C. Hazlitt. London, 1871. 4 v. 8°.

Contents. Vol. 1. Preface. — Origin of romantic fiction in Europe. — Lais of Marie de France. — Introduction of learning into England. — Gesta Romanorum. — Seven sages; by T. Wright. 2. Anglo-Saxon period to Chaucer. 3. Chaucer to Surrey. 4. Sixteenth century.

— Mons Catharinæ, prope Wintoniam; poema. London, 1760. 4°. (A 69)

— Poetical works. 5th ed.; added, memoirs of his life and writings by R. Mant. Oxford, 1802. 2 v. 8°.

— Poems. (*In* **Anderson**, R. Brit. poets, v. 11. 1795.)

— Poems. (*In* **Chalmers**, A. Eng. poets, v. 18. 1810.)

— Poems. (*In* **Campbell**, T. Brit. poets, v. 7. 1819.)

— Remarks on Spenser's [poetry]. (*In* **Spenser**, E. Works, v. 2. 1805.)

— *and others.* Essays on Gothic architecture. 2d ed. London, 1802. 8°.

— Austin, W. S., *jr.* (*In his* Lives of the poets-laureate. 1853.)

— Carey, H. F. (*In his* Lives of Eng. poets. 1846.)

Warton Club. [Publications.] London, 1855. 8°.

Namely. History of Fulk Fitz-Warine; ed. by T. Wright.

Warville, Jean Pierre Brissot de. *See* **Brissot de Warville, J. P.**

Warwick, *Rev.* Arthur. Spare minutes. London, 1821. 16°.

Warwick, Robert E. Operation of poor laws. (*In* **Nat. Assoc. Prom. Soc. Sci.** Trans., 1862, 63.) — Treatment of the vagrant poor of the metropolis. (*In* 1866.)

Warwick, Wm. Atkinson, *ed.* *See* **Cambridge University.** Cambridge Univ. reg. for 1843.

Warwick, *Earls of.* Description of Beauchamp Chapel and of the monuments of the Earls in the Chapel. London, 1796. f°.

Warwick County, *Eng.* Wedge, J. General view of the agriculture of the County of Warwick. London, 1794. 4°. (W 75)

— Brewer, J. N. Warwickshire. (*In* **Beauties of Eng. and Wales**, v. 15, pt. 2. 1814.)

— Cooke, G. A. (*In his* Topography of Gr. Brit., v. 16. 182–.)

— White, W. All round the Wrekin. London, 1860. 8°.

See also **Coventry**; — **Stratford-upon-Avon.**

Warwick, Wybrandt van. Historische verhael vande reyse gedaen inde Oost Indien onder het beleydt van W. van Waerwijck als Admirael ende S. de Weert als Vice-Admirael, 1602. (*In* **Commelin**, I. Begin, v. 1. 1646.)

Note. For other accounts of the same voyage, *see* **Purchas.** Pilgrimes, v. 1. 1625; — **Harris**, J. Col., v. 1. 1705; — *and, Germ.*, **Allgemeine** Hist., v. 8. 1751.

Was sich der Wald erzält; von G. zu Putlitz. Boston, [18—]. 8°. (E 24)

Waser, Kaspar. Niceron, J. P. (*In his* Mém., v. 24. 1733.)

Washbourn, John. Bibliotheca Gloucestrensis; a col. of tracts rel. to the county and city of Gloucester. Gloucester, 1825. 4°.

Contents. **Webb**, J. Hist. introd., with notes. — **Corbet**, J. Hist. relation of military government of Gloucester. — **True** relation of late attempt made upon town of Ciceter, Jan. 7, 1642. — **Particular** relation of action before Cyrencester in Glocestershire, taken in on candlemas day, 1642, by the army under Prince Rupert. — **Relation** of the taking of Ciceter, Feb. 2, 1642. — **Petition** of inhabitants of Cyrencester, presented to his Majesty at Oxford; with his Majestie's answer thereunto. — **Victorious** and fortunate proceedings of Sir Wm. Waller and his forces in Wales, and other places since they left Malmsbury; a letter from Sir W. Waller and Sir A. Haslerig. — **True** relation of late fight betweene Sir Wm. Waller's forces and those sent from Oxford; with manner of Sir W. Waller's retreat to Bristol. — **Dorney**, J. Briefe and exact relation of most materiall, *etc.*, passages that hapned in the late siege laid before Glocester. — **True** relat. of the late exped. of Robert Earle of Essex for relief of Gloucester; with descript. of fight at Newbury. — **Foster**, H. True relation of marchings of regiments of trained bands of London, *etc.*, for reliefe of Glocester, Aug. 23 to Sept. 28. — **True** relation of severall passages which have happened to our army since it advanced towards Glocester, with manner of reliefe. — **Backhouse**, R. True relation of a wicked plot intended and still on foot against Glocester to betray the same into the hands of the cavaliers. — **Full** and exact relation of victorious proceedings of Col. Massy, governeur of Gloucester, May 7 to May 25, 1644. — **Great** victory obtained by Collonel Massey at storming of Sir J. Winter's house. — **Great Brit.** *Parliament.* Foure ordinances: 1st, for raising and maintaining of horse and foot garrison of Glocester; 2d, 3d, for a weekly assessment on Glocester, and continuance of the assessment; 4th, concerning Currans; — Ordinance for uniting certain churches, and for maintenance of preaching-ministers in Glocester. — Appendix.

Washbourne, Henry, *pub.* Book of family crests. 5th ed. London, 1847. 2 v. (v. 1 w.). 16°.

— Catalogue of books. London, 1834. 8°. (B 1669)

Washbourne, Thomas, *D.D.* Poems; ed. with memorial-introduction and notes, by A. B. Grosart. [Auburn,] 1868. 16°. (Fuller worthies' lib.)

Washburn, Alvan H. Old and new methods; address at the dedication of Academy Hall, Leicester Academy, Oct. 29. Boston, 1853. 8°. (B 1587)

Washburn, Charles A. History of Paraguay; with notes of personal observations. Boston, 1871 [1870]. 2 v. 8°.

Washburn, Emory. Address, festival of the bar of Worcester Co., Mass., Feb. 7. Worcester, 1856. 8°. (B 1589)

— Address, Mass. Charit. Mech. Assoc., Sept. 26, 1860. (*In* **Mass. Charit. Mech. Assoc.** 9th exhibition. 1860.)

— Address, 200th anniver. of the incorporation of Bridgewater. (*In* **Bridgewater.** Celebration. 1856.)

— Anniversary address, Boston Young Men's Christian Union, Nov. 26, 1855. Boston, 1856. 8°. (B 1588)

— Anniversary of the Mass. Temperance Soc.; annual address. Boston, 1839. 8°. (B 1653)

— Extinction of slavery in Massachusetts. (*In* **Mass. Hist. Soc.** Col., v. 34. 1858.)

— Historical sketches of the town of Leicester. Boston, 1860. 8°.

— Politica civil como un ramo de educacion en las escuelas. (*In* **Sarmiento**, D. F. Escuelas. 1866.)

— Political influence of school masters. (*In* **Amer. Inst. of Instr.** Lectures, 1835.)

— Professional training as an element of success and conservative influence; lecture, Jan. 11. Boston, 1861. 8°. (B 1430)

— Sketches of the judicial history of Massachusetts, 1630-1775. Boston, 1840. 8°.
— Slavery as it once prevailed in Massachusetts. (*In* **Massachusetts Hist. Soc.** Lectures, 1869.)
— Transfer of the colony charter of 1628 from Eng. toi Mass. (*In* **Mass. Hist. Soc.** Proc., 1858-60.) — Origin and sources of the bill of rights declared in the constitution of Mass. (*In* 1864-65.)
Washburn, Israel. Kansas and the Lecompton constitution; speech, Jan. 7. Wash., 1858. 8°. (**B 1509**)
— Plan for shortening the transit between N. Y. and London; speech, March 10, European and N. American railway. Wash., 1852. 8°. (**B 1505**)
— President's message and the slavery question; speech, Dec. 10. Wash., 1856. 8°. (**B 1480**)
— The Republican party; speech, Jan. 10. Wash., 1859. 8°. (**B 1508**)
— The Sandwich Islands; speech, Jan. 4. Wash., 1854. 8°. (**B 1506**)
— Speech on the bill to organize territorial governments in Nebraska and Kansas, Apr. 7. Wash., 1854. 8°. (**B 1509**)
Washburn, James. KNAPP, S. L. (*In his* Biog. sketches. 1821.)
Washburn, Peter T. Reports. *See* **Vermont.** *Adj.-Gen.*
Washburn, *Rev.* Royal. Evils which threaten our country; sermon, Amherst, fast day, Apr. 9. Amherst, 1829. 8°. (**B 1259**)
Washburn, Wm. Tucker. Fair Harvard. N. Y., 1869. 12°.
Washburn & Co. Amateur cultivator's guide. Boston, [1867]. 8°.
Washington, *pseud.* To the people of the U. S. on the choice of a President. Boston, 1812. 8°. (**B 442, W 4**)
Washington, B., *M.D.* Observations on yellow fever. *n.t.p.* [18—.] 8°. (**B 1104, E 59**)
Washington, Bushrod. BINNEY, H. B. Washington. Phila., 1858. 8°.
Washington, George, *Pres. of the U. S.* Writings, selected from the original mss.; with a life of the author. Boston, 1837. 12 v. 8°.

Contents. Vol. 1. Life. 2. Corresp., Mar. 1754-May 1775. 3. June 1775-July 1776. 4. July 1776-July 1777. 5. July 1777-July 1778. 6. July 1778-Mar. 1780. 7. Mar. 1780-Apr. 1781. 8. Apr. 1781-Dec. 1783. 9. Dec. 1783-Apr. 1789. 10. May 1789-Nov. 1794. 11. Nov. 1794-Dec. 1799. 12. Speeches to Congress. — Messages. — Proclamations. — Addresses. — Appendix: Correspondence on agriculture, *etc.* — Indexes.

— *Germ.* Leben und Briefwechsel Georg Washingtons; hrsg. von F. von Raumer. Lpz., 1839. 2 v. 8°.

Contents. Vol. 1. Leben. 2. Auszüge aus Washingtons Schriften.

— Address to his fellow citizens on declining being a candidate for their future suffrage. Boston, 1796. 8°. (**W 13b**)
— *Same.* (*In* **Abbott**, A. Eulogy. 1800. **B 1914, E 48**)
— *Same.* Address to the people of U. S. *n.t.p.* [18—?] 8°. (**B 741**)
— *Same.* Salem, 1800. 8°. (**E 109**)
— *Same.* (*In* **Forbes**, E. Eulogy. 1800; — **Frisbie**, L. Eulogy. 1800; — **Morse**, J. Prayer and sermon. 1800; — *and in* **West**, S. Greatness the result of goodness. 1800.)
— *Same.* Farewell address. *n.t.p.* [1796.] 8°. (**B 1914**)
— *Same.* (*In* **Mass.** Constitution, *etc.* 179-.)
— *Same.* Albany, 1812. 12°.
— *Same.* (*In* **Freeman's** guide. 1812; — *and in* **Moore**, F. Amer. eloq., v. 1. 1864.)
— *Same.* N. Y., 1850. f°.
— *Same.* Valedictory address, on declining being candidate for presidency of U. S. *n.t.p.* [18—?] 8°. (**B 173, 2510, E 162**)
— *Same. n.p.*, 1812. 32°.
— *Same.* (*In* **Kirkland**, J. Discourse. 1800. **B 173, 2510, E 162, W 50**)
— *Same.* Versification of W.'s Farewell address; by a gentleman of Portsmouth, N.H. [J. M. Sewall]. 1798. 4°. (**B 650**)
— Col. of speeches to Congress, *etc.*; also, address to the President with his answer; with app. cont. the Circular letter to the governors of the several states, *etc.* Bost., July, 1796. 12°.
— *Same, with a correction.* Boston, 1796. 16°.
— Diary, Oct. 1, 1789 to Mar. 10, 1790; [ed. by B. J. Lossing]. N. Y., 1858. 8°.
— Diary, 1789-91; with his journal of a tour to the Ohio, 1753; ed. by B. J. Lossing. N. Y., 1860. 12°.
— Epistles, domestic, confidential, and official, [including the spurious letters]. N. Y., 1796. 8°.
— Farewell address. *See, above,* 'Address'.
— Inaugural address, 1789. (*In* **Moore**, F. Amer. eloq., v. 1. 1864.)
— Journal, [Apr. 2-June 27, 1854]. (*In* **France.** Memorial cont. a summary view of facts. 1757. **B 618, D 53, 56**)
— Journal of W. sent by R. Dinwiddie to the commandant of the French forces on the Ohio, [Oct. 31, 1753-Jan. 16, 1754]; with a new map. Williamsburgh *printed*, London *reprinted* 1754. 12°. (**B 922**)
— Resignation and address, in a circular letter to the President of New Hampshire. Exeter, 1783. 4°.
— *Another copy.* (**B 14**)
— *Same, entitled* Last official address; [with] papers rel. to half-pay. Hartford, 1783. 8°. (**B 1005, 1092**)
— *Same, entitled* Col. of papers, *etc.* Boston, 1783. 4°. (**B 518**)
— Last will and testament of Washington. Boston, 1800. 8°. (**B 2509, W 55**)
— *Same.* Phila., 1800. 8°. (**E 61**)
— Letter to Gen. Burgoyne. (*In* **Burgoyne**, J. Substance of speeches. 1778.)
— Letter to Gen. Knox, 1789. (*In* **Maine Hist. Soc.** Col., v. 4. 1856.)
— Letter to Gov. Hamilton rel. to surrender of the fort in the forks of Monongahela to the French, 1754. (*In* **Mass. Hist. Soc.** Col., v. 6. 1799.) — Letter to J. Williams, 1795. (*In* Proc., 1866-67.)
— Letters to A. Young, cont. an account of his husbandry. London, 1801. 8°. (**W 12**)
— Letters to A. Young and Sir J. Sinclair; an account of his husbandry and of the rural economy of the U. S. Alexandria, 1803. 8°.
— Letters to his friends in 1776, in which is set forth a view of Amer. politics. London, 1777. 8°. (**B 385**)
— *Same.* Phila., 1795. 8°. (**B 356**)
— *Same.* With J. Duché's letter to Washington, and answer by J. Parke. London, 1778. 8°. (**B 364, C 74, 106**)
— Letters to J. Belknap. (*In* **Mass. Hist. Soc.** Proc., 1858-60.)
— Letters [fac-simile] to Sir J. Sinclair on agricultural and other interesting topics. London, 1800. 4°.
— Official letters to Congress during the war between the Colonies and Gr. Britain. London, 1795. 2 v. 8°.

Contents. Vol. 1. June 1775-Dec. 1776. 2. Jan. 1777-Dec. 1778.

— *Same.* Boston, 1795. 2 v. 8°.
— Political legacies; [with] an app. cont. account of his death, with biog. outline of his life. Boston, 1800. 8°.

Contents. Dedication to Mrs. Washington. — App't to command of the army, 1775. — Order on cessation of hostilities. — Circular letter to the governors of the several states, 1783. — Address of Congress on acknowledgment of his services. — Answer. — Farewell address to the army. — Address to Congress on resigning his commission. — Answer. — Inaugural speech to Congress, 1789. — Valedictory address to his fellow citizens. — Letter to Pres. Adams on accepting command of the army, 1798. — Gen. Marshall's address to the speaker of the House on the death of W. — President's message to Congress, enclosing Col. Lear's letter, announcing the death of W. — Gen. Marshall's second address. — Resolutions of Congress resp. suitable honors to the memory of W. — Condolence from the House to the Pres. — Answer. — Condolence from the Senate to the Pres. — Answer. — Resolutions of Congress for perpetuating the memory of W. — Gen. Lee's Eulogy before the nat. legislature. — President's proclamation. — Acc't of the last illness of W. — Funeral. — President's message to Congress communicating Mrs. Washington's letter. — Biog. outline of W. — Anon. address to the army, 1783. — W.'s address in answer.

— Resignation and address, 1783. *See, above,* Last official address.
— Revolutionary orders of W. issued during 1778, 80, 82; selected from the mss. of J. Whiting; ed. by H. Whiting. N. Y., 1844. 8°.
— Selections from correspondence of W. and J. Anderson. Charlestown, 1800. 8°. (B 594, 971, 1879)
— Unpublished letters to Hon. Meshech Weare and others. (*In* N. H. Hist. Soc. Col., v. 2. 1827.)
— Valedictory address. *See, above,* Address.

WORKS ABOUT WASHINGTON.

— BINNEY, H. Inquiry into the formation of W.'s 'Farewell address'. Phila., 1859. 8°.
— FAC SIMILES of the memorial stones of the last English ancestors of W. in the church of Brington, Northamptonshire, Eng.; placed in the State House, Mass. Boston, 1862. 8°.
— MAZZEI, P. Du général Washington et du marquis de la Fayette, relativement à la Société de Cincinnatus. (*In his* Recherches sur les Etats-Unis, v. 4. 1788.)
— NORTHMORE, T. W.; or, Liberty restored; poem. Balt., 1809. 12°.
— - *Same.* Balt., 1812. 12°.
— ODE in honor of the troops under Gen. W. who turned the tide of fortune against Britain. Albany, 1800. 8°. (C 116)
— POETICAL epistle to W.; annexed, sketch of W.'s life. London, *reprin.* 1780. 4°. (A 32, B 651, W, 30)
— UNITED STATES. *27th Cong. 3d sess.* Proceedings in the House on presentation of the sword of Washington and staff of Franklin, Feb. 7. Wash., 1843. 8°. (B 1499)
— WASHINGTON; a national poem. Pt. 1. *n.p.*, [184-]. 8°. (W 49)
— WASHINGTONIANA. Lancaster, 1802. 8°.

Contents. Biog. sketch. — Aikin, —. Tribute. — Eulogium by Gen. H. Lee, — W. Jackson, — S. Chaudron, — Dr. W. Linn, — F. Ames, — G. Morris, — W. C. Frazer, — G. Bedford, — J. Vining, — D. Ramsay, — G. Frelinghuysen, — C. P. Sumner, — S. Bayard, — W. Griffith, — R. Messenger, — S. S. Smith, — S. White, — D. M'Keehan, — R. Davidson, — J. Davis, — U. Ogden, — J. Croes, — E. C. Dick, — L. Fontanes. — Character of W. from a London paper. — Chastellux, F. J., *marquis* de. Portrait. — Brissot de Warville, J. P. Sketch from his 'Travels'. — Caldwell, C. Extract from a poem. — Paine, R. T., *Jr.* Tribute. — Lines from a London paper. — Death of W.; from a London paper. — *Appendix.* Washington, G. Circular letter; — Farewell address to the armies; — Address to the people on retiring from public life; — Letter to the Pres. on accepting the appointment of Com. in Chief; — Last will. — U. S. *Army.* Address of the officers to Cong., Dec. 1782. — Washington, G. Letter to Cong. rel. to the anon. letters. — 1st, 2d anonymous letter. — Washington, G. Speech to the officers rel. to the anon. letters; — Letter to the Pres. of Cong. on the same.

— WASHINGTONIANA. Balt., 1800, *privately reprinted* N. Y., 1865. 8°.

Contents. Biog. sketch of W. — App't to the army. — Orders on the cessation of hostilities. — Circular letter. — Address of Cong. acknowledging his services. — Answer. — Farewell orders to the army. — Answer. — Address to Cong. on resigning his com. — Answer. — Inaugural speech to Congress, 1789. — Valedictory address. — Letter to Pres. Adams on accepting command of the army, 1798. — Death. — Gen. Marshall's address to the House on the death of W. — President's message to Cong. inclos. Col. Lear's letter announcing the death of W. — Gen. Marshall's 2d address. — Resolutions of Cong. resp. honors to the memory of W. — Address of condolence from the House to the Pres. — Answer. — Address of condolence from the Senate. — Answer. — Resolutions of Cong. for perpetuating the memory of W. — President's proclamation. — Gen. Hamilton's introd. to his orders resp. the funeral solemnities by the army. — Resolves of Cong. resp. the obs. of Feb. 22, 1800. — President's 2d proclamation. — Acc't of the last illness and death of W. — Funeral. — President's message communicating Mrs. Washington's letter. — Tributes to the memory of W. in different parts of the U. S. and of Europe. — Fugitive pieces on W.

— WASHINGTON'S birthday; an historical poem with notes. Albany, 1812. 4°. (W 80)

See also U. S. *President*; — *also* Mt. Vernon Ladies' Assoc.; — *also* Northmore, T. Washington; — Thackeray, W. M. The Virginians. 1859.

Administration, military and civil.

— ADAMS, C. F. Remarks on the appointment of Washington to the command of the army. (*In* Mass. Hist. Soc. Proc., 1858-60.)
— CONDUCT of Washington compared with that of the present administration. Boston, 1813. 8°. (B 453)
— *Same.* FACTS and documents relating to the state of the controversy between Amer. and Gr. Brit. Boston, 1813. 8°. (B 453, 1000)
— DUANE, W. Letter to W. [with] strictures, on his address of Sept. 17, 1796; by J. Dwight [pseud.]. Phila., 1796. 8°. (B 356, 628)
— FIVE minutes answer to Paine's letter to W. London, 1797. 8°.
— *Another copy.* (B 343)
— GIBBS, G. Memoirs of the administration of W. and J. Adams; ed. from the papers of O. Wolcott. N. Y., 1846. 2 v. 8°.
— GUIZOT, F. P. G. Essay on the character and influence of W. in the Revolution of the U. S.; [tr. by G. S. Hillard]. Bost., 1840. 8°.
— - *Same.* Washington; tr. by H. Reeve. London, 1840. 12°.

Note. Prepared as an introduction to the Fr. abridgment of Sparks's ed. of W.'s Writings.

— HAVEN, C. C. Thirty days in New Jersey; Washington and his army in 1776, 77. Trenton, 1867. 8°.
— KENNEDY, P. Answer to Paine's letter to W. London, 1797. 8°. (B 525, 619)
— - *Same.* 3d ed. London, 1797. 8°.
— - *Same.* Phila., 1798. 8°. (W 60)
— MONUMENTS of patriotism; col. of documents connected with [his] military command and civil administration; [with] an eulogium on [his] character by W. Jackson. Phila., 1800. 8°.

Contents. Resolution of Congress to appoint a general. — Choice of W. — President's information to W. of his election. — Answer. — Com. appointed to draught a commission, *etc.* — Commission. — Extracts from W.'s letters resp. the evacuation of Boston. — Resolution of thanks by Congress to W., *etc.* — Communication to Congress resp. his refusal of a letter from Lord Howe; Congress approve. — Orders to the army. — Address to the officers conc. anon. papers, *etc.* — Proc. of the officers. — Circular letter. — Orders to the army on the cessation of hostilities. — Resolution by Congress in honor of W. — Address of the Pres. of Congress to W. — Reply. — Farewell orders to the armies. — Answer of the officers. — W.'s address to the Pres. of Congress, and resignation of his com. — President's reply. — Speeches, *etc.*, 1st-4th Congress. — Address to the people of the U. S. — Messages. — Proclamations. — Letter to the Sec. of State declaring certain letters to be forgeries. — Letter on accepting command of the army, 1798, to the Pres. of the U. S. — Eulogium on the character of W. by W. Jackson.

— MONUMENTS of W.'s patriotism. 4th ed. Wash., 1844. f°.

Contents. Fac simile of letters to the publisher. — Ancestry of W. — Chronol. statement of the events of his life. — Lines by Rev. W. Jay. — Monumental inscription. — Facsimile of W.'s acc't of pub. expenditures, 1775-83. — Appointed Com.-in-Chief. — His acceptance, commission. — Circular letter. — Resolution of Cong. to erect an equest. statue of W. — Visits Princeton by request of Cong. — Farewell address to the army. — Takes leave of the officers in N. Y. — Speech on resigning his com. — Inaugurated Pres. of the U. S. — Proclamation for a day of thanksgiving. — Farewell address to the people of the U. S. — Letter accepting command of the army, 1798. — Oration on the death of W. by Gen. H. Lee. — Const. of the U. S.

— NEW England patriot; a candid comparison of the principles and conduct of the Washington and Jefferson administrations, *etc.* Boston, 1810. 8°. (B 142, 437, 525)
— PAINE, T. Letter to W. on affairs public and private. Phila., 1796. 8°. (B 356, 641, W 60)
— PRESIDENT II.; observations on the late official address of W. Newark, 1796. 8°. (W 50)
— PROMINENT political acts of W. (*In* U. S. *Constitution.* The constitution, *etc.* 1846.)
— REMARKS occasioned by the late conduct of W. as Pres. of the U. S. Phila., 1797. 8°. (B 397)

Biography.

— BANCROFT, A. Essay on the life of W. Worcester, 1807. 8°.
— - *Same.* London, 1808. 8°.
— - *Same.* Boston, 1825-26. 2 v. 12°.
— Βίος, μεταφρασθεὶς ἐκ τοῦ Ἀγγλικοῦ ὑπὸ Ν. Δραγουμη. Ἐν Ἀθήναις, 1856. 8°.
— BIOGRAPHICAL memoirs of W. New Haven, 1809. 12°.
— *Same.* Barnard, Vt., 1813. 12°.
— BIOGRAPHICAL memoirs of W. 4th ed. Brattleborough, 1811. 16°.
— *Same.* Brattleborough, 1814. 8°.
— BROUGHAM, H., *Lord.* (*In his* Hist. sketches, ser. 2. 1839.)
— CORRY, J. Life of W. 1st Amer. ed. N. Y., 1807. 12°.
— CUSTIS, G. W. P. Recollections of W.; with memoir of the author by his daughter; and notes by B. J. Lossing. N. Y., 1860. 8°.
— EDMONDS, C. R. Life and times of W. London, 1835-36. 2 v. 16°. (Fam. lib., v. 53, 54.)
— - *Same.* 2d ed. London, 1838. 2 v. 16°.
— ELSNER, H. Das Leben Washingtons. (*In his* Befreiungskampf. 1835.)
— EVERETT, E. Life of W. N. Y., 1860. 12°.
— GIRAULT, A. N. Vie de W. 10e éd. Phila., 1840. 12°.
— GLASS, F. Life of W., [in Latin prose]; ed. by J. N. Reynolds. N. Y., 1835. 12°.
— HEADLEY, J. T. Life of W. N. Y., 1856. 8°.
— - Washington and his generals. N. Y., 1847. 2 v. 8°.
— IRVING, W. Life of W. N. Y., 1855-59. 5 v. 8°.
— - *Same.* N. Y., 1856-59. 5 v. 12°.
— - *Same, on large paper.* N. Y., 1855-57. 4 v. 4°.
— - *Same.* (*In his* Works, v. 17-21. 1861.)
— KIRKLAND, C. M. Memoirs of W. N.Y., 1857. 12°.
— LIFE of W. Bridgeport, 1815. 18°.
— LIFE of W. New ed. Phila., *Amer. S. S. Union*, [1842]. 12°.
— MALDEN, H. (*In his* Disting. men of modern times, v. 4. 1838; v. 40 of Lib. ent. knl.)
— MARSHALL, J. Life of W. Phila., 1804-07. 5 v. 8° *and* Atlas.
— - *Same.* 2d ed. rev. Phila., 1832. 2 v. 8° *and* Atlas.
— - *Germ.* Lebensbeschreibung. Hamburg, 1805. 2 v. 8°.
— MEMORY of W.; a sketch of his life, and the national testimonials of respect; also, col. of eulogies and orations. Newport, 1800. 12°.
— MILITARY and civil life of W. N. Y., 1849. 8°. (Amer. biog. lib. W 49)
— MORSE, J. Biog. sketch of W. (*In his* Prayer and sermon. 1800. E 162, W 50)
— PARKER, T. (*In his* Historic Americans. 1870.)
— PAULDING, J. K. Life of W. N. Y., [1836]. 2 v. 12°. (Harper's fam. lib., v. 75, 76.)
— - *Same.* N. Y., 1836. 2 v. 12°.
— RAMSEY, D. Life of W. N. Y., 1807. 8°.
— - *Same.* 3d ed. Balt., 1814. 8°.
— - *Spanish.* La vida de W.; tr. por E. Barry. Filadelfia, 1826. 8°.
— RÉMUSAT, C. de. Vie, correspondance, et écrits de W. (*In* Revue d. D. Mondes, jan. 1840.)
— SCHROEDER, J. F. Life and times of W.; illust. by A. Chappel. N. Y., [1857]. 2 v. 4°.
— SKETCH.] (*In* Longacre, J. B., *and* Herring, J. Nat. portr. gal., v. 1. 1837.)
— SKETCH.] (*In* Patriarch, The. 1841. W 49)
— SPARKS, J. Life of W. (Vol. 1 *of* Washington, G. Writings. 1837.)
— - *Same, abridged.* Auburn, 1851. 2 v. in 1. 12°.
— - *Same.* Boston, 1852. 8°.
— - *Germ.* Leben. (Vol. 1 *of* Washington, G. Leben. 1839.)
— UPHAM, C. W. Life of W., in the form of an autobiography. Boston, 1840. 2 v. 8°.
— VENEDEY, J. Georg Washington; ein Lebensbild. Freiburg im Breisgau, 1861. 12°.
— WEEMS, M. L. History of the life and death of W. Georgetown, [1800]. 8°. (W 11)
— - Life of Washington. 10th ed. Phila., 1814. 8°.
— - *Same.* 29th ed. Frankford, 1826. 12°.
— - *Same.* Phila., 1833. 8°.
— - *Same.* Phila., 1837. 12°.
— WILSON, T. (*In his* Biog. Am. mil. heroes, v. 1. 1817.)

Biographical miscellany, Character, Portrait, etc.

— AMPÈRE, J. J. (*In* Revue d. D. Mondes, mai 1855.)
— CALDWELL, C. Character of W. Phila., 1801. 8°. (W 11, 52)
— CELEBRATION of W.'s birthday in Rome and Naples, Feb. 22, 1866. *n.p., n.d.* 8°.
— CLARK, W. G. Address on the characters of Lafayette and Washington, before the Wash. Soc. of Lafayette Coll., July 4. Phila., 1840. 8°. (B 1578)
— ENTERTAINING anecdotes of W. Boston, 1833. 12°.
— *Same.* Boston, 1839. 12°.
— FOX, C. Portrait of W. as he appeared while reviewing the continental army on Boston Common, 1776; hist. of the portrait and documentary evidence in proof of correctness of the likeness. Boston, 1851. 8°.
— GIST, C. Journal of a visit with Maj. Washington to the French commander on the Ohio. (*In* Mass. Hist. Soc. Col., v. 25. 1836.)
— LOSSING, B. J. Mount Vernon and its associations, hist., biog., and pictorial. N. Y., 1859. 8°.
— M'GUIRE, E. C. Religious opinions and character of W. 2d ed. N. Y., 1847. 12°.
— MEMORIALS of W. (*In* Young people's book, Nov. 1841. W 49)
— NOTT, S. Principles and character of W. (*In his* Lessons. 1841. C 209)
— ODE suggested by Rembrandt Peale's national portrait of W. Phila., 1824. 8°. (W 11)
— PETERS, R. Facsimile of Gen. W.'s hand writing, and sketches of his private character. *n.t.p.* [1811.] 8°. (W 11)
— PICKELL, J. New chapter in the early life of W., in connection with the history of the Potomac Company. N. Y., 1856. 8°.
— QUINCY, J. Description of the gorget of W. (*In* Mass. Hist. Soc. Proc., 1858-60.)
— QUÉNARD, P. (*In his* Portraits, v. 1. 1796.)
— REIMANN, E. Die Anfänge Washingtons [-1775]. (*In* Historische Zeitschrift, v. 4. 1860.)
— RITNER, J. Vindication of W. from the stigma of adherence to secret societies, Mar. 8, 1837. Boston, 1841. 8°. (B 1499, E 57)
— RUSH, R. Washington in domestic life; from original letters and ms. Phila., 1857. 8°.
— TUCKERMAN, H. T. Character and portraits of W. N. Y., 1859. 4°.
— - *Same, without the essay on portraits.* (*In his* Essays biog. and crit. 1857.)
— WARREN, C. H. Washington not a marshal of France. (*In* Mass. Hist. Soc. Proc., 1858-60.)
— WEBSTER, D. Character of W.; speech, 22 Feb., 1832. (*In his* Works, v. 1. 1851.)

Birthday, Death, Eulogies, etc.

— ACCOUNT of the death of Washington. (*In* Ulster County gazette, Jan. 4, 1800. W 49)
— ALSOP, R. Poem sacred to the memory of W. Hartford, 1800. 8°. (B 2510, E 162, W 11, 55)
— BAILEY, E. Triumphs of liberty; prize ode, Feb. 22. Boston, 1825. 8°. (B 1715)
— EULOGIES. *See 1st col.* MEMORY.
— EULOGIES and orations on W. Bost., 1800. 8°.
Contents. Lee, H. Oration at the request of Congress, Dec. 26, 1799. — Minot, G. R. Eulogy, Boston, Jan. 9,

1800. — **Sewall**, J. M. Eulogy, Portsmouth, N. H., Dec. 31, 1799. — **Morris**, G. Oration, New York, Dec. 31, 1799. — **Paine**, R. T. Eulogy, Newburyport, Jan. 2, 1800. — **Brooks**, J. Eulogy, Medford, Mass., Jan. 13, 1800. — **Ramsay**, D. Oration, Charleston, S. C., Jan. 15, 1800. — **Blake**, G. Masonic eulogy, St. John's Lodge, Feb. 4, [1800]. — **Ames**, F. Oration, Boston, Feb. 8, 1800. — **Bigelow**, T. Eulogy, before the Free-Masons, Boston, Feb. 11, 1800. — **Davis**, J. Eulogy, Boston, Feb. 19, 1800, Amer. Acad. of Arts and Sci. — **Linn**, W. Eulogy, Feb. 22, 1800, N. Y. Soc. of the Cincinnati. — **Smith**, J. Oration, Exeter, Feb. 22, 1800. — **Blyth**, J. Oration, All Saints' Parish, S. C., Feb. 22, 1800. — **Parker**, I. Oration, Portland, Feb. 22, 1800. — **Mason**, J. M. Oration, Feb. 22, 1800, by appointment of a number of the clergy of New York. — **Jackson**, W. Eulogium, Pennsylvania Society of the Cincinnati, Feb. 22, 1800. — **Sumner**, C. P. Eulogy, Milton, Feb. 22, 1800. — **Dunham**, J. Oration, Oxford, Mass., Jan. 15, 1800. — **Kirkland**, J. T. Discourse, Dec. 29, 1799.

— FUNERAL elegy for Feb. 22. *n.p.*, [18-]. obl. 8°. (W 49)

— HOLDEN, O. Sacred dirges, hymns, and anthems commemorative of the death of W. Boston, [1800]. f°.

— HOUGH, F. B. Washingtoniana; or, memorials of the death of W. Roxbury, 1865. 2 v. 8°.

— HYMNS and odes on the death of Washington, adapted to Feb. 22; [compiled by G. Richards?]. Portsmouth, 1800. 8°. (W 49)

— LEYDEN. GENOOTSCHAP KUNST WORDT DOOR ARBEID VERKREEGEN. G. Washington, lierzang. *n.p.*, [17–]. 4°.

— LINN, J. B. The death of W.; a poem. Phila., 1800. 8°. (W 55)

— LOVE, C. Poem, death of W. In 2 books. Alexandria, 1800. 12°.

— — *Another copy.* (C 146)

— LUNT, G. Washington and our own times; a lecture, Feb. 22. Boston, 1861. 12°. (C 273)

— ORATION in memory of the virtues of W., Feb. 22. N. Y., 1800. 8°. (W 55)

— POPKIN, J. S. The death of W. (*In* **Felton**, C. C. Memorial. 1852.)

— UNION BRIGADE. Proceedings on the death of W.; with Austin's prayer, and Capt. White's oration. *n.p.*, 1800. 8°. (E 61)

— PUBLIC expressions of grief for the death of W., Dorchester, [Feb. 22]. *n.p.*, [1800]. 8°.

— ROGERS, W. Prayer, Feb. 22, Phila., before the Penn. Soc. of the Cincinnati. Phila., 1800. 8°. (W 55)

— SKETCH of a discourse [on] the death of W. Dublin, 1800. 8°. (W 55)

— SPEECHES and other proc. at the pub. dinner in honor of the centennial anniv. of W.; with [his] farewell address. Wash., 1832. 8°. (B 1790, W 49)

— STRICKAND, W. Tomb of Washington at Mt. Vernon; added, His farewell address. Phila., 1840. 8°.

Note. The Library has also eulogies, addresses, orations, and sermons delivered upon the death of Washington by **Alden**, T., at Portsmouth, 1800 (B 268, 556, 916, E 48); — **Alexander**, C., Mendon, 1799 (E 162, W 50); — **Ames**, F., Boston, 1800 (B 138, 1721, 2510, E 61, W 55); — **Baldwin**, T., Boston, 1799 (B 173, W 50); — **Barnard**, T., Salem, 1799 (B 873, E 109); — **Bayard**, S., New Rochelle, 1800 (E 61, W 55); — **Beers**, W. P., Albany, 1800 (B 2511, E 48, W 80); — **Bigelow**, T., Boston, 1800 (E 61, W 52); — **Blake**, G., Boston, 1800 (B 142, 1839, 2510, E 61); — **Bowers**, J., Pittston, 1800 (A 38); — **Brooks**, J., Medford, 1800 (B 872, E 162, W 55); — **Buckminster**, J., Portsmouth, 1799 (W 50); — **Burrill**, G. R., Providence, 1800 (B 937, W 55); — **Chaudron**, S., Phila., 1800 (E 61, W 55); — **Croes**, J., Woodbury, 1800 (W 50); — **Cumings**, H., Billerica, 1800 (W 52); — **Davis**, J., Boston, 1800 (A 72, B 627, 2510, E 48, W 52); — **Dehon**, T., Newport, 1799 (E 162); — **Dunham**, J., Oxford, 1800 (E 48, W 55); — **Fisher**, N., Salem, 1799 (E 109); — **Fiske**, T., Cambridge, 1799 (B 173, W 50); — **Fontanes**, L., Paris, 1800 (E 48); — **Foster**, J., Cambridge, 1799 (B 173, W 50); — **Frisbie**, L., Ipswich, 1800 (B 222, E 48, W 52); — **Green**, A., Malden, 1800 (B 173); — **Harris**, T. M., Dorchester, 1799 (E 162); — **Holcombe**, H., Savannah, 1800 (B 318); — **Holmes**, A., 1799 (B 846, E 162, W 50); — **Keith**, I. S., Charleston, 1800 (*In his* Sermons. 1800); — **Kirkland**, J. T., Boston, 1799 (B 173, 2510, E 162, W 50); — **Lee**, *Maj. Gen.* H., Washington, 1800 (*In* **Moore**, F. Amer. eloquence; *also* B 142, 2510, E 61, W 55); — **MacWhorter**, A., Newark, 1799 (W 50); — **Miller**, S., New York, 1799 (B 2510, E 61); — **Minot**, G. R., Boston, 1800 (*In* **Moore**, F. Amer. eloq., v. 1; *also* B 138, 853, 2510, E 61, W 52); — **Morris**, G., N. Y., 1799 (B 2511, E 48, W 55); — **Morse**, J., Charlestown, 1799 (E 162, W 50); — **Osgood**, U., Newark, 1799; Belville, 1800 (W 52); — **Osgood**, D., Medford, 1799 (B 173, 229, E 162, W 50); — **Paine**, R. T., *Jr.*, Newburyport, 1800 (*In his* Works. 1812; *also* B 87, 1879, 2510, E 61, W 52); — **Patten**, W., Newport, 1799 (B 204, E 61); — **Payson**, P., Chelsea, 1800 (B 87, W 50); — **Pierce**, J., Brookline, 1800 (B 1914, E 48); — **Porter**, D., Spencertown, 1799, 1800 (C 61); — **Porter**, E., Roxbury, 1800 (B 229, E 48, W 52); — **Ramsay**, D., Charleston, 1800 (E 61, W 50); — **Sewall**, J. M., Portsmouth, 1799 (E 48, W 52); — **Smith**, S. S., Trenton, 1800 (B 2511, D 2, E 48, W 11, 55); — **Spaulding**, J., Salem, 1799 (E 109); — **Spring**, S., Newburyport, 1799 (B 955, W 50); — **Stillman**, S., Bost., 1799 (E 162); — **Story**, J., Marblehead, 1800 (B 61, E 61, W 52); — **Strong**, N., Hartford, 1799 (B 173, E 162); — **Thatcher**, T. C., Lynn, 1800 (E 61); — **Trumbull**, B., North Haven, 1799 (W 50); — **Ware**, H., Hingham, 1800 (B 172, 234, W 50); — **West**, S., Boston, 1799 (B 173, 846, E 162, W 50)

For other eulogies, addresses, orations, and sermons on Feb. 22, *see* **Abbot**, A., Haverhill, 1800 (B 1914, E 48); — **Allen**, J., Western, 1800 (B 555); — **Andrews**, E. W., Newburyport, 1816 (B 941, W 49); — **Andrews**, J., Newburyport, 1800 (B 937, W 52); — **Atherton**, C. H., Amherst, 1800 (B 627, E 48); — **Backus**, H. T., Norwich, 1832 (B 1572); — **Bancroft**, A., Worcester, 1800 (W 52); — **Barnes**, D., Scituate, 1800; — **Bartlett**, J., Charlestown, 1800 (B 955); — 1813 (B 937, W 49); — **Bascom**, J., Orleans, 1800 (W 55); — **Bates**, I. C., Northampton, 1812 (B 416, W 49); — **Bender**, H. R., Homer, 1813 (B 1572); — **Bigelow**, T., Boston, 1800 (W 52); — **Bishop**, S. G., Pittsfield, *N. H.*, 1800; — **Bradford**, A., Wiscasset, 1800 (E 61, W 52); — **Braman**, I., Rowley, 1800 (E 48); — **Briggs**, G. W., Salem, 1862 (B 1572); — **Broom**, J., N. Y., 1854 (B 1572); — **Burroughs**, C., Portsmouth, 1832 (B 1052); — **Caldwell**, C., Phila., 1810 (B 436, W 4); Lexington, 1832 (W 49); — **Carroll**, J., Baltimore, 1800 (W 50); — **Clack**, F. H., Emmettsburg, 1845 (B 1572); — **Cleaveland**, M., Windham, 1800 (B 937); — **Crafts**, W., Charleston, 1812 (W 49); — **Cunningham**, W., *Jr.*, Lunenburg, 1800 (E 162, W 52); — **Curtis**, B. R., Deerfield, 1832 (B 1572); — **Dana**, D., Newburyport, 1800 (B 1006, W 50); — **Dana**, J., Ipswich, 1800 (B 219, W 50); — **Dickins**, A., Phila., 1800 (E 48, W 52); — **Dunham**, J., Winsor, 1812 (B 410); 1814 (B 937, W 49); — **Elliott**, S., Brattleboro, 1812 (W 4); — **Dwight**, T., New Haven, 1800 (W 80); — **Ellis**, G. E., Charlestown, 1857 (B 1572); — **England**, J., *Bp. of Charleston*, Charleston, 1838 (*In his* Works, v. 4. 1849.); — **Erskine**, D. S., Edin., 1811 (B 787, W 11); — **Flint**, A., Hartford, 1800 (B 173); — **Flint**, J., Cohasset, 1832 (B 1828); — **Forbes**, E., Gloucester, 1800 (B 917, E 48); — **Fox**, T. B., Newburyport, 1832 (B 1572); — **Frelinghuysen**, F., New Brunswick, 1800 (W 55); — **Gleason**, B., Wrentham, 1800 (E 48, W 55); — **Gray**, F. C., Boston, 1832 (B 1052, 1721, 1804, 1808, 1828, W 49); — **Griffith**, W., Burlington, 1800 (E 61, W 55); — **Hanson**, C. W., Balt., 1811 (B 416); — **Heath**, U. S., Balt., 1812 (B 416); — **Hitchcock**, E., Providence, 1800 (B 204, E 61, W 50); — **Holley**, M., Canandaigua, 1812 (B 416); — **Holmes**, A., Cambridge, 1800 (B 173, W 50); — **Houdin**, M. G., Albany, 1800 (A 30); — **Huse**, J., Warren, 1800 (E 48); — **Jackson**, W., Phila., 1800 (B 2510, E 61, W 11, 45, 52); — **Johnson**, J., Westminster, 1832 (B 1572); — **Johnson**, J. B., Albany, 1800 (E 48); — **Kemp**, J., Easton, 1800 (E 61); — **Kendall**, J., Plymouth, 1800 (B 173, E 48); — **Knapp**, S. L., Newburyport, 1812 (B 937, W 49); — **Langdon**, C., Castleton, 1800 (E 162); — **Lee**, E., Sheffield, 1800 (E 162); — **Lincoln**, S., Plymouth, 1832 (B 1571, W 49); — **Lindsley**, P., Nashville, 1832 (B 1064); — **Linn**, W., New York, 1800 (B 2510, E 61, W 11, 52); — **Lisle**, H. M., Hingham, 1800 (E 162, W 52); — **Madison**, J., Williamsburg, 1800 (B 1006, W 50); — **Magaw**, S., Phila., 1800 (E 61); — **Marsh**, E. G., Wethersfield, 1800 (B 1006); — **Mason**, J. M., N.Y., 1800 (B 2510, E 61); — **Merrick**, P., Brookfield, 1800 (B 555); — **Messenger**, R., Old York, 1800 (E 48); — **Mitchell**, A. R., N. Yarmouth, 1800 (W 49); — **Morison**, W., Londonderry, 1800 (B 323); — **Morrell**, T., Baltimore, 1800 (W 50); — **Mycall**, J., Harvard, 1800 (E 162); — **Niles**, S., Abington, 1800 (E 162); — **Parish**, E., Byfield, 1800 (E 48, 61); — **Pickman**, B., Salem, 1797 (W 50); — **Pitman**, J., Providence, 1832 (B 1572); — **Pierce**, J., Brookline, 1800 (B 1914, E 48); — **Reed**, W. B., Phila., 1844 (B 1572); — **Richards**, G., Portsmouth, 1800 (E 48); —

Roberdeau, I., Johnsonbury, 1800 (W 55); — **Roche**, E., Wilmington, 1800 (E 48); — **Russell**, J. M., Boston, 1800 (B 937); — **Sanders**, D. C., Burlington, Vt., 1800 (A 30); — **Smith**, Jeremiah, Exeter, 1800 (E 162); — **Story**, I., Sterling, 1800 (E 162); — **Sumner**, C. P., Milton, 1800 (B 2510, E 61, W 52); — **Taggart**, S., Colrain, 1800 (E 48, W 50); — **Tappan**, D., Cambridge, 1800 (*In* Willard, J. Address in Latin. 1800); — **Thacher**, P., Boston, 1800 (B 173, 867, E 162, W 50); — **Thacher**, T., Dedham, 1800 (E 162); — **Tomb**, S., Newbury, 1800 (E 48); — **Tuckerman**, J., Boston, 1800 (B 61, 87, 872, E 61, W 55); — **Tufts**, C., Weymouth, 1800 (B 87, E 48, W 55); — **Ullmann**, D., New York, 1841 (B 1572); — **Vining**, J. Phila., 1800 (E 61, W 52); — **Wadsworth**, B., Danvers, 1800 (B 627, E 48); — **Waterman**, N., Bozrah. 1800 (B 555); — **Wetmore**, W., Castine, 1800 (E 61); — **Wheeler**, D. E., N. Y., 1851 (B 1572); — **White**, D. A., Methuen, 1800 (E 48); — **Whitney**, P., Northborough, 1800 (B 1078); — **Whitwell**, B., Augusta, 1800 (E 162); — **Willard**, J., Cambridge, 1800 (A 19, B 234, 867, 2510, E 61, W 50, 80); — **Wilson**, W. D., Littleton, 1839 (B 1572).

Eulogies on W. on other occasions by Clark, W. G., Easton, Pa., 1840 (B 1578); — **Holmes**, A., Cambridge, 1813 (B 457, 754, W 49); — **Winthrop**, R., Boston, 1859 (B 1611); — **Winthrop**, R. C., Wash., 1848 (B 1666).

Library.

— BOSTON ATHENÆUM. Subscribers for the purchase of a collection of books most of which formerly belonged to W. MS.

— - *Same, an incomplete list.* MS.

— - List of books formerly belonging to W., including books from the library at Mt. Vernon and books rel. to W. in the library of the Boston Athenæum, Boston, 1860. MS.

— WALL, W. L., & Co. Catalogue of rare books, incl. 200 from the library of W. *n.p.*, [1863]. 8°.
Note. The 200 were *not* from W.'s library.

Monument, Medals.

— AUTHENTIC account of the proc., July 4, with regard to laying the corner stone of the Washington monument in Baltimore; and biog. sketch of W. Balt., 1815. 8°.

— SNOWDEN, J. R. Description of the medals of W., *etc.*, in the Museum of the Mint. Phila., 1861. 4°.

— WASHINGTON MONUMENT ASSOCIATION. Proceedings to erect a monument [to] Gen. Washington; [with a ms. list of the subscribers. Boston, 1811.] f°.

— - *Same, without the list.* Boston, 1811. 16°. (C 64)

Writings.

— PAPERS rel. to the valedictory address of Pres. W. (*In* **Penn. Hist. Soc.** Mem., v. 1. 1826.)

— SPARKS, J. Remarks on a 'Reprint of the original letters from W. to Reed during the Revolution. Boston, 1853. 8°. (B 1601)

— - Reply to Lord Mahon and others on the mode of editing the Writings of W. Camb., 1852. 8°.

— - *Same.* Also, Review of Lord Mahon's 'History of the Amer. Revolution'. London, 1852. 8°.

— - *Another copy.* (B 1601)

Washington, *Capt.* John. Naval architecture and life-boats. (*In* **Soc. of Arts.** Lectures, 1851, 52.)

Washington, Jno. M. KERN, E. M. Map of the route pursued in 1849 by the U. S. troops under J. M. Washington, in an expedition against the Navajos Indians. Santa Fé, 1849.

Washington, *Mrs.* Martha Dandridge. [SKETCH.] (*In* **Longacre**, J. B., *and* **Herring**, J. Nat. portr. gal., v. 1. 1837)

Washington, Wm. Augustine, *Brig. Gen.* [SKETCH.] (*In* **Longacre**, J. B., *and* **Herring**, J. Nat. portr. gal., v. 3. 1836.)

Washington, Wm. Henry. Speech, bill to provide revenue from imports, *etc.* Wash., 1842. 8°. (B 1174)

Washington, *D.C.* Proceedings of the Corporation and citizens of Washington, on the occasion of the death of John Quincy Adams who died Feb. 23. Washington, 1848. 8°. (B 1207)

— *Public Schools.* CHANDLER, J. R. Address pub. sch. celebration, Aug. 1. Wash., 1850. 8°. (B 1205)

Description.

— WINCHESTER, E. Description of W. (*In his* Oration. 1792. B 349)

— OBSERVATIONS on the Potomack and Washington. N. Y., 1794. 8°. (B 628, C 73, W 18)

— LAMBERT, W. Abstracts of calculations to ascertain the longitude of the Capitol in W. from Greenwich. Wash., 1817. 4°. (A 44)

— - *Same.* (*In* **Amer. Phil. Soc.** Trans., n. s., v. 1. 1818.)

— FORCE, P. Directory for the public offices, the library, offices, *etc.*, in the Capitol. Wash., 1820. 12°. (D 17)

— ELLIOT, S. A. Washington pocket almanac, 1824-29. Wash., *n.d.* 6 v. 12°.

— VARNUM, J. B., *Jr.* Seat of government of the U. S. N. Y., 1848. 8°.

— - *Same.* 2d ed. Wash., 1854. 8°.

— BOHN, C. Hand-book of W. Wash., 1861. 12°.

— VARNUM, J. B., *Jr.* Washington sketch book. N. Y., 1864. 12°.
Note. This is a revised edition of 'The seat of gov.' 1848, *see above.*

— BARNARD, J. G. Report; defenses of W. Wash., 1871. 4°.

History.

— WILLIAMS, J. S. History of the invasion and capture of W., [1813, 14]. N. Y., 1857. 12°.

— INGRAHAM, E. D. Sketch of events which preceded the capture of W. by the British, Aug. 24, 1814. Phila., 1849. 8°.

— U. S. *13th Cong. 3d sess.* Report of committee to inquire into the causes and particulars of the invasion of the city of W. by the British forces, Aug. Wash., 1814. 8°.

— SPECTATOR, *pseud.* Enquiry respecting the capture of W. by the British. Wash., 1816. 8°. (B 455)

— REMARKS on 'An enquiry', *etc.* Balt., 1816. 8°. (B 455)

— GOBRIGHT, L. A. Recollection of men and things at W., [1834-68]. Phila., 1869. 16°.

— U. S. *Quarter-Master Gen.* Names of soldiers interred in the national cemeteries at W., Aug. 3, 1861 - June 30, 1865. Wash., 1865. 8°. (Roll of honor, no. 1. B 1954)

— POLLARD, E. A. The rival administrations in Richmond and Wash., Dec. 1863. Richmond, 1864. 8°.

— ADAMS, F. C. Siege of W., D. C., [1864. Fiction.] N. Y., 1867. 8°.

Miscellaneous.

— CRITO, *pseud.* Letters on the commercial representation and the seat of government; [in favor of Phila. as the capital]. Phila., 1807. 8°. (B 433)

— WINDER, W. H. Government building corner of F. and 17th streets. Wash., 1849. 8°. (B 1502)

— - Cost of government buildings; reasons for buying corner of F and 17th streets. *n.t.p.* [1849.] 8°. (B 1507)

— BALL, E. Speech, profligate expenditures upon public buildings, May 26. Wash., 1856. 8°. (B 1508)

CONVENTIONS, AND OTHER PUBLIC MEETINGS.

— PROCEEDINGS and speeches at a meeting held Jan. 13, 1832, for promoting the cause of temperance in the U. S. Wash., 1832. 8°. (B 1278)

— *Same.* *n.t.p.* [1832.] 12°. (C 204)

— PROCEEDINGS at a meeting for prom. the cause of temperance in the U. S., Washington, Feb. 24. Wash., 1833. 8°. (B 1278, 1783)

— PROCEEDINGS of the opponents of the administration, at public meetings, Feb. 15, 18, 1840; with addr. of P. R. Fendall. *n.t.p.* [Wash., 1840.] 8°. (B 1497)

— PROCEEDINGS of a convention of the friends of African colonization, May 4. Wash., 1842. 8°. (B 1484)

See also **National Academy of Sciences**; — **Smithsonian Institution.**

Washington, *Mass.* KNIGHT, C. History of Washington. (*In* **Field, D. D.** Hist. of Berkshire, pt. 2. 1829.)

Washington, *Mt.* HEYDEN, G. History of Egremont. (*In* **Field, D. D.** Hist. of Berkshire, pt. 2. 1829.)

— PACKARD, A. S., *Jr.* Insect fauna of the summit of Mt. Washington as compared with that of Labrador. (*In* **Amer. Assoc.** Proc., v. 16. 1868.)

— HITCHCOCK, C. H., *and others.* Mt. Washington in winter; experiences of a scientific expedition, 1870-71. Boston, 1871. 16°.

Washington; a national poem. Pt. 1. Boston, 1843. 8°. (B 1177)

Washington; or, Liberty restored; a poem. *See* **Northmore, T.**

Washington Academy, *Salem.* Plan of the theological seminary. Salem, N. Y., 1819. 8°. (B 675)

Washington Asylum, *D. C.* ADDRESS to the guardians, by a physician. Wash., 1827. 8°. (B 937)

Washington Benevolent Society of Mass. For addresses and orations before the Soc. *see* **Andrews, E.** (B 941, W 49); — **Bartlett, J.** (B 937); — **Quincy, J.** (B 937); — **Budd, T. A.** (B 937); — **Dunham, J.** (B 937)

Washington College, *Hartford, Conn.* Statement of the course of study and instruction; with a catalogue of officers and students. Hartford, 1835. 8°. (B 1088)

— CONSIDERATIONS suggested by the establishment of a second college in Connecticut. Hartford, 1824. 8°. (B 566)

Washington College, *Md.* Account of the College. Phila., 1784. 8°. (W 31)

Washington College, *Va.* JUNKIN, G. History. (*In his* Christianity the patron of literature and science. 1849. B 1581)

Washington Co., *Me.* WALLING, H. F. Topographical map. N. Y., 1861.

Washington Co., *Miss.* PROCEEDINGS of a meeting of citizens. Wash., 1803. 8°. (U. S. 7th Cong. 2d sess. B 502)

Washington Co., *Vt.* WALLING, H. F. Map. 1858.

Washington federalist; Jan. 3 - June 20. Georgetown, D. C., 1809. f°.

Washington (*Pa.*) **Female Seminary.** WILLARD, E. Address to the pupils. Pittsburgh, 1844. 8°. (B 1205)

Washington gazette. Feb. 1 - June 17. Wash., 1822. f°.

See also **City of Washington gazette**, Feb. 5, 1819. (W 80)

Washington Islands. *See* **Marquesas Islands.**

Washington Literary, Scientific, and Military Gymnasium, *Georgetown, D. C.* 2d semi-annual report. Georgetown, 1828. 8°. (B 1100)

Washington Monument Assoc. Proceedings to erect a monument in honour of W.; [with a ms. list of the subscribers. Boston, 1811]. f°.

— *Same, without the list.* Boston, 1811. 16°. (C 64)

Washington Society. Address to the people of S. C. [on nullification]. Charleston, 1832. 8°. (B 1067)

Washington Soc. of Alexandria. For oration before the Soc., *see* **Thomas, J. H.** Oration. 1807. (B 243, C 104)

Washington Territory. COX, R. Adventures on the Columbia River; incl. six years on the Rocky Mts., *etc.*, [1812-16]. London, 1831. 2 v. 8°.

— SWAN, J. G. The northwest coast; or, Three years' residence in Washington Territory, [1853-55]. N. Y., 1857. 12°.

— GIBBS, G. Reconnaissance of the country lying upon Shoal Water Bay and Puget Sound; geology of the central portion of Washington Territory. — Rept. on Indian tribes, [1854]. (*In* **U. S.** *War Dept.* Reports of explorations for R. R. to the Pacific, 1853-54, v. 1. 1855.)

— COOPER, J. G., *and others.* National history of Washington Territory, *etc.* N. Y., 1859. 4°.

— LECONTE, J. T., *M. D.* Report on the insects of Washington Territory. (*In* **Cooper, J. G.** Nat. hist. of Wash. Terr. 1859.)

— HITTELL, J. S. (*In his* Resources of California. 1866.)

Washington theological repertory. Vol. 1-8. Jan. - Mar., May - Dec. 1820; Jan. - May, July - Aug., Oct. - Dec. 1821; July, Nov., Dec., 1822; Jan. - July 1823; Jan., Mar. - Dec. 1824; Jan. - April, June - Dec. 1825; Jan., Feb., Apr. - June, Aug. - Dec. 1826; Jan. - Dec. 1827. Washington, 1820-27. 8 v. 8°.

— *Same.* New ser. Vol. 1-2. Feb. - May, July, Dec. 1828; Apr., Mar. 1829. Wash., 1828-29. 2 v. 8°.

Washington Total Abstinence Society. Address of the government to the society and the public. Boston, 1842. 8°. (B 1280)

Washington University, *St. Louis, Mo.* Inauguration, April 23. Boston, 1857. 8°.

Contents. **Eliot,** *Rev. Dr.* W. G. Introductory remarks. — Address by **J. D. Low,** — **J. How,** — **S. Treat,** — Rev. **T. M. Post.** — **Eliot,** W. G. Remarks. — **Everett, E.** Inaugural address on academical education.

Washingtonian Home. HARRISSON, D. A voice from the Washingtonian Home; hist. of the Home in Boston for the reformation of the inebriate; with a sketch of the temperance reform in America. Boston, 1860. 8°.

Washingtons, The; by J. N. Simpkinson. London, 1860. 8°.

Washoe. BROWNE, J. R. A peep at Washoe. (*In* **Harper's** mag., v. 22. 1860-61.)

Wasner, de, *and others.* Letter to His Majesty's principle secretaries of state by the ministers of the Roman Catholick princes and states residing here, *etc.* London, 1746. 8°. (B 57)

Wasps. DISDERI, S. Vespæ Gallicæ historia. (*In* **Turin. Ac. d. Sci.** Mem., v. 22. 1816.)

Wassermensch, Der; von L. Tieck. (*In his* Gesam. Novellen, v. 5. 1853.)

Wassilief, W. *See* **Vassilief, V.**

Wasson, David Atwood. Essay; the relation of social science to religion. (*In* **Free Religious Assoc.** 2d an. meeting. 1869.)

— Religion divorced from theology; farewell disc. Groveland, Aug. 29. 2d. ed. Boston, 1852. 8°. (B 1304)

— Sacrificial religion; installation sermon before Groveland Independent Church, May 1. Boston, 1853. 8°. (B 1324)

— The universe no failure; sermon, Worcester, Nov. 4, 1855. Worcester, 1856. 8°. (B 1304)

Waste land. ROBINSON, J. Letter to Sir J. Sinclair, Apr. 5, 1794, [on the improvement of waste lands]. London, 1794. 4°. (W 48)

Wastel, Peter. Vindiciarum libri tres quibus Joanni opera hactenus incognita instruunter. (*In* **Joannes** *Hierosolymitanus.* Opera, v. 2. 1643.)

Wasting diseases of infants and children. *See* **Smith, E.**

Wat Tyler; a dramatic poem. 1817. *See* **Southey, R.** (C 67)

Watch and ward; by H. James, Jr. (*In* **Atlantic** monthly, v. 28. 1871.)

Watches. *See* **Chronometers**; — **Time-keepers.**

Watchman and reflector. *See* **Christian watchman.**

Watchwords for little soldiers; stories on Bible texts; by S. H. Foster. Boston, *Sunday School Soc.*, 1868. 16°.

Watelet, Claude Henri, *and* **Levesque, P. C.** Beaux-arts. Paris, 1788-91. 2 v. *and* Plates, 1805. 4°. (Encyc. méthod., v. 32, 33.)

Contents. Vol. 1. A - Peintres. 2. Peintres modernes - Y. — Dictionnaire de la pratique des beaux arts A - V.

— *Same.* Dictionnaire des arts de peinture, sculpture, et gravure. Paris, 1792. 5 v. 8°.

Contents. Vol. 1. A - D. 2. E - G. 3. H - Pass. 4. Pat - Pei. 5. Pen - Y.

— CATALOGUE [de ses] livres, la vente 22 mai 1786. Paris, 1786. 8°. (B 887)

— VICQ D'AZYR, F. (*In his* Œuvres, v. 2. 1805.)

Water, Jonas Willem. Oratio de studio historiæ ecclesiasticæ, *etc.* Lugd. Bat., 1785. 4°. (B 1399)

Water. LAVOISIER, A. L. De la nature des eaux d'une partie de la Franche-Comté, *etc.* — Resultat des expériences faites sur les eaux. — Sur la nature des eaux de la ville de Rouen. [177-.] (*In his* Œuvres, v. 3. 1865.)

— PRIESTLEY, J. Experiments and observations rel. to the principle of acidity, the composition of water, *etc.* *n.t.p.* [1788.] 4°. (A 21)

— TISSANDIER, G. L'eau. [1867.] 2e éd., illustré de vignettes. Par., 1869. 12°. (Bibl. des merv.)
— - *Eng.* The wonders of water; ed. with add. by S. de Vere. N. Y., 1872 [1871]. 8°.
See also **Aqueducts; — Artesian wells; — Fountains; — Hydraulics; — Hydrogeology; — Hydromechanics; — Ocean springs.**

Water *in medicine.* SMITH, J. Curiosities of common water in curing distempers. [1723.] 5th ed., with add., by R. Thoresby and others. London, *printed*, Boston, *reprinted* 1725. 8°. (C 81)
— SIMS, J. Tentamen med. inaug. de usu aquæ frigidæ interno. Edinburgi, 1774. 8°. (B 1562)
— CURRIE, J. Medical reports on the effects of water in fever, *etc.* [1797.] Phila., 1808. 8°.
— - Abridgement of [his] work on the use of water. Augusta, [1799]. 8°. (D 38, 59)
☞ For the water-cure of Priessnitz and his followers *see* **Hydropathy.**

Water-babies, The; a fairy tale by C. Kingsley; with illust. New ed. London, 1869. 12°.
Note. From **Macmillan's mag.,** v. 6-7. 1862-63; reprinted in Littell's living age, v. 75. 1862.

Water colors. SOCIETY OF PAINTERS IN WATER COLORS. The 5th exhibition. London, 1809. 4°. (A 6)
— NICHOLSON, F. Practice of drawing and painting landscape from nature in water colours. London, 1820. 4°.
— SOCIETY OF PAINTERS IN WATER COLOURS. Gallery. London, [1831]. f°.
— SERIES of progressive lessons to elucidate the art of flower painting in water colours. Phila., 1835. 4°.
— SELECTION of the Spanish and Venetian schools at the new Water-Colour Gallery. London, 1841. 12°. (B 1743)

Water-cure. *See* **Hydropathy.**

Water cure in America; ed. by a water patient. N. Y., London, 1848. 8°.

Water supply. HECQUET, A. Recherches hydrologiques sur l'arrondissement d'Abbeville, suivies de trois cartes hydrologiques. (*In* **Abbeville. Soc. Imp. d'Emul.** Mém., 1867-68.)
— MACADAM, S. What is the relation of water supply in large towns to the health of the inhabitants? (*In* **Nat. Assoc. Prom. Soc. Sci.** Trans., 1868.)
See also **Hydraulics;** — *also* the names of places which have water works, as **Boston; — Glasgow; — London; — Marley; — Paris; — Philadelphia; — Portsea Island.**

Water-Witch, The; by [J. F. Cooper]. Phila., 1831. 2 v. 12°.
— *Same.* Illustr. by Darley. N. Y., 1864. 8°.
— *Same.* Rev. ed. N. Y., 1851. 12°.

Waterbury, *Conn.* BRONSON, H. History of W. Waterbury, 1858. 8°.
— CATALOGUE of the Silas Bronson library of Waterbury, Conn. Waterbury, 1870. 8°.

Waterford, *Me.* RIPLEY, L. Description and history of W., 1803. (*In* **Mass. Hist. Soc.** Col., v. 9. 1804.)

Waterhouse, Benjamin, *M.D.* The botanist; lectures on natural history; with a discourse on the principle of vitality. Boston, 1811. 8°.
— Cautions to young persons conc. health, Camb., Nov. 20, 1804. *n.p.*, 1805. 8°. (B 427)
— *Same.* 5th ed. Camb., 1822. 8°. (B 1353, 1565)
— Circular letter to the surgeons in the 2d military dept. of the U. S. army [on dysentery]. Camb., 1817. 12°. (D 39)
— Dissertatio med. de sympathia. Lugd. Bat., 1780. 4°. (A 6)
— An essay conc. whooping-cough; with obs. on the diseases of children. Boston, 1822. 8°.
— Essay on Junius and his letters; life of W. Pitt, *etc.* Boston, 1831. 8°.
— Heads of a course of lectures on natural history. Camb., 1810. 8°. (B 436)
— Journal of a young man of Mass., captured at sea by the British, May 1813. 2d ed. Boston, 1816. 12°.
— Ms. letter repelling a charge of plagiarism. (*Appended to* **Swinden, J.** Junius. 1833.)
— Mss. notes of lectures from the library of W. [1846.] 5 v. MS.
— Oratio inaug. quam in Academia Harvardiana habuit, 1783. Cantab., 1829. 4°. (A 32)
— The principle of vitality; disc., June 8, before the Humane Soc. of Mass. Boston, 1790. 4°. (A 19, 72)
— Prospect of exterminating the small-pox; history of the variolæ vaccinæ or kine-pox, commonly called cow-pox. Camb., 1800. 8°. (B 736, 821)
— *Same.* Pt. 2. Camb., 1802. 8°. (B 812)
— Rise, progress, and present state of medicine; discourse, Concord, July 6, 1791; before the Middlesex Med. Assoc. Boston, 1792. 8°. (B 418, 1891)
— Synopsis of a course of lectures on the theory and practice of medicine. Boston, 1786. 8°. (B 471, 1891)
— Vorsichtsregeln zur Erhaltung der Gesundheit der Jünglinge. Wien, 1808. 8°. (B 813)

Waterhouse, George Robert. Mammalia. (*In* **Darwin, C.** Zoology of the voyage of Beagle, v. 2. 1838.)
— Natural history of marsupialia or pouched animals. (*In* **Jardine,** *Sir* W. Nat. lib., Mam., v. 11. 1841.)
— *and* **Johnston, A. K.** Geographical division and distribution of the orders of rodentia and ruminantia. (*In* **Johnston, A. K.** Physical atlas. 1856.)

Waterhouse, Nicholas. Results of emigration. (*In* **Nat. Assoc. Prom. Soc. Sci.** Trans., 1858.) — Local examinations of universities. — Suggestions for the next census. (*In* 1859.)

Waterhouse, Sylvester. Resources of Missouri. St. Louis, 1867. 8°.

Watering places. GUIDE to watering and sea-bathing places. New ed. London, 1816. 12°.
— BLANCHARD, E. L. Adam's illustrated guide to the watering-places of England. London, 1848. 16°.
Note. For an account of any particular place see the name of that place.

Waterland, Daniel, *D.D., Archdeacon of Middlesex.* Answer to Dr. Whitby's 'Reply' resp. his 'Disquisitiones modestæ'. Camb., 1720. 8°. (B 112)
— Case of Arian-subscription considered. Camb., 1721. 8°. (B 112)
— Farther vindication of Christ's divinity; in answer to [S. Clark's] 'Observations on Waterland's second defence'. London, 1724. 8°. (B 112)
— Regeneration explained, with a view of the doctrine of justification. Phila., 1829. 12°.
— *Same.* 2d Amer. ed. Newbt., 1832. 12°. (D 63)
— Remarks on S. Clark's exposition of the church catechism. 2d ed. London, 1730. 8°. (C 232)
— *Same.* 3d ed. London, 1730. 8°.
— The sacramental part of the eucharist explained in a charge to the clergy of Middlesex. London, 1739. 8°. (B 27)
— Scripture vindicated; in answer to [Tindal's] 'Christianity as old as the creation'. Pt. 1. London, 1730. 8°. (B 116)
— Sermons. (*In* **Family** lectures. 1791.)
— Some remarks on a 'Reply to the "Defence of the 'Letter to Dr. Waterland'"', *etc.* Lond., 1732. 8°. (B 119)
— BEASLEY, F. Vindication of the argument, a priori in proof of the being and attributes of God, from the objections of Dr. Waterland. Phila., 1825. 8°. (W 1)
— CHUBB, T. (*In his* Some observ., *etc.* 1735. C 228)
— CLARKE, S. The modest plea, *etc.*, continued; or, A brief and distinct answer to Dr. Waterland's queries rel. to the doctrine of the trinity. — Observations on W.'s second defense of his queries. (*In his* Works, v. 4. 1738.)
— DICKINSON, J. Remarks on W.'s 'Regeneration'. (*In his* Nature of regeneration. 1743. C 48)
— EMLYN, T. Observations on the notions of W. (*In his* Works, v. 1, 2. 1746.)
— MIDDLETON, C. Defence of the 'Letter to Dr. W.' against the cavils of the author of the 'Reply'. London, 1732. 8°. (B 119, 261)
— - Letter to W. containing remarks on his 'Vindication of Scripture'. London, 1731. 8°. (B 119)
— MORGAN, T. Letter to W. on his defence of the Athanasian hypothesis. London, 1722. 8°. (B 114)
— PEARCE, L. Reply to the 'Letter to W.' 2d ed. London, 1732. 8°. (B 119)
— SYKES, A. A. True foundations of natural and revealed religion; reply to W. London, 1730. 8°.

— WETMORE, J. Letter occasioned by [J.] Dickinson's remarks on W.'s 'Regeneration'. N. Y., 1744. 8°. (C 4)
— WILLIAMS, P., *D.D.* Reply to "Remarks on some 'Observations [by Dr. Williams] addr. to the author of the letter to Waterland'." London, 1734. 8°. (B 119)
— *Funeral sermon on.* 1741. *See* Seed, J. (B 1227)

Waterloo, Battle of. CARTE et plan pour la campagne de 1815. [18—.] f°.

Namely. Carte du pays compris entre Charleroy, Namur, et Bruxelles. — Plan du champ de bataille de Waterloo.

— EATON, C. A. Narrative of a residence in Belgium during the campaign of 1815, and visit to the field of W. London, 1817. 8°.
— FRAZER, A. S. Letters written during the Peninsular and Waterloo campaigns, [1815]; ed. by E. Sabine. London, 1859. 8°.
— MERCER, C. Journal of the Waterloo campaign, 1815. London, 1870. 2 v. 8°.
— TYLER, *Lieut.* The Battle of Waterloo taken on the spot after the action, 18th June 1815. London, 1815. MAP.
— SCOTT, J. Journal of a tour to Waterloo and Paris, with Sir W. Scott, 1815. London, 1842. 12°.
— SCOTT, *Sir* W. Paul's letters to his kinsfolk, [1815]. (*In his* Prose works, v. 5. 1839.)
— DESCRIPTION of the field of battle, and disposition of the troops, *etc.* *n.p.*, 1816. 8°. (B 692)
— CRAAN, W. B. Hist. account of the Battle of Waterloo. Brussels, 1817. 8°. (B 1141)
— GIFFORD, C. H. Battle of W. (*In his* Hist. of the wars [of] the French Revolution. 1817.)
— MUDFORD, W. Historical account of the Battle of Waterloo. London, 1817. 4°.
— NARRATIVE of the battles of Quatre Bras, Ligny, and Waterloo. (*In* **Memorials** of the late war, v. 2. 1828; v. 28 of Constable's miscel.)
— HEAD, *Sir* F. B. Memorandum on Mr. Alison's statement. [1843.] (*In his* Descriptive essays, v. 2. 1857.)
— CHARRAS, J. B. A. Histoire de la campagne de 1815. Lpz., 1857. 8°.
— - Atlas spécial. Brux., 1863. 8°.
— HOOPER, G. Waterloo; the downfall of the first Napoleon. London, 1862. 8°.
— CHESNEY, C. C., *and* REEVE, H. Waterloo lectures; study of the campaign of 1815. London, 1868. 8°.

See also Colbourne, *Sir* J., *Lord Seaton*; — Grouchy, A. F. E., *marquis* de; — Napoleon I.; — Wellesley, A., *Duke of Wellington.*

Waterloo, Stories of; by W. H. Maxwell. London, 1854. 12°.

Waterloo, suite du conscrit de 1813; [par] Erckmann et Chatrian. 8e éd. Paris, [1865]. 12°.
— *Eng.* Waterloo. N. Y., 1869. 12°.

Waterlos, Lambertus. Annales Cameracenses, 1099–1170. (*In* **Pertz.** Mon. Germ., Scr., v. 16. 1859.)

Waterman, —. The wren and eagle in contest; or, A short method with the Unitarian nobility; by Aquæ Homo. Boston, 1819. 8°. (B 272)

Waterman, *Rev.* Elijah. The noble convert; sermon, May 28. Bridgeport, 1809. 8°. (B 869)

Waterman, *Rev.* Jotham. Fraternal affection and neighbourly kindness; sermon, Plymouth, N. Carolina, Feb. [22], 1818, also at Ipswich, Feb. [22], 1819. Boston, 1819. 8°. (B 286)
— Two better than one: sermon, Dec. 4, A. L. 5805, installation of King Hiram's Lodge, in Provincetown. Boston, 1806. 8°. (B 334)

Waterman, Nehemiah. Oration, Bozrah, Feb. 22. Windham, 1800. 8°. (B 555)

Waterman, T. T. Lecture on the Christmas festival. Prov., 1835. 8°. (B 1776)
— *Same.* 2d ed. Prov., 1835. 8°. (C 226)

Waterman, Thomas. Address, Concord, July 4. Amherst, 1806. 8°. (B 457)

Waterman, The; a ballad opera. *See* **Dibdin,** C.

Watermelon. SALISBURY, J. H. Analysis of the watermelon. (*In* **Amer. Assoc.** Proc., v. 6. 1852.)

Watermen and Lightermen, Company of. Constitutions, by-laws, *etc.* London, 1730, *repr.* 1790. 8°.
— Laws and constitution of the company. [London,] 1742. 8°.

Waterous, Timothy, Timothy, *Jr.*, *and* Zachariah. The battle-axe; aimed for the final destruction of priestcraft. 2d ed. Groton, 1841. 8°.

Waters, Abigail. HUNTINGTON, J. Memoirs of W.; sermon on her death. Boston, 1817. 18°.

Waters, Alderman Thomas Houghton, *M. D.* Diseases of the chest. Lond., Liverpool, 1868. 8°.

Waters, E. S. Genealogical table of the sovereigns of France. — First voy. to Japan. (*In* **Essex Inst.** Hist. col., v. 2. 1860.) — Materials for a history of the Ropes family. (*In* v. 7–9. 1865–68.)

Waters, Francis, *D. D.* Salvation and prosperity; sermon before the annual conference of the Md. district of the M. E. Church, April 3. Balt., 1839. 8°. (B 1463)

Waters, Samuel. Brief description of a gospel church. Worcester, 1818. 8°. (B 273)
— Meditations on Abraham's conduct in sending his servant to take a wife for his son. Worcester, 1793. 8°. (B 1360)
— Sermon, Worcester jail. Worcester, 1817. 8°. (B 334)

Waterston. *See also* **Watterston.**

Waterston, Robert. DEANE, C. Brief memoir of W. Boston, 1869. 8°. (E 85)

Waterston, *Rev.* Robert Cassie. Address at the 3d convention of the W. Newton State Normal School, July 26. Boston, 1848. 8°. (B 1589)
— Address before the Sunday School Soc. of Newburyport at their 3d anniv. Boston, 1835. 8°. (B 1121)
— Address on pauperism, Feb. 4. Boston, 1844. 8°. (B 1197, 1733)
— Address, life and character of T. Sherwin, Feb. 16, before the English High School Association, *etc.* Boston, 1870. 8°.
— Christianity applied to cities; discourse, dedication of the Preble Chapel, Portland. Boston, 1851. 8°. (B 1310)
— Condition of the insane in Massachusetts. Boston, 1843. 8°. (B 1179.)
— The diffusive nature of Christianity; address bef. the S. S. Soc. Boston, 1840. 12°. (C 211)
— Discourse, dedication of the chapel of the Church of the Saviour, Apr. 19. Boston, 1846. 8°. (B 1310, 1735)
— Discourse, life and character of J. Q. Adams, Feb. 27. Boston, 1848. 8°. (B 1206, 1207)
— Discourse, life and character of J. Story. Boston, 1845. 8°. (B 1734)
— The dying archer. (*In* **Boston** book, 3d col. 1841.)
— Farewell discourses in Boston, May 2. Boston, 1852. 8°. (B 1304)
— The keys of the kingdom of heaven; sermon. Boston, 1844. 8°. (B 1194, 1304)
— On moral and spiritual culture in early education, before the Amer. Inst. of Instr., Aug. Boston, 1836. 8°. (B 1121)
— *Same.* (*In* **Amer. Inst. Instr.** Lect., 1855.)
— Poem before the Mercantile Library Association, 25th anniversary, Oct. 15. Boston, 1845. 8°. (B 1234, 1582, 1734, 1960)
— Thoughts on moral and spiritual culture. Boston, 1842. 16°.

Contents. Introduction. — Childhood. — Growth of the mind. — Religious education. — Diffusion of Christianity through Sunday schools. — Moral and spiritual culture in day schools. — Address before the teachers of Boston. — Influences of home. — Culture of the imagination. — Love of nature. — Death of children. — Conclusion.

— The Thursday lecture, discourse, Boston, Dec. 14, 1843. Boston, 1844. 8°. (B 1184, 1591)
— To Scotland; a poem. (*In* **Boston** book, 4th col. 1851.)
— True position of the Church in rel. to the age; discourse, dedication of the Church of our Saviour. Boston, 1847. 8°. (B 1310)
— The widow's son; a sketch from real life. Boston, 1843. 8°. (B 1177, 1234)
— Various papers and remarks.] (*In* **Mass. Hist. Soc.** Proc., 1871–76.)

Waterston, Wm. Cyclopædia of commerce, *etc.* New ed.; with essay on commerce by J. R. McCulloch. London, 1846. 8°.

Waterton, Charles. Essays on natural history, chiefly ornithology; with an autobiog. of the author. London, 1838. 16°.
— Wanderings in South America, the northwest of the U. States, and the Antilles, in 1812, 16, 20, 24; with instructions for the preservation of birds, *etc.* London, 1825. 4°.
— *French, extract.* Voyages à travers l'Amérique du Sud, *etc.* (*In* **Montémont, A.** Bibl. univ., v. 41. 1835.)
Watertown, *Conn.* BRONSON, H. History of W. (*In his* Hist. of Waterbury. 1858.)
Watertown, *Mass.* FRANCIS, C. Historical sketch of W., [1630-1830]. Camb., 1830. 8°.
— BOND, H. Genealogies of families of the early settlers of W.; appended, the early history of the town. Boston, 1855. 2 v. 8°.
— HARRIS, W. T. Epitaphs in the old burying-ground in Watertown; with notes by E. D. Harris. Boston, 1869. 4°.
See also **Waverly Co. in Watertown.**
Watertown, *Mass.* **Congregational Society.** FRANCIS, C. Three discourses. Camb., 1836. 8°. (**B 1308**)
Watertown, *Mass.* **Council of Churches.** TRUE account of the result of the council of 14 churches at W., May 1, 1722; [with C. Mather's letter to Ireland, and the reports]. Boston, [1723]. 8°. (**B 662**)
Watertown, *Wisc.* BALLOU, D. W. First grave in the city of Watertown. (*In* **Wisconsin State Hist. Soc.** Col., v. 4. 1859.)
Watertown Washington Total Abstinence Soc., *Mass.* First quarterly report. Boston, 1841. 8°. (**B 1280**)
Watery war, The; [poem]. 1808. *See* **Benedict, D.** (**C 69**)
Watford, R. de. *See* **Robert** *de Watford.*
Wathen, George Henry. Arts, antiquities, and chronology of antient Egypt; from observations in 1839. London' 1843. 8°.
Watkins, —. History of the Amer. Revolution. 1822. *See* **Neal, J.**
Watkins, Francis. [Plan of a steam engine made by W. London, 1751.] (**E 55**)
Watkins, John. Universal biog. and historical dictionary. London, 1800. 8°.
Watkins, Wm. Henry. Correspondence with R. S. Coxe, and a brief statement of explanatory facts. Wash., 1833. 8°. (**B 1074, 1101**)
Watkins, Wm. J. Our rights as men; address before the legislative com. on the militia, Feb. 24. Boston, 1853. 8°. (**B 1506**)
Watmough, Edmund C. Scribblings and sketches, diplomatic, piscatory, and oceanic; by a fisher in small streams. Phila., 1844. 12°.
Contents. A fortune founded on a hurricane. — A burial by the sea-side. — The first and last speech of a tyro. — Von Yearling Heiffer. — A great battle off the Havanna. — Steam against sails. — Scenes and incidents between home and China. — Diplomatic correspondence. — Official correspondence. — Letters from Isaac Walton. — An incident of the war of 1812.
Watson, Alexander. Lecture, April 2, before the members of the Albany Female Academy. Albany, 1845. 8°. (**B 1205, 1589**)
Watson, Christopher Knight. The life and genius of Molière. (*In* **Cambridge essays,** 1855.)
Watson, Elkanah. Address, 1817. (*In* **Morris, J.** Address. 1817. **B 445, 1138**)
— Address to the members of the Berkshire Agricultural Society, Sept. 24, 1811. *n.t.p.* [Pittsfield, 1811.] 12°. (**B 450, 658**)
— History of the rise, progress, *etc.*, of canals in N. Y., and of agricultural societies. Albany, 1820. 8°.
— DEANE, W. R. Biographical sketch of W., with a genealogy of the Watson family. Albany, 1864. 8°. (**B 1692**)
— MEMOIR of W. (*In* **Munsell, J.** Collections on the hist. of Albany, v. 1. 1865.)
— MEN and times of the Revolution; or, Memoirs of E. Watson, incl. journals of travels, 1777-1842; ed. by W. C. Watson. N. Y., 1856. 8°.
Watson, *Col.* George, *Funeral sermon on.* 1800. *See* **Kendall, J.** (**B 908, 1007**)

Watson, Gustave. Remarks. (*In* **Free Religious Assoc.** 2d ann. meeting. 1869.)
Watson, Henry. Account of a gouty body. — Account of a large aneurism in the abdominal portion of the aorta. — Account of dissection of [a] subject. — Case of ascites. (*In* **Soc. Prom. Med. Knowl.** Med. com., v. 1. 1784.) — Case of hernia femoralis. — Contraction of the fore-arm and fingers. (*In* v. 2. 1790.)
Watson, Henry C. Yankee tea party; or, Boston in 1773. Phila., 1852. 12°.
Watson, James. National education and educational tests. — Measures required for the improvement of the low parts of Glasgow. (*In* **Nat. Assoc. Prom. Soc. Sci.** Trans., 1860.)
Watson, James Madison. Hand-book of calisthenics and gymnastics. N. Y., 1864. 8°.
Watson, John, *ed. See* **Gentleman's and citizen's almanack,** 1745.
Watson, *Rev.* John. Apology for his conduct, yearly, on Jan. 30; with a sermon, 1755. London, [1755]. 8°. (**B 579**)
Watson, John, *M.D.* The medical profession in ancient times; anniversary discourse before the N. Y. Academy of Medicine, Nov. 7, 1855. N. Y., 1856. 8°.
— Lecture on practical education in medicine, Nov. 3. N. Y.,1846. 8°. (**B 1565**)
Watson, John. Theory and practice of weaving by hand and power. Phila., 1864. 8°.
Watson, John Fanning. Annals of Philadelphia and Pennsylvania in the olden time. Phila., 1857. 2 v. 8°.
— Indian treaty for the lands now the site of Phila., and the adjacent country. (*In* **Penn. Hist. Soc.** Mem., v. 3, pt. 2. 1836.)
Watson, *Rev.* John Lee. BOSTON. TRINITY CHURCH. Proceedings of the treatise of the Greene foundation rel. to the resignation of J. L. W. Boston, 1846. 8°. (**B 1735**)
Watson, *Rev.* John Selby. Biographies of J. Wilks and W. Cobbett. Edin., London, 1870. 8°.
— Life of G. Fox. London, 1860. 12°.
— Life of R. Porson. London, 1861. 8°.
— Life of W. Warburton. London, 1863. 8°.
— The reasoning power in animals. N. Y., 1869. 8°.
Watson, Joseph. Instruction of the deaf and dumb; with a vocabulary. London, 1809-10. 2 v. 8°.
Watson, Marston. DAVIS, J. Biog. notice. (*In* **Mass. Hist. Soc.** Col., v. 8. 1802.)
Watson, Ralph. Brief statement of a life and ship preserver invented by R. W. London, 1827. 8°. (**B 1741**)
Watson, Richard, *D. D., Bp. of Llandaff, b.* 1737, *d.* 1816. Address to young persons after confirmation. 1st Amer. ed. Bost., 1797. 18°.
— Address to the people of Gr. Brit. Phila., 1798. 8°. (**B 597**)
— Anecdotes of the life of W., by himself; published by his son. London, 1817. 4°.
— *Same.* Phila., 1818. 8°.
— Apology for Christianity; letters to E. Gibbon. 2d ed. Camb., 1777. 4°.
— *Same.* 1st Amer. ed. Prov., 1794. 8°.
— *Same.* Phila., 1796. 8°. (**B 522**)
— Apology for the Bible; letters to T. Paine. Boston, 1796. 12°.
— *Same.* 2d ed. Phila., 1796. 8°. (**B 1373**)
— Charge to the clergy of Landaff, June 1791. London, 1792. 4°. (**A 58, 59**)
— Charge to the clergy of Landaff, June. London, 1802. 4°. (**A 58**)
— Chemical essays. Dublin, 1791. 2 v. 8°.
Contents. Vol. 1. Rise and progress of chemistry. — Terms and operations used in chemistry. — Saline substances. — Fire, sulphur, and phlogiston. — Origin of subterraneous fires. — Vitriols, and the reputed transmutation of iron into copper. — Nitre or saltpetre, and the application of its acid to the inflammation of oils, *etc.* — Manner of making saltpetre in Europe. — Manner

of making saltpetre in the E. Indies. — Time when gunpowder was discovered. — Composition and analysis of gunpowder. — Common salt. — Salt and nitre as manures. — Saltness and temperature of the sea. — Fresh water procurable from sea water by congelation and distillation. — Calcareous earth. — Clay, marle, and gypseous alabaster. — Pit coal. — Bitumens and char-coal. — Quantity of water evaporated from the surface of the Earth in hot weather. — Water dissolved in air. — Cold produced during the evaporation of water, *etc.* — Degrees of heat in which water begins to part with its air, and boils. — Water in a solid state, *etc.* — Derbyshire lead ore. — Smelting of lead ore in D. — Silver extracted from lead. — Red and white lead. 2. Lapis caliminaris, blende, zinc, brass. — Orichalcum. — Gun metal, *etc.* — Tinning copper, tin, pewter. — Tinning iron, *etc.* — Gilding in ormulu; use of quicksilver in extracting gold and silver from earths; Boerhave's experiments on quicksilver; silvering looking-glasses, *etc.* — Transmutability of water into earth. — Westmoreland slate, *etc.* — Sulphur wells at Harrowgate. — Phenomena attending the solution of salts. — Subjects of chemistry and their general division. — Effects of the great cold in Feb. 1771. — Experiment with a thermometer, the bulb of which was painted black and exposed to the direct rays of the Sun. — Plan of a course of chemical lectures. — Institutionum chemicarum in prælectionibus acad. explicatarum pars metallurgicæ [*sic*].

— Collection of theological tracts. 2d ed London, 1791. 6 v. 8°.

Contents. Vol. 1. **Taylor, J.** Scheme of Scripture divinity, formed upon the plan of the divine dispensations. — **Allix, P.** Reflexions upon the books of the Scripture to establish the truth of Christian religion. 2. **Lardner, N.** History of the Apostles and Evangelists. 3. **Brett, T.** Dissertation on the ancient versions of the Bible. — **Johnson, A.** Historical account of the several English translations of the Bible, and the opposition they met with from the Church of Rome. — **Beausobre, I. de,** *and* **L'Enfant, J.** Introduction to the reading of the Scriptures; for young students in divinity. — **Taylor, S.** Key to the apostolic writings; or, An essay to explain the gospel scheme and the principal words and phrases the Apostles have used in describing it. — **Chandler, S.** Plain reasons for being a Christian. 4. **Locke, J.** Reasonableness of Christianity, as delivered in the Scripture. — **Clarke, S.** Boyle lecture sermons, 1705; discourse conc. the unchangeable obligations of natural religion, and the truth and certainty of the Christian revelation. — **Smith, J.** Discourse on prophecy. — **Barrington, J. S.,** *Vict. Barrington.* Essay on the teaching and witness of the Holy Spirit. — **Benson, G.** Essay conc. inspiration; — Essay conc. the unity of sense. 5. **Hartley, D.** Of the truth of the Christian religion. — **Addison, J.** Of the truth of the Christian religion. — **Lardner, N.** Argument for the truth of Christianity. — **Macknight, J.** All the actions recorded in the Gospels are probable; — Of the argument for the truth of the Christian religion arising from the conversion of the world to Christianity. — **Benson, G.** Essay on the man of sin; from B.'s 'Paraphrase and notes on St. Paul's epistles'. — **West, G.** Observations on the history and evidence of the resurrection of Christ. 6. **Secker, T.** Eight charges delivered to the clergy of the dioceses of Oxford and Canterbury; added, Instructions to candidates for orders. — **Ostervald, J. F.** Treatise conc. the causes of the present corruption of Christians, and the remedies thereof. — **Fowler, E.** The design of Christianity.

— Institutionum chemicarum pars metallurgica. Cantab., 1768. 8°. (B 993)

— Letter to J. Eliot on being elected a member of the Mass. Hist. Soc., 1807. (*In* **Mass. Hist. Soc.** Col., v. 11. 1814.)

— Letter to the Archbp. of Canterbury. New ed. Dublin, 1783. 8°. (W 19)

— *Same.* 3d ed. (*In* **Pamphleteer,** 1816; v. 8 of B 838)

— On orichalcum. (*In* **Literary and Phil. Soc. of Manchester.** Mem., v. 2. 1789.)

— Principles of the Revolution vindicated; sermon before the Univ. of Cambridge, May 29. Camb., 1776. 4°. (B 1262)

— Sermon before the Lords, Jan. 30. 2d ed. London, 1784. 4°. (A 19)

— Sermon before the Soc. for the Suppression of Vice, May 3. London, [1804]. 8°. (B 1862)

— Sermon before the stewards of the Westminster Dispensary, Apr. 1785. 3d ed. Lond., 1793. 8°. (B 1858)

— Sermon before the University of Cambridge, Feb. 4, general fast. 2d ed. Camb., 1780. 4°. (B 1263)

— Sermon before the Univ. of Cambridge. Oct. 25, anniversary of [the] accession of George III. Camb., 1776. 4°. (B 1263)

— Sermon; the testimony of the Spirit. (*In* **Suddards, W.** British pulpit, v. 1. 1837.)

— CUMBERLAND, R. Letter to [W.] on his letter to the Abp. of Canterbury. London, 1783. 8°. (B 1964)

— GLYNN, R. C. Narrative concerning the late frenzy of R-ch-rd W-ts-n. London, 1781. 4°. (A 32)

— HEROIC epistle to W. London, 1780. 4°. (A 47)

— JONES, J. Vindication of the Bishop of Landaff's 'Apology for the Bible'. London, 1797. 8°. (C 231)

Watson, *Rev.* Richard, *b.* 1781, *d.* 1833. JACKSON, T. Memoirs of W. N. Y., 1836. 8°.

Watson, Robert, *M.D.* Life of Fletcher of Salton. (*In* **Fletcher, A.** Political works. 1798.)

Watson, Robert. History of the reign of Philip II. of Spain. Dublin, 1777. 2 v. 8°.

Contents. Vol. 1. 1527–76. 2. 1576–98.

— History of the reign of Phillip III., King of Spain. Dublin, 1783. 8°.

Note. Called vol. 3. The first four books are by W.; the last two by William Thompson.

Watson, Robert Grant. History of Persia, [1800]–58. London, 1866. 8°.

Watson, Robert Spence. The industrial schools' act. (*In* **Nat. Assoc. Prom. Soc. Sci.** Trans., 1867.)

Watson, Samuel, *ed.* *See* **Gentleman's** and citizen's almanack. 1788.

Watson, Samuel. ACCOUNT of the case of W. (*In* **Chase, S. P.** Address, *etc.* 1845. **B 1476**)

Watson, Samuel M. BRYNE, D. P. Exposition of the medical treatment of S. M. W. Boston, 1841. 12°. (C 271)

Watson, Thomas, *b.* 1560, *d.* 1592. Poems; ed. by E. Arber. London, 1870. 16°. (English reprints.)

Contents. The passionate centurie of love. — Melibœus sive Ecloga in obitum, *etc.* — An eclogue upon the death of the right Hon. Sir F. Walsingham. — The teares of fancy; or, Love disdained.

— The 'Εκατομπαθία; or, Passionate centurie of love. Repr. from the orig. ed. of 1581. London, 1869. 4°. (Spencer Soc., v. 6.)

— The nymphs to their May queen. — Sonnet. (*In* **Campbell, T.** Brit. poets, v. 2. 1819.)

Watson, Thomas, *d. about* 1689. Body of practical divinity; sermons on the Assembly's catechism; with a supplement of sermons; add., The art of divine contentment. *t.p.w.* [1692.] 4°.

— Redemption through the blood of Jesus set forth in five sermons; pub. by J. H. Meyer. London, 1780. 8°.

— Sermon, Aug. 17, 1662. (*In* **Farewell** sermons of Nonconformist ministers. 1816.)

Watson, Thomas, *and others.* Youth's arithmetical guide. Phila., 1805. 12°.

Watson, Wm., *Treasury Keeper of the Court of Common Pleas.* Compleat collection of the rules and orders of the Court of Common Pleas at Westminster, 1654–1736. [Lond.,] 1736. 8°.

Watson, Wm., *barrister at law.* Treatise on the law of partnership. Phila., 1807. 8°.

Watson, Wm., *Prof. in the Mass. Inst. of Technology.* New method of investigating plane curves. (*In* **Amer. Assoc.** Proc., v. 13. 1860.)

Watson, Wm., *Sheriff of Aberdeen.* Aberdeen industrial school.—Crime of Aberdeenshire for ten years preceding 1860. (*In* **Nat. Assoc. Prom. Soc. Sci.** Trans., 1860.) — Treatment of young offenders. (*In* 1861.) Criminal statistics and criminal legislation. — Law of evidence as affecting the administration of justice in sheriff courts. — Monitorial system of elementary instruction, *etc.* (*In* 1863.)

Watson, Winslow Cossoul. Military and civil history of the Co. of Essex, N.Y., its physical geography, *etc.*, an acc. of the northern wilderness, and military annals of Crown Point and Ticonderoga. Albany, 1869. 8°.

— Pioneer hist. of the Champlain Valley; account of the settlement of the town of Willsborough by W. Gilliland, with his journal. memoir, *etc.* Albany, 1863. 8°.

Watson and Pritchell. Plans, *etc.*, for the lunatic asylum at Wakefield. York, 1819. f°.

Watson family. DEANE, W. R. Biographical sketch of E. Watson, with a genealogy of the Watson family. Albany, 1864. 8°. (B 1962)

Watsons, The; by J. Austen. (*In* **Austen-Leigh, J. E.** Memoir. 1871.)

Watt, Alexander. Electro-metallurgy practically treated. London, *Weale*, 1860. 12°.

Watt, Hugh. Practice of banking in Scotland and England. London, 1833. 8°. (B 1073)

Watt, James, *b.* 1736, *d.* 1819. ARAGO, D. F. J. Notice biog. (*In his* Œuvres, v. 1. 1854.)

— - *Eng.* Life of W. Edin., 1839. 8°.

— BROUGHAM, H., *Ld.* (*In his* Lives of men of letters, v. 1. 1845.)

— MALDEN, H. (*In his* Distinguished men of modern times, v. 4. 1838; v. 40 of Lib. ent. knl.)

— MUIRHEAD, J. P. Origin and prog. of [his] mechanical inventions. Lond., 1854. 3 v. 8°.

— PROCEEDINGS of the public meeting for erecting a monument to J. W. London, 1824. 8°.

— SMILES, S. (*In his* Brief biog. 1861.)

— - Lives of Boulton and Watt. Lond., 1865. 8°.

Watt, James, *Jr.*, *b.* 1769, *d.* 1848. [Various articles.] (*In* **Lit. and Phil. Soc. of Manchester.** Mem., v. 3. 1790.)

Watt (*Lat.* **Vadianus**), Joachim von. NICERON, J. P. (*In his* Mém., v. 37. 1737.)

Watt, John James. Encyclopedia of surgery, medicine, midwifery, *etc.*; added, abridged trans. of Cullen's 'Nosology'. London, 1806. 12°.

Watt, Peter. Theory and practice of joint-stock banking. N. Y., 1836. 12°. (C 297)

Watt, Robert, *M.D.* Bibliotheca Britannica; a general index to British and foreign literature. Edin., 1824. 4 v. 4°.

Contents. Vol. 1. Authors: A-H. 2. I-Z. 3. Subjects: A-H. 4. I-Z.

— Cases of diabetes, consumption, *etc.*; with observations on the history and treatment of diseases in general. Paisley, 1808. 8°.

— Treatise on chincough; subjoined, an inquiry into the relative mortality of diseases of children. Glasgow, 1813. 8°.

Watteau, Antoine. Figures de caractères, de paysages, et d'études, dessinées d'après nature. 1r vol. Paris, [17—]. f°.

— GONCOURT, E. *and* J. (*In their* Portraits. 1857.)

— SKETCH. (*In* **Men** and women of France, v. 3. 1852.)

Wattenbach, Wilhelm. Die Germanisirung der östlichen Grenzmarken des deutschen Reichs. (*In* **Historische Zeitschrift**, v. 9. 1863.)

Watterston. *See also* **Waterston.**

Watterston, George. The child of feeling; comedy. George Town, 1809. 18°. (D 15)

Watteville, *baron* Oscar de. Globes, cartes, appareils pour l'enseignement de la géographie. (*In* **France.** *Com. Imp. de l'Expos. de* 1867. Rapports, v. 13.)

Watton, Wm. Reflections on the [hypothesis] of W. (*In* **Tindal, M.** Letter [on] the trinity. 1694. B 96)

Watts, Alaric Alexander. Poetical sketches and other poems. 4th ed. London, 1827. 16°.

See also **Literary** souvenir for 1832; — **Cabinet** of modern art for 1842.

Watts, *Mrs.* Anna Mary (Howitt). Art student at Munich. Boston, 1854. 16°.

— A school of life. Boston, 1855. 16°.

Watts, Elizabeth. Poultry; an original and practical guide to their breeding, rearing, feeding, and exhibiting. London, 1867. 16°.

Watts, George Burghall. Inter-oceanic communications across the Isthmus of Panama. (*In* **Amer. Geog. Statist. Soc.** Bul., v. 1. 1854.)

Watts, George Frederick. ATKINSON, J. B. Criticism on W. (*In his* Eng. painters of the present. 1871.)

Watts, Henry. Dictionary of chemistry and the allied branches of other sciences. London, 1863-68. 5 v. *and* Suppl. 1872. 8°.

— *tr. and ed. See* **Wurtz, A.** History of chemical theory, *etc.* 1869.

Watts, Isaac, *D.D.* Works; ed. by D. Jennings and P. Doddridge. London, 1753. 6 v. 4°.

Contents. Vol. 1. Sermons, with hymns. — The world to come; or, Discourses on the joys and sorrows of departed souls, *etc.* 2. Evangelical discourses. — Death and heaven. — Strength and weakness of human reason. — Humility represented in the character of St. Paul. — A defence against self-murder. — Holiness of times, places, and people. — A caveat against infidelity. — The harmony of all religions which God ever prescribed. — The doctrine of the passions explained and improved. — The love of God and its influence on the passions. — An essay on charity schools. — Sermons on reformation of manners and religious improvement of public events. 3. A humble attempt toward the revival of practical religion. — A guide to prayer. — Instruction for children and youth by catechisms. — Prayers for the use and imitation of children. — A short view of the Scripture history. — Questions for students and young Christians. — Orthodoxy and charity united. — Self-love and virtue reconciled only by religion. — The Redeemer and the Sanctifier. 4. The Psalms of David imitated in the language of the New Testament. — Hymns and spiritual songs. — An essay on psalmody. — Divine songs, for the use of children. — Horæ lyricæ. — Reliquiæ juveniles. — Remnants of time employed in prose and verse. — The art of reading and writing English correctly. 5. Logic. — The improvement of the mind. — An essay on education. — The knowledge of the heavens and the earth made easy. — Philosophical essays. — Ontology. 6. The rational foundation of a Christian church. — A new essay on civil power in things sacred. — The ruin and recovery of mankind. — Essay on the freedom of will in God and in creatures. — The Christian doctrine of the trinity. — Seven dissertations on the trinity. — Useful and important questions conc. Jesus the son of God freely proposed and answered, and the glory of Christ as God-Man displayed.

— Additional hymns to the supplement of Winchell's Watts. Boston, 1832. 12°. (C 190)

— Beauties of Dr. W.; [with] his life. Elizabeth-Town, 1796. 12°.

— Catechisms for children; added, prayers and hymns. 2d Brattleboro' ed. *n.p.*, 1823. 16°. (D 33)

— Christian psalmody; Watts's psalms and hymns abridged. *t.p.w* [Salem, 1814.] 12°.

— Discourse on the way of instruction by catechisms, and the best manner of composing them. 3d ed. corr. Boston, 1748. 12°.

— Divine and moral songs for children. (*In* **New England Tract Soc.** Tracts, v. 2. 1814.)

— Extracts from [his] writings rel. to the trinity. Boston, [18—]. 12°. (C 242)

— First sett of catechisms and prayers, [for] children under seven or eight years. 7th ed. Boston, 1748. 12°.

— The glory of Christ as God-Man displayed. Boston, 1795. 8°.

— Horæ lyricæ and divine songs; with memoir by R. Southey. Boston, 1854. 16°.

— Hymns and spiritual songs. Boston, 1801. 12°.

— *Same.* Whitehall, 1801. 12°.

— *Same.* Norwich, [17—]. 18°.

— Hymns taken chiefly from W.'s col. (*Appended to* **Bible.** *O.T.* New version of the Psalms. 1757.)

— Imitation of the Psalms of David, corr. and enl. by J Barlow; add., a col. of hymns. 4th ed. Hartford, [1785]. 12°.

— Improvement of the mind; also posthumous works; pub. by D. Jennings and P. Doddridge. Edin., 1801. 8°.

Contents. Directions for the attainment of useful knowledge. — Communication of useful knowledge. — Discourse on the education of youth. — Remnants of time employed in prose and verse.

— *Same.* [With a prayer.] Bost., 1812. 2 v. 18°.

— Letter to C. Mather conc. Neal's 'History of New England'. (*In* **Mass. Hist. Soc.** Col., v. 5. 1798.) — Letter to a friend in New England, May 8, 1734. (*In* v. 20. 1823.)

— Logic; or, The right use of reason. Phila., 1789. 12°.

— *Same.* Edin., 1805. 12°.

— A new essay on civil power in things sacred. London, 1739. 8°. (B 582)

— Philosophical essays. 2d ed. Lond., 1734. 8°.

Contents. Enquiry and debate conc. space. — Of substance, and of solid extension and a thinking power, as the two only original substances. — Of the original of our perceptions and ideas. — Innate ideas and propositions natural and moral. — Enquiry whether the soul thinks always. — Power of spirits to move bodies; of their being in a place and removing from it. — The departing soul. — Resurrection of the same body. — Production, nourishment, and operations of plants and animals. — Sun-beams and star-beams. — On some metaphysical subjects. — Rem. on chapters of Locke's 'Essay on the human understanding'.

— Poems. (*In* **Anderson, R.** Brit. poets, v. 9. 1795.)

— Poems. (*In* **Chalmers, A.** Eng. poets, v. 13. 1810.)

— Poems. (*In* **Campbell, T.** British poets, v. 5. 1819.)

— Prayers for use of children. London, 1755. 12°.

— Preservative from the sins and follies of childhood and youth; added, catalogue of Scripture names. 5th ed. Boston, 1748. 12°.

— *Same. n.t.p.* [London, 17—.] 12°. (C 250)

— Psalms and hymns set to new music, by E. Miller; with an app. containing the most favorite tunes, also an introduction to psalmody, *etc.* London, [17—]. 2 v. 4°.

— *Same.* Arrangement of his psalms, hymns, and spiritual songs, by J. M. Winchell. 2d ed., *etc.* Boston, 1820. 12°.

— *Same.* With a supplement of 300 hymns, *etc.* Boston, 1832. 12°.

— Psalms, hymns, spiritual songs, [and] occasional hymns. Dedham, 1811. 3 v. 12°.

— *Same, without occasional hymns.* [With] select hymns by S. Worcester, *etc.* New ed. Boston, 1847. 12°.

— Psalms of David. Boston, 1801. 12°.

— *Same.* Norwich, [17—]. 18°.

— Psalms of David, with hymns, *etc.* Northampton, 1799. 12°.

— *Same.* Boston, 1812. 2 pts. 12°.

See also 'Imitation of the Psalms'.

— Second sett of catechisms and prayers [for] children from 7 to 12. 7th ed. Boston, 1748. 12°.

— Sermons on various subjects, with a hymn suited to each subject. 7th ed. Boston, 1746. 2 v. 12°.

Note. Continuous pagination.

— Short view of the whole of Scripture history in questions and answers. 9th ed. London, 1769. 12°.

— Ulla i katikisma; or, Child's catechism in Choctaw. 2d ed. revised. Boston, 1835. 12°. (E 34)

— Wiconi owihanke wannin tanin kin; 2d catechism in Dakota. Boston, 1837. 12°. (E 34)

— A wonderful vision. Indianapolis, 1832. 16°. (D 20)

— Gibbons, T. Memoirs of I. W. Lond., 1780. 8°.

— Howe, S. Abridgement of Watt's lyric poems. Northampton, 1798. 8°. (B 994)

— Johnson, S. (*In his* Works, v. 11. 1806; *and* Lives of eminent English poets, v. 2. 1810.)

— Life of W.; chiefly selected from D. Gibbons. London, [18—]. 18°.

— Milner, T. Life, times, and correspondence of W. London, 1834. 8°.

— Willmott, R. A. (*In his* Lives of the English sacred poets, v. 2. 1853.)

Watts, John, *d.* 1717, *Funeral sermon on.* 1718. *See* **Baxter, J.** (C 4)

Watts, John, *M. D.* Diss. med. inaug. de morbo coxario. Edin., 1809. 8°. (B 822)

Watts, John. The facts of the cotton famine. London, 1866. 8°.

Watts, Stephen. Essay on the reciprocal advantages of perpetual union between Gr. Brit. and her Amer. colonies. (*In* **Four Dissertations,** *etc.* 1766. B 389)

Watts, Thomas. On M. Manavit's 'Life of Cardinal Mezzofanti. (*In* **Philological Soc.** Trans., 1854.)

Watzke, Philipp Anton. Ein Tag aus meiner Praxis; Parallelen zwischen Allöopathie und Homöopathie. Lpz., 1866. 8°.

Wau-Bun, the 'early day' in the northwest. *See* **Kinzie,** *Mrs.* J. H.

Wauchope (*Lat.* **Vauchopius**), George. De magistratibus veteris populi Rom. (*In* **Schryver, P.** Respub. Rom. 1626; — *and in* **Sallengre, A. H.** Nov. thes. antiq. Rom., v. 3. 1719.)

Waud, Samuel Wilkes. Treatise on algebraical geometry. Lond., 1835. 8°. (Lib. Usef. knowl.)

Waugh, Alex. Sermon, the nature of prayer. (*In* **Suddards, W.** Brit. pulpit, v. 2. 1836.)

Waugh, John, *Bp. of Carlisle.* Sermon, Westminster, Jan. 30, anniv. of the martyrdom of Charles I. London, 1724. 8°. (B 602)

Waukesha County, *Wis.* Walling, H. F. Map. 1859.

Wauquelin, Jehan. Merveilles d'Inde. (*In* **Berger de Xivrey, J.** Traditions tératologiques. 1836.)

Waurin, Jehan de. Anchiennes chronicques d'Angleterres; choix de chapitres inéd. Paris, 1858-63. 3 v. 8°. (Soc. de l'Hist. de France.)

Contents. Vol. 1. Albine-1444. 2. 1442-69. 3. Préface. — Notice sur Wavrin. — 1469-71. — Pièces justificatives. — Histoire de Charles dernier duc de Bourgogne.

Note. This edition omits the portions of the chronicle which relate exclusively to England, and those which were borrowed from Froissart, Monstrelet, and other chroniclers.

— Recueil des croniques et anchiennes istories de la Grant Bretaigne; ed. by W. Hardy. London, 1864-79. 3 v. 8°. (Chron. and mem.)

Contents. Vol. 1. Albina-A.D. 688. 2. 1399-1422. 3. 1422-31.

— *Eng.* Col. of chronicles, *etc.*; tr. by W. Hardy. Vol. 1: Albina - A. D. 688. London, 1864. 8°. (Chron. and mem.)

Waverley; by Sir W. Scott. Edin., 1814. 3 v. 12°.

— *Same.* Boston, 1833. 2 v. 12°.

— *Same.* (*In his* Waverley novels, v. 1, 2. 1829.)

Waverley Abbey. Annales, 1-1291. (*In* **Luard, H. R.** Annales monastici, v. 2. 1865.)

Waverley anecdotes; illust. of the novels of W. Scott. Boston, 1833. 2 v. 12°. (Works, v. 99-100.)

Waverley Company in Watertown, *Mass.* Plan of lands. 1854.

Waverley magazine and literary repository; M. A. Dow, ed. Vols. 14-17. Boston, [1857-58]. 4 v. f°.

Waverley novels. *See* **Scott,** *Sir* W.

Waves. Lyman, C. S. New form of wave apparatus. (*In* **Amer. Assoc.** Proc., v. 16. 1868.)

Wawne, G. Barker. Sermon; it is better to go from the house of mourning than to the house of feasting. (*In* **Beard, J. R.** Sermons. 1832.)

Way, Lewis, *of Stanstead.* Letter to the Ld. Bp. of St. Davids'. London, 1818. 8°. (B 688)

— Sermon. (*In* **London Soc. for Prom. Christ. among the Jews.** 9th report, 1817. (B 1002, 1033)

Way, Lewis. Decorative pavement tiles. (*In* **Archæol. Inst. of Gr. Brit.** Illust. hist. of Bristol. 1853.)

Way of escape from temporal evils and eternal death. Boston, 1836. 18°.

Way of the world, The; a comedy; by W. **Congreve.** (*In his* Works, v. 2. 1788.)

Way to be rich and respectable; addressed to men of small fortune. 4th ed. London, [18—]. 8°. (B 756)

Way to do good; by J. Abbott. N. Y., 1855. 12°. (Young Christian series.)

Way to keep him, The; a comedy. *See* **Murphy, A.**

Wayland, Francis, *D. D., Pres. of Brown University, d.* 1865. Address, June 23, to G. S. Comstock and others as missionaries to the heathen. Boston, 1834. 8°. (B 1239)

— Address, dedication of the new school-house, North Prov., Oct. 31. Pawtucket, 1846. 8°. (B 1647)
— The affairs of R. Island, discourse, Providence, May 22. Boston, 1842. 8°. (B 1304)
— *Same.* 3d ed. Prov., 1842. 8°. (B 1647)
— Article on the debts of U. S. Boston, 1844. 8°. (B 1647)
— Certain triumph of the Redeemer; sermon, May 9. N. Y., 1830. 8°. (B 1304, 1647)
— Claims of whalemen on Christian benevolence; discourse, Nov. 20, 1842. New Bedford, 1843. 8°. (B 1647)
— Discourse, dedication of Manning Hall, the chapel and library of Brown University; [dependence of science upon religion]. Prov., 1835. 8°. (B 1164, 1310)
— Discourse in commemoration of the life of Hon. N. Brown, Nov. 3. Boston, 1841. 8°. (B 1209, 1647)
— Discourse in commemoration of W. G. Goddard. Prov., 1846. 8°. (B 1216, 1647)
— *Same.* (*In* Goddard, W. G. Political writings, v. 2. 1870.)
— Discourse, opening of Providence Athenæum, July 11. Prov., 1838. 8°. (B 1164, 1585, 1696)
— Discourse, Providence, July 21, thanksgiving. 2d ed. Prov., 1842. 8°. (B 1254, 1647)
— Doctrine of expediency. (*In* Robinson, E. Bibliotheca sacra. 1843. B 1647)
— Duties of an American citizen; two discourses, Apr. 7. Boston, 1825. 8°. (B 288)
— *Same.* 2d ed. Boston, 1825. 8°. (B 295)
— Duty of obedience to the civil magistrate; three sermons. Boston, 1847. 8°. (B 1304)
— The education demanded by the people of the U. S.; discourse, Union Coll., July 25, 1854, 50th anniv. of the presidency of E. Nott. Boston, 1855. 8°. (B 1577)
— Elements of moral science. N. Y., 1835. 8°.
— Elevated attainments in piety; sermon, N. Y., Dec. 17, 1832, ordination of W. R. Williams. N. Y., 1833. 8°. (B 1324, 1781)
— Encouragements to religious effort; sermon, May 25. Phila., 1830. 8°. (B 1647, 1920)
— Introductory lecture. (*In* Amer. Instit. Instr. Lectures, 1830; 1854.)
— Letters on the ministry of the gospel. Boston, 1863. 16°.
— The limitations of human responsibility. Boston, 1838. 12°.
— Memoir of the life and labors of A. Judson. Boston, 1853. 2 v. 12°.
— Memoirs of the Christian labors of Th. Chalmers. Boston, 1864. 12°.
— On modern collegiate studies. (*In* Youmans, E. L. Modern culture. 1867.)
— Moral conditions of success in the promulgation of the gospel; address, Boston, June 29. Boston, 1834. 8°. (B 1239, 1647)
— Moral dignity of the missionary enterprise; sermon before the Boston Baptist Foreign Mission Soc., Oct. 26, and before the Salem Bible Translation Soc., Nov. 4, 1823. Boston, 1824. 8°. (B 1353)
— *Same.* 2d ed. Boston, 1824. 8°. (B 301, 1647, 1784, W 1)
— *Same.* 7th ed. Boston, 1827. 8°. (B 288)
— Moral law of accumulation; substance of two discourses, Providence, May 14. Prov., 1837. 8°. (B 1647)
— Notes on the principles and practice of Baptist churches. N. Y., 1857. 12°.
— Occasional discourses. Boston, 1833. 12°.
— Sermons to the churches. N. Y., 1858. 12°.
— University sermons; sermons delivered in the chapel of Brown University. 3d ed. Boston, 1850. 12°.
— WAYLAND, F. *and* H. L. *See next entry.*

Wayland, Francis, *the younger, and* H. L. Memoir of F. Wayland, D. D. N. Y., 1867. 2 v. 16°.

Wayland, Heman Lincoln. *See previous entry.*

Wayland, John. Inquiry into the policy, humanity, and effects of the poor-laws. London, 1807. 8°.

Wayland, John, *D.D.* The promotion of literary taste a duty binding upon educated men; address, Aug. 6. Geneva, 1845. 8°. (B 1647)

Waylen, *Rev.* Edward. Ecclesiastical reminiscences of the U. S. N. Y., 1846. 8°.

Waymouth, George. Voyage to Virginia. (*In* Harris, J. Col. of voy., v. 1. 1705.)
— Voyage towards the North West. (*In* Harris, J. Col. of voy., v. 1. 1705; — *and in* Rundall, T. Narr. of voy. toward the N. W. 1849. Hakluyt Soc., v. 5.)
— McKEEN, J. Remarks on [W.'s] voy. to the coast of Maine, 1605. (*In* Maine Hist. Soc. Col., v. 5. 1857; *also* B 1601)
— ROSIER, J. A true relation of his voyage, 1605; with remarks by G. Prince. Bath, 1860. 8°.
— — *Another copy.* (B 1601)
— — *Same.* (*In* Mass. Hist. Soc. Col., v. 28. 1843.)
— WILLIS, W. Comments on his voyage. (*In* Maine Hist. Soc. Col., v. 5. 1857.)

Wayne, *Gen.* Anthony. Orderly book of the northern army, Oct. 1776 - Jan. 1777; ed. by J. Munsell. Albany, 1859. 4°. (Munsell's hist. ser., v. 3.)
— ARMSTRONG, *Gen.* J. Life of W. (*In* Sparks, J. Amer. biog., v. 4. 1835.)
— BOYER, *Lieut.* Journal of W.'s campaign against the N. W. Indians, July 28 - Nov. 2, 1794. (*Appended to* Jacob, J. J. Biog. sketch of M. Cresap. 1866.)
— DAWSON, H. B. Assault on Stony Point, July 16, 1779. (*In his* Gleanings, pt. 11. 1863.)
— HEADLEY, J. T. (*In his* Washington, v. 1. 1847.)
— SKETCH.] (*In* Longacre, J. B., *and* Herring, J. Nat. portr. gal., v. 1. 1837.)
— WILSON, T. (*In his* Biog. of American military and naval heroes, v. 1. 1817.)

Wayne, Anthony. To the Democratic Party of Penn. on the next presidential election. Phila., 1841. 8°. (B 1498)

Wayne, Isaac. Timber at Valley Forge. (*In* Phila. Soc. Prom. Agric. Mem., v. 3. 1814.)

Waynflete, Wm. CHANDLER, R. Life of W. London, 1811. 8°.

Ways and means. *See* Colman, G., *the younger.*

Ways of man. *See* Sampson, E.

Ways of the hour, The; by [J. F. Cooper]. N. Y., 1850. 12°.
— *Same.* Illust. by Darley. N. Y., 1864. 8°.

Wazstenense diarium, 1344-1545. (*In* Fant, E. M. Scriptores rerum Svec., v. 1. 1818.)

We four in Normandy; by D. M. M. Craik. (*In* St. Paul's mag., v. 7. 1870-71.)

We girls; a home story by Mrs. A. D. T. Whitney. Boston, 1870. 8°.

Weak points; a farce, by J. B. Buckstone. (*In* Webster's act. nat. dr., v. 4. 1838.)

Weakest goeth to the wall, The; a comedy. *See* Webster, J.

Weakness and inefficiency of the government of the United States; by a late American statesman. London, 1863. 8°.

Weaknesses, The, of Brutus exposed; or, Some remarks in vindication of the constitution proposed by the federal convention; [by P. Webster]. Phila., 1787. 8°. (B 65, 614)

Weal and woe in Garveloch; by H. Martineau. Boston, 1833. 18°. (Illustrations of polit. econ.)

Weald of Kent. FURLEY, R. History of the Weald of Kent, with an outline of the history of the County; also physical features, by H. B. Mackerson. Ashford, London, 1871-74. 2 v. in 3 pts. 8°.
— MARKHAM, G. Inrichment of the Weald of K. (*In his* A way to get wealth. 1676.)

Weale, John. Bibliotheca architectonica. 1825. *See* Priestley & Weale.
— Catalogue of books on architecture and engineering. London, 1854. 4°
— Divers works of early masters in Christian decoration. London, 1846. 2 v. f°.

Contents. Vol. 1. Introd. — Biog. notice of A. Dürer; with selections from his diary. — Biog. notice of W. Wohlgemuth, — B. Pirckmeyer, — A. Krafft. — Painted and stained glass. — Biog. sketches of D. and W. Crabeth. — Descr. of the windows in the Ch. at Gouda. — Hist. notice of the Ch. of St. Jacques, Liége. — Descr. and arr. of the plates. 1, 2. Colored plates of ancient painted and stained glass windows from St. George's Chapel, Windsor, — Ch., *etc.*, at Limbourg, — Ch. of St. Jacques, Liége, — Ch. of Gouda, — Ch. at W. Wickham, Kent, — York.

— Quarterly papers on architecture. London, 1844–45. 4 v. 4°.

Contents. Vol. 1. **Moore, G.** Essay. — **Browne, R. P.** Greenwich Union poor-house. — **Morrison, J.** Life of W. V. Morrison. — **Stained** glass at York. — **Primative** churches of Norway. — **Schayes, A. G. B.** Treatise on the pointed style of architecture in Belgium; tr. by H. Austin. (*Also in* v. 2.) — **Gessert,** *Dr.* **M. A.** Art of painting on glass; tr. by W. Pole. — **Painted** glass windows in Church at Gouda in Holland. — **Illuminated** Scriptural painted miniatures and capital letters of the 14th and 15th centuries. — **Temple** Church, London, with plan. — **Papworth, J. W.** Artistic ecclesiastical decoration. — **Bell,** —, *and* **Gould,** —. Selection of painted and stained glass from York. — **Walker, T. L.** Historical account of the Church of St. Margaret. — Ch. of **St. James** at Liége. — Dedication of the volume to the Earl of Lincoln. 2. **Present** condition and prospects of architecture in England. — **Waller, J. G.** Painted or stained glass from West Wickham. — **Curtis, O. B.** Same from Winchester Cathedral. — **Leeds, W. H.** Outlines and characteristics of different architectural styles. — **Memoir** of the Hall of the Middle Temple. — **Architectural** and ornamental illust. of the Church of St. Jacques at Liége. — **Temple** Church, its interior restorations and decorations. — **Queen Mary and Philip** II. of Spain. — **Alphabet** of the 14th cent. — **Miniature** of St. Augustine with capital letters of the 14th cent. — **Gloria,** *etc.*, in the Gregorian chant and letters. — **Suckling** papers on the ancient architecture and antiquities of England. — **Carter, O. B.** Beaulieu Abbey. — **Smirke, S.** Temple Church. — **Symbolic** colours. (*Also in* v. 3.) — **Penton** Meusey Church. — **East** window of choir Winchester Cathedral. — **West Wickham** Church, St. Christopher. — **Monograms,** *etc.* — **Winchester** Cathedral painted glass. — Dedication to J. **Fergusson.** 3. **Carter, O. B.** Headbourn Worthy Ch. — **Suckling** papers, County of Essex. — **Ancient** ecclesiastical decorations. — **St. Jacques** plan. — On **desecration.** — **Wrightwick, G.** Ancient and modern English Gothic architecture. (*Also in* v. 4.) — **Rood** loft at Compton Basset Church, Wilts. — **Ashpitel, A.** De la Zouch cross. — **Winchester** Cathedral painted glass. — **Descriptive** catalogue of plates. — Dedication to Rev. **A. Suckling.** 4. **Smith, C. H.** Lithology. — **Carter, O. B.** Bishopstone Church. — **Whichcord, J.** Hist. and antiquities of the Collegiate Ch. of All Saints. — **Polychromatic** decoration of the Middle Ages. — **Review** of the Oxford Gothic Architectural Soc. Pub. — **Clutton, H.** Examples of ecclesiastical perpendicular roofs. — **Withers, R. I.** Architectural antiquities of the Ch. of Holy Cross; — Examples of encaustic tiles from Beaulieu Abbey. — **Fromberg, E. O.** Introd. essay on the art of painting on glass; tr. by H. J. Clarke. — **Mylne, R.** Brief account of the basilicas at Rome. — Dedication to E. Smirke.

— Quarterly papers on engineering. London, 1844–46. 5 v. 4°.

Contents. Vol. 1. **Hughes, S.** Memoir of J. Brindley. — Memoir of W. **Chapman.** — The **dredging** machine. — **Schuyler, R.** *and* **G. L.** Account of the engines of the Russian steam frigate of war, Kamschatka. — **Gill, J.** Hints on some improvements of the steam engine. — **Notices** of works of engineering in the preceding Michaelmas quarter. — **Simms, F. W.** On setting out the widths of ground required for the works of a railway or canal. — **Hughes, S.** Memoir of W. Jessop. — **Vetch,** *Capt.* **J.** Advantages of employing a framework of malleable iron in the construction of jetties and breakwaters. — **Notices** of books on engineering published to Christmas quarter. 2. **Mallet, R.** Report on the railroad constructed from Kingstown to Dalkey in Ireland. — **Gill, J.** Sketch of a novel method of applying the atmospheric pressure to railways by means of pneumatic locomotive engines. — Memoir of **S. Clegg.** — **Péclet, E.** Treatise on heat. — **Bury,** —, *and others.* Dredging. — **Higgins, W. M.** Harbours of the south-eastern coast; — Restoration of the Herne Bay pier. — **Examples** of engineering in the U. S. — **Vetch, J.** Havens of safety. — **Rennie, J.** Report on Holyhead and Port Dynllaen harbours. — **Pole, W.** Investigation of the comparative loss by friction in beam and direct action steam engines. — **Clarke, H.** Engineering of Holland. — **Wood, G.** Review of the circumstances which have affected the consumption of fuel in the locomotive engines of the Liverpool & Manchester railway. — **Macneill,** *Sir* **J.** Report on the atmospheric railway. 3. **Péclet, E.** Treatise on heat; tr. — **Page, T.** Report on the harbours of Holyhead and Porth-dynllaen. — **Boswall,** *Capt.* Description of a model plan for the construction of a spacious harbour in connexion with Granton pier. — **Construction** of the iron roof of the new house of Parliament. — **Hughes, S.** Paper on slate quarries. — **Woolf, A.** Patent steam engine. — **Sargent, J. O.** Lectures on American steam navigation. — **Arago, D. F. J.** Report on atmospheric railways. — **Cast** iron permanent bridge across the Nevka at St. Petersburg. — **Law, H.** Memoir of the Thames Tunnel. — **Neville, J.** Inquiry into the fall necessary in the cross sections of roads, *etc.* — **Péclet, E.** Treatise on heat considered in its application; tr. — **Clarke, H.** On the manufacture of bricks and tiles in Holland. 4. **Hydrostatic** and hydraulic docks. — **Meryon, J.** Ancient and present state of the harbour of Rye. — **Harris, T.,** *Jr.* Application of atmospheric pressure to railways. — **Bashforth, F.** Attempt to explain some of the circumstances observed by Mr. Provis at the Menai bridge during stormes. — **Egan, C.** Law of French and English patents. — **Atmospheric** railways. — **Rennie, J.** Experiments on the power of water-wheels. — **Barlow, W. H.** Construction of oblique bridges. 5. **Progress** of machinery and manufactures in Gr. Brit. from the Saxon era to the reign of Queen Anne. — **Peacocke, B. A.** Practical and experimental researches in hydraulics. — **Law, A.** Memoir of the Thames Tunnel. — **Mallet, R.** Report of the Inst. of France upon E. Arnollet's system of atmospheric railways. — **Thorman, R.** Taunus railway. — **Murray, J.** Description of a wet dock and other works.

— Rudimentary dictionary of terms used in architecture, art, engineering, mining, *etc.* London, 1849–54. 4 pts. in 1 v. 12°.

— Series of rudimentary works. London, 1850–60. 152 v. 12°.

Namely. Vol. 1. **Fownes, G.** Rudimentary chemistry. 1854. 2. **Tomlinson, C.** Introduction to the study of natural philosophy. 1853. 3. **Portlock, J. E.** Rudimentary treatise on geology. 1854. 4, 5. **Varley, D.** Rudimentary treatise on mineralogy. 3d ed.; with treatise on rocks by J. D. Dana. 1856. 6. **Tomlinson, C.** Rudimentary mechanics. 1855. 7. **Harris,** *Sir* **W. S.** Rudimentary electricity. 1854. 7*. **Harris,** *Sir* **W. S.** Rudimentary treatise on galvanism; and principles of animal and voltaic electricity. 1856. 8–10. **Harris,** *Sir* W. S. Rudimentary magnetism. 1850. 11, 11*. **Highton, E.** Electric telegraph: its history and progress. 1852. 12. **Tomlinson, C.** Pneumatics. 1854. 13–15.* **Law, H.** Rudiments of civil engineering; and rudiments of hydraulic engineering by G. R. Burnell. 1852–55. 16. **Leeds, W. H.** Rudimentary architecture. 1854. 17. **Bury, T. T.** Rudimentary architecture; styles of archit. of various countries. 1856. 18, 19. **Garbett, E. L.** Principles of design in archit. 1850. 20, 21. **Pyne, G.** Treatise on perspective. 1852. 22. **Dobson, E.** Rudiments of art of building. 1854. 23, 24. **Dobson, E.** Manufacture of bricks and tiles. 1850. 25, 26. **Dobson, E.** Treatise on masonry and stonecutting. 1856. 27, 28. **Field, G.** Rudiments of painter's art; or, Grammar of colouring. 1850. 29. **Dempsey, G. D.** Treatise on drainage of districts and lands. 1854. 30. **Dempsey, G. D.** Treatise on drainage of towns and buildings. 1854. 31. **Swindell, J. G.** Treatise on well-digging, boring, and pump-work. 3d ed., by G. R. Burnell. 1854. 32. **Heather, J. F.** Treatise on mathematical instruments. 1856. 33. **Glynn, J.** Construction of cranes and machinery. 1854. 34. **Lardner, D.** The steam engine. 1856. 35. **Burgoyne,** *Sir* **J.** On blasting and quarrying of stone. 1856. 36–39. **Weale, J.** Rudimentary dictionary of terms used in architecture, *etc.* 1849–50. 40. **Gessert, M. A.** Art of painting on glass or glass staining; with appendix on the art of enamelling, *etc.* 1851. 41. **Fromberg, E. O.** Essay on the art of painting on glass. 1851. 42. **Allen, C. B.** Treatise on cottage building. 1854. 43. **Dempsey, G. D.** Tubular and other iron girder bridges, *etc.* 1850. 44. **Dobson, E.** Treatise on foundations and concrete works. 1850. 45. **Burnell, G. R.** Treatise on limes, cements, mortars, concretes, mastics, plastering, *etc.* 1856. 46. **Law, H.** Art of constructing and repairing common roads; with general survey of the principal metropolitan roads, by S. Hughes. 1855. 47–49. **Stevenson, A.** Treatise on the history, construction, and illumination of lighthouses. 1850. 50. **Gibbons, D.** Law of contracts for works and services. 2d ed. 1857. 51–53. **Peake, J.** Rudiments of naval architecture. 1855. 54. **Kipping, R.** Rud. treat. on masting, mast-making, and rigging of ships. 8th ed. 1863. 55, 56. **Greenwood, J.** Rudimentary treatise on navigation. 1856. 57–58. **Tomlinson, C.** Treatise on warming and ventilation. 1850. 59. **Armstrong, R.** Rudimentary treatise on steam boilers. 1856 60, 61. **Baker,** T. Land and engineering surveying. 1857. 62. **Stephenson,** R. M. Railways. 1850. 62*. **Chattaway,** E. D. Railways; their capital and dividends. 1855–56. 63–65. **Andrews,** G. H. Treatise on agricultural engineering. 1852. 66. **Donaldson,** J. Clay lands and loamy soils. 1852. 67, 68. **Denison,** E. B. Clock and watch making; with a chapter on church clocks. 1850. 69, 70. **Spencer,** C. C. Rudimentary and practical treatise on music. 1854. 71. **Spencer,** C. C. Rudiments of the art of playing the pianoforte. 1853. 72–75*. **Woodward,** S. P. Manual of mollusca; or, Treatise of recent and fossil shells. 1851. 76, 77. **Heather,** J. F. Elementary treatise on descriptive geometry. 1851. 77*. **Prideaux,** T. S. Economy of fuel. 1853. 78, 79. **Sewell,** J. Elem. treatise on steam and locomotion. 1852–53. 78*. **Dempsey,** G. D. Locomotive engine in all its phases. 1856. 79*. **Dempsey,** G. D. Atlas of engravings to illust. locomotive engine. 1856. 4°. 79**. **Halleur,** G. C. H. Art of photography; with pract. hints by F. Schubert; tr. by G. L. Strauss. 1854. 80, 81. **Murray,** R. Rudimentary treatise on marine engines and steam vessels. 1858. 80*, 81*. **Wiggins,** J. Practice of embanking lands from the sea. 1852. 82, 82*. **Glynn,** J. Power of water. 1853. 83. **Haddon,** J. Rudimentary book-keeping and commercial phraseology. 1854. 82**, 83*, 83 bis. **Hughes,** S. Treatise on gas-works, *etc.* 1853. 82***. **Hughes,** S. Treatise on water-works for the supply of cities and towns. 1856. 83**. **Tomlinson,** C. Construction of locks. 1853. 83 bis. **Bland,** W. Hints on form of ships and boats. 1856. 84. **Young,** J. R. Rudimentary treatise on arithmetic. 1856. 84*. **Young,** J. R. Key to rudimentary treatise on arithmetic. 1853. 85. **Hipsley,** W. Equational arithmetic applied to questions of interest, annuities, *etc.* 1854. 86, 87. **Haddon,** J. Elements of algebra. 1855. 86*, 87*. **Young,** J. R. Key and companion to rudimentary algebra. 1856. 88, 89. **Law,** H. Elements of Euclid; with additional propositions, essay on logic, *etc.* 6th and 4th ed. 1873. 2 v. 90. **Hann,** J. Analytical geometry and conic sections. 1850. 91, 92. **Hann,** J. Elements of plane trigonometry. 1854. 93. **Baker,** T. Mensuration, *etc.* 1856. 94, 95. **Law,** H. Logarithms. 1856. 96. **Main,** R. Rudimentary astronomy. 1852. 97. **Baker,** T. Principles and practice of statics and dynamics. 1851. 98, 98*. **Baker,** T. Elements of mechanism. 1852. 99, 100. **Jeans,** H. W. Navigation and nautical astronomy. 1853. 101. **Woolhouse,** W. S. B. Elements of differential calculus. 1854. 101*. **Woolhouse,** W. S. B. Measures, weights, and moneys of all nations. 1856. 102. **Cox,** H. Rudimentary treatise on integral calculus. 1852. 103. **Hann,** J. Examples on integral calculus. 1850. 104. **Haddon,** J. Examples of solutions in differential calculus. 1851. 105. **Kirkman,** T. P. First mnemonical lessons in geometry, algebra, and trigonometry. 1852. 106. **Cotsell,** G. Treatise on ships' anchors. 1856. 107. **Gr. Brit.** *Parl.* Metropolitan building act; ed., with notes, *etc.*, by D. Gibbons and R. Hesketh. 1859. 108, 108*. **Gr. Brit.** *Parl.* Metropolis local management acts; and amendment act 1862; with notes, *etc.* 1862. 109. **Gr. Brit.** *Parl.* Nuisance removal and diseases prevention amendment act; with notes, *etc.* 1855. 110. Six legislative enactments for guidance of contractors, merchants, and tradesmen. 1858–59. 111. **Bland,** W. Exper. essays on the principles of construct. of arches, piers, buttresses, *etc.* 1862. 112. **Raspail,** F. V. Domestic medicine; ed. by G. L. Strauss. 1853. 113. **Taubert,** *Capt.* Use of field artillery on service; tr. by H. H. Maxwell. 1856. 113*. **Marey,** G. S. Memoir on swords; tr. by H. H. Maxwell. 1860. 114. **Abel,** C. D. Element. principles of construct., and on working of machinery. 1860. 115. **Abel,** C. D. Atlas of plates illust. the preceding. 1860. 4°. 116. **Smith,** T. R. Acoustics of public buildings. 1861. 117. **Fenwick,** T. Subterraneous surveying and magnetic variation of the needle; also, Method of conducting subterraneous surveys without the use of the needle; by T. Baker. 118, 119. **Stevenson,** D. Civil engineering of North America. 1859. 120, 120*. **Burnell,** G. R. Rudiments of hydraulic engineering. 1858–59. 121, 122. **Frisi,** P. Treatise on rivers and torrents; tr. by J. Garstin. 1861. 123. **Robison,** J., *and* **Tredgold,** T. Principles of construction in carpentry and joinery. 1859. 123*. **Robison,** J., *and* **Tredgold,** T. Atlas of engravings to accompany the preceding. 1859. 124. **Robison,** J., *and others.* Principles of construct. in carpentry and joinery of roofs. 1859. 125, 126. **Williams,** C. W. Combustion of coal and prevention of smoke. 1858. 127. **Richardson,** T. A. Art of architectural modelling in paper. 1859. 128, 129. **Vitruvius Pollio,** M. Architecture; tr. by J. Gwilt. 1860. 130. **Gordon,** G., *Earl of Aberdeen.* Inquiry into principles of beauty in Grecian architecture. 131. **Millers',** merchants', and farmers' ready reckoner. 1861. 132. **Brooks,** S. H. On erection of dwelling-houses. 1860. 133. **Lamborn,** R. H. On metallurgy of copper. 1860. 134. **Lamborn,** R. H. Metallurgy of silver and lead. 1861. 135. **Watt,** A. Electro-metallurgy practically treated. 1860. 136. **Haddon,** J. Rudimentary arithmetic. New ed., rev. by A. Arman. 1862. 137. **Arman,** A. Key to preceding. 1862. 138. **Bond,** R. Handbook of the telegraph. 1862. 139. **Baker,** T. Mathematical theory of the steam engine. 1862. 140, 141. **Burn,** R. S. Outlines of modern farming. 1863. 142. *Wanting.* 143. **Tomlinson,** C. Experimental essays. 1863. 144. **Brenan,** J. Composition and punctuation. 1863. 145. *Wanting.* 146. **Burn,** R. S. Outlines of modern farming. Vol. 5. 1865. 147. **Arman,** A. Stepping stone to arithmetic. 1864. 148. **Arman,** A. Key to the stepping stone to arithmetic. 1865. 149–151. *Wanting.* 152. **Playford,** F. Practical hints for investing money, *etc.* 1864.

— Theory, practice, and architecture of bridges. London, 1843. 2 v. *and* Plates 2 v. 8°.

Contents. Vol. 1. **Hann,** J. Theory of bridges. — **Gauthey,** E. M. Papers on bridges. — **Moseley,** H. Theory of the arch. — **Hughes,** T. Foundations of bridges. — **Hill,** L. Acc. of Hutcheson bridge, Glasgow. — **Stevenson,** R. Specification of Hutcheson bridge. — **Dredge,** J. Mathematical principles of his suspension bridge. — **Colquhoun,** *Sir* J., *and* **Dredge,** J. Contract for erect. suspension bridge upon Dredge's principle, at Balloch Ferry, Dumbartonshire. — **Specification** of material. 2. **Hosking,** W. Essay and practical treatises on the theory and architecture of bridges. — **Trubshaw,** J. Specification of the Chester Dee bridge. — **Isherwood,** B. F. Description of timber bridges, *etc.*, on the Utica and Syracuse R. R. — Descrip. of plates. — General index. 3, 4. Plates.

Weale, W. H. James. Hans Memlinc; notice of his life and works. London, *Arundel Soc.*, 1865. 8°.

Wealth, Wealth of nations. *See* **Political Economy.**

Wear River. ARMSTRONG, *Sir* W. G., *and others.* Industrial resources of the Tyne, Wear, and Tees. 2d ed. London, 1864. 8°.

Weare, Meshech. Letter to Messrs. Langdon & Peabody, delegates to Congress, Nov. 1779, and to Col. Peabody, March 1780, on the state of the currency. (*In* **New Hamp. Hist. Soc.** Col., v. 2. 1827.) — WINGATE, P. Sketch of W. (*In* v. 5. 1837.)

Weare, Nathaniel, *councilor of N. H.* Letter to Maj. R. Pike, Mar. 15, 1689-90. (*In* **New Hamp. Hist. Soc.** Col., v. 1. 1824.) — BELL, S. D. Brief notice of W. (*In* v. 8. 1866.)

Wearg, Clement. Replies, *etc.* 1723. *See* **Reeve,** T. (A 56)

Wearmouth, Benedictine House of. *See* **Monk-Wearmouth, Benedictine House of.**

Wearyfoot common; by L. Ritchie. (*In* **Chambers' journ.,** n.s., v. 1. 1854; — *and in* **Littell's** living age, v. 41-42. 1854.)

Weather. MILLS, J. Essay on the weather. London, 1770. 8°. (B 747)

— MARSHALL, W. Experiments and observations conc. agriculture and the weather. London, 1779. 4°.

— ALLING, J. Register of the weather for 25 years, ending 1810. New Haven, 1810. 8°. (B 993)

— BUTLER, T. B. Philosophy of the weather and guide to its changes. N. Y., 1856. 12°.

— THOMAS, W. H. B. Indications of weather as shown by animals and plants. (*In* **American Assoc.** Proc., v. 7. 1856.)

— FITZ ROY, R. Weather book. Lond., 1863. 8°.

— JACKSON, R. E. S. Influence of weather upon disease and mortality. (*In* **Roy. Soc. of Edin.,** v. 23. 1864.)

— LOOMIS, E. Influence of the moon upon the weather. (*In* **Amer. Assoc.** Proc., v. 17. 1869.)

See also **Meteorology.**

Weathercock, The; by J. T. Allingham. (*In* **Minor dr.,** v. 5.)

Weatherhead, George Hume, *M.D.* Essay on the diagnosis between erysipelas, phlegmon, and erythema; with an app. touching the probable nature of puerperal fever. London, 1819. 8°.

— Philosophical rambler; or, Obs., *etc.*, in France and Italy. London, 1834. 8°.

See also **Almanacs.** BRITISH telescope, 1737, 40–49. (E 72)

Weaver, Wm. A. Reply to a pamphlet by T. Allen. Wash., 1842. 8°. (B 1449)

Weaving. Duncan, J. Practical essays on the art of weaving. Glasgow, 1808. 8°.

— Michel, F. Recherches sur le commerce, la fabrication des étoffes de soie, d'or, d'argent pendant le Moyen Age. Par., 1852-54. 2 v. 4°.

— Watson, J. Theory and practice of weaving by hand and power. Phila., 1864. 8°.

See also **Framework knitters**; — **Hand loom weavers**; — **Lace**; — **Pneumatic loom.**

Webb, *Rev.* Benjamin. Present scope and future gain of the Christian life; discourse, Truroe, Oct. 8, 1732, death of R. Avery. Boston, 1733. 8°. (C 310)

Webb, Benjamin. The complete annuitant; tables. London, 1762. 16°.

Webb, Charles. Belphegor the mountebank; a drama. (*In* **Sargent, E.** Mod. stand. dr., v. 43.)

Webb, Daniel. Inquiry into the beauties of painting. 4th ed. London, 1777. 16°.

— Selections from M. Pauw; with additions. Bath, 1795. 8°.

Webb, Edward. Evidences of the Scythian affinities of the Dravidian languages; condensed from R. Caldwell's comparative Dravidian grammar. (*In* **Amer. Orient. Soc.** Journ., v. 7. 1862.)

Webb, Elizabeth. Letter to A. W. Boehm, with his answer. Phila., 1781. 8°. (B 201)

Webb, George James. Common school songster. Boston, 1842. 4°.

— Massachusetts collection of psalmody; by the Boston Handel and Haydn Soc. Boston, 1840. obl. 8°.

— Purity of tone. (*In* **Russell, W.** Orthophony. 1848.)

— Salve regina; from the 'Cantica ecclesiastica'. (*In* **Dwight, J. S.** Journal of music, 1860.)

Webb, James Watson. Slavery and its tendencies; letter to the N. Y. courier and inquirer. Wash., 1856. 8°. (B 1480)

Webb, *Rev.* John. Brief discourse at the ordination of a deacon. Boston, 1731. 8°. (B 66, 78, 235)

— Christ's suit to the sinner while he stands and knocks at the door; sermon, Boston, Oct. 13. Boston, 1741. 8°. (C 18)

— Duty of a degenerate people; sermon, June 18; [fast-day, North Church]. Boston, 1734. 12°. (C 11, 51)

— Duty of ministers to work the works of Him that sent them; sermon, death of W. Waldron. Boston, 1727. 8°.

— *Other copies.* (B 83, 281)

— Government of Christ; sermon, election, May 31. Boston, 1738. 8°. (B 145, 178, 181, 183)

— Great concern of New England; sermon, [Thursday lecture]. Boston, 1730. 8°. (B 63, C 11)

— Greatness of sin; sermon [before the execution of] J. Ormsby and M. Cushing; with an appendix by W. Cooper. Boston, 1734. 8°. (D 3)

— Seasonable warning against bad company-keeping; discourse. Boston, 1726. 8°. (C 18)

— Sermon at lecture, Nov. 15. Boston, 1722. 8°. (C 11)

— Sermon, Newbury, funeral of J. Hinton. London, 1720. 8°. (B 175)

— Young man's duty explained and pressed upon him; sermon to a soc. of young men. Boston, 1718. 8°. (B 81, C 51)

— *Funeral sermon on.* 1750. *See* **Eliot, A.** (B 312)

Webb, *Rev.* John, *d.* 1869. Historical introduction. (*In* **Washbourn, J.** Bibliotheca Gloucestrensis. 1825.)

Webb, Maria. The Penns and Penningtons of the 17th century in their domestic and religious life; also, notices of T. Ellwood, with some of his unpublished verses. London, 1867. 12°.

Webb, Philipp Carteret. Short account of Danegeld; with particulars relating to William the Conqueror's survey. London, 1756. 4°. (E 13)

— Short account of some particulars concerning Domesday book. London, 1756. 4°. (E 13)

Webb, Richard D. Life and letters of Captain J. Brown. London, 1861. 16°.

— National anti-slavery societies in Eng. and the U. S.; strictures on a 'Reply to charges against the Amer. and Foreign Anti-Slavery Soc.', *etc.*, by L. Tappan. Dublin, 1852. 8°. (B 1479)

Webb, *Lieut.* Thomas. Military treatise on the appointments of the army; with a short treatise on military honor. Phila., 1759. 12°.

Webb, Thomas Hopkins, *M. D.* Accounts of a discovery of antiquities at Fall River, Mass.; with remarks by C. C. Rafn. (*In* **Copenhagen. Kong. Nord. Oldsk. Selsk.** Mém., 1840-44.)

— Information for Kansas immigrants. 13th ed. Boston, 1857. 12°.

— *Same.* 14th ed. Boston, 1857. 12°. (C 266)

— Papers on Prof. Rafn. (*In* **Mass. Hist. Soc.** Proc., 1864-65.)

— Remarks on the cholera. 1832. *See* **Mauran, J.** (B 1569)

— Rheumatism, its causes and treatment; Fiske fund prize diss., June 1836. Boston, 1837. 8°. (B 1565)

— Mass. Hist. Soc. Proc. of the Soc. on the death of W. (*In their* Proc., 1866-67.)

Webb, Thomas Smith. Freemason's monitor; or, Illustrations of masonry. Albany, 1797. 12°.

— *Same.* New and illust. ed. by G. W. Chase. Boston, 1859. 32°.

— Deane, P. Euology on W., Aug. 19. Boston, 1819. 8°. (B 556)

— Hunt, W. G. Masonic eulogy on the character of W., Sept. 1. Lexington, 1819. 8°. (B 555)

Webb family. Vinton, J. A. (*In his* Giles memorial. 1864.)

Webbe, Edward. The rare and most wonderful thinges which E. W. hath seene in his trauailes in Jerusalem, Dammasko, *etc.*; and in Jewrie, Egipt, *etc.*, 1590; ed. by E. Arber. London, 1868. 16°. (English reprints, v. 2.)

Webbe, Wm. Discourse on English poetrie, 1586; ed. by E. Arber. London, 1870. 16°. (English reprints, v. 12.)

Webber, Charles Wilkins. Gold mines of the Gila. N. Y., 1849. 2 v. (paged continuously). 12°.

— Old Hicks the guide; adventures in the Camanche country in search of a gold mine. N. Y., 1848. 12°.

Webber, George. Discourse at the celebration of the centenary of Wesleyan Methodism, Oct. 25. Portland, 1839. 8°. (B 1326)

Webber, Horace Hervey. Confederation of British North America. 1866. *See* **Bolton, E. C.**

Webber, S. Singular growth of a potato. (*In* **Amer. Assoc.** Proc., v. 4. 1851.)

Webber, Samuel, *Pres. of Harvard College*, *b.* 1759, *d.* 1810. Eulogy at the funeral of J. Willard. (*In* **Lathrop, J.** Prayer. 1804. B 203, 234, 425, 852)

— Mathematics; from the best authorities. 2d ed. Camb., 1808. 2 v. 8°.

— Observations of an annular eclipse of the Sun, Cambridge, Apr. 3, 1791. (*In* **Amer. Acad. of Arts and Sci.** Mem., v. 2. 1793.)

— *Funeral sermon on.* 1810. *See* **Ware, H.** (B 435, 911)

Webber, Samuel, *M.D.* Introduction to English grammar on an analytical plan. Camb., 1832. 12°.

— Logan; an Indian tale. Camb., 1821. 18°.

— War; a poem. Camb., 1823. 12°. (C 119)

Weber, Albrecht Friedrich. Die neuern Forschungen über das alte Indien. (*In* **Historisches** Taschenbuch, 1855.)

— Zwei vedische Texte über Omina und Portenta. (*In* **Berlin. Akad. d. Wiss.** ad. Abh., 1858.) — Ueber die Vajrasûcî, Demantnadel, des Açvaghosha. (*In* 1859.) — Die vedischen Nachrichten von den naxatra Mondstationen. (*In* 1860, 61.) — Ueber den Vedakalender, Namens Jyotisham. (*In* 1862.) — Die Râma-Tâpanîya Upanishad. (*In* 1864.) — Ein Fragment der Bhagavatî. (*In* 1865, 66.) — Ueber die Krishnajanmâshtamê. (*In* 1867.)

— Whitney, A. D. Views of Biot and Weber respecting the relations of the Hindu and Chinese systems of asterisms. — Reply to Weber. (*In* **Amer. Orient. Soc.** Journ., v. 8. 1866.)

Weber, Georg. Germanien in den ersten Jahrh. seines geschichtlichen Lebens, mit Biographie. Berlin, [1862]. 8°. (Schmidt, F. Deutsche nat. Bibl., v. 1.)

— Geschichte der deutschen Literatur. Lpz., 1847. 8°.

— Milton's prosaische Schriften über Kirche, Staat, und öffentliches Leben seiner Zeit; ein literarisches und publicistisches Charakterbild aus der englischen Revolution. (*In* **Historisches** Taschenbuch, 1852-53.) — Jean Froissart und seine Zeit; Streiflichter aus das Literatur- und Gesellschaftsleben des spätern Mittelalters. (*In* 1870.)

— Outlines of universal history; tr. from the German by M. Behr; revised with add. of the hist. of the U. S., by F. Bowen. 2d ed. Boston, 1853. 8°.

— Vollständiges Namen- und Sachregister zu Schlosser's 'Geschichte des 18ten Jahrhunderts', 2e, 3e Aufl. Heidelb., 1849. 8°.

Weber, Henry Wm. Illustrations of northern antiquities. Edin., 1814. 4°.

Contents. Antient Teutonic poetry and romance. — Das Heldenbuch. — Der Niebelungen Lied. — Die Klage. — Popular heroic and romantic ballads; tr. by R. Jamieson. — Abstract of the Eyrbiggia-Saga; by W. Scott.

— Metrical romances of the 13th, 14th, and 15th centuries; with introduction, notes, and glossary. Edin., 1810. 3 v. 8°.

Contents. Vol. 1. Introduction. — **Kyng Alisaunder.** — Sir Cleges. — **Marie de France.** Lay le Freine. 2. **Richard** Cœur de Lion. — The **Lyfe** of Ipomydon. — **Amis** and Amiloun. 3. **Sandabad.** Proces of the seuyn sages: The Pinnote-tree and its ympe; — The knight and his grehonde; — The bore and the herd; — Ypocras and his neveu; — The father murdered by his son; — The husband shut out; — The king and his stiward; — The old wise man and his wife; — Cressus, the riche man; — The magpie; — Herowdes and Merlin; — The sheriffe, his widow, and the knight; — Of maister Gemes; — The two dreams; — The ravens. — **Octouian** imperator. — **Sir Amadas.** — The **hunting** king of the hare. — Notes. — Glossary.

Weber, J. Edward. Hydatids of the liver; operation and cure. N. Y., 1852. 8°. (B 1565)

Weber, Joseph. Mémoires concernant Marie Antoinette. *See* **Lally-Tolendal,** T. G., *marquis* de.

Weber, Karl von. Ein Schuss im Walde, 1603. (*In* **Historisches** Taschenbuch, 1860.)

Weber, Karl Maria Friedrich Ernst, *Freiherr* von. Der Freischütz. London, 1849. 12°. (E 7)

— Der Freyschütz [for the piano]. (*In* **Dwight,** J. S. Journal of music, 1861.)

— Letters. (*In* Nohl, L. Letters of musicians. 1867.)

— Blaze de Bury, H. (*In* **Revue** d. D. Mondes, juil. 1846, jan. 1867.) — Scudo, P. (*In* av., oct. 1857.)

— Weber, M. M. *See the next entry.*

Weber, Max Maria, *Freiherr* von. Carl Maria von Weber; life of an artist; tr. by J. P. Simpson. London, 1865. 2 v. 8°.

Weber's Volks-Kalendar für 1854. Lpz., [1853]. 4°.

Webster, A., *D.D.* Education; address before the Linnæan Assoc. of Penn. Coll., Apr. 18. Gettysburg, 1853. 8°. (B 1579)

Webster, Alexander, *D.D.* Heathens professing Judaism, *etc.*; substance of two sermons, Edinburgh, thanksgiving for the victory at Culloden. Edin., 1746. 8°. (B 26)

Webster, *Mrs.* Augusta. Portraits. 2d ed. Lond., 1870. 16°.

Contents. Medea. — Circe. — The happiest girl in the world. — A castaway. — A soul in prison. — Tired. — Coming home. — In an almshouse. — An inventor. — A dilettante. — The manuscript of S. Alexius.

Webster, Benjamin. Acting national drama. London, 1837-38. 5 v. 12°.

Contents. Vol. 1. **Knowles,** J. S. Bridal; a tragedy. — **Planché,** S. R. Two Figaros; a musical comedy. — **Coyne,** J. S. Queer subject; a farce. — **Webster,** B. Modern Orpheus; farce. — **Ball,** E. F. Walter Tyrrel; drama. — **Webster,** B. My young wife and old umbrella; farce. — **Dance,** C. Country squire; an original comedy. — **Morton,** J. M. Sentinel; a musical burletta. — **Planché,** J. R. A peculiar position; farce. — **Blink,** G. Tiger at large; comic burletta. — **Peake,** R. B. Middle Temple; farce. — **Planché,** J. R., *and* **Dance,** C. Riquet with the tuft; burletta. 2. **Power,** T. St. Patrick's eve. — **Peake,** R. B. A quarter to nine; Blanche of Jersey; — The bottle imp. — **Planché,** J. R. Court favor. — **Morton,** J. M. The spitfire. — **Lover,** S. Rory O'Moore. — **Dance,** C. Advice gratis. — **Morton,** J. M. The original: — Barbers of Bassora. — **Mathews,** C. Why did you die? — **Coyne,** J. S. Valsha. — **Dance,** C. Bengal tiger. 3. **Planché,** J., *and* **Dance,** C. Puss in boots. — **Mathews,** C. The ring-doves; — Black domino. — **Buckstone,** J. B. Our Mary Anne; — Shocking events. — **Bayly,** T. H. The culprit. — **Reynolds,** J. H. Confounded foreigners. — **Selby,** C. The dancing barber. — **Coyne,** J. S. All for love; or, the lost pleiad. — **Bayly,** T. H. Spitalfield's weaver. — **Selby,** T. The rifle brigade. — **Haynes,** J. T. Angeline. — **Mathews,** C. Truth. 4. **Bayly,** T. H. You can't marry your grandmother. — **Peake,** R. B. Spring lock. — **Selby,** C. The valet de sham. — **Hall,** *Mrs.* C. S. The groves of Blarney. — **Planché,** E. The hasty conclusion. — **Peake,** R. B. The Meltonians. — **Buckstone,** J. B. Weak points. — **Dance,** C. Naval engagements. — **Bayly,** T. H. British legion. — **Buckstone,** J. B. The Irish lion. — **Peake,** R. B. Lying in ordinary. 5. **Buckstone,** J. B. Married life. — **Lover,** S. White horse of the peppers. — **Peake,** R. B. Gemini. — **A'Becket,** G. A. The artist's wife. — **Buckstone,** J. B. A lesson for ladies. — **Macfarren,** G. A. The devil's opera. — **Bayley,** T. H. Tom Noddy's secret; — Forty and fifty. — **Dance,** C. Sons and systems. — **Planché,** J. R. Printer's devil. — **Selby,** C. Ask no questions. — **Mayhew,** H., *and* Baylis, A. But, however. — **Sterling,** E. Nicholas Nickleby. — **Bayly,** T. H. One hour; or, The carnival ball.

— Dead heart, The; a drama. (*In* **Sargent,** E. Mod. stand. dr., v. 43.) — Giralda; a comic drama. (*In* v. 36.)

— The golden farmer; a domestic drama. (*In* **Minor** drama, v. 1.)

Webster, Benjamin Franklin. Annals of the Army of the Cumberland. Phila., 1863. 8°.

Webster, Charles. Facts tending to show the connection of the stomach with life, disease, and recovery. London, 1793. 8°. (B 815)

Webster, Daniel. Works. Boston, 1851. 6 v. 12°.

Contents. Vol. 1. Biog. memoir, by E. Everett. — Speeches on various public occasions, 1820-43. 2. 1840-51. 3. Speeches in the convention to amend the constitution of Mass. — Speeches in Congress, 1815-33. 4. 1834 - March 30, 1840. 5. May 18, 1840-50. — Legal arguments and speeches to the jury, 1817-21. 6. 1824-48. — Diplomatic and official papers. — Miscellaneous letters. — Index.

— Address at Andover, Nov. 9. Boston, 1843. 8°. (B 1500)

— Address at the completion of Bunker Hill Monument, June 7. Boston, 1843. 8°. (B 1700, 1764)

— Address at the laying of the corner stone of Bunker Hill monument. Boston, 1825. 8°. (B 568, 1662, 1730, 2006)

— *Another copy.* Boston, *Tappan and Dinnet,* 1843. 8°. (B 1764)

— *Same.* Let it rise till it meet the Sun in his coming, *etc.* Boston, 1843. 8°. (B 1700)

— *Same.* (*In* **Moore,** F. American eloquence, v. 2. 1864.)

— Address at the laying of the corner stone of the addition to the Capitol, July 4. Wash., 1851. 8°. (B 1612)

— Address before the federal gentlemen of Concord, July 4. Concord, 1806. 8°. (B 421)

— Address before the N. Y. Hist. Soc., Feb. 23. N. Y., 1852. 8°. (B 1607)

— Address before the Washington Benevolent Soc., Portsmouth, July 4. Portsmouth, [1812]. 8°. (B 415)

— Argument for Dartmouth College.] *n.t.p.* [181-.] 8°. (B 446)

— Argument in trial of J. F. Knapp. (*In* **Moore,** F. Amer. eloquence, v. 2. 1864.)

— The Austro-Hungarian question; correspondence between Hülsemann and W. Wash., 1851. 8°. (B 1505)

— Correspondence [with] Ld. Ashburton; on the Mc Leod's case; on the Creole case; on impressment. *n.p.*, [1842]. 8°. (B 1499, 1871)

— Discourse, commemoration of the lives and services of J. Adams and T. Jefferson, Faneuil Hall, Aug. 2. Boston, 1826. 8°. (B 556, 1206, 1646, 1668, 1730, 1755, 1797, 2006, 2013)

— Discourse, Plymouth, Dec. 22, 1820, in commemoration of the first settlement of New England. Boston, 1821. 8°. (B 568, 1646)

— *Same.* 3d ed. Boston, 1825. 8°. (B 1730)

— *Same.* 4th ed. Boston, 1826. 8°. (B 2010)

— Duties of American mothers. (*In* **Boston** book, 3d col. 1841.)

— Extracts from speeches on slavery, with his compromise speech, Mar. 7, 1850, and the Boston memorial drawn up by W. Boston, 1861. 8°. (B 1481)
— Fatal secret. (*In* **Boston** book, 4th col. 1851.)
— Letter to Hülsemann. (*In* **Kossuth**, L. SKETCH. 1851.)
— Opinion in relation to the title of the Duke of Alagon. (*In* **White**, J. M. Opinions, *etc.* 1837.)
— Private correspondence of W.; ed. by F. Webster. Boston, 1857. 2 v. 8°.
— Protest against expunging; speech in Senate, Jan. 16. Wash., 1837. 8°. (B 1496, 1718)
— Remarks to the ladies of Richmond, Va., Oct. Boston, 1840. 12°. (C 178)
— Remarks upon that part of the President's message [rel.] to revenue and finances, Dec. 16, 17. Wash., 1840. 8°. (B 1147, 1497, 1823)
— Selections from the writings of W. (*In* **Blake**, L. Constitutional text book. 1854.)
— Specie circular; speech, Senate, Dec. 21, 1836. *n.t.p.* [Wash., 1836.] 8°. (B 1496)
— Speech; a defence of the Christian religion and of the religious instruction of the young; case of S. Girard's will, Feb. 10. N. Y., 1844. 8°. (B 1646)
— Speech at Abington, Oct. 9. *n.t.p.* [1848.] 8°. (B 1502, 1668)
— Speech at Marshfield, Sept. 1; and speech on the Oregon bill, in the Senate, Aug. 12. Boston, 1848. 8°. (B 1516, 1668)
— Speech at the National Repub. Conven. in Worcester, Oct. 12. Boston, 1832. 8°. (B 1646, 1721, 1723, 1882, 2006)
— Speech at the Whig State Convention, Sept. 23, 1846. (*In* **True** Whig sentiment of Mass. 1846. B 1502)
— Speech in answer to Calhoun, Mar. 22, 1838. [Wash., 1838.] 8°. (B 1129, 1723, 1751, 1791)
— Speech in reply to Calhoun on the bill to provide for the collection of duties on imports, Feb. 16. Wash., 1833. 8°. (B 1495, 1810)
— *Same.* (*In* **Calhoun**, J. C. Speeches on the enforcing bill. 1833; — *and in* **Political** register, supplement. 1833. B 1495)
— Speech in reply to Hayne [on] the resolution of Mr. Foot in rel. to pub. lands, Jan. 26. Wash., 1830. 8°. (B 1494, 1792)
— *Same.* 2d speech in the Senate, Jan. 26, 1830; with sketch of preceding debate on the resolution respect. sale of pub. lands, with W.'s last remarks. Boston, 1830. 8°. (B 1836)
— *Same.* (*In* **Hayne**, R. S. Speeches of H. and W. 1849; — *and in* **Moore**, F. American eloquence, v. 2. 1864.)
— Speech, Jan. 14, 1814, bill for filling the ranks of the regular army, *etc.* Alexandria, 1814. 8°. (B 669, 2530)
— Speech on moving for leave to introduce a bill to continue the Bank of the U. S. for 6 years, Mar. 18. Wash., 1834. 8°. (B 1810)
— Speech on public lands, *etc.*, Jan 20. Wash., 1830. 8°. (B 1792, 1831, 2006)
— Speech on slavery, March 7. Boston, 1850. 8°. (B 1478)
— *Same, with portrait.* [Another ed.] Boston, 1850. 8°. (B 1486)
— *Same.* Speech on Mr. Clay's resolutions. Boston, 1850. 8°. (B 1668)
— *Same.* (*In* **Calhoun**, J. C. Speeches on slavery. 1850. B 1486)
— Speech on the compromise bill, July 17, 1850. *n.t.p.* [Wash., 1850.] 8°. (B 1504)
— Speech on the currency and the new plan for collecting pub. moneys, Sept. 28, 1837. Wash., 1837. 8°. (B 1777, 2010)
— Speech on the distribution of surplus revenue, May 31. Wash., 1836. 8°. (B 1777, 2009)
— Speech on the Greek Revolution. Wash., 1824. 8°. (B 1755, 1789)
— *Same.* Boston, 1824. 8°. (B 554, 2010)
— Speech on the north-eastern boundary. (*In* **Gallatin**, A. Mem. on the north-eastern boundary. 1843.)
— Speech on the Panama mission, 14 Apr. Wash., 1826. 8°. (B 554)
— *Same.* (*In his* Works, v. 3. 1851.)
— Speech on the president's protest, May 7. Wash., 1834. 8°. (B 1810)
— Speech on the President's veto of the bank bill, July 11. Boston, 1832. 8°. (B 926, 1064, 1646, 2009, E 95)
— 2d speech on the sub-treasury bill, Mar. 12. [Wash., 1838.] 8°. (B 1129, 1646, 1723, 1751, 1791, 2010)
— *Same.* Speech on the sub-treasury bill, Mar. 12, and his speech, 22d March, in answer to J. C. Calhoun. Wash., 1838. 8°. (B 1732)
— Speech on the tariff bill, July 25. Wash., 1846. 8°. (B 1514)
— Speech on the three millions appropriation, and appropriation bill for fortifications. Wash., 1836. 8°. (B 1113, 1721, 2008)
— Speech on the war with Mexico, Senate, Mar. 23. Boston, 1848. 8°. (B 1510)
— Speech to the young men of Albany, May 28. Wash., 1851. 8°. (B 1505)
— Speech upon the tariff, April. Wash., 1824. 8°. (B 554, 1789, 1804, 2010)
— *Same.* Boston, 1824. 8°. (B 1702)
— Speeches and forensic arguments. Boston, 1830. 8°.
— *Same.* (Vol. 1, 2, 8th ed.) Boston, 1844, 43. 3 v. 8°.
Contents. Vol. 1. 1820-30. 2. 1831-Feb. 26, 1835. 3. Aug. 25, 1835-40.
— Speeches at a dinner given to [him] by the Reform convention of Maryland, Annapolis, March 25. Wash., 1851. 8°. (B 1505)
— Speeches, Buffalo, Syracuse, and Albany, May. N. Y., [1851]. 8°. (B 1668)
— Speeches of Calhoun and W. on the enforcing bill. Boston, 1833. 8°.
— Adams, C. F. Appeal from the new to the old Whigs, in consequence of the Senate's course, and particularly of W.'s speech upon the executive patronage bill. Boston, 1835. 8°. (A 43)
— Address to the Antimasonic Republicans of Mass. in favor of D. Webster for President. *n.p.*, [1836]. 8°. (B 1496)
— Allen, W. H. Eulogy on the character and services of W. Phila., 1853. 8°. (B 1727)
— Appeal to the Whig National Convention in favor of the nomination of W. N. Y., 1848. 8°. (B 1502)
— Ashmun, G. Speech in reply to the attack of C. J. Ingersoll upon W., Apr. 27. Wash., 1846. 8°. (B 1502)
— Boardman, H. A. Disc. on the life and character of W. Phila., 1852. 8°. (B 1726)
— Clark, J. Seventy-fourth anniv. of the birthday of W., Boston, Jan. 18. Boston, 1856. 8°. (B 1729)
— Creole case and W.'s despatch, with comments of the N. Y. American. N. Y., 1842. 8°. (B 1499)
— Curtis, G. T. Life of W. N. Y., 1870. 2 v. 8°.
— - Speech on the presidential election, Oct. Boston, 1852. 8°. (B 1506)
— Everett, E. Biog. memoir of the public life of W. (*In* **Webster**, D. Works, v. 1. 1851.)
— Graham, S. Letter to W. on the compromises of the constitution. Northampton, 1850. 8°. (B 1504)
— Hayne, R. Y. Defence of the South! reply to Mr. W. Charleston, 1830. 8°. (B 1066)
— Heywood, J. H. Disc. on the life and services of W. Louisville, Ky., 1852. 8°. (B 1728)
— Hillard, G. S. Memorial of W. Boston, 1853. 8°.
— Inauguration of the statute of W., Sept. 17. Boston, 1859. 8°.
— Jay, W. Reply to W. in a letter to W. Nelson. Boston, 1850. 12°. (B 1486)
— - *Same.* Letter to W. Nelson on W.'s speech. N. Y., 1850. 12°. (C 262)
— Jeffries, J. Acc. of the last illness of W., *etc.* From the Amer. journ. of med. sci., Jan. Phila., 1853. 8°. (B 1729)
— Junius Americanus. Review of a discourse [on] the death of W., by T. Parker. Boston, 1853. 8°. (B 1729)
— Knapp, S. L. Memoir of the life of W. N. Y., 1831. 12°.
— - *Same.* 2d ed. rev. N. Y., 1835. 12°.
— Lanman, C. Private life of W. N. Y., 1852. 12°.
— Lester, C. E. (*In his* Gallery of illustrious Americans. 1850.)
— Loring, J. S. (*In his* Hundred Boston orators. 1852.)
— March, C. W. Life of W. (*In his* Reminescences of Congress. 1850.)
— Maury, S. M. (*In her* Statesmen of America. 1847.)
— Maynard, H. Disc. [on] the life and services of W., Jan. 1. Knoxville, Tenn., 1853. 8°. (B 1729)
— Newburyport. Citizens. Letter to W. in rel. to his speech of March 7, and his reply. Wash., 1850. 8°. (B 1504)
— New Hampshire State Society of the Cincinnati. (*In* **New Hamp. Hist. Soc.** Col., v. 6. 1850.)
— Parker, J. Daniel Webster as a jurist. Camb., 1853. 8°. (B 1727)

— PARKER, T. Discourse, death of W., Oct. 31, 1852. (*In his* Speeches, v. 1. 1855.)
— - Speech in the old Cradle of Liberty, Mar. 25. Boston, 1850. 8°. (B 1968)
— PARTON, J. (*In his* Famous Americans of recent times. 1867.)
— PHILLIPS, W. Review of W.'s speech on slavery. Boston, 1850. 8°. (B 1478)
— PROCEEDINGS of two meetings to protest against the nomination of Gen. Scott and to recommend W., July 7, 14. Boston, 1852. 8°. (B 1506)
— REFORM CONVENTION OF MARYLAND. Speeches deliv. at a dinner given to W. by the R. C. M., Mar. 25. Wash., 1851. 8°. (B 1505)
— SAMSON, G. W. The providence of God in raising up great and good men as our rulers. Boston, 1853. 8°. (B 1726)
— SANBORN, R. S. Eulogy on the intellectuality of W. West Randolph, 1852. 8°. (B 1727)
— SEVENTY-second anniv. of the birthday of W., N. Y., Jan. 18. N. Y., 1854. 8°. (B 1729)
— SIMMONS, A. E. Spiritualism; communications from W. and others. Woodstock, 1852. 8°. (B 1200)
— SKETCH.] (*In* **Longacre, J. B.,** *and* **Herring, J.** Nat. portr. gal., v. 1. 1837.)
— SPEAR, C. Incidents of W. in relation to the late mission to England. Boston, 1853. 8°. (B 1729)
— SPEECHES and addresses on the presentation of the name of W. as president, [Boston, Nov. 25, 1851]. Boston, 1852. 8°. (B 1506)
— STUART, M. Conscience and the constitution; with remarks on the speech of W. Boston, 1850. 8°. (B 1486, 1478, 1668)
— - Webster's Andover address and polit. course while Sec. of State. Essex Co., 1844. 8°. (1197, 1500, 1646)
— TAFT, A. Oration on the life and public services of W. Cincin., 1853. 8°. (B 1727)
— TEFFT, B. F. Webster and his masterpieces. Auburn, 1854. 3 v. 12°.
— - Daniel Webster; his life and character. Rochester, 1852. 8°. (B 1727)
— U. S. *29th Cong. 1st sess.* Alleged official misconduct of the late Sec. of State; report of the committee of the House, June 9. Wash., 1846. 8°. (B 1502)
— - *32d Cong. 1st sess.* Obituary addresses. Wash., 1853. 8°.
— VAN RENSSELAER, C. New Jersey's tribute to Massachusetts; eulogy on W., Nov. 4; with app. cont. funeral ceremonies at Marshfield. Burlington, 1852. 8°. (B 1726)
— VAN SANTVOORD, C. Discourse on Daniel Webster. — Samuel Johnson and Daniel Webster. (*In his* Discourses on special occasions. 1856.)
— WALKER, T. Oration on the life and pub. services of W. Cincin., 1852. 8°. (B 1726)
— WEBSTER UNION WHIG CONVENTION. Address and proceedings of the friends of W. in Mass. Convention. Boston, 1852. 8°. (B 1506, 1668)
— WHIPPLE, E. P. (*In his* Essays, v. 1. 1848.)
— WHIPPLE, J. Disc. [on] the life and services of W., Nov. 23. Providence, 1852. 8°. (B 1726)
— WHITMAN, J. W. Report of the trial of T. Lyman for libel on W. Boston, 1828. 8°. (B 949)
— WILKINS, P. Letter to W. cont. an examination of his claims to be supported by Mass. as a candidate for the presidential chair. Bost., 1836. 8°. (B 1496)
— *Addresses on the death of W. See* **Adams, N.** (B 1729); — **Allen, W. H.** (B 1727); — **Bartol, C. A.** (B 1726); — **Butler, C. M.** (B 1728); — **Cheever, T. P.** (B 1727); — **Choate, R.** (B 1727); — **Choules, J. O.** (B 1728); — **Cleaveland, E. L.** (B 1726); — **Davis, T. T.** (B 1726); — **Drake, C. D.** (B 1727); — **Eastburn, M.** (B 1726); — **Eells, W. W.** (B 1728); — **Haven, J.** (B 1727); — **Hitchcock, R. D.** (B 1728); — **Ketchum, H.** (B 1727); — **King, T. S.** (B 1726); — **Kirk, E. N.** (B 1726); — **Lawrence, E. A.** (B 1728); — **Lothrop, S. K.** (B 1727, 1729); — **Lunt, W. P.** (B 1128, 1728, E 280); — **McCoy, A.** (B 1729); — **Mason, C.** (B 1726); — **Mayo, A. D.** (B 1728); — **Parker, T.** (B 1728); — **Perley, I.** (B 1727); — **Pope, L.,** *Jr.* (B 1727); — **Rawlings, A.** (B 1728); — **Richards, G.** (B 1726); — **Rogers, E. P.** (B 1727); — **Sanborn, E. D.** (B 1728); — **Skinner, O. A.** (B 1726); — **Stearns, J. F.** (B 1728); — **Stearns, W. A.** (B 1726); — **Stone, A. L.** (B 1727); — **Webster, G. W.** (B 1729); — **Weiss, J.** (B 1728); — **Wiley, C.** (B 1728); — **Woods, H. W.** (B 1726); — **Woods, L.,** *Jr.* (B 1728)
Note. All published in 1852, except Allen, Choate, Ketchum, McCoy, Parker, Pope, Rogers, Stone, and Webster, which were in 1853, and another edition of McCoy, was in 1856.

Webster, Edward. On a declaratory code. (*In* **Nat. Assoc. Prom. Soc. Sci.** Trans., 1859.) — Transfer of freehold estates in England and Wales by voluntary registration of title. (*In* 1861.)
Webster, Ezekiel. Defence of the national administration; address to the people of N. H.; by Cato. Concord, 1828. 8°. (B 1494)
Webster, Fletcher. Oration before the authorities of the city of Boston, July 4. Boston, 1846. 8°. (B 1201)
— HILLARD, G. S. Biography of W. (*In* **Higginson, T. W.** Harvard mem. biog., v. 1. 1866.)
— LORING, J. S. (*In his* Hundred Boston orators. 1852.)
Webster, *Rev.* **Geo. W.** Sermon to the 1st Independent Cong. Soc. of Wheeling, Va., on the death of D. Webster. 2d ed. Wheeling, 1853. 8°. (B 1729)
Webster, Harriet F., *Funeral sermon on.* 1853. *See* **Newell, W.** (B 1227)
Webster, J. P. Lorena; words by **H. D. L. Webster.** Augusta, [186-]. 4°. (E 171)
— Paul Vane; or Lorena's reply; words by **H. D. L. Webster.** Macon, [186-]. 4°. (E 171)
Webster, James, *of the County of Perth.* General view of the agriculture of Galloway. Edinburgh, 1794. 4°. (W 77)
Webster, James, *of the Inner Temple.* Travels through the Crimea, Turkey, and Egypt, 1825-28; incl. particulars of the last illness and death of the Emperor Alexander, and of the Russian conspiracy in 1825. London, 1830. 2 v. 8°.
Webster, James, *M.D.* Lecture introductory to the course on anatomy and physiology in the Geneva Med. College, Oct. Geneva, [1840]. 8°. (B 1565)
— Reply to Dr. [J.] Eberle. *n.p.*, [1827]. 8°. (B 1448)
Webster, John. Dramatic works; ed. by W. Hazlitt. London, 1857. 4 v. (v. 1, 2 w.). 12°.
Contents. Vol. 1, 2. *Wanting.* 3. Devil's law-case. — Appius and Virginia. — Monuments of honor. — A monumental column. — Odes. 4. Cure for a cuckold. — Induction to The malcontent. — Thracian wonder. — The weakest goeth to the wall.
— Appius and Virginia. (*In* **Old plays,** v. 6. 1816; — *and in* **Lamb, C.** Spec. of dram. poets. 1854.)
— The devil's law case. (*In* **Lamb, C.** Spec. of dram. poets. 1854.)
— Dutchesse of Malfy. (*In* **Scott,** *Sir* **W.** Anc. Brit. drama, v. 3. 1810; — *and in* **Lamb, C.** Spec. of dram. poets. 1854.)
— The malcontent; augmented by Marston. (*In* **Dodsley, R.** Old plays, v. 4. 1825; — *and in* **Marston, J.** Works, v. 2. 1856.)
— White devil; or, Vittoria Corombona. (*In* **Scott,** *Sir* **W.** Anc. Brit. dr., v. 3. 1810; — *and in* **Dodsley, R.** Col. of plays, v. 6. 1825.)
— - *Same, extract.* (*In* **Campbell, T.** Brit. poets, v. 3. 1819.)
— *and* **Rowley, W.** Thracian wonder. (*In* **Old plays,** v. 6. 1816.)
— DURHAM, S. A. (*In his* Lives of literary and scientific men of Gr. Britain, v. 2. 1857. Lardner. Cab. cyc., v. 2.)
Webster, John, *M.D.* Essay on epidemic cholera. London, 1832. 12°.
Webster, John White. Description of the Island of St. Michael. Boston, 1821. 8°.
— Manual of chemistry on the basis of Brande's. 2d ed. Boston, 1828. 8°.
— *Same.* 3d ed. Boston, 1839. 8°.
— Notes. (*In* **Liebig, J. J.** Animal chemistry. 1842.)
— *ed. See* **Boston** journal of philosophy and the arts.
— AWFUL disclosures rel. to the Parkman tragedy. [Boston,] 1849. 8°. (B 1757)
— BEMIS, G. Report of the case of J. W. Webster indicted for the murder of G. Parkman. *n.p.*, 1850. 8°.
— COMPLETE report of the trial of W. for the murder of G. Parkman. *n.p.*, 1850. 8°. (B 1757)
— PARKMAN murder, The; trial of W. Boston, [1850]. 8°. (B 1445, 1757)
— REVIEW of the Webster case; by a member of the N. Y. bar. N. Y., 1850. 8°. (B 1445)
— SPOONER, L. Illegality of the trial of W. Boston, 1850. 8°. (B 1445)
— STONE, J. W. Report of the trial of W. Boston, 1850. 8°.
— - *Another copy.* (B 1445)

— TRIAL of W. [Boston,] *Boston herald steam press.*, 1850. 8°. (B 1445, 1757)
— TRIAL of W., reported for the Boston daily times. Boston, 1850. 8°. (B 1445)
— TRIAL of W., reported for the Boston journal. Boston, 1850. 8°. (B 1445)
— TRIAL of W., reported for the N. Y. daily globe. N. Y., 1850. 8°. (B 1445)

Webster, *Rev.* Josiah. Mystery of godliness; sermon, Thomaston, June 15, installation of J. Lord. Newburyport, 1809. 8°. (B 334)
— Sermon, July 10, ordination of J. W. Dow, Tyringham, Mass. Stockbridge, 1811. 8°. (B 334, 1856)

Webster, *Mrs.* M. M. Pocahontas, a legend; with historical and traditionary notes. Phila., 1840. 12°.

Webster, Nathan B. Meteorograph, an automatic meteorological register. (*In* **Amer. Assoc.** Proc., v. 8. 1855.)

Webster, Noah. Address at the laying of the corner stone of the charity institution, Amherst; and sermon, by D. A. Clark. Boston, 1820. 8°. (B 1237)
— Address before the Hampshire, Franklyn, and Hampden Agricultural Soc. Northampton, 1818. 8°. (B 994)
— American dictionary of the English language. N. Y., 1828. 2 v. 4°.
— *Same.* New Haven, 1841. 2 v. 8°.
— *Same.* Rev. by C. A. Goodrich. Springfield, 1848. 4°.
— *Same.* Rev. by C. A. Goodrich. Springfield, 1859. 4°.
— *Same.* Rev. by C. A. Goodrich and N. Porter. Springfield, 1864. 4°.
— American selection of lessons in reading and speaking; the 3d part of a grammatical institute of the English language. 8th ed. Boston, 1796. 12°.

Contents. Lessons in reading. — Lessons in speaking. Dialogues. — Poetry.

— Collection of essays and fugitiv [*sic*] writings on moral, historical, political, and literary subjects. Boston, 1790. 8°.

Contents. Education of youth in America. — Principles of guvernment and commerce. — Bills, or declarations of rights. — Guvernment. — Manners, guvernment, and debt of the U. S. — Enquiry into the origin of the words domesday, parish, parliament, *etc.* — Divisions of property, guvernment, education, religion, *etc.*, in the U. S.

— Compendious dictionary of the English language. Hartford, 1806. 12°.
— Dissertation on the English language; with an essay on a reformed mode of spelling; with Dr. Franklin's arguments on that subject. Boston, 1789. 8°.
— Dissertation on the supposed change in the temperature of winter. — Number of deaths in the Episcopal Church in N. Y. in each month for ten years. — On the decomposition of white lead paint. — Origin of mythology. (*In* **Conn. Acad.** of **Arts.** and **Sci.** Mem., v. 1, pt. 1. 1810.)
— Effects of slavery on morals and industry. Hartford, 1793. 8°. (B 774)
— Elementary spelling book. Concord, 1840. 12°.
— *Same.* 3d Southern ed. Macon, 1865. 12°.
— Elements of useful knowledge. (Vol. 1, 5th ed., 2, 3d ed.) Vol. 1, N. Y., 1810, 2, 3, New Haven, 1808, 06. 3 v. 12°.

Contents. Vol. 1, 2. Historical and geographical account of the United States. 3. Historical and geographical accounts of Europe, Asia, and Africa, and New Holland.

— *Same.* Vol. 2. Historical and geographical account of the U. S. 3d ed. [Hartford,] 1809. 12°.
— Experiments respecting dew. (*In* **Amer. Acad.** Mem., v. 3. 1809.)
— Grammatical institute: pt. 2 cont. a comprehensive grammar. 4th ed. Hartford, [1787]. 12°.
— History of animals. New Haven, 1812. 12°.
— History of the U. S.; prefixed, a brief account of our English ancestors, and of the conquest of S. America by the Spaniards. New Haven, 1832. 12°.
— Improved grammar of the English language. New Haven, 1839. 12°.
— Letter to D. Ramsay [on] errors in Johnson's Dictionary, and other lexicons. N. Haven, 1807. 12°. (C 104)
— Letter to Gen. Hamilton, occasioned by his letter to Pres. Adams. *n.t.p.* [1800.] 8°. (B 401, 593, 1699, 2516)

Note. Anonymous; ascribed to N. Webster by Josiah Quincy.

— Letter to J. Pickering on his Vocabulary. Boston, 1817. 8°. (B 445)
— Manual of useful studies. Phila., 1846. 16°.
— Miscellaneous papers on political and commercial subjects: To the president of the U. S. on his administration; Rights of neutral nations; Value of the American commerce to Gr. Brit.; Sketch of the history of banks and insurance cos. in the U. S. New York, 1802. 8°. (B 403)
— Oration, Amherst, July 4. Northampton, 1814. 8°. (B 457)
— Oration, New Haven, July 4, 1798. New Haven, [1798]. 8°. (B 342)
— Oration, New Haven, July 4. New Haven, 1802. 8°. (B 557)
— A collection of papers on political, literary, and moral subjects. New York, 1843. 8°.

Contents. Revolution in France. — Rights of neutral nations. — Supposed change of temperature in modern winters. — Origin of the first bank in the U. S. — Letter from Washington respecting the last campaign in the Revolution. — Corresp. with Madison. — Origin of the copy-right laws of the U. S. — Vindication of the treaty with Gr. Brit., 1795. — Origin of Amherst Coll., Mass. — Addr. on agriculture. — Letter to D. Webster. — Ans. of the Ho. of Reps., Mass., to the Governor's address. — Letter to S. Lee. — Reply to a letter of D. McClure. — Letter to a young gentleman commencing his education. — Form of association for young men. — Modes of teaching the Eng. language. — Origin of the Hartford Convention, 1814. — Brief history of political parties. — State of Eng. philology.

— The peculiar doctrines of the Gospel explained and defended. Portland, 1811. 18°.
— *Another copy.* (B 608)
— Philosophical and practical grammar of the Eng. language. New Haven, 1807. 12°.
— Political progress of Britain. Pt. 1. 2d ed. Phila., 1794. 8°. (B 628)
— The prompter; or, A commentary on common sayings, *etc.* Windsor, 1827. 32°.
— Reply to Mellen's 'Remarks'. (*In* **Mass. Hist. Soc.** Col., v. 3. 1794.)
— Revolution in France, its progress and effects. N. Y., 1794. 8°. (B 628, 741)
— Series of books for systematic instruction in the English language. *n.t.p.* [18—.] 8°. (B 1063)
— Sketches of American policy under different heads. Hartford, 1785. 8°. (A 2)
— Ten letters to J. Priestley in answer to his letters to the inhabitants of Northumberland. New Haven, 1800. 8°. (B 613)
— Theory of vegetation. (*In* **Amer. Acad.** Mem., v. 2. 1793.)
— COBB, L. Critical review of the orthography of Webster's series of books for systematic instruction in the English language. N. Y., 1831. 8°. (B 1020)
— MELLEN, J. Remarks on Mr. Webster's calculation on lives. (*In* **Mass. Hist.** Soc. Collections, v. 3. 1794.)
— OBSERVATIONS on a letter from N. Webster, Jr., published in the Panoplist. New Haven, 1809. 8°. (B 431, 2017)
— SKETCH.] (*In* **Longacre,** J. B., *and* **Herring,** J. Nat. portr. gal., v. 2. 1835.)

Webster, Pelatiah. Dissertation on the political union and constitution of the thirteen U. S. Phila., 1783. 8°. (B 515)
— A plea for the poor soldiers; essay to demonstrate that the soldiers, *etc.*, have not been paid, ought to be paid, *etc.* Phila., 1790. 8°. (B 625)
— *Same.* New Haven, *reprinted* 1790. 8°. (B 1488)

— Polit. essays on the nature and operation of money, pub. finances, *etc.* Phila., 1791. 8°.
Contents. Danger of too much circulating cash in a state, *etc.* — Free trade and finance. — Strictures on tender-acts. — Essay to examine and state the true interest of Pennsylvania with respect to paper currency. — Economy, policy, and resources of the thirteen states. — Nature, authority, and uses of the office of a financier-general. — Rem. on the resolution of council, 2d May, 1781, *etc.* — Strictures on a publication in the Freeman's journal, May 16, 1781, signed Timoleon. — Strictures on two publications in the Freeman's journal, May 30, signed Phocion and Impartial. — Polit. union and constitution of the U. S., *etc.* — Free trade and finance. — Plea for poor soldiers, *etc.* — Review of the two foregoing essays. — Seat of the federal government, *etc.* — Rem. on the address of sixteen members of the Assembly of Penn. to their constituents, *etc.* — Weaknesses of Brutus exposed, *etc.* — Essay on credit. — Strictures on the net produce of the taxes of Gr. Brit., 1784. — Test acts imposed with penalties. — Extent and value of our Western unlocated lands, *etc.* — Scales of depreciation of Continental money. — Chron. table of remarkable events.

— Weaknesses of Brutus exposed; or, Some remarks in vindication of the Constitution. Phila., 1787. 8°. (B 65, 614)

Webster, Redford. Observations on the Amherst question. *n.t.p.* [1825.] 8°. (B 976)

Webster, Samuel, *D.D., of Salisbury.* Account of an oil-stone found at Salisbury. (*In* **Amer. Acad.** Mem., v. 1. 1785.)

— Blessedness, *etc.*; discourse, Newbury, Mar. 26, 1792, interment of J. Tucker. Boston, 1793. 8°. (B 334)

— Justification by the free grace of God; two sermons, June, 1761, March, 1765. Boston, 1765. 8°. (B 147)

— Ministers labourers together with God, *etc.*; sermon, Oct. 2, 1771, ordination of S. Webster, Jr., in Temple. Salem, 1772. 8°. (B 75, 1311)

— *Same.* (*In* **Blood,** H. A. History of Temple. 1860.)

— Misery and duty of an oppressed and enslaved people; sermon, July 14 [fast-day]. Boston, 1774. 8°. (B 47, 235, 840)

— Sermon, election. Boston, 1777. 8°. (B 146, 180, 186, 868)

— Soldiers and others directed and encouraged, *etc.*; sermon, March 25, Salisbury. Boston, 1756. 8°. (B 47, 64, 148, 235)

— Winter evening's conversation on original sin. Boston, 1757. 8°. (B 41, 269)

— The 'Winter evening's conversation' vindicated against P. Clark, in 'A summer morning's conversation'. Boston, [1757]. 8°. (B 41, 269)

— Young children declared by Christ members of his church; two discourses, Sept. 20, 1772. Salem, 1773. 8°. (B 147, 235, 862)

— *Same.* Boston, 1780. 4°. (A 2)

— Bellamy, J. Letter to the author of the 'Winter evening's conversaton'. Boston, 1758. 8°. (B 41)

— Clark, P. Defence of the 'Summer-morning's conversation'; against [W.'s] "'Winter evening's conversation' vindicated". Boston, 1760. 8°. (B 912)

— — Scripture doctrine of original sin defended; in a 'Summer-morning's conversation'; [with] remarks on a 'Winter-evening's conversation'. Boston, 1758. 8°. (B 41)

— *Funeral sermon on.* 1796. *See* **Cary,** T. (B 215)

Webster, Samuel, *of Temple, N. H.* Rabshakeh's proposals; sermon, Groton, Feb. 21, 1775. (*In* **Blood,** H. A. History of Temple. 1860.)

Webster, Stephen Peabody. Oration before the Phi Beta Kappa, Aug. 21. Hanover, 1804. 8°. (B 435)

Webster, Thomas, *prof. of geol., d.* 1844. Encyclopædia of domestic economy. From the last London edition with notes by D. M. Reese. N. Y., 1845. 8°.

Webster, Thomas, *civil engineer.* On relative temperature and density of elastic fluids. (*In* **Inst. of Civil Engin.** Trans., v. 1. 1842.)

Webster, Thomas, *barrister-at-law.* Amendment of the [patent] law. 2d ed. London, 1852. 8°. (B 1433)

— Letters patent and copyright of designs. 3d ed. London, 1851. 8°.

— Minutes of evidence and of proceedings on Liverpool and Birkenhead dock bills, 1848–52. London, 1853. 8°.

— Port and docks of Birkenhead; with maps, plans, sections, *etc.* London, 1848. 8°.

— Protection of property in intellectual labour, *etc.*, by amendment of laws of patent right. (*In* **Nat. Assoc. Prom. Soc. Sci.** Trans., 1859.) — Concentration of courts and offices of judicature. — Patent right. (*In* 1862.) — On the palace of justice; its site and approaches, and the arrangements of the courts and offices of judicature. (*In* 1865.)

Webster, Wm. Preface. (*In* **Skinner,** F. Life of G. Monk. 1724.)

Webster, Wm. H. B. Narrative of a voyage to the southern Atlantic Ocean, 1828–30. London, 1834. 2 v. 8°.

Weckherlin, Georg Rodolf. Auserlesene Gedichte. (Vol. 4 *of* **Mueller,** W. Bibliothek deutscher Dichter. 1823.)

Weddell, James. Voyage towards the South Pole, 1822–24. London, 1825. 8°.

— *French, abridged.* Voyage. (*In* **Montémont,** A. Bibl., v. 21. 1834.)

Wedderburn, Alexander, *Baron Loughborough.* Brougham, H., *Ld.* (*In his* Statesmen of the time of Geo. III., v. 1. 1839.)

— Townsend, W. C. (*In his* Lives of twelve eminent judges, v. 1. 1846.)

Wedderburn, John Walter. The naturalist in Bermuda. 1859. *See* **Jones,** J. M.

Wedderburn, *Rev.* Robert. Letter to S. Herchell conc. the origin of the Jewish prophecies of their expected Messiah. 2d ed. London, [18—]. 8°. (B 1681)

Wedding, The; a comedy. *See* **Shirley,** J.

Wedding day, The; a comedy. *See* **Fielding,** H.

Wedding day, The; a farce. *See* **Inchbald,** *Mrs.* E.

Wedding gown, The; by D. Jerrold. (*In his* Writings, v. 8. 1854.)

Wedding ring. Maskell, J. The wedding ring; its history, literature, and the superstitions respecting it. London, 1868. 12°.

Wedel, August Carl Emil Claussen. Motivirte Entscheidung des Streits über Nationalität, Staatsrecht, und Staatsuccession in Schleswig und Holstein. Phila., 1848. 8°.

Wedel (*Lat.* **Wedelius**), Georg Wolfgang. Niceron, J. P. (*In his* Mém., v. 7. 1729; *and, Germ.*, v. 7. 1753.)

Wedenberg, Adolf Fridrik. Varietas ciborum. (*In* **Linné,** C. Amœn. acad., v. 7. 1769.)

Wedge, John. General view of the agriculture of the Co. of Warwick. London, 1794. 4°. (W 75)

Wedge, Thomas. General view of the agriculture of the County of Chester. London, 1794. 4°. (W 73)

Wedgwood, Hensleigh. Dictionary of English etymology. London, 1859–65. 3 v. in 4 pt. 8°.
Contents. Vol. 1. A–D. 2. E–P. 3. Q–Z.

— *Same.* Ed. by G. P. Marsh. Vol. 1: A–D. N. Y., 1862. 8°

— Origin of language. London, 1866. 16°.

— Several articles.] (*In* **Philolog. Soc.** Proc., 1842–53; Trans., 1854–63.)

Wedgwood, Josiah. Description of the Portland vase. London, 1790. 4°.

— Boardman, J. Catalogue of cameos, intaglios, medals, *etc.*, formed in various kinds of terra cotta. Liverpool, 1817. 8°.

— — *French, with omissions and additions.* Catalogue de camées, intaglios, médailles, *etc.* *n.d.*, 1788. 8°. (B 882)

— Gladstone, W. E. Wedgwood; an address. London, 1863. 8°.

— Meteyard, E. Life of W.; with sketch of the art of pottery in England. London, 1865–66. 2 v. 8°.

Wedgwood, Julia. Female suffrage, chiefly with regard to its indirect results. (*In* **Butler,** J. E. Woman's work. 1869.)

Wedgwood family. Meteyard, E. A group of Englishmen, 1795–1815; records of the younger Wedgwoods and their friends. London, 1871. 8°.

Wednesday's Club. Dialogues upon the union of Great Britain, and upon the redemption of the national debt and taxes, 1706 and 1718. (*In* **Paterson,** W. Writings, v. 1, 2. 1859.)

Wee Davie; by N. Macleod. London, 1865. 16°.

Weech, Friedrich von. Kaiser Ludwig der Bayer und Pabst Clemens VI. (*In* **Historische** Zeitschrift, v. 12. 1864.) — Französische Zustände während der hundert Tage und der Occupation. (*In* v. 16. 1866.)

Weeden, John. *See* **Trevett** *vs.* **Weeden.** (B 626)

Weeds. WILKINSON, *Lady* C. C. Weeds and wild flowers, their uses, legends, and literature. London, 1858. 12°.

Week day book for boys and girls; by the eds. of the popular library. Boston, 1835. 18°.

Week in a French country house, A; by A. K. Sartoris. (*In* **Littell's** living age, v. 93. 1867.)

Week in Wall street, A. N. Y., 1841. 12°.

Week on the Concord and Merrimac Rivers, A. *See* **Thoreau,** H. D.

Weekes, James Eyre. The five traitors; a song. (*In* **Campbell,** T. Brit. poets, v. 5. 1819.)

Weekly. For names of newspapers beginning with this word *see* the word following.

Weekly character, The. No. 1: The character of a pope. London, 1679. 4°. (B 12)

Weekly instructor. *See* **Hogg's** weekly instructor.

Weekly messenger. *See* **Mrs. A. S. Colvin's** weekly messenger. 1828.

Weekly monitor; a series of essays on moral and religious subjects; by a layman. Nos. 1–40. Phila., Charleston, 1810. 8°.

Weekly political review of H. R. Yorke. Vol. 6; Jan.–June 1809. [London, 1809.] 8°.

Weekly register, The. *See* **Niles'** weekly register.

Weekly visitant. *See* **Visitant,** Weekly.

Weeks, *Rev.* Holland. Discourse, interment of J. B. Preston and sketch of his life. Salem, 1813. 8°. (B 1222)

— The Lord's words are spirit and life; discourse, Abington, Mass., May 21. Boston, 1820. 8°. (B 1008)

Weeks, John M. History of Salisbury, Vt. Middlebury, 1860. 12°.

Weeks, Lemuel W. Address, opening of the Chamber. (*In* **Milwaukee.** *Chamber of Commerce.* Commercial hist. 1859.)

Weeks, Wm. Raymond, *D. D.* Dialogue on the atonement. (*In* **Park,** E. A. The atonement. 1859.)

— Withholding suitable support from the ministers of religion is robbing God; sermon, Plattsburgh, N. Y., Sept. 26, 1813. Albany, 1814. 8°. (B 1305)

Weems, Mason L. The drunkards' looking glass. 2d ed. *n.p.*, 1813. 8°. (B 1278)

— God's revenge against murder; a tragedy performed by Ned Findley. 2d ed. Augusta, 1807. 8°. (B 426)

— *Same.* 4th ed. Phila., 1808. 8°. (B 469)

— *Same.* Balt., 1814. 8°. (W 4)

— History of the life and death of G. Washington. Georgetown, [1800]. 8°. (W 11)

— *Same.* Life of G. Washington. 10th ed. Phila., 1814. 8°.

— *Same.* Frankford, 1826. 12°.

— *Same.* Phila., 1833. 8°.

— *Same.* Phila., 1837. 12°.

— Hymen's recruiting serjeant; or, The maid's and bachelor's friend. Phila., 1802. 4°. (A 33)

— Life of Franklin. Phila., 1835. 12°.

— Life of Penn. Phila., 1836. 12°.

— *and* **Horry,** P. Life of Gen. F. Marion. Phila., 1816. 12°.

Weemse, John. Exposition of the ceremoniall laws of Moses. London, 1636. 4°.

— Exposition of the judiciall laws of Moses. London, 1636. 4°.

— Treatise of the foure degenerate sonnes. London, 1636. 4°.

Ween, Cornelius van. Reise nach Ostindien. (*In* **Allgemeine** Hist., v. 8. 1751.)

Weerdt, Sebald van. Historische verhael van de reyse gedæn inde Oost-Indien onder het beleydt van W. Wærwijck ende S. de Weert, 1602. (*In* **Commelin,** I. Begin, v. 1. 1646.)

Note. For other accounts of his voyage. *See* **Purchas.** Pilgrimes, v. 1. 1625; — **Harris,** J. Col., v. 1. 1705; — *and*, *Germ.*, **Allgemeine** Hist., v. 12. 1754.)

— Kort ende waerachtigh verhael van't gheene seeckere vijf schepen van Rotterdam in 't jaer 1598. (*In* **Commelin,** I. Begin, v. 1. 1646.)

— *Eng.* (*In* **Col.** of voy. by the Dutch E. I. Co. 1703.)

Note. For accounts of the same voyage, *see* **Harris,** J. Col., v. 1. 1705, 1764; — *and* **Kerr,** R. Col., v. 10. 1824.

Weerth, Johann von. *See* **Werth,** J. von.

Weethee, J. P. Battle of Armageddon; or, The word of God against the world. 2d ed. Boston, 1849. 18°.

Weever, John. Ancient funerall monuments within Gr. Brit. and Ireland. Lond., 1631. f°.

— *Same.* London, 1767. 4°.

Wegele, Franz Xaver. Wilhelm v. Grumbach. (*In* **Historische** Zeitschrift, v. 2. 1859.) — Elisabeth von Thüringen. (*In* v. 5.) — Alexis von Tocqueville. (*In* v. 20. 1868.)

Wegeler, Franz Gerhard, *and* **Ries,** F. Notices biog. sur L. van Beethoven; tr. par A. F. Legentel. Paris, 1862. 18°.

Wegelin, Jakob Dominik. *See* **Weguelin,** J. D.

Wegener, Kaspar Frederik. Ueber die unzertrennliche Verbindung Schleswigs mit Dänemark in staatsrechtlicher Beziehung. Copenhagen, 1848. 8°.

Węgierski, Tomasz Kajetan. Poezye. W Lipsku, 1837. 16°. (Bobrowicz, J. N. Bibl. klass. Polsk., v. 29.)

Weguelin, Jakob Dominik. Caractères historiques des empereurs romains, Auguste jusqu'à Maximin. Berlin, 1768. 2 v. 8°.

— Le différend entre les patriarches Photius et Ignace. — Plan raisonné d'une hist. univ. et diplomatique de l'Europe depuis Charlemagne jusqu'en 1740. (*In* **Sérieys,** A. Bibl., v. 5. 1811.) — Sur J. A. de Thou. (*In* v. 6. 1811.)

— Sur la philosophie de l'histoire. (*In* **Berlin. Ak. d. Wiss.** Abh., 1776.) — Sur le patriarche Photius. (*In* 1777.) — Sur la psychologie de Tacite. 1779.) — Sur l'art caractéristique, moral, et politique de Tacite. — Sur les biog. de Plutarque. (*In* 1780.) — Sur l'histoire considérée comme la satire des travers du genre humain. — Sur S. Athanase. (*In* 1782.) — Sur les notions claires et obscures, distinctes et confuses en fait d'histoire. — Sur J. A. de Thou. (*In* 1783, 85.) — Sur le cours périodique des événemens. — Sur la nomenclature politique. (*In* 1785.) — Sur la probabilité historique. (*In* 1786.)

Weguelin, Jean Philippe. Nouveaux dialogues françois et russes. Moscou, 1810. 8°.

Wehm, Zacharias. ANDRESEN, A. (*In his* Der deutsche Peintre-Graveur, v. 3. 1866.)

Wehner, Paul Matthias. RAMBACH, F. E. (*In* **Niceron,** J. P. Nachrichten, v. 19. 1759.)

Wehrhan, Robert, *and* **Wraxall,** *Sir* F. C. L. Memoirs of Queen Hortense. Lond., 1862. 2 v. 8°.

Weiberfeind, Der; Posse von C. Lebrun. (*In* **Kotzebue,** A. Almanach, v. 22. 1824.)

Weiberg, Caspar Dieterich. SCHWACHE Ausdrücke der Wehmuth über den Tod Weibergs. [Phila., 1790.] 8°. (D 36)

Weibliche Jakobiner-Klubb, Der; von A. v. Kotzebue. (*In his* Theater, v. 2. 1840.)

Weichsel, Fd. Fr. Die erwerbende Verjährung. Magdeburg, 1825. 8°.

— — Zusätze. Magdeburg, 1825. 8°.

Weidlich, Christoph. Vollständiges Verzeichniss aller aus der Universität zu Halle herausgekommener juristischen Disputationen und Programmen; nebst Succession aller Rechtsgelehrten und deren Biographien. Halle, 1789. 8°.

Weigel, Johann Adam Valentin. Geographische, naturhistorische, und technologische Beschreibung des Herzogthums Schlesien. Berlin, 1800. 8°. (C 156)

Weigel, Johann August Gottlob. Apparatus literarius, sive Index librorum quos empturientibus offert. Lps., 1807–09. 3 v. 8°.

Weigel, Rudolph. Catalog der [hinterlassenen] Kunst-Sammlung. 1e Hälfte. Lpz., 1867. 8°.

— Kunstcatalog. 1es–35n Abth. (1e Abth., 3e Aufl.; 2e Abth., 2e Aufl.) Lpz., 1849, 43, [36]–66. 5 v. 8°.

— Die Kupferstiche, Handzeichnungen, und Kunstbibliothek nachgelassen durch C. Rolas du Rosey. le Hälfte: Original Radirungen und Stiche. Lpz., 1864. 8°.
Note. With a half title 'Die Sammlungen für Kunst u. Wissenschaft. 3. Abth., Die Kupferstiche', *u. s. w.*

Weigel, Theodor Oswald. Catalogue de la libraire ancienne. 2e-4e supplément. Lpz., [185-]. 8°.
— Katalog des antiquarischen Lagers. Lpz., 1865. 8°.
— Katalog des Bücherlagers. les Supplement. Lpz., [185-]. 8°.
— 9r-12r Katalog naturwissenschaftlicher Werke aus dem antiq. Lager. Lpz., [1861]. 8°.

Weightman, Richard Hanson. To the Congress of the U. S. requesting the passage of a bill declaring N. Mexico one of the U. S. on certain conditions. Wash., 1851. 8°. **(B 1505)**

Weights and measures. Mariana, J. De ponderibus et mensuris. Toleti, 1599. 8°.
— Greaves, J. Disc. of the Roman foot and denarius. [1647.] (*In his* Miscel. works, v. 1. 1737; — *and in* Churchill, O. *and* J. Col. of voy., v. 2. 1744.)
— Seller, J. A pocket book cont. severall choice col. in arithmetick, astronomy, *etc.* London, [1677]. 16°.
— Greaves, J. Origin and antiq. of English weights, and measures. [1706.] 2d ed. London, 1745. 12°.
— Hayes, R. Negociator's magazine; or, Monies, weights and measures. [1719.] 8th ed. London, 1754. 8°.
— Fréret, N., *d.* 1749. Sur les mesures longues des anciens. (*In his* Œuvres, v. 15. 1796.)
— Hyde, T. Epistola de mensuris et ponderibus Serum seu Sinensium. (*In his* Syntagma, v. 2. 1767.)
— Whitehurst, J. Attempt towards obtaining measures of length, *etc.*, from the mensuration of time. London, 1787. 4°.
— — *Same.* (*In his* Works. 1792.)
— U. S. *Dept. of State.* Report of the Sec. on establishing a uniformity in the weights, measures, and coins of the U. S. N. Y., 1790. 8°. **(W 17)**
— Keith, G. S. Tracts on weights, measures, and coins. London, 1791. 4°. **(W 51, 71)**
— Beccaria, C. B. di. Riduzione delle misure di lunghezza all' uniformità per lo stato di Milano. (*In* Econ. class. ital., pte. mod., v. 12. 1804.)
— Gibbon, E. Diss. sur les anciennes mesures du Bas Empire. (*In his* Miscel. works, v. 3. 1815.)
— Calculator, *pseud.* Observations on the report of the committee of weights and measures. — Mercator, *pseud.* Sketch for a new division and subdivision of monies, weights, and measures. (*In* Pamphleteer, 1814; v. 4 of **B 838**)
— Mendo Trigozo, S. F. de. Sobre os pesos e medidas portuguezas, e sobre a introducção do systema metro-decimal. (*In* Lisbon. Ac. d. Sci. Mem. econ., v. 5. 1815.)
— British metre and its derivatives; sketch of a proposed reformation in the Brit. measures, weights, and coins. — Gr. Brit. *Commissioners on Weights and Measures.* 1st Report. (*In* Pamphleteer, 1820; v. 16 of **B 838**)
— Adams, J. Q. Report upon weights and measures. Wash., 1821. 8°. (House doc., 109.)
— Gosselin, P. F. J. Différens systèmes métriques linéaires de l'antiquité. (*In* Paris. Inst. *Ac. d. Inscr.* Mém., v. 6. 1822.) — Mongez, A. Sur les mesures romaines gravées sur un rocher près de Terracine. (*In* v. 7. 1824.)
— Balbo, P. Del metro sessagesimale, antica misura egizia, rinnovata in Piemonte. (*In* Turin. Ac. d. Sci. Mem., v. 29-31. 1825-27.)
— Metrology universalized; or, A proposal to equalize weights and measures. London, 1828. 8°. **(B 981)**
— Hussey, R. Weights, measures, and money of the ancients. Oxford, 1836. 8°.
— Walckenaer, C. A., *and* Jomard, E. F. Sur un pied romain trouvé dans la forêt de Maulevrier en 1834. (*In* Paris. Inst. *Ac. d. Inscr.* Mém., v. 12, pt. 1. 1836.) — Dureau de la Malle, A. J. C. A. Le système métrique des Romains. (*In* v. 12, pt. 2. 1836.)
— Boeckh, A. Untersuchungen über Gewichte, Münzfüsse, und Masse des Alterthums. Berlin, 1838. 8°.
— Siebold, P. F. von. Künste und Wissenschaften. (*In his* Nippon, v. 4. 1852.)
— Woolhouse, W. S. B. Measures, weights, and moneys of all nations. London, *Weale,* 1856. 12°.
— Hare, R. A method of forming small weights. (*In* Smithsonian Inst. Report, 1858.)
— Taylor, J. The battle of the standards. London, 1864. 8°.
— International Committee on Weights, Measures, *etc.* Extracts from report. (*In* U. S. *Com. for the Paris Expos.*, 1867. Reports, v. 1.)
— Lyman, B. S. On the link of Gunter's chain as the unit of a decimal system of weights and measures. (*In* Amer. Assoc. Proc., v. 15. 1867.)
— Lapparent, M. de. Poids et mesures. (*In* France. *Com. Imp. de l'Expos. de* 1867. Rapports, v. 2.)

Dictionary.

— Alexander, J. H. Dictionary of weights and measures. Balt., 1857. 8°.

Tables.

— Borel, F. Tableaux de comparison des poids de commerce, mesures, *etc.*, des nations étrangères avec celles de Russie. St. Pétersbourg, 1807. f°.
— Gutteridge, W. Tables of all measures of capacity used in Gr. Britian. Lond., 1825. 12°.
See also Congius; — Decimal system; — Scales.

Weihnacht-Abend; von J. L. Tieck. (*In his* Gesam. Novellen, v. 5. 1853.)

Weik, Johann. Californien wie es ist, oder Handbuch von Californien. Phila., Lpz., 1849. 16°.

Weil, Gustav. Die Assassinen. (*In* Historische Zeitschrift, v. 9. 1863.) — Zur Literatur der Geschichte der Kreuzzüge. (*In* v. 24. 1870.)
— Biblical legends of the Mussulmans. London, 1846. 12°.
— Geschichte der Chalifen. Mannheim, Stuttgart, 1846-62. 5 v. 8°.
Contents. Vol. 1. 632-750. 2. 749-945. 3. 945-1258. 4. 1258-1390. 5. 1390-1517.
— Mohammed der Prophet, sein Leben und seine Lehre. Stuttgart, 1843. 8°.

Weiland, P. Ter bevorderinge van Lambertus Nolst. *n.p.*, [17—?]. 4°. **(A 48)**

Weill, Alexandre. La guerre des paysans. Paris, 1847. 18°.
— Histoire de la grande guerre des paysans. 3e éd. Paris, 1860. 12°.

Weimar. Stahr, A. W. J. Weimar und Jena; ein Tagebuch. Oldenburg, 1852. 2 v. 12°.
— Wacksmuth, E. W. F. Weimars Musenhof, 1772 bis 1807. Berlin, 1844. 8°.

Weimar. Deutsche Shakespeare-Gesellschaft. Einladung zur Theilnahme an der Deutschen Shakespeare-Gesellschaft. [Weimar? 18—]. 4°. **(A 67)**

Weiner, Hans. Andresen, A. (*In his* Der deutsche Peintre-Graveur, v. 2. 1865.)

Weiner, Peter. Chorographia Bavariæ. *n.p.*, [1579].

Weingart, E. Verzeichniss einer Sammlung von 4000 Dissertationen, *u.s.w.* Erfurt, [186-]. 4°.

Weingarten. Annales Weingartenses, 792-936. (*In* Pertz, G. H. Mon. Germ. hist., Scr., v. 1. 1826.) — Annales Weingartenses Welfici, 1101-81. (*In* v. 17. 1861.)

Weinhart, Benj. Gottfried. Topographische Geschichte der Stadt Dresden, und der Gegenden. Dresden, 1777. 4°.

Weinland, David Friedrich. Names of animals and and plants, with ref. to the origin of languages, *etc.* — Digestive apparatus of the acanthocephala. (*In* Amer. Assoc. Proc., v. 10, pt. 2. 1857.) — Two human cestoidea new to science. — Method of comparative animal psychology. (*In* v. 12. 1859.)

Weinmann, Johann Wilhelm. DIETERICH, J. G. N., *and* BIELER, A. C. Phytanthoza iconographia, oder Vorstellung etl. von W. Weinmann gesamml. Pflantzen; in lat. and deutscher Sprache. Regenspurg, 1737-45. 4 v. f°.

Note. Vol. 1, 2 by Dieterich; v. 3, 4 by A. C. Bieler. Vol. 1 has a preface by A. Haller giving a history of illustr. works on botany pub. in Germany or by German authors.

Weinreich, Caspar. Danziger Chronik. (*In* **Hirsch, T.** Scr. rerum Prus., v. 4. 1870.)

Weir, *Rev.* Archibald. Conciliation and comprehension; charity within the Church and beyond. (*In his* Church and age. 1870.)

— St. Petersburg and Moscow. (*In* **Galton, F.** Vacation tourists. 1861.)

— *and* Maclagan, W. D., *ed.* The Church and the age; essays on the principles and present position of the Anglican Church. London, 1870. 8°.

Contents. Introduction. — **Hook, W. F.** Anglican principles. — **Ellicott, C. J.** The course and direction of modern religious thought. — **Irons, W. J.** The State, the Church, and the synods of the future. — **Tyrwhitt, R. St. J.** The religious use of taste. — **Burrows, M.** The place of the laity in church government. — **How, W. W.** Private life and ministrations of the parish priest. — **Haddan, A. W.** English divines of the sixteenth and seventeenth centuries. — **Sadler, M. F.** Liturgies and ritual. — **Frere, B.** Indian missions. — **Barry, A.** The Church and education. — **Maclagan, W. D.** The Church and the people. — **Weir, A.** Conciliation and comprehension; charity within the Church and beyond.

Weir, George. Historical and descriptive skethes of the town and soke of Horncastle. London, 1822. 12°.

Weir, Robert Walter. [DESCRIPTION of] picture of the embarkation of the pilgrims from Delft Haven, painted by W. N. Y., 1843. 8°. (B 1603)

Weir, Thomas. HICKES, G. Account of the trial of Maj. Weir. (*In* **Somers, J.** Col. of tracts, v. 8. 1813.)

Weis, Johann Nepomuk. Urkunden des cistercienser-Stiftes Heiligenkreuz im Wiener Walde. Wien, 1856-59. 2 v. 8°. (Fontes rerum Austr., 2. Abth., 11., 16. Bd.)

Contents. Vol. 1. 1136-1296. 2. 1300-96.

Weisbach, Julius. Principles of the mechanics of machinery and engineering. 1st Amer. ed. ed. by W. R. Johnson. Phila., 1848-49. 2 v. 8°.

Weise, Adam. Albrecht Dürer und sein Zeitalter. Lpz., 1819. 8°.

Weise, Christian. Gedichte. (*In* **Mueller, W.** Bibl. deutscher Dichter, v. 14. 1838.)

Weiske, Benjamin Gotthold. Pleonasmi Græci. Lps., 1807. 8°.

Weismann, Ehrenreich. Lexicon Latino-Germanicum et Germanico-Latinum. 8a ed. Stuttg., 1725. 4°.

Weiss, Charles. L'Espagne, depuis le règne de Philippe II jusqu'à l'avenement des Bourbons. Paris, 1844. 2 v. 8°.

Contents. Vol. 1. 1556-1665. 2. 1665-1700.

— Histoire des refugiés protestants de France. Paris, 1853. 2 v. 12°.

Contents. Vol. 1. Hist. des Protestants de France de l'édit de Nantes jusqu'à la révocation par Louis XIV. — Les refugiés dans le Brandebourg, — en Angleterre, — en Amérique. 2. Les refugiés en Hollande, — en Suisse, — en Danemark, en Suède, et en Russie.

Weiss, François Rodolphe de. Principes philosophiques, politiques, et moraux. Genève, 1806. 2 v. 8°.

Contents. Vol. 1. Introduction. — Des passions. — Vertus sociales. 2. Ebauche d'un sage. — De la société civile. — Religion naturelle.

Weiss, *Rev.* John. American religion. Boston, 1871. 12°.

— Address. (*In* **Free Religious Assoc.** 2d ann. meeting. 1869.)

— Discourse, death of D. Webster, New Bedford, Nov. 14, 1852. Boston, 1853. 8°. (B 1728)

— Discourse, death of E. Peabody, N. Bedford, Dec. 7. N. Bedford, 1856. 8°. (B 1594)

— Life and correspondence of T. Parker. London, 1863. 2 v. 8°.

— *Same.* Amer. ed. N. Y., 1864. 2 v. 8°.

— Northern strength and weakness; address, national fast, April 30. Boston, 1863. 16°. (B 1593)

— Our private and public stewardship; discourse, Watertown. Camb., 1845. 8°. (B 1305)

— Reform and repeal; sermon on fast-day, Apr. 6; and legal anarchy, sermon, June 4, rendition of A. Burns. Boston, 1854. 8°. (B 1260)

— Unity and peace; sermon, Worcester, Jan. 10, 1847. Worcester, [1847]. 8°. (B 1305)

Weiss, Mathias. Roméo et Julie; tragédie. (*In* **Junker, G. A.**, *and* **Liébault, —.** Théâtre allemand, v. 4. 1785.)

Weiss, Siegfried. Mémoire diplomatique sur la Prusse, l'Autriche, Schleswig Holstein, *etc.* Brux., Paris, 1865. 8°.

Weisse, J. A. Key to the French langauge. Boston, 1842. 24°.

Weissenburg. Annales Weissemburgenses, 765-846. (*In* **Pertz, G. H.** Mon. Germ., Scr., v. 1. 1826.) — 708-1147. (*In* v. 3. 1839.)

Weizsäcker, Julius. Die pseudo-isidorische Frage in ihrem gegenwärtigen Stande. (*In* **Historische Zeitschrift,** v. 3. 1860.)

Wékey, Sigismund. Grammar of the Hungarian language; with exercises and specimens of poetry. London, 1852. 8°.

Welch, Benjamin, *M. D.* Annual address, Med. Institution of Yale Coll., Jan. 27. N. Haven, 1853. 8°. (B 1565)

Welch, Charles Alfred. Biography of C. H. Wheelwright. (*In* **Higginson, T. W.** Harvard mem. biog., v. 1. 1866.)

Welch, Jonathan A. Address before Windham County Peace Society, Feb. 13. Brooklyn, Conn., 1828. 8°. (B 938)

Welch, Moses Cook, *D.D.* An excellent spirit, [*etc.*]; sermon, Hartford, May 14. Hartf., 1812. 8°. (B 294, 334)

Welch, Oliver. American arithmetic. 3d ed. Exeter, [1814]. 12°.

— *Same.* Improved. Boston, [1834]. 12°.

Welch Indians. *See* **Welsh Indians.**

Welch traveller, The; or, The unfortunate Welchman; by H. Crouch, 1671; ed. by J. O. Halliwell. London, 1860. 16°.

Welch. *See also* **Welsch**; — **Welsh.**

Welchman, Edward. Defence of the Church of Eng. from the charge of schism and heresie laid against it by the vindicator of the deprived bishops [H. Dodwell]. London, 1693. 4°. (B 4)

Welcker, Friedrich Gottlieb. Alte Denkmäler erklärt. Göttingen, 1849-64. 5 v. 8° *and* Plates 4°.

Contents. Vol. 1. Die Giebelgruppen u. andre griechische Gruppen u. Statuen. 2. Basreliefe und geschnittne Steine. 3. Griechische Vasengemälde. 4. Wandgemälde. 5. Statuen, Basreliefe, und Vasengemälde.

— Die Composition der polygnotischen Gemälde in der Lesche zu Delphi. (*In* **Berlin. Ak. d. Wiss.** Abh., 1847.) — Der Felsaltar des höchsten Zeus oder das Pelasgikon in Athen, bisher genannt die Pnyx; nach der Entdeckung des H. R. Ulrich's in Athen. (*In* 1852.)

— Epische Cyclus oder homerischen Dichter. Bonn, 1835-49. 2 v. 8°. (Supplementband d. Rhein. Mus.)

Contents. Vol. 1. Der epische Cyclus. — Die Homerischen Dichter. 2. Die Gedichte des troischen Kreises. — Gedichte des thebischen Kreises. — Die übrigen Gedichte des epischen Cyclus.

— Griechische Götterlehre. Göttingen, 1857-63. 3 v. 8°.

— Griechischen Tragödien. Bonn, 1839-45. 3 pts. 8°. (Suppl.band d. Rhein. Mus.)

Contents. Pt. 1. Einleitung. — Tragiker vor Æschylus. — Æschylus. — Sophokles. 2. Euripides. — Vergleichende Uebersicht der Tragödien des Æschylus, Sophokles, Euripides. 3. Die übrigen Tragiker bis auf Alexander. — Tragödien unbekannter Verfasser. — Dichter ausserhalb Athens. — Die Tragödien nach Alexander. — Die griechisch-römischen und die römischen Tragödien. — Allgemeine Zusammenstellung der griech. u. röm. Tragödien. — Zusätze. — Register.

— Kleine Schriften. Bonn, 1844-61. 4 v. 8°.

Contents. Vol. 1. Namen. 1823. — Ueber den Linos. 1830. — Der Elegos. 1836. — Archilochos. 1816. — Die Zwölfkämpfe des Herakles bey Pisander. 1833. — Der Delphin des Arion und die Kraniche des Ibykos. 1833. — Sappho. 1828. — Alkäos. 1830. — Stesichoros. 1829. — Ibykos. 1834. — Anakreon. 1835. — Epicharmos. 1829. — Ein Vers aus einer Iliupersis des Æschylus bey Aristophanes. 1831. — Ein Stoff der alten Attischen Komödie. 1830. — Das ABCbuch des Kallias in Form einer Tragödie. 1833. — Die späteren Thebaïden, auch die des Statius. 1832. — Ueber den Ursprung des Hirtenlieds. 1820 oder 1821. — Unächtheit der Rede des Lysias gegen den Sokratiker Aeschines. 1834. — Ueber die unächten Lydiaka von Xanthos. 1830. — Herakides Pontikos περὶ πολιτειῶν. 1837. 2. Ueber die Lage des homerischen Ilion. 1843. — Aöden u. Improvisatoren. 1820 od. 1821. — Die Molionen und die Aloiden in der Ilias. 1822. — Die homerischen Phäaken u. die Inseln der Seligen. 1832. — Sappho von einem herrschenden Vorurtheil befreyt. 1816. — De Erinna et Corinna poetriis; adj. est Melinnus, vulgo Erinnæ Lesbiæ, carmen in Romam. 1816. — Pindar. 1833. — Ueber den Plan einzelner Gesänge des Pindar. 1834. — Des Dionysios Chalkus elegische Verse. 1836. — Æsop; eine Fabel. 1839. — Ueber den Ajas des Sophokles. 1829. — Die Anakreonteen. 1835. — Prodikos der Vorgänger des Sokrates. 1832. — Hesychius. 1834. 3. Chiron der Phyllride; Der Pelion. 1831. — Medea oder die Kräuterkunde bei den Frauen; Ephyra. 1831. — Wundheilkunst der Heroen bei Homer. 1832. — Seuchen von Apollon. 1832. — Innere Heilkunde; Podalirios. 1832. — Einfluss der Luft und der Winde. 1832. — Epoden oder das Besprechen. — Incubation; Aristides der Rhetor. — Lykanthropie ein Aberglaube und eine Krankheit. — Entbindung. 1833. — Schneiden und Brennen. — Anatomie. — Die Aerzte. — Lamina argentea. 1835. — Inscriptio Megarensis. 1843. — Inscriptio Spartana. 1844. — Isisinschrift in Andros. 1843. — Krissäische Inschrift. 1843. — Grab und Schule Homers in Ios und die Betrügereien des Grafen Pasch von Krienen. 1844. — Inschrift von Phanagoria. 1817. — Aus der Anzeige von K. O. Müllers Handbuch der Archäologie die vorangehenden allgemeinen Bemerkungen. 1834. — Ueber die archäologische Kritik und Hermeneutik. 1834. — Schatzhäuser oder Grabmäler in Mykenä und Orchomenos. 1834. — Der kleine Tempel auf der Spitze des Bergs Ocha in Euböa. — Fr. Jacobs über den Reichthum der Griechen an plastischen Kunstwerken und die Ursachen desselben. 1811. — L. Schorn über die Studien der griechischen Künstler. 1819. — Ueber die Sitte der Alten die Sculptur zu bemalen. 1839. — Die enkaustische Malerei. 1836. — Die Enkaustik ein Gemälde. 1833. — Zwei Gemälde des Protogenes bei Plinius. 1837. — Der Ajas und die Medea von Timomachos. 1829. — Die Alexanderschlacht bei Issos. 1834. — Griechische Künstlergeschichte; Silligs Catalogus artificum. 1827. — Die Therikleia mit Thierfiguren verzierte Becher. 1838. — Endöos. — Ueber das Zeitalter des Gitiadas. 1833. 4. Ueber die Bedeutung der Philologie. 1841. — Alte Autoren in Bezug auf die Lage Ilions. 1857. — Der homerische Margites. 1856. — Alcmanis fragm. de Tantalo; eiusdem fragm. de sacris in summis montibus peractis et alia. 1855. — Ueber die beiden Oden der Sappho. 1856. — Der Æschylus Schutzflehende, Ægypter und Danaiden. 1845. — Zu des Æschylus Schutzflehenden. 1858. — Œdipodee und Tebais. 1861. — Ueber die Perser des Æschylus. 1837. — Philoktetes oder Ilions Zerstörung. 1837. — Die Heliaden des Æschylus. 1828. — Der erste Monolog des sophokleischen Ajas. 1860. — Theokrits vierte Idylle. 1833. — Die Akropolis von Athen. 1843. — Denkmal des Sesostris. 1843.

— Wandgemälde aus Pompeji und Herculanum, mit Text von K. O. und W. Mueller. *See* **Ternite**, W.

Welcker, Karl Theodor. Das Staats-Lexikon. 1856-65. *See* **Rotteck**, K. W. von.

Weld, Allen Hayden. Classical instruction. (*In* **Amer. Instit. of Instr.** Lect., 1844.)

— English grammar. 50th ed. Portland, 1846. 12°.

— Latin lessons and reader. 2d ed. Andover, 1845. 16°.

Weld, *Mrs.* Angelina Emily (Grimké). Letter to the woman's rights convention at Syracuse, Sept. 1852. (*In* **Woman's rights tracts.** 1854. B 1667)

Weld, C. M. Address as president, 1862. (*In* **Mass. Hom. Med. Soc.** Publ., 1862.)

Weld, Charles Richard. History of the Royal Society. London, 1848. 2 v. 8°

— Statistical companion for 1850. *See* **Banfield**, T. C.

— Two months in the Highlands, Orcadia, and Skye. London, 1860. 8°.

— A vacation in Brittany. London, 1856. 12°.

— Vacations in Ireland. London, 1857. 8°.

Weld, Daniel, *Funeral sermon on.* 1852. *See* **King**, T. S. (B 1227, 1247)

Weld, *Rev.* Ezra. Discourse, Apr. 25, [fast] day. Boston, 1799. 8°. (B 857)

— Sermon at a singing lecture, Braintree, May 21, 1788. Springfield, 1789. 8°. (B 285)

— Sermon. Christian union, Wrentham, May 22, at public fast. Boston, 1794. 8°. (B 235)

— Sermon, Sept. 23, ordination of J. French. Boston, [1772]. 8°. (B 276)

Weld, *Rev.* Habijah. Note on Attleborough. (*In* **Mass. Hist. Soc.** Col., v. 11. 1814.)

Weld, Horatio Hastings. Corrected proofs. Boston, 1836. 12°.

— Sacred quotations from the poets. Phila., 1854. 8°.

Weld, Isaac. Travels through North America, 1795-97. London, 1799. 2 v. 8°.

Weld, J. H. Fourth experiment of living. 13th ed. Boston, 1837. 18°.

Weld, *Mrs.* Mary Anne. *See* **Fitzherbert**, *Mrs.* M. A.

Weld, Theodore Dwight. American slavery as it is; testimony of a thousand witnesses. N.Y., 1839. 8°.

— The Bible against slavery; inquiry into patriarchal and Mosaic systems of human rights. *n.p.*, [184-]. 8°. (B 1471)

Welde, Thomas. Short story of the rise, reign, and ruine of the Antinomians, *etc.*, that infected the churches of New England, *etc.* London, 1644. 4°.

Welding, *Sir* Anthony. *See* **Weldon**, *Sir* A.

Weldon, *Sir* Anthony. Brief history of the Kings of England, particularly those of the House of Stuart. London, 1755. 4°. (B 579)

Note. The title page bears the name of Sir A. Welding, Bart. This is a reprint of his 'A cat may look upon a king. Amst., 1714.'

— Court and character of King James; add., Court of King Charles. (*In* **Secret** history of the court of James I., v. 1. 1811.) — Perfect description of the people and country of Scotland. (*In* v. 2.)

Note. The 'Perfect description' is 'by James Howell, generally attributed to Sir Anthony Weldon'. — *Catalogue of the Advocates' Library.*

— AULICUS coquinariæ; in answer to 'Court of K. James'. (*In* **Secret** history of the court of James I. 1811.)

Note. The 'Aulicus is attributed to Wm. Sanderson and to Peter Heylin'.

Well-chapels. BLIGHT, J. T. Remarks on the well-chapels of Cornwall. — JEWITT, L. Add. notices of the Cornish well-chapels. (*In* **Reliquary**, v. 2. 1861-62.)

Well dressing. WATTS, *Mrs.* A. M. H. Well-dressing at Tissington. (*In* **Reliquary**, v. 3. 1862-63.)

Well spent sous; or, Bibles for the poor negroes; tr. from the French by J. Porter. New Haven, 1830. 8°. (B 1359)

Wellbeloved, Charles. Charge. (*In* **Robberds**, J. G. Services, ordination P. P. Carpenter. 1841. B 1745.)

— Devotional exercises for the use of young persons. 2d Amer. ed. [Boston,] 1824. 12°.

Wellborn, C. J. Catalogue of the State Library of Georgia. Milledgeville, 1859. 8°.

Wellborn, M. J. To the voters of the 2d Congressional district of Georgia. [Wash.? 1850.] 8°. (B 1507)

Weller, Emil. Annalen der poetischen National Literatur der Deutschen, 16., 17. Jahrhundert. Freiberg, 1862-64. 2 v. 8°.

— Die falschen und fingirten Druckorte. Lpz., 1858. 8°.

— Die falschen und fingirten Druckorte. 2e Aufl. Lpz., 1864. 2 v. 8°.
Note. Vol. 2 has the 2d title, 'Dictionnaire des ouvrages français'.
— Index pseudonymorum. 2e Ausg. Lpz., 1862. 8°.
— - Nachträge. Lpz., 1857. 8°.
— - Neue Nachträge. Lpz., 1862. 8°.
— - Neue Nachträge. Glauchau, Lpz., 1867. 8°.
— Repertorium typographicum; die deutsche Literatur in ersten Viertel des sechzehnten Jahrhunderts. Nördlingen, 1864. 8°.
Note. Also entitled 'Panzers Annalen. 3r Theil'.

Weller, George, *D.D.* Letter to the members of the Protestant Episc. Ch. in Nashville, containing a reply to to a publication of S. Miller. Nashville, 1836. 8°. (B 1360)

Weller, Jacob. Grammatica Græca nova ante ab A. Tellero quod ad dialectos attinet completa ab ipso auctore novis notis; præter obs. C. Daumii acc. L. Bosii brevissima syntaxis et accentuum ratio; ed. J. F. Fischerus. Lips., 1781. 8°.
— Fischer, J. F. Animadversionum ad J. Welleri grammaticam Græcam specimen. Lps., 1798-1801. 4 v. 8°.
Note. I-III; [Spec. III, ed. C. T. Kuinoel].

Weller, John B. Speech on the loan bill, July 10. Wash., 1841. 8°. (B 1663)
— Speech on the U. S. fiscal bank bill, Aug. 4, 1841. *n.t.p.* [1841.] 8°. (B 1664)

Weller, Karl Heinrich. Traité des maladies des yeux; tr. par F. J. Riester; notes par L. Jallat. Paris, 1832. 2 v. 8°.

Welles, Arnold, *Jun.* Address to the members of the Mass. Char. Fire Soc., June 2. Boston, 1797. 8°. (B 669)

Welles, Gideon. Report in relation to armored vessels. *See* **U. S.** *Navy Dept.*

Welles, Noah. Patriotism described, *etc.*; sermon, Hartford, May 10. New London, 1764. 8°. (B 334)
— Vindication of the validity of Presbyt. ordination, as set forth in Chauncy's sermon and Welles' discourse, in answer to the exceptions of J. Leaming, in his 'Defence', *etc.* New Haven, 1767. 8°. (B 293)
— Leaming, J. Defence of the Episcopal government of the church; [with] remarks on two late sermons on Presbyterian ordination. New York, 1766. 8°. (B 293)

Welles, Wm. H. Speech, Senate, Apr. 1, 1816, on the bank bill *.n.t.p.* [1816.] 8°. (B 455)

Wellesley, Arthur, 1*st Duke of Wellington*. Correspondence with T. Raikes. Lond., 1861. 8°.
— Despatches, correspondence, and memoranda; ed. by his son in contin. of a former series. London, 1867-80. 8°.
Contents. Vol. 1. 1819-22. 2. 1823-25. 3. 1825-27. 4. 1827-28. 5. 1828-29. 6. 1829-30. 7. 1830-31. 8. 1831-32.
— Dispatches, 1799-1818; compiled by J. Gurwood. New ed. Lond., 1837-38. 12 v. 8°.
Contents. Vol. 1. 1794-1803. 2. 1803-04. 3. 1804-05. 4. 1805-09. 5. 1809-10. 6. 1810. 7. 1810-11. 8. 1811-12. 9. 1812. 10. 1812-13. 11. 1813-14. 12. 1814-15.
— General orders, 1809-15; comp. by J. Gurwood. London, 1832. 8°.
— Index to the despatches of W.; in three parts; by J. Gurwood. London, 1839. 8°.
— Selections from despatches and general orders; comp. by J. Gurwood. London, 1841. 8°.
— Speech. (*In* **Copley**, J. S. Summary of the session. 1836. B 1118)
— Supplementary despatches and memoranda; ed. by his son. London, 1858-65. 12 v. 8°.
Contents. Vol. 1. 1797-1800. 2. 1800-01. 3. 1801-03. 4. 1803-08. 5. 1807-09. 6. 1807-10. 7. 1810-13. 8. 1813-14. 9. 1814-15. 10. 1815. 11. 1815-17. 12. 1817-19.
Note. Vol. 5 has the title-page 'Civil correspondence and memoranda'.
— Batty, R. Campaign in the western Pyrenees, *etc.*, 1813-14. London, 1823. 4°.
— Binney, T. Wellington as warrior, senator, and man. London, 1852. 18°.
— Brialmont, A. H. Life of W.; with add. by G. R. Gleig. London, 1858-60. 4 v. 8°.
— Brown, J. R. Ode, death of W. London, 1853. 8°. (B 1452)
— Capefigue, J. B. H. R. (*In his* Diplomatists of Europe. 1845.)
— Evans, S. Sonnets on the death of W. Camb., 1852. 8°. (B 1461)
— Gore, M. Lecture, character of W. London, 1852. 8°. (B 1461)
— Jackson, B., *and* Scott, C. R. Military life of W. London, 1840. 2 v. 8°.
— James, G. P. R. Oration on W. Boston, 1853. 8°. (B 1227)
— Jones, *Sir* J. T. Journals of sieges carried on by the army under W. in Spain, 1811-14; with notes and add.; also, memoranda rel. to the lives [of Torres Vedras], thrown up to cover Lisbon in 1810. 3d ed. by H. D. Jones. London, 1846. 3 v. 8°.
— Letter relating to the Wellington and Nelson tribute. *n.t.p.* [1839.] 8°. (B 1852)
— Maurel, J. The Duke of Wellington, his character, actions, and writings; preface by Lord Ellesmere. London, 1853. 12°.
— Maxwell, W. H. Life, military and civil, of Wellington. London, *Bohn*, 1852. 8°.
— Memoir of W.; from the 'Times'. Lond., 1852. 8°.
— Military and political life of W. London, 1852. 8°.
— Military history of W. in India. London, 1852. 8°.
— Phillips, C. A. B. Historical sketch of W. Brighton, 1852. 8°. (B 1461)
— Redding, C. (*In his* Personal reminis., v. 2. 1867.)

Wellesley, Henry, *D.D.* Library [rich in Italian literature], sold, Nov. 1866. Lond., [1866]. 8°.

Wellesley, Richard Colley, 2*d Earl of Mornington, afterward Marquess Wellesley.* Despatches, minutes, and correspondence during his administration in India; ed. N. Martin. (Vol. 1, 2d ed.) London, 1840, 36-37. 5 v. 8°.
Contents. Vol. 1. 1798-99. 2. 1799-1802. 3. 1802-05. 4. 1798-1804. 5. 1804-05.
— Memoirs and correspondence; ed. by R. R. Pearce. London, 1846. 3 v. 8°.
Contents. Vol. 1. 1760-1803. 2. 1798-1808. 3. 1808-42.
— Military plans for [his] history of the Marhatta war. London, 1804. 4°.
— Speech. (*In* **Chapman**, N. Select speeches, v. 4. 1808.)
— Substance of speech, Jan. 21, on a motion for an address to His Majesty. Dublin, 1794. 8°. (B 1890)
— Authentic correspondence and documents explaining the proceedings of the Marquess Wellesley and Earl of Moira, in the recent negotiations for the formation of an administration. London, 1812. 8°. (B 789)
— Bayne, P. (*In his* Essays. 1871.)
— Brougham, H., *Ld.* (*In his* Statesmen in the time of George III., v. 3. 1843.)

Wellesley, Wm. Pole Tylney Long, *Viscount Wellesley, Earl of Mornington.* The Irish question considered in its integrity. Dublin, 1844. 8°.

Wellesley, Province of. Cameron, J. (*In his* Malayan India. 1865.)

Wellfleet, *Mass.* Pratt, E. Hist. of W., [1763-1844.] (*In his* Comprehensive hist. of Eastham. 1844.)
— Whitman, L. Topographical description of W., [1793]. (*In* **Mass. Hist. Soc.** Col., v. 3. 1794.) — Account of creeks and islands in W., [1794]. (*In* v. 4. 1795.) — Note on W., [1802]. (*In* v. 8. 1802.)

Wellford, Beverley R. Address before the Medical Society of Virginia, April. Richmond, 1852. 8°. (B 1565)

Wellington, Arthur Wellesley, *Duke of*. *See* **Wellesley, A.**

Wellington, *Rev.* Charles. Sermon, commemoration of the fiftieth anniv. of his ordination, Feb. 25. Boston, 1807. 8°. (B 1326)

Wellington, *Rev.* Charles, *of Templeton*. Sermon, Templeton; interment of L. Rice. Boston, 1822. 8°. (B 1224)

— Sermon, Templeton, Jan. 29, after the decease of J. Howe. *n p.*, 1843. 8°. (B 1218)

Wellington, Jeduthan, *Lt.-Col.* Mass. *Gen. Court.* Report of committee in the court martial of J. W. *n t.p.* [1808.] 8°. (B 1858)

Wellington, Timothy, *M.D.* Biog. notice of W. (*In* **Mass. Med. Soc.** Med. comm., v. 8. 1854.)

Wells, Charles Thomas. Examination of the question of anæsthesia, on [his] memorial. *n.p.*, 1853. 8°. (B 1567)

Wells, Daniel. Argument on the trial of W. Wyman, at Lowell. Greenfield, 1844. 8°. (B 1441)

— Examination of the message of the Gov. to the Senate, Mar. 28. Boston, 1833. 8°. (B 1088, 1768)

Wells, David Ames. Things not generally known. N. Y., 1857. 12°.

— Distribution of manganese. — Existence of organic matter in stalactites and stalagmites, forming crystallyzed amorphous crenate of lime. — Origin of stratification. (*In* **Amer. Assoc.** Proc., v. 6. 1852.)

See also **United States.** *Special Comm. of the Revenue* (p. 3096); — *also* **Annual** of scientific discovery, 1850–71.

Wells, Eleazar Mather Porter, *D. D.* Discourse, death of Wm. Appleton. Boston, 1862. 8°. (B 1244)

— Preparations for death; lecture, Boston, in Lent, 1852. *n p.*, [1852]. 8°. (B 1305)

— Sermon, death of Ann C. Butler. [Boston, 1858?] 8°. (B 1209)

Wells, Edward, *D.D.* Elementa arithmeticæ numerosæ et speciosæ. [Ed. alt.?] Londini, 1726. 8°.

— Letter to Clarke, in answer to his 'Letter'. Oxford, 1713. 8°. (B 28)

— A new sett of [41] maps both of ancient and present geography. London, [169–]. f°.

— Remarks on Clarke's introduction to his Scripture doctrin of the trinity. Oxford, 1713. 8°. (B 28)

— A specimen of an help for the more easy understanding of the Scriptures. Oxford, 1709. 4°. (B 15)

— A treatise of ancient and present geography. Oxf., 1701. 8°.

— Young gentleman's trigonometry, mechanics, and optics. 2d ed. London, 1731. 8°.

— Clarke, S. Letter to W. in answer to his 'Remarks'. London, 1714. 8°. (B 28)

— – *Same.* (*In his* Works, v. 4. 1738.)

Wells, *Rev.* George Wadsworth. Two discourses to the 1st parish in Kennebunk, Oct. 21, 1838. Kennebunk, 1839. 8°. (B 1305)

— *Funeral sermon on.* 1843. *See* **Bartol, C. A.** (B 1227)

Wells, Henry. The American express in its relation to the city of Buffalo. Albany, 1863. 8°. (B 1605)

Wells, Horace, *M. D.* Wales, J. Discovery by H. Wells of the applicability of nitrous oxyd gas, ether, *etc.* Hartford, 1852. 8°. (B 1567)

— Testimony in relation to the claims of W., with evidence explanatory thereto. (*In* Morton, W. T. G. Statements. 1853.)

Wells, J. Soelberg. Treatise on diseases of the eye. London, 1869. 8°.

Wells, John. Oration before the young men of the city, New York, July 4. N. Y., 1798. 12°. (B 1202)

Wells, John Doane, *Eulogy on.* 1830. *See* **Childs, H. H.** (B 1227, 1247)

Wells, Nathaniel. Topog. description of Wells, County of York. (*In* **Mass. Hist. Soc.** Col., v. 3. 1794.)

Wells, Nathaniel Armstrong. Picturesque antiquities of Spain. London, 1846. 8°.

Wells, Samuel Adams. Oration at Boston, July 5. Boston, 1819. 8°. (B 558, 1662)

— Loring, J. S. (*In his* Hundred Boston orators. 1852.)

Wells, Seth Y. Summary view of millennial church or united soc. called Shakers. *See* **Green, C.**

Wells, *Mrs.* Shepard. Forman. *Rev.* J. G. (*In* **Brockett, L. P.** Woman's work in the civil war. 1867.)

Wells, Thomas Spencer. Diseases of the ovaries. Vol. 1. London, 1865. 8°.

Wells, Walter. Water power of Maine. *See* **Maine.** *Hydrographic Survey.*

413. (21. 10. 81)

Wells, Wm. Excerpta quædam e scriptoribus Latinis. Bostonii, 1810. 8°.

Wells, Wm., *D.D.* Observations taken from an address in Brattleborough. *n.t.p.* [18–.] 12°. (B 659)

— Some communications first published in the Brattleborough paper. Brattleboro', 1816. 8°. (B 265)

See also **Belsham, T.** American Unitarianism. 1815. (B 266)

Wells, Wm. Charles, *M.D.* Essay on dew. 2d ed. London, 1815. 8°.

— Two essays. London, 1818. 8°.

Contents. Memoir of W. by himself. — Essay upon single vision with two eyes. — Exper. and obs. on several subjects in optics. — Essay on dew. — Letter to Ld. Kenyon. — Acc. of a female of the white race, part of whose skin resembles that of a negro.

Wells, Wm. Harvey. Grammar of the English language. 154th thous. Boston, 1854. 12°.

— Self-reliance. (*In* **Amer. Inst. Instr.** Lectures, 1852.)

Wells, Wm. Vincent. Explorations and adventures in Honduras, *etc.* N. Y., 1857. 8°.

— Life and public services of S. Adams. Boston, 1865. 3 v. 8°.

Contents. Vol. 1. 1722–72. 2. 1772–78. 3. 1778–1804.

Wells, *Me.* Wells, N. Topog. descrip. of W. (*In* **Mass. Hist. Soc.** Col., v. 3. 1794.)

— Hubbard, J., *and* Greenleaf, J. Account of W., 1825. (*In* **Maine Hist. Soc.** Col., v. 1. 1865.)

Wells. Swindell, J. G. Well-digging, boring, and pump-work. 3d ed., rev. by G. R. Burnell. London, *Weale*, 1854. 12°.

See also **Artesian wells; — Boring; — Well-dressing.**

Wells Cathedral. Architectural Photographic Association. Architectural details from Wells Cathedral and the precinct buildings. London, [186–?]. f°.

— – Descriptive account of the sculptures of the west front; extracted from the 'Iconography of the west front'; by C. R. Cockerell. London, 1862. 4°.

Note. To accompany the photographs.

— – Photographs from the sculptures in the west front. London, 1862. 8°.

— Britton, J. History and antiquities of the Cathedral. London, 1824. 4°.

— Freeman, E. A. History of the Cathedral. London, 1870. 16°.

Wellsted, J. Raymond. Travels to the city of the Caliphs, along the shores of the Persian Gulf and the Mediterranean. Lond., 1840. 2 v. 8°.

— *Germ.* Reisen in Arabien; deutsche Bearbeitung hrsg. mit Anmerkungen und einem Excurs über himjaritische Inschriften von E. Rödiger. Halle, 1842. 2 v. 8°.

Wellsted. *See also* **Welsted; — Welsteed.**

Wellwood, *Sir* Henry Moncrieff. Account of the life and writings of J. Erskine. Edin., 1818. 8°.

— Sermons. 2d ed. Edin., 1807. 8°.

Welman, Oliver Deming, *Funeral sermon on.* 1803. *See* **Muir, J.** (B 174)

Welsch. *See also* **Welch; — Welsh.**

Welsch, Georg Hieronymus. Commentarius in Ruzname naurus sive Tabulæ æquinoctiales novi Persarum et Turcarum anni; acc. Dissertatio de earundem usu. August. Vindel., 1676. 4°.

— Specimen supplementorum ad bibliothecam Gesnero-Simlero-Frisianano. (*In* **Schelhorn, J. G.** Amœn. lit., v. 6. 1727.)

Welsch, James. Two voy. to Benin beyond Guinea, 1588–90. (*In* **Green, J.** Col. of voy., v. 1, 2. 1745; — *in* **Moore, J. H.** New col. of voy., v. 1. 1778; — *in* **Hakluyt, R.** Col. of voy., v. 2. 1810; — *and in* **Kerr, R.** Col. of voy., v. 7. 1824.)

Welsch, John. Letters to R. Boyd of Trochrig, 1607–19. (*In* **Wodrow Soc.** Miscellany, v. 1. 1844.)

Welser, Marcus. Epistola. (*In* **Schelhorn, J. G.** Amœn. lit., v. 3. 1730.) — Antiquorum quæ Aug. Vind. extant monumentorum supplementum. — Monumentorum Augustan. supplementum. (*In* v. 5. 1726.)

— Examen de la liberté originaire de Venise; avec harangue de Louis Hélian contre les Vénitiens; tr. par Amelot de la Houssaye. Ratisbonne, 1677. 12°.

— Mantissa III. monumentorum vetustorum Romanorum. (*In* **Beck, M. F.** Monumenta. 1686.)

— NICERON, J. P. (*In his* Mém., v. 24. 1733.)

Welsford, Henry. Mithridates minor; an essay on language. London, 1848. 8°.

— Origin and ramifications of the English language; preceded by an inquiry into the primitive seats, migrations, and settlements of the principal European nations. Lond., 1845. 8°.

Welsh. *See also* **Welch**; — **Welsch.**

Welsh, Benjamin. Blood letting in the epidemic fever of Edinburgh. Edin., 1819. 8°.

Welsh, David. Account of the life and writings of T. Brown. Edin., 1825. 8°.

Welsh, Jane Kilby. Familiar lessons in mineralogy and geology. Boston, 1832. 2 v. 12°.

Welsh, John. YOUNG, J. Life of W., minister of Ayr. Edin., 1866. 8°.

Welsh, Thomas, *M. D.* Curious facts respecting worms. (*In* **Mass. Med. Soc.** Med. comm., v. 1. 1808.) — Dissertation on heat and cold. — Report on spotted or petechial fever. (*In* v. 2. 1813.)

— Oration, Mar. 5, to commemorate the tragedy of Mar. 5, 1770. Boston, [1783]. 4°. (**A 6**)

— *Same.* (*In* **Orations.** 1785. **B 614**)

— LORING, J. S. (*In his* Hundred Boston orators. 1852.)

Welsh, Wm. Report of a visit to Spotted Tail's tribe of Brulé Sioux Indians, *etc.* Phila., 1870. 8°.

Welsh girl, The; a comedy. *See* **Planche**, *Mrs.* E.

Welsh Indians. BURDER, G. The Welch Indians; papers resp. a people whose ancestors emigrated from Wales in 1170. Lond., [1797]. 8°.

— - *Another copy.* (**W 84**)

— WILLIAMS, J. Enquiry into the truth of tradition conc. the discovery of America by Prince Madog, 1170. London, 1791. 8°.

— - *Another copy.* (**W 84**)

— - Farther observations on the discovery of America by Prince Madog; [with] account of Welsh Indians. London, 1792. 8°.

— - *Another copy.* (**W 84**)

Welsted, Leonard. From his Summum bonum. (*In* **Campbell, T.** Brit. poets, v. 5. 1819.)

Welsteed, Wm., *Funeral sermon on.* 1729. *See* **Colman, B.** (**B 19, 84, C 310**)

Welsteed, *Rev.* Wm., *d.* 1753. Dignity and duty of the magistrate; sermon, election, May 29. Boston, 1751. 8°. (**B 145, 180, 184, 274**)

— *Funeral sermon on.* 1753. *See* **Mather, S.** (**B 228**)

Welt und Zeit. (1r Th., 2e Aufl.) Germanien, 1816–18. 3 v. 8°.

Weltevreden, *Java.* GIBSON, W. M. The prison of W., *etc.* N. Y., 1855. 12°.

Welton, Thomas A. Composition of populations of large towns. (*In* **Nat. Assoc. Prom. Soc. Sci.** Trans., 1857.)

Welwood, Andrew. Meditations representing a glimpse of glory; or, Gospel discovery of Emmanuel's land. Bost., *reprinted* 1744. 12°.

Welwood, James, *M.D.* Memoirs of the most material transactions in Eng. for the last hundred years preceding the revolution in 1688. 2d ed. London, 1700. 8°.

— Answer to K. James's Declaration, May 8. London, 1689. 4°. (**B 5**)

Wemms, Wm., *and others.* TRIAL for the murder of C. Attucks [and others], 5th Mar. Boston, 1770. 12°. (**C 77**)

— *Same.* Boston, 1807. 8°. (**B 948**)

Wemyss, Francis Courtney, *ed.* The modern standard drama, v. 10, 12, 13. *See* **Sargent, E.**

Wemyss, Thomas. Job and his times; and a new version, with notes, *etc.* London, 1839. 8°.

— Symbol dictionary. (*In* **Jenks, W.** Comprehensive commentary, v. 6. 1838.)

Wenceslas, *St.*, *Duke of Bohemia*, *b.* 907, *d.* 936. CHRISTIANUS *de Scala.* (*In* **Acta** sanct., v. 47. 1867.)

Wenceslas IV., *King of Bohemia, and Emp. of Germany*, *b.* 1361, *d.* 1419. ANONYMUS de origine Taboritarum et de morte Wenceslai IV. (*In* **Vienna. Ak. d. Wiss.** Fontes rer. Austr., Abth. 1., B. 2. 1856.)

Wenck, Woldemar. Die wittenberger Capitulation von 1547. (*In* **Historische** Zeitschrift, v. 20. 1868.)

Wenckstern, Otto von. History of the war in Hungary, 1848–49. London, 1859. 16°.

— Memoir on the rights of Schleswig and Holstein. London, 1848. 8°.

Contents. **Introductory** remarks. — **Bunsen, C. C. J.,** *Freiherr* von. Memorial on the constitutional rights of Schleswig and Holstein, *etc.*, 1848. — **Gruner, V.** Mem. on the Danish question, 1846. — **Schleswig-Holstein.** Mem. of the provisional government addressed to Lord Palmerston. — **Collection** of docs. rel. to the Danish question. — **Map** of Schleswig and Holstein.

Wendeborn, Friedrich August. View of England towards the close of the 18th cent.; tr. from the German by the author. Dublin, 1791. 2 v. 12°.

Wendelin (*Lat.* **Wendelinus**), Gottfried. Aries seu aurei velleris encomium. [Colophon:] Antverpiæ, 1632. 4°.

Wendell, Abraham. CASE of W. of the brig Kremlin of N. Y. arising from an outrage perpetrated by him upon W. Bell, first officer of said brig in Havana, July 1838. [Wash., 1840.] 8°. (**B 1448, E 256**)

— TRIST, N. P. Reply to the resolutions at a meeting in Boston on the case of W. [Wash., 1840?] 8°. (**B 1159, E 256**)

Wendoverus, Rogerus. *See* **Rogerus** *de Wendover.*

Wendt, Johann Amadeus. De philosophia Cyrenaica. (*In* **Goettingen. Ges. d. Wiss.** Comm., 1832–37.)

— Wilhelm Nesen; eine Erinnerung aus der Reformationszeit. (*In* **Reformations** Almanach, v. 3. 1821.)

Wenham, *Mass.* MANSFIELD, D. The sanctuary a blessing; sermon, dedication of the new meeting-house of the Cong. Soc., Dec. 20, 1843. Andover, 1844. 8°. (**B 1194**)

Wenlock of Wenlock; by T. E. Wilks. (*In* **Sargent, E.** Mod. stand. dr., v. 17.)

Wensley, by E. Quincy. (*In* **Putnam's** mag., v. 2. 1853.)

Wentworth, Benning, *Gov. of N. H.* Letter to J. Wentworth, June 14, 1767. (*In* **New Hamp. Hist. Soc.** Col., v. 3. 1832.) — Order for raising men in 1759. (*In* v. 6. 1850.)

Wentworth, Charles Watson, *2d Marquis of Rockingham.* KEPPEL, G. T., *6th Earl of Albemarle.* Memoirs of the Marq. of Rockingham and his contemporaries. London, 1852. 2 v. 8°.

Wentworth, John, *Lieut. Gov. of N. H.*, *b.* 1672, *d.* 1730. Lieut. Gov. W.'s commission. 1717. — GR. BRIT. *King.* (*In* **New Hamp. Hist. Soc.** Col., v. 1. 1824.) — Instructions to T. Atkinson, commissioner to Canada in 1724. (*In* v. 6. 1850.)

Wentworth, *Sir* John, *Gov. of N. H.*, *Lieut. Gov. of Nova Scotia*, *b.* 1737, *d.* 1820. Letter to Col. T. W. Waldron, 1768. (*In* **New Hampshire Hist. Soc.** Col., v. 3. 1832.) — Letter, Jan. 17, 1777. (*In* v. 5. 1837.)

Wentworth, John, *Jr.*, *b.* 1745, *d.* 1787. SKETCH of W. (*In* **New Hampshire Hist. Soc.** Col., v. 5. 1837.)

Wentworth, John, *b.* 1815. The Wentworth genealogy. Boston, 1870. 2 v. 8°.

— WHEELER, H. G. Biog. sketch of J. Wentworth. (*In his* History of Congress, v. 2. 1848.)

Wentworth, Tappan. Speech on the Kansas and Nebraska question, May 18. Wash., 1854. 8°. (**B 1509**)

Wentworth, Thomas, *of Lincoln's Inn*, *b.* 1567, *d.* 1627. Office and duty of executors. London, 1676. 8°.

Wentworth, *Sir* Thomas, *Earl of Strafford*, *b.* 1593, *d.* 1641. Two speeches in Parliament, 1628. (*In* **Somers, J.** Col. of tracts, v. 4. 1810.)

— FORSTER, J., *and* COURTENAY, T. P. (*In their* Lives of eminent British statesmen, v. 2. 1836.)

— MACDIARMID, J. (*In his* Lives of Brit. statesmen, v. 2. 1820.)

— RUSHWORTH, J. Tryal of Thomas, Earl of Strafford. 2d ed. London, 1700. f°.
— SKETCH, with some letters.] (*In* Precept and example. 1825.)
Wentworth, Thomas, *of Chicago*. Speech on the Kansas and Nebraska question, May 18. Wash., 1854. 8°. (**B 1509**)
Wentworth family of New Hampshire. GENEALOGICAL notice. (*In* **New Hampshire Hist. Soc.** Col., v. 5. 1837.)
— WENTWORTH, J. Wentworth genealogy. Boston, 1870. 8°.
Wentworth, Charles, The history of; [by **A. Bancroft**]. London, 1770. 3 v. 12°.
Wentworth Grange, Five days entertainments at; by F. T. Palgrave. London, 1868. 8°.
Wepfer, Johann Jakob. Observationes anatomicæ de apoplexia. Amst., 1681. 8°.
— Observationes de affectibus capitis. Scaphusii, 1727. 4°.
— NICERON, J. P. (*In his* Mém., v. 11. 1730; *and, Germ.*, v. 10. 1854.)
Wept of the Wish-Ton-Wish, The; drama. (*In* **Sargent**, E. Mod. stand dr., v. 20.)
Wept of Wish-Ton-Wish, The; by [**J. F. Cooper**]. Phila., 1829. 2 v. 12°.
— *Same.* Illust. by Darley. N. Y., [1859]. 8°.
Wer weiss wozu das gut ist; von A. v. **Kotzebue**. (*In his* Theater, v. 31. 1841.)
Werburgh *or* **Werburge**, *Saint*. BRADSHAW, H. The holy lyfe and history of Saynt Werburge; ed. by E. Hawkins. London, 1848. 4°. (Chetham Soc., v. 15.)
Werdenhagen, Johann Angelius. De rebus publicis Hanseaticis. Pars 3. Lugd. Bat., 1631. 12°.
— De S. Rom. Imperii circulis tractatus. Amst., 1636. 24°.
Werder, *Prussia*. JANSON, O. Tractuum [*sic*] Borrussiæ ab incolis Werder appellati delineatio. *n.p.*, [16—.] (**E 78**, no. 269a)
Werdet, Edmond. Extrait de l'hist. du livre en France; études bibliographiques sur la famille des Didot, 1713-1864. Paris, 1864. 8°.
— De la librairie française. Paris, 1860. 18°.
Were-wolves. GOULD, S. B. Book of were-wolves. London, 1865. 8°.
Werlauff, Eric Christian. [Several papers.] (*In* **Copenhagen. K. Com. f. Olds. Opb.** Antiq. Ann., v. 1., pt. 1, v. 2, pt. 1, v. 3, pt. 1, v. 4, pt. 2. 1812-27.)
Wermüller *or* **Vierdmüller**, Otto. How a Christen man oughte to behave hymselfe in the daũger of death. (*In* **Coverdale, M.** Remains. 1846.)
Werne, Ferdinand. Expedition to discover the sources of the White Nile, 1840-41; from the German, by C. W. O'Reilly. London, 1849. 2 v. 12°.
Werner, Abraham Gottlob. CUVIER, G. L. C. F. D. (*In his* Eloges hist., v. 2. 1819.)
— JARDINE, *Sir* W. (*In his* Naturalists' lib. Entomol., v. 3. 1835.)
Werner, Friedrich Ludwig Zacharias. Martin Luther; oder Die Werke der Kraft; eine Tragödie. Berlin, 1807. 8°.
— Vierundzwanzigste Februar; eine Tragödie. Lpz., Altenburg, 1815. 18°.
— CARLYLE, T. (*In his* Crit. essays, v. 1. 1860.)
Werner, Karl. Geschichte der katholischen Theologie. München, 1866. 8°. (**Munich. Ak. d. Wiss.** Gesch. d. Wiss.)
Werner. *See* **Byron, G. G. N.**, *Lord Byron*.
Wernerian Natural History Society. Memoirs. Edin., 1811-38. 7 v. 8°.
Contents. Vol. 1. **Jameson**, *Prof.* R. Contemporaneous veins. — **Thomson**, T. Analysis of fluor-spar. — **Brown**, R. On the asclepiadeæ. — **Montagu**, G. Account of five rare species of British fishes. — **Laskey**, J. Elucidation respecting the pinna ingens in Pennant's 'British zoology'. — **Jameson**, *Prof.* R. Mineralogical queries. — **Ogilby**, J. Transition greenstone of Fassney. — **Fleming**, *Rev.* J. Description of a small-headed narwal cast ashore in Zetland. — **Jameson**, *Prof.* R. Colouring geognostical maps. — **Fleming**, J. Mineralogical account of Papa Stour, one of the Zetland Islands. — **Montagu**, G. Observations on some peculiarities observable in the structure of the gannet; — Account of a species of fasciola which infests the trachea of poultry. — **Neill**, P. Some account of a fin-whale stranded near Alloa. — **Maughan**, R. List of the rarer plants observed in the neighbourhood of Edinburgh. — **Scoresby**, W., *Jr.* Meteorological journals kept during voyages from Whitby to Greenland and back again, 1807-09. — **Edmondston**, *Dr.* A. Obs. on the natural and medical history of the Zetland sheep. — **Macknight**, *Dr.* T. Mineralogy and local scenery of certain districts in the Highlands of Scotland. — **Laskey**, J. Account of North British testacea. — **Barclay**, *Dr.* J. Remarks on some parts of the animal that was cast ashore on the Island of Stronsa, Sept. 1808. — **Jameson**, *Prof.* R. Topaz of Scotland. — **Imrie**, *Lieut.-Col.* Remarks upon the pudding or conglomerate rock which stretches along the south front of the Grampian Mts. — **Jameson**, *Prof.* R. Strontian lead-glance formation; — Cryolite. — **Ogilby**, *Dr.* J. Veins that occur in the newest flœtz-trap formation of East Lothian. — **Bald**, R. Coal formation of Clackmannanshire. — **Thomson**, *Dr.* T. Gaseous combinations of hydrogen and carbon. — **Neill**, P. List of fishes found in the Frith of Forth, and rivers and lakes near Edinburgh. — **Jameson**, *Prof.* R. Catalogue of animals of the class vermes found in the Frith of Forth. — **Stewart**, C. List of insects found in the neighborhood of Edin. — **Scoresby**, W., *Jr.* Account of the balœna mysteceetus or Greenland whale. — **Yule**, *Dr.* J. Summary of experiments and obs. on the germination of the gramineæ. — **Mackenzie**, T. Account of the coal formation at Durham. — **Scoresby**, W., *Jr.* Meteorological obs. on a Greenland voyage, 1810. — **Mackenzie**, C. Analysis of compact felspar from Pentland Hills. 2. **Mackenzie**, C. Mineralogy of the Ochil Hills. — **Imrie**, *Lieut.-Col.* —. Geological account of the southern district of Stirlingshire. — **Thomson**, *Dr.* T. Chemical analysis of a specimen of magnetic iron ore from Greenland. — **Leach**, W. E. Description of a swordfish found in the Frith of Forth, June 1811; — Obs. on the genus squalus of Linné. — **Montagu**, G. Essay on sponges. — **Macknight**, T. Mineralogical description of Tinto. — **Fleming**, *Rev.* J. Account of the rocks which occur in the neighbourhood of Dundee; — Mineralogy of St. Andrews. — **Scoresby**, W., *Jr.* Obs. on a Greenland voyage in 1811; — Meteorological journal kept during a Greenland voyage, 1812. — **Hisinger**, W. Analyse de la spath perlée. — **Jameson**, *Prof.* R. Outline of the mineralogy of the Pentland Hills; — Conglomerated or brecciated rocks; — Porphyry; — Mineralogical obs. and speculations. — **Edmondston**, *Dr.* A. Obs. on the natural history of the colymbus immer. — **Fleming**, *Rev.* J. Contributions to the British fauna. — **Thomson**, *Dr.* T. Description and analysis of a new species of lead-ore from India. — **Barclay**, *Dr.* J. Notice concerning the structure of the cells in the combs of bees and wasps. — **Scoresby**, W., *Jr.* Greenland or polar ice. — **Fleming**, *Rev.* J. Mineralogy of the redhead in Angusshire. — **Dacosta**, H. M. Description of a specimen of native iron found in the Leadhills. — **Grierson**, *Dr* J. Mineralogical obs. in Galloway. — **Macknight**, *Dr.* T. Lithological obs. on the vicinity of Loch-Lomond; — Description of Ravensheugh. — **Gray**, *Ld.* Hints regarding the coincidence which takes place in the pressure of the atmosphere at different latitudes and at nearly the same time. — **Montagu**, G. Account of several new and rare species of fishes taken on the south coast of Devonshire. — **Stevenson**, R. Obs. upon the alveus or general bed of the German Ocean and British Channel. — **Macknight**, *Dr.* T. Geol. remarks on the Cartlane craig. — **Brown**, T. Account of the Irish testacea. — **Barclay**, *Dr.* J. Remarks respecting the causes of organization. — **Leach**, W. E. Genera and species of eproboscideous insects; — Arrangement of æstrideous insects. — **Wilson**, J. Obs. on some species of genus falco of Linnœus. — **Jameson**, *Prof.* R. Geognosy of the Lothians. 3. **Traill**, *Dr.* T. S. Obs. on the anatomy of the orang outang. — **Brewster**, *Sir* D. Connection between the primitive forms of crystals and the number of their axes of double refraction. — **Montagu**, G. Description of a species of delphinus. — **Fleming**, *Dr.* J. Mineralogy of the neighbourhood of Cork. — **Macknight**, *Dr.* T. Mineralogical notices and observations. — **Bald**, R. Additional obs. on the coal field of Clackmannanshire. — **Grierson**, *Rev.* J. Account of some sandstone petrifactions found near Edinburgh. — **Traill**, *Dr.* T. S. Description of the simia sagulata or jacketed monkey. — **Fleming**, *Dr.* J. Water rail. —

Traill, *Dr.* T. S. Description of a new species of felix from Guyana. — **Fleming**, *Dr.* J. On the water rail. — **Butter**, *Dr.* J. Account of the change of plumage exhibited by many species of female birds at an advanced period of life. — **Neill**, P. Account of some fossil remains of the beaver found in Perthshire and Berwickshire. — **Jameson**, *Prof.* R. Rocks of sandside in Caithness; — Geognosy of East Lothian. — **Holder**, *Dr.* R. Account of the effects of the juice of the papaw tree in intenerating butchers'-meat. — **Dick**, T. L. Travelled stone near Castle-Stewart. — **Campbell**, J. Abstract of a paper on the scale of being. — **Dewar**, *Dr.* H. Nutrition of cuticle, nails, hair, feathers, and plants. — **Swainson**, W. Obs. on the genus picus of Linnæus. — **Don**, D. Descrip. of new and rare native plants found in Scotland. — **Jameson**, *Prof.* R. Rocky Mt. sheep of the Americans. — **Stevenson**, R. Bed of the German Ocean or North-Sea. — **Brewster**, *Sir* D. Additional obs. on the connection between the primitive forms of minerals and the number of their axes of double refraction. — **Greville**, R. K. Account of some of the cryptogamous plants of Devonshire. — **Barclay**, D., *and* **Neill**, P. Account of a beluga killed in the Frith of Forth. — **Greville**, R. K. New species of fucus found in Devonshire. — **Fleming**, *Dr.* J. British species of the genus beroe. — **Don**, D. Descrip. of new plants from Nepaul. — **Greville**, R. K. New species of potentilla from Greenland. — **Traill**, T. S. Acc. of the lutra vittata and of the viverra poliocephalus. — **Greville**, R. K. Leaves, capsule, and root of buxbaumia aphylla. — **Young**, *Rev.* G. Singular fossil skeleton found at Whitby. — **Wilson**, J. Physiological notice concerning the early state of the common frog. — **Murray**, J. Luminosity of the sea. — **Deuchar**, J. Explanation of an apparatus suggested by Col. Yule for discharging ordnance upon Mr. Forsyth's plan. — **Adie**, A. Descrip. of two new philosophical instruments; — Descrip. of an instrument for ascertaining the specific gravity of bodies without the use of weights or calculation. — **Deuchar**, J. Continuation of an account of some experiments performed with an apparatus for discharging ordnance. **4. Haidinger**, W. Crystallisations of copper pyrites. — **Notice** of the attempts to reach the sea by Mackenzie's River since the expedition of Sir A. Mackenzie. — **Adam**, *Dr.* J. Geological notices rel. to the district between the Jumna and Nerbuddah, *etc.* — **Bald**, R. Notices regarding the fossil elephant of Scotland. — **Greville**, R. K. Descrip. of seven new Scottish fungi. — **Macritchie**, *Rev.* W. Meteorological journal kept at Clunie, 1809–20. — **Greville**, R. K. Descrip. of a new species of grimmia found in Scotland. — **Boué**, *Dr.* A. Geognosy of Germany. — **Greville**, R. K., *and* **Arnott**, G. A. W. Arrangement of the genera of mosses, with characters and obs. — **Baird**, J. Short account of the rocks in the neighbourhood of St. John's, Newfoundland. — **Edmondston**, L. Obs. on the snowy owl. — **Wauchope**, *Capt.* R. Meteorological and hydrographical notes. — **Anderson**, G. Account of the small district of primitive rocks near Stromness in the Orkney Islands. — **Edmondston**, L. Account of a new species of larus shot in Zetland; — Additional acc. of the Iceland gull. — **Macgillivray**, W. Notice relative to two varieties of nuphar lutea. — **Anderson**, G. Geognostical sketch of part of the great glen of Scotland. — **Edmondston**, L. Obs. on the immer goose of Zetland. — **Greville**, R. K. Descrip. of two new plants found in Scotland. — **Grierson**, J. Observ. on the natural history of the mole. — **Vetch**, *Capt.* Account of the Island of Foula. **5. Knox**, *Dr.* R. Account of the foramen centrale as seen in the eyes of certain reptiles. — **Edmondston**, L. Obs. on the lesser guillemot, *etc.* — **Knox**, *Dr.* R. Obs. on the anatomy of the duck-billed animal of New South Wales. — **Greville**, R. K., *and* **Arnott**, G. A. W. Tentamen methodi muscorum. — **Miller**, M. Register of the weather at Corfu. — **Knox**, R. Additional obs. rel. to the foramen centrale of the retina in reptiles. — **Marshall**, H. Contributions to a natural and economical history of the coco-nut tree. — **Knox**, *Dr.* R. Obs. on organs of digestion and their appendages, *etc.* — **Coldstream**, J. Account of a series of thermometrical obs. at Leith. — **Arnott**, G. A. W. Notice of a journal of a voyage from Rio de Janeiro to the coast of Peru, by W. Jameson. — **Knox**, *Dr.* R. Origin and characteristic differences of the native races [in] So. Africa. — **Don**, D. Monograph of the genus pyrola. — **Macgillivray**, W. Descrip., *etc.*, of the different species of the genus larus. — **Atkinson**, J. Geographical distribution of plants in Yorkshire. — **Fleming**, *Rev. Dr.* J. New British species of spantangus. **6. Don**, G. Monograph of the genus allium. — **Scot**, *Rev.* D. Saphan of the Hebrew scriptures. — **Grant**, R. E. Structure of the eye of the sword-fish. — **Whitham**, H. Notice regarding a vein of asphaltum. — **Macgillivray**, W. New species of ornithorynchus. — **Grant**, R. E. Obs. on the anatomy of the paca of Brazil. — **Buchanan**, T. Comparative anatomy of the organ of hearing. — **Young**, *Rev.* G. Fossil remains of quadrupeds, *etc.* — **Grant**, R. E. Anatomy of the perameles nasuta from New Holland. — **Jameson**, W. Meter. journal from the mouth of the Rio de la Plata to the coast of Chili, 1822. — **Menteath**, J. S. Memoir on the geology of the Snowdon range of mts. — **Hamilton**, F. Commentary on the second book of the 'Herbarium Amboinense'. — **Craigie**, D. Anatomical peculiarities of the sturgeon. — **Watt**, M. Obs. on the aranea geometrica, *etc.* — **Traill**, T. S. Descrip. of a silurus known by the name of gilbacke; — New species of cephalus. — **Fleming**, J. Remarks on the genus scissurella of M. D'Orbigny. — **Gregg**, S. T. Optical illusion called the fairy islands. — **Scot**, D. On the question whether domestic poultry were bred among the ancient Jews. — **Wilson**, J. Origin of domestic poultry. — **Scot**, *Rev.* D. Okrub of the ancient Hebrews. — **Macgillivray**, W. Species of arvicola. — **Scot**, *Rev.* D Mustard plant mentioned in the gospels. — **Duncan**, J. Catalogue of coleopterous insects found in the neighbourhood of Edin. — **Macgillivray**, W. Phenogamic vegetation of the River Dee. — Appendix. **7. Cunningham**, R. J. H. Geology of the Lothians. — **Parnell**, R. Natural and economical history of the fishes of the river district of the Frith of Forth.

Wernherus, *St.*, *d.* 1287. VITA. (*In* **Acta** sanct., v. 11. 1866.)

Wernherus, *episc. Merseburgensis*, *d.* 1093. VITA. (*In* **Pertz**, G. H. Mon. Germ., Scr., v. 14. 1861.)

Wernicke *or* **Wernike**, Christian. Gedichte. (*In* **Mueller**, W. Bibl. deutsche Dichter, v. 14. 1838.)

Wernyhora, wieszcz Ukraiński; przez M. Czaykowski. Paryż, 1838. 2 v. 8°.

Werth *or* **Weerth**, Johann von. CUST, E. (*In his* Lives of the warriors of the 30 years' war, v. 2. 1865.)

Werther, Leiden des jungen; von J. W. von Goethe. (*In his* Werke, v. 12. 1817; — Sämmtliche Werke, v. 3. 1854.)

— *Eng.* Sorrows of Werther. Chiswick, 1823. 32°.

Werwing, Jonas. Konung Sigismunds och Carl den IX.des historier; utg. af A. A. v. Stiernman. Stockholm, 1746–47. 2 v. 4°.

— - Bilagor. Stockholm, 1747. 4°.

Wescher, Karl. Etude sur le monument bilingue de Delphes. (*In* **Paris. Inst.** *Ac. d. Inscr.* Div. sav., 1e sér., v. 8. 1869.)

Wesel. ABBILDUNG Wesel mit dero umbligenden Orten. *n.p.*, [16—]. (E 78, no. 156b)

— MAP. Amst., [17—]. (E 60)

Weser, Daniel. Hirudo medicinalis. (*In* **Linné**, C. Amœn. acad., v. 7. 1769.)

Wesley, Charles. Charles Wesley seen in his finer and less familar poems; ed. by F. M. Bird. N. Y., 1867. 12°.

— Epistle to J. Wesley. London, 1755. 8°. (B 1883)

— Sacred poetry selected from [his] works; with selections from his version of the Psalms. N. Y., 1864. 8°.

— JACKSON, T. Life of W. comprising a review of his poetry. London, 1841. 2 v. 8°.

— MOORE, H. (*In his* Life of J. Wesley, *etc.*, v. 1. 1824.)

— WHITEHEAD, J. (*In his* Life of W., v. 1. 1793.)

Wesley, John. The almost Christian; sermon. London, 1784. 8°. (W 44)

— Calm address to our American colonies. London, [1775]. 12°. (B 390)

— *Same.* New ed. corr. and enl. London, [1775]. 12°. (C 114)

— Calm address to the inhabitants of England. London, 1777. 12°. (B 390)

— Collection of hymns. N. Y., 1830. 16°.

— Compendium of natural philosophy. New ed., by R. Mudie. London, 1836. 3 v. 16°. (Fam. lib., v. 56–58.)

— Concise history of England to the death of George II. London, [1775]–76. 4 v. 12°.

— Explanatory notes upon the New Testament. 11th ed. London, 1831. 2 v. 8°.

— Extract of W.'s journal, from his embarking for Georgia [Oct. 18, 1730] to his return to Lond. [Jan. 29, 1738]. 5th ed. Lond., 1775. 12°.

— Extract of W.'s journal, from Feb. 1, 1737 to his return from Germany, 1738. 5th ed. London, 1775. 12°.
— Extract of W.'s journal from Aug. 12, 1738 to Nov. 1, 1739. London, 1788. 8°.
— The great assize; sermon. London, 1783. 12°. (W 44)
— The important question; sermon. London, 1783. 8°. (W 45)
— Lectures on the new heavens and new earth. (*In* Time of the end. 1856.)
— Preservation against unsettled notions in religion. *t.p. mut.* [1770.] 12°.
— Serious address to the people of England. London, 1778. 8°. (B 662)
— Sermon, death of G. Whitefield, Nov. 18, 1770. Boston, 1771. 8°. (B 235)
— Sermon, original sin. Bath, 1783. 8°. (W 45)
— Sermon, salvation by faith. London, 1783. 8°. (W 44)
— Sermons on several occasions. Lond., 1845. 8°.
— Some observations on liberty; occasioned by a late tract. London, 1776. 12°. (B 390)
— Thoughts upon slavery. 3d ed. London, 1774. 12°. (B 390)
— *Same.* (*In* Benezet, A. Potent enemies of America. 1774. B 390)
— CONSTITUTIONAL answer to Wesley's 'Calm address to the American colonies'. London, 1775. 12°. (B 390, C 114)
— EVANS, C. Letter to Wesley, occasioned by his 'Calm address to the American colonies'. New ed. London, 1775. 12°. (B 390, C 114)
— - Reply to Fletcher's Vindication of Wesley's 'Calm address'. Bristol, [1776]. 8°. (C 112)
— FEW thoughts [on] Methodism; [with] answer to a late pamphlet of W. against Erskine. Edin., 1766. 12°. (C 24)
— FLETCHER, J. W. Vindication of Wesley's Minutes; or First check to Antinomianism. (*In his* Works, v. 1. 1802.)
— FREE grace indeed! Letter to J. Wesley relating to his sermon [on] free grace. London, *printed*, Boston, *reprinted* 1741. 16°. (C 24)
— HAMPSON, J. Memoirs of J. Wesley. Sunderland, 1791. 3 v. 12°.
— HERVEY, J. Aspasio vindicated in reply to Wesley's 'Preservative against unsettled notions, *etc.* *n.p.*, 1764. 12°.
— - *Same.* (*In his* Works, v. 4. 1825.)
— LETTER to W. in vindication of absolute unconditional election, particular redemption, special vocation, and final perseverance. London, 1743. 8°. (D 67)
— LETTERS [1-4] to W. *n.t.p.* [17—.] 8°. (D 67)
— LOFFT, C. Observations on Wesley's second 'Calm address'; remarks on constitution, *etc.*; plan of peace. London, 1777. 12°. (B 390)
— MALDEN, H. (*In his* Disting. men of modern times, v. 3. 1838; v. 39 of Lib. ent. kn.)
— MR. Wesley's principles detected: a defence of the pref. to the Edin. ed. of 'Aspasio vindicated' in answer to Kershaw's 'Earnest appeal'. Edin., 1765. 12°. (C 24)
— MOORE, H. Life of W.; [with] life of C. Wesley, and memoirs of their family. London, 1824-25. 2 v. 8°. (C 46)
— OLIPHANT, *Mrs.* M. O. W. J. Wesley, the reformer. (*In her* Hist. sketches, v. 2. 1869.)
— NATURE and fitness of things; or, The perfection of God a standing rule to try all doctrine and experience by; poem offered to the consideration of J. Wesley. 2d ed. London, 1752. 8°. (C 192)
— PALMER, S. Vindication of the Dissenters, in answer to W.'s Defence of his Letter. London, 1705. 4°.
— RÉMUSAT, C. de. W. et le méthodisme. (*In* Revue d. D. Mondes, jan. 1870.)
— SHIRLEY, W. Narrative of W.'s conference, Bristol, Aug. 6. 2d ed. Bath, 1771. 8°. (B 256)
— SOUTHEY, R. Life of W.; the rise and progress of Methodism. London, 1820. 2 v. 8°.
— - *Same.* N. Y., 1820. 2 v. 8°.
— - *Same.* London, 1846. 2 v. 8°.
— TAYLOR, J. Wesley and Methodism. London, 1851. 12°.
— TOPLADY, A. M. Letter to W. [on] his pretended abridgment of Zanchius on predestination. 2d ed. London, 1771. 8°. (B 1371)
— WHITEFIELD, G. Letter to W. in answer to his sermon entitled 'Free grace'. Boston, 1740. 16°. (C 51, 60)
— WHITEHEAD, J. Life of W.; [with] account of his ancestors, *etc.* London, 1793-96. 2 v. 8°.
— *Funeral sermon on.* 1791. *See* Whitehead, J. (B 235)

Wesley, W. H. The iconography of the skull. (*In* Anthropological Soc. Mem., v. 2. 1866.)

Wesleyan Methodist Church. DORSEY, D. B. Review of an address signed by W. Wilkins. Balt., 1827. 8°. (B 1395)

Wesleyan Methodists. YERIWANONTONTHA ne ne Wesleyan Methodists. [In the Mohawk language.] Lynn, Mass., 1834. 12°. (E 33)

Wesleyan University, *Middletown, Conn.* Catalogue of the corporation, faculty, and students. *n.p.*, [1833]. 8°. (B 1722)
— SPRAGUE, W. B. Address before the Literary Soc. of Wesleyan Univ., July 31. Albany, 1848. 8°. (B 1738)

Wessel, Caspar. Kort over Siæland. *n.p.*, 1770-77. 5 maps. (E 66)

Wesselhœft, Conrad. Annual address, 1862: Homœopathy and some of its leading features. (*In* Mass. Homœop. Med. Soc. Publ. 1862.) — Cases of dysentery. (*In* 1864.)

Wesselhœft, Robert, *M.D.* Descr. of the Brattleboro hydropathic establishment. Brattleboro, 1848. 8°. (B 1549)
— Medical and philosophical communications. (*In* Green Mountain Spring, v. 1, 2. 1846, 47.)

Wesseling, Pieter. Lectio publica. (*In* Valckenær, L. C. Diatribe. 1806.)
— Observationum variarum libri duo. Amst., 1727. 8°.
— Probabilium liber singularis, in quo præter alia insunt vindiciæ verborum Joannis 'Et Deus erat verbum'. Ultrajecti, 1731. 8°.

West, Benjamin, *Prof. of Brown Univ.*, *b.* 1730, *d.* 1813. Account of the observations in Providence of the eclipse of the Sun, Apr. 23, 1781.) — On the extraction of roots. (*In* Amer. Acad. Mem., v. 1. 1785.)

West, *Sir* Benjamin, *b.* 1738, *d.* 1820. Gallery of pictures painted by W., engr. by H. Moses; [text by R. H. London, 1811.] 4°.
— CAREY, W. Critical description of 'Death on the pale horse', painted by W. London, 1817. 8°.
— CUNNINGHAM, A. (*In his* Lives of British painters, v. 2. 1830, Fam. lib., v. 5. 18—; Harper's fam. lib., v. 18.)
— DESCRIPTION of 'Death on the pale horse'. London, 1820. 4°. (A 32)
— DESCRIPTION of [his] picture, 'Christ healing the sick in the Temple'. London, 1811. 12°. (B 653)
— *Same.* Phila., 1817. 8°. (B 692, W 4)
— DESCRIPTION of W.'s 'Christ rejected'. London, 1820. 8°. (B 954)
— GALT, J. Life, studies, and works of W. London, 1820. 2 v. 8°.
— - The life and studies of W. prior to his arrival in Eng. Phila., 1816. 8°.
— MCQUIN, A. D. Description of 'Christ rejected by the Jews'. Phila., 1830. 8°. (B 954)

West, Benjamin, *of New Hampshire*, *b.* 1746, *d.* 1817. KNAPP, S. L. (*In his* Biog. sketches. 1821.)

West, Charles, *M.D.* Lectures on the diseases of infancy and childhood. 3d ed. London, 1854. 8°.

West, Charles E. Earthquake in western New York. (*In* Amer. Assoc. Proc., v. 12. 1859.)

West, Edward. Legacy; discourse of the perfect man. London, 1679. 8°.

West, Gilbert. Allegorical description of vertu; fr. The abuse of travelling. (*In* Campbell, T. Spec. of Brit. poets, v. 5. 1819.)
— Education; a poem. London, 1751. 4°.
— Defence of the Christian revelation; obs. on the history and evidences of the resurrection of Jesus Christ, by W.; and Obs. on the conversion and apostleship of St. Paul, by G. Lyttelton. London, 1748. 8°.
— *Same.* (*In* Watson, R. Theol. tracts, v. 5. 1791.)
— *Same.* Edinburgh, 1839. 8°. (B 1399)

— Poems; [with] life of W. by Dr. Johnson. (*In* **Chalmers, A.** Eng. poets, v. 13. 1810.)
— Poetical works; prefixed [a] life. (*In* **Anderson, R.** Brit. poets, v. 9. 1795.)
— CRICHTON, A. (*In his* Converts from infidelity, v. 1. 1827. Constable's miscel., v. 6.)
— DISSERTATION on the observations of the history of the resurrection. (*In* **Supernaturals** examined. 17—.)
— JOHNSON, S. (*In his* Works, v. 11. 1806; *and* Lives of Eng. poets, v. 2. 1810.)

West, *Mrs.* Jane. Letters to a young man on his entrance into life. Charlestown, 1803. 2 v. 12°.
— The loyalists; a historical novel. Boston, 1813. 2 v. 12°.

West, John, *Chaplain to Hudson's Bay Co.* Substance of a journal during a residence at the Red River Colony, 1820–23. 2d ed; with a journal of a mission to the Indians of New Brunswick, Nova Scotia, and Canada, 1825–26. London, 1827. 8°.

West, John, *of the Univ. of St. Andrews.* Elements of conic sections; revised and improved. N. Y., 1820. 8°.

West, Nathaniel, *Jr.* Establishment in national righteousness, and present causes for thanksgiving; sermon, Brooklyn, N. Y., Nov. 28. N. Y., 1861. 8°. (B 1592)

West *or* Weste, Richard. The booke of demeanor. (*In* **Furnivall,** F. J. The babees boke. 1868. Early Eng. Text Soc.)

West, Richard, *D.D., d.* 1716. Sermon before the House of Commons, at St. Margarets, Westminster, Jan. 30. London, 1710. 8°. (B 27)
— *Same.* Dublin, 1710. 8°. (C 79)

West, Richard, *d.* 1726. Opinion as to the king's right to the woods in the province of Maine. (*In* **Maine Hist. Soc.** Col., v. 2. 1847.)

West, Richard, *d.* 1742. Poetical works; prefixed [a] life. (*In* **Anderson,** R. Brit. poets, v. 10. 1795.) — Ad amicos. (*In* **Campbell,** T. Specimens of Brit. poets, v. 5. 1819.)

West, Samuel, *D. D., b.* 1730, *d.* 1807. Anniversary sermon, Plymouth, Dec. 22, 1777. Boston, [1778]. 8°. (B 65)
— *Same.* Boston, 1778. 12°. (C 22)
— Essays on liberty and necessity; arguments of Edwards and others considered. Vol. 1 Boston, v. 2 New Bedford, 1793–95. 2 v. 8°.
Contents. Vol. 1. Introduction. — Nature of liberty. — Volition is not properly an effect which has a cause. — Divine prescience does not imply the necessity of future events. 2. Introd. — Objections answered, and the nature of action and volition considered. — Moral agency, *etc.* — Shewing that the Deity's permitting and over-ruling sin is a proof that men have a self-determining power. — The Deity not the positive cause of sin. — Postscript. — Appendix.
— *Another copy.* (C 128)
— *Same.* Pt. 1. Boston, 1793. 8°. (B 191, 2509, C 251)
— *Same.* Pt. 2. New Bedford, 1795. 8°. (B 246)
— Letter concerning Gay Head. (*In* **Amer. Acad.** Mem., v. 2. 1793.)
— Sermon, Dec. 3, 1788, ordination of J. Allyn, Duxbury. Salem, 1789. 8°. (B 163)
— Sermon, election. Boston. 1776. 8°. (B 180, 185, 868)
— *Same.* (*In* **Thornton,** J. W. Pulpit of the Amer. rev. 1860.)

West, Samuel, *b.* 1738, *d.* 1808. The Christian soldier; sermon, artillery election. Boston, 1794. 8°. (B 177, 179)
— Greatness the result of goodness; sermon, death of Washington; [with addr. of Washington declining the presidency]. Boston, [1800]. 8°. (B 173, 846, E 162, W 50)
— Sermon, Boston, March 12, at his installment. Boston, 1789. 8°. (B 169, 911)
— Sermon, Dedham, occasioned by the death of two young men. Boston, 1785. 8°. (B 335)
— Sermon, general election. Boston, 1786. 8°. (B 49, 182 186)
— Sermon, ordination of J. Newell, Stow, Oct. 11, 1774. Boston, 1775. 8°. (B 911, 1311)
— Sermon, thanksgiving day, Feb. 19. Boston, 1795. 8°. (B 843, 911)
— Two discourses [fast day], Needham, Apr. 7. Boston, 1785. 8°. (B 200)
— THACHER, T. Biog. memoir of W. [Boston,] 1808 8°. (B 209, 867, 908)
— *Funeral sermon on.* 1808. *See* **Lathrop,** J. (B 209 282, 853, 908)

West, Stephen, *D.D.* Animadversions on 'Th duty and obligation of Christians to marry only i the Lord'. Fish-kill, 1779. 8°. (B 80)
— Essay on moral agency; containing remark on [J. Dana's] "Examination of Edward' 'Enquiry on freedom of will' ". New Ha ven, [1772]. 8°.
— *Another copy.* (B 59)
— *Same.* With an app. 2d ed. Salem, 1794. 8
— Evidence of the divinity of Christ. Stockbridge 1816. 8°. (B 260)
— Grace a necessary qualification for the gospel ministry sermon. Stockbridge, 1795. 8°. (B 1007)
— Introduction. (*In* **Hopkins,** S. Sketches, *etc.* 1805.
— Scripture doctrine of the atonement. Stock bridge, 1809. 12°.
— Sermon, ordination of E. G. Swift, Sept. 26, 1810 Stockbridge, 1811. 8°. (B 1356)
— Sermons, Mosaic account of the creation, *etc.* Stock bridge, 1809. 8°. (B 335)
— Vindication of the principles and conduct of th church in Stockbridge in excluding from their com munion one of their members for marrying a per son immoral and profane. Hartford, 1780. 8°. (] 80, 133)
— DANA, J. Examination, *etc.*; with strictures o W.'s 'Essay on moral agency'. New Haven 1773. 8°.
— *Another copy.* (B 247)
— HUNTINGTON, J. [Reply to W.'s 'Vindication'.] Hart ford. 1780. 8°. (B 80)
— HYDE, A. Sketches of the life, ministry, and writ ings of W. Stockbridge, 1819. 8°. (B 1461)

West, Wm. First, second pt. of symboleography London, 1632, 27. 2 v. 4°

West & Johnstone, *booksellers.* Descriptive cata logue. Richmond, [186–]. 8°.

West, The (*i.e.* the western part of the Unite States).

Antiquities.

— ASHE, T. Memoirs of mammoth and other bone found [near] the Ohio, Wabash, and Illinois Rivers Liverpool, 1806. 8°. (B 685)
— PRIEST, J. American antiquities and discoveries in the West. Albany, 1835. 8°.

Commerce and Internal improvement.

— PROCEEDINGS of sundry citizens of Baltimore con vened for devising the most efficient means of im proving the intercourse between that city and th Western states. Balt., 1827. 8°. (B 953)
— DEARBORN, H. A. S. Letters [1-4 only] on the inter nal improvements and commerce of the West. Bos ton, 1839. 8°. (B 1605, 1748)
— HENSHAW, D. Letters on the internal improvement and commerce of the West. Boston, 1839. 8°. (I 1136, 1142, 1605, 1748)
— WEST vindicated, The; review of the address of J Tallmadge before the American Institute, Oct. 26 1841; by a western New Yorker. Buffalo, 1842. 8 (B 1586)
— STEWART, A. Speech in favor of western improve ments. [Wash., 1844.] 8°. (B 1174)
— EVANSVILLE CONVENTION FOR THE PROTECTION O WESTERN INTERESTS. Proc., Nov. 19. Evans ville, 1850. 8°. (B 1504)
— DE BOW, J. D. B. Industrial resources of th southern and western states. New Orleans 1852–53. 3 v. 8°.
See also **Prairies, American.**

Description and Travels.

— SIMPSON, J. H. Coronado's march in search of th 'seven cities of Cibola', [1540]. (*In* **Smithsonian Inst.** Ann. report, 1869.)
— SAGEAN, M. Extrait de la relation [de ses avantures et voyage, [168–]. Nouvelle York 1863. 8°.

— M'Clung, J. A. Sketches of Western adventure, 1755-94. Dayton, Ohio, 1854. 8°.

— Carver, J. Three year's travels through North America, 1766-68. [2d ed.] Phila., 1784. 8°.

— - *Same*. Boston, 1797. 12°.

— - *Same*. 3d ed. London, 1781. 8°.

— - *Same*. (*In* Moore, J. H. New col. of voy., v. 2. 1778?)

— Brackenridge, H. M. Recollections of persons and places in the West, [1786-1810]. Phila., [1834]. 12°.

— Finley, J. B. Autobiography; or, Pioneer life in the West, [1788-1845]. Cincin., 1853. 12°.

— Imlay, G. Topographical disc. of the western territory of N. America. 3d ed., with add. London, 1797. 8°.

— Perrin du Lac, F. M. Voyage dans les deux Louisianes, Missouri, l'Ohio, et les provinces qui le bordent, 1801-03. Lyon, 1805. 8°.

— Michaux, F. A. Voyage à l'ouest des monts Alléghany, 1802. Paris, 1804. 8°.

— - *Eng*. Travels to the west of the Alleghany Mts., 1802. London, 1805. 8°.

— Harris, T. M. Journal of a tour northwest of the Alleghany Mts., 1803. Boston, 1805. 8°.

— Allen, P. History of the expedition under Lewis and Clark, across the Rocky Mts., *etc.*, 1804-06. Phila., 1814. 2 v. 8°.

— Gass, P. Journal of voy., *etc.*, from the mouth of the Missouri to the Pacific Ocean, 1804-06. Pittsburgh, 1807. 12°.

— Ashe, T. Travels in America, 1806, for exploring the Rivers Alleghany, Monongahela, Ohio, and Mississippi. Lond., 1808. 3 v. 16°.

— Ker, H. Travels through the western interior of the U.S., 1808-16. Elizabethtown, 1816. 8°.

— Bradbury, J. Travels in the interior of America, 1809-11. Liverpool, 1817. 8°.

— Thomas, D. Travels through the western country, 1816. Auburn, 1819. 12°.

— Brown, S. R. Western gazetteer; or, Emigrant's directory. Auburn, N. Y., 1817. 8°.

— Flint, J. Letters from America, cont. obs. on the climate, *etc.*, of the western states, [1818-20]. Edin., 1822. 8°.

— Darby, W. Emigrant's guide to the western and southwestern states and territories. N. Y., 1818. 8°.

— Evans, E. Pedestrious tour through the western states and territories [in] 1818. Concord, N. H., 1819. 12°.

— James, E. P. Account of an expedition from Pittsburg to the Rocky Mts., 1819-20, under Maj. S. H. Long. Phila., 1823. 2 v. 8° *and* Atlas 4°.

— Dana, E. Geographical sketches of the western country. Cincin., 1819. 12°.

— Hall, J. Letters from the West, [1820-28]. London, 1828. 8°.

— Cumings, S. The western navigator. Phila., 1822. 2 v. (v. 1, a folio vol. of maps, w.). 8°.

— Keating, W. H. Narrative of an exped. to the source of St. Peter's River, *etc.*, under Maj. S. H. Long, 1823. Phila., 1824. 2 v. 8°.

— - *Same*. London, 1825. 2 v. 8°.

— Pattie, J. O. Personal narr., during an exped. from St. Louis [to] the Pacific, [1824-26]; ed. by T. Flint. Cincin., 1833. 8°.

— Flint, T. Condensed geography and history of the western states. Cincin., 1828. 2 v. 8°.

— Atwater, C. Remarks on a tour to Prairie du Chien [and] Washington, 1829. Columbus, 1831. 12°.

— Kinzie, *Mrs.* J. H. Wau Bun, the 'early day' in the north-west, [1830-33]. 2d ed. Chicago, 1857. 8°.

— Marcy, R. B. Thirty years of army life on the border, [183·-186·]. N. Y., 1866. 8°.

— Hoffman, C. F. A winter in the West, [1833-34]. N. Y., 1835. 2 v. 12°.

— Parker, A. A. Trip to the West and Texas, 1834-35. 2d ed. Concord, 1836. 18°.

— Martineau, H. Retrospect of western travel, [1834]. London, 1838. 3 v. 12°.

— Parker, S. Journal of an exploring tour beyond the Rocky Mts., 1835-37. Ithaca, N. Y., 1838. 12°.

— Peck, J. M. New guide for emigrants to the West. Boston, 1836. 16°

— Steele's western guide-book. 5th ed. Buffalo, 1836. 24°.

— Hall, J. Notes on the western states. Phila., 1838. 12°.

— Ruxton, G. F. Life in the far West, [184-]. (*In* Blackwood's mag., v. 63-64. 1848.)

— Schoolcraft, H. R. The rise of the West; or, A prospect of the Miss. Valley; a poem. N. Y., 1841. 8°. (C 190)

— Haskins, R. W. New England and the West. Buffalo, 1843. 8°. (C 265)

— Disturnell, J. Western traveller. N. Y., 1844. 16°.

— Domenech, E. Seven years in the deserts of N. Amer., [1846-52]. London, 1860. 2 v. 8°.

— Lanman, C. Summer in the wilderness; a canoe voyage up the Missisippi and around Lake Superior, [1846]. N. Y., 1847. 12°.

— Conclin, G. New river guide; or, Gazetteer of towns on the western waters, 1848. Cincin., 1850. 8°.

— Curtiss, D. S. Western portraiture, and emigrants' guide. N. Y., 1852. 12°.

— Moellhausen, B. Diary of a journey from the Mississippi to the Pacific, [1853-54]; introd. by A. v. Humboldt; tr. by Mrs. P. Sinnett. London, 1858. 2 v. 8°.

— Heap, G. H. Central route to the Pacific; expedition of Beale and Heap from Missouri to California, 1853. Phila., 1854. 8°.

— Richardson, A. D. Beyond the Mississippi, 1857-67. Hartford, 1867. 8°.

— Gillmore, P. Hunter's adventures in the great West, [186-]. London, 1871. 8°.

— Burton, R. F. City of the saints; across the Rocky Mts. to California, [1860]. London, 1861. 8°.

— - *Same*. N. Y., 1862. 8°.

— Fergusson, D. Report on the country between Tucson and Lobos Bay. Wash., 1863. 8°. (37th Cong., spec. sess. Ex. doc. 1.)

— Bowles, S. Across the continent; a journey to the Rocky Mts., *etc.*, [1865]. Springfield, 1865. 12°.

— Campbell, J. L. The great agricultural and mineral West; guide. Chicago, 1866. 8°.

— Palmer, W. J. Report of surveys across the continent, in 1867-68, for a route extending the Kansas Pacific R. W. to the Pacific Ocean. Phila., 1869. 8°.

— Dodge, M. A. Wool-gathering. Bost., 1867. 16°.

— Keim, De B. R. Sheridan's troopers on the borders; a winter's campaign on the plains, [1868-69]. Phila., 1870. 8°.

— COFFIN, C. C. The seat of empire, [1869]. Boston, 1870. 12°.
— LUDLOW, F. H. The heart of the continent; travel across the plains, and in Oregon, with an examination of the Mormon principle. N. Y., 1870. 8°.

See also Mississippi Valley; — North West boundary of the U. S.; — North West Territory; — Pacific Railroad; — Prairies, American; — Rocky Mts.; — South West, The; — *also* the names of the different states and territories; — *also* the following works of fiction: Hall, J. Legends of the West; — Hall, B. R. The new purchase; — Kirkland, C. M. Western clearings; — Cary, A. Clovernook.

Geology.

— U. S. *Commissioner of Mining Statistics.* Statistics of mines and mining in the states and territories west of the Rocky Mountains; [1st, 2d,] 4th, 6th report by R. W. Raymond. Wash., 1869–74. 4 v. 8°. (41st Cong. 2d sess. Ho. Ex. doc. 207)
— - *Corps of Engineers.* Geological exploration of the 40th parallel; C. King, geologist. Wash., 1870–77. 6 v. 8° *and* 2 Atlases f°.

History.

— BARBER, J. W., *and* HOWE, H. All the western states and territories, their history, *etc.*, [1512–1867]. Cincin., 1867. 8°.
— HOWE, H. Historical collections of the great West, [1512–1850]. Greenville, Tenn., 1855. 2 v. 8°.
— PERKINS, J. H. Annals of the West, [1512–1850]. 2d ed., rev. and enl., by J. M. Peck. St. Louis, 1850. 8°.
— HALL, J. Romance of western history, [1535–1812]. Cincin., 1857. 8°.
— BRADFORD, W. J. A. History, [1624–1846]. (*In his* Notes. 1846.)
— PARKMAN, F. The discovery of the great West, [1643–89]. Boston, 1869. 8°. (France and England in N. A., pt. 3.)

See also Western Sanitary Commission.

Literature.

— COGGESHALL, W. T. Poets and poetry of the West; with biog. and crit. notices. Columbus, 1860. 8°.

Missions.

— MILLS, S. J., *and* SMITH, D. Report of a missionary tour west of the Alleghany Mts., [1814–15]. Andover, 1815. 8°.

Politics.

— IMPARTIAL enquiry, An, into the right of the French King to the territory west of the Mississippi. London, [176–]. 8°.
— *Another copy.* (B 603)
— PAINE, T. Public good; an examination into the claims of Va. to the vacant western territory, and the right of the U. S. to the same; [with] proposals for laying out a new state. Phila., 1780. 8°. (B 702, W 21)
— LEARNED, J. D. View of the policy of permitting slaves west of the Mississippi, [1819]. Balt., 1820. 8°. (B 537)

Religious affairs.

— SCHERMERHORN, J. F., *and* MILLS, S. J. Correct view of that part of the U. S. west of the Allegany Mts. with regard to religion and morals, [1812–13]. Hartford, 1814. 8°. (B 454)
— CHASE, P. A plea for the West, [in behalf of relig. and learning]. Phila., 1826. 8°. (B 1603)
— - *Same.* Boston, 1827. 8°. (B 964, 1662)
— BEECHER, L. A plea for the West. 2d ed. Cincin., 1835. 12°.
— ADDRESS to the people of the Eastern States on the western country, its moral and religious wants. Boston, 1842. 12°. (C 220)

West Boston Society. *See* Boston (p. 348).

West Brookfield Anti-Slavery Society. Correspondence [with] Rev. M. Chase. *n.p.*, 1842. 12°. (C 261)

West Cambridge Temperance Soc. DAMON, N. Remarks on the importance of obedience to law, *etc.*, Dec. 30, 1839. Boston, 1840. 8°. (B 1280)

West country intelligence, Nov. 19, 1715; May 1, 1716. No. 4–61, 63–67. Glasgow, 1715–16. 53 nos. 4°. (C 281)
Note. For previous nos. *see* Glasgow courant.

West end; by D. Boucicault. (*In* Sargent, E. Mod. stand. dr., v. 30.)

West India Dock Co. At a general court of proprietors, *etc.*; report from a committee on the conduct of the Co's. concerns. *n.p.*, 1809. 8°. (B 1747)
— COMPARATIVE view of the wet docks in Wapping and the Isle of Dogs for the West India trade. [London,] 1797. 8°. (B 1747)
— FAIRBURN, J. Abstract of an act for making a canal and wet docks for the West India trade in the Isle of Dogs. London, [1799]. 8°. (B 1747)
— LETTER to the Ld. Mayor, on the intended new docks to be established at Wapping; with app. cont. extract from the rept. of a committee of W. I. merchants resp. landing and delivering sugar at the legal quays. London, 1796. 8°. (B 1747)
— OBSERVATIONS on the W. I. dock salaries. London, 1804. 8°. (B 1747)
— To G. Hibbert [on] his speech for making wet docks and other works at the Isle of Dogs. *n.p.*, [1799]. 8°. (B 1747)
— TRIAL, J. and G. Cowell *vs.* G. Smith, Treasurer, upon cooperage on rums; [added] Mr. Garrou's speech. London, 1804. 8°. (B 1747)
— WEST INDIA PLANTERS AND MERCHANTS. Report of committee on a bill for forming wet docks at the port of Lond.; [also rept. of W. I. Merchants resp. the landing sugar at the legal quays, 1793]. London, 1797. 8°.

West India Planters and Merchants. *See previous entry.*

West Indian, The; a comedy. *See* Cumberland, R.

West Indies. *Commerce.*

— THOMAS, D. Historical account of the rise and growth of the W. I. collonies, and of the great advantages they are to England in resp. to trade. London, 1690. 8°.
— LETTER from a merchant of London to W---- P---- upon the affairs and commerce of N. America and the W. I. London, 1757. 8°. (B 742)
— BUTEL-DUMONT, G. M. Histoire et commerce des Antilles angloises. [Paris,] 1758. 12°.
— GLOVER, R. Substance of the evidence on the petition [of] the West India planters and merchants to the Ho. of Com., March 16, 1775. London, [17—]. 8°. (C 148, W 35)
— - *Same.* London, 1775. 8°. (W 32)
— GALLOWAY, J. Cool thoughts on the value of the Amer. colonies and the West Indies to the British Empire. London, 1780. 8°. (B 638, 1635)
— SOCIETY OF SHIP-OWNERS OF GR. BRITAIN. Collection of reports, *etc.*, on the trade of Gr. Britain in the W. I. and America, [1784–1806]. London, 1807. 8°.
— EDWARDS, B. Thoughts on the late proc. of gov. resp. the trade of the W. I. Islands with the U. S. London, 1784. 8°. (B 702, 1638, 2517)
— - *Same.* 2d ed. London, 1784. 8°. (B 462)
— STEVENSON, J. Address to B. Edwards, on his 'Thoughts on the late proc. of government, resp. the trade of West India with the U. S., also observations on 'Considerations on the intercourse between H. M.'s sugar colonies and the U. S.' London, 1784. 8°. (B 463)
— LOWE, J. Inquiry into the state of the British West Indies. 2d ed. London, 1807. 8°. (B 1419)
— SOFTLY, brave Yankees! or, The West Indies rendered independent of America. London, 1807. 8° (B 671)
— YOUNG, *Sir* W. W. I. common-place book; compiled from Parliamentary and official documents. London, 1807. 4°.
— GR. BRIT. *Parl.* Acts [relating to trade with the W. Indies, 45, 48 Geo. III. Wash., 1818.] 8°. (15 *Cong., 1st sess. Ho.* B 1536)

— EAST and West India sugar; refutation of the claims of the W. I. colonists to a protecting duty on E. India sugar. London, 1823. 8°.

See also **Bahama Islands**; — **Curaçao**; — **Great Britain.** *Colonies*; — **Grenada.**

Description and Travels.

— N., N. Exact descr. of the W. I., [-1655]. *See* **Spanish Amer.** (p. 2826).

— HERRERA, A. de. Descr. de las Indias Occid., [-1601]. *See* **Spanish Amer.** (p. 2826).

— CASAS, B. de las. Voy., *etc.*, que les Espagnoles ont fait dans les Indes Occid., [-1542]. *See* **Spanish Amer.** (p. 2826).

— ANGHIERA, P. M. d'. De orbe novo decades octo, [-1526]. Paris, 1587. 12°. (With map.)

Note. For other editions *see* **Anghiera, P. M. d'.**

— CARADOC *of Llancarvan.* Voyage and discovery of the West Indies by Madoc, 1170. (*In* **Hakluyt, R.** Col. of voy., v. 3. 1810.)

— SUMMARY of the discoveries and settlements of the Spaniards in the W. I., [1506-18]. (*In* **Kerr, R.** Col. of voy., v. 3. 1824.)

— VOYAGES to the W. Indies, 1516-97. (*In* **Hakluyt, R.** Col. of voy., v. 3-4. 1810-11.)

— HAWKINS, *Sir* J. Voyage to the W. I., 1562. — Voy. to Guinea and the Indies of Nova Hispania, 1564. — Third voy. to Guinea and the W. I., 1567-68. (*In* **Hakluyt, R.** Col. of voy., v. 3. 1810.) — Last voy. to the W. I., 1595. (*In* v. 4. 1811.)

— VOYAGES to the W. I., [1593-1605]. (*In* **Harris, J.** Col. of voy., v. 1. 1705.)

— CHAMPLAIN, S. Brief discours des choses plus remarquables que C. a recouneues aux Indes Occidentalles, [1599-1602]. (*In his* Œuvres, v. 1. 1870.)

— - *Eng.* Narrative of a voyage to the W. I. and Mexico, 1599-1602. London, 1859. 8°. (Hakluyt Soc., v. 23.)

— ACOSTA, J. Naturall and morall historie of the East and W. I. London, 1604. 8°.

— REISEN und Niederlassungen auf den Antillen, [1630-92]. (*In* **Allgemeine Hist.**, v. 17. 1759.)

— LAET, J. de. Novus orbis seu descriptionis Indiæ Occidentalis libri. Lugd. Bat., 1633. f°.

— - *French.* L'histoire du Nouveau Monde, ou description des Indes Occidentales. Leyde, 1640. f°.

— GAGE, *Father* T. New survey of the W. I., *etc.*, [1648]. 2d ed. Lond., 1655. f°.

— - *Same.* 4th ed., with map. Lond., 1699. 8°.

— DU TERTRE, J. B. Histoire générale des Isles de S. Christophe, Guadeloupe, *etc.* Paris, 1654. 4°.

— ROCHEFORT, C. de. Histoire naturelle et morale des îles Antilles de l'Amérique. Roterdam, 1658. 4°.

Note. Attributed also to L. de Poincy.

— COREAL, F. Voyage aux Indes Occidentales, 1666-97. Amst., 1722. 3 v. 12°.

— EXQUEMELIN, A. O. Historie der boecaniers van America, [1666-95]. Amst., 1700. 4°.

Note. For other versions *see* **Exquemelin, A. O.**

— BLOME, R. Description of Jamaica, with other islands and territories in America to which the English are related, [1671]. London, 1672. 16°.

— - *Same, extracts.* (*In* **Anderson, W. W.** Description of Jamaica. 1851.)

— VRIES, S. de. Curieuse aenmerckingen der bysonderste Oost en W. I. verwonderenswaerdige dingen. Utrecht, 1682. 4 v. 4°.

— CAPINÉ, L. de. Aanhangsel behelzende een reyse na de Spaansche West-Indien, benevens de expeditie der Franschen op Cartagena, 1697, [1688-97]. (*In* **Hennepin, L.** Nieuwe ontdekkinge. 1702.)

— LABAT, J. B. Nouveau voyage aux isles de l'Amérique, [1693-1705]. Paris, 1722. 6 v. 12°.

— OLDMIXON, J. (*In his* British empire, v. 2. 1708; 1741.)

— CARRANZA, D. G. A geographical description of the coasts, harbours, and seaports of the Spanish West Indies; tr. by C. Smith. London, 1740. 8°. (C 313)

— BOSSU, N. Nouveaux voyages aux Indes Occidentales, [1751-66]. 2e éd. Paris, 1768. 2 v. 12°.

— NATURAL and civil history of the French dominions in North and South America; maps by T. Jefferys. London, 1760. 2 v. f°.

— JEFFERYS, T. Description of the Spanish islands and settlements on the coast of the W. I.; with maps. London, 1762. 4°.

— YOUNG, *Major.* Some obs. [on] the nature of our new W. I. colonies. London, 1764. 8°. (B 702)

— NORTH American and W. I. gazetteer. 2d ed. London, 1778. 12°.

— ALCEDO Y BEXARANO, A. de. Diccionario geog. hist. de las Indias Occident. Madrid, 1786-89. 5 v. 4°.

— - *Eng.* Geographical and historical dictionary of America and the W. I.; with add. by G. A. Thompson. London, 1812-15. 5 v. 4°.

— PINCKARD, G. Notes on the W. I., [1795-97]. London, 1806. 3 v. 8°.

— WINTERBOTHAM, W. (*In his* Hist. view of the U. S., v. 4. 1796.)

— MCKINNEN, D. Tour through the British W. I., 1802-03. London, 1804. 8°.

— ST. CLAIR, T. S. Residence in the W. I. and America, [1806-08]. London, 1834. 2 v. 8°.

— HEATHER, W. New W. I. pilot. 2d ed. London, 1806. 8°.

— DERROTERO de las islas Antillas de las costas de tierrafirme y de las del Senõ Mexicano. Madrid, 1810. 4°.

— WATERTON, C. Wanderings in S. America and the Antilles, 1812, 16, 20, 24. London, 1825. 4°.

— TRAVELLER'S guide to Madeira and the W. I., [1814]. Haddington, [1817]. 8°.

— LEWIS, M. G. Journal of a W. I. proprietor, [1815-17]. London, 1834. 8°.

— COLERIDGE, H. N. Six months in the W. I., 1825. Lond., 1837. 16°. (Fam. lib., v. 42.)

— FERRARIO, G. Descrizione dell' archipelago di Colombo. (*In his* Costume, v. 17. 1829.)

— ALEXANDER, J. E. Transatlantic sketches, [1831]. London, 1833. 2 v. 8°.

— HALLIDAY, *Sir* A. The W. I., [1833-35]. London, 1837. 12°.

— MADDEN, R. R. Twelvemonth's residence in in the W. I., [1833-34]. Lond., 1835. 2 v. 12°.

— MARTIN, R. M. [British] possessions in the W. I. (Vol. 2 *of his* Hist. of the British colonies. 1834.)

— WEST India sketch book. Lond., 1834. 2 v. 12°.

— WINTER in the W. I. and Florida. N. Y., 1839. 12°.

— GURNEY, J. J. Familiar letters to H. Clay, describing a winter in the W. I. N. Y., 1840. 8°.

— DAVY, J. The W. I. before and since slave emancipation, *etc.*, [1845-48]. London, 1854. 8°.

— DAY, C. W. Five years' residence in the W. I., [1846-51]. London, 1852. 2 v. 12°.

— WILLIS, N. P. Health trip to the tropics, [1852]. N. Y., 1854. 12°.

— TROLLOPE, A. West Indies and the Spanish Main, [1859]. 4th ed. London, 1860. 8°.

— CAMPBELL, J. G. E. H. D. S., *Marquis of Lorne.* A trip to the tropics and home through America, [1866]. London, 1867. 8°.

— KINGSLEY, C. At last; a Christmas in the W. I., [1869-70]. London, N. Y., 1871. 8°.
— - Letters from the tropics. (*In* Good words, v. 11. 1870.)
— DELITSCH, O. Westindien und die Südpolar-Länder. Lpz., 1871. 8°. (Wappäus. Handbuch der Geog., 1e B., 4e Abth.)

Maps.

— BLAEU, W. Insulæ Americanæ in Oceano Septentrionali. [Amst., 16—.] (E 78, no. 322)
— ENGLISH pilot. Pt. 4: [Charts of the coasts of N. America and W. I.]. London, 1707. f°.
— *Same.* Book 4: W. I. navigation from Hudson Bay to the Amazones. London, 1742. f°.
— JEFFERYS, T. The West India Islands in 17 maps. London, 1775. f°.
— - Complete pilot for the W. I. Lond., [178-]. f°.
— - The W. I. atlas. London, 1794. f°.
— LA ROCHETTE, L. S. de. Gen. chart of the W. I. London, 1796. (E C7)
— NEW atlas of the British W. I. to accompany the Phila. ed. of Edwards's W. I. Phila., 1806. 4°.
— WINDWARD passage between the islands of Jamaica, Hispaniola, and Cuba. London, 1795. (E 67)

See also Antigua; — Bahama Islands; — Barbadoes; — Bermuda; — Buccaneers; — Caribee Islands; — Cuba; — Curaçao; — Fort Royal; — Grenada; — Guadeloupe; — Hayti; — Jamaica; — Leeward Islands; — Martinique; — Nieves; — Port Royal; — Porto Rico; — St. Christopher's Island; — St. Croix; — St. Eustatius Island; — St. Lucia; — St. Martin, Island of; — St. Michael, Island; — St. Thomas Island; — St. Vincent Island; — Santo Domingo; — Spanish America; — Tobago; — Trinidad.

Ethnography.

See Caribee Islands (LA BORDE),

History.

— REGNAULT, E. Histoire des Antilles [-1845]. Paris, 1849. 8°. (Univers.)
— SOUTHEY, T. Chronological history of the W. I., [-1816]. London, 1827. 3 v. 8°.
— EDWARDS, B. History of the British colonies in the W. I., [-1793]. 4th ed. London, 1807. 3 v. 8°.
— - *Same, abridged.* London, 1798. 8°.
— - *French.* Histoire civile et commerciale des Indes Occidentales; suivie d'un tableau hist. de St. Dominique; par [F. Soulès]. 2é ed. Paris, 1804. 8°.
— CASAS, B. de las. La découverte des Indes Occid. par les Espagnols, [-1541]. *See* Spanish Amer. (p. 2827).
— ANGHIERA, P. M. d'. Sommario della Historia dell' Indie Occidentali, [-1515]. (*In* Ramusio, G. B. Navig., v. 3. 1565.)
— BOYER-PEYRELEAU, E. E. Les Antilles françaises, [1506-1825]. 2e éd. Paris, 1825. 3 v. 8°.
— CLODORÉ, J. de. Relation de ce qui s'est passé dans les isles et terre ferme de l'Amérique pendant la dernière guere avec l'Angleterre, et depuis, en exécution du traitté de Breda, [1665-69]. Paris, 1671. 2 v. 12°.
— CATHCART, J. Letter to E. Vernon, Vice-Admiral, conc. some gross misrepresentations in 'Original papers rel. to the exped. to Cuba', [under Gen. Wentworth, 1741]. London, 1744. 8°.
— - *Another copy.* (B 1707)
— GARDINER, A. Relation de l'expédition aux Indes Occidentales contre la Martinique, avec la réduction de la Guadelupe, [1758-59]. 3e éd. Birmingham, 1762. 4°. (A 17)
— EDWARDS, B. History of the war in the W. I., 1793-94. (*In his* Hist. survey of the Island of St. Domingo. 1801.)
— WILLYAMS, C. Account of the campaign in the W. I. in 1794. London, 1796. 4°.

See also Barbadoes; — Cuba; — Great Britain. *Colonies.* — Guadeloupe; — Hayti; — Jamaica; — Martinique; — Porto Rico; — St. Christopher's Island; — St. Lucia; — Santo Domingo; — Spanish America; — Trinidad; — *also* Slavery. *General and misc. works. Note.* (p. 2748).

Labor.

— SPENCE, W. Radical cause of the present distresses of the West India planters pointed out. London, 1807. 8°. (B 671)
— GREAT BRITAIN. *House of Com.* Report on W. I. colonies. [London, 1842.] f°.
— CASE of the free-labour in the British colonies; submitted to the Brit. legislature [by a sub-committee of the Nat. Assoc. for Protection of Industry]. London, 1852. 8°.
— SEWELL, W. G. Ordeal of free labor in the British W.I., [1859-60]. N.Y., 1861. 12°.

See also Politics; — *also* Slavery. *General and Misc. works. Note* (p. 2748).

Laws.

— REVIEW of the laws of the U. S., Brit. Provinces, and W. I. London, 1790. 8°.

Medicine.

— DICKINSON, N. Observations on the yellow fever. London, 1819. 8°.
— WILSON, J. Memoirs of W. I. fever. London, 1827. 8°.
— BARTON, W. P. C. Hints for naval officers in the W. I. Phila., 1830. 12°.
— EVANS, W. J. Clinical treatise on the endemic fevers of the W. I. London, 1837. 8°.
— TULLOCH, A. M. Sickness and mortality among the troops in the W. I. (*In* Statist. Soc. Journ., v. 1. 1838-39.)

Missions.

— PELLEPRAT, P. Relation des missions de la Compagnie de Jésus dans les isles de l'Amérique Méridionale, [1638-55]. Paris, 1655. 8°.
— LETTRES par des missionaires, [1725-43]. (*In* Lettres édifiantes, v. 7. 1810; v. 7, 8. 1809; v. 1, 2. 1838, 43.)

Natural history.

— OVIEDO Y VALDÉS, G. H. de. Sumario de la natural historia de las Indias, [1527]. (*In* Barcia, A. G. Historiadores, v. 1. 1749; — *and in* Vedia, E. de. Hist. prim. de Indias, v. 1. 1858; v. 22 of Aribau. Bibl.)
— PISO, W. De Indiæ utriusque re naturali et medica. Amst., 1658. f°.
— FRANCISCI, E. Ost- und west-indischer wie auch cinesischer Lust- und Stats-Garten. Nürnberg, 1668. f°.
— FEUILLÉE, L. Journal des observations physiques, mathematiques, et botaniques sur les côtes orientales de l'Amérique Méridionale et aux Indes Occidentales, [1708-11]. Paris, 1725. 4°.
— NATURAL history of the Antilles. (*In* Natural and civil history of the French dominions in America. 1760.)
— DESCOURTILZ, M. E. Voyages d'un naturaliste en St. Yago de Cuba et à S. Domingue. Paris, 1809. 3 v. 8°.

Politics.

— CONSIDERATIONS on the state of the sugar islands, by a W. I. planter. London, 1773. 8°. (B 1706)
— MALOUET, P. V. Lettere à M. S. D., membre du Parlement sur l'intérêt de l'Europe au salut des colonies de l'Amérique. Londres, 1797. 8°. (B 731)
— CRISIS of the sugar colonies; enquiry into the objects and probable effects of the French exped. to the W. I. London, 1802. 8°. (B 685, 782)

— MARRYATT, J. Concessions to America the bane of Britain; cause of the distressed situation of Brit. colonial interests. London, 1807. 8°. (B 671)
— MEDFORD, M. Oil without vinegar, and dignity without pride; or, British, American, and W. I. interests considered. 2d ed., with add. London, 1807. 8°. (B 671)
— PERMANENT and effectual remedy for the evils [of] the British W. I. London, 1807. 8°. (B 671)
— BOURNE, —. British W. I. colonies in connection with slavery, emancipation, *etc.*, [1847]; introd. by S. Bourne. London, 1853. 8°. (B 1482)

See also **Slavery.** *General and miscel. works. Note* (p. 2748); — *also* **Great Britain.** *Colonies*; — **Guadeloupe**; — **Hayti**; — **Jamaica.**

Slavery.

For works rel. to slavery and emancipation in the the W. I., *see* **Slavery.** *General and miscellaneous works. Note* (p. 2748).

Social condition.

— CARMICHAEL, *Mrs.* A. C. Domestic manners and social condition of the population of the W. I. London, 1833. 2 v. 12°.
— PRINCE, *Mrs.* N. G.' The W. I.; progress of Christianity, education, *etc.*, among the colored population. Boston, 1841. 12°. (C 258)
— The UNDERHILL, E. B. The West Indies; their social and religious condition, [1860–61]. London, 1862. 8°.

Statistics.

— GR. BRIT. *Colonial Office.* (*In their* Reports [on] the past and present state of colonial possessions, v. 1. 1861.)

West Indische Compagnie. ASHER, G. M. Bibliographical and hist. essay on the books, *etc.*, rel. to New Netherland and the Dutch W. I. Co., *etc.* Amst., 1854–67. 4°.
West Lothian County, *Scotland.* TROTTER, J. General view of the agriculture of the County of W. Lothian. Edin., 1794. 4°. (W 77)
West Newbury. COFFIN, J. Sketch of the history of Newbury, Newburyport, and West Newbury. Boston, 1845. 8°.
West Newton State Normal School. GANNETT, E. S. Address, 4th convention of the graduates and members of the W. N. State Normal School, July 24. Boston, 1850. 8°. (B 1205, 1589)
West-Point. *See* **United States.** *Department of War* (p. 3107).
West Point scrap book, The; by Lieut. O. E. Wood. N. Y., 1871. 8°.
West Riding of York Pauper Lunatic Asylum. 13th, 15th, 18th–23d reports of the director. Wakefield, 1832–34, 1837–42. 9 v. 8°. (B 1766)
West Roxbury, *Mass.* LAWRIE, T. Historical discourse to the South Evangelical Church, West Roxbury. Boston, 1861. 12°. (C 208)
West Springfield. LATHROP, J., *D.D.* Stedfastness; [historical] sermon, in the 1st Parish, Aug. 25. Springfield, 1796. 8°. (B 1325)
— - *Same.* West Springfield, 1797. 12°. (C 32, 145)
West Stockbridge, *Mass.* FIELD, D. D. History of Stockbridge. (*In his* Hist. of Berkshire, pt. 2. 1829.)
West Virginia. *Adjutant General.* Annual report, 1864. Wheeling, 1865. 8°.
— DE HAAS, W. History of the early settlement and Indian wars of Western V., [1584-1791]. Wheeling, 1851. 8°.
— DODDRIDGE, J. Notes on the settlements and and Indian wars of West Virginia and West Pennsylvania, 1763–83. Wellsburgh, 1824. 12°.
— DODGE, J. R. West V.; its farms and forests, mines and oil-wells. Phila., 1865. 12°.
— *Map.* HUTCHINS, T. Western Va. London, 1778. (E 68)

See also **Crawford, W.**; — *also* **Indiana,** *a tract in West Virginia.*

Westborough, *Mass.* PARKMAN, E. Account of Westborough, Mass., 1767. (*In* **Mass. Hist. Soc.** Col., v. 10. 1809.)
Westbrook, Otis. Letter to W. Dummer, Mar. 1722/23. (*In* **Mass. Hist. Soc.** Col., v. 18. 1819.)
Westchester County, *N. Y.* BOLTON, R. History of the Co. of Westchester. N. Y., 1848. 8°.
— - History of the Prot. Episc. Ch. in W. Co., 1693–1853. N. Y., 1855. 8°.
Westchnienie pobożne za dynastya Czartokysrick [*sic*] w Polsce. [W Paryżu,] 1840. 12°. (E 81)
Westcott, *Rev.* Brooke Foss. General survey of the history of the canon of the New Testament during the first four centuries. Camb., 1855. 8°.
— General view of the history of the English Bible. London, Camb., 1868. 8°.
Westcott, Thompson. Life of J. Fitch. Phila., 1857. 12°.
— Names of persons who took the oath of allegiance to Pennsylvania, 1777–89; with a history of the test laws of Pennsylvania. Phila., 1865. 8°.
Weste, R. *See* **West, R.**
Westenberg, Johann. Comitatus Bentheim et Steinfurt; G. Blaeu exc. [Amst., 16—.] (E 78, no. 158)
Westenberg, Johann Ortwin. Principia juris secundum ordinem digestorum seu pandectarum. Ed. alt. Berol., 1823. 2 v. 8°.
Westenra, Warner Wm., *Ld. Rossmore.* Letter on Catholic emancipation. (*In* **Pamphleteer,** 1828; v. 29 of B 838)
Westergaard, Niels Ludwig. Connexion between Sanscrit and Icelandic. — Boucles de la dernière période du paganisme. — Deciphering of the second Achæmenian or Median species of arrow-headed writing. (*In* **Copenhagen. Kon. Nord. Oldsk. Selsk.** Mém., 1840–44.)
Western, Charles Callis, *Ld. Western.* Observations on the speech of W. Huskisson, June 11, 1822, on W.'s motion conc. resumption of cash payments. Lond., 1823. 8°. (B 1677)
— Speech on the distressed state of the agriculture of the United Kingdom. (*In* **Pamphleteer,** 1816; v. 7 of B 838) — Letter on the cause of our present embarrassment and distress, and the remedy. (*In* 1826; v. 27.)
Western and Atlantic Rail-Road. GEORGIA. *House of Rep.* Report of committee on the Western and Atlantic R. R. *n.t.p.* [1862.] 8°.
Western Association of Universalists, *N. Y.* Minutes of the proceedings, 1812–13. *n. p.*, 1813. 12°. (B 657)
Western Australian Association. 1st report. London, 1836. 8°. (B 1743)
Western clearings; by Mrs. C. M. Kirkland. N. Y., 1845. 16°.
Western Education Soc. of New York. Report of the directors to the first annual meeting. Utica, 1819. 8°. (B 448, 1041)
Western flying post; or, Sherborne and Peovil mercury and general advertiser; May 18. Sherborne, 1807. 8°. (E 198)
Western Hemisphere. ANVILLE, J. B. B. de. Map. [Paris,] 1786. f°. (E 65)
Western herald and Steubenville gazette; May 11. Steubenville, 1822. f°. (E 181)
Western Inland Lock Navigation Co. Report of a committee appointed to explore the Western waters in N. Y. for the purpose of prosecuting the inland lock navigation, 1792. (*In* **N. Y.** *Sec. of State.* Doc. hist., v. 3. 1850.)
Western Islands. *See* **Azores.**
Western Islands of Scotland. *See* **Hebrides.**
Western messenger. Vol. 2–8; 1836–41. Vol. 2–6, Louisville, 7–8, Cincin., 1837–41. 7 v. 8°.
Western monthly review; [ed.] by T. Flint; May 1827–30. Vol. 1–3. Cincinnati, 1828–30. 3 v. 8°.
Western National Armory. CINCINNATI CITIZENS. Proceedings of a public meeting on the Western National Armory, Sept. 30. Cincin., 1841. 8°. (B 1498)
Western navigation. *See* **Cumings, S.**

Western Railroad Corporation. 1st ann. rept. with act of incorporation and by-laws. Boston, 1836. 8°. (B 1116, 1125) — 2d ann. report. Boston, 1837. 8°. (B 1718, 1771)
— Reports of the engineer. 1836-37. Springfield, 1838. 8°. (B 1771)
— Proceedings, Nov. 23; [with] an address to the people of Mass. on the application for a loan of the state credit. Boston, 1837. 8°. (B 1771) — Dec. 12; incl. an address, *etc.* Boston, 1838. 8°. (B 1136, 1748) — Mar. 12. Boston, 1840. 8°. (1150, 1164) — Jan. 21. Boston, 1842. 8°. (B 1180)
— MASS. *Commissioners of Internal Improvements.* Report of commissioners for a survey of routes for a railway from Boston to Albany. Boston, 1828. 8°. (B 901)
— BLISS, G. Historical memoir of the Western R. R., [1833-56]. Boston, 1863. 8°.
— BRIEF statement of facts in rel. to the Western R. R., Feb. 6, 1841. [Boston, 1841.] 8°. (B 1180)
— GUILD, W. Chart and description of the Boston and Worcester and Western R. Rs. Boston, 1847. 8°.
— BOSTON. BOARD OF TRADE. Report of the select committee on the controversy between the Boston, Worcester, and Western R. Rs. Boston, 1862. 8°. (E 127)

Western Reserve College. Catalogue of the officers and students, Dec. 1832. *n.p.*, [1832]. 8°. (B 1722)

Western review and miscellaneous magazine. Lexington, Ky., 1819-21. 3 v. 8°.

Western Sanitary Commission. Daily countersign; published for the Mississippi Valley Sanitary Fair, May 17 - June 4, 1864. St. Louis, 1864. 4°.
— FORMAN, J. G. The Western Sanitary Commission; its history, labors, *etc.* St. Louis, 1864. 8°.

Western University of Penn. System of education, *etc.* Pittsburgh, 1822. 8°. (B 534)

Westfield Academy. BATES, W. G. Address, laying of the corner stone, July 31. Springfield, 1857. 8°. (B 1612)
— STARR, P. Address, Aug. 14. Northampton, 1844. 8°. (B 1205)

Westgarth, Wm. Australia, its rise, progress, and present condition. Edin., 1861. 12°.
— Australian gold discovery. (*In* **Nat. Assoc. Prom. Soc. Sci.** Trans., 1861.)
— Colony of Victoria; its history, commerce, and gold mining; with remarks on the other Australian colonies, *etc.* London, 1864. 8°.
— Victoria and the Australian gold mines in 1857; with notes on the overland route from Australia via Suez. London, 1857. 8°.

Westhemer, Bartholomew. Conciliatio patrum et conciliorum cum Sacra Scriptura. *t.p.w.* [Tiguri? 1563?] 8°.

Westindier, Der; von A. v. **Kotzebue.** (*In his* Theater, v. 33. 1841.)

Westlake, John. The Church in the colonies. (*In* **Clay, W. L.** Essays on church policy. 1868.)
— International aspects of bankrupt laws. (*In* **Nat. Assoc. Prom. Soc. Sci.** Trans., 1861.) — Extradition of criminals. (*In* 1866.)

Westmacott, *Capt.* G. E. Indian commerce and Russian intrigue; present and future of our Indian empire. [London,] 1838. 8°. (B 1149)

Westmacott, P. On engineering. (*In* **Armstrong,** *Sir* W. G. Industrial resources. 1864.)

Westmacott, Richard. Handbook of sculpture, ancient and modern. Edin., 1864. 8°.
— Sculpture. (*In* **Smedley, E.,** *and others.* Encyc. metrop., v. 5. 1845.)
— Sculpture in Westminster Abbey. (*In* **Archæological Inst. of Gr. Brit.** Old London. 1867.)

Westman, Hab'k O., *pseud.* Transactions of the Soc. of Lit. and Scientific Chiffonniers: The spoon. N. Y., 1844. 8°.

Westmeath, *Marquis of.* *See* **Nugent,** G. T. J.

Westmeston Church. CAMPION, C. H. Mural paintings in Westmeston Church. (*In* **Sussex Archæol. Soc.** Col., v. 16. 1864.)

Westminster, Matthew of. *See* **Matthæus** *Westmonasteriensis.*

Westminster, *Eng.* CROUCH, N. Historical remarks on London and W., to 1681. New ed. Westminster, 1810. 4°.
— SAUNDERS, G. Results of an inquiry conc. the situation and extent of Westminster at various periods, [951-1725]. (*In* **Archæologia,** v. 26. 1836.)
— PITT, W., *and* FOX, C. J. Speeches, June 8, upon the Westminster scrutiny [at the election of Fox]. London, 1784. 8°.
— SOANE, J. A brief statement of the proceedings resp. the new law courts at Westminster. London, 1828. f°.
— *Maps.* SMITH, C. New plan of W. London, 1810.
— - STRANGER'S guide to London and Westminster. London, *E. Mogg*, 1815.

Westminster, *Mass.* Celebration of the 100th anniv. of the incorp. of W.; address by C. Hudson, poem by W. S. Haywood. Boston, 1859. 8°.
— HAYWOOD, W. S. Poem. Boston, 1860. 8°. (B 1233)

Westminster, *Mass.* **Cong. Church.** RICH, A. J. Historical discourse on the 125th anniv. Springfield, 1869. 8°.

Westminster, *Vt.* **Cong. Church.** WHITE, P. H. Sermon, Westminster, 100th anniv. of the Congregational Church. Bellows Falls, 1867. 8°.

Westminster Abbey. CRULL, J. Antiquities of St. Peter's or the abbey church of Westminster; cont. inscriptions, with the lives, marriages, *etc.*, of eminent personages therein reposited, and their coats of arms. 3d ed. London, 1722. 2 v. 12°.
— BRAYLEY, E. W. History and antiquities of the abbey church of St. Peter; illust. by J. P. Neale. London, 1818-23. 2 v. 4°.
— MOULE, T. Antiquities in Westminster Abbey; eng. from drawings by G. P. Harding. London, 1825. f°.
— SCOTT, G. G. The chapter-house of Westminster. — WESTMACOTT, R. On the sculpture in Westminster Abbey. (*In* **Archæological Inst. of Gr. Brit.** Old London. 1867.)
— STANLEY, A. P. Historical memorials of Westminster Abbey. London, 1868. 8°.
— - Supplement to the 1st and 2d eds. London, 1869. 8°.

Westminster Assembly of Divines. Answer to the 'Reasons of the dissenting brethren against the propositions conc. ordination'. (*In* **Gr. Brit.** *Parl.* Reasons. 1648.)
— Confession of faith, the larger and shorter catechisms; with the sum of saving knowledge, covenants, national and solemn league, directories, *etc.* Glasgow, 1766. 8°.
— Assembly's catechism, with notes; or, The shorter catechism; with an explication of difficult words, by I. Watts. [1730.] 6th ed. Boston, 1748. 12°.
— - Shorter catechism. Newburyport, 1804. 12°. (C 58)
— - *Same.* (*In* **New England Tract Soc.** Tracts, v. 2. 1814.)
— - Scripture catechism; the [shorter] catechism, with Scriptural questions and answers, by M. Henry. N. Y., Andover, 1835. 12°.
— - Shorter catechism; with notes, [mostly of Dr. Watts]. (*In* **Emerson, J.** Evangelical primer. 1844.)
— - *Indian, Stockbridge dialect.* Assembly's shorter catechism. *n.t.p.* [18—.] 16°. (E 33)
— HETHERINGTON, W. M. History of the Westminster Assembly of Divines, [1531-1654]. 3d ed. Edin., London, 1856. 8°.

— REASONS presented by the dissenting brethren [Th. Goodwin and six others] against certain propositions conc. Presbyteriall government; and the proofs of them voted by the Assembly, with the answer to those reasons. London, **1648.** 4°.
— FLAVEL, J. Exposition of the Assemblies [shorter] catechism, *etc.* **1688.** (*In his* Works, v. 2. 1701.)
— BROWN, J. Exposition of the Assembly's [shorter] catechism. [17—.] 8th ed. London, 1824. 12°. (C 250)
— PIKE, S. Present thoughts of the Assembly's shorter catechism; letter on J. Griffith's pref. to his new ed. Boston, 1768. 8°. (C 6)
— VINCENT, T. Explicatory catechism, explanation of the Assembly's shorter catechism. Northampton, **1805.** 12°.

Westminster Association. Address by ministers on the duty of family religion; with forms of prayer. Charlestown, 1801. 12°.

Westminster Bridge. LABELYE, C. Description of W. bridge. [London, 1751.] 8°. (B 705)

Westminster Greek grammar. *See* **Busby,** R.; — **Camden,** R.

Westminster magazine; May, Aug., 1783. *n.p.*, [1783]. 8°. (B 1749)

Westminster Palace. BRAYLEY, E. W., *and* BRITTON, J. History of the ancient Palace and late Houses of Parliament at Westminster. London, **1836.** 8°.
— GULLICK, T. J. Descriptive handbook for the national pictures in the Westminster Palace. London, **1865.** 8°.
— *St. Stephen's Chapel.* PEARCE, Z. Sermon, Westminster, at a jubilee kept by members of the Collegiate Church. London, 1760. 4°. (A 59)
— - TOPHAM, J. Some account of the Chapel; [with a description of plates by Sir H. C. Englefield. Lond., *Soc. of Antiq.*, 1795.] f°.
— - MACKENZIE, F. Architectural antiquities of St. Stephen's. London, **1844.** f°.
— *Westminster Hall.* Foss, E. Tabulæ curiales; or, Tables of the superior courts, **1066-1864.** London, 1865. 8°.
— - SMIRKE, S. Letter on the architectural history of Westminster Hall. (*In* **Archæologia,** v. 26. 1836.) — ON four illuminations representing the Courts of Chancery, King's Bench, Common Pleas, and Exchequer. (*In* v. 39, pt. 2. 1863.)
— - FOSS, E. Westminster Hall. (*In* **Archæological Inst. of Gr. Brit.** Old London. 1867.)

Westminster review. London, 1824-51. 56 v. (v. 25, 26 w.). 8°.
Note. Vol. 1-24 called the Westminster review; 25, 26, The London review; 27-33, The London and Westminster review; 34-45, The Westminster review; 46-56, The Westminster and foreign quarterly review.
The library has not v. 1-2 of the London review; the combined London and Westminster reviews were called '3 and 25', *etc.*, as far as '7 and 29', but in the next volume the double numbering was discontinued and a number was given (32) which included the two vols. of the London review.
— - General index, 1st-13th v. Lond., 1832. 8°.
— New series: Westminster review. London, 1852-81. 60 v. 8°.

Westminster School. HIST. of Westminster School. (*In* **Ackermann,** R. Hist. of the colleges of Winchester. 1816.)

Westmoreland, *Eng.* FERGUSON, R. The Northmen in Cumberland and Westmoreland. London, 1856. 8°.
— GILPIN, W. Mountains and lakes of Cumberland and Westmoreland, 1772. 3d ed. London, 1792. 2 v. 8°.
— WILKINSON, J. Select views in Cumberland, Westmoreland, Lancashire. Lond., 1810. f°.
— WILLS and inventories. (*In* **Raine,** J. Wills. 1853. Surtees Soc., v. 26.)
See also **Lakes of England.**

Weston, Ann W. Report of the 21st national anti-slavery bazaar. Boston, 1855. 12°. (C 262)

Weston, Daniel C. Scenes in a vestry; account of the late controversy in the South Parish Congregational Church in Augusta. Augusta, 1841. 12°.

Weston, Edward. Apology for the conduct of a late celebrated second-rate minister, 1729-46. London, 1746. 8°. (B 1519)

Weston, Edward Payson. Bowdoin poets. Brunswick, 1840. 12°.
Contents. F. Barbour. — C. H. Browne. — N. Cleaveland. — W. G. Crosby. — W. Cutter. — D. Dole. — A. Dunning. — E. Flagg. — H. W. Fuller, Jr. — B. A. G. Fuller. — H. J. Gardner. — C. L. Hemans. — E. Kellogg, Jr. — G. W. Lamb. — H. W. Longfellow. — G. F. Magoun. — F. Mellen. — I. M'Lellan, Jr. — E. Peabody. — C. H. Porter. — N. L. Sawyer. — S. Smith. — J. B. L. Soule. — G. F. Talbot. — B. B. Thatcher. — C. W. Upham. — C. H. Upton. — R. H. Vose. — W. B. Walter. — E. P. Weston. — R. Wyman.
— The pedestrian; journal of incidents on a walk from Boston to Washington. N. Y., 1862. 8°.
— Reports. *See* **Maine.** STATE. *Superintendent of Common Schools* (p. 1840).
— Strength and beauty in the education of our daughters. (*In* **Amer. Inst. of Instr.** Lectures, 1855.)

Weston, Ezra, *Jr.* Address before the Mass. Horticultural Soc. Boston, 1836. 8°. (E 9)

Weston, George. CLAPP, H. A. (*In* **Higginson,** T. W. Harvard mem. biog., v. 2. 1866.)

Weston, George Melville. The progress of slavery in the U. S. Wash., 1857. 12°.

Weston, James. New short hand grammar; [including a dictionary and observations]. London, 1749. 8°.

Weston, Jonathan D. History of Eastport and vicinity. Boston, 1834. 8°.

Weston, Nathan. Oration, July 4, 1810, before the repub. citizens of Augusta and neighboring towns. Hallowell, [1810]. 8°. (B 415)

Weston, Richard. Gardener's and planter's calendar. 2d ed., cor. and enl. Lond., 1778. 12°.
— Tracts on practical agriculture and gardening. 2d ed. impr. London, 1773. 8°.

Weston, Silas. Four months in the mines of California; or, Life in the mountains. 2d ed. Prov., 1854. 8°. (B 1600)

Weston, Stephen. The praise of Paris; or, Sketch of the French capital. London, 1803. 8°.

Weston, Wm. Report on introducing the water of the Bronx into New York. [N. Y.,] 1799. 8°. (B 526)

Weston, *Mass.* BOND, H. Genealogies of families of Weston. (*In his* Genealogies of families of Watertown. 1855.)
— KENDAL, S. Sermon, Jan. 12, a century since the incorporation of the town. Cambridge, 1813. 8°. (B 275)

Westphalia. HAMELMANN, H. Opera genealogico-historica de Westphalia et Saxonia inferiori, [-**1600**]. Lemgoviæ, 1711. 4°.
— *Maps.* GIGAS, J. Westphalia, G. Blaeuw exc. [Amst., 16—.] (E 78, no. 153)
— - MAP. *n.p.*, [16—]. (E 78, no. 152b)
— - HOMANN, J. B. Circuli Westphaliæ tabula. Norbergæ, [17—]. (E 94)
— - VISSCHER, N. Westphaliæ circulus. Amst., [17—]. (E 64, no. 22)
— - CERCLE de Westphalie, Le. Nuremberg, 1756. (E 94)
See also **Osnaburg.**

Westphalia, Peace of. BOUGEANT, G. H. Histoire des guerres et des négociations qui précédèrent le traité de Westphalie, [**1517-1648**]. Paris, 1767. 3 v. 4°.
— HULLE, A. von. Icones legatorum qui ad pacem constit. monasterium Westphalorum convenerunt. Antwerpiæ, **1691.** f°.
— BERNARD, M. The Congress of Westphalia. (*In his* Four lectures. 1868.)

Westropp, Hodder M. Analogous forms of implements among early races. (*In* **Anthropological Soc.** Mem., v. 2. 1866.)

— Rock carvings. (*In* **International Cong. of Prehist. Archæology.** Trans., 1868.)

Westward for smelts; by Kit of Kingstone; ed. by J. O. Halliwell. London, 1848. 8°. (Percy Soc., v. 22.)

— *Same, extract.* The tale told by the fishwife of Stand on the Green. (*In* **Collier, J. P.** Shakespeare's library, v. 2. 1843.)

Westward ho! a tale; by [J. K. Paulding]. N. Y., 1832. 2 v. 12°.

Westward ho! or, Voyage and adventures of Sir Amyas Leigh; by C. Kingsley. Camb., 1855. 3 v. 16°.

Note. Reviewed by E. Montégut in **Revue** d. D. Mondes, déc. 1855.

Westward hoe. *See* **Dekker**, T., *and* **Webster**, J.

Westward hoe for Avalon, in the New-found-land. *See* **Whetbourn,** R.

Westwood, John Obadiah. Arcana entomologica. London, 1841-45. 2 v. 8°.

— Genera of diurnal lepidoptera. *See* **Doubleday, E.**

— Introd. to the modern classification of insects; founded on natural habits and corresponding organizations. Lond., 1839-40. 2 v. 8°.

— Notes. (*In* **Koellar,** V. Treatise on insects. 1840.)

Wet days at Edgewood; by [D. G. Mitchell]. N. Y., 1865. 12°.

Note. Previously published in v. 11-14 of the **Atlantic** monthly as 'Wet weather work'.

Wet weather work. *See previous entry.*

Wetenhall, Edward. Letter to a friend [on] the surrender of Mons. London, 1691. 4°. (**B 4**)

Wetherald, Thomas. Sermons. Balt., 1826. 8°.

Wetherell, Elizabeth, *pseud. See* **Warner,** S.

Wetherell, Thomas May. Sermon before the Lord Mayor, *etc.*, Sept. 29. London, 1835. 4°. (**B 1250**)

Wetherill, Charles M. Modern theory of chemical types. (*In* **Smithsonian Inst.** Reports, 1863.) — Ozone and antozone. (*In* 1864.) — Plan of a research upon the atmosphere. (*In* 1866.)

Wetherill, Samuel, *and others.* Address to the people of Penn. *n.p.*, [18—]. 8°. (**B 1106**)

Wethersfield. Phelps, R. H. Some account of the state prison at Wethersfield. (*In his* History of Newgate of Conn. 1860.)

Wetmore, Alphonso. Gazetteer of Missouri; with map. St. Louis, 1837. 8°.

Note. Map wanting.

Wetmore, *Rev.* James. Appendix. (*In* **Beach,** J. Calm vindication. 1749.)

— Letter occasioned by Dickinson's remarks on Waterland's 'Regeneration'. N. Y., 1744. 8°. (**C 4**)

— Prefatory address. (*In* **Englishman** directed in the choice of his religion. 1748. **B 661, 1906**)

— Vindication of the professors of the Church of England in Connecticut, against N. Hobart. Boston, 1747. 8°. (**C 25**)

— Hobart, N. Serious address to the Episcopal separation in N. Eng. [on] W.'s 'Vindication'. Boston, 1748. 8°. (**C 19**)

Wetmore, James Carnahan. Wetmore family of America and its collateral branches. Albany, 1861. 8°.

Wetmore, Thomas Fletcher. Inaugural dissertation on the puerperal fever. N. Y., 1795. 8°. (**B 823**)

Wetmore, Wm. Oration on Washington, Feb. 22, 1800. Castine, [1800]. 8°. (**E 61, W 55**)

Wetmore, Wm. S. Memorial of the revenue bond-holders of the late republic of Texas. *n.t.p.* [1850.] 8°. (**B 1516**)

Wetmore family. *See, above,* **Wetmore,** J. C.

Wetstein. *See* **Wettstein.**

Wette, Wilhelm Martin Leberecht de. Human life; tr. by S. Osgood. Boston, 1842. 2 v. 12°. (Ripley, G. Spec. of for. lit., v. 12-13.)

— Introduction to the canonical books of the New Test.; tr. from the 5th ed. by F. Frothingham. Boston, 1858. 8°.

— Lehrbuch der historische-kritischen Einleitung in die kanonischen und apokryphischen Bücher des Alten Testamentes. 5e Ausg. Berlin, 1840. 8°.

— *Eng.* Introduction to the Old Testament; tr. and ed. by T. Parker. Bost., 1843. 2 v. 8°.

— Theodore; tr. by J. F. Clarke. Boston, 1841. 2 v. 12°. (Ripley, G. Spec. of for. lit., v. 10, 11.)

— Ueber den Verfall der protestantischen Kirche in Deutschland, und die Mittel ihr wieder aufzuhelfen. (*In* **Reformations** Almanach, v. 1. 1817.) — Ueber den sittlichen Geist der Reformation in Beziehung auf unsere Zeit. (*In* v. 2. 1819.)

— Ripley, G. View of the opinions of De Wette. (*In his* The latest form of infidelity. 1840.)

Wetterau, *Hesse Darmstadt.* Wetteravie; die Wetteraw. *n.p.*, [16—]. (**E 78,** no. 161)

Wetterstrand, Bernard Gottlieb. Die Macht der Zeit; Lustpiel, von A. v. **Kotzebue.** (*In his* Almanach, v. 20. 1822.)

Wettstein *or* Wetstein, Johann Jakob. Adnotatio ad 1 Joan. v. 7. (*In* **Burgess,** T. Adnotationes Millii. 1822.)

— Prolegomena in Nov. Test.; notas adj. J. S. Semler. Halæ Magd., 1764. 8°.

Wettstein, Johann Rudolf, *b.* 1614, *d.* 1684. Niceron, J. P. (*In his* Mém., v. 2. 1727; *and Germ.*, v. 2. 1750.)

Wettstein, Johann Rudolph, *b.* 1647, *d.* 1711. Pro Græca et genuina linguæ Græcæ pronunciatione orationes. 2a ed. Basil., 1686. 8°.

Contents. De linguæ Græcæ pronunciatione. — De federibus. — De fide Helvetica. — De exilii miseria. — De exilii solatio. — Pro fide Helvetica. — De accentibus Græcorum. — De fato scriptorum Homeri.

Wetzel, Lewis. De Haas, W. Biographical sketch of L. W. (*In his* History of the early settlements and Indian wars of Western Virginia. 1851.)

Wetzstein, Johann Gottfried. Ausgewählte griechische und lateinische Inschriften, gesammelt auf Reisen in den Trachonen und um das Haurângebirge. (*In* **Berlin. Ak. d. Wiss.** Abh., 1863.)

Wever, R. Lusty-Juventus; a morality. (*In* **Hawkins,** T. Origin of English dr., v. 1. 1773.)

Wex, Friedrich Carl. Zur Geschichte der schweriner Gelehrtenschule; eine Hinweisung auf das am 4. Aug. 1853 zu feiernde 300jährige Jubiläum. Schwerin, 1853. 4°.

Wexford. Vallancey, C. Language, manners, and customs of an Anglo-Saxon colony in the baronies of Forth and Bargie, County of Wexford, 1167-69. (*In* **Roy. Irish Acad.** Trans., v. 2. 1788.)

Wey, Francis Alphonse. Londres il y a cent ans. Paris, 1859. 12°.

Weyden, Rogier van der. Michiels, A. R. van der Weyden, sa biographie. (*In* **Gazette** des beaux arts, v. 21. 1866.)

Weyer, Florence. The honesty and true zeal of the king's witnesses vindicated against [the] protestations of O. Plunkett. London, 1681. f°. (**A 50**)

Weyer, Jean Sylvain van der. Choix d'opuscules. 1e-4e sér. Londres, 1863-76. 4 v. 8°.

Contents. Vol. 1. Le roi Cobden. 1863. — Lettres sur les Anglais qui ont écrit en français. 1854. — Discours sur l'histoire de la philosophie. 1827. — Moyen facile et économique d'être bienfaisant proposé aux jeunes gens, et suivi de pensées diverses. 1828. — Lettre à E. Münch. 1829. 2. Simon Stevin et M. Dumortier. 1845. — Le marquis de Sy et M. de Poupar. — De la littérature de l'exil. 1857. — Lettre à lord Aberdeen. 1832. — La Hollande et la conférence. 1833. — Dissertation sur le devoir. 1823. 3. Introd. — Coup d'œil sur la philosophie d'Hemsterhuis. — Lettre sur la révolution belge. — Essai sur l' 'Enseignement universel' de Jacotot. — Les jacotins et leur antagoniste; satire. — Il faut savoir dire non; petit traité de morale et de politique, [avec] appendice [d'extraits]. — *Articles de critique littéraire.* Du jésuitisme anciens et moderne, par de Pradt. — La philosophie; considérations générales. — Tablettes belges. — Littérature. — Dénonciations aux cours royales rel. au système religieux et politique signalé par le comte Montlosier. — Esquisse sur C. Victor de Bonstetten. — Analyse du mémoire de N. G. Van Kampen. — Six mois en Russie, par M. Ancelot. — Réponse à C. Froment. — De la multiplicité des livres. — Principe de littérature par le baron Massias. — Epigrammes en vers. 4. Lettre d'un vieux bibliophile belge à P. Namur. — Complément de l'ouvrage de Namur sur les ana. — Observ. sur quelques ana par l'éditeur. — Maximes et réflexions morales. — Les aveugles, la ministère, et l'opposition. — L'autorité, la petite ville, *etc.*; lettre à un ministre belge.

— The Queen and the Duchess of Nemours. — Les pendules de Thiers et le cuisinier de Van de Weyer; lettre au Times. — Van de Weyer, publiciste; par A. Le Roy. — Un fondateur de la monarchie belge, S. Van de Weyer; par A. Laugel. — S. Van de Weyer; par E. Van Bemmel. — Self-forgetfulness; a sermon, by Rev. W. B. Turner, in remembrance of W. — In memoriam.

Weyermann, Albrecht. Nachrichten von Gelehrten, Künstlern, und andern merkwürdigen Personen aus Ulm. Ulm, 1798. 8°.

Weyhe-Eimke, Arnoldo di. PICCOLOMINI, E. Sopra le recerche e i guidizi del barone di Weyhe-Eimke int. alla personalità storica del M. Piccolomini nel Wallenstein di Schiller. (*In* **Archivio** stor. ital., 3a ser., v. 14. 1871.)

Weyman, George Washington. Analysis of bituminous coal ash. (*In* **Amer. Assoc.** Proc., v. 6. 1852.)

Weymouth, George. CUSHMAN, D. Attempt to show that the islands and river now called St. George were those visited by Weymouth. (*In* **Maine Hist. Soc.** Col., v. 6. 1859.)

Weymouth, Richard. Notes and glossary. (*In* **Grosseteste,** R. Castel off love. 1864. Philol. Soc. Early Eng. vol.)

— Numerous articles.] (*In* **Philological Soc.** Trans., 1856, 60-61, 62-63, 70-72.)

Weymouth, *Mass.* GOD'S voice crying to the inhabitants of Weymouth and the neighboring towns. *n.p.*, 1752. 8°. (B 265)

Weymouth. 2d Church. BAYLEY, S. Clerical intolerance; brief statement of proceedings of the 2d Church against S. B. Boston, 1824. 12°. (C 236)

Weymouth. South Parish. Report of the committee of inquiry [on] their reasons for declining the assistance of the North Parish in the ordination of W. Tyler. *n.p.*, [1819]. 8°. (B 538, 1393)

Whale, Theophilus. STILES, E. (*In his* Hist. of the judges. 1794.)

Whale fishery. COFFIN, P. Progress of the whale fishery at Nantucket, [1690-1785]. (*In* **Mass. Hist.** Soc. Col., v. 3. 1810.) — STATE of cod and whale fisheries in Mass., 1763. (*In* v. 8. 1802.)

— OBSERVATIONS on the whale fishery. *n.p.*, [1789]. 8°. (W 17)

— ANDRADA Y SILVA, J. B. de. Sobre a pesca das baleas, e extraccaõ do seu azeite. (*In* **Lisbon. Ac. d.** Sci. Mem. econ., v. 2. 1790.)

— SCORESBY, W. Account of the Arctic regions and whale fishery. Edin., 1820. 2 v. 8°.

— — Journal of a voyage to the northern whale fishery. Edin., 1823. 8°.

— WHALE fishery. (*In* **Holbrook,** J. Scientific tracts, v. 1. 1831.)

— MACY, O. Hist. of Nantucket and the whale fishery. Boston, 1835. 8°.

— GRINNELL, J. Speech on the tariff; with statistical tables of the whale fishery of the U. S. Wash., 1844. 8°. (B 1174)

— BROWNE, J. R. Etchings of a cruise; appended, a brief history of the whale fishery. Boston, 1846. 8°.

— SEWARD, W. H. The whale fishery and American commerce in the Pacific Ocean; speech, July 29. Wash., 1852. 8°. (B 1506, 1608)

See also **Maurice,** J., *vs.* **Judd,** S. W.

Whales. HAMILTON, R. Natural history of the ordinary cetacea or whales. Edin., 1837. 16°. (Jardine, *Sir* M. Nat. lib., v. 26.)

See also **Cetacea**; — **Whale fishery.**

Whaley *or* **Whalley,** *Col.* Edward. FELT, J. B. Papers relating to Whalley and Goffe, 1661-78. (*In* **Mass. Hist. Soc.** Col., v. 27. 1838.)

— PHILAGATHOS, *pseud.* Poem commemorative of W. Boston, 1793. 8°. (B 352, 609, 628)

— STILES, E. (*In his* History of three of the judges of Charles I. 1794.)

Whaley, *Rev.* John. Journey to Houghton Hall; poem. (*In* **Walpole,** H. Ædes Walpolianæ. 1767.)

Whalley, George H. RITCHIE, J. E. (*In his* Brit. senators. 1869.)

Whalley, Lawson, *M. D.* Vindication of the University of Edinburgh as a school of medicine. (*In* **Pamphleteer,** 1819; v. 13 of B 838)

Whalley, P. Notes. (*In* **Jonson,** B. Works. 1756.)

Whalley, Thomas Sedgewick, *D.D.* Journals and correspondence; ed. with memoir, by H. Wickham. London, 1863. 2 v. 8°.

Whalley Abbey. Coucher book; or, Chartulary of Whalley Abbey; ed. by W. A. Hulton. [Manchester,] 1847-49. 4 v. 4°. (Chetham Soc., v. 10, 11, 16, 20.)

Wharton, *Rev.* Charles Henry, *D.D.* Remains; with a mem. by G. W. Doane. Phila., 1834. 2 v. 12°.

Contents. Vol. 1. Memoir. — Sermons. — Selected papers. 2. Letter to the Roman Catholics of Worcester. — Address to the Roman Catholics of the U. S. by J. Carroll. — Reply to [C.'s] address. — Short answer to the appendix to the 'Cath. question in America'. — Rem. on Dr. O'Gallagher's 'Reply' to the 'Short answer'.

See also **Quarterly** theological magazine, v. 3, 4.

Wharton, Francis, *D.D.* The silence of Scripture. Boston, 1867. 16°.

— Treatise on theism and on modern skeptical theories. Phila., 1859. 12°.

— A willing reunion not impossible; thanksgiving sermon, Brookline, Nov. 26. Boston, 1863. 8°. (B 1592)

Wharton, *Sir* George, *ed.* *See* **Almanacs.** CALENDARIUM Carolinum (p. 53).

Wharton, George M. Answer to Binney's reply to 'Remarks on B.'s treatise on the habeas corpus'. Phila., 1862. 8°. (B 1724)

— Remarks on Binney's treatise on the writ of habeas corpus. 2d ed. Phila., 1862. 8°. (B 1724)

Wharton, Grace, *pseud.* *See* **Thomson,** *Mrs.* K. B.

Wharton, Henry, *Rector of Chartham.* Excerpta ex vita ms. H. Whartoni a seipso scripta. (*In* **D'Oyly,** G. Life of W. Sancroft. 1821.)

— NICERON, J. P. (*In his* Mém., v. 15. 1731; *and, Germ.*, v. 11. 1754.)

Wharton, John. Tentamen physiologico-medicum inaugurale de mania. Edin., 1806. 8°. (B 138, 814)

Wharton, Philip, *Duke of Wharton.* Speech, Ho. of Lords, on the bill [against] Francis late Bp. of Rochester. London, 1723. f°. (A 56)

Wharton, Philip, *pseud.* *See* **Thomson,** J. C.

Wharton, Richard. Patent to land on the Androscoggin, 1686; with depositions of J. Reding and others. (*In* **Maine Hist.** Soc. Col., v. 3. 1853.)

Wharton, Richard. Fables from Dante, Berni, *etc.*, imitated in English heroic verse. London, 1804. 8°.

Wharton, Thomas. GODDARD, W. Conduct of W. delineated. (*In his* The partnership, *etc.* 1770. B 618)

Wharton, Thomas I. Address at the opening of the New Hall of the Athenæum of Philadelphia, October 18, 1847; [with an appendix, cont. the address of the President Samuel Breck at the laying of the Corner Stone, November 1845]. Phila., 1847. 8°. (B 1585)

— Discourse, Oct. 24, before Soc. for the Commem. of the Landing of Wm. Penn. Phila., 1826. 8°. (B 1097)

— Memoir of W. Rawle, read Feb. 22, 1837; with a letter from P. S. Du Ponceau to the author containing his recollections of Rawle's life and character. (*In* **Penn. Hist. Soc.** Mem., v. 4, pt. 1. 1840.)

— Oration, July 4. Phila., 1827. 8°. (B 1097)

Wharton, Wm. H. Texas; address in N. York, Apr. 26. N. Y., 1836. 8°. (E 11)

Wharves. BOWDITCH, N. I. Wharf property; or, The law of flats. Boston, 1852. 8°. (B 1431)

What a curse! or, Johnny Hodges the blacksmith; [by L. M. Sargent]. Boston, 1835. 24°. (D 24)

— *Same.* 4th ed. Boston, 1835. 24°.

What banks are constitutional? *n.p.*, [184-?]. 8°. (B 1543)

What d'ye call it? by J. Gay. (*In* **Col.** of most esteemed farces, v. 5. 1792.)

What happened after the battle of Dorking. N. Y., 1871. 12°.

What is our situation and what our prospects? by an American. *n.p.*, [1798]. 8°. (W 10)

What next? farce, by T. Dibdin. (*In* **London** stage, v. 4.)

What she could; [by S. Warner]. N. Y., 1871. 16°.

What think ye of the Congress now? *See* **Chandler,** T. B. (B 343, W 21)

What will he do with it; by Sir E. L. Bulwer Lytton. Lpz., *Tauchnitz*, 1857-58. 4 v. 16°.

— *Same.* N. Y., 1859. 8°.

Note. From **Blackwood's** mag., v. 81-85. 1857-59.

What you will. *See* **Marston,** J.

Whateley, Thomas, *surgeon*. Account of exfoliation of the internal surface of the tibia. (*In* **Soc. Prom. Med. Knowl.** Med. com., v. 2. 1790.)

Whately, E. Jane. Life and correspondence of R. Whately. London, 1866. 2 v. 8°.

— Selection of English synonyms. 1st Amer. ed. enl. from 2d Lond. ed. Bost., 1852. 12°.

Whately, *Rev.* Edward. On the life and writings of J. Foster the essayist. (*In* **Afternoon** lectures, v. 1. 1863.) — Romeo and Juliet. (*In* v. 5. 1869.)

Whately, Richard, *Archbp. of Dublin*. Address, recent changes in the system of Irish national education. 2d ed. London, 1853. 8°. (E 3)

— Address to the clergy on the use and abuse of the present occasion for beneficence. 2d ed. London, 1847. 12°. (E 3)

— Address to the national school teachers, members of the established church. Dublin, 1847. 8°. (E 3)

— Annotations. (*In* **Paley, W.** View of the evidences of Christianity. 1859.)

— Charge to the clergy of the dioceses of Dublin and Kildare. Dublin, 1847. 8°. (E 3)

— Charges and other tracts. London, 1836. 8°.
Contents. Charge to the clergy of Dublin, 1834. — Charge to the clergy of D., 1835. — Address to the clergy of D. on confirmation, 1832. — Address to the clergy of D. on confirmation, 1834. — Address to the inhabitants of D. and vicinity resp. the Lord's Day. — National education in Ireland. — Appeal in behalf of the Assoc. for Discountenancing Vice, *etc.* — Tithes in Ireland. — Jew's relief bill. — Obs. on presenting a petition to the Ho. of Lords from the clergy of Kildare, rel. to Church reform.

— Christian saints as described in the New Testament; discourse. Dublin, 1848. 8°. (E 3)

— Dissertation on the rise, progress, and corruptions of Christianity. (*In* **Encyclopædia Britannica**, 8th ed., v. 1. 1853.)

— Easy lessons on money matters. 13th ed. London, 1853. 24°.

— Easy lessons on reasoning. 7th ed. London, 1853. 12°.

— Elements of logic. 9th ed. London, 1848. 8°.

— *Same.* (*In* **Smedley, E.,** *and others.* Encyc. metrop., v. 1. 1845.)

— Elements of rhetoric. Camb., 1832. 12°.

— *Same.* 4th ed. Oxford, 1832. 8°.

— *Same.* With add. Boston, 1843. 12°.

— *Same.* (*In* **Smedley, E.,** *and others.* Encyc. metrop., v. 1. 1845.)

— Essays on dangers to Christian faith. London, 1839. 8°.
Contents. Dangers from injudicious modes of preaching. — Danger from neglect of instruction in Christian evidences and from party spirit among Christians. — Danger of an erroneous imitation of Christ's teaching. — Best mode of conveying Scriptural instruction. — Jesus despised as a Nazarene. — Treason of Judas.

— Essays. [1st series:] On the peculiarities of the Christian relig. 2d ed. Oxford, 1827. 8°.
Contents. Future state. — Declaration of God in His Son. — Love towards Christ as a motive for obedience. — Practical character of revelation. — Example of children as proposed to Christians.

— Essays. 2d ser.: On some of the difficulties in the writings of the apostle Paul and other parts of the N. T. 6th ed. London, 1849. 8°.
Contents. Introduction. — Love of truth. — Difficulties and value of St. Paul's writings. — Election. — Perseverance and assurance. — Abolition of the Mosaic law. — Imputed righteousness. — Apparent contradictions in Scripture. — Mode of conveying moral precepts in the N. T. — Influence of the Holy Spirit. — Self-denial.

— Essays. 3d ser.: On the errors of Romanism having their origin in human nature. 4th ed. London, 1850. 8°.
Contents. Introduction. — Superstition. — Vicarious religion. — Pious frauds. — Undue reliance on human authority. — Persecution. — Trust in names and privileges.

— *Same.* Errors of Romanism. Lond., 1830. 8°.

— Example of children as proposed to Christians; 5th of the Essays [1st ser.]. London, 1846. 8°. (E 3)

— Historic doubts rel. to N. Buonaparte. (*In* **Pamphleteer**, 1826; v. 27 of **B 388**)

— *Same.* From 4th London ed. Camb., 1832. 12°. (**B 1060**)

— *Same.* 4th Amer. from 11th London ed. Boston, 1853. 16°.

— Infant baptism considered. 2d ed., with add. London, 1850. 8°.

— Introductory lessons on Christian evidences. 13th ed. London, 1853. 24°.

— *French.* Leçons faciles sur l'évidence du christianisme. Lausanne, 1840. 12°. (**E 170**)

— *Greek.* Ἀποδείξεις τοῦ χριστιανισμοῦ. Σμύρνῃ, 1846. 16°. (**E 170**)

— *Ital.* Letture popolari sull' evidenza del christianesimo. Lugano, 1841. 16°. (**E 170**)

— *Swedish.* Inledning till bewisen för Christna religionen. Stockholm, 1853. 24°. (**E 170**)

— Introductory lessons on the British constitution. London, 1854. sm. 12°.

— Introductory lessons on the history of religious worship. 2d ed. London, 1849. 24°.

— The Kingdom of Christ. 2d ed. London, 1842. 8°.
Contents. Christ's account of His person and the nature of His kingdom. — Constitution of a Christian church, *etc.*

— Lectures on political economy. Lond., 1831. 8°.

— Lectures on the characters of [the] apostles. London, 1851. 12°.

— Lectures on the Scripture revelations resp. good and evil angels. London, 1851. 12°.

— Letter to a clergyman on religious controversy. Dublin, 1850. 12°. (E 3)

— Letter to the lord lieutenant of Ireland rel. to the re-establishment of the bishoprick of Kildare, in union with that of Leighlin. Lond., 1842. 8°. (E 3)

— Logic. *See, above,* Elements of logic.

— Miscellaneous remains from his common-place book; ed. by E. J. Whately. Lond., 1864. 8°.

— Preparation for death; a lecture. London, [185-]. 12°. (E 3)

— Protective measures; in behalf of the established church; a charge. London, 1851. 8°. (E 3)

— Rhetoric. *See, above,* Elements of rhetoric.

— Scripture doctrine conc. the sacraments. London, 1857. 12°.

— Search after infallibility; discourse. Dublin, 1847. 8°. (E 3)

— Sermons on festivals and other occasions. 3d ed. enl. London, 1854. 8°.

— Speech on a bill for the removal of disabilities from the Jewish persuasion; with remarks on objections to that measure; also, a petition rel. to church reform. 2d ed. London, 1834. 8°. (E 3)

— Substance of a speech on the motion for a committee on Irish poor laws. London, 1847. 8°. (E 3)

— Thoughts on church government. London, 1844. 8°. (E 3)

— Thoughts on secondary punishments; app., articles on transportation and colonization. London, 1832. 8°.

— Thoughts on the Sabbath. London, 1854. 8°.

— Use and abuse of party feeling, *etc.*; sermons, Bampton lecture, 1822; added, five sermons preached before the Univ. of Oxford. 3d ed. London, 1833. 8°.

— View of the Scripture revelations concerning a future state. London, 1853. 12°.

— What are the arts in the cultivation of which the moderns have been less successful than the ancients. (*In* **Oxford** prize essays, v. 2. 1836.)

— Joly, H. E. Questions deducible from the 'Introd. lessons', *etc.* London, 1849. 24°.

— Martineau, H. (*In her* Biog. sketches. 1869.)

— Whately, E. J. Life and correspondence of W. London, 1866. 2 v. 8°.

Whately, Thomas, *Sec. to the Treasury.* Remarks on the 'Budget'. (*In* **Collection** of scarce tracts, v. 1. 1788. **B 604**) — Considerations on the trade and finances of this kingdom. (*In* v. 2. 1787. **B 605**)

Whately, *Mass.* TEMPLE, J. H. Early ecclesiastical history of W. Northampton, 1849. 8°.
Whatley, Robert. Letter to a bencher of the Inner Temple, [Sir P. King], writ in 1713. 2d ed. London, 1729. 8°. (B 118)
Whatley, Stephen. England's gazetteer. London, 1751. 3 v. (v. 2, 3 w.). 12°.
Wheare, Degory. NICERON, J. P. (*In his* Mém., v. 19. 1732; *and, Germ.*, v. 15. 1757.)
Wheat. BRAND, J. Determination of the average depression of the price of wheat in war. London, 1800. 8°.
— SINCLAIR, *Sir* J. Result of an inquiry into the nature of the blight, rust, and mildew. Edin., 1809. 8°. (W 9)
— STERNBERG, P. Treatise on the raising of wheat. Albany, [1811]. 8°. (B 666)
— BANKS, J. Remarks on the mildew of wheat and the choice of seed corn. (*In* Pamphleteer, 1816; v. 8 of B 838)
— HUDSON, C. Speech, wheat trade of the country, Feb. 26. Wash., 1846. 8°. (B 1514)
Wheat and tares. (*In* Fraser's mag., v. 61–62. 1860.)
Wheatfield. CHUBBE, J. History and antiquities of the ancient villa of W. (*In his* Miscel. tracts, v. 1. 1770.)
Wheatley, C. *See* Wheatly, C.
Wheatley, Henry Benj. Round about Piccadilly and Pall Mall. London, 1870. 8°.
Wheatley, John. Remarks on currency and commerce. London, 1803. 8°. (B 1414)
— Thoughts on the object of a foreign subsidy. London, 1805. 8°. (B 1414)
Wheatley, Phillis. *See* Peters, *Mrs.* P. W.
Wheatley & Adlard. Catalogue of the library, sold by W. and A., Dec. 9, 1829; [partly priced. Lond., 1829.] 8°. (B 1618)
— Catalogue of library, sold by W. and A., July 22. [London, 1830.] 8°. (B 1618)
Wheatley mine. SMITH, J. L. Minerals of the Wheatley mine. (*In* Amer. Assoc. Proc., v. 9. 1856.)
Wheatly, Charles. Rational illustration of the Book of common prayer; [with] add. Boston, 1837. 8°.
Wheaton, Abby. Memoir of R. Wheaton; with selections from his writings. Bost., 1854. 12°.
Wheaton, Henry. Address at the opening of the New York Athenæum, Dec. 14. N. Y., 1824. 8°. (B 567, W 4)
— *Same.* 2d ed. N. Y., 1825. 8°.
— Anniv. discourse before the N. Y. Hist. Soc., 1820. N. Y., 1821. 8°. (B 939)
— *Same.* (*In* New York Hist. Soc. Col., v. 3. 1821.)
— Elements of international law. Phila., 1836. 8°.
— *Same.* 2d annotated ed. by W. B. Lawrence. Boston, 1863. 8°.
— *Same.* 8th ed. by R. H. Dana, Jr. Boston, 1866. 8°.
— *Chinese.* Tr. by W. A. P. Martin. Peking, 1864. 8°.
— Enquiry into the validity of British claim to right of search. Phila., 1842. 8°.
— History of the law of nations, to 1842. N. Y., 1845. 8°.
— History of the Northmen. London, 1831. 8°.
— Life of W. Pinkney. (*In* Sparks, J. Amer. biog., v. 6. 1836.)
Note. From 'Life, writings, *etc.*, of Pinkney', and also from an article on that work in the N. Amer. review.
— Life, writings, and speeches of W. Pinkney. Boston, 1826. 8°.
— The progress and prospects of Germany; a discourse before the Phi Beta Kappa Soc. of Brown Univ., Prov., Sept. 1. Boston, 1847. 8°. (B 1652)
— Scandinavia. *See* Crichton, A.
— OUR relations with England, *etc.*; [a review of W.'s 'Enquiry', *etc.*]. From the June no. of the Southern literary messenger. *n.p.*, [1842]. 8°. (B 1475)
Wheaton & Donaldson *vs.* Peters & Grigg. HOPKINSON, J. Opinion in the case. Phila., 1833. 8°. (B 1440)
Wheaton, Joseph. Sermon, Jan. 6, funeral of Miss S. Emmons. Boston, 1823. 8°. (B 283)
— Statement to Congress.] *n.t.p.* [1820?] 8°. (B 531)

415. (2. 11. 81.)

Wheaton, Nathaniel Sheldon, *D.D.* Discourse, St. Paul's epistle to Philemon, Dec. 22, 1850. Hartford, 1851. 8°. (B 1305, 1478)
— Happiness or misery the result of choice. (*In* Prot. Episc. pulpit, v. 4. 1834. B 1776)
— Journal of a residence in London, *etc.*, and a tour in France and Scotland. Hartford, 1830. 12°.
Wheaton, Robert. Memoir of W., [by A. Wheaton], with writings. Boston, 1854. 12°.
Wheel of fortune, The. *See* Cumberland, R.
Wheel of the law. *See* Alabaster, H.
Wheeler. *See also* Wheler.
Wheeler, A. C. Chronicles of Milwaukee. Milwaukee, 1861. 8°.
Wheeler, A. O. Eye witness. Boston, 1865. 12°.
Wheeler, Betsy. *See* Wheeler, E. (B 427)
Wheeler, C. A. Sportascrapiana. London, 1867. 8°.
Wheeler, Charles Henry. Essential elements in American education. (*In* Amer. Inst. of Instr. Lect., 1852.)
Wheeler, Charles Stearns. DAVIS, W. A. Biog. notice of W. Boston, 1843. 8°. (B 1461)
Wheeler, David Everett. Discourse at the request of the Order of United Americans, Feb. 22. N. Y., 1851. 8°. (B 1572)
Wheeler, Ephraim. Report of the trial of E. W. for rape on B. Wheeler, Lenox, Sept. Stockbridge, 1805. 8°. (B 427)
Wheeler, Henry G. History of Congress. N. Y., 1848. 2 v. 8°.
Wheeler, J. A. Handbook of anatomy for artists. London, [18—]. 18°.
Wheeler, J. Talboys. Analysis and summary of Herodotus. 2d ed. London, *Bohn*, 1852. 8°.
— Analysis and summary of Thucydides. London, *Bohn*, 1855. 8°.
— The geography of Herodotus explained and illustrated from modern researches. London, 1854. 8°.
— History of India from the earliest ages. London, 1867–76. 4 v. 8°.
Contents. Vol. 1. The Vedic period and the Mahá Bhárata. 2. The Ramayana and the Brahmanic period. 3. Hindú; Buddhist; Brahmanical revival. 4, pt. 1. Mussulman rule.
— Introduction. (*In* Bholanauth Chunder. Travels of a Hindoo. 1869.)
— Life and travels of Herodotus; an imaginary biography. London, 1855. 2 v. 8°.
— Madras *vs.* America; handbook to cotton cultivation. N. Y., 1866. 8°.
Wheeler, Jacob D. Introductory lecture upon criminal jurisprudence. N. Y., 1827. 8°. (B 1431)
Wheeler, John, *D. D.* Address before the Porter Rhetorical Soc., Theological Seminary, Andover, Sept. 1834. Andover, 1836. 8°. (B 1239)
— Discourse, death of Wm. H. Harrison, Burlington, April 23. Windsor, 1841. 8°. (B 1217)
— Discourse, July 6, funeral of J. Marsh. Burlington, 1842. 8°. (B 1221, 1246)
— Historical discourse, address by J. R. Spalding, and poem, by Rev. O. G. Wheeler, on the semi-centennial anniv. of the University of Vermont. Burlington, 1854. 8°.
Wheeler, John H. Historical sketches of North Carolina, 1584–1851. Phila., 1851. 2 v. 8°.
Wheeler, *Rev.* Joseph. Account of Harvard, 1767. (*In* Mass. Hist. Soc. Col., v. 10. 1809.)
Wheeler, *Mrs.* Mercy. LORD, B. Humble importunity victorious; sermon on the deliverence of Mrs. W. Boston, 1743. 8°. (C 21)
Wheeler, *Rev.* Orville Gould. Poem. (*In* Wheeler, J. Historical discourse; semi-centennial anniv. of the Univ. of Vermont. 1864.)
Wheeler, Thomas. Narrative of an expedition with Capt. E. Hutchinson into the Nipmuck Country and to Quaboag, 1675. (*In* New Hampshire Hist. Soc. Col., v. 2. 1827.)
Wheeler, Wm. DWIGHT, T. Discourse on [his] life and character, July 17. New Haven, 1864. 8°. (B 1639)

Wheeler, Wm. Adolphus. Dictionary of noted names of fiction, pseudonyms, *etc.* London, 1866. 8°.

— First lessons in reading. 1866. *See* **Soule, R.**

— Manual of English pronunciation and spelling. 1861. *See* **Soule, R.**

Wheeler, *Mrs.* Zerviah. WILSON, J. Sermon, July 25, death of Mrs. W. Prov., 1802. 8°. (B 335)

Wheeler. *See also* **Wheler.**

Wheeling, *Va.* MATHERS, W., *Chairman.* Report of a meeting of workingmen, on forming a settlement in Illinois. *n.t.p.* [1830.] 8°. (B 1854)

Wheelock, *Rev.* Edwin Miller. Harper's Ferry and its lesson; sermon for the times. 2d ed. Boston, 1859. 12°. (C 211)

— The human soul; discourse, Dover, N. H. Boston, 1858. 8°. (B 1505)

— Inspiration; discourse, Dover, N. H. Boston, 1857. 8°. (C 211)

— Literal interpretations; lecture, Dover. Boston, 1858. 8°. (C 211)

Wheelock, Eleazar, *D.D.* Brief narrative of the Indian charity school in Lebanon. London, 1766. 8°. (B 629)

— *Same.* 2d ed. London, 1767. 8°.

— Letter to the Provincial Congress at Exeter, 1775. (*In* **N. H. Hist. Soc.** Col., v. 2. 1827.)

— Plain narrative of the design, progress, and present state of the Indian charity school at Lebanon. Boston, 1763. 8°.

— *Another copy.* (B 417)

— - 1st-5th] continuation. Vol. 1, Boston, 2, *n.p.*, 3, N. Hampshire, 4, 5, Hartford, 1765-75. 5 v. 8° *and* 4°.

Contents. Vol. 1. Nov. 27, 1762 - Sept. 3, 1765. 2. 1768-71. 3. May 6, 1771 - Sept. 10, 1772. 4. Sept. 26, 1772 - Sept. 26, 1773. 5. Sept. 26, 1773 - Feb. 20, 1775.

— 2d contin. [1768-71.] *n.t.p.* [1771.] 4°. (B 196)

— 3d contin. [May 6, 1771 - Sept. 10, 1772.] N. H., 1773. 4°. (W 31)

— 4th contin. [Sept. 26, 1772 - Sept. 26, 1773.] Hartford, 1773. 4°. (W 31)

— 5th contin. [Sept. 26, 1773 - Feb. 20, 1775.] Hartford, 1775. 4°. (W 25)

— Letter to [J.] Davenport. 1744. *See* **Williams, S.** (C 51)

— MCCLURE, D., *and* PARISH, E. Memoirs of W. Newburyport, 1811. 8°.

Wheelock, *Rev.* James R. Farewell sermon to the Congregational Church and Soc., Newport, N. H., Mar. 2. Windsor, Vt., 1823. 8°. (B 1238)

Wheelock, John, *Pres. Dartmouth Coll.* Eulogium on J. Smith. Hanover, 1809. 8°. (B 87, 435, 911)

— *Funeral sermon on.* 1817. *See* **Allen, S.** (B 357)

Wheels. CAMUS, C. E. L. Treatise on the teeth of wheels, *etc.*; tr. from the French. [1749.] London, 1806. 8°.

— SHELDRAKE, T. Theory and properties of inclined plane wheels. London, 1811. 8°.

— WILLIS, R. On the teeth of wheels. (*In* **Instit. of Civ. Engin.** Trans., v. 2. 1842.)

Wheelwright, *Mrs.* Anne. APTHROP, E. Character and example of a Christian woman; discourse, death of Mrs. W. Boston, 1765. 4°. (A 3)

Wheelwright, Charles Apthorp. Poems, including versions of the Medea and Octavia of Seneca. London, 1810. 8°.

Wheelwright, Charles Henry. WELCH, C. A. (*In* **Higginson, T. W.** Harvard memorial biog., v. 1. 1866.)

Wheelwright, *Rev.* John. Sermon, Boston, fast day, 16th of Jan. 1636/37. Reprinted from Mass. Hist. Soc., Proc., 1866-67; ed. by C. Deane. Camb., 1867. 8°.

— *Same.* [Ed. by H. B. Dawson.] Morrisania, 1867. 8°.

— INDIAN deeds to W. and others. — PLUMER, W. Remarks on the authenticity of the Wheelwright deed. (*In* **N. Hamp. Hist. Soc.** Col., v. 1. 1824.) — FARMER, J. Communication resp. the Wheelwright deed. (*In* v. 2. 1827.)

Wheelwright, Wm. Statements and documents rel. to the establishment of steam navigation in the Pacific. London, 1838. 8°. (B 1742)

Wheildon, Wm. Willder. Memoir of S. Willard, architect and superintendent of Bunker Hill Monument. Boston, *Bunker Hill Mon. Assoc.*, 1865. 8°.

— Remarks on the supposed open sea in the Arctic regions. (*In* **Amer. Assoc.** Proc., v. 14. 1861.) — Remarkable case of freezing fresh water in pipes submerged in salt water. (*In* v. 19. 1871.)

Wheland, Wm. Narrative of the horrid murder and piracy on board the schooner Eliza by three foreigners. London, [18—]. 8°. (B 774)

Wheler. *See also* **Wheeler.**

Wheler *or* **Wheeler**, *Sir* George. Voyage d'Italie, *etc.*, 1724. *See* **Spon, J.**

Wheler, Robert Bell. Guide to Stratford-upon-Avon. Stratford-upon-Avon, 1814. 12°.

— History and antiquities of Stratford-upon-Avon. Stratford-upon-Avon, [18—]. 8°.

Whelpley, James D., *and* **Storer, J. J.** HUNT, T. S. On the metallurgical system of Messers. Whelpley and Storer. (*In* **Amer. Assoc.** Proc., v. 15. 1867.)

Whelpley, *Rev.* Philip Melancthon. Sermon, N. Y., in behalf of the United For. Miss. Soc., May 11. N. Y., 1823. 8°. (B 301)

Whelpley, *Rev.* Samuel (*pseud.* **Philadelphus**). Compend. of history. Vol. 1. 10th ed., with corr. and add. by J. Emerson. N. Y., 1835, 30. 2 v. 12°.

— Letters addressed to C. Strong, showing that retaliation, capital punishments, and war are prohibited by the Gospel. N. Y., 1816. 8°.

— *Same.* 2d ed. Phila., 1817. 8°.

— EMERSON, J. Questions to W.'s 'Compend of history'. 10th ed. N. Y., 1829. 12°.

Whelpley, *Rev.* Samuel W. Address before the Peace Society of Hartford County. Hartford, 1830. 8°. (B 1786)

When I was a little girl; illust. by L. Frölich; by [Miss E. Tabor]. 2d ed. London, 1871. 16°.

When will the day come. *See* **Mass. Temperance Society.**

Whetstone, George. Censure of a loyal subject. (*In* **Collier, J. P.** Illust. of early Eng. lit., v. 1. 1863.)

— History of Promos and Cassandra. (*In* **Collier, J. P.** Shakespeare's library, v. 2. 1843.)

— A mirror of treue honour, *etc.* (*In* **Park, T.** Helliconia, v. 2. 1815.)

— Rocke of regard; [ed. by J. P. Collier. London, 18—.] 4°.

Contents. Castle of delight. — Garden of unthriftinesse. — Arbour of vertue. — Ortcharde of repentance.

Whewell, Wm., *D.D.* Analytical statics; suppl. to the 4th ed. of an elementary treatise on mechanics. Camb., 1833. 8°.

— Astronomy and general physics with ref. to natural theology. London, 1833. 8°. (Bridgewater treatises, v. 3.)

— Elementary treatise on mechanics. Vol. 1. Camb., 1819. 8°.

— Elements of morality. London, 1848. 2 v. 16°.

— General bearing of the Great Exhibition on the progress of arts and sciences. (*In* **Soc. for the Encouragement of Arts.** Lectures, 1st ser. 1851.)

— History of the inductive sciences. London, 1837. 3 v. 8°.

Contents. Vol. 1. Hist. of the Greek school philosophy with reference to physical science. — Hist. of the physical sciences in ancient Greece. — Hist. of Greek astronomy. — Hist. of physical science in the Middle Ages. — Hist. of formal astronomy after the stationary period. 2. Hist. of mechanics, including fluid mechanics. — Hist. of physical astronomy. — Hist. of acoustics. — Hist. of optics, formal and physical. — Hist. of thermotics and atmology. 3. Hist. of electricity. — Hist. of magnetism. — Hist. of galvanism. — Hist. of chemistry. — Hist. of mineralogy. — Hist. of systematic botany and zoology. — Hist. of physiology and comparative anatomy. — Hist. of geology.

— Influence of the hist. of science upon intellectual education. (*In* **Roy. Inst. Gr. Brit.** Lectures on education. 1855; — *and in* **Youmans, E. L.** Modern culture. 1867.)

— Lectures on the history of moral philosophy. New ed., with add. lectures. Camb., 1862. 8°.
— Novum organum renovatum. 2d part of the Philosophy of the inductive sciences. 3d ed. London, 1858. 8°.
— Philosophy of discovery. London, 1860. 8°.
Note. The 'History' and the 'Philosophy' were reviewed by Sir J. F. W. Herschel, in the Quar. rev., v. 68; repr. in his Essays. 1857.
— Philosophy of the inductive sciences. New ed., with corr., add., and app. London, 1847. 2 v. 8°.
— Plurality of worlds; with introd. by E. Hitchcock. Boston, 1854. 12°.
— Preface to [Mackintosh's] Dissertation on the progress of ethical philosophy. (*In* **Encycl. Brit.**, v. 1. 1853.)
— On the principles of English university education including thoughts on the study of mathematics. 2d ed. London, 1838. 12°.
— Tides. (*In* **Herschel, J. F. W.** Manual of scientific enquiry. 1851.)
— Brewster, *Sir*. D. More worlds than one; [answer to 'Plurality of worlds']. N. Y., 1854. 12°.
— Martineau, J. Whewell's 'Morality' and Whewell's 'Systematic morality'. (*In his* Essays, philosophical and theological, v. 2. 1868.)
Which is the man; a comedy, by Mrs. H. P. Cowley. (*In* **London** stage, v. 2.)
Which is the wiser; by M. Howitt. N. Y., 1842. 18°.
Which of the two; comedietta, by J. M. Morton. (No. 105 *of* **De Witt's** acting plays.)
Which should John have helped? a conversation between Dame Europa and Mrs. Fairplay. 2d ed. Lond., 1871. 16°. (E 158)
Which will have him? a vaudeville; tr. by J. A. Woodward. (No. 62 *of* **Spencer's** univ. stage.)
Whichcord, John, *Jr.* History and antiquities of the Collegiate-church of All Saints. (*In* **Weale, J.** Quarterly papers on architecture, v. 4. 1845.)
Whichcote, Benjamin, *D.D.* Select aphorisms. (*In* **Moral** tracts. 1820.)
Whig, The. *See* **Independent** Whig.
Whig almanac, The, and politician's register, 1845. *n.t.p.* [N. Y., 1844.] 12°. (C 199)
See also **Tribune** almanac.
Whig and Tory; [a play,] by B. Griffin. *n.p.*, [1720]. 8°. (B 475)
Whig Club. Resolutions and declarations of the Club. *n.p.*, [1789]. 4°. (W 70)
— Goddard, W. The prowess of the Whig Club, and the manœuvres of Legion. Balt., [1777?]. 16°. (B 662, W 46)
Whig Party in Mass. *State Central Committee.* To the electors of Mass. recommending Edw. Everett as Governor.] *n. p.*, [1837]. 8°. (B 1814)
— *State Convention*, Boston, Sept. 23, 1846. The true Whig sentiment of Mass. [Bost., 1846.] 8°. (B 1502)
— - Worcester, Oct. 2, 1855. Proceedings. Boston, *J. H. Eastburn's press*, 1855. 8°. (B 1507)
— - *Another ed.* Boston, *Office of the Boston courier*, 1855. 8°. (B 1507)
— *Middlesex Co.* To the electors of the courts. *n.p.*, 1838. 8°. (B 1496)
See also **Boston.** **Whig party.** (p. 346).
Whig text book; or, Democracy unmasked. Wash., [1844]. 8°. (B 1500)
Whigs, American. Dissertation on the rise, progress, *etc.*, of the parties of Whigs and Tories. Boston, 1773. 8°. (B 611)
— Hall, B. F. Republican party, 1796-1832; the Whig and Democratic parties during the interregnum, *etc.* N. Y., 1856. 12°.
— Appeal from the new to the old Whigs, in consequence of the Senate's course, Webster's speech upon the executive patronage bill. Boston, 1835. 8°. (A 43)
— Kennedy, J. P. Defence of the Whigs. N. Y., 1844. 18°.
Whigs, English. Squire, F. Universal benevolence; sermon, wherein is a farther justification of principles of Whigs. London, 1714. 8°. (B 161)
— Withers, J. Whigs vindicated. London, 1715. 8°. (B 756)
— Character of an independent Whig. 2d ed. London, 1719. 8°. (B 668)
— Plain matter of fact; or, Whiggism the bulwark of these kingdoms. London, 1742. 8°. (B 760)
— Burke, E. Appeal from the new to the old Whigs rel. to the 'Reflections on the French Revolution'. London, 1791. 8°.
— - *Same.* 2d ed. London, 1791. 8°. (B 1408)
— - *Same.* Dublin, 1791. 8°. (W 61)
— - *Same.* N. Y., 1791. 8°. (B 1537)
— Vassall, H. R., *Lord Holland.* Memoirs of the Whig party, [1800-08]. Lond., 1852. 2 v. 8°.
— Erskine, T. Defences of the Whigs. — Letter to the author of 'A reply to the short defence of the Whigs'. (*In* **Pamphleteer**, 1819; v. 15 of B 838)
— Short defence of the Whigs. London, 1819. 8°. (B 1673)
— Parr, S. Notes on Rapin's 'Dissertation on Whigs and Tories. (*In his* Works, v. 3. 1828.)
— Cox, H. Whig and Tory administrations, [1855-68]. London, 1868. 8°.
Whildin, J. R. Memoranda on the strength of materials used in engineering construction. N. Y., 1860. 12°.
Whimsicalities; by T. Hood. Phila., 1845. 12°.
Whipple, *Gen.* Amiel W. Extracts from the preliminary report of W. upon the route near the 35th parallel, *etc.* — Pt. 1-4 of report upon the route near the 35th parallel. (*In* **United States.** *War Dept.* Reports of explorations for a R.R. to the Pacific, 1853-54, v. 3.) — Pt. 5, 6. (*In* v. 4.) — Nos. 2-5 of pt. 6. (*In* v. 10.)
— Physical data resp. the southern part of California included in the line of boundary between San Diego and the mouth of the River Gila; with notices of the Dieguños and Yuma Indian tribes. (*In* **Schoolcraft, H. R.** Hist. and statist. information resp. the history, *etc.*, of the Indian tribes, v. 2. 1852.)
— Report of explorations for a railway from the Mississippi to the Pacific. [Wash., 1854.] 8°. (33d Cong. 2d sess. Sen. 18.)
Whipple, Charles King. Chapter of theological and religious experience. Boston, 1858. 16°. (D 29)
— Relation of the Amer. Board of Commissioners for Foreign Missions to slavery. Bost., 1861. 12°.
— *Another copy.* (C 259)
Whipple, Edwards. Sermon, Deerfield, Feb. 10, installation of B. Rice. Deerfield, 1819. 8°. (B 1324)
Whipple, Edwin Percy. Character and characteristic men. Boston, 1866. 12°.
Contents. Character. — Eccentric character. — Intellectual character. — Heroic character. — The American mind. — The English mind. — Thackeray. — Hawthorne. — Everett. — King. — Agassiz. — Washington and the principles of the Revolution.
— Essays and reviews. N. Y., 1848. 2 v. 12°.
Contents. Vol. 1. Macaulay. — Poets and poetry of America. — Talfourd. — Words. — James's novels. — Sydney Smith. — Webster. — Neal's History of the Puritans. — Wordsworth. — Byron. — English poets of the 19th cent. — Vagaries of volition. 2. Old English dramatists. — South's sermons. — Romance of rascality. — The croakers of society and literature. — British critics. — Choate. — Coleridge as a philosophical critic. — Prescott's histories. — Prescott's Conquest of Peru. — Shakspeare's critics. — Sheridan. — Appendix.
— Lectures on subjects connected with literature and life. Boston, 1850. 8°.
Contents. Authors in their relations to life. — Novels and novelists: C. Dickens. — Wit and humor. — The ludicrous side of life. — Genius. — Intellectual health and disease.
— Literature of mirth. (*In* **Boston** book, 4th col. 1841.)
— Literature of the age of Elizabeth. Boston, 1869. 8°.
Contents. Characteristics of the Elizabethan literature. — Marlowe. — Shakespeare. — Ben Jonson. — Minor Elizabethan dramatists. — Heywood, Middleton, Marston, Dekkar, Webster, and Chapman. — Beaumont and Fletcher, Massinger, and Ford. — Spenser. — Minor Elizabethan poets. — Phineas and Giles Fletcher, Daniel, Drayton, Warner, Donne, Davies, Hall, Wotton, and Herbert. — Sidney and Raleigh. — Bacon. — Hooker.

— Oration before the municipal authorities of Boston, July 4. Boston, 1850. 8°. (B 1201)
— Success and its conditions. Boston, 1871. 12°.
Contents. Young men in history. — The ethics of popularity. — Grit. — The vital and the mechanical. — The economy of invective. — The sale of souls. — Tricks of imagination. — Cheerfulness. — Mental and moral pauperism. — The genius of Dickens. — Shoddy. — J. A. Andrews.
— Washington and the principles of the Revolution; oration, Boston, July 4. Boston, 1850. 8°. (B 1725)
— LORING, J. S. (*In his* Hundred Boston orators. 1852.)
Whipple, John. STRANG, J. Confession of S., who was convicted for the murder of J. Whipple. Albany, 1827. 8°. (B 561)
Whipple, John, *LL.D.* Discourse in commemoration of the life and services of D. Webster, Nov. 23. Prov., 1852. 8°. (B 1726)
— Importance of usury laws. From the Banker's mag., March. [Boston, 1850.] 8°. (B 1545)
— *Same.* Free trade in money; or, Note shaving the great cause of fraud, poverty, and ruin. Boston, 1855. 8°. (B 1515)
— Report. *See* **Rhode Island.** *General Assembly* (p. 2508).
Whipple, Joseph. History of Acadie, Penobscot Bay and River, *etc.* Bangor, 1816. 8°.
— *Same.* Geographical view of the district of Maine, *etc.* Bangor, 1816. 8°. (B 455)
Whipple, Wm. SANDERSON, J. (*In his* Biography of the signers, v. 5. 1824.)
Whipple, Wm. J. Masonic address before Corinthian Lodge, Concord, June 24, 5819. Concord, 1819. 8°. (B 555)
Whirlpools. DISSERTAZIONE sopra il quesito come si generino i vortici orizzontali e verticali appiè degli argini in corrosione. Mantova, 1786. 4°. (A 17)
Whisperer, The. *See* **Moore, W.**
Whispering gallery, Our; by J. T. Fields. (*In* **Atlantic** monthly, v. 27, 28. 1871.)
Whist. SCOTT, *Gen.* The rules of whist. 6th ed. London, 1810. 16°. (C 64)
— MATTHEWS, T. Advice to the young whist player. From 2d London ed. Boston, 1812. 12°. (C 57)
— *Same.* Whist and short whist. N. Y., 1857. 24°.
— YOUNG, *Maj.* Short whist. [1835.] (*In* **Matthews, T.** Whist. 1857.)
— BUNBURY, H. C. The whist player; laws and practice of short whist. London, 1856. 16°.
Note. Now known *not to be* by Bunbury.
— BALDWIN, J. L. Laws of short whist. 2d ed. with add. London, [1871]. 16°.
— POLE, W. Theory of the modern scientific game of whist. 2d ed. London, 1871. 16°.
Whistelo, Alexander, *vs.* N. Y. **Commissioners of the N. Y. Alms-House.** Case of bastardy, Mar. 6. N. Y., 1801. 8°. (B 408)
Whistlecraft, Wm. *and* Robert, *pseud.* Prospectus and specimen of an intended national work. (*In* Frere, J. H. Works, v. 1. 1872 [1871].)
Whiston, John, *and* **White**, B. Catalogue of [books to] be sold, Feb. 6, 1755. [London, 1755.] 8°. (B 878)
Whiston, Wm. Accomplishment of Scripture prophecies. Camb., 1708. 8°. (Boyle lectures.)
— *Same.* (*In* **Boyle** lecture sermons, v. 2. 1739.)
— Account of Dr. Sacheverell's proc. in order to exclude him from St. Andrew's church in Holborn. Lond., 1710. 8°. (B 135)
— Account of the exact time when miraculous gifts ceased in the Church. London, 1749. 8°. (B 247)
— Astronomical principles of religion, natural and revealed; with a pref., Of the temper of mind necessary for the discovery of divine truth, *etc.* London, 1725. 8°.
— Elements of Euclid, [books I.-VI., XI. and XII.]; with theorems out of Archimedes, by A. Pacquet. 6th ed. London, 1747. 8°.
— Essay on the Revelation of St. John; also two dissertations, with a collection of Scripture prophecies rel. to the times after the coming of the Messiah. Camb., 1706. 4°.
— Letter to the Earl of Nottingham [on] the eternity of the Son of God and of the Holy Spirit. London, 1719. 8°. (B 28)
— Memoirs. London, 1753. 2 v. 8°.
Contents. Vol. 1, 2. Memoirs; by himself. 2. Lectures on the late meteors and earthquakes, and on the future restoration of the Jews. — The liturgy of the Ch. of Eng. reduced nearer to the primitive standard.
— New theory of the Earth; its creation, the deluge, and general conflagration. London, 1696. 8°.
— Prælectiones astronomicæ; acc. tabulæ. Cantab., 1707. 8°.
— Primitive Christianity revived. London, 1711-12. 5 v. 8°.
Contents. Vol. 1. **Whiston**, R. Hist. preface; — App.; — 2d app.; — Suppl.; — Dissertation upon the epistles of Ignatius. — **Ignatius** *Antiochenus.* Epistles. — **Eunomius.** Apologetik. 2. **Clemens** *Romanus.* Constitutions of the apostles. 3. **Whiston**, R. Essay on the apostolical constitutions. 4. **Whiston**, R. Acc. of the faith of the two first centuries. — App. to 4th vol. — **Bible.** *Esdras.* Second book. 5. **Clemens** *Romanus.* Recognitions. — **Whiston**, R. App. cont. obs. on Dr. Clarke's 'Scripture doctrine of the trinity'; — App. cont. farther acc. of the convocation's and other proceedings against W.
— DODWELL, W. Eternity of future punishment; answer to W.; two sermons before the Univ. of Oxford, Mar. 21, 1741. Oxford, 1743. 8°. (B 311)
— GRABE, J. E. Essay upon two Arabic mss., and the doctrine of the apostles said to be extant in them, wherein W.'s mistakes are proved. Oxford, 1711. 8°.
— E., H. Answer to Dr. Clark and W. Whiston conc. the divinity of the Son and Holy Spirit. London, 1729. 8°. (B 149)
— EDWARDS, J. Some observations on Whiston's 'Primitive Christianity'. London, 1712. 8°. (C 229)
— EXAMINATION of Apology for W.'s 'Liberty of writing'. (*In* **Examination** of a late 'Discourse'. 1724. E 154)
— FINCH, H. Answer to W.'s letter to him on the eternity of the Son of God. 9th ed. London, 1721. 8°. (B 28)
— N., N. Will-with-a-Wisp; or, The grand ignis fatuus of London; letter conc. the articles lately exhibited against W. London, 1714. 8°. (B 30)
— SCRIPTURE account of the eternity of heaven and hell; reply to W. Whiston's 'Eternity of hell torments'. London, 1742. 8°. (B 35)
— TRYAL of W. for defaming and denying the holy Trinity. 3d ed. London, 1740. 8°. (B 576)
Whitaker, Edgar K. Address, Medfield, before the Norfolk Co. Washington Total Abst. Soc., July 4. Boston, 1846. 8°. (B 1281)
Whitaker, Edward. Letter to [S. Colledge] upon his bill being sent to Oxford. *n.t.p.* [London, 1681.] f°. (A 50)
Whitaker, Edward Wm. Sermon, Feb. 25, 1795, fast [day]. Chertsey, [1795]. 4°. (B 1258)
Whitaker, *Rev.* Epher. Sermon, funeral of D. M. Lord, Aug. 29. Boston, 1861. 8°. (B 1246)
Whitaker, *Rev.* John. The course of Hannibal over the Alps ascertained. London, 1794. 2 v. 8°.
— History of Manchester; in four books. [Book 1.] 2d ed. corr. London, 1773. 2 v. 8°.
Contents. Book 1. The Brit. and Roman-Brit. period.
— POWNALL, T. Remarks on crticisms by W. [in his 'Course of Hannibal'], *etc.*, on 'Notices of antiquities in the Provinca Romana of Gaul'. (*In his* Antiquarian romance. 1795.)
Whitaker, Jonathan. Sermon, Walpole, Mar. 10. Dedham, 1816. 8°. (B 1126)
Whitaker, Joseph. *See* **Almanacs.** ALMANACK, 1869-72.
Whitaker, Nathaniel, *D.D.* Antidote against Toryism; or, The curse of Meroz; discourse, Salem. Newburyport, 1777. 12°. (W 44)
— Brief history of the settlement of the 3d Church in Salem, 1769, and of the usurpation of an ecclesiastical council, 1784. Salem, 1784. 8°. (B 34, 2517)
— Confutation of two tracts, 'Vindication of the N. Eng. churches' and 'The churches quarrel espoused', by J. Wise. Boston, 1774. 8°. (B 253)
— Funeral sermon, death of G. Whitefield, Oct. 17, 1770. Salem, [1770]. 8°. (B 17, 235)

— Mutual care of the members, *etc.*; sermon, Groton, June 9, 1784. Salem, 1785. 8°. (B 335)
— Reward of Toryism; discourse, Salem, May. Newburyport, 1783. 8°. (B 335)
— Two sermons on the doctrine of reconciliation; with an answer to a dialogue wrote to discredit the main truths, *etc.*, by W. Hart. Salem, 1770. 8°. (B 132, 253, 911)
— CLEVELAND, J. The Rev. N. Whitaker's neighbor is come and searcheth him; or, A brief defence of the late council's result against the Dr.'s charges. Salem, 1784. 8°. (B 194)
— GATCHEL, S. Contrast to Rev. N. W. his confutation of Rev. J. Wise. Danvers, 1778. 8°. (B 253)
— HART, W. False propositions collected out of sundry discourses by W. and Mr. Hopkins. New London, 1769. 8°. (C 198)
— - Letter to W. [on] his misrepresentations of Hart's 'Brief examination', *etc.* New London, 1771. 8°. (B 1357, 1903)

Whitaker, Thomas Dunham. Loidis and Elmete; or, An attempt to illustrate the districts described in those words by Bede, in the County of York. Leeds, 1816. f°.
— Notes and add. (*In* **Thoresby**, R. Ducatus Leodiensis. 1816.)

Whitaker, Wm., *D.D.* Disputation on Holy Scripture against the Papists, espec. Bellarmine and Stapleton; ed. by W. Fitzgerald. Camb., 1849. 8°. (Parker Soc.)
— Prælect. de concilijs, contra Bellarminum; opera Allenson, adj. est alia prælectio. Cantab., 1600. 8°.
— Prælect. de ecclesia contra Bellarminum; opera Io. Allenson; acc. ejusdem ult. concio ad clerum, cum descriptione vitæ authore A. Assheton. Cantab., 1599. 4°.
— Prælect. de Romano pontifice adv. Bellarminum; opera Allenson. Hanoviæ, 1608. 8°.
— Tractatus de peccato originale. Cantab., 1600. 8°.
— CYGNÆ cantio; last public discourse of W.; prefixed, account of [his] life, death, *etc.* Camb., 1772. 8°. (B 1883)

Whitaker, Wm. J. Drawing a means of education. (*In* **Amer. Inst. of Instr.** Lect., 1852.)

Whitbourne, Richard. Westward hoe for Avalon, in the New-found-land; ed. by T. Whitburn. London, 1870. 16°.

Whitbread, John. Letter to Ld. Holland on the situation of Spain. 2d ed. London, 1808. 8°. (B 724)

Whitbread, Samuel. Pref. letter. (*In* **Young**, S. Cases of cancer. 1816.)

Whitby, Daniel, *D.D.* Answer to Dr. Snape's 2d letter to B. Hoadley. London, 1717. 8°. (B 101)
— Considerations for taking the oath of allegiance to Wm. and Mary. London, 1689. 4°. (B 6)
— Discourses. Worcester, 1801. 8°.
— Historical account of some things rel. to the nature of the English government. London, 1690. 4°. (B 6)
— Last thoughts. (*In* **Sparks**, J. Col. of essays, v. 2. 1823.)
— Paraphrase and commentary on the New Testament. London, 1760. 2 v. (v. 1 w.). f°.
— *Same.* 10th ed. London, 1808. 2 v. 4°.
— NICERON, J. P. (*In his* Mém., v. 21. 1733; *and*, *Germ.*, v. 16. 1758.)
— WATERLAND, D. Answer to Whitby's "Reply resp. his 'Disquisitiones modestæ'". Camb., 1720. 8°. (B 112)

Whitcomb, Samuel, *Jr.* Address before the Working Men's Soc. of Dedham, Sept. 7. Dedham, 1831. 8°. (B 1586)

Whitcomb, Wm. C. Discourse on the recapture of fugitive slaves, Stoneham, Nov. 3. Boston, 1850. 8°. (B 1485)

White. *See also* **Whyte.**

White, —. Relation de Terre-Neuve. (*In* **Bernard**, J. F. Recueil de voyages, v. 3. 1716.)

White, Abijah, *Funeral sermon on.* 1804. *See* **Harris**, T. M. (B 316)

White, Adam. Collection of documents on Spitzbergen and Greenland. London, 1855. 8°. (Hakluyt Soc.)

Contents. Introduction. — **Martens**, F. Voyage into Spitzbergen and Greenland; — App., list of the animals of S. — **La Peyrère**, I. de. Relation du Groënland. — **Pellham**, E. God's power and providence shewed in the deliverance of eight Englishmen left in Green-land, 1630, *etc.*

White, Albert. Speech, reply to Mr. Holmes, on the principles which divide the two parties, Feb. 8. Wash., 1843. 8°. (B 1499)

White, Alexander. Dying confession. (*In* **American** bloody register. 1784. B 657)
— *Sermon on his execution.* 1785. *See* **Hilliard**, T. (B 225)

White, Andrew. Relation of the colony of the Lord Baron of Baltimore in Maryland. (*In* **Force**, P. Col. of tracts, v. 4. 1846.)

White, Andrew Dickson. Cornell University; origin and plan. (*In* **Spencer**, S. Scenery of Ithaca. 1866.)
— Letter to Wm. H. Russell on passages in his 'Diary north and south'. From the London ed. Syracuse, 1863. 8°.

White, Blanco. *See* **White**, Joseph Blanco.

White, Charles, *surgeon, of Manchester.* Account of the regular gradation in man and in different animals and vegetables. Lond., 1799. 4°.
— Cases in surgery; with Essay on the ligature of arteries, by J. Aikin. London, 1770. 8°.
— Swelling of the lower extremities of lying-in women. 2d ed. London, 1792. 8°.
— Treatise on management of pregnant and lying-in women. 1st Worcester ed. Worcester, 1793. 8°.
— Various articles.] (*In* **Lit. and Phil. Soc. of Manchester.** Mem., v. 1, 2, 5. 1789-98.)
— SMITH, S. S. Remarks on certain strictures by C. White in a series of discourses, Manchester. (*In his* Essay. 1787; 1810.)

White, Charles. Remarks on the preservation of the teeth, with directions for using [his] absorbent tooth powder. [Boston, 1816.] 12°. (D 38)

White, Charles, *b.* 1793. Almacks revisited. London, 1828. 3 v. 12°.

White, Charles, *D.D.*, *Pres. of Wabash Coll.* Address at his inaug. as President of Wabash College. Indianapolis, 1842. 8°. (B 1580)
— Duties of educated young men of the West; address to candidates for the baccalaureate, July 20. Indianapolis, 1842. 8°. (B 1580)
— Essays in literature and ethics. 2d ed. Boston, 1853. 12°.

Contents. Religion an essential part of all education. — Independence of mind. — Goodness indispensable to true greatness. — A pure and sound literature. — Political rectitude. — Western colleges. — Contributions of intellect to religion. — The practical element in Christianity. — The conservative element in Chr stianity. — Protestant Christianity adapted to be the religion of the world. — Characteristics of the present age. — Literary responsibility of teachers.

— Literary responsibility of teachers. (*In* **Amer. Inst. Instr.** Lect., 1838.)
— Sermons; Man ruined; Man recovered. (*In* **National** preacher, v. 22. 1848.)
— HOWARD, T. A. Charge on his inaug. as Pres. of Wabash College, July 19. Indianapolis, 1842. 8°. (B 1580)

White, Charles Abiathar. Report. *See* **Iowa.** *Geological Survey.*

White, *Rev.* Charles I. Life of Mrs. E. A. Seton. N. Y., 1853. 12°.

See also **United States** Catholic magazine and monthly.

White, Daniel Appleton. Address before the Essex Co. Lyceum. Salem, 1830. 8°. (B 1051)
— Address before the Soc. of the Alumni of Harvard Univ., Aug. 27. Camb., 1844. 8°. (1197, 1734, 1738)
— Address, consecration of Harmony Grove Cemetery, Salem, June 14. Salem, 1840. 8°. (B 1150, 1697)
— Address to the Merrimack Humane Soc., Newburyport, Sept. 3. Newburyport, 1805. 8°. (B 399, 871)
— Eulogy on J. Pickering, delivered before the American Acad. of Arts and Sci., Oct. 28, 1846. Camb., 1847. 8°. (B 1222, 2544)
— *Same.* (*In* **Amer. Acad.** Mem., n.s., v. 3. 1848.)
— Eulogy on N. Bowditch. Salem, 1838. 8°. (B 1209, 1654, 1814)

— Eulogy on Washington, Methuen. Haverhill, 1800. 8°. (E 48)
— Mem. of the Plummer family. (*In* **Plummer Hall.** Proceedings. 1858.)
— New England Congregationalism in its origin and purity. Salem, 1861. 8°.
— View of the jurisdiction and proceedings of the courts of probate in Mass. Salem, 1822. 8°.
— Briggs, G. W. Memoir of D. A. White. (*In* **Essex** Inst. Hist. col., v. 6. 1864.)
— Felt, J. B. Reply to [his] New England Congregationalism. Boston, 1861. 8°.
— Walker, J. Memoir of D. A. White. (*In* **Mass. Hist. Soc.** Proc., 1862–63.)

White, E. E., *ed.* *See* **Ohio** educational monthly.

White, E. L. On the disorder familiarly termed a cold. London, 1807. 16°.
— *Same.* [Ed.] with annotations by J. Stuart. Phila., 1808. 12°.

White, Edward L., *and* **Gould**, J. E. The harmonia sacra; a new collection of anthems, choruses, *etc.*; added, The Episcopal Church service. Boston, [1851]. obl. 8°.

White, Elijah. View of Oregon Territory. [Wash., 1846.] 8°.

White, Elipha. Introductory lecture. (*In* **American Inst.** of **Instr.** Lectures, 1837.)

White, *Mrs.* Elizabeth, *Funeral sermon on.* 1798. *See* **Allen**, T. (B 174)

White, Francis. Replie to Jesuit Fisher's answere to certain questions propounded by James I. London, 1624. f°.

White, George. Historical collections of Georgia. 3d ed. N. Y., 1855. 8°.
— Statistics of Georgia. Savannah, 1849. 8°.

White, George Savage. Memoir of S. Slater. 2d ed. Phila., 1836. 8°.

White, Gilbert. Natural hist. of Selborne. New ed. London, 1825. 2 v. 8°.
— *Same.* N. Y., 1847. 12°. (Harper's fam. lib., v. 147.)
— *Same.* With add. by Sir W. Jardine and ed. by E. Jesse. London, *Bohn*, 1851. 8°.

White, *Rev.* Henry. Early history of New England. 7th ed. Concord, 1842. 12°.

White, Henry, *of N. Haven.* History of the Cutler Lot. — New Haven Colony. (*In* **New Haven Colony Hist. Soc.** Papers, v. 1. 1865.)

White, Henry. The Massacre of St. Bartholomew. London, 1868. 8°.

White, Henry Kirke. Poetical works; with memoir by Sir N. H. Nicolas. Boston, 1854. 16°.
Contents. Memoir of W. — Miscel. poems. — Odes. — Sonnets. — Ballads, songs, and hymns. — Tributary verses.
— Remains; with life by R. Southey. 1st Amer. from 4th London ed. Phila., 1811. 2 v. 12°.
Contents. Vol. 1. Acc. of the life of W. by R. Southey. — Poems inserted in the life. — Poems inserted in the letters. — Tributary verses. — Poems written before the publication of Clifton Grove. 2. To my lyre. — Clifton Grove. — Gondoline. — Survey of the heavens. — Lines by a lover at the grave of his mistress. — My study. — To an early primrose. — Sonnets. — Poems written during or after the publication of Clifton Grove. — Sonnets. — Poems of a later date. — Fragments. — Prose compositions. — Melancholy hours. — Reflections.
— Beauties of W.; selections from his poetry and prose; by A. Howard. Boston, 1826. 12°.
— Cary, H. F. (*In his* Lives of the Eng. poets. 1846.)

White, *Rev.* Hugh. A small performance entitled Philotheos. Richmond, 1806. 12°. (C 69)

White, *Rev.* Hugh, *of Dublin.* The Gospel promotive of true happiness. Dublin, 1843. 16°.

White, Hugh Lawson. Letter to the legislature of Tenn. resigning the office of senator of the U. S. Wash., 1840. 8°. (B 1497)
— Speech, Jan. 7, on Mr. Giles' bill for enforcing the embargo laws. Wash., 1809. 8°. (B 410, 1193, 2019)
— Longacre, J. B., *and* Herring, J. (*In their* Nat. portr. gal., v. 4. 1839.)
— Maury, A. P. Address on the life and character of W. Franklin, [Tenn.,] 1840. 8°. (B 1227)
— Maury, S. M. (*In her* Statesmen of America. 1847.)
— U. S. *4th Cong. 2d sess.* Report of the committee to whom were re-committed the petition of H. L. White, Jan. 17. *n.p.*, [1797]. 8°. (W 65)

White, *Rev.* J. S. The wheat and the chaff; discourse, Worcester. Hartford, 1852. 8°. (B 1305)

White, James, *veterinary surgeon.* Treatise of veterinary medicine. 8th ed. (Vol. 2, 3d ed.) London, 1807, 06. 2 v. 12°.

White, James, *b.* 1806, *d.* 1862. Eighteen Christian centuries. 2d ed. Edin., 1859. 8°.
— Feudal times. (*In* **Sargent**, E. Mod. standard dr., v. 6.)
— History of France from the earliest times to 1848. 2d ed. Edin., London, 1860. 8°.
— King of the Commons. (*In* **Sargent**, E. Mod. stand. dr., v. 4.)

White, *elder* James. Life incidents in connection with the great advent movement. Vol. 1. Brattle Creek, Mich., 1868. 12°.

White, James, *M. P.* Ritchie, J. E. (*In his* British senators. 1869.)

White, James Clarke. Introd. lect. before the Med. and Dental Schools of Harv. Univ., Nov. 2. Boston, 1870. 8°. (H 8)

White, James P., *M. D.* Life of S. Bard. (*In* **Gross**, S. D. Lives of eminent American physicians. 1861.)
— Remarks on the construction of obstetrical forceps. Buffalo, 1849. 8°. (B 1565)

White, John. Voy. to Virginia, 1590. (*In* **Hakluyt**, R. Col. of voy., v. 3. 1810.)

White, *Rev.* John, *of Dorchester, Eng.*, *b.* 1574, *d.* 1648. Instructions for the plantation of N. E. (*In* **Mass. Hist. Soc.** Proc., 1864–65.)
— Planter's plea; or, The grounds of plantations examined and usual objections answered. (*In* **Force**, P. Col. of tracts, v. 2. 1838.) — Extract. (*In* **Young**, A. Chron. of Mass. 1846.)
— *Same.* London, 1630. 8°. (B 13)
— Shattuck, L. Memorials of the Whites. (*In* **Mass. Hist. Soc.** Col., v. 32. 1854.)

White, John, *called* Century **White**, *b.* 1590, *d.* 1645. Shattuck, L. Memorials of the Whites. (*In* **Mass. Hist. Soc.** Col., v. 32. 1854.)

White, *Rev.* John, *of Gloucester*, *b.* 1677, *d.* 1760. New England's lamentations; added, reasons for adhering to our platform, *etc.* Boston, 1734. 8°. (B 665)
— *Same.* 2d ed. Boston, 1734. 8°. (D 3)
— Secret prayer inculcated and encouraged; sermon, Gloucester, Dec. 1717; with a preface of I. Mather. Boston, 1719. 8°. (C 50)
— *and others.* Testimony of New Eng. ministers met at Boston, Sept. 25, 1725. Boston, 1745. 8°. (B 247)

White, John, *Vicar of Nayland, d. about* 1760. Defence of 'Three letters to a gentleman dissenting from the Church of Eng.', against the dissenting gentleman's [Towgood's] answer to W.'s three letters. London, 1746. 8°. (B 124)
— *Same.* 2d ed. London, 1748. 8°. (B 1897)
— 2d defence of the Three letters. *n.t.p.* [17—.] 8°. (B 247)
— Letter conc. the lives of Churchmen and Dissenters. 3d ed. London, 1746. 8°.
— Towgood, M. Dissent from the Ch. of England fully justified. 3d ed. Lond., 1765. 12°.
— - *Same.* 11th ed. Boston, 1768. 12°. (C 185)
— - Dissenting gentleman's answer to Mr. W.'s 'Three letters'. 5th ed. Boston, 1748. 8°.
— - *Another copy.* (B 1897, C 305)
— - The dissenting gentleman's 2d letter to W. in answer to his 'Three letters'; with postscript containing remarks on W.'s defence of his 'Three letters'. London, 1747. 8°. (B 124)

White, John. *See* **White**, M. Case. 1818. (B 340)

White, John, *Lieut. U. S. N.* History of a voyage to the China Sea. Boston, 1823. 8°.

White, John, *pilot, of N. Y.* Charges against H. Cahoone, commander of the revenue cutter Alert. N. Y., 1825. 8°. (B 1099)

White, *Rev.* John, *of Dedham*, *b.* 1788, *d.* 1852. Address before the Dedham Soc. for Suppression of Intemperance, Feb. 10. Dedham, 1817. 8°. (B 357)
— Centennial disc. before the Cong. Soc., Dedham, Jan. 17. Dedham, 1836. 8°. (B 1139)

— Sermon, nature and extent of Christian liberty. Dedham, 1828. 8°. (B 1127)
— Sermon, Nov. 3, 1821, interment of S. Palmer. Dedham, 1822. 8°. (B 283, 1127)
— *Funeral sermon on.* 1852. *See* **Lamson, A.** (B 1227, 1247, E 41)

White, John, *teacher at Edinburgh, b.* 1786, *d.* 1857. Practical system of mental arithmetic. Phila., 1818. 8°.
— *Another copy.* (B 1835)

White, John, *Fellow of Queen's Coll., Oxford.* Sketches from America. London, 1870. 8°.
Contents. Canada. — A picnic to the Rocky Mountains. — The Irish in America.

White, John B. Oration, Charleston, Mar. 4. Charleston, 1815. 8°. (B 457)

White, John Duncan, *alias* **Marchant,** C. Trials of White and Curtis for the murder of Selfridge and Jenkins. Boston, 1827. 8°. (B 1442, 1794)

White, John Silas. Address, inaug. of C. W. Eliot. *See* **Harvard College.** *President.* (H 10)

White, Joseph, *of Buck's County, Penn., b.* 1712. FRIENDS, SOC. OF, *Penn.* Memorial of W. (*In* **Churchman,** J. Account, 1781.)

White, Joseph, *D.D., b.* 1746, *d.* 1814. Ægyptiaca. Pt. 1: History of Pompey's pillar. Oxford, 1801. 4°.
— Sermons, Bampton lecture, 1784. 2d ed.; added, sermon, Oxford, July 4. London, 1785. 8°.
— GABRIEL, R. B. Facts rel. to [his] Bampton lecture. London, [1789?]. 8°.
— LETTER to R. B. Gabriel in answer to 'Facts'. London, 1789. 8°.
— PRIESTLEY, J. (*In his* Importance of free inquiry. 1785. B 236)

White, Joseph, *M.D.* Annual address, 1816. (*In* **Med. Soc. of the State of N. Y.** Trans., 1816. B 1559)
— 1817. (*In* 1817. B 816)

White, Joseph. WHITMAN, J. W. Trial of G. Crowninshield, J. J. Knapp, *Jr.*, and J. F. Knapp for the murder of W. Boston, 1830. 8°. (B 1404, E 272)

White, Joseph. Address before the alumni of Williams Coll., Aug.; with poem by E. W. B. Canning. Boston, 1855. 8°. (B 1576)
— Reports, 25th–40th, 1862–77. *See* **Mass.** *Board of Educ.*

White, *Rev.* Joseph Blanco. Answer to some remarks on 'The law of anti-religious libel' reconsidered; with an app. on the true meaning of an epigram of Martial. Dublin, 1834. 8°. (B 1371)
Note. The author's name was originally José Maria White y Crespo but popularly changed in Spain into José Maria Blanco y Crespo.
— Evidence against Catholicism. 1st Amer. ed. Georgetown, 1826. 12°.
— Letters from Spain; by L. Doblado. London, 1822. 8°.
— Life; by himself; with correspondence; ed. by J. H. Thom. London, 1845. 3 v. 12°.
— ENGLAND, J., *Bp. of Charleston.* Letters on the calumnies of W. (*In his* Works, v. 1. 1849.)
— REDDING, C. (*In his* Personal reminisc., v. 3. 1867.)

White, Joseph M. Case stated; [grant of land to P. F. Renaut, in Louisiana]. *n.t.p.* [New Orleans, 183-?] 16°. (B 1440)
— Exposition historical and legal of the title of C. Mitchell and others to lands in Florida. Wash., 1834. 8°. (B 1088)
— *and others.* Legal opinions in relation to the title of the Duke of Alagon. N. Y., 1837. 8°. (B 1431)

White, Joshua E., *M.D., of Savannah.* Hist. of Ann Moor, *etc.* Savannah, 1812. 8°. (B 443, W 10)
— Letters on England. Phila., 1816. 2 v. 8°.

White, Levi. History of Sandisfield. (*In* **Field, D. D.** History of Berkshire, v. 2. 1829.)

White, *Mrs.* Margaret E. (Harding), *ed. See* **Harding,** C.

White, Marvin *and* J., *vs.* **Skinner,** R., in error. Respondent's case. Troy, 1818. 8°. (B 340)

White, *Rev.* Moses C. Chinese local dialects reduced to writing. (*In* **Amer. Orient. Soc.** Journ., v. 4. 1854.) — Notice of] 'A guide to conversation in English and Chinese languages', by S. Hernisz, [also of] 'Discoveries in Chinese', by S. P. Andrews. (*In* v. 5. 1856.)

White, N. Address at the interment of T. Amory. 1774. (*In* **Flexman, R.** Sermon. 1774. B 128, 1242)

White, Nathaniel. Trial. *See* **Williams,** J. Trial. 1819.

White, *Rev.* Pliny Holton. Sermon, Westminster, Vt., on the one hundreth anniv. of the Congregational Church; with a historical paper by A. Stevens. Bellows Falls, 1867. 8°.
— The Windsor convention, July 2, 1777; adoption of the constitution. (*In* **Vt. Hist. Soc.** Col., v. 1. 1870.)

White (*Lat.* **Vitus**), Richard. NICERON, J. P. (*In his* Mém., v. 24. 1733.)

White, Richard Grant. National hymns. N. Y., 1861. Large 12°.
— The new gospel of peace; according to St. Benjamin. N. Y., 1866. 12°.
— Shakespeare's scholar; historical and critical studies of his text, *etc.*, with an examination of Collier's folio of 1632. N. Y., 1854. 8°.
— Words and their uses; a study of the English language. N. Y., 1870. 8°.
Note. From the **Galaxy,** v. 3–8. 1867–69.
— Poetry of the civil war. N. Y., 1866. 16°.

White, Robert. Madeira, its climate and scenery; ed. by J. Y. Johnson. 2d ed. Edin., 1857. 12°.

White, *Capt.* Samuel. Oration, death of Washington, 1800. (*In* **Union Brigade.** Proceed. 1800. E 61)

White, Samuel. Speech, Jan. 7, [on the embargo]. *n.p.*, [1809]. 8°. (B 410)
— Speech on the bill interdicting all intercourse between the U. S. and St. Domingo, Feb. 20, 1806. *n.p.*, [1806]. 8°. (B 429, 2519, W 86)
— Speech on the embargo laws, Nov. 22. *n.p.*, [1808]. 8°. (B 410, 2019)

White, Samuel, *M.D.* Address on insanity, before the N. Y. State Med. Soc., Feb. 5. Albany, 1844. 8°. (B 1568)

White, *Lieut.* Steele. Oration, July 4. Savannah, 1810. 8°. (B 415)

White, Thomas. Taking of two Spanish ships bound for W. Indies, 1592. (*In* **Green,** I. Col. of voy., v. 1. 1745; — **Hakluyt,** R. Col. of voy., v. 3. 1810; — *and in* **Kerr,** R. Col. of voy., v. 7. 1824.)

White (*Lat.* **Anglus ex Albiis** *or* **Candidus,** *Ital.* **Bianchi,** *also* **Richworth, Rushworth,** *or* **Blackloe** *or* **Vitus**), Thomas, *d.* 1676. CHILLINGWORTH, W. Answer to some passages in Rushworth's 'Dialogues'. (*In his* Works, v. 3. 1838.)

White, Thomas, *Bp. of Peterborough, b.* 1630, *d.* 1698. STRICKLAND, A. (*In her* Lives of the seven bishops. 1866.)

White, Thomas. Sermons. London, 1817. 8°.

White, *Rev.* Thomas Henry. Fragments of Italy and the Rhineland. London, 1841. 12°.

White, W. A. A. Catalogue of [his] hist., topog., and numismat. library, sold. London, 1848. 8°. (B 1619)

White, Walter. All round the Wrekin. London, 1860. 8°.
— Eastern England, from the Thames to the Humber. London, 1865. 2 v. 8°.
— On foot through Tyrol in the summer of 1855. London, 1856. 8°.
— July holiday in Saxony, Bohemia, and Silesia. London, 1857. 8°.
— A Londoner's walk to Land's End, and a trip to the Scilly Isles. 2d ed. Lond., 1861. 12°.
— A month in Yorkshire. 4th ed. London, 1861. 12°.
— Northumberland and the Border. London, 1859. 8°.

White, Wm. Letter to Gov. Winthrop, 1648. (*In* **Mass. Hist. Soc.** Col., v. 14. 1816.)

White, Wm. GR. BRIT. *Parl. Lords.* Report of the lord's committees on the writ of error depending in the House of Peers; M. Ashby plaintiff, W. White and others defendants. London, 1704. f°. (A 56)

White, Wm., *surgeon, of Bath.* On diseases of the liver. Bath, 1808. 8°.
— Observations on strictures of the rectum. 3d ed., impr. Bath, 1820. 8°.
— Further observations on strictures of the rectum, *etc.* Bath, 1822. 8°.

White, Wm., *Bp. of Penn.* Address, commencement of the General Theolog. Seminary of the Prot. Episc. Ch., June 27. N. Y., 1828. 8°. (B 1574)
— Address before the trustees, *etc.*, of the General Theolog. Seminary, July 30. N. Y., 1824. 8°. (B 1574)
— Charge to the Clergy of the Prot. Episc. Ch. in Penn. Phila., 1807. 8°. (B 291)
— Commentaries suited to occasions of ordination. N. Y., 1848. 12°.
— Of the gospel; sermon, New Haven, Oct. 27, consecration of T. C. Brownell. N. Haven, 1819. 8°. (B 276)
— Integrity of the Christian doctrine, *etc.*; sermon, New Haven, May 22. N. Y., 1811. 8°. (B 335)
— Lecture. *n.t.p.* [1842.] 8°. (B 1295)
— Memoirs of the Prot. Episc. Ch. in the U. S. Phila., 1820. 8°.
— *Same.* 2d ed. N. Y., 1836. 8°.
— Review of the question of a personal assurance of pardon of sin. Phila., 1818. 8°. (B 286)
— Sermon, character, *etc.*, of the gospel ministry, Baltimore, May 18. N. Y., 1808. 8°. (B 335)
— Sermon, duty of civil obedience as required in Scripture, Apr. 25. Phila., 1799. 8°. (W 53)
— Sermon, reciprocal influence of civil policy and religious duty, Phila., Feb. 19, [thanksgiving day]. Phila., 1795. 8°. (W 38, 54)
— SKETCH.] (*In* **Longacre, J. B.,** *and* **Herring, J.** Nat. portr. gal., v. 1. 1837.)

White, Wm. Statement of facts relative to the late proceedings in Harvard Coll. Boston, 1807. 8°. (C 251)

White, *Capt.* Wm. The murdered king of Oude; letter to Sir J. C. Hobhouse. London, [1838]. 8°. (B 1151)

White, Wm., *of Hampstead, Eng.* Emanuel Swedenborg; his life and writings. London, 1867. 2 v. 8°.

White, Wm. Augustus. Lyrics. Boston, 1841. 12°.
— NOTICE of W. (*In* **Wisconsin. State Hist. Soc.** Col., v. 3. 1857.)

White, Wm. Charles. Avowals of a Republican. Worcester, 1813. 8°. (B 453)
— Compendium and digest of the laws of Massachusetts. Boston, 1809–11. 4 v. 8°.
— Oration. Boston, July 4. Boston, 1809. 8°. (B 416, 457, 558)
— Oration, Hubbardston, July 4. Boston, 1810. 8°. (B 415)
— Oration, Rutland, Mass., July 5. Worcester, 1802. 8°. (B 1006)
— Oration, Worcester, July 4. Worcester, 1804. 8°. (B 416)
— LORING, J. S. (*In his* Hundred Boston orators. 1852.)

White, Wm. H. Essay. (*In* **Judd, O.** Manual of flax-culture. 1865.)

White. *See also* **Whyte.**

White family. KELLOGG, A. S. Memorials of elder John White, and his descendants. Hartford, 1860. 8°.

White chief, The; a legend of North Mexico; by Mayne Reid. N. Y., [1856]. 12°.

White devil; a drama. *See* **Webster, J.**

White greyhound, The. (*In* **Montgomery,** *Miss* **M. M.** Lights, *etc.*, v. 2. 1833.)

White hoods; by A. E. Bray. London, 1845. 16°. (Novels, v. 10.)

White horse of the Peppers; by S. Lover. (*In* **Minor** drama, v. 3; — *and in* **Webster, B.** Acting nat. dr., v. 5. 1838.)

White Knight's library. *See* **Churchill, G. S.,** *Marq. of Blandford.*

White lady or spirit of Avenel; romantic opera. Boston, 1833. 12°. (C 286)

White lead. WEBSTER, N. On the decomposition of white lead paint. (*In* **Conn. Acad. Arts and Sci.** Mem., v. 1, pt. 1. 1810.)
— BOULLAY, —, *and others.* Rapport sur la fabrique de céruse de Clichy. [Paris, 1813.] 8°. (C 87)

White Mts. WILLEY, B. G. History of the White Mountains. New ed. by F. Thompson. N. Y., 1870. 12°.
— ALDEN, T. Indian names of the White Hills and Piscataqua River. (*In* **Mass. Hist. Soc.** Col., v. 12. 1814.)
— BIGELOW, J. Some account of the White Mountains of N. H. [Boston, 1816.] 8°. (B 455)
— MOORE, J. B. Account of a storm and avalanches at the White Mts., 1826. (*In* **New Hampshire Hist. Soc.** Col., v. 3. 1832.)
— OAKES, W. Scenery of the White Mountains; with plates from drawings of I. Sprague. Boston, 1848. 4°.
— ROUTES to the White Mountains and Lake Winnipiseogee; with descriptions and maps. Boston, 1851. 16°. (C 277)
— BECKETT, S. B. Guide-book of the [Grand Trunk R. R.] including a description of the White Mountains. Portland, 1853. 12°.
— COMPLETE guide to the White Mountains. Boston, 1857. 24°. (C 277)
— KING, T. S. White Hills, their legends, landscape, and poetry. Boston, 1860. 8°.
— - *Same.* Boston, 1871. 8°.
— EASTMAN, S. C. White Mountain guide book. 3d ed. Concord, 1863. 16°.
— VOSE, G. L. Tracts of ancient glaciers in the White Mts.; geological structure of portions of that group. (*In* **Amer. Assoc.** Proc., v. 16. 1868.)
See also **Grand Trunk R. R.**

White, red, and black; sketches of American society. *See* **Pulszky, F. A.** *and* **T.**

White Republican, *pseud.* North and South. 1863. *See* **Fuller, H.**

White rose; by A. E. Bray. London, 1846. 16°. (Novels, v. 4.)

White rose, The; by G. J. W. Melville. (*In* **Fortnightly** review, v. 7–9. 1867–68.)

White rose, The; a word for the House of York; by W. B. London, 1680. f°. (A 52)

White Russia. RYPIŃSKI, A. Bialoruś; kilka słów o poezii prostego ludu téj naszéj Polskiéj prowincii; o jego muzyce, śpiéwie, tańcach, *etc.* Paryż, 1840. 16°.

White Sea. HAMEL, *Dr.* J. England and Russia; the voyages of J. Tradescant the elder, Sir H. Willoughby, R. Chancellor, Nelson, and others to the White Sea, *etc.*; [about 870–1835]; tr. by J. S. Leigh. London, 1854. 8°.
— OTHERE. Voyage, [870]. (*In* **Kerr, R.** Col. of voy., v. 1. 1824.)
— ALLISON, T. Voy. from Archangel, 1697. (*In* **Pinkerton, J.** Voy., v. 1. 1808.)
— MILNER, T. Notice of the White Sea. (*In his* Baltic. 1854.)
See also **Russia.**

White slave, The; [Archy Moore, with additions]; by R. Hildreth. Boston, 1852. 12°.

White slavery, a new emancipation cause; by W. Burton. Worcester, 1839. 12°.

White swelling. CROWTHER, B. Observations on white swelling. London, 1808. 8°.
— FORD, E. Observations on disease of the hip; also, white swelling of the knee. London, 1810. 8°.

Whitebread, Thomas, *and others.* True speeches before their execution at Tyburn, June 20. London, 1679. f°. (A 49)

Whitefield, George. Works. London, 1771. 4 v. 8°.
Contents. Vol. 1–2. Letters, 1842–53. 3. Letters to the inhabitants of Savannah. — An account of the Orphan-house in Georgia. 4. Answer to the Bishop of London's last pastoral letter. — Letter to the religious societies of England. — Letter to the inhabitants of Maryland, Virginia, North and South Carolina. — Letter to some church-members of the presbyterian persuasion in answer to certain scruples lately proposed. — Letter to Wesley in answer to his sermon entitled Free-grace. — Vindication and confirmation of the remarkable work of God in New England. — Brief account of the occasion, process, and issue of a late trial at the assize, Gloucester, March 3, 1743, between some of the people called Methodists, plaintiffs, and certain persons of Winchinhampton, defendants. — Answer to the first part of an anonymous pamphlet, 'Observations upon the conduct and behaviour of a certain sect, usually distinguished by the name of Methodists'. — Letter to the Rev. T. Church, in answer to his serious and expostulatory letter to Whitefield. — Answer to the second part of an anonymous pamphlet. — Remarks upon a late charge against enthusiasm, delivered by Richard, Lord Bishop of Litchfield and Coventry, to the clergy of that diocese, 1741. —

Letter to the president and professors, tutors and Hebrew instructor of Harvard College, in Cambridge. — Remarks on a pamphlet entitled 'The enthusiasm of Methodists and Papists compared'. — Expostulatory letter to Count Zinzendorff. — Address to persons of all denominations. 1756. — Preface to the serious reader on behalf of the Rev. S. Clarke's edition of the Bible. — Observations on some fatal mistakes in a book entitled 'The doctrine of grace', *etc.*, by William, Lord Bishop of Gloucester. — A recommendatory preface to the works of Bunyan. — Letter to the Rev. Dr. Durell, Vice-chancellor of the University of Oxford. — Observations on select passages of Scripture turned into catechetical questions. — Law gospelized; an attempt to render Mr. Law's 'Serious call' more useful to the children of God. — Preface to a new edition of the homilies. — Prayers.

— Account of Lent and other processions at Lisbon. London, 1768. 12°. (C 59)

— Account of money received and disbursed for the Orphan-house in Georgia. London, 1741. 8°. (B 735)

— Answer to the 1st and 2d part of 'Observations upon the conduct of the Methodists'. Boston, 1744. 3 pt. 4°. (B 583)

— Brief account of the first part of the life of W., by himself. Boston, 1740. 12°. (C 52)

— Britain's mercies and Britain's duty; sermon, Aug. 24, on the suppression of the late rebellion. 2d ed. Boston, 1746. 8°. (B 74, 160)

— Collection of papers, *etc.*; [by and about W.]. *n.p.*, [1740]. 8°. (B 251)

— Directions how to hear sermons. 3d ed. Boston, 1740. 12°. (B 63)

— Eighteen sermons; taken in short hand and transcribed by J. Gurney, rev. by A. Gifford. Newburyport, 1797. 8°.

— *Same.* N. Y., 1809. 12°.

— Journal of a voyage from London to Savannah, Georgia [Dec. 28, 1737 - Dec. 4, 1738]. 5th ed. London, 1739. 8°.

Contents. Pt. 1. London to Gibraltar. 2. Gibraltar to Savannah. 3. Savannah to London.

— *Same.* Parts 1, 2. 6th ed. London, 1743. 8°. (B 18)

— *Same.* Pt. 3. 2d ed. London, 1739. 8°. (B 18)

— Continuation from his arrival at London to his departure from thence on his way to Georgia, [Dec. 8, 1738 - June 3, 1739]. 2d ed. London, 1739. 8°.

— *Same.* 2d ed. London, 1744. 8°. (B 18)

— Continuation during the time he was detained in England by the embargo, [June 4 - Aug. 3, 1739]. 3d ed. London, 1739. 8°.

— *Another copy.* (B 18)

— Continuation from his embarking after the embargo to his arrival at Savannah, [Aug. 4, 1739 - Jan. 9, 1739/40]. 2d ed. Lond., 1740. 8°.

— *Another copy.* (B 18)

— Continuation after his arrival at Georgia to a few days after his second return from Phila., [Jan. 11, 1739/40 - June 6, 1740]. London, 1741. 8°.

— *Another copy.* (B 18)

— Continuation from a few days after his return to Georgia to his arrival at Falmouth; [June 25, 1740-] March 11, 1741; 7th journal. London, 1741. 8°.

— *Same.* 2d ed. London, 1744. 8°. (B 18)

— Continuation of [his] journal from Savannah, June 25, to his departure from Stanford for N. Y. [Oct. 29, 1740]. Boston, 1741. 8°. (C 52)

— Continuation of [his] journal [from Rye to 'On board the Minerva', Oct. 30, 1740 - Jan. 18, 1741]. *n.t.p.* [1741.] 8°. (C 51)

— Continuation of his journal, from his arrival at Savannah, May 7, to his arrival in England, Dec. 8, 1741. Boston, 1741. 8°. (C 51)

— Letter to Dr. Chauncy on some passages rel. to W. in his 'Seasonable thoughts'. Boston, 1745. 4°. (B 583)

— Letter to Dr. Durell occasioned by a late expulsion of six students from Edmund Hall. London, 1768. 8°. (B 21, 859)

— *Same.* Boston, 1768. 8°. (B 514, C 12)

— Letter to J. Wesley [on] his sermon, 'Free grace'. Boston, 1740. 8°. (C 51, 60)

— Letter to some Presbyterians rel. to passages in his sermons and writings. Boston, 1740. 8°. (B 44)

— Letter to the President, *etc.*, of Harv. Coll.; in answer to [their] Testimony. Boston, 1745. 4°. (B 45, 583)

— Sermons; added, prayers. Vol. 11. Phila., 1740. 18°.

— Short address to persons of all denominations; occasioned by the alarm of an intended invasion. 5th ed. London, 1756. 8°. (B 194)

— *Same.* 6th ed. Boston, 1756. 8°. (B 64)

— Some remarks on a late pamphlet, 'The state of religion in New Eng. since W.'s arrival there'. 2d ed. Glasgow, *printed* 1742, Boston, *reprinted* 1743. 8°. (C 51)

— Some remarks upon a late charge against enthusiasm by the Bp. of Litchfield. Boston, 1745. 4°. (B 583)

— ANDREWS, J. R. George Whitefield, a light rising in obscurity. London, 1864. 8°.

— APPLETON, N. God and not ministers to have the glory; two discourses occasioned by the powerful preaching of W. Boston, 1741. 8°. (B 850)

— BATE, J. Methodism displayed; or, Remarks upon Whitefield's answer to the Bp. of London's last pastoral letter. London, [1740?]. 8°. (B 1361)

— BISSET, J. Letter containing remarks upon [an] apology for the Presbyterians in Scotland who keep communion with Whitefield. 2d ed. Glasgow, 1743. 8°. (C 172)

— C - - - - D, A., *and* C., J. J. Letter to Foxcroft; examination of his 'Apology'. Boston, 1745. 4°. (B 583)

— CHANLER, I. Character of W. (*In his* New converts. 1740. C 172)

— CHAUNCY, C. Letter to W. vindicating 'Seasonable thoughts on the state of religion in New England'. Boston, 1745. 8°. (B 150)

— CLEAVELAND, J. A twig of birch for Billy's breech; letter to W. Hobby, being a correction for his folly lately published in 'A defence of the conduct of W.' Boston, 1745. 4°. (B 583, 1096)

— CROSWELL, A. Answer to Garden's first three letters to W.; with Garden's treatment of Whitefield. Boston, 1741. 8°. (C 25)

— CUSHING, C., *and others.* A letter from two associations of ministers in the country to the associated ministers of Boston, rel. to the admission of W. into their pulpits. Boston, 1745. 4°. (B 583)

— EDWARDS, J. Expostulatory letter to T. Clap, in reply to his letter [on] W. Boston, 1745. 8°. (C 43)

— EELLS, N. Letter to the 2d Church in Scituate; reasons why he doth not invite W. into his pulpit. Boston, 1745. 8°. (C 44)

— FOXCROFT, T. Apology in behalf of W. Boston, 1745. 4°. (B 70, 583)

— - Some thoughts on evangelic preaching; sermon, Oct. 23. Boston, 1740. 8°. (B 67, 223)

— GARDEN, A. Six letters to W.; with Whitefield's answer. 2d ed. Boston, 1740. 8°. (B 34)

— GILLIES, J. Memoirs of W. N. Y., 1774. 12°.

— GLEDSTONE, J. P. Life and travels of W. London, 1871. 8°.

— HARVARD COLLEGE. Testimony of the President, professors, tutors, and Hebrew instructor against W. Boston, 1744. 8°. (B 44, 1119)

— HENCHMAN, N. Reasons for declining to admit W. into his pulpit. Boston, 1745. 8°. (C 80, 172)

— HOBBY, W. Inquiry into the itinerancy and conduct of W. Boston, 1745. 4°. (B 583)

— K., L. Letter to W., calling on him to vindicate his conduct. [Boston, 1744.] 8°. (B 34)

— - *Same.* 2d ed. corr. [Boston, 1744.] 8°. (B 44)

— PATERSHALL, R. Pride humbled; or, Mr. Hobby chastised; being some remarks on [his] Defence of the conduct of W. Boston, 1745. 4°. (B 583)

— PICKERING, T. Letter to W., touching his relation to the Church of Eng. Boston, 1745. 4°. (B 70, 583)

— PRESCOTT, B. Letter to W. Boston, 1745. 4°. (B 583)

— PRINCE, T., *and* CHAUNCY, C. Correspondence. (*In* Mass. Hist. Soc. Col., v. 32. 1854.)

— SEWARD, W. Journal of a voyage from Savannah to Philadelphia and from Philadelphia to England. London, 1740. 8°.

— SHURTLEFF, W. Letter to those in the ministry who refuse to admit W. into their pulpits. Boston, 1745. 4°. (B 583)

— STATE of religion in New England, since W.'s arrival there; with reply to W.'s 'Remarks on the 1st ed.' 2d ed. Glasgow, 1742 8°.

— STEPHEN, *Sir* J. The evangelical succession. (*In his* **Essays** in ecclesiastical biog., v. 2. 1850.)
— TESTIMONY of an assoc. of laymen at Boston resp. the present times. Boston, 1745. 4°. (B 583)
— TESTIMONY of an association of ministers convened at Marlborough, Jan. 22, 1744/5, against W.; also of ministers in the Co. of Bristol. Boston, 1745. 8°. (B 1080)
— VINDICATION of W. against the charges some have lately endeavored to fix upon him. Boston, 1745. 8°. (C 86)
— WIGGLESWORTH, E. Letter to W. [in] reply to his answer to the College testimony against him; [with E. Holyoke's] answer to W. Boston, 1745. 4°. (B 70, 583)
— *Funeral sermons on*. 1770. *See* **Parsons, J.** (B 654); — **Pemberton, E.** (B 73, 854); — **Wesley, J.** (B 235); — **Whitaker, N.** (B 17, 235)
See also **Revival.**

Whitefield, John, *D.D.* Christian liberty; sermon, Aug. 1, 1724. Camb., 1725. 8°. (B 602)

Whitefoord, Caleb. LIFE. (*In* **Soc. of Anc. Scots.** Lives of Scottish poets, v. 3. 1822.)

Whitegift, John. *See* **Whitgift, J.**

Whitehall. SMIRKE, S. Notices of the Palace of Whitehall. (*In* **Archæologia,** v. 25. 1854.)
— THOMSON, *Mrs.* A. T. Whitehall and its predecessors. (*In her* Recollections of literary characters, v. 1. 1854.)

Whitehead, Charles. Richard Savage; a romance. London, 1842. 3 v. 12°.
Note. From **Bentley's** miscel., v. 10-12. 1840-42.

Whitehead, Charles E. Wild sports in the South. N. Y., 1860. 12°.

Whitehead, George. Gospel salutation recommended to Friends. London, 1719, *reprinted* Phila., 1827. 16°. (C 16)
— IMPRISONMENT of W. (*In* **Hookes, E.** Due order of law. 1680. C 284)

Whitehead, James, *M.D.* Transmission from parents to offspring of some forms of disease. 2d ed. London, 1857. 8°.

Whitehead, John, *M.D.* Life of J. Wesley; with life of C. Wesley. London, 1793-96. 2 v. 8°.
— Sermon, Mar. 9, funeral of J. Wesley. London, 1791. 8°. (B 235)
— REMARKS on [his] 'True narrative', *etc.* London, 1792. 12°. (C 69)

Whitehead, Paul. Honour; a satire. Lond., 1747. 4°. (A 71)
— The hunting song. (*In* **Campbell, T.** Brit. poets, v. 6. 1819.)
— Poems. (*In* **Anderson, R.** Brit. poets, v. 10. 1795; — *and in* **Chalmers, A.** Eng. poets, v. 16. 1810.) —
— The state dunces. Pt. 1, 2. London, 1733. f°. (A 45)

Whitehead, Wm. Creusa. (*In* **Bell, J.** British theatre, v. 34. 1797; — *and* **Scott,** *Sir* W. British drama, v. 1., pt. 2. 1804.)
— Observations on the shield of Æneas. (*In* **Virgilius Maro, P.** Works, v. 3. 1763.)
— Poems. (*In* **Anderson, R.** Brit. poets, v. 11. 1795; — *and* **Chalmers,** A. Eng. poets, v. 17. 1810.)
— Roman father. (*In* **Bell, J.** Brit. theatre, v. 3. 1795; — *in* **London** stage, v. 3. 1826; — *and in* **Scott,** *Sir* W. British dr., v. 1, pt. 2. 1804.)
— School for lovers. (*In* **Bell, J.** Brit. theatre, v. 7. 1791; — *and in* **Scott,** *Sir* W. British dr., v. 2, pt. 2. 1804.)
— Trip to Scotland. (*In* **Collection of the most esteemed farces,** v. 6. 1792.)
— AUSTIN, W. S., *Jr.*, *and* J. R. (*In their* Lives of the poets-laureate. 1853.)

Whitehead, Wm. Adee. Biographical sketch of W. Franklin. (*In* **New Jersey Hist. Soc.** Proc., v. 3. 1848-49.) — Robbery of the treasury of E. Jersey in 1768, and contemporaneous events. (*In* v. 5. 1850-51.) — East Jersey under the proprietary governments. (*In* Col., v. 1. 1846.)
— Contributions to the early history of Perth Amboy; with sketches of men and events in New Jersey during the provincial era. N. Y., 1856. 8°.

Whitehead, *Rev.* **Wm. Baily.** Letter on the expected parliamentary provision in furtherance of general education. (*In* **Pamphleteer,** 1820; v. 16 of B 838) — Prosecutions of infidel blasphemers briefly vindicated. (*In* 1823; v. 22.)

Whitehurst, John. Works. London, 1792. 4°.
Contents. Memoirs, by C. Hutton. — An inquiry into the original state and formation of the Earth. — An attempt toward obtaining invariable measures of length, capacity, and weight, from the mensuration of time, *etc.* — An appendix to the attempt. — Three papers from the philosophical transactions: Thermometrical observations at Derby; — An account of a machine for raising water, at Oulton in Cheshire; — Experiments on ignited substances.
— Attempt towards obtaining invariable measures of length, *etc.*, from the mensuration of time. London, 1787. 4°.
— Enquiry into the original state and formation of the Earth; with obs. on the strata of Derbyshire. London, 1792. 4°.
— Observations on the ventilation of rooms, *etc.*; [ed. by **R. Willan**]. London, 1794. 4°.

Whiteing, Richard, *tr.* Wonderful escapes. 1871. *See* **Bernard, F.**

Whitelaw, James, *and others.* History of the city of Dublin. London, 1818. 2 v. 4°.

Whitelock. *See also* **Whitlock.**

Whitelocke, Whitelock, *or* **Whitlock,** *Sir* Bulstrode. Journal of the Swedish ambassy, 1653-54, from England, Scotland, and Ireland; with app. of original papers. London, 1772. 2 v. 4°.
— *Same.* New ed. by **H. Reeve.** London, 1855. 2 v. 8°.
— Memorials of English affairs, Charles I. to the restoration of Charles II. London, 1682. f°.
— *Same.* New ed. Oxford, 1853. 4 v. 8°.
— WHITELOCKE, R. H. Memoirs of W. London, 1860. 8°.
— WOOLRYCH, H. W. (*In his* Lives of eminent serjeants-at-law, v. 1. 1869.)

Whitelocke, *Sir* **James.** Liber famelicus; ed. by **J. Bruce.** London, 1858. 4°. (**Camden Soc.,** v. 70.)

Whitelocke, John. TRIAL by court-martial, 28th Jan. London, 1808. 8°.
— *Another ed.* London, 1808. 8°. (B 721)

Whitelocke, R. H. Memoirs of B. Whitelocke. London, 1860. 8°.

Whiteman (*Lat.* **Leucander**), Andrew. Voyage to Palæstina, 1020. (*In* **Hakluyt, R.** Col. of voy., v. 2. 1810.)

Whiter, *Rev.* **Walter.** Etymologicon magnum; or, Universal etymological dictionary, on a new plan. Pt. 1. Camb., 1800. 4°.
— Etymologicon universale; or, Universal etymological dictionary; in which it is shewn that consonants are alone to be regarded in discovering the affinities of words; that languages are derived from the Earth, *etc.* Camb., 1822-25. 3 v. 4°.
Note. Vol. 1, 2 paged continuously.
— Specimen of a commentary on Shakespeare. London, 1794. 8°.
Contents. Notes on 'As you like it'. — Attempt to explain passages of S. on a new principle of criticism derived from Locke's doctrine of the association of ideas.

Whiteside, James. Essays and lect. Dubl., 1868. 16°.
Contents. Life and death of the Irish parl. — The city of Rome and its vicissitudes. — Goldsmith, his friends and critics. — The homely virtues. — The Church in Ireland.
— Italy in the nineteenth century. 2d ed. London, 1849. 3 v. 12°.
— Landed estates court. — Progress of legislation in our criminal law. (*In* **Nat. Assoc. Prom. Soc. Sci.** Trans., 1861.)
— RITCHIE, J. E. (*In his* British senators. 1869.)

Whitewater, *Wis.* LEONARD, J. A. Sketch of W. (*In* **Wisconsin Hist. Soc.** Col., v. 3. 1857.)

Whitfield, Henry. The light appearing more and more; or, Farther discovery of the state of the Indians in N. E. [London, 1651,] *reprinted* N. Y., *Sabin*, 1865. 4°.
— *Same.* (*In* **Mass. Hist. Soc.** Col., v. 24. 1834.)

— Strengt' out of weakness; further progress of the Gospel among the Indians. [London, 1652,] *reprinted* N. Y., *Sabin*, 1865. 4°.
— *Same.* (*In* Mass. Hist. Soc. Col., v. 24. 1834.)

Whitgift, John, *Archbp. of Canterbury*. Works. Camb., 1851-53. 3 v. 8°. (Parker Soc.)
Contents. Vol. 1-3. Defence of the answer to the admonition against the reply of T. Cartwright. 3. Memoir of J. W. — Sermons. — Letters.
— Perspectiva communis. Coloniæ, 1592. 4°.
— CARTWRIGHT, T. Reply to an answer of W. againste the admonition to the Parliament. *n.p.*, [*about* 1574]. 4°.
— GARROW, D. W. (*In his* Hist. of Croydon. 1818.)
— PAULE, *Sir* G. Life of W. London, 1699. 8°.
— - *Same.* (*In* Wordsworth, C. Eccles. biog., v. 3. 1839.)
— STRYPE, J. Life and acts of W. Oxford, 1822. 3 v. 8°.

Whitgreave, Thomas. Narrative. (*In* **Hughes, J.** Boscobel tracts. 1857.)

Whither, George. LAMB, C. (*In his* Works, v. 3. 1870.)

Whithington, N. *See* **Withington, N.**

Whiting, Augustus, *M.D.* NOTICE of W. (*In* **Mass. Med.** Soc. Med. comm., v. 11. 1867.)

Whiting, Calvin, *Funeral sermon on.* 1795. *See* **Palmer, S.** (B 325)

Whiting, Henry, *Brig.-Gen.* Discourse. — Remarks on supposed tides, *etc.*, of N. Amer. lakes. (*In* **Historical** and scientific sketches of Michigan. 1834.)
— Life of Z. M. Pike. (*In* **Sparks, J.** Amer. biog., v. 15. 1845.)
— Ontwa, the son of the forest. N. Y., 1822. 8°.
— *ed.* Revolutionary orders of Washington. *See* **Washington, G.**

Whiting, John. Persecution exposed; memoirs rel. to the sufferings of W. and many others of the people called Quakers, with memoirs of many eminent Friends deceased. 2d ed. London, 1791. 8°.

Whiting, Lyman. Address before the Soc. for the Prom. of Collegiate and Theological Education at the West. Boston, 1855. 8°. (B 1609)

Whiting, Nathan. *See* **Pinniger, D.** Trial. 1808. (B 474)

Whiting, *Rev.* Samuel. Discourse, Windsor, Oct. 12. Rutland, 1797. 8°. (B 177, 335)
— Oration, Sheffield, July 4. Stockbridge, 1796. 8°. (B 416, 421)

Whiting, *Rev.* Thurston. Oration, Thomaston, July 4, 1798. Hallowell, [1798]. 4°. (B 650)

Whiting, Wm. Abstract of an argument in behalf of the remonstrants against the erection of a bridge across Chelsea Creek. Boston, 1854. 8°. (E 202)
— Address to the members of the New Eng. Hist. Geneal. Soc., Jan. 12. Boston, 1853. 8°. (B 1692)
— Argument, Boston Gas Light Company *vs.* W. Gault. Boston, 1848. 8°. (B 1456, E 202)
— Argument, E. Johnson *et al. vs.* P. Low *et al.* Boston, 1848. 8°. (E 202)
— Argument, R. Winans *vs.* O. Eaton *et al.*, for an alleged infringement of his patent for the eight-wheeled railroad car. Boston, 1853. 8°. (E 202)
— Memoir of J. Harrington. Boston, 1854. 12°.
— *Same.* (*In* **Harrington, J.** Sermons. 1854.)
— Report of the argument in the case of A. L. Brooks *et al. vs.* J. Fisk and N. G. Norcross, upon Woodworth's planing machine. Boston, 1854. 8°. (E 202)
— Speech before the legislative committee on the application of J. C. Tucker *et al.* for the charter for the Mystic River Railroad, *etc.* Boston, 1851. 8°. (E 202)
— War powers under the constitution of the U. S. 10th ed. Boston, 1864. 8°.

Whitington. *See* **Whittington.**

Whitlaw, Charles. Reply to Dr. Hosack's inaug. address before the Medical Society of the Co. of N. Y., July 12, 1824. Phila., 1825. 8°. (B 968)
— West London Medicated Vapour Bath Inst.; also address to the British and American public. London, 1842. 8°. (B 1565)

Whitley, Nicholas. Application of geology to agriculture, *etc.* London, 1843. 8°.

Whitlock. *See also* **Whitelock.**

Whitlock, Henry. Sermon, June 2, at the institution of Rev. P. Chase. Hartford, 1812. 8°. (B 1007)

Whitlock, Samuel. Address, effects of war and peace, July 4. Rutland, 1827. 8°. (B 1102)

Whitman, Benjamin. Index to the laws of Massachusetts to 1796. Worcester, 1797. 12°.

Whitman, Benjamin, *Jr.* Heroes of the North; or, Battles of Lake Erie and Champlain; poems. Boston, 1816. 8°. (B 455)

Whitman, *Rev.* Bernard. Answer to 'E. Pearsons' letter to the candid'. Boston, 1832. 8°. (E 277)
— Discourse on Christian union, installation of A. Ballou, Mendon, May 3, 1832. Bost., 1833. 8°. (B1324)
— *Same.* 3d ed. Boston, 1831. 12°. (A. U. A. 1st ser., no. 33, C 168, v. 3.)
— On Christian salvation. Boston, 1830. 8°. (C 211)
— Discourse on denying the Lord Jesus. 2d ed. Boston, 1827. 12°. (C 211)
— Discourse on regeneration. Boston, 1828. 8°. (C 211, D 64)
— Discourse on the limited influence of the gospel. Boston, 1829. 8°. (C 211)
— Letter to an orthodox minister on revivals of religion. Boston, 1831. 12°. (C 184)
— *Same.* 2d ed. Boston, 1831. 12°. (C 226)
— *Same.* 3d ed. Boston, 1831. 12°. (D 64)
— Reply to the 'Review of W.'s letters to Prof. Stuart'. Boston, 1831. 8°. (B 1022, E 277)
— Sermon; continual rejoicing. (*In* **Liberal** preacher, v. 4. 1834.)
— Thanksgiving discourse on the means of increasing public happiness. Bost., 1828. 12°. (B 1253, D 64)
— Two letters to [M.] Stuart, on religious liberty. Boston, 1830. 8°. (B 1843, 2017)
— *Same.* 2d ed. Boston, 1831. 8°. (B 1020, E 277)
— BALFOUR, W. Letter to W. on the term Gehenna. Boston, 1834. 12°.
— REVIEW of [B.] Whitman's letters to [M.] Stuart on religious liberty. 2d ed., with app. Boston, 1831. 8°. (B 1022, 1780)

Whitman, *Rev.* Elnathan. Sermon [on the death of] E. Dorr. Norwich, 1773. 8°. (B 174)

Whitman, George H. Essay on the congress of nations; [signed Hamilton]. (*In* **Amer. Peace Soc.** Prize essays. 1840.)

Whitman, *Rev.* Jason. Change experienced in becoming truly religious. Dover, 1834. 12°. (C 226)
— Christian aims; sermon at the induction of C. H. A. Dall, Needham, Feb. 7. Boston, 1847. 8°. (B 1324)
— The hard times; discourse, Jan. 1. Portland, 1837. 8°. (B 1168, 1305)
— Home preparation for school. (*In* **Amer. Inst. Instr.** Lectures, 1846.)
— Inquiry into the Scriptural authority for the doctrine of the two natures of Christ. *n.t.p.* [Dover, 18—.] 12°. (C 226, D 62)
— Religious excitements not the result of special divine influence; sermon, ordination of E. H. Edes, Eastport, Nov. 15, 1831. Boston, 1832. 8°. (C 212, D 62)
— MUZZEY, A. B. Memorial of W., and address at his funeral. Boston, 1848. 8°. (B 1227)
— *Funeral sermon on.* 1848. *See* **Dorr, T. H.** (B 1227)

Whitman, John Winslow. Report of trial, Boston, Dec. 16 and 17, of T. Lyman for libel on D. Webster. Boston, 1828. 8°. (B 949)
— Trial of G. Crowninshield, J. J. Knapp, Jr., and J. F. Knapp for the murder of J. White. Boston, 1830. 8°. (B 1404, E 273)
Note. The above contains the trial of J. F. Knapp only.
— *Same, without the introduction.* *n.t.p.* Boston, 1830. 8°. (E 273)
— Trial of the case of the Commonwealth *vs.* D. L. Child for libel on J. Keyes. Bost., 1829. 8°.
— *Another copy.* (B 949)

Whitman, Levi. Jesus Christ the resurrection and the life; discourse, interment of C. Upham. Boston, 1786. 8°. (B 1090)
— Sermon, Oct. 6, 1786. interment of I. Lewis. Boston, 1787. 8°. (B 335, 1090)
— Topographical description of Wellfleet. (*In* **Mass. Hist. Soc.** Col., v. 3. 1810.) — Account of creeks and islands in Wellfleet. (*In* v. 4. 1795.) — Note on Wellfleet. (*In* v. 8. 1802.)

Whitman, *Rev.* Nathaniel. Being defamed, we entreat; thanksgiving discourse, Nov. 26, 1829. Boston, 1830. 8°. (B 1253)
— Sermon; claims of the Lord's supper to a practical observance. (*In* **Liberal** preacher, new ser., v. 1. 1831.)

— Unitarianism sound doctrine; sermon, Waltham, ordination of B. Whitman, Feb. 15. Camb., 1826. 8°. (B 1324)

Whitman, *Rev.* Samuel. Christ the son of God; sermon, Oct. 5, 1819, at a session of the Mountain Assoc. 2d ed. Goshen, Mass., 1820. 8°. (B 1328)

— Nature and design of the baptism of Christ; sermon, Goshen. Northampton, 1800. 8°. (B 1305)

— Two sermons, ordination of W. Hallack, Plainfield, July 11. Northampton, 1792. 8°. (B 1315)

Whitman, *Mrs.* Sarah, *wife of* Levi, *Funeral sermon on.* 1803. *See* **Shaw,** P. (B 854)

Whitman, Walt. Leaves of grass. N. Y., 1856. 12°.

— *Same.* Boston, 1860–61. 12°.

Whitman, Wm. E. S., *and* **True,** C. H. Maine in the war of the Union. Lewiston, 1865. 8°.

Whitman, Zechariah Gardner. Address before the Harmonick Club, Boston, Dec. 21, 1808. Boston, 1809. 8°. (B 399)

— Historical sketch of the Ancient and Honorable Artillery Company. Boston, 1820. 8°.

— History of the Ancient and Honorable Artillery Company. 2d ed. Boston, 1842. 8°.

Whitmarsh, *Miss* Caroline Snowden, *and* **Guild,** A. E. Hymns of the ages. 1st–3d ser. Boston, 1871, 65. 3 v. 8°.

Whitmarsh, Joseph A. LETTER to the jurors empannelled to try the indictment against [him] for libel. Boston, 1838. 4°. (B 1435, 1770)

Whitmore, Wm. Henry. Account of the Temple family; with notes and pedigree of the family of Bowdoin. Boston, 1856. 8°.

— The Andros tracts; a collection of pamphlets and official papers; with notes and a memoir of Sir E. Andros. Boston, *Prince Soc.*, 1868. 3 v. 4°.

Contents. Vol. 1. **Andros,** T. Memoir of Sir E. Andros. — Introduction. — **Byfield,** N. Account of the late revolution. — Declaration of the inhabitants of **Boston.** — **Palmer,** J. Impartial account. — **Rawson,** E., *and* **Sewall,** S. The revolution in New England justified. — **Andros,** E. Proclamation of Jan. 10, 1688–89. — **Stoughton,** W., *and others.* Narrative of Andros's proceedings. — **List** of authorized fees. 1686. — **Charges** against Andros and others; from the mss. in the Massachusetts archives. — **Faireweather,** J., *and* **Williams,** N. Treatment of the prisoners at Castle Island, Boston. — Petition of the inhabitants of **Maine** against the revolution. — **Willard,** S. Discourse on the ceremony of laying the hand on the Bible in swearing. — **C.,** S. Further quæries upon the present state of the New-English affairs. — Index. 2. **Whitmore,** W. H. Increase Mather. — Introduction. — **Mather,** I. Narrative of the miseries of New-England, with the addresses of the clergy of London, and of the non-conformist ministers to the Prince of Orange, 1688; — The present state of the New-English affairs; [from the original broadside], 1689; — A vindication of New-England, containing the first petition of the Boston Episcopalians, 1690. — Petition of the inhabitants of **Charlestown**; [reprinted from Frothingham's history]. 1689. — **Bulkeley,** G. The people's right to election. 1689. — **Mather,** I. New-England vindicated, in reply to certain considerations, 1689. — **Ashurst,** H., *and others.* Answer of the Massachusetts agents to Randolph; [from the mss. in Mass. archives]. 1690. — **Short** discourse against restoring the charters, in reply to 'New-England vindicated'. 1689. — **Mather,** I. A brief relation of the state of New-England, containing a letter from Abraham Kirk, and a translation of Mather's 'De successu evangelii apud Indos'. 1689. — **Report** of the proceedings against Andros, before the privy-council; [from the manuscript at the state paper office, London]. 1690. — **B.,** A. An account of the revolution in New-England. 1689. — **D.,** C., [*probably* Edward **Randolph**]. New-England's faction discovered. 1690. — **Mather,** I. Reasons for the confirmation of the charters. 1690. — The humble address of the publicans of **New-England**, containing the second petition of Boston Episcopalians. 1691. — **Mather,** I. Account of the agents of New England, 1691; with an extract from a letter from the London ministers. — **Mather,** I. Address to the inhabitants, prefixed to his sermon before the General Court. 1693. — **Letter** of the London ministers. 1691. — **Mather,** I. Reply to Calef. 1701. — **Mather,** C. Political fables. — **List** of members of the Prince Society. — Index. 3. Introd. — **Considerations** against the charter. — **Abstract** of laws of New England. — **Andros,** *Sir* E. Report of his administration. — **Original** documents. — **Papers** rel. to Andros's administration. — **Mather,** C. Memoirs of I. Mather. — **Appeal** to the men of New England, 1689. — **Papers** rel. to Randolph. — The **Prince** Soc. — Index.

— Brief genealogy of the descendants of W. Hutchinson and T. Oliver. Boston, 1865. 4°.

Note. Repr., with add. fr. the N. E. hist. and geneal. register.

— Brief genealogy of the Usher family of New England. Boston, 1869. 8°. (B 1962)

— The cavalier dismounted; essay on the origin of the founders of the thirteen colonies. Salem, 1864. 8°.

— Early painters and engravers of New England. (*In* **Mass. Hist. Soc.** Proc., 1866–67.)

— The Hall family, settled at Medford, Mass. Boston, 1855. 8°.

— Handbook of American genealogy. Albany, 1862. 4°.

— The Massachusetts civil list, 1630–1744. Albany, 1870. 8°.

— Memoir of T. Prince and list of his publications. (*In* **Boston.** *Public Library. Prince Lib.* Catalogue. 1868.)

— Notes on the manor and family of Whitmore. Boston, 1856. 8°.

— Record of the descendants of F. Whitmore, of Cambridge. Boston, 1855. 8°.

— Register of families settled at Medford. Boston, 1855. 8°.

Note. Reprinted from the 'History of Medford by C. Brooks'.

Whitmore, Wm. W. Letter on the corn laws. (*In* **Pamphleteer,** 1827; v. 28 of **B 838**)

— Letter to the agriculturists of the County of Salop, June 5. 2d ed. London, [1841]. 12°. (C 180)

— OBSERVATIONS on the corn-laws, addressed to W. W. Whitmore. (*In* **Pamphleteer,** 1827; v. 28 of B 838) — REMARKS on the state of the corn question; app. to 'Observations on the corn laws', addressed to W. W. Whitmore. (*In* 1828; v. 29 of B 838)

Whitney, *Mrs.* Adeline Dutton (Train). Faith Gartney's girlhood. 12th ed. Boston, 1865. 12°.

— The Gayworthys; a story of threads and thrums. 5th ed. Boston, 1865. 12°.

— Hitherto; a story of yesterdays. Boston, [1869]. 12°.

— Mother Goose for grown folks. New enl. ed. Boston, [1870]. 12°.

— Patience Strong's outings. Boston, 1869. 12°.

— Real folks. Boston, 1872. 8°.

— A summer in Leslie Goldthwait's life. Boston, 1869. 12°.

— We girls; a home story. Boston, 1870. 16°.

— Zerub Throop's experiments. Boston, 1871. 16°.

Note. From Old and new, v. 3. 1871.

Whitney, Anne. Poems. N. Y., 1859. 12°.

Whitney, Daniel S. American slavery; echoes and glimpses of prophecy. Boston, 1859. 16°. (D 37)

Whitney, Eli. OLMSTED, D. Memoir of W. New Haven, 1846. 8°.

— *Another copy.* (B 1461)

Whitney, *Rev.* Frederick Augustus. Address at the consecration of Evergreen Cemetery, Brighton. Boston, 1850. 8°. (B 1609)

— Address on temperance, Brighton, Dec. 21, 1845. Boston, 1846. 8°. (B 1281)

— Address; The Christian mother, Brighton, funeral of Mrs. S. P. Champney; with an appendix, containing a general notice of the Champney and Park families. Boston, 1855. 8°. (B 1211)

— Death of little children; sermon, Brighton, Sept. 19. Boston, 1847. 8°. (B 1305)

— The early New-England home; thanksgiving sermon. [Reprinted from the Monthly religious mag.] Boston, 1846. 8°. (B 1254)

— Historical sketch of the old Church, Quincy, Mass. Albany, 1864. 8°.
Note. From **New England** histor. and geneal. register.

Whitney, *Rev.* George. Commemorative discourse, Quincy, May 25; 2d centennial of the incorporation of the town; with an appendix. Boston, 1840. 8°.
— *Other copies.* (**B 1164, 1697, 1822**)
— The common lot; sermon, death of W. H. Harrison, Apr. 18. Boston, 1841. 8°. (**B 1217, 1878**)
— The moral and religious uses of mechanical exhibitions; sermon, Jamaica Plain, Sept. 24. Boston, 1837. 8°. (**B 1305, 1696**)
— Voices of the dead; sermon, Jamaica Plain, Dec. 20. Boston, 1840. 8°. (**B 1305**)
— *Funeral sermon on.* 1842. *See* **Putnam, G.** (**B 1227, 1247**)

Whitney, John Prescott. Silver mining regions of Colorado; with some account of the processes for working gold ores. N. Y., 1865. 12°.

Whitney, Josiah Dwight. Cave in Calaveras County, Cal. (*In* **Smithsonian Inst.** Report, 1867.)
— Geological survey of Illinois. *See* **Illinois.** *Geological Survey.*
— Metallic wealth of the U. S. described and compared with that of other countries. Phila., 1854. 8°.
— Occurrence of the ores of iron in the azoic system. — Remarks on the geology of the north shore of Lake Superior. (*In* **Amer. Assoc.** Proc., v. 9. 1856.)
— *and* **Foster, J. W.** Various articles.] (*In* **Amer. Assoc.** Proc., v. 5. 1851.)

Whitney, Lorenzo H. History of the war for the preservation of the Federal Union. Vol. 1. Phila., 1863. 8°.

Whitney, Moses, *Funeral sermon on.* 1803. *See* **Harris, T. M.** (**B 203**)

Whitney, *Gen.* Moses, *Funeral sermon on.* 1860. *See* **Pike, R.** (**B 1227**)

Whitney, *Rev.* Peter, *of Northborough, b.* 1744., *d,* 1816. Account of a singular apple-tree producing fruit of opposite qualities. (*In* **Amer. Acad. of Arts and Sci.** Mem., v. 1. 1785.)
— Christ's ambassadors, *etc.*; sermon, Feb. 5, ordination of P. Whitney, Jr., Quincy. Boston, 1800. 8°. (**B 166, 235, 1313**)
— Death gain to Christians; discourse, Shrewsbury, Feb. 16, funeral of Mrs. L. Sumner. Worcester, 1810. 8°. (**B 1007**)
— Duty of praising the works of God, *etc.*; discourse, Northborough, June 1. Worcester, 1796. 8°. (**B 335**)
— History of the County of Worcester, Mass. Worcester, 1793. 8°.
— Topographical and historical description of Sudbury. — East Sudbury. (*In* **Mass. Hist. Soc.** Col., v. 14. 1816.)
— Weeping and mourning at the death of eminent persons; sermon, Northborough, death of G. Washington. Brookfield, 1800. 8°. (**B 1078**)
— WHITNEY, P., *Jr.* Biographical notice of W. (*In* **Mass. Hist. Soc.** Col, v. 17. 1818.)

Whitney, *Rev.* Peter, *of Quincy, b.* 1770, *d.* 1843. Discourse, interment of J. Adams, July 7. Boston, 1826. 8°. (**B 1206**)
— Discourse, Quincy and Hingham; fast[day], July 23. Boston, 1812. 8°. (**B 335**)
— Discourse, Quincy, Oct. 19, interment of Hon. R. Cranch and wife. Boston, 1811. 8°. (**B 335**)
— Sermon, Aug. 7, ordination of P. Lincoln, Gloucester. Boston, 1805. 8°. (**B 335, 1314**)
— Sermon on the Lord's day succeeding the interment of Madam A. Adams, Nov. 1, 1818. Boston, 1819. 8°. (**B 335**)
— Sermon, Quincy, Jan. 1. Quincy, 1837. 8°. (**B 1305**)
— *Funeral sermon on.* 1843. *See* **Lunt, W. P.** (**B 1184**)

Whitney, *Rev.* Phineas. Sermon, interment of Z. Adams. Charlestown, 1801. 8°. (**B 174**)
— Sermon, Jan. 1, ordination of N. B. Whitney, Hingham. Boston, 1800. 8°. (**B 166, 235, 1314**)

Whitney, Reuben M. Memorial to the Ho. of Representatives, U. S., in relation to the charges against him as witness before the com. of investigation into the Bank of the U. S. Wash., 1832. 8°. (**B 1059, 1541**)

Whitney, Sarah Coffin, *Funeral sermon on.* 1810. *See* **Gurney, J.** (**B 316**)

Whitney, Wm. Dwight. Compendious German grammar. N. Y., 1869. 12°.
— Language and the study of language; twelve lectures. N. Y., 1867. 8°.
— Lectures on the principles of linguistic science. (*In* **Smithsonian Inst.** Report, 1863.)
— Main results of the later vedic researches in Germany. (*In* **Amer. Orient. Soc.** Journ., v. 3. 1853.) — On the history of the vedic texts. (*In* v. 4.) — Contributions from the Atharva-veda to the theory of Sanskrit verbal accent. — On the Avesta or the sacred scriptures of the Zoroastrian religion. — Notice of 'Vergleichendes accentuationssystem von F. Bopp'. (*In* v. 5.) — On Lepsius's standard alphabet. (*In* v. 7. 8.) — On the views of Biot and Weber respecting the relations of the Hindu and Chinese systems of asterisms, with Müller's views. — Reply to Weber on the asterismal system. (*In* v. 8.) — The Tâittiriya-prâtiçâkhya; with its commentary. — The Tribhâsyaratna; text, translation, and notes. (*In* v. 9. 1871.)

Whiton, James M. Railroads and their management. Concord, 1856. 8°. (**B 1758**)

Whiton, John Milton, *D.D.* Brief notices of Antrim. (*In* **New Hamp. Hist. Soc.** Col., v. 4. 1834.)
— The Gospel minister; sermon, ordination of S. H. Tolman, Shirley, Oct. 25, 1815. New Ipswich, 1816. 8°. (**B 1324**)

Whittaker, Wm. *See* **Whitaker, W.**

Whittelsey, *Rev.* Samuel. Regards due to the eminent and useful; disc., death of J. Hall. Boston, 1730. 8°. (**C 5**)
— Sermon, ordination of S. Whittelsey, Jr.; with charge by N. Chauncey. Boston, 1739. 8°. (**B 77**)
— Woful condition of impenitent souls in their separate state; sermon, Apr. 4. Boston, 1731. 8°. (**B 235**)

Whittemore, David. TRIAL of S. M. Mayo and W. Love for the murder of W. Augusta, 1807. 8°. (**B 344**)

Whittemore, George. Fox, T. B. (*In* **Higginson, T. W.** Harvard memorial biog., v. 1. 1866.)

Whittemore, Thomas. Biography of H. Ballou. (*In* **Ballou, H.** Valedictory discourse. 1851. **B 1282**)
— Life of H. Ballou. Boston, 1854-55. 4 v. 12°.
— Modern history of universalism from the era of the Reformation to the present time. Boston, 1830. 12°.
— Notes and illustrations of parables of the New Testament. Rev. ed. Boston, 1834. 12°.
— Oration, Milford, Mass., 4th of July. Boston, 1821. 8°. (**B 944**)
— Plain guide to universalism. Boston, 1840. 8°.
— Report of a discussion on endless misery. 1833. *See* **Braman, M. P.** (**C 243**)

Whitten plaster. SMITH, J. C. Account of the Whitten plaster. (*In* **Conn. Acad. of Arts and Sci.** Mem., v. 1, pt. 1. 1810.)

Whitteron, John. Comparative health of forge men. (*In* **Nat. Assoc. Prom. Soc. Sci.** Trans., 1859.)

Whittier, John Greenleaf. Among the hills, and other poems. Boston, 1869. 16°.
— Barbara Frietchie. (*In* **Murdock, J. E.** Patriotism in poetry and prose. 1865.)
— Child life; a collection of poems. Boston, 1872 [1871]. 8°.
Contents. Infancy. — Out of doors. — Legendary. — Pictures, fancies, and memories. — Miscellaneous. — Hymns.
— Introduction. (*In* **Woolman, J.** Journal. 1871.)
— Justice and expediency; or, Slavery, with a view to its abolition. Haverhill, 1833. 8°. (**B 1473**)
— *Same.* (*In* **Anti-slavery** reporter, v. 1. 1833. **B 1473**)
— Kathleen. — The Yankee Zincali. (*In* **Boston** book, 4th col. 1850.)
— Leaves from Margaret Smith's journal, 1678-79. Boston, 1849. 16°.
— Miriam, and other poems. Bost., 1871 [70]. 16°.
— Old portraits and modern sketches. Boston, 1850. 12°.
Contents. Bunyan. — T. Ellwood. — J. Nayler. — A. Marvell. — J. Roberts. — S. Hopkins. — R. Baxter. — W. Leggett. — N. P. Rogers. — R. Dinsmore.
— Poems. Boston, 1856. 8°.
— Poems during the progress of the abolition question. Boston, 1837. 16°.

— Poetical works. Bost., 1857. 2 v. (v. 2 w.). 16°.
Contents. Vol. 1. Poems. — Legendary. — Voices of freedom. — Miscellaneous.

— Prose works. Boston, 1866. 2 v. 12°.
Contents. Vol. 1. Margaret Smith's journal. — J. Bunyan. — T. Ellwood. — J. Nayler. — A. Marvell. — J. Roberts. — S. Hopkins. — R. Baxter. — W. Leggett. — N. P. Rogers. — R. Dinsmore. 2. Utopian schemes and political theorists. — Peculiar institutions of Mass. — Carlyle on the slave question. — England under James II. — The two processions. — Evangeline. — Chapter of history. — Fame and glory. — Fanaticism. — The border war of 1708. — Great Ipswich fright. — Lord Ashley and the thieves. — Mirth and medicine. — Pope night. — The better land. — The poetry of the North. — The boy captives. — The black men in the Revolution and War of 1812. — My summer with Dr. Singletary. — Charms and fairy faith. — Magicians and witch folk. — Agency of evil. — The little iron soldier. — The city of a day. — Patucket falls. — Hamlet among the graves. — Yankee gypsies. — The world's end. — Swedenborg. — First day in Lowell. — Taking comfort. — The beautiful. — Lighting up. — The Scottish reformers. — The training.

— Sketch of the life of Brainard. (*In* **Brainard, J. G. C.** Literary remains. 1832.)

— Snow-bound; a winter idyl. Boston, 1866. 16°.

— Songs of labor, and other poems. Boston, 1856. 16°.

— The tent on the beach, and other poems. Boston, 1867. 12°.

— In war time, and other poems. Boston, 1864. 16°.

Whittingham, Bernard. Notes on the late expedition against the Russian settlements in Eastern Siberia. London, 1856. 8°.

Whittingham, Wm., *Dean of Durham.* A brief discourse of the troubles begun at Frankforte, 1554, about the Book of common prayer and ceremonies. London, 1846. 8°.

— *Same.* (*In* **Phenix,** v. 2. 1708.)

— Life of W.; from a ms. in Antony Wood's collection; ed. by M. A. E. Green. Westminster, 1870. 4°. (Camden Soc., v. 104.)

Whittingham, Wm. Rollinson, *D.D.* Annual sermon before the Board of Missions of the Prof. Episc. Ch., June 17. N. Y., 1840. 8°. (B 1330)

— Priesthood in the church; two discourses, Baltimore, ordination, of T. J. Wyatt and J. N. McJilton, [and] H. V. Johns. 2d ed. Balt., 1843. 8°. (B 1324)

— True glorying; sermon, Baltimore, April 16. Balt., 1848. 8°. (B 1305)

Whittington, Nicholas. Obs. during the 10th voyage of the E. I. Co. (*In* **Kerr, R.** Col., v. 9. 1824.)

Whittington, *Sir* Richard. Bourne, H. R. F. (*In his* English merchants, v. 1. 1866; — *and his* Famous London merchants. 1869.)

Whittle, James, *and* **Laurie,** Richard Holmes. New traveller's companion; survey of the roads in England, Wales, and Scotland. 8th ed. London, 1818. 8°.

Whittle, John Lowry. Several articles.] (*In* **Nat. Assoc. Prom. Soc. Sci.** Trans., 1863, 67.)

Whittlesey, *Col.* Charles. Ancient human skulls and other bones in a cave near Elyria, O. — Superficial deposits of the N. W. part of the U. S. — Equivalency of the rocks of N. E. Ohio, and the Portage, Chemung, and Hamilton rocks of N. Y. (*In* **Amer. Assoc.** Proc., v. 5. 1851.) — Drift cavities or potash kettles of Wisconsin. — Origin of the azoic rocks of Michigan and Wisconsin. (*In* v. 13.) — Ice movements of the glacial era in the valley of the St. Lawrence. (*In* v. 15.) — Abstract of remarks upon the occurrences of iron in masses. — Depression of the ocean during the ice period. (*In* v. 16.) — Evidences of the antiquity of man in the U. S. (*In* v. 17. 1869.)

— Description of ancient works in Ohio. (*In* **Smithsonian Inst.** Contrib., v. 3. 1852.) — Fluctuations of level in the North American lakes. (*In* v. 12; — *also in* **Amer. Assoc.** Proc., v. 11. 1858.) — Ancient mining on the shores of Lake Superior. (*In* v. 13. 1863; — *also in* **Amer. Assoc.** Proc., v. 11. 1858.)

— Description of part of Wisconsin south of Lake Superior. (*In* **United States.** *Geological Survey.* Report of a survey of Wisconsin. 1852.)

— Justice to the memory of J. Fitch. Cincin., 1845. 8°. (B 1456)

— Life of J. Fitch. (*In* **Sparks,** J. Amer. biog., v. 16. 1845.)

— Recollections of a tour through Wisconsin in 1832. (*In* **Wisconsin Hist. Soc.** Col., v. 1. 1855.) — The Cass manuscripts. (*In* v. 3. 1857.)

— Weapons and military character of the race of the mounds. — The physical geology of eastern Ohio. (*In* **Boston Soc. of Nat. Hist.** Mem., v. 1. 1866-69.)

Whittlesey, Elisha. Address before the Tallmadge Colonization Soc., July 4. Ravenna, 1833. 8°. (B 1483)

Whittlesey, Elisha D. Remarks upon the British exped. to Danbury, 1777, as narrated in Marshall's Life of Washington. (*In* **New York Hist. Soc.** Col., 2d ser., v. 2. 1849.)

Whittlesey, Frederick. Address at the 3d fair of the mechanics of Western N. York. Rochester, 1841. 8°. (B 1586)

Whittock, Nathaniel. Construction and decoration of the shop fronts of London. London, 1840. 4°.

Whitty, *Mrs.* A mother's journal during the last illness of her daughter, S. Chisman; with preface by J. Taylor. Boston, 1821. 16°.

Whitty, Edward Michael. Knaves and fools; a satirical novel of London life. N. Y., 1857. 12°.

Whitwell, Benjamin. Address to the Mass. Char. Fire Soc., May 27. Boston, 1814. 8°. (B 669)

— Eulogy on Washington, Augusta. Hallowell, Me., 1800. 8°. (E 162)

— Oration, Boston, 4th of July. Boston, 1814. 8°. (B 945)

— Loring, J. S. (*In his* Hundred Boston orators. 1852.)

Whitwell, Samuel. Oration to the Soc. of the Cincinnati in Mass., July 4. Boston, 1789. 8°. (A 38)

— Loring, J. S. (*In his* Hundred Boston orators. 1852.)

Whitwell, *Rev.* Wm. Discourse, Dec. 17, 1769. Boston, 1770. 8°. (B 147)

— Discourse, Marblehead, Jan. 29, 1770, funeral of J. Barnard. Salem, [1770]. 8°. (B 17)

Whitwell, Wm. A. Epistle to the Romans. *See* **Bible.** *Romans* (p. 289).

Whitwell & Seaver. Catalogue of a collection of French medical and other scientific books. Boston, 1837. 8°. (B 1770)

— Catalogue of valuable books to be sold Nov. 11. [Boston, 1837.] 8°. (B 1770)

Whitwell, Bond & Co. Catalogue of books to be sold May 25. Boston, 1837. 8°. (B 1770)

Whitwill, Mark. Local preliminary jurisdiction in cases of application to Parliament. (*In* **Nat. Assoc. Prom. Soc. Sci.** Trans., 1860.) — Private bill legislation. (*In* 1862.)

Whitworth, Charles, *Lord Whitworth, d.* 1725. Account of Russia, 1710. (*In* **Dodsley, R.** Fugitive pieces, v. 2. 1761.)

Whitworth, *Sir* Charles. State of the trade of Great Britain, in its imports and exports, 1697-[1776]. London, 1776. f°.

Whitworth, Joseph. Miscellaneous papers on mechanical subjects. London, 1858. 8°.
Contents. Plane metallic surfaces or true planes. — Uniform system of screw threads. — Address to the Institution of Mechanical Engineers, Glasgow, 1856. — Standard decimal measures of length. — Rifled fire-arms. — N. Y. Industrial Exhibition, 1853.

— New York Industrial exhibition; special report. London, 1854. 8°.

Whitworth, T. Apology for deism. London, 1820. 8°. (B 1681)

Who breaks pays; by [Mrs. W. C. Jenkin]. London, 1861. 2 v. 16°.

Who is the heir; by M. Collins. (*In* **Dublin** univ. mag., v. 64-66 1864-65.)

Who is who? a farce; by T. Williams. (No. 98 *of* **De Witt's** acting plays.)

Who's afraid? or, All about the row in Dame Europa's school; by an Eton boy. London, [18—]. 16°. (E 158)

Who's the dupe; by Mrs. H. Cowley. (*In* **London** stage, v. 1.)

Who's who in 1851, 53, 55, 59; ed. by C. H. Oakes. London. [1851-59]. 4 v. 16°.

Who's who? or, All in a fog: farce. *See* **Williams, T. J.**

Who speaks first? by C. Dance. (*In* **Minor** drama, v. 5.)

Whole duty of man, Author of the. Works. 2d impression. Oxford, Lond., 1687. 2 pts. f°.
Contents. Pt. 1. Whole duty of man; with private devotions. — The causes of the decay of Christian piety. — The gentleman's calling. 2. The ladies' calling. — The government of the tongue. — Art of contentment. — The lively oracles given to us; or, The Christians birthright.
Note. Each tract has a separate title-page.
— *Same.* 3d impression. Oxford, Lond., 1695. 2 pts. f°.
— Causes of the decay of Christian piety. London, 1707. 16°.
— Gentleman's calling. London, 1696. 8°.
— Ladies' calling. New ed. London, 1787. 8°.
— The new whole duty of man; made easy for the present age; with devotions. Trenton, 1809. 8°.

Whole world's temperance convention, Metropolitan Hall, N. York, Sept. 1, 2. N. Y., 1853. 8°. (**B 1667**)

Whom shall we hang; the Sebastopol inquiry. London, 1855. 8°.

Whooping-cough. BUTTER, W. Treatise on the kink-cough. London, 1773. 8°. (**B 865**)
— ANIMADVERSIONS on [Butter's] Treatise. London, 1774. 8°. (**B 865**)
— WATERHOUSE, B. Essay on whooping cough, *etc.* Boston, 1822. 8°.

Why are we at war with Russia? a letter to the Earl of Aberdeen; by an East Anglian. London, 1854. 8°. (**B 1534**)

Why did you die? a petite comedy, by C. J. Mathews. (*In* **Webster, B.** Acting nat. dr., v. 2. 1838.)

Why Johnny didn't interfere; answer to 'The fight at Dame Europa's school'. London, 1871. 16°. (**E 158**)

Why Paul Ferroll killed his wife; by C. W. Clive. N. Y., 1862. 12°.

Whymper, Edward. Ascent of Mont Pelvoux. (*In* **Ball, J.** Peaks, passes, *etc.*, 2d ser., v. 2. 1862.)
— Scrambles amongst the Alps, 1860-69. London, 1871. 8°.
— *Same.* 2d ed. London, 1871. 8°.

Whymper, Frederick. Travel and adventure in Alaska; [with] app. cont. Indian dialects, *etc.* N. Y., 1869. 8°.

Whyte. *See also* **White.**

Whyte, A. Bruce. Histoire des langues romanes et de leur littérature jusqu'au 14e siècle. Paris, 1841. 3 v. 8°.

Whyte, Adam. Political preaching, *etc.*; letter to W. Dun. Glasgow, 1792. 8°. (**B 1860**)

Whyte, James. Simile. (*In* **Campbell, T.** Spec. of Brit. poets, v. 7. 1819.)

Whytt, Robert, *M.D.* Works. Edin., 1768. 4°.
Contents. Essay on the vital and involuntary motions of animals. — Inquiry into the causes which promote circulation in the small vessels of animals. — Obs. on the sensibility of the parts of men and other animals. — Account of experiments with opium. — Essay on the virtues of lime-water and soap in the cure of the stone. — Appendix to the above, cont. cases of H. Walpole, *etc.* — Essay on the strength of different lime-waters. — Postscript on Lord Walpole's case. — Obs. on the virtue of the Carlsbad waters, *etc.* — Instance of electrical virtue in cure of palsy. — Obs. on the nature of disorders called nervous, hypochondriac, or hysteric. — Cases of effects of blisters in coughs. — Obs. on dropsy in the brain. — *Appendix.* Acc. of an epidemic at Edinburgh, 1758. — Extracts of letters [on] use of the sublimate in cure of phagedænic ulcers.
— Essay on vital and other involuntary motions. Edin., 1751. 8°.
— SELLER, W. Memoir. (*In* **Roy. Soc. of Edin.** Trans., v. 23. 1864.)

Wiadomości krajowe i emigracyjne pismo historyczne i literackie. No. 1-21, 23-29, 31-36. Paryż, 15 lutego-22 grudnia, 1837. 8°. (**E 84**)

Wiard, Norman. Great guns; the cause of their failure and the true method of constructing them. N. Y., 1863. 8°.

Wibald, *abbot of Stablo and Corvey.* Epistolæ. — Notæ Stabulenses. (*In* **Jaffé,** P. Bibl. rer., v. 1. 1864.)

Wiborg, *Ridder.* (*In* **Copenhagen.** *K. Com. f. Olds. Opb.* Antiq. Ann., v. 3, pt. 2. 1820.)

Wiboroda, *St., d.* 925. HARTMANNUS. Vita S. W. — HEPIDANNUS. Vita. (*In* **Acta** sanct., v. 14. 1866.)

Wicbertus. SIGEBERTUS *Gemblacensis.* (*In* **Pertz, G. H.** Mon. Germ., Ser., v. 8. 1848.)

Wiccamicus, *pseud.* Elegy on the death of G. Canning. London, 1827. 12°. (**C 201**)

Wicheringe, Barthold. Groninga dominium; G. Blaeuw excudit. Amst., [16—]. (**E 78,** no. 66)

Wichern, Immanuel. LIEFDE, J. de. The Rauhe Haus at Horn. (*In his* Romance of charity. 1867.)
— STEVENSON, W. F. (*In his* Praying and working. 1862.)

Wichmann, Burchard von. BULGARIN, T. W. Erinnerung an W. (*In his* Werke, v. 1. 1828.)

Wichmann, Gottfried Joachim. Heman über die Unsterblichkeit der Seele nach mosaischen Grundsätzen; in drei Gesprächen. Lpz., 1773. 16°.

Wicked justice, The, outwitted; and the remarkable dream of his grand-daughter. London, [17—?]. 12°. (**C 248**)

Wickes, *Rev.* Thomas. The Son of man. Boston, *Amer. Tract Soc.*, [1868]. 16°.

Wickham, Henry Lewis, *and* **Cramer,** J. A. Dissertation on the passage of Hannibal over the Alps. 2d ed. London, 1828. 8°.

Wickham, *Rev.* Hill. Memoir and notes. (*In* **Whalley,** T. S. Journals and correspondence. 1863.)

Wickham, Wm. Correspondence; ed. by his grandson W. Wickham. London, 1870. 2 v. 8°.
Contents. Vol. 1. 1761-96. 2. 1797-1800.

Wickliffe, Robert. Circular to his constituents. *n.t.p.* [1841?]. 8°. (**B 1498**)
— Machiavel's polit. discourses upon the 1st decade of Livy. Louisville, 1840. 8°. (**B 1498**)
— Reply to R. J. Breckenridge. Lexington, 1841. 8°. (**B 1449**)
— *and others.* Supplement to the Kentucky reporter; address of the Fayette County corresponding committee on the proc. in the Senate of Kentucky against the President, Secretary of State, and members of Congress. Lexington, [1828]. 8°. (**E 1106**)
— BRECKINRIDGE, H. J. Speech; reply to W. upon resigning his seat as senator. Lexington, 1840. 8°. (**B 1475**)
— MARSHALL, T. F. Letters in favor of the constitutionality of the law of 1833 prohibiting the importation of slaves into [Kentucky]; reply to W., *etc.* *n.t.p.* [Louisville, 1840.] 8°. (**B 1473**)
— THIRD defence of R. J. Breckinridge, against the calumnies of W. Balt., 1843. 8°. (**B 1449**)

Wicklow mountains, The; by **J. O'Keeffe.** (*In his* Dramatic works, v. 2. 1798.)

Wickram, Joerg. Rollwagenbüchlein. Lpz., 1865. 16°. (Kurz, H. Deutsche Bibliothek, v. 7.)

Wicksteed, Thomas. Effective power of high-pressure expansive condensing steam engines. (*In* **Inst. of Civil Engin.** Trans., v. 1, 2. 1842.)

Wiclif, John. Select English works; ed. by T. Arnold. Oxford, 1869. 3 v. 8°.
Contents. Vol. 1. Sermons on the Gospels for Sundays and festivals. 2. Sermons on the ferial Gospels and Sunday epistles. — Væ octuplex. — Mynystris in the Chirche. 3. Super cantica sacra. — The ten comaundementis. — The pater noster. — Ave Maria. — The Apostles' creed. — The five outer wits. — The seven deadly sins. — The seven werkys of mercy bodyly and gostly. — Five questions on love. — The sufficiency of Holy Scripture. — Wedded men and wifis. — De stipendiis ministrorum. — A short rule of life. — Simonists and apostates. — Church temporalities. — De precationibus sacris Lincolniensis. — Vita sacerdotum. — De pontificum Romanorum schismate. — The grete sentence of curs. — The Church and her members. — Fifty heresies and errors of friars. — De blasphemia. — De apostasia. — Seven heresies. — Octo in quibus seducuntur simplices Christiani. — The twenty-five articles. — The eucharist. — Letter to Pope Urban. — Petition to the King and Parliament.
— Apology for Lollard doctrines; with introd. and notes by J. H. Todd. London, 1842. 4°. (Camden Soc., v. 20.)
— BOEHRINGER, F. Johannes von Wykliffe. (*In his* Die Kirche Christi in Biographieen, 2r B., 4e Abth., 1. H. 1856.)

— Fox, T. (*In* **Wordsworth,** C. Ecclesiastical biog., v. 1. 1839.)
— Gilpin, W. (*In his* Lives of the reformers. 1814.)
— Hus, J. Tenor appellationis ab Archiepiscopo Pragensi, contra combustionem librorum Wicleff. — Actus pro defensione libri Wicleff de trinitate. — Replica contra J. Stokes Wicleñ calumniatorem. — Defensio Wicleff. (*In his* Historia et monumenta, v. 1. 1715.) — Oxford University. Testimonium Universitatis Oxoniensis de doctrina et vita Wicleff. (*In* v. 2. 1715.)
— King, W. Reflections upon Varillas's 'History of heresy' as far as relates to W. (*In his* Works, v. 1. 1776.)
— Malden, H. (*In his* Distinguished men of modern times, v. 1. 1838. Lib. ent. knl., v. 37; v. 1. 1840. Harper's fam. lib., v. 123.)
— Milman, H. H. (*In his* Hist. of Latin Christianity, v. 6. 1855.)
— Netter, T. Fasciculi zizaniorum magistri J. Wyclif cum tritico; ed. by W. W. Shirley. London, 1858. 8°. (Chron. and mem.)
— Pauli, R. (*In his* Pictures of old England. 1861.)
— Vaughan, R. Life and opinions of W. London, 1828. 2 v. 8°.

Wicquefort, Abraham van. Rights, privileges, *etc.*, of embassadors. 2d ed. London, 1740. f°.
— Niceron, J. P. (*In his* Mém., v. 38. 1737.)

Widdrington, Wm., *4th Baron of Widdrington.* Answer to articles of impeachment. (*In* **Several answers.** 1716.)

Wide, wide world; by E. Witherell [S. Warner]. N. Y., 1851. 2 v. 12°.

Widely different account of the fight in Dame Europa's school; by an old boy. London, 1871. 16°. **(E 158)**

Wido. *See* **Guido.**

Widow, The; by **F. Beaumont** and **J. Fletcher.** (*In their* Works, v. 4. 1844.)

Widow, The. (*In* **Dodsley,** R. Col. of old plays, v. 12. 1827.)

Widow, The; by **T. Middleton.** (*In his* Works, v. 3. 1840.)

Widow, The; a drama, by **B. Jonson** and others. (*In* **Scott,** *Sir* W. Anc. Brit. dr., v. 3. 1810.)

Widow hunt, A; comedy, by J. S. Coyne. (No. 12 *of* **De Witt's** acting plays.)

Widower, The; by J. P. Smith. N. Y., 1871. 12°.

Widows. *See* **Suttee.**

Widow's son, The; a sketch from real life, by R. C. Waterston. Boston, 1843. 8°. **(B 1177)**

Widow's tears; by G. Chapman. (*In* **Dodsley,** R. Col., v. 6. 1780.)

Widow's victim, The; by C. Selby. (*In* **Minor** dr., v. 3.)

Widukind. Res gestæ Saxonicæ, 919–973. (*In* **Pertz,** G. H. Mon. Germ., Scr., v. 3. 1849.)

Wie das Volk spricht; sprichwörtliche Redensarten. 4e verm. Aufl. Stuttgart, 1862. 16°.

Wied-Neuwied, Maximilian Alexander Philipp, *Prinz* von. *See* **Maximilian Alexander Philipp,** *Prinz von Wied-Neuwied.*

Wiedemann, Christian Rudolf Wilhelm. Modern English poems. Vol. 2. Kiel, 1816. 8°.
Contents. Vol. 2. **Byron,** G. G. N., *Baron Byron.* Lara. — **Scott,** *Sir* W. Lady of the lake. — **Carr,** *Sir* J. Miscel. poems. — **Wordsworth,** W. Poems. — **Scott,** *Sir* W. Field of Waterloo. — **Byron,** G. G. N., *Baron Byron.* Ode to N. Buonaparte.

Wiedenbrueck. Moeser, J. Stiftung des Collegiatstifts in W. (*In his* Sämmt. Werke, v. 9. 1858.)

Wiederkehrende griechische Kaiser, Der; von **L. Tieck.** (*In his* Gesam. Novellen, v. 6. 1853.)

Wieer, Wm. Chauncy, C. The horrid nature of murder; sermon, Nov. 19, execution of W. Wieer. Boston, 1754. 8°. **(C 43)**

Wiegmann, Rudolph. Andresen, A. (*In his* Die deutschen Maler Radirer, v. 2. 1867.)

Wieland, Christoph Martin. Sämmtliche Werke. Lpz., 1824–26. 49 v. 16°.
Contents. Vol. 1. Die Natur der Dinge. — Moralische Briefe. 2. Anti-Ovid. — Der Frühling. — Erzählungen: Balsora; — Zemin und Gulindy; — Serena; — Der Unzufriedne; — Melinde; — Selim und Selima. — Briefe von Verstorbenen an hinterlassene Freunde. 3. Prüfung Abrahams. — Hymne auf Gott. — Psalmen. — Erinnerungen an eine Freundin. — Kritik der Zeit über Wielands Werke in dessen erster Periode. 4. Cyrus. — Araspes und Panthea. 5, 6. Don Sylvio von Rosalva. 7. Nadine. — Erdenglück. — Celia an Damon. — Komische Erzählungen: Diana und Endymion; — Das Urtheil des Paris; — Aurora und Cefalus. — Bruchstücke von Psyche. — Aspasia. — Kombabus, oder was ist Tugend? — Das Leben, ein Traum. 8. Idris und Zenide. — Ueber romantische Poesie, Mährchen, und Feen-Mährchen. 9–11. Geschichte des Agathon. 12. Musarion. — Die Grazien. — Der verklagte Amor. — Koxkox und Kikequetzel. 13. Nachlass des Diogenes von Sinope. — Gedanken über eine alte Aufschrift. 14. Der neue Amadis. 15. Der neue Amadis. — Kritik über Wieland's Werke in dessen zweyter Periode. 16, 17. Der Goldne Spiegel. 18. Geschichte des weisen Danischmend. 19, 20. Geschichte der Abderiten. 21. Die erste Liebe. — Sixt und Klärchen. — Liebe und Liebe. — Das Wintermährchen. — Das Sommermährchen. — Geron der Adeliche. — Schach Lolo. 22. Pervonte, oder die Wünsche. — Der Vogelsang oder die drei Lehren. — Klelia und Sinibald. — Hann und Gulpenheh. — Die Wasserkufe. — Gedichte an Olympia. 23, 24. Oberon. — Ueber das romantische Epos. 25. Lady Johanna Gray. — Klementina von Porretta. — Die Wahl des Herkules. — Alceste. 26. Rosemunde. — Pandora. — Singgedicht. — Das Urtheil des Midas. — Ueber Wieland's dramatische Werke. — Nachtrag zur Geschichte der schönen Rosemunde. 27. Bonifaz Schleichers Jugendgeschichte. — Der Stein der Weisen. — Die Salamandrin und die Bildsäule. — Göttergespräche. — Gespräche im Elysium. 28. Menander und Glycerion. — Krates und Hipparchia. 29. Das Hexameron von Rosenhain. 30. Sympathien. — Gesicht des Mirza. — Gesicht von einer Welt unschuldiger Menschen. — Platonische Betrachtungen über den Menschen. — Was ist eine schöne Seele? — Was ist Wahrheit? — Filosofie als Kunst zu leben und Heilkunst der Seele betrachtet. 31. Ueber J. J. Rousseau. — Reise des Priesters Abulfauaris ins innere Afrika. — Bekenntnisse des Abulfauaris. — Ueber die Ausbildung der menschlichen Gattung. — Ueber die Abnahme des menschlichen Geschlechts. — Auszüge aus Jacob Forsters Reise um die Welt. 32. Gebrauch der Vernunft in Glaubenssachen. — Hang der Menschen an Magie zu Glauben. — Euthanasia. 33, 34. Peregrinus Proteus. — Antworten auf die Anfragen eines vorgeblichen Weltbürgers. 35. Agathodämon. 36–39. Aristipp. 40. Stilpon. — Göttliche Recht der Obrigkeit. — Athenion, genannt Aristion. — Beitrag zu Deutschlands höchstem Flor. — Gespräche über einige neueste Weltbegebenheiten. — Mark-Aurel an die Römer. — Eine Lustreise ins Elysium. — Göttergespräche. — Sechs Antworten auf sechs Fragen. — Rechte und Pflichten der Schriftsteller. — Das Geheimniss des Kosmopoliten-Ordens. 41. Französische Revoluzion. 42. Gespräche unter vier Augen. 43. Die pythagorischen Frauen. — Ehrenrettung der Aspasia, Julia, und Faustina.—Nikolas Flamel, Paul Lukas, und der Derwisch von Brussa. — Alexander Dow's Nachrichten von den Fakirn in Ostindien. — Briefe über eine Anekdote aus J. J. Rousseau's Leben. — Ueber die ältesten Zeitkürzungsspiele. — Die Aeropetomanie. — Die Aeronauten. 44. Timoklea. — Theages. — Verhältniss des Angenehmen und Schönen zum Nützlichen. — Sendschreiben an einen jungen Dichter. — Die Kunst aufzuhören. — Die sterbende Polyxena des Euripides. — Was ist Hoch-deutsch? — Die Titanomachie. 45. Die Bunkliade. — Ueber das deutsche Singspiel. — Die Perspektiv in den Werken der griechischen Maler. — Ueber die Ideale der griechischen Künstler. 46–49. Miscellaneen.
— Geschichte der Abderiten. Carlsruhe, 1783. 2 v. 8°.
— Histoire du sage Danischmend. (*In* **Biblioth.** univ. des romans, Nouv., v. 38. 1801.) — Royaume de Zatoïaba. (*In* v. 50. 1801.) — La pierre philosophale. (*In* v. 69. 1803.) — Les graces. (*In* v. 75. 1803.)
— History of Agathon; trans. London, 1773. 4 v. 12°.
— Neueste Gedichte, 1770–1777. Neue Aufl. Carlsruhe, 1777. 8°.
— Oberon; ein Gedicht. Carlsruhe, 1782. 8°.
— *Eng.* Oberon; [tr.] by W. Sotheby. 2d ed. London, 1805. 2 v. 16°.
— *Same.* 1st Amer. from 3d London ed. Boston, 1810. 2 v. 12°.
— Philosophy considered as the art of life. — Letter to a young poet. — On the relation of the agreeable and the useful. — From the dialogues of the gods. (*In* **Hedge,** F. H. Prose writers of Germany. 1848.)
— Böttiger, C. W. C. M. Wieland nach seinen eigenen Aeusserungen. (*In* **Historisches** Taschenbuch, 1839.)

— Goethe, J. W. von. Rede zum Andenken Wielands. (*In his* Sämmt. Werke, v. 4. 1854.)
— Wranitzky, P. Oberon, König der Elfen; ein Singspiel nach Wielands Oberon. Berlin, 1792. 8°. (D 14)
Wieland; or, The transformation, by C. B. Brown. Boston, 1827. 12°. (Novels, v. 1.)
Wieland der Schmied. (*In* **Simrock, C.** Heldenbuch, v. 4. 1843.)
Wien. *See* **Vienna.**
Wier's Cave, *Va.* Jones, C. Description of Wier's Cave. Albany, 1815. 8°. (B 444)
Wiertz, Antoine. Laveleye, E. de. (*In* **Revue** d. D. Mondes, déc. 1866.)
Wiese, Ludwig Adolf. German letters on English education; tr. by W. D. Arnold. London, 1854. 16°.
— Das höhere Schulwesen in Preussen. Berlin, 1864-74. 3 v. 8°.
Wiesel, Pauline, *geb.* Cesar. Briefe. (*In* **Varnhagen von Ense,** K. A. Aus dem Nachlass, v. 2. 1867.)
Wiesener, —. L'ile de Crète de [G.] Perrot. (*In* **Paris.** Soc. de Géog. Bul., 5e sér., v. 14. 1867.)
Wiesinger, J. T. August. Biblical commentary on the New Testament, v. 5, 6. *See* **Olshausen, H.**
Wiessner, J. Meteorological observations and results in the District of Columbia. (*In* **Smithsonian Inst.** Report, 1857.)
Wiet, Emile. Itinéraire en Albanie et en Roumélie. (*In* **Paris.** Soc. de Géog. Bul., 5e sér., v. 16. 1868.)
Wietersheim, Karl August Wilhelm Eduard von. Historische Erinnerungen aus Friaul und Dalmatien. (*In* **Historische** Zeitschrift, v. 13. 1865.)
Wife. Wife, The; advice and directions for all conditions of the marriage state. 1st Amer. ed. Boston, 1806. 12°.
— Alcott, W. A. The young wife; or, Duties of women in the marriage relation. [1837.] 8th ed. Boston, 1839. 16°.
See also **Marriage.**
Wife, The; a tale of Mantua; by J. S. **Knowles.** (*In his* Select works, v. 2. 1833.)
Wife for a month, A; by F. **Beaumont** and J. **Fletcher.** (*In their* Works, v. 9. 1845.)
Wife of two husbands, The; a drama, by W. Dunlap. N. Y., 1804. 16°. (D 43)
Wife's secret, The; [a] play, by G. W. Lovell. (No. 55 *of* **Spencer's** univ. stage.)
Wife's sister, The; by Mrs. Hubback. London, 1851. 3 v. 12°.
Wife's story. (*In* **Littell's** living age, v. 47. 1855.)
Wiffen, Benjamin Barron. Life and writings of Juán de Valdes; with trans. of his cx considerations, by J. T. Betts. Lond., 1865. 8°.
Wiffen, Jeremiah Holme. Essay on Spanish poetry. — Life of Garcilasso de la Vega. (*In* **Vega,** G. de la. Works. 1823.)
— Historical memoirs of the House of Russell, from the time of the Norman conquest. London, 1833. 2 v. 8°.
— Life of Tasso. (*In* **Tasso,** T. Jerusalem delivered, v. 1. 1826; 1846.)
Wigan, Alfred. A model of a wife; farce. (No. 51 *of* **De Witt's** acting plays.)
Wigan, Arthur Ladbroke. The duality of the mind; structure, functions, and diseases of the brain. London, 1844. 8°.
Wigan, Horace. Always intended; a comedy. (No. 25 *of* **Spencer's** univ. stage.)
Wigand *von Marburg.* Chronik. (*In* **Hirsch,** T. Script. rer. Pruss., v. 2. 1863.) — Zwei Fragmente der Reimchronik. (*In* v. 4. 1870.)
Wiggers, Gustav Friedrich. Versuch einer pragmatischen Darstellung des Augustinismus und Pelagianismus nach ihrer geschichtlichen Entwickelung. Hamb., 1833. 2 v. 8°.
Wiggers, Julius. Kirchengeschichte Mecklenburgs. Parchim, Ludwigslust, 1840. 8°.
— Kirchliche Statistik. Hamburg u. Gotha, 1842-43. 2 v. 8°.
Wiggin, C. P. MacLean and Lawrence's sectional map of Kansas Territory. Pittsburgh, 1857.

Wiggins, John. The practice of embanking lands from the sea a means of profitable employment of capital. London, *Weale*, 1852. 12°.
Wigglesworth, Edward, *D.D., b.* 1693, *d.* 1765. The blessedness of the dead who die in the Lord; sermon, Apr. 6, upon the news of the death of T. Hollis, of London. Boston, 1731. 8°. (B 234, 867, C 310)
— Discourse conc. the duration of the punishment of the wicked in a future state, Apr. 24. Boston, 1729. 8°. (B 78, 86, 234, 867)
— The doctrine of reprobation; substance of lectures in Harvard Coll. Boston, 1763. 8°. (B 51, 143, 234, 599, 1238)
— Enquiry into the truth of the imputation of the guilt of Adam's first sin to his posterity. Boston, 1738. 8°. (B 35, 234)
— Faithful servant of Christ rewarded; sermon [on] B. Wadsworth. Boston, 1737. 8°. (B 79)
— Letter to G. Whitefield in reply to his answer to the college testimony against him and his conduct; added the President's [E. Holyoke's] answer to things charged upon him by G. W. as inconsistencies. Boston, 1745. 4°. (B 70, 583)
— A seasonable caveat against believing every spirit; two lectures, Camb., Apr. 22, 29. Boston, 1735. 8°. (B 234, C 44)
— Some distinguishing characters of extraordinary and ordinary ministers of Christ; two lectures, Harvard Coll., Nov. 12, 19. Boston, 1754. 8°. (C 44)
— Some evidences of divine inspiration of the Scriptures of the Old Testament; lecture, Harvard Coll., June 24. Boston, 1755. 8°. (B 37, 147, 1305)
— Some thoughts upon the infallibility claimed by the Church of Rome; Dudleian lecture, Cambridge, May 11. Boston, 1757. 8°. (B 51, 67, 152, 234)
— The sovereignty of God; two lectures, at Harvard Coll. Boston, 1741. 8°. (C 16)
— *Funeral sermon on.* 1765. *See* **Appleton, H.** (B 17, 212, 850); — **Taylor, J.** (B 17, 212, 471, 850)
Wigglesworth, Edward, *D. D., b.* 1732, *d.* 1794. Authority of tradition considered; [Dudleian lecture,] Harvard College, Nov. 5, 1777. Boston, 1778. 8°. (B 67, 145, 152, 200, 234)
— Calculations on American population. Boston, 1775. 8°. (B 350)
— Comparative view of thermometrical and barometrical observations at Cambridge. — Observations on the longevity of the inhabitants of Ipswich and Hingham. (*In* **Amer. Acad.** of **Arts** and **Sci.** Mem., v. 1. 1785.) — Table shewing the probability of the duration, the decrement, and the expectation of life in Mass. and N. H. (*In* v. 2. 1793.)
— Hope of immortality; discourse, death of J. Winthrop, Camb. Boston, 1779. 8°. (B 172, 234, 335)
Wigglesworth, Edward. Sketch of the Boston Athenæum. *n.t.p.* [Boston, 1839.] 8°. (E 130)
— *Same.* (*In* **Amer.** quarterly register, Nov. 1839. B 1819)
— Encyclopædia Americana. 1829-33. *See* **Lieber, F.**
Wigglesworth, *Rev.* Michael. The day of doom. N. Y., 1867. 12°.
— Sermons.] MS.
— Dean, J. W. Sketch of the life of W. Albany, 1863. 8°.
Note. From the N. E. genealogical register.
— - *Same.* 2d ed. Albany, 1871. 8°.
Wigglesworth, *Rev.* Samuel. Blessedness of such as trust in Christ; discourse, Ipswich, Mar. 20, [fast] day. Boston, 1755. 8°. (B 335, C 43)
— Essay for reviving religion; sermon, election, May 30. Boston, 1733. 8°. (B 86, 145, 180, 183)
— God's promise to an obedient people of victory; discourse, Ipswich, May 25, [to] soldiers going against Crown Point. Boston, 1755. 8°. (B 335, C 43)
— Pleasures of religion; sermon to a soc. of young men, Ipswich. Boston, 1728. 8°. (C 7)
— View of the inestimable treasure of the Gospel; sermon, Ipswich, Jan. 5, after the funeral of J. Rogers. Boston, 1746. 8°. (B 234)
— *and* **Chipman,** J. Remarks on some points of doctrine [of] W. Balch. Boston, 1746. 4°. (B 24, 45)
— Balch, W. Vindication of some points of doctrine; answer to the 'Remarks' of Wigglesworth and Chipman. Boston, 1746. 8°. (B 45)
Wigham, Eliza. The anti-slavery cause in America, and its martyrs. London, 1863. 8°.
Wight, Andrew. Catalogue of the library of W., sold by J. E. Cooley, June 6. New York, 1864. 8°.

Wight, Danforth Phipps, *M.D.* Memoir of T. Wight of Dedham; with genealogical notices of his descendants, 1637–1840. Boston, 1848. 12°.
— Seaman's medical guide. Boston, 1834. 12°.
Wight, Orlando Williams. The romance of Abelard and Heloise. N. Y., 1853. 12°.
Wight, Samuel F. Adventures in California and Nicaragua, in rhyme. Boston, 1860. 8°.
Wight, Thomas. WIGHT, D. P. Memoir of W. Boston, 1848. 12°.
Wight family. *See, above,* Wight, D. P.
Wight, Isle of. PENNANT, T. Journey from London to the Isle of Wight, [1787]. London, 1801. 2 v. 4°.
— HASSELL, J. Tour of the Isle of Wight, 1790. (*In* **Pinkerton**, J. Col. of voy., v. 2. 1808.)
— GILPIN, W. Picturesque beauties of the I. of W., [1798]. (*In his* Picturesque scenery. 1808.)
— BRAYLEY, E. W., *and* BRITTON, J. (*In* **Beauties of** England, v. 6. 1805.)
— STERLING, J. Isle of Wight, [1828]. (*In his* Essays, v. 2. 1848.)
— BRETTELL, T. Guide to the Isle of Wight. London, 1840. 12°.
— MANTELL, G. A. Geological excursions round the Isle of Wight, [1847]. 3d ed. London, *Bohn*, 1854. 8°.
— NEY, J. N., *prince de la Moskowa.* L'isle de Wight. (*In* **Revue** d. D. Mondes, oct., nov. 1857.)
— HANDBOOK for Surrey, Hampshire, and the Isle of Wight. London, *Murray*, 1865. 12°.
— *Map.* BELLIN, J. N. Carte réduite de l'Isle de Wight et costes voisines. *n.p.*, 1762. (E 87, no. 12.)
Wightman, Joseph M. Annals of the Boston primary school committee to its dissolution, 1818–55. Boston, 1860. 8°.
— Address, dedication of Mechanics' Hall. (*In* **Mass.** Charit. Mechan. Assoc. Dedication. 1860. B 1587)
— *ed.* *See* **Young** mechanic.
Wightwick, George. Remarks on Chubb's 'True gospel of Jesus'. London, 1740. 8°. (B 40, 117)
Wightwick, George. Ancient and modern English Gothic architecture. (*In* **Weale**, J. Quarterly papers on archit., v. 2-4. 1843–45.)
Wigoleis vom Rade. (*In* **Simrock**, K. Deutschen Volksbücher, v. 3. 1846.)
Wigwam, The, and the cabin; by [W. G. Simms]. 1st ser. N.Y., 1845. 12°.
Wikoff, Henry. Adventures of a roving diplomatist. N. Y., 1857. 12°.
— A New Yorker in the foreign office, and his adventures in Paris. London, 1858. 12°.
Wilars *de Honecourt.* Facsimile of the sketch-book of W.; with commentary, *etc.*, by J. B. A. Lassus and J. E. J. Quicherat; tr. and ed. by R. Willis. London, 1859. 4°.
Wilberforce, Edward. Social life in Munich. London, 1863. 12°.
Wilberforce, Robert Isaac. Doctrine of the eucharist. 3d ed. London, 1854. 16°.
— *and* **Wilberforce**, S. Life of W. Wilberforce. London, 1838. 5 v. 8°.
— TAYLOR, J. True doctrine of the eucharist; in refutation of Wilberforce's book. London, 1855. 8°.
Wilberforce, Samuel, *successively Bp. of Oxford and Westminster.* Preface. (*In* **Hopkins**, M. Hawaii. 1862; 1869.)
— Preface. (*In* **Replies** to 'Essays and reviews'. 1862.)
— A reproof of the American church, from [his] History of the Protestant Episc. Church in America. N. Y., 1846. 8°. (B 1476)
— BERRY, P. Review of the Bp. of Oxford's counsel to the American clergy. Wash., 1848. 8°. (B 1477)
— CAMPBELL, G. D., *Duke of Argyll.* The two-fold protest; letter to the Bishop of Oxford. London, 1851. 8°. (B 1232)
— K., C. E. The Bishop of Oxford and Dr. Hampden. London, 1848. 12°. (B 1231)

Wilberforce, Wm. Letter on the abolition of the slave trade to the free holders of Yorkshire. London, 1807. 8°.
— *Same.* 3d ed. London, 1807. 8°. (B 723)
— Letter to Talleyrand on the slave trade, 1814. (*In* **Pamphleteer**, 1815; v. 5 of B 838)
— *French.* Lettre à Talleyrand Périgord, au sujet de la traite des nègres; tr. de l'anglaise. Londres, 1814. 8°. (C 90)
— Practical view of the prevailing religious system of professed Christians. 5th ed. London, 1797. 12°.
— *Same.* 4th Amer. ed. Boston, 1815. 12°.
— Speech, 2d April 1792, on abolition of the slave trade. (*In* **Chapman**, N. Select speeches, v. 5. 1808.)
— Substance of speeches on the clause in the E. India bill for promoting the religious instruction of the natives of India. (*In* **Pamphleteer**, 1814; v. 3 of B 838)
— BAYNE, P. (*In his* Christian life. 1855.)
— BELSHAM, T. Review of W.'s 'Practical view of the prevailing religious system of professed Christians', *etc.* London, 1800. 12°. (Unit. Soc. Prom. Christ. Knowl. Tracts. C 142)
— - *Same.* 3d ed. London, 1813. 8°.
— BROUGHAM, H., *Ld.* (*In his* Statesmen in the time of George III., v. 1. 1839.)
— CLARKSON, T. Strictures on W. and S. Wilberforce's life of W. London, 1838. 8°.
— COLQUHOUN, J. C. Wilberforce, his friends and times. London, 1866. 8°.
— GAMBIER, J. (*In his* Memorials. 1861.)
— EDWARDS, B. Speech at a free conference between the council and assembly of Jamaica, Nov. 19, on Wilberforce's propositions [on] the slave trade. Kingston, 1789. 8°. (B 682, W 16)
— HARFORD, J. S. Recollections of W. London, 1864. 8°.
— MALDEN, H. (*In his* Disting. men of mod. times, v. 4, 1838; v. 40 of Lib. ent. knowl.; v. 2. 1840; v. 124 of Harper's fam. lib.)
— SMITH, W. Letter to W. on the proposed abolition of the slave trade. London, 1807. 12°. (C 114)
— STEPHEN, *Sir* J. (*In his* Essays on eccles. biog., v. 2. 1850.)
— WILBERFORCE, S. *and* R. I. Life of W. London, 1838. 8°.
— *Funeral sermon on.* 1833. *See* **D'Arblay**, A. C. L. (B 1228)
Wilbraham, Frances M. Recollections of Hursley vicarage. (*In* **Yonge**, C. M. Musings over the 'Christian year'. 1871.)
Wilbraham, *Mass.* STEBBINS, R. P. Address, centennial celebration of Wilbraham, 1863. Boston, 1864. 8°.
Wilbrandt, Adolf. Hölderlin, der Dichter des Pantheismus. (*In* **Historisches** Taschenbuch. 1830.)
Wilbrandus *or* **Willebrandus** *comes Hallermendus ab Oldenborg.* Itinerarium Terræ Sanctæ. (*In* **Byzant.** hist. scr., v. 23. 1733.)
Wilbur, Hervey, *D.D.* Discourse, religious education of youth, Homer, Oct. 11. 2d ed. Boston, 1814. 8°. (B 285, 335)
— Female piety demanding assistance; two sermons, Bradford, Jan. 5. Haverhill, 1812. 8°. (B 1305, 1785)
— The pilgrims; sermon, Wendell, Dec. 22, 1820. Wendell, 1821. 8°. (B 1571)
— Short Biblical catechism. 2d ed. with Assembly's catechism. Exeter, 1812. 12°. (C 57)
— *Same, without the* Assembly's catechism. Exeter, 1813. 12°.
Note. The answers in the ed. of 1812 are chiefly references to the Bible.
Wilbur, Homer, *pseud.* Melibœus-Hipponax; the Biglow papers. *See* **Lowell**, J. R.
Wilbur, Jedidiah, *Funeral sermon on.* 1816. *See* **Pomeroy**, J. L. (B 328)
Wilcke, Christian Daniel. Politia naturæ. (*In* **Linné**, C. Amœn. acad., v. 6. 1763.)
Wilcocke, Samuel Hull, *M. D.* History of the viceroyalty of Buenos Ayres. Lond., 1807. 8°.
— A new and complete dictionary of the Eng. and Dutch languages in two parts. London, 1798. 2 v. 8°.
Contents. Vol. 1. English-Dutch. 2. Nederduitsch-Englich.

Wilcocks, Joseph. Roman conversations; a short description of the antiquities of Rome. 2d ed. London, 1797. 2 v. 8°.

Wilcoks, Thomas. A choice drop of honey from the rock Christ. 10th ed. Boston, 1743. 12°. (C 120)

Wilcox. *See also* Willcox.

Wilcox, Cadmus Marcellus. Rifles and rifle practice. N. Y., 1861. 12°.

Wilcox, *Rev.* Carlos. Sermon; unreasonableness and danger of indecision. (*In* National preacher, v. 2. 1827.)

Wilcox, Daniel. FIELD, The, cleared of [W.'s] 'Noble stand'. London, 1720. 8°. (B 110)

Wild, Charles. Specimens of eccles. architecture of the Middle Ages, from cathedrals of England. London, [1828-31]. f°.

Wild (*Lat.* Ferus), Johann. Opuscula varia. Lugd., 1567. 8°.

Contents. In tria posteriora libri primi Esdræ capita. — In historiam Evangelicam, de muliere peccatrice. — In Jonam prophetam. — In parabola Luc. 15 de filio prodigo, cum aliis tribus in provinciali synodo Moguntinensi habitis. — In Psalmum 31 et 66. — In Salomonis Ecclesiasten. — In threnos Hieremiæ. — Examen ordinandorum, cum expositione canonis Missæ. — Precationum formulæ.

— NICERON, J. P. (*In his* Mém., v. 26. 1734.)

Wild Dick and good little Robin; [by L. M. Sargent]. Boston, 1833. 24°. (D 18)

Wild gallant, The; a comedy; by J. Dryden. (*In his* Works, v. 2. 1808.)

Wild-goose-chase, The; by F. Beaumont and J. Fletcher. (*In their* Dram. works, v. 5. 1778.)

Wild huntress, The; by M. Reid. (*In* Chambers' journal, n.s., v. 14. 1860.)

Wild Ireland; by B. Donbavand. Phila., 1871. 8°.

Wild Irish boy; by D. J. Murphy [pseud. for C. R. Maturin]. N. Y., 1808. 2 v. 12°.

Wild Irish girl; by Miss Owenson [Lady S. Morgan]. Phila., 1822. 2 v. 18°.

Wild Nell, the White Mountain girl; by Mrs. H. J. Moore. N. Y., 1860. 12°.

Wild oats; by J. O'Keeffe. (*In his* Dram. works, v. 2. 1798; — *and in* Sargent, E. Mod. stand. drama., v. 31.)

Wild scenes in the forest; by C. F. Hoffman. London, [1838?]. 2 v. in 1. 12°.

Wild sports of the West; [by W. H. Maxwell]. London, 1822. 2 v. 8°.

— *Same.* New ed. London, 1850. 16°.

Wild western scenes; by J. B. Jones. New ser. Richmond, 1863. 12°.

Wilda, Wilhelm Eduard. Geschichte des Strafrechts der Germanen. Halle, 1842. 8°.

— Das Gildenwesen im Mittelalter. Berlin, [1831]. 8°.

Wildberg, Christian Friedrich Ludwig. Bibliotheca medicinæ publicæ. Berolini, 1819. 2 v. 4°.

Note. Vol. 1 has the second title-page, Bibliotheca medicinæ forensis; 2 is Bibliotheca medicinæ politicæ.

Wildberger, John. Orthopædic institution for the cure of every species of deformity of the human frame, in Bamberg, Bavaria. *n.t.p.* [Bamberg, 1852.] 4°. (A 63)

Wilde, George C. Oration, July 4. Newburyport, 1823. 8°. (B 1168)

Wilde, *Sir* James Plaisted. Address on jurisprudence and amendment of the law. (*In* Nat. Assoc. Prom. Soc. Sci. Trans., 1864.)

Wilde, John. Address to the Soc. of the Friends of the People. London, 1793. 8°.

Wilde, Richard Henry. Conjectures and researches concerning the love, madness, *etc.*, of Torquato Tasso. N. Y., 1842. 2 v. 12°.

— Hesperia; a poem; ed. by [W. C. Wilde]. Boston, 1867. 12°.

— Poems. (*In* Campbell, T. Brit. poets, v. 4. 1819.)

— REUMONT, A. Necrologia di Wilde. (*In* Archivio stor. ital., app., v. 6. 1848.)

Wilde, Samuel Sumner, *Funeral sermon on.* 1855. *See* Peabody, E. (B 1228)

Wilde, *Sir* Wm. Robert. The closing years of Dean Swift's life. Dublin, 1849. 8°.

Wilden, Die; Singspiel. *See* Allairac. (D 14)

Wilder, Burt Green, *M.D.* Extra digits. (*In* Mass. Med. Soc. Pub., v. 2, no. 3. 1867.)

— On morphology and teleology, especially in the limbs of mammalia. (*In* Boston Soc. of Nat. Hist. Mem., v. 1, pt. 1. 1866-68.)

Wilder, Charles, *M.D.* Pulmonary consumption. (*In* Mass. Med. Soc. Med. comm., v. 7. 1848.) — BIOGRAPHICAL notice of W. (*In* v. 8. 1854.)

Wilder, David. History of Leominster, 1701-1852. Fitchburg, 1853. 12°.

Wilder, *Rev.* H. A. Description of Natal. (*In* Amer. Geog. Statist. Soc. Bul., v. 1, pt. 3. 1854.)

Wilder, John. Epigrammata numismate annuo dignata, Cantab. *n.p.*, 1823. 8°. (B 1236)

Wilder, Marshall Pinckney. Address before the Hampshire Agric. Soc., Oct. 22, 1851; with transactions of the Society. Amherst, 1851. 8°.

— Addresses [before] the New Eng. Hist. Geneal. Soc., Jan. 1, 16, 1868-72, with reports of proceedings. Boston, 1868-72. 5 pam. 8°. (B 1962)

— *and others.* Culture and products of the vine. (*In* U. S. *Commissioners for Paris Expos.*, 1867. Reports, v. 3.)

Wilder, Sampson Vryling Stoddard. Records from [his] life. N. Y., [1865]. 12°. (Amer. Tract Soc.)

Wilderness, *Va.* U. S. *Quartermaster Gen.* Roll of honor II: Names of soldiers found on the battle-field of the Wilderness, Va. Wash., 1865. 8°. (B 1954)

Wildes, George, *et al.*, *vs.* Parker, T. D. AUSTIN, I. J. Argument for the plaintiffs on the special plea in bar of the jurisdiction. *n.t.p.* [1840.] 8°. (B 1440)

Wildes, *Rev.* George Dudley (?) Address at 50th anniv. of the N. England Guards. (*In* Boston N. E. Guards. Proc., 1862.)

— Memoir of Capt. W. Nichols. (*In* Essex Inst. Hist. col., v. 6. 1864.)

Wildfang, Der; von A. v. Kotzebue. (*In his* Theater, v. 6. 1840.)

Wildrake, *pseud.* The cracks of the day. [London, 1841.] 8°.

Wilds, Wm. Art of building cottages and houses for the humbler classes. London, 1835. 8°.

Wiley, *Rev.* Charles. 'Honor to whom honor'; discourse, commemorative of D. Webster, Oct. 31, in the Reformed Dutch Church. Utica, 1852. 8°. (B 1728)

Wiley, Henry Gustavus, *M. D.* BIOGRAPHICAL notice of W. (*In* Mass. Med. Soc. Med. comm., v. 7. 1848.)

Wiley, John. *See* American book circular. 1843.

Wilfred Cumbermede; by G. Macdonald. (*In* St. Paul's mag., v. 7-8. 1870-71; — *and in* Littell's living age, v. 108, 109. 1871.)

Wilfrid I., *St.*, *Abp. of York*, *d.* 709. EADMERUS *Cantuariensis.* (*In* Acta sanct., v. 12. 1866.)

— LIFE of St. Wilfrid. (*In* Lives of the Eng. saints, v. 8. 1844.)

Wilhelm de derde. *See* Rotgans, L.

Wilhelm Meisters Lehrjahre; von J. W. von Goethe. (*In his* Werke, v. 3, 4. 1816; *and in his* Sämmt. Werke, v. 3. 1854.) — Wilhelm Meisters Wanderjahre. (*In his* Werke, v. 26. 1821; *and in his* Sämmt. Werke, v. 3. 1854.)

— *Eng.* Wilhelm Meister's apprenticeship and travels; [tr. by T. Carlyle]. Boston, 1828. 3 v. (v. 1 w.). 18°.

— *Same.* New ed. London, 1842. 3 v. 8°.

— *Same, in part.* Wilhelm Meister's travels. (*In* Carlyle, T. German romance, v. 4. 1827.)

Wilhelmes *of Tudela.* *See* Guilelmus *Tudelensis* (p. 1298).

Willhemi, *properly* Zechmeister, Alexander Victor. Einer muss heirathen: Lustspiel, von W.; Eigensinn, Lustspiel von R. Benedix. Boston, 1865. 8°.

Wilhelmina, *sister of Frederic the Great.* *See* Frederica Sophia Wilhelmina, *daughter of* Frederic William, *of Prussia, Markräfin von Baireuth.*

Wilhelmina Dorothea Carolina, *Queen Consort of Geo.* II. MATHER, S. Funeral disc., Mar. 23, 1737/38. Boston, 1738. 8°. (B 228, 853)

Wilhelmus. *See* Guilelmus (p. 1298).

Wilhite, Abram, *and others.* Investigator; or, A defence of the order, government, and economy of the United Society called Shakers against sundry charges and legislative proceedings; by the society of believers at Pleasant Hill, Ky. Lexington, Ky., 1828, *repr.* N. Y., 1846. 12°.

Wilken, Friedrich. Andronikus Komnenus. (*In* **Historisches** Taschenbuch, 1831.)

— Geschichte der alten heidelbergischen Büchersammlungen. Heidelberg, 1817. 12°.

— Ueber die Partheyen der Rennbahn, vornehmlich im byzantinischen Kaiserthum. (*In* **Berlin. Ak. d. Wiss.** Abh., 1827-1830; — *and in* **Historisches** Taschenbuch, 1830.)

— Rerum ab Alexio I, Joanne, Manuele, et Alexio II Comnenis gestarum libri quatuor. Heidelbergæ, 1811. 8°.

— Ueber die Verfassung, den Ursprung, und die Geschichte der Afghanen. (*In* **Berlin. Ak. d. Wiss.** Abh., 1818-19.) — Ueber die Verhältnisse der Russen zum byzantinischen Reiche in dem Zeitraume vom 6n bis zum 12n Jahrhundert. (*In* 1829.) — Ueber die venetianischen Consuln zu Alexandrien im 15n, 16n Jahrhunderte. (*In* 1831.) — Geschichte der Sultane aus dem Geschlechte Bujeh nach Mirchond. (*In* 1835.)

Wilker, George, *Jun.*, *Funeral sermon on.* 1817. *See* **Cushing**, J. (B 1651)

Wilkes, —, *D.D.* CORDNER, J. Christ the son of God; disc., review of [W.'s] sermon 'Who is Christ'. Montreal, 1851. 8°. (B 1286)

Wilkes, Charles, *Rear. Adm. U. S. N.* Charts of George's Shoal and Bank. N. Y., 1837. 1 sheet.

— Effects of the areas of oceanic temperatures. (*In* **Amer. Assoc.** Proc., v. 5. 1851.) — Zodiacal light. (*In* v. 11. 1858.)

— Narrative of the U. S. exploring expedition, 1838-42. *n.p.*, 1845-58. 23 v. (v. 7, 8, pt. 1, 11, 13, 14, 16-19, 21-23 w.). f° *and* 4°, *and* 10 (4 w.) Atlases f°.

Note. For contents *see* **United States.** *Exploring Expedition* (p. 3064).

— *Another ed. of* Vol. 1-5. Phila., 1850. 5 v. 8°.

— *Same.* London, 1852. 2 v. 8°.

— *Another ed. of* Vol. 9. New ed., by J. C. Hall. London, *Bohn*, 1851. 8°.

— Synopsis of the exped.; added, list of officers and scientific corps. Wash., 1842. 8°.

— *vs.* **S. Dinsman.** *n.p.*, 1848. 8°. (B 1440)

— HEADLEY, J. T. (*In his* Farragut and our naval commanders. 1867.)

Wilkes, George. McClellan from Ball's Bluff to Antietam. N. Y., 1863. 8°.

Wilkes, John, *b.* 1727, *d.* 1797. Correspondence; [with] memoirs, by J. Almon. London, 1805. 5 v. 12°.

Contents. Vol. 1. 1727-81. 2. 1763-66. 3. 1762-69. 4. 1769-84. 5. 1768-97.

— Letter to J. Hancock, May 15, 1783. (*In* **Mass. Hist. Soc.** Proc., 1864-65.)

— Letter to S. Johnson. [London,] 1770. 8°. (B 591)

— Letter to the Duke of Grafton. 3d ed. London, 1767. 8°. (B 674)

— Observations on the papers relative to the rupture with Spain. London, 1762. 8°. (B 746)

See also **North Briton**, The.

— AUTHENTICK account of the proceedings against W. London *printed*, Boston *reprinted* 1763. 8°. (B 592, 698, 762)

— BRITANNIA'S intercession for the deliverance of W. 6th ed. London *printed*, Boston, *reprinted* 1769. 8°. (C 70)

— BROUGHAM, H., *Ld.* (*In his* Statesmen of the times of George III., v. 3. 1843.)

— DYSON, J. Case of the late election for Middlesex. — GRENVILLE, G. Speech on the motion for expelling W. — LETTER to Grenville in answer to his speech. — LETTER on the public conduct of W. — FAIR trial of the important question. (*In* **Col. of scarce tracts**, v. 3. 1787. B 606)

— HISTORICUS, *pseud.* The sham-patriot unmasked. Concord, 1805. 8°. (B 427)

— JOHNSON, S. The false alarm. London, 1770. 8°. (B 591)

— REFLECTIONS on the case of Wilkes and on the rights of the people to elect their own representatives; added, the case of Walpole. London, 1768. 8°. (B 591)

— WATSON, J. S. Biographies of J. Wilkes and W. Cobbett. Edin., 1870. 8°.

Wilkes, John. Universal British directory. 1797. *See* **Barfoot**, P.

Wilkes. *See also* **Wilks.**

Wilkes' spirit of the times; Sept. 13, 1862 - Dec. 24, 1864. N. Y., 1862-64. 2 v. f°.

Wilkeson, Samuel. Concise history of the commencement, progress, *etc.*, of the American colonies in Liberia. Wash., 1839. 8°. (B 1484)

Wilkie, *Rev.* D. On length and space. (*In* **Lit. and Hist. Soc. of Quebec.** Trans., v. 2. 1831.)

Wilkie, *Sir* David. Quelques extraits de sa correspondance. (*In* **Gazette** des beaux-arts, v. 27. 1869.)

— CUNNINGHAM, A. Life of W. London, 1843. 3 v. 8°.

— DESROSIERS, J. (*In* **Gazette** des beaux-arts, v. 24. 1868.)

— HAYDON, B. R. (*In his* Lectures on painting, v. 2. 1846.)

— THOMSON, Mrs. K. B. (*In her* Recollections of literary characters, v. 2. 1854.)

— TUCKERMAN, H. T. (*In his* Biog. essays. 1857.)

Wilkie, Francis B. Davenport, past and present. Davenport, 1858. 8°.

Wilkie, James. Plea for short apprenticeships. (*In* **Nat. Assoc. Prom. Soc. Sci.** Trans., 1863.)

Wilkie, Wm., *D.D.* Fables. London, 1768. 8°.

— Poems. (*In* **Anderson**, R. Works of Brit. poets, v. 11. 1795; — *and in* **Chalmers**, A. Works of the Eng. poets, v. 16. 1810.)

— LIFE. (*In* **Soc. of Anc. Scots.** Lives of Scottish poets, v. 2, pt. 4. 1822.)

Wilkins, Charles, *of Kentucky.* Account of an exsiccated body found in a cave in Kentucky. (*In* **Amer. Antiq. Soc.** Trans., v. 1. 1820.)

Wilkins, Charles. WOOLRYCH, H. W. (*In his* Lives of serjeants-at-law, v. 2. 1869.)

Wilkins, David, *D.D.* De lingua Coptica. (*In* **Chamberlayne**, J. Oratio Dominica. 1715.)

Wilkins, Edward G. P. Young New York; a drama. (*In* **Sargent**, E. Mod. stand. drama, v. 24.)

Wilkins, George. The miseries of inforced marriage. (*In* **Scott**, *Sir* W. Brit. drama, v. 2. 1810; — *and in* **Dodsley**, R. Col. of old plays, v. 5. 1825.)

Wilkins, George, *Archdeacon of Nottingham.* Body and soul. 1st Amer. from 3d London ed. Phila., 1824. 2 v. 12°.

— BROWNE, J. H. Sixth letter to W. in reply to 'Evangeline'. London, 1823. 8°. (B 1362)

Wilkins, *Col.* Henry St. Clair. Reconnoitering in Abyssinia. London, 1870. 8°.

Wilkins, Isaac. Alarm to the Legislature of N. York, occasioned by political disturbances in North America; addressed to the General Assemby. N. Y., 1775. 8°. (B 377)

Wilkins, John, *Bp. of Chester.* Discourse concerning a new world and another planet, in 2 books. London, 1640. 12°.

Note. The first book has the title page, 'Discovery of a new world, *etc.*, 3d impress. corr. and enl.'; the second has a separate pagination.

— Discourse concerning the gift of prayer. London, 1667. 16°.

— Essay towards a real character and a philosophical language; appended, an alphabetical dict. by W. Lloyd. London, 1668. f°.

— Mathematical and philosophical works. London, 1802. 2 v. 8°.

Contents. Vol. 1. Life of the author and acc. of his writings. — The discovery of a new world; or, That the moon may be a world. — Discourse on a new planet; or, That the earth may be a planet. 2. Mercury, the secret and swift messenger. — Mathematical magic; or, The wonders of mechanical geometry. — Abstract of an essay towards a real character.

— Sermons. 2d ed. London, 1701. 8°.
— NICERON, J. P. (*In his* Mémoires, v. 4. 1728; *and*, *Germ.*, v. 4. 1751.)
Wilkins, John. Account of the gathering on Braddock's field. (*In* Ward, T. The insurrection in 1794. 1858. Penn. Hist. Soc. Mem., v. 6.)
Wilkins, John H. Civilization. (*In* **Sargent, E.** Mod. stand. dr., v. 13.)
Wilkins, John Hubbard. Elements of astronomy; with questions. 2d ed. Boston, 1823. 8°.
— Remarks on supplying Boston with pure water. 2d ed. Boston, 1845. 8°. (B 1191, E 128)
Wilkins, Peter. Letter to D. Webster, containing an exam. of his claims to be supported by Mass. as a candidate for the presidential chair. Boston, 1836. 8°. (B 1496)
Wilkins, Samuel J. Bible acrostics. London, 1839. 12°.
Wilkins, W. Walker. Political ballads of the 17th and 18th centuries; annotated. London, 1860. 2 v. 8°.
Wilkins, Wm. The antiquities of Magna Græcia. Cambridge, 1807. f°.
— Introduction. (*In* **Vitruvius Pollio, M.** Civil architecture. 1812.)
— Remarks on the inscription from Athens. (*In* **Walpole, R.** Memoirs rel. to Turkey. 1817.)
Wilkins, Wm. DORSEY, D. B. Review of an 'Address', professing to be a vindication of the Baltimore conference; added, a Reply to the same address by a member of the conference. Balt., 1827. 8°. (B 1395)
Wilkinson, *Lady* Caroline Catherine (Lucas). Weeds and wild flowers; their uses, legends, and literature. London, 1858. 12°.
Wilkinson, Charles Henry, *M. D.* Elements of galvanism, in theory and practice. London, 1804. 2 v. 8°.
Wilkinson, *Rev.* Henry. Babylon's ruine Jerusalem's rising; sermon, to House of Com., 25 Oct., fast. London, 1644. 8°. (B 161)
Wilkinson, J. H. Remarks on cutaneous diseases. London, 1822. 8°. (B 829)
Wilkinson, *Gen.* James. Memoirs of my own times; with atlas. Phila., 1816. 4 v. 8°.
Contents. Vol. 1. 1776–92. 2. 1793–1812. 3. 1813–15.
— AGRESTIS, *pseud.* Short review of the late proceedings at New Orleans on suspending the writ of habeas-corpus. Richmond, 1807. 8°. (B 433)
— ARGUMENTS and decisions on the motion for the attachment of W. (*In* **Burr**, A. Trial, v. 1. 1807.)
— CLARK, D. Deposition in relation to the conduct of W. Wash., 1808. 8°. (W 86)
— - Proofs of the corruption of W. and his connexion with A. Burr. Phila., 1809. 8°.
— - *Another copy.* (B 409)
— MEMOIRS of W. Vol. 2. Wash., 1810. 8°. (B 451)
— ORLEANS TERRITORY. *Ho. of Rep.* Debate on the conduct of W. N. Orleans, 1807. 8°.
— - *Another copy.* (B 433)
— PLAIN tale, justifying the character of W.; by a Kentuckian. N. Y., 1807. 8°. (B 433)
Wilkinson, James John Garth. Homœopathic principle applied to insanity; proposal to treat lunacy by spiritualism. London, *reprinted* Boston, 1857. 8°. (B 1200, 1568)
— Tracts for the new times. No. 2: Science for all. N. Y., 1847. 8°. (B 1470)
— *Same.* No. 3: Popular sketch of Swedenborg's philosophical works. N. Y., 1847. 8°. (B 1470)
Wilkinson, *Sir* John Gardner. Colour, and the necessity for a general diffusion of taste. London, 1858. 8°.
— Dalmatia and Montenegro. London, 1848. 2 v. 8°.
— The Egyptians in the time of the Pharaohs; also introd. to the study of Egyptian hieroglyphs, by S. Birch. London, 1857. 8°.
— The fragments of the hieratic papyrus at Turin. London, 1851. 8° *and* Plates f°.
— Handbook for Egypt. New ed. London, *Murray*, 1858. 12°.
— Manners and customs of the ancient Egyptians. (Vol. 1, 2d ed.) London, 1842, 37. 3 v. 8°.
— *Same.* 2d series. London, 1841. 2 v. 8°.
— *Same.* Supplement: Index and plates. London, 1841. 8°.
— Modern Egypt and Thebes. London, 1843. 2 v. 8°.
— Topography of Thebes, and general view of Egypt, with customs of the ancient Egyptians. London, 1835. 8°.
Wilkinson, Joseph. Select views of Cumberland, Westmoreland, and Lancashire. London, 1810. f°.
Wilkinson, Josiah. Report. (*In* **Gr. Brit.** *Educ. Comm.* Reports [on] state of popular education, v. 3. 1861.)
Wilkinson, Robert. Plan of Toyola. Lond., 1798. (E 67)
Wilkinson, S. Voyages and adventures of Teach, called Black Beard, the pirate; with an account of the Roman, Algerine, and West-India pirates. Boston, 1808. 12°. (C 158)
Wilkinson, T. T. The Lancashire geometers and their writings. (*In* **Lit. and Phil. Soc. of Manchester.** Mem., 2d ser., v. 11. 1854.) — Account of the early mathematical and philosophical writings of Dr. Dalton. — Memoir of Rev. J. Lawson. (*In* v. 12. 1855.)
Wilkinson, Tate. MANNERS, N. Remarks on the memoirs of W. (*In his* Attempt to illust. 1791.)
Wilkinson, Thomas. Some account of the last journey of J. Pemberton to the Highlands and other parts of Scotland. From Lond. ed. Phila., 1811. 8°. (C 156)
Wilks, Edward D. J. Educational clauses of the factory acts, *etc.* (*In* **Nat. Assoc. Prom. Soc. Sci.** Trans., 1859.) — Public elementary education. (*In* 1860.)
Wilks, Jonathan. Practical scheme for the reduction of the public debt and taxation without individual sacrifice. (*In* **Pamphleteer**, 1822; v. 20 of B 838)
Wilks, Mark. The flower faded; a short memoir of C. Cuvier; with reflections by J. A. James. N. Y., 1838. 16°.
Wilks, *Mrs.* Mary, *Funeral sermon on.* 1732. *See* **Foster**, J. (B 314)
Wilks, Matthew, *Funeral sermon on.* 1829. *See* **Collison**, G. (B 1228); — **Hill**, R. (B 1228)
Wilks, *Rev.* Samuel Charles. Christian essays. Boston, 1829. 12°.
Contents. True and false repose in death. — Full assurance of understanding. — Full assurance of faith. — Full assurance of hope. — Christian obedience. — Form and power of religion. — Sources of error in opinion. — False modesty in religion. — Affection between ministers and their flock. — Natural and revealed religion. — The influence of a moral life on our judgment in matters of faith.
— Essay on the influence of a moral life on our judgment in matters of faith. Boston, 1823. 8°. (B 273, 1781)
Wilks, Thomas Egerton. Bamboozling; a farce. (*In* Minor drama, v. 3.)
— Roll of the drum; drama. (No. 77 *of* **De Witt's** acting plays.)
— Seven clerks; drama. (*In* **Sargent, E.** Mod. stand. drama, v. 15.) — Wenlock of Wenlock. (*In* v. 17.) — Ben the boatswain; a nautical drama. (*In* v. 19.) — Michael Erle; drama. (*In* v. 31.) — Raffaelle the reprobate. (*In* v. 36.)
Wilks, Washington. E. Irving; an ecclesiastical and literary biography. London, 1854. 16°.
— English criticism on President Lincoln's anti-slavery proclamation and message. *n.t.p.* [London, 1863.] 16°.
— The half-century; its history, political and social. 2d ed., revised and enl. Lond., 1853. 8°.
Wilks. *See also* **Wilkes.**
Will *the rover, pseud.* Rambles in Chili and life among the Araucanian Indians, 1836. Thomaston, 1851. 8°.
Will. KLEIN, E. F. Ueber die Abhängigheit des ganzen Menschen-Werthes von der Energie des Willens. (*In* **Berlin. Ak. d. Wiss.** Abh., 1801-02.)
— BAIN, A. The emotions and the will. London, 1859. 8°.
— HUGHES, T. The human will; its functions and freedom. London, 1867. 8°.
See also **Liberty of the Will**; — **Necessity.**

Will Adams, the first Englishman in Japan; by W. Dalton. London, 1861. 8°.

Will he escape? by P. Fitzgerald. (*In* Gentleman's mag., n.s., v. 3-5. 1869-70.)

Will o' the Wisp, *ship*. Gr. Britain. *Parl.* Correspondence respecting the seizure of the British schooner 'Will o'the Wisp' by the United States' ship of war 'Montgomery', at Matamoros, June 3, 1862. London, 1863. f°. (N. A. papers, no. 12.)

Will Summer's last will and testament. *See* Nash, T.

Will-with-a-wisp; or, The grand ignis fatuus of London; by [N. N.]. London, 1714. 8°. (B 30)

Willan, Robert, *M.D.* Cutaneous diseases. Vol. 1. London, 1808. 4°.

— Diseases in Lond., 1796-1800. Lond., 1801. 12°.

— Miscellaneous works; ed. by A. Smith. London, 1821. 8°.

Contents. Inquiry into the antiquity of the small-pox, measles, and scarlet fever. — Reports on the diseases in London. — Detached papers on medical subjects collected from various periodical pub.: Case of abstinence; — Case of obstruction of the bowels; — Singular termination of dropsy; — Obs. on the use of arsenic in intermittent fevers; — Cases of ischuria renalis in children.

— Remarkable case of abstinence. (*In* Soc. Prom. Med. Kn. Med. comm., v. 2. 1790.)

— Vaccine inoculation. London, 1806. 4°.

Willard, *Mrs.* Emma C. (Hart). Address to the public, proposing a plan for improving female education. Albany, 1819. 8°. (B 447)

— *Same.* 2d ed. Middlebury, 1819. 8°. (B 447)

— Address to the pupils of the Washington Female Seminary. Pittsburgh, 1844. 8°. (B 1205)

— Advancement of female education; a series of addresses. Troy, 1833. 8°. (B 1100)

— Ancient geography as connected with chronology, and preparatory to the study of anc. hist.; compiled from D'Anville [and others]; added, problems on the globes to accompany the modern geography, by W. C. Woodbridge. Hartford, 1822. 12°.

— *Same.* Rev. ed. Hartford, 1844. 12°.

— Atlas to accompany a system of universal history. Hartford, 1836. 4°.

— History of the United States or Republic of America. 4th ed. N. Y., 1831. 8°.

Willard, Jacob. Oration, July 4, before the inhabitants of Marblehead. Salem, 1812. 8°. (B 415)

Willard, Joseph, *President of Harvard College, b.* 1738, *d.* 1804. Address in Latin by W.; and a discourse in Eng. by D. Tappan before the Univ. in Camb., Feb. 21, in commemoration of Washington. *n.p., S. Etheridge,* 1800. 8°. (B 234, 867, 2510, E 61, 212)

— *Same.* [Another ed.] *n.p.*, 1800. 4°. (A 19, W 80)

— Duty of the good and faithful soldier; sermon, Mendon, Mar. 25. Boston, 1781. 8°. (B 306)

— Memoir containing observations of a solar eclipse, Oct. 27, 1780, made at Beverly, *etc.* — Method of finding the altitude and longitude of the nonagesimal degree of the ecliptic. — Observations made at Beverly, to determine the variation of the magnetical needle. — Table of the equations to equal altitudes for the latitude of the Univ. of Camb., with an account of its construction and use. (*In* Amer. Acad. of Arts and Sci. Mem., v. 1. 1785.) — Observations of the transit of Mercury over the Sun's disc, Nov. 5, 1789. (*In* v. 2. 1793.)

— Sermon, May 13, funeral of T. Hilliard. Boston, 1790. 8°. (B 254, 867)

— Sermon, Oct. 16, 1793, ordination of H. Packard. Boston, 1794. 8°. (B 234)

— Sermon, ordination of J. McKeen, Beverly. Salem, 1785. 8°. (B 911)

— Thanksgiving sermon, Boston, Dec. 11, 1783. Boston, 1784. 8°. (B 67, 234)

— *Funeral sermon on.* 1804. *See* Holmes, A. (B 203, 226, 286, 425, 852); — Pearson, E. (B 73, 398, 854, 1238)

Willard, Joseph, *the younger, b.* 1798, *d.* 1865. Address, commemoration of the 200th anniversary of the incorporation of Lancaster, Mass. Boston, 1853. 8°.

— Address to the members of the bar of Worcester Co., Mass., Oct. 2, 1829. Lancaster, 1830. 8°.

— *Another copy.* (B 932)

— Memoir of Wm. Lincoln. (*In* Mass. Hist. Soc. Col., v. 30. 1849.)

— Memoir of Samuel Willard. Boston, 1839. 8°. (B 1144, 1461)

— *Same.* (*In* Amer. quarterly register, Nov. 1839. B 1819)

— Naturalization in the American colonies. (*In* Mass. Hist. Soc. Proc., 1858-60.) — On a 'Plan for the general arrangement of the militia of the U. S.', by Gen. Knox; [with plan]. (*In* 1862.) — Washburn, E. Remarks on the death of W. (*In* 1864-65.) — Brooks, C. Memoir of J. W. (*In* 1866-67.)

— Willard memoir; or, Life and times of Simon Willard; with notices of his descendants, *etc.* Boston, 1858. 8°.

Willard, Joseph, *son of the preceding.* Biography of S. Willard. (*In* Higginson, T. W. Harvard mem. biog., v. 1. 1866.)

Willard, Josiah. Letter to W. Bollan relative to the failure of the Crown Point expedition. (*In* Mass. Hist. Soc. Col., v. 6. 1800.)

— Oliver, P. Poem sacred to the memory of J. Willard. Boston, 1757. 4°. (B 650)

— *Funeral sermon on.* 1756. *See* Prince, T. (C 164)

Willard, Katharine. Mather, C. El-Shaddai; essay on all supplied in an alsufficient Saviour; death of W. Boston, 1725. 8°. (C 9)

Willard, Paul. Oration, Charlestown, Mass., 4 July. Boston, 1821. 8°. (B 944)

Willard, Samuel, *D.D., Vice-President of Harvard College, b.* 1640, *d.* 1707. Body of divinity. Boston, 1726. f°.

— Brief discourse conc. the ceremony of laying the hand on the Bible in swearing. London, 1689. 4°.

— *Same.* (*In* Whitmore, W. H. Andros tracts, v. 1. 1868. Prince Soc.)

— Character of a good ruler; [election] sermon. Boston, 1694. 8°. (D 5)

— Checkered state of the gospel church; sermon, [fast-day,] Sept. 18. Boston, 1701. 8°. (C 43, 50)

— Christian's exercise by Satan's temptations; substance of several sermons. Boston, 1701. 8°. (D 7)

— Fear of an oath; or, Cautions about swearing; sermon, Jan. 30, 1700. Boston, 1701. 8°. (C 51)

— The fountain opened; or, The admirable blessings to be dispensed at the national conversion of the Jews. 3d ed. (*Appended to* Sewall, S. Phænomena, *etc.* 1727.)

— *Another copy.* (B 257)

— Israel's true safety; sermon, Mar. 15, [fast-day]. Boston, 1704. 8°. (C 55, D 6)

— Morality not to be relied on for life; sermon, May 23. Boston, 1700. 12°. (C 7)

— Mourner's cordial against excessive sorrow. Boston, 1691. 12°.

— *Another copy.* (D 5)

— Ne sutor ultra crepidam; or, Brief animadversions upon the N. E. Anabaptist's late narrative. Boston, 1681. 4°. (B 234, 653)

— Principles of the Protestant religion. 1690. *See* Allen, J. (C 1, D 8)

— Reply to G. Kieth [*sic*] in answer to his 'Refutation of a dangerous opinion maintained by S. Willard'. Boston, 1703. 12°. (C 1)

— Sinfulness of worshipping God with men's institutions; sermon. Boston, 1691. 8°. (D 5)

— Some brief sacramental meditations. 2d ed. Boston, 1743. 16°.

— Some miscellany observations on our present debates respecting witchcrafts; by P. E. and J. A. Phila., 1692. 4°. (B 654)

— Thanksgiving sermon, Boston, Dec. 1705. London, 1709. 8°. (B 86, 335)

— Willard, J. Memoir of S. Willard. Boston, 1839. 8°. (B 1144, 1461)

— *Same.* (*In* Amer. quarterly register, Nov. 1839. B 1819)

— *Funeral sermon on, with poem by* B. Coleman. *See* Pemberton, E. (D 4)

Willard, Samuel, *D.D., of Deerfield, b.* 1775, *d.* 1859. Affectionate remonstrance against a frequent abuse of the pulpit and the religious press. Greenfield, 1856. 8°. (B 1360, 1591)

— Comments on 'An address to the Christian public, in two parts', *etc.* Greenfield, 1814. 8°. (C 86)
— Essays on the philosophy of instruction. Greenfield, 1829. 12°. (D 11)
— History of the rise, progress, *etc.*, of the rupture which now divides the Cong. clergy of Mass.; discourse, Deerfield, Sept. 22. Greenfield, 1858. 8°.
— *Another copy.* (B 1326)
— Hymns; with musical directions. Greenfield, 1824. 12°.
— Introduction to the Latin language. Boston, 1835. 12°.
— Remarks on the Strictures of J. Lyman, on 'Comments', *etc.* Greenfield, [1814]. 8°. (C 86)
— Rhetoric; or, The principles of elocution and rhetorical composition. Boston, 1830. 18°.
— Sacred poetry and music reconciled; a col. of hymns. Boston, 1830. 12°.
— Sermon, Oct. 27, 1808, opening of Northampton bridge. Northampton, 1808. 8°. (C 869)
— Sermon on Christian fidelity. (*In* **Liberal preacher**, v. 1. 1828.)
— Valedictory discourse, Deerfield, Sept. 20, 1829. 2d ed. Boston, 1831. 8°. (B 1305)
— CHANDLER, A. Review of an historical sermon, Sept. 22, 1857, by W. Greenfield, 1859. 8°.
— LYMAN, J. Strictures upon the Comments of W. on 'A counterpart'. Greenfield, 1814. 8°. (C 86)
— RESULTS of two ecclesiastical councils; W.'s confession of faith, *etc.* Greenfield, Mass., 1813. 8°. (C 86)

Willard, Sidney, *Prof.*, *b.* 1780, *d.* 1856. Hebrew grammar. Camb., 1817. 8°.
— Memories of youth and manhood. Camb., 1855. 2 v. 16°.
— Sermon: Christian perseverance. (*In* **Liberal preacher**, n.s., v. 5. 1836.)

Willard, *Maj.* Sidney, *b.* 1831, *d.* 1862. WILLARD, J. (*In* **Harvard** mem. biog., v. 1. 1866.)
— *Tribute to W.* 1862. *See* **Bartol**, C. A. (B 1594)

Willard, Simon, *Maj.* NEW HAMPSHIRE. *Council.* Letter to him, 1675. (*In* **New Hampshire Hist.** Soc. Col., v. 3. 1832.)
— WILLARD, J. Life and times of S. W. Boston, 1858. 8°.

Willard, Simon. Columbian union and Columbian constitution; an amendment to the constitution of the U. S. Albany, 1815. 8°.

Willard, Solomon. Plans and sections of the obelisk on Bunker's Hill; with the experiments made in quarrying the granite. Boston, 1843. 4°.
— Report on the cost of stone for the rail-road [to Prov.]. [Boston, 1823.] 8°. (B 1796)
— WHEILDON, W. W. Memoir of W. Boston, 1865. 8°.

Willard, Sylvester D. Annals of the Med. Soc. of the Co. of Albany, 1806–51; with biog. sketches. Albany, 1864. 8°.
— Annual address before the Med. Soc. of the Co. of Albany, Nov. 8. Albany, 1859. 8°. (B 1565)
— Biographical memoir of T. Spencer. Albany, 1858. 8°. (B 1565)
— Biographical memoirs of the physicians of Albany Co., June 9; address. Albany, 1857. 8°. (B 1565)
— Diphtherite, its presence in Albany. Albany, 1859. 8°. (B 1565)
— Hist. address before the Med. Soc. of the Co. of Albany, Nov. 11, 1856, at its semi-centennial anniversary. Albany, 1857. 8°. (B 1565)

Willard family. *See* **Willard**, J.

Williats, Charles. Religion of Nature proved to be a mere idol. (*In* **Scholar** armed, v. 1. 1800.)

Willcox. *See also* **Wilcox**.

Willcox, *Rev.* Wm. H. Hope for the country; fast-day sermon. Boston, 1863. 8°. (B 1593)

Willdenow, Karl Ludwig. True principles of botany and of vegetable physiology; tr. from the German. Edin., 1805. 8°.

Willebrandus. *See* **Wilbrandus**.

Willehad *or* **Wilhead**, *St.* ANSCHARIUS, *Bp.* Vita W. (*In* **Pertz.** Mon. Germ., Scr., v. 2. 1829.)

Willelmus *monachus.* Venerabilis Benedicti Clusensis abbatis vita. (*In* **Sardinia.** Mon. hist. pat., Scr., v. 5. 1848.)

Willelmus *Parvus.* *See* **Guilelmus** *Parvus de Newburg.*

Willeram, *abbas Eberspergensis.* Paraphrasis gemina in Canticum canticorum. *See* **Bible.** *Song of Solomon* (p. 280).

Willes, Richard. History of travayle in the West and East Indies, augm., *etc.*, by W. 1577. *See* **Eden**, R.

Willets, Georgiana. MOORE, F. (*In his* Women of the war. 1866.)

Willett, Marinus. *See, below,* **Willett**, W. M.

Willett, Ralph. MERLY library; catalogue of [his] library, sold 1813. Lond., [1813]. 8°.
Note. Added, prices of the books in the library of W.

Willett, Wm. M. Narrative of the military actions of Marinus Willett; taken chiefly from his own ms., by his son. N. Y., 1831. 8°.

Willey. *See also* **Wylie**.

Willey, Benj. G. History of the White Mts. New ed., by F. Thompson. N. Y., 1870. 12°.

Willey, *Rev.* Isaac. Memoir of D. Barker. (*In* **New Hamp. Hist. Soc.** Col., v. 4. 1834.)

Willey family. UPHAM, T. C. Acc. of the destruction at the White Mts., 1826. (*In* **New Hamp. Hist.** Soc. Col., v. 3. 1832.)

William I, *of England, the Conqueror.* Laws. (*In* **Gr. Brit.** *Commissioners on the Public Records.* Anc. laws. 1840.)
— ABBOTT, J. History of William the Conqueror. New York, 1854. 16°.
— CHRISTIEN *de Troyes.* Du roi Guillaume d'Angleterre. — DIT du Guillaume d'Angleterre, Le. (*In* **Michel**, F. Chron. anglo-normandes, v. 3. 1840.)
— DUCHESNE, A. Historiæ Anglicanæ circa tempus conquestus Angliæ selecta monumenta excerpta ex 'Historiæ Normannorum scriptoribus antiqui'; cum notis a F. Maseres. London, 1807. 4°.
— GUILLAUME *de Poitiers.* Gesta Guillelmi ducis Normannorum et regis Anglorum. (*In* **Maseres**, F. Hist. Angl. 1807.)
— — *French.* Vie de Guillaume-le-conquérant. (*In* **Guizot**, F. P. G. Col. des. mém., v. 29. 1826.)
— NAPIER, C. J. William the Conqueror; a historical romance; ed. by Sir W. Napier. London, 1858. 12°.
— WEBB, P. C. Short account of Danegeld; with further particulars relating to Will[iam] the Conqueror's survey. London, 1756. 4°. (E 13)

William II., *of England, Rufus.* STRICKLAND, A. (*In her* Lives of the bachelor kings of England. 1861.)

William III., *of England.* Collection of speeches, messages, *etc.*; added, the English declaration of rights. London, 1712. 8°.
— *Another copy.* (B 755)
— Letters. *See, below,* GRIMBLOT, P.
— ARRAIGNMENT, tryal, and condemnation of Sir W. Parkins for the conspiracy to assassinate William III. London, 1696. f°. (A 56)
— BEAMONT, W. Jacobite trials at Manchester in 1694. [Manchester,] 1853. 4°. (Chetham Soc., v. 28.)
— CHEVALIER, N. Histoire par médailles de Guillaume III. Amsterdam, 1692. f°.
— COLLECTION of state tracts on the revolution of 1688 and reign of Wm. III.; with a history of the Dutch war in 1672. London, 1705-07. 3 v. f°.
— COMBER, T. Vindication of the revolution in England, 1688, and of the characters of William and Mary. London, 1758. 8°. (B 579)
— CUST, *Sir* E. (*In his* Lives of the warriors who have commanded armies, v. 1. 1869.)
— DILWORTH, W. H. History of William III. *n.p.*, 1758. 12°.
— GRIMBLOT, P. Letters of William III. and Louis XIV., 1697–1700. Lond., 1848. 2 v. 8°.
Contents. Vol. 1. 1697–98. 2. 1698–1700.

— Histoire de Guillaume III. Amsterdam, 1793. 2 v. 12°.
— Hulsius, H. Jura Guilielmi III. in regna Angliæ asserta. Lugd. Bat., 1697. 4°.
— Impartial account of the conspiracy to assassinate W. London, 1696. 4°. (B 654)
— Kane, R. Campaigns of W.; with remarks by Gen. Kane. (*In* Muller, J. System of camp-discipline. 1757.)
— Malden, H. (*In his* Disting. men of modern times, v. 2. 1838; v. 38 of Lib. ent. kn.)
— Ranke, L. Aus dem Briefwechsel Wilhelms III. (*In his* Eng. Gesch., v. 7. 1868.)
— Reflections upon the late conspiracy to murther His Majesty in Flanders. London, 1692. 4°. (B 4)
— Rotgans, L. Wilhem de derde; in heldendicht beschreven. Utrecht, 1698–1700. 2 v. 8°.
— Somerville, T. History of political transactions and of parties, from the Restoration to the death of Wm. Dublin, 1793. 8°.
— Trevor, A. H., *Viscount Dugannon.* Life and times of W. London, 1835. 2 v. 8°.
— Vernon, J. Letters illustrative of the reign of W.; ed. by G. P. R. James. London, 1841. 3 v. 8°.
— *Funeral sermon on.* 1712. *See* Fleetwood, W. (E 211)
See also Landen, Battle of.

William IV., *of Eng.* The highly important speech [of W.] to Parl. *n.t.p.* [1835.] Broadside. (A 66)
— The reform act, 1832; correspondence of Earl Grey with W. London, 1867. 8°.
— Grenville, R., *2d Duke of Buckingham.* Memoir of the courts and cabinets of William IV. and Victoria. London, 1861. 2 v. 8°.
— Wright, G. N. Life and reign of W. London, 1837. 2 v. 8°.

William I., *of Nassau, Prince of Orange, the silent.* Apology or defence, in answer to proclamation and proscription of him by the King of Spain. (*In* Phenix, v. 1. 1707.)
— Correspondance, suivie de pièces inédites sur l'assassinat de ce prince, *etc.*; par M. Gachard. Bruxelles, 1850–66. 5 v. 8°.
— Boettiger, R. W. Wilhelm's von Oranien Ehe mit Anna von Sachsen. (*In* Historisches Taschenbuch, 1836.)
— Praet, J. v. Essays on the political history of the 15th–17th cent.; ed. by Sir E. Head. London, 1868. 8°.

William IV., *of Orange.* Ranke, F. L. von. Briefwechsel Friedrich des Grossen mit dem Prinzen Wilhelm IV von Oranien und mit Anna. (*In* Berlin. Ak. d. Wiss. Abh., 1868.)

William, *Duke of Gloucester, Funeral sermon on.* 1708, 1712. *See* Fleetwood, W. (E 211)

William *of Malmesbury.* *See* Guilelmus *Malmesburiensis.*

William *of Newburgh.* *See* Guilelmus *Parvus de Newburgh.*

William *of Tudela.* *See* Guilelmus *Tudelensis.*

William *of Tyre.* *See* Guilelmus *Tyrius.*

William *of Worcester.* *See* Guilelmus *Worcestrius.*

William *of Wykeham.* Cockerell, C. R. The architectural works of William of Wykeham. (*In* Archæol. Inst. of Gr. Brit. Proceedings at the annual meeting at Winchester. 1845, 1846.)
— Cunningham, A. (*In his* Lives of British painters, *etc.*, v. 4. 1831. Fam. lib., v. 7.)
— Lowth, R. Life of William of Wykeham. Oxford, 1777. 8°.

William and Henry; an occasional dialogue, [by J. Gretton]. *n.t.p.* [1768.] 4°. (A 19)

William and the Werwolf. *See* William *of Palerne.*

William Augustus, *Duke of Cumberland.* Haldane, J., *and* Leslie, J. Declaration against the invasion of Scotland. (*In their* Active testimony. 1749. C 24)
— Historical memoirs of William Augustus. London, 1767. 8°.

William Cooper and his family; or, Christian principles exemplified. Boston, 1827. 16°. (C 249)

William Engs, *ship.* Case of the crew, embracing the inquiry, who is R. R. Madden? [Wash., 1840.] 8°. (B 1166, E 256)
— Reply of N. P. Trist to the resolutions at a meeting in Boston on the cases of Capt. A. Wendell, Jr., and the crew of the ship Wm. Engs. [Wash., 1840.] 8°. (B 1159, E 256)

William Fitzherbert, *St., Archbishop of York.* Life of W. (*In* Lives of the Eng. saints, v. 5. 1844.)

William Henry and his friends; by Mrs. A. M. Diaz. Boston, 1872. 16°.

William Henry letters, The; by Mrs. A. M. Diaz. Boston, 1870. 8°.

William of Palerne, Romance of; [or] William and the Werwolf; tr. from the French, added a fragment of Alisaunder, tr. from the Lat.; ed. by W. W. Skeat. London, 1867. 8°. (Early Eng. Text Soc., ex. ser., v. 1.)

William Ratcliff; von H. Heine. (*In his* Sämmtl. Werke, v. 2. 1856.)

William Rufus, *King of England.* *See* William II., *of England.*

William Tell. *See* Knowles, J. S.

William Tell. *See* Schiller, F.

William Tell! with a vengeance! a burlesque. *See* Byron, H. J.

William the conquerer; by Gen. Sir C. Napier; ed. by W. Napier. London, 1858. 12°.

William the cottager. N. Y., 1848. 12°.

William Wyrcestre redivivus; notices of church architecture in the 15th century. Bristol, 1823. 4°.

Williams. *See also* Willyams.

Williams, —. Catalogue of a collection of books, sold by W., Nov. 26, 1829. London, [1829]. 8°. (B 1618)
— Catalogue of books, sold by Williams, June 5, 1830. London, [1830]. 8°. (B 1618)

Williams, *Rev.* A. D. Fugitive slave law; discourse, Pawtucket, Dec. 8, 1850. Prov., 1851. 8°. (B 1305)

Williams, *Rev.* Abraham. Sermon, election. Boston, 1762. 8°. (B 181, 185)
— Sermon on James v. 9. Boston, 1766. 8°. (B 814)

Williams, Amos A. Correspondence [on the branch bank at Baltimore. Balt., 1819.] 12°. (C 197)

Williams, Arthur John. Upon what principle should local courts be constituted with ref. to the extent of jurisdiction and system of procedure? (*In* Nat. Assoc. Prom. Soc. Sci. Trans., 1865.) — Is it desirable to reorganize our courts, and if so, on what system? (*In* 1868.)

Williams, *Rev.* Avery. Discourse, Lexington, Mar. 31. Boston, 1813. 8°. (B 335)

Williams, Benj. Samuel. The orchid growers' manual. London, 1852. 8°.

Williams, C. C. Natural language of the organs. (*App. to* Graves, J. M. Phrenology. 1838.)

Williams, *Mrs.* Catherine R. Biography of revolutionary heroes. Prov., 1839. 12°.
Contents. Life of W. Barton. — Life of T. Olney.

Williams, *Sir* Charles Hanbury. Works; with notes by H. Walpole, Earl of Orford. London, 1822. 3 v. 16°.
— Curious pieces. (*In* New foundling hospital for wit. 1768, 69–72.)
— Ode, to a great number of great men, newly made. (*In* Campbell, T. Brit. poets, v. 5. 1819.)

Williams, Charles James Blasius, *M.D.* Rational exposition of the physical signs of diseases of the lungs and pleura. Phila., 1830. 8°.

Williams, Charles Wye. Elementary treatise on the combustion of coal and the prevention of smoke; appendix, report on the Newcastle steam coal. Lond., *Weale,* 1858. 12°.
— Heat, in its relations to water and steam. London, 1860. 8°.
— Preparation, properties, and uses of turf and turf coke. (*In* London. Inst. of Civil Engineers. Trans., v. 3. 1842.)

Williams, Chauncy K. Centennial celebration of the settlement of Rutland, Vt. Rutl., 1870. 8°.

Williams, Cynric R. Tour through the Island of Jamaica, 1823. 2d ed. London, 1827. 12°.

Williams, D. E. Life and correspondence of Sir T. Lawrence. London, 1831. 2 v. 8°.

Williams, Daniel, *D.D.*, *b.* 1664, *d.* 1716. Questions previous to the ordination of S. Clarke, *etc.* London, 1713. 8°. (B 42)

— BIBLIOTHECÆ quam D. Williams bono publico legavit catalogus. Ed. 2a. Londini, 1801. 8°.

— CATALOGUE of the library in Red Cross St. founded pursuant to the will of D. Williams. London, 1841. 2 v. 8°.

Note. Vol. 2 cont. tracts and pamphlets.

— PAPERS relating to W., and the trust estab. by his will. London, 1816. 16°. (C 256)

Williams, David, *Funeral sermon on.* 1804. *See* **Harris**, T. M. (B 203, 399)

Williams, *Rev.* David, *b.* 1738, *d.* 1816. Essays on public worship, patriotism, and projects of reformation. London, 1773. 12°.

— Lectures on politeness, giving a beautiful display of nature and her laws. 2d ed. London, 1819. 8°.

Note. The 1st and perhaps only ed. of this work, published in 1789, has the title 'Lectures on political principles', *etc.* The title alone appears to be new.

— Lessons to a young prince, by an old statesman, on the present disposition in Europe to a general revolution; with The mode of studying and profiting by the 'Reflections on the French Revolution, by E. Burke'. 5th ed. Dublin, 1791. 12°.

— *Same.* 6th ed. London, *reprinted* N. Y., 1791. 8°. (B 774, 2504)

Williams, David R. Speech, 9th Dec., in the Ho., on [submission] to the late edicts of Gr. Brit. *n.t.p.* [1808.] 8°. (C 83)

Williams, Ebenezer, *Funeral sermon on.* *See* **Williams**, S. (B 1194)

Williams, Edmund. TRIAL. (*In* **Trials** at large. 1745. E 86)

Williams, Edward. Virgo triumphans; or, Virginia in generall; incl. the fertile Carolina, and the Island of Roanok. Lond., 1650. 12°.

Williams, *Rev.* Edward. Discourse; the influence of relig. practice upon our enquiries after truth. Shrewsbury, 1791. 8°. (B 1346)

— Memoir of J. Owen. (*In* **Owen**, J. Exposition, v. 1. 1811.)

— Predestination to life; sermon, Sheffield, April 18, 1804. 2d ed., corr. and enl. London, 1805. 8°. (B 1351)

Williams, Edwin. Addresses and messages of the Presidents of the U. S., 1789–1846; with a memoir of each and a hist. of their administrations; also the constitution of the U. S., and a selection of documents, *etc.* N. Y., 1846. 2 v. 8°.

Note. Called usually 'Statesman manual'.

Williams, Eleazer, *Funeral sermon on.* 1743. *See* **Williams**, S. (C 45)

Williams, Eliphalet, *D.D.* The ruler's duty and honor; sermon, death of W. Pitkin, Oct. 3, 1769. Hartford, 1770. 8°. (C 5)

Williams, *Col.* Elisha, *Pres. of Yale Coll.* Essential rights of Protestants; seasonable plea for liberty of conscience. Boston, 1744. 8°. (B 249)

— SHORT memoirs of W. (*In* **Lockwood**, J. Man mortal, *etc.* 1756. B 227)

— *Funeral sermon on.* 1756. *See* **Lockwood**, J. (B 227)

Williams, *Col.* Ephraim, *b.* 1715, *d.* 1755. FITCH, E. Life and character of W. (*In* **Mass. Hist. Soc.** Col., v. 8. 1802.)

Williams, Ephraim, *d.* 1835. Report of cases argued and determined in the Supreme Court of Mass., 1806–22. (Vol. 1, 2d ed.) Boston, 1816, 11, 08–23. 17 v. 8°.

Note. Vol. 2–17 are ed. by D. H. Tyng.

Williams, Folkestone. *See* **Williams**, R. F.

Williams, Frederick, *and others.* Mémoire pour F. W., *etc.*, chargeurs particuliers sur le navire américain 'The brothers'. [Paris, 180–.] 4°. (A 7)

Williams, Gilbert T. Sermon, Rowley, May 2, on [his] dismission. Haverhill, 1813. 8°. (B 1305)

Williams, *Mrs.* H. Dwight. *See* **Williams**, M. N.

Williams, Helen Maria. Letters containing a sketch of the politics of France, May 31, 1793 – July 28, 1794. London, 1795. 3 v. 12°.

— Letters from France. N. Y., 1793. 4 v. (v. 1, 2 w.). 12°.

— *Same.* [Vol. 1.] 1st Amer. ed. Boston, 1791. 12°. (C 63)

— *Same.* 2d Amer. ed. N. Y., 1794. 4 v. 12°.

— Nouveau voyage en Suisse [1798]; tr. par J. B. Say. 2e éd. Paris, 1802. 2 v. 8°.

— Peru; a poem. London, 1784. 4°.

— Political and confidential correspondence of Lewis XVI.; with observations on each letter. London, 1803. 3 v. 8°.

Williams, Henry. Remarks on banks and banking. Boston, 1840. 8°. (B 1515)

Williams, Henry. Address to the Legislature. (*In* **Deerfield.** WAIT, D. R., *and others.* Petition. 1850. B 1596)

Williams, Henry Willard, *M. D.* Address before the Suffolk District Med. Soc., Apr. 30. Boston, 1853. 8°. (B 1565)

— Ophthalmic report. *See* **Boston.** *City Hospital.* 1870 (p. 340).

— Our eyes and how to take care of them. Boston, 1871. 16°.

Note. From the **Atlantic** monthly, v. 27, 28. 1871.

— Recent advances in ophthalmic science. Boston, 1866. 16°.

— On treatment of iritis without mercury. Boston, 1856. 8°. (B 1565)

Williams, *Rev.* Isaac. Christian liberty. — Short address on the nature and constitution of the church of Christ. (*In* **Tracts** for the times, v. 1. 1840.) — On reserve in communicating religious knowledge. (*In* v. 4.) — Indications of a superintending Providence in the preservation of the prayer-book and in the changes which it has undergone. (*In* v. 5. 1840.)

— A few remarks on the charge of the Ld. Bp. of Gloucester on no. 80 and 87. Oxford, 1841. 8°. (B 1377)

— Oxford theology; reserve in communicating religious knowledge. N. Y., 1865. 12°. (Tracts for the times, no. 80. B 1377)

— Thoughts in past years. 6th ed. Oxford, 1852. 32°.

Williams, J. Fletcher. Bibliography of Minnesota. St. Paul, 1870. 8°.

Note. From Minn. Hist. Soc. Col., v. 3, pt. 1.

— History of the newspaper press of St. Paul, Minn. [St. Paul, 1871.] 8°.

Williams, J. J. Isthmus of Tehuantepec; with maps. N. Y., 1852. 2 v. 8°.

Williams, J. M. Biog. outline of G. Washington. (*In* **Washington**, G. Political legacies. 1800.)

Williams, James. Letters on slavery from the old world; [proof sheets]. Nashville, 1861. 18°.

Williams, Jane. Memoir of Rev. T. Price. (*In* **Price**, T. Literary remains, v. 2. 1855.)

Williams, John, *Abp. of York*, *b.* 1582, *d.* 1650. Gr. Britain's Salomon; sermon, funeral of King James, 1625. (*In* **Somers**, J. Col. of tracts, v. 2. 1809.)

— PHILIPS, A. Life of Williams. Cambridge, 1700. 8°.

Williams, John, *Bp. of Chichester*, *b.* 1634, *d.* 1709. Answer to the address presented to the ministers of the Church of England. London, 1698. 4°. (B 1397)

— Difference between the Church of England and the Church of Rome. (*In* **Cardwell**, E. Tracts on points at issue, v. 3. 1837.)

— On divine revelation. 1697. (*In* **Boyle** lecture sermon. 1739.)

— Vindication of a discourse [by E. Stillingfleet] concerning the unreasonableness of a new separation on account of the oaths. London, 1691. 4°. (B 4)

— *Same.* (*In* **Collection** of state tracts, v. 1. 1705.)

— Vindication of the sermons of J. [Tillotson on] the divinity of our Saviour, and of [E. Stillingfleet's] sermon on the 'Mysteries of the Christian faith', from [T. Firmin's] 'Considerations on the explications of the doctrine of the Trinity'; with a letter from G. Burnet. London, 1695. 4°. (B 96)

— MATHER, I. Some remarks on [W.'s] pretended answer to a discourse on common-prayer worship. Boston, 1712. 8°. (C 14)

— VINDICATION of the answer to the popish address. London, 1688. 4°. (B 1397)

Williams, *Rev.* John, *of Deerfield, b.* 1664, *d.* 1729. The redeemed captive; annexed, sermon, Dec. 5, 1706. 3d ed.; appendix, by [S.] Williams and [T.] Prince. Boston, 1758. 8°. (C 5)

Note. The sermon has a separate title-page.

— *Same.* Sermon. [4th ed.] *mut. and t.p.w.* [Springfield, 1793.] 16°.

— DEERFIELD captive, The. 2d ed. Greenfield, 1834. 24°.

— WILLIAMS, S. W. Biographical memoir of W. Greenfield, 1837. 12°.

— *Funeral sermon on.* 1729. *See* **Foxcroft, T.** (B 223)

Williams, *Rev.* John, *minister at Bridwell Chapel.* Address. (*In* **Toulmin, J.** Promise of Christ's presence. 1792. B 961)

Williams, *Rev.* John, *of Sydenham, b.* 1726, *d.* 1798. Enquiry into the truth of the tradition concerning the discovery of America by Prince Madog, about 1170. London, 1791. 8°.

— *Another copy.* (W 84)

— Further observations; cont. the acc. of Gen. Bowles of a Welsh tribe of Indians. London, 1792. 8°.

— *Another copy.* (W 84)

— Serious and earnest address to gentlemen who opposed the late application of the Protestant dissenting ministers to Parl. London, 1773. 8°. (B 907)

Williams, John (*pseud.* Anthony **Pasquin**). The Hamiltoniad; or, An extinguisher for the royal faction of New England. Boston, [1804]. 8°. (B 425)

— *Same.* N.Y., 1862, *reprinted* 1865. 8°. (Hamilton club, no. 3.)

Note. 'To perpetuate the infamy of J. Park'.

— Life of A. Hamilton. Boston, 1804, *reprinted* N. Y., 1865. 8°. (Hamilton Club, no. 1.)

— Life of the Earl of Barrymore. London, 1793. 8°.

— The pin basket. London, 1796. 4°.

Williams, John, *mineral engineer.* Nat. hist. of the mineral kingdom. 2d ed. by J. Millar. Edin., 1810. 2 v. 8°.

Williams, John, *b.* 1757, *d.* 1810. WOOLRYCH, H. W. (*In his* Lives of eminent serjeants-at-law, v. 2. 1869.)

Williams, John, *of Pitmaston.* The climate of Gr. Britain; the change in 50 years. London, 1806. 8°.

Williams, John, *b.* 1789, *d.* 1819. LIVES and confessions of J. W., F. Frederick, J. P. Rog, and P. [called N.] Peterson. Boston, [1819]. 8°. (B 344, 1462)

— TRIAL of J. W., F. Frederick, J. P. Rog, N. Peterson, and N. White, for murder on the high seas. Boston, 1819. 8°. (B 344, 559)

Williams, John, *of the Inner Temple.* The laws of trade and commerce. London, 1812. 8°.

Williams, John, *M. P.* SUGDEN, E. B. Letter to J. Williams, in reply to his observations on the abuses of the Court of Chancery. (*In* **Pamphleteer,** 1825; v. 25 of B 838)

Williams, John, *Archdeacon of Cardigan, b.* 1792, *d.* 1858. Essays on various subjects. London, 1858. 8°.

Contents. Carn Goch in Caermarthenshire. — On the early intercourse between the Eastern and Western worlds, and on Celtic coins. — One source of the non-Hellenic portion of the Latin language. — The Virgilian cosmogony. — On the Aristotelian expression Μετὰ τὰ φυσικά. — A selection from archæological papers. — Extracts from archæological letters. — Extract from an unpublished archæological paper. — On the megalithic structures in Auvergne. — Primitive tradition; letter to the ed. of the Edinburgh review. — Antiquity of Celtic coins. — A few obs. on certain very ancient traditions among certain primitive nations. — Ancient Phœnicians and their language. — The written records of the Cumri. — On the difference between the Cumraeg and the Gaeleg. — On the great ethnological theory. — Antiquity of certain Welsh manuscripts.

— Life and actions of Alexander the Great. London, 1829. 16°. (Fam. lib., v. 7.)

— *Same.* N. Y., 1843. 16°. (Harper's fam. lib., v. 7.)

— Two essays on the geography of ancient Asia. London, 1829. 8°.

Williams, John, *of Mansfield.* Memoir of T. Belsham. London, 1833. 8°.

Williams, *of London Miss. Soc.* Missionary enterprises in the South Sea Island, [1821–33]. 1st Amer. ed. N. Y., [183–?]. 12°.

— CAMPBELL, J. The martyr of Erromanga; life and character of W. 2d ed. Lond., 1842. 8°.

— YONGE, C. M. (*In her* Pioneers and founders. 1871.)

Williams, John, *oculist.* HOBAN, J. Speech [at the trial] of J. W. for obtaining money by false pretences. Wash., 1837. 8°. (B 1824)

Williams, John, *Bp. of Conn., b.* 1817. Academic studies; inaug. disc, Trinity Coll. Hartford, 1849. 8°. (B 1576)

— Charge to the clergy of the diocese of Connecticut, New Haven, June 13. Hartford, 1865. 8°. (B 1591)

— Christian scholar; address before the Ho. of Convocation of Trinity Coll., Aug. 5. Hartford, 1846. 8°. (B 1576)

— The Church's rule of fasting; sermon. Middletown, 1842. 8°. (B 1305)

Williams, *Sir* John Bickerton. Life and character of S. Savage. Boston, 1821. 12°.

— Memoir of the life, character, and writings of M. Henry. Boston, 1830. 12°.

Williams, John Lee. Territory of Florida; sketches of the topog., civil and nat. hist., *etc.* N. Y., 1837. 8°.

Williams, John Mason. Address, death of P. O. Thacher, and proceedings of the municipal court. Boston, 1843. 8°. (B 1226)

— Extracts from a charge to the grand jury, Northampton. Northampton, 1838. 8°. (B 1435)

— Sketch of the character of S. Howe. Worcester, 1828. 8°. (B 1218, 1793)

Williams, John S., *Brigade Major and Inspector, Columbian Brigade, in the war of* 1812. History of the invasion and capture of Washington. N. Y., 1857. 12°.

Williams, John S., *Brig. Gen. C. S. A.* Report of operations in East Tennessee, Sept. 27 – Oct. 15, 1863. Richmond, 1864. 8°.

Williams, Jonathan, *Funeral sermon on.* 1737. *See* **Chauncy, C.** (B 307, E 153)

Williams, *Brig.-Gen.* Jonathan, *b.* 1750, *d.* 1815. Plan for fortifying the narrows between Long and Staten Islands. N. Y., 1807. 8°. (B 444)

— Thermometrical navigation. From Amer. philos. trans., with add. and improv. Phila., 1799. 8°.

— *Another copy.* (B 526)

— SKETCH.] (*In* **Longacre, J. B.,** *and* **Herring, J.** Nat. portr. gal., v. 1. 1837.)

Williams, Joseph. Considerations on the Amer. war. London, 1782. 4°. (A 20)

Williams, Joseph, *of Kidderminster.* Extracts from [his] diary, meditations, *etc.*; [ed. by B. Fawcett]. New ed. London, 1825. 24°.

Williams, Joseph R. Oration before the citizens of New Bedford, July 4. New Bedford, 1835. 8°. (B 1204)

Williams, Martha, *Funeral sermon on.* 1816. *See* **Willson, L.** (B 960, 1228)

Williams, *Mrs.* Martha Noyes, *wife of* H. Dwight. A year in China; with narrative of capture and imprisonment, when homeward bound, on board the rebel pirate Florida. N. Y., 1864. 16°.

Williams, Monier. Indian epic poetry; lectures. Oxford, [1862]. London, 1863. 8°.

— Practical grammar of the Sanskrit language. 2d ed. Oxford, 1857. 8°.

Williams, Montague, *and* **Burnand, F. C.** The Turkish bath; a farce. (No. 5 *of* **Spencer's** universal stage.)

Williams, Montgomery. Wrought iron roofs at Pembroke. (*In* **Gr. Brit.** *Corps of Roy. Engin.* Papers, v. 9. 1847.)

Williams, Moses. Cracked jug; or, Five answers to neighbor Parley's five letters, cracking his Fifteen gallon jug; by 'Neighbor Smith'. Boston, 1838. 12°. (B 1279)

Williams, Nassau. Introductory lecture on political economy. (*In* **Pamphleteer**, 1828; v. 29 of **B 838**)

Williams, Nathan, *D.D.* Carefully to observe, *etc.*; sermon, Stafford, July 4. Hartford, 1793. 8°. (B 335)

— Enquiry concerning the design and importance of Christian baptism and discipline. 2d ed. Boston, 1792. 8°. (B 259)

— Order and harmony, *etc.*; sermon, in Tolland, fast [day], Apr. 17. Hartford, 1793. 8°. (B 335)

Williams, Nathaniel, *M.D.* The method of practice in the small-pox; with observations on inoculation. Boston, 1752. 8°. (C 70)

— *Funeral sermon on.* 1738. *See* **Prince**, T. (B 329)

Williams, Nathaniel. To the Baltimore bar [on his removal from the office of counsel to the Baltimore branch of the Bank of the U. S. Balt., 1819.] 12°. (C 197)

Williams, Otho Holland, *Brig.-Gen.* [SKETCH.] (*In* **Longacre**, J. B., *and* **Herring**, J. Nat. portr. gal., v. 2. 1835.)

Williams, Peter, *Jr.* Discourse, death of P. Cuffe, Oct. 21. N. Y., 1817. 8°. (B 283)

Williams, Philip, *D.D.* Reply to "Remarks on some 'Observations [by W.] addressed to the author of the Letter to Dr. Waterland'", *etc.* London, 1734. 8°. (B 119)

— MIDDLETON, C. Remarks on some 'Observations', *etc.* London, 1733. 8°. (B 119)

Williams, Reuel. Speech on the bill to provide for the northeastern boundary. Wash., 1838. 8°. (B 1496)

— POOR, J. A. Memoir of W. [Camb.,] *privately printed* 1864. 8°.

Williams, Richard. The poore man's pittance. London, 1868. 8°. (Ballad Soc., v. 2., pt. 1.)

Contents. The fall and complaynte of Anthonie Babington. 1586. — The life and deathe of Roberte, Lorde Deverox, Earle of Essex. 1601. — Acclamatio patrie. 1604.

Williams, Robert. Medicine. (*In* **Smedley**, E., *and others.* Encyc. metrop., v. 7. 1845.)

Williams, Robert Folkestone. Historical sketch of the art of sculpture in wood to the present time; with notices of works now in Europe and account of their designers. London, 1835. 16°.

— Lives of the English cardinals. London, 1868. 2 v. 8°.

Contents. Vol. 1. *Introduction.* The papacy. — Anglo-Saxon church. — *Eng. cardinals of the 12th century.* N. Breakspear. — Adrian IV. — R. le Poule. — B. Breakspear. — H. de Bosham. — Doubtful and obscure cardinals. — *13th, 14th centuries.* S. Langton. R. Curzon. — R. Somercote. — John of Toledo. — R. Kilwardby. — T. Joyce. — S. Langham. — A. Eston. — Doubtful and obscure cardinals. — Chaucer a promoter of the pre-Lutheran reformation. — Appendix. 2. *15th century.* Philip Repingdon. — English opinion in Bohemia. — R. Hallam. — H. Beaufort. — J. Kemp. — T. Bourchier. — J. Morton. — *16th century.* C. Bainbridge. — T. Wolsey. — Rome and the English cardinal.

— Memoirs and correspondence of F. Atterbury; with notice of his contemporaries. London, 1869. 2 v. 8°.

— Memoirs of Sophia Dorothea, consort of George I. London, 1845. 2 v. 8°.

— Shakspeare and his friends. Phila., 1839. 3 v. 12°.

Williams, *Sir* Roger, *d.* 1595. Actions of the Lowe Countries. (*In* **Somers**, J. Col. of tracts, v. 1. 1809.)

Williams, Roger. Bloudy tenent of persecution for cause of conscience discussed in a conference between Truth and Peace, and Mr. Cotton's Letter examined and answered; ed. by E. C. Underhill. London, 1848. 8°. (Hanserd Knollys Soc.)

— *Same.* Ed. by S. L. Caldwell. Prov., R. I., 1847. 4°. (Narragansett Club, v. 3.)

— The bloody tenent yet more bloody; ed. by S. L. Caldwell. Prov., 1870. 4°. (Narragansett Club, v. 4.)

— Experiments of spiritual life and health, and their preservatives. London, 1652 *reprinted* [Providence, 1863]. 4°.

— G. Fox digg'd out of his burrowes; or, An offer of disputation made 1672 to F. Boston, 1676. 4°

— Key into the languages of America. London, *printed* 1643, *reprinted by the R. I. Hist. Soc.*, [Prov., 1827]. 8°.

— *Same.* Ed. by J. H. Trumbull. (*In* **Narragansett Club.** Pub., v. 1. 1866.)

— *Same, with omissions.* 1643. (*In* **Mass. Hist. Soc.** Col., v. 3. 1810.) — Letter to Major Mason. (*In* v. 1.) — Letter to Governor Bradstreet. 1682. (*In* v. 18.) — Seven letters, 1636-38. (*In* v. 21.) — Petition to the General Court of Mass. (*In* v. 34. 1858.)

— Mr. Cotton's letter lately printed, examined, and answered; ed. by R. A. Guild. (*In* **Narragansett Club.** Pub., v. 1. 1866.) — Queries of highest consideration; ed. by R. A. Guild. (*In* v. 2. 1867.)

— COTTON, J. The bloudy tenent washed and made white in the bloud of the Lambe; added, a reply to Williams' answer to Mr. Cotton's letter. London, 1647. 4°.

— - Letter, and Williams' reply; ed. by R. A. Guild. (*In* **Narragansett Club.** Pub., v. 1. 1866.) — Answer to Master R. Williams. (*In* v. 2. 1867.)

— EDDY, D. C. R. Williams and the Baptists; an historical discourse. Boston, 1861. 12°.

— ELTON, R. Life of W. Prov., 1853. 12°.

— FOX, G., *and* BURNYEAT, J. A new England fire-brand quenched; answer to 'G. Fox digg'd out of his burrow'. *n.p.*, 1678. 4°.

— GAMMELL, W. Life of W. (*In* **Sparks**, J. Amer. biog., v. 14. 1845.)

— GUILD, R. A. Biographical introd. to the writings of W. (*In* **Narragansett Club.** Pub., v. 1. 1866.)

— HINMAN, R. R. Charges and banishment of W. (*In his* Blue laws. 1838.)

— JOHNSON, L. D. The spirit of W. Boston, 1839. 16°.

— KNOWLES, J. D. Memoir of W. Boston, 1834. 12°.

Williams, Rowland, *D.D.* Broadchalke sermon-essays. London, 1867. 16°.

Contents. The testimony of nature. — The Mosaic law. — David and Absalom. — Pure religion. — What is man? — The authority of Christ's teaching. — The blood of Jerzeel. — The Holy Spirit. — The atonement. — The mediatorship of the law and of the gospel. — The Holy Trinity. — The song of the ark and the psalms of war. — Providence and prayer. — Transfiguration and conversion. — Absolution. — The great gulf. — The prophetic Christ.

— Bunsen's Biblical researches. (*In* **Essays** and reviews. 1860.)

— The Hebrew prophets translated afresh. London, 1866. 2 v. 8°.

Contents. Vol. 1. The prophets of Israel and Judah during the Assyrian Empire. 2. Hebrew prophets during the Babylonian and Persian Empires.

— Holy Scripture. — Servants of God speaking as moved by the Holy Ghost. — The spirit and the letter; or, The truth and the book. (*In* **Noyes**, G. R. Col. of theological essays. 1867.)

— ROSE, H. J. Bunsen, the critical school, and Dr. Williams. (*In* **Replies** to Essays and reviews. 1862.)

— STEPHEN, J. F. Defence of W. before the Arches Court. London, 1862. 8°.

Williams, Samuel, *Funeral sermon on.* 1763. *See* **Rogers**, N. (B 73)

Williams, Samuel, *Prof.*, *b.* 1743, *d.* 1817. Account of a very uncommon darkness in New England, May 19, 1780. — Astronomical observations in Mass. — Memoir on the latitude of the Univ. at Cambridge. — Observations and conjectures on the earthquakes of New England. (*In* **Amer. Acad. of Arts** and Sci. Mem., v. 1. 1785.)

— Discourse on love of country, thanksgiving, 1744. Salem, 1775. 8°. (B 47, 335, 862)

— Discourse, Rutland, Oct. 9. Rutland, 1794. 8°. (B 335)

— Influence of Christianity, *etc.*; disc., Nov. 10, 1779, ordination of J. Prince, Salem. Bost., 1780. 8°. (B 335)

— Natural and civil history of Vermont, 1724-91. Walpole, N. H., 1794. 8°.
— *Same, enlarged.* [To 1806.] 2d ed. Burlington, 1809. 2 v. 8°.
— Regeneration the most important concern, with directions, *etc.*, from the holy Scriptures; two sermons. Boston, 1766. 8°. (B 72)
— Sermon, Jan. 13, ordination of T. Barnard, Jr., in Salem. Salem, 1773. 8°. (B 75, 860, 911)

Williams, Samuel. Flax-growing in Seneca Co., N. Y. (*In* **Moore**, D. D. T. Manual of flax culture. 1863.)

Williams, Samuel G. CATALOGUE of the library of W., sold. Boston, 1837. 8°. (B 1616)

Williams, *Rev.* Samuel Porter. Duties of congregations to their pastors; sermon, Newburyport, installation of D. Dana, May 24. Salem, 1826. 8°. (B 1324)
— Faithful minister's monument; sermon, funeral of Rev. J. Giles, Newburyport, Oct. 1. Newburyport, 1824. 8°. (B 1353)
— The good minister; discourse, Newburyport, installation of the author. Newburyport, 1821. 8°. (B 1237, 1324, 1784)
— Walking in God's name; sermon before the Educ. Soc. of the Young Men of Boston, Jan. 25. Newburyport, 1824. 8°. (B 1329)

Williams, Samuel Wells. The middle kingdon; a survey of the Chinese Empire. N. Y., 1848. 2 v. 12°.
— Note on Japanese syllabaries. (*In* **Amer. Orient. Soc.** Journ., v. 2. 1851.)
— Present position of the Chinese Empire in respect to the extension of trade and intercourse with other nations. (*In* **Amer. Ethnol. Soc.** Trans., v. 2. 1848.)
— Ying Hwa Yun-fu Lih-kiâi; an English and Chinese vocabulary, in the court dialect. Macao, 1844. 8°.
— MACY, W. A. The tonic dictionary of the Chinese language by W. (*In* **Amer. Orient. Soc.** Journal, v. 6. 1860.)

Williams, Simon. Introduction. (*In* **Blackwell**, T. Forma sacra. 1774.)

Williams, Solomon, *D.D.*, *b.* 1700, *d.* 1776. Glorious reward of wise and faithful teachers; sermon, ordination of J. Eliot. Boston, 1730. 8°. (B 925)
— Power of prayers; sermon, Mansfield, Aug. 4, 1741. Boston, 1742. 8°. (C 18, 53)
— Relations of God's people to him; thanksgiving sermon, Lebanon, Nov. 15, 1759. New London, 1760. 8°. (C 18)
— Servants of Christ ought to be quickened to diligence; funeral sermon, Mansfield, Sept. 23, 1742, [on] E. Williams. Boston, 1743. 8°. (C 45)
— Substance of two discourses, Sept. 13, 1741, on the death of J. Woodward and the deliverance of S. Gray. New London, 1742. 12°. (C 202)
— True state of the question conc. qualifications necessary to lawful communion; answer to J. Edwards' 'Humble inquiry'. Boston, 1751. 4°. (B 24)
— Vindication of the gospel-doctrine of justifying faith; answer to A. Croswell's 'What is Christ to me if He is not mine', [and] reply to his answer to G. Firmin's 'Eight arguments'. Boston, 1746. 4°. (B 24)
— Word of God preached; discourse, Pomfret, Apr. 22, 1753, death of E. Williams. Boston, 1754. 8°. (B 1194)
— *and* **Wheelock**, E. Two letters to J. Davenport, which were the principal means of his late retraction. Boston, 1744. 8°. (C 51)
— CROSWELL, A. Second defence of the doctrine of justifying faith; reply to the exceptions of S. Williams against 'What is Christ to me if He is not mine'. Boston, 1747. 8°. (B 24, 45)
— EDWARDS, J. Misrepresentations corrected and truth vindicated in reply to W.'s 'True state of the question', *etc.* (*In his* Works, v. 1. 1808.)

Williams, *Rev.* Solomon, *b.* 1752, *d.* 1834. Historical sketch of Northampton, from its first settlement; sermon, thanksgiving, Apr. 13. Northampton, 1815. 8°. (B 335, 1788)
— Sermon, Northampton, Jan. 5. Northampton, 1802. 8°. (B 335)
— Three sermons, Northampton, Mar. 30 and fast day, Apr. 4. Northampton, 1805. 8°. (B 1788)

Williams, Stephen, *D.D.* Names of persons taken captive at Deerfield, Feb. 1703/4; names of the slain; account of the mischief done [by Indians] in Deerfield, to the death of J. Williams. (*In* **Williams**, J. Redeemed captive. 1758.)
— Journal during his captivity. (*In* **Williams**, S. W. Biog. memoir of J. Williams. 1837.)
— *Funeral sermon on.* 1782. *See* **Breck**, R. (B 305)

Williams, Stephen West, *M.D.* Biog. memoir of Rev. J. Williams; with a sketch of Deerfield and account of the Indian wars; app., cont. the journal of S. Williams, and other papers relating to Indian wars. Greenfield, 1837. 12°.
— Genealogy and hist. of the family of Williams in America; partic. of descendants of R. Williams of Roxbury. Greenfield, 1847. 12°.
— Memoir of W. S. Williams. (*In* **Mass. Med. Soc.** Med. com., v. 4. 1829.) — Medical history of the Co. of Franklin. (*In* v. 7. 1848.)

Williams, T., *dramatist.* *See* **Williams**, Thomas J.

Williams, Theodore. Academical stenography; a simplified system of short hand. London, [1826]. 8°.

Williams, *Rev.* Theodore. CATALOGUE of the library of W. sold, 1827; [with ms. prices]. London, [1827]. 8°.

Williams, Thomas, *M.D.* Complete dictionary of arts and sciences. 1764-65. *See* **Croker**, T. H.

Williams, Thomas, *M.D.*, *of Deerfield*, *b.* 1718, *d.* 1775. WILLIAMS, S. W. Notice of W. (*In* **Mass. Med. Soc.** Med. comm., v. 4. 1829.)

Williams, Thomas. The age of infidelity; in answer to T. Paine's 'Age of reason'. Boston, 1794. 12°. (B 159, C 86)
— *Same.* Pt. 2; in answer to the 2d pt. of the 'Age of reason'. London, 1796. 8°.

Williams, Thomas. ERSKINE, T., *and* KYD, S. Speeches on the trial of W. for publishing Paine's 'Age of reason'; with Ld. Kenyon's Charge. 2d ed. London, [1797]. 8°. (C 253)
— *Same.* Phila., 1797. 8°. (B 631)

Williams, *Rev.* Thomas, *of Providence*, *b.* 1779. Discourse for April. Prov., 1816. 8°. (B 1126)
— The domestic chaplain. Hartford, 1839. 12°.
— The greatest sermon that ever was preached. 2d ed. New England, 1825. 8°. (B 1126)
— The official character of N. Emmons; sermon on his death. Boston, 1840. 8°. (B 1214)
— *Same.* Rhode Island ed. Prov., 1841. 8°. (B 1214)
— Sermon on the conclusion of the 2d century from the settlement of R. I. and Prov. Plantations. Prov., 1837. 8°. (B 1305)

Williams, Thomas J. Cabman no. 93; or, Found in a four wheeler; farce. (No. 24 *of* **De Witt's** acting plays.)
— Dandelion's dodges; farce. (No. 4 *of* **De Witt's** acting plays; — *and* no. 23 *of* **Spencer's** universal stage.)
— Dunducketty's picnic; or, On and off; farce. (No. 16 *of* **Spencer's** univ. stage.)
— I've written to Browne. (No. 17 *of* **Spencer's** univ. stage.)
— Larkins' love letters; farce. (No. 34 *of* **De Witt's** acting plays.)
— My turn next; farce. (No. 20 *of* **Spencer's** univ. stage.)
— Nursey chickweed; farce. (No. 45 *of* **Spencer's** univ. stage.)
— Old gooseberry; farce. (No. 52 *of* **Spencer's** univ. stage.)
— One too many for him; farce. (No. 33 *of* **De Witt's** acting plays.)
— Race for a widow; farce. (No. 33 *of* **Spencer's** univ. stage.)
— A silent protector; farce. (No. 37 *of* **De Witt's** acting plays.)
— Smashington Goit; or, Peace and quiet; farce. (No. 9 *of* **Spencer's** univ. stage.)
— An ugly customer; farce. (No. 58 *of* **Spencer's** univ. stage.)
— Who's who? or, All in a fog; farce. (No. 53 *of* **Spencer's** univ. stage; — *and* no. 98 *of* **De Witt's** acting plays.)
— *and* **Harris**, A. Ruth Oakley; drama. (*In* **Sargent**, E. Mod. stand. dr., v. 36.)

Williams, Thomas Walter. Digest of statute law, 9 Henry III.-30 Geo. III. Lond., 1791. 2 v. 8°.
Contents. Vol. 1. A-K. 2. L-W.

Williams, Timothy S., *Funeral sermon on.* 1849. *See* **Sprague**, W. B. (B 1738)

Williams, W. Appletons's new and complete U. S. guide book. N. Y., 1850. 2 v. 12°.

Williams, W. B. Sermon; Ephraim's idolatry and its consequences. (*In* **Suddards**, W. British pulpit, v. 1. 1837.)

Williams, Wm. Speech upon the electing of him speaker in Parliament, Mar. 21. London, 1680. f°. (A 54)
— Manning, J. A. (*In his* Lives of the speakers. 1851.
Williams, *Rev.* Wm., *of Hatfield*, *b.* 1665, *d.* 1741. Death of a prophet lamented; sermon, Northampton, Feb. 13, interment of S. Stoddard. Boston, 1729. 8°. (B 235, C 310)
— Directions [for] a true conversion. 2d ed. Boston, 1738. 12°. (C 11, 82)
— Great concern of Christians to preserve the doctrine of Christ; sermon, Watertown, June 11, ordin. of Warham Williams. Boston, 1723. 12°. (B 242, C 11, 51)
— Great duty of ministers; sermon, convention, May 26. Boston, 1726. 8°. (B 244, C 11)
— Plea for God; election sermon, May 27. Boston, 1719. 12°. (C 6)
— Work of ministers, *etc.*; sermon, Deerfield, Nov. 8, 1732, ordin. of J. Ashley. Bost., 1733. 8°. (B 335)
Williams, *Rev.* Wm., *of Weston*, *b.* 1688, *d.* 1753. God the strength of rulers; sermon, election, May 27. Boston, 1741. 8°. (B 145, 183)
— Martial wisdom recommended; sermon, artillery election, June 6. Boston, 1737. 8°. (B 145)
— The office of gospel ministers; sermon, Sutton. Oct. 15, ordination of D. Hall. Boston, 1729. 12°. (C 11)
— Serious consideration, that God will visit men for sin, *etc.*; sermon, Cambridge, Sept. 15, execution of P. Kennison. Boston, 1738. 8°. (B 235)
Williams, Wm., *b.* 1717, *d.* 1791. Marwnad ar farwolaeth y parchedig W. Williams, a fu farw, Ionawr 11. Caerfyrddin, 1791. 12°. (C 300)
Williams, Wm., *b.* 1731, *d.* 1811. Sanderson, J. (*In his* Biog. of the signers, v. 4. 1820.)
Williams, Wm., *Bp. of Waipu.* Christianity among the New Zealanders. Lond., 1867. 8°.
Williams, Wm. Mattieu. Fuel of the sun. London, 1870. 8°.
— Teaching of social economy. (*In* Nat. Assoc. Prom. Soc. Sci. Trans., 1857.)
— Through Norway with a knapsack, [1855]. 2d ed. London, 1859. 8°.
Williams, Wm. R., *D.D.* Increase of faith necessary to the success of Christian missions; sermon before the Board of Managers of the Baptist General Convention, N. Y., April 30. N. Y., 1834. 8° (B 1651)
— Sermon, death of A. Lincoln. (*In* Lincoln, A. Our martyr president. 1865.)
Williams, Wm. Stoddard. Williams, S. W. Memoir of W. (*In* Mass. Med. Soc. Med. comm., v. 4. 1829.)
Williams family. Williams, S. W. Geneal. and history of the W. family in America. Greenfield, 1847. 12°.
Williams. *See also* Willyams.
Williams & Norgate. Foreign catalogues, Oct. 1855 - June 57. London, *n.d.* 8°.
Contents. Classical catalogue. — Theological. — French. — German. — Suppl. map-cat. — Linguistic. — Scientific and medical.
Williams College, *Williamstown, Mass.* Catalogue of officers and students for 1839/40. Troy, 1839. 8°. (B 1165)
— *Same.* 1876/77, 78/79-80/81. N. Adams, 1876-80. 4 v. 8°.
— Catalogue of the library. Boston, 1852. 8°.
— *Same.* North Adams, 1875. 8°.
— Catalogus senatus academici, *etc.*, 1871, 72, 74, 75, 78. Oppidi Gulielmi, 1871-78. 5 v. 8°.
— General catalogue of the officers, alumni, *etc.* [Boston,] 1880. 8°.
— Inauguration of Pres. P. A. Chadbourne, July 27, 1872. Williamstown, 1872. 8°.
Note. Received too late to be entered in the previous part of the Catalogue.
— Laws. Stockbridge, 1795. 4°. (B 654)
— Obituary record. *n.p.*, 1877-81. 5 v. 8°.
— Publications of the presidents and professors, 1793-1876. 8°. North Adams, 1876. 8°. (E 343)
— Report of the examining committee, June. North Adams, 1874. 8°. (E 343)
— Report of Board of Visitors. North Adams, 1879. 8°. (E 343)
— Re-union of the class of 1850. N. Y., 1880. 8°. (E 343)
— Durfee, C. History of Williams College. Boston, 1860. 8°.
— - Williams biographical annals. Bost., 1871. 8°.
— Everett, E. Speech in support of the memorial of Harvard, Williams, and Amherst Colleges, Boston, Feb. 7. Camb., 1849. 8°. (B 1738)
— Fitch, E. Hist. sketch of Williams Coll. (*In* Mass. Hist. Soc. Col., v. 8. 1802.)
— Wells, D. A., *and* Davis, S. H. Sketches of Williams College. Williamstown, 1847. 8°.
— White, J. Address before the alumni, Aug. 14. Boston, 1855. 8°. (B 1576)
Williamsburg, *N. Y.* Stiles, H. R. Hist. of the village and city of W. (*In his* Hist. of Brooklyn, v. 2. 1869.)
Williamsburg, *Va.* Lewis, *Gen.* A. Orderly book of the Amer. army at W., under L., 1776; from the ms., with notes and introd., by C. Campbell. Richmond, 1860. 4°.
— Burns, J. R. Battle of W. N. Y., 1865. 24°.
Williamson, *Rev.* Abraham. Letters to a millenarian. N. Y., 1852. 12°.
Williamson, *Lieut.-Col.* George, *Funeral sermon on.* 1812. *See* Clark, G. (B 1242)
Williamson, George, *M.D.* Military surgery. London, 1863. 8°.
— Notes on the wounded from the mutiny in India; with description of the preparation of gun-shot injuries in the museum at Fort Pitt. London, 1859. 8°.
Williamson, Hugh, *M.D.* Anniv. discourse, 1810. (*In* N. Y. Hist. Soc. Col., v. 2. 1814.)
— Climate of America compared with that of the eastern continent. N. Y., 1811. 8°.
— Of comets. (*In* Lit. and Phil. Soc. of N. Y. Trans., v. 1. 1815.)
— History of North Carolina. Phila., 1812. 2 v. 8°.
— Hosack, D. Biog. memoir of W. N. Y., 1820. 8°. (B 570)
— - *Same.* (*In* N. Y. Hist. Soc. Col., v. 3. 1821; — *and in his* Essays, v. 1. 1824.)
Williamson, James. Dissertations. (*In* Eucleides. Elements. 1781-88.)
Williamson, Joseph. Castine, and the old coins found there. (*In* Maine Hist. Soc. Col., v. 6. 1859.)
Williamson, Passmore. Cannon, A. Proceedings on writ of habeas corpus in case of U. S. ex rel. J. H. Wheeler *vs.* W. Phila., 1856. 8°.
— Narrative of facts in the case of W. Phila., 1855. 12°. (C 259)
Williamson, Peter. Wilson, H., *and* Caulfield, J. Memoirs and anecdotes of W., remarkable for his captivity. (*In their* Book of wonderful characters. 1870.)
Williamson, *Lieut.* Robert S. Report of a survey in California for a railway route from the Mississippi to the Pacific, 1853. [Washington, 1854.] 8°. (U. S. 33d Cong. 1st sess. Ho. Doc. 129.)
— Report of explorations in California for R. R. routes to connect with the routes near the 35th and 32d parallels. (*In* United States. *War Dept.* Reports of explorations for a R. R. to the Pacific. 1853-54, v. 5. 1856.)
— Use of the barometer on surveys and reconnaissances; [with appendix]. N. Y., 1868. 4°. (U. S. Corps of Engineers. Prof. papers, no. 15.)
Williamson, Thomas, *M.D.* On certain causes affecting the origin of diseases in towns. (*In* Nat. Assoc. Prom. Soc. Sci. Trans., 1863.)
Williamson, Thomas S., *M.D.* Dacotas of the Mississippi. (*In* Schoolcraft, H. R. Hist. and statist. information. v. 1. 1851.)
Williamson, Wm. Crawford. On some microscopical objects found in the mud of the Levant; with remarks on the mode of formation of calcareous and infusorial siliceous rocks. (*In* Lit. and Phil. Soc. of Manchester. Mem., v. 8. 1848.)
Williamson, Wm. Cross. Ode before the H. L. of I. O. of O. F. (*In* Harvard College. *Societies.* Oration. 1849. H 13)
Williamson, Wm. Durkee. History of Maine, 1602-1820. Hallowell, 1832. 2 v. 8°.

— Notice of Orono, a chief at Penobscot. — Indian tribes in New England. (*In* **Mass. Hist. Soc.** Col., v. 29. 1846.)

Williamstown, *Mass.* KELLOGG, E. History of W. (*In* **Field,** D. D. History of the Co. of Berkshire, pt. 2. 1829.)

— NOBLE, M. Centennial discourse, Nov. 19. No. Adams, 1865. 8°.

Willibaldus, *Bishop of Aichstadt.* Travels, 721-727. (*In* **Wright,** T. Early travels in Palestine. 1848.)

— LIFE of W. (*In* **Lives** of the Eng. saints, v. 2. 1844.)

Willibaldus, *Presbyter.* De vita vel passione beatissimi martyris Bonifacii. (*In* **Pertz,** G. H. Mon. Germ., Scr., v. 2. 1829; — *in* **Bonifacius,** *St.* Opera, v. 2. 1844; — *in* **Jaffé,** P. Biblioth. rer. Germ., v. 3. 1866; — *and in* **Acta** sanct., v. 21. 1867.)

— VITA W. (*In* **Acta** sanct., v. 29. 1867.)

Willich, A. F. M., *M.D.* Lectures on diet and regimen. From 2d London ed. Boston, 1800. 2 v. 12°.

— *Same.* From 3d London ed. N. Y., 1801. 8°.

— Lectures on the physical education of children. (*In* **Struve,** C. A. Phys. ed. of children. 1801.)

Willich, Charles M. Annual suppl. to the tithe commutation tables for 1846. London, 1846. 4°. (**A 65**)

Willihelmus, *abbas Hirsaugiensis.* HAIMO. Vita. (*In* **Pertz.** Mon. Germ., Scr., v. 12. 1856.)

Willihelmus, *archæp. Moguntinus.* MEMORIÆ. (*In* **Jaffé,** P. Bibl. rer. German., v. 3. 1866.)

Willis, Browne. Additions. (*In* **Ecton,** J. Thes. rer. eccles. 1763.)

Willis, Francis. Translations. (*In* **Miscellany** poems. 1685.)

Willis, Francis, *M.D.* Treatise on mental derangement. London, 1823. 8°.

Willis, *Rev.* James. Prize essay on the commutation of tithes. (*In* **Pamphleteer,** 1816; v. 8 of **B 838**)

Willis, John. Inaugural dissertation on astringents. Phila., 1795. 8°. (**C 271**)

Willis, John R. List of birds of Nova Scotia; from notes made by Blakiston and Bland. (*In* **Smithsonian Inst.** Report, 1858.)

Willis, Lemuel. Semi-centennial address, celebration of the 50th anniversary of the dedication of the Universalist church, Salem. Salem, 1859. 8°.

Willis, *Rev.* Martin Wyman. Discourse on Christian doctrine. Bath, Me. Bath, 1853. 8°. (**B 1306**)

Willis, Nathaniel Parker. Complete works. N. Y., 1846. 8°.

Contents. Pencillings by the way. — Letters from under a bridge. — Dashes at life with a free pencil. — High life in Europe. — American life. — Inklings of adventure. — Loiterings of travel. — Ephemera. — Lecture on fashion. — Poetical works. — Sacred poems. — Poems of fashion. — The Lady Jane; novel in rhyme. — Miscellaneous poems. — Tortesa, the usurer. — Bianca Visconti; or, The heart overtasked.

— L'Amérique pittoresque; gravures faites sur les dessins de W. H. Bartlett; tr. de l'anglais par L. de Bauclas. Londres, 1840. 2 v. 4°.

— The annoyer. — Lines on leaving Europe. — Unwritten music. (*In* **Boston** book, 3d col. 1841.) — Minute philosophies. (*In* 4th col. 1851.)

— The convalescent. N. Y., 1859. 12°.

— Famous persons and places. Auburn, 1855. 12°.

Contents. Letters. — Second visit to England. — Eglinton tournament. — Talks over travel. — Letters from Eng. and the continent, 1845, 46. — The requested letter. — Nature criticised by art. — Jenny Lind. — The Kossuth day. — Death of Lady Blessington. — Moore and Barry Cornwall. — Jane Porter. — Ole Bull's Niagara. — Dr. Lardner's lecture.

— Fugitive poetry. Boston, 1829. 8°.

— Fun jottings; or, Laughs I have taken a pen to. N. Y., 1853. 12°.

Contents. Larks in vacation. — Meena Dimity. — Mrs. Passable Trott. — The spirit-love of Ione S—. — The ghost ball at Congress Hall. — Pasquali, the tailor of Venice. — The widow by brevet. — Nora Mehidy. — The marquis in petticoats. — Tom Fane and I. — The poet and the mandarin. — The Countess of Nyschriem and the handsome artist. — The inlet of peach blossoms. — The belle of the belfry. — The female ward. — The pharisee and the barber. — Mabel Wynne. — The bandit of Austria. — My one adventure as a brigand. — Count Pott's strategy. — The power of an injured look. — Mrs. Flimson. — From Saratoga.

— Health trip to the tropics. N. Y., 1854. 12°.

— Hurry-graphs; or, Sketches of scenery, celebrities, and society. N. Y., 1851. 12°.

Contents. Letters. — Old Whitey and Gen. Taylor. — The late President. — E. Everett. — Emerson. — Calhoun and Benton. — Fanny Kemble Butler. — Webster under the spell of Jenny Lind's music. — Sir H. Bulwer. — S. Lover. — Mrs. Anna Bishop. — Fields, the Amer. Moxon. — Grace Greenwood. — F. Cooper. — Schroeder and Fay. — Steffanoni. — F. Bremer. — Lieut. Wise. — Alboni. — Sir W. Don. — Parodi's Lucrezia Borgia. — Truffi. — E. Poe. — Whipple. — G. P. Morris. — Irving. — Jenny Lind. — Fashion and intellect in New York. — Want of married belles. — Married ladies and their daughters. — Usages of society. — Society and manners in N. Y. — Manners at watering-places. — Opera manners. — Wedding etiquettes. — Society news. — Usages, etiquette, *etc.* — Society this winter. — Shawl aristocracy. — Suggestion for the opera. — Coming opera season. — May day in N. Y. — Are operas moral, *etc.*? — Evening access to N. Y. information and amusement.

— Inklings of adventure. N. Y., 1836. 2 v. 12°.

Contents. Vol. 1. Pedlar Karl. — Niagara, Lake Ontario, St. Lawrence. — The Cherokee's threat. — F. Smith. — Edith Linsey. — Scenes of fear. — Incidents on the Hudson. 2. The Gipsy of Sardis. — Tom Fane and I. — Larks in vacation. — A log in the Archipelago. — Miscel. papers.

— Lecture on fashion before the N. Y. Lyceum, June. N. Y., 1844. 8°. (**A 64**)

— Letters from under a bridge, and poems. London, 1840. 4°.

— Life here and there. N. Y., 1850. 12°.

Contents. Edith Lindsey. — Scenes of fear. — Incidents on the Hudson. — Pedlar Karl. — Niagara, Lake Ontario, St. Lawrence. — The Cherokee's threat. — F. Smith. — Leaves from the heart book of Ernest Clay. — Beauty and the Beast. — Miss Jone's son. — Lady Rachel. — Wigwam *versus* Almack's.

— Out-doors at Idlewild. N. Y., 1855. 12°.

— Paul Fane. N. Y., 1857. 12°.

— Pencillings by the way. N. Y., 1852. 12°.

— People I have met. N. Y., 1850. 12°.

Contents. A revelation of a previous life. — The phantom head upon the table. — Getting to windward. — Two buckets in a well. — Light Vervain. — Brown's day with the Mimpsons. — Mr. and Mrs. Follett. — Lady Ravelgold. — Kate Crediford. — Beware of dogs and waltzing. — Flirtation and fox-chasing — The revenge of the Signor Basil. — Love and diplomacy. — The madhouse of Palermo. — An up-town crisis. — The icy veil. — Born to love pigs and chickens. — Those ungrateful Blidgimses. — Belles of New York.

— Poems, sacred, passionate, and humourous. N. Y., 1864. 12°.

— Romance of travel. N. Y., 1840. 12°.

Contents. Lady Ravelgold. — Paletto's bride. — Violanta Cesarina. — Pasquali. — The bandit of Austria. — Oonder Hoofden. — The picker and piler. — Stratford-on-Avon. — Charlecote.

— Rural letters and thoughts at leisure. N. Y., 1849. 12°.

Contents. Letters from under a bridge. — The four rivers. — Letter to the unknown purchaser and next occupant of Glenmary. — Glenmary poems. — Invalid rambles in Germany, 1845. — Letters from watering-places. — A plain man's love.

— Summer cruise in the Mediterranean. N. Y., 1859. 12°.

Willis, Richard Storrs. Sketch of Mendelssohn. (*In* **Lampadius,** W. A. Life of Mendelssohn. 1865.)

Willis, *Rev.* Robert, *b.* 1800. Architectural history of Canterbury Cathedral. London, 1845. 8°.

— On the teeth of wheels. (*In* **Instit. of Civil Engin.** Trans., v. 2. 1842.)

— On machines and tools for working in metal and other materials. (*In* **Society for the Encouragement of Arts.** Lectures, 1st ser. 1852.)

Willis, Robert, *M.D.* Benedict de Spinoza; his life, correspondence, and ethics. London, 1870. 8°.

Willis, Thomas, *M.D.* Opera omnia. Genevæ, 1676. 4°.

Contents. Same as the Amst. ed. of 1682, *omitting* De anima brutorum *and what follows.*

— *Same.* Stud. G. Blasii. Amstel., 1682. 4°.

Contents. De fermentatione. — De febribus. — De urinis. — Cerebri anatome, nervorumque descriptio et usus. — De morbis convulsivis. — De scorbuto. — Affectionum quæ dicuntur hystericæ et hypochondriacæ pathologia spasmodica vindicata. — De sanguinis incalescentia. — De motu musculari. — De anima brutorum. — De medicamentorum operationibus in corpore humano.

— De anima brutorum. Londini, 1672. 16°.

— Niceron, J. P. (*In his* Mémoires, v. 15. 1731; *and, Germ.*, v. 11. 1754.)

Willis, Wm. Address before the New Bedford Aux. Soc. for the Suppression of Intemperance. New Bedford, 1819. 8°. (B 994, 998)

Willis, Wm., *of Portland.* Documentary history of the State of Maine. Portland, 1869. 8°. (Maine Hist. Soc. Col., 2d series, v. 1.)

— History of the law; the courts, and lawyers of Maine. Portland, 1863. 8°.

— History of Portland; with notices of neighboring towns. Portland, 1831. 8°.

— *Same.* 2d ed., rev. and enl. Portland, 1865. 8°.

— *Same.* Pt. 1. (*In* **Maine Hist. Soc.** Col., v. 1. 1865.)

— Notice of W. Ladd. — Account of a settlement on Sheepscot River. (*In* **Maine Hist. Soc.** Col., v. 2. 1847.) — Address at Augusta Feb. 2, 1855. — Language of the Abnaquies. (*In* v. 4.) — Inaugural address, cont. biographical notices of former presidents, 1857. (*In* v. 5.) — Remarks on coins found at Portland, 1849 and at Richmond's Island, 1855. — Scotch-Irish immigration to Maine, and a summary history of Presbyterianism. (*In* v. 6. 1859.)

— Summary history of Portland. (*In* **Smith, T.** Journal. 1849.)

Willis, *Rev.* Zephaniah. Description of Kingston, Mass. (*In* **Mass. Hist. Soc.** Col., v. 13. 1815.)

— *Funeral sermon on.* 1847. *See* **Pope, A. R.** (B 1228)

Willis (G.) & Sotheran (H.). Catalogue of books on sale, 1858, 59, 62. London, 1858–62. 3 v. 8°.

— Catalogue of 30,000 volumes. Lond., 1866. 8°.

— Willis's price current: Catalogue of books on sale. No. 190–200; Christmas no. London, 1863. 12 v. 4°.

Willis Family. Morse, A. (*In his* Genealog. register, v. 2. 1859.)

Willison, *Rev.* John. Looking to Jesus. Boston, 1743. 12°. (C 4)

— Sacramental meditations and advices. Newburyport, 1794. 12°.

— The young communicant's catechism. N. Y., 1839. 18°.

Williston, *Rev.* Noah. Sermon, ordination of D. H. Williston, Turnbridge, June 26, 1793. Hanover, 1794. 8°. (B 1324)

Williston, Seth, *D.D.* Discourses on the Sabbath. New Haven, 1847. 12°.

— The parable of the sower; two sermons. N. Y., 1834. 8°. (B 1306)

— Slavery not a scriptural ground of division in efforts for salvation of the heathen. N. Y., 1844. 12°. (C 258)

Willm, Joseph. Secondes lectures françaises. Paris, 1832. 12°.

Willmore, Graham, *and* **Beedell, E.** Mercantile and maritime guide. Glasgow, 1856. 8°.

Willmott. *See also* **Wilmot.**

Willmott, Robert Aris. The Christian's harvest home; sermon, Bear Wood, funeral of J. Walter. London, 1847. 8°. (B 1227)

— Gems of epistolary correspondence; selected from the best English authors. London, 1846. 8°.

— The jasper clouded and the rainbow round the throne; sermon, June 2. London, 1844. 8°. (B 1346)

— Journal of a summer time in the country. N. Y., 1852. 12°.

— Lives of the English sacred poets. 2d ed. London, 1839–53. 2 v. 16°.

Contents. Vol. 1. Introduction. — Sir J. Davies. — G. Sandys. — G. Fletcher. — P. Fletcher. — G. Wither. — R. Herrick. — T. Heywood. — F. Quarles. — J. Quarles. — G. Herbert. — Wm. Habington. — H. Vaughan. — R. Crashaw. — H. More. — J. Beaumont. — Flatman. — Additional notes. 2. J. Milton. — T. Ken. — I. Watts. — E. Young. — R. Blair. — Sir R. Blackmore. — Parnell. — Addison. — Gray. — C. Smart. — W. Cowper. — J. Hurdis. — W. H. Roberts. — J. Grahame. — R. Heber. — Additional notes.

— Memoir of George Herbert. (*In* **Herbert, G.** Poetical works. 1855.)

Willock, John. The abbot of Crossraguell and W.'s correspondence, at Ayr, 1559. (*In* **Wodrow Soc.** Miscel., v. 1. 1844.)

Willock, John. Voyages and adventures of W. Phila., 1798. 12°.

Willock, Wm. Alexander, *D.D.* Junior classes of elementary schools. (*In* **Nat. Assoc. Prom. Soc. Sci.** Trans., 1861.)

Willoughby, *Sir* Hugh. Voyage to Russia and Siberia, [1553–81]. (*In* **Harris, J.** Col. of voy., v. 1. 1705; — *in* **Pinkerton, J.** Col. of voy., v. 1. 1808; — *in* **Hakluyt, R.** Col. of voy., v. 1. 1809; — *and in* **Hamel, J.** England and Russia. 1854.)

Willoughby, Sarah, *Funeral sermon on.* 1839. *See* **Pierce, I. B.** (B 1228)

Willoughby, Lady, Diary of; by **H. M. Rathbone.** London, 1844–48. 2 v. 4°.

— *Same.* Part 1. N. Y., 1845. 16°.

Willow copse, The; by D. Boucicault. (*In* **Sargent, E.** Mod. stand. drama, v. 3.)

Wills, Alfred. 'The Eagle's Nest', a summer home among the Alps. London, 1860. 8°.

— Passage of the Fenêtre de Salena. (*In* **Ball, J.** Peaks and passes. 1859.)

Wills, Archibald, *pseud.* Poem on door-keeping, [and other poems]. Raleigh, 1808. 8°. (B 450)

Wills, *Lieut. Gen* Charles. The case of Col. G. Burston, with respect to the dispute between him and W. London, 1720. 8°. (B 1454)

Wills, Frank. Ancient English ecclesiastical architecture. N. Y., 1850. 4°.

Wills, *Rev.* James. Essay upon Mr. Stewart's explanation of certain processes of the human understanding. (*In* **Roy. Irish Acad.** Trans., v. 19. 1841.) — Essay on accidental association. (*In* v. 21.) — The law of spontaneous and voluntary association. (*In* v. 22.) — Dreams. (*In* v. 23. 1856.)

Wills, John A. Address before the Philological Inst., Dec. 8. Pittsburgh, 1843. 8°. (B 1306, 1585)

Wills, Obadiah. Vindication of a treatise, Infant-baptism asserted and vindicated by Scripture and antiquity; answer to H. D'Anvers. London, 1675. 8°.

Wills, W. G. David Chantrey. (*In* **Temple Bar**, v. 13–16. 1864–66.)

Wills, Wm. John. A successful exploration through the interior of Australia; ed. by W. Wills. London, 1863. 8°.

— Great Britain. *Parliament.* Australian exploring exped. [by] Burke and Wills. [London,] 1862. f°.

Wills. Swinburn, H. Treatise of testaments and last wills. London, 1590. 4°.

— Spelman, H. Of the original of testaments and wills. [1633.] (*In his* English works. 1727.)

— Gr. Britain. *Parl.* Act for amend. of the law [respecting] wills; with remarks by R. T. Fisher. London, 1837. 12°.

— — *Another copy, without the 'Remarks'.* (B 1452)

Collections.

— Nicolas, N. H. Testamenta vetusta; illust. of manners, customs, *etc.*, Henry II.–Elizabeth. London, 1826. 2 v. 8°.

— Raine, J. Wills and inventories of the northern counties of England from the 11th century. Lond., 1835. 8°. (Surtees Soc., v. 2.)

— - Testamenta Eboracensia; or, Wills registered at York from 1300 downwards. London, 1836-69. 4 v. 8°. (Surtees Soc., v. 4, 30, 45, 53.)
— EDWARDS, H. Collection of curious bequests. London, 1842. 8°.
— TYMMS, S. Wills and inventories from the registers of Bury St. Edmunds' and Sudbury. London, 1850. 4°. (Camden Soc., v. 49.)
— RAINE, J. Wills and inventories from the registry of the archdeaconry of Richmond. London, 1853. 8°. (Surtees Soc., v. 26.)
— PICCOPE, G. J. Lancaster and Cheshire wills and inventories. Manchester, 1857-61. 3 v. 4°. (Surtees Soc., v. 33, 51, 54.)
— RAINE, J. Wills and inventories from the registry at Durham. London, 1860. 8°. (Surtees Soc., v. 38.)
— NICHOLS, J. G., *and* BRUCE, J. Wills from Doctor's commons; proved in the court of Canterbury, 1495-1695. London, 1863. 4°. (Camden Soc., v. 83.)
Note. For single wills *see* **Boylston, T.**; — **Carroll, C.**; — **Churchill, S.**; — **Dearborn, B.**; — **Tenison, T.**
See also **Executors.**

Willsborough, *N.Y.* WATSON, W. C. (*In his* Pioneer history of the Champlain Valley. 1863.)

Willson. *See also* **Wilson.**

Willson, Byron Forceythe. The old sergeant, and other poems. Boston, 1867. 12°.

Willson, *Rev.* Edmund Burke. Address, Petersham, commemoration of its 100th anniversary, 1854. Boston, 1855. 8°.
— *Another copy.* (B 1599)
— The bad Friday; sermon, W. Roxbury, Sunday after the return of A. Burns. Boston, 1854. 8°. (B 1306, 1485)

Willson, Edward James. Examples of Gothic architecture in England; by A. Pugin; [text] by W. Vol. 1. London, 1831. 4°.
— Specimens of Gothic architecture in England; by A. Pugin; [text] by W. (Vol. 1, 3d ed., 2, 2d ed.) London, 1825-26. 2 v. 4°.

Willson, *Rev.* James M. The deacon; inquiry into the nature, duties, *etc.*, of the office of deacon. Phila., 1841. 8°.

Willson, James Renwick, *D.D.* Address on African slavery, Fayetteville, Sept. 14. Chambersburg, 1837. 8°. (B 1474)
— On the atonement. Phila., 1817. 8°.

Willson, *Rev.* Luther. The character and effects of Christian love; sermon, death of Mrs. M. Williams. Prov., 1816. 8°. (B 960, 963, 1228)
— Remarks upon a sermon preached in Brooklyn, Conn., Aug. 24, 1817, by W. Preston. Boston, 1818. 8°. (B 264)
— Review of eccl. proc. in the Cong. church, Brooklyn, *etc.* Worcester, 1818. 8°. (B 270)

Willson, Marcius. History of the United States. 14th thous. N. Y., 1847. 12°.

Wilughby, Francis. Ornithologiæ libri tres; ed. J. Rains. Londini, 1676. f°.
— Relation of a voyage through Spain. (*In* **Ray, J.** Obs. made in a journey through the Low Countries, 1673; — *and in* **Harris, J.** Col. of voy., v. 2. 1705; 1764.)
— MEMOIR of W. (*In* **Jardine, W.** Naturalist's lib. Orn., v. 13. 1843.)

Willyams. *See also* **Williams.**

Willyams, *Rev.* Cooper. Campaign in the W. Indies, 1796. London, 1796. 4°.
— Voyage up the Mediterranean under Nelson; with a descr. of the Battle of the Nile. London, 1802. 4°.

Wilmer, James. Memoirs. Balt., 1792. 8°. (W 45)
— Sermon, doctrine of the New Jerusalem Church. Balt., 1792. 8°. (W 33)

Wilmer, James Jones. Address to the citizens of the U. S. on national representation. Balt., [1796]. 8°. (W 60)
— Consolation; a replication to T. Paine and others on theologics. Phila., 1794. 8°. (W 33)

Wilmer, John. The modern vassal. Boston, [1849]. 8°.
Note. From **Littell's** living age, v. 23. 1849.

Wilmer, Richard H., *Bp. of Ala.* Future good the explanation of present reverses; sermon, Mobile and elsewhere in Ala. Charlotte, 1864. 16°.

Wilmer, Wm. Holland, *D.D.* Discourse, June 24, anniversary of St. John the Baptist. Alexandria, 1820. 8°. (W 4)

Wilmington, *Delaware.* FERRIS, B. History of W., to [1845]. (*In his* Hist. of orig. settlements on the Delaware. 1846.)
— MONTGOMERY, E. Reminiscences of W. Phila., 1851. 8°.

Wilmington daily commercial. Wilmington, Del., 1867-76. 15 v. f°.

Wilmingtons, The; by [Mrs. A. C. Marsh Caldwell]. N. Y., 1850. 8°.

Wilmot. *See also* **Willmot.**

Wilmot, *judge.* Speech at the Bible meeting, and lecture on the Catacombs. St. John, N. B., 1859. 8°. (B 1360)

Wilmot, *Sir* Eardley Eardley. Letter on the increase of crime. (*In* **Pamphleteer,** 1828; v. 29 of B 838)

Wilmot, John, *2d Earl of Rochester.* Poems, and tragedy of Valentinian. London, 1696. 8°.
— Poems. (*In* **Chalmers, A.** Works of the Eng. poets, v. 8. 1810.)
— Poetical works; with life. (*In* **Anderson, R.** Brit. poets, v. 6. 1795.)
— Songs. (*In* **Campbell, T.** Spec. of Brit. poets, v. 4. 1819.)
— BURNET, G., *Bp.* Life of John, Earl of Rochester. London, 1820. 12°.
— - *Same.* Dublin, 1681. 4°.
— - *Same.* London, 1724. 8°. (B 745)
— - *Same.* Some account, *etc.* 2d Amer. ed. Boston, 1803. 18°.
— - *Same.* Boston, 1812. 12°.
— - *Same.* (*In* **Wordsworth, C.** Eccl. biog., v. 4. 1839.)
— CRICHTON, A. (*In his* Converts from infidelity, v. 1. 1827. Constable's miscel., v. 6.)
— JOHNSON, S. (*In his* Works, v. 9, 1806; *and* Lives of Eng. poets, v. 1. 1810.)
— PARSONS, R. Sermon, funeral of the Earl of R. (*Appended to* **Burnet, G.** Life of R. 1820.)

Wilmot, *Sir* John Eardley, *b.* 1709, *d.* 1792. [SKETCH, with some letters.] (*In* **Precept** and example. 1825.)
— CAMPBELL, J. Life of Sir E. Wilmot. (*In his* Lives of Chief Justices of Eng., v. 2. 1849.)
— MEMOIRS of Sir J. E. Wilmot. Lond., 1802. 4°.
— ROSCOE, H. Life of W. (*In his* Lives of eminent Brit. lawyers. 1833; v. 2. 1841.)

Wilmot, *Sir* John Eardley Eardley, *b.* 1748, *d.* 1815. Short defence of the opposition. London, 1778. 8°.
— Present mode of budding and grafting fruit trees. (*In* **Soc. Prom. Useful Arts in N. Y.** Trans., v. 4, pt. 2. 1819.)

Wilmot, *Sir* John Eardley Eardley. Reminiscences of T. A. Smith. London, 1860. 8°.
— Criminal appeal. (*In* **Nat. Assoc. Prom. Soc. Sci.** Trans., 1867.)

Wilmot, Robert. Tancred and Gismunda. (*In* **Dodsley, R.** Col. of old plays, v. 2. 1825.)

Wilmot family, The; by Mrs. Drummond. Edin., 1848. 18°.

Wilmot proviso. JENKINS, T. Speech on the Wilmot proviso, Feb. 13. Wash., 1847. 8°. (B 1502)

Wilmot. *See also* **Willmott.**

Wilson, *Commissary.* Orderly book; expedition of the British and provincial army, under Maj.-Gen. J. Amherst, against Ticonderoga and Crown Point, 1759. Albany, 1857. 4°.

Wilson, Alexander, *M.D., Prof., d.* 1786. WILSON, P. Biog. account of A. Wilson. (*In* **Roy. Soc. of Edin.** Trans., v. 10. 1826.)

Wilson, Alexander, *b.* 1766, *d.* 1813. American ornithology; the natural history of the birds of the U. S. Phila., 1808-14. 9 v. 4°.

— *and* **Bonaparte**, C. L. Amer. ornithology; ed. by R. Jameson. Edin., 1831. 4 v. 16° (Constable's miscel., v. 68-71.)

— Bonaparte, C. L. Observations on the nomenclature of W.'s ornithology. Phila., 1826. 8°.

— Memoir of W. (*In* **Jardine,** *Sir* W. Naturalist's lib., Orn., v. 14. 1843.)

— Paton, A. P. Wilson, the ornithologist; a new chapter in his life. London, 1863. 8°.

— Peabody, W. B. O. (*In* **Sparks,** J. Amer. biog., v. 2. 1834.)

Wilson, Alexander Philip. Febrile diseases. Winchester, 1803-04. 4 v. 8°.

— Observations on the use and abuse of mercury, and on the precautions necessary in its employment. Winchester, 1805. 8°. (B 823)

Wilson, Andrew, *M.D.* Observations on the action of morbid sympathies. Edin., 1818. 8°.

Wilson, Andrew, *graduate of Edin. Univ.* Infanti perduti. (*In* **Edinburgh** essays, 1857.)

Wilson, Andrew. The ever victorious army; history of the Chinese campaign under Gordon and the suppression of the Tai-Ping rebellion. London, 1868. 8°.

Wilson, Arthur. History of James I. (*In* **Kennet,** W., *and* **Hughes,** J. Complete hist. of Eng. 1796.)

Wilson, *Mrs.* Augusta J. (Evans). Macaria; or, Altars of sacrifice. 2d ed. Richmond, 1864. 8°.

Wilson, Benjamin, *F. R. S.* Series of experiments on phosphori and their prismatic colors; new properties of light; also two memoirs of J. B. Beccaria. London, 1776. 4°.

Wilson, Benjamin O. *and* George C. Botanic materia medica. Boston, 1850. 8°.

Wilson, Bird, *D.D.* Address before the trustees, *etc.*, of of the General Theological Seminary of the Prot. Episc. Ch. in the U. S., Nov. 13. N. Y., 1823. 8°. (B 1574)

— Sermon in the chapel of the Seminary of the Prot. Episc. Ch. in the U. S., Dec. 9, 1827. N. Y., 1828. 8°. (B 957)

Wilson, Charles. Memoirs of W. Congreve. London, 1730. 8°.

Wilson, Charles. Gout and rheumatism. 3d ed., enl. London, 1823. 8°.

Wilson, Charles, *ed.* The art of sail-making as practised in the royal navy. 4th ed. corr. London, 1843. 8°.

Wilson, *Capt.* Charles Wm. Ordnance survey of Jerusalem; [plates]. *See* **Gr. Brit.** *Ordnance Survey.*

— Ordnance survey of Jerusalem. — Sea of Galilee. (*In* **Morrison,** W. Recovery of Jerusalem. 1871 [1870].)

Wilson, *Mrs.* Cornwell Baron. *See* **Wilson, M. C. B.**

Wilson, Daniel, *Bp. of Calcutta, b.* 1778, *d.* 1858. Common sense. (*In* **Oxford** English prize essays, v. 2. 1836.)

— Defence of the Church Miss. Soc. against the objections of J. Thomas. (*In* **Pamphleteer,** 1818; v. 11 of B 838)

— Divine authority of the Lord's day asserted. Boston, 1831. 12°.

— Farewell discourse. (*In* **Suddards,** W. Brit. pulpit, v. 1. 1837.)

— Sermon. (*In* **Lond. Soc. Prom. Christianity Amongst the Jews.** 8th report. 1816. B 1033)

— Yonge, C. M. (*In her* Pioneers and founders. 1871.)

Wilson, *Rev.* Daniel, *of Islington, son of preceding.* Scott, W. Letter to W. on his 'Appeal to the evangelical members of the Church of England'. 4th ed. London, 1850. 8°. (B 1231)

Wilson, Daniel, *Prof. in Univ. Coll., Toronto.* Chatterton; a biog. study. London, 1869. 8°.

— Indications of ancient customs, suggested by certain cranial forms. (*In* **Amer. Antiq. Soc.** Proc., 1863.)

— On physical ethnology. (*In* **Smithsonian Inst.** Report, 1862.)

— Prehistoric annals of Scotland. 2d ed. London, 1863. 2 v. 8°.

— Prehistoric man; researches into the origin of civilization in the old and new world. London, 1862. 2 v. 8°.

— Supposed uniformity of cranial type throughout all varieties of the Amer. race. (*In* **Amer. Assoc.** Proc., v. 11. 1858.)

Wilson, Erasmus. *See* **Wilson, W. J. E.**

Wilson, F. A., *and* **Richards**, A. B. Britain redeemed and Canada preserved. London, 1850. 8°.

Wilson, George. Mortimer, J. Trial of W. (*In his* Report of trials. 1830. B 949)

Wilson, *Prof.* George, *b.* 1818, *d.* 1859. Chemical final causes. (*In* **Edinburgh** essays. 1857.)

— Life and works of H. Cavendish. London, *Cavendish Soc.*, 1851. 8°.

— Progress of the telegraph; introductory lecture on technology for 1858-59. Camb., 1859. 8°.

— *and* **Geikie**, A. Memoir of E. Forbes. Camb., 1861. 8°.

— Wilson, J. A. Memoir of W. Lond., 1862. 8°.

Wilson, George C. Botanic materia medica. 1850. *See* **Wilson, B. O.**

Wilson, Henn. Trow's N. Y. city directory, 1854/55, 58. 61, 62, 64, 66, 72/73. N. Y., 1854-72. 7 v. 12°.

Note. 1872/73 has the title 'Wilson's business directory of N. Y. city'.

Wilson, Henry. Surveying improved. 4th ed; added, Geodœsia accurata, by W. Hume. London, 1755. 8°.

Wilson, *Capt.* Henry. Keate, G. An account of the Pelew Islands; from the journals, *etc.*, of W., 1783. 2d ed. London, 1788. 4°.

— *Same, abridged.* (*In* **Shipwrecks** and disasters, v. 3. 1812.)

Wilson, Henry, *Vice Pres. U. S.* Aggressions of the slave power; speech, reply to J. Davis, Jan. 26. Wash., 1860. 8°. (B 1481)

— Defence of the Republican party; speech on the president's message, Dec. 19, 1856. Wash., 1857. 8°. (B 1507)

— History of the anti-slavery measures of the 37th and 38th Congress., 1861-64. Boston, 1864. 12°.

— Speech, bill to abolish slavery in the District of Columbia, March 27. Wash., 1862. 8°. (B 1481)

— Speech, President's message on the Lecompton constitution, Feb. 3, 4. Wash., 1858. 8°. (B 1509)

— Speech, reply to Mr. Douglas on the petition of the Kansas legislature and a question of veracity settled for B. F. Hallet, Apr. 14. Wash., 1856. 8°. (B 1508, 1509)

— State of affairs in Kansas; speech, Feb. 18. Wash., 1856. 8°. (B 1509)

— Suppression of the slave trade; speech, Senate, May 21. Wash., 1860. 8°. (B 1481)

— Territorial slave code; speech in the Senate, Jan. 25. Wash., 1860. 8°. (B 1481)

— Stowe, H. B. (*In her* Men of our times. 1868.)

Wilson, Henry, *and* **Caulfield**, J. The book of wonderful characters; memoirs and anecdotes of remarkable and eccentric persons in all ages and countries. London, [1870]. 8°.

Contents. F. Battalia, the stone eater. — N. Bentley, the well-known Dirty Dick. — Bertholde, prime minister to Alboinus. — Miss Biffin, born without arms. — J. Boruwlaski, the Polish dwarf. — T. Britton, the musical small-coal man. — J. Broughton, a notorious pugilist. — E. Brownrigg, executed for cruelty and murder. — M. Buchinger, the little man of Nuremberg. — J. Capper, the enemy of flies. — B. M. Carew, king of the beggars. — J. Clark, the posture-master. — T. Cooke, the notorious Islington miser. — D. Cuerton and his astonishing feats. — Baron D'Aguilar, of Starvation Farm. — D. Dancer, the remarkable miser. — J. Darney, a character in Cumberland. — D'Eon, the Chevalier, who passed as a woman. — C. Desseasau, the vain dwarf. — H. Dimsdale, mayor of Garrat. — C. Domery, the remarkable glutton. — S. Dunstan, mayor of Garrat. — M. East, alias J. How. — Eaters of iron; W. Reeves and J. Cummings. — J. Elwes, the remarkable miser. — T. H. Everitt, the enormous baby. — M. Finch, queen of the gipsies. — E. Fleigen, who lived on the smell of flowers. — Fire and poison eaters, *etc.*; Richardson, De Hightrehight, R. Powell. — Jemmy Gordon, an eccentric character of Cambridge. — J. Hall, the rope dancer. — Miss Harvey, the beautiful Albiness. — Miss Hawtin, born without arms. — S. House, the patriotic publican. — E. Hoyle, of Sowerby, Yorkshire. — J. Hudson, dwarf to Charles I. — T. Hudson, remarkable for his misfortunes. — H. Jenkins, the modern Methusaleh. — H. C. Jennings, the remarkable virtuoso. — W. Kingston, born without arms. — D. Lambert, of surprising corpulency. — T. Laugher, commonly called 'Old Tommy'. — — H. Lemoine, an eccentric bookseller. — J. Lewson, an eccentric old lady. — W. Lolkes, the Dutch dwarf. — M. Lovat, who crucified himself. — F. Marchand, the great water-spouter. — M. M'Avoy, the blind girl. — S. M'Donald, commonly called Big Sam. — A. Moore, the fasting woman. — G. Morland, a celebrated painter. — Nice New, a well-known-character at Reading. — Old Boots, of Ripon in Yorkshire. — T. Parr, who died at the age of 152 years. — Peter the wild boy of the woods of Hamelin. — F. Powell, the astonishing pedestrian. — Lord Rokeby, of singular eccentricity. — G. Romondo, an eccentric mimic. — C. A. Seurat, the living skeleton. — J. Smith, better known by the name of Buckhorse. — J. Southcott, an extraordinary fanatic. — W. Stevenson, a notorious beggar. — M. A. Talbot, the female sailor. — Madam Teresia, the Corsican fairy. — S. Terry, the Botany Bay Rothschild. — Toby, a begging impostor. — F. Trouvillou, the horned man. — B. Urslerin, the hairy-faced woman. — J. Valerius, born without arms. — Miss Whitehead, the bank nun. — R. Williams, commonly called the Monster. — P. Williamson, remarkable for his captivity. — T. Wood, the abstemious miller. — E. Woodcock, buried in snow nearly eight days.

Wilson, *Rev.* Henry Bristow. Schemes of Christian comprehension. (*In* **Oxford** essays, 1857.)

— Séances historiques de Genève. — The national church. (*In* **Essays** and reviews. 1860.)

— Speech before the committee of the Privy Council in the cause of Wilson *vs.* Fendall. London, 1863. 8°.

Wilson, Horace Hayman. Works. London, 1862–70. 10 v. 8°.

Contents. Vol. 1, 2. The religion of the Hindus. 3-5. Sanskrit literature. 6-10. The Vishńu Puráńa. — Index.

— History of British India, 1805-35. London, 1848. 3 v. 8°.

— Introduction to the grammar of the Sanskrit language. 2d ed. London, 1847. 8°.

— Select specimens of the theatre of the Hindus; tr. from the original Sanskrit. 2d ed. London, 1835. 2 v. 8°.

Contents. Vol. 1. Preface. — Treatise on the dramatic system of the Hindus. — List of Hindu plays. — *Dramas from the orig. Sanskrit.* The Mrichchakati, or the toy-cart. — Vikrama and Urvasé, or the hero and the nymph. — Uttara Ráma Cheritra, or contin. of the hist. of Ráma. 2. Málatí and Mádhava, or the stolen marriage. — Mudrá Rákshasa, or the signet of the minister. — Retnávali, or the necklace. — Appendix, cont. short accounts of different dramas.

Note. For other trans. *see* **Kalidasa**; — **Puráńa**; — **Veda.**

— Several articles.] (*In* **Philological Soc.** Proc., 1842-44.)

— Several articles.] (*In* **Med. and Phys. Soc. of Calcutta.** Trans., v. 1-3. 1825-27.)

— CATALOGUE of [his] library, sold. [London, 1861.] 8°.

Wilson, James, *b. abt.* 1742, *d.* 1798. Works; ed. by B. Wilson. Phila., 1804. 3 v. 8°.

Contents. Vol. 1, 2, 3. Lectures on law. 3. On the history of property. — Considerations on the nature and extent of the legislative authority of the Brit. Parl., 1774. — Speech in the convention for the province of Penn., 1775. — Oration, 4 July, 1778, Phila. — Speech on choosing the members of the senate by electors, 31 Dec. 1789. — Speech, 19 Jan. 1790, in the convention of Penn., for amending the constitution of the State. — Charge delivered to the grand jury in the circuit court of the U. S. for the district of Va., May 1791. — Considerations on the Bank of N. A., 1785.

— Considerations on the nature and extent of the legislative authority of the Brit. Parl. Phila., 1774. 8°. (B 359, 377)

— Introd. lecture to a course of law lectures; with a plan of the lectures. Phila., 1791. 8°. (B 465)

— Vindication of the colonies, 1775. — Speech on the federal constitution. (*In* **Moore,** F. Amer. eloquence, v. 1. 1864.)

— SANDERSON, J. (*In his* Biog. of the signers, v. 6. 1824.)

Wilson, James, *D.D., of Falkirk.* Defence of public or social worship, in a letter to G. Wakefield. Stockport, 1792. 8°. (B 1371)

Wilson, *Rev.* James, *of Providence, b.* 1759, *d.* 1839. Letters to E. S. Ely on Calvinism. Boston, 1814. 8°.

— Oration, Providence, 4th July. Prov., 1804. 8°. (B 944)

— Sermon, July 25, death of Mrs. Z. Wheeler. Prov., 1802. 8°. (B 335)

Wilson, *Capt.* James, *b.* 1760, *d.* 1814. CRICHTON, A. (*In his* Converts from infidelity, v. 2. 1827. Constable's miscel., v. 7.)

— DAVENPORT, R. A. Escape of W. (*In his* Narratives, v. 1. 1840. Fam. lib., v. 74.)

— GRIFFIN, J. Memoirs of W. *n.t.p.* [London, 1815.] 8°.

— — *Same.* With app. Boston, 1822. 8°.

— SMITH, W. Interesting circumstances in the life of W. (*In his* Voyage in a missionary ship. 1813.)

Wilson, James, *M.D.* Lectures on the blood and vascular system. London, 1819. 8°.

— Lectures on the structure and physiology o the skeleton and diseases of the bones and joints. London, 1820. 8°.

— Lectures on the urinary and genital organs of the human body. London, 1821. 8°.

— Observations on incurvations of the spine arising from the softness of the bones. London, 1821. 8°. (B 827, 829)

— Pharmacopœia chirurgica; or, Manual of chirurgical pharmacy. London, 1814. 12°.

Wilson, James, *F.R.S.E., of Woodville, b.* 1795, *d.* 1856. Sketches of the natural history of the North American regions. (*In* **Tytler,** P. F. Progress of discovery. 1832. Edin cab. lib. 1846. Harper's fam. lib., v. 53.)

— Voyage round the coast of Scotland. Edin., 1842. 2 v. 12°.

— Zoology of Africa. (*In* **Murray,** H. Narr. of discov. in Africa. 1844. Harper's fam. lib., v. 16.)

— Zoology of India. (*In* **Murray,** H. Account of Brit. India. 1832. Harper's fam. lib., v. 49.)

— HAMILTON, J. Memoirs of W. Lond., 1859. 8°.

Wilson, James Grant. Life and letters of F. G. Halleck. N. Y., 1869. 12°.

Wilson, *Gen.* James H. ANDREWS, C. C. Operations of [his] cavalry in Alabama. (*In his* History of the campaign of Mobile. 1867.)

Wilson, James Maurice. On teaching natural science in schools. (*In* **Farrar,** F. W. Essays on a liberal education. 1868.)

Wilson, James Patriot, *D.D.* Easy introduction to the Hebrew language. Phila., 1812. 8°.

Wilson, Jasper. Letter commercial and political to W. Pitt. 2d ed. enl. London, 1793. 8°. (B 612)

— The lie direct! refutation of the proclamation of Pres. Jefferson. London, 1807. 8°. (B 671)

Wilson, Jessie Aitken. Memoirs of G. Wilson. 3d thous. London, Camb., 1862. 8°.

Wilson, Job. An inquiry into the nature and treatment of spotted fever. Bost., 1815. 8°.

Wilson, John, *minister in Boston, b.* 1588, *d.* 1667. M'CLURE, A. W. Lives of J. Wilson, *etc.* Boston, 1846. 12°. (Lives of the chief fathers of N. England, v. 2.)

— MATHER, C. Johannes in eremo; memoirs rel. to the lives of J. Cotton, J. Wilson, *etc.* Boston, 1695. 16°.

— MEMORIA Wilsoniana; life of W. *n.t.p.* [1667.] 16°. (C 62)

Wilson, John, *b.* 1720, *d.* 1789. Life. (*In* **Soc. of Ancient Scots.** Lives of Scottish poets, v. 3, pt. 5. 1822.)

Wilson, John, *surgeon*. Cutaneous diseases. 2d ed. London, 1814. 8°.

Wilson, John. Report, 1819. *See* **South Carolina.** *Civil and Military Engineer.*

Wilson, John, *Prof.* (*pseud.* Christopher North), *b.* 1785, *d.* 1854. Works; ed. by J. F. Ferrier. Edin., Lond., 1855-58. 12 v. 8°.

Contents. Vol. 1-4. Noctes Ambrosianæ. 5-8. *Essays critical and imaginative.* 5. Streams. — Meg Dod's cookery. — There is death in the pot. — Gymnastics. — Cruikshank on time. — Health and longevity. — Early rising. — Old North, and young North. — The man of ton. — The loves of the poets. — Education of the people. — The young lady's book. — Days departed. — Wordsworth. 6. Christopher at the Lakes. — Tennyson's poems. — Mem. of Sir H. Blackwood. — Amer. poetry; W. C. Bryant. — Poetry of E. Elliott. — On the punishment of death. — Anglimania. 7. The genius and character of Burns. — Speech at the Burns festival. — Christopher on Colonsay. — Coleridge's poet. works. — Tupper's Geraldine. — De Berenger's Helps and hints. — Macaulay's Lays of anc. Rome. — A few words of Shakespeare. 8. Homer and his translators. — Greek drama: the Agamemnon of Æschylus. 9-10. *Recreations of Christopher North.* 9. Christopher in his sporting jacket. — Tale of expiation. — Morning monologue. — The field of flowers. — Cottages. — An hour's talk about poetry. — Inch-Cruin. — A day at Windermere. — The moors. — Highland snow-storm. — The holy child. — Our parish. 10. May-day. — Sacred poetry. — Christopher in his aviary. — Dr. Kitchiner. — Soliloquy on the seasons. — A few words on Thomson. — The snowball bicker of Pedmont. — Christmas dreams. — Our winter quarters. — Stroll to Grassmere. — L'envoy. — Remarks on the scenery of the Highlands. 11. Tales: Lights and shadows of Scottish life. — Trials of Margaret Lyndsay. — The foresters. 12. Poetical works: The isle of palms. — The city of the plague. — The convict. — Miscel. poems. — Sonnets. — Lines to the memory of Rev. J. Grahame. — Troutbeck Chapel. — A churchyard dream. — The magic mirror. — The children's dance. — An evening in Furness Abbey. — Unimore. — Edderline's dream. — A recommendation of the study of the remains of anc. Grecian and Roman architecture, sculpture, and painting.

— The city of the plague, and other poems. Edin., 1816. 8°.

— The foresters. N. Y., 1825. 12°.

— Lights and shadows of Scottish life. Boston, 1822. 12°.

— Recreations of Christopher North. Phila., 1845. 8°. (Mod. Brit. essayists, v. 4.)

Note. For contents *see*, above, Works, v. 9-10.

— Trials of Margaret Lindsay. Boston, 1823. 12°.

— *pseud.* Letters on Shakespeare. (*In* **Imitation of** cel. authors. 1844.)

— *and others.* Noctes ambrosianæ; with mem. and notes by R. S. Mackenzie, Aug. 1819 - Feb. 1835. N. Y., 1854. 5 v. (v. 2 w.). 12°.

Note. From **Blackwood's** mag., v. 11-37. 1822-35.

— GORDON, *Mrs.* Christopher North; a memoir of W. Edin., 1862. 2 v. 8°.

— - *Same.* With introd. by R. S. Mackenzie. N. Y., 1863. 8°.

— MARTINEAU, H. (*In her* Blog. sketches. 1869.)

— PATTERSON, R. H. In memoriam. (*In his* Essays. 1862.)

— TUCKERMAN, H. T. The magazine-writer. (*In his* Characteristics of lit., 2d ser. 1851.)

Wilson, John, *M.D.* On yellow fever. London, 1827. 8°.

Wilson, John, *D.D.* The lands of the Bible visited and described. Edin., London, 1847. 2 v. 8°.

Wilson, John, *printer*, *b.* 1802, *d.* 1868. Concessions of Trinitarians. Manchester, 1842. 8°.

— Scripture proofs and scriptural illustrations of Unitarianism. 3d ed. rev. London, 1846. 8°.

— Shaksperiana; catalogue of books, pamphlets, *etc.*, rel. to Shakspeare. London, 1827. 12°.

— Treatise on Eng. punctuation. 14th ed. Boston, 1862. 12°.

- Unitarian principles confirmed by trinitarian testimonies. Boston, *A. U. A.*, 1855. 12°.

Wilson, John, *prof. of Agric. in Univ. of Edin.* Agricultural products and implements. (*In* **Soc. for Encouragement of Arts, Manufactures and Commerce.** Lectures, 2d ser. 1853.)

Wilson, John, *farmer, of Edington Mains.* British farming. Edin., 1862. 8°.

Wilson, John. Liverpool Co-operative Provident Assoc. (*In* **Nat. Assoc. Prom. Soc. Sci.** Trans., 1858, 62.) — [Several articles.] (*In* 1865.)

Wilson, John, *pseud.* *See* **Ratford, J.**, *alias* **J. Wilson.**

Wilson, *Rev.* John Leighton. Comparative vocabularies of some of the principal negro dialects of Africa. (*In* **Amer. Orient. Soc.** Journ., v. 1. 1847.)

— Western Africa. N. Y., 1856. 12°.

— DWIGHT, T. Sketch of the Mpongwes and their language; from information by W. (*In* **American Ethnol. Soc.** Trans., v. 2. 1848.)

Wilson, Joseph. History of mountains, geography, and mineralogy. London, 1807-10. 3 v. 4°.

Contents. Vol. 1. List of the mountains of Europe, — Asia, — Africa, — America. 1, 2. Europe. 3. European islands. — Asia. — Asiatic islands. — Africa. — Islands of Africa. — America. — Islands of America.

Wilson, Joseph M., *ed.* *See* **Presbyterian historical almanac**, 1858/59, 61-63. 67.

Wilson, Joshua Lacy, *D.D.* War the work of the Lord, *etc.*; sermon, May 14. Cincin., 1812. 8°. (B 335, C 145)

Wilson, *Mrs.* Margaret Cornwall Baron. Memoirs of [the] Duchess of St. Albans. Phila., 1840. 2 v. 12°.

— Volume of lyrics. London, 1840. 12°.

Wilson, Matthias. Mercy and truth; or, Charity maintained by Catholics; [with an answer by W. Chillingworth]. (*In* **Chillingworth, W.** Works, v. 1, 2. 1838.)

Wilson, Richard, *b.* 1713, *d.* 1782. CUNNINGHAM, A. (*In his* Lives of Brit. painters, v. 1. 1829; Fam. lib., v. 1. 18—; Harper's fam. lib., v. 17.)

Wilson, Richard, *D.D.* System of plane and spherical trigonometry; added, a treatise on logarithms. Camb., 1831. 8°.

Wilson, *Gen. Sir* Robert. MAYNE, W. Narrative of the campaigns of the Loyal Lusitanian Legion, under W., 1809-11. Lond., 1812. 8°.

Wilson, Robert. Enquiry into the causes of the high prices of corn and labour. Edin., 1815. 8°. (B 1675)

Wilson, Robert, *M.D.* Poems. Boston, 1856. 16°.

Wilson, Robert. On what principle should a bankrupt law be founded. (*In* **Nat. Assoc. Prom. Soc. Sci.** Trans., 1866.)

Wilson, Robert Anderson. Mexico and its religion, with incidents of travel, 1851-54. N. Y., 1855. 12°.

— New history of the conquest of Mexico. Phila., 1859. 8°.

— TICKNOR, G. Papers discussing the merits of Prescott's and Wilson's histories. *n.p.*, 1861. 8°. (B 1601)

— - Remarks on 'A new history of the conquest of Mexico'. (*In* **Mass. Hist. Soc.** Proc., 1858-60.)

Note. The first paper of the preceding work.

Wilson, *Sir* Robert Thomas. Brief remarks on the character of the Russian army; campaigns in Poland, 1806-07. London, 1810. 4°.

— Enquiry into the present state of the military force of the British Empire, *etc.*; address to W. Pitt. Lond., 1804. 8°. (B 719)

— History of the British expedition to Egypt; with maps. 4th ed. London, 1803. 2 v. 8°.

— *Same.* Phila., 1803. 8°.

— Narrative of events during the invasion of Russia by Napoleon; ed. by H. Randolph. London, 1860. 8°.

— Private diary during the campaigns of 1812-14; from the invasion of Russia to the capture of Paris; ed. by H. Randolph. London, 1861. 2 v. 8°.

Contents. Vol. 1. 1812-13. 2. 1813-14.

— Sketch of the military and political power of Russia in 1817. N. Y., 1817. 8°.

— FORGUES, P. E. D. Le gén. R. Wilson au camp russe, 1812. (*In* **Revue d. D. Mondes**, jan. 1861.)

— NICHOLSON, —. Trial of Wilson, Bruce, and Hutchinson for assisting in the escape of Gen. Lavalette; prefixed, biog. mem. of W. London, 1816. 8°. (**B 1673**)

— RANDOLPH, *Rev.* H. Life of W.; from autobiographical memoirs, *etc.* London, 1862. 2 v. 8°.

Wilson, Samuel. Account of the province of Carolina in America. London, 1682. 4°.

— *Same.* (*In* **Carroll**, B. R. Hist. col., v. 2. 1836.)

Wilson, *Rev.* Samuel. Christ the great propitiation; sermon; added, Remarks on 'A vindication of Mr. Foster's account of the late Earl of Kilmarnock. 2d ed. London, 1746. 8°. (**B 1895**)

— *Funeral sermon on.* 1750. *See* **Gill, J.** (**B 1242**)

Wilson, Samuel, *of Kentucky.* Chelys Hesperia; carmina quædam anniversaria. Lexingtoniæ, 1825. 8°. (**B 1107**)

Wilson, Samuel Farmer. History of the American Revolution. 3d ed. Balt., 1838. 12°.

Wilson, *Rev.* Thomas, *d.* 1621. Complete Christian dictionary, continued by J. Bagwell, enlarged and digested into one alphabetical dictionary by A. Simson. London, 1678. f°.

Wilson, Thomas, *Bp.*, *b.* 1663, *d.* 1755. Form of excommunication. — Form for receiving penitents. (*In* **Tracts** for the times, v. 1. 1833.) — Meditations on his sacred office. (*In* v. 1, 2. 1833–40.)

— Knowledge and practice of Christianity made easy to the meanest capacities. 2d ed., with add. London, 1741. 12°.

— *Same, with alterations.* 1st Amer. ed., from 8th London ed. Camb., 1815. 12°.

— Maxims of piety and of Christianity. Bath, London, 1815. 12°.

— Sacra privata; private meditations and prayer. 2d Camb. ed. Camb., 1808. 12°.

— *Same.* N. Y., 1837. 12°. (**C 240**)

— Sermon on fraud. 1st Amer. ed. Camb., 1805. 12°. (**C 16**)

Wilson, *Rev.* Thomas, *b.* 1747, *d.* 1813. Miscellanies of W.; with memoirs of his life by T. R. Raines. London, 1857. 4°. (Chetham Soc., v. 45.)

Contents. Memoirs. — Poetical specimens. — Correspondence. — Miscel. pieces.

Wilson, Thomas, *of Phila.* Biography of Amer. military and naval heroes. N. Y., 1817–19. 2 v. 12°.

Contents. Vol. 1. J. Warren. — R. Montgomery. — D. Morgan. — I. Putnam. — N. Biddle. — F. Marion. — J. Barry. — J. Manly. — Baron de Kalb. — J. P. Jones. — W. Heath. — A. Wayne. — C. Lee. — G. Washington. — N. Greene. — E. Preble. — T. Truxtun. — H. Mercer. 2, Z. M. Pike. — L. Covington. — J. Chrystie. — W. H. Allen. — J. C. Aylwin. — W. Burrows. — J. Lawrence. — R. M. Johnson. — O. H. Perry. — J. Jones. — S. Decatur. — C. Morris. — D. Porter. — W. Bainbridge. — L. Warrington. — G. Croghan. — T. Macdonough. — W. Carroll. — J. Brown. — A. Jackson. — E. W. Ripley. — W. Scott. — I. Hull. — J. Rodgers. — A. C. Ludlow. — J. Biddle. — H. Dearborn.

Wilson, *Rev.* Thomas, *of Palmer.* Historical address, Palmer, July 5, 1852. Lowell, 1855. 8°.

Wilson, Walter, *d.* 1847. Memoirs of D. De Foe. London, 1830. 3 v. 8°.

Wilson, Walter. Rise and progress of manufactures at Hawick. (*In* **Nat. Assoc. Prom. Soc. Sci.** Trans., 1863.)

Wilson, Wm. Missionary voyage to the southern Pacific Ocean, 1796–98, in the Duff; with a disc. on the geog. and history of the South Sea Islands; [also] the natural and civil state of Otaheite. London, 1799. 4°.

Wilson, Wm., *of Dumfries.* Collection of poems. Edin., 1803. 8°. (**B 575**)

Wilson, *Rev.* Wm. Blessedness of a nation whose God is Jehovah; sermon. Pittsburgh, 1840. 8°. (**B 1306**)

Wilson, Wm., *of Carmylie.* Believing prayer heard and answered. (*In* **Free** Church pulpit. 1853.)

Wilson, Wm. On hats. (*In* **Armstrong**, *Sir* W. G. Industrial resources of the Tyne. 1864.)

Wilson, Wm. Dexter. Discourse on slavery before the Anti-Slavery Soc., Littleton, N. H., Feb. 22. Concord, 1839. 18°. (**B 1572**)

Wilson, Wm. James Erasmus, *M.D.* Diseases of the skin. 6th ed. London, 1867. 8°.

— On the revival of the eastern bath in Britain. (*In* **Nat. Assoc. Prom. Soc. Sci.** Trans., 1860.)

— System of human anatomy. New Amer. from an enl. London ed., by W. H. Gobrecht. Phila., 1859. 8°.

— Thermo-therapeia; the heat cure. Boston, [186-]. 8°. (**C 271**)

— Three weeks' scamper through the spas of Germany and Belgium. London, 1858. 8°.

Wilson, Wm. Rae. Records of a route through France and Italy. London, 1835. 8°.

— Travels in Norway, Sweden, *etc.* London, 1826. 8°.

— Travels in Russia. London, 1828. 2 v. 8°.

Wilson; nouvelle anglaise. (*In* **Biblioth.** univ. des romans, Nouv., v. 63. 1802.)

Wiltes, Earldom of. FINLASON, W. F. Case of the earldom of Wiltes. (*In his* Dissertation on the history of hereditary dignities. 1869.)

Wilton, Joseph. CUNNINGHAM, A. (*In his* Lives of Brit. painters, v. 3. 1830. Fam. lib., v. 6; Harper's fam. lib., v. 19.)

Wilton, Samuel, *D.D.* Apology for the renewal of an application to Parliament by the Protestant dissenting ministers. London, 1773. 8°. (**B 906**)

— Sermon, death of J. Longhurst, June 18, 1769; with the funeral oration, June 16. London, 1770. 8°.

— Sermon, Feb. 7, for the school in Bartholomew-Close. London, 1770. 8°.

— PALMER, S. Brief memoirs of S. Wilton. *n.p.*, [1805]. 8°. (**B 267**)

— *Funeral sermon on.* 1778. *See* **Hill, N.**; — **Palmer, S.**

Wilton, Thomas, *Funeral sermon on, with address by* A. Booth. 1776. *See* **Gibbons, T.**

Wilton, *N. H.* PEABODY, E. Address at the centennial celebration. Boston, 1839. 8°.

— - *Another copy.* (**B 1697**)

Wilton Harvey; by C. M. Sedgwick. (*In her* Tales. 1844.)

Wilton-House. KENNEDY, J. Description of the antiquities and curiosities in W.; with the anecdotes and remarks of Thomas, Earl of Pembroke. New ed. Sarum, 1786. 4°.

— NEWTON, C. T. Notes on the sculptures at Wilton House. (*In* **Archæol. Inst. of Gr. Brit.** Memoirs illust. of the hist. of Wiltshire. 1851.)

Wiltsch, Johann Elieser Theodor. Handbook of the geography and statistics of the Church; tr. by J. Leitch, with preface by F. D. Maurice. London, 1868. 2 v. 8°.

Contents. Vol. 1. 750 B.C. - 1073 A.D. 2. 1073–1517.

Wiltshire, *Eng.* MARSHALL, W. Dairy management of North Wiltshire. [1789.] (*In his* Rural economy of Glocestershire. 1796.)

— DAVIS, T. General view of the agriculture of the County of Wilts. London. 1794. 4°. (**W 75**)

— BRITTON, J. Wiltshire. (*In* **Beauties** of England and Wales, v. 15. 1814.)

— COOKE, G. A. Topographical and statistical description of W. London, [182-?]. 18°.

— ARCHÆOL. INST. OF GR. BRIT. Memoirs illust. of the hist. of W., 1849. London, 1851. 8°.

— HANDBOOK for Wiltshire, Dorsetshire, and Somersetshire. New ed. London, *Murray*, 1859. 12°.

See also **Malmesbury.**

Wily, John. Treatise on the propagation of sheep, the manufacture of wool, and the cultivation of flax. Williamsburg, 1765. 12°. (**W 46**)

Wily beguiled; a comedy. (*In* **Hawkins**, T. Origin of the Eng. drama, v. 3. 1773.)

Wiman, Johannes. Euphorbia. (*In* **Linné**, C. Amœn. acad., v. 3. 1764.)

Wimbleton. Caley, J. Survey of the manor of Wymbledon, al. Wimbleton. (*In* **Archæologia**, v. 10. 1792.)

Wimborn Minster. Remarks. (*In* **Archæolog. Inst. of Gr. Brit.** Mem. illust. hist. of Wiltshire. 1851.)

Wimpey, Joseph. On œconomical registers. (*In* **Lit. and Phil. Soc. of Manchester.** Mem., v. 1. 1789.)

Wimpffen, François Alexandre Stanislaus, *baron* de. Voyage to St. Domingo, 1788–90; tr. by J. Wright. London, 1817. 8°.

Wimpheling *or* **Wympfeling** (*Lat.* **Wimphelingius**), Jakob. Niceron, J. P. (*In his* Mém., v. 38. 1737.)

Winans, Ross, *vs.* **Eaton, Gilbert, & Co.** Testimony of defendants; [eight wheel cars]. Syracuse, 1852. 12°.

— Cannon, A. Argument of W. Whiting in the case. Boston, 1853. 8°. (**E 202**)

Winchell, Alexander. Geology of the Choctaw Bluff. (*In* **Amer. Assoc.** Proc., v. 7. 1856.) — Notes on the geology of middle and southern Alabama. — Statistics of some artesian wells of Alabama. (*In* v. 10.) — The fruit-bearing belt of Michigan. — Stromatoporidæ; their structure and zoological affinities. (*In* v. 15.) — Isothermals of the lake region. (*In* v. 19. 1871.)

— *and* Marcy, O. Enumeration of fossils collected in the Niagara limestone at Chicago, Ill. (*In* **Boston Soc. Nat. Hist.** Mem., v. 1. 1866–69.)

Winchell, *Rev.* James Manning. Arrangement of the psalms, hymns, *etc.*, of I. Watts. 2d ed. Boston, 1820. 12°.

— *Same.* [With] add. Boston, [1832]. 12°.

— Jubilee sermons; two discourses exhibiting an hist. sketch of the 1st Baptist Church, Boston, 1665–1818. Boston, 1819. 8°. (**B 286**)

— *Same.* 2d ed. Boston, 1820. 8°. (**B 287**)

— *Funeral sermon on.* 1820. *See* **Baldwin, T.** (**B 1007**)

Winchester, *Bp. of. See* **Cooper,** T.; — **Hoadly,** B.; — **Sumner,** C. R.; — **Tomline,** G. P.

Winchester, *Rev.* Elhanan. Divinity of Christ proved from the Scriptures of the Old and New Testament. *n.p.*, [17—]. 8°. (**B 194, 247, 1703**)

— Oration on the discovery of Amer. 2d ed., with a descr. of the city of Washington. London, 1792. 8°. (**B 349, 585**)

— Ten letters to T. Paine in answer to his 'Age of reason'. Boston, 1794. 12°.

— *Same.* 2d ed. N. Y., 1795. 12°. (**W 44**)

— Thirteen hymns suited to the present times. 2d ed. Balt., 1776. 12°. (**W 46**)

— The three woe trumpets; substance of two discourses. 2d ed. London, [1793]. 8°. (**B 284**)

— *Same.* Boston, 1794. 8°. (**B 240**)

Winchester, *Gen.* James. Atherton, W. Narrative of the suffering and defeat of the N. W. army under W., [1813]. Frankfort, Ky., 1842. 12°.

— Darnell, E. Journal cont. an acc. of the sufferings, *etc.*, of Kentucky volunteers and regulars, commanded by W., 1812, 13. Phila., 1854. sm. 12°.

Winchester, *Eng.* History and antiquities of Winchester, [B.C. **892**–A.D. **1772**]. Winton, **1773.** 2 v. 12°.

— Old usages of the cite of Wynchestre. [13—.] (*In* **Smith, T.** Eng. gilds. 1870.)

— Archæol. Instit. of Gr. Brit. Proceedings at the annual meeting at Winchester, **1845.** London, 1846. 8°

Winchester, Monastery of. Annales, 519–1277. (*In* **Annales** monastici, v. 2. 1865. Chron. and mem.)

Winchester Cathedral. Britton, J. History and antiquities of the cathedral church of Winchester. London, **1817.** 4°.

— Curtis, O. B. Painted or stained glass from Winchester Cathedral. — East window of choir. — Painted glass. (*In* **Weale, J.** Quarterly papers on arch., v. 2. 1844.) — Winchester Cathedral painted glass. (*In* v. 3. 1845.)

Winchester College. Ackerman, R. History of the colleges of Winchester, Eton, *etc.*, [**1382–1816**]. London, 1816. 4°.

— Clarke, L. Letter to H. Brougham in reply to strictures on Winchester College. Winchester, **1818.** 8°.

— Bowles, W. L. Vindiciæ Wykehamicæ; or, Vindication of Winchester College. (*In* **Pamphleteer,** 1819; v. 13 of **B 838**)

— M., R. B. School life at Winchester Coll. London, **1866.** 8°.

Winchester. County Hospital. Clarke, A. Sermon before the Governors of the Hospital, Oct. 18, 1736. 2d ed. London, 1737. 8°. (**C 216**)

Winchester republican, political, agricultural, and miscellaneous; May 18. Winchester, 1822. f°. (**E 181**)

Winckelmann. *See also* **Winkelmann.**

Winckelmann, Johann Joachim. Werke. Dresden, 1808–25. 11 v. 8°.

Contents. Vol. 1. Kurzer Abriss von W.'s Leben. — Schriften über die Nachahmung der alten Kunstwerke. — Kleine Aufsätze über Gegenstände der alten Kunst aus Zeitschriften. — Anmerkungen über die Baukunst der Alten; hrsg. von C. L. Fernow. 2. Schriften über die herculanischen Alterthümer. — Abhandlung von der Fähigkeit der Empfindung des Schönen. — Versuch einer Allegorie; hrsg. v. C. L. Fernow. 3–6. Geschichte der Kunst des Alterthums; hrsg. v. H. Meyer und J. Schulze. 3. Von dem Ursprunge der Kunst, und den Ursachen ihrer Verschiedenheit unter den Völkern. — Von der Kunst unter den Ægyptern, Phöniziern, und Persen. — Von der Kunst der Hetrurier und ihrer Nachbarn. 4. Von der Kunst unter den Griechen. 5. Von der Bekleidung. — Von der mechanischen Theile der griechischen Kunst. — Wachsthum und Fall der griechischen Kunst. 6. Geschichte der Kunst des Alterthums nach den äussern Umständen der Zeit unter den Griechen. 7. Trattato preliminare oder vorläufige Abhandlung vor dem Werk: Monumenti antichi inediti; hrsg. v. H. Meyer u. J. Schulze. 8. Ein allgemeines Sachregister, und die Verzeichnisse der in sämmtlichen Banden erwähnten Künstler und Schriftsteller; bearbeitet von C. G. Siebelis. 9–11. Briefe; hrsg. von F. Förster. 9. 1747–61. 10. 1761–66. 11. 1766–68.

— Alte Denkmäler der Kunst, aus dem ital. übers. von F. L. Brunn. Berlin, 1791–92. 2 v. f°.

Contents. Vol. 1. Vom Ursprunge der Kunst. — Von der Kunst unter den Egyptern. — Von der Kunst unter den Hetruriern. — Von der Kunst der Zeichnung unter den Griechen, und von der Schönheit. 2. Von den Zeiten vor dem trojanischen Kriege. — Vom trojanischen Kriege. — Griechische und römische Geschichte. — Sitten, Gebräuche, und Kunste.

— Histoire de l'art chez les anciens; tr. de l'allemand par Huber, et revue par Jansen. Paris, 1802–03. 3 v. 4°.

Contents. Vol. 1. Mém. sur la vie et les ouvrages de W., par Huber. — Eloge de W., par Heyne. — De l'origine de l'art et des causes de sa diversité chez les peuples qui l'ont cultivé. — De l'art chez les Egyptiens, les Phéniciens, et les Perses. — De l'art chez les Etrusques et chez les peuples circonvoisins. — De l'art chez les Grecs. — Hist. des progrès de l'art, par A. R. Mengs. — De l'ivoire chez les anciens, *etc.*, par Heyne. — Des limites de la peinture et de la poésie, *etc.*, par Lessing. — Mém. sur deux momies qui se trouvent dans le cabinet électoral d'antiques à Dresde. — Lettre de milord Montagu à W. — Des Etrusques et des époques de l'art chez ce peuple, par Heyne. — Sur les différentes causes de la perfection à laquelle l'art parvint chez les Grecs, *etc.*, par Heyne. — Des distinctions véritables et supposées qu'il y a entre les faunes, les satyres, *etc.*, par Heyne. 2. De l'art chez les Grecs. — De l'art chez les Romains. — Des révolutions de l'art. — Obs. sur l'architecture des anciens. — Obs. sur le temple de Girgenti. 3. Lettre du père Paolo sur l'origine et l'antiquité de l'architecture. — De la peinture chez les anciens, par B. Rode et A. Riem. — De la toreutique chez les anciens, par Heyne. — Obs. de Heyne sur quelques passages de l'histoire de l'art. — Obs. de Lessing sur l'Histoire de l'art par W.

— History of ancient art; tr. by G. H. Lodge. Boston, 1856, 49–73. 4 v. 8°.

Contents. Vol. 1. Life of W. — The origin of art, and the causes of its difference among different nations. — Art among the Egyptians, Phœnicians, and Persians. — Art of the Etruscans and their neighbors. 2. Art among the Greeks. 3. Drapery. — The mechanical part of Greek art. — The rise and fall of Greek art. 4. Hist. of anc. art in its relation to the external circumstances of the times among the Greeks. — Greek art among the Romans. — Greek art under the Romans.

— Receuil de lettres sur les découvertes faites à Herculanum, à Pompeii, à Stabia, à Caserte, et à Rome. Paris, 1784. 8°.

— JUSTI, K. Ueber die Studien Wincklemann's in seiner vorrömischen Zeit. (*In* **Historisches** Taschenbuch, 1866.)

— KLETKE, G. H. Winckelmann's Biographie. (*In his* Walhalla. 1854.)

Winckelmann, Johann Justus. Der americanischen neuen Welt Beschreibung. Oldenburg, 1664. 4°.

Winckelmann. *See also* **Winkelmann.**

Winder, John Singleton. Report. (*In* **Gr. Brit.** *Educ. Comm.* Reports [on] the state of popular education, v. 2. 1861.)

Winder, W. H. Cost of government buildings; reasons for buying the building corner of F and 17th streets. Wash., 1849. 8°. (B 1507)

— The government building corner of F and 17th streets. Wash., 1849. 8°. (B 1502)

Windham, Thomas. ALDIE, J. Originall of the first voyage for traffique into the kingdom of Morocco in Barbary in 1551. (*In* **Hakluyt,** R. Col. of voy., v. 2. 1810.)

— THOMAS, J. Second voyage to Barbary, 1552, [by] W. (*In* **Greene,** J. Col. of voy., v. 1. 1745; — *in* **Hakluyt,** R. Voyages, v. 2. 1810; — *in* **Kerr,** R. Col. of voy., v. 7. 1824; — *and in* **Walckenaer,** C. A. Col. de voy., v. 1. 1842.)

— VOYAGE to Guinea and Benin, 1553. (*In* **Eden,** R. Histoire of travayle. 1577; — *in* **Green,** J. Col. of voy., v. 1. 1745; — *in* **Moore,** J. H. New col. of voy., v. 1. 1778; — *in* **Hakluyt,** R. Voy., v. 2. 1810; — *in* **Kerr,** R. Voy., v. 7. 1824; — *and in* **Walckenaer,** C. A. Voy., v. 1. 1842.)

— REISE nach der Barbarey, Guinea, und Benin. (*In* **Allgemeine Hist.,** v. 1. 1748.)

Windham, *Hon.* Wm. Diary, 1784–1810; ed. by Mrs. H. Baring. London, 1866. 8°.

— Speech on the report of an address to the throne approving the preliminaries of peace with France. London, 1801. 8°. (B 715)

— Speeches in Parliament. London, 1812. 3 v. 8°.
Contents. Vol. 1. Acc. of W.'s life, by T. Amyot. — Speeches, 1785–1801. 2. 1801–06. 3. 1806–10. — Definitive treaty, May 3, 13, 1802.

— BROUGHAM, H., *Ld.* (*In his* Statesmen in the time of George III., v. 1. 1839.)

— HOLCROFT, T. Letter to W. on the intemperance and dangerous tendency of his public conduct. London, 1795. 8°. (B 1406)

Windham Co., *Conn.* **Associated Ministers.** Letter to the people in the Socs. in said Co. Boston, 1745. 4°. (B 45, 248)

Windham Co., *Conn.* **Association of Cong. Churches.** SHERMAN, J. View of the proceedings in the Co. of Windham, Conn. Utica, 1806. 8°. (B 239)
See also next entry but one.

Windham Co., *Conn.* **Consociated Churches.** Result of a council at Scotland. Boston, 1747. 4°. (B 248)

Windham County. *Conn.* **Eastern Association of Cong. Churches.** The churches warned to stand fast in the liberties wherewith Christ has made them free, in an appeal rel. to an act of the Gen. Assoc. of Conn. respecting the Eastern Assoc. of Windham. Norwich, 1810. 8°. (B 247, 1079)

Windham Co. Peace Society. *See* **Peace Soc. of Windham Co.** (B 1093)

Windisch-Graetz, Alfred Candid Ferdinand, *Fürst* von. Der Winter-Feldzug, 1848-49, in Ungarn. Wien, 1851. 8°.

Windisch-Graetz, Joseph Nikolas, *Reichsgraf* von. De la peine de mort et de la torture. *n.p.,* [1801]. 8°. (C 95)

Windmills. BEATSON, R. Essay on the comparative advantages of vertical and horizontal windmills. London, 1798. 8°. (B 1901)

Winds, Wm. Tuttle, J. F. Biog. sketch of W. (*In* **New Jersey Hist. Soc.** Proc., v. 7. 1855.)

Winds. BACON, F. Historia ventorum. [1622.] (*In his* Works, v. 2. 1857.)

— ALEMBERT, J. L. d'. Réflexions sur la cause générale des vents. Paris, 1747. 4°.

— ROMME, C. Tableaux des vents, des marées, et des courans; avec des réflexions. Paris, 1806. 2 v. 8°.

— COFFIN, J. H. Report on the winds of the northern hemisphere. — MAURY, M. F. Winds and currents of the ocean. (*In* **Amer. Assoc.** Proc., v. 1. 1849.) — COFFIN, J. H. Instrument for determining the variation and duration of winds. (*In* v. 2.) — MAURY, M. F. Geol. agency of the winds. (*In* v. 6.) — BACHE, A. D. Winds of the western coast of the U. S. (*In* v. 11.) — COFFIN, J. H. Winds of the southern hemisphere. — SCHOTT, C. A. Abstract of results of obs. for direction and force of the winds, at Van Rensselaer Harbor, N. Greenland, by the second Grinnell expedition, 1853–55. (*In* v. 13. 1860.)

— *Map.* BELLIN, J. N. Carte des variations de la boussole et des vents généraux dans les mers. *n.p.,* 1765. (E 87, no. 2)
See also **Air;** — **Cyclones;** — **Meteorology;** — **Monsoons;** — **Storms;** — **Tornadoes.**

Windship, Charles Williams, *M.D.* Discourse on religion and doctrines before the 1st Soc. of Free Inquirers in Boston. Boston, 1829. 8°. (B 1360)

— Introductory discourse on the phenomena of vitality or laws of mobility in animal bodies, 1817. Boston, 1818. 8°. (E 59)

Windsor. *See also* **Winsor.**

Windsor, *Rev.* Lloyd. Inquiry into the ministerial commission. N. Y., 1844. 12°.

Windsor, Thomas. Report on ophthalmic medicine and surgery. (*In* **New Sydenham Soc.** Biennial retrospect, 1865–66.) — Report on surgery. (*In its* Year book of medicine and surgery. 1862–64.)

Windsor, *Conn.* STILES, H. R. History of ancient Windsor, [1614–1859]; also genealogies, *etc.* N. Y., 1859. 8°.

— — Supplement. Albany, 1863. 8°.

— M'CLURE, D. Settlement and antiquities of W., [1635–1797]. (*In* **Mass. Hist. Soc.** Col., v. 5. 1816.)

Windsor, *England.* TIGHE, R. R., *and* DAVIS, J. E. Annals of Windsor, [1065–1857]. London, 1858. 2 v. 8°.

— BICKHAM, G. Curiosities of Windsor Castle. (*In his* Deliciæ Britannicæ. 17—.)

— MELA *Britannicus, pseud.* Letter on the works in progress at Windsor. London, 1827. 8°.

— ROYAL Windsor guide; with an account of Eton. New ed. Windsor, [184-]. 16°. (D 70)

— RITCHIE, L. Windsor Castle and its environs. London, 1840. 8°. (Heath's pict. ann.)

— TAYLOR, W. F. Guide to Windsor, Eton, *etc.* London, [186-]. 16°.

Windsor, *Mass.* DORRANCE, G. History of Windsor, [1762–1827]. (*In* **Field,** D. D. History of the Co. of Berkshire, v. 2. 1829.)

Windus, —. ROSSETTI, W. M. (*In* **Atkinson,** J. B. English painters of the present day. 1871.)

Windus, John. Journey to Mequinez, 1721. London, 1725. 8°.

— *Same.* (*In* **Knox,** J. Col. of voy., v. 6. 1767; — *in* **Pinkerton,** J. Col. of voy., v. 15. 1814; — *and in* **Moore,** J. H. New col., v. 1.)

Wines. *History.* HENDERSON, A. History of ancient and modern wines. Lond., 1824. 4°.

— REDDING, C. History and description of modern wines. London, 1833. 8°.

— — *Same.* 3d ed., with add. and corr. London, *Bohn,* 1851. 8°.

— DENMAN, J. L. The vine and its fruit; more especially in relation to the production of wine; hist. and descr. account of the grape. London, 1864. 8°.

— CHARLETON, W. Mysterie of vintners. [1662.] (*In his* Two discourses. 1669.)

— BIDET, N. Traité sur la vigne; sur le vin. [1752.] 2e éd. Paris, 1759. 2 v. 12°.

— MAUPIN, —. L'art de faire le vin. Paris, 1772. 12°.

— ST. PIERRE, L. de. Art of planting, *etc.,* the vine, also making wines, *etc.* Lond., 1772. 12°.

— CHAPTAL, J. A. Treatise upon wines [1801]; tr. by J. H. Sargent. Charleston, 1811. 16°.

— SAMPAYO, —, de. Observations chimiques sur l'art de faire le vin rouge; extr. du Journ. d'écon. rurale et domestique. *n.t.p.* [Paris, 1808?] 8°. (B 805)
— WORTHINGTON, R. Invitation to the inhabitants of Eng. to the manufacture of wines. Worcester, 1812. 8°. (B 690)
— BULOS, —. Art of wine making. (*In* Fisher, S. I. Obs. on the European vine. 1834.)
— PARSONS, B. The wine question settled. London, 1841. 8°. (C 204)
— REDDING, C. Every man his own butler. 3d ed. enl. with important wine statistics. London, 1853. 16°.
— MULDER, G. J. Chemistry of wine; ed. by H. B. Jones. London, 1857. 16°.
— CRAMPTON, R. S. The wine of the Bible and the Bible use of wine; a sermon. N. Y., 1859. 8°. (B 206)
— JULLIEN, H. Nouveau manuel du sommelier, ou Instruction sur la manière de soigner les vins [1859]; rev., corr., et aug. par C. E. Jullien. 7e éd. Paris, 1860. 18°. (Manuels-Roret.)
— GUYOT, J. Culture de la vigne et vinification. [1860.] 2e éd. Paris, 1861. 8°.
— REDDING, C. French wines and vineyards, and the way to find them. London, 1860. 8°.
— SHAW, T. G. Wine, the vine, and the cellar. London, 1863. 8°.
— KIRWAN, A. V. Host and guest; a book about dinners, wines, and desserts. Lond., 1864. 8°.
— DRUITT, R. Report on cheap wines, *etc.* London, 1865. 8°.
— MEAD, P. B. Elementary treatise on American grape culture and wine-making. N. Y., 1867. 8°.
— TEISSONNIÈRE, —. Vins. — CHÉDIEU, E. Production des vins en Amérique et dans les colonies anglaises. (*In* France. *Com. Imp. de l'Expos. de* 1867. Rapports, v. 11.)
— FLAGG, W. J. Three seasons in European vineyards. N. Y., 1869. 12°.
— ANSTIE, F. E. On the uses of wines in health and disease. N. Y., 1870. 12°.
See also Barley; — Wine.

Wine and walnuts; or, After dinner chit-chat, by E. Hardcastle [pseud.]. *See* Pyne, W. H.

Winer, Johann Georg Benedict. Grammatik des neutestamentlichen Sprachidioms. 4e Aufl. Lpz., 1836. 8°.
— *Same.* 5e Aufl. Lpz., 1844. 8°.
— *Eng.* Grammar of idioms of the Greek language of the N. T. Phila., 1840. 8°.
— Handbuch der theologischen Literatur. 3e sehr erweiterte Aufl. Lpz., 1838–40. 2 v. 8°.
— *Same.* 1s Ergänzungsheft zur 3n Aufl. Lpz., 1842. 8°.

Wines, *Rev.* Abijah. The merely amiable, moral man no Christian; discourse. Portland, 1828. 8°. (B 1306)
— The perfection of the divine government, *etc.*; sermon, ordination of B. Sawyer, Cape-Elizabeth, Nov. 22. Portland, 1809. 8°. (B 1849)

Wines, Enoch Cobb, *D.D.* Commentaries on the laws of the ancient Hebrews. New York, 1855. 8°.
— Girard College. (*In* Amer. Inst. Instr. Lect., 1842.)
— Peep at China in Dunn's Chinese collection. Phila., 1839. 8°.
— Two years and a half in the navy, 1829–31. Phila., 1832. 2 v. 12°.
— *and* Dwight, T. W. Report on the prisons and reformatories of the U. S. and Canada. Albany, 1867. 8°.

Winfrid, *Arbp. of Mayence.* *See* Bonifacius, *St.*

Wing, John, *ed.* Almanac, 1837, 40–49. *See* Almanacs.

Wing, Vincent. Ephemerides of the cœlestial motions, 1659–71. London, 1658. 8°.

Wing-and-wing; by J. F. Cooper. Rev. ed. N. Y., 1851. 12°.
— *Same.* Illust. by Darley. N. Y., 1863. 12°.

Wingate, George W., *auth.?* *See* Last campaign. 1864.

Wingate, Paine. Sketch of M. Weare. (*In* New Hamp. Hist. Soc. Col., v. 5. 1837.)

Winged figures. GERHARD, E. Ueber die Flügelgestalten der alten Kunst. (*In* Berlin. Ak. d. Wiss. Abh., 1839.)

Wingfield, Anthony. Voy. to Spaine and Portugal, 1589. (*In* Hakluyt, R. Col. of voy., v. 2. 1810.)

Wingfield, Edward Maria. Discourse of Virginia; ed. by C. Deane. (*In* Amer. Antiq. Soc. Archæol. Amer., v. 4. 1860.)
— *Same.* *Privately reprinted*, Boston, 1860. 8°.

Wings. *See* Flying.

Winibald, *abbot of Heidenheim.* LIFE of W. (*In* Lives of the English saints, v. 2. 1844.)

Winifred Bertram and the world she lived in; by [Mrs. E. R. Charles]. N. Y., 1866. 12°.

Winkel, Francis Gray. Reflexiones sobre el comercio de trigo, 1761. (*In* Valladares, A. Seman., v. 34. 1790.)

Winkelmann. *See also* Winckelmann.

Winkelmann, Eduard. Kaiser Heinrich VI. (*In* Historische Zeitschrift, v. 18. 1867.) — Ueber die neuesten Schriften zur Geschichte der Ostseeprovinzen. (*In* v. 23. 1890.)

Winkles, H. *and* B. Architectural and picturesque illustrations of the cathedral churches of England and Wales; with descriptions by T. Moule. (Vol. 3, new ed. with the add. of the Manchester Cathedral.) Lond., [1835]–51. 3 v. 8°.

Winkley, *Rev.* Samuel Hobart. An enemy within the lines. (*In* Amer. Unit. Assoc. Tracts. Army ser. 1865.)

Winkworth, Catherine. Christian singers of Germany. London, [1869]. 16°.
— Lyra Germanica. 2d ed. London, 1856. 8°.

Winkworth, Stephen. Col d'Argentière. (*In* Ball, J. Peaks, passes, 2d ser., v. 1. 1862.)

Winkworth, Susanna, *trans.* *See* Niebuhr, B. G. LIFE; — Tauler, J. HISTORY.

Winlock, Joseph. Difference of personal equation in transit observations of the sun and of the fixed stars. (*In* Amer. Assoc. Proc., v. 8. 1855.)
— *and* Bartlett, J. [New method of chess notation. Boston, 1858.] 4°.

Winnard, Jane M. The strange gentleman. (*In* Sharpe's mag., v. 14–15. 1851.)

Winnebago Indians. MEMOIR conc. the peace made by M. de Ligney [or Signey] with the chiefs of the Foxes, Sauks, and Winnebagos, June 7, 1726. — HASKINS, R. W. Legend of the Winnebagos. (*In* Wisconsin State Hist. Soc. Col., v. 1. 1855.)
— OCANGRA aramee wawakakara; [Rom. Cath.] prayer book. Detroit, 1833. 16°. (E 54)

Winnington, Thomas. Apology for the conduct of a late celebrated second rate minister, 1729–46; written by himself. London, [1746]. 8°. (B 1519)

Winnipiseogee Canal. Report of the committee appointed by the directors, rel. to the proposed canal. Dover, 1826. 8°. (B 1796)

Winnipiseogee, Lake. Routes to the White Mountains and Lake Winnipiseogee; with descriptions and maps. Boston, 1851. 16°. (C 277)
— COMPLETE guide to Lake Winnipiseogee. Boston, 1857. 24°. (C 277)

Winnipiseogee Lake Cotton and Woolen Manufac. Co. *See* Parker, J. A., *vs.* Winnipiseogee Lake Cotton and Woolen Manufac. Co.

Winsbeckius. Paræenesis ad filium. (*In* Schilter. Thes. antiq. Teut., v. 2. 1727.)

Winslow, Edward, *Gov. of Plymouth Colony.* Brief narration of the true grounds or cause of the first planting of New England. (*In* Young, A. Chronicles. 1841.)
— Good newes from New Eng. (*In* Mass. Hist. Soc. Col., v. 8, 19. 1802–22; — *and in* Young, A. Chron. of the pilgrims. 1841.)
— *Same, abridged.* (*In* Purchas, S. Pilgrimes, v. 4. 1625.)
— Journal of a plantation settled at Plymouth, 1621. *See* Bradford, W.
— New England's salamander discovered. (*In* Mass. Hist. Soc. Col., v. 22. 1830.)
— MOORE, J. B. (*In his* Memoirs of American governors, v. 1. 1846.)

Winslow, Edward Lee. Oration before the Fayetteville Independent Light Infantry Co. on the semi-centennial anniv. of the corps. Fayetteville, 1843. 8°. (B 1599)

Winslow, Forbes, *M.D.* Light; its influence on life and health. London, 1867. 16°.
— Obscure diseases of the brain and disorders of the mind. London, 1860. 8°.
— Physic and physicians; exhibiting the life of the most celebrated medical men of former days, with memoirs of eminent living London physicians. London, 1839. 2 v. 12°.
— Plea of insanity in criminal cases. Boston, 1843. 12°.
— *Another copy.* (B 1568)
— *ed. See* **Journal** of psychological medicine and mental pathology.

Winslow, Harriet. Morning and night. (*In* **Boston** book, 4th col. 1850.)

Winslow, *Mrs.* Harriet Wadsworth (Lathrop). Winslow, M. Memoir. N. Y., [184–]. 18°.

Winslow, Hubbard, *D.D.* Appropriate sphere of woman; discourse, July 9. Bost., 1837. 8°. (B 1306)
— Dangerous tendency to innovations and extremes in education. (*In* **Amer. Inst. of Instr.** Lect., 1834.) — Study of language. (*In* 1847.)
— Eulogy on the late Prof. E. A. Andrews, LL.D. Boston, 1858. 8°. (B 1208)
— Means of the perpetuity and prosperity of our republic; oration, Boston, July 4. Boston, 1838. 8°. (B 1201, 1814)
— Rejoice with trembling; discourse, thanksgiving, Nov. 30. Boston, 1837. 8°. (B 1253)
— *Same.* 2d ed. Boston, 1838. 8°. (B 1126)
— The relation of natural science to revealed religion; address before the Bost. Nat. Hist. Soc., June 7. Boston, 1837. 8°. (B 1583)
— Woman as she should be; also, woman in her social and domestic character, by Mrs. J. Sandford. From 2d London ed. Boston, 1838. 16°.
— Loring, J. S. (*In his* Hundred Boston orators. 1852.)
— Strictures on W.'s thanksgiving sermon. Boston, 1838. 8°. (B 1253)

Winslow, Isaac. Old and new tariffs compared; with observations on the effect of high duties on revenue and consumption. Boston, 1820. 4°. (A 35)

Winslow, Jacques Bénigne. Exposition anatomique de la structure du corps humain. Amst., 1732. 4 v. (v. 3, 4 w.). 12°.
— *Eng.* Anatomical exposition; tr. by G. Douglas. 3d ed. London, 1749. 2 v. 4°.

Winslow, *Gen.* John. Letter to the Earl of Halifax, rel. to his conduct, *etc.*, on the Ticonderoga expedition, 1756. (*In* **Mass. Hist. Soc.** Col., v. 6. 1800.)

Winslow, *Commodore* John A. Headley, J. T. (*In his* Farragut and our naval commanders. 1867.)

Winslow, Josiah, *Gov. of Plymouth Colony.* Moore, J. B. (*In his* Memoirs of American governors, v. 1. 1846.)

Winslow, Miron, *D.D.* Comprehensive Tamil and English dictionary. Madras, 1862. 4°.
— Hints on missions to India. N. Y., 1856. 12°.
— Memoir of Mrs. H. L. Winslow. N. Y., [184–]. 18°.
— Sermon previous to the sailing of W. [and others] as missionaries to Ceylon. Andover, 1819. 8°. (B 300, 1785)

Winsor. *See also* **Windsor.**

Winsor, Justin. History of Duxbury, Mass.; with a genealogical register. Boston, 1849. 8°.
— Songs of the unity. 1859. *See* **Hepworth**, G. H.

Winstanley, *Rev.* Calvin. Vindication of certain passages in the common Eng. version of the New Testament; addr. to G. Sharp. Camb., 1819. 8°. (B 538)

Winstanley, John. Poems by W.; with many others by ingenious hands. Dublin, 1742. 8°.

Winstanley, Wm. England's worthies, from Constantine the Great. London, 1684. 8°.

Winston, Charles. Painted glass at Bristol, Wells, *etc.* (*In* **Archæol. Inst. of Gr. Brit.** Mem. illust. of the hist. of Bristol. 1851.)

Winter, Johann. *See* **Guinter, J.**

Winter, John. Cliffe, E. [Voyage of] W. to Magellanica. (*In* **Callander, J.** Terra Australis cognita, v. 1. 1766; — *and in* **Hakluyt**, R. Col. of voy., v. 4. 1811.)
— *Same, in part.* Voyage after parting from Sir F. Drake. (*In* **Kerr, R.** Collection of voyages, v. 10. 1824.)

Winter, Lucrezia Wilhelmine (Merken) van. Germanicus; poëme. Amst., 1787. 8°.

Winter, Robert, *D.D.* Address, interment of G. Burder. (*In* **Fletcher, J.** Christian's hope of mercy. 1832. B 1243)

Winter, Wm. E. Booth in twelve dramatic characters. Boston, 1872 [1871]. 4°.

Winter evenings. *See* **Knox, V.**

Winter evening's conversation, A, upon the doctrine of original sin; [by S. Webster]. Boston, 1757. 8°. (B 41)

Winter in London; a novel, by T. S. Surr. N. Y., [1806]. 2 v. 12°.

Winter in the West, A; [by C. F. Hoffman]. N. Y., 1835. 2 v. 12°.

Winter in the West Indies and Florida; by an invalid. N. Y., 1839. 12°.

Winter nights; or, Fire-side lucubrations; by N. Drake. London, 1820. 2 v. 12°.

Winter studies and summer rambles in Canada. *See* **Jameson, A.**

Winter with the swallows, A. *See* **Edwards, M. B.**

Winterbotham, Henry Self Page. Ritchie, J. E. (*In his* British senators. 1869.)

Winterbotham, Wm. Historical, geographical, *etc.*, view of the U. S., and of the European settlements in America and the W. Indies. 1st Amer. ed. N. Y., 1796. 4 v. 8°.
Contents. Vol. 1. History, 1492–1789. 2. N. E. states. — Middle states. — Territory N. W. of the Ohio. 3. Southern states. — Advantages peculiar to the U. S. — Prospects, *etc.*, of an European settler in the U. S. 4. British settlements in Amer. — Spanish dominions in Amer. — Portuguese settlement in S. Amer. — French possessions in S. Amer. — Dutch possessions in S. Amer. — Aboriginal Amer. — Amazonia. — Patagonia. — W. I. Islands. — Hist. of Amer. quadrupeds. — Hist. of the birds of Amer. — Reptiles of Amer. — Treaties between Amer. and foreign nations.
— Trial, Exeter, July 15, 1793, for seditious words. 2d ed. London, 1794. 8°. (B 714)

Winter-green, The, for 1844; ed. by J. Keese. N. Y., [1843]. 16°.

Winter's tale, The. *See* **Shakespeare, W.**

Winterslow. *See* **Hazlitt, W.**

Winthrop, Fitz John, *Funeral sermon on.* 1710. *See* **Mather, C.** (B 29)

Winthrop, Grenville Temple, *Lieut. Col.* Trial of W., by a court martial on charges preferred against him by W. H. Sumner, in pursuance of orders from Governor L. Lincoln. Boston, 1832. 8°.

Winthrop, James. Account of the transit of Mercury observed at Camb., Nov. 12, 1782. (*In* **Amer. Acad. of Arts and Sci.** Mem., v. 1. 1785.) — Barometical observations and remarks made during a tour to Lake Champlain. — Geometrical methods of finding any required series of mean proportionals between given extremes. — Rule for trisecting angles geometrically. (*In* v. 2. 1793.)
— Appendix to the New Testament. Camb., 1809. 12°.
— Attempt to arrange in the order of time those Scripture prophecies yet remaining to be fulfilled. Cambridge, 1803. 8°. (B 153, 284)
— Attempt to translate the prophetic part of the Apocalypse of St. John into familiar language. Boston, 1794. 8°. (B 132, 190, 235, 284)
— Description of the County of Middlesex. (*In* **Mass. Hist. Soc.** Col., v. 1. 1792.) — Biographical memoir of W. Fiske. (*In* v. 9.) — Memoir of J. Sullivan. (*In* v. 11. 1814.)
— Systematic arrangement of several Scripture prophecies rel. to Anti-Christ. Boston, 1795. 8°. (B 190)
— Bradford, A. Biog. notice of J. Winthrop. (*In* **Mass. Hist. Soc.** Col., v. 20. 1823.)

Winthrop, John, *Gov. of Mass.*, *b.* 1587, *d.* 1649. Journal of the transactions and occurrences in the settlement of Mass. and the other New England colonies, 1630-44; ed. by N. Webster. Hartford, 1790. 8°.

— *Same, entitled* History of New England, 1630-49; with notes by J. Savage. Boston, 1825-26. 2 v. 8°.

— *Same*. New ed. Boston, 1853. 2 v. 8°.

— A model of Christian charity; written on board the Arabella. (*In* **Mass. Hist. Soc.** Col., v. 27. 1838.)

— Drake, S. G. Review of Winthrop's 'Journal' as edited by J. Savage. Boston, 1854. 8°.

— Holmes, A. Notes on a newly discovered ms. journal of W. (*In* **Mass. Hist. Soc.** Col., v. 14. 1816.)

— Moore, J. B. (*In his* Memoirs of Amer. governors, v. 1. 1846.)

— Winthrop, R. C. Life and letters of W. Boston, 1864-67. 2 v. 8°.

— — *Same*. (*In* **Mass. Hist. Soc.** Col., v. 36-37. 1863-65.)

Winthrop, John, *1st governor of Conn.*, *b.* 1605, *d.* 1676. Letter respecting the payment of expenses for obtaining the charter of Connecticut, 1662. (*In* **Conn. Hist. Soc.** Col., v. 1. 1860.)

— Dreuillettes G. Epistola ad J. Wintrop. Neo-Eboraci, *J. M. Shea*, 1869. 8°.

— Wolcott, R. Brief account of the agency of W. in the court of Charles II. (*In* **Mass. Hist. Soc.** Col., v. 4. 1795.) — **Mass.** *Governor*. Instructions from the Massachusetts to W., to treat with the Pequots. (*In* v. 23. 1833.)

Winthrop, John, *F. R. S.*, *d.* 1747. Account of the winter of 1717. (*In* **Mass. Hist. Soc.** Col., v. 2. 1810.)

— Selections from an ancient catalogue of objects of natural history formed in New England by W. From the Amer. journal of sci., v. 47. New Haven, 1844. 8°. (B 1189)

Winthrop, John, *prof. at Harvard Coll.*, *b.* 1714, *d.* 1779. Cogitata de cometis. Londini, 1767. 8°. (B 670)

— Lectures on earthquakes. Boston, 1755. 8°. (A 76, B 393)

— Relation of a voyage from Boston to Newfoundland for the observation of the transit of Venus, June 6. Boston, 1761. 8°. (B 393, 670)

— Two lectures on comets. Boston, 1759. 8°. (B 393, 643, 670)

— *Same*. Also, an Essay on comets by A. Oliver; with sketches of lives of Winthrop and Oliver; and a suppl. rel. to the comet of 1811, [by J. Davis]. Boston, 1811. 12°.

— *Other copies*. (B 643, 670)

— Two lectures on the parallax and distance of the sun as deducible from the transit of Venus, March. Boston, 1769. 8°. (B 393, 670)

— *Funeral sermon on*. 1779. *See* Langdon, S. (B 320); — Sewall, S. (B 70); — Wigglesworth, E. (B 172, 234, 335)

Winthrop, Robert Charles. Address. (*In* **Mass. Hist. Soc.** Proc., 1855-58. B 1960)

— Address at the Music Hall, fast day, Apr. 7, before the Young Men's Christian Assoc. Boston, 1859. 8°. (B 1588)

— Address at the opening of the grand musical festival, Boston Music Hall, May 21. Boston, 1857. 8°. (B 1960)

— Address at the opening of the new rooms of the Provident Assoc. in the Bureau of Charity, [May 19]. [Boston, 1869.] 8°. (B 1960)

— Address before the Association of the Alumni of Harvard College, July 22, 1852. Camb., 1852. 8°. (B 1960)

— Address before the Boston Mercantile Lib. Assoc., 25th anniv., Oct. 15. Boston, 1845. 8°. (B 1582, 1734, 1960)

— Address before the Maine Hist. Soc., Bowdoin Coll., Sept. 5. Boston, *Redding & Co.*, 1849. 8°. (B 1539, 1960)

— *Same*. Boston, *Ticknor, Reed, & Fields*, 1849. 8°. (B 1610)

— Address before the New England Soc. in N. Y. City, Dec. 23, 1839. Boston, 1840. 8°. (B 1697, 1819)

— Address on the occasion of the laying of the corner stone of the Public Library of Boston, Sept. 17. Boston, 1855. 8°. (B 1960)

— Addresses and speeches on various occasions [1839-51]. Boston, 1852. 8°.

Contents. The pilgrim fathers, Dec. 23, 1839. — The influence of commerce, Oct. 15, 1845. — National monument to Washington, July 4, 1848. — Life and services of J. Bowdoin, Sept. 5, 1849. — Free schools and free governments, Dec. 20, 1838. — The Bible, May 28, 1849. — Compensation for the destruction of the Ursuline Convent, Mar. 12, 1835. — Testimony of infidels, Feb. 11, 1836. — Protection to domestic industry, Feb. 15, 1837. — Congratulations to the Whigs of N. Y., Nov. 22. — The sub-treasury system, Mar. 26, 1838. — Votes of interested members, Feb. 19, 1840. — Reply to a vote of thanks, Mar. 21. — Proceeds of the public lands, July 2, 1841. — Policy of discriminating duties, Dec. 30. — Imprisonment of free colored seamen, Jan. 20, 1843. — Safe keeping of the public moneys, Jan. 25. — Credit of Mass. vindicated, Oct. 12. — Right of petition, Jan. 23, 1844. — Oregon question and the Treaty of Washington, March 18. — Annexation of Texas, Jan. 6, 1845. — Great Britain and the U. S., Feb. 1. — Arbitration of the Oregon question, Jan. 3, 1846. — River and harbor improvements, March 12. — Wants of government and the wages of labor, June 26. — Whig predictions and Whig policy, September 23. — War with Mexico, Jan. 8, 1847. — Conquest of Mexican territory, Feb. 22. — Address on taking the chair as speaker of the House, December 6. — Death of J. Q. Adams, Feb. 24, 1848. — Horticulture, September 22. — City of Wash., December 20. — Reply to a vote of thanks, Mar. 4, 1849. — Personal vindication, Feb. 21, 1850. — Death of J. C. Calhoun, April 1. — Admission of Cal. and the adjustment of the slavery question, May 8. — Death of Pres. Taylor, July 10. — Death of D. P. King, July 27. — To the people of Boston, July 30. — Boundary of New Mexico and Texas, Aug. 14. — Protest against the admission of Cal., Aug. 14. — The fugitive slave law, Aug. 19. — The Ottoman Empire, Nov. 4. — Religious instruction of the young, Apr. 27, 1851. — The American revolution, July 4. — Railroad jubilee, Sept. 19. — Agriculture, Sept. 24. — The mechanic arts, Oct. 1. — Agricultural education, Oct. 9. — Mass. in 1775, Oct. 29.

— Addresses and speeches on various occasions, 1852-67. Boston, 1867. 8°.

Contents. Religious instruction for the young, May 27, 1852. — Nomination of W. Scott for the Pres. of the U. S., June 29. — Obligations and responsibilities of educated men, July 22. — American agriculture, Oct. 15. — Electoral vote of Mass., Dec. 1. — Groton massacre in 1781, Sept. 6, 1853. — The coalition in Mass., Sept. 28. — Archimedes and Franklin, Nov. 29. — Algernon Sydney, Dec. 21. — Repeal of the Missouri Compromise, Feb. 23, 1854. — Death of J. Davis, Apr. 26. — Increased circulation of religious books, May 31. — Boston mechanics and Boston patriots, Oct. 11. — Historic glories of the Empire State, Nov. 20. — Dedication of the Winthrop School, Feb. 24, 1855. — Death of A. Lawrence, Aug. 20. — Boston Public Library, Sept. 17. — The fusion of parties in Mass., Oct. 15. — Agriculture of the U. S., Oct. 26. — National politics, Sept. 3, 1856. — Inaug. of the statue of Franklin, Sept. 17. — The presidential question, Oct. 24. — The worthies of Ct., Jan. 14, 1857. Opening of the Dowse library, Apr. 9. — Music in N. E., May 21. — The Cincinnati Soc., May 27. — Welcomes to Va. and Md., June 17. — The alumni of Harvard, July 17. — Central charity bureau, Oct. 8. — Boston Provident Association, Dec. 22. — Dedication of the Public Library, Boston, Jan. 1, 1858. — Boston Light Infantry, June 16. — Music in the schools, July 27. — Memory of T. Dowse, Dec. 9. — Death of the historian Prescott, Feb. 1, 1859. — Christianity neither sectarian nor sectional the remedy for social and political evils, Apr. 7. — Luxury and the fine arts, May 13. — The presidential election 1860, Sept. 25, 1860. — Tribute to Hon. N. Appleton, Aug. 8, 1861. — The flag of the union, Oct. 8, 1861. — Tribute to Hon. W. Appleton, Feb. 18, 1862. — Tribute to Pres. Felton, Mar. 13. — Tracts for the soldiers, May 27. — African colonization, May 28. — A star for every state and a state for every star, Aug. 27. — Irish recruits, Sept. 9. — The church as affected by the war, Oct. 9. — A flag to the 43d, Nov. 5. — Washington's birthday, Feb. 22, 1863. — Tribute to Crittenden, Aug. 13. — Concordia, Oct. 14. — Death of Lord Lyndhurst, Nov. 12. — Birthday of Shakespeare, Apr. 14, 1864. — More tracts for the camp, May 24. — The officers of the Russian fleet, June 7. — Death of J. Quincy, June 14. — The nomination of McClellan, Sept. 17. — Presidential election of 1864, Oct. 18. — The policy of the opposition, Nov. 2. — A home for the sailors, Nov. 9. — Death of E. Everett, Jan. 18, 1865. — Tribute to E. Everett, Jan. 30. — The fall of Richmond, Apr. 4. — Death of Pres.

Lincoln, Apr. 20. — 600th birthday of Dante, May 11. — Tribute to G. Livermore, Sept. 14. — Tribute to J. Sparks Apr. 3, 1866. — Jubilee of Amer. Bible Soc., May 10. — Death of Gen. Scott, June. — G. Peabody, Mar. 22, 1867. *Appendix: Letters.* Repeal of the Missouri compromise. — Policy of the old line Whigs. — Conciliation and forbearance to avert a conflict. — The national union convention at Phila., 1866.

— Admission of California; speech on the President's message transm. the constitution of California, May 8. Wash., 1850. 8°. (B 1516, 1700)

— Algernon Sydney; a lecture before the Boston Mercantile Lib. Assoc., Dec. 21. Boston, 1854. 8°. (B 1582)

— American agriculture; address before the Bristol Co. Agric. Soc., Taunton, Oct. 15, 1852. Boston, 1853. 8°. (B 1960)

— Archimedes and Franklin; lecture before the Mass. Charitable Mechanic Assoc., Nov. 29. Boston, 1853. 8°. (B 1960)

— Eulogy, funeral of G. Peabody, Peabody, Mass., Feb. 8. 2d ed. Boston, 1870. 8°. (B 1960)

— Interpretation of the title 'Knight of the golden melice'. (*In* **Mass. Hist. Soc.** Proc., 1858–60.)

— Introductory address. (*In* **Everett**, E. Eulogy on T. Dowse. 1859.)

— Introd. lecture on the early hist. of Massachusetts, Lowell Institute. Boston, 1869. 8°. (B 1960)

— Letter] on fusion. [Boston? 1855.] 8°. (B 1960)

— Life and letters of J. Winthrop. Boston, 1864–67. 2 v. 8°.

— *Same.* (*In* **Mass. Hist. Soc.** Col., v. 36, 37. 1863–65.)

— Luxury and the fine arts in some of their moral and historical relations; address in aid of the fund for Ball's equestrian statue of Washington, May 13. Boston, 1859. 8°. (B 1611)

— Massachusetts and its early history. (*In* **Mass. Hist. Soc.** Lect., 1869.) — Memoir of N. Appleton. (*In* Proc., 1860–62.)

— *Same.* With introd. and app. Boston, 1861. 8°.

— Oration at the inauguration of the statue of B. Franklin in his native city, Sept. 17. Boston, 1856. 8°. (B 1611, 1960)

— *Same.* (*In* **Shurtleff**, N. B. Mem. of the inaug. of of the statue of Franklin. 1857.)

— Oration, July 4, laying the corner stone of the national monument to the memory of Washington. Wash., 1848. 8°. (B 1510, 1612, 1666, 1738)

— Oration on the 250th anniv. of the Pilgrim Fathers at Plymouth, Dec. 21, 1870. Boston, 1871. 8°. (B 1960)

— *Same.* Boston, *privately printed* 1871. 4°.

— Remarks, Dec. 9, [on] the governments established in the conquered provinces of Mexico. Wash., 1846. 8°. (B 1510)

— Remarks on Mr. Fraser. (*In* **Mass. Hist. Soc.** Proc., 1860–62.)

— Remarks on the distribution bill, July 2. [Wash., 1841.] 8°. (B 1167, 1498)

— Remarks on the revenue bill, July 28. Wash., 1841. 8°. (B 1498)

— Speech at New London, Conn., Oct. 18. — Speech at the great ratification meeting, in Union Square, Sept. 17. (*In* **Hand-book** of the Democracy. 1864.)

— Speech at the Whig convention, Sept. 23. (*In* **True** Whig sentiment of Mass. 1846. B 1502)

— Speech in the Mass. Ho. of Rep. on the resolutions relating to the sub-treasury system, Mar. 26. [Boston, 1838.] 8°. (B 1496, 1732, 1751, 1814, 2010)

— Speech on the annexation of Texas, Jan. 6. Wash., 1845. 8°. (B 1174, 1510)

— Speech on the Mexican War, Jan. 8. Wash., 1847. 8°. (B 1510)

— Speech on the Oregon question, Mar. 18. Wash., 1844. 8°. (B 1516)

— Speech on the Oregon question, Feb. 1. Wash., 1845. 8°. (B 1197, 1516)

— Speech on the Oregon question, Jan. 3. Wash., 1846. 8°. (B 1516)

— Speech on the President's message, Feb. 21. Wash., 1850. 8°. (B 1516)

— Speech on the resolution to refer that part of the Pres. message rel. to the tariff to the com. on manufactures, Dec. 30, 1841. Wash., 1842. 8°. (B 1174, 1513)

— Speech on the resolution that the exchequer plan ought not to be adopted, Jan. 25. Wash., 1843. 8°. (B 1499, 1668)

— Speech on the right of petition, Jan. 23, 24. Wash., 1844. 8°. (B 1174, 1500, 1668)

— Tributes to the memory of E. Everett. Boston, 1865. 8°. (B 1594)

— Washington and the Union. (*In* **Boston** book, 4th col. 1850.)

— *and others.* To the electors of Mass. *n.p.*, [1837]. 8°. (B 1751)

— Loring, J. S. (*In his* Hundred Boston orators. 1852.)

— Maury, M. (*In her* Statesmen of America. 1847.)

— Mr. Winthrop's vote on the war bill. Boston, 1846. 8°. (B 1501)

— Wheeler, H. G. Biog. sketch of R. C. Winthrop. (*In his* History of Congress, v. 1. 1848.)

Winthrop, Theodore. The canoe and the saddle; and Isthmiana. Boston, 1863. 12°.

— Cecil Dreeme. Boston, 1862. 12°.

— Edwin Brothertroft. Boston, 1862. 12°.

— John Brent. Boston, 1862. 12°.

— Life in the open air. (*In* **Atlantic** monthly, v. 10. 1862.)

— *Same.* And other papers. Boston, 1863. 12°.
Contents. Life in the open air; Katahdin and the Penobscot. — Love and skates. — New York Seventh regiment; our march to Washington. — Washington as a camp. — Fortress Monroe. — Brightly's orphan; a fragment. — The heart of the Andes.

Winthrop, Thomas Lindall, *and* **Everett**, E. Address for the relief of the Greeks. *n.t.p.* [Boston, 1823.] 8°. (B 568, 937, 1836)

— *and others.* Address in behalf of the Juvenile Library Co. of Richmond. Richmond, 1823. 8°. (B 568)

— *and others.* Memorial of the inhabitants of Boston on the subject of the Greeks, Jan. 5. Wash., 1824. 8°. (18th Cong. 1st sess. B 942)

— Folsom, G. Memoir of T. L. Winthrop. (*In* **Amer. Antiq. Soc.** Archæol. Amer., v. 3. 1857.)

— Jenks, W. Memoir of W. (*In* **Mass. Hist. Soc.** Col., v. 32. 1854.)

Winthrop, Wm. Maltese antiquities. (*In* **Amer. Orient. Soc.** Journ., v. 2. 1851.)

Winthrop, *Me.* Thurston, D. Brief history of W., 1764–1855. Portland, 1855. 12°.

Winthrop papers. (*In* **Mass. Hist. Soc.** Col., v. 29, 30, 36, 37, 39, 41. 1846–71.)

Wintle, Thomas. Daniel. *See* **Bible.** *Daniel* (p. 281).

Winton, Andrew. *See* **Wyntown**, A.

Wintringham, Clifton. Inquiry on some parts of the animal structure. London, 1740. 8°.

Wintringham, Eliza. Trial of W. Parkinson for assault and battery upon W. N. Y., 1811. 8°. (B 439)

Winwood, *Sir* Ralph. Memorials of affairs of state, reigns of Elizabeth and James I.; col. from his papers by E. Sawyer. Lond., 1725. 3 v. f°.
Contents. Vol. 1. 1596–1602. 2. 1603–08. 3. 1609–13.

Wipo, Wippo, *or* **Witpo**. Proverbia. — Tetralogus Heinrici regis. — Vita Chuonradi II. imperatoris. (*In* **Pertz**, G. H. Mon. Germ. hist., Scr., v. 11. 1854.)

— Pertz, G. H. Ueber Wipo's Leben und Schriften. (*In* **Berlin. Ak. d. Wiss.** Abh., 1851.)

Wiréen, W. E. Praktisk Vägledning i Navigations-Vetenskapen. Carlshamn, 1850. 12°.

Wirgman, Thomas. Principles of the Kantesian or transcendental philosophy. (*In* **Pamphleteer**, 1824; v. 23 of B 838)

Wirrwarr, Der; oder, Der Muthwillige; von A. v. **Kotzebue.** (*In his* Theater, v. 15. 1841.)

Wirt, Wm. Celebration in Baltimore of the triumph of liberty in France; with address by W. Balt., 1830. 8°.

— Discourse on T. Jefferson and J. Adams, Oct. Wash., 1826. 8°. (B 1730, W 12)

— *Same.* (*In* **Moore**, F. Amer. eloquence, v. 2. 1864.)

— Extract from the argument in the Cherokee case. — Speech in the trial of A. Burr. (*In* **Moore**, F. Amer. eloq., v. 2. 1864.)

— Letters of the British spy in Virginia. 5th ed. Balt., 1813. 32°.

— *Same.* Newburyport, 1804. 18°.

— Sketches of the life and character of Patrick Henry. Phila., 1818. 8°.

— Two principal arguments on the trial of Aaron Burr. Richmond, 1808. 12°.

— Kennedy, J. P. Discourse, Baltimore, life and character of W. Balt., 1834. 8°. (B 1228)

— Memoirs of W. Phila., 1849. 2 v. 8°.

— Sketch.] (*In* **Longacre**, J. B., *and* **Herring**, J. Nat. port. gallery, v. 1. 1837.)

— SOUTHARD, S. L. Discourse, professional character and virtues of Wirt. Wash., 1834. 8°. (B 1228)

Wirtemburg. *See* **Würtemburg.**

Wirth, Johann Georg August. Die politisch-reformatorische Richtung der Deutschen im 16. u. 19. Jahrhundert. Belle-Vue, 1841. 8°.

Wirtzung, Christoph. General practise of physicke; tr. by I. Mosan. London, 1605. 8°.

Wisbuy, *Gothland.* Ordonnances. (*In* **Cleirac, E.** Us et coustumes de la mer. 1661.)

Wiscasset, *Me.* BRADFORD, A. Description of W. (*In* **Mass. Hist. Soc.** Col., v. 7. 1801.)
See also **Freemasons.**

Wisconsin. *Adjutant Gen.* Annual report, 1861, 62, 64. Madison, 1861–65. 3 v. 8°.
Note. Report for 1864 includes reports of Q. M. Gen. and Surg. Gen.

— - Army list. (*In* **Smith, G. B.** Official army list of the volunteers of Western States. 1862.)

— *Governor* (W. A. Barstow). Annual message. Madison, 1855. 8°.

— *Legislature.* General laws, 1859–61. Madison, 1859–61. 3 v. 8°.

— *State Geologist.* Annual report of the geological survey of Wis.; by J. G. Percival. Madison, 1856. 8°.

Antiquities.

— LAPHAM, I. A. Antiquities of W. (*In* **Smithsonian Inst.** Contrib., v. 7. 1855.)

— BARRY, W. Antiquities of W. (*In* **Wisconsin Hist. Soc.** Col., v. 3. 1857.) — LAPHAM, I. A. The man-shaped mounds of Wisconsin. (*In* v. 4. 1859.)
See also **Pepin, Lake.**

Botany.

— LAPHAM, I. A. Plants of W. (*In* **Amer. Assoc.** Proc., v. 2. 1850.)

— PARRY, C. C. Systematic catalogue of plants of W., *etc.* (*In* **U. S.** *Geological Survey.* Report of a geolog. survey of Wisconsin. 1852.)

Boundary.

— VINTON, S. F. North-eastern boundary of W. (*In* **Wisconsin Hist. Soc.** Col., v. 4. 1859.)

Description.

— WHITTLESEY, C. Recollections of a tour through W., 1832. (*In* **Wisconsin Hist. Soc.** Col., v. 1. 1855.)

— LAPHAM, I. A. Geographical and topographical description of W. Milwaukee, 1844. 16°.

— - *Same, entitled,* Wisconsin, its geography and topography. 2d ed. Milwaukee, 1846. 12°.

— CHAPMAN, S. Hand-book of W. 2d ed. Milwaukee, 1855. 16°.

— GREGORY, J. Industrial resources of Wisconsin. Milwaukee, 1855. 16°.

— EDWARDS, T. O. The progress, condition, and prospects of Wisconsin. (*In* **Wisconsin State Hist. Soc.** Col., v. 2. 1856.) — ELLIS, A. G. The 'upper Wisconsin' country. — QUINER, E. B. Resources of north-eastern Wisconsin. — WISCONSIN and her internal navigation. (*In* v. 3. 1857.) — LAPHAM, I. A. Public land surveys, and the latitude and longitude of places in Wisconsin. (*In* v. 4. 1859.)

— RITCHIE, J. S. Wisconsin and its resources. [1857.] 3d rev. ed. Phila., 1858. 12°.

— *Map.* SUYDAM, J. V. Map of Wisconsin territory. N. Y., 1839.

See also **Baraboo Valley**; — **Calumet Co.**; — **Madison**; — **Milwaukee Co.**; — **Pierce Co.**; — **Prairie du Chien**; — **West, The**; — **Whitewater.**

Geology.

— U. S. *Geological Survey.* Geological reconnoissance, 1835. Wash., 1836. 8°.

— FEATHERSTONHAUGH, G. W. Account of the lead and copper deposits in Wisconsin, [1837]. (*In his* Canoe voyage up the Minnay Sotor. 1847.)

— U. S. *Geological Survey.* Report of geological survey of Wisconsin, Iowa, and Minnesota, [1847–50]; with plates. Phila., 1852. 2 v. 4°.

— WHITTLESEY, C. Drift cavities or potash kettles of Wisconsin. (*In* **Amer. Assoc.** Proc., v. 13. 1860.)

History.

— GRIGNON, A. Seventy-two years' recollections of Wisconsin, [-1857]. (*In* **Wisconsin Hist. Soc.** Col., v. 3. 1857.) — BAIRD, H. S. Early history and condition of Wisconsin, [-1836]. (*In* v. 2. 1856.)

— SMITH, W. R. History of Wisconsin, [-1836]. Madison, 1854. 2 pts. in 3 v. (pt. 1, v. 2 never published). 8°.
Contents. Pt. 1, v. 1. Historical, 1634–1836. Pt. 2, v. 3. Documentary, 1639–1848.

— BRUNSON, A. Early history of W., [-1832]. (*In* **Wisconsin Hist. Soc.** Col., v. 4. 1859.) — WITHERELL, B. F. H. Reminiscences of the north-west, [1807–28]. (*In* v. 3.) — LOCKWOOD, J. H. Early times and events in W., [1816–40]. (*In* v. 2. 1856.) — TENNEY, H. A. Early times in W., [1818–38]. (*In* v. 1. 1855.) — CHILDS, E. Recollections of Wisconsin, 1820–52. — BAIRD, H. S. Recollections of the early history of northern Wisconsin, [1824–36]. (*In* v. 4. 1859.) — PARKINSON, D. M. Pioneer life in W., [1827–32]. (*In* v. 2. 1856.) — CHAPMAN, C. B. Early events in the Four Lake country, [1828–39]. (*In* v. 4. 1859.) — PRATT, A. F. Reminiscences of W., [1834–38]. (*In* v. 1. 1855.)

— LOVE, W. D. Wisconsin in the rebellion, [1861–65]. Chicago, 1866. 8°.
See also **Green Bay**; — **Green Co.**; — **Madison**; — **Milwaukee**; — **Monroe Co.**; — **New London.**

Names.

— BRUNSON, A. Wisconsin geographical names. (*In* **Wisconsin State Hist. Soc.** Col., v. 1. 1855.)

Natural history.

— PRATTEN, H. Systematic catalogue of birds of Wisconsin and Minnesota. (*In* **U. S.** *Geological Survey.* Report of a geological survey of Wisconsin, *etc.* 1852.)

— HOY, P. R. On the amblystoma luridum, a salamander inhabiting W. (*In* **Smithsonian Inst.** Report, 1854.)

Wisconsin almanac and annual register for 1856; comp. by J. W. Hunt. Milwaukee, [1855]. 12°.

Wisconsin Indians. SHEA, J. G. Indian tribes of W. (*In* **Wisconsin State Hist. Soc.** Col., v. 3. 1857.)

Wisconsin Soldiers Aid Society. FORMAN, *Rev.* J. G. Notice. (*In* **Brockett, L. P.** Woman's work in the civil war. 1867.)

Wisconsin State Agricultural Society. Transactions, 1854–59, 71–76. Vol. 4, 5, 10–14. Madison, [1858]–76. 7 v. 8°.

Wisconsin State Historical Society. Report and col. for 1854–58, 77–79. Vol. 1–4, 8. Madison, 1855–79. 5 v. 8°.
Contents. Vol. 1. **Whittlesey, C.** Green Bay in 1726. — **Gorrell, J.** Journal at Green Bay, 1761–63. — **Biddle, J. W.** Recollections of Green Bay, 1816–17. — **Whittlesey, C.** Recollections of a tour in Wisconsin in 1832. — **Haskins, R. W.** Legend of the Winnebagoes. — **Tenney, H. A.** Early times in Wisconsin. — **Cammuck, T.** Sketch of Calumet County. — **Haseltine, I. S.** Sketch of Richland Co. — **Brunson, A.** Wisconsin geographical names. — **Hathaway, J.** Indian names. — **Calkins, H.** Indian nomenclature of northern Wisconsin, *etc.* — **Pratt, A. F.** Reminiscences of Wisconsin. — Circular: Objects of collection desired by the Soc. 2. **Wright, H. A.** Eulogies on Wright, McLane, and Sully. — **Baird, H. S.** Annual address: Early history and condition of Wisconsin. — **Lockwood, J. H.** Early times and events in Wisconsin. — **Shaw, J.** Personal narrative. — **Brunson, A.** Memoir of Hon. T. P. Burnett. — **Parkison, D. M.** Pioneer life in Wisconsin. — **Bracken, C.,** *and* **Parkison, P.** Pekatonica battle controversy. — **Parkison, P.** Strictures on Gov. Ford's history of the Black Hawk War. — **Bracken, C.** Further strictures on Ford's history of the Black Hawk War. — **Ellis, A. G.** Some account of the advent of the N. Y. Indians into Wisconsin. — **Lothrop, J.** Sketch of the early history of Kenosha Co. — **Taylor, S.** Wisconsin; its rise and progress, with notices of Mineral Point and Richland Co. — **Robinson, C. D.** Legend of the Red Banks. — **Edwards, T. O.** Progress, condition, and prospects of Wisconsin. 3. Introduction. — **Calkins, E. A.** Eulogies on J. G. Percival. — Notices of Wm. A. White. — **Law, J.** Early Jesuit missionaries in the North west. — **Shea, J. G.** Indian tribes of Wisconsin.

— The **Cass** manuscripts; tr. by C. Whittlesey. — **Brunson,** A. Ancient mounds or tumuli in Crawford Co. — **Barry,** W. Antiquities of Wisconsin. — **Grignon,** A. Seventy-two years' recollections of Wisconsin. — **Witherell,** B. F. H. Reminiscences of the North West. — **Morse,** R. F. The Chippewas of Lake Superior. — **Frank,** M. Early history of Kenosha. — **Mygatt,** W. First settlement of Kenosha. — **Stewart,** J. W. Early history of Green Co. — **Leonard,** J. A. Sketch of Whitewater. — **Ellis,** A. G. The Upper Wisconsin country. — **Gibbs,** O., *and* **Young,** C. E. Sketch of Prescott and Pierce County. — **Hall,** T. D. Hudson and its tributary region. — **Lawson,** A. G. New London and surrounding country. — **Quiner,** E. B. Resources of north-eastern Wisconsin.— **Wisconsin** and its internal navigation. — **McBride,** D. Lemonweir River. — **Baraboo** Valley, a dairy region. — **Cruzat,** *Don* F. Message to the Sauks and Foxes. — **Draper,** L. C. Public libraries of Wisconsin. — Corrections and additions. **4.** Introductory. — **Smith,** J. Y. Annual address. — **Childs,** E. Recollections of Wisconsin. — **Baird,** H. S. Recollections of the early history of Northern Wisconsin. — **Brunson,** A. Early history of Wisconsin. — **Holton,** E. D., *and others.* Commercial history of Milwaukee. — **Commuck,** T. Sketch of the Brothertown Indians. — **Marsh,** C. The Stockbridges. — **Konkapot,** L., *Jr.* Last of the Mohegans. — Death of S. W. **Quinney.** — **Quinney,** J. W. Speech on Stockbridge traditionary history; — Memorial to Congress. — **Rublee,** H. Early times in Sheboygan Co. — **Chapman,** C. B. Early events in the Four Lake country. — **Vinton,** S. F. North-eastern boundary of Wisconsin. — **Lapham,** I. A. Public land survey; — Latitude and longitude of Wisconsin; — Man-shaped mounds of Wisconsin. — **Brunson,** A. Death of Tecumseh. — **Kingston,** J. T. Death of Tecumseh. — **Ballou,** D. W., *Jr.* First grave in Watertown. — **McMillan,** M. Early settlement of La Crosse and Monroe Counties. — **Graham,** J. D. On the latitude and longitude of Milwaukee, Prairie du Chien, Racine, and Madison. **8.** Introd. — Objects of col. — Index of papers. — **Houghton,** J. Ancient copper mines of Lake Superior. — **Slafter,** *Rev.* E. F. Prehistoric copper implements. — **Draper,** L. C., *and others.* Ancient copper implements. — **Brown,** *Rev.* E. Pictured cave of La Crosse Valley. — **Rice,** J. A. Add. notes on the La Crosse cave. — **Sulté,** B. Notes on J. Nicolet. — **Butler,** J. D. Early historic relics of the Northwest. — Tradition of the **Fox Indians,** 1730. — **Langlade** papers, 1737–1800. — **Schoolcraft,** H. R. Incident of Chegoimegon, 1760. — **Porlier,** L. J. Capture of Mackinaw, 1763. — **Moran,** E., *and others.* Green Bay and the frontiers, 1763–65. — **Strong,** M. M. Indian wars of Wisconsin. — **Tanner,** E. Wisconsin in 1818. — **Bristol,** *Mrs.* M. A. B. Reminiscences of the North-West. — **Clark,** S. Early times at Fort Winnebago. — **Ellis,** *Gen.* A. G. Recollections of E. Williams. — **Draper,** L. C. Add. notes on E. Williams. — **Kingston,** J. T. Early exploration and settlement of Juneau Co. — **Luchsinger,** J. Swiss colony of New Glarus. — **Tschudy,** J. J. Add. notes on New Glarus. — **Draper,** L. C. Wisconsin necrology, 1876–78. — Add. and corr. — General index.

Note. There is a list of officers and an annual report in each volume.

Wisdom of our fore-fathers, The, recommended to the present times. London, 1745. 8°. (B 746)

Wise, *Rev.* Daniel. Adam and Christ contrasted; discourse. Fall River, 1849. 8°. (C 211)

— Young lady's councellor. 8th thous. N. Y., 1852. 12°.

— Young man's councellor. 10th thous. N. Y., 1852. 12°.

Wise, Henry Alexander, *Gov. of Va.* American slavery; eloquent and elaborate vindication of the system; letter to a Boston clergyman. 1854. *Newspaper cutting.* (B 149)

— Correspondence with L. M. Child. Boston, 1860. 12°. (C 263)

— Message. 1859. *See* **Virginia.** *Governor.*

— Seven decades of the Union; memoir of J. Tyler. Phila., 1872 [1871]. 8°.

— Speech on the causes of the loss of the fortification bill of the last session. Jan. 22. Wash., 1836. 8°. (B 1113, 1777, 1791, 2009)

— Speech on the treasury note bill, Jan. 27–29. Wash., 1841. 8°. (B 1167, 1497).

— *and* **Peyton,** B. Speeches rel. to the agents of the Treasury and the deposite banks, Apr. 14 and 19. Wash., 1836. 8°. (B 1777)

— Savage, J. (*In his* Our living represent. men. 1860.)

Wise, Henry Augustus. Captain Brand of the Centipede. N.Y., 1864. 8°.

— Los Gringos; an inside view of Mexico and California, with wanderings in Peru, Chili, and Polynesia. N. Y., 1849. 12°.

Wise, *Rev.* Isaac M. The outlines of Judaism. (*In* **Free Religious Assoc.** 2d ann. meeting. 1869.)

Wise, *Rev.* Jeremiah. Prayer for ministers needful; sermon, ordination of J. Pike, Summersworth, Dover, Oct. 28, 1730. Boston, 1731. 8°. (C 22)

— Rulers the ministers of God for the good of their people; [election] sermon, May 28. Boston, 1729. 8°. (B 86, 183)

Wise, John, *d.* 1725. Churches' quarrel espoused. 2d ed. Boston, 1715. 16°.

— *Same.* Boston, 1772. 8°.

— *Another copy.* (B 82)

— *Same.* (*In his* Vindication. 1772.)

— Vindication of the government of New England churches. Boston, 1772. 8°.

— *Another copy.* (B 82)

— *Same.* Boston, 1772. 8°.

Note. This is the 2d edition published in this year. It contains, continuously paged, but with separate title-pages, 'The churches' quarrel espoused', 'Platform of church discipline agreed upon by the synod, Cambridge'. Pp. 165–180 are 'An extract from J. White's lamentations'; 232–271, 'Confession of faith consented unto, Boston, 1680'.

— Gatchel, S. Contrast to Rev. N. Whitaker, his confutation of Rev. J. Wise. Danvers, 1778. 8°. (B 253)

— Whitaker, N. Confutation of two tracts, 'Vindication of the N. Eng. churches' and 'Churches quarrel espoused', by J. Wise. Boston, 1774. 8°. (B 253)

Wise, John. System of aeronautics. Phila., 1850. 8°.

— Hare, R. On J. Wise's obs. resp. a thunder-storm during an aerial voyage, June 3, 1852. (*In* **Smithsonian Inst.** Report, 1854.)

Wise, John Richard. The New Forest, its history and its scenery. London, 1863. 4°.

Wiseman, Nicholas, *Cardinal.* Essays on various subjects. London, 1853. 3 v. 8°.

Contents. Vol. 1. Two letters on some parts of the controversy conc. the genuineness of 1 John v. 7. — Catholic versions of Scripture. — Parables of the N. Testament. — Miracles of the N. T. — Letters to J. Poynder upon Popery in alliance with heathenism. — Authority of the Holy See in S. Amer. — Eccles. organization. — The fate of sacrilege. — Prayer and prayer-books. — National holidays. — Minor rites and offices of the Church. — Anc. and mod. Catholicity. — The actions of the N. T. 2. The Hampden controversy. — Tracts for the times, pt. 1. — Froude's Remains. — The High Church theory of dogmatical authority. — Tracts for the times, pt. 2: Anglican claims of apostolical succession. — Tracts for the times, pt. 3: The Catholic and Anglican churches. — The Anglican system. — Protestantism of the Anglican Church. — Unreality of Anglican belief. — Position of the High Church theory at the close of 1847. — The fourth of October. 3. Papers on hist., antiq., and art. — Boniface VIII. — St. Elisabeth of Hungary. — Acc. of the council at Constantinople, 1166. — Writings of St. Ephrem. — Acc. of a recently discovered Christian inscription.— Rem. on lady Morgan's statement regarding St. Peter's chair. — The Roman Forum. — Christian art. — Spanish and Eng. national art. — Superficial travelling. — Italian guides and tourists. — Religion in Italy. — Italian gesticulation. — Early Italian academies. — Sense *v.* science.

— Fabiola; or, The church of the catacombs. N. Y., 1855. 12°.

— Horæ Syriacæ, seu commentationes et anecdota res vel litteras Syriacas spectantia. Tom. 1. Romæ, 1828. 8°.

Contents. De objectionibus contra sensum litteralem verborum eucharistiæ sacramentum institutientium, ex indole linguæ Syriacæ instauratis. — Symbolæ philologicæ ad historiam versionum Syriacarum Veteris Fœderis, Particula 1a, de versionibus generatim; deinde de peschito. — Particula, 2a recensionem Karkaphensem nunc primum describens. — Fragmentum Syriacum chronologiam 18æ dynastiæ Ægyptorum illustrans.

— Inaugural discourse at 1st session of the Academia, June 29, 1861. — Truth of supposed legends and fables. (*In* **Manning,** A. E. Essays on relig. and literature. 1865.)

— Lectures on the doctrines and practices of the Catholic Church. Dublin, 1867. 12°.
— Pastoral letter, Oct. 7, 1850. (*In* Cooper, C. P. Anc. Brit. churches. 1851. (E 107)
— Recollections of the four last Popes. London, 1858. 8°.
Namely. Pius VII., Leo XII., Pius VIII., Gregory XVI.
— Sermons, lectures, and speeches during a tour in Ireland, 1858. Dublin, 1859. 16°.
— Twelve lectures on the connexion between science and revealed religion. 4th ed. London, 1851. 2 v. 12°.
— GAVAZZI, A. My recollections of the last four popes and of Rome in their times; answer to Dr. W. London, 1858. 8°.

Wiseman, Richard. Chirurgical treatises. 5th ed. London, 1719. 2 v. 8°.

Wishart, George, *Bp. of Edinburgh*, *b.* 1609, *d.* 1671. Memoirs of J. Graham, Marquis of Montrose; tr. from the Latin. Edin., 1819. 8°.

Wishart, *Rev.* George. Times of public distress; sermons, Nov. 1745, on the present rebellion. Edin., 1745. 8°. (B 1902)

Wishart, Wm., *D.D.* Certain and unchangeable difference betwixt moral good and evil; sermon before the Socs. for Reformation of Manners, at Salter's Hall, July 3. London, 1732. 8°. (B 1861)
— Charity the end of the commandment, *etc.*; sermon, Apr. 19. Edin., 1731. 8°. (B 1861)
— Essay on the inefficiency of a death-bed repentance. Birmingham, 1817. 8°. (C 232)

Wislizenus, A. Memoir of a tour to northern Mexico with Col. Doniphan, 1846–47. Wash., 1848. 8°. (U. S. 30th Cong. Sen. doc. 26.)

Wisner, Benjamin Blydenburg, *D.D.* Benefits and claims of sabbath schools. Boston, 1830. 8°. (C 211)
— History of the Old South Church, Boston; four sermons. Boston, 1830. 8°.
— *Other copies.* (B 1326, 1781, 2538)
— Influence of religion on liberty; disc. in commemoration of the landing of the Pilgrims, Dec. 22, 1830. Boston, 1831. 8°. (B 1571)
— Memoirs of Mrs. S. Huntington. 3d ed. Boston, 1829. 12°.
— Moral condition and prospects of the heathen; sermon, Boston, before the For. Miss. Soc., Jan. 1. Boston, 1824. 8°. (B 301)
— Proper mode of conducting missions to the heathen; sermon before the Soc. for Prop. the Gospel among the Indians, Nov. 5. Boston, 1829. 8°. (B 1150)
— Sermon, death of Mrs. M. Phillips, May 18. Camb., 1823. 8°. (B 283)
— Sermon, death of W. Phillips, June 3. Boston, 1827. 8°. (B 960, 1780)
— *Funeral sermon on.* 1835. *See* Fay, W. (B 1228)

Wisner, *Rev.* Wm. Candid examination of certain doctrines [of] the friends of sabbath mails. Ithaca, 1829. 8°. (B 1374)

Wiss, Johann David. *See* Wyss, J. D.

Wissett, Robert. Treatise on hemp; its cultivation in Europe, Asia, *etc.*; with app. by Lord Somerville. London, 1808. 4°.

Wissowatius, Andreas. Narratio compendiosa quomodo in Polonia a Trinitariis reformatis separati sint Christiani Unitarii; acc., Historia de spiritu Belga. — Epistola exhibens vitæ ac mortis A. Wissowatii nec non ecclesiarum Unitariorum ejus tempore historiam. (*In* Sand, C. von der. Bibl. Anti-trin. 1684.)

Wistar, Caspar, *M.D.* Account of two heads found in the morass called the Big Bone Lick. — Case of disease in which one side of the thorax was at rest while the other performed the motion of respiration in the usual way. — On those processes of the ethmoid bone which form the sphenoidal sinuses. (*In* Amer. Phil. Soc. Trans., n.s., v. 1. 1818.)
— System of anatomy. Phila., 1811. 2 v. 8°.
— HOSACK, D. Tribute to the memory of W. N. Y., 1818. 8°. (B 357)
— MORRIS, C. Life of C. Wistar. (*In* Gross, S. D. Lives of eminent Amer. physicians. 1861.)
— SKETCH.] (*In* Longacre, J. B., *and* Herring, J. Nat. portr. gal., v. 2. 1835.)
— *Eulogium.* 1818. *See* Tilghman, W. (B 357, 1828, W 4)

Wiswall, Hattie. BROCKETT, L. P. (*In his* Woman's work in the civil war. 1864.)

Wit. *See also* Witt; — Witte.

Wit, Friedrich de. Insula Candia ejusque fortificatio. Amst., [16—]. (E 78, no. 254)

Wit and humor. COLLINS, A. Discourse conc. ridicule and irony in writing. Lond., 1729. 8°.
— — *Another copy.* (B 1365)
— PRESTON, W. Essay on ridicule, wit, and humour. (*In* Roy. Irish. Acad. Trans., v. 2. 1788.)
— KETT, H. Flowers of wit; a col. of bon-mots. Boston, 1815. 2 v. 18°.
— BYERLEY, T., *and* ROBERTSON, J. C. (*In their* Percy anecdotes, v. 10. 1823.)
— FOURNIER, E. L'esprit dans l'histoire. [1856.] 3e éd., augm. Paris, 1867. 12°.
— COBBE, F. P. The humour of various nations. (*In her* Hours of work and play. 1867.)
— DINAUX, A. M. Les sociétés badines, bachiques, *etc.*; leur histoire; rév. par G. Brunet. Paris, 1867. 2 v. 8°.
See also Epigrams; — *also* English wit and humour; — Oriental literature. *Collections.* (GALLAND).

Wit, New foundling hospital for. *See* New.

Wit and science, Moral play of; ed. by J. O. Halliwell. London, 1848. 8°. (Shakespeare Soc., v. 42.)

Wit at several weapons; by F. Beaumont and J. Fletcher. (*In their* Dram. works, v. 9. 1778; Works, v. 4. 1844.)

Wit bought; or, Life and adventures of Robert Merry; by S. G. Goodrich. N. Y., 1844. 18°.

Wit without money; by F. Beaumont *and* J. Fletcher. (*In their* Dram. works, v. 2. 1778; *and* Works, v. 4. 1844.)

Witch, The; a tragi-comedy by T. Middleton. (*In his* Works, v. 3. 1840.)

Witch Hampton Hall. (*In* In lodgings at Knightsbridge. 186–.)

Witch of Edmonton, The; a tragedy, by J. Ford. (*In his* Dram. works, v. 3. 1869.)

Witch of Edmonton, The; by W. Rowley and others. (*In* Lamb, C. Spec. of dram. poets. 1854.)

Witchcraft, Magic, Sorcery. *Bibliography.*
— GRÆSSE, J. G. T. Bibliotheca magica et pneumatica. Lpz., 1843. 8°.

General histories.

— ENNEMOSER, J. History of magic; tr. from the Germ. by W. Howitt; added, stories of apparitions, *etc.* London, 1854. 16°.
— MAURY, L. F. A. La magie et l'astrologie dans l'Antiquité et au Moyen Age. 3e éd. Paris, 1864. 16°.
— SCOTT, *Sir* W. Letters on demonology and witchcraft. N. Y., 1848. 16°. (Harper's fam. lib., v. 11.)
— UPHAM, C. W. *See next page.*

Middle ages and later.

— FORMEY, J. H. S. Recherches sur les anciennes procédures contre les sorciers. (*In* Sérieys, A. Bibl. acad., v. 4. 1811.)
— GLANVILL, J. *See next page.*
— HUTCHINSON, F. Historical essay conc. witchcraft. London, 1718. 8°.
— LOWELL, J. R. Witchcraft. (*In his* Among my books. 1870.)
— LECKY, W. E. H. On magic and witchcraft. (*In his* Rationalism in Europe, v. 1. 1865.)
— MACKAY, C. The witch mania. (*In his* Memoirs of popular delusions, v. 2. 1852.)
— MICHELET, J. La sorcière. 4e éd. Brux., Lpz., 1863. 12°.
— ROSKOFF, G. Periode der gerichtlichen Hexenverfolgung, [1230–1787]. (*In his* Geschichte des Teufels, v. 2. 1869.)
— WRIGHT, T. Narratives of sorcery and magic, [1324–1711]. 2d ed. Lond., 1851. 2 v. 12°.

Histories of shorter periods, with some other works, chronologically arranged.

— PARTHEY, G. F. C. Zwei griechische Zauberpapyri des Berliner Museums. (*In* **Berlin. Ak. d. Wiss.** Abh., 1865.)

— BOISSARD, J. J. De divinatione et magicis præstigiis [antiquis]. Oppenheimii, [17—]. f°.

— CONTEMPORARY narrative of the proceedings against A. Kyteler prosecuted for sorcery in **1324**; ed. by T. Wright. London, 1843. 4°. (Camden Soc., v. 24.)

— BEIGEL, H., *ed.* Examination and confession of witches at Chelmsford, Co. of Essex. London, **1566**, *reprinted* 1864. 8°.

— DARREL, J. Strange and grievous vexation by the devil of seven persons in Lancashire, and W. Somers of Nottingham, **1600**. (*In* **Somers, J.** Col. of tracts, v. 3. 1810.)

— GIFFORD, G. Dialogue of witches and witchcraft, **1603**; [ed. by T. Wright]. London, 1842. 8°. (Percy Soc., v. 8.)

— PERKINS, W. The damned art of witchcraft. **1608**. (*In his* Workes, v. 3. 1613.)

— DELRIO, M. A. Disquisitionum magicarum libri VI. Moguntiæ, **1612**. 4°.

— POTTS, T. Discovery of witches in the County of Lancaster [**1613**]; [with the triall of 19 witches, Aug. 17, 1612; and the triall of J. Preston at Yorke. Manchester,] 1845. 4°. (Chetham Soc., v. 6.)

— — *Same.* (*In* **Somers, J.** Col. of tracts, v. 3. 1810.)

— DRAKE, S. G. Annals of witchcraft in New England and elsewhere in the United States, **1636-1728**. Boston, 1869. 4°. (Woodward's hist. ser., v. 8.)

— WITCHCRAFT in New Hampshire, **1656**. (*In* **New Hampshire Hist. Soc.** Col., v. 1. 1824.)

— HINMAN, R. R. Witchcraft, [**1663-88**]. (*In his* Blue laws of New Haven Colony. 1838.)

— GLANVILL, J. Sadducismus triumphatus; evidence conc. witches and apparitions; 1st, their possibility, 2d, their real existence. [**1681**]. 4th ed. with add. London, 1726. 8°.

— BRATTLE, T. Account of witchcraft in the County of Essex, **1692**. (*In* **Mass. Hist. Soc.** Col., v. 5. 1816.)

— CALEF, R. More wonders of the invisible world, [**1692-97**]; added, a postscript rel. to 'The life of Sir W. Phips'. London, 1700, Salem, *reprinted* 1796. 12°.

— — *Same, entitled* The wonders of the invisible world displayed. New ed. Bost., 1828. 12°.

— — *Same.* (*In* **Fowler, S. P.** Salem witchcraft. 1861; —*and in* **Drake, S. G.** Witchcraft delusion, v. 2, 3. 1865.)

— CHANDLER, P. W. Trials for witchcraft, 1692. (*In his* American criminal trials, v. 1. 1841.)

— DRAKE, S. G. The witchcraft delusion in N. Eng., its rise, progress, and termination as exhibited by C. Mather in 'The wonders of the invisible world' [1693], and by R. Calef in his 'More wonders of the invisible world', [1697]; with preface, introd., and notes. Roxbury, 1866. 3 v. 4°.

— FOWLER, S. P. Salem witchcraft; comprising 'More wonders of the invisible world, by R. Calef; and 'Wonders of the invisible world', by C. Mather. Salem, 1861. 12°.

— GODDARD, D. A. The Mathers weighed in the balances and found not wanting. Boston, 1870. 12°.

— LONGFELLOW, H. W. Giles Corey of the Salem Farms. [1692.] (*In his* New England tragedies. 1868.)

— MATHER, C. Wonders of the invisible world; account of the tryals of witches executed in Eng.; added, Farther account, by I. Mather, [1692]. London, 1862. 8°.

— — Autograph letter on witchcraft. [1692] (*In* **Lit. and Hist. Soc. of Quebec.** Trans., v. 2. 1831.)

— POOLE, W. F. The Mather papers; Cotton Mather and Salem witchcraft. Bost., 1868. 12°.
Note. From the **Boston** d. Advertiser, Oct. 28.

— — Cotton Mather and Salem witchcraft. Boston, 1869. 8°.
Note. Repr. from the North Amer. rev.

— — Cotton Mather and witchcraft; two notices of Mr. Upham his reply. Boston, London, 1870. sm. 4°.

— RECANTATION of confessors of witchcraft. [1692.] (*In* **Mass. Hist. Soc.** Col., v. 13. 1815.)

— WOODWARD, W. E. Records of Salem witchcraft, 1691-92. Roxbury, 1865. 4°. (Woodward's hist. ser., v. 1, 2.)

— SALEM witchcraft; extracts from the records of the church in Danvers rel. to the dissensions occasioned by the prosecutions for witchcraft, *etc.*, [1692-94]. (*In* **Mass. Hist. Soc.** Col., v. 23. 1833.)

— THACHER, J. Acc. of witchcraft at Salem, 1692. (*In his* Essay on demonology. 1831.)

— UPHAM, C. W. Lectures on witchcraft; comprising a history of the delusion in Salem, 1692. Boston, 1832. 12°.

— — Salem witchcraft, [1691-92]; with account of Salem Village and history of witchcraft and kindred subjects. Boston, 1867. 2 v. 8°.

— WILLARD, S. Some miscellany observations on witchcrafts. Phila., 1692. 4°. (B 654)

— TURELL, E. Detection of witchcraft. [1720.] (*In* **Mass. Hist. Soc.** Col., v. 20. 1823.)

— DE FOE, D. System of magic. [1728.] (Vol. 12 *of his* Works. 1840.)

See also **Essex Inst.** Hist. col., *passim*; — *also* **Demonology**; — **Devil**; — **Magic, Natural**; — **Necromancers**; — **Occult sciences**; — **Possession.**

Witchcraft; a tragedy, by J. Baillie. (*In her* Dram. and poet. works. 1851.)

Witching times. (*In* **Putnam's** mag., v. 8-10. 1856-57.)

With, Emile. Railroad accidents; their causes, and means of preventing them, with an introduction by A. Perdonnet; tr. from the French, with an app. by G. F. Barstow. Boston, 1856. 8°.

With Gen. Sheridan in Lee's last campaign; by a staff officer. Phila., 1866. 12°.

Wither, George. Hallelujah; or, Britain's second remembrancer; introd. by E. Farr. London, 1857. 16°.

— Hymns and songs of the Church; ed. by E. Farr. London, 1856. 12°.

— Juvenilia; poems contained in the col. of his Juvenilia [of] 1626 and 1633. [Manchester,] 1871. 3 v. 4°. (Spenser Soc., v. 9-11.)

— Poems. (*In* **Campbell, T.** Brit. poets, v. 4. 1819.)

— BRYDGES, *Sir* S. E., *Bart.* (*In his* Brit. bibliographer, v. 1. 1810.)

— WILLMOTT, R. A. (*In his* Lives of the English sacred poets, v. 1. 1839.)

Witherell, B. F. H. Reminiscences of the north-west. (*In* **Wisconsin State Hist. Soc.** Col., v. 3. 1857.)

Witherell, *Mrs.* E. C. FORMAN, *Rev.* J. G. (*In* **Brockett, L. P.** Woman's work in the civil war. 1867.)

Withering, Wm. Arrangement of British plants according to the Linnæan system. 3d ed. Birmingham, London, 1796. 4 v. 8°.

Withers, *Rev.* **John.** Defence of the 'True and impartial account of the conference in Exon', [against] Agate's reply. Exon, 1707. 8°. (B 105)

— History of resistance as practised by the Ch. of Eng. (*In* **Somers, J.** Col. of tracts, v. 12. 1814.)

— The pestilence abroad; sermon, March 1, 1720. London, 1721. 8°. (B 120)

— Plain reasons for dissenting from the Ch. of Eng., *etc.* 3d ed., with add. London, 1717. 8°. (B 29)

— *Same.* 18th ed. Boston, 1725. 8°. (C 185)

— Truth try'd; or, Agate's 'Plain-truth' proved an untruth. Part 2. Exon., 1709. 8°. (B 105)

— The Whigs vindicated, the objections against them answered. London, 1715. 8°. (B 756)

— AGATE, J. The plain truth; an answer to Withers's 'Defence'. Pt. 2. Exon, 1708. 8°. (B 105)
— - Reply to W.'s Account of a conference at Exon. *t.p.w.* [1707.] 4°. (B 105)
See also Caveat against Anabaptists, *etc.* 1714. (B 105, 659)

Withers, R. J. Ancient antiquities of the Church of the Holy Cross, Brinstead. — Examples of encaustic tiles from Beaulieu Abbey. (*In* Weale, J. Quarterly papers on archit., v. 4. 1845.)

Witherspoon, John, *D.D.* Works. Phila., 1802. 4 v. 8°.
Contents. Vol. 1. Funeral discourse on W., by J. Rodgers. — Essay on justification, [with] a letter to Rev. J. Hervey. — Treatise on regeneration. — Sermons. 2. Sermons. 3. A pastoral letter from the synod of New York and Philadelphia. — Sermons. — Address to the students of the senior class, Sept. 23, 1775. — Serious inquiry into the nature and effects of the stage. — Letter respecting play-actors. — Ecclesiastical characteristics. — Serious apology for the 'Ecclesiastical characteristics'. — The history of a corporation of servants. — Lectures on moral philosophy. — Lectures on eloquence. 4. Introductory lecture on divinity. — Letters on education. — Letters on marriage. — Address to the inhabitants of Jamaica and other West-India islands in behalf of the College of New-Jersey. — Essay on money, with remarks on the advantages, *etc.*, of paper admitted into general circulation. — Speech in the synod of Glasgow when accused of being the author of the 'Ecclesiastical characteristics'. — An humble supplication to such of the nobility and gentry of Scotland as are elders of the church and members of the General Assembly. — Speech in the General Assembly on the transportation of Dr. C—. — Letter sent to Scotland for the Scots magazine. — Ignorance of the British with respect to America. — Reflections on the present state of public affairs and on the duty and interest of America. — Thoughts on American liberty. — On the controversy about independence. — On conducting the American controversy. — Aristides. — Part of a speech in Congress, on the conference proposed by Lord Howe. — Speeches in Congress: on the convention with Gen. Burgoyne; on a motion for paying the interest of loan-office certificates; on the finances; upon the confederation; on the appointment of plenipotentiaries. — On the proposed market in Gen. Washington's camp. — Address to Gen. Washington. — Memorial and manifesto of the United States. — On the contest between Great-Britain and America. — On the affairs of the United States. — Obs. on the improvement of America. — Supplication of J. R. — Recantation of B. Towne. — Description of the State of New-Jersey. — A few reflections on the federal city. — On the Georgia constitution. — The Druid, originally published in numbers periodically.
— Absolute necessity of salvation through Christ; sermon before the Soc. in Scotland for Prop. Chr. Knowl., Edinburgh, Jan. 2. Edin., 1758. 8°. (B 1922)
— Address to the inhabitants of Jamaica in behalf of the College of New Jersey. Phila., 1772. 8°. (B 739)
— Charge of sedition and faction against good men, *etc.*; sermon. Boston, *reprinted* 1811. 12°. (C 211)
— Christian magnanimity; sermon, Princeton, [with] an addr. to the senior class. Princeton, 1787. 8°. (B 859)
— Dominion of Providence over the passions of men; sermon, Princeton, May 17, 1776, general fast; added, addr. to natives of Scotland in Amer. Phila., 1776. 8°. (B 235, 2503)
— *Same, sermon only.* Lond., *reprinted* 1778. 8°. (B 388)
— Ministerial character and duty. — Man in his natural state. — Inducement to come to Christ. (*In* Austin, D. American preacher, v. 1. 1791.) — Seeking a competency in the wisdom of Providence. — The danger of prosperity. — The danger of adversity. (*In* v. 2.) — Trust in God. (*In* v. 3. 1791.)
— Serious apology for 'Ecclesiastical characteristics'. Edin., 1763. 8°. (B 256)
— Sermon, religious educ. of children. Elizabeth-Town, 1789. 8°. (B 336)
— Speech on conference with Lord Howe. — Remarks on confederation. — Speech on convention with Burgoyne. — Speech on appointment of plenipotentiaries. — Speech on loan office certificates. — Portion of speech on finances. (*In* Moore, F. Amer. eloquence, v. 1. 1864.)
— SANDERSON, J. (*In his* Biog. of the signers to the declaration of independence, v. 5. 1824.)
— *Funeral sermon on.* 1795. *See* Rodgers, J. (W 39)

Withington, Leonard, *D.D.* Cobwebs swept away, *etc.*; sermon, fast day, Apr. 6, Newbury. Newburyport, 1837. 8°. (B 1306)
— Emulation in schools. (*In* Amer. Inst. of Instr. Lect., 1833.)
— Puritan morals defended; discourse, dedication of Crombie St. Ch. Salem, 1832. 8°. (B 1310)
— Sermon, annual election. May 25. Boston, 1831. 8°. (B 1052, 1804, 2011)
— Sermon, 200th anniv. of the First Church in Newbury on its present site, Oct. 20. Newburyport, 1846. 8°. (B 1306)
— Solomon's Song. *See* Bible. *Song of Solomon* (p. 280).
— The soul of man; sermon, Salem, Apr. 22. Salem, 1832. 8°. (B 1306)
— Take warning; sermon, Newbury and Newburyport, Aug. 22 and 29. Newburyport, 1830. 8°. (B 1168)
— Thanksgiving sermon, Newbury, Nov. 28, 1850. 2d ed. Newburyport, 1851. 12°. (B 1254)
— Vibrations in theology. (*In* Essex North Assoc. Contrib. 1865.)

Withington, Nicholas. Travels in the East Indies. (*In* Cockburn, J. Faithful account. 1740.)

Withington, Oliver Wendell. The pilgrim; poem before the Associate Alumni of the Univ. of Vermont, Aug. Boston, 1849. 8°. (B 1234, 1467)

Withington, Wm. Sermon; the reward sought, obtained. (*In* Protestant Episcopal pulpit, v. 1. 1831.)

Withrington, Robert. SARRACOLL, J. Voyage of W. for the South Sea. (*In* Burney, J. Discoveries in the South Sea, v. 2. 1806; — *and in* Hakluyt, R. Col. of voy., v. 4. 1811.)

Withy, George. CANDIDATUS, *pseud.* Letter to G. Withy; reflections on [his] sermon in Burlington. Phila., 1822. 12°. (C 161)

Witiko; eine Erzählung; von A. Stifter. Pest, 1865-67. 3 v. 8°.

Witness. SAMPSON, W. The Catholic question in Amer.; case of the people *vs.* D. Phillips and wife; whether a Roman Catholic clergyman be compellable to disclose secrets of confession. N. Y., 1813. 8°.
— FROST, C. Considerations on the propriety of making a remuneration to witnesses in civil actions for loss of time. (*In* Pamphleteer, 1816; v. 7 of B 838)
— PARKMAN, S. Relations of the medical witness with the law and lawyer. From the Amer. journ. of med. sci., Jan. Phila., 1852. 8°. (B 1559)

Witness, The; a collection of original and selected pieces, Jan.-June 1809. Boston, [1809]. 12°.

Wits, The; a drama, by Sir W. Davenant. (*In* Scott, *Sir* W. Anc. Brit. dr., v. 1. 1810; — *and* Dodsley, R. Old plays, v. 8. 1825.)

Wits and beaux of society. *See* Thomson, K. B. *and* J. C.

Wits common-wealth; or, A treasury of divine, moral, *etc.*, sentences; by [J. Bodenham]. Newly corr. and enl. London, 1722. 8°.

Witsen, Nicolaus. Aeloude en hedendaegsche Scheeps-bouw en bestier. Amst., 1671. f°.
— Extract from 'Noord en Oost Tartarye'. (*In* Major, R. H. Early voyages to Terra Australis. 1859.)

Witsius, Hermann. Essay on the use and abuse of reason in matters of religion; tr. by J. Carter. Norwich, 1795. 8°. (B 1360)

Witt. *See also* Wit.

Witt, August. Der preussische Landtag im Februar 1813; nach den im Archive der Generallandschaftsdirection von Ostpreussen aufbewahrten Acten des Landtags von 1813 und nach mündlichen Mittheilungen des Staatsministers von Schön. (*In* Historisches Taschenbuch, 1857.)

Witt, Cornelis de. Thomas Jefferson; étude historique sur la démocratie américaine. 3e éd. Paris, 1861. 12°.

Witt, *Mme.* Henriette (Guizot) de. A French country family; tr. by D. M. Craik. N. Y., 1868. 12°.
— The Lady of Latham; being the life and letters of Charlotte de la Trémoille Countess of Derby. London, 1869. 8°.
— Motherless; or, A Parisian family; [tr. by D. Craik]. N. Y., 1871. 8°.

Witt, Jan de. Lettres et négociations entre W. et les plénipotentiaires des Provinces Unies des Pais-Bas aux cours de France, d'Angleterre, *etc.*, 1652-69, cont. les négoc. de G. Borrel en France, 1653-59; tr. Amst., 1725. 4 v. 12°.
Contents. Vol. 1. 1652-59. 2. 1660-64. 3. 1664-66. 4. 1667-69.

— *and others.* True interest and political maxims of the republick of Holland and West-Friesland. London, 1702. 8°.
— BARNWELL, R. G. Sketch of the life and times of W. N. Y., 1856. 12°.
— CROWE, E. E., *and* JAMES, G. P. R. (*In their* Lives of eminent for. statesmen, v. 3. 1836.)
— MALDEN, H. (*In his* Dist. men of mod. times, v. 2. 1838, Lib. ent. knowl., v. 38; v. 1. 1840, Harper's fam. lib., v. 123.)
— PETER, H. (*In* Historische Zeitschrift, v. 13. 1865.)
— SIMONS, P. Witt und seine Zeit; aus dem Holländischen übers. von F. Neumann. Erfurt, 1835-36. 2 v. 8°.
Witt, Jan de, *son of preceding.* CATALOGUS bibliothecæ, libris quæsitis a Joanne de Witt. Dordraci, [1701]. 2 v. in 4 pts. 12°.
Witte. *See also* Wit.
Witte, Henning. Diarium biographicum, in quo scriptores sec. XVII præcipui adducuntur. Gedani, 1688. 4°.
Witte, Karl. Dante-Forschungen, altes und neues. Berlin, 1869. 8°.
Wittenberg. MEYNER, A. M. Geschichte der Stadt Wittenberg, [-1845]. Dessau, 1845. 8°.
— WENCK, W. Die Wittenberger Capitulation von 1547. (*In* Historische Zeitschrift, v. 20. 1868.)
Wittenberg Universität. Liber decanorum facultatis theologicæ Academiæ Vitebergensis; ex autographo ed. C. E. Foersteman. Lips., 1838. 8°.
— Soteria Saxonum duci Johanni Georgio quum Silesiam Lusatiamque pacasset persoluta. Wittenb., [1622]. 4°.
Contents. Oratio panegyrica in honorem J. Georgii, a F. Balduino. — Panegyricus J. Georgii ab A. Buchnero.
Wittenmeyer, Annie. BROCKETT, L. P. (*In his* Woman's work in the civil war. 1867.)
Wittich, Federico Guglielmo. L'ultima campagna de' Francesi in Germania. Napoli, 1816. 8°. (B 802)
Wittich, Wm. On the former and present condition of the elementary schools in Prussia. (*In* Cent. Soc. of Educ., v. 1. 1837.) — On the seminaries for schoolmasters for the working classes in Prussia. (*Ib.* v. 2. 1838.)
— The geography of America and the West Indies. 1841. *See* Long, G.
Wittich Wielands Sohn. (*In* Simrock, K. J. Heldenbuch, v. 4. 1843.)
Wittings, André. *See* Vésale, A.
Wittje, G. Die wichtigsten Schlachten, Belagerungen, und verschanzten Lager, 1708-1855. Lpz., Heidelb., 1861. 2 v. 8°.
Wittmer, Johann Michael. ANDRESEN, A. Leben und Werken. (*In his* Die deutschen Maler-Radirer. v. 2. 1867.)
Wittstein, Georg Christoph. Etymologisch-botanische Handwörterbuch. 2e Ausgabe. Erlangen, 1856. 8°.
Wittwe, Die, und das Reitpferd; von A. v. Kotzebue. (*In his* Theater, v. 6. 1840.)
Wittwe, Die, und der Wittwer; oder Treue bis in den Tod; Lustspiel von Holbein. (*In* Kotzebue, A. von. Almanach, v. 20. 1822.)
Wittwer, Wilhelm Constantin. Briefe über A. von Humboldts Kosmos, 4r Theil. 1859. *See* Cotta, B. von.
Witty fair one, The; a play, by J. Shirley. (*In his* Dram. works, v. 1. 1833.)
Witwicki, Stefan. Poezije. Paryż, 1836. 18°.
— Wieczory pielgrzyma, rozmaitości moralne, literackie, i polityczne. Paryż, 1837. 2 v. 16°.
Wives. CHILD, L. M. Biographies of good wives. Boston, 1833. 12°. (Ladies' fam. lib., v. 3.)
— DIXON, W. H. Spiritual wives. London, 1868. 2 v. 8°.
Wives and daughters; by Mrs. E. C. Gaskell. (*In* Cornhill mag., v. 10-13. 1864-1866; — *and in* Littell's living age, v. 85-88. 1865-66.)
Wives as they were and maids as they are; a comedy, by Mrs. E. Inchbald. (*In* London stage, v. 2.)
Wives' excuse, The; or, Cuckolds make themselves; a comedy, by T. Southerne. (*In his* Works, v. 1. 1721.)
Wives of England. *See* Ellis, S.
Wix, Edward. Six months of a Newfoundland missionary's journal. London, 1836. 12°.
Wizard of the wave, The; by J. T. Haines. (*In* Sargent, E. Mod. stand. dr., v. 27.)
Woad. LASTEYRIE, C. P. de. Treatise on the culture, preparation, hist., and analysis of pastel or woad; tr. from the French by H. A. S. Dearborn. Boston, 1816. 12°.
Woart, John. Address at the funeral of J. W. Ingraham. Boston, 1848. 8°. (B 1219)
Woburn, *Mass.* SEWALL, S. History of Woburn, 1640-1860; with a sketch of the author, by C. C. Sewall. Boston, 1868. large 12°.
Woburn, *Mass.* Congregational Church. CHICKERING, J. Discourse to the Cong. Soc. in Woburn, at the dedication of their meeting-house. Charlestown, 1809. 8°. (B 307)
— BENNETT, J. Permanence of the pastoral office; sermon on the 25th anniv. of the author's ordination. Boston, 1846. 8°. (B 1325)
Woburn, *Mass.* Council. 1746. Council of Six Churches upon request of Rev. E. Jackson, pastor, and the First Church. *n.t.p.* [1746.] 4°. (B 24)
Woburn Agricultural and Manufacturing Company. 1st an. report. Boston, 1836. 8°. (B 1718)
Wodehouse, John. *Earl of Kimberley.* [SKETCH.] (*In* Gladstone government, The. 1869.)
Wodrow, Robert. Correspondence; ed. by T. M'Crie. Edin., *Wod. Soc.*, 1842-43. 3 v. 8°.
Contents. Vol. 1. 1709-14. 2. 1715-22. 3. 1723-31.
Wodrow Society. Publications. Edin., 1842-55. 26 v. 8°.
Namely. Woodrow, R. Correspondence; ed. by T. M'Crie. 3 v. — Row, J. History of the Kirk of Scotland. — Melvill, J. Autobiography and diary; ed. by R. Pitcairn. — Bruce, R. Sermons, with life by R. Wodrow; ed. by W. Cunningham. — Calderwood, D. History of the Kirk of Scotland; ed. by T. Thomson. 8 v. — Rollock, R. Select works; ed. by W. M. Gunn. 2 v. — Laing, D. Miscellany of the Wodrow Soc. (Confession of faith of the churches of Switzerland; tr. from the Latin by G. Wishart. 1536. — Melville, J. Certamen cum Lutheranis, Saxoniæ habitum. Bononiæ, 1530. — Historie of the estate of Scotland, July 1558-Apr. 1560. — Kennedy, Q., *Abbot of Crosraguell.* Ane compendius tractive, *etc.* 1558. — Davidson, J. Ane answer to the Compendius tractive. Edinburgh, 1563. — Kennedy, Q. Letter to James Arbp. of Glasgow, with the correspondence of the Abbot and J. Willock, at Ayr, 1559. — Carswell, J., *and others.* Letters to J. Campbell of Kinyeancleuch, Ayrshire. — Forme and maner of buriall used in the kirk of Montrois. — Pontanus, R. Parvus catechismus, carmine iambico. Andreapoli, 1573. — Register of ministers and readers in the kirk of Scotland, from the book of the assi[illegible]iation of stipends. 1574. — Church of Scotland. *Gen. Assembly.* Supplication to the regent Earl of Morton, Apr. 1578. — Haddington. Presbytery. Subscription to the second book of discipline, Sept. 1591. — Edinburgh. Presbytery. Act appointing two ministers to the Lords at Falkirk, 12th Aug. 1578. — Carmichael, J. Letters and papers, 1584-86. — Account of the death and funeral of J. Lawson, minister of Edinburgh. 1584. — Edinburgh. Presbytery. Visitations of the kirk of Holyroodhouse. — Vindication of the Church of Scotland, in reply to Dr. Bancroft's sermon at Paul's Cross, London, Feb. 1588/9. — Ane forme of sindrie maters to be usit in the Eldership, 1589-1592. — Davidson, J. A short forme of evening and morning prayer. 1595. — Welsch, J., *minister of Ayr.* Letters to R. Boyd of Trochrig, 1607-19. — Hume, A. Ane afold admonition to the ministerie of Scotland. 1609. — Church of Scotland. *Gen. Assembly.* The forme and maner of ordaining ministers and consecrating of archbishops and bishops. 1620.) — Tweedie, W. K. Select biographies. 2 v. — Scot, W. Narration. — Forbes, J. Records. Knox, J. Works; ed. by D. Laing. 4 v. — Blair, R. Life; ed. by T. M'Crie. — Ferme, C. Logical analysis of the epistle of Paul to the Romans, tr. by W. Skae; and Commentary on the same epistle by A. Melville in Latin; ed. by W. L. Alexander.
Woechentliche Unterhaltungen für Liebhaber deutscher Lektüre in Russland; hrsg. von J. F. Recke. No. 1-52. Mitau, 1805. 2 v. 8°.

Woestyn, Eugène. Guerre d'Orient; les victoires et conquêtes des armées alliées. Paris, 1856. 2 v. 8°.

Wohlau. *Map.* SCULTETUS, J. Ducatus Silesiæ Wolanus; J. Jansson exc. [Amst., 16—.] (E 78, no. 135)

Wohlgemuth, Michael. WEALE, J. (*In his* Divers works of early masters, v. 1. 1846.)

Wola, *fort near Warsaw.* SWITKOWSKI, T. Owzięciu Woli dnia 6 Września 1831. Paryż, 1833. 8°. (E 83)

Wolcott, *Mrs.* Cornelia F., *Funeral sermon on.* 1850. *See* Robbins, C. (B 1539)

Wolcott, John, *M.D.* (*pseud.* Peter Pindar). Works. Dublin, 1795. 2 v. 8°.

Contents. Vol. 1. Epistle to the reviewers. — Lyric odes to the Royal Academicians for 1782–86. — Farewell odes for 1786. — The Lousiad. — Epistle to J. Boswell. — Bozzy and Piozzi. — Ode upon ode. — Apologetic postscript to Ode upon ode. — Instructions to a celebrated laureat. — Brother Peter to brother Tom. — Peter's prophecy. — Peter's pension. — Sir J. Banks and the Emperor of Morocco. — Epistle to a falling minister. 2. Subjects for painters. — Expostulatory odes. — Epistle to J. Nichols. — A Rowland for an Oliver. — Advice to the future laureat. — Epistle to J. Bruce. — The rights of kings. — Odes to Paine. — The remonstrance. — More money. — Odes of importance. — The tears of St. Margaret. — A pair of lyric epistles to Ld. Macartney. — Odes to Kien Long. — Epistle to the Pope. — Pathetic odes to the Duke of Richmond. — Celebration.

— *Same.* Prefixed, account of [W.'s] life. Boston, 1811. 24°.

— Expostulatory odes to a great duke and little lord. Dublin, 1789. 8°. (B 1850)

— Instructions to a celebrated laureat, alias The progress of curiosity, alias, A birthday ode, *etc.* 8th ed. N.Y., 1788. 8°. (B 743)

— The Lousiad, canto v. and last. Dublin, 1796. 8°. (B 352)

— Pindariana; or Peter's portfolio. London, 1794. 4°.

— Poetical epistle to Boswell, on his 'Tour to the Hebrides'. New ed. London, 1786. 4°. (A 47)

— Poetical serious epistle to the Pope; also, a pair of odes. Dublin, 1793. 8°. (B 352)

— Tears and smiles; a miscel. collection of poems. London, 1801. 12°.

— GIFFORD, W. Epistle to P. Pindar. *n.t.p.* [1800.] 12°. (B 613)

Wolcott, Oliver. Address to the people on the report of a comm. of the Ho. of Reps. to examine and report whether monies have been applied to the objects for which they were appropriated. Boston, 1802. 8°. (B 531, 622, 2514, W 11)

— *Same.* Hartford, *reprinted* 1802. 8°. (B 1489)

— British influence on the affairs of the U. S. proved and explained. Boston, 1804. 8°. (B 424)

— Memoirs of the administrations of Washington and J. Adams; edit. from papers of Washington by G. Gibbs. N. Y., 1846. 2 v. 8°.

Contents. Vol. 1. 1789–97. 2. 1797–1801.

— Remarks on the present state of currency, credit, commerce, and national industry. N. Y., 1820. 8°. (B 563)

— SANDERSON, J. (*In his* Biography of the signers to the declaration of independence, v. 3. 1823.)

— *Funeral sermon on.* 1797. *See* Backus, A. (B 303, W 54)

Wolcott, Roger, *Gov. of Conn.* Account of J. Winthrop's agency in obtaining a charter for Conn. (*In* Mass. Hist. Soc. Col., v. 4. 1795.)

— Journal at the siege of Louisbourg, 1745. (*In* Conn. Hist. Soc. Col., v. 1. 1860.)

— Letter to N. Hobart, [on the Cong. churches]. *n.p., n.d.* [Boston, 1761.] 4°. (B 248)

— Poetical meditations; pref. by J. Bulkley. New London, 1725. 16°.

— *Funeral sermon on.* 1767. *See* Perry, J. (B 258)

Wolcott, *Rev.* Samuel. Address at the consecration of Rock Hill Cemetery, Foxborough. Prov., 1853. 8°. (B1609)

Wolcott, *Conn.* BRONSON, H. History of W. (*In his* Hist. of Waterbury. 1858.)

Woldemar, *elector of Brandenburg.* BECMANN, B. L. Sur le mariage de l'électeur Woldemar. (*In* Berlin. Ak. d. Wiss. Abh., 1752.)

Woldemar; von F. H. Jacobi. (Vol. 5 *of his* Werke. 1820.)

Wolf, Caspar. *See* Gesner, C. De stirpium, *etc.* 1587.

Wolf, Christian Wilhelm Friedrich August. Prolegomena ad Homerum. Vol. 1. Ed. 2a. Hal. Sax., 1859. 8°.

Wolf, Ferdinand Joseph. Le Brésil littéraire; histoire de la littérature brésilienne. Berlin, 1863. 8°.

— Floresta de rimas modernas castellanas; con noticias biograficas y criticas. Paris, 1837. 2 v. 8°.

Contents. Vol. 1. Advertencia del editor. — Introduccion. — I. de Luzan. — J. de Pitillas. — N. F. de Moratin. — J. de Cadalso. — V. G. de la Huerta. — T. de Iriarte. — F. M. de Samaniego. — F. G. de Salas. — L. de Arroyal. — L. conde de Noroña. — J. M. Valdes. — G. M. de Jovellanos. — D. Gonzales. 2. J. I. de la Casa. — J. P. Forner. — N. Cienfuegos. — M. J. Quintana. — F. S. Barbero. — J. N. Gallego. — L. F. de Moratin. — M. de Arjona. — J. M. Roldan. — F. de Castro. — J. B. de Arriaza. — P. de Xérica. — A. Lista. — F. Martinez de la Rosa. — J. J. de Mora. — A. de Saavedra, duque de Rivas. — M. Breton de los Herreros.

— Ueber die Romanzen-Poesie der Spanier. Wien, 1847. 8°.

Wolf, George, *Gov.* [SKETCH.] (*In* Longacre, J. B., *and* Herring, J. Nat. portr. gal., v. 2. 1835.)

Wolf, Hieronymus. Annotationes ad Demosthenem. (*In* Schaefer, G. H. Apparatus criticus. 1824–33.)

— Vita ab ipsomet conscripta. (*In* Reiske, J. J. Orat. Gr., v. 8. 1773.)

— PASSOW, F. H. Wolfs Jugendleben, 1516–36. (*In* Historisches Taschenbuch, 1830.)

Wolf *or* Wolff, Johann Christian, *Freiherr* von. Philosophia rationalis sive logica. Ed. 3a emend. Francof., 1740. 4°.

— Briefwechsel zwischen Leibnitz und W.; hrsg. von C. I. Gerhardt. (*In* Leibnitz, G. W. Gesam. Werke, v. 7. 1860.)

— RAMBACH, F. E. (*In* Niceron, J. P. Nachrichten, v. 20. 1760.)

Wolf, Johann Christoph. Bibliotheca Hebræa; acc. J. Gaffarelli Index codicum cabbalisticorum mss. quibus J. Picus Mirandulanus usus est. Hamburgæ, Lipsiæ, 1715–27. 3 v. 4°.

— Curæ philologicæ et criticæ [in Novum Testamentum]. Basileæ, 1741. 3 v. 4°.

Wolfborough, *N.H.* LOWELL, C. Note on W. (*In* Mass. Hist. Soc. Col., v. 13. 1815.)

Wolfe, *Rev.* Charles. Remains of W. [1st Amer. ed.] Hartford, 1828. 12°.

Contents. Memoir, by J. A. Russell. — Jugurtha incarceratus. — Battle of Busaco. — Burial of Sir J. Moore. — Spanish song. — The grave of Dermid. — Songs. — The frailty of beauty. — The college course. — Patriotism. — Fragments of a speech. — Farewell to Lough Bray. — Song. — The Dargle. — Birthday poem. — Song. — To a friend. — Speech, May, 1821. — Sermons. — Appendix: Obs. on religious poetry. — Jesus raising Lazarus. — Death of Abel. — Græcia capta ferum victorem cepit. — Principiis obsta. — Ira furor brevis est. — Miscel. thoughts.

— *Same.* 9th ed. London, 1847. 12°.

Wolfe, *Maj.-Gen.* James. GLEIG, G. R. (*In his* Lives, v. 2. 1831. Lardner. Cab. cyc., v. 18.)

— JONES, J. A. Haverhill; [fictitious] memoirs of an officer in the army of W. London, 1831. 3 v. 12°.

— SABINE, L. Address before the New England Historical Genealogical Society, Sept. 13, 1859, the 100th anniv. of the death of W. Boston, 1859. 8°.

— — *Another copy.* (B 1962)

— WRIGHT, R. Life of W. London, 1864. 8°.

Wolfe, John Reissberg. Improved method of extraction of cataract. London, 1868. 8°.

Wolfe, Udolpho. Proofs of the purity and medical properties of [his] aromatic schnapps. N. Y., 1853. 8°. (C 271)

Wolfenbuettel. Annales Guelferbytani, 740–826. (*In* Pertz, G. H. Mon. Germ., Scr., v. 1. 1826.)

Wolfenbuettelsche Fragmente; [von H. S. Reimarus]. (*In* Lessing, G. E. Sammtl. Schriften, v. 5, 6, 13. 1818, 1793.)

Wolfert's Roost, and other papers; by W. Irving. N. Y., 1855. 12°.
— *Same.* (Vol. 16 *of his* Works. 1860.)
Wolff. *See also* Wolf.
Wolff, August. Den nordamerikanske Borgerkrig. Kjöbenhavn, 1867. 8°.
Wolff, Elizabeth (Bekker), *and* Deken, A. Historie van mejuffrouw Sara Burgerhart. 2e druk. 's Gravenhage, 1783. 2 v. 8°.
Wolff, Jens. Sketches and obs. taken on a tour through a part of the South of Europe. London, 1801. 4°.
Wolff, *Rev.* Joseph, *D.D.* Narrative of a mission to Bokhara, 1843-45, to ascertain the fate of Col. Stoddart and Capt. Conolly. N. Y., 1845. 8°.
— Researches and missionary labours among the Jews, Mohammedans, and other sects, 1831-34. 1st American ed. Phila., 1837. 12°.
— Travels and adventures. 2d ed. London, 1860-61. 2 v. 8°.
Wolff, Pius Alexander. Precjoza, drama liryczne, przeł. przez J. D. Minasowicza. Warszawa, 1835. 16°. (Teatra Warszawskie, pt. 2, v. 5.)
Wolffhart, Konrad. *See* **Lycosthenes,** K.
Wolfhelmus *Brunwilarensis.* CONRADUS *Brunwilarensis.* Vita. (*In* **Pertz,** G. H. Mon., Scr., v. 14. 1854.)
Wolfherius. Vita Godehardi episcopi Hildeneshelmensis. (*In* **Pertz.** Mon. Germ., Scr., v. 11. 1854.)
Wolfius, Christianus. *See* **Wolf,** J. C. von.
Wolfram *von Eschenbach.* Parzival und Titurel; hrsg. von K. Bartsch. Lpz., 1871-72. 3 v. 8°.
— LACHMANN, K. K. F. W. Ueber den Eingang des Parzivals. (*In* **Berlin. Ak. d. Wiss.** Abh., 1835.)
Wolfram, Ludwig Friedrich. Vollständiges Lehrbuch der gesammten Baukunst. Stuttgart, Wien, 1833-45. 3 v. in 11 pts. 4°.
Wollaston, *Rev.* Francis. Address to the clergy of the Church of England, *etc.*, in the matter of subscription. London, 1772. 8°. **(B 905, 1371)**
— Fasciculus astronomicus; obs. of north circumpolar regions. London, 1800. 4°.
— CURSORY observations on 'An address to the clergy'; by a layman. London, 1773. 8°. **(B 1371)**
Wollaston, Wm. Religion of nature delineated. 6th ed. London, 1738. 4°.
— NICERON, J. P. (*In his* Mém., v. 42. 1741.)
Wollaston, Wm. Hyde, *M.D.* MALDEN, H. (*In his* Disting. men, v. 4. 1838; v. 40 of Lib. ent. knl.)
Wolle, Christoph. Collectio quatuor de verbis Græcorum mediis dissertationum L. Kusteri, J. Clerici, E. Schmidii, denique quartam exemplis cum sacris tum profanis illuminatam ipse adiecit. Lips., 1733. 8°.
— Dissertatio crit. de eo quod pulchrum est in vers. Castellionis. (*In* **Bible.** *Whole. Latin.* Biblia ex Castellionis interp. 1734, p. 270 of this Catalogue)
— Examen regularum hermeneuticarum ab A. Calmeto commendatarum; acc. De genuina locutionum sacrarum comparativarum ac superlativarum explanatione. Lips., 1733. 8°.
Wolleben, Johannes. Compendium theologiæ Christianæ. Ed. 2a. Amst., 1637. 24°.
— *Same.* Ed. nov. Amst., 1642. 24°.
— *Same.* *t.p.w.* [17—.] 12°.
Wollrath, Johan Gustaf. Horticultura academica. (*In* **Linné,** C. Amœn. acad., v. 4. 1759.)
Wollstonecraft, Mary. *See* **Godwin,** *Mrs.* Mary (W.), p. 1167.
Wolowski, Franciszek. Coup d'œil sur la législation polonaise. [Paris, 1838.] 8°. **(E 83)**
— Podróż do Szwajcaryi i Włoch, 1825. Paryż, 1845. 8°.
— Zycie. Paryż, 1844. 8°. **(E 84)**
Wolowski, Louis François Michel Raymond, *son of the preceding.* La Banque d'Angleterre et les banques d'Ecosse. Paris, 1867. 8°.
— Echange et monnaie. (*In* **Thévenin, E.** Association polytechnique, 3e sér. 1866.)
— Etudes d'économie politique et de statistique. Paris, 1848. 8°.
— Rapport sur le concours rel. à l'administration de Colbert. (*In* **Paris. Inst.** *Ac. d. Sci. Mor.* Mém., v. 10. 1860.) — Rapport sur le concours rel. à l'histoire de la Ligue Hanséatique. (*In* v. 12. 1865.)
— Several articles.] (*In* **Revue** d. D. Mondes, août 1857 - sept. 1868.)
Wolseley, *Sir* Charles. Liberty of conscience asserted and vindicated; [with] 2d part, Liberty of conscience the magistrates interest. 2d ed., corr. London, 1668. 4°. **(B 1)**
Wolseley, Richard, *chairman.* Collection of documents expressive of public opinion on the utility and importance of the ordnance memoir of Ireland. Dublin, 1844. 8°.
Wolsey, Thomas, *Cardinal.* CAVENDISH, G. Life of W.; with notes by S. W. Singer. Chiswick, 1825. 2 v. 8°.
— - Life of W. (*In* **Wordsworth,** C. Eccles. biog., v. 1. 1839.)
— CAMPBELL, J. (*In his* Lives of the Lord Chancellors, v. 1. 1845.)
— FIDDES, R. Life of W. London, 1724. f°.
— - *Same.* 2d ed. London, 1726. f°.
— FORSTER, J., *and* COURTENAY, J. P. (*In their* Lives of eminent Brit. statesmen, v. 1. 1831.)
— GALT, J. Life of W. 3d ed. Edin., 1824. 12°.
— GROVE, J. History of the life and times of W. 2d ed. Vol. 1. London, 1748. 8°.
— PAULI, R. Cardinal Wolsey und das Parlament von 1523. (*In* **Historisches** Zeitschrift, v. 21. 1869.)
— REUMONT, A. Il cardinale Wolsey e la Santa Sede. (*In* **Archivio** stor. ital., app., v. 9. 1853.)
— THOMSON, *Mrs.* K. B. Life of W. (*In* **Soc. Dif. Usef. Knl.** Lib. usef. knl. Lives of eminent persons. 1833.)
— WILLIAMS, F. (*In his* Lives of Cardinals, v. 2. 1868.)
Wolstan. Navig. into the East Sea or Sound of Denmarke. (*In* **Hakluyt,** R. Col. of voy., v. 1. 1809.)
Wolstenholme, Elizabeth C. The education of girls, its present and its future. (*In* **Butler,** J. E. Woman's work. 1869.)
— What better provision ought to be made for education of girls of the upper and middle classes? (*In* **Nat. Assoc. Prom. Soc. Sci.** Trans., 1865.)
Woltmann, Alfred. Holbein und seine Zeit. Lpz., 1866-68. 2 v. 8°.
— *Eng.* Holbein and his time; tr. by F. E. Bunnètt. London, 1872 [1871]. 4°.
Woltmann, Carl Ludwig von. HEEREN, A. H. L. (*In his* Historische Werke, v. 6. 1823.)
Woltmann, Reinhard. Theory and description of a ventilator for airing vessels, with remarks on airing vessels, *etc.*, suspected of infection; [in English and German]. Hamb., 1805. 8°.
Wolverhampton. PRESBYTERIANS and Independents; observations on the results of the legal principles in the Lady Hewley and Wolverhampton cases. London, [18—]. 8°. **(B 1395)**
— LEE, T. E. Remarks on an app. to an 'Appeal to the public', in the case of the old church, Wolverhampton. *n.t.p.* [1819.] 8°. **(B 1395)**
Wolzogen, Alfred, *Freiherr* von. Raphael Santi, his life and his works; tr. by F. E. Bunnètt. London, 1866. 8°.
— Schiller's Beziehungen zu Eltern, Geschwistern, und der Familie von Wolzogen; aus den Familien-Papieren mitgetheilt. Stuttgart, 1859. 8°.
— Wilhelmine Schröder-Devrient; ein Beitrag zur Geschichte des musikalischen Dramas. Lpz., 1863. 8°.
Wolzogen, Jan Ludvik. Opera. Irenopolis, 1656. f°

Contents. Commentarius in Matth., Mar., Luc., Joh., Acta, Epist. Jacobi, Judæ. — Præparatio ad utilem SS. Litterarum lectionem, in qua de natura religionis Christianæ agitur. — Tres conciones in Joh. xvii. 3. — Compendium religionis Christianæ. — Declaratio duarum contrariarum sententiarum de uno Deo Patre et de uno Deo in essentia et tribus personis. — Annotationes ad J. Slichtingii quæstiones de magistratu, bello, et defensione. — Annotationes in Meditationes metaphysicas R. Discartis. — Responsio ad J. Slichtingii Annotationes in Annotationes de magistratu.

Wolzogen, Ludvik, *son of the preceding*. BROWN, J. Libri duo [contra] Wolzogium. Amst., 1670. 12°.

Woman. *General works.*

— THOMAS, A. L. Essai sur le caractère, les mœurs, et l'esprit des femmes dans les différens siécles. [1772.] (*In his* Œuvres complètes, v. 4. 1802.)

— ALEXANDER, W. History of women from the earliest antiquity. London, 1779. 2 v. 4°.

— BYERLEY, T., *and* ROBERTSON, J. C. (*In their* Percy anecdotes, v. 20. 1822.)

— JAMESON, *Mrs.* A. M. Characteristics of women. [1832.] 3d ed. enl. London, 1836. 2 v. 8°.

— DISCUSSION on the character, education, prerogatives and moral influence of woman. Boston, 1837. 16°.

— WALKER, A. Woman physiologically considered as to mind, morals, marriage, *etc.* N.Y., 1840. 12°.

— LEGOUVÉ, J. W. E. G. Histoire morale des femmes. [1848.] 4e éd. Paris, 1864. 12°.

— NICHOLS, T. L. Women in all ages and nations. N. Y., 1849. 12°.

— CRAIK, *Mrs.* D. M. M. A woman's thoughts about women. London, 1858. 16°.

— MICHELET, J. La femme. 3e éd. Par., 1860. 12°.

— GONCOURT, E. L. A. H. de *and* J. A. H. de. La femme au 18e siècle. Paris, 1862. 8°.

— KOLTZOF-MASSALSKY, H. G., *princesse*. Des femmes, par une femme. Paris, 1865. 2 v. 8°.

— DALL, *Mrs.* C. H. The college, the market, and the court; or, Woman's relation to education, labor, and law. Boston, 1867. 8°.

— BUTLER, J. E. Woman's work and woman's culture; a series of essays. London, 1869. 8°.

Biography.

— TIXIER DE RAVISI, J. De memorabilibus et claris mulieribus diversorum scriptorum opera. Parisiis, S. *Colenæus*, 1521. f°.

— SCUDERY, M. de. Female orators; or, The courage and constancy of divers queens, *etc.* [1665]; tr. London, 1714. 16°.

— MENAGE, G. Historia mulierum philosopharum. Lugd., 1690. 12°.

— BETHAM, M. Biographical dictionary of celebrated women. London, 1804. 8°.

— HAYS, M. Female biography; memoirs of celebrated women. 1st Amer. ed. Phila., 1807. 3 v. 8°.

— JAMESON, *Mrs.* A. M. Memoirs of the loves of the poets. [1829.] Boston, 1833. 2 v. 12°.

— - Memoirs of the beauties of the court of Charles the Second. [1833.] London, 1838. 2 v. 8°.

— SAINTE-BEUVE, C. A. Portraits of celebrated women [1844]; tr. by H. W. Preston. Boston, 1868. 16°.

— HALE, S. J. Woman's record; or, Sketches of distinguished women, with selections. N. Y., 1853. 8°.

— SKETCHES of women of the time. (*In* Men of the time. 1856, 1862, 1865, 1868.)

— REMARKABLE women of different nations and ages. 1st ser. Boston, 1858. 12°. (Lib. of biog.)

— ELLET, *Mrs.* E. F. Women artists in all ages and countries. London, 1859. 8°.

— ALGER, W. R. The friendships of women. [6th ed.] Boston, 1870. 8°.

See also Queens; — Singers; — Wives; — *also* English poetry. *Bibliography*; — France. *Biography*; — France. *Literature* (*History*); — France. *Revolution* (JACOB) p. 1045; — Germany. *Literature* (*Hist.* ROBINSON) p. 1139; — Great Britain. *Biography*; — Italy. *Biography*; — United States. *Female biography* (p. 3110); — United States. *Literature* (*Coll.*) p. 3132; — *also* Chaucer, G. A legende of goode women.

The chief separate biographies of women in the Library are those of Adams, H.; — Albany, L. M. C., *ctsse. d'*; — Alexandra Feodorovna, *Empress of Russia*; — Agrippina; — Anne, *Queen of Eng.*; — Anne *of Austria, Queen of France*; — Anthony, S.; — Arblay, F. B., *Mme.* d'; — Bearn, P., *comtesse* de; — Beauclerk, H. M., *duchess of St. Albans*; — Bethune, *Mrs.* J.; — Bonny, A.; — Borgia, L., *duchessa di Ferrara*; — Broglie, A. I. G. de Staël-Holstein, *duchess* de; — Byron, A. I.; — Cameron, J., *pseud.*; — Canning, E.; — Caroline Amelia Elizabeth, *Queen of George* IV.; — Caroline, *wife of Christian* VII. *of Denmark*; — Caterina Fieschi Adorno, *St., called* St. Catharine of Genoa; — Catharine II., *Empress of Russia*; — Catharine de' Medici; — Cenci, B.; — Charlotte Augusta, *Princess of Wales*; — Chevreuse, M. de R., *duchesse* de; — Chimay, T. C., *princesse* de; — Christina, *Queen of Sweden*; — Churchill, S., *Duchess of Marlborough*; — Clapp, M. E.; — Clarke, *Mrs.* M. A.; — Clayton, C., *Viscountess Sundon*; — Cleopatra, *Queen of Egypt*; — Colonna, V., *marchesa di Pescara*; — Colquhoun, *Lady* J.; — Cooper, M.; — Corday d'Armont, M. A. C. de; — Créqui, R. C. de F., *marquise* de; — Cuvier, S. L. C.; — Darc, J.; — Dashkof, E. R. W.; — Davidson, *Mrs.* M. M.; — Delany, *Mrs.* M. G. P.; — Dimmick, *Mrs.* C. M.; — Dorothea, *St.*; — Du Barry, M. J. G. de V., *comtesse*; — Du Cayla, L. V., *comtesse*; — Dyson, J. A. P.; — Elizabeth, *Queen of Bohemia*; — Elizabeth, *Q. of Eng.*; — Elizabeth *de Valois, Q. of Spain*; — Elizabeth *of York, Q. of Henry* VII. *of Eng.*; — Elizabeth, *sister of Louis* XVI.; — Epinay, *Mme.* L. F. P.; — Estrées, G. d'; — Falletti, *marchesa* G.; — Felt, *Mrs.* A. A.; — Fitzherbert, *Mrs.* M. A.; — Frederica Sophia Wilhelmina, *Markgräfin von Baireuth*; — Fry, E.; — Gannett, *Mrs.* D. S.; — Gardiner, M., *Countess of Blessington*; — Genlis, S. F. D. de St. A., *comtesse* de; — Godolphin, *Mrs.*; — Godwin, *Mrs.*; — Grubb, S.; — Guyon, J. M. B. de la M.; — Hamilton, *Lady* E.; — Hamlin, *Mrs.* H. A. L.; — Hastings, S. S., *Countess of Huntington*; — Haven, *Mrs.* A.; — Hortense, *Queen of Holland*; — Huntington, *Mrs.* S.; — Inchbald, *Mrs.* E.; — Joanna I., *Q. of Naples*; — Jordan, *Mrs.* D. B.; — Josephine, *Emp. of the French*; — Judson, *Mrs.* A. H.; — Judson, *Mrs.* E. C.; — Junot, L. P., *duchesse d'Abrantès*; — Koltzof-Massalsky, H. G., *Princess* (*pseud.* Dora *d'Istria*); — Lafarge, *Mme.* M.; — Lafayette, *Mme.* M. A. F. N. de; — Lamballe, M. T. L. de S. C., *princesse* de; — La Vallière, F. L. de la B. le B., *duchesse* de; — L'Enclos, A., *called* Ninon de; — Longueville, A. G. de B.-C., *duchesse* de; — Louisa, *wife of Charles Edward the Pretender*; — Louise Juliane, *Electress Palatine*; — Lyon, M.; — Mackenzie, A., *Countess of Balcarras*; — Maclean, *Mrs.* L. E.; — Maintenon, F. d'A., *marquise* de; — Malibran, M. F. G.; — Margaret, *Q. of Navarre*; — Maria Theresa; — Marie Antoinette de Lorraine, A. J. J.; — Marie de l'Incarnation; — Marie de Medicis; — Mary I., *Q. of Eng.*; — Mary, *Q. of Scots*; — Mary, *Duchess of Burgundy*; — Matilda, *gran contessa di Toscana*; — Mawson, J.; — Meszlenyi, *Mme.* S. K.; — Mitford, M. R.; — Montagu, A. P. D. de N., *marquise* de; — Montespan, F. A. de R. de N., *marquise* de; — Montpensier, A. M. L. d'O., *duchesse* de; — More, *Mrs.* H.; — Nesle, *Mlles.* de; — Nicholls, *Mrs.* C. B.; — Orléans, H. L. E., *princesse de Mecklenbourg-Schwérin*; — Ossoli, S. M. F., *marchesa* d'; — Peters, *Mrs.* P. W.; — Parabère, M. M. de la V., *comtesse* de; — Plater, E., *Gräfin*; — Polignac, Y. M. G. de P., *duchesse* de; — Pompadour, J. A. P., *marquise* de; — Pulszky, T.; — Quincy, E. S. M.; — Rachel, E.; — Ramsay, *Mrs.* M. L.; — Read, M.; — Recamier, *Mme.* J. A.; — Renée, *of France, Duchess of Ferrara*; — Ritchie, *Mrs.* A. C. O. M.; — Rochechouart de Montemart, M. M. G. de; — Robinson, *Mrs.* M. D.; — Rochefort, T., *comtesse* de; — Roland de la Platière, *Mme.* M. J. P.; — Rumpff, E.; — Russell, R. W. V., *Lady*; — Sablé, M. de L., *marquise* de; — Savage, *Mrs.* S.; — Schimmelpenninck, M. A.; — Schomberg, *Mme.* M. de H., *duchesse* de; — Schuyler, *Mrs.* C.; — Sedgwick, C. M.; — Seton, *Mrs.* E. A.; — Sevigné, M. de R. C., *marquise* de; — Sheridan, *Mrs.*

F.; — Siddons, *Mrs.* S.; — Sieveking, A. W.; — Sigourney, *Mrs.* L. H.; — Smith, *Mrs.* S. L.; — Sorel, A.; — Staal, M. J. C. de L., *baronne* de; — Stael Holstein, A. L. G. N., la *baronne* de; — Stanhope, *Lady* H.; — Stanly, C.; — Stuart, *Lady* A.; — Suffolk, *Countess of*; — Swetchine, *Mme.* A. S. S.; — Walburga, *Abbess of Heidenheim*; — Ward, *Mrs.* H. L.; — Ware, *Mrs.* M. L.; — Warens, L. E. de la T. du P., *baronne* de; — Waters, A.; — Wiboroda, *St.*; — Winslow, *Mrs.* H. W.; — Wordsworth, M.; — Xanthippe; — Zenobia, *Queen of Palmyra*.

Character and duties, etc.

— La Tour-Landry, G. de. The book of the knight of La Tour Landry [1372]; tr. from the French and ed. by T. Wright. London, 1868. 8°. (Early Eng. Text Soc.)
— Passi, G. I donneschi diffetti. [1598.] 2a impres. Venetia, 1601. 8°.
— Ladies calling, The; in two parts. (*In* Whole duty of man, Works of the author. 1687. 1695.)
— *Same.* New ed. London, 1787. 8°.
— Excellent woman, The, described. London, 1692. 8°.
— Roussel, P. Système physique et morale de la femme. [1775.] 7e éd. Paris, 1820. 8°.
— Women invited to war; or, A friendly add. to the honourable women of the U. S. Bost., 1787. 8°. (B 1360)
— Schlegel, K. W. F. von. Ueber die Darstellung der weiblichen Charaktere in den griechischen Dichtern. 1794. (*In his* Sämmtl. Werke, v. 4. 1846.)
— Card, H. Condition and character. [1810.] *See Social condition* (p. 3353).
— Jamieson, J. The beneficent woman; sermon, Leith, Mar. 10. Edin., 1811. 8°. (B 319)
— Aspland, R. Beneficial influence of Christianity on the character and condition of the female sex; sermon. London, 1812. 8°. (B 1098)
— Wilbur, H. Female piety demanding assistance; two sermons, Bradford, Jan. 5. Haverhill, 1812. 8°. (B 1305)
— Crocker, H. M. Observations on the real rights of women; with their appropriate duties, *etc.* Boston, 1818. 12°.
— — *Another copy.* (B 1023)
— Clark, D. A. The wise builder; sermon, Amherst, May 3. Boston, 1820. 8°. (B 287)
— Cary, *Mrs.* V. Letters on female character. 3d ed. Hartford, 1831. 12°.
— Richardson, J. Sermon, dignity and duty of woman, Apr. 22, 1832. Hingham, 1833. 8°. (B 1300)
— Sandford, *Mrs.* J. Woman in her social and domestic character. [1832.] 5th ed. London, 1837. 16°.
— — *Same.* (*In* Winslow, H. Woman as she should be. 1838.)
— Hofmanowa, K. z T. Pamiątka po dobréy matce. (*In her* Wybor pism, v. 1. 1833.)
— Sketches and anecdotes of female character. Boston, 1833. 12°.
— Philanthropos, *pseud. for* W. Ladd. Duty of females to promote the cause of peace. Boston, 1836. 8°. (B 1169)
— Ellis, *Mrs.* S. S. The women of England, their social duties and domestic habits. [1838.] N. Y., 1839. 12°.
— Winslow, H. Woman as she should be, *etc.* Boston, 1838. 18°.
— Woman's rights and duties with relation to their influence on society and her own condition; by a woman. Lond., 1840. 2 v. 12°.
— Hay, P. C. Female excellence; discourse, Geneva, Sept. 5. Geneva, N. Y., 1841. 8°. (B 1293)
— Ellis, *Mrs.* S. S. The daughters of England, their position in society, character, and responsibilities. London, [1842]. 8°.
— — The mothers of England; their influence and responsibility. [1843.] N. Y., 1844. 8°.
— — The wives of England, their relative duties, domestic influence, and social obligations. Author's ed. N. Y., 1843. 8°.
— Mann, H. A few thoughts on the powers and duties of woman. Syracuse, 1853. 16°.
— Hardinge, E. The place and mission of woman. Boston, 1859. 8°. (B 1200)
— Ruskin, J. Of queen's gardens; [on woman's education]. (*In his* Sesame and lilies. 1865.)
— Linton, *Mrs.* E. L. Ourselves; a series of essays on women. [1867.] 2d ed. London, N. Y., 1870. 16°.
— Beecher, *Miss* C. E. Woman's profession as mother and educator. Philadelphia, 1872 [1871]. 12°.

See also Girls; — Marriage; — Mother; — Young woman; — *also General works* (p. 3351).

Crime.

— Benoiston de Chateauneuf, J. Sur la condition des femmes et des jeunes filles détenues et libérées. (*In* Paris. Inst. *Ac. d. Sci. Mor.* Mém., v. 6. 1850.)
— Stallard, J. H. The female casual and her lodging. London, 1866. 8°.
— Ford, C. R. Efforts on behalf of criminal women. (*In* Nat. Assoc. Prom. Soc. Sci. Trans., 1868.)
— Woods, C. H. Woman in prison. N. Y., 1869. 12°.

See also Infanticide; — Prostitution; — *also General works* (p. 3351).

Education.

See Female education (p. 971).

Labor, Professions.

— Case of the seamstresses. Phila., 1830. 8°. (B 1115)
— Tuckerman, J. Essay on the wages paid to females for their labour. Phila., 1830. 12°. (C 511)
— Cooke, P. Female preaching unlawful and inexpedient; sermon. Lynn, 1837. 8°. (C 206)
— Appeal to the Medical Society of Rhode Island in behalf of woman as midwife. *n.p.*, 1850. 12°. (C 267)
— Gregory, S. Letter to ladies in favor of female physicians. Boston, 1850. 8°. (B 1553)
— Lee, L. Woman's right to preach the Gospel; sermon. Syracuse, N. Y., 1853. 8°. (B 1667)
— Jameson, *Mrs.* A. M. Communion of labour; social employments of women. London, 1856. 12°.
— Milne, J. D. Industrial employment of women in the middle and lower ranks. [1857.] Revised ed. London, 1870. 8°.
— Brown, W. S. Capability of women to practice the healing art; a lecture. Boston, 1859. 8°. (B 1549)
— Dall, *Mrs.* C. W. H. Woman's right to labor; or, Low wages and hard work; three lectures, 1859. Boston, 1860. 16°.
— Simon, J. F. S. S. Le salaire et le travail des femmes. (*In* Revue d. D. Mondes, fév., août, nov. 1860, mars 1861.)
— Lagrange, L. Du rang des femmes dans les arts. (*In* Gazette des beaux-arts, v. 8. 1860.)
— Penny, V. Employments of women. Boston, 1863. 12°.
— Baker, R. S. Social results of the employment of girls and women in manufactories and work-shops. (*In* Nat. Assoc. Prom. Soc. Sci. Trans., 1868.)

See also General works (p. 3351).

Law.

— Gide, P. Etude sur la condition privée de la femme dans le droit ancien et moderne. Paris, 1867. 8°.
— Schellhaffer, H. G. De origine juris circa mulieres diversi. Lps., [1738]. 4°.
— Mignet, F. A. A. Du droit de succession des femmes au Moyen Age. (*In* Paris. Inst. *Ac. d. Sci. Mor.* Mém., v. 4. 1844.)
— Woman's rights tracts. Nos. 1-10. *n.p.*, [1845-52]. 8°. (B 1667)
— May, S. J. Rights and condition of women. Syracuse, [1846]. 8°. (B 1297)
— — *Same.* 3d ed. *n.t.p.* [Syracuse, 1846.] 8°. (B 1667)
— Mill, J. S. Enfranchisement of women. [1851.] (*In his* Dissertations, v. 2. 1859.)

— HIGGINSON, T. W. Woman and her wishes; essay. Boston, 1853. 8°. (B 1667)

— NORTON, *Mrs.* C. E. S. S. English laws for women in the 19th cent. London, 1854. 8°.

— STANTON, *Mrs.* E. C. Address adopted by the State Woman's Rights Convention, Albany, Feb. 14, 15. Albany, 1854. 8°. (B 1667)

— DALL, *Mrs.* C. W. H. Woman's rights under the law. Boston, 1861. 16°.

— ASSOLANT, A. Le droit des femmes. 2e éd. Paris, 1868. 12°.

— COOKSON, W. S., *and others.* Is it desirable to amend the present law which gives the personal property and earnings of the wife to her husband, *etc.* (*In* **Nat. Assoc. Prom. Soc. Sci.** Trans., 1868.)

— MILL, J. S. Subjection of women. 2d ed. London, 1869. 8°.

— AMOS, S. Difference of sex as a topic of jurisprudence and legislation. London, 1870. 8°.

— REPLY to J. S. Mill on the subjection of women. Phila., 1870. 8°.

— BAUDRILLART, H. J. L. L'agitation pour l'émancipation des femmes en Angleterre et aux Etats-Unis. (*In* **Revue** d. D. Mondes, oct. 1872.)

See also **India.** *Law*; — **Salic laws**; — **Woman's suffrage**; — *also General works* (p. 3351).

Medicine.

— ALBERTUS *Magnus.* De secretis mulierum; de virtutibus herbarum, *etc.* Lugd., 1596. 32°.

— CHURCHILL, F. Essays on the puerperal fever and other diseases peculiar to women. [1602–1846.] London, 1849. 8°. (Sydenham Soc.)

— ROONHUYSE, H. van. Heel-konstige aanmerkkingen betreffende de gebreekken der vrouwen. Amst., 1663. 12°.

— ASTRUC, J. Treatise on the diseases of women. [1760.] Vol. 1. London, 1762. 8°.

— ROUSSEL, P. *See Character.* 1775.

— DOEVEREN, G. van. De cognoscendis mulierum morbis. Ed. alt. Lugd. Bat., 1777. 8°.

— HAMILTON, A. Management of female complaints and of children. N. Y., 1792. 12°.

— GARDIEN, C. M. Traité d'accouchemens, des maladies des femmes, *etc.* Paris, 1807. 4 v. 8°.

— CLARKE, C. M. Diseases of females attended by discharges. London, 1814–21. 2 v. 8°.

— CAPPE, C. Thoughts on the desirableness of ladies visiting the female wards of hospitals and lunatic asylums. (*In* **Pamphleteer**, 1816; v. 8 of B 838)

— HALL, M. Cases of a serious morbid affection, chiefly occurring after delivery, miscarriage, *etc.* London, 1820. 8°. (B 827)

— DEWEES, W. P. Diseases of females. Phila., 1826. 8°.

— - *Same.* 3d ed., corrected. Phila., 1831. 8°.

— GOOCH, R. Account of some of the most important diseases peculiar to women. [1829.] 2d ed. London, 1831. 8°.

— - *Same.* Pref. essay by R. Ferguson. London, 1859. 8°. (New Sydenham Soc.)

— ADDISON, T. Disorders of females connected with uterine irritation. London, 1830. 8°.

— - *Same.* (*In his* Col. of published writings. 1868.)

— LEE, R. Researches on the pathology and treatment of some of the diseases of women. London, 1833. 8°.

— HALE, E. Sore mouth of nursing women. — JACKSON, J. Paruria retentionis peculiar to women. (*In* **Mass. Med. Soc.** Med. comm., v. 5. 1836.)

— CHURCHILL, F. Outlines of diseases of females. Phila., 1839. 8°.

— ASHWELL, S. Diseases peculiar to women. London, 1844 [1840–44]. 8°.

— - *Same.* [Pt. 1.] Boston, 1843. 8°. (Libr. of pract. med., v. 13.)

— BLUNDELL, J. Diseases of women; ed. by T. Castle. Phila., 1840. 8°. (Dunglison's Amer. med. lib.)

— TILT, E. J. Diseases of women. [1850.] 2d ed. London, 1853. 8°.

— CHAPMAN, J. Functional diseases of women. London, 1863. 8°.

— HEWITT, G. Diagnosis and treatment of diseases of women. London, 1863. 8°.

— MCCLINTOCK, A. H. Clinical memoirs on diseases of women. Dublin, 1863. 8°.

— HUTCHINSON, J. Surgical diseases of women. (*In* **Holmes, T.** Syst. of surg., v. 4. 1864.)

— BARNES, R. Report on midwifery and diseases of women and children. (*In* **New Sydenham Soc.** Bien. retrospect, 1865–70.)

— BERNUTZ, G., *and* GOUPIL, E. Clinical memoirs on diseases of women; tr. and ed. by A. Meadows. London, 1866–67. 2 v. 8°. (New Sydenham Soc.)

— LEWIS, D. Our girls. N. Y., 1871. 12°.

— STORER, H. R. The causation, course, and treatment of reflex insanity in women. Boston, N. Y., 1871. 8°.

See also **Chlorosis**; — **Fecundity**; — **Midwifery**; — **Ovaries**; — **Pregnancy**; — **Puerperal fever**; — **Uterus**; — **Vagina.**

Social condition and political rights.

— KNOX, J. First blast of the trumpet against the monstrous regiment of women. 1558. (*In his* Works, v. 4. 1855.)

— GODWIN, *Mrs.* M. W. Wrongs of woman. (*In her* Posthumous works, v. 1, 2. 1798.)

— SÉGUR, A. J. P. de. Les femmes, leur condition, et leur influence dans l'ordre social. Paris, 1803. 3 v. 12°.

— CARD, H. Condition and character of women. [1810.] (*In his* Literary recreations. 1811.)

— CHILD, *Mrs.* L. M. Brief history of the condition of women in various ages and nations. [1832.] 5th ed. N. Y., 1845. 2 v. 12°.

— YOUNG, S. Influence of women on the social states. Albany, 1837. 8°. (B 1588)

— MORGAN, *Lady* S. Woman and her master. London, 1840. 2 v. 8°.

— GRAVES, *Mrs.* A. J. Woman in America. N. Y., [1842]. 16°. (Harper's fam. lib., v. 166.)

— OZANAM, A. F. De l'ascendant des femmes dans la société chrétienne. (*In his* Dante. 1845.)

— PARKER, T. Sermon, public function of woman. Boston, 1853. 8°. (B 1667)

— - *Same.* (*In his* Speeches, v. 2. 1855.)

— OSSOLI, S. M. F., *marchesa* d'. Woman in the nineteenth century. 3d thous. Boston, 1855. 12°.

— M'ELHERAN, J. Condition of women and children among Celtic and other nations. Boston, 1858. 12°.

— DODGE, *Miss* M. A. A new atmosphere. Boston, 1865. 16°.

— MODERN women; a reprint of articles in the Saturday review; with introd. by Mrs. L. G. Calhoun. [1866–68.] N. Y., 1868. 12°.

— DODGE, *Miss* M. A. Woman's wrongs; a counterirritant. Boston, 1868. 16°.

— FULTON, J. D. The true woman; added, Woman *vs.* ballot. Boston, 1869. 16°.

— LECKY, W. E. H. Position of women. (*In his* European morals, v. 2. 1869.)

— CLAFLIN, T. C. Constitutional equality a right of woman, with her duties to herself. N. Y., 1871. 8°.

— DODGE, *Miss* M. A. Woman's worth and worthlessness. N. Y., 1872 [1871]. 12°.

— LYTTON, E. G. E. L. B., *Baron Lytton.* The coming race. Edin., London, 1871. 8°.

— - *Same.* N. Y., 1871. 12°.

See also **Rome** (Anc.): *Social antiq.* (SANTINELLI) p. 2545; — *also General works* (p. 3351).

Miscellaneous.

— EVELYN, J. Mundus muliebris; or, The ladies dressing room unlocked, and her toilette spread, in burlesque. **1690.** (*In his* Miscel. writings. 1825.)

— HUMBOLDT, K. W. Ueber die männliche und weibliche Form. [1795.] (*In his* Gesam. Werke, v. 1. 1841.)

— GENLIS, S. F. D. de St. A., *comtesse* de. De l'influence des femmes sur la littérature française. [1811.] (Vol. 71-72 *of her* Œuvres. 1826.)

— AFTERNOON of unmarried life, The. From the London ed. N. Y., **1859.** 12°.

— DUDEVANT, *Mme.* A. L. A. D. Pourquoi les femmes à l'Académie. Paris, **1863.** 8°.

— LUDLOW, J. M. Woman's work in the Church; historical notes on deaconesses and sisterhoods. London, **1865.** 16°.

— COURTHOPE, W. J. Ludibria lunæ; or, The wars of the women and the gods; an allegorical burlesque. London, **1869.** 8°.

— GREG, W. R. Why are women redundant? (*In his* Literary and social judgments. 1869.)

— REED, J. Man and woman, equal but unlike. Boston, 1870. 12°.

See also **Amazons**; — **Marriage**; — **Mother**; — **Old maids**; — **Young women**; — *also the next entry.*

Woman and her Saviour in Persia; by a returned missionary [Rev. T. Laurie]. Bost., 1863. 12°.

Woman-captain, The; a comedy, by **T. Shadwell.** (*In his* Dram. works, v. 3. 1720.)

Woman hater, The; by **F. Beaumont** and **J. Fletcher.** (*In their* Dram. works, v. 10. 1778.)

Woman killed with kindness, A; by **T. Heywood.** (*In* **Dodsley, R.** Col. of plays, v. 7. 1780; 1825; — *in* **Scott,** *Sir* W. Anc. Brit. dr., v. 2. 1810; — *and in* **Lamb,** C. Spec. dram. poets. 1854.)

Woman in the moone, The; by **J. Lyly.** (*In his* Dram. works, v. 2. 1858.)

Woman in white, The; by **W. Collins.** N. Y., 1861. 8°.

Note. From **All** the year round, v. 2-3. 1859-60.

Woman of business, The; or, The lady and the lawyer; by **M. Savage.** N. Y., 1870. 8°.

Note. From the **Fortnightly** review, v. 11-13. 1869-70.

Woman who dared, The; by **E. Sargent.** Boston, 1870. 12°.

Woman's journal; Jan. 8, 1870 - Dec. 30, 1874. Boston, 1870-74. 5 v. f°.

Woman's kingdom, The; by [*Mrs.* **D. M. M. Craik**]. N. Y., 1869. 8°.

— *Same.* (*In* **Good** words, v. 9. 1868; — *and in* **Harper's** mag., v. 36-38. 1867-69.)

Woman's love and the world's favor; by **E. Phipps.** Phila., 1840. 2 v. 12°.

Woman's prize, The; by **F. Beaumont** and **J. Fletcher.** (*In their* Dram. works, v. 8. 1778.)

Woman's record; sketches of distinguished women to 1850. *See* **Hale, S. J.**

Woman's rights. *See* **National Woman's Rights Convention**; — **Woman.** *Legal rights*; — **Woman.** *Social condition*; — **Woman's suffrage.**

Woman's rights and duties; by a woman. London, 1840. 2 v. 12°.

Woman's rights tracts. Nos. 1-10. *n.p.*, [1845-52]. 10 pam. 8°. (B 1667)

Namely. No. 1. **May, S. J.** The rights and condition of women; sermon, 1845. — 2. **Phillips, W.** Speech at Worcester, Oct. 15, 16, 1851. — **Coe,** *Mrs.* Extract from speech. — **Foster, A. K.** Speech. 3. **Davis,** *Mrs.* **P. W.** Education of females. — **Martineau, H.** Letter. 4. **Enfranchisement** of women. — **Hunt, H. K.** Taxation without representation. 5. **Smith,** *Mrs.* E. O. Sanctity of marriage. 6. **Nichols,** *Mrs.* C. I. H. Responsibilities of woman. 7. **Gage,** *Mrs.* M. E. J. Speech, Sept. 1852. 8. **Weld, A. G.** Letter to the Convention. 9. **May, S. J.** Letter. 9. **Rose,** *Mrs.* E. L. Speech, Oct. 1850. 10. **Stanton,** *Mrs.* E. C. Letter, Oct. 1850; — Letter, Sept. 1852.

Woman's rights tracts, no. 1-5. Boston, 1854. 12°.

Contents. **Phillips, W.** Speech, Worcester, Oct. 1851. — **Parker, T.** Public function of woman; a sermon. — **Enfranchisement** of women; from **Westminster** and foreign quarterly review, July 1851. — **Higginson, T. W.** Woman and her wishes. — **Nichols,** *Mrs.* C. I. H. Responsibilities of woman.

Woman's suffrage. BUSHNELL, H. Women's suffrage; the reform against nature. N. Y., **1869.** 12°.

— FAIR play to women. (*In* **Radicalism** in religion, philosophy, *etc.* **1858.**)

See also **Woman.** *Law*; — **Woman.** *Social condition* (FULTON) p. 3353.

Woman's wit; or, Love's disguises. *See* **Knowles, J. S.**

Woman's wit; or, The lady in fashion; a comedy, by **C. Cibber.** (*In his* Dram. works, v. 1. 1777.)

Woman's worth and worthlessness; by **Gail Hamilton.** *See* **Dodge, M. A.**

Womb. *See* **Uterus.**

Women; [an early English poem]. (*In* **Adam** *of Cobsam.* The wright's chaste wife. 1865.)

Women beware women; a tragedy, by **T. Middleton.** (*In his* Works, v. 4. 1840; — **Old** plays, v. 5. 1780; — *and in* **Lamb,** C. Specimen. 1808; 1854.)

Women of England. *See* **Ellis,** *Mrs.* **S.**

Women of the American Revolution. *See* **Ellet,** *Mrs.* **E. F.**

Women; or, Pour et contre, by [**C. R. Maturin**]. Phila., 1818. 2 v. 12°.

Women pleas'd; by **F. Beaumont** and **J. Fletcher.** (*In their* Dram. works, v. 8. 1778.)

Women rule; a comedy, [by **J. W. Huff**]. Phila., 1868. 8°.

Wonder, The; a comedy, by **Mrs. S. Centlivre.** (*In* **Bell,** J. Brit. theatre, v. 2. 1797; — **Scott,** *Sir* W. Brit. dr., v. 2, pt. 2. 1804; — *and in* **Sargent,** E. Mod. stand. dr., v. 37.)

Wonder-book. *See* **Hawthorne, N.** Tanglewood tales.

Wonder of a kingdom. *See* **Dekker, T.**

Wonder of women, The; or, The tragedie of Sophonisba; by **J. Marston.** (*In his* Works. v. 1. 1856; — *and in* **Lamb,** C. Spec. of dram. poets. 1854.)

Wonder stories for children; by **H. C. Andersen.** N. Y., 1870. 8°.

Wonder-working providence. *See* **Johnson, E.**

Wonderful appearance of an angel, devil, and ghost in Boston, Oct. 14-16. Boston, 1774. 8°. (B 655)

Wonderful characters. *See* **Wilson, H.,** *and* **Caulfield, J.**

Wonders. WAKEFIELD, P. Mental improvement; or, Beauties and wonders of nature and art. [1794.] 3d Amer. ed. Phila., 1814. 12°.

— HUTTON, W. Wonders of nature and art. London, **1823.** 12°.

— SEARS, R. Wonders of the world in nature, art, and mind. N. Y., **1843.** 8°.

— GLIMPSES of the wonderful. N. Y., **1846.** 4°.

Wonders of the invisible world. *See* **Mather, C.**

Wonders of the invisible world, More. *See* **Calef, R.**

Wonders of the little world; or, A general history of man. *See* **Wanley, N.**

Wonders of the year 1716. Nottingham, 1716. 8°. (C 285)

Wondrous tale of Alroy; by **B. Disraeli.** (*In his* Works, v. 2. 1845.)

— *Same.* Miriam Alroy. Phila., [18—]. 8°.

— *Same.* Alroy. (*In his* Novels and tales, v. 1. 1866.)

Wood, *Capt.* —. Voyage through the Streights of Magellan, *etc.* (*In* **Hacke, W.** Col. of voy. 1699.)

— *Germ.* Reise durch die Magellanische Strasse. (*In* **Allgemeine** Hist., v. 12. 1754.)

Wood, Alphonso. Account of six new species of plants. (*In* **Amer. Assoc.** Proc., v. 7. 1856.)

— Class-book of botany. Boston, 1845. 12°.

Wood, *Rev.* Amos. Sermon, June 5, [election day]. Portsmouth, N. H., 1794. 8°. (B 336)

Wood, Anthony à. Athenæ Oxonienses. London, 1691-92. 2 v. f°.

Contents. Vol. 1. 1500-1640. 2. 1641-90.

— *Same.* 2d ed., cor. and enl. with the addition of above five hundred lives. London, 1721. 2 v. f°.

— *Same.* With Fasti Oxonienses. New ed., with add. by P. Bliss. London, 1813-20. 4 v. 4°.

Note. The 'Fasti' have a separate paging and title. The 1st part, 1500-1640, is appended to v. 2 of the 'Athenæ', the 2d part, 1641-91, to v. 4 of the 'Athenæ', following the general Index.

— Letter to I. Mather, 1690, [rel. to the Athenæ Oxonienses]. (*In* **Mass. Hist. Soc.** Col., v. 17. 1818.)

— Life, by himself, pub. by T. Hearne; continued to his death. (*In* **Huddesford, W.** Lives, v. 2. 1772.)

Wood, Benjamin. Voyage into the East Indies; from letters of Alcasar de Villa Señor. (*In* **Purchas.** Pilgrimes, v. 1. 1625; — **Harris, J.** Compleat col., v. 1. 1705; — **Green, J.** Col., v. 1. 1745; — **Kerr, R.** Col., v. 8. 1824; — *and, Germ., in* **Allgemeine Hist.**, v. 1. 1748.)

Wood, *Rev.* Benjamin, *b.* 1772, *d.* 1849. Centennial address, Sutton, Mass., June 25. Boston, 1835. 8°. (B 1882)

— Labourers needed in the harvest of Christ; sermon, Sutton, Mar. 18. Worcester, 1812. 8°. (B 285)

— Sermon delivered at the ordination of S. W. Colbourne, West Cong. Society, Taunton. Sutton, 1809. 8°. (C 212)

— Sermon delivered at Upton, Apr. 24, at the interment of Mrs. Rachel Ruggles. Worcester, 1811. 8°. (B 1007)

— Sermon, delivered at Upton, June 1. Worcester, 1846. 8°. (B 1326)

Wood, Edmund Gough de Salis. The supernatural. (*In* **Shipley, O.** Church and the world. 1868.)

Wood, Fernando. Address on the genius, *etc.*, of A. Hamilton. N. Y., 1856. 8°. (B 1218)

— Speech on U. S. fiscal bank bill. Wash., 1841. 8°. (B 1664)

Wood, George. Marrying too late. N. Y., 1857 [1856]. 8°.

— Modern pilgrims. Boston, 1855. 2 v. 12°.

Wood, George B., *M.D.* Address at a meeting of the American Medical Assoc., Detroit, May. Phila., 1856. 8°. (B 1565)

— Address at the centennial celebration of the Penn. hospital. Phila., 1851. 8°.

— Address to the medical graduates of the Univ. of Pa. Phila., 1836. 8°. (B 1565)

— History of the University of Pennsylvania, from the origin to 1827. (*In* **Penn. Hist. Soc.** Mem., v. 3, pt. 2. 1836.)

— Introd. lectures and addresses on medical subjects. Phila., 1859. 8°.

Contents. Pharmaceutical addresses. — Lectures introd. to the course on materia medica and pharmacy in the Univ. of Penn. — Lectures on the theory and practice of medicine. — Lectures giving the results of professional observation abroad. — Addresses to the medical graduates of the Univ. of Penn. — Biog. memoirs: Life and character of J. Parrish; — Mem. of S. G. Morton.

— Lecture introd. to the course of materia medica and pharmacy in the Univ. of Penn., 1836/37. Phila., 1836. 8°. (C 271)

— *and* Bache, F. Dispensatory of the United States of America. 10th ed. Philadelphia, 1854. 8°.

— - *Same.* 12th ed. rev. Phila., 1865. 8°.

Wood, H. Early life of Jesus; serm. to the children of the 1st Cong. Soc., Tyngsborough, Dec. 25. Boston, 1841. 18°. (C 16)

Wood, *Mrs.* Ellen Price, *wife of* Henry. East Lynne; or, The Earl's daughter. Richmond, 1864. 8°.

— Lady Adelaide's oath. (*In* **Temple Bar**, v. 17-19. 1866-67.)

— Oswald Cray. (*In* **Good words**, v. 5. 1864.)

— *pseud.* Selina Sedilia. (*In* **Harte, B.** Condensed novels. 1871.)

Wood, *Rev.* Horatio. Address on temperance, Salisbury, N. H., Apr. 3. Concord, 1833. 8°. (B 1278)

— Gospel truths; sermon before the Unitarian Soc. in Franklin and Salisbury, Nov. 1833. Camb., 1834. 8°. (B 1306)

Wood, Horatio C., *Jr.* On the collection of specimens of myriapods, phalangidæ. (*In* **Smithsonian Inst.** Reports, 1866.)

Wood, Hutton. Collection of decrees by the Court of Exchequer in tithe-causes. London, 1798-99. 4 v. 8°.

Wood, J. B., *M.D.* Address at the 4th ann. meeting of the Homœopathic Med. Soc. of Chester Co., Oct. W. Chester, 1861. 8°. (B 1565)

Wood, Jacob. Defence of universalism; examination of the arguments and objections advanced by J. W. Tucker in an address against the doctrine of universal restoration. Newburyport, 1816. 8°. (B 263)

— Letter to J. Kelley, cont. remarks on 'Solemn and important reasons against becoming an Universalist'; also 'Additional reasons', *etc.* Haverhill, 1816. 8°. (B 263)

— Sermon, Townsend, Feb. Worcester, 1818. 8°. (B 286)

Wood, Jacob A., *M.D.* Pott's disease; or, Angular curvature of the spine. N. Y., 1859. 8°. (B 1565)

Wood, James. Parable of the ten virgins, illust. in six sermons. London, 1722, *reprinted* Amherst, 1830. 12°.

Wood, James, *D.D.*, *d.* 1839. Elements of algebra. 2d ed. Camb., 1798. 8°.

Wood, *Capt.* John. Voy. for the discov. of N.-E. passage, 1676. (*In* **Harris, J.** Col. of voy., v. 1. 1705.)

— - *French.* Journal de W. allant à la découverte d'un passage par le Nord-Est, 1676. (*In* **Bernard, J. F.** Recueil de voy., v. 2. 1716.)

— - *Germ.* Reise gegen Nordwest und Nordost. (*In* **Allgemeine Hist.**, v. 17. 1759.)

— - Supplement to his north east voyage; navigations and observations northwest of Greenland. (*In* **Harris, J.** Col. of voy., v. 1. 1705.)

Wood, John, *architect, of Bath, d.* 1754. Origin of building; or, The plagiarism of the heathens detected. Bath, 1741. f°.

Wood, John, *d.* 1822. Correct statement of the various sources from which the hist. of the administration of J. Adams was compiled, and the motives for its suppression by Col. Burr; with obs. on 'A narrative by a citizen of N. Y.' [J. Cheetham]. 2d ed. corr. with notes. N. Y., 1802. 8°. (B 622)

— Full exposition of the Clintonian faction and the Soc. of the Columbian Illuminati. Newark, 1802. 8°. (B 622)

— Full statement of the trial and acquittal of A. Burr. Alexandria, 1807. 8°. (B 433)

— General view of the history of Switzerland. Edin., 1799. 8°.

— History of the administration of J. Adams. N. Y., 1802. 8°.

— Letter to A. Addison, in answer to his 'Rise and progress of revolution'. Phila., 1801. 12°. (B 657)

— Observations on 'A narrative by a citizen of N. Y.' N. Y., 1802. 8°. (B 622)

— Cheetham, J. Narrative of the suppression by Col. Burr, of the 'History of the administration of J. Adams'. N. Y., 1802. 8°.

— - *Another copy.* (B 1885)

— - *Same.*, 2d ed. rev. and corr. N. Y., 1802. 8°. (B 622)

— Warren, *pseud.* Antidote to J. Wood's poison. N. Y., 1802. 8°. (B 622)

Wood, John, *of Edin. Sessional Sch.* Account of Edinburgh Sessional School and other parochial institutions for education. 2d ed. Edin., Boston, *reprinted* 1830. 12°.

Wood, *Capt.* John, *Indian navy.* Personal narrative of a journey to the source of the River Oxus, 1836-38. London, 1841. 8°.

Wood, John Arthur. Chronological table of and index to the statutes, to 1869. London, 1870. 8°.

Wood, *Rev.* John George. Common objects of the microscope. London, 1861. 16°.

— Homes without hands. London, 1865. 8°.

— Insects at home; being a popular account of insects, their structure, habits, and transformations. N. Y., 1872 [1871]. 8°.

— Our garden friends and foes. London, N. Y., 1864. 8°.

Wood, Joseph. Schott, A. Results of observations taken at Marietta by W. (*In* **Smithsonian Inst.** Contrib., v. 16. 1871.)

Wood, Nicholas. On coal. (*In* **Armstrong,** *Sir* W. G. Indust. resources of the Tyne, *etc.* 1864.)

— Treatise on railroads. London, 1825. 8°.
— *Same.* [2d ed., with additions.] London, 1831. 8°.

Wood, *Lieut.* Oliver E. The West-Point scrap-book. N. Y., 1871. 8°.

Wood, Robert. Les ruines de Balbec. Londres, 1757. f°.
— Account of Palmyra and Balbec. (*In* **Knox, J.** Col., v. 6. 1767.)

Wood, *Rev.* S. Common schools in Mass., N. York, and Pennsylvania. (*In* **Central Soc. of Educ.** Publications, v. 3. 1839.)
— Letters from the U. S. From the Christian reformer, *n.p.*, [1838]. 8°. (**B 1603**)

Wood, Samuel, *D.D.*, *Funeral sermon on.* 1836. *See* **Price,** E. (**B 1840**)

Wood, Silas. Sketch of the first settlement of several towns on Long Island. Brooklyn, 1824. 8°.

Wood, Thomas, *LL.D.* Institute of the laws of England; in four books. 9th ed. London, 1763. f°.

Wood, Thomas, *M.D.* Inquiry concerning the primitive inhabitants of Ireland. Cork, 1821. 8°.
— On the mixture of fable and fact in the early annals of Ireland. (*In* **Royal Irish Acad.** Trans., v. 13. 1818.)

Wood, Wilkes. Oration, Middleborough, June 4. New Bedford, 1795. 8°. (B 936)

Wood, Wm., *d.* 1639. New England's prospect. London, 1639. 4°.
— *Same.* 3d ed. Boston, *reprinted* 1764. 8°. (**B 618, 1838**)
— *Same.* Boston, *reprinted* 1865. 4°. (Prince Soc.)
— *Same.* Chapters 1, 10. (*In* **Young, A.** Chronicles of Massachusetts. 1846.)

Wood, Wm., *letter-carrier.* MANAGEMENT of inland letter-carrier's superannuated fund. London, 1815. 8°. (B 1682)

Wood, Wm., *F. R. S.* General conchology; or, Description of shells arranged according to the Linnean system; with plates. Vol. 1. London, 1815. 8°.
— Illustrations of the Linnæan genera of insects. London, 1821. 2 v. 16°.
— Index testaceologicus; or, Catalogue of shells, British and foreign. London, 1825. 8°.
— - Supplement. London, 1828. 8°.

Wood, Wm., *M.D.* Essay on the structure and functions of the skin. Edin., 1832. 8°.

Wood, Wm. B. Personal recollections of the stage. Phila., 1855. 8°.

Wood, Wm. H. Moral responsibility of teachers. (*In* **Amer. Inst. of Instr.** Lectures. 1842.)

Wood, *Sir* Wm. Page. Address on jurisprudence and the amendment of the law. — On charitable trusts. (*In* **Nat. Assoc. Prom. Soc. Sci.** Trans., 1859.)
— Convocation. *See* **Thesiger,** *Sir* F. (**B 1376**)

Wood, Wm. W. Descriptions of four new species of the Linnæan genus blennius and a new exocetus. — Description of a new species of salamander. — Two species of Linnæan lacerta and construction of new genus cyclura. (*In* **Acad. Nat. Sci. of Phila.** Journ., v. 4, pt. 2. 1825.)

Wood. *See* **Forests**; — **Timber**; — **Trees.**

Wood dealer's companion; containing a wood measure; by L. Dimick. Glen's Falls, N. Y., 1845. 8°.

Wood engraving. PAPILLON, J. M. Traité historique et pratique de la gravure en bois. Paris, **1766.** 2 v. 8°.
— GOTZMANN, J. D. F. Aelteste Geschichte der Xylographie und der Druckkunst überhaupt; besonders in Anwendung auf den Bilddruck. (*In* **Historisches** Taschenbuch, 1837.)
— CHATTO, W. A. Treatise on wood engraving; with 300 illustrations by J. Jackson. 2d ed. Lond., **1861.** 8°.
— BERJEAU, J. B. Catalogue illustré des livres xylographiques. Londres, **1865.** 8°.
— GILKS, T. The art of wood engraving. London, **1866.** 18°.

See also **Cruikshank,** G.; — **Duerer,** A.; — **Holbein,** H.; — *also* **Doré,** G.; — **Millais,** J. E.; — *also* **Art journal**; — **Art union**; — **Punch.**

Wood family. MORSE, A. (*In his* Genealogical register, v. 1. 1855.)

Wood Leighton; by M. Howitt. Phila., 1837. 3 v. 12°.

Woodall, John. Surgeon's mate; or, Military and domestic surgery. London, 1655. f°.

Woodbridge, *Rev.* Ashbel. Sermon, election, Hartford, 1752. New London, 1753. 12°. (**B 63**)
— *Funeral sermon on.* 1758. *See* **Lockwood, J.** (**B 227, 853**)

Woodbridge, Jerusha, *Funeral sermon on.* 1799. *See* **Lockwood, W.** (**B 1096**)

Woodbridge, *Rev.* John. Address before the alumni of Williams Coll., Sept. 3. Hartford, 1823. 8°. (**B 1576**)
— The jubilee of New England; sermon, Hadley, Dec. 22, 1820. Northampton, 1821. 8°. (**B 275, 1788**)
— Sermon; God's respect to the lowly. — Pride abased by the Gospel. (*In* **National** preacher, v. 2. 1827–28.)

Woodbridge, Sylvester. Farewell sermon, Jan. 6, Ashfield. Northampton, 1816. 8°. (**B 336**)

Woodbridge, *Rev.* Timothy. Autobiography of a blind minister; including sketches of the men and events of his time. Bost., 1856. 8°.
— Oration, Great Barrington, July 4. Stockbridge, 1809. 8°. (**B 421**)

Woodbridge, *Rev.* Wm. Illustration of some difficult passages of Scripture on the doctrine of absolute predestination; sermon. Middletown, 1805. 8°. (**B 911**)
— Key to the Eng. lang. Middletown, 1801. 16°.
— Sermon, care of the soul, No. Killingworth. Middletown, 1798. 8°. (B 48)

Woodbridge, Wm. Channing, *b.* 1795. System of modern geography. Hartford, 1844. 12°.
— Vocal music. (*In* **Amer. Inst. of Instr.** Lectures, 1830.) — On schoolrooms. (*In* 1831.) — On the best method of teaching geography. (*In* 1833.)

Woodburne, John. Tryal and condemnation of W. for felony in slitting the nose of Edward Crispe. *See* **Coke,** A. 1722. (**A 56**)

Woodbury, Augustus. Character and influence of American civilization; oration, Lowell, July 4. Lowell, 1855. 8°. (**B 1573**)
— Major General A. E. Burnside and the 9th army corps. Prov., 1867. 8°.
— We ought to obey God rather than men; sermon, Concord, N. H., Nov. 3. Concord, 1850. 8°. (**B 1306**)

Woodbury, Benjamin, *Funeral sermon on.* 1728. *See* **Sewall, J.** (**B 231, C 172**)

Woodbury, *Capt.* Daniel Phineas. Treatise on the various elements of stability in the well-proportioned arch, *etc.* N. Y., 1858. 8°. (U. S. Corps of engineers. Prof. papers, no. 7.)

Woodbury, Fanny. Writings; ed. by J. Emerson. Boston, 1815. 12°.

Woodbury, J. H. On the hypodermic use of homœopathic remedies. (*In* **Mass. Homœop. Med. Soc.** Publ., 1864.)

Woodbury, Levi. Writings. Bost., 1852. 3 v. 8°.
Contents. Vol. 1. Biographical notice. — Speeches. — Reports. — Gubernatorial message, speeches, and reports on state topics. — Occasional letters and speeches on important subjects. — Appendix. 2. Judicial. 3. Literary.
— Anniversary address before the New Hampshire Hist. Soc., 1845. (*In* **New Hamp. Hist. Soc.** Col., v. 6. 1850.)
— Annual address before the National Institute, Jan. 15. Wash., 1845. 8°. (**B 1583**)
— Eulogy on the life, character, and public services of J. K. Polk. Boston, 1849. 8°. (**B 1222**)
— Oration, Hanover, N. H., before the Handel, Middlesex, *etc.*, musical societies, Aug. 27. Amherst, 1812. 8°. (**B 1589**)

— Remarks on the bill for relief of surviving officers of the Revolution. Wash., 1828. 8°. (B 971)
— Report, present system of keeping and disbursing the public money. [Wash., 183-.] 8°. (B 1494)
— Speech in relation to a board of exchequer. Wash., 1842. 8°. (B 1663)
— Speech on the capital of the fiscal bank, July 10. Wash., 1841. 8°. (B 1664)
— Speech on the judiciary bill, in the Senate, April 11, 1826. *n.t.p.* [1826.] 8°. (W 13a)
— Tables and notes on cultivation, manufacture, and foreign trade of cotton. Wash., 1836. 8°. (24th Cong. 1st sess. Ho. Doc. 146.)
— SKETCH.] (*In* Longacre, J. B., *and* Herring, J. Nat. portr. gal., v. 2. 1835.)
— LORING, J. S. (*In his* Hundred Boston orators. 1852.)

Woodbury, Peter P., *and others*. History of Bedford, N. H. Boston, 1851. 8°.

Woodbury, W. H. Shorter course with the German language. N. Y., 1852. 12°.

Woodchester. LYSONS, S. Roman antiquities at Woodchester. London, 1797. f°.

Woodcock's little game; a comedy farce, by J. M. Morton. (No. 11 *of* De Witt's acting plays.)

Woodcroft, Bennet. Brief biographies of inventors of machines for textile fabrics. London, 1863. 8°.

Woodcuts. *See* Wood engraving.

Woodcutter of the Lebanon; by [J. R. Macduff]. N. Y., 1854. 12°.

Woodd, Basil. Advice to youth. 2d ed. London, [18—]. 12°. (C 232)

Woodeson, Richard. Elements of jurisprudence. Dublin, 1792. 8°.

Woodfall, Wm., *and others*. An impartial report of the debates, 4th sess. 17th Parl. of Great Brit., 1794 - 4th sess. 18th Parl., [1800]. London, 1794-1800. 23 v. 8°.
Note. Each sess. has a separate numbering of the vols.
— Parliamentary register; or, Impartial report of the debates, 2d sess. 1st Parl. of the United Kingdom - 2d sess. 2d Parl., [1801-04]. London, 1802-04. 10 v. 8°.
Note. Each sess. has a separate numbering of the vols.

Woodforde, James. On dyspepsia; with observ. on hypochondriasis and hysteria. 2d ed. London, 1821. 12°.

Woodhead, Abraham. ATTERBURY, F. Answer to 'Some considerations on the spirit of Luther'. Oxford, 1687. 4°.
— SMALRIDGE, G. Reflections on the historical part of Church government, pt. 5. Oxford, 1687. 4°. (B 91)

Woodhead, Henry. Memoirs of Christina, Queen of Sweden. London, 1863. 2 v. 8°.

Woodhouse, John. Funeral sermon, death of Mrs. J. Papillon. London, 1698. 16°. (C 164)

Woodhouse, John. RARE English portraits; catalogue of [his] collection, sold Nov. 24. [London,] 1803. 8°. (B 1621)

Woodhouse, John Chappel. Apocalypse. *See* Bible. *Revelation* (p. 291).
— Evidence for the authenticity, *etc.*, of the Apocalypse stated and vindicated from the objections of J. D. Michaelis. London, 1802. 8°.
— *Same.* Dissertation on the divine origin of the book. (*In* Bible. *Revelation.* The Apocalypse. 1805.)

Woodhouse, Robert. An elementary treatise on astronomy. Camb., 1812. 8°.
— A treatise on astronomy, theoretical and practical. New ed. Cambridge, 1821-23. 2 v. 8°.
— Treatise on plane and spherical trigonometry. 2d ed. corrected and enlarged. Cambridge, 1813. 8°.

Woodhouselee, *Lord*. *See* Tytler, A. F.

Woodhull, Alfred Alexander. Catalogue of the surgical section of the U. S. Army Medical Museum; prepared under the direction of the Surg. Gen. U. S. Army [J. K. Barnes]. Wash., 1866. 4°.

Woodhull, Nathaniel. ONDERDONK, H. Capture and death of W.; letters to J. F. Cooper. [Cuttings from Home journal. N. Y., 1848.]

Woodlawn Cemetery, *N. Chelsea and Malden*. FULLER, H. W. Boston, 1856. 8°.

Woodlock, Ellen, *and* Atkinson, S. Irish poor in workhouses. (*In* Nat. Assoc. Prom. Soc. Sci. Trans., 1861.)

Woodman, Cyrus. Memoir of P. Coffin. (*In* Maine Hist. Soc. Col., v. 4. 1856.)

Woodman, *Miss* Hannah J. Sibylline leaves; or, The mirror of fate; a col. of poems. Boston, 1846. 18°.

Woodman, Jabez C. Reply to W. T. Dwight on spiritualism. Portland, 1857. 8°. (B 1200)

Woodman, Joseph. Sermon, June 3, annual election of New Hampshire. Concord, 1802. 8°. (B 336)

Woodman, The; a comic opera; by B. Dudley. (*In* London stage, v. 4.)

Woodman, The; by G. P. R. James. New York, [1849]. 8°.

Woodman, The. *See* Channing, W. E.

Woodruff, Hezekiah North. Life and character of a gospel minister; sermon, Boston, ordination of C. Brown. Boston, 1795. 8°. (B 911)

Woodruff, Hiram. The trotting horse of America; how to train and drive him; with reminiscences of the trotting turf; ed. by C. J. Foster; including an introd. notice by G. Wilkes, and a biog. sketch by the editor. N. Y., Boston, 1868. 12°.

Woodruff, J., *reporter*. The sequestration cases before Hon. A. G. Magrath, in the district court for South Carolina, Oct. term, 1861. [Charleston, 1861?] 8°.

Woodruff, *Mrs.* J. L. M. My winter in Cuba; by W. M. L. Jay [pseudon.]. N. Y., 1871. 12°.

Woodruffe the gardener. (*In* Household words, v. 1. 1850.)

Woods, *Mrs.* Abby, *Funeral sermon on.* 1846. *See* Stuart, M. (B 1228)

Woods, Alva. Baccalaureate address, Dec. 17, commencement of the University of Alabama. [Tuscaloosa,] 1836. 12°. (B 1581)
— Discourse, Transylvania Univ., Oct. 13. Lexington, 1828. 8°. (B 936)
— Valedictory address at the close of the 7th collegiate year of the Univ. of Alabama. Tuscaloosa, 1837. 8°. (B 1129)

Woods, Caroline H. Woman in prison. N. Y., 1869. 12°.

Woods, Edward. Forms of locomotive engines. (*In* Instit. of Civil Engin. Trans., v. 2. 1842.)

Woods, *Rev.* Henry W. The fading leaf an emblem of man's frailty; sermon, Newton Lower Falls, Oct. 31, the Sunday after the death of D. Webster. Boston, 1852. 8°. (B 1726)

Woods, John. McBRIDE, J. (*In his* Pioneer biography, v. 1. 1869.)

Woods, Joseph. Letters of an architect from France, Italy, and Greece. London, 1828. 2 v. 4°.

Woods, Julian E. Tenison. History of the discovery and exploration of Australia. London, 1865. 2 v. 8°.

Woods, Leonard, *D.D.*, *b.* 1774, *d.* 1854. Works. Boston, 1851. 5 v. 8°.
Contents. Vol. 1-3. Lectures to young men preparing for the ministry. 4. Letters to Unitarians. — Reply to Dr. Ware's 'Letters to the Unitarians and Calvinists'. — Remarks on Dr. Ware's answer. — Letters to Dr. N. W. Taylor. — Examination of the doctrine of perfection. — *Appendix.* Letter to Mr. Mahan. — Dissertation on miracles. — Course of study. 5. Letters to young ministers. — Philosophy of the mind. — Remarks on cause and effect in connection with fatalism and free agency. — Reply to 'Inquirer'. — Effi-

cacy of the word of God. — Sermon on the death of S. Abbot, — S. Spring, — Rev. S. Worcester, — M. Brown, — J. Evarts, — Rev. E. Porter, — Rev. J. H. Church, — Mrs. P. Farrar, — H. Newell. — Sermon at the ordination of J. W. Ellingwood, — J. Idle, — J. Hawes, — A. Woods, — B. Woodbury, — N. Hewitt, — T. M. Smith. — Sermons in the Chapel of the Theological Seminary.
— Address on the opening of the new hall of the medical school of Maine, Feb. 21. Brunswick, 1862. 8°. (B 1565, 1587)
— Discourse on sacred music, Sept. 10. Salem, 1804. 8°. (B 171)
— The grand theme of the Christian preacher; sermon, ordination of B. B. Wisner, Feb. 21. Andover, 1821. 8°. (B 278)
— The heaven of Christians; sermon, funeral of P. Farrar, Jan. 26. Andover, 1848. 8°. (B 1245)
— Importance of a minister's reputation; sermon, installation of W. Hewit, Bridgeport, Conn., Dec. 1, 1830. Andover, 1831. 8°. (B 1064)
— Letters to Unitarians; occasioned by the sermon of W. E. Channing at the ordination of J. Sparks. Andover, 1820. 8°. (B 337)
— Love of popularity; sermon, Feb. 23, installation of W. Fay, in Charlestown. Charlestown, 1820. 8°. (B 278)
— A minister's final account; sermon, ordination of J. Hawes, Hartford, March 14. Hartford, 1818. 8°. (B 277, 336)
— The mourning husband; discourse, funeral of Mrs. Church, Apr. 15, 1806. Boston, 1807. 12°. (C 202)
— Reply to Dr. Ware's letters to Trinitarians and Calvinists. Andover, 1821. 8°. (B 337)
— Sermon before the Anc. and Hon. Artil. Co., Boston, June 6. Boston, 1808. 8°. (B 211)
— Sermon before the Mass. Miss. Soc., May 26. Boston, 1812. 8°. (B 1330)
— Sermon, Boston, May 29. Boston, [1823]. 8°. (B 280)
— Sermon, Boston, Oct. 28, ordination of A. Woods. Boston, [1821]. 8°. (B 278)
— Sermon, death of J. Evarts, Andover, July 31. Andover, 1831. 8°. (B 1214, 1780, 1828)
— Sermon, death of S. Worcester, July 12. Salem, 1821. 8°. (B 283, 1237)
— Sermon; duties of the rich. (*In* National preacher, v. 1. 1826.) — Sermon, funeral of J. H. Church. (*In* v. 14. 1840. B 1840)
— Sermon, in remembrance of Mrs. H. Newell, who died at the Isle of France, Nov. 30, 1812; [with] memoirs of her life. Boston, 1814. 8°. (B 336)
— Sermon, June 9, Falmouth, Mass., ordination of B. Woodbury. Andover, 1824. 8°. (B 1324)
— Sermon, March 9, funeral of S. Spring. Newburyport, 1819. 8°. (B 279, 283, 1237, 1789)
— Sermon, May 3, funeral of S. Abbot. Boston, 1812. 8°. (B 336, 1238)
— Sermon; nature and influence of faith. Andover, 1826. 8°. (B 1306)
— Sermon, ordination of J. W. Ellingwood, Nov. 4, 1812; J. Ide, Nov. 2, 1814; and W. Eaton, Aug. 30. Andover, 1815. 8°. (B 336)
— *Same.* Sermon, ordination of W. Eaton, Fitchburg, Aug. 30. Andover, 1815. 8°. (B 1651)
— Sermon, Salem, Feb. 6, ordination of S. Newell, A. Judson, S. Nott, G. Hall, and L. Rice, missionaries to Asia. Boston, 1812. 8°. (B 336, 1849, 1875)
— Sermon, Theol. Seminary, Andover, Feb. 1, death of H. Lyman, S. Munson, H. H. Post, L. Baker and C. Lord. Andover, 1835. 8°. (B 1220, 1246)
— A testimony against the publications of Marcus [on the council]. Newburyport, 1806. 8°. (D 2)
— Theology of the Puritans. Boston, 1851. 8°.
— Two sermons on profane swearing, April 4. Newburyport, 1799. 8°. (B 846)
— Usefulness of the sacred office; sermon, March 9, funeral of Rev. S. Spring. Newburyport, 1819. 8°. (B 279, 283, 1237, 1789)
— ALLEN, G. The Andover fuss; or, Dr. Woods *vs.* Dr. Dana on the imputation of heresy against Prof. Park, *etc.* Boston, 1853. 8°. (B 1394)
— BUSH, G. Reply to Woods' lectures on Swedenborgianism. N. Y., 1847. 8°.
— DEFENCE of Dr. Woods; remarks illustrative of his letter to Unitarians. Boston, 1820. 8°. (B 337)
— LETTER to Dr. Woods [on] his address to Unitarians; by a layman. Boston, 1820. 8°. (B 338)
— WARE, H. Answer to Dr. Woods' reply, in a second series of letters to Trinitarians and Calvinists. Camb., 1822. 8°. (B 338)
— - Letters to Trinitarians and Calvinists, occasioned by Dr. Woods' 'Letters to Unitarians'. Camb., 1820. 8°. (B 338, 2538)
— - Postscript to the second series of letters to Trinitarians and Calvinists, in reply to Dr. Woods on those letters. Camb., 1823. 8°. (B 338)

Woods, Leonard, *Jr., D.D., b.* 1807. Address on the life of P. Cleaveland before the Maine Hist. Soc. Portland, 1859. 8°. (B 1211, 1455)
— *Same.* (*In* **Maine Historical Society.** Col., v. 6. 1859.)
— Eulogy on D. Webster, Portland, Nov. 17. Brunswick, 1852. 8°. (B 1728)
See also **Literary** and theological review.

Woods, Wm. The twins; altered from Shakespeare's 'Comedy of errors'. (*In* **Collection** of most esteemed farces, v. 4. 1792.)

Woods. *See* **Forests.**

Woodstock, *Vt.* STREETER, R. Mirror of Calvinistic fanatical revivals; or, J. Burchard & Co. during a protracted meeting in Woodstock; added, 'Preamble and resolution' of the town. Woodstock, 1835. 12°. (C 200)

Woodstock, *Vt.* **Friends of a Protective Tariff in the County of Windsor.** Memorial and resolutions, March 15, 1842. *n.t.p.* [1842.] 8°. (B 1513)

Woodstock and Stonington Baptist Associations. Circular letters from the Associations to their churches. *n.p.*, 1807. 8°. (B 431)

Woodstock; or, The cavalier; by Sir W. Scott. Phila., 1826. 2 v. 12°.
— *Same.* (*In his* Works, v. 39, 40. 1829.)

Woodville, Elizabeth, *Queen of Edward* IV. STRICKLAND, A. (*In her* Queens of Eng., v. 3. 1840.)

Woodville, Wm. Observations on the cow-pox. London, 1800. 8°. (B 821)
— COMPARATIVE statement of facts and obs. rel. to the cow-pox pub. by Drs. Jenner and W. London, 1800. 8°. (E 272)
— HIGHMORE, A. Address previous to the funeral of Wm. Woodville. [London, 1805.] 8°. (B 1228)

Woodward, Ashbel. Historical address. (*In* **Franklin,** *Conn.* Celebration of 150th anniv. 1869.)

Woodward, Augustus B. Considerations on the executive government of the United States. Flatbush, 1809. 8°. (B 411)
— Considerations on the government of the territory of Columbia. No. 1-6. Wash., 1801. 4°. (B 651)
— *Same.* No. 7. Alexandria, 1802. 8°. (B 422)
— *Same.* No. 8. Wash., 1803. 8°. (B 422)
— Considerations on the substance of the Sun. Wash., 1801. 8°. (B 393)
— Supplement to the representation of the case of O. Pollock. Wash., 1803. 8°. (B 1459)

Woodward, Bernard Bolingbroke. History of Wales. London, 1852. 2 v. 8°.

Woodward, Cyrus, *Funeral sermon on.* 1782. *See* **Woodward,** S. (B 867, 911)

Woodward, David. Narrative cont. an account of a captivity among the Malays in the island of Celebes; app., containing narratives of escapes from shipwrecks, *etc.* London, 1804. 8°.

Woodward, Ebenezer, *M.D.* OBITUARY. (*In* **Mass. Med. Soc.** Med. comm., v. 11. 1866.)

Woodward, *Judge* George W. KEMBLE, F. A. Views of Judge Woodward and Bp. Hopkins on slavery; illustrated from the Journal of a residence on a Georgian plantation. [Phila., 1863.] 8°. (B 1481)

Woodward, J. M. On the manufacture of needles and fish-hooks. (*In* **Timmins,** S. Resources of Birmingham. 1866.)

Woodward, James W. Sermon, May 24, 1813, funeral of E. Burroughs. Boston, 1814. 8°. (B 336)

Woodward, John, *M.D., b.* 1665, *d.* 1728. Essay towards a natural history of the Earth, *etc.* 3d ed. London, 1723. 8°.
— ARBUTHNOT, J. Examination of W.'s 'Account of the deluge', *etc.* (*In his* Miscellaneous works, v. 2. 1751.)

Woodward, John, *Funeral sermon on.* 1741. *See* **Williams,** S. (C 202)

Woodward, John Anson. The anonymous kiss; a vaudeville. (No. 64 *of* **Spencer's** univ. stage.)
— Bouquet; a commedietta. (No. 54 *of* **Spencer's** univ. stage.)
— Madame is abed; a vaudeville. (No. 63 *of* **Spencer's** univ. stage.)
— Which will have him? a vaudeville. (No. 62 *of* **Spencer's** univ. stage.)

Woodward, Joseph Janvier, *Assist. Surg., U.S.A.* Catalogue of the medical section of the U. S. Army Medical Museum; prepared under the direction of the Surgeon-General. Wash., 1867. 4°.

— Hospital steward's manual. Philadelphia, 1862. 12°.

— Report on the extent and nature of the materials for the preparation of a medical history of the rebellion. (*In* **United States.** *Surgeon General.* Circular, no. 6. 1865.) — Report on epidemic cholera in the army of the United States during the year 1866. (*In* no. 5. 1867.) — Report on epidemic cholera and yellow fever in the army of the United States during the year 1867. (*In* no. 1. 1868.)

Woodward, Josiah. Copy of a letter from the pastors and professors of the Church and Academy at Geneva to the King of Prussia; his answer, together with the manner of the joint administration of the Lord's supper by Lutheran and Calvinist ministers. London, 1708. 4°.

— The divine original and incomparable excellency of the Christian religion asserted and vindicated. 1710. (*In* **Boyle** lecture sermons, v. 2. 1739.)

Woodward, Richard, *Bp. of Cloyne.* Observations on the indecent and illiberal strictures against [him] contained in a pamphlet lately published under the title of 'Mr. O'Leary's defence'. Dublin, 1787. 8°. (B 860)

— The present state of the Church of Ireland; subjoined, some reflections on the impracticability of a proper commutation for tithes, and a general account of the insurrections in Munster. Dublin, 1787. 8°.

— *Same.* 7th ed., with additions. London, 1787. 8°. (B 762)

— Butler, J. Justification of the tenets of the Roman Catholic religion, and refutation of the charges brought against its clergy by [W.]. Lond., 1787. 8°. (B 149)

— Campbell, W. Vindication of the principles of the Presbyterians of Ireland. 2d ed. London, 1787. 8°. (B 1363)

— O'Leary, A. Defence of [his] conduct and writings during the disturbances in Munster; in answer to the insinuations of R. Woodward. London, 1787. 8°. (B 341)

Woodward, Samuel. Help of the Lord in signal deliverances to be acknowledged; sermon, Lexington, commemoration of Apr. 19, 1775. Boston, 1779. 8°. (B 235, 840)

— Office, *etc.*, of a watchman of Israel; sermon, ordination of J. Wheeler, Harvard, Dec. 12, 1759. Boston, 1760. 8°. (B 275)

— Sermon, ordination of J. Marsh, Jan. 12, 1774. New Haven, [1774]. 8°. (B 144, 911)

— Submission to the Providence of God; sermon, Sept. 15, 1782, death of C. Woodward. Boston, 1783. 8°. (B 867, 911)

— Thanksgiving sermon, Oct. 9, 1760; reduction of Montreal, and the entire conquest of Canada. Boston, 1760. 8°. (B 146, 911)

Woodward, Samuel Bayard, *M.D.* Essays on asylums for inebriates. [Worcester, 1838.] 8°. (B 1748)

— Hints for the young in rel. to the health of body and mind. Boston, 1856. 24°. (D 39)

— Biographical notices of W. (*In* **Mass. Med. Soc.** Med. comm., v. 8. 1854.)

Woodward, Samuel P. Manual of the mollusca; or, Treatise of recent and fossil shells; illust. by N. N. Waterhouse and J. W. Lowry. London, *Weale*, 1851-56. 3 pt. 12°.

Woodward, Thomas. Columbian Plutarch; an exemplification of distinguished American characters. Phila., 1819. 12°.

Contents. Columbus. — Vesputius. — J. Cabot. — S. Cabot. — J. Cartier. — J. Smith. — J. Robinson. — G. Calvert. — L. Calvert. — W. Penn. — J. Bartram. — A. Benezet. — J. Warren. — N. Greene. — B. Franklin. — J. Hancock. — D. Rittenhouse. — A. Wayne. — G. Washington. — P. Henry. — S. Adams. — A. Hamilton. — G. Wythe. — F. Ames. — B. Rush. — D. Ramsay. — H. Adams. — T. Jefferson.

Woodward, Wm. Elliot. Bibliotheca Americana; catalogue of the library of W. Bost., 1869. 8°.

— Historical series. Roxbury, *privately printed* 1864. 8 v. (v. 5-7 w.). 4°.

Namely. Vol. 1, 2. Records of Salem witchcraft. 3, 4. Hubbard, W. Hist. of the Indian wars in New Eng. 5-7. *Wanting.* 8. Drake, S. J. Annals of witchcraft in N. Eng.

Woodward, Wm. H. Treasurer's report. (*In* **Documents** rel. to Dartmouth Coll. 1816.)

— Farrar, T. Report of the case of the trustees of Dartmouth College against W. H. W. Portsmouth, [1819]. 8°.

— New Hampshire. *Superior Court.* Opinion in the case of Dartmouth Coll. *vs.* W. H. W. Concord, 1818. 8°. (B 263)

— Perkins, C. Eulogy. Hanover, 1818. 8°. (B 1194)

Woodworth, Abner. Meteorite in Mexico. (*In* **Smithsonian Inst.** Report, 1867.)

Woodworth, John. Reminiscences of Troy, from its settlement to 1807. Albany, 1853. 8°.

Woodworth, Samuel. The forest rose; a drama. (*In* **Sargent**, E. Mod. stand. dr., v. 41.)

— Poems, odes, songs, and other metrical effusions. N. Y., 1818. 16°.

Woodworth, Westerlo. Oration before the Young Men's Association, July 4. Albany, 1834. 8°. (B 1203)

Wool, John Ellis, *Major General.* Savage, J. (*In his* Our living representative men. 1860.)

Wool.

— *History.* Bischoff, J. Comprehensive history of the woollen and worsted manufacture and of sheep. London, 1842. 2 v. 8°.

— — Samuel Brothers. Wool and woolen manufactures of Gr. Britain; hist. sketch. London, 1859. 8°.

— — Taylor, W. C. The hand-book of silk, cotton, and woollen manufactures. London, 1843. 16°.

— Adams, N. J. de. Nuevo reglamento para las fabricas de seda y de lana. [1759.] (*In* **Valladares, A.** Seman. erud., v. 11. 1788.)

— Wily, J. Treatise on the propagation of sheep, the manufacture of wool, *etc.* Williamsburg, 1765. 12°. (W 46)

— Turnor, E. Short view of the proceedings of committees [on] the intended petition for a limited exportation of wool. [1781, 82.] (*In* **Pamphleteer**, 1821; v. 23 of **B 838**)

— Contrast, The; comparison between our woollen, linen, cotton, and silk manufactures. London, 1782. 8°. (B 1536)

— Robbins, A. C. Account of the first woollen manufactory in the U. S. [1783.] (*In* **Maine Hist. Soc.** Col., v. 4. 1856.)

— Wansey, H. Wool encouraged without exportation; practical observations on wool and the woollen manufacture. London, 1791. 8°. (W 41)

— Holroyd, J. B., 1*st Earl of Sheffield.* On the trade in wool and woollens. 1809-12. (*In* **Pamphleteer**, 1814; v. 3 of B 838) — Report at the meeting at Lewes Wool Fair. [1813.] (*In* 1814; v. 4 of B 838)

— McDuffie, G. Speech on the woollens' bill. Wash., 1827. 8°. (B 1831)

— Benton, C., *and* Barry, S. F. Statistical view of the number of sheep [in the New England and Middle States]; and account of the principle woolen manufactories. Camb., 1837. 12°.

— Gr. Brit. *Inspector Gen. of Exports and Imports.* Account of the quantity of sheep and lambs' wool imported [and] exported, [also] an account of British manufactures exported in 1839. [Lond., 1840.] f°. (E 45)

— Collamer, J. Speech on wool and woolens. Wash., 1844. 8°. (B 1174)

— Boston. Board of Trade. Report on wool, 1858, 1859, 1863. Boston, [1859]-64. 8°. (E 127)

— Baines, E. The woolen manufacture of England. [1858.] (*In* **Statistical Society.** Journal, v. 22. 1859.)

— Turgan, J. Filature de laine de Davin. (*In his* Les grandes usines de France, v. 2. 1863.)

— REYBAUD, M. R. L. Rapport sur la condition des ouvriers qui vivent de l'industrie de la laine. (*In* **Paris. Instit.** *Ac. d. Sci. Mor.* Mémoires, v. 12. 1865.)
— FRANCE. *Com. Imp. de l'Exposition de* 1867. (*In their* Rapports du jury, v. 4.) — MOLL, L. Laines. (*In* v. 6.)
— MUDGE, E. R., *and* HAYES, J. L. Report upon wool and manufactures of wool. (*In* **U. S.** *Com. Paris Expos.* 1867. Reports, v. 6. 1868.)
— HAMILTON, A. Wool supply. (*In* **Statist. Soc.** Journ., v. 33. 1870.)

See also **Manufactures**; — **Sheep**; — **Shetland wool**; — **Textile fabrics**; — **Worsted.**

Wool manufacturers. *See* **Nat. Assoc. of Wool Manufacturers.**

Wool gathering. *See* **Dodge, M. A.**

Woolams, J. Le cuisinier anglais. 1810. *See* **Collingwood, F.**

Wooler, J. P. Founded on facts; farce. (No. 88 *of* **De Witt's** acting plays.)
— Locked in; comedietta. (No. 109 *of* **De Witt's** acting plays.)
— Marriage at any price; original farce. (No. 63 *of* **De Witt's** acting plays.)
— Orange blossoms; a comedietta. (No. 97 *of* **De Witt's** acting plays.)
— Sisterly service; original comedietta. (No. 43 *of* **De Witt's** acting plays.)

Wooley, Charles. Two years journal in New York, and part of its territories in America, 1679. New ed. with an introd. and notes, by E. B. O'Callaghan. N. Y., 1860. 8°. (Gowans' Bibl. Amer., v. 2.)

Woolhouse, W. S. B. Elements of the differential calculus. 2d ed. London, *Weale*, 1854. 12°.
— Essay on eclipses. (*In* **Nautical** almanac, 1836.)
— Measures, weights, and moneys of all nations; and an analysis of the Christian, Hebrew, and Mahometan calendars. London, *Weale*, 1856. 12°.

Woolley, *Rev.* William. Cure for canting; or, The grand impostors of St. Stephen's and Surrey Chapels unmasked; letter to R. Hill. London, 1794. 8°. (**B 777**)

Woolman, John. Works. London, 1775. 8°.
Contents. Life and travels. — Pure wisdom and human policy. — Labor. — Schools. — The right use of the Lord's outward gifts. — On serving the Lord in our outward employments. — The example of Christ. — Merchandizing. — Divine admonitions. — Loving our neighbors. — On a sailor's life. — Silent worship. — An epistle.
— Journal; with an introd. by J. G. Whittier. Boston, 1871. 12°.

Woolridge, J. Systema horti-culturæ; art of gardening. 3d ed. with add. London, 1688. 16°.

Woolrych, Humphrey Wm. Four letters on the bill for a general registry of deeds rel. to real property. London, 1833. 8°. (**B 1529**)
— Life of Sir E. Coke. London, 1826. 8°.
— Lives of eminent serjeants-at-law of the English bar. London, 1869. 2 v. 8°.
Contents. Vol. 1. Sir J. Maynard. — J. Row. — W. Bendloes. — E. Plowden. — W. Fleetwood. — Sir W. Methold. — N. Barham. — Sir J. Hecle. — Sir J. Davys. — Sir R. Hitcham. — Sir F. More. — Sir T. Crew. — J. Hoskins. — R. Callis. — Sir J. Glanville. — B. Whitelocke. — Sir H. Finch. — W. Conyers. — Sir J. Kelyng. — Sir T. Hardres. — T. Conyers. — Sir T. Skipwith. — Sir N. Bond. — Sir J. Tremaine. — Sir J. Trenchard. — Sir G. Strode. — Sir W. Thompson. 2. Sir J. Darnal. — T. Carthew. — C. Boynthon. — J. Hooke. — Sir H. Chauncey. — W. Salkeld. — Sir J. Darnal, Jr. — J. Toller. — Sir J. Chesshyre. — W. Hawkins. — M. Skinner. — T. Barnardiston. — E. Leeds. — W. Wynne. — Sir S. Prime. — W. Whitaker. — E. Willes. — J. Glyn. — W. Davy. — G. Hill. — J. Adair. — G. Bond. — J. Williams. — S. Heywood. — J. Lens. — Sir A. Peel. — A. Onslow. — B. J. Sellon. — Sir S. Shepherd. — C. Wilkins.
— Memoirs of Judge Jeffreys. London, 1827. 8°.
— Punishment of death. (*In* **Nat. Assoc. Prom. Soc. Sci.** Trans., 1857.)

Woolsey, Georgiana M. BROCKETT, L. P. (*In his* Woman's work in the civil war. 1867.)

Woolsey, Jane Stuart. Hospital days. N. Y., 1870. 8°.
— BROCKETT, L. P. (*In his* Woman's work in the civil war. 1867.)

Woolsey, Theodore Dwight. The death of a young man; sermon, Yale College, June 1, death of A. Hebard. N. Haven, 1851. 8°. (**B 1218**)
— The equilibrium between physical and moral truth. (*In* **Boston** lectures. 1870.)
— Essay on divorce and divorce legislation with special reference to the United States. N. Y., 1869. 12°.
— Introduction to the study of international law. Boston, 1860. 12°.
— *Same.* 2d ed. revised and enlarged. N. Y., 1864. 8°.
— Nature and sphere of police power. (*In* **Amer. Soc. Sci. Assoc.** Journ., v. 3. 1871.)
— Religion of the present and of the future. N. Y., 1871. 12°.
— Remarks on a letter from J. L. Porter, of Damascus, containing Greek inscriptions. (*In* **Amer. Orient. Soc.** Journ., v. 5. 1856.)

Woolsey, Wm. W., *and others.* Brief view of the law rel. to transactions between principals and agents. *n.p.*, 1825. 8°. (**B 544**)

Woolston, Thomas. Defence of his discourse on the miracles of our Saviour. Pt. 2. London, 1730. 8°. (**B 1711**)
— BOWMAN, W. Defense of our Saviour's miracle of cursing the fig-tree, in answer to Woolston's discourse. London, 1721. 8°. (**E 124**)
— BROWNE, S. A fit rebuke to a ludicrous infidel; remarks on Woolston's 5th discourse on the miracles. London, 1732. 8°. (**B 117**)
— DISCOURSE on the mystery and hist. of the Scriptures, and nature and use of miracles; occas. by Woolston's discourses on miracles. London, 1739. 8°. (**E 124**)
— EXPOSTULATORY letter to T. W. on account of his late writings; by a clergyman. London, 1730. 8°. (**B 1864**)
— GARDINER, W. Short answer to a long rabbinical letter supposed to be wrote to Mr. W. London, 1730. 8°. (**C 230**)
— LARDNER, N. Vindication of three of our Saviour's miracles; in answer to the objections of T. W. London, 1729. 8°. (**B 1864**)
— *Same.* (*In his* Works, v. 11. 1788.)
— LIFE of W.; with an account of his writings. London, 1733. 8°.
— NICERON, J. P. (*In his* Mém, v. 40. 1739.)
— PEARCE, Z. Miracles of Jesus vindicated [against W.'s Objections]. 2d ed. London, 1729. 3 pts. 8°. (**B 1864**)
— SHERLOCK, T. Tryal of the witnesses of the resurrection of Jesus; [in which] T. Woolston's 'Objections' are considered. 4th ed. London, 1729. 8°. (**B 1864**)
— STEBBING, H. Defence of the Scripture history; in answer to W.'s 5th disc. on the Saviour's miracles. London, 1730. 8°. (**B 117, 124**)

Woolton, John, *Bp. of Chester.* Christian manual; or, Of the life and manners of the true Christian. Camb., *Parker Soc.*, 1851. 8°.

Woolworth, James M. Nebraska in 1857. Omaha, 1857. 12°.

Wooster, *Maj.-Gen.* David. Statisticks of New Haven, 1774. (*In* **Mass. Hist. Soc.** Col., v. 12. 1814.)
— HEADLEY, J. T. Maj.-Gen. W. (*In his* Washington, v. 2. 1847.)
— P., T. D. Wooster. (*In* **Longacre, J. B.,** *and* **Herring, J.** Nat. portr. gal., v. 2. 1835.)

Wooten, H. V., *M.D.* Character; valedictory address at the Memphis Medical Coll., Feb. Memphis, 1853. 8°. (**B 1565**)

Worcester, *2d Marq. of.* *See* **Somerset, E.**

Worcester, Henry A. The sabbath. Boston, 1840. 16°.

Worcester, *Rev.* Isaac R. Discourse occasioned by the recent duel at Washington, Littleton, N. H., fast day, Apr. 12. Concord, 1838. 8°. (**B 1840**)

Worcester, Jonathan Fox. Memorial of the class of 1827, Dartmouth College. 2d ed. enlarged. Hanover, 1869. 8°.

Worcester, Joseph Emerson. Comprehensive pronouncing and explanatory dictionary of the English language. 2d ed. N. Y., 1831. 12°.
— *Same.* Universal and critical dictionary. Boston, 1846. 8°.
— *Same, abridged.* Comprehensive, pron., and explan. dictionary. Rev. and enl. Boston, 1848. 12°.
— *Same.* Dictionary. Rev. with add. Boston, 1851. 12°.
— *Same.* Pronouncing, explanatory, and synonymous dictionary. Boston, 1855. 8°.
— *Same.* Dictionary. Boston, 1860. 4°.
— *Same.* Boston, 1864. 4°.
— Elements of geography. Boston, 1819. 12°.
— *Same.* Improved ed. Boston, 1840. 12°.
— *Same.* Rev. ed. Boston, 1846. 12°.
— Elements of history, ancient and modern; with historical charts. 2d ed. Boston, 1826. 12°.
— *Same.* Boston, 1832. 12°.
— *Same.* New ed. revised and enlarged. Boston, 1850. 12°.
— Epitome of modern geography. Boston, 1820. 12°.
— Gazetteer of the United States. Andover, 1818. 8°.
— A geographical dictionary; or, Universal gazetteer, ancient and modern. Andover, 1817. 2 v. 8°.
— Historical atlas. 4th ed. Boston, 1830. f°.
— *Same.* 7th ed. Boston, 1835. f°.
— *Same.* New ed. Camb., 1852. f°.
— Remarks on longevity and the expectation of life in the U. S., rel. more particularly to N. H. (*In* **Amer. Acad.** Mem., n.s., v. 1. 1833.)
— Sketches of the Earth and its inhabitants. Boston, 1823. 12°.

Worcester, Leonard. Appeal to Rev. S. Aiken conc. his 'Appeal to the churches'. Montpelier, Vt., 1821. 8°. (**B 1393**)
— Discourse on the Alton outrage, Peacham, Vt., Dec. 17, 1837. Concord, 1838. 8°. (**B 1840**)
— Letters and remarks [on] a sermon by A. Bancroft, in opposition to the doctrine of election. Worcester, 1795. 8°. (**B 272**)
— Sermon, Oct. 15. Windsor, Vt., 1809. 8°. (**B 870**)

Worcester, Noah. Appeal to the candid. No. 1. *n.t.p.* [17—.] 8°. (**B 1360**)
— Bible news of the Father, Son, and Holy Spirit. Concord, 1810. 8°.
— *Other copies.* (**B 141, 261**)
— Candid discussion of the subject of close communion, addressed to T. Baldwin. Worcester, 1794. 8°. (**B 523**)
— Coup d'œil raisonné sur la guerre. Londres, 1822. 8°. (**B 542**)
— The doctrine of pronouns applied to Christ's testimony of himself. Boston, 1827. 12°. (A. U. A. 1st ser. 15. **C 168**, v. 2.)
— Friendly review of remarkable extracts relative to the sufferings of Christ. Cambridge, 1832. 8°. (**C 226, D 62**)
— Impartial inquiries resp. the progress of the Baptist denomination. Worcester, 1794. 8°. (**B 522**)
— Impartial review of testimonies in favor of the divinity of the Son of God. Concord, 1810. 12°. (**C 81, 226**)
— Letter to Rev. T. Baldwin. Concord, 1791. 8°. (**C 315**)
— The peace catechism; by Philo Pacificus. Boston, 1816. 8°. (**C 56**)
— A remedy for schism; conference between Ariel and Clement. Brooklyn, [18—]. 8°. (**C 226**)
— Respectful address to the Trinitarian clergy rel. to their manner of treating opponents. Boston, 1812. 12°. (**C 84, D 63**)
— Solemn reasons for declining to adopt the Baptist theory and practice. Concord, 1807. 8°. (**C 238**)
— *Same.* 2d ed. Charlestown, 1809. 12°. (**C 109**)
— *Same.* 4th ed. N. Y., 1809. 8°. (**B 1852**)
— Solemn review of the custom of war; by Philo Pacificus. 5th ed. Camb., 1816. 8°. (**B 542, 1274**)
— *Same.* Prov., 1818. 8°. (**B 1786**)
— *Same.* 11th Amer. ed. rev. Boston, 1833. 8°. (**B 1088, 1165, 1768, 1786, 1843, 1888, 2016**)
— Some difficulties for solution; letter to Rev. J. Murray conc. his 'Origin of evil', *etc.* Newburyport, 1786. 8°. (**B 150**)
— Thoughts on the personality of the word of God. Boston, 1836. 12°. (**C 200**)
See also **Friend** of peace.
— Andros, T. Bible news of the Father, Son, and Holy Ghost as reported by N. Worcester not correct. Boston, 1813. 8°. (**B 263**)
— Channing, W. E. Tribute to the memory of W.; discourse. Boston, 1837. 8°. (**B 1228, 1247, 1806, 1880**)
— Farley, S. Letters to N. Worcester, on his 'Bible news'. Windsor, 1813. 12°. (**C 222, 241**)
— Kinne, A. Essay on the Sonship of Christ; with remarks on [N. Worcester's] 'Bible news'. Boston, 1814. 12°. (**C 85**)
— Letters on 'Bible news'.] *n.t.p.* [181-.] 8°. (**B 260**)
— Life. (*In* **Lives** of disting. shoemakers. 1849.)
— Ware, H., *Jr.* Memoirs of Worcester; with preface and notes by S. Worcester. Boston, 1844. 8°.

Worcester, *Rev.* Samuel, *d.* 1821. The Christian mourning with hope; sermon on the death of Mrs. Emerson; annexed, [her] writings, with a sketch of her life. Boston, 1809. 12°. (**C 109**)
— The Christian's confidence; sermon. funeral of R. Anderson, Feb. 15. Boston, 1814. 8°. (**B 336**)
— *Same.* Boston, 1809. 12°. (**C 109**)
— The commission and the object of the gospel minister; sermon, Apr. 26, ordination of W. Cogswell. Dedham, 1815. 8°. (**B 336**)
— Courage and success to the good; discourse, Aug. 20 [fast-day], on account of the war with Gr. Brit.; also discourse, Aug. 9, 1812, [martyrdom of St. Stephen]. Salem, 1812. 8°. (**B 336**)
— Discourse before the New Jerusalem Church, Boston, Christmas, 1818. Boston, 1819. 8°. (**B 1306**)
— The drunkard a destroyer; discourse, May 30. Boston, 1817. 4°. (**B 336**)
— Facts and documents exhibiting a summary view of the ecclesiastical affairs in Fitchburg. Boston, 1802. 8°. (**B 199, C 12**)
— The foundation of God sure and sealed; sermon. July 31, installation of E. D. Griffin. Boston, 1811. 8°. (**B 336**)
— Kingdom of the Messiah; sermon before the For. Miss. Soc. of Salem and vicinity, Jan. 6. Salem, 1813. 8°. (**B 1330**)
— Knowledge of Christ supremely important; sermon, June 8, installation of J. Webster, Hampden, N. H. Salem, 1808. 8°. (**B 864**)
— Letter to W. E. Channing on his letter to S. C. Thatcher, rel. to the review in the Panoplist of Amer. Unitarianism. Boston, 1815. 8°. (**B 266, 298, 2537**)
— 2d letter to W. E. Channing on Unitarianism. 2d ed. Boston, 1815. 8°. (**B 298, 2537**)
— *Same.* 3d ed. Boston, 1815. 8°. (**B 266**)
— 3d letter to Channing on Unitarianism. Boston, 1815. 8°. (**B 266**)
— Martyrdom of St. Stephen. *See, above,* 'Courage and success'.
— Messiah of the Scriptures, The; sermon, Salem, Apr. 8. Boston, 1808. 8°. (**B 243, 245**)
— Oration, New Ipswich, July 4. Amherst, N. H., 1796. 8°. (**B 342, 421**)
— Paul on Mars Hill; sermon, June 21, ordination of S. J. Mills [and others], missionaries. Andover, 1815. 8°. (**B 336**)
— Select hymns. (*In* **Watts**, I. Psalms and hymns. 1847.)
— Righteousness conducive to happiness; sermon, Reading, Apr. 15. Salem, 1804. 8°. (**B 1886**)
— Sermons on various subjects, practical and doctrinal. Salem, 1823. 8°.
— Substance of a discourse; martyrdom of Stephen. (*In his* Courage and success. 1812. **B 336**)
— The testimony of Jehovah sure and perfect; sermon, Salem, before the Bible Soc. of Salem, June 10. Salem, 1818. 8°. (**B 336, 1327**)
— True liberality; sermon, Oct. 23. Andover, 1816. 8°. (**B 336, 1329**)
— Two discourses on the perpetuity of God's covenant with Abraham and his seed. Salem, 1805. 8°. (**B 911, 1238**)

— Wisdom of God; sermon before the Mass. Miss. Soc. at their 10th annual meeting, Boston, May 30. Boston, 1809. 8°. (B 911)
— CHANNING, W. E. Remarks on Worcester's letter to Channing on the 'Review', *etc.* Boston, 1815. 8°. (B 266, 298)
— - Remarks on Worcester's 2d letter to Channing on American Unitarianism. Boston, 1815. 8°. (B 266, 298, 2537)
— CURSORY remarks on Worcester's 2d letter on the trinity; by a layman. Boston, 1815. 8°. (B 266)
— LOWELL, J. Are you a Christian or a Calvinist? suggested by 'Review of American Unitarianism', and Worcester's 'Letter to Channing'; by a layman. Boston, 1815. 8°. (B 266, 1388, 2537)
— NARRATIVE of the relig. controversy in Fitchburg; with comments [on] 'Facts and documents', *etc.* Worcester, 1804. 12°. (B 207, C 12, 32)
— NORTON, J. Candid and conciliatory review of the late corresp. of Worcester with Channing on Unitarianism; by a serious inquirer. Boston, 1817. 8°. (B 266)
— REVIEW of Amer. Unitarianism. From the Panoplist. *n.t.p.* [Boston, 1815.] 8°. (B 266)
— *Funeral sermon on.* 1821. *See* Cornelius, E. (B 283); — Woods, L. (B 283, 1237)

Worcester, Samuel. Fourth book of lessons for reading. *t.p.w.* [1834.] 12°.
— Third book for reading and spelling. 107th ed. Boston, 1844. 12°.

Worcester, *Rev.* Samuel Austin. Remarks on the principles of the Cherokee language. (*In* Schoolcraft, H. R. Hist. information respecting the history of the Indian tribes, pt. 2. 1852.)
— *and* Boudinot, E. Cherokee hymns. 2d ed. enl. New Echota, 1830. 24°. (D 13)
— *vs.* State of Georgia. UNITED STATES. *Supreme Court.* Opinion at Jan. term, 1832, by Chief Justice Marshall, *etc.* Washington, 1832. 8°. (B 1064, 1831, 1854, W 1801, 1805)

Worcester, Samuel Melancthon. Discourse, first centennial anniv. of the Tabernacle Church, Salem, Apr. 26. Salem, 1835. 8°. (B 1738)
— Memorial of the Old and New Tabernacle, Salem, Mass. Boston, 1855. 12°.
— New England's glory and crown; discourse, Plymouth, Dec. 22, 1848. 2d ed. Boston, 1849. 8°. (B 1571)
— Our country and our work; discourse at the Tabernacle, June 18. Salem, 1843. 8°. (B 1306)
— A review of the result of an ecclesiastical council convened at Salem, Mass., Dec. 4, 1849, *etc.* Boston, 1850. 8°. (B 1393)
— Tribute to the memory of J. Punchard; sermon, Feb. 16. Boston, 1857. 8°.

Worcester, Thomas. Appeal to the testimony of Christ with respect to what dishonors him; discourse. Boston, 1810. 8°. (B 336)
— Call for Scripture evidence that Christ is God; letter to S. Spring. Boston, 1811. 12°. (C 84, 150, D 63)
— Conversion of the jailor, and his baptism, with his household; sermon, Salisbury, Oct. 1. Concord, 1805. 8°. (B 1306)
— A discourse, Boston, thanksgiving. Boston, 1864. 8°. (B 1592)
— Discourse the Sunday following the death of W. Parsons. Boston, 1847. 8°. (B 1222)
— Distressing judgments, *etc.*; sermon, Salisbury, N. H., Jan. 4. Concord, 1813. 8°. (B 961)
— Jesus said unto him, follow me; discourse before the Boston Soc. of the New Jerusalem. Camb., 1822. 8°. (B 285, 1126)
— Letter to [W. Harris], moderator of the N. Hampshire Association. Boston, 1812. 12°. (C 84, 236)
— The most plain sense of Scripture the test of opinions; two unanswered letters to [W. Harris]. Boston, 1812. 12°. (C 84, 149)
— New chain of plain argument against Trinitarianism. Boston, 1817. 8°. (B 265)
— Our Savior's divinity in primitive purity; sermon on the divine sonship of Christ. Concord, 1810. 8°. (B 336)
— The record, *etc.*; concise view of the glory of Christ. Concord, 1811. 12°. (C 61)
— Sermons illustrative of the influence of a life according to the commandments, *etc.* Boston, 1824. 12°. (C 211)
— BARRETT, B. F. Plain letter to W., touching the author's intercourse with [him]. N. Y., 1864. 12°.

Worcester, Wm. *of.* *See* Guiliemus *Worcestrius.*
Worcester, *Bp of.* *See* Gauden, J.; — Hurd, R.; — Latimer, H.; — Maddox, I.
Worcester. *See also* Wooster.

Worcester, *England.* Ordinances, constitucions, and articles of the cyte of Worcestre. (*In* Smith, J. T. English gilds. 1870.)
— GREEN, V. History and antiquities of the city and suburbs of Worcester. London, 1796. 2 v. 4°.

Worcester, *Eng.* Cathedral. *See* Worcester, See of (NOAKE); — Worcester, See of.

Worcester (*Eng.*), Priory of. Annales prioratus de Wigornia, 1-1377. (*In* Luard, H. R. Annales monastici, v. 4. 1869.)
— Registrum sive Liber irrotularius et consuetudinarius prioratus beatæ Mariæ Wigorniensis; with introd. and notes by W. H. Hale. Londini, 1865. 4°. (Camden Soc., v. 91.)
See also, below, Worcester, See of (NOAKE).

Worcester (*Eng.*), See of. BRITTON, J. History and antiquities of the see and cathedral church of W. London, 1836. 4°.
— NOAKE, J. Monastery and cathedral of W. London, 1866. 16°.

Worcester, *Mass. Free Public Library.* Catalogue of the circulating department. Worcester, 1861. 12°.
— - *Same.* Worcester, 1870. 8°.
— LINCOLN, W. History of W., [1664]-1836. Worcester, 1837. 8°.
— - *Same.* Worcester, 1862. 8°.
— BARTON, W. S. Epitaphs from the cemetery on Worcester common, [1727-1824]. Worcester, 1848. 8°.
— PAINE, T., *and others.* Topog. descrip. of W. (*In* Mass. Hist. Soc. Col., v. 1. 1792.)
— HERSEY, C. History of Worcester, 1836-61. (*Appended to* Lincoln, W. Hist. of W. 1862.)
— - WORCESTER in 1850. Worcester, 1850. 16°.
— HOWLAND, H. J. The heart of the commonwealth; or, Worcester as it is. Worcester, 1856. 4°.
— MARVIN, A. P. History of Worcester in the war of the rebellion, [1861-64]. Worcester, 1870. 8°.
See also American Antiquarian Soc.

Worcester, *Mass.* Association of Ministers. A catechism, in three parts. 9th ed. Boston, 1837. 12°. (D 33)
— New catechism. 3d ed. Worcester, 1810. 24°. (D 13)

Worcester, *Mass.* 1st Church. Origin of the difficulties; and result of an ecclesiastical council to investigate charges against C. A. Goodrich. Worcester, 1820. 8°.
— *Another copy.* (B 270)
— AUSTIN, S. Protest against the proceedings of the 1st Church. Worcester, 1821. 8°. (B 538)
— REMARKS on the late publications of the 1st Church in Worcester, rel. to the 'Origin and progress of difficulties' in that church. Worcester, 1821. 8°. (B 270, 538)

Worcester, *Mass.* 2d Church. BANCROFT, A. Sermon, termination of 50 years of his ministry. Worcester, 1836. 8°. (B 1325)
— - The world passeth away, *etc.*; sermon before the 2d Christian Church and Soc. in W., Jan. 6. Worcester, 1811. 8°. (B 304)
— HILL, A. Minister and parish; discourse, 25th anniv. of his ordination. Worcester, 1852. 8°. (B 1319, 1325)
— - Pastor's record; sermon before the 2d Cong. Society, Mar. 28. Camb., 1867. 8°.

Worcester, *Mass.* Calvinist Church. BROOKFIELD ASSOCIATION. Communication to the Council which ordained L. I. Hoadly. Worcester, 1824. 8°. (B 1394)

Worcester, *Mass.* Convention of Friends of Peace, 1812. Proceedings of a convention of delegates from forty-one towns. Worcester, 1812. 8°. (B 441)

Worcester, *Mass.* Convention of Ministers. Proceedings on slavery. Worcester, 1838. 8°. (B 1475)

Worcester. State Lunatic Asylum. *See* Mass. *State Lunatic Hospital*, p. 1897.

Worcester. Whig State Convention. *See* Whig Party in Mass.

Worcester, *ship*. CASE of Capt. T. Green, commander of the ship Worcester, and his crew, tried and condemned for pyracy and murther in the High Court of Admiralty of Scotland. London, 1705. 4°. (B 1434)

Worcester almanac and directory; by H. J. Howland, 1844–69, 73. Worcester, 1844–73. 16 v. 16°.

Worcester County, *Mass.* *House of Correction.* Account of expenses, Feb. 1819 - March 1825. Boston, 1826. 8°. (B 1768)

— WHITNEY, P. History of W. Co. Worcester, 1793. 8°.

— FISKE, O. Epidemics in the County, 1796. (*In* Mass. Med. Soc. Med. comm., v. 2. 1813.)

— WORCESTER CO. COMMITTEE. Account of the proposed canal from Worcester to Providence, [with] report of engineer and remarks on inland navigation. Worcester, 1822. 8°. (B 902)

— HARTWELL, C., *and* HITCHCOCK, E., *Jr.* Description of certain mineral localities, chiefly in the northern part of Worcester and Franklin Cos., in Mass. (*In* Amer. Assoc. Proc., v. 2. 1850.)

— CHOATE, R. Argument for the division of Worcester County, on petition of O. L. Huntley and others, before the legislative committee, April. Boston, 1854. 8°. (B 1596)

— BOUTWELL, G. S. Argument on the petitions for the division of Middlesex and Worcester Counties, before the legislative committee, March 25. *n.t.p.* [Boston, 1855.] 8°. (B 1596)

— WALLING, H. F. Map. 1857.

See also Baptists, *Worcester Co., Mass.*; — Evesham; — Worcester.

Worcester Co. Committee. An acc. of the proposed canal from Worcester to Providence; [with] report of engineer and remarks on inland navigation. Worcester, 1822. 8°. (B 902)

Worcester magazine; April 1786 - March 1788. Worcester, 1786–88. 4 v. 8°.

Worcester magazine and historical journal. Vol. 1, 2, Oct. 1825 - Apr. 1826. Worcester, 1826. 2 v. 8°.

Worcester North Agricultural Society. Transactions, 1863. Fitchburg, 1863. 8°.

Worcestershire, *Eng.* POMEROY, W. T. General view of the agriculture of the County of Worcester. London, 1794. 4°. (W 75)

— LAIRD, F. C. Worcestershire. (*In* Beauties of England and Wales, v. 15. 1814.)

— HANDBOOK for travellers in Worcestershire, *etc.* London, *Murray*, 1867. 12°.

Word. *See* Holy Spirit; — Logos.

Word in season, A; or, The soldier's widow; [by L. M. Sargent]. 7th ed. Boston, 1835. 24°.

Word of the spirit to the Church; [by C. A. Bartol]. Boston, 1859. 12°.

Word to Federalists and to those who love the memory of Washington. *n.p.*, [1810]. 8°. (B 436, 971, 2019)

Word to the wise, A; by H. Kelly. (*In* Bell's Brit. theatre, v. 30. 1797.)

Word within-doors, A; or, A reply to 'A word without-doors'. *n.t.p.* [168-?] f°. (A 54)

Worde, Wynkyn de. The boke of kervynge. 1413 [1513]. (*In* Furnivall, F. J. The babees book. 1868.)

Worden, John. Chemical articles. (*In* Sutton, T. Dict. of photography. 1858.)

Worden, John Lorimer. HEADLEY, J. T. (*In his* Farragut and our naval commanders. 1867.)

Words. WHITE, R. G. Words and their uses. N. Y., 1870. 8°.

Note. From the Galaxy, v. 3–8. 1867–69.

See also English language; — Etymology; — Grammar; — Language; — Rhetoric.

Words for the hour; by [J. W. Howe]. Boston, 1857. 16°.

Words of a believer. *See* La Mennais, H. F. R. de.

Words of Christ, The, recorded by the Evangelists; [by G. Field]. New ed. rev. Lond., 1847. 8°.

Words of counsel to men of business; by a man of business. *n.p.*, [1856]. 8°. (B 1507)

Wordsworth, Charles. On Shakspeare's knowledge and use of the Bible. London, 1864. 8°.

Wordsworth, Christopher, *b.* 1774, *d.* 1846. Christian institutes; a series of discourses and tracts selected, arranged, and illustrated with notes. 2d ed. London, 1842. 4 v. 8°.

Contents. Vol. 1. Evidences of natural and revealed religion. — Natural law. — Principles of Christianity. 2. Sundry articles of the creed, and other topics of Christian doctrine. 3. Principles of society and of government, civil and ecclesiastical. 4. Polemical theology. — Popery. — Puritanism. — Non-conformity.

— Ecclesiastical biography. 3d ed. London, 1839. 4 v. 8°.

Contents. Vol. 1. Introduction. — Inett, R. British church and the Anglican; — King Henry II. and Archbishop Becket; — National churches; — Papal usurpations on rights of the civil government; — King John, the barons, and Pope Innocent III.; — Papal usurpations in church and state. — Bentley, R. Doctrinal corruptions of popery. — Fox, J. J. Wickliffe. — Wm. Thorpe; — Lord Cobham; — Supplementary extracts; — Invention of printing; — Chaucer and Gower; — Progress of reformation and of persecution; — Martin Luther. — Erasmus, D. Dean Colet. — Cavendish, G. Cardinal Wolsey. 2. Fox, J. T. Bilney; — Sir T. More; — Wm. Tindall; — Cromwell, Earl of Essex; — J. Rogers; — Bp. Hooper; — Rowland Taylor; — Bp. Latimer. 3. Fox, J. Bp. Ridley; — Archbishop Cranmer. — Strype, J. T. Mountain. — Biog. of Bp. Jewel. — Carleton, G., *Bp.* B. Gilpin. — Walton, I. R. Hooker. — Paul, *Sir* G. Archbishop Whitgift. — Walton, I. J. Donne. 4. Walton, I. G. Herbert; — Sir H. Wotton. — Peckard, P. N. Ferrar. — Hall. J. Biog., by himself. — Fell, *Bp.* J. H. Hammond. — Walton, I. Bp. Sanderson. — Baxter, R. Biog. by himself. — Burnet, *Bp.* G. Sir Matthew Hale; — J. Wilmot, Earl of Rochester. — Biog. of Archbp. Tillotson.

— King Charles I. the author of Icôn basilikè. Camb., London, 1828. 8°.

— Who wrote Εἰκὼν βασιλική? London, 1824. 8°.

— - Documentary supplement. London, 1825. 8°.

Wordsworth, Christopher, *the son*, *Bp. of Lincoln.* Athens and Attica. Lond., 1855. 12°.

— Interpretation of Scripture. (*In* Replies to 'Essays and reviews'. 1862.)

— The invasion of Russia by Napoleon. — Carmen Latinum. — Epigrammata. — Senarii Græci. (*In* Cambridge Univ. Prolusiones. 1828. B 1236)

— Journal of a tour in Italy. London, 1863. 2 v. 8°.

— Memoirs of Wm. Wordsworth. London, 1851. 2 v. 8°.

— Pompeian inscriptions. New ed. London, 1846. 8°.

— Theophilus Anglicanus; or, Instruction conc. the Church and the Anglican branch of it. 6th ed. London, 1850. 8°.

Wordsworth, J. C. Surgical instruments and apparatus. (*In* Holmes, T. Syst. of surg., v. 4. 1864.)

Wordsworth, *Mrs.* Mary. MARTINEAU, H. (*In her* Biog. sketches. 1869.)

Wordsworth, Wm. Poetical works. Boston, 1824. 4 v. 12°.

Contents. Vol. 1. Preface. — Essay; suppl. to preface. — Preface to Lyrical ballads. — Poems referring to childhood and early youth. — Juvenile pieces. — Poems founded on the affections. — Poems of the fancy. 2. Poems of the imagination. — Miscellaneous sonnets. 3. The River Duddon; a series of sonnets. — Poems of sentiment and reflection. — On the naming of places. — Inscriptions. — Poems ref. to old age. — Epitaphs and elegiac poems. — Ecclesiastical sketches. — Memorials of a tour on the continent. 4. The excursion.

— *Same.* [Ed. with life by J. R. Lowell.] Boston, 1854. 7 v. 16°.

Contents. Vol. 1. Sketch of W.'s life. — Poems written in youth. — Poems referring to childhood. — Poems founded on the affections. 2. Poems on the naming of places. — Poems of the fancy. — Poems of the imagination. — Miscel. sonnets. 3. Mem. of a tour in Scotland, 1803, 1814. — Poems dedicated to national independence and liberty. — Tour on the continent, 1820. — Mem. of a tour in Italy, 1837. — The River Duddon. — Yarrow revisited, and other poems. 4. The white doe of Rylestone. — Eccles. sonnets. — Evening voluntaries. — Poems composed during a tour in 1833. — Poems of sentiment and reflection. — Sonnets dedicated to liberty and order. — Sonnets upon the punishment of death. 5. Miscel. poems. — Inscriptions. — Selections from Chaucer, modernized. — Poems referring to old age. — Epitaphs and elegiac pieces. — Appendix, prefaces, *etc.* 6. The excursion. 7. The prelude. — Appendix.

— The prelude; or, Growth of a poet's mind. London, 1850. 8°.

— AUSTIN, W. S., *Jr.*, *and* R. J. Life of W. (*In their* Lives of the poets-laureate. 1853.)

— BRIMLEY, G. Wordsworth's poems. (*In his* Essays. 1860.)

— DE QUINCEY, T. (*In his* Lit. reminiscences. 1851.)

— - Poetry of W. (*In his* Essays on the poets. 1853.)

— FONTENAY, A. (*In* **Revue** d. D. Mondes, août 1835.)

— GRAVES, R. P. Recollections of W. and the Lake country. (*In* **Afternoon** lectures, 1867–68.)

— HORNE, R. H. W. Wordsworth and L. Hunt. (*In his* New spirit of the age, v. 1. 1844.)

— HUTTON, R. H. Wordsworth and his genius. (*In his* Essays, v. 2. 1871.)

— MASSON, D. (*In his* Essays. 1856.)

— PHILLIPS, G. S. Memoirs of W., by January Searle. London, 1852. 8°.

— ROBERTSON, F. W. Lecture on W. (*In his* Lectures and addresses. 1859.)

— SHAIRP, J. C. (*In his* Studies. 1868.)

— WHIPPLE, E. P. (*In his* Essays, v. 1. 1848.)

— WILSON, J. (*In his* Essays crit., v. 1. 1856.)

— WORDSWORTH, C. Memoirs of W. London, 1851. 2 v. 8°.

Work, Alanson. THOMPSON, G. Prison life and reflections; narrative of the arrest, imprisonment, *etc.*, of Work, Burr, and Thomson, *etc.* 3d ed. Hartford, 1849. 12°.

Work, Working classes. *See* **Labor and Laboring classes** (p. 1646–47).

Work and play; or, Literary varieties. *See* **Bushnell, H.**

Workhouse. DUPPA, B. F. Education of pauper children in union workhouses. (*In* **Cent. Soc. of Educ.** Pub., v. 3. 1839.)

Working Brothers. Spiced slaw for southern digestion, and other papers, by J. J. Delchamps; with the constitution of the order. [Dish 1–3.] Mobile, 1863. 8°.

— *Same.* Dish no. 3. Mobile, 1862. 8°.

Working farmer, The; devoted to agriculture, *etc.*; ed. by J. J. Mapes; Feb. 1849 – Feb. 1855. Vol. 1–6. N. Y., 1850–54. 6 v. f°.

Workingman's companion; results of machinery. London, 1831. 18°.

Workingmen's Party. BERRIAN, H. Brief sketch of the origin of the party in N. Y. *n.p.*, [1840]. 8°. (B 1822)

— EVERETT, E. Lecture, Oct. 6, before the Charlestown Lyceum. Boston, 1830. 8°. (1761, 1793, 1884, 2009)

Workman, James. Letter to the citizens of the County of Orleans. New Orleans, 1807. 8°. (B 433)

— CASE of Mr. Workman for an alleged contempt of the Superior Court of the territory of Orleans. Phila., [1809]. 8°. (B 444)

— TRIALS of Workman and Col. L. Kerr for planning an expedition [against] Mexico. New Orleans, 1807. 12°. (C 104)

Workman, William. Progress of medical science. (*In* **Massachusetts Medical Society.** Medical communications, v. 8. 1854.)

Workman, The, and the franchise. *See* **Maurice, F. D.**

World. EDWARDS, J. Conc. the end for which God created the world. (*In his* Two dissertations. 1765.)

— HUGHES, T. S. Remarks on 'An essay on the eternity of the world'. (*In* **Pamphleteer,** 1826; v. 26 of B 838)

— *Maps.* BLAEU, J. Nova totius terrarum orbis tabula. *n.p.*, [16—]. (E 78, no. 4)

— - KÆR, P. Nova totius terrarum orbis tabula. Amst., [16—]. (E 78, no. 3)

— - RUDOLPHUS. Nova orbis terrarum delineatio. Norimb., 1630. (E 78, no. 5)

— - SEPTENTRIO; [map of the northern part of the world]. *n.p.*, [16—]. (E 78, no. 312)

— - VISSCHER, N. J. Meridies. [Amst.,] 1650. (E 78, no. 314)

See also **Astronomy; — Atlas; — Cosmogony; — Cosmography; — Earth; — Plurality of worlds; — Voyages round the world.**

World, The, for 1753–55; by Adam Fitz-Adam [E. Moore]. London, [1753–55]. 3 v. f°.

— *Same.* (Vol. 26–29 *of* **Chalmer's.** British essayists. 1802; — *and in* **Harrison's** British classics, v. 7. 1787.)

World, The; July 1860 – Dec. 1876. N. Y., 1869–76. 33 v. f°.

World before the deluge. *See* **Figuier, G. L.**

World in a village, The; by J. O'Keeffe. (*In his* Dram. works, v. 4. 1798.)

World tost at tennis, The; by T. Middleton. (*In his* Works, v. 5. 1840.)

World without souls; [by J. W. Cunningham]. 2d Boston ed. Boston, 1810. 12°.

Worlde, The, and the chylde. (*In* **Dodsley,** R. Col. of old plays, v. 12.)

Worlds, Plurality of. *See* **Plurality of worlds.**

World's progress; dictionary of dates. *See* **Putnam, G. P.**

Wormald, Thomas, *and* **McWhinnie, A. M.** Anatomical sketches and diagrams. London, 1843. 4°.

Wormeley, Mary Elizabeth. Amabel; a family history. N. Y., 1853. 12°.

Wormeley, *Miss* Katharine Prescott. United States Sanitary Commission; its purposes and its work. Boston, 1863. 12°.

— BROCKETT, L. P. (*In his* Woman's work in the civil war. 1867.)

Worms, Emile. Histoire commerciale de la Ligue Hanséatique. Paris, 1864. 8°.

Worms, Henry, *is said to be the author of* 'The Austro-Hungarian Empire and the policy of Count Beust. 1870'. (*See* p. 266, BEUST.)

Worms, *Germany.* ANNALES Wormatienses, 873–1366. (*In* **Pertz,** G. H. Monumenta Germaniæ historica, Scr., v. 17. 1861.)

Worms, *Germany.* **Kirche des Heiligen Paulus.** MOLLER, G. (*In his* Denkmäler. 1831.)

Worms. SAMUELSON, J., *and* HICKS, J. B. Humble creatures; the earthworm and house-fly. London, 1858. 12°.

Worms (intestinal). CHAMBERLAINE, W. Efficacy of cowhage in diseases occasioned by worms. [1784.] 9th ed. London, 1804. 12°.

— WELSH, T. Curious facts resp. worms. [1789.] (*In* **Massachusetts Medical Society.** Medical comm., v. 1. 1808.)

— BRERA, V. R. Maladies vermineuses; tr. et aug. par J. Bartoli et Calvet. [1802.] Paris, 1804. 8°.

— - A treatise on verminous diseases, *etc.*; tr. from French with add. by J. G. Coffin. Boston, 1817. 8°.

— FISHER, J. Observations on worms in the human body. [1806.] (*In* **Mass. Med. Soc.** Med. comm., v. 1. 1808.)

— RUDOLPH, C. A. Entozoorum sive vermium intestinalium historia naturalis. [1808–10.] Parisiis, Argent., Amst., 1810. 3 v. 8°.

— SIEBOLD, C.T. von. On tape and cystic worms; with an introd. on the origin of intestinal worms; tr. by T. H. Huxley. [1854.] London, 1857. 8°. (Sydenham Soc.)

— BENEDEN, P. J. van. Mémoire sur les vers intestinaux. (*In* **Paris. Inst.** *Ac. d. Sci.* Suppl. aux Comptes rendus, v. 2. 1861.)

— STURGIS, F. R. Human cestoids. Camb., 1867. 8°.

See also **Acanthocephala.**

Worms de Romilley, P. Pièces détachées de machines, paliers, embrayages, déclics, appareils de graissage, compteurs, dynamomètres, modèles et dessins de machines. — Machines servant à élever les fardeaux, grues, montecharges, crics, courroies. — Moteurs hydrauliques. (*In* **France.** *Com. Imp. de l'Expos. de* 1867. Rapports du jury, v. 9.)

Wornum, Ralph Nicholas. Analysis of ornament; the characteristics of styles; an introd. to the study of the history of ornamental art. 3d ed. London, 1869. 8°.
— Descriptive and historical catalogue of the the pictures in the National Gallery; with biog. notices of the painters: Foreign schools. 43d ed. London, 1866. 8°.
— *Same.* 56th ed. London, 1870. 8°.
— Epochs of painting. London, 1847. 12°.
— Lectures on painting by the Royal Academicians, J. Barry, J. Opie, H. Fuseli. London, *Bohn*, 1848. 8°.
— Life and works of Holbein. London, 1867. 4°.

Worrall, W. Pro bono civitate; discourse [on] the application of the clergy for an increase of stipend. Glasgow, 1827. 12°. (C 200)

Worsaae, Jens Jacob Asmussen. Account of the Danes and Norwegians in England, Scotland, and Ireland. London, 1852. 8°.

Worship. DUPUIS, C. F. Origines de tous les cultes. Paris, l'an III [1795]. 3 v. *and* Plates. 4°.
— - *Same.* Paris, l'an III [1795]. 7 v. 8°.
— DISCOURSE on divine worship. *t.p.w.* [16—.] 12°.
— BRADSHAW, W. Treatises on worship and ceremonies. London, 1660. 4°.
— BARCLAY, R., *and others.* On worship. [1690–1805.] *n.t.p.* [18—.] 8°. (B 1360)
— KING, W. Discourse conc. the inventions of men in the worship of God. [1704.] 5th ed. London, 1712. 4°. (B 15)
— NIEDEK, M. B. van. De populorum veterum et recentiorum adorationibus. Amstelædami, 1713. 8°.
— MOODY, J. Practical disc. conc. the benefit of communion with God in his house. Boston, 1746. 8°. (C 164)
— FOTHERGILL, G. The reasons and necessity of publick worship; sermon, Mar. 8. Oxford, 1753. 8°. (B 56)
— GILL, J. Attendance in places of religious worship; two sermons, Oct. 9, 1757. London, 1757. 8°. (B 1895)
— ESSAYS on public worship, patriotism, and projects of reformation. London, 1773. 16°. (C 219)
— FARMER, H. Worship of human spirits. London, 1783. 8°.
— EXTRACTS conc. the importance of religion and public worship to civil society; [from Mrs. Barbauld and others. 1785–1819.] Hallowell, 1820. 12°. (C 222)
— WAKEFIELD, G. Enquiry into the expediency of public or social worship. 3d ed. London, 1792. 8°. (E 207)
— BARBAULD, A. L. A. Remarks on G. Wakefield's 'Enquiry'. London, 1792. 8°. (B 1361)
— - *Same.* 2d ed. London, 1792. 8°. (E 207)
— - *Same.* Thoughts on public worship. (*In* Sparks, J. Col. of essays, v. 4. 1824.)
— POPE, J. Divine worship founded in nature; with remarks on Wakefield's arguments against divine worship. London, 1792. 8°. (E 207)
— WILSON, J. Defence of public or social worship; letter to G. Wakefield. Stockport, 1792. 8° (B 1371)
— KINGHORN, J. Public worship considered and enforced. London, 1800. 12°. (C 231)
— DEWEY, O. A letter on devotion at church. From the Christian examiner, v. 4, no. 4. Boston, 1827. 12°. (C 241)
- WHATELEY, R. Introductory lessons on the history of religious worship. [1847.] London, 1849. 24°.
— MANN, H. Religious worship in England and Wales; abridged from [his] report, 1851. 5th thous. rev. London, 1854. 8°.

See also Family worship; — Hymns; — Prayer; — Psalmody; — Religions; — Religious ceremonies; — Ritualism; — Temples.

Worship of animals. *See* Zoological mythology.

423. (28. 12. 81.)

Worsley, Israel. View of American Indians. London, 1828. 12°.

Worsley, S. Serious reflections on the present state of Amer. affairs; sermon, fast-day, Dec. 13. London, [1776]. 8°. (B 1257)

Worsted manufacture. FORBES, H. Worsted, alpacca, and mohair manufactures of Eng. (*In* Soc. of Arts. Lect., 1851, 52.)
— JAMES, J. History of worsted manufacture in England. London, 1857. 8°.

Wortabet, Gregory M. Syria and the Syrians; or, Turkey and its dependences. London, 1856. 2 v. 12°.

Worth, Gorham A. Random recollections of Albany, 1800–08. 3d ed. with notes by [J. Munsell]. Albany, 1866. 8°.

Worth, James. An account of the insect destructive to peach trees. (*In* Acad. of Nat. Sci. Journ., v. 3. 1823.)

Worthen, Augustus H. Geological survey. *See* Illinois. *Geological Survey.* 1866.
— Occurrence of fish remains in the carboniferous limestone of Illinois. (*In* Amer. Assoc. Proc., v. 10. 1857.) — Remarks on the discovery of a terrestrial flora in the mountain limestone of Illinois. (*In* v. 13. 1860.) — Remarks on the relative age of the Niagara and Lower Helderberg groups. (*In* v. 19. 1871.)

Worthies of England, History of. *See* Fuller, T.

Worthington, A. W. Importance of natural history as a branch of education. (*In* Nat. Assoc. Prom. Soc. Sci. Trans., 1859.)

Worthington, Hugh. An approved pastor; charge, Daventry, Feb. 25, ordination of J. Runnels. London, 1762. 8°. (B 1349)
— Two letters adapted to the present conjuncture. London, 1758. 8°. (B 1868)

Worthington, J. H. Sermon; the new year. (*In* Beard, J. R. Sermons to be used in families. 1832.)

Worthington, James T. Essay on the rise and progress of political communities. (*In* Ohio Hist. Phil. Soc. Trans., v. 1, pt. 2. 1838.)

Worthington, John, *D.D., master of Jesus College, Cambridge.* Diary and correspondence; ed. by J. Crossley. Vol. 1, 2, pt. 1. [Manchester,] 1847–55. 2 v. 4°. (Chetham Society, v. 13, 36.)

Contents. Vol. 1. 1632–61. 2. 1661–67.
— A form of sound words; a Scripture catechism. 6th ed. London, 1733. 8°. (B 243)
— New and complete whole duty of man. New ed., rev. London, [1787?]. 8°.

Worthington, Richard. Invitation to the inhabitants of Great Britain to the manufacture of wines from fruits of their own country. Worcester, 1812. 8°. (B 690)

Worthington, Thomas. Letter, inclosing an ordinance passed by the convention of Ohio, *etc.* [Wash.,] 1802. 8°. (B 502)

Worthington, Thomas, *of Manchester.* Dwellings of the working-classes. (*In* Nat. Assoc. Prom. Soc. Sci. Trans., 1866.)

Worthington, W. G. D. Speech on the Jew bill, in the House of Delegates, Maryland. (*In* Brackenridge, H. M. Speeches. 1829.)

Note. The initials are given in the book as J. W. D. on p. 101.

Worthington, *Mass.* SECULAR and ecclesiastical history of W. Albany, 1853. 8°.

Note. With a ms. note, 'This was written during one of my college vacations. J. C. R.' The Ecclesiastical history is by J. H. Bisbee.

Wortman, Tunis. Oration on the influence of social institution upon human morals, before the Tammany Soc., May 12. N. Y., 1796. 8°. (B 352)

Wortley, *Lady* Emmeline Stuart. Travelling sketches in rhyme. London, 1835. 8°.

See also Keepsake, The, for 1837.

Wotton, *Sir* Henry. Elements of architecture. 1624. (*In* Somers, J. Col. of tracts, v. 3. 1810.)
— *Same, abridged.* Ground-rules of architecture. (*In* Leybourn, W. Mirror of archit. 1708.)
— Observations, by way of parallel, of Robert, Earl of Essex, and George, Duke of Buckingham. 1641. (*In* Somers, J. Col. of tracts, v. 4. 1810.)

— Poems; ed. by A. Dyce. London, 1842. 8°. (Percy Soc., v. 6.)
— Poems. (*In* **Campbell**, T. Brit. poets, v. 3. 1819.)
— WALTON, I. (*In his* Lives. 1796; v. 1. 1832; — *and in* **Wordsworth**, C. Eccles. biog., v. 4. 1839.)

Wotton, Wm. De confusione linguarum Babylonica. (*In* **Chamberlayne**, J. Diss. 1715.)
— TINDAL, M. Defence of 'The rights of the Christian Church' against a late visitation sermon by W. Wotton. London, 1707. 8°. (B 83)

Wounded, The. MOYNIER, G. Droit des gens; étude sur la Convention de Genève pour l'Amélioration du Sort des Militaires Blessés dans les Armées en Campagne, 1864, 68. Paris, 1870. 8°.

Wounds. WYER, E. On covering with skin parts recently exposed. [1784.] (*In* **Mass. Med. Soc.** Med. comm., v. 1. 1808.)
— BELL, J. Nature and cure of wounds. [1795.] 1st American ed. Walpole, N. H., 1807. 2 v. 8°.
— STEVENS, A. H. Clinical lecture on the primary treat. ment of injuries. N. Y., 1837. 8°. (B 1562)
— MOORE, C. H. Wounds of vessels. — PAGET, J. Wounds. (*In* **Holmes**, T. Syst. of surg., v. 1. 1860.)
— GAY, G. H. A few remarks on the primary treatment of wounds received in battle. Boston, 1862. 8°. (B 1553)

See also **Gun-shot wounds; — Strap, Adhesive; — Surgery.**

Wounds of civil war; by T. Lodge. (*In* **Dodsley**, R. Col. of plays, v. 8. 1780.)

Wouwer *or* **Wowerius**, Jan van der. Assertio Lipsiani donari adversus Gelastorum suggillationes. (*In* **Lipsius**, J. Opera, v. 1. 1675.)
— De polymathia tractatio. [Basil.,] *ex bibliopolio Frobeniano*, 1604. 4°.
— *Same.* (*In* **Gronovius**, J. Thes. Gr. antiq., v. 10. 1701.)
— NICERON, J. P. (*In his* Mem., v. 6. 1728; *and, Germ.*, v. 6. 1752.)

Woven of many threads; [by Mrs. C. V. Hamilton]. Boston, 1871. 8°.

Woverius, Wowerius, Johannes, *See* **Wouwer, J.**

Wrangel, Karl Gustaf. CUST, E. (*In his* Lives of the warriors of the 30 years' war, v. 2. 1865.)

Wrangell, *Admiral* Ferdinand von. Narrative of an expedition to the Polar Sea, 1821–23; ed. by E. Sabine. London, 1840. 8°.
— *Same.* N. Y., [1841]. 16°. (Harper's fam. lib., v. 148.)

Wrangham, Francis, *Archdeacon of Cleveland.* Joseph made known to his brethren; prize poem. Camb., 1812. 8°. (A 48)
— The pleiad; evidences of Christianity. Edin., 1828. 18°. (Constable's miscel., v. 26.)
— Poem on the restoration of learning in the East. Camb., 1805. 8°. (A 48)
— Sermon, translation of the Scripture, *etc.*, before the University, May 10. Camb., 1807. 4°. (B 1263)

Wranitzky, Paolo. Oberon, König der Elfen; ein Singspiel nach Wielands Oberon. Berlin, 1792. 8°. (D 14)

Wratislaw, Wenceslas, *Baron.* Adventures of Wratislaw in Constantinople, 1599; tr. from the Bohemian by A. H. Wratislaw. London, 1862. 8°.

Wraxall, *Sir* Frederick Charles Lascelles. Armies of the great powers. London, 1859. 12°.
— Backwoodsman; or, Life on the Indian frontier. Boston, 1866. 12°.
— Life and times of Caroline Matilda, Queen of Denmark. London, 1864. 3 v. 8°.
— Memoirs of Queen Hortense. 1862. *See* **Wehrhan, R.**

Wraxall, *Sir* Nathaniel William, *Bart.* Historical memoirs of my own time. London, 1815. 2 v. 8°.

Contents. Vol. 1. 1772–80. 2. 1781–84.

— Posthumous memoirs of his own time. London, 1836. 3 v. 8°.

Contents. Vol. 1. 1784–85. 2. 1786–87. 3. 1788–89.

— Tour round the Baltic. 4th ed. London, 1807. 8°.

Wray, John. Dangers of an entire repeal of the bank restriction act. 2d ed. (*In* **Pamphleteer**, 1819; v. 13 of B 838)

Wreath, The; a collection of poems. Hartford, 1824. 18°.

Wreck ashore, The; by J. B. Buckstone. (*In* **Sargent**, E. Mod. stand. dr., v. 33.)

Wreck of the Golden Mary. (*In* **Littell's** living age, v. 52. 1857.)

Wrecked in port; by E. Yates. (*In* **All** the year round, v. 21, n.s., v. 1-2. 1868–69.)

Wrede, H. New instructions for the German flute. London, [17—]. obl. 4°.

Wreford, J. R. Sermon; the parable of Nathan. (*In* **Beard**, J. R. Sermons. 1832.)

Wrekin and vicinity. WHITE, W. All round the Wrekin. London, 1860. 8°.

Wren, *Sir* Christopher. CUNNINGHAM, A. (*In his* Lives of British painters, v. 4. 1831. Fam. lib., v. 7.)
— ELMES, J. Memoirs of the life and works of W. London, 1823. 4°.
— - Wren and his times. London, 1852. 8°.
— KER, H. B. Life. (*In* **Soc. Diff. Usef. Kn.** Lib. of usef. kn. Lives of eminent persons. 1833.)
— MALDEN, H. (*In his* Distinguished men of modern times, v. 3. 1838. Lib. ent. kn., v. 39.)

Wren, Roger. Sentiments of the humours of the times. Boston, 1763. 8°. (B 976, 1005)

Wren, Walter. Voyage of Capt. Fenner to the Islands of Cape Verde, 1566. (*In* **Green**, J. Collections, v. 1. 1745.)

Wren of the Curragh, The. Reprinted from the Pall Mall gazette. London, 1867. 16°.

Wrench, *Rev.* Jacob George. What measures are required for the further improvement of the Universities of Oxford and Cambridge? (*In* **Nat. Assoc. Prom.** Soc. Sci. Trans., 1868.)

Wrenne, G., *and others.* Voyage to Persia, 1563. (*In* **Hakluyt**, R. Col., v. 1. 1809.)

Wrentham, *Mass.* BEAN, J. Sermon, Oct. 26, 1773, first century since the town was incorporated. Boston, 1774. 8°. (B 304)
— MANN, J. Account of the surprise and defeat of Indians near Wrentham. (*In* **Mass. Hist.** Soc. Col., v. 10. 1809.)

Wrentham. Church of Christ in North Parish. Report of committee on the reply of M. Thacher to their request to administer to them the Lord's supper; also facts exhibited to the eccl. council, Dec. 14, 1830. Boston, 1831. 16°. (C 236)

Wrestling. DUERER, A. Die Ringkunst des deutschen Mittelalters, mit 119 Ringerpaaren; herausgegeben von K. Wassmannsdorff. Lpz., 1870. 8°.

Wrey, J. W. Restoration of the criminal to society. (*In* **National Assoc. Prom. Soc. Sci.** Transactions, 1857.)

Wright, Andrew, *printer.* Report of the trial of W. on an indictment for libels against Gov. Strong. Northampton, 1806. 8°. (B 989)

Wright, Andrew, *of the Inner Temple.* Court-hand restored; or, The student's assistant in reading old deeds, charters, records, *etc.* 8th ed. London, 1867. 4°.

Wright, Austin H. Looking unto Jesus; sermon, Oroomiah, Persia, Oct. 11, 1857, death of Mrs. M. A. Rhea. Boston, 1858. 8°. (B 1247)

Wright, Benj. Report rel. to the survey of the New York and Erie R. R. *n.t.p.* [1835.] 8°. (B 1771)

Wright, Caleb. Constructive method of projecting solar eclipses. (*In* **Amer. Assoc.** Proc., v. 8. 1855.)
— Lectures on India. 5th ed. Boston, 1851. 8°.

Wright, Crafts J. Journal of the Conference Convention, Washington, Feb. Washington, 1861. 8°.

Wright, E. Perceval. Molluscoida. — Rotifera. — Annelida. — Scolecida. — Echinodermata. — Cœlenterata. — Protozoa. (*In* **Record** of zoological lit., v. 3. 1867.)

Wright, Edward. Cruizing voyage by George, Earl of Cumberland, to the Azores, 1589. (*In* **Green**, J. Col. of voy., v. 1. 1745; — *and in* **Hakluyt**, R. Col. of voy., v. 2. 1810.)
— Some observations made in travelling through France, Italy, *etc.*, 1720-22. London, 1730. 2 v. 4°.
Wright, Elizur. Be happy. (*In* **Boston** book, 4th col. 1841.)
— Description of an air-pump invented by [himself]. —Dissertation on the production of vapor. (*In* **Conn. Acad. of Arts and Sci.** Mem., v. 1, pt. 1. 1810.)
— Perforations in the 'Latter-day pamphlets'. No. 1. Boston, 1850. 8°.
— Valuation tables on the combined experience rate of mortality. Boston, 1853. f°.
Wright, Frances (*Mme.* d'Arusmont). Biography, notes, and political letters. N. Y., 1844. 2 nos. 12°. (C 255)
Contents. No. 1. Biography and letters. 2. Political letters.
— Lecture on existing evils and their remedy. N. Y., 1829. 8°. (B 1854)
— Views of society and manners in America, 1818-20. London, 1821. 8°.
— M'Calla, W. L. Examination of W.'s system of knowledge. *n.t.p.* [1829.] 8°. (B 1854)
— Young, W. Twelve letters to young men on the sentiments of F. Wright and R. D. Owen. Phila., 1830. 8°. (B 1358, 1854)
Wright, Francis, *vs.* **Wardle**, G. L. Trial to recover £1,914, the amount of articles sent to Mrs. Clarke. London, [1809]. 8°. (B 667)
Wright, *Rev.* George. Conversion of the world consequent upon the improvement of the Church; sermon before the Society in Scotland for Propagating Christian Knowledge, June 3, 1819. Edin., 1820. 8°. (B 1642)
Wright, George, *b.* 1802. Biographical notice of W. (*In* **Mass. Medical Society.** Med. comm., v. 9. 1860.)
Wright, George Newham. China; scenery, architecture, *etc.*, illust. by T. Allom. London, [1843]. 4 v. 4°.
— Life and reign of William iv. London, [1837]. 2 v. 8°.
Wright, Henry Clarke. Christian communion with slave-holders, will the alliance sanction it? letters to J. A. James and R. Wardlaw. 3d thous. Rochdale, 1846. 12°. (C 257)
— Empire of the mother over the character and destiny of the race. Boston, 1863. 12°.
— Farewell letter to the com. of the Glasgow Emancipation Soc. Glasgow, 1847. 12°. (C 257)
— Funeral discourse, death of Miss J. Griffin. *n.p.*, 1852. 16°. (C 202)
— Human life; [autobiography]. Boston, 1849. 12°.
— Natick resolution; or, Resistance to slaveholders the right and duty of slaves and freemen. Boston, 1859. 12°. (C 263)
— The self-abnegationist; or, The true king and queen. Boston, 1863. 12°.
Wright, Hezekiah Hartley. Desultory reminiscences of a tour through Germany, Switzerland, and France. Boston, 1838. 8°.
Wright, Hiram A. Atwood, J. P. Eulogy on W. (*In* **Wisconsin Hist. Soc.** Col., v. 2. 1856.)
Wright, J. M. F., *of Trinity Coll., Camb.* Solutions of the Cambridge problems, 1800-20. London, 1825. 2 v. 8°.
Wright, J. Skirrow. Employment of women in factories in Birmingham. (*In* **Nat. Assoc. Prom. Soc. Sci.** Trans., 1857.) — New trades in Birmingham, *etc.* (*In* 1862.)
— The jewellery and gilt-toy trades. (*In* **Timmins**, S. Resources. 1866.)
Wright, James, *b. about* 1644, *d. about* 1715. Historia histrionica; hist. acc. of the Eng. stage. (*In* **Dodsley**, R. Col. of old plays, v. 1. 1825.)
Wright, *Rev.* James, *Minister at Maybole.* Discourse, duties of a minister of the gospel, ordination of S. Young, Mar. 8. Edin., 1780. 8°. (B 1860)
Wright, James Edward. Biography of C. L. Alden. — Biography of S. G. Emerson. (*In* **Higginson**, T. W. Harvard memorial biog., v. 2. 1866.)
Wright, John. The American negotiator; or, The various currencies of the British colonies in America, as well the islands as the continent; the currencies of Nova Scotia, *etc.* 3d ed. London, 1767. 8°.
Wright, John, *and* **Hall**, J. Catalogue of plants growing without cultivation in the vicinity of Troy. Troy, 1836. 8°. (B 1138)
Wright, John C. Speeches on the resolution calling for information rel. to the selection of newspapers for the publication of the laws. Wash., 1827. 8°. (B 1731)
Wright, John Harvey. Inaugural dissertation on croup. Northampton, 1838. 8°. (B 1565)
Wright, John S. Chicago; past, present, future. 2d ed. Chicago, 1870. 8°.
— Reply to C. G. Loring upon reconstruction. Boston, 1867. 8°.
Wright, John Turner. Rope making. — Hemp and twine. (*In* **Timmins**, S. Resources of Birmingham. 1866.)
Wright, L. The practical poultry keeper; a complete and standard guide to the management of poultry. London, New York, 1867. 12°.
Wright, L. B., *M.D.* Guide to health; the liquid cathartic. N. Y., [185-]. 12°. (D 38)
Wright, Luther. Sermon, Medway, Nov. 4, 1813, close of a century since the incorporation of the town. Dedham, 1814. 8°. (B 1306)
Wright, M. B. Introductory address at the Medical College of Ohio, Nov. Cincin., 1847. 8°. (B 1565)
Wright, Nathaniel H. Boston; or, A touch at the times; poem. Boston, 1819. 8°. (B 447)
— The fall of Palmyra, and other poems. Middlebury, 1817. 24°.
Wright, P. C., *solicitor.* In chancery, U. S. Circuit Court, Eastern district of Louisiana, M. C. Gaines *vs.* Relf, Chew, and others; brief for complainant. New Orleans, 1850. 8°. (E 229)
Wright, Phineas, *Funeral sermon on.* 1802. *See* **Adams**, M. (B 213)
Wright, R. W. The vision of judgment; or, The South Church; by Quevedo Redivivus, Jr. N. Y., 1867. 12°.
Wright, Richard. Answer to Why are you not a Trinitarian. 1st Amer. from 2d Liverpool ed. *n.p.*, 1816. 12°. (B 665, C 82)
— Catechism, in which the most important parts of religion are taught. 2d ed. Liverpool, 1808. 12°. (C 250)
— Essay on the nature and discipline of a Christian Church. — Necessity and utility of adhering to first principles in religion. — Salvation of sinners by the free grace of God. (*In* **Philadelphia. 1st Unitarian Society.** Collection of pieces. 1810.)
Wright, Robert, *Bp. of Lichfield and Coventry, d.* 1643. Speech spoken before the bar of the House of Commons, 1641. (*In* **Somers**, J. Col. of tracts, v. 4. 1810.)
Wright, *Sir* Robert, *d.* 1689. Campbell, J. Life of Sir R. Wright. (*In his* Lives of Chief Justices of England, v. 2. 1849.)
Wright, Robert. Lloyd, J. Address to the citizens of Kent and Queen Anne's Counties, in answer to R. Wright. Annapolis, [1794]. 8°. (W 62)
Wright, Robert. Life of Maj. Gen. James Wolfe. London, 1864. 8°.
— A memoir of Gen. J. Oglethorpe. London, 1867. 8°.
Wright, Robert S. The golden treasury of ancient Greek poetry. Oxford, 1867. 16°.
Wright, Robert Temple. Medical students of the period. Edin., 1867. 12°.
Wright, Samuel. Change of times and seasons considered; sermon, Oct. 20. London, 1724. 8°. (B 602)
— Human virtues; or, Col. of rules of Scripture. London, 1730. 8°. (B 1864)
— Lordship of Christ considered as it extends to the dead and living; two sermons, July 28 and Aug. 11. 2d ed. London, 1724. 8°. (B 602)

— The occasional preacher. No. 2: Aggravated folly of them that despise, *etc.*; sermon. London, 1741. 8°. (B 128)

— Scripture and tradition; sermon, Salter's-Hall. London, 1735. 8°. (B 33)

Wright, Samuel Osgood. THATCHER, B. B. Memoir of W. Boston, 1834. 16°.

Wright, Sarah A. Clara Hollinbrook the beauty of Fairfax. N. Y., 1863. 12°.

Wright, Silas. Speech on the permanent prospective pre-emption bill. Wash., 1841. 8°. (B 1663)

— HAMMOND, J. B. Life and times of W. Syracuse, 1848. 8°.

— JENKINS, J. S. Lives of the governors of New York. Auburn, 1851. 8°.

— LESTER, C. E. Memoir of W. (*In his* Gallery of illustrious Americans. 1850.)

— *Funeral sermon on.* 1847. *See* **Sprague,** W. B. (B 1228)

Wright, *Rev.* Thomas. Sermon, ordination of I. Smith, Sidmouth, Devon; added, disc. by J. Ward, *etc.* Taunton, 1778. 8°. (B 66, 1312)

Wright, Thomas. New chart of the Gulf of St. Lawrence. London, 1790. f°. (E 68)

Wright, Thomas. History of the Walcheren remittent fever. London, 1811. 8°.

Wright, Thomas, *minister of Borthwick, Scotland.* Good life; from [his] 'True plan of a living temple'; with an introd. essay by J. Brazer. Boston, 1836. 8°.

Wright, Thomas, *b.* 1810. Anecdota literaria; illust. the literature and history of England in the 13th century. London, 1844. 8°.

— Biographia Britannica litteraria: Anglo-Norman period. London, 1846. 8°.

— *Same.* Anglo-Saxon period. London, 1842. 8°.

— Caricature history of the Georges. London, [1868]. 8°.

— The Celt, the Roman, and the Saxon. 2d ed. London, 1861. 8°.

— Early travels in Palestine. London, *Bohn*, 1848. 8°.

Contents. Introd. — **Adamnan,** *Abbot of Iona.* Travels of Arculf. — **Willibaldus,** *Bishop of Eichstädt.* — **Bernard** *the Wise.* — **Saewulf.** — **Snorri Sturluson.** Saga of Sigurd. — **Benjamin,** *of Tudela.* — **Mandeville,** *Sir* J. — **Bertrandon de le Brocquière.** — **Maundrell,** H.

— England under the House of Hanover; from caricatures, *etc.* 2d ed. Lond., 1848. 2 v. 8°.

— Essays on archæological subjects, and on questions connected with the history of art, science, and literature in the Middle Ages. London, 1861. 2 v. 12°.

Contents. Vol. 1. Remains of a primitive people in the south-east corner of Yorkshire. — Ancient barrows or tumuli in East Yorkshire. — Curious forms of sepulchral interment in E. Yorkshire. — Treago, and the large tumulus found at St. Weonards. — Ethnology of S. Britain at the period of the extinction of the Roman government in the island. — Origin of the Welsh. — Anglo-Saxon antiquities, with reference to the Faussett collection. — True character of the biographer Asser. — Anglo-Saxon architecture illustrated from illuminated ms. — Literary history of Geoffrey of Monmouth's History of the Britons, and of the romantic cycle of King Arthur. — Saints' lives and miracles. — Antiquarian excavations and researches in the Middle Ages. 2. On the ancient map of the world preserved in Hereford Cathedral. — History of the English language. — On the abacus, or mediæval system of arithmetic. — Antiquity of dates expressed in Arabic numerals. — Rem. on an ivory casket of the beginning of the 14th century. — Carvings of the stalls in cathedral and collegiate churches. — Illustrations of questions rel. to architectural antiquities: Mediæval architecture illustr. from illuminated ms.; — Mediæval bridge builders; — Remains of proscribed races in mediæval and modern society as explaining peculiarities in old churches. — Origin of rhymes in mediæval poetry, and its bearing on the authenticity of the early Welsh poems. — Hist. of the drama in the Middle Ages. — Literature of the trobadours. — History of comic literature during the Middle Ages. — Satirical literature of the Reformation.

— Essays on the literature, superstitions, and history of England in the Middle Ages. London, 1846. 2 v. 8°.

Contents. Vol. 1. Anglo-Saxon poetry. — Anglo-Norman poetry. — Chansons de geste. — Proverbs and popular sayings. — Anglo-Latin poets of the 14th cent. — Abelard and the scholastic philosophy. — Dr. Grimm's German mythology. — National fairy mythology of England. — Popular superstitions of modern Greece. 2. Friar Rush and the frolicsome elves. — Observations on Dunlop's History of fiction. — History and transmission of popular stories. — Poetry of history. — Adventures of Hereward the Saxon. — Story of Eustace the monk. — History of Fitz Fulke Warine. — Popular cycle of the Robin Hood ballads. — Conquest of Ireland by the Anglo-Norman. — Old English political songs. — Scottish poet Dunbar.

— Historical introduction. (*In* **Fairholt,** F. W. Miscel. graphica. 1857.)

— History and antiquities of London. *See* **Allen,** T.

— History and topography of the County of Essex. London, 1836. 2 v. 4°.

— History of caricature and the grotesque in literature and art; with illust. Lond., 1865. 4°.

— History of domestic manners and sentiments in England during the Middle Ages. London, 1862. 4°.

— History of Ireland. Lond., [1848-52]. 3 v. 8°.

Contents. Vol. 1. To 1643. 2. 1644-1798. 3. 1798-1853.

— Introduction and notes. (*In* **Malory,** *Sir* T. History of Arthur. 1858.)

— Letters relating to the suppression of monasteries; ed. from the originals in the British Museum. London, 1843. 4°. (Camden Soc., v. 26.)

— Narratives of sorcery and magic. 2d ed. London, 1851. 2 v. 12°.

Contents. Vol. 1. Introd. — Story of the Lady Alice Kyteler. — Further political usage of the belief in sorcery; the Templars. — Sorcery in France; the citizens of Arras. — The lord of Mirabeau and Pierre d'Estaing, the alchemist. — The earlier medieval type of the sorcerer; Virgil the enchanter. — The later medieval types of the magician; friar Bacon and Dr. Faustus. — Sorcery in Germany in the 15th century; the Malleus maleficarum. — Witchcraft in Scotland in the 16th century. — King James and the witches of Lothian. — Magic in England during the age of the Reformation. — The English magicians, Dr. Dee and his followers. — The witches of Warboys. — The poetry of witchcraft. — Witchcraft in France in the 16th century. — Pierre de Lancre, and the witches of Labourd. — Magic in Spain; the auto-da-fé of Logrono. 2. Adventures of Dr. Torralva. — Trial of the Earl and Countess of Somerset. — La maréchale d'Ancre. — Louis Gaufridi. — The Ursulines of Loudun. — The Lancashire witches. — Witchcraft in England during the earlier part of the 17th century. — Witchcraft under the Commonwealth; Matthew Hopkins, the witchfinder. — Witchcraft in Germany in the earlier part of the 17th century. — The witches in Scotland under king James after his accession to the English throne. — Confessions of Isobel Gowdie. — The witches of Mohra in Sweden. — Sir Matthew Hale and Chief Justice Holt. — The doings of Satan in New England. — Conclusion.

— Political ballads published in England during the Commonwealth. Lond., 1841. 8°. (Percy Soc., v. 3.)

— Political condition of the Eng. peasantry during the Middle Ages. (*In* **Archæologia,** v. 30. 1844.)

— Political poems and songs rel. to English hist. from Edward III. to Richard III. London, 1859-61. 2 v. 8°. (Chron. and mem.)

Contents. Vol. 1. 1327-1480. 2. 1400-1483.

— Political songs of Eng., from the reign of John to that of Edward II. London, 1839. 4°. (Camden Soc., v. 6.)

— Popular treatises on science written during the Middle Ages. London, 1841. 8°. (Hist. Soc. Sci., v. 2.)

Contents. **Anglo-Saxon** manual of astronomy. — **Than,** P. de. Livre des créatures; — The bestiary. — **English** verses on popular science.

— Preface and index. (*In* Neckam, A. De naturis rerum. 1863.)
— Queen Elizabeth and her times. London, 1838. 2 v. 8°.
— St. Patrick's purgatory; essay on legends of purgatory, hell current during the Middle Ages. London, 1844. 8°.
— Selection of Latin stories. London, 1842. 8°. (Percy Soc., v. 8.)
— The seven sages. (*In* Warton, T. History of Eng. poetry, v. 1. 1871.)
— Songs and carols of the 15th century. London, 1847. 8°. (Percy Soc., v. 23.)
— Specimens of lyric poetry composed in England in the reign of Edward I.; ed. from ms. London, 1842. 8°. (Percy Soc., v. 4.)
— Specimens of old Christmas carols. London, 1841. 8°. (Percy Soc., v. 4.)
— Wanderings of an antiquary, chiefly upon the traces of the Romans in Britain. London, 1854. 8°.
— *and* Evans, R. H. Historical and descr. account of the caricatures of J. Gillray. London, 1851. 8°.

Wright, Wm. Address to persons afflicted with deafness. London, 1820. 12°.
— Varieties of deafness and diseases of the ear. London, 1829. 8°.

Wright, Wm. Aldis. *See* Journal of philology. 1868-69.

Wright's chaste wife, The; a merry tale, by Adam of Cobsam; ed. by F. J. Furnivall. London, 1865. 8°. (Early Eng. Text Soc.)

Wrightson, Richard Heber. History of modern Italy, [1793]-1850. London, 1855. 8°.

Wrigley, T. Effects of recent legislation on British paper manufacture. (*In* Nat. Assoc. Prom. Soc. Sci. Trans., 1863.)

Writer, The; a series of original essays, moral and amusing; [by G. Bradford]. Boston, 1822. 12°.

Writers to His Majesty's Signet. *See* Society of the Writers to His Majesty's Signet.

Writing. *History.* Astle, T. Origin and progress of writing and printing. 2d ed. London, 1803. 4°.
— - Baring, D. E. Clavis diplomatica; specimina veterum scripturarum. Hanoviæ, 1737. 4°.
— - De Vere, M. S. History of writing. (*In his* Comparative philology. 1853.)
— - Sankey, W. S. Conjectures on the origin of the Oriental practice of writing from right to left, deduced from the names and forms of the Hebrew characters. (*In* Roy. Irish. Acad. Trans., v. 13. 1818.)
— Maronier, J. Excempel-boek. [Amst.?,17—?] obl. 8°.
— Davy, C. Conjectural obs. on the origin and progress of alphabetic writing. London, 1772. 8°.
— Fisher, G. Instructor; or, Young man's best companion; spelling, reading, writing arithmetic. 22d ed. Edin., 1773. 12°.
— - *Same.* London, 1799. 12°.
— Wright, A. Court-hand restored. [1773.] 8th ed. London, 1867. 4°.
— Jenkins, J. Art of writing reduced to a plain and easy system. Book 1. Boston, 1791. 4°. (B 654)
— - *Same.* Camb., 1813. 8°.
— Maimieux, J. de. Pasigraphie; l'art d'écrire de manière à être lu dans toute autre langue. Paris, 1797. 4°.
— Buchanan, C. Writing-master and accountant's assistant. Glasgow, 1798. 4°.
— Mulhaueser, —. Manual of writing founded on Mulhaüser's method. [1829.] London, 1842. 8°.
— Rapp, A. W. Complete system of scientific penmanship. [1831.] Phila., 1832. 4°.
— Dearborn, N. American text book for letters. [3d ed.] Boston, [1846]. 8°.

See also Notæ Tyronianæ; — Phonography; — Stenography; — Tachygraphy.

Writing on the wall; by T. and J. M. Morton. (*In* Sargent, E. Mod. stand. dr., v. 12.)

Wroe, Caleb. The improvement and perfection of our faith; sermon. London, 1722. 8°. (B 120)

Wroniecki, Antoni. Sprawa piesza. Księga 1; 2, część 1. W Paryżu, 1834-36. 2 pt. 18°.

Wrottesley, John, *Baron Wrottesley.* Navigation. (*In* Soc. Diff. Usef. Kn. Lib. usef. kn. Nat. phil., v. 3. 1834.)

Wuellerstorf-Urbain, B. von. *See* Novara, Voyage of the.

Wuertemberg. Stælin, C. F. Wirtembergische Geschichte. Vol. 1: Schwaben und Südfranken, bis 1080. Stuttg., Tüb., 1841. 8°.
— Le Bas, P. Histoire et description, [B.C. 58 - A.D. 1841]. (*In his* Etats de la Confédération Germanique. 1842.)
— Vehse, E. Geschichte der Höfe der Häuser Baiern, Würtemberg, *u.s.w.*, [1503-1847]. (*In his* Geschichte der Deutschen Höfe, v. 26. 1853.)
— *Map.* Wirtenberg. *n.p.*, [16—]. (E 78, no. 97)
— - Visscher, J. N. Amst. Bat., [17—]. f°.

Wuertemberg. Evangelische Consistorium. Entwurf eines Gesangbuches. 2e Aufl. Stuttg., Tüb., 1840. 8°.

Wueste, Die; von A. v. Kotzebue. (*In his* Theater, v. 36. 1841.)

Wuestenfeld, Theodor. Delle falsificazioni di alcuni documenti concernenti la storia d'Italia. (*In* Archivio stor. ital., n.s., v. 10, pt. 1. 1859.) — Odorici, F. Osservazioni a proposito di un lavoro di W. sulle 'Falsificazioni'. (*In* v. 10, pt. 2. 1859.) — Cantù, C. Di alcune falsificazioni storiche e del signor Wuestenfeld. (*In* v. 12, pt. 1. 1860.)

Wulfen, Franz Xaver, *Freiherr* von. De plumbo spatoso Carinthiaco; ex Germanico idiomate in Latinum transtulit J. Eyerel. Vind., 1791. 4°.

Wulfilas. *See* Ulfilas.

Wulframnus, St., *Ep. Senonensis.* Jonas *Fontanellensis.* Vita S. Vulfranni. (*In* Acta sanct., v. 9. 1865.)

Wulfstan. Alfred, *King of England.* Wulfstan's voyage in the Baltic. (*In his* Descr. of Europe. 1855; — *and in* Kerr, R. Col. of voy., v. 1. 1824.)

Wullenweder, Jürgen. Barthold, F. W. Jürgen Wullenweber von Lübeck oder die Bürgermeisterfehde. (*In* Historisches Taschenbuch, 1835.)

Wulstan, *Bishop of Worcester.* Life. (*In* Lives of the Eng. saints, v. 5. 1844.)

Wunderlich, Karl August. Handbuch der Pathologie und Therapie. 2e verm. Aufl. Stuttg., 1852-56. 4 v. in 6 pts. 8°.

Contents. Vol. 1. Die allgemeinsten Grundsätze, Begriffe, und Thatsachen der Pathologie und Therapie. — Die allgemeine Ætiologie, Hygiene, und Jamatologie. — Die allgemeine pathologische Physiologie. 2. Die Erkrankungsformen der Gewebe. 3. Die Formen der topischen Erkrankungen. 4. Specielle Anomalien der Constitution und Erkrankungsformen mit multiplen Localisationen. — Autogenetische Constitutionskrankheiten.

— On the temperature in diseases; tr. from 2d German ed., by W. B. Woodman. London, 1871. 8°. (Sydenham Soc., v. 49.)

Wunderlichkeiten; von L. Tieck. (*In his* Gesam. Novellen, v. 9. 1853.)

Wundersuechtigen, Die; von L. Tieck. (*In his* Gesam. Novellen, v. 7. 1853.)

Wurdemann, William. Modification of apparatus for the registration of time for astronomical purposes. (*In* Amer. Assoc. Proc., v. 5. 1851.)

Wurdiman, F. Notes on Cuba. Boston, 1844. 12°.

Wurm, I. Archiv für Ophthalmologie; General-Register zu Band 1-10. Breslau, 1868. 8°.

Wurmsser von Vendenheym, Hans Jacob. Relation of a journey with Lewis Frederick, Duke of Wirtemberg, 1610. (*In* Rye, W. B. England as seen by foreigners. 1865.)

Wurtz, Charles Adolphe. History of chemical theory, from the age of Lavoisier to the present time; tr. and ed. by H. Watts. London, 1869. 12°.

Contents. Introduction. — Lavoisier. — Dalton and Gay-Lussac. — Berzelius. — Laurent and Gerhardt. — Theories of the present day. — Notes.

— Introduction to chemical philosophy, according to modern theories; tr. by W. Crookes. London, 1867. 16°.

Wurtz, Henry. Availability of the green sand of N. J. as a source of potash and its compounds. — New method of decomposing silicates in the process of analysis. — Troostite of New Jersey. (*In* **Amer. Assoc. Proc.,** v. 4. 1851.) — Action of nitric acid in the cold upon some metallic solutions, with new methods of obtaining pure compounds of larium, strontium, and cadmium. — Chemical examination connected with a bullet embedded in the lung of a man. — Detection of nitric acid in solution, *etc.* — Improvement in the preparation of hard minerals for analysis. — Investigation of the action of nitric acid upon the metallic chlorides. — Modes of increasing the heat of the mouth blowpipe. — Occurrence of cobalt and nickel in Gaston Co., N. C. — Preliminary notice of an investigation upon the action of hot chlorohydric acid upon some metallic nitrates. — Preparation of some pure sulphates. — Suggestions regarding economical applications of glycerine. (*In* v. 12.) — New chemical relations of metallic aluminum. (*In* v. 17.) — On the grahamite of West Virginia, and the New Colorado resinoid. — Investigation of flame temperatures in their reference to composition and luminosity. — Studies in chemical geogony. (*In* v. 18. 1870.) — HUNT, T. S. Leucine and its homologous rel., with some critical remarks upon the late researches of Mr. Wurtz. (*In* v. 2. 1850.)

Wurzbach von Tannenberg, Constant. Biographisches Lexikon des Kaiserthums Oesterreich, 1750 bis 1850. Wien, 1856–80. 41 v. 8°.

Contents. Vol. 1. A-Bl. 2. Bn-Cord. 3. Cors-Eger. 4. Egerv-Fuc. 5. Fug-Es. 6. Eu-Habsburg, Ludwig. 7. Habsburg, Magdalena-Hartl. 8. Hartm-He. 9. Hi-Hy. 10. J-Karoli. 11. Karoly-Ki. 12. Kl-Kor. 13. Kos-Lag. 14. Lai-Len. 15. Leo-Lom. 16. Lon-Marl. 17. Maro-Mes. 18. Met-Moli. 19. Moll-My. 20. Nab-Ode. 21. O'Do-Pere. 22. Perg-Podh. 23. Podl-Prok. 24. Proo-Rasc. 25. Rasn-Rheder. 26. Rhedey-Rosena. 27. Rosenb-Rz. 28. Saa-Saw. 29. Sax-Schim. 30. Schin-Schm. 31. Schn-Schröt. 32. Schrött-Schwic. 33. Schwarzenberg. — Schwin-Seidl, Johann. 34. Seidl, Joseph-Sina. 35. Sinac-Sonne. 36. Sonnk-Stade. 37. Stadi-Steg. 38. Steh-Stie. 39. Stif-Streel. 40. Streer-Susc. 41. Susi-Sze.

Wurzburg. Annales Wirziburgenses, 687–1480. (*In* **Pertz,** G. H. Monumenta Germaniæ historica, Scr., v. 2. 1829.)

— MONUMENTA episcopatus Wirziburgensis, [788–1287]. (*In* **Munich. K. Ak. d. Wiss.** Mon. Boica, v. 37. 1854.)

— ANNALES Herbipolenses, 1125–1215. (*In* **Pertz,** G. H. Mon. Germ. hist., Scr., v. 16. 1859.)

Wuthering Heights; by Ellis Bell [E. Brontë]. N. Y., 1862. 12°.

— *Same.* And Agnes Grey, by Acton Bell [A. Brontë]. New ed. rev., with a biog. notice of the authors, a selection from their lit. remains and a preface by Currer Bell [C. B. Nichols]. Lpz., *Tauchnitz,* 1851. 2 v. 16°.

Wuttig, Gustav Wilhelm. Novus index. *See* **Kayser,** C. G. Index, v. 13–17.

Wuttke, Johann Karl Heinrich. Der Kampf der Freiheitsmänner und der Geistlichen in Belgien in den letzten Jahrzehnten des vorigen Jahrhunderts. (*In* **Historische** Taschenbuch, 1864.)

— Die Volkerschlacht bei Leipzig. Berlin, 1863. 8°. (Schmidt, F. Deutsche National-Bibliothek, v. 11.)

Wyandot Indians. *See* **Huron Indians.**

Wyandotte; by [J. F. Cooper]. Phila., 1843. 2 v. 12°.

— *Same.* Illust. by F. O. C. Darley. N. Y., 1859. 12°.

Wyat, Wyatt, *or* **Wiat,** *Sir* Thomas, *the elder.* Works. (Vol. 2 *of* **Howard,** H. Works. 1816.)

Contents. Preface. — Mem. of W. — Essay on the poems. — Poems. — Penitential psalms. — Sonnets, rondeaux, and odes. — Letters to his son. — Oration. — Letters and official correspondence. — App. — Notes. — List of contents of the Harington ms. — Contents of the Duke of Devonshire's ms. — Different readings given by the Yelverton ms. of W.'s Declaration and oration. — Glossary.

— Poetical works; prefixed, life of W. (*In* **Anderson,** R. Brit. poets, v. 1. 1793.)

— Poetical works; ed. with memoir, [by F. J. Child]. Boston, 1854. 12°.

Contents. Memoir. — Songs and sonnets. — Rondeaux. — Odes. — Poems. — Songs and epigrams. — Satires. — Penitential psalms. — Sir Antonie Sentleger of Sir T. Wyatt.

— Poems. (*In* **Chalmers,** A. Eng. poets, v. 2. 1810.)

— Poems. (*In* **Campbell,** T. Brit. poets, v. 2. 1819.)

— Songes and sonettes. (*In* **Tottel,** R. Miscel. 1870.)

Wyat, *Sir* Thomas, *the younger.* Chronicle of the rebellion of W. (*In* **Mary I.** CHRONICLE. 1850. Camden Soc., v. 48.)

Wyatt, Matthew Digby. Art of illuminating; illustrated by borders, initial letters, *etc.*; chromolithographed by W. R. Tymms; with an essay and instructions by W. London, [18—]. 8°.

— An attempt to define the principles which should determine form in the decorative arts. (*In* **Soc. of Arts.** Lectures, 1851, 52.)

— Fine art; a sketch of its history, theory, practice, and application to industry. London, N. Y., 1870. 8°.

— Industrial arts of the 19th century at the Exhibition of 1851. London, 1851. 2 v. f°.

— Metal work and its artistic design. London, 1852. f°.

— Notices of sculpture in ivory; with catalogue of select examples by E. Oldfield. London, *Arundel Soc.*, 1856. 4°.

— *and* **Waring,** J. B. Byzantine and Romanesque court. — Mediæval, Renaissance, and Italian courts. (*In* **Crystal Palace Company.** Fine arts courts, v. 2. 1854.)

Wyatt, *Mrs.* Sophia (Hayes). Autobiography of a landlady of the old school. Boston, 1854. 12°.

Wyatt, *Sir* Thomas. *See* **Wyat,** T.

Wyatt, Thomas, *A.M.* Description of the national medals of America presented to the officers of the wars of the Revolution and 1812. N. Y., 1854. 12°.

Wyatt, William, *d.* 1683. Sermon to those who have been pupils of St. Paul's School, London, St. Paul's Day. London, 1679. 8°. (B 1346)

Wyatt, *Rev.* Wm. Edward. Review of J. Sparks' letters on the Prot. Episc. Church, in reply to W.'s sermon. Balt., 1820. 8°. (B 339)

— Sermon, doctrines of the Prot. Episc. Church, U. S. Balt., 1820. 8°. (B 290, 1306)

Wycherly *or* **Wycherley,** Wm. Works. London, 1713. 8°.

Contents. Plain dealer. — Country wife. — Gentleman dancing-master. — Love in a wood.

— Country girl. (*In* **Bell,** J. British theatre, v. 13. 1797.)

— Letters to and from W. (*In* **Pope,** A. Works, v. 7. 1806.)

— Plain dealer. (*In* **Bell,** J. Brit. theatre, v. 23. 1797; — *and in* **Scott,** *Sir* W. Brit. dr., v. 2. 1810.)

— DUNHAM, S. A. (*In his* Lives, v. 3. 1838. Lardner. Cab. cyc., v. 15.)

Wychowaniu mlodzieży Polskiej, O. [Paryż, 184–.] 8°.

Wychwood. AKERMAN, J. Y. View of the ancient limits of the forest of Wychwood. (*In* **Archæologia,** v. 37. 1857.)

Wycliffe, J. *See* **Wiclif,** J.

Wydowse, Thomas. Report on Hudson's voyage. (*In* **Harris,** J. Col. of voy., v. 1. 1705.)

Wye River. Gilpin, W. Observations on the River Wye, 1770. 3d ed. London, 1792. 8°.
— - *Same.* 5th ed. London, 1800. 8°.
Wyer, Edward. Advantages of covering with the skin parts recently exposed. — On lymphatic distention of the lower extremities of women in the puerperal state. (*In* **Massachusetts Medical Society.** Medical comm., v. 1. 1808.)
Wyet, Silvester. Voyage of the Grace of Bristoll up into the Gulfe of St. Laurence, 1594. (*In* **Hakluyt,** R. Col. of voy., v. 3. 1810.)
Wyeth, John B. Oregon; or, A journey to the Pacific. Camb., 1833. 12°.
Wyeth, Nathaniel J. Indian tribes of the South Pass of the Rocky Mts.; the Salt Lake basin; the valley of the Great Säaptin or Lewis River and the Pacific coasts of Oregon. (*In* **Schoolcraft,** H. R. Historical and statistical information resp. the hist., *etc.*, of the Indian tribes of the U. S., v. 1. 1851.)
Wyk, J. van. Verhandeling over de Nederlandsche ontdekkingen in Amerika, Australië, de Indiën, en de Poolanden. 1827. *See* **Bennet,** R. G.
Wykeham, Wm. of. *See* **William** *of Wykeham.*
Wykes *or* **Wikes,** Thomas. Chronicon, 1066–1289. (*In* **Luard,** H. R. Annales monast., v. 4. 1869.)
Wyld. *See also* **Wild**; — **Wilde**; — **Wylde.**
Wyld, George. Ventilation by means of the kitchen fire. (*In* **Nat. Assoc. Prom. Soc. Sci.** Trans., 1857.)
Wyld, James. Geographical and mineralogical notes to accompany Wyld's map of the gold regions of California. London, 1849. 8°. (B 1516)
— Gold fields of Australia; notes on the distribution of gold throughout the world. 2d ed. London, [1851]. 8°.
Wylde, James. Magic of science. Lond., 1861. 8°.
Wylde, S. T. Letter to the clergy of Somersetshire, rel. to undue marriages. (*In* **Pamphleteer,** 1813; v. 1 of B 838)
Wylder's hand; by J. S. Le Fanu. (*In* **Dublin univ. mag.,** v. 61-63. 1863-64.)
Wyle, Nicolaus von. Transzlatzion oder tütschungẽ etlicher bücher. [Coloph.:] Strassb., 1510. f°.
Contents. **Pius** II. Euriolo und Lucrecia. — **Boccaccio,** G. Guiscardo und Sigismunda. — **Pius** II. Wider die band der liebe. — **Poggio Bracciolini,** G. F. Trost dem Cosimo de Medicis; — Ob der wirt den gesten oder gest dẽ wirt danckẽ sollẽ; — Ob eim alten man gebühr ein wyb zenemen. — **Wie** durch ratt und wyszheit der athenenser der grosz Allexander gesenfftiget ward; Æschines, Demas, und Demosthenes miteinander redende. — **Bernardus** *Claræveallensis, St.* Von huszhalten. — **Haemmelin,** F. Wem das armusen zegeben sey. — **Pius** II. Was frucht kommt von lernung der schrift. — **Poggio Bracciolini,** G. F. Wie Jeronimus in Concyly zu Costentz verbrant. — **Pius** II. Von der künginfrawglück. — **Lucianus** *Samosatensis.* Von dem guldin esel. — **Wylie,** N. von. Von dem adel; usz alten historien. — **Petrarca,** F. Trostung in leyd usz vernunfft. — **Wylie,** N. von. Von lobwürdigen frawen; usz alten historien. — **Poggio Bracciolini,** G. F. Ein red vor dem Concyly der Cardinellen als babst Nicholaus ward erwelet. — **Wylie,** N. von. Von gebührlichen tyteln.
Wylie, A. On the Nestorian tablet of Se-gan Foo. (*In* **Amer. Orient. Soc.** Journ., v. 5. 1856.)
Wylie, Wyley. *See also* **Wiley**; — **Willey.**
Wyll, The, of the deuyll, and last testament. (*In* **Collier,** J. P. Early Eng. lit., v. 1. 1863.)
Wyman, Edward. Influence of the social relations in the West upon professional usefulness and success. (*In* **Amer. Inst. of Instr.** Lectures, 1850.)
Wyman, Jeffries. Anatomy of the nervous system of rana pipiens. (*In* **Smithsonian Inst.** Contrib., v. 5. 1853.)
— Description of a portion of the lower jaw and a tooth of the mastodon andium; also of a tooth and fragment of the femur of a mastodon from Chile. *n.p.*, [1855]. 4°. (A 67)
— Description of the osteology of the troglodytes gorilla. (*In* **Savage,** T. S. Descr. of the gorilla. 1847.)
— Fossil mammals of Chile. (*In* **U. S.** *Navy Dept.* Naval astronom. exped., v. 2. 1855.)
— Observations on crania. Boston, 1868. 8°.
— Observations on the development of raia batis. (*In* **Amer. Acad.** Mem., n.s., v. 9. 1867.)
Wyman, Morrill. Practical treatise on ventilation. Camb., 1846. 8°.
— Progress in school discipline; corporal punishment in public schools. Camb., 1867. 8°.
— Reality and certainty of medicine. (*In* **Mass. Med. Soc.** Med. comm., v. 10. 1866.)
— Valerianate of morphia. (*In* **Amer. Assoc.** Proc., v. 2. 1850.) — Batrachian reptile from the coal formation. — Note on the teeth of an elephant discovered near Zanesville, Ohio. (*In* v. 10, pt. 2. 1857.)
Wyman, Rufus. Annual discourse before the Mass. Med. Soc., 1830; mental philosophy as connected with mental disease. (*In* **Mass. Med. Soc.** Med. comm., v. 5. 1836.)
Wyman, Thomas Bellows, *Jr.* Genealogy of the name and family of Hunt. Bost., 1862. 4°.
Wyman, Wm. Trial. *See* **Wells,** D.
Wymondham. Woodward, S. Account of some discoveries made in excavating the foundations of Wymondham Abbey, *etc.* (*In* **Archæol.,** v. 26. 1836.)
Wyncoop, Henry. Cyder making. — Acct. of a crab apple orchard. (*In* **Phil. Soc. Prom. Agric.** Mem., v. 3. 1814.)
Wyndham, *Mrs.* Anne. Claustrum regale reseratum; or, King Charles II.'s concealment at Trent. (*In* **Hughes,** J. Boscobel tracts. 1857.)
Wyndham, *Sir* Wm. Speech. (*In* **Chapman,** N. Select speeches, v. 1. 1808.)
Wynds. *See* **Glasgow** (p. 1160).
Wyneken, Fr. Spruchbuch zum kleinen catechismus Lutheri. Balt., 1849. 8°. (C 250)
Wynkelmann. *See* **Wincklemann**; — **Winkelmann.**
Wynn, Charles W. W. Argument upon the jurisdiction of the House of Commons to commit, in cases of breach of privilege. London, 1810. 8°. (B 1418)
Wynn, John, *Bp.* Sermon before the Soc. for Prop. of Gospel, *etc.*, St. Mary-le-Bow, 1724. London, 1725. 8°. (A 31)
Wynne, Edward. Eunomus; or, Dialogues concerning the law and constitution of England. 2d ed. London, 1785. 4 v. 8°.
Wynne, James. Influence of the gulf stream upon the summer climate of the Atlantic coast. (*In* **Amer. Assoc.** Proc., v. 11. 1858.)
— Memoir of S. Maj. Ringgold. Balt., 1847. 8°. (B 1459)
— Private libraries of New York. N. Y., 1860. 8°.
— Typhus fever at the Baltimore almshouse in 1850-51. Pages 417-425 *of* **Amer.** journal of med. sci., n.s., v. 23. 1852. (B 1565)
Wynne, John Huddleston. General history of the British Empire in America. London, 1770. 2 v. 8°.
Contents. Vol. 1. 1492-1748. 2. 1748-62.
Wynne, Robert, *D.D.* Case of the oaths stated. London, 1689. 4°. (B 6, 1397)
— Unity and peace the support of church and state; sermon before the Ho. of Com., Jan. 31. London, 1704. 4°. (B 1465)
Wynne, Wm. Defence of Francis, late Bp. of Rochester at the bar of the Ho. of Lords, May 9, 11. London, 1723. f°. (A 56)
Wynpersse, Dionysius van de. Proof of the true and eternal godhead of Jesus Christ; tr. by T. Bell. Edin., 1795. 8°. (B 194)
Wynter, Andrew. Curiosities of civilization. From the Quarterly and Edinburgh reviews. 3d ed. London, [1860]. 8°.
Contents. Advertisements. — Food and its adulterations. — The zoological gardens. — Rats. — Lunatic asylums. — The London commissariat. — Woolwich arsenal. — Shipwrecks. — Lodging, food, and dress of soldiers. — The electric telegraph. — Fires and fire insurance. — The police and the thieves. — Mortality in trades and professions.
— Our social bees. London, 1865-66. 2 v. 8°.
Contents. Hedging against fate. — London omnibuses. — The water supply of London. — Buried history. — How to buy your own house or land. — The Thames embankment. — Our furniture. — 'Our once fat friend'. — My first deal in horse-flesh. — Horses and horse copers. — Dipsomania; or, Thirst madness. — Our great iron-workers. — Machine tool-makers. — The school of cookery. — Sweets for the million. — Death in the match-box. — A few words on our meat. — Human wasters. — The city companies. — Photo-sculpture. — 'Old clo'.' — Longevity. — The foundling hospital. — A word about wines. — Distinguished settlers from abroad. — False hair; where it comes from. — A sermon on precious stones. — Our lifeboats. — The birth of the steam-engine. — The flesh worm disease.

— Subtle brains and lissom fingers. Lond.,1863. 8°.
Contents. The buried Roman city in Britain. — Dining-rooms for the working classes. — 'Silvertown'. — Railways and city population. — Advertising. — A day with the coroner. — Vivisection. — The English in Paris. — The new hotel system. — The 'Times' newspaper of 1798. — The restoration of our soil. — The under-sea railroad. — Half hours at the Kensington Museum. — Oh! the roast beef of Old England. — Mudie's circulating library. — Physical education. — Fraudulent trade marks. — Advice by a retired physician. — Superstition; where does it end? — The clerk of the weather. — The new counterblast to tobacco. — Portsmouth dockyard. — Air traction. — Village hospitals. — Illuminations. — Railways the great civilizers. — Boat-building by machinery. — On taking a house. — The effects of railway travelling upon health. — Photographic portraiture. — The workingmen's flower show. — Doctors' stuff. — Messages under the sea. — Small-pox in London. — Town telegraphs. — Hospital distress. — The bread we eat. — Excursion trains. — Early warnings. — Poems.

Wyntown, Wintoun, Wyntoune, Wynton, *or* Winton, Andrew. De orygynale cronykil of Scotland; pub., with notes, *etc.*, by D. Macpherson. London, 1795. 2 v. 8°.
Contents. Vol. 1. To 1285. 2. 1286–1408.
— Irving, D. (*In his* Lives of Scot. poets, v. 1. 1804.)
— Life. (*In* **Soc. of Anc. Scots.** Lives of Scot. poets, v. 1, pt. 1. 1822.)
— Tytler, P. F. (*In his* Lives of Scot. worthies, v. 2. Fam. lib., v. 30.)

Wyoming, *pseud.* Letters on the presidential election, and in favour of A. Jackson. Phila., 1824. 8°. (B 1492)

Wyoming. Chapman, J. A. Sketch of the history of Wyoming, [1742–1830]; added, appendix, cont. a statistical acct. of the valley and adjacent country. Wilkesbarre, Penn., 1830. 12°.
— Miner, C. History of Wyoming, [1742–84]. Phila., 1845. 8°.
— Pickering, T. Letter cont. a narrative of the outrage on him at Wyoming, [1818]. Salem, 1819. 8°. (B 448)
— Stone, W. L. Poetry and history of Wyoming, [1742–99]. N. Y., Lond., 1841. 12°.
— - *Same.* 3d ed. with index. Albany, 1864. 12°.

Wypisy do teoryi jazdy. *n.p.*, [184-?]. 8°. (E 84)

Wyrcester, William of. *See* **Guilelmus** *Worcestrius.*

Wyre. Denham, H. M. Directions for navigating the sea-reach of the Wyre. Liverp., 1840. 8°.

Wyse. *See also* **Wise.**

Wyse, *Sir* Thomas. Education in the United Kingdom. (*In* **Central Soc. of Educ.** Papers, v. 1. 1837.) — Lyceum system in America. (*In* v. 2. 1838.) — Present state of Prussian education. (*In* v. 3. 1839.)
— Education reform. Vol. 1. London, 1836. 8°.
— Blanchard, L. (*In his* Saunders' portraits, v. 1. 1838.)
— Redding, C. (*In his* Personal reminiscences of eminent men, v. 1. 1867.)

Wyse child, The, and the Emperor Adrian; dialogue resembling that of Solomon and Saturn; ed. by J. O. Halliwell. London, 1860. 16°.

Wyss, Johann David. Le Robinson suisse; ou, Journal d'un père de famille naufragé avec ses enfants; tr. de l'allemand; [contin. par J. P. P. de B. de C., baronne de Montolieu]. 5e éd. Paris, 1825, 24. 5 v. 12°. (Montolieu. Œuvres.)
— The Swiss family Robinson; or, Adventures of a father and mother and four sons in a desert island. Phila., 1868. 12°.
Note. This is usually attributed to Johann Rudolph Wyss. On the authorship *see* **Kayser,** C. G. 'Bücher-Lexicon'. 1750–1832, v. 6, p. 302, and 'Notes and queries', v. 18 (2d ser., v. 6), p. 289.

Wyssheid en zotheid; zinnespel. Amst., 1699. 4°.

Wyszowaty, A. Narratio quomodo in Polonia a Trinitariis reformatis separati sint Christiani Unitarii cum app. Historia de spiritu Belga. — Epistola exhibens historiam vitæ ac mortis A. Wissowatii. (*In* **Sand,** C. von der. Bibliotheca anti-trinitariorum. 1684.)

Wytfliet, Cornelius. Descriptionis Ptolemaicæ augmentum, sive Occidentis notitia. 2a ed. aucta. Duaci, 1603. f°.

Wyth, John. Portraits to the life and manners of the inhabitants of that part of Amer. called Virginia, 1585–88. *Publ.* 1590, *repub.* N.Y., 1841. 8°. (Pt. 1 of Graphic sketches, *etc.*)

Wythe, *pseud.* The power of Congress over the District of Columbia. N. Y., 1838. 8°. (B 1756)
— *Same.* Anti-slavery examiner, no. 5. 4th ed. N. Y., 1838. 8°. (B 1654)

Wythe, George. Sanderson, J. (*In his* Biog. of the signers to the Declaration of Independence, v. 2. 1820.)

Wyttenbach, Daniel Albert. Opuscula. Lugd. Bat., 1821. 2 v. 8°.
Contents. Vol. 1. Epistola critica ad D. Ruhnkenium. — Dedicatio ex ed. libelli Plutarchei de sera numinis vindicta. — Præf. ex eadem editione. — Oratio de conjunctione philosophiæ cum elegantioribus literis. — Præf. partis primæ Bibliothecæ criticæ. — De obitu Burmanni. — Oratio de philosophia, auct. Cicerone. — Præf. partis quintæ Biblioth. crit. — Dedicatio ex libro Præceptorum philosophiæ logicæ. — Præf. ex eodem libro. — De obitu Ernesti. — De obitu Schraderi. — Oratio de vi et efficacia historiæ ad studium virtutis. — Præf. partis nonæ Bibl. crit. — Præf. ex prima ed. Selectorum principum historicorum. — Præf. ex ed. Plutarchi Moralium, v. 1. — Præf. Animadversionum in Plutarchi Moralia. — Disputatio de libro de Puerorum educatione. — Præf. vitæ D. Ruhnkenii. — Vita D. Ruhnkenii. — Additamentum ad eandem. — De obitu Valckenarii. 2. Epistola ad P. G. van Heusde. — Epistola ad Boschium. — De obitu Villoisoni. — De obitu Santenii. — Prolegomena ex ed. Phædonis Platonici. — Præf. ex 2a ed. Selectorum principum historicorum. — Epistola ad Lyndenum. — De obitu Saxii, Hanæ, Jægeri, et Bangii.—De obitu Wynperssii et Ravii. — Præf. libri primi Miscellaneæ doctrinæ. — Mem. Sanctocrucii. — Addenda ad hanc memoriam. — Annot. ad J. Bakii librum de Posidonio. — Proptrepticus. — Diatribe de Philoxenis. — Mem. G. L. van Wassenaer. — Præf. libri tertii Miscel. doctrinæ. — Parentalia. — Disputatio de Unitate Dei. — De immortalitate anima. — Index utriusque voluminis. — Addenda et emendanda.
— Bibliotheca critica. Amstel., 1779–1808. 3 v. 8°.
— Selecta principum historicorum Herodoti, Thucydidis, Xenophontis, Polybii illustres loci, Plutarchi vitæ Demosthenis et Ciceronis. Ed. altera. Amst., 1808. 8°.
— Vita D. Ruhnkenii. Lugd. Bat., 1799. 8°.
— *Same.* (*In* **Lindemann,** F. Vitæ duor. vir. 1822.)
— Mahne, W. L. Vita W.; ed. et Wyttenbachii epist. adj. F. T. Friedemann. Brunswigæ, 1825. 8°.

Wyttenbach, *Mme.* Jeanne (Galien). Ὁ Ἀλέξις μεταφρασθεὶς ἀπὸ τὴν Γαλλικὴν γλῶσσαν. Ἐν Παρισίοις, 1823. 12°. (B 940)

Wyvern mystery. (*In* **Dublin** university magazine, v. 73–74. 1869.)

Wyvill, Christopher, *dean of Rippon.* An assize sermon, York, Mar. 8. London, 1686. 4°. (B 1351)
— Duty of honoring the King; sermon, Feb. 6. York, 1686. 4°. (B 1272)

Wyvill, *Rev.* Christopher, *rector of Black Notley.* Apology for the petitioners for liberty of conscience. London, 1810. 8°. (B 1916)
— Correspondence of W. with Pitt. Pt. 1. 2d ed. Newcastle, 1796. 8°. (W 60)
— Intolerance the disgrace of Christians not the fault of their religion. 2d ed. Lond., 1809. 8°. (B 241, 1916)
— Letter to the Hon. W. Pitt. 2d ed. York, [1793]. 8°. (B 996)
— Letters on the proposed reformation of the Parl. of Ireland; also address to the freeholders of Yorkshire. York, 1783. 4°. (A 19)
— More discussion in favour of liberty of conscience. 3d ed. London, 1809. 8°. (B 241, 1916)
— Political papers. York, [1794]. 6 v. 8°.
Contents. Vol. 1. 1779–82. 2. 1782–85. 3. 1783–85. 4. 1782–86. 5. 1792–98. 6. 1798–1805.
— Secession from Parliament vindicated. York, 1799. 8°. (B 996)
— State of the representation of England on the principles of Mr. Pitt in 1785. 2d ed. York, 1794. 8°. (B 1524)

Wzokhilain, Peter Paul. *See* **Osunkhirhine,** P. P.

X. Sulle consorterie delle arti edificative in Venezia. (*In* Archivio stor. ital., n.s., v. 6, pt. 1. 1857.)

Xanctoigne, Jean Alphonse de. LITERARY AND HIST. SOC. OF QUEBEC. Voyages de découverte au Canada, 1534–42, par X., *etc.* Quebec, 1843. 8°.

Xanten. ANNALES Xantenses, 640–874. (*In* Pertz, G. H. Mon. Germ. hist., Scr., v. 2. 1829.)

— PERTZ, G. H. Ueber das Xantener Recht. (*In* Berlin. Ak. d. Wiss. Abh., 1846.)

Xanthippe. ZELLER, E. Zur Ehrenrettung der Xanthippe. (*In his* Vorträge. 1865.)

Xanthus *historicus*. Lydiaca. — Magica. — De Empedocle. (*In* Mueller, C. Fr. hist. Gr., v. 1. 1841.)

Xanthus *poeta*. *See* Bergk, T. Poet. lyr. Gr., p. 739.

Xanthus, *Lycia*. BIRCH, S. Observations on the Xanthian marbles recently deposited in the British Museum. (*In* Archæologia, v. 30. 1843.)

— FELLOWS, C. The Xanthian marbles; their acquisition and transmission to England. London, 1843. 4°.

Xaraquemada, Joan. Informe sobre las cosas de Chile. — Cartas. (*In* Gay, C. Hist. de Chile segun documentos, v. 2. 1852.)

Xauregui. *See* Jauregui y Aguilar, J. de.

Xaverius, *Elector of Saxony*. Mühlen-Ordnung vor die Stadt Colditz und dasige, an der Mulde gelegene Amts-Mühle, d. d. 10. Junii, 1766. (*Appended to* Leupold, J. Theatr. mach. mol., v. 3. 1788.)

Xavier, *St.* Francis. *See* Francisco Xavier, *St.*

Xayra, o la fé triunfante del amor y cetro; tragedia francesa. (*In* Huerta, V. G. de la. Tragedias. 1783?)

Xenagoras. Fragm. (*In* Mueller, C. Fr. hist. Gr., v. 4. 1851.)

Xenarchus. Fragm. (*In* Meineke, A. Fr. com. Gr., v. 3. 1840.)

Xenion. Fragm. (*In* Mueller, C. Fr. hist. Gr., v. 4. 1851.)

Xeno. Fragm. (*In* Meineke, A. Fr. com. Gr., v. 4. 1841.)

Xenocles. Fragm. (*In* Nauck, A. Trag. Gr. fr. 1856; — *and in* Wagner, F. W. Fr. Eurip. 1846.)

Xenocrates. Fragm. (*In* Mueller, C. Fr. hist. Gr., v. 4. 1851.)

Xenomedes *Chius*. (*In* Mueller, C. Fr. hist. Gr., v. 2. 1848.)

Xenophanes. Fragm. (*In* Bergk, T. Poet. lyr. Gr. 1853.)

— ARISTOTELES. Traité sur Melissus, Xenophane, et Gorgias. (*In his* Œuvres: Traité de la production. 1866.)

Xenophilus. Fragm. (*In* Mueller, C. Fr. hist. Gr., v. 4. 1851.)

Xenophon *Atheniensis*. Opera omnia. Gotha, 1828–58, 52, 41. 4 v. 8°. (Bibl. Gr., v. 7–10.)

Contents. Vol. 1. Cyropædia; ed. F. A. Bornemann. 2. Commentarii de Socrate; ed. R. Kühner. 3. De expeditione Cyri; rec. R. Kühner. 4. Ed. L. Breitenbach. 4, sect. 1. Œconomicus. 4, sect. 2. Agesilaus. 4, sect. 3. Hiero. 4, sect. 3, [pt. 2]. Hellenica.

— Quæ extant; rec. et interp. est I. G. Schneider. (Vol. 1, ed. 3a; 2, ed. 2a; 3, ed. nova; 4, ed. maior.) Lpz., 1838–40, 25–49, 29, 15–38. 6 v. in 7 pts. 8°.

Contents. Vol. 1. Cur. F. A. Bornemann. 1, pt. 1. De Cyri disciplina, lib. I–V. 1, pt. 2. VI–VIII. — Indices. 2. De expeditione Cyri commentarii. — De Scilluntio agro Xenophonti a Lacedæmoniis donato. — Porsoni adnot. 3. Historiæ Græcæ lib. VII; rec. I. G. Schneider. 4. Rec. F. A. Bornemann. Memorabilia. — Apologia. 5. Rec. I. G. Schneider. Œconomicus. — Convivium. — Hiero. — Agesilaus. 6. Rec. G. A. Sauppe. De auctoritate et integritate libri De republica Lacedæmoniorum disputatio B. Weiskii. — De republica Lacedæmoniorum. — De republica Atheniensium. — De reditibus sive vectigalibus civitatis Atheniensis augendis. — De re equestri. — De magistri equitum officio. — De venatione. — Arrhiani sive Xenophontis Atheniensis de venatione libellus.

— Scripta quæ supersunt; Græce et Latine. Parisiis, *Didot*, 1853. 8°.

— Illustres loci. (*In* Wyttenbach, D. Selecta princip. hist. 1808.)

— *French*. Œuvres complètes; trad. nouv. avec introd. et des notes par E. Talbot. Paris, 1859. 2 v. 16°.

Contents. Vol. 1. Introd. — Mémoires sur Socrate. — De l'économie. — Apologie de Socrate. — Le banquet. — Hiéron. — De l'équitation. — Le commandant de cavalerie. — De la chasse. — Histoire grecque. 2. Expédition de Cyrus et retraite des dix mille. — Cyropédie, ou éducation de Cyrus. — Agésilas. — Gouvernement des Lacédémoniens. — Gouvernement des Athéniens. — Les revenues. — Lettres.

Separate works.

— De æquivocis. (*In* Nanni, G. Berosi lib. 1612.)

— Commentarii; recog. L. Dindorfius. Ed. 2a. Lips., *typis Teubneri*, 1858. 16°.

— *Eng*. Memoirs of Socrates; with the defence of Socrates; tr. by S. Fielding. London, 1788. 8°.

See also, below, 'Anabasis'.

— De Cyri expeditione libri VII in usum scholarum seorsim excusi. Argent., 1561. 8°.

— *Same*. A T. Hutchinson. Ed. 4a. Cantab., 1785. 4°.

— Κύρου ἀναβάσεως βίβλια ἕπτα; juxta ed. T. Hutchinson; acc. var. lect. et index Græcitatis ex ed. Zeunii. Oxon., 1805. 8°.

— Narrative of the expedition of Cyrus and of the retreat of the ten thousand; ed. by A. Crosby. Boston, 1844. 12°.

— Κύρου ἀνάβασις; mit Anmerk. hrsg. von K. W. Krüger. 4e Aufl. Berlin, 1854. 8°.

— Expeditio Cyri; recens. L. Dindorfius. Ed. 4a. Lips., *typis Teubneri*, 1859. 16°.

— *Eng*. Expedition of Cyrus; tr. with notes by E. Spelman. 3d ed. Camb., 1776. 2 v. 8°.

— — The Anabasis and the Memorabilia of Socrates; tr. by J. S. Watson; with a geographical commentary by W. F. Ainsworth. London, *Bohn*, 1859. 8°.

— De Cyri institutione; notas Stephani, Leunclavii, Porti, et Mureti, var. lect. delectum indicesque adj. T. Hutchinson. [Gr. et Lat.] Ed. 6a. Londini, 1765. 8°.

— *Same*. [Gr. et Lat.] Ed. 9a. Londini, 1790. 8°.

— *Same*. [Gr. et Lat.] Ed. 1a Amer., cura J. Watts. Phila., 1806. 8°.

— Cyropædia. Ed. ster. cur. C. H. Weise. Lips., 1828. 24°.

— Institutio Cyri; recens. L. Dindorfius. Ed. 4a. Lpz., *in ædibus Teubneri*, 1858. 16°.

— *Eng*. Cyropædia; or, The Institution of Cyrus; tr. by M. A. [Cooper]. London, 1803. 8°.

— — *Same*. Phila., 1810. 8°.

— — The Cyropædia and the Hellenics; tr. by J. S. Watson and H. Dale. London, *Bohn*, 1855. 8°.

— — *Same*. London, *Bohn*, 1859. 8°.

— *Latin*. *See, above*, 'De Cyri'.

— Defence of the Athenian democracy; tr. from the Greek [by H. J. Pye]. London, 1794. 8°. (B 710)

— Discours sur la manière d'augmenter les revenues d'Athènes. — Sur la république lacédémone; tr. par C. V. Saint-Real. (*In his* Œuvres, v. 7. 1757.)

— Historia Græca; rec. L. Dindorfius. Ed. 2a. Lips., *typis Teubneri*, 1859. 16°.

— *Eng*. History of the affairs of Greece; tr. by W. Smith. London, 1770. 4°.

See also, back, 'The Cyropædia'.

— *Germ.*, *extract*. Rede des Phliasiers Patrokles in Athen, als nach der Schlacht bei Leuktra die Thebaner die Spartaner hart bedrängten. (*In* Seume, J. G. Spaziergang nach Syrakus, v. 3. 1817.)

— Λόγος περὶ ἱππικῆς. — Ἱππαρχικός. — Κυνηγετικός, acc. veterum testimonium de Xenophonte. Ὀξόνια, 1693. 8°.

— Memorabilia. *See, back*, 'Commentarii'.

— Œconomicus. — Apologia Socratis. — Symposium. — Hiero. — Agesilaus, cum animad. I. A. Bachii. Lips., 1749. 8°. (E 29)

— *Same.* [Cum] epistolarum fragm. et Bachii suisque notis explicavit J. C. Zeunius. Lips., 1782. 8°.

— *French.* La mesnagerie; tr. par E. de La Boetie. (*In his* Œuvres complètes. 1846.)

— Scripta minora; recog. L. Dindorfius. Ed. 2a. Lps., *typis Teubneri*, 1858. 16°.

Contents. Œconomicus. — Convivium. — Hiero. — Agesilaus. — Respublica Lacedæmoniorum. — Respublica Atheniensium. — De vectigalibus liber. — Hipparchicus. — De re equestri. — Cynegeticus. — Apologia Socratis.

— *Eng.* Minor works; tr. by J. S. Watson. London, *Bohn*, 1857. 8°.

Contents. Agesilaus. — Hiero. — Œconomicus. — The banquet. — Apology of Socrates. — On the Lacedæmonian government. — On the Athenian government. — On improving the revenues of Athens. — Horsemanship. — Hipparchicus. — Hunting. — Fragments of letters.

— Grant, *Sir* A. Xenophon. Phila., 1871. 12°. (Collins. Ancient classics for Eng. readers.)

— **Melanchthon**, P. Interpretatio orationis Critiæ contra Theramenem, narrationis Prodici de Hercule. (*In his* Opera, v. 17. 1851.)

Xenophon *Ephesius.* De amoribus Anthiæ et Abrocomæ. (*In* **Erotici** scr. 1856; 1859.)

Note. For Eng., French, and Ital. trans. *see* **Erotici** (p. 923).

— *Germ.* Anthia und Abrokomas. (*In* **Bürger**, G. A. Sämmtliche Werke, v. 5. 1823; 1835.)

Xenophon *historicus.* Fragm. (*In* **Mueller**, C. Fr. hist. Gr., v. 3. 1849.)

Xérès, Francisco. Relation véridique de la conquête du Pérou et du Cuzco. (*In* **Ternaux-Compans**, H. Voy., v. 4. 1837.)

— *Ital.* Relatione della conquista fatta da F. Pizarro del Peru. (*In* **Ramusio**, G. B. Rac., v. 3. 1565.)

Xérica, Pablo de. Poesias. (*In* **Wolf**, F. J. Floresta de rimas, v. 2. 1837.)

Xersès; tragédie, par P. J. **Crébillon**. (*In his* Œuvres, v. 2. 1824.)

Xerxes. Abbot, J. History of Xerxes the Great. N. Y., 1854. 16°.

Xiężna i paż, komedya; przeł. z franc. przez L. Zuczkowską. Warszawa, 1834. 16°. (Teatra Warszawskie, pt. 2, v. 1.)

Ximena; or, The heroic daughter; a tragedy by C. **Cibber**. (*In his* Dram. works, v. 3. 1777.)

Ximenes, Juan. Vita S. Paschalis Baylon. (*In* **Acta** sanct., v. 17. 1866.)

Ximenes de Cisneros, Francisco, *Card.* Instruccion al arzobispo Tortoza, al sujeto de la llegada de Carlos v. á España. (*In* **Valladares**, A. Seman. erud., v. 20. 1789.)

— Las historias del origen de los Indios di Guatemala; tr. de la lengua quiché; aument. con introd. y annot. por C. Scherzer. London, 1857. 8°.

— **Arnao**, V. G. Elogio del card. de Cisneros. (*In* **Madrid.** Ac. de la **Hist.** Mem., v. 4. 1805.)

— Baudier, M. History of the administration of X.; tr. by W. Vaughan. Lond., 1679. 8°.

— **Crowe**, E. E., *and* **James**, G. P. R. (*In their* Lives of foreign statesmen, v. 1. 1833. Lardner. Cab. cyc.)

— **Fléchier**, E. (*In his* Œuvres complètes, v. 2, pt. 1. 1782.)

— **Lavergne**, L. de. (*In* **Revue** d. D. Mondes, mai 1841.)

— Marsollier, J. Histoire du ministère du card. Ximenès, Nouv. éd. Paris, 1739. 2 v. 12°.

Ximenez, Andrés, Descripcion del monast. de S. Lorenzo del Escorial. Madrid, 1764. f°.

— De studiis philosophicis et mathematicis. Vol. 1. Matriti, 1789. 8°.

Ximenez y Fernandez, Pedro. El piscator de tejas arriba. Madrid, 1759. 4°. (B 1896)

Ximeno, *Don.* Pregunta [sobre los diezmos]. (*In* **Valladares**, A. Seman. erud., v. 16. 1788.)

Xylander (*Germ.* **Holtzmann**), Wilhelm. **Niceron**, J. P. (*In his* Mém., v. 19. 1732; *and, Germ.*, v. 15. 1757.)

Xystus. *See* **Sextus** *Pythagoræus.*

Y., B. The modern practice of the Court of Exchequer. London, 1731. 8°.

Y., W. Twelve letters to young men on the sentiments of F. Wright and R. D. Owen. Phila., 1830. 8°. (B 1358, 1854)

Yacht voyage to Norway, Denmark, and Sweden. *See* **Ross**, W. A.

Yachting. *See* **Boat.**

Yaçna. Burnouf, E. Commentaire sur le Yaçna. Tome 1. Paris, 1833. 4°.

Yahveh Christ. *See* **Mac Whorter**, A.

Yair, James. Account of the Scotch trade in the Netherlands and of the staple port in Campvere. London, 1766. 8°.

Yakama Indians. *See* **Shahaptan Indians.**

Yakkun Nattannawa, a Cingalese poem; The practices of a capua or devil priest; and Kolan Nattannawa, Cingalese poem; tr. by J. Callaway. London, *Orient. Tr. Fund.*, 1829. 8°.

Yalden, Thomas. Poems; prefixed a life of Y. (*In* **Anderson**, R. Brit. poets, v. 7. 1795; — *and in* **Chalmers**, A. Eng. poets, v. 11. 1810.)

— **Johnson**, S. (*In his* Lives of Eng. poets. 1779; — Lives of eminent Eng. poets, v. 2. 1810; — *and* Works, v. 10. 1806.)

Yale, Cyrus. Address before the Adelphic Union Soc. of Williams Coll., Sept. 4. Williamstown, 1827. 8°. (B 1576)

— Life of the Rev. J. Hallock. 2d ed. Hartford, 1830. 12°.

— Mutual love between a minister and people; sermon, ordination of H. Goodwin, New Marlborough, Mass., Jan. 4. Hartford, 1826. 8°. (B 1133)

Yale College.

Note. Several pamphlets are inserted here which were received too late to be entered under their authors but will be found in the supplement.

Alumni.

Note. In 1841 an association was formed intended to include all the living alumni of Yale.

— Catalogue of the works of art exhibited in the Alumni building, 1858. New Haven, 1858. 8°.

— Addresses and proc., [with] oration by Dr. Bushnell, at the commemorative celebration, July 26, 1865, in honor of the Alumni who were in the service during the recent war; with the names in the Roll of honor. New Haven, 1866. 8°.

— Some statements resp. the late progress and present condition of the Univ., 1868-81. *n.p.*, [1868-81]. 14 v. 8°.

— **Yale** College and the late meeting of the Alumni. Reprinted from the New Englander, Apr. 1869. *n.p.*, [1869]. 8°.

This Library has addresses before the Alumni by the following authors: 1842, **Silliman**, B.; — 1843, **Bushnell**, H.; — 1844, **Dwight**, W. T.; — 1848, **Bacon**, L.; — 1850, **Woolsey**, T. D.; — 1856, **Dana**, J. D.; — 1860, **Sprague**, W. B.; — 1861, **Sturtevant**, J. M.; — 1863, **Stillé**, C. J.

See also Biography.

Annuals.

— Yale banner. Vol. 40. New Haven, 1881. 8°.

— Yale naught-ical almanac, 1873. *n.p.*, *n.d.* 8°.

Biography.

— Obituary record of the graduates deceased during the academical year ending July 1860-81. *n.p.*, [1860-]81. 22 v. 8°.

Note. Collected in two vols. 1860-70, 1871-80, with a separate title-page and suppl. for each vol. The first 18 nos. are not printed, that for 1860 being 'no. 1 of the printed series and no. 19 of the whole record'.

Catalogues.

— Catalogue of the graduates, 1702-1827. New Haven, 1827. 8°.

Annual catalogues.

— Catalogue, 1814, 17-18, 20-81/82. New Haven, 1814-81. 66 v. 8°.

— *Same.* 1840/41. *n.p.*, 1841. 8°. (B 1172)

Triennial catalogues.

— Catalogus senatus acad. et eorum qui munera et officia gesserunt, 1780-1880. In Novo Portu, 1781-1880. 33 v. 8°.

Note. 1778 was the first in octavo form and is very rare.

— *Same.* Novi-Portus, 1808. 8°. (B 140)
— *Same.* Novi-Portus, 1814. 8°. (B 946)
— *Same.* Novi-Portus, 1817. 8°. (B 1012)
— *Same.* Novi-Portus, 1844. 8°. (B 1195)

Classes.

1802.

— Brief memoirs of the members; by D. D. Field, [class historian]. *n.p.*, 1863. 8°.

1814.

— The past and the present; semi-centennial address, July 27, by S. B. Ruggles. N. Y., 1864. 8°.

— Dwight, T. Decisions of questions discussed by the senior class. N. Y., 1833. 12°.

1819.

— Meeting at Yale Coll., July 27, 1859; with biog. notices; [by J. Edwards]. Troy, 1861. 8°.

1821.

— Proc. at their meeting, Yale Coll., Aug. 19; with record of the class; [H. White, sec.]. New Haven, 1846. 8°.

1822.

— Record of meetings, Yale Coll., 1862, 67; with biog. sketches; [H. Herrick, sec.]. New Haven, 1869. 8°.
— Summary of the record of the class to 1860. *n.p.*, [1860]. 8°.

1826.

— Biog. sketch of the class; by S. Haines. Utica, 1866. 8°.

1832.

— Biog. memoranda; by [E. E. Salisbury, sec.]. New Haven, 1880. 8°.

1833.

— 2d decennial meeting, July 27, 1853; [S. W. S. Dutton, sec.]. New Haven, 1854. 8°.
— 3d record of the class; [by G. E. Day]. New Haven, 1870. 8°.

1834.

— History; with biog. sketches; [by H. C. Kingsley]. New Haven, 1875. 8°.

1835.

— Biog. and historical record; [by T. A. Thacher]. New Haven, 1881. 8°.

1837.

— Statistics, 1837-50; with a notice of their meeting, Yale Coll., Aug. 15; [B. Silliman, sec.]. New Haven, 1850. 8°.
— Record; with a notice of their meeting, 1872, and biog. notices. 6th issue. New Haven, 1873. 8°.

1839.

— Poem, by L. W. Smith, and oration, by R. P. Cutler, before the senior class, July 3. N. Haven, 1839. 8°. (B 1233)

1840.

— Statistics; with a notice of their meeting, Yale Coll., July 25, 1860; with a poem, by G. H. Hollister. New Haven, 1860. 8°.

1841.

— Biog. and historical record; [S. W. Barnum, sec.]. N. Y., 1867. 8°.
— - Suppl. New Haven, 1879. 8°.

1842.

— Biog. record; [by R. W. Wright]. New Haven, 1878. 8°.

1845.

— Record; by the sec. [O. Crane]. New York, 1881. 8°.

1848.

— Statistics, Aug. 1848 - July, 1852. New Haven, 1852. 8°.
— Statistics; by H. M. Colton, sec. New Haven, 1869. 8°.

1849.

— Report of the secretary [T. Dwight]. New Haven, 1859. 8°.
— Record of the graduated members; prepared for the meeting, June 25, 1879; [T. E. Harrison, sec.]. New Haven, 1880. 8°.

1850.

— Biog. record; by the class committee. New Haven, 1877. 8°.

1851.

— Statistics; by W. W. Winthrop, sec. Boston, 1854. 8°.

1852.

— 2d biog. record; by D. C. Gilman. New Haven, 1862. 8°.
— Record; [by D. C. Gilman, sec.]. New Haven, 1868. 8°.

1853.

— Statistics; by W. T. Gilbert, sec. New Haven, 1857. 8°.

1854.

— Statistics; by M. N. Whitmore, sec. N. Haven, 1858. 8°.
— Appendix to the class [record, 1867]. New Haven, 1875. 8°.

1855.

— Decennial report; by H. N. Cobb, sec. N. Y., 1866. 8°.

1856.

— Record; by H. E. Pardee, sec. New Haven, 1867. 8°.
— Report and hist. record; by H. N. Cobb, sec. Fishkill, 1876. 8°.

1857.

— Statistics of the class; by D. C. Eaton, sec. N. Y., 1861. 8°.
— Biog. record; with an account of the decennial meeting. New Haven, 1870. 8°.

1858.

— First septennial meeting; with a biog. record; W. P. Bacon, sec. New Haven, 1865. 8°.

1861.

— Poem, [by E. R. Sill], and valedictory oration [by S. Shearer, Jr.], June 19. New Haven, 1861. 8°.
— Triennial meeting; with a biog. record and statistics; [by W. D. Sheldon, sec.]. New Haven, 1864. 8°.
— Decennial record. Cleveland, 1872. 8°.
— - Supplement, 1871-76. New Haven, 1877. 8°.

1864.

— Triennial meeting; with the biog. record and statistics; [C. G. Rockwood, sec.]. New Haven, 1868. 8°.

1866.

— Triennial meeting; with the biog. record and statistics. New Haven, 1869. 8°.

1867.

— Report of the triennial meeting, New Haven, July 20, 1870; with biog. statistics. New Haven, 1870. 8°.

1868.

— Baccalaureate sermon; by Pres. Woolsey, July 19. New Haven, 1868. 8°.

1869.

— Report of the triennial meeting, and biog. record of the class; [E. Heaton, sec.]. New Haven, 1873. 8°.

1870.

— Report of the triennial meeting of the class; with biog. notices; [M. F. Tyler, sec.]. New Haven, 1874. 8°.

Chapel.

— Yale college; two sermons; on leaving the old chapel, [and] on entering the new; by N. Porter. New Haven, 1876. 8°.

Church.

— Clap, T. Religious constitution of colleges, especially Yale College. New-London, 1754. 8°. (B 739)
— Fisher, G. P. Discourse; hist. of the Church in Yale College during the first cent. of its existence, Nov. 22, 1857. N. Haven, 1858. 8°.

Commencement.

— Order of exercises, Sept. 8, 1819. New Haven, [1819]. 8°. (B 447)

Corporation.

— Laws. *See State and College* (Conn. *Gen. Assemb.* Acts).

Directories.

— Addresses, June 1872. *n.p.*, [1872]. 12°.
— Directory. 2d ed. New Haven, 1881. 12°.

Financial affairs.

— GALE, B. Letter shewing that the taxes of Yale College, are stated higher than necessary to defray the annual expences. New Haven, 1759. 8°. (B 739)
— KINGSLEY, J. L. Remarks on the present situation of Yale College; for the consideration of its friends and patrons. *n.t.p.* [1818.] 8°. (B 566)

History.

— WOOLSEY, T. D. Hist. discourse before the graduates, Aug. 14, 1850; 150 years after the founding. New Haven, 1850. 8°.
— BALDWIN, E. Annals of Yale College. 2d ed. New Haven, 1838. 8°.
— CLAP, T. Annals of Yale College, 1700–66. New Haven, 1766. 8°. (C 113)

See also President, etc. Progress, *etc.* (*below*).

Law School.

This Library has an oration before the School by D. H. Chamberlain. 1875.

Laws.

— Laws enacted by the President and Fellows. New Haven, 1787. 8°. (B 739)
— *Same.* Enacted Oct. 1795. New Haven, 1800. 8°.
— *Same.* New Haven, 1808, 11, 17, 22, 25, 32, 35, 37, 43, 48, 50, 52, 54, 56, 58, 60, 62, 64–66, 68, 70, 73. 23 v. 8°. and (1873) 12°.

Library.

— Laws. *n.t.p.* [1872.] 8°.
— Catalogue of most valuable books in the Library. *n.t.p.* [1742.] 8°. (B 609)
— Catalogue of books. New Haven, 1808. 8°. (B 881)
— *Same.* New Haven, 1823. 8°. (B 1138)

See also Numismatics.

Miscellaneous.

— MONUMENTAL gratitude attempted in a poetical rel. of the danger of several of the members of Yale Coll. in passing the Sound, Aug. 20, 1726. New London, 1727. 8°. (B 662)
— HUBBARD, J. Benefactors of Yale Coll., a poetical attempt. Boston, 1733. 8°. (B 355)
— Z., A. Reply to a pamphlet, 'The answer of the friend in the West,' *etc.* *n.p.*, 1755. 4°. (B 652)
— FRIENDLY remarks to the people of Conn. upon their College and schools. *n.p.*, 1799. 12°. (B 615)
— DAY, J., *and* KINGSLEY, J. L. Calculation of the longitude of Yale Coll. (*In* Conn. Acad. of Arts and Sci. Mem., v. 1, pt. 3. 1813.)
— GILMAN, D. C. Bishop Berkeley's gifts to Yale Coll. (*In* N. Haven Colony Hist. Soc. Papers, v. 1. 1865.)
— BAGG, L. H. Four years at Yale; by a graduate of '69. New Haven, 1871. 8°.

Numismatics.

— Catalogue of the coins in the College Library. New Haven, 1863. 8°.

Picture Gallery.

— Catalogue of paintings in the south room of the Trumbull gallery. New Haven, 1835. 8°.
— *Same.* *n.t.p.* [1859.] 8°.
— Catalogue of paintings by Col. Trumbull. 3d ed. New Haven, 1852. 8°.
— *Same.* 5th ed. New Haven, 1864. 8°.

See also Alumni (Catalogue of the works of art), p. 3374.

President.

— Addresses [by T. D. Woolsey, T. A. Thacher, H. M. Sanders, and N. Porter], inaug. of N. Porter, Oct. 11. N. Y., 1871. 8°.
— Report to the Fellows, Oct. 1880–81. *n.t.p.* [1880–81.] 2 v. 8°.
— Progress and changes in the last fifteen years; report to the Soc. of the Alumni, June 28, 1881. *n.t.p.* [1881.] 8°.

School of Engineering.

— Plan of reorganization; by W. A. Norton. *n.t.p.* [18—.] 8°.

School of the Fine Arts.

— 1st, 3d annual exhibition. New Haven, 1867–71. 2 v. 8°.
— STURGIS, R. Manual of the Jarves collection of early Italian pictures; catalogue, with biog. notices of the artists, *etc.*, forming a guide to the study of early Christian art. New Haven, 1868. 8°.
— Catalogue; winter exhibition. New Haven, 1871. 8°.
— Catalogue of the Jarves collection sold by auction in the galleries, Nov. 9. Boston, 1871. 8°.
— Exhibition of Allston's 'Jeremiah' about to be opened at the School. From the New Haven Palladium, Nov. 30. [1866 *or* 67 *or* 68.] Broadside.

Scientific School.

— CONN. *Gen. Assemb.* Report of the joint standing committee on education [on] the petition of the President and Fellows on the establishment of professorships. Hartford, 1847. 8°.
— Appeal in behalf of the School. New Haven, 1856. 8°.
— Proposed plan for a complete organization of the School. New Haven, 1856. 8°.
— GILMAN, D. C. Scientific education the want of Connecticut. *n.t.p.* [1856.] 8°.
— PORTER, J. A. Plan of an agricultural school. *n.p.*, 1856. 8°.

Sheffield Scientific School.

— 1st–15th annual report. New Haven, 1866–81. 15 v. 8°.
— Anniversary [programme], July 15, 1867. *n.p.*, [1867].
— Aim and object of scientific education in the school; [by W. D. Whitney]. From the annual report for 1867/8. New Haven, 1869. 12°.
— Circular.] Evening lectures to mechanics. 1868. Broadside.
— Evening lecture to mechanics; 3d course, 1868, programme. Broadside.
— Exercises of the graduating class, July 19, 1869, July 18, 1870. *n.p.*, [1869–70]. 2 pam.
— The profession of the mechanical or dynamical engineer; inaug. address, Oct. 5, by W. P. Trowbridge. New Haven, 1870. 8°.
— The Sheffield Sci. School as considered by the governors and lieut.-governors of Conn. New Haven, 1870. 8°.
— The Sheffield Sci. School described. N. Y., 1870. 12°.
— The Sheffield Sci. School: what it is not, what it is, what it may be. New Haven, 1870. 12°.

The Library has an oration before the School by C. S. Lyman, 'Scientific education in its relations to industry. 1867.'

See also Scientific School.

Societies.

Association of the Alumni.
See Alumni (p. 3374).

Brothers in Unity.

— POOLE, W. F. Index to subjects in reviews and other periodicals; prepared for the Brothers in Unity. N. Y., 1848. 8°.
— Catalogue of the library. New Haven, 1851. 8°.
— Catalogue of the Society. New Haven, 1854. 8°.
— Prize debate in the senior class, Jan. 15, 1859; question, Does a republic offer a better field for statesmanship than a monarchy. [1859.] Broadside.

Linonian Society.

— Catalogue of the library. New Haven, 1846. 8°.
— *Same.* June. New Haven, 1860. 8°.

Φ Β Κ.

— Catalogue, 1808, 13, 18, 21, 26, 29, 32, 35, 38, 41, 47, 52. New Haven, 1808–52. 12 pam. 8°.

Note. This Library has the following Phi Beta Kappa orations, *etc.*: 1802, On chemistry and botany, by E. Ives; — 1822, On the study of history, by J. G. Percival; — 1827, On the progressive state of the present age, by D. Olmsted; — 1831, J. Kent; — 1833, E. Everett; — 1839, H. Humphrey; — 1840, A. Barnes; — 1842, S. H. Dickson; — 1843, W. B. Sprague; — 1844, W. Hall; — 1846, D. D. Barnard; — D. March; — 1847, L. Ray; — S. North; — 1848, C. B. Haddock; — 1849, A. Smith; — 1850, J. W. Andrews; — 1851, A. B. Street; — Influence of the pulpit and the bar, by D. Lord; — 1853, The problem of the philosophy of history, by H. B. Smith; — 1854, W. H. Seward; — 1861, Poem, by C. Bissell; — 1862, The true and the false, by C. Tracy;

— The stars and stripes, poem, by C. D. **Helmer**; — 1868, How to build a nation, by J. P. **Thompson**; — Yale revisited, poem, by G. T. Dole; — 1869. The college as an element of the state, by E. **Washburne**; — The clocks of Gnoster-town; or, Truth by majority; poem, by E. R. Sill.

State and College.

— DANA, S. W. Yale College subject to the General Assembly. New Haven, 1784. 8°. (B 739)
— LETTER to the Council-Board of Conn., shewing that Yale College is of high importance to the state, *etc.* New Haven, 1766. 8°. (B 651)
— CONNECTICUT. *Gen. Assem.* Acts; with other permanent documents. New Haven, 1871. 8°.
— - *Same.* 2d ed. New Haven, 1878. 8°.

Theological Department.

— General catalogue. New Haven, 1838. 8°.
— *Same.* 1822–72. New Haven, 1873. 8°.
— Addresses [of T. D. Woolsey and J. M. Hoppin], at the inaug. of the professors, Sept. 15. New Haven, 1861. 8°.
— Addresses [of L. Bacon, and others], laying of the corner-stone of Divinity Hall, Sept. 22. New Haven, 1869. 8°.
— The theological department essential in a university; address, by S. Harris. at his inaug. as Dwight professor, Oct. 10. New Haven, 1871. 8°.
— Semi-centennial anniversary of the Divinity School, May 15–16. New Haven, 1872. 8°.

Treasurer.

— Report, 1879–81; by H. C. Kingsley. *n.t.p.* [1879–81.] 3 v. 8°.

Trumbull Gallery.
See Picture Gallery.

Winchester Observatory.

— Report of the Board of Managers; appended, report of the astronomer. *n.p.*, [1881]. 8°.

Yamacraw Indians. JONES, C. C., *Jr.* Historical sketch of Tomo-Chi-Chi, Mico of the Yamacraws. Albany, 1868. 8°.

Yamassee war in S. Carolina. (*In* **Carroll**, B. R. Hist. col., v. 2. 1836.)

Yandell, Lunsford P. Distribution of the crinoidea in the Western States. (*In* **Amer. Assoc.** Proc., v. 5. 1851.)
— M'DOWELL, W. A. Reply to Yandell's rejoinder rel. to cure of consumption. Louisville, Ky., 1844. 8°. (B 1557)

Yáñez y Ribera, Jeronimo, *de Alcala.* El donado hablador Alonso, mozo de muchos amos. (*In* **Rosell**, C. Nov. post. a Cervantes, v. 1. 1851.)

Yang-Tsze-Kiang, *river.* BLAKISTON, T. W. Five months on the Yang-Tsze. London, 1862. 8°.
— GR. BRITAIN. *Parl.* Correspondence resp. the opening of the Yang-Tze-Kiang River to foreign trade. London, 1861. f°.

Yankee, The; Jan. 3, 1812 – Dec. 24, 1813; Jan. 7, 1814 – Dec. 30, 1819. Bost., 1812–19. 5 v. f°.
Note. From Apr. 5 to Dec. 30, 1819 called 'Boston Yankee'.

Yankee among the nullifiers; autobiography by Elnathan Elmwood [Asa Greene]. N. Y., 1833. 16°.

Yankee and Boston literary gazette; n. s., July – Dec. 1829. Boston, 1829. 8°.

Yankee chronology. *See* **Dunlap**, W. (C 6)

Yankee tea party; by H. C. Watson. Phila., 1852. 12°.

Yankees. CONFEDERATE, The; [the history and character of the Yankees], by a South Carolinian. Mobile, 1863. 12°.

Yankey in England; a drama in five acts; by [D.] Humphreys. *n.p.*, [1815]. 8°. (B 666)

Yankey in London, The; letters by an American to friends in Boston. Vol. 1. N. Y., 1809. 12°. (C 107)

Yankies' war-hoop, The; or, Ld. North's Te-deum; [verses] by an American. London, 1775. 4°. (A 28)

Yanosky, J. L'Afrique chrétienne et domination des Vandales en Afrique. (*In* **Avezac-Macaya**, M. A. P. d'. Afrique. 1844.)

— Carthage. 1835. *See* **Dureau de la Malle**, A. J. C. A.
— Italie ancienne. 1850–51. *See* **Duruy**, V.
— *and* **David**, J. A. Syrie ancienne et moderne. Paris, 1848. 8°. (Univers.)

Yaradee; a plea for Africa. *See* **Freeman**, F.

Yardley, E. Practical exposition on baptism and confirmation, and on the communion service of the Church of England. Lond., 1811. 12°.

Yarmouth, *Eng.* NALL, J. G. Great Yarmouth; a handbook. London, 1866. 16°.

Yarmouth, *Mass.* ALDEN, T. Memorabilia of Yarmouth. (*In* **Mass. Hist.** Soc. Col., v. 5. 1816.)
— FREEMAN, J. Note on the south parts of Yarmouth and Barnstable. 1802. (*In* v. 8. 1802.)

Yarnall, Ellis, *et al.* *See* **Evans**, J. (B 239)

Yarranton, Andrew. SMILES, S. (*In his* Industrial biog. 1863.)

Yarrell, Wm. History of British fishes. London, 1836. 2 v. 8°.
— - Supplement. London, 1839. 8°.

Yate, *Rev.* Wm. Account of New Zealand and the formation and progress of the Church Missionary Society's mission to the northern island. London, 1835. 12°.

Yates. *See also* **Yeates.**

Yates, Andrew. Charity the evidence of piety; sermon, Sept. 13. Hartford, 1812. 8°. (B 336)

Yates, Christopher C., *M.D.* Exposition of a most villainous attempt at extortion. *n.t.p.* [1817.] 8°. (B 449)
— Observations on Asiatic or spasmodic cholera. 2d ed. N. Y., 1832. 8°. (B 1565)

Yates, Edmund Hodgson. Black sheep; a novel. Lpz., *Tauchnitz*, 1867. 2 v. 12°.
Note. Repub. from **All** the year round, v. 16, 17. 1866–67; *also in* **Every** Saturday, v. 2, 3. 1866–67.
— Broken to harness. (*In* **Temple Bar**, v. 10–13. 1864–65.)
— Land at last. (*In* v. 14–17. 1865–66.)
— Wrecked in port. (*In* **All** the year round, v. 21, n. s., v. 1–2. 1868–69.)
— *and* **Harrington**, N. H. Hit him, he has no friends; farce. (No. 31 *of* **Spencer's** univ. stage.)
— FORGUES, E. (*In* **Revue** d. D. Mondes, juin 1867.)

Yates, *Rev.* J. F. God and the king; discourse. Pittsfield, 1862. 8°. (B 1593)

Yates, James, *b.* 1789. Vindication of Unitarianism; reply to Wardlaw's Discourse, 'Principal points of the Socinian controversy'. Boston, 1816. 8°.
— Sequel to 'Vindication of Unitarianism', reply to Wardlaw's 'Unitarianism incapable of vindication'. Liverpool, 1817. 8°.
— *Another copy.* (B 1017)
— WARDLAW, R., *D.D.* Unitarianism incapable of vindication; a reply to Yates's 'Vindication'. Andover, 1817. 8°.
— *Funeral sermon on.* 1826. *See* **Shepherd**, W. (B 1228)

Yates, James, *M.A.* Irregularities of the versification of Homer. (*In* **Philological** Soc. Trans., 1856.)
— Observations on Lord Russell's bill for registering births, deaths, and marriages in England. London, 1836. 8°. (B 1529)
— Observations on the statue of the dying gladiator at Rome. (*In* **Archæol. Inst.** of Gr. Brit. Memoirs illust. hist. of Bristol. 1853.)

Yates, John, *D.D.* Modell of divinitie, catechistically composed. London, 1622. 4°.

Yates, John Ashton. Letters on the distresses of the country. 2d ed. London, 1817. 8°.

Yates, John V. N., *and* **Moulton**, J. W. History of the State of N. Y., incl. aboriginal and colonial annals. Vol. 1, pt. 1. N. Y., 1824. 8°.
— CASE of Yates, decided in the Supreme Court of N. Y., Aug. term, 1809. *n.t.p.* 8°. (B 458)

Yates, Joseph C. JENKINS, J. S. (*In his* Lives of the governors of N. Y. 1851.)

Yates, Peter W. Address, Schenectady, Dec. 27, 1783, festival of St. John the Evangelist. Albany, 1784. 12°. (W 19)

Yates, Richard. Sermon [to] the Royal Humane Society, April 12; with an app. on resuscitation, by the Society. London, 1807. 8°. (B 336)
— COURTIER, P. L. (*In his* Pulpit, v. 1. 1809.)

Yates, Robert. Secret proc. and debates of the convention at Phila., 1787, for forming the Constitution of the U. S.; from notes taken by Y.; including the genuine information laid before the legislature of Maryland by L. Martin; also other historical documents. Albany, 1821. 8°.
— *Same.* Wash., 1836. 8°.
— *Same.* Richmond, 1839. 8°.
Yates, Thomas. Pewter and britannia metal trade. (*In* **Timmins**, S. Resources of Birmingham. 1866.)
Yates, W. H. Temptations and dangers to youth of both sexes in London. (*In* **Nat. Assoc. Prom. Soc. Sci.** Trans., 1864.)
Yates, Wm., *and* **Maclean**, C. View of the science of life; on the principles of J. Brown; [also] treatise on mercury, and a dissert. on epidemic and pestilential diseases by C. Maclean. Dover, [N. H.,] 1801. 8°.
Yates, Wm., *b.* 1792, *d.* 1845. Essay on Sanscrit alliteration. (*In* **Asiatic researches**, v. 20, pt. 1.) — Review of the Naishadha Charita, a Sanscrit poem, by Shrí Harsha. (*In* pt. 2. 1836.)
— Sanscrit reader. Calcutta, 1822. 8°.
Yatman, Matthew. Animal electricity; origin and identity of the electric and galvanic fluids. 2d ed., with add. London, [1805]. 8°. (B 817)
Yawry Bay. Fisher, R. Map. London, 1794. (**E 67**)
Yaws. Adams, J. (*In his* Morbid poisons. 1807.)
Yeadon, Richard. Amenability of northern incendiaries as well to southern as to northern laws. Charleston, 1835. 8°. (B 1474)
— Speech at the Pilgrim celebration, Plymouth, Aug. 1. N. Y., 1853. 8°. (B 1571)
Yeaman, George H. The study of government. Boston, 1871. 8°.
Yeamans family. Sumner, W. H. (*In his* Memoir of I. Sumner. 1854.)
Year. Ideler, L. Ueber die bei den morgenländischen Völkern gebräuchlichen Formen des julianischen Jahrs. (*In* **Berlin. Ak. d. Wiss.** Abh., 1816–17.)
See also **Chronology.**
Year and a day, A. (*In* **Blackwood's** mag., v. 105–106. 1869.)
Year at the shore, A. *See* **Gosse**, P. H.
Year-books. Year-book, The; an astronomical and phil. annual; by M. Conant. Boston, 1836. 12°.
— Year-book of facts in science and art; by [J. Timbs]. London, 1840–80. 41 v. 16°.
— *Same.* Extra volume: Year-book of facts in the International Exhibition, 1862. London, 1862. 16°.
— Year-book of daily recreation and information; by W. Hone. London, 1841. 8°.
— Antiquarian and architectural year-book for 1844. London, 1845. 8°.
— Congregational year-book, 1850, 53. London, 1850–53. 2 v. 8°.
— American congregational year-book. N. Y., 1854–59. 6 v. 8°.
— Yearly journal of trade, 1854/55, 56; by C. Pope. London, 1854–56. 2 v. 8°.
— Year-book of the Unitarian churches, 1855–58, 67–77. Boston, *A. U. A.*, 1855–77. 15 v. 12°.
— Churchman's year book; or, Eccles. annual register, 1856. London, 1856. 12°.
— Year-book of the nations for 1856; by E. Burritt. N. Y., 1856. 12°.
— American educational year-book, 1857–58. Boston, 1857–58. 2 v. 12°.
— Year-book of medicine, surgery, *etc.*, 1859–63; ed. by G. Harley, and others. London, *New Syd. Soc.*, 1859–64. 5 v. 8°.
Note. Afterwards called 'Biennial retrospect'.
— Year-book of agricultural facts, 1861; ed. by R. S. Burn. Edin., 1862. 12°.
— Statesman's year-book, 1864–81. London, [1864–81]. 17 v. 16°.
— Year books of Edward I.; ed. and tr. by A. J. Horwood. London, 1866, 73, 63, 64, 79. 5 v. 8°. (Chron. and mem.)
Contents. Vol. 1. 20, 21 Edward I. 2. 21, 22. 3. 30, 3. 4. 32, 33. 5. 34, 35.
— Christian year book, The. London, 1867–68. 2 v. 8°.
— Churchman's year-book, The; with kalendar, 1871; comp. by W. S. Perry. Hartford, 1871. 8°.
— Hunt's merchants' magazine year-book, 1871. N. Y., 1871. 8°.
See also **Annuals.**
Year in Spain, A; by [A. S. Mackenzie]. Boston, 1829. 8°.
— *Same.* London, 1831. 2 v. 12°.
Year nine; by [Mrs. A. Manning]. London, 1858. 12°.
Year of consolation. *See* **Kemble**, F. A.
Yearly journal of trade, 1854/55, 56; by C. Pope. London, 1854–56. 2 v. 8°.
Yeast; a problem, by C. Kingsley. New York, 1851. 12°.
Note. Reprinted from **Fraser's** mag., v. 38. 1848.
Yeates. *See also* **Yates.**
Yeates, Jasper. Hamilton, W. Report of the trial of Yeates, *etc.* London, 1805. 8°.
Yeates, Thomas. Hebrew grammar. London, 1804. 8°.
Yeats, Grant David. Early symptoms of water in the brain. London, 1815. 8°.
Yeats, J. Human growth in towns. (*In* **Nat. Assoc. Prom. Soc. Sci.** Trans., 1863.) — On national exodus; its consequences and results. (*In* 1864.)
Yeddo, *or* **Yedo**. *See* **Jeddo.**
Yellow fever. Hillary, W. Yellow fever. [1759.] (*In his* Obs. on the changes of air, *etc.* 1811.)
— Currie, W. Treatise on yellow fever. Phila., 1794. 8°. (B 816)
— Chisholm, C. Essay on the fever introduced into the W. I. Islands from Boulam. Phila., 1799. 8°.
— - *Same.* 2d ed. enlarged. London, 1801. 2 v. 8°.
— Rush, B. 2d address to the citizens of Phila.; [with] proofs of the domestic origin of yellow fever, *etc.* Phila., 1799. 8°. (B 832)
— Tytler, J. Treatise on the plague and yellow fever. Salem, 1799. 8°.
— Washington, B. Observations on yellow fever. *n.t.p.* [18—.] 8°. (B 1104, E 59)
— Brown, S. Nature, origin, and progress of the yellow fever. Boston, 1800. 8°.
— - *Other copies.* (B 419, 832, 924, 1877)
— Caldwell, C. Address to the Phila. Medical Soc. on the analogies between yellow fever and true plague. Phila., 1801. 8°. (B 470)
— Ruston, T. A collection of facts interspersed with obs. on the yellow fever. Pt. 1. Phila., 1804. 8°. (B 470, 832)
— Dalmas, A. Sur la fièvre jaune. Paris, 1805. 8°.
— Woltman, R. Ueber die Propagation des Gelben-Fiebers. (*In his* Theory and description of a ventilator. 1805.)
— Bancroft, E. N. Essay on yellow fever, *etc.* [1806, 07.] London, 1811. 8°.
— - Sequel to an Essay on yellow fever. London, 1817. 8°.
— Assalini, P. Yellow fever, plague, *etc.*; tr. by A. Neale; added, letter on yellow fever, by G. Pinchard. N. Y., 1806. 12°.
— Chisholm, C. Letter to J. Haygarth on the infectious nature of this distemper in Granada and the U. S. London, 1809. 8°.

— Miller, E., *d.* 1812. Cursory obs. on yellow fever. (*In his* Medical works. 1814.)

— Pym, W. Obs. upon the Bulam fever. London, 1815. 8°.

— Armstrong, J. Yellow fever. [1816.] (*In* **Boott, F.** Life, *etc.*, of J. Armstrong. 1833.)

— Burnet, W. Account of the Mediterranean fever. London, 1816. 8°.

— Doughty, E. Yellow or Bulam fever in Jamaica and Cadiz. London, 1816. 8°.

— Dickinson, N. Obs. on the yellow fever. London, 1819. 8°.

— Spalding, L. Reflections on yellow fever periods; or, Investigation of the question, whether the yellow fever can originate amongst us. N. Y., 1819. 8°. (B 832, 1716)

— Boston. Board of Health. Interesting account of plague, yellow fever, *etc.* Boston, 1820. 8°. (B 832, 1754, E 59)

— Osgood, D. Letter on the yellow fever of the West Indies. N. Y., 1820. 8°. (B 826)

— Chabert, J. L. Réflexions médicales sur la maladie spasmodico-lipyrienne, vulgairement appelée fièvre jaune. Nouvelle Orléans, 1821. 8°.

— Jackson, R. Yellow fever on south coasts of Spain. London, 1821. 8°.

— Caldwell, C. Dissertation resp. the origin, contagion, and general philosophy of yellow fever. [1823.] (*In his* Med. and phys. mem. 1826.)

— O'Halloran, T. Remarks on the yellow fever of the south and east coasts of Spain. London, 1823. 8°.

— Romaine, B. Observations, reasons, and facts disproving importation and also contagion in yellow fever. N. Y., 1823. 8°. (B 832)

— Palloni, G. Se la febbre gialla sia o no un contagio. Livorno, 1824. 8°.

— Wilson, J. Memoirs of West Indian fever commonly called yellow fever. London, 1827. 8°.

— Chervin, N. Sur la contagion ou non contagion de la fièvre jaune. Paris, Londres, 1829. 8°.

— Simons, T. Y. Essay on the yellow fever. Charleston, 1851. 8°. (B 1562)

— Howard Association of Norfolk. Report to contributors who gave aid in behalf of sufferers from yellow fever in 1855. Phila., 1857. 8°.

— Anderson, T. Handbook for the yellow fever, *etc.* London, 1866. 16°.

— Woodward, J. J. Report on epidemic cholera and yellow fever. (*In* **United States.** *Surgeon General.* Circular, no. 1. 1868.)

Note. For accounts of the yellow fever in various cities *see* **Charleston** (p. 531); — **Gibraltar** (p. 1148); — **Newport** (p. 2131); — **Philadelphia** (p. 2314).

Yellow mask, The. (*In* **Household words**, v. 11. 1855.)

Yellowplush, Charles J., *pseud.* Yellowplush correspondence; by W. M. Thackeray. Phila., 1838. 8°.

— *Same.* Memoirs of C. J. Yellowplush; by W. M. **Thackeray.** (*In his* Miscellanies, v. 2. 1856.)

— *Same.* Yellowplush papers; by W. M. Thackeray. N. Y., 1864. 12°.

Note. From **Fraser's mag.**, v. 16–21. 1837–40.

Yellowstone River. Raynolds, W. F. Report on the exploration of the River. Wash., 1868. 8°.

Yelverton, Therèse, *Viscountess Avonmore.* Zanita; a tale of the Yo-Semite. N. Y., 1872. 8°.

Yemen. Sjögren, A. J. Ueber die älteren Wohnsitze der Jemen; ein Beitrag zur Geschichte der tschudischen Völker in Russland. (*In* **St. Petersburg. Ac. Sci.** Mém., 6e sér., v. 1. 1832.)

Yemeniz, N. Catalogue de la bibliothèque de Y.; préc. d'une notice par C. [Roux de Lincy; la vente, mai 1867]. Paris, 1867. 8°.

Yenikale, Straits of. Lenormant, C. Sur les antiquités du Bosphore Cimmérien. (*In* **Paris. Inst.** *Ac. d. Inscr.* Mém., v. 24, 1e pt. 1861.)

Yeoman, Thomas H. Consumption of the lungs; revised by [C. E. Ware]. Boston, 1850. 12°.

Yeomans, John William. History of Adams; [also] history of Clarksburg. (*In* **Field, D. D.** History. 1829.)

— Sermon, annual election, Jan. 1. Boston, 1834. 8°. (B 1085, 1695, 1830)

Yerbury, *Mrs.* **Frances,** *Funeral sermon on.* 1752. *See* **Billingsley, S.** (B 128)

Yerrington, James M. W. Report of the case of G. C. Hersey indicted for the murder of B. F. Tirrell. Boston, 1862. 8°.

Yes and no; a tale by C. H. Phipps. Phila., 1828. 2 v. 12°.

Yesso *or* **Jesso Island.** Rinsifé. Descr. du pays des Yeso. (*In his* San kokf tsou ran to sets. 1832.)

— Relation de la découverte de la terre de Jesso en 1643; tr. du hollandois. (*In* **Bernard, J. F.** Rec. de voy., v. 3. 1716.)

Yesterday, to-day, and forever; a poem. *See* **Bickersteth, E. H.**

Yezidis. Layard, A. H. The Yezidis, or devil worshippers. (*In his* Nineveh. 1849; 1867.)

Yo et les principes de 89; [par] H. Pessard; fantaisie chinoise; préface de Prevost Paradol. Brux., 1866. 8°.

Yo por vos, y vos por otro; comedia. *See* **Moreto y Cabaña, A. de.** (E 111)

Yoakum, H. History of Texas; with app. N. Y., 1856. 2 v. 12°.

Contents. Vol. 1. 1685–1835. 2. 1835–46.

Yonge, Charles Duke. An English-Greek lexicon; ed. by H. Drisler. N. Y., 1870. 8°.

— History of England to the peace of Paris, 1856. London, 1857. 12°.

— History of France under the Bourbons. London, 1866–67. 4 v. 8°.

Contents. Vol. 1. 1589–1643. 2. 1643–1715. 3. 1715–87. 4. 1787–1830.

— History of the British navy. London, 1863. 2 v. 8°

Contents. Vol. 1. 700–1801. 2. 1801–62.

— Life and administration of R. Banks, 2d Earl of Liverpool. London, 1868. 3 v. 8°.

Contents. Vol. 1. 1770–1814. 2. 1814–19. 3. 1820–28.

Yonge, Charlotte Mary. Beechcroft. N. Y., 1869. 12°.

— Book of golden deeds. Cambridge, Mass., 1865. 16°.

Contents. What is a golden deed? — Alcestis and Antigone. — The cup of water. — How one man has saved a host. — The pass of Thermopylæ. — The rock of the capitol. — The two friends of Syracuse. — The devotion of the Decii. — Regulus. — The brave brethren of Judah. — The chief of the Arverni. — Withstanding the monarch in his wrath. — The last fight in the Colisæum. — Shepherd girl of Nanterre. — Leo the slave. — The battle of the Blackwater. — Guzman el Bueno. — Faithful till death. — What is better than slaying a dragon? — The keys of Calais. — Battle of Sempach. — The constant prince. — Carnival of Perth. — Crown of St. Stephen. — George the triller. — Sir Thomas Moore's daughter. — Under Ivan the Terrible. — Fort St. Elmo. — The voluntary convict. — Housewives of Löwenburg. — Fathers and sons. — The soldiers in the snow. — Gunpowder perils. — Heroes of the plague. — The 2d of September. — The Vendéens. — Faithful slaves of Haiti. — The petitioners for pardon. — Children of Blentarn Ghyll. — Agostina of Zaragoza. — Casal novo. — The mad dog. — The Monthyon prizes. — The loss of the Drake and the Magpie. — Fever at Osmotherly. — The chieftainess and the volcano. — Discipline. — The rescuers. — The rescue party. — The children in the wood of the far South.

— The caged lion. N. Y., 1870. 12°.

— The castle builders. N. Y., 1864. 12°.

— The clever woman of the family. N. Y., 1865. 8°.

Note. From **Littell's living age**, v. 82–85. 1864–65.

— Countess Kate. 3d ed. Boston, 1866. 12°.

— The daisy chain. N. Y., 1856. 2 v. 12°.
Note. See, below, 'The trial'.
— Danvers papers. London, 1867. 16°
— The dove in the eagle's nest. New York, 1866. 12°.
Note. From Macmillan's mag., v. 12–13. 1865-67.
— Dynevor Terrace. London, 1857. 2 v. 16°.
— Friarswood post-office. N. Y., 1865. 16°.
— The gain of a loss. London, 1866. 3 v. 8°.
— The heir of Redcliffe. N. Y., 1871. 2 v. 12°.
— History of Christian names. London, 1863. 2 v. 8°.
— Hopes and fears; or, Scenes from the life of a spinster. London, 1860. 2 v. 16°.
Note. From Littell's living age, v. 64-68. 1860-61.
— Kenneth; or, The rear guard of the Grand Army. N. Y., 1855. 12°.
— The lances of Lynwood. N. Y., 1856. 12°.
— Landmarks of history: Ancient history. 1st American ed. from 5th London ed. Phila., 1863. 12°.
— Marie Thérèse Lamourous; a biog. abridged from the French [of the abbé Pouget]. London, 1858. 16°.
— Musings over 'The Christian year'; and 'Lyra innocentium, with recollections of Keble by friends. N. Y., 1871. 8°.
— Pioneers and founders. London, 1871. 12°.
Contents. J. Eliot. — D. Brainerd. — C. F. Schwartz. — H. Martyn. — W. Carey and J. Marshman. — Judson family. — T. Middleton, R. Heber, Dr. Wilson. — S. Marsden. — J. Williams. — A. Gardiner. — C. F. Mackenzie.
— The pupils of St. John the divine. London, 1868. 12°.
— The six cushions. Boston, 1870. 16°.
— A store house of stories. London, 1870. 8°.
Contents. The history of Philip Quarll. — Goody Twoshoes. — The governess. — Jemima Placid. — The perambulations of a mouse. — The village school. — The little queen. — History of little Jack.
— The trial; more links of the daisy chain. N. Y., 1864. 2 v. 12°.
— The two guardians; or, Home in this world. N. Y., 1866. 12°.
— The young step-mother; or, Chronicle of mistakes. N. Y., 1862. 2 v. 12°.

Yonge, Francis. Narrative of proc. of the people of S. Carolina in 1719. (*In* Carroll, B. R. Hist. col., v. 2. 1836; — *and in* Force, P. Collection of tracts, v. 2. 1836.)

Yonge, Philip, *Bp. of Bristol.* Sermon, Feb. 13, general fast. London, 1761. 4°. (B 1257)

Yonge, Walter. Diary, written at Colyton and Axminster, Co. Devon, 1604–28; ed. by G. Roberts. London, 1848. 4°. (Camden Soc., v. 41.)

Yonkers gazette. *See* **Gazette.**

Yonne, Département de l'. QUANTIN, M. Répertoire archéologique du Département de l'Yonne; Paris, 1868. 4°. (Répert. archéol. de la France.)

Yorick *figlio di Yorick, pseud.* Viaggio attraverso l'esposizione ital. del 1861. Ed. 2a. Firenze, 1861. 16°.

Yorick, *Mr., pseud. See* **Sterne, L.**

York, *Archbp. of.* **Blackburn, L.**; — **Dawes, W.** *See* **Herring, T.**; — **Hutton, M.**; — **Markham, W.**; — **Sandys, E.**; — **Sharp, J.**; — **Thompson, W.**; — **Williams, J.**

York, *Duke of. See* **James II.**; — **Frederic,** *Duke of York.*

York, Brantley. Analytical, illustrative, and constructive grammar of the Eng. language. 3d ed. Raleigh, 1862. 8°.
— English grammar as adapted to southern schools. 3d ed. Raleigh, 1864. 8°.

York, *Eng.* *Antiquities and History.*
— LOCKWOOD, H. F., *and* CATES, A. H. History of the ancient fortifications of York. London, 1834. 4°.
— CAVE, H. Antiquities of York. Lond., 1813. 4°.
— DRAKE, F. Eboracum; history and antiquities of the city of York, [to **1736**]. London, 1736. 2 pt. f°.
— RAINE, J. Testamenta Eboracensia; or, Wills registered at Y., illust. of the hist., manners, language, *etc.*, of the province of Y., **1300–[1509.]** London, Durham, 1836–69. 4 v. 8°. (Surtees Soc., v. 4, 30, 45, 53.)

Ecclesiastical affairs.

— DIXON, W. H. Fasti Eboracenses; lives of the archbishops of York; ed. and enl. by J. Raine. Vol. 1. London, 1863. 8°.
— EATON, D. Narrative of the proc. of the Society of Baptists in York. 3d ed. London, 1823. 12°.

Lunatic Asylums.

See **Retreat, The, near York**; — **West Riding of York Pauper Lunatic Asylum**; — **York Lunatic Asylum.**

York, *Eng.,* **Diocese of.** EGBERT, *Archbp. of York.* Pontifical; [ed. by W. Greenwell]. Durham, 1853. 8°. (Surtees Soc., v. 27.)

York, *Maine.* SEWALL, D. Topographical description of York. (*In* Mass. Hist. Soc. Col., v. 3. 1810.)

York, House of. B., W. The white rose; a word for the House of York, vindicating the right of succession. London, 1680. f°. (A 52)
— SPELMAN, E. History of the civil wars between York and Lancaster; continued by G. W. Lemon. Lynn, 1792. 8°.

York, Cumberland, *and* **Lincoln Counties,** *Me.* Proceedings of two conventions to consider the expediency of a separate government in Maine, [1786]. (*In* Mass. Hist. Soc. Col., v. 4. 1795.)
— Address of a convention from 20 towns and 5 plantations to the people on their separation from Mass. Portland, [1795]. 12°. (B 613)

York Cathedral. BRITTON, J. History and antiquities of the Cathedral of York. London, 1819. 4°.
— FRÈRE, E. B. De livres de liturgie des églises d'Angleterre, York, *etc.* Rouen, 1867. 8°.
— FABRIC rolls of York Minster; [ed. by J. Raine, Jr.]. Durham, 1859. 8°. (Surtees Soc., v. 35.)

York Lunatic Asylum. HIGGINS, G. Abuses at the Asylum. Doncaster, 1814. 8°.
— - Evidence taken before a committee of the House of Commons resp. the Asylum at York; with notes, and a letter to the committee. Doncaster, 1816. 8°.

Yorke, Charles. Letters to W. Warburton. (*In* Warburton, W. Letters. 1809.)
— *and* **Leake, W. M.** Egyptian monuments in the British Museum and other collections. (*In* Royal Soc. of Lit. Trans., v. 1. 1827.)
— PARLIAMENTARY opinions, *etc.* London, 1788. 8°. (B 761)

Yorke, *Rev.* Grantham. Some account of the Birmingham Free Industrial School. (*In* Nat. Assoc. Prom. Soc. Sci. Trans., 1868.)

Yorke, Henry Redhead. These are the times that try men's souls; letter to J. Frost. London, [1793]. 12°. (D 55)
— Thoughts on civil government; addressed to the disfranchised citizens of Sheffield. London, 1794. 12°. (D 55)
— CAMPBELL, J. (*In his* Lives of the admirals. 1817.)
See also **Weekly** political review of H. R. Yorke. Vol. 6.

Yorke, Philip, *1st Earl of Hardwick.* Two speeches of a late Lord Chancellor. London, 1770. 8°. (B 1632)

Yorke, Philip, *2d Earl of Hardwick.* Miscellaneous state papers. London, 1778. 2 v. 4°.
Contents. Vol. 1. 1501–1625. 2. 1625–1726.

— *and others.* Athenian letters. London, 1798. 2 v. (v. 2 w.). 4°.
Note. These letters are by P. Yorke, C. Yorke, G. H. Rooke, J. Green, D. Wray, J. Heaton, Dr. Heberden, H. Coventry, J. Lawry, Mrs. C. Talbot, T. Birch, and Dr. Salter.

— Cooksey, R. Life and character of P. Yorke. Worcester, 1791. 4°.

Yorkshire, *Eng.* *Agriculture.*

— Best, H. Rural economy in Yorkshire in 1641; farming and account books; [ed. by C. B. Robinson]. London, 1857. 8°. (Surtees Soc., v. 33.)

— Marshall, W. Rural economy of Yorkshire. London, 1788. 2 v. 8°.

— Leatham, I. General view of the agriculture of the East Riding of Yorkshire and the Ainsty of the city of York. London, 1794. 4°. (W 75)

— Rennie, G., *and others.* General view of the agriculture of the West Riding of Yorkshire. London, 1794. 4°. (W 75)

Antiquities.

— Wright, T. Some ancient barrows or tumuli opened in E. Yorkshire. — Some curious forms of sepulchral interment found in East Yorkshire. — Remains of a primitive people in the S. E. corner of Yorkshire. (*In his* Essays on archæol., v. 1. 1861.)

Bibliography.

— Boyne, W. Yorkshire library; a bibliographical account of books rel. to the County of York. London, 1869. 4°.

Description.

— Kirkby, J. de. Survey of the County of York [1284–85]; commonly called Kirkby's inquest; also Inquisitions of Knights' fees, the Nomina villarum for Yorkshire, and an app.; ed. by R. H. Skaife. Durham, 1867. 8°. (Surtees Soc., v. 49.)

— Bigland, T. Yorkshire. (*In* Beauties of England and Wales, v. 16. 1812.)

— White, W. A month in Yorkshire. London, 1861. 16°.

— Hand-book for travellers in Yorkshire. London, *Murray*, 1867. 12°.

See also Ackworth School; — Bridlington Priory; — Doncaster; — Howard Castle; — Pontefract Castle; — York.

History and Politics.

— Dugdale, W. Visitation of the County of Yorke, 1665–66. London, 1859. 8°. (Surtees Soc., v. 36.)

— Wyvill, C. Political papers respecting the attempt of the County of Y. and other districts, 1779–[1802] to effect a reformation of the Parliament of Gr. Brit. York, [1794–1808]. 6 v. 8°.

Language and Literature.

— Ingledew, C. J. D. The ballads and songs of Yorkshire; with notes and glossary. London, 1860. 16°.

See also Craven.

Yorkshire question; or, Petition or address to the people of England. London, [1781]. 8°. (B 766)

Yorkshire Soc. Schools for Boarding the Children of Indigent Yorkshire Parents. Report of the committee, *etc.* London, 1838. 8°. (E 56)

Yorkshire tragedy, A. (*In* Scott, *Sir* W. Anc. Brit. dr., v. 1. 1810.)

Yorktown, *Va.* Journal of the siege of Yorktown. (*In* Mass. Hist. Soc. Col., v. 9. 1804.)

— Edge, F. M. Maj. Gen. McClellan and the campaign on the Yorktown peninsula. London, 1865. 12°.

Yorktown; an historical romance. Boston, 1826. 2 v. 12°.

Yosemite Valley. Kneeland, S. The wonders of the Yosemite Valley and California. Boston, 1871. 8°.

See also California.

You can't marry your grandmother; comedy, by T. H. Bayly. (*In* Webster, B. Acting nat. dr., v. 4.)

Youatt, Wm. Cattle, their breeds, management, and diseases. London, 1834. 8°. (Soc. Diff. Usef. Knowl.)

— The complete grazier. 11th ed. enl., by R. S. Burn. London, 1864. 8°.

— The dog. (*In* Knight, C. Farmer's lib., v. 2. 1849.)

— The horse; with a treatise on draught. London, 1831. 8°.

— *Same.* (*In* Knight, C. Farmer's lib., v. 1.)

— Sheep, their breeds, management, and diseases; added, The mountain shepherd's manual. London, 1837. 8°. (Lib. usef. knowl.)

Youcan. *See* Alaska.

Youmans, Edward Livingston. Correlation and conservation of forces; a series of expositions. N. Y., 1865. 12°.
Contents. Introduction. — Grove, W. R. Correlation of physical forces. — Helmholtz, H. L. F. Interaction of natural forces. — Mayer, J. R. Rem. on the forces of inorganic matter; — Celestial dynamics; — Rem. on the mechanical equivalent of heat. — Faraday, M. Some thoughts on the conservation of force. — Liebig, J. J. Connection and equivalence of forces. — Carpenter, W. B. Correlation of the physical and vital forces.

— Modern culture; its true aims and requirements. London, 1867. 8°.
Contents. Tyndall, J. Study of physics. — Daubeny, C. G. B. Study of chemistry. — Henfrey, A. Botany. — Huxley, T. H. Zoology. — Paget, J. Physiology. — Whewell, W. Educational history of science. — Faraday, M. Education of the judgment. — Hodgson, W. B. Study of economic science. — Spencer, H. Political education. — Masson, D. College-education and self-education. — Youmans, E. L. Scientific study of human nature. — Herschel, S. J. University studies. — Paget, G. E. General influence of scientific culture. — Spencer, H. Order of discovery in the progress of knowledge. — Draper, J. W. Deficiencies of clerical education. — Seguin, E. Physiological basis of primary education. — Wayland, F. Modern collegiate studies. — De Morgan, A. Thoroughness of intellectual attainment. — Forbes, E. Educational uses of museums. — Albert, *Prince.* Educational claims of science. — Hill, T. Cultivation of the senses. — Smith, G. Classical and modern culture. — Acland, H. W. Early physiological study. — Macaulay, T. B. Study of classical languages. — Evidence before the public schools commission, by Dr. W. B. Carpenter, — Sir C. Lyell, — Dr. M. Faraday, — Prof. R. Owen, — Dr. J. Hooker.

Young, *Dr.* —. Salt, H. Essay on Y.'s and Champollion's phonetic system of hieroglyphics. London, 1825. 8°.

Young, *Maj.* Short whist. (*In* Mathews, T. Whist. 1857.)

Young, *Major,* —, *of the Wilts militia.* Some obs. which may afford a just idea of the nature, importance, and settlement of our new West India colonies. London, 1764. 8°. (B 702)

Young, Alexander, *b.* 1800, *d.* 1854. Address, ordination of W. Newell, Cambridge, May 19. Camb., 1830. 8°. (B 959)

— The beneficent woman; discourse, May 23, death of Mrs. C. G. Prescott. Boston, 1852. 8°. (B 1247)

— Chronicles of first planters of the colony of Mass. Bay, 1623–36. Boston, 1846. 8°.
Contents. White, J. Brief relation of the planting of this colony. — Hubbard, W. Narrative of the discovery and first planting of Mass. — Governor and Company of Mass. Bay. Original records of the Gov. and Co. — Cradock, M. Letter to Capt. J. Endicott. — Governor and Co. of Mass. Bay. 1st and 2d letters of instructions to Endicott and his council; — Form of government for the colony; — Allotment of the lands;

— Oaths of office for Gov. and council; — Agreement with the ministers. — **Higginson**, F. Journal of his voyage and New England's plantation. — **General** considerations for planting New England. — **Agreement** at Cambridge. — **Governor and Company of Massachusetts Bay**. Letter to Higginson and Endicott; — Request to their brethren in the Church of England. — **Dudley**, T. Letter to the Countess of Lincoln. — **Clap**, R. Memoirs. — **Charlestown**. Early records. — **Wood**, W. Description of Massachusetts. — **Cotton**, J. Life and letters. — **Whiting**, S. Life of J. Cotton. — **Cotton**, J. Letter to his wife; — Letter to the Bishop of Lincoln; — Reasons for his removal to New England. — **Mather**, R. Journal. — **Thacher**, A. Narrative of his shipwreck. — **Shepard**, T. Mem. of his own life.

— Chronicles of the Pilgrim fathers of the colony of Plymouth, 1602–1625. Boston, 1841. 8°.
Contents. **Bradford**, *Gov.* W. History of Plymouth colony. — **Bradford**, *Gov.* W., *and* **Winslow**, E. Journal. — **Cushman**, R. Discourse. — **Winslow**, E. Relation; — Brief narration. — **Bradford**, *Gov.* W. Dialogue; — Memoir of Elder Brewster. — **Robinson**, J., *and others*. Letters.

— The church, the pulpit, and the Gospel; discourse, ordination of G. E. Ellis, Charlestown, Mar. 11. Boston, 1840. 8°. (B 1324)

— Congregationalism vindicated; sermon, May 13. Boston, 1846. 8°. (B 1306)

— Discourse, life and character of Rev. J. T. Kirkland, May 3. Boston, 1840. 8°. (B 1163, 1219, 1246, 1654, 1822, 1963)

— Discourse, ordination of J. W. Thompson, Natick, Feb. 17. Boston, 1830. 8°. (B 959)

— Discourse, sins of the tongue. Boston, 1829. 8°. (B 956)

— *Same.* 2d ed. Boston, 1829. 12°. (C 145)

— *Same.* (*In* **Liberal** preacher, v. 3. 1830.)

— Discourse, 20th anniversary of his ordination, Jan. 19. Boston, 1845. 8°. (B 1326)

— Evangelical Unitarianism adapted to the poor. Boston, 1830. 12°. (C 145)

— The good merchant; discourse, Mar. 26, decease of W. Parsons. Boston, 1837. 8°. (B 1126, 1718)

— The good parishioner; discourse, June 8, death of B. Rich. Boston, 1851. 8°. (B 1223, 1247)

— Library of old English prose writers. Camb., 1831–34. 9 v. 12°.
Contents. Vol. 1. **Fuller**, T. Holy and profane states. 2. **Sidney**, *Sir* P. Defence of poesy. — **Selden**, J. Table-talk. 3. **Browne**, *Sir* T. Miscel. works. 4. **Feltham**, O. Resolves, divine, moral, and political. 5, 6. **Walton**, I. Lives of Donne, *etc.* 7. **Latimer**, H. Select sermons. 8. **Taylor**, J. Selections from the Works of T. 9. **More**, *Sir* T. Utopia; — Life of Richard III.

— The stay and the staff taken away; discourse, death of Hon. Wm. Prescott, Dec. 15. Boston, 1844. 8°. (B 1194, 1222)

— The varieties of human greatness; discourse on N. Bowditch, Mar. 25. Boston, 1838. 8°. (B 1133, 1751, 1806)

— Robbins, C. (*In* **Mass. Hist. Soc.** Col., v. 32. 1854.)

— *Funeral sermon on.* 1854. *See* **Ellis**, G. E. (B 1228); — **Gannett**, E. S. (B 1228)

Young, Arthur. The advantages which have resulted from the establishment of the Board of Agriculture; substance of a lecture, May 26. London, 1809. 8°. (W 9)

— The constitution safe without reform; cont. remarks on 'The commonwealth in danger', by J. Cartwright. London, 1795. 8°. (B 1406)

— Course of experimental agriculture. Dublin, 1771. 4 v. 8°.

— Farmer's calendar; re-written by J. C. Morton. 2d ed. London, N. Y., 1862. 8°.

— General view of the agriculture of the County of Suffolk. London, 1794. 4°. (W 75)

— General view of the agriculture of the County of Sussex. London, 1793. 4°. (W 75)

— The husbandry of three British farmers, Bakewell, Arbuthnot, and Ducket. London, 1811. 8°. (W 9)

— Inquiry into the rise of prices in Europe, comp. with that in Eng., during the last 25 years. (*In* **Pamphleteer**, 1815; v. 6 of B 838)

— Observations on the present state of waste lands of Gr. Britain. London, 1773. 8°. (B 1704)

— Potatoes. (*In* **Phil. Soc. Prom. Agric.** Mem., v. 3. 1814.)

— Proposals to the legislature for numbering the people. London, 1771. 8°. (B 1704)

— Rural economy; essays on the practical parts of husbandry; added, The rural Socrates, by [J. G.] Hirzel. 3d ed. Burlington, 1792. 8°.
Contents. Of that proportioned farm which is the most profitable. — Best method of conducting a farm of arable land. — Method of conducting a farm of grass land. — Of the means of keeping, the year round, the most cattle on a given quantity of land. — Consid. on the economical conduct of such as make agriculture their business or amusement. — Cheapest way of manuring land. — Comparative profit of cultivating different soils. — Management of the borders of arable fields. — New husbandry. — Experimental agriculture. — Periodical publications conc. rural economies.

— A tour in Ireland, 1776–79. Dublin, 1780. 2 v. 8°.

— *Same, abstract.* (*In* **Pinkerton**, J. Col. of voy., v. 3. 1809.)

— Travels, 1787–89; with a view of ascertaining the cultivation, wealth, *etc.*, of France. Bury St. Edmund's, 1792. 4°.

— *Same.* 2d ed. London, 1794. 2 v. 4°.

— *Same.* Dublin, 1793. 2 v. 8°.

— *Same.* (*In* **Pinkerton**, J. Col. of voy., v. 4. 1809.)

— Cartwright, J. The commonwealth in danger; with remarks on late writings of A. Young. London, 1795. 8°.
See also **Annals** of agriculture.

Young, Bennett H. Benjamin, L. N. The St. Albans raid; report of the proceedings on the demand of the United States for the extradition of Young and others. Montreal, 1865. 8°.

Young, Brigham. Waite, *Mrs.* C. V. The Mormon prophet and his harem. Camb., 1866. 16°.

Young, C. E. Sketch of Prescott, and Pierce County. 1857. *See* **Gibbs**, O.

Young, Charles. The Amazon and Rio Madeira. (*In* **Galton**, F. Vacation tourists. 1861.)

Young, Charles Augustus. Spectrum observations at Burlington, Iowa, during the eclipse of Aug. 7, 1869. — New method of observing the first contact of the moon with the sun's limb at a solar eclipse, by the spectroscope. (*In* **Amer. Assoc.** Proc., v. 18. 1869.) — Method of determining the level error of the axis of a meridian instrument. (*In* v. 19. 1870.)

Young, Charles Frederick T. Fires, fire engines, and fire brigades. London, 1866. 8°.

Young, Charles Mayne. Young, J. C. Memoir of C. M. Young. London, N. Y., 1871. 8°.

Young, David. The contrast; a poem. Elizabeth-town, 1804. 12°. (B 657)

Young, Edward, *Dean of Salisbury*. Sermons on several occasions. Vol. 1. London, 1706. 8°.

Young, Edward, *son of the preceding*. Works. London, 1798. 3 v. 12°.
Contents. Vol. 1. Mem. of Y. — Night thoughts. — A paraphrase on part of the book of Job. — Verses occasioned by that famous piece of crucifixion by Michael Angelo. — On the death of Queen Anne, and the accession of King George. — Letter to Tickell. — Resignation. 2. The Centaur not fabulous; six letters to a friend on the life in vogue. — The foreign address; occasioned by the British fleet and the posture of affairs. — Busiris, king of Egypt; tragedy. — The revenge; tragedy. — The brothers; tragedy. 3. Poem on the last day. — The force of religion; or, Vanquished love. — Love of fame the universal passion. — A true estimate of human life. — Conjectures on original composition in a letter to the author of Sir Charles Grandison. — Ocean; an ode, to which is prefixed an ode to the King, and a discourse on the ode. — Sea piece. — Epistles. — Some thoughts occasioned by the present juncture. — The instalment. — The merchant; an ode on the British trade and navigation.

— Works; with life. London, 1813. 3 v. (v. 3 w.). 8°.
Contents. Vol. 1. Life of Dr. Young. — The complaint; or, Night thoughts. 2. Poem on the last day. — Force of religion; or, Vanquished love. — Love of fame the universal passion. — Ode to the King, on his encouragement of the sea service. — Epistles. — Paraphrase on part of the book of Job. — Ocean; an ode. — Sea piece. — Busiris, king of Egypt; tragedy.

— Brothers. (*In* Bell, J. British theatre, v. 30. 1797; — *and in* Scott, *Sir* W. British drama, v. 1, pt. 2. 1804.)

— Busiris, king of Egypt. (*In* Bell, J. Brit. theatre, v. 29. 1797.)

— The centaur not fabulous. 1st Boston from 3d London ed., 1755. Boston, 1805. 12°.

— The complaint; or, Night thoughts on life, death, and immortality. N. Bedford, 1808. 12°.

— *Same.* N. Y., 1824. 18°.

— Extracts from Night thoughts. — Extracts from Satires. (*In* **Campbell**, T. Brit. poets, v. 6. 1819.)

— Jüngster Tag; übersetzet [von S. Grynæus]. (*In* **Grynæus**, S. Vier auserlesene Meisterstücke. 1757.)

— Poems; with a life of the author, by S. Johnson. (*In* **Chalmers**, A. Eng. poets, v. 13. 1810.)

— Poetical works; with a life of the author. (*In* **Anderson**, R. Brit. poets, v. 10. 1795.)

Namely. The last day. — The force of religion. — Love of fame. — Ocean; an ode. — Paraphrase on part of the book of Job. — Miscellanies. — Reflections on the public situation of the kingdom. — The complaint, or Night thoughts. — Resignation. — On the late Queen's death, and His Majesty's accession to the throne. — The instalment. — Epistles. — Sea-piece: The British sailor's exultation; His prayer before engagement. — Imperium pelagi.

— Poetical works; [ed. by F. J. Child]. Boston, 1871, 54. 16°.

Contents. Vol. 1. Life, by J. Mitford. — The complaint; or, Night thoughts. 2. The last day. — The force of religion; or, Vanquished love. — Love of fame the universal passion. — Ocean; an ode; prefixed, an ode to the King; and a discourse on ode. — Paraphrase on part of the book of Job. — On Michael Angelo's famous piece of the crucifixion. — To Addison on the tragedy of Cato. — Historical epilogue to the Brothers, a tragedy. — Epitaph on Lord Aubrey Beauclerk in Westminster Abbey, 1740. — Epitaph at Welwyn, Hertfordshire. — Letter to Tickell on the death of Addison. — Reflections on the public situation of the kingdom. — Resignation. — On the late Queen's death, and His Majesty's accession to the throne. — The instalment. — Epistle to George Lord Lansdowne. — Epistles to Pope. — Epistle to Sir R. Walpole. — The old man's relapse. — Verses sent by Lord Melcombe to Young.

— Resignation; [a poem]. Boston, 1803. 12°. (D 20)

— Revenge. (*In* Bell, J. Brit. theatre, v. 8. 1797; — **London** stage, v. 1; — *and in* **Scott**, *Sir* W. Brit. drama, v. 1. 1804.)

— BELL, R. (*In his* Lives of literary men. of Gr. Brit., v. 2. 1839. Lardner. Cab. cyc.)

— JOHNSON, S. (*In his* Works, v. 11. 1806; — *and* Lives of eminent Eng. poets, v. 2. 1810.)

— WILLMOTT, R. A. (*In his* Lives of the Eng. sacred poets, v. 2. 1853.)

Young, Edward, *M.A.*, *of Trinity College, Camb.* Pre-Raffaellitism; enquiry into newly asserted principles connected with art. London, 1857. 8°.

Young, Edward Daniel. The search after Livingston; diary during the investigation of his reported murder; rev. by H. Waller. London, 1868. 16°.

Young, Edward James. Memoir of S. A. Smith. (*In* **Smith**, S. A. Christian lessons. 1866.)

— Words commemorative of H. Bigelow, M.D., Jan. 25, 28, Newton. Boston, 1866. 8°. (B 1639)

Young, *Rev.* George. Catalogue of the library of Y., sold. London, 1848. 8°. (B 1619)

Young, *Sir* George. The House of Commons in 1833. (*In* **Essays** on reform. 1867.)

Young, George Renny. British North American colonies. London, 1834. 8°.

— Colonial literature, science, and education. Vol. 1. Halifax, 1842. 12°.

Contents. Introd. to general literature and science. — Nat. systems of education in the Old and New World. — Colonial education. — On the public speaking of ancient and modern times. — Education in Upper Canada. — Education in Newfoundland.

Young, J. S. Address to Congress on the protection of American labor. Portsmouth, 1849. 8°. (B 1514)

Young, *Rev.* James. Life of J. Welsh, Minister of Ayr; with a biog. sketch of the author [by J. Anderson]. Edin., 1866. 8°.

Young, *Rev.* John. Essays. 5th ed. Phila., 1798. 12°. (C 77)

Contents. Government. — Revolutions. — The British constitution. — Kingly government. — Parliamentary representation and reform. — Liberty and equality. — Taxation. — The present war and the stagnation of credit.

Young, John. Letters on agriculture in Nova Scotia. Halifax, 1822. 8°.

Young, John. Prints from Y.'s galleries of English noblemen, *etc.*; impressions in 1827. *n.p.*, [1827]. f°.

Young, John, *LL.D.*, *d.* 1829. Lectures on intellectual philosophy; ed. with a memoir [of Y.] by W. Cairns. Glasgow, 1835. 8°.

Young, John, *b.* 1802, *d.* 1852. JENKINS, J. S. (*In his* Lives of the governors of New York. 1851.)

— COMPLIMENTARY dinner to him at the Irving House, Jan. 18; correspondence and speeches. N. Y., 1851. 8°. (B 1505)

Young, *Rev.* John, *LL.D.* The Christ of history. London, 1855. 8°.

— *Same.* N. Y., 1857. 12°.

Young, John, *M.P.P.* Letters to F. Lemieux on Canadian trade and navigation, and to the citizens of Montreal on the commerce of the city and the means of its further development. Montreal, 1855. 8°. (B 1605)

Young, John Clark. Sermon; the sinfulness, folly, and danger of delay. (*In* **Akers**, T. P. Col. of sermons. 1851.)

Young, John Radford. Concise exposition of the method of instructing the deaf and dumb. London, 1826. 12°.

— Elementary essay on the computation of logarithms. 2d ed. London, 1835. 12°.

— Elements of the integral calculus. London, 1831. 12°.

— Key and companion to [Haddon's] Rudimentary algebra. 2d ed. London, *Weale*, 1856. 12°.

— Nutrition and digestion. (*In* **Caldwell**, C. Medical theses, v. 1. 1805.)

— Rudimentary treatise on arithmetic. 3d ed. London, *Weale*, 1856. 12°.

— - Key. London, *Weale*, 1853. 16°.

Young, Julian Charles. Memoir of C. M. Young. London, N. Y., 1871. 8°.

Young, Lambton J. H. Sea-fishing as a sport. London, 1865. 8°.

Young, *Mrs.* Marianne. Our camp in Turkey, and the way to it. London, 1854. 12°.

Young, *Rev.* Matthew. Ancient Gaelic poems resp. the race of the Fians; col. in the Highlands of Scotland in 1784. — Synthetical demonstration of the rule for the quadrature of simple curves. — Extraction of cubic and other roots. (*In* **Roy. Irish Acad.** Trans., v. 1, 1787.) — Modes of demonstration by which the velocity of spouting fluids has been investigated a priori. (*In* v. 2.) — Origin and theory of the Gothic arch. (*In* v. 3. — Demonstration of Newton's theorem for the correction of spherical errors in object glasses of telescopes. (*In* v. 4.) — Precession of the equinoxes. — Velocity with which fluids issue from apertures. — Force of testimony in establishing facts contrary to analogy. — Number of the primitive colorific rays in solar light. (*In* v. 7. 1800.)

Young, Moses. STATEMENT of the case of Y. on his Memorial now depending before Congress. *n.t.p.* [Wash., 1804.] 8°. (B 1461)

Young, Patrick. Nonnullæ in secundum marmor Oxoniense conjecturæ. (*In* **Maittaire**, M. Marm. Arund. 1732.)

Young, Peter. Truth and Calvinism contrasted; letter to J. Curtis. Concord, 1818. 12°. (C 118)

Young, Robert. SPRAT, T. Relation of the wicked contrivance of S. Blackhead and R. Young against the life of several persons, *etc.* The Savoy, 1692. 2 pts. 4°. (B 93)

— - *Same.* 2d pt. The Savoy, 1693. 4°. (B 93)

Young, Robert. Essay on the powers and mechanism of nature. London, 1788. 8°.

— Examination of the 3d and 4th definitions of the 1st book of Newton's Principia. London, 1787. 8°. (B 768)

Young, Samuel. Cases of cancer; pref., letter by S. Whitbread. London, 1816. 8°.
— Inquiry into the nature and action of cancer; a mode of curing that disease by natural separation. London, 1805. 12°.
— Use of the adhesive strap in surgery of wounds. London, 1808. 4°.

Young, Samuel. Lecture on civilization, before the Young Men's Assoc. of Saratoga Springs, Mar. 8. Saratoga Springs, 1841. 8°. (B 1588)
— Suggestions on the best mode of promoting civilization, *etc.*; lect. before the Young Men's Assoc. in Albany, Jan. 24. Albany, 1837. 8°. (B 1588)

Young, Thomas, *D.D.* An answer to a booke entitvled 'An humble remonstrance', in which the originall of episcopacy is discussed. 1641. *See* **Marshal**, S.
— Hope's incouragement; sermon, House of Commons, fast, Feb. 28, 1643. London, 1644. 8°. (B 11)

Young, Thomas, *M.D.* Loring, J. S. (*In his* Hundred Boston orators. 1852.)

Young, Thomas, *b.* 1773, *d.* 1829. Miscellaneous works. London, 1855. 3 v. 8°.

Contents. Vol. 1. Vision. — Mechanism of the eye. — Outlines of experiments and inquiries resp. sound and light. — Cycloidal curves. — Music. — Letter to Nicholson, respecting sound and light. — Theory of light and colours. — Acc. of some cases of the production of colours not hitherto described. — Experiments and calculations relative to physical optics. — Reply to the animadversions of the Edinburgh reviewers. — Harmonic sliders. — Review of Laplace's mem. 'Sur la loi de la réfraction extraordinaire dans les cristaux diaphanes'. — Review of the 'Mém. de physique et de chimie de la Société d'Arcueil'. — Review of Malus, Biot, Seebeck, and Brewster, on light. — The article 'Chromatics', from the supplement to the Encyclopædia Britannica. — Rem. on the measurement of minute particles, especially those of the blood and of pus. — Selections from correspondence relating to optical subjects. — Theoretical investigations to illustrate the phenomena of polarisation. — Cohesion of fluids. — The article 'Cohesion' from the supplement to the Encyc. Brit. — Cohesion of fluids. — Hydraulic investigations. — Functions of the heart and arteries. — Rem. on the employment of oblique riders and on other alterations in the construction of ships. — A numerical table of elective attractions. — A review of Sir H. Davy's Elements of chemical philosophy. 2. Appendix to Capt. Kater's Account of experiments for determining the length of the pendulum. — Probabilities of error in physical observations, and on the density of the Earth. — Postscript on atmospherical refraction. — Extension of the inverse series for the computation of refraction. — A finite and exact expression for the refraction of an atmosphere nearly resembling that of the Earth. — Hist. sketch of the various solutions of the problem of atmospherical refraction. — Computation of the effect of terrestrial refraction in the actual condition of the atmosphere. — Rem. on Laplace's latest computation of the density of the Earth. — Astronomical measurements of the ancients. — Estimate of the effect of the terms involving the square of the disturbing force on the determination of the figure of the Earth. — Simple determination of the most ancient epoch of astronomical chronology. — Resistance of the air. — Considerations on the reduction of the length of the pendulum to the level of the sea. — Computations for clearing the compass of the regular effect of a ship's permanent attraction. — Brief investigation of the properties of the geodetic curve. — A simple rectification of the geodetic curve. — Calculation of the rate of expansion of a supposed lunar atmosphere. — Concise method of determining the figure of a gravitating body revolving round another. — Calculation of the direct attraction of a spheroid, and demonstration of Clairault's theorem. — Equilibrium and strength of elastic substances. — Propositions on waves and sound. — Investigation of the pressure sustained by the fixed supports of flexible substances. — Pressure of semifluid and cohesive substances. — Structure of covered ways. — Friction of wheelwork and on the forms best suited for teeth. — Selections from the article 'Bridge', in the suppl. to the Encyc. Brit. — A portion of the article 'Carpentry', from the suppl. to the Encyc. Brit. — Theory of tides, including the consideration of resistance. — The article 'Tides', from the suppl. to the Encyc. Brit. — Extracts rel. to the theory of the tides, from Brande's Quarterly journal of science. — An algebraical expression for the value of lives. — Formula for expressing the decrement of human life. — Principle of compound interest. — Letter to W. Morgan, on the experience of the Equitable Society. — Practical comparison of the different tables of mortality. — Practical application of the doctrine of chances to the subdivision of risks. — Addendum to the article on annuities. — Review of 'An essay on dew and several appearances connected with it'. — Weights and measures. — Description of a new species of opercularia. — Habits of spiders; on passages in Aristotle and Aristophanes, and an illustration of the Fabrician system. — Biographies of men of science: H. Cavendish; — S. Tennant; — Sir B. Thompson, Count Rumford; — R. Watson, Bp. of Llandaff; — A. F. de Fourcroy; — J. Ingenhousz; — J. Robison; — D. G. S. T. de G. de Dolomieu; — C. A. Coulomb; — J. C. Borda; — C. M. de la Condamine; — J. L. Lagrange; — P. de Fermat; — J. Dollond; — S. L. Malus; — J. J. Le F. de Lalande; — J. H. Lambert; — N. Maskelyne; — G. Atwood. 3. Ancient Egyptian mss. with translation of the Rosetta inscription. — Correspondence rel. to the Rosetta inscription. — Egypt. — Inscription on the paw of the great sphinx. — Obs. on a Greek ms. on papyrus. — Correspondence upon hieroglyphical subjects. — Discoveries in hieroglyphic literature. — Correspondence upon hieroglyphical subjects. — Advertisement to Y.'s Egyptian dictionary. — The article 'Languages', from the suppl. to the Encyclopædia Britannica. — The article 'Herculaneum'. — Lives of eminent scholars: J. H. Tooke; — G. Wakefield; — J. Bryant; — R. Porson.

— Course of lectures on natural philosophy and the mechanical arts. London, 1807. 2 v. 4°.
— Historical and practical treatise on consumptive diseases. London, 1815. 8°.
— Medical literature; including practical nosology. London, 1813. 8°.
— Arago, D. F. J. (*In his* Œuvres, v. 1. 1854; — *and in* **Revue** d. D. Mondes, déc. 1835.)
— - Eulogy on T. Young. (*In* **Smithsonian Inst.** Report, 1869.)
— Peacock, G. Life of Y. London, 1855. 8°.

Young, Thomas. Carpentry. (*In* **Ashpitel**, A. Treatise on architecture. 1867.)

Young, W. A. History of N. and S. America, W. Indies, and the American Islands; rise and progress of the present American disputes. London, 1776. 2 v. 12°.

Young, William. Portugal in 1828. London, 1828. 8°.

Young, *Maj.* Wm. Manœuvres; or, Practical observations on the art of war. London, [1770]. 12°.

Young, *Rev.* Wm., *d.* 1757. Latin-English and English-Latin dictionary. 9th ed. Dublin, 1793. 8°.

Young, *Sir* Wm., *b.* 1815. History of Athens. 3d ed. enl. London, 1804. 8°.
— Tour through the Islands of Barbadoes, St. Vincent, Antigua, *etc.* (*In* **Edwards**, B. Hist. survey. 1801.)
— West-India common-place book; shewing the interest of Gr. Brit. in its sugar colonies. London, 1807. 4°.

Young, Wm. Smut in wheat. (*In* **Phil. Soc. Prom. Agric.** Mem., v. 1. 1808.) — Oat pasture and improvement of soils. — Salivary defluxions in horses. (*In* v. 2. 1811.)

Young, Wm. J. Cloud bursts. (*In* **Smithsonian Inst.** Report, 1867.)

Young, The. Mather, C. Youth under a good conduct; a short essay to render young people happy. Boston, 1704. 24°. (C 4)
— Gentleman, R. Addresses to youth. [1767–92.] 2d ed. Kidderminster, 1793. 12°.
— Dodd, W. The beauties of history; selected for the instruction of youth. Boston, 1796. 16°.
— Young Christian's pocket book. N.Y., [18—]. 12°.
— Parental legacies. Boston, 1804. 12°.
— Instructions chrétiennes pour les jeunes gens. Québec, 1807. 12°.
— *Same.* Nouv. éd. Avignon, 1808. 12°.
— Woodd, B. Advice to youth. 2d ed. London, 1807. 12°. (C 232)
— Gentleman, R. Address to young people. Boston, 1812. 12°. (D 28)

— WILBUR, H. Discourse on the religious education of youth. 2d ed. Boston, 1814. 8°. (B 335)
— POTTER, W. Essays moral and religious. Phila., 1817. 12°.
— MCALL, R. S. Addresses to the young. [1818.] London, 1842. 12°.
— PARENT'S monitor and teacher's assistant; comp. by A. Bullard. Vol. 2. Boston, 1829. 18°.
— BURTON, W. Best mode of fixing the attention of the young. (*In* Amer. Inst. of Instr. Lectures, 1835.)
— STONE, M. The young Christian's assistant to prayer. Brookfield, 1835. 12°.
— YOUNG folks of the factory; their duties and dangers. London, *Religious Tract Society*, 1840. 12°.
— PERCIVAL, T.? Parental instructions for young persons of either sex, selected mainly from the writings of an eminent physician. N.Y., 1846. 12°.
— SMITH, M. H. Counsels addressed to the young. 3d ed. Wash., 1846. 8°.
— MUZZEY, A. B. The blade and the ear. Boston, 1865. 12°.

See also Boy; — Education; — Girls; — Young men; — Young women.

Periodicals.

— PARENT'S gift; or, Youth's magazine; 1830, 31. Vol. 1, 2. Phila., [1830, 31]. 2 v. 16°.
— YOUTH'S cabinet; by F. C. Wordworth. Vol. 1-3. N. Y., 1846-48. 3 v. 8°.
— YOUTH'S companion; May 15, 1840 - Dec. 25, 1845; May 6, 1847 - Apr. 27, 1848; May 3, 1849 - Dec. 30, 1858. Boston, 1840 - 58. 20 v. f°.

Note. May 15, 1840 - May 7, 1841, 4°.

— YOUTH'S friend, The; 1838, 39. Phila., *Amer. S. S. U.*, [1838], 39. 2 v. 16°.

Young & Minns, *printers*. DEFENCE, before the committee of the Ho. of Representatives. Boston, 1805. 8°. (B 424)

Young admiral, The; a comedy by J. Shirley. (*In his* Works, v. 3. 1833.)

Young cadet; by Mrs. B. Hofland. Boston, 1829. 18°.

Young Christian series. *See* Abbott, J.

Young Christian's pocket book. N. Y., [18—]. 18°. (Prot. Episc. S. S. Union.)

Young collegian, The; a farce; by T. W. Robertson. (No. 54 *of* De Witt's acting plays.)

Young duke, The; by [B. Disraeli]. N. Y., 1831. 2 v. 12°.
— *Same.* (*In his* Works, v. 1. 1845.)

Young emigrants, The; by Mrs. S. A. L. Sedgwick. Boston, 1830. 12°.

Young folks of the factory; their duties and dangers. London, 1840. 12°.

Young Ladies' Literary and Missionary Assoc. of N. Hampton Female Seminary. 6th annual report, with constitution, *etc.*, 1839-40. Boston, 1840. 8°. (B 1165)

Young man's guide; [by W. A. Alcott]. Boston, 1833. 18°.

Young man's offering. Boston, 1848. 12°.

Young mathematician's guide. *See* Ward, J.

Young mechanic; ed. by B. W. Light and others; Jan. 1832 - Feb. 1836. Boston, 1832-36. 4 v. 8°.

Note. Vol. 3 called 'The mechanic', v. 4 'The Boston mechanic'.

Young men. MATHER, W. Young man's companion. [1710.] 24th ed., with add., by J. Barrow. London, 1775. 12°.
— GENTLEMAN, R. Addresses to youth. [1767-92.] 2d ed. Kidderminster, 1793. 12°.
— FORDYCE, J. Addresses to young men. [1777.] Boston, [17—]. 2 v. 12°.
— TEGG, T. Young man's book of knowledge. 1st Amer. from 20th London ed. N. Y., [1800]. 12°.
— WEST, *Mrs.* J. Letters to a young man on his entrance into life. Charlestown, 1803. 2 v. 12°.
— ADVICE to young men; or, A guide to gain esteem and estate. From the London ed. Boston, 1823. 12°.
— ALCOTT, W. A. The young man's guide. [1832.] Boston, 1833. 18°.
— - *Same.* 18th ed. Boston, 1848. 12°.
— MUZZEY, A. B. The young man's friend. [1836.] 2d ed. Boston, 1838. 12°.
— LIVERMORE, A. A. Lectures to young men. [1846.] New ed. Boston, 1847. 16°.
— WISE, D. The young man's counsellor. [1850.] 10th thous. N. Y., 1852. 12°.
— ELIOT, W. G. Lectures to young men. [1853.] 4th ed. Boston, 1854. 16°.

See also Young, The.

Young Men's Colonization Society of Pennsylvania. TYSON, J. R. Discourse before the Society, *etc.*, Oct. 24. Phila., 1830. 8°. (B 1483)

Young Men's League. Address to the citizens of Boston, *etc.*, 1853. *n.t.p.* 12°. (C 203)

Young Mens' Missionary Soc. of New York. 3d annual report. N. Y., 1818. 8°. (B 1043)
— History of the Society. [N. Y.,] 1817. 8°. (B 449)

Young merchant, The. 2d ster. ed. Boston, 1840. 18°.

Young music teacher and other tales; by T. S. Arthur. Phila., 1847. 18°.

Young New York; by G. P. Wilkins. (*In* Sargent, E. Mod. stand. dr., v. 24.)

Young patroon, The; or, Christmas in 1690; by P. H. Myers. N. Y., 1849. 12°.

Young people's book, The, Nov. 1841; ed. by J. Frost; [cont. 'Memorials of Washington']. Phila., 1841. 8°. (W 49)

Young prince, A; by A. I. Thackeray. (*In her* Five old friends. 1868.)

Young seer, The; by E. F. Dagley. London, 1834. 16°.

Young ship-builders of Elm Island, The; by E. Kellogg. Boston, 1871. 8°.

Young step-mother; [by C. M. Yonge]. N. Y., 1862. 2 v. 12°.

Young wife, The; by W. A. Alcott. Boston, 1837. 16°.

Young women. JACKSON, L. Letter to a young lady conc. the Christian life. 2d ed. London, 1758. 12°.
— INSTRUCTIONS for a young lady, *etc.* Edin., 1773. 12°.
— GREGORY, J. A father's legacy to his daughters. [1774.] Boston, 1822. 18°.
— - *Same.* (*In* Ladies' pocket library. 1787.)
— - *Same.* (*In* Parental legacies. 1804.)
— - *Same.* (*In* Trusler, J. Principles of politeness. 1806.)
— - *Same.* With a French trans. Paris, 1793. 12°.
— MURRY, A. Mentoria; or, Young ladies' instructor. [1778.] 10th ed. Lond., 1800. 12°.
— BARBAULD, *Mrs.* A. L. A legacy for young ladies. 2d ed. London, 1826. 12°.
— - *Same.* Boston, 1826. 12°.
— FARRAR, *Mrs.* E. The young lady's friend. Boston, 1836. 12°.
— MUZZEY, A. B. The young maiden. [1840.] 12th ed. Boston, 1850. 16°.

— Beekman, *Miss* J. The juvenile offering; letters to young ladies. Utica, **1850**. 12°.
— Wise, D. The young lady's counsellor. [**1851**.] 8th thous. 1852. 12°.
— Eliot, W. G. Lectures to young women. [**1853**.] 4th ed. Boston, 1854. 16°.
See also **Young, The.**

Younge, *Rev.* Hercules. Select odes of Anacreon and translations from other authors. London, 1802. 12°.
Contents. Anacreon. — Bion. — Moschus. — Catullus. — Horace. — Phocylides.

Youngs, Benjamin Seth. Testimony of Christ's second appearing; general statement of all things pertaining to the church in this latter-day. 2d ed. Albany, 1810. 8°.
— *Same.* 3d ed. Union Village, 1823. 8°.
— *Same.* 4th ed. [Albany? 1854.] 8°.

Your five gallants; by T. **Middleton.** (*In his* Works, v. 2. 1840.)

Your life's in danger; farce, by J. M. Morton. (No. 34 *of* **Spencer's** univ. stage.)

Youth and womanhood of Helen Tyrrel; by the author of 'Brampton rectory', *etc.* London, 1854. 8°.

Youth of the old dominion; by S. Hopkins. Boston, 1856. 12°.
Note. Fiction; but written with 'a scrupulous regard to historic truth'.

Youth under a good conduct; [by C. Mather]. Boston, 1704. 24°. (C 4)

Youthful queen, The; by Shannon. (*In* **Sargent, E.** Mod. stand. dr., v. 25.)

Youth's cabinet; by F. C. Wordworth. Vol. 1-3. N. Y., 1846-48. 3 v. 8°.

Youth's companion; May 15, 1840 - Dec. 25, 1845; May 6, 1847 - Apr. 27, 1848; May 3, 1849 - Dec. 30, 1858. Boston, 1840-58. 20 v. f°.
Note. May 15, 1840 - May 7, 1841, 4°.

Youth's friend, The; 1838, 39. Phila., *Amer. S. S. U.*, [1838,] 39. 2 v. 16°.

Youth's friendly monitor; or, The affectionate school-master. *n.t.p.* [17—.] 12°. (C 246)

Youth's history of the civil war in the U. S., 1861-65. N. Y., 1866. 16°.

Youth's keepsake, The. Boston, 1830. 18°.

Youth's manual; containing the catechism of the Protestant Episcopal Church, with form of prayer. Boston, 1816. 12°. (C 58)

Youth's miscellaneous sketch book, The. Boston, 1829. 12°.

Ypres. Beaulieu, S. de P., *seigneur* de. Plan de la ville d'Ipres. Amst., [16—]. (E 60)

Yriarte, Charles Emile. Les types parisiens. — Les clubs. (*In* **Paris** guide, v. 2. 1867.)

Yriarte. *See* **Iriarte.**

Yrujo, Carlos Martinez de. Letter to T. Pickering. [Phila.,] 1797. 8°. (B 465, 1000)

Ysbrants. Ides, E. Travels from Muscovy to China. (*In* **Harris, J.** Col. of voy., v. 2. 1764.)

Yu kiao li; Les deux cousines; roman, tr. [avec] commentaire par S. Julien. T. 2, 2e éd. Paris, 1864. 2 v. 16°.
— *Same, abstract of ch. i-iv.* (*In* **Tu-Li-Shin.** Narrative. 1821.)

Yucatan. *Antiquities.*
— Landa, D. de. Relation des choses de Y., [**1566**]; texte espagnol et traduction française; précédés d'un essai sur les sources de l'histoire du Mexique, *etc.*, par Brasseur de Bourbourg. Paris, 1864. 8°.
— Stephens, J. L. Incidents of travel in Central America, Chiapas, and Y., [**1839-40**]. 12th ed. N. Y., 1844. 2v. 8°.
— Catherwood, F. Views of ancient monuments in Central America and Yucatan. N. Y., **1844**. f°.

Description.
— Diaz, J. Itinerario de la armada del rey catolico à la isla de Yucatan, **1518**. (*In* **Ternaux-Campans, H.** Voy., v. 10. 1838; — *and in* **Icazbalceta, J. G.** Col. de doc., v. 1. 1858.)
— Norman, B. M. Rambles in Y., [**1841-42**]. N. Y., 1843. 8°.
— Stephens, J. L. Incidents of travel in Y. N. Y., **1843**. 2 v. 8°.
— Map. London, 1787. (E 68)
See also **Campeachy; — San Salvador; — Yzamal.**

Ethnology.
— Gallatin, A. Notes on the semi-civilized nations of Mexico, Yucatan, and Central Amer. (*In* **Amer. Ethnolog. Soc.** Trans., v. 1. 1845.)

History.
— Fancourt, C. St. J. History of Yucatan to the close of the 17th cent. London, 1854. 8°.
— Case of His Majesty's subjects settled on the coast of Yucatan in the Bay of Honduras. London, 1789. 4°. (A 20)

Language.
See **Maya language.**

Yule, *Col.* Henry. Cathay and the way thither; a collection of medieval notices of China. London, 1866. 2 v. 8°. (Hakluyt Soc., v. 36, 37.)
Contents. Vol. 1. Preliminary essay on the intercourse of China and the western nations previous to the discovery of the sea-route by the Cape. — Supplementary notes. — **Odorico** *da Pordenone.* Cathay and the way thither. 1316-30. — **Giovanni** *da Monte Corvino, and others.* Letters and reports of missionary friars from Cathay and India. 1292-1338. 2. **Raschid-ad-din.** Cathay under the Mongols; extracted from Rashidud-din's hist., circa 1300-07. — **Pegolotti, F. B.** Notices of the land route to Cathay, *etc.*, circa 1330-40. — **Marignolli, G. de'**, *Bp. of Bisagno.* Recollections of eastern travel. 1338-53. — **Ibn-Batuta.** Travels in Bengal and China. — **Goës, B. de.** The journey of G. from Agra to Cathay. 1602-07. — App. — Latin text of Odoric. — Old Italian text of Odoric. — Transcript from the ms. of of the first two chapters of Pegolotti.
— Narrative of the mission sent by the governor-general of India to the court of Ava in 1855. London, 1858. 4°.

Yule, T. Present mode of constructing a breakwater, *etc.* (*In* **Great Britain.** *Corps of Roy. Engin.* Papers, v. 8. 1845.)

Yule-tide stories; col. of Scandinavian and North German popular tales and traditions; ed. by B. Thorpe. London, *Bohn*, 1853. 8°.

Yung Lun Yuen. History of the pirates who infested the China Sea, 1807-10; tr. by C. F. Neumann. (*In* **Neumann, C. F.** Tr. fr. the Chinese.)

Yvan, Melchior. L'insurrection en Chine. *See* **Callery, J. M.**

Yve, *comtesse* d'. Gaudefroy, L. F. A. Description bibliographique d'une col. de livres de la bibliothèque de la comtesse d'Y. Brux., 1819-20. 2 v. 8°.

Yver, Pierre. Catalogue des estamps [de] Rembrandt. 1797. *See* **Bartsch, A.**

Yverdun. Nott, J. Papers on the Yverdun waters. (*In his* Chem. dissertation. 1793. B 816)

Yves d'Evreux, *le père.* Voyage dans le nord du Brésil, 1613-14; publié avec une introduction et des notes, par F. Dénis. Lpz., Paris, 1864. 16°.

Yvetot. Vertot, R. A. de V. d'A. Sur l'origine du royaume d'Yvetot. (*In* **Sérieys, A.** Bibl. acad., v. 6. 1811.)

Yvo, *St.* *See* **Ivo**, *St.*

Y-Worth, W. Chymicus rationalis; or, The fundamental grounds of the chymical art. London, 1692. 8°.

Yzamal, *Yucatan.* Schott, A. Remarks on the 'cara gigantesca' of Yzamal in Yucatan. (*In* **Smithsonian Inst.** Report, 1869.)

Z., *da Livorno*. Meditazioni poetiche del signor Lamartine. — Il golfo di Baia. — Invocazione all' Armonia. — Ad un illustre poeta francese. — Versi in morte di Giovinetto pittore. (*In* **Poeti ital.** contemp. 1843.)
Z., A. Reply to 'The answer of the friend in the West', *etc.* *n.p.*, 1755. 4°. (B 652, 739)
Z., A. Debate between M. Byles and the brethren of the Church [in New London]. New London, 1768. 4°. (C 128)
Z., A. Presbyterian ordination doubtful; letter in 2 parts. *n.p.*, 1819. 8°. (B 666)
— Pt. 2. *t.p.w.* [1819.] 8°. (B 1776)
Z (*Greek letter*). HALDEMAN, S. S. Investigation of the power of the Greek Z by means of phonetic laws. (*In* **Amer. Assoc.** Proc., v. 7. 1856.)
Zaccaria, Francesco Antonio. Lo stato presente o sia la relazione della corte di Roma; giá pub. da G. Lunadoro; ora ritoccata ed illustrata da F. A. Zaccaria. Roma, 1774. 2 v. 12°.
Zaccheus. COLMAN, H. Sermon, character, and conduct of Z. *n.p.*, 1810. 8°. (B 243, 912, C 109)
Zacchia, Laudisio, *Bp.*, *nunzio a Venezia*. LUDOVISI, L., *card.* Istruzione [a] Z. (*In* **Archivio stor.** ital., n. s., v. 7, pt. 1. 1858.)
Zach, Franz Xaver, *Freiherr* von. Nouvelles tables d'aberration et de nutation pour 1404 étoiles. Marseilles, 1812. 8°.
— - Supplément. Marseilles, 1813. 8°.
— Tables abrégés et portatives de la lune. Florence, 1809. 8°.
— Tabulæ motuum solis; acc. fixarum præcipuarum catalogus novus ex observ. 1787–90. Gothæ, 1792. 4°.
See also **Algemeine** geographische Ephemeriden; — **Correspondance** astronomique; — **Monatliche** Correspondenz.
Zachariae, Theodor Maximilian. Philosophische Rechtslehre oder Naturrecht und Staatslehre. 2e Aufl. Breslau, 1835. 8°.
— Opusculum philosophiæ naturalis metallorum cum annot. N. Flamelli. (*In* **Zetzner,** L. Theatr. chem., v. 1. 1613; — *and in* **Manget,** J. J. Biblioth. chem., v. 2. 1702.)
Zacuto (*Lat.* **Zacutus** *Lusitanus*), Abraham ben Samuel. Praxis medica. Lugd., 1637. 8°.
Zadig. *See* **Voltaire.**
Zadith ben Hamuel. Tabula chimica, marginalibus adaucta. (*In* **Zetzner,** L. Theatr. chem., v. 5. 1622; — *and in* **Manget,** J. J. Biblioth. chemica, v. 2. 1702.)
Zadyg, Sowieść Woltera, przez J. Szymanowski. (*In his* Pisma. 1836. Bobrowicz. Bibl. klass. polsk., v. 26.)
Zagales de Genil, Los; zarzuela pastoral por R. de la Cruz y Cano. (*In his* Teatro, v. 6. 1788.)
Zafar, Ibn. *See* **Ibn Zafar, Ibn Abi Muhammad.**
Zahn, Joannes. Specula physico-mathematico-historica. Norimb., 1696. 3 v. f°.
Contents. Vol. 1. Mundi mirabilis œconomia. 2. Geocosmi sive mundi terrestris notabilia. 3. Microcosmi sive hominis notabilia.
Zahn, Johann Karl Wilhelm. Ornamente aller klassischen Kunst-Epochen. Berlin, 1854. obl. 8°.
— Der schönsten Ornamente und Gemälde aus Pompeji, Herkulanum, und Stabiæ. Berlin, 1827–59. 3 v. f°.
Zaidee; a romance, by Mrs. Oliphant. Boston, 1866. 8°.
— *Same.* (*In* **Blackwood's** mag., v. 76–78, 1854–55; — *and in* **Littell's** living age, v. 44–48. 1855–56.)
Zaire; tragédie. *See* **Voltaire,** F. M. A. de.
Zaire River. *See* **Congo River.**
Zakrzewska, Marie E., *M.D.* Introductory lecture before the New England Female Medical College, Nov. 2. Boston, 1859. 8°. (B 1565)
Zaluski, Andrzej Chrysostom, *Graf.* NICERON, J. P. (*In his* Mém., v. 13. 1730.)
Zamariel, *pseud.* *See* **Chandieu,** A. la R. de.
Zambezi. LIVINGSTONE, D. *and* C. Narrative of an expedition to the Zambezi. London, 1865. 8°.
Zamor; a tragedy. *n.t.p.* [18—.] 16°. (D 43)
Zamora, Antonio de. El hechizado por fuerza. (*In* **Huerta,** V. G. de la. Theatro, pt. 1, v. 2. 1735; — *and in* **Ochoa,** E. de. Tesoro del teatro esp., v. 5. 1838.)
— *Same.* No hay plazo que no se cumpla ni deuda que no se pague, y convidado de piedra. — Mazariegos y Monsalves. — Cada uno es linaje aparté, y los Mazas de Aragon. (*In* **Mesonero Romanos,** R. de. Dram. post. a Lope de Vega, v. 2. 1859; v. 49 of Aribau Bibl.)
Zamora, Bartolomé de. *See* **Salazar,** M. de.
Zamora y Coronado, José Maria. Biblioteca de legislacion ultramarina. Madr., 1844. 2 v. 8°.
Zamoyski, Andrzej, *Count.* MAZADE, C. de. (*In* **Revue** d. D. Mondes, déc. 1862.)
Zamoyski (*Lat.* **Zamoscius**), Jan Sarius. De senatu Romano. (*In* **Grævius.** Thes. antiq. Rom., v. 1. 1694.)
Zampa; opera komiczna; przez A. H. J. Duveyrier; przeł. z Franc. przez J. Jasinskiego. Warszawa, 1834. 16°. (**Teatra** Warszawskie, pt. 1, v. 6.)
Zampieri, Antonio. Vita di C. Catari. (*In* **Crescimbeni,** G. M. Vite, v. 2. 1710.)
— PAPOTTI, T. (*In his* Elogi d'illust. Imolesi. 1841.)
Zampieri, Camillo. FABRONI, A. (*In his* Vitæ Ital., v. 12. 1785.)
— PAPOTTI, T. Elogi di Z. (*In his* Elogi d'illust. Imolesi. 1841.)
Zampieri, Domenico *called* **Domenichino.** Œuvre du D., avec une description. (*In* **Toulongeon,** F. E. Man. du Mus. Fr., v. 2. 1802.)
— Pitture nel palazzo Costaguti; inc. da D. Cunego. Romæ, 1777. f°.
— BELLORI, G. P. (*In his* Vite dei pittori, v. 2. 1821.)
Zan, Bernhard. ANDRESEN, A. (*In his* Der deutsche peintre-graveur, v. 3. 1866.)
Zancaroli (*Lat.* **Zancarolus**), Basilico. Antiquitatum civitatis Fori Julii libri 4. (*In* **Grævius.** Thes. antiq. Ital., v. 6, pt. 4. 1722.)
Zanchi, Basilio. NICERON, J. P. (*In his* Mém., v. 41. 1740.)
Zanchi (*Lat.* **Zanchius**), Girolamo. Operum theologicorum tomus 7, 8. *n.p.*, 1605. f°.
Contents. Vol. 7. Epistola ad Philippum seniorem Lantgravium, in qua continetur historia, de prioris dissidii Argentinensis ortu, *etc.* — Supplicatio. — Consensus inter theologos et professores in ecclesia et schola Argẽtinensi, 1563. — Theses. — Prelectiones de fine seculi. — De perseverantia sanctorum. — De libro vitæ. — De gradibus nostræ salutis. — De prædestinatione locus. — De impiorum excæcatione atque induratione. — Locus de redemptione Ecclesiæ. — De Christo advocato. — De peccatorum remissione. — De studio Christiani hominis. — Παρέκβασις de vitandis peccatis seruãdaque lege Dei. — Ad calumnias responsio. — Theses. — De prædestinatione sanctorum. — De cœna Domini. — Epistola ad Christophorum Ehemium. — Oratio de aperiendis in ecclesia scholis. 8. De incarnatione filii Dei. — Tractatus de S. Scriptura. — De religione christiana fides. — In confessionem observationes. — Compendium præcipuorũ capitũ doctrinæ christianæ. — Ad Ariani libellum Antithesis doctrinæ Christi et Antichristi de uno vero Deo, responsio. — Ad partem Prodomi Vichelmi Holderi responsio.
— TOPLADY, A. Letter to J. Wesley; [on] his pretended abridgment of Zanchius on predestination. 2d ed. London, 1771. 8°. (B 1371)
Zanchi (*Lat.* **Zanchus**), Giovanni Crisostomo. De Orobiorum origine, situ, ac Bergomi rebus antiquis. (*In* **Grævius.** Thes. antiq. Ital., v. 3, pt. 1. 1704.)
Zander, Adolf, *and* **Geissler,** A. Die Verletzungen des Auges; mit besonderer Rücksicht auf die Bedürfnisse des praktischen Arztes und Wundarztes. Lpz., Heidelb., 1864. 8°.
Zandt, C. C. v. Poem. (*In* **Randall,** G. M. Address. 1857.)
Zane, Ebenezer. DEHASS, W. Biog. sketch of E. Zane. (*In his* History of the early settlements and Indian wars of Western Virginia. 1851.)
Zane, Jacopo. AGOSTINI, G. degli. (*In his* Notiz. degli scr. viniz., v. 2. 1754.)
Zane, Lorenzo. AGOSTINI, G. degli. (*In his* Notiz. deg. scr. viniz., v. 1. 1752.)
Zane, Matteo. Relazione di Z., 1584. (*In* **Venice.** Relaz. deg. ambasc. ven., ser. 1, v. 5. 1861.)
Zane, Sarah. Opinion of the circuit court of the U. S. on the will of Z. Phila., 1834. 8°. (B 1439)
Zanelli, Domenico. REUMONT, A. La Bibilioteca Vaticana dalla sua origine fino al presente. (*In* **Archivio** stor. ital., n.s., v. 8, pt. 1. 1858.)

Zanetini, Geronimo de. Conclusio et comprobatio alchymiæ. (*In* **Zetzner**, L. Theatrum, v. 4. 1613.)

Zanetti, Alexandre. Premier siècle de la calcographie; ou Catalogue raisonné des estampes du cabinet de L. Cicognara; avec une append. sur les nielles: Ecole d'Italie. Venise, 1837. 8°.
Note. For Ecoles allemande, flamande, et française *see* **Albrizzi**, C.

Zanetti, Antonio Maria. Della pittura veneziana. Ed. 2a. Venezia, 1792. 2 v. 18°.
— Varie pitture a fresco de' principali maestri veneziani. Venezia, 1760. f°.

Zanetti, Luigi. Poesie. (*In* **Gamba**, B. Rac. di poesie in dial. venez. 1845.)

Zangemeister, Karl Freidrich Wilhelm. Inscriptiones parietariæ Pompeianæ, Herculanenses, Stabianæ; acc. vasorum fictilium ex eisdem oppidis erutorum inscriptiones ed. a R. Schœne. Berolini, 1871. f°. (Corpus ins. Lat., v. 4.)

Zanguebar. Ferrario, G. (*In his* Costume ant. e mod., v. 15. 1829.)
— Hoefer, J. C. (*In his* Afrique australe, *etc.* 1848. Univers.)

Zanita; a tale of the Yo-Semite; by T. Yelverton. N. Y., 1872. 8°.

Zannichelli, Gian Girolamo. Istoria delle pianti che nascono ne' lidi intorno a Venezia. Venezia, 1735. f°.
— Niceron, J. P. (*In his* Mém., v. 24. 1733.)

Zanoja, Giuseppe. Sermone sulle pie disposizioni testamentarie. (*In* **Poeti** ital. contemp. 1843.)

Zanon, Antonio. Lettere scelte sull' agricoltura, sul commercio, e sulle arti. — Apologia della mercatura. — Dell' utilità morale, economia, e politica delle Accad. di Agric., Arti, e Commercio. (*In* **Econ.** class. ital., pte mod., v. 18, 19. 1804.)

Zanoni; by [Sir E. Bulwer Lytton]. N. Y., 1842. 2 v. 12°.
— *Same.* Lpz., *Tauchnitz*, 1842. 16°.

Zanotti, Eustachio. **Fabroni**, A. (*In his* Vitæ Ital., v. 12. 1785.)

Zanotti, Francesco Maria. Carmina. (*In* **Volpi**, G. A. Carmina. 1725.)
— Lettere. (*In* **Raccolta** di prose e let., v. 1. 1830.)
— Tre orazioni sulle belle arti. (*In* **Milizia**, F. Opere, v. 9. 1827.)
— Fabroni, A. (*In his* Vitæ Ital., v. 5. 1779.)

Zanotti, GiamPietro Cavazzoni. Didone. (*In* **Raccolta** di trag., v. 1. 1825.)
— Lettere. (*In* **Raccolta** di prose e let., v. 1. 1830.)

Zanth, Karl Ludwig. Architecture moderne de la Sicile. *See* **Hittorf**, J. I.

Zanzibar. Browne, J. R. Notes of a sojourn on the Island of Zanzibar. (*In his* Etchings of a whaling cruise. 1846.)
— Germain, A. Note sur Zanzibar et la côte orientale d'Afrique. (*In* **Paris. Soc. de Géog.** Bul., 5e sér., v. 16. 1868.)
— Osgood, J. B. F. Notes of travel; or, Recollections of Zanzibar and other eastern ports. Salem 1854. 12°.

Zapata, Luis. Canto del poema de Carlo famosa. (*In* **Sedana**, J. J. L. de. Parnaso esp., v. 8. 1774.)

Zapatero, El, y el rey; drama. (*In* **Zorrilla y Moral**, J. Obras, v. 2. 1852.)

Zapf, Georg Wilhelm. Annales typographiæ Augustanæ, 1466–1530; acc. F. A. Veith diatribe de origine et incrementis artis typographiæ in Augusta Vindelicorum. Aug. Vind., 1778. 4°.

Zapolya; a Christmas tale, by S. T. Coleridge. (*In his* Poetical works, v. 2. 1835.)

Zappettini, Stefano. Vocabolario bergamasco-italiano. Bergamo, 1859. 18°.

Zappi, Faustina Maratti. Sonetti. (*In* **Gironi**, R. Rac. di lir. ital. 1808.)
— Sonetti. (*In* **Poeti** ital. contem. 1843.)

Zappi, GiamBattista Felice. Sonetti, canzoni, *ec.* (*In* **Poesie** di div. aut. 1782.)
— Sonetti, canzone. (*In* **Gironi**, R. Rac. di lir. ital. 1808.)
— Fabroni, A. (*In his* Vitæ Ital., v. 16. 1795.)
— Papotti, T. (*In his* Elogi d'illust. Imolesi. 1841.)

Zara; tragedia; por R. de la **Cruz y Cano**. (*In his* Teatro, v. 6. 1788.)

Zara; tragedy. *See* **Hill**, A.

Zaragoza. *See* **Saragossa.**

Zarah, Christianity before Judaism. *See* **Fayerman**, F.

Zárate, Augustin de. Historia del descubrimiento y conquisto del Peru. (*In* **Barcia**, A. G. Hist. de las Indias, v. 3. 1749; — *and in* **Vedia**, E. de. Hist. prim., v. 2. 1862; v. 26 of Aribau. Bibl.)
— *Eng.* History of the discovery and conquest of Peru by Pizarro. (*In* **Kerr**, R. Col. of voy., v. 4, 5. 1824.)
— *French.* Histoire de la découverte et de la conquête de Pérou; tr. de la langue espagnol par S. D. C. Paris, 1716. 2 v. 8°.

Zárate, Fernando Jacinto de. Egloga. — Romances. (*In* **Sedana**, J. J. L. de. Parnaso esp., v. 8. 1774.)
— La escala de la Garcia. (*In* **Comedias** nuevas, v. 35. 1671.)
— Mudarse por mejorarse. (*In* **Ochoa**, E. de. Tesoro del teatro esp., v. 5. 1838.)
— *Same.* — La presumida y la hermosa. — Quien habla mas obra menos. — El valiente Campuzano. (*In* **Mesonero Romanos**, R. de. Dram. post. a Lope de Vega, v. 1. 1858; v. 47 of Aribau. Bibl.)

Zárate, Francisco Lopez de. La invencion de la cruz. (*In* **Ochoa**, E. de. Tesoro de los poemas esp., 1840.)

Zárate, Hernando de. Discursos de la paciencia cristiana. (*In* **Escritores** del siglo 16, v. 1. 1853; v. 27 of Aribau. Bibl.)

Zarathustra. *See* **Zoroaster.**

Zarco, Juan Gonçalvez. Voyage to Africa. (*In* **General** col. of voy. by the Portuguese. 1789.)

Zaretti, Angelo. Lossetti, *avvocato.* Vite di Z. (*In* **Amato**, G. d'. Panteon, v. 2. 1851.)

Zastrow, Heinrich Adolf. Histoire de la fortification permanente; tr. de l'allemand, par Neuens. Liége, 1846. 8° *and* Atlas obl. f°.

Zauberring, Der; von F. B. de la Motte Fouque. 2e Aufl. Nürnberg, 1816. 3 v. 16°.

Zauberschloss, Das; von J. L. Tieck. (*In his* Gesam. Novellen, v. 5. 1853.)

Zavala, Lorenzo de. Manifiesto de los principios politicos [de] J. R. Poinssett. Mexico, 1828. 8°. (B 1848)

Zavaleta, Juan de. La Margarita preciosa. *See* **Calderon de la Barca.**

Zayas y Sotomayor, María de. El castigo de la miseria. (*In* **Rosell**, C. Nov. post. a Cervantes, v. 2. 1854; *and*, *Eng.*, Spanish novelists, v. 2. 1832.)
— La fuerza del amor. — El juez de su causa. — Tarde llega el desengaño. (*In* **Rosell**, C. Nov. post. a Cervantes, v. 2. 1854.)

Zayde; histoire espagnole, par M. S. **La Fayette**. (*In her* Œuvres, v. 1. 1820.)

Zazzera, Francesco. Narrazioni tratte dai giornali del governo di Don P. Girone, duca d'Ossuna. (*In* **Archivio** stor. ital., v. 9. 1846.)

Zbawieniu Polski, O. Lipsk, 1862. 16°. (E 81)

Zealand, Province of. Vosmeer, M. Principes Hollandiæ et Zelandiæ, cum iconibus. Antverp., 1578. f°.
— Objects of the expedition; account of the islands of Walcheren, Beveland, Schowen, and Cadsand. London, 1809. 8°. (B 785)
— Andersen, A. Tour in Zealand, 1802; by a native of Denmark. London, 1805. 18°.
— *Maps.* Blaeu, W. Flandria et Zeelandia. [Amst., 16—.] (E 78, no. 41)
— — Zeelandia. [Amst., 16—.] (E 78, no. 43)
— — Conynenberg, J. (*In his* Eng. coasting pilot. 1700.)
— — Wessel, C. Kort over Siæland. *n.p.*, 1770–77. 5 maps. (E 66)
— — Zeelandia insula. *n.p.*, [16—]. (E 78, no. 177)

Zecchi, Giovanni. Collezione dei monumenti sepolcrali del cimitero di Bologna. Bologna, 1825–27. 4 v. 8°.

Zechariah. *See* **Bible** (p. 282).

Zedler, Johann Heinrich. Grosses vollständiges universal Lexicon aller Wissenschaften und Künste; nebst einer Vorrede [von] J. P. von Ludewig. Halle, Lpz., 1732–50. 64 v. f°.
Note. Ed. by J. A. von Franckenstein, P. D. Longolius, and others.
Contents. Vol. 1. A–Am. 2. An–Az. 3. B–Bi. 4. Bl–Bz. 5. C–Ch. 6. Ci–Cz. 7. D.

8. E. 9. F. 10. G-Gl. 11. Gm-Gz. 12. H-He. 13. Hi-Hz. 14. I. 15. K. 16. La-Leir. 17. Leis-Lm. 18. Lo-Lz. 19. Ma. 20. Mb-Mh. 21. Mi-Mt. 22. Mu-Mz. 23. N-Net. 24. Nev-Nz. 25. O. 26. P-Pb. 27. Pe-Ph. 28. Pi-Pg. 29. Pr-Pz. 30. Q-Reh. 31. Rei-Ri. 32. Ro-Rz. 33. S-San. 34. Sao-Schla. 35. Schle-Schwa. 36. Schwe-Senc. 37. Send-Si. 38. Sk-Spie. 39. Spif-Sth. 40. Sti-Sulm. 41. Suin-Tarn. 42. Taro-Teutsch. 43. Teutscher-Th. 44. Ti-Trao. 45. Trap-Tz. 46. U-Veq. 47. Ver-Vers. 48. Vert-Vis. 49. Vit-Un. 50. Vo-Urh. 51. Uri-Uz. 52. W-War. 53. Was-Weh. 54. Wei-Wend. 55. Wene-Will. 56. Wief-Wilk. 57. Will-Wn. 58. Wo-Woo. 59. Wor-Wuq. 60. Wur-Zar. 61. Zas-Zet. 62. Zeu-Zi. 63. Zk-Zul. 64. Zum-Zz.

Zedlitz, Joseph Christian, *Freiherr* v. Gedichte. (*In* **Album** österreichischer Dichter. 1858.)

Zedner, —. Catalogue of the Hebrew books. *See* **British Museum.**

Zeen-ud-Deen. *See* **Zin-ud-Din.**

Zei, Raffaello. FINZI, M. (*In* **Amato**, G. d'. Panteon, v. 2. 1851.)

Zeigler, J. M. Geographischer Atlas über alle Theile der Erde. Berlin, 1851. f°.

Zeiller, Martin. Itinerarium Italiæ. Franck. a. M., 1640. f°.

Zeisberger, *Rev.* David. Grammar of the language of the Lenni Lenape or Delaware Indians; tr. by P. S. Du Ponceau. (*In* **Amer. Phil. Soc.** Trans., n.s., v. 3. 1830.)

— SCHWEINITZ, E. de. Life and times of Zeisberger, the apostle of the Indians. Phila., 1870. 8°.

Zeising, Adolf. Meister Ludwig Tieck's Heimgang. Frankf. a. M., 1854. 8°.

Zeitgenossen. *See* **Reumont**, A. v.

Zeitschrift der Deutschen morgenländischen Gesellschaft. Lpz., 1847-80. 34 v. 8°.

— Wissenschaftlicher Jahresbericht über die morgenländischen Studien, 1859-61. [Suppl. zum 20n Bd.] Lpz., 1868. 8°.

Zeitschrift für Astronomie; hrsg. von B. von Lindenau und J. G. F. Bohnenberger. Tüb., 1816-18. 6 v. 8°.

Zeitschrift für bildende Kunst; hrsg. von C. v. Lützow. 1r Bd., 1.-6. Heft. Berlin, Lpz., Wien, 1866. f°.

Zeitschrift für die Alterthumswissenschaft; hrsg. von T. Bergk und J. Cæsar. Vol. 1, 2 Marburg, 3-9 Cassel, 10-15 Wetzlar, 1843-57. 15 v. 4°.

Zeitschrift für geschichtliche Rechtswissenschaft; hrsg. von F. C. von Savigny, C. F. Eichhorn, und J. F. L. Göschen. Berlin, 1815-31. 7 v. 8°.

Zeitschrift für populäre Mittheilungen aus dem Gebiete der Astronomie und verwandter Wissenschaft; hrsg. von C. A. F. Peters. Altona, 1860-63. 2 v. 8°.

Zelder van Beveren, Gerardus van. Catalogus librorum, in omni fere scientiarum genere, præcipue juridico. Hag.-Com., 1796. 8°. (B 894)

Zelina; by C. A. Somerset. (*In* **Sargent**, E. Mod. stand. dr., v. 37.)

Zeller, Eduard Gottlob. Die Philosophie der Griechen in ihrer geschichtlichen Entwicklung. Tüb., 1856-62, 52. 3 v. 8°.

Contents. Vol. 1. Allgemeine Einleitung. — Vorsokatische Philosophie. 2, 1. Sokrates und die Socratiker. — Plato und die alte Akademie. 2, 2. Aristoteles und die alten Peripatetiker. 3. Die nacharistotelishe Philosophie.

— *Eng.* Socrates and the Socratic schools; tr. by O. J. Reichel. London, 1868. 8°.

— - Stoics, Epicureans, and Sceptics; tr. by O. J. Reichel. London, 1870. 12°.

— Vorträge und Abhandlungen geschichtlichen Inhalts. Lpz., 1865. 8°.

Contents. Die Entwicklung des Monotheismus bei den Griechen. — Pythagoras und die Pythagorassage. — Zur Ehrenrettung der Xanthippe. — Der platonische Staat in seiner Bedeutung für die Folgezeit. — Marcus Aurelius Antoninus. — Wolff's Vertreibung aus Halle, der Kampf des Pietismus mit der Philosophie. — J. G. Fichte als Politiker. — Schleiermacher. Zum zwölften Februar. — Das Urchristenthum. — Die tübinger historische Schule. — F. C. Bauer. — Strauss und Renan.

— Der platonische Staat in seiner Bedeutung für die Folgezeit. (*In* **Historische** Zeitschrift, v. 1. 1859.) — J. G. Fichte als Politiker. (*In* v. 4. 1860.) — Zur Würdigung der ritschl'schen Erläuterungen. (*In* v. 8. 1862.) — Strauss und Renan. (*In* v. 12. 1864.) — Lessing als Theolog. (*In* v. 23. 1870.)

Zeller, Jules Sylvain. Epoque du Moyen Age. (*In* **Geffroy**, M. A., *and others.* Rapports. 1867.)

See also **Année** historique, L', 1859-62.

Zell's popular encyclopedia. *See* **Colange**, L.

Zelmire; tragédie, par P. L. B. de Belloy. (*In his* Œuvres, v. 1. 1811.)

Zelos hasta los cielos, Los, y desdichada Estefania. *See* **Guevara**, L. V. de. (E 116)

Zelos son bien y ventura; comedia, por F. Godinez. (*In* **Comedias** nuevas, v. 35. 1671.)

Zeloso estremeño, El; por M. de **Cervantes Saavedra.** (*In his* Novelas exemp., v. 2. 1783.)

Zelter, Karl Friedrich. Briefwechsel zwischen Goethe und Zelter, 1796-1832. Berlin, 1833-34. 6 v. 8°.

Contents. Vol. 1. 1796-1811. 2. 1812-18. 3. 1819-24. 4. 1825-27. 5. 1828-30. 6. 1830-32.

Zeluco; by J. Moore. Boston, 1792. 8°.

Zémine et Almanzor; en un acte; by A. R. **Le Sage.** (*In his* Œuvres, v. 16. 1823.)

Zémire et Azor; comédie-ballet; by J. F. **Marmontel.** (*In his* Œuvres complettes, v. 16. 1787.)

Zend. TYCHSEN, T. C. De religionum Zoroastricarum apud exteras gentes vestigiis. (*In* **Goettingen. Ges. d. Wiss.** Comm., 1793.)

Zend language. RASK, E. Remarks on the Zend language. (*In* **Royal Asiatic Soc.** Trans., v. 1. 1827.)

— BOPP, F. Ueber die Zahlwörter der Zendsprache. (*In* **Berlin. Ak. d. Wiss.** Abh., 1833.)

— LEPSIUS, K. R. Das ursprüngliche Zendalphabet. (*In* **Berlin. Ak. d. Wiss.** Abh., 1862.)

— JUSTI, F. Handbuch der Zendsprache; altbactrisches Wörterbuch; Grammatik; Chrestomathie. Lpz., 1864. 4°.

Zendavesta. *See* **Avesta.**

Zendrini, Antonio. Briefwechsel zwischen Leibniz [und] Zendrini. (*In* **Leibnitz**, G. W. v. Gesam. Werke, 3. Folge, 4. Bd. 1859.)

Zenger, F. X. Ueber das vadimonium der Römer. Landshut, 1826. 12°.

Zenger, John Peter. BRIEF narrative of the case and tryal of Z. *n.t.p.* [Boston, 1738.] 4°.

— *Same.* *n.t.p.* Boston, 1799. 8°. (B 598)

— *Same.* Added the trial of W. Owen. London, 1765. 8°. (B 674, 1632)

— CHANDLER, P. W. Trial. (*In his* Amer. criminal trials, v. 1. 1841.)

Zenis. Fragm. (*In* **Mueller**, C. Fr. hist. Gr., v. 4. 1851.)

Zenker, Julius Theodor. Bibliotheca orientalis; manuel de bibliographie orientale. Lpz., 1846-61. 2 v. 8°.

Zeno *Rhodius.* Fragm. (*In* **Mueller**, C. Fr. hist. Gr., v. 3. 1849.)

Zeno, Antonio, *d. about* 1405. *See* **Zeno**, N. *and* A.

Zeno, Antonio. In concionem Periclis et Lepidi ex libro primo Thucydidis et Sallustii commentarius. Venetiis, 1569. 4°.

Zeno, Apostolo. Lettere. 2a ed. Venezia, 1785. 6 v. 8°.

Contents. Vol. 1. 1693-1708. 2. 1708-19. 3. 1719-24. 4. 1724-34. 5. 1734-39. 6. 1739-50.

— Lettere. (*In* **Raccolta** di prose let., v. 1. 1830.)

— M. A. C. Sabellici vita. (*In* **Istorici** venez., v. 1. 1718.) — Vita di P. Paruta. (*In* v. 3.)

— Poesie drammatiche. Orleans, 1785-86. 11 v. 8°.

Contents. Vol. 1. Gl' inganni felici. — Il Narciso. — I rivali generosi. — Eumene. — Faramondo. 2. Temistocle. — Lucio Vero. — Griselda. — Venceslao. — Aminta. 3. Pirro. — Teuzzone. — Svanvità. — L'amor generoso. — Engelberta. 4. Scipione nelle Spagne. — Merope. — Ifigenia in Aulide. — Atenaide. — Alessandro

Severo. 5. L. Papirio. — Sirita. — Ormisda. — Meride e Selinunte. — Nitocri. 6. Andromaca. — Gianguir. — Euristeo. — Semiranide. — I due dittatori. 7. Imeneo. — Ornospade. — Mitridate. — C. Fabbrizio. — Enone. 8. Sisara. — Tobia. — Naaman. — Giuseppe. — David. — Le profezie evangeliche d'Isaia. — Gioaz. — Il Batista. — Gionata. — Nabot. — Daniello. — David umiliato. — Sedecia. — Gerusalemme convertita. — San Pietro in Cesarea. — Gesu' presentato nel tempio. — Ezechia. 9-11. Composte insieme con P. Pariati. 9. Artaserse. — Antioco. — Ambleto. — Statira. 10. Flavio Anicio Olibrio. — Astarto. — Sesostri. 11. Costantino. — Don Chisciotte. — Alessandro in Sidone. — Psiche.

— FABRONI, A. de. (*In his* Vitæ Ital., v. 9. 1782.)

See also **Giornale** de' letterati d' Italia.

Zeno, Caterino. Commentarii del viaggio in Persia et delle guerre persiane. (*In* **Ramusio**, G. B. Nav., v. 2. 1573.)

Zeno, Jacopo. Vita C. Zeni, 1334–1418. (*In* **Muratori**, L. A. Rer. Ital. scr., v. 19.)

— AGOSTINI, G. degli. (*In his* Notizie degli scrittori viniz., v. 1. 1752.)

— NICERON, J. P. (*In his* Mém., v. 21. 1733; *and*, *Germ.*, v. 16. 1758.)

Zeno, Nicolò *and* A. MARCOLANI, F. Dello scoprimento dell' isola Frislanda, Eslanda, Engrouelanda, Estotilanda, et Icaria. (*In* **Ramusio**, G. B. Navigation, v. 2. 1573; — *and*, *Eng.*, *in* **Hakluyt**, R. Col. of voy., v. 3. 1810; — *and in* **Kerr**, R. Col. of voy., v. 1. 1824.)

— ZURLA, P. Dissertazione intorno ai viaggi settentrionali di N. et A. Zeno. Venez., 1808. 8°.

Zeno, Pietro Caterino. Vita di B. Nani. (*In* **Istorici** veneziane, v. 8. 1720.) — Vita del senatore M. Foscarini. (*In* v. 10. 1722.)

Zenobia, *Queen of Palmyra*. Fragm. (*In* **Mueller**, C. Fr. hist. Gr., v. 3. 1849.)

— MUENTER, F. De numo plumbeo Zenobiæ, reginæ orientis, et æneo Palmyreno. (*In* **St. Petersburg. Ac.** Sci. Mem., v. 9. 1819–20.)

— DELRIO, M. A. Antiquitates Tiburtinæ. — Villa Zenobiæ. (*In* **Grævius**. Thes. antiq. Ital., v. 8, pt. 4. 1723.)

— JAMESON, *Mrs.* A. (*In her* Memoirs of celeb. female sovereigns, v. 1. 1831.)

Zenobia; di P. **Metastasio**. (*In his* Opere, v. 6. 1782.)

Zenobia; tragedy. *See* **Murphy**, A.

Zenobia; or, The fall of Palmyra; romance, by W. Ware. N. Y., 1839. 2 v. 12°.

Zenobius. Proverbia, Gr. et Lat. (*In* **Schott**, A. Adagia. 1612.)

Zenobius *Florentinus*, *St.*, *Bp.* ANTONINUS *Florentinus*. Vita S. Z. (*In* **Acta** sanct., v. 19. 1866.)

Zenodotus *epigrammaticus*. Fragm. (*In* **Nauck**, J. A. Trag. Gr. fr. 1856.)

Zenodotus *Trœzenius*. Fragm. (*In* **Mueller**, C. Fr. hist. Gr., v. 4. 1851.)

Zenus, Antonius. *See* **Zeno**, A.

Zephaniah. *See* **Bible**. MINOR PROPHETS (p. 281).

Zerbrochene Krug, Der; von H. v. **Kleist**. (*In his* Gesam. Schriften, v. 2. 1863.)

Zerdusht. *See* **Zoroaster**.

Zero, *pseud.* Succinct review of the American contest. London, [1782]. 8°.

Zerstreuten, Die; von A. v. **Kotzebue**. (*In his* Theater, v. 24. 1841.)

Zerub Throop's experiment; by **Mrs. A. D. T. Whitney**. Boston, 1871. 16°.

Note. From Old and new, v. 3. 1871.

Zesen, Philipp C. van. Gedichte. (*In* **Mueller**, W. Biblioth. deutsch. Dichter, v. 13. 1837.)

— Leo Belgicus [seu] Narratio reipublicæ fœderatarum Belgii regionum. Amst., *Elzevir*, 1660. 12°.

Zestermann, August Christian Adolf. Memoir on the European colonization of Amer. in ante-historic times. [From the Proc. of the Amer. Ethnol. Soc.] *n.p.*, 1851. 8°. (B 1601)

Zeter, Jacob van. Parvus mundus. Francof., 1618. 4°.

Zetetic sermon. Boston, [183-?]. 12°. (C 180)

Zetland Islands. *See* **Shetland Islands**.

Zetzner, L. Theatrum chemicum, præcipuos selectorum auctorum tractatus de chemiæ et lapidis philosophici continens. Argent., 1613–61. 6 v. 8°.

Contents. Vol. 1. **Vaux**, R. de. De veritate et antiquitate artis chemicæ. — **Fanianus**, J. C. De artis alchemiæ veterum auctorum et præsertim jurisconsultorum judicia; — De arte metallicæ metamorphoseos: — Testamentum novum Arnoldi à Villanova. — **Moufet**, T. Dialogus apologeticus de jure et præstantia chemicorum medicamentorum; — Epistolæ quædam medicinales. — **Hoghelande**, T. De alchemiæ difficultatibus. — **Dorn**, G. Clavis totius philosophiæ chemisticæ; — Liber de naturæ luce physica, ex Genesi desumta; — De transmutationibus metallorum; — Genealogia mineralium atque metallorum. — **Penot**, B. G. De vera præparatione et usu medicamentorum chemicorum tractatus varii. — **Trevisano**, B. De chemico miraculo quod lapidem philosophiæ appellant. — **Zacharius**, D. Opusculum philosophiæ naturalis metallorum; cum annotationibus N. Flamelli. 2. **Claveus**, G. Apologia chrysopœiæ et argyropœiæ adversus T. Erastum. — **Du Wés**, G. Dialogus inter naturam et filium philosophiæ; — Tabula diversorum metallorum vocabula quibus usi sunt veteres ad artem celandam explicans. — **Ripley**, *Sir* G. Duodecim portarum epitome, duobus modis concinnata. — **Albertus** *Magnus*. De mineralibus. — **Holland**, I. Fragmentum de opere philosophorum. — **Penot**, B. G. Quæstiones tres de corporali mercurio; — Ad varias quæstiones responsio; — LVII canones de opere physico; — Vera mercurii ex auro extractio; — Chrysorrhoas, sive De arte chemica dialogus. — **Duchesne**, J. Ad J. Auberti Vendonis de ortu et causis metallorum epistolam responsio. — **Dee**, J. Monas hieroglyphica. — **Ventura**, L. Liber de conficiendi lapidis philosophici ratione. — **Pico della Mirandola**, J. F. De auro. — **Bacon**, R. Speculum alchemiæ. — **Richardus** *Anglicus*. Correctorium; — Rosarius minor, de rerum metallicarum cognitione. — **Albertus** *Magnus*. De alchymia. — **Pantheus**, J. A. Ars et theoria transmutationis metallicæ. 3. **Incerti** auctoris De magni lapidis compositione et operatione. — **Aristoteles** *chemicus*. De perfecto magisterio. — **Arnaldus** *de Villa Nova*. Lumen luminum, seu flos florum; — Practica. — **Efferarius** *monachus*. De lapide philosophorum secundum verum modum effor-mando; — **Thesaurus** philosophiæ. — **Lullius**, R. Praxis universalis magni operis. — **Odomarus**, M. Practica; — De argento in aurum verso; — De marchasita; — De arsenico; — De sale alkali; — An lapis philosophorum valeat contra pestem; — Vetus epistola de metallorum materia et artis imitatione. — **Rupescissa**, J. de. Liber de confectione veri lapidis philosophorum. — **Augurello**, G. A. Chrysopœia carmine conscripta. — **Thomas** *Aquinas*. Secreta alchemiæ magnalia; — Thesaurus alchemiæ secretissimus. — **Rupescissa**, J. de. Liber lucis. — **Lullius**, R. Clavicula et apertorium. — **Holland**, I. De lapide philosophico. — **Vogel**, E. Liber de lapidis physici conditionibus. — **Balbian**, J. v. Tractatus septem de lapide philosophico. — **Grever**, J. Secretum. — **Alanus**. Philosophi dicta de lapide philosophico. — **Barnard**, N. Commentariolum in quoddam epitaphium Bononiæ studiorum; — Processus chemici aliquot; — Tigri chemica; — Quadriga aurifera; — Theosophiæ palmarium, sive Auriga chemicus; — Epistola de occulta philosophia; — Dicta sapientum. 4. **Lullius**, R. Theoria et practica; — Compendium animæ transmutationis artis metallorum. — **Artefius**. Clavis majoris sapientiæ. — **Helias** *artista*. Nova disquisitio. — **Zanetini**, G. de. Conclusio et comprobatio alchymiæ. — **Happel**, N. N. De auro philosophico; — Carmen Apollineum Helianum. — **Lavinus**, W. Tractatus de cœlo terrestri. — **Happel**, N. N. Aphorismi Basiliani, sive Canones hermetici, de spiritu, anima et corpore, medio, majoris et minoris mundi. — **Brenta**, A. Variarum philosophorum sententiarum perveniendi ad lapidem benedictum collectanea. — **Claveus**, G. De triplici præparatione auri et argenti; — De recta et vera ratione progignendi lapidis philosophici, seu salis argentifici et aurifici. — **Sendivogius**, M. De lapide philosop.; — Ænigma philosophicum ad filios veritatis; — Dialogus Mercurii, Alchymistæ, et Naturæ. — **Aureliæ** occultæ philosophorum partes duæ. — **Arnaldus** *de Villa Nova*. Speculum alchymiæ; — Carmen; — Ad Bonifacium VIII. quæstiones essentiales quam accidentales. — **Philosophi** anonymi de secretissimo antiquorum philosophorum arcano. — **Propositiones** XXII in quibus veritas totius artis chemiæ comprehenditur. — **Lasnioro**, J. de. Tractatus aureus de lapide philosophorum. — **Trithemius**, J. Tractatus chemicus nobilis. — **Hermes** *Trismegistus*. Tractatus vere aureus de lapidis philos. secreto. — **Lagneus**, D. Harmonia philosophorum chemicorum. — **Albertus** *Magnus*. De concordantia philosophorum in lapide philosophico; — Compositum de compositis; — Liber octo capitulorum de lapide philosophorum. — **Avicenna**. Ad regem Hasen epistola de re recta; — Lapidis philos. declaratio filio suo Alboali. — **Guilelmus** *Tecenensis*. Lilium de spinis evulsum. — **Ortholanus**. Practica vera alchymiæ probata et experta sub A.D. 1358. — **Lumen** juvenis experti novum, id est, tractatus in quo nominat lapidem philosophicum. — **Valentinus**, M. Opus præclarum ad utrumque. — Incerti auctoris tractatulus super hæc verba, Studio namque florenti. — **Opus** ad album. — **Thomas** *Aquinas*. Liber lilii benedicti. — **Innominati** authoris tractatulus super verba Mer fugi dum bibit. — **Opus** breve ad Rubeum cum sole per aquas fortes. — **Silento**, P. de. Opus. — **Anonymi** tractatus ad rubrum et album. — **Eck**, P. Clavis philosophorum. **5. Turba** philosophorum. — **In** turbam philosophorum sermo. — **Allegoriæ** sapientum, et distinctiones XXIX supra librum Turbæ. — **Micreris**. Tractatus suo discipulo Mirnesindo, ex manuscripto itidem. — **Plato**. Libri quartorum, seu stellici, cum commento Hebuhabes Hamed, explicati ab Hestole. — **Kalid**. Liber secretorum alchimiæ; — Liber trium verborum. — **Zadith**. Tabula chimica, marginalibus adaucta. — **Menens**, G. Aurei velleris libri tres. — **Anonymi** veteris philosophi consilium conjugii, seu de massa solis et lunæ libri III. — **Boni**, P. A. Margarita novella correctissima. — **Scott**, M. De natura solis et lunæ. — **Rodargirus**, L. Pisces zodiaci inferioris, vel de solutione philosophica, cum ænigmatica totius lapidis epitome. — **Alphonso** X., *of Castile*. Liber philosophiæ occultioris. — **Aristoteles** *chemicus*. Tractatus de lapide philosophico. — **Epistola** de lapide philosophico. — **Thomas** *Aquinas*. Tractatus sextus de esse et essentia mineralium. — **Alvetanus**, C. De conficiendo divino elixire, sive lapide philosophico; — Animadversiones chimicæ quatuor. — **Bacon**, R. Epistola de secretis operibus artis et naturæ, et nullitate magiæ, cum notis. — **Horn**, C. De auro medico philosophorum dialogus scholasticus. **6. Vigenère**, B. De igne et sale. — **Collesson**, J. Idea perfecta philosophiæ hermeticæ. — **Anonymi** philosophi Galli instructio patris ad filium de arbore solari. — **Christophorus** *Parisiensis*. Elucidarius seu artis transmutatoriæ summa major cum app. — **La Brosse**, —. De compositione sulphuris et menstrui vegetabilis seu de auro potabili. — **Grasseus**, J. Dicti arca arcani artificiosissimi de summis naturæ mysteriis. — **Anonymus** de auro potabili. — **Cruce**, R. Responsiones. — **Ortel**, A. Commentator in novum lumen chymicum M. Sendovogii. — **Trognianus**, G. Scripta de lapide. — **Blaven**, A. v. De auro potabili epistola. — **Ortel**, A. Discursus de præcedenti epistola. — **Anonymus** de principiis artis hermeticæ. — **Plinius Secundus**, C. Excerpta ex libro aromatici philos. — **Excerpta** ex interlocutione Mariæ et Aaron. — **Ortel**, A. Interpretatio verborum Mariæ. — **Pontanus**, J. Epistola de lapide. — **Ortel**, A. Commentatio in Epistolam Pontani. — **Haymo**. Epistola de lapidibus philosophicis. — **Alvetanus**, C. Epistola de lapide. — **Astronomia** inferior. — **Rithmi** de lapide. — **Concordantia** gloriæ mundi. — **Pezel**. Opus singulare ex Theophrasto redivivo. — **Sententiæ** ex duello equestri Mercurii, Solis, et Martis. — **Rithmi** de lapide. — **Mysterium** occultæ naturæ anonymi discipuli J. Grassei. — **Monte**, G. de. Descriptio philosophici adrop; — Calcinatio metallorum; — De ovo philosophorum. — **Holland**, I. De spiritu urinæ. — **Chartier**, J. Scientia plumbi s cri. — **Polemann**, J. Novum lumen medicum de mysterio sulphuris philosophorum. — **Saltzthal**, S. De potentissima philosophorum medicina universali. — **Hermes** *Trismegistus*. Tabula smaragdina. — **Rochas**, H. de. Tractatus de observationibus novis et vera cognitione mineralium et de illorum qualitatibus et virtutibus antehac incognitis.

Zeuner, Charles. The feast of the tabernacles; an oratorio, music by C. Zeuner, words by H. Ware, Jr., May 3, 1837. [Boston, 1837.] 12°. (B 1770)

Zeus. *See* **Jupiter**.

Zeuxis. (*In* **Bergk**, T. Poet. lyr. Gr. 1853.)

Zia e la nipote, La; commedia, da **G. Giraud**. (*In his* Opere, v. 11. 1842.)

Ziegler, Anton. Historische Memorabilien des In- und Auslandes aus mehreren Jahrhunderten gesammelt. Wien, 1840. 4°.

Ziegler, J. M. Geographischer Atlas über alle Theile der Erde [in 24 Blättern]. Berlin, 1851. f°.

Ziemann, Adolf. Altdeutsches Elementarbuch. 1r Abth. Quedlinb., Lpz., 1833. 2 v. 8°.

Contents. Abth. 1. Grundriss zur Buchstaben- und Flexionslehre des Altdeutschen, nebst einem Wurzelverzeichniss. Abth. 2. Altdeutsches Lesebuch.

Ziervogel, Samuel. Rhabarbarum. (*In* **Linné**, C. Amœn. acad., v. 3. 1764.)

Zieten, J. J. *See* **Ziethen**, H. J.

Ziethen, Hans Joachim. **Blumenthal**, L. J. L. v. Life of Gen. Zieten; tr. from the German by B. Beresford. Berlin, 1803. 2 v. 8°.

Zigeunerin, Die, wahr zu sagen. Quedlinb., Lpz., 1856. 8°.

Zigzagging amongst Dolomites. London, 1871. obl. f°.

Ziliolo, Vettore. **Agostini**, G. degli. (*In his* Not. deg. scr. viniz., v. 2. 1754.)

Zillah; by [H. Smith]. N. Y., 1829. 2 v. 12°.

Zilli, Carlo. Poesie inedite. (*In* **Gamba**, B. Rac. di poesie in dial. venez. 1845.)

Zimenes, *Cardinal*. *See* **Ximenes de Cisneros**, F.

Zimmermann, Carl. Denkschrift über den Lauf des Oxus zum Karabugas-Haff des Caspischen Meeres und über die Strombahn des Ochus, oder Tedshen der Neueren, zur Balkan-Bay; nebst einem Anhang Nachrichten über die turanischen Länder, *u.s.w.*; [mit Karten]. Berlin, 1845. 4°.

— Geographische Analyse eines Versuches zur Darstellung des Kriegstheaters Russlands gegen China. Berlin, 1840. 4°.

Note. Without the Atlas.

— Geographische Analyse der Karte von Inner-Asien. Berlin, 1841. 8°.

Note. Without the Atlas.

Zimmermann, Clemens von. **Andresen**, A. (*In his* Die deutschen Maler-Radirer, v. 3. 1866.)

Zimmermann, Eberhard August Wilhelm von. Essai de comparison entre la France et les Etats Unis. Lpz., 1797. 2 v. 8°.

— A political survey of the present state of Europe. London, 1787. 8°.

— *Same*. Dublin, London, 1788. 8°.

Zimmermann, Edward. Report of 4th meeting of German jurists. (*In* **Nat. Assoc. Prom. Soc. Sci.** Trans., 1863.)

Zimmermann, Jacob. Exercitatio de atheismo Platonis. — Meditatio de præstantia religionis Christianæ collata cum philosophia Socratis. — Vindiciæ dissertationis de atheismo Platonis contra N. H. Gundlingium. (*In* **Schelhorn**, J. G. Amœn. lit., v. 9, 11, 13. 1728–30.)

Zimmermann, Johann Georg. Briefwechsel. (*In* **Herder**, J. G. von. Aus Herders Nachlass, v. 2. 1857.)

— Essay on national pride; pref., memoirs by S. H. Wilcocke., N. Y., 1799. 8°.

— Reflections on men and things; tr. from a French ms. London, 1799. 8°.

— *Same*. Aphorisms and reflections on men, morals, and things. London, 1800. 14°.

— Solitude; its influence upon mind and heart; from the French [trans.] of J. B. Mercier. Albany, 1796. 8°.

Zimmermann, Matthias. **Niceron**, J. P. (*In his* Mém., v. 36. 1736.)

Zimorowicz, Szymon. Sielanki. W Lipsku, 1836. 16°. (Bobrowicz. Bibl. klass. Polsk., v. 27.)

Zinc. **Fuchs**, E. (*In* **France**. *Com. Imp. de l'Expos. de* 1867. Rapports, v. 5.)

Zincali, The. *See* **Borrow**, G.

Zincke, Foster Barham. Last winter in the United States. London, 1868. 8°.

— Bearings of circumstances on education. (*In* **Nat. Assoc. Prom. Soc. Sci.** Trans., 1859.)

Zinckgref, Julius Wilhelm. Gedichte. (*In* **Muller**, W. Bibliothek deutscher Dichter, v. 7. 1825.)

Zinkeisen, Johann Wilhelm. Geschichte des Osmanischen Reiches in Europa. Hamburg, Gotha, 1840–63. 7 v. *and* Register v. J. H. Möller. 8°. (Heeren u. Ukert. Europ. Staat.)

— Versailles. (*In* **Historisches** Taschenbuch, 1837.) — Die orientalische Frage in ihrer Kindheit; eine geschichtliche Studie zur vergleichenden Politik. (*In* 1856–56.) — Der Westen und der Norden im dritten Stadium der orientalischen Frage. (*In* 1858.) — Das vierte Stadium oder das jüngste Jahrhundert und die Zukunft der orientalischen Frage. (*In* 1859.)

Zin-ud-din. Tohfut-ul-Mujahideen; an historical work in the Arabic language; tr. by M. J. Rowlandson. London, *Oriental Tr. Fund.*, 1833. 8°.

Zinzendorf, *Graf* Nikolaus Ludwig von. BOVET, F. The banished count; or, Life of Z.; tr. from the French by J. Gill. Lond., 1865. 8°.

— CROWE, E. E., *and* JAMES, G. P. R. (*In their* Lives of eminent foreign statesmen, v. 5. 1838. Lardner. Cab. cyc.)

— RITTER, A. History of the Moravian Church in Phila., with notices of Z. Phila., 1857. 8°.

— SPANGENBURG, A. G. Life of Z. London, 1838. 8°.

— THOLUCK, F. A. G. (*In his* Vermischte Schriften, v. 1. 1839.)

Zinzerling, Justus. Description of England, circa 1610. (*In* **Rye, W. B.** England as seen by foreigners. 1865.)

Zion's ioy in her king comming in his glory. *n.p.*, 1643. 4°. (B 13)

Zipoli, Perlone, *pseud.* *See* **Lippi, L.**

Zirardini, Antonio. MORDANI, F. (*In* **Hercolani, A.** Biog. rom., v. 2. 1835.)

Zirardini, Giuseppe. L'Italia litteraria ed artistica; 100 ritratti con cenni storici. Parigi, 1850. 8°.

Zirclaria *or* **Tirkler,** Thomasin von. Account of the Italian guest; ed. by E. Oswald. (*In* **Gilbert,** *Sir* **H.** Queene Elizabethe's achademy. 1859. Early Eng. Text Soc. Ex. ser., v. 8.)

Zisca. GILPIN, W. (*In his* Lives of J. Wicliff, *etc.* 1814.)

Zita, *St.* VITA. (*In* **Acta** sanct., v. 12. 1866.)

Zito, Bartolomeo. Difesa de 'La Vaiasseida di G. C. Cortese'. (*In* **Cortese,** G. C. La Vaiasseida. 1628.)

Zito, Maria. La bilancia critica. (*In* **Tasso,** T. Opere, v. 21. 1828.)

Zittau. GUBEN, J. von. Jahrbücher des zittauischen Stadtschreibers. (*In* **Goerlitz. Oberlaus. Ges. der Wiss.** Scr., v. 1. 1839.)

Zittel, Karl Alfred. Fossile Mollusken und Echinodermen. (*In* **Hochstetter,** F. von, *and others.* Novara, geol. Th., v. 1, pt. 2. 1864.)

Zixilanus, *Bp. of Toledo.* *See* **Cixila.**

Zjednoczonych, *Brothers.* Zbratnienie pismo poświęcone sprawie Polskiej. Paryż, 1847. 8°. (E 83)

Zlatagorskoi, E. Essai d'un dictionnaire des homonymes de la langue franç. avec la tr. allemande, russe, et anglaise. Lpz., 1862. 8°.

Zobeide, La; tragedia fiabesca, da C. **Gozzi.** (*In his* Opere, v. 2. 1772.)

Zober, Ernst Heinrich. Zur Geschichte des stralsunder Gymnasiums. Stralsund, 1839–48. 3 v. 4°.

Zobi, Antonio. Cronaca degli avvenimenti d'Italia nel 1859. Firenze, 1859–60. 2 v. 8°.

— Memorie economico-politiche, 1737–1859. Firenze, 1860. 2 v. 8°.

Contents. Vol. 1. Memorie economico-politiche. 2. Sommario di documenti officiali a dimostrazione delle Memorie economico-politiche.

— Storia civile della Toscana, 1737–1848. Firenze, 1850–52. 5 v. 8°.

Contents. Vol. 1. 1737–65. 2. 1765–91. 3. 1791–1814. 4. 1814–46. 5. 1847–48.

Zodiac. ANTIQUITY of the Indian zodiac. (*In* **Asiatick** researches, v. 2. 1801.)

— COLEBROOKE, H. T. Indian and Arabian divisions of the Zodiack. (*In* **Asiatick** researches, v. 9. 1809; *and in his* Misc. essays, v. 2. 1837.)

— IDELER, C. L. Ueber den Ursprung des Thierkreises. (*In* **Berlin. Ak. d. Wiss.** Abh., 1838.)

— MOLLIEN, E. Recherches sur le zodiaque indien. (*In* **Paris. Inst.** *Ac. d. Inscr.* Div. sav., 1e sér., v. 3. 1853.)

— BURGESS, E. On the origin of the lunar division of the zodiac represented in the Nakshatra system of the Hindus. (*In* **Amer. Orient. Soc.** Journ., v. 8. 1866.)

See also **Denderah**; — **Esneh.**

Zodiacal light. JONES, G. Observations on the zodiacal light, Apr. 2, 1853 – Apr. 22, 1855, on the U. S. steam-frigate Mississippi. Wash., 1856. 4°. (Vol. 3 of U. S. Japan exped.)

— OLMSTED, D. Observations on the zodiacal light. (*In* **Amer. Assoc.** Proc., v. 6. 1852.) — WILKES, C. Zodiacal light. (*In* v. 11. 1858.) — JONES, G. Recent observations on the gegenschein or completed arch of the zodiacal light. (*In* v. 13. 1860.)

Zoé, ou L'amant prêté; comédie-vaudeville. *See* **Scribe, A. E.** (E 22)

Zoeckler, Otto. Biblical account of creation and natural science. (*In* **Bremen** lectures. 1871.)

— Hieronymus: sein Leben und Wirken aus seinen Schriften dargestellt. Gotha, 1865. 8°.

Zoellner, Johann Friedrich. Ueber den Versuch einer Theodicee. (*In* **Berlin. Ak. d. Wiss.** Abh., 1790–91.) — Ueber den Stand der Natur. — Giebt es im menschlichen Leben ein Uebergewicht des Guten oder des Bösen? (*In* 1792–97.)

Zoe's brand. New ed. London, [1868]. 8°.

Zohrab, the hostage; by [J. Morier]. N. Y., 1833. 2 v. 12°.

Zoilus *Amphipolita.* Fragm. (*In* **Mueller, C.** Fr. hist. Gr., v. 2. 1848.)

Zola, Emile. Le vœu d'une morte. Paris, 1867. 18°.

Zolfo, Il. *See* **Masini, V.**

Zółkowski, Aloyzy. Momus. Kraków, 1836. 3 v. 16°.

Zollickoffer, Wm. Treatise on the use of prussiate of iron or prussian blue in intermitting and remitting fevers. Frederick, Md., 1822. 8°. (B 526)

Zollikofer, Georg Joachim. Sermons on the education of children; prefixed a sermon on parental example, by G. Warker. Boston, 1809. 12°.

— *Another copy, without W.'s sermon.* Boston, 1809. 8°. (B 189)

— Seven sermons on the Reformation; tr. by W. Tooke. Boston, 1809. 8°.

— *Other copies.* (B 136, 189)

Zollverein. KIRCHENPAUER, G. H. Der Handelstractat vom 21. Jan. 1839 und der deutsche Nordseehandel. Hamburg, 1839. 8°. (B 1145)

— BOWRING, J. Report on the Prussian commercial union. London, 1840. f°.

— PASSY, H. Rapport rel. aux associations commerciales allemandes. (*In* **Paris. Inst.** *Ac. d. Sci. Mor.* Mém., v. 3. 1841.)

Zon, Angelo. SAGREDO, A. Necrologia. (*In* **Archivio** stor ital., app., v. 6. 1848.)

Zonæus. De figuris. (*In* **Spengel, L.** Rhetores Gr., v. 3. 1856.)

Zonaras, Joannes. Annales. (*In* **Byzant.** hist. scr., v. 10. 1729.)

— Annales; ex rec. M. Pinderi. (*In* **Niebuhr.** Byzant. hist. script., v. 42–43. 1841–44.)

— Lexicon; illustravit J. A. H. Tittmann. Lips., 1808. 2 v. 4°.

Zoological geography. MAURY, L. F. A. La géographie zoologique. (*In* **Revue** d. D. Mondes, nov. 1859.)

— *Eng.* Zoological geography. (*In* **Amer. Geog. and Statist. Soc.** Journal, v. 2, pt. 1. 1860.)

Zoological journal; ed. by T. Bell, J. G. Children, J. de C. Sowerby, and G. B. Sowerby; March 1824–34. London, 1825–35. 5 v. 8°.

Zoological mythology. LOUANDRE, C. L'épopée des animaux: Zoologie fantastique; cycle relig. et moral. (*In* **Revue** d. D. Mondes, déc. 1853.) — Cycle chevaleresque et satirique. (*In* jan. 1854.)

— KOLLOFF, E. Die sagenhafte und symbolische Thiergeschichte des Mittelalters. (*In* **Historisches** Taschenbuch, 1867.)

— SPENCER, H. Origin of animal worship. (*In his* Recent discussions. 1871.)

Zoological notes and anecdotes; by [S. Holt]. London, 1852. 12°.

Zoological psychology. WEINLAND, D. F. Method of comparative animal psychology. (*In* **Amer. Assoc.** Proc., v. 12. 1859.)

Zoological Society, *London.* BENNETT, E. T. Gardens and managerie of the Zoological Society delineated. Chiswick, 1830–31. 2 v. 8°.

Contents. Vol. 1. Quadrupeds. 2. Birds.

Zoology. *Bibliography.*

— SWAINSON, W. Taxidermy with the biog. of zoologists and notices of their works. London, 1840. 16°. (Lardner. Cab. cyc., v. 119.)

— AGASSIZ, L. Bibliographia zoologiæ et geologiæ; ed. by H. E. Strickland and Sir W. Jardine. Lond., *Ray Soc.*, 1848–54. 4 v. 8°.

— CARUS, J. V., *and* ENGLEMANN, W. Bibliotheca zoologica. Lpz., 1861. 2 v. 8°.

— RECORD of zoological literature. London, 1865–81. 16 v. 8°.

— EDWARDS, H. M. Rapport sur les progrès récents des sciences zoologiques en France. Paris, 1867. 8°. (Rec. de rapports.)

Classification.

See General and miscellaneous works, especially HUNTER, J., *d.* 1793; — FLEMING. 1822; — SWAINSON, W. 1835; — AGASSIZ, L. 1859; — HUXLEY, T. H. 1869.

General and miscellaneous works.

— ARISTOTELES, *fl.* B.C. 384. De animalibus. *See* **Aristoteles** (p. 135).

— ÆLIANUS, C., *fl. about* 130 A. D. De natura animalium libri XVII; [Gr. et Lat.]; cur. A. Gronovio. Londini, 1744. 2 v. 4°.

— NICANDER *Colophonius, fl.* 11*th cent.* Theriaca; [Gr., cum vers. Lat.] interp. J. Gorræo. Paris, 1557. 4°.

— - Theriaca et Alexipharmaca. (*In* **Poetæ** bucolici. 1851.)

— PHILE *or* PHILES, M., *d.* 1340. De animalium proprietate; [ed.] a J. C. De Pauw cum vers. Lat. G. Bersmanni. Traj. a. R., 1730. 4°.

— - *Same.* (*In* **Poetæ** bucolici. 1851.)

— GILLES, P. Ex Æliani historia, item ex Porphyrio, Heliodoro, *etc.*, libri XVI de vi et natura animalium. Lugd., 1535. 8°.

— ACXTELMEIER, S. R. Ebenbild der Natur. Augspurg, 1699. 8°.

— BEUDANT, F. S. Mémoire sur la structure des parties solides des mollusques, des radiares, *etc. n.t.p.*, [17—.] 4°. (A 17)

— SWEDENBORG, E. Economy of the animal kingdom [1741]; tr. by A. Clissold. Boston, 1868. 2 v. 8°.

— HASSELGREN, N. The Swedish Pan. [1749.] (*In* **Stillingfleet**, B. Miscellaneous tracts. 1759.)

— FORSKÅL, P., *d.* 1763. Descr. animalium, avium, *etc.*, ed. C. Niebuhr. Hauniæ, 1775. 4°.

— LINNÉ, C. von. Animal kingdom of Linnæus as pub. by Gmelin, with, add., *etc.*, by R. Kerr. [1766.] Vol. 1. 1792. 4°.

— HUNTER, J. Observations on certain parts of the animal œconomy. [1786.] 2d ed. London, 1792. 4°.

— SHAW, G. Naturalist's miscellany; figures by F. P. Nodder. London, 1790–1813. 24 v. 8°.

— NECKER, N. J. de. Phytozoologie philosophique, dans laquelle on démontre comment le nombre des genres et des espèces, concernant les animaux et les végétaux, a été limité et fixé par la nature. Neuwied, 1790. 8°.

— SMELLIE, W. Philosophy of natural history; introd. by J. Ware. [1790.] Boston, 1824. 8°.

— - *Same.* 2d ed. Boston, 1827. 8°.

— - *Same.* Stereotype ed. Boston, 1836. 12°.

— KERR, R. The animal kingdom or Zoological system of Linnæus; with add. Vol. 1, pts. 1, 2; Mammalia and birds. London, 1792. 4°.

— HUNTER, J., *d.* 1793. Classification of animals. (*In his* Essays, v. 1. 1861.)

— REIMARUS, H. S. Betrachtungen über die Triebe der Thiere. Hamburg, 1798. 8°.

— SHAW, G. General zoology; contin. by J. F. Stephens. London, 1800–26. 14 v. in 28. 8°.

— STEWART, C. Elements of natural history. London, 1801–02. 2 v. 8°.

— RAY, P. A. F. Zoologie universelle et portative, avec un nouv. suppl. red. par L. F. Jauffret. Paris, 1804. 4°.

— SHAW, G. Lectures at the Royal Zoological Institution in 1806–07. London, 1809. 2 v. 8°.

— HOWITT, S. New work of animals; designed from Æsop, Gay, and Phædrus. London, 1811. 4°.

— WEBSTER, N. The history of animals. New Haven, 1812. 12°.

— BROWNELL, P. Inaugural dissertation on animal heat; submitted to the Med. Inst. of the state of N. Y., *etc.*, Apr. 12. *n.p.*, 1814. 8°. (B 812, 1877)

— LEACH, W. E. Zoological miscellany; illust. by R. P. Nodder. London, 1815–17. 3 v. 8°.

— CUVIER, G. L. C. F. D. Le règne animal distribué d'après son organisation. Paris, 1817. 4 v. 8°.

— - *Same.* Nouv. éd., [v. 4, 5 par P. A. Latreille]. Paris, 1829–30. 5 v. 8°.

— - *Eng.* The animal kingdom; with add. by E. Griffith. London, 1827–35. 16 v. *and* Plates 11 v. 8°.

— - *Same.* [Vol. 4 by P. A. Latreille;] tr. with add. by H. M'Murtrie. N. Y., 1831. 4 v. 8°.

— - *Same.* Tr. and abr. by H. M'Murtrie. London, 1834. 8°.

— SWAINSON, W. Zoological illustrations. London, 1820–33. 2 ser. in 6 v. 8°.

— HINTON, J. R. Elements of natural history; or, Introd. to systematic zoology. London, [182–?]. 4°.

— FLEMING, J. Philosophy of zoology; or, Structure, functions, and classification of animals. Edin., 1822. 2 v. 8°.

— BINGLEY, W. Animal biography; or, Popular zoology. 6th ed. London, 1824. 4 v. 12°.

— RICHARDSON, J., *and others.* Zoölogy of Beechy's voyage; 1825–28. Lond., 1839. 4°.

— DUMÉRIL, A. M. C. Zoologie. (Vol. 2 *of his* Elémens des sciences nat. 1825.)

— LATREILLE, P. A. Familles naturelles du règne animal. Paris, 1825. 8°.

— HOEVEN, J. van der. Handbook of zoology [1827–33]; tr. by W. Clark. London, 1856–58. 2 v. 8°.

— GRANT, R. E. Essay on the study of the animal kingdom; introd. lect. at London Univ., Oct. 23. London, 1828. 8°.

— GRAY, J. E. Spicilegia zoologica. Pt. 1. London, 1828. 4°.

— GUÉRIN-MÉNEVILLE, F. E. Ichnographie du règne animal de G. Cuvier. Paris, 1829–44. 3 v. 8°.

— GOODRICH, S. G. Peter Parley's tales of animals. Boston, 1830. 12°.

— LAMARCK, J. B. P. A. de M. Philosophie zoologique. Nouv. éd. Paris, 1830. 2 v. 8°.

— TRIMMER, *Mrs.* M. Natural history of quadrupeds, birds, fishes, *etc.* [1830.] Abridged. Boston, 1836. 12°.

— DARWIN, C. R. Zoology of the voyage of H. M. S. Beagle under command of Capt. Fitzroy, 1832–36. London, 1840–43. 3 v. 4°.

— GEOFFROY-SAINT-HILAIRE, I. Recherches zoologiques et physiologiques sur les variations de la taille chez les animaux et dans les races humaines. (*In* **Paris. Inst.** *Ac. de Sci.*, v. 3. 1832.)

— JARDINE, *Sir* W. The naturalist's library. Edin., 1833–43. 40 v. 16°.

— Mongez, A. Sur les animaux promenés ou tués dans les cirques. (*In* Paris. Inst. *Ac. d. Inscr.* Mém., v. 10. 1833.)

— Kirby, W. Power, wisdom and goodness of God as manifested in the creation of animals London, **1835.** 2 v. 8°. (Bridgewater treat., no. 7.)

— Kishemanito muzinaigun, *etc.*, Bible stories and nat. history [in Chippewa]. Bost., 1835. 12°.

— Swainson, W. Geog. and classification of animals. London, 1835. 16°. (Lardner. Cab. cyc., v. 106.)

— Geoffrey Saint Hilaire, I. La zoologie. (*In* Revue d. D. Mondes, av. 1837.)

— Bachman, J. Observations on the changes of colour in birds and quadrupeds. (*In* Amer. Phil. Soc. Trans., n.s., v. 6. 1839.)

— Forster, T. Philozoia; or, Moral reflections on the condition of the animal kingdom. Brussels, 1839. 8°.

— Griscom, J. H. Animal mechanism and physiology. N. Y., 1839. 18°. (Harper's fam. lib., v. 85.)

— Pictorial museum of animated nature. London, *C. Knight and Co.*, [184–]. 2 v. 4°.

— Edwards, H. M. Manual of zoology; tr. by R. Knox. [**1841.**] 2d ed.; with add. obs., ed. by C. C. Blake. London, 1863. 16°.

— Geoffroy Saint Hilaire, I. Essais de zoologie générale; mémoires et notices sur la zoologie générale. Paris, 1841. 8°.

— Jones, T. R. General outline of the animal kingdom and comparative anatomy. London, 1841. 8°.

— Hetzel, P. J., *ed.* Scènes de la vie des animaux. Paris, **1842–44.** 2 v. 8°.

Note. Satirical stories in which the characters are represented as animals.

— Gosse, P. H. Introduction to zoology. London, [**1844**]. 2 v. 12°.

— Jones, T. R. Natural history of animals. Vol. 1. London, **1845.** 8°.

— South, J. F. (*In* Smedley, E., *and others.* Encyc. metrop., v. 7. 1845.)

— Patterson, R. Zoology for schools. Pt. 1: Invertebrate animals. London, **1846.** 12°.

— Agassiz, L. J. R., *and* Gould, A. A. Principles of zoology. [**1848.**] Boston, 1853. 12°.

— Broderip, W. J. Zoological recreations. New ed., with add. London, **1849.** 12°.

— Humboldt, A. von. Das nächtliche Thierleben im Urwalde. (*In his* Ansichten der Natur, v. 1. 1849.)

— - *Eng.* Nocturnal life of animals in the primeval forest. (*In his* Aspects of nature, v. 1. 1849; — *and in his* Views of nature. 1850.)

— Maunder, S., *d.* **1849.** Treasury of natural history. 2d ed. London, 1849. 12°.

— Banvard, J. Library series. Boston, **1850.** 8 v. 24°.

— Broderip, W. J. Leaves from the note book of a naturalist. [1850.] London, 1852. 12°.

— Loudon, *Mrs.* J. W. The entertaining naturalist. New ed. rev. and enl. London, 1850. 16°.

— Owen, R. Zoology. (*In* Herschell, J. F. W. Manual of sci. enquiry. 1851.)

— Holt, S. Zoological notes and anecdotes. London, **1852.** 12°.

— U. S. *War Dept.* (*In their* Reports of explorations for a R. R. to the Pacific, 1853-1854. 1855–60.)

— Burmeister, H. Vergangenheit und Gegenwart des Thierreichs. — Vom Werth thierischer Geschöpfe. (*In* Geologische Bilder. 1855.)

— Dallas, W. S. Zoology. (*In* Orr, W. S. Circle of the sciences, v. 2, 3. 1855.)

— - Tenby; a sea-side holiday. Lond., **1856.** 12°.

— Buckland, F. T. Curiosities of natural history. [**1857.**] N. Y., 1859–60. 2 ser. 16°.

— - *Same.* 2d ser. London, 1860. 16°.

— Ogilvie, G. The master-builder's plan; or, The principles of organic architecture as indicated in the typical forms of animals. London, **1858.** 8°.

— Agassiz, L. Essay on classification. London, **1859.** 8°.

— Ware, J. Philosophy of natural history; on the plan and retaining portions of the work of W. Smellie. Boston, **1860.** 12°.

— Boner, C. Forest creatures. London, **1861.** 8°.

— Agassiz, L. J. R. The structure of animal life. [**1862.**] N. Y., 1866. 8°.

— Wood, J. G. Our garden friends and foes. London, **1864.** 8°.

— Pouchet, F. A. The universe [**1865**]; tr. N. Y., 1870. 12°.

— Tenney, S. Manual of zoology. N. Y., 1865. 12°.

— Meunier, V. Les grandes chasses. [**1866.**] 2e éd. Paris, 1869. 16°. (Bibl. des merv.)

— Tenney, S. *and* A. A. Natural history of animals. N. Y., 1866. 12°.

— Huxley, T. H. Introduction to the classification of animals. London, **1869.** 8°.

— Blanchard, E. Les animaux disparus depuis les ages historiques. (*In* Révue d. D. Mondes, oct. 1870.)

— Alcock, T. Zoology; or, Four plans of animal creation. (*In* Science lectures for the people. 1st ser. 1871.)

Medicine.

— Bosche, G. V. D. Historia medica; animalium natura et medica utilitas. Brux., 1639. 4°.

Study.

— Huxley, T. H. The study of zoology. (*In his* Lay sermons. 1870.)

Periodicals.

See also Bibliography (p. 3329).

— Annals of natural hist. or Mag. of zoology, *etc.*, [1st]-3d ser. London, 1838-67. 60 v. 8°.

— Museum of Comparative Zoology, *Cambridge, Mass.* Bulletin. Boston, 1863-81. 8 v. 8°.

— - Illustrated catalogue. No. 1-8. Camb., 1865–75. 8 nos. 4°.

See also **Anatomy; — Comparative anatomy; — Comparative physiology; — Domestication; — Instinct; — Menageries; — Microscope, — Natural history; — Natural selection; — Taxidermy; — Veterinary art; — Zoological geography; — Zoological mythology; —**

also **Amphibia; — Animalculæ; — Ass; — Beaver; — Branchipidæ; — Bull frog; — Camels; — Cat; — Cattle; — Chimpanzee; — Coral; — Cows; — Crustacea; — Domestic animals; — Elephant; — Entomology; — Felinæ; — Game; — Goose; — Gorilla; — Hog; — Horse; — Ichthyology; — Infusoria; — Invertebrata; — Mammalia; — Marsupialia; — Mastodons; — Mollusca; — Monkeys; — Opossum; — Orang-outang; — Ornithology; — Quadrupeds; — Rat; — Reindeer; — Reptiles; — Ruminantia; — Vertebrata; — Zoöphytes; —**

also **Africa; — California; — Chili; — Christiania; — France; — Georgia; — Germany; — Gr. Britain; — Iceland; — Illinois; — India; — Jamaica; — Labrador; — Magellan, Strait of; — Massachusetts; — Moray Co.,** *Scotland*; **— New England,** *Nat. hist.*; **— New York; — North America; — Ocean; — Wisconsin.**

also **American Assoc. for Adv. of Science.**

Zoonomia, Popular lectures on. *See* **Garnett, T.**
Zoonomia of Darwin, Observations on the. *See* **Brown, T.**
Zoonomia; or, The law of animal life. *See* **Hall, M.**
Zoonomia; or, The laws of organic life. *See* **Darwin, E.**

Zoophytes. Solander, D. Natural hist. of zoöphytes collected by J. Ellis. Lond., **1786.** 4°.

— JOHNSTON, G. History of the British zoophytes. Edin., 1838. 8°.
— VAN CLEVE, J. W. Fossil zoophytes of Western Ohio. (*In* Amer. Assoc. Proc., v. 1. 1849.)
See also Ocean.

Zophiel; or, The bride of seven. *See* **Brooks**, *Mrs.* M. G.

Zopyrion. Fragm. (*In* **Mueller**, C. Fr. hist. Gr., v. 4. 1851.)

Zopyrus *Byzantius.* Fragm. (*In* **Mueller**, C. Fr. hist. Gr., v. 4. 1851; — *and in* **Nauck**, A. Tr. Gr. fr. 1856.)

Zoraida; tragedia, por N. A. de Cienfuegos. (*In* **Ochoa**, E. de. Tesoro del teatro esp., v. 5. 1838.)

Zorm, Peter. Erörterung der dunckelsten Schrift-Stellen im N. Test. Cölln a. R., 1711. 8°.

Zornlin, Rosina M. Outlines of physical geography. London, 1851. 24°.

Zoroaster, Zarathustra, *or* **Zerdusht.** Magica oracula. (*In* **Maximus**, V. De dictis factisque mem., v. 2. 1823. Bibl. class. Lat.)
— Oracula magica, cum schollis Plethonis et Pselli; ed. studio J. Opsopœi. (*In* **Gallæus**, S. Sybillina oracula. 1689.)
— HYDE, T. Zoroastris vita, *etc.* (*In his* Historia religionis veterum Persarum. 1760.)
— LETTRE à A*** [Anquetil] du P*** [Perron] dans lequel est compris l'examen de sa traduction des livres attribués à Zoroastre. Londres, 1771. 8°. (**B 680**)
— MEINERS, C. De Zoroastris vita, institutis, doctrina, et libris. (*In* **Goettingen. Ges. d. Wiss.** Comm., 1777.) — De Z. vita, inventis, et scriptis. (*In* **1778.**) — Tertia de Zoroastre commentatio, in qua præsertim in eorum quas Anqestilius sub Z. nomine vulgavit librorum antiquitatem atque auctoritatem inquiritur. (*In* **1779.**)
See also **Avesta.**

Zorrilla y Moral, José. Obras. Nueva ed. corr. Paris, 1852. 2 v. 8°.
Contents. Vol. 1. Biografia, por I. de Ovejas. — Prologo. — Composiciones diversas. — Recuerdos y fantasias. — Cantos del trovador. — Vigilias del Estio. — La azucena silvestre, leyenda religiosa del siglo IX. — El desafio del diablo, leyenda tradicional. — Un testigo de bronce, leyenda tradicional. 2. *Obras dramaticas.* Vivir loco y morir mas; capricho dramático. — Mas vale llegar á tiempo que rondar un año; comedia. — Ganar perdiendo; comedia. — Cada cual su razon; comedia. — Lealtad de una muger y aventuras de una noche; comedia. — El zapatero y el rey, 1a y 2a parte; drama. — El eco del torrente; drama. — Los dos vireyes; drama. — Apoteósis de Don Calderon de la Barca. — El molino de Guadalajara; drama. — Sanche García; composicion trágica. — Cain, pirata; cuadro de introduccion al drama titulado un año y un dia. — Un año y un dia; drama. — La gran comedia de el caballo del rey Don Sancho. — La mejor razon, la espada; comedia original escrita sobre una de Moreto. — Don Juan Tenorio; drama religioso-fantástico. 1a parte, 2a parte. — El puñal del godo; drama. — Sofronia; tragedia. — La oliva y el laurel; alegoría. — La copa de márfil; espectáculo trágico. — El alcalde Ronquillo; ó El diablo en Valladolid; drama.
— Apuntes biograficos de Lafuente Alcantara. (*In* **Lafuente Alcantara**, M. Hist. de Granada, v. 1. 1852.)
— Translations; [by S. Eliot. Boston, 1846.] 8°.

Zorzi, Giorgio. COMPENDIO dei dispacci, 1627–29. (*In* **Barozzi**, N., *and* **Berchet**, G. Relazioni degli stati europei, ser. 2, v. 2. 1859.)

Zorzi, MarcAntonio. Epigrammi. — Canzonetta. (*In* **Gamba**, B. Raccolta di poesie in dial. venez., 1845.)

Zosimus, *of Panopolis, fl. about 3d cent.* **KOPP, H.** (*In his* Beitr. z. Gesch. d. Chem. 1869.)

Zosimus, *Comes, fl. about 5th cent.* Historia; [cum comment. hist. I. F. Reitemeieri, cum annot. C. G. Heynii;] ex rec. I. Bekkeri. (*In* **Niebuhr.** Byzant. hist. ser., v. 30. 1837.)
— *Same.* Lib. I, II. [Gr. et Lat.] (*In* **Herodianus.** Hist. lib. 1611.)
— *Eng.* New history of Z., with the notes of the Oxford ed.; pref. Leunclavius's Apology; newly Englished. London, 1684. 8°.
— *Same.* Tr. from the Greek, with the notes of Oxford ed. London, 1814. 8°.

Zosiny; sielanka, przez F. D. Kniaźnin. (*In his* Dziela, v. 4. 1837. Bobrowicz, J. N. Bibl. klass. Polsk., v. 35.)

Zouch, Thomas. Life of I. Walton. (*In* **Walton**, I. Lives 1796.)

Zoylus (*Span.* Zoyl), *St. of Cordova.* VIDA y martyrio. — IN natali; vita; miracula. (*In* **Florez**, H. Esp. sagrada, v. 10. 1753.)

Zriny; Trauerspiel, von T. Koerner. (*In his* Poet. Nachlass, v. 1. 1823. Sämmt. Werke. 1861.)

Zschokke, Johann Heinrich Daniel. Ausgewählte historische Schriften. Aarau, 1830. 16 v. 16°.
Contents. Vol. 1. Lebensgeschichtliche Umrisse. — Erinnerungen aus Rhaetien. — Burgerkrieg in der Ital. Schweiz. 2. Aufruhr von Stans. 2, 3. Kampf und Untergang schweizerischen Berg- und Waldkantone. 3. Metapolitische Ideen. — Bemerkungen zu dem Nibelungen Liede. — Meinungskampfe des deutschen Volkes im 19. Jahrh. 4. Klio's Winke. — Europens Niedergang Amerika's Aufgang. 5. Ausbreitung des Christenthums auf dem Erdball. — Verhältniss der Freimaurerei zu Kirche und Staat. — Vom Asylrecht. 6–13. Baierische Geschichte. 6. 590 B.C. – 911 A.D. 7. 911–1253. 8. 1253–1347. 9. 1348–1508. 10. 1508–1632. 11. 1633–1726. 12. 1726–77. 13. 1777–99. 14–15. Geschichte des Freistaates der drei Bünde im hohen Rhätien. 14. 600 B.C.–1620. 15. 1620–1815. 16. Des Schweizerlands Geschichte, 100 B.C.–1815.
— The fool of the nineteenth century. *See, below,* Incidents of social life amid the European Alps.
— Gryzon, albo czarodziejska dolina; tłumacz. p. W. G. W Warszawie, 1830. 2 v. 12°.
— Incidents of social life amid the European Alps; tr. by L. Strack. New York, 1844. 12°.
Contents. Florian; the fugitive of the Jura. — Marble and Conrad. — Olivier Flyeln; a fool of the 19th century. — Hortensia.
— *Same, entitled,* The fool of the nineteenth century, and other tales. N. Y., 1845. 12°.
— Labour stands on golden feet; tr. by J. Yeats. N. Y., [187-]. 8°.
— Meditations on death and eternity; tr. by F. Rowan. London, 1862. 8°.
— Meditations on life and its religious duties; tr. by F. Rowan. London, 1863. 8°.
— The military campaigns of a man of peace. — The fugitive of the Jura. (*In* **Montgomery**, *Miss* M. M. Lights and shadows of German life, v. 1. 1833.) — It is very possible! (*In* v. 2. 1833.)
— Novellen und Dichtungen. Aarau, 1858. 17 v. 16°.
Contents. Vol. 1. Alamontade. — Harmonius. — Der Eros, oder Ueber die Liebe. — Die Herrnhuter-Familie. 2. Diocletian in Salona. — Blätter aus dem Tagebuch des armen Pfarr-Vikars von Wiltshire. — Die Verklärungen. — Kleine Ursachen. — Jonathan Frock. 3. Ein Narr des 19. Jahrhunderts. — Die weiblichen Stufenjahre. — Der Millionär. — Der todte Gast. — Der Fürstenblick. — Das Loch im Aermel. 4. Addrich im Moos. 5. Der Freihof von Aarau. 6. Der Flüchtling im Jura. — Die Gründung von Maryland. — Die Irrfahrt des Philhelenen. — Florette, oder Die erste Liebe Heinrichs IV. — Maryam in der Wüste. 7. Die Prinzessin von Wolfenbüttel. — Agathokles. — Der Pflanzer in Cuba. — Hermingarde. 8. Der Pascha von Buda. — Der Creole. — Der Feldweibel. — Das blaue Wunder. 9. Das Abenteuer der Neujahrsnacht. — Die Walpurgisnacht. — Der Blondin von Namur. — Kriegerische Abenteuer eines Friedfertigen. — Die Bohne. — Die Nacht in Brczwezmcisl. — Das Bein. — Es ist sehr möglich! — Erzählungen im Nebel. — Die isländischen Briefe. 10. Rückwikungungen, oder Wer regiert denn? — Der zerbrochene Krug. — Herrn Quints Verlobung. — Hans Dampf in allen Gassen. — Tantchen Rosmarin. — Die Reise wider Willen. — Der Abend vor der Hochzeit. — Das Wirthshaus zu Cransac. 11. Die Rose von Disentis. — Die Liebe der Ausgewanderten. — Schulze von Celle und Cäcilie. 12. Lyonel Harlington. — Die Lampe des Anaxagoras und die russische Fürstin. — An Euphrasien über den Nachruhm. — Der König von Akim. — An Rosalis. 13. Das Pfarrhaus. — Die Erbschaft. — Ein Buckliger. — Julius, oder Die zwei Gefangenen. — Julius, oder Die Bibliothek das Oheims. — Julius, oder Die Mansarde. — Das Thal von Trient. — Elisa und Widmer. — Der Col d'Anterne. — Das Abenteuer am See von Gers. 14. Bilder aus dem häuslichen Leben. — Schweizer-Skizzen. — Olavides. — Der Besuch im Marienbade. 15. Wie man lieben muss. — Abellino. — Gedichte. 16. Das Goldmacherdorf. — Meister Jordan. — Die Branntweinpest. 17. Spruch und Schwank des Schweizerboten.

— La princesse de Wolfenbuttel; tr. en français par Madame de Montolieu. Paris, 1820. 12°.
— Schweizerlands Geschichte; 9e vermehrte Ausg. mit Fortsetzung der neuern Geschichte von E. Zschokke. Aarau, 1853. 16°.
— HEDGE, F. H. (*In his* Prose writers of Germany. 1848.)

Zuazo, Alonso de. Carta al L. de Figueroa. (*In* **Icazbalceta**, J. G. Col. de doc., v. 1. 1858.)

Zubly, John Joachim, *D.D.* Law of liberty; sermon on Amer. affairs at the opening of the Provincial Congress of Georgia; with account of struggles of Swisserland. Phila., 1775. 8°. (B 47, 362)
— Letter, 1773. (*In* **Mass. Hist. Soc.** Proc. 1864-65.)
— The nature of faith; sermon, with [an app. showing the doctrine of the Protestants in the article of faith, and] some vindication of Hervey against J. Bellamy. Savannah, 1772. 12°. (C 126)
— Stamp-act repealed; sermon, Savannah, June 25. Georgia, 1766. 4°. (B 258)

Zubr, Mikołay. HOFMANOWA, K. z T. (*In her* T. Wybór pism, v. 4. 1833.)

Zuchold, Ernst Amandus. Bibliotheca chemica; Verzeichniss der auf dem Gebiete der Chimie 1840-58 erschienenen Schriften. Gött., 1859. 8°.
— Bibliotheca theologica; Verzeichniss der auf dem Gebiete der evangelischen Theologie 1830-62 in Deutschland erschienenen Schriften. Göttingen, 1864. 2 v. 8°.
Contents. Vol. 1. A-K. 2. L-Z.
— Novus index. 1853-54. *See* **Kayser**, C. G. Index.
See also **Bibliotheca** historico-naturalis, physicochemica, et mathematica.

Zuendt, Matthes. ANDRESEN, A. (*In his* Der deutsche Peintre-Graveur, v. 1. 1864.)

Zugemauerte Fenster, Das; von A. v. **Kotzebue**. (*In his* Theater, v. 26. 1841.)

Zulime; tragédie, par F. M. A. de **Voltaire**. (*In his* Col. des œuvres, v. 5. 1768; — Théâtre complet, v. 3. 1788; v. 4. 1813.)

Zulma; par A. L. G. Staël-Holstein. (*In* **Biblioth.** univ. des romans, Nouv., v. 59. 1802.)

Zulménie et Volsidor. *See* **Dorat**, C. J.

Zulus. IRELAND, W. Historical sketch of the Zulu mission in S. Africa. Boston, *A. B. C. F. M.*, [186-]. 8°. (E 10)
— WALMSLEY, H. M. Ruined cities of Zulu Land. London, 1869. 2 v. 8°.

Language and Literature.

— BRYANT, J. C. The Zulu language. — GROUT, L. The Zulu and other dialects of Southern Africa. (*In* **Amer. Orient. Soc.** Journ., v. 1. 1847.) — Essay on the phonology and orthography of the Zulu and kindred dialects in Southern Africa. (*In* v. 3. 1853.)
— CALLAWAY, C. Nursery tales, traditions, and histories of the Zulus, in their own words, with a tr. into English, and notes. Vol. 1. Natal, London, 1868. 8°.

Zuma; suivi de La belle Paule, Zénéïde, Les roseaux du Tibre, La veuve de Luzi; par Mad. de Genlis. Paris, 1817. 16°.
— *Same*. (*In* **Genlis**, S. F. D. de. Œuvres. 1826.)

Zumalacarregui, Tomas. HENNINGSEN, C. F. The most striking events of a twelvemonth's campaign with Z., in Navarre and the Basque Provinces. London, 1836. 2 v. 8°.

Zumpt, August Wilhelm. De C. T. Zumptii vita et studiis narratio; acc. C. T. Z. orationes Latinæ sex. Berolini, 1851. 8°.
— Grammar of the Latin language. 2d Amer. from latest German ed. N. Y., 1831. 8°.

Zumpt, Karl Gottlob (*Lat.* Timotheus). Ueber die Abstimmung des römischen Volks in comitiis centuriatis oder über die Verbindung der beiden Eintheilungen des römischen Volks nach Classen und Centurien und nach Tribus. — Ueber den M'. Curius, der den Velinus abgeleitet. (*In* **Berlin. Ak. d. Wiss.** Abh., 1836.) — Ueber Ursprung, Form, und Bedeutung des Centumviralgerichts in Rom. (*In* 1837.) — Ueber die römischen Ritter und den Ritterstand in Rom. — Ueber den Unterschied der Benennungen Municipium, Colonia, Præfectura im römischen Staatsrecht. (*In* 1839.) — Ueber den Stand der Bevölkerung und die Volksvermehrung im Alterthum. (*In* 1840.) — Ueber den Bestand der philosophischen Schulen in Athen und die Succession der Scholarchen. (*In* 1842.) — Commentationis de legibus judiciisque repetundarum pars I. (*In* 1845.)
— ZUMPT, A. W. De C. T. Zumptii vita et studiis; acc. C. T. [Z.] orationes Latinæ sex. Berolini, 1851. 8°.

Zúñiga, Francesillo de. Cronica. (*In* **Castro**, A. de. Curios. bibliog. 1855; v. 36 of Aribau. Bibl.)

Zurcher, Fréderic, *and* **Margollé**, Elié. Les ascensions célèbres aux plus hautes montagnes du globe; fragments de voy. rec., tr., et mis en ordre. Paris, 1867. 16°. (Biblioth. des merv.)
— Les glaciers. Paris, 1868. 16°. (Biblioth. des merv.)
— Volcans et tremblements de terre. 2e éd. Paris, 1868. 16°. (Biblioth. des merv.)
— *Eng.* Volcanoes and earthquakes, from the French, by Mrs. N. Lockyer. London, 1868. 8°.
— Les météores. 1867. — *Eng.* Meteors, ærolites, storms, and atmospheric phenomena. 1870. *See* **Margollé**, E.

Zur-Eich, Hans Jacob. Africanische Reissbeschreibung in die Landschaft Fetu. (*Appended to* **Spöri**, F. C. Amer. Reiss-beschreibung. 1677.)

Zurich (*Lat.* **Tigurum**). SCHELHORN, J. G. Commentatio in antiqua monumenta in agro Tigurino. 1724. (*In his* Amœn. lit., v. 7. 1727.) — BREITINGER, J. J. Suppl. ad Commentationem in antiqua monumenta in agro Tigurino 1724 eruta. (*In* **Schelhorn**, J. G. Amœn. lit., v. 9. 1728.)
— *Map*. MERCATOR, G. Argow cum parte merid. Zurichgow. *n.p.*, [16—]. (E 78, no. 34)
— - MAP. *n.p.*, [17—]. (E 60)

Zurich. Institut des Aveugles et des Sourds-Muets. Rapport par H. d'Orelli; tr. de l'allemand par H. Mousson. Zurich, 1835. 8°. (B 1152)

Zurich letters. ROBINSON, H. Ser. 1, 2: Correspondence of English Bishops and others with Helvetian reformers. Camb., 1842-45. 2 v. 8°. (Parker Soc.)
Contents. Vol. 1. 1558-79. 2. 1558-1602.
— *Same*. Ser. 3, 4: Letters relative to the English reformation. Camb., 1846-47. 2 v. 8°. (Parker Soc.)

Zurita, Alonzo de. Memorial de Z. (*In* **Icazbalceta**, J. G. Col. de doc., v. 2. 1866.)
— Rapport sur les classes de chefs de la Nouv.-Espagne. (*In* **Ternaux-Compans**, H. Voy., v. 11. 1840.)

Zurita *or* **Curita**, Jerónimo. Anales de la corona de Aragon; con una apologia de A. de Moráles. Caragoça, 1669, 10, 69, 68, 70, 04. 7 v. f°.
Contents. Vol. 1. 710-1313. 2. 1304-1409. 3. 1410-51. 4. 1452-92. 5. 1492-1504. 6. 1504-16. — Apologia de A. de Moráles. 7. Index.

Zurla, Placido. Dissertazione intorno ai viaggi settentrionali di Nicolò ed Antonio Zeni. Venezia, 1808. 8°.

Zurueckkunft des Vaters, Die; von A. v. **Kotzebue**. (*In his* Theater, v. 12. 1840.)

Zurueckkunft aus Surinama, Die; von A. G. A. **Müllner**. (*In his* Spiele für die Bühne, v. 1. 1818.)

Zutphen. BLAEU, W. Geldria ducatus et Zutfania comitatus. Amst., [16—]. (E 78, no. 55)
— Zutphania comitatus. [Amst., 16—.] (E 78, no. 63)
— MAP. Amst., [17—]. (E 60)

Zuyder-Zee. CARTE des entrées du Suyder-Zée et de l'Embs avec les isles, bancs, et costes comprises entre la Hollande et la Frise orientale. *n.p.*, [17—]. (E 87, no. 17.)

Zwei Familien; Schauspiel, von E. v. Bauernfeld. Wien, 1840. 8°. (E 14)

Zwei Nichten für Eine; von A. v. **Kotzebue**. (*In his* Theater, v. 30. 1841.)

Zweiflerin, Die; von A. G. A. **Müllner**. (*In his* Spiele für die Bühne, v. 2. 1820.)

Zweihundert Bildnisse und Lebensbeschreibungen berühmter deutscher Männer. 2e Aufl. Lpz., 1857. 16°.

Zwetl *or* **Zwettel.** Cistercienser-Kloster. Das 'Stiftungen-Buch' des Cistercienser-Klosters; hrsg. von J. von Frast. Wien, 1851. 8°. (Fontes rer. Austr., 2. Abth., 3. Bd.)

— ANNALES Zwetlenses, 1-1386. — Kalendarium, 1243-1458. (*In* Pertz, G. H. Mon. Germ. hist., Scr., v. 9. 1851.)

Zwick, Henry Augustus, *and* **Schill**, J. G. Calmuc Tartary; or, A journey from Sarepta, 1823. London, 1831. 8°.

Zwiefalten. ANNALES Zwifaltenses, 1-1503. (*In* Pertz, G. H. Mon. Germ. hist., Scr., v. 10. 1852.)

Zwinger, Gustav Philipp. ANDRESEN, A. (*In his* Die deutschen Maler-Radirer, v. 4. 1870.)

Zwinger, Jacob. Græcarum dialectarum hypotyposis. (*In* Scapula, J. Lexicon Gr.-Lat. 1628; v. 2 1816.)

Zwierkowski, W. Zywot generala K. Małachowskiego. Paryż, 1845. 8°.

Zwingli, Ulrich *or* Huldreich. Werke. 1e vollständige Ausgabe durch M. Schuler und J. Schulthess. Zürich, 1828-42, 36, 30-42. 8 v. 8°.

Contents. Vol. 1-2. *Die deutschen Schriften*: *Lehr- u. Schutzschriften.* **1.** 1522-24. Von erkiesen und fryheit der spysen. — Von ärgernuss und verböserung. Ob man gwalt hab die spysen zů etlichen zyten verbieten. — Ein fründlich bitt und ermanung etlicher priester der eidgnossenschaft, dass man das heilig evangelium predigen nit abschlahe. — Von klarheit und gewüsse oder unbetrogliche des worts gottes. — Ein predig von der ewig reinen magd Maria. — Handlung der versammlung in Zürich 29. jenners von wegen des heiligen evangelii zwüschend der botschaft von Costenz und Zwingli sammt gemeiner priesterschaft des statt Zürich. — Uslegen und gründ der schlussreden oder artiklen durch Zwingli, Zürich 19. jenners 1523 usgangen. — Von göttlicher und menschlicher gerechtigheit; ein predge. — Acta oder gschicht, wie es uf dem gespräch 26-28 wynmonats in Zürich ergangen ist, anbetreffend die götzen und die mess. — Ein kurze christenliche ynleitung, die ein eersamer rat der statt Zürich den seelsorgern und prädicanten zůgesandt habend damit sy die evangelische warheit einhellig fürohin verkündind und jren underthonen predigind. — Ratschlag von den bildern und der mess. — Christenlich antwurt burgermeisters und rates zů Zürich dem herren Hugen, bischofen zů Costenz, über die underricht beider artiklen der bilder und mess. — Der hirt, wie man die waren christenlichen hirten und widerum die falschen erkennen sölle. **2**, 1. *Zum Behufe des Ueberschritts*, 1525-28, *betref. die Täuferey*, *u. betref. die streitige Abendmahlslehre*, 1526-27. Antwurt Valentino Compar. Vom evangelio, was es sye. — Von den leereren, wie vil jnen zů glouben sye. — Von den bilderen, und wie an denen die schirmir und stürmer missleerend. Vom fegfür, das keins syn mag. — Die Disputation zu Bern. — Zwo predigen zů Bern. — Vom touf, vom widertouf und vom kindertouf. — Von dem predigamt. — Ueber doctor Balthazars toufbüchlin. — Welche ursach gebind zů ufrüren, welches die waren ufrührer sygind, und wie man zů christlicher einigheit und friden kommen möge. — Ein klare underrichtung vom nachtmal Christi. — Antwurt über doctor Strussen büchlin das nachtmal Christi betreffende. **2**, 2. *Abendmahlslehre*, 1527-28, *liturgische u. poetische*, *u. vermischte kleinere meistens politische*, 1522-July 1526. Fründlich verglimpfung über die predig Luthers wider die schwärmer. — Dass dise wort Christi 'Das ist min lychnam, ewiglich den alten einigen sinn haben werdend, und Luther mit sinem lezten bůch sinen und des papsts sinn gar nit geleert noch bewärt hat. — Ueber Luthers bůch, bekenntnuss genannt, antwurt. — Liturgisches. — Poetische Schriften. — Ein göttlich vermanung an die ältisten eidgnossen zů Schwyz. — Entschuldigung etlicher Huldrychen Zwingli zůgelegter artiklen, doch unwarlich. — Anmerkungen uf der dry bischofen fürtrag. — Ein epistel über die ungegründten geschrift J. Gebwylers die er zů beschirmung der römischen kilchen und jro erdachten wesens hat lassen usgon. — Ein trüw vermanung an die frommen eidgenossen, das sy sich nach jrer vordren bruch und gestalt leitind, damit sy die untrüw und gefärd jrer fygenden nit beleidigen mög. — Ein flyssige und kurze underrichtung. — Was mit den münchen zů Zürich gehandlet werden soll. — Gůtachten im Ittingerhandel — Allen christlichen brüdern zů Ougspurg. Vor Leo Juds widerfechtung wider Mathys Kretzen zů Ougspurg falsche mess und priestertum, ouch dass das brot und wyn des fronlychnams und blůts Christi kein opfer sye. — Fürtrag vor dem rat zů Zürich, da er demselben die übergab der hohen und nideren gerichten im namen des stifts zum grossen münster anzeigt. — Ueber die gevatterschaft, dass sy die ee nit hindren soll noch mag. — Predigen wider die pensionen 1521 und 1525. — Ueber die usschliessung von dem abendmal. — Ordnung und ansehen, wie hinfür zů Zürich in der statt über eelich sachen gericht soll werden. — Wie sich die münch ze Rüti mit lesen und hören der heiligen gschrift halten söllind. — Ueber den zehenden und die beschwerden der landlüten von Zürich. — Ueber den Kornmarkt, die Pfründen der Geistlichen und die Hausarmen. — Aussage über die Wiedertäufer vor den Nachgängern. — Antwurt von rät zů Zürich an den rat von Bern über den antrag dass Zürich die mess wider ufrichte. — Gutachten in den Verhandlungen des Raths von Zürich mit dem Papst wegen des rückständigen Soldes und der Religionsanderung 1526. — *Schriften Zwinglis durch die Disputation zu Baden veranlasst.* J. Eggen missive den eidgnossen boten zů Baden überschickt, *etc.* — Ueber solchs Zwinglis verantwurt. — Zwinglis antwurt dem eersamen rat zů Zürich ylends ggeben über anzeigen Eggen geschrift und nüner orten anschlag zů Frowenfeld beschehen. — Ein kopy beeder fründlicher geschrift und gleitbriefs, die ein eersamer grosser rat zů Zürich Joh. Eggen, doctorn zůgeschickt, darüber Zwingli sin antwurt. — Zwinglis Bedenken wegen der Disputation zu Baden. — Ein fründliche gschrift an gmein eidgnossen der 12 orten. — Ein sandbrief Fabri an Zwinglin von wegen der künftigen disputation. Ueber den ungesandten sandbrief Fabers. — An der Eidgenossen Boten zu Baden. — Das gleit, das die 7 ort gen Zürich gschickt. — Die ander geschrift an doctor Joh. Faber. — Die erst kurze antwurt über Eggen siben schlussreden. — Die ander antwurt über etlich antwurten, die Egg uf der disputation ze Baden ggeben hat. — Der eidgenossen boten an den rat von Zürich. — Zwingli an der eidgenossen boten zu Baden versammlet. — Ein kurze gschrift warnende vor dem unchristlichen fürnemen Fabers. — Die dritte geschrift wider Faber über das erdicht büchlin, das er nüw zytung genennet. — Musikalischer Anhang. **2**, 3. *Schriften apologetischen, kirchlichen, geschichtlichen, grossentheils politischen Inhalts*, 1526-31. Ein christenliche epistel von etlichen predigen, so doctor B. Sattler gethon hat. — Der ander sandbrief. — Trachtung Z. in Geroldseggs handel. — Ratchlag miner herren der vier verordneten sammt den dry lütpriesteren wegen der disputation zuo Bern. — Entwürfe auf die erste Synode zu Zürich. — Vorrede zu Schwenkfelds 'Anweisung, dass die Opinion der leiblichen Gegenwart unsers Herrn im Brot ist wider den Inhalt der ganzen Schrift'. — Vom Bildersturm zu St. Johann im Toggenburg. — Ursachen, warum man sich mit den stätten Costanz, Lindow, Strassburg, *etc.*, in ein burgrecht ynlassen sölle. — Gutachten, den Abbt und das Kloster Sant Gallen betreffend. — Rathschlag über den Krieg. — Entwürfe zu Friedensartikeln. — Das Religionsgespräch zu Marburg. — Wie sich Luther, *etc.*, und Z., *etc.*, in der summa christenlicher leer glychförmig ze syn befunden habend uf dem gespräch jüngst zuo Marburg in Hessen 1529. — Ein Stück des Gesprächs zwischen Luther und Z. — Scheda manu Oecolampadii transmisit. — Anbringen uf künftigen burgertag. — Trachstuck in Loubenbergers und Surgensteiners sachen. — Was von Venedig gekommen. — Schreiben von Burgermeister und heimlichen Räthen von Zürich an die Gesandten zu Wyl. 1530. — Schreiben von Burgermeister und heimlichen Räthen von Zürich an Bern. 1530. — Beschluss des Rathes von Zürich wegen der Pfarrbesoldungen und Kirchegüter, von Z. verfasst, 1530. — Supplikation und begeren der prädikanten ze Zürich an die ratsboten der christlichen stätten. — Z. im Nahmen der Prädikanten von Strassburg, Zürich, Bern, und Basel an die 5 Orte der Eidgenossenschaft. — Ursachen, um deren willen Philipp, landgraf in Hessen, in das christliche burgrecht ufzenemen. — An Burgermeister Röust und Stadtschreiber in Zürich, jetzt Boten zu Basel. — Instrucktion für Walenstad. — Schreiben der geheimen Räthe von Zürich an den geheimen Rath zu Strassburg wegen den Schmalkaldischen Vereinigung und wegen der Confession vom Nachtmahl. — Zuschrift der geheimen Räthe von Zürich an die von Basel. — Geheime Rathschläge gegen die 5 Orte auf den künftigen Burgertag. — Was Zürich und Bern not ze betrachten sye in dem fünfortischen handel. — Trachtungen des künftigen tags, dass man dise meinung den heimlichen, *etc.*, nach gelegenheit fürtrage vor dem tag, damit sy dess gerüster kommind, *etc.* — Supplikation Etlicher der Gemeinde zu Rappersweil. 3-8. *Scripta Latina.* **3.** *Didact. et apol.*, 1521-26. Concilium cujusdam ex animo esse consultum cupientis et Pontificis dignitati et christianæ religionis tranquillitati. — Epistola ad Erasmum Fabricium de actis legationis ad Tigurinos missæ. — Supplicatio quorundam apud Helvetios Evangelistarum ad Hugonem episcopum Constantiensem ne se induci patiatur ut quidquam in præjudicium evangelii promulget, *etc.* — Apologeticus Archeteles quo respondetur parænesi ab episcopo Constantiensi ad senatum Præpositura Figurinæ quem Capitulum vocant missæ. — Suggestio deliberandi super propositione Hadriani Pontificis Romani Neroborgæ facta ad principes Germaniæ. — De canone missæ epichiresis. — De canone missæ libelli apologia. — Adversus H. Emserum canonis missæ adsertorem apologia. — De vera et falsa religione. — Subsidium sive coronis de Eucharistia. — In catabaptistarum strophas elenchus. — Responsio brevis ad epistolam amici haud vulgaris in qua de eucharistia quæstio tractatur. — Amica exegesis, id est expositio eucharistiæ negotiii ad Lutherum. — Quæstiones de sacramento baptismi a docto quodam propositæ Z. — Ad M. Alberum Rutlingensium Ecclesiasten de cœna Domini. — Ad J. Bugenhagii Pomerani epistolam responsio. — Ad F. Lambertum ac omnes qui in fide sinceri sunt fratres Argentorati. — De peccato originali declaratio ad Urbanum Rhegium. — Ad T. Billicani et U. Rhegii epistolas responsio. **4.** *Didactica et apologetica ab* 1526 *ad obitum auctoris, ceteraque varia poetica, pædagogica, philologica, hist.*; *acc. sermones vulgares in Psalmos.* Ad Carolum Romanorum imperatorem Germaniæ comitia Augustæ celebrantem fidei Z. ratio. — Ad illustrissimos Germaniæ principes Augustæ congregatos de convitiis Eccii epistola — Christianæ fidei a Z. prædicatæ brevis et clara expositio ab Z. paulo ante mortem ejus ad regem christianum scripta hactenus a nemine excusa et nunc primum in lucem edita. — Ad illustrissimum Cattorum principem Philippum sermonis de providentia Dei anamnema. — Toggenburgii ineducatum bovis fabulosum centimetrum currentium rerum commenticium. — Quo pacto ingenui adolescentes formandi sint, praeceptiones pauculæ. — Præfatio Geminii ad linguarum candidatos præfixa editioni Pindari Cæporino-Cratandrinæ 1526 et epistola ejusdem ad lectorem editioni illi epilogi loco annexa. — De gestis inter Gallos et Helvetios ad Ravennam, Papiam, aliisque locis, et conventu apud Thermas Helveticas 1512. — De colloquio Marburgensi relationes Latine scriptæ. — In Zuinglii Sermones in Psalmos et Prophetas præfatio Schuleri. — Liber Psalmorum sermonibus vulgaribus illustratus **5.** *Exegetica Vet. Test.* Annotationes in Genesin. — In Exodum. — Enchiridion Psalmorum ex Hebraica veritate patriæ linguæ pariter et Latinitati donatum. — Complanatio Iesaiæ Latina. — Apologia complanationis Iesaiæ. **6**, pt. 1. *Exegetica Vet. Test. residua, ac Evangelia.* Complanatio Jeremiæ prophetæ. — Annotationes in Evang. Matthaei. — In Evang. Marci. — In Evang. Lucæ. — In Evang. Joannis. **6**, 2. *Exeg. Nov. Test.* Brevis commemoratio mortis Christi ex quatuor Evangelistis. — Historia resurrectionis et ascensionis Christi. — In Epist. ad Romanos annotationes. — In priorem ad Corinthios annotationes. — In posteriorem ad Corinthios annotationes. — In Epist. ad Philippenses annotationes. — In Epist. ad Colossenses annotationes. — In I, II, Epist. ad Thessalonicenses annotationes. — In Epist. Jacobi expositio. — In Epist. ad Hebræos expositio. — In Epist. Joannis canonicam expositio. **7, 8.** *Epistolæ.* 7. 1510-26. 8. 1527-31.

— CHRISTOFFEL, R. Zwingli; or, The rise of the Reformation in Switzerland; life of the reformer; trans. by J. Cochran. Edin., 1858. 2 v. 8°.

— HESS, J. G. Vie de Z. Paris, 1810. 8°.

— - *Eng.* Life of Z.; tr. by L. Aiken. London, 1812. 8°.

Zwischen den Schlachten; von B. Björnson. (*In his* Dramatische Werke, v. 2. 1866.)

Zwischen Himmel und Erde; von O. Ludwig. 3e Aufl. Berlin, 1862. 16°.

Zwolle. MAP. Amst., [17—]. (E 60)

Zymoses. CUTTER, B. Brief reports of zymoses of 1857 and of 1858. (*In* **Mass. Med. Soc.** Med. Comm., v. 9. 1860.)

THE EDITOR TO THE PROPRIETORS.

In 1856 it was decided to prepare and print a catalogue of the Boston Athenæum Library. It was to resemble in its general features the catalogue of the Mercantile Library Association of Boston prepared by Mr. W. F. Poole and issued two years before; that is, it was to be a "dictionary" catalogue (one in which authors and titles are mingled in a single alphabet), and each title was to occupy only one line. The making of it, I have been told, was entrusted to several young men. They were intelligent and industrious; one of them, at least, has since made his mark in the world; but they had never had any instruction in cataloguing, probably had never been trained even in accuracy of copying. Sometimes they took the title from the back of the book, sometimes from the title-page, sometimes from the half-title, and sometimes, apparently, from their own imaginations. They omitted freely, of course, and they altered the order of words for the purpose of omitting, and of the words which they retained they abbreviated the greater part to the verge of unintelligibility. They spent no time on the investigation of authors' full names or in the discovery of the authors of anonymous and pseudonymous books, nor did they trouble themselves about cataloguing rules. Their chief object must have been quick work; their writing, therefore, was often illegible or ambiguous by reason of haste; their copying was often faulty, especially in names and dates; and their classification, made at a glance, was subject to such errors as putting Osmont's "Dictionnaire typographique des livres rares" under Printing, where it no more belongs than Brunet or any other bibliographical work, and Romayne "De puris generatione" (on the formation of *pus*) under Baths, as if it were a treatise on the use of pure water, and Condorcet's "Analyse appliqué à la probabilité des décisions rendues à la pluralité des voix" under Decisions, and Lancelot's "Jardin des racines grecs" under Botany, and the "Geographische Carte von *gantz* Deutschland" among the maps of 'Ghent (in French Gand).' The result, if it had been printed, would have been one of the most remarkable catalogues ever issued. Of course, working so rapidly, these writers got over a great deal of ground; the worse they worked, the more they did, leaving a larger crop of errors for others to uproot, and the nearer the catalogue seemed to completion the farther off it really was.

At last the suspicion that all was not right appears to have arisen, and in 1862 the full control of the work was transferred to Mr. Charles R. Lowell, who had been employed upon it from 1857. He was a gentleman who will always be remembered with regard by all who knew him for his unfailing courtesy and his remarkable devotion to the interests of the Library. He was a lover of books, and familiar with the Athenæum from his earliest years, and he took up the task and pursued it almost as a labor of love. His best course would have been to throw the work of his predecessors into the fire and begin anew. But unfortunately he also was without experience. Not knowing what a catalogue ought to be he was not shocked at the material which came into his hands; besides, most of the errors were not, like those which I have instanced, on the surface, and it was only after several years that he acquired the habit of assuming every title of his predecessors to contain some mistake. He continued, therefore, on their lines. But Mr. Lowell, though without the special training of a cataloguer, had a sympathy with students, and the instincts of a lifelong reader. He found that the catalogue, as it had been made, was a very unsatisfactory assistant to researches in the library. He began to study the somewhat scanty literature of cataloguing, and to introduce the ideas which he there found into his practice. As the work was evidently too much for one person, he was allowed a copyist to assist him, and then another, and finally a third. They catalogued the books that had not been reached before, and they copied the titles left by his predecessors, some of them, but unfortunately not all, after correction. As time went on, and his ideas extended, he had his own early titles altered and copied, and later still these slips were rewritten to introduce new improvements. In some places this happened five or six times. Each time the matter improved, but the form was exposed to all the chances of mistake which accompany the most skilful copying. * After 8 years of this labor the catalogue was supposed to be, and at first sight was nearly ready for printing. But in fact different portions were in very different states of preparation. Reminiscences of the early masters were still to be found here and there; of the rest, part was in Mr. Lowell's first manner, other parts in some one of his later styles; and it would have been very difficult for an outsider to say which was which. In Washington Allston's "Feast of Belshazzar" one distinguishes at a glance the original figures from the unfinished products of the second design. But a catalogue is more like a panorama than a picture; it cannot be seen as a whole, and only close scrutiny and laborious comparison of part with part can detect all its incongruities of method.

Mr. Lowell was busily engaged in removing defects which he alone knew of, when in June 1870 he suddenly died, and the unfinished work came into the hands of the present editor. I had been engaged chiefly upon a catalogue constructed upon an

* Thus, to take a few out of hundreds of instances, Ibn Batuta became John Batuta; Wilson, Winslow; Lossing, Jennings; Lincoln and Rutland Counties was altered into Lincoln and Rutland Cosmetics; Busby's grammar appeared as Reldemerta Grammatices, Græces-Latinæ, Metricum; French accents rarely appeared at all; Cardinal Newman's famous "Development of Christian doctrine" was given as Development of Christian character and put under the heading Christian character; the "Civil and ecclesiastical rites used by the Hebrews" became their "ecclesiastical rights".

entirely different plan (that of Harvard College Library). Fearful of yielding too much to my preference for that plan, I began with the intention of making as few changes as possible. There was, moreover, at that time, a very strong desire for immediate publication. "For years", as one of the Trustees wrote a little later, "the Proprietors had had no other catalogue than the separate and disjointed strips which had been insecurely attached to the insecure sheets of sundry loose and unwieldy volumes". The prevalent feeling was, as the Library Committee reported in 1872, "it is better to have *soon* a printed catalogue which, though perhaps incomplete and somewhat incongruous in its arrangement, will yet be a useful guide to the Library, than to wait for years in order to obtain one that will suit all the requirements of the bibliographic art". It was decided, therefore, to take the catalogue as it was, or rather as it was supposed to be, to revise certain groups of titles that had been selected by Mr. Lowell as especially needing examination, and to begin to print in a year and a half.

In that time much was to be done. The Catalogue was in this condition. About 87,000 volumes and 5300 bound pamphlets had been entered upon it under the authors' names, and under that word of the title which best expressed the subject of the book. In a considerable number of cases among the English books, but less frequently among the foreign, the cataloguer had also made an entry under some word expressive of the subject of the book, even when that did not clearly appear from the title. The volumes received during the 18 months (4800) were to be included, also the 583 volumes and 1286 pamphlets of the Washington Library, and 30,000 other bound pamphlets. In other words the catalogue was to be enlarged more than one-third. It became evident, too, before long that some other preliminary work was needed. Christian names were not generally given in full; different persons of the same name needed to be distinguished; the edition was hardly ever noted; the imprint was frequently omitted, especially under subjects; when the publication of a set of volumes had extended over several years, only the date of the first volume was given; many dates had been altered in copying; the number of volumes was often erroneously given, especially where two or more volumes were bound in one. Entries were still frequently divided between two synonymous headings (as Birds and Ornithology). The greater part of the "contents" of sets of volumes had not yet been written; "analysis", that is, reference to the parts of collected works and of the publications of societies, and the like, though it had been made with remarkable minuteness for the works issued by American historical societies, had not yet been carried much farther; it was necessary to find out just how far it went and to complete it *; reference from the titles of plays, poems, and other works in English was not complete, and in the foreign languages had been very sparingly inserted. In fact the catalogue so far as then made was chiefly suited to an English-reading community. It was finally found necessary to go through the whole library, as well as could be done while the books were in circulation, with a view of finding works likely to have been imperfectly entered in the catalogue and having them treated properly.

It will be seen that a large part of the material was new. When the "style" came to be considered it was found best to make that entirely new. It is impossible to explain this without using technical language. There were several styles of subject-entry in the catalogue; the prevailing one resembled the index of Low's "English catalogue", being an alphabetical mixture of authors and titles, rather than of authors and subjects. Of course the two correspond to a certain extent; the same entry is often at once a title- and a subject-entry. But the style which had been used emphasized the title quality, the style which was now substituted for it emphasized the subject quality; the first is better suited for the man in search of a book whose name he knows, the second is made in the interest of the man who wants a book on a certain topic. † Besides this change, the larger subjects, such as Architecture, Art, Bible, Great Britain, France, United States, and other large countries, were carefully subdivided. The punctuation and the capitalization were entirely altered, and a variety of type was adopted to express certain distinctions of meaning in the briefest possible way. Many titles were abridged, others, being imperfect or ambiguous, were lengthened. This revision though it required from one to half-a-dozen changes, in each of nearly a quarter of a million of entries, was not all. Some cross-references had been made, but with no completeness, because that is one of the last things

* I cannot let this clause pass without remarking on the greatly increased value given to the catalogue by the unusual fulness of these analytical references. Some of them may seem unnecessary; we may grudge the time they take to make and the space they occupy; but our almost daily experience shows us that many works which have cost large sums of money would stand upon the shelves untouched, useless, did not analytical references call the attention of inquirers to the fact that in those volumes they will find matter bearing upon the points which they are investigating. I do not in the least underrate the value of bibliographies and of the bibliographical helps which it is becoming the excellent custom to annex to treatises of all sorts, but every one knows that there are not enough of them and that they do not adequately meet the needs of library work. Whether it is worth while to have a catalogue, and further whether it is worth while to have an analytical catalogue are questions which can best be answered by those who use them or who have attempted without them to assist students in the use of a large library. I do not understand how any person who day by day sees the difficulties of research can fail to give an affirmative answer. In fact I do not know any such person who does. One would as soon expect to hear a sea-captain call in question the utility of charts and compass.

† This difference, which necessarily is merely alluded to here, will be found set forth at length in "Public libraries in the U. S., special report of the Bureau of Education", Pt. 1, p. 536-539.

to be done before going to press. If properly made from each subject to all the less extensive headings which in a "systematic" catalogue would be classed under that subject, but in the dictionary catalogue are dispersed through the alphabet, these cross-references do away to some extent with the evils of this dispersion, and enable the dictionary catalogue to combine some of the advantages of a synoptical view of the whole field, which is the characteristic of the classed plan, with the great advantage of ready reference, which belongs to the alphabetical arrangement. Other kinds of cross-references, such as those between similar classes and between synonymous class names are also indispensable but had as yet rarely been made. As there are over 6000 subject-headings in the catalogue the task of pointing out their proper connections according to their various relationships was not slight.

All this revision and addition could not be crowded into eighteen months; its extent has been mentioned to dispose the reader to leniency if he should find that some part of it was inadequately performed, and if in the hurry some errors were made with one hand of the very kind which we were trying to eradicate with the other. Various things were done with the consciousness that they were only makeshifts. What could be put off (as the writing of "Contents", alteration of the "style", the verification of suspicious titles) was left to be finished during the printing. Those who have charge of similar work will do well to avoid imitating this example. Let them send the copy to the printer not when they are ready to begin but when they are ready to end. Little or no time is saved by the opposite course. A catalogue that is absolutely ready can be carried through the press with great rapidity in any large printing office; but one which, like the present, is made while it is printing, will not only move slowly, but is in great danger of inconsistencies and errors. This is particularly the case when the want of preparation consists in erroneous classification. Repeatedly we have come across works which did not belong where we found them but should have gone under some heading that had already been printed.* Moreover any change made in one place may require corresponding changes to be made in several others, some of which may have been fixed in the printed page. But the incompleteness of the material was not at that time fully known, and even if it had been, it may be a question whether a thorough preliminary revision would have been justified under the circumstances. Undoubtedly the result would have been a better catalogue; but with no fixed date set for printing, there would have been a constant temptation to attempt too much, and to introduce refinements whose expense would not be justified by their practical utility. In cataloguing *c'est le dernier pas qui coûte.*

Jan. 1, 1872, therefore, was taken as the limit beyond which no new book should be added. † In the next four months many experiments were made to determine the best form of page and arrangement of type; the paper, type, and material needed in a small printing office were bought, so that the type might be set in the building by compositors in our own employ, a method which I should decidedly recommend in a similar case. (The press work has been done by John Wilson and Sons, of Cambridge.) On the 1st of May 1872 the printing began; it has stretched over nine years of working time and nine months of vacation. ‡

I have said that we had not designed to print an exceptionally good catalogue but simply one that should be as useful as we could make it, and that could be finished in about four years. But the sheets, as they were sent out to various persons, elicited warm encomiums, founded rather, it is to be feared, upon what was thought to be aimed at, than upon what had been accomplished. It was plain that more was expected than we had intended to give, and less would be pardoned than we had supposed. Because it had been pronounced to be so good we were impelled to make it better, especially as the absolute necessity of certain improvements was becoming more and more evident. §

* For examplé, Bigot's three reports on the "mission abnaquoise" not put under Abnaki but under North America; G. W. Dasent's "Tales from the North", which is a translation of Asbjörnsen and Moe's "Norske Folkeeventyr", not entered under Asbjörnsen; several works on Hydraulics hidden away under Mechanics because their titles spoke of the mechanics of fluids; Bartlett's "Annihilation" [of the wicked] first appearing under Future life.

† When the concluding or continuing volumes of sets have been procured since this date, the volumes have been included in the catalogue, if the part containing their author-entry had not already been printed. Analytical references to authors and subjects contained in such volumes have not generally been made, with the exception of a few works which had nearly reached their completion when the printing began.

‡ I should be very ungrateful did I not acknowledge the services of the young ladies who have assisted me in the preparation of the copy for the press. They have all taken great interest in the work and have expended upon it long, hard, and intelligent labor, without which it would have been impossible to double the rate of progress during the last two years, and at the same time to elaborate and partly apply in the library a new system of classification. I should particularly mention Miss E. F. Knowles who, originally engaged simply to read proof, in time came to take a large and of late the largest share in the preparation of the copy.

§ One defect not suspected at first, made itself known after a time, at first accidentally, then as the result of inquiry. Either from original failure to catalogue books properly, or from the loss of slips, there was under subjects a very frequent absence of titles that should have been found there. After the first few there is probably no subject heading of any importance that has not received considerable additions as the work was passing through the press. Thus under England and English 512 titles were added to 786 already on the Catalogue. In Theology there were 337 new titles and 283 old. The addition was made by an examination of the shelves in the appropriate alcoves, and as the books were all the time in circulation, some may have been missed; this danger was in a measure obviated by a collation (as careful as time would allow) of the manuscript with the subject catalogue of the Congressional Library, and of the proof with the excellent card catalogue of Harvard

Something of this could be done as the printing went on slowly. The funds of the Athenæum did not warrant quicker procedure, and the Catalogue failed to meet with that pecuniary support among the Proprietors which might have been expected from the often expressed impatience to obtain it which had led to the printing. Perhaps it was just as well that there should be this delay. It has given time, not indeed to make the Catalogue perfect, as is shown by the copious list of errata prefixed to each volume, but to remove numberless faults and to introduce some improvements. *

The additions to the Library since 1872 have been entered upon a card-catalogue of a similar plan, except that in accordance with a practice which is growing in favor, and has been incorporated in the rules of the American Library Association and of the Library Association of the United Kingdom, the works of British noblemen have been entered under their titles, and not as heretofore, under their less known family names. After the arrangement of the library on a more exact and more satisfactory classification, which is now going on, the shelf-lists will in effect be, for all those who come to the library, a systematically classed catalogue; and as the unbound pamphlets will be thrown into a precisely parallel arrangement, although kept in a separate place, they will form their own classed catalogue. The library will then need only an alphabetical subject-index to the classes, a brief author-index to the unbound pamphlets, and suitable guides to the shelves, to be provided with every facility for consultation.

CHARLES A. CUTTER.

College Library.

The "separate slips insecurely attached to insecure sheets" must have been occasionally torn off altogether and lost, for we occasionally came across fragments of partially torn slips. These latter could be usually completed with a little ingenuity, even when there was no more left of them than in the three following cases:

tolomeo Colleoni. Bergamo, 1732. 4°.

Sir W.

30. [crossed out] 76.2 [followed by part of another figure].

But the lost slips of course were gone irretrievably, and when the books to which they had belonged turned up there was no resource but to catalogue them upon the Supplement.

* Some time after the first volume of the Catalogue was issued, I was asked by the United States Commissioner of Education to prepare an essay on cataloguing for the Special report on libraries which formed part of his exhibit at the Centennial Exposition, and was afterwards widely distributed. To fill a gap in library literature a collection of "Rules for a dictionary catalogue" was added, in which many things which I had been accustomed to do as it were by instinct or experimentally, were set down systematically with statements, and now and then with discussions, of the reasons for them. Some of those who have studied and used the "Rules" may wonder why they have not been applied thoroughly in the Catalogue. The reasons are: (1) in some matters it would have been too costly to change Mr. Lowell's work; (2) the "Rules" show the result of experience acquired in printing the first 1300 pages of the Catalogue, and in some matters they advocate a practice better than the one adopted in the beginning, which, however, had to be followed to the end, for the sake of uniformity; (3) in other cases, where uniformity was of less importance a change was made, and it will be found that the "Rules" have been followed in the last two-thirds, though not before. The most important change introduced was the arrangement of titles under subject headings not in the alphabetical order of the authors' names but in the chronological order of publication, or, in historical subjects, of the period treated of in the book. This arrangement consumes considerable time in the making, but it is far superior to the other in the assistance it offers to investigation.

www.ingramcontent.com/pod-product-compliance
Lightning Source LLC
LaVergne TN
LVHW021306110826
845150LV00003B/502

* 9 7 8 1 4 2 5 5 5 8 6 1 1 *